February 29–March 3, 2012
Raleigh, North Carolina, USA

Association for Computing Machinery

Advancing Computing as a Science & Profession

SIGCSE'12

Proceedings of the 43rd ACM Technical Symposium on Computer Science Education

Sponsored by:

ACM SIGCSE

Association for
Computing Machinery

Advancing Computing as a Science & Profession

The Association for Computing Machinery
2 Penn Plaza, Suite 701
New York, New York 10121-0701

Copyright © 2011 by the Association for Computing Machinery, Inc. (ACM). Permission to make digital or hard copies of portions of this work for personal or classroom use is granted without fee provided that copies are not made or distributed for profit or commercial advantage and that copies bear this notice and the full citation on the first page. Copyright for components of this work owned by others than ACM must be honored. Abstracting with credit is permitted. To copy otherwise, to republish, to post on servers or to redistribute to lists, requires prior specific permission and/or a fee. Request permission to republish from: permissions@acm.org or Fax +1 (212) 869-0481.

For other copying of articles that carry a code at the bottom of the first or last page, copying is permitted provided that the per-copy fee indicated in the code is paid through www.copyright.com.

Notice to Past Authors of ACM-Published Articles
ACM intends to create a complete electronic archive of all articles and/or other material previously published by ACM. If you have written a work that has been previously published by ACM in any journal or conference proceedings prior to 1978, or any SIG Newsletter at any time, and you do NOT want this work to appear in the ACM Digital Library, please inform permissions@acm.org, stating the title of the work, the author(s), and where and when published.

ISBN: 978-1-4503-1098-7

Additional copies may be ordered prepaid from:

ACM Order Department
PO Box 30777
New York, NY 10087-0777, USA

Phone: 1-800-342-6626 (USA and Canada)
+1-212-626-0500 (Global)
Fax: +1-212-944-1318
E-mail: acmhelp@acm.org
Hours of Operation: 8:30 am – 4:30 pm ET

ACM Order Number: 457120

Printed in the USA

Message from the SIGCSE Chair

It is my pleasure to welcome you to the 43rd SIGCSE Technical Symposium on Computer Science Education (SIGCSE 2012). With a diverse technical program and over 1100 attendees from around the world, you are participating in the premiere technical conference on computer science education. I hope that you will find this event an opportunity to hear influential keynote addresses, to learn about new resources and pedagogy, to renew friendships, to meet future collaborators, and to have fun and learn a lot.

SIGCSE 2012 is sponsored by the ACM Special Interest Group on Computer Science Education (the SIGCSE organization). The SIGCSE organization consists of approximately 2600 members, whose interests in improving computer science education are probably similar to your own. Many of these members are also volunteers who carry out the various activities associated with the SIGCSE organization. Chief among the volunteers responsible for the SIGCSE 2012 symposium are Laurie Smith King and Dave Musicant, symposium co-chairs, who have worked for over two years on this conference. Laurie and Dave selected and steered a committee of 27 colleagues in organizing all aspects of this event. Included in the organizing committee are members, on whom we depend year in and year out, to handle conference registration (Lynn Degler, Cary Laxer, and Larry Merkle), to manage the conference database (John Dooley and Henry Walker) and to coordinate with exhibitors and sponsors (Susan Rodger). On behalf of the SIGCSE organization I thank all of the members of the committee for their countless contributions.

I also thank all of the conference supporters and exhibitors, who enhance this event by their presence. Without their participation, this conference would not be as memorable.

I encourage you, the reader, to consider becoming more involved in the SIGCSE community and the workings of the SIGCSE organization. I encourage you to attend in the annual SIGCSE Business meeting on Friday afternoon, from 5:10 to 5:55p.m., in room 302A. This is an opportunity to meet the members of the SIGCSE board: Daniel Joyce (vice chair), Doug Baldwin (treasurer), Susan Rodger (secretary) and at-large members Tiffany Barnes, Mark Guzdial and Amber Settle. Most importantly, it is an opportunity to learn more about how the organization works – a first step in becoming more involved.

Enjoy the conference!

Renée McCauley
College of Charleston
SIGCSE Chair, 2010-2013

Message from the Symposium and Program Chairs

Welcome to the proceedings of the 43rd ACM Technical Symposium on Computer Science Education, or SIGCSE 2012, where you will find the archival record of over one hundred papers as well as multiple other session formats that document the latest in computer science education: research, tool building, teaching, curriculum and philosophy. Reflecting our location in North Carolina's renowned *Research Triangle*, this year's conference features the three themes of "Teaching, Learning, and Collaborating" throughout the sessions. Teaching, learning, and collaborating occur inside and outside of the classroom, and among various combinations of students, academics, industry professionals, and others.

We are pleased to announce the winners of the two annual SIGCSE awards. Professor Harold (Hal) Abelson of Massachusetts Institute of Technology will receive the SIGCSE award for Outstanding Contribution to Computer Science Education, and will provide Friday's keynote address. Jane Prey of Microsoft Research will accept the SIGCSE Award for Lifetime Service to the Computer Science Education Community and speak at our First Timer's Lunch. In addition, we've invited speakers to deliver two more keynote presentations. Frederick P. Brooks, Jr., from University of North Carolina at Chapel Hill, will deliver Thursday's keynote address titled "*The Teacher's Job is to Design Learning Experiences; not Primarily to Impart Information.*" Fernanda Viégas and Martin Wattenberg from Google's "Big Picture" visualization group will jointly address Saturday's luncheon with "*Through the Looking Glass: Talking about the World with Visualization.*"

Symposium statistics are presented below. Many thanks to the authors, reviewers, and Program Committee members whose enormous and vital service generated this program. This year's program includes the usual wide selection of events, including the First-Timer's Lunch and Evening Reception on Thursday and the SIGCSE luncheon on Saturday. Our exhibit hall features a number of exhibitors showcasing the latest in hardware, software tools, textbooks and educational programs and research. We continue to offer accessibility at SIGCSE 2012 for the deaf and hard of hearing.

Proposal type	*Accepted*	*Received*	*Acceptance Rate*
Paper	100	289	35 %
Panel/Special Session	24	53	45 %
Workshop	36	78	46 %
Poster	48	109	44 %
Birds of a Feather	36	46	78 %

We are excited about the variety of pre-symposium events that we will be offering. As of the press deadline for this overview, meetings on the following topics will occur on Wednesday: Teaching Open Source, Career Mentoring, SIGCAS Open Meeting, Teaching Ethics in Computer Science, and Computing Accreditation. Near the end of the symposium on Saturday, top undergraduate and graduate students will present their work at the ACM SIGCSE Student Research Competition, managed by Ann Sobel. SIGCSE 2012 will also see the return of robots through a new venue, "The SIGCSE Playground: Experience It!" Many thanks go to Jennifer Kay and Douglas Blank for organizing this event.

Our sincere thanks go out to the people who made this Symposium extraordinary. First, our symposium committee: Carl Alphonce, Adrienne Decker, Lynn Degler, John Dooley, Mary Anne Egan, Susan Fox, Michael T. Helmick, Olaf Hall-Holt, John Harrison, Sarah Heckman, Catherine Lang, Steven Huss-Lederman, Cary Laxer, Chuck Leska, Lester I. McCann, Scott McElfresh, Larry Merkle, Brad Miller, Briana Morrison, Kris Nagel, Sarah Monisha Pulimood, Susan Rodger, Kimberly Voll, and Henry Walker. Additional thanks go to our Associate Program Chairs who provided meta-reviews for papers: Joel Adams, Doug Baldwin, Tim Bell, Sheila Castañeda, Tim Fossum, Mark Guzdial, Sherri Goings, Nancy Kinnersley, Lori Pollock, and Sami Rollins. We'd also like to thank all of our student volunteers who help us with all of the small details.

In difficult economic times, we extend a *very* grateful thank you to our supporters, vendors, exhibitors and in-kind donors whose participation literally make the symposium possible. We especially thank Microsoft, Google, and Intel as platinum supporters, SAP University Alliances as a silver supporter, and Oracle for funding an ice cream break. Special thanks go to Dorothea Heck and her team at D. Lawrence Planners for coordinating an outstanding exhibition and to Susan Rodger, our amazing supporter/exhibitor liaison.

We thank SIGCSE President Renée McCauley and the entire SIGCSE Board for their support and guidance, and acknowledge the contributions of SIGCSE Symposium Site Coordinators Bob Beck and Scott Grissom, as well as Ashley Cozzi of ACM. Lisa Tolles of Sheridan Printing Company brought all materials together. The City of Raleigh provided valuable information and prizes through their excellent Convention and Visitor's Bureau, with special thanks to Julie Brakenbury. We were supported at the Raleigh Convention Center by Tim Greene, Mara Craft, Dave Chapman, Mason Hotaling, Dan Capps (of Centerplate Catering), and Michael Murphy (of American AV); at the Raleigh Marriott City Center Hotel by Sasha Armour and Thomas Kelville; at the Sheraton Raleigh Hotel by Kevin Johnson; and at the Clarion Raleigh Hotel State Capital by Tricia Nelson.

Special thanks to our home institutions for providing needed resources: College of the Holy Cross, Carleton College, Colorado School of Mines, and Rochester Institute of Technology. We genuinely hope you enjoy the Symposium and find the SIGCSE 2012 Proceedings of use for your work now and your future projects and activities.

Symposium Chairs

Laurie Smith King
College of the Holy Cross

David R. Musicant
Carleton College

Program Chairs

Tracy Camp
Colorado School of Mines

Paul Tymann
Rochester Institute of Technology

Table of Contents

Session 11: Paper – Games

Session Chair: Adrienne Decker *(Rochester Institute of Technology)*

Session 12: Paper – Professional Experiences

Session Chair: Sarah Heckman *(North Carolina State University)*

Session 13: Paper – A Session with a View

Session Chair: Don Goelman *(Villanova University)*

Session 14: Paper – Pedagogy: Programming

Session Chair: Saquib Razak *(Carnegie Mellon University)*

Session 15: Panel

Session Chair: Rebecca Bates *(Minnesota State University, Mankato)*

Session 27: Paper – Summer Experiences

Session Chair: Kinnis Gosha *(Morehouse College)*

Session 28: Paper – Software Engineering

Session Chair: Ariel Ortiz *(Tecnologico de Monterrey, Campus Estado de Mexico)*

Session 29: Special Session

Session Chair: Owen Astrachan *(Duke University)*

Session 30: Special Session

Session Chair: Pat Yongpradit *(Springbrook High School)*

Session 31: Special Session

Session Chair: Michael Kölling *(University of Kent)*

Session 32: Paper – Collaborative Learning

Session Chair: Adrian German *(Indiana University)*

Session 33: Paper – Curriculum Issues

Session Chair: Colleen Lewis *(University of California, Berkeley)*

Session 34: Paper – Active Learning I

Session Chair: Robert England *(Transylvania University)*

Session 35: Paper – Communication Skills

Session Chair: James Early *(SUNY Oswego)*

Session 36: Special Session

Session Chair: Suzanne Westbrook *(National Science Foundation)*

Session 37: Panel – Teaching Outside the Text

Session Chair: Lester Wainwright *(Charlottesville High School)*

Session 38: Special Session

Session Chair: John Impagliazzo *(Hofstra University)*

Session 39: Paper – Projects

Session Chair: Jeff Gray *(University of Alabama)*

Session 40: Paper – Alice and Scratch

Session Chair: Kelly Powers *(Advanced Math & Science Academy Charter School)*

Session 41: Paper – Active Learning II

Session Chair: Douglas Kranch *(North Central State College)*

Session 42: Paper – Non-majors

Session Chair: Derek Schuurman *(Redeemer University College)*

Session 43: Special Session

Session Chair: Nick Parlante *(Stanford University)*

Session 44: Special Session

Session Chair: Amy Briggs *(Middlebury College)*

Session 45: Panel

Session Chair: Wendy DuBow *(University of Colorado)*

Session 46: Paper – High School Collaborations

Session Chair: Tim Bell *(University of Canterbury)*

Session 47: Paper – Parallelism and Concurrency

Session Chair: Jodi Tims *(Baldwin-Wallace College)*

Session 48: Paper – Mobile Computing

Session Chair: Cyndi Rader *(Colorado School of Mines)*

Session 54: Paper – OS and Distributed Computing

Session Chair: William Mongan *(Drexel University)*

Session 55: Paper – Curricular Innovations and Research

Session Chair: Michael Hewner *(Duke University)*

Session 56: Paper – CS Education Research

Session Chair: Yana Kortsarts *(Widener University)*

Plenary Session

Session Chair: Laurie Smith King *(College of the Holy Cross)* and Dave Musicant *(Carleton College)*

Workshops

Poster Session 1

Poster Session 2

Birds-of-a-Feather

SIGCSE 2012 Symposium Committee

Laurie Smith King, Symposium Co-Chair
College of the Holy Cross

David R. Musicant, Symposium Co-Chair
Carleton College

Tracy Camp, Program Co-Chair
Colorado School of Mines

Paul Tymann, Program Co-Chair
Rochester Institute of Technology

Doug Baldwin, Associate Program Chair
SUNY Geneseo

Sherri Goings, Associate Program Chair
Carleton College

Joel Adams, Associate Program Chair
Calvin College

Tim Fossum, Associate Program Chair
SUNY Potsdam

Nancy Kinnersley, Associate Program Chair
University of Kansas

Lester I McCann, Workshops
University of Arizona

Brad Miller, Publications
Luther College

Larry Merkle, Registration
Wright State University

Kris Nagel, Posters
Georgia Gwinnett College

Steven Huss-Lederman, Student Volunteers and Activities
Beloit College

Henry Walker, Database Administrator
Grinnell College

Michael T. Helmick, Webmaster
Google

Sara Monisha Pulimood, Kids Camp Coordinator
The College of New Jersey

Susan Rodger, Supporter/Exhibitor Liaison
Duke University

Ann Sobel, Student Research Competition
Miami University (Ohio)

Briana Morrison, Pre-Conference Event Liaison
Southern Polytechnic State University

Sheila Castaneda, Associate Program Chair
Clarke University

Lori Pollock, Associate Program Chair
University of Delaware

Tim Bell, Associate Program Chair
University of Canterbury

Chuck Leska, Associate Program Chair
Randolph-Macon College

Sami Rollins, Associate Program Chair
University of San Francisco

Mark Guzdial, Associate Program Chair
Georgia Institute of Technology

Chuck Leska, Panels and Special Sessions
Randolph Macon College

Adrienne Decker, Workshops
Rochester Institute of Technology

Cary Laxer, Registration
Rose-Hulman Institute of Technology

Lynn Degler, Registration
Rose-Hulman Institute of Technology

Olaf Hall-Holt, Birds-of-a-Feather
St. Olaf College

Scott McElfresh, Treasurer
Wake Forest University

Mary Anne Egan, Student Volunteers and Activities
Siena College

John Dooley, Database Administrator
Knox College

Carl Alphonce, Evaluations
University at Buffalo, SUNY

Susan Fox, Kids Camp Coordinator
Macalester College

Catherine Lang, International Liaison
Swinburne University

John Harrison, K-12 Liaison
Princess Ann High School

Sarah Heckman, Local Arrangements
NC State University

Kimberly Voll, Publicity / Social Networking
University of British Columbia

SIGCSE 2012 Board-Sponsored Pre-Symposium Events

Career Mentoring Workshop

Susan Rodger, *Duke University*; Sheila Casteneda, *Clarke College*; Dave Reed, *Creighton University*

The goal of the Career Mentoring Workshop is to provide critical mentoring information for instructors, pre-tenure faculty and graduate students in Computer Science and Engineering who are interested in an academic career. The day-long workshop, to be held on Wednesday, February 29, will be co-located with the SIGCSE 2012 conference in Raleigh. Tentative topics will include: Mentoring, Teaching Strategies, Getting Started with Research / Finding Funding / Research with Undergraduates, Promotion and Tenure, Time Management, and Balancing Priorities (i.e., teaching vs. research vs. service). February 29, 8:00am to 5:00pm

Upcoming Events

ITiCSE 2012

Technion Campus
Haifa, Israel
July 3-5, 2012
www.iticse12.org.il/htmls/home.aspx

Conference Chair
Tami Lapidot – *Technion, Israel*
Judith Gal-Ezer – *The Open University, Israel*

ICER 2012

Auckland, New Zealand
September 10-11, 2012
http://icer-conference.org/

General Chair
Alison Clear, *Christchurch Polytechnic Institute of Technology*

SIGCSE 2013

Denver, Colorado, USA
March 6-9, 2013
http://sigcse.org/sigcse2013/

Symposium Co-Chairs
Paul Tyman, *Rochester Institute of Technology*
Tracy Camp, *Colorado School of Mines*

CALL FOR PARTICIPATION

SIGCSE 2013: The Changing Face of Computing The 44th ACM Technical Symposium on Computer Science Education

March 6-9, 2013, Denver, Colorado, USA

http://www.sigcse.org/sigcse2013

SIGCSE 2013 continues our long tradition of bringing together colleagues from around the world to present papers, panels, posters, special sessions, and workshops, and to discuss computer science education in birds-of-a-feather sessions and informal settings. The SIGCSE Technical Symposium addresses problems common among educators working to develop, implement and/or evaluate computing programs, curricula, and courses. The symposium provides a forum for sharing new ideas for syllabi, laboratories, and other elements of teaching and pedagogy, at all levels of instruction.

Submissions in line with the conference theme, "The Changing Face of Computing", are ideal. The theme focuses our attention on how computing is changing, and how we must change in education to address the changes in computing.

PAPERS
Papers describe an educational research project, classroom experience, teaching technique, curricular initiative, or pedagogical tool. Two versions of a submission are required: a full version having author names and affiliations and an anonymous version for use in reviewing. Papers will undergo a blind reviewing process and must not exceed six pages. Authors will have approximately 25 minutes for their presentations, including questions and answers.

PANELS
Panels present multiple perspectives on a specific topic. To allow each panelist sufficient time to present his or her perspective and still enable audience participation, a panel will normally have at most four panelists, including one moderator. Panel submissions should include a list of the panelists, their affiliations, and a description of the topic, with brief position statements from panelists. Proposals with more than four panelists must provide a statement connecting the extra panelist to the effectiveness of the panel and must convincingly show that each panelist will be able to speak, and the audience able to respond, within the session time. Panel abstracts must not exceed two pages. A panel session is approximately 75 minutes.

SPECIAL SESSIONS
Special sessions are your opportunity to customize and experiment with the SIGCSE conference format. Possible special sessions include a seminar on a new topic, a committee report, or a forum on curriculum issues. More generally, they must be 75 minutes in length, held in standard conference spaces, and justifiably distinct from the panel, paper, and poster tracks. Within those constraints, the form is yours to design. Special session abstracts must not exceed two pages.

WORKSHOPS
Workshops offer participants opportunities to learn new techniques and technologies designed to foster education, scholarship, and collaborations. A workshop proposal (including abstract) must not exceed two pages. Proposals must specify equipment needs (e.g., participant-supplied laptops, room configurations, and A/V equipment) and any limitation on the number of participants. Workshops are scheduled for a three-hour session and do not conflict with the technical sessions.

BIRDS OF A FEATHER SESSIONS
Birds of a Feather (BOF) sessions provide an environment for colleagues with similar interests to meet for informal discussions. A maximum one-page description (including abstract) is requested to describe the informal discussion topic. A/V equipment will not be provided for these sessions. Approximately 45 minutes are allocated to each BOF topic.

POSTERS
Posters describe computer science education materials or research, particularly works in progress. Proposals (including abstract) are limited to two pages. Poster demonstrations are scheduled to permit one-on-one discussion with conference attendees, typically during session breaks. Prepared handouts are encouraged in order to share your work.

STUDENT RESEARCH COMPETITION
Research from all areas of computer science is considered for awards in two categories of competition: graduate and undergraduate. All submissions must represent a student's individual research contribution and a student must be an ACM student member to qualify for awards and travel grants. Entry due date is September 30, 2012.

Association for Computing Machinery
Advancing Computing as a Science & Profession

SIGCSE
ACM Special Interest Group on Computer Science Education

IMPORTANT DUE DATES

Friday, September 7, 2012: *Paper, Panel, Special Session, and Workshop submissions*
Monday, October 29, 2012: *Birds of a Feather and Poster submissions*

PROGRAM COMMITTEE

Symposium Chairs

Tracy Camp
Colorado School of Mines
tcamp@mines.edu

Paul Tymann
Rochester Institute of Technology
ptt@cs.rit.edu

Program Chairs

J.D. Dougherty
Haverford College
jd@cs.haverford.edu

Kris Nagel
Georgia Gwinnett College
knagel@ggc.edu

Panels and Special Sessions

Sue Fitzgerald
Metropolitan State University
sue.fitzgerald@metrostate.edu

Workshops

Susan Haller
SUNY Potsdam
hallersm@potsdam.edu

Lester I. McCann
The University of Arizona
mccann@cs.arizona.edu

Publications

Joel Adams
Calvin College
adams@calvin.edu

Database Administrators

John Dooley
Knox College
jdooley@knox.edu

Henry Walker
Grinnell College
walker@cs.grinnell.edu

Registration

Lynn Degler
Rose-Hulman Institute of Technology

Cary Laxer
Rose-Hulman Institute of Technology

Larry Merkle
Computational Optimization Services

sigcse2013-registration@cs.rit.edu

Posters

Jodi Tims
Baldwin-Wallace College
jltims@bw.edu

Birds Of A Feather

Jian Zhang
Louisiana State University
zhang@csc.lsu.edu

Student Volunteers and Student Activities

Steven Huss-Lederman
Beloit College
huss@beloit.edu

Steven Wolfman
University of British Columbia
wolf@cs.ubc.edu

Webmasters

Dan Bogaard
Rochester Institute of Technology
dsbics@rit.edu

Steve Zilora
Rochester Institute of Technology
sjzics@rit.edu

Treasurer

Scott Grissom
Grand Valley State University
grissom@gvsu.edu

Evaluations

James Early
SUNY Oswego
earlyjp@cs.oswego.edu

Kids' Camp

Susan Fox
Macalester College
fox@macalester.edu

Kimberly Voll
University of British Columbia
kvoll@cs.ubc.ca

Support/Exhibitor Liaison

Susan Rodger
Duke University
rodger@cs.duke.edu

Pre-Conference Events Liaison

Adrienne Decker
Rochester Institute of Technology
amdigm@rit.edu

K-12 Liaison

Marilyn Cadenhead
School of Science and Engr. Magnet
mcadenhead@dallasisd.org

Ria Galanos
Centennial High School
galanos@fultonshools.org

International Liaison

Catherine Lang
Swinburne University of Technology
clang@swin.edu.au

Local Arrangements

Jody Paul
Metropolitan State College of Denver
jody@acm.org

Student Research Competition

Ann Sobel
Miami University (Ohio)
sobelae@muohio.edu

Association for Computing Machinery
Advancing Computing as a Science & Profession

SIGCSE
ACM Special Interest Group on Computer Science Education

Recipients of the SIGCSE Award for Outstanding Contributions to Computer Science Education

1981 **William F. Atchison**, *University of Maryland*

1982 **Alan Perlis**, *Yale University*

1983 **Karl V. Karlstrom**, *Prentice-Hall*

1985 **Elliot I. Organick**, *University of Utah*

1986 **Donald Knuth**, *Stanford University*

1987 **Niklaus Wirth**, *ETH, Zurich*

1988 **Grace Murray Hopper**, *Rear Admiral, USN, Digital Equipment Corp.*

1989 **Edsger W. Dijkstra**, *The University of Texas at Austin*

1990 **Curriculum '68 Committee**:
William F. Atchison, Samuel D. Conte, John Hamblen, Thomas E. Hull, Thomas A. Keenan, William B. Kehl, Edward J. McClusey, Silvio O. Navarro, Werner Rheinboldt, Earl J. Schweppe, William Viavant, David M. Young, Jr.

1991 **David Gries**, *Cornell University*

1992 **Daniel D. McCraken**, *City College, City University of New York*

1993 **Alan C. Kay**, *Apple Computer*

1994 **Norman E. Gibbs**, *Software Engineering Institute*

1995 **Robert M. Aiken**, *Temple University*

1996 **Nell B. Dale**, *The University of Texas at Austin*

1997 **Andrew Tannenbaum**, *Vrije University*

1998 **William A. Wulf**, *University of Virginia and National Academy of Engineering*

1999 **Peter J. Denning**, *George Mason University*

2000 **Andries Van Dam**, *Brown University*

2001 **Allen B. Tucker**, *Bowdoin College*

2002 **Elliot Soloway**, *University of Michigan*

2003 **Eric Roberts**, *Stanford University*

2004 **Mordechai Ben-Ari**, *Weizmann Institute of Science*

2005 **Kim Bruce**, *Williams College*

2006 **Richard Pattis**, *Carnegie Mellon University*

2007 **Judith Gal-Ezer,** *Open University of Israel* and **John Hughes**, *University of Technology, Sydney*

2008 **Randy Pausch,** *Carnegie Mellon University*

2009 **Elliot B. Koffman,** *Temple University*

2010 **Sally Fincher,** *University of Kent, Canterbury*

2011 **Matthias Felleisen,** *Northeastern University*

2012 **Harold (Hal) Abelson,** *Massachusetts Institute of Technology*

Recipients of the SIGCSE Lifetime Service Award

1997 **Richard Austing**, *University of Maryland*
1998 **Della Bonnette**, *University of Southwestern Louisiana*
1999 **Robert Aiken**, *Temple University*
2000 **James E. Miller**, *University of Southern Mississippi*
2001 **Lillian N. (Boots) Cassel**, *Villanova University*
2002 **Joe Turner**, *Clemson University and Zayed University*
2003 **Harriet Taylor**, *National Science Foundation and Louisiana State University*
2004 **Bruce Klein**, *Grand Valley State University*
2005 **Andrew McGettrick**, *University of Strathclyde*
2006 **Joyce Currie Little**, *Towson State University*
2007 **John Impagliazzo**, *Hofstra University*
2008 **Dennis Frailey**, *Raytheon Corporation*
2009 **Michael J. Clancy**, *University of California, Berkeley*
2010 **Peter Denning**, *Naval Postgraduate School*
2011 **Gordon Davies**, *Open University*
2012 **Jane Prey**, *Microsoft Research*

SIGCSE 2012 Reviewers

Safurah Abdul Jalil, *University of Auckland*
Adel Abunawass, *University of West Georgia*
Ernest Ackermann, *University of Mary Washington*
Donald Acton, *University of British Columbia*
Raman Adaikkalavan, *Indiana University South Bend*
Victor Adamchik, *Carnegie Mellon University*
Elizabeth S. Adams, *James Madison University*
Joel Adams, *Calvin College*
Robert Adams, *Grand Valley State University*
Paul Addison, *Ivy Tech Community College*
Rajeev Agrawal, *North Carolina A & T State University*
Shakil Akhtar, *Clayton State University*
Paul Albee, *Central Michigan University*
Richard Allen, *St. Olaf College*
Vicki Almstrum, *University of Texas at Austin*
Hana Alnuaim, *King Abdulaziz University*
Carl Alphonce, *University at Buffalo, The State University of New York*
Jamal Alsabbagh, *Grand Valley State University*
Christine Alvarado, *Harvey Mudd College*
Peter Anderson, *Rochester Institute of Technolgy*
Ruth Anderson, *University of Washington*
Peter Andreae, *Victoria University of Wellington*
Stefan Andrei, *Lamar University*
Danner Andrew, *Swarthmore College*
Peter Andrews, *Eastern Illinois University*
Steven K. Andrianoff, *St. Bonaventure University*
Karen Anewalt, *University of Mary Washington*
Barbara Anthony, *Southwestern University*
Florence Appel, *Saint Xavier University*
Antonio Araujo, *Universidade do Porto*
Michal Armoni, *Weizmann Institute of Science*
Tom Armstrong, *Wheaton College*
David Arnow, *Brooklyn College*
Charles Ashbacher, *Charles Ashbacher Technologies*
John Avitabile, *College of Saint Rose*
John Aycock, *University of Calgary*
Pavel Azalov, *Penn State*
Isabel Azevedo, *ISEP*
Serhat Azgur, *Bilkent University*
Dinabandhu Bag, *National Institute of Technology*
Mark Bailey, *Hamilton College*
Laura Baker, *St. Edward's University*
Doug Baldwin, *SUNY Geneseo*
Catherine Bareiss, *Olivet Nazarene University*
Ian Barland, *Radford University*
David Barnes, *University of Kent*
Tiffany Barnes, *University of North Carolina at Charlotte*
Lewis Barnett, *University of Richmond*
N. Dwight Barnette, *Virginia Tech*
John Barr, *Ithaca College*
Valerie Barr, *Union College*
Martin Barrett, *East Tennessee State University*
Joao Barros, *Instituto Politecnico de Beja - ESTIG*
Phillip Barry, *University of Minnesota*
Carlos Barto, *Universidad Nacional de Cordoba*
Rebecca Bates, *Minnesota State University Mankato*
Michael Bauer, *University of Hawaii - Leeward Community College*
Robert Beck, *Villanova University*
Byron Weber Becker, *University of Waterloo*
Andrew Begel, *Microsoft Research*
John Beidler, *Univ. of Scranton*
Tim Bell, *University of Canterbury*
Mordechai Ben-Ari, *Weizmann Institute of Science*
Jens Bennedsen, *Aarhus School of Engineering*
Chris Bennett, *University of Maine Farmington*
Seth Bergmann, *Rowan University*
Mikael Berndtsson, *University of Skovde*
Gian Mario Besana, *CTI DePaul University*
Anne Beug, *California Polytechnic State University*
Ivona Bezakova, *Rochester Institute of Technology*
Marie Bienkowski, *SRI International*
William Birmingham, *Grove City College*
Judith M Bishop, *Microsoft Research*
M. Brian Blake, *University of Notre Dame*
Stephen Bloch, *Adelphi University*
Michael Blumenstein, *Griffith University*
Steven Bogaerts, *Wittenberg University*
Esmail Bonakdarian, *Franklin University*
William Booth, *Baylor University*
James Bowring, *College of Charleston*
Stefan Brandle, *Taylor University*
Evelyn Brannock, *Georgia Gwinnett College*
Anna Bretscher, *University of Toronto at Scarborough*
Monica Brockmeyer, *Wayne State University*
Renee Bryce, *Utah State University*
Dennis Brylow, *Marquette University*
Joel Brynielsson, *Royal Institute of Technology*
Suzanne Buchele, *Southwestern University*
Duane Buck, *Otterbein University*
Everett Bull, *Pomona College*
David Bunde, *Knox College*
Barry Burd, *Drew University*
Darci Burdge, *Nassau Community College*
Kevin Burger, *Arizona State University*
Ben Burrell, *Randolph-Macon College*
Vicky Bush, *University of Gloucestershire*
Mary Elaine Califf, *Illinois State University*
Andre Paul Calitz, *Nelson Mandela Metropolitan University*
Johan Calu, *KHBO*
Tracy Camp, *Colorado School of Mines*
Daniel Canas, *Wake Forest University*
Roxanne Canosa, *Rochester Institute of Technology*
Angela Carbone, *Monash University*
James Caristi, *Valparaiso University*
Andrew Carle, *University of California, Berkeley*
Martin Carlisle, *US Air Force Academy*
Janet Carter, *University of Kent at Canterbury*
Lori Carter, *Point Loma Nazarene University*
Jeffrey Carver, *University of Alabama*
Lori Case, *University of Waterloo*
Steven Case, *University of the Virgin Islands*
Lillian N. Cassel, *Villanova University*
Sheila Castaneda, *Clarke University*
Tim Chamillard, *University of Colorado at Colorado Springs*
Albert Chan, *Fayetteville State University*
Maiga Chang, *Athabasca University*

Mahesh Chaudhari, *Arizona State University*

Ranjan Chaudhuri, *Eastern Michigan University*

Tom Cheatham, *Middle Tennessee State Univ.*

Jimmy Chen, *Salt Lake Community College*

Peng-Wen Chen, *Oriental Institute of Technology*

Ping Chen, *University of Houston-Downtown*

Robert Chen, *Framingham State University*

Tzu-Yi Chen, *Pomona College*

Wei Kian Chen, *Champlain Cpllege*

Li-hsiang Cheo, *William Paterson University of New Jersey*

Chia-Chu Chiang, *University of Arkansas at Little Rock*

Donald Chinn, *University of Washington, Tacoma*

Jayan Kurian Chirayath, *Royal Melbourne Institute of Technology*

David Chiu, *Washington State University, Vancouver*

Radhouane Chouchane, *Columbus State University*

James Church, *University of Mississippi*

Vincent Cicirello, *Richard Stockton College*

John Cigas, *Park University*

Dawn Cizmar, *University of Texas at Austin (retired)*

Michael Clancy, *University of California, Berkeley*

Peter Clarke, *Florida International University*

Tony Clear, *Auckland University of Technology*

Daniel Cliburn, *University of the Pacific*

Joe Clifton, *University of Wisconsin, Platteville*

Osvaldo Clua, *Universidad de Buenos Aires*

Marge Coahran, *Dickinson College*

Avi Cohen, *Ministry of Education*

james Cohoon, *University of Virginia*

Ben Coleman, *Moravian College*

Tim Comber, *Southern Cross University*

Randy Connolly, *Mount Royal University*

Phillip Conrad, *University of California, Santa Barbara*

Robert Cook, *Georgia Southern University*

Peter Cooper, *Sam Houston State University*

Stephen Cooper, *Stanford University*

jean f. coppola, *pace university*

David Cordes, *University of Alabama*

Jose L. Cordova, *University of Louisiana at Monroe*

Thomas Cortina, *Carnegie Mellon University*

Monica Costa, *IPCB*

Mary Courtney, *Pace University*

Annemieke Craig, *Deakin University*

Michelle Craig, *University of Toronto*

Al Cripps, *Middle Tennessee State Univ.*

James Cross, *Auburn University*

Joyce Blair Crowell, *Belmont University*

Diana Cukierman, *Simon Fraser University*

Jose Cunha, *New University of Lisbon*

Steve Cunningham, *Brown Cunningham Associates*

Edwin P. Curran, *University of Ulster*

Pamela Cutter, *Kalamazoo College*

Quintin Cutts, *University of Glasgow*

Mohammad Dadfar, *Bowling Green State University*

Lucia K Dale, *Sewanee*

Nell Dale, *University of Texas at Austin, retired*

Andrew Dalton, *Western Carolina University*

Mats Daniels, *Uppsala University*

Douglas Dankel, *University of Florida*

Lawrence D'Antonio, *Ramapo College of New Jersey*

Andrea Danyluk, *Williams College*

Stephen Davies, *University of Mary Washington*

Janet Davis, *Grinnell College*

Renzo Davoli, *University of Bologna*

Susan Dean, *UMUC - Europe*

Hannah Mary Dee, *Grenoble Institute of Technology*

Katherine Deibel, *University of Washington-Seattle*

Stavros Demetriadis, *Aristotle University of Thessaloniki*

Peter DePasquale, *The College of New Jersey*

Molisa Derk, *Dickinson State University*

Yogesh Deshpande, *University of Western Sydney*

Lucia Dettori, *DePaul University*

Kamyar Dezhgosha, *University of Illinois at Springfield*

Martin Dick, *RMIT University*

Suzanne W. Dietrich, *Arizona State University*

Wei Ding, *University of Massachusetts-Boston*

Adair Dingle, *Seattle University*

William Doane, *Bennington College*

Zachary Dodds, *Harvey Mudd College*

Aijuan Dong, *Hood College*

John Dooley, *Knox College*

Brian Dorn, *University of Hartford*

John Dougherty, *Haverford College*

Maureen Doyle, *Northern Kentucky University*

Peter Drexel, *Plymouth State University*

John Duncan, *Indiana University*

James Early, *SUNY Oswego*

J. Philip East, *University of Northern Iowa*

Jeffrey Edgington, *University of Denver*

Stephen Edwards, *Virginia Tech*

Mary Anne Egan, *Siena College*

Roger Eggen, *University of North Florida*

Kurt Eiselt, *University of British Columbia*

Joseph Ekstrom, *Brigham Young University*

Hala ElAarag, *Stetson University*

Ahmed El-Deeb, *Nile University*

Heidi J. C. Ellis, *Western New England College*

Stephanie Elzer, *Millersville University*

Richard Enbody, *Michigan State University*

Alec Engebretson, *Doane College*

Gerald Engel, *University of Connecticut, Stamford*

Ed C. Epp, *Intel Corp.*

Barbara Ericson, *Georgia Tech*

Daniel Ernst, *Cray, Inc.*

John Estell, *Ohio Northern University*

Yadran Eterovic, *Pontificia Universidad Catolica de Chile*

Henry Etlinger, *Rochester Institute of Technology*

Barry Fagin, *US Air Force Academy*

Daisy Fan, *Cornell University*

Homma Farian, *SUNY Geneseo*

David Farrell, *Glasgow Caledonian University*

Dave Feinberg, *The Wellington School*

Alan Fekete, *University of Sydney*

Maria Feldgen, *Universidad de Buenos Aires*

Ernest Ferguson, *Northwest Missouri State University*

Roger Ferguson, *Grand Valley State University*

Francesc J. Ferri, *Universitat de Valencia*

Georgios Fesakis, *University of the Aegean*

Ronald Finkbine, *Indiana University Southeast*

Sue Fitzgerald, *Metropolitan State University*

Robin Flatland, *Siena College*

Samantha Foley, *Oak Ridge National Laboratory*
Jeffrey Forbes, *Duke University*
Timothy Fossum, *SUNY College at Potsdam*
Kent Foster, *Winthrop University*
Edward Fox, *Virginia Tech*
Susan Fox, *Macalester College*
Charles Frank, *Northern Kentucky University*
Robert Franks, *Central College*
Karen Fraser, *University of Ulster*
Andre Freire, *University of York*
Bill Freitas, *The Lawrenceville School*
Frank Friedman, *Temple University*
Ines Friss de Kereki, *ORT Uruguay University*
S. Jane Fritz, *St. Joseph's College*
Daniel Frost, *University of California, Irvine*
Mohammad Fuad, *Winston-Salem State University*
Kenneth Funk, *Kirkwood Community College*
Jacob Furst, *DePaul University*
Galal Galal-Edeen, *Cairo University*
Angel Garcia-Beltran, *Universidad Politecnica de Madrid*
Charlie Garrod, *Swarthmore College*
Alessio Gaspar, *University of South Florida Polytechnic*
Dick Gayler, *Kennesaw State University*
Rick Gee, *Okanagan College*
Edward Gehringer, *North Carolina State University*
Joe Geigel, *Rochester Institute of Technolgy*
Edward M. Gellenbeck, *Central Washington University*
Jill Gerhardt, *Richard Stockton College of New Jersey*
Adrian German, *Indiana University*
Judith Gersting, *Indiana University Purdue & University at Indianapolis*
Paul Gestwicki, *Ball State University*
Lila Ghemri, *Texas Southern University*
J Paul Gibson, *T&M Sud Paris*
Mark Goadrich, *Centenary College of Louisiana*
Don Goelman, *Villanova University*
Sherri Goings, *Carleton College*
Michael Goldwasser, *Saint Louis University*
Michael Goldweber, *Xavier University*
Evan Golub, *University of Maryland*
Mercedes Gomez-Albarran, *Dep. Ingenieria del Software e Inteligencia Artificial*
Marco Antonio Gomez-Martin, *Universidad Complutense de Madrid*
Pedro Pablo Gomez-Martin, *Universidad Complutense de Madrid*
Aaron Gordon, *Metropolitan State College of Denver*
Peter Gorny, *University of Oldenburg*
Jean Goulet, *Universite de Sherbrooke*
Michael Gousie, *Wheaton College (MA)*
Mary Granger, *George Washington University*
Cary Gray, *Wheaton College*
Larry Griffith, *Westfield State University*
Scott Grissom, *Grand Valley State University*
Paul Gross, *Washington University in St. Louis*
Andrew Grover, *Thiel College*
Mario Guimaraes, *Zayed University*
Jiang Guo, *California State University, Los Angeles*
Mark Guzdial, *Georgia Institute of Technology*
Bruria Haberman, *Holon Institute of Technology & The Weizmann Institute of Science*
Max Hailperin, *Gustavus Adolphus College*
Susan Haller, *SUNY Potsdam*
Ranette Halverson, *Midwestern State University*
John Hamer, *University of Auckland*
Nadeem Hamid, *Berry College*
Brian Hanks, *BFH Educational Consulting*
Stuart Hansen, *University of Wisconsin - Parkside*
Mindy Hart, *Purdue University*
Thanos Hatziapostolou, *CITY College - University of Sheffield*
Jessen Havill, *Denison University*
Christopher Haynes, *Indiana University*
Orit Hazzan, *Technion -- Israel Institute of Technology*
Sarah Heckman, *North Carolina State University*
Phillip Heeler, *Northwest Missouri State University*
Cecily Heiner, *Southern Utah University*
James Heliotis, *RIT*
Keith Hellman, *Colorado School of Mines*
Michael Helmick, *Google*
David Hemmendinger, *Union College*
Dean Hendrix, *Auburn University*
Tyson Henry, *California State University, Chico*
Katherine Herbert, *Montclair State University*
Matthew Hertz, *Canisius College*
Jose R. Hilera, *University of Alcala*
Curtis Hill, *Valley City State University*
Rachelle Kristof Hippler, *Bowling Green State University*
Gregory Hislop, *Drexel University*
William Hochstettler, *Franklin*
Mark A. Holliday, *Western Carolina University*
Joe Hollingsworth, *Indiana University*
Christopher Homan, *Rochester Institute of Technology*
William Hooper, *Belmont University*
Charles Hoot, *Oklahoma City University*
Cay Horstmann, *San Jose State University*
Hoda Hosny, *The American University in Cairo*
Mahmood Hossain, *Fairmont State University*
Shahadat Hossain, *University of Lethbridge*
Dwight House, *Fayetteville State University*
David Hovemeyer, *York College of Pennsylvania*
Brian Howard, *DePauw University*
James Howatt, *Luther College*
Trudy Howles, *Rochester Institute of Technology*
Michelle Hribar, *OHSU*
Wen-Jung Hsin, *Park University*
Chenglie Hu, *Carroll University*
Meriel Huggard, *Trinity College, Dublin*
James Huggins, *Kettering University*
Janet Hughes, *University of Dundee*
Richard Hull, *Lenoir-Rhyne University*
Dalton Hunkins, *St. Bonaventure University*
Frances Hunt, *Educational Testing Service*
Kenny Hunt, *University of Wisconsin - La Crosse*
Michelle Hutton, *Stanford University*
Deborah Hwang, *University of Evansville*
Jorge Eduardo Ibarra-Esquer, *Universidad Autonoma de Baja California*
Lubomir Ivanov, *Iona College*
Sridhar Iyer, *Indian Institute of Technology, Bombay*
Clemente Izurieta, *Montana State University*
Letizia Jaccheri, *Norwegian University of Science and Technology*
Jana Jackova, *Slovak University of Technology in Bratislava*
Matthew Jadud, *Allegheny College*

Mark Jaeger, *Baker College*
David Janzen, *California Polytechnic State University, San Luis Obispo*
Ciera Jaspan, *Carnegie Mellon University*
Giti Javidi, *Virginia State University*
Jam Jenkins, *Valdosta State University*
Mike Jipping, *Hope College*
David John, *Wake Forest University*
Chris Johnson, *University of Wisconsin, Eau Claire*
Colin Johnson, *University of Kent at Canterbury*
Julie Johnson, *Vanderbilt University*
Edward Jones, *Florida A&M University*
Anthony Joseph, *Pace University*
Mike Joy, *University of Warwick*
Daniel Joyce, *Villanova University*
Maria Jump, *King's College*
Edward Jung, *Southern Polytechnic State University*
Alan Kaminsky, *Rochester Institute of Technology*
Pankaj Kamthan, *Concordia University*
Debbie Kaneko, *Old Dominion University*
Ville Karavirta, *Aalto University*
Elizabeth Katz, *Millersville University*
David Kauchak, *Middlebury College*
David G. Kay, *University of California, Irvine*
Jennifer Kay, *Rowan University*
Judy Kay, *University of Sydney*
Fereydoun Kazemian, *Rochester Institute of Technology*
Petros Kefalas, *University of Sheffield*
Charles Kelemen, *Swarthmore College*
Thomas Kelliher, *Goucher College*
Andreas Kerren, *Linnaeus University*
Mark Kerstetter, *Western Michigan University*
Arshia Khan, *The College of St. Scholastica*
Sami Khuri, *San Jose State University*
Nancy Kinnersley, *University of Kansas*
David Klappholz, *Stevens Institute of Technology*
Myungsook Klassen, *California Lutheran University*
Frank Klassner, *Villanova University*
Carsten Kleiner, *University of Applied Sciences & Arts Hannover*
Jane Kochanov, *Pennsylvania State University - Capital College*
James Kolasa, *Bluegrass Community and Technical College*
Michael Kolling, *University of Kent*
April Kontostathis, *Ursinus College*
Yana Kortsarts, *Widener University, Chester*
David Kosbie, *Carnegie Mellon University*
Janet Kourik, *Webster University*
Nicholas Kraft, *The University of Alabama*
Joan Krone, *Denison University*
Jan Kruger, *Unisa School for BusinessLeadership*
Marja Kuittinen, *University of Joensuu*
Amruth Kumar, *Ramapo College of New Jersey*
Deepak Kumar, *Bryn Mawr College*
Durgesh Kumar, *DRDO*
Benjamin Kuperman, *Oberlin College*
Stan Kurkovsky, *Central Connecticut State University*
Zachary Kurmas, *Grand Valley State University*
Clif Kussmaul, *Muhlenberg College*
Lynn Lambert, *Christopher Newport University*
H. Chad Lane, *University of Southern California*
Catherine Lang, *Swinburne University of Technology*
Matthew Lang, *Moravian College*
Joan Langdon, *Bowie State University*
Yedidyah Langsam, *Brooklyn College of CUNY*
Mick Lantis, *Purdue University North Central*
David Largent, *Ball State University*
brian larkins, *Coastal Carolina University*
Eric Larson, *Seattle University*
Mary Last, *self-employed*
Robert Law, *Glasgow Caledonian University*
Deirdre Lawless, *Dublin Institute of Technology*
Barry Lawson, *University of Richmond*
Lucas Layman, *Fraunhofer USA*
Alina Lazar, *Youngstown State University*
Christopher League, *Long Island University*
Cathie LeBlanc, *Plymouth State College*
Mark LeBlanc, *Wheaton College*
Arthur Lee, *Claremont McKenna College*
Byong Lee, *Bennett College*
Cynthia Lee, *University of California, San Diego*
Gilliean Lee, *Lander University*
Chi Un Lei, *University of Hong Kong*
David Levine, *St. Bonaventure University*
Anany Levitin, *Villanova University*
Gary Lewandowski, *Xavier University*
John Lewis, *Virginia Tech*
Weidong Liao, *Shepherd University*
Billy Lim, *Illinois State University*
Janne Lindqvist, *Carnegie Mellon University*
Panagiotis Linos, *Butler University*
Jiang-Jiang Liu, *Lamar University*
Jigang Liu, *Metropolitan State University*
Peter Liu, *Seneca College*
William S. Lloyd, *University of West Georgia*
Kate Lockwood, *California State University, Monterey Bay*
Sergio F. Lopes, *University of Minho*
Salvador López-Mendoza, *Universidad Nacional Autónoma de México*
Chris Lueer, *Amazon.com*
Andrew Luxton-Reilly, *The University of Auckland*
William Lyle, *Murray State University*
Ian Macdonald, *Victoria University*
Bonnie MacKellar, *St John's University*
Peter Macpherson, *Rogers State University*
Joaquim Madeira, *University of Aveiro*
John S. Mallozzi, *Iona College*
Bill Manaris, *College of Charleston*
Ted Markowitz, *University of New Haven*
Mercedes Marques, *University Jaume I*
Fred Martin, *University of Massachusetts -- Lowell*
Kenneth Martin, *University of North Florida*
Manuel Martins Barata, *ISEL - Instituto Superior de Engenharia de Lisboa*
Dave Mason, *Ryerson University*
Bruce R. Maxim, *University of Michigan-Dearborn*
Bruce Maxwell, *Colby College*
Christopher Mayfield, *James Madison University*
Lester McCann, *The University of Arizona*
Robert McCloskey, *University of Scranton*
O. William McClung, *Nebraska Wesleyan University*
Jeffrey McConnell, *Canisius College*
Frank McCown, *Harding University*
W. Michael McCracken, *Georgia Institute of Technology*
Sean McCulloch, *Ohio Wesleyan University*
Chris McDonald, *The University of Western Australia*
Charlie McDowell, *University of California, Santa Cruz*
Scott McElfresh, *Wake Forest University*
James McGuffee, *St. Edward's University*

Hugh McGuire, *Grand Valley State University*

Tim McGuire, *Sam Houston State University*

Michael McMillan, *Pulaski Technical College*

Bonita McVey, *St. Norbert College*

Pedro Medeiros, *Universidade Nova de Lisboa*

Lisa Meeden, *Swarthmore College*

Gloria Melara, *California State University, Northridge*

Antonio Jose Mendes, *University of Coimbra*

Susan Mengel, *Texas Tech University*

Suzanne Menzel, *Indiana University*

Joseph Mertz, *Carnegie Mellon University*

Panagiotis Metaxas, *Wellesley College*

Jose Carlos Metrolho, *Polytechnic Institute of Castelo Branco*

Timothy Meyer, *Edinboro University of Pennsylvania*

Mark Meysenburg, *Doane College*

Lisa Michaud, *Merrimack College*

Gail Miles, *Lenoir-Rhyne College*

Bradley Miller, *Luther College*

James Miller, *Bradley University*

James Miller, *University of Alberta*

Keith Miller, *University of Illinois at Springfield*

Afsaneh Minaie, *Utah valley University*

Joe Miro, *Universitat de les Illes Balears*

Susan Mitchell, *University of Maryland, Baltimore County*

Roland Mittermeir, *Universität Klagenfurt*

Sriram Mohan, *Rose-Hulman Institute of Technology*

William Mongan, *Drexel University*

Sara Miner More, *McDaniel College*

Nelma Moreira, *University of Porto*

Patricia Morreale, *Kean University*

Briana Morrison, *Southern Polytechnic State University*

Srikanth Mudigonda, *Saint Louis University*

Laurie Murphy, *Pacific Lutheran University*

Michael Murphy, *Concordia University Texas*

Keitha Murray, *Iona College*

William Myers, *Belmont Abbey College*

Kristine Nagel, *Georgia Gwinnett College*

Mario Nakazawa, *Berea College*

Nannette Napier, *Georgia Gwinnett College*

Tom Naps, *University of Wisconsin - Oshkosh*

Krish Narayanan, *Eastern Michigan University*

Pavol Navrat, *Slovak University of Technology*

Rance Necaise, *College of William and Mary*

Robert Neufeld, *McPherson College - Emeritus*

Tia Newhall, *Swarthmore College*

Lijun Ni, *Georgia Institute of Technology*

Jaime Nino, *Univ. of New Orleans*

Robert Noonan, *College of William and Mary*

Cindy Norris, *Appalachian State University*

Linda Null, *Penn State University*

William Oblitey, *Indiana University of Pennsylvania*

Rainer Oechsle, *University of Applied Sciences, Trier*

Keith O'Hara, *Bard College*

Chris Okasaki, *USMA*

Edward Okie, *Radford University*

Amos Olagunju, *St. Cloud State University*

Joseph Oldham, *Centre College*

Nina Onesti, *Indiana University*

Lawrence Osborne, *Lamar University*

Youwen Ouyang, *California State University at San Marcos*

Barbara Owens, *Southwestern University*

Jill Pala, *Girls Preparatory School*

Greta Pangborn, *Saint Michael's College*

Iraklis Paraskakis, *University of Sheffield*

Abelardo Pardo, *Carlos III University of Madrid*

Crist'obal Pareja-Flores, *Universidad Complutense de Madrid*

Young Park, *Bradley University*

Brenda C. Parker, *Middle Tennessee State University*

David Parker, *Salisbury University*

Jeff Parker, *Harvard Extension*

Rembert Parker, *Anderson University*

James Paterson, *Glasgow Caledonian University*

Elizabeth Patitsas, *University of Toronto*

Laurie Patterson, *University of North Carolina Wilmington*

Richard E. Pattis, *University of California, Irvine*

Jody Paul, *MSCD*

Thaddeus Pawlicki, *University of Rochester*

Arnold Pears, *Uppsala University*

Ramanee Peiris, *University of Dundee*

Eileen Peluso, *Lycoming College*

Bin Peng, *Southwestern College*

Manuel A. Perez-Quinones, *Virginia Tech*

Teresa Peterman, *Grand Valley State University*

Andrew Petersen, *University of Toronto Mississauga*

John Peterson, *Western State College*

Noel Petit, *Augsburg College*

Chrisila C. Pettey, *Middle Tennessee State University*

Charles Pheatt, *Emporia State University*

Vreda Pieterse, *University of Pretoria*

Nelishia Pillay, *University of KwaZulu-Natal*

Francois Pitt, *University of Toronto*

Tony Pittarese, *East Tennessee State University*

Paul Piwowarski, *University of Kentucky*

Chris Plaue, *The University of Georgia*

Shannon Pollard, *Elon University*

Lori Pollock, *University of Delaware*

Wayne Pollock, *Hillsborough Community College*

Irene Polycarpou, *Colorado School of Mines*

Elvira Popescu, *University of Craiova*

Jeffrey Popyack, *Drexel University*

Lori Postner, *Nassau Community College*

George J. Pothering, *College of Charleston*

Annu Prabhakar, *University of Cincinnati*

Jon Preston, *Southern Polytechnic State Unviersity*

Roger Priebe, *Texas State University - San Marcos*

Philip Prins, *Seattle Pacific University*

William Pugh, *Univ. of Maryland*

Sarah Monisha Pulimood, *The College of New Jersey*

Semmy Purewal, *University of North Carolina at Asheville*

John Rabung, *Randolph-Macon College*

Cyndi Rader, *Colorado School of Mines*

John Rager, *Amherst College*

Imad Rahal, *College of Saint Benedict & Saint John's University*

Rajendra Raj, *Rochester Institute of Technology*

Muthu Ramachandran, *Leeds Metropolitan University*

Bina Ramamurthy, *University at Buffalo, SUNY*

Saquib Razak, *Carnegie Mellon University*

Eliseo Reategui, *Universidade Federal do Rio Grande do Sul*

Samuel Rebelsky, *Grinnell College*

Michael Redmond, *La Salle University*

David Reed, *Creighton University*

Donna Reese, *Mississippi State University*
Susan Reiser, *UNC Asheville*
Dan Resler, *Virginia Commonwealth University*
Eugene K. Ressler, *United States Military Academy*
Loren Rhodes, *Juniata College*
Catherine Ricardo, *Iona College*
Michael Rieck, *Drake University*
Charles Riedesel, *University of Nebraska - Lincoln*
Suzanne Rivoire, *Sonoma State University*
Steven Robbins, *University of Texas at San Antonio*
Christian Roberson, *Plymouth State University*
Eric Roberts, *Stanford University*
Stefan Robila, *Montclair State University*
Susan H. Rodger, *Duke University*
Ken Rodham, *Brigham Young University*
Guido Roessling, *Technische Universitaet Darmstadt*
Sami Rollins, *University of San Francisco*
Joel Ross, *University of California, Irvine*
John Ross, *Indiana University Kokomo*
Jerry Roth, *Vanderbilt University*
Krishnendu Roy, *Valdosta State University*
Martin Ruckert, *Munich University of Applied Sciences*
Anthony Ruocco, *Roger Williams University*
Paulo Rupino da Cunha, *University of Coimbra*
Adrian Rusu, *Rowan University*
Amalia Rusu, *Fairfield University*
Rebecca Rutherfoord, *Southern Polytechnic State University*
Mihaela Sabin, *University of New Hampshire*
Roberta Evans Sabin, *Loyola College*
Shazia Sadiq, *The University of Queensland*
Mehran Sahami, *Stanford University*
Samuel Sambasivam, *Azusa Pacific University*
Ian Sanders, *University of the Witwatersrand*
William Sanders, *University of Hartford*
Pete Sanderson, *Otterbein University*
André Santos, *Lisbon University Institute*
Vijayalakshmi Saravanan, *Ryerson University , Canada & VIT University*
Amit Sawant, *NetApp*
Suzanne Schaefer, *University of California, Los Angeles*
christelle scharff, *Pace University*
Stephen Schaub, *Bob Jones University*
Walter Schilling, *Milwaukee School of Engineering*
Diane Schwartz, *California State University Northridge*
leslie schwartzman, *UIS*
Dino Schweitzer, *United States Air Force Academy*
Otto Seppälä, *Aalto University*
Amber Settle, *DePaul University*
Behrooz Seyed-Abbassi, *University of North Florida*
Cliff Shaffer, *Virginia Tech*
Victor R.L. Shen, *National Taipei University*
Ching-Kuang Shene, *Michigan Technological University*
Mark Sherriff, *University of Virginia*
Sen Shilad, *Macalester College*
Yasuto Shirai, *Shizuoka University*
Keith Shomper, *Cedarville University*
charles shub, *University of Colorado at Colorado Springs*
Scott Sigman, *Drury University*
Gavin Sim, *Uni of Central Lancashire*
Maria Simi, *Universita di Pisa*
Beth Simon, *University of California, San Diego*
Oberta Slotterbeck, *Hiram College*
William Slough, *Eastern Illinois University*
Joslyn Smith, *Florida International University*
Peter Smith, *California State University - Channel Islands*
Robert Snapp, *University of Vermont*
Peter Sommerlad, *HSR Rapperswil*
Joel Sommers, *Colgate University*
Raja Sooriamurthi, *Carnegie Mellon University*
Jonathan Sorenson, *Butler University*
Barry Soroka, *Cal Poly Pomona*
Jaime Spacco, *Knox College*
Greg Speegle, *Baylor University*
David Spooner, *Rensselaer Polytechnic Institute*
Carol Spradling, *Northwest Missouri State University*
Nathan Sprague, *James Madison University*
Denbigh Starkey, *Montana State University*
Mark Stehlik, *Carnegie Mellon University*
Josh Steinhurst, *Bucknell University*
Ben Stephenson, *University of Calgary*
Daniel Stevenson, *University of Wisconsin - Eau Claire*
Khadija Stewart, *DePauw University*
Evelyn Stiller, *Plymouth State University*
Vojislav Stojkovic, *Morgan State University*
Christopher Stone, *Harvey Mudd College*
Jeffrey Stone, *Pennsylvania State University*
Forrest Stonedahl, *Centre College*
Fred Strickland, *South University*
Kristina Striegnitz, *Union College*
Catherine Stringfellow, *Midwestern State University*
Lena Stromback, *Department of Computer and Information Science*
Deborah Sturm, *College of Staten Island CUNY*
Dario Suarez Gracia, *Universidad de Zaragoza*
Jose Such, *Technical University of Valencia*
Leigh Ann Sudol, *Carnegie Mellon University*
John R. Sullins, *Youngstown State University*
Fred Sullivan, *Wilkes University*
Wayne Summers, *Columbus State University*
Valerie Summet, *Emory University*
Weiqing Sun, *University of Toledo*
Ken Surendran, *Southeast Missouri State University*
Jerry Talton, *Stanford University*
Joo Tan, *Kutztown University*
Stewart Tansley, *Microsoft Research*
Blair Taylor, *Towson University*
James Teresco, *Siena College*
Allison Elliott Tew, *Georgia Institute of Technology*
William Thacker, *Winthrop University*
Lynda Thomas, *Aberystwyth University*
Megan Thomas, *California State University Stanislaus*
Rebecca Thomas, *Bard College*
Stan Thomas, *Wake Forest University*
Alfred Thompson, *Microsoft*
Jodi Tims, *Baldwin-Wallace College*
Fergus Toolan, *University College Dublin*
Gloria Childress Townsend, *DePauw University*
Christian Trefftz, *Grand Valley State University*
Deborah Trytten, *University of Oklahoma*
Shengru Tu, *University of New Orleans*
David S. Tucker, *Midwestern State Univ.*
William Turner, *Wabash College*
Sharon M. Tuttle, *Humboldt State University*
Hakan Tuzun, *Hacettepe University*

Suleyman Uludag, *The University of Michigan - Flint*
Susan D. Urban, *Texas Tech University*
Timothy Urness, *Drake University*
Jaime Urquiza-Fuentes, *Rey Juan Carlos University*
Ian Utting, *University of Kent at Canterbury*
Jan Vahrenhold, *Technische Universität Dortmund*
Ignatios Vakalis, *California Polytechnic and State University*
David Valentine, *Slippery Rock University*
James Vallino, *Rochester Institute of Technology*
Robert Van Camp, *Marietta College*
Tammy Van De Grift, *University of Portland*
Ian van der Linde, *Anglia Ruskin University*
Brad Vander Zanden, *University of Tennessee*
Asaf Varol, *Wilkes University*
Yaakov Varol, *University of Nevada Reno*
Jorge Vasconcelos, *Johns Hopkins University*
Troy Vasiga, *University of Waterloo*
Kam Vat, *University of Macau*
Steven Vegdahl, *University of Portland*
Nanette Veilleux, *Simmons College*
J. Angel Velazquez-Iturbide, *Universidad Rey Juan Carlos*
Gabriela Vilanova, *National Patagonia Austral University*
Tamar Vilner, *The Open University of Israel*
Kimberly Voll, *University of British Columbia*
Ken Vollmar, *Missouri State University*
David Voorhees, *Le Moyne College*
Rosita Wachenchauzer, *Universidad de Buenos Aires*
Paul Wagner, *University of Wisconsin - Eau Claire*
Sally Wahba, *Clemson University*
Gursimran Walia, *North Dakota State University*
Ellen Walker, *Hiram College*
Henry Walker, *Grinnell College*
Xinli Wang, *Michigan Technological University*
Xueyi Wang, *Northwest Nazarene University*
Xusheng Wang, *Winthrop University*
Karen Ward, *University of Portland*
Stan Warford, *Pepperdine University*
Richard Wasniowski, *California State University Dominguez Hills*
Thomas Way, *Villanova University*
Scott Weiss, *Mt. St. Mary's University*
Stephen Weiss, *University of North Carolina at Chapel Hill*
Emily Wenk, *Penn State York*
Linda Werner, *University of California, Santa Cruz*
Roger West, *University of Illinois at Springfield*
Curt White, *DePaul University*
Elizabeth White, *George Mason University*
Laurie White, *Mercer University*
Howard Whitston, *University of South Alabama*
Paul Wiedemeier, *The University of Louisiana at Monroe*
Sheila Wiggins, *retired*
Linda Wilkens, *Providence College*
Judith Williams, *William Penn University*
Craig Wills, *Worcester Polytechnic Institute*
Linda Wilson, *Texas Lutheran University*
Michael Wirth, *University of Guelph*
Lee Wittenberg, *GW Software*
Walter Wolf, *Rochester Institute of Technology*
Christine Wolfe, *Ohio University*
Rosalee Wolfe, *DePaul University*
David Wolff, *Pacific Lutheran University*
Greg Wolffe, *Grand Valley State University*
Steven Wolfman, *University of British Columbia*
Ursula Wolz, *Olin College of Engineering*
Gary Wong, *The Community College at Lingnan University*
David Wonnacott, *Haverford College*
Karl Wurst, *Worcester State University*
Stelios Xinogalos, *University of Macedonia*
Dianna Xu, *Bryn Mawr College*
T. Andrew Yang, *University of Houston - Clear Lake*
Arthur Yanushka, *Christian Brothers University*
Ken Yasuhara, *University of Washington*
Dowming Yeh, *National Kaohsiung Normal University*
Juang Yih-Ruey, *Jinwen University of Science & Technology*
Duane Yoder, *University of West Georgia*
Alison Young, *Christchurch Polytechnic Institute of Technology*
Kwok-Bun Yue, *University of Houston-Clear Lake*
Timothy Yuen, *UTSA*
Marsha Zaidman, *University of Mary Washington*
Carol Zander, *University of Washington, Bothell*
Alan Zaring, *Ohio Wesleyan University*
Julie Zelenski, *Stanford University*
Dean Zeller, *Art Institute of Jacksonville*
Jinghua Zhang, *Winston-Salem State University*
Lynn Ziegler, *St. John's University*
Uta Ziegler, *Western Kentucky University*
Stephen Zilora, *Rochester Institute of Technology*
Guy Zimmerman, *Bowling Green State University*
Jill Zimmerman, *Goucher College*
Daniel Zingaro, *University of Toronto*
Fani Zlatarova, *Elizabethtown College*

Association for
Computing Machinery

Advancing Computing as a Science & Profession

The Association for Computing Machinery
2 Penn Plaza, Suite 701
New York, New York 10121-0701

Copyright © 2011 by the Association for Computing Machinery, Inc. (ACM). Permission to make digital or hard copies of portions of this work for personal or classroom use is granted without fee provided that copies are not made or distributed for profit or commercial advantage and that copies bear this notice and the full citation on the first page. Copyright for components of this work owned by others than ACM must be honored. Abstracting with credit is permitted. To copy otherwise, to republish, to post on servers or to redistribute to lists, requires prior specific permission and/or a fee. Request permission to republish from: Publications Dept., ACM, Inc. Fax +1 (212) 869-0481 or <permissions@acm.org>.

For other copying of articles that carry a code at the bottom of the first or last page, copying is permitted provided that the per-copy fee indicated in the code is paid through the Copyright Clearance Center, 222 Rosewood Drive, Danvers, MA 01923 (USA).

Notice to Past Authors of ACM-Published Articles
ACM intends to create a complete electronic archive of all articles and/or other material previously published by ACM. If you have written a work that has been previously published by ACM in any journal or conference proceedings prior to 1978, or any SIG Newsletter at any time, and you do NOT want this work to appear in the ACM Digital Library, please inform permissions@acm.org, stating the title of the work, the author(s), and where and when published.

ISBN: 978-1-4503-1098-7

Additional copies may be ordered prepaid from:

ACM Order Department
PO Box 30777
New York, NY 10087-0777, USA

Phone: 1-800-342-6626 (USA and Canada)
+1-212-626-0500 (Global)
Fax: +1-212-944-1318
E-mail: acmhelp@acm.org
Hours of Operation: 8:30 am – 4:30 pm ET

ACM Order Number: 457120

Printed in the USA

Message from the SIGCSE Chair

It is my pleasure to welcome you to the 43rd SIGCSE Technical Symposium on Computer Science Education (SIGCSE 2012). With a diverse technical program and over 1100 attendees from around the world, you are participating in the premiere technical conference on computer science education. I hope that you will find this event an opportunity to hear influential keynote addresses, to learn about new resources and pedagogy, to renew friendships, to meet future collaborators, and to have fun and learn a lot.

SIGCSE 2012 is sponsored by the ACM Special Interest Group on Computer Science Education (the SIGCSE organization). The SIGCSE organization consists of approximately 2600 members, whose interests in improving computer science education are probably similar to your own. Many of these members are also volunteers who carry out the various activities associated with the SIGCSE organization. Chief among the volunteers responsible for the SIGCSE 2012 symposium are Laurie Smith King and Dave Musicant, symposium co-chairs, who have worked for over two years on this conference. Laurie and Dave selected and steered a committee of 27 colleagues in organizing all aspects of this event. Included in the organizing committee are members, on whom we depend year in and year out, to handle conference registration (Lynn Degler, Cary Laxer, and Larry Merkle), to manage the conference database (John Dooley and Henry Walker) and to coordinate with exhibitors and sponsors (Susan Rodger). On behalf of the SIGCSE organization I thank all of the members of the committee for their countless contributions.

I also thank all of the conference supporters and exhibitors, who enhance this event by their presence. Without their participation, this conference would not be as memorable.

I encourage you, the reader, to consider becoming more involved in the SIGCSE community and the workings of the SIGCSE organization. I encourage you to attend in the annual SIGCSE Business meeting on Friday afternoon, from 5:10 to 5:55p.m., in room 302A. This is an opportunity to meet the members of the SIGCSE board: Daniel Joyce (vice chair), Doug Baldwin (treasurer), Susan Rodger (secretary) and at-large members Tiffany Barnes, Mark Guzdial and Amber Settle. Most importantly, it is an opportunity to learn more about how the organization works – a first step in becoming more involved.

Enjoy the conference!

Renée McCauley
College of Charleston
SIGCSE Chair, 2010-2013

Message from the Symposium and Program Chairs

Welcome to the proceedings of the 43rd ACM Technical Symposium on Computer Science Education, or SIGCSE 2012, where you will find the archival record of over one hundred papers as well as multiple other session formats that document the latest in computer science education: research, tool building, teaching, curriculum and philosophy. Reflecting our location in North Carolina's renowned *Research Triangle*, this year's conference features the three themes of "Teaching, Learning, and Collaborating" throughout the sessions. Teaching, learning, and collaborating occur inside and outside of the classroom, and among various combinations of students, academics, industry professionals, and others.

We are pleased to announce the winners of the two annual SIGCSE awards. Professor Harold (Hal) Abelson of Massachusetts Institute of Technology will receive the SIGCSE award for Outstanding Contribution to Computer Science Education, and will provide Friday's keynote address. Jane Prey of Microsoft Research will accept the SIGCSE Award for Lifetime Service to the Computer Science Education Community and speak at our First Timer's Lunch. In addition, we've invited speakers to deliver two more keynote presentations. Frederick P. Brooks, Jr., from University of North Carolina at Chapel Hill, will deliver Thursday's keynote address titled "*The Teacher's Job is to Design Learning Experiences; not Primarily to Impart Information.*" Fernanda Viégas and Martin Wattenberg from Google's "Big Picture" visualization group will jointly address Saturday's luncheon with "*Through the Looking Glass: Talking about the World with Visualization.*"

Symposium statistics are presented below. Many thanks to the authors, reviewers, and Program Committee members whose enormous and vital service generated this program. This year's program includes the usual wide selection of events, including the First-Timer's Lunch and Evening Reception on Thursday and the SIGCSE luncheon on Saturday. Our exhibit hall features a number of exhibitors showcasing the latest in hardware, software tools, textbooks and educational programs and research. We continue to offer accessibility at SIGCSE 2012 for the deaf and hard of hearing.

Proposal type	*Accepted*	*Received*	*Acceptance Rate*
Paper	100	289	35 %
Panel/Special Session	24	53	45 %
Workshop	36	78	46 %
Poster	48	109	44 %
Birds of a Feather	36	46	78 %

We are excited about the variety of pre-symposium events that we will be offering. As of the press deadline for this overview, meetings on the following topics will occur on Wednesday: Teaching Open Source, Career Mentoring, SIGCAS Open Meeting, Teaching Ethics in Computer Science, and Computing Accreditation. Near the end of the symposium on Saturday, top undergraduate and graduate students will present their work at the ACM SIGCSE Student Research Competition, managed by Ann Sobel. SIGCSE 2012 will also see the return of robots through a new venue, "The SIGCSE Playground: Experience It!" Many thanks go to Jennifer Kay and Douglas Blank for organizing this event.

Our sincere thanks go out to the people who made this Symposium extraordinary. First, our symposium committee: Carl Alphonce, Adrienne Decker, Lynn Degler, John Dooley, Mary Anne Egan, Susan Fox, Michael T. Helmick, Olaf Hall-Holt, John Harrison, Sarah Heckman, Catherine Lang, Steven Huss-Lederman, Cary Laxer, Chuck Leska, Lester I. McCann, Scott McElfresh, Larry Merkle, Brad Miller, Briana Morrison, Kris Nagel, Sarah Monisha Pulimood, Susan Rodger, Kimberly Voll, and Henry Walker. Additional thanks go to our Associate Program Chairs who provided meta-reviews for papers: Joel Adams, Doug Baldwin, Tim Bell, Sheila Castañeda, Tim Fossum, Mark Guzdial, Sherri Goings, Nancy Kinnersley, Lori Pollock, and Sami Rollins. We'd also like to thank all of our student volunteers who help us with all of the small details.

In difficult economic times, we extend a *very* grateful thank you to our supporters, vendors, exhibitors and in-kind donors whose participation literally make the symposium possible. We especially thank Microsoft, Google, and Intel as platinum supporters, SAP University Alliances as a silver supporter, and Oracle for funding an ice cream break. Special thanks go to Dorothea Heck and her team at D. Lawrence Planners for coordinating an outstanding exhibition and to Susan Rodger, our amazing supporter/exhibitor liaison.

We thank SIGCSE President Renée McCauley and the entire SIGCSE Board for their support and guidance, and acknowledge the contributions of SIGCSE Symposium Site Coordinators Bob Beck and Scott Grissom, as well as Ashley Cozzi of ACM. Lisa Tolles of Sheridan Printing Company brought all materials together. The City of Raleigh provided valuable information and prizes through their excellent Convention and Visitor's Bureau, with special thanks to Julie Brakenbury. We were supported at the Raleigh Convention Center by Tim Greene, Mara Craft, Dave Chapman, Mason Hotaling, Dan Capps (of Centerplate Catering), and Michael Murphy (of American AV); at the Raleigh Marriott City Center Hotel by Sasha Armour and Thomas Kelville; at the Sheraton Raleigh Hotel by Kevin Johnson; and at the Clarion Raleigh Hotel State Capital by Tricia Nelson.

Special thanks to our home institutions for providing needed resources: College of the Holy Cross, Carleton College, Colorado School of Mines, and Rochester Institute of Technology. We genuinely hope you enjoy the Symposium and find the SIGCSE 2012 Proceedings of use for your work now and your future projects and activities.

Symposium Chairs

Laurie Smith King
College of the Holy Cross

David R. Musicant
Carleton College

Program Chairs

Tracy Camp
Colorado School of Mines

Paul Tymann
Rochester Institute of Technology

Table of Contents

Session 6: Paper – K-6 Collaborations

Session 7: Paper – Tools

Session 8: Panel

Session 9: Special Session

Session 10: Panel

Session 11: Paper – Games

Session Chair: Adrienne Decker *(Rochester Institute of Technology)*

Session 12: Paper – Professional Experiences

Session Chair: Sarah Heckman *(North Carolina State University)*

Session 13: Paper – A Session with a View

Session Chair: Don Goelman *(Villanova University)*

Session 14: Paper – Pedagogy: Programming

Session Chair: Saquib Razak *(Carnegie Mellon University)*

Session 15: Panel

Session Chair: Rebecca Bates *(Minnesota State University, Mankato)*

Session 16: Panel

Session Chair: Leisa D. Thompson *(University of Virginia)*

Session 17: Special Session

Session Chair: Christopher Hundhausen *(Washington State University)*

Session 18: Paper – Broadening Participation

Session Chair: Kristine Nagel *(Georgia Gwinnett College)*

Session 19: Paper – Online Collaboration

Session Chair: Charles Leska *(Randolph-Macon College)*

Session 20: Paper – Middle School Collaborations

Session Chair: Catherine Lang *(Swinburne University of Technology)*

Session 21: Paper – New Tricks for the Classroom

Session Chair: Julian Mason *(Duke University)*

Session 27: Paper – Summer Experiences

Session Chair: Kinnis Gosha *(Morehouse College)*

Session 28: Paper – Software Engineering

Session Chair: Ariel Ortiz *(Tecnologico de Monterrey, Campus Estado de Mexico)*

Session 29: Special Session

Session Chair: Owen Astrachan *(Duke University)*

Session 30: Special Session

Session Chair: Pat Yongpradit *(Springbrook High School)*

Session 31: Special Session

Session Chair: Michael Kölling *(University of Kent)*

Session 32: Paper – Collaborative Learning

Session Chair: Adrian German *(Indiana University)*

Session 33: Paper – Curriculum Issues

Session Chair: Colleen Lewis *(University of California, Berkeley)*

Session 34: Paper – Active Learning I

Session Chair: Robert England *(Transylvania University)*

Session 35: Paper – Communication Skills

Session Chair: James Early *(SUNY Oswego)*

Session 36: Special Session

Session Chair: Suzanne Westbrook *(National Science Foundation)*

Session 37: Panel – Teaching Outside the Text

Session Chair: Lester Wainwright *(Charlottesville High School)*

Session 38: Special Session

Session Chair: John Impagliazzo *(Hofstra University)*

Session 39: Paper – Projects

Session Chair: Jeff Gray *(University of Alabama)*

Session 40: Paper – Alice and Scratch

Session Chair: Kelly Powers *(Advanced Math & Science Academy Charter School)*

Session 41: Paper – Active Learning II

Session Chair: Douglas Kranch *(North Central State College)*

Session 42: Paper – Non-majors

Session Chair: Derek Schuurman *(Redeemer University College)*

Session 43: Special Session

Session Chair: Nick Parlante *(Stanford University)*

Session 54: Paper – OS and Distributed Computing

Session Chair: William Mongan *(Drexel University)*

Session 55: Paper – Curricular Innovations and Research

Session Chair: Michael Hewner *(Duke University)*

Session 56: Paper – CS Education Research

Session Chair: Yana Kortsarts *(Widener University)*

Plenary Session

Session Chair: Laurie Smith King *(College of the Holy Cross)* and Dave Musicant *(Carleton College)*

Workshops

Poster Session 1

Poster Session 2

Birds-of-a-Feather

SIGCSE 2012 Symposium Committee

Laurie Smith King, Symposium Co-Chair
College of the Holy Cross

David R. Musicant, Symposium Co-Chair
Carleton College

Tracy Camp, Program Co-Chair
Colorado School of Mines

Paul Tymann, Program Co-Chair
Rochester Institute of Technology

Doug Baldwin, Associate Program Chair
SUNY Geneseo

Sherri Goings, Associate Program Chair
Carleton College

Joel Adams, Associate Program Chair
Calvin College

Tim Fossum, Associate Program Chair
SUNY Potsdam

Nancy Kinnersley, Associate Program Chair
University of Kansas

Lester I McCann, Workshops
University of Arizona

Brad Miller, Publications
Luther College

Larry Merkle, Registration
Wright State University

Kris Nagel, Posters
Georgia Gwinnett College

Steven Huss-Lederman, Student Volunteers and Activities
Beloit College

Henry Walker, Database Administrator
Grinnell College

Michael T. Helmick, Webmaster
Google

Sara Monisha Pulimood, Kids Camp Coordinator
The College of New Jersey

Susan Rodger, Supporter/Exhibitor Liaison
Duke University

Ann Sobel, Student Research Competition
Miami University (Ohio)

Briana Morrison, Pre-Conference Event Liaison
Southern Polytechnic State University

Sheila Castaneda, Associate Program Chair
Clarke University

Lori Pollock, Associate Program Chair
University of Delaware

Tim Bell, Associate Program Chair
University of Canterbury

Chuck Leska, Associate Program Chair
Randolph-Macon College

Sami Rollins, Associate Program Chair
University of San Francisco

Mark Guzdial, Associate Program Chair
Georgia Institute of Technology

Chuck Leska, Panels and Special Sessions
Randolph Macon College

Adrienne Decker, Workshops
Rochester Institute of Technology

Cary Laxer, Registration
Rose-Hulman Institute of Technology

Lynn Degler, Registration
Rose-Hulman Institute of Technology

Olaf Hall-Holt, Birds-of-a-Feather
St. Olaf College

Scott McElfresh, Treasurer
Wake Forest University

Mary Anne Egan, Student Volunteers and Activities
Siena College

John Dooley, Database Administrator
Knox College

Carl Alphonce, Evaluations
University at Buffalo, SUNY

Susan Fox, Kids Camp Coordinator
Macalester College

Catherine Lang, International Liaison
Swinburne University

John Harrison, K-12 Liaison
Princess Ann High School

Sarah Heckman, Local Arrangements
NC State University

Kimberly Voll, Publicity / Social Networking
University of British Columbia

SIGCSE 2012 Board-Sponsored Pre-Symposium Events

Career Mentoring Workshop

Susan Rodger, *Duke University*; Sheila Casteneda, *Clarke College*; Dave Reed, *Creighton University*

The goal of the Career Mentoring Workshop is to provide critical mentoring information for instructors, pre-tenure faculty and graduate students in Computer Science and Engineering who are interested in an academic career. The day-long workshop, to be held on Wednesday, February 29, will be co-located with the SIGCSE 2012 conference in Raleigh. Tentative topics will include: Mentoring, Teaching Strategies, Getting Started with Research / Finding Funding / Research with Undergraduates, Promotion and Tenure, Time Management, and Balancing Priorities (i.e., teaching vs. research vs. service). February 29, 8:00am to 5:00pm

Upcoming Events

ITiCSE 2012

Technion Campus
Haifa, Israel
July 3-5, 2012
www.iticse12.org.il/htmls/home.aspx

Conference Chair
Tami Lapidot – *Technion, Israel*
Judith Gal-Ezer – *The Open University, Israel*

ICER 2012

Auckland, New Zealand
September 10-11, 2012
http://icer-conference.org/

General Chair
Alison Clear, *Christchurch Polytechnic Institute of Technology*

SIGCSE 2013

Denver, Colorado, USA
March 6-9, 2013
http://sigcse.org/sigcse2013/

Symposium Co-Chairs
Paul Tyman, *Rochester Institute of Technology*
Tracy Camp, *Colorado School of Mines*

CALL FOR PARTICIPATION

SIGCSE 2013: The Changing Face of Computing The 44th ACM Technical Symposium on Computer Science Education

March 6-9, 2013, Denver, Colorado, USA

http://www.sigcse.org/sigcse2013

SIGCSE 2013 continues our long tradition of bringing together colleagues from around the world to present papers, panels, posters, special sessions, and workshops, and to discuss computer science education in birds-of-a-feather sessions and informal settings. The SIGCSE Technical Symposium addresses problems common among educators working to develop, implement and/or evaluate computing programs, curricula, and courses. The symposium provides a forum for sharing new ideas for syllabi, laboratories, and other elements of teaching and pedagogy, at all levels of instruction.

Submissions in line with the conference theme, "The Changing Face of Computing", are ideal. The theme focuses our attention on how computing is changing, and how we must change in education to address the changes in computing.

PAPERS

Papers describe an educational research project, classroom experience, teaching technique, curricular initiative, or pedagogical tool. Two versions of a submission are required: a full version having author names and affiliations and an anonymous version for use in reviewing. Papers will undergo a blind reviewing process and must not exceed six pages. Authors will have approximately 25 minutes for their presentations, including questions and answers.

PANELS

Panels present multiple perspectives on a specific topic. To allow each panelist sufficient time to present his or her perspective and still enable audience participation, a panel will normally have at most four panelists, including one moderator. Panel submissions should include a list of the panelists, their affiliations, and a description of the topic, with brief position statements from panelists. Proposals with more than four panelists must provide a statement connecting the extra panelist to the effectiveness of the panel and must convincingly show that each panelist will be able to speak, and the audience able to respond, within the session time. Panel abstracts must not exceed two pages. A panel session is approximately 75 minutes.

SPECIAL SESSIONS

Special sessions are your opportunity to customize and experiment with the SIGCSE conference format. Possible special sessions include a seminar on a new topic, a committee report, or a forum on curriculum issues. More generally, they must be 75 minutes in length, held in standard conference spaces, and justifiably distinct from the panel, paper, and poster tracks. Within those constraints, the form is yours to design. Special session abstracts must not exceed two pages.

WORKSHOPS

Workshops offer participants opportunities to learn new techniques and technologies designed to foster education, scholarship, and collaborations. A workshop proposal (including abstract) must not exceed two pages. Proposals must specify equipment needs (e.g., participant-supplied laptops, room configurations, and A/V equipment) and any limitation on the number of participants. Workshops are scheduled for a three-hour session and do not conflict with the technical sessions.

BIRDS OF A FEATHER SESSIONS

Birds of a Feather (BOF) sessions provide an environment for colleagues with similar interests to meet for informal discussions. A maximum one-page description (including abstract) is requested to describe the informal discussion topic. A/V equipment will not be provided for these sessions. Approximately 45 minutes are allocated to each BOF topic.

POSTERS

Posters describe computer science education materials or research, particularly works in progress. Proposals (including abstract) are limited to two pages. Poster demonstrations are scheduled to permit one-on-one discussion with conference attendees, typically during session breaks. Prepared handouts are encouraged in order to share your work.

STUDENT RESEARCH COMPETITION

Research from all areas of computer science is considered for awards in two categories of competition: graduate and undergraduate. All submissions must represent a student's individual research contribution and a student must be an ACM student member to qualify for awards and travel grants. Entry due date is September 30, 2012.

Association for Computing Machinery
Advancing Computing as a Science & Profession

SIGCSE
ACM Special Interest Group on Computer Science Education

IMPORTANT DUE DATES

Friday, September 7, 2012: *Paper, Panel, Special Session, and Workshop submissions*
Monday, October 29, 2012: *Birds of a Feather and Poster submissions*

PROGRAM COMMITTEE

Symposium Chairs

Tracy Camp
Colorado School of Mines
tcamp@mines.edu

Paul Tymann
Rochester Institute of Technology
ptt@cs.rit.edu

Program Chairs

J.D. Dougherty
Haverford College
jd@cs.haverford.edu

Kris Nagel
Georgia Gwinnett College
knagel@ggc.edu

Panels and Special Sessions

Sue Fitzgerald
Metropolitan State University
sue.fitzgerald@metrostate.edu

Workshops

Susan Haller
SUNY Potsdam
hallersm@potsdam.edu

Lester I. McCann
The University of Arizona
mccann@cs.arizona.edu

Publications

Joel Adams
Calvin College
adams@calvin.edu

Database Administrators

John Dooley
Knox College
jdooley@knox.edu

Henry Walker
Grinnell College
walker@cs.grinnell.edu

Registration

Lynn Degler
Rose-Hulman Institute of Technology

Cary Laxer
Rose-Hulman Institute of Technology

Larry Merkle
Computational Optimization Services

sigcse2013-registration@cs.rit.edu

Posters

Jodi Tims
Baldwin-Wallace College
jltims@bw.edu

Birds Of A Feather

Jian Zhang
Louisiana State University
zhang@csc.lsu.edu

Student Volunteers and Student Activities

Steven Huss-Lederman
Beloit College
huss@beloit.edu

Steven Wolfman
University of British Columbia
wolf@cs.ubc.edu

Webmasters

Dan Bogaard
Rochester Institute of Technology
dsbics@rit.edu

Steve Zilora
Rochester Institute of Technology
sjzics@rit.edu

Treasurer

Scott Grissom
Grand Valley State University
grissom@gvsu.edu

Evaluations

James Early
SUNY Oswego
earlyjp@cs.oswego.edu

Kids' Camp

Susan Fox
Macalester College
fox@macalester.edu

Kimberly Voll
University of British Columbia
kvoll@cs.ubc.ca

Support/Exhibitor Liaison

Susan Rodger
Duke University
rodger@cs.duke.edu

Pre-Conference Events Liaison

Adrienne Decker
Rochester Institute of Technology
amdigm@rit.edu

K-12 Liaison

Marilyn Cadenhead
School of Science and Engr. Magnet
mcadenhead@dallasisd.org

Ria Galanos
Centennial High School
galanos@fultonshools.org

International Liaison

Catherine Lang
Swinburne University of Technology
clang@swin.edu.au

Local Arrangements

Jody Paul
Metropolitan State College of Denver
jody@acm.org

Student Research Competition

Ann Sobel
Miami University (Ohio)
sobelae@muohio.edu

Association for Computing Machinery
Advancing Computing as a Science & Profession

SIGCSE
ACM Special Interest Group on Computer Science Education

Recipients of the SIGCSE Award for Outstanding Contributions to Computer Science Education

1981 **William F. Atchison**, *University of Maryland*

1982 **Alan Perlis**, *Yale University*

1983 **Karl V. Karlstrom**, *Prentice-Hall*

1985 **Elliot I. Organick**, *University of Utah*

1986 **Donald Knuth**, *Stanford University*

1987 **Niklaus Wirth**, *ETH, Zurich*

1988 **Grace Murray Hopper**, *Rear Admiral, USN, Digital Equipment Corp.*

1989 **Edsger W. Dijkstra**, *The University of Texas at Austin*

1990 **Curriculum '68 Committee**:
William F. Atchison, Samuel D. Conte, John Hamblen, Thomas E. Hull, Thomas A. Keenan, William B. Kehl, Edward J. McClusey, Silvio O. Navarro, Werner Rheinboldt, Earl J. Schweppe, William Viavant, David M. Young, Jr.

1991 **David Gries**, *Cornell University*

1992 **Daniel D. McCraken**, *City College, City University of New York*

1993 **Alan C. Kay**, *Apple Computer*

1994 **Norman E. Gibbs**, *Software Engineering Institute*

1995 **Robert M. Aiken**, *Temple University*

1996 **Nell B. Dale**, *The University of Texas at Austin*

1997 **Andrew Tannenbaum**, *Vrije University*

1998 **William A. Wulf**, *University of Virginia and National Academy of Engineering*

1999 **Peter J. Denning**, *George Mason University*

2000 **Andries Van Dam**, *Brown University*

2001 **Allen B. Tucker**, *Bowdoin College*

2002 **Elliot Soloway**, *University of Michigan*

2003 **Eric Roberts**, *Stanford University*

2004 **Mordechai Ben-Ari**, *Weizmann Institute of Science*

2005 **Kim Bruce**, *Williams College*

2006 **Richard Pattis**, *Carnegie Mellon University*

2007 **Judith Gal-Ezer,** *Open University of Israel* and **John Hughes**, *University of Technology, Sydney*

2008 **Randy Pausch,** *Carnegie Mellon University*

2009 **Elliot B. Koffman,** *Temple University*

2010 **Sally Fincher,** *University of Kent, Canterbury*

2011 **Matthias Felleisen,** *Northeastern University*

2012 **Harold (Hal) Abelson,** *Massachusetts Institute of Technology*

Recipients of the SIGCSE Lifetime Service Award

1997 **Richard Austing**, *University of Maryland*

1998 **Della Bonnette**, *University of Southwestern Louisiana*

1999 **Robert Aiken**, *Temple University*

2000 **James E. Miller**, *University of Southern Mississippi*

2001 **Lillian N. (Boots) Cassel**, *Villanova University*

2002 **Joe Turner**, *Clemson University and Zayed University*

2003 **Harriet Taylor**, *National Science Foundation and Louisiana State University*

2004 **Bruce Klein**, *Grand Valley State University*

2005 **Andrew McGettrick**, *University of Strathclyde*

2006 **Joyce Currie Little**, *Towson State University*

2007 **John Impagliazzo**, *Hofstra University*

2008 **Dennis Frailey**, *Raytheon Corporation*

2009 **Michael J. Clancy**, *University of California, Berkeley*

2010 **Peter Denning**, *Naval Postgraduate School*

2011 **Gordon Davies**, *Open University*

2012 **Jane Prey**, *Microsoft Research*

SIGCSE 2012 Reviewers

Safurah Abdul Jalil, *University of Auckland*
Adel Abunawass, *University of West Georgia*
Ernest Ackermann, *University of Mary Washington*
Donald Acton, *University of British Columbia*
Raman Adaikkalavan, *Indiana University South Bend*
Victor Adamchik, *Carnegie Mellon University*
Elizabeth S. Adams, *James Madison University*
Joel Adams, *Calvin College*
Robert Adams, *Grand Valley State University*
Paul Addison, *Ivy Tech Community College*
Rajeev Agrawal, *North Carolina A & T State University*
Shakil Akhtar, *Clayton State University*
Paul Albee, *Central Michigan University*
Richard Allen, *St. Olaf College*
Vicki Almstrum, *University of Texas at Austin*
Hana Alnuaim, *King Abdulaziz University*
Carl Alphonce, *University at Buffalo, The State University of New York*
Jamal Alsabbagh, *Grand Valley State University*
Christine Alvarado, *Harvey Mudd College*
Peter Anderson, *Rochester Institute of Technolgy*
Ruth Anderson, *University of Washington*
Peter Andreae, *Victoria University of Wellington*
Stefan Andrei, *Lamar University*
Danner Andrew, *Swarthmore College*
Peter Andrews, *Eastern Illinois University*
Steven K. Andrianoff, *St. Bonaventure University*
Karen Anewalt, *University of Mary Washington*
Barbara Anthony, *Southwestern University*
Florence Appel, *Saint Xavier University*
Antonio Araujo, *Universidade do Porto*
Michal Armoni, *Weizmann Institute of Science*
Tom Armstrong, *Wheaton College*
David Arnow, *Brooklyn College*
Charles Ashbacher, *Charles Ashbacher Technologies*
John Avitabile, *College of Saint Rose*
John Aycock, *University of Calgary*
Pavel Azalov, *Penn State*
Isabel Azevedo, *ISEP*
Serhat Azgur, *Bilkent University*
Dinabandhu Bag, *National Institute of Technology*
Mark Bailey, *Hamilton College*
Laura Baker, *St. Edward's University*
Doug Baldwin, *SUNY Geneseo*
Catherine Bareiss, *Olivet Nazarene University*
Ian Barland, *Radford University*
David Barnes, *University of Kent*
Tiffany Barnes, *University of North Carolina at Charlotte*
Lewis Barnett, *University of Richmond*
N. Dwight Barnette, *Virginia Tech*
John Barr, *Ithaca College*
Valerie Barr, *Union College*
Martin Barrett, *East Tennessee State University*
Joao Barros, *Instituto Politecnico de Beja - ESTIG*
Phillip Barry, *University of Minnesota*
Carlos Barto, *Universidad Nacional de Cordoba*
Rebecca Bates, *Minnesota State University Mankato*
Michael Bauer, *University of Hawaii - Leeward Community College*
Robert Beck, *Villanova University*
Byron Weber Becker, *University of Waterloo*
Andrew Begel, *Microsoft Research*
John Beidler, *Univ. of Scranton*
Tim Bell, *University of Canterbury*
Mordechai Ben-Ari, *Weizmann Institute of Science*
Jens Bennedsen, *Aarhus School of Engineering*
Chris Bennett, *University of Maine Farmington*
Seth Bergmann, *Rowan University*
Mikael Berndtsson, *University of Skovde*
Gian Mario Besana, *CTI DePaul University*
Anne Beug, *California Polytechnic State University*
Ivona Bezakova, *Rochester Institute of Technology*
Marie Bienkowski, *SRI International*
William Birmingham, *Grove City College*
Judith M Bishop, *Microsoft Research*
M. Brian Blake, *University of Notre Dame*
Stephen Bloch, *Adelphi University*
Michael Blumenstein, *Griffith University*
Steven Bogaerts, *Wittenberg University*
Esmail Bonakdarian, *Franklin University*
William Booth, *Baylor University*
James Bowring, *College of Charleston*
Stefan Brandle, *Taylor University*
Evelyn Brannock, *Georgia Gwinnett College*
Anna Bretscher, *University of Toronto at Scarborough*
Monica Brockmeyer, *Wayne State University*
Renee Bryce, *Utah State University*
Dennis Brylow, *Marquette University*
Joel Brynielsson, *Royal Institute of Technology*
Suzanne Buchele, *Southwestern University*
Duane Buck, *Otterbein University*
Everett Bull, *Pomona College*
David Bunde, *Knox College*
Barry Burd, *Drew University*
Darci Burdge, *Nassau Community College*
Kevin Burger, *Arizona State University*
Ben Burrell, *Randolph-Macon College*
Vicky Bush, *University of Gloucestershire*
Mary Elaine Califf, *Illinois State University*
Andre Paul Calitz, *Nelson Mandela Metropolitan University*
Johan Calu, *KHBO*
Tracy Camp, *Colorado School of Mines*
Daniel Canas, *Wake Forest University*
Roxanne Canosa, *Rochester Institute of Technology*
Angela Carbone, *Monash University*
James Caristi, *Valparaiso University*
Andrew Carle, *University of California, Berkeley*
Martin Carlisle, *US Air Force Academy*
Janet Carter, *University of Kent at Canterbury*
Lori Carter, *Point Loma Nazarene University*
Jeffrey Carver, *University of Alabama*
Lori Case, *University of Waterloo*
Steven Case, *University of the Virgin Islands*
Lillian N. Cassel, *Villanova University*
Sheila Castaneda, *Clarke University*
Tim Chamillard, *University of Colorado at Colorado Springs*
Albert Chan, *Fayetteville State University*
Maiga Chang, *Athabasca University*

Mahesh Chaudhari, *Arizona State University*
Ranjan Chaudhuri, *Eastern Michigan University*
Tom Cheatham, *Middle Tennessee State Univ.*
Jimmy Chen, *Salt Lake Community College*
Peng-Wen Chen, *Oriental Institute of Technology*
Ping Chen, *University of Houston-Downtown*
Robert Chen, *Framingham State University*
Tzu-Yi Chen, *Pomona College*
Wei Kian Chen, *Champlain Cpllege*
Li-hsiang Cheo, *William Paterson University of New Jersey*
Chia-Chu Chiang, *University of Arkansas at Little Rock*
Donald Chinn, *University of Washington, Tacoma*
Jayan Kurian Chirayath, *Royal Melbourne Institute of Technology*
David Chiu, *Washington State University, Vancouver*
Radhouane Chouchane, *Columbus State University*
James Church, *University of Mississippi*
Vincent Cicirello, *Richard Stockton College*
John Cigas, *Park University*
Dawn Cizmar, *University of Texas at Austin (retired)*
Michael Clancy, *University of California, Berkeley*
Peter Clarke, *Florida International University*
Tony Clear, *Auckland University of Technology*
Daniel Cliburn, *University of the Pacific*
Joe Clifton, *University of Wisconsin, Platteville*
Osvaldo Clua, *Universidad de Buenos Aires*
Marge Coahran, *Dickinson College*
Avi Cohen, *Ministry of Education*
james Cohoon, *University of Virginia*
Ben Coleman, *Moravian College*
Tim Comber, *Southern Cross University*
Randy Connolly, *Mount Royal University*
Phillip Conrad, *University of California, Santa Barbara*
Robert Cook, *Georgia Southern University*
Peter Cooper, *Sam Houston State University*
Stephen Cooper, *Stanford University*
jean f. coppola, *pace university*
David Cordes, *University of Alabama*
Jose L. Cordova, *University of Louisiana at Monroe*
Thomas Cortina, *Carnegie Mellon University*
Monica Costa, *IPCB*
Mary Courtney, *Pace University*
Annemieke Craig, *Deakin University*
Michelle Craig, *University of Toronto*
Al Cripps, *Middle Tennessee State Univ.*
James Cross, *Auburn University*
Joyce Blair Crowell, *Belmont University*
Diana Cukierman, *Simon Fraser University*
Jose Cunha, *New University of Lisbon*
Steve Cunningham, *Brown Cunningham Associates*
Edwin P. Curran, *University of Ulster*
Pamela Cutter, *Kalamazoo College*
Quintin Cutts, *University of Glasgow*
Mohammad Dadfar, *Bowling Green State University*
Lucia K Dale, *Sewanee*
Nell Dale, *University of Texas at Austin, retired*
Andrew Dalton, *Western Carolina University*
Mats Daniels, *Uppsala University*
Douglas Dankel, *University of Florida*
Lawrence D'Antonio, *Ramapo College of New Jersey*
Andrea Danyluk, *Williams College*
Stephen Davies, *University of Mary Washington*
Janet Davis, *Grinnell College*
Renzo Davoli, *University of Bologna*
Susan Dean, *UMUC - Europe*
Hannah Mary Dee, *Grenoble Institute of Technology*
Katherine Deibel, *University of Washington-Seattle*
Stavros Demetriadis, *Aristotle University of Thessaloniki*
Peter DePasquale, *The College of New Jersey*
Molisa Derk, *Dickinson State University*
Yogesh Deshpande, *University of Western Sydney*
Lucia Dettori, *DePaul University*
Kamyar Dezhgosha, *University of Illinois at Springfield*
Martin Dick, *RMIT University*
Suzanne W. Dietrich, *Arizona State University*
Wei Ding, *University of Massachusetts-Boston*
Adair Dingle, *Seattle University*
William Doane, *Bennington College*
Zachary Dodds, *Harvey Mudd College*
Aijuan Dong, *Hood College*
John Dooley, *Knox College*
Brian Dorn, *University of Hartford*
John Dougherty, *Haverford College*
Maureen Doyle, *Northern Kentucky University*
Peter Drexel, *Plymouth State University*
John Duncan, *Indiana University*
James Early, *SUNY Oswego*
J. Philip East, *University of Northern Iowa*
Jeffrey Edgington, *University of Denver*
Stephen Edwards, *Virginia Tech*
Mary Anne Egan, *Siena College*
Roger Eggen, *University of North Florida*
Kurt Eiselt, *University of British Columbia*
Joseph Ekstrom, *Brigham Young University*
Hala ElAarag, *Stetson University*
Ahmed El-Deeb, *Nile University*
Heidi J. C. Ellis, *Western New England College*
Stephanie Elzer, *Millersville University*
Richard Enbody, *Michigan State University*
Alec Engebretson, *Doane College*
Gerald Engel, *University of Connecticut, Stamford*
Ed C. Epp, *Intel Corp.*
Barbara Ericson, *Georgia Tech*
Daniel Ernst, *Cray, Inc.*
John Estell, *Ohio Northern University*
Yadran Eterovic, *Pontificia Universidad Catolica de Chile*
Henry Etlinger, *Rochester Institute of Technology*
Barry Fagin, *US Air Force Academy*
Daisy Fan, *Cornell University*
Homma Farian, *SUNY Geneseo*
David Farrell, *Glasgow Caledonian University*
Dave Feinberg, *The Wellington School*
Alan Fekete, *University of Sydney*
Maria Feldgen, *Universidad de Buenos Aires*
Ernest Ferguson, *Northwest Missouri State University*
Roger Ferguson, *Grand Valley State University*
Francesc J. Ferri, *Universitat de Valencia*
Georgios Fesakis, *University of the Aegean*
Ronald Finkbine, *Indiana University Southeast*
Sue Fitzgerald, *Metropolitan State University*
Robin Flatland, *Siena College*

Samantha Foley, *Oak Ridge National Laboratory*
Jeffrey Forbes, *Duke University*
Timothy Fossum, *SUNY College at Potsdam*
Kent Foster, *Winthrop University*
Edward Fox, *Virginia Tech*
Susan Fox, *Macalester College*
Charles Frank, *Northern Kentucky University*
Robert Franks, *Central College*
Karen Fraser, *University of Ulster*
Andre Freire, *University of York*
Bill Freitas, *The Lawrenceville School*
Frank Friedman, *Temple University*
Ines Friss de Kereki, *ORT Uruguay University*
S. Jane Fritz, *St. Joseph's College*
Daniel Frost, *University of California, Irvine*
Mohammad Fuad, *Winston-Salem State University*
Kenneth Funk, *Kirkwood Community College*
Jacob Furst, *DePaul University*
Galal Galal-Edeen, *Cairo University*
Angel Garcia-Beltran, *Universidad Politecnica de Madrid*
Charlie Garrod, *Swarthmore College*
Alessio Gaspar, *University of South Florida Polytechnic*
Dick Gayler, *Kennesaw State University*
Rick Gee, *Okanagan College*
Edward Gehringer, *North Carolina State University*
Joe Geigel, *Rochester Institute of Technolgy*
Edward M. Gellenbeck, *Central Washington University*
Jill Gerhardt, *Richard Stockton College of New Jersey*
Adrian German, *Indiana University*
Judith Gersting, *Indiana University Purdue & University at Indianapolis*
Paul Gestwicki, *Ball State University*
Lila Ghemri, *Texas Southern University*
J Paul Gibson, *T&M Sud Paris*
Mark Goadrich, *Centenary College of Louisiana*
Don Goelman, *Villanova University*
Sherri Goings, *Carleton College*
Michael Goldwasser, *Saint Louis University*
Michael Goldweber, *Xavier University*
Evan Golub, *University of Maryland*
Mercedes Gomez-Albarran, *Dep. Ingenieria del Software e Inteligencia Artificial*
Marco Antonio Gomez-Martin, *Universidad Complutense de Madrid*
Pedro Pablo Gomez-Martin, *Universidad Complutense de Madrid*
Aaron Gordon, *Metropolitan State College of Denver*
Peter Gorny, *University of Oldenburg*
Jean Goulet, *Universite de Sherbrooke*
Michael Gousie, *Wheaton College (MA)*
Mary Granger, *George Washington University*
Cary Gray, *Wheaton College*
Larry Griffith, *Westfield State University*
Scott Grissom, *Grand Valley State University*
Paul Gross, *Washington University in St. Louis*
Andrew Grover, *Thiel College*
Mario Guimaraes, *Zayed University*
Jiang Guo, *California State University, Los Angeles*
Mark Guzdial, *Georgia Institute of Technology*
Bruria Haberman, *Holon Institute of Technology & The Weizmann Institute of Science*
Max Hailperin, *Gustavus Adolphus College*
Susan Haller, *SUNY Potsdam*
Ranette Halverson, *Midwestern State University*
John Hamer, *University of Auckland*
Nadeem Hamid, *Berry College*
Brian Hanks, *BFH Educational Consulting*
Stuart Hansen, *University of Wisconsin - Parkside*
Mindy Hart, *Purdue University*
Thanos Hatziapostolou, *CITY College - University of Sheffield*
Jessen Havill, *Denison University*
Christopher Haynes, *Indiana University*
Orit Hazzan, *Technion -- Israel Institute of Technology*
Sarah Heckman, *North Carolina State University*
Phillip Heeler, *Northwest Missouri State University*
Cecily Heiner, *Southern Utah University*
James Heliotis, *RIT*
Keith Hellman, *Colorado School of Mines*
Michael Helmick, *Google*
David Hemmendinger, *Union College*
Dean Hendrix, *Auburn University*
Tyson Henry, *California State University, Chico*
Katherine Herbert, *Montclair State University*
Matthew Hertz, *Canisius College*
Jose R. Hilera, *University of Alcala*
Curtis Hill, *Valley City State University*
Rachelle Kristof Hippler, *Bowling Green State University*
Gregory Hislop, *Drexel University*
William Hochstettler, *Franklin*
Mark A. Holliday, *Western Carolina University*
Joe Hollingsworth, *Indiana University*
Christopher Homan, *Rochester Institute of Technology*
William Hooper, *Belmont University*
Charles Hoot, *Oklahoma City University*
Cay Horstmann, *San Jose State University*
Hoda Hosny, *The American University in Cairo*
Mahmood Hossain, *Fairmont State University*
Shahadat Hossain, *University of Lethbridge*
Dwight House, *Fayetteville State University*
David Hovemeyer, *York College of Pennsylvania*
Brian Howard, *DePauw University*
James Howatt, *Luther College*
Trudy Howles, *Rochester Institute of Technology*
Michelle Hribar, *OHSU*
Wen-Jung Hsin, *Park University*
Chenglie Hu, *Carroll University*
Meriel Huggard, *Trinity College, Dublin*
James Huggins, *Kettering University*
Janet Hughes, *University of Dundee*
Richard Hull, *Lenoir-Rhyne University*
Dalton Hunkins, *St. Bonaventure University*
Frances Hunt, *Educational Testing Service*
Kenny Hunt, *University of Wisconsin - La Crosse*
Michelle Hutton, *Stanford University*
Deborah Hwang, *University of Evansville*
Jorge Eduardo Ibarra-Esquer, *Universidad Autonoma de Baja California*
Lubomir Ivanov, *Iona College*
Sridhar Iyer, *Indian Institute of Technology, Bombay*
Clemente Izurieta, *Montana State University*
Letizia Jaccheri, *Norwegian University of Science and Technology*
Jana Jackova, *Slovak University of Technology in Bratislava*
Matthew Jadud, *Allegheny College*

Mark Jaeger, *Baker College*
David Janzen, *California Polytechnic State University, San Luis Obispo*
Ciera Jaspan, *Carnegie Mellon University*
Giti Javidi, *Virginia State University*
Jam Jenkins, *Valdosta State University*
Mike Jipping, *Hope College*
David John, *Wake Forest University*
Chris Johnson, *University of Wisconsin, Eau Claire*
Colin Johnson, *University of Kent at Canterbury*
Julie Johnson, *Vanderbilt University*
Edward Jones, *Florida A&M University*
Anthony Joseph, *Pace University*
Mike Joy, *University of Warwick*
Daniel Joyce, *Villanova University*
Maria Jump, *King's College*
Edward Jung, *Southern Polytechnic State University*
Alan Kaminsky, *Rochester Institute of Technology*
Pankaj Kamthan, *Concordia University*
Debbie Kaneko, *Old Dominion University*
Ville Karavirta, *Aalto University*
Elizabeth Katz, *Millersville University*
David Kauchak, *Middlebury College*
David G. Kay, *University of California, Irvine*
Jennifer Kay, *Rowan University*
Judy Kay, *University of Sydney*
Fereydoun Kazemian, *Rochester Institute of Technology*
Petros Kefalas, *University of Sheffield*
Charles Kelemen, *Swarthmore College*
Thomas Kelliher, *Goucher College*
Andreas Kerren, *Linnaeus University*
Mark Kerstetter, *Western Michigan University*
Arshia Khan, *The College of St. Scholastica*
Sami Khuri, *San Jose State University*
Nancy Kinnersley, *University of Kansas*
David Klappholz, *Stevens Institute of Technology*
Myungsook Klassen, *California Lutheran University*
Frank Klassner, *Villanova University*
Carsten Kleiner, *University of Applied Sciences & Arts Hannover*
Jane Kochanov, *Pennsylvania State University - Capital College*
James Kolasa, *Bluegrass Community and Technical College*
Michael Kolling, *University of Kent*
April Kontostathis, *Ursinus College*
Yana Kortsarts, *Widener University, Chester*
David Kosbie, *Carnegie Mellon University*
Janet Kourik, *Webster University*
Nicholas Kraft, *The University of Alabama*
Joan Krone, *Denison University*
Jan Kruger, *Unisa School for BusinessLeadership*
Marja Kuittinen, *University of Joensuu*
Amruth Kumar, *Ramapo College of New Jersey*
Deepak Kumar, *Bryn Mawr College*
Durgesh Kumar, *DRDO*
Benjamin Kuperman, *Oberlin College*
Stan Kurkovsky, *Central Connecticut State University*
Zachary Kurmas, *Grand Valley State University*
Clif Kussmaul, *Muhlenberg College*
Lynn Lambert, *Christopher Newport University*
H. Chad Lane, *University of Southern California*
Catherine Lang, *Swinburne University of Technology*
Matthew Lang, *Moravian College*
Joan Langdon, *Bowie State University*
Yedidyah Langsam, *Brooklyn College of CUNY*
Mick Lantis, *Purdue University North Central*
David Largent, *Ball State University*
brian larkins, *Coastal Carolina University*
Eric Larson, *Seattle University*
Mary Last, *self-employed*
Robert Law, *Glasgow Caledonian University*
Deirdre Lawless, *Dublin Institute of Technology*
Barry Lawson, *University of Richmond*
Lucas Layman, *Fraunhofer USA*
Alina Lazar, *Youngstown State University*
Christopher League, *Long Island University*
Cathie LeBlanc, *Plymouth State College*
Mark LeBlanc, *Wheaton College*
Arthur Lee, *Claremont McKenna College*
Byong Lee, *Bennett College*
Cynthia Lee, *University of California, San Diego*
Gilliean Lee, *Lander University*
Chi Un Lei, *University of Hong Kong*
David Levine, *St. Bonaventure University*
Anany Levitin, *Villanova University*
Gary Lewandowski, *Xavier University*
John Lewis, *Virginia Tech*
Weidong Liao, *Shepherd University*
Billy Lim, *Illinois State University*
Janne Lindqvist, *Carnegie Mellon University*
Panagiotis Linos, *Butler University*
Jiang-Jiang Liu, *Lamar University*
Jigang Liu, *Metropolitan State University*
Peter Liu, *Seneca College*
William S. Lloyd, *University of West Georgia*
Kate Lockwood, *California State University, Monterey Bay*
Sergio F. Lopes, *University of Minho*
Salvador López-Mendoza, *Universidad Nacional Autónoma de México*
Chris Lueer, *Amazon.com*
Andrew Luxton-Reilly, *The University of Auckland*
William Lyle, *Murray State University*
Ian Macdonald, *Victoria University*
Bonnie MacKellar, *St John's University*
Peter Macpherson, *Rogers State University*
Joaquim Madeira, *University of Aveiro*
John S. Mallozzi, *Iona College*
Bill Manaris, *College of Charleston*
Ted Markowitz, *University of New Haven*
Mercedes Marques, *University Jaume I*
Fred Martin, *University of Massachusetts -- Lowell*
Kenneth Martin, *University of North Florida*
Manuel Martins Barata, *ISEL - Instituto Superior de Engenharia de Lisboa*
Dave Mason, *Ryerson University*
Bruce R. Maxim, *University of Michigan-Dearborn*
Bruce Maxwell, *Colby College*
Christopher Mayfield, *James Madison University*
Lester McCann, *The University of Arizona*
Robert McCloskey, *University of Scranton*
O. William McClung, *Nebraska Wesleyan University*
Jeffrey McConnell, *Canisius College*
Frank McCown, *Harding University*
W. Michael McCracken, *Georgia Institute of Technology*
Sean McCulloch, *Ohio Wesleyan University*
Chris McDonald, *The University of Western Australia*
Charlie McDowell, *University of California, Santa Cruz*
Scott McElfresh, *Wake Forest University*
James McGuffee, *St. Edward's University*

Hugh McGuire, *Grand Valley State University*
Tim McGuire, *Sam Houston State University*
Michael McMillan, *Pulaski Technical College*
Bonita McVey, *St. Norbert College*
Pedro Medeiros, *Universidade Nova de Lisboa*
Lisa Meeden, *Swarthmore College*
Gloria Melara, *California State University, Northridge*
Antonio Jose Mendes, *University of Coimbra*
Susan Mengel, *Texas Tech University*
Suzanne Menzel, *Indiana University*
Joseph Mertz, *Carnegie Mellon University*
Panagiotis Metaxas, *Wellesley College*
Jose Carlos Metrolho, *Polytechnic Institute of Castelo Branco*
Timothy Meyer, *Edinboro University of Pennsylvania*
Mark Meysenburg, *Doane College*
Lisa Michaud, *Merrimack College*
Gail Miles, *Lenoir-Rhyne College*
Bradley Miller, *Luther College*
James Miller, *Bradley University*
James Miller, *University of Alberta*
Keith Miller, *University of Illinois at Springfield*
Afsaneh Minaie, *Utah valley University*
Joe Miro, *Universitat de les Illes Balears*
Susan Mitchell, *University of Maryland, Baltimore County*
Roland Mittermeir, *Universität Klagenfurt*
Sriram Mohan, *Rose-Hulman Institute of Technology*
William Mongan, *Drexel University*
Sara Miner More, *McDaniel College*
Nelma Moreira, *University of Porto*
Patricia Morreale, *Kean University*
Briana Morrison, *Southern Polytechnic State University*
Srikanth Mudigonda, *Saint Louis University*
Laurie Murphy, *Pacific Lutheran University*
Michael Murphy, *Concordia University Texas*
Keitha Murray, *Iona College*
William Myers, *Belmont Abbey College*
Kristine Nagel, *Georgia Gwinnett College*
Mario Nakazawa, *Berea College*
Nannette Napier, *Georgia Gwinnett College*
Tom Naps, *University of Wisconsin - Oshkosh*
Krish Narayanan, *Eastern Michigan University*
Pavol Navrat, *Slovak University of Technology*
Rance Necaise, *College of William and Mary*
Robert Neufeld, *McPherson College - Emeritus*
Tia Newhall, *Swarthmore College*
Lijun Ni, *Georgia Institute of Technology*
Jaime Nino, *Univ. of New Orleans*
Robert Noonan, *College of William and Mary*
Cindy Norris, *Appalachian State University*
Linda Null, *Penn State University*
William Oblitey, *Indiana University of Pennsylvania*
Rainer Oechsle, *University of Applied Sciences, Trier*
Keith O'Hara, *Bard College*
Chris Okasaki, *USMA*
Edward Okie, *Radford University*
Amos Olagunju, *St. Cloud State University*
Joseph Oldham, *Centre College*
Nina Onesti, *Indiana University*
Lawrence Osborne, *Lamar University*
Youwen Ouyang, *California State University at San Marcos*
Barbara Owens, *Southwestern University*
Jill Pala, *Girls Preparatory School*
Greta Pangborn, *Saint Michael's College*
Iraklis Paraskakis, *University of Sheffield*
Abelardo Pardo, *Carlos III University of Madrid*
Crist'obal Pareja-Flores, *Universidad Complutense de Madrid*
Young Park, *Bradley University*
Brenda C. Parker, *Middle Tennessee State University*
David Parker, *Salisbury University*
Jeff Parker, *Harvard Extension*
Rembert Parker, *Anderson University*
James Paterson, *Glasgow Caledonian University*
Elizabeth Patitsas, *University of Toronto*
Laurie Patterson, *University of North Carolina Wilmington*
Richard E. Pattis, *University of California, Irvine*
Jody Paul, *MSCD*
Thaddeus Pawlicki, *University of Rochester*
Arnold Pears, *Uppsala University*
Ramanee Peiris, *University of Dundee*
Eileen Peluso, *Lycoming College*
Bin Peng, *Southwestern College*
Manuel A. Perez-Quinones, *Virginia Tech*
Teresa Peterman, *Grand Valley State University*
Andrew Petersen, *University of Toronto Mississauga*
John Peterson, *Western State College*
Noel Petit, *Augsburg College*
Chrisila C. Pettey, *Middle Tennessee State University*
Charles Pheatt, *Emporia State University*
Vreda Pieterse, *University of Pretoria*
Nelishia Pillay, *University of KwaZulu-Natal*
Francois Pitt, *University of Toronto*
Tony Pittarese, *East Tennessee State University*
Paul Piwowarski, *University of Kentucky*
Chris Plaue, *The University of Georgia*
Shannon Pollard, *Elon University*
Lori Pollock, *University of Delaware*
Wayne Pollock, *Hillsborough Community College*
Irene Polycarpou, *Colorado School of Mines*
Elvira Popescu, *University of Craiova*
Jeffrey Popyack, *Drexel University*
Lori Postner, *Nassau Community College*
George J. Pothering, *College of Charleston*
Annu Prabhakar, *University of Cincinnati*
Jon Preston, *Southern Polytechnic State Unviersity*
Roger Priebe, *Texas State University - San Marcos*
Philip Prins, *Seattle Pacific University*
William Pugh, *Univ. of Maryland*
Sarah Monisha Pulimood, *The College of New Jersey*
Semmy Purewal, *University of North Carolina at Asheville*
John Rabung, *Randolph-Macon College*
Cyndi Rader, *Colorado School of Mines*
John Rager, *Amherst College*
Imad Rahal, *College of Saint Benedict & Saint John's University*
Rajendra Raj, *Rochester Institute of Technology*
Muthu Ramachandran, *Leeds Metropolitan University*
Bina Ramamurthy, *University at Buffalo, SUNY*
Saquib Razak, *Carnegie Mellon University*
Eliseo Reategui, *Universidade Federal do Rio Grande do Sul*
Samuel Rebelsky, *Grinnell College*
Michael Redmond, *La Salle University*
David Reed, *Creighton University*

Donna Reese, *Mississippi State University*
Susan Reiser, *UNC Asheville*
Dan Resler, *Virginia Commonwealth University*
Eugene K. Ressler, *United States Military Academy*
Loren Rhodes, *Juniata College*
Catherine Ricardo, *Iona College*
Michael Rieck, *Drake University*
Charles Riedesel, *University of Nebraska - Lincoln*
Suzanne Rivoire, *Sonoma State University*
Steven Robbins, *University of Texas at San Antonio*
Christian Roberson, *Plymouth State University*
Eric Roberts, *Stanford University*
Stefan Robila, *Montclair State University*
Susan H. Rodger, *Duke University*
Ken Rodham, *Brigham Young University*
Guido Roessling, *Technische Universitaet Darmstadt*
Sami Rollins, *University of San Francisco*
Joel Ross, *University of California, Irvine*
John Ross, *Indiana University Kokomo*
Jerry Roth, *Vanderbilt University*
Krishnendu Roy, *Valdosta State University*
Martin Ruckert, *Munich University of Applied Sciences*
Anthony Ruocco, *Roger Williams University*
Paulo Rupino da Cunha, *University of Coimbra*
Adrian Rusu, *Rowan University*
Amalia Rusu, *Fairfield University*
Rebecca Rutherfoord, *Southern Polytechnic State University*
Mihaela Sabin, *University of New Hampshire*
Roberta Evans Sabin, *Loyola College*
Shazia Sadiq, *The University of Queensland*
Mehran Sahami, *Stanford University*
Samuel Sambasivam, *Azusa Pacific University*
Ian Sanders, *University of the Witwatersrand*
William Sanders, *University of Hartford*
Pete Sanderson, *Otterbein University*
André Santos, *Lisbon University Institute*
Vijayalakshmi Saravanan, *Ryerson University , Canada & VIT University*
Amit Sawant, *NetApp*
Suzanne Schaefer, *University of California, Los Angeles*
christelle scharff, *Pace University*
Stephen Schaub, *Bob Jones University*
Walter Schilling, *Milwaukee School of Engineering*
Diane Schwartz, *California State University Northridge*
leslie schwartzman, *UIS*
Dino Schweitzer, *United States Air Force Academy*
Otto Seppälä, *Aalto University*
Amber Settle, *DePaul University*
Behrooz Seyed-Abbassi, *University of North Florida*
Cliff Shaffer, *Virginia Tech*
Victor R.L. Shen, *National Taipei University*
Ching-Kuang Shene, *Michigan Technological University*
Mark Sherriff, *University of Virginia*
Sen Shilad, *Macalester College*
Yasuto Shirai, *Shizuoka University*
Keith Shomper, *Cedarville University*
charles shub, *University of Colorado at Colorado Springs*
Scott Sigman, *Drury University*
Gavin Sim, *Uni of Central Lancashire*
Maria Simi, *Universita di Pisa*
Beth Simon, *University of California, San Diego*
Oberta Slotterbeck, *Hiram College*
William Slough, *Eastern Illinois University*
Joslyn Smith, *Florida International University*
Peter Smith, *California State University - Channel Islands*
Robert Snapp, *University of Vermont*
Peter Sommerlad, *HSR Rapperswil*
Joel Sommers, *Colgate University*
Raja Sooriamurthi, *Carnegie Mellon University*
Jonathan Sorenson, *Butler University*
Barry Soroka, *Cal Poly Pomona*
Jaime Spacco, *Knox College*
Greg Speegle, *Baylor University*
David Spooner, *Rensselaer Polytechnic Institute*
Carol Spradling, *Northwest Missouri State University*
Nathan Sprague, *James Madison University*
Denbigh Starkey, *Montana State University*
Mark Stehlik, *Carnegie Mellon University*
Josh Steinhurst, *Bucknell University*
Ben Stephenson, *University of Calgary*
Daniel Stevenson, *University of Wisconsin - Eau Claire*
Khadija Stewart, *DePauw University*
Evelyn Stiller, *Plymouth State University*
Vojislav Stojkovic, *Morgan State University*
Christopher Stone, *Harvey Mudd College*
Jeffrey Stone, *Pennsylvania State University*
Forrest Stonedahl, *Centre College*
Fred Strickland, *South University*
Kristina Striegnitz, *Union College*
Catherine Stringfellow, *Midwestern State University*
Lena Stromback, *Department of Computer and Information Science*
Deborah Sturm, *College of Staten Island CUNY*
Dario Suarez Gracia, *Universidad de Zaragoza*
Jose Such, *Technical University of Valencia*
Leigh Ann Sudol, *Carnegie Mellon University*
John R. Sullins, *Youngstown State University*
Fred Sullivan, *Wilkes University*
Wayne Summers, *Columbus State University*
Valerie Summet, *Emory University*
Weiqing Sun, *University of Toledo*
Ken Surendran, *Southeast Missouri State University*
Jerry Talton, *Stanford University*
Joo Tan, *Kutztown University*
Stewart Tansley, *Microsoft Research*
Blair Taylor, *Towson University*
James Teresco, *Siena College*
Allison Elliott Tew, *Georgia Institute of Technology*
William Thacker, *Winthrop University*
Lynda Thomas, *Aberystwyth University*
Megan Thomas, *California State University Stanislaus*
Rebecca Thomas, *Bard College*
Stan Thomas, *Wake Forest University*
Alfred Thompson, *Microsoft*
Jodi Tims, *Baldwin-Wallace College*
Fergus Toolan, *University College Dublin*
Gloria Childress Townsend, *DePauw University*
Christian Trefftz, *Grand Valley State University*
Deborah Trytten, *University of Oklahoma*
Shengru Tu, *University of New Orleans*
David S. Tucker, *Midwestern State Univ.*
William Turner, *Wabash College*
Sharon M. Tuttle, *Humboldt State University*
Hakan Tuzun, *Hacettepe University*

Suleyman Uludag, *The University of Michigan - Flint*
Susan D. Urban, *Texas Tech University*
Timothy Urness, *Drake University*
Jaime Urquiza-Fuentes, *Rey Juan Carlos University*
Ian Utting, *University of Kent at Canterbury*
Jan Vahrenhold, *Technische Universität Dortmund*
Ignatios Vakalis, *California Polytechnic and State University*
David Valentine, *Slippery Rock University*
James Vallino, *Rochester Institute of Technology*
Robert Van Camp, *Marietta College*
Tammy Van De Grift, *University of Portland*
Ian van der Linde, *Anglia Ruskin University*
Brad Vander Zanden, *University of Tennessee*
Asaf Varol, *Wilkes University*
Yaakov Varol, *University of Nevada Reno*
Jorge Vasconcelos, *Johns Hopkins University*
Troy Vasiga, *University of Waterloo*
Kam Vat, *University of Macau*
Steven Vegdahl, *University of Portland*
Nanette Veilleux, *Simmons College*
J. Angel Velazquez-Iturbide, *Universidad Rey Juan Carlos*
Gabriela Vilanova, *National Patagonia Austral University*
Tamar Vilner, *The Open University of Israel*
Kimberly Voll, *University of British Columbia*
Ken Vollmar, *Missouri State University*
David Voorhees, *Le Moyne College*
Rosita Wachenchauzer, *Universidad de Buenos Aires*
Paul Wagner, *University of Wisconsin - Eau Claire*
Sally Wahba, *Clemson University*
Gursimran Walia, *North Dakota State University*
Ellen Walker, *Hiram College*
Henry Walker, *Grinnell College*
Xinli Wang, *Michigan Technological University*
Xueyi Wang, *Northwest Nazarene University*
Xusheng Wang, *Winthrop University*
Karen Ward, *University of Portland*
Stan Warford, *Pepperdine University*
Richard Wasniowski, *California State University Dominguez Hills*
Thomas Way, *Villanova University*
Scott Weiss, *Mt. St. Mary's University*
Stephen Weiss, *University of North Carolina at Chapel Hill*
Emily Wenk, *Penn State York*
Linda Werner, *University of California, Santa Cruz*
Roger West, *University of Illinois at Springfield*
Curt White, *DePaul University*
Elizabeth White, *George Mason University*
Laurie White, *Mercer University*
Howard Whitston, *University of South Alabama*
Paul Wiedemeier, *The University of Louisiana at Monroe*
Sheila Wiggins, *retired*
Linda Wilkens, *Providence College*
Judith Williams, *William Penn University*
Craig Wills, *Worcester Polytechnic Institute*
Linda Wilson, *Texas Lutheran University*
Michael Wirth, *University of Guelph*
Lee Wittenberg, *GW Software*
Walter Wolf, *Rochester Institute of Technology*
Christine Wolfe, *Ohio University*
Rosalee Wolfe, *DePaul University*
David Wolff, *Pacific Lutheran University*
Greg Wolffe, *Grand Valley State University*
Steven Wolfman, *University of British Columbia*
Ursula Wolz, *Olin College of Engineering*
Gary Wong, *The Community College at Lingnan University*
David Wonnacott, *Haverford College*
Karl Wurst, *Worcester State University*
Stelios Xinogalos, *University of Macedonia*
Dianna Xu, *Bryn Mawr College*
T. Andrew Yang, *University of Houston - Clear Lake*
Arthur Yanushka, *Christian Brothers University*
Ken Yasuhara, *University of Washington*
Dowming Yeh, *National Kaohsiung Normal University*
Juang Yih-Ruey, *Jinwen University of Science & Technology*
Duane Yoder, *University of West Georgia*
Alison Young, *Christchurch Polytechnic Institute of Technology*
Kwok-Bun Yue, *University of Houston-Clear Lake*
Timothy Yuen, *UTSA*
Marsha Zaidman, *University of Mary Washington*
Carol Zander, *University of Washington, Bothell*
Alan Zaring, *Ohio Wesleyan University*
Julie Zelenski, *Stanford University*
Dean Zeller, *Art Institute of Jacksonville*
Jinghua Zhang, *Winston-Salem State University*
Lynn Ziegler, *St. John's University*
Uta Ziegler, *Western Kentucky University*
Stephen Zilora, *Rochester Institute of Technology*
Guy Zimmerman, *Bowling Green State University*
Jill Zimmerman, *Goucher College*
Daniel Zingaro, *University of Toronto*
Fani Zlatarova, *Elizabethtown College*

The Teacher's Job is to Design Learning Experiences; Not Primarily to Impart Information

Frederick P. Brooks, Jr.
Kenan Professor of Computer Science
University of North Carolina at Chapel Hill
brooks@c.s.unc.edu

Abstract
The primary job of the teacher is to make learning happen; that is a design task. Most of us learned most of what we know by what we did, not by what we heard or read. A corollary is that the careful designing of exercises, assignments, projects, even quizzes, makes more difference than the construction of lectures. A second corollary is that project courses that go deeply into narrow aspects of a subject seem to stick longer and deeper than approaches aiming at comprehensive coverage. How to strike a balance? I've taught a first software engineering laboratory course 22 times, and an advanced computer architecture course about ten times. Here are some techniques that work for me.

Categories and Subject Descriptors
K.3.2 [**Computers and Education**]: Computer and Information Science Education – *Computer science education*

General Terms
Experimentation

Copyright is held by the author/owner(s).
SIGCSE'12, February 29–March 3, 2012, Raleigh, North Carolina, USA.
ACM 978-1-4503-1098-7/12/02.

Computer Science Curriculum 2013: Reviewing the Strawman Report from the ACM/IEEE-CS Task Force

Mehran Sahami (moderator)
Stanford University
Computer Science Department
sahami@cs.stanford.edu

Steve Roach
University of Texas at El Paso
Computer Science Department
sroach@utep.edu

Ernesto Cuadros-Vargas
San Pablo Catholic University
School of Computer Science
ecuadros@ucsp.edu.pe

David Reed
Creighton University
Department of Journalism, Media & Computing
davereed@creighton.edu

Categories and Subject Descriptors
K.3.2 [**Computers and Education**]: Computer Science Education; Curriculum

General Terms
Documentation, Design, Standardization.

Keywords
Computing Curricula 2013: Computer Science, CS2013.

1. SUMMARY
Beginning over 40 years ago with the publication of Curriculum 68 [1], the major professional societies in computing—ACM and IEEE-Computer Society—have sponsored various efforts to establish international curricular guidelines for undergraduate programs in computing. As the field has grown and diversified, so too have the recommendations for curricula. There are now guidelines for Computer Engineering, Information Systems, Information Technology, and Software Engineering in addition to Computer Science. These volumes are updated regularly with the aim of keeping computing curricula modern and relevant.

In the Fall of 2010, work on the next volume in the series, Computer Science 2013 (CS2013), began. Considerable work on the new volume has already been completed and a first draft of the CS2013 report (known as the Strawman report) will be complete by the beginning of 2012. This panel seeks to update and engage the SIGCSE community in providing feedback on the Strawman report, which will be available shortly prior to the SIGCSE conference.

The rapid evolution and expansion of the computing field and the growing number of topics in computer science has made regular revision of curricular recommendations necessary. The integration of computing with other disciplines creates additional opportunities for defining innovative computing curricula. Balancing this topical growth with the need to keep recommendations realistic and implementable in the context of undergraduate education is particularly challenging. As a result, it is important to engage the broader computer science education community in a dialog to better understand new opportunities, local needs, and novel successful models of computing curriculum.

The last complete Computer Science curricular volume was released in 2001 [3] and was followed by a review effort that concluded in 2008 [2]. While the review helped to update some of the knowledge units in the 2001 volume, it was not aimed at producing an entirely new curricular volume and deferred some of the more significant questions that arose at the time. The Computer Science 2013 effort seeks to provide a new volume reflecting the current state of the field. In particular, it highlights promising future directions through revisiting and redefining the knowledge areas in CS, rethinking the essentials necessary for a CS curriculum, and identifying working exemplars of courses and curricula along these lines.

The high-level themes on which the CS2013 effort is based include:

- *The "Big Tent" view of CS* – As CS expands to include more multi-disciplinary work and new programs of the form "Computational X" are developed, it is important to embrace an outward looking view in computing that sees CS as a discipline actively seeking to work with and integrate into other disciplines.
- *Managing the size of the curriculum* – Although the field of Computer Science continues to grow unabated, it is simply not feasible to proportionately expand the size of the curriculum. As a result, CS2013 seeks to re-evaluate what are considered essential topics in computing so as to make room for new topics without requiring more total instructional hours than the prior CC2001 guidelines. The circumscription of curriculum size in necessary to promote more flexible models for curricula without losing the essence of a rigorous CS education.
- *Actual course exemplars as opposed to stylized course guidance* – CS2001 took on the significant challenge of providing descriptions of stylized courses incorporating the knowledge units defined in that report. While this was a valiant effort, it was felt in retrospect that such course guidance

Copyright is held by the author/owner(s).
SIGCSE'12, February 29–March 3, 2012, Raleigh, North Carolina, USA.
ACM 978-1-4503-1098-7/12/02.

did not have much impact on actual course design. As a result, CS2013 plans to take a different approach: identifying existing successful courses and curricula as fielded exemplars of how relevant knowledge units can be addressed in actual programs. This bears similarity to the report by CRA-E [4], although that report focused on preparing students for research careers.

- *Institutional needs* – CS2013 aims to provide curricular models suitable in a broad range of contexts, understanding that curricula exist in the context of specific institutional needs, goals, and resource constraints. As a result, CS2013 allows for explicit flexibility in curricular structure through a *tiered* set of core topics, where a small set of Tier 1 topics are considered essential for all CS programs, but individual programs have flexibility with regard to their coverage of Tier 2 topics.

Work so far on the CS2013 effort has primarily focused on updating the Body of Knowledge in computer science, organized around 18 Knowledge Areas, outlined below:

- Algorithms and Complexity (AL)
- Architecture and Organization (AR)
- Computational Science (CN)
- Discrete Structures (DS)
- Graphics and Visual Computing (GV)
- Human-Computer Interaction (HC)
- Information Assurance and Security (IAS)
- Information Management (IM)
- Intelligent Systems (IS)
- Networking and Communications (NC)
- Operating Systems (OS)
- Platform-Based Development (PBD)
- Parallel and Distributed Computing (PD)
- Programming Languages (PL)
- Software Development Fundamentals (SDF)
- Software Engineering (SE)
- System Fundamentals (SF)
- Social and Professional Issues (SP)

In a departure from previous curricular efforts, CS2013 reorganizes coverage of introductory programming in an area now called Software Development Fundamentals (previously called Programming Fundamentals), and defines a new area called Systems Fundamentals that captures cross-cutting systems-level concepts. Additionally, specific developments in the field in the past decade (such as the pervasiveness of parallel computing and the need for better understanding computer security) have given rise to the development of knowledge areas in Parallel and Distributed Computing, Information Assurance and Security, and a reorganization of topics in Networking and Communications. Finally, the rise of platform-specific development (for example mobile computing and game consoles) is also addressed through the new Platform-Based Development area. Discussion of these new knowledge areas, changes in existing knowledge areas, and the larger-scale suggestions around curricular structure will provide numerous topics for engagement during this panel.

As mentioned previously, the goal of this panel is not simply to provide an update on the current thinking and state of CS2013, but to actively engage the community in the discussions and work that will eventually manifest into the final published volume. Holding this panel at SIGCSE is an important step in further engendering that engagement in a broad forum. Indeed, the CS2013 effort has already reached out to a number of communities, holding presentations at SIGCSE-11 [5], CSEET-11, FIE-11, FCRC-11, EAAI-11, as well as being involved in curricular discussions at SIGCOMM-11 and SPLASH-11. We believe that SIGCSE-12 will be the most relevant venue to provide the *first* discussions on the complete CS2013 Strawman draft, which will be available shortly before the conference.

2. MEHRAN SAHAMI

Mehran Sahami is co-chair of the Steering Committee for the Computing Curricula 2013: Computer Science volume. He is an Associate Professor and Associate Chair for Education in the Computer Science Department at Stanford University, where he led a redesign of the undergraduate Computer Science curriculum.

3. STEVE ROACH

Steve Roach is co-chair of the Steering Committee for the Computing Curricula 2013: Computer Science volume. He is an Associate Professor in the Department of Computer Science at the University of Texas at El Paso. He was involved in Computing Curriculum Software Engineering 2004 and the Graduate Software Engineering 2009 efforts.

4. ERNESTO CUADROS-VARGAS

Ernesto Cuadros-Vargas is a member of the Steering Committee for the Computing Curricula 2013: Computer Science volume. He is a Professor of Computer Science and Dean of the School of Engineering and Computing at San Pablo Catholic University in Arequipa, Peru. He is Executive Secretary of the Latin American Center on Computer Science and former President of the Peruvian Computing Society.

5. DAVID REED

David Reed is a member of the Steering Committee for the Computing Curricula 2013: Computer Science volume. He is an Associate Professor and Director of the Computer Science Program at Creighton University. He is currently on the Board of Directors of the Computer Science Teachers Association and served as Chief Reader for the AP CS exam from 2004-2008.

6. REFERENCES

[1] ACM Curriculum Committee on Computer Science. 1968. Curriculum 68: Recommendations for Academic Programs in Computer Science. *Comm. ACM* 11, 3 (Mar. 1968), 151-197.

[2] ACM/IEEE-CS Joint Interim Review Task Force. 2008. Computer Science Curriculum 2008: An Interim Revision of CS 2001, Report from the Interim Review Task Force. http://www.acm.org/education/curricula/ComputerScience2008.pdf

[3] ACM/IEEE-CS Joint Task Force on Computing Curricula. 2001. ACM/IEEE Computing Curricula 2001 Final Report. http://www.acm.org/sigcse/cc2001.

[4] CRA-Education Committee. 2010. Creating Environments for Computational Researcher Education. http://www.cra.org/uploads/documents/resources/rissues/CRA-E-Researcher-Education.pdf

[5] Sahami, M., Guzdial, M., McGettrick, A., and Roach, S. 2011. Setting the Stage for Computing Curricula 2013: Computer Science – Report from the ACM/IEEE-CS Joint Task Force. In *Proc. SIGCSE '11*, 161-162.

Scrum Across the CS/SE Curricula: A Retrospective

Charles Wallace
Michigan Technological University
Houghton, MI 49931
wallace@mtu.edu

Sriram Mohan
Rose-Hulman Institute of Technology
Terre Haute, IA 47803
mohan@rose-hulman.edu

Douglas Troy
Miami University
Oxford, OH 45056
troyda@muohio.edu

Mark E. Hoffman (Moderator)
Quinnipiac University
Hamden, CT 06518
mark.hoffman@quinnipiac.edu

Summary

Scrum is one of the many *agile* approaches to software development that have been widely adopted over the past decade. Agile processes allow developers to embrace under-defined problems in complex environments where change in requirements is inevitable. The key agile features of Scrum are a flexible, adaptive schedule; democratic, collaborative teams; and frequent, iterative project and process reviews [2]. While students may engage with Scrum in the context of software development, the characteristics that suit many software problems to an agile approach also describe the student learning environment: complexity (new and unfamiliar concepts), under-defined problem space (students don't know what they don't know), short timeframe with frequent meetings (terms and class meetings), and inevitable change (apply new knowledge). This makes Scrum not only a software development strategy but a general learning strategy. Scrum facilitates frequent and iterative practice with timely feedback, development of mastery, and self-direction [1].

In this panel, the participants will describe how their students learn and practice Scrum in a software development context, how they use it to manage student projects outside the software development context, and how Scrum provides opportunities to integrate communication skills into the Computer Science (CS) and Software Engineering (SE) curricula. As participants in the NSF-funded CPATH II project (NSF Grants 0939122 and 0939081) "Incorporating Communication Skills Throughout Computer Science and Software Engineering Curricula," each panelist has developed Scrum-based assignments that exercise the skills of reading, writing, speaking, and teaming. The participants will discuss the design of these assignments and their experiences with them to date.

Categories and Subject Descriptors

K.3.2 [**Computer and Education**]: Computer Science Education

General Terms

Documentation, Design, Management

Copyright is held by the author/owner(s).
SIGCSE'12, February 29–March 3, 2012, Raleigh, North Carolina, USA.
ACM 978-1-4503-1098-7/12/02.

Keywords

Scrum, software development, curriculum, communication skills

1. Douglas Troy

I use Scrum as the primary organizational strategy in our introductory software engineering course, CSE 201, which is targeted to sophomores. The course is a broad introduction to the software life cycle including a semester-long project to make the concepts concrete. Students enter CSE 201 having completed two semesters (CS1 and CS2) of programming in Java including object-oriented programming but little in the way of teamwork and communications. The teamwork and communications skills used in Scrum in CSE 201 introduce students to the human side of our discipline. I have also found that the short iterations and constant feedback helps students to create higher quality and more sophisticated projects than I, or they, would have imagined possible before using Scrum.

I typically engage an external client who has a real problem to solve. The past two years the client has been the Miami Tribe from which Miami University gets its name. The Miami Tribe and Miami University sponsor a culture and language reclamation project called the Myaamia Project. My CSE 201 students develop interactive web-based games and activities to help Miami Tribe families to learn the Myaamia language in their homes. At the start of the semester the client has a general idea of what they want to accomplish, but the requirements are vague. Furthermore, the client wants the students to suggest alternative approaches and to offer creative ideas. Thus, it is impossible to define complete project requirements before beginning design and implementation. The iterative Scrum process is a natural fit for this environment, allowing the requirements to evolve through repeated team presentations, demos, and frequent feedback from the client. This process is a great immersive introduction to communicating with variety of audiences (client, peers, instructor) and team work.

Before using Scrum projects were typically not completed by the end of the semester. With Scrum projects have been delivered and are in use by the client. Short two-week iterations with frequent builds and demos provide the structure and motivation that drive the project toward completion. One challenging aspect of the course is that each team is implementing a portion of the project, all of which need to be integrated into the final product. This encourages teams to work together and problem-solve, but I am still working out how to manage a Scrum of Scrums. Overall, Scrum is a natural fit for the learning environment, it works, and has helped me to achieve better results and more motivated students than in the past.

2. Sriram Mohan

We have had great success in incorporating a wide variety of agile techniques such as Scrum, TDD, and Kanban in our curriculum.

Scrum has been used for the past four years in our sophomore level class (CSSE 333) titled Introduction to Database Systems. This course follows 2 quarters of introductory software development classes that utilize Python and Java and a class on data structures typically taught using Java. These prior classes are built around a term project with fixed weekly deadlines. Students are exposed mainly to good design techniques and the notion of project management is not captured. The only agile methodology that students use on a regular basis is Pair Programming.

An important learning objective of using Scrum in CSSE 333 is to educate students on simple management techniques such as Feature Selection, Cost Estimation and Scheduling. Students work on a 6-week final project (about 150 hours) and are tasked with the development of an information system. Specific functionality and objectives of the information system (web based e-commerce system, video game, etc.) are subject to certain minimum complexity constraints, but are decided by each team based on their interests.

Each team has complete freedom in deciding their internal organization and workload arrangement. Each team is expected to meet with the instructor on a weekly basis, to discuss the project progress. To ensure that the teams are making adequate progress, each team will demonstrate the current status of the project at the end of each week. During the meeting, each team will: a) Demonstrate the progress made during the previous week and b) Identify and confirm the user scenario that will be demonstrated during next week's meeting

The use of Agile techniques has greatly enhanced student learning and provides students with a hands-on opportunity to develop their management techniques. Students showcase a mastery of these techniques in a follow-up course on Software Quality Assurance, wherein students are required to use Scrum or other similar agile techniques in conjunction with Test Driven Development. We have also seen a near universal adoption of Agile methodologies in our Junior and Senior Project classes, where students have the freedom to choose and implement any methodology to manage their yearlong software projects for an external client.

3. Charles Wallace

One of the things I find remarkable about Scrum is its emphasis on *reflection*, both at the project level and the process level. It is not simply encouraged but explicitly built into the process, through daily stand-ups and sprint retrospectives. Other activities, such as task estimation and computing velocity, require developers to look back and consider the lessons learned from prior experience.

I feel that reflection is especially important for the senior students in my capstone project course. I think of a capstone course as operating on two levels. At one level, it is a project, where the goal is to achieve what the client needs. At a higher level, it is an opportunity for students to reflect on the process: what things do they do when they "work on the project", how do these things help, and what could be done differently and better. While I can preach the virtues of reflection, it has been difficult to make students put aside the project temporarily and spend time thinking about what they have learned. Scrum makes this easier by *reifying* reflection: it is an honored activity, performed every day and as the culmination of every sprint.

I have developed some assignments to enhance the reflective opportunities afforded by the capstone project. These assignments ask students to reflect on the communicative aspects of the project: how they plan and carry out communication with one another and with their clients, and how other Scrum teams do things differently. The assignments vary in the genres and heuristics they use, so students get experience contemplating and describing the communication in their project in different ways. I think they have been effective in helping me to fulfill my job as not only a project manager but a facilitator of deeper learning.

4. Mark Hoffman

Scrum has been used for the past three years in our first-semester, sophomore-level course (CSC 225) titled Introduction to Software Development. The course follows a two-semester, introductory programming sequence where students use a scripting language (e.g., Python, Ruby, or Scala) in CS1 and use Java in CS2. Typical projects in the introductory courses are designed for single students or occasionally small teams. The focus of these courses is on problem solving. CSC 225 introduces students to the issues of an ongoing project that requires a team to develop. The course is not a comprehensive Software Engineering course; instead, students learn about developing software experientially by actually developing a good-sized, ongoing project.

Prior to using Scrum, a traditional linear process resembling Waterfall was used. Students were required to submit documents in stages over the semester. Because the process was linear, students were not able to reflect, revise, and reapply what they had experienced. Project results relied on negative lessons more heavily than desirable. Scrum, instead, has yielded much better results by allowing students to refine and reapply what they learn. For example, when a team selects an item from the backlog they need to estimate its cost in time and developers. Since students have no experience estimating, their "guesses" are wildly inaccurate. For the students this is an under-defined and complex task. Over the course of four, two-week Scrum Cycles, students begin to develop an understanding of the issues involved in estimating and the need to monitor progress.

One of the critical objectives of CSC 225 is to introduce students to the "soft" skills integral to software development. These include teaming (working in small, collaborative teams), speaking (presenting in a variety of situations from formal presentations to informal explanations), and writing (process and software documentation). Participation in the CPATH project has provided the opportunity to redesign the course and integrate critical communication skills. Assignments evaluate not only the technical skills but also the communication skills. For each assignment, rubrics detail the criteria and levels of achievement expected. Scrum easily facilitates reflection and evidence of achievement through an iterative, self-directed process.

5. REFERENCES

[1] S. Ambrose, M. Bridges, M. DiPietro, M. Lovett, and M. Norman, *How Learning Works: 7 Research-Based Principles for Smarter Teaching*, Jossey-Bass, 2010.

[2] K. Schwaber and M. Beedle, *Agile Software Development with Scrum*, Prentice Hall, 2002.

The Role of Interdisciplinary Computing in Higher Education, Research and Industry

Lillian (Boots) Cassel
Dept. of Computing Sciences
Villanova University
Villanova, PA 19085
+1 610 519 7341
cassel@acm.org

Ursula Wolz
Franklin. W. Olin College of Engineering
Needham MA
+1 609 213 7682
Ursula.Wolz@olin.edu

Categories and Subject Descriptors
K.3.2 [**Computing Milieux**] Computer and Information Science Education
K. 4.0 Computers and Society

General Terms
Human Factors

Keywords
Interdisciplinary computing.

1. SUMMARY
At SIGCSE 2010 program directors from the National Science Foundation held a panel [1] on the potential for Interdisciplinary Computing. As an outgrowth of that session, via an EAGER grant (OCI-1058623), ***Toward a Climate for Interdisciplinary Computing***, a group of individuals drawn from a range of universities and from industry met in January 2011 and April 2011 to discuss the nature of interdisciplinary computing, its importance both for computing and for other disciplines, obstacles to the further emergence of interdisciplinary computing and ways in which these obstacles might be overcome. This session will provide an opportunity for the SIGCSE community to participate in this discussion.

2. OBJECTIVES
Interdisciplinary studies are emerging as both necessary and expedient in the academy [2]. I During this special session the facilitators provide a brief summary of the outcomes of January and April meetings along with those from a meeting scheduled for November 2011.

Copyright is held by the author/owner(s).
SIGCSE'12, February 29–March 3, 2012, Raleigh, North Carolina,USA.
ACM 978-1-4503-1098-7/12/02.

Through these meetings the following questions have emerged:

- Why interdisciplinary computing is important.
- Why should it be nurtured,
- How can it be nurtured?

These questions spawned a more detailed set of questions that are for which we are beginning to develop answers:

- What spectra are we looking at for professional and student interdisciplinary work?
- What are the indicators of successes in industry and academia that we want to replicate?
- What are the categories of interdisciplinary work?
- Why is interdisciplinary work important?
- Where does it exist?
- How does it exist in both industry and academia?
- What are the major contributors to a climate for interdisciplinary computing?
- What are the most significant obstacles to interdisciplinary collaboration, both in general and with respect to interdisciplinary computing?
- What success stories provide good exemplars for new activities and programs?
- What failures provide good examples of pitfalls to avoid?
- What needs to happen to make more successful interdisciplinary computing experiences happen?

These questions called for examples of collaborations that seem to be successful, evaluating real observable results. But we also needed to articulate setbacks, negative outcomes, and impediments. Meeting participants provided the initial set of examples and pointers that are leading to more data.

During this special session we will review our results to date, and ask attendees to participate in the round-table analysis experience held during our meetings.

3. SESSION OUTLINE
This 75 minute session will be scheduled as follows:

- An overview and summary of prior meetings will take approximately 20 minutes and will include instructions for round table discussion. Participants will be asked to join groups of 5 to 8 related to a particular topic.

- Participants, in groups of 5 to 8 will spend 30 minutes addressing specific questions related to the topics.
- The remaining time will be used for a full group discussion including short reports selected from the groups.

Topics will include domain areas where interdisciplinary computing is robust (e.g. astrophysics, biology, media), where it is emerging (e.g. journalism, humanities) as well as broader topics such as the undergraduate experience, interdisciplinary computing in industry, motivation for faculty and institutions.

Prepared worksheets will facilitate and focus the discussion. Materials will also be available on line, and participants can both receive and submit materials electronically. More than one group can focus on a pre-defined topic. Participants will be able to put forth their own focus as well within the constraints the three basic questions listed in section 1.

The facilitators, as well as meeting participants who attend SIGCSE will circle the room to keep the discussion focused and identify significant outcomes. We anticipate five to ten co-facilitators from the 100 who will have attended our meetings prior to SIGCSE 2012.

4. EXPECTATIONS

Expectations for this session are to:

1. That the SIGCSE community will provide commentary on the outcomes of the meetings on interdisciplinary computing and suggest an agenda for anticipated fourth meeting.
2. The SIGCSE community will provide real data (via the round table discussions) that begin to address the questions raised in section 2. These materials will be incorporated into future reports of this project.
3. The summary discussion at the end of this session will provide insight into next steps. In particular it will provide guidance on recommendations to NSF on how to support interdisciplinary computing in educational, research and industrial settiongs.

5. ACKNOWLEDGMENTS

This work supported by the National Science Foundation under Grant No. OCI-1058623, any opinions, findings, and conclusions or recommendations expressed here are those of the authors and do not necessarily reflect the views of the National Science Foundation."

6. REFERENCES

[1] Amoussou, G., Boylan M. and Peckham J. (2010) Inderdiscipliary computing education for the challenges of the future" *Proceedings of the 41st ACM Technical Symposium on Computer Science Education,* (March 10-13, Milwaukee, WI USA)

[2] Davis, J. R. (1995). Interdisciplinary courses and team teaching: New arrangements for learning. Phoenix, AZ: American Council on Education and Oryx Press

Sustainability Themed Problem Solving In Data Structures And Algorithms

Ali Erkan*
aerkan@ithaca.edu
Ithaca College
401B Williams Hall
Ithaca, NY 14850, U.S.A.

Tom Pfaff†
tpfaff@ithaca.edu
Ithaca College
311A Williams Hall
Ithaca, NY 14850, U.S.A.

Jason Hamilton‡
jhamilton@ithaca.edu
Ithaca College
252 Cntr. Nat. Sci.
Ithaca, NY 14850, U.S.A.

Michael Rogers§
mrogers@ithaca.edu
Ithaca College
265 Cntr. Nat. Sci.
Ithaca, NY 14850, U.S.A.

ABSTRACT

During the past two years, we have been creating curricular material centered around complex problems rooted in sustainability. Since multidisciplinary learning is one of our primary goals, these projects are most meaningful when they connect students from different disciplines working toward a common understanding. However, strong disciplinary components present in their solutions also allow us to frame these projects from strictly disciplinary perspectives; in this paper, we show how they can be used for increased engagement in the context of data structures and algorithms. In an earlier publication, we presented a project for computer science students to analyze the changes in the size and the ice-concentrations of the Arctic. In this paper, we review two new ones to explore (i) the structural characteristics of the western part of the U.S. power-grid, and (ii) challenges of sustainably harvesting fish.

Categories and Subject Descriptors

K.3.2 [**Computers and Education**]: Computer and Information Science Education—*Computer science education*; J.2 [**Physical Sciences And Engineering**]: Earth and atmospheric sciences; E.1 [**Data Structures**]: Arrays, graphs and networks, lists, stacks, and queues

General Terms

Algorithms, Measurement, Experimentation

Keywords

Scientific computing, active learning

*Associate Professor of Computer Science.

†Associate Professor of Mathematics.

‡Associate Professor of Environmental Science and Studies.

§Associate Professor of Physics.

Permission to make digital or hard copies of all or part of this work for personal or classroom use is granted without fee provided that copies are not made or distributed for profit or commercial advantage and that copies bear this notice and the full citation on the first page. To copy otherwise, to republish, to post on servers or to redistribute to lists, requires prior specific permission and/or a fee.
SIGCSE'12, February 29–March 3, 2012, Raleigh, North Carolina, USA.
Copyright 2012 ACM 978-1-4503-1098-7/12/02 ...$10.00.

1. INTRODUCTION

Most significant problems of the 21st century require systems thinking. Consequently, we are now witnessing the growing importance of producing professionals with the skills to collaborate across disciplinary boundaries [17, 12]. Unfortunately, despite individual efforts and contributions (such as [10] and [20] for Computer Science), Science, Technology, Engineering, and Math (STEM) education in general has not been evolving sufficiently fast [2] and is therefore in need of additional attention to address the deficit [18].

We (four faculty members of our institute representing Computer Science, Mathematics, Biology, and Physics) are working on creating an NSF supported framework to address an undergraduate component of this deficit [7]. Specifically, we are focusing on the problems encountered in sustainability and formulating a method for them to be addressed by students from different disciplines. Since our curricular products are meant to work seamlessly within existing disciplinary and administrative structures of higher education, our approach is to be contrasted with others that require new resources, such as those proposed in [19, 21, 3] (for STEM education) and [15] (for computational sciences).

Our sustainability themed modules are built around real-world problems too complex to belong to a single discipline. Students from participating courses address these problems using their disciplinary techniques and produce technical reports to convey their findings; in the process, they also read technical reports coming from their peers from other disciplines. At the end of a module, students respond to

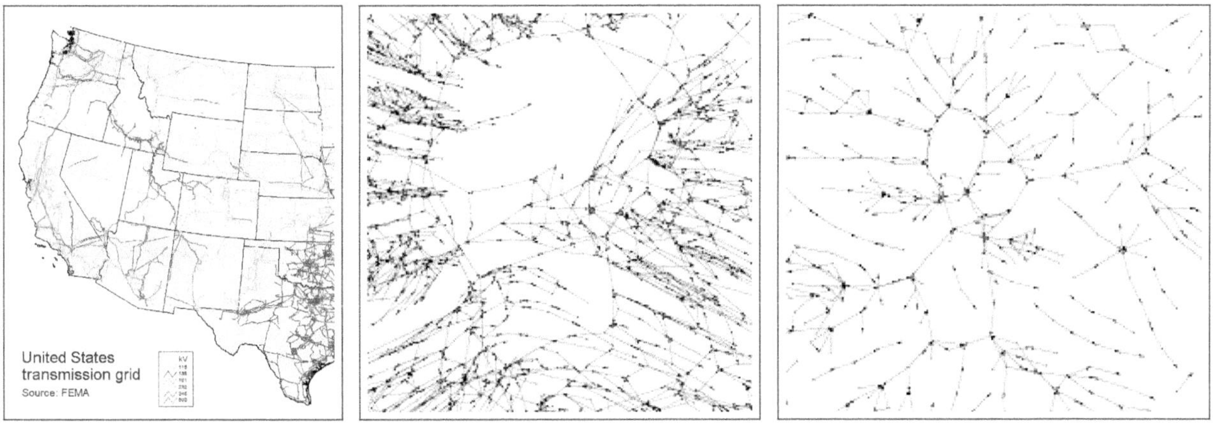

(a) Western power grid (b) Graph view (c) Effect of 2000 node deletions

Figure 1: *Figure 1a is a high-level geographic view of the transmission (AKA power) grid of the United States, as of 2005 [9]. Figure 1b (rendered by GraphViz of http://www.graphviz.org, based on a slightly modified version of the topological data from [23]) is a fragment of a graph view of the western section of the power grid, which has 4940 nodes and 6594 edges. Figure 1c is a fragment of the state of the graph after 2000 randomly chosen nodes are removed, leaving behind a set of disconnected components. The transformation of the graph from its state in 1b to that in 1c (iteratively, one node at a time, as done in [1]) is the basis of our structural analysis.*

module based questions that go beyond conventional disciplinary boundaries. Both our own experience as well as those reported in the literature [6] confirm that engagement through such real-world contexts leads to deeper learning.

In [4], we outlined the Computer Science (CS) perspective of our climate themed first module that explores the future of polar bears. In this paper, we outline two new modules for two other significant aspects of sustainability. For each, we arrange the subject matter in four parts: (i) how the underlying question creates a CS project; (ii) how the project relates to conventional CS topics; (iii) project details, particularly pertaining to implementation; (iv) a general discussion regarding its use in class. The power grid module (outlined in section 2) is for CS students to understand the structural characteristics and vulnerabilities of the United States electrical power grid. The fish harvesting module (outlined in section 3) is for CS students to understand the consequences of over-harvesting fish stocks. Both projects are designed to engage students in the Data Structures and Algorithms (DS&A) context of a conventional CS curriculum. The student responses we received after the first trials of these modules are reported in section 4.

The curricular material behind both modules (as well as instructor resources) will be available for dissemination via our project portal at http://www.ithaca.edu/mse.

2. POWER GRID PROJECT

One of the infrastructural problems facing the U.S. is the state of its electrical power grid. Considered to be one of the most monumental constructions of the country, this massive network has not gone through all the upgrades it needs to remain reliable. In addition to historic failures such as the northeast blackout of 2003, the number of non-disaster-related blackouts is on the rise. As individuals become more dependent on it for dealing with hotter summers, electric cars, etc., it has been approaching its operating capacity. Furthermore, since it is not monitored by a real-time system, it is not equipped to prevent regional failures from propagating into national blackouts. Therefore, understanding its current state and determining the best way in which it can be upgraded is a significant task for engineers and scientists.

For a sustainability point of view, our power grid project is designed for CS students to understand the power grid from a structural perspective and to start making inferences about the ways in which it may fail. From a computing point of view, the project is based on graphs, specifically to understand structural integrity when the directed acyclic graph topic of articulation points do not apply.

• **DS&A Question**: What are the structural vulnerabilities of the U.S. power grid? Does it have single points (or small clusters) of failure? How would it fragment as its components fail?

• **DS&A Connection**: As shown in figure 1, the power-grid is a network; therefore, when expressed as a collection of *nodes* (generators, transmission junctions, etc) and *edges* (transmission lines), it is a *graph.* The consideration of single points of failure relates to the topic of *articulation points*; the consideration of small-clusters, on the other hand, is a generalization of the same topic.

• **DS&A Project**: A complete understanding of the vulnerabilities of the power grid requires comprehension of a wide range of topics; transmission properties of the wires, load generation characteristics of the users, transformer limits, etc, are all intertwined in determining how the system operates (or fails). Therefore, it is important to note that the focus of the DS&A project is only on what can be inferred from the structure of the grid.

Topological descriptions of actual power grids are available from the WWW. For example, a graph ML representation of the Western U.S. power grid, as analyzed in [24], can be downloaded from [23] in GraphML form. Since the algorithms needed to process the structure of this grid require internal representation, a graph implementation (built by students) is needed as well. The search for articulation

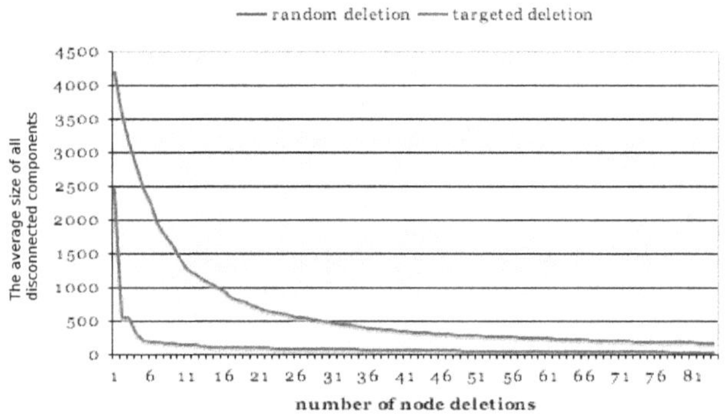

(a) Average disconnected component size

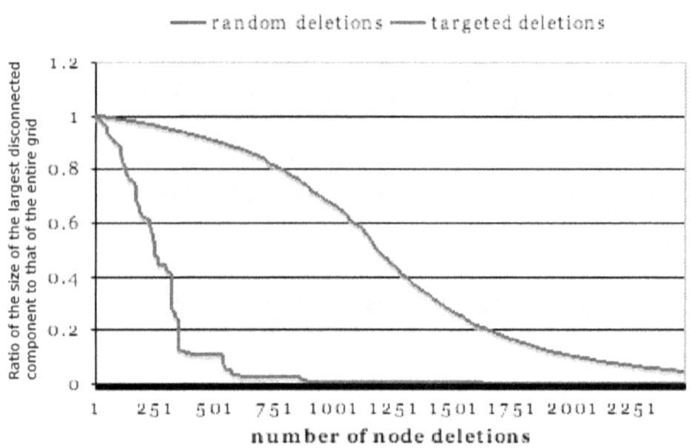

(b) "Largest component size" to "graph size" ratio

Figure 2: *Structural failure analysis for the Western U.S. power grid. Figure 2a shows the average size of all disconnected components while figure 2b shows the ratio of the size of the largest disconnected component to that of the entire grid. For both, random node removal (displaying a smoother curve) leads to a slower disintegration than adversarial node removal (displaying a more jittery curve by virtue of the particular numbers of edges of the maximally interconnected nodes chosen for removal).*

points is based on the associated directed acyclic graph algorithm provided in any standard textbook.

Much like many of the real-world networks (and unlike the artificial graphs included in textbooks for reinforcement exercises), it is extremely unlikely for an actual power grid to have an articulation point for understandable design reasons. Instead, we see clusters of highly-interconnected nodes that collectively form articulation "super-nodes". What makes the project interesting in many ways is requiring students to deal with this road-block either when they encounter it on their own or after a guided discussion. In our experience, the best solution to get a sense of the structure of the grid (particularly in terms of how it would fall apart as its nodes fail) is to use the technique employed in [1] which is basically an iterative removal of nodes from the underlying graph while computing at each iteration the (a) average size of the resulting disconnected components, and (b) the ratio of the largest disconnected component size to that of the entire graph size. The selection of the node to be removed (done once per iteration) can be *random* (meaning any of the remaining nodes is equally likely to be chosen next) or *adversarial* (meaning the node with the most number of edges is always chosen next).

Figure 2a shows the average disconnected component size of the western U.S. power grid while figure 2b shows the scaled size of the largest component of the grid. In both cases, the adversarial node failure model (rendered in red, displaying punctuated sequences of drops) leads to a dramatic disintegration of the structure while the random model (rendered in blue, displaying smoother plot-lines) shows the same tendency at a slower rate. Based on these results, students realize (through their own results) that despite the absence of articulation points, the power grid has structural vulnerabilities.

• **Discussion**: As it commonly happens with real-world problems, students generate new questions and new insights during the course of their work. In the power-grid project, we encountered two that confirmed deeper learning.

In terms of the implementation of the graph structure, students initially tend to use an adjacency list built as a singly linked list of singly linked lists. This arrangement is efficient for the construction of the graph but, for the removal of a node, the entire node set must be traversed to determine which incoming edges must also be discarded. Since node removal is done so frequently in the analysis behind figures 2a and 2b, students realize the inefficiency of their original design and feel compelled to reimplement their graph in an undirected manner[1] (i.e. with edges as well as reverse edges). This reduces the complexity of the node removal from big-O of the number of nodes down to big-O of the number of edges of the maximally interconnected node.

In terms of the real-world context, students question the realism of the random vs adversarial methods of node removal. They realize that if a node in a highly interconnected cluster fails, then power will most likely be rerouted over neighboring nodes. If these nodes are operating close to capacity, then they will probably be pushed beyond capacity. Since nodes of such clusters will have similar in- and out-degrees (almost by definition since it is the similar edge density among these nodes that gives rise to the formation of the cluster), the failed-node selection sequence will follow an edge density pattern. Consequently, the sequence will be more accurately modeled with the adversarial selection model.

3. FISH HARVESTING PROJECT

Due to unsustainable practices, the world's fish stocks are in a perilous state. For example, as shown in figure 3 and studied in [13, 22, 14, 8], the Atlantic Cod stocks of the east cost have collapsed between 1970 and 1992. Since a substantial percentage of the world's population get their nourishment from the sea [5], proper fish harvesting is an important resource management issue for the world.

From a sustainability point of view, our fish harvesting project is an attempt for CS students to get familiar with this problem and to understand that if we do not use our natural resources within their tolerance limits, we are bound to deplete them. From a computing point of view, the project is based on creating a discrete event simulation for exploring population dynamics subject to harvesting disruptions:

[1]During our trial, a few groups worked on this modification, providing us anecdotal evidence of their interest.

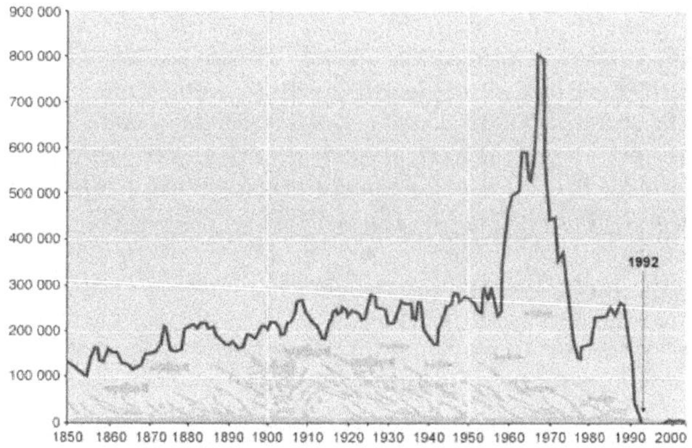

Figure 3: *The collapse of the Atlantic Cod stocks of the east cost of Newfoundland by 1992 [26]. The y-axis is fish landing in tons.*

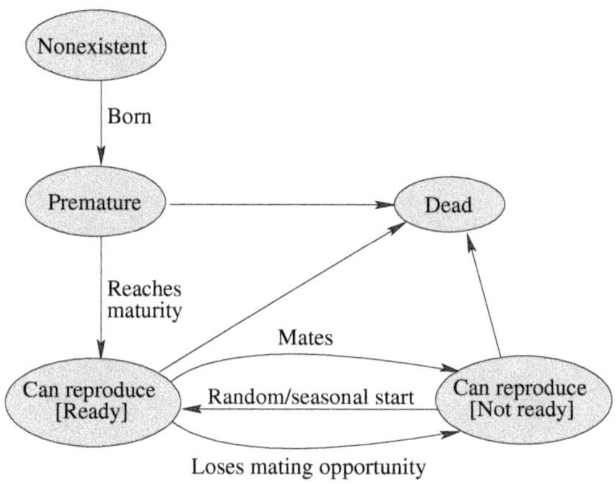

Figure 4: *A (very) simplified representation of the states occupied by a fish throughout its life. The "`Nonexistant`", "`Premature`", and "`Dead`" states are self-explanatory. Maturity is broken into the "`Can reproduce:[Ready]`" and "`Can reproduce:[Not Ready]`" states to incorporate the realism that once a fish reaches maturity, it will not be mating at all times (e.g. when it is outside of the mating season).*

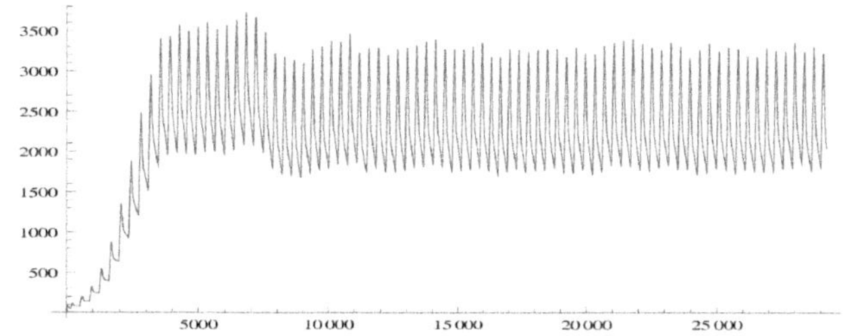

(a) Harvest rate of 5% of population

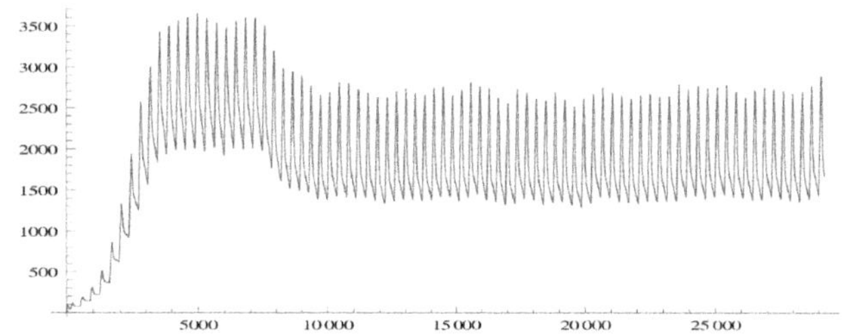

(b) Harvest rate of 10% of population

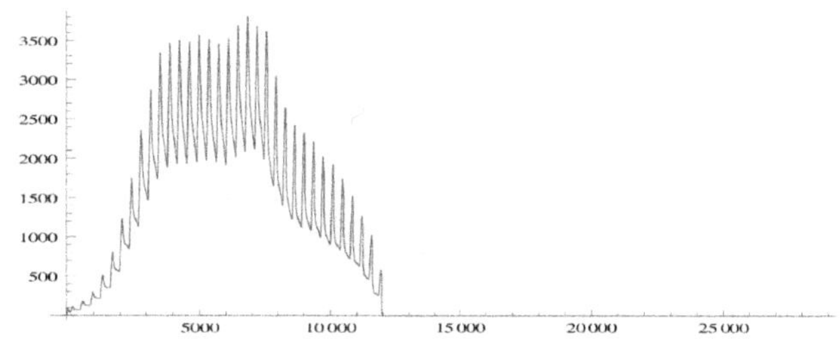

(c) Harvest rate of 15% of population

Figure 5: *Population size (y-axis) as a function of time in units of days (x-axis). In all three cases, the simulation starts with 3000 fish. The harvest rates are 5%, 10%, and 15% in figures 5a, 5b, and 5c, respectively.*

• **DS&A Question**: How sensitive is nature to the changes in our fish-harvesting practices? What kind of resilience can we expect when the extent of harvesting is not modulated by the size of the fish population?

• **DS&A Connection**: The system built by students is a conventional discrete event simulator[2]. Events are generated based on a very simple *finite state machine* (FSM) representation of fish; figure 4 shows the states as well as the possible transitions between these states. Discrete events that represent births, deaths, mating, etc, are all managed by a *priority queue* where priority is based on time; specifically, the closer the event is in the future, the higher the priority. The actual functionality of the priority queue is provided by a *heap* data structure. Depending on the sophistication of the simulation, the project may also use *hash tables* for managing sets of fish such as those that are premature, those that are reading for mating, etc.

• **DS&A Project**: The design of a discrete event simulation system is basically a matter of creating a collection of fish FSMs and letting them interact according to a simple set of rules (such as males proactively initiating mating); all durations (such as the time it takes for a fish to reach puberty) are determined by suitable probabilistic distributions. Aside from the "`Nonexistent`" and "`Dead`" states that delimit the existence of a particular fish, the simulated fish life consists of some period of prematurity followed by cycling between two states that determine when the fish can or cannot reproduce after reaching maturity. The primary result of the simulation is to represent fish population as a function of time.

• **Discussion**: This project is difficult in the sense that simulation errors are hard to detect; a subtle timing error produces reasonable yet incorrect results instead of crashing the program. Therefore, one option is to provide a solution with a missing piece that is to be provided by the students (such as the heap structure to manage the data and the operations associated with the priority queue). Regardless, given the huge numbers of events generated and executed,

[2]This section is only for highlighting how the project intersects with the standard topics from data structures and algorithms. More information on discrete event simulations can be found in CS2 (e.g. [25]) and CS7 textbooks.

students get a different perspective on what it takes to claim correctness on their result.

As in the power grid module, students' increased engagement leads to new questions and new insights in the project. For example, students question whether discrete event simulation is the only way one could model nature; the continuous model in [16, section 2.2] leads to an interesting discussion if the students already have some comprehension of differential equations. In our class, the time it takes to cycle between the "`Can reproduce:[Ready]`" and "`Can reproduce:[Not Ready]`" states was also considered to be a hook to create the effect of seasonal mating. If the timer that controls when a fish can transition from "`Can reproduce:[Not Ready]`" to "`Can reproduce:[Ready]`" is a probabilistic function of a master cyclic event marking the start of mating seasons, offspring are then created around the same time. If, on the other hand, the timer is determined independently, then there is no general pattern as to when offspring are produced. This difference turns out to have an effect on the perceived resilience of the fish population. When mating is seasonal, harvesting has a more detrimental effect on population if done soon after the production of a wave of offspring.

Figure 5 contains three population-vs-time plots from one of the student produced simulations. While each represents a different simulation, they are all based on an initial fish population of 3000. However, they differ by the periodic harvesting rate. Specifically, the harvest rate in figures 5a, 5b, and 5c are 5%, 10%, and 15%, respectively. Despite being based on a fairly simple model, it is interesting to see how the 15% rate depletes the fish population. This is indeed consistent with the real world where small changes can cause big differences, making it hard to sustainably harvest fish.

4. STUDENT RESPONSES

We have been gathering assessment data to capture students' reactions to our projects and to understand the extent of change in their perspectives. Parts of these findings have been included in [4, 7] and all will be reported once we have the necessary longitudinal components. However, during the 2010-2011 academic year, the students in the Algorithms class became the first group to experience all three modules: Polar Bear, Power Grid, and Fish Harvesting. Immediately after a presentation of 21st century problems and a discussion on our corresponding multidisciplinary approach, we asked them to anonymously express their thoughts; the following are *all* the responses we received (14 out of 16), in *unedited* form (i.e. with grammatical/spelling errors). The consistency of the students' appreciation is encouraging:

- "*Your point of view exactly reflects what I have in mind when it comes to undergrad studies. I am taking so many and so different classes and majors because eventually when I go into the work force I want to have as many different points of view.*"
- "*I really like hearing educators talk about how education should/will change to adjust to the times. I only wish every educator was on board. Without that, it will be pretty hard to make any serious changes in the way our education works.*"
- "*Examining problem solving like this has opened my mind to the larger problems I may face post-college - yet at the same time the problems are daunting and intimidate me as a relatively new programmer.*"
- "*Learning advanced problem solving skill is probably the most important thing I can learn. Programming languages can be easily picked, but learning how to think is much harder.*"
- "*I enjoyed the discussion alot it seemed organized and allowed for a good discussion. It is interesting to apply things from classes to bigger problems in realistic ways, and to see that our programming was purposeful is meaningful. I enjoy talking and discussing issues from an interdisciplinary perspective and allowing for not only computer science thinking, but also appreciation of classes.*"
- "*I was surprised how difficult problems could really be. I always like a new way to look at things and this way seems very logical and effective. I am glad we did this.*"
- "*As I am concerned about these "21st century problems", I feel that incorporating them into class is a good idea. I think it will not only help us improve our computer science skills but it will help us become better aware of these issues. I think our generation needs to help (or be the ones to actually) solve these problems and beginning with a small problem now will prepare us for the future.*"
- "*I believe that these topics are absolutely essential for computer scientists (and others) to be addressing.*"
- "*I think humanity is going downhill and there isn't enough being done to solve the major problems that relate to everyone. I thought the presentation was great and I hope that I can contribute to solving these problems in the future.*"
- "*I find it interesting how much fixing these global 21st century problems can be related down to Computer Science, and the skills needed to be a programmer in a world with constantly shifting programming laguages and needs. But with glaciers instead of programming languages.*"
- "*As the problems of the world become more complicated because the "easy" problems have already been solved, it is necessary to integrate these easy, solved problems into more complex, more useful tools that can solve greater problems.*"
- "*I think what we are doing right now is very interesting, I just want to see more examples and know if anyone has made an animation of a complex system.*"
- "*This discussion is beneficial to us because it shows us how we are going to think when all of our problems aren't structured like they are in school. Even though we may not be able to use this knowledge immediately, we will probably end up thinking this way when we try to tackle other problems.*"
- "*I think what we talked about is very intriguing but it's also kind of scary becuase there are so many problems that are becoming worse at a rate that's even too fast for computers to keep up with/solve & people could end up destroying this earth in the next few generations. Talking about this also made me realize a little more about how creative & unique this major is because often times I find myself very tunnel visioned, focusing & dwelling on things like syntax etc... Great discussion.*"

5. CONCLUSIONS

Given the most significant challenges of the 21st century, sustainability offers important guiding principles to produce solutions. Since these principles do not neatly fall within the boundaries of any one discipline, we believe a multidisciplinary approach is the right way to introduce them into education. And since this introduction cannot be done at the cost of producing disciplinary experts, multidisciplinary sustainability themed problems must be exercised in the context of disciplinary education. The participation of computing students in our three modules (two outlined in sections 2 and 3, one in [4]) allow CS students to learn core computing concepts as well as understand global climate, energy, and food matters.

Finding meaning in what they do is one of the strongest motivators for students [11]. In our experience, the meaning students find at the heart of sustainability themed problems brings out a different kind of commitment in them. As stated in one of the student comments in section 4, the big picture is less about programming languages and more about solving problems that matter to everyone.

6. ACKNOWLEDGMENTS

This work is supported by the NSF DUE #0837721 grant. The portal for our work is `http://www.ithaca.edu/mse`. The plots shown in figures 2a and 2b were produced by Pat Haggerty (class of 2011). The plots shown in figures 5a, 5b, and 5c were produced by Isaac Wagner (class of 2016), Colleen Muldowney (class of 2013) and Naomi Kaduwela (class of 2013).

7. REFERENCES

[1] R. Albert, H. Jeong, and A.-L. Barabasi. Error and attack tolerance of complex networks. *Nature*, 406:378, 2000.

[2] N. R. C. Board on Sustainable Development, Policy Division. *Our Common Journey: a transition toward sustainability.* National Academies Press, 1999.

[3] D. Deremer and K. G. Herbert. An interdisciplinary undergraduate science informatics degree in a liberal arts context. *SIGCSE Bull.*, 38(1):179–183, 2006.

[4] A. Erkan, J. Hamilton, T. Pfaff, and M. Rogers. Use of satellite imagery in multidisciplinary projects. In *SIGCSE '10: Proceedings of the 41th SIGCSE technical symposium on Computer Science education*, pages 32–37, New York, NY, USA, 2010. ACM.

[5] Food and A. O. of the United Nations. Recent trends and possible consequences for world fisheries and aquaculture. `http://www.fao.org/DOCREP/003/X8002E/x8002e07.htm`.

[6] M. Guzdial and E. Soloway. Teaching the nintendo generation to program. *Commun. ACM*, 45(4):17–21, 2002.

[7] J. G. Hamilton, M. Rogers, T. J. Pfaff, and A. Erkan. Multidisciplinary collaborations in the traditional classroom: Wrestling with global climate change to improve science education. *Transformations: The Journal of Inclusive Scholarship and Pedagogy*, XXI(1):89–98, Spring-Summer 2010.

[8] R. Hilborn and E. Litzinger. Causes of decline and potential for recovery of atlantic cod populations. *The Open Fish Science Journal*, (2):32–38, 2009.

[9] G. E. N. Institute. U.S. transmission lines. `http://geni.org/globalenergy/library/national_energy_grid/united-states-of-america/americannationalelectricitygrid.shtml`, 2005.

[10] D. T. Kaplan. Teaching computation to undergraduate scientists. *SIGCSE Bull.*, 36(1):358–362, 2004.

[11] L. Layman, L. Williams, and K. Slaten. Note to self: make assignments meaningful. In *Proceedings of the 38th SIGCSE technical symposium on Computer science education*, SIGCSE '07, pages 459–463, New York, NY, USA, 2007. ACM.

[12] J. Lubchenco. Entering the century of the environment: A new social contract for science. *Science*, 279:491–497, 1998.

[13] R. A. Myers, H. J. A., and B. N. J. Hypotheses for the decline of cod in the North Atlantic. *Marine Ecology Progress Series*, 138:293–308, 1996. http://www.int-res.com/abstracts/meps/v138/p293-308/.

[14] R. A. Myers, J. A. Hutchings, and N. J. Barrowman. Why do fish stocks collapse? The example of cod in Atlantic Canada. 7(1):91–106, 1997. doi: 10.1890/1051-0761(1997)007[0091:WDFSCT]2.0.CO;2.

[15] J. L. Noyes. A first course in computational science: (why a math book isn't enough). In *SIGCSE '02: Proceedings of the 33rd SIGCSE technical symposium on Computer science education*, pages 18–22, New York, NY, USA, 2002. ACM.

[16] W. G. on Re-Evaluation of Biological Reference Points for New England Groundfish. Re-evaluation of biological reference points for New England groundfish. Technical report, Northeast Fisheries Science Center, 2002. Ref. Doc. 02-04; 395 pages.

[17] M. e. A. Palmer. Ecological science and sustainability for the 21st century. *Frontiers in Ecology and the Environment*, 3(4-11), 2005.

[18] M. R.A., R. DeHaan, and J. Schuck, editors. *Improving Undergraduate Instruction in Science, Technology, Engineering, and Mathematics: Report of a Workshop.* 2003. Steering Committee on Criteria and Benchmarks for Increased Learning from Undergraduate STEM Instruction, Committee on Undergraduate Science Education, National Research Council.

[19] G. M. Schneider. Computational science as an interdisciplinary bridge. *SIGCSE Bull.*, 31(1):141–145, 1999.

[20] R. Sedgewick and K. Wayne. *Introduction to Programming in Java: An Interdisciplinary Approach.* Addison-Wesley, 2008.

[21] A. B. Shiflet. Computer science with the sciences: an emphasis in computational science. *SIGCSE Bull.*, 34(4):40–43, 2002.

[22] A. Sinclair. Recent declines in cod species stocks in the Northwest Atlantic. *Northwest Atlantic Fisheries Organization Scientific Council Studies*, 24:41–52, 1996. http://www.nafo.int/publications/frames/science.html.

[23] D. Watts and S. Strogatz. Western states power grid of the United States. `http://www-personal.umich.edu/~mejn/netdata/`, 1998.

[24] D. J. Watts and S. H. Strogatz. Collective dynamics of small-world networks. *Nature*, 393:440–442, 1998.

[25] M. Weiss. *Data Structures and Problem Solving using Java.* Addison Wesley, fourth edition, 2010. ISBN: 0-321-54140-5.

[26] M. E. A. X. Collapse of Atlantic Cod stocks of the east cost of Newfoundland in 1992. http://maps.grida.no/go/graphic/collapse-of-atlantic-cod-stocks-off-the-east-coast-of-newfoundland-in-1992, 2005.

Metaphors and Analogies for Teaching Algorithms*

Michal Forišek
Department of Computer Science
Comenius University, Bratislava, Slovakia
forisek@dcs.fmph.uniba.sk

Monika Steinová
Department of Computer Science
ETH Zurich, Switzerland
monika.steinova@inf.ethz.ch

ABSTRACT

In this paper we explore the topic of using metaphors and analogies in teaching algorithms. We argue their importance in the teaching process. We present a selection of metaphors we successfully used when teaching algorithms to secondary school students. We also discuss the suitability of several commonly used metaphors, and in several cases we show significant weaknesses of these metaphors.

Categories and Subject Descriptors

K.3.2 [**Computer Science Education**]: Algorithms

General Terms

Algorithms

1. INTRODUCTION

Metaphors and analogies are an important tool in learning unfamiliar concepts. Many authors agree that they can be used not only to communicate the relevant properties of the new concept, but also to facilitate developing new conceptual structures – new mental models and new abstractions [13]. (Kindly refer to the appendix for an explanation of differences between metaphors and analogies.) Abstraction of knowledge is, in some sense, the holy grail of both research and education. A famous example: Among chicken, often a "stronger" chicken pecks a "weaker" one, but not vice versa. Biologists observing chicken groups discovered that this is not always a transitive relation. Surprisingly, it was still always possible to find a linear "pecking order" in which each chicken pecked the next one. The surprise ended with Landau's proof [18] that every tournament graph contains a Hamiltonian path – the existence of a pecking order is a mathematical certainty, not a biological property.

For teaching programming, [5] empirically shows that good explanatory analogies, characterized by clarity and a systematic approach, positively influence all factors, including program comprehension, program composition, and time needed for the given tasks. Metaphors in programming and Computer Science (CS) were also presented and analyzed in [27, 7, 28]. Many nice metaphors and analogies useful for teaching CS to young kids can be found in [2, 29].

Metaphors and analogies can be used in all levels of education, starting with the complete basics. For instance, it is well known that a "labeled box" metaphor for a variable in a program helps explain the potentially confusing "x=x+1" statement. But there is no real upper bound on subject difficulty – metaphors are also used in graduate courses at universities. For instance, amortized time complexity is often explained using the physical metaphor of potential energy [8], and zero-knowledge proofs can be illuminated using the beautiful Ali Baba's cave metaphor [24].

One caveat when using metaphors and analogies in education is that they are very sensitive to cross-cultural aspects [12, 16], and also to cross-gender aspects – e.g., "car analogies" are commonly used in engineering courses and textbooks such as [6]. These tend to be less suitable for female students. Another source of difficulties with metaphors is that the target never matches the source perfectly. The inherent danger is that a subject will use the metaphor to infer incorrect conclusions about the target, and additionally have high confidence in these conclusions. This danger must be foreseen and mitigated by the educator. In Section 7 of this paper we identify several false and/or misleading metaphors and analogies that are widely used in practice.

The danger of flawed metaphors cannot be avoided completely. Spolsky [25] quotes several prominent cases where simple abstractions fail in unexpected ways. One of the examples is iterating over a simple 2D array (a table). The array is a mathematical abstraction that allows us to visualize the operations done with the actual data in memory. When working just with this abstraction it seems that iterating in row major order should be the same as in column major order – either way we process each element once. But in practice this is not the case: row major order is usually a order of magnitude faster due to caching. (It is faster to process data in the order in which it is stored in physical memory.) Spolsky concludes that becoming a proficient programmer is getting harder and harder, even though we have higher and higher level programming tools with better and better abstractions.

Many scientists, famously including Dijkstra in [11], warn against misleading metaphors. Dijkstra explains that CS represents a major breakthrough, hence often "the analogies

*The research is partially supported by Hasler Stiftung.

Permission to make digital or hard copies of all or part of this work for personal or classroom use is granted without fee provided that copies are not made or distributed for profit or commercial advantage and that copies bear this notice and the full citation on the first page. To copy otherwise, to republish, to post on servers or to redistribute to lists, requires prior specific permission and/or a fee.
SIGCSE'12, February 29 – March 3, 2012, Raleigh, North Carolina, USA.
Copyright 2012 ACM 978-1-4503-1098-7/12/02 ...$10.00.

become too shallow, and the metaphors become more misleading than illuminating". Still, nowadays we already have many good metaphors in CS. Their existence can be seen as a measure of our scientific progress – we already managed to fill in many of the gaps perceived by Dijkstra. In fact, one of our results is a good metaphor we successfully used to explain Dijkstra's very own shortest paths algorithm.

We also agree with Dijkstra in that we are convinced that a rigorous formal approach to CS can never be replaced by simply inferring from the metaphors. The metaphors can only provide intuition and insight that makes formal reasoning easier. Dijkstra also argues that anthropomorphic metaphors (e.g., programs "knowing" or "wanting" things) should be avoided at all costs. His argument is that adoption of these metaphors prevents a departure from operational semantics – the programmer is forced to think about the flow of the computational process, without the possibility of an abstraction. In the example scenario given by Dijkstra such problems are plausible indeed. We are not using any anthropomorphic metaphors in our paper.

Paper outline. The paper is organized as follows: Section 2 contains several new metaphors for simple algorithmic concepts. An explanation of Dijkstra's algorithm for shortest paths via a physical metaphor is contained in Section 3. In Sections 4 and 5 we give metaphors for a few geometry problems and for the Knuth-Morris-Pratt substring search algorithm, respectively. In Section 6 we describe our experience with using our new metaphors in education. The paper is concluded by Section 7 where widely used false or misleading concepts are discussed. In Appendix A we define and explain the terminology used in this paper.

2. METAPHORS FOR SIMPLE CONCEPTS

Here we illustrate our intended usage of metaphors on simple examples that do not deserve a separate section. Still, all of these examples are meaningful and in our experience their proper use significantly improves the teaching process.

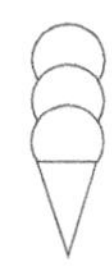

The stack. When explaining the data structure *stack* (LIFO memory – last in, first out) we realized that many of the students already have a deep understanding of the same principle. In Slovakia ice cream is customarily served as shown in the figure on the right. The vendor takes an empty cone and adds the scoops as they are requested. However, such a cone needs to be eaten from top to bottom, hence to eat the flavors in the desired order, kids are required to place the order in reverse.

(Note that this metaphor is culturally biased, as it only works in countries where kids have the prior experience. Just explaining it with pictures tends to be useless. Also note that the metaphor can be extended to less trivial stack operations, for instance the cone offers "read access" to all its elements, just like a stack stored in an array.)

The queue. The most common metaphor for a queue is the checkout line in a supermarket. This metaphor can be found in many textbooks, for instance [15]. While this metaphor is nice to introduce the "first in, first out" principle, it is woefully inadequate when it comes to an actual implementation of the queue and its time complexity – based on the way actual queues work, the student is coaxed into thinking that it is necessary to move all elements each time we process the first one. Therefore we prefer to follow this metaphor by a better one. In practice we can easily find examples of smarter queuing. For instance, there are waiting rooms with a machine that dispenses tickets with numbers. You take a ticket, sit down anywhere and wait until your number comes up. This corresponds to a queue implemented in an array. (Actually, a cyclic array. The tickets commonly reuse numbers 000 to 999 repeatedly.)

There are also other examples of smart queuing. For instance, in some cultures the doctor's office has a waiting room that serves as a queue. Upon entering the room you just ask who is the last in line, remember them and then take any available seat. When the person before you gets called into the office, you are the next one to go in. This closely resembles the linked list implementation of a queue.

Alternately, we sometimes present the correct queue implementation as a "think out of the box" puzzle after the checkout line metaphor. The solution: instead of moving everyone in the checkout line, move the cash register.

Topological sorting. Our favorite metaphor for the topological sorting problem is *getting dressed.* There are many non-trivial dependencies between various pieces of clothing. Their graph can easily be constructed by students and it is a good example for a test run of the algorithm. The intuitive approach "put on anything you already can" actually translates to a correct algorithm.

3. DIJKSTRA'S ALGORITHM

In this section we present a metaphor that helps our students (including secondary school students) create a deep mental model of Dijkstra's shortest path algorithm.

The input for Dijkstra's algorithm is a graph with positive edge lengths and one marked vertex s. The algorithm computes the shortest paths from s to each other vertex of the graph. We will now give its brief overview, for more details see [8, 10]. The algorithm proceeds as follows: Let the *distance value* of vertex v be the smallest known distance from the vertex s to v. These values are stored in the array D; the value $D[v]$ is updated whenever a smaller distance to v is discovered. Initially, all $D[v]$ are infinite except for $D[s] = 0$. Each vertex v is in one of two states: visited (meaning that $D[v]$ is final) or unvisited. Initially, all vertices are unvisited. The algorithm then repeats the following steps:

1. Let u be an unvisited vertex with the smallest distance value, i.e., the closest unvisited vertex to the vertex s.
2. The vertex u becomes visited and thus $D[u]$ is final.
3. For each edge uv: update $D[v]$ if the path via u to v is shorter. (Its length is $D[u]$ + length of uv.)
4. If there are unvisited vertices left, continue with step 1.

There is a well-known metaphor related to the shortest path problem: the balls-and-string metaphor. Each vertex of the graph corresponds to a small ball. The balls are connected by strings with lengths proportional to edge lengths. To find the shortest path between s and t, one just grabs the corresponding two balls and tries to pull them apart. This process stops when some strings between the balls become stretched. These strings then form the shortest path. One textbook mentioning this metaphor is [10], but the metaphor is not actively used in algorithm presentation.

We will show how to augment the metaphor by adding the aspect of gravity. This will intuitively model all necessary properties of the algorithm. Similar insights can then lead to new algorithm design, as in [22]. The way we use our new metaphor can be summarized as follows:

If we take the balls-and-strings gadget and let it hang by the ball s, ball depths correspond to their shortest distances *from the ball s. Dijkstra's algorithm computes their depths by discovering and processing the balls from top to bottom, while it builds the gadget on the fly.*

Now in more detail: Imagine the gadget hanging by the ball s. Due to gravity, some strings from s to other balls become stretched simultaneously. The strings with no slack form precisely all shortest paths from s to other vertices. To find the shortest distances from s, it is sufficient to determine how the gadget looks like in its stable state, hanging by the ball s. It can now be shown that Dijkstra's algorithm corresponds to examining this gadget from top to bottom. For added clarity, we will *build* the gadget, adding balls and strings as we go, focusing on its behavior thanks to gravity.

We start by fixating the single ball s (with no strings attached yet) on the top of a vertical wall. This matches the initialization of Dijkstra's algorithm. We then process the gadget from top to bottom. Whenever we encounter a ball, we add all its remaining strings (and the balls on their other end, if necessary) to the gadget. Remember that string lengths are proportional to edge lengths.

By observing the physical properties of the gadgets we can make one important observation: Imagine that you are adding a piece of string between two balls. Obviously, this can never pull a ball *further downwards*. The only two cases: either the string is long enough and the balls remain where they were, or the string pulls the deeper ball upwards. This intuition is reflected in the algorithm – processing edges in step 3 can only decrease the distances in the array D. (Note that at any moment the values in D directly correspond to current ball depths, measured from the top of the wall.)

The other observation we need: adding a string somewhere *does not influence anything above it*. Once again, this is obvious thanks to intuition from physics. How does this property help us here? Whenever we encounter a ball, we know that the unfinished part of the gadget currently lies below the ball only – and therefore this ball is in its final position. (This corresponds to the step 2 of the algorithm. Adding the strings from this ball is step 3.)

4. COMPUTATIONAL GEOMETRY

Thanks to the close connection between geometry and physics, many involved geometric concepts can be explained more easily when appealing to intuition from physics. One classic metaphor commonly used in computational geometry is "rubber band as a two-dimensional convex hull": Imagine the points as pegs on a board and take a closed rubber band that contains them all. If you let the rubber band go, it will contract until it hits some of the pegs, eventually stabilizing itself as the convex hull of the point set. Rubber bands are an excellent metaphor, because from real life experience we know how they behave: they contract whenever possible. We discovered that many proofs and algorithms in computational geometry can be stated in terms of local optimizations, hence the rubber band metaphor can be used.

Shortest path with obstacles. As a first example, consider a two-dimensional shortest path problem in a plane with obstacles. (This is a very important problem with applications in motion planning, see chapter 13 in [3].) The number of possible paths is infinite, even uncountable. The algorithms for this problem are based on reducing the possible paths to a finite set of candidates. To do so, one has to prove that the shortest path always consists of several special segments, each segment being either a straight line or copying the boundary of an obstacle.

A formal proof of this claim can be based on local optimizations: if we can locally improve a path, it is not the shortest one. The intuition behind this proof is captured by a rubber band metaphor. Imagine that you are looking for the shortest path from point A to point B. We will show that the shortest path must have the shape described above. To see why, take a rubber band, fix one of its ends at A and, keeping the other end in hand, walk to B using any path you like. Of course, the rubber band will try to contract. Once you reach B, it will be at most as long as your path was, and it will have the desired shape.

Distance between line segments. One of the basic problems in computational geometry is to determine the shortest straight-line distance between two line segments. In two dimensions this problem is simple, as there are only three distinct cases to consider. However, the problem becomes much more involved in three dimensions and students often miss some of the cases. Notably, in one tricky case the shortest path does not contain any segment endpoint – it is a line segment orthogonal to both given segments.

With rubber band intuition, the three-dimensional case becomes no harder than the two-dimensional one. Imagine each line segment as a railroad track. Place one tiny railroad car on each segment and connect them by a rubber band. The rubber band will try to contract, thereby pulling the cars along the tracks. And while the rubber band pulls them, their distance is decreasing. Hence in the optimal configuration, when the cars are closest to each other, none of them can be pulled any further. This means that each railroad car is either stuck at the end of its segment, or the rubber band is perpendicular to that car's segment.

Polygon triangulation. Our last example contains a combination of two metaphors: gravity and our favorite rubber band. We will show an intuitive proof of an involved geometric theorem with many practical consequences: every polygon completely contains one of its diagonals (and hence has a triangulation). In addition to being easy to visualize, our proof is constructive and leads to an efficient algorithm.

To prove the claim, place the polygon on a vertical wall. The polygon has at least one convex angle. Pick one and rotate the polygon so that both sides of this angle point downwards and no edge is horizontal. Take a lead ball on the end of a rubber band, fix the other end of the band to our vertex and drop the ball. Clearly, it will fall straight down until it hits a side of the polygon, and then slide along the side until it reaches a vertex. At this moment, look at the rubber band. If it is straight, it is the diagonal we are looking for. Otherwise, start at the initial vertex and look for the first obstacle it hits. This has to be some other vertex, and the rubber band piece between them is the diagonal.

5. KNUTH-MORRIS-PRATT

The Knuth-Morris-Pratt algorithm (KMP, see chapter 32 in [8]) is one of the most frequently used linear time algorithms for the task of locating a given substring N (the "needle") in a longer string H (the "haystack"). We will denote the lengths of these strings n and h. We developed a physical metaphor for the algorithm that both illuminates how the algorithm works and simplifies its bug-free implementation. Additionally, our metaphor is also useful when analyzing the time complexity of the algorithm.

We will assemble a large gadget consisting of balls falling down a series of tubes. Conceptually, the gadget resembles a finite automaton. The gadget will have n blocks – one containing each letter of N, from top to bottom. An example for the word $N =$ `COCOA` is shown on the right. Each block contains a switch. If the switch is on, a ball coming from above will continue downwards, as in the first and third block in the figure; otherwise, the ball will be redirected to drop out of the gadget. The switch is controlled by a gnome. Whenever he hears his letter, he turns the switch on, and whenever he hears any other letter, he turns it off.

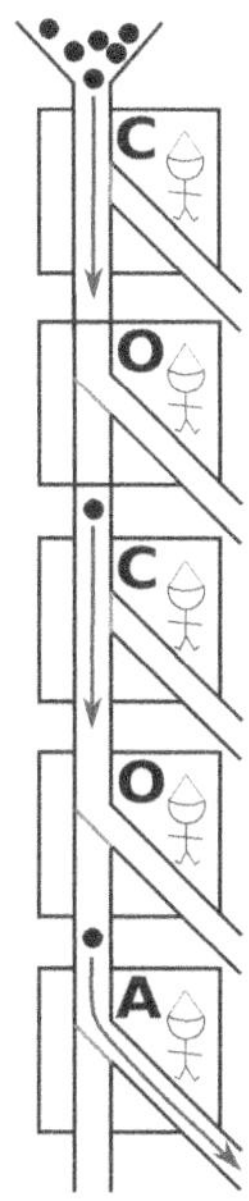

Our time units will be called *ticks*. In a single tick each ball travels through one block of the gadget. To look for the string N in a given string H, we will use our gadget as follows: Once per tick we read aloud the next letter of H and drop a new ball into the gadget. The letter is always heard by all the gnomes.

The figure shows the state of the gadget immediately after reading the last letter of the string `OCOCOC`. Switches are already set according to the last `C`. During the next tick, three balls will travel as shown by the arrows.

Here is the summary of why this is a suitable metaphor for KMP: *Simulating the entire gadget corresponds to the naive string matching algorithm. KMP then achieves speedup by only keeping track of the number of blocks cleared by the currently bottommost ball.*

For the naive string matching, just note that each occurrence of N in H corresponds to a ball successfully traversing the entire gadget and dropping out the bottom after the last letter of the occurrence was read. Then, the core idea of KMP is that we just need to follow the bottommost ball – the one closest to success. With our metaphor it is easy to prove that we do not lose any information by doing so: If we know that the lowest ball b already passed k blocks, we can determine the last k letters we read from H. These uniquely determine the paths taken by all balls thrown in after b.

To make the simulation efficient, we need one more piece of information. What if the bottommost ball drops out of the machine? The next ball above it now becomes the bottommost one. Thus we need to precompute the information "if the bottommost ball is here, where is the one above it?" This is precisely the "failure function" precomputed during the first phase of KMP, and it is closely related to the back-links in a deterministic finite automaton for locating N.

Finally, the metaphor can illustrate the non-trivial proof of KMP's time complexity: our entire simulation consists only of two types of steps: "move the bottommost ball" and "jump to the next ball above", and each of these can be executed at most h times.

6. PRACTICAL EXPERIENCE

The metaphors presented in Sections 2 to 5 of this paper were used in teaching various groups of students in years 2000 through 2010. In most of the cases, the students' age group was 15 to 19 and the algorithm lectures were given by the authors as a part of an extra-curricular activity for talented kids interested in CS. In all cases, we analyzed whether and/or how using these metaphors helped our students. We observed that the explanations that were accompanied by suitable metaphors were much more successful than ones given without metaphors. With our metaphors we usually saw deeper understanding of the topic in most students. The main way in which this was observed was by asking them to *think* in terms of the newly acquired knowledge. Below, we give concrete accounts how this thinking was directly influenced by the presence of the metaphor in various cases.

For Dijkstra's shortest path problem, we followed the presentation by a series of questions that tested the students' understanding. Here are several of these questions: "What happens to the shortest path tree in a graph if we add another edge to the graph? How would you recompute the new tree? Why does the algorithm require edge lengths to be non-negative? Can you find an instance with a negative edge where the algorithm fails?" Many of these questions are non-trivial; in our experience even university students who passed an introductory algorithm course often have trouble answering them. Our students, having the physical metaphor, were very successful in answering these questions.

Here are examples of similar questions for the KMP substring search: "How is the failure function related to the periods of the substring (the 'needle')? What is the time complexity? Can you prove it?" Additionally, having the metaphor, many of the students were able to independently discover the Aho-Corasick algorithm – a generalization of KMP that searches for multiple patterns at once.

With KMP we observed one additional, very significant difference. Implementations of this algorithm are notoriously prone to off-by-one errors. Before we introduced the metaphor, we routinely observed these in implementations by our students. However, in implementations by students knowing the metaphor these errors are virtually non-existent.

We also note that our KMP metaphor can be easily introduced as a kinaesthetic activity in which each student plays the role of one of the gnomes.

7. MISLEADING METAPHORS

In daily computer usage we can find many metaphors that are confusing for many users. For years, in MacOS a common way to eject a CD-ROM drive was to drag its icon to Trash. The "desktop" and "trash" metaphors were so strong that many users were anxious about losing their data when "dragging the CD to trash" [14]. Stephenson [26] gives another example, so common that proficient computer users do not even realize that it is a metaphor: the words "document" and "save". When we document something in the real world, we make fixed, permanent, immutable records of it – but computer documents are mutable. And if we "save" something in real life, we protect it from harm. But every time you hit "save" on your computer, you annihilate the previous version of the document – the one you supposedly "saved" before. In our research we focused on flawed metaphors that are used both in teaching and in designing algorithms. For this paper, we identified multiple such cases.

Queue. We already mentioned one in Section 2: the "checkout line" metaphor happily used to illustrate the queue. As we explained above, this concept should only be used as an analogy to the FIFO principle. It is not a suitable metaphor, because it leads to incorrect reasoning about the time complexity of operations with the data structure.

Russian dolls ("Matryoshkas"). These nesting dolls are commonly used as metaphors for two distinct concepts: for recursion and for nesting of data structures [9]. In our experience both usages turned out to be problematic. With recursion, the main caveat is that each of the dolls always directly contains at most one smaller doll – this sometimes caused false impression that a function can only make one recursive call. With nested data structures, the main misconception arising from the metaphor was that the structures have to be of the same type.

Soap and Steiner trees. The last two topics in this section have very much in common. In both of them we document situations where researchers draw false analogies between physical experiments and CS concepts. In some cases their readers then misinterpret those analogies as metaphors, which leads them to wildly inaccurate conclusions about the difficulty of problems solved by computer scientists.

In a classic science experiment two parallel glass plates with pegs between them are dipped into soapy water. After the plates are taken out of the water, a soap film will form between the pegs. Once it reaches a stable state, we will see a soap film network connecting all the pegs. This stable configuration of the soap film has properties similar to the optimal solution for the *Steiner tree problem.* This is a well-known NP-hard problem. Given a set of points in the plane (pegs), their Steiner tree is the shortest collection of line segments that connects all of them. Note that this problem differs from the spanning tree problem, as here we are allowed to create new points where the segments meet.

Due to mistakenly identifying the soap film contraction with solving the Steiner tree problem, several researchers published this claim in their papers. There even was a paper[1] claiming that P=NP and "proving" it via soap bubbles.

It is true that to minimize surface tension, the soap film always contracts into a shape resembling the optimal Steiner tree. However, soap contraction is *not* a suitable metaphor for solving the Steiner tree problem. As shown by Aaronson in [1], the final configuration of the soap is just a local minimum of the energy function, not necessarily the global one. The behavior of soap film should just be used as an analogy to explain one heuristic approach to approximating the Steiner tree. However, there are more suitable metaphors for such approximation algorithms, e.g., "hill climbing".

Animals "solving" hard problems. Simulating the behavior of an animal colony is a frequently used and well researched meta-heuristic for designing approximation algorithms that tend to perform reasonably well for some practical instances of hard optimization problems [21]. Taking inspiration from nature is surely a good idea. However, we noticed that too often the readers (and sometimes also the researchers) interpret the behavior of the animal colony in question as an actual metaphor for the computation, which often leads to incorrect conclusions.

In a recent publication by Reid et al. [23] the authors transform an instance of a classical three disc Towers of Hanoi problem to a physical maze in which the paths from start to exit correspond to solutions of the Towers of Hanoi instance. The authors then let ants navigate the maze to get to a food source. The experiment showed that the ants were able to find the shortest path in the maze, and they were able to adjust the solution if a simple obstacle was added.

The actual biological experiment is scientifically sound. However, the authors then claim that "ants are capable of solving dynamic optimization problems" (i.e., they can optimally solve optimization problems and even adjust the solutions as the instance changes). This is obviously false for optimization problems as known in CS. For n discs the optimal solution of the problem needs exactly $2^n - 1$ moves, which produces an exponentially large maze – unexplorable by any ant colony, real or simulated. The observed results cannot be related to optimal solutions for real optimization problems. At best, they are just another confirmation that studies of ants may help improve heuristic algorithms.

In [20] the authors descibe an experiment on discovering flowers and route optimization by bumblebees. The reoptimization occurred whenever the flowers' locations were manually changed. In the last section of the study authors relate the observed behavior to the famous and provably NP-hard Traveling Salesman Problem (TSP, see [8]) and its dynamic version; they suggest that bumblebees can find an optimal solution for this problem. However, the study [20] never even confirms that the bumblebees' solution in the experiments is indeed always globally optimal, and not just a local optimum. The experiment was done with only four flowers, with no attempt at a generalization for more vertices. And what is even worse, this result was then incorrectly adopted in online articles [19] and [4] that generalized the suggestion to a bold claim that bees can efficiently solve TSP.

We the computer scientists are at least partially responsible for this confusion. One part of the problem here is that the hardness of many optimization problems is pretty subtle. For instance, a person who is not a computer scientist can form an approximate mental model of TSP – "visit all locations as quickly as you can", and also a model of ant colony behavior – "try varying the path and if you find a better one, stick with it". For a computer scientist, these are two very different concepts. We understand that the difficulty of the optimization problem lies in computing its globally optimal solution, or at least in finding a *provably* good approximation. But to a person without a CS background, ant colony behavior can be a very strong metaphor for solving the optimization problem. From this metaphor the person often infers incorrect conclusions about the optimization problem. It should be our duty to clarify such confusion when it occurs, and to look for ways how to prevent it in the future.

8. CONCLUSION

In our paper we presented multiple metaphors that we developed to teach algorithms. To our best knowledge, the metaphors are original, and our experience shows that they are indeed an efficient tool: they help students to form correct mental models, and these mental models lead to deeper understanding of the topics. We also showed that careless usage of flawed metaphors can easily mislead the students, and that it is easy to draw false conclusions based on such flawed metaphors. Teachers should carefully consider the suitability of metaphors before using them. Finally, we stress that metaphors and analogies are just a didactic tool that can help the teacher give a better explanation. They should not (and in principle cannot) replace a formal approach. Instead, they should supplement the formal presentation, helping the students to grasp and visualize it.

9. REFERENCES

[1] Aaronson, S.: NP-complete Problems and Physical Reality. Electronic Colloquium on Computational Complexity (ECCC) 12 (2005)

[1]Bringsjord, S., Taylor, J.: P=NP. arXiv:cs/0406056v1 (2004). It was never published in a peer-reviewed journal.

[2] Bell, T., Fellows, M., Witten, I.: CS Unplugged: Off-line activities and games for all ages (1998).

[3] de Berg, M., Cheong, O., van Kreveld, M., Overmars, M. Computational Geometry: Algorithms and Applications (3rd ed.). Springer-Verlag (2008)

[4] Boyle, R.: Bees solve hard computing problems faster than supercomputers. PopSci (2010).

[5] Chee, Y. S.: Applying Gentner's theory of analogy to the teaching of computer programming. Int. J. of Man-Machine Studies 38, 347–368 (1993)

[6] Cohoon, J. P., Davidson, J. W.: C++ Program Design: An intro to programming and object-oriented design (3rd ed.). McGraw-Hill (2002)

[7] Colburn, T. R., Shute, G. M.: Metaphor in Computer Science. Journal of Applied Logic 6, 526–533 (2008)

[8] Cormen, T. H., Leiserson, C. E., Rivest, R. L., Stein, C.: Introduction to Algorithms (3rd ed.). The MIT Press (2009)

[9] Danzig, N.: Introduction to Computer Science – C++. Available online: `http://www.danzig.us/cpp/` (2009)

[10] Dasgupta, S., Papadimitriou, C., Vazirani, U.: Algorithms. McGraw-Hill (2006)

[11] Dijkstra, E. W.: On the cruelty of really teaching Computer Science. Comm. of the ACM 32 (1989)

[12] Duncker, E.: Cross-cultural usability of the library metaphor. Proceedings of JCDL 2002, pp. 223–230, ACM (2002)

[13] Gentner, D., Stevens, A. L. (eds.).: Mental Models. L. Erlbaum Assoc. (1983)

[14] Hübscher-Younger, T.: Understanding algorithms through shared metaphors. CHI EA '00 on Human factors in computing systems, pp. 83–84, ACM (2000)

[15] Keogh, J. E., Davidson, K.: Data structures demystified. McGraw-Hill (2004)

[16] Keränen, J.: Using metaphors in Computer Science education – cross cultural aspects. Tech. report, CS Department, Univ. of Joensuu (2005)

[17] Lakoff, G., Johnson, M.: Metaphors We Live By. Univ. of Chicago press (2003)

[18] Landau, H. G.: On dominance relations and the structure of animal societies III. Bull. of Mathematical Biophysics 15, 143–148, Springer, New York (1953)

[19] Levey, S.: Tiny brained bees solve a complex mathematical problem. Queen Mary Univ. of London Media Centre (2010)

[20] Lihoreau, M., Chittka, L., Raine, N. E.: Travel optimization by foraging bumblebees through readjustments of traplines after discovery of new feeding locations. The American Naturalist 176, 744–757, The University of Chicago Press (2010)

[21] Monmarché, N., Guinand, F., Siarry, P. (eds.).: Artificial Ants. Wiley-ISTE (2010)

[22] Narváez, P., Siu, K., Tzeng, H.: New Dynamic SPT Algorithm Based on a Ball-and-String Model. ACM Transactions on Networking 9, 706–718, ACM (2001)

[23] Reid, C. R., Sumpter, D. J. T., Beekman, M.: Optimisation in a natural system: Argentine ants solve the Towers of Hanoi. J. of Exper. Biol. 214 (2011)

[24] Quisquater, J. J., Guillou, L., Annick, M., Berson, T.: How to explain zero-knowledge protocols to your children. Proceedings of CRYPTO 1989, pp. 628–631, Springer-Verlag New York (1989)

[25] Spolsky, J.: The Law of Leaky Abstractions. Joel on Software (2002).

[26] Stephenson, N.: In the beginning... was the command line. Harper Perennial (1999)

[27] Waguespack, L. J.: Visual Metaphors for Teaching Programming Concepts. Proceedings of SIGCSE 1989, pp. 141–145, ACM (1989)

[28] Woollard, J.: The rôle of metaphor in the teaching of computing; towards a taxonomy of pedagogic content knowledge. PhD. Thesis, Univ. of Southampton (2004)

[29] Yim, K., Garcia, D. D., Ahn, S.: Computer Science Illustrated: engaging visual aids for CS education. Proc. of SIGCSE 2010, pp. 465–469, ACM (2010)

APPENDIX

A. TERMINOLOGY

The terms *analogy* and *metaphor* are often misused in practice. To avoid the confusion, we provide definitions and a few examples. For a more detailed treatment of these topics we recommend [17]. An *analogy* is a cognitive process in which a subject transfers information from one particular object to another. The word *analogy* can also be used as a noun describing the similarity between the two particular objects. A sample analogy: CPU is the brain of the machine. It takes input data, processes it and produces outputs.

A (conceptual) *metaphor* is a cognitive process that occurs when a subject seeks understanding of one idea (the target domain) in terms of a different, already known idea (the source domain). The subject creates a conceptual mapping between the properties of the source and the target, thereby gaining new understanding about the target. The metaphor can be conveyed by any means of communication, not only by words. For an *anthropomorphic metaphor (personification)* the source domain is a living being, usually a human. Sample metaphors: calling the workspace in a graphic environment "desktop", calling breadth-first search "flood fill". Personifications are common in colloquial speech of computer scientists, for instance in the expressions "the program is running", "the compiler needs to see a semicolon there", "the client machines periodically ask the server", etc.

By definition every metaphor is an analogy, but not vice versa. In an analogy, only some of the properties of the source are transferred to the target; these properties may be explicitly stated as a part of the analogy. In a good metaphor, the target and source should match on all relevant properties, enabling us to infer information about the target in terms of the source. For example, the analogy "the CPU is the brain" is a poor metaphor – it is impossible to think about the CPU in terms of what we know about our brains. In classroom setting, such poor metaphors may lead to unnecessary confusion.

An *abstraction* is a process by which a subject derives more general, higher level knowledge from patterns observed in multiple particular objects. For example, pseudocode is an abstraction from various imperative programming languages, and the strategy of looking for a greedy algorithm is an abstraction of observing concrete problems for which particular greedy algorithms work.

Detecting and Understanding Students' Misconceptions Related to Algorithms and Data Structures

Holger Danielsiek
holger.danielsiek@udo.edu

Wolfgang Paul
wolfgang.paul@udo.edu

Jan Vahrenhold
jan.vahrenhold@udo.edu

Faculty of Computer Science, Technische Universität Dortmund
44227 Dortmund, Germany

ABSTRACT

We describe the first results of our work towards a concept inventory for Algorithms and Data Structures. Based on expert interviews and the analysis of 400 exams we were able to identify several core topics which are prone to error. In a pilot study, we verified misconceptions known from the literature and identified previously unknown misconceptions related to Algorithms and Data Structures. In addition to this, we report on methodological issues and point out the importance of a two-pronged approach to data collection.

Categories and Subject Descriptors: K.3.2 [Computers and Education]: Computer and Information Science Education

General Terms: Algorithms.

Keywords: Misconceptions, Concept Inventories, CS1/2.

1. INTRODUCTION

Studies concerning first-year students' software design and programming abilities show that a considerable number of students do not know how to program at the end of their introductory computer-science courses [12]. To make matters worse, related studies show this problem to persist throughout whole university careers and that a sizeable portion of graduating students still do not know how to design software or to program properly [4, 11]. This phenomenon clearly requires a multicausal explanation, but at least some of the causes can be linked to students' misconceptions.

Concept inventories are standardized assessment tools that help in the analysis of students' concepts or misconceptions regarding a collection of accepted conceptual frameworks. While previous studies mainly focussed on misconceptions related to programming or (object-oriented) modelling, little attention has so far been paid to misconceptions related to modelling and analyzing a problem's structure and solution, i.e., to the field of Algorithms and Data Structures.

Permission to make digital or hard copies of all or part of this work for personal or classroom use is granted without fee provided that copies are not made or distributed for profit or commercial advantage and that copies bear this notice and the full citation on the first page. To copy otherwise, to republish, to post on servers or to redistribute to lists, requires prior specific permission and/or a fee.
SIGCSE'12, February 29–March 3, 2012, Raleigh, North Carolina, USA.
Copyright 2012 ACM 978-1-4503-1098-7/12/02 ...$10.00.

Previous Work.

Most work on misconceptions in Computer Science, e.g. [5, 9, 13, 14, 16], is related to object-orientation which is not the focus of our study. In contrast, only few observations have been made about misconceptions related to algorithms. Seppälä *et al.* [15] present a study of the build-heap algorithm that was conducted using algorithm simulation exercises, and Ginat, in a series of articles, e.g. [6], elaborates on conceptual difficulties with solving puzzles.

Concept inventories in Computer Science (or rather pilot versions) have been described for Digital Logic [8] and (the programming part of) CS1 [10, 16]. Goldman *et al.* [7] describe the application of a multi-stepped Delphi process to identify sets of topics fundamental to CS1-related programming, Discrete Mathematics, and Logic Design. Building upon this work, Herman *et al.* [8] work towards a concept inventory for Digital Logic. Similarly, Kaczmarczyk *et al.* [10] report on misconceptions related to memory models and the assignment of data in the context of the declaration of primitives. Tew and Guzdial [16] report on a "validated assessment of fundamental CS1 concepts" where the main focus is on abstracting over heterogeneous programming languages encompassing a wide variety of textbooks. Almstrum *et al.* [1] report on a working group focussed on concept inventories. They give a comprehensive introduction to the terminology and propose and outline a comprehensive approach to developing a concept inventory.

2. DESIGN OF A CONCEPT INVENTORY

In developing a concept inventory for Algorithms and Data Structures, we closely follow the process proposed by Almstrum *et al.* [1]: After an initial phase devoted to identifying fundamental concepts (using input from various sources such as instructors or papers), two possible paths can be taken to develop pilot multiple-choice items. The first, direct way is to generate distractors based upon the suggestion of subject matter experts, have an instructor administer an alpha version of these items, and perform a frequency analysis to determine common misconceptions. The second, more involved way is to create the test items in a feedback-loop on the basis of student-based investigations using open-ended questions. In the final phase the instrument is administered, its validity is assessed using statistical methods, and it is iteratively revised on the basis of statistical analyses.

Scope of the Study.

We report on the first two stages of this process, i.e. the identification of fundamental concepts and the development

Topic	Reference(s)
Call-by-Value	[16]
Class vs. Object	[5, 9, 13, 16]
Constructors	[13]
Exception Handling	beyond scope
Heaps	[15]
Heap vs. Binary Search Tree	(this paper)
Interface vs. Abstract Class	beyond scope
Visibility under Inheritance	beyond scope
Visibility (Inheritance & Packages)	beyond scope

Topic	Reference(s)
Asymptotic Runtime	[7]
Breadth-First-Search	beyond scope
Divide-and-Conquer	(this paper)
Dynamic Programming	(this paper)
Heap vs. Binary Search Tree	(this paper)
Invariants	[7]
Shortest-Path Algorithms	beyond scope
Topological Sorting	beyond scope
Tree Traversal	beyond scope

"beyond scope": omitted due to space constraints

Figure 1: Topics investigated for the CS111$_O$ (left) and CS103$_O$ (right) course. References indicate the first reference to this topic as a source for errors and (if applicable) studies on misconceptions related to the topic.

and evaluation of open-ended questions. This pilot study was conducted accompanying the *Introduction to Programming* course and the *Algorithms and Data Structures* course as offered to first-year students at the TU Dortmund during the winter term 2010/2011 and the summer term 2011. Since the topics covered in *Introduction to Programming* are comparable to the ones in CS111$_O$ [2, p. 175f.], we refer to this course as CS111$_O$. Similarly, we refer to the *Algorithms and Data Structures* course as CS103$_O$ [2, p. 174]. This hybrid of a two- and three-course introduction [2, p. 25] can be explained by the slightly different schedule at the TU Dortmund: Both courses were comprised of 180 mins. of class time and 90 mins. of recital sessions and (mandatory) lab sessions each per week. With fifteen weeks per semester, this results in 45 hours of class time and 45 hours of extra sessions in total. Approximately 250 students registered for the recital sessions of both CS111$_O$ and CS103$_O$.

Identifying Fundamental Concepts.

In a first step, we examined 400 written exams for the introductory Computer Science courses (217 exams for the CS111$_O$ course, winter term 2009/2010, and 183 exams for the CS103$_O$ course, summer term 2010) to identify errors made by a significant percentage of students or topics with an apparent difficulty. In addition, we ran expert interviews with the faculty members teaching these courses to identify topics of central importance to the respective courses. For our study, we then selected the topics given in Figure 1. Anticipating Section 3, an item is set in boldface if significant misconceptions could be verified (w.r.t. previous work) or detected for the first time during our study.

Developing Pilot Multiple-Choice Items.

In the pilot phase reported upon, we decided to simultaneously follow both paths suggested by Almstrum *et al.* [1]. Along the lines of the first path we designed flash test items for all topics; these flash tests were administered during two parallel recital sessions in the week after the topic was discussed in class. Each recital session was attended by 8 students on average. The flash tests consisted of one or two multiple-choice items with exactly one correct answer and distractors chosen based upon the relevant literature (if applicable) or designed based upon errors observed during the evaluation of the exams. In addition, students were asked to name solutions they did not choose but considered, i.e. students could, say, choose answer 1 because they thought it the most promising, but could indicate that they thought answer 4 to be the second most probable. The results from these flash tests were used to filter out topics that did not appear to be the source of (significant) misconceptions. In our case, we could rule out, e.g., *visibility under inheritance* and *tree traversal*.

Following also the second path proposed by Almstrum *et al.* [1] and in line with previous studies, e.g. [5, 10], we conducted think-aloud interviews with students. For each of the courses, we interviewed 23 students whose participation in this study was voluntarily and not compensated for. Each (open-ended) question asked in the interview was restricted to one topic and one specific concept so as to minimize the influence of related topics and concepts.

3. RESULTS FOR SELECTED TOPICS

Due to space constraints, we present results for only three topics: heaps vs. binary search trees, invariants, and dynamic programming.[1] The first topic was chosen because the "heapsort" test item in the CS111$_O$ final exam (winter term 2009/2010) was not answered by 33 out of 217 students (which was the highest number among all items in this exam) and the average score (43%) for this item was the lowest of all items in this exam. The second topic (invariants) was selected by the instructor for the CS103$_O$ course as a topic of central importance, and the third item (dynamic programming) had the lowest average score (35%) and highest "no attempt" rate (64/183) in the two CS103$_O$ exams offered at the end of the summer term 2010.

3.1 Heaps and Binary Search Trees

The first step towards understanding the difficulties apparent from the low success rates for the heapsort items was to verify whether the students worked with the correct formal definition of a heap. To this end, we presented CS111$_O$ students with a flash test item comprised of several definitions for ordered trees including max-heap (the structures used in class), min-heap, and binary search tree (which was not formally defined in class at this point). Of the twelve students participating, six gave the correct answer, four selected the definition of a min-heap, and only one selected the definition of a binary search tree; one student selected both the min- and max-heap definition. For cross-validation, we presented the students with five binary trees on the same set

[1]The evaluation of the CS111$_O$ topics related to object-orientation confirmed findings from previous studies [5, 9].

of nodes and asked them to identify the only tree that represented a heap. Nine out of twelve students gave the correct answer, whereas the three remaining students selected a tree that fulfilled the order property but was not left-complete (two of these students also selected the right answer and said they were unsure which of the two answers was right). At this point, misconceptions could neither be detected from the flash tests nor from the recital or lab sessions.

We revisited this topic after binary search trees had been discussed (which was about six weeks later; at this point four students had dropped the class, i.e. $n = 8$). In a flash test item, we asked the students to determine, for each of the four trees given in Figure 2 (top), whether the tree was a heap, a binary search tree, neither, or both. We also conducted the same test with eight CS103$_O$ students after the course had covered dictionary operations on binary search trees.

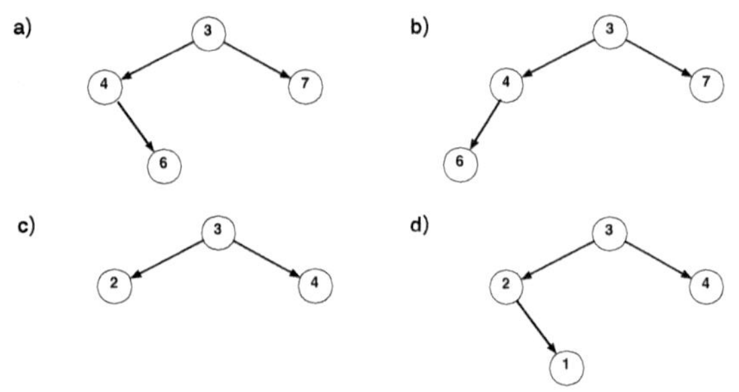

	n	(a)	(b)	(c)	(d)	all
CS111$_O$	8	25%	63%	50%	88%	25%
CS103$_O$	8	63%	88%	88%	88%	50%

Figure 2: Heaps, trees, and search trees (top) and percentage of correct classifications (bottom).

The answers given in these flash test (Figure 2, bottom) indicate that there are issues with understanding the structural property of a heap and that (a) seems to be a good distractor. They also indicate that the order property seemed to be well-understood. The think-aloud interviews conducted with a total of 23 CS103$_O$ students, however, revealed that this understanding was not always of an active nature.

Student A correctly states that a heap is a binary tree. Asked for the definition of a binary tree, however, he reveals the misconception that every binary tree is a *search* tree.

A: *A heap is, er* [laughs], *a heap is a tree with an ordering and, er, that's hard to explain. Er, a binary tree.*

$\mathcal{I}$: *Let's talk about binary trees, shall we?*

A: *Binary trees are trees, all of them, which have, have two children, that's indicated by the word binary already, two, er, children, or two child nodes, at most that is, we could also have null. Er, and the child node, the one that's stuck to the left, is smaller than the the node itself and the one, the one stuck on the right has a bigger value than the node itself and that's than kept up recursively and then we get, if we keep hanging on to that thought, far, far, far down on the left the smallest one, the smallest element; far, far, far on the bottom on the right is the biggest element.*

The interview with another student (Student B) revealed the same misconception; moreover, this student indicated how he would construct a heap, namely by insertion.

B: *Yes, the heap was like this, er. We put the first number into the root and then we take the second number and we check whether it's bigger, er, than the root. If it's bigger, we write the number down on the right side, and if its smaller, then we write it down on the left side. And then we take the next number and do the same again starting with the root, we check whether it's bigger. If it's smaller, we go to the left again. And then we take a look at the next. If this one is smaller again then we will go to the left again of this one and to the right if its bigger.*

The central new insight with respect to heaps is that students – even though they seem to have a rather good passive knowledge of the formal definition of a heap – tend to conflate heaps with binary search trees. Since the vast majority of students that attempted to solve the heapsort test item in the CS111$_O$ exam visualized the intermediate steps of the algorithm, this adds another significant cause for errors. This conflation could not be observed in the previous study on misconceptions related to heapsort [15] since this study used a visual learning environment that took care of all graphical representations. In addition, the structural property of a heap (being left-complete) was found to be not always present in the flash tests and was not mentioned in any of the think-aloud interviews.

3.2 Invariants

The instructor for the CS103$_O$ course (summer 2011) mentioned during the expert interview that he intended to put a special emphasis on invariants. This topic had not been part of previous final exams as a stand-alone item, and thus we agreed upon testing it separately during our study.

Flash Tests.

In coordination with the instructor for CS103$_O$, we also designed a flash test item concerning invariants which then was administered to a group of nine students in the recital session overseen by the second author. At this point in time, students had already worked on exercises related to invariants, and this topic had been discussed in a previous recital session. Each of the students was given a small iterative program which computes the arithmetic series $\sum_{i=1}^{n} i$ (Figure 3, left). They were then given four possible invariants (Figure 3, right) and asked to identify the correct one.

Only two out of nine students were able to identify the correct, i.e. second, answer. Three students chose the first invariant. Two students chose the fourth invariant and two students could not be tied down to a specific choice at all.

Think-Aloud Interviews.

Since the flash test was inconclusive, we tried to find out why the majority of students was not able to identify the correct invariant. For this, we conducted a total of 23 think-aloud interviews where we presented the same program and asked the participants how they would prove the program's formal correctness. Six interviewees had participated in the flash test and therefore knew the test item already.

During the interviews, 15 out of the 23 students directly stated that they required a loop invariant and four students mentioned this term after the for-loop in the program had been pointed out. The last four students could be set back on track by mentioning the term "loop invariant". No stu-

Input: A natural number $n \in \mathbb{N}$
Output: $n \cdot (n+1)/2$

$sum \leftarrow 0$
for $i \leftarrow 1$ **to** n **do**
    $sum \leftarrow sum + i$
return sum

1. Let $1 \le j \le i$ be the number of executed iterations of the for-loop. The invariant $A(j)$ states that $sum = j \cdot (j+1)/2$ after the j-th iteration.
2. Let $1 \le j \le n$ be the number of executed iterations of the for-loop. The invariant $A(j)$ states that $sum = j \cdot (j+1)/2$ after the j-th iteration.
3. Let $i \le j \le n$ be the number of executed iterations of the for-loop. The invariant $A(j)$ states that $sum = j \cdot (j+1)/2$ after the j-th iteration.
4. Let $0 \le j \le n$ be the number of executed iterations of the for-loop. The invariant $A(j)$ states that $sum = j \cdot (j+1)/2$ before the j-th iteration.

Figure 3: "Invariants" flash test. Students were given the algorithm (left) and four possible invariants (right).

dent seemed to have more than a vague idea of "invariant" as no one had internalized a formal definition. Some did not give a correct answer right away but were able to get there by systematically checking the scope of the invariant counter against the domain of the program's counter variable.

C: *Because we start here with 1 and ... yes, we continue until less-or-equal to n with this loop.*

D: *... does it have to start with 0 or with 1 ... yes, the loop starts with 1, so we have to take the second one.*

Students E and F could not really give an explanation why either the second or the fourth alternative should be correct; unfortunately, their reasoning steered them wrong:

E: *Er ... everything with an i and i < j is somehow nonsense, because this has to be true for the loop as such, I guess that true. That's also the reason why we can start with null and where I ...* [pauses] *now, why I start with 1 ...* [pauses] *... I don't have to, er ...* [pauses] *... could also take this one ...* [pauses] *normally I write down some numbers or ... No, it's the second. The second one could, ... this one is actually better, because we have $j \le 1$, so after the first iteration, er ...* [pauses] *I'm a bit ... puzzled at the moment, I have to say. I guess I'll take the fourth one.*

F: *No, the third one has to be wrong. Bigger than i can't be true, bigger than n is also ... so it's either the second or the fourth. I guess it has to be the fourth one than, because here we're starting with 0.*

Student G seemed to have the intuitive notion that a valid loop invariant would be useful for a formal induction proof as it could be used as an induction hypothesis.

G: *I guess, I would choose the last one, because, yes, basically we have to be able to prove that such invariants, that they ... I mean, that they are already true when we enter, er, that they are true. So, I would say that ... that for the zeroth loop iteration this has also to be true. This means that ... so to say, that this has also to be true before the loop.*

The think-aloud interviews show that students profit from some kind of drill-and-practice effect (invariant were a central part of the course) concerning the formal proof of correctness for iterative programs, as 15 out of the 23 students directly mentioned loop invariants as the tool of choice. When being asked to make active use of their knowledge in a flash test or interview, the students show a lack of both procedural and conceptual knowledge.

3.3 Dynamic Programming

As mentioned above, the examination of the CS103$_O$ final exams revealed significant difficulties with test items related to dynamic programming. Since a prominent error made in unsuccessful attempts was to try to write a recursive program, we hypothesized that students were trying to directly use the recursive *definition* of the value of an optimal solution they came up with for solving the problem recursively.

The chapter on dynamic programming in the textbook used for the CS103$_O$ course very prominently describes the steps for developing a dynamic-programming algorithm and explicitly requires to "recursively define the value of an optimal solution" and then to "compute the value of an optimal solution in a bottom-up fashion" [3, p. 323]. However, the very same chapter begins as follows:

> "Dynamic programming, like the divide-and-conquer method, solves problems by combining the solutions to subproblem." [3, p. 323]

Notwithstanding the perfect validity of this statement, it mentions in the same breath two algorithmic approaches that are contrasted immediately afterwards ("In contrast, dynamic programming is applicable when the subproblems are not independent [...]." [3, p. 323]).

In a two-pronged approach, we thus attempted to both identify possible difficulties with modelling the optimal solution and to find out whether a possible conflation of dynamic programming with divide-and-conquer (possibly additionally) prevented students from correctly answering the items in the final exams.

Flash Tests.

In a first flash test administered after the first time dynamic programming was addressed in class (but before the lab and recital sessions) we investigated the students' understanding of *divide-and-conquer*. At this point, no misconceptions could be detected.

Due to the apparent difficulty of dynamic programming, we administered two flash tests in which students were given a correctly structured dynamic-programming algorithm and asked to complete the two assignments needed to update the current field based upon solutions to subproblems. Each algorithm was presented with a full written description of the problem setting, a specification of the input and output, and the initialization of first row and column of the lookup table (with comments) – see Figure 4 for an example. The first optimization problem was to compute the minimum number of coins needed to represent a given amount of money, and the second optimization problem (given one week later) was a knapsack-type problem asking for the maximum-value set of weighted items whose total weight did not exceeding some given threshold. Both flash tests were administered before dynamic programming was part of the lab sessions.

The results of the flash tests (given in Figure 5) seem to imply that a much better understanding was observed with

Input: An array $D[1,\ldots,k]$ with the k coins' denominations and a positive number n.
Output: Minimum number of coins needed to represent n cents.

```
1: C ← new int[1,...,k][1,...,n]        ▷ Result C with k rows and n columns
2: for i ← 1 to k do C[i][1] ← 0        ▷ First column: no coins for 0 cents
3: for j ← 1 to n do C[1][j] ← j  ▷ First row: use j one-cent coins for j cents.
4: for i ← 1 to k do
5:     for j ← 1 to n do
6:         if j < D[i] then FILL IN ASSIGNMENT FOR C[i][j]
7:         else FILL IN ALTERNATIVE ASSIGNMENT FOR C[i][j]
8: return C
```

Options for Line 6:

1. $C[i][j] \leftarrow 0$
2. $C[i][j] \leftarrow C[i-1][j-1]$
3. $C[i][j] \leftarrow C[i-1][j]$
4. $C[i][j] \leftarrow C[i][j-1]$

Options for Line 7:

1. $C[i][j] \leftarrow min\{C[i-1][j-1], 1+C[i][j-D[i]]\}$
2. $C[i][j] \leftarrow min\{C[i-1][j], C[i][j-D[i]]\}$
3. $C[i][j] \leftarrow min\{C[i-1][j], 1+C[i][j-D[i]]\}$
4. $C[i][j] \leftarrow min\{C[i][j], C[i][j-D[i]]\}$

Figure 4: Dynamic-programming algorithm for representing n cents using k different types of denominations.

Item	n	(a)	(b)	(c)	(d)	none
Coins (1st line)	20	5	1	**8**	5	1
Coins (2nd line)	20	1	6	**5**	6	2
Knapsack (1st line)	7	2	**4**	1	0	0
Knapsack (2nd line)	7	1	0	**6**	0	0

Figure 5: Distribution of answers for the dynamic-programming items (marked: correct answer).

the second test. There exist at least two (non-exclusive) interpretations: The first interpretation is that even without the lab sessions, a training effect took place. The second interpretation relates to the second problem itself: Due to the nature of the problem, the algorithm and the possible solutions included several references to weight, capacities, and values, i.e. the code itself presented a clear indication that multiple criteria were to be considered. In contrast, it cannot be ruled out that the "cleaner" and "simpler" code of the first problem hid away some of the complexity of the problem and did not present a strong enough stimulus. It remains thus open to investigate how to factor in the modelling and description complexity of an algorithm.

Think-Aloud Interviews.

By design, flash tests using multiple-choice items cannot capture the *process* of modelling and solving a problem using dynamic programming. Thus, these tests could not give any hints as to why students failed when trying to solve problems in final exams. As mentioned above, we observed a large number of attempts to write recursive solutions, furthermore, the concept of dynamic programming is often mentioned in connection with divide-and-conquer.

In a second phase, well after the administration of the flash tests, we interviewed a total of 23 CS103O students with open-ended questions regarding both divide-and-conquer and dynamic programming. While these questions had been designed to determine a possible conflation of divide-and-conquer and dynamic programming, they also served to detect misconceptions regarding the *divide-and-conquer* paradigm.

Several students were under the impression that divide-and-conquer algorithms are designed to obtain a logarithmic running time, i.e. that the height of the recursion tree is equal to the running time of the algorithm:

> H: *... and the, er, advantage of this, er, method divide-and-conquer is that we have a runtime ... or, yes we get a, er, usually we get a runtime of logarithmic nature. I mean, we get a ... a structure with a specific height and in the end this height is the logarithm of ... of the size of the original problem.*

Another student apparently conflated "problems of the same size" and "two identical problems for the same data":

> I: *... and, er, a profitable runtime is only possible, if the smaller subproblems are ... only if, er, the subproblems are pretty much the same. So if I have two subproblems, I don't have to, er, solve both problems.*

The interviews indeed confirmed the hypothesis that students tried to implement a recursive algorithm to compute the value of an optimal solution. Several interviews explicitly mentioned "recursive algorithms" or "recursion". At times, students realized that their conception obviously had flaws but were unable to resolve the cognitive conflicts.

> J: *Put simply, dynamic programming is writing all of the results of a recursive algorithm into one table. So we try to, er, to reduce redun... er, we try to save the results of single recursive method calls and to use them to get more quickly to the final result. With quicker I mean: It's less of a fuzz to ... to do it this way.*

> K: *Dynamic programming is, er, ... the way I got it, a sort of recursion, er, and we have a some data that so far, er, is complicated or consumes a lot of memory ... needs a lot of memory to solve, er ... and now, we sort of ... er, need less, er ... memory to solve it. But actually now, er, ... we sort of ... er, need more memory to solve it, because we sort of store new stuff.*

One student was able correctly reason about using dynamic programming but still insisted on implementing the algorithm recursively.

> L: *Yes, if the subproblems are overlapping, then we would, if we do it strictly recursively, do lots of calculations several times. That would be much too inefficient. That's why we save them and always reference to them. This way we can use them and then this gets considerably faster. But this of course isn't the solution to all ... I mean, we can't solve $\mathcal{NP}$-problems this way, I mean. This isn't the solution to all problems, I mean.*

It should be noted that only six of the 23 students mentioned an "iterative" approach to solving the problem and that only four students mentioned the term "bottom-up".

In a second interview question, the participants were given the (conceptually) correct solution to the "coin representation" problem from the flash tests. The participant were then asked to fill in the blank lines for how to update the table and the solution. Only if students could not come up with a correct answer by themselves, they were given four possible answers each and were asked to explain which one they considered the right answer.

Despite having worked with dynamic-programming algorithms during the lab sessions, only two out of the 23 students were capable of interpreting the code and complementing the missing lines by themselves. Many students were struggling with the general approach of dynamic programming, e.g. several students were not aware (despite of the specification of the output, see Figure 4) of the fact that the program was computing the number of coins necessary to change a certain amount of money and not the denomination of the coins to be used:

M: *Okay, er ... so, if the amount of money j is smaller than the denomination D_i, then this cell has to ... this cell must be ... then this column ... so we actually just have a value of one cent. This amount of money can't be changed with a 2-cents coin, so we have to note down a zero. $C[i][j]$ has to be zero that's, er, the only valid value for this cell.*

For some of the participants, interpreting the bottom-up style in which the values of the two-dimensional table were used seemed to be very hard. They tended towards looking for data in the wrong places:

N: *... because the program uses this denomination and then looks up the value in the cell to the left minus the value of the current denomination and adds a one for the additional coin.*

O: *We are looking for a smaller solution but plus the current one, but not plus one but plus the current denomination.*

We conclude that there is not a single source of confusion when it comes to dynamic programming. Students struggle with orthogonal problems that include both the (conceptual) modelling of the problem and its optimal solution and the conflation of divide-and-conquer and dynamic programming.

4. SUMMARY

Our central contribution to the body of knowledge related to misconceptions consists of the conflation of heaps and binary search trees, the difference in passive and active knowledge of how to use invariants, and the conflation of divide-and-conquer and dynamic programming.

On the methodological side, the main insight from our study is that the two paths suggested by Almstrum *et al.* [1] lead to different but mutually complementing results. Conducting think-aloud interviews with open-ended questions allowed us in many cases to reveal common misconceptions, e.g. students believing that dynamic programming can be characterized as storing recursively computed results in a table. Asking the right questions, however, was facilitated by the flash tests as these gave us invaluable clues to which parts of concept definitions students definitely did or did not understand and remember. By establishing a weekly routine of in-class flash tests, we could promptly establish whether or not test items were capable of identifying problematic topics and could follow up on these with interviews.

Finally, we observe that not only the algorithmic (procedural) content of a test item but also the inherent modelling complexity of a solution needs to be taken into account when designing and evaluating test items related to algorithms.

Acknowledgments

This work was partially funded by the Deutsche Telekom Stiftung under the name *dort*MINT. We thank Jörg Gödel for his help with transcribing the interviews.

5. REFERENCES

[1] V. L. Almstrum, P. B. Henderson, V. J. Harvey, C. Heeren, W. A. Marion, C. Riedesel, L.-K. Soh, and A. E. Tew. Concept inventories in computer science for the topic discrete mathematics. *SIGCSE Bulletin*, 38(4):132–145, Dec. 2006.

[2] C. Chang, P. J. Denning, J. J. Cross II, G. Engel, R. Sloan, D. Carver, R. Eckhouse, W. King, F. Lau, S. Mengel, P. Srimani, E. Roberts, R. Shackelford, R. Austing, C. F. Cover, G. Davies, A. McGettrick, G. M. Schneider, and U. Wolz. Computing Curricula 2001: Computer Science. *Journal on Educational Resources in Computing*, 1, 2001. Article 1, 240 pp.

[3] T. H. Cormen, C. E. Leiserson, R. L. Rivest, and C. Stein. *Introduction to Algorithms*. MIT Press, Cambridge, MA, 2nd ed., 2001.

[4] A. Eckerdal, R. McCartney, J. E. Moström, M. Ratcliffe, and C. Zander. Can graduating students design software systems? In *Proc. 37th SIGCSE Symp. Computer Science Education*, pp. 403–407. 2006.

[5] A. Eckerdal and M. Thuné. Novice Java programmers' conceptions of "object" and "class", and variation theory. In *Proc. 10th ITiCSE Conf. Innovation and Technology in Computer Science Education*, pp. 89–93. 2005.

[6] D. Ginat. The baffling CS notions of "as-if" and "don't-care". In *Proc. 41st SIGCSE Symp. Computer Science Education*, pp. 385–389. 2010.

[7] K. Goldman, P. Gross, C. Heeren, G. L. Herman, L. C. Kaczmarczyk, M. C. Loui, and C. Zilles. Identifying important and difficult concepts in introductory computing courses using a Delphi process. In *Proc. 39th SIGCSE Symp. Computer Science Education*, pp. 256–260. 2008.

[8] G. L. Herman, M. C. Loui, and C. Zilles. Creating the digital logic concept inventory. In *Proc. 41th SIGCSE Symp. Computer Science Education*, pp. 102–106. 2010.

[9] S. Holland, R. Griffiths, and M. Woodmann. Avoiding object misconceptions. In *Proc. 28th SIGCSE Symp. Computer Science Education*, pp. 131–134. 1997.

[10] L. C. Kaczmarczyk, E. R. Petrick, J. P. East, and G. L. Herman. Identifying student misconceptions of programming. In *Proc. 41st SIGCSE Symp. Computer Science Education*, pp. 107–111. 2010.

[11] C. Loftus, L. Thomas, and C. Zander. Can graduating students design: revisited. In *Proc. 42nd SIGCSE Symp. Computer Science Education*, pp. 105–110. 2011.

[12] M. McCracken, V. Almstrum, D. Diaz, M. Guzdial, D. Hagan, Y. B.-D. Kolikant, C. Laxer, L. Thomas, I. Utting, and T. Wilusz. A multi-national, multi-institutional study of assessment of programming skills of first-year CS students. *SIGCSE Bull.*, 33:125–180, 2001.

[13] N. Ragonis and M. Ben-Ari. A long-term investigation of the comprehension of OOP concepts by novices. *Computer Science Education*, 15(3):203–221, Sept. 2005.

[14] K. Sanders, J. Boustedt, A. Eckerdal, R. McCartney, J. E. Moström, L. Thomas, and C. Zander. Student understanding of object-oriented programming as expressed in concept maps. In *Proc. 39th SIGCSE Symp. Computer Science Education*, pp. 332–336. 2008.

[15] O. Seppälä, L. Malmi, and A. Korhonen. Observations on student misconceptions – a case study of the build-heap algorithm. *Computer Science Education*, 16(3):241–255. 2006.

[16] A. E. Tew and M. Guzdial. Developing a validated assessment of fundamental CS1 concepts. In *Proc. 41st SIGCSE Symp. Computer Science Education*, pp. 97–101. 2010.

A C-based Introductory Course Using Robots

David Cowden
Grinnell College
Grinnell, Iowa 50112 U.S.A.
+1 215-326-9336
cowdenda@grinnell.edu

April O'Neill
Grinnell College
Grinnell, Iowa 50112 U.S.A.
+1 641-269-9059
oneilla@grinnell.edu

Erik Opavsky
Grinnell College
Grinnell, Iowa 50112 U.S.A.
opavskye@grinnell.edu

Dilan Ustek
Grinnell College
Grinnell, Iowa 50112 U.S.A.
ustekdil@grinnell.edu

Henry M. Walker
Grinnell College
Grinnell, Iowa 50112 U.S.A.
+1 641-269-4208
walker@cs.grinnell.edu

ABSTRACT

Using robots in introductory computer science classes has recently become a popular method of increasing student interest in computer science. This paper describes the development of a new curriculum for a CS 2 course, *Imperative Problem Solving and Data Structures*, based upon Scribbler 2 robots with standard C. The curriculum contains eight distinct modules with a primary topic theme, readings, labs, and project at the end. Each module resulted from collaboration among former CS 2 students and a faculty member, utilizing an iterative process with revisions. Each lab includes a survey to obtain student feedback that will allow the course to evolve and better fit the needs of future CS 2 students. All materials discussed here are available online for use by others.

Categories and Subject Descriptors

*K.3.2 [**Computers and Education**]: Computer and Information Science Education – computer science education, curriculum*

General Terms

Design, Experimentation, Languages

Keywords

Robots, course materials, lab-based course, collaborative learning, modules

1. INTRODUCTION

This paper describes an innovative approach for incorporating robots within the context of a second course of a three-course multi-paradigm introductory sequence to computing. In summary, this work has at least four vital characteristics:

- Scribbler 2 robots are introduced in the context of imperative problem solving and C, in order to fit within a multi-paradigm sequence;
- The course is divided into eight modules, each with readings, labs, and a project; and each module highlights capabilities of the robots;
- Each module was developed by a faculty member working with upper-level students, so the instructor could provide pedagogical guidance, and the students could encourage applications that would interest introductory students; and
- For each class meeting, a feedback/evaluation process is tied to the readings and labs to help the refinement of course materials over several semesters.

Both the software environment (using C that links to C++ object code) and all course materials are publicly available (via launchpad.net [11, 12] and the course home page [15], respectively). Thus, faculty interested in experimenting with robots within C-based courses have a complete collection of materials to start with.

The rest of this paper describes this course and the process of developing it in some detail. Section 2 describes the multi-paradigm context of the course, the selection of C, and the motivation for an application-oriented theme. Since a standard C interface was not available for the Scribbler 2 robot, Section 3 outlines the work needed to adapt a Myro-C++ package from the University of Tennessee at Knoxville [12], so that students can write their CS 2 programs in standard C. Section 4 reviews the goals, pedagogy, and organization for this lab-based course, and Section 5 reviews the process of developing both the C interface and the course modules. Since the Myro-C++ package was already available from launchpad.net [12], the development group wanted the C-based materials (called MyroC) to also be available on launchpad.net [11], and Section 6 describes some resulting interactions with Launchpad. The paper concludes with a consideration of next steps (Section 7), acknowledgments (Section 8), and references (Section 9).

2. CONTEXT: ROBOTS & C IN CS 2

In recent years, many computing educators have experimented with connecting problem-solving and programming with application themes in introductory computing courses. For example, [1, 2, 11] describe experiments using media computation to motivate students; [4, 6, 12] discuss the use of robots, and [10] describes music as an application area. These experiments regularly demonstrate considerable success in engaging students and encouraging them to try another computing course.

Permission to make digital or hard copies of all or part of this work for personal or classroom use is granted without fee provided that copies are not made or distributed for profit or commercial advantage and that copies bear this notice and the full citation on the first page. To copy otherwise, or republish, to post on servers or to redistribute to lists, requires prior specific permission and/or a fee.
SIGCSE'12, February 29–March 3, 2012, Raleigh, North Carolina, USA.
Copyright 2012 ACM 978-1-4503-1098-7/12/02...$10.00.

As another theme for introductory computing, many schools utilize a multi-paradigm approach for introductory computing, following curricular recommendations from the ACM [5, sections 3.2.4 and 9.1.5] and the Liberal Arts Computer Science Consortium [7]. For example, [13] describes several approaches for functional problem solving within Scheme in the first course. In particular, within [13], Rebelsky and Davis describe the use of media computation and image processing as an extremely successful application area for a CS 1 course that emphasizes functional problem solving and Scheme.

With this attention to application areas for CS 1 within a multi-paradigm context, relatively little discussion has focused on an application area for the second course in the sequence. Specifically, for the course described here, any application area needed to meet these criteria:

- CS 1 covers functional problem solving, Scheme, and media computation, so an application area for CS 2 should complement this prerequisite work.
- CS 2 focuses on imperative problem solving.
- CS 2 explores C and low-level details including data allocation, memory allocation, and data representation.

Altogether, the use of robots with programming in C naturally fits this framework. Further, the course should not place extensive emphasis on hardware construction, since building robots would likely detract from the central theme of imperative problem solving with C.

In reviewing available platforms, the Scribbler 2 robot seemed a natural choice, because it is widely used at the introductory level [4, 12] and extensive materials are available to support courses using Python [4, 6] and C++ [8]. Unfortunately, neither the Scribbler 2 nor other platforms seemed to have mature environments for programming in C.

A natural development path, therefore, seemed to base software development on the Myro-C++ materials from the University of Tennessee at Knoxville [12] and develop a C interface that could call compiled C++ materials that utilize 'extern "C"' directives.

With a clean and clear C library, work then could focus on the development of course materials.

3. USE OF C

Out of the box, the robots are not ready for classroom use with C. Our group extended and refined the available material so the robots would function in alignment with the desired course curriculum. The following subjects were considered when revising the robot functionality.

3.1 Choice of the C Programming Language

We chose to use C with the robots in order to constrain students to a strict imperative problem solving approach as indicated by the course title and description. This is highly compatible with previous courseware since C was the language of choice for our prior CS 2 course. Although it would have been possible to use the C subset of C++, we used strict C to retain the pure nature of the standard C specification and to remove extra features that might distract students from the imperative nature of standard C.

3.2 Drawing Upon Existing C++ Material

The de facto implementation of the IPRE Scribbler communication protocol is provided by roboteducation.org in the Python programming language [4]. To adapt the robots for use in an imperative programming course using C, we had two options: write our own implementation of the library, or adapt the publicly available C++ version from the University of Tennessee at Knoxville [3]. Since C++ supports 'extern "C" ' function declarations, the most logical approach was to simply wrap existing C++ member functions of the robot class with C-style functions that mask all object-oriented interactions from the user.

3.3 Definition of MyroC

Using the 'extern "C" ' keyword, it is possible to write a C header for a C++ library. When the header containing 'extern "C" ' declarations is included, the compiler creates function symbols C can link against. Although our header file allows students to call procedures in standard C, the underlying library is implemented in C++ and can reference C++ objects in other C++ libraries. For example, if we want to enable the user to get the name of the robot, we simply provide an 'extern "C" ' function that calls the robot object's getName member function. Our function then converts the C++ string returned by robot.getName() to a C string and returns a pointer to the first character in the string.

In certain cases it was necessary to discard the extra level of abstraction provided by a higher level language such as C++ in order to make functionality compatible with standard C. As shown by the previous example, users have no notion of objects or that a robot has the function getName, etc. The C++ library also utilizes smart pointers. Smart pointers, the C++ solution to memory management, delete the data they point to if they are the last reference to that data when they fall out of scope. Since the smart pointers are implemented as objects that override the unary dereference operator, it was necessary to discard the notion of smart pointers altogether and simply return normal pointers to the C caller.

Finally, it is possible to retain objects on the C++ side and pass pointers to those objects back to the C caller. For example, rather then re-write all the Picture class member functions to operate on raw picture data, any time a picture was created we kept the entire class on the heap and simply passed its location on to the caller. Later, the caller can pass that pointer back to the library and it can be treated as the C++ class that it is. This method of interchanging objects between C and C++ is accomplished with a simple typedef. Since the size of a pointer is consistent between the two languages, a struct with the same name as the C++ class can be declared. The C compiler now knows there is a struct named Picture (in the given example) but does not know how big that struct is. This is acceptable because we are only passing pointers to the struct; which the compiler does know the size of.

4. COURSE PLANNING

Initial explorations with the Scribbler 2 suggested that the robots would interest many students and be a valuable addition to the CS 2 course. Subsequent course planning considered how the inclusion of robots would fit with curricular goals, course organization, and pedagogical considerations.

4.1 Curricular Goals and Course Topics

The initial work of integrating the Scribbler 2 into the course required identifying the following course goals:

- Introduce imperative problem solving and data structures;
- Teach the fundamentals of programming robots;
- Provide students with the opportunity to gain and practice knowledge of the C programming language;
- Increase interest in continuing the study of computer science;
- Describe elements of the representation of integers, floating-point numbers, characters, and other data structures; and
- Introduce concepts and skills related to a Linux environment.

Some main topics for the course are:

- *Imperative problem solving:* top-down design, common algorithms, assertions, invariants;
- *C programming:* syntax and semantics, control structures, functions, parameters, macro-processing, compiling, linking, program organization;
- *Concepts with data:* data abstraction, integer and floating-point representation, string representation, arrays, unions, structures, linked list data structures, stacks, and queues;
- *Machine-level issues:* data representation, pointers, memory management; and
- *GNU/Linux operating system:* commands, bash scripts, software development tools.

4.2 Use of Modules

Course organization and development proceeded in two stages, the second of which was successful. At first, we tried appending Scribbler 2 activities to existing labs on each topic, but this approach did not provide a coherent structure for the course or fully utilize the robots' potential.

Instead, we organized topics required for CS 2 course into eight groups, called modules. For each module, we identified readings for each topic, outlined laboratory activities, constructed possible examples (i.e., C programs), and devised a project that would integrate the topics of that module. Next we arranged the topics within each module and the order of the modules from foundational concepts to more advanced uses of imperative problem solving. With this framework, we considered how each module would fit within an overall day-by-day semester schedule.

Each module has a unifying theme, lasts six or seven class days, and utilizes a common format. On the first day of each module, the instructor introduces the topics to be covered over the course of the module, demonstrates examples of programs using those concepts, and may begin discussing the fundamentals of one or more topics. For each of the next few days, students are assigned readings on the topic for the next lab, and the class periods are a mixture of lectures and laboratory practice of the topics introduced on each day. Near the end of the module, students have one to two class periods to work on an assigned project that integrates most or all of the concepts discussed in the module as well as concepts introduced in previous modules. Projects for several modules are closely related to previous ones, in order to reinforce the connectedness of the topics and review previous material. Overall, the modules are designed to introduce course topics to the students, discuss and practice the topics, and then review and apply the knowledge gained.

4.3 Pedagogical Considerations

Much of the course planning and materials development was guided by considerations of how and what students learn. Some important elements of pedagogy include:

- Lab-based approach: the overall course includes about 35 laboratory sessions;
- Student practice in solving problems: numerous exercises build experience with imperative problem solving;
- Sequencing of topics: complex topics are spread over several days;
- Emphasis on pair programming: the course encourages collaboration on lab activities and projects (in and out of class);
- Range of lab activities: laboratory exercises include an introduction to the topic, simple usage (including student descriptions/commentaries), writing code, testing, comparing approaches, and identifying advantages and disadvantages of various implementations;
- Readings: in-class lab activities are supported by readings from a textbook and/or Web-based materials; and
- Projects: a final activity integrates previous work.

4.4 Semester Outline

Table 1 illustrates how central topics in imperative problem-solving were mapped into new modules that also allow exploration of the Scribbler 2 robots. In addition, the course includes three in-class hour tests, a day for end-of-course evaluations, and a three-hour final exam. A more complete outline may be found at [15].

5. PROJECT DEVELOPMENT

The development process included initial experimentation, development of a C interface, writing C programs, designing modules, and writing the course materials. As part of the development work, we presented our work to colleagues throughout the summer to get feedback on our work.

The development of materials represented a collaborative effort between students and faculty. Two students had recently taken the course, so they understood perspectives of the target audience. Two other students had a greater amount of technical experience. The faculty member contributed technical background, coordinated the project, and provided pedagogical and curricular perspectives.

5.1 Initial Experimentation

After conducting experiments in Python with the Scribbler 2 robots, we concluded that some important capabilities included obtaining sensor data, beeping in different frequencies, moving back and forth, turning, taking photos with the built-in camera on the robot, and manipulating these photos.

5.2 Development of the C Interface

Given that Scribbler 2 robots had a library in C++, and CS 2, *Imperative Problem Solving and Data Structures,* would be taught using C, our next step was to make a wrapper library that translated C++ into C so that the CS 2 students could write programs in C, and the robot could execute them. This resulted in the first draft of MyroC.cpp and its header file MyroC.h. MyroC was a continuous effort throughout the project. We kept track of the revisions that were released of Myro-Cpp and if there was something that was of use to us, we updated our MyroC. This was occasionally problematic, since some components of the Myro-Cpp revisions did not compile with our MyroC. The final version of MyroC was not written before the project concluded, since Myro-Cpp was updated several times with new functions that were beneficial for our use, although documentation was improved many times before end of the project.

5.3 Writing C Programs

After we were able to compile C programs for the robot to follow, we tested MyroC for every function to make sure they all worked as intended. We then began writing demonstration programs for range of robot capabilities such as moving to avoid objects, dancing, playing various songs, and controlling the robot using command line arguments.

Table 1: Semester Outline for Imperative Problem Solving and Data Structures

Module	Days Allocated	Overall Theme	Summary and Main Topics
0	7	*Introduction: Play a song*	the Linux environment, elements of a C program, introduction to Scribbler 2
1	6	*Motion (+song, motion)*	variables, types, conditions, loops, Scribbler 2 motion
2	6	*Motion and sensors*	1-dimensional arrays, testing, functions, parameters, values, addresses, & operator, Scribbler 2 sensors
---	3	*Data representation*	integer and floating point representation
3	6	*Deepen understanding of imperative problem solving and C*	characters, strings, input and output
4	6	*Image Processing*	2-dimensional processing, transforming a pixel, transforming a picture
5	6	*Music Composition*	musical notes as frequency/duration structs, pointers, linked lists
6	6	*Storage/retrieval Patterns*	stacks, queues, Bash scripts
7	6	*Integrated Robotics*	files, command-line arguments, robot motion with logging

5.4 Initial Approach

When we were familiar with the Scribber 2's capabilities, and had written various programs aligned with the topics of the course, we tried rewriting the previously existing labs to include the robots. The structure of this course alternated lecture, lab, lecture, lab, etc. However, this approach did not give a view of the capabilities of the robots. The use of robots seemed forced rather than natural.

5.5 A Better Approach: Modules

As a second approach, we organized the course into 8 modules. A module, as we defined it, would each last approximately two weeks, and would comprise a part of the course that would begin with lecture and examples, continue with a few days of labs, and end with more extensive projects that would require the students to use cumulative knowledge to complete.

After deciding on the structure of the course, and making a day-by-day schedule of the topics and their labs, we wrote the various components of the modules in pairs; all of the readings and labs were written in HTML format.

5.6 Writing the Course Materials

Students worked in different pair groupings to develop multiple iterations of each module. The approach to writing modules included 4 steps:

1. A pair made a module outline containing readings that corresponded to each topic, links to the labs and a final project.
2. The pair wrote a first draft of each lab, project, and reading.
3. Each pair reviewed their work with the faculty leader.
4. The authoring pair then gave the module to others, who had not seen it, for a test run. The test run was performed by recording the time each lab took, and giving the authors comments and suggestions the testers had on each aspect of the module.
5. The authors performed the final revisions, resulting in a final draft of the module.

By the end of development, modules, readings, examples, labs, and projects were all collected into one course website, [15].

These materials are available to students in the course as well as to other computer scientists doing work in related fields, and educators wanting to teach the same course with these robots.

6. INTERACTIONS WITH LAUNCHPAD

To benefit as many people as possible, our work, consisting of the MyroC library, header specification, Makefile, and README, is publicly available through Launchpad.net on the world wide web, though a secure connection, at [11]. References to the course material can also be found there as well.

Launchpad was chosen because it is the home of the Myro-C++ project, which MyroC utilizes. Launchpad also boasts support for a variety of bug tracking solutions and effectively keeps track of all users' contributions to a project. Further, Launchpad's ease of use and welcoming nature factored into the decision on where to host our code.

7. CONCLUSIONS/NEXT STEPS

Previous work [4, 6, 8, 14] has shown that robots can raise student interest in computer science and potentially bring more students into the major. Our curriculum shows that the course can be structured around the use of robots and still cover all of the fundamental concepts of imperative problem solving, supported by the C programming language.

We have developed programming support and curricular materials for the use of robots in the teaching of CS 2 *Imperative Problem Solving and Data Structures* with the C programming language. Programming support includes a rich C-callable header file and corresponding implementation (in C++) that allows students to write imperative programs in standard C and link to a C++ library. This C-based header and implementation is packaged as a MyroC project that is available online on Launchpad and provides support for most features available with Scribbler 2 robots using the IPRE fluke dongle.

The CS 2 curriculum with robots, which includes modules, readings, labs, and projects, is also available online, and is currently being field tested in a classroom setting. The full package of 55 C programs and 57 Web pages is available from the authors for use for any instructors who wish to teach an introductory course in computer science with robots in the C language at [15].

The innovative development process for these materials demonstrates the effectiveness of collaboration among former CS 2 students and a faculty member. The former CS 2 students provide deeper insight into the needs of future CS 2 students, while the faculty member provided guidance and experience in the development and writing of a course. The full collaboration allowed an iterative review of all materials, including extensive testing of the MyroC package.

As current students field test the labs and projects, they will submit reviews on the material describing whether it is too long, too short, too confusing, etc., following the style of short lab surveys suggested in [9]. The material will then be revised by former CS 2 students and the faculty member to better fit the needs of future CS 2 students. Future iterations of the curricular materials will also be made available online as they are developed.

Field testing will also allow the MyroC package to continually evolve, and updates to our Launchpad materials will be made accordingly. For example, there are several features left to implement, such as a graphics library and greater control over the various sensors on the Scribbler 2 and fluke dongle.

Overall, we believe that our existing MyroC materials provide a solid base for CS 2 which uses robots in the context of imperative problem solving and C. Through an integrated feedback mechanism, we expect our publicly-available materials will continue to evolve.

8. ACKNOWLEDGMENTS

We would like to thank Dr. John Stone, who provided technical assistance with the interaction of the robots and the network, and Mr. John Hoare of the University of Tennessee at Knoxville, who developed the MyroC++ library. Finally, none of the work over the summer would have been possible without the funding provided by Grinnell College.

9. REFERENCES

[1] Guzdial, Mark, "A Media Computation Course for Non-Majors", *ACM SIGCSE Bulletin*, 35 (3), September 2003, 104-108.

[2] Guzdial, Mark, et al, "Variations on a theme: Role of Media in Motivating Computing Education", *ACM SIGCSE Bulletin/SIGCSE 2010*, 42 (1), March 2010, 66-67.

[3] Hoare, John, Myro-cpp, home page at http://web.eecs.utk.edu/~jhoare/Myro-cpp/Myro-cpp, retrieved August 21, 2011.

[4] Institute for Personal Robots in Education (IPRE), *Main Page*, http://wiki.roboteducation.org/Main_Page, accessed August 21, 2011.

[5] Interim Review Task Force, *Computer Science Curriculum 2008: An Interim Revision of CS 2001*, ACM/IEE, December 2008.

[6] Kumar, Deepak, *Learning Computing with Robots (Uses Python + Scribbler or Scribbler* 2), textbook available at http://wiki.roboteducation.org/Introduction_to_Computer_Science_via_Robots, Fall 2011.

[7] Liberal Arts Computer Science Consortium, "A 2007 Model Curriculum for a Liberal Arts Degree in Computer Science", *Journal on Educational Resources in Computing (JERIC),* 7 (2), June 2007.

[8] MacLennan, Bruce, *Learning Computing With Robots in C++*, (based on Kumar's Python-based text), textbook available at http://web.eecs.utk.edu/~mclennan/Classes/102/LCRcpp/index.html, January 2011.

[9] Metaxas, Panagiotis, *Applied Ancient Wisdom: Lessons from an experiment in CS2 (and not only)*, slides with Stella Kavavouli, presentation to the Liberal Arts Computer Science Consortium, Holland, MI, July 23, 2011.

[10] Misra, Ananya, Douglas Blank, and Deepak Kumar, "A Music Context for Teaching Introductory Computing", ACM *SIGCSE Bulletin/ ITiCSE 2009,* 41 (3), September 2009, 248-252 .

[11] Myro C Developers, *Myro C: A C Implementation for Scribbler 2 Robots*, https://launchpad.net/myro-c, August 21, 2011.

[12] Myro C++ Developers, *C++ Port of Myro*, https://launchpad.net/myro-c++, August 21, 2011.

[13] Rebelsky, Samuel, Janet Davis, Richard Brown, and Brian Harvey, Whither scheme?: 21st century approaches to scheme in CS1", ACM *SIGCSE Bulletin/SIGCSE 2009*, 41 (1), March 2009, 551-552.

[14] Summet, Jay, et al, "Personalizing CS1 with Robots", *ACM SIGCSE Bulletin/SIGCSE 2009*, 41 (1), March 2009, 433-437.

[15] Walker, Henry M., *CSC 161: Imperative Problem Solving and Data Structures Home Page,* http://www.cs.grinnell.edu/~walker/courses/161.fa11/, Fall, 2011.

dLife: A Java Library for Multiplatform Robotics, AI and Vision in Undergraduate CS and Research

Grant Braught
Department of Mathematics and Computer Science
Dickinson College
Carlisle, PA USA
+1 (717) 245-1401
braught@dickinson.edu

ABSTRACT

dLife is a free and open-source Java library that supports undergraduate education and research involving robotics, artificial intelligence, machine learning and computer vision. The design of dLife addresses many concerns raised by experience reports in the CS education literature including a shortened code/test/debug cycle, ready access to robot sensor information and close integration with a robotic simulation system. Full support is currently provided for the following robots: Finch, Hemisson (or Khepera Jr.), Sony Aibo, Khepera 2, Khepera 3, and Pioneer 3, with more in development. Easily extensible packages support classroom and research applications using neural networks, genetic algorithms, reinforcement learning and computer vision.

Categories and Subject Descriptors

I.2.9 [**Artificial Intelligence**]: Robotics – *Autonomous vehicles*; K.3.2 [**Computers and Education**]: Computer and Information Science Education – *Computer science education*;

General Terms

Design, Experimentation, Human Factors, Languages.

Keywords

Mobile robotics, Java, machine vision, neural networks, genetic algorithms, reinforcement learning.

1. INTRODUCTION

The use of robotics in computer science education has received significant and steadily increasing attention during the past decade. Over that time the number, variety, capabilities and price range of commercially available robotic hardware targeted for use in education and research has expanded greatly. As the choices in robotic hardware increased the choices of programming languages, libraries and APIs for programming them have increased as well. For example, Lego NXT robots can now be programmed in at least C/C++, C#, Matlab, Ada, Java, Ruby, Python, Visual Basic, Haskell and LabView [10]. Further, there are several different APIs to choose from in many of the most popular languages. This variety of choices has made it much easier for instructors to match a selected robotic hardware platform with a preferred programming language and an API that is appropriate for the target audience (e.g. CS1, Artificial Intelligence or research experience). However, when there is a desire to employ a variety of different robotic platforms without the overhead of teaching multiple programming languages, environments and/or APIs the array of choices shrinks significantly.

Permission to make digital or hard copies of all or part of this work for personal or classroom use is granted without fee provided that copies are not made or distributed for profit or commercial advantage and that copies bear this notice and the full citation on the first page. To copy otherwise, or republish, to post on servers or to redistribute to lists, requires prior specific permission and/or a fee.
SIGCSE'12, February 29–March 3, 2012, Raleigh, North Carolina, USA.
Copyright 2012 ACM 978-1-4503-1098-7/12/02...$10.00.

dLife is one of a small but growing number of libraries that are designed to support programming a range of robotic hardware platforms using the same language and API across multiple levels of the CS curriculum. In addition, dLife has been designed to meet the broadly held ideal that when used in core CS courses robotics should be an engaging application of the course content and as such should not present technical hurdles that detract from the course [3,6,9,11]. The next section briefly describes and compares several robotics libraries. The core of the paper then presents a tour of dLife, highlighting a selection of its key features. Following, the description of dLife some examples of how the author has used dLife the curriculum are presented. Finally, a preview of several new features that are being developed and a summary are given.

2. RELATED WORK

A number of libraries now exist that allow a variety of different robotic hardware platforms to be programmed using the same language, environment and API. Some of the most robust, well-known and full-featured libraries are Microsoft Robotics Studio, Tekkotsu, Robot Operating System (ROS), URBI (Universal Real-Time Behavior Interface), and Player. All of these libraries have been developed for use in academic research and/or industrial robotics applications and make excellent choices for courses focused on robotics or for use in research projects. However, their programming models and APIs would be unfamiliar to most instructors and inaccessible to students at the introductory level. Further, even in upper division courses where robots are being used to engage other topics (e.g. Artificial Intelligence) the overhead of learning these libraries would necessarily squeeze out other important topics.

Two other libraries, like dLife, have been developed specifically for both teaching and research. They are thus accessible to students at the introductory level, applicable at the upper level with minimal overhead and also powerful enough for use in research.

The Pyro (Python Robotics) [3] project produced the first library in this space. Pyro is distributed free and open-source and supports programming of a variety of different robots using a common API in Python. A number of features central to Pyro's educational mission have had a significant influence on the design of dLife. User programs that control robots in Pyro run on a host computer and communicate wirelessly with the robots. This removes concerns about processing power and storage space. It also eliminates the time consuming process of downloading a program to the robot each time it is to be tested. Pyro is tightly integrated with several robot simulators, allowing controllers to run seamlessly on a physical robot or its simulator. In combination these two features reduce the time required for students to iterate the code/test/debug cycle and make it possible for students to continue to work outside of class time and/or without access to a physical robot. A number of recent reports on the use of robots in the classroom have continued to emphasize the importance of a short code/execute/debug cycle and the availability of simulators as important for student engagement with robots [2,4,6,7,8]. Pyro automatically provides GUI visualizations for many robot sensor values, making them easily available to students for design and debugging purposes, which may help ease some frustrations that are commonly reported by students [1, 2]. Finally, Pyro has a direct/reactive programming model that is easy for introductory students to grasp, while providing other models (finite state machines and subsumption) for more advanced applications. Much of Pyro's development effort has recently shifted to Myro and Calico [12] which together support several robots for use at the introductory level with programming in a variety of languages including Python, Ruby, Lisp Scheme, F#, and Boo.

The second library in this space is Webots [15], which supports programming a wide variety of robots in C, C++, Java, Python, Matlab, or URBI. Like Pyro, Webots also provides good sensor visualization and tight integration with a robot simulator. Webots supports both downloading programs to physical robots and remote control of robots via wireless networking. Unlike Pyro and dLife, however Webots is a closed-source commercial package with a current price of just over $400 USD for an academic license and in excess of $4000 USD for a commercial license. While Webots commercial nature may bring a richer feature set, higher quality and more reliable support, its cost will often be prohibitive for classroom use. This cost may become an even larger factor with a number of educators now beginning to advocate that introductory students each have their own robot and development environment.

As compared to the libraries just reviewed dLife presents a unique combination of attributes. As compared to the research/industrial libraries, dLife presents an environment and an API that is accessible to introductory students, while also supporting more advanced applications. In the education space, dLife provides a free and open-source alternative to Webots and a Java alternative to Pyro. In addition, dLife currently supports a larger selection of robots, provides more tightly integrated simulator support and more complete sensor visualization than Pyro.

3. DLIFE TOUR

3.1 dLife's Robots

dLife currently supports seven educational and research robots across a wide range of prices, features and sizes. In approximate order by the cost of the base unit the supported robot platforms are: Finch, Hemisson† (or Khepera Jr. †), Sony Aibo, Khepera 2†, Khepera 3†, and Pioneer 3†. The robots marked with a † are also supported in simulation by dLife through the Player/Stage system. For each platform, dLife supports the sensors and effectors included with the base unit as well as many of the available add-ons. Full documentation of the features supported for each robot can be found in standard Javadoc format on the dLife web site at www.dickinson.edu/~braught/dlife.

3.2 The dLife Control Center

The Control Center, shown in Figure 1, provides the simplest way to write, compile and execute robot controllers using the dLife library. The Control Center runs on a host PC and communicates wirelessly with the robots to send commands and receive sensor data. When started the Control Center contains tabs (along the right side) for information about dLife (*Info*), a console that displays standard output and standard error generated by executing robot controllers (*Console*), and an integrated Java editor and compiler (*Code*, active in Figure 1). The *Robot* drop-down at the top-left of the window contains a list of all of the robots (both physical and simulated) that are supported by dLife and is used to select the type of robot to be controlled. The *Controller* button opens a file chooser that is used to select a controller for the robot. In dLife terminology, a controller is a user-written sub-class of the `dlife.robot.Controller` class (see section 3.3 for more details).

Users manage the execution of a controller using the buttons at the bottom of the Control Center. A click on the *Start Up* button establishes a connection to the robot and performs any required initialization. Dialog boxes are displayed to collect connection information such as domain name, IP address or bluetooth name from the user; hiding the complexity of establishing these connections. The controller can be executed by clicking the *Run* button or single stepped using the *Step* button. The *Shut Down* button closes the connection to the robot.

Figure 1. The dLife Control Center shown with the integrated Java editor and compiler tab active.

When a controller is started up a tab automatically appears in the Control Center for each sensor and effector that is used by the controller. Each tab contains a GUI that provides the user with a visualization of the sensor or effector. The GUIs for several sensors and effectors are shown in Figure 2. The visualizations for sensors show live sensor readings from the robot and are updated several times per second. Visualizations for effectors can be used to manually control the robot; for example, moving the robot, opening and closing a gripper or pan/tilt/zooming a camera. Double clicking a tab opens it in its own window, allowing multiple GUIs to be viewed simultaneously.

Visualizations such as those in Figure 2 benefit students in a number of ways. Students new to robotics are able to learn about the robot, moving it about manually and observing the sensor values. Students creating controllers can use the GUI controls to try out actions manually (e.g. finding useful pan/tilt/zoom values for a camera) and to observe key sensor values (e.g. infrared proximity sensor values at a specific distance from an obstacle). Then, because there is a direct correspondence between the dLife API and the visualizations the actions performed manually in the GUI are readily translated into program statements. For example, when moving the robot with the Motion GUI, values for translation and rotation speed are shown. These values can then be used directly in method calls that control the movement of the robot (see Figure 3). Students debugging controllers can place the robot in a problematic situation and observe the relevant sensor values as they single step their controller. These types of experiences help to address student frustrations that have been reported with sensor and motor accuracy and consistency [1] and with difficulties obtaining information from the robot [2].

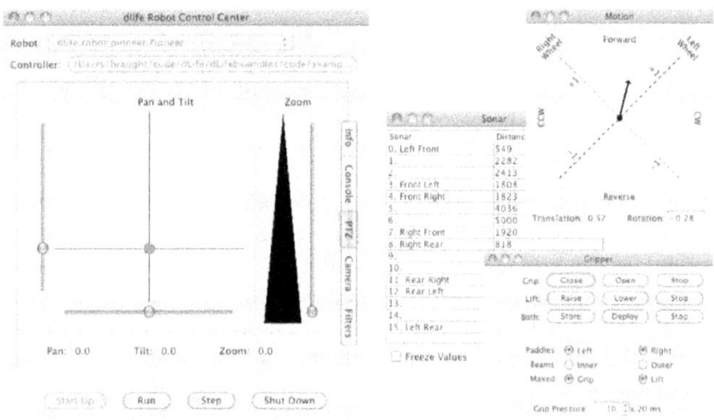

Figure 2. GUI visualizations for a few common sensors and effectors in the Control Center (left) and opened in their own windows (right).

The dLife library also includes tight integration with the Player/Stage robot simulation system [14] and strives to achieve Dodds' "ideal educational toolset [comprising] both a simulator and robot hardware with identical programming APIs"[6]. For many of the robots supported by dLife controllers can be run both in simulation and on a physical robot without modification. All that is required is a single mouse action to change the *Robot* drop-down from the physical robot to the Player/Stage version of the robot. This type of close integration with a simulator has been argued as necessary for student engagement by shortening the code/test/debug cycle [2, 8] and by enabling students to continue their work outside of class when they may not have access to physical robot hardware [5].

3.3 Robot Controllers in dLife

The dLife Control Center is able to load and execute robot controllers that are sub-classes of the abstract `dlife.robot.Controller` class. The source code for a simple controller is shown in Figure 3. Each sub-class of `Controller` must implement two methods: `startUp` and `step`. The `startUp` method is executed when the user clicks the *Start Up* button in the Control Center. Its job is to create objects representing the sensors and effectors that will be used by the controller and to add them to the robot. The `step` method is executed either once when the user clicks the *Step* button or continuously when the *Run* button is clicked. Its job is to control the robot's behavior by reading its sensors and issuing commands to its effectors. This model of control is very similar to one that has been used effectively in Pyro [3].

In Figure 3, the `startUp` method creates objects representing the differential drive and the infrared proximity sensors for the Hemisson robot and adds each to the robot. The act of adding the sensors and effectors to the robot causes their GUI's to be displayed in the Control Center. A wide range of classes modeling the sensors and effectors of each supported robot are available in dLife. The `step` method in Figure 3 retrieves the value of the proximity sensor located at the front of the robot (index 0) and checks to see if its value is greater than 10, indicating the presence of a nearby obstacle. The value of 10 used here was determined by placing the robot near obstacles and using the sensor visualizations described earlier. If there is an obstacle the differential drive mechanism is instructed to move with no translation (first argument) and to rotate clockwise at half speed (second argument). Otherwise the drive is instructed to move forward at half speed with no rotation. This controller almost achieves obstacle avoidance as it moves the robot around. However, it will occasionally hit an obstacle along one of its sides. Giving this controller to students, showing them its failures and asking them to improve it has proven to be an excellent way to get them engaged quickly.

```
import dlife.robot.*;
import dlife.robot.hemisson.*;

public class FirstController extends Controller {
  private HemissonProximitySensor prox;
  private HemissonDifferentialDrive drive;

  public void startUp(Robot r) {
    drive = new HemissonDifferentialDrive();
    r.addDevice(drive);
    prox = new HemissonProximitySensor();
    r.addDevice(prox);
  }

  public void step() {
    if (prox.getValue(0)>10) { // prox 0 is front
                               //  larger = closer

      drive.move(0.0, -0.5);   // rot cw 1/2 speed
                               //  <0 = CW
    }                          //  >0 = CCW
    else {
      drive.move(0.5, 0.0);    // fwd 1/2 speed
                               //  <0 = backward
    }                          //  >0 = forward
  }
}
```

Figure 3. A controller that causes a Hemisson robot to turn clockwise at half speed if an obstacle is detected in front of it, and to move forward at half speed otherwise.

In situations where a more sophisticated form of control is necessary, dLife provides a range of options. A finite state controller allows the definition of states, each with its own `step` method. This method controls the robot when the state is active and specifies transitions between states. This type of control simplifies the creation of context dependent behaviors and sequencing of actions. A subsumption controller simplifies the creation of behavior-based controls. If the provided controllers are not sufficient, greater flexibility can be achieved by using dLife's robot, sensor and effector classes in stand-alone Java programs.

3.4 Vision Support

Increasingly, even low-cost robots designed for classroom use are coming equipped with color cameras. The video input provided by these cameras holds the potential for incorporating object location, object identification and landmark based mapping and navigation into assignments. For example, if the location of an object is readily available, introductory students can focus on the use of conditional execution to have the robot track the object. If landmarks are easily located and identified, intermediate students can focus on the use of graph data structures and search algorithms for navigation. If objects are readily located and identified, advanced students can focus on constructing representations and using heuristic search or reasoning algorithms for planning. However, the details of the necessary vision processing for these tasks can often pull focus from the main point of the assignments. To reduce the chances of this happening significant effort has been devoted to providing dLife with a robust, powerful, easy to use vision system.

The dLife vision system uses the common metaphor of applying a linear chain of filters to a sequence of images. Each filter in the chain can modifiy each image before passing it on to the subsequent filter (e.g. blurring or edge enhancement). In addition, some filters extract information from the image making it available to the programmer (e.g. object locations and sizes). Figure 4 shows the GUI that dLife provides for managing the chain of filters. Controls in the GUI make it easy to add/remove/reorder filters. The filter chain shown in Figure 4 can be used to find an object in an image based upon its colors. The GaussianFilter first blurs the image making its colors more uniform. The MatchFilter then colors regions of the image that match a list of specified colors. Finally the BlobFilter extracts information about contiguous regions of a given color. The effects of this chain of filters, with the MatchFilter tuned to match the colors of a Coca-Cola can, is illustrated in Figure 5. Note that dLife's Camera GUI (Figure 5) displays both the raw and filtered images, allowing the user to see what the robot is seeing and to directly observe the effects of the applied filters.

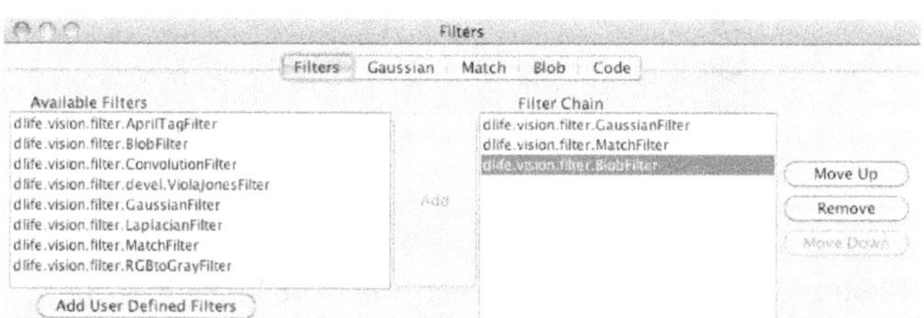

Figure 4. The GUI for managing the chain of filters in the dLife vision system.

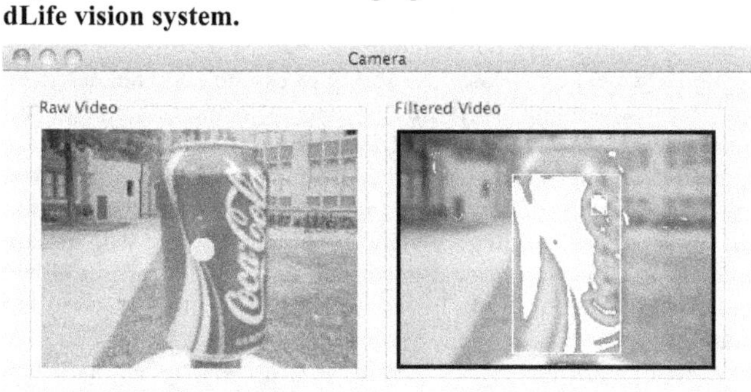

Figure 5. The dLife Camera GUI displaying the effects of the filter chain from Figure 4. The GaussianFilter blured the colors, the MatchFilter painted the matched pixels yellow and the BlobFilter painted white bounding boxes around the identified blobs. A user-written controller used information extracted by the BlobFilter to paint the cyan circle in the raw video image.

When a Camera device is being used, a *Filters* tab, containing the GUI from Figure 4, appears in the Control Center. This GUI contains a tab for each filter currently in the chain (e.g. *Gaussian*, *Match*, *Blob*). The tab for each filter contains a GUI that can be used to configure and/or observe the data extracted by the filter. For example, Figure 6 shows the GUI for configuring the MatchFilter. The controls in this GUI can be used to specify the colors to be matched. Alternatively, the user can click and/or drag on the raw or filtered images to select the colors to be matched.

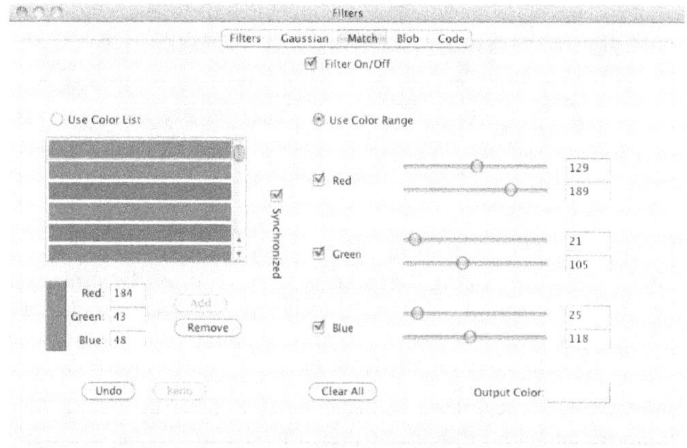

Figure 6. The GUI for configuring the MatchFilter. Individual colors to match can be specified on the left or ranges of RGB values to match can be specified on the right. Colors to be matched may also be added by clicking and/or dragging on the raw or filtered video (see Figure 5).

As another example of a filter GUI, Figure 7 shows the GUI for the BlobFilter. It contains a data table showing all of the information about the blobs that the filter extracted from the image. The data shown in Figure 7 are the results extracted from the image in Figure 5. In addition, the blob filter GUI allows the user to tune the filter by specifying the color of the blobs to identify, the minimum number of contiguous pixels to consider a blob and the number of blobs to draw in the *Filtered Video* window.

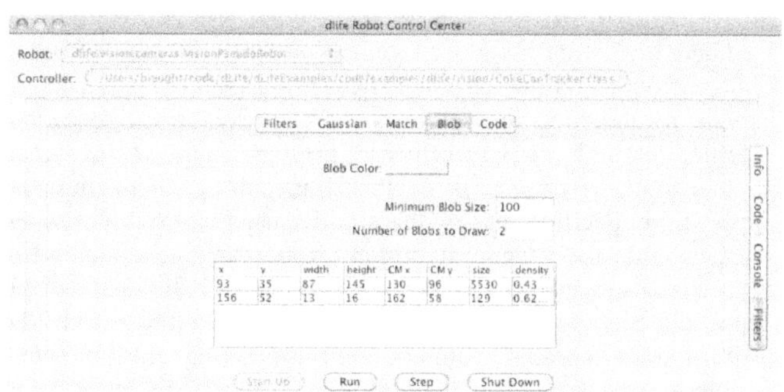

Figure 7. The GUI for the BlobFilter. The data table displays the information extracted from the images (e.g. blob location, center of mass, size and density). This data is available to user-written controller code via methods in the dLife API.

dLife provides a number of other useful filters that perform edge enhancement, face detection, grayscale conversion and detection of AprilTag fedicial markers [13]. As a final example of dLife's vision system, Figure 8 shows the effects of dLife's AprilTagFilter. This filter almost trivializes the challenging task of locating and identifying landmarks and objects. Each point or object of interest is tagged with one of hundreds of unique 2-dimensional bar codes, called AprilTags. The filter identifies the location and ID number of each tag that it finds in the image. The AprilTagFilter, like the BlobFilter, has a GUI that displays all of the information collected about the tags and an API that makes it available to controllers.

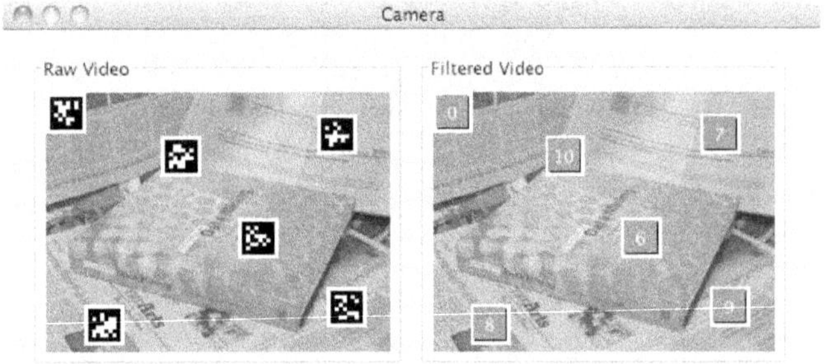

Figure 8. The AprilTag filter locates and identifies 2-dimensional bar codes that can be used to simplify landmark or object detection and identification. The location and ID number of each recognized tag is available to user-written controllers through the dLife API.

Once the GUIs just described have been used to fine-tune a filter chain for an application, dLife makes it easy to use that chain in a user-written controller. The *Code* tab (visible in Figures 4, 6 and 7) displays the Java code necessary to implement the filter chain, which can be copy and pasted into a controller. The controller can then access the information extracted by filters through the dLife API. For filters such as the BlobFilter or AprilTagFilter, one method returns the rows of the data table as an iterable collection of objects. The objects in the collection then provide methods for retrieving the values in each column of the row (e.g. the x and y coordinates of the blob).

3.5 Other Features

In addition to the robotics and vision features described in detail above, dLife includes a number of other features and design elements worth mention.

3.5.1 Artificial Intelligence and Machine Learning

Packages for neural networks, genetic algorithms and TD based reinforcement learning are included in dLife. These packages support its classroom and research use in artificial intelligence and machine learning areas. All three of these packages are designed so that students can focus on the conceptually interesting and application specific parts of the algorithms. For example, when working with the genetic algorithms (GA) package students use dLife classes to specify the representation of an individual as well as the selection and reproduction operators that will be used. The dLife classes represent common gene types (e.g. bits, integers, doubles), reproductive operators (e.g. probabilistic mutation, one-point crossover) and selection operators (e.g. fitness proportional, tournament). Then for each problem to be solved, students create a task specific fitness function that is able to evaluate the quality of an individual. The GA package deals with the more mundane tasks of creating an initial population of random individuals, evaluating the population of individuals using the defined fitness function, advancing the population to the next generation and tracking statistics about the population. The neural network (NN) package supports feed-forward, backpropagation, Elman and CMAC neural networks. When using neural networks dLife allows students to focus on defining the network structure and constructing the training sets to be used. The reinforcement-learning (RL) package supports Q-Learning, R-Learning and SARSA policies. Here dLife allows students to focus on selecting an appropriate sensory state and actions, choosing an action selection model (e.g. epsilon-greedy) and computing the reinforcement signal for each action that is taken.

3.5.2 A Microworld Simulation

dLife contains a microworld simulation named Simple World, shown in Figure 9. In the Simple World a robotic agent (center), directed by a user-written controller, like those used for physical robots, attempts to move about consuming food (cheese) while avoiding predators (dragons), poison (flasks) and obstacles (rocks). Agents receive life force for consuming food and lose life force for consuming poison, colliding with predators and obstacles, and for each action that they take. The simple world agent has a very small set of discrete sensor values (4 sensors, 3 values each) and actions (3 possible actions - forward, turn left, turn right). This makes Simple World well suited for exploring topics such as automated reasoning, reinforcement learning (e.g. Q-Learning) and the evolution of neuro-controllers; all tasks that are typically more difficult with the (approximately) continuous sensor values and effector parameters of most robotic hardware.

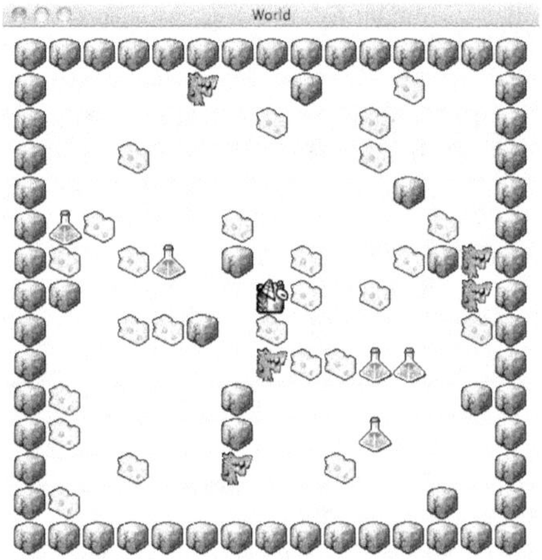

Figure 9. The Simple World microworld included in dLife.

3.5.3 Extensibility

While dLife supports a wide range of robots and AI/ML techniques there are many more out there. Recognizing that this would always be the case, the ability to extend and enhance dLife has been a primary dLife design goal from the beginning. For example, the classes for all of the supported robots and devices derive from base classes that provide reusable communication code, connection dialog boxes and GUI widgets for visualization. In most cases, adding a new robot or device will require surprisingly little effort. For example, support for the Finch robot's differential drive, including the GUI control required less than 20 lines of new code. Similarly, new sources of video, new vision filters, new GA operators, new NN types and new reinforcement-learning polices can be added with relatively little code by extending abstract base classes containing much of the necessary infrastructure.

3.5.4 Documentation and Examples

An extensive set of documentation and illustrative working examples accompanies dLife. Comprehensive Javadoc documentation describes each robot platform, the API for the robot and the classes representing each of its devices. A Quick Start guide is given for each robot, describing the fastest way to get the robot up and running under dLife control. In most cases, a first time user can download dLife and be running a sample controller on a robot in less than 15 minutes. Working sample programs are included to illustrate the use of every supported robot and every dLife package (e.g. the nn, ga and rl packages). This documentation is well suited for use by upper-class undergraduates and instructors, and can serve as the basis for generating simplified instructions for beginning students.

4. USES OF DLIFE

dLife as been used at a variety of levels of the curriculum both as a small component of a course and as the primary platform for assignments. One class of First-Year Seminar students was introduced to robotics, dLife and conditional statements and successfully programmed line following behaviors within two 75-minute class periods. Upper level CS majors in an artificial intelligence course completed the same task in less than 45 minutes including a brief introduction to dLife and robotics. In another offering of artificial intelligence, dLife and robotics were used extensively throughout the course. Assignments in this course addressed feature extraction for obstacle avoidance, vision processing for object tracking, A* search for path planning and neural networks for wall following. dLife was also used in a course on Artificial Life as the primary platform for assignments exploring genetic algorithms, neural networks and the evolution of neuro-controllers.

Outside of the classroom dLife has supported a range of independent implementation and research projects by undergraduate students. The successful implementation projects to date are mentioned in the acknowledgements below. With new robots and devices becoming available all the time, the potential for dLife based student implementation projects seems limitless. Student independent research projects have included: a genetic algorithm based robot localization algorithm; an approach to improving the performance of robot controllers evolved in simulation when run on physical robots; a study of self-adaptive mutation rates in co-evolving neuro-controllers for a game of robot tag; and the use of reinforcement learning to select robot actions that satisfy evolved desires.

5. CONTINUING WORK

The development of dLife is an ongoing project and a number of forthcoming features will likely be of interest. Support for a variety of popular robots is currently being developed, including: Lego NXT, the Parallax Scribbler+iPRE Fluke, and the Parrot ARDrone Quadrocopter. In addition, an interface between dLife and Scratch BYOB is being developed. This interface will allow all of the robots supported by dLife to be controlled by Scratch BYOB programs.

6. SUMMARY

The dLife Java library has been designed to allow students to engage CS course content through robotics without getting bogged down in unnecessary technical details. It has been used with non-majors and advanced CS students as well as in a variety of undergraduate research projects. Some key dLife features include wireless control, tight integration with simulation, GUIs for observing, controlling and configuring devices, powerful and easy to use support for computer vision and a built in editor/compiler. Brought together within the Control Center these features help to shorten the code/execute/debug cycle, reduce the complexities typically associated with programming robots and encourage experimentation. The dLife software, documentation and a complete set of working examples can be obtained under the GNU GPLv3 from http://users.dickinson.edu/~braught/dlife.

7. ACKNOWLEDGMENTS

I would like to acknowledge the contributions that my students at Dickinson have made to dLife. Russell Toris developed the Khepera 3 support and the interface to the Player/Stage simulation system. Kent Carmine, Nate Mitchell, Alex Diehl, Luke Maffey and Mike Olasin all contributed to the Aibo support. Lewis Flanagan developed the Elman Neural Network. I would also like to thank Tom Lauwers at BirdBrain Technologies for lending me a Finch, and Doug Blank with IPRE for lending me a Scribbler+Fluke while I develop(ed) support for them in dLife.

8. REFERENCES

[1] Apiola, M. et al. 2010. Creativity and intrinsic motivation in computer science education: experimenting with robots. In *ITICSE 2010*, 199-203.

[2] Barnes, D. 2002. Teaching introductory Java through LEGO MINDSTORMS models. *SIGCSE Bull.* 34, 1 (February 2002), 147-151.

[3] Blank, D. et al. 2005. Pyro: A python-based versatile programming environment for teaching robotics. *J. Educ. Resour. Comput.* 3(4). Article 1.

[4] Burhans D., et al., 2006. "Introductory computer science with robots," in *proceedings of the 21st national conference on Artificial intelligence - Volume 2*, 1962-1963.

[5] Challinger, J. 2005. Efficient use of robots in the undergraduate curriculum. In *SIGCSE 2005*, 436-440.

[6] Dodds Z., et al. 2006. Components, curriculum, and community: Robots and robotics in undergraduate AI education. *AI Magazine* 27(1). 11-22.

[7] Dodds, Z., et al., 2004. "Teaching robot localization with the Evolution ER1," *Accessible Hands-on Artificial Intelligence and Robotics Education.* 18–23.

[8] Fagin, B. and Merkle, L. 2002. Quantitative analysis of the effects of robots on introductory Computer Science education. *J. Educ. Resour. Comput.* 2(4). Article 2.

[9] Kumar, A. 2004. Three years of using robots in an artificial intelligence course: lessons learned. *J. Educ. Resour. Comput.*, 4(3). Article 2.

[10] Lego Mindstorms NXT. Retrieved August 28, 2011, from Wikipedia:http://en.wikipedia.org/wiki/Lego_Mindstorms_NXT.

[11] Moorman, K. and Parks, D. Using Robots in Undergraduate AI Courses at Small Universities. In FLAIRS 2010, 311-316.

[12] Myro Development. Retrieved August 28, 2011, from IPRE Wiki: http://wiki.roboteducation.org/Myro_Development.

[13] Olson, E. AprilTag: A robust flexible visual fiducial system. In Proceedings of the IEEE International Conference on Robotics and Automation, 2011.

[14] Player Project. Retrieved August 28, 2011, from Source Forge: http://playerstage.sourceforge.net/

[15] Webots: robot simulator. Retrieved August 28, 2011, from Cyberbotics: http://www.cyberbotics.com.

Seven Big Ideas in Robotics, and How To Teach Them

David S. Touretzky
Computer Science Department
Carnegie Mellon University
Pittsburgh, PA 15213
dst@cs.cmu.edu

ABSTRACT

Robotics is widely recognized as an interdisciplinary mixture of engineering and computer science, but the latter component is not well represented at many undergraduate institutions. The sophisticated technologies that underlie perception, planning, and control mechanisms in modern robots need to be made accessible to more computer science undergraduates.

Following the curriculum design principles of Wiggins and McTighe (*Understanding by Design*, 2nd Ed.), I present seven big ideas in robotics that can fit together in a one semester undergraduate course. Each is introduced with an essential question, such as *"How do robots see the world?"* The answers expose students to deep concepts in computer science in a context where they can be immediately demonstrated. Hands-on labs using the Tekkotsu open source software framework and robots costing under $1,000 facilitate mastery of these important ideas. Courses based on parts of an early version of this curriculum are being offered at Carnegie Mellon and several other universities.

Categories and Subject Descriptors

K.3.2 [**Computer and Information Science Education**]: Computer science education, Curriculum; I.2.9 [**Robotics**]: Commercial robots and applications

General Terms

Algorithms, Design

Keywords

computer vision, path planning, kinematics, Tekkotsu

1. INTRODUCTION

Mobile robots provide a compelling context for introducing students to a wide range of computing topics, including machine perception, heuristic search, software engineering, and geometry and linear algebra [13]. But many computer science departments still aren't teaching serious robotics at the undergraduate level. Those that do offer a robotics elective are all too often teaching a high school curriculum where students assemble primitive robots from parts kits and program simple-minded reactive controllers. This paper is a call to action: we *can* make sophisticated robot technologies accessible to undergraduates. Doing so will help them develop into better computer scientists.

In this paper I present seven "big ideas" in robotics that can fit together in a one semester course for junior or senior level computer science majors. Following the *Understanding by Design* methodology of Wiggins and McTighe [17], each big idea is introduced with an essential question, such as *"How do robots see the world?"* The answers to these questions involve deep computer science concepts, some of which can only be fully mastered in graduate classes. But exposing undergraduates to these ideas – at an appropriate level – can broaden their understanding of computer science and encourage them to learn more. All of these ideas are implemented in the Tekkotsu software framework [11, 12] and can be demonstrated on commercially available, fully-assembled robots costing less than $1,000.

Courses based on parts of an early version of this curriculum are being offered at Carnegie Mellon and several other universities, including members of the ARTSI Alliance, a consortium of historically black colleges and universities and major research universities that is working to become a national resource for robotics education [2]. Course materials are available on the web at wiki.Tekkotsu.org.

2. THE TEKKOTSU "CREW"

The guiding principle advocated here is that students should be exposed to the richness of robotics algorithms and representations from the beginning, which precludes their implementing everything themselves from scratch. Instead they should be provided with a comprehensive software framework on which to build. The Tekkotsu framework includes a collection of interacting software modules known as the "Crew" [15] that students use to explore the big ideas to be described below. The Crew presently has four components:

- The **Lookout** manages the robot's sensor package and controls the "head" if one is present. Typically the head is a pan/tilt with a video camera.
- The **MapBuilder** [14] is responsible for vision, and for maintaining egocentric (body-centered) and allocentric (world-centered) maps of the environment.

Permission to make digital or hard copies of all or part of this work for personal or classroom use is granted without fee provided that copies are not made or distributed for profit or commercial advantage and that copies bear this notice and the full citation on the first page. To copy otherwise, to republish, to post on servers or to redistribute to lists, requires prior specific permission and/or a fee.
SIGCSE'12, February 29–March 3, 2012, Raleigh, North Carolina, USA.
Copyright 2012 ACM 978-1-4503-1098-7/12/02 ...$10.00.

- The **Pilot** [16] handles localization and navigation.
- The **Grasper** [9] is responsible for manipulation, for those robots that include an arm.

Tekkotsu programmers issue requests to the Crew to achieve desired effects. The Crew modules are responsible for determining how to satisfy these requests, which may require invocation of complex algorithms such as path planners or inverse kinematics solvers. These algorithms are also directly accessible to students, and can be explicitly invoked when students want to explore them in detail. But under normal circumstances students work at a higher level of abstraction and leave these details to the Crew.

3. SEVEN QUESTIONS AND THE SEVEN BIG IDEAS

3.1 How Do Robots Know What To Do?

Big idea: Autonomous robot behaviors are **mechanisms** constructed from carefully designed algorithms and representations.

Underlying technology: event-based architectures and hierarchically structured, parallel state machines.

Learning goal: students will be able to think algorithmically about robot behavior.

Specific skills: students will be able to decompose a behavior into a series of states and transitions, draw state machine diagrams by hand, translate between graphical and textual state machine notations, make appropriate use of fork and join operations, visualize the execution of a state machine using Tekkotsu's Storyboard tool, and locate and describe errors in state machine definitions.

3.2 How Do Robots See The World?

Big idea: Robots use sophisticated but imperfect **computer vision algorithms** to deduce real world object representations from arrays of pixels.

Underlying technologies: basic vision algorithms (e.g., Hough transforms), AprilTags [10], SIFT (Scale-Invariant Feature Transform) [7], face detection, and more.

Learning goal: students will be familiar with both the capabilities and limitations of state of the art machine perception algorithms.

Specific skills: students will be able to use the MapBuilder to demonstrate the function of several built-in vision algoirithms, and use these components effectively in robotics applications.

3.3 How Do Robots Know Where They Are?

Big idea: Robots estimate their position and orientation in the world using a combination of **odometry**, **visual landmarks**, and other types of sensory information.

Underlying technology: particle filters.

Learning goal: students will understand the uses and limitations of odometry and visual landmarks, the basic principles of particle filters, and how particle filters are used for localization.

Specific skills: students will be able to demonstrate effective robot navigation behavior by arranging landmarks appropriately in the environment and invoking the Pilot's localization mechanism as needed to determine their robot's position.

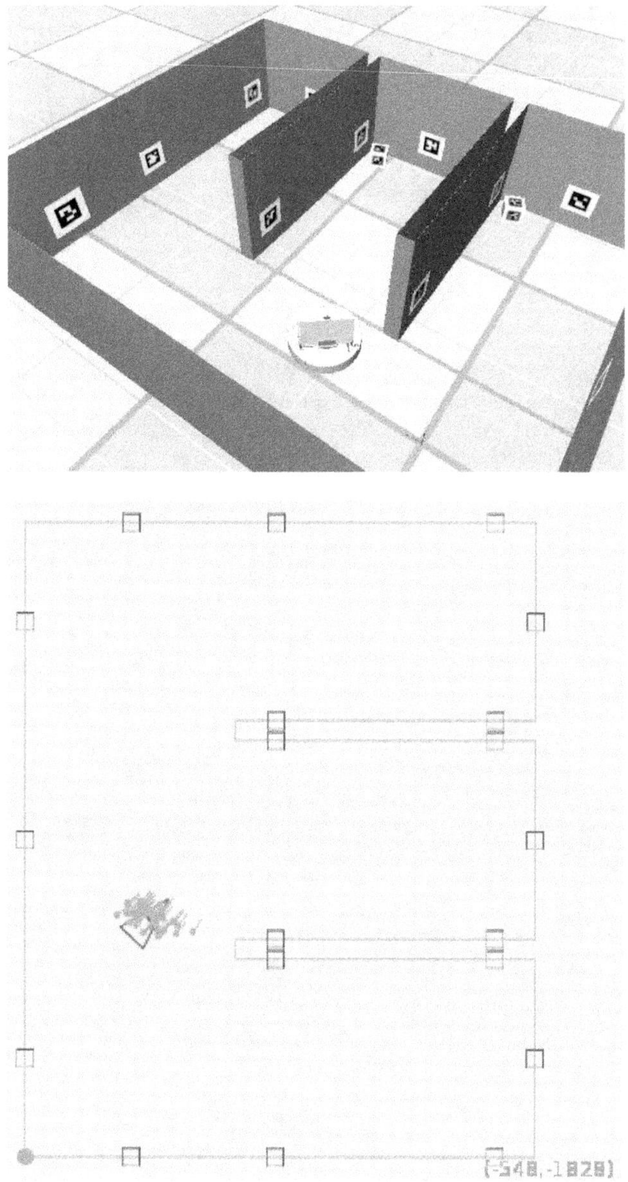

Figure 1: Top: Robot wandering in an E-shaped maze with AprilTag landmarks. Bottom: robot's estimated position and heading shown by a blue triangle; particle cloud shows each particle's position and heading value.

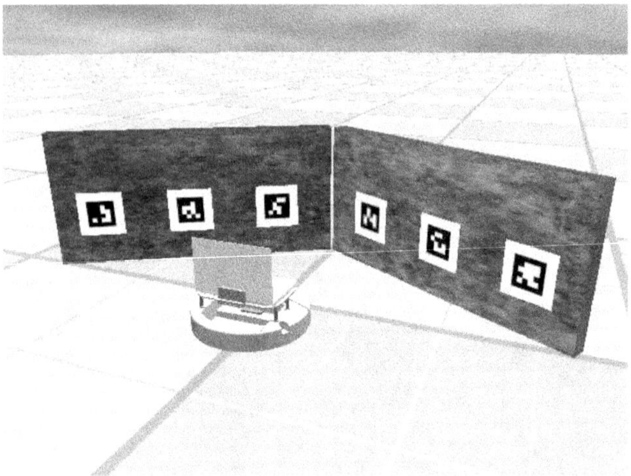

Figure 2: Starting position of the robot relative to a vee-shaped barrier in the Mirage simulator. The real-world version of the barrier uses two sheets of posterboard at a 120° angle.

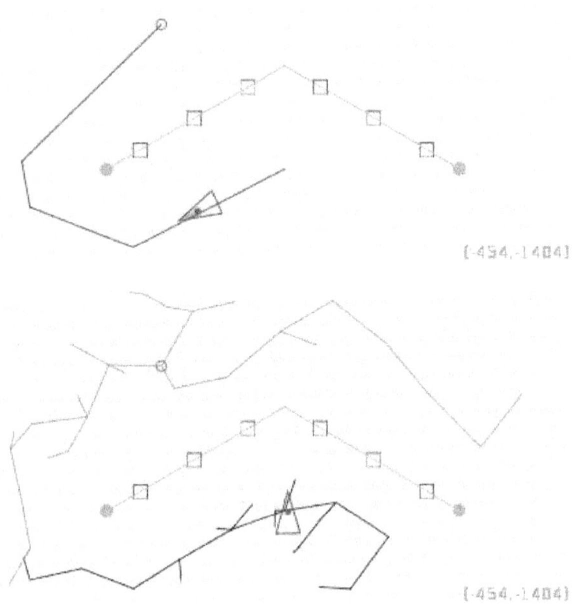

Figure 3: Top panel: world map with barrier and AprilTags; the path planned by the Pilot is shown in blue, and the goal location marked with a red circle. The robot is following the path. Bottom panel: how the path planner works. Once search trees from the start location (black) and goal location (green) meet in the RRT-Connect algorithm, the path can be extracted and then smoothed, yielding the blue line in the top panel.

3.4 How Do Robots Know Where To Go?

Big idea: Robots navigate through the world using a **path planner** to search for routes around obstacles and an **execution monitor** to ensure that the robot stays on the path.

Underlying technology: RRTs (Rapidly-exploring Random Trees) [6].

Learning goal: students will understand the concept of a stochastic search algorithm, how the RRT-Connect algorithm is used for path planning, and how planning can fail.

Specific skills: students will be able to invoke one of the Pilot's path planners to plan and execute paths through environments containing obstacles.

3.5 How Do Robots Control Their Bodies?

Big idea: Robots describe their bodies as **kinematic trees** and use **kinematics solvers** to translate between joint angles and body coordinates.

Underlying technology: kinematic description files, forward and inverse kinematics solvers.

Learning goal: students will understand kinematic descriptions expressed as trees of joints and links, and how kinematics solvers use this representation when translating between world coordinates and joint coordinates.

Specific skills: students will be able to construct and visualize kinematic descriptions using Tekkotsu's DH Wizard tool, and invoke kinematics solvers via the Lookout or Grasper to produce desired robot motions.

3.6 What Can We Do When A Robot Becomes Too Complex For One Person To Fully Understand It?

Big idea: Robots are complex software systems that employ standard **abstraction** and **software engineering** techniques to **manage complexity**.

Underlying technologies: tools such as modular design, coding standards, doxygen (automatically generated documentation), standard libraries, etc.

Specific skills: students will be able to search and navigate through the extensive online Tekkotsu documentation (over 3500 web pages), make appropriate use of abstraction mechanisms (e.g., write classes that inherit from predefined node types, or create appropriate enumerated types for state machine signaling), produce code that conforms to Tekkotsu coding conventions, and give a picture of the modular organization of Tekkotsu in terms of directories and namespaces.

3.7 How Do We Calculate the Quantities Needed To Make A Robot Function?

Big idea: Geometry, trigonometry, and linear algebra are the **mathematical underpinnings** of much of robotics.

Underlying technology: Tekkotsu's angular arithmetic classes and **fmat** matrix/vector manipulation package.

Learning goal: students will understand frames of reference, angular and vector arithmetic, homogeneous coordinates, coordinate transformation matrices, and how these concepts are applied in robotics.

Specific skills: students will be able to solve simple kinematics problems using Tekkotsu's built-in kinematics solvers and matrix/vector classes.

4. HOW TO TEACH THESE IDEAS

The first stage of the *Understanding by Design* process is to define the learning goals, big ideas, and essential questions, as listed above. The second stage, which will not be covered here, is to plan for assessment by deciding what constitutes acceptable evidence that students have met the learning goals. The third stage is to choose specific instructional activities that will lead students to achieve these learning goals. For most of the big ideas, a seven-step framework similar to the WHERETO schema of Wiggins and McTighe [17] or the framework of Bransford et al. [3] can be used to guide instruction. Here is how this framework would be applied to the third big idea in our list, localization:

- **Motivate:** Introduce an essential question and big idea: How do robots know where they are?
- **Demonstrate:** Show the technology students will learn about, e.g., set out some landmarks and demonstrate the robot using them to keep track of its position as it moves. How did it do that?
- **Explain:** Provide a high level explanation of how the technology works, e.g., describe particle filters and how they're used by the Pilot for localization.
- **Visualize:** Give students a way to see the algorithm in action, e.g., show them how to display the particles the Pilot is using, and observe how the particles change as the robot moves (Figure 1).
- **Experiment:** Guide students to play with the technology to test its accuracy and uncover its limitations. For example, how does the particle filter respond if you move one of the landmarks? How does it cope with ambiguous (visually identical) landmarks?
- **Apply:** Show students how to apply the technology in programs they write themselves. Example: show them how to ask the Pilot to use specific landmarks for localization, and how to obtain the robot's position estimate from the particle filter.
- **Review:** Ask students to summarize what they've learned about particle filters and localization, and to demonstrate mastery by answering quiz questions and solving small problems.

Algorithm visualization (step 4) is the most technically demanding of the seven steps, since it requires software enhancements, but most of this work has already been done for Tekkotsu. Figure 1 shows the particle filter's state made visible using a tool called the SketchGUI [14]. The robot is visualized using the Mirage simulator. AprilTags [10] on the walls of the maze serve as landmarks.

Tekkotsu includes an extensive collection of visualization tools, such as the Storyboard, which generates and displays a state machine execution trace, and the DH Wizard, which displays the kinematic structure of a robot. To take one more example: when the Pilot is navigating from the robot's starting position (Figure 2) to a goal location on the other side of a vee-shaped barrier, the planned path is automatically displayed as a blue line (Figure 3, top); also note the tight particle cloud. The bottom panel shows the search tree constructed by the path planner using the RRT-Connect algorithm [6]. Figure 2 was generated by the Mirage simulator, and Figure 3 by the SketchGUI tool. Students can pose their own path planning problems and see the results visualized automatically using this tool.

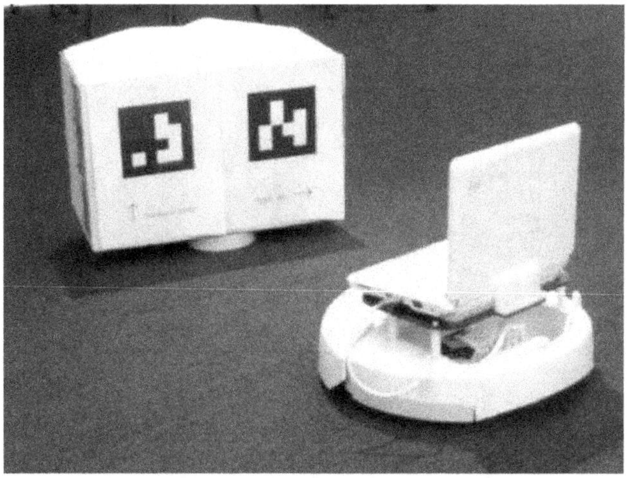

Figure 4: A challenge problem using pairs of AprilTags to guide the robot.

Guided experimentation (step 5) is also difficult to do well, and we expect to explore many variations on this activity over the next few years. For example, we recently developed an activity called Particle Filter Bingo in which students use Tekkotsu to participate in a competitive simulation of robot localization. It's fun, but we don't know yet whether this activity achieves its intended effect of reinforcing student understanding of how particles are evaluated by a particle filter.

5. WHAT CAN STUDENTS DO?

Figure 4 shows part of a challenge task from the 2011 ARTSI Student Robotics Competition. Students had to program their robot to read and follow instructions to make its way around a complex course they had not seen before. The instructions consisted of pairs of AprilTags describing a distance to travel and a direction to turn to reach the next instruction pair in the sequence. The task combines vision, navigation, and state machine control. Some student teams who completed this task had taken or were presently enrolled in a Tekkotsu-based robotics elective, but other teams learned in less formal settings, using the material on the wiki.

A high school student who learned Tekkotsu programming in a summer enrichment program was able to program a Chiara hexapod robot to approach an electronic piano keyboard, visually locate the keys, and play Ode to Joy with its right front leg (Figure 5). This work combined computer vision algorithms with kinematics calculations. The student's video explaining how his software worked received an award at the 2011 Association for the Advancement of Artificial Intelligence conference [5].

Other student projects have included chasing and swatting a ball in a maze, and playing tic-tac-toe using the Grasper to calculate arm trajectories for moving the pieces. A masters student programmed a robot to play chess on a real chessboard [4].

6. BARRIERS TO IMPLEMENTATION

The Tekkotsu software and curriculum materials are freely available on the web, so the cost of adoption is limited to the

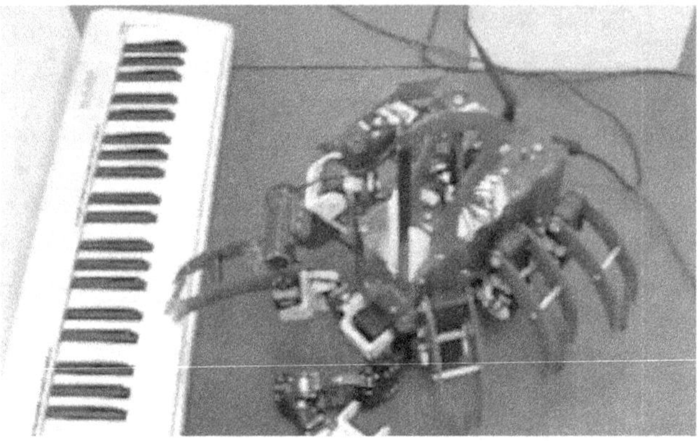

Figure 5: Chiara hexapod robot programmed by a high school student to play Ode to Joy.

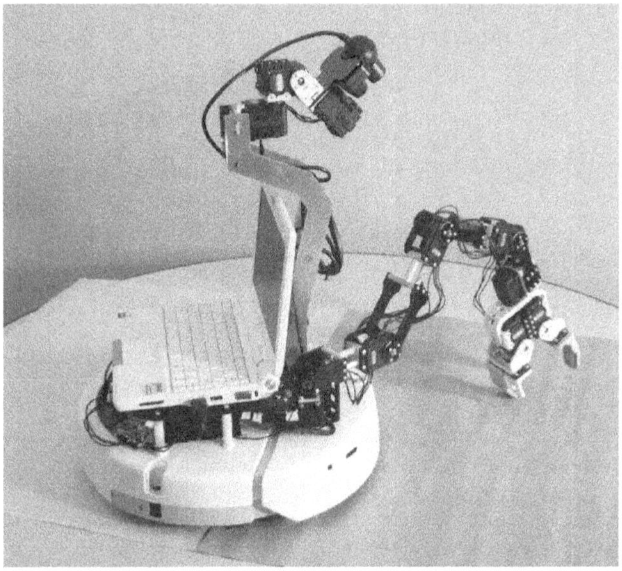

Figure 6: Calliope prototype with pan/tilt camera and 5 degree-of-freedom arm. A version with a Microsoft Kinect in place of the webcam is under development.

hardware cost of the robots. One of the biggest barriers to improving undergraduate robotics courses since the demise of the Sony AIBO has been the lack of capable but affordable robots. The iRobot Create mobile base provides excellent price/performance but is not a complete solution due to its lack of sensors and on-board computing power. Fortunately, several good options are now available that place an Ubuntu Linux netbook atop a Create. The Calliope from RoPro Design costs $900 for the basic model and is available from RobotShop.com with Tekkotsu pre-installed. Versions with a pan/tilt and an arm (Figure 6) are planned for 2012. The Turtlebot from Willow Garage, and the Bilibot, which originated from a group at MIT, both sell for roughly $1200 and include a Microsoft Kinect as the camera. Both come with ROS, the Robot Operating System from Willow Garage [18]. The Bilibot also includes a 2 degree of freedom arm. All three designs are open source.

Although these platforms are admittedly more expensive than LEGO or VEX kits, fewer are needed, because they are interchangeable and can thus easily be shared. Four robots are recommended for a class of 8 to 12 students.

We've recently begun supplying students with bootable 8GB flash drives that have Ubuntu, Tekkotsu, and the Mirage simulator pre-installed. This allows students to use their personal laptops for robotics assignments without altering their hard drive in any way.

While some work can be done in simulation, students will still need ample laboratory time to interact with physical robots. And the robots need space to run around in. This is perhaps the hardest barrier to overcome, as space is at a premium at many schools. The ideal arrangement is a dedicated lab with keycard access so students can have unrestricted access to the robots. Some schools instead opt to have designated periods each day for the laboratory to be open with a faculty member or graduate student present.

A final issue is lack of a textbook specific to this curriculum. At present, instructors are using the labs and tutorials on the Tekkotsu wiki as their primary source, with supplementary material of their own choosing. A popular supplementary textbook has been Mataric's *Robotics Primer* [8].

The curriculum design presented here could potentially be used with other software frameworks that provide particle filters, path planners, and visualization tools, such as ROS. Tekkotsu's design philosophy differs from ROS [12], e.g., Tekkotsu provides tightly-integrated components and uses a shared memory model for simplicity, while ROS emphasizes modularity (at the cost of increased complexity) and uses a networking model for scalability. Both seek to provide services to robot programmers based on state of the art algorithms.

7. DISCUSSION

Robotics courses using the Tekkotsu framework have been taught for six years at Carnegie Mellon, and for several years at ARTSI Alliance-affiliated schools including Norfolk State University, Florida A&M University, Hampton University, Winston-Salem State University, Jackson State University, and the University of the District of Columbia. Tekkotsu and the associated curriculum materials have both evolved substantially over this time. The curriculum described here, which is the new target for both Carnegie Mellon and the ARTSI Alliance, is partially implemented now and will be completed over the next few years.

7.1 What Do Students Gain?

Besides learning about robotics, students gain several other important things in a course of this type:

Appreciation for mathematics. We require CS majors to take a lot of math, but almost none of it is used in their CS courses. For many, especially those who have not taken computer graphics, robotics may be their only opportunity to apply trigonometry and linear algebra to real computing problems. For some students, robotics will actually be their introduction to linear algebra.

Mastery of advanced programming concepts. Many students report that learning Tekkotsu has made them better C++ programmers by helping them understand features such as templates, multiple inheritance, operator overloading, functors, and namespaces. These topics are often introduced superficially in undergraduate courses, using only toy examples. Since they are used extensively in Tekkotsu, students can see how they are actually employed in "industrial strength" software.

Software engineering skills. Robotics provides a compelling context for teaching software engineering because students are being asked to delve into and extend a software system far more complex than anything they could expect to write from scratch themselves. Baltes and Anderson, describing a mixed reality infrastructure for robotics instruction, have likewise observed that working on robotics assignments gave students useful software engineering experience [1].

7.2 Common Misconceptions

Certain misconceptions about robotics must be corrected for CS education to move forward [13]:

Robotics is not about building robots. Not for computer scientists, anyway. We don't expect our students to build their own laptops. Why should they be trying to build robots, when the robots they ought to be using are more complex than any laptop? Leave the construction to industry. CS students' time is best spent learning to program the most capable robots we can provide them with.

Robotics is not just a vehicle for teaching CS1, and robot programming involves more than writing simple reactive controllers. As computer science faculty become more familiar with the rich intellectual content of robotics and the tools for teaching this material to undergraduates, they will be less likely to trivialize the subject.

7.3 More Big Ideas

Some additional big ideas that could be taught to undergraduates include:

- **Human-robot interaction:** *How should robots behave around people?*
- **Multi-robot coordination:** *How can robots work together?*
- **Task-level planning:** *How can robots formulate plans for solving complex problems?*

These topics would be difficult to fit into the one semester course outlined in this paper, but would be good choices for the second half of a two-semester robotics sequence.

8. ACKNOWLEDGMENTS

This research was supported in part by National Science Fondation awards DUE-0717705 and CNS-1042322. I am grateful to Sharon Carver at Carnegie Mellon for introducing me to the *Understanding by Design* methodology and for several very helpful discussions. I would also like to thank the faculty and students of the ARTSI Alliance for their insights and feedback regarding the Tekkotsu framework and curriculum.

9. REFERENCES

[1] J. Baltes and J. E. Anderson. Leveraging mixed reality infrastruture for robotics and applied AI instruction. In *Proceedings of EAAI-10: The First Symposium on Educational Advances in Artificial Intelligence*, Menlo Park, CA, 2010. AAAI Press.

[2] C. Boonthum-Denecke, D. S. Touretzky, E. J. Jones, T. Humphries, and R. Caldwell. The ARTSI Alliance: Using robotics and AI to recruit African-Americans to computer science research. In *Proceedings of FLAIRS-24*. AAAI Press, 2011.

[3] J. D. Bransford, A. L. Brown, and R. R. Cocking. *How people learn: Brain, Mind, Experience, and School.* National Academy Press, Washington, DC, 2000.

[4] J. Coens. Taking Tekkotsu out of the plane. Master's thesis, Carnegie Mellon University, Computer Science Department, 2010. Available at http://reports-archive.adm.cs.cmu.edu/anon/2010/CMU-CS-10-139.pdf.

[5] A. Iyengar. Chiara robot plays the piano, 2011. Video available at aivideo.org or `http://www.youtube.com/watch?v=-e8zmGypBDg`.

[6] J. J. Kuffner and S. M. LaValle. RRT-connect: an efficient approach to single-query path planning. In *ICRA'2000*, 2000.

[7] D. G. Lowe. Object recognition from local scale-invariant features. In *ICCV 2*, pages 1150–1157, 1999.

[8] M. J. Mataric. *The Robotics Primer (Intelligent Robotics and Autonomous Agents).* The MIT Press, Cambridge, MA, 2007.

[9] G. V. Nickens, E. J. Tira-Thompson, T. Humphries, and D. S. Touretzky. An inexpensive hand-eye system for undergraduate robotics instruction. In *SIGCSE 2009*, pages 423–427, 2009.

[10] E. Olson. AprilTag: A robust and flexible multi-purpose fiducial system. Technical report, University of Michigan April Laboratory, 2010. Available at http://april.eecs.umich.edu/papers/details.php?name=olson2010tags.

[11] Tekkotsu robotics development framework, 2011. http://Tekkotsu.org.

[12] E. J. Tira-Thompson and D. S. Touretzky. The Tekkots robotics development environment. In *Proceedings of ICRA-2011*, Shanghai, China, 2011.

[13] D. S. Touretzky. Preparing computer science students for the robotics revolution. *Communications of the ACM*, 53(8):27–29, August 2010.

[14] D. S. Touretzky, N. S. Halelamien, E. J. Tira-Thompson, J. J. Wales, and K. Usui. Dual-coding representations for robot vision in Tekkotsu. *Autonomous Robots*, 22(4):425–435, 2007.

[15] D. S. Touretzky and E. J. Tira-Thompson. The Tekkotsu "crew": Teaching robot programming at a higher level. In *Proceedings of EAAI-10: The First Symposium on Educational Advances in Artificial Intelligence*, Menlo Park, CA, 2010. AAAI Press.

[16] O. Watson and D. S. Touretzky. Navigating with the Tekkotsu Pilot. In *Proceedings of FLAIRS-24*. AAAI Press, 2011.

[17] G. Wiggins and J. McTighe. *Understanding by Design.* Pearson Education, Upper Saddle River, NJ, expanded 2nd edition, 2005.

[18] Willow Garage. ROS: Robot Operating System, 2011. http://ros.org.

Design and Evaluation of a Braided Teaching Course in Sixth Grade Computer Science Education

Arno Pasternak
Fritz-Steinhoff-Gesamtschule Hagen and
Technische Universität Dortmund
44227 Dortmund, Germany
arno.pasternak@cs.tu-dortmund.de

Jan Vahrenhold
Technische Universität Dortmund
Faculty of Computer Science
44227 Dortmund, Germany
jan.vahrenhold@cs.tu-dortmund.de

ABSTRACT

We report on the design and evaluation of the first year of a Computer Science course in lower secondary education that implements the concept of *braided teaching* [7]. Besides being a proof-of-concept, our study demonstrates that students can indeed be taught Computer Science (as opposed to Information and Communication Technology) as early as in sixth grade while at the same time not falling behind with respect to Information Technology Literacy. We present quantitative and qualitative results and argue that Computer Science can be taught just like any other science subject worth full curriculum credit.

Categories and Subject Descriptors: K.3.2 [Computers and Education]: Computer and Information Science Education

General Terms: Design, Experimentation.

Keywords: Lower Secondary Computer Science Education, Braided Teaching, Computer Science vs. ICT

1. INTRODUCTION

A recent study [10] conducted by the ACM and the CSTA reveals that in contrast to the crucial role Computer Science and the technologies enabled by it plays in the 21st century (see also [11]), Computer Science as a subject of study still plays a minor if non-existent role in K-12 education. While the study presents comprehensive data only for the U.S., reports from other countries (e.g. [1, 5, 12]) indicate that there are only few success stories in general.

One important conclusion that can be drawn from this study is that policymakers are not technology-oblivious *per se*: 73% of the school districts in the U.S. have adopted a curriculum that aims at *Information and Communication Technology* (ICT) *skills* [10, p. 44]. In contrast, only 37% of the districts have adopted a curriculum that goes beyond this and aims at *concepts* in *Computer Science* [10, p. 37].

Permission to make digital or hard copies of all or part of this work for personal or classroom use is granted without fee provided that copies are not made or distributed for profit or commercial advantage and that copies bear this notice and the full citation on the first page. To copy otherwise, to republish, to post on servers or to redistribute to lists, requires prior specific permission and/or a fee.
SIGCSE'12, February 29–March 3, 2012, Raleigh, North Carolina, USA.
Copyright 2012 ACM 978-1-4503-1098-7/12/02 ...$10.00.

As part of their "National Call to Action" the authors of the study request to "develop courses to implement new computer science standards" [10, p. 14] and present efforts from the states of Georgia and Texas. The authors emphasize that a "rudimentary knowledge of computing" is insufficient in the digital age; instead, they demand Computer Science to be taught "on a continuum from basic computing concepts that can be attained at elementary and middle school levels to deeper knowledge, skills, and practices more appropriate for secondary school" [10, p. 25].

An established way of teaching "a continuum of concepts" is along what is known as Bruner's *spiral curriculum* [2]. In the case of Computer Science in lower secondary education, we have proposed to follow this approach in what we termed *braided teaching* [7]: a contextualized approach to course design that organizes topics along *strands* which then are taught in an interleaved way and along a spiral curriculum (see [7] and the references therein for a discussion of this concept and related work).

DEFINITION 1. *A* strand *is a sequence of items addressed in class that satisfies the following criteria: (1) The items can be assigned to a well-defined subject matter (by their structure or their content). (2) The subject matter is identifiable and recognizable to the students throughout the sequence. (3) The subject matter is being presented from more than one point of view or embedded in more than one context. (4) The sequence of items is addressed in more than one teaching unit.*

Two questions left open are whether this concept can be instantiated in practice and whether positive effects can be observed. We report on the first year of a prototypical implementation of the concept and, based upon qualitative and quantitive evidence, affirmatively answer both questions.

2. DESIGN AND IMPLEMENTATION OF A BRAIDED TEACHING COURSE

One of the major impediments in implementing and evaluating Computer Science courses in lower secondary education is that in the authors' state these courses are not worth full curriculum credit and that thus the student population in these courses is somewhat biased. Fortunately, the administration at the Fritz-Steinhoff-Gesamtschule allowed for a prototypical implementation of a Computer Science course in sixth grade that is worth the same (i.e. full) curriculum credit as Mathematics, Physics, Biology, and Chemistry. In general, students choose one elective course at the beginning of sixth grade; this course is one of French, Italian, Natural Sciences (a combined course on Physics, Biology, and Chemistry), or Employment Studies. Each of these courses is taught for 120 mins. per week and fully counts towards the final exams, i.e. failing such a course has the same effect as failing Mathematics or English. In support of our research, a Computer Science course was added to the list of electives. In 2010/2011, 27 students enrolled in this course.

2.1 Overview of the Curriculum

The course reported upon was designed according to the principles of *braided teaching* we proposed in an earlier article [7] and taught by the first author, an in-service teacher who has taught Computer Science, Mathematics, and Physics at the Fritz-Steinhoff-Gesamtschule for over two decades. The course was organized along the following five strands:

Programming: Statements, sequences, control structures, variables and assignment, procedures, functions, ...

(Semi-)Structured Data: HTML, XHTML, SVG, XML, XSLT/XPath, ...

Typed Systems: Organizing and dispatching by type, e.g. classes in programming languages, or file types in an operating system.

Multimedia: Raster graphics, vector graphics, sound, ...

Operating Systems: Elementary functions, GUI-based applications, shell, remote access, ...

Again in line with our original proposal, we used `Tcl/Tk` [6] as the programming language for this course – see our previous article for the rationale behind this. In accordance with the school's policy regarding the use of free and open software, the course was instantiated using a Linux environment. It should be noted that this choice also helped establishing equity since the vast majority of students had access to computers at home which ran some version of a Windows operating system (see Section 3.1 for more comments).

2.2 Details of the Implementation

The break-down of the curriculum for the first year of the braided teaching curriculum into teaching units and their association with the strands is shown below:

Strand \ Unit	1	2	3	4	5	6
Programming	■			■	■	■
(Semi-)Structured Data		■				
Typed Systems	■		■			
Multimedia				■	■	■
Operating Systems		■	■		■	

In the remainder of this section, we outline all teaching units and verify that each strand is indeed a strand according to Definition 1. Criterion (1) (*well-defined subject matter*) is verified easily by the above description of the strands and since criterion (2) (*easily recognizable by the students*) also depends on the way the teacher is presenting the material, only criteria (3) and (4) remain to be verified. The above table shows that even in the first year three of the five strands appear in more than one block of teaching units, so, extrapolating to the second and third year of the course, we can assume that the fourth criterion is fulfilled. This leaves us with criterion (3) (*more than one point of view/context*) which is indeed crucial for ensuring that students do not fall for the misconception of a many-to-one or even one-to-one relationship between concepts and contexts.

Unit 1: Buttons and Labels (5 Weeks).

An obvious requirement for contextualized teaching is that students should be familiar with the context itself. A common body of knowledge for all students in sixth grade is the computer and interaction with the computer, e.g. launching a web browser, a word processor, or a game, and it seems natural to start with the computer itself as context.

While students experience the GUI as the primary (if not sole) interface between the user and the machine, they do not preceive the GUI as anything but a "black box". Thus, their first encouter with Computer Science is to open this box and to use `Tcl/Tk` to build a "launch button".

```
button .opera   -text "start Opera" -command opera
pack .opera
```

Ultimately, as part of the *Programming* strand, students come to realize that all commands executed inside a computer can be represented in textual form.

With moderate effort students can design (mockup) a GUI which resembles the GUI they see in their everyday lives.

The second part of this unit involves creating an array of buttons and labels used to display each student's weekly timetable. At this point, students learn that the GUI is composed of different types of components, i.e. the course visits the *Typed Systems* strand.

Unit 2: Creating a Web Page (5 Weeks).

Following up on the first unit's last topic, the goal of the second unit is to enable each student to create a small web page displaying his/her timetable (thus making contact with the *(Semi-)Structured Data* strand). At this point, students realize that it becomes necessary to convert the `Tcl/Tk` output into an image that can be put on the web page. Since, in contrast to most environments of other interpreted languages, the `Tcl/Tk`-console also allows to execute commands of the underlying operating system, the course can move to the *Operating Systems* strand rather effortlessly.

Using the `import` command provided by `ImageMagick`, students can interactively capture the section of the screen displaying their timetable and save it as a `.jpg`-file.

```
import -pause 10 timetable.jpg
```

The outcome of this first encounter with the *(Semi-)Structured Data* strand is an understanding of the (hierarchical) constructs used in defining a simple web page and the markup languages' syntax. A typical markup of a web page created by the students looks as follows:

```
<html>
  <head><title>Lisa's Timetable</title></head>
  <body>
    <center>
      <h1>Lisa's Timetable (Grade 6)</h1>
      <img width="90%" src="timetable.jpg">
    </center>
  </body>
</html>
```

Unit 3: Files, Directories, and Trees (3 Weeks).

As the students create more web pages (possibly using their own images) the need for organizing the corresponding files becomes evident. Students realize that their files should be easy to access, even if the class takes place in a different lab. The concepts of *file*, *directory*, and *tree* are introduced. In particular, students create different representations of directory trees and learn how to translate each of these representations into commands for the operating system level. Students learn how to create directories and to navigate in a directory tree, reacting to situational conditions and teacher inputs. The different types of entries in a directory (files and folders) and the different subtypes of files present a new view on the *Typed Systems* strand.

Unit 4: Drawing in Tcl/Tk (8 Weeks).

In the fourth unit, the *Programming* strand is touched upon for the second time. According to Definition 1(3), it is mandatory to present this strand embedded in a different context. The course does so by having the students create simple vector graphics using `Tcl/Tk`-commands thus also embarking on the *Multimedia* strand.

The graphics are created either from instructions verbally given by the teacher or trying to reproduce simple drawings handed out to the students. In either situation, students are asked to write a `Tcl/Tk`-script that executes the appropriate drawing on the canvas. To do this, it is necessary to analyze which components – in the beginning merely lines – make up a picture and then to translate them into a sequence of corresponding instructions.

Finally, students move on to (describe and) create their own graphics which allows them to practice modelling skills required in Computer Science as well as in Geometry.

Unit 5: Raster and Vector Graphics (6 Weeks).

In the previous unit, students created, described, and programmed line drawings using `Tcl/Tk`. In the second unit, they created a screenshot from a `Tcl/Tk`-window and used the resulting `.jpg`-file as part of their web page. At this point, the students merely used the `.jpg`-file without having been taught about the concept of *raster graphics*.

Following a spiral curriculum and continuing along the *Multimedia* strand, the fifth unit revisits the second and fourth unit, formally introduces the concepts of raster and vector graphics and points out the differences between these two types. In this unit, students work with `.xpm`-files instead of `.jpg`-files for a variety of reasons: First and foremost, the `X PixMap` format is a textual representation of an image, and thus an `.xpm`-file can be opened and modified using any text editor. Secondly, research on misconceptions has shown that students tend to conflate a concept and its instantiation if only one (type of) instantiation is considered, and thus presenting a second file format helps preventing a conflation between *raster graphics* and *file format used for representing a raster graphic*. Finally, concepts in operating systems (such as extensions and associated actions) present themselves quite naturally.

During this unit, students work to produce a (vector) graphic in `Tcl/Tk` (see Unit 4), export this into an `.xpm`-file, modify it using a text editor, and finally view the result using a graphics viewer. In addition to the strands covered in Unit 4, this unit also revisits the *Operating Systems* strand and presents – as discussed above – a new perspective.

Unit 6: Variables (5 Weeks).

Piaget observes that "the building up of formal relations begins at about 11 or 12 years" [8, p. 162]. Thus it is adequate to introduce the concept of variable in sixth grade. To facilitate the transgression from (according to Piaget) the "concrete operational phase" to the "formal operational phase", it is helpful to introduce the formal construct of variables by using them for "storing" (representations of) concrete, real-world objects.

As a result of the previous unit(s), students have a variety of images created by themselves, and in addition to this, students are provided with a collection of images. These pictures are stored in a directory on the file server. Students are taught how to load a picture into a variable and to work with such variables, e.g. how to draw (on the `Tcl/Tk` canvas) multiple copies of the picture stored in a single variable. Again, the playfulness of sixth graders is build upon, and students create pictures of, e.g. villages with streets, cars, trees, and houses.

This unit lies in both the *Multimedia* and *Programming* strand. As a follow-up, students will learn to use loops for scripts which produce animated films on the `Tcl/Tk` canvas.

3. EVALUATION

The main goal of our evaluation was to investigate whether students were able to understand the Computer Science concepts taught during the course of the first year. We also evaluated the students' knowledge of ICT topics that were not part of the course and investigated possible changes in attitude towards topics in Computer Science and ICT.

3.1 Exams and Homework Exercises

A standard indicator of students' knowledge of subjects taught in class is their performance in exams. As pointed out before, the course in question was designed from scratch and thus no exams from previous courses could be reused. Over the duration of one year, four written exams of sixty minutes each were administered. The distribution of the grades is given in Figure 1.

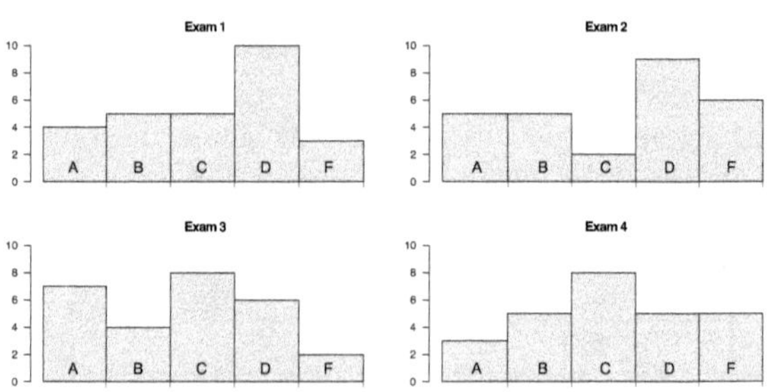

Figure 1: Histogram of the grades for all exams.

The first exam's histogram exhibits a slight imbalance towards less perfect grades but is not unusual for first exams in Sciences where students still have to struggle with the effect of the first contact with a new Science subject. The second exam, however, shows a rather dramatic shift towards a bimodal distribution. At this point, we realized that the school's general policy not to require extensive homework exercises in Sciences should be overruled in favor of giving a student more opportunities to recapitulate and practice. Since even as of today, one cannot assume every student to have access to a computer at home that provides an environment comparable to the one in school, we decided to provide more but only paper-and-pencil homework exercises.

Not unexpectedly, the results from the third exam show a boost for almost all students which can be directly attributed to more practice activities due to the increased volume of homework activities. The distribution of the fourth exam is almost exactly what one would expect.

Examples.

The fact that students in sixth grade are relatively young poses a particular problem for exams in Computer Science: on the one hand, students work with texts in some (programming or markup) language – in our case `Tcl/Tk`, HTML, or shell commands – on the other hand, they often still struggle with the language of instruction (both in speaking and in writing). While these problems have been found to occur more often with non-native speakers (roughly a third of the students), another, even more challenging problem is that ICT and Computer Science terminology has permeated everyday language in a way that causes ambiguities and imprecisions that cannot be (detected and resolved) until one has obtained a full understanding of the (scientific) meaning. Thus, it is necessary to ban test items which demand a translation from one language level to another.

Humans think in images – real images or concepts – while the computer manipulates (character) strings. Often the last step of running a program is to visualize the results of a computation. Conversely, modelling in Computer Science ultimatly can be seen as transforming ideas (with interim stages) into a textual form. Thus, one type of test item was to let students draw a picture of the result from running a `Tcl/Tk`-script or rendering a page described in HTML:

Joe has created the following three images:

`me.jpg` `bike.jpg` `train.jpg`

He now uses HTML for a markup of his webpage:

```
<html>
  <head><title>Joe's Webpage</title></head>
  <body>
    <center>
      <h1>Joe's gorgeous webpage</h1>
      Here's my new webpage. Do you like it?<br>
      That's me:<br>
      <img width="30%" src="me.jpg"><br>
      <h2>Things I like:<br>
      <img width="25%" src="bike.jpg">
      <img width="25%" src="train.jpg">
      <br>
      Biking and trains.
    </center>
  </body>
</html>
```

How does this page look like in a web browser?

As children at this age like to paint and draw the inverse type of test items is possible (and highly popular): Write a `Tcl/Tk`-script for drawing a given picture or use HTML for a markup of a given web site.

---

1. Using paper and pencil, draw a picture of a chair and a desk using three straight lines for each.
2. Write a `Tcl/Tk`-script to have the computer draw your picture.

3.2 Final Grades

Finally, we compare the distribution of the students' final grades (which are computed from both the written exams and in-class assessment) for Computer Science, Mathematics, and Natural Sciences. The distribution (Figure 2) shows that the grades in Mathematics follow an almost perfect Gaussian distribution (again, this is not surprising given the long tradition of Mathematics Education) while the grades in both Computer Science and Natural Sciences exhibit a bimodality. What is interesting, though, is that there are very few "borderline pass" cases in Computer Science, i.e. that the "fail" grades were clearly separate from "pass" grades. This rebuts some of the concerns raised by parents prior to the course, namely that a course in a "new" subject would affect their children's chances of passing the final exam.

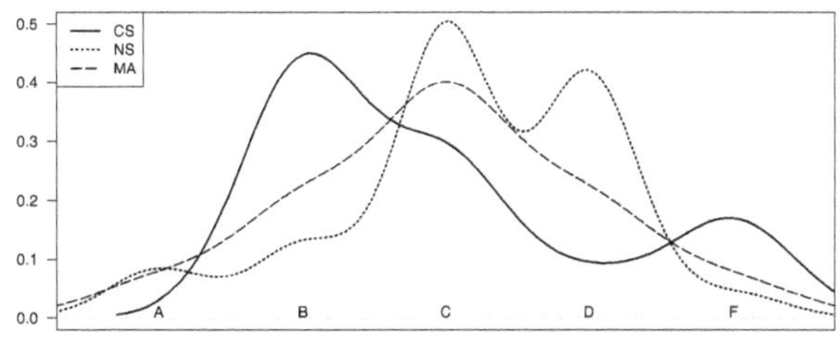

Figure 2: Grade distributions: Mathematics (MA) Natural Sciences (NS), and Computer Science (CS).

3.3 Quantitative and Qualitative Analysis

The evaluation of the students' knowledge of factual and procedural knowledge in Computer Science was measured by pre- and post-test adminstration of Likert-type scale questionnaires and supported by semi-structured interviews using think-aloud surveys. Additionally, we gathered data about the students' attitudes towards Computer Science.

Control Groups.

For all questionnaires and surveys, we used two control groups. The *external* control group (CG_{ext}, $n = 117$) consisted of students from ICT courses at two other schools in the same school district and age group. Their teachers were informed of the *braided teaching* concept, the course's design, and the fact that questionnaires and surveys were to be administered well in advance of the beginning of the respective courses. Due to the repeated adminstration of the same questionnaires, a "teaching to the test"-effect could not be precluded. To prevent such an effect to occur for the first author who was teaching the study group (BT, $n = 27$), the items for which interviews were performed were selected by the second author at the end of the course based upon the curricula of both the BT and the CG_{ext} group.

At Fritz-Steinhoff-Gesamtschule, students in fifth grade are required to take a 360 mins. teaching unit on text processing, spreadsheets, and the school's intranet. To measure the effects of this teaching unit and to verify that the student population was not different across the three schools, we used an *internal* control group (CG_{int}, $n = 27$) in sixth grade that did not select Computer Science as an elective.

Questionnaires.

Due to the different foci of the courses and the fact that the CG_{int} control group did not receive either Computer

"Yes/No/Don't Know" Item	Pre-Test		Post-Test	
	BT/ CG_{int}	BT/ CG_{ext}	BT/ CG_{int}	BT/ CG_{ext}
I know what a variable is.	0.33	0.54	0.000*	0.000*
I know what a vector graphic is.	0.29	0.40	0.001	0.000*
I know what a directory tree is.	0.19	0.15	0.01	0.001
I know what a directory is.	0.21	0.21	1.0	0.25
One can use a variable to store a value.	0.84	0.47	0.005	0.28

Figure 3: Self-assessment of the study group relative to each of the control groups (p-values for the χ^2-test).

Science or (additional) ICT training, all items in the questionnaires allowed for an "I don't know what this question is about" answer. Each questionnaire consisted of three parts:

(i) 29 "yes/no/don't know"-type items (including cross-validating items) that aimed at the self-assessment of factual knowledge (e.g. "I know what an 'operating system' is" or "Variables can be used to store values").

(ii) 20 Likert-type items that aimed at the self-assessment of abilities (e.g. "I know how to use a word processing system" or "I know my way around in the WWW") and attitudes towards programming (e.g. "Programming is important in Computer Science" or "If a program works, it is not important how it was programmed").

(iii) 21 Likert-type items that aimed at personal experiences and attitudes towards Computer Science (e.g. "I'm using a computer many times a week", "I enrolled for this course because my parents made me to", "Boys are more successful in Computer Science than girls").

Due to space constraints, we only report on the evaluation of a few of the items related to factual knowledge, i.e. taken from the first part of the questionnaire. These items asked the students to assess whether they knew what a certain concept in Computer Science or ICT is.

Figure 3 summarizes the statistical evaluation of the self-assessment in pre- and post-test questionnaires. For each setting, we used a χ^2-test for the hypothesis that the BT group and either of the two control groups responded according to the *same* distribution. For none of the items, the evaluation of the pre-test significantly substantiated a *rejection* of this hypothesis, i.e., the groups' responses could not be discriminated. The evaluation of the *post-test*, however, showed that seven out of ten times, the hypothesis has to be rejected with a very high level of significance ($p \leq 0.01$). In decreasing order of significance, these items pertain to *variables*, *vector graphics*, and *directory trees*. Since the results are statistically significant for both the comparison with CG_{int} and CG_{ext}, we can conclude that the students in the BT group have a higher confidence in their level of knowledge (for instance, the distribution of "yes:no:don't know" (in percent) for the "vector graphics" item was 78:11:11 for the BT group while it was 31:54:15 for CG_{int} and 22:39:39 for CG_{ext}). The items for which no statistically significant difference could be observed pertain to *directories* (i.e. a concept students might be acquainted with from their everyday use of a computer) and the question of whether it is possible to use a variable to store a value (see next section).

Interviews.

To validate the student's self-assessments, a total of 54 interviews was conducted during the last week of the school-year. 19 interviews were conducted in the BT course and 35 interviews were conducted in the CG_{ext} and CG_{int} group. The participants from the CG_{ext} and CG_{int} groups were selected by their respective teachers, thus we can safely assume that the level of knowledge represented in these interviews does not underestimate the average level of the group.

The interviews touched upon the following topics: (i) files and directories, (ii) text processing, (iii) variables, and (iv) graphics. Of these, topics (i), (iii), and (iv) are part of the braided teaching curriculum, and topics (i), (ii), and (iv) are part of the "ICT Literacy" part of the "Information and Communication Technology in Secondary Education" curriculum of the UNESCO [3, Units A2, A3, and A6].

We classified the interviews addressing a certain topic w.r.t. whether the topic was unknown or known. If it was known, follow-up questions were evaluated to classify how much (no/partial/full) understanding was evident.

For the "variable" concept (for which the difference in self-assessment was strongest), the interviews confirmed a strong difference between BT and the control groups

variable	n	unknown	no	partial	full
BT	18	17%	28%	22%	33%
CG_{int} + CG_{ext}	18	100%	0%	0%	0%

A similar confirmation was made for the "vector graphics" concept; this item, however, also revealed an even more prominent difference in self-assessement (where 78% stated they knew the concept) and external evaluation (where 56% were found not to know the concept by name). This astonishing difference in combination with the fact that the students were rather well able to *work* with vector graphics in the exams (see above) prompts us to revisit the respective teaching unit to ensure that the concept as such is presented and contrasted with raster graphics much prominently.

To examine the effects of the BT course on the knowledge of ICT concepts, we included a question related to "directory trees"; also, we asked the students how they would (in a word processing systems) transform a left-aligned text into a centered text. For this question, we provided printouts of the text in left-aligned and centered form. Both items ("subdirectories"/"centering") are explicitly mentioned in the UNECSO ICT curriculum [3, p. 59/61].

directory tree	n	unknown	no	partial	full
BT	13	38%	15%	23%	23%
CG_{int}	12	58%	33%	8%	0%
CG_{ext}	4	75%	0%	25%	0%

The responses to the first question showed that students from the BT group showed a much deeper understanding of the hierarchical concept represented by a directory tree – an indication that Computer Science indeed augments the understanding of an ICT concept.

As mentioned in Section 2.2, one goal of our course was to open the "black box" as which a computer and the software is perceived. To our (pleasant) surprise, the success w.r.t. this goal became evident when evaluating the responses to the "text centering" question which had been designed to verify the hypothesis that Computer Science and ICT could be distinguished by, e.g., the procedural knowledge w.r.t. using a word processing system. We classified the responses according to whether students suggested to manually insert white spaces, to change the justification to *centered*, or both.

centering	n	no idea	white space	justify	both
BT	14	0%	21%	43%	36%
CG_{int}	12	34%	25%	41%	0%
CG_{ext}	19	21%	42%	31%	4%

While a significant percentage of students in each of the groups suggested the appropriate solution, it is striking to observe that the BT group was the only group where every student interviewed could solve the problem and almost 80% chose the appropriate answer. The answers to this item indicate that students were in fact able to *transfer* a concept (justification) from a plain-text markup language (HTML) to the use of GUI in a word processing system.

Gender Issues.

Reports on in-class and outreach activities imply that one crucial factor influencing the recruitment of female students is to debunk (negative) stereotypes and to do this as early as possible in the students' careers – see, e.g., [4]. We followed up on (part of) a recent study by Taub *et al.* [9] and included one item in the third part of the questionnaire that asked for an assessment of the hypothesis that boys are more successful in Computer Science than girls.

Group	n	Pre-Test	Post-Test	p-value
BT (female)	8	2.38 (1.77)	2.11 (1.76)	0.019
CG_{int} (female)	13	3.08 (1.16)	2.17 (1.03)	0.014
BT (male)	19	3.00 (1.38)	3.14 (1.74)	0.003
CG_{int} (male)	14	3.11 (1.27)	2.21 (1.48)	0.005

Figure 4: "Boys are more successful in Computer Science than girls.": mean/std. deviation (six-level scale) and p-value for Wilcoxon's signed rank test.

The statistical evaluation (Figure 4) of the students' responses supports the following observations and hypotheses: (1) The pre-test shows that female students who chose the BT course revealed a stronger disagreement with the hypothesis than any of the other groups, i.e. a *non-negative* attitude towards Computer Science can exist even in fifth grade and prior to any contact with Computer Science – and this attitude can be capitalized on. (2) Over the course of one year, *all* groups significantly changed their attitude towards the gender issue; this supports the hypothesis that outreach activities should target middle schoolers. (3) Except for the male students in the BT group, the results in the post-test were almost identically distributed. This allows for the following interpretations: (3.1) Female students in the BT course positively experienced their abilities and validated their already strong disagreement. (3.2) Male students in the BT course also positively experienced their abilities and were led to a slightly stronger agreement. (3.3) All students in the CG_{int} group did not have any contact with Computer Science, and thus external factors such als "growing up" and the influence in other subjects, e.g. Mathematics, lead to a uniform shift towards disagreement.

The disagreement with the hypothesis is stronger than reported by Taub *et al.* [9]. Whether this is due to the course design (Computer Science vs. Computer Science Outreach) or to external factors (see above) remains to be investigated. In fact, the result that all groups except the male students in the BT group were led to stronger disagreement raises the question whether such external factors (possibly including the male(!) teacher as a role model) are predominant.

Summary.

The evaluation of the first year of our *braided teaching* course is encouraging: we have demonstrated that a Computer Science course worth full curriculum credit can be successfully implemented in sixth grade and that statistically significant results related to both factual and procedural knowledge as well as to attitude can be observed. Besides continuing the course described, future work will focus on long-term effects and on revisiting the teaching material with a stronger focus on conceptual knowledge.

Acknowledgments

The support of the colleagues teaching the CG_{ext} courses as well as of the administration of the Fritz-Steinhoff-Gesamtschule was essential for this project. The authors thank Holger Danielsiek, Rebecca Doherty, Jörn Gödel, and Wolfgang Paul for their help with evaluating the questionnaires and with conducting and transcribing the interviews.

4. REFERENCES

[1] T. Bell, P. Andreae, and L. Lambert. Computer science in New Zealand high schools. In*Proc. 12th Australasian Computing Educ. Conf.*, pp. 15–22, 2010.

[2] J. S. Bruner. *The Process of Education.* Harvard University Press, Cambridge, MA, 1960.

[3] Y. Buettner, C. Duchâteau, C. Fulford, P. Hogenbirk, M. Kendall, R. Morel, and T. van Weert. Information and communication technology in secondary education: A curriculum for schools. UNESCO, Paris, 2000.

[4] S. Graham and C. Latulipe. CS girls rock: Sparking interest in computer science and debunking the stereotypes. In *Proc. 34th SIGCSE Symp. Computer Science Education*, pp 322–326, 2003.

[5] O. Hazzan, J. Gal-Ezer, and L. Blum. A model for high school computer science education: the four key elements that make it! In *Proc. 39th SIGCSE Symp. Computer Science Education*, pp. 281–285. 2008.

[6] J. K. Ousterhout. *Tcl and the Tk Toolkit.* Addison-Wesley, Reading, MA, 1994.

[7] A. Pasternak and J. Vahrenhold. Braided teaching in secondary CS education: Contexts, continuity, and the role of programming. In *Proc. 41st SIGCSE Symp. Computer Science Education*, pp. 204–208. 2010.

[8] J. Piaget. *The Psychology of Intelligence.* Routledge Chapman & Hall, London/New York, 2nd ed., 2001.

[9] R. Taub, M. Ben-Ari, and M. Armoni. The effect of CS unplugged on middle-school students' views of CS. In *Proc. 14th SIGCSE Conf. Innovation and Technology in Computer Science Education*, pp. 99–103. 2009.

[10] C. Wilson, L. A. Sudol, C. Stephenson, and M. Stehlik. Running on empty: The failure to teach K-12 computer science in the digital age. ACM/CSTA, 2010.

[11] J. M. Wing. Computational thinking. *Communications of the ACM*, 49(3):33–35, Mar. 2006.

[12] A. H. Yahya. The interaction between high school curriculum and first year college courses: The case of computing. In *Proc. 41st SIGCSE Symp. Computer Science Education*, pp. 406–410. 2010.

EcoSim: A Language and Experience Teaching Parallel Programming in Elementary School

Chris Gregg Luther Tychonievich James Cohoon Kim Hazelwood

Department of Computer Science
University of Virginia
PO Box 400740
Charlottesville, VA 22904

ABSTRACT

Traditional introductory programming classes teach sequential programming using a single-threaded programming model. It is typical to wait until a student has developed proficiency in sequential programming before teaching parallel programming. As computer hardware becomes increasingly parallel, there is a greater need for software engineers who are proficient in designing parallel programs, and not just by "parallelizing" sequential designs. Teaching parallelism first is an important step towards educating tomorrow's programmers.

We present an overview of a five-day introductory parallel programming course. We taught the course to nine and ten year-olds with no prior programming experience. Our course utilized a fundamentally parallel language we designed for the course, one with a near-natural language syntax that exposed the parallel processors throughout the code. This language, coupled with an interactive online programming environment, allowed us to teach a wide range of parallel programming concepts in a very limited timeframe.

We also present examples of student-written code that demonstrates their understanding of some basic parallel programming concepts, and we describe the overall course goal and specific lesson plans geared towards teaching students how to "think parallel."

Categories and Subject Descriptors

D.3.2 [**Concurrent Programming**]: Language Classifications—*concurrent, distributed, and parallel languages*; K.3.2 [**Computers and Education**]: Computer and Information Science Education—*computer science education, curriculum*

General Terms

Languages, Design, Human Factors

Keywords

Concurrent languages, parallel languages, instructional design, introductory programming, pedagogy, education, readability, elementary school, K-12

Permission to make digital or hard copies of all or part of this work for personal or classroom use is granted without fee provided that copies are not made or distributed for profit or commercial advantage and that copies bear this notice and the full citation on the first page. To copy otherwise, to republish, to post on servers or to redistribute to lists, requires prior specific permission and/or a fee.
SIGCSE'12, February 29–March 3, 2012, Raleigh, North Carolina, USA.
Copyright 2012 ACM 978-1-4503-1098-7/12/02 ...$10.00.

1. INTRODUCTION

Introductory programming classes are often taught using languages designed primarily for single-threaded applications. Multi-threaded or parallel programming concepts are considered advanced. It is rare that students learn about parallel programming before a second or third programming course. Traditionally, many colleges and universities in the U.S. provided only a single parallel programming course, often as a senior-level undergraduate elective. When students do learn parallel programming, many have difficulties transitioning from a sequential-programming mentality to a parallel programming mentality. One manifestation of this difficulty is that parallel programming is considered "hard" by many students and instructors alike [9].

As parallel platforms become more common, parallel programming skills are becoming increasingly important. Within the last five years, multicore computing has become the *de facto* standard on desktops and laptops. General Purpose GPU (GPGPU) computing has matured such that multi-core GPUs can be programmed with minimal extensions to traditional languages such as C++ and Python [5]. These trends are expected to continue in coming years [7]. To take full advantage of this increasing parallelism, programmers must understand traditional parallel concepts such as race conditions, atomicity, synchronization, and deadlock. Beyond those skills, they must also be able to look at computing problems and devise solutions that utilize parallel processes. Parallel programming requires a change in mindset as well as practice, adopting new models of what activities are "easy" and "hard" to guide the development of algorithms that can be executed efficiently by highly-parallel hardware.

Rather than strive to correct existing sequential programming habits, we developed an introductory parallel programming course specifically targeting novice programmers. The class, titled "Programming the Computers of the Future," was offered during a five-day weekend enrichment program to students from the 4th and 5th grade (9 and 10 years old). The choice of this age group was primarily based on the opportunity we had to teach novice programmers, but pedagogically the methodology we describe could be applied to any group of beginner programmers. None of the students in our classes had significant prior programming experience. Each class period was two hours long. A week elapsed between each class, during which the students could access the programming development environment online to continue learning independently, although no out-of-classroom assignments were given.

Our course was designed around three objectives.

```
a plant has
  a position
  size, a number
  a color

create 10 plant and for each
  do in order
    replace the plant's color with green
    replace the plant's size with 10
```

Figure 1: A simple *EcoSim* program to define and create ten green "plants" on the screen.

- Introduce the students to basic parallel programming ideas using multiple processors.
- Help the students develop a mental model of what programming is and what computers do.
- Teach the students to "think parallel" about computing problems.

We measured these objectives through exit surveys, informal interactions with individual students, and by inspecting the code produced by each student. Structured assessment was not possible within the enrichment program structure.

The course used a programming language of our own design, called *EcoSim*[1]. *EcoSim* uses an English-like syntax and makes parallelism both pervasive and visible to the user. We also developed an online environment in which students could write and run code from any computer. This environment gives each students step-by-step feedback on the behavior of each emulated processor. Figure 1 shows an example *EcoSim* program that defines and draws ten green "plants" on the screen, where the plants are represented by circles of radius 10. Figure 4 shows the *EcoSim* development environment, which includes a code window, settings, a console window with output messages, and a window for graphical objects.

2. ECOSIM

We looked for four characteristics in the language we used in our course[2]:

Visibly Parallel: We wanted a language that was parallel unless requested otherwise. We also wanted the idea of parallel processors executing the instructions to be emphasized throughout the language and visible in the runtime environment.

Self-Explanatory: We did not want to have to translate what code meant. We didn't want to re-define symbols like "=" or to introduce new symbols or words. We also wanted all elements of the language to be accessible at the 4th-grade level.

Web-Based: We wanted the students to be able to work at home without installation. This meant building on top of either Javascript or Flash, the only tools we could count on all the students having already installed.

Engaging: We wanted every program the students wrote to interest them. Every program should be graphical, with text reserved for diagnostic information.

[1] *EcoSim* is so-named because we envisioned students using it to program *eco*logical *sim*ulations.

[2] We considered, but rejected, a fifth characteristic: a "complete" language. As an enrichment course, we did not anticipate being a gateway into serious software development. In hindsight, this may have been a poor choice.

Since we were aware of no language having all four desired characteristics, we created our own. We designed the syntax and semantics, wrote a type-checking parser, interpreter, and runtime environment in Javascript. We also created an interactive environment using HTML and CSS, with the HTML5 Canvas element providing graphical output.

2.1 The EcoSim Runtime

The *EcoSim* environment has three basic interfaces: the code entry pane, a status window listing the results of parsing and the behavior of each processor, and a graphical display of the state of each object. The graphical display automatically draws a circle for each object that had a defined position and size in the student's code. By automating the display we were able to focus on core programming concepts rather than teaching about a graphics API.

In addition to the user interface, the *EcoSim* runtime provides the following:

A fixed number of virtual processors.
At each processing step the interpreter assigns to each processor a task; this task is displayed both in the code pane and in the status window.

A shared work queue for ongoing tasks.
Processors pull jobs off this queue in a random order and insert any unfinished work back on the queue at the end of each step.

A global list of objects of each type.
Each object is placed on a global list of objects of its type when it is instantiated. These lists are used to handle "`for each`" and "`for some`" constructs.

A collision tracker and set of collision handlers.
The code may provide handlers for collisions of objects with position and size. These are given to the processors if the work queue is empty.

A set of idle tasks.
If the work queue is empty and there are no collisions to handle, the remaining processors are given jobs from a set of low-priority tasks.

The runtime is aware of four types: number, color (HTML-compliant color names), comparison (boolean values; used only behind the scenes to type-check guard expressions), and position (a pair of numbers, x and y). User-defined types are built out of these parts.

2.2 The EcoSim Language

Three principles guided our design of *EcoSim*'s language constructs: "audience: processor", "self-describing syntax", and "anonymous by default." The first two are directly parallel our first two objectives: we wanted the processors to be visible throughout the language and the language to be self-explanatory. We added the third principal, defaulting to anonymity, to reduce students' need to come up with names for variables, simplifying the programming process. We hoped it would also reduce the likelihood of conflict over limited, named computing resources, but this kind of conflict did not arise in any class example.

Rather than provide a full description of the language that grew out of these principles, we provide a few elements that typify our design choices and rely on *EcoSim*'s self-describing character to render later code examples understandable.

2.2.1 Statements

The first operator we considered was the assignment operator. We had discovered in previous interactions with CS1 students that the syntax used in "`x = x + 1`" was often confusing. We brainstormed ways we might explain that operation, things like "x is redefined; it's new value is $1 +$ the old value of x," but most were too verbose or failed the "audience: processor" principle. We finally settled on "`replace x with old x + 1`", which we implemented as two rules: an assignment syntax of "`replace` *lvalue* `with` *rvalue*" and a requirement that the word "`old`" precede rvalue variables that also appear in the lvalue.

Similar processes resulted in "`while(1 < 2)`" becoming "`as long as 1 < 2`", "`else`" being replaced with "`otherwise`", and "`double x = 3`" becoming "`start x as 3`". We replaced the membership operator (commonly "`.`" or "`->`") with the more English-like "`'s`" (as in "`baz's position's x`"). We also implemented type inference to create a statically-typed language without needing to declare variable types.

The runtime keeps a list of objects of each type (see §2.1); we add to these lists by writing "`create` *number type*" and remove with a "`destroy`" command. We can access objects either by grabbing one randomly selected object:

```
for some number
  destroy the number
```

or by accessing all of them in parallel:

```
for each number
  replace the number with the old number + 1
```

2.2.2 Blocks

Blocks caused us some difficulty with our "self-explanatory" goal because they largely don't exist in spoken language. We decided to go with indentation as more readable than delimited blocks, but neither we nor our students were entirely happy with this choice.

The basic notion behind a block is "do each of these things once", followed by a list of statements. We distinguished different kinds of blocks based on their sequentiality and atomicity. This gives the four blocks types "`do in order`", "`do in any order`", "`do atomically in order`", and "`do atomically in any order`". Atomic blocks implicitly lock all of the variables they accesses. "In order" blocks can handle only a single processor, while multiple processors can execute the statements of an "in any order" block simultaneously.

Examples of blocks are provided in Figures 1, 2, and 3.

2.2.3 Definitions

We observed that structures, properties, and subroutine definitions are describing "what we mean by X" rather than "you should do X". We thus decided that, per the "audience: processor" principle, we should word these to inform, not direct, the processor.

For example, to introduce a structure type named "plant" with a named field "size", an anonymous position field, and two anonymous colors, we write

```
a plant has
  size, a number
  a position
  2 color
```

We can also define properties for plants:

```
a plant's age is the plant's size − 5
a plant's trunk is the plant's 2nd color
```

Properties are always single expressions and are accessed exactly like fields. Multiple fields (such as "`color`" above) can only be accessed by compile-time ordinals like "`5th`"; you cannot write "`the plant's` *n*`th color`" for variable n.

Subroutines are defined with a "how to":

```
how to add a number years to a plant
  replace the plant's size with the plant's old size
     + the number
```

Calling a subroutine is straightforward:

```
for some plant
  add 3 years to the plant
```

Because this syntax for defining and calling subroutines is context sensitive, it is not easy to achieve using most parser techniques. Our parser type-checks and builds the symbol table as it goes, so when we parse a line "`how to` *words*" we already know which of the words identify types and which are unbound words naming the subroutine. Similarly, we know from context that "`the plant`" is a value and thus that we are calling a method named "add ___ years to ___" and not "add ___ years to the plant".

2.2.4 Handlers

The last element of the language we want to identify is collision handlers and idle operations.

```
when a bulldozer hits a plant
  destroy the plant
when bored
  create a plant
```

Again, these are worded to address the processor in a self-explaining way. They prevent the need for an explicit simulation loop and make event-oriented programming straightforward. Multiple "`when bored`" declarations were permitted, with the runtime selecting between them at random.

The general structure of our collision handlers would have worked with arbitrary predicates, such as "`when a plant's size > 7`". We chose not to expose this generality to the students because they could easily write their own single-object predicates already and collisions covered all of the multi-object interactions we expected in an ecological simulation.

3. COURSE OVERVIEW

The pilot course we created was for fourth and fifth grade students in an enrichment program that is run through our university. We designed the course and *EcoSim* concurrently, for an audience of self-selected primary school students with no prior formal programming experience.

3.1 Ecosystem in Parallel

The original conception of the pilot course was, simply, "Let's teach fourth and fifth graders about parallel programming." To streamline our lessons we decided to structure our examples around a single theme. The theme we selected was "ecosystems" because it is familiar to students at that level, inherently parallel, easy to visualize, and allows for a wide range of example applications. By the end of the course students had simulated ecosystems ranging from simple growing plants to complex interactions between diurnal locally-seeding plants, competing herbivores and hunters, carnivorous and poisonous plants, and other more imaginative fantasy elements.

Students quickly learned the importance of initial conditions and parameters, both from a computational perspective and a scientific one. For example, students found that starting ten thousand herbivores in a field with only ten plants both results in over-grazing and starvation and slows the computer to a crawl as it looks for each object's collisions. We spent a number of classes discussing the remote St. Matthew Island in Alaska, where a herd of reindeer overpopulated and subsequently died out [14, 17]. With the *EcoSim* model the students were able to adjust the parameters and look for an equilibrium that would have allowed the reindeer to survive.

3.2 Getting the Students to "Think Parallel"

We began each class period with a conversation and activity introducing a new parallel programming concept. Table 1 shows the group activities we conducted and their associated parallel processing concept or concepts. During and after each activity, we discussed the associated concept, and in most cases we then wrote a simple program in *EcoSim* that demonstrated the idea.

For example, on the first day of class we introduced the students to the difference in computational time between parallel and sequential processes by having them sort themselves by height. First, we allowed the students to line themselves up by height, all at once (the parallel method), and we timed this; it took roughly forty-five seconds for a class of eighteen. Next, we re-randomized the class and assigned one student to be the "processor," in charge of sorting the students. Unsurprisingly, this took roughly twice as long, leading to a fruitful discussion on why parallel processing can be faster. We then showed the students that *EcoSim* allows a programmer to set the number of processors that will be used to run the program and had the students experiment with the speedups resulting from multiple processors.

After the opening class discussion we would transition to programming exercises. Each student would sit at a computer with *EcoSim* loaded into their web browser, and they were able to type out the examples as we wrote them on the overhead projector. For example, after the race condition activity, we wrote the programs in Figure 2. These programs demonstrate a race condition stemming from allowing multiple processors to replace the moths' color in an arbitrary order. When the "In order" program runs, all of the moths end up black at the end, but when the "In any order" program runs, an indeterminate number of moths end up black and the remainder are gray. This outcome was unexpected for many of the students, and we allowed them to experiment with the code, trying out other conditions to explore the idea more fully.

The ability to step through code in the *EcoSim* environment allowed students to see how the computer followed their instructions. For example, if *EcoSim* is set to use two processors for the "In order" program from Figure 2, the students see that individual "moths" changing color two at a time. Often when students were surprised at some result of program behavior we would step though the code, discussing how each processor's actions effected the simulation.

In order:

```
a moth has
    a position
    a color
a moth's size is 50

create 10 moth and for each
    do in order
        replace the moth's color with gray
        replace the moth's color with black
```

In any order:

```
a moth has
    a position
    a color
a moth's size is 50

create 10 moth and for each
    do in any order
        replace the moth's color with gray
        replace the moth's color with black
```

Figure 2: Example *EcoSim* programs that demonstrate race conditions. In the "in order" program, all moths end up black, while in the "out of order" program the final color is dependent on a race condition.

3.3 The Use of Example Programs

As with any programming course, example programs played an important role in teaching our course. Because this course was the first time most of the students had seen any programming language at all, we decided to provide a scaffolding in the form of example programs that they could look at and modify. *EcoSim* has a "Load Example" button that brings up a listing of programs written by the instructors. Many times during class we would have students pay attention to the projector as we typed in the code for a program. Once they saw our initial work, we would have them load the example instead of typing it out. This provision saved time (not all pre-teens are fast typists), and it also allowed us to start the whole class at the same point in a program's development. In some cases we gave them example programs that were missing a line or two and asked them to fill in the details themselves. We encouraged the students to modify the programs as well. Students that completed programming tasks before others in the class were able to modify the example programs, write their own programs, or return to programs they had been working on previously.

Another reason we relied on example programs was to build a compendium of programs that the students could go back and look at if they did not remember the details of a particular topic. Frequently, we would direct the students to previously covered examples.

3.4 Student Assessment

Because this course was an ungraded enrichment class, we did not perform formal assessments (e.g., tests or deadline-based homework). However, we reviewed the students' work regularly and gave feedback often. At the beginning of each hour of class, we asked whether anyone had something they wanted to show the class. Many students enjoyed displaying their work on the projector and seemed motivated to create interesting programs they could share with the rest of the class. Some students showed off work that they completed on their own at home during the week between classes, which we highly encouraged.

All student work is captured in a MySQL database that we were able to review regularly. Each time a student clicks on the "Setup Code" (which parses the code and reports errors), the current program is saved, and all versions are retained. Therefore, we were able to look at a students progress, including how many attempts they made at fixing syntax errors and how they went about writing their programs. We used this analysis to determine where we needed to review; e.g., once we realized how much trouble the students had with understanding indentation and blocks, we modified our lesson plan to include a review and further examples.

Concept	Group Activity
Parallel speedup	Students sort themselves, and then one student sorts everyone.
Locks / Atomicity	Everyone shares a pen to write on the whiteboard to increment a number.
Race Conditions	Students roll dice until they get a six, read a number off the board, increment it, roll more dice, and call out the new number, which is written on the board.
Divide and Conquer	All students start with a number, and half hand to their neighbor to add together. This continues until one student has the total sum.

Table 1: Group activities.

```
when bored
  for each pacman
    do in any order
      move the pacman's position a random number
          between 10 and 50 right
      move the pacman's position a random number
          between 10 and 50 left
      move the pacman's position a random number
          between 10 and 50 up
      move the pacman's position a random number
          between 10 and 50 down

when a pacman hits a ghost
  destroy the pacman
```

Figure 3: Part of one student's "Pacman" program, that demonstrates a competent understanding of the programming language and its parallel programming structure.

4. STUDENT WORK AND OUTCOMES

During the course the students had an opportunity to modify example programs and write their own applications. We analyzed the database of student programs to perform basic analysis of each student's programming process. Students worked on between twelve and thirty-two separate programs each, with a mean of twenty programs per student. We observed that the students who worked on more programs tended to be the ones who picked up the material the fastest in class, and were also more likely to work on programs at home. The students' programs ranged from simple five-line examples to over 150-line simulations of complex ecosystems. In addition, some students created novel programs that demonstrated proficient understanding of the language. Figure 3 shows part of one student's novel "Pacman" program, demonstrating that some students were able to use the programming elements discussed in class in a novel, parallel context.

As with any introductory programming course, students can get frustrated with the debugging process. When a student clicks on the "Setup Code" button in *EcoSim*, the parser reports the first parse error (if one or more exist) and highlights the offending line number. Over the duration of the course, it took the students an average of 4.2 attempts to fix a program that had errors. If a student gave up on a program with errors by starting or opening a different program, he or she attempted an average of 8.3 times to fix the error before giving up.

On the last day of class, the students demonstrated their work to their parents and siblings. We had each student to prepare a program that showcased their own work—either one they created on their own or an example from class that they modified significantly. They enthusiastically demonstrated their programs, including various modifications to the St. Matthew Island ecosystem, programs that had snow

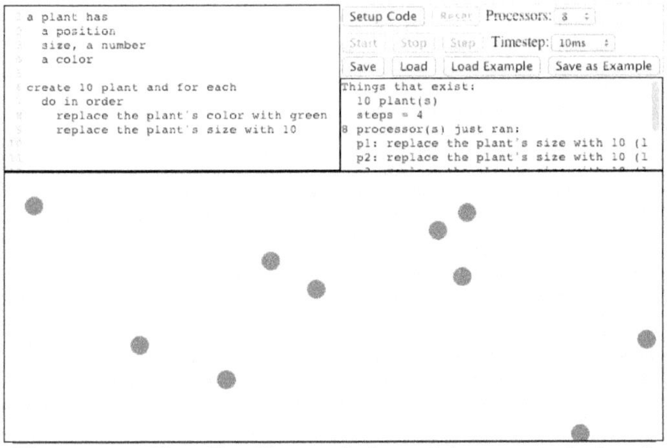

Figure 4: The *EcoSim* web-based integrated development environment hosted at `http://ecosimulation.com`. Code is written and debugged in the top left window, settings are on the top right, a console with runtime and debug information is below the settings, and the main window shows the graphical output of the program.

"fall" on the screen and accumulate at the bottom, simulations of mice searching for cheese, etc.

5. RELATED WORK

Parallel computing is not new, dating back to 1955 and the IBM 704 [12]. Today, multicore desktop and laptop computers are ubiquitous—when novice programmers write their first code today, it is often running on a parallel computer. In order to make the most efficient use of these computers, parallel programming is necessary.

There are numerous programming languages available for desktop parallel programming. Many of these languages are extensions, libraries, or APIs built on top of sequential languages such as C or Fortran (e.g., OpenMP, CUDA, OpenCL, Intel Thread Building Blocks, pthreads, Cilk, Co-array Fortran, and Unified Parallel C), requiring a novice programmer to first become proficient in a sequential language before tackling the parallel programming concepts. While this does not necessarily hinder a student's overall programming ability, parallel programming tends to receive less emphasis than simply learning the sequential aspects of the language.

There are languages designed specifically for parallel programming, but they tend have advanced syntax and are targeted towards students already proficient at programming in general (e.g., X10 [8], Go [4], and ParaSail [21]). Novice programmers would almost certainly find it difficult to learn one of these languages as an introduction to programming.

Several researchers have investigated teaching parallel programming concepts at the undergraduate level [13, 18, 23] and at least one at the secondary school level [22]. These studies targeted both first and second year students using openly available parallel programming languages (e.g., OpenMP, MPI, and CUDA). A common result was that students were motivated more by concrete examples of parallel code and significant classroom programming time rather than by abstract concepts delivered in a lecture. We likewise utilized concrete examples and in-class programming time.

Parallel concepts could be taught using groups of robots. However, robotics packages aimed at younger students such as Mindstorms [19], PicoCricket [2], and Arduino [1] focus on single-processor single-robot programming tasks.

Several successful languages have been designed to have English-like syntax, including COBOL [3], AppleScript [6], and Wolfram Alpha [15]. Like *EcoSim*, each was designed to accessible to non-programmers and each targets a relatively narrow set of possible use cases. None are targeted toward teaching parallel programming concepts.

An alternative to "readable" languages is to use a graphical rather than textual representation of the program. Recent examples of graphically-represented languages that are aimed at children include Alice [10], Scratch [16], Greenfoot [11], and Kodu [20]. While an exhaustive survey of graphical programming languages was impractical, we were unaware of any that did not require installation and were suitable for teaching core parallel programming concepts.

6. CONCLUSIONS

We have demonstrated that it is possible to teach elementary school students parallel programming, even if they are completely novice programmers. We were able to teach basic programming skills as well as concepts such as race conditions, atomicity, locks, and the speedups that can be obtained by using multiple processors. None of our students had any difficulty with parallelism, and most were able to explain core parallel concepts to their parents at the end of the course.

To facilitate learning in our course, we

- designed a unique, English-like parallel programming language and associated visual web interface;
- provided a curriculum that taught programming through a parallel lens; and
- utilized learning activities, think-pair-share discussions, and individual guided exploration to teach each concept.

We found the students eagerly learned the *EcoSim* language. Despite some trouble with the notion of indented blocks, most students were able to successfully write significant programs without difficulty.

Parallel programming does not have to be difficult to teach or learn, and it is a skill that will become even more important as computers continue to become more parallel in the future.

Acknowledgments

This work was supported in part by NSF grants BPC-0739259, BPC-104282, CNS-0747273, CSR-0916908, and CNS-0964627; and awards from Microsoft and Google. We would like to thank the University of Virginia Saturday and Summer Enrichment Program for the opportunity to teach *Programming the Computers of the Future* during the winter 2011 session. We are grateful to the students in the class for their enthusiasm for the subject. We would also like to thank the anonymous reviewers for their helpful comments and suggestions.

7. REFERENCES

[1] Arduino. Available: http://arduino.cc.

[2] Picocricket. Available: http://picocricket.com.

[3] *General Information Manual, IBM Commercial Translator.* IBM Corporation, New York, 1959.

[4] The go programming language. http://golang.org, accessed on August 6, 2011.

[5] Archives for programming languages. http://gpgpu.org/tag/programming-languages, accessed on July 31, 2011.

[6] Apple, Inc. Applescript overview. http://developer.apple.com/library/mac/documentation/AppleScript/Conceptual/AppleScriptX/AppleScriptX.pdf, accessed on August 9, 2011.

[7] K. Asanovic, R. Bodik, J. Demmel, T. Keaveny, K. Keutzer, J. Kubiatowicz, N. Morgan, D. Patterson, K. Sen, J. Wawrzynek, D. Wessel, and K. Yelick. A view of the parallel computing landscape. *Communcations of the ACM*, 52:56–67, October 2009.

[8] P. Charles, C. Grothoff, V. Saraswat, C. Donawa, A. Kielstra, K. Ebcioglu, C. von Praun, and V. Sarkar. X10: an object-oriented approach to non-uniform cluster computing. *SIGPLAN Not.*, 40:519–538, October 2005.

[9] C. R. Cook, C. M. Pancake, and R. Walpole. Are expectations for parallelism too high?: a survey of potential parallel users. In *Proceedings of the 1994 ACM/IEEE conference on Supercomputing*, pages 126–133. ACM, 1994.

[10] S. Cooper, W. Dann, and R. Pausch. Alice: a 3-d tool for introductory programming concepts. *J. Comput. Small Coll.*, 15:107–116, April 2000.

[11] P. Henrickson. A direct interaction tool for object-oriented programming education. Master's thesis, University of Southen Denmark, Maersk Mc-Kinney Moller Inst. for Production Technology, 2004.

[12] R. Hockney and C. Jesshope. *Parallel computers 2: Architecture, programming, and algorithms*, volume 2. Taylor & Francis, 1988.

[13] D. Johnson, D. Kotz, and F. Makedon. Teaching parallel computing to freshman. In *Conference on Parallel Computing for Undergraduates*, pages 1–7, 1994.

[14] D. Klein. The introduction, increase, and crash of reindeer on St. Matthew Island. *The Journal of Wildlife Management*, pages 350–367, 1968.

[15] W. A. LLC. Wolfram|Alpha: Computational knowledge engine. http://www.wolframalpha.com, accessed on August 9, 2011.

[16] J. Maloney, M. Resnick, N. Rusk, B. Silverman, and E. Eastmond. The scratch programming language and environment. *ACM Transactions on Computing Education*, November 2010.

[17] S. McMillen. St. matthew island. http://www.recombinantrecords.net/2011/02/09/st-matthew-island, accessed on August 6, 2011.

[18] C. Nevison. Parallel computing in the undergraduate curriculum. *Computer*, 28(12):51–56, December 1995.

[19] S. Papert. *Mindstorms: children, computers, and powerful ideas.* Basic Books, Inc., New York, NY, USA, 1980.

[20] K. T. Steele. Kodu language and grammar specification. http://research.microsoft.com/en-us/projects/kodu/kodugrammar.pdf, August 2010.

[21] S. T. Taft. Designing parasail, a new programming language. http://parasail-programming-language.blogspot.com, accessed on Auguet 9, 2011.

[22] S. Torbert, U. Vishkin, R. Tzur, and D. J. Ellison. Is teaching parallel algorithmic thinking to high school students possible?: one teacher's experience. In *Proceedings of the 41st ACM technical symposium on computer science education*, SIGCSE '10, pages 290–294. ACM, 2010.

[23] J. Tourino, M. Martin, J. Tarrio, and M. Arenaz. A grid portal for an undergraduate parallel programming course. *Education, IEEE Transactions on*, 48(3):391–399, aug. 2005.

Building Upon and Enriching Grade Four Mathematics Standards with Programming Curriculum

Colleen M. Lewis
Graduate School of Education
University of California, Berkeley
Berkeley, CA 94720
colleenl@eecs.berkeley.edu

Niral Shah
Graduate School of Education
University of California, Berkeley
Berkeley, CA 94720
niralshah@gmail.com

ABSTRACT

We found that fifth grade students' scores on Scratch programming quizzes in a summer enrichment course were highly correlated with their scores on a standardized test for mathematics. We identify ways in which the programming curriculum builds upon target skills from the *Mathematics Content Standards for California Public Schools*. We hypothesize that the programming curriculum leveraged and enriched students' mathematics content knowledge.

Categories and Subject Descriptors

K.3.2 **[Computers and Education]:** Computer and Information Science Education—*computer science education*

General Terms

Human Factors

Keywords

Scratch, middle-school, mathematics, computational thinking

1. INTRODUCTION

Methods for predicting college students' success in a programming course have been hotly debated for decades (see [15] for a review). The current study investigated correlations between young students' standardized test scores and their performance in a programming course. However, rather than aiming to predict success, the intention of the present study is to uncover dependencies between a middle school programming curriculum in a language called Scratch and grade-specific mathematical content.

We found students' scores on the Grade 4 California Mathematics Standards Test predicted performance on programming quizzes in a summer enrichment program, which was statistically significant at the 1% level. Our hypothesis that students' scores on the Grade 4 California English-Language Arts Standards Test would be correlated with performance on programming quizzes was not confirmed.

2. PREVIOUS RESEARCH

For decades, research has attempted to correlate students' non-programming and programming performance. Simpson [16] in 1973 published a bibliography of more than 150 papers, which attempted to identify methods for selecting computing staff. In summarizing the set of papers, Simpson noted that: "They mainly report on correlations of test scores with either course grades or supervisor ratings and almost all conclude that further research is required." (p. 2) [16]. For example, in 1985 Butcher and Muth [2] developed a model to attempt to predict performance in a computing course based upon ACT test scores. They reported a high level of false negatives; approximately one-third of the students that they predicted would not be successful in the undergraduate program were in fact successful.

In 2006 Simon *et al.* [15] reported that "the results achieved by students in programming courses do not correlate well with their other academic results." (p. 190) [15]. Further, Rountree *et al.* argued that "despite the attention given to this topic, a reliable means of predicting the success of students who enter an introductory programming course remains elusive." (p. 101) [13].

This long line of research opens up questions regarding the complexity of transferring knowledge between non-programming and programming domains, which is part of our ongoing research program [21]. However, the current paper does not seek to predict performance in a computing course. We hypothesize that mathematical content standards in the early grades are more aligned with the mathematical content embedded within our programming curriculum and seek to investigate this hypothesis. Based upon this hypothesis we predict that students' performance on mathematics standardized tests in elementary school would be correlated with performance on programming quizzes.

A second feature that separates the current work from related correlational research is that, as others note [12], [21], much of previous work has looked for predictors of programming aptitude, assuming the existence of an innate ability for computer science. But we reject this assumption regarding innate ability as unsubstantiated and reiterate its potentially negative effects on student learning. Of greater relevance is previous research using programming to support content learning in another domain.

The most recent and visible example of using programming as a tool for mathematics learning is the Bootstrap project [14] [19]. This project uses a functional programming environment to teach game development and programming to students as young as 11 [14]. The curriculum is designed to introduce and support the development of students' competencies in "algebra, coordinate geometry, and simple modeling" [19]. Unfortunately, there appear to be no studies to date assessing students' transfer of this mathematical content knowledge between the programming and non-programming domains.

The Bootstrap project builds upon earlier examples where programming was used as a tool for mathematics learning. In the 1980's Sutherland [17] and Noss [10] showed students could develop conceptual understanding of variables through

Permission to make digital or hard copies of all or part of this work for personal or classroom use is granted without fee provided that copies are not made or distributed for profit or commercial advantage and that copies bear this notice and the full citation on the first page. To copy otherwise, or republish, to post on servers or to redistribute to lists, requires prior specific permission and/or a fee.
SIGCSE '12, February 29–March 3, 2012, Raleigh, North Carolina, USA.
Copyright 2012 ACM 978-1-4503-1098-7/12/02...$10.00.

programming in Logo. In another example from 1992, Harel & Papert [8] were successful in supporting the learning of fractions in a Logo programming environment with fourth grade students. Students in the treatment group learned Logo with the goal of developing software to teach younger children about fractions. Students in the control group spent the same amount of time learning Logo and completed the same two-month mathematics unit on fractions. However, students in the treatment group demonstrated greater mastery of both the Logo and fractions content.

These previous research projects are examples of a broader trend of using programming "microworlds" [11] to explore non-programming content. For example, Abelson and diSessa [1] authored a textbook using Logo programming as a tool for teaching introductory and college level geometry. diSessa [7] mapped the ways in which programming microworlds could empower new ways of learning and knowing physics. diSessa [7] describes the general idea of "computational literacy", a precursor to "computational thinking" [18], in which programming can function as a new literacy (like algebra), reshaping scientific communication. As diSessa claims: "Not only can new inscription systems and literacies ease learning, as algebra simplified the proofs of Galileo's theorems, but they may also rearrange the entire intellectual terrain." (p. 19) [7]. We build upon this existing body of work to support non-programming content learning using programming as a medium.

3. METHODS

3.1 Classroom Context

Forty-seven students in the summer of 2011 were enrolled in a summer enrichment program for students entering the sixth grade and agreed to participate in a research study. Of these students, approximately 30% were female. These students were divided between two classes that were co-taught by the authors, each of whom have a degree in computer science. One of the instructors had taught the course twice in the same enrichment program [20] [22]. The other instructor had five years of experience teaching high-school math, but had never taught programming.

The course introduced programming in Scratch [20], Snap [9], and Logo [8], with the majority of 36 hours of class spent using Scratch. Although students frequently drew on their mathematical knowledge, the course was designed to teach students programming constructs from these languages, and was not specifically designed around mathematics content. Students programmed on their own computers. Each day, students were assigned a partner and were expected to discuss any questions with their partner before asking an instructor [22]. Details regarding the curriculum (available at www.colleenmlewis.com/scratch/) and pedagogical techniques developed for teaching young students programming can be found in a previous publication regarding the course [22].

3.2 Sources of Data

3.2.1 Standardized Test Scores

Participants in the research were given the option to submit the numerical scores for a recent standardized test given in the state of California (CA). Students' most recent CA state test was taken during their fourth grade year, in April of 2010. The tests are designed to assess students' performance relative to the state's content standards for the particular grade. Students receive a score between 150 (low) to 600 (high) for the Mathematics and English-Language Arts component separately.

A score below 300 is described as "Below Basic" and demonstrates "little or flawed understanding" for the content area assessed. A score between 300 and 349 is described as "Basic" and demonstrates "partial and rudimentary understanding". A score between 350 and 400 (or 392 for English-Language Arts) is described as "Proficient" and demonstrates "competent and adequate understanding". Above this score is described as "Advanced" and demonstrates "comprehensive and complex understanding."

Twenty-two of the forty-seven students who agreed to participate in the study submitted test scores. The summer enrichment program was designed for academically advanced students and the submitted test scores show their performance was well above the state average. On the 2010 administration, only 42% and 36% of fourth graders in California received a score of "Advanced" in Mathematics and English-Language Arts respectively [4]. In contrast, in the study population, 100% and 95% of students received a score of "Advanced" for Mathematics and English-Language Arts respectively. Figure 1 shows a scatter plot for the scores submitted by study participants. In our sample, 95% of students had an equal or higher score for Mathematics than English-Language Arts. Figure 2 shows box plots of the two sets of scores.

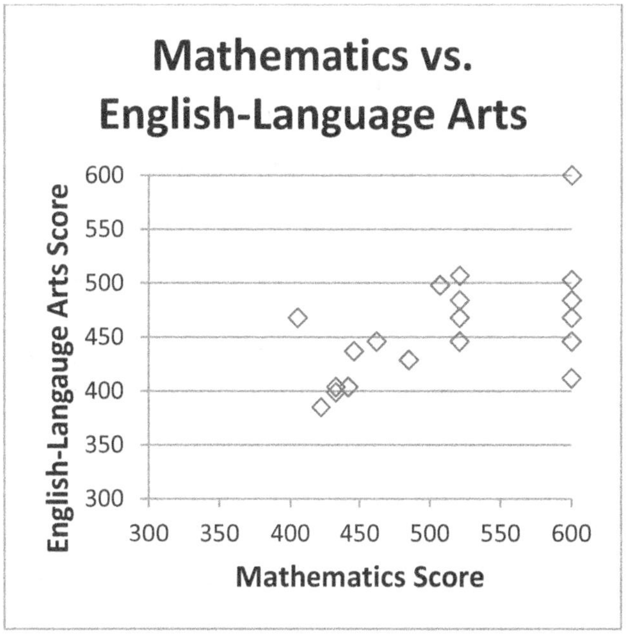

Figure 1. Scatter plot of Mathematics and English-Language Arts scores from participants' Grade 4 CA Standards Tests.

3.2.2 Programming Quizzes

The 36 hour programming course occurred on 12 days during the summer of 2011. On the 2nd through 10th days of instruction, students took paper-based quizzes assessing their knowledge of the programming content from the previous day. With the exception of one quiz, the questions were consistent between this study and a previous study [22], which includes a representative question from each quiz. Quiz questions were graded with one point for most questions; no partial credit was given. Each quiz had between 11 and 19 points, and each quiz point was weighted equally when calculating students' average quiz performance. Quizzes lasted on average 15 minutes and there were a total of 148 points possible across all quizzes.

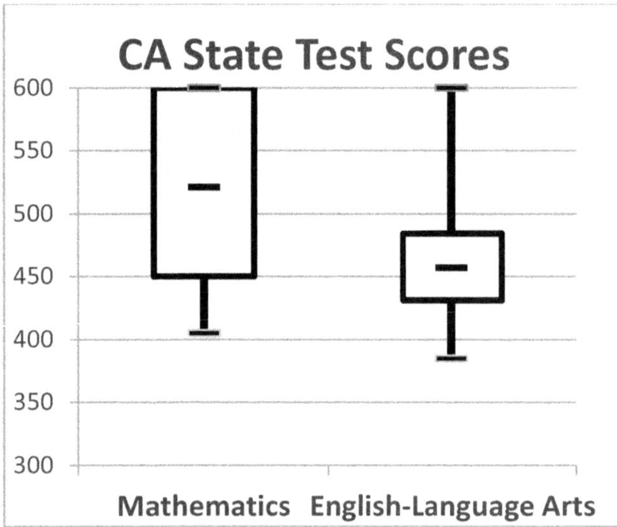

Figure 2. Box-plot of Mathematics and English-Language Arts scores from participants' Grade 4 CA Standards Tests.

The majority of the questions appearing on the programming quizzes had mathematical content, identified as the use of variables, mathematical computation, or geometric relationships. We hypothesized that questions without such mathematical content may have a different pattern of correlation with students' mathematics scores. A portion of one such non-mathematical question is shown in Figure 3, which asks students to identify scripts that "work like this one". The question also included six additional scripts, two of which are equivalent to the first script shown in Figure 3. For reference, two incorrect answers are shown below in Figure 3.

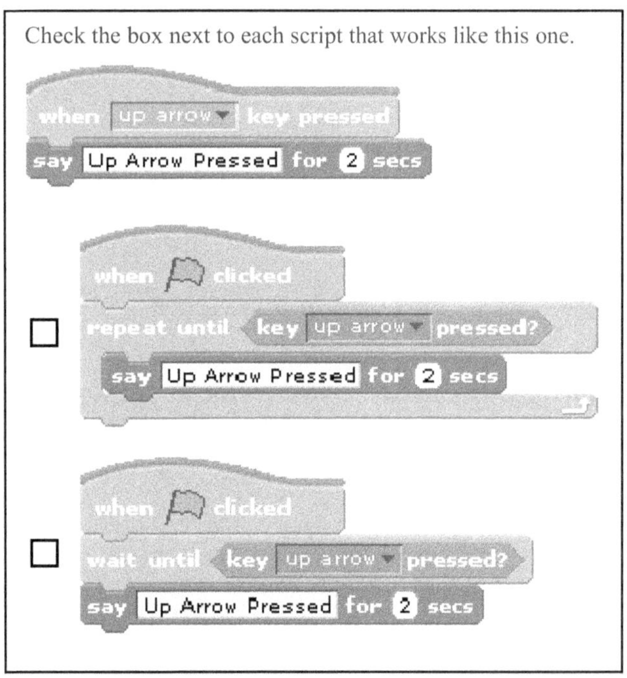

Figure 3. Question taken from the 9th programming quiz with two incorrect answers.

3.3 Analytical Methods

This study employed both quantitative and qualitative methods for interpreting patterns in students' CA state test scores and programming quiz performance. We investigated three hypotheses using t-tests and a standard statistical significance level of 0.05.

- Are students' scores on programming quizzes correlated with their reported scores on the CA Grade 4 Mathematics Test?
- Are students' scores on programming quizzes correlated with their reported scores on the CA Grade 4 English-Language Arts Test?
- When controlling for students' English-Language Arts scores, are students' scores on non-mathematical components of the programming quizzes correlated with their reported scores on the CA Grade 4 Mathematics Test?

To better understand the data we identified overlap between content covered on the Grade 4 California Mathematics Standards and the programming content of daily quizzes. This additional qualitative analysis of the mathematics standards [5] and example questions [3] may provide insight regarding the results of the statistical tests.

4. QUANTITATIVE RESULTS

We found that students' test scores in mathematics were highly correlated with performance on the programming quizzes in the summer enrichment course ($t=3.461$, $p=0.0025$), significant at the 1% level. The line of best fit shows that for a 50 point increase in mathematics score (ranging from 150 to 600) the student will answer correctly an additional 20 points out of the 148 total quiz points. Figure 4 shows a scatter plot and line of best fit comparing the 22 students' scores in mathematics and their average quiz performance in the summer enrichment program after completing the fifth grade.

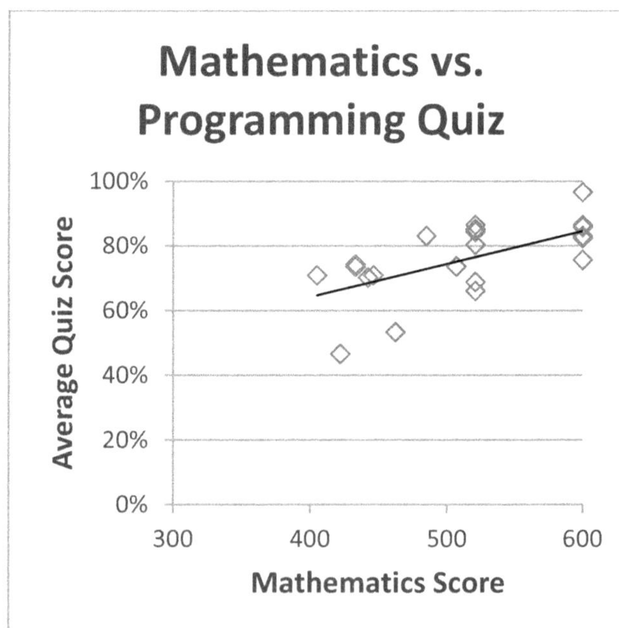

Figure 4. Scatter plot of students' Mathematics scores versus average quiz performance.

Testing the second hypothesis, we could not reject the null hypothesis that students' scores on the English-Language Arts component of their grade four test were not correlated with their performance on quizzes within the enrichment program ($t = 1.288$, $p=0.213$). Figure 5 shows a trend for higher English-Language Arts scores to be associated with higher average quiz performance; however this trend is not statistically significant at the 5% level. When both the Mathematics and English-Language Arts components are included in the linear model, the statistical significance of the English-Language Arts component drops ($t = -0.217$, $p = 0.830$), while the Mathematics component remains significant at the 1% level ($t = 3.020$, $p = 0.007$).

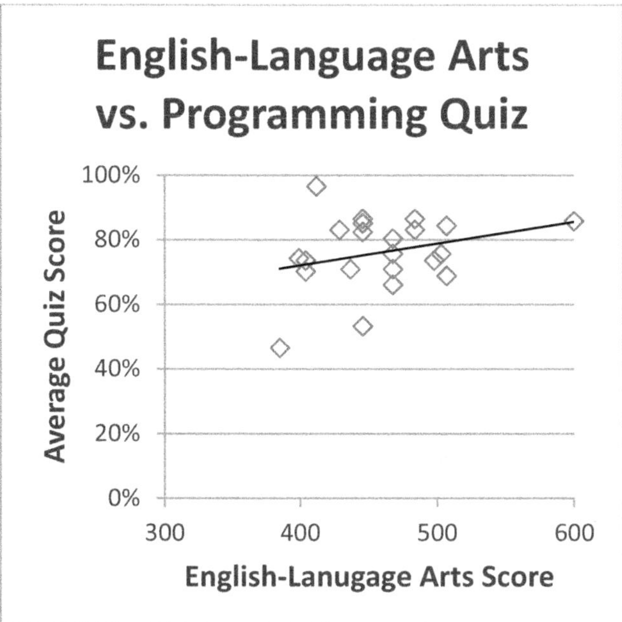

Figure 5. Scatter plot of students' English-Language Arts scores versus average quiz performance.

Investigating the third hypothesis, we found that when controlling for students' scores on the English-Language Arts component, the Mathematics scores were not a statistically significant predictor of performance on non-mathematical quiz questions ($t = 1.357$, $p = 0.191$), such as the question shown in Figure 3.

5. QUALITATIVE ANALYSIS: MATHEMATICS CONTENT STANDARDS

The Grade 4 California Mathematics Standards are summarized as: "By the end of grade four, students understand large numbers and addition, subtraction, multiplication, and division of whole numbers. They describe and compare simple fractions and decimals. They understand the properties of, and the relationships between, plane geometric figures. They collect, represent, and analyze data to answer questions." [5].

In grade four students are assessed within five content areas, "Number Sense," "Algebra and Functions," "Measurement and Geometry," "Statistics, Data Analysis, and Probability," and "Mathematical Reasoning." These content areas are subdivided into a total of 14 sub-areas, which are further subdivided into 54 standards. The authors estimate that more than 35% of the CA state standards for grade four apply to the curriculum used in our 36-hour summer enrichment program. We expect that in these cases the curriculum would both build upon the students' mathematical content knowledge and reinforce or enrich that knowledge.

As it is not possible in this venue to identify every instance of overlap within the 54 content standards for grade four, we provide three representative examples comparing questions taken from a set of released test questions for Grade Four Mathematics [3] and questions from the programming quizzes.

5.1 Example 1: Algebra and Functions

The question shown in Figure 6 was taken from a previous Grade 4 CA Mathematics Standards Test. It exemplifies the following content standard within the "Algebra and Functions" content area (Standard #1.5): "Understand that an equation such as $y = 3x + 5$ is a prescription for determining a second number when a first number is given." [3]. The question shown in Figure 7 was taken from the third quiz in the programming curriculum, and similar to the question in Figure 6, it also requires students to consider an underlying linear relationship. That is, to make a closed polygon in Scratch the character must turn a total of 360 degrees. For a regular polygon with N sides, the character should turn $360 \div N$ degrees between each side. Thus, the number of repetitions needed to create a 10-sided shape must be equal to 10.

This quiz question was considered equivalent to Standard #1.5 because students have to use the given value (*i.e.*, "10") to determine the value of the second number (*i.e.*, the measure of the turning angle). Admittedly, the quiz question in Figure 7 requires additional knowledge not required by the question shown in Figure 6. For example, the second blank (the number of steps to move) is a free variable that determines the size of the 10-sided shape. Also, the linear relationships in this question are tacit, which poses an additional obstacle for students. These additional steps would not be possible if the students had not been introduced to ideas of "Turtle Geometry" [1] and we hypothesize that this represents an advanced application of the mathematical competence described in the CA standard.

Question CSM01966 [3]: Look at the problem below.

$$\square = \Delta + 4$$

If $\Delta = 7$, what is $\square$?
A 3
B 7
C 11
D 14

Figure 6. Reproduction of a released question CSM01966 from previous grade four Mathematics test.

Fill in the blanks below to draw a 10 sided shape.

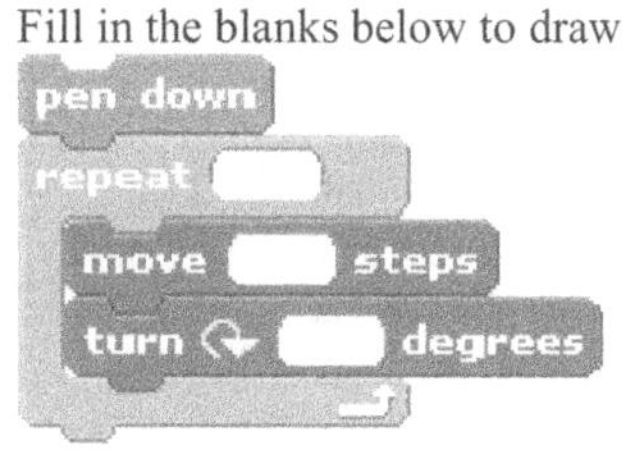

Figure 7. Question taken from the third programming quiz.

5.2 Example 2: Algebra and Functions

Figure 8 shows a reproduction of a released question from the grade four examinations in mathematics. This question assesses a second standard within the area "Algebra and Functions", which is described as "Use parentheses to indicate which operation to perform first when writing expressions containing more than two terms and different operations." [3]. Similarly, the question shown in Figure 9, taken from the second programming quiz, requires students to perform the correct ordering of operations.

The question in Figure 9 places additional requirements on students in interpreting the sequencing of events, but a possible solution requires a similar mathematical calculation. For example a correct solution to calculate the final value of tempo could include the following expression: 55 + (3x2) + (5x(-3)) + (4x1)

Question CSM10837 [3]: Anna bought 3 bags of red gumballs and 5 bags of white gumballs. Each bag of gumballs had 7 pieces in it. Which expression could Anna use to find the total number of gumballs she bought?

```
A (7x3) + 5 =
B (7x5) + 3 =
C 7 x (5+3) =
D 7 x (5x3) =
```

Figure 8. Reproduction of a released question CSM10837 from previous grade four Mathematics test.

What is the value of tempo after we double click on the script below?

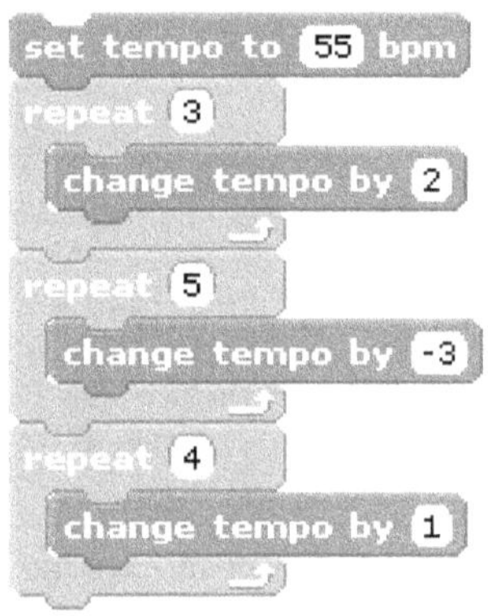

Figure 9. Question taken from the second programming quiz.

5.3 Example 3: Measurement and Geometry

In supporting mathematical understanding, Scratch was particularly effective at promoting understanding of geometric relationships. One of the standards within the area "Measurement and Geometry" states: "Know the definitions of a right angle, an acute angle, and an obtuse angle. Understand that 90°, 180°, 270°, and 360° are associated, respectively with 1/4, 1/2, 3/4, and full turns." [5]. The only released question regarding this standard tested the definition of obtuse angle. However, multiple programming quiz questions directly related to students' understanding of the angles 90°, 180°, 270°, and 360°.

Figure 10 shows a question that requires the student to trace the motion of a character in Scratch. The character begins facing right, which is represented in Scratch as the direction 90°. The character then traces the shape of a square and then re-traces two of the sides of the squares.

The character starts at the arrow, facing the same direction as the arrow. Draw what the character draws when you double click the script. Draw the final position and direction of the character with an arrow.

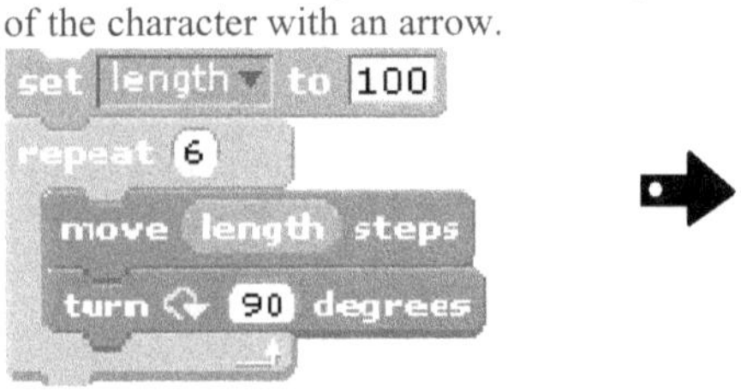

Figure 10. Question taken from the fourth programming quiz.

6. THREATS TO VALIDITY

In addition to threats to validity identified by the testing agency [4], only 47% of students that agreed to participate in the study submitted CA test scores from 2010. To investigate if there was bias introduced between students that did and did not submit test scores, we compared the average quiz performance between the populations using a Mann-Whitney test and found no significant difference on performance on in-class quizzes between the population that did and did not submit test CA state test scores ($z = 1.255$, $p = 0.210$). Figure 11 shows the distribution of average quiz performance between the two populations.

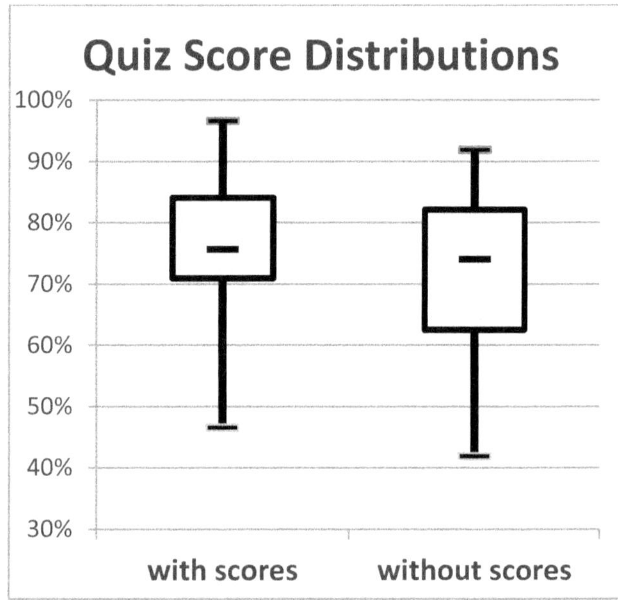

Figure 11. Box plot of average performance on quizzes between students that did and did not submit state test scores.

This paper proposes the hypothesis that the overlap in content between the fourth grade standards and the programming content accounts for the correlations observed. It is possible that these correlations existed within the study for another reason. For example, perhaps CA state exam scores correlate with students' learning efficacy and learning efficacy alone accounted for the difference in performance within the population.

7. CONCLUSION

The current study contributes to the line of research looking for non-programming predictors of performance in programming courses by investigating correlations within a middle-school programming course for the first time. However, the primary contribution is articulating the ways in which mathematics content in the early grades can be built upon and reinforced or enriched through programming curriculum.

While we did not find students' English-Language Arts scores to be correlated with students' quiz performance, there is reason to believe that the students' programming competence would be mediated by their competence assessed by the English-Language Arts test. Students frequently engaged in discussion regarding complex Scratch programs and read information in the online curriculum used in the course. The Grade Four English-Language Arts Standards state: "Students read and understand grade-level-appropriate material. They draw upon a variety of comprehension strategies as needed (*e.g.*, generating and responding to essential questions, making predictions, comparing information from several sources)." [6].

Researchers have found that prior academic performance, for example in mathematics, is not correlated with performance in an introductory programming course [15]. We hypothesize that this underestimates the extent to which students can and should use content knowledge from mathematics when learning to program. The examples shown here indicate that mathematics that is relevant to students in grade four has remarkable overlap with content from a middle-school programming curriculum in Scratch.

While the programming curriculum was designed to challenge students in learning the programming content, it appears that there was significant reliance on mathematical content knowledge. It is possible that limitations in students' mathematical competence constrained their access to the programming content. While we hope to help all students be successful learning the programming content, there may be realistic constraints imposed by the mathematical nature of computer programming. Ultimately we are encouraged by the opportunity to reinforce and enrich students' understanding of the mathematical content through the programming curriculum.

8. ACKNOWLEDGMENTS

We would like to thank the students and staff of the summer enrichment program. In particular we appreciate the hard work of our undergraduate teaching assistant, Ian Ornstein, who contributed substantially to the teaching and organization of the course. The research reported here was supported in part by a grant from the National Science Foundation (Award #1044106) and through the Institute of Education Sciences pre-doctoral training grant R305B090026 to the University of California, Berkeley. The opinions expressed are those of the authors and do not represent views of the National Science Foundation, the Institute of Education Sciences, or the U.S. Department of Education.

9. REFERENCES

[1] Abelson, H. & diSessa, A. A. (1980) Turtle Geometry: The Computer as a Medium for Exploring Mathematics. MIT Press, Cambridge, MA.

[2] Butcher D. F. and Muth W. A. (1985). Predicting performance in an introductory computer science course. *Communications of the ACM*, 28 (3) 263-268.

[3] California Department of Education Assessment and Accountability Division. (2009). California Standards Test - Released Test Questions - Math Grade 4 http://www.cde.ca.gov/ta/tg/sr/documents/cstrtqmath4.pdf

[4] California Department of Education Assessment and Accountability Division. (2011). California Standards Tests Technical Report Spring 2010 Administration. http://www.cde.ca.gov/ta/tg/sr/documents/csttechrpt2010.pdf

[5] California State Board of Education (1997). Mathematics Content Standards for CA Public Schools

[6] California State Board of Education (1997). English-Language Arts Content Standards for California Public Schools - Kindergarten Through Grade Twelve.

[7] diSessa, A. (2000). Changing minds: Computers, learning, and literacy. Cambridge, MA: MIT Press.

[8] Harel, I., & Papert, S. (1992). Software design as a learning environment. In D. P. Balestri, S. C. Ehrmann, & D. L. Ferguson (eds.) Learning to design, designing to learn: using technology to transform the curriculum. 35-70. Taylor and Francis. Washington DC.

[9] Harvey, B., & Mönig, J. (2010). Bringing 'No Ceiling' to Scratch: Can one language serve kids and computer scientists? Constructionism, 2010, 1–10.

[10] Noss, R (1986). Constructing a conceptual framework for elementary algebra through Logo programming. Educational Studies in Mathematics, 17(4), 335-357.

[11] Resnick, M. (1994). Turtles, Termites and Traffic Jams: Explorations in Massively Parallel Microworlds, MIT Press, Cambridge, MA.

[12] Robins, A. (2010). Learning edge momentum: a new account of outcomes in CS1. *Computer Science Education,* 20(1), 37-71.

[13] Rountree, N., Rountree, J., Robins, A., Hannah, R., (2002) Interacting Factors that Predict Success and Failure in a CS1 Course. *Inroads*, 34, 101–104.

[14] Shanzer, E. (N.D.) Bootstrap. www.bootstrapworld.org

[15] Simon, Fincher, S., Robins, A., Baker, B., Box, I., Cutts, Q., de Raadt, M., Haden, P., Hamer, J., Hamilton, M., Lister, R., Petre, M., Sutton, K., Tolhurst, D. & Tutty, J. (2006), Predictors of success in a first programming course, in *Proc. Eighth Australasian Computing Education Conference* (ACE2006), ACS, pp. 189-196.

[16] Simpson, D. (1973). Psychological testing in computing staff selection: a bibliography. *SIGCPR Computer Personnel Research*, 4, 1-2, 1973, 2-5.

[17] Sutherland, R. (1989). Providing a computer based framework for algebraic thinking. Educational Studies in Mathematics, 20 (3), 317-344.

[18] Wing, J. M. (2006) Computational thinking. *Communications of the ACM, 49(3).* 33-35.

[19] Yoo, D., Schanzer, E., Krishnamurthi, S., & Fisler, K. (2011) WeScheme: The Browser is Your Programming Environment. *ITiCSE 2011.* Darmstadt, Germany.

[20] Lewis, C. M. (2010). How programming environment shapes perception, learning and goals: Logo vs. Scratch, *ACM SIGCSE Bulletin. 41(1)*, 346-350.

[21] Lewis, C. M. (2011) Integrating Students' Prior Knowledge into Pedagogy. *Proceedings of the International Computer Science Education Research Workshop.* Providence, RI. 139-140.

[22] Lewis, C. M. (2011). Is pair programming more effective than other forms of collaboration for young students? *Computer Science Education. 21(2).* 105-134.

Calico: A Multi-Programming-Language, Multi-Context Framework Designed for Computer Science Education

Douglas Blank[1], Jennifer S. Kay[2], James B. Marshall[3], Keith O'Hara[4], and Mark Russo[1]

[1]Computer Science Department
Bryn Mawr College
Bryn Mawr, PA (USA)
(1) 610-526-6501
dblank@brynmawr.edu

[2]Computer Science Department
Rowan University
Glassboro, NJ (USA)
(1) 856-256-4593
kay@rowan.edu

[3]Computer Science Department
Sarah Lawrence College
Bronxville, NY (USA)
(1) 914-395-2673
jmarshall@slc.edu

[4]Computer Science Program
Bard College
Annandale-on-Hudson, NY
(1) 845-752-2359
kohara@bard.edu

ABSTRACT

The Calico project is a multi-language, multi-context programming framework and learning environment for computing education. This environment is designed to support several interoperable programming languages (including Python, Scheme, and a visual programming language), a variety of pedagogical contexts (including scientific visualization, robotics, and art), and an assortment of physical devices (including different educational robotics platforms and a variety of physical sensors). In addition, the environment is designed to support collaboration and modern, interactive learning. In this paper we describe the Calico project, its design and goals, our prototype system, and its current use.

Categories and Subject Descriptors

K.3.2 [**Computers and Education**]: Computer and Information Science Education – *computer science education.*

General Terms

Design, Experimentation, Languages.

Keywords

CS1, computer science education, integrated development environment, IDE, pedagogy, programming languages, robots.

1. INTRODUCTION

Today there are many new and exciting programming environments and contexts available for learning about computing. For example, Alice [8] and Scratch [10] provide drag-and-drop, no-syntax-errors programming environments, and DrRacket (formerly DrScheme) offers an award-winning integrated error display and logging system for Scheme [11]. Likewise, there are many exciting pedagogical contexts for learning about computer science, including media computation [6], story-telling, game development, AI, robotics, visualization, and art. Unfortunately, these contexts are often tied to a specific programming environment, which limits their availability to only those willing to work in that programming environment. Similarly, picking a specific programming environment often limits which contexts one can explore. Ideally, educators should be free to choose the most appropriate programming languages and, independently, the most appropriate themes and contexts for their courses. The choice of programming language should not limit the context, nor should the choice of context limit the programming language.

The Calico project is designed to provide a single framework for multiple programming environments and multiple contexts so that instructors and institutions need not limit their pedagogical choices [3]. Thus, within a single framework, teachers can smoothly transition students from one programming paradigm to another. For example, perhaps an instructor would like students to begin with a Scratch-like language [16] and then move to Python. Or perhaps the instructor might wish to start with Python and move to Scheme. Both of these transitions are possible in Calico without changing the computing context, whether it be art, game development, visualization, or any number of other possibilities.

Calico comprises four main components: an interface for multiple programming languages; an interface for multiple libraries for exploring different computing contexts; an interface for peer-to-peer communication; and an integrated editor. The language interface allows for the execution of individual language expressions or entire program files, and for the sharing of data and functions across languages. The library interface enables program modules to appear as native objects within all of the available languages. This provides a foundation for exploring computing contexts, such as graphics and robotics, in a language-independent manner. The communication interface provides functionality that enables users to easily exchange information among themselves. Finally, the editor provides a common framework for editing programs in any language, be it graphical or text-based.

We have developed a prototype version of Calico (Figure 1) that provides well-tested support for the Python programming language and a personal robotics context (called Myro) for introductory computing, as well as preliminary support for several other languages and contexts. Calico runs on Linux, Macintosh, and Windows. This paper describes the prototype version of Calico, which is currently being piloted in five Fall 2011 CS courses, as well as our broader goals and vision for the system.

In the ongoing development of the Calico framework, our overall goals are to "raise the ceiling" by including a variety of more sophisticated pedagogical contexts and programming languages, to "lower the floor" by including support for an intuitive

Permission to make digital or hard copies of all or part of this work for personal or classroom use is granted without fee provided that copies are not made or distributed for profit or commercial advantage and that copies bear this notice and the full citation on the first page. To copy otherwise, or republish, to post on servers or to redistribute to lists, requires prior specific permission and/or a fee.
SIGCSE'12, February 29–March 3, 2012, Raleigh, North Carolina, USA.
Copyright 2012 ACM 978-1-4503-1098-7/12/02...$10.00.

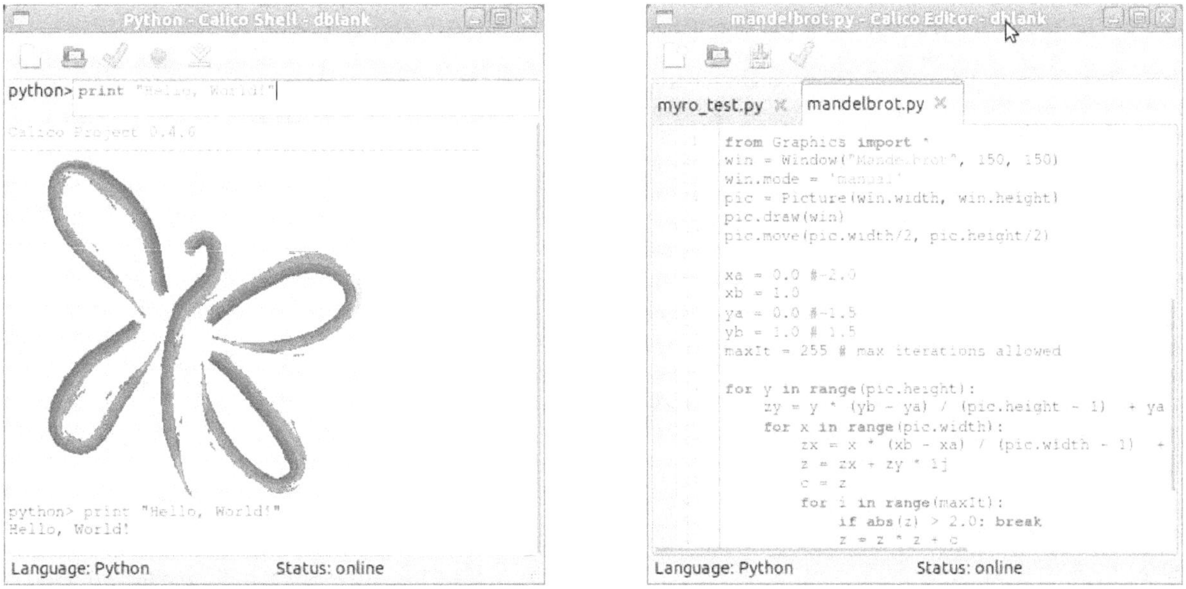

Figure 1: Prototype of the Calico shell (left) and editor (right).

visual programming language for beginners, and to "widen the doorway" by including contexts beyond those typically found in traditional computer science, such as scientific visualization and art.

2. A MULTI-LANGUAGE ENVIRONMENT

Users interact with each supported language through the Calico Shell. The shell provides a place for text-based language expressions to be entered and evaluated interactively, with the results available for immediate inspection. In many ways, the shell is very similar to other interactive interfaces, such as IDLE, DrRacket, Jython Environment for Students (JES), and many others going back to the read-eval-print loop of Lisp. However, Calico offers three significant improvements over these other interfaces: Calico is completely language-agnostic, users can easily switch between a variety of available languages, and different languages can share data and functions.

Our Calico prototype currently fully supports Python as a scripting language for students to use. Beyond support for Python, there is preliminary support for Ruby, F# (similar to OCaml), Boo (Python with types), and Scheme. The shell is language-agnostic in that it is not tied specifically to any programming language. Languages are dynamically loaded on startup through a simple, standard interface. Once Calico is started, users may switch between loaded languages through a simple key combination (*e.g.*, Control+5 might be Python, and Control+6 Ruby).

Of course, most users will probably only use a single language at a time; however, users can mix data structures and functions from different languages together. Furthermore, the sharing of data and functions requires no extra overhead. For example, data need not be "marshaled" (or copied) in order to be accessed by different languages. In addition, functions defined in one language appear native to each of Calico's supported languages, even if they involve very different types of execution mechanisms.

As an example, the following Calico Scheme program defines a recursive function for testing whether an integer is even:

```
scheme> (define is-even?
          (lambda (n)
            (cond
              ((= n 0) #t)
              ((= n 1) #f)
              ((< n 0) (is-even? (- n)))
              (else (is-even? (- n 2))))))
Ok
```

In this example, *is-even?* is local to Scheme. However, this function can easily be made available to other Calico languages. The following code adds the function *even* to the global environment, turning the Scheme function *is-even?* into a function callable from other Calico languages:

```
scheme> (define! even (func is-even?))
Ok
```

The user can then dynamically switch to Python, and call the *even* function as if it were a native Python function:

```
python> even(9998)
True
```

Conversely, functions defined in Python can be utilized by Scheme programs in a similar fashion. However, an essential aspect of Calico's Scheme implementation (and most others, as well) is that it is properly tail-recursive. The effective depth of Scheme's call stack is limited only by the amount of system memory available, unlike in many other languages, such as Python or Java, which impose a limit on the maximum depth of the stack.

Other Calico languages, however, can take advantage of Scheme's flexibility. For example, the above *even* function called from Python will work for arguments of any size, whereas a function defined in Python equivalent to *is-even?* will crash for arguments above a certain size, depending on the depth limit of Python's call stack, even though the function is tail-recursive. (The argument 9998 shown above, for instance, causes CPython 2.7.2 to crash.) In fact, whether or not a function is tail-recursive is irrelevant, since Scheme imposes no limit on the recursion depth either way. This example shows that Python can directly exploit the power of Scheme in Calico.

In addition to supporting a variety of different languages, Calico makes it easy for educators to modify either the syntax or semantics of a language, or to create a completely new language. Both of these options have been largely unavailable to educators in the past. Because a language is a plugin, and is written in the same manner as any Calico library (discussed below), adding a new text-based or graphical language is a simple matter of adding a single file to the system. This file defines what to do when Calico is asked to evaluate a snippet of code such as an expression or group of statements, and also what is necessary to run an entire program file. Additional functionality can also be included if desired, but little else is necessary for the language to appear in Calico's menu. To fully integrate the language into Calico, the system needs to define a method for accessing the global environment that is shared across all languages.

Calico incorporates a layer for language designers called the Dynamic Language Runtime (DLR). This layer is an open source set of functions to help designers create programming languages using modern techniques [4]. Open source versions of Python and Ruby have already been developed using the DLR. This layer is also the mechanism that allows Calico's languages to share data and functions.

The syntax and semantics of Calico's version of Python has been refined for pedagogical purposes. For example, the *print* function of Python 3 has been selected over the *print* statement of earlier versions, and Python's new *with* statement has been included. Of course, these are minor changes, but instructors have the ability to change any aspect of a language in principle. This gives instructors fine-grained control over the languages they use, and frees them from having to rely strictly on the choices made by language designers. Of course, this could potentially have adverse effects, by splintering a language into many incompatible versions. On the other hand, this could allow new variations of a language to emerge that would not otherwise be possible.

2.1 A Visual Programming Language

To demonstrate the flexibility of the Calico system to incorporate new languages, we are developing a blocks-oriented, drag-and-drop visual programming language for Calico called Jigsaw (Figure 2). This new language will closely follow the lead of Scratch [16], a visual programming language primarily for children from the Lifelong Kindergarten Group at the MIT Media Lab. Visual programming tools like Scratch have been very successful at making computer programming accessible to K-12 and undergraduate students [9].

Students will be able to execute a Jigsaw program directly in the graphical environment with the built-in Jigsaw language interpreter. Alternatively, the system will be able to translate a visual program into the equivalent source code for several textual languages integrated into the Calico environment. The translator will build a bridge from the high-level programming concepts represented by Jigsaw blocks to specific language implementations. The student will thus be able to see directly how an abstract programming concept can be expressed concretely in multiple ways.

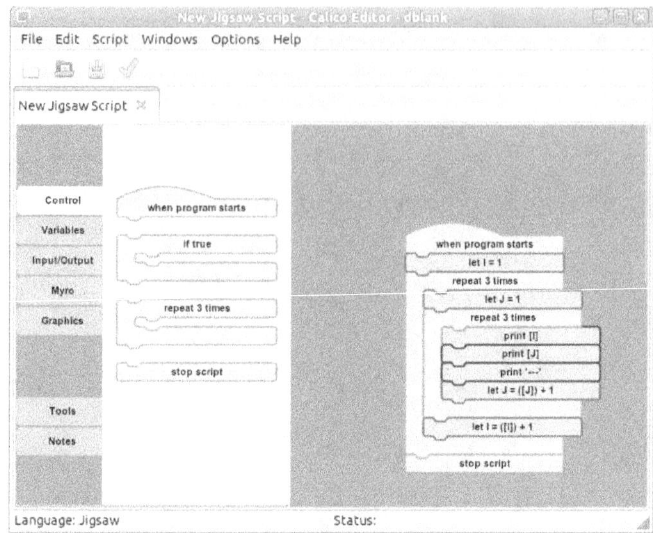

Figure 2: The Jigsaw visual programming environment.

Jigsaw will include block palettes that encapsulate the rich array of computing contexts available to all Calico programming languages. Calico's common environment and shared libraries will greatly facilitate the integration of new contexts as Jigsaw block sets, as well as the process of translating a Jigsaw program to the equivalent source code in multiple textual languages.

Jigsaw will be extended in several ways to further enhance students' ability to visualize computer programming. Graphical extensions to Jigsaw will include interactive design and manipulation of data structures, a stepping debugger with the ability to inspect and modify multiple levels of execution scope within a Jigsaw program, and a facility to create and deploy code-your-own blocks for others to use.

Experience has shown that new students often cling tightly to the syntax of the language that they are learning. So one may not want to expose introductory students to too many languages at once. We suspect, however, that starting with a visual programming language and migrating to Python in CS1 would be beneficial to students. This hypothesis can be easily tested with Calico.

3. MULTI-CONTEXT COMPUTING

We consider a *context* to be a unifying theme used to drive student motivation. A context should be supported by well-designed curricular materials and libraries, and perhaps also by appropriate physical devices. Currently Calico supports two contexts: the Myro robotics library for the Scribbler robot with the IPRE Fluke extension [2, 14, 17], and a 2D Graphics library with optional support for physics simulations, including gravity.

A Calico library only needs to be written once, but appears as if it were implemented for each of the supported languages. For example, the Myro library appears as a native Python module inside Python, as a native Ruby module inside Ruby, and so on. We have written programs in several languages using Myro commands to control a robot, and have created a number of 2D graphics demos as well. As an example, the following programs demonstrate using the Graphics library in four Calico languages: Python, Scheme, F#, and Ruby.

```
# Python Graphics Example
import Graphics
win = Graphics.Window("Hello")
line = Line((0,0), (100,100))
line.draw(win)
```

```
;; Scheme Graphics Example
(using "Graphics")
(define win (Graphics.Window "Hello"))
(define line (Graphics.Line (Graphics.Point 0 0)
                            (Graphics.Point 100 100)))
(line.draw win)
```

```
// F# Graphics Example
module MyModule
let win = Graphics.Window("Hello")
let line = new Graphics.Line(new Graphics.Point(0,0),
                             new Graphics.Point(100,100))
line.draw(win)
```

```
# Ruby Graphics Example
win = Graphics::WindowClass.new("Hello")
line = Graphics::Line.new(Graphics::Point.new(0,0),
                          Graphics::Point.new(100,100))
line.draw(win)
```

The Graphics library is written once in standard C#, following some basic guidelines, and then compiled on any platform to a shared library. This shared library is then placed into a folder of the Calico Project, which makes it available to all of the supported languages. As can be seen from the above examples, the library provides a native interface for each language. It is important to note that there is no additional "glue" or "wrapper" code necessary to use a library. In addition, the library is not dependent upon the language that is using it, nor the operating system. In this manner, the compiled library can be used as-is with future languages or operating systems that have not yet been created. This will greatly facilitate the maintainability of the entire project as time goes on.

The Myro robot library implements a well-tested API developed by the Institute for Personal Robots in Education (IPRE) [7]. This API has been ported by others to many languages, including C++, C, and Java. We are currently deploying Calico within a "robots first" CS1 setting. The 2D Graphics library is designed to support many different uses. For example, it can serve as a replacement for Zelle's Python Tkinter-based graphics library [18]. Of course, since it is written as a generic Calico library, it is available to all of the Calico languages, not just Python. We would also like for it to eventually provide the functionality of Processing's 2D graphical library [15]. Combined with the drag-

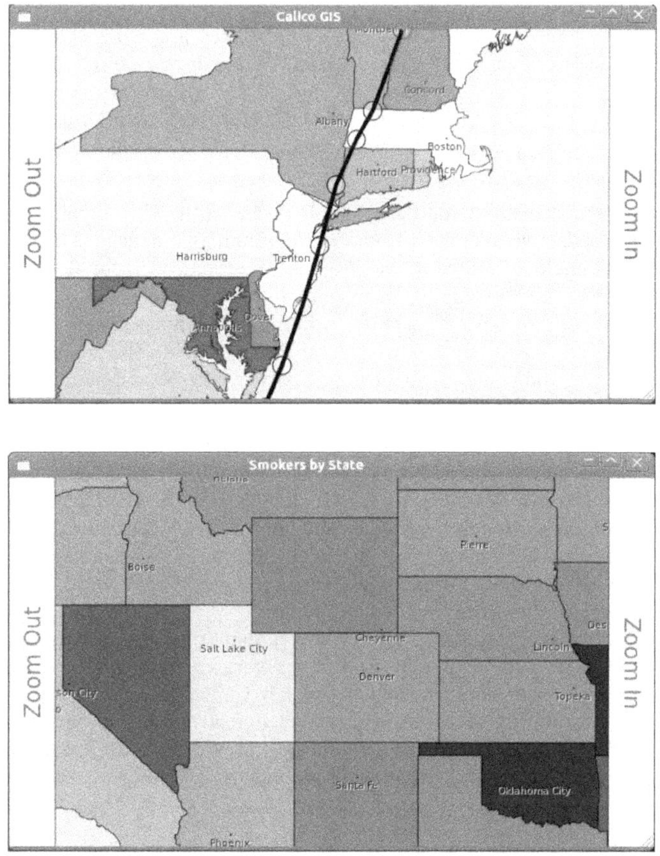

Figure 3: Examples created with Calico's 2D Graphics library.

and-drop Jigsaw language, Calico could also be used as an alternative to Scratch. Or with its Scheme support, it might serve as an alternative to NetLogo.

The 2D Graphics library currently has support for basic drawing functionality, including shapes, turtle graphics, and image processing. In addition, the library also has a selection of "modes" for top-level windows to operate in. For example, "auto mode" will automatically update a window's contents as soon as possible, but without overloading the system; "manual mode" leaves the updating of graphics completely under the user's control; and "physics mode" imbues all shapes with physical properties such as mass and velocity under the influence of gravity. Physics mode allows for many interesting explorations into topics typically outside the scope of introductory computer science courses. For example, students can easily write their own version of the game "Angry Birds", using nothing more than standard graphical shapes and turning on physics mode.

To augment the Calico 2D Graphics library, we have also included in Calico a set of real world data. For example, we have included the regions of each US state in longitude/latitude format. Combining this with some supporting code for mapping longitude/latitude points to a window coordinate system allows students to easily create interesting visualizations. For example, one can plot the path of an active hurricane, or visualize by state the percentage of adult smokers (see Figure 3). The top image shows the path of Hurricane Irene plotted using a Calico function to map longitude and latitude to (*x*, *y*) window coordinates. The bottom image shows a visualization of the adult smoking population of various states. The darker the color of the state, the higher the percentage of smokers in the state. States are represented by polygons of longitude/latitude pairs that are drawn using Calico's Polygon class. More generally, this library will make it easy for students to learn to manipulate and experiment with "big data" within many different contexts, using graphical visualizations as the primary tool.

One of the main design goals of Calico is the separation of the pedagogical context from the programming language. This has the benefit of allowing one group of educators to focus their resources on developing interesting libraries and contexts, independently of other researchers working on language issues. Thus, the hope is to create many reusable components (languages, libraries, and contexts) that can be easily integrated and maintained within a single framework.

Calico contexts may also incorporate the use of special hardware and other devices. Inexpensive sensors and effectors are increasingly available for use in the classroom. Hardware like Arduino microcontrollers [1], the Microsoft Kinect camera, and the iRobot Create robot are relatively inexpensive and allow students to write programs that interact with the real world. This physical presence can make students' programs seem more relevant and engaging, as they are "authentic" problem domains. Our goal is to make cutting edge hardware accessible to all levels of the computing curriculum through Calico's Devices library. For example, students using Calico in a creative computation class will be able to access the depth images provided by the Kinect, or to drive a Create mobile robot around using a simple, standard API.

3.1 An IDE for Interaction and Collaboration

Learning a different programming language should not entail learning a completely different development environment. Too often, each language comes with its own extra baggage of IDE, libraries, and supporting framework. Educators should be free to focus the student's attention on the ideas that matter, rather than on getting students up to speed in yet another new, unfamiliar environment. For example, the fact that Scheme uses functions and recursion as opposed to loops and mutable state is important; using the F5 key to run the program as opposed to some other key or menu option is not important. The Calico IDE has a fast, robust, extensible color syntax highlighter for all available languages, and allows switching between languages with a keystroke. Students can interactively enter commands in the currently selected language and see the results immediately. Any further improvements made to the IDE will automatically carry over to all of Calico's programming languages and contexts.

In addition to the shell and editor windows, Calico's interface also has a third component, called Chat. The Chat window appears as a typical chatroom interface, and uses Extensible Messaging and Presence Protocol (XMPP) as the back-end protocol for communicating messages between the users' computers and the server. The integrated chat interface allows students and teachers to communicate in a more modern medium. However, and perhaps more importantly, the XMPP connection can be used in ways other than as a chat interface. This provides a general mechanism for moving information between Calico clients. For example, we are currently exploring what we call "code blasting". Using Calico, teachers will have the ability to blast code to students such that it shows up directly in their Calico editors. This will make it easy for them to immediately try out the examples being discussed in class. Likewise, students will be able to blast their assignments to their teachers, or perhaps blast code to each other. In addition, we have outlined plans to develop further support for interactive collaboration in Calico, so that two students could work together, even if they are in different locations.

Finally, Calico is designed to incorporate the functionality of Personal Response Systems (often referred to as "clickers"), which can be used to provide interactivity in a classroom. Interactivity can be an effective way to enhance learning, even with larger class sizes. At this stage, we plan on implementing only a basic "quick poll" functionality. The instructor could initiate a question on the fly, perhaps with a multiple-choice answer selection, in order to gauge students' comprehension of a particular topic. Students would each receive the quick poll via a pop-up dialog in Calico, where they would select one of the choices. Afterwards, the instructor could display a bar chart of the group's responses, leaving individuals anonymous. The class could then either discuss the topic further, or move on to the next topic, depending on overall student understanding.

3.2 Technical Details

Calico is designed to run identically on Linux, Macintosh, and Windows. In order to satisfy our cross-platform goal, we decided to implement the system on a virtual machine (VM). We considered two popular virtual machines: Java and .NET. Unfortunately, .NET only runs under Windows. However, an open source implementation of .NET exists, called Mono, which runs on all three target operating systems. Like Java, Mono includes both an object-oriented language/compiler and a virtual machine/runtime. However, although many languages can run on the Java VM, no common infrastructure exists, other than the VM itself, for each language implemented on the VM. This makes it difficult for different languages to share environments, data structures, objects, or functions. On the other hand, .NET and Mono have a framework for implementing languages called the Dynamic Language Runtime (DLR), and there already exist several languages written for the DLR, including Python and Ruby. The DLR contains many tools and technologies for implementing languages, along with support for making languages interoperable. Also, Java lacks a complete, robust, and official open source implementation. In contrast, .NET's Common Language Infrastructure (CLI) has been clearly defined by Ecma standards #334 and #335 [5], and is protected by a promise from Microsoft not to sue [12]. The Mono virtual machine implements the Ecma standards. We have put a high value on Calico having a complete and open source "stack" of software layers, and for these reasons we decided to select the CLI as implemented by Mono as the basis of our system.

Calico is designed to be easy to maintain and modify over time. The main Calico interface is written in IronPython, which has the advantage of allowing the interface to be easily altered without recompiling. For example, one can change Calico's menus by simply editing a text file. Those changes are then reflected immediately on all platforms. We also selected Gtk as the graphical toolkit, as it is very robust and consistent across operating systems and has good documentation. The libraries are written in C# for speed. However, these libraries require only a single compilation on each operating system, after which they run identically on all platforms with any of the supported languages.

4. CONCLUSION

With Calico, one can pick the operating system, programming language, and context independently. Working within the Calico IDE, instructors and students can switch between different programming languages with ease while exploring a given context. Having the IDE and libraries be language-agnostic will make it easy to incorporate new, yet-to-be-invented languages into the system without having to reinvent all of the necessary supporting infrastructure, and without the need for adapting existing contexts to work with the new languages.

It would be ideal if improvements to one educational IDE—DrRacket's Scheme environment, say—could also benefit students using other languages. However, currently each such project is developed largely in isolation, and it is very difficult to apply advances in one environment to another. By providing an extensible, common framework spanning many programming languages and paradigms, enhancements to the environment or to a context benefit all of the languages, thereby creating a vibrant ecosystem for pedagogical development.

As another example, computer science students typically study a variety of programming languages in a comparative manner in a junior-level programming languages course. Calico would be an excellent tool for side-by-side language comparison in such a course. But why wait until the junior year? Why not do this type of side-by-side comparison early in a computing curriculum? If switching languages were as easy as pressing a key, what pedagogical benefits would that offer the students? We hope to explore these questions through Calico.

In summary, we hope that Calico will provide a long-term, robust framework that can be used to create and sustain a community of researchers, educators, and students working together.

5. ACKNOWLEDGMENTS

An early version of this project was funded by NSF DUE grant #0920539 (Blank and O'Hara). Initial funding for the Myro project was provided for Blank and O'Hara by Microsoft Research. We would also like to thank Deepak Kumar for his support on this project. Finally, we would like to acknowledge the six institutions currently testing Calico: Bard College, Boston College, Bryn Mawr College, the Baldwin School, Macalester College, and Rowan University.

6. REFERENCES

[1] Banzi, M. 2008. *Getting Started with Arduino*. O'Reilly Media / Make. December 2008.

[2] Blank, D. 2006. Robots make computer science personal. *Communications of the ACM* 49, 12, 25-27.

[3] Calico Project Home Page. http://calicoproject.org. Retrieved 9/2/2011.

[4] Dynamic Language Runtime. http://dlr.codeplex.com. Retrieved 9/2/2011.

[5] Ecma Standards. http://www.mono-project.com/ECMA. Retrieved 9/2/2011.

[6] Guzdial, M. 2003. A media computation course for non-majors. In *Proceedings of the 8th Annual Conference on Innovation and Technology in Computer Science Education*. ITiCSE '03. ACM, New York, NY, 104-108.

[7] Institute for Personal Robots in Education. http://roboteducation.org. Retrieved 9/2/2011.

[8] Kelleher, C., Pausch, R., and Kiesler, S. 2007. Storytelling Alice motivates middle school girls to learn computer programming. In *Proceedings of the SIGCHI Conference on Human Factors in Computing Systems*. CHI '07. ACM, New York, NY, 1455-1464.

[9] Malan, D. and Leitner, H. 2007. Scratch for budding computer scientists. *SIGCSE Bulletin (39)* 1, 223-227.

[10] Maloney, J., Resnick, M., Rusk, N., Silverman, B., and Eastmond, E. 2010. The Scratch programming language and environment. *Transactions on Computing Education* 10, 4, Article 16 (Nov. 2010).

[11] Marceau, G., Fisler, K., and Krishnamurthi, S. 2011. Measuring the effectiveness of error messages designed for novice programmers. In *Proceedings of the 42nd ACM Technical Symposium on Computer Science Education*. SIGCSE '11. ACM, New York, NY, 499-504.

[12] Microsoft Community Promise. 2007. http://www.microsoft.com/interop/cp. Retrieved 5/17/2011.

[13] NSF. 2003. Beyond LEGOs: Hardware, Software, and Curriculum for the Next Generation Robot Laboratory. NSF CCLI award #0231363.

[14] NSF. 2009. Personal Robots for CS1: Next Steps for an Engaging Pedagogical Framework. NSF CCLI award #0920539.

[15] Reas, C., Fry, B., and Maeda, J. 2007. *Processing: A Programming Handbook for Visual Designers and Artists*. MIT Press.

[16] Resnick, M., Maloney, J., Monroy-Hernandez, A., Rusk, M., Eastmond, E., Brennan, K., Millner, A., Rosenbaum, E., Silver, J., Silverman, B., and Kafai, Y. 2009. Scratch: programming for all. *Communications of the ACM* vol. 52 no. 11 (Nov. 2009), 60-67.

[17] Summet, J., Kumar, D., O'Hara, K., Walker, D., Ni, L., Blank, D., and Balch, T. 2009. Personalizing CS1 with robots. In *Proceedings of the 40th ACM Technical Symposium on Computer Science Education*. SIGCSE '09. ACM, New York, NY, 433-437.

[18] Zelle, J. 2003. *Python Programming: An Introduction to Computer Science*. Franklin, Beedle, and Associates.

How a Language-based GUI Generator Can Influence the Teaching of Object-Oriented Programming

Prasun Dewan
University of North Carolina
Department of Computer Science
Chapel Hill, NC 27599
001-919-962-1823
dewan@unc.edu

ABSTRACT

A language-based direct-manipulation user-interface generator automatically creates a visualization of an object directly from its class, allows users to edit the visualization, and invokes methods in the object in response to these edits. Such a generator can change, and we argue, improve the lectures and assignments on programming conventions, methods, state, constructors, preconditions, MVC, polymorphism, graphics, structured objects, loops, concurrency, and annotations. We have built such a generator, which has several novel features for teaching such as interactive instantiation of a class, interactive invocation of methods and constructors that take arbitrary arguments, visualization of objects representing records, sequences, table and graphics, use of preconditions to disable/enable user-interface elements, and automatic generation of model threads. We have been working on and using such a generator for teaching CS 1 and CS 2 for about a decade.

Categories and Subject Descriptors

D.1.5 [**Programming Techniques**] – Object-oriented programming.

General Terms

Documentation, Design, Human Factors, Standardization

Keywords

MVC, User-interface generator, preconditions, concurrency

1. INTRODUCTION

Instructors of introductory programming are faced today with two main choices: use an interpretive functional language such as Scheme or ML; or use a compiled object-based programming language such as C# or Java. Though decreasing in popularity, the first choice continues to be a valid alternative because it allows students to write functions, and hence focus on programming logic, from day one. Once they have written a function, they can see what it does by simply calling it interactively – the interpreter performs the messy tasks of mapping user-input to function calls and displaying return values of these calls, freeing them from learning about I/O altogether. Object-oriented programming requires the teaching of either console I/O or (user-interface) toolkits. Usually the latter variation is chosen as it allows the creation of graphical user-interfaces (GUIs). In comparison to the functional-language-with-interpreter approach, the OO-programming-with-toolkit approach is the more popular choice because it teaches the powerful and practical concepts of object-based programming and allows generation of GUIs.

The BlueJ [1] and Dr. Java systems have shown a path to overcome this problem by allowing methods of objects to be invoked interactively. However, these systems have two related problems. First, they come with their own programming environments. Second, they support command-based interaction, wherein a user manipulates an object by entering a command and parameters, using the command line and/or menus/dialogue boxes. A more modern alternative is to support direct-manipulation user-interfaces [2], where a user interacts with an object by editing a visual representation of it. Such interfaces are not only more compelling to the students, but also can intuitively display complex concepts. These two problems are related as programming environments mimic the interaction style offered by programming languages.

User-interface generation [3] seems to offer a solution to this problem. It is based on the insight that certain types of conventional program values can be automatically visualized by certain kinds of user-interface objects. For instance, any primitive type can be displayed as a string, an int as a slider, an enum as a combo-box or spinner, a record as a form, and an array, sequence, and map as a list, table, or tree. It is possible to edit these visualizations to change the underlying values.

However user-interface generation is apparently at odds with object encapsulation – it requires knowledge of the structure of the visualized object, while encapsulation hides these details. Two workarounds have been tried to overcome this problem. One is to require programmers to manually create an explicit description of the object structure in a non object-oriented language (e.g. [4]). This description must be manually mapped to the implementation of the object, which is an error prone and tedious task. Moreover, it is hard enough to teach programming to students in one language – one cannot expect them to use and learn two very different languages simultaneously. The second workaround is to break encapsulation and require programmers to declare object components as public variables [5], which essentially asks programmers to do conventional programming in an object-oriented language.

What is required, thus, is a generator that overcomes the apparent difficulty above to create an editable visualization of encapsulated objects directly from the descriptions of these objects in a

Permission to make digital or hard copies of all or part of this work for personal or classroom use is granted without fee provided that copies are not made or distributed for profit or commercial advantage and that copies bear this notice and the full citation on the first page. To copy otherwise, or republish, to post on servers or to redistribute to lists, requires prior specific permission and/or a fee.
*SIGCSE'*12, February 29–March 3, 2012, Raleigh, North Carolina, USA.
Copyright 2012 ACM 978-1-4503-1098-7/12/02...$10.00.

standard programming language. We refer to such a generator as a language-based direct-manipulation GUI generator. In this paper, we describe how we have adapted and applied the author's research on such a generator for Java, to the teaching of programming in CS 1 and CS 2 classes. The difference between the two classes in our university is that students in CS 2 are required to have seen some programming before, which may not have been object-oriented. Thus, students in both classes are introduced to object-oriented programming. Freshmen take both classes, and usually the majors take CS 2.

2. STATELESS OBJECTS

When ObjectEditor is used, the first program students see is not the traditional "hello world" printer. Instead it is a stateless class that implements a mathematical function (Figure 1). Students in CS1 see a class without a package declaration, while those in CS2 see the packaged version shown here. Without ObjectEditor, students would have to use a main method to exercise the function. But this approach has the well-known problem that it uses the concepts of arrays of static methods, arrays, and string – none of which CS 1 students know on day one. Thus, they have to be presented the main method as a magic recipe.

Figure 2 shows how the functional language interpreter approach has been adapted in ObjectEditor. Among other items, the tool provides the "new(String)" menu item (a), which can be selected to create a form allowing the entry of the name of a class to be instantiated (b). The result of pressing the button on the form is creation and visualization of a new instance of the entered class (c). The class provides the menu, ABMICalculator, containing the single item, "Calculate BMI (double, double)", which can be selected to create a form to enter the parameters of the corresponding method. Pressing the button invokes the method, and displays a visualization of the Double result (e). This visualization allows interactive invocation of the Double methods on the result (e). The student can use this facility to interactively explore the functionality of a Double. As we see above, Fig 2(a) and (b) are very similar to 2(c) and (d), respectively. The reason is that in Figure 2(a), ObjectEditor is used to visualize and edit itself. In general, the visualization of an object of class C creates a menu named C with items for invoking the methods of the class (Figure 2(a, c, e)). Selecting a menu item creates a form to enter the parameters of the corresponding method, and creates a visualization of the result of the method (Figure 2(c, e)).

Interactive class instantiation and object editing allow CS 1 students to write and test a useful function on the first day. In addition, they allow method invocation to be learnt at an intuitive level – assigning actual parameters to formal parameters defined by a method declaration is essentially filling items in a form to request a service that defines the structure of the form and reads the filled values. This analogy is made concrete by ObjectEditor. Furthermore, the names of method menu items such as "new(String)" and "Calculate BMI (double, double)" make the abstract idea of a method signature concrete to both CS 1 and 2 students. Students see that a signature is useful to distinguish between different methods. Finally, both CS 1 and 2 students also use ObjectEditor to test the functionality of an object without multiple iterations of the run-modify program steps. To try out different values of the parameters of a method, they do not have to write modify a main class that calls the method. They can simply call the method repeatedly with different parameters

```
package examples.objects;
public class ABMICalculator{
    public double calculateBMI(double weight, double height) {
        return weight/(height*height);
    }
}
```

Figure 1 Writing a Function on Day 1 in CS 1

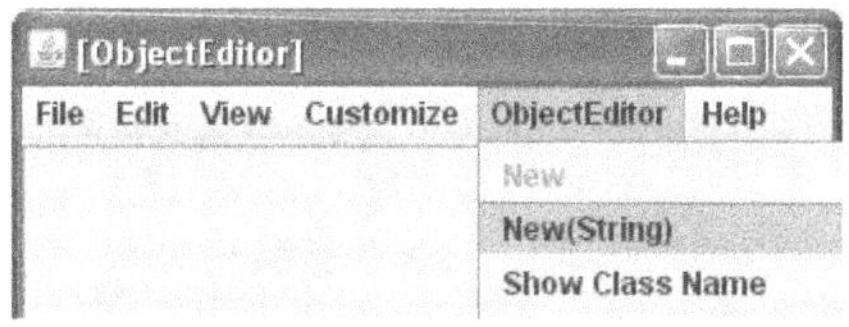

(a) Running ObjectEditor and Selecting New Item

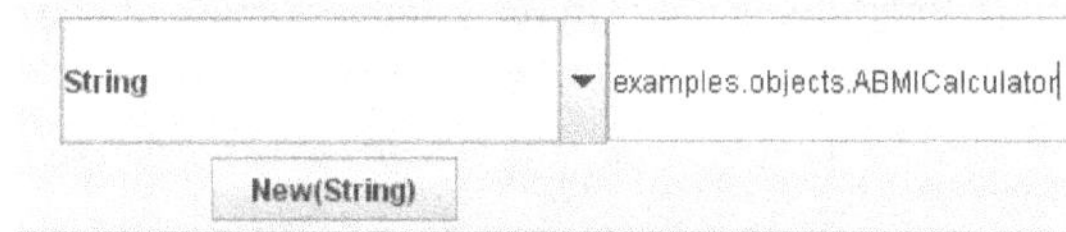

(b) Filling class name and pressing New(String)

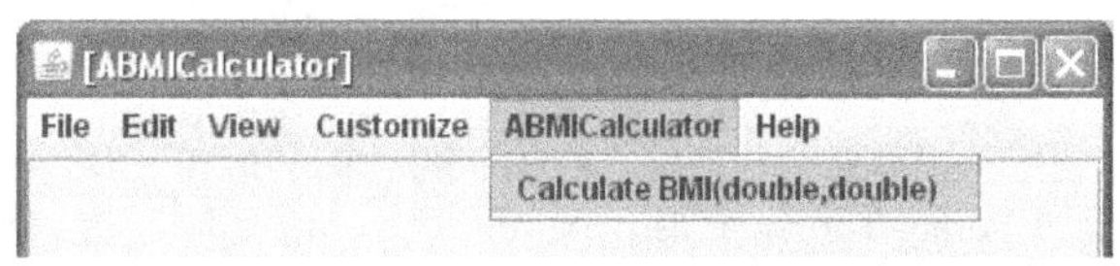

(c) The result of new, and selecting Calculate BMI(double)

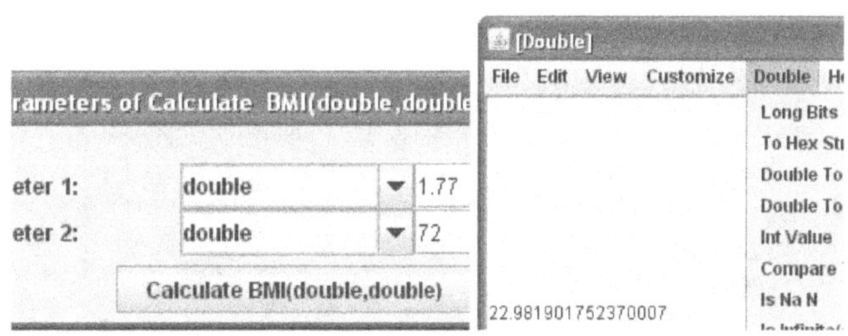

(d) Method Actual Parameters (e) Method Return Value

Figure 2 Interactive Object Instantiation and Manipulation

CS 2 students do not use the ObjectEditor for creating and displaying an object. Instead, they do so directly from a main method, as shown in Figure 3.

```
public class ABMICalcluatorDriver{
    public static main (String[] args) {
        ObjectEditor.edit(new ABMICalculator());
    }
}
```

Figure 3 Creating and Displaying an Object from Code

CS 1 students are also shown this code. Those who feel comfortable living with the mysteries of the main method are allowed to use it – others wait until main methods are taught, which happens after arrays and static members are explained.

Once students learn how to define and invoke functions, they can be taught functional programming to the depth desired by the instructor. At some point, however, state must be introduced.

3. BEANS AND CONSTRUCTORS

To motivate state, we take a stateless object, such as the example above, and point out the effort required to specify all actual parameters of a method in each invocation of it, even if some of these invocations share some of these values. For example, the height parameter must be specified in each of the two invocation of the calculateBMI method shown in Figure 4, even though it does not change.

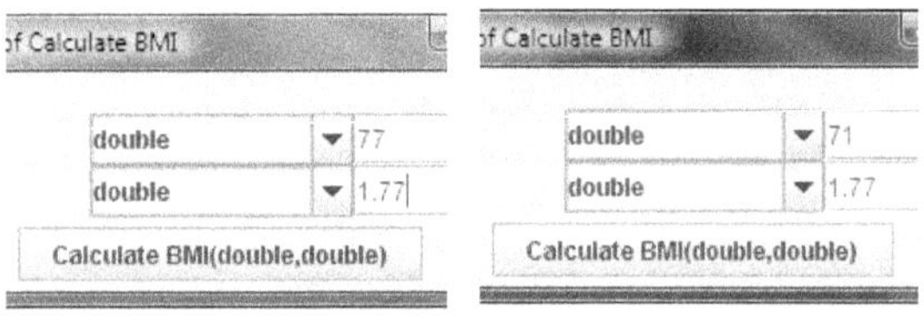

Figure 4 The problem of re-entering height

We then take a stateful version of some stateless object to show how values can be remembered. The code and visualization of the stateful version of the BMI calculator class is shown in Figure 5. The figure shows how the seemingly impossible problem of breaking up an encapsulated object can be addressed. The generation process, which students understand intuitively, is formally explained in terms of Java Bean conventions for defining getters and setters of typed properties. They are able to derive on their own that getters are invoked to display property values and setters to reflect user edits to them. They are able to understand that programming conventions make the code understandable to both humans and tools such as ObjectEditor.

```
public class ABMISpreadsheet {
  double height;
  double weight;
  public ABMISpreadsheet(double initHeight, double initWeight) {
    height = initHeight;
    weight = initWeight;
  }
  public double getHeight() {
    return height;
  }
  public void setHeight(double newHeight) {
    height = newHeight;
  }
  public double getWeight() {
    return weight;
  }
  public void setWeight(double newWeight) {
    weight = newWeight;
  }
  public double getBMI() {
    return weight/(height*height);
  }
}
```

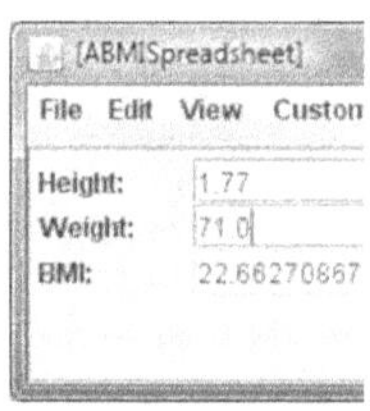

Figure 5 Displaying Bean Properties

As we see in Figure 5, a stateful object can have constructors, which can also be invoked interactively. If a class has more than one constructor, then when it is instantiated using ObjectEditror (Figure 2(a)), a menu of all of its constructors is displayed to the user (Figure 6, top window) Choosing one of these results in a form similar to the one created to invoke any method (Figure 6, bottom window). Invocation of the constructor results is the newly created instance to be shown. As we see here, ObjectEditor concretely visualizes the abstract idea of multiple constructors and their use in initializing objects.

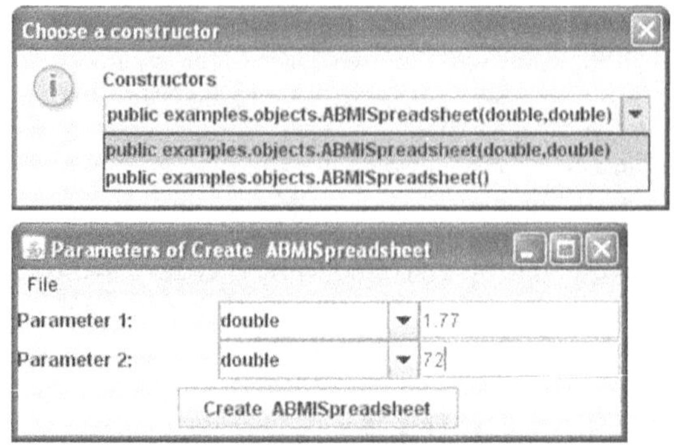

Figure 6 Interactive Constructor Invocation

ObjectEditor also makes the distinction between stateless and stateful objects very clear. Different stateless instances of a class all look the same, and have no main window to display the components of the instance, while different stateful instances of a class have main windows that can diverge based on the constructor used and methods called on them. Once students see state, they are shown that executing the Show Class Name command in ObjectEditor (Figure 2(a)), allows a property to be displayed that remembers the last class they entered. As we see later, students use preconditions to themselves dynamically display properties or enable menu items.

4. DYNAMIC TYPES & POLYMORPHISM

Not all stateful objects use Bean conventions. Essentially, Bean conventions allow decomposition of an encapsulated object that implements a conventional record type. Students also create and/or use objects that represent arrays, (variable-length) sequences, sets, and (hash) tables – four other important data types taught in CS 1 and 2 classes. Arrays are language-defined, so they pose no problem – the predefined constructs for setting and getting their elements can be used to create editable visualizations of them. One approach to handling sequences, sets, and tables is to require these to be instances of predefined interfaces such as the Java Set, List and Map interfaces, respectively. However, this approach has two related problems. First, it does not give students experience in implementing their own interfaces for these types. Second, predefined interfaces may contain too few or many methods for a particular application. In both classes in our institution, they make extensive use of history objects, which are sequences that allow addition but not replacement or insertion of elements. The Java List interface provides the union of all methods that may be used in sequences, and thus cannot support various kinds of constrained sequences

Therefore, as for records, we rely on conventions for defining dynamic objects. We have taken two steps to address the fact that no standard Bean-like conventions have been defined for these and other types discussed below. (a) We allow conventions to be defined by the instructor – the exact details are beyond the scope of his paper. (b) We have defined conventions based on popular Java types. For example, we recognize an object as a variable-length readonly sequence of type <ElementType> if it defines the following two methods:

```
int size();
<ElementType> get(int index)
```

Here the words in angle brackets are placeholders. If a class also defines the following optional method:

<AnyType> set(int index, , <ElementType> element)

then the elements of the sequence can be edited by the user. We define several other conventions for sequences and other dynamic types, which are details we omit because of space constraints

Figure 7 shows the use of the convention above to visualize and edit an instance of a Java vector. It also brings out another use of ObjectEditor – visualization of the abstract concept of polymorphism. Figure 7(a) visualizes a new, and hence empty, instance of a Vector. Suppose we call add(Object) to add a new element to this instance (Figure 7(b)). As we saw when we invoked the calculateBMI() method, a dialogue box is displayed to enter the actual parameter of the method. However, there is an important difference – the type of the parameter is an object type rather than a primitive type. Unlike a primitive type, an object type is a polymorphic type in that it can stand for a set of types, which includes all types that have an IS-A relationship with it. Therefore, before entering the parameter value, the user must first specify the class of the parameter. ObjectEditor allows the user to type the exact class name. It also provides a drop down menu listing commonly-used predefined class names that have an IS-A relationship with the declared type and those the user has explicitly entered in previous invocations of the method. In this example, the user selects the String class as the parameter type (Figure 7 (b)) and then enters the actual string to be used as the parameter (Figure 7(c)). The new string is then displayed as a dynamic element of the Vector (Figure 7(d)).

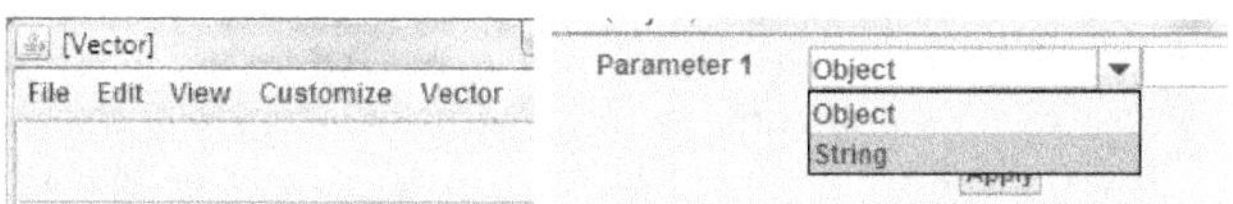

(a) Empty Vector (b) Polymorphic type

(c) Entering value of chosen type (c) New element added

Figure 7 Vector and Polymorphic Add

One of the first questions students ask when they encounter ObjectEditor is "why is the type field a combo-box"? They are told to wait until they are taught polymorphism, and once this abstract anticipated concept is covered, they can visualize it as a combo-box representing a type choice.

In this example, the value of the chosen type is atomic in that it can be entered by directly editing the parameter text field. To be complete, ObjectEditor should also be able to handle arbitrary parameter types, which could include structured types such as ABMISpreadsheet or Vector. Figure 8 shows how a structured value is entered. In this example, we use an extended version of ABMISpreadsheet of Figure 5, which has two additional properties, BMIClassification (enum) and OverWeight (bool), respectively, and an additional method, RestoreWeightAndHeight, which resets the height and weight to their initial values.

Let us call the Vector add(Object) method again, but this time, let us enter ABMISpreadsheet as the class of its parameter (Figure 8(a)). As this type is structured, it has no standard parsable String representation ObjectEditor instantiates such a parameter class and recursively creates an editor for the new instance (Figure 8(b)). We can now use this editor to manipulate the object (Figure 8(c)), and execute the File→Done command to commit the parameter value (not shown here). At this point, the edited object is assigned as the actual parameter of the dialogue box, with its string representation (that is, the return value of the toString() method defined on all objects) being shown as the parameter value (not shown here). The user can then press the button in the parameter dialogue box to invoke the add(Object) method. The visualization of Vector changes to show the new item (Figure 8(d)). This, such interaction shows the relationship between structured parameter types in the code and cascaded dialogue boxes in the user interface.

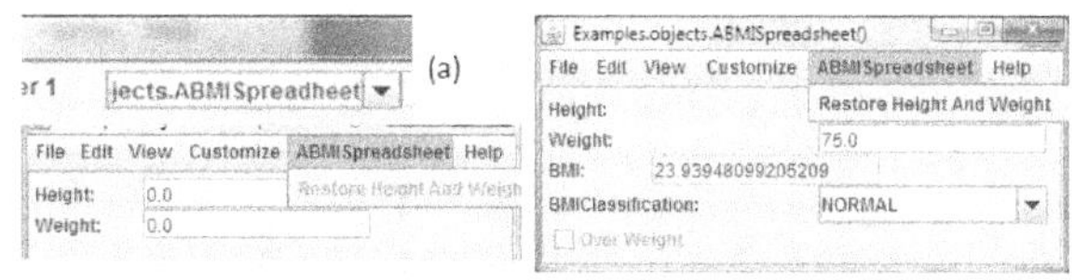

(b) Initial Param Value (c) Edited Param Value

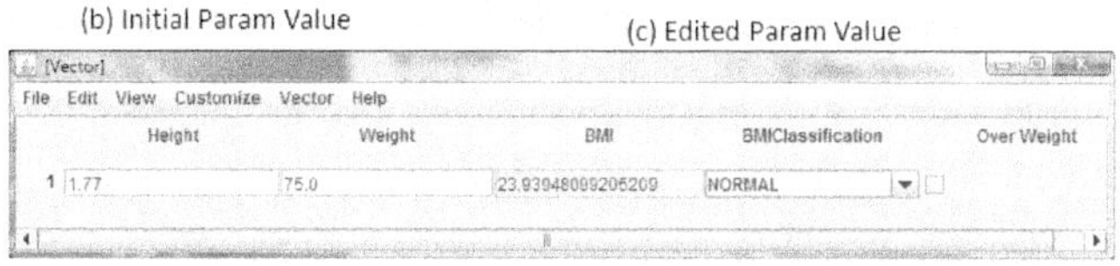

(d) Vector display after Parameter Value Committed and Method Invoked

Figure 8 Entering Structured Parameter Value

5. PRECONDITIONS

Yet another important abstract concept visualized by ObjectEditor is the concept of preconditions. Consider an arbitrary target method whose signature is decomposed as follows:

<AnyType> <M>(<T_1> p_1, <T_2> p_2, …,<T_n> p_n)

A method with the signature:

public boolean pre<M>(<T_1> p_1, <T_2> p_2, … <T_n> p_n)

is considered its precondition method. Thus, the following method:

```
boolean preGetBMI() {return height >= 0 && weight >= 0}
```

is the precondition method of the target method:

```
public double getBMI() {
    assert preGetBMI();
    return weight / (height*height);
}
```

If a target method is a getter for some property P, then ObjectEditor does not display P until its precondition method returns false. If a target method is not a getter or a setter, then it is shown in the method menu ObjectEditor creates for the class of the object. The menu item for the method, however, is not enabled until the corresponding precondition method returns true. It is because of these two rules that the BMI, BMIClassification, and OverWeight properties are not shown when the height or weight are 0 (Figure 8(b)), and the RestoreWeightAndHeight menu item is disabled if the height and weight have their initial values (Figure 8(b)). The impact of preconditions on disabling and enabling of widgets have encouraged our CS 1 and 2 students to use assertions in the manner shown above. Before ObjectEditor, students have disliked putting assertions in code, mainly because they did not see concrete benefit of doing so.

6. GRAPHICS

It is attractive to teach students about (2-D) graphics objects such as Point, Line, and Rectangle for several reasons. First they are familiar with some of these concepts from earlier geometry courses. Second they form excellent examples to show that there might be multiple useful representation of the same real-world object – for example, a rectangle may be represented by two diagonally opposite end points or an end point and a width and height. Third, they form the basis of projects displaying graphics.

To provide the last benefit, ObjectEditor displays a graphics object by the image it represents in a 2-D plane, relying again, on (customizable by the instructor) programming conventions to determine the kind of the graphics object. These conventions are layered on top of the Bean conventions. A class whose name contains the substring Point and defines the X and Y named int properties (using Bean conventions) is recognized as a point type. A type whose name contains the substring "Line"/ "Rectangle"/"Oval"/"Text"/"Image" and defines the X, Y, Width, and Height integer properties is recognized as a line/rectangle/oval/text/image-file type These four properties define the bounding rectangle of the object. The label and image types must, in addition, define a String property giving the text to be used as the label and the name of the file to be used as the image, respectively. All of these types can define several additional optional properties such as Color that determine attributes of the shapes.

Figure 8 shows the code for the type Line and two visual representation of an instance of the type. Both user-interfaces display the geometric shape the object represents. The top user-interface also contains an optional tree window showing a textual representation of the object, which is useful for debugging purposes.

```
public interface Line {
  public int getX();
  public void setX(int newX);
  public int getY();
  public void setY(int newY);
  public int getWidth();
  public void setWidth(int new
  public int getHeight();
  public void setHeight(int new
}
```

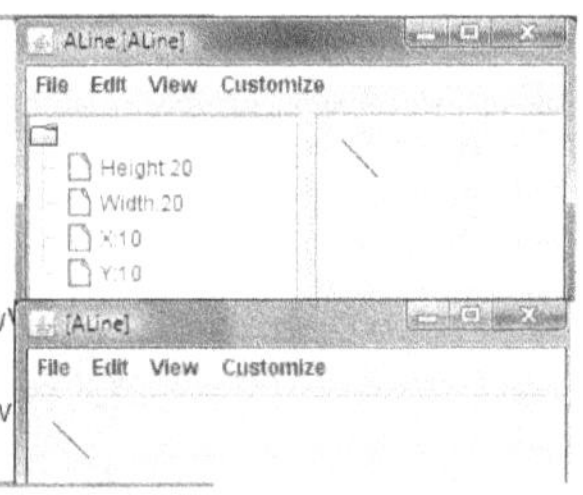

Figure 9 Graphics Object With Two Visualizations

We see above a single graphics object displayed in the graphics window. In general, a visualized object can be decomposed into a tree based on the Bean, sequence, set, and table patterns (we currently do not support arbitrary graphs). All graphics objects in this tree reachable from the top-level object visualized are displayed in the graphics window. In addition to the graphics window, ObjectEditor also creates a tree window to the left of the graphics window (Figure 9) and a main window on top of the graphics window (Figure 11(a)). The tree without the graphics objects is displayed in the main window, and the whole tree displayed in the tree window. ObjectEditor provides user-interface commands and API calls to hide/show these three optional windows.

7. INCREMENTAL COMPOSITION

Developers can incrementally build the tree of desired objects. At each stage in this development, ObjectEditor provides a user-interface to visualize and interact with the part of the tree developed so far. This, in turn, has allowed both CS 1 and 2 students to implement assignments that add up to a large semester project. Figure 10 (a-d) shows some of the stages in a Spreadsheet CS 2 project. First students developed an evaluator of expressions involving only numbers (a). Then this evaluator became a part of an expression list (b), which then became part of an expression matrix (c), which finally became a spreadsheet in which expressions involved both numbers and variables (d). Similarly, Figure 10(e-h) shows some of the stages in a Halloween CS 2 simulation project. An atomic graphic object representing a candy (e), is composed into a sequence of candies and added to a candy container (f), which is composed with a stick avatar representing a candy taker (g), which is then composed with a sequence of houses with candy (h).

8. INCREMENTAL COMPOSITION

Developers can incrementally build the tree of desired objects. At each stage in this development, ObjectEditor provides a user-interface to visualize and interact with the part of the tree developed so far. This, in turn, has allowed both CS 1 and 2 students to implement assignments that add up to a large end-semester project. Figure 10(a-d)shows some of the stages in a Spreadsheet project - First they developed an evaluator of expressions involving only numbers (a). Then this evaluator became a part of an expression list (b), which then became part of an expression matrix (c), which finally became a spreadsheet in which expressions involved both numbers and variables (d). Similarly, Figure 10(e-h) shows some of the stages in a Halloween CS 2 simulation project. An atomic graphic object representing a candy e), is composed into a sequence of candies and added to a candy container(f), which is composes with a stick avatar representing a candy taker(g), which is then composed with a sequence of houses with candies(h).

A project-based approach is particularly appropriate to teach object-oriented programming as the benefits of such programming are more evident in such projects. Our CS 1(2) students typically create projects with twenty (forty) different classes and interfaces. They are able to do create such large projects because they do not have to worry about details of input/output. This approach has also excited students, as many students go beyond the sample project provided by the professor as a guide, as seen by comparing Figures 10(h) and (i).

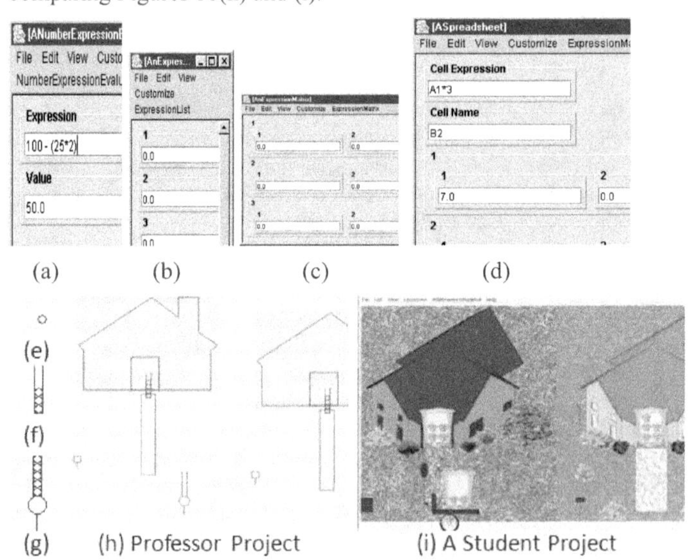

Figure 10 Composing Assignments into Projects

9. TOOLKITS AND Model View Controller

The use of ObjectEditor does not preclude the teaching of toolkits. The tool can work as a set of training wheels that are later removed when students were taught to create their own user-interface classes. The objects visualized by it are essentially models whose views and controllers are provided by it. These models can later be attached, unchanged, to custom views and controllers written using a toolkit. For example, in one of the CS 1 classes, students first created a turtle-graphics model that was automatically manipulated by ObjectEditor (Figure 11(a)) and then created their own view and controller to interact with the unchanged model (Figure 11 (b)). Thus, students concretely see the power of MVC and separation of concerns

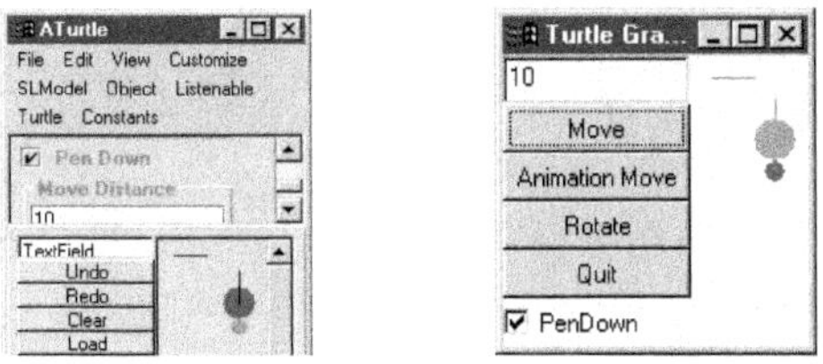

(a) Generated UI (b) Custom UI

Figure 11 Replacing ObjectEditor UI with Custom UI

10. ANIMATION AND THREADS

It is attractive to animate actions on graphics objects, such as a turtle moving to its next position and a candy moving from the container of a house to that of the avatar. Such an animation involves writing a loop of the kind shown in Figure 12.

```
public synchronized void animateMoveX(
   int increment, int steps, int pauseTime) {
    for (int step = 0; step < steps; step++) {
      sleep(pauseTime);
      moveX(increment);
    }
}
```

Figure 12 Asynchronous Animation Loop

The animate method will not achieve the desired effect if ObjectEditor waits for it to complete. For the animation to work, this method must be active concurrently with the paint() method in ObjectEditor, which draws the animating object on the screen. If the two methods were executed serially, one after the other, then the paint method would be executed before or after the animate method is called, when the animating point is always at its resting position. Thus, it would never show any of the positions the object takes while the method is executing

By default, ObjectEditor executes a programmer-defined method as part of the thread that handles events and paints. It forks a new thread for invoking a method if the method does not return a value and the keyword **synchronized** appears in its header, as shown above. Even in a manual implementation of an animating user interface, an animation method should have this keyword to prevent concurrently executing painting and animation methods from stepping on each other's toes as they access shared data structures. Thus, ObjectEditor does not require this keyword to be used in a way that is inconsistent with the semantics of the animation method. CS 2 students write their own threads for animation, and see animation as an application of concurrency. CS 1 students see it as an application of loops.

11. ANNOTATIONS

ObjectEditor allows extensive facilities for customizing the user-interface, which is beyond the scope of this paper, and are not advertised to the students unless they specifically ask for them. ObjectEditor uses annotations to specify values of customizable attributes. To illustrate, one feature many students ask is a way to influence the (a) stacking order of overlapping properties in the graphics window, and (b) order of properties in the main and tree windows. These two orders can be specified by annotating the getter method for the property with the annotation:

@Position(int)

where the parameter gives the position of the property.

Annotations are also used to document or override the kind of data type implemented by an object. For example, a class implementing line conventions can be associated with the annotation:

@StructurePattern(StructurePatternNames.LINE_PATTERN)

to indicate that it implements a Line graphics type. Such an annotation allows ObjectEditor to determine if the class follows the conventions of a Line graphics type, and give errors otherwise, which is useful when students are learning the conventions. Thus, ObjectEditor provides a setting to motivate and explain to them the concept of annotations.

12. SUMMARY

Some of the ideas in ObjectEditor are in other tools. BlueJ and Dr. Java allow command-based invocation of methods, and the Java BeanBuilder allows visualizing and editing of Beans with primitive properties. ObjectEditor goes beyond these tools by supporting interactive invocation of methods and constructors that take arbitrary arguments, visualization of objects representing records, sequences, table and graphics, use of preconditions to disable/enable user-interface elements, and automatic generation of model threads. In the limited space available to us, we have shown that it can change, arguably for the better, lectures and exercises on programming conventions, methods, state, constructors, preconditions, MVC, polymorphism, graphics, structured objects, loops, concurrency, and annotations. It is difficult to objectively evaluate its teaching benefits. The complexity of some of the projects illustrated here is evidence that it helps students improve their understanding of these concepts. This work is the culmination of about ten years of refinement and use of ObjectEditor (by four instructors at our university), and we finally feel confident to advertise its capabilities to the public.

13. ACKNOWLEDGMENTS

This research was funded in part by NSF grants IIS 0712794 and IIS-0810861.

14. REFERENCES

[1] Barnes, D.J. and M. Kölling, *Objects First with Java: A Practical Introduction Using BlueJ*. 2008: Prentice Hall.

[2] Shneiderman, B., *Direct Manipulation: A Step Beyond Programming Languages*. IEEE Computer, Aug 1983.

[3] Dewan, P. and M. Solomon, *An Approach to Support Automatic Generation of User Interfaces*. ACM TOPLAS October 1990.

[4] Nichols, J., et al. Huddle: Automatically Generating Interfaces for Systems of Multiple Connected Appliances. in Proc. UIST, 2006.

[5] Engelson, V., D. Fritzon, and P. Fritzon. Automatic Generation of User Interfaces from Data Structure Specification and Object-Oriented Models. in ECOOP '96.

CodeWave: A Real-Time, Collaborative IDE for Enhanced Learning in Computer Science

Jason Vandeventer
University of North Carolina Wilmington
601 South College Road
Wilmington, NC 28403
jmv8649@uncw.edu

Benjamin Barbour
University of North Carolina Wilmington
601 South College Road
Wilmington, NC 28403
beb1512@uncw.edu

ABSTRACT

Computer science instructors often rely on the final version of a program for assessment and feedback. This ignores the process the student used to arrive at the final program. When the instructor has the ability to observe real-time development progress of each student, they are better equipped to provide appropriate and timely feedback. CodeWave, a software program developed at the University of North Carolina Wilmington looks to alleviate these issues.

CodeWave is a real-time, collaborative Integrated Development Environment with traditional features such as syntax highlighting and non-traditional features such as integrated messaging and logged playback. CodeWave enhances productivity by integrating many common tools students and instructors use during the programming process. Communication is effortless and allows a user to specify a point in the code as a link in the message body. Log playback provides the ability to review the entire development process. In this paper, we describe the software program we developed to enhance learning in computer science programming courses.

Categories and Subject Descriptors

H.5.3 [**Information Interfaces and Presentation**]: Group and Organization Interfaces; K.3.1 [**Computers and Education**]: Computer Uses in Education; D.2 [**Software Engineering**]: Miscellaneous

General Terms

Human Factors

Keywords

Collaboration, Distance Learning, IDE, Asynchronous Interaction

Permission to make digital or hard copies of all or part of this work for personal or classroom use is granted without fee provided that copies are not made or distributed for profit or commercial advantage and that copies bear this notice and the full citation on the first page. To copy otherwise, to republish, to post on servers or to redistribute to lists, requires prior specific permission and/or a fee.
SIGCSE'12, February 29–March 3, 2012, Raleigh, North Carolina, USA.
Copyright 2012 ACM 978-1-4503-1098-7/12/02 ...$10.00.

1. INTRODUCTION

Computer science programming courses are challenging for a variety of reasons, both for students and instructors. Students learning to program for the first time are often not aware of all of the tools and resources available to them. Students rely on instructor notes, textbooks, and on-line resources. When they face an issue and cannot resolve it using those resources, they require assistance from a knowledgeable source. This can be the instructor, but at many universities instructors of introductory programming courses often have teaching assistants (TA). TAs are available to assist students, grade assignments, and develop coursework [15]. If a student needs assistance outside the office hours of their instructor or TA, they must either wait or use a communication medium such as email. Email is disconnected, slow, and for larger assignments can be very cumbersome.

Instructors often find grading programming assignments challenging. They cannot review the process the student used when approaching the problem, how they handled debugging, or whether they received unauthorized assistance. They are forced to evaluate the students' performance solely on their final product. This is not beneficial to the development of the student [19]. Programming is a process, not a final product. If an instructor cannot assess the student's programming process, they cannot offer appropriate assistance to enable improvement. If a student is only being graded on their final product, they can lose motivation when they fall behind schedule. Many students may even choose to forgo turning in the assignment, since they will not benefit from incomplete work [11]. A tool that would allow an instructor to view the progress of a student, both in real-time and after completion, could ease the challenging aspect of grading and increase the development of the student's entire programming process.

Students use a variety of tools when developing code. These tools range from Integrated Development Environments (IDE) to messaging services. A common issue students face is using disconnected tools for development and communication. Students can program in an IDE, communicate and share files via email or instant messaging, use screen-sharing software, and coordinate multiple versions of the same file across several machines. Using multiple programs and coordinating member responsibilities can reduce productivity. Progress can become confusing to follow due to this disconnected process.

Section 2 explains the motivation behind the project. Section 3 describes current issues in computer science programming courses. Section 4 covers the software program the author's have developed as a solution to these issues. Section 5 describes future work and Section 6 concludes with a discussion of related works.

2. MOTIVATION

The motivation of CodeWave is to offer a real-time, collaborative IDE for students and instructors. The IDE integrates the traditional workspace, which includes syntax highlighting and other common features, with non-traditional features such as messaging, instant messaging, and log playback. This integration provides students with the majority of the tools they need to complete an assignment. It offers the instructor the ability to observe individual student progress, review group workload statistics, and reduces the time required to assist students. Communication is effortless and allows a user to specify a point in the code as a link in the message body. Log playback provides the ability to review the entire development process.

3. DESCRIPTION OF PROBLEM

Most computer science education courses use Integrated Development Environments (IDEs) as tools for programming. Students use these tools to assist them in writing code. Many IDEs, such as Microsoft's Visual Studio, Apple's Xcode, and Eclipse, provide syntax highlighting, debugging tools, and code completion [7], among other features. The problem with the use of IDEs in an educational environment is that, by default, IDEs typically do not take into account a collaborative approach [4]. They lack many tools which would make collaboration, either by instructor and students, or between group members much more efficient.

3.1 Individual Assignments

On an individual assignment, a student works by themselves to finish a programming project and turns in the final program to the instructor. The instructor cannot see the process the student used to arrive at the final product and can only deduce the process they used to get there. If there are complex errors, the instructor may not be able to determine where the errors occur. The instructor also has no way of confirming that the work submitted is that solely of the student. In the worst case scenario, a student who cannot get their program to work may just forgo turning it in. This is problematic because many students may be very close to the correct answer, and in need of just a little more assistance. However, they would end up receive no credit or reduced credit and may become discouraged for future projects [11].

3.2 Group Assignments

In group assignments, a student works with other students to complete a programming assignment. The two main difficulties students face with this type of project are communicating and meeting issues and work distribution issues [4]. In both secondary school and university settings these communication issues are affected by other class schedules, jobs, extra-circular activities, and a lack of communication skills. Group programming is typically complex from a logistics standpoint and as a result, there can be a lack of quality and an uneven work distribution. Many instructors base grades in a group project on the quality of the final product and a peer assessment system [17, 18, 5]. This is unfair to students who were required to do the majority of the work to compensate for the uneven work distribution or risk a poor grade for an incomplete project [14].

3.3 Distance Learning

Distance Learning is a growing area in education and this is especially true in computer science, given the nature of the field [12]. Unfortunately, many students are finding distance learning in computer science programming courses difficult due to the lack of assistance from instructors and an inability to properly communicate with other group members. Classroom-based courses allow students to ask specific questions and show their code to an instructor. They also have the ability to visit a teaching assistant or the instructor during office hours. Distance learning students do not have this ability [3]. In group projects, it is very possible that students in a distance learning class will never meet their group members in person. As with the group assignment, distance learning success can be hampered by communication and meeting difficulties.

3.4 Tools for Educators

There are very few computer science specific tools for educators that facilitate interactive, collaborative learning. Instructors cannot typically see how a student arrived at their final program and need a tool that allows them to view the final project and the history of development. When an instructor is attempting to assist a student outside of their class or office hours, the primary method of communication is typically email. Email communication requires a student to attach their program to the message. Multiple exchanges between the instructor and student can become very difficult to follow. A single software program that allows the instructor to simultaneously review code and communicate with students would be very beneficial to both the instructor and student [13]. It would reduce the time the instructor requires to assist the student in a timely manner.

3.5 Plagiarism

Plagiarism in computer programming takes many forms and is difficult to define. Formal languages do not afford the same level of creative license as natural languages. Most would agree that presenting someone else's work as a student's own is clear plagiarism but beyond that, specifically in early education, many instructors may disagree. Collusion, reverse engineering, translation, and code generation, may be acceptable in an introductory course [8]. Some instructors may decide that no external help is allowed and any use of code not originally authored by the student is unacceptable. Other instructors may encourage the exploitation of any available resources to complete a project.

One of the most difficult tasks is to determine if a student received unauthorized assistance and to what extent. In group projects, it can be difficult to determine code ownership and should any member plagiarize code, accountability and responsibility falls on the entire group. However, if students are given the ability to cite the sources of their information and are tracked in their usage of that information, the lines between acceptable collusion and other potential forms of plagiarism can become less blurry. If an instructor has the ability to observe the development process, rather than just the final product, plagiarism concerns could be greatly reduced by offering an extra dimension for detection [20].

3.6 Source Control

Current source control programs, such as CVS, Subversion, and Git, allow more than one individual access to the same file. Their purpose is to manage access and concurrent versions software development projects throughout the development lifecycle. These systems however were not developed with the needs of an educational program in mind [16, 21]. They allow access to a file, but do not allow individuals to work asynchronously on the same document. Problems in efficiency and productivity arise when using source control systems in relatively short-term group projects. A real-time collaborative IDE where individuals can work on the same file at the same time, with enhanced locking features, would allow for a more efficient system that could greatly enhance productivity.

4. CODEWAVE

CodeWave is a language independent, real-time collaborative Integrated Development Environment designed to improve learning of software programming. CodeWave offers integrated syntax highlighting for a large variety of popular languages. Its primary goal is to provide instructors with the tools they need to properly assess a student's progress in all areas of the software development process, not just the final product. Other goals include offering better assistance to students by making communication with instructors and other students easier and more efficient, as well as offering mechanisms for tracking development progress.

CodeWave was developed at the University of North Carolina Wilmington as an answer to the challenges faced by students learning to program code. It was written in C# and is based on AvalonEdit, a component of the open source IDE project SharpDevelop. It is composed of two parts, a server that manages security and communication, and a traditional IDE client.

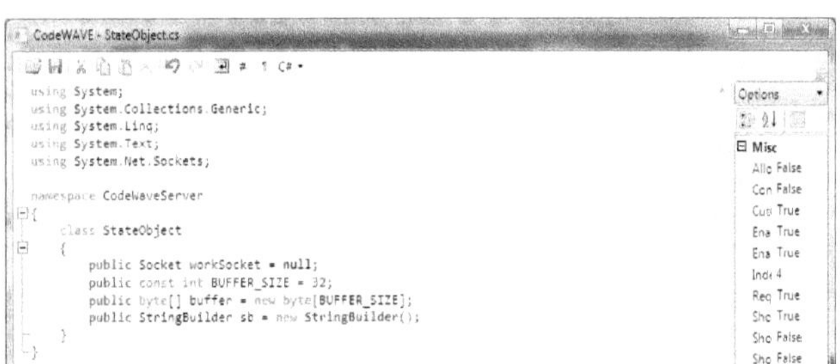

Figure 1: Early Screenshot of the IDE

4.1 Permissions and Organization

CodeWave uses a permission system for files on the server. When a new file is created by an instructor, the instructor is the "owner". An owner has read/write/delete privileges. They can then specify read, write, or read/write permissions for other users. When a student creates a file, the instructor and the student are both listed as an "owner". Either can then specify access privileges for other students. If a student is in more than one class using the software, they are required to choose the instructor for the related class from a drop down menu.

Each file has an associated XML data file that contains information about the organization of that file such as code ownership/permissions, annotations, and edit log. Sections of code that have been edited by a specific user are "owned" by that user.

4.2 Real-time editing

The benefits of real-time editing in a group environment are numerous. It is common practice for students in group projects to divide responsibilities and program separately, and then combine each of their sections. CodeWave's real-time editing feature allows users to see where other students are working and the changes being made. This reduces the time required for a project and increases productivity [13].

4.3 Recording/Playback

By generating a recording of each keystroke, instructors and students may playback a chronological replay of the development process at any speed. The playback feature uses a scrubber bar mechanism, much like those found in popular video players. CodeWave's scrubber controls the playback of logged changes. The user dictates the speed of the log playback and the playback is read-only. By adding a logging feature to students' deliverables, an instructor can quickly answer the questions of whether or not a student is commenting during development or waiting until afterwards. They also have the ability to observe whether or not the student is catching errors and debugging them properly. Related to the subject of plagiarism, having a record of each keystroke will make it easier to see if a student used copy and paste from an outside source.

With the information provided by the playback system, an instructor can better tailor their methods to the needs of the students. For example, one of the most valuable skills a programmer can learn is the ability to debug theirs or others' code. If an instructor simply receives the final working copy, there is no way to measure how many mistakes the student made along the way or how they went about solving those problems. Knowing the point in the development process where the student went wrong may help to quickly assess areas the student may need to focus on. If the instructor is noticing that many students are producing similar errors, they can review the topic in class.

Recordings may also be distributed as packaged lectures and include annotations created during programming. This allows students to see the process the instructor used which has been shown to significantly increase learning potential and student motivation [1]. Another advantage to this is the instructor can purposely make errors and debug them. With traditional methods, such as slide presentations or screen capture software, this is very difficult and tedious to do. In CodeWave, this is a very simple process for the instructor, the result is very beneficial to the student, and unlike many other IDEs, CodeWave does not require a third-party tool for this feature.

Recordings can also be used by group members to see in detail the work done by their group members. Playback is available at any point and is especially useful when coming back to a project after changes have been made by others. Since the color-specific name tag denotes the user, it is easy for a user to see what was changed and by whom. This facilitates better communication when speaking to group members. A user can specify a location and line number in the playback.

4.4 Instructor Feedback

"Providing feedback is the most common method that teachers typically use to encourage and motivate students." [22].

Integrated instructor feedback is one of the biggest advantages of CodeWave over other IDEs. Instructors have the ability to set up program skeletons, record programming lectures, offer support via messaging and instant messaging, work real-time, side-by-side with students, view a student's programming assignment from beginning to end using the playback feature, see group workload statistics, and grade an assignment based on more than just the final product. Group workload statistics include the percentage of code contributed per user, the amount of time spent editing, and code ownership distribution. CodeWave integrates all of these features into one IDE and helps an instructor offer more assistance in less time. This productivity translates directly into success for students, as they can receive timely support that will help them achieve the goals set for them by the instructor [10].

4.5 Annotations

CodeWave allows students and instructors to annotate code. Annotations in text are colored to match the owner, based off of the owner's unique name tag color. Instructors have the ability to annotate sections of the code with an explanation for a grade. With this advanced annotation system, it is very easy to document the code itself, as well as communicate about the code in a non-message-related medium. For instance, a student can leave a note for a group mate about a section of code they are both working on in the code itself, rather than an email message referencing the code.

4.6 Code Locking

To make sure that two users are not working on the same line at the same time, a simple locking mechanism has been implemented. The program gives priority to the user who was working on the line first, unless they have been inactive for 2 minutes. Just like block commenting is a feature of many IDEs, "block locking" is a feature of CodeWave. This will allow a user to work on a specific section of code and restrict access to others. There are many situations in which this may be useful. To ensure that a code block doesn't remain inaccessible to users, after 20 minutes of inactivity, a block of locked code will be released. Also, when the user logs out the block of locked code will automatically be released.

4.7 Messaging and Notification Center

Codewave provides direct integration of messaging and instant messaging system, as well as a notification center. Users have the ability to send messages to one another without leaving the development environment. One of the main advantages of this is the ability to reference a specific line in the code with a link. Being able to send a message in the software program simplifies the communication process by eliminating the difficulties of using personal email accounts for communications on programming projects. It also helps save time by not requiring a user to use a separate application for communication. The benefits of instant messaging are similar and have the added benefit of instantaneous support or communication. For instance, an instructor or a teaching assistant can hold office hours from any location and be available to help via instant message. When given a link to a specific line in a file, with one click they can look at the code and assist the student. As described in the background section, communication difficulties is one of the main issues facing group work. An integrated service specific to the context is one of the best ways to help fix this communication issue. Instant messaging availability settings can be modified in order to limit distractions.

CodeWave's notification center informs a user of new messages and new files they have permission to access. It also informs them of changes to their files since their last login.

4.8 Source Control

Traditional source control systems operate with a disconnected check-in/check-out system. They require several steps, either with third-party utilities or command line applications, to create a project, import skeleton code, check-in/out a project, update and commit that project, and correct any errors along the way [9]. These skills are important to learn as a future team member. In the introductory stages of learning, however, they may complicate the process.

CodeWave on the other hand is a connection-based source versioning system. Rather than downloading a copy of a file and merging it back to a server, all files are stored and manipulated directly on the server and require a constant connection to perform updates. Versioning is maintained at the keystroke resolution via the log and playback system. It is possible at any time to roll back to any point in the history of the document. To accomplish this efficiently, CodeWave employs a custom TCP/IP sockets-based communication protocol that seamlessly translates asynchronous transmissions to synchronous document updates.

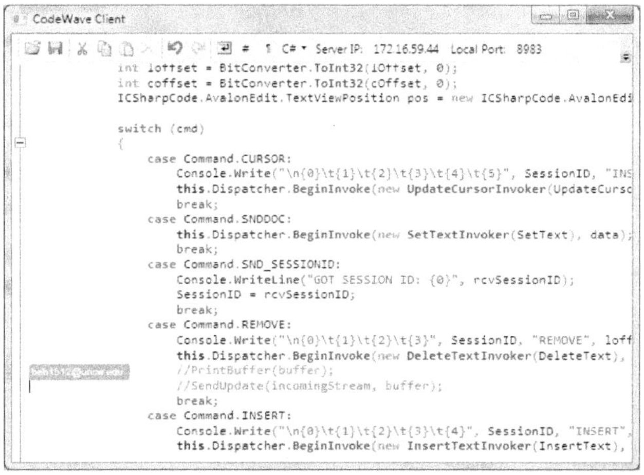

Figure 2: Screenshot of IDE with User Name Tag

4.9 Distance Learning

Built in collaboration, annotation, and logging provide solutions to many of the problems facing students enrolled in distance education courses. It maintains the ability to conduct connected instruction through real-time collaboration and disconnected support through messaging and annotations. Group projects, often omitted from distance learning curriculum due to the difficulty in connecting students together, are supported by the same instructor-student collaboration features.

5. FUTURE WORK

The software program was initially developed during a software engineering course in the Computer Science department at the University of North Carolina Wilmington. Due to time constraints, not all of the features listed in this paper were implemented. The next step is to develop "CodeWave 2.0", a program that will contain all of the features described in this paper. Once it has been developed, the authors would like to have it used on a test-basis by an introductory programming course and by a secondary level programming course. The feedback from first-time programmers, those familiar with programming, and the instructor of the course will go a long way in either confirming our belief that this program enhances learning in computer science programming courses or it will highlight areas of improvement. It is the author's opinion that we will receive a little of both.

6. RELATED WORKS

CodeWave is based on functions demonstrated in Google's "Google Wave" technology in which users can communicate in real-time. The system is designed to facilitate open and immediate discussion blending the best of email, instant messaging, and collaboration. It will allow users to modify and mark files in an organized manner [4]. It is not designed to work with structured documents such as coding environments. The technology is however, highly conducive to use in the software development world.

In [20], an anti-plagiarism plug-in for Eclipse is described that tracks the process of individual software development over time as a method to improve detection of plagiarism. [2] describes another plug-in for Eclipse, Ripple, that enables pair programming through instant messaging, synchronized views, and session logging. It is specific to the Java language and only supports the pair programming paradigm of one editor and one viewer. A custom IDE for novice programmers, Gild, supporting collaboration is described in [21] in which code sharing through CVS, coordination, and communication are integrated features. Communication supports asynchronous and synchronous as well as messages anchored in the document [6].

7. REFERENCES

[1] J. Bennedsen and M. E. Caspersen. Revealing the programming process. *SIGCSE Bull.*, 37:186–190, February 2005.

[2] K. E. Boyer, A. A. Dwight, R. T. Fondren, M. A. Vouk, and J. C. Lester. A development environment for distributed synchronous collaborative programming. *SIGCSE Bull.*, 40:158–162, June 2008.

[3] S. Carr. Online psychology instruction is effective but not satisfying, study finds. *Chronicle of Higher Education*, March 2000.

[4] L.-T. Cheng, C. R. de Souza, S. Hupfer, J. Patterson, and S. Ross. Building collaboration into ides. *Queue*, 1:40–50, December 2003.

[5] D. Chinn. Peer assessment in the algorithms course. *SIGCSE Bull.*, 37:69–73, June 2005.

[6] E. F. Churchill, J. Trevor, S. Bly, L. Nelson, and D. Cubranic. Anchored conversations: chatting in the context of a document. In *Proceedings of the SIGCHI conference on Human factors in computing systems*, CHI '00, pages 454–461, New York, NY, USA, 2000. ACM.

[7] P. J. Denning. Acm president's letter: smart editors. *Commun. ACM*, 24:491–493, August 1981.

[8] J. P. Gibson. Software reuse and plagiarism: a code of practice. *SIGCSE Bull.*, 41:55–59, July 2009.

[9] L. Glassy. Using version control to observe student software development processes. *J. Comput. Small Coll.*, 21:99–106, February 2006.

[10] M. Heo. A learning and assessment tool for web-based distributed education. In *Proceedings of the 4th conference on Information technology curriculum*, CITC4 '03, pages 151–154, New York, NY, USA, 2003. ACM.

[11] T. Jenkins. The motivation of students of programming. *SIGCSE Bull.*, 33:53–56, June 2001.

[12] J. Kleinman and E. B. Entin. Comparison of in-class and distance-learning students' performance and attitudes in an introductory computer science course. *J. Comput. Small Coll.*, 17:206–219, May 2002.

[13] J. T. Langton, T. J. Hickey, and R. Alterman. Integrating tools and resources: a case study in building educational groupware for collaborative programming. *J. Comput. Small Coll.*, 19:140–153, May 2004.

[14] T. Lorenzen, J. Santore, D. Glassman, and J. Baltikauskas. No slacker on team programming projects. *SIGCSE Bull.*, 39:117–118, December 2007.

[15] J. Peckham, L. DiPippo, J. Reynolds, J. Paris, P. Monte, and P. Constantinidis. A first course in computer science: the discipline is more than programming. *J. Comput. Small Coll.*, 15:220–227, April 2000.

[16] K. L. Reid and G. V. Wilson. Learning by doing: introducing version control as a way to manage student assignments. *SIGCSE Bull.*, 37:272–276, February 2005.

[17] J. Sitthiworachart and M. Joy. Effective peer assessment for learning computer programming. *SIGCSE Bull.*, 36:122–126, June 2004.

[18] H. H. Smith, III and D. L. Smarkusky. Competency matrices for peer assessment of individuals in team projects. In *Proceedings of the 6th conference on Information technology education*, SIGITE '05, pages 155–162, New York, NY, USA, 2005. ACM.

[19] M. Ulloa. Teaching and learning computer programming: a survey of student problems, teaching methods, and automated instructional tools. *SIGCSE Bull.*, 12:48–64, July 1980.

[20] P. Vamplew and J. Dermoudy. An anti-plagiarism editor for software development courses. In *Proceedings of the 7th Australasian conference on Computing education - Volume 42*, ACE '05, pages 83–90, Darlinghurst, Australia, Australia, 2005. Australian Computer Society, Inc.

[21] D. Čubranić and M. A. D. Storey. Collaboration support for novice team programming. In *Proceedings of the 2005 international ACM SIGGROUP conference on Supporting group work*, GROUP '05, pages 136–139, New York, NY, USA, 2005. ACM.

[22] H.-T. Yeh. The use of instructor's feedback and grading in enhancing students' participation in asynchronous online discussion. In *Proceedings of the Fifth IEEE International Conference on Advanced Learning Technologies*, ICALT '05, pages 837–839, Washington, DC, USA, 2005. IEEE Computer Society.

A Stratified View of Programming Language Parallelism for Undergraduate CS Education

Richard Brown (Moderator)
St. Olaf College
rab@stolaf.edu

Joel C. Adams
Calvin College
adams@calvin.edu

David P. Bunde
Knox College
bunde@knox.edu

Jens Mache
Lewis & Clark College
jmache@lclark.edu

Elizabeth Shoop
Macalester College
shoop@macalester.edu

SUMMARY

It is no longer news that undergraduates in computer science need to learn more about parallelism. CS graduates who enter the computing workforce without substantial knowledge of parallel computing do so at their peril, since all new computers feature multi-core processors, with the number of cores expected to increase exponentially over time [3]. Also, our work and home lives have grown dependent on web services fueled by distributed parallel computing on cloud platforms.

Students learn parallel computing well through hands-on exercises and projects using programming languages with support for parallelism [4]. The range of options for parallel programming is truly staggering, involving hundreds of languages. How can a CS instructor make informed choices among all the options?

This panel provides a guided introduction to parallelism in programming languages and their potential for undergraduate CS education, organized into four progressive categories:

- low-level libraries and features that are close to the hardware and operating system;
- higher-level libraries and features, providing a layer of abstraction or management;
- programming languages that incorporate parallelism; and
- frameworks for productive parallel programming.

The four panelists, who direct NSF-funded projects on languages and instructional materials for teaching parallelism and/or led a recent international study on adding parallelism to undergraduate CS curricula [4], will present representative examples in their categories, then present viewpoints on how those categories relate to coursework, curriculum, and trends in parallelism.

A wiki accompanies this panel, with references on relevant language resources and curricular materials (hopper.macalester.edu/groups/sigcse2012languageparallelism/).

Categories and Subject Descriptors

D.3.2 [**Programming Languages**]: Language classifications – *Concurrent, distributed, and parallel languages.*

General Terms

Languages, Design, Performance.

Keywords

Programming languages, parallel computing, parallelism, education.

Copyright is held by the author/owner(s).
SIGCSE'12, February 29–March 3, 2012, Raleigh, North Carolina, USA.
ACM 978-1-4503-1098-7/12/02.

1. RICHARD BROWN (MODERATOR)

Dick Brown co-directs (with panelist Shoop) the CSinParallel project (csinparallel.org) for producing and sharing modular materials for incrementally adding parallelism to existing undergraduate computer science courses [6]. He has directed the creation of parallel platform resources, including the MistRider virtual cluster [5] and the WebMapReduce interface to Hadoop map-reduce computing [9]. A longtime director of CS at St. Olaf, he serves as an executive board member of the EAPF (eapf.org).

Brown will briefly review the goals of the session (3-4 min), introduce each panelist (10 min each), and moderate discussion.

2. JENS MACHE

Jens Mache is Professor of Computer Science at Lewis & Clark College. He has taught parallelism to undergraduates since 2001. He and panelist Bunde direct an NSF TUES project about teaching parallel computing with activity-based laboratories.

Statement: One way to introduce concurrency is through "low-level" multi-threaded programming (in C/C++, Java, or Python). These programs include explicit instructions for parallelism: each core executes an explicitly assigned task, all cores synchronize, they execute another task, and so on. Even though threads are unlikely to work in most CS 1 courses, they fit well into OS, networking, and system programming types of courses. Moreover, CUDA and OpenCL enable the use of graphics processing units (GPUs) for general purpose parallel computing. Unlike current CPUs, many GPUs already have hundreds of cores. All of these approaches give students the ability to map tasks to threads as well as more explicitly manage memory, potentially allowing high performance and helping students learn about the hardware.

I will present an overview, as well as selected examples from teaching materials.

3. JOEL ADAMS

Joel Adams is Professor and Chair of the Department of Computer Science at Calvin College, and has been teaching his students about concurrency and parallelism for 20 years. To provide platforms for his students to experience the benefits of distributed parallelism, he has designed and built a variety of Beowulf clusters, ranging from the personal cluster *Microwulf* [1] to the terascale interdisciplinary science cluster *Dahl* [2].

Statement: A relatively easy way to introduce parallelism into the computer science curriculum is through high-level libraries that add parallel capabilities to a sequential language. OpenMP and

MPI are prominent examples, among many others. Such libraries provide abstraction mechanisms that simplify process/thread creation, communication, management, synchronization, and destruction, freeing a student (and software engineer) to focus on parallel algorithm development, debugging, and tuning. Some make it quite easy to add parallelism to legacy applications. Many of these libraries can also be used with different languages (e.g., C, C++, Fortran, Python), allowing a typical software engineer to incorporate parallelism into her projects without having to learn a new language.

I will present an overview of libraries that support shared-memory parallelism and distributed-memory parallelism; and will present selected examples from teaching materials as illustrations.

4. DAVID BUNDE

David Bunde is Assistant Professor of Computer Science at Knox College. He has taught concurrency and parallelism in a variety of courses. He and panelist Mache have written about the need for higher-level approaches in parallel education [7] and now direct an NSF TUES project developing this approach.

Statement: One can also teach parallelism and concurrency by using languages with high-level constructs to manage them. As with a library-based approach, these languages seek to let the programmer focus on algorithms, with some low-level details being handled by the compiler or run-time system. In fact, many parallel languages are close relatives of traditional sequential languages to simplify adoption. The language-based and library-based approaches differ in that a parallel language can add new keywords and constructs rather than needing to fit its form entirely within the structure of the base language.

There is a tremendous variety of parallel programming languages to select from. Many are created by extending a base language with mechanisms for lightweight task creation; Charm++ and Cilk extend C++, Habanero Java extends Java, and Scala is a Java-like but functionally-flavored language. Other functional language options are Erlang, Haskell, and occam. Some languages rely more heavily on the compiler by including high-level operations that it parallelizes; examples include loops and reductions in Chapel and the use of math symbols in Fortress.

I will present a brief overview of these options, exploring a couple in greater depth and describing our experiences at Knox. With so many language choices, the goal is to be a "commercial" so attendees become aware of interesting options, with more detailed information available on the wiki.

5. ELIZABETH SHOOP

Libby Shoop co-directs (with moderator Brown) the CSinParallel project (csinparallel.org) [6]. She teaches several courses in the CS curriculum, ranging from the introductory level to computer systems organization, software development, and parallel and distributed systems. She is developing a parallel computing course structured according to OPL patterns (parlab.eecs.berkeley.edu/wiki/patterns/patterns).

Statement: The technologies of data-intensive scalable computing on cloud platforms provide an ever-expanding array of web services that have become staples in the computing consumer market. Scalable map-reduce frameworks as described in [8] lie behind most of the web services we have come to expect. The open-source Hadoop framework (hadoop.apache.org), Yahoo-initiated software that makes it possible for tiny startups with good ideas to launch new web services on rented cloud computing resources, is equally available as a teaching platform for undergraduate CS students. We have been teaching these technologies to students as early as the introductory course [9].

Map-reduce is not the only pattern of parallel computing that might be encapsulated in a convenient framework, although it is the first to have such great success. I will present several other patterns that might be encapsulated in frameworks, and ask the community to consider whether interfaces to such frameworks might become available for languages of the future, or even be integrated into them.

6. ACKNOWLEDGMENTS

Brown and Shoop are supported by NSF DUE-0941962/0942190. Bunde and Mache are supported by NSF DUE-1044299/1044932.

7. REFERENCES

[1] J. Adams, T. Brom. Microwulf: A Beowulf Cluster For Every Desk. *Proc. 39th ACM Technical Symp. Computer Science Education* (SIGCSE 2008), pp. 121-125.

[2] J. Adams, K. Hoogeboom, and J. Walz, A Cluster for CS Education in the Multicore Era, *Proc. 42nd ACM Technical Symp. Computer Science Education* (SIGCSE 2011), pp. 27-31.

[3] Asanovic, K., Bodik, R. et al. A view of the parallel computing landscape. *CACM.* 52, 10 (2009), pp. 56-67.

[4] Brown, R., Shoop, E., Adams, J., et al. Strategies for Preparing Computer Science Students for the Multicore World. *Proc. 15th Annual Conf. Innovation and Technology in Computer Science Education (ITiCSE 2010) Working Group Reports*, pp. 97-115.

[5] Brown, R.A. Hadoop at home: large-scale computing at a small college. *Proc. 40th ACM Technical Symp. Computer Science Education* (SIGCSE 2009), pp. 106-110.

[6] Brown, R., Shoop, E. Modules in community: Injecting more parallelism into computer science curricula. *Proc. 42nd ACM Technical Symp. Computer Science Education* (SIGCSE 2011), pp. 447-452.

[7] D.P. Bunde and J. Mache. Teaching concurrency beyond HPC. Position paper presented at *1st Workshop on Curricula in Concurrency and Parallelism*, OOPSLA, 2009.

[8] Dean, J. and Ghemawat, S. MapReduce: Simplified Data Processing on Large Clusters. *Operating System Design and Implementation* (OSDI 2004), pp. 137-150.

[9] Garrity, P., Yates, T., Brown, R., Shoop, E. WebMapReduce: An accessible and adaptable tool for teaching map-reduce computing. *Proc. 42nd ACM Technical Symp. Computer Science Education* (SIGCSE 2011), pp. 183-188.

Demystifying Computing with Magic

Daniel D. Garcia
University of California, Berkeley
777 Soda Hall
Berkeley, CA 94720-1776
+1 510-642-9595
ddgarcia@cs.berkeley.edu

David Ginat
Tel-Aviv University
Sharet Building; Ramat Aviv
Tel-Aviv, Israel
+972 3-640-8151
ginat@post.tau.ac.il

SUMMARY

One man's "magic" is another man's engineering.
– Robert A. Heinlein

One of the most important tasks an introductory computing student must do is to form a mental model of how the computer works. This could be as specific as understanding the read-evaluate-print loop of an interpreter, or as general as believing that the computer works predictably and deterministically. However, some have fuzzy mental models, or worse, sincerely believe that the computer works unpredictably, "by magic" [2]. We seek to demystify computing for these students using analogy, by showing them something that even magic itself isn't really mystical, it is just computation.

Magic is one of the most colorful examples of "unplugged" (i.e., without-computer, active learning) activities. It adds a unique facet in that it holds a *hidden secret* that an audience can be challenged to unfold. Once solved, students are often enthusiastic to perform the magic in front of others. In this session, we will share a variety of magic tricks whose answer is grounded in computer science: modulo arithmetic, permutations, algorithms, binary encoding, probability, etc. For each trick, we will have an interactive discussion of its underlying computing fundamentals, and tips for successful showmanship. Audience participation will be critical, for helping us perform the magic, discussing the solution, and contributing other magic tricks.

Categories and Subject Descriptors
K.3.2 [**Computer and Information Science Education**]: Computer Science Education

General Terms
Algorithms, Design, Human Factors, Theory

Keywords
Computational thinking, magic, card tricks, unplugged activities

1. OBJECTIVE
Magic is a lot of fun. Yet, it can be more than fun – it can be used to illustrate and teach scientific and mathematical notions, including those of computer science [1, 3, 4, 5]. Our objective in this special session is to offer an approach to embed magic in teaching as an unplugged exercise. Magic may be employed for illustrating particular notions, by challenging the students to figure out the idea behind the trick, then elaborating on these notions and relating them to the studied material. Students may also be encouraged to practice the magic, and even perform in front of the class. In our primary experience, students (majors and non-majors) are enthusiastic to take part. Such an activity may provide valuable assimilation of notions in an original and motivating way.

Copyright is held by the author/owner(s).
SIGCSE'12, February 29–March 3, 2012, Raleigh, North Carolina, USA.
ACM 978-1-4503-1098-7/12/02.

2. OUTLINE
The session will be an interactive seminar. It will include motivation, illustrations, audience participation, and conclusion. The general structure will be as follows.

- **Rationale.** The relevance of magic, as a special unplugged activity, will be described, and presented. An emphasis will be put on magic's baffling impact on one hand, and the enthusiastic characteristic to discover the secret – on the other.
- **Aspects and illustrations.** We will display several magic tricks. The presentations will sometimes involve volunteers from the audience. The secrets behind the presented magic will be related to various CS principles, e.g., binary representation, invariants, modulo arithmetic, permutation, algorithms, information theory, and more. Suggestions will be offered on how one may elaborate on the underlying CS notions following a magic presentation.
- **Audience participation.** The audience will participate in three ways. Volunteers may take part in some presentations. The audience will be challenged to discover the secrets. Audience participants may offer further, enriching, unplugged ideas for magic, including those presented, and will be invited to perform them, if they wish.
- **Suggestions for educators.** Pedagogical lessons of ways to embed magic will be displayed and discussed. We will share our experience with students, who like to perform (sometimes more than once) in front of their friends. This yields active assimilation of studied principles.

Here are but five of the magic tricks we will perform, and the youngest group that could solve the tricks on their own with no hints. We will have more ready to present, if time permits.

2.1 The 11th Variation
The magician places 21 cards in a grid of 3 columns by 7 rows, and asks the volunteer to choose a card but only reveal which column it is in. The dealer picks up all the cards (by columns, with the chosen column in the middle) and re-creates the same grid by laying the cards down by rows. The process (indicate column, pick up the cards, re-create grid) is repeated twice more.

The dealer then picks up the cards, holds them behind her back, and (without looking) produces the chosen card.

Youngest group: Jr. High School (~12 years old)

Lesson: Permutations and algorithms.

2.2 Beatles Encoder

While the magician's assistant is off-stage, the audience flips 4 coins randomly and places them on a table, left-to-right. The audience then chooses a random Beatle (John, Paul, Ringo, or George). The magician turns over *exactly one* of the coins and leaves the room. The assistant returns and names the Beatle.

Youngest group: High School (~18 years old)

Lesson: Encoding and decoding data (i.e., information theory).

2.3 Magic Hats

Three magicians stand on the stage, and people from the audience will put one hat on each of the three. Before putting the hats on, the audience will write a number (1, 2 or 3) on each hat. Thus, the three numbers on the hats may be, for example: 3 3 3, or 3 2 2, or 1 2 1, or 1 2 3. Then, each of the three magicians will look at the hats of the two others, and write on a paper a guess of his hat's number. No signs are allowed between the magicians, and they will all write their guesses on paper at the same time. The written guesses will be shown to the audience, and at least one of them will always be right!

Youngest group: University (~20 years old)

Lesson: Basic properties of integer arithmetic.

2.4 Guess the Value

The magician takes the deck and makes piles of cards face down with varied numbers of cards in each pile. She is then blindfolded. The audience is asked to choose any three piles and return the remaining cards to the magician, who holds them behind her back. She asks the audience to turn the top cards from any two of the piles over, and say the value of these cards out loud. She then confidently declares the value of the remaining top card.

Youngest group: Jr. High School (~12 years old)

Lesson: Simple algebra and algorithms.

2.5 Josephus Flavius Circle Game

The audience stands in a circle. The magician scans the group and stands behind one particular person. Starting with the tallest person in the room and working clockwise, every other person is asked to sit down until there is one person left ... which is exactly where the magician is standing.

Youngest group: High School (~18 years old)

Lesson: Induction and recursion.

2.6 Guess My Age

The magician hands an audience member six pieces of paper with 32 (seemingly random) numbers written on each, and tells the volunteer to return the cards that have their birthday age on them. The magician quickly scans the cards and correctly states the age.

Youngest group: Grade School (~10 years old)

Lesson: Binary numbers.

3. EXPECTATIONS

The intended audience for the special session is the broad community of computing educators, especially those who enjoy magic but have not used it in their classes or during occasions of unplugged computing outreach. They will hear (and hopefully, contribute) some classic tricks, the computing fundamentals behind them, tips for showmanship, and how to direct a follow-up discussion.

4. SUITABILITY

Our presentation is interactive and engaging, with active audience participation. Anyone in attendance who knows magic tricks based on computing fundamentals is encouraged to contribute. A special session affords and encourages this unique format with the most audience involvement.

5. REFERENCES

[1] Computer Science Unplugged. *Error Detection.* http://csunplugged.org/error-detection

[2] Clancy, M. Misconceptions and attitudes that interfere with learning to program. In *Computer Science Education Research*, s. Fincher and M. Petre, eds. Taylor and Francis Group, London, 2004, 85–100.

[3] Curzon, P. and McOwan, P. W. 2008. Engaging with computer science through magic shows. In *Proceedings of the 13th Annual Conference on innovation and Technology in Computer Science Education* (Madrid, Spain, June 30 - July 02, 2008). ITiCSE '08. ACM, New York, NY, 179-183. doi.acm.org/10.1145/1384271.1384320

[4] Ginat, D., Garcia, D., and Gasarch, W. 2002. Aha! an illuminating perspective. In *Proceedings of the 33rd SIGCSE Technical Symposium on Computer Science Education* (Cincinnati, Kentucky, February 27 - March 03, 2002). SIGCSE '02. ACM, New York, NY, 1-2. doi.acm.org/10.1145/563340.563342

[5] The Magic of Computer Science website. www.cs4fn.org/magic/

Community-Based Projects for Computing Majors: Opportunities, Challenges and Best Practices

Jeffrey A. Stone (Moderator)
Pennsylvania State University
Schuylkill Haven, PA 17972 USA
stonej@psu.edu

Bonnie MacKellar
St. John's University
Queens, NY 11439
mackellb@stjohns.edu

Elinor M. Madigan
Pennsylvania State University
Schuylkill Haven, PA 17972 USA
emm17@psu.edu

Janice L. Pearce
Berea College
Berea, KY 40404
jan_pearce@berea.edu

OVERVIEW

The use of community-based projects has been recognized as having pedagogical and experiential value for computing majors (e.g. [3], [4], [5], [6]). Community-based projects can be valuable learning experiences for computing majors as well as for faculty and community partners. However, these types of projects do present challenges for faculty and should be aligned with desired course outcomes. This panel will discuss the use of community-based projects from multiple perspectives. The expectation is that the panel will serve as a forum for the participants to share the opportunities, challenges, pedagogical motivations, and best practices obtained from prior experience. Exemplar projects will be highlighted. The panel also hopes the session motivates the audience to share their own experiences and sparks the interest of those faculty members who may have no prior experience with community-based projects.

Categories and Subject Descriptors

K.3.2 **[Computers and Education]**: Computer and Information Science Education – Computer Science Education.

General Terms

Human Factors.

Keywords

Community Projects, Experiential Learning, Service Learning.

1. JEFFREY A. STONE

Community-based projects provide a rich set of opportunities for computing students to exercise the non-technical "soft" skills they will need in their post-graduation careers. The use of community-based clients with multiple stakeholders and ill-structured problems provide students a chance to hone their communication, collaboration, client relations, and project management skills. In terms of technical skills, these types of projects can be tailored to different course learning objectives. System design, systems development, requirements gathering, interface design, documentation writing, and testing of implemented systems are just a few possibilities afforded by community-based projects. For faculty, community-based projects provide an opportunity to cultivate university-community relationships and to bring positive attention to campus computing programs.

Successful community-based projects can benefit both students and the community partners. At our campus, many of the community-based projects undertaken by students would not otherwise be feasible due to limited technical and economic resources. Consequently, community partners benefit from the resources, knowledge, and solutions the students provide. For students, these types of projects can lead to extended involvement through internships or post-graduate employment. Perhaps most importantly, community-based projects provide an opportunity for students to see the actual value and importance of the IT solutions they create. Allowing students to work on multiple community-based projects – such as digital histories, Web site design, or emergency planning management systems – provides a firm grounding in the challenges and obstacles faced in real-world IT projects. This experience also allows students to see the wider social impact of their work.

In this panel session I plan to discuss some of the opportunities provided by community-based projects, both to the students and faculty as well as to the community partners themselves. Specific projects used at our campus will be highlighted.

2. ELINOR M. MADIGAN

When choosing community partners, faculty need to keep their student's abilities in the forefront of their decisions. There will be a 'training' period for the students, where the faculty will teach students how to interact with their community partner. Faculty must also train community partners. These partners must be reminded that students are not professionals. The projects are a learning opportunity and, as a result, community partner expectations concerning the scope of work need to be realistic. Managing the expectations of both populations (students and community) can be very challenging.

Communication between students and their community partner needs to be monitored. Faculty presence 'in the loop' is a critical success factor for any project. Faculty need to be aware of – and provide contingency plans for – risk factors such as lack of

Copyright is held by the author/owner(s).
SIGCSE'12, February 29–March 3, 2012, Raleigh, North Carolina, USA.
ACM 978-1-4503-1098-7/12/02.

response from a community partner, students starting projects but not being able to finish and expectations not being met. The most successful projects are ones where the community partner is patient, communicates well and can scale back requirements when needed. In this panel I will discuss these and other challenges related to the use of community-based projects.

3. BONNIE MACKELLAR

The Humanitarian Free and Open Source (HFOSS) program is an initiative that was started by three schools in Connecticut – Trinity College, Wesleyan University, and Connecticut College. Its mission is to involve faculty and students at a wide range of schools in open source projects that solve problems faced by humanitarian organizations. My school, St John's University, was able to participate in this project as a chapter school this year. Through funding and support from HFOSS, as well as a mentor from Google Crisis Response, we involved students on an Android project aimed at volunteer firefighter companies and other first responders. During the 10 weeks that they worked on it, the students produced a working prototype that is being used as a demo for real firefighters. In addition, the students participated in a Random Hacks of Kindness hackathon where volunteer software developers gather to help prototype technology solutions to humanitarian problems. We plan to continue work on this project during the upcoming year and are also planning to involve other humanitarian organizations, such as the local Ronald McDonald House.

From our perspective as a chapter school, the HFOSS initiative works well as a model for involving faculty and students in projects for non-profit organizations. HFOSS provides a great deal of support, both formally through its workshops and symposia, and informally through extensive mentoring. In addition, St John's University, which is strongly committed to service learning, maintains the Vincentian Institute for Social Justice (VISA), which serves as a liaison with non-profit, community organizations for faculty who want to incorporate service projects into their courses. We are working with them to find other community organizations that have software projects that need to be done.

Many faculty members are afraid to take on collaborative projects with community organizations because these efforts are notoriously time-intensive, or because they do not know how to find community organizations. I believe that one best practice for encouraging faculty/student collaboration with community organizations is through organized initiatives which support and nurture faculty as they incorporate service learning into their courses. In this panel session, I plan to discuss how our involvement with HFOSS, a helpful mentor from Google, and support from our VISA office jumpstarted us into collaborative software development with community organizations.

4. JANICE L. PEARCE

For the fourth consecutive year, Berea College has been selected for the President's Higher Education Community Service Honor Roll for engaging its students, faculty and staff in meaningful service that achieves measurable results in the community [1]. The CS curriculum at Berea College incorporates community-based projects at several points in our major curriculum. These CS projects range in size from hour-long outreach events at the public library to course-long service-learning projects in which students design and implement a web site, database, or software package for a community partner.

In our CS0-level service-learning website design course, students work in two-student teams with a community partner organization to create or enhance a community partner website. This allows us both to introduce the notions of pair-programming early and also to help students develop skills in communicating directly with a client. In another CS0-level course we offer an overview of robotics. This CS0-level course requires students to take robots on a "roadshow" to children in the wider community. Our Database Systems course is an upper-level service-learning course in which students work in teams of four to design and build a database for a community partner organization. Finally, in our Senior Projects capstone course, a significant number of students have opted to develop a software project for a community partner.

In each case, our primary motivation for the addition of these various community-based projects has been to add educational value to the CS course, while our secondary motivations include engaging students more deeply, helping students to see the social relevance of the discipline of CS, and helping students develop skill in teamwork and interacting with a client. These community-based projects are almost universally viewed positively by students with some students even indicating that the service component was the most valuable part of their college career. Through reflection and assessment, we find that students gain deeper understanding of course content as well as the importance of civic engagement. Over time and with the help and resources of our Berea's Center for Excellence in Learning through Service (CELTS) office, we have improved our techniques for incorporating and evaluating reflection and the quality of the student-partner interactions into our course grading structures, which has additionally served to help students to appreciate how we value of these components of the courses. In addition, one surprising benefit we have realized from the community-based outreach in CS0 is an increase in the number of students continuing from the CS0-level course into CS1. [2]

5. REFERENCES

[1] Corporation for National & Community Service. 2011 *President's Higher Education Community Service Honor Roll.* http://www.learnandserve.gov/about/programs/higher_ed_honorroll.asp.

[2] Pearce, J. 2011. Requiring outreach from a CS0-level robotics course. *J. Comput. Sci. Coll.* 26, 5 (May 2011), 205-212.

[3] Sanderson, P. 2003. Where's (the) computer science in service-learning? *J. Comput. Small Coll. 19*, (October 2003), 83-89.

[4] Scorce, R. 2010. Perspectives concerning the utilization of service learning projects for a computer science course. *J. Comput. Small Coll.* 25, (January 2010), 75-81.

[5] Stone, J. & Madigan, E. 2011. Experiences with community-based projects for computing majors. *J. Comput. Sci. Coll.* 26, 6 (June 2011), 64-70.

[6] Tan, J. & Phillips, J. 2005. Incorporating service learning into computer science courses. *J. Comput. Small Coll.* 20, (April 2005), 57-62.

The Five Year Evolution of a Game Programming Course

Gillian Smith and Anne Sullivan
Center for Games and Playable Media
University of California, Santa Cruz
Santa Cruz, CA 95064, USA
{gsmith, anne}@soe.ucsc.edu

ABSTRACT

This paper presents lessons learned from five years of teaching a game design and programming outreach course. This class is taught over the course of a month to high school students participating in the California Summer School for Mathematics and Science (COSMOS) at the University of California, Santa Cruz. Over these five years we have changed everything in the course, from the overall project structure to the programming language used in the class. In this paper we discuss our successes and failures, and offer recommendations to instructors offering similar courses.

Categories and Subject Descriptors

K.3.2 [**Computers and Education**]: Computer and Information Science Education – *Computer science education*

General Terms

Design, Human Factors.

Keywords

Game development, outreach, high school, CS education.

1. INTRODUCTION

Computer games resonate strongly with high school students, with 99% of American teenage boys and 94% of American teenage girls playing video games [7]. Game design is a highly interdisciplinary field, incorporating advanced computer science concepts such as artificial intelligence, computer graphics, and HCI as well as skills from art and design. This paper describes the evolution of a game programming course taught in the California State Summer School for Mathematics and Science (COSMOS) program at the University of California, Santa Cruz. COSMOS is a summer enrichment program for high school students who are hoping to pursue STEM fields when they attend college. In this program, we teach students how to create their own games during an intensive, month-long course. The authors have been involved in teaching the course since its inception in 2007.

COSMOS is split into 9 different clusters based on topic. Each cluster is made up of 18-20 students who are between 9th and 12th grades. Our cluster, *Design of Fun: From Concept to Code*, focuses on teaching computer game development and programming skills. Over the last five years, we have taught 88 students: 40 women and 48 men. These students have a mixture of programming experience, ranging from never having used a computer to having completed AP Computer Science. However, all the students are typically skilled in mathematics and science, and are highly motivated to learn how to create their own games. Some students consider themselves "core" gamers and invest multiple hours per day playing AAA titles (i.e. big budget, high quality games), others play mostly casual online games, and some students express an interest in game design but do not play many games themselves. The goal of the course is to instill in students core CS1 programming skills and a desire to further study computer science and/or game design in university.

Our course focuses equally on teaching fundamental programming skills and providing students with a foundation for how to play, discuss, and analyze games critically. These goals are symbiotic; games have previously been shown as a great motivational force for learning computer science [5][10]. The iterative nature of game design motivates students to reflect on the code they've written, and the procedural thinking and concrete instantiation of abstract ideas that is required when programming feeds back into the iterative game design loop. We have previously described the structure of the game design portion of the class and our recommendations for structuring a game design course [15]; this paper focuses entirely on the programming portion of the course, called *Technologies of Fun*.

The focus on creating a project in a short time period, as well as the variety in experiences and backgrounds of our students provides a unique set of challenges and opportunities for us as instructors. We have tried a number of different teaching methods, learning a great deal about how to effectively teach game programming to a high school audience. We will look at these throughout the paper, presenting what we have learned over the five years this program has been offered. We will first explain changes made in the design of the course itself: the programming languages used, programming instruction methods, and some of the techniques we have used to effectively teach to a mixed-skill classroom. We will then discuss the project portion of the course: dealing with student expectations, assignment format, and prototyping. Finally, we present our recommendations for other instructors involved in similar efforts to teach both game design and programming.

2. COURSE DESCRIPTION

The programming portion of the game design cluster, *Technologies of Fun* is an interactive, projects-based course in which the students program their own small games. The course is designed to teach students the skills required to design and develop their own game over the course of the month-long class. We assume that students entering the course will have no prior programming knowledge; therefore, the goal is to give them a fast-paced course in fundamental programming skills needed for game programming. *Technologies* also includes some short lectures that discuss more advanced concepts, such as 3D graphics and artificial intelligence, most of which will not be used in the students' games. The aim of this is to get students excited about computer science and interested in learning more when they get to college.

Permission to make digital or hard copies of all or part of this work for personal or classroom use is granted without fee provided that copies are not made or distributed for profit or commercial advantage and that copies bear this notice and the full citation on the first page. To copy otherwise, or republish, to post on servers or to redistribute to lists, requires prior specific permission and/or a fee.
SIGCSE'12, February 29–March 3, 2012, Raleigh, North Carolina, USA.
Copyright 2012 ACM 978-1-4503-1098-7/12/02...$10.00.

2.1 Class Structure

Technologies of Fun is taught in a three-hour block, four days per week for the four weeks of the program. The remaining time in the week is taken up with the game design course [15], and a transferable skills course that teaches research and presentation skills. We took an activities-based approach when teaching programming. Students had access to laptops during lectures, and the first hour of lecture was structured to introduce a new programming concept with brief breaks during which students could experiment with the new material. The other two hours were spent with students working on the projects while the instructor and teaching assistants (TAs) supervise and answer any questions.

Students are encouraged to share their progress with the class by presenting their work at various milestones, or showing how they have solved a particularly challenging problem. They could also share code with each other through a cluster wiki[1], which served as a home for lecture materials and assignment descriptions.

In the last two weeks of the program, there is very little time devoted to lecturing, as students need to work full time on their projects. Lectures become more impromptu: they are only held when it becomes clear that a number of students are struggling with the same general problem, such as adding music to their game, or implementing side-scrolling animation.

2.2 Project Structure

As a requirement for completing the COSMOS program, students must present a project to their teachers and classmates at their home institution. To accommodate this, the majority of our program is focused on enabling the students to produce a complete game. The games are created entirely by the students using programming and design concepts that they have learned in class. All of the games that students create are 2D games with original graphics. Examples of student-produced games include a puzzle platformer where the player shifts between two different worlds; a space-themed, column-based, tower defense game; a game where the player uses the Wiimote to control a net for catching ghosts in a graveyard; and a puzzle game where the player must shape the path of sushi around various obstacles from a refrigerator to a hungry boy.

The project is structured as a series of deliverable assignments. The first assignment is a game pitch in which the student describes a general setup of the game, a narrative hook and a brief overview of the game interaction. Game pitches are used to assign teams, and the teams decide which of their game pitch or combination of pitches they will pursue. The next assignment is for the team to create a design document which discusses their proposed project in much more detail. The students were then required to take the core mechanic (main type of interaction with the game) and create a paper prototype to test this mechanic. A paper prototype is a paper-based representation of the game, and is created to quickly test concepts. Once the core mechanic has been tested and adapted through the paper prototype, the students are then allowed to create a computational prototype. From there the students expand and create their fully realized game.

3. COURSE EVOLUTION

In the last five years we have taught three different programming languages and game engines and changed our teaching methodology. Each year we have reduced the amount of time we are lecturing, and increased the amount of time the students participate in activities, giving even more activity time closer to the end of the course when they focus on their projects. Lectures are also more interactive, with the instructor programming live in front of the students, so they can follow the process and see how small code changes lead to different results.

3.1 Programming Language Choice

We have used three different programming languages in the five years of the program: Python with the Pygame library[2] in 2007 and 2008, Java with the Greenfoot [6] framework in 2009, and finally Processing [12] in 2010 and 2011. We intend to continue using Processing in this course for the foreseeable future. There were many different factors that played into our decision for which programming language to use, including ease of learning, applicability to future computer science courses, and engine support. We also had to bear in mind that most students in the class would have never programmed before.

Visual programming environments such as Scratch [13], Alice [2], and GameMaker[3] are used by many programs that are similar to ours [3][1][18]. There are a few different reasons that we have chosen to use a traditional language instead. Firstly, one of the goals of COSMOS is to give students an experience similar to what they will have in a university, where traditional programming languages are usually used in introductory courses. We also felt that many of the well-established visual environments are targeted at audiences younger than high school students; Scratch and Alice in particular are have audiences as young as elementary school students [17]. Finally, we wanted students to learn programming skills that could be easily applied to domains outside of game design or interactive graphics.

3.1.1 Python and Pygame

Python was initially chosen due to Pygame's support for simple 2D games and recent reports of Python's suitability for introductory programming [11]. Its interactive shell is particularly useful for teaching simple programming concepts such as mathematical operators, variables, and lists. The original instructor for the course also built a game engine that sat atop Pygame, which added support for sprites, animated sprites, collision detection, Bluetooth-connected gamepads and Wiimotes, and particle systems. For the two years that we used this setup, we found that students with no programming experience could make their own animated scenes in the first week of class. However, by the beginning of week three, most students were struggling with their projects. Many of them started their games writing code without a complete understanding of how it worked; as their understanding caught up with them, they would feel overwhelmed by the poor design decisions they had made earlier in the project.

We can expect this to happen for introductory students using any programming language; however, Python had some disadvantages that exacerbated the problem. While it's a fairly simple language to learn, Python is overly supportive of the programmer making mistakes. For example, we frequently found students who had defined functions inside of while loops and then received confusing scoping errors, or who didn't understand that identifiers are case sensitive, and so they were assigning values into different variables than they were reading later. It became clear that we

---

[1] http://www.sokath.com/cosmos2011/doku.php

[2] http://www.pygame.org/

[3] http://www.yoyogames.com/gamemaker

needed to use a language that provides more structure and the safety of static typing and explicit variable declaration: the compiler can provide much more rapid feedback than periodic support from TAs.

3.1.2 *Java and Greenfoot*

In 2009, in response to the problems we faced with Python, we decided to use Java as our programming language, supported by the Greenfoot framework for making games. Those students who came into class with programming experience had typically learned Java in their high school computer science classes, and we expected that any students who continued studying computer science after the program would be most likely to learn Java in their introductory courses. Greenfoot offered a number of helpful features for students: ease of drawing graphics, mouse and keyboard callbacks, and collision detection are all built-in. There was an observed improvement in the quality of code the students were writing in Java when compared to Python, as the compiler could catch more errors and give helpful messages pointing to where the error occurred.

However, there were a number of problems introduced by the use of Greenfoot as well. Many students were confused by heavy Java syntax such as import statements, class declarations, and especially the type-casting required for collision detection. Greenfoot also forced us to teach object-oriented programming and the concept of inheritance from the first day of instruction. This proved too abstract and difficult a concept, especially for those students who had limited experience with using a computer.

A benefit of using Python that we lost moving to Greenfoot was that students could write simple procedural code for drawing an image on the screen with only a few lines of code, and could immediately see the results of their work. To achieve the same effect in Greenfoot required editing two different files: the *world* that the object would live in, and the *actor* itself. Students also felt confused over the graphical interface accompanying the scenario; it proved helpful for testing how objects interacted with each other, but students were confused over when they could use that interface versus when they needed to programmatically specify the location of different objects.

3.1.3 *Processing*

These lessons led to our decision to use Processing starting in 2010. Processing is a Java-based language and environment that is intended for creating interactive art and rapid prototyping. It was clear from 2009 that a Java-like language is an appropriate choice for the course, but we needed a simpler point of entry. Processing makes it easy to draw shapes and pictures to the screen and have a user interact with them: it takes a single line of code to draw a rectangle to the screen, and two lines to make that rectangle be a different color. The availability of many different small art projects written in Processing[4] also encouraged students to experiment; for the first time in teaching the course, we allowed students to take code from other sources (with appropriate attribution) and use it in their games. We only required that they be able to loosely explain how it worked. This kept students excited during class, which motivated them to learn not only from their instructors but also from each other. We saw many instances of one student learning how to make a certain effect in their program and then that effect appearing in different variations across other students' programs.

[4] http://www.openprocessing.org

Processing also has the benefit of allowing a gentle introduction to object-oriented programming, just as Python provided. Students who were not prepared to understand more complicated programming concepts could opt-out and use purely procedural programming; those who were ready to use objects (often those who had already taken a computer science course) could do so with no problems.

3.2 Programming Instruction

This section discusses the various approaches we've used, from unstructured programming activities to highly structured mandatory assignments. Our main goal has been to balance the students' desires to be creative with a structure that ensures everyone learns the core programming concepts.

3.2.1 *Freeform Programming*

In 2007 and 2008, we took a freeform approach to the programming course. We did not give any assignments; rather, the first week was spent teaching core programming concepts which students could apply however they wished, followed by three weeks of individual and small group instruction as needed, while students worked on their games. In the first week, many students chose to make small animations as introductory scenes for their final games; others began haphazardly constructing pieces of a game, such as movement logic and simple collisions. All of the students had code that they had written on the first day of class in their final games.

This approach to teaching introductory programming has a number of disadvantages, many of which seem obvious in retrospect. Perhaps the most problematic result was that students were stuck with any mistakes or poor design decisions made early on in the project. Students were reluctant to throw away their work and start afresh, even when encouraged to do so by instructors, due to concern that they would not be able to re-create their efforts.

However, there was also one major advantage to this lack of structure: students were continually motivated to learn, due in large part to the creative control they had over their projects [14]. For example, instead of learning about control flow in the abstract, they learned about it because they needed to solve a particular problem they were having in their project.

3.2.2 *Mandatory Mini-Game Assignment*

In 2009, we decided that the disadvantages of a freeform project far outweighed the advantages, and added a programming activity at the beginning of the class, which students were required to complete before they could start working on their game projects.

This small project was the same for each student: a simple game where the player controls a hippopotamus moving around a maze collecting all the flowers before leaving. The game taught students almost all the major concepts they would need to be able to build their own games: drawing, keyboard input, collision detection with maze walls and flowers, variables to store information about player state, functions and classes. This was fairly successful: by the time students were making their own games, they could look back on their old code to see patterns for how to solve their current problems.

However, the students were not nearly as excited or motivated by the example game as they had been in previous years. Creativity and ownership over their work was clearly very important to them.

3.2.3 Creativity in Small Assignments

In 2010 and 2011 we combined our two prior strategies by instituting a required individual project in the first week, but allowing students to choose what that project was within certain constraints: it had to involve keyboard or mouse input, at least three objects had to exist on screen and those objects must be connected in some way, at least one of the objects was required to move around the screen, and the objects must change color over time. Students generally enjoyed working on their "three points in space" assignment, but still learned all of the major techniques they would need for making their games.

We also introduced a second assignment to combat a common problem we had seen in prior classes—students did not comment their code, and struggled to integrate different sections of code with each other. The second assignment was to modify somebody else's three points assignment in a meaningful way, e.g. adding a new object that interacted with existing ones, changing the colors, or changing how objects moved around the world. The students were not allowed to communicate with each other for this assignment; they were required to declare the change they wanted to the instructors, then read their classmate's code and make the modification themselves. This assignment was extremely effective in teaching the value of commenting code, and seemed to improve each student's understanding of programming concepts by forcing them to read and understand code not in their own style.

Only after completing these two individual assignments were students allowed to work together on their games. While this meant that students started work on their game projects half a week later than in prior iterations of the course, we feel that their improved programming skills made up for the loss of time.

3.3 Handling a mixed-skill classroom

COSMOS accepts high school students from all over California. Our youngest students have been only 13 years old, and our oldest have been 18 years old. This diversity in students naturally leads to a mixed-skill classroom in terms of both programming and mathematics ability, although we do require that all students have completed high school Algebra II. Some students, particularly from the less affluent areas of the state, have no access to computer science courses and limited access to computers. Others have already taken an Advanced Placement (AP) Computer Science course and are looking for further challenges.

Over the five years of our program, we have used a number of different techniques to teach to a mixed-skill classroom. A successful approach has been to create additional content for advanced students to work through while others are learning the basics of programming. The students are encouraged to quietly work through the activities on these handouts while the rest of the class is listening to the lecture, and ask their questions during the group's programming time. Activities have included drawing with splines, the basics of 3D graphics, and programming an artificial intelligence to play Tic-Tac-Toe against a human.

In 2011, we introduced an activity called "Make It Fun", based on a similar activity suggested by Steve Swink [16]. We provided students with source code for a simple maze game with procedurally generated levels. The player controls a ship and navigates the ship around the maze with the arrow keys, collecting coins. This activity was designed to appeal to students at three different skill levels. Those who were just getting started learning programming could read the source code, but choose only to change the values for variables controlling the appearance of the maze, the number of walls and coins in the maze, the size of the ship, and how quickly the ship moves. Intermediate students could choose to modify behavioral aspects of the code, such as changing the control scheme for the ship or adding code for what happens when the player wins or loses. More advanced students could delve into the procedural level generator, which required an understanding of three-dimensional arrays, loops, and random generation. The students greatly enjoyed this assignment as they were in control of making their first game, and the ability to immediately see changes to a game based on even the smallest code changes was a useful learning exercise.

4. PROJECT EVOLUTION

We have also made numerous changes to the design of the class project, to meet the goal of having students spend more time in the design phase before committing their ideas to code, and to ensure that every student learns how to program. To accomplish this, we added multiple prototyping steps to the project and instituted rules about when students were allowed to focus on the aesthetic aspects of the project such as art and music.

4.1 Calibrating Student Expectations

Each year we have become more emphatic about setting up the expectations of the students. Many of the students expect to create AAA-like games using some of the industry-standard 3D game engines. Given time constraints and the amount of learning required, it is more likely that they will instead create a far simpler, unpolished 2D game. Unless expectations are calibrated early, there is a certain amount of frustration and growing disappointment that happens as the student progresses through the course.

In 2007, our first year, we mentioned our expectations as we assigned the game project in the second week of the course. In 2011, we told students at the first day orientation and showed examples of previous games on the first day of class to allow them time to realign their expectations before they were required to create a design document. We found that the game designs showed more creativity and innovation in game mechanics and puzzles instead of being focused on realistic graphics or physics. Keeping the students focused on a 2D game also discouraged re-implementation of their favorite games, which was a common issue in the first and second years of the program.

4.2 Physical Prototypes

One of the major changes we made to the class is a move from the traditional waterfall method to an iterative design process [19]. A key concept in the iterative design process is the use of prototypes to be able to playtest the game design at many stages during game creation. We first introduced a computational prototype (discussed in Section 3.4), which was quite successful. Building on this success, in 2010 we added a requirement to build a playable physical prototype to the project.

When a prototype was not required, students would begin coding directly from their design documents. This would often lead to a situation where the students would be unable to make changes to their code in the last week as the code had evolved in a way that made it quite brittle. Building a physical prototype requires the students to think through mechanics of the game instead of designing on the fly while they were programming. By requiring a physical prototype even before coding, it meant that the students designed the code in a much more stable fashion as they reflected on concrete play experiences. The design would still change as they coded, but they were approaching the code in a much more structured way.

Physical prototypes have a couple of benefits. Firstly, they are simple to build which allows rapid iteration and refinement. When the students did not build prototypes, they would work through a design idea from start to finish without being able to try out their game mechanics until the game was mostly complete. This left very little time and flexibility for changes if the mechanics did not work out in practice. With the prototypes, students were able to try out and modify their game mechanics multiple times before they ever started coding.

Physical prototyping also allowed the students to make design progress while still learning the programming language. Each prototype was played by other students in the class, who gave feedback on parts that they found confusing or difficult. Most students found that they needed to make changes to their game design to address the issues the other students had, and all students made changes purely based on their experience designing the prototype.

4.3 Computational Prototype

Our students often have difficulty with understanding where to start with making their games. In the first two years of COSMOS we addressed the problem by asking students to list all of the tasks required for them to complete their games, and then assign a priority to each of these tasks. Instructional staff would then go through these lists with the students, adding further details and commenting on the stated priorities. However, even with instructor assistance, the list was always incomplete, unwieldy, and rarely referred to after its creation.

In 2009, we adopted Fullerton et al.'s recommendation of digitally prototyping early in the design process [4] by instituting a computational prototype assignment. We required students to identify a core mechanic of their game and prototype it. They were required to complete this prototype and show it to instructors, and then create a list of remaining tasks on the game. We found that by requiring students to make a concrete implementation of their core game design, teams were able to better communicate their ideas to each other and all team members were on the same page throughout the rest of the project. This reduced group tension due to creative differences.

There were also a number of cases where building the prototype changed the direction of the game. For example, one game made in 2010 began in a written concept as a rogue-like dungeon crawler where the character had a limited field of view. After computationally prototyping their movement mechanics, the group decided to change their game to better explore this single mechanic by turning it into a game of exploration and collection rather than adding a number of other mechanics to create a turn-based dungeon crawler with fog of war. Although the redesigned game was much simpler, it allowed the students the opportunity to fully explore this mechanic through many different level designs, rather than shallow exploration of many different mechanics.

4.4 Ensuring equal division of work

One of the goals of our cluster is to have students create a game that they can be proud of and feel that they own; to this end, we found it important to ensure that all of the art and music in their games were made by themselves or their peers. We cautioned against using freely available art from internet sources and advised that even if they felt their art was poor, their games would look better with consistent amateur art versus inconsistent professional art. In the first three years, this had the unfortunate side effect that many teams began worrying about art assets for their games entirely too early in the design process–frequently before core game concepts had even been determined. It also led to a seemingly natural split in teams, where one member would become responsible for art and another responsible for code. Additionally, while mixed-gender teams constituted only about 20% of the overall teams every year, in each mixed-gender team the female student was always the artist and the male student was always the programmer. This situation was extremely concerning; in a computer science focused course, half of our students weren't practicing any programming, and women, a highly under-represented group in computer science [9], were being left out of programming activities.

In 2010 we instituted a requirement that no work be done on the art or music before the final five days of class. While this decision met with resistance at first, students quickly embraced the notion of using programmer art -- rectangles and circles -- and instead exploring their game designs more deeply. The "no art" requirement, combined with assigning teams such that students in teams had equivalent skill levels, was extremely effective in addressing this problem. With no clear division of labor, the inexperienced students were naturally inclined to participate in pair programming, which has been shown to improve results in introductory students [8], and more advanced students learned how to efficiently divide programming tasks. It also meant that each student had continuous input over the evolution of their game, improving their sense of ownership over the final product. In 2011, we relaxed this requirement and allowed students to create art and music earlier in the course, but only during their homework time. This allowed students to make incremental progress on the art for their game and experiment with different animation techniques while also requiring all students to be involved in programming.

5. DISCUSSION

Based on our experiences developing this course, we have drawn up a set of concrete recommendations for similar game design programs to follow:

A programming language should be chosen that minimizes programmer errors and maximizes creative potential. We found the most success when students used a language that can catch the majority of their programming errors at compile-time. The language should also support ease of creative experimentation. For example, a clear benefit we saw in Processing was how easy it was to get started with drawing shapes to the screen and having those shapes move; this framework meant that students could learn how to program through experimentation, such as changing the color and movement patterns of shapes. Later, this led to an ability to focus on testing out different game mechanics, thus maximizing their creative potential.

An iterative approach to game design allows students to build better games more efficiently. Although prototyping is a time-consuming process, our experience has shown that it is worth requiring prototyping stages early in the students' design process; prototyping not only helps to refine the game design, it also ensures that students are communicating their ideas effectively and that everyone in the group understands what they are making.

Design activities and assignments to have multiple entry points to support learning in students at multiple skill-levels. The "make it fun" activity described in Section 2.3 was hugely successful in teaching programming concepts to all students because it had multiple entry points, from editing variable values to changing complex behavior. Similarly, the three-points assignment is successful because it allows every student the opportunity to work at their own pace; beginning students can complete simple versions of the assignments while more advanced students can explore their creativity further. Giving students creative control over their assignments motivates them to learn more. For example, instead of being taught about if statements in the abstract, students typically ask the instructor how they can make a shape turn around when it hits the edge of the screen.

5.1 Future Plans

Technologies of Fun suffers from a strict time limit: four weeks of classes, even at 3 hours/day, is an extremely short period in which to teach programming skills and mentor students creating their games. This time limitation stops us from making some desired changes to the course, such as requiring students to make multiple computational prototypes that stand separate from their main game code. However, we would like to experiment with requiring two separate, smaller game projects as opposed to a single large project. The majority of the code for the game is written in the middle two weeks of the course—the beginning is devoted largely to teaching game programming, and the end is devoted to polishing games and presenting them to their peers. Also, much of the programming effort in the latter half of those two weeks is in fixing bugs introduced by naïve design choices made in the first few days. By creating two games, students would have the opportunity to learn from their mistakes in the first game and apply those lessons to a second game.

This paper has presented our lessons learned from five years of iteration designing and teaching a month-long intensive game programming course. As the program has matured, we believe it has become much stronger, with more innovative games produced by more prepared students. We hope that the lessons presented here will help other instructors in designing their own outreach programs and courses that use game design to teach computer science concepts.

6. ACKNOWLEDGMENTS

COSMOS is a program under the UC Office of the President, run by the Educational Partnership Center, and funded by both the state of California and by private sponsors. The authors would like to acknowledge the efforts of Jim Whitehead (UCSC), Nathan Whitehead (NVIDIA), and Heather Logas (UCSC) as former instructors for the Structure of Fun and Technologies of Fun courses, respectively. Finally, we would like to thank the cluster's Teacher Fellows, Takeshi Kaneko and Thomas May, for their insight into teaching methodology, and all of the UCSC COSMOS staff for their support.

7. REFERENCES

[1] Carmichael, Gail. Girls, Computer Science, and Games. *SIGCSE Bulletin*, 40, 4 (2008), 107-110.

[2] Cooper, Stephen, Dann, Wanda, and Pausch, Randy. Teaching Object-First in Introductory Computer Science. In *Proceedings of the 34th SIGCSE Technical Symposium on Computer Science Education* (Reno, NV, USA 2003), 191-195.

[3] Doran, Katelyn, Boyce, Acey, and Finkelstein, Samantha. Reaching Out with Game Design. In *Proceedings of the Fifth International Conference on the Foundations of Digital Games (FDG '10)* (Monterey, CA, USA 2010), 250-251.

[4] Fullerton, Tracy. *Game Design Workshop: A Playcentric Approach to Creating Innovative Games*. Morgan Kaufmann, Burlington, MA, USA, 2008.

[5] Guzdial, Mark and Soloway, Elliot. Teaching the Nintendo Generation to Program. *Communications of the ACM*, 45, 4 (April 2002), 17-21.

[6] Henriksen, Poul and Kölling, Michael. greenfoot: Combining Object Visualisation with Interaction. In *Companion to the 19th Annual ACM SIGPLAN Conference on Object-Oriented Programming Systems, Languages, and Applications (OOPSLA)* (Vancouver, BC, Canada 2004), 73-82.

[7] Lenhart, Amanda, Kahne, Joseph, Middaugh, Ellen, Macgill, Alexandra, Evans, Chris, and Vitak, Jessica. *Teens, Video Games and Civics*. Pew Internet, Pew Research Center, 2008.

[8] McDowell, Charlie, Werner, Linda, Bullock, Heather, and Fernald, Julian. The Effects of Pair-Programming on Performance in an Introductory Programming Course. In *Proceedings of the 33rd SIGCSE Technical Symposium on Computer Science Education* (Cincinnati, KY, USA 2002), 38-42.

[9] NCWIT. *The NCWIT Scorecard: A Report on the Status of Women in Information Technology*. URL: http://www.ncwit.org/scorecardflash/, 2010.

[10] Overmars, Mark H. Teaching Computer Science through Game Design. *IEEE Computer*, 37, 4 (April 2004), 81-83.

[11] Ranum, David, Miller, Bradley, Zelle, John, and Guzdial, Mark. Successful Approaches to Teaching Introductory Computer Science Courses with Python (Special Session). In *Proceedings of the 37th SIGCSE Technical Symposium on Computer Science Education* (Houston, TX, USA 2006).

[12] Reas, Casey and Fry, Benjamin. Processing: A Learning Environment for Creating Interactive Web Graphics. *ACM SIGGRAPH 2003 Web Graphics* (2003).

[13] Resnick, Mitchel, Maloney, John, Monroy-Hernández, Andrés et al. Scratch: Programming for All. *Communications of the ACM*, 52, 11 (November 2009), 60-67.

[14] Romeike, Ralf. Applying Creativity in CS High School Education - Criteria, Teaching Example, and Evaluation. In *7th Baltic Sea Conference on Computing Education Research* (Koli National Park, Finland 2007).

[15] Sullivan, Anne and Smith, Gillian. Lessons in Teaching Game Design. In *Proceedings of the 2011 International Conference on the Foundations of Digital Games (FDG 2011)* (Bordeaux, France June 2011).

[16] Swink, Steve. *Tune: A Game about Game Design*. September 2006. Retrieved September 2, 2011 from http://www.steveswink.com/tune/

[17] Utting, Ian, Cooper, Stephen, Kölling, Michael, Maloney, John, and Resnick, Mitchel. Alice, Greenfoot, and Scratch -- A Discussion. *ACM Transactions on Computing Education*, 10, 4 (2010).

[18] Werner, Linda, Denner, Jill, Bliesner, Michelle, and Rex, Pat. Can Middle-Schoolers Use Storytelling Alice to Make Games? Results of a Pilot Study. (Orlando, FL 2009), Proceedings of the Fourth International Conference on the Foundations of Digital Games (FDG '09), 207-214.

[19] Zimmerman, Eric. Play as Research: The Iterative Design Process. In Laurel, Brenda, ed., *Design Research: Methods and Perspectives*. MIT Press, Cambridge, MA, USA, 2003.

Programming, PWNed: Using Digital Game Development to Enhance Learners' Competency and Self-Efficacy in a High School Computing Science Course

Katie Seaborn
York University
4700 Keele Street
Toronto, ON M3J 1P3
1-416-736-5978
kseaborn@yorku.ca

Magy Seif El-Nasr
Northeastern University
360 Huntington Avenue
Boston, MA 02115
1-847-372-4489
magy@neu.edu

David Milam
Simon Fraser University
250 - 13450 – 102nd Avenue
Surrey, BC V3T 0A3
1-778-782-8180
dma35@sfu.ca

Darren Yung
Frank Hurt Secondary
13940 77th Avenue
Surrey, BC V3W 5Z4
1-604-590-1311
yung_d@frankhurt.ca

ABSTRACT
Games are an important part of popular culture and have successfully engaged audiences from different age groups [8]. This has caused many educators to start thinking of different ways to infuse game-based techniques (playing or construction) to enhance education. Over the past five years, there has been several research efforts on curriculum development and the evaluation of game construction and playing methods to promote STEM (Science Technology, Engineering and Mathematics) concepts to middle and high school students. In this paper, we report on a new study following the lead of previous efforts. In particular, we were granted a block within Frank Hurt High School by the Surrey school district for which to develop a game construction-based curriculum as a basis for computer science education within the school, replacing a traditional computer science class. From February till June 2011 students were taught elementary programming using *GameMaker*, a digital game development tool. In addition to collecting students' overall impressions, we also evaluated students' technical competency (using tests) and self-efficacy (using surveys) at the start and end of the semester. Our findings show that the curriculum had a positive, statistically significant effect on concept comprehension, which suggests that the curriculum was effective for understanding computer science and game design concepts. In this paper we present the course structure, methods, and evaluation as a contribution.

Categories and Subject Descriptors
K.3.1 [**Computers and Education**]: Computer Uses in Education – *computer-assisted instruction (CAI)*; Computer and Information Science Education – *computer science education, curriculum.*

General Terms
Design, experimentation, theory.

Keywords
Games and learning, game design curriculum, computer science curriculum, constructionist learning.

Permission to make digital or hard copies of all or part of this work for personal or classroom use is granted without fee provided that copies are not made or distributed for profit or commercial advantage and that copies bear this notice and the full citation on the first page. To copy otherwise, or republish, to post on servers or to redistribute to lists, requires prior specific permission and/or a fee.
SIGCSE'12, February 29–March 3, 2012, Raleigh, North Carolina, USA.
Copyright 2012 ACM 978-1-4503-1098-7/12/02...$10.00.

1. INTRODUCTION
The past decade has seen an influx in the use of the digital games medium for learning. The genre of games for learning, or "serious games," has come into fruition following the medium's move beyond its entertainment origins into the education and scholarly spheres [18]. Researchers are investigating how and in what ways games can be used to support and inspire learning [6]. This is particularly relevant to computer science and mathematics pedagogy, as a nascent network of educators for game-based learning suggests [4]. Educational perspectives on games and learning have been investigated, including instructionist and constructionist pedagogy [10]. Serious games exemplify instructionist learning, where learners gain knowledge through playing a game. Constructionist approaches require creation as part of the learning process.

The problem of using a constructionist approach to learning is that constructing games from scratch is hard and an extremely tedious process. As a result, numerous projects have investigated the development of tools that allow students to construct game or narrative experiences quickly while learning STEM-based concepts. Examples of such projects are *Scratch* [13], *Alice* [5] and *Stagecast* [16], to mention a few. In addition, the game industry has responded to the desires of fans and ultimately, if indirectly, in support of the education community by offering promising avenues for game-based construction. Now, many commercial games (like Blizzard's *Starcraft* and *Warcraft* series) provide opportunities for players to customize or build on the default gaming experience. For example, by allowing players access to environment map editors or the underlying game engine, players can now modify the maps and create their own map designs. Thus, modding and the use of game engines (such as *GameMaker*, *Unity*, or *Unreal Engine*) in classrooms have started to be investigated for their value in teaching computer science and related concepts [15].

Game-based constructionist approaches to pedagogy are *slowly* gaining stead. Academics and educators have traditionally favored game-based instructionist approaches to pedagogy [10], despite the clear success and (empirically underexplored) qualitative benefits of constructionist approaches [1, 9, 11, 12, 14, 19]. These previous works have evaluated the use and benefits of constructionist approaches for understanding of, retention of, and interest in computer science, mathematical, and related concepts. Further, while previous work evaluated and reported on the motivation and engagement benefits of this approach [9, 12], no studies have empirically evaluated competency in programming and specifically the transfer of programming competency using a game construction curriculum.

In this paper, we report on a high school computer science and game design curriculum we developed over years of conducting game construction camps for kids. The curriculum was adapted to be administered within a high school classroom setting as part of the computer science course curriculum in collaboration with the teacher who previously taught the course using traditional methods. The course embodied the constructionist perspective of learning through digital game development supported by a diverse team of instructors, learning modules, and digital game creation software. This paper has several contributions. First, we present this curriculum as a case study of a game construction approach to learning computer science concepts within a high school setting. Second, we present methods and results of self-efficacy and competency measures to show the effectiveness of this approach. We believe that our methods may be reused by other researchers, and that this curriculum can be adapted and repurposed for high schools around the world.

2. BACKGROUND

Yasmin Kafai is known for her extensive and long-standing work on constructionist approaches to learning, particularly involving digital game creation [9]. In her first study, Kafai recruited sixteen students for her "Game Design Project," in which teams created an original digital game that would teach younger children about the mathematical concept of fractions, while at the same time enriching their own knowledge of fractions. This six month project involved students in learning game development and programming in the Logo language. This study resulted in several significant findings. First, Kafai found that the efforts of students paralleled those of professional game design teams, including brainstorming, scoping, problem-solving, teamwork, time management and flexibility in development—all soft skills transferable to domains outside of game design and development. Second, Kafai found empirical support for the benefits of the constructionist approach, which she summarizes as follows: (1) technical fluency, which involves knowledge of use and encourages significant applications and novel uses, and (2) entrance into digital prosumer (professional-consumer, producer-consumer) culture. We argue that (1) should also include game design fluency, as findings from our and others' [12] research suggest.

Rajaravivarma [12] also developed an introductory college-level computer science course that involved game creation as a means of understanding the abstract computer science concepts novice students are known to struggle with. The findings from her study echoed those found in Kafai's work. In particular, she notes how the inherently motivating quality of the game medium encouraged learning in the face of difficulty. However, she didn't empirically validate competency or self efficacy effects.

Another work using the game construction approach is that of Sullivan and Smith, who have iteratively developed a game design class over the course of four years [17]. This class, called "Video Games: The Design of Fun, from Concept to Code," is part of the California State Summer School for Mathematics and Science (COSMOS), which aims to introduce high school students to college-level curricula in the STEM line of disciplines: science, technology, engineering and mathematics. The course is divided into two intertwining streams: structure, focus on game theory and technology, focus on STEM concepts. Students work in small teams to create a 2D computer game, and learn how to create their own art assets as well as how to program. Their findings over the course of four years were a list of considerations for the design of game development curricula, some of which are as follows: appropriate choice of programming language, especially one that "minimizes programmer errors and maximized creative potential" is important; activity-oriented classes can bridge the abstract-concrete gap. While there are many positives, the researchers note one persistent challenge: ensuring equal division of labor among the student teams. They found that students would gravitate and stick to certain roles, in particular that girls found themselves taking on the artist role, which was of great concern to the researchers, who advocate for the increased presence of females in STEM disciplines. Their solution was to implement an initial "no-art" rule and rely on students' natural inclination to work in pairs while programming. In our curriculum (presented below), we offer a new solution: rotating roles of artist, designer and programmer over the course of the semester with requirement of three game modules (thus balancing the roles with the modules).

Werner, Campe and Denner developed an NSF-supported after-school program for middle school-aged girls called "Girls Creating Games" to increase their information technology (IT) fluency through game creation [20]. IT fluency is defined as a combination of possessing contemporary IT skills (IT literacy), knowledge of fundamental IT concepts, and intellectual capabilities (non-IT but IT-relevant, like sustained reasoning). In contrast to literacy, fluency means not only learning *how to use* technology, but *using* technology in *novel* and *creative* ways. They found that their twelve-week project-based program was beneficial to students' engagement with IT and acquisition of IT fluency. The program was structured around collaborative work and pair programming; 85% of students preferred to work in pairs over the duration of the program. They assessed IT fluency and literacy by participation, making the assumption that students who participated in activities and used tools acquired a minimal competency level with the skill or tool. By this measure, the program was a success. All students and pairs of students completed a fully functioning game by the end of the program and were able to demonstrate many aspects of IT fluency.

Werner and colleagues conducted a two-week game development summer camp to increase middle school students' information technology (IT) fluency [21]. They used *Storytelling Alice* (SA), a visual, 3D animation-based game creation tool, to engage students in single and paired projects. Their findings show that SA was engaging and conducive to increasing students' technological fluency. They found that 74% of the games students produced displayed at least two components of technological fluency. A further 52% showcased students' understanding of parallelism, a programming concept known to be very difficult to learn; the authors suggest that the 3D aspect of the SA programming environment aided students' understanding of this concept.

In addition to game construction using engines, Seif El-Nasr et al. [15] have explored the use of game modding, or modifying commercial games, for educational purposes, particularly with respect to increasing information technology literacy. They developed a game modding course for middle and high school girls with the goal of introducing this overlooked audience to IT and having them attain five basic IT competencies: the ability to engage in sustained reasoning; the ability to manage complexity; the ability to test a solution; the ability to manage problems in faulty situations; and the ability to organize, navigate and evaluate information structures and their content [22]. The course was successful in increasing the motivation and self-efficacy of girls, as well as teaching these IT competencies.

The games for learning movement is gradually coming to embrace constructionist approaches, even while the instructionist perspective continues to dominate [10]. However, one main issue with previous work in this area is the lack of evaluation methods and results demonstrating competency and transfer of STEM-based concepts. This paper situates itself as a contribution towards game-based constructionist methods, but also addresses the issue of transfer and competency measures and results.

In addition to work on the constructionist approach, researchers are investigating the design of technology to target STEM-based learning. An example is Boyce and Barnes, who redesigned a piece of mathematical learning software called Virtual Bead Loom (VBL) to increase its potential by augmenting it with game-based elements [3]. Their tool, the BeadLoom Game, provided puzzles that required learners to understand and use mathematical concepts like Cartesian coordinates to re-create digital images constructed of virtual beads. The BeadLoom Game was tested in two five-day long summer camps comprised of twenty middle school students each. They found that students enjoyed the tool, and reported on statistically significant learning gains. Their findings argue for the continued implementation of game elements to motivate students in learning mathematical concepts.

3. THE DIGITAL GAME DEVELOPMENT CLASS

The curriculum we designed exposed students to the world of game development. We introduced students to the game industry and development fundamentals followed by three team-based modules. Each module consisted of four phases, each five weeks in duration. Teams of three produced a unique game for each module; each member was responsible for one of three roles: Designer, Artist or Programmer. Students changed roles each module in order to gain and practice the skills associated with each role.

3.1 Curriculum Structure

The curriculum's four phases are outlined as follows:

Phase 1: Game Pitch. Once the team agrees on a game idea, a pitch presentation is created. The purpose of the pitch is for the team to visually conceptualize their game and to explain and present it to an audience made up of peers and instructors. The audience is then able to ask and seek clarification from the team about their game concept.

Phase 2: Design Conceptualization and Specification. This module's main deliverable is the high-level design document. This document includes specific details on the requirements of the game. It is meant to ensure that all members of the team know what needs to be completed for the game. The specifics of the game's rules, actions, and art assets and progression details are all outlined in this document.

Phase 3: Prototyping and Testing. This phase includes several stages of prototype development and testing, analysis and iteration. The main deliverable of this phase is several prototypes and testing results, which are all presented in Phase 4.

Phase 4: Final Game Demonstration and Presentation. In the final presentation, the designer and team summarizes the process that the team went through to make their game, including the challenges that they faced and may or may not have overcome, and what they learned during the process of creating the game. A live demonstration of their game is also given. Screen shots from students' final games are shown in Fig 1.

The high school teacher was in class daily as the primary instructor. Due to the collaborative nature of this course, we augmented the teacher's instruction with the instruction and presence of three researchers and educators from Simon Fraser University.

3.2 Roles and Responsibilities

Three roles were established and circulated through all members of the team through the three modules. Thus, each student took on a unique role for each module, allowing them to learn the responsibilities and skills required of each role. The roles were: Design, Art, and Programming.

The Designer was responsible for creating team documents and acted as team leader, ensuring that the project was on track. The Designer also guided brainstorming sessions on game concepts. The Programmer was responsible for transforming the game idea from the design document to a playable game. This included programming all activities, actions and reaction in the game. The Artist was responsible for producing the graphics, including backgrounds, sprites and animations, for the game. The Artist was encouraged to use digital art tools, like Adobe Photoshop, to create original graphics for their game.

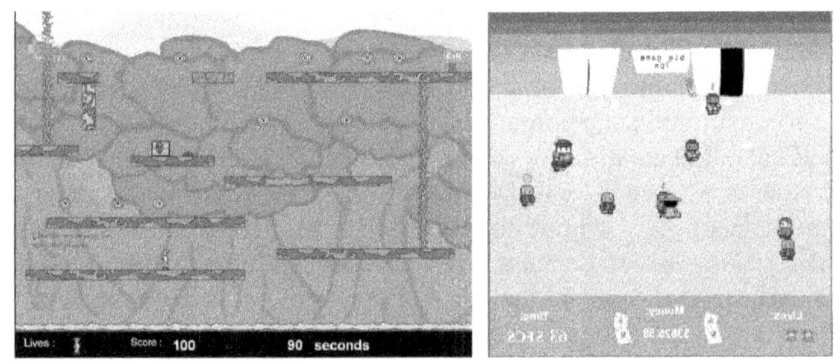

Figure 1. Screen shots from two different student games.

3.3 Programming Language and Design Tools

Students used *GameMaker 8* by YoYo Games to develop their games. This programming environment features a simple graphical user interface, ideal for novice programmers. However, it also requires students to think in terms of programming constructs, by hiding the syntax through visual blocks and thus allowing students to understand semantics first. If students need to do more complex operations, they do need to write simple scripts using a scripting tool, which is similar to Java Script in syntax. Students were also trained on the use of audio and visual tools like Adobe Photoshop, Illustrator, Flash, Audacity and/or the GIMP to create additional resources.

4. EVALUATION

We conducted a study over the course of one six-month semester. Twelve high school students, one female, were recruited upon entrance into the class, which was offered as an elective high school class within Frank Hurt School. To evaluate the effectiveness of the digital game development-based curriculum, we used an assessment questionnaire administered at the beginning and end of the course. In particular, we assessed three aspects: (a) self-efficacy with respect to learning computer science and game design concepts, (b) perception of helpfulness of class activities, and (c) understanding of computer science concepts. In addition, we also collected qualitative feedback on students' impressions of the course through an optional anonymous online survey comprised of multiple choice and open-ended questions. Students were offered gear and gadgets from Simon Fraser University for participating in the class and study.

4.1 Measures, Instruments and Analysis

A pre- and post-course assessment questionnaire was assigned in-classroom. The pre-test (63 questions) differed from the post-test (54 questions) only in that it included a demographics section (the results are summarized in Table 1).

Table 1. Participant demographics

Prior programming experience	Yes, a lot	2	17%
	Yes, a little	4	33%
	Unsure	4	33%
	No	2	17%
Taken programming course	Yes	4	33%
	Unsure	1	8%
	No	7	58%
Plays digital games	Yes, a lot	7	58%
	Yes, sometimes	5	42%
	Rarely	0	0%
	Never	0	0%
Social environment of game-play	Mostly with friends	1	8%
	Equally both	5	42%
	Mostly alone	6	50%
	Only alone	0	0%
Spoken publicly or lead a presentation	Yes	8	67%
	Unsure	1	8%
	No	3	25%
Used PowerPoint or similar	Yes	12	100%
	Unsure	0	0%
	No	0	0%
Worked in a group on a project	Yes	10	83%
	Unsure	1	8%
	No	1	8%
Experience sketching, drawing or painting	Yes	5	42%
	Unsure	3	25%
	No	4	33%
Used a digital tool to draw	Yes	9	75%
	Unsure	1	8%
	No	2	17%

The questionnaires were comprised of three parts: (1) feelings and attitudes towards programming, (2) activities and learning, and (3) a competence assessment, comprised of questions on three aspects of game development: computer science, game design, and digital art. Students were given a total of 1.5 hours to answer the assessment each time.

The 10 questions in (1) measured self-efficacy, particularly confidence and enjoyment with programming via a 5-point Likert scale. This instrument was derived from [7] and [2]. Examples include: Do you believe that programming is a simple subject? Do you fear programming? I am sure I could learn programming.

The 7 questions in (2) measured students' perceptions of the helpfulness of pedagogical tools, such as class activities and materials, for their learning via a 5-point Likert scale derived from [7]. It included such topics as lecture slides, projects, and feedback from instructors. Examples include: Which of the following class activities help you learn the most? The exercises. The game projects. Lecture slides uploaded on Moodle.

The 29 questions in (3) measured students' understanding of course content, and were comprised of multiple choice and short answer questions on computer science, game design and digital art concepts. The instruction team in conjunction with a master's student at Simon Fraser University constructed questions to specifically assess competence and transfer. The questions were based on the high school teacher's previous assessment instrument and thus ensure transfer of concepts and learning objectives needed within the Surrey High School. Figure 2 shows one question within the test.

We used several methods to analyze the data from these questionnaires and tests. Responses from parts (1) and (2) were nonparametric and so a Wilcoxon Signed Rank test was used for each set. Responses from (3) were parametric and so a paired samples *t*-test was used to compare pre- and post data.

```
Which of the following correctly displays the
sum of 20 and 44 in a dialog box?
(a) show_message('20' + '44');
(b) show_message('20 + 44');
(c) show_message(string(20+44));
(d) show_message(string(20) + string(44));
```

Figure 2. An example computer science assessment question.

4.1.1 End-of-Term Survey

An 18-question survey was delivered electronically to students after the end of the semester. Students were elicited for anonymous feedback and their impressions on the course via yes-and-no and open-ended questions. The survey had a total of five respondents (a 42% response rate).

5. RESULTS

5.1 Assessment

5.1.1 Confidence

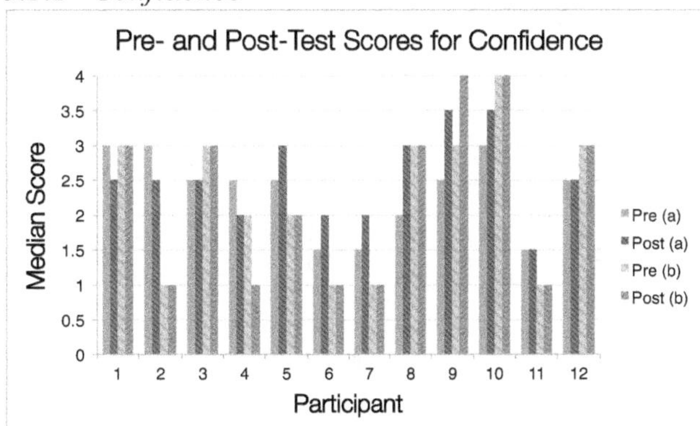

Figure 3. Pre- and post-test results for confidence.

A Wilcoxon Signed Rank test for the first set of confidence questions showed that there was no improvement in scores over time, Z = -1.311, $p = .190$. A Wilcoxon Signed Rank test for the second set of confidence questions showed that there was no improvement in scores over time, Z > .0005, $p = 1.000$. See Fig 3.

5.1.2 Enjoyment

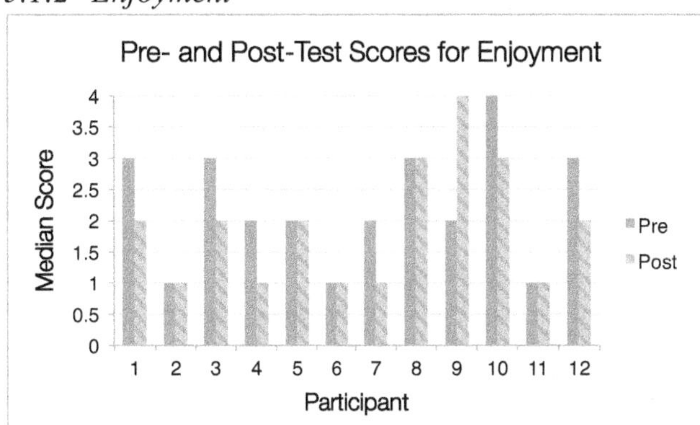

Figure 4. Pre- and post-test results for enjoyment.

A Wilcoxon Signed Rank test for the enjoyment questions showed that there was no improvement in scores over time, Z = -1.265, $p = .206$. See Fig 4.

5.1.3 Helpfulness of Class Activities and Materials

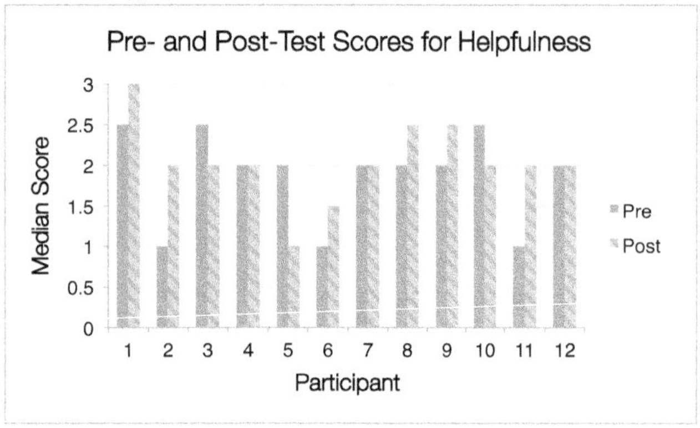

Figure 5. Pre- and post-test results for helpfulness.

A Wilcoxon Signed Rank test for the perceived helpfulness of activities and materials questions showed that there was no improvement in scores over time, Z = -.921, p = .357. See Fig 5.

5.1.4 Assessment of Programming Concepts

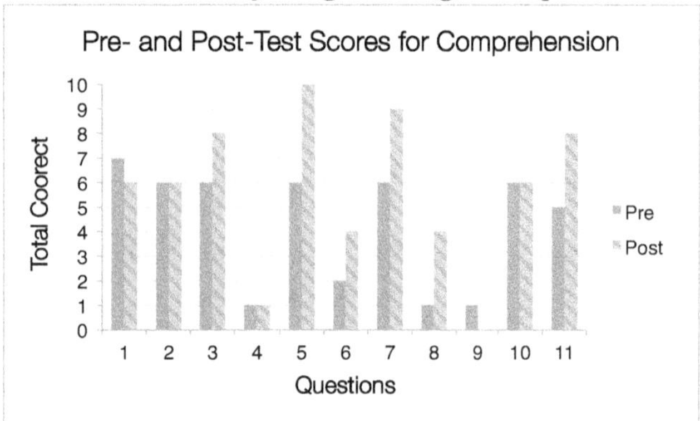

Figure 6. Pre- and post-test scores for comprehension.

A paired samples t-test showed that there was a significant improvement in assessment scores over time, $t(10)$ = -2.507, p = .031. See Fig 6.

5.2 Survey

5.2.1 Yes-or-No Questions

Three students reported spending an average of 7.3 hours per week working on their game projects; two reported an average of 24 hours per week. No student agreed that their choice in games changed because of this course. All students agreed they would work in a team to create a game again and desired to become professional game developers or designers; three students agreed that this course influenced their decision to pursue a career in the game industry, and two did not. All students indicated that they would be continuing to take game courses after high school.

5.2.2 Open Ended Questions

Regarding what they learned about game development, students reported that they underestimated the effort, knowledge and time required for making games. Two students pointed out the impact of effective communication and team work; one student wrote, "There is so much planning involved and tons and tons of communication, team work and effort that needs to be put in." On their strengths as novice game creators, two students noted their skills in both programming and problem solving, while two others noted their skills in creating art assets; these last two noted that they would like to improve upon their programming skills in answer to the question "What are some things you would like to improve upon?" On working with teams, three students stressed the importance of having reliable team members and good communication; one student reported having a "perfect" team. Those inspired by this course to become a game designer or developer noted that the course exposed them to the game design process, how the industry works, and the realities of the project cycle. In a final commentary section, one student requested that the amount of time allotted for the course should be increased to a full year. One student stated that the course was "excellent" and another wrote that it was "[the] greatest experience in my school years."

6. DISCUSSION

6.1 Self-Efficacy

The inferential results for confidence, enjoyment and the helpfulness of class activities and materials show that the digital game development-based approach to learning computer science, game design and digital art concepts did not have a significant effect on students' self-efficacy. This result is surprising because it does not reflect our and other researchers' impressions from previous similar studies. However, in the optional post-course survey, over half (60%) indicated that the course influenced their decision to pursue a career in the games industry as designers or developers, and all students (100%) indicated that they would continue taking digital game development courses in post-secondary education. A review of the demographics data shows that the majority of students were unsure of their programming experience and had not taken programming classes before. This, in conjunction with findings from previous research, suggests that the digital game development-based approach did, in fact, affect self-efficacy, despite a lack of statistical significance.

Qualitative findings from studies conducted by Kafai [9] and Rajaravivarma [12] indicated that the games-based constructionist approach is highly motivating, which suggested an effect on self-efficacy. In spite of our quantitative results, our qualitative findings support this notion as well. Responses to the open-ended questions in the post-course survey suggest that students came to recognize the realities of the game design and development cycle, including the importance of scoping, teamwork and communication. Students also recognized their strengths and weaknesses and, in conjunction with what the survey's quantitative data state, were nonetheless inspired to improve upon their weaknesses, and continue taking computer science and game design-related courses in post-secondary education.

The authors and class teacher believe students' self-efficacy of programming concepts was also positively influenced by switching roles and playtesting with peers. Switching between programming, technical artistry, and game design roles gave students hands-on experience with art, code, and game structures, thereby providing a different point of view in each module. These roles required team cooperation to plan, build assets, and code, which are interlocking components of the game creation process. In addition, playtesting with peers allowed teams to reflect on their hard work. Valuable feedback from students in the same role, but from different teams, gave hints on how to enhance the game experience. This feedback boosted team motivation to refine the game, including programming.

6.2 Learning

The statistically significant inferential results for the assessment of programming concepts show that the digital game development-based approach was effective for students' comprehension of computer science subjects. Although we do not have a control to compare with, these results advocate for the constructionist perspective of learning and call for future research in which traditional instructionist pedagogy is compared to the games-based constructionist approach.

6.3 Limitations

A number of limitations limit the generalizability of our findings. The sample size of twelve is low; however, this issue will be obviated as more data is collected in subsequent semesters and following the curriculum's implementation in other schools. The data favors a male perspective, which prevents us from distinguishing gender effects, if they exist; we hope that exposure and recruitment will in time increase the enrollment rate of girls. Finally, we were not able to compare to a control because of a lack of scholastic resources and the limitations and ethically disconcerting aspects of other approaches. For example, a split approach to the curriculum, in which students would first learn computing science via traditional methods, and then via digital game-based development, is highly susceptible to learning effects; offering a traditional class and a digital game development class presents issues due to individual variability, and is ethically questionable concerning equity in accessibility to learning strategies.

7. CONCLUSION

The reimagining of the digital game medium affords a number of trajectories for its use as a learning tool. In this paper, we presented a computer science and game design curriculum optimized for high school level pedagogy, which featured a constructionist approach to learning through a digital game development-based format. We conducted a study that assessed students' self-efficacy for learning these concepts. Pre- and post-assessments revealed that despite no significant inferential results, qualitative findings and a significant improvement in comprehension scores show that self-efficacy was positively affected by the games-based constructionist approach. Our findings support the continued implementation of digital game development-based formats for learning computer science and game design concepts, and call for longitudinal research to further elucidate its affect on self-efficacy. Future iterations of this workshop are being scheduled within different schools and locations. We believe more data is needed to further generalize our findings. We also believe a comparative study is important and will attempt to pursue one in the future.

8. ACKNOWLEDGMENTS

This research is funded by GRAND NCE. Our thanks to Frank Hurt Secondary School principle Gloria Sarmento for supporting and accommodating this research. Our thanks to Bardia Aghabeigi for the computer science segment of the assessment.

9. REFERENCES

[1] Barnes, T., Richter, H., Powell, E., Chaffin, A. and Godwin, A. 2007. Game2Learn: building CS1 learning games for retention. *SIGCSE Bull.* 39, 3 (2007), 121-125.

[2] Bishop-Clark, C., Courte, J. and Howard, E.V. 2006. Programming in Pairs with Alice to Improve Confidence, Enjoyment, and Achievement. 34, 2 (2006), 213-228.

[3] Boyce, A. and Barnes, T. 2010. BeadLoom Game: using game elements to increase motivation and learning. *Proceedings of the Fifth International Conference on the Foundations of Digital Games* (Monterey, California, 2010), 25-31.

[4] Clua, E., Feijó, B., Rocca, J., Schwartz, J., Graças, M. das, Perlin, K., Tori, R. and Barnes, T. 2006. Game and interactivity in computer science education. *ACM SIGGRAPH 2006 Educators program* (Boston, Massachusetts, 2006), 2.

[5] Cooper, S., Dann, W. and Pausch, R. 2000. Alice: a 3-D tool for introductory programming concepts. *J. Comput. Small Coll.* 15, 5 (2000), 107-116.

[6] Gee, J.P. 2007. *What Video Games Have to Teach Us About Learning and Literacy*. Palgrave Macmillian.

[7] Georgantaki, S. and Retalis, S. 2007. A Learning Research Informed Design and Evaluation of a Web-Enhanced Object Oriented Programming Seminar. *Journal of Information Systems Education*. 18, 2 (2007), 243-253.

[8] Jenkins, H. 2006. *Fans, Bloggers and Gamers: Essays on Participatory Culture*. New York University Press.

[9] Kafai, Y.B. 1995. *Minds in Play: Computer Game Design as a Context for Children's Learning*. Lawrence Erlbaum Associates, Inc.

[10] Kafai, Y.B. 2006. Playing and Making Games for Learning. *Games and Culture*. 1, 1 (Jan. 2006), 36-40.

[11] Lieberman, D.A. 1997. Interactive Video Games for Health Promotion: Effects on Knowledge, Self-Efficacy, Social Support, and Health. *Health Promotion and Interactive Technology*. Routledge. 103-120.

[12] Rajaravivarma, R. 2005. A games-based approach for teaching the introductory programming course. *SIGCSE Bull.* 37, 4 (2005), 98-102.

[13] Resnick, M., Maloney, J., Monroy-Hernández, A., Rusk, N., Eastmond, E., Brennan, K., Millner, A., Rosenbaum, E., Silver, J., Silverman, B. and Kafai, Y. 2009. Scratch: programming for all. *Commun. ACM*. 52, 11 (2009), 60-67.

[14] Seif El-Nasr, M. and Maygoli, T. 2010. Understanding the Underlying Patterns: Teaching Scientific Thinking through Building Games. *International Journal of Science in Society*. (2010), in press.

[15] Seif El-Nasr, M. and Smith, B.K. 2006. Learning through game modding. *Comput. Entertain.* 4, 1 (2006), 7.

[16] Smith, D.C., Cypher, A. and Tesler, L. 2000. Programming by example: novice programming comes of age. *Commun. ACM*. 43, 3 (2000), 75-81.

[17] Sullivan, A. and Smith, G. Lessons from COSMOS: Four Years of Iteration on a Game Design Class.

[18] Susi, T., Johannesson, M. and Backlund, P. 2007. *Serious games – An overview*. University of Skövde.

[19] Thomas, R., Cahill, J. and Santilli, L. 1997. Using an Interactive Computer Game to Increase Skill and Self-Efficacy Regarding Safer Sex Negotiation: Field Test Results. *Health Education & Behavior*. 24, 1 (1997), 71-86.

[20] Werner, L.L., Campe, S. and Denner, J. 2005. Middle school girls + games programming = information technology fluency. *Proceedings of the 6th conference on Information technology education* (Newark, NJ, USA, 2005), 301-305.

[21] Werner, L., Denner, J., Bliesner, M. and Rex, P. 2009. Can middle-schoolers use Storytelling Alice to make games?: results of a pilot study. *Proceedings of the 4th International Conference on Foundations of Digital Games* (Orlando, Florida, 2009), 207-214.

[22] Yucel, I., Zupko, J. and El-Nasr, M.S. 2006. IT Education, Girls and Game Modding. *Interactive Technology and Smart Education*. 3, 2 (2006), 143-156.

A Learning Objective Focused Methodology for the Design and Evaluation of Game-based Tutors

Michael John Eagle
University of North Carolina at Charlotte
9201 University City Blvd.
Charlotte, NC USA
mjeagle@uncc.edu

Tiffany Barnes
University of North Carolina at Charlotte
9201 University City Blvd.
Charlotte, NC USA
tiffany.barnes@uncc.edu

ABSTRACT

We present the *Game2Learn* methodology for the design and evaluation of educational games with a focus on well-defined learning objectives and empirical verification. This integrative process adapts ideas from educational design, intelligent tutoring systems, classical test-theory, and interaction and game design, and agile software development. The methodology guides researchers through the steps of the design process, including identification of specific learning objectives, translation of learning activities to game mechanics, and the empirical evaluation of the final product. This methodology is particularly useful for ensuring successful student research experiences or software engineering courses.

Categories and Subject Descriptors

K.8 [**General**]: Games; D.2 [**Software Engineering**]: Design—*Methodologies*

General Terms

Design, Experimentation, Human Factors

Keywords

Game Design, Design Methods, Educational Games, Serious Games, Empirical Evaluation

1. INTRODUCTION

Engaging undergraduates in research is a powerful technique that improves self-efficacy and retention in computing programs[21]. We have employed the *Game2Learn* methodology presented here to engage UNC Charlotte students in research, by creating, and conducting small studies on, educational games. We have found that the development of serious games, or those with non-entertainment purposes, imposes many design challenges over "just for fun" games. For students to get the most out of the design and development process, and for their games to be effective, there is a need to have a specific methodology to design and evaluate effective games for learning.

The *Game2Learn* methodology seeks to produce quality games, that produce learning, as well as quality students, who have learned about software engineering, human computer interaction, and research methods. The methodology can be used by students, young researchers, and professors who are interested in starting a serious game project. We specifically target computer science educational games since our students know this material, and their games can benefit younger students in computing [1, 10]. However, we have also modified the methodology for other serious game projects [5].

While games could transform education, most educational game developers have produced games without any theory of learning or underlying body of research [23], and most educational games for computing have only been evaluated anecdotally [25]. There are few "hard and fast" research findings for educational video games [16]. The *Game2Learn* methodology leverages practices from educational psychology, cognitive science, and traditional educational knowledge to increase the likelihood that student-created games will promote learning in measurable ways. Even good games will fail to reveal their full potential without adequate study design, therefore our methodology provides support for rigorous empirical evaluation. Students using the methodology perform higher-quality studies, with games specifically designed for learning, and evaluation instruments and studies designed to detect learning gains.

1.1 The *Game2Learn* Project

The *Game2Learn* project promotes educational games designed and developed *by* students *for* students. The benefit of this process is twofold: the students *designing* the games gain valuable research and development experience; the students *playing* the games receive new and innovative study tools. While the *Game2Learn* project concentrates preimarily on computing education, the principles listed here are useful for any type of educational game.

We draw on four years of our experience in supporting 50 undergraduate research projects and 15 graduate student projects in developing and evaluating educational software and games, and our experience in teaching courses with over 140 students in five game development courses and three courses in intelligent tutoring systems. Our methodology provides a stepping-stone to the creation of effective educational games by undergraduate students. *Game2Learn* has developed over 17 educational games, helped uncover aspects of games that aid in education, shown positive learn-

Permission to make digital or hard copies of all or part of this work for personal or classroom use is granted without fee provided that copies are not made or distributed for profit or commercial advantage and that copies bear this notice and the full citation on the first page. To copy otherwise, to republish, to post on servers or to redistribute to lists, requires prior specific permission and/or a fee.
SIGCSE'12, February 29–March 3, 2012, Raleigh, North Carolina, USA.
Copyright 2012 ACM 978-1-4503-1098-7/12/02 ...$10.00.

ing gains for six games, and has shown impressive retention into graduate computing programs [2, 10].

One of the goals of the *Game2Learn* methodology is to introduce undergraduate students to scientific research, as poorly crafted evaluation sabotages the chances for meaningful discovery. Student developers often have little or no experience in performing human research, in teaching, or in predicting what they can make in a single semester. For example, in the early stages of the *Game2Learn* project, many students set out to build games that taught broad computing concepts. While this is ideally possible, in one semester students can only produce about 30 minutes of learning material — which must be sufficiently focused to be effective. Early students' evaluation measures such as pretests and posttests read like comprehensive computer science exams. After these early setbacks, we determined that the *Game2Learn* project needed to incorporate evaluation of the educational objectives at its core.

Following this methodology provides a systematic process that has worked in practice for the development and evaluation of educational games. Like Carver's checklist [4], the *Game2Learn* methodology provides a way to integrate student development and studies into teaching and research goals. The methods described here can also aid in and encourage scientific studies on video games.

2. OBJECTIVE DRIVEN DESIGN

The *Game2Learn* methodology incorporates agile software development processes, rapid prototyping and playtesting cycles as suggested by Fullerton, et al [14], and task centered interaction design [18]. We augment these techniques with specific interventions for the unique challenges posed by educational games and their evaluation. We measure success in terms of improved learning including pre- to post-learning gains, transfer learning, and retention. We also measure student attitudes via surveys on satisfaction, motivation, frustration, and persistence when using our games.

The *Game2Learn* methodology is an integrative approach that allows students to be creative while developing games to achieve specific *learning objectives*. The steps in this process are similar to those for the development of general educational activities, but is integrated here with task-centered interaction design [18] applied in an agile way. Along with these design processes, we encourage students to develop games that are primarily interactive, challenging, and have immediate feedback. These guidelines help ensure that the developed games promote cognitive changes in students.

We require that *Game2Learn* prototypes teach an important computing concept (or promote another important goal), provide a meaningful interaction that supports direct skill transfer, allow learners to visualize abstract concepts; provide obvious and immediate feedback, be easy to acquire and install, and record all play interactions in a log. Our games, developed in six to 12 months, target 30–60 minutes of play time to facilitate usage in lab, homework, and research settings.

The phases in our process are: **Target**, **Observe**, **Design-Prototype**, **Translate**, and **Evaluate**.

An inherent risk in game development is that developers often have fixed ideas of what a game is or should be which prevents a focus on the learning objective that is central to the success of an educational game [13]. However, the nature of learning itself provides enjoyment to learners [22], particularly when that learning meets the characteristics of flow. Flow occurs when a person (1) has a chance of completing the task, (2) is able to concentrate, (3) has clear goals and immediate feedback, (4) exercises control, and (5) has a deep but effortless involvement [9].

Our own projects have suffered when developers focus on creating a particular kind of game, rather than on immersing players in a flow experience that helps them meet their learning goals. For example, developers may create a game and then simply tack on a flash-card style educational component. This can result in a game that acts like homework with play used as a reward but with little to no educational value. We have therefore shifted our process to first focus on the "who, what, and why." Without this focus developers design the projects for themselves rather than for the users and the users' needs. Of course, the design of educational games goes beyond designing usable interactive interfaces; the goal is to encourage both learning and fun at once. Developers must pay careful attention to enable effortless interaction with a game without removing the challenges that provide for learning.

2.1 Target: Identify users and needs

Educational game developers must first select a target audience for their product. Once developers choose a target audience, such as students in a particular class, it is important to choose content that is both important and challenging for students to learn. A number of strategies can be used to ensure that a topic of value is chosen, including: (1) researching learning in the field, (2) interviewing or observing instructors, or (3) observing tutors and students interacting, or (4) interviewing students or professionals reflecting on prior learning. In addition, a community of educators in the field may also have shared resources for problems and exercises that meet important learning objectives in an area. When all of these sources agree on a topic, it is likely that students can most benefit from an alternative way of learning.

In this critical step of the creative process, developers engage in better understanding the problem domain and previous work on educational solutions. We recommend a combination of literature search, classroom observation, and engagement in or observation of tutoring sessions where developers observe a number of metaphors and methods for communicating the target content, paying particular attention to areas where the most confusion is occurring for students. Ideally, developers engage in individual tutoring, observing what works and what does not. This is similar to a software engineering approach, where software engineers observe users in their natural environment looking for areas of inefficiency and opportunities to streamline processes [12].

2.1.1 Target Learning Objectives: Choosing tasks

Of particular importance in this stage is the precise identification of the outcomes that learners should be able to achieve once the content is learned. In this stage, developers are writing learning objectives as teachers do for lessons or curricula, where outcomes should be observable and measurable. However, for the development of an educational game, it is important not only to identify measurable outcomes, but also to operationalize them into specific problems students will be able to solve. This corresponds to choosing representative tasks in task-centered design.

Table 1: Example post-test questions

Q1	Given this declaration: int Num[7]=1,9,7,3,11,5,13; What are the values of the expressions below? Num[2] Num[7] Num[4] Num[2]+Num[5]

Q2	Given the following code segment:
	`int x=7; int Num[3][2];`
	`for ( int j = 0; j <= 2 ; j++ )`
	`  for ( int k = 0; k <= 1 ; k++ )`
	`    { Num[j][k] = x; x++; }`
	What are the values in the last row of Num?

To make this goal concrete, developers encapsulate the learning objectives by designing the post-test that students should be able to complete after playing the educational game. Developers can design these post-tests by using class and textbook exercises, or exam questions. Questions should attempt to measure the depth of the student's knowledge; we recommend development of questions that consider the difficulty level based on Bloom's Taxonomy of Educational Objectives [3]. We also recommend that researchers use guidelines for effective question design such as those by Piontek [20]. Researchers should also design questions for collection and grading.

Once the post-test is created, it should be verified before use by consulting other researchers and educators. Designers can also perform independent validity research by administering the post-test along with some other measure (which has its own evidence for validity,) and looking for correlations between the tests. Table 1 shows examples of reasonable test questions for a game for teaching loops and arrays.

Like test-driven programming and curriculum development, this approach ensures a focus on the desired outcomes for the game, rather than on features that may make a game fun, but perhaps not effective for learning. If the content of the test is valuable and something that students need to learn, then students should not be able to answer the post-test correctly without a well-designed learning activity. A post-test enables communication with educators, who can help with the design and evaluation of the post-test. This requirement also helps ensure that the activities in the game are valid; that is, that the games teach what they claim to. This is of particular value when the goal is to convince educators to use game interventions in their courses.

After the post-test is verified and validated by educators, researchers should create a isomorphic pre-test; items on this test are phrased in exactly the same way but with alterations in problem parameters, so that students cannot simply memorize answers from pre- to post-test. Test designers may also wish to experiment with alternate forms, tests with items that are not precisely the same but test the same concepts; however, doing this requires reliability studies to ensure the interchangeability of the two test forms. As such, it might be better suited for replication studies; in situations when questions are difficult to alter; or when question memorization is determined to be a threat to the study. Crocker has written an introduction to test theory that can help interested readers learn more about test-design, reliability, and validity [8].

2.2 Observe

This stage highlights the differences between the game developers and the target audience. Student game developers with limited experience in teaching may or may not have experienced the so-called expert blind spot [19], where experts are systematically incorrect at understanding student difficulties. Our techniques are adapted from interaction design practices to provide developers with an understanding of the target audience.

With the construct and the target audience in mind, developers observe instructors and attend tutoring sessions to see what metaphors and methods are currently used to teach, paying particular attention to gaps in the target audience's knowledge. We encourage student developers to become tutors for their target audience, since tutors must actively create analogies and experiences to help learners construct new knowledge. Direct communication with the target audience provides opportunities to understand what problems learners have in understanding the target material.

We also encourage think-aloud protocols [24] where learners think out loud about their problem-solving process. This can help reveal whether the post-test requires additional questions to show intermediate stages of learning, and whether the target questions are appropriate for the audience. Detailed notes or recordings of the think-alouds will allow for a cognitive analysis of problem solving, identification of gaps in knowledge, and provide insight into the game design. In later stages, these think-alouds can be compared with in-game think-alouds to determine whether the game supports learning processes.

Another aspect of observation is collecting information about what's been done before to meet the same goal. Before students begin the game design process, they review and discuss articles in game and educational research. Students also play previously created games and train for human studies with the university internal review board. When possible these new students assist senior students with the later stages of evaluation for existing games.

The observation phase also includes examining other approaches. Developers should look for games, assignments, and online learning materials that are effective for the target material. Common methods for problem solving should be noted for incorporation into the design.

2.3 Design-Prototype: Build and Test

The next phase in task-centered interaction design is "Design" — where a rough idea is outlined. We do ask students to do a short pitch on their games, but move quickly on to very small physical prototypes to test our their ideas. Since students are not experienced at design, they are unlikely to come up with effective designs right away. So, the next phase of development is to create small interactive prototypes that can assist learners in the chosen task. An analysis of the prior observed metaphors, instructional practices, and thought processes of students should inform these prototypes. We recommend particular attention to creating interactions that can make an abstract process more concrete for learners. The opportunity for direct manipulation of artifacts in games is one potential benefit of using games for education.

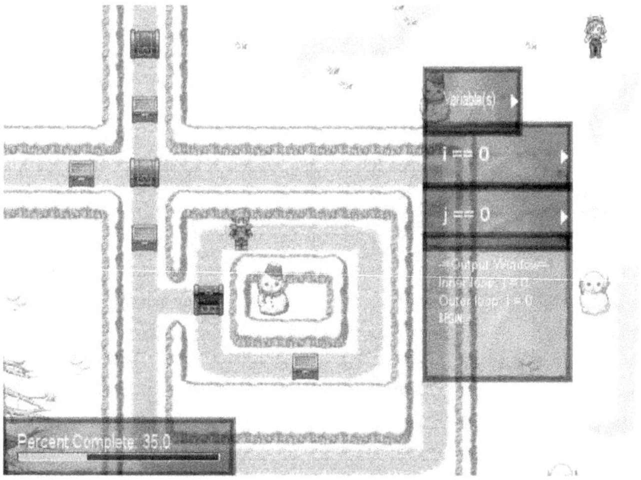

Figure 1: Example of game-play derived from a paper-based prototype. The student must guide the game character though a physical representation of a nested for-loop.

Figure 2: A 2D array is represented as a grid of snowmen. The player must use nested for-loops in order to complete the task.

For example: attempting to describe nested-loop behavior might result in two circles drawn around each other, each representing a loop; or, torn paper cutouts with numbers lined up to show the sorting process of an array. The target audience should use the prototypes; researchers should document the successful and unsuccessful mechanics. Using a think-aloud protocol at this stage can help identify problems with the mechanics and rules that may need to be added to improve learning. The problems learners should solve with the prototype should be analogous to those developed for the post-test.

As the prototype is refined to represent the learning task, developers should document the rules, materials, and mechanics that allow interactive feedback, immersive engagement, and challenges that allow for exploration of correct and incorrect conceptions of the construct. When the construct is particularly abstract, an interactive visualization can help. For example, in a prototype for nested loops, one developer drew two nested circles, and traced program execution over the loops. Another paper- based prototype involved students placing index cards in a grid representing an array. Having learners demonstrate an understanding of these metaphors can reveal and correct misconceptions the developers may have about where learner difficulties occur.

For example, in performing the index-card based array task the tutor uncovered that students became confused between the integer *values* of the array and the integer *index* of the array. To alleviate the student confusion the tutor replaced the array data with pictures.

2.4 Translate: Build interactive versions

After a working prototype that facilitates learning is developed, we then translate the prototype into a video game. If needed, developers can refer to Gunter's text on serious game design paradigms [15] for help on how to apply the instructional methods and prototypes within a video game, always keeping the educational construct and post-test in mind. To be effective for learning, the game environment must promote the same behaviors that are needed to solve the post-test. Developers iteratively build testable parts of the prototype, with frequent feedback from learners, other developers, and instructors.

At this stage, we recommend conducting informal play testing and think-alouds with target audience members to ensure that the game is an effective translation of the specific learning goals. Developers should make changes to the game interface and controls using feedback collected from the observation of players, keeping in mind that making controls "easier" could detract from learning.

Figure 1 shows one level of *Wu's Castle*, a direct translation of tracing nested loops on paper into a game task where the player traverses a nested loop maze [11]. Another level, as shown in Figure 2, translates an index-card based tutoring activity into a game task where players position game characters into one- and two-dimensional arrays.

2.5 Evaluate

There are two phases to game verification once pilot tests show that learners can use and play the game. The first phase is to conduct a formal, lab-based or "in vitro" quasi-experimental study to determine the potential learning gains for the game. The second phase is to perform an "in vivo" controlled study in a realistic setting, such as a classroom, to compare the game effects with other learning methods. The difference between these is quite important with regard to the internal and external validity of the research. The controlled lab setting offered by in vitro studies strengthens internal validity, while the real-world setting of an in vivo study increases the external validity of the research. The *Game2Learn* program seeks to place developed games into the classroom. This means we want to ensure that the games created have positive learning effects in real world situations.

2.5.1 Pilot quasi-experimental study

While play testing and informal evaluation are part of the game design process, a formal quasi-experimental preliminary evaluation incorporating a pre-test, game treatment, post-test design can demonstrate the potential for learning gains when using the newly constructed game. This step is important for building rigorous practices for educational game design and evaluation. This will in turn improve adoption of the developed games into the classrooms by providing solid evidence to educators of the game's validity.

Based on our theoretical foundation, we assume that learning results in discrete movement from one learning state to another. We therefore measure learning through changes in behavior, within subjects, before and after playing the educational game. Through the analysis and reporting of practical significance and effect sizes, educational game researchers can help contribute to a clearer understanding of the impact of games on education. Practical significance, not to be confused with statistical significance, is a judgment call that researchers make concerning the practical implications of a treatments effect.

In educational research, there exist practical significance guidelines, which allow us to make recommendations for sample sizes for educational game research studies. On a bell curve, a change of half a standard deviation (Cohen's $d = .5$), could be equivalent to a letter grade, so we use this as a threshold for practical significance. Feedback, such as that from student tutors, has an effect size of $d = 0.5$ [6]. Mastery learning has also produced effect sizes of $d = 0.5$, while expert tutors have been known to reach effect sizes of $d = 2$ [17]. Cognitive tutors, incorporating mastery learning, and intelligent feedback, have been able to approach the effectiveness of expert tutors [7]. These numbers provide good metrics for what an educational game should be able to accomplish. Educational games should aim for results similar to non-expert tutors, that is at least $d = .5$ for when compared to traditional instruction. When not comparing between groups, the within-subject effect size should aim for an effect size around $d = 1$. Games that include mastery learning techniques and intelligent feedback could achieve higher effect sizes. This is an area of future research; researchers are encouraged to report effect sizes of their studies to aid in future meta-reviews of game-treatment effect sizes. These are only guidelines to practical significance in educational games; it is ultimately up to the researcher to interpret the practical significance of the results.

With knowledge of the expected effect sizes, it is possible to run an a priori power analysis; with this, we can determine an appropriate number of subjects for studies. Assuming a within- subjects effect size of $d = 1$, the number of study participants needed to achieve a power of .8 on a two-tailed dependent mean t- test, with $\alpha = 0.05$, $\delta = 2.80$, we can calculate the following: $n = (\frac{\delta}{d})^2 = (\frac{2.80}{1})^2 = 10$.

This shows that a study must have at least 10 participants to have an 80% chance of detecting an effect in the population, assuming that an effect exists. Because of this, a preliminary study must require at least 10 participants. However, we recommend that researchers plan for more study participants than they need, as participant dropout rates, or other errors decrease the amount of useable data. Researchers should interpret the results of such studies with caution, and should primarily use these to ensure the proper development of the game. Researchers must also take care to ensure that the study pool is a true representation of the target audience. For preliminary studies, it is likely that researchers will recruit volunteer study participants, which can confound the results due to participant characteristics. While a one-group within-subjects experiment is not the most compelling evidence, it can offer insight into the games effectiveness; if a smaller effect-size is found, the preliminary study can inform the researcher about appropriate participant numbers for later controlled studies.

2.5.2 Controlled study

Once a preliminary study provides evidence of a positive within-subject learning effect, the next step is to compare the game with a traditional educational activity. This between-subjects controlled experimental design requires larger numbers of participants, since the difference between groups will not be as large as the difference within subjects. For an 80% chance of discovering an effect with a Cohen's d of .5, on a between-subjects, two-tailed t-test, requires two groups of 64 study participants (128 total); a larger effect size of $d = 1$ would only require 17 participants per group.

We note that, when a researcher believes that the educational game will be more useful for learning than a traditional activity they should provide the game treatment to all learners at the conclusion of the formal study, so that all participants may benefit. Another way to address this issue to use a crossover, or switching replications, research design, where each participant engages in both activities, half with the game first and half with the traditional activity, with tests administered before any activities, between the two, and after both, for all participants. This ensures equal access to both types of activities while providing insight into the impact of using your new game before or after a traditional educational activity.

Pilot study results can help convince instructors to try the prototype educational game as a required assignment in a class. Since our goal is to create new games that educators can use to enhance learning in courses, this is the ideal, realistic measure of game performance. In our prior studies, we have been able to show that a game developed using this methodology can be more effective in teaching computing, and have more lasting effects on learning, than a traditional programming assignment [11].

3. CONCLUSION

This work provides a methodology for a learning objective focused design process for educational games, and methods for study of these games to maximize the chances for learning and detection of that learning. Although our specific environment is the development of educational games by undergraduate and graduate students in short six to 12 month periods, we believe our methodology to be useful for guiding the design of educational games. Development teams tend to have values about what belongs in games, which can be in direct conflict with building learning games that appeal to, and are effective for, a broad audience [13]. Our methodology helps educational game development teams communicate and focus on learning outcomes, and supports the development of research studies that will detect significant learning gains for these games if they exist. This allows limited development teams to tackle the challenging task of creating educational games, while helping them to avoid the pitfalls of many teams working in this multidisciplinary field.

Games developed using the *Game2Learn* methodology, vetted by empirical studies, can support the growing calls for stronger evaluation in educational games; while also educating and inspiring young researchers. Larger numbers of educational game studies and publications will provide the ability to run meta-reviews and find important factors such as the practical significance measures of game-based assignments. Researchers can follow this methodology to develop games to enhance the field, while educators can implement the methodology in classroom and research labs to provide quality undergraduate research.

4. REFERENCES

[1] T. Barnes, E. Powell, A. Chaffin, and H. Lipford. Game2Learn: improving the motivation of CS1 students. In *Proceedings of the 3rd international conference on Game development in computer science education*, pages 1–5, Miami, Florida, 2008. ACM.

[2] T. Barnes, H. Richter, E. Powell, A. Chaffin, and A. Godwin. Game2Learn: building CS1 learning games for retention. In *Proceedings of the 12th annual SIGCSE conference on Innovation and technology in computer science education*, pages 121–125, Dundee, Scotland, 2007. ACM.

[3] B. S. Bloom. *Taxonomy of educational objectives; the classification of educational goals.* Longmans, Green, New York, 1956.

[4] J. C. Carver, L. Jaccheri, S. Morasca, and F. Shull. A checklist for integrating student empirical studies with research and teaching goals. *Empirical Softw. Engg.*, 15:35–59, February 2010.

[5] A. Chaffin and T. Barnes. Lessons from a course on serious games research and prototyping. In *Proceedings of the Fifth International Conference on the Foundations of Digital Games*, FDG '10, pages 32–39, New York, NY, USA, 2010. ACM.

[6] P. A. Cohen, J. A. Kulik, and C.-L. C. Kulik. Educational Outcomes of Tutoring: A Meta-Analysis of Findings. *American Educational Research Journal*, 19(2):237–248, 1982.

[7] A. T. Corbett. Cognitive computer tutors: Solving the two-sigma problem. In *Proceedings of the 8th International Conference on User Modeling 2001*, UM '01, pages 137–147, London, UK, 2001. Springer-Verlag.

[8] L. A. J. Crocker. *Introduction to Classical and Modern Test Theory.* Holt, Rinehart and Winston, Orlando, FL, 1986.

[9] M. Csikszentmihalyi. *Creativity: Flow and the Psychology of Discovery and Invention.* Harper Perennial, 1997.

[10] T. Dahlberg, T. Barnes, A. Rorrer, E. Powell, and L. Cairco. Improving retention and graduate recruitment through immersive research experiences for undergraduates. In *Proceedings of the 39th SIGCSE technical symposium on Computer science education*, pages 466–470, Portland, OR, USA, 2008. ACM.

[11] M. Eagle and T. Barnes. Evaluation of a game-based lab assignment. In *Proceedings of the 4th International Conference on Foundations of Digital Games*, pages 64–70, Orlando, Florida, 2009. ACM.

[12] H. Erdogmus and O. Tanir. *Advances in software engineering : comprehension, evaluation, and evolution.* Springer, New York, 2002.

[13] M. Flanagan and H. Nissenbaum. A Game Design Methodology to Incorporate Social Activist Themes. *CHI -CONFERENCE-*, 1:181–190, 2007.

[14] T. Fullerton, C. Swain, and S. Hoffman. *Game Design Workshop: Designing, Prototyping, and Playtesting Games.* CMP Books, 2004.

[15] R. F. Gunter, G. A. Kenny and E. H. Vick. A case for a formal design paradigm for serious games. *The Journal of the International Digital Media and Arts Association*, 3(1):93–105, 2006.

[16] J. Kirriemuir, A. McFarlane, and N. Futurelab. *Literature review in games and learning : a report for NESTA Futurelab.* NESTA Futurelab, Bristol, 2004.

[17] C.-L. C. Kulik. Effectiveness of Mastery Learning Programs: A Meta-Analysis. *Review of Educational Research*, 60(2):265–299, 1990.

[18] C. Lewis and J. Rieman. Task-centered user interface design. *Text*, 2002(December):14–19, 2008.

[19] M. J. Nathan and A. Petrosino. Expert Blind Spot Among Preservice Teachers. *American Educational Research Journal*, 40(4):905–928, 2003.

[20] M. Piontek. Best practices for designing and grading exams. Technical report, Center for Research on Learning and Teaching, Ann Arbor, MI, 2008.

[21] J. A. Polack-Wahl and K. Anewalt. Learning strategies and undergraduate research. In *Proceedings of the 37th SIGCSE technical symposium on Computer science education*, pages 209–213, Houston, Texas, USA, 2006. ACM.

[22] M. Prensky. Digital game-based learning. *Comput. Entertain.*, 1(1):21–21, 2003.

[23] D. W. Shaffer, K. R. Squire, R. Halverson, and J. P. Gee. Video games and the future of learning. *Phi Delta Kappan*, 87(2):104–111, 2005.

[24] M. W. van Someren and et al. *The Think Aloud Method: A Practical Guide to Modelling Cognitive Processes.* Academic Press, Inc., 525 B Street, Suite 1900, San Diego, CA 92101 ($48)., 1994.

[25] C. G. v. Wangenheim and S. Forrest. To Game or Not to Game? *IEEE Software*, 26:92–94, 2009. IEEE Software.

Course Guides: A Model for Bringing Professionals into the Classroom

Thomas Gibbons
The College of St. Scholastica
1200 Kenwood Avenue
Duluth, MN 55811
tgibbons@css.edu

ABSTRACT

A new model, professional course guides, describes how practicing professionals can be brought into the classroom as student mentors and integrated into the course material. This new model is compared to existing models for student interactions with practicing professionals including guest speakers, adjunct faculty, and program mentors.

Categories and Subject Descriptors

K.3.2 [**Computer and Information Science Education**]: Computer & Information Science Education – Information Systems Education, Curriculum.

General Terms

Design, Experimentation, Human Factors.

Keywords

Professional practice, industry/academic collaboration, information systems, classroom management, mentors, systems analysis and design.

1. INTRODUCTION

In the last decade, the importance of exposing Information System (IS) students to real world perspectives has been repeatedly highlighted. See (Grant, Malloy, Murphy, Foreman, & Robinson, 2010) and (Kamoun & Selim, 2007) for summaries. Most agree that the question is not whether students need to explore real world perspectives, but what methods are most effective at this.

A new model, professional course guides, describes how practicing professionals can be brought into the classroom as student mentors and integrated into the course material. This new model is compared to existing models for student interactions with practicing professionals including guest speakers, adjunct faculty, and program mentors. Challenges to implementing the new model are identified and the performance of the new model is assessed in a Systems Analysis and Design undergraduate course.

2. PRACTICING PROFESSIONALS IN EDUCATION

Different disciplines bridge the gap between the college student and the practicing profession in different ways. Nursing curriculums use clinical experiences to refine nursing skills and give students a chance to observe professionals in the workplace. Education curriculums use student teaching to place students alongside practicing teachers in the classroom. Computing curriculums have used less formal methods for bridging the gap between school and professional practice. Generally computing curriculums have relied on a blend of the following methods:

Guest Speakers: One simple way to bring practicing professionals into the classroom is simply to invite them in as a guest speaker. As shown by Kamoun and Selim, the benefits of bringing IT professionals into the classroom as guest speakers include discovery of new IT career opportunities and an increase in students' positive attitudes towards the IT profession (Kamoun & Selim, 2007). Their work also suggests that increased benefits could result from tying guest speaker topics more closely to the course learning outcomes. Work from other disciplines, including accounting (Metrejean, Pittman, & Zarzeski, 2002) and hospitality and tourism (McCleary & Weaver, 2008), suggests faculty and practicing professionals also benefit from guest speaker events through mutual interactions.

Adjunct Faculty: The use of part-time or adjunct instructors has been growing at most colleges and universities (Bettinger & Long, 2010). While some adjunct faculty members do not have professional experience, a number of them are working professionals who take time out of their day to teach. These teachers generally infuse the courses they teach with real world examples that help bridge the school-profession gap. But finding working professionals who also have the skills needed in teaching remains a challenge because, "expertise in a particular domain does not guarantee that one is good at helping others learn it" (Tenenberg, 2010).

Mentors: Mentors are generally practicing professionals who meet with students multiple times during a given time period. Examples of these include computing identity mentoring (Boyer, Thomas, Rorrer, Cooper, & Vouk, 2010) and web based professional mentoring (Williams, 2009). Work has also been done to create a framework to measure the effectiveness of different mentoring methods (Pamuk & Thompson, 2009) in the hopes to identify the needed components of a mentoring program which is beneficial to the student, the professional, and the college. One of the challenges of mentoring systems is that they are generally removed from the classroom and so cannot focus on specific course learning outcomes.

Curriculum Development: While not directly interacting with students, practicing professionals have been a standard part of most school's program review process through serving on

Permission to make digital or hard copies of all or part of this work for personal or classroom use is granted without fee provided that copies are not made or distributed for profit or commercial advantage and that copies bear this notice and the full citation on the first page. To copy otherwise, or republish, to post on servers or to redistribute to lists, requires prior specific permission and/or a fee.
SIGCSE'12, February 29–March 3, 2012, Raleigh, North Carolina, USA.
Copyright 2012 ACM 978-1-4503-1098-7/12/02...$10.00.

advisory boards. While not all colleges use advisory boards with working professionals, a large percentage of the top IT programs in the nation make use of professionals in this way (Benamati, Ozdemir, & Smith, 2010). An alternative to the standard curriculum advisory board has been developed. The Industry Fellows model pairs a faculty member with a practicing professional focused on refining and delivering the curriculum for a single course (Tenenberg, 2010). In this model, the industry professional not only advises the faculty member on the curriculum, but also joins regularly in the classroom as a co-lecturer. But where advisory boards generally look at the entire curriculum, industry fellows focus on a single course.

The last two methods for bridging the gap between school and industry do not rely on bringing practicing professionals into the classroom, but instead send students out into the workplace.

Internships: The first of these are internships or co-ops where students work, frequently for pay, in the industry. Many companies have formal summer internship programs or co-op programs that last a semester or more—see Surakka & Malmi, 2002, for a comparison of different work programs. Students completing internship or co-op programs have shown an increased understanding of the computing profession (Stanton, Guzman, & Fagnot, 2006).

Applied class projects: A hybrid approach combining some elements of an internship with some elements from the traditional classroom is the applied projects course. These courses are often the capstone course in a computing curriculum. A good overview of this model and how it fits in with current model curriculums is in (Grant, et al., 2010). Similarly, (Rusu, Rusu, Docimo, Santiago, & Paglione, 2009) present a case study of using the applied class project in a software engineering course.

3. PROFESSIONAL COURSE GUIDES

The concept of a course guide is a practicing professional who acts as a mentor within a particular course. Unlike typical mentors, who generally interact outside the curriculum, course guides can be integrated closely into the course and learning outcomes. Like guest speakers, course guides can help relate the course material to the professional setting, but by interacting with the same student over time, they can build up a relationship with that student and understand the student better.

The author developed and tested the professional course guide model in a Systems Analysis and Design undergraduate course. Alumni who were practicing professionals were recruited to be course guides. Because they were volunteering their time, careful limits were placed on the requirements for participation. Guides were asked to participate in five 20-minute web conferences with their assigned students over a twelve week period. The course schedule was altered, replacing 40 minutes of lecture every other week with course guide related activities.

The course was taught in a computer lab which included web conferencing equipment, web cams, and microphone/earphone headsets for each student. Each course guide also needed a computer with a microphone and preferably a webcam. Web conferencing software was also set up with a separate web conferencing room for each course guide.

Questions covering the current course material were developed and shared with the students and guides before each course session involving the course guides. During the sessions, students spent 20 minutes web conferencing with the guides and discussing the questions. With 18 students and 12 course guides, each course guide was assigned to one or two students.

Students conferenced with the same guides over the 12 week period, allowing them to build knowledge about the company where the guide worked and the projects and activities the guide was involved in. Each week one discussion question was included of a more general nature, allowing the students to learn more about the course guides and the environment where they worked.

After 20 minute web conferencing sessions with the course guides, the students spent 15 minutes sharing responses with the rest of the class. This allowed students to compare their guides' response with others and discuss how different companies' development methodologies varied.

4. CHALLENGES TO SUCCESS

During the development and implementation of this model, three primary challenges were identified. The first was handling times when the technology failed by using redundancy. Redundant technology does not guarantee student and guide attendance, so plans also were needed for times when the students or guides failed to participate. The final challenge was in the recruitment of the practicing professionals to serve as course guides. This section describes the simple steps taken to overcome each of these challenges.

4.1 Challenges of Technology Failure

When technology is a key component of your classroom activities, it is important to have a plan in place to handle technology failures. While this project used a robust network with tested web conferencing software, technology failures were still anticipated and did occur. These were commonly related to the microphone and earphones used by both students and guides, though we did also experience scheduled network downtime at some guide sites.

To provide redundant communication, each guide provided a cell phone number that could be used as a backup communication device if the web conferencing system failed. Most students also had cell phones available for use, but an additional phone was provided as a backup for the few students without cell phones. This allowed students to simply call their guides when the technology failed and carry on the session via the cellular network. While this back-up plan allowed communication to continue, it did provide only audio and not video conferencing.

4.2 Absent Guides or Students

Because of the one-to-one assignment of some students to guides, it was also crucial to have a plan in place for when either guides or students were absent. Guides would generally reply to an email sent out before each session if their schedule did not allow them to participate, but sometimes a guide was simply preoccupied and did not connect to the session or answer a cell phone call. While students are known for skipping classes, attendance on days with course guide sessions was very high, as students knew that it was their responsibility to meet with their assigned guides. Still there were times when students could not attend the classes.

To accommodate the absences of either students or guides, we did not use an exact one-to-one mapping of guides to students. Instead, the number of guides was approximately 2/3 the number of students. This meant that some guides were assigned two students to work with. This provided the flexibility needed to dynamically reassign students and guides to handle absences. For the first five minutes of each session, students discussed a general ice breaker question with the guides. This allowed time to determine which students and guides were missing and reassign students to guides on the fly. When a guide was unavailable, students were temporarily reassigned to a different web conferencing room with a different guide. When a guide did not have a student to work with, one student from a pair of students assigned to a different guide was reassigned to the guide without a student. While this may sound complicated, it worked rather well using a simple shared spreadsheet to track the 12 web conferencing rooms and whether there were guides and students in each room during the first five minutes of each session.

4.3 The Challenge of Recruiting Guides

Another challenge to the project's success is recruiting enough course guides. As noted by (Williams, 2009) one of the keys to recruiting practicing professionals as guides or mentors is to carefully limit the required time commitment. Course guides were given specific days and times they were needed during recruitment and the time requirements were limited to 20 minutes every other week. Use of desktop web conferencing equipment also meant that many course guides had to connect to the class directly from their offices, thus eliminating travel time needed for face-to-face interactions.

Another challenge to recruiting guides or mentors from alumni is simply being able to contact alumni. The author's work with course guides supports William's position (Williams, 2009) that maintaining strong alumni connections facilitates the successful recruitment of mentors or guides. The growing use of social media networks has strengthened the faculty's ability to stay connected with alumni.

5. ASSESSMENT OF THE MODEL

The assessment of the course guide model looks at how well the model achieved the three different objectives:

1. Increase student understanding of the professional work environment and prepare students for their future internships and careers.
2. Increase the engagement of alumni in the academic process, providing them an avenue for recruiting promising students while strengthening the relationship and possible future support from these alumni.
3. Provide an avenue whereby faculty can validate the relevance of a course's curriculum with professional practice.

At the end of the course, students were given an anonymous survey to assess the first objective. As shown in Figure 1, over 90% of the students found course guides helpful and worth the use of class time.

Comments from the anonymous survey also show that students felt the course guides helped give them a better understanding of the professional work environment:

- "It was really helpful to talk to a person who is actually in the workforce to see how they use the information that we have been learning in their everyday life. It was also helpful to develop a professional contact that we can go to in the future with questions or concerns."
- "A real world experience was very needed as we complete different units of the course."
- "I liked the experience that the course guides brought. I liked their knowledge that they had."

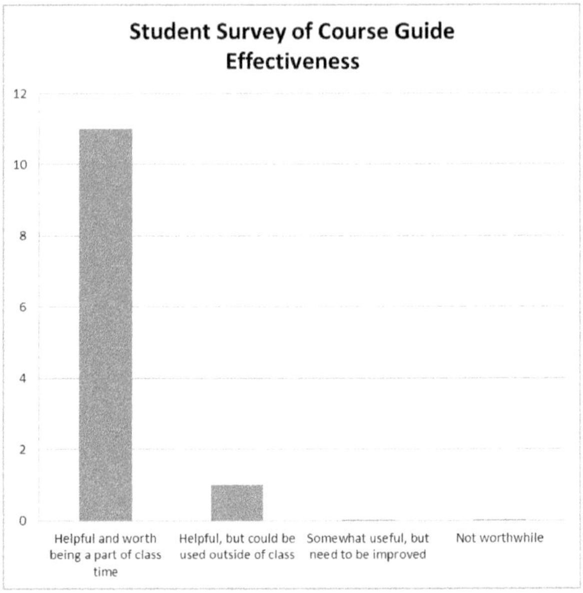

Figure 1

- "I really liked being able to talk to someone that has work experience so then I can get their input on what really goes on in the work place. It was a great experience!!"
- "Hearing what it was like out in the real world and hearing how the material we are learning is used in an organization."
- "They gave a significant amount of information that we were able to relate to. It was a nice change of pace rather than listening to power points every day."
- "I really liked that they were able to share their real world experiences with us and how what we're learning is actually used in their jobs."
- "I really enjoyed having the course guides available to us. Having the guide really helped put what we are learning into perspective with how she uses it daily at her job."
- "Hearing the stories from people who have had these experiences from real life."

The second objective is to increase the engagement of alumni. In recruiting alumni to participate as course guides, a number of them gave anecdotal feedback that they and their company felt that participating would help recruit students as future employees. In today's job market, many companies are struggling to fill openings with qualified candidates and are making recruitment a priority goal. Many of the course guides also expressed that they found being a course guide personally rewarding and provided a nice way for them to share their expertise and help mentor a student.

One qualitative measure of whether practicing professionals found being course guides rewarding is their interest in future opportunities to participate as course guides. Of the twelve course guides, ten expressed a desire to participate again in the future, one had a change of employment and responsibilities that prevented him from participating in the future, and one course guide did not want to commit to future participation. The fact that over 80% of course guides wanted to participate again in the future is strong evidence that they found the activity rewarding at both a professional and personal level.

The final objective was to give the teacher the chance to validate the course material. A majority of the material in a Systems Analysis and Design course focuses on understanding the processes professionals use to analyze an existing software system and designing and implementing an updated version of the software. Student questions for course guides generally focused on if the guides used any of the techniques discussed in class over the previous two weeks. Students would obviously question the relevancy of topics covered in class that were not used by any course guides.

This process allowed the author to validate certain course material, while questioning the relevancy of other course material. The feedback of course guides in the classroom followed by a student discussion sharing insight from different course guides is similar to Just-in-Time Teaching (Davis, 2009). While not following the JITT framework, the use of course guides forces the instructor to modify course material on a tight time frame. It was not uncommon for guides to bring up the use of certain methodologies or tools and then spend the remaining time period discussing these topics with students.

The use of course guides also brought into question the relative importance of different topics in the course and the amount of time devoted to each. In this particular course, none of the course guides were using Use Cases or other UML techniques, though significant class time was spent on these topics. On the other hand, many of the course guides stressed the importance of testing and discussed different testing methods. Future offerings of this course will likely reflect this by increasing the time spent on testing methodologies and reducing the time spent on Use Cases and other UML techniques.

6. COSTS OF THE MODEL

If this model increases student understanding of their future profession and allows the teacher to validate the course curriculum, what are the costs of implementing this model?

Time: This model requires additional teacher preparation time to contact prospective course guides and to assign students to guides. The model also requires class time to be freed up for the course guides which may require removing material from the course. The author was able to replace class time dedicated to reviewing material with time with course guides, which also served to review material. There was additional time needed for each guided session to prepare questions and contact guides, but this time displaced time normally spent preparing a lecture or other classroom activity.

Equipment: This model made use of a computer lab with microphones, earphones and webcams. This equipment may be available at many institutions, but that is not guaranteed. The author's institution received a grant allowing for updating a computer lab for this model. In the future, institutions may replace desktop web conferencing with video conferencing via smart phones or tablets.

Professionals: A key component of this model is access to practicing professionals. Alumni were asked to volunteer their time as course guides and no reimbursement was given to guides, except for small thank you gifts. The professionals did see some benefits to their companies through interactions with prospective employees. Limits on the time requirements allowed the professionals to see a balance between the time costs of serving as course guides and the recruiting benefits.

7. CONCLUSION

Although most agree that students need to have more interactions with real world professionals, there is less agreement on the best ways to achieve this. While guest speakers bring practicing professionals into the classroom, the single contact between one guest speaker and many students prevents a personalized mentor relationship from developing and provides a single point to compare course material with professional practice. Adjunct faculty, who are also practicing professionals, are able to mentor students over an entire course and build multiple ties between course material and professional practice, but it is challenging to find adjunct instructors who have the skill set to be successful in both the profession and the classroom. The use of practicing professionals as student mentors provides a way to build relationships between students and the professionals outside the classroom. While this makes it easier to find mentors than adjunct faculty, removing the professionals from the classroom makes it difficult for the students to compare course material with professional practice.

A new model, professional course guides, demonstrates how practicing professionals can be brought into the classroom as student mentors. Because of the repeated interactions, students can build a mentoring relationship with the professionals. The interactions between students and their guides can also be tied closely to the course material, since this relationship exists within the context of a specific course. Since there are multiple interactions between students and guides, students can compare course material with professional practice over the entire course and see how a working professional's use of course material varies over time.

Assessment of the model shows that students felt the class time spent with course guides was more valuable than class time spent on lectures and hands on assignments. The professional course guides felt that the time spent mentoring students was valuable for both recruiting future employees and personally providing guidance to students. This also provided a clear method for the teacher to validate the course material through regular feedback from practicing professionals on the relevancy of the weekly topics.

8. ACKNOWLEDGMENTS

I am grateful to the Securian Foundation for supporting the development of this model including the laboratory updated web conferencing hardware and software. I am grateful to the course guides who were willing to participate in this program and the students of the Systems Analysis and Design course. My thanks are also extended to all the others who supported me in this endeavor.

9. REFERENCES

[1] Benamati, J. H., Ozdemir, Z. D., & Smith, H. J. (2010). Aligning undergraduate IS curricula with industry needs. *Commun. ACM, 53*(3), 152-156.

[2] Bettinger, E. P., & Long, B. T. (2010). Does Cheaper Mean Better? The Impact of Using Adjunct Instructors on Student Outcomes. *Review of Economics and Statistics, 92*(3), 598-613. doi: http://www.mitpressjournals.org/loi/rest

[3] Boyer, K. E., Thomas, E. N., Rorrer, A. S., Cooper, D., & Vouk, M. A. (2010). *Increasing technical excellence, leadership and commitment of computing students through identity-based mentoring.* Paper presented at the Proceedings of the 41st ACM technical symposium on Computer science education, Milwaukee, Wisconsin, USA.

[4] Davis, J. (2009). *Experiences with just-in-time teaching in systems and design courses.* Paper presented at the Proceedings of the 40th ACM technical symposium on Computer science education, Chattanooga, TN, USA.

[5] Grant, D. M., Malloy, A. D., Murphy, M. C., Foreman, J., & Robinson, R. A. (2010). Real World Project: Integrating the Classroom, External Business Partnerships and Professional Organizations. *Journal of Information Technology Education, 9,* IIP-167-IIP-196.

[6] Kamoun, F., & Selim, S. (2007). A Framework towards Assessing the Merits of Inviting IT Professionals to the Classroom. *Journal of Information Technology Education, 6,* 81-103.

[7] McCleary, K. W., & Weaver, P. A. (2008). The Effective Use of Guest Speakers in the Hospitality and Tourism Curriculum. *Journal of Teaching in Travel & Tourism, 8*(4), 401-414.

[8] Metrejean, C., Pittman, J., & Zarzeski, M. T. (2002). Guest speakers: reflections on the role of accountants in the classroom. *Accounting Education, 11*(4), 347-364.

[9] Pamuk, S., & Thompson, A. D. (2009). Development of a technology mentor survey instrument: Understanding student mentors' benefits. [Article]. *Computers & Education, 53*(1), 14-23.

[10] Rusu, A., Rusu, A., Docimo, R., Santiago, C., & Paglione, M. (2009). *Academia-academia-industry collaborations on software engineering projects using local-remote teams.* Paper presented at the Proceedings of the 40th ACM technical symposium on Computer science education, Chattanooga, TN, USA.

[11] Stanton, J., Guzman, I., & Fagnot, I. (2006). *Internships and occupational commitment of college students in IT-related majors.* Paper presented at the Proceedings of the 2006 ACM SIGMIS CPR conference on computer personnel research, Claremont, California, USA.

[12] Surakka, S., & Malmi, L. (2002). Work experience vs. co-operative education program. *SIGCSE Bull., 34*(4), 44-47.

[13] Tenenberg, J. (2010). *Industry fellows: bringing professional practice into the classroom.* Paper presented at the Proceedings of the 41st ACM technical symposium on Computer science education, Milwaukee, Wisconsin, USA.

[14] Williams, R. (2009). *Work in progress - professional mentoring for CS students.* Paper presented at the Proceedings of the 39th IEEE international conference on Frontiers in education conference, San Antonio, Texas, USA.

Towards a Better Capstone Experience

Sriram Mohan
Rose-Hulman Institute of Technology
5500 Wabash Avenue
Terre Haute, Indiana
mohan@rose-hulman.edu

Stephen Chenoweth
Rose-Hulman Institute of Technology
5500 Wabash Avenue
Terre Haute, Indiana
chenowet@rose-hulman.edu

Shawn Bohner
Rose-Hulman Institute of Technology
5500 Wabash Avenue
Terre Haute, Indiana
bohner@rose-hulman.edu

ABSTRACT

The computer science capstone experience is designed to bridge the gap from university expectations to those of industry. Yet trying to solve this problem with a single course sequence, even one spanning the senior year, has some shortcomings, in terms of learning outcomes which can be achieved, and also instructional strategies that can be employed. We describe here an alternative plan which first provides a junior year of practice on a client-based project integrated with learning design and other related topics, followed by a senior year in which students can work more independently to hone these skills on a harder year-long project with another client. This two-year sequence, with scaffolding provided at first that is gradually removed, has proven to be especially effective in preparing undergraduates for a career in the software industry. The approach also integrates well with the need for these students to become proficient at working in engineering teams.

General Terms

Design

Categories and Subject Descriptors

K.3.2 [**Computer and Information Science Education**]: [Curriculum]

Keywords

Software Engineering, Capstone, Education, Curriculum

1. INTRODUCTION

Industry practitioners often express concern that software engineering and computer science degrees do not adequately prepare students for a professional career. This is a concern, given a sizable majority of CS students join the workforce on graduation. Universities in response have strengthened their programs to expose students to current trends in a rapidly changing field - chiefly by using the senior project or a similar capstone experience. In spite of the many advantages of the capstone experience, there are some shortcomings that need to be addressed. These can be analyzed from two perspectives - a) Learning Outcomes and b) Instructional Strategy.

Learning outcomes Some common core learning outcomes associated with the capstone experience include:

- Demonstrate the necessity for life long learning.
- Apply relevant professional, communication and social skills.
- Understand and apply relevant technical skills to design and develop a software solution.
- Demonstrate the ability to succeed in a software design experience similar to the real world.

An informal survey of several course instructors reveals a common concern - the capstone experience has become a sink for various educational outcomes that cannot be met elsewhere in the curriculum[1]. While one can argue that the capstone experience is a natural fit for other learning outcomes, it must be noted that these can distract from core learning outcomes. Examples of such additional outcomes are mature decision making, design, testing, construction, requirements, ethics and teamwork.

Instructional Strategy Schools have implemented the capstone experience in several ways including a) a traditional two semester, year long software engineering course, and b) a project-based learning approach. Project-based learning approaches have traditionally revolved around the use of either a) a simulated client - the instructor acting as a client, and b) a real client with a real need.

Each of the above approaches has distinct merits and demerits. The learning outcomes to be met by the capstone experience determine the instructional strategy and the approach to be employed for the capstone. For instance, if the chief outcome is to provide students with an experience that is similar to the real world, the use of project-based learning with a real client is often preferred as the optimal strategy. As Walker et. al point out [11] "the process of software development is learnt by developing software under conditions similar to those used in industry". The importance of using real clients is further confirmed by [3] and [6]. The use of the senior capstone experience creates a situation when approached from an instructional design perspective- students have just one chance to learn, reflect and apply the various concepts they have learnt before graduation.

This raises an interesting research question. **Is there a better educational strategy?** We analyzed this question

Permission to make digital or hard copies of all or part of this work for personal or classroom use is granted without fee provided that copies are not made or distributed for profit or commercial advantage and that copies bear this notice and the full citation on the first page. To copy otherwise, to republish, to post on servers or to redistribute to lists, requires prior specific permission and/or a fee.
SIGCSE'12, February 29–March 3, 2012, Raleigh, North Carolina, USA.
Copyright 2012 ACM 978-1-4503-1098-7/12/02 ...$10.00.

from an instructional design perspective and made several systemic changes to our curriculum. In this paper, we provide an overview of the instructional strategies that we have used, the changes that we made to our curriculum and the results from our experience over the last three years and the improvements we have observed.

2. INSTRUCTIONAL DESIGN

We practice **Test First Teaching** [2], an extreme programming technique applied to Instructional Design. Test First Teaching encourages the course designer to first identify the outcome and assessment technique. The outcome we had in mind was a simple one - we wanted our students to engage in a software development process in a manner similar to industry professionals. We wanted our students to be able to analyze and understand the given problem, the client and the technologies available, and to identify strategies, processes and plans for producing said software within the available time frame and within any budgetary constraints that were imposed by the client. We felt that it was important for our students to have enough design experience and be able to reflect on their past experience in class projects and internships to identify the best way to proceed in any given situation [1]. In effect, we wanted to avoid the capstone experience from becoming a "trial by fire" - an experience that can set up a student team for failure. We had a different idea in mind.

A quick detour into the world of cognitive psychology leads us to **Metacognition** [8]. Metacognition - the art of thinking about thinking - has been popular in the field of educational strategy. It refers to the ability to control and reflect on activities such as planning, monitoring, evaluating the progress of a task - all vital to the success of a software professional. Metacognition also plays a critical role in successful life-long learning. Students who demonstrate these meta cognitive abilities have a higher level of performance and are known to complete their work in an efficient manner. Researchers in instructional design have identified several strategies that can be used to instruct these vital skills to students. Most of these strategies involve providing the student with both the knowledge of the skills concerned and experience or practice in using these strategies. "Simply providing knowledge without experience or vice versa does not seem to be sufficient" [7].

A strategy that has grown in popularity is **Cognitive Scaffolding** [10]. This instructional strategy is built around the idea of an expert guiding the development of a student by providing support structures that the learner can use to advance to the next level of learning. The scaffolds are temporary and are removed gradually as the student's confidence and skill level increases. The objective is for the student to reach a skill level that enables them to master the task independently [4].

As a capstone project is a team project, **Cooperative Learning** is key to it's success. Teaching is not provided by the instructor only; team members play a substantial role in teaching each other what they learn. Cooperative learning is the instructional use of small groups so that students work together to maximize their own and each other's learning [5]. This can be contrasted with competitive learning (where students compete for the highest grade, or other tangible reward). Yet, teams sometimes experience challenges (e.g., strong students feel they carry too much load while weaker students feel they are not listened to or considered unimportant). The way to get the most out of cooperative learning is to start with requisite cognitive scaffolding for class exercises and projects, and systematically remove the scaffolding as the knowledge matures in the students to a point that they can take more responsibility for perpetuating their learning without the scaffolding inhibiting their progress.

How does this all fit in? We envisioned a curriculum that would implement the above strategies and thus would better advance our students through their capstone experience.

- To enhance the meta cognitive skills that are critical to their success, we desired a capstone experience wherein our students would practice software development in a manner similar to the real world. We wanted our students to demonstrate to the faculty that they had the ability to **independently** lead the planning, design, development, testing and deployment of a software solution that met the client's need's.
- To ensure that students had all the core communication skills (teaming, writing, listening, speaking and reading) and the right mix of cooperative learning experiences, we enriched our freshman and sophomore curriculum to incorporate these strategies.[2]
- We built a scaffolding experience as a part of our junior sequence to help the students gain the elicitation, design, software construction, quality assurance and maintenance skills that are critical to a successful capstone experience.

3. CURRICULUM

It is important to understand the educational context within which we implemented the changes. We are a four year engineering college with an emphasis on undergraduate education. Currently our department offers undergraduate programs in computer science and software engineering. As a part of these programs, graduating software engineering students are required to complete a year long senior capstone experience. This experience requires students to work on teams of about four students on a project for a client to understand the need for, design, and develop a system that meets the identified needs, and to deliver and refine the system in response to feedback about those needs. Past examples of clients include companies like Microsoft, Omni Software, Turner Broadcasting, Mayo Clinic, Naval Surface Warfare Center, etc.

3.1 Key Elements of Cooperative Learning

The following five elements are essential to any cooperative learning experience.[5]

1. Positive interdependence: Team members rely on one another to achieve the goals. Team members "sink or swim together." If any team member fails to do

[1]The assessment technique was the success of a team's solution.

[2]Our students work on team projects in every core course and are taught the basic skills that are necessary to have a good teaming experience, techniques to lead teams, techniques to participate in effective meetings, techniques to collaborate effective and techniques to offer constructive feedback to their team members.

their part, everyone suffers consequences - therefore, this engenders commitment to one another to work towards success.

2. Individual or group accountability: All team members are held accountable for doing their share of the work as well as for mastery of all of the material.
3. Promotive (face-to-face) interaction: This occurs when team members share resources, support, encourage, and recognize each other's efforts to learn. Although some of the group work may be parceled out and done individually, some must be done interactively, with group members providing feedback, challenging reasoning and conclusions, and perhaps most importantly, teaching and encouraging one another.
4. Requisite interpersonal and collaborative skills: Team members are encouraged to develop and practice effective leadership, decision-making, communication, trust-building, and conflict management skills.
5. Group processing: Team members set group goals, periodically assess what they are doing well as a team, and identify changes they will make to function more effectively in the future.

3.1.1 How did we implement cooperative learning?

Practicum deepens the understanding for students. Approaches to providing practicum experience for CS and SE students included (in order of sophistication):

- A series of homework assignments: These are designed and directed at understanding the various facets of developing software artifacts (project plan, requirements specification, architecture, design, etc.). The advantage to this is that everyone has the same deliverables and it can be readily designed to accentuate course outcomes. It works best for a single course. The down side is that it takes a lot of design of the assignments and conditioning for the students to make it look anything like a real-world experience with clients and team members. Further, there is effort expended to ensure that the students' deliverables are not shared or copied between students; hence, it is not a good cooperative learning exercise (it lacks elements 3, 4, and 5 of cooperative learning listed above).
- An individual project assignment: This individual assignment is to develop software for the class project where everyone gets the same project, but students do not collaborate. The advantage to this is that everyone has the same deliverables and it can be readily designed to accentuate course outcomes. It works best for a single software engineering course, but can be staged across multiple courses .

  The downside is that it takes a lot of design of the assignment deliverables and conditioning of the students to make it look anything like a real-world experience with clients and team members. In this case, staging the reviews of the artifacts replaces the homework assignment grading and can be accommodated with project milestones. Again, there is effort expended to ensure that the students' deliverables are not shared or copied between students; hence, it is not a good cooperative learning exercise (it lacks elements 3, 4, and 5 of cooperative learning listed above).
- Team project assignment: This is a project assignment to develop a specific software product with a team of three to five project members where everyone gets the same project, but the students do collaborate. The main advantage to this is that the project can be more substantive and representative of challenges in the real-world environment. Everyone has the same deliverables and it can be readily designed to accentuate course outcomes. It works well for both a single course and for a multiple course sequence in software engineering.

  The downside is that it still takes a lot of design of the assignment deliverables and conditioning for the students to make it look similar to a real-world project with clients. In this case, staging the reviews of the artifacts replaces the homework assignment grading and can be accommodated with project milestones. Again, because the same system is to be delivered, effort must be expended to ensure that the student teams' deliverables are not shared or copied between teams. Meeting and advising teams can be challenging - particularly with teams that have members that choose to be laggard or disruptive. This is a good cooperative learning exercise, but additional activities for evaluation of team members must be incorporated.
- A team project for a client - This assignment is to develop a software product with a team of three to five project members for a specific client. In this case the deliverables will be specific to a real client who along with the project must be managed. This is where things get challenging for the instructor and students, but potentially very rewarding for the student. The main advantage to this is that the project is more real-world and representative of the challenges of real projects. Each team has a different client and different delivery set tailored to the client. Everyone has the same general deliverables, but they are specific and may not be easily designed to accentuate course outcomes (however, team and client engagement outcomes may be much better served). The students get more of the impact of working with teams and managing the project, the client, and the product as the project evolves. It works best for a multiple software engineering course sequence.

  The main downside is that the acquisition, selection, and distribution of the projects to the teams is a substantial effort. Further, meeting with teams and organizing for successful delivery of these projects can be challenging - particularly with teams that have members that choose to be laggard or disruptive. In grading the project outcomes, client and team member perspectives must be incorporated along with additional activities for evaluation of team and team member performance.

  Note also that not all clients are created equal - on the most agreeable side is an on-campus client who understands the educational objectives of the project and is likely to manage well to student expectations. However, they seldom offer a real-world experience. On the most industrial side, the conflicts can arise with mismanaged expectations where the client does not understand or fully agree with educational objectives, but the students see the opportunity to work with a new technology or relevant project. This is a good cooperative learning exercise, but all of these and more must be addressed when having student projects for real clients.

We implemented our cooperative learning exercise via the junior project experience - an activity that is utilized to provide our scaffold. More details are available in the next section.

3.2 Scaffolding our way to success

To help educate students on the skills necessary for a successful senior capstone experience and to provide them with a sound background in software engineering, we require our students to take a series of courses on the following subject areas:

1. Quality Assurance
2. Requirements Engineering and Human Computer Interaction (HCI)
3. Project Management
4. Design
5. Construction, Maintenance and Evolution
6. Formal Methods

Over the past couple of years, in order to create an experience similar to those faced by software professionals and to provide our students with more opportunities to work with real clients, we reorganized some of the above courses into a Junior Design Sequence. The courses that comprise the junior design sequence share a common project (similar in idea and execution to that of the senior capstone experience). These courses[3] include the following:

1. Requirements Engineering and HCI
2. Project Management
3. Design
4. Construction, Maintenance and Evolution

3.2.1 Junior Project

The Junior Project is the first chance for many of these students to participate in developing a system that requires more than a single summer internship or academic term. In addition to the work that the team will do to understand and implement the requirements, they will also be learning about a variety of important techniques for:

1. Gathering, analyzing, and documenting requirements;
2. Developing prototypes;
3. Describing designs and evaluating design trade-offs;
4. Developing and evolving quality software that can be maintained over time.

This additional learning occurs in regular classes involving lectures, case studies, homework, and exams. This combination of acquiring new knowledge and applying it to a real world project provides a great balance and a scaffold for our students to learn the skills necessary for a successful software development experience. With this in mind, we decided to utilize a three-tier learning model to provide numerous opportunities for our students to practice and develop a mastery of these vital skills. The three tier model includes the following:

1. Tier 1 - In-class Elicitation
2. Tier 2 - Elicitation via Homework Projects
3. Tier 3 - Elicitation through Junior Design

You can find more details of the this scaffolding experience in [9].

It must be noted that students in the computer science program have the option of pursuing either a senior capstone experience or a senior thesis to complete their graduation requirements. However, irrespective of this choice, the computer science students are required to participate in the junior design sequence through the following courses

1. Requirements Engineering and HCI
2. Design

To align the Junior Projects with the classes the students are taking, we follow a hybrid process. This begins with classical requirements elicitation and documentation, where the students also learn to interact with project stakeholders and hone their verbal and written communication skills. The teams then move into a more iterative development process, regularly delivering successively more refined systems and documentation.

The junior projects tend to have a smaller scope than a traditional senior capstone experience. And because the requirements phase is more structured, Junior Projects can sometimes accommodate projects that might be less clearly defined at the outset. For Junior Projects we favor proposals that can be implemented using object-oriented languages and systems. This constraint supports the educational outcomes of our Software Design course, which emphasizes object-oriented design patterns.

3.2.2 Junior Project Schedule

In general, work on the junior projects is done using an agile lifecycle model once requirements and a prototype are done. As the teams progress through their junior year, the scaffolding for learning new material progressively is removed. By the time they get to spring term, the topics discussed in class are applied directly to their project. Thus, the projects evolve into being more and more like problem-based-learning activities.

The schedule for delivery of each of the junior projects is kept flexible over the school year for two reasons:

1. **Project issues:** Some projects inevitably turn out to be less complex than anticipated, and some turn out to be unsuitable for unforeseen reasons. Examples of the second situation would be that the client loses interest or changes the requirements completely after the term where students elicit these. Such projects need to be completed early, and the students on those teams reassigned to other projects.
2. **Course organization:** As mentioned before, the software requirements course and the design course are required for both our computer science majors and our software engineering majors. The third course, software construction and evolution, is required only of the latter. During 2010-11 academic year, for example, the number of students working on the projects thereby dropped from 45 to 28 for the final term. The number of projects which therefore can be completed during that term is typically less than the number from the prior term.

[3]It must be noted, that software engineering students would have received a background in quality assurance fundamentals including test-driven development, metrics and quality assurance before they begin the junior sequence.

3.2.3 Senior Project

Students will work together on Senior Project teams of about four students over one academic year[4], September through May. During that time they will work with the client to understand their needs, design and develop a system that meets the needs to the best of their abilities as entry level software engineers and computer scientists, and deliver and refine the system in response to the client's feedback. Expectations for professionalism, communication and team responsibilities are very high.

The senior project represents a culmination of their undergraduate experience, as they apply their newly acquired engineering skills to a real-world project. To help them refine those skills, the student team is responsible for managing their own process. They will work with the client to determine the management approach and software engineering process most likely to result in a successful project. This includes understanding the organization's needs, creating and maintaining a project plan, managing their schedule and risks, and communicating with the client.

Throughout the process, a faculty member will serve as the team's advisor. This advisor will meet weekly with the team to discuss their progress, review their project plan and risk assessment, and make sure the team is maintaining clear lines of communication with their client. Communication includes regular interaction via weekly meetings. Based on the needs, the team will also produce technical documents such as requirements specifications, design documents, and test plans. To come up to speed on any existing systems and required technologies, the team will also invest time in reading and understanding provided documentation and any other relevant information.

A key element of the team's educational experience is developing an appreciation for the importance of professionalism. We request the client to work with the team to help them understand the importance of client relationships, intellectual property issues, and professional ethics. Of course, the team's advisor will also be providing consistent coaching in this area. Our students greatly appreciate the interaction with their project clients and the chance to develop and deliver a significant project that meets a real need.

3.2.4 Senior Project Schedule

In Senior Project, student teams work almost autonomously, with a faculty adviser they give a progress report to each week. They also interact at about the same frequency with their external client. The project life cycles normally are "agile" and the clients may begin to see partially completed products before the end of the first term. Officially, the teams are expected to provide a real "release 1" product that the client can use, by the end of the second term. During the third (spring) term, they then do a "maintenance turn" on their product, fixing the things the client asks to have added or changed from their first release. Thus, by the end of the school year, they have delivered a product that really works to the client's satisfaction.

Artifacts turned in for senior project are determined by a combination of the needs of the client and also our being able to "prove" that they are capable of demonstrating the skills of software development. Thus, for example, they need to maintain living documents describing their requirements, design, testing, and project plan, whether the client asks for these or not.

Our ability to let the teams work so independently is based on their having had the prior, junior year project experience. We do run the weekly status meetings as they are in industry, asking them to start with what was promised that week, and ending with how their current position translates to eliminating risks of final completion. Even in these faculty-participating meetings, the students do the talking and we largely ask any questions we believe they have not answered.

[4]It must be noted that by the time the students start their senior project, all scaffolding is removed.

4. LESSONS LEARNT AND EMERGENT PATTERNS

We have evaluated our sequence of courses over the last three years. Our students agree that the two year sequence of projects was beneficial to their learning. They specifically were happy with the ability to work on two real world projects and said "they were better prepared to start in the industry". Clients and faculty have seen substantial improvements in the teams successes and the resulting projects have routinely outperformed the projects from the previous years. We have seen several patterns of learning emerge in our attempt to better prepare students. These include:

- **Value:** We have been successful in implementing multi-term client-based projects over two years of our CS and SE curricula. The integration with coursework, their junior year, has strengthened the students' perception of the value of software process and best practices. They have been able to see this value by using the lessons in these areas on a larger-than-usual, multi-term project. The repeat of this experience their senior year, on an even more difficult software development, gives the students strong skills toward working in industry, something that 90% of them go on to do as a career.
- **Student maturity:** The CS and SE major students taking this program have been seasoned by a succession of prior courses where they did extensive team project work. In addition, about half of them have outside work experience by this time, in co-ops and internships. We believe that by the time they get to their junior year, they are ready for a multi-term project with an outside client. This belief has been born-out now after three years of trials: Almost all of the junior projects have been a success. In addition, the senior projects have become more difficult, and yet the student teams have been increasingly successful at completing these to their clients' satisfaction as well.

Importance of project selection: We have found that the nature of the projects used during the students' junior year is even more important to the students' learning than it is for their senior project experience. This is because these projects are closely integrated with specific course content about software engineering:

1. Requirements: Because the students are learning about the value of eliciting and managing requirements well, as these projects begin, the projects should have requirements which pose some difficulty in getting right, the way most real projects are. Thus, projects do not

work as well, if they are "canned" or if the client has a more crisp than usual picture of what they want, during initial conversations with the students.

2. Design: Because the second junior year course using the project is about object-oriented software design, the project needs to be one where this can be done in a sophisticated way, so that students can test the design ideas from the course in their project. For example, if the project is written in C, or has little complexity to it, the students do not have an opportunity to test their developing OO design skills.

3. Construction: In the third term of their junior year, the software engineering students continue on to complete these projects, in a course on software construction and evolution. The project needs to have work still remaining on it, and work done earlier which now needs to be revised. It also should be amenable to practices such as test-first, so that the students can remove software dependencies and do unit testing as they evolve the design.

Infrastructure Developing the processes, the timelines, the contacts, the marketing material and the like for acquiring projects, if done effectively, will entail many hours of work. In the Spring term, we use an online proposal system for potential clients to submit their proposals (keeping the proposals relatively uniform for comparison and managing the proposers' expectations). Then there is a selection process for the projects (ranging from 40-60 projects from which only 8-10 will be selected). Students self-select their team members (for the senior project) and submit a team list. While the students are given an opportunity to select their top three choices, faculty do a preliminary evaluation of the projects to consider the best fit for the project goals. Once the student selections are made, a faculty committee identifies the best-fit projects for teams and produce a draft selection. For those students that didn't form teams, the program director forms their teams. The students are then given a chance to respond to the selections and any adjustments are made accordingly. The teams are introduced to their clients and encouraged to follow-up during the summer to prepare for their year-long effort in their senior year. Note the level of infrastructure needed so far and the projects haven't even started yet .

For each project, resources (hardware, software, space on the servers, etc.) must be acquired and allocated. For each project, the software processes, artifacts, and plans, must be established and agreed upon. The weekly meetings must be run and the inevitable hurdles of software projects must be cleared as the project proceeds. Each term there are reviews of the relevant artifacts and presentations of status and prototype demonstrations. At the end of the year, there is a project exposition that is held for clients, faculty, students, and administration to come see the results of the projects delivered for the year. All of this requires dedication and coordination across multiple organizations. Despite the long hours that this entails, it is probably one of the best educational experiences we give our students and one that has lasting payoff.

5. CONCLUSION

The start of larger, multi-term software development experiences with outside clients for a CS or SE major's junior year has been demonstrated here to be a success. Most of these projects completed to the satisfaction of their clients, as the junior year students learned the fundamentals of requirements gathering, project management, design and software construction. These same students were then even more successful at taking on even harder projects for industry their senior years, as a part of their capstone experience. The use of cooperative learning and the presence of a scaffold boosted the students learning and resultant performance appreciably.

Certain factors need to be in place for this more advanced start to work, at moving students toward industry-level activity. The students involved worked on team projects in CS courses starting in their freshman years, so that they had some maturity in integrating group work with learning material in their major. They did not have to learn to use positive interdependence at the same time as software design. We also were careful at selecting projects matching the needs of the junior students as they applied successive topics to these. One can imagine that being cautious this way in junior project selection in a way frees the students their senior year to focus on some specialized type of project, without fear that they never demonstrated the ability to achieve some major skill area. For example, as seniors they could pick a project for which requirements were more well defined, because they already demonstrated requirements-eliciting skills in their junior year.

It is important in applying our approach to consider the instructors' own familiarity with the recommended teaching techniques, such as test-first teaching, teaching through reflection, cooperative learning, and problem-based learning combined with scaffolding. The authors expect that this paper will help open discussion of alternatives to the popular strategy of the one-year capstone experience. There may be other fruitful directions in addition to our program of preceding the senior year project with a junior-level one that has scaffolding to link it to the theory of software development.

6. REFERENCES

[1] Computer science, final report, the joint task force on computing curricula. *IEEE Computer Society*, 2001.

[2] M. Ardis and C. Dugas. Test-First Teaching: Extreme Programming Meets Instructional Design in Software Engineering Courses. *ASEE/IEEE FIE*, 2004.

[3] R. Bruhn and J. Camp. Capstone course creates useful business products and corporate-ready students. *ACM SIGCSE Bulletin*, 2004.

[4] H. Hartman. Scaffolding & cooperative learning. *Human learning and instruction*, 69, 2002.

[5] D. Johnson, R. Johnson, and K. Smith. *Active Learning: Cooperation in the College Classroom.* 1998.

[6] H. Koppelman and B. van Dijk. Creating a realistic context for team projects in HCI. *ACM SIGCSE Bulletin*, 2006.

[7] J. Livingston. Effects of metacognitive instruction on strategy use of college students. 1996.

[8] J. Metcalfe and A. Shimamura. *Metacognition: Knowing about knowing.* The MIT Press, 1994.

[9] S. Mohan and S. Chenoweth. Teaching requirements engineering to undergraduate students. 2011.

[10] K. Porayska-Pomsta and H. Pain. Providing cognitive and affective scaffolding through teaching strategies: applying linguistic politeness to the educational context. In *Intelligent Tutoring Systems*, pages 18–21. Springer, 2004.

[11] E. Walker and O. Slotterbeck. Incorporating realistic teamwork into a small college software engineering curriculum. *J. of Computing Sciences in Colleges*, 2002.

An Open Co-op Model for Global Enterprise Technology Education: Integrating the Internship and Course Work

Jeffrey Saltz*
JPMorgan Chase
270 Park Ave
New York, NY 10017
Jeffrey.S.Saltz@Chase.com

Jae C. Oh
EECS Dept.
Syracuse University
Syracuse, NY 13214
jcoh@syr.edu

ABSTRACT

We present an open co-op program called Global Enterprise Technology Immersion Experience (GET IE) developed by JPMorgan Chase & Co. and Syracuse University. The new program creates a global enterprise focus in technology-oriented academic majors, integrated with hands-on experiential work-based learning to provide a context in which students are stimulated to utilize their classroom experience. The program includes a two-semester paid internship component that can be seamlessly incorporated with the existing computer science curriculum at Syracuse and else where. The internship's unique pedagogical innovation is to simultaneously provide the students academic course work that is integrated within a students extended internship and provides relevant problems in global enterprise technology. The curricula is "open" in the sense that other institutions and companies can join the consortium to enrich choices for the students and foster cross-fertilization of curricula activities. The program, in effect, creates a domain specific next generation co-op program that complements typical computer science curricula with a skill-set that is required for creating very large, global enterprise applications for technically and socially diverse organizations.

Categories and Subject Descriptors

K.3.2 [**Computers and Education**]: Curriculum

Keywords

Large global enterprise applications, real-world experience curriculum, open-coop consortium model

1. INTRODUCTION

In this paper, we present the Global Enterprise Technology Immersion Experience (GET IE) program developed by JPMorgan Chase & Co. and Syracuse University. The new program provides a global enterprise focus in technology-oriented academic majors and integrates course work with hands-on experiential learning. GET IE is open to multiple academic institutions and companies, and in effect, creates a domain specific next generation co-op consortium. To prepare students for successful careers in large-scale, technology-leveraged global operating environments, the program consists of a two semester long paid internship integrated with interdisciplinary coursework. Students are encouraged to take the program starting from the Spring semester of their junior year and finish the program at the end of subsequent summer. GET IE provides a unique opportunity for students to take courses while simultaneously working at their internship site location. Therefore, the courses and internship create a rich synergy in student learning.

In May 2011, we organized a workshop inviting participants from various academic institutions and companies to share results to date and encourage other institutions to follow our model. Universities and companies can join the GET IE consortium as well as establish their own program by modeling our effort. The program is designed to grow by enabling students at other academic institutions to participate via a semester away framework, where faculty from other institutions are not required to teach courses within the program, but rather, focus on helping their students understand how courses within the program map to graduation requirements. Currently several academic institutions and companies are involved in the program consortium including: Syracuse University, U. Delaware, Ohio State University, Rutgers, JP Morgan Chase, IBM, Ernst & Young, Nationwide Insurance, and GE.

This paper has three major contributions. We will discuss each of the following contributions at length in the following sections.

- Creating a synergistic effect: GET IE interweaves internship and course work together.
- A holistic and comprehensive approach to teaching large scale enterprise systems: In previous work, the issue was addressed by adding one on-campus course. GET IE integrates the classroom and internship for two-semesters, starting with one-week "boot-camp."
- Open-ness of the program: GET IE provides the opportunity for additional academic institutions and companies to join the consortium. It also provides a model for a new consortium to be created.

Finally, this paper is organized as follows. Section 2 presents the motivation of this work. Section 3 discusses related work and how previous work and this work are different. In Section 4, four key challenges in designing a curriculum are reviewed. Section 5 discusses key components of the GET IE program. In Section 6, we present the academic learning objectives of the program, and how the new curricula components integrate with the traditional computer science (CS) curriculum at Syracuse University. Section

*Also a University Professor at Syracuse University

Permission to make digital or hard copies of all or part of this work for personal or classroom use is granted without fee provided that copies are not made or distributed for profit or commercial advantage and that copies bear this notice and the full citation on the first page. To copy otherwise, to republish, to post on servers or to redistribute to lists, requires prior specific permission and/or a fee.
SIGCSE'12, February 29–March 3, 2012, Raleigh, North Carolina, USA.
Copyright 2012 ACM 978-1-4503-1098-7/12/02 ...$10.00.

7 presents a case study of the GET IE program. The case study reports on results of the first three years of the GET IE program, with students participating from several universities and industry partners. Finally, in Section 8, we discuss dissemination of the program and how the program can grow to include additional universities and companies.

2. MOTIVATION

Today's graduates typically have a solid foundation in all key areas of software engineering and the software development life cycle. However, most students have been exposed to these concepts "in the small," where the concepts are best explained and understood. Due to this *teaching in the small-scale,* new hires with a typical CS undergraduate degree often go through a substantial period of learning to put their undergraduate education into a real-world context. In particular, an understanding of a global enterprise perspective is crucial for today's technology oriented professionals [2]. Unfortunately, there is little to no preparation for this kind of skill in a typical CS undergraduate curriculum. As a result, most large companies need to train their college hires in many of the domains that are critical for the success of those new hires. In fact, it is a common concern that today's graduates do not have the skill sets required for large scale enterprise software development for global scale companies [6, 2, 4].

We believe that any solution to the above mentioned skills gap should leverage experiential learning. Experiential learning enables students to get true exposure to large production environments, and also supports one of the desirable characteristics of graduates recommended by the ACM/IEEE Curriculum 2008 [1]:

> "Significant project experience. To ensure that graduates can successfully apply the knowledge they have gained, all students in CS programs must be involved in at least one substantial software project."

We developed GET IE to provide students with hands-on experiential learning blended with course work and real-world problems.

3. RELATED WORK

In this section, we discuss some of the previous educational efforts to bring large scale global enterprise concepts into CS curricula. In addition, we discuss the importance of *experiential learning* in preparing students for the real-world. We also will elucidate the difference between our curriculum and previous efforts.

3.1 Large Scale Computing Education

While the need for teaching large scale enterprise systems has been previously noted [3], faculty have typically attempted to close this curricula gap via the creation of a specific enterprise technology course [9, 7]. For example, Lidtke et al [5] discuss a curriculum component that is designed to prepare students for developing large scale systems from the very beginning of the system design and specifications to development of communication skills necessary for such a work environment. University faculty and industry representatives worked together to develop this course. In another example, Davis et al [4] discuss enterprise integration in business education, not necessarily only in technology education. The paper discusses a business centric method for enterprise integration for a course at the senior undergraduate level at the University of New Brunswick. Cameron et al [3] also argues that in enterprise systems education, both technical and business aspects of the systems development must be taught to fulfill the pedagogical requirements for such a curriculum component. Several others discuss similar themes for courses in their papers [7, 9, 8].

Developing software for large global enterprises requires an understanding of how scale may impact software requirements, hardware and software architectures, and the project management of the large team. These concepts are not easily incorporated within a single course, and in addition, many faculty members do not have deep domain expertise in these areas. Furthermore, creating a course that leverages an enterprise computing environment is extremely difficult, due to the fact that universities cannot afford to acquire equipment at the same scale as used within large companies, making it difficult to offer enterprise computing courses that demonstrate the true challenges introduced with scale [4, 8].

3.2 Experiential Learning

A program that tries to prepare students for working in large scale enterprises needs to leverage experiential learning, which has been shown to be a key part of how one educates students in the domain of large scale enterprise computing. For example, Cameron et al [2] discuss an experiential learning model for teaching enterprise-level software development and for integrating such learning components into existing curricula. The paper emphasizes human-level communication and collaboration skills and advocates that the experiential learning paradigm better addresses the educational needs of today's rapidly changing technological fields.

In addition, several industry-academia collaborations have existed for co-op and internship developments. There are, of course, different reasons for such collaborations. For example, the University of Washington (UW) and Boeing collaboration [10] attempts to develop a senior-level software engineering capstone course that reflects the needs of Boeing. The collaboration aimed to develop a new paradigm for teaching large complex information systems within the context of an industry environment. Senior level students at UW were given opportunities to work on industry defined projects (i.e., provided by Boeing). As an evaluative result, all of the participated students responded positively to the surveys about the course. This is one of the well-known examples of academia-industry collaborations in developing curriculum components for teaching enterprise-level software engineering. Another example is the Arizona State University and American Express collaboration started in 1997 [10].

In most CS curricula, including Syracuse University, a software engineering oriented capstone course serves the goal of exposing students to an experiential learning opportunity. In Syracuse, we have CIS453 and CIS454 as a two-semester sequence for teaching software design, specification, and implementation. Students are to conceive a group project in the beginning of the sequence, and to take the entire software development cycle through the semesters. However, the GET IE Program goes far beyond what is possible within a capstone course as explained below.

4. KEY CHALLENGES

In this section, we discuss several key challenges that motivate essential components of the GET IE program. The single most important goal of the GET IE program is to complement the existing CS curriculum with the right set of pedagogical components so that the graduates will be ready for global scale companies upon their graduation. Specifically, the curriculum was designed such that it could integrate with our existing CS curricula.

In answering the question "What are the pedagogical improvements that needs to be made to the current CS curriculum to support the understanding of a large systems issues?," one must first understand the key gaps in the current CS education. The following list summarizes the key gaps in the current typical CS curriculum relating to large scale "GET-systems":

- *Traditional CS curricula lacks integration of theory and practice over multiple aspects of software engineering:* There exists a deeper integration within each specific course but not across an entire curriculum. Traditionally capstone courses serve this purpose; however, they usually have another focused purpose–bringing different computer science topics together, especially focused on a system perspective. For example, we believe that developing global-scale software requires not only technical knowledge but also understanding business drivers.
- *It is difficult to provide a proper context in an academic setting for a global enterprise practice:* Without a close collaboration between an academic institution and an industry partner, providing such a context would be challenging.
- *The challenge of providing large scale enterprise computing courses/modules/labs/environments:* This challenge not only includes technological requirements but also cultural challenges and people skills.

We discuss how the GET IE program addresses these challenges in the following sections.

5. KEY COMPONENTS OF GET IE

To properly address the key challenges discussed above, we introduce the following key components to the design of GET IE. Specifically, our new model has three main components:

- Work & School challenges are integrated: Course projects are specifically designed to be applicable in the work context. Since faculty are interacting with students extensively during their work assignments, this interaction enables faculty to more effectively support the student's integrated education across both classroom and work-based learning.
- Extended work time (7+ months): This enables students to work on "real" problems at work.
- Using multiple forms of "classroom learning": This augments face-to-face instruction during the residency with distance-based learning methods while students work (ex. online web discussions/blogs and weekly synchronous conference calls).

5.1 Technology for Large-scale Systems

One of the major differences between a global scale enterprise system and a smaller-scale system is the amount of data that needs to be managed. For example, for a global banking corporation, a question such as "How do we design our system to support 100 million accounts?" will introduce a significantly different software and hardware architecture discussion as compared to a system that needs to support 1,000 accounts. In particular, we need to look at the large scale systems across multiple, related perspectives:

- *Application Architecture of Enterprise Systems:* For instance, how will the system scale as the amount of data and the number of instances increase as well as the geographical locations covered widen?
- *Hardware and Network architectures:* For example, how to evaluate different computing architectures - ranging from wintel clusters to mainframe computing environments?
- *Non-functional requirements:* For example, availability, scalability and the need to support a highly available system even during a disaster recovery scenario.
- *Building and running Large Systems:* Skills needed to work within a software development team are different when working on large globally distributed development teams (the software development life cycle is fundamentally very different on a 10 person or 300 person team).

5.2 Effective Communication Skills

Software development within large enterprises, with a globally distributed and diverse workforce, requires effective communication skills–as increased collaboration, coordination and communication are required within project management roles, as well as other roles, ranging from software development to quality assurance. Effective communication is a required component of most CS curricula, and is part of the ABET accreditation criteria.

We developed a course that can help students practice communicating effectively within a global enterprise. The focus includes skills such as how to elicit requirements from end users, how to effectively present a software idea to a group of people with varying levels of technical and business expertise, how to provide an "elevator pitch" on a key issue or opportunity. We have found that practicing these skills within a traditional classroom setting is not nearly as effective (and motivating to students) as having the chance to practice these skills within a work environment, with oversight and coaching from a university instructor.

5.3 Integrating industry participation

The GET IE program enables students to work full-time within a global enterprise for 8 months, while at the same time, taking a full course load. Students learn about large scale computing by working within large scale technology-driven enterprises. In addition, the courses within the IE program leverage the fact that students are working while taking courses (the GET IE courses are only open to students within the IE program).

6. GET IE COURSES

The GET IE program consists of two required core courses, one (of two) core elective, as well as additional electives selected by each student. Each course is designed to address the unique needs to support globally scaled enterprise systems, as well as leveraging the work context to which the students have access and experience.

6.1 Core Courses

Students work across the following two courses in one common innovative project. The project involves: (1) Developing an IT-enabled innovative proposal; (2) Developing a change plan to implement the proposal; and (3) Presenting the idea to managers in host organization.

- **IT enabled innovation and change in Global Enterprises:** Students understand how to develop a strategic approach to technology innovation and change; understand organizational implications of innovation; and present innovative ideas to senior management. Students work to understand how to use IT to solve a problem or create a competitive advantage. The solution must consider technical obstacles, organizational challenges to adoption, as well as financial considerations. Finally, must integrate key challenges of their idea across the systems development life cycle.
- **Communication Practicum:** This course starts during the January residency and continues through the spring semester; it covers presentation, networking and meeting skills and focuses on practical guidance drawing on the student's own experiences within the work environment.

6.2 Core Electives

Students select one of the following two courses, and work across the two courses on a single project. At the end of the course, they present their joint project results to industry experts.

- **Enterprise Systems Strategies and Architectures:** Build a foundational understanding of the application architectures that comprise enterprise computing environments. Topics covered include enterprise multi-tier architectures and messaging to support those architectures, achieving highly available and scalable systems, transaction processing and an overview of enterprise databases (relational and non-relational).
- **Modeling and Optimization in a Global Enterprise:** Use quantitative modeling and computational thinking to solve business problems. The course covers modeling techniques such as pivot tables, simulation, and linear programming.

6.3 Electives

Students are encouraged to take additional elective courses, which change from year to year, but often include courses such as:

- **GET IE Internship:** This course, which is taken during spring semester, provides a faculty supervisor in addition to the internship manager. Students complete a learning contract with their on-site manager and jointly review progress with the faculty advisor.
- **Enterprise technologies:** Coverage of technical architectures and infrastructure management issues that comprise enterprise computing environments. Focus on identifying and solving large complex problems and using large scale computing systems to deploy enterprise solutions. Hands-on development using enterprise technologies.
- **Leadership and Ethics:** Understand the difference between management and leadership and how ethics and leadership are intertwined. Gain insight into leadership styles (yours and others), through reflection on actions observed in large-scale and complex global work environments.

6.4 Mapping to Existing CS Requirements

The BSCS program at Syracuse University balances theory and practice. The curriculum is well-balanced with algorithms, math, and theory courses as well as systems and software engineering. The requirements for the program of study are divided into three categories: general education, mathematics, and major. The general education category has requirements in writing (6 credits), presentation skills (3 credits), natural science and engineering (18 credits), and a requirement for courses offered by the College of Arts and Sciences or the College of Visual and Performing Arts (21 credits requirements and 9 credits of free electives). The major category has two parts–the computer science core (33 credits), and the upper-division electives (18 credits). Students are also required to take 15 or 16 credit hours of mathematics courses.

The curriculum committee sees the GET IE program as a great complimentary curriculum component to the current BSCS program in providing an excellent experience in real-world large-scale software design and development. SU's BSCS curriculum follows the ABET accreditation criteria and we believe that most CS programs could benefit from GET IE, and could easily integrate the GET IE courses into their program of study.

The GET IE program is designed to fit well with Syracuse University's undergraduate computer science program, enabling computer science students participating in GET IE to graduate in the normal 4 year time frame. In order to smoothly incorporate the GET IE program into the existing SU Computer Science curriculum with minimal effort, the BSCS curriculum committee allows:

- 6 credits of upper-division technical electives (IT enabled innovation, Enterprise Systems Strategies & Architectures, or Enterprise technologies)
- 3 credits for communication skills (GET Communication Practicum)
- 3 credits Ethics (Leadership and Ethics)[1]
- 0-6 credits of humanity / electives (student dependent)

7. CASE STUDY

The GET IE program started with 8 students in 2009, and has doubled in size each year, with the most recent class having 31 students. From the beginning, student feedback has been consistently positive, as has been the feedback from our industry partners. In terms of educational background, students have participated in the GET IE program across a variety of majors (but most of the students are either CS or IS/MIS majors). This section analyzes the first three years of the GET IE program along three dimensions:

- The value of the *next generation co-op* model (compared to the traditional co-op model)
- Does the program fill the GET Curricula gaps?
- Ability to establish a multi-school collaboration (openness)

7.1 GET IE Timeline

The GET IE program starts in early January with a *one-week intensive residency*. Then the students work for 16-weeks at their place of work. During this 16-week work period, students are also taking two courses: IT-Enabled Innovation and the Communication Practicum, through a hybrid educational model that leverages online learning (ex. discussion forums, online recorded lectures), with synchronous distributed discussions (ex. phone calls, chat) and the face-to-face discussions held during the initial January residency.

After this initial work period, a one-week of vacation is scheduled, followed by a second weeklong residency, where students complete a course on Modeling or Enterprise Systems. After this second residency, students complete a 10-week summer work period. In this period, as well as during the spring work period, students can choose to take an optional elective course.

Finally, after the regular GET IE schedule, students can take an optional two-week EuroTech trip and earn an additional 3 credits by visiting interns and other global technology organizations - to compare and contrast their experience in the united states with those from other countries(from a corporate, technology and internship perspective).

7.2 GET IE Learning Opportunities

GET IE contrasts with a traditional co-op program, where students alternate between school and work internships. In the traditional co-op model, students need to synthesize the learning from their academic classes and internships without specific support from faculty or industry mentors. However, we take experiential learning to the next level by combining course work and internship experience into an integrated experience, creating pedagogical synergy between these two components. Unlike the previous

[1]Students can waive the required ethics course, ECS 392 (Ethical Aspect of Engineering and Computer Science), if they take the *leadership and ethics* course within the GET IE program (via a course petition). SU's BSCS curriculum committee is reviewing the possibility of granting the credits for ECS 392 to students who take the GET IE program without the need for submitting a petition.

efforts discussed in Section 3, our enterprise systems education requires students to take courses relevant to the topics in parallel with a two-semester internship. Students are required to work in groups and to apply the theory learned in the course work to internship work. This pedagogical methodology tightly couples and inter-weaves the materials from the classes with practical hands-on projects on an everyday basis.

7.2.1 *Unique Course related learning opportunities*

The structure of the GET IE program enables several unique learning opportunities that are typically are not possible during a regular semester due to the demands imposed to both faculty and students. Specifically:

- Intensive residencies (in Jan and May) are leveraged to simulate the "stress" of a deadline within the work environment. This intensive work environment not only builds student confidence (so that students are better prepared for the demands within the work environment), but is also used for "team-building" of the cohort (since, when students are working, they are located across many work locations).
- Two coordinated courses (Business Modeling & Optimization and Enterprise Architectures) share an integrated project. For the project, which is the design of a cost effective enterprise system, students need to leverage expertise gained within both courses. The project is evaluated on different criteria for each course (ex. technical architecture or the business model for the value of the project). The project is then presented to industry experts for feedback and review.
- Two Integrated courses (IT enabled Innovation and Communication Practicum) are integrated so that a common innovative project is assigned across the two courses. The project, *developing an IT-enabled innovative proposal and a change plan to implement the proposal*, is presented to managers in the host organization. The presentations include an "elevator pitch," a written presentation and an oral presentation.

7.2.2 *Examples of leveraging the work context*

Large scale computing concepts were easily framed within the work context. Some examples include:

- How does one "put into production" a large IT system–in addition to analyzing potential technical architectures, what are the financial costs, benefits and value of that IT system?
- How can new technology be leveraged within the corporation–including analysis of financial and organizational challenges?
- How can one thrive productively in large global teams and how can one understand cultural nuances across a global team?

In addition, the work context was leveraged as a unique way to introduce specific learning opportunities. For example, early within the internship, students needed to network to explore different possible IT innovation ideas and explain their ideas to get feedback/refinements of their idea. At the same time, they needed to create a software architecture and implementation plan for their idea, and have it critiqued by mentors within the company. This opportunity enables students to practice effective communication as well as improving their understanding of large scale systems, and how they are created within large enterprises.

7.3 Evaluating the next generation co-op model

Table 1 shows the results of a survey from the most recent GET IE cohort of 31 students. They results show that significant improvement (as perceived by the students and their managers) was achieved during the GET IE internship (i.e. the improvement in score from the start of the program). Specifically, during GET IE, students improved across all questions, with the largest increase in competency being in understanding corporate culture (note that students and managers provided a score in the range of 1 to 5 for each question, with 5 being the best).

In addition to obtaining the quantitative information discussed in Table 1, we also obtained general impressions of the GET IE program. As can be seen from some of the student responses listed below, students appreciated the integration of school and work, as well as noted the learning achieved during the program.

- "GET provided a almost perfect combination of school work and work work."
- "I have learned more here than I ever will in the classroom."
- "Best opportunity I have come across in my college career."
- "I loved the experience. I love the idea of taking classes during an extended internship. I can't imagine many internships being better than this one."
- "It has been one of the most amazing experiences of my life to date. Our ability to network and learn is far better than being trapped in a college classroom."
- "The GET internship experience was intellectually stimulating and rewarding."

7.3.1 *Does GET IE address the Key Challenges?*

In Section 4, we presented the key challenges in designing a global enterprise technology curriculum. We now discuss how the GET IE program addresses each of these challenges and how the key gaps in the typical computer science curriculum relating to large scale "GET-systems" is addressed within GET IE:

- *Traditional CS curricula lacks integration of theory and practice over multiple aspects of software engineering:* GET IE provides theory and practice learning opportunities through courses taken during the internship and the work experience provided by the internship, respectively. These two components are interwoven to create unique synergistic effects. As can be seen in Table 1, the GET IE curricula deliveries learning outcomes that are required to succeed within a large scale global enterprise.
- *It is difficult to provide a proper context in an academic setting for a global enterprise practice:* IBM, in conjunction with JPMorgan Chase & Co. and Syracuse university, have created a large scale computing environment that is available to all students participating in the program. In addition, the combination of the extended internship work period (7+ months), combined with the faculty support provides a unique context for learning that was noted many times by students within the program, some of the comments were noted in the student feedback section.
- *The challenge of providing large scale enterprise computing courses/modules/labs/environments:* This challenge is addressed via a combination of methods. First, the large scale computing environment at Syracuse University was leveraged for some of the courses (for students from all schools). In addition, students shared their work experiences, hence providing insight into other computing environments. Finally, with respect to cultural and people skills, this was addressed via specific courses and course projects that required students to work with many people within their host company.

Table 1: Mean Improvements in Abilities as Perceived by Students and Managers

Questions	Students			Managers		
	Beginning	End	Improvement	Beginning	End	Improvement
Present effective, well organized material	2.6	4.0	1.4	2.0	3.3	1.3
Communicate and collaborate	2.4	4.1	1.7	2.0	3.3	1.3
Understand how scale impacts the team	1.9	3.7	1.8	1.4	2.7	1.3
Understand enterprise architectures	2.2	4.0	1.8	1.4	2.6	1.1
Understand how scale impacts the solution	2.2	4.0	1.8	1.6	2.4	0.9
How to achieve IT-enabled innovation	2.3	4.0	1.7	1.4	3.3	1.9
How to propose innovative IT projects	1.9	4.0	2.1	1.4	2.9	1.5
Understand corporate culture	2.1	4.1	2.0	1.4	3.4	2.0

7.4 Lessons Learned

It is important to note that GET IE is open to students from any university, and students can intern at any large technology-focused company. From a university perspective, in addition to Syracuse University, other schools that have participated, or have specific plans to participate in 2012 include the University of Delaware, The Ohio State University, Boston College and Rutgers University. In addition to JPMorgan Chase & Co. , other companies that have participated, or have specific plans to participate in 2012 include IBM, Erst & Young, Cisco, Nationwide Insurance, Bloomberg, and GE. Getting additional schools to participate is highly dependent on the University being able to map the GET IE courses to existing student majors, as well as a University's willingness to participate in a "semester away" program,

Another related challenge identified was how to attract more students to the IE program. For some undergraduate computer science majors, it may be hard to see themselves working for a financial company or a perceived non "high-tech" company. Students often initially are interested in well-known computer companies such as Google, Microsoft, and Apple. Educating students about technology needs in such companies is a challenge.

8. DISSEMINATION AND FUTURE PLANS

On May 25th, 2011, SU and JPMorgan Chase & Co. organized a workshop on GET IE, partially funded by NSF. There were representatives from more than 30 universities that attended the workshop and many were interested in having their students participate in the GET IE program. The workshop brought professors, administrators, and industry participants together in a forum to discuss the challenges and opportunities in our industry-academia collaboration. There were several break-out discussion sessions on how to make a multi-university, multi-company collaboration work, how to attract students to the immersion experience program, and what are the best majors for such a program. In particular, the main theme of the workshop was about the openness of the GET IE program. Participating institutions were welcomed to join the effort or create their own program based on our field-tested model. We have established a point of contact and email list of the participants for further collaboration and exchange of ideas.

In discussing the skill gaps of newly hired computer science college graduates, industry representatives continued to consistently note the lack of focus on large scale enterprise skills. Based on our accumulating experience, we will continue to increase the number of students, universities and companies participating in GET IE.

9. ACKNOWLEDGMENTS

Senior Associate Dean Robert Heckman (Syracuse University) has been instrumental in launching and helping to run the GET IE program. His insight has been invaluable to the program. Professor Rajiv Ramnath (Ohio State) has been very helpful in working with Computer Science students from OSU. In addition, JP Morgan Chase's support of GET has been critical to the success of programs such as GET IE. Finally, we would also like to acknowledge the faculty and staff from Syracuse University and the University of Delaware that have helped create and deliver the course content.

10. REFERENCES

[1] ACM and I. C. Society. Computer Science Curriculum 2008: Computer Science Curriculum 2008: Computer science curriculum 2008: An interim revision of CS 2001. Technical report, ACM/IEEE, 2008.

[2] Cameron and Purao. Enterprise integration: An experiential learning model. Information Systems Education Journal, 8(38), 2010.

[3] B. H. Cameron. Enterprise systems education: new directions & challenges for the future. In Proceedings of the 2008 ACM SIGMIS CPR conference on Computer personnel doctoral consortium and research, SIGMIS CPR '08, pages 119–126, New York, NY, USA, 2008. ACM.

[4] C. Davis. Enterprise integration in business education: Design and outcomes of a capstone erp-based undergraduate e-business management course. Journal of Information Systems Education, 15(3), 2004.

[5] D. K. Lidtke and G. Stokes. An information systems-centric curriculum, iscc '99. Journal of Systems and Software, 49(2-3):171 – 175, 1999.

[6] M. C. Mulder, D. Lidtke, and G. E. Stokes. Enterprise enhanced education: an information technology enabled extension of traditional learning environments. SIGCSE Bull., 29:355–359, March 1997.

[7] J. V. Nickerson. Teaching the integration of information systems technologies. IEEE Transactions on Education, 49(2):271–277, 2006.

[8] G. W. Prigge. University-industry partnerships: What do they mean to universities? Industry and Higher Education, 19(3), 2005.

[9] A. Wegmann. Theory and practice behind the course designing enterprise-wide it systems. In Business and IT Alignment with SEAM. Proceedings of 1st International Workshop on Requirements Engineering for Business Need, and IT Alignment, page 496, 2004.

[10] K. A. Williams. Educating the next generation of information specialists: industry and university collaborative learning pilot project. SIGCSE Bull., 29:350–354, March 1997.

Integrating Video Components in CS1

Tamar Vilner
The Open University of Israel
Computer Science Dept.
108 Ravutski St.
Raanana, Israel
tami@openu.ac.il

Ela Zur
The Open University of Israel
Computer Science Dept.
108 Ravutski St.
Raanana, Israel
ela@openu.ac.il

Ronit Sagi
The Open University of Israel
The Evaluation Dept.
108 Ravutski St.
Raanana, Israel
ronitsa@openu.ac.il

ABSTRACT

The Open University of Israel (OUI) is a distance learning university. Our CS1 course is taught through video-taped lectures that cover the study material. In addition, students may participate in face-to-face group meetings in study centers located all over the country and taught by tutors. There is a special group called *Ofek*, in which the tutor is located in a studio and the lesson is broadcast over the internet. Students enrolled in this group participate from their home PCs. The taped *Ofek* sessions as well as the lectures are stored on the course website, and students can watch them whenever convenient. We conducted a study to investigate students' viewing habits and the relationship between viewing and the success rate in the course.

Categories and Subject Descriptors

K.3.1 [**Computers and Education**]: Computer Uses in Education – *distance learning.*

General Terms

Human Factors.

Keywords

CS1, Video, taped lectures, distance learning

1. BACKGROUND

1.1 The Open University of Israel

The Open University of Israel (OUI) is a distance learning university which offers a variety of undergraduate programs and several graduate programs [19].

The OUI is similar to other universities in its pursuit of excellence and its commitment to superior scientific and scholastic standards. However, it differs in that it is open to all those who wish to study a single course or a number of courses, or to pursue a full program of study towards a Bachelor's degree.

The method of study practiced in the OUI is distance learning and self-study. The study material is mainly based on a course book especially designed for self-study or on a well-known textbook on the topic of the course.

Students must submit assignments, exercises and other tasks during the semester, on which they receive a grade and feedback. They must also pass the final examination of the course.

Permission to make digital or hard copies of all or part of this work for personal or classroom use is granted without fee provided that copies are not made or distributed for profit or commercial advantage and that copies bear this notice and the full citation on the first page. To copy otherwise, or republish, to post on servers or to redistribute to lists, requires prior specific permission and/or a fee.

SIGCSE'12, February 29–March 3, 2012, Raleigh, North Carolina, USA.

Copyright 2012 ACM 978-1-4503-1098-7/12/02...$10.00.

Each course also includes a face-to-face component in the form of small group tutorials. At tutorial meetings, the tutors provide additional examples, answer the students' questions, etc. Attending the tutorial sessions is not mandatory, but is highly recommended.

To improve its distance teaching, the OUI also makes use of web-based technologies, which provide a wealth of learning materials and continuous contact with faculty and other students in the course.

1.2 CS1 at the OUI

1.2.1 Topics and Units

At the OUI, CS1 is similar to introductory courses at other universities, and includes the topics recommended in *Computing Curricula 2008* [11] which is an interim revision of *CS1 2001* [10].

The course covers the following topics: basic logic, algorithms and problem solving, fundamental data structures, fundamental programming constructs, recursion, fundamental computing algorithms, basic computability, the main topics of OO programming such as encapsulation and information hiding, classes and objects, inheritance, and polymorphism. To some extent, we also teach software design, including fundamental design concepts and principles, design for reuse, etc. At many universities and colleges this wide range of topics is divided into two courses: CS1 and CS2.

Computer science is known as a difficult field of study, one that requires a great deal of mathematics. Because of the OUI's open admissions policy, CS1, which is among the students' first mathematics courses, serves as a filter. The course helps students to find out whether they are capable of coping with academic studies in CS. About 600 students enroll in the course each semester. Many of them, unfortunately, fail. Indeed, the percentage of dropouts from this and other introductory courses is relatively high – in some courses reaching about 50%. In addition, fewer than 60% of those who take the final exam pass it.

The main component of study in CS courses is usually a textbook. However, our CS1 course is based on 20 videotaped lectures (about 42 hours), each covering a unit of study. The lectures include all the material covered in the course. The lecturer is Prof. Jeffrey Rosenschein of the CS department of the Hebrew University of Jerusalem.

We also provide a specially developed study guide containing additional explanations, as well as exercises and solutions. The book *Java Software Solutions*, by Lewis and Loftus [12], is used as a reference book. The book is in English, while the rest of the materials are in Hebrew.

In a paper [5], we described a study that we conducted to determine how the students respond to the new and different method, which uses videotaped lectures instead of textbooks, in terms of both learning and technical operation. The findings show that this method of study is at least as efficient as the traditional one based on books. The students' attitude to the new study method was positive and supportive.

1.2.2 Face-to-Face Meetings

Like all the other courses taught at the OUI, CS1 also includes face-to-face meetings held at OUI study centers throughout the country. The tutorials are offered in a "regular" mode – two-hour meetings every other week, or an "intensive" mode, which includes weekly three-hour meetings. Attending the tutorial sessions is not mandatory, but is highly recommended, and the students indeed tend to attend.

To help students who live far from a study center, or those who cannot attend face-to-face meetings, there is a special group called *Ofek*. For this group, an instructor teaches from a studio on the OUI campus and the lesson is broadcast over the internet. The students enrolled in this group participate from their home PCs. If they want to answer the instructor's questions or to ask questions of their own, they can use chat or telephone the studio. Only students enrolled in this special group may participate in the live broadcasts. However, students in all other groups can watch the recorded *Ofek* sessions. They cannot play an active role in these meetings but they can see and hear the instructor, and hear the questions and the answers. There are links to the recorded *Ofek* sessions on the course website, so students can watch them whenever convenient. These sessions are held weekly, which means that there are about 45 hours of recorded sessions.

1.2.3 CS1 Website

All OUI courses have websites that serve as interactive learning environments. The websites provide two types of communication channels – an administrative channel (including course schedule, office hours of the teaching team, and e-mail addresses of the team and the students) and an academic channel that includes a message board, discussion forums and enrichment materials. These include various types of supplementary study materials, exercises and exams for self-evaluation, demonstrations, sample exams, feedback on assignments, links to the recorded lectures and videotaped tutorial sessions, as well as to relevant websites, etc.

1.3 Integrating Technology into CS1 – Related Work

It is well known that teaching CS1 is very difficult. Failure and dropout rates are usually high, and many students find it very hard to grasp the notion of solving problems algorithmically. Like many other researchers, we are looking for ways to make the course materials more accessible for the students. Many papers describe using visualization in CS1 to simplify the course material (for example, see [3, 9]). Another method is the integration of friendlier programming tools, such as Alice and Scratch [6, 14, 20, 23]. We have tried integrating Greenfoot into the course [21]. Other researchers have reported on pair-programming as way to simplify programming activities [16]. Research has shown that effective online discussions support good online learning, by facilitating the exchange of information among students and enabling tutor intervention when necessary [15, 22].

In this study, we investigated the delivery mode of the CS1 course materials. Today, a wide range of audiovisual materials are digitized by educational institutions and made available online [17]. Fritze and Nordkvelle's paper compares how lectures are being performed in different technologies. They found that "taped lectures are more stringent and content oriented, while live-lectures are time consuming and more focused on establishing dialogues with students [4]. Bell et al. describes a system that automatically captures and indexes audio and video streams of traditional university lectures. They tried it on CS1 students, and found that "Early in the trial, many students expressed an intention to use the system, but few did. Late in the course, many students stated that they urgently needed the system for revision, but even fewer used it. At the same time, lecture attendance appeared to be lower than normal. They hypothesize that the availability of a flexible alternative to lectures removed the necessity of attending lectures, and that students deceived themselves about their intentions to catch up using the digital medium." [1]. Some papers have described the effectiveness of the video mode of delivery in university courses [7] and in computer science courses [8, 13]. These papers suggest an alternate delivery mode to avoid difficulties in teaching large classes or in order to save money. Smith & Fidge [18] used prerecorded lectures for teaching introductory programming and found a weak quantitative correlation between students' use of the prerecorded material and their final grades. However, they found that the students' perception of the study materials improved.

2. THE STUDY

The purpose of this study was to observe to what extent students view the video components in the CS1 course and to determine whether there is a relationship between the amount of viewing and success in the course. In addition, we wanted to examine the students' attitudes toward the video components.

2.1 Research Questions

1. **Viewing the video components of the course** – When do students watch the taped lectures and the recorded *Ofek* sessions? Do they primarily view the tapes before the deadlines for submitting assignments, or throughout the entire semester? Are there any specific lectures or meetings that are viewed more than others? Can this be characterized?
2. **Correlation between watching habits and final grade** – Is there a correlation between the intensity of watching the lectures and the *Ofek* sessions and success in the course?
3. **Attitudes toward the recorded *Ofek* sessions** – To what extent are students satisfied with the *Ofek* components? The different ways of learning from these meetings – when and how do the students watch the videos? What do they do while watching? Do the students watch the *Ofek* sessions instead of or in addition to going to their own face-to-face meetings?

2.2 Research Population

The research population included 629 students who took CS1 in the fall semester of 2010, of whom 45 were in an *Ofek* group.

2.3 Research Instruments

- The university database, which includes data on assignment submission and grades, and on final exams in all courses.
- Lists of times that students watched the video components. Every time a student entered the course website and viewed a video lecture or an *Ofek* session, this was listed. We examined all these lists.
- A specially designed questionnaire including about 50 closed items, with room for remarks. The questionnaire examined

students' satisfaction and their attitudes toward the *Ofek* sessions, preferences, habits and ways of learning, and watching the *Ofek* component. The questionnaire was emailed to all the students; only 144 (23%) responded.

3. RESULTS

3.1 Viewing Habits

During the semester, the students have to submit 8 assignments, every other week. We saw that usually, the students begin watching the lectures and the *Ofek* session that deals with the material covered on the assignment about 2 weeks before the submission date. We noticed that there is one peak a week before the deadline, and another, even higher, peak, the day before and on the due date.

Figure 1 shows the mean number of views both of *Ofek* sessions and of the lectures, in the days before the submission deadline.

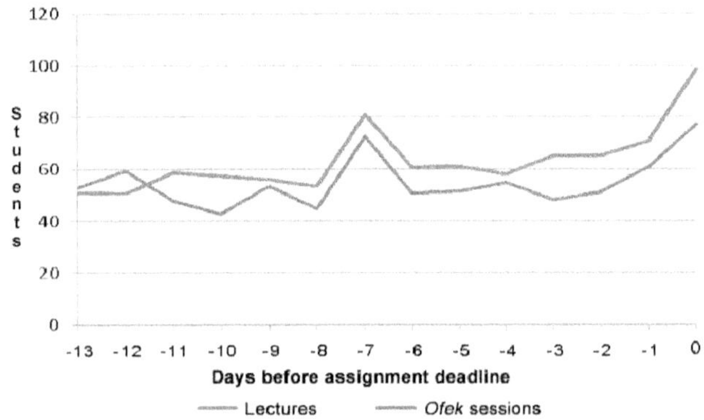

Figure 1. Mean number of views before the assignment submission deadline

Figure 2 summarizes of the percentage of students who watched the different lectures and *Ofek* sessions which related to the units of study covered. More students watch the lectures than the *Ofek* sessions. From the pedagogical point of view, this is a positive finding, since the lectures contain the course material while the *Ofek* sessions serve to explain and clarify points in the lectures.

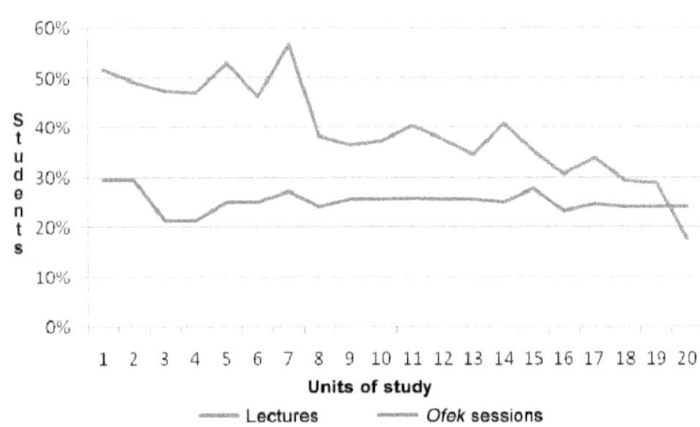

Figure 2. Percentage of students who viewed lectures and *Ofek* sessions

The figure shows a decrease in the number of students who viewed the lectures, which reflects the high dropout rate. It is interesting to see that while there is a decrease in viewing the lectures, viewing of the *Ofek* sessions remains more or less stable. This finding caused us to examine whether there is a difference in watching habits (1) between students enrolled in the *Ofek* group and the other students and (2) between students enrolled in "regular" mode and the "intensive" mode of face-to-face meetings.

Table 1 presents the mean number of clips viewed by students in the *Ofek* group vs. the other groups. We found that there is no significant difference between the total number of views (lectures and *Ofek* sessions): p=0.178.

Table 1. Views by the *Ofek* group vs. the other groups

Technology		Lectures	Ofek	Total
***Ofek* group**	**Mean**	8.64	17.64	26.29
	N	45	45	45
	SD	8.28	15.27	19.84
Other groups	**Mean**	13.84	7.86	21.70
	N	584	584	584
	SD	14.29	13.08	22.15

Table 2 presents the mean number of clips viewed by the students in the intensive tutorial mode vs. the regular mode.

Table 2. Views by the regular groups vs. intensive groups

Face-to-face meetings		Lectures	Ofek	Total
Intensive tutorials	**Mean**	13.54	8.89	22.44
	N	504	504	504
	SD	13.79	13.34	21.55
Regular tutorials	**Mean**	13.18	7.22	20.40
	N	125	125	125
	SD	14.89	14.00	23.79

We found that there is no significant difference in the total number of clips viewed, between students enrolled in the regular and the intensive mode of face-to-face meetings (p=0.36). This finding surprised us, since we expected students enrolled in the regular mode, who don't have many face-to-face meetings, to watch the *Ofek* sessions much more frequently.

We examined whether there were specific lectures or *Ofek* sessions which were watched more, or less, than others, and whether this could be characterized. As shown in Figure 2, unit 5 and unit 7 are relatively highly viewed. Units 1-4 deal with Karel the Robot [2], which serves as an introduction to Object Oriented concepts. Unit 5 is when students begin to study the Java language: types, variables, expressions, etc. Unit 7 begins to introduce OO topics: classes and objects, methods, encapsulation etc. It is a long and difficult unit, and many students drop out of the course after it. Unit 20 is not mandatory, so many students skip it.

3.2 Correlation between Viewing Habits and Final Grade

3.2.1 Defining the Different Groups According to their Viewing Habits

We divided the student population into three groups according to the number of clips (lectures and *Ofek* sessions) that they viewed during the semester. For this purpose, we defined 3 levels of viewing for the 20 lectures: "low" (students who viewed 0-5 lectures); "medium" (students who viewed 6-14 lectures); and "high" (students who viewed more than 14 lectures). In addition, we defined 3 levels of viewing for the 15 *Ofek* sessions: "low" (students who viewed 0-3 sessions); "medium" (students who viewed 4-9 sessions); and "high" (students who viewed more than 9 sessions).

Table 3 shows the distribution of students in the three groups for lectures and for *Ofek* sessions, as well as the interactions between the groups.

Table 3. Distribution of the three groups (N = 629)

			Lectures			
			Low	**Medium**	**High**	**Total**
***Ofek* sessions**	**Low**	N	209	102	63	374
		%	33.3%	16.2%	10%	59.5%
	Medium	N	41	51	40	132
		%	6.5%	8.1%	6.4%	21%
	High	N	26	51	46	123
		%	4.1%	8.1%	7.3%	19.5%
	Total	N	276	204	149	629
		%	43.9%	32.4%	23.7%	100.0%

Figure 3 shows the distribution of the groups when counting students whose viewing level was low, medium or high, for **either** lectures or *Ofek* sessions.

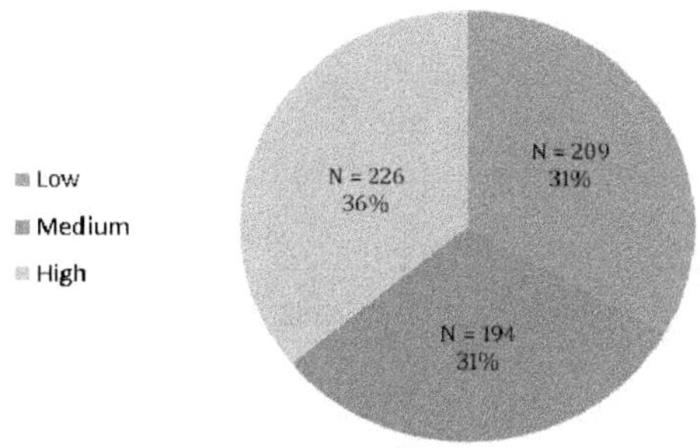

Figure 3. Distribution of students in the three groups

3.2.2 Correlation between Viewing Level and Taking the Final Exam

We have found that many students drop out during the semester and therefore never take the final exam (about 40%). We were interested to see if there is a connection between the viewing level and taking the final exam. Table 4 shows the distribution of students who took the final exam, according to their viewing level. The Pearson chi-square test showed that there is a significant relationship between the two.

Table 4. Relationship between viewing level and taking the final exam (N=629)

Took final exam		Viewing level			
		Low	**Medium**	**High**	**Total**
Yes	**N**	93	97	191	381
	%	14.8%	15.4%	30.4%	60.6%
No	**N**	116	97	35	248
	%	18.4%	15.4%	5.6%	39.4%
Total	**N**	209	194	226	629
	%	33.2%	30.8%	35.9%	100.0%

$\chi^2 = 85.932$, df = 2, p = 0.00

The table shows that 44% of the students (93 of 209) who were in the "low" group took the final exam; 50% (97 of 194) of those in the "medium" group took the exam, and 85% (191 of 226) of those in the "high" group took the exam. We found that there is a significant difference in the proportions of the students who attend the final exam in the different groups (p=0.00). This is not surprising, because clearly students who drop out in the middle of the semester stop watching the lectures and *Ofek* sessions. Multiple comparisons (Bonferroni's test) showed that there is a significant difference between the low group and the high group, and between the high group and the medium group, but no significant difference between the low group and the medium group.

This relationship is illustrated in Figure 4, which shows the distribution of students who took the final exam, by group.

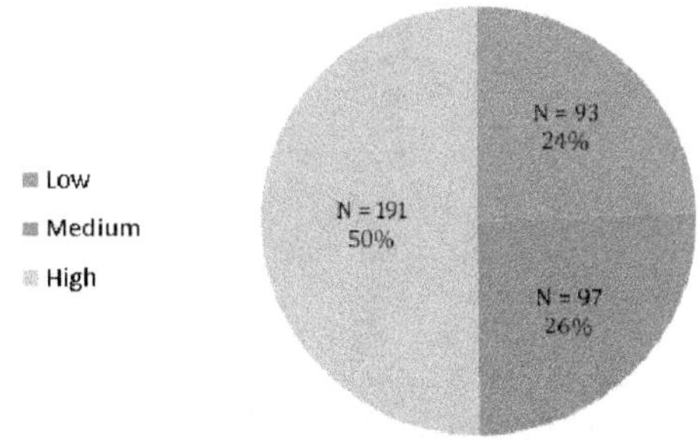

Figure 4. Distribution of students who took the final exam

The figure shows that fully half of those who took the exam were in the "high" viewing level group.

3.2.3 Correlation between Viewing Level and Passing the Final Exam

We were also interested to see whether there is a connection between the viewing level and passing the final exam. Table 5 presents the distribution of the students who passed or failed the final exam according to their viewing level. A Chi-Square test showed no significant relationship between the two.

Table 5. Relationship between viewing level and passing the final exam (N=380)

Exam result		Viewing level			
		Low	**Medium**	**High**	**Total**
Passed	**N**	32	46	86	164
	%	8.4%	12.1%	22.6%	43.2%
Failed	**N**	61	51	104	216
	%	16.1%	13.4%	27.4%	56.8%
Total	**N**	93	97	190	380
	%	24.5%	25.5%	50.0%	100.0%

$\chi^2 = 3.964$, df = 2, p = 0.138

In contrast to the previous result, this finding was surprising. We expected to see differences between the groups.

When examined via ANOVA, the mean exam grades among all the students who took the final exam showed no significant differences between the three groups, as indicated in Table 6.

Table 6. Mean final exam grades

Viewing level	N	Mean	SD
Low	93	60.72	27.718
Medium	97	51.33	28.128
High	190	54.17	27.867
Total	380	55.05	28.035

p=0.06

Only students who submit all the required assignments and pass the final exam can pass the course. We therefore checked whether there is a connection between the viewing level and the final grade in the course, among students who passed the exam. Again, we found no significant relationship, as shown in Table 7.

Table 7. Mean final course grades

Viewing level	N	Mean	SD
Low	60	80.05	11.069
Medium	50	78.20	10.266
High	104	79.99	10.366
Total	214	79.59	10.523

p=0.568

These results were also surprising. One would expect that the more students watch the video clips during the course, which actually represent the course material, the better prepared they are for the assignments and the exam, and this would increase their chances of passing the exam and getting a higher grade. In the discussion section, we will discuss these findings and try to explain them.

3.3 Attitudes toward *Ofek* Sessions

To examine the third research question, we used a specially designed questionnaire which examined students' satisfaction and their attitudes toward the *Ofek* sessions, preferences, habits and ways of learning, and watching the *Ofek* component.

As mentioned above, only 144 (of 629) students (23%) returned the questionnaire administered at the end of the semester.

The questionnaire included 51 questions, most closed, and some had room for remarks. It was a detailed questionnaire that dealt with many aspects that relate to *Ofek* meetings. This section summarizes the responses to questions relevant to this study.

One question asked why students who signed up for face-to-face meetings rather than for the *Ofek* group did so. Their responses were as follows (they could choose more than one statement):

- 38% mentioned the importance of direct interaction with the tutor and the other students;
- 32% noted that they knew that they could watch the taped *Ofek* sessions on the course website;
- 8% said that watching the videos (instead of going to a face-to-face meeting) demands self discipline;
- 9% were worried about technical problems.

In parallel, we asked the students in the *Ofek* group why they chose that group. Their answers follow:

- 73% mentioned the convenience of the technology, which helps to adjust the learning process to personal constraints;
- 66% said that *Ofek* enables one to study at one's own pace;
- 40% noted that they had had good previous experience with studying via *Ofek*;
- 33% said that the fact that they could sit at home and not travel to the study center saved time and money;

In addition, we asked about students' learning methods as they watched the taped *Ofek* meetings;

- 80% said that they reviewed material that was unclear to them;
- 66% stopped the tape in order to answer the questions and exercises presented by the tutor;
- 42% summarized the tutorial sessions;
- 34% wrote down topics and concepts they wanted to review again;
- 10% said that after watching the session, they posted questions on the discussion forum of the course website regarding topics they didn't understand.
- 64% of the students reported that they watched the *Ofek* meetings to complement the face-to-face meetings they attended at the study centers, while 36% watched *Ofek* sessions instead of going to face-to-face meetings.

Table 8 summarizes general attitudes toward the *Ofek* sessions by ranking statements on a scale of 1 (do not agree) to 5 (agree strongly).

Table 8. Attitudes toward *Ofek* sessions

Statements	Mean	SD
Studying through *Ofek* can be a positive experience	4.48	0.82
A face-to-face meeting is more effective than an *Ofek* video	3.39	1.17
I would like a series of taped *Ofek* sessions in every course I take	4.77	0.63
It is very important to interact directly with the tutor during the live broadcast of *Ofek* sessions	4	1
Watching the *Ofek* video can improve the understanding of the study material	4.65	0.66
An *Ofek* meeting can replace a face-to-face meeting	3.41	1.42

4. DISCUSSION AND CONCLUSIONS

Our results show that there is a relationship between students' level of viewing (lectures and *Ofek* sessions) and how many take the final exam. The more video clips they watch, the more likely they are to take the final exam. Since students who drop out of the course will not continue to view the course material, this result is reasonable.

One important finding from this study is that there is no proof that watching the video components improves the learning process. We found that there is no correlation between the number of clips viewed and the success rate in CS1. This is quite a surprise since one would think that because the course material is conveyed via Prof. Rosenschein's lectures, if students don't hear the lectures, how can they pass the course? And yet, we saw that even students who were in the "low" viewing group, i.e., didn't see clips at all (or saw very few), passed the exam with the same mean scores as students in the "high" viewing group. Smith and Fidge [18] reported a similar finding: The use of prerecorded 'mini' lectures had no discernible effect on improving students' grades.

This seemingly illogical finding can be explained by the fact that the most important component of learning in CS courses is exercising. Students can read a lot of books on the course material or hear lectures, but if they don't practice by themselves, and solve a lot of algorithmic problems by programming them and running them on the computer, they won't be able to pass the course.

In addition, it is possible that many "low" viewing students went to the face-to-face meetings in the study centers, and learned the material from the tutors. A well-known disadvantage of distance learning is the lack of face-to-face interaction with both teachers and students. Many of our students may have attended the face-to-face meetings to make up for this.

Yet, as the questionnaire results show, many students find the video components very useful. They would like to have these components in every course they take. It is very convenient for students to have a component that they can review until they understand. Smith and Fidge [18] also found that students appreciated the effort put into the prerecorded 'mini' lectures and felt much better about the study materials.

As we are a distance learning institution, we feel obligated to have video components in every course we teach. Many of our students live far from study centers, and most are part time students, so they miss tutorial sessions from time to time. The video components help the students to overcome these difficulties.

5. ACKNOWLEDGMENTS

We would like to thank Boaz Mermelstein and Dr. Tsily Raz-Liebermann of *Shoham* – The Open University Center for Technology in Distance Education.

6. REFERENCES

[1] Bell, T., Cockburn, A., McKenzie, B., & Vargo, J. 2001. Digital Lectures: If You Make Them, Will Students Use Them? Constraints on Effective Delivery of Flexible Learning Systems, *Interactive Multimedia Electronic Journal of Computer-Enhanced Learning*, retrieved May 10, 2007, from http://imej.wfu.edu/articles/2001/2/06/index.asp .

[2] Bergin, J., Stehlik, M., Roberts, J., Pattis, R., *Karel J. Robot: A gentle introduction to the art of object-oriented programming in Java*, Dream Songs Press, 2005.

[3] Buck, D. 2011. GUIGraph: Editing Live Object Diagrams for GUI Generation Enables New Pedagogy in CS1/2, ITiCSE 2011 – *Proceedings of the 16th Annual SIGCSE Conference on Innovation and Technology in Computer Science Education*, June 2011, 193-197.

[4] Fritze y. & Nordkvelle Y. T. 2003. Comparing Lectures: Effects of the Technological Context of the Studio, *Education and Information Technologies*, 8(4), 327-343.

[5] Gal-Ezer, J., Vilner, T. & Zur, E. The Professor on Your PC: A Virtual CS1 Course, *Inroads SIGCSE Bulletin*, September 2009, 41(3), 191-195.

[6] Garlick, R. & Cankaya E.C. Using Alice in CS1: a quantitative experiment, ITiCSE 2010 – *Proceedings of the 15th Annual SIGCSE Conference on Innovation and Technology in Computer Science Education*, June 2010, 165-168.

[7] Goodwin, R. & Williams, N. Flexible Learning: Maximizing Flexibility in a Subject with Large students Numbers, *ACE 2004 – Proceedings of the Six Australian Computing Education Conference*, Darlinghurst, Australia, 2004, 77-82.

[8] Hermann, N., Popyack, J. L., Char, B. & Zoski, P. Assessment of a Course Redesign: Introductory Computer Programming Using Online Modules, *SIGCSE 2004 - Proceedings of the 35th SIGCSE Technical symposium on Computer Science Education*, 2004, 66-70.

[9] Hunhausen, C. D. & Brown, J. L. Personalizing and Discussing Algorithms within CS1 Studio Experiences: An Observational Study, *ICER 2005 - Proceedings of the first international workshop on Computing education research*, October 2005, 45-67.

[10] IEEE Computer Society/ACM Task Force, *Computing curricula 2001* (CC-2001), http://www.computer.org/education/cc200/final

[11] IEEE Computer Society/ACM Task Force, *Computing curricula 2008* (CS2008), http://www.acm.org//education/curricula/ComputerScience2008.pdf

[12] Lewis, J., and Loftus, W., *Java software solutions*, Pearson Education, 2009.

[13] Malan, D. J. Podcasting Computer Science E-1, *SIGCSE 2007 - Proceedings of the 38th SIGCSE Technical symposium on Computer Science Education*, 2007, 389-393.

[14] Maloney, J., Resnick, M., Rusk, N., Silverman, B., & Eastmond, E. The Scratch Programming Language and Enviroment, *ACM Transactions on Computing Education , 2010, 10* (4), 16:1-16:15.

[15] Mazzolini, M. and Maddison, S., Sage, guide or ghost? The effect of instructor intervention on student participation in online discussion forums, *Computers & Education*, 40, 3, 2003, pp. 237-253.

[16] McDowell, C. Werner, L. Bullock, H. & Fernald, J. The effect of Pair-Programming on Performance in an Introductory Programming Course, *SIGCSE 2002 - Proceedings of the 33rd SIGCSE Technical symposium on Computer Science Education*, 2002, 38-42.

[17] Report based on the findings of a Study Designed and Funded by Copyright Clearance Center and Conducted by Intelligent Television with the Cooperation of New York University, Video Use and Higher Education: Options for the Future, June 2009. http://library.nyu.edu/about/Video_Use_in_Higher_Education.pdf

[18] Smith, G. & Fidge, C. On the Efficacy of Prerecorded Lectures for Teaching Introductory Programming, *ACE 2008 – Proceedings of the Tenth Australian Computing Education Conference*, Wollongong, Australia, 2008, 129-136.

[19] The Open University of Israel website: http://www-e.openu.ac.il/

[20] Utting, I., Cooper, S., Kolling, M., Maloney, J. & Resnick, M. Alice, Greenfoot and Scratch – a Discussion, *TOCE - Transaction on Computing education*, 2010, Vol. 10, issue 4, 1-11.

[21] Vilner, T., Zur, E. & Tavor, S. Integrating Greenfoot into CS1 – a Case Study, *ITiCSE 2011 - Proceedings of the 16th Annual SIGCSE Conference on Innovation and Technology in Computer Science Education*, July 2011.

[22] Wallace, F. L. and Wallace, S. R., Electronic office hours: A component of distance learning, *Computers & Education*, 37, 3-4, 2001, 195-209.

[23] Ward, B., Marghitu, D., Bell, T. & Lambert, L. Teaching Computer Science Concepts in Scratch and Alice, *Journal of computing Sciences in Colleges*, 2010, Vol 26, issue 2, 173-180.

Development and Evaluation of Indexed Captioned Searchable Videos for STEM Coursework

Tayfun Tuna[1]
ttuna@uh.edu

Jaspal Subhlok[1]
jaspal@uh.edu

Lecia Barker[2]
lecia@ischool.utexas.edu

Varun Varghese[1]
vkvarghese@uh.edu

Olin Johnson[1]
johnson@cs.uh.edu

Shishir Shah[1]
shah@cs.uh.edu

ABSTRACT

Videos of classroom lectures have proven to be a popular and versatile learning resource. This paper reports on videos featuring Indexing, Captioning, and Search capability (ICS Videos). The goal is to allow a user to rapidly search and access a topic of interest, a key shortcoming of the standard video format. A lecture is automatically divided into logical indexed video segments by analyzing video frames. Text is automatically identified with OCR technology enhanced with image transformations to drive keyword search. Captions can be added to videos. The ICS video player integrates indexing, search, and captioning in video playback and has been used by dozens of courses and 1000s of students. This paper reports on the development and evaluation of ICS videos framework and assessment of its value as an academic learning resource.

Categories and Subject Descriptors

H.5.2 **[Information Interfaces And Presentation]:** User Interfaces - *Evaluation/methodology* H.3.1 **[Information Storage and Retrieval]**: Content Analysis and Indexing *-Indexing method* I.4. **[Image Processing And Computer Vision]**: Segmentation-*Edge and feature detection* I.7.5 **[Document and Text Processing]:** Document Capture- *Optical character recognition (OCR)*

General Terms

Design, Experimentation, Measurement, Performance

Keywords

Assessment, Educational Technologies, Lecture Videos, OCR, Text Segmentation, Video Indexing, Video Search

1. INTRODUCTION

Video of classroom lectures is a versatile learning resource. It is often made available as additional material for a conventional course, as the core of distance learning coursework, or posted publicly for community learning or as reference material. Evidence of the popularity of lecture videos includes thousands of complete courses posted on portals such as MIT OpenCourseware and Apple's iTunes University. At the University of Houston, video lectures have been widely used for over a decade to enhance STEM coursework. Typically Tablet PCs, which allow free mixing of prepared (PowerPoint) viewgraphs with hand annotations and illustrations, are employed for teaching and simultaneous recording of lectures. Advantages include excellent resolution, as the video consists of PC screen shots, and low video production cost, as no camera or operator is needed. The videos typically show whatever the professor is projecting on the screen (e.g., PowerPoint slides, animations, annotations, formulas, algorithms, or drawings) and the instructor's voice. Prior research has established that the recorded Tablet PC lectures are a powerful resource on par with a textbook and the classroom.

A major weakness of these recorded lecture videos is the inability to quickly access the content of interest in a video lecture. This is intuitively clear and also established by our surveys and student interviews. This paper reports on **ICS videos**: videos enhanced with *Indexing, Captioning,* and *Search* capability that are designed for quick access to video content. **Indexing** adds logical index points, each in the form of a snapshot representing a video segment that can be accessed directly; **Captioning** adds the text of the video lecture in a separate panel; **Search** enables identification of video segments that match a keyword provided by the user.

The central technical goal of this project is automatic conversion of standard videos to ICS Videos. Index points are identified automatically with analysis of video frames. Search framework is based on the adoption of OCR technologies enhanced with a suite of image transformations to identify text on video frames. The accuracy and efficiency of indexing and search procedures are presented in the paper. Currently, captioning is done manually. All aspects are integrated in a unified ICS Video player.

The ICS video framework has been used by dozens of STEM courses and 1000s of students at the University of Houston, a large public university system. Captioned videos have been tested and evaluated with project partners at the Texas School for the Deaf. Results are reported from extensive assessment of ICS video usage carried out with student surveys and instructor interviews. The research presented clearly demonstrates that i) Tablet PC based video lectures are an extremely important student resource, ii) The framework developed to enhance videos with indexing and search features is efficient, effective, and a significant improvement over the state of the art, and iii) Indexing and search capability significantly enhance the value of lecture

Permission to make digital or hard copies of all or part of this work for personal or classroom use is granted without fee provided that copies are not made or distributed for profit or commercial advantage and that copies bear this notice and the full citation on the first page. To copy otherwise, or republish, to post on servers or to redistribute to lists, requires prior specific permission and/or a fee.
SIGCSE'12, February 29–March 3, 2012, Raleigh, North Carolina,USA.
Copyright 2012 ACM 978-1-4503-1098-7/12/02...$10.00.

[1] Department of Computer Science, University of Houston, Houston, TX 77204

[2] School of Information, University of Texas, Austin, TX 78701

videos. The video framework developed is freely available to academic institutions.

2. RELATED WORK

Because of limited space, we only list representatives of the main directions of related work. The idea of capturing videos of classroom lectures and other presentations, and making them available electronically, has been in widespread use for several years. These videos are generally recorded by camera(s) operated by professionals or installed in the lecture/presentation rooms [3]. Navigating between video chunks, using annotations and hyperlinks is discussed in [9,11]. An index structure-based method to efficiently search short video clips in large video collections is presented in [17]. OCR engines and text localization has been used for indexing videos [8].

The key features of the work presented in this paper that differentiates it from most previous work are i) automation of segmentation of videos, ii) deployment of image transformations with OCR for enhanced video search, iii) an approach based on video frame analysis that is independent of any hardware or presentation technology, v) focus on recordings from Tablet PC screens, and v) large-scale evaluation of student outcomes.

3. ICS VIDEOS

This section discusses the technology and evaluation of the key components of ICS videos; indexing, search, captioning and the video player. The technical aspects of this work are reported in more detail in related work [17].

3.1 Indexing

In the context of ICS videos, indexing is the task of dividing a lecture video into segments that contain different topics. This task is accomplished by first identifying all *transition points* where the scene in the video changes significantly. A subset of these transition points is selected as *index points,* which represent the beginning of the video segments as presented to the user.

Detection of transition points is based on a comparison of successive frames in the video. Corresponding pixels in successive frames are considered to be different if they differ by a minimum *RGB threshold* when the RGB values of the pixels are compared. Successive frames constitute a transition point if the fraction of pixels that are different based on the RGB criteria exceeds a minimum threshold, which we refer to as the *transition point threshold.* The reason for using thresholds to identify transition points is that frames corresponding to the same scene in practice (e.g., exactly the same viewgraph) also have minor differences in the RGB spectrum that must be ignored to avoid false transition points. The threshold values are chosen empirically after evaluation of a large number of diverse lectures. Figure 1 illustrates a transition point in a sequence of video frames.

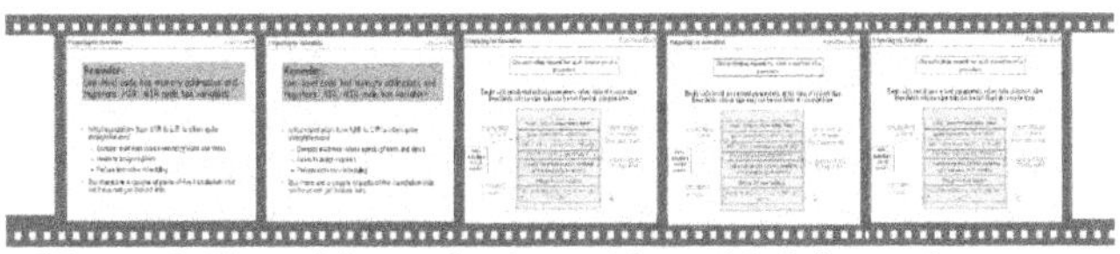

Figure 1. Transition point in a video: third frame is a new transition point

Comparing pairs of all successive frames in a video is rather inefficient and time consuming. We apply two methods to speed up this process: *Employing Jumping Interval* and *Binary Search.*

Employing Jumping Interval: In a video lecture, scene transitions are relatively infrequent. With this optimization, instead of comparing successive frames, the current frame is compared to a frame that is one *Jumping Interval* ahead. If the two frames are identical, then in all likelihood, the frames between them are also identical. Hence the search marker is moved up by a *Jumping Interval* and the frames between them are not processed. If the current frame and the frame one *Jumping Interval* ahead are different, then the frames between them are compared sequentially starting from the current frame to identify all transition points. Essentially, in a long sequence of identical frames, most comparisons between successive frames are skipped.

Binary Search: This procedure starts by splitting the video into two segments – from the first frame to the middle frame and from the middle frame to the last frame. For each of these segments, the first and the last frame are compared. If they are identical, then it is assumed that the segment contains no transition points and if they are different, the segment is again subdivided into two segments and the procedure is applied recursively. When a segment size of one is reached, a transition point is identified.

Employment of a jumping interval and binary search substantially improves performance but there is a chance that a legitimate transition point may be missed. This happens when the first and last frame in a segment are identical masking transition points inside the segment. A common reason for this to happen is when the instructor goes back and forth between viewgraphs while explaining a topic in a lecture. For evaluation we selected 20 different videos prepared by 15 different instructors. These videos were selected for their diversity in templates and color styles. The courses being taught were from the Computer Science, Biology, and Earth and Atmospheric sciences departments. Figure 2 and Figure 3 present results of experiments with this video suite.

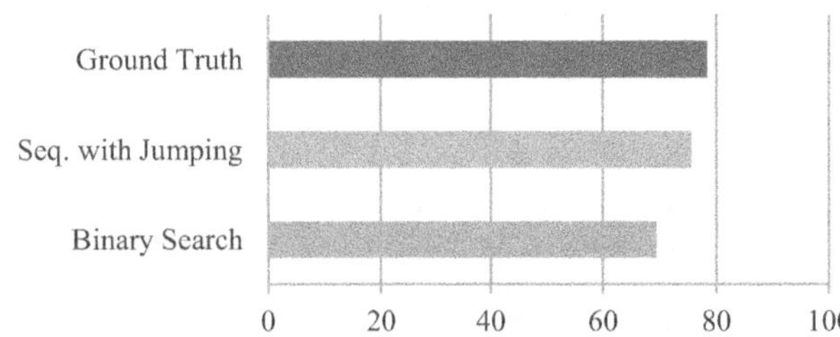

Figure 2. Average number of transition points detected with different methods in a lecture video

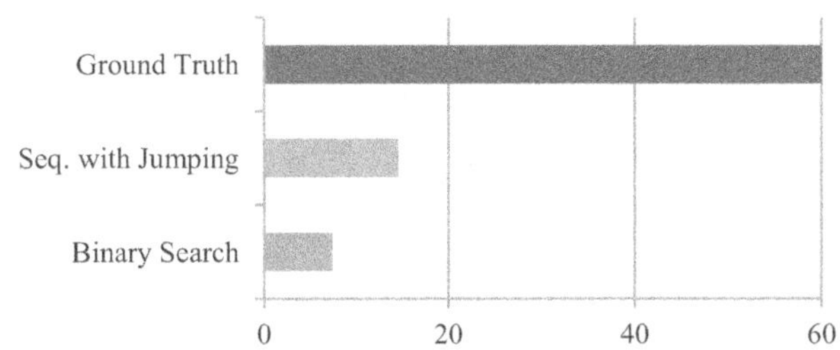

Figure 3. Average time (mins) for indexing an hour of video

Figure 2 shows the number of transition points detected on average in a video and Figure 3 shows the average processing time for indexing an hour of video. We note that a few transition points are indeed missed due to the optimizations. However, the cost of losing a few transition points is outweighed by the significant benefit of improved execution time.

The algorithms discussed above typically find all slide transitions in a lecture video with very few false positives. However, a video may have a large number of such transition points; over 100 is not unusual when an instructor writes frequently on the Tablet PC screen. To make indexing more meaningful and easier to use, we need to identify a smaller number of index points from the detected transition points. For this purpose a filtering algorithm is applied to eliminate unwanted transition points. The algorithm takes the number of index points desired and the minimum time gap between successive index points as parameters, and then applies iterative elimination. The basic idea is to repeatedly find the closest pair of remaining transition points on the timeline and eliminate one from the pair. When there is a cluster of transition points on the timeline, the algorithm ensures that a representative is included as an index point. The transition points are eliminated until their number has reached the desired number of index points, and the time difference between the remaining transition points has exceeded the predefined minimum time gap. The remaining transition points are retained as index points.

3.2 Keyword Search

Keyword search is the process of identifying all video segments where a particular keyword exists. The framework to support keyword search is as follows. The indexer creates the video segments as well as the transition point frames. Text on these frames is detected and stored in a database. The ICS Video Player loads the keywords from this database along with the corresponding video. When a user searches for a keyword, the player presents a series of index points that allow the user to navigate to the corresponding video segments. This process requires that all the text contained in the images corresponding to the transition points be identified. This can be accomplished by the use of Optical Character Recognition (OCR) tools, an approach investigated in [10]. After a comprehensive analysis of available OCR tools that could be integrated for use with the ICS Video Project, we opted to use the MODI (Microsoft Office Document Imaging) toolset. We found that OCR tools generally have limited effectiveness at recognizing text in the presence of 1) certain text and background color and shade combinations, 2) text mingled with colorful shapes, and 3) small and exotic fonts. To increase the detection efficiency of text on video frames, we used simple image processing techniques for image enhancement (IE) prior to the application of OCR tools. IE operations employed include segmentation of text, enlargement with interpolation, and color inversion.

Segmentation of text involves defining and extracting the text regions in an image. For text segmentation, we first convert the color image to a binary black and white image by using Simple Image Statistics based thresholding[14]. Then by using a dilation operation, which allows for growth of separate objects and joining of objects, we build words from characters. After that we employ Sobel edge detection. Lastly, we use blob extraction to extract standalone objects in the image using connected components labeling algorithm. Enlargement with interpolation is implemented for the segmented blocks. By this operation, small size text is enlarged so that some of it becomes visible to OCR engines. Segmentation of text and enlargement is illustrated in Figure 4. Color inversion is done separately by altering the RGB values of images, aimed at increasing the contrast between the text and background. Image enhancement procedures often lead to new text being recognized, but can also prevent the recognition of other text. Hence OCR engines are applied to the original images as well as the enhanced images and the union of the results is taken.

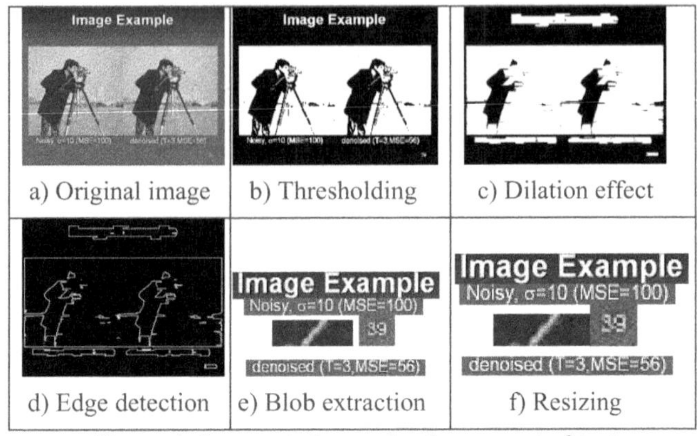

Figure 4. Segmentation and enlargement of text

To test the OCR Tools and the impact of IE procedures, we evaluated 1387 different images that are selected by the indexer from 20 diverse videos discussed in the previous section. Images in these videos contain 20,007 unique words, 27,201 total words (of more than 1 character length) for a total of 144,613 characters.

Experimental results, presented in Figure 5, show that the search accuracy of three distinct OCR engines, Tesseract, GOCR and MODI, improved, with an increase of 9% on average with IE transformations. The maximum accuracy obtained by applying all OCR engines with image enhancements was 97.1%. Alternately stated, the miss rate was 8.9% for the best single OCR engine, 5.2% for all OCR tools combined, and 2.9% for all OCR engines combined with image enhancement.

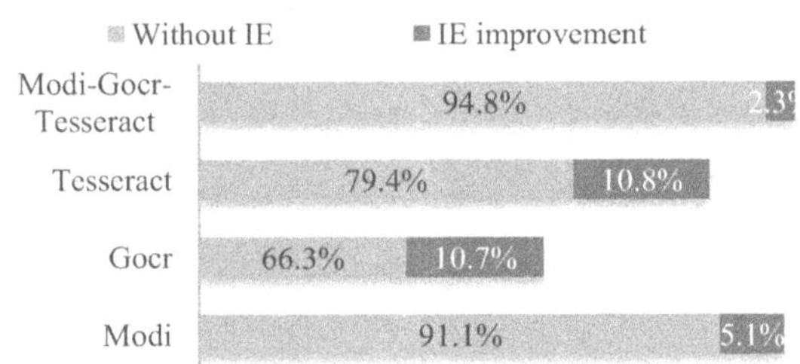

Figure 5. Search accuracy rate of OCR tools

Image enhancement provided this accuracy improvement, but increased the processing time significantly, partly because OCR engines have to be applied on the original and the enhanced images. Nonetheless, the processing time remains modest for a typical video. On average it is in the range of 2-3 minutes for an hour long video on a typical desktop. Image enhancement also doubled the false positives detected by OCR engines, i.e., more words were detected that were not actually present in the video. This often happens when an OCR engine misses a character in a word, leading to false identification of a different word. Since the main aim of the text recognition is to let the user find words of interest, the "extra words" resulting from false positives are unlikely to diminish the functionality in a meaningful way.

3.3 Captioning

Captioning consists of adding synchronized text blocks matching the audio stream, which typically consists of the instructor's speech as well as student interactions. Captioning was motivated by the need to have video lectures available to the deaf, although it also has significant potential for improving the experience of hearing and foreign language students. Ideally, captioning should be automatic based on speech recognition technology, which has been known to work well in many scenarios. However, our preliminary investigation revealed that available speech recognition tools were not satisfactory for technical lectures. The key reasons were the preponderance of technical jargon and abbreviations. We believe that a number of techniques can be used to make speech recognition practical, in particular training speech recognition software with instructors, dictionaries of technical terms, and a GUI for correction of speech errors. However, this has not yet been investigated systematically so we will not discuss further. The ICS video player does support manually transcribed captions. We have prepared lecture material for testing and evaluation for the Texas School for the Deaf and are in the process of preparing diverse course material with captions. We expect to report on these in the future.

3.4 ICS Video Player

ICS Video Player is a Flash-based player capable of playing standard H.264 encoded streaming media. The player is made up of video playback component, Index Panel, Timeline with selectable index, Search box, Search results display, and Caption display, as illustrated in Figure 6.

Figure 6. A snapshot of ICS Video Player

Index Display: An index panel is situated on the left side of the player, as shown in Figure 6. Index points are listed vertically in the index panel and each has an index title, a screenshot of the video at that point of time, and index time *in hh:mm:ss*. Users can select any index point from the list and the video starts playing from the selected index point. The bottom part of the player has a panel comprised of the timeline, indicating the progress of the video playback, along with index points arranged by their time locations. Users can skip to any part of the video by selecting the desired position in the timeline. The image screenshot corresponding to the index point is displayed as a pop-up when the mouse cursor is placed over an index point bar, providing a visual display of the segment represented by the index point.

Search Display: A search box is located on the top right corner of the video player. In order to execute a search, a user types the keywords in the search box. All index segments that contain the search term are displayed as results. The matching keyword, number of matches in the segment, the index title, and the index image are also displayed. The search feature is illustrated in Figure 6; two video segments represented by index points are presented as matches for the search term "granite." Clicking on the search images displayed will start the video from that point.

Caption Display: Captions are displayed as an overlay at the bottom of the video and in a separate caption window. The caption window displays the start time of the caption together with the caption text. The most recent caption is added to the bottom of the list. Users can scroll and read the previously displayed captions. The captions can be turned on or off by clicking the appropriate button on the player. A visual display is omitted due to lack of space.

4. EXPERIENCE AND ASSESSMENT

The usage of ICS videos framework is widespread at the University of Houston campus. For example, in the Spring 2011 semester, raw statistics show that 34 courses employed ICS videos for instruction. 314 new video lectures were uploaded, (and many of the existing video lectures from earlier semesters were also accessed). There were a total of over 23,000 video accesses by the students throughout the semester. Students in many (but not all) courses participated in the assessment of videos.

The evaluation described below adds to a small, but expanding, literature on the value of capturing classroom lectures as videos. Most studies show that students willingly use video lectures to their advantage when they are available [1,5,12,15,16].

We have assessed ICS Video use to develop an understanding of the overall perceived value of the video lectures and the value added, if any, by providing indexing and search. Surveys were administered over three years in six semesters; all but the original pilot survey were administered online. The original pilot survey was developed in part based on the open-ended questionnaire in our previous work [16] that motivated this project. The surveys asked about the nature and frequency of usage, strength of need, value, preparation for the class, expected grade, and several individual difference variables, including hours worked to earn income, credit hours taken, hours of studying per week, commute time, marital status, number of dependents, and demographic information. In this paper we report the key findings from the two most recent terms, Spring 2010 and Spring 2011 in regard to general video usage, and specifically on indexing and search tools. The procedures and detailed results from the survey are made available online through *icsvideos.cs.uh.edu.*

4.1 Survey Procedures and Sample

Surveys were administered in the last week of the semester. Participating faculty representing 18 courses sent a link to their students, resulting in 1167 usable surveys (Spring 2010 N=612, Spring 2011 N=555). About half of students in the sample were in freshman biology courses (53%), though not primarily freshmen themselves. The remaining courses were in computer science, chemistry, geology, and mathematics. Undergraduates were widely distributed across levels, with 17% freshmen, 23% sophomores, 31% juniors, and 29% seniors and post-baccalaureate. A majority (60%) of the undergraduates sampled were female, because of high percentage of women in the biology courses (67%). The sample is also ethnically diverse: 27% were Eastern or Southeastern Asian; 24% were White; 16% were Asian Indian; 14% were Latin American; and 7% were African American. In addition, although the majority of the students are

American citizens or permanent residents (96%), about 30% speak English as a second language. Most of them rate their English competence as good.

The survey was conducted at the University of Houston, where there are many demands on students' time. Students reported a mean one-way commute time to campus between 30-45 minutes. Most of the students (57%) work to support themselves, with about 7% working 36 or more hours per week. A larger fraction of students in this sample work as compared to students nationally: 46% of full-time students, compared to 41% nationally.

The surveyed students are committed to their education. The majority of respondents felt that going to class was important and were very concerned about their course grade and their grade point average in general.

4.2 Summary of Overall Findings

Instructors posted anywhere between 8 and 30 videos per course. About 84% of students responded that they had used the videos.

4.2.1 Videos Strongly Valued for Learning, Grades

A series of survey items asked students to agree or disagree, or to rate the importance of certain aspects of the videos. Responses indicated strikingly high value for the videos. Table 1 shows evaluation by the students who viewed at least one video. Students found the videos helpful for clarifying material, for reviewing, and for studying for quizzes and tests. Additionally, most of the students agreed that having access to videos was important to them for the individual class (72% agreed strongly) and rated the videos very important for getting the grade they hoped for (64% felt it was very important; mean of 3.5 on a 4-point scale for this item).

Table 1. Perceived value of videos

Survey Item	N	Mean (6-pt scale)	Std. Dev.
Lecture videos help me to clarify material that was not clear in class.	825	5.45	.826
Lecture videos are useful for reviewing.	841	5.63	.693
Having access to lecture videos for this class is important to me.	837	5.61	.774
The lecture videos helped me to study for quizzes or tests.	829	5.51	.842

Students were asked to rate several content sources for their importance in their learning for the class, and these ratings are shown Figure 7. The most highly rated were "professor's lecture notes" (84% of students) and lecture videos (63% of students), followed by notes they themselves take. The lowest in relative importance were the textbook and other reading sources.

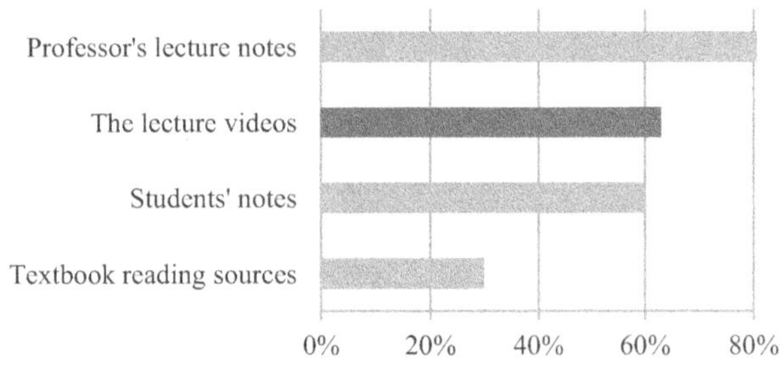

Figure 7. Student ratings of learning resources: Percentage of students that consider the resource "very important"

4.2.2 Index Use Correlated with Increased Value of Videos

A test of significance was conducted to compare index users' perceptions of the value of the lecture videos to non-index users' perceptions of value. In order to conduct the test, a scale variable, Overall Attitude Toward Videos, was computed by combining the six variables discussed above (Lecture videos help me to clarify material that was not clear in class; Lecture videos are useful for reviewing; Having access to lecture videos for this class is important to me; The lecture videos helped me to study for quizzes or tests; How important was use of the lecture videos for this class for getting the grade you hoped for? Rating of the importance of lecture videos for learning in this class). Students who had used the indexing feature scored higher on average on the Overall Attitudes Toward Video scale than students who had not used the indexing feature ($t(616) = -3.284$, $p < .001$). To estimate the magnitude of the value added by the index, the effect size was calculated using Cohen's *d*. A small to moderate effect ($d = 0.265$) was found.

4.2.3 Index was Helpful, Easy to Use

A series of forced-answer questions were intended to provide an understanding of the usefulness of the indexing tool. Among the 299 students who had used the indexing feature, response was very positive:

- 97% felt that the index was helpful
- 89% said they knew immediately what to do with the index (a proxy for the construct "intuitive")
- 96% felt the placement of information and images made the index easy to use
- 90% thought the time intervals were appropriate for the lecture

In open-ended comments, students stated that using the indexing feature saved them time (e.g., "I didn't have to wade through the rest of lecture just to answer one question") and helped them to get back to studying after interruptions (e.g., "sometimes I would have to pause the lecture to take care of other responsibilities that I had to attend too, and when I was ready to come back to the lecture I'd pick up exactly where I was at. It was great!").

4.2.4 Search Tool Less Used, But Valued

Relatively few students (46) responding to the 2011 survey had used the search tool. In hindsight, perhaps this is not surprising: the students were never informed that search existed or what it meant, the search icon did not stand out in the interface, and the search feature was not usable for part of the semester for technical reasons. A series of forced-answer statements asked students to evaluate the search tool. Most respondents found the tool easy to use (96%), found the search results easy to use (97%), and felt that the search tool helped them find the part of the video they were looking for most of the time (70%). Students usually knew which words to enter into the search box to find the segment of the video they were looking for (72%). Although these results are strong, they are still preliminary, given the small sample size.

4.2.5 More Class Attendance, More Video Use

A fear often reiterated in literature on making lecture videos available is that the students will be less likely to go to class, using the videos as a substitute [1,2,5,7,12,13]. That fear was not substantiated in our findings for STEM coursework, in any of the terms. Most (86%) students strongly agreed that it was important for them to go to class, whether or not the video lectures were available, and 67% reported that they had attended 75-100% of classes. In addition, class attendance was positively and significantly correlated with video use ($r(1019) = .234$, $p < .000$).

5. DISCUSSION AND FUTURE WORK

The underlying significance of this and related research is that video is a dynamic and versatile resource, not a poor substitute for a classroom. The videos were valuable for students who attended classes, were primarily used for reviewing and clarifying concepts, and had little impact on class attendance. In this regard, we hope some of the following major directions of work will be pursued by the community or educational vendors:

- Enabling instructors to customize videos with easy interfaces for selection of indexes and other basic editing and manipulation.
- One touch operation from starting of recording a lecture to it being posted online for students.
- With mobile devices becoming increasingly common, understanding what modifications need to be made to make use on mobile devices attractive.
- Enhancement and automation of captioning to make video material more useful to the deaf students.
- Making infrastructure for ICS or similar video technology widely available to STEM instructors.

6. CONCLUSIONS

This paper reports on technologies developed for Indexed, Captioned, and Searchable videos and their usage for STEM coursework. We demonstrated that automated indexing and search frameworks are effective and efficient. The ICS Videos framework underwent large scale deployment and assessment and was a success in all respects. The videos were judged by students to be very valuable and employed for diverse purposes such as clarifying and reviewing material and preparing for exams. Indexing and search features were considered very helpful and easy to use. This work points to a new and innovative direction for effective use of videos in STEM coursework. The framework developed is freely available to educational institutions.

7. ACKNOWLEDGMENTS

Partial support for this work was provided by the National Science Foundation's Division of Undergraduate Education under the Course, Curriculum, and Laboratory Improvement (CCLI) program with Award No. DUE-0817558. Any opinions, findings, and conclusions or recommendations expressed in this material are those of the authors and do not necessarily reflect the views of the National Science Foundation.

We would also like to acknowledge the contributions of several members of the ICS Videos group: Gautam Bhatt, Zhigang Deng, Salvador Baez-Franseschi, Pradeep Krishnan, and Joann Li.

8. REFERENCES

[1] Abowd, G. D. 2010. Classroom 2000: An experiment with the instrumentation of a living educational environment. *IBM Systems Journal*, *38*(4), 508–530.

[2] Bell, T., Cockburn, A., McKenzie, B., & Vargo, J. 2001. Flexible delivery damaging to learning? Lessons from the Canterbury Digital Lectures Project. In *ED-MEDIA 2001: Proceedings of the World Conference on Educational Multimedia, Hypermedia and Telecommunications* (pp. 117–122).

[3] Bianchi, M. 2004. Automatic video production of lectures using an intelligent and aware environment. In *Proceedings of the 3rd international conference on Mobile and ubiquitous multimedia* (MUM '04). ACM, New York, NY, USA, 117-123. DOI=10.1145/1052380.1052397 http://doi.acm.org/10.1145/1052380.1052397

[4] Brecht, H. D., & Ogilby, S. M. 2008. Enabling a comprehensive teaching strategy: Video lectures. *Journal of Information Technology Education, 7.*

[5] Chandra, S. 2007. Lecture video capture for the masses. *ACM SIGCSE Bulletin*, *39*(3), 276–280.

[6] The Condition of Education 2011. (2011, May 26). National Center for Education Statistics. http://nces.ed.gov/pubsearch/pubsinfo.asp?pubid=2011033

[7] Keengwe, J. 2007. Faculty integration of technology into instruction and students' perceptions of computer technology to improve student learning. *Journal of Information Technology Education*, *6*(1), 169–179.

[8] Lienhart R and Effelsberg, W. 2000. Automatic text segmentation and text recognition for video indexing. *Multimedia Syst.* 8, 1 (January 2000), 69-81. DOI=10.1007/s005300050006 http://dx.doi.org/10.1007/s005300050006

[9] Ma, W., Lee, Y., Du, D. H. C., and McCahill, M. P. 1998. Video-Based Hypermedia for Education-on-Demand. *IEEE MultiMedia* 5, 1 (January 1998), 72-83. DOI=10.1109/93.664744 http://dx.doi.org/10.1109/93.664744

[10] Merler, M. and Kender, J.R. 2009. Semantic keyword extraction via adaptive text binarization of unstructured unsourced video, *IEEE International Conference on Image Processing, Cairo, Egypt,* Nov. 2009 .

[11] Microsoft Project Tuva, http://research.microsoft.com/apps/tools/tuva/

[12] Odhabi, H., & Nicks-McCaleb, L. 2011. Video recording lectures: Student and professor perspectives. *British Journal of Educational Technology*, *42*(2), 327-336.

[13] Phillips, R., Gosper, M., McNeill, M., Woo, K., Preston, G., & Green, D. 2007. Staff and student perspectives on web based lecture technologies: Insights into the great divide. In *ICT: Providing choices for learners and learning. Proceedings of the Australasian Society for Computers in Learning in Tertiary Education (ASCILITE) Conference. Singapore, Dec* (pp. 2–5).

[14] Simple Image Statistics Threasholding, http://www.aforgenet.com/framework/docs/html/39e861e0-e4bb-7e09-c067-6cbda5d646f3.htm.

[15] Soong, S. K., Chan, L. K., Cheers, C., & Hu, C. 2006. Impact of video recorded lectures among students. *Who's Learning*, 789–793.

[16] Subhlok, J., Johnson, O., Subramaniam, V., Vilalta, R., & Yun, C. 2007. Tablet PC video based hybrid coursework in computer science. *Proceedings of the 38th SIGCSE technical symposium on Computer science education - SIGCSE '07* (p. 74). Presented at the Proceedings of the 38th SIGCSE technical symposium, Covington, Kentucky, USA.

[17] Tuna, T., Subhlok, J., Shah, S. 2011. Indexing and Keyword Search to Ease Navigation In Lecture Videos, *Applied Imagery Pattern Recognition Workshop, Washington, DC, Oct 2011.*

[18] Yuan,J., Duan L., Tian Q., and Xu C. 2004. Fast and robust short video clip search using an index structure. In *Proceedings of the 6th ACM SIGMM international workshop on Multimedia information retrieval (MIR '04)*. ACM, New York, NY, USA, 61-68. DOI=10.1145/1026711.1026722 http://doi.acm.org/10.1145/1026711.1026722

Metaview: A Tool for Learning About Viewing in 3D

James R. Miller
Electrical Engineering and Computer Science
1520 W. 15 Street; 2001 Eaton Hall
Lawrence, KS 66045
1-785-864-7384
jrmiller@ku.edu

ABSTRACT
Metaview is an interactive tool that helps to teach concepts related to nested 3D coordinate systems, especially in the context of defining and establishing views of 3D scenes in common graphics APIs like OpenGL and Direct3D. We describe the context in which nested coordinate systems arise in the study of graphics programming, then we relate the common conceptual difficulties students typically experience when studying and trying to put this material into practice. We then describe the role that metaview plays in helping to overcome these problems. Space allows us only to describe its core uses in these areas; several of its additional features are briefly listed at the end. Metaview is packaged with a set of built-in 3D models used to demonstrate major concepts. In addition, external and/or student-programmed models are easily imported into the tool. Metaview can be run anywhere, anytime using Java Web Start. The latest released version of the tool can be executed from http://people.eecs.ku.edu/~miller/JOGL/metaview.jnlp. We are currently working on a port to OpenGL ES targeted for portable smart devices such as tablet computers.

Categories and Subject Descriptors
K.3.1 [**Computers and Education**]: Computer Uses in Education – *distance learning*

K.3.2 [**Computers and Education**]: Computer and Information Science and Education – *computer science education; self-assessment*

General Terms
Design, Experimentation, Human Factors.

Keywords
Computer-aided Learning; Educational Technology; Computer-Graphics; Self-paced learning.

1. INTRODUCTION
Learning how to employ a 3D graphics API like OpenGL [10] or Direct3D [8] to generate specific desired views of 3D models seems to be a difficult skill for typical upper level undergraduates to master. Users of turnkey 3D modeling systems frequently experience analogous challenges when trying to understand how to build, view, and animate a 3D model. Especially problematic is the case when a 3D model (or the piece of it in which we are currently interested) has unequal dimensions with respect to the coordinate axes and/or is not near the origin of the coordinate system. In such cases, the graphics programmer must understand and bring to bear a solid understanding of how the various coordinate systems used by the graphics engine (most notably, the *world* and *eye* systems whose definitions are reviewed below) are specified as well as how they relate to one another and to the coordinate system of the display device.

Our Introduction to Computer Graphics course is targeted towards senior undergraduates, although there will typically be some beginning graduate students as well. No prior knowledge of computer graphics is assumed. There is no formal laboratory associated with the course, however students complete about four programming projects that require increasingly sophisticated uses of OpenGL. After quite a few years teaching this course, a number of conceptual problems related to viewing in 3D have been observed to cause high levels of frustration for students. This paper describes the design and use of metaview, an interactive graphics tool designed to help students achieve a deeper understanding of viewing in 3D in the context of a conventional graphics API.

Before they begin using the metaview tool described here, students learn about basic 2D graphics concepts including defining geometry, using window-viewport transformations, modeling transformations, handling events, creating animations, and so forth. The first two projects allow them to use these concepts in practice, and they generally do very well. However, the transition to 3D is a significant one. Lectures and assigned readings from the text (currently [1]; formerly [6]) describe the major concepts, but experience has shown that, even when warned about the quantum jump in difficulty they will see with their first 3D project, many students ignore this, only to achieve high levels of frustration as they labor late into the night a day or so before the due date.

Of course an enormous amount of related information and examples can be easily located on the internet, but as noted in [5], this more often than not simply serves to confuse them even more because the examples often include certain advanced features not yet discussed in class that have non-obvious side effects and/or additional requirements that students don't notice or don't understand.

Spending meaningful time learning concepts and completing projects is vitally important to mastering the material [11]. The

Permission to make digital or hard copies of all or part of this work for personal or classroom use is granted without fee provided that copies are not made or distributed for profit or commercial advantage and that copies bear this notice and the full citation on the first page. To copy otherwise, or republish, to post on servers or to redistribute to lists, requires prior specific permission and/or a fee.
SIGCSE'12, February 29–March 3, 2012, Raleigh, North Carolina, USA.
Copyright 2012 ACM 978-1-4503-1098-7/12/02...$10.00.

goal of this effort was therefore to provide an easy-to-use interactive learning tool that is accessible whenever and wherever students find themselves working that can help them over some of the major stumbling blocks in 3D modeling and viewing, for example, achieving expected views of 3D objects, both when generating still images as well as animated sequences such as 3D walk-throughs.

When helping the student make the connection between the viewing abstraction and a programming construct, a specific graphics API had to be chosen. Two obvious candidates were OpenGL [10] and Direct3D [8]. Moreover, two styles are common in OpenGL: classical v2.1 with routines like *gluLookAt*, and the more modern v3.3 and later in which *gluLookAt* and many other routines have been deprecated along with the fixed function pipeline. There is a 1-1 mapping between the viewing-related functions in OpenGL 2.1 and their counterparts in Direct3D. Moreover, even in OpenGL 3.3, it is common for programmers to use their own versions of analogous routines. In the end, we chose to use generic names and formal parameter calling sequences, based loosely on the OpenGL 2.1 conventions since we use OpenGL in classes here. Obviously it is trivial to alter these mappings for other environments.

2. RELATED WORK

Significant real estate is allocated in common textbooks to the development of an intuition for viewing in 3D (e.g., [1, 6, 10]). A typical textbook starting point for this intuition is to introduce and develop a camera analogy. Figures illustrate moving the camera around, sometimes with attached depictions of coordinate system axes, and snapping pictures. Sometimes the development of the intuition is intermixed with the mathematics and/or computer code representing one way to carry out the operations.

Since the presentation is static in the textbook, students are of course unable to try different viewing orientations or incorporate their own models. Experience with metaview has shown that the ability to interact with the viewing abstraction seems to enhance the ability to master the relationships among the coordinate systems. Coupled with a small set of key text displays that are kept in sync as the student directly manipulates key graphical abstractions, this knowledge is then more quickly transferred to an understanding of how to use a given graphics API to achieve desired views.

An early inspiration for the tool described here came from illustrations in [6] in which photographs of hands holding tinker toys were used in an attempt to make the relationship among the various coordinate systems concrete. After trying that exact technique once in class here, it was obvious that it was helpful to have a physical abstraction that was not restricted to the pages of the textbook. At the same time, it was also obvious that so much more could be done if the abstraction were a bit more flexible and embedded in a more powerful interactive framework.

The birth and evolution of metaview began shortly thereafter, now just over a decade ago. It started as a simple C++-based OpenGL program with a single object (the "XYZCube" that is now a part of the startup screens), using the GLUI [9] for interactive controls. The initial goal was to make the tinker toy idea a bit more interactive as well as to make some visuals for lectures and handouts. After the first couple of years, I noticed students being more engaged in those lectures and asking better questions. Some of the feedback I received was that they wanted to be able to run the program themselves outside of class and incorporate their own (or at least other) models. Unfortunately, it had never been designed for use by anyone other than the instructor, and it was incomplete and idiosyncratic in operation.

After spending some time making the tool a bit more robust and intuitive, I made it available on the machines allocated to the course. This proved useful, but was not nearly as effective as had been hoped, largely because by that time students were increasingly using their own machines and resisted trips to the lab just to use this tool. The answer seemed to be to make it available on their machines, but that immediately led to innumerable problems related to different operating systems and a host of configuration issues.

The emergence of Java, Java OpenGL (JOGL), and Java Web Start led to what ultimately proved to be a viable solution. The original tool was completely redesigned and redeveloped in Java/JOGL, using Swing for the GUI. Many additional features were added (and continue to be added) as well, and the result is the version described in this paper.

While this evolution of metaview was occurring, other interactive tools appeared. Three-dimensional modeling toolkits including Maya [2] and Blender [3] had appeared, providing the ability to create and animate elaborate 3D models. Instructors at a few universities had started to use these and similar tools to present, teach, and explore these concepts in an interactive setting.

We learned more recently of two other comprehensive interactive educational systems that were evolving over the same period of time. The Brown University Computer Graphics Research Group is actively developing the Exploratory Project [4]. The long-term goal is to develop a rich set of learning modules for a variety of topics. Their current products include tools for teaching 3D graphics concepts such as those presented here.

The system described by Hunkins [7] consists of a set of interactive OpenGL-based programs used to illustrate and teach 3D graphics concepts such as those targeted by metaview. The version described in [7] is written in C++ using the C binding to OpenGL 2.1 and is supported on Windows machines. Hunkins referred to development of a Java-JOGL version as well [7].

3. MAIN CONTRIBUTIONS OF THIS EFFORT

As noted in the previous section, there are many books, articles, and online tutorials that include static pictures and descriptions of this process. There are also some interactive tools that have been employed. Unique aspects of metaview include:

- It can be used as a platform independent and completely turnkey system. The application downloads and launches automatically via Java web start following, for example, clicking on a link in a web page. This avoids platform-specific installation issues and involvement of system administrators. It also makes it readily accessible to non-programmer users. Access to the metaview system is freely available to anyone.
- In addition to using numerical spinner controls, students can directly manipulate the graphical abstractions of the viewing parameters. They can click and drag the eye, the center of attention, and all the other parameters reviewed and discussed below. Regardless of whether students type new values or directly manipulate the graphical abstractions, both are kept in sync by the system. Direct manipulation of certain quantities (e.g., the view frustum) is correctly constrained to maintain its

proper orientation with respect to the eye coordinate system. Other quantities are unconstrained, but they are allowed to be constrained. Constraining how the eye point can be dragged, for example, allows it to be moved around without altering the direction of the reference line of sight.

- In addition to normal orthogonal and perspective viewing, metaview helps students learn the mechanics of stereoscopic viewing by presenting a pair of eye points, each with its own view frustum along with the two resulting left and right eye images.
- The projection plane position is unrestricted. Metaview allows the plane to be positioned anywhere inside the view volume. This helps students understand and control phenomena like motion parallax in animations.
- In addition to the models that come bundled with metaview, users can import their own models into the metaview framework, either by importing a Wavefront *obj* file or by writing a simple pair of classes whose structure is documented along with a complete example in the greeting page that appears when the application starts. The latter is especially helpful for students when trying to understand how to focus on arbitrary portions of their own models.
- While originally developed to illustrate how viewing in standard interactive 3D APIs worked, the tool can also be used for a variety of other purposes such as visualizing issues related to aliasing and antialiasing and understanding how the ray tracing rendering paradigm works.

4. COORDINATE SYSTEMS AND TRANSFORMATIONS

Before presenting the educational aspects of the metaview tool and describing its use in class, some basic concepts must be established so that the features of metaview will make sense to the reader. Virtually all modern graphics APIs utilize multiple coordinate systems. During rendering, vertices of primitives are transformed from one coordinate system to the next until pixels on the display covered by the primitives are determined. The typical progression of coordinate systems through which each vertex passes is, in order: modeling coordinates, world coordinates, eye coordinates, normalized projection coordinates, and device (pixel) coordinates. The names used by specific graphics APIs vary somewhat, but conceptually they all use this same sequence. The definition and use of the systems of primary interest to us here is briefly reviewed below.

Modeling coordinate systems employ application-defined units (e.g., centimeters, angstroms) and provide a basic reference frame in which subcomponents of a model can be defined by assuming a simple placement and orientation with respect to the modeling system axes. A complete model can be assembled by creating a hierarchy of modeling coordinate systems by successively placing one or more systems inside of a parent system. The highest level modeling coordinate system is called the world coordinate system. Note that the geometry of this model is view-independent.

Once this view-independent model geometry has been defined, creating a view of the model can be imagined as representing it in a different coordinate system whose axes have specific relationships with respect to the view and display device. This is typically accomplished in two stages using two successive coordinate systems. The first is called the eye coordinate system and is defined so that a reference line of sight is along the negative z-axis; the x- and y-axes are parallel to the horizontal and vertical display device directions, respectively. The transformation from world coordinates to eye coordinates is a rigid one that simply re-orients and translates the model while preserving the basic application units (e.g., centimeters). A subsequent transformation accounts for the field of view, a desired 3D to 2D projection method (e.g., orthogonal or perspective), and a mapping to a logical device coordinate viewport region.

For a variety of reasons, the field of view is defined in the eye coordinate system; not in world coordinates. This seemingly simple fact is one of the major sources of confusion experienced by students, and it is therefore one of the more important intuitions that metaview seeks to solidify.

When defining the view-independent structure of the model, a graphics programmer is typically concerned only with modeling and world coordinates, including how the various component modeling systems are placed inside of one another. Students generally have relatively little conceptual difficulty with this step. On the other hand, significant conceptual difficulties often arise in the next step as the programmer tries to generate desired views by creating an appropriate world coordinate to eye coordinate transformation and then using the resulting eye coordinate system to define an appropriate projection system. It was to help with the intuition and development of these two transformations that metaview was originally designed.

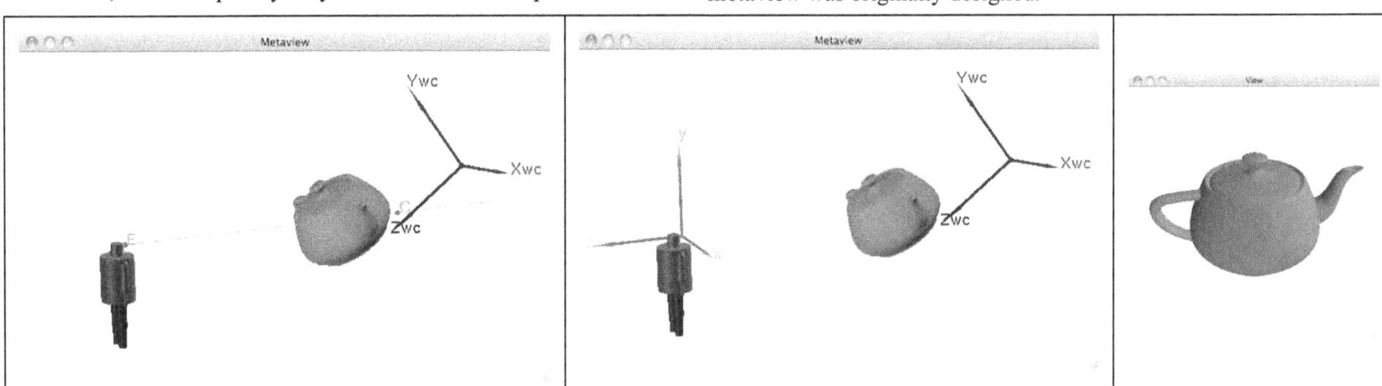

Figure 1(a): Positioning the eye (E) of a viewer and looking towards a center of attention (C). Both E and C are defined in the *world coordinate system*, shown here in blue.

Figure 1(b): From E, C, and the orientation of the viewer, the graphics system can automatically compute the *eye coordinate system*, shown here in yellow.

Figure 1(c): The view of the teapot as seen by our robot observer.

4.1 Defining the World to Eye Coordinate System Transformation

The physical analogy involves someone standing at some position in thc world coordinate space, looking towards another point in the same space. This defines the reference line of sight mentioned above. See Figure 1(a) in which we use a robot model as an abstraction of our viewer or observer.

The *reference line of sight* is directed from the eye point towards the center of attention and becomes the negative *z*-axis of the eye coordinate system, and the position of the observer (more precisely, the position of the observer's eye) becomes the origin of the eye coordinate system as shown in Figure 1(b). What the robot viewer will see is shown in Figure 1(c).

For monoscopic views, the eye can be imagined as either the left or the right eye; for stereoscopic views, we generate two eye coordinate systems and two views, one for each eye. With this background on coordinate systems and transformations between them, we can begin our description of how metaview contributes to the educational experience of students in graphics classes.

5. STUDENT LEARNING OBJECTIVES

Generating desired views of a 3D model is surprisingly hard for beginning graphics programmers. It is even harder if the desired view represents some arbitrary subset of their model. Oftentimes it is straightforward for students to create basic views of simple models because they can arrange to have the world and eye coordinate systems being very similar to one another. When this happens, it is almost irrelevant whether certain information is given in one frame or the other, and in any event, simple trial and error parameter tweaking quickly yields a reasonable view. Unfortunately the students are left at this point without a real understanding of what they have done or why it worked. Worse yet, they often create such nearly identical systems without realizing it. Then when they need to make a change – for example, to focus on some detail in some remote location of their model – they are totally baffled when the result is a blank screen. They then revert to trial and error parameter tweaking using their intuition, usually just making things worse. These problems are often exacerbated if their model happens to have quite different dimensions along the three world coordinate axes as illustrated in some of the examples below.

The primary learning objective, then, was to help students more quickly and efficiently master these concepts. The approach was to provide an interactive tool with a variety of built-in self-test features with built-in checks for correctness so that students could access and learn anytime and anywhere. More specifically, the learning objectives included:

- Develop the intuition surrounding how an observer relates to a world coordinate system, how this relationship determines the relationship between the world and eye coordinate systems, and the significance of the fact that the view frustum is defined in eye, not world, coordinates. It is over this latter point that students especially stumble.
- Understand how to apply knowledge of the relationships mentioned in the previous objective to an actual graphics API (in our case, OpenGL [10]) so that desired views can be easily and naturally generated.
- Understand how several other important imaging concepts relate. Included are: parallel versus perspective projections, controlling the amount of perspective distortion, impact of placement of the projection plane on effects like motion parallax in animations, image generation by projection versus by ray tracing, aliasing and antialiasing.
- Encourage students to engage in meaningful self-assessment of their understanding of these concepts in a variety of ways:
    - Find and generate specific views of objects hidden in the metaview program.
    - Directly insert their own arbitrarily complex model (either implemented in code or imported from a file) into the metaview framework to explore how to create desired views of all or parts of it.

6. TOOLS, METHODS, AND EXERCISES DEVELOPED

When the program starts, the user sees the three windows shown in Figure 2. The window on the bottom is a tabbed Control Panel with several exploration, annotation, and self-test features. The tab initially shown is a general greeting that begins with an explanation of the motivation and context for the metaview tool. This greeting explains that the window on the left (labeled "View") always contains a rendering of a 3D scene with some assumed line of sight, field of view, and projection type. The window on the right (labeled "Metaview") is a visual abstraction of how the view on the left was determined. It goes on to explain that the robot is an abstraction of the viewer, and the "View" image on the left is what the robot "sees" when viewing the model as indicated. The "Metaview" window contains a static text label at the bottom explaining to the user that the world coordinate axes are shown in blue, while the eye coordinate system axes are in yellow. This text will be suppressed in the rest of the figures in the paper. There are also dynamic text labels on the bottom of the "View" window that will be discussed later.

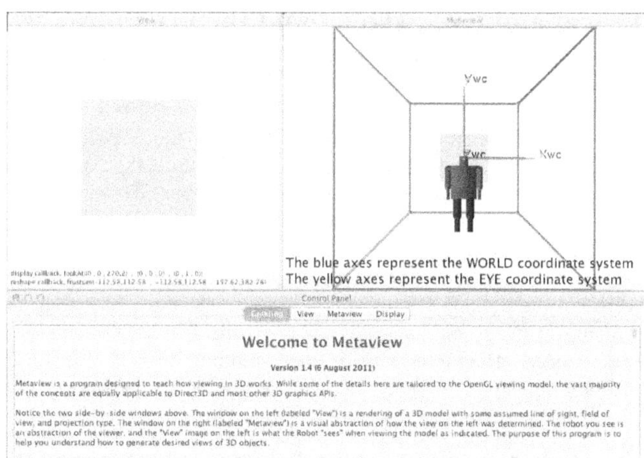

Figure 2: The three windows of the metaview program when the program launches.

The basic interactive controls are also described in the greeting tab. Included is a description of how the mouse works in the metaview window and what controls are to be found in the other tabs of the control panel.

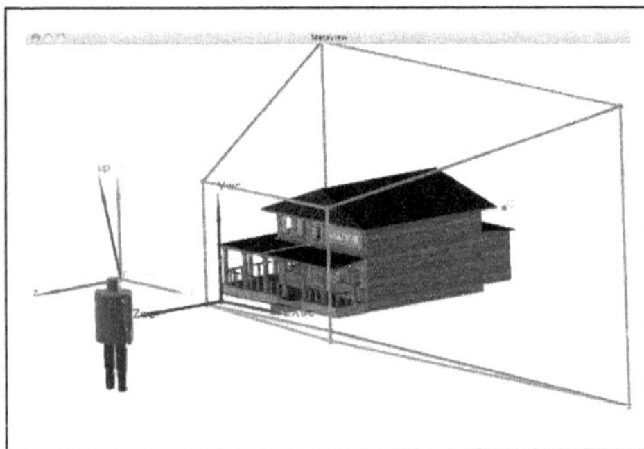

Figure 3(a); E, C, up define the Eye Coordinate System

Figure 3(b): The "View" from 3(a)

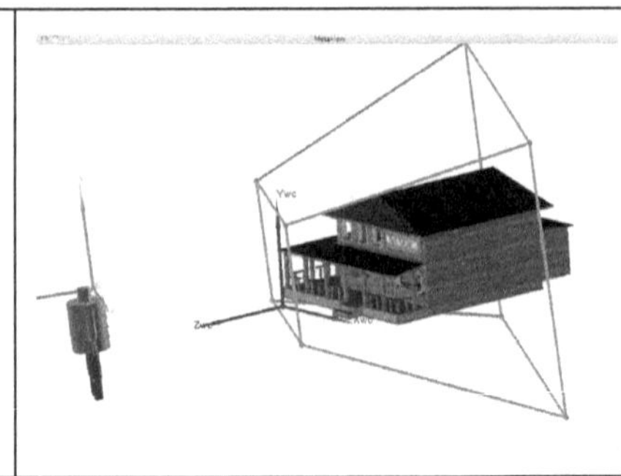

Figure 3(c): Interactively dragging the observer to another location

Figure 3(d): The "View" after the direct manipulation in (c).

6.1 Tools for Visualizing Relationships among World and Eye Systems and the Frustum

In their initial study of 2D graphics, students learn about the *world coordinate window*, a rectangular subset of the *xy*-plane such that only that portion of a model inside the window will actually appear on the display. The analog in 3D is the view frustum, drawn as a yellow truncated pyramid in Figure 3(a). While the basic role is the same (i.e., only that part of our 3D scene lying inside the frustum will appear on the display), the important difference is that the frustum is defined in the eye coordinate system in 3D. (It actually is defined in eye coordinates in 2D as well, but the default 3D-related view parameters are such that the typical 2D programmer is not aware of the fact.) As mentioned earlier, internalizing and truly understanding this fact is often difficult for students. The metaview approach to conveying this idea is discussed next.

Three quantities uniquely define the eye coordinate system: the eye point (E), the center of attention (C), and an orientation determined by a so-called "**up**" vector. The component of the "**up**" vector perpendicular to the reference line of sight determines the positive y direction of the eye coordinate system. Once the programmer provides E, C, and **up** (e.g., as shown in Figure 3(a)) the graphics system computes the x, y, and z eye system axis directions – also shown in Figure 3(a) – which determine the orientation of the "View" image shown in Figure 3(b).

One exercise students perform is to modify the viewing parameters by direct manipulation. For example, starting with the configuration in Figure 3(a), the student can grab the observer and drag it around in world coordinate space (Figure 3(c)). What is observed while doing so is that (i) the *xyz* eye coordinate axes move rigidly along with the observer, and (ii) the frustum also rigidly moves with the observer and eye coordinate system. Meanwhile, the "View" image in the "View" window always shows what the observer currently sees (Figure 3(d)). Continuously updated text labels at the bottom of the View window show "lookAt" and projection function parameters corresponding to the current position of the observer. Even though the frustum moves with the observer, the students see that only the numeric values for "lookAt" actually change while dragging the observer around. The combination of these observations clarifies the meaning of and cements the idea that the view frustum is defined in eye coordinates.

The role of the **up** vector is also sometimes hard for students to grasp. For example, the fact that it is just a reference direction used to determine the actual eye coordinate system y axis – i.e., **up** is not necessarily equal to y – is confusing. Its role is to fix the degree of freedom corresponding to a rotation of the viewer about the eye coordinate system z-axis. Starting with the situation depicted in Figure 4(a), for example, the student observes that certain types of changes to the **up** vector have no effect on the eye coordinate system (and hence the view frustum) whatsoever. Specifically, any changes to the **up** vector that do not change the plane containing E, C, and **up**, and that leave the **up** vector on the same side of the line of sight in that plane will have no effect. Compare Figure 4(a) to Figure 4(b). The **up** vectors differ, but the resulting eye coordinate systems are the same, hence the resulting image (Figure 4(c)) is the same in either case. Changes that do not alter the plane, but lead to the **up** vector being in the opposite half of the plane turn the observer on its head (Figure 4(d)), producing the view of Figure 4(e).

7. DISCUSSION

Space constraints limit the features of metaview we can discuss. In addition to the core features described, metaview facilitates an understanding of different projection types; what influences and how to control the amount of perspective distortion; stereoscopic viewing in which two frustums and two View images are presented; aliasing and antialiasing techniques; ray tracing; and issues related to parallax. Moreover, students can easily add their own models to metaview, either programmatically or via Wavefront *obj* files.

In addition, there are several exploration, self-test, and self-assessment features in the Control Panel tabs that could not be completely described here. For example, several models are

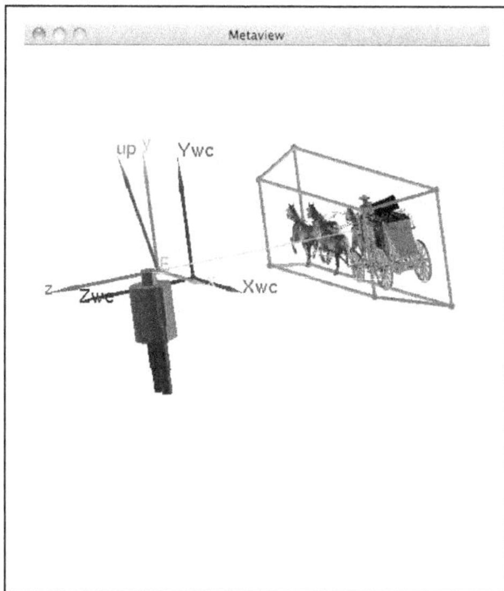

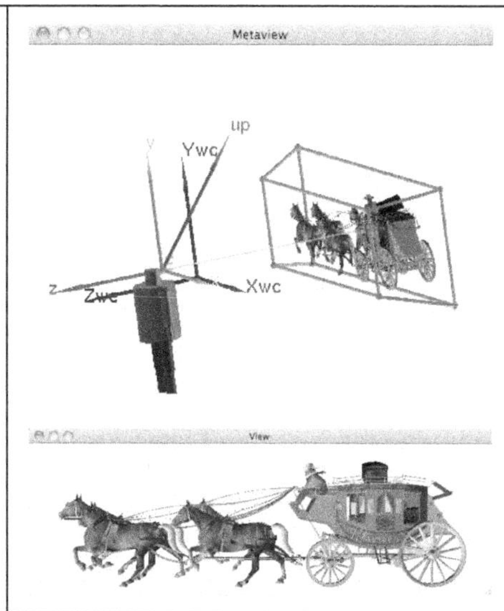

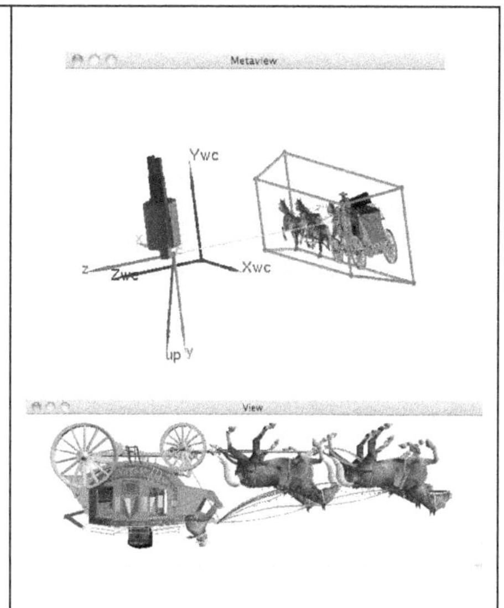

Figure 4(a): The original viewing parameters.

Figure 4(b): (TOP) An up vector change that has no effect

Figure 4(c): (BOTTOM) "View" for settings shown in both 4(a) and 4(b)

Figure 4(d): An up vector setting that flips the viewer upside down.

Figure 4(e): (BOTTOM) "View" for settings shown in Figure 4(d)

"hidden" in the environment. Students can query the world coordinate bounding box for such objects and then test their understanding by manually setting viewing and projection parameters to try to obtain specified views of the hidden objects. For example, "generate a view of the rear of the castle, using an approximate line of sight from the red turret towards the flag".

While no formal user study has been performed, we have solicited anonymous feedback from students from the past few offerings of the course. The feedback has generally been positive, exposed some bugs that have been corrected, and led to some useful usability improvements, both to the metaview program itself as well as to a web site often used in conjunction with the program.

8. FUTURE DIRECTIONS

While the Java Web Start mechanism used for launching the program has proven to be very effective, the emergence of portable smart devices like tablets has made it clear that an OpenGL ES version should be developed. Such devices do not currently support (and may never support) Java Web Start, hence design for an OpenGL ES port is underway.

Also underway is design and development for functionality that will allow interactive placement of light sources of various types. Among other things, goals include understanding the implications of light source placement in various coordinate systems, most notably world versus eye.

9. ACKNOWLEDGMENTS

The work described here was supported in part by the National Science Foundation under Grant No. 0633016. Any opinions, findings, and conclusions or recommendations expressed in this material are those of the author and do not necessarily reflect the views of the National Science Foundation. I would also like to thank the creative and mostly anonymous designers that make their models freely available for use without restriction. The saloon and stagecoach models used here were obtained from www.sharecg.com. Other such models are packaged with various versions of metaview, and the "Info" display for those models acknowledges their source.

REFERENCES

[1] Angel, E. 2012. *Interactive Computer Graphics: A Top-Down Approach With Shader-Based OpenGL*. Addison-Wesley, Boston, MA. (6th edition).

[2] Autodesk. 2011. *Autodesk Maya*. Retrieved October 16, 2011 from http://usa.autodesk.com/maya.

[3] Blender. 2011. *Blender*. Retrieved October 16, 2011 from http://www.blender.org.

[4] Brown. 2011. *Exploratories*. Retrieved October 16, 2011 from http://www.cs.brown.edu/exploratories.

[5] Colace, F. and De Santo, M. 2010. Ontology for E-Learning: A Bayesian Approach. *IEEE Transactions on Education* 53 (May 2010), 223-233.

[6] Foley, J. D., van Dam, A., Feiner, S. K., and Hughes, J. F. 1990. *Computer Graphics: Principles and Practice*. Addison-Wesley, Reading, MA, (2nd edition).

[7] Hunkins, D. 2011. *Computer Graphics: An Interactive Introduction with OpenGL*. Retrieved October 16, 2011 from http://cgems.inesc.pt/ModuleInfo.aspx?id=79.

[8] Luna, D. 2008. *Introduction to 3D Game Programming with DirectX 10*. Wordware Publishing, Inc., Plano, Texas.

[9] Rademacher, P. 2011. *GLUI User Interface Library*. Retrieved October 16. 2011 from http://www.cs.unc.edu/~rademach/glui/.

[10] Schreiner, D., Woo, M., Neider, J., and Davis, T. 2008. *OpenGL Programming Guide*. Addison-Wesley, Boston, MA. (6th ed.).

[11] Wolf, T. 2010. Assessing Student Learning in a Virtual Laboratory Environment. *IEEE Transactions on Education* 53 (May 2010), 216-222.

Mediated Transfer: Alice 3 to Java

Wanda Dann
Computer Science Department
Carnegie Mellon University
Pittsburgh, PA 15213
1-412-268-9959
wpdann@andrew.cmu.edu

Dennis Cosgrove
Human Computer Interaction Institute
Carnegie Mellon University
Pittsburgh, PA 15213
1-412-268-4074
dennisc@cs.cmu.edu

Don Slater
Computer Science Department
Carnegie Mellon University
Pittsburgh, PA 15213
1-412-268-4370
dslater@cs.cmu.edu

Dave Culyba
Human Computer Interaction Institute
Carnegie Mellon University
Pittsburgh, PA 15213
1-412-268-4074
dculyba@andrew.cmu.edu

Steve Cooper
Computer Science Department
Stanford University
Stanford, CA 94305
1-650-723-9798
coopers@stanford.edu

ABSTRACT

In this paper, we describe a pedagogy for an undergraduate programming course using Alice 3 and Java. We applied the educational theory of mediated transfer to develop a new version of the Alice system and accompanying instructional materials. The pedagogy was implemented and tested over two years. Student test scores in experimental, treatment course sections showed dramatic improvement over scores in comparable non-treatment sections.

Categories and Subject Descriptors

K.3.2 [**Computer and Information Science Education**]: Computer Science Education

General Terms

Measurement, Experimentation, Human Factors

Keywords

Alice, Java, Mediated transfer

1. INTRODUCTION

In this project, we developed and tested a pedagogy (teaching techniques and instructional materials) for a college level first-year programming course that uses Alice 3 and Java. Alice takes advantage of the high level of interest and motivation students find in video games and animated films. Since its release in 2004, Alice 2 and other highly innovative visualization tools have been increasingly adopted in college-level courses, particularly in courses for non-majors and in CS0. In addition, we have recently seen a wide-spread adoption in K-12 schools as an educational tool for introducing computational thinking and fundamental programming concepts. We want to build on this framework and encourage students to continue learning computing in AP CS and CS1 courses. (CS1 is defined here as a typical undergraduate, first course in programming with standard curriculum concepts [1].) Java is a widely used language of instruction in first-year college programming courses and is the language choice in the current AP Computer Science course.

Permission to make digital or hard copies of all or part of this work for personal or classroom use is granted without fee provided that copies are not made or distributed for profit or commercial advantage and that copies bear this notice and the full citation on the first page. To copy otherwise, or republish, to post on servers or to redistribute to lists, requires prior specific permission and/or a fee.
SIGCSE'12, February 29–March 3, 2012, Raleigh, North Carolina, USA.
Copyright 2012 ACM 978-1-4503-1098-7/12/02...$10.00.

In terms of technology, we built Alice 3 and a custom plugin for a Java integrated development environment (IDE) that translates the Alice 3 abstract syntax tree (AST) into Java code. In terms of pedagogy, we developed a tailored set of instructional materials that integrates the Alice problem solving strategy (originally introduced using Alice 2 [5]) with support for mediated transfer teaching techniques known as "bridging" and "hugging." This Alice 3 to Java approach is designed to enable students and instructors to transfer concepts learned in the context of Alice animations to programming in Java.

We conducted a two year study of the effectiveness of this Alice 3 to Java approach in terms of student achievement. Our hypothesis was that using explicit mediated transfer with Alice 3 would improve student achievement in learning Java in a CS1, one-semester course while still maintaining the strengths of the approach originally introduced with Alice 2 in a pre-CS1 course, (i.e., a course preparing students for CS1).

2. EDUCATIONAL TOOLS

Multiple tools and pedagogic approaches are available for teaching Java programming at the high school and undergraduate college level. In this section, we describe Alice and two well-known tools for teaching/learning Java. The purpose is merely to clarify the distinctions between Alice 3 and some currently available tools that have some visual component for teaching Java.

2.1 Alice

Alice is a programming environment specifically designed as a teaching/learning tool to enable novice programmers to create animations and games using 3D worlds [16, 17]. In Alice, hundreds of 3D models (e.g., people, animals and props) are provided in a gallery of Java classes. Instances of these classes are created to populate a virtual world. The Alice IDE provides a drag-and-drop editor (not text-entry) to create program code that animates these objects, thereby eliminating the possibility of novice programmers creating syntax errors. Alice was designed by studying how novices try to describe the motions of objects in a 3D world, and then modifying Alice to reflect these observed expectations [18]. Alice makes use of program visualization and enables students to immediately see how their animation programs run, enabling students to easily understand the relationship between each individual programming statement and the corresponding behavior of objects in their animation.

2.2 BlueJ

BlueJ [20] is an educational tool used in teaching with an objects-first methodology. BlueJ is a text-entry Java IDE in which the user generally starts with a predefined set of classes. The class structure is presented graphically, in UML-like fashion. The user can create objects and invoke methods on these objects to illustrate their behavior. Later, users may create their own classes. (BlueJ provides a graphical representation of these classes as well.)

2.3 Greenfoot

Greenfoot[12] is an interactive environment that enables students to develop 2D graphic applications such as simulations and games. Greenfoot works with a text-entry Java IDE. At its most fundamental level, Greenfoot has two built-in classes, *World* and *Actor*. The user creates a program in Greenfoot by declaring sub-classes of Actor and then implementing an *act* method, in standard Java, for each sub-class. Execution of a Greenfoot program consists of a built-in main loop that iteratively calls each actor's *act* method.

3. PREVIOUS WORK

Alice 2 has been used successfully as an intervention to draw at-risk students into computing [4, 5, 6]. At-risk students were defined as those students who had demonstrated less success in math and/or those who had little previous programming experience. A textbook [5] was developed and pilot tested in introductory computer programming courses (pre-CS1) offered at Saint Joseph's University and Ithaca College. Additionally, a detailed set of curricular materials [8], including several different curricular models (with complete lecture notes), laboratory exercises, solutions, exams, assignments, sample student projects, and other material, was created.

The primary results of this investigation [14] were:

- The average grade for at-risk students exposed to Alice was a 3.0 GPA in CS1, which is comparable to the grades of students who were at no risk or low risk. The average grade for at-risk students not exposed to Alice was a 1.2 GPA in CS1.
- 88% of at-risk students exposed to Alice enrolled in CS2 after CS1. Only 47% who were not exposed to Alice enrolled in CS2. ($p < .05$, chi-squared)

Investigators in this study concluded that the Alice approach doubled retention rates of at-risk students and increased achievement by at least one letter grade.

Other investigators have performed studies in various courses and reached supportive conclusions. For example, Mullins, Whitfield, and Conlon [15] concluded: "Retention data shows that the incorporation of Alice into the programming sequence has increased the number of students that pass the courses and decreased the number of withdrawals. Also, the number of students enrolling in Alice has increased by 10% as the number of majors has dropped by 50%."

Instructional materials have been designed for and tested with pre-CS1 and pre-AP courses. Over the last six years, dozens of Alice professional development workshops have been conducted in which the curricular materials and the Alice approach for pre-CS1 and pre-AP were presented.

In National Science Foundation-sponsored workshops [9], surveys were used to obtain feedback from participants regarding their intended target audience and their plans for using Alice 2 in their courses. One clear survey result was a significant demand for curriculum and instructional materials that could be used to blend the Alice approach with Java in a "regular CS1" course. The primary reason for this demand is the reality of reduced budgets and limited resources in collegiate Computer Science departments, which limits their ability to offer a pre-CS1 course. Community colleges face similar problems and are further burdened by the constraints of a 2-year curriculum and the need to adhere to articulation agreements.

To respond to this demand, a major question had to be answered: How can we use Alice to teach/learn fundamental programming concepts in an engaging context and then apply those same concepts in a text-based Java environment? Early attempts to start with Alice 2 and then move to a professional programming language in the same course demonstrated that "new techniques are needed to improve student confidence during the transition from Alice's graphical, syntax free, storytelling environment to object-oriented textual programming."[19] This observation was confirmed in course sections instructed in Spring, 2006, by one of the investigators in this study.

Three textbooks have been published in an effort to address this issue [2, 3, 13]. In each of these texts the authors (including an investigator in this study) use Alice 2 examples to introduce a programming concept and then a traditional Java program that uses the same concept. Of particular importance is the study that underlies the Alice and Media Computation textbook.[3] An experimental study was conducted by Cooper, co-author of the text, at Saint Joseph's University. Eight high-risk students (3rd quartile of math background) were taught using a back and forth approach (Alice, Media Comp, Alice, Media Comp, etc.). All students successfully finished the course and 4 of the students (3 of whom are women) switched their major to CS. The results of this study involved a starting n too small for research publication and Cooper took a position at NSF prior to being able to replicate the study. The experimental results, however, were encouraging to the investigators and the study strengthened our motivation to create a version of Alice that would support the ability to transfer an Alice animation directly into Java code.

4. MEDIATED TRANSFER

The goal of an Alice 3 to Java approach is to take advantage of Alice in developing an intuitive understanding of both object-oriented and fundamental programming concepts and then transfer the Alice program directly into Java and programming in a text-based IDE. By using the exact same example in both Alice and Java, we can better mediate a transfer of concept.

4.1 Educational Theory

Educational theorists are adamant that learning should be transferable. [7, 11, 21] That is, what is learned in one context should be employable in another context. Although we may expect transfer of learning, it does not necessarily occur "on its own."

A good illustration is the following anecdote [21]: A Physics professor presented and solved this problem in lecture: "A ball weighing 5 kg is dropped from the top of a building that is 100 meters high. How many seconds later does the ball hit the ground." Then, this problem was on the next exam: "A hole in the ground is 150 meters deep. A ball weighing 7 kg is dropped into the hole. How long does it take for the ball to reach the bottom of the hole?" One student complained to the professor that the problem was unfair because "We didn't have any hole problems!"

While we might dismiss this as just a funny story to tell our colleagues, it is actually a common student experience in many problem-solving disciplines. In our experience, it is not unusual to observe students who are bewildered and not at all sure of how to begin designing and implementing program code for an assigned project, even though a similar problem was previously demonstrated in lecture/presentation.

4.2 Teaching for Transfer

The art of teaching for transfer, known as "mediating transfer," is an active research field [7, 11, 21]. Perkins (Harvard Graduate School of Education)[21] and Salomon (University of Arizona) [21] define two broad categories of techniques that teach for transfer. The first category is "bridging," in which the teacher helps students build a bridge from the context in which a concept was learned into other potential contexts. Bridging is in the form of meanings, generalizations, and insights. The second category is "hugging," in which the teacher makes the learning situation more like the situations in which transfer is expected.

In this Alice to Java approach, we apply a "bridging technique" of using analogies, and the reasons for them, to encourage students to abstract the concept and recognize other contexts in which it may be applied. For example, in Alice we introduce the concept of parameter data types by writing a procedure to have a dragon fly toward a target object, a given distance, in a given amount of time. The target object's data type is Person and the distance and amount of time are each of type Double. We then discuss the example with students, using the analogy of ordering a pizza on their cell phone. The waiter taking an order will ask for the size of the pizza (Double), whether or not it is to be delivered (Boolean), and so forth. Each of these items is a different data type. Then, we ask students to work in pairs to brainstorm other situations where information must be supplied in order to carry out some action. The idea is to integrate into Alice to Java instructional materials the use of techniques that teach for transfer. Using analogies and encouraging students to develop their own generalization of a concept in different contexts is just one example of a bridging technique.

Fortunately, using bridging techniques in instructional materials is software independent. Further, many teachers already use these techniques in their teaching styles. However, using a "hugging technique" for transitioning from Alice to Java implies that writing a program in Alice needs to be more like writing a program in Java. Clearly, this means the Alice software must undergo changes – but at what cost? Alice allows students to assemble programs using a drag-and-drop editor. An advantage of the drag-and-drop editor is that students can focus their attention on understanding a fundamental programming construct without the initial distraction and frustration of syntax details.

To maintain a drag-and-drop IDE and also "hug" Java, Alice 3 has been designed to provide a set of preference options that allows the student to view Java code with greater syntax details than in Alice 2. (Note: Alice 2 had a similar option, but the code was "Java-like," whereas Alice 3's Java display is a far more accurate representation.) Figure 1 illustrates the preference options for Java code in Alice 3. Figure 2 illustrates the Java code, with all parentheses, quotes, commas, and semicolon syntax detail.

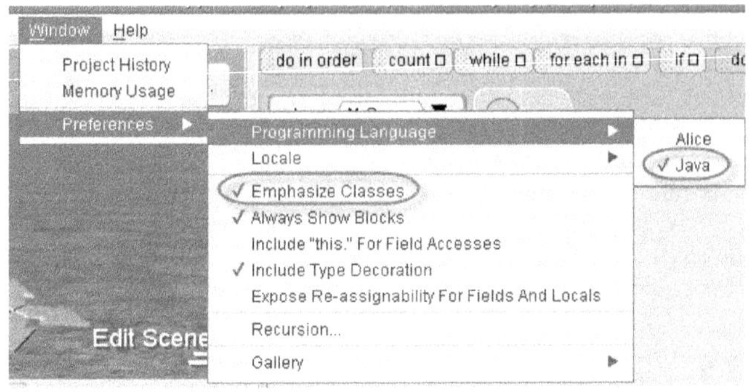

Figure 1. Java options in Alice 3

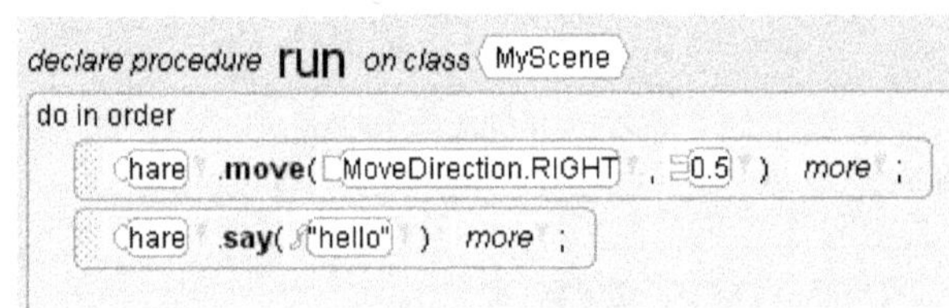

Figure 2. Java code in Alice 3

We found that the more accurate representation of Java code in Alice 3 is a step in the right direction, but it is not sufficient to truly "hug" a Java text-editor environment. For more effective transfer, we developed a plugin for NetBeans (an open source Java IDE[10]) that allows students to transfer their Alice project directly into Java, as illustrated in Figure 3.

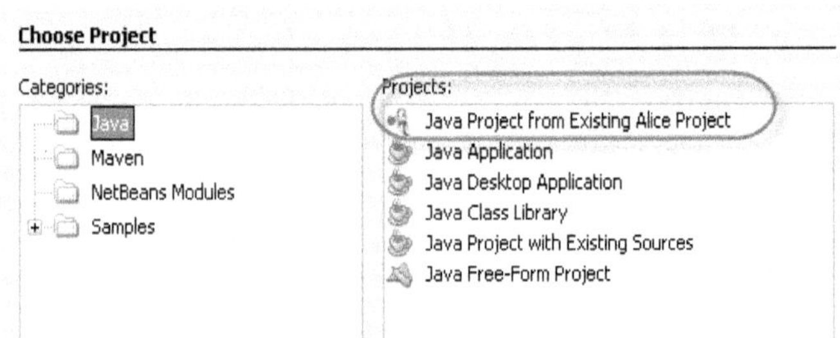

Figure 3. Transferring an Alice Project to Java

When a student transfers their own Alice project from Alice 3 to a Java IDE, the context does not change. They are still working with the same animation program as was created in Alice but now the code can be modified using traditional text editing. Figures 4 and 5, below, show an example of student code for the following assignment:

Build a commercial for Bug's Gym, where a frog catches a bug and gets a surprise when the bug grabs the frog's tongue, lifts the frog off the ground, and carries it away to drop in a nearby pond. The commercial message is "Learn how to handle bullies at Bug's Gym."

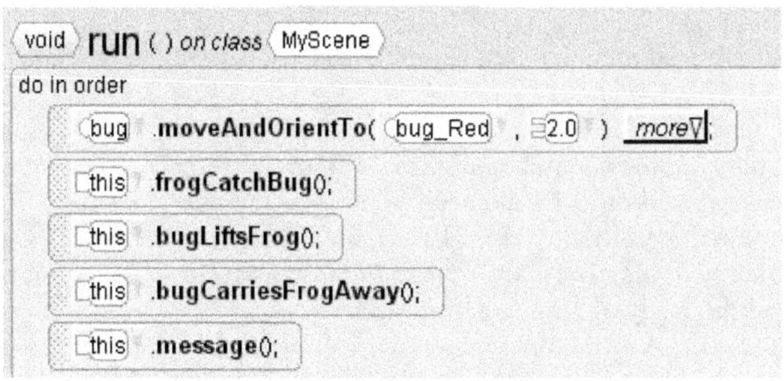

Figure 4. Alice 3 code for Bug's Gym

```
public void run() {
      bug.moveAndOrientTo( bug_Red, 2.0);
      this.frogCatchBug( bug);
      this.bugLiftsFrog();
      this.bugCarriesFrogAway();
      this.message();
}
```

Figure 5. Alice 3 code transferred to NetBeans

With each transfer of code from Alice 3 to a Java IDE, the instructor uses "hugging" techniques to directly connect Alice code to Java code. For example, both Alice 3 and Java IDE are displayed on a projector and lines are literally drawn from Alice statements to equivalent Java statements. Then, students are given a previously unseen Alice code segment and asked to write (on paper) the equivalent code in Java. In this same lab exercise, students are also asked to modify the code in the Java IDE to add a second frog and, at runtime, ask the user to select which frog that will perform the actions with the bug. This modification is done in the Java IDE with text-entry and requires that some methods be modified to use parameters.

5. TESTING AND EVALUATION

5.1 Historical Data

For comparison purposes, historical data was collected from a final exam originally administered in the Carnegie Mellon University (CMU) 15-100 course sections in the Spring semester, 2006. At that time the CMU 15-100 course was a course in Java programming and students in the course included both majors and non-majors. Course instruction consisted of three 50-minute lectures/presentations and one 50 minute recitation/lab session per week.

Because final exams and summaries are kept on file for at least 3 years, access to a historical record of raw scores, broken into the topic sections of the exam (Parts 1–6) as well as final scores (total 100 possible points) were available. Student identities were protected as no student names were included in the summary.

The content of questions in each part is listed here:

- Part 1: Expression evaluation (arithmetic, Boolean, String)
- Part 2: Control Structures (conditionals, iteration)
- Part 3: Arrays of Primitives
- Part 4: Work with a class definition
- Part 5: Work with arrays of objects
- Part 6: Write code in a class

For this study, we selected all course sections in which Alice 2 was introduced during the first two weeks of the course, before switching over to Java for the remainder of the course. Mediated transfer techniques were not used, as Alice 2 did not have the capability of supporting a direct transfer to Java.

Students in the selected class sections include both majors and non-majors, although more than 70% were non-majors. We collected data only from these sections of the CMU 15-100 course because other sections did not use Alice 2 and we were specifically testing for the effect of mediated transfer in a one-semester course. Other variants in demographics, such as sections specifically for majors and sections with a majority of majors, also contributed to this selection process.

Table 1 summarizes the historical data from that exam in the sections selected for the study. The number of students tested was 67 (n = 67).

Table 1. Historical Achievement Data, Spring 2006 (Java Only)

	Part 1	Part 2	Part 3	Part 4	Part 5	Part 6	Total
Points	7.45 / 10	6.84 / 15	9.42 / 15	14.7 / 20	9.21 / 20	13.2 / 20	60.8 / 100
Percent	**74%**	**46%**	**63%**	**74%**	**46%**	**66%**	**61%**

Table 2. Experimental Achievement Data, Fall 2009 (First Trial Alice to Java)

	Part 1	Part 2	Part 3	Part 4	Parts 5 & 6	Total
Points	13.06 / 15	17.46 / 20	16.3 / 20	21.26 / 25	16.88 / 20	84.96 / 100
Percent	**87%**	**87%**	**81%**	**85%**	**84%**	**85%**

Table 3. Second Trial, Fall 2010 (Second Trial Alice to Java)

	Part 1	Part 2	Part 3	Part 4	Parts 5 & 6	Total
Points	13.1 / 15	16.0 / 20	16.5 / 20	21.75 / 25	14.54 / 20	81.52 / 100
Percent	**87%**	**80%**	**83%**	**87%**	**73%**	**82%**

5.2 First Trial

In the Fall semester of 2009, experimental sections of CMU 15-101 were offered. The course instructors used the Alice 3 to Java mediated transfer approach and curricular materials. Course instruction time for 15-101 was the same as the previous 15-100 course consisting of three 50-minute "lectures/presentations" and one 50-minute "recitation/lab" per week. One of the participating instructors had also taught the 15-100 course in 2006 and was familiar with the standard course content.

At the conclusion of the Fall 2009 semester, students in 15-101 took the same exam (with the modification that topics in Parts 5 & 6 were merged to use a 3D animation example as a basis for the questions). The number of students tested in Fall 2009 was 50, most of whom were non-majors and had little if any prior programming experience (n = 50). The data shown in Table 2 summarizes results in the Fall 2009 semester. There was no significant difference in student scores between sections taught by the one instructor and sections taught by a second instructor.

Table 2 indicates that Parts 5 & 6 were merged. As described above, Parts 5 & 6 of the original exam (Spring 2006) were blended into Part 5, using a programming example for an Alice 3 animation. Although the program is for an animation, it was written on paper in Java. Students were asked to write their code in Java (as on the original exam). Even with these disclaimers, we are uncomfortable making any claims with regard to Parts 5 and 6 of the exam. For the purpose of full disclosure, Tables 1, 2, and 3 include all data for all Parts. For the purpose of comparison, however, Figures 5 and 6 below will display only Parts 1 – 4.

The best (most scrupulous) evaluation of this data is to compare percentage scores where Part 1 is compared to Part 1, Part 2 to Part 2, and so forth. Comparisons of respective parts of the exam show a consistent gain of at least 10 % (one letter grade) and the gain in Part 2 is nearly double, as can be seen Figure 5. An ANOVA analysis of the data yielded $p < 0.001$ for each Part of the exam as well as for the Total scores.

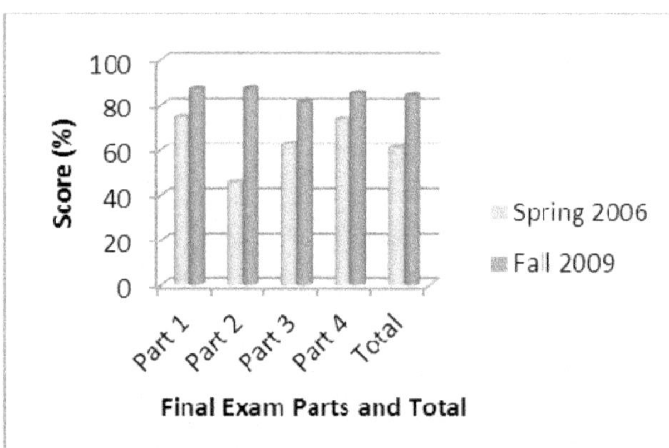

Figure 5. Comparison of Parts, Spring 2006 and Fall 2009

5.3 Second Trial

The data collected and analyzed in Fall 2009 showed a clear increase in scores in the respective parts of the exam. Being wary about making broad claims based on a single trial run of the instructional materials and curriculum, we made a decision to extend the study and run a second trial.

In the Fall 2010 semester, an experimental section of CMU's 15-101 (Alice to Java) course was conducted once again, using instructional materials developed in this project. The number of students involved in this iteration was 28 (n = 28). As in the first trial (Fall 2009), the students were primarily non-majors and had little or no previous programming experience. To control as many other factors as possible, the same instructors taught the courses and used the same instructional approach. Further, course instruction time for 15-101 remained consistent, three 50-minute instruction sessions and one 50-minute recitation/lab sessions per week.

The evaluative exam was administered for this test group and raw scores and percentages for this iteration are listed in Table 3. Again, all raw data is reported, for purposes of full disclosure. An ANOVA analysis of the data yielded $p < 0.001$ for each Part of the exam as well as for the total scores.

5.4 Summative Comparison

The exam score data can be interpreted as a guide to the achievement of students in the treatment course. In each semester, the final exam was written in "pure Java." That is, all questions were stated and all answers were written using Java.

Two trials were run to obtain reliable data for comparison, one in Fall of 2009 and one in Fall of 2010. The original exam (Spring 2006) was taken by a diverse group of students, including both majors and non-majors (though the majority was non-majors). The exam taken in Fall 2009 and in Fall 2010 was taken almost entirely by non-majors. Figure 6 summarizes the results of the two trial runs with the historical data.

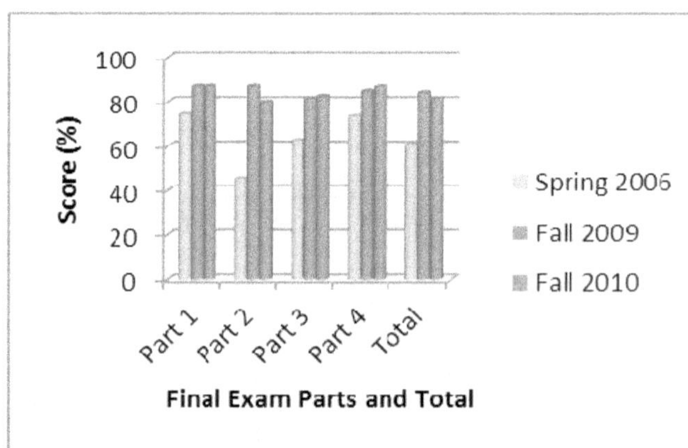

Figure 6. Summative comparison

In the summative comparison for Parts 1 – 4, average student scores (expressed in percentage) in Fall 2009 and 2010 sections were consistent. This provides evidence that the test results are reliable. In viewing the overall scores, student achievement in the experimental sections averaged at least one letter grade above those in the control course sections in Spring 2006. This result provides evidence to support our hypothesis. Our hypothesis was that using explicit mediated transfer would improve student achievement in learning Java in a CS1, one-semester course while still maintaining the strengths of the approach originally introduced with Alice 2 as a pre-CS1 course.

Of particular interest is the large increase in scores in Part 2 of the exam. The focus of questions in Part 2 is Control Structures (conditionals and iteration). We do not have evidence as to the specific cause of this jump in scores in this part of the exam. This suggests a topic for future study.

In summary, data collection and analysis indicates that using explicit mediated transfer techniques, supported by Alice 3's ability to transfer code directly to Java, has a statistically significant, positive impact on students' learning Java.

5.5 Other findings and future work

Although this study was focused on evaluating the effectiveness of an Alice 3 to Java approach using mediated transfer, other findings are noteworthy.

One finding is that for transfer of concept, inheritance needs to be more fully implemented in Alice 3. The lack of fully implemented inheritance constrains the ability to illustrate inheritance concepts in Alice and then mediate a transfer of those concepts to Java.

A second finding is that transferring Alice code containing concurrency and events to Java results in complex code that forces the introduction of inner classes early in the curriculum. But, inner classes are not a common topic in a CS1 course.

These two findings are catalyzing revisions in Alice 3 and will form the basis of future work.

6. ACKNOWLEDGMENTS

This work is based on upon work supported, in part, by the National Science Foundation under grants: DUE #1007631 and DUE #0903271.

Any opinions, findings, and conclusions or recommendations expressed in this material are those of the author(s) and do not necessarily reflect the views of the National Science Foundation.

7. REFERENCES

[1] ACM Joint Task Force for Computing Curricula. 2005. Computing Curricula 2005. Retrieved September 2, 2011 from http://www.acm.org/education/education/curric_vols/

[2] Adams, J. 2007. *Alice in Action with Java.* Thompson Course Technology: Boston, MA.

[3] Dann, W., Cooper, S., and Ericson, B. 2009. *Exploring Wonderland: Java Programming Using Alice and Media Computation.* Prentice-Hall: Upper Saddle River, NJ.

[4] Cooper, S., Dann, W., & Pausch, R. 2003. Teaching objects-first in introductory computer science. *Proceedings of the 34th SIGCSE technical symposium on Computer science education* (Reno, Nevada, USA).ACM Press.

[5] Dann, W. P., Cooper, S., & Pausch, R. 2005. *Learning to program with Alice.* Prentice-Hall: Upper Saddle River, NJ.

[6] Dann, W., Dragon, T., Cooper, S., Dietzler, K., Ryan, K., & Pausch, R. 2003. Objects: Visualization of behavior and state. Proceedings of the 8th annual conference on innovation and technology in computer science education, Thessaloniki, Greece, 84-88.

[7] Forgarty, R.; Perkins, D.; & Barell, J. 1991. *The Mindful School: How to Teach for Transfer.* Palatine, IL: IRI/Skylight Publishing.

[8] Alice 2 instructional materials . Retrieved September 2, 2011 from http://www.aliceprogramming.net

[9] Alice workshops – 2011. Retrieved September 2, 2011 from http://www.aliceprogramming.net/workshop2011.html

[10] NetBeans download. Retrieved September 2, 2011 from http://netbeans.org/downloads/

[11] Ip, Alex. Transfer of Learning. Retrieved September 2, 2011 from http://www.cdtl.nus.edu.sg/ideas/iot18.htm.

[12] Kolling, M. 2009. *Introduction to Programming with Greenfoot:.* Prentice-Hall: Upper Saddle River, NJ.

[13] Lewis, J. and DePasquale. 2008. *Programming with Alice and Java.* Addison Wesley: Boston, MA.

[14] Moskal, B., Lurie, D., & Cooper, S. 2004. Evaluating the effectiveness of a new instructional approach. *Proceedings of the 35th SIGCSE technical symposium on Computer Science Education.* (Norfolk, Virginia).

[15] Mullins, P., Whitfield, D., and Conlon, M. 2008. Using Alice 2.0 as a first language. *Journal of Computer Science in Colleges,* 24(3), 136-143.

[16] Pausch, R., & Forlines, C. 2000. Alice: Model, paint & animate — easy-to-use interactive graphics for the web. *SIGGRAPH Comput. Graph., 34*(2), 42-43.

[17] Pierce, J., Cobb, T., & Pausch, R. 1998. Alice. *ACM SIGGRAPH 98 Conference abstracts and applications.* (Orlando, Florida, United States).

[18] Pierce, J. S., Christiansen, K., Cosgrove, D., Conway, M., Moskowitz, D., Stearns, B., et al.1998. Alice: Easy to learn interactive 3d graphics, *CHI 98 conference summary on* Human factors in computing systems. (Los Angeles, California, USA).

[19] Powers, K., Ecott, S. and Hirshfield, L. 2007. Through the looking glass: teaching CS0 with Alice. *Proceedings of the 38th SIGCSE technical symposium on Computer Science Education.* (Covington, Kentucky, USA).

[20] Rolling, M. & Rosenberg, J., Guidelines for teaching object orientation with Java. 2001. In *Proceedings of the 6th annual conference on Innovation and Technology in Computer Science Education* (Canterbury, England, June, 2001), 33-36.

[21] Salomon, G., & Perkins, D. 1988, September. Teaching for transfer. *Educational Leadership*, 22-32.

Over-Confidence and Confusion in Using Bloom for Programming Fundamentals Assessment

Richard Gluga
School of Information Technologies
The University of Sydney
NSW 2006 Australia
richard@gluga.com

Judy Kay
School of Information Technologies
The University of Sydney
NSW 2006 Australia
judy.kay@sydney.edu.au

Raymond Lister
School of Software
University of Technology Sydney
NSW 2006 Australia
raymond.lister@uts.edu.au

Sabina Kleitman
School of Psychology
The University of Sydney
NSW 2006 Australia
sabinak@psych.usyd.edu.au

Tim Lever
Electrical & Information Engineering
The University of Sydney
NSW 2006 Australia
tim.lever@sydney.edu.au

ABSTRACT
A computer science student is required to progress from a novice programmer to a proficient developer through the programming fundamentals sequence of subjects. This paper deals with the capturing and representation of learning progression. The key contribution is a web-based interactive tutorial that enables computer science educators to practice applying the Bloom Taxonomy in classifying programming exam questions. The tutorial captures participant confidence and self-explanations for each Bloom [5] classification exercise. The results of an evaluation with ten participants were analyzed for consistency and accuracy in the application of Bloom. The confidence and self-explanation measures were used to identify problem areas in the application of Bloom to programming fundamentals. The tutorial and findings are valuable contributions to future ACM/IEEE CS curriculum revisions, which are expected to have a continued emphasis on Bloom [1].

Categories and Subject Descriptors
K.3 [Computers & Education]: Computer & Information Science Education – Computer Science Education

General Terms
Algorithms, Management, Measurement, Design, Human Factors.

Keywords
programming, CS1/2, Bloom, maturity, competence, confidence, learning progression, assessment, pedagogy.

1. INTRODUCTION
Benjamin Bloom himself once said that the original Bloom Handbook [5] was "one of the most widely cited yet least read books in American education" [4]. The taxonomy is a behavioral classification system of educational objectives. The framework specifies six categories, namely, Knowledge, Comprehension, Application, Analysis, Synthesis and Evaluation. Knowledge is the simplest behavior, with each category thereafter being more sophisticated. That is, a Knowledge level objective or assessment task requires a student to simply recall information from memory. In contrast, a Synthesis level task requires students to apply what they have learnt to create new and unique works. A very brief description of the categories follows (adapted from [4]):

- *Knowledge* – recalling of information
- *Comprehension* – interpreting, translating or reordering of concepts, applying a given abstraction
- *Application* – identifying an appropriate abstraction to solve a problem without being prompted
- *Analysis* – breaking down a problem or communication into parts and identifying the relationships between the parts
- *Synthesis* – Identifying and putting together abstractions to create a new and unique artifact or solution to a non-trivial problem
- *Evaluation* – Commenting on the validity of a work with respect to implicit or explicit criteria

The ACM/IEEE Computer Science Curriculum [2] specifies learning objectives based on the revised Bloom Taxonomy [1]. As an example, the Programming Fundamentals / Data Structures knowledge area specifies the following nine learning objectives (the italicized verbs are indicative of the Bloom levels):

- *Describe* the representation of numeric and character data.
- *Understand* how precision and round-off can affect numeric calculations.
- *Discuss* the use of primitive data types and built-in data structures.
- *Describe* common applications for each data structure in the topic list.
- *Implement* the user-defined data structures in a high-level language.
- *Compare* alternative implementations of data structures with respect to performance.
- *Write* programs that use each of the following data structures: arrays, strings, linked lists, stacks, queues, and hash tables.
- *Compare* and contrast the costs and benefits of dynamic and static data structure implementations.

Permission to make digital or hard copies of all or part of this work for personal or classroom use is granted without fee provided that copies are not made or distributed for profit or commercial advantage and that copies bear this notice and the full citation on the first page. To copy otherwise, or republish, to post on servers or to redistribute to lists, requires prior specific permission and/or a fee.
SIGCSE'12, February 29–March 3, 2012, Raleigh, North Carolina, USA.
Copyright 2012 ACM 978-1-4503-1098-7/12/02...$10.00.

- *Choose* the appropriate data structure for modeling a given problem.

These objectives show a spread of competence levels ranging from Bloom Knowledge (*describe*) to Bloom Synthesis and Evaluation (*write, implement, compare & contrast*). The ACM/IEEE CS 2013 curriculum is also expected to use a variant of Bloom's Taxonomy, consisting of only three categories: Knowledge, Application and Evaluation [1].

Using Bloom's Taxonomy to classify objectives and assessment items is not straightforward. Oliver et al. [19] invited four teaching academics to categorize some assessment questions on the original Bloom Taxonomy scale. For the example question presented in the paper, the four participating lecturers each came up with a different Bloom classification, ranging from Knowledge to Analysis. Whalley et al. [22] found the use of Bloom's taxonomy for rating the cognitive complexity of programming MCQ's "challenging even to an experienced group of programming educators." They attributed the difficulty to either some deficiency in Bloom, or "the author's current level of understanding of how to apply the taxonomy."

Thompson et al. [21] attempted to contextualize the revised Bloom Taxonomy to computer science. They ran an experiment where five participants were asked to analyze six first-year computer science final exam papers and categorize each question on the Bloom scale. The results showed significant disagreement between the rankings performed by different participants. This was attributed to some having implicit knowledge of how the subject was taught, and hence having a better understanding of the cognitive processes of the students undertaking the exam papers. Thompson et al. [21] however did not discuss the participants' prior knowledge of the Bloom Taxonomy, or its application in a computer science context. It was only after the participants had a chance to collaborate and discuss each classification that they reached consensus on each exam question.

On the basis of our reading of the above work, we concluded that academics seeking to use Bloom's Taxonomy need to be trained. To this end, our contribution described in this paper is a computer science contextualized web-based tutorial on the Bloom Taxonomy with interactive examples, user self-explanation and self-reflection. The tutorial is a useful resource in training computer science educators on the application of Bloom in classifying programming assessment questions. The results from the evaluation of this tutorial are useful in identifying where Bloom is used inconsistently due to different assumptions about the learner or learning context, different interpretations of the Bloom categories, or a misunderstanding of the categories. The tutorial and Bloom insights are important inputs to future work on measuring learner progression in computer science and future ACM/IEEE CS curriculum revisions.

2. METHOD

ProGoSs (Program Goal Progression) is an online web-based system built as part of our research on curriculum mapping and measuring learning progression in higher education. In this experimental setup, participants were invited to login into the system and take our interactive Bloom tutorial. A detailed discussion on the design and content of this tutorial is provided in [9]. The following is an overview of the tutorial structure as background for the evaluation study results presented here.

The tutorial commenced with a pre-survey asking the participants to self-rate their own confidence, based on their existing knowledge, in being able to correctly classify programming exam questions using the Bloom Taxonomy. We will refer to this confidence judgment as the Initial Confidence score (IC), which was measured as a percentage, with 100% indicating complete confidence.

After the pre-survey, participants read a description of each Bloom Taxonomy category. The descriptions were adapted from [4] but contextualized with wording relevant to programming fundamentals. Each category was described and illustrated with an example in a tab-based layout as in Figure 1.

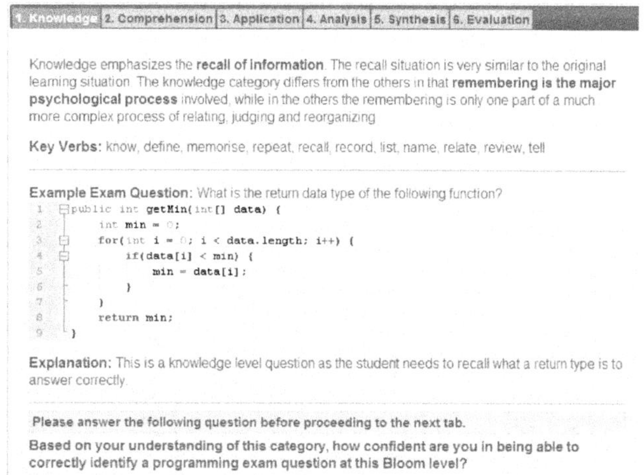

Figure 1: Tutorial Category Description

After reading each description and example, the participants self-rated their confidence in being able to apply the Bloom category in classifying programming questions. We call these Prediction Confidence (PC) scores. These were expressed as a percentage for each Bloom category. Participants moved from one tab to the next to read and rate each category.

Participants were next asked to classify twelve example examination questions, such as the one shown in Figure 2. Participants were encouraged to scroll back to refer to the tabbed category definitions if needed, which remained present at the top of the page. For each example, the participants classified the exam question on the Bloom scale. Participants had to self-rate their confidence in each classification (On-Task Confidence), provide a justification for each classification, and comment on any uncertainties in their classification choice. This was done in accordance with work by Chi M.T.H and colleagues [18] showing that "Eliciting self-explanations improves understanding". After providing this feedback for each example, participants were presented with the nominated classification and justification for the example, and given the opportunity to comment further on the classification.

The Bloom classifications of our twelve example questions were nominated by the authors of this paper, one of which is a computer science academic with an active research interest and publication record in the application of Bloom to the grading of programming fundamentals [16][17]. Out of the twelve example questions, three were targeted as Knowledge, two as Comprehension, two as Application, two as Analysis, one as Synthesis and two as Evaluation. Uneven numbers were used so that participants would not be able to guess the last few example questions by discerning the pattern and counting answers.

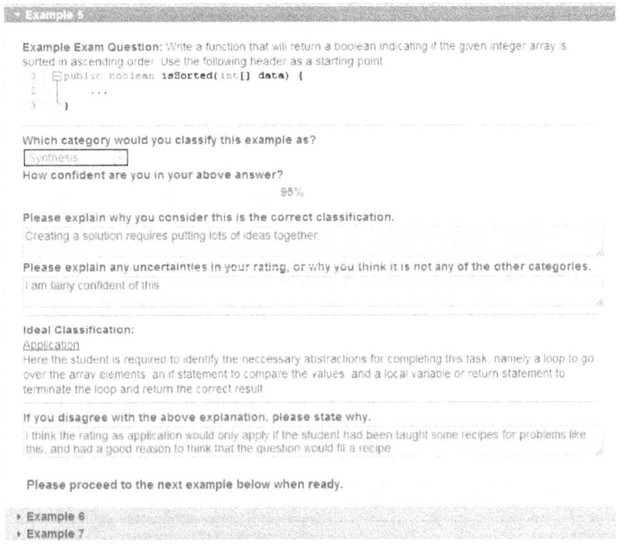

Figure 2: Tutorial Example Question

The order in which the questions were presented was random, with the same sequence used for all participants.

After completing all twelve examples, participants were asked to self-rate their Final Confidence (FC) in being able to classify programming questions using the Bloom taxonomy in future attempts. Participants were also asked to comment upon whether they found the tutorial useful and efficient at increasing their ability to apply Bloom in computer science.

3. RESULTS

3.1 Participants

A total of ten participants completed our interactive tutorial and assessment classifications. These consisted mostly of computer science graduate teaching assistants and one computer science professor, all of whom had extensive experience in teaching introductory programming. The experiment took roughly sixty minutes to complete, although no time-limit was given.

3.2 Initial Confidence

The average participant Initial Confidence (IC) score was 30%. This was the confidence of participants in being able to apply Bloom in classifying programming questions *before* taking our tutorial.

3.3 Prediction Confidence, On-Task Confidence and On-Task Accuracy

Figure 3 shows the six Bloom categories along the horizontal axis. Each category is sub-divided into three columns. These are, from left to right, Prediction Confidence, On-Task Confidence and On-Task Accuracy. The average participant Prediction Confidence (PC) scores after reading our initial tabbed Bloom category descriptions ranged between 67% and 71%. The On-Task Accuracy is the percentage of participants who classified each of the examples with the same Bloom category as our nominated classification (i.e., answered 'correctly').

Results indicate that for each category On-Task Confidence judgment was higher than Prediction Confidence judgment. This indicates that participants felt more capable about applying the Bloom taxonomy after reading the initial category descriptions.

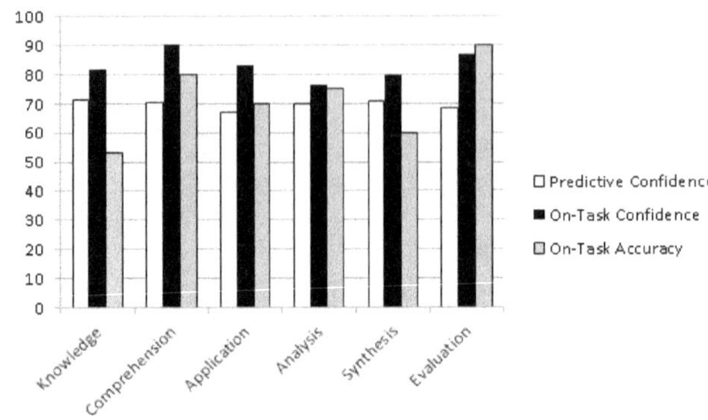

Figure 3: Prediction Confidence, On-Task Confidence and On-Task Accuracy

On-Task confidence judgments had a more homogeneous range (between 77% for the Analysis and 90% for the Comprehension categories) than the relevant On-Task Accuracy scores (ranging between 53% for the Knowledge and 90% for the Evaluation categories). However, for only two categories – Evaluation and Analysis – the On-Task Confidence levels matched the On-Task Accuracy Scores (their difference, referred to as Bias scores, were -3% and 2% respectively). In all other categories, a different degree of overconfidence (confidence exceeds the actual accuracy) is evident: 28% (for Knowledge), 20% (for Synthesis), 13% (for Application) and 10% (for Comprehension). This indicates that, despite their subjective feeling of confidence, participants had difficulty correctly classifying the items for these four categories, especially Knowledge and Synthesis. Importantly, the high degrees of overconfidence for the Knowledge category strongly suggests that these examples, and/or the use of this Bloom category, may also be 'tricky' or misleading (see [12][13][8][14] for reviews), suggesting a need to reconsider the selection of examples that evaluate this category in future studies. The use of On-Task Confidence judgments provided the novel and additional information allowing such diagnostics.

3.4 Confusion Matrix

Figure 4 is a confusion matrix that shows all of the participant classifications for each example. Along the left, as rows, is the nominated classification. Along the top are the actual participant classifications. Each cell has the question number, followed by a colon and then by a character code that indicates if the participant:

- was 'correct' (C) (i.e., participant classification matched our nominated classification);
- incorrect but agreed with our nominated explanation after being shown the answer (A);
- incorrect but still disagreed with our explanation after being shown the answer (D);
- incorrect and did not agree or disagree with our explanation after seeing the answer (N).

To illustrate, we nominated Example 11 as an Application task. Five participants classified this correctly, as shown in the Application/Application cell (11:CCCCC). Of the other five participants, one believed it to be a Knowledge task and disagreed with our explanation (11:D); one believed it to be a Comprehension task and neither agreed nor disagreed with our explanation (11:N); one believed it to be an Analysis task and further disagreed with our explanation (11:D); and two initially believed it to be a Synthesis task but consequently agreed with our explanation (11:AA).

(Participant Classifications)

(Our Classifications)	Knowledge	Comprehension	Application	Analysis	Synthesis	Evaluation
Knowledge	2:CCCCCCCCC 7:CCCCCCC	2:A 7:A	9:DADAN	7:N 9:A	9:NAAN	
Comprehension	5:D	5:CCCCCCCCC 6:CCCCCCC	6:DA 7:A	6:N		
Application	11:D	11:N	1:CCCCCCCCC 11:CCCCC	11:D	1:D 11:AA	
Analysis		4:AN		4:CCCCCCCC 10:CCCCCCC		10:NNA
Synthesis			8:ANN	8:N	8:CCCCCC	
Evaluation				3:NN		3:CCCCCCCC 12:CCCCCCCCCC

Legend:

C correct (matching) classification
D non-matching and participant does not agree with our justification
N non-matching and participant neutral (does not agree or disagree with our justification)
A non-matching and participant agrees with our justification
[thick-bordered box] thick border used to section bloom into 3 bands
<number>: the number of the example (ie. Example 1 to Example 12)

Figure 4: Confusion Matrix

The shaded cells represent 'correct' answers (i.e., our nominated classifications). The thick-bordered cells represent the clustering of Bloom into three categories as proposed for the ACM/IEEE CS 2013 revised curriculum [2]. This highlights participants who answered incorrectly, but were still within the correct band grouping. Participant answers outside of the thick-bordered cells are undesirable, as they represent a greater distance in classifications (i.e., more severe inconsistency).

3.5 Final Confidence and Participant Feedback

After completing the twelve examples, the average participant Final Confidence score was 75.0% (an increase from the 30.8% Initial Confidence before starting the tutorial). This non-trivial increase of 44.2% of confidence could be attributed largely to the training they experienced during the Bloom tutorial.

All participants responded positively in the final feedback question. The common trend in these comments was that the category descriptions were good for gaining a basic grasp, but the interactive examples with explained justifications were very useful in solidifying their understanding.

4. DISCUSSION

Most of the participants had limited exposure to Bloom prior to taking the tutorial, hence the low average Initial Confidence of 30.8%. Only three participants had an Initial Confidence greater than 30%. These were a computer science professor, an educational researcher and a computer science postdoc researcher. After reading the initial descriptions of the Bloom categories, participant Predictive Confidence increased to around 70% across all Bloom categories. This was a good indicator that the category descriptions were helpful to those with very limited prior understanding of Bloom.

The chart in Figure 3 shows participants were on average overly confident in their classifications, however. The largest difference between confidence and accuracy is in the Knowledge category. This was caused by Example 9 in particular (discussed below).

The tutorial confidence matrix shows every participant classification for every example and how it differed from our nominated classification. Again the biggest discrepancy here appears in the Knowledge row, namely for Example 9. Our nominated classification for this was Knowledge, yet no participants picked this. The participant classifications were four Synthesis, five Application and one Analysis. Example nine was a question that asked students to write a SortedMap implementation "*as discussed in lectures and practiced in tutorials*". Since the question suggests that students have had repeated practice at this particular exercise, we argue that it is a Knowledge level task. From reading the participant feedback comments, five agreed with this explanation after being shown the justification, three did not comment, and two disagreed on the basis that a student would not be able to memorize that much code and would thus have to use abstractions to implement the algorithm (and hence why these two participants picked the Application level). The example highlights the tight dependence on knowledge of the teaching context to correctly classify exam questions using Bloom. That is, different assumptions about the teaching context, and different assumptions about how the student can derive the answer, lead to vastly different classifications (Knowledge and Synthesis are at opposite ends).

Additionally, the disagreements (D) in the confusion matrix stemmed mostly from one participant. S/he had a somewhat higher than average Initial Confidence (40%), perhaps bringing preconceptions about Bloom and its use in this context. The self-explanations left by this participant gave well-reasoned arguments. For example, we classified the task to write a function that returns the minimum value in an array as Application; the student solution should traverse an array and update the minimum, both very familiar and practiced elements by the end of a second programming subject. Importantly, there is little potential for diverse, correct solutions. However, this participant appeared to take the perspective of a very novice programmer, and argued it was a Synthesis task, as the student needs to think about many abstractions and put them together into something that is not immediately obvious to them. This again highlights that Bloom classifications are dependent on the teaching context and learner context.

5. CONCLUSION AND FUTURE WORK

The Bloom Taxonomy is a framework for specifying the sophistication of learning objectives, but it is often misunderstood. We thus created an interactive tutorial to train computer science educators on how to apply Bloom in classifying programming questions and evaluated the results.

Our evaluation of the interactive tutorial showed that the tutorial was effective in developing participants' confidence in identifying the level of performance involved in programming fundamentals exam questions. The evaluation also confirmed previously documented ambiguities in the application of Bloom to cases where knowledge about the learning context is required for accurate classification. Participant self-reflection and self-explanation revealed other reasons as to why different people make different classifications, namely due to pre-conceived misunderstandings of the categories, or different interpretations about the complexity of tasks and sophistication required to solve them.

Our evaluation can be repeated with a greater participant pool and greater number of examples. This would give a clearer insight into the degree of classification inconsistency arising from assumptions about the learning context, as opposed to a misunderstanding of Bloom. What is also becoming apparent is that a seeming Synthesis level task for one programmer, may be more like an Application or Knowledge level task for another. That is, writing a function to, say, return the minimum value in an array, may require a lot of thought and problem solving ability for a novice who derives a solution from first principles. For an experienced programmer however, the solution may be strikingly obvious and be largely automated, hence requiring very little cognitive ability.

Our work was motivated by the wide use of Bloom in defining curriculum, particularly in the case of programming fundamentals [2] and our concerns about the reliability with which it was being used. This paper makes a contribution in presenting an online Bloom tutorial and reporting its evaluation. We believe that our ProGoSs system's Bloom tutorial is the first such system that helps teachers of programming fundamentals have greater understanding of Bloom, as a foundation for more systematic design of teaching and learning materials and assessment of how well student learning matches the intended learning goals.

6. ACKNOWLEDGMENTS

We would like to thank the Smart Services CRC for partially sponsoring this project and our colleagues who gave their time to test the tutorial.

7. REFERENCES

[1] ACM/IEEE 2013 Computing Curriculum, http://www.118.ifip.info/wise/wise7/resources/cs2013.ppt

[2] ACM/IEEE Computer Science Curriculum 2008, http://www.acm.org/education/curricula/ComputerScience2008.pdf

[3] Anderson, L. W., & Krathwohl, D. R. (Eds.). Airasian, P. W., Cruikshank, K. A., Mayer, R. E., Pintrich, P. R., Raths, J. and Wittrock, M. C. (2001). A taxonomy for learning, teaching and assessing: A revision of Bloom's Taxonomy of Educational Objectives. New York: Allyn Bacon Longman.

[4] Anderson, W.L., Sosniak, A.L, Bloom, B.S. (1994). Bloom's taxonomy: a forty-year retrospective. Chicago: University of Chicago Press

[5] Bloom, B.S. (Ed.) (1956) Taxonomy of Educational Objectives: Handbook I: Cognitive Domain, Longmans, Green and Company.

[6] Centre for the Advancement of Teaching and Learning, University of Western Australia (2005). A Basic Guide to Writing of Student Outcome Statement. Retrieved 24 August 2011 from http://www.catl.uwa.edu.au/current_initiatives/obe/outcomes

[7] Centre for Learning and Professional Development, University of Adelaide (2011). Writing learning objectives. Retrieved 24 August 2011 from http://www.adelaide.edu.au/clpd/curriculum/objectives/

[8] Gigerenzer, G., Hoffrage, U., & Kleinbolting, H. (1991). Probabilistic Mental Models - a Brunswikian theory of confidence. *Psychological Review, 98*(4), 506-528.

[9] Gluga. R., Kay. J., Lister, R., Kleitman. S., Lever. T. (2012). Coming to terms with Bloom: an online tutorial for teachers of programming fundamentals. Proc. Fourteenth Australasian Computing Education Conference (ACE2012), Melbourne. Pp. TBA

[10] Gluga, R., Kay, J., and Lever, T (2010). Modeling long term learning of generic skills. In V. Aleven, J. Kay, and J. Mostow, editors, ITS2010, Proceedings of the Tenth International Conference on Intelligent Tutoring Systems, pages 85-94. Springer, 2010.

[11] Gluga, R., Kay, J. (2009) Largescale, long-term learner models supporting flexible curriculum definition. In Proceedings of the Workshop on Scalability Issues in AIED, held in conjunction with AIED2009, pages 10-19, 2009.

[12] Harvey, N. (1997). Confidence in Judgment. *Trends in Cognitive Sciences, 1* (2), 78-82.

[13] Juslin, P. (1994). The overconfidence phenomenon as a consequence of informal experimenter-guided selection of almanac items. *Organizational Behaviour & Human Decision Processes, 57* (2), 226-246.

[14] Kleitman, S., & Stankov, L. (2001). Ecological and person-oriented aspects of metacognitive processes in test-taking. *Applied Cognitive Psychology, 15* (3), 321-341.

[15] Learning and Teaching Centre, Macquarie University (2008). Writing learning outcomes. Retrieved 24 August 2011 from http://www.mq.edu.au/ltc/about_lt/assess_docs/writing_learn_out.pdf

[16] Lister, R., (2001), Objectives and objective assessment in CS1. In Proceedings of the thirty-second SIGCSE technical symposium on Computer Science Education (SIGCSE '01). ACM, New York, NY, USA, 292-296.

[17] Lister, R. and Leaney, J. (2003). Introductory programming, criterion-referencing, and bloom. In Proceedings of the 34th SIGCSE technical symposium on Computer science education (SIGCSE '03). ACM, New York, NY, USA, 143-147.

[18] Michelene T. H. Chi , Nicholas De Leeuw , Mei-hung Chiu, Christian Lavancher (1994). Eliciting self-explanations improves understanding. Journal of Cognitive Science. Pp. 439-477. Vol. 18.

[19] Oliver, D., Dobele, T., Greber, M., and Roberts, T. 2004. This course has a Bloom Rating of 3.9. Proc. Sixth Australasian Computing Education Conference. Volume 30 (ACE '04), Raymond Lister and Alison Young (Eds.), Vol. 30. Australian Computer Society, Inc., Darlinghurst, Australia, Australia, 227-231.

[20] Sheard, J., Carbone, A., Lister, R. and Simon, B. (2008), Going SOLO to assess noice programmers. Proc. of the 13th annual conference on Innovation and technology in computer science education (ITiCSE2008), pp. 209-213, Vol. 40.

[21] Thompson, E., Luxton-Reilly, A., Whalley, J.L., Hu, M., Robbins, P. (2008). Bloom's Taxonomy for CS Assessment. Proc. ACE2008 Tenth Conference on Australasian Computing Education. Vol. 78

[22] Whalley, J., Lister, R., Thompson, E., Clear, T., Robbins, P., Kumar, P.K.A. and Prasard, C. (2006). An Australasian Study of Reading and Comprehension Skills in Novice Programmers, using the Bloom and SOLO Taxonomies. Eighth Australasian Computing Education Conference (ACE2006), Hobart, Australia. CRPIT, 52, pp. 243-252. ACM International Conference Proceeding Series, Vol. 165. http://crpit.com/confpapers/CRPITV52Whalley.pdf

Modeling How Students Learn to Program

Chris Piech[1], Mehran Sahami[1], Daphne Koller[1], Stephen Cooper[1], Paulo Blikstein[2]
[1]Computer Science Department, [2]School of Education
Stanford University
Stanford, CA. 94305
{piech, sahami, koller, coopers}@cs.stanford.edu, paulob@stanford.edu

ABSTRACT
Despite the potential wealth of educational indicators expressed in a student's approach to homework assignments, *how* students arrive at their final solution is largely overlooked in university courses. In this paper we present a methodology which uses machine learning techniques to autonomously create a graphical model of how students in an introductory programming course progress through a homework assignment. We subsequently show that this model is predictive of which students will struggle with material presented later in the class.

Categories and Subject Descriptors
K.3.2 [**Computer and Information Science Education**]: Computer Science Education.

General Terms
Algorithms, Measurement, Experimentation, Languages

Keywords
Probabilistic Graphical Models, Hidden Markov Model, Program Dissimilarity Metric, Intelligent Tutor, Student Progress Model

1. INTRODUCTION
In analyzing student learning in introductory programming courses, there is a wealth of information not only in the final products (i.e., programs) that students submit for evaluation, but also in the development *path* they took to produce their programs. In traditional settings, the data on how students developed their programs over time is either not available or not analyzed. In this work, we show that temporal traces of the development paths taken by students in an introductory programming class can be mined to build graphical models that compactly capture the common major milestones in such development paths. More significantly, we show that these models also carry predictive capability in that the paths students take in these models are correlated with their future performance in the class.

We gathered and analyzed the development paths for students in Stanford's CS1 course, which begins with an initial assignment in Karel the Robot that is subsequently followed by five or six Java programming assignments. While students' final submitted solutions to course assignments can be used to identify which individuals need extra assistance or are struggling with the material, there are surprisingly a substantial number of novice programmers who do not grasp important core concepts, but are able to somehow still produce a fully functional final solution to the first programming assignment. As a result, the submitted work is devoid of any indication that the student actually needs help. Though the student's solution might not contain obvious warning signs of missed concepts, there tends to be evidence of such misunderstandings hidden in the development *path* by which the student arrived at his/her final solution.

It is easy to claim that understanding how students progress through an assignment allows educators to better identify students that need interventions. It is difficult to implement a process to record and analyze students' progress. Manual observation and analysis of students as they program raises privacy concerns, and it is tedious and difficult to personally interpret raw snapshots of student code over time, especially in large courses. Rather, we take an automated approach, developing machine learning techniques that can be applied to code snapshots captured periodically by an instrumented IDE. Our machine learning algorithm produces a finite state machine of development "milestones" that provide a high-level graphical view of student development paths through an assignment. Such graphical models help provide a better understanding of how novice programmers go about solving a problem. More significantly, these models allow us to then cluster students into groupings that are predictive of students' future performance. We applied this technique to one of the problems given as part of the first programming assignment in our CS1 class. This problem, dubbed "Checkerboard Karel", requires that Karel the Robot produce a checkerboard pattern of beepers in his world.

As we show later in this paper, the patterns that our machine learning algorithm found in *how* students solved the Checkerboard Karel problem were more informative at predicting how well students would perform on the class midterm than the grades students received on the assignment. We demonstrate that the algorithm captured a meaningful general trend in how students were solving this programming problem by using the model generated from student development traces in the spring offering of the course to predict student performance in the subsequent summer term. While our results initially focus on a programming problem in the limited domain of Karel the Robot, we show the more general applicability of our methodology by applying our algorithm to a Java assignment in which students write an open-ended version of the graphical arcade game Breakout (also known as Brick Breaker).

There are many potential applications for high-level representations of student progress in programming assignments. These include using such models to track the progress of new students and suggest possible interventions if it has been determined that the development path the student is on is not likely to lead to a positive outcome. Similarly, such information can be logged, compiled, and relayed to the course instructor to

Permission to make digital or hard copies of all or part of this work for personal or classroom use is granted without fee provided that copies are not made or distributed for profit or commercial advantage and that copies bear this notice and the full citation on the first page. To copy otherwise, or republish, to post on servers or to redistribute to lists, requires prior specific permission and/or a fee.
SIGCSE'12, February 29–March 3, 2012, Raleigh, North Carolina, USA.
Copyright 2012 ACM 978-1-4503-1098-7/12/02...$10.00.

help provide a more accurate picture of the concepts in the course with which the students are truly struggling.

As mentioned previously, our machine learning algorithm autonomously produces a probabilistic finite state machine representation of how students in the class traversed through various "milestones" in the Karel assignment. The patterns that the machine learning algorithm finds provide insight into what programming motifs are common for students who would struggle later on in the course, and also provides a visualization of how the class as a whole approached the Karel assignment.

The main results presented in this paper are:

- the development of machine learning methods that build models of high-level student development pathways in programming assignments,
- the application of these methods to a large set of student trace data by which the algorithm is successfully able to autonomously extract novel features of a student's progress over the course of an assignment, and
- the use of these features to predict students' future performance in the class as measured by their midterm grades.

The novelty of this work stems from:

- the collection of a unique dataset of student development trace data,
- the presentation of an application of unsupervised machine learning concepts to a new domain, and
- the potential pedagogical insights that can be gained from the model generated by the machine learning algorithm. This research is particularly pertinent to large lecture-based classes and online courses.

2. RELATED WORK

This research expands upon previous attempts to find a symbolic representation of student progress. Reiser [19] made the argument that development of an autonomous system that could understand a student's current state as the student solves a programming problem would have profound educational implications.

Spohrer and Soloway [27] tried to represent how students learned to program through an investigation of the bugs in the students' code. Students' programs were examined as soon as their code cleanly compiled (and was thus devoid of syntax errors), and their bugs identified and categorized. The decision to analyze student bugs as soon as their code compiled cleanly was reasonable, given that it would not have been possible to analyze all intermediate versions of students' code as the analysis was done by hand. Their strategy was limited in that it would not be useful for trying to analyze the students who solve a problem one part at a time (those initial clean compiles would not include much of the overall solution), and they did not observe the progression of student code development throughout the assignment.

There has been work on studying students' progress at a more fine-grained level, by focusing on specific programming language constructs. These constructs include variables [23], conditionals [10], looping [25], and methods [12]. The assumption in many of these studies is that student progress can be understood through difficulties with specific programming constructs.

Many researchers have attempted to determine students' mental models of computers and computing (see [13] as an interesting early example), using various qualitative techniques such as phenomenography [1, 3]. Because such studies tend to be in-depth and time-consuming, the number of participants tends to be quite small.

The task of constructing a dynamic student model has had a resurgence with the introduction of artificial intelligence algorithms. In a paper on coached problem solving using Bayesian networks, Conati [5] demonstrated the potential of using an expert crafted graphical model for tutoring students learning physics. However, in Conati's work, as in many instances of supervised learning applied to constructing a dynamic student model, it is noted that supervised learning is limited by the laborious process of expert graphical model construction and the lack of transferability of these expert generated models from one program to another.

Recent research has used automated log analysis analyze student programs, especially trying to distinguish novices and experts. Blikstein [30, 31, 32] used thousands of time-stamped snapshots of students' code and found markedly diverse strategies between experienced and novice programmers. By mining snapshots from code repositories, Berland and Martin [29] found that novice students' developed successful program code by following one of two progressions: planner and tinkerer. Planners found success by carefully structuring programs over time, and tinkerers found success by accreting programs over time. Students were generally unsuccessful if they didn't follow one of those paths.

This common limitation in the state of the art for dynamic student modeling highlights the need for an unsupervised (i.e., fully autonomous) approach. However, despite the apparent utility of a fully autonomous system, little work has been done to apply unsupervised learning algorithms.

3. DATA COLLECTION

Over the summer of 2010 we modified the Integrated Development Environment (IDE)—Eclipse—used by students in Stanford's CS1 course so that it would log snapshots, a complete version of the student's program at that point in time, every time a student compiles a project (which the students must do before they can run their program) and commits that snapshot to a local *git* repository. When the student submits the final version of their assignment, they can elect (opt-in) to also submit the full git repository of their progress (i.e., code snapshots) in developing their solution. For this investigation we analyzed data from two assignments, Checkerboard Karel and Breakout, described below.

Checkerboard Karel: Karel the Robot is used in the first week of CS1 to teach students basic program flow and decomposition. The particular variant of the Karel programming language we use is a Java-based language [20], which most notably does not include variables or parameters. In this assignment the students were asked to make Karel the Robot place beepers in a checkerboard fashion with an alternating pattern of beepers and no beepers, filling up the whole world. The full solution needs to work on any sized Karel world. It is hard to get an algorithm to work on worlds with an odd number of columns, particularly so if there is only one column. At this point in the course most students struggle with understanding nested while loops and how to identify pre and post conditions for their methods and loops.

Breakout: This assignment asks students to implement a classic arcade game [16]. The students need to write an animation loop, incorporate mouse events and keep track of game state. It is the third assignment given in CS1 and the first large programming project written in Java using the ACM graphics library [28].

We collected repositories from $N = 370$ Karel assignments (238 from spring 2011 and 132 from summer 2011). For each student we had on average 159 snapshots of them programming checkerboard Karel with a standard deviation of 82 snapshots. Each snapshot was time-stamped and could be run through a simulator to record errors or to test functionality. We also analyzed Breakout repositories from $N = 205$ students all of which were from winter 2011 where the snapshot count per student had a mean of 269, and a variance of 153. To protect the privacy of our students we removed students' names from all snapshots. We chose to capture snapshots when the student compiled/saved as we thought this would be the best interpretation of a "unit" of work.

4. DATA ANALYSIS

4.1 Program Distance Metric

For the machine learning algorithm to build a model of how students progress through an assignment, it needs to compare two programs against one other and determine the extent to which the two pieces of code should be considered similar. Specifically, the algorithm used requires that we calculate a real number that accurately reflects the degree to which two programs are dissimilar. We considered three algorithms for calculating dissimilarity:

1. Bag of Words Difference: We built histograms of the different key words used in a program and used the Euclidean distance between two histograms as a naïve measure of the dissimilarity. This is similar to distance measures of text commonly used in information retrieval systems [22].

2. Application Program Interface (API) Call Dissimilarity: We ran each program with standard inputs and recorded the resulting sequence of API calls. We used Needleman-Wunsch global DNA alignment [14] to measure the difference between the lists of API calls generated by the two programs. Intuitively, we think of the sequence of API calls made in the program to be the "DNA" of that program, and we are comparing the DNA of two programs to determine their dissimilarity. We note that we modified the Needleman-Wunsch algorithm to allow for gap penalties which varied based on the API call that was matched with the gap.

API calls are a particularly good representation of Karel programs because the Karel programs do not store variables—and as a result an assignment's entire functionality is expressed in terms of simple API calls (e.g., turnLeft, move, etc,). This metric is more difficult to implement for full Java programs. For example, Breakout makes graphics API calls but with parameters that change the nature of the API call. This makes it more difficult to create a single token that fully captures the effect of any call.

3. Abstract Syntax Tree (AST) Change Severity: We built AST representations of both programs and calculated the summation of Evolizer abstract change severities as described by Gall *et al* [9]. The Evolizer change severity score calculates the minimum number of rotations, insertions and deletions that need to be applied to the AST of one program to transform it into the AST of another program. It uses an analysis of each syntax tree to weight how significantly an edit changes the AST.

All of our dissimilarity metrics were normalized by sum of the distances between the programs and the "starter" code (the small amount of code students may have been given initially as part of their assignment framework). To evaluate each metric we had a group of five advanced computer science students with teaching experience (whom we subsequently refer to as "experts") label a set of snapshot pairs as either similar or different and measured how well the distance metrics could replicate the expert labels.

Table 1. Distance Metric Evaluation

Metric	*Percent Accuracy*
1. Bag of Words	55%
2. API Calls	86%
3. AST Change	75%

The experts were asked to assess similarity based on a rubric having them identify major and minor stylistic and functional differences between pairs of programs. We selected 90 pairs of programs, capturing a spectrum of similar, dissimilar and slightly similar code. For the checkerboard Karel assignment the API Call Dissimilarity performed best (see Table 1) with an accuracy of 86% ($p < 10^{-8}$ relative to chance). The set of pairs mislabeled by the Bag of Words and AST Change Severity largely overlapped with the set of pairs where the human experts disagreed.

While the distance metrics seemed to accurately measure the dissimilarity between code snapshots, they are biased towards assigning low dissimilarity score to snapshots from the same student. To account for this bias, we modified all of our algorithms to never use the dissimilarity value computed from two snapshots that originated from the same student.

The distance metric used to build our model was a weighted sum of the AST Change metric and a set of API Dissimilarity scores (each generated by running the programs with a different input world). We built a Support Vector Machine [6] trained to classify the human labeled data using the different distance metrics as features. The values used to weight the distance measures in our composite dissimilarity score were the weights assigned to each distance measure by the Support Vector Machine.

4.2 Modeling Progress

The first step in our student modeling process was to learn a high level representation of how each student progressed through the checkerboard Karel assignment. To learn this representation we modeled a student's progress as a Hidden Markov Model (HMM) [17]. The HMM we used (see Figure 1) proposes that at each snapshot, a student is in a "high-level milestone," referred to as a *state*. While we cannot directly observe the state (it is a *latent* variable), we can observe the source code of the snapshot, which is a noisy sensor of the latent variable. Example states could be "the student has just started" or "the student has gotten Karel to checker all worlds except for worlds with a single column." Note that these states need not be explicitly labeled in the model. They are autonomously induced by our learning algorithm given the student trace data provided. The HMM is parameterized by the probabilities of a student going from one state to another and the probability that a given snapshot came from a particular milestone. A HMM is a relevant model of student progress because programming is generally an incremental process. The milestone where a student is at a given time is not independent of the milestone that he/she was at in the previous time step. The HMM explicitly captures this dependency.

Modeling student progress as a HMM makes the over-simplifying Markov assumption that the future state of a student is independent of past states that the student was in given that we know the individual's current state. While this assumption is not entirely correct (a student's current state alone does not capture what they learned from experience), this statistical simplification is still useful for finding patterns and making predictions while maintaining algorithmic tractability. Similarly this HMM assumes a relatively constant rate of change between observations. Realizing that a commit/save is a coarse representation of a unit of work, and that there are notably different patterns in commit rates among different students, we smooth out the difference in commit rates using dynamic time warping [18] to better match the underlying assumptions of the model.

Learning a HMM is identical to learning a finite state machine (FSM) of how students transition through the high-level milestones. Each state from the HMM becomes a node in the FSM and the weight of a directed edge from one node to another provides the probability of transitioning from one state to the next.

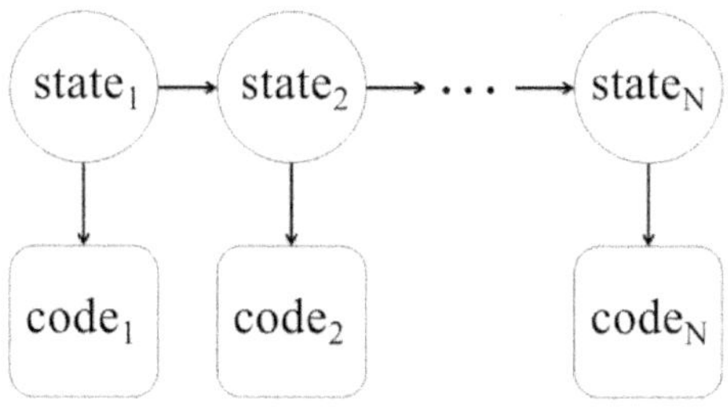

Figure 1. The program's Hidden Markov Model of state transitions for a given student. The node "code$_t$" denotes the code snapshot of the student at time *t*, and the node "state$_t$" denotes the high-level milestone that the student is in at time *t*. N is the number of snapshots for the student.

In order to learn the HMM we must identify three variables:

1. The finite set of high-level $States = \{s_1 \cdots s_k\}$ or milestones that a student could be in. A state is defined by a set of snapshots where all the snapshots in the set came from the same milestone.
2. The transition probability, $P(State^{(t+1)}|State^{(t)})$, of being in a state given the state you were in in the previous unit of time.
3. The emission probability, $P(Code^{(t)}|State^{(t)})$, of seeing a specific snapshot given that you are in a particular state. To calculate the emission probability we interpreted each of the states as emitting snapshots with normally distributed dissimilarities. In other words, given the dissimilarity between a particular snapshot of student code and a state's "representative" snapshot, we can calculate the probability that the student snapshot came from a given state using a Normal distribution based on the dissimilarity.

While it would be possible to learn all three variables in the HMM in a single Expectation Maximization (EM) algorithm [8], for computational ease the process is divided into two phases: learning the assignment states and learning the transition and emission probabilities.

To compute the set of high-level states (the different milestones of the assignment), we sampled two thousand snapshots chosen from the Karel training dataset (distributed evenly over students and evenly over time) and clustered the sample using K-Medioids [11]. K-Medioids is a variation of K-Means clustering where centroids are represented by the median code snapshot instead of being a numerical average of the set of examples in the cluster, as it is not possible to construct a synthetic "average" code snapshot. In a similar vein to the Buckshot algorithm [7], we initialized K-Mediods using cluster labels from Hierarchical Agglomerative Clustering.

Once we had established the set of states (i.e., milestones) of an assignment, we used an EM algorithm to simultaneously compute both the transition and emission probabilities in the state diagram. To initialize the algorithm, we calculate the probabilities under the assumption that all state variables are independent of one another. In the expectation step of EM, the best guess at the progress of a student through the HMM was made using the forward-backwards algorithm [17]. The EM algorithm resulted in a probabilistic assignment to the state variables for *each* student at each point in time, and also provided estimates for parameters to the HMM reflecting the state diagram induced from data over all students in the class.

4.3 Finding Patterns in Paths

The final step in our algorithm was to find patterns in how the students were transitioning through the HMM. To find these patterns we clustered the paths that students took through the HMM. To cluster the paths we ran the K-Means algorithm over the space of HMM, using a method developed by Smyth [24]. For each student we constructed a HMM to represent their state transitions—these *per student* models also incorporated prior probabilities based on the HMM developed using data from the whole class. We measured dissimilarity between two students as the symmetric (i.e., averaged) probability that student A's trajectory could be produced by student B's HMM and vice versa. Using this distance measure, we then clustered all the student paths to create groupings of students based on the characteristics of their entire development path for the assignment.

5. RESULTS

Clustering on a sample of 2000 random snapshots from the training set returned a group of well-defined snapshot clusters (see Figure 2). The value of K that maximized silhouette score (a measure of how natural the clustering was) was 26 clusters. A visual inspection of these clusters confirmed that snapshots which clustered together were functionally similar pieces of code.

When we repeated this process with a different set of random snapshots, 25 of the 27 clusters were the same, indicating that the results were quite stable and that the patterns found were not due to chance. Moreover, a manual examination of the states of the induced HMM revealed that they made intuitive sense. The class-wide state machine showed that there were several "sink" states—milestones where the students clearly had serious functional problems. Interestingly, once a student transitioned to such a state, the student had a high probability of remaining there through several code updates. For each "sink" state, the state machine showed how significant the sink state was and what transition most students took to get out of that state. Such revelations can be quite useful for determining how to appropriately aid students who may have encountered significant difficulties in programming an assignment, as revealed by the trajectory taken in the student's development path.

In addition to finding patterns in students' development progress, which can be indicative of a student's need for help (and the means for providing such help), we also wanted to determine the predictive power of such data mining in the early identification of students who may have more difficulty with computing generally. To this end, we sought to measure the extent to which student development trajectories on their first assignment in the course could be used to determine the performance of those students on the midterm exam (generally 3 to 4 weeks later in the term).

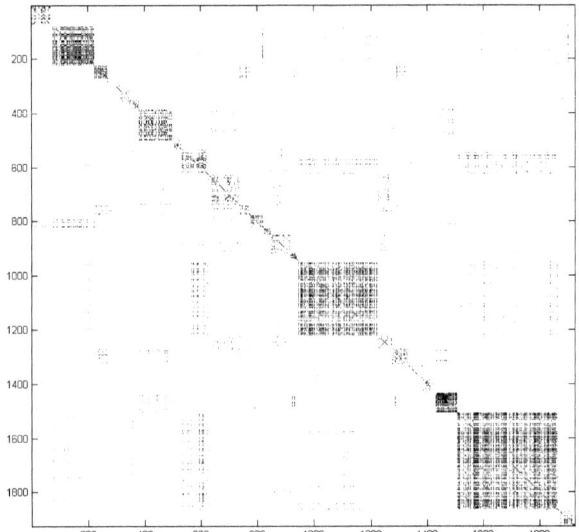

Figure 2. Dissimilarity matrix for clustering of 2000 snapshots. Each row and column in the matrix represents a snapshot and the entry at row i, column j represents how similar snapshot i and j are (dark means more similar)

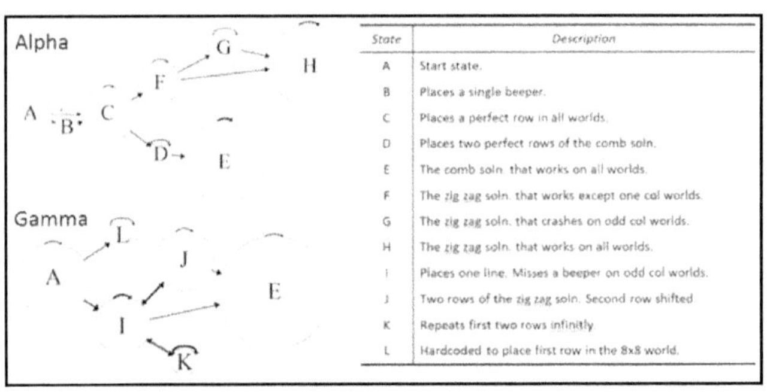

Figure 3. Visualization of finite state machines for Alpha and Gamma clusters of students.

Table 2. Delineation of Alpha, Beta and Gamma clusters

Metric	*Alpha*	*Beta*	*Gamma*
Num Students (count)	84	108	46
Midterm score (percent)	$\mu = 73.3$, $\sigma = 20.0$	$\mu = 71.4$, $\sigma = 26.2$	$\mu = 65.4$, $\sigma = 23.2$
Time (days)	$\mu = 8.2$, $\sigma = 2.0$	$\mu = 9.1$, $\sigma = 1.8$	$\mu = 9.3$, $\sigma = 1.9$
Karel score (percent)	$\mu = 91.2$, $\sigma = 7.0$	$\mu = 88.6$, $\sigma = 6.9$	$\mu = 88.3$, $\sigma = 7.6$

We clustered students' development paths into three groups (see Table 2), hereafter referred to as *alpha*, *beta* and *gamma*. The group that a student was clustered into was indeed predictive of the student's midterm grade. The distinction between the *alpha* and *gamma* groups was particularly large, having a mean midterm score difference of 7.9%. The difference in midterm performance between the *alpha* and *gamma* groups is statistically significant, yielding a p value of 0.04 using a two-tailed t-test.

A visualization of the finite state machine for the *alpha* group versus that for the *gamma* group (Figure 3) shows that there are clear differences in both the types of states that the two groups visit and the pattern of how students transition between states. Qualitatively, the *gamma* group can be described as getting stuck into several sink states and then making a direct transition from a semi-working program to a fully functional program. The *alpha* group seems to make smaller but steadily positively accretive steps towards the solution.

Seeking to understand the generality of such models in their application to future (out of sample) students, we classified the students who took the class in the *summer* quarter into the *alpha*, *beta* and *gamma* groups, which were induced from students taking the class during the prior quarter. The *alpha* group (N = 30) had midterm scores $\mu = 69.7$, $\sigma = 14.1$ and the *gamma* group (N = 42) had midterm scores $\mu = 63.3$, $\sigma = 15.4$. Again, we found a statistically significant difference between the mean midterm scores of these groups as a two-tailed t-test yielded a p value of 0.08. This result shows that the induced models are quite robust, as they capture patterns in development paths that are not specific to a single class of students, but generalize across student development behavior between classes (that also had different instructors). We believe this generality of the induced models has the potential to not only provide predictive capability in helping address student difficulties in programming, but also yielding deeper insights regarding fundamental misunderstandings of programming that transcend the details of one particular class.

We used the same algorithm, with the AST dissimilarity metric instead of the API dissimilarity metric, to build a model of how students progressed through Breakout. Interestingly there was a more articulated trajectory that most students followed—this could be as a result of clear objectives laid out in the assignment handout or it could reflect that the students at this point in the course are more mature programmers. Clustering of the paths that students took through the assignment resulted in two groups of students that had a 6.9 difference of means for their midterm scores, with a student TTest score of 0.06. Since the Breakout samples were collected in a different quarter than the Karel samples, we could not test the extent to which the groups of students discovered through analyzing in breakout correlated to the groups of students discovered through the Karel assignment.

6. DISCUSSION

The process of building the Karel state machine provided several pedagogical insights into the introductory computer science class. We found that by analyzing students' development paths, rather than simply their final grade, on an assignment, we discovered a higher correlation with students' understanding of the material, as reflected by their midterm scores. We believe the underlying reason for this phenomenon is that there is greater variability in student development paths than their final program outcomes. The development path provides important information regarding students' understanding of concepts beyond simply their final product. We seek to explore this issue in further work to better understand the degree to which data from student development paths reflects measurable understanding of programming concepts. We believe this line of investigation is not only quite promising with respect to providing a data-driven methodology for improving programming instruction and pedagogy, but also for gaining deeper insight into learning in general.

The success of the model also implies more subtle insights. The construction of the Karel state machine relied on two substantial assumptions: that a dynamic time-warped commit reflected a unit of work and that in generating the state transitions the future is independent of the past given the present. Building the assignment state machine based on these assumptions does not prove the assumptions are correct. It does demonstrate a tractable scheme for model construction that is fine-grained enough to capture important trends while not providing enough degrees of freedom in the model to overfit the training data.

Our results also show the generality of patterns found in student programming paths. For example, we analyzed programming paths by students in CS1 in two different quarters, taught by different instructors, yet observed similar patterns of student development paths in both courses. Such observations lead us to believe that there are further insights regarding program development that can be gleaned from our models. Moreover, this generality indicates that such models may be more broadly applicable as a means for predicting the sorts of interventions that would most benefit novice programmers and provide guidance as to when such interventions would be useful to provide. As reflected in our empirical results showing the correlation between development paths from the first assignment in CS1 and students' midterm scores, we believe that these models can be successful for identifying students in need of early intervention.

This model could potentially provide further insight into whether or not students need interventions, as many schools offer various open and closed laboratory opportunities to students who may need help. By understanding what students have tried and their projected path, this model provides an indication whether students need help at the time that they seek it, or if a student should ponder the problem a bit more without external help.

7. REFERENCES

[1] Booth, S. 1992. Learning to program: A phenomenographic perspective. Gothenburg, Sweden: Acta Universitatis Gothoburgensis.

[2] Bowman, M., Debray, S. K., & Peterson, L. L. 1993. Reasoning about naming systems. *ACM Trans. Program. Lang. Syst.* 15, 5 (Nov. 1993), 795-825.

[3] Bruce, C., Buckingham, L., Hynd, J., McMahon, C., Roggenkamp, M., & Stoodley, I. 2004. Ways of experiencing the act of learning to program: A phenomenographic study of introductory programming students at university. *Journal of Information Technology Education*, 3, 143-160.

[4] Brusilovsky, Peter. 2000. Adaptive hypermedia: From intelligent tutoring systems to web-based education. LNCS.

[5] Conati, C., Gertner, A. S., VanLehn, K., & Druzdzel, M. J. 1997. On-line student modeling for coached problem solving using Bayesian networks. *Proceedings of the 6th Int'l Conference on User Modeling (UM-96)*, 231-242.

[6] Cristianini, N. & Shawe-Taylor, J. 2000. An introduction to support vector machines and other kernel-based learning methods. Cambridge University Press.

[7] Cutting, D., Karger, D., Pedersen, J., & Tukey, J. 1992. Scatter/gather: A cluster-based approach to browsing large document collections. *Proc. 15th SIGIR*, 1992.

[8] Dempster, A.P., Laird, N.M., & Rubin, D.B. 1977. Maximum likelihood from incomplete data via the em algorithm. *J. of the Royal Statistical Society B*, 39 (1): 1–38.

[9] Gall, Harald et al. 2009. Change analysis with evolizer and changedistiller, *Software, IEEE.*

[10] Hoc, J-M. 1984. Do we really have conditional statements in our brains? *Proceedings of the 2nd European Conference on Readings on Cognitive Ergonomics - Mind and Computers*, G. van der Veer, M. Tauber, T. Green, and P. Gorny (Eds.), Springer-Verlag, London, UK, 92-101.

[11] Kaufman, L. and Rousseeuw, P.J. 1990. Finding groups in data: An introduction to cluster analysis, Wiley.

[12] Kessler, C. & Anderson, J. 1988. Learning flow of control: Recursive and iterative procedures. In [26], 229-260.

[13] Kurland, D. & Pea, R. 1983. Children's mental models of recursive logo programs. *Proceedings of the 5th Annual Conference of the Cognitive Science Society*, NY, 1-5.

[14] Needleman S. & Wunsch C. 1970. A general method applicable to the search for similarities in the amino acid sequence of two proteins. *Journal of Molecular Biology.*

[15] Paine, Carina. 2001. How students learn to program: Observations of practical tasks completed. *Proceedings of the IEEE International Conference on Advanced Learning Technologies (ICALT '01).*

[16] Parlante, N.,Wolfman, S., McCann, L., Roberts, E., Nevison, C., Motil, J., Cain, J., & Reges, S. 2006. Nifty assignments. *SIGCSE Bull.* 38, 1 (March 2006), 562-563.

[17] Rabiner, L.R., & Juang, B,H. 1986. Introduction to hidden markov models. *IEEE ASSP Magazine*, 3(1):4–16, 1986.

[18] Rabiner, L.R., & Juang, B,H. 1993. Fundamentals of speech recognition. Prentice-Hall, Inc.

[19] Reiser , B., Anderson , J., Farrell, R. 1985. Dynamic student modelling in an intelligent tutor for LISP programming, *Proceedings of the 9th int'l joint conference on AI*, 8-14.

[20] Roberts, Eric. Karel Learns Java. Available from: http://www.stanford.edu/class/cs106a/cs106a_spring11/book/karel-the-robot-learns-java.pdf Accessed 9/1/2011.

[21] Sagar, Tobias et al. 2006. Detecting similar java classes using tree algorithms. *Proceedings of the 2006 international workshop on mining software repositories (MSR '06).*

[22] Salton, G., Wong, A., & Yang, C. S. 1975. A vector space model for automatic indexing. *CACM*, 18: 613-620.

[23] Samurcay, R. 1988.The concept of variable in programming: Its meaning and use in problem-solving by novice programmers. In [26], 161-178.

[24] Smyth, P. 1997. Clustering sequences with hidden markov models. Advances in Neural Information Processing Systems, volume 9, 648-654. The MIT Press.

[25] Soloway,E., Bonar,J., Ehrlich,K. 1983. Cognitive strategies and looping constructs: an empirical study. *CACM*, 26, 11, 853-860.

[26] Soloway E. & Spohrer, J. 1988. Studying the novice programmer. L. Erlbaum Assoc. Inc., Hillsdale, NJ, USA.

[27] Spohrer, J. & Soloway, E. 1986. Analyzing the high frequency bugs in novice programs. *Papers presented at the first workshop on empirical studies of programmers*, E. Soloway and S. Iyengar (Eds.). Ablex Publishing, Norwood, NJ, USA, 230-251.

[28] ACM Graphics library. Available from: http://www-cs-faculty.stanford.edu/~eroberts/jtf/ Accessed 9/1/2011.

[29] Berland, M. & Martin, T. 2011. Clusters and patterns of novice programmers. *AERA*, New Orleans, LA.

[30] Blikstein, P. & Worsley, M. (2011). Learning analytics: Assessing constructionist learning using machine learning. *AERA*, New Orleans, LA.

[31] Blikstein, P. (2011). Using learning analytics to assess students' behavior in open-ended programming tasks. *Proc. of the Learning Analytics Knowledge Conference*, Banff.

[32] Blikstein, P. 2008. An Atom is known by the company it keeps. Unpublished PhD. dissertation, Northwestern University, Evanston, IL.

Science Fiction in Computer Science Education

Rebecca Bates (moderator)
Minnesota State University, Mankato
Mankato, MN 56001
+1-507-389-5587
bates@mnsu.edu

Judy Goldsmith
University of Kentucky
Lexington, KY 40526
+1-859-257-4245
goldsmith@cs.uky.edu

Rosalyn Berne
University of Virginia
Charlottesville, VA 22904
+1-434-924-6098
rwb@virginia.edu

Valerie Summet
Emory University
Atlanta, GA 30322
+1-404-727-0546
valerie@mathcs.emory.edu

Nanette Veilleux
Simmons College
Boston, MA 02115
+1-617-521-2705
veilleux@simmons.edu

SUMMARY

The use of science fiction (SF) to engage students in computer science learning is becoming more popular [1-6]. There is ample material available to help both undergraduate and graduate students make connections between technical content and human experience, from *Star Trek* to *The Hitchhiker's Guide to the Galaxy* to *2001: A Space Odyssey* to *I, Robot* and many others. Fiction can be included in technical courses or used to draw students into the field in introductory classes. The panelists, who represent a range of schools, perspectives and classes, will present brief overviews (5-8 minutes) of how they have used science fiction to engage students in technical topics as well as ethical and societal issues related to computing. After the overviews, there will be plenty of time for discussion of examples used within the community and ways to make connections between science fiction and particular classes or topics. We will be gathering additional examples from the discussion and making them available online.

Categories and Subject Descriptors

K.3.2 [**Computer and Information Science Education**]: Computer science education

General Terms

Human Factors

Keywords

Science fiction, computer science education methods.

1. REBECCA BATES

In the context of a teaching-focused, comprehensive university, I have developed an undergraduate general education course on Artificial Intelligence and Science Fiction (CS 201W), which meets the requirements for literature, ethics and writing intensive classes. The course traces the historical imagining of AI technology in science fiction, giving a context for the technical developments and societal expectations of technology. Students can grapple with ethical issues in the relative comfort of an alien world, while learning about state-of-the-art technology and developing their writing skills. The course has also been taught for graduate students with the option of completing a technical project, with required connections to literature, or a creative project, with required connections to technology.

Copyright is held by the author/owner(s).
SIGCSE'12, February 29–March 3, 2012, Raleigh, North Carolina, USA.
ACM 978-1-4503-1098-7/12/02.

Science fiction is incorporated through weekly movies, television episodes, novels and short stories. History and point of view can be shown through comparison of movies such as *The Computer Wore Tennis Shoes,* a Disney movie released in 1969, *TRON,* another Disney movie released in 1982 (the same time as *WarGames)* and the TRON sequel released in 2010. Related essays by philosophers and scientists are included to help provide real-world context and analysis. Explicitly stated in the course is the importance of creativity in computer science and the relationship between "traditional" creativity and technical creativity. Student reaction to this class, as well as to fiction reading assignments in other introductory classes, has been very positive, in part because students are able to connect something they (often) love to their future career. This has implications for retention and long-term persistence in the field. (See [7] for more information about the course.)

2. JUDY GOLDSMITH

CS 463 is a senior-level elective, Introduction to Artificial Intelligence. The students are usually juniors and seniors, though formally, non-CS graduate students can take the class for credit. (So far, none have.) The University of Kentucky is a Research 1 university, and has the strongest CS research program in the state. The students who take the course can program reasonably well in at least one programming language. The graded work for the class consists of significant programming assignments (specified), plus the students' individual choices of midterm and final papers, projects and presentations.

For the midterm and final, the students can review science fiction (book, movie, or TV show) with significant AI, write a survey paper on an AI topic, implement an AI algorithm from the research literature, present a research paper to the class, or even write a short story with AI content. The two general constraints are that they can't choose the same option for midterm and final, and they must submit a proposal and negotiate the details with the professor. The most popular option is the SF review. The proposal consists of the SF work and the relevant AI theme. The negotiations lead to a suitable work, and corresponding bibliography of research papers (at least 3 peer-reviewed papers or chapters of advanced textbooks) on the AI topic of interest.

Suitable work is broadly defined. I try to steer students away from instances of "AI" that have no technical content, and to warn them if they choose overtly sexual material. (For example, one student complained that there was too much sexual content in Marge Piercy's *He, She, and It.*) I provide a list of suggestions, which is deliberately weighted toward female authors, e.g. Nalo

Hopkinson's *Midnight Robber*, Melissa Scott's *The Jazz*, and Joan Slonczewski's *Daughters of Elysium* and *Brain Plague*.

It has been my experience that students are often contrarian, seeking out more obscure AI themes. This keeps the papers fresh, and is encouraged. One of the difficulties for students is that the contrarian urge leads them away from my areas of expertise, so they are left to track down the research themselves. I teach them how to use CiteSeer and Google Scholar, but it is still real work to track down relevant and readable papers.

Overall, this is a popular assignment. Students like the sense of agency, and the chance to explore a small corner of the research world. (See [8] for more information about the course.)

3. ROSALYN BERNE

STS 2500, "Ethics, Science Fiction and The Future" is a course I have been teaching at the University of Virginia's School of Engineering and Applied Sciences. Most amazing is how consistently engineering students express concern over the possible loss of control of artificial intelligences. Fueled by science fiction itself, these concerns lead many of them to attest that engineering design which allows for autonomous decision making by artificially intelligent machines is destined to seek independence from human beings, most likely becoming a threat to our existence. The focus of my research is the ethical, cultural, and societal implications of the emergence and convergence of nanotechnology, bio-technology, information technology and cognitive sciences. I am particularly interested in the role and function of moral imagination, mythology and religious belief in conceptualizations pertaining to ethics in technological development. These I have explored and discussed in the book *Nanotalk: Conversations with Scientists and Engineers about Ethics, Meaning and Belief in the Development of Nanotechnology* [9], and continue in the science fiction novel *Waiting in the Silence* (under review for publication).

4. VALERIE SUMMET

CS 190 is a freshman seminar course at Emory University based on robotics. Every department is required to offer seminar courses for first year students only. These courses offer small group learning experiences and should include components to foster a liberal arts education such as critical thinking, writing and communication skills, and interactive learning experiences. The course includes basic programming in Python, roughly following the IPRE robotics curriculum with Scribbler Robots [10]. In addition, the course includes current news articles, science fiction stories, and research readings. In particular, I use science fiction stories like Bierce's "Moxon's Master" and Silverberg's "The Macauley Circuit" to foster discussion about society's perceptions of robotics and AI. The students discuss the technology portrayed in the stories (often in very outdated terms) and whether the situations could "really happen" given the current state of technology. These discussions help students to refine technical topics related to robotics and AI, which are the subject of further writing assignments. These assignments hone students' academic research, writing, and public speaking skills.

5. NANETTE VEILLEUX

HON 101/102 at Simmons College, a women's liberal arts college, is a learning community that pairs two professors from different fields with a single cohort of incoming freshman in the Honors program. My partner was a visual artist who has worked extensively in digital media; I introduced computational linguistics. We found that science fiction was an excellent means of allowing students to abandon their preconceived notions of very basic aspects of encoding information. Most notably, the famous "Darmok and Jalad at Tanagra" Star Trek episode engendered a discussion on the nature of representation, a topic that first year students had not fully considered. (Developmentally, they are at the "one-truth" stage)

More recently, I have developed a curriculum for IT 101, Living in a Digital Society, which is an information technology fluency course and serves the college to provide a basic level of technological competency, primarily to non-CS students. As an innovation this fall, I have used several science fiction texts (e.g., *Super Sad True Love Story*, G. Shteyngart , "We Were Out of Our Minds with Joy", D. Marusek) to push students to examine their relationships with devices, most noticeably those that they anachronistically refer to as "phones". The readings are paired with an exercise that requires students to isolate themselves from remote communication devices and applications for several hours and report on the adjustments they made in response. My goal is to use the texts and exercises to begin discussion on the place technology has in our lives, the skills we need to understand and control it, and the opportunities and trade-offs it requires.

6. ACKNOWLEDGMENTS

Our thanks to the late Don Sanderson for conversations about science fiction and CS education at SIGCSE 2011.

7. REFERENCES

[1] Sanderson, D. 2004. Using science fiction to teach computer science. *Proc. WWW@10*. Terra Haute, IN, 9/30-10/1/2004.

[2] Want, R. 2008. The seeds of inspiration. *IEEE Pervasive Computing 7,* No. 3, 2-3.

[3] Schmitz, M., C. Endres and A. Butz. 2007. A survey of human-computer interaction design in science fiction movies. *Proc. 2nd Internat'l Conf on Intelligent Technologies for Interactive Entertainment*, 7:1-10.

[4] VanderLeest, S. 2000. Perspectives on technology through science fiction. *Proc. American Society for Engineering Education Annual Conference and Exposition.*

[5] Layton, D. 2010. Using the college science fiction class to teach technology and ethics: themes and methods. *Proc. American Society for Engineering Education Annual Conference and Exposition.*

[6] Schurr, N., P. Varakantham, E. Bowring, M. Tambe and B. Grosz. 2007. Asimovian multiagents: applying laws of robotics to teams of humans and agents. *Proc. 4th Internat'l. Conf. on Programming Multi-agent Systems,* 41-55.

[7] Bates, R. 2011. AI & SciFi: teaching writing, history, technology, literature and ethics. *Proc. American Society for Engineering Education Annual Conference and Exposition.*

[8] Goldsmith, J. and N. Mattei. 2011. Using science fiction in AI classes. *Proc. EAAI-11: The Second Symposium on Educational Advances in Artificial Intelligence.*

[9] Berne, R. 2005. *Nanotalk: Conversations with Scientists and Engineers about Ethics, Meaning and Belief in the Development of Nanotechnology*, Lawrence Erlbaum Associates.

[10] Summet, J., Kumar, D., O'Hara, K., Walker, D., Ni, L., Blank, D., Balch, T. 2009. Personalizing CS1 with Robots, *Proc. SIGCSE,* 433-437.

Initiatives to Support Systemic Change for Women in Undergraduate Computing

Leisa D. Thompson (Moderator)
National Center for Women & IT (NCWIT)
University of Virginia
1-210-883-6204
leisadthompson@gmail.com

Lecia J. Barker
NCWIT
School of Information
University of Texas
Austin, TX
1-512-232-8364
lecia@ischool.utexas.edu

Rita Manco Powell
NCWIT
University of Pennsylvania
Philadelphia, PA
1-215-898-0051
rpowell@cis.upenn.edu

Catherine E. Brawner
NCWIT
Research Triangle Educational Consultants
Raleigh, NC
1-919-782-4427
rtecinc@bellsouth.net

Tom McKlin
NCWIT
The Findings Group, LLC
Atlanta, GA
1-404-788-4506
tom@theFindingsGroup.com

Categories and Subject Descriptors
K.3.2. Computers and Education. Computer and Information Science Education.

General Terms
Human Factors

Keywords
Recruitment, Retention, Gender, Women, Diversity, Systemic Change.

SUMMARY

The National Center for Women & Information Technology (NCWIT) Extension Services for Undergraduate Programs (ES-UP) has created a large group of trained consultants (ESCs) and clients who are passionate about women's participation in computing. This panel will describe how our ESCs and clients have worked together to effect change and will show outcomes from our activities over the past three years.

The ES-UP recruited, motivated, and guided 34 diverse undergraduate computing departments to engage in systemic reform that increases enrollment, retention, and graduation of women. Each of these departments is committed to participating in a process that follows the best expert advice for essential steps toward positive organizational change.

Table 1: Characteristics of ES-UP Client Institutions

Carnegie Classification	Research University: 26 4-year College: 3 Master's College: 4 Engineering School (4-year): 1
Control	Private: 12 Public: 22
Special Populations	Women's College: 2 Minority-Serving Institution: 2
Size	Small: 5 Medium: 4 Large: 24
U.S. Region	Far West 7 Midwest 8 Southeast 5 Southwest, Rockies 5 New England, Middle Eastern 8

Copyright is held by the author/owner(s).

SIGCSE'12, February 29–March 3, 2012, Raleigh, North Carolina, USA.
ACM 978-1-4503-1098-7/12/02.

The process for working with university departments involved a baseline study to understand the recruitment and retention history of women in the department and the factors that might support or hinder increased participation of women in the department; strategic planning with departmental leadership targeting the most pressing actions the department could take; and establishing metrics to measure the success of those efforts. Some institutions also administered the "Student Experience of the Major" (SEM) survey [1] to understand the factors underlying low participation among women in the department. This analysis fed into the strategic planning [2, 3] and revealed an initial set of actions the department could take. Thus, many of our client institutions are showing positive increases in women's enrollments, retention, and graduation rates.

Our model of systemic reform in undergraduate computing includes a focus on the events and practices women experience directly and those that indirectly affect their outcomes. The components of the model shown in Figure 1 derive from research on women in undergraduate computing, research on change in higher education, and research and theories of communication and marketing [4, 5]. The components include recruitment, pedagogy, curriculum, institutional policies, evaluation, and student support. Each of these components can affect the others in one way or another and should therefore be assessed when trying to increase women's representation.

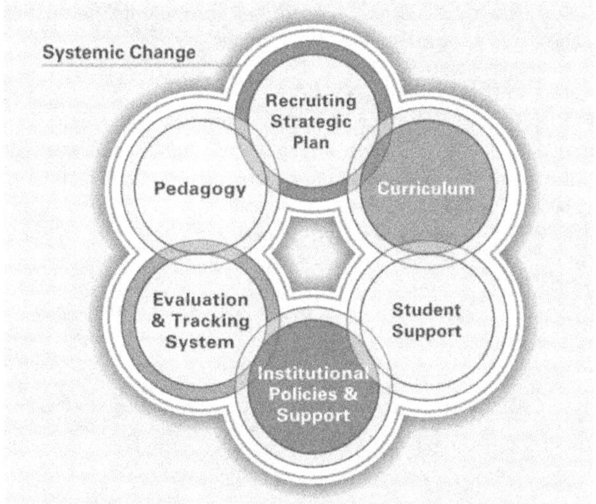

Figure 1: Systemic Change in Undergraduate Computing

NCWIT ES-UP advocates a research-based approach to sustained change. Reform initiatives should:

- Integrate teaching methods that create inclusive, collaborative environments in early curriculum.
- Successfully implement a strategic recruiting plan for creating an enduring pipeline of diverse students with appropriate competencies.
- Help students understand how their classes and other experiences (internships, REUs, etc.) contribute to their future identities as computing professionals.
- Align assignments and coursework with student interests and career goals.
- Foster everyday positive student-student and student-faculty interactions that contribute to a sense of belonging in the departmental community.
- Include visible, high-level administrative support and resources for sustained implementation and evaluation.
- Ensure that efforts to diversify are positively reinforced within the reward structure for promotion and tenure.
- Evaluate efforts to identify what works and what doesn't work; make mid-course corrections to increase success; and communicate findings for increased support and replication by others.

1. LEISA D. THOMPSON

As Director of Research and Consultation for ES-UP, Dr. Thompson will briefly describe some of the resources ES-UP has developed to assist the consultants. She will also be the moderator and introduce the other panelists.

2. LECIA J. BARKER

As co-PI for this project, Dr. Barker will discuss the systemic change model, the importance of strategic planning for recruitment and retention, and describe combined outcomes of ES-UP client departments.

3. RITA MANCO POWELL

Dr. Powell is a consultant and representative at the University of Pennsylvania. She will discuss different initiatives in curriculum, increased student/student and student/faculty interaction, and outreach to high school girls that her department has implemented with a corresponding increase in women's enrollments, graduation rates, and a decrease in attrition in computer science.

4. CATHERINE E. BRAWNER

NCWIT has developed numerous resources for Extension Services consultants and their clients to use together to evaluate the conditions for undergraduate computer science students, particularly underrepresented populations (women and minorities). Dr. Brawner will discuss how her clients, large, state-supported research universities with substantial engineering colleges, have used the information provided by the NCWIT Student Experience in the Major survey and Entry survey to assess and modify their planning and practices.

5. TOM McKLIN

Dr. McKlin will discuss one client's outcomes from strategic planning and how they are on their way to becoming a national exemplar for diversity in computing and information technology, by working on goals to accelerate recruitment and retention of women. He will describe the process this department took to set goals, actions they took with administrators and faculty, and their processes for measuring near-term outcomes.

6. ACKNOWLEDGMENTS

This material is based upon work supported by the National Center for Women and Information Technology with funding from the National Science Foundation under grant number HRD-0533565. Any opinions, findings, and conclusions or recommendations expressed in this material are those of the authors and do not necessarily reflect the views of the National Science Foundation or other supporting organizations.

7. REFERENCES

[1] Barker, L.J.,McDowell, C. & Kalahar, K. Exploring factors that influence computer science introductory course students to persist in the major. In *SIGCSE '09 Proceedings of the 40th ACM Technical Symposium on Computer Science Education* (Chattanooga, TN USA, March 4-7,2009) ACM, New York, NY, 153-157. DOI= http://dl.acm.org/citation.cfm?doid=1508865.1508923

[2] National Center for Women & Information Technology. (2009). Strategic Planning for Retaining Women in Undergraduate Computing. Retrieved October 15, 2011 from http://www.ncwit.org/pdf/StrategicPlanning_RetainingWorkbook.pdf

[3] National Center for Women & Information Technology. (2010). Strategic Planning for Recruiting Women into Undergraduate Computing: High Yield in the Short Term. Retrieved October 15, 2011 from http://www.ncwit.org/pdf/NCWIT_Recruiting_Workbook_2009.pdf

[4] Cohoon, J.M. and Aspray, W. A critical review of the research on women's participation in postsecondary computing education. In *Women and information technology: Research on underrepresentation*. MIT Press, Cambridge, MA, 2006, 137-180.

[5] Boyce, M. Organizational Learning Is Essential to Achieving and Sustaining Change in Higher Education. *Innovative Higher Education 28*, 2 (2003), 119-136.

Transforming the CS Classroom with Studio-Based Learning

N. Hari Narayanan,[1] Christopher Hundhausen,[2] Dean Hendrix,[1] Martha Crosby[3]

[1]Computer Science & Software Engineering Department, Auburn University, Auburn, AL 36849

[2]School of Electrical Engineering and Computer Science, Washington State University, Pullman, WA 99164

[3]Department of Information and Computer Sciences, University of Hawaii at Manoa, Honolulu, HI 96822

naraynh@auburn.edu, hundhaus@wsu.edu, dh@auburn.edu, crosby@hawaii.edu

SUMMARY

The studio-based learning (SBL) model aims to promote learning in a social and collaborative context by having learners construct, iteratively refine, and critically review design artifacts under the guidance of instructors and disciplinary experts. Recognizing the potential of SBL to foster the development of not only technical design skills, but also increasingly-coveted communication and collaboration skills, we have been adapting the approach for computing education, implementing it in various courses, and evaluating its impact over the past 5 years. This effort now involves 26 computing courses at 15 institutions in seven states. To our knowledge, this represents the most systematic implementation and evaluation of a pedagogy for computing education to date. This special session will introduce SBL to the SIGCSE community and facilitate a discussion and exchange of ideas. In addition to oral and poster presentations of the SBL model and its evaluation results, the session will feature "war stories" from teachers who have applied the model to their courses and hands-on activities to help attendees apply SBL to their courses.

Categories and Subject Descriptors

K.3.1 [**Computers and Education**] Computer Uses in Education - *collaborative learning*; K.3.2 [**Computers and Education**]: Computer and Information Science Education – *curriculum.*

General Terms

Design, Experimentation.

Keywords

Design crits, evaluation, pedagogy, studio-based learning.

1. BACKGROUND

The studio-based learning (SBL) model has been the centerpiece of architecture and fine arts education for over a century. Based on sociocultural learning theory, SBL aims to promote learning in a social and collaborative context by having students design and construct artifacts, and then present their artifacts to others in so-called "design crits." The purpose of these design crits is to enable students to obtain critical feedback from peers, teachers and other experts, ultimately helping students to refine and improve their designs and acquire disciplinary skills.

Copyright is held by the author/owner(s).

SIGCSE'12, February 29–March 3, 2012, Raleigh, North Carolina, USA.

ACM 978-1-4503-1098-7/12/02

With support from the NSF CPATH program, we have been adapting this approach for computing education [4], implementing it in several courses, and systematically evaluating its impact over the past five years. The SBL model was implemented in CS0, CS1, CS2 and CS3 at Auburn University, Washington State University and the University of Hawaii at Manoa during 2007-10 academic years. In addition, the model is currently being implemented in 26 computing courses at 15 institutions in seven states during the 2010-12 academic years.

So far, approximately 1600 computing majors have experienced SBL in 33 courses at 15 institutions. Quantitative data on student performance and qualitative data on student perceptions and attitudes have been collected from all studio and traditional versions of courses for comparison purposes. Data analyses to date indicate that students in studio courses learn as much or more than students in the same courses taught in the traditional way [1,3]. Perhaps more importantly, students in studio courses have shown higher levels of motivation and engagement than students in traditional courses [1,3]. Since SBL requires significant amounts of classroom time, we have been developing the Online Studio-Based Learning Environment (OSBLE), a free and open source environment that facilitates asynchronous SBL activities in courses where face-to-face SBL activities are not feasible [2]. More details on our efforts and research results may be found at www.studiobasedlearning.org.

2. OBJECTIVE

The proposed special session has three objectives: (a) to introduce the SIGCSE audience to the SBL model and the emerging body of research on its use and impact in computing education; (b) to share and discuss "war stories" from teachers who have used the approach; and (c) to provide practical guidance to audience members who would like to explore the use of SBL in their own courses. The session will be organized with atypical elements such as "war stories" and hands-on "studio sessions," as well as elements drawn from more traditional conference sessions such as presentations and posters. These will be combined in an engaging way to meet our objectives.

We believe that introducing SBL to the broad SIGCSE audience through a special session is important for at least three reasons. First, though enrollment has started to climb after a precipitous decline, attrition is still a major problem in computing disciplines. Based on the affective impact of SBL that we have documented, there is reason to believe that SBL may help educators address this problem. Second, SBL is a flexible instructional model that is adaptable to lower-division and upper-division, small and large, and lecture and lab courses. Hence, we believe it will be attractive to SIGCSE attendees. Finally, this session will enrich the conference by highlighting the fruits of educational research from one of the most systematic implementation and evaluation efforts of a computing pedagogy to date.

3. SESSION OUTLINE

The special session will consist of six elements: (1) tutorial-style quick presentations; (2) stories from the trenches; (3) discussions involving the audience and a panel of SBL practitioners; (4) question-and-answer (Q & A) periods; (5) hands-on curriculum redesign activities involving experienced SBL teachers and interested attendees; and (6) informative posters around the room.

First 20 minutes: The session will begin with an introduction to SBL that will be presented in three five-minute quick tutorial-style talks to answer the following questions for attendees. (1) What is SBL? (2) Why should I be interested in SBL? (3) How do I apply SBL in my course? These will be followed by a five-minute Q & A period. There will be three posters in the room that provide more details on each of these questions, which attendees can inspect throughout the session.

Next 40 minutes: The next part of the session will consist of three 10-minute stories presented by teachers, selected from our cohort of 18 SBL faculty. They will recount their experiences: how they turned their course into a studio course and its highlights, the benefits and limitations of SBL that they observed in comparison with the traditional style in which they previously taught, and personal advice and tips on how to turn a traditional computing course into a more effective studio course. These will be followed by a 10-minute Q & A period. Posters with more details on these studio courses will be available in the room.

Final 15 minutes: At least seven experienced SBL educators (the four authors and the three teachers from our cohort of 18 SBL faculty) will be present. Three of us will form a panel during this final session to take questions from the audience and initiate discussions. The others will provide a hands-on course and curriculum redesign experience for interested educators in the audience. We will identify audience members interested in the hands-on experience at the outset, and form one or more groups that will sit separately in the session room or in a public area to work out initial curriculum designs for studio versions of the courses taught by these audience members. These hands-on design sessions have the potential to continue beyond the end of the special session. Participants will be invited to attend the BOF session entitled "Enriching Computing Instruction with Studio-Based Learning," which will take place immediately after this session. In addition, they can arrange additional meetings with SBL faculty during the rest of the conference.

The proposed session involves significant audience interaction and elicitation of audience feedback. Forty percent of the time will be devoted to interaction with attendees. Besides, attendees will be free to view posters displayed on the walls of the room throughout the session. In addition to the aforementioned six posters, we will display posters with SBL evaluation results and student comments. Another unique aspect is that audience members who are interested in exploring the use of SBL in their own courses will have the opportunity to work closely with members of our team on the design of SBL versions of their own courses during the special session, afterwards at the BOF and during the rest of the conference, and even later through the SBL community portal designed for online discussions and resource sharing (www. studiobasedlearning.org).

4. EXPECTATIONS

We expect that the audience will consist of a mix of (a) instructors who have used another collaborative learning technique in their courses and are curious about SBL, and (b) instructors who wish to learn more about collaborative learning in general and SBL in particular, and how they might benefit their own courses. The session will cover SBL at various levels to suit a wide variety of attendees. For the merely curious, the first part of the session will provide an overview of SBL and its impact as revealed through observation and formal evaluation. For the more interested, the second part will provide real experiences from practitioners. For the inspired, the final part will be a starting point for transforming their courses—an effort in which they can expect continued support from us during and after the conference.

5. SUITABILITY FOR SPECIAL SESSION

Our proposed special session consists of a mix of several different types of activities: presentations, experience reports, discussions, Q & A periods, hands-on activities and posters. This mix is not accommodated by any of the regular SIGCSE sessions. We have been developing and refining these kinds of sessions in annual faculty development workshops since 2008. Based on our experiences, and resonant with the interactive nature of the SBL method, we believe that this mix of activities is the most appropriate means of meeting our stated objectives.

6. ACKNOWLEDGMENTS

This special session is based on research conducted as part of a multi-university project supported by NSF under CPATH Awards CNS 0939055, 0939017 and 0939157. We gratefully acknowledge the contributions of all teachers involved, as well as the other members of the research team—Margaret Ross, Michael Trevisan, and Rita Vick.

7. REFERNCES

[1] Hendrix, D., Myneni, L., Narayanan, N. H. and Ross, M. Implementing studio-based learning in CS2. In *Proc. ACM SIGCSE Symposium*, ACM Press, New York, 2010, 505-509.

[2] Hundhausen, C.D., Agrawal, A. and Ryan, K. The design of an online environment to support pedagogical code reviews. In *Proc. ACM SIGCSE Symposium*, ACM Press, New York, 2010, 182-186.

[3] Hundhausen, C.D., Agrawal, A., Fairbrother, D. and Trevisan, M. Does studio-based instruction work in CS 1? An empirical comparison with a traditional approach. In *Proc. ACM SIGCSE Symposium*, ACM Press, New York, 2010, 500-504.

[4] Hundhausen, C. D., Narayanan, N. H. & Crosby, M. E. (2008). Exploring studio-based instructional models for computing education. In *Proc. ACM SIGCSE Symposium*, ACM Press, New York, 2008, 392-396.

Making Turing Machines Accessible to Blind Students

Pilu Crescenzi
Dip. di Sistemi e Informatica
Università di Firenze
Viale Morgagni 65
50134, Firenze, Italy
pierluigi.crescenzi@unifi.it

Leonardo Rossi
Dip. di Sistemi e Informatica
Università di Firenze
Viale Morgagni 65
50134, Firenze, Italy
leonardo.rossi@gmail.com

Gianluca Apollaro
Dip. di Sistemi e Informatica
Università di Firenze
Viale Morgagni 65
50134, Firenze, Italy
gianluca.apollaro@libero.it

ABSTRACT

In this paper we describe how we tried to make the well-known JFLAP Turing machine simulator accessible to blind students taking a theoretical computer science course. Software accessibility is an important topic for both legal and ethical reasons: in our case, however, we also wanted to make the accessible software usable by blind students in cooperation with the other students, in order to encourage the integration of the blind students within the rest of the class. For this reason, the accessible version of the JFLAP Turing machine simulator that we developed is as much similar as possible to and fully compatible with the original one. In the paper, we also report some very satisfactory preliminary validation results that indicate how the new software can really make Turing machines accessible to blind students.

Categories and Subject Descriptors

F.1.1 [**Models of Computation**]: Computability theory; F.1.1 [**Models of Computation**]: Bounded-action devices (e.g., Turing machines, random access machines); K.4.2 [**Social Issues**]: Assistive technologies for persons with disabilities

General Terms

Experimentation, Human Factors, Theory

Keywords

Software accessibility, Turing machines, Computability

1. INTRODUCTION

Theoretical Computer Science (in short, *TCS*) is a third-year course of the Computer Science Bachelor program at our university. The course deals with the theories of computability, formal languages, and computational complexity, and it requires as a prerequisite a second-year course on formal languages and compilers. In particular, in the first part of the TCS course the students are introduced to the notion of Turing Machines (in short, TMs) and to the classical results concerning language decidability and reducibility between languages (in other words, Chapters 3, 4, and 5 of the well-known book by Sipser [11]).

The first author started teaching the TCS course in the fall semester of 2005. Since 2006 he decided to use a TM simulator in order to define, to execute, and to debug TMs (indeed, from 2006 to 2008 a laboratory exam was also included as part of the final grade). In particular, during the first two years a simulator developed by the teacher himself was used, while starting from 2008 the teacher decided to switch to the well-known JFLAP application [10], which included both a TM graphical editor and a TM execution environment. At the end of 2007, the students were asked to fill a brief survey evaluating the usefulness of using the TM simulator. In particular, the students were asked to say whether they agreed with the following statements.

1. The simulator is useful to follow the lectures.
2. The simulator is useful to study at home.
3. A theoretical computer science course must use a TM simulator.

The students' answers are summarized in the following table.

Statement	Fully disagree	Disagree	Agree	Fully agree
1	0	1	14	10
2	0	0	5	20
3	0	0	14	11

The same survey was asked to be filled by the students of the next year (that is, the first year JFLAP was used). The students' answers are summarized in the following table.

Statement	Fully disagree	Disagree	Agree	Fully agree
1	0	0	5	15
2	0	1	2	17
3	0	0	9	11

As it can be seen, almost all students thought that using a TM simulator is useful and that such a simulator should be adopted by the teacher of a theoretical computer science course. As a consequence of these results, the first author has continued using the JFLAP simulator in the next three years he taught the TCS course (and he will use it even the

Permission to make digital or hard copies of all or part of this work for personal or classroom use is granted without fee provided that copies are not made or distributed for profit or commercial advantage and that copies bear this notice and the full citation on the first page. To copy otherwise, to republish, to post on servers or to redistribute to lists, requires prior specific permission and/or a fee.

SIGCSE'12, February 29–March 3, 2012, Raleigh, North Carolina, USA.

Copyright 2012 ACM 978-1-4503-1098-7/12/02 ...$10.00.

next semester). Moreover, JFLAP is strongly integrated with the course lecture notes in which all TM examples are implemented within JFLAP (including a full implementation of the universal TM).

Two years ago, however, a new challenge arose while teaching the TCS course, due to the fact that one of the students was blind. The teacher immediately contacted the developers of JFLAP, in order to know whether this situation had already been considered: unfortunately, the answer was negative. It is worth noting that JFLAP includes a zoom-in feature: this feature can be useful for visually impaired students, but of course does not solve the accessibility problem for blind students.

On the ground of the two previously described surveys, we thought that it was very important to allow the blind student to enjoy the possibility of creating and testing TMs. Moreover, we wanted to let him cooperate with the other sighted students while developing TMs, so that this activity could turn out to be a further motivation for integrating with the rest of the class. Hence, we concluded that the best solution would have been to make the tool used by the sighted students (that is, JFLAP) accessible also to the blind student. Fortunately, the JFLAP developers made the simulator source code freely available [7], so that we could decide to modify the TM simulator module of JFLAP in order to make it accessible.

This paper describes this modification and reports some preliminary results concerning its utilization. In particular, in Section 2 we review the components of the JFLAP TM simulator which turned out to be not accessible, while in Section 3 we describe how we decided to solve these accessibility problems and we report some quite satisfying experimental results. We will then report, in Section 4 the problems that arose when we tried to let the accessible JFLAP tool be used by another first-year blind student, we will describe the current version of the accessible JFLAP tool which solved these problems, and, once again, we report some preliminary satisfying experimental results. We finally conclude in Section 5 by describing the most interesting directions that we intend to follow in the near future.

1.1 Related work

As far as we know, the problem of making Turing machines accessible to blind users has never been analyzed in the past, even though, of course, the problem of software accessibility has been one of the most important topic in software development since the very beginning of the information and communication technology (see, for example, [2]). The work most similar to what we are going to describe in this paper is [12], where the authors describe a graphical program that allows students, both sighted and visually impaired, to develop and test finite state automata. Since a TM can be represented as a graph (see the next section), the system described in [4] is also related to our work: this system, indeed, displays a drawn graph on a tablet PC and uses auditory cues to help a blind user navigate the graph. For what concerns the cooperation between sighted and blind students, it is worth mentioning [17], where the authors review work on assistive interfaces concerning how collaboration between sighted and blind might be supported. Moreover, one of the most recent papers on the problem of teaching computer science to visually impaired students is [5], where perspectives of both professors and a severely visually impaired student are presented. From a different perspective, finally, our work is also related to projects on tactile graphics (which are images that are designed to be touched rather than looked at), such as the Tactile Graphics Assistant developed at the University of Washington [6], which addresses making print-versions of graphs and diagrams accessible to blind users.

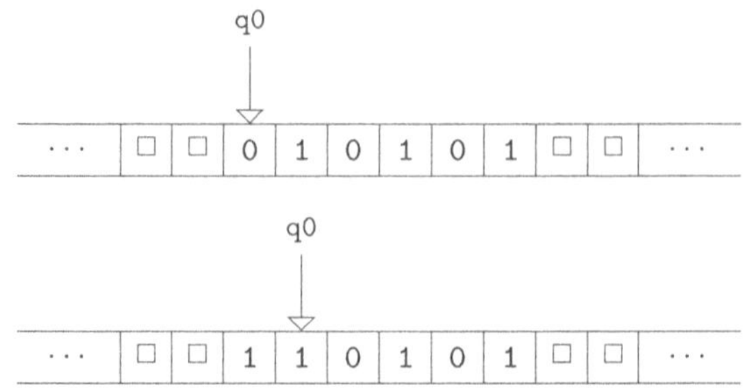

Figure 1: The execution of a step of a TM

1.2 Preliminaries

The TM is a very simple model of computation introduced by Alan Turing in 1936 [13]. It consists of an infinite tape subdivided into cells, each containing one symbol of a specific alphabet (see Figure 1). At each step, the TM is in a specific state and reads the content of a specific cell (in the upper part of the figure, the state is $q0$ and the read symbol is 0): depending on its state and on the symbol contained in the read cell, the TM executes an instruction according to which it can modify this symbol, enter a new state, and move its reading head to a cell adjacent to the current one (in the lower part of the figure, the state is not changed, the written symbol is 1, and the head moved to the right). The execution of the TM ends whenever a final state is reached or whenever there is no instruction specified for the current combination of state and symbol. The set of instructions of a TM can be either described by means of a transition table or by a means of a transition graph (see Figure 2): this latter representation is the one adopted by JFLAP.

2. JFLAP ACCESSIBILITY ANALYSIS

JFLAP is a very powerful tool for experimenting with the theory of formal languages and the theory of computability. This application allows the user to work with several different models of computation, among the others finite state automata, pushdown automata, and TMs. As we said in the introduction, we were mainly interested to the TM simulation environment included in JFLAP, since this was the module used while teaching the first part of the TCS course. In order to make this module accessible to blind

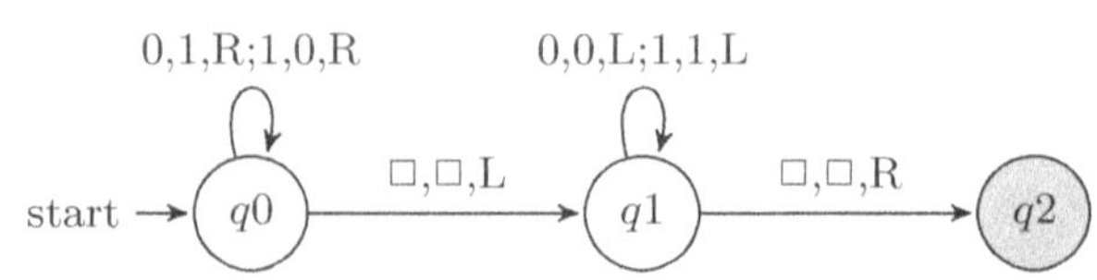

Figure 2: An example of a transition graph of a TM

Figure 3: The editor toolbar of JFLAP

students, we then analyzed which activities of the module itself turned out to be not accessible even if the user made use of a general-purpose screen reader (such as JAWS [9]) .

2.1 The TM editor

Even if, by appropriately making use of the Java Accessibility API [8], a screen reader can recognize and describe the toolbar of the TM editor of JFLAP (see Figure 3), once a tool has been selected and activated, the blind user is stuck, since all the operations (apart from the undo/redo operations) have to interact with the drawing area below the toolbar, which is clearly not accessible to a blind user. Moreover, JFLAP allows a user to modify some properties of a state of a Turing machine by right clicking on the corresponding node: a blind user does not know where this node is located within the drawing area and there is no way of cyclically visiting all the states of the machine. For the very same reason, creating a transition of the TM is an operation which is not accessible to a blind user, since it requires to left click on the starting state and to drag the mouse until reaching the ending state of the transition. In other words, the editing of a TM within JFLAP is almost fully not accessible.

2.2 The TM execution

Even if the JFLAP `Fast run` operation turned out to be almost accessible to a blind user, this operation is not very useful in order to debug a TM, since it allows the user to specify an input string and to simulate the TM until the end of the execution without giving any information about the intermediate configurations. The `Step run` operation is instead much more useful, since it allows the user to examine the TM execution one step after the other. However, this latter operation is not accessible to blind users since the graphical elements representing the transition graph of the TM and the current machine configuration cannot be recognized and described by the screen reader. Finally, JFLAP implements a `Multiple run` operation which allows the user to execute the same TM on different inputs: the output of this operation is a table containing an input column and and a result column. Unfortunately, the description of the content of a table is not always realized in a perfect way by a screen reader: for example, JAWS reads the elements of the table by first specifying, for each of them, the row and the column indices (which turned out to be quite frustrating).

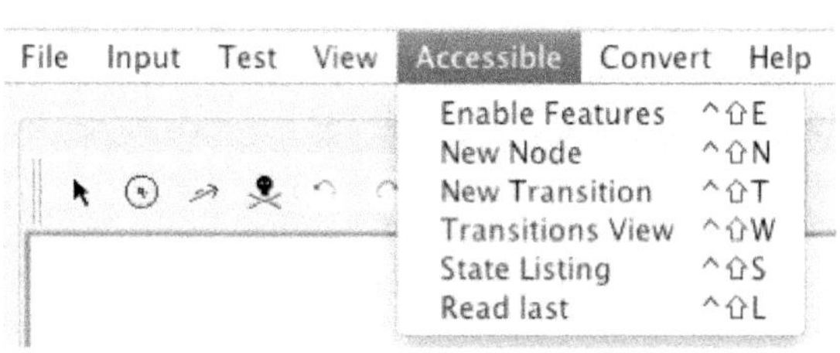

Figure 4: The new menu of the accessible JFLAP

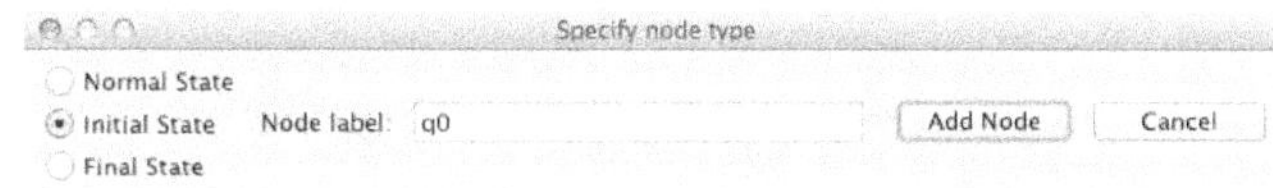

Figure 5: The new node window

3. ACCESSIBLE JFLAP (VERSION 1)

As we said in the introduction, our goal was to modify the current version of JFLAP in order to obtain a new version of the TM editor tool which could be used by blind students without, however, changing too much the original graphical user interface of the tool itself. To this aim, the first version of the accessible JFLAP has been developed by making use of keyboard shortcuts and by integrating the original general-purpose screen reader (such as JAWS) with an *ad hoc* screen reader integrated in the JFLAP code. The keyboard shortcuts and the ad hoc screen-reader can be activated by means of the keyboard shortcut `ctrl-shift-e` or by means of the first item of a new menu, called `Accessible`, which contains one item for any keyboard shortcut (see Figure 4).

3.1 The ad hoc screen reader

The ad hoc screen-reader has been realized by making use of the `FreeTTS` speech synthesis system, which is entirely written Java [16]. This system is based upon `Flite`, which is a small run-time speech synthesis engine developed at Carnegie Mellon University [3]. We have chosen `FreeTTS` both because it could be easily integrated within the JFLAP source code (which is written in Java) and because of its very good performances (see [15]). As we will see in the next section, this choice has also allowed us to solve other problems that arose while experimenting the accessible JFLAP TM simulation tool with another blind student. Note that all messages read by the ad hoc screen reader can be read again by using the keyboard shortcut `ctrl-shift-l`.

3.2 The accessible TM editor

The accessible JFLAP TM simulation tool implements an additional way of creating a new machine state which can be activated by typing the keyboard shortcut `ctrl-shift-n`. By selecting this feature a new window is created which allows the user to specify the type of the new state and its label (see Figure 5). The blind user can interact with this window either by making use of a general-purpose screen reader (such as JAWS) or, in case this screen-reader is not activated, by making use of the ad hoc screen reader. Note that every time a new node is created the transition graph is redrawn by invoking one of the automatic layout algorithms already implemented in JFLAP: this clearly allows the blind user to better cooperate with another student while creating the machine. Similarly, a new way of creating a new transition has a been also added to the JFLAP TM simulation tool: even in this case, a window is created that allows the user to specify the starting state, the list of read symbols, the corresponding list of written symbols, the head move-

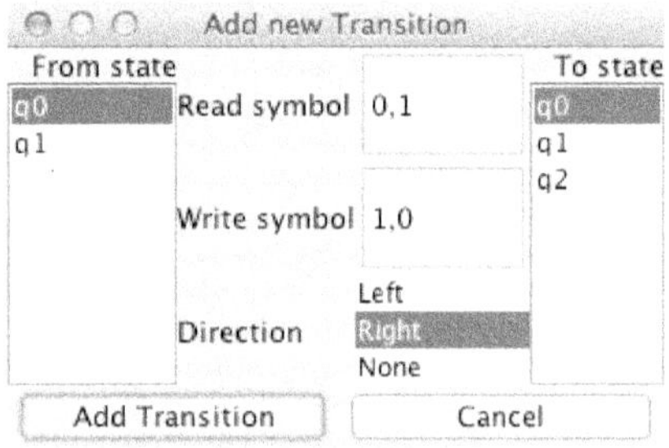

Figure 6: The new transition window

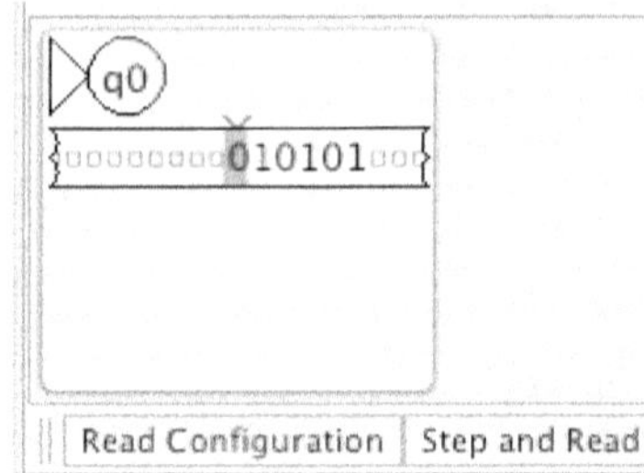

Figure 8: The step-by-step accessible execution

ment, and the ending state of the transition (see Figure 6). Note that, in order to make the transition creation process faster, the user can specify a comma separated list of read and/or written symbols (indeed, we think that this feature might be useful even for sighted users). Finally, both the states and the transitions of a machine can be listed and edited (see Figure 7): in the case of the transitions, however, we decided to not allow the user to modify a transition but just to delete it (and eventually create a new one).

3.3 The accessible TM execution

All three execution modes of JFLAP have been modified in order to make them accessible. In the case of the `Fast run` operation, we just simplified the input string window by avoiding the possibility of opening an input file: the result of the execution is either read by the general-purpose screen reader or by the ad hoc screen reader. The `Step run` operation, instead, has been almost fully implemented by making use of the ad hoc screen reader. In particular, two new buttons have been added to the graphical user interface which allows the user to let the application read the current configuration and to advance by one step and read the next configuration (see Figure 8). A configuration is read by first saying which is the current state, and by then listing the symbols in the tape: the symbol currently read by the machine is distinguished from the other symbols by saying that it is selected. For example, the configuration shown in the figure would cause the ad hoc screen reader to pronounce the following phrase: `Current state is q0. The tape is 0 selected, 1, 0, 1, 0, 1`. Finally, the `Multiple run` graphical user interface has been simplified in order to make it accessible (see Figure 9). The user is allowed to insert one input after the other and to add them to the input list: after pressing the run button, beside each input it is specified whether it has been accepted. Moreover, each line of the list is colored in green or red: even if this feature is clearly not useful for blind users, it turns out to be valuable whenever the blind user is cooperating with another user who is not blind.

3.4 Validation results

In order to validate the accessibility of the new version of JFLAP, we asked the blind student to solve nine exercises that were proposed within a TM competition that took place at the University of Pisa, Italy. The results were very satisfying. Indeed, the student was able to solve all the exercises within two hours and twenty-three minutes. The solution times range between two and a half minutes (required to develop a machine deleting all leftmost zeros of a decimal integer number) and twenty-nine minutes (required to develop a machine dividing by two an integer represented in unary notation).

4. NEW ACCESSIBILITY PROBLEMS

At the beginning of the last academic year, we planned to further validate the accessibility of the new version of JFLAP by asking a first-year blind student of the Computer Science program at our university to follow a crash course on TMs and to then solve some simple exercises. However, we immediately realized that the just developed accessible JFLAP application presented the following problems in order to be used by the blind student.

- The platform adopted by the first-year student was a Mac OS X machine instead of a Windows machine. This implied that the general-purpose screen reader (that is, `VoiceOver`) was different and it did not work exactly the same as JAWS (which was the screen reader used by the third-year blind student).

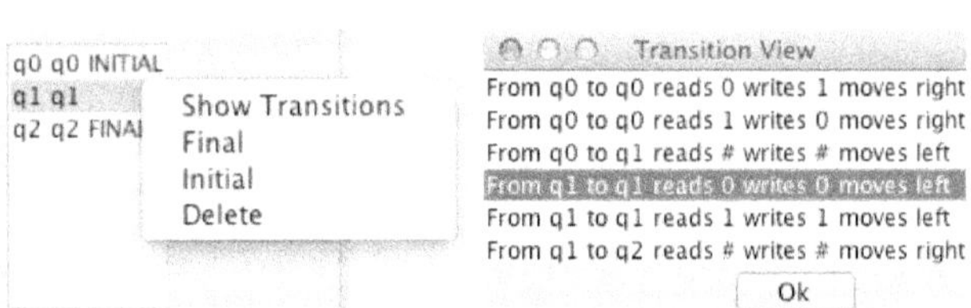

Figure 7: The state and the transition list windows

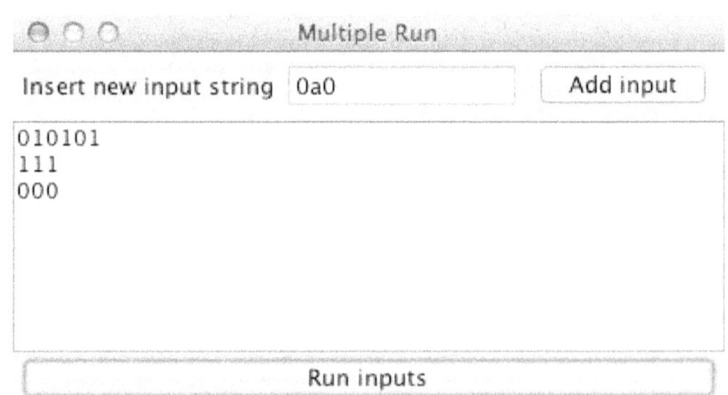

Figure 9: The multiple input accessible execution

- The new student was more used to utilize a Braille keyboard device than a screen reader software. This implied that all the features of our application that were based on the general-purpose screen reader (such as, for instance, the open and save items of the `File` menu) were not available anymore.

- The first-year student was not so comfortable with the English language (indeed, at our university the students are only assumed to take the English course before the end of the three-year program).

4.1 Accessible JFLAP (version 2)

The language problem was quite easily solved by making use of a variation of the `FreeTTS` library, called `MLFreeTTs`, which is a multi-language version of the original text-to-speech system [1]. Currently, `MLFreeTTS` supports both English and Italian, but it should be possible to extend it to other languages (see the next section). Moreover, in order to let the user decide which language has to be used, we utilized the internationalization feature of the Java language.

The problem of the Braille device could have been solved by managing the output of the application in order to send it directly to the Braille keyboard. However, it is clear that such a solution would have been specific for the device used by the student: a different device would have required a modification of the source code. As a consequence, we decided to further modify the accessible JFLAP application in order to make it dependent only on the ad hoc screen reader. This implied a substantial reprogramming of the application, since all the operations (such as file opening and saving) that were directly managed by the general-purpose screen reader had to be recoded in order to be managed by our ad hoc screen reader. On the other hand, such a solution also solved the platform dependency problem, since the entire application (which is written in Java) is now platform-independent. Of course, in order to not interfere with the JFLAP application, the general-purpose screen reader has now to be deactivated before launching the accessible JFLAP.

4.2 Validation results

Once again we tried to validate the accessibility of our application by asking the first-year blind student to develop three very simple TMs. It is worth noting that, due to logistic reasons, we had to perform this experiment with a version of the application in which the execution features were not yet implemented: in other words, the student could define the machines without testing them. Even in this case, however, the results were quite satisfying, since the student could develop the three machines. One of them was correct, another one was almost correct (apart from the fact that the head was not positioned to the beginning of the output string), and the last one contained a very simple error that would have been certainly corrected if the execution modes had been available.

5. FUTURE DIRECTIONS

In this paper, we have described an accessible version of the well-known JFLAP software, which allows blind students to develop and test TMs in cooperation with other sighted students. We have also presented some quite satisfactory preliminary validation results that, in our opinion, support the following future action plan (in order of difficulty).

- It is essential to validate our software in a more extensive way. The TMs are such a simple model of computation that we think this can be done not only by referring to computer science students but to any blind user who is interested to learn this model of computation (such as, for instance, philosophy students).

- One of the main goal of our project was to make the accessible application as much similar as possible to the original one, in order to allow a blind student to cooperate with other sighted students. It is now time to validate our tool from a cooperation point of view, by letting pairs of students (one blind and one sighted) work on it.

- We focused our attention on TMs. However, JFLAP is a very powerful tool for experimenting with many other models of computation. It is then natural to plan to extend the accessibility features to this other models.

- So far, the accessible JFLAP is available in English and in Italian. Of course, it would be nice to add support for a language other than these two (after all, JFLAP has been downloaded by people in 161 of the 193 countries in the world). This is not a trivial task as it requires a lexicon for the new language as well as various statistical data about it: however, the `MLFreeTTS` system should make this goal reasonably attainable.

6. ACKNOWLEDGMENTS

This research was partially supported by funds of the "DISCO" PRIN National Research Project. The authors are very grateful to the developers of JFLAP, who made the source of this excellent tool freely available.

7. REFERENCES

[1] F. Battaglia. *MLFreeTTS*. Available at `visilab.unime.it`.

[2] E. Bergman and E. Johnson. **Towards accessible human-computer interaction**. *Advances in human-computer interaction*, 5, 87–113, 1995.

[3] A.W. Black and K.A. Lenzo. **Flite: a small fast run-time synthesis engine**. *Proc. ISCA Workshop on Speech Synthesis*, 2001.

[4] R.F. Cohen, A. Meacham, and J. Skaff. **Teaching graphs to visually impaired students using an active auditory interface**. *Bull. SIGCSE*, 38, 279–282, 2006.

[5] M.E. Califf, M. Goodwin, and J. Brownell. **Helping him see: guiding a visually impaired student through the computer science curriculum**. *Proc. SIGCSE*, 444–448, 2008.

[6] C. Jayant, M. Renzelmann, D. Wen, S. Krisnandi, R.E. Ladner, and D. Comden, **Automated Tactile Graphics Translation: In the Field** *Proc. SIGACCESS*, 75–82, 2007.

[7] JFLAP. Available at `www.cs.duke.edu/csed/jflap`

[8] Oracle SDN. *Java SE Desktop Accessibility*. Available at `java.sun.com/javase/technologies`

[9] Freedom Scientific. *Jaws for Windows. Quick start guide*. Available at `www.freedomscientific.com`.

[10] S.H. Rodger and T.W. Finley. *JFLAP: An Interactive Formal Languages and Automata Package* Jones & Bartlett Publishers, 2006.

[11] M. Sipser. *Introduction to the Theory of Computation (2nd ed.)*. Massachusetts Institute of Technology, 2006.

[12] M. Stallmann, S. Balik, R. Rodman, S. Bahram, M. Grace, and S. High **ProofChecker: An Accessible Environment for Automata Theory Correctness Proofs**. *Proc. ITICSE*, 48–52, 2007.

[13] A.M. Turing. **On Computable Numbers, with an Application to the Entscheidungsproblem**. *Proceedings of the London Mathematical Society*, 42, 230–265, 1936.

[14] Università deli Studi di Pisa. *Gara nazionale di programmazione della machine di Turing*. Available at `mdt.unipi.it`.

[15] W. Walker, P. Lamere, and P. Kwok. **FreeTTS: a performance case study**. SMLI TR-2002-114. Sun Microsystems, 2002.

[16] W. Walker, P. Lamere, and P. Kwok. *FreeTTS*. Available at `freetts.sourceforge.net`

[17] F. Winberg and J. Bowers. **Assembling the Senses: Towards the Design of Cooperative Interfaces for Visually Impaired Users**. *Proc. CSCW*, 332–341, 2004.

Toward an Emergent Theory of Broadening Participation in Computer Science Education

David C. Webb
University of Colorado at Boulder
249 UCB
Boulder, CO 80309
+1 (303) 492-0306
dcwebb@colorado.edu

Alexander Repenning
University of Colorado at Boulder
430 UCB
Boulder, CO 80309
+1 (303) 492-1349
ralex@cs.colorado.edu

Kyu Han Koh
University of Colorado at Boulder
430 UCB
Boulder, CO 80309
+1 (303) 495-0357
kohkh@colorado.edu

ABSTRACT

A fundamental challenge to computer science education is the difficulty of broadening participation of women and underserved communities. The idea of game design and game programming as an activity to introduce children at an early age to computational thinking in a motivational way is quickly gaining momentum. A pedagogical approach called Project First has allowed the Scalable Game Design project to reach a large group of middle schools students including a large percentage of female (45%) and underrepresented (48%) students. With over 4000 students in inner city, remote rural, and Native American communities Scalable Game Design has investigated the impact on students' interest level of pedagogical approaches employed by teachers such as mediation and scaffolding. Findings suggest strong gender effects based on classroom scaffolding approaches. For instance, girls are substantially less likely to be motivated through scaffolding based on direct instruction. Conversely, guided discovery scaffolding approaches are highly motivating to the point where they can even overcome other negative predictors such as small girls to boys class participation ratios. This paper introduces the project, discusses different scaffolding approaches and presents data connecting gender specific motivational levels with scaffolding approaches.

Categories and Subject Descriptors

K.3.2 [**Computers and Education**]: Computers and Information Science Education – *pedagogical approaches, gender differences.*

General Terms

Measurement, Experimentation, Human Factors.

Keywords

Student interest, guided discovery, teacher-directed instruction.

1. Introduction

One of the central questions still being asked by computer science educators is whether instructional experiences should start with programming techniques (e.g., loops, if-then-else statements, etc.) stressing notions of program control before moving to the design of projects, or visa-versa. Of course, while some knowledge of programming methods is required to design interesting programs, what is the differential impact on student motivation of a more directive approach compared to a guided discovery approach? Results from the implementation of a game and simulation design curriculum suggest instruction incorporating a more guided discovery approach may address a motivation gap that we identified between middle school girls and boys.

Permission to make digital or hard copies of all or part of this work for personal or classroom use is granted without fee provided that copies are not made or distributed for profit or commercial advantage and that copies bear this notice and the full citation on the first page. To copy otherwise, or republish, to post on servers or to redistribute to lists, requires prior specific permission and/or a fee.
SIGCSE'12, February 29–March 3, 2012, Raleigh, North Carolina, USA.
Copyright 2012 ACM 978-1-4503-1098-7/12/02...$10.00.

The Scalable Game Design project [1] context in which this study took place involved the implementation of instructional units to support student design of games and science simulations using AgentSheets [2], as a way to motivate student interest in computer science courses and careers. To broaden the participation of middle school, we recruited teachers and schools in diverse settings, such as urban, remote rural and Native American communities, including schools serving significant proportions of low-income students. Embedded in existing computing education and science, technology, engineering and mathematics (STEM) courses, the project curriculum introduces students to computational thinking (CT) through game design and then advances to STEM simulation design (e.g., forest fire, predator-prey models, etc.). Teacher participation was supported by a two-week summer institute completed prior to classroom implementation of game and simulation design units.

High levels of interest by teachers resulted in rapid project diffusion, as the proposed goal of reaching 1120 students in 3 years was exceeded in the first implementation semester and is estimated to reach over 5000 students by the end of the project.

The integration of the curriculum into existing courses resulted not only in very high participation by female (45%) and underrepresented minority students (48%) in terms of course enrollment, but also high levels of motivation, as expressed by students' interest in taking another game design class: 74% of boys, 64% of girls (100% for some schools); 71% of white, 69% of minority students.

However, further analysis of student motivation with respect to gender ratios and the manner in which teachers implemented design units revealed emergent factors influencing student interest. This paper outlines the relationship of these factors and the potential contribution of a pedagogical theory of broadening student participation in K-12 computer science education.

2. Conceptual Framework

Improving students' interests in computer science education will require different approaches than the current set of middle grades options where students are exposed to business software and Internet use. Problems with the computer science pipeline extend into US high schools that typically offer Advanced Placement (AP) courses to represent the CS discipline. This type of curriculum is usually focused on programming, and fails to provide motivating applications. Courses of this nature do not attract many students and are even less successful in attracting women and minorities [3]. Even though there has been a modest increase in CS majors since 2009 [4], the rapid decline in student interest over the past decade leaves the number of CS majors at half the level of its peak in 2004. In spite of the recent national attention given to STEM education, computer science is rarely included as part of the national discourse. Fortunately, curricular responses to this *Computer Education Problem*[1] are already in play [5]. However, because of the systemic nature of the problem a revision to curriculum will be a necessary but insufficient response. We would argue that a renewed vision for computer science pedagogy may be a more critical part of the solution to the problem.

Our proposed vision for CS pedagogy, focuses on the differences between "our project-first" and "more traditional principals first" approaches. Our pedagogical approach allows students to learn the necessary CT principles just-in-time. The fundamental idea of the Project-first approach can be illustrated through what we call the *Zones of Proximal Flow* (ZPF), which combines Csikszentmihalyi's notion of Flow [6] with Vygotsky's notion of the Zone of Proximal Development (ZPD) [7]. Flow is an ideal condition for learning, and illustrates the importance of attending to the affordances and limitations of particular forms of mediation, as well as the need for social and technical scaffolding to advance learning. The ZPD can be understood as an orchestration of participation in a rich set of carefully designed practices where forms of assistance and tool use are strategically employed.

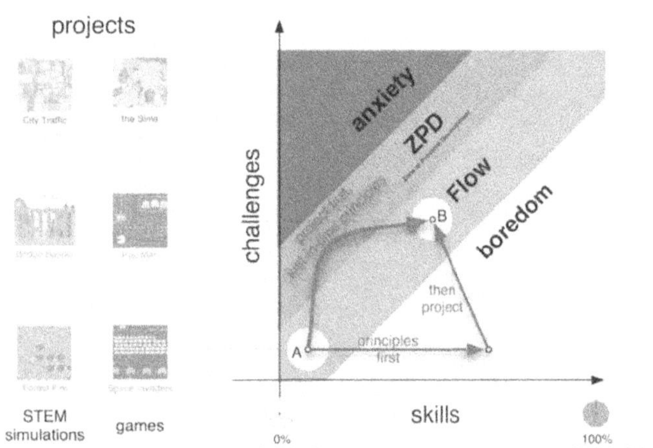

Figure 1. The Zones of Proximal Flow, a combination of Vygotzky's Zone of Proximal Development and Csikszentmihalyi's Flow.

[1] Defined here as the systemic challenge to improved computer science education. With all due respect, we acknowledge the similarities between the Computer Education Problem and Jim Kaput's [8] articulation of The Algebra Problem, "...the intolerably poor outcomes of our highly dysfunctional, late, abrupt, isolated, and superficial approach to school algebra, and our collective inability to move beyond it." (p. 2).

In the *Zones of Proximal Flow* diagram in Figure 1, the horizontal axis represents students' computational thinking (CT) skills and the vertical axis represents the level of the design challenge that would be intrinsic to a certain game or STEM simulation. CT skills are measured through a Computational Thinking Pattern Analysis (CTPA), which utilizes principles of latent semantic analysis to identify programmed computational thinking patterns [9]. As student acquisition of skills advances in response to the challenges, an ideal path in the flow region would progress from the origin to the upper right.

Within this diagram, pedagogical approaches can now be described as instructional trajectories connecting a skill/challenge starting point (A) with destination point (B) in the Zones of Proximal Flow diagram. In many traditional CS education models, a *principles-first* approach would introduce students to a number of concepts such as AI search algorithms that may, or may not, be relevant for future projects. At some later stage, students receive the challenge of making a project such as a Pacman-like game.

The acquisition of skills without the context of concrete challenges is not a bad pedagogical model, especially at the undergraduate CS level, but it runs the risk of seeming irrelevant, hence boring, for a broader audience of younger students if it does not go hand-in-hand with project based approaches [10]. This assertion is consistent with the Flow model and with our own observations in classrooms. Instead of decoupling the acquisition of principles and the applications of these principles to a project, the project-first approach combines *just-in-time CT skill acquisition* with *application* to produce a tangible artifact.

This project-first approach allows students with less experience and expertise to engage in practices and use tools otherwise not generally available to them. In restructuring computing education in ways that ratchet up the possibilities of zones of proximal flow to emerge, instances of unrealized learning will be minimized. The navigation of the skill/challenges space can be supported by teachers through different scaffolding approaches discussed in the next two sections.

2.1 Teacher-Directed Instruction

Teacher-Directed Instruction (direct instruction) is an approach where scaffolding is oriented toward an adult-defined endpoint or goal and, thus, provides limited opportunities to draw on students' repertoires of practice, or the cultural and knowledge toolkit that students develop across their learning trajectories. In a number of instances, the scaffolding can take on a form of hypermediation [11] in which excessive, non-strategic, and unnecessary assistance impedes rather than supports the learning goal. Teachers might use online tutorials in a lockstep fashion with all students expected to proceed together one step at a time to maintain control of the classroom. Rigidly following a tutorial with no room for deviation not only affects levels of engagement and motivation, but also student ownership, as they have little opportunity to embellish or personalize their game or simulation.

The result is a collection of practically identical artifacts for which there is no significant degree of ownership for students. This type of scaffolding may be good for introduction of something new to novices in the form of explicit instruction cases where game design is used in non-elective classes and where student's background and interest may vary widely or in classrooms with a large numbers of students and short class periods. In other words this can still be appropriate when game design is used in non-elective classes, or classrooms with large numbers of students.

2.2 Guided Discovery

When scaffolding is implemented as guided discovery, that is, when forms and degree of mediation are regulated to provide just enough assistance to support students' mastery of CT concepts, students tend to remain in the flow zone. In line with the concept of the Zones of Proximal Flow, the instructional trajectory organizes students' present activity in ways that build future psychological functions [12], including computational thinking. Instead of focusing on prescriptive steps explaining how to use the tool, teachers set more general goals for building the same game, but include discussions of why and how something should be done. Guided discovery still includes bits of formal instruction, but teacher regulation of mediation provides students more freedom to explore design options. Students' ability to personalize their design contributes to student ownership, which in turn could bolster levels of motivation.

3. Method

The project discussed in this paper was designed to investigate the potential impact on the IT workforce by stimulating interest in computer science at the middle school level. The main goal of this project is to increase opportunities for computer science education in public schools by motivating and educating students about computer science through game design starting at the middle school level. The strategy to maximize exposure includes the integration of computer science education into existing required courses such as exploratory wheels offered at most middle schools. Middle schools are excellent places for increasing and broadening the participation in computer science especially in regions where extracurricular options (e.g. after-school programs, summer camps) are financially problematic. To serve a wide spectrum of communities, we work with teachers and schools from urban, rural, suburban and remote/tribal regions. An important goal is to develop local resources and capacity for sustainability through the involvement of IT students from local community colleges.

The primary evaluation question for the project was to monitor the impact of the game and simulation design experience on students' attitudes and dispositions towards computer-based design experiences, computer classes, and related future pursuits. Data were collected before the unit and after the unit, creating matched pre and post data for each student. For the purposes of this paper, we focus on the following data: 1) students' self-reported interest in similar experiences, 2) gender ratios for each teacher, and 3) observation of teacher practice.

3.1 Classroom Implementation

During the first year of the project, most teachers recruited into the project had not implemented a game design unit with their students. Teachers participated in a one-week summer institute to learn the interface and complete the activities they would use with their students. These institutes and game design units stressed, implicitly at first, an approach that focuses immediately on making a complete game project. For instance, a teacher starting an activity would jump into making a game project with the student in the first hour of instruction even if the students had no background in programming whatsoever.

For the purposes of this report, it is important to recognize that the first year of the Scalable Game Design (SGD) project was the initial implementation of this software and design-oriented curriculum approach for most teachers. Issues encountered with the first implementation of a technology related unit could include problems with the school network, the need to debug and troubleshoot errors encountered during class, and teachers' limited awareness of potential student difficulties.

In Year 2 teachers were asked to extend the game design unit beyond Frogger, and have students design at least one more game (e.g., Pacman, Space Invaders) which required the programming of more advanced computational thinking patterns such as collaborative diffusion and choreography. Many of the teachers also implemented a unit in which students designed a math/science simulation (e.g., ant foraging, predator-prey ecosystem, etc). The duration between the administration of the pre- and post-unit surveys in Year 2 was, therefore, longer and the programming content was more sophisticated compared to Year 1.

After students completed their games they uploaded their program to a Scalable Game Design Arcade (SGDA). This student product repository allows students to play and download any uploaded game. Students can also post feedback to students who designed games, through comments and ratings.

3.2 Participant Demographics

During the Year 1 administration of the student motivation surveys, we collected 2,371 pre-unit responses and 1,299 post-unit responses. From the overall set we filtered out responses in which the student did not identify their teacher, reducing the respective sets to 2,070 pre-unit and 1,210 post-unit surveys. Using a simple matching of student initials, teacher, and birth date, we reduced the set of data to 894 matched pairs of pre and post unit responses (which is 43.8% of all pre-unit responses) from 13 middle grades teachers. Some teachers' data were not included here since they only administered the pre-unit survey and neglected to administer the post-unit survey before students moved onto a different course. In addition to these reasons, student numbers reported here do not represent all students who completed the Scalable Game Design units since participation in the administration of the surveys was also dependent on parental consent.

Of these 907 matched responses from the Year 1 administration of the student motivation surveys, 47.8% of the responses were from girls and 52.2% were from boys. With respect to self-reported ethnicity, 53.2% were White, 43.0% Hispanic or Latina/o, 13.5% Black, 10.5% Native American, and 6.2% Asian/Pacific Islander. This method of collecting ethnicity was aligned with the census and the new federal requirements from the U.S. Department of Education, therefore these percentages represent a duplicate count for some students. Students' grade level was 48% 6th grade, 29% 7th grade, and 22% 8th grade.

During the Year 2 administration of the student motivation surveys, by mid-February 2011 we had collected 1,241 pre-unit responses and 885 post-unit responses. Using a simple matching of student initials, teacher, and birth date, we reduced the set of data to 544 matched pairs of pre and post unit responses (which is 43.8% of all pre-unit responses). At the time the post-unit survey data were collected, teachers were still completing a unit and had yet to administered post-unit surveys to their students. (For the sake of comparison, by mid April we had collected 2,140 pre-unit and 1460 post-unit surveys.)

Of the responses for the Year 2 administration of the post-unit student motivation surveys, 526 responses from 13 teachers remained after similar filtering and matching procedures used for Year 1 data. 44.3% of the responses were from girls and 55.7%

were from boys. With respect to self-reported ethnicity, 52.3% of were White, 43.3% Hispanic or Latina/o, 15.9% Black, 11.4% Native American, and 6.5% Asian/Pacific Islander. In comparison to Year 1, the ethnic distribution in Year 2 showed slight increases in participation by Black and Native American students. Students' grade level was 35.7% 6th grade, 37.2% 7th grade, and 24.3% 8th grade. With respect to their reported primary language in the home 81.6% spoke English as their first language, and 18.4% spoke Spanish or some other language.

3.3 Classroom Observations

As part of the support provided to teachers, the evaluation and design team visited most of the classrooms during the initial and subsequent iterations of implementing game design and STEM simulation units. During SGD planning meetings, we discussed and documented the observed practices of teachers and consequently developed a crude categorization scheme for pedagogy that identified teacher practice as primarily teacher-directed or guided discovery. In a few instances of limited classroom visitations, we used teachers' self-reported Lesson Log data and student products to determine the extent to which students were simply following instructions in related tutorials or if they were given opportunities to develop products demonstrating allowances for student creativity and ownership (e.g., opportunities to adapt methods or design their own game).

4. Results

As part of the student motivation survey given after students completed game and simulation design units, students were asked to respond to the statement, "I want to take another game design course." Students reported their interest using a four point Likert scale ranging from Strongly Disagree to Strongly Agree. Using the matched data from all survey responses, we disaggregated counts of boys and girls for each teacher and found the percentage of girls and boys who responded Agree or Strongly Agree to the statement. In addition to the total number of responses per teacher, we also found the ratio of girls to boys for each teacher.

4.1 Year 1 Comparisons

As shown in Table 1, responses for Year 1 data show the majority of girls and boys were interested in taking another game design

Table 1: Percent of boys and girls interested in taking another game design class by teacher, number of students, and ratio of boys to girls in Year 1 survey group.

TEACHER	GIRLS	BOYS	N	RATIO (G : B)
A	50%	71%	134	51 : 49
B	77%	91%	74	41 : 59
C	88%	90%	52	62 : 38
D	63%	77%	114	47 : 53
E	63%	94%	35	49 : 51
F	75%	65%	35	54 : 46
G	67%	86%	10	30 : 70
H	50%	57%	30	53 : 47
I	71%	80%	58	43 : 57
J	85%	85%	65	40 : 60
K	68%	71%	178	39 : 61
L	59%	64%	91	64 : 36
M	28%	80%	18	44 : 56
Average	65%	78%	894	

class. The mean percent of students who were interested in taking another game design class, using teacher as the unit of analysis, was 65% of girls and 78% of boys (this difference in means was statistically significant at the $p < 0.05$ level). Out of 13 teachers, 11 groups of students showed a greater interest among boys, one teacher's group showed greater interest among girls, and one group showed equal interest between boys and girls. With respect to enrollment ratios per teacher, eight teachers had a boy-to-girl ratio favoring boys and five teachers had a gender ratio favored girls.

An interesting relationship that also emerged in the Year 1 data was found among teachers who had boy-to-girl ratios with large differences favoring boys (see last column for teachers B, G, I, J, K & M). Four of these teachers also had differences in student interest in future game design class favoring boys (i.e., B, G, I & M). This pattern suggested that student enrollment ratios could have a differential effect on student interest. Two other teachers in this group (i.e., K and J) also had enrollment ratios favoring boys without the same differences in interest.

Of the two teachers K and J, we observed that Teacher J demonstrated a guided discovery approach with students, which we surmised could be a possible factor in the negligible difference in interest between boys and girls (in spite of the 40:60 girl-to-boy gender ratio that would typically suggest a potential difference in interest favoring boys). Although we recognize that data for 13 teachers should be interpreted with caution, we continued to monitor this relationship in the Year 2 data.

4.2 Year 2 comparisons

In the second year of the project we continued to administer student motivation surveys to students before and after completion of a multi-week unit. In contrast to Year 1, the unit activities involved the design of one or more games and a STEM simulation during the 2010-11 school year. Typical simulations included a

Table 2: Percent of boys and girls interested in taking another game design class by teacher, number of students, and ratio of boys to girls in Year 2 survey group.

TEACHER	GIRLS	BOYS	N	RATIO (G : B)
N	44%	73%	152	36 : 64
O	67%	93%	24	38 : 63
P	71%	70%	37	46 : 54
Q	76%	86%	93	53 : 47
R	50%	50%	14	29 : 71
S	38%	57%	31	55 : 45
T	100%	67%	9	67 : 33
U	67%	86%	15	47 : 53
V	0%	82%	20	40 : 60
W	71%	88%	15	13 : 87
X	85%	90%	47	57 : 43
Y	100%	70%	12	17 : 83
Z	79%	75%	28	46 : 54
AA	52%	55%	29	38 : 62
Average	64%	74%	526	

Note: To protect teacher confidentiality teacher labels for Year 1 data do not correspond to teacher labels for Year 2 data.

viral outbreak, a forest fire simulation, and predator-prey models. Similar to the Year 1 post-unit survey, students were asked if they wanted to take another game design course after completing the unit.

The same filtering and matching methods used with Year 1 data were applied with the Year 2 data, and any data entries that did not have a pre/post match were discarded. This reduced the set of all responses from 2033 combined responses to 1052 responses (i.e., 526 matched).

As with Year 1 results, as shown in Table 2 the majority of boys and girls in almost all classes were interested in taking another game design class (see Table 8). In contrast to Year 1 however, these differences in means (64% girls v. 74% boys) were not statistically significant.

In addition, the exclusion of one teacher (V) results in a mean difference of only 5% (69% girls v. 74% boys).

Out of data for 14 teachers, 9 groups showed a greater interest among boys, 4 groups showed greater interest among girls, and one class showed equal interest between girls and boys. The summary means combined with the distribution of survey results suggests that Year 2 saw a greater balance in interest between boys and girls. Similar to Year 1 results, large differences favoring boys might be attributed to either a greater boy-to-girl ratio (e.g., teachers N, O, U, V, & W) coupled with over-reliance on direct instruction (e.g., teachers N and V). The influence of gender differences on students' continued interest appears to be ameliorated by teachers who demonstrated pedagogical approaches characterized by guided discovery (i.e., teachers R, Z, AA). Figure 2 offers a visual comparison of gender differences in student interest in taking similar courses. The results from Table 2 appear as a double bar graph for each teacher. It is worth noting the relative positive interest across all groups regardless of gender, as well as the relative similarity in interest between genders for several of the teachers (e.g., P, Q, R, X, Z, AA).

4.3 Students' written responses

Included in the post-unit student motivation surveys were open-ended prompts requiring students to submit a written response. To further analyze students' experiences with the game and simulation design units, we coded student responses to an open response prompt that asked students: *How did this experience make you think differently about ways to use computers?*

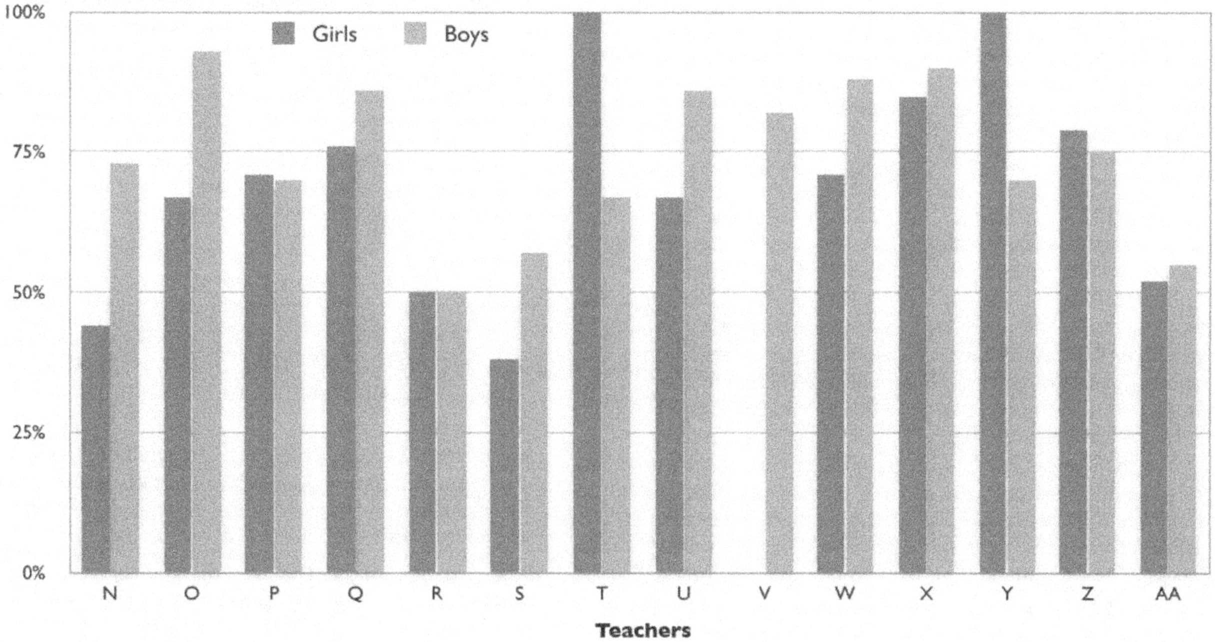

Figure 2: Gender distribution of student interest by teacher: Student interest in taking another game design class.

From a sample of 425 responses to this prompt, we coded responses as positive, neutral, or negative. For this sample, 65% (n_{Male}=152, n_{Female}=124) were coded as a positive response, 21% (n_{Male}=37, n_{Female}=54) were neutral, 7% (n_{Male}=17, n_{Female}=14) were interpreted as negative, and 6% (n_{Male}=7, n_{Female}=20) of the responses were blank. A sample of responses for each of these categories is included below.

4.3.1 *Positive statements*

Positive attributions of students' self-reported experience included new insights, recognition of computer processes, descriptions of how computers could be used to support design, and increased self-confidence. The brief list included below is representative of the types of responses coded as positive.

- *Now I know what computer programmers do. I never knew you could do this stuff.*
- *I never thought that computers could be not for super smart people but now i know you don't have to be super smart!*
- *It made me think if this then this*
- *Agent Sheets makes me want to make more complex games and take more computer classes.*
- *It made me think that I don't have to use other people's games on the computer i can just create my own.*
- *Agent Sheets opened up a new process in using the computer, using cause and effect to make an action.*
- *It made me feel less hopeless with computers*

With respect to students' interest in future engagement in similar activities, we assert that self-reported new learning and a sense of increased internal locus of control [13] can serve as powerful and enduring motivators supporting future pursuit of computer-based design.

4.3.2 Neutral statements

For a statement to be coded as neutral, the response needed to include an expression of prior similar experience or no change in the ways computers work.

- *It didn't really make me think differently about ways to use the computer. I already know a lot about website design.*
- *I don't think it made me think differently about computers because it was just a computer program that teaches us how to create games... that was pretty much all that it did.*

4.3.3 Negative statements

Negative attribution of the experience suggested that the student may be less inclined to pursue future computer courses or career pathways. Although we don't necessarily see individual recognition of challenge or identity development as negative, per se, it is negative with respect to the CS pipeline.

- *I use to think computers were so easy, but not no more [sic].*
- *That I should not make computer games for living.*

When students were asked how the experience changed their understanding of computers, the percentage of positive attributions for a sample of participating students was approximately the same percentage of students who were interested in taking another game design class (i.e., 65%).

5. Discussion

When comparing students' interests in taking another game design class to gender ratio enrollments in courses, an intriguing pattern emerged. When girl-to-boy enrollment ratios for a teacher approached 40:60, there appeared to be a notable gender difference, favoring boys, with respect to students interested in taking another game design class. This gender difference may be exacerbated when the observed instruction is teacher directed and highly prescriptive. In some cases, these gender differences in student interest were reduced or completely eliminated for teachers who utilized a guided discovery approach. Given the limited number of teachers and classrooms that have been used as the basis for this conjecture, further research at greater scale is warranted that can examine the effects of pedagogy on gender differences towards computer science education.

In general, two thirds of participating students had positive responses to both the "course taking" prompt and the "understanding computers" prompt. To ensure broader participation with respect to girls, pedagogy may have a stronger impact on student attitudes. Such findings have implications for giving greater attention to pre-service education opportunities in computer science and professional development opportunities to support student ownership, creativity and access to the zone of proximal flow.

6. ACKNOWLEDGMENTS

This work is supported by the National Science Foundation under Grant Numbers DLR-0833612 and IIP-0848962. Any opinions, findings, and conclusions or recommendations expressed in this material are those of the authors and do not necessarily reflect the views of the National Science Foundation.

7. REFERENCES

[1] A. Repenning, D. C. Webb, A. Ioannidou. 2010. Scalable Game Design and the Development of a Checklist for Getting Computational Thinking into Public Schools. *The 41st ACM Technical Symposium on Computer Science Education* (SIGCSE 2010). Milwaukee, WI: ACM Press. doi:10.1145/1734263.1734357

[2] A. Repenning. 2011. Making Programming more Conversational. In *Proceedings of the IEEE Symposium on Visual Languages and Human-Centric Computing*. Los Alamitos, CA. doi:10.1109/VLHCC.2011.6070398

[3] National Science Foundation, Division of Science Resources Statistics. May 2004. *Women, Minorities, and Persons with Disabilities in Science and Engineering*. Arlington, VA NSF 04-317.

[4] S. Zweben. 2011. Undergraduate CS Degree Production Rises; Doctoral Production Steady: 2009-2010 Taulbee Survey. *Computing Research News,* 23(3): 6-21.

[5] J. Goode. 2010. Connecting K-16 curriculum & policy: making computer science engaging, accessible, and hospitable for underrepresented students. *Science Education,* 41(2): 22-26.

[6] M. Csikszentmihalyi. 1990. *Flow: The Psychology of Optimal Experience*. New York: Harper Collins Publishers.

[7] L. S. Vygotsky. 1978. *Mind in Society: The Development of Higher Psychological Processes*. Cambridge, Massachusetts: Harvard University Press.

[8] J. J. Kaput & M. Blanton. 1999. "Algebraic reasoning in the context of early mathematics: Making it implementable on a massive scale," Paper presented at the Annual Meeting of the American Educational Research Association, Montreal, Canada. Retrieved December 6, 2011 from http://www.eric.ed.gov/PDFS/ED441663.pdf

[9] A. Basawapatna, K. H. Koh, A. Repenning, D. C. Webb, K. Marshall. 2011. Recognizing Computational Thinking Patterns. In *Proceedings of the 42nd ACM technical symposium on Computer science education*. Dallas, TX. doi:10.1145/1953163.1953241

[10] J. S. Krajcik and P. Blumenfeld. 2006. "Project-based Learning," in *The Cambridge Handbook of the Learning Sciences*, R. K. Sawyer, Ed. Cambridge: Cambridge University Press.

[11] K. Gutiérrez and L. Stone. 2002. "Hypermediating literacy activity: How learning contexts get reorganized," in *Contemporary Perspectives in Early Childhood Education*. vol. 2, O. Saracho and B. Spodek, Eds. Greenwich, Conn: Information Age Publishing, pp. 25-51.

[12] M. Cole. 1996. *Cultural psychology: A once and future discipline*. Cambridge, Mass.: Belknap Press of Harvard University Press.

[13] H. M. Lefcourt. 1966. Internal versus external control of reinforcement: A review. *Psychological Bulletin, 65*(4): 206–20. doi:10.1037/h0023116. PMID 5325292.

Exploring Formal Learning Groups and their Impact on Recruitment of Women in Undergraduate CS

Julie Krause
Colorado School of Mines
Golden, CO
+1 303-384-2465
jkrause@gmail.com

Irene Polycarpou
Colorado School of Mines
Golden, CO
+1 303-273-3462
ipolycar@mines.edu

Keith Hellman
Colorado School of Mines
Golden, CO
+1 303-273-3820
khellman@mines.edu

ABSTRACT
As percentages of women in computing jobs and university programs decline, recruiting and retaining women in the field of Computer Science (CS) becomes increasingly important. Undergraduate CS programs, and more specifically, introductory-level CS courses, offer an opportunity to introduce women to CS studies. Furthermore, learning experiences in introductory CS courses can be pivotal in shaping female students' perceptions of CS. Collaborative learning, in various forms, is an instructional construct that has been shown to be effective in recruiting and retaining women in undergraduate CS programs. In this paper we present an exploratory study on *formal learning groups* and their potential to attract and maintain female students' interest in CS studies.

Categories and Subject Descriptors
K.3.2 [**Computers and Education**]: Computer and Information Science Education– *Computer science education.*

General Terms
Design, Experimentation

Keywords
Computer science education, introduction to computer science, collaborative learning, formal learning groups, gender, women, recruitment, retention

1. INTRODUCTION
Representation of women in Computer Science (CS) degree programs is low at a national level. According to the most recent Taulbee Survey conducted by the Computing Research Association, females obtained 13.8% of CS degrees in 2010 [18].

The issue of low participation in the CS major is of particular concern at our University, Colorado School of Mines (CSM), a small engineering school, where approximately 13% of the undergraduate students enrolled in the CS program are female. Moreover, this percentage is lower than the percentage of students enrolled at CSM who are female, which is approximately 25%.

Permission to make digital or hard copies of all or part of this work for personal or classroom use is granted without fee provided that copies are not made or distributed for profit or commercial advantage and that copies bear this notice and the full citation on the first page. To copy otherwise, or republish, to post on servers or to redistribute to lists, requires prior specific permission and/or a fee.
SIGCSE'12, February 29–March 3, 2012, Raleigh, North Carolina, USA.
Copyright 2012 ACM 978-1-4503-1098-7/12/02...$10.00.

While percentages of women in CS-related careers and degree programs remain low, there is great need for women in the field. For example, having women in the workplace and academic environments promotes diversity. Diversity, particularly in a technical field, brings varied talents, contributions and perspectives, and increases creativity and innovation [7]. These all contribute to improved technology development. To increase the number of women in CS-related careers, more women must obtain CS degrees and recruitment/retention efforts must continue.

Students are drawn to CS based on positive early experiences [17]; therefore introductory-level courses in undergraduate CS degree programs offer the opportunity to recruit more women into the field and represent an environment in which efforts to retain women are critical. The use of group learning in various implementations has been shown to improve recruitment and retention of women in CS studies [4, 8, 11, 12, 13, 15]. At CSM we incorporate collaborative learning into our introductory CS course (CSCI 101) via formal learning groups [10]. This paper describes formal learning groups as they are used in our course, as well as a summary of students' perceptions of formal learning groups as related to students' intent to continue CS studies.

2. RECRUITMENT/RETENTION & COLLABORATIVE LEARING

2.1 Recruiting and Retaining Women in Undergraduate CS
Studies over the past two decades have shown that there are numerous factors contributing to the fact that women have a lower participation rate in CS than men, including women's perceptions that CS is intimidating, feelings of discouragement, and underestimation of their own abilities in science and math [5, 6, 7]. Another factor that has been identified as a cause for low numbers of women in CS is disinterest in the field due to its perceived lack of opportunities for social interaction [3, 5, 6, 7]. Given the prevalence of these factors, recruiting and retaining more women in CS may require instruction that promotes confidence and social opportunities for all students, particularly female students.

Instructional methods that have shown to be effective in recruiting women into and retaining women in CS programs include techniques that can be incorporated into introductory-level CS courses, such as presenting CS in meaningful real-world contexts [3], using activities that promote creativity [16], broadening the scope of introductory CS instruction beyond programming alone [1], and using group learning [8].

2.2 Collaborative Learning as a Recruiting and Retention Tool

The National Center for Women & Information Technology (NCWIT) identifies integration of collaborative learning in early curriculum as one of the key pedagogical practices for retaining undergraduate students in computing [14].

To understand motivations behind the use of collaborative learning in modern education, other types of learning goals must first be understood. In addition to *collaborative* learning in which students share learning goals, there are two other types of learning: *individualistic* learning in which students have their own goals and do not share goals with others, and *competitive* learning in which students work against one another to accomplish a goal that can only be reached by one (or only a few) student(s) [9, 10]. In *collaborative* learning, benefiting the self benefits others, whereas benefiting the self does not affect others or deprives others in individualistic and competitive learning, respectively [10]. When more students learn as a result of one student achieving a goal, there is a clear victory. Therefore, collaborative learning has advantages over individualistic and competitive learning.

Among collaborative learning constructs that have been shown to have success at retaining women in university-level CS studies are pair programming and peer-led team learning.

Results from studies conducted by Nagappan et al. [12] and McDowell et al. [11] showed that in introductory CS courses, more female students who participated in pair programming completed and passed those courses than those who did only individual programming. In addition, the study by McDowell et al. tracked students' majors after their first year and found that more female students in the pair programming group pursued CS-related majors (46% of the paired group vs. 11% of the non-paired group) [11].

In peer-led team learning, all students in a course are invited to attend a program where groups get together regularly (weekly, for example) and work on assigned problem-solving activities under the guidance of an undergraduate "peer leader" who is trained by and follows direction from the course instructor [15]. While there are differences between peer-led team learning and formal learning groups, such as the presence of one designated / trained team leader, and the fact that the sessions are optional rather than required for coursework, successful aspects of peer-led team learning may also benefit formal learning groups. Studies at eight universities of differing sizes and status (e.g., private vs. public), used peer-led team learning in CS courses over a period of about five years and evaluated its efficacy in retaining students in their CS programs [8]. Results of their evaluation were promising in that students had positive responses to the peer-led team learning experience, there was a significant improvement in retention of students in the course (i.e., completing the course; not necessarily retention in the CS major), and female students' grades in the course were significantly better if they were involved in peer-led team learning.

In-class collaborative learning is yet another approach that may be used to improve female participation in CS studies. Collaborative learning in the college classroom may take the form of single group problem-solving sessions or discussions. It may also take the form of formal learning groups in which students remain with the same group members over a period of multiple weeks [10]. Group assignments may be either graded or un-graded; to promote retention of female students in CS studies, it is recommended that students be given opportunities to collaborate on both graded and un-graded assignments [13]. The results of a study conducted by Chase & Okie [4] suggest that the use of formalized collaborative learning in the classroom can improve completion and pass rates for female students in an introductory CS course. Their course used cooperative learning groups simultaneously with peer instruction which is a construct that appears to be similar to peer-led team learning.

According to Barker et al. [2], incorporating collaborative environments into CS curricula "lead to the development of peer networks, better self-assessments of progress, greater retention in the major, and often, improved learning." (p. 155). Given that collaborative learning in the CS curriculum has the potential to address some of the well-known factors in low female involvement in CS, there is motivation to further explore collaborative learning as a means to improve recruitment and retention of female students in the CS program at CSM, as was intended by our study.

2.3 Formal Learning Groups

Formal learning groups, which we are investigating through our study, are a specific type of collaborative learning that has been used in college courses since before the 1990's. The prevalence of their use in CS courses is not currently known to be high, but they are being implemented in other fields.

Formal learning groups, as defined and outlined by Johnson, Johnson & Smith [10] offer the opportunity for students to work collaboratively with other students, under the guidance of an instructor, in the following manner:

- Group sessions may be problem-solving oriented or investigative, where students break up tasks to learn content or solve problems on their own and later teach one another what they have learned. This type of learning group is typically used to introduce specific content.
- The same groups of students work together over a period of time (e.g., several days to several weeks).
- A key role of the instructor when using formal learning groups is to guide students; the instructor is "uncovering the material with the students" rather than giving material directly to them, as in a traditional lecture format.
- "Positive interdependence," or the notion that students rely on one another's successes in order to succeed themselves, is important in the success of formal learning groups. Positive interdependence can be achieved by giving all students the same reward for the whole group's performance (e.g., awarding all students the same grade for their performance on a task as a group) or by giving all students the same goal to achieve (e.g., requiring all students to learn the same material).
- "Individual accountability," or a requirement that the performance of each individual in the group be assessed, helps to prevent single students from sitting out while other members of the group do the work, and helps to encourage all students to be engaged. Techniques for supporting individual accountability include calling on one student to respond for the group, and giving individual assessments where grades or other outcomes impact the group.

3. CSCI 101 AT CSM

Our investigation explores formal learning groups in the Introduction to Computer Science (CSCI 101) course at CSM, and their effects on recruiting and retaining women in CS. Formal learning groups have been used in the course since it was first introduced at CSM, which was in Fall 2010. Students who register for the course include CS majors as well as non-majors and students without a declared major. The course is offered every Fall and Spring semester. An estimated 200-400 students enroll in the course each academic year. Currently, classes have 40 to 60 students each. During Spring 2011 when our study was conducted, approximately 20% of the students enrolled in the course were female.

CSCI 101 is designed to provide an introduction to the field of CS, especially for students who are new to the field. The course incorporates instruction on a broad variety of CS concepts, as well as computer programming in Python. Enrollment in the course does not require any prior experience in computer programming. CSCI 101 incorporates formal learning groups as a primary instructional approach.

Formal learning group work in the course involves both problem-solving activities and sessions in which students teach one another concepts they have learned through individual out-of-class work (learning group assignments). Groups are comprised of roughly five students each. During each class period, students are presented with a learning group assignment and are given time to divide up problems among group members. Each group member is then responsible for investigating specific topics and completing related problems. Groups are encouraged to duplicate coverage on completion of problems between two or more students. A session in which group members teach one another and discuss their respective findings occurs during the beginning of the following class. As a motivation for students to be invested in teaching their peers, a portion of each student's course grade is dependent on their group members' performance on individually completed quizzes. Groups change approximately three to four times during the course. Currently, first-round learning groups are chosen at random and subsequent learning groups are "randomly assigned," but with the additional metrics that:

1. Groups with duplicate pairings from previous rounds are discouraged.
2. Randomized groups with a similar distribution of member ability levels, gauged from programming assignments and previous learning group scores, are favored.

As a result of the randomization, group formations typically include differing combinations of females and males, and CS majors and non-majors. Note that during the first two semesters of CSCI 101, including the semester in which data for this study were collected, there were upperclass CS majors taking the course due to a change in the CS program bulletin which allowed them to take CSCI 101 (15% of the students enrolled in Spring 2011 were upperclass CS majors). The presence of such students in the groups presented a different dynamic within the learning groups than is expected in subsequent semesters.

4. STUDY DESCRIPTION

Our exploratory study was designed to identify the impact of formal learning groups on female students in terms of their intent to pursue further studies in CS.

The investigation included the collection of self-reported data related to 1) students' change in perception of learning groups after participating in them throughout CSCI 101, 2) how students rank learning groups with respect to other learning methods utilized in the course, 3) students' change in intent to pursue CS studies, and 4) learning groups' impact on students' intent to study CS. Data collection entailed surveys, as well as individual interviews and focus groups.

4.1 Participants

All students registered in CSCI 101 during Spring 2011 (20 females and 82 males) were given the opportunity to volunteer to participate. Students were encouraged to participate via announcements during class. 15 female students and 61 male students completed both the pre-survey and the post-survey. All survey data reported in the results presented in this paper refer to the responses of these 76 individuals.

4.2 Survey Instruments

A pre-survey and post-survey were developed for the purpose of identifying changes from the beginning to the end of the semester in items such as students' intent to study CS and attitude toward formal learning groups. Additionally, students were surveyed at the end of the semester regarding their rank of learning groups among other instructional methods used in the course, and if/how learning groups had an impact on students' intent to study CS.

Surveys included Likert-type scale questions, yes/no questions, rank questions, and open-ended questions. The Likert-type scale questions represented a four-point scale with the following answers: strongly disagree, disagree, agree, and strongly agree (the "undecided" response was not provided to the students).

Exploratory surveys were conducted during the Fall 2010 semester for the purpose of improving survey questions' clarity.

4.3 Interviews and Focus Groups

Individual interviews and focus groups were conducted to obtain more detailed insights from students. Students were asked to discuss their perceptions of learning groups in CSCI 101, including their views on how learning groups compared to traditional learning methods, which aspects of learning groups they liked and disliked, and impacts learning groups may have had on their intent to study CS.

The interviews and focus groups were approximately 20 to 30 minutes long and were semi-structured; a set of questions were asked to guide the discussion, but participants were given the opportunity to speak openly and provide additional details.

The interview and focus group participants were selected at random. All female students were invited to participate in an interview or a focus group, and whether they were selected for an interview or focus group was random; a total of 12 female students participated in one or the other. The number of male students selected was chosen to match the number of female participants. For each gender, four interviews and two focus groups were conducted. The focus groups were intended to have four students each. Due to the absence of two male students, however, both male focus groups had only three students each.

5. RESULTS

Data were analyzed quantitatively, as well as qualitatively to obtain a greater depth of understanding of students' perceptions about formal learning groups. Since there were only 15 female students for which to analyze numerical data, our quantitative analysis includes descriptive statistics.

5.1 Change in Perception of Learning Groups

We measured students' perception of learning groups as "fun" at the beginning of the semester and then again at the end of the semester after students had experienced the learning groups. Students were asked to rate the following statement on a Likert-type scale on the pre- and post-surveys:

> "I will have fun (had fun) working in formal learning groups in CSCI 101."

Students were given a description of formal learning groups on the first day of the semester, prior to completing the pre-survey.

On average, students entered CSCI 101 with positive expectations that learning groups would be fun (> 1.5 on the scale of 0 to 3) and left the course with positive perceptions as well. Female students' ratings increased slightly after taking CSCI 101, while male students' ratings decreased slightly (see Table 1).

Table 1. Average responses, on a four-point Likert scale, where 0 is Strongly Disagree and 3 is Strongly Agree, regarding the statement "I will have fun (had fun) working in formal learning groups in CSCI 101."

	Before CSCI 101	After CSCI 101	Change
Females	1.53	1.87	0.33
Males	1.75	1.67	- 0.08
All Students	1.71	1.71	0.00

Table 2 shows the number and percentage of female students, male students, and all students combined, whose change in perception of learning groups as "fun" was negative, zero, or positive. More female students showed a positive change than showed a negative change, whereas fewer male students showed a positive change than a negative change.

Table 2. Students with negative, zero, and positive change in their opinion that learning groups would be / were fun.

	Negative Change	Zero Change	Positive Change
Females	3 (20.0%)	5 (33.3%)	7 (46.7%)
Males	19 (31.1%)	28 (45.9%)	14 (23.0%)
All Students	22 (28.9%)	33 (43.4%)	21 (27.6%)

5.2 Rank of Formal Learning Groups with Other Instructional Methods

After taking CSCI 101, students were asked to rank formal learning groups among four other instructional methods used in CSCI 101, two of which are traditional instructional methods (textbook and lecture), one of which is commonly used in CS instruction (programming), and one of which is less common and only took place a few times over the semester (playing/watching content-related computer games). The questions stated:

> "Rank the following in CSCI 101 in terms of **how much you learned** from each of them, on a scale of 1 to 5 where 1 is the one from which you learned the most and 5 is the one from which you learned the least:"
>
> "Rank the following in CSCI 101 in terms of **how much you enjoyed learning** from each of them, on a scale of 1 to 5 where 1 is the one you enjoyed the most and 5 is the one you enjoyed the least:"
>
> Choices: "Reading Textbook," "Participating in Learning Groups," "Observing Lecture," "Programming in Python," and "Playing/Watching Course-Specific Video Games"

40% of the female students ranked learning groups as the method from which they learned the most. This percentage is higher than the percentage of females who ranked learning groups as either 2nd, 3rd, 4th, or 5th. The same is also the case for ranking the instructional method from which they enjoyed learning the most. Figure 1 and Figure 2 show the percentages of students for each ranking (highest to lowest) regarding how much students learned from, and how much they enjoyed learning in, learning groups.

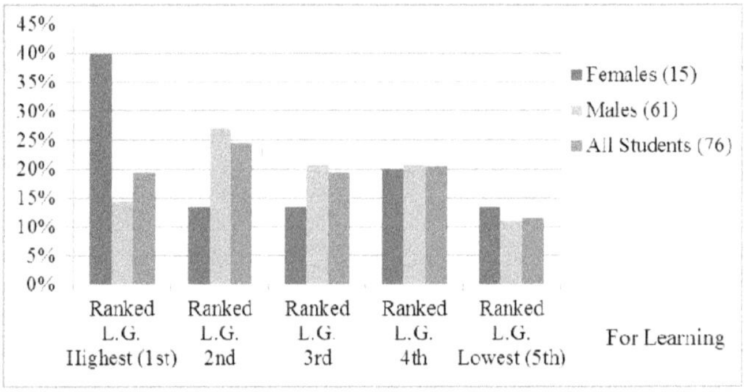

Figure 1. Percentage of students who ranked learning groups 1st through 5th among five instructional methods used in CSCI 101, in terms of *how much they learned* from each method.

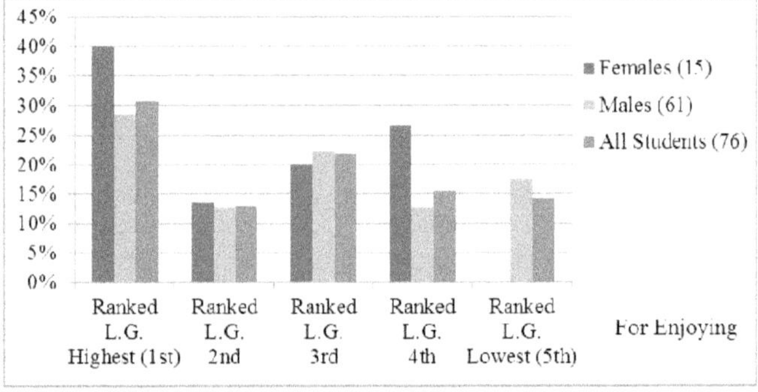

Figure 2. Percentage of students who ranked learning groups 1st through 5th among five instructional methods used in CSCI 101, in terms of *how much they enjoyed learning* from each method.

It should be noted that although 40% of female students and 19% percent of all students combined ranked "Participating in Learning Groups" as the method from which they *learned* the most (as shown in Figure 1), even more students (40% of females and 39% of all students combined) ranked "Reading Textbook" as the method from which they learned the most. Unlike a more traditional course, where reading assignments are given with the content subsequently recapitulated in lecture, the reading assignments in CSCI 101 are directly linked to questions in the learning group assignments. The high textbook ranking may be related to the fact that reading the text was an integral part of the learning group assignments.

When students were asked at the end of the semester (via surveys, interviews, or focus groups) how learning groups compared to traditional learning methods such as lectures and textbooks, students who reported in favor of learning groups indicated reasons such as:

- Feeling more comfortable participating in a small group than in front of a whole class (e.g., "It was easier to participate in a small group, that way like when you say something, not everyone's looking at you.")
- Experiencing additional motivation from having an impact on others (e.g., "I learn and work best when my peers are depending on me.")
- Gaining additional interactive instruction (e.g., "Sometimes [learning groups] were really helpful in allowing me to learn things that I didn't understand. Someone else would explain it to me in a different way than the book explains, and I'd grasp an understanding.")

Students who reported learning groups negatively in comparison to other learning methods indicated reasons such as:

- Having the potential for learning incorrectly (e.g., "If two people get the same question wrong, the whole group adopts a false understanding.")
- Possibility of having unproductive groups (e.g., "We always went off topic.")

5.3 Changes in Intent to Study CS

To determine whether changes had taken place in students' intent to study CS, we asked students via pre- and post-surveys to what extent they intended to pursue CS studies. Students were asked:

> "Are you considering further studies in CS in any of the categories below? If so, select all categories you are considering. If not, select 'None'."
>
> The provided categories were "Major in CS," "Minor or ASI (Area of Special Interest) in CS," "Taking additional CS courses without pursuing a CS major/minor/ASI," and "None."

Changes from the pre-survey and post-survey were noted for each student for each of the four categories. The category of strongest interest is the CS Major category.

While the majority of female students reported no change in their interest in majoring in CS, one female student who had not reported an interest in a CS Major prior to taking CSCI 101 did report an interest after taking CSCI 101, and no female students lost interest in a CS Major after taking CSCI 101 (see Table 3). The majority of male students also reported no change. There were an equal number of male students who showed a loss and a gain in interest to major in CS. Changes in whether a student indicated interest in a CS Major, for female students, male students, and all students combined, are outlined in Table 3.

Table 3. Students who gained interest in CS Major, retained interest in CS Major, retained no interest in CS Major, or lost interest in CS Major.

	Gained Interest in Major	Retained Interest in Major	Retained No Interest in Major	Lost Interest in Major
Females	1 (6.7%)	7 (46.7%)	7 (46.7%)	0 (0.0%)
Males	3 (4.9%)	36 (59.0%)	19 (31.1%)	3 (4.9%)
All Students	4 (5.3%)	43 (56.6%)	26 (34.2%)	3 (3.9%)

The high occurrence of students retaining the intent to major in CS may be partly due to the upperclass CS majors in the course.

5.4 Formal Learning Groups' Impact on Intent to Study CS

In a survey given at the end of the semester, students were asked the following question:

> "Did working in learning groups have any impact on your intent to pursue further studies in Computer Science? Please Explain."

Student responses were categorized as "no" (learning groups did not have impact on intent to study CS), and "yes" (learning groups did have impact on intent to study CS). Some responses were unclear or unanswered. Most female and male students indicated that learning groups did not have an impact on their intent to pursue additional CS studies. Table 4 summarizes responses for female students, male students, and all students combined.

Table 4. Student responses when asked if learning groups had an impact on intent to pursue further CS studies.

	Did Not Have Impact	Had Impact	Unanswered/ Unclear
Females	10 (66.7%)	2 (13.3%)	3 (20.0%)
Males	47 (77.0%)	8 (13.1%)	6 (9.8%)
All Students	57 (75.0%)	10 (13.2%)	9 (11.8%)

In examining the "yes" responses to determine whether students who reported an impact from learning groups experienced a positive or negative impact, those responses were further categorized in terms of positive vs. negative impact. We defined "positive" as an indication that the learning groups had a positive impact on the student's intent to study CS (i.e., the student had more interest in studying CS), and "negative" as an indication that the learning groups had a negative impact on the student's intent to study CS (i.e., the student had less interest in studying CS). Students primarily indicated that learning groups had a positive impact on their intent to pursue CS studies, although no specific themes emerged as to why.

Female students' responses: The explanations of the two female students who responded that learning groups had impacted their intent to study CS were both positive.

Positive explanations from female students were:

> "I got to hear my group members' thoughts on the computer science major and I liked what I heard."

"I enjoy computer science more now that I realize how interesting it can be - a lot of people in the groups do really cool things with their computers."

Male students' responses: Of the explanations of the eight male students who responded that learning groups had impacted their intent to study CS, four were positive, two were negative, and two were neither positive nor negative.

Examples of **positive** explanations from male students included:

"[I] realized how much fun I could have in a career working with other people interested in comp. sci."

"I liked working with other people who had the same major."

An example of a **negative** explanation from a male student was:

"Yes because I realize how little I know about computer science."

6. CONCLUSIONS AND FUTURE WORK

In this paper, we have presented the results of an exploratory study on students' perception of formal learning groups in CSCI 101 at CSM. The results of our study showed that many female students who took the course reported that they learned from and enjoyed formal learning groups. While there is not an indication that formal learning groups in CSCI 101 had a direct impact on female students' intent to pursue CS studies, students' reported perceptions of learning groups indicate that they generally had a positive impact. Students generally found learning groups fun and there were aspects of them that students reported as beneficial in their motivation to participate. To strengthen our findings and to answer questions that arose from our study, further investigation of formal learning groups in introductory CS courses is needed.

As part of our future research we plan to conduct studies on assessing the impact that specific learning group formations (e.g., different combinations of females/males, majors/non-majors, etc.) have on female students. We intend to continue the use of formal learning groups in CSCI 101, and plan to continue collection of data on students' perceptions of learning groups to facilitate the repetition of a similar study after upperclass CS students are no longer participating in the course. Moreover, we plan to follow students through their studies to report any changes in their enrollment in the CS program.

7. ACKNOWLEDGMENTS

The authors gratefully acknowledge the support of NCWIT in the form of external funding (NCWIT Academic Alliance Seed Fund Award supported by Microsoft Research) and The John U. and Sharon L. Trefny Curriculum and Development Program at CSM in the form of internal funding.

We would also like to thank all of the students who took the time to participate in our study.

8. REFERENCES

[1] Alvarado, C., & Dodds, Z. 2010. Women in CS: an evaluation of three promising practices. *SIGCSE'10*. ACM, New York, NY, 57-61.

[2] Barker, L. J., McDowell, C., & Kalahar, K. 2009. Exploring factors that influence computer science introductory course students to persist in the major. *SIGCSE'09*. ACM, New York, NY, 153-157.

[3] Biggers, M., Brauer, A., & Yilmaz, T. 2008. Student perceptions of computer science: a retention study comparing graduating seniors vs. CS leavers. *SIGCSE'08*. ACM, New York, NY, 402-406.

[4] Chase, J. D., & Okie, E. G. 2000. Combining cooperative learning and peer instruction in introductory computer science. *SIGCSE'00*. ACM, New York, NY, 372-376.

[5] Cottrell, J. 1992. I'm a stranger here myself: a consideration of women in computing. *ACM SIGUCCS XX*, 71-76.

[6] Fisher, J., & Margolis, A. 2002. *Unlocking the clubhouse: women in computing.* MIT Press, Cambridge, MA.

[7] Hill, C., Corbett, C., & St. Rose, A. 2010. *Why so few? women in science, technology, engineering, and mathematics*. Research Report. AAUW, Washington, DC.

[8] Horwitz, S., & Rodger, S. H. 2009. Using peer-led team learning to increase participation and success of under-represented groups in introductory computer science. *SIGCSE'09,* ACM, New York, NY, 163-167.

[9] Hymel, S., Zinck, B., & Ditner, E. 1993. Cooperation versus competition in the classroom. In *Exceptionality Education Canada Vol. 3*. 103-128.

[10] Johnson, D., Johnson, R., & Smith, K. 1991. *Active learning: cooperation in the college classroom.* Interaction Book Company, Edina, MN.

[11] McDowell, C., Werner, L., Bullock, H. E., & Fernald, J. 2006. Pair programming improves student retention, confidence and program quality. *Commun. ACM.* 49, 8 (Aug. 2006), 90-95.

[12] Nagappan, N., Williams, L., Ferzli, M., Wiebe, E., Yang, K., Miller, C. & Balik, S. 2003. Improving the CS1 experience with pair programming. *SIGCSE'03,* ACM, New York, NY, 359-362.

[13] NCWIT, 2011. Promising Practice Catalog. Retrieved November 14, 2010 from http://www.ncwit.org/images/practicefiles/PPCatalog2011_Version05092011_WEB.pdf.

[14] NCWIT, Barker, L., & Cohoon, J.M. 2009. Key Practices for Retaining Undergraduates in Computing. Retrieved November 14, 2010 from http://www.ncwit.org/pdf/KeyPracticesRetainingUndergraduatesComputing_FINAL.pdf.

[15] NCWIT, Barker, L., & Cohoon, J.M. 2008. Promising Practices Sheet: Retaining Women through Collaborative Learning. Retrieved November 14, 2010 from http://www.ncwit.org/images/practicefiles/PeerLedTeamLearning_RetainingWomenCollaborativeLearning_Practice.pdf.

[16] Rich, L., Perry, H., & Guzdial, M. 2004. A CS1 course designed to address interests of women. *SIGCSE'04.* ACM, New York, NY, 190-194.

[17] Tillberg, H. K., & Cohoon, J. M. 2005. Attracting women to the CS major. In *Frontiers*. 126-140.

[18] Zweben, S. 2011. CRA Taulbee Survey Report 2009-2010. http://www.cra.org/uploads/documents/resources/taulbee/CRA_Taulbee_2009-2010_Results.pdf.

Perspectives on Active Learning and Collaboration: JavaWIDE in the Classroom

Jam Jenkins
Valdosta State University
Valdosta, GA, USA
cjjenkins@valdosta.edu

Evelyn Brannock
Georgia Gwinnett College
Gwinnett, GA, USA
ebrannoc@ggc.edu

Thomas Cooper
The Walker School
Marietta, GA, USA
thomas.cooper@thewalkerschool.org

Sonal Dekhane
Georgia Gwinnett College
Gwinnett, GA, USA
sdekhane@ggc.edu

Mark Hall
University of Wisconsin - Marathon County, WI, USA
mark.hall@uwc.edu

Michael Nguyen
Emory University
Atlanta, GA, USA
michael.nguyen@emory.edu

ABSTRACT

The Java Wiki Integrated Development Environment (JavaWIDE) is an innovative environment that promotes active learning and collaboration in programming courses. This paper surveys how JavaWIDE's features have been used to promote active and collaborative learning in both traditional and distance education (synchronous) in four different environments: high school, summer enrichment courses, and at two- and four-year colleges. The authors describe the context of each teaching and learning environment and the parts of JavaWIDE that are particularly well suited in each context. After discussing the active learning and collaboration techniques employed, student responses to the experience are summarized. This collection of case studies illustrates how the concurrent editing, shared environment awareness and other features of JavaWIDE can be used to promote active learning and collaboration within a heterogeneous set of teaching and learning environments.

Categories and Subject Descriptors

D.2.6 [**Software**]: Programming Environments – *integrated environments, interactive environments.*

General Terms

Design, Experimentation, Human Factors, Languages.

Keywords

JavaWIDE, concurrent editing, distance education, tutoring, web-based IDE, collaboration, active learning, case study, Java, CS0, CS1, introductory programming.

1. INTRODUCTION

Active learning and cooperative learning have been used successfully in introductory programming courses to promote retention and pass rates [1-3]. Examples of using these techniques include using enhanced clickers for providing instantaneous feedback, incorporating short student exercises within the lecture, and using short in-class exercises such as Think-Pair-Share, pair programming, group projects and others [4-9].

The Java Wiki Integrated Development Environment (JavaWIDE) is designed to support the active classroom and collaboration by supporting synchronous group programming via concurrent editing and shared environment awareness. While tools exist for supporting group programming [10-13], these tools have not been widely adopted at the introductory programming level.

JavaWIDE simplifies the adoption process by providing a zero-install web-based environment that scales well. There are currently over 120 JavaWIDE sites for schools from around the world, all supported by a single server and site administrator. This paper describes how and why JavaWIDE has been used at four different levels (high school, summer camp, two-year and four-year colleges) and in a combination of traditional co-located classrooms and in distance education. These four different use cases drawn from actual experience demonstrate how JavaWIDE can support promoting active learning and collaboration in a heterogeneous set of environments.

2. JAVAWIDE OVERVIEW

The Java Wiki Integrated Development Environment (JavaWIDE) is a web-based development environment built for collaboration and ease of use. The initial version of JavaWIDE was created in 2007 in an effort to eliminate the need for installing an IDE while including the collaborative features of a wiki. Since this time JavaWIDE has been enhanced to include many commonly desired features such as code completion, syntax highlighting, automatic indentation, code formatting, auto-import, code refactoring, integrated Java API documentation and others. In addition, the web-based interface allows the inclusion of other features uncommon to development environments including the automatic posting of all source code and executable programs, integration with social networking sites, and a shared codebase (allows everyone to see, use and modify code on the system).

Perhaps the most innovative features are the integration of concurrent editing and shared environment awareness. Using the follow feature it is possible for one user to automatically open all of the files another user currently has open. As the "followed"

Permission to make digital or hard copies of all or part of this work for personal or classroom use is granted without fee provided that copies are not made or distributed for profit or commercial advantage and that copies bear this notice and the full citation on the first page. To copy otherwise, or republish, to post on servers or to redistribute to lists, requires prior specific permission and/or a fee.
*SIGCSE'*12, February 29–March 3, 2012, Raleigh, North Carolina, USA.
Copyright 2012 ACM 978-1-4503-1098-7/12/02...$10.00.

user subsequently opens additional files, these same files open automatically within the "follower's" view of files. Moreover, as each user edits the file, the updates appear immediately on all users who have the same file open. Users do not need to take turns editing – everyone can edit whenever and wherever they would like. This feature is called concurrent editing. All of the cases that follow made extensive use of the concurrent editing and the shared environment awareness (the follow feature).

The sections that follow are use cases describing actual experiences of using JavaWIDE to promote active learning and collaboration. Each use case is composed of three subsections. The first subsection will describe the educational atmosphere in which JavaWIDE was used. These vary by level, length of instruction and whether the course was in the traditional classroom, delivered entirely online through synchronous distance education, or some combination of these two. The second subsection describes the type of active learning and collaboration activities included within the course and how JavaWIDE supported them. The third subsection in each use case gives quantitative and qualitative feedback from students about the activities and JavaWIDE itself.

3. HIGH SCHOOL PERSPECTIVE

3.1 Environment for using JavaWIDE

Many high school AP Computer Science classes are small, sometimes with less than 10 students. One of the experiences that AP students should have is that of collaborating with others and completing team-based work. This is obviously difficult with a limited number of students. In spring 2010, seven high schools participated in a project called the Computer Science Collaborative [14]. The purpose of this project was to implement and assess innovative techniques to allow collaboration and teamwork at a distance.

The project needed a technological infrastructure that could allow the geographically distributed groups to collaborate in as natural an environment as possible. This included at a minimum two-way group voice communication and data sharing, in addition to the ability of collaboratively editing code. Elluminate, a webinar system, was used to provide the voice communications, an interactive whiteboard, and recording capability. Several options were available for sharing and editing the code.

JavaWIDE was selected for its ability to support collaborative code editing. It also reduced the need for version control because files were stored online in a central location. Moreover, JavaWIDE allowed us to participate in synchronous lessons. These programming lessons were truly collaborative rather than just cooperative. They allowed students and teachers to participate in developing algorithms at the same time and more easily help each other. The marriage of a webinar system and JavaWIDE provided a way for students to communicate with each other, to collaborate on programming in real time, and for us to document the process for research purposes.

3.2 Active Learning & Collaboration

During the project, students participated in several synchronous distance education lessons. The instructors used JavaWIDE to make the lessons interactive. In our cyber-icebreaker, students used turtle graphics to draw lines, make the pen lift up and down, and change the color of the pen. Many students attempted to draw their initials. Students were then placed into breakout rooms and asked to collaborate on writing basic methods to draw a shape or a word related to a computer science principle. During the time students were becoming familiar with using the webinar system and JavaWIDE, instructors monitored students' progress by using JavaWIDE's follow feature. Using this and the concurrent editing feature, each student's work could be monitored at a distance.

Over the course of the project, students participated in programming increasingly difficult fractals found in natural system using recursive algorithms. These methods were applied to four different fractals. In the first case students were given a lecture on recursive methods, provided the pseudo-code for a fractal tree and shown how to code the fractal tree in JavaWIDE. In each subsequent case, students were given less information in an effort to promote active discussion, problem solving and algorithm development. The other lessons on fractals over the course of this project included programming a Koch Curve, which students were asked to extend to create a coastline fractal and a Sierpinski Triangle, which students were asked to extend to create a sea coral or sponge-like structure. In the final project, student groups were asked to apply what they learned in the online large group sessions to create a fractal of their own design. Recorded sessions, presentations and documents for the project can be found on the project website.

Between each large group session, student groups were asked to meet online to collaborate on programming the fractal that was discussed in the large group session and to extend it to an environmental or biological system. Each group consisted of 5-7 students, one from each participating school. In two instances, groups had 2 students from the same school. Students were divided into groups based on their computational thinking skills and previous programming experience.

In each online small group meeting, the instructor-mentor was in charge of taking attendance and making sure that the session was recorded. The peer leader was in charge of conducting the session, while the instructor monitored the meetings. The peer leaders were instructed to use a form of the Think-Pair-Share (TPS) model to facilitate the development of each algorithm [15]. Student groups posted their solutions to their site in JavaWIDE and shared their solution with other groups at the next online large group meeting.

3.3 Student Response

During the course of the collaborative project students were asked to keep a reflection log. In addition, teachers provided written feedback at the end of the project. Below are excerpts from students' logs and from teachers who participated in this project. These responses indicate a very positive experience collaborating using JavaWIDE and that some minor tweaks are needed in its interface.

<u>Students</u>

"The tools have been very helpful [JavaWIDE, Elluminate, Google Docs]. We were all able to write code in one class on JavaWide and I shared my desktop and talked through questions with my teammates while we were writing code."

"JavaWide is a ridiculously cool idea. Being able to have our whole group work on the same file is very useful."

<u>Teachers</u>

"JavaWide is great with the ability to share code and work at the same time without a program on the computer. The lag issues are minor but somewhat annoying."

"I really like the potential of having students editing one file together in one session; I have already begun to use it in class. Its file management system is not intuitive for such things as saving multiple versions of a file or moving a file from one place to another."

4. ENRICHMENT PERSPECTIVE

4.1 Environment for using JavaWIDE

In summer 2011, a one-week summer enrichment course was offered, entitled the Cooperative Online Game Programming Course. The purpose of this course was two-fold: first to prepare AP teachers to deliver engaging synchronous online distance education, and second to improve the preparation of and motivate students entering AP Computer Science. During the first week the course was offered to an AP teacher and teaching assistant. During the second week the teacher and assistant offered the course to a group of 14 students entering AP Computer Science.

By recognizing motivation as a primary problem of online learning, the Cooperative Online Game Programming Course (COGPC) used a pedagogical model that emphasized online presence of the instructor, related learning to students' personal goals, and fostered student collaboration. JavaWIDE facilitated the implementation of this model in several key ways.

First, the group editing part of JavaWIDE allowed the instructors to design activities promoting student interdependence. This interdependence helped build the online community in the brief period of the single week in which the course was delivered entirely at a distance.

Second, JavaWIDE eliminated a large amount of technical issues by providing a tool that does not need to be installed or configured, and works across web browsers and operating systems.

Third, the mode of communication in JavaWIDE between instructor and students enabled the instructor to be more accessible and responsive to students, and increased the perceived quality of the class and the effectiveness of the instructor. The features used in this communication included the 'follow' feature and the concurrent editing.

4.2 Active Learning & Collaboration

The integration of JavaWIDE into the COGPC allowed for the following active learning techniques to be utilized:

Leading question: Questions were framed to guide the students questioned to respond with a particular obvious answer as expressed in generating Java code. These answers were then explored in further depth which ultimately concluded with answers that were not so explicit, fostering cognitive dissonance, and/or self-questioning on the part of the students.

Brainstorming: This method of collaborative problem solving involved all members of the class spontaneously contributing code as ideas are generated.

Student-created art and video game: Students were encouraged to create abstract art and a video game in groups as contexts for extending their understanding of key course-specific concepts. This sort of exercise encouraged students to ask each other: What would a good game/program look like? How should the art/game be created? What are the strengths and weaknesses of various approaches? JavaWIDE provided an excellent resource for this sort of learning.

Problem-based learning: The COGPC enrichment course utilized this pedagogical strategy based on constructivist learning theory that simultaneously develops both problem solving strategies and disciplinary knowledge bases and skills by placing students in the active role of problem solvers.

Student creative construction: Based on a set of criteria that were determined in the course and informed by course materials, students created an abstract art piece and a video game. Students worked collaboratively producing an artistic product. In the process of creative expression, students learned basic programming skills.

4.3 Student Response

Before and after the course all students were asked to rate their level of agreement (1 is strongly disagree, 5 is strongly agree) for questions related to using JavaWIDE, interest and preparation for the Advanced Placement Computer Science course, and perceptions on group work. Out of 14 the students in the course, 13 agreed to participate in the study. All but one student (12) answered questions in the pre-survey, and all 13 answered questions in the post-survey.

The numbers following the questions indicate the average level of agreement before and after the course.

1. I know how to use JavaWIDE. (1.25, 4.54)
2. I feel confident that I will do well in the Advanced Placement Computer Science course this fall.(4.33, 4.46)
3. I am excited about taking Advanced Placement Computer Science this fall. (4.58, 4.62)
4. I feel well prepared to take Advanced Placement Computer Science.(3.58, 4.62)
5. Working with groups has benefits over working individually. (3.83, 4.15)
6. I can learn more by working with others than I can by working alone. (3.75, 4.31)
7. Working in groups is often frustrating. (2.83, 2.08)
8. Some people in a group always end up doing all of the work while others hardly do anything. (3.50, 2.85)
9. On computer related projects, I prefer working in groups over working individually. (3.58, 3.85)
10. I am interested in game programming and collaborative team programming. (4.17, 4.08)

Overall the student responses are positive and indicate students had a positive first experience with collaborative programming. Particularly, the changes in questions 5-9 all show an improved perception of group work after taking the course.

Below are some of the comments from students after the course:

"It was not what i was expecting at all. I enjoyed it a lot more than I expected to and my partner was a great help "

"It made complicated programs easy to do."

"I really enjoyed the class, and it has opened my eyes to an enjoyable career path."

"I had a lot of fun participating in this program. I learned a lot and I hope to keep in touch with all the instructors involved."

"I learned a lot about how to program. Especially on how to program in Java. I learned how to cooperate with people in programming and I got to experience programming with others. Very fun experience."

"It was a fun and informative course. I would have preferred more classes or more time."

5. TWO-YEAR COLLEGE

5.1 Environment for using JavaWIDE

The thirteen 2-year University of Wisconsin (UW) Colleges serve students over the entire state of Wisconsin [16]. The computer science (CS) program in the UW Colleges is designed to be easily transferable to the 4-year institutions within the UW System. The nationwide decline in CS enrollments reported in the 2003-2004 Taulbee Survey [17] has affected the UW System, and has been particularly hard on the 2-year UW – Colleges (UWC), which are relatively small campuses, with a combined enrollment of 12,452 students.

In addition, 70% of our students are in the bottom 50% of their high school rank. The majority of our students enroll to prove that they can achieve at the University level in order to be accepted at a 4-year University. Currently, CS2 and CS3 are only offered via distance education once per year for all campuses.

Seven of the campuses have enrollment so low in computer science that we had to offer a distance education CS1 course to support the smaller campuses. Each of the distance education campuses has between 1-5 students enrolled in the lecture component of the CS1 course. These students face isolation fears due to low number of students available to discuss problems and to an instructor who is not on the same campus.

The UW-Colleges provide funding for the CS1 DE (distance education) lecturer while each campus had to hire a local lab instructor. Some campuses had difficulty hiring a local Java instructor or had financial issues with paying an instructor for small enrollments. The computer science department firmly believes that CS1 students need the face to face presence for the CS1 labs.

During spring 2011, these problems forced two campuses with combined CS1 enrollment of 8 students to drop the CS curriculum from their campus. The UW-Colleges administration along with the computer science department chair made the decision that the CS1 DE course must be able to offer not only the lecture via DE but also the labs for spring 2012. The CS department insisted on having final approval on exactly how the CS1 labs would be offered and still emphasized the necessity of maintaining the ability of DE students to show code and ask questions of the lab instructor. These DE labs must also take into consideration the type of students that would take this course. Retention of CS1 students is very critical for CS2 and CS3 when you start with small enrollments in CS1.

As I looked at the guidelines established by the UW Colleges for teaching the general concepts for the CS1 course, the emphasis that course coverage for designing algorithms should take at least a minimum of six hours. And the reality is that every programming assignment typically forces students to design a totally different algorithm. In order to be successful in this course, for the students and the professor, somehow, someway, the critical thinking skills of students have to be improved. Improvements in critical thinking along with the understanding of the basic control structures will allow students to be successful writing simple programs using any language. It is obvious that more time on task can be very helpful for developing these critical thinking skills.

5.2 Active Learning & Collaboration

In early January, 2011, I was first introduced to JavaWIDE. Very quickly it became obvious that this tool would be perfect for dealing with programming issues for DE students. There wasn't enough time to get familiar with the IDE and implement this feature into my spring 2011 CS1 DE course as part of the syllabus. So about 4 weeks into the semester, I started offering optional programming sessions picking random assignments chosen by myself or students, usually from the back of the textbook. These assignments would mimic the upcoming lab assignment. We would meet on Monday and Wednesday using JavaWIDE from 5-7 pm and students could join one or both sessions. Attendance varied as attendance ranged from five to fourteen students, with certain students attending both sessions.

We used D2L Online rooms (Elluminate) so we could use the VoIP feature for students who had microphones and headphones. Other students would use the chat feature of JavaWIDE. We would start using the whiteboard feature to discuss the objects in the assignment to create UML diagrams for these objects. Then we moved to JavaWIDE to start programming. I allowed students to pick which methods for the object that they wanted to program, and for those students that did not get methods, they were assigned certain methods to watch and help fix any syntax errors. At first, this approach seemed very chaotic as control was lost to the students in the development process. If students struggled, they could ask questions, and at times, I asked for all programming to stop so we could discuss the issue. Students would provide the answers and then "chaotic programming" would start again.

If there were questions, students could ask out loud but some students preferred using chat to ask the question. I would verbally tell the group what the question was and ask for responses. Inevitably students would provide the correct response. If we started using a Java API that we had not discussed in class, I told the students to google to find out the answer. They would copy and paste into JavaWIDE their ideas and we would discuss them. This approach seemed to open doors for students to ask questions if they were not sure about any part of the code. At the end of the first pass at writing the code for the object, coding would stop and we would do "code inspections" starting at the top to the bottom and ask questions to see if the code makes sense as a method and as part of the object.

It was very interesting using this approach as I felt at times more of a conductor than a teacher as we wrote this piece of music (algorithm). After two hours though, I was mentally drained trying to keep up with student's ideas and questions. Since I worked in the commercial world prior to becoming a teacher, I firmly believe in introducing good programming practices and style early into the semester so students could understand these practices and be able to write "good code", or as I sometimes label it "pretty programming." As we went on, students who would be watching students write a method would start modifying the code to enforce these good practices like descriptive variable names. And if there was a dispute, we would discuss different variable names and then vote which one we would use. As part of my teaching, I tell students they are NOT writing code for themselves, they are writing code for the next programmer, and that programmer was usually me.

At times, we would take the previous week's source code and add new features to the code that were being discussed in the lectures so that we would not have to start over from scratch. This approach showed students that the software development process is cyclical and that "good code" can be made even better as new knowledge is gained.

Using group assignments or peer-programming can be beneficial for at-risk students to increase their success rate. However, the remote distances between students make this near impossible.

5.3 Student Response

JavaWIDE allowed the development of a different type of lab. Instead of having traditional closed labs and students work individually on their assignments, we will use this 2 hour lab to develop a different programming assignment but one which is similar to the current lab. At the end of the lab, students are allowed to keep the electronic copy of the in-class lab source code. Instead of having one lab time for the DE students, multiple sections will be offered to keep student numbers lower for each session of the in-class labs. This will allow each student to have more participation in each session. There will be a pre-lab assignment where students will have to "discover" the objects and methods in each lab assignment and these assignments must be turned in prior to the lab. The assessment rubric for these pre-labs will be very low-key as they will get a "Exceed expectations" (bonus points), "Meets expectations" (passing grade) and "Does not meet expectations" grade. This will be part of the overall lab grade for their assignments.

"JavaWide was very fun, the interactivity demanded you to know your stuff, and if you didn't you were shown how. I feel that Javawide was more valuable than the slideshows, but the slideshows taught much needed vocabulary at the same time, so it is hard to say which is the most important."

"This course was very good overall and as a first timer to programming I surely learned quite a lot. I think less time should be used on the lectures and more time should be spent on using the JavaWide program. I learned basically all of my coding skills from JavaWide and it helped me get practice in and it helped me see what things I was doing wrong. JavaWide is more hands on which is better for the learning experience overall in my opinion. I wouldn't know as much as I do today if it wasn't for the use of JavaWide. The program should be used more next semester and I think it should be mandatory."

"The use of Javawide was also very helpful in learning how to program."

6. FOUR-YEAR COLLEGE

6.1 Environment for using JavaWIDE

Georgia Gwinnett College (GGC) is an open access, four-year, liberal arts college. GGC requires two ITEC courses in their core curriculum of all graduating students. The first is an Introduction to Computing and the students may choose their second from Digital Media and Introduction to Programming. Therefore, Introduction to Programming is a general education course that contains many non-majors in the enrollment.

Because many students are not majors, and owning a computer is not a requirement, finding access to properly configured and installed computers on which students can program is a challenge. Instead of offering individual technical support to students and asking for installed software in labs and school computers, it was easier to use JavaWIDE since the interface is entirely browser based (i.e. requires no installation). As long as the students have an Internet connection available and a browser they have the capability to code, compile and test. JavaWIDE supports Google Chrome, Firefox, IE, and Safari browsers and can be run on the Mac, PC and Linux operating systems. The no installation, easy to use environment is in bold contrast to many of the other client desktop IDEs, such as Eclipse and Dr. Java that require the correct installation of the JDK and the IDE software. JavaWIDE requires no requests to the Office of Educational Technology, making the life of the instructor and the support personnel's lives easier!

Many students find object oriented coding paradigms difficult to grasp at first, and the non-linear execution of the code tends to be confusing. Many times students will follow what has happened in class, but then find they cannot reproduce the results on their own at home. Using JavaWIDE, they find it very helpful that they can view all of the coding completed in class, without having to download it. JavaWIDE documents all revisions and keeps track of who changes what and when. This feature also aids the instructor if cheating is suspected, as all changes are stamped with a user name.

6.2 Active Learning & Collaboration

Active learning begins on day one when the instructor employs JavaWIDE. On the first day of class students actually produce their very first program and they are encouraged to share this program with friends or family via JavaWIDE's integrated social networking capability. This provides immediate positive feedback and gratification on the very first day of class.

The fact that students can concurrently edit the same source file together, much like in Google Docs, in class supports an extremely interactive environment. Students can pose a problem, then they work on a solution in concert. The professor is not the driver of the keyboard, but the facilitator and motivator.

Another active learning technique used is to talk about the problem, break it up into workable pieces (i. e. methods) and assign groups of students the different pieces in class. This is especially useful when teaching the concepts of parameters and method invocation; these concepts become imminently clear. The concurrent editing also allows the instructor the offers the students remote tutoring.

6.3 Student Response

To evaluate the effectiveness of JavaWIDE in the classroom students were recruited to participate in end of course surveys. 30 students participated in the survey in Fall 2009, 15 in Fall 2010 and 44 in Spring 2011. All 100% of the students participating in the surveys said that they had a computer and access to the Internet at home. This result is significant in that JavaWIDE requires students to have access to a browser and an Internet connection, which all of them have readily available at home.

In spring 2011, we asked students to choose from two different options given specific scenarios:

- 2% preferred to download the programs and then use them in a stand-alone, desktop IDE instead of accessing the program code on the Internet.
- 7% preferred to take notes in class, while 55% preferred to access the step-by-step revisions of the program on-line.

- 38% reported equal satisfaction with both in-person tutoring and online tutoring (a feature offered by JavaWIDE).
- 58% preferred the revision-tracking feature of JavaWIDE instead of having to manually do version control in many of the novice programming IDEs.
- 62% preferred the concurrent editing feature, allowing students and instructor to solve problems together, to other IDEs that do not support collaboration in such a fashion.

In summary, the student responses to features of JavaWIDE and its usefulness in learning programming were positive. When given various scenarios and options to choose from, the students invariably picked JavaWIDE features over features of other IDEs.

7. CONCLUSION

The high school, summer enrichment, and two-year and four-year colleges comprise a heterogeneous set of environments, all with different needs but with the same desire to include active learning and collaboration in the introductory programming experience. JavaWIDE was selected as one of the tools that would support this type of learning while also meeting the other goals and restraints of the course/project. In each environment the ability to use JavaWIDE without installation or configuration eased adoption.

JavaWIDE supported a wide range of collaboration and active learning activities, primarily by using the concurrent editing and the follow feature. These allowed instructors to monitor student progress on individual and small group work, allowed students to participate in creating example code, and to work together.

The student responses to the active learning and collaboration were largely quite positive. Students enjoyed being able to work together and share code easily. In student comments during and after the course, students enjoyed receiving help, not only from their teachers but also their classmates.

8. ACKNOWLEDGMENTS

Our thanks to all of our students who agreed to participate in the surveys before, during and after our courses, and to the John & Mary Franklin Foundation for supporting the Cooperative Online Game Programming Course.

9. REFERENCES

[1] Graciela Gonzalez. 2006. A systematic approach to active and cooperative learning in CS1 and its effects on CS2. In *Proceedings of the 37th SIGCSE technical symposium on Computer science education* (SIGCSE '06). ACM, New York, NY, USA, 133-137.

[2] Leland L. Beck and Alexander W. Chizhik. 2008. An experimental study of cooperative learning in cs1. In *Proceedings of the 39th SIGCSE technical symposium on Computer science education* (SIGCSE '08). ACM, New York, NY, USA, 205-209.

[3] Patricia Lasserre and Carolyn Szostak. 2011. Effects of team-based learning on a CS1 course. In *Proceedings of the 16th annual joint conference on Innovation and technology in computer science education* (ITiCSE '11). ACM, New York, NY, USA, 133-137.

[4] Dino Schweitzer, Jeff Boleng, and Lauren Scharff. 2011. Interactive tools in the graphics classroom. *In Proceedings of the 16th annual joint conference on Innovation and technology in computer science education* (ITiCSE '11). ACM, New York, NY, USA, 113-117.

[5] Jeffrey J. McConnell. 2005. Active and cooperative learning: more tips and tricks (part II).*SIGCSE Bull.* 37, 4 (December 2005), 34-38.

[6] Charlie McDowell, Linda Werner, Heather E. Bullock, and Julian Fernald. 2006. Pair programming improves student retention, confidence, and program quality. *Commun. ACM* 49, 8 (August 2006), 90-95.

[7] Laurie Williams. 2007. Lessons learned from seven years of pair programming at North Carolina State University. *SIGCSE Bull.* 39, 4 (December 2007), 79-83.

[8] Steven Robbins. 2011. Beyond clickers: using ClassQue for multidimensional electronic classroom interaction. In *Proceedings of the 42nd ACM technical symposium on Computer science education* (SIGCSE '11). ACM, New York, NY, USA, 661-666.

[9] Roy P. Pargas. 2006. Reducing lecture and increasing student activity in large computer science courses. In *Proceedings of the 11th annual SIGCSE conference on Innovation and technology in computer science education* (ITICSE '06). ACM, New York, NY, USA, 3-7.

[10] Kenroy G. Granville and Timothy J. Hickey. 2009. CollabEd: A Platform for Collaboratizing Existing Editors. In *Proceedings of the 2009 International Conference on Mobile, Hybrid, and On-line Learning* (ELML '09). IEEE Computer Society, Washington, DC, USA, 90-96.

[11] DocShare Plugin for Eclipse. 2011. Retrieved August 2011 from http://wiki.eclipse.org/DocShare_Plugin

[12] Stephan Salinger, Christopher Oezbek, Karl Beecher, and Julia Schenk. 2010. Saros: an eclipse plug-in for distributed party programming. In *Proceedings of the 2010 ICSE Workshop on Cooperative and Human Aspects of Software Engineering* (CHASE '10). ACM, New York, NY, USA, 48-55.

[13] Max Goldman, Greg Little, and Robert C. Miller. 2011. Collabode: collaborative coding in the browser. In *Proceeding of the 4th international workshop on Cooperative and human aspects of software engineering* (CHASE '11). ACM, New York, NY, USA, 65-68.

[14] Thomas Cooper. 2011. Computer Science Collaborative. Retrieved August 2011 from http://sites.google.com/site/cscollaborative

[15] Lyman F. 1981. The responsive classroom discussion. In: *Mainstreaming Digest*, edited by Anderson AS. College Park, MD: Univ. of Maryland College of Education.

[16] UW System, Two-Year Campuses. 2011. Retrieved August 2011 from http://www.wisconsin.edu/campuses/twoyear.htm

[17] Zweben, S., 2003-2004 Taulbee Survey, *Computing Research News*, Vol. 17/No.3, May 2005. http://www.cra.org/CRN/articles/may05/taulbee.html

How Well Do Online Forums Facilitate Discussion and Collaboration Among Novice Animation Programmers?

Christopher Scaffidi, Aniket Dahotre, Yan Zhang
Oregon State University, Corvallis, OR, USA
{cscaffid, dahotrea, zhangya} @onid.oregonstate.edu

ABSTRACT

Animation programming is a widely-respected approach for helping students to learn programming skills, and online forums are a widely-used approach for helping students to interact with one another. But in what ways, if any, does combining animation programming with online forums lead to useful discussion and collaboration among learners? To answer this question, we analyzed online forum discussions among people who were learning to create animation programs using the Scratch programming environment. We discovered that specific kinds of online posts were more likely than others to be followed by discussion, and we found that the ensuing collaboration often involved the exchange of design ideas and feedback within small groups of users. These findings reveal opportunities for enhancing online forums and surrounding tools so they more effectively facilitate discussion, collaboration, and ultimately development of programming skills.

Categories and Subject Descriptors

K.3.2 [**Computers and Education**]: Computer and Information Science Education – *Computer Science Education*

General Terms

Human Factors, Languages.

Keywords

Novice programming environments, Scratch, forums.

1. INTRODUCTION

Beginning with the Logo environment in the 1960's, animation programming has proven highly effective for motivating students to learn how to program [12]. Over the past fifty years, various other animation programming environments such as KidSim [3], AgentSheets [13], and Alice [2] have appeared, each offering new features for engaging students, for easing creation of animations, and for creating new kinds of animations.

Representing a recent iteration in this series of tools, the Scratch programming environment also provides a website, including online forums, where learners can publish animations and can form collaborative partnerships [10][15]. Scratch's website is not the first of its type (e.g., AgentSheets has had one [16]), but it is by far the largest, with nearly 900,000 users as of late 2011 [11].

Permission to make digital or hard copies of all or part of this work for personal or classroom use is granted without fee provided that copies are not made or distributed for profit or commercial advantage and that copies bear this notice and the full citation on the first page. To copy otherwise, or republish, to post on servers or to redistribute to lists, requires prior specific permission and/or a fee.
SIGCSE'12, February 29–March 3, 2012, Raleigh, North Carolina, USA.
Copyright 2012 ACM 978-1-4503-1098-7/12/02...$10.00.

Scratch's design was initially motivated by social constructionism [10]. Constructionism posits that learning happens "especially felicitously in a context where the learner is consciously engaged in constructing a public entity, whether it's a sand castle on the beach or a theory of the universe" [12]. The Scratch website is aimed at providing this context, with animations serving as "public entities" to anchor discussion and collaboration. Prior studies have uncovered several anecdotes about how these online discussions have led to the formation of virtual "companies"—collaborations where learners produce jointly-owned animations as a team [15].

To date, however, there has been no attempt to statistically analyze the process by which useful discussion and, eventually, collaboration come about in this online community. In particular, we do not know which kinds of online forum posts are effective at initiating useful discussions, and we even lack information about what collaboration really *means* in this context; the companies mentioned above might merely be the tip of the iceberg, so to speak. For example, it is possible that in addition to the formation of actual companies, learners might use the forums to share code or to exchange and challenge design ideas.

A better understanding of website usage would be helpful for guiding enhancements of the Scratch environment as well as the instruction of learners. For example, if certain kinds of posts to the site are particularly useful for stimulating discussion and collaboration, then the website could encourage users to make these kinds of posts when they seek collaborative programming partners. Moreover, a clearer understanding of what forms of collaboration actually take place would make it possible to prepare learners with realistic expectations of what responses they can anticipate. Information about site usage would also facilitate the design of new tools. For example, if learners are using the forum to exchange code fragments or images, then it might be feasible to create a system that harvests these materials from the forums, in order to facilitate reuse by other learners in the future.

Therefore, we statistically and qualitatively analyzed discussions in the Scratch forums to answer two research questions:

- Do different kinds of initiating posts lead to differences in ensuing discussions?
- What kinds of collaboration take place via the forums?

Section 2 summarizes Related Work, including earlier studies focused on Scratch and other tools in the classroom. Section 3 describes our methods for acquiring and analyzing data. Section 4 presents our results, which reveal that specific kinds of online posts were more likely than others to be followed by discussion, and that the ensuing collaboration often involved the exchange of design ideas and feedback within small groups of users. Finally, Section 5 discusses conclusions and implications for future work.

2. RELATED WORK

Seymour Papert, the lead inventor of the early Logo animation-programming language, argued that creating animations and showing them to other people, or even creating them with other people, can speed the learning process [12]. Some proponents of this approach argue that a social context boosts learning because it enables less proficient programmers to adopt ideas and practices of more competent programmers, while more proficient programmers refine their own knowledge by helping others [12][14][15]. Thus, a crucial element of a learning environment based on this social constructionist approach is a context whereby discussion eventually leads to collaborative interactions, particularly the creation of jointly owned ideas and artifacts.

Numerous studies have confirmed that animation tools can indeed serve as effective platforms for teaching a wide variety of skills in clubs, classrooms, and other teacher-facilitated settings. These include skills related to programming primitives [9], algorithm design [2], and problem-solving [13]. Animation programming is also effective at motivating people to continue programming after they leave the classroom [3]. For these and many other reasons, K-12 teachers have responded favorably to training on how to apply animation programming environments in their classrooms [7]. Moreover, university faculty have begun investigating how to use Scratch as a tool to interest college freshmen in computer science and to train them in programming skills [8][18].

Yet one of the most interesting ways in which Scratch is *different* from prior animation programming environments is that it includes a massive *online* community aimed at bringing the benefits of social constructionism to a wider audience *beyond the classroom* [9][10]. Repositories for other tools (e.g., AgentSheets and Alice) are much smaller. Indeed, neither a study comparing Logo with Scratch, nor another study comparing Alice with Scratch, found statistical differences suggesting that Scratch was superior for teaching basic programming skills through classes (and, in fact, students who learned with Logo obtained slightly higher confidence than those who learned with Scratch) [1][6]. It is the *website* that makes Scratch so distinctive, particularly in the sense of being based on *social* constructionism.

This website contains several features intended to help users learn and collaborate with one another [11]. For example, the front page provides a list of highly-rated animations that users have posted, which other users can download and remix. In addition, users can comment on posted animations; in a previous study, we found that some comments contained suggestions that might have helped animation programmers learn how to create better animations [4]. However, we did not uncover any cases where these comments led to users working together on animations, but this could be because this form of collaboration would require lengthier communication than is convenient through the website's features for commenting on existing animations.

We hypothesize that collaborative communication is instead taking place via the online Scratch forums, which are designed to support lengthy, detailed discussions. Specifically, because users can start a forum discussion that is not connected to any existing animation, we suspect that users could be creating forum discussions as a way of initiating companies aimed at creating new animations. Considering the putative role of animations as "public entities" that anchor discussions [12], we particularly suspect that forum discussions centered on existing animations might serve as a venue for planning collaborations aimed at producing more complex or engaging animations. Our goal in this paper is therefore to investigate what kinds of online forum posts lead to lengthy discussion, as well as what kinds of collaborative interaction are revealed by forum discussions.

3. METHODOLOGY

3.1 Identifying forums for analysis

Historically, the Scratch website has included 19 primary forums. These include 13 forums that were written in English and were active in late 2010 when we began our study, as well as 6 forums that had been deactivated by MIT but were still publicly visible. We did not have the necessary foreign language skills to analyze 14 additional small forums that were either written in another language or oriented toward porting Scratch to other languages.

We manually reviewed several dozen posts from each of these 19 primary forums and assigned each forum to a category (Table 1). We found that 11 forums (shown in the first three rows of Table 1) were generally focused on showing off an existing animation in order to get praise or other feedback, asking for help figuring out a problem with programming, or proposing of a new animation, typically with a request for collaboration. In the other 8 forums, almost all posts were textual word games unrelated to Scratch programming. For example, in one variation of the "alphabet game," one person stated the username of a user, and the next person in the discussion had to state a username that began with the last letter of the first username, and so on. Consequently, we chose to focus the remainder of our study on the 36886 distinct discussions in the 11 Show Off, Trouble, and Collab Request forums, which together held 58% of all posts.

3.2 Acquiring data for analysis

In late 2010, we wrote a program that retrieved all discussions from the 11 Scratch forums of interest, then saved the discussions in text files. In 2011, we wrote additional programs that parsed these files and computed three groups of variables.

For each discussion, we computed one group of four variables that characterized the initiating-post that started the discussion. First, our program recorded whether the discussion was in a Show Off, Trouble, or Collab Request forum (yielding variable *frm_catg).* Second, our program recorded whether the initiating post included a

Table 1. Distribution of 19 primary Scratch forums, which together contained 689,556 posts

Forum category	Discussions of...	For example...	# forums	# discussions	# posts	% of posts
Show Off	Advertising existing animations	Announcement of a new game	2	19891	214151	31%
Trouble	Asking for technical help	Difficulty using loops	5	11940	100138	15%
Collab Request	Ideas for new animations	Proposal of a new game	4	4979	83188	12%
Word Games	Clever uses of words	Alphabet game	2	2027	234488	34%
Suggestions	Ideas to improve Scratch	New way of sorting forum posts	1	3436	30790	4%
Welcome	Information for newcomers	MIT announcements to users	2	1680	23828	3%
Research & Ed	Academic research and education	Scratch @ MIT Conference posts	3	366	2973	0.4%

hyperlink to a particular animation, which could serve the role of a "public entity" to stimulate and anchor learning as posited by social constructionism (variable *has_anim*). Third, our program recorded whether the initiating-post mentioned three words that reflect Scratch terminology for certain forms of collaboration (variable *collab_word)*: (1) "company," denoting a team that jointly owns animations, (2) "gallery," denoting a web page where companies post their animations, and (3) "clan," denoting a collection of characters that appear in multiple animations, often with a shared story arc. We learned that the first two words were Scratch user jargon from existing research literature (e.g., [9][10][15]); while searching the forum to confirm for ourselves that people actually do use the first two words in practice, we discovered "clan" as another relevant term. Fourth, our program recorded whether the discussion was started by a community manager, which we considered to be a member of the MIT Scratch research team or a site moderator (variable *mgr)*.

The second group of four variables characterized the discussion that ensued in response to the initiating post. Specifically, these response variables were the total number of replies by other users (variable *n_replies)*, the total number of distinct users participating in the discussion (*n_users)*, the total number of hyperlinks included in replies to reference existing animations (*n_anim)*, and the total number of times "company," "gallery," or "clan" were mentioned in replies (*n_collab_words)*.

Finally, in preparation for exploring the overall collaborative structure of the community (across discussions) and for finding potentially collaborative users whose interactions we could study, we computed a third group of variables each associated with a user. We used a standard social network analysis methodology, wherein we generated a directed graph with one node per user [17]; in our graph, we created a directed edge X → Y if user X ever replied to a discussion initiated by user Y. Thus, our variable for each user identified the list of outgoing edges. To support visualization, we only used data from the 4 Collab Request forums for constructing the graph.

3.3 Analysis methods

Statistical analysis: To investigate if characteristics of initial posts affected ensuing discussions, we applied multiple linear regression to each variable in the second group above (response variables), using variables in the first group as predictor variables. To characterize the community's overall collaborative structure, we used the third group of (user-level) variables describing the graph edges to compute three fundamental social network statistics: average in-degree, the number of weakly connected components, and the number of strongly connected components.

Qualitative analysis: We applied qualitative analysis to investigate what collaboration typically entailed. We used the social network graph to identify clusters of users that had a moderately high in-degree, then manually examined and categorized 30 randomly-selected discussions initiated by these users. To categorize discussions, we used a grounded theory approach, which is a bottom-up (data-driven) approach requiring the researcher to identify appropriate categories (codes) based on observations rather than attempting to impose an externally-determined categorization scheme [5]. For each discussion, we identified a category that described the entire conversation. A second researcher then independently used the category definitions to recategorize the same discussions. We found that we had 100% agreement on these 30 discussions, indicating high reliability for category assignment.

4. RESULTS

4.1 Do different kinds of initiating posts lead to differences in ensuing discussions?

For each response variable, multiple linear regression was significant (at $P<0.01$), indicating a relationship between discussions and their initiating posts. Within each regression, there was a statistically significant relationship (at $P<0.01$) between the response variable and most or all of the individual predictor variables (Figure 1, next page).

Forum category (frm_catg)

As explained in Section 3.1, the forum category generally reflected the purpose of the post that initiated the discussion. Posts in the Collab Request forums were typically proposals of a new animation idea, usually with an explicit request for feedback. Our analysis showed that posts in these forums received more discussion on average than posts in the other forums, which were largely devoted to showing off existing animations or asking for help with implementing an animation. In particular, compared to the posts in the other two categories of forums, Collab Request posts received 88% more replies from 33% more users, with 101% more mentions of animations and 160% more mentions of words related to Scratch collaboration terminology.

Inclusion of a link to an existing animation (has_anim)

We found that 23% of discussion-initiating posts included a hyperlink to an existing animation, but including a link did not have a clearly positive effect on the discussion. In fact, posts that included a hyperlink actually had responses from 7% *fewer* distinct users than posts that omitted such a hyperlink. Including a hyperlink in the initial post did correspond to a 127% increase in the number of hyperlinks provided in subsequent replies.

To understand why links to animations did not stimulate discussion as we expected based on social constructionism, we informally reviewed several dozen discussions initiated by posts that included hyperlinks to animations. We found many cases where the initial post just provided a link to an animation with little detail about what the animation did or why other users should take an interest. Ensuing discussions had few lengthy responses; some provided a link to another animation that a user claimed was preferable. In fact, some "responses" were actually posts by the same initiator with the word "bump"—i.e., they were intended just to move the discussion back to the top of the forum's topic list by updating the discussion's timestamp. Conversely, in other discussions, initial posts included a detailed description of the linked animation and specific requests for feedback. In such cases, replies included questions, compliments, complaints, and suggestions. In short, posting a link to an animation was not enough to stimulate discussion unless if the post also described the animation and explicitly invited particular feedback.

Use of collaboration-related terminology (collab_word)

The 4% of discussion-initiating posts that used the words "company," "gallery," and "clan" were associated with higher levels of our response variables than posts which omitted these words. In particular, posts that used these words received 36% more replies and 76% more links to animations in replies. The initiating posts that used these words did not receive responses from more distinct users on average; instead, they obtained more responses per user who did reply.

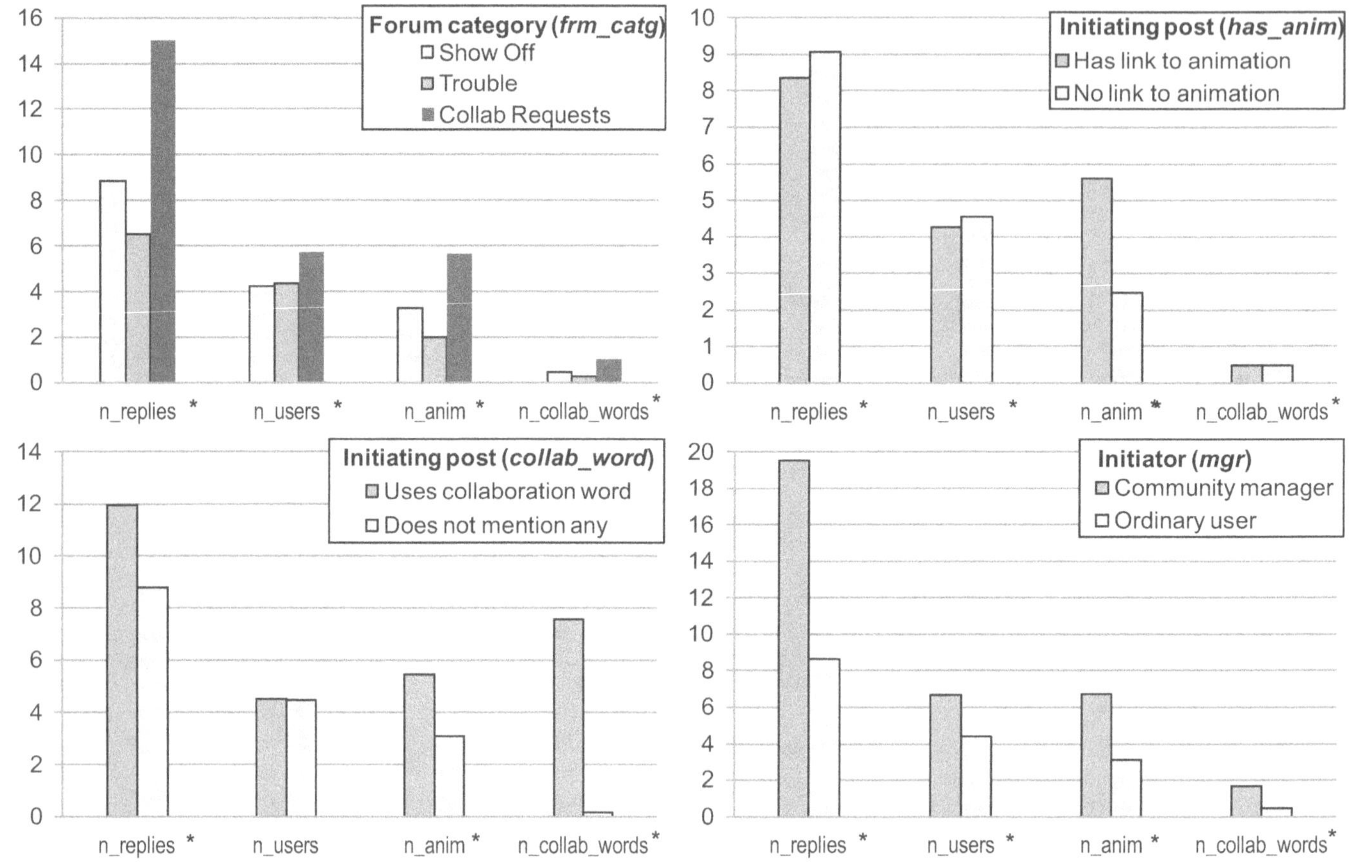

Figure 1. Each chart above shows how the four response variables (*n_replies, n_users, n_anim, n_collab_words*) varied depending on the value of an initiating-post variable (*frm_catg, has_anim, collab_word, mgr*). Asterisks indicate statistically significant pairwise relationships (at P<0.01) between the response variable and the initiating-post variable of that chart.

We informally examined a sample of discussions initiated with mentions of these words and found that they were typically started with an announcement of a new company, along with a general invitation that other users could join if desired. Other users would then reply with agreement to join or reasons why they could not join. The person who initiated the discussion would usually welcome each person one by one to the fledgling company and negotiate a role for that person. We did not see even a single instance where any company organizer turned away a volunteer.

Whether the initiator is a community manager (mgr)

Overall, ordinary user posts initiated 98% of all discussions, and 76% of ordinary user posts received at least one reply. However, we found that community managers (MIT researchers and community moderators) typically received far more response than ordinary users did: 126% more replies, replies from 51% more distinct users, 116% more links to animations in replies, and 269% more mentions of collaboration-related words.

These results greatly exceeded our expectation of this variable's impact on ensuing discussion. We reviewed several dozen posts and found that many explicitly asked users to provide anecdotes about how Scratch was succeeding. For example, one discussion in the "Show and tell" forum that garnered over 1200 replies was created to harvest suggestions for animations that should be advertised on the website's homepage.

4.2 What kinds of collaboration take place via the forums?

Overall community structure

Using our graph of user interactions within the Collab Request forums, we computed several important statistics that characterize social networks [17]. The average in-degree for the 2074 user nodes was only 6.27, meaning that only a few people ever responded to any given user on average. We found 101 weakly connected components (where each pair of nodes in a component is connected via edges ignoring directedness), indicating an average of 20.5 persons per weak component. In other words, each user's friend-of-a-friend network included fewer than two dozen people that they might incidentally meet (and collaborate with) through a person already known. Meanwhile, the number of strongly connected components was 1484 (where each pair of nodes in a component is connected both directions via directed paths), or an average of 1.40 users per component. This indicated that each user had a bi-directional connection to an average of only 0.40 other people. Together, these statistics suggest a fragmented community, with any collaboration likely taking place within small groups consisting of a few people.

Figure 2 provides a visualization of this social network. For visual clarity, undirected edges are shown here between user X and user Y if at least 20% of X's posts are in discussions started by Y, or vice versa. This illustration reveals approximately 200 small

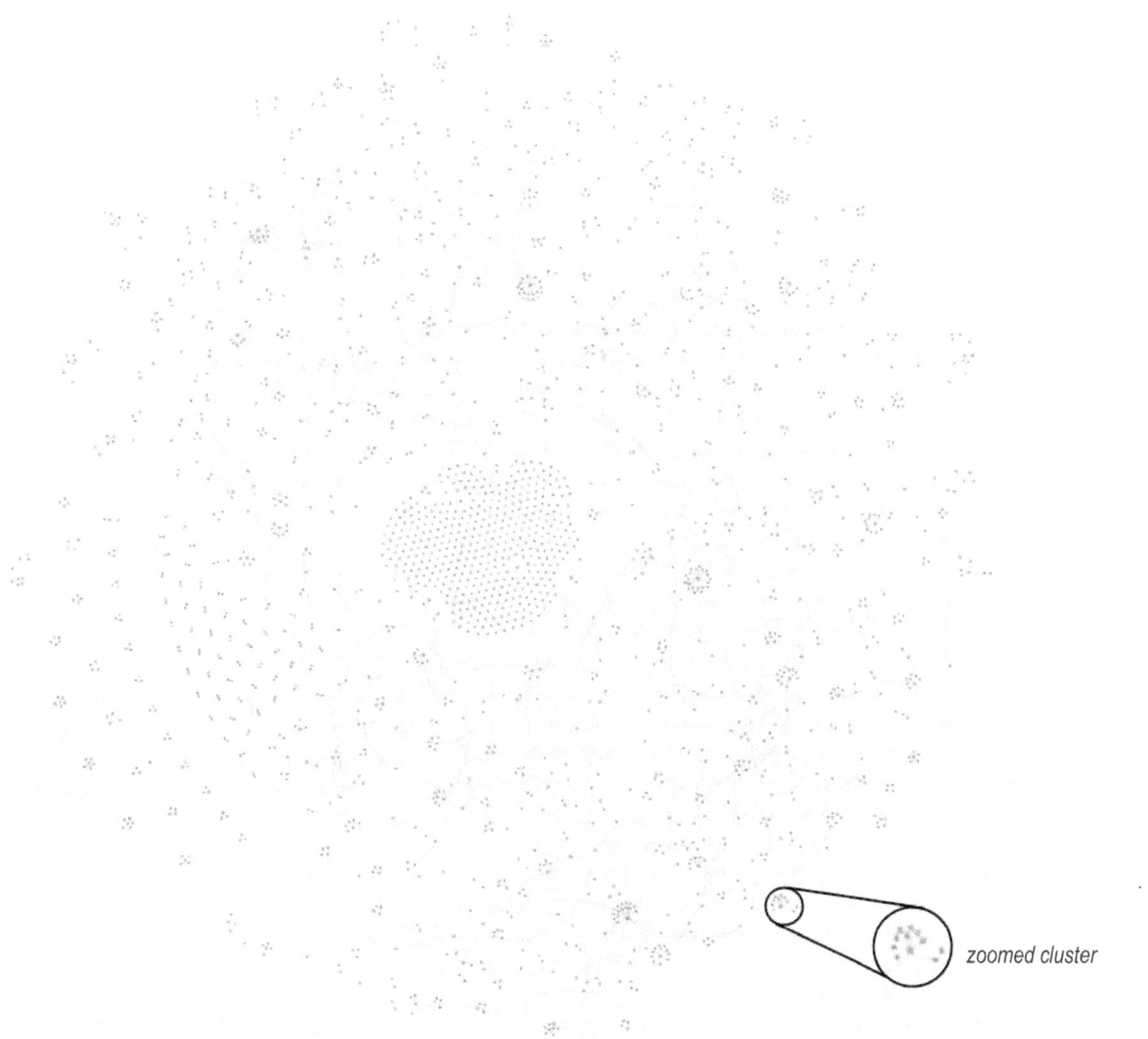

Figure 2. This illustration is a simplified depiction of the social network graph that we used to analyze user interactions in the Collab Request forums. Each node represents a user, with undirected edges (here) indicating that at least 20% of one user's posts were in response to discussions started by another user.

clusters of users, with at most approximately 20 users per cluster. Approximately half of these clusters, shown in the lower-left corner of the figure, were unconnected to any other users within the network—these were isolated clusters where users mostly responded to one another but not to the rest of the community. The remaining half of the clusters had some linkage to the larger community.

Interestingly, many clusters exhibited a leader-follower structure: clusters usually had a central user who interacted with multiple users, most of whom in turn only interacted with the central user. When we refered back to our full directed graph, we saw that most nodes in each cluster generally had outgoing edges pointing to the central user, meaning that their posts were typically replies to discussions initiated by the cluster's central user.

The other interesting feature of this graph was that 10% of the nodes appeared in the center, unconnected to any other nodes. Approximately half of these were users who made one or more post but never received any reply, and who never replied to another user's post. The other half of the users in the center lacked edges because posts were spread over too many users, thus not meeting the 20% cutoff used for edges in this visualization.

In short, this figure illustrates that the community has many small clusters of users, and it further reveals that interaction within clusters often has a leader-follower structure.

Specific forms of collaborative interaction

To investigate what forms of collaboration might occur within these interactions, we manually reviewed discussions started by users who had a moderate in-degree in our full graph. Because we wanted to find users who were collaborating yet not atypical in the sense of being unusually collaborative, we focused on users whose in-degree was approximately in the 80th percentile. This corresponded to an in-degree of 10 or 11. We then categorized 30 randomly-selected discussions initiated by these users.

We found that although 11 of these 30 discussions dealt with non-Scratch topics (such as music or politics), the remaining 19 involved some form of Scratch-centric collaboration:

- *Requests for media* (3 discussions): Three discussions were started by a request for images or sounds. In each case, another person provided the needed media.
- *Requests for animation ideas* (4): Four discussions were initiated with a request for ideas about what kind of animation

would be an interesting project to create. In three of these cases, several users offered ideas in response.

- *Requests for feedback on existing animations* (2): In two cases, users asked for feedback on existing animations. In both cases, a few users did offer feedback.
- *Requests for participation in a new company* (2): One user proposed an online newspaper, and another proposed starting a company to make games. A few users responded with tentative interest, but no company actually resulted.
- *Tips* (2): One discussion consisted of an unsolicited suggestion about how to make a helicopter game, with no response. The other asked for help with compressing audio, to which other users said that Scratch does it automatically.
- *Forum meta-discussions* (4): Four discussions were about the forums. For example, one was an announcement by a user that he was about to become the person with the most posts. In response, other users commented that he is now jinxed, and that they expect him to quit or be banned from the forums like two other people who previously held the record.
- *Community meta-discussion* (2): Two discussions centered on ways to change the larger online Scratch community. One user proposed a new economy, where users receive "credits" for contributing to others' animations or for advertising other users' work. The other discussion focused on a new website created to replace or supplement the MIT Scratch site. In this alternate site, users can now post Scratch animations as well as other kinds of content such as music, and they can engage in live chat with other community members. In response, some users have migrated to the new site.

5. DISCUSSION AND IMPLICATIONS

An educational approach based on social constructionism depends critically on fostering discussion and collaboration among learners. We found, for the most part, that the Scratch forums facilitate discussion, as over 76% of ordinary users' posts received at least one reply (and an average of 8.7 replies). We uncovered several characteristics of forum posts that were statistically related to, and might have caused, higher response. In particular, explicit requests for collaboration obtained more response than just showing off an existing animation. When users did include links to existing animations, it appeared to be helpful if they also provided details about the animation and an explicit request for particular feedback. We discovered that when collaboration occurred, it took many forms (though we did not observe any successful company formation). Collaborative interactions included exchange of media, discussion of animation ideas, and proposals of ways to improve the forum and community. Such exchanges occurred in the context of an extremely fragmented community, where users interacted with relatively few other users (even across multiple discussions).

These results suggest four opportunities for improving the Scratch forums and surrounding computational environment. These suggestions might apply to other animation environments (e.g., AgentSheets, Alice) as well as Scratch. First, if a user includes a link to an animation, the website could remind the user that it is helpful to describe the animation and to explicitly state what forms of feedback are desired. Second, to further reinforce the relationship between discussions and animations, the programming tool could be tightly integrated with the forums. For example, when a user opens an animation for editing, the tool could provide a screen for reading forum discussions that mention the animation, as well as a screen where the user could write new forum posts to request collaboration on parts of the animation. Third, the tool could also be integrated with the other section of the website where users write pithy comments about animations.

Finally, another opportunity for improving the Scratch environment is apparent in what we did *not* observe: discussions that led to direct collaborative creation of code. The forums, programming tool, and other parts of the environment could be improved to better facilitate learning through collaborative programming. For example, forums could be enhanced with a new kind of "project-coordination page" where users can coordinate as they work on parts of an animation. Further studies could then investigate the extent to which this and other new features enable novice animation programmers to collaborate with, and ultimately learn from, one another.

6. REFERENCES

[1] Adams, J. 2010. Scratching middle schoolers' creative itch. *SIGCSE Symp. on Comp. Sci. Ed.*, 356-360.

[2] Cooper, S., Dann, W., and Pausch, R. 2000. Developing algorithmic thinking with Alice. *Information Systems Educators Conference*, 506-539.

[3] Cypher, A., Smith, D, and Tessler, L. 2001. Novice programming comes of age. *Your Wish is My Command,* Morgan Kaufmann, 7-20.

[4] Dahotre, A, Zhang, Y, and Scaffidi, C. 2010. A qualitative study of animation programming in the wild. *Symp. on Empirical Software Engineering and Measurement*, 1-10.

[5] Glaser, B., and Strauss, A. 1967. *The Discovery of Grounded Theory: Strategies for Qualitative Research*, Aldine Publishers.

[6] Lewis, C. 2010. How programming environment shapes perception, learning and goals: Logo vs. Scratch. *SIGCSE Symp. on Comp. Sci. Ed.*, 346-350.

[7] Liu, J, *et al.* 2011. Introducing computer science to K-12 through a summer computing workshop for teachers. *SIGCSE Symp. on Comp. Sci. Ed.*, 389-394.

[8] Malan, D, and Leitner, H. 2007. Scratch for budding computer scientists. *SIGCSE Symp. on Comp. Sci. Ed.*, 223-227.

[9] Maloney, J, *et al.* 2008. Programming by choice: Urban youth learning programming with Scratch. *SIGCSE Symp. on Comp. Sci. Ed.*, 367-371.

[10] Maloney, J, *et al.* 2010. The Scratch programming language and environment. *ACM Trans. Computing Education, 10*, 4, 1-16.

[11] MIT Scratch website, http://scratch.mit.edu

[12] Papert, S. 1991. *Constructionism*, Ablex Publishing.

[13] Repenning, A. 1993. *Agentsheets: A tool for building domain-oriented dynamic, visual environments.* PhD Dissertation, Dept. of Comp. Sci., University Colorado-Boulder.

[14] Repenning, A., Ioannidou, A., and Ambach, J. 1998. Learn to communicate and communicate to learn. *Journal of Interactive Media in Education, 98*, 7, 1-50.

[15] Resnick, M, *et al.* 2009. Scratch: Programming for everyone. *Communications of the ACM.* 52, 11, 60-67.

[16] Stahl, G., Sumner, T., and Repenning, A. 1995. Internet repositories for collaborative learning: Supporting both students and teachers. *Conf. Computer Support for Collaborative Learning*, 321-328.

[17] Wasserman, S, and Faust, K. 1994. *Social Network Analysis: Methods and Applications*, Cambridge University Press.

[18] Wolz, U, et al. 2009. Starting with Scratch in CS 1. *SIGCSE Symp. on Comp. Sci. Ed.*, 2-3.

Classroom Salon: A Tool for Social Collaboration

Ananda Gunawardena*
Carnegie Mellon University
5000 Forbes Ave.
Pittsburgh, PA 15213-3890
Phone: (412) 268-1559
guna@cs.cmu.edu

John Barr†
Ithaca College
953 Danby Rd.
Ithaca, NY 14850-7000
Phone: (607) 274-3579
barr@ithaca.edu

ABSTRACT

Classroom Salon is an on-line social collaboration tool that allows instructors to create, manage, and analyze social networks (called *Salons*) to enhance student learning. Students in a *Salon* can cooperatively create, comment on, and modify documents. *Classroom Salon* provides tools that allow the instructor to monitor the social networks and gauge both student participation and individual effectiveness. This paper describes *Classroom Salon*, provides some use cases that we have developed for introductory computer science classes and presents some preliminary observations of using this tool in several computer science courses at Carnegie Mellon University.

Categories and Subject Descriptors

K.3.1 [**Computers Uses in Education**]: Collaborative learning; K.3.2 [**Computer and Information Science Education**]: Computer Science Education—*complexity measures, performance measures*; J [**Computer Applications**]: Miscellaneous—*Social Networks*

General Terms

Management

Keywords

Social Networking, Collaborative Documents, Assessment

1. INTRODUCTION

1.1 Social Media

Since the heydays of electronic bulletin boards (bbs) in the late 1970's, computer networks have been used for social purposes. Today, with the rise of Facebook, twitter, and YAHOO! Sites and with the introduction of Google+, social network/media systems (SNS) have become part of the fabric of student culture.

With student interest in computer science courses dropping and with challenges in engaging students in the classroom, it is tempting to use SNS to enhance instruction. There are many examples and projects that have incorporated SNS in the classroom and many tools have been created or adapted to this purpose. Hardy et. al. [7] studied the characteristics of Web 2.0 applications (and thus SNS) that students find appealing. Greenhow [5] investigated student use of social networks and concluded that such networks provided significant support for creative endeavors and school-related tasks. Other papers have examined SNS and related technology [3] and tools [6]. Though all of these researchers identify many diverse features that appeal to students, common characteristics include simplicity (in the user interface), flexibility, the power to personalize their environment (i.e., to form identity), and the establishment of social connections.

Unfortunately, SNS in the wild are difficult to adapt for the classroom. Many of the characteristics of SNS that make them popular with students also make them hard to harness productively for education. For example, instructors need to organize and manage the educational process and to assess the effectiveness of the techniques used and the degree of participation of students. As Egert et. al. note [3], it is difficult to balance the usability and social needs of the students with the technical demands of the application or the educational needs of the instructor. Even Google+'s introduction of circles, though a step in the direction of manageability, cannot provide the control over the learning process that instructors often need.

1.2 Classroom Salon

`Classroom Salon` is a tool designed to meet the needs of instructors while providing students with the usability and power over social connections that they are use to in SNS. It arose out of earlier work by Adamchik et. al. [1] on a content-delivery system for tablet computers called *Adaptive Book*. Research on *Adaptive Book* led to insights into the delivery, management, annotation, and presentation of documents that form the basis of `Classroom Salon`. `Classroom Salon` is now used by over 8000 teachers and students in disciplines ranging from the humanities to the sciences as a collaborative annotation and analysis tool.

Classroom Salon is built around the concept of a `Salon`, an on-line area where students can interact with each other and collaborate on documents. The name `Salon` was chosen

*Associate Teaching Professor of Computer Science
†Associate Professor of Computer Science

Permission to make digital or hard copies of all or part of this work for personal or classroom use is granted without fee provided that copies are not made or distributed for profit or commercial advantage and that copies bear this notice and the full citation on the first page. To copy otherwise, to republish, to post on servers or to redistribute to lists, requires prior specific permission and/or a fee.
SIGCSE '12, February 29-March 3, 2012, Raleigh, North Carolina, USA.
Copyright 2012 ACM 978-1-4503-1098-7/12/02 ...$10.00.

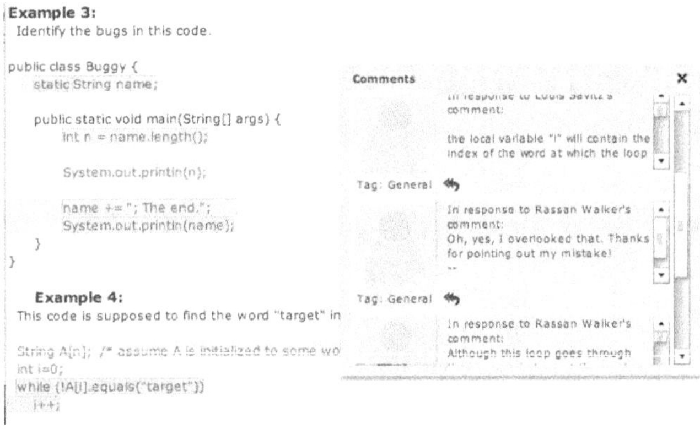

Figure 1: Debugging Code

to reflect the ideals of the 18th Century French Salons where people gathered to socialize and to learn. Our hope is that students will find Classroom Salon an inviting setting to both socialize *and* learn.

`Classroom Salon` has three principal components: `Salons`, `documents`, and the `Dashboard`. `Salons` are online spaces where students can interact. Every registered user of `Classroom Salon` can create `Salons`. A `Salon` can be open to anyone or it can be by invitation only. The goal is to give students the same usability and flexibility to create and maintain social relations as they find in an SNS. At the same time, instructors are free to guide students into `Salons` to leverage the student's social inclinations for the purpose of learning. An instructor, then, can make a `Salon` that is open to the entire class, to just a subset of the class, or to the whole world. Instructors can also remove, either temporarily or permanently, students from a Salon. Similarly, students can choose to make `Salons` with just their friends or unrestricted `Salons` where anyone can join and ask questions.

Once a `Salon` has been formed, documents can be created or uploaded and associated with the `Salon`. Documents are the centerpiece around which students interact. A document can be a program, a piece of text such as a lab assignment, a textbook, or a series of questions. Questions can be embedded in the documents or they can be added separately.

The members of a `Salon` can interact over documents in many ways. They can highlight text and comment on it or they can view or reply to other people's comments or edit an old comment they have made. If the document owner has provided `tags`, a student may "tag" their response. Members can answer questions associated with the document and can look at other students responses, if the instructor allows this. It's also possible to look at just the answers that a single person or a set of people have posted. Students can reply to comments via an email and can vote on comments that they think were "most helpful",

One of the more useful features of a `Salon` is the analytical tools that accompany documents. These tools exist in a feature called the `dashboard`. The `dashboard` allows the owner of a `Salon` to see all of the annotations on a document and to graph statistics related to the annotations. The `Salon` owner, for example, can view pie charts that show how much each `Salon` member contributed, percentages of responses categorized by tag, or how many responses individual members made to questions.

We envision several different ways to use `Salons`. For example, programs with bugs can be placed into a Salon. Students in the Salon can be asked to find the bugs and can comment on others' suggestions. Questions about the code can be associated with the program and the instructor can choose to let students see other students' responses and comment on them. As students comment on the program (Figure 1), the answers begin to converge on a correct explanation of the bug. Other uses for `Salons` are detailed in section 4 below.

Our goal is to provide an environment in which students can collaborate on coursework in familiar ways. At the same time, instructors can use these social interactions as a pedagogical tool that enables and motivates student learning. Instructors can also use the analytical tools in `Classroom Salon` to assess engagement and learning without living their lives on the SNS.

2. BACKGROUND

2.1 Uses of Social Networks in Learning

Several papers have suggested using social networks in computer science classes. Alt et. al. [2], for example, advocated for the inclusion of social networking modules into CS0 classes, and Purewal [10] built a complete CS0 course around SNS. Both of these papers, however, used available SNS and did not attempt to leverage the SNS as learning systems.

Greenhow [5] performed a broader investigation of SNS use among students from low-income families and concluded that SNS have significant potential to enhance learning among these students. She is currently exploring an informal learning environment , called `Hot Dish`, located within Facebook. Our work differs from this work in that we have created a SNS specifically designed for managing the learning process.

2.2 Tools

There have been several surveys of tools available for online collaborative learning. Hamer et. al. [6] performed a survey of tools currently available (as of 2010) to support online collaborative learning in computer science. This study identified over 25 tools for collaborative activities such as peer review, dialogue and discussion, annotation, and making links. Though many of these tools have social networking characteristics, none are designed principally, as Classroom Salon is, as a SNS.

Egert et. al. [3] performed an extensive comparison between SNS and courseware/course management systems (C/CMS) to determine the degree of similarity between them. They charted the technical, social, and usability attributes of systems for enabling and supporting collaboration. They concluded that there is no direct mapping between SNS and C/CMS and that it will be difficult to have prior solutions in SNS map onto C/CMS systems. This, however, is exactly what `Classroom Salon` is designed to do: provide a SNS system with the manageability of C/CMS systems.

In addition to these overviews, there has been research into using Web 2.0 technology to enhance collaboration in particular areas. Ferretti et. al [4], for example, produced a system that focused on collaboration around media annotation and Hoffman et. al. [8] created a web-based system

Figure 2: The opening screen of Classroom Salon

for encouraging active code reading skills. Neither of these tools enabled the general SNS activities that are built into `Classroom Salon`.

Ram et. al. [11] presented `OpenStudy`, a large-scale open social learning community. OpenStudy is a broad on-line social community based on Web 2.0 technologies that allows students to post questions and receive responses from anyone in the world. It does not, however, provide for the management of these communities to the same degree as `Classroom Salon`.

Finally, the tool `piazza` (*http://piazza.com/*)has become very popular recently. `Piazza` is a web-based tool designed for education that allows participants to ask and answer questions in a social media context. Though powerful in many respects, `piazza` does not offer the text annotation or analytic tools that `Classroom Salon` offers and thus serves a different, though overlapping, purpose.

In conclusion, while there are many tools that enable on-line collaboration and many tools that provide for on-line classroom management, we have not found systems that carefully combine these capabilities as well as `Classroom Salon`. `Classroom Salon` provides the possibility of truly leveraging students' social habits for pedagogical purposes in a unique way.

3. OVERVIEW OF CLASSROOM SALON

In this section we describe the capabilities of `Classroom Salon` and demonstrate how social networks can be established and documents shared in this environment. We also describe the `Dashboard` which provides access to the analytic tools of `Classroom Salon`.

To become a member of `Classroom Salon` a student or instructor must first register. Anyone can register by going to the `Classroom Salon` web site at http://www. classroomsalon.org. Figure 2 shows the screen that a user will see when they log in. There are three main options for a user: they may create or join a `Salon`, create a document, or edit their profile. The following sections will detail these options and will also describe the `Dashboard`, the set of analytical tools for a document.

3.1 Profiles

Every `Classroom Salon` member has a profile. Currently the only information available in the profile is the the member's name, email, password and an image. The image is displayed beside the member's responses and serves to personalize the user's experience. We plan to add other personalization features to `Classroom Salon` in the future.

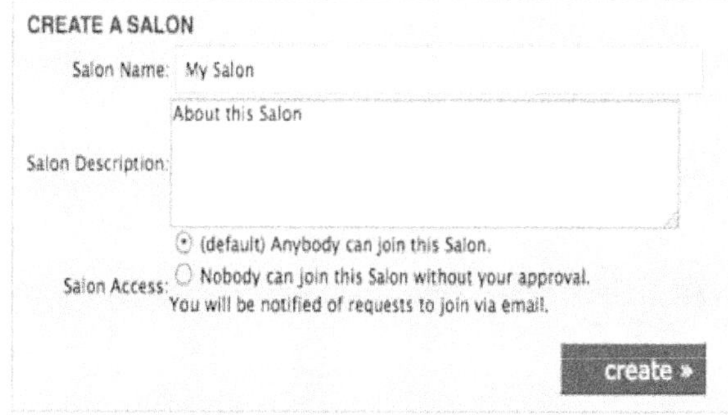

Figure 3: Creating a Salon

3.2 Creating Salons

`Salons` are created by clicking on the "Start a Salon" link in the left hand menu of the screen shown in Figure 2. When this link is chosen, the creator is given the option to name the `Salon` and either open the `Salon` to everyone or to require users to request access to the `Salon`. See Figure 3.

In the main window of `Classroom Salon` you can choose to view all of the `Salons` that you belong to by clicking on the `My Salons` link in the left hand menu. Choosing a `Salon` brings you to a configuration page where the `Salon`'s members can be managed, email messages can be sent to members, and documents can be managed.

3.3 Documents

Once a `Salon` has been created, documents can be created and associated with the `Salon`. On the main page there is a link `Create a Document`. Clicking on this link takes the user to a document creation page. On this page you can directly enter text or import it from a file on your computer, give the document a name, or require a password for the document. Text that is entered can be formatted and links can be embedded. Documents can be a set of questions, a reading with questions embedded, or a piece of computer code that students have to understand and annotate. In `Classroom Salon` every conversation must be based on a document, thereby creating a context for all conversations. This differentiates `Classroom Salon` from many of the other discussion forums.

Once a document has been created, it will be accessible from the main menu under the menu option `My Documents`. Clicking on this link shows a listing of all documents that the user has created. The gear icon next to the document name in this listing gives the user access to a document configuration page (Figure 4). Here questions and tags may be added to a document and the document may be associated with a `Salon`. If the document needs to be associated with several `Salons`, it may be copied from this menu and each copy can be associated with a separate `Salon`. The duplication functionality allows reuse of the same content from semester to semester with or without annotations. `Salon` documents can also carry hotspots of the document (based on user interactions) from semester to semester allowing users to benefit from collective intelligence of those who came before.

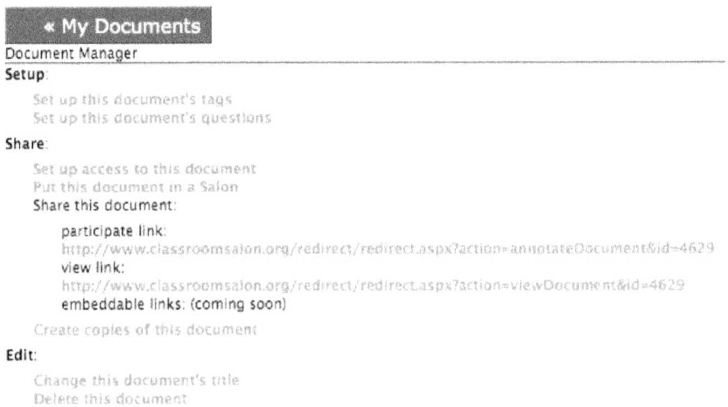

Figure 4: Configuring Documents

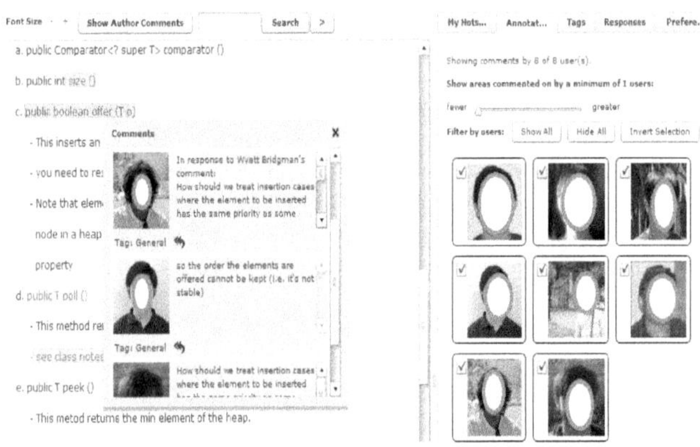

Figure 5: Documents and Modes

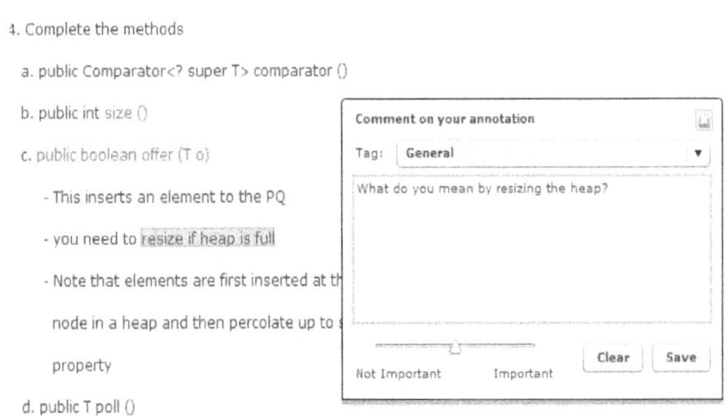

Figure 6: Annotating

3.4 Modes

Once a **Salon** has been created and one or more documents associated with it, members of the **Salon** can access a document and interact with it (Figure 5). Document pages have three modes, view mode, participate mode, and dashboard mode. The view mode allows students to see other student's comments and reply to them. The panel on the left of Figure 5 shows a document with several comments. In this figure, the user has single-clicked on a highlighted comment and is viewing comments that other users have made. If the current user had made one of the comments, an edit button would be available. Right now, the user is able to reply to any of the comments.

In the right panel is a tabbed area that gives the user some options for viewing responses. Currently, the **Annotations** tab is clicked and the user can see images (if they were uploaded) of all the people who have commented on the document. By clicking in the checkbox in the upper left corner of each image, a user can choose whether to view that person's comment. The **tag** tab allows a user to see annotations based on their tag and the **hotspots** tab lets the user see where she has commented and to identify who else has commented on those same places. The **Responses** tab allows the user to see responses to questions associated with the document while the **Preferences** tab allows users to determine which comments to show. amount of overlap in highlighted words or number of highlighted words.

In **participate mode** users can highlight text and annotate it and also answer questions associated with the document. In Figure 6, the user is annotating a section of highlighted text.

3.5 Dashboard

One of the most powerful features of **Classroom Salon** is the ability to view statistics about document annotations. This is done through a mode called the **dashboard**. In dashboard mode you can view all annotations that have been made on a document in a **Salon** that you created or you can view charts on the annotations grouped by members of the **Salon**, by tags, or by density. Figure 7 shows two charts that can be viewed in the **dashboard**. The first chart displays the percentage of comments made by each user in the **Salon**. The **Salon** owner can choose which members to include in this chart. The chart on the right of Figure 7 displays a graph of the number of *helpful*tags that members have given to other members. The **dashboard** can also display a chart that graphs who made responses to questions. The **ashboard** is a great way for an instructor to "get to know" the student.

A final feature is **breadcrumbs**. When a **Salon** member responds to a question, they can highlight text in the document to support their answer. Each piece of highlighted text is called a *breadcrumb*. When viewing responses in the **dashboard**, **Salon** owners can also view the breadcrumbs that a member used in forming their response.

4. TECHNIQUES

There are many different approaches to using that Classroom Salon in a class. In the simplest approach it can be used for collaborative analysis of documents or code. For example, a **Salon** can be used as a depository of lab specifications. Students can annotate the document with comments or questions. Instructors, TAs or other students can address

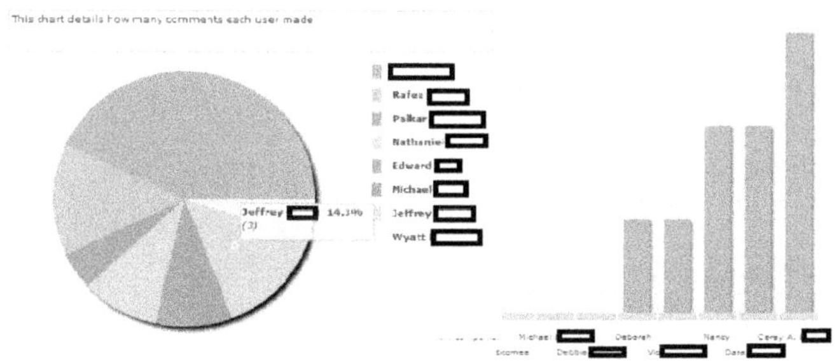

Figure 7: Dashboard charts

the questions and provide insight. Comments and questions are made right on the specification and particularly useful comments can be tagged. We found in our studies, that hundreds of questions that are typically raised in discussion forums can be resolved with just a few clarifications in the context of the document with *zero* redundancy of threads.

Though this is a natural use for `Salons`, it is not much different than a wiki. More insightful applications of `Salons` would encourage active participation of students in learning. In this section we describe three techniques that we have found to be effective in engaging students, code analysis and collaborative summaries.

4.1 Learning by debugging

Debugging programs individually, especially for beginning students, can be a frustrating and time consuming task. Swigger et. al. [12] examined the possibility that students might improve their assembly language programming ability through repeated exposure to common programming errors. Their conclusion in their 1988 study was that students' abilities were not appreciatively affected.

We have found in our preliminary studies, however, that group debugging in a social context does mitigate much of the frustration of debugging while still enhancing learning. We hypothesize that contemporary students are more attuned to input from their social circle (as Greenhow [5] found in her study) and thus will learn more effectively from debugging in a social context.

In this approach code with deliberate bugs is loaded into a `Salon`. Obviously students cannot run or compile the code, instead we ask them to walk through the code and try, as a group, to find the bugs in the program. Students are encouraged to identify bugs by highlighting the problematic sections of code and adding an annotation describing the problem. Other students comment on the annotation, extending the explanation or disputing it. Students are given a period of time to converge on one correct explanation of each bug. If students are unable to reach a consensus, the instructor will put the correct code into the `Salon` and add her annotations to the incorrect code.

4.2 Summary example

We have also successfully asked students to create documents summarizing a set of lectures. Each week one student in a private Salon is responsible for adding the summary document with some related questions. Other students in the `Salon` are required to annotate the summary by adding missing material, correcting mistakes, and providing clarifying comments. In our studies this approach seem to work well with little overhead to instructor. However, being able to monitor student activities through the `dashboard` allows the instructor to guarantee student engagement.

4.3 Learning through questions

A third technique that we have employed is to have students in a `Salon` post a solution (either a program or an algorithm) to a programming problem. The student also provides questions about the code. The other students in the Salon provide responses to the questions and annotate the code with suggestions and comments. This is an example of active code reading as advocated by Hoffman et. al. [8] and Kumar [9], but in a SNS context.

5. EXPERIENCE

5.1 The Experiment

In this section we describe some preliminary observations after using `Classroom Salon` in two CS2 classes in Spring and Summer 2011. The goal of this experiement is to determine whether collective intelligence generated from collaborative annotation visualization actually helps students reduce code errors and debugging time.

In the Spring 2011 semester, one lecture of CS2 at Carnegie Mellon University (CMU) with 42 students was involved in this project. In the experiment, students used `Classroom Salon` in odd numbered assignments to discuss concepts and common errors in a social setting before attempting to complete the programming assignment individually. For even numbered assignments we used the traditional approach of completing the assignment after lectures covering the concepts. In all cases, we asked students to record the time to design, program, and debug their code.

In Summer 2011, we used `Classroom Salon` in a CS2 class of 32 students at CMU with the same approach but also added a discussion forum to see if we could improve on the quality of discussions as a result of using `Classroom Salon`. We found that `Classroom Salon` could replace traditional discussion forums with hundreds of redundant discussion threads with just a few clarifying comments on the document. This was the result of `Classroom Salon's` novel ability to clarify questions in the context of the document as shown in Figure 5.

5.2 Data

We collected the following data points at the end of summer 2011 for all odd numbered assignments with a Salon component.

1. percentage of annotations generated by a student in a Salon.
2. Number of helpful votes received by a student for his comments.
3. Number of times a student change the response as a result of seeing others responses.
4. Number of attempts at changing Salon responses before reaching group consensus on the correct answer.
5. The amount of time spent on the assignment as reported by the student.

On all even numbered assignments without a Salon component we collected the amount of time spent on the assignment as reported by the student.

Our data collection was completed at the end of Summer 2011 and as of this writing we are analyzing the large amount of annotations, responses, student influences in Salons and how they may or may not related to improved performance in assignments. We are currently gathering data in our Fall 2011 CS2 classes at CMU. For Fall 2011, 180 students in one section of CS2 are using `Classroom Salon` to enhance their understanding of the class concepts. A second control section of CS2 with 120 students at the same institution is using only traditional teaching methods. In addition, a second institution, Ithaca College, is performing the same experiment using `Classroom Salon` in CS1 in Fall 2011 with a class of 23 students and a control group of 25 students. We hope to present our analysis of spring, summer and fall data in early 2012.

6. FUTURE WORK

Much work remains to be done on `Classroom Salon`. We are working on several enhancements to make the user interface more assessable and the assessment tools more effective. For example, we will be incorporating annotation feeds so that a `Salon`'s members can easily see when new annotations are made. We are also expanding profile options so that students can better personalize their presence in a `Salon`.

We are also making many enhancements to the assessment tools including a time line tool. Instructors will be able to move a slider across a time axis and see the amount and quality (as judged by "helpful" tags) of annotations at different points in time. This will enable instructors to gauge a student's involvement over time instead of cumulatively.

7. CONCLUSIONS

SNS have become an integral part of contemporary student culture. Unfortunately, it is messy and time consuming to use public SNS like Facebook for educational purposes. This paper has described `Classroom Salon`, an SNS designed for education that provides students with a familiar and compelling social network and yet gives instructors the management and assessment tools needed to effectively use SNS for teaching. Our experience so far indicates that this approach is effective and productive. We also believe that computer science, a discipline where students have traditionally worked in isolation, can benefit from the collective intelligence of the group. Our approach encourages collaboration as a way to generate group intelligence that eventually benefits the individual student's performance in computer science classes.

8. ACKNOWLEDGMENTS

We would like to acknowledge the many people who made `Classroom Salon` possible. In particular, we would like to acknowledge Dev Doshi, Aaron Tan and Rupen Paul who provided technical leadership for `Classroom Salon`. In addition we would like to acknowledge Prof. David Kaufer, for his vision of Classroom Salon. This work supported in part by NSF grant DUE-0942721.

9. REFERENCES

[1] V. Adamchik and A. Gunawardena. Adaptive book: Teaching and learning environment for programming education. In *Proceedings of the International Conference on Information Technology: Coding and Computing (ITCC'05) - Volume I - Volume 01*, pages 488–492, Washington, DC, USA, 2005. IEEE Computer Society.

[2] C. Alt, O. Astrachan, J. Forbes, R. Lucic, and S. Rodger. Social networks generate interest in computer science. *SIGCSE Bull.*, 38:438–442, March 2006.

[3] C. A. Egert, S. Jacobs, and S. B. Barnes. When social worlds collide: Charting the intersection of social media and courseware/course management systems. In *Proceedings of the 3d International Conference on Online Communities and Social Computing: Held as Part of HCI International 2009*, OCSC '09, pages 452–461, Berlin, Heidelberg, 2009. Springer-Verlag.

[4] S. Ferretti, S. Mirri, L. A. Muratori, M. Roccetti, and P. Salomoni. E-learning 2.0: you are we-lcome! In *Proceedings of the 2008 international cross-disciplinary conference on Web accessibility (W4A)*, W4A '08, pages 116–125, New York, NY, USA, 2008. ACM.

[5] C. Greenhow. Social networking and education: emerging research within cscl. In *Proceedings of the 9th international conference on Computer supported collaborative learning - Volume 1*, CSCL'09, pages 454–458. International Society of the Learning Sciences, 2009.

[6] J. Hamer, H. C. Purchase, A. Luxton-Reilly, and J. Sheard. Tools for "contributing student learning". In *Proceedings of the 2010 ITiCSE working group reports on Working group reports*, ITiCSE-WGR '10, pages 1–14, New York, NY, USA, 2010. ACM.

[7] N. Hardy, M. Pinto, and H. Wei. The impact of collaborative technology in it and computer science education: harnessing the power of web 2.0. In *Proceedings of the 9th ACM SIGITE conference on Information technology education*, SIGITE '08, pages 63–64, New York, NY, USA, 2008. ACM.

[8] D. M. Hoffman, M. Lu, and T. Pelton. A web-based generation and delivery system for active code reading. In *Proceedings of the 42nd ACM technical symposium on Computer science education*, SIGCSE '11, pages 483–488, New York, NY, USA, 2011. ACM.

[9] A. N. Kumar. Data space animation for learning the semantics of c++ pointers. *SIGCSE Bull.*, 41:499–503, March 2009.

[10] T. S. Purewal, Jr. Social networking: the new computer fluency? In *Proceedings of the 41st ACM technical symposium on Computer science education*, SIGCSE '10, pages 112–116, New York, NY, USA, 2010. ACM.

[11] A. Ram, H. Ai, P. Ram, and S. Sahay. Open social learning communities. In *Proceedings of the International Conference on Web Intelligence, Mining and Semantics*, WIMS '11, pages 2:1–2:6, New York, NY, USA, 2011. ACM.

[12] K. M. Swigger and L. F. Wallace. A discussion of past programming errors and their effect on learning assembly language. *J. Syst. Softw.*, 8:395–399, December 1988.

Bringing the Breadth of Computer Science to Middle Schools

Elizabeth Carter
Lehigh University
19 Memorial Drive West
Bethlehem, PA 18015 USA
908-319-1150
eec209@lehigh.edu

Glenn Blank
Lehigh University
19 Memorial Drive West
Bethlehem, PA, 18015 USA
484-727-8224
glennblank@gmail.com

Jennifer Walz
Harrison Morton Middle School
137 North 2nd Street
Allentown, PA, 18012 USA
484-765-5700
walzj@allentownsd.org

ABSTRACT

In order to garner more student interest in the pursuit of computer science as both a major and a career path, K-12 students need to be made aware of what computer science is and what it is about earlier in their education. Although students in many high schools can pursue introductory programming, high school is arguably too late to interest students who may have developed ill-informed attitudes about computer science. This paper documents curricular items developed for and taught to an audience of mixed ability 6th through 8th graders taking a local Technology Education class that attempts to showcase some of the more interesting, less stereotypical, aspects of computer science using a breadth approach in an effort to encourage interest in the field.

Categories and Subject Descriptors

K.3.2 [**Computer and Information Science Education**]: Computer Science Education

General Terms

Documentation, Human Factors

Keywords

K-12 Education, Curricula, Computer Science Education, STEM

1. INTRODUCTION

Despite many initiatives to introduce real computer science within the sphere of K-12 education, the field has yet to be incorporated as a mainstream subject within the curricula or standards of many school districts. While many schools may have middle school oriented Information Science or Information Technology courses, the material for many of these courses still tends to be dominated by word processing, using the Internet for research, and creating PowerPoint documents. Some curricula go further, teaching a course in Technology Education that aims to broadly discuss STEM (Science, Technology, Engineering, and Mathematics) topics with an emphasis on engineering, physical science, and/or web design. Students in these classes not only will not learn what computer science is about, they will also leave the class with misconceptions about what computer science actually is. These misconceptions may discourage able students from pursuing its study by making the field seem boring, frivolous, or otherwise "not for them."

Permission to make digital or hard copies of all or part of this work for personal or classroom use is granted without fee provided that copies are not made or distributed for profit or commercial advantage and that copies bear this notice and the full citation on the first page. To copy otherwise, or republish, to post on servers or to redistribute to lists, requires prior specific permission and/or a fee.
SIGCSE'12, February 29—March 3, 2012, Raleigh, North Carolina, USA.
Copyright 2012 ACM 978-1-4503-1098-7/12/02...$10.00.

Although students may have the opportunity to pursue Computer Science in High School or on their own time, mainstreaming the field and concepts at the middle school level would likely contribute greatly to the number of college Computer Science majors, help increase the number of women and minorities pursuing CS, and help reduce gendered and other minority based attrition.

This paper describes efforts to bring computer science into the middle school classroom in order to encourage an interest in the field and show younger students what real world computing is about. Topics of interest to undergraduate computer science students were chosen and made accessible to an audience of 6th through 8th grade students at Harrison Morton Middle School in Allentown, Pennsylvania in conjunction with LVSTEM (an NSF GK-12 project). At this school, Technology Education is a required elective taught to all students (regardless of ability level or special needs identification) on a rotation basis, with each rotation lasting 9 weeks. The following sections discuss an overview of other research regarding bringing computer science into the K-12 classroom, the Harrison Morton Technology Education pre-existing curriculum, the method of delivery for the new material, the topics and content covered, and a discussion of resultant qualitative results.

2. OVERVIEW

There have been several different approaches to introducing K-12 students to computer science while remaining within the curricular demands placed on K-12 education by state and national standards. Many of these efforts have a similar construction. Some introduce an expert figure directly into the classroom, some teach the existing faculty of the school the material and how to teach it to their students. Others take an afterschool program or summer camp approach where the expert and/or the existing faculty teach the material either alone or cooperatively. Frequently tools for programming interactive multimedia artifacts are used including Flash, Scratch, and Alice [9, 11, 8]. Others may take a robotics-oriented approach, using Lego MINDSTORMS or another novice robotics environment.

2.1 Related Work

The authors of [11] took the after school program approach, utilizing Scratch in order to ameliorate middle school students to computing. Their study focused on interactive journalism via an afterschool program where the students composed a more modern, multimedia based, school newspaper. Goals of this work included changing student perspectives on computer programming while showing students the similarities between news reporting and software design. The study also aimed to empower the students and demonstrate that programming can be fun and social as opposed to current computer stereotypes. Their methodology consisted mainly of integrating computer science into existing curricula and activities via language arts [11]. Scratch was utilized due to the fact that it is syntax free, removing many of the difficulties introduced by teaching programming and computer science at the same time to a group of novice students. The syntax free nature of Scratch also enabled the students to have a more positive, hands-on, first experience with computer science [11].

Another study, discussed in [9], utilized Flash as a tool to introduce computer science concepts while dispelling existing field stereotypes. Specifically, the work aimed to encourage students entering high school to get a taste of computing and programming without becoming overwhelmed by the syntactical issues of more traditional programming languages. Students gained hands on experience with a tool that enables novices to quickly and easily develop custom animations. After creating these animations, students were motivated to learn some ActionScript in order to program their animations to stop and be interactive, responding to button control.

Flash has been used successfully within two local high schools, Liberty and Freedom, and within Lehigh University's Launch-IT summer program [9]. Previously, these high schools introduced students to computing as word processing, Powerpoint, and simple spreadsheets. Students and parents complained to administrators, who were thus open to a change. The Flash curricula was introduced first as two weeks of animations, then adding a third week of ActionScript programming [9]. Some projects that the students were required to complete over the course of this work included creating an animated sunrise/sunset scene and animating a ball to move across the screen. Ending on a successful note, this work was able to show a positive increase in interest, knowledge, and confidence regarding computer science among all demographic groups involved, notably females and other minorities, who signed up in record numbers for newly created advanced Flash courses. [9].

Another work, given by [8], focused on working directly with a younger audience of 4th through 6th graders. The authors of this study created Alice environments and provided workshops for a larger range of K-12 teachers on how to use Alice 3D in order to help them incorporate it (and, consequently, computer science education) into their classrooms. Specifically, the paper delineated tutorials, sample worlds, and templates built using Alice to facilitate integration into standard curricula by existing teachers. Specific Alice 3D worlds described involved math and music classes, including: a game for reinforcing certain mathematical concepts; a programming project where students were given a template and had to complete the program by providing certain mathematical calculations; and animations of certain mathematical concepts that students exhibited difficulty in understanding [8].

A different approach is to encourage student interest in computer science through the use of robotics. Some of this work has been done at the same middle school as concerns this paper. A paper by Rieksts and Blank documents efforts to interest students in STEM fields through the introduction of a Mars simulation environment replete with 1/6th replicas of the actual Mars Rovers used by NASA to explore the surface of Mars. Specifically, an old boiler room in the school was converted into a simulation of the Mars surface, complete with rough terrain (through the application of poured concrete) and an artistic mural replicating the Martian horizon. Students in the second floor Technology Education classroom view the rovers and room via ceiling and rover mounted cameras and control them with software built by Rieksts [6].

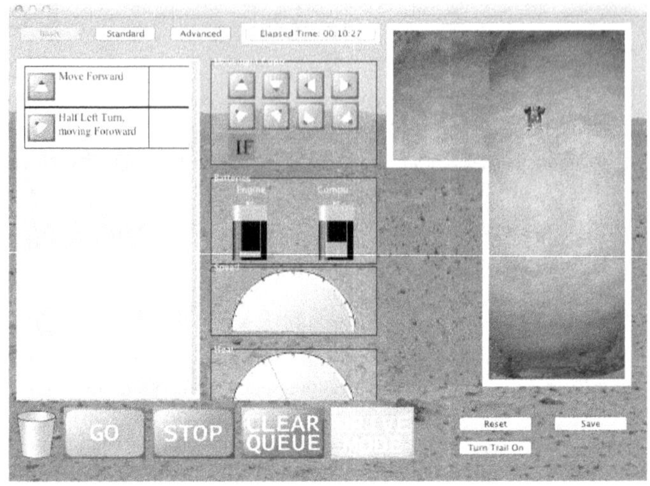

Figure 1: Rover Control Interface

Some other robotics initiatives include a Duke initiative to introduce the RoboCupJunior competition to middle school students using Lego MINDSTORMS NXT [5], an initiative from Columbia University to encourage inner-city New York students to enhance local math and science education using Lego MINDSTORMS and the RoboLab programming environment [2], and a study combining robotics and GPS receivers to teach STEM concepts [4].

Although all the material above describes successful methodologies for introducing computer science to a pre-collegiate audience, none of these approaches were applicable to the environment the authors of this paper were faced with. Our lessons had to fit completely within a 9 week time period, twice a week, and not require individual or group workstations. With these constraints (common to most middle schools in our region), it was not plausible to teach any appreciable programming knowledge to this audience. An additional concern was that the method of instruction had to be sustainable – easily integrated into the curriculum by the existing teacher after the funding supporting the Graduate Fellow was exhausted. Our methodology, unique from the preceding examples, was to focus on introducing the breadth of computer science, thereby teaching as much computing knowledge as possible within the described classroom limitations.

2.2 Previous Curriculum at Harrison Morton Middle School

Within in the Harrison Morton Classroom, the preexisting curriculum differed by grade level and concentrated on basic computer skills, engineering, and physics. 6th graders taking the class were taught word processing and keyboarding (i.e. typing skills). The 7th grade curriculum consisted of a West Point Bridge Design module and two K'nex engineering modules, exhibiting a curricular focus on engineering. The first K'nex module focused on students creating a launcher with K'nex pieces in order to achieve distance and accuracy when launching a projectile. The second of these activities involved students creating freestanding bridges with K'nex pieces. Finally, the 8th grade curriculum consisted of three modules, all based on physics and Newton's three laws of motion: a Newton car module, an egg drop module, and a hero engine module.

Although all of the modules contained within this preexisting curriculum are important to Technology Education, computer science was not actually present in the material. With the approval and assistance of the existing technology education instructor, the modules described in following sections were integrated into this curriculum with little loss of existing material.

2.3 Methodology

Over the course of an academic year, 6th through 8th grade students were introduced to some of the more interesting topics available within an undergraduate Computer Science curriculum by an NSF GK-12 graduate fellow from the LVSTEM program (www.lehigh.edu/stem) introduced material to the students in twice weekly sessions within the existing Technology Education curriculum at Harrison Morton Middle School in Allentown Pennsylvania with the participation and assistance of the regular classroom teacher. The existing curriculum for this particular class covers many areas of STEM with the heaviest focus on engineering. Computer Science curricular items were integrated within the existing curriculum, concentrating on topics that were either predicted to be of interest to the students or that they explicitly requested. Technology education is taught within the Pennsylvania School District as a Related Arts class on par with Art and Music on a rotation basis. The implication of this rotational schedule is that the graduate fellow saw some students over two different rotations, requiring an extension to the original, single rotation, lesson materials that built on the material presented during the first rotation.

Additionally, as an LVSTEM GK-12 fellow, the graduate student was expected to bring ideas relevant to their research into the middle school. The goal of the project is for the graduate student to be able to present their ideas to a broader audience while exposing students within the K-12 pipeline to cutting edge work. In order for the middle school students to understand these ideas, certain background knowledge was required.

The materials developed consisted of two sequences of lessons covering a total of six topics from undergraduate computer science. Topics presented include the Internet, Computer Security, Cryptography, Artificial Intelligence, Video Game Design, and Computer Architecture. Lessons were taught in a loose Socratic style in order to encourage student participation and ownership of the material. These lessons were constrained by a 45-minute class period; because of this some lessons were taught over the course of multiple class sessions. The following sections describe each of these lessons in detail including their goals, what computer science concepts were taught, and a qualitative evaluation of student information retention and resulting interest in Computer Science.

3. CLASSROOM ENVIRONMENT AND LIMITATIONS

Due to room renovations within the middle school where these lessons were presented, certain lessons were developed for presentation in any room (with or without student laptops). For example, the Internet lesson described below discusses that a single, entire class, web page was developed as opposed to individual student websites. This decision was motivated by the fact that the first few times this lesson was taught class was held in the school auditorium, therefore laptops were not considered a viable option. This lesson would work just as well with students each creating their own page or working in groups of 2 to 3, as seen in the discussion of the second Internet lesson. The reader will note that some of the lessons below have a part 1 and a part 2; part 2 was taught to students received for a second rotation.

4. CURRICULAR ITEMS

The material described below was taught with the permission and review of the regular classroom teacher over the course of the 2009-2010 school year, with the regular classroom teacher adding content to the lessons both while they were being taught and when the graduate student was not in the classroom. Full lesson plans were developed for each topic described, including where the lesson would fit within Pennsylvania state standards. Additionally, all but two of the lessons described have associated PowerPoint presentations that were used to help teach the lessons. All lesson materials for these lessons can be downloaded from http://lvstem.cse.lehigh.edu/ecdc.php. Questions or issues with using this site or downloading lessons should be directed to the first author of this paper.

4.1 Lesson Set 1

4.1.1 The Internet

The first lesson focused on the Internet—starting with a topic already familiar and interesting to the students, and expanding on that interest. The lesson began by asking the students "What is the Internet?" Varying answers were received, mainly centering around the Internet being a place to talk to other people, play video games, and listen to music. Then, an actual definition for the Internet was given. This definition was expanded to a discussion on computer networks, a brief overview of the TCP/IP protocol and protocols in general, and IP addressing. Computer networking and connection establishment had the students enact two ends of a network connection. One student would request the connection, the other student would acknowledge and accept, thereby illustrating the three-way-handshake concept utilized by TCP/IP. We introduced IP addressing by likening IP addresses to house addresses, and illustrating how a device's IP address changes when the device changes networks.

Next, a tutorial on HTML examined what HTML is and why it is necessary, the basic structure of an HTML document, and how to form correct tags. After teaching the students some basic markup and document structure, the instructor helped the class as a whole successfully develop a simple HTML web page, which the class was able to view at the end of the period and then discuss more advanced improvements they would like to make to the site had they had the time.

4.1.2 Computer Security

Several lessons developed for this classroom were developed according to observed student interest. This lesson evolved from questions students posed during the Internet lesson regarding computer viruses and computer security. The goals of this lesson were to teach the students about common computer security threats, how to avoid those threats, and how to keep themselves safe on the Internet. This lesson was structured mostly as an open Q&A, with some guided topics of discussion according to the above lesson goals. During the Q&A, most of the students' questions were related to avoiding viruses, removing viruses after the fact, whether a certain behavior their computer exhibited indicated that the computer had a virus, whether or not the instructor could hack, and whether or not the instructor could teach the students how to hack (to which the answer was no). Guided discussion topics included where computer viruses come from, what a hacker is, why hackers exist, and the three main types of hackers (white hat, grey hat, black hat). Students were taught that they should avoid opening attachments from people they do not trust or that look suspicious and that they should avoid suspicious looking websites. Additionally, the instructor discussed the dangers of talking to strangers on the Internet and how easily strangers can trick other Internet users by pretending to be someone trusted by the user. An example was given where the instructor selected a celebrity most opposite themselves and described a situation where, if they knew enough about the celebrity, they could pretend to be that person over the Internet without the user knowing otherwise.

4.1.3 Cryptography

The Cryptography lesson was created to fit within existing Pennsylvania state mathematics standards in order to illustrate the connection between Computer Science and Mathematics. This topic combines history, mathematics, and Computer Science in unique ways that appealed to student interests. Cryptography and Computer Security also have the added benefit of being concrete applications of Computer Science that have been popularized through television and other media—thus these subfields can help overcome some of stereotypes about Computer Science generally.

This lesson was the first to require multiple class periods to complete, taking as long as 3 periods depending on student ability. Historical information on Cryptography was presented first, discussing the origins of Cryptography and the related art of Steganography. Of the history presented, the students were most interested in a steganographic method invented by Giovanni Porta which involved creating a clear ink made of alum and vinegar, then using this ink to write on a hard boiled egg [10]. This ink would seep through the pores of the egg and react with the underlying albumin, transferring the message through the shell while leaving no visible trace on the shell itself.

After discussing steganography and its historical significance, cryptography was introduced. While discussing the history of cryptography, students exhibited some confusion about why it was necessary. A reenactment centering on Julius Caesar—loosely based on the Code Book's description of the invention of the Caesar Shift cipher—was created to illustrate the need for cryptography. Several volunteers from the class were selected to be either part of Caesar's army or an opposing army. Then, one student from each 'army' was selected to be a messenger for that group that would have to cross the classroom into 'enemy territory.' First, one messenger student was given a plaintext message that they had to deliver across the class, hidden inside a book and thereby employing very basic steganography. That student was then 'captured' by the opposing army and their message was found and read. Then the other messenger student received an encrypted message encoded with the Caesar Shift cipher. That student then had to deliver their message across the classroom and was also captured; however, since their message was encoded the 'enemy army' was unable to read the message—effectively illustrating the usefulness cryptography.

Once students understood the historical significance of cryptography, they learned three encryption schemes. Both substitution and transposition ciphers were discussed with a focus on substitution, specifically Caesar Shift, Affine, and Vigenère. Encryption was taught for all three but decryption and frequency analysis were only discussed for Caesar Shift given time constraints and the mathematical ability of the class.

While learning the Caesar Shift cipher, students created decoder circles according to a template found on the National Council of Teachers of Mathematics web site [3].

After assembling the circles, the class performed encryption and decryption with known keys. Once this skill was mastered the lesson moved on to frequency analysis in order to show students attacks on encrypted texts where the key is unknown. Once students were able to apply this concept, the mathematical formulation for Caesar Shift was taught and applied (ciphertext letter = plaintext letter + k mod 26). The rest of the lesson correlated increasingly difficult ciphers to creating increasingly difficult math problems by showing that the Affine cipher applies a multiplicative factor to the formula for a regular shift cipher and Vigenère employs a series of shifts based off of a code word.

4.1.4 Artificial Intelligence

Artificial Intelligence is one of the more difficult, most interesting, and popularized areas of computer science. This lesson was developed in line with expressed student interest—one student saw the graduate fellow's textbook for a class on intelligent agents and wanted to know more about the subject. Therefore this set of lessons brought graduate level material to the middle school level.

The focus of the lesson was the concept of rationality and how to determine if an artificial entity is behaving rationally. This lesson entailed defining and explaining agents, sensors, actuators, percepts, the agent's environment, and what a task environment is. Percepts and actuators were illustrated by pointing to parts of the teacher that fulfill those roles (i.e., eyes as sensors, arms as actuators). Both actual robots and software bots were discussed, the latter exemplified by Amazon.com's suggestion engine. Also, concepts of performance measure and utility were discussed.

One activity developed for this lesson was created to illustrate the concepts of performance measure and utility further while clarifying the level of detail required to program an agent (or, any program). The activity involved the students programming the teacher to walk. Students would begin with commands like "walk forward," to which the instructor would prompt for more details before moving. After a few tries the students would realize that they had to give commands like "lift left foot", "move left foot forward 1 foot in length", "drop left foot" and then repeat with the right foot. An entertaining aspect of this activity is that, after the students understood the simple 'teacher-bot' language, almost every class tried to program the teacher to walk out the door.

The lesson next required students to determine if an agent was acting rationally by defining the agent's task environment in terms of actuators, sensors, environment, and performance measure (i.e. PEAS specification). Clips from *Short Circuit 2, The Muppets Take Manhattan,* and *Muppet Treasure Island* were used; the students had to define if the agent was behaving rationally in a given situation.

The last part of the lesson articulated the previously mentioned graduate level material. Specifically, the material involved interagent dependencies in multiagent systems. Independent, mutual, reciprocal, and unilateral relationships were illustrated, as before, with a movie clip.

4.1.5 Video Game Design

When asked, the students requested a lesson about video games so, a lesson on video game design was created based on material from an undergraduate class on video game AI. One goal of this lesson was to show that many different fields go into the development of a video game and that, if the students were truly interested in making video games when they grew up, they didn't necessarily have to study computer science. Conversely, the computer science aspects of video game creation were also discussed for those students who *were* interested in pursuing computer science as a field of study when they got older.

Topics discussed included different genres of video games, what goes into making a video game, the skill set involved in each step, programming realistic character motion, a brief history on video game AI, and a discussion of how to create a good artificially intelligent opponent. The discussion on programming realistic character motion was facilitated via a promotional video for the video game Band Hero, where the creation of Taylor Swift's in game character was explained. Also discussed under this topic were the concepts of polygons and texture mapping, as they were mentioned in the video clip shown. When discussing game AI discussion topics included the goals of early arcade game AI, what scripted AI is, and creating a good AI opponent.

4.1.6 Reinforcement of Lesson Set 1

Because Technology Education within the school district is presented in a related arts class and not a core subject, tests are not really given nor is homework really assigned. In light of this, the material was reinforced by an in class review game structured after the game show Jeopardy! where the winning students received small prizes.

The class was divided into 3 to 6 groups depending on class size and each group played as though they were a single Jeopardy! contestant. Categories included the Internet, Security, Cryptography, and AI. All clues came from material taught in class lessons and discussion sessions. The final Jeopardy! question was also AI based and came from the graduate level AI material presented, students were required to identify the interagent dependency described in the clue. Further discussion of the review game can be found in the discussion section.

4.2 Lesson Set 2

4.2.1 The Internet, part 2

The goal for this lesson was to expand on the first Internet lesson and expose the students to more professional web site development. For this lesson the students worked in groups on laptops and were provided instruction on how to use an industry standard web development tool - Visual Studio, via a free trial of Visual Web Developer. The class discussed what goes into a good website by considering what they liked about sites they frequented on the Internet, especially what about those sites made them more appealing. After this the instructor introduced the students to the tag structure of an ASP.NET web page, showing how it differs from simple HTML but also explaining that the ASP.NET content gets converted to HTML content when a client loads the page. The tag structure of ASP.NET also required an explanation of client-server interactions. After receiving this information, the students worked in groups to create websites with assistance from the instructor

4.2.2 Artificial Intelligence, part 2

Many students expressed a desire to actually make a video game. Given that the students had no programming background and that the graduate student instructor was only in their classroom twice a week, teaching the students enough programming skills to create a video game was infeasible. Instead, the instructor adapted an undergraduate level homework assignment centered on an open source project called Robocode[7]. Robocode is a Java based video game environment where AI agents battle each other. Each agent gets one tank and that tank must be controlled within the environment to destroy the other tanks. Generally, the last tank standing wins although the scoring is more complicated than this. Tanks can move forwards or backwards, turn left or right, fire, and perform other similar actions. Supported events include getting hit, hitting another tank, running into the wall, and more. Students were placed into about 4 groups, depending on class size, and given a worksheet delineating the commands that a tank could be given but in English. Students then developed a small script in the edited language of the worksheet and handed those scripts in to the instructor. The instructor then coded the students' scripts and started a tournament. This lesson was generally completed within a single 45-minute period if time was well managed and the number of student groups was limited.

4.2.3 Computer Architecture

A lesson on computer architecture was created in order to introduce students to the hardware of the computer. This lesson began by having the students first try to define what a computer is and identify what devices they use everyday are non-obviously computers. Following this guessing session was the actual definition for computer, a simplified description of how the processor works and what it interacts with, and the internal pieces of the processor. Depending on the perceived attention and ability of the class, logic gates were also discussed and simple logic circuits were developed by the class on the board corresponding to simple logic statements. Then the rest of the class was spent showing students the hardware in an older unidentified desktop machine, a broken 2005 model MacBook, and a recent model of Dell laptop. The instructor removed parts from the machines, explaining what each piece's function was. Additionally, if there was time, an television clip from a 1980's TV show was used to show what the interface to early computers was like, highlighting the fact that a GUI interface was then nonexistent.

5. QUALITATIVE RESULTS

Student material retention and interest in presented subject areas were qualitatively evaluated over the course of the school year in which these lessons were taught. Students received for a first rotation were taught the following lessons in this order: The Internet, Computer Security, Cryptography, AI, Video Game Design, Review game. Students received for a second rotation received the second set of materials in varying order but usually started with the Advanced Internet lesson. Additionally, the Video Game Design lesson was developed further into the school year, so that lesson occasionally was taught to second rotation students who did not receive it in the first rotation.

Observed levels of information retention were encouraging. Although tests, homework, and other standard methods of determining material retention were not applicable due to afore mentioned classroom limitations, material retention was qualitatively observed by both the visiting graduate student and the existing classroom teacher. The graduate student employed two methods to determine material retention. The more formal of these methods centered on the review game.

As mentioned earlier in this paper, the review game emulated the popular trivia game show Jeopardy! The game board was created using a PowerPoint document the existing classroom teacher had used before and was edited to contain categories for each of the subjects taught in the first set of lessons with five questions each, with question values ranging from 100 to 500 points. During the course of the review game the existing teacher and visiting graduate student collectively took on the role of host, with student groups "buzzing in" by raising their hands. The existing teacher and graduate student monitored student retention via their progress within the game. Although students exhibited some difficulty remembering the vocabulary associated with the materials taught, they displayed an unexpectedly high level of retention with the actual concepts.

Additionally, there was an unexpected amount of information loss among the students for certain multi-lesson topics. Retention rate variability may have several causes. First, the graduate student was only present in the class twice a week and not contiguously. For lessons that required multiple class sessions to teach, the disruption in subject matter may have caused a drop in retention. Another possible factor is the difficulty of the material. The most severe drops in retention were observed in the Cryptography and first AI lessons, which contained the most difficult material and incurred the most discontinuity.

Student interest and enthusiasm for the material varied by grade level. After observing the students' voluntary participation in the materials, we note that all three grade levels displayed interest from the outset, with 6th grade students exhibiting the highest and most enduring enthusiasm. The 7th grade group approached the material more maturely and though they exhibited a general interest in the subject and participated in class discussions, they were less overtly excited about the material (as would be expected from their age group). The 8th grade students were the hardest group to interest of the three. This last group responded best to the more interactive activities, like the Robocode lesson and the advanced Internet lesson.

As of the end of the 2009-2010 school year, the classroom teacher (and third author) requested the materials for the lessons described in this paper in order to adopt them within their curriculum going forward. Given the positive acceptance of the material by most of the students and the existing classroom teacher, it is believed that the idea of taking a breadth first approach to introducing younger students to computer science could be a beneficial avenue for introducing younger students to the field of computer science as a whole. The approach described throughout this paper has the benefit of opening the students' eyes to the possibilities inherent in the field while avoiding the adoption of stereotypes showing computing as a solitary, programming dominated field of study.

However, over the course of this experience we reached the conclusion that 6th grade appears to be too late to gain a student's lasting interest in the subject without additional outside encouragement. Over the course of the 2010-2011 school year many students who had been interested as 6th or 7th graders exhibited a strong disinterest in pursuing the field further. Our hypothesis is that the changing social pressures inherent when progressing through middle school negated much of the ground gained during the 2009-2010 school year. Therefore, the lead author of the paper proposes to pursue a similar initiative with younger students and a more formal evaluation.

6. ACKNOWLEDGMENTS

We would like to thank the faculty and administration at Harrison Morton Middle School for their cooperation and enthusiasm for the LVSTEM and Launch-IT programs. Additionally we would like to thank Dr. Henry Odi, Co-Director of the LV STEM and Launch-IT projects, for his invaluable help. LV STEM and Launch-IT are sponsored by NSF grant numbers 0639664 and 0624553, respectively. The Pennsylvania Infrastructure Technology Alliance (PITA) also provided supplementary funding for this project. Any opinions, findings and conclusions or recommendations expressed in this material are those of the authors and do not necessarily reflect the views of the National Science Foundation or PITA.

7. REFERENCES

[1] Franz, D. and Elmore, B.B. 2009. Work in progress – collaborative outreach to "atrisk" middle school students using LEGO robotics. In *Frontiers in Education Conference, 2009. FIE '09. 39th IEEE,* vol., no., pp.1-2 18-21 Oct 2009. Doi: 10.1109/FIE.2009.5350549

[2] Goldman, R., Eguchi, A., and Sklar, E.. 2004. Using educational robotics to engage inner-city students with technology. In *Proceedings of the 6th international conference on Learning sciences* (ICLS '04). International Society of the Learning Sciences 214-221.

[3] Schmid, D. 2008. Illuminations: Code Crackers. Retrieved January, 13, 2010 from http://illuminations.nctm.org/LessonDetail.aspx?id=L587.

[4] Nugent, G., Barker, B., Grandgenett, N. and Adamchuk, V. 2009. The use of digital manipulatives in K-12L robotics, GPS/GIS and programming. In *Frontiers in Education Conference,* 2009 (FIE '09). *39th IEEE.* 2009, 1-6 Oct 2009. Doi: 10.1109/FIE.2009.5350828

[5] Osborne, R. B., Thomas, A. J., and Forbes, J.R.N. 2010. Teaching with robots: a service-learning approach to mentor training. In *Proceedings of the 41st ACM technical symposium on Computer science education* (SIGCSE '10). ACM, New York, NY, USA, 172-176. DOI=10.1145/1734263.1734321 http://doi.acm.org.ezproxy.lib.lehigh.edu/10.1145/1734263.1734321

[6] Rieksts, I. and Blank, G. D. 2008. Inspiring future IT professionals with Mars rovers. *J. Comput. Sci. Coll.* 23, 5 (May 2008), 44-51.

[7] Robocode. Retrieved January, 24, 2010 from http://robocode.sourceforge.net/

[8] Rodger, S. H., Bashford, M., Dyck, L., Hayes, J., Liang, L., Nelson, D., and Qin, H. 2010. Enhancing K-12 education with alice programming adventures. In *Proceedings of the fifteenth annual conference on Innovation and technology in computer science education* (ITiCSE '10). ACM, New York, NY, USA, 234-238. DOI=10.1145/1822090.1822156 http://doi.acm.org.ezproxy.lib.lehigh.edu/10.1145/1822090.1822156

[9] Sands, M., Evans, J., and Blank, G. D. 2010. Widening the K-12 pipeline at a critical juncture with Flash™. *J. Comput. Small Coll.* 25, 6 (June 2010), 181-190.

[10] Singh, S. *The Code Book.* Knopf Doubleday Publishing Group, New York, NY, 2000.

[11] Wolz, U., Stone, M., Pulimood, S. M., and Pearson, K.. 2010. Computational thinking via interactive journalism in middle school. In *Proceedings of the 41st ACM technical symposium on Computer science education* (SIGCSE '10). ACM, New York, NY, USA, 239-243. DOI=10.1145/1734263.1734345 http://doi.acm.org.ezproxy.lib.lehigh.edu/10.1145/1734263.173434

Integrating Hard and Soft Skills: Software Engineers Serving Middle School Teachers*

Richard Burns, Lori Pollock, and Terry Harvey
Computer and Information Sciences
University of Delaware
Newark, DE 19716
{burns,pollock,harvey}@cis.udel.edu

ABSTRACT

We have developed and implemented, over four semesters, a model for engaging computer science majors in service learning for teachers of grades 6-8 at a K-8 school in an underserved community. This paper describes the design of a course focused on interweaving software engineering practice, service learning, and development of "soft" professional skills. CS student teams partner with middle school teacher teams to create learning games for classrooms, and then conduct classroom instruction and observation. We report on our results from evaluating the experience of CS students and middle school teachers through pre-post surveys, evaluator observation of student demo presentations and classroom instruction, focus groups, and student reflective journals.

Categories and Subject Descriptors

K.3.2 [**Computing Milieux**]: Computers and Education-Computer science education

General Terms

Human Factors

Keywords

service learning, software engineering, soft skills, studio-based classroom, reflective journaling, problem-based learning

1. INTRODUCTION

We are embracing the challenges in broadening participation of computing in middle schools of underserved communities as opportunities for university computer science students to develop valuable technical and communication skills. Our central theme is that middle school teachers can be significantly supported in their quest to integrate computing into their teaching with the help and role models of carefully mentored undergraduate software development teams, who in turn gain from collaborative learning [1, 7, 12], software engineering practice with a real client [11, 10], peer leader experiences [5], and an opportunity to experience first-hand the potential impact of their computing expertise in helping others [4, 3]. The service experience may in turn improve underrepresented participation in computing at the college level [8].

The authors have partnered with a local, 2400-student, K-8 school in a city with one of the highest crime and poverty rates in Pennsylvania. The partner school received a generous donation of XO laptops designed for the One-Laptop-per-Child program which targets the world's poorest children [9]. We have developed a pilot program that leverages the low-cost, networked XO laptops to help their teachers integrate computational thinking into middle school math, science, language arts, and social studies in a sustainable way.

The program is highlighted by: (1) development of *computational thinking activities* and *increased collaborative and differentiated learning opportunities* to enable computing-based learning in middle school, (2) a *service learning* course for CS majors, with *collaborative development teams* matched with the teachers and led by *peer leaders* to develop XO learning activities and apply good *software engineering practice* with *a real client*, and (3) continuous *software and professional development customized to teachers' student learning goals*, with biannual teacher-focused workshops for training and collaborating. This paper describes the first two of these efforts.

We have developed a service learning course in computer science, with the goal of engaging computer science majors (sophomore or later) by partnering with middle school teachers to integrate XO-based computing into their teaching. Our goals for using service learning with undergraduates are: to effectively learn fundamentals of software engineering via a service context; increasing overall learning, enthusiasm, confidence in technical abilities and communication skills; and delivering a final educational software product that incorporates learning components and is useful to the partner school. We also strive to create awareness about the challenges and strategies of technology in education, the role and impact of assessment in education, and the range and difference of learning styles and how to target each through soft-

*This material is based on work supported by the National Science Foundation Grant CNS-0940501. Thanks to our evaluators Kathy Pusecker and Manuel Torres, learning specialists Cecily Selling and Jon Manon, and service learning coordinator Sue Serra.

Permission to make digital or hard copies of all or part of this work for personal or classroom use is granted without fee provided that copies are not made or distributed for profit or commercial advantage and that copies bear this notice and the full citation on the first page. To copy otherwise, to republish, to post on servers or to redistribute to lists, requires prior specific permission and/or a fee.
SIGCSE'12, February 29–March 3, 2012, Raleigh, North Carolina, USA.
Copyright 2012 ACM 978-1-4503-1098-7/12/02 ...$10.00.

ware. Service learning participation has been shown to have a particularly positive impact on minorities and women [8].

We pair student teams with middle school teachers (the clients) to develop educational software. These teams are guided by "peer leaders" who have taken the course previously. The partnership targets middle school students (grades 6-8) and math, science, language arts, and social studies teachers. While our students work closely with the teachers, middle school students will be the ultimate users of the learning software, providing feedback directly to our students and through teachers on the developed software, noting robustness, usability, user-friendliness, and fun. Specifically, the goal is to design a piece of educational software which both facilitates learning and also is "replayable". The authors, as instructors in the course and supervisors of the partnership, are committed to steering both the CS students and middle school teachers away from projects that do not incorporate educational learning components in their final product. For example, projects such as building a website, creating an automated quiz grader, or facilitating web-based testing were discouraged. As a result, we believe that our course is primarily service learning for education.

We have taught four semesters of the course (Fall 2009, Spring 2010, Fall 2010, Spring 2011) so far. This paper describes the course components, logistics and lessons learned, evaluation, and guidance to other instructors interested in developing a similar course at their institution.

2. COURSE COMPONENTS

Table 1 shows the general timetable for organizing the three major components of software engineering, service learning and soft skills lessons into a 14-week semester course. Both service learning and teaching of soft skills are interleaved with the software engineering process. Attention is paid to each major component during every week of the semester. We use pedagogies that we found to be successful in our earlier independent study course: collaborative teamwork, open-ended project, weekly presentations, continuous revision, and reflective journaling. Each subsection details some uses of these pedagogies for providing a practical software engineering experience, service learning with an educational partner, and development of soft skills along with technical skills.

2.1 Software Engineering

Our main software engineering goal is to provide students with a practical experience in the software engineering process including client introduction and requirements gathering and analysis, software design creation and critique, iterative design, implementation, testing, client use and feedback, and revision [6, 11, 10]. Our first activity is to form the CS student teams to be matched with middle school teachers. Each semester, we have had enough students to create 3-5 teams of 4 students each. Students complete a questionnaire on the first day of class which we use to construct teams based on schedule availability and balanced by programming experience, CS background, confidence, and self-rating of communication skills.

Students are presented with the challenge of designing, implementing, and deploying a learning game to meet their teachers' objectives for the middle school students in mind. The first challenge is learning the XO platform, and how to program in Python for the XO, including GUI programming and working with a database on a remote server. Students complete coding assignments and help each other master the intricacies of programming interactive software with Python on the XO.

Student teams take responsibility for coding and presenting various aspects of Python to each other. Discussions of advanced Python language features which are critical to master in order to provide youth-friendly user interfaces and exploit the collaborative capabilities of the XO laptops (such as GUIs, animation/motion/display buffering, events, etc.) are typically augmented by the instructors to ensure that they are discussed in enough detail. We also discovered that a review of OO design principles is helpful at this stage. Python learning is capped by reviewing the previous semesters' products and fixing any bugs found after release.

We discuss requirements gathering and analysis, storyboarding, and how to formulate and utilize use cases, as an initial step in software design and engineering. The design presentations and critiques integrate studio-based learning into the classroom environment. Teams present their hand-drawn storyboards, example screen shots, and use cases portraying the proposed flow of their game to the class. The presentations also focus on how learning at higher levels of Bloom's taxonomy will be incorporated into the game. The student audience then critiques (and compliments) the presentation and brainstorm ways to improve the game. After initial rounds, we invite an outside panel to offer additional perspectives from their collective technical experience at the K-12 levels in differentiated instruction and incorporating learning into pedagogies. This iterative development and critique continues throughout the semester.

Following several teacher (client) meetings, prototypes, and iterative development and critique, the implementations evolve to alphas and then to betas. The betas are first tested by the CS instructors and the other teams. We provide feedback, and minor revisions (hopefully only minor!) are determined and implemented given the time constraints. This effectively becomes the final version of the learning game due to the semester constraints. A final presentation and demo to invited guests, and partner school classroom distribution and in-situ observation conclude the semester.

2.2 Service Learning

An unusual aspect of our course is that it integrates a software engineering learning experience into a service learning experience to benefit an underrepresented group. This provides our undergraduates with multiple clients (middle school teachers and students) and the opportunity to see their final product deployed in a classroom, all in a learning context outside of the university.

At the start of the semester, we discuss the XO Laptop program, our partnership with the middle school, and assign readings from popular media about the current successes and failures of the XO Laptop program worldwide. Our Service Learning office facilitates discussions on service learning features and pitfalls, and reviews preconceptions about middle school learning environments and underprivileged communities.

The student teams take their first trip off-campus to observe the middle school classroom using the XOs and meet privately with their teacher team. The CS team objective is to gain an understanding of the learning challenges and context in the partner school. The CS students must con-

Table 1: Week-by-week timetable for Software Engineering (SE), Service Learning (SL), and Soft Skill development (SS) over 14-week course with partner school (PS)

Week	Software Engineering (SE)	Service Learning (SL)	Soft Skills (SS)
1	familiarize with XO laptop and existing software; form teams	obtain competence in PS' computing technology; discuss and begin journaling	introduce students, peer leaders, and team members; discuss teamwork, peer review, critiquing
2,3	research programming concepts that are believed to be important; teach each other main Python programming language features, and how to bundle and distribute "activities" on XO laptop	introduce context of XO: One Laptop Per Child (OLPC); discuss potential cultural differences in community partner (PS); discuss middle school learning environments	prepare for first teacher meeting; facilitate discussion about communicating w/non-tech; goals/strategies for meeting; team presentation of Python features
4,5	demo advanced Python programming (gui, graphics, animation, events); server-client protocols and databases; IDE integration; versioning; review OO design patterns	observe PS students using XO; meet PS teachers and gain understanding of PS students' learning challenges; report out on teacher meetings; follow-up with email to teachers	thank and politely request follow-up meeting with community partner; collaborate and communicate as a team
6,7	gather and analyze requirements; present software design as storyboards and use cases; iterative redesign	brainstorm initial game ideas; understand that individuals have different learning styles; map designs into Bloom's taxonomy; identify state requirements which guide PS lessons	give and receive peer critique; write reflective journal entries on PS and team experiences; discuss how to demo software, communicate and sell ideas to teachers
8,9	develop prototypes; test and iterate; demo alpha version (on emulator); consider change from client feedback	schedule and conduct design critique meeting with teachers; review feedback from PS teachers	prepare and present a report in class that emphasizes teams' proposed handling of teacher feedback
10,11	test; present progress reports; discuss remaining challenges; critique peers; demo beta version	schedule final demo and classroom observations with teachers; develop observation goals	prepare and present a demo with a progress report on the status of their learning game
12,13	test peers' games and submit feedback; debug minor bugs; port; overcome hardware issues; fine-tune final version (on XO laptop)	demo final version to PS teachers; deploy final version in classroom and observe its use by PS students	collaborate with entire class to prepare an overall class-wide project presentation; rehearse to clock
14	share with CIS faculty and peers; package final version for future distribution by others	report out on classroom observation experiences in class; bundle final product with documentation to PS teachers	present in a formal presentation forum to a strongly technical audience

sider the objectives and challenges of both the middle school teachers and their students during the design phases; both audiences are critical to a successful product.

During the brainstorming and software design phase, we invite a learning specialist from a local K-12 school to explain that individuals can have different learning styles (e.g. visual, auditory, kinesthetic) and that an educational game needs to consider the strengths and limitations that a user may have. We also discuss Bloom's taxonomy [2] of learning objectives: remember, understand, apply, analyze, evaluate, create. We are interested in creating learning games that reach the analytical and evaluation objectives, and we discuss this with our students. To date our products are mostly skills practice (apply). This is partially due to the difficulty of designing and making fun analysis/evaluation games in ten weeks.[1]

A major objective of our partner school is for their students to demonstrate competence in learning areas via a strong performance on the state assessment exam. Thus undergraduates spend some time researching the state assessment exams and understanding the concepts they cover, so that our brainstorming can lead to a learning game that caters to multiple learning styles, reaches as many learning levels as possible, and is conceptually relevant to the state assessment for the targeted grade level.

[1]We are improving in this regard, and will report in a future paper.

2.3 Soft Skills

A significant component throughout the course is "soft skills" development. Students learn how to handle team management issues, effectively present their design ideas, carefully and constructively critique others' ideas, conduct useful and persuasive demos of their software, good reflective journal entries, and communicate with a non-technical teacher client and middle school students living in a high crime, high poverty community.

We use various techniques to increase the self-awareness of our students' soft skills and challenge them to improve. For example, each semester students typically have the false impression that they can prepare minimally and still successfully initiate and lead a meeting with their teacher team to brainstorm a semester project. However, before their first teacher meeting, each student team is put into a role play situation where the authors play the non-technical middle school teacher who is quite knowledgeable about their teaching and middle school students. During the role-play, most students typically stumble on: facilitating an introduction or ice-breaker, communicating the goals of the partnership and the current meeting, avoiding computer science lingo and acronyms, and/or establishing a back-and-forth dialogue to brainstorm educational learning game possibilities. This role play takes many of our students outside of their comfort zone. We then assist students in identifying a list of goals for the initial meeting, and a corresponding set of strategies to achieve the goals. We then have a series of smaller role-plays to practice specific techniques.

We also dedicate several class sessions preparing for the client meeting, culminating in a one-page summary of the objectives and lists for requirements gathering during the meeting, and a CS team profile document to leave with the teacher. Students confidently leave their initial teacher meetings with an understanding of the teacher's goals, a sense of where the middle school students struggle in learning, a broad idea of the lesson schedules for the year, and ideas on how technology could be incorporated in the classroom. Back at the university we evaluate the meeting in terms of goals met.

Students also hone their communication skills as they work in teams, present their ideas and projects to the whole class, give and receive critiques, write in their reflective journals and demo their software to assorted audiences. They practice how to communicate technically as well as non-technically, and it is fun for us to watch the dramatic improvement over the semester. For many of our students, this is the first time they have discussed what makes communication successful, and the course emphasis reinforces the importance of building good communication skills.

3. COURSE LOGISTICS

3.1 Class Time, Assignments and Assessment

We have varied the weight of each grade component over time, but the over-riding importance of the project has been constant. Weekly project presentations are an excellent opportunity for feedback from peers and faculty. In our experience, peer feedback is much more powerful – students work much harder to please their team and peer audience than they would work for a grade from faculty. These widely varied components all contribute to the success of each team and their project; if any piece is done poorly, their entire project suffers.

60% Learning Game Project.

Weekly Presentations: Each presentation begins with the goal slide from the previous week, along with a list of successes, challenges, and a DONE/NOT DONE rating. This style makes it fairly simple to assign intermediate project grades to software engineering deliverables, e.g. storyboards, code, tests. After discussion of successes, challenges, and decisions, new goals are set for the following week. The quality of the presentation and participation are also noted.

Customer Relations: We use subjective evaluation by the faculty on a team's work with the middle school teachers.

Peer Evaluation Factor: Individuals use an online questionnaire to evaluate themselves and other team members along six continua: contributing in meetings, team communication, timely task completion, design and correctness, doing their share, and overall. Individual ratings are averaged and a zero-sum project grade factor is calculated for each team member relative to the team average rating. Thus a strong team member could be assigned a factor of 1.10, while a weaker team member could receive a .90 factor. Faculty reserve the right to intervene if these factors seem out of line, but we have not yet had to do so.

15% Class Participation. Participation is crucial to the design of the course, so students are held accountable for contributing to e.g. discussions, role plays, and critiquing sessions. Intermediate feedback about this grade can be delivered in journal comments or directly. This is a subjective grade assigned by faculty in consultation with peer leaders.

15% Reflective Journal. An important component of service learning is directed-reflection, which connects what students learn in the classroom with their experience of real-world conditions [3]. We have found that students need time to reflect on what they are experiencing, as most are being put into situations very different from their own experiences. Reflection on learning is also a pedagogical technique used to promote the higher order cognitive skills of analysis, synthesis, and evaluation, i.e., critical thinking.

Students maintain a directed reflective journal as a private wiki. We also lead discussions on effective journaling. Students are given a set of default questions to structure their entries ("How well is your team working together?"), and additional journal questions are communicated during class based on discussions or presentations ("Explain three aspects of this CS course in terms of Bloom's Taxonomy."). For full credit, students write two entries per week. Peer leaders, and sometimes faculty, read and comment in private journals as a means of delivering feedback and encouraging meta-analysis of individual, team, and class performance. Journal feedback gives us a way to acknowledge and support individuals outside of the classroom. This is a subjective grade assigned by peer leaders in consultation with faculty.

10% Quizzes and Labs. We give a small set of quizzes on programming topics, software engineering, and other discussions from class, e.g. learning styles and Bloom's taxonomy, and small labs on Python. These help students gauge their progress, and can serve as an indicator for instructors trying to understand team dynamics.

3.2 Partnering with the School

Working with middle school teachers has been enlightening. Busy teachers with established curricula and very full schedules are still willing to spend extra time to have our students visit. Our initial contacts with the partner school were all through the administration. Administration was protective of their teachers and did not want, for example, to have us peppering them with email. Communication turnarounds were sometimes two weeks. Once we established relations with individual teachers, communication sped up significantly (but only rarely is within 24 hours).

The middle school teachers do not have much experience with educational software outside of quizzes, so all of our early projects were skills tests that assigned a numeric grade. To change this, we taught our students that they would have to *sell* their more interesting project ideas to the teachers. This resulted in more interesting meetings and software.

Each CS student visits the partner school 3-5 times. Scheduling visits is tricky given students' and teachers' conflicting schedules. Our class does not have the benefit of any "open" service learning day. Driving time to the school is an hour round trip, and the trip would probably not be worthwhile if meetings and observations were less than two hours on-site. This means that each trip is at minimum a three hour commitment. Students car-pool each other[2]. Early visits are typically by the whole class, while later visits are scheduled by teams with their teachers. Having teams negotiate meetings with their teachers adds a level of professionalism to

[2]In one semester, visits were so difficult to negotiate that project teams were formed around carpools.

the process. Sometimes multiple teachers are willing to provide more critique than an individual teacher at the client meetings, especially when the ratio of teachers-to-students is closer to 1:1.

4. EVALUATION

The program evaluation was designed to measure how well the program goals were met each semester, as well as to provide qualitative feedback on the course for continuing improvement.

Program Goals and Expected Outcomes. Our goals for the CS students each semester were to (1) increase knowledge/experience in software engineering, (2) build team management skills, (3) increase technical knowledge of the discipline, (4) improve problem solving skills, (5) improve communication skills with non-technical clients, (6) design and implement a project addressing a community problem, (7) increase enthusiasm for CS, (8) increase awareness of potential impact of applying technical expertise, and (9) increase confidence in ability to succeed in CS.

Evaluation Instruments. The University's Office of Educational Assessment (OEA) developed evaluation instruments and collected and analyzed data for the surveys. This included pre and post surveys of the computer science students enrolled in the course each semester. OEA also attended the final demo presentations of the learning software created by the students each semester and wrote reports on their observations of the students products and informal conversations with them. OEA also joined the students a few times in their middle school classroom instruction sessions and provided a report on their observations of the middle school students, CS students, and teachers during those sessions. OEA also conducted a focus group study in Spring 2011 of the students who participated in the course in the third semester, Fall 2010. The instructors monitored and analyzed the reflective journals of the service learning students. In addition, CS students completed peer evaluations of their team members periodically throughout the semester.

Results and Discussion. Table 2 shows results from pre-post surveys for the last two semesters.

Software Engineering Skills - Questions 4 through 7 are targeted at gaining student perceptions on their software engineering skills before and after this course experience. For question 4, "teach myself a new programming language", there was an in increase from 89% to 100% in "strongly agree" and "agree" responses. For question 7, "be able to develop software to meet a client's needs", there was an increase from 68% to 95% in "strongly agree" and "agree" responses. Interestingly, the percent of students who "strongly agreed" and "agreed" that they would work well with their peers decreased from 95% to 85%. This may reflect students' first experience with a team and a large project[3]. For question 5, "be able to talk to and question non-computer science clients to meet their needs", there was an increase from 95% to 100% in "strongly agree" and "agree" responses, and the percentage who responded "strongly agree" increased 39%.

Two students wrote in their reflective journals:

> "It was also interesting to work with the teachers because it added a whole new dimension to programming that I'm not used to. Some of our work was scrapped ...I guess that just shows what it would be like in the real world."

> "Storyboarding the game is pretty interesting. I've never done anything like that before, and its sort of fun. Plus it really makes you think about what feature you are going to have, and which ones you will have to cut. Its also a challenge to figure out how you are going to transition smoothly from one aspect to the next, and arrange everything on one screen."

Service Learning and its Impact - Questions 8 are 9 are targeted at gaining student perceptions on working for or seeking paid work for a non-profit. The results are mixed. While the percentage of "strongly agree" to "agree" responses decreased between the pre and post survey, the results for "strongly agree" increased.

Overall, the undergraduate students stated they had a positive experience working with their assigned teachers. Our evaluator reported these responses from CS students at the final demo:

> "These CS students reported that it was easy to develop a rapport with the teachers since they were only a few years older than the CS undergrads. They reported that the teachers were excited to work with this team. The CS students said the teachers had many ideas and informed this team specifically of the area of study (math, such as fractions and decimals) they wanted their game to be based upon, and the skills the game would be used to enhance."

> "The CS students said interacting with teachers was a lot easier than they thought it would be. After the initial contact, they felt comfortable in communicating with the teachers."

> "This team said it was easy to talk with and interact with their specific teacher. This CS student said that although his teacher was not "tech savvy" she was still actively engaging with CS undergrads on this project."

In a May report from the evaluator's interviews of CS students, she reports: "All but one [student] reports feeling like they were helping a community that needs their skills and that made them feel good about themselves. All but one reported feeling like they would continue to think about volunteering their skills."

Soft Skills - Questions 1, 2, and 3 provide insight into both service learning impact and soft skills development. Overall, the experience with working with teachers actually decreased their confidence in teaching teachers how to use laptops in the classroom. This may reflect the fact that students weren't expecting to have to instruct teachers in using XO laptops, which use a variant of the GNU/Linux OS. However, their confidence in teaching middle school students to operate laptops with unique software increased from 74% to 90% in "strongly agree" and "agree" responses.

[3]Our introductory courses now incorporate more teamwork.

Table 2: Pre/Post Survey Results from 19 responses and the latest 2 semesters of data. Students responded using a 5-point scale: AA=Strongly Agree, A=Agree, N=Neither Agree nor Disagree, D=Disagree, DD=Strongly Disagree. Out of 100 percent.

Survey Question: I am confident that I can and will ...		AA	A	N	D	DD
1. Teach Middle School Teachers how to use laptops in their classrooms	pre	47	53	0	0	0
	post	35	50	10	0	5
2. Teach Middle School Students to operate laptops with unique software	pre	26	48	26	0	0
	post	35	55	10	0	0
3. Interact with underrepresented middle school students	pre	26	53	16	5	0
	post	30	50	15	5	0
4. Teach myself a new programming language	pre	68	21	11	0	0
	post	70	30	0	0	0
5. Be able to talk to and question non Computer Science clients to meet their needs	pre	26	69	5	0	0
	post	65	35	0	0	0
6. Work very well with my peers to serve a client	pre	16	79	5	0	0
	post	35	50	15	0	0
7. Be able to develop software to meet a client's needs	pre	26	42	32	0	0
	post	45	50	5	0	0
8. Volunteer my computer knowledge to help a non-profit after I graduate	pre	21	42	32	1	5
	post	40	15	40	5	0
9. Seek out paid work with a non-profit business	pre	5	26	53	11	5
	post	20	10	60	10	0
10. Seek out employment with a for-profit business after graduating	pre	42	32	26	0	0
	post	65	25	10	0	0

5. GUIDANCE TO OTHER EDUCATORS

We conclude with what we believe are the key lessons learned from these four semesters:

- The most powerful learning moment in the course is when teams watch real middle school students use their software. Both triumphs and failures are greatly magnified. We found that having this moment early helps teams address issues before semester end.
- In general, soft skills that are explicitly discussed or role-played in class ("How do you introduce your ideas to a teacher?") are vastly more successful than those communicated via lecture.
- Role playing takes time, but is efficient. It forces students to confront their skills, or lack thereof.
- Brainstorming the characteristics of good and bad critique, and then pointing out examples of good critique, helps students learn how to critique. It is important to verbally praise good critiques when they happen.
- Coordinating with teachers is easiest using direct communication between teachers and their matched teams, with oversight from instructors. Students should provide a written list of goals before each interaction.
- Debriefing after community interactions should be done as soon as possible, with full class discussion followed by individual reflective journaling.
- Journaling improves individualized student communication with instructors.
- For the end-of-semester presentation, students should do a timed dress rehearsal and get class feedback.

6. REFERENCES

[1] *Greater Expectations: A New Vision for Learning as a Nation goes to College*. Association of American Colleges and Universities, 2002.

[2] B. Bloom, M. Englehart, E. Furst, W. Hill, and D. Krathwohl. *Taxonomy of educational objectives: The classification of educational goals*. Longman Group, United Kingdom, 1956.

[3] R. G. Bringle and J. A. Hatcher. Reflection in service-learning: Making meaning of experience. *Educational Horizons*, pages 179–185, 1999.

[4] D. Cone and S. Harris. Service-learning practice: Developing a theoretical framework. *Michigan Journal of Community Service Learning*, 3:31–43, 1996.

[5] B. J. Duch, S. E. Groh, and D. E. Allen, editors. *The Power of Problem-based Learning: A Practical 'How To' for teaching Undergraduate Courses in Any Discipline*. Stylus Publications, 2001.

[6] J. Liu, J. Marsaglia, and D. Olson. Teaching software engineering to make students ready for the real world. *Jouranl of Computing Sciences in Colleges*, 18:43–50, 2002.

[7] B. J. Millis and P. G. Cottell. *Cooperative Learning For Higher Education Faculty*. American Council on Education, 1998.

[8] W. Oakes. *Service-learning in Engineering:A Resource Guidebook*. Campus Compact, 2004.

[9] OLPC. One laptop per child. http://laptop.org/en/.

[10] J. A. Polack-Wahl. Incorporating the client's role in a software engineering course. *30th SIGCSE Technical Symposium on Computer Science Education*, pages 73–77, 1999.

[11] C. P. Rosience and J. A. Rosiene. Experiences with a real software engineering client. *Frontiers in Education Conference*, 2006.

[12] L. Springer, M. E. Stanne, and S. S. Donovan. Effects of small-group learning on undergraduates in science, mathematics, engineering, and technology: A meta-analysis. *Review of Educational Research*, 69:21–51, 1999.

The Fairy Performance Assessment: Measuring Computational Thinking in Middle School

Linda Werner
University of California
Santa Cruz, CA
831-459-1017
linda@soe.ucsc.edu

Jill Denner
ETR Associates
4 Carbonero Way
Scotts Valley, CA 95066
831-438-4060
jilld@etr.org

Shannon Campe
ETR Associates
shannonc@etr.org

Damon Chizuru Kawamoto
Brown University
chchchez@aol.com

ABSTRACT
Computational thinking (CT) has been described as an essential capacity to prepare students for computer science, as well as to be productive members of society. But efforts to engage K-12 students in CT are hampered by a lack of definition and assessment tools. In this paper, we describe the first results of a newly created performance assessment tool for measuring CT in middle school. We briefly describe the context for the performance assessment (game-programming courses), the aspects of CT that are measured, the results, and the factors that are associated with performance. We see the development of assessment tools as a critical step in efforts to bring CT to K-12, and to strengthen the use of game programming in middle school. We discuss problems and implications of our results.

Categories and Subject Descriptors
K.3.2 [Computers and Education]: Computer and Information Science Education – *Computer science education.*

General Terms
Measurement.

Keywords
Assessment, Computational Thinking, Game Programming, Middle School, Pair Programming, Alice.

1. INTRODUCTION
Computational thinking (CT) was first described by Papert [10], and then pioneered by Wing [16]. At its core, it is closely related to scientific reasoning defined as the specification of a problem, use of resources for inquiry and hypothesis generation, model building and experimentation to test hypotheses, and the evaluation of evidence [4] [17]. Additional features of CT include creating artifacts and automation. Little is known about the development of CT in K-12, although recent articles begin to describe what it looks like [3][6].

Permission to make digital or hard copies of all or part of this work for personal or classroom use is granted without fee provided that copies are not made or distributed for profit or commercial advantage and that copies bear this notice and the full citation on the first page. To copy otherwise, or republish, to post on servers or to redistribute to lists, requires prior specific permission and/or a fee.
SIGCSE'12, February29–March 3, 2012 Raleigh, North Carolina, USA.
Copyright 2012 ACM 978-1-4503-1098-7/12/02...$10.00.

One factor that limits the uptake of CT into K-12 is the lack of assessments. The ACM and CSTA report titled "Running on Empty: Failure to Teach K-12 Computer Science in the Digital Age" [15] states "Assessments for computer science education are virtually non-existent." To our knowledge, the only existing measures of pre-college CT were created by Repenning et al [11] yet there have been numerous recent reports of measures of computer science conceptual understanding thought to be useful in the acquisition of CT including [5][12][13].

The purpose of this study was to develop and test a CT performance assessment for middle school students, and to understand why there is variation across students, in order to develop and strengthen efforts to engage K-12 students in CT. The study was conducted in computer game programming classes held after school and during electives. Classes were randomly assigned to either solo or pair programming conditions, based on research that shows programming with a partner is beneficial in terms of retention and performance to both male and female university students learning to program [17]. We predicted that some of these benefits would be observed from pair programming over solo programming for middle school students too.

Prior work provides the basis for both the type of assessment we designed and for the choice of attributes we used in our search for which factors explain variance in students' CT. Most relevant to our choice for assessment style is the work by Webb [14] who reports success with a post-test assessment used in after-school classes of 24 middle school students creating 3D games with AgentCubes, a programming environment designed for youth. Webb used five faulty scenarios to assess his students' skill in CT. He observes that the administration of equivalent pre- and post-test assessments "for software-dependent instruction is problematic as student fluency requires some degree of familiarity with the software." Problems arise because students could take hours to become familiar enough with the programming environment so that working on the assessment would make sense. Webb's faulty scenarios are based on programming patterns the students learn in class but are interspersed with faults. Most important for our choice for attribute analysis is the work by Linn [9] who is an early investigator in the area of assessment of problem solving skills among novice programmers. Linn described the Chain of Cognitive Accomplishments [9], which includes three links: Comprehension: understand programs and be able to make small changes to single program instructions; Design: build programs from collections of patterns and use procedural skills to combine these patterns to solve problems; and Problem Solving: learn transferable problem-solving skills and use them in new and different formal systems. In this paper, we use Linn's three-link chain metaphor to describe the different cognitive demands in our assessment, and to interpret variation in our results.

2. METHOD

2.1 Participants

The data described in this paper were collected over two years as part of a study of how game creation and pair programming can promote CT. A total of 325 students with parental consent participated in classes at seven public schools along the central California coast. Participation in all parts of the study was voluntary and we are reporting on 311 students who submitted a Fairy assessment. In year 1, 78 students participated in after-school classes, and in year 2, 37 participated in after-school and 196 in elective technology classes. More than half of the students (57%) were in the pair condition; however, due to absences, only 21% of the total were partnered all the time, and 23% most of the time.

Of the 311 students, 36% were female; they ranged in age from 10-14 years (mean=12), 52% were white, 37% were Latino/a, and 75% spoke English or primarily English at home. Twenty five percent had mothers with educational levels of high school or lower, and 39% of mothers had completed a university degree.

2.2 Procedure

Students used one of the two programming environments in the Alice [2] series developed at Carnegie Mellon. In year 1, students used Storytelling Alice (SA), and in year 2 they used Alice 2.2 because SA is only available on PCs, which were limited at our partner schools. In the rest of this paper, we will refer to both SA and Alice 2.2 as Alice unless it is necessary to distinguish between the two. Alice allows users to control characters in 3D environments using drag-and-drop programming, a language that is closely related to Java, and many other modern imperative programming languages. Most code is written in the methods of objects that have properties that store state and functions that return values. Each property, method, and function is attached to an object, with World being the global object. The event system in Alice is primarily used to handle user interactions, such as mouse clicks, although it can also handle in-World events, such as when the value of a variable changes.

Students engaged with CT in a three-stage progression called Use-Modify-Create[6] over approximately 20 hours during a semester. In the first half of the semester, students worked through a series of self-paced instructional exercises built to provide scaffolding, which we call "challenges." During the last half of the course, the students freely designed and developed their own games. Most students completed 8 to 10 of 11 required challenges, though some completed up to six additional optional challenges. In our courses where pair programming was used, two students shared one computer, with one driving (controlling the mouse and keyboard) and the other navigating (checking for bugs, consulting resources, and providing input). We asked students to reverse roles approximately every 20 minutes. At the end of the semester, students were given up to 30 minutes to *individually* complete the Fairy Assessment described below. The data collectors and the instructions did not refer to it as a test or assessment, but we told students we designed it to help us know what students learned in the classes. While working on the assessment, students could ask for clarification of instructions only.

2.3 Measures

Students completed an on-line survey at the beginning and end of the semester. The items include demographic questions about age, gender, race/ethnicity, language spoken at home, mother's and father's use of computers at work, grades on last report card, and favorite subject at school. Additional questions measure confidence with computers (e.g., I feel confident about my ability to use computers), attitude toward computers (e.g., I would like to learn more about computers), frequency and type of computer use, and simple Alice content knowledge (8 multiple-choice items with screen shots of images and sample code). Classroom teachers collected attendance data that we used to compute total number of hours attended, as well as total number of hours that students in the paired condition worked with a partner. The parent completing the consent form reported parent education levels.

3. THE FAIRY ASSESSMENT

We created the Fairy Assessment as an Alice program to analyze two of the three parts of CT identified by the Carnegie Mellon Center for Computational Thinking (CMCCT): thinking algorithmically, and making effective use of abstraction and modeling. We did not include an assessment task to measure considering and understanding scale, the third part of CT as identified by the CMCCT, since we did not include scale topics in our set of required challenges and few students experimented with aspects of scale in their games. In Year 1, we gave some of the directions on paper; we gave other directions via game character dialog. In Year 2, in an effort to standardize the instructions, all directions were communicated both via game character dialog and repeated as itemized text instructions displayed at the bottom of the program screen throughout the exercise. The top level of the program is a sequence of method calls each containing a series of Alice primitive control statements and built-in method calls. See Figure 1.

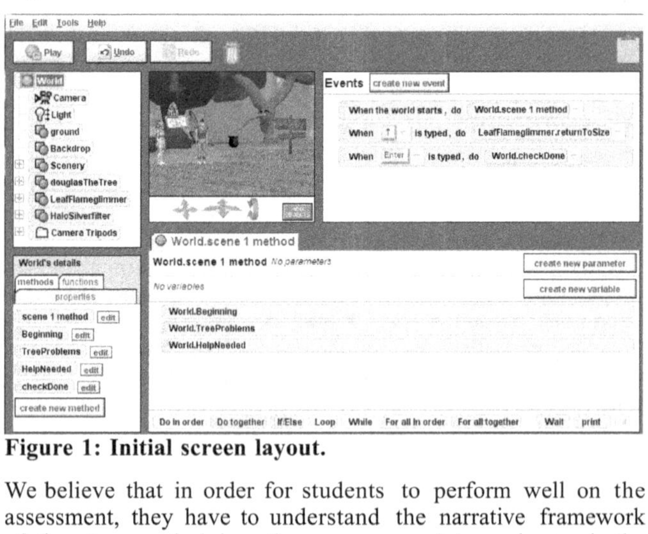

Figure 1: Initial screen layout.

We believe that in order for students to perform well on the assessment, they have to understand the narrative framework of the story underlying the program and to understand the existing program instructions that create that framework. The assessment features two fairies: HaloSilver (female) and LeafFlame (male). When the student plays the program, they see HaloSilver talking, and LeafFlame talking about walking into a forbidden forest where he shrinks to one-half his original size because of a magic spell. He asks for help because he's stuck in the forest and can't fly (also the result of a magic spell). Figure 2 is a screen shot showing LeafFlame walking into the forbidden forest. We designed three separate and independent assessment tasks with varying levels of difficulty so that failure in any one task did not dictate failure in any other. We designed the tasks to measure aspects of algorithmic thinking and abstraction and modeling. The following is an overview of each task.

Figure 2: LeafFlame walking into forbidden forest.

Task 1 instructions say to program HaloSilver so that she turns to watch LeafFlame as he walks into the forbidden forest; the turning should take the same amount of time that it takes LeafFlame to talk. Students that do this correctly understand the basic narrative framework of the story and can correctly place instructions within a given finite sequence of instructions (algorithm). They also recognize the need to modify a method parameter: the length of time of execution of an instruction (abstraction and modeling). We assigned full credit for this task (10 points) if students recognized the need for concurrent execution of this new turn method call along with an existing LeafFlame walk method call into the forest and if the instruction length was modified appropriately. We assigned students 4 points (partial credit) if HaloSilver turned somewhere in the vicinity of LeafFlame's walk. Both of these solutions suggest the student has achieved the first link in Linn's chain of cognitive accomplishments because he/she understands someone else's program code enough to make simple changes or additions.

In Task 2, HaloSilver asks the student to repair the program; HaloSilver says, "Make pressing the up arrow work right and return LeafFlame to his original size." We expected Task 2 to be the most difficult. To solve task 2, students need to think algorithmically and understand that event handlers alter a program's default execution sequence. They need to recognize the presence of an event handler for the up arrow and verify it is not working correctly. Correcting the method called in the 'up arrow event handler' (LeafFlame's returnToSize method) shows algorithmic thinking because it shows the student understands how to read, interpret, and correct or replace the conditional logic in this method. See Figure 3. We assigned credit of from 2 to 8 points for partial solutions. For example, in one solution attempt, a student added another event handler for the up arrow that called one of LeafFlame's built-in methods: resize with parameter set to '2'. If this code was present **and** the initial handler removed, this solution would have earned the student 10 points because it would clearly demonstrate a cognitive accomplishment including the second link in Linn's chain of cognitive accomplishments: build programs from collections of patterns and use procedural skills to combine these patterns to solve problems. Unfortunately, the student left both up arrow event handlers in the program; indicative of movement into the second link of Linn's chain.

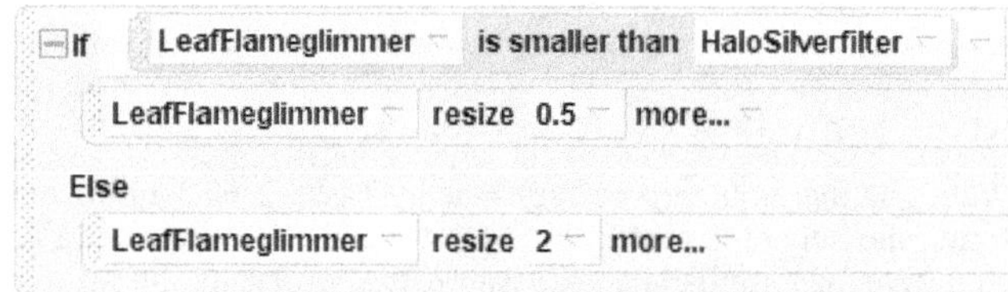

Figure 3: Faulty logic of returnToSize method.

For Task 3, HaloSilver asks students to help LeafFlame fly out of the forest toward her; she says, "Make clicking on LeafFlame bring him to me and FLY out of the forest!" See Figure 4.

Figure 4: HaloSilver providing instructions.

To solve task 3, again students need to think algorithmically and understand that events alter the program's default execution sequence. This required students to recognize the need for, and then add another event handler. The complexity of Task 3 was high because the intended method call for this event handler ('flyAway') uses two parameters: 'to whom to fly' and 'number of times to fly.' Students need to think on another level of abstraction and navigate the object tree to locate LeafFlame and his built-in methods. The students must also have an understanding of abstraction to use the method 'flyAway towardWho numberOfTimes,' and analyze it in a detailed level to determine values for the parameters. Within-program feedback told the student if he or she was successful in helping LeafFlame: LeafFlame's size and position are checked. Partial credit of 8 points was assigned to students who created a 'mouse-click-on-LeafFlame' event handler calling one of LeafFlame's built-in methods: 'move toward' with parameter 'toward-who' set to HaloSilver. This solution makes LeafFlame move, but not 'fly,' out of the forest toward HaloSilver. Full credit of 10 points was assigned to a very creative solution: the student created a new method local to LeafFlame where LeafFlame's wings' flapped as he hopped up and down which made him appear to fly toward HaloSilver. The student called this method in a 'mouse-click-on-LeafFlame' event handler.

Successful solutions to Tasks 2 and 3 use knowledge of programming patterns, or segments of non-contiguous code that together form a complex computational construct. The use of a programming pattern is an example of a design skill that Linn [9] calls templates. She writes, "Templates are stereotypic patterns of code that use more than a single language feature. Templates perform complex functions such as sorting names alphabetically or summing a set of numbers. Templates can be used each time a given task is encountered. A large repertoire of templates enables the programmer to solve many problems without creating new code." The patterns we expected from our students include event handling, complex conditional use, and use of methods with multiple parameters. Partial scores of 4 in either of these two tasks constitute movement into the second link in Linn's chain of cognitive accomplishments.

We argue that non-zero performance in Tasks 2 or 3 represents some movement toward the second link in the chain of cognitive accomplishments because it shows that the student has a partial understanding of someone else's code and can modify portions of programming patterns to accomplish the tasks. The second link involves the design of a program using templates and skill in combining these templates. Completely understanding Task 2 requires code understanding, fault identification, code modification to remove the fault and places the student at the beginning of the third link in the chain.

4. DATA ANALYSIS

Two of the paper's authors scored the students' solutions to the Fairy Assessment. We graded each task on a scale from zero to ten, with partial credit possible, resulting in a maximum score of 30. The scorers discussed discrepancies and came to an agreement on all students' scores. The scoring rubric is available upon request from the first author.

The tasks were summarized separately, and although the average score on each task varied, the three task scores were significantly correlated (range is from r=.30 to r=.45). In this paper, we combined the task scores into a single total Fairy score for some analyses. We used bivariate analyses using t-tests and correlations to identify key factors from the pre- and post-survey data that were related to total Fairy scores.

5. RESULTS AND DISCUSSION

Mean (and standard deviation - σ) scores for the Fairy Assessment are given in Table 1.

Table 1. Fairy Assessment Scores, n=311

Task	Mean (σ)
1 (comprehension)	6.03 (3.87)
2 (comprehension, design, problem solving)	4.54 (4.73)
3 (comprehension, design)	5.93 (4.34)
Total score	16.50 (9.95)

Student performance was highest on Task 1, which measures comprehension, and lowest on Task 2, which measures comprehension, design, and complex problem solving skills using debugging. There was great variation in scores: 30 students submitted an unchanged program and were assigned a score of zero on all three tasks, while 40 students had perfect scores on all three tasks. There was not a significant difference between average scores for students from year 1 using SA (mean=16.13, standard deviation (sd)=9.38, n=78) and year 2 using Alice 2.2 (mean=16.63, sd=10.15, n=233).

Pair programming was found to be significantly positively related to assessment scores at the $p<0.01$ level: the more time a student spent with a partner while learning and programming a game, the higher their individual score on the assessment (r=.17). Since some students missed some classes, we maintained records of amount of time in a paired state while learning and programming their games. Several pre- and post-survey factors were significant at the $p < 0.05$ level. Several parental factors were positively related to total score: parent education (r=.31), and having a mother (yes mean=19.01, sd= 9.10; no mean=14.96, sd=10.18) and/or father (yes mean=19.79, sd=8.60; no mean=14.08, sd=10.31) that works with computers. In addition, students scored higher if they also reported speaking more English at home (r=.30). Several student factors at post-survey were positively correlated with Fairy Assessment scores: interest in taking a computer science class in high school (r=.14), grades in school (r=.25), frequency of computer-use across locations (r=.13), confidence with computers (r=.26), attitude toward computers (r=.18), and Alice content knowledge measured at post-survey time (r=.54). Total scores were not related to gender, student age, hours of attendance in the class, or their frequency of creating things using the computer outside this class.

The findings suggest that the Fairy assessment is a promising strategy for assessing CT during middle school. First, it was motivating: all but 30 of the students that worked on it submitted a modified program. Fourteen students were absent on the day of the assessment; there were no refusals. Webb [14] found similar results with the use of his assessment requiring trouble-shooting skills to debug faulty scenarios. He found middle school-aged students to be engaged for up to 45 minutes on his assessment.

Our results also suggest that the assessment was successful in picking up a range of CT across students, and a variety of types of CT across the three tasks. Mean scores for Task 2 were lowest, because it required students to debug the conditional logic in the method in the 'up arrow' event handler. Not all students completed challenges that taught conditional logic; this may have contributed to the lower scores on this task. Our findings are similar to what Linn [9] found in her sample of middle school students using BASIC: more progress was made in comprehension than in design. As a comparison, her assessment also did not address the third link in the chain of cognitive accomplishments.

The data provide some explanation of why student performance varied. For example, the scores for students in elective classes were higher (mean=17.94, sd=9.64) than those taking the class after school (mean=14.05, sd=10.02). The data confirm that this was not due to differences in SA and Alice 2.2. However, it may be related to the improved instructions for year 2 when all the in-school classes were held or to the higher levels of parent education among students in year 2. Another possible explanation is that students working in an in-school environment may be more attentive, more concerned about performance and grading, and therefore, learn more or try harder on an assessment.

Students that worked using pair programming scored higher than those that programmed alone. Additionally, we found the more time with a partner was related to higher CT performance. This is important because it tells us that pair programming was an effective technique to use for engaging middle school students in CT. Some educators express concern about whether both students benefit or whether the weaker student lets the stronger student work and reap the educational benefits. We found that both students, regardless of initial ability, scored higher than students that worked alone. This finding is consistent with what has been reported by researchers of pair programming at the university level [17]. Our results differ from those of Lewis [8] who gave daily quizzes to students entering sixth grade enrolled in a 3-week summer camp. She found statistically significantly greater variation in quiz scores between the students that shared one computer over the variation between students that worked on their own computer with help from an assigned collaborator to discuss problems. However, Lewis' study was of a very small number of students (40) and partners switched roles every 5 minutes instead of the longer time period we used. More research needs to be done to determine the circumstances under which pair programming benefits learning in middle school, however it appears to be useful for improved performance on the Fairy Assessment.

Not surprisingly, parent capacity was also related to students' scores on the assessment. The two measures, parent education and use of computers at work, indicate socioeconomic resources as well as exposure to computing outside of school were positively associated with assessment score. There were some students who did well on the assessment, even though their parents had low education and did not use computers at work. More detailed case studies are needed to understand the factors that helped some students with lower parent capacity to score high on the assessment.

Several behavioral factors were related to scores. More frequent computer use and higher grades on their last report card were related to higher performance on the Fairy Assessment. This suggests that students with greater access to computers, and those that do better academically, also engage in higher levels of CT. Similarly, students who are interested in taking a computer science class in high school score higher. These findings are not surprising, and unfortunately without a pre-test of the Fairy Assessment we cannot tell if the more advanced and interested students improved more over time, or started out at a higher level of CT.

Similar to results found by Levine and Donitsa-Schmidt [7] in a study of grade 7-12 students, we found confidence with computers to be an important predictor of performance. This may be due to a willingness to persist in the face of a challenging task, or to just having more experience. In our sample, confidence was also significantly correlated with frequency of computer use, and further analyses are needed to determine the relative importance of each of these factors. Levine and Donitsa-Schmidt suggest that confidence also predicts attitudes, which was another significant predictor of students' scores.

Some limitations of our study are that we are reporting bivariate associations that do not let us make conclusions about the relative importance of each factor. Many of these variables (significant and not significant) are highly correlated, and multi-level modeling is necessary to tease out the interrelationships. Another limitation is that the data collected from pairs is not independent, which violates certain statistical assumptions. Similarly, mean scores varied greatly across the seven school groups, and the interdependence of these scores is not taken into account. These types of data require more sophisticated dyadic data analysis, and multi-level modeling. Our next step is to conduct these analyses.

Another limitation of this study is the lack of a test of construct validity—whether the Fairy Assessment really measures the aspects of CT that we claim. To this end, we compared students' Alice content knowledge measured at post-survey and found it was positively related to performance on the Fairy Assessment. These knowledge questions assessed a student's understanding of someone else's program code, which is the first link in Linn's chain of cognitive accomplishments, and a key aspect of each of the tasks of the Fairy Assessment.

While the Fairy Assessment itself may not be generalizable to learning environments not using Alice, others who are trying to measure CT can easily adapt this assessment. Each task should be designed to measure certain aspects of CT (e.g., in our case we measured algorithmic thinking and abstraction and modeling), and certain links in the chain of cognitive accomplishments. Care must be taken to describe the assessment tasks in language that is consistent with the style used by the game characters. The tasks should be described to students without suggesting the use of specific program constructs (that would test programming syntax knowledge but not higher levels of knowledge needed for CT) but instead by describing requirements the solution must meet using the context of narrative of the game's virtual world. We believe we have done some of this with our Fairy Assessment.

It is possible that, with the current drag-and-drop programming interfaces that prevent syntactic errors, middle school students could complete a course using one environment (for example, Alice), and then work on an assessment using another environment (for example, Scratch). This would allow us to more accurately assess whether students accomplished the third link in the chain of cognitive accomplishments.

6. CONCLUSIONS AND FUTURE WORK

Elective technology and computer game courses for middle school students are a promising strategy to introduce CT to a broad population. This is an important step towards engaging groups that are currently underrepresented in the computer science community. However, without the ability to assess whether and how such programs can engage students in CT, they will likely never see widespread adoption.

In this paper, we continue the work pioneered by others in addressing the issue of CT by middle school students. We still have quite a few things to learn about the definition and assessment of CT in middle school youth. We are currently analyzing the 'challenges,' self-paced instructional materials, to identify aspects of CT that are taught in each of the challenges. We are also working on analysis of the log files to identify steps in students' solutions, which includes trying to understand what they tried before reaching a final solution, and their 'intent'. The Fairy Assessment logs can show us whether students place the correct instruction at the correct program location in one attempt or if they make multiple attempts. We want to look closer at the students' Fairy Assessments to determine if mistakes are indicative of CT misunderstandings or reflect specific issues in the mechanics of Alice programming. We are also experimenting with a translation of the Fairy Assessment into a Scratch version, which was recently implemented in two different Scratch courses. The Scratch assessment has three tasks that are very similar to those in the Fairy Assessment. We hope to report on these experiments soon. Also, we are looking at the results of other assessment methods used in this study. These include looking for evidence of CT in the students' games (identifying programming constructs and CT patterns similar to those described in [5] [12][11] and in the logs captured during game creation. Finally, we are coding videotapes of the pairs working together to see if the quality of interaction while students were learning Alice and making their games affects how well individual students do on the assessment.

7. ACKNOWLEDGMENTS
Our thanks go to the teachers and administrators at our seven schools, specifically Anne Guerrero, Shelly Laschkewitsch, Don Jacobs, Sue Seibolt, Karen Snedeker, Susan Rivas, and Katie Ziparo. Thanks also to teaching assistants, Will Park and Joanne Sanchez; and to Eloy Ortiz and Pat Rex, whose vital support was necessary to run this program. Thanks to all of the students who participated. Finally, thanks to Barb Ericson, Irene Lee, Clayton Lewis, Fred Martin, Alex Repenning, David Webb, Teale Fristoe, and Caitlin Sadowski for help on early drafts of this paper. This research is funded by a grant from NSF 0909733 "The Development of Computational Thinking among Middle School Students Creating Computer Games." Any opinions, findings, conclusions or recommendations expressed in this material are those of the authors and do not necessarily reflect the views of the National Science Foundation.

8. REFERENCES

[1] ACM K-12 Task Force Curriculum Committee. A Model Curriculum for K-12 Computer Science: Final Report of the ACM K-12 Task Force Curriculum Committee, http://www.csta.acm.org/Curriculum/sub/ACMK12CSModel.html.

[2] Alice website, September 1, 2011. www.alice.org.

[3] Barr, V. and Stephenson, C., 2011. Bringing computational thinking to K-12: what is Involved and what is the role of the computer science education community? ACM Inroads 2, 1, 48-54.

[4] Bransford, J.D. and Donovan, M.S., 2005. Scientific inquiry and how people learn. In National Research Council, How students learn: History, mathematics, and science in the classroom. Washington DC: The National Academies Press.

[5] Denner, J., Werner, L. and Ortiz, E., 2012. Computer games created by middle school girls: Can they be used to measure understanding of computer science concepts? Computers & Education, 58(1), 240-249.

[6] Lee, L., Martin, F., Denner, J., Coulter, B., Allan, W., Erickson, J., Malyn-Smith, J., and Werner, L., 2011. Computational thinking for youth in practice. ACM Inroads 2, 1, 32-37.

[7] Levine, T. and Donitsa-Schmidt, S., 1998. Computer use, confidence, attitudes, and knowledge: A causal analysis, Computers in Human Behavior, Volume 14, Issue 1, 125-146.

[8] Lewis, C., 2011. Is pair programming more effective than other forms of collaboration for young students? Computer Science Education Vol. 21, No. 2, 105-134.

[9] Linn, M. C., 1985. The Cognitive Consequences of Programming Instruction in Classrooms. Educational Researcher, Vol. 14, No. 5, pp. 14-16+25-29 at http://www.jstor.org/stable/1174202.

[10] Papert. S., 1993. Mindstorms: Children, Computers, and Powerful Ideas. 2nd ed. NY: Basic Books.

[11] Repenning, A., Webb, D., and Ioannidou, A., 2010. Scalable Game Design and the Development of a Checklist for Getting Computational Thinking into Public Schools. SIGCSE '10, 265-269.

[12] Rodger, S.H., Hayes, J., Lezin, G., Qin, H., Nelson, D., Tucker, R., Lopez, M., Cooper, S., Dann, W., and Slater, D., 2009. Engaging middle school teachers and students with Alice in a diverse set of subjects. SIGCSE Bull. 41, 1, 271-275.

[13] Stolee, K.T. and Fristoe, T., 2011. Expressing computer science concepts through Kodu game lab. In Proceedings of the 42nd ACM technical symposium on Computer science education (SIGCSE). ACM, New York, NY, USA, 99-104.

[14] Webb, D.C., 2010 Troubleshooting assessment: an authentic problem solving activity for it education, Procedia - Social and Behavioral Sciences, Volume 9, World Conference on Learning, Teaching and Administration Papers, pp. 903-907.

[15] Wilson, C., Sudol, L., Stephenson, C., and Stehlik, M., 2010. Running on Empty: The Failure to Teach K-12 Computer Science in the Digital Age. ACM Available as: http://www.acm.org/runningonempty/fullreport.pdf.

[16] Wing, J., 2006. Computational Thinking. CACM vol. 49, no, 3. March 2006, pp. 33-36.

[17] Werner, L., Hanks, B., & McDowell, C., 2004. Pair programming helps female computer science students. ACM Journal of Educational Resources in Computing, 4(1).

[18] Zimmerman, C., 2005. The development of scientific reasoning skills. Accessed on Sept. 1, 2011 from www7.nationalacademies.org/bose/Corinne_Zimmerman_Final_Paper.pdf.

Running Students' Software Tests Against Each Others' Code: New Life for an Old "Gimmick"

Stephen H. Edwards, Zalia Shams, Michael Cogswell, and Robert C. Senkbeil
Department of Computer Science
Virginia Tech
114 McBryde Hall (0106)
Blacksburg, VA 24061
{edwards,zalia18,cogswell,rcsvt}@cs.vt.edu

ABSTRACT

At SIGCSE 2002, Michael Goldwasser suggested a strategy for adding software testing practices to programming courses by requiring students to turn in tests along with their solutions, and then running every student's tests against every other student's program. This approach provides a much more robust environment for assessing the quality of student-written tests, and also provides more thorough testing of student solutions. Although software testing is included as a regular part of many more programming courses today, the all-pairs model of executing tests is still a rarity. This is because student-written tests, such as JUnit tests written for Java programs, are now more commonly written in the form of program code themselves, and they may depend on virtually any aspect of their author's own solution. These dependencies may keep one student's tests from even compiling against another student's program. This paper discusses the problem and presents a novel solution for Java that uses bytecode rewriting to transform a student's tests into a form that uses reflection to run against *any* other solution, regardless of any compile-time dependencies that may have been present in the original tests. Results of applying this technique to two assignments, encompassing 147 student programs and 240,158 individual test case runs, shows the feasibility of the approach and provides some insight into the quality of both student tests and student programs. An analysis of these results is presented.

Categories and Subject Descriptors

K.3.2 [**Computers and Education**]: Computer and Information Science Education; D.1.5 [**Programming Techniques**]: Object oriented Programming; D.2.5 [**Software Engineering**]: Testing and Debugging—testing tools.

General Terms

Design, Experimentation, Languages, Verification.

Keywords

Test-driven development, automated assessment, software testing, programming assignments, test coverage, reflection, bytecode transformation.

Permission to make digital or hard copies of all or part of this work for personal or classroom use is granted without fee provided that copies are not made or distributed for profit or commercial advantage and that copies bear this notice and the full citation on the first page. To copy otherwise, or republish, to post on servers or to redistribute to lists, requires prior specific permission and/or a fee.
SIGCSE'12, February 29–March 3, 2012, Raleigh, North Carolina, USA.
Copyright 2012 ACM 978-1-4503-1098-7/12/02...$10.00.

1. INTRODUCTION

Ten years ago at SIGCSE 2002, Michael Goldwasser presented an interesting strategy for including software testing in programming courses that was centered on having students submit tests along with their code, and then *running every student's software tests against every other student's program code* [2]. He described how the results of the all-pairs execution of tests could be used as part of student grading. He also discussed several advantages to this strategy, including some anticipated benefits for the students involved.

While the original proposal may be best remembered for the tournament-style scoring approach it suggests to "[provide] a bit of light-hearted motivation to course work," it has other positive effects as well. Running one student's tests against everyone else's solution provides a more robust mechanism for evaluating the quality of those tests, and can also reward students who are struggling with their own implementations for the effort they have put into testing. Similarly, running one student's program against everyone else's tests provides a more robust mechanism for evaluating the quality of that solution, possibly revealing bugs that might be missed by instructor-written tests. Furthermore, once students see how the class performs overall—and how they performed individually—both in terms of solutions passing other tests, and in terms of test suites detecting failures in other programs, they gain a whole new perspective on the value of testing *and* on the presence of hidden bugs in their own code. When students only see the results of their own tests (and possibly their instructor's), they often have an overly inflated sense of the quality of their own programs. As an educator who has used this technique in the classroom, I appreciate the eye-opening effect it has on students. Students take away a greater realization of the density of bugs in code they write, as well as their own ability to write tests that find defects in other solutions.

At the time of Goldwasser's paper, relatively few universities included writing software tests as a student activity in their core programming courses, and this "gimmick" was a novel idea for getting both students and instructors interested in practical software testing in the classroom. Including software testing in programming courses has come a long way in ten years, however. Today, many universities regularly include software testing as part of programming assignments in core courses. It is common to see unit testing covered in CS1 and CS2 textbooks, and most IDEs that students use have built-in support for automatically running software tests in some form. Despite this, the all-pairs model of executing those tests is not typically used. The reason is that *a technical obstacle makes it infeasible* to run one student's tests against another's code in many common classroom situations, such as when students are programming in Java and using JUnit (or a similar framework) to write software tests.

The technical obstacle hinges on the fact that software tests written by students for most object-oriented programs are written in the form of program code using an appropriate unit testing framework. Because of the nature of unit testing, student-written tests may make use of (and thus depend on) internal features of their own design. In a compiled language, this fact often means one student's tests *will not even compile* against another student's solution. In interpreted languages, it may mean tests fail with runtime errors that do not reveal defects, but instead reveal different internal choices between student solutions.

This paper describes this technical issue in more detail, along with a Java-specific solution we have developed. This novel solution uses bytecode rewriting to transform one student's tests into a form that can be applied to any other student's code while avoiding the key problems. In addition, we present the evaluation results of employing this technique on a CS1 programming assignment and on a CS2 programming assignment.

2. RELATED WORK

Rather than making software testing the subject of a single advanced course, many educators have argued for incorporating it throughout the programming activities in the typical computer science curriculum. Embracing this idea, Goldwasser described running each student's software tests against all other students' programs [2]. In his approach a student submits a program and a test set. All of the submitted programs are then executed against all of the submitted test sets as an automated batch activity. The percentage of test sets passed by a given program is recorded and may be used as a portion of the student's grade. Similarly, of all student-written implementations that have had flaws detected, the percentage that failed to pass a given test set is recorded as well, and may be used as a port of that student's grade. Similar competitive approaches have also been described [3] [4].

At the same time, automated assessment tools for evaluating student programs have explored software testing as well. Web-CAT [5] and ASSYST [6] are the mostly used such assessment tools. Web-CAT can measure the code coverage (statement coverage, decision coverage, or a combination of the two) of student-written tests submitted as part of an assignment. Web-CAT can also execute instructor-provided reference tests, and for some languages (such as Java) provides static analysis tools that can assess code style, adherence to coding standards, and some structural aspects of commenting conventions. Depending on the instructor's preferences, student scores can include how many reference tests are passed, how much code coverage is achieved by the student-written tests, and the results of static analysis. For a compiled language where software tests are provided in the form of program code (as with Java and JUnit tests), reference tests will not compile against student solutions that fail to provide all the features required in the assignment or that have incorrect operation signatures. As a result, no capability for all-pairs test execution is available.

ASSYST also provides support for executing instructor-written reference tests against student submissions, as well as support for measuring code coverage (i.e., statement coverage) of student solutions when the instructor-written tests are executed. This system also can evaluate the run-time efficiency of a program by the amount of CPU time consumed, it's code complexity, and its style. Moreover, weightings can be assigned to particular aspects of tests using ASSYST.

Marmoset [1] is another automated grading system that focuses on Java assignments. It evaluates student programs against two test sets: 1) public test sets, where students see all results, and 2) "release" test sets provided by the instructor—that is, private instructor-written reference tests. The public test sets are available publicly to students and feedback from running public test sets are provided to students immediately. However, release test sets can be run only if a submission passes all the public tests. The results from release test sets are delayed and limited. Marmoset uses code coverage from the release test sets and from the student's own test sets. This system also provides students with information about their programs using the static program analysis tool FindBugs [7].

All three systems, Web-CAT, ASSYST and Marmoset, use some form of code coverage analysis. As an alternative, Aaltonen *et al.* [8] propose using mutation analysis to assess the quality of student-written tests in Java assignments. Mutation analysis seeds simple programming errors in source code—in this case, in the student's own solution—and then runs the student-written tests to see if the seeded defects are detected. This approach appears to provide a deeper perspective on the adequacy of the student-written tests, going well beyond code coverage metrics, but it has not been used in a live classroom. Further, some limitations may make it impractical to use for real-time feedback generation, although it appears feasible for use in batch-style analysis of student submissions. Aaltonen et al. do not consider all-pairs analysis for this approach, perhaps because of the issues discussed in this paper.

BugHunt [9] is a web based tutorial for students to learn how to write unit tests. It provides existing code containing known defects for students to "find" using testing. Though this work does not address the all-pairs model of employing student-written tests, it does aim directly at including software testing in courses, and helps students learn from their mistakes through an interactive feedback system.

3. THE ROOT OF THE PROBLEM

As described in Section 1, the primary technical obstacle preventing all-pairs test execution in many of today's classrooms stems from changes in software testing technology during the past ten years. As test-driven development (TDD) [10][11] became well known with the rise of extreme programming (XP), XUnit-style testing frameworks were developed for many languages. JUnit (http://junit.org), the testing framework for Java, is perhaps the most well known of these, and it has seen growing use in the classroom during the past decade. It is now the most common Java testing framework presented in Java programming textbooks.

XUnit-style software tests, including JUnit tests, are written in program form in the same language as the software under test. Normally, writing such tests requires no significant expertise beyond that required for writing the software being tested, and tests can be written and managed with the same tools used to produce the source code to be tested. This has caused a significant change in the way software tests are written in many classrooms.

Unfortunately, the nature of such software tests violates one of Goldwasser's principal observations [2]:

> Because students will be submitting test sets that are to be run (automatically) on other students' submissions, a standardized format for describing the tests must be established in the assignment description. The overwhelming conclusion is to rely on a textual interface for program input.

In other words, student tests must be written to a consistent interface or API in order to be "interchangeable" across submissions. They must be expressed in a "black box" form that is devoid of any dependencies on how a particular solution is constructed. Goldwasser notes the potential for tragic failure if a student make mistakes in understanding or implementing the test input format, or the part of their solution that handles reading/parsing such input. He even suggests that where possible the instructor provide all students with an appropriate front-end implementing the standardized testing interface to preempt such issues.

Because XUnit-style tests are written as additional classes (or modules) in the same programming language as the software under test, they may refer to any visible feature of the code itself. This means that students may write tests that use or depend on any visible features, whether or not those features happen to be required by the assignment (and are thus present in all solutions) or happen to be personal design decisions (that are not transportable). Many such differences may be specific to a particular "unit" (class or module) within the program rather than to the program as a whole (more common, since many/most tests are unit tests, and may include "white box" information). Further, software tests that include dependencies on features of the software being tested that are not present in *all* solutions typically *will not even compile* against other student solutions where those features happen to be missing (or are designed differently). This is true in JUnit tests written for Java.

Requiring student submissions to take the form of a complete program with "a textual interface for program input" provides a uniform mechanism for executing tests, regardless of the internal design choices made by any particular student. Further, it allows tests to be run against any solution, even if that solution happens to be missing significant required features entirely, or only a partial implementation of others. JUnit (or, more generally, XUnit) tests do not work that way because of their nature.

Thus, if we wish to execute each student's tests against every other student's solution, and students are writing JUnit-style test cases against Java solutions, we must devise a way to ensure a uniform interface against which tests can be executed that insulates test sets against any differences between solutions or divergence from the assignment requirements, and also insulates any student solution from extraneous dependencies in any given test set.

Note that, in fact, **similar issues already exist with instructor-written reference tests**. In automated grading systems that run JUnit-style instructor reference tests against student solutions, the same constraints apply. Reference tests should depend only on features specified in the assignment. If they happen to have extraneous dependencies (such as dependencies on internal features of an instructor's personal solution, but which are not described in the assignment), they will fail to compile against student solutions that do not provide identical features. In general, however, most instructors are willing to take on the responsibility of writing tests that avoid dependencies on features that are not explicit in an assignment ("hidden" requirements implied by the structure of reference tests). Nevertheless, the problem is essentially the same.

Further, student solutions that fail to conform to the requirements of the assignment—say, by omitting some required elements, or getting the type signature wrong on others—cannot be assessed using such reference tests because such a solution is not compile-time-compatible with the tests. As a result, such a partial or incomplete submission would have no results for performance against reference tests, and most grading systems would assign no credit for the corresponding portion of the assignment grade.

4. A SOLUTION USING BYTECODE REWRITING

In our experiences using Web-CAT, some educators have adopted strategies for coping with reference tests that may not compile against partial or incomplete student submissions. Over the past eight years, the solution that has proven the most robust and effective is extreme: instructors write JUnit reference tests that perform all manipulation of student classes and objects using reflection so that they have no direct compile-time dependencies on any particular solution. Java reflection can be complicated and error-prone to use, but we use a library of methods that completely encapsulates the details of using reflection underneath a powerful, streamlined interface ideal for writing test actions. As a result, test cases written using this library are no longer than their non-reflective equivalent, but they have no compile-time dependencies on the software under test.

When purely reflective test cases are run against a student submission, any missing or incorrect features in a student's solution no longer cause issues at compile-time. Instead, the test set will compile and run against any student submission. Those individual test cases in the test set that depend on features that are missing or indirectly declared in the student's work simply fail at run-time, while other test cases run normally. This allows the portion of the student's work that was completed to be assessed, even if other required features are missing. Our reflection library provides appropriate diagnostic messages for test cases that fail because of missing or broken features, reporting to the student the specific class and/or method that is missing or incorrectly declared.

Although reflection has a reputation for being costly at run-time (it definitely does add overhead), experiences with this approach suggest that the overhead is very modest compared to the I/O overhead involved in loading classes and generating test result output. Using reflection in test cases on Web-CAT, for example, has not significantly increased the time required for assessing student submissions.

Unfortunately, expressing all actions through this alternative interface is a significant extra burden for anyone writing tests—it is certainly inappropriate for imposing on students. Indeed, the burden is large enough for educators that only those who have significant experience writing test cases employ the technique. The technique is extremely effective, however, and instructors who do employ it are strongly committed to continue because of its benefits. The nature of this burden then raises two questions: is there an *automated* way to execute normal (non-reflective) JUnit tests in this way, and if so, could we employ it on student-written tests as well?

The answer to both questions is: yes.

4.1 The Strategy

First, we note that test sets that depend on the internal details on one particular solution can still be *compiled*—if compiled against the particular solution they were written for. For example, one student's tests will compile against his or her own code if they compile at all, and so we need not worry about syntactically invalid test sets. Similarly, instructors typically provide their own implementation to double-check reference test sets, so the reference tests will compile against this.

Thus, the strategy involves these steps:

1. Compile JUnit tests against the solution provided alongside them (i.e., written by the same author) when they are first received (an action that existing automated grading systems already perform).
2. *Transform* the bytecode in the .class files from the compiled version of a test set so that it performs all manipulation of the solution's class(es) using reflection. In other words, use a tool to automatically convert the "plain" JUnit tests into purely reflective tests.
3. Run transformed versions of test sets against other solutions as needed, now that the test sets have no compile-time dependencies of the software to be tested.

This strategy leverages the fact that the compiled form of Java code, i.e., bytecode for the Java Virtual Machine, is relatively easy to read, manipulate, and write with other programs. If, from one compiled copy of the test set we can generate an alternative version that uses Java reflection, we can obtain the benefits of using reflection without any of the burden of writing the tests in that style by hand.

If we run one student's tests against another's code, however, we now have to consider three possible outcomes for a single test case (rather than just pass/fail):

1. The test case may pass successfully.
2. The test case may fail inside the reflection infrastructure, indicating that some dependency in the test case was not met correctly by the code being tested, a situation we can call a *reflection mismatch.*
3. The test case may fail in some other way, indicating incorrect behavior of the software under test.

We may wish to handle reflection mismatches differently depending on the nature of the test set. If we are running a reference test against a student solution, and therefore assume the reference test only contains dependencies specified in the assignment, then a reflection mismatch is a mistake on the student's part and can be handled the same as other failures. However, if we are running a student-written test against another student's code, a reflection mismatch may instead indicate an "impedance mismatch" between the test and the code. The test may have an implicit dependency on something not required in the assignment, *or* the code may fail to correctly provide some necessary feature.

Fortunately, there is a simple way to differentiate—we can simply run the student's tests on the instructor-written implementation (the one used to double-check the reference tests). Student tests that pass against the reference solution can be presumed *valid*—that is, they do not possess student-specific dependencies and check for results that are consistent with the assignment. Student tests that produce reflection mismatches against the reference solution can be presumed *student-specific*—since they depend on some features of their original author's code that was missing in the reference solution. Finally, student tests that fail against the reference implementation can be presumed *invalid*, since they encode different behavioral expectations than those embodied in the reference solution.

4.2 The Implementation

The key mechanism in the implementation of this strategy is the bytecode transformer. Bytecode rewriting has been employed in a number of aspect-oriented programming tools and a number of robust libraries for this task exist. For our implementation, we chose to use Javassist [12], which provides an API that is well suited for the transformation task at hand. Javasist provides a mechanism for expressing bytecode translations in the form of Java source-level code snippets laced with substitution variables. Javassist uses its own compiler internally to produce the new bytecode that corresponds to such a pattern.

Using these features, we implemented a Javassist-based bytecode transformer that can load each of the class files that comprise a test set, replacing each constructor call, method call, and field access on any object of the class(es) under test with a corresponding action from our streamlined reflection interface. The modified form of each class file is then written out to disk for use whenever that test set needs to be executed.

Translation can occur at different times. For our purposes it is most convenient to translate the class files for a test set when the code is first submitted and save them, since they potentially will be used multiple times. Alternatively, translation could be performed later. By writing a custom class loader, it is even possible to perform translation dynamically on demand, but such flexibility is not necessary in this context.

5. EVALUATING THE SOLUTION

To evaluate the practicality of this solution, we applied it to two solutions and test sets written by students in separate assignments in two different courses.

5.1 A CS1-level Assignment

First, we examined a CS1 assignment from Fall 2007 where students implemented their own "virtual pet" (an assignment inspired by Grant Braught at Dickinson College). The assignment provided an abstract base class and a state machine description of the required behavior. Students wrote their own implementation of the state machine along with their own software tests.

In the semester under consideration, 46 students completed the assignment. We used our bytecode translator to convert all of the corresponding test sets to reflective versions. The 46 test sets consisted of 463 individual test cases. Test sets ranged in size from five test cases to 15, with a mean of 10.1 and median of 9.

The reflective versions of all test sets were run against an instructor-provided reference solution. Of the 463 test cases, 405 (87.5%) were passed by the reference solution and were thus valid. 27 test cases (5.8%) were invalid, with incorrect expected behaviors. In most cases, this appeared to result from students who did not understand the required state machine behavior and instead had tests that reflected the behavior of their own (incorrect) solution. Just 12 students authored the 27 invalid test cases. Most of those students wrote test sets that had only one invalid test case, and only two students wrote test sets containing more than two invalid test cases.

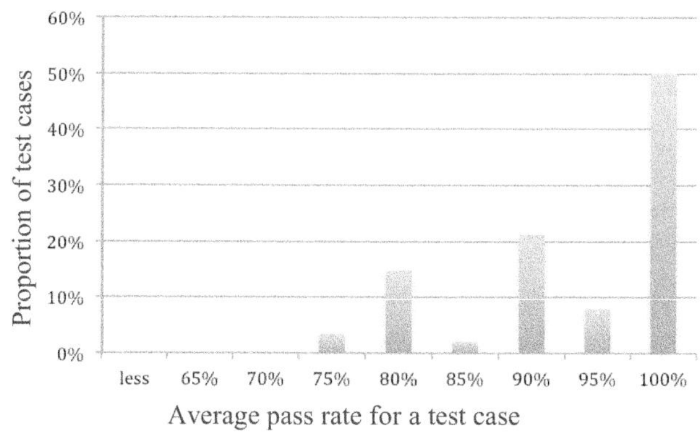

Figure 1: Distribution of pass rates for test cases in the CS1 assignment.

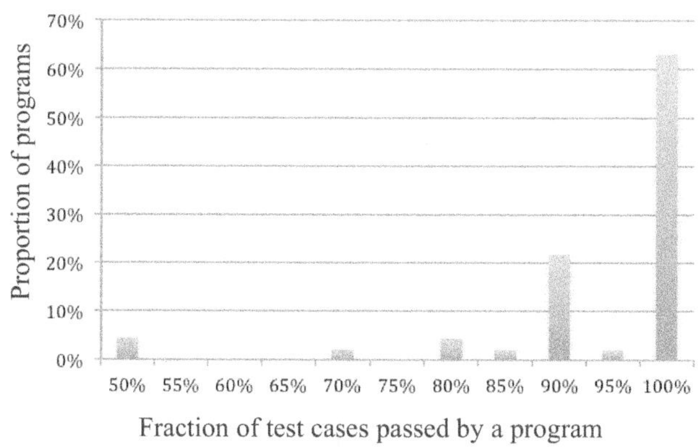

Figure 2: Distribution of program performances in the CS1 assignment.

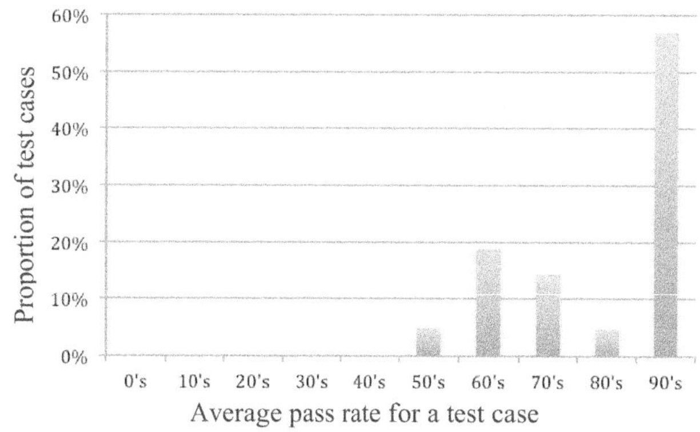

Figure 3: Distribution of pass rates for test cases in the CS2 assignment.

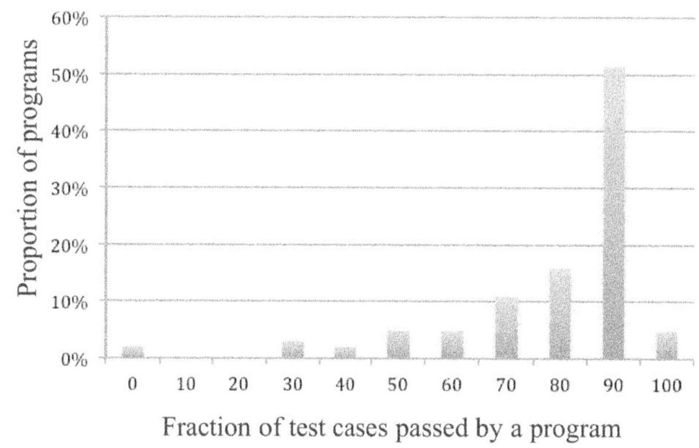

Figure 4: Distribution of program performances in the CS2 assignment.

Among the 463 test cases, just 31 (6.7%) produced reflection mismatches on the reference solution and were thus student-specific. These test cases came from just four students, and the reflection mismatches resulted from calls to custom methods or custom overloaded constructors that those students chose to provide in their own solutions.

Next, all 46 test sets were run against all 46 solutions and the results were compiled, a process that took approximately 30 minutes. The translated bytecode performed as expected. The results for those individual test cases that were judged invalid or student-specific were removed, as were the results from each student's tests on his or her own code. This resulted in a total of 18,225 test case outcomes over the entire population.

Of the 405 valid test cases remaining, the average pass rate across all 46 solutions was 94.4%, with the distribution shown in Figure 1. While just over 50% of test cases failed to find any defects (were passed by *all* programs), the remaining test cases written by students varied in effectiveness and did uncover defects in many other submissions. Every test case was passed by at least 65% of submissions, however. In fact, the average portion of the test cases passed by a solution was also 94.4%, with the distribution shown in Figure 2. Here we see that 63% of the submissions passed every test case written by every student, and every submission passed at least 50% of the test cases. These high pass rates are typical of an assignment that students perform well on, as was the case here. Also, **no** valid test cases produced reflection mismatches, indicating that there were no situations where any student's solution failed to provide a feature required in the assignment.

5.2 A CS2-level Assignment

Employing the strategy on a CS1 assignment established its feasibility. However, the simplicity of the CS1-level assignment left less room for divergence among student tests and solutions. To get a better feel for how this strategy would work in a larger situation, we also examined a CS2 assignment from Spring 2011. This assignment required students to write two different implementations of a generic queue interface in Java—one using a linked representation and one using an array-based implementation. In addition to basic queue operations, students were also required to implement `equals()`, `hashCode()`, `clone()`, `toString()`, and `iterator()`. Students were also required to write their own software tests and were graded in part on the statement coverage and decision coverage they achieved.

In the semester under consideration, 101 students completed the assignment. We used our bytecode translator to convert all of the corresponding test sets to reflective versions. The 101 test sets consisted of 2155 individual test cases. Test sets ranged in size from eight test cases to 33, with a mean of 21.3 and median of 22.

The reflective versions of all test sets were run against an instructor-provided reference solution. Of the 2155 test cases, 2001 (92.9%) were valid, 126 test cases (5.8%) were invalid, and 28 (1.3%) were student-specific. The 126 invalid test cases came from 96 suites, 92 of which contained just one invalid test case. The student-specific test cases came from just three students.

Next, all 101 test sets were run against all 101 solutions and the results were compiled, a process that took approximately two hours. The translated bytecode performed equally well in this larger scale situation. The results for test cases that were judged invalid or student-specific were removed, along with the results from each student's tests on his or her own code. This resulted in a total of 200,100 test case outcomes over the entire population.

Of the 2001 valid test cases, the average pass rate across all 101 solutions was 83.5%. The distribution of test case pass rates is shown in Figure 3. This distribution is more typical of challenging program tasks, and illustrates that students on the whole are quite capable of writing test cases that will reveal bugs. On average, a given test case was failed by 16.5% of student solutions, indicating defects in those programs. Unlike the CS1 assignment, there were *no* test cases that were passed by every program, in part because two programs were so poorly constructed that nearly every valid test produced a reflection mismatch (one could only be run against three valid test cases, and passed just two, while the other was only compatible with 22 test cases and passed just four).

A similar pattern emerges in the distribution of test case pass rates, however. Over half the test cases were consistently passed by nearly all the programs, while the other half were much more likely to reveal defects.

The performance of the programs themselves was also more representative of a challenging assignment, as shown in Figure 4. The average portion of the test cases passed by a solution was also 83.5%. Only five student programs passed all valid test cases. However over half the class passed 90% or more of the test cases, with a rapid drop-off in number of students for successively lower test case pass rates.

6. CONCLUSION

From the results, it is clear that it is indeed possible to remove compile-time dependencies automatically, replacing them with dynamic resolution using reflection. This resolves the primary obstacle to all-pairs execution of student-written tests that exists in many courses today, in the context of JUnit tests for Java programs (similar techniques can be applied in other languages where reflection or interpretation is available). Furthermore, the exact same technique can be applied to reference tests written by instructors for automated grading. This brings a further advantage of making those reference tests more resilient, allowing partial, incomplete, or poorly formed assignments to be tested to the extent possible without requiring any effort on the part of instructors.

This strategy resurrects the viability of Goldwasser's approach to including software tests in programming assignments, both for the purposes of making the testing task more interesting and meaningful and also making the assessment of test quality more comprehensive. As a result, we plan to deploy this strategy on Web-CAT for reference tests so that existing courses can take advantage of the benefits to reference testing transparently, without any effort on the part of instructors. We also plan to provide automated support for all-pairs test execution so that instructors using Web-CAT who wish to use Goldwasser's approach can do so without any additional preparation or effort in building infrastructure or compiling results.

7. REFERENCES

[1] J. Spacco and W. Pugh, "Helping students appreciate test-driven development (TDD)," presented at the Companion to the 21st ACM SIGPLAN symposium on Object-oriented programming systems, languages, and applications, Portland, Oregon, USA, 2006.

[2] M. H. Goldwasser, "A gimmick to integrate software testing throughout the curriculum," presented at the Proceedings of the 33rd SIGCSE Technical Symposium on Computer Science Education, ACM, New York, NY, pp. 271-275, 2002.

[3] M. Hauswirth, *et al.*, "The JavaFest: a collaborative learning technique for Java programming courses," presented at the Proceedings of the 6th international symposium on Principles and practice of programming in Java, Modena, Italy, 2008.

[4] W. Marrero and A. Settle, "Testing first: emphasizing testing in early programming courses," *SIGCSE Bull.*, vol. 37, pp. 4-8, 2005.

[5] S. H. Edwards, "Rethinking computer science education from a test-first perspective," presented at the Companion of the 18th annual ACM SIGPLAN conference on Object-oriented programming, systems, languages, and applications, Anaheim, CA, USA, 2003.

[6] D. Jackson and M. Usher, "Grading student programs using ASSYST," *SIGCSE Bull.*, vol. 29, pp. 335-339, 1997.

[7] B. Cole, *et al.*, "Improving your software using static analysis to find bugs," presented at the Companion to the 21st ACM SIGPLAN symposium on Object-oriented programming systems, languages, and applications, Portland, Oregon, USA, 2006.

[8] K. Aaltonen, *et al.*, "Mutation analysis vs. code coverage in automated assessment of students' testing skills," presented at the Proceedings of the ACM international conference companion on Object oriented programming systems languages and applications companion, Reno/Tahoe, Nevada, USA, 2010.

[9] S. Elbaum, *et al.*, "Bug Hunt: Making Early Software Testing Lessons Engaging and Affordable," presented at the 29th International Conference on Software Engineering (ICSE), pp. 688-697, 2007.

[10] Beck, K. Aim, fire (test-first coding). *IEEE Software*, 18(5): 87-89, Sept./Oct. 2001.

[11] Beck, K. *Test-Driven Development: By Example*. Addison-Wesley, Boston, MA, 2003.

[12] S. Chiba and M. Nishizawa, "An easy-to-use toolkit for efficient Java bytecode translators," presented at the Proceedings of the 2nd international conference on Generative programming and component engineering (GPCE '03), Springer-Verlag New York, Inc., New York, NY, USA, pp. 364-376, 2003.

Group Note-Taking in a Large Lecture Class: Design, Implementation, and Evaluation of a Low-Cost Universal Design Practice

Christopher Plaue, Sal LaMarca, and Shelby H. Funk
Department of Computer Science
The University of Georgia
Athens, GA 30602
[plaue, lamarca, shelby] @ cs.uga.edu

ABSTRACT

Large introductory-level classes provide a cost-efficient approach for universities to serve many students at once, but also present several challenges to learning (e.g., poor visual angles). In addition, more students with declared, undeclared, or undiagnosed learning disabilities are entering the college and university systems. In the spirit of universal design, we created a group note-taking system in our large introductory computer science course to increase interaction amongst students, promote good note-taking strategies, and provide study resources to all students while also fulfilling the role of accommodating for students with learning disabilities. We show that the section of the course taught with our intervention performed significantly better on their final examination compared to a course taught without the intervention. We report that students enjoyed increased interactions with their peers, and that one third of the class self-reported an increase in their note-taking skills. Furthermore, our intervention only required minimal cost to the institution, and no financial cost to students, and is easily implemented in any size class.

Categories and Subject Descriptors

K.3.2 **[Computer and Information Science Education]**;
K.4.2 **[Social Issues]** *Assistive technologies for persons with disabilities*

General Terms

Measurement, experimentation

Keywords

Universal design, teamwork, introductory coursework, note-taking

1. INTRODUCTION

Many universities and colleges use large introductory-level lecture classes as a low-cost way of providing instructional resources to a large number of students. However, large lecture classes may contain several disadvantages, including a general lack of engagement amongst students, increased distractions, and challenging visual and audio characteristics (e.g., poor viewing angles or lack of a sound system.) Furthermore, many of these courses contain new or first-year students, and the large lecture format does not easily provide for opportunities for students to network and engage their classmates, leading to a sense of isolation [20, 21].

A further challenge to instructors of these large courses is the increasing number of students with declared learning disabilities, estimated to have tripled between 1978 and 1998 [12]. NSF considers disabled populations to be underserved within computing [13]. Cavender et al. note that the Taulbee Report, the main demographic report for computer science, does not track the number of students with learning disabilities [6], but 5 to 15% of the student population is estimated to have some form of learning disorder [18]. These statistics, however, may not include numbers of students who opt not to declare their disability, are embarrassed by the declaration process, may not even be aware they have a learning disorder, or are unable to afford diagnosis.

Instructors of all courses including large lectures, have a responsibility to provide students with disabilities equal access to resources. As a result, many institutions have disability resource offices that work with students to provide appropriate accommodations. One accommodation is for the university to hire a note-taker. Note-takers are an effective accommodation since many learning-disabled individuals have great difficulty in organizing information [10]. In particular, much research has investigated the impact of various note-taking strategies on the learning-disabled [16]. Boyle and Weishaar reported that learning-disabled students who learn strategies for note-taking scored significantly higher on measures of free and long-term free recall than those using conventional note-taking [3].

While teaching such strategies and techniques has benefits, it is impractical for a large-lecture course instructor to incorporate these lessons into an often-standardized curriculum. While it may be possible to provide these strategies outside of class, this would not impact students who have not declared their disability, do not know that they have a disability, or are unable to afford the cost of diagnosis, which is $500 at our institution.

In this article, we present the design, implementation, and evaluation of a group note-taking component for a large introductory-level computer science course for non-majors (CS-0). We chose note-taking as a vehicle for universal design [4] in the classroom. Students take notes and publicly publish them to classmates to provide resources to all students, which are especially of value to those with learning disabilities. We opted to make the note-taking intervention a group-based project to

Permission to make digital or hard copies of all or part of this work for personal or classroom use is granted without fee provided that copies are not made or distributed for profit or commercial advantage and that copies bear this notice and the full citation on the first page. To copy otherwise, or republish, to post on servers or to redistribute to lists, requires prior specific permission and/or a fee.
SIGCSE'12, February 29-March 3, 2012, Raleigh, North Carolina, USA.
Copyright 2012 ACM 978-1-4503-1098-7/12/02...$10.00.

promote the development of social and academic networks in the large-lecture classroom.

Much research within the computer science education community examines the benefits of active learning (e.g., [1, 8]). Furthermore, research also examines the importance of gaining feedback in large lecture classes through mechanisms such as the Personal Response System (aka "clickers") [5]. Our work builds upon this literature by describing a low-cost active learning process of note-taking.

2. CSCI 1100 Course Overview

CSCI 1100 is a computer science service course (i.e., CS-0) at The University of Georgia, providing a survey of topics within computer science. Students are exposed to core concepts of computing hardware, software, networking, databases, and HTML/CSS principles. They also gain exposure to special research topics such as artificial intelligence, user-interface design, visual analytics, and social networking. The class meets for 50-minute large-lectures on Mondays and Wednesdays, and then meets for 100-minutes of laboratory time (labs are capped at 24 students) on another day. A full-time faculty member teaches the lecture portion of the course while graduate teaching assistants teach labs.

CSCI 1100 enrolls 150-180 students during a typical fall or spring semester. During Spring 2011, 68% of the students were female, and the most popular majors of students in the course included psychology (21%) and childhood and family development (14%). Since CSCI 1100 does not count towards any university requirements, the vast majority of students taking this course are doing so as part of a major-specific requirement. Also, 58% of the students surveyed in this class stated that they were not interested in taking any additional computer sciences courses, indicating that students are indeed required to take this course and are not electing to do so on their own.

3. NOTE-TAKING INTERVENTION

The note-taking intervention was largely based on large lecture note-taking strategies outlined in SciTrainU [19], an inter-college research initiative in developing and promoting universal design practices. We designed our note-taking strategy to leverage the benefits of teamwork. Cooperative learning strategies can improve students' academic success and enjoyment. Moreover, compared to students who work individually, students who work in teams are significantly more likely to agree that a course achieved its learning objectives [22]. Group note-taking satisfies three of the Chickering and Gameson's principles for good practice in education: developing reciprocity and cooperation amongst students, encouraging active learning, and respecting diverse talents and ways of learning [7].

We explicitly sought to incorporate best-practices for teamwork, including smaller group sizes, rotating roles between participants, having accountability via peer review, and providing built-in mechanisms to manage issues. Our strategy for introducing note-taking into the CS-0 course included:

- randomly assigning up to five individuals per team (*small group sizes*)
- half of the teams are tasked to take notes in a given week as well as develop study & review questions for material covered in class and in the textbook
- teams taking notes and creating study questions are divided into the roles of two note-takers, one study question generator, and one compiler who organizes, proofreads, and posts the notes publicly
- roles within each team change each note-taking week (*rotate roles)*
- teams not taking notes in a given week are tasked to review and grade the notes posted by the other teams (*external peer reviews)*
- teams also evaluate their team members' performance (*internal peer reviews)*

In a given week, the teams taking notes posted their notes and study/review questions to the course management system by 11PM on Friday evening. Teams evaluating other teams completed their reviews by 11PM of the following Wednesday evening. In addition, team members complete their internal peer reviews to give the instructor and TA feedback by 11PM on Sunday evening.

The note-taking intervention replaced three individual homework assignment grades (worth 75-points or 9% of the students' grade). In a week that students were tasked to review other teams' notes, students used a "needs improvement", "meets expectations", and "exceptional" grading criteria, which corresponded to scores of 1, 2.5, and 3 points, respectively. Individuals used this criterion to grade the posted notes for content/clarity, organization of notes, and quality of study questions. Grades were based on the average of all peer evaluation scores for a given week. In addition, students received 3.5 points for completing their evaluations of other teams' notes. A maximum of 75-points could be obtained. To further motivate students in the note-taking assignment, we provided an incentive of a full-letter grade boost to the team who had the highest-rated notes at the end of the semester.

3.1 Fall 2010 Pilot Testing

Our initial deployment of the group note-taking assignment occurred during Fall 2010. Our main goals were to explore the logistics of coordinating 31 teams and to gauge student reaction to the assignment. The only additional teaching resource required was the appointment of one graduate teaching assistant to the lecture portion of the course to help coordinate teams.

We experienced a series of setbacks during our pilot run that impacted the ability to carry out the note-taking intervention, mainly due to limitations of the course management system (CMS) and our strategy for assigning groups. Our CMS was Vista Learning System, and we used the discussion boards and assessment features for the group note-taking project. A combination of bugs in the CMS and generally poor response time negatively impacted the ability for teams to upload their notes or save student responses to peer evaluations. Furthermore, our institution experienced a week-long outage of the CMS which caused hardship and difficulties for teams coordinating their note-taking for the week.

Team members were randomly assigned to each group. Unfortunately, we found this assignment method resulted in students communicating only electronically. The instructor and TA received many complaints about team members, so they began a lecture mid-semester by requesting all teams sit with each other during class. Only three teams (out of 31) were able to do so; the rest did not have any idea who their teammates were. We discovered that when teams had been communicating solely via online communication, they often used harsh words. This

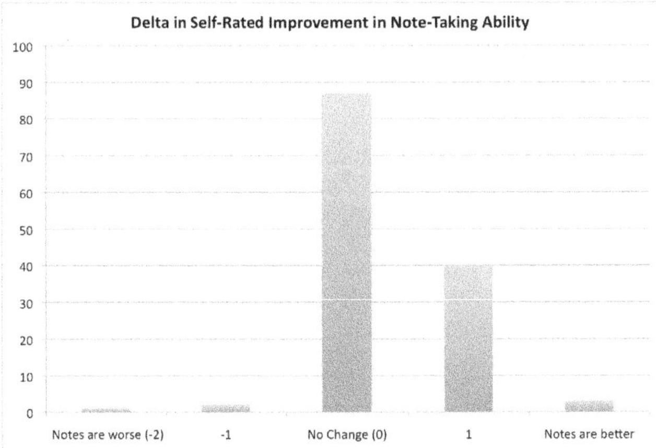

Figure 1: Number students' survey responses indicating improvement (if possible) in note-taking skills.

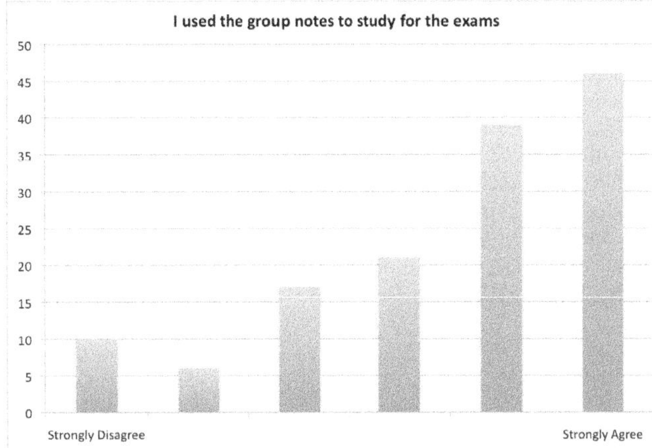

Figure 2: Number of students' survey responses indicating use of group notes to study for exams.

corresponds to existing body of literature that shows that anonymous communication can be aloof [9] and unfriendly [17]. In addition, the instructor and TA were inundated by reports of non-participation amongst group members. Accusations of non-participation were handled on a case-by-case basis, and represented a significant investment of time and energy to resolve.

3.2 Spring 2011 Evaluation Period

We ameliorated the issues with the CMS and group assignments for Spring 2011. First, team members were no longer randomly assigned from students across the entire lecture. Rather, we randomly assigned 34 teams of up to five individuals based on students who had the same weekly lab session. This forced students to physically be in an environment with fewer people at least once a week, allowing for face-to-face interaction.

We built our own Web-based peer review system using an Apache Tomcat JSP server that reliably recorded participation into a MySQL database. Benefits of using our own system allowed us to streamline the process of students rating their teammates, record additional information such as time-stamps, and also reduce the overhead of modifying the CMS to meet our needs. We also had students review their teammates each week to inform the instructor and TA about students who were not participating.

During this phase, every time a group note-taking assignment was completed, students would individually access the website to anonymously rate the participation of other students in their group. The ratings were done on a scale of 1 ("needs improvement") to 5 ("Exceptional"). The internal peer reviews were kept anonymous to students while the instructor and teaching assistant had full information about survey responses.

We also slightly modified the grading criteria we used. In Spring 2011, external peer reviewers could select "needs improvement", "met expectations", or "exceptional" to rate organization, content, and study questions. These ratings corresponded to assigning points of 1.5, 3.5, and 4.25, respectively.

Overall, the group note-taking intervention required minimal effort for the instructor and TA. The creation of the Web-based peer review system took one TA only 20 hours to create. We note that this is a one-time cost. The only other additional resource needed for deploying the group note-taking intervention was again assigning a teaching assistant to the lecture portion of the class. There were no additional grading responsibilities since students were grading each other's notes.

4. RESULTS

We collected information using a variety of quantitative and

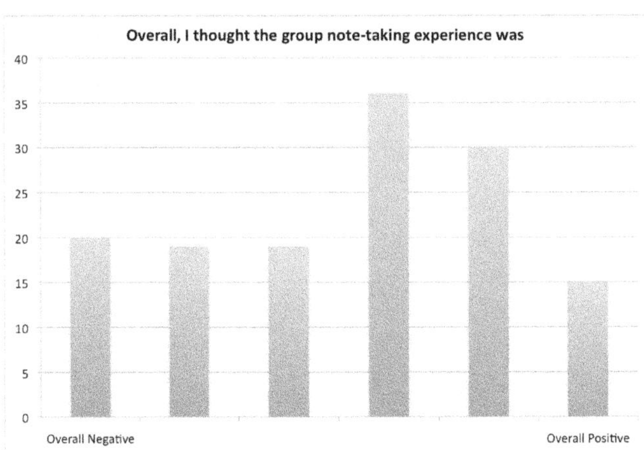

Figure 3. Number of students' responses indicating overall positive or negative experiences with group note-taking.

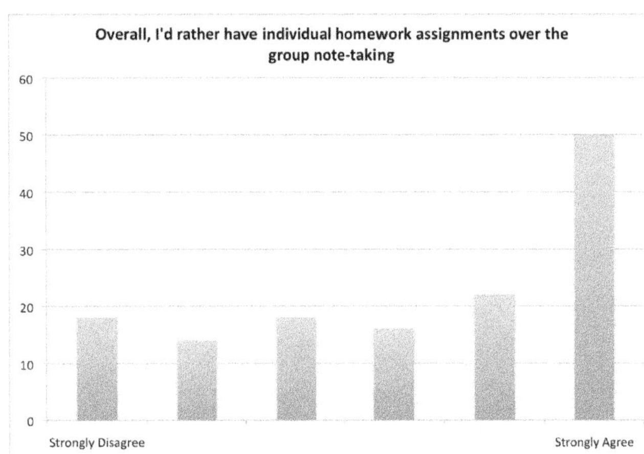

Figure 4. Number of students' responses indicating overall preference for individual assignments.

Table 1: Grouped positive and negative themes in students' impressions of the group note-taking intervention.

Positive aspects of participating in group note-taking	Negative aspects of participating in group note-taking
(66) Used for Studying / Resources	(54) Unequal Distribution of Work
(63) Increased Social/Class Network	(31) Confusion over Deadlines
(42) Acquired New Skills / Abilities	(30) Group Member Can Impact Grade
(28) Provided Academic Support System	(35) Communication & Coordination Issues
(20) Reduced Workload	(12) Peer Review System Flawed/Biased
(16) Broadened Perspectives	(15) Workload too High
(10) Forced to Read Textbook	(14) Felt Project was Busy Work
(4) Reward for Best Notes	(14) Personality Conflicts
	(4) Forced to Attend Lecture

(#) represents number of responses grouped under each theme in a class of 143 students

qualitative measures. We logged all peer reviews for each week, recorded teams' ratings for other teams' published notes and study questions, and compared exam performance of the experimental Spring 2011 course to the results of a conventional Spring 2010 section. We also deployed a survey at the end of the semester to capture overall impressions of the group note-taking project. This survey contained a mix of Likert ratings and free-response questions asking students to list two positive and negative aspects of group note-taking. We analyzed free-response questions using an affinity diagramming technique to establish themes, and used descriptive and inferential measures for other data.

Overall, students in the note-taking section scored significantly higher on their final exam than those in the conventional section ($F(1,299)=8.10$, $p=.005$). However, exam scores did not differ significantly between the two sections for the two midterm exams.

We analyzed our Likert-based survey data using descriptive statistics. Of those students who did not initially rate their note-taking abilities as being perfect (that is, they felt there was no room for improvement), 32.3% of the students indicated an increase in their ability to take notes after completing CSCI 1100 (Figure 1). 65.4% did not believe that their note-taking ability changed in the course, and only 3 students indicated that their note-taking ability was negatively impacted by the course.

Overall, 76.4% of the students indicated that they used the group notes in some form to study for the exams (Figure 2), implying that these resources were indeed of universal design. This was echoed in the free response statements, where the highest number of responses (66) about positive experiences with group note-taking centered on the benefits of having additional resources for studying: *"[group notes were] a good resource for exam time and a good way to make yourself keep up with the class."*

Students were evenly distributed in their impressions of the group note-taking experience (Figure 3), with 58.2% expressing a positive view and 41.7% indicating a negative view. Many students (63.7%) indicated they would have preferred an individual homework assignment over group notes (Figure 4), mainly because they also indicated that they felt that they did more than their fair share of work within groups (Figures 5, 6). This was echoed in the free-response comments, where the number one theme amongst the comments was an unequal distribution of work. Comments included, *"Not everyone did their fair share" or "if someone did not do what they needed to do, it left others with more work."* However, the actual internal peer review grades assigned by teammates paints a different picture (Figure 7). We discuss this in the next section.

Other frequent positive comments about group note-taking noted the benefits of the assignment facilitating networking in the class (63 comments). Remarks included, *"I had fun working with classmates"* and *"I got to know people I wouldn't have otherwise."* Other frequent positive comments about the intervention included the benefits of new skills or abilities (42), having a built-in academic support system to ask for clarifications

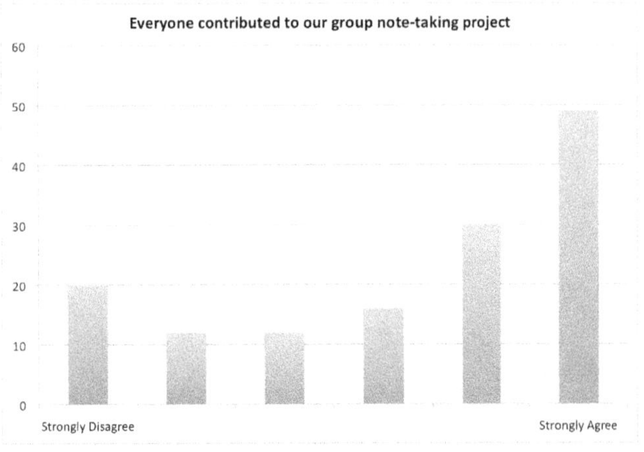

Figure 5. Number of students' survey responses indicating group contributions.

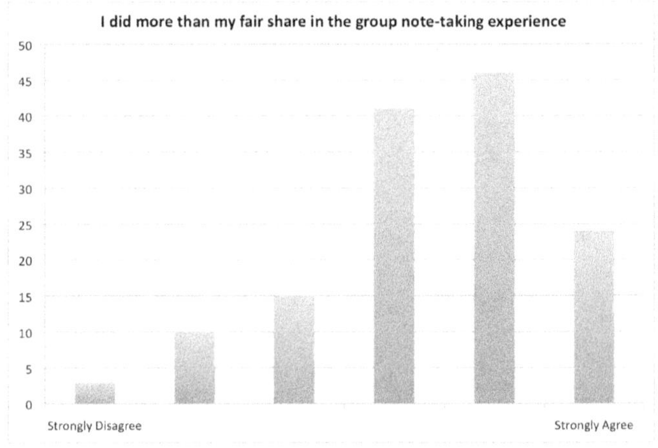

Figure 6. Number of survey responses indicating individual contributions to the group project.

or help (28), and the division of workload (20). Furthermore, 16 students also commented on an appreciation for discovering other students' perspectives on the course material: "*It helped me think of ways to better explain certain concepts*" and that group notes were an "*opportunity to learn something in a different way*" through the group notes.

A frequent gripe of students revolved around confusion regarding deadlines. One student remarked, "*it was easy to forget to do group reviews*" and many others said one of the most negative aspects of group note-taking was, "*forgetting to do evaluations.*" Also, students did not care for the deadline for group note postings at 11 PM on Friday: "*11PM on Friday as a due date is not a good time*" and "*Friday night isn't really convenient for weekends when you're going out of town.*"

Many students also expressed a fear that their group note-taking process would negatively impact their grades: "*Bad grades effect everyone in the group even if I did my part and no one else did theirs.*" Another common complaint about group note-taking was the difficulty of communicating and coordinating amongst team members.

5. DISCUSSION

Our findings illustrate that group note-taking is a promising universal design intervention for a large CS-0 course. We discuss several themes emerging from our findings:

Minimal Cost Intervention for Universities and Students: Financial considerations impact not only the college or university, but also students and their families. Georgia's public school system contains 36.2% rural campuses [11]. This is the third-largest rural student population in the United States. 74.3% of students from rural areas are living at poverty levels [11]. At our institution, 34.4% of undergraduates receive need-based financial aid [14] (including 24.9% of undergraduates receiving need-based Federal Pell Grants). We also note that a state scholarship program for academic achievement provides tuition assistance to 72.2% of undergraduates [15]. Thus, financial considerations of students are important to consider for any classroom innovation. Unlike requiring the purchase a response clicker or additional texts, our innovation does not impose additional financial costs on students.

Furthermore, we believe that financial hardships are a limiting factor in understanding how much of the student population is learning-disabled. At our institution's disability resource office, an official diagnosis of a learning disability is required for students to receive accommodations in the classroom. Testing for learning disabilities at our institution is about $500. This cost may be a huge financial encumbrance for many of our students.

Finally, we note that our note-taking intervention was of minimal cost to the university. The only additional resource required was a single TA assigned to the lecture portion of the course. Smaller-sized courses may not require any additional resources.

Generalizability of Claims: We acknowledge that many factors can influence academic performance in the classroom, such as individual differences, social trends, or unauthorized publishing of previous examinations. To minimize confounding variables, we made the two courses as identical as possible using the same textbooks, lecture slides, and examinations. To avoid having previous semesters' examinations being posted publicly, we did not return examinations to students (but students were encouraged to visit office hours to go over their exams). We strongly believe

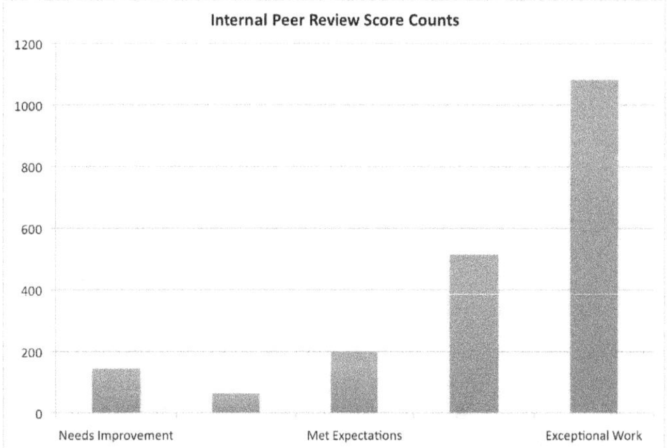

Figure 7. Number of internal peer review scores issued over the semester to teammates.

that note-taking was an effective resource for a non-trivial number of students in the course, as indicated by self-reporting and final examination scores.

Significant Improvement on Final Exam: Students in the note-taking course were able to outperform their counterparts only on the final examination, and not either of the two mid-semester examinations. We believe this may be attributed to two factors. First, the final examination was a cumulative exam, resulting in a greater amount of material being covered. We hypothesize that the public availability of group notes and study guides helped more students effectively study and manage large amounts of information. Second, the material taught after the second exam contained lectures of special topics on computer science, many of which were not in the textbook. We hypothesize that the group notes and study guides were a valuable resource for students reviewing these topics for the final exam.

Perception versus Reality of Grade Impact: As shown in Table 1, many individuals indicated one of the negative aspects of group note-taking was how other students' performance could negatively impact individual grades. This is echoed in Figure 4, where 63.8% of respondents indicated a preference toward individual homework assignments over the group project. We compared the students' grades with and without the group notes components and found that 80.8% of students' final grades did not change; 8.2% of students' grades went down one step (e.g., A to A-minus), 10.3% of students grades went up one step (e.g., B-minus to B), and 0.7% of students' grades went down two steps (e.g., B-plus to B-minus). Thus, the *actual* negative impact on course grades was minimal.

Mismatch Between Survey and Actual Evaluations: During the self-evaluations, a majority of individuals indicated they felt like they did more than their fair share of work during the semester. However, the actual ratings captured during the internal peer review process largely indicated that team members were doing their fair share throughout the semester. We believe this disparity resulted from students being generous during internal peer reviews to avoid "throwing a team member under the bus", either for fear of reprisals or it negatively impacting their grades. In addition, students were aware that the instructor and teaching assistant had access to the internal peer review information, although ratings were kept confidential and anonymous within the teams. Conversely, the cloak of anonymity may facilitate individuals being harsher than during face-to-face interactions [2].

6. FUTURE WORK

In the future, we plan to administer surveys specifically to students with disabilities. In the current study, we showed significant improvements in learning outcomes for the general population (presumably including learning disabled individuals), but we were unable to focus our research on students with disabilities. Earlier, we discussed the difficulties in gathering information about students with disabilities, and we plan to explore methods of identifying and reporting on students with disabilities in our research, including those who have not been diagnosed by our disability resource office.

We also observed that some students had a negative impression of the note-taking intervention because they were concerned that other students could negatively impact their grade. We note that our findings correspond to other researchers' observations that students often resist team projects due to prior negative experiences. We intend to mitigate these negative impacts in two ways. First, we will inform students that group note-taking had an overall positive effect on student grades—very few were negatively impacted and those impacts were small. Second, in future semesters, we will maintain averages with and without group note-taking grades, demonstrating the degree to which the group assignments impact grades.

7. CONCLUSION

In this paper, we describe the design, implementation, pilot testing, and evaluation of a group note-taking intervention in a large CS-0 course. Our specific contributions include:

- A classroom intervention that is of minimal cost to students, institutions, and instructors.
- A universal design mechanism that provides notes and study guides for all students, including those with declared, undeclared, or undiagnosed learning disabilities (an under-served population within computing).
- Quantitative evidence indicating that students in the group note-taking process scored significantly higher on a final examination than students in a conventional course.
- Survey results indicating that 32% of individuals self-reported an increase in their note-taking abilities.
- Students reported benefits such as meeting individuals they would normally have met or interacted with had the group note-taking project not been implemented.

8. ACKNOWLEDGMENTS

The research presented in this article is part of SciTrain U, and the authors would like to especially thank the following individuals associated with the SciTrain project: Stephen Rehberg, Brendan Leahy, Margaret Totty, and Melissa Ann Crane.

9. REFERENCES

[1] Anderson, R., Anderson, R., Davis, K.M., Linnell, N., Prince, C. and Razmov, V., Supporting active learning and examples based instruction with classrom technology. in *SIGCSE '07*, (2007), ACM Press, 69-73.

[2] Bernstein, M.S., Monroy-Hernandez, A., Harry, D., Andre, P. and Vargas, G,. 4chan and /b/: an analysis of anonymity and ephemerality in a large online community. *AAAI Weblogs and Social Media*. Retrieved August 1, 2011 from http://www.aaai.org/ocs/index.php/ICWSM/ICWSM11/paper/view/2873

[3] Boyle, J.R. and Weishaar, M. The effects of strategic notetaking on the recall and comprehension of lecture information for high school students with learning disabilities. *Learning Disabilities Research & Practice*, *16* (3). 133-141.

[4] Burgstahler, S. and Cory, R. *Universal design in higher education: From principles to practice*. Harvard Education Press, Boston, 2008.

[5] Caldwell, J.E. Clickers in the large classroom: Current research and best-practice tips. *CBE Life Sci Ed*, *6* (1). 9-20.

[6] Cavender, A.C., Richard, R.E. and Rother, R.I., The summer academy for advancing deaf and hard of hearing in computing. In *SIGCSE '10*, ACM Press, 514-518.

[7] Chickering, A.W. and Gamson, Z.F. Seven principles for good practice in undergraduate education. *AAHE Bulletin*, *3* (7). 3-7.

[8] Gehringer, E.F. and Miller, C.S., Student-generated active-learning exercises. in *SIGCSE '09*, ACM Press, 81-85.

[9] Hiltz, S.R., Johnson, K. and Turoff, M. Experiments in group decision making communication process and outcome in face-to-face versus computerized conferences. *Human Communications Research*, *13* (2). 225-252.

[10] Hughes, C.A. and Suritsky, S.K. Note-taking skills of university students with and without learning disabilities. *Journal of Learning Disability*, *27* (1). 20-24.

[11] Johnson, J. and Strange, M. Why rural matters 2009: State and regional challenges and opportunities, 2009.

[12] National Council on Disability. People with Disabilities and Postsecondary Education, 2003.

[13] National Science Foundation. Women, minorities, and persons with disabilities in science and engineering (04-31), National Science Foundation, 2007.

[14] Office of Institutional Research. The University of Georgia Common Data Set, 2010.

[15] Office of Institutional Research. The University of Georgia Fact Book, 2010.

[16] Saski, J., Swicegood, P. and Carter, J. Notetaking formats for learning disabled adolescents. *Learning Disability Quarterly*, *6* (3). 265-272.

[17] Short, J., Williams, E. and Christie, B. *The social psychology of telecommunications*. Wiley, London, 1976.

[18] Snyder, T.D. and Dillow, S.A. Digest of Education Statistics 2010 (NCES 2011-015). National Center for Education Statistics, Institute of Education Sciences, U.S. Department of Education., Washington, D.C., 2011.

[19] The Center for Assistive Technology and Environmental Retrieved August 1, 2011 from http://www.catea.gatech.edu/scitrainU/.

[20] Tinto, V. Classrooms as communities: Exploring the educational character of student persistence. *The Journal of Higher Education*, *68* (6). 599-623.

[21] Weaver, R.R. and Qi, J. Classroom organization and participation: College students' perceptions. *Journal of Higher Education*, *76* (5). 570-601.

[22] Wilson, M.E. Teaching, learning, and the millenial students. *New Directions for Student Services*, *1004* (106). 59-71.

Following a Thread: Knitting Patterns and Program Tracing

Michelle Craig
Dept. of Computer Science
University of Toronto
mcraig@cs.toronto.edu

Sarah Petersen
sarah@sarahpetersen.net

Andrew Petersen
Dept. of Mathematical and Computational Sciences
University of Toronto Mississauga
andrew.petersen@utoronto.ca

ABSTRACT

This paper presents observations about teaching program tracing to novices drawn from a study of knitting patterns. Due to changes in audience, knitting patterns have evolved from vague, chatty discourse written for experts to precise, line-by-line procedures that are akin to programs. The modern knitting community has developed numerous conventions for articulating iteration, expressing conditions, and documenting design decisions. "Executing" one of these patterns is analogous to tracing, since the knitter must demonstrate understanding of the instructions. We argue that the conventions adopted by knitters to make their patterns more understandable to non-experts provide useful insight to computer scientists teaching novices. Our observations suggest that phrasing conditions as termination cases ("until" instead of "while") and partially unrolling loops may help beginners understand code and that some structures, like parameters to functions, may be unfamiliar because they have no common analog.

Categories and Subject Descriptors

K.3.2 [**Computer Science Education**]: Computer and Information Science Education

General Terms

Languages, Human Factors

Keywords

tracing, novice programming, nonmajors

1. INTRODUCTION

The struggles of students learning how to read and write code are well documented. Numerous authors within the computer science community have proposed explanations for these difficulties and provided suggestions for how to more effectively teach programming skills [1, 18]. This work takes on added urgency as a number of non-computing disciplines recognize the need for computing skills and ideas. For example, Dorn has considered how to assist an end-user community of graphic designers with no formal CS training who regularly use computational ideas in their work [3].

At the same time, many non-computing disciplines have developed computational ideas and formalisms without the involvement of traditionally trained computer scientists. In addition to considering what computer scientists have to offer to other disciplines, we believe it worthwhile to explore what these disciplines can teach the CS education community. In the study described in this paper, we consider how knitting patterns resemble programs and discuss what the computational formalisms developed by the knitting community can teach us about tracing code. To be clear, we are not advocating teaching novice programmers to knit. Instead, we are interested in what the knitting community can teach us about learning to program.

1.1 Why Knitting?

In introductory programming courses, recipes are often cited as an example of algorithms, but they lack many important attributes of computer programs: the instructions are largely written in plain English and involve no variables and limited iteration. In contrast, knitting is a craft with extensive hand-execution (or tracing) of a complex set of instructions. A knitter follows a written pattern, normally in the absence of its author, to produce a result. The pattern itself contains a number of algorithmic structures including loops, conditionals, sub-routines, and assertions. To our knowledge, although mathematicians recognize mathematical thought in fiber arts and have been producing knitted mathematical objects[1], no one has seriously considered knitting as analogous to tracing a computer program.

Knitting became a fashionable pastime around 1835, as marked by a surge in published books and booklets [10]. Patterns gradually evolved to their modern, step-by-step form with the first list of abbreviations published in 1906. Although knitting was often taught in school during the late 19th and early 20th centuries, many of today's knitters are self-taught from books, websites, and other online resources [21], resulting in a need for clear, understandable patterns which can be used by non-experts. Modern knitting patterns typically consist of detailed, line-by-line instructions. Some training is still assumed since patterns do not usually include instructions for the most basic operations, but the novice portion of the audience has little to no

Permission to make digital or hard copies of all or part of this work for personal or classroom use is granted without fee provided that copies are not made or distributed for profit or commercial advantage and that copies bear this notice and the full citation on the first page. To copy otherwise, to republish, to post on servers or to redistribute to lists, requires prior specific permission and/or a fee.
SIGCSE'12, February 29–March 3, 2012, Raleigh, North Carolina, USA.
Copyright 2012 ACM 978-1-4503-1098-7/12/02 ...$10.00.

[1] `http://www.toroidalsnark.net/mathknit.html`

training in following the algorithmic instructions. In this paper, we investigate the conventions developed by this established, non-technical, female-dominated field for conveying algorithmic instructions to novices to trace.

1.2 Related Work

Several studies show that students without computing training have already developed related problem solving and reasoning skills that CS instructors should use [13, 4, 6]. Small changes to syntax that take advantage of novices' familiarity with conventions in natural languages can increase understanding of programming constructs [11]. Simon et al. noted that students prefer post-test loops [15], and VanDeGrift et al. found that students better understood conditionals if they were reworded as "use both or neither" [19].

However, prior experience with processes described in natural languages has also been cited as a source of errors. Fidge and Teague found evidence of common programming errors in natural language solutions to problems [5], and Bonar et al. studied how resorting to knowledge of instructions in a natural language generates bugs. In particular, they claim that misconceptions with "while" are rooted in its natural meaning [1, 2]. ("while" continues to cause problems 25 years later [7].) Pea investigated programming misconceptions and concluded that humans like to believe that the language executing the program, like a human listening to dialogue, has intuitive powers [12]. In the case of knitting patterns, this is true, since a human is "executing" the program directly.

CS educators have long advocated explicit instruction in hand-tracing [16], and several studies have examined the relationship between learning to write code and learning to read and hand-trace the execution of code [8, 20]. While the assertion that reading is a prerequisite skill for writing is unconfirmed [9, 14], learning to read code and hand-execute a program is a non-trivial skill that CS students must master.

2. METHODOLOGY

We selected a sample of 20 knitting patterns: the top 10 patterns across all categories and the top 10 sock patterns as classified on Ravelry, an online knitting community with over one million members.[2] The lists of popular patterns are continually updated based on user interest. To select a sample of high-quality patterns, we chose the most popular patterns on the assumption that patterns would not be popular if they were too unclear or contained many mistakes. We chose sock patterns in addition to the overall popular patterns because socks are well-understood but complex garments. The two authors who are experienced knitters expected that sock patterns in particular would contain algorithmic structures of interest to this study.

All three authors analyzed patterns separately and then compared findings to catalogue the algorithmic structures identified. We discussed how the instructions match or differ from structures that would be used in a computer program with the aim of identifying similarities *and* differences.

3. OBSERVATIONS

A knitting pattern can be viewed as a program (specific, detailed instructions) or an algorithm (a description of how to accomplish a task). Most modern patterns are programmatic, with detailed line-by-line instructions, but a few provide more general directions, often with opportunities for customization. The knitting community refers to the latter as "recipes". In our sample, three patterns were recipe-like rather than programmatic.

Most patterns loosely follow the same format. The common sections are listed in Table 1. The order is not fixed, and all sections are optional.

3.1 Documentation

Knitting patterns contain a lot of documentation: text that is not strictly required for tracing. There is generally a high-level description of the item and often a picture. At some point in the instructions, most patterns we examined include a stitch count even though it was redundant information. For example, the hat pattern Turn a Square[3] states "You will ... now have a total of 104 stitches on your needle." This information does not guide the knitter in producing the proper output. Instead, it can be interpreted like an assert statement, allowing the knitter to confirm that the pattern has been traced correctly thus far. We observed another knitting "assert" in Wise Hilda's Basic Ribbed Sock[4] which says "RS [right side] is facing for next row" and affirms that the knitter didn't add or skip an entire row. Turn a Square also provides informational documentation within the program: "Trapping the carried yarns in this way will create a secure and clean finish on the inside of your fabric." This is the form of internal documentation we strive to get our students to write; it explains *why* the program contains a particular instruction rather than just restating it.

Some knitting patterns provide instructions in two different ways: written step-by-step instructions and a row-by-row chart with symbolic representations of different stitches. This provision of redundant directions allows the knitter to follow their preferred pattern style, and also provides a way for novices to double-check their understanding of the chart using the longer, wordy instructions.

3.2 Conditionals

The majority of conditionals encountered in knitting patterns could be statically determined before tracing begins. For example, patterns with multiple similar pieces, such as left and right socks or sleeves, might include different instruction sections for only the segments which vary between pieces, and a pattern written for multiple sizes may contain sections which pertain to specific sizes. Multi-size patterns also typically express stitch counts for the various sizes as lists of counts "k 20[24,30]"; by convention, the knitter knows that if she is making the nth size, she always picks the nth count from the list. For all of these variations, knitters can (and many do) skim the entire pattern and circle the parts that will apply to their desired instantiation of the pattern before starting to trace.

The sample patterns contain a few conditionals that can only be evaluated while knitting. One common example is the instruction to continue knitting until the piece measures

[2] `http://www.ravelry.com`.

[3] J. Flood. 2008. Turn a Square. Retrieved Aug 18, 2011 from `http://www.ravelry.com/patterns/library/turn-a-square`

[4] K. Atherly. 2006. Wise Hilda's Basic Ribbed Sock. Retrieved Aug 18, 2011 from `http://www.ravelry.com/patterns/library/basic-ribbed-socks`

Pattern Section	Corresponding Program Element
List of materials, with or without examples such as a specific yarn or needle size	Setup/config
Specification of gauge	Setup/config
Measurements of finished item	Global constant
Prose instructions providing guidance about how to interpret the rest of the pattern. These may be found at the beginning or interleaved row-by-row.	Programmer-level documentation
Row-by-row instructions and/or charts	Main program code

Table 1: Correspondences between Knitting Patterns and Computer Programs

the desired length. Another execution-time conditional is an option that can be exercised "if you have enough yarn." A variety of other customizations could also be considered conditionals, such as the suggestion in the Monkey sock pattern[5] to increase the height of the heel if needed. Turn a Square advises "switching to DPNs [a type of needle] when necessary" without explaining when this will be necessary. This last type of conditional assumes a fair amount of sophistication on the part of the reader and is algorithmic rather than strictly programmatic.

3.3 Iteration

A piece of knitted fabric is a 2D array of arrays, possibly of varying length. Two main types of iteration occur in these patterns. Within-row loops instruct the knitter to repeat an instruction over a set of stitches within the same row. Often the loop is executed over the entire row, but it might also be a subset of a row.[6] Table 2 lists the within-row loop forms encountered in the 20-pattern sample. More interesting are loops which range over multiple rows of knitting, present in 100% of the patterns in our sample for a total of 144 loops. The types of multi-row loops that we observed are enumerated in Table 3.

Half (51%) of the loops in our sample are counted loops, usually with the body first and instructions to repeat it a specified number of times second. In a few cases, the count is first, e.g., the instruction, "Work a 10 row twisted rib cuff (knit 1 tbl, purl 1)" for the cuff of a sock.[7]

Only 40% of the general patterns in our sample include a conditional loop, while 100% of the sock patterns did, probably because socks are customized based on the length of the intended wearer's foot. Every conditional loop in our sample provides the body before a terminating condition. i.e., the loops are all "repeat <body> until <cond>" rather than "while <cond> do <body>" or "do <body> while <cond>." One could imagine a pattern saying, "Until the work measures x inches, keep repeating k1,p1" or "keep repeating rows 1-4 while you still have yarn" but none of the patterns in our sample ever take this form.

One pattern, the original Baby Surprise Jacket[8], contains implicit conditional loops: several lines of instructions (essentially an unrolled loop body) establish a sequence to be repeated, followed by the condition upon which the knitter should switch to the next step, but no words such as repeat or continue are used. Termination conditions for conditional loops are typically based on the size of the work in progress or stitch count. Notably, for all the loops that specify a condition, a *terminating*, rather than *continuing*, condition is specified.

Instructions that could conceivably be written as a loop are sometimes unrolled. (An "unrolled loop" has been transformed into a sequence of repeated statements to eliminate the terminating condition. See Figure 4 for an example.) We also observed five "partially unrolled" loops where more than one repetition is presented, presumably to make the pattern clear to the reader. Fully or partially unrolled loops comprised 13% of all loops in our sample. 55% of the patterns contain at least one unrolled loop.

Unlike loops in computer programs, knitting loops are only specified if they will be executed at least once. When a pattern might not need to execute the body of the loop at all, the pattern uses a conditional section to isolate the loop in only the instantiation(s) of the pattern that require it. More generally, edge cases are often left unspecified because they would never occur in real life. For example, there are no rows with zero or an infinite number of stitches.

3.4 Subroutines

Individual steps in a knitting pattern such as knit (`k`), purl (`p`) or cast on (`CO`) form the building blocks of the craft and are similar to both atomic programming language operations or subroutines. They are rarely explained in patterns. It is assumed that the reader already knows how to execute them or will consult another reference. There are also often different ways to accomplish one of these steps, and it is usually left to the knitter to choose a method. This is similar to our use of abstract data types. For example, an algorithm may require a queue but not specify its implementation. In a knitting pattern, the designer may specify if a particular version should be chosen, e.g., "using the long-tail cast on method, CO 32 stitches" but in the absence of a specification the knitter is free to choose.

The knitting community makes extensive use of standard abbreviations (e.g., `ssk`, `k2tog`, `m`) for slightly more complex operations. Some patterns define these abbreviations even though they are standard, perhaps in acknowledgement of the novice component of their audience. Another set of standard terminology are a set of prose terms that describe well-understood stitch arrangements such as "stockinette" or "ribbing" which even a fairly novice knitter can translate into a sequence of knits and purls.

3.5 Parameters

Figure 1 gives an example of some more complicated operations from Bella's Mittens.[9] Consider the first four abbreviations, written in bold font with an English description followed by step by step directions. The directions for the four

[5]C. A. 2006. Monkey. Retrieved Aug 18, 2011 from `http://www.knitty.com/ISSUEwinter06/PATTmonkey.html`

[6]Such instructions over a whole row could also be viewed as vector operations, e.g., knit all the stitches in a row.

[7]T. Seppälä. 2009. Kalajoki. Retrieved Aug 18, 2011 from `http://www.ravelry.com/patterns/library/kalajoki`

[8]E. Zimmerman. 1968. The Opinionated Knitter, Newsletter #21. Schoolhouse Press.

[9]M.Henault. 2008. Bella's Mittens. Retrieved Aug 18, 2011 from `http://subliminalrabbit.blogspot.com/2008/12/bellas-mittens-updated-pattern.html`

Name	Description	Examples
Implicit	One simple instruction which applies to the entire row	k
Counted	Do something a specified number of times	k12 [k1 k2tog] 5 times Repeat from * 5 times
Repeat until	Repeat something until a condition becomes true	Knit the rest of the row k until 3 stitches before the end of the row [k4 yo] to marker

Table 2: Within-Row Loop Examples: Iteration within a Single Line

Name	Description	Examples	Count (% of loops in sample)
Counted	Repeat one or more rows a specified number of times	k 5 rows Repeat rows 1 through 4 seven more times Work 20 rows of k1p1 ribbing	74 (51%)
Repeat until	Repeat the specified rows until the termination condition is met	Repeat rows 1-4 until the piece measures 2 inches Work in pattern until work measures 5 inches	51 (35%)
Unrolled loops	Fully unrolled or several unrolled repetitions followed by a loop	Row 1: ssk, k 20, k2tog Row 2: ssk, k18, k2tog Row 3: ssk, k16, k2tog Continue in this manner until 6 stitches remain	19 (13%)

Table 3: Multi-Row Loop Examples and Counts: Iteration over Multiple Rows

ABBREVIATIONS
6-st LC: 6-stitch left-leaning cable. Slip three stitches to cable needle and hold in front; knit next three stitches; knit three stitches from cable needle.
6-st RC: 6-stitch right-leaning cable. Slip three stitches to cable needle and hold in back; knit next three stitches; knit three stitches from cable needle.
6-st LPC: 6-stitch left-leaning cable. Slip three stitches to cable needle and hold in front; purl next three stitches; knit three stitches from cable needle.
6-st RPC: 6-stitch right-leaning cable. Slip three stitches to cable needle and hold in back; knit next three stitches; purl three stitches from cable needle.
M1R: From the back, lift loop between stitches with left needle, knit into front of loop.
M1L: From the front, lift loop between stitches with left needle, knit into back of loop.

Figure 1: Example of standard abbreviations used in Bella's Mittens

cables are almost identical and are common abbreviations in the knitting community. A computer scientist would have defined a single subroutine with two boolean parameters - the first to indicate front vs. back and second to indicate knit vs. purl. The names of the abbreviations mimic this symmetry, and at first glance, one might think that the variation in the names is similar to having a subroutine name that essentially encodes the variables. However, the choice of `L/R` in the names shows that this isn't the intent. Left (`L`) and right (`R`) don't reflect the variation in the instructions but rather the difference in the end result of the operation. If the names were to reflect the instruction variations, the abbreviations would be called `6-st C FK` (6-stitch cable front knit), `6-st C BK`, `6-st C FP` and `6-st C BP`. The next two abbreviations are also a matched pair and exhibit the same naming property where the `R` and `L` represent the result rather than the variation in the instructions.

When a designer uses a custom stitch arrangement, the pattern defines the subroutine by specifying the name and

Lace Pattern (Worked in the round over a multiple of 11 sts)
Round 1: K all sts.
Even-Numbered Rounds 2-24: K all sts.
Odd-Numbered Rounds 3-11: K2, ssk, k2tog, k3, yo, k1, yo, k1] to end.
Round 13: K all sts.
Odd-Numbered Rounds 15-23: [K3, yo, k1, yo, k3, ssk, k2tog] to end.
Repeat Rounds 1-24 for Lace Pattern.

Figure 2: Example of subroutine definition in Spring Forward where row numbers are used as labels

the instructions, often before the actual instructions to begin knitting are given. Unlike novice programmers, who are occasionally unclear about whether defined procedures should be executed on definition, novice knitters know that they can't execute the subroutine at this point in the pattern because they don't have stitches on the needle yet. Figure 2 shows an example from Spring Forward.[10]

Subroutines are not always defined before the pattern begins; our pattern set also included examples where small subroutines are defined the first time they are executed. For example, Wise Hilda's Basic Ribbed Sock, excerpted in Figure 3, labels a particular row "Toe decrease row" and refers back to this row by the name. The reader is meant to understand that this "toe decrease row" is to be executed at this point, not simply defined for later use.

Some patterns label specific rows for later reference, while others explicitly number every row and reference the numbers. Figure 2 displays an interesting variation: numbered rows of instructions are not defined in completely sequential order. Instead, the pattern specifies a set of row numbers followed by the instructions for each row in the set. Following this pattern is like using a look-up table: the knitter looks up each row in turn and completes them in order.

[10]L. Welch. 2008. Spring Forward. Retrieved Aug 18, 2011 `http://knitty.com/ISSUEsummer08/PATTspringforward.html`

Toe decrease round: Knit to three stitches before start of instep, k2tog, k2, ssk; k to 3 sts before end of instep, k2tog, k2, ssk, k to end of round.
Work 3 rounds even.
Work a decrease round followed by 2 even rounds, twice. [6 rounds total]
Work a decrease round followed by 1 even round, three times. [6 rounds total]
Work decrease rounds until 8 stitches remain.

Figure 3: Example of subroutine defined during execution in Wise Hilda's Basic Ribbed Sock

1. K34, sl 1, K2 tog, psso, K86, sl1, K2 tog, psso, K34.
2. and all even-numbered rows, KNIT.
3. K33, sl 1, K2 tog, psso, K84, sl1, K2 tog, psso, K33.
5. K32, sl 1, K2 tog, psso, K82, sl1, K2 tog, psso, K32.
7. K31, sl 1, K2 tog, psso, K80, sl1, K2 tog, psso, K31.

See what you are doing? You are decreasing 2 at each marked stitch, making 2 diagonal lines, and 2 corners.

Figure 4: Example of unrolled loop with the designer's prose summary of the loop in the original Baby Surprise Jacket pattern

3.6 Variables

We did not observe any variables in the sample patterns. This may be because understanding variables is challenging for people without formal training, because there are easier ways to convey the same instructions, or because knitting patterns just don't have a need for variables. To explore this question we re-read the patterns looking for examples where a computer scientist giving instructions for the same process might have used a variable. We found one situation where using a variable could have been an option: the unrolled loops present in half of our patterns could be re-written in a shorter form by using one or more variables. However, since many knitters find it convenient to check off rows of a pattern as they complete them, there may be limited benefit to compressing many lines into a shorter form.

One pattern in our sample, the Baby Surprise Jacket, was originally published in 1968, when it consisted only of algorithmic instructions that guided the knitter through the key points in the construction of the pattern. The pattern was re-released in 2009[11] due to customer demand for a more detailed version of this popular pattern. The original contains three partially unrolled repeat-until loops where the designer gave several rows in sequence and then expected the knitter to follow the established pattern until specifically instructed to move on to the next step. Figure 4 shows an excerpt of this pattern with several unrolled loops steps followed by a plain English summary. The re-released version consists of one completely unrolled loop, providing step-by-step instructions for all 97 lines of the pattern. However, the loop could be written with a single counter used to reduce the number of stitches knit at the beginning, middle, and end of each row.

4. DISCUSSION

The conventions for expressing algorithmic structures in knitting patterns evolved gradually and organically within the knitting community. Their development and continued use within this diverse community indicates that these structures are easily understood by knitters without any particular computational background. They provide insight into the challenges faced by novice programmers and suggest methods for making code more accessible to novices.

Correctly interpreting loop conditionals is challenging for novice programmers. The patterns only include conditional loops that use a terminating condition (in contrast to while loops that use a continuing condition), suggesting that the knitting community finds it easier to interpret the former. This observation suggests that novice programmers might also find "repeat-until" more natural than "do-while." Interestingly, despite the importance of termination conditions in the study of correctness, the CS literature doesn't typically differentiate between "do-while" or "repeat-until" loops. The latter is considered a version of the former, which suggests that computer scientists underestimate the difficulty of switching between the two perspectives.

This observation may explain why some students in introductory courses overuse "break" to terminate "while" and "for" loops [17]. If a conditional that evaluates a termination condition is inserted into a "while" loop, the resulting structure is equivalent to "repeat-until." Unfortunately, most CS1 instructors are tied to a particular language chosen for other pedagogical reasons, but where the language of instruction makes it available, this observation suggests that instructors might be better off starting with the "repeat-until" loop. In languages without this structure, explicitly evaluating the termination condition and negating it may be an option, though this method risks increasing the cognitive load the novice programmers are handling.

When tracing loops, beginning programmers also have difficulty understanding exactly when the condition is evaluated. One situation that occurs several times in our pattern sample illuminates this. In Spring Forward, the knitter is instructed to, "Continue in pattern until work measures approx. 2 inches less than desired length to end of toe. End with Round 12 or 24 of Lace Pattern if possible." The Lace Pattern itself is 24 rows, and the instruction to "Continue in pattern" tells the knitter to keep repeating these 24 rows until the work reaches the right length. However, the extra note makes it clear that the exit condition is not only evaluated every 24 rows but effectively constantly. For aesthetic reasons, the author would prefer that the knitter exit the loop after Round 12 or Round 24, but if the condition became true between these rounds, the knitter might decide to exit at that time to produce a better-fitting sock. This implies that loop conditionals are commonly understood to be evaluated constantly. In a programming context, this would lead to the misconception that a loop can cease executing at any point – not just at the top or bottom of the loop.

5. CONCLUSIONS

Many researchers have studied the challenges faced by novice programmers. We approached this issue from a new direction and sought insights about reading code from outside the CS community. We observed and described algorithmic formalisms developed by the knitting community to convey instructions to both novices and experts in their field.

When teaching tracing, CS instructors can use our observations to provide examples that students will find easier to read. For example, knitters use assert statements ex-

[11]Schoolhouse Press Pattern #5. Elizabeth Zimmerman's A-B-C-SJ Adult, Baby and Child's Surprise Jacket. 2009. Schoolhouse Press.

tensively to confirm correct execution and to discover errors before they propagate. Assert statements added to programs can provide the same benefits to beginning programmers learning to trace code. Knitting patterns also sometimes use unrolled or partially unrolled loops to help the reader understand the progression; CS instructors could use a similar strategy to demonstrate program execution. Finally, variables and return values were not present in knitting patterns, perhaps because they have no common analog, shedding light on why these constructs are often difficult for novice program tracers and suggesting that data flow needs to be emphasized while learning to trace.

Several of our findings corroborate work on the benefits and challenges brought by the natural language understanding of certain constructs. For example, repeat <body> until <condition> is the preferred conditional loop form in knitting patterns, and in both conditional and counted loops, knitters prefer loops where the body is stated first. We speculate that both of these preferences follow from normal English usage. We suggest that when the language of instruction allows, instructors should consider teaching repeat-until loops first. This structure naturally forces at least one execution of the loop body, but initial examples can be chosen that require the body of the loop to be executed at least once. Later examples can transition to standard "while" loops or, as is done in knitting patterns, a conditional can be used to avoid the loop completely.

We also found situations where relying on the conventions of natural language might add to a novice programmer's confusion. For example, some knitting patterns contain loop conditions that are effectively evaluated continuously rather than just once per iteration. Instructors should emphasize the differences between natural languages and programming languages when they cannot be avoided and adjust the way that a programming language is introduced when an understanding of natural language will aid in comprehension.

6. REFERENCES

[1] J. Bonar and E. Soloway. Uncovering principles of novice programming. In *Proc. 10th ACM SIGACT-SIGPLAN Symposium on Principles of Programming Languages*, pages 10–13, 1983.

[2] J. Bonar and E. Soloway. Preprogramming knowledge: a major source of misconceptions in novice programmers. *Human-Computer Interaction*, 1:133–161, June 1985.

[3] B. Dorn, A. E. Tew, and M. Guzdial. Introductory computing construct use in an end-user programming community. In *Proc. IEEE Symposium on Visual Languages and Human-Centric Computing*, pages 27–32, 2007.

[4] A. Eckerdal, M. Thuné, and A. Berglund. What does it take to learn 'programming thinking'? In *Proc. 1st International Workshop on Computing Education Research*, pages 135–142, 2005.

[5] C. Fidge and D. Teague. Losing their marbles: syntax-free programming for assessing problem-solving skills. In *Proc. 11th Australasian Conference on Computing Education*, volume 95, pages 75–82, 2009.

[6] J. P. Gibson and J. O'Kelly. Software engineering as a model of understanding for learning and problem solving. In *Proc. 1st International Workshop on Computing Education Research*, pages 87–97, 2005.

[7] L. C. Kaczmarczyk, E. R. Petrick, J. P. East, and G. L. Herman. Identifying student misconceptions of programming. In *Proc. 41st Technical Symposium on Computer Science Education*, pages 107–111, 2010.

[8] R. Lister, E. S. Adams, S. Fitzgerald, W. Fone, J. Hamer, M. Lindholm, R. McCartney, J. E. Moström, K. Sanders, O. Seppälä, B. Simon, and L. Thomas. A multi-national study of reading and tracing skills in novice programmers. *SIGCSE Bulletin*, 36:119–150, June 2004.

[9] M. Lopez, J. Whalley, P. Robbins, and R. Lister. Relationships between reading, tracing and writing skills in introductory programming. In *Proc. 4th International Workshop on Computing Education Research*, pages 101–112, 2008.

[10] A. L. Macdonald. *No idle hands: the social history of American knitting*. Ballantine Books, 1988.

[11] L. A. Miller. Natural language programming: styles, strategies, and contrasts. *IBM Systems Journal*, 20:184–215, June 1981.

[12] R. Pea. Language-independent conceptual "bugs" in novice programming. *Journal of Educational Computing Research*, 2:25–36, 1986.

[13] C. Schulte and J. Magenheim. Novices' expectations and prior knowledge of software development: results of a study with high school students. In *Proc. 1st International Workshop on Computing Education Research*, pages 143–153, 2005.

[14] Simon, M. Lopez, K. Sutton, and T. Clear. Surely we must learn to read before we learn to write! In *Proc. 11th Australasian Conference on Computing Education*, volume 95, pages 165–170, 2009.

[15] B. Simon, T.-Y. Chen, G. Lewandowski, R. McCartney, and K. Sanders. Commonsense computing: what students know before we teach (episode 1: sorting). In *Proc. 2nd International Workshop on Computing Education Research*, pages 29–40, 2006.

[16] E. Soloway. Learning to program = learning to construct mechanisms and explanations. *Comm. of the ACM*, 29:850–858, September 1986.

[17] E. Soloway, J. Bonar, and K. Ehrlich. Cognitive strategies and looping constructs: an empirical study. *Comm. of the ACM*, 26:853–860, November 1983.

[18] E. Soloway and J. C. Spohrer. *Studying the Novice Programmer*. L. Erlbaum Associates Inc., 1988.

[19] T. VanDeGrift, D. Bouvier, T.-Y. Chen, G. Lewandowski, R. McCartney, and B. Simon. Commonsense computing (episode 6): logic is harder than pie. In *Proc. 10th Koli Calling International Conference on Computing Education Research*, pages 76–85, 2010.

[20] A. Venables, G. Tan, and R. Lister. A closer look at tracing, explaining and code writing skills in the novice programmer. In *Proc. 5th International Workshop on Computing Education Research*, pages 117–128, 2009.

[21] Y. Wakefield. A Brief History. Retrieved Aug 27, 2011 from `http://miniknittingstuff.com/history.htm`.

From Computational Thinking to Computational Values

Hal Ableson
Professor of Electrical Engineering and Computer Science
Massachusetts Institute of Technology
hal@mit.edu

Abstract

SIGCSE members love the beauty of computational thinking. They know the joy of bringing those ideas to young people. That love for computational thinking entails respect for the computational values that empower people in the digital world. For academics, those values have been central to the flowering of computing as an intellectual endeavor.

Today, those values are increasingly threatened by stresses from both within and outside academia: squabbles over who owns academic work, increasingly stringent and overreaching intellectual property laws, and the replacement of open computing platforms by closed applications and walled-garden application markets.

In this talk I'll describe some things we've done at MIT to support computational values, like open publication of all our course materials, our faculty policy on open publication of academic research, and our recently announced initiative for open online instruction based on non-proprietary software platforms. I'll discuss Creative Commons licensing and Free Software, and the importance of tinkerability for empowering citizens in an information society. And I'll describe App Inventor for Android, a new programming tool motivated by the vision that all of us us can experience mobile computing as creators using tools that we can control and reshape, rather than only as consumers of packaged applications.

Categories and Subject Descriptors

K.3.2 [**Computers and Education**]: Computer and Information Science Education – *Computer science education*

General Terms

Experimentation

Copyright is held by the author/owner(s).
SIGCSE'12, February 29–March 3, 2012, Raleigh, North Carolina, USA.
ACM 978-1-4503-1098-7/12/02.

Teaching Mathematical Reasoning across the Curriculum

Joan Krone [moderator]
Denison University
211 Olin Hall
Granville, OH 43023
+1 740-587-6484
krone@denison.edu

Doug Baldwin
SUNY Geneseo
1 College Circle
Geneseo, NY 14454
+1 585-245-5659
baldwin@geneseo.edu

Jeffrey C. Carver
University of Alabama
2019A Shelby Hall
Tuscaloosa, AL 35487
+1 205-348-9829
carver@cs.ua.edu

Joseph E. Hollingsworth
Indiana University Southeast
4201 Grant Line RD
New Albany, IN 47119
+1 812-941-2425
jholly@ius.edu

Amruth Kumar
Ramapo College of New Jersey
505 Ramapo Valley Road
Mahwah, NJ 07430
+1 201-684-7712
amruth@ramapo.edu

Murali Sitaraman
Clemson University
100 McAdams Hall
Clemson, SC
+1 864-656-3444
MSITARA@clemson.edu

Summary [Joan Krone]

It is all too often the case that CS students learn concepts of mathematical reasoning in a required discrete math course, but fail to apply what they have learned to their CS courses. This may occur because the courses are taught in different departments with little communication between faculty members, so that different terminology may be used in the math course from what is used in the CS curriculum, making it seem as though these two areas are not connected. Even when discrete math faculty collaborate with CS course instructors, students may not carry over what they learned into their CS curriculum.

Here we discuss ways in which the panel members have incorporated mathematical reasoning into a variety of courses, encouraging and supporting students to apply and enhance their reasoning skills in productive ways across the entire CS curriculum.

Joan Krone has been teaching computer science at Denison University for 22 years, and has made it a teaching priority to help students apply mathematical reasoning skills to all of their CS courses. She is co-author of the text **Essential Mathematics for Computer Science.**

1. Discrete Structures [Doug Baldwin]

The "three-fold" course sequence at SUNY Geneseo was designed in the 1990s to consciously introduce students to three methods of inquiry: the design of algorithms and programs; mathematical analysis of algorithms, and empirical analysis of algorithms. Over the years this sequence has evolved from being Geneseo's introduction to computer science into being the backbone of the intermediate computer science curriculum, where it has grown to include the mid-level design and analysis of algorithms course. The basic sequence, however, is still being taught, with over a decade of success.

Copyright is held by the author/owner(s).
SIGCSE'12, February 29–March 3, 2012, Raleigh, North Carolina, USA.
ACM 978-1-4503-1098-7/12/02.

In its current form, the sequence begins in CS2. While this course concentrates on advanced object oriented programming and elementary data structures, it also introduces the study of algorithms and their performance, and teaches the use of asymptotic notation to describe performance. The heart of the sequence is a unique course that could be considered "CS2.5." It teaches the design and analysis of recursive data structures and algorithms with a strong dose of mathematical analysis: correctness proofs, particularly by induction, recurrence relations, summations, formal treatment of asymptotic notation, etc. The final course in the sequence examines advanced algorithm design techniques, and teaches discrete probability as a tool for algorithm analysis (e.g., expected execution times, probabilistic correctness of randomized algorithms). Note that all of these courses teach the mathematical techniques they use; they do not assume mathematical knowledge from elsewhere.

Crucial to this sequence is the idea that intellectual paradigms for doing computer science—notably mathematical reasoning—are taught in computer science courses by computer scientists. Students thereby see and experience the interplay between paradigms and how they mutually reinforce one another in computer science. This avoids many of the problems students have motivating real engagement with material taught outside of computer science and with integrating that material into their understanding of computer science.

Doug Baldwin is a professor of computer science at SUNY Geneseo. He was one of the lead developers of Geneseo's "three-fold" introductory/intermediate computer science course sequence. In addition to computer science education, his professional interests include computer graphics and visualization, and programming languages and methods.

2. Data Structures [Joe Hollingsworth]

On my campus the past few years, I have had the good fortune to teach discrete math, advanced data structures, and algorithms analysis courses. Additionally, I have recently spent a significant amount of time formulating specific learning outcomes related to math reasoning across the curriculum. These two experiences have provided a good perspective on the curriculum alignment and assessment issues we face when attempting to integrate mathematical reasoning across the undergraduate computer science curriculum. I have recently developed short video podcasts intended for my data structures students that demonstrate the process for developing and proving the verification conditions for an imperative operation. I look forward to assessing the impact of such videos on student learning.

Hollingsworth serves as a Professor of Computer Science at Indiana University Southeast where he has been since 1992. He also serves as the director of the IU Southeast teaching and learning center for faculty. His primary interests are related to software engineering. Specifically, he is interested in the technical details related to how to better engineer software, how to better teach these details to undergraduates, how to assess what is taught, and finally, how to put into practice what he preaches (recently he has worked on smart-phone apps).

3. Programming Languages [Amruth Kumar]

Formal methods as a topic is a natural progression from BNF grammars and analysis of dynamic semantics, topics that I cover in the upper-level Programming Languages course. In fall 2011, I introduced RESOLVE (an integrated specification and programming language) tutorials as a self-study component of the course, as an additional opportunity for students to hone their formal reasoning skills. This is the course in which students are introduced to functional and logic-based paradigms of programming, and to lesser extent, event-driven programming. Additional exposure to formal reasoning skills brings better balance to the content covered in the course.

At our institution, each course must have an associated "unsupervised" experiential learning component. Formal methods were introduced as the experiential learning component in the course. Students were asked to work with two tutorials, one on mathematical reasoning and another on formal specifications, during the two halves of the semester. They were asked to solve a mandatory problem each on the midterm and the final exam to demonstrate their understanding of this material.

Results of these self-learning exercises will be presented during the panel.

Amruth Kumar is Professor of Computer Science at Ramapo College of New Jersey. His interests include Intelligent Tutoring Systems, Evidence-based Teaching and Learning, Programming Languages and Introductory Computer Science. He has been developing online tutors for introductory Computer Science called problets (problets.org) and finds the idea of online tutors for formal methods very appealing and timely.

4. Software Engineering [Jeffrey C. Carver and Murali Sitaraman]

The Software Engineering course at the University of Alabama is taken by second semester sophomores or first semester juniors. It is primarily a theoretical course in that there is no semester long project. The course touches on all of the basic concepts in Software Engineering as outlined in the textbook by Roger Pressman. We augment some of the topics with additional external materials. Topics covered in the spring and fall 2011 offerings include formal specifications, mathematical reasoning, and proofs of correctness using formal contracts. The students complete a homework assignment in which they create reasoning tables and verification conditions, and prove correctness of portions of code.

Dr. Jeffrey Carver is an Assistant Professor in the Department of Computer Science at the University of Alabama. Previously, he was an Assistant Professor in the Department of Computer Science and Engineering at Mississippi State University. He received his PhD in Computer Science from the University of Maryland. His main research interests include empirical software engineering, software quality, software inspections, software architecture, and human factors in software engineering. He is a Senior Member of the IEEE and the ACM.

The software engineering course at Clemson is a typical one in that it covers requirements analysis, design & specification, implementation, quality assurance, and maintenance topics. However, it emphasizes component-based implementations that are connected through formally-specified contracts that are based on mathematical models, such as strings and sets. In a team project, members develop different components independently strictly based on interface specifications (given to them by the instructor) and integrate them with no rewriting; whether the integration succeeds or fails, they understand the value of formal contracts. The course at Clemson, like the one at Alabama, also teaches them how to reason mathematically about the correctness of components, helping students see that the mathematics they learn is directly useful in establishing software correctness. The student projects use a web-based reasoning environment available at www.cs.clemson.edu/group/resolve/ to reinforce the concepts.

Sitaraman is a Professor in the School of Computing at Clemson. has been teaching software engineering courses for over 20 years, and his interests span research, educational, and practical aspects of software engineering. He has led workshops and Bbirds-of-a-Feather sessions at SIGCSE on topics related to mathematical thinking.

Teaching HS Computer Science As If the Rest of the World Existed

Design, Implementation and Rationale for a HS Pre-APCS Curriculum of Interdisciplinary Central-Problem-Based Units that Model Real-World Applications

Scott R. Portnoff

Downtown Magnets High School
1081 West Temple Street
Los Angeles, CA 90012
(213) 481-0371
srport@alum.mit.edu , srp4379@lausd.net

SUMMARY

The presentation, an interim report, will focus on the design, implementation and rationale for a pre-APCS HS curriculum of Interdisciplinary Central-Problem-Based units that model real-world applications. In a typical multi-week unit, students use an existing complex software application to explore a specific problem, e.g. configuring SDSC Biology Workbench to build a phylogenetic (evolutionary) tree for various animal species after determining the degree of homology between protein or DNA sequences obtained from online genomic and protein databases. Students then build a small-scale version of the program – focusing on 1 or 2 algorithms – using Processing, Excel, BYOB or Alice. This approach allows students a glimpse into the inner workings of such programs, and affords them both context and practical potential for their projects. Back-stories from film and literature (e.g. Inherit the Wind) place problems within an historical and social context so that students will understand both their importance and the contribution CS can make to their solution. Unit topics have come from the fields of Astronomy (Galileo's discoveries), Bioinformatics (evolution), Molecular Modeling (DNA double helix), Political Science (women's suffrage/ Florida 2000 Presidential election), Environmental Science, Music (visualization software like Synthesia), and Holocaust Studies (IBM's active hardware and programming support for Hollerith machine technology used in the Nazi extermination programs).

Categories and Subject Descriptors

K.3.2 Computer and Information Science Education
Subjects: Computer Science Education; Curriculum

General Terms

Algorithms, Design, Standardization, Theory

Keywords

K-12 Instruction, pre-APCS, Curriculum, Interdisciplinary, Central Problem, Gender / Diversity, Increasing Enrollment

Copyright is held by the author/owner(s).
SIGCSE'12, February 29–March 3, 2012, Raleigh, North Carolina, USA.
ACM 978-1-4503-1098-7/12/02.

SESSION OBJECTIVE

The session will address how an interdisciplinary ICPB pre-APCS curriculum might increase overall enrollments of HS students taking CS courses. The session will be a seminar in which the author will give a presentation followed by Q&A.

SESSION OUTLINE

Two major problems have plagued Computer Science education at both the secondary and post-secondary levels for at least the last two decades: (1) low enrollment numbers and (2) a severe gender imbalance. Educational commentators and researchers since 1990 have speculated that curriculum issues might be a major factor contributing to gender imbalances. They argued for an educational paradigm that included real-world contexts, with inclusion of social and humanistic values. Although statistical evidence suggests that gender imbalances at the high school level may simply be an artifact of very low enrollment numbers overall, this does not invalidate the remedy these educators proposed; in fact, their proposed solution may be an essential piece for boosting enrollment numbers for all secondary students in CS.

CS as an academic field also has a public relations problem: the popular perception is that its major applications are limited to gaming, social networking, hand-held devices and the Internet. Worse, this limited view of the scope of CS is reinforced by CS educators and decision-makers themselves. Even though CS has wide application across the academic, commercial and social spectrums, very little, if any, of this content makes its way into curricula.

Since mathematics is the academic field closest to CS, it may be instructive to look at its curricular models, specifically IMP (Interactive Mathematics Project). In the 1990s, NSF funded the creation of this alternative HS math curriculum, a 4-year program of problem-based mathematics that replaces the traditional Algebra I / Geometry / Algebra II / Trigonometry / Precalculus sequence. Each IMP unit has a specific mathematical focus and is structured around a complex central problem into which other topics are brought in as needed for its solution. Because the prominence of CS stems from its facility as an applied science, curricula easily could lend themselves to model significant problems in many cross-curricular settings. In contrast to IMP, whose extensions of central problems to real-world situations are often a stretch, examples for modeling problems outside of CS are abundant.

Units either taught or planned include the following[1]:

1. ***Around the World in 24 Days*** (BYOB), in which students create a simulation to visualize the phenomenon described at the end of Jules Verne's book: that a traveler circum-navigating the globe traveling east will experience 1 day more than those remaining at the starting point.
2. ***Galileo's Revolution*** (Alice), in which students create both Copernican and Ptolemeic models of the Solar System and observe whether they account for (a) the phases of Venus and (b) Mars' retrograde motion.
3. ***The Right to Vote*** (BYOB), in which students write a program to tally sample results of the 2000 presidential election using Palm Beach's flawed butterfly ballot.
4. ***The DNA Double Helix*** (BYOB), in which students learn the mathematics behind computer graphics ops (translation, rotation, scaling, mirroring) in order to write a 2-D molecular modeling application for the 4 DNA bases and position them to visualize the hydrogen bonding between the opposing anti–parallel strands of the double helix.
5. ***Bioinformatics/Evolution*** (Excel): Construction of Phylo-genetic trees from genomic and protein databases, modeled after SDSC Biology Workbench. Other candidates: DNA Fragment Assembly (used in the Human Genome Project); SNP (Single Nucleotide Polymorphism) Mapping of Genes; Population Genetics
6. ***Music*** (Processing): Music Visualization Software, such as *Synthesia* or *Music Animation Machine*.
7. ***Geography/Geology***: Trip Routing: Dijkstra's algorithm; GPS: Triangulation.
8. ***History/Holocaust Studies***: IBM's active support for Nazi Germany's extermination programs through its punch card and Hollerith machine technologies.

Each central problem was also placed within a social context. In the solar system unit, students studied Bertolt Brecht's play Life of Galileo, whose major conflict is scientific truth vs. authority/convenience. The Right to Vote included not only study of the 2000 election, but of the early 20th-century women's suffrage movement. The back-story for the DNA Double Helix unit was the history of the complex interactions between Watson / Crick and Rosalind Franklin, whose x-ray diffraction data was crucial to construction of their DNA model, but to whom they never gave credit. The historical and literary content is not simply tacked on: as an integral part of each unit, it places each problem within a social / historical context, and helps explain why solving the central problem is important in the first place.

Consideration must be given as to whether such units will cover the requisite CS standards. Were there recognized standards, or standardized pre-APCS courses, one might be able to respond. Although CSTA has proposed standards, there are three problems with its objectives and outlines. First, it is a top-down approach, which – lacking any research to support it – consists simply of educated guesses. Second, the standards are topics without contexts; it is inadequate to stipulate *Iteration*, without specifying which of dozens of types of tasks to which this concept can be applied. Third, algorithms are dealt with on only the most rudimentary level. The author would argue that a curriculum such as the one described in this proposal, given a broad enough range of fields and problems, might be a ***source*** for deciding what might be the specific concepts and skills we want to teach at the high school level. Moreover, a curriculum composed of central problems explored in depth lends itself to unforeseen, but fascinating, sub-problems that crop up on the way to crafting the larger solutions.

Programming Standards can be divided into at least 4 levels:

1. ***Coding***: Programming Language Concepts.
2. ***Structure***: Organization, Modularization, Method Hierarchy.
3. ***Abstraction***: Object-Oriented Model.
4. ***Algorithms***: Object-Oriented Problem-Solving Strategies

The sub-problems encountered so far in the ICPB units are more often on the levels of ***Abstraction*** and ***Algorithms***, and turn out to be the more powerful and engaging ideas in each unit. Studying these sub-problems and ideas can give rise to specific standards CS educators may never have previously considered.

The largest obstacle to implementing a course of ICPB units in an introductory course is students' lack of a programming foun-dation; without such, the programming concepts in each unit will remain opaque. For many pedagogical reasons, students must gain competence in applying programming concepts from Day 1. This year, the author has structured the freshman introductory course as one semester of programming in ***Processing***, to be followed by a semester of ICPB units. The expectation is that student retention into the 2nd-year course – which will continue the presentation of ICB units – will increase.

EXPECTATIONS

Participants should take home the importance of ***CONTEXT*** – on many levels – in a HS pre-APCS curriculum. The thrust of the arguments made in this proposal is to give students a broad awareness of the range of fields in which CS has application so that they can put the Programming Language concepts they learn into a larger context. The proposal also advocates placing these cross-curricular problems within a social and historical context so that students will understand the importance of the problems and the contribution CS can make to their solution. Even on a more nuts-and-bolts level, CS education needs to give students a map for how programming concepts fit within a broader programming context vis-à-vis accessing OS tasks. The alternative is the current educational paradigm that caters to the traditional CS demographic, and still leaves most students finishing the APCS-A course with (a) few ideas, if any, for how the knowledge they've learned can be realistically applied; and (b) little perspective on how what they've learned fits into the larger picture of CS programming. Students are therefore left with few external incentives to explore subsequent CS courses.

SUITABILITY FOR SPECIAL SESSION

This proposal was awarded a SIGCSE Special Projects Grant in the August 2011 cycle. The presentation will be an interim report. The full proposal may be found at:

http://www.hebrewworks.com/HS-CS-Education/SIGSCE/SIGCSE-Special-Projects-Grant-Proposal.pdf

[1] The curricular materials can be accessed at the URL below:

ECS-BYOB Moodle Course:
http://dmhsport.mdl.gnomio.com/course/view.php?id=2
Click on the ***Login as a guest button***.
Enrollment Key: ***portnoffBYOB***

Funding the Challenges in Computing

Guy-Alain Amoussou
National Science Foundation
Arlington Boulevard
1-703-292-5108
gamousso@nsf.gov

Scott Grissom
Grand Valley State University
Allendale, MI 49401
1-616-331-2088
grissom@gvsu.edu

SUMMARY

What are the perceived challenges by the computing education and research communities? After small groups discuss this question, we will compare and contrast these perceived challenges to the current trend in proposals submitted and funded by the National Science Foundation's (NSF) Transforming Undergraduate Education in STEM (TUES) program. The intention is to create awareness for all involved and to broaden the range of proposals submitted to the NSF.

Categories and Subject Descriptors

K.3.2 [**Computer and Information Science Education**]: Computer Science Education

General Terms

Human Factors

Keywords

Computing challenges, Funding trends, NSF

1. OVERALL OBJECTIVE OF THE SESSION

The computing education and research community is faced with various challenges. Various organizations have reported their views and recommendations about how the computing education and research communities should move forward. Some of these reports include the ACM / IEEE curriculum recommendations for computer science and software engineering [1, 2], the 2009 ACM Future of Computing Education Summit [3], the 2009 Rebooting Computing Summit [4], an exploration of the current state of information assurance education [5], a inquiry of computing as a science [6], trends in computing employment [7] and a shifting perspective on computing's future [8]. The report of the computing education summit lays out the following six challenges: revising the computer science curriculum; diversity of the students in computing; professional development and lifelong learning; pedagogy; defining computing; and promoting computing. Their recommendations suggest strategies related to measurement and research of different audiences and participants; establishment of university/industry partnerships; cross-computing engagements and collaboration; changing the university; improving public relations; and consistent policy [3].

Copyright is held by the author/owner(s).
SIGCSE'12, February 29–March 3, 2012, Raleigh, North Carolina, USA.
ACM 978-1-4503-1098-7/12/02.

A legitimate question one might ask is how these reports and recommendations are embraced by the larger computing community. Another more pressing question is the degree to which these reports and recommendations are an accurate representation of the challenges that are faced by the broader computing community.

The participants and leaders of this special session will examine the challenges identified by the computing education community and the grant resources made available to help address them. After examining data on grant proposals submitted to the NSF TUES program, participants will discuss whether the historical record of proposals addresses a good representation of the challenges identified by the broader community. More precisely, are the grant proposals submitted and eventually funded adequately addressing the perceived computing challenges in both the short and long term? Are the "right" problems being tackled in the proposals submitted and are we investing appropriately in projects that impact computing education and research?

The goal of this session is to openly engage both participants and moderators in the analysis of proposal submission and funding trends. This will provide an opportunity to assess gaps and how to address them.

Ultimately, we intend to create awareness about what the computing needs are and what proposals are being submitted and funded. This will serve as a call to action to all involved by encouraging the submission of proposals that address an expanded set of challenges and investment in projects with lasting impact.

2. OUTLINE OF THE SESSION

The session will be structured as follows:

- Short introductory comments by the moderators (5minutes).
- Participants will discuss in breakout sessions, what are their perceived challenges in computing and report out (25 minutes).
- Leaders will present an analysis of an ongoing data collection about the NSF TUES (and former Course Curriculum and Laboratory Improvement - CCLI) proposals submitted and funded since 2000 (15 minutes).
- Panel moderators will facilitate discussion of the questions by a, with active participation of the audience (30 minutes).

The following sample questions are proposed for the conversation:

- What challenges are worth investing in to impact computing education research?
- Besides NSF what sources of funding should address these challenges?
- What partnerships should be formed to successfully secure funding for key challenges?
- What other questions should we be asking to better address the challenges within the computing education community?

3. EXPECTATIONS

The expected outcomes of this conversation are to create and increase awareness about the ongoing challenges in computing and computing education research, to encourage innovation, and to broaden the range of proposals submitted to and funded by the NSF TUES program.

4. INTENDED AUDIENCE

The intended audience includes computing faculty, new or experienced investigators, leaders in the computing communities, and industry members. We expect a broad representation of participants.

5. REFERENCES

[1] ACM Curricula Recommandations, http://www.acm.org/education/curricula-recommendations, 2008 (accessed December 8, 2011).

[2] ACM/IEEE-CS Curriculum Guidelines for Undergraduate Degree Programs in Software Engineering, http://sites.computer.org/ccse/, 2004 (accessed December 8, 2011).

[3] ACM Future of Computing Education Summit, http://www.acm.org/education/future-of-computing-education-summit/, 2009 (accessed Dec. 8, 2011).

[4] Rebooting Computing Summit, http://www.rebootingcomputing.org, 2009 (accessed December 8, 2011).

[5] Cooper et All, An exploration of the current state of information assurance education, ITiCSE, 2009.

[6] Denning , P.J., Is Computer Science Science, Communications of the ACM April 2005.

[7] Wright, B., Employment, trends, and training, Occupational Outlook Quarterly, Spring 2009.

[8] Grimson, E., A Shifting Perspective on Computing's Future, Computing Research News, November 2011.

6. PRESENTERS SHORT BIOGRAPHY

Dr. Guy-Alain Amoussou is currently serving as a Program Officer in the Division of Undergraduate Education at the NSF. He is a Professor of Computing Science at Humboldt State University (HSU), a California State University. As a faculty at HSU, he was awarded six grants from NSF alone to support his interdisciplinary research and education related projects. Three of these NSF awards focused exclusively on attracting under-represented populations in computing and to undergraduate research. Two additional NSF awards from the Science of Design and the Small Business Technology Transfer programs supported his research. At NSF, he contributed to initiate the analysis of the CCLI/TUES portfolio. Currently, he manages projects in the following programs: Transforming Undergraduate Education in STEM (TUES), Federal Cyber Service: Scholarship for Service (SFS) and Scholarships in Science Technology, Engineering, and Math (S-STEM).

Dr. Scott Grissom is currently a Professor of Computer Science at Grand Valley State University and spent two years as an NSF Program Officer (2009-2011). He was awarded as a faculty five grants from NSF that were mainly focused on algorithm visualization and repository of reusable teaching resources for computer science educators. During his time at NSF, he led an effort to analyze ten years of funding decisions for the NSF Course, Curriculum and Lab Improvement program (now called TUES). The goal was to determine if there are known challenges that are not currently being funded or even addressed by proposals submitted by the CS education community.

Creative Coding and Visual Portfolios for CS1

Ira Greenberg
Center of Creative Computation
Dept. of Comp. Sci. & Engineering
Southern Methodist University
Dallas, TX (USA)
igreenberg@smu.edu

Deepak Kumar
Department of Computer Science
Bryn Mawr College
Bryn Mawr, PA (USA)
(1) 610-526-7485
dkumar@brynmawr.edu

Dianna Xu
Department of Computer Science
Bryn Mawr College
Bryn Mawr, PA (USA)
(1) 610-526-6502
dxu@brynmawr.edu

ABSTRACT
In this paper, we present the design and development of a new approach to teaching the college-level introductory computing course (CS1) using the context of art and creative coding. Over the course of a semester, students create a portfolio of aesthetic visual designs that employ basic computing structures typically taught in traditional CS1 courses using the *Processing* programming language. The goal of this approach is to bring the excitement, creativity, and innovation fostered by the context of creative coding. We also present results from a comparative study involving two offerings of the new course at two different institutions. Additionally, we compare our results with another successful approach that uses personal robots to teach CS1.

Categories and Subject Descriptors
K.3.2 [**Computers and Education**]: Computer and Information Science Education-*computer science education.*

General Terms
Design, Experimentation.

Keywords
CS1, computer science, education, pedagogy, creative coding, art, visual portfolio, Processing.

1. INTRODUCTION
Many theories have been put forward to explain the waning CS enrollments. While there is little agreement on a single cause or solution, there is some consensus that Computer Science has an image problem [Yardi & Bruckman 2007, Guzdial 2009]. The most wired and computationally involved student population ever perceives Computer Science as tedious, antisocial and irrelevant. A lagging response by CS departments to modify less relevant pedagogical approaches, perhaps too fettered to the mathematical and engineering legacy of the discipline [Hillberg & Meiselwitz 2008] does little to improve the image.

The contextualized approach to introduce students to Computer Science has gained momentum and recognition in recent years. Notable efforts include media computation [Guzdial 2004], robots [Summet et al 2009], games/animation [Moskal et al 2004, Bayless & Stout 2006], and music [Beck et al 2011]. Arguments in favor of teaching CS1 in context are persuasive, and may provide a much needed trigger for sustained student interest well beyond the introductory courses [Kay 2011, Guzdial 2010].

We present the design and development of a new context to teaching CS1, using generative art and creative coding. Over the course of a semester, students create a portfolio of aesthetic visual designs that employ basic computing structures typically taught in traditional CS1 courses using the *Processing* programming language [Processing Group]. The goal of this approach is to present computing as a medium of creativity and nurture an accessible, engaging environment that attracts a modern, diverse student body that appreciates the excitement, creativity, and innovation that computing brings.

In this paper we present results from a comparative study involving two parallel offerings of the new course at two different institutions, Bryn Mawr College and Southern Methodist University (SMU). Additionally, we compare our results with another successful approach that uses personal robots to teach CS1.

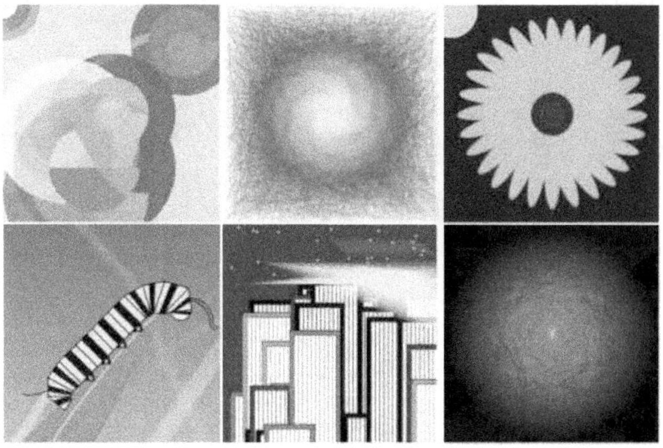

Figure 1: Student artwork in Bryn Mawr and SMU classes

1.1 Related Work
There have been various attempts at incorporating graphics and creativity in introductory computing courses, one of the earliest being Niguidula & van Dam [N&vD 1987]. Perhaps the most successful efforts to date are those of Guzdial using media computation as a context [Guzdial 2004, 2009, Guzdial & Ericsson 2006] and using Alice to introduce non-majors to computing [Cooper et al 2003, Moskal et al 2004]. These

Permission to make digital or hard copies of all or part of this work for personal or classroom use is granted without fee provided that copies are not made or distributed for profit or commercial advantage and that copies bear this notice and the full citation on the first page. To copy otherwise, or republish, to post on servers or to redistribute to lists, requires prior specific permission and/or a fee.
SIGCSE'12, February 29–March 3, 2012, Raleigh, NC, USA.
Copyright 2012 ACM 978-1-4503-1098-7/12/02...$10.00.

approaches have since been expanded into CS1 courses with documented success [Balter & Bailey 2010]. Other notable efforts in this arena include a course taught by Prof. Ursula Wolz (at The College of New jersey) on *Introduction to Interactive Multimedia*, the Artbotics project which also uses robotics to engage students in creating creative artifacts [Yanco et al 2007] and the *Computational Thinking* course at Colby College taught by Professor Bruce Maxwell, which uses Python and Turtle Graphics for 2D graphics as a medium of creativity, expression, communication and experimentation. Despite its appeal, the concept of generative art and creative computing are relatively underutilized in creating introductory computing curricula.

Besides Processing there are several other projects that are focused on creating design and art using computational techniques [VVVV, PD, Zimmer 2009, Scratch, Resnick 2007a, 2007b, Maloney et al 2008, Monroy-Hemandez & Resnick 2008, Panda3D, Arduino, Wiring]. Most of these projects either build on the context of robotics and creativity, or are still in early development stages (still in alpha-releases). Their uses in formal computing education are mostly localized to the development groups and their institutions or their immediate communities (not in Computer Science). However, they represent an exciting direction for bringing computing to a much larger community of students and practitioners.

2. CREATIVE CODING & PROCESSING

The concept of creative coding offers a different conceptual lens to the task of programming and computing. Our approach is firmly grounded in the innovative and rigorous explorations of the *Aesthetics + Computation Group*, headed by Prof. John Maeda, at the MIT Media Lab [Maeda 1999, 2004]. Maeda's group explored computation, including pedagogy, from the context of the arts classroom. We believe that the lessons learned and ultimately tools that have been created have a very direct bearing on the discussion of CS pedagogy and ultimately enrollment and retention. John Maeda is both a formally trained artist and computer scientist, who pioneered an approach to "Creative coding" that radically *recontextualized* computer code–from an applied math notation to a creative medium, on par with charcoal, paint, clay, etc. Lessons learned from these explorations led to the design of the *Processing* language [Reas & Fry 2006, 2007].

```
nematodeStage1
/* Nematode - Stage 1
Ira Greenberg, January 7, 2004
*/
int width = 500, height = 300;
float radius = 0, thickness = .35, amp = .5, angle = 0.
float y = height/2;

size (width, height);
background(255);
strokeWeight(.2);
smooth();
noFill();

for (int i=0; i<width; i++) (
  stroke(65, 10, 5);
  translate(2, y);
  ellipse(-radius/2, -radius/2, radius*.75, radius);
  y = sin(radians(angle+=5))*amp;
  radius += thickness;
  if (i==width/4)
    thickness*=-1;
}
```

Figure 2: Nematode program

Processing is a robust and full-featured language that has use both in the classroom and beyond; it is used widely in industry and growing quickly in popularity. Factors contributing to its growing popularity include: it is integrated into Java; it is stable; it has a very flat learning curve; it has a simple, intuitive, and easy-to-use IDE; it is fun to work with; it is open source and easily extendable; and runs on all popular computing platforms.

Figure 3: Nematode Sketch (see Figure 2 for program listing)

Processing was designed for the construction of 2D and 3D visual forms. Its IDE is light-weight, but well-suited for the kind of rapid proto-typing needed for dynamic visual work. Novice programmers respond well to programming environments where small snippets of code can be quickly tested and minimal effort is needed to run code. Despite the ease with which beginners take to Processing, it is a full featured programming language capable of rendering stunning graphics and animations, ones that rival the capabilities of OpenGL and other standard Graphics libraries, with little learning curve and much less actual code. For example, Figure 2 shows a complete Processing program [Greenberg 2007] which generated the sketch in Figure 3. It comes as no surprise that Processing is being embraced by academia–from departments of Art and Design and Architecture; to the Sciences, for visualization; to computer science departments, to teach CS1. In addition, Processing is built on top of Java, but uses a simplified syntax and graphics programming model. It is fully integrated in that straight Java code can be embedded freely in any Processing program/sketch, and every Processing program/sketch can be exported to a Java applet as well as a Java application for Linux, Mac and Windows.

3. COURSE DESIGN

Our pilot offering consisted of the following topics, in the order of presentation during the semester:

Course Introduction: What is computing? Algorithms, programming. What is creative computing? Creative computing examples.

Drawing Primitives: point, line, shapes, color, curves, text, images, 3D objects.

Interactivity and Simulation: I/O, mouse and keyboard events, animation and gaming, simple physics.

Control Structures: Syntax, variables and data types, expressions, conditionals, loops.

Functions: Procedural abstraction, modularity, parameters, return values.

Mathematical Concepts: Coordinate systems, polar-coordinates, basic trigonometry and geometry.

Arrays & Objects: Introduction to reference types; arrays, ArrayLists and indexing; introduction to OOP, including encapsulation, inheritance and polymorphism.

Creative Coding Concepts: Transformations, including translate, rotate and scale; iteration and randomization; algorithmic drawing; introduction to image processing.

Text, Data & Visualization: Strings, displaying text, fonts; file I/O; introduction to data mining; acquiring, parsing, filtering and cleaning data; visualization design.

Each topic was structured around 1-2 weeks of lectures and laboratory exercises followed by a creative coding assignment. Figure 1 shows some example student work. Over the course of a semester students built a visual portfolio of their work, exhibited it in a public website (www.openprocessing.org) where they could also watch and interact with the work of others, and learned the core concepts in computing. A larger collaborative project (virtual fish tank) between the students of the two partner institutions Bryn Mawr College and SMU was given mid-semester. Instructors provided an interface (the fish tank) where students shared code (fish class, physics class, etc) and learned team programming. The course culminated in a final design project where students chose, designed, and built a data visualization artifact of their own interest. These design projects ranged from visualizations of box office movie earnings, weather data, restaurant reviews (Zagat), aural data (music), demographics, etc. Some students also built games and animations.

As we continue to develop the structure of such a course we are examining ways in which we can reorganize the course content, both from design and computing perspectives. We are currently engaged in creating a set of structured instructional materials that reflect our course design. These materials will be tested in the coming year and also made available for wider adoption.

3.1 Assessment

Assessment of the students included traditional instruments such as quizzes, exams and presentations and also critiques. The critique process comes out of the arts classroom, where students and the instructor openly discuss individual projects. In the arts classroom, student work is assessed primarily through a formal analysis of design and aesthetic principles. In the Processing CS1 classroom, discussions included both technical aspects of the projects, such as a review of the source code, and also basic aesthetic issues. The aesthetic issues, as listed in any introductory design book [Rowena & Hannah 2002], included factors such as symmetry, repetition, contrast, balance, focal point, rhythm, emphasis, movement, pattern, variety, unity, etc.

One of the main benefits of utilizing the critique process was increased student engagement. Students were consistently motivated to improve their programs following the critique. This invariably led to a rethinking of both technical and aesthetic factors. In addition, students were motivated to auto-didactically learn beyond the course curriculum to extend their classroom projects.

3.2 Statistics and Early Results

In the fall semester of 2010, two CS1 classes were offered, one at each partner institution involving a total of 39 students (23 at Bryn Mawr and 16 at SMU). Both classes were capped and pre-registration numbers far exceeded available seats (closed at 45 when the cap was 23) at Bryn Mawr and lotteries were conducted. In the spring semester of 2011, Bryn Mawr offered two sections (each capped at 23) of the Processing-based CS1 due to demand, again both sections required lotteries. Bryn Mawr was not able to offer more sections due to staffing constraints.

The success of the Processing-based CS1 has led SMU to start offering an entire curriculum, including a three-course introductory sequence starting with a Processing-based CS1 and a new minor and major in creative computing. A new graduate program is also being built.

4. EVALUATION

Survey results from our pilot classes show that our approach is successful and appears particularly appealing to women. Note the enrollment trends (quoted in section 3.2) and survey results for Bryn Mawr, an all-women's institution.

4.1 Cross-institutional Comparisons

Identical surveys were collected from pilot classes at both Bryn Mawr College and SMU, which are very different institutions. Bryn Mawr is a small all-women's liberal arts college with 1,300 undergraduate students while SMU offers a more conventional CS and Engineering program with a much larger student body (11,000 total with 6,000 undergraduates). SMU also offers an Introduction to CS for Non-majors (CS0) while Bryn Mawr does not, making SMU's CS1 less likely to attract non-majors, particularly non-STEM majors. Bryn Mawr's CS1 tends to be 90% non-majors or undecided.

In addition, near identical surveys were also given to traditional Java-based CS1 sections running concurrently at SMU as a control, with two art and/or Processing specific questions taken out. A total of 21 Bryn Mawr Processing CS1 students, 11 SMU Processing CS1 students and 39 SMU non-Processing Java-based CS1 students returned the surveys for the Fall 2010 semester. We had additional data collected from the Spring 2011 sections, but we did not have sufficient time to perform the data analysis in time for this paper. We also did not calculate Chi-square because these results are early and we have a relatively small sample size.

From the Fall 2010 data we observe the following:

- Students in the Processing sections appear more positively inclined to take additional CS courses. 42.86% at Bryn Mawr and 45.45% at SMU said yes to another CS class versus 28.21% non-Processing students at SMU (see Figure 6). We would like to point out the significance of the 42.86% at Bryn Mawr, where the majority of students in the CS1 are non-majors taking the class to fulfill the quantitative requirement of the college and thus the 'yes' is unlikely to be influenced by required course sequences in the major or minor. This is borne out by the answers to whether they expect to ever have to write another program in any language after this class. 61.9% of the Bryn Mawr students said no (see Figure 8). Also interesting were the answers to why they took this class. 76.77% of Bryn Mawr students said they were just checking to find out what CS is all about, versus 27.27% at SMU, which again clearly indicates SMU required course sequences.
- Students in the Processing sections are more likely to spend extra time on a homework assignment for "fun". 85.71% of Bryn Mawr students and 72.72% of SMU students reported spending extra time on at least one homework because it was cool, versus 30.77% non-Processing students at SMU (see Figure 4).
- Students in the Processing sections indicate strong tendency to talk to friends not in the class about the class. 80.96% at Bryn Mawr and 65.64% at SMU agreed or strongly agreed.
- Students in the Processing sections at both institutions disagree that CS and programming are the same thing. 52.38% at Bryn Mawr and 54.55% at SMU disagreed or strongly disagreed.
- SMU students exhibit stronger confidence in knowledge and technical knowhow (compared to peer in class) than Bryn Mawr students. Although Bryn Mawr's distribution approximates the normal curve, possibly influenced by the all-

female student body and is likely also a more accurate depiction of relative knowledge of peers.

- SMU students also exhibit stronger confidence in math and science abilities, which is partly explained by the higher number of intended CS majors in the class. It may also have a strong correlation to gender rather than actual ability.
- Students at both institutions are quite positive about technology and trying new tools/products, with the SMU students indicating stronger tendencies.

4.2 Comparing with Another Contextualized Approach (Robots)

The Computer Science Department at Bryn Mawr College was part of the IPRE institution [Blank 2006, Kumar 2008, Summet et al 2009] that developed the personal robots approach to CS1. We have various data collected on other contextualized approaches from Bryn Mawr and Georgia Tech during the robot-based CS1 endeavors and this forms the basis for comparison. Different surveys were given out as the IPRE project evolved and they did not all contain questions comparable to our surveys. In this particular paper, we are comparing to survey data collected in the Spring 2007 (22 returned surveys) [IPRE 2007] and Spring 2008 (24 returned surveys) classes of CS1 with robots taught at Bryn Mawr, where equivalent or near equivalent questions were asked. Those were the first and second years of the IPRE project.

We would like to point out that this comparison is not intended to show which contextualized approach is better or worse. While the authors are reassured that the data supported that the new art/creative coding context is doing at least as well as another more established context, the important point is that bringing context, any context to CS1 makes a dramatic difference for student motivation and engagement on all levels, and we direct the readers' attention to the contrast of both contextualized approaches with the traditional approach.

The positive effects on student motivation demonstrated by other contextualized approaches continued consistently in our art/creative coding-based approach. Similar to results obtained from CS1 with robots, students showed strong tendency to spend extra time on assignments because they enjoyed it (see Figure 4).

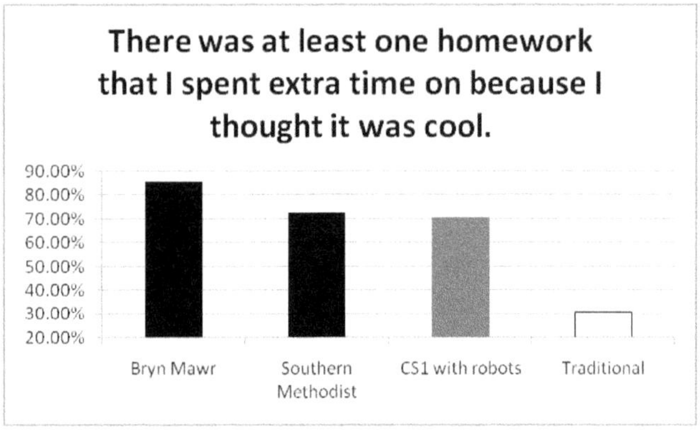

Figure 4: % of students responding Agree or Strongly Agree

As shown in Figure 5, students responded very favorably to the context of art and more found it appealing than robots. Note in Figure 4, the third data point was for the question "I enjoyed using the robot in class". We do not have a comparison data point for the traditional approach as this is a context-specific question and was taken out in the surveys given to the traditional sections.

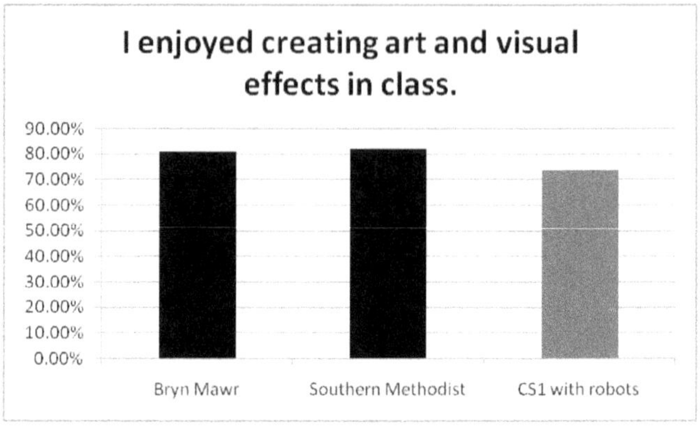

Figure 5: % of students responding Agree or Strongly Agree

Figure 6 shows that the art/creative coding context was very effective in initiating student interest and influencing students to consider taking a further course in Computer Science.

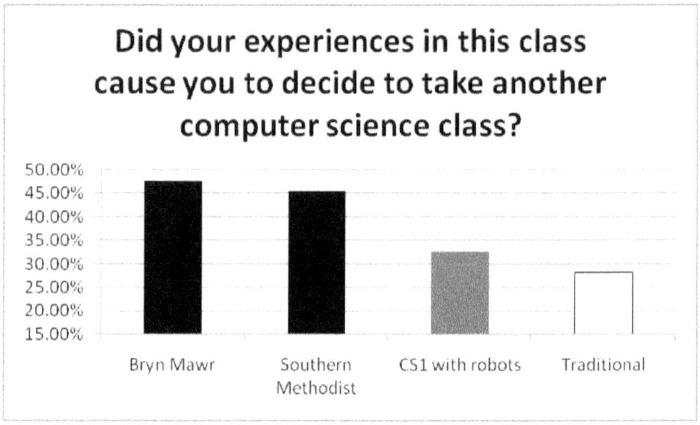

Figure 6: % of students responding Yes

Lastly, Figure 7 shows that 42.86% Bryn Mawr students indicated that they wrote additional Processing programs not assigned for this class, compared to 37.5% of students saying so for the robot approach. The SMU responses were comparable to the robot approach, at 36.36%. 28.21% of the traditional section responded Yes.

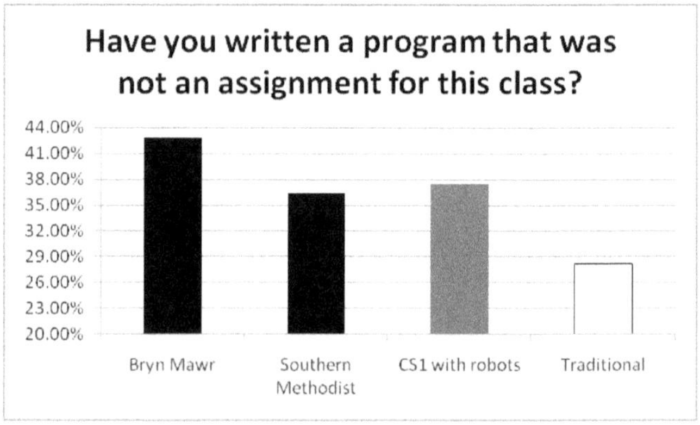

Figure 7: % of students responding Yes

Correlated with the responses to the question shown in Figure 8, we would like to point out that 61.9% of the Bryn Mawr students did not expect that they would ever have to write another program in any language after this class (likely non-STEM majors), yet the same Bryn Mawr students also showed the most interest in creating self-initiated programming projects outside of class. We believe this is a particularly encouraging sign that the art and creative coding context attracts and motivates women.

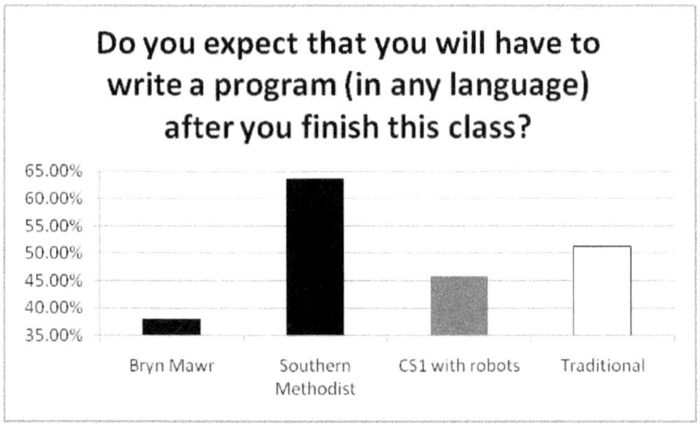

Figure 8: % of students responding Yes

5. FUTURE WORK

We continue to offer Processing-based CS1 in the 2011-2012 academic year at both institutions, using the opportunities to refine our course design and accumulate more course materials and student feedback. As we collect more survey data and build a more significant sample size, we will run more statistical analysis and look at cross-institutional differences as well as gender differences more closely. We will be conducting longitudinal studies to look at retention and enrollment numbers in CS2 and beyond. We are very excited about the development of the creative computing curriculum at SMU, which to our knowledge is the first of its kind nationwide.

As we continue to develop more course materials, they will be made freely available via our website. We are also writing a textbook for CS1 that showcases our approach and we are planning to wrap it up in time for the Spring 2012 classes. We hope that our dissemination efforts will attract signification adoption in peer institutions.

ACKNOWLEDGMENTS

The authors would like to thank Douglas Blank, Steve Cooper, Jennifer Burg, Eric Eaton, Ben Fry, Mark Guzdial, Darrel Ince, James Kiper, John Lee, Bruce Maxwell, Suku Nair, Jeffrey Nyhoff, Mark Russo, Daniel Shiffman, Allison Tew, Eugene Wallingford and Ursula Wolz for their support, encouragement, and assistance in several phases of this project. This project is supported in part by the National Science Foundation award DUE-0942626, Bryn Mawr College and Southern Methodist University and National Science Foundation award CCF-0939370.

6. REFERENCES

[1] Arduino. Web site: www.arduino.cc/

[2] Balter & Bailey 2010. Olle Balter and Duane Bailey. Enjoying Python, processing, and Java in CS1. *ACM Inroads, V(1)No.4*. ACM Press, December 2010.

[3] Bayless & Stout 2006. Jessica D. Bayless and Sean Strout. Games as a "Flavor" of CS1. In *proceedings of SIGCSE 2006*. ACM Press, 2006.

[4] Beck et al 2011. Robert E. Beck, Jennifer Burg, Jesse M. Heines, and Bill Manaris. Computing and Music: A Spectrum of Sound. *Special Session, SIGCSE 2011*. Dallas, TX, March 2011.

[5] Blank & Kumar 2003. Douglas Blank and Deepak Kumar. Patterns of Curriculum Design. In Cassel & Reis (editors), *Informatics Curricula and Teaching Methods*. Kluwer Academic Publishers/IFIP, 2003.

[6] Blank 2006. Douglas Blank. Robots make computer science personal. *Communications of the ACM*, 49(12), December 2006.

[7] Cooper et al 2003. Stephen Cooper, Wanda Dann, Randy Pausch. Teaching Objects-first in Introductory Computer Science. In *Proceedings of SIGCSE 2003*. ACM Press 2003.

[8] Greenberg 2007. Ira Greenberg. *Processing: Creative Coding and Computational Art*. Friends of Ed, 2007.

[9] Guzdial 2004. Mark Guzdial. *Introduction to computing and programming with Python: A Multimedia Approach*. Prentice-Hall, 2004.

[10] Guzdial & Ericsson 2006. Mark Guzdial and Barbara Ericsson. *Introduction to computing and programming with Java: A Multimedia Approach*. Prentice-Hall, 2006.

[11] Guzdial 2009. Mark Guzdial. Teaching Computing to Everyone. *Communications of the ACM (CACM)* 52(5):31-33. ACM Press, May 2009.

[12] Guzdial 2010. Mark Guzdial. Does Contextualized Computing Education Help?. *ACM Inroads, V(1)No.4*. ACM Press, December 2010.

[13] Hillberg & Meiselwitz 2008. J. Scott Hilberg, Gabriele Meiselwitz, Undergraduate fluency with information and communication technology: perceptions and reality, In *Proceedings of the 9th ACM SIGITE conference on Information technology education*, October 16-18, 2008, Cincinnati, OH, USA

[14] IPRE 2007. Institute for Personal Robots in Education. *IPRE 2007 Annual Report*. Institute for Personal Robots in Education (IPRE), 2007.

[15] Kay 2011. Jennifer Kay. Contextualized Approaches to Introductory Computer Science: The Key to Making Computer Science Relevant or Simply Bait and Switch?. In *Proceedings of SIGCSE 2011*. ACM Press, 2011.

[16] Kumar 2008. Deepak Kumar (editor). *Learning Computing With Robots*. Institute for Personal Robots in Education (IPRE), 2008.

[17] Maeda 1999. John Maeda. *Design By Numbers*. The MIT Press, 1999.

[18] Maeda 2004. John Maeda. *Creative Code*. Thames & Hudson Press, 2004

[19] Maloney et al 2008. Maloney, J., Peppler, K., Kafai, Y., Resnick, M., and Rusk, N. (2008). Programming by Choice: Urban Youth Learning Programming with Scratch. In *Proceedings of SIGCSE 2008*. ACM Press 2008

[20] Monroy-Hemandez & Resnick 2008. Monroy-Hernández, A. and Resnick, M. (2008). *Empowering kids to create and share programmable media*. Interactions, March-April 2008.

[21] Moskal et al 2004. Barb Moskal, Deborah Lurie, Stephen Cooper. Evaluating the Effectiveness of a New Instructional Approach. In *Proceedings of SIGCSE 2004*. ACM Press, 2004.

[22] Niguidula & van Dam 1987: David A. Niguidula and Andries van Dam. *Pascal on the Macintosh: A Graphical Approach*. Addison Wesley, 1987.

[23] Panda3D. Web Site: www.panda3d.org.

[24] PD. Pure Data. Web site: www.puredata.info.

[25] Processing Group. Main portal for all things Processing. Web site: www.processing.org.

[26] Resnick, M. (2007a). All I Really Need to Know (About Creative Thinking) I Learned (By Studying How Children Learn) in Kindergarten. In *Proceedings of the SIGCHI Conference on Creativity and Cognition*, Washington, D.C.

[27] Resnick, M. (2007b). Sowing the Seeds for a More Creative Society. In *Learning and Leading with Technology*, 2007.

[28] Reas & Fry 2006. Casey Reas and Ben Fry. Processing Code: Programming within the Context of Visual Art and Design. In *Aesthetic Computing*. Paul A. Fishwick (editor). The MIT Press, 2006.

[29] Reas & Fry 2007. Casey Reas and Ben Fry. *Processing: A Programming Handbook For Visual Designers and Artists*. The MIT Press, 2007.

[30] Rowena & Hannah 2002. Rowena Kostellow and Gail Hannah. *Elements of Design and the Structure of Visual Relationships*. Princeton Architectural Press, 2002.

[31] Scratch. Web Site: www.scratch.org.

[32] Shiffman 2008. Daniel Shiffman. *Learning Processing: A Beginner's Guide toProgramming Images, Animation, and Interaction*. Morgan Kauffman Publishers, 2008.

[33] Summet et al 2009. Jay Summet, Deepak Kumar, Keith O'Hara, Daniel Walker, Lijun Ni, Doug Blank, Tucker Balch. Personalizing CS1 with Robots. In *Proceedings of ACM SIGCSE 2009*. March 2009.

[34] VVVV. A Multimedia Toolkit. Web site: www.vvvv.org.

[35] Wiring. Web site: www.wiring.org.co/

[36] Yanco et al. Holly A. Yanco, Hyun Ju Kim, Fred G. Martin and Linda Silka . *Artbotics:* Combining Art and Robotics to Broaden Participation in Computing. *2007 Workshop on Research in Robots for Education at the Robotics Science and Systems*. 2007.

[37] Yardi & Bruckman 2007. Sarita Yardi and Amy Bruckman.What is computing? bridging the gap between teenagers' perceptions and graduate students' experiences. In *Proceedings of the Third international Workshop on Computing Education Research* (Atlanta, Georgia, USA, September 15 - 16, 2007). ICER '07.

[38] Zimmer 2009. Frank Zimmer. *loadbang - Programming Electronic Music in Pd*. Wolke Publishing House, 2009.

Stepping Up to Integrative Questions on CS1 Exams

Daniel Zingaro
Ontario Institute for Studies in Education
University of Toronto
daniel.zingaro@utoronto.ca

Andrew Petersen
Dept. of Mathematical and Computational Sciences
University of Toronto Mississauga
andrew.petersen@utoronto.ca

Michelle Craig
Dept. of Computer Science
University of Toronto
mcraig@cs.toronto.edu

ABSTRACT

In this paper, we explore the use of sequences of small code writing questions ("concept questions") designed to incrementally evaluate single programming concepts. We report on a study of student performance on a CS1 final examination that included a traditional code-writing question and four intentionally corresponding concept questions. We find that the concept questions are significant predictors of performance on both the corresponding code-writing question and the final exam as a whole. We argue that concept questions provide more accurate formative feedback and simplify marking by reducing the number of variants that must be considered. An analysis of responses categorized by the students' previous programming experience suggests that inexperienced students have the most to gain from the use of concept questions.

Categories and Subject Descriptors

K.3.2 [**Computer Science Education**]: Computer and Information Science Education

General Terms

Measurement

Keywords

novice programming, exams, CS1

1. INTRODUCTION

Learning how to program requires understanding a challenging set of concepts and skills, each of which requires significant time and effort to develop. In an introductory programming course, each student's programming abilities develop gradually over the term, and as these abilities become more robust, the student is able to undertake and complete increasingly complex tasks. The ability to handle these tasks is related to self-efficacy, so providing structured, accurate feedback and acknowledging and rewarding progress are crucial. However, assessments in introductory programming often require students to complete large pieces of code, and the danger is that students who cannot successfully complete a program will be unable to identify how much they do know and where they need to improve.

The way in which a student represents a problem has a direct bearing on the problem's difficulty for that student [2]. Both novices and experts begin solving a problem by deciding to which "category" the problem belongs, then use knowledge associated with that category to form a solution. Unfortunately, novices often categorize by using surface features of the problem, rather than an understanding of the underlying principles or core concepts. In a physics study, novices (first-semester mechanics students) grouped conceptually-unrelated problems based on similar objects or physics terms in the problem text [2]. A corresponding study in computing found similar results: when given a list of 27 problem specifications and asked to sort them based on solution type, novices grouped them by application area (e.g., business, operating systems), whereas experts grouped them on the basis of the algorithm required in their solution.

More recently, it has been argued that students have difficulty seeing the "big picture" of a problem, tending instead to focus on individual components or line-by-line explanations [5, 10]. According to the SOLO taxonomy [1], such students are working at a multistructural level rather than a relational level. For example, students are often unable to explain the purpose of a small piece of code, even when presented in multiple choice format [12].

That students often evoke suboptimal problem representations and fail to abstract from the given problem statement suggests a particular difficulty with large, integrative code-writing questions on tests and exams. Due to the high proportion of such questions, our final exams may not afford students a reasonable opportunity to demonstrate what they know. Code-writing questions intended to target specific concepts may involve many more concepts than expected, and fragile understanding of any of these concepts leads to poor performance overall [7]. Here, we contend that code-writing questions are difficult for novices because they require the students not only to use many concepts, but also to know which of those concepts to use in the first place.

In this paper, we consider an alternative to large, integrative code-writing questions: sequences of small questions that target individual concepts by asking students to write fragments of code. We argue that such questions allow for more fine-grained measures of student ability, and that they

Permission to make digital or hard copies of all or part of this work for personal or classroom use is granted without fee provided that copies are not made or distributed for profit or commercial advantage and that copies bear this notice and the full citation on the first page. To copy otherwise, to republish, to post on servers or to redistribute to lists, requires prior specific permission and/or a fee.
SIGCSE'12, February 29–March 3, 2012, Raleigh, North Carolina, USA.
Copyright 2012 ACM 978-1-4503-1098-7/12/02 ...$10.00.

can serve as powerful indicators of performance on integrative questions.

2. RELATED WORK

Using published lists of CS concepts [9, 4], Petersen et al. [7] investigated the number of concepts embodied in typical CS1 final exam questions. In a sample of fifteen CS1 final exams, the authors found that 59% of exam marks were devoted to code-writing questions. On average, each such question required students to understand and use four "significant" concepts (excluding, for example, fundamental syntactic and structural concepts). It appears that programming questions are, at least in terms of the number of concepts, more difficult than instructors expect.

In a similar study, Sheard et al. [11] sought to develop a classification scheme with which to categorize CS1 exams on a number of dimensions. The authors found that it was quite difficult to agree on whether a question was easy, medium, or hard. Furthermore, the authors tended to identify large numbers of concepts per question; they provide an anecdote describing the identification of fourteen topics for a single multiple choice question. These results therefore show that other question styles can also test students simultaneously on many topics.

As CS1 teachers, our goal is to help students ultimately write code. Yet, code-writing has been found to be the most difficult of a hierarchy of tasks that includes code reading and tracing, explaining, and writing [14]. Researchers have therefore investigated the utility of these other types of questions in terms of predicting performance on code-writing questions. For example, Lopez et al. [6] found in a final exam that performance on two types of questions — tracing code containing a loop, and explaining code — accounted for 46% of the variance exhibited in the code-writing portion. In a similar study, Venables et al. found that "explain" questions accounted for 49% of the variance on the writing questions, but that much of this predictive power is restricted to students who received maximum points on the "explain" questions. When these students were removed, only 6% of variance was explained [13]. Tracing questions accounted for a similar percentage of variance, but in contrast to the "explain" questions, the linear relationship applies to students who fall *below* a certain threshold on the tracing questions. That is, those who do poorly on tracing do poorly on code-writing, but doing well on tracing does not imply doing well on code-writing.

Parsons problems have also been suggested as a tool to assess requisite code-writing knowledge. In a Parsons problem, students are provided with a random permutation of the lines of code required to solve a problem and must reorder that code correctly. Often, a superset of the code lines is provided, where each line must be selected from a pair of similar lines. Research has found that performance on Parsons problems is highly correlated with code-writing but not with code-tracing [3]. In addition, inter-rater reliability on marking a Parsons problem was substantially higher than agreement when marking a code-writing question. Rubrics for Parsons problems require fewer cases than code-writing rubrics and have better-defined marking criteria.

The ease and accuracy by which Parsons puzzles can be marked suggests that such puzzles can serve as a source of consistent feedback for students. Yet, there is evidence that solving a Parsons puzzle does not necessarily mean that students can write code. In a qualitative interview study, students were given a Parsons puzzle and, once they solved it correctly, were asked to write that solution code from scratch. Many students were unable to do so, suggesting that heuristic or contextual cues can be used to solve a Parsons puzzle without fully understanding the solution [3]. In addition, since the code is already "on the page", students are not themselves writing any code.

In this paper, we are interested in the use of focused code-writing tasks where students write small amounts of code. Our goal is to be able to test concepts in relative isolation, limiting larger design or problem-solving requirements. We are also interested in providing consistent and accurate formative feedback to students about their mastery of individual concepts.

3. STUDY CONTEXT

In the fall of 2010, we conducted a study to investigate the utility and appropriateness of small code-writing questions on CS1 written examinations. Our goal was to test understanding of single concepts (such as being able to loop over a list, use an if-statement, or use variable assignment) with very little distraction or dependence on other concepts. However, topics in CS1 are graduated in the sense that it is hard to imagine being able to write code that uses an accumulator without first understanding a looping structure. Therefore, when we could not target what we considered to be an important concept directly, we created several graduated questions leading up to that concept. Each such question contains a short statement of the problem and typically requires one to five lines of code. We refer to these questions as **concept questions** and, in some cases, labeled them with the concept being evaluated.

Our full study evaluated responses on term test and final exam questions from four CS1 courses with a total of 642 consenting undergraduate students. Each student provided information about their previous programming experience and their intentions to major in CS. The exams and tests included concept questions and standard code-writing questions, as well as a mix of code-explaining and tracing questions.

This paper reports on five questions (one code-writing and four concept questions) on one final exam. The concept questions were intentionally written to match the concepts tested in the code-writing question. In addition, the students had encountered similarly-styled concept questions on a test given earlier in the term, which should reduce any effect caused by unfamiliarity with a new type of question.

The exam was graded out of 73 marks, including 11 marks for concept questions, 22 marks for tracing, 30 marks for code-writing, 3 marks for code-explaining, and 6 marks for sorting algorithms. Of the 193 students initially registered in the course, 112 (58%) provided consent to include their data in the study. A total of 123 students completed the term work and final exam; of these, 77 (63%) provided consent. Our consenting subset averaged 70% on the exam; the entire class averaged slightly lower at 67%. All questions on the exam were graded by the course instructor.

3.1 The Questions

The code-writing question we studied and one possible solution are presented in Figure 1. We refer to this question as

A list of students and their assignment marks has the following format. Each element of the list is a tuple where the first element is the student ID and the second element is a list of marks. Here is an example:

```
marks = [('dan11', [76,80,67]), ('jane23', [81,90,69]),
         ('jones11', [77,79,55])]
```

In the list of assignment marks, element 0 corresponds to assignment 0. Every assignment is out of 100 marks.
Complete `calc_average` so that it works according to the docstring.

```
def calc_average(a_num, marks):
    '''Return the average mark on assignment a_num for
    all students in list marks.
    Precondition: marks contains an assignment
    corresponding to a_num.'''
```

```
    total = 0.0
    for student in marks:
        total += student[1][a_num]
    return total / len(marks)
```

Figure 1: The code-writing (*write*) question with solution entered into the answer box.

write. While this question does not require much code (not much more than the concept questions introduced later), students must understand several concepts and, as importantly, identify the need for specific programming structures and integrate them. They must use a loop to iterate over the tuples in the outer list, be able to use list-indexing, and understand the idea of nesting inner lists within the tuples. They must maintain an accumulator inside their loop (i.e., by using an expression) and, following the loop, divide that accumulator by the length of the list (another expression). Though the function header is given, elements of function structure remain pertinent: students must include a `return` statement and understand that the parameters are accessible as variables within the function.

This question was marked using an additive scheme worth a total of five marks. Students earned one mark for each for: looping through the list, initializing and updating the accumulator, indexing a tuple's second element (dealing with the nested structure), and accessing the correct assignment in the inner list. They earned 0.5 marks each for: a `return` statement and dividing the accumulator by the number of marks. Syntax issues were generally ignored.

To target isolated elements of **write**, we created four concept questions worth one mark each. They appear in sequence in Figure 2 with sample correct solutions provided in the answer boxes. The bold font labels describing what is required in each question (e.g., **Accessing a List Element**) were included on the examination paper.

The first of these concept questions asks whether students can index a list in isolation, and the second determines whether students can perform a basic loop over a list. We anticipated that this would be the combined minimum knowledge required to make any progress whatsoever on **write**. The third concept question adds one level of nesting to a list, and the fourth introduces the idea of an accumulator. Together, the latter two questions capture what we think of as the core of **write**. For the remainder of the paper, we refer to these concept questions as **access**, **iterate**, **nest**, and **accumulate**, respectively.

Accessing a List Element. Write a single Python statement to follow the code below that prints the value `'corn'` by accessing the third element from the list `food`.

```
food = ['peas', 'carrots', 'corn', 'potatoes']
```

```
print food[2]
```

Iterating Over a List. Assume you have the Python variable `friends` that refers to a list of strings. Write Python code to print each element of the list on a separate line.

```
for friend in friends:
    print friend
```

Nested Lists. Python list `L` is a list of lists that could look as shown below. Using a `for` loop, extract and print the second element of each of the sublists of `L`, each on its own line. For example, if `L` were set as follows:

```
L = [ ['a', 'this_one', 'b'], ['c', 'that_one', 'd'] ]
```

your `for` loop would print:

```
this_one
that_one
```

```
for sublist in L:
    print sublist[1]
```

Accumulating from a List. Assume you have the Python variable `prices` that refers to a list of floating point numbers. Write Python code to print the total of all the elements in `prices` without using the built-in `sum` function.

```
total = 0.0
for price in prices:
    total += price
print total
```

Figure 2: The *access*, *iterate*, *nest*, and *accumulate* concept questions. Solutions have been entered into the answer boxes.

Most concept questions were marked as 0 (incorrect) or 1 (correct). On **accumulate**, 12 students received 0.5 for either omitting the final print statement, not initializing the accumulator, or including extraneous code such as an unnecessary type cast.

4. RESULTS

4.1 Performance by Quartile

Table 1 presents student performance for each of the five questions of interest. The average for the class and the average for each quartile is presented. The quartiles are based on total exam mark.

The average on the final exam (over all questions) was 70%. The questions we studied covered the most basic material on the exam, so they each have substantially higher

	write	access	iterate	nest	accum-ulate
Mean	4.09 (82%)	0.95	0.95	0.79	0.90
Q1	2.69 (54%)	0.94	0.81	0.39	0.72
Q2	4.39 (88%)	0.875	1.0	0.8	0.93
Q3	4.34 (87%)	1.0	1.0	0.95	0.92
Q4	4.80 (96%)	1.0	1.0	1.0	1.0

Table 1: Average performance on each question for the class as a whole (Mean) and for each quartile as determined by the total exam mark.

averages than this. The marks cannot be compared directly since **write** includes marks for all four components as well as some structures not evaluated by the concept questions. However, unsurprisingly, the average for **write** was lower than almost all of the concept questions. **nest** had a slightly lower average, suggesting that the concept of nesting is, as expected, particularly difficult.

The quartile data gives some indication of the types of problems experienced by various achievement groups in the class. For example, the students in the lowest quartile (Q1) perform very poorly on **write**, but perform well on **access** and **iterate**. It is likely that, for these students, a combination of the larger context of **write** and trouble with nesting and accumulating leads to poor performance on the larger code-writing task. However, the second quartile was able to perform well on **write** despite relatively lower performance on **nest**. This suggests that despite being at the core of the question, nesting is not well represented in the final mark for the question.

4.2 Performance of Subgroups

As explained earlier, we experienced difficulty in targeting concepts that seemed to have necessary prerequisites. In **accumulate**, for example, we additionally tested their ability to write a loop over the list. One can imagine an alternative, where we provide students the skeleton of a loop and ask them to write the one-line accumulator assignment inside. Doing so would likely "give away" **iterate**.

We believe that our concept questions, therefore, are hierarchical, in the sense that **nest** and **accumulate** require the use of the concepts evaluated in **access** and **iterate**. We expect this claim to be borne out in student performance on **write**.

First, we expect that students who cannot answer **iterate** will fail to make much progress on **write**. Only three of the 77 students answered **iterate** incorrectly; on **write**, they obtained scores of 2.5, 2.5, and 0. Based on the marking rubric, these students received some marks on **write** by completing non-central aspects of the question like initializing a variable that could be used as an accumulator and by including a `return` statement.

Turning to **accumulate**, 2 students scored 0, 12 students scored 0.5, and 63 students scored 1. Students could obtain a 0.5 for making a small syntax mistake. On **nest**, 16 students scored 0 and 61 scored 1. The performance of these groups on the **write** question is broken down in Table 2. Among those students who answered both **nest** and **accumulate** correctly, the average mark on **write** was 4.44. **Nest** and **accumulate**, therefore, appear to be a prerequisite for **write** but are not wholly sufficient. That is, **write** includes "more" than the sum of its major concepts. The relationship between **nest** and **accumulate** is less clear; one is not necessarily a prerequisite for the other, though **nest** in general appears to be more difficult.

accumulate Score (# students)	0 (2)		0.5 (12)		1 (63)	
nest Score (# students)	0 (2)	1 (0)	0 (6)	1 (6)	0 (8)	1 (55)
Mean **write** Score	1.25	N/A	2.33	4.33	3.53	4.44

Table 2: Performance on *nest* and *accumulate* is indicative of performance on *write*. *accumulate* is the more difficult of the two questions.

4.3 Predicting Performance

Writing code is the major determinant of whether a student passes CS1, and the widespread use of integrative code-writing questions [7, 11] suggests that CS1 instructors believe they are important assessments of student understanding. We are therefore interested in measuring the extent to which concept questions measure what is measured by writing questions.

To address this, we performed a multiple regression with **iterate**, **nest**, and **accumulate** as independent variables, and **write** as the dependent variable. (**access** was dropped from this and all future regressions since it did not contribute to predictive power.) A power transform on **write** was required to create normally-distributed residuals. Assumptions of homoscedasticity (non-significant Breusch-Pagan test) and imperfect multicolinearity (VIF = 1.29) were tenable.

The three concept questions explained approximately 37% of the variance in the code-writing question ($F = 14.2$, $p = 0$, R-squared = 0.37, adjusted R-squared = 0.34); each of **iterate** and **nest** on its own was a significant predictor (**accumulate** was weakly significant). A nonparametric Fisher's exact test of independence, which is resistant to small sample sizes, confirms that scores on the concept questions (all correct vs. at least one mark lost) and **write** (80% and greater vs. below 80%) are significantly dependent ($p = 0$). This relationship is very similar to results from Venables et al. [13] reported earlier. That is, when targeting the key concepts of a code-writing question, it appears that our concept questions, like tracing and explaining questions, significantly relate to code-writing questions.

Since the three concept questions were selected because of their connection to the concepts evaluated by **write**, this strong relationship is perhaps unsurprising. However, the remainder of the final exam tested other concepts, many of which we perceived to be more complex than the ones tested by **write**. We therefore ran a multiple regression using the same independent variables but with the final exam mark (minus the contributions of the three concept questions) as the dependent variable. Here, performance on the three concept questions accounts for about 45% of variance on the rest of the final exam mark ($F = 21.51$, $p = 0$, R-squared = 0.47, adjusted R-squared = 0.45). In addition, we find that **write** is only slightly more predictive on the remainder of the final exam mark than are the concept questions ($F = 75.27$, $p = 0$, R-squared = 0.50, adjusted R-squared = 0.49). Together, these results suggest that our concept questions capture a component of ability that is also being measured by the rest of the exam.

Many students answered all three concept questions correctly, and correspondingly did very well on **write** (on average, 4.47 out of 5). To investigate whether our relationships hold with weaker students, we dropped all students who scored a perfect three out of three on the concept questions, and ran a multiple regression of the remaining concept question scores against **write**. We find a significant linear relationship ($F = 5.39$, $p = 0.007$, R-squared = 0.46, adjusted R-squared = 0.37). This is in contrast to other published comparisons of question types where a linear relationship to code-writing is nonexistent when the high-performers are removed [13]. This may be due to our concept questions requiring code-writing skills, even if they don't require the ability to compose multiple structures.

As a final analysis, we were interested in the extent to which the three concept questions predicted performance on the three other code-writing questions on the exam. The first such code-writing question used the same setup as **write**, but asked students to write a function to add one new mark for each student. Unfortunately, scores on this question were extremely negatively skewed, and normality of residuals could not be attained. The second question asked students to apply a list of weights to assignment marks in order to return a new tuple mapping students to overall assignment grade. The linear relationship was weak (accounting for 20% of the variance); only **nest** was a significant predictor. Finally, the third question required the use of dictionaries to keep a count of the number of each character existing in a supplied string. The linear relationship accounted for 41% of the variance, this time with both **iterate** and **nest** as significant predictors. It appears that our concept questions can predict performance on code-writing questions built to evaluate different, unrelated concepts. Some of the necessary concepts, like iteration, are shared by these other code-writing questions, but neither nesting nor the use of an accumulator was required. The nature of this relationship requires future work.

4.4 Discussion

Our concept questions were significant predictors of both **write** and final exam performance as a whole. In addition, **write** predicted final exam performance only slightly better than our concept questions. Based on these results, we suggest two hypotheses.

First, like explanation or tracing questions, concept questions correlate well with code-writing performance [13]. On the surface, this is perhaps unsurprising, as our concept questions do require some code to be written, as compared to explain and trace questions. Yet, the amount of code written for the concept questions is so small that one could argue that it hardly reflects a "genuine" exam code-writing question, or that such concept questions are so easy as to fail as predictors of anything. Instead, we have found that performance on concept questions tells us much about the performance on more integrative code-writing questions.

Second, concept questions are testing only a subset of what the code-writing questions are testing. Since the major concepts required by **write** are embodied in the concept questions, we suggest that any difference in performance between concept questions and **write** is due to a synthesis or design component. In **write**, students are not only required to understand concepts, but to know which of those concepts to use in the first place, and how to synthesize them in a coherent way. Poor performance on **write** is therefore ascribable to fragile concept knowledge, a failure at the design stage, or a combination of the two. Concept questions help us make progress toward disentangling these sources of difficulty.

In this way, we suspect, but have not tested, that concept questions will be more useful than integrative questions in terms of providing formative feedback to students. There is some wizardry involved in arriving at a student's mark using a typical code-writing rubric [3]. Students can sometimes earn a majority of marks on integrative questions through correct "boilerplate" code (like setting up accumulators and return statements) that is nevertheless distant from the question's intended target. Rubrics for concept questions, on the other hand, can be as simple as awarding a mark for a correct answer, or possibly half a mark if the question is readily separable into two independent pieces.

Even if students are given the marking scheme for a typical question, we suspect that they will struggle to determine exactly where marks were lost or what can be done to increase their performance on the next assessment. Our concept questions are labeled with the very concept that they test. Getting a 0 on a concept question therefore carries with it both the realization that they have answered incorrectly, and a cue to the area on which the student should focus.

5. IMPACT OF EXPERIENCE

In a study on the relationship between self-efficacy and mental models and learning to program, Ramlingam et al.[8] demonstrate that self-efficacy is influenced by previous programming experience and in turn affects course performance. These authors claim that instructors of introductory programming can increase student performance through activities that directly affect self-efficacy. They advocate that instructors "must challenge students but not overwhelm them with complex programming tasks that undermine their self-efficacy" and further suggest that "students need to incrementally build up a history of success at increasingly difficult tasks."

We postulated that the large integrative code-writing tasks may be overwhelming for beginning programmers and that the use of independent concept questions would help students to demonstrate success on the pieces of content that they had mastered. To the extent that this is true, concept questions may serve as affirmations of progress.

While all students in our study were learning to program, students arrive in their first programming course with a spectrum of previous experience. We wondered if the ability to integrate the individual concepts was a skill that developed only after a certain amount of time or exposure to writing code. Perhaps the differences between the performance on independent concept questions and integrative questions would depend on the student's level of programming experience. To study this, we included the question, "Before this course, have you had any experience programming in any computer language?" on the survey accompanying the participant consent form.

The 46 experienced students in our consenting group did very well on both **write** and on the concept questions. They averaged 4.39 on **write**, and between 90% and 98% on each concept question. A regression line for these students confirms that those who do well on concept questions do well on code-writing ($F = 6.79$, $p = 0.0008$, R-squared = 0.33, adjusted R-squared = 0.28).

A regression line explains a similar amount of variance for the inexperienced subset. Yet, these inexperienced students did correspondingly more poorly, averaging 3.64 on **write**, 0.90 on **access**, 0.97 on **iterate**, but only 0.61 on **nest** and 0.84 on **accumulate**. We hypothesize that this increased variance in concept scores supports the utility of these questions as diagnostic tools. A Fisher's test of independence is inconclusive, though it weakly confirms that scores on the concept questions (all correct vs. at least one mark lost) and **write** (at least 80% vs. below 80%) are not significantly dependent ($p = 0.06$). The corresponding Fisher's test on the experienced students was highly significant ($p = 0$). This result suggests that, particularly for inexperienced students, code-writing questions are more difficult than what might be expected by conceptual performance alone. We hypothesize that, while some inexperienced students obtain conceptual knowledge, they have not had sufficient time during which to be able to flexibly use that knowledge to solve new problems in an exam situation.

We also hypothesize that our concept questions help us address the call of Ramlingam et al.[8] to allow novices to build confidence based on what they know. Our results indicated that inexperienced students did well on some of the concept questions, even in the face of poor performance on **write**. We believe, in the case of term tests, that such successes can be important for increasing self-efficacy. Even though novices might not be able to write code on a first term test, we do wish to acknowledge what they **have** learned.

6. CONCLUSION

Traditional code-writing exam questions seem to require a mastery of several concepts, plus the ability to design with or synthesize those concepts. Rubrics for such questions are difficult to create and use and, we suggest, equally confusing as a formative feedback mechanism. Students receive marks for peripheral code in addition to code that satisfies the question's purpose; the mark received therefore may not alert students to core misunderstandings. We propose that single-concept questions — questions targeting one concept, or adding one concept over a previous concept question — are more effective formative feedback tools. We have shown that such questions correlate strongly with code-writing questions and the final exam mark, suggesting that what they target is a significant component of what we care to test. That concept questions are less predictive for inexperienced students suggests a disconnect between conceptual knowledge and code-writing ability for these students. Our tentative suggestion is that some (but not all) of the code-writing questions on tests can be replaced by concept questions, more clearly separating concept-understanding from larger problem-solving and design considerations. We of course believe that all of these abilities are important outcomes of CS1, but we assert that questions targeted to each skill are more indicative of specific abilities than questions testing these skills in tandem.

7. REFERENCES

[1] J. B. Biggs and K. F. Collis. *Evaluating the quality of learning: The SOLO taxonomy (Structure of the Observed Learning Outcome)*. Academic Press, 1982.

[2] M. Chi, P. Feltovich, and R. Glaser. Categorization and representation of physics problems by experts and novices. *Cognitive Science*, 5:121–152, 1981.

[3] P. Denny, A. Luxton-Reilly, and B. Simon. Evaluating a new exam question: Parsons problems. In *Proceedings of the Fourth International Workshop on Computing Education Research*, pages 113–124, 2008.

[4] K. Goldman, P. Gross, C. Heeren, G. L. Herman, L. Kaczmarczyk, M. C. Loui, and C. Zilles. Setting the scope of concept inventories for introductory computing subjects. *Transactions on Computer Education*, 10(2):1–29, 2010.

[5] R. Lister, B. Simon, E. Thompson, J. L. Whalley, and C. Prasad. Not seeing the forest for the trees: novice programmers and the SOLO taxonomy. *SIGCSE Bulletin*, 38(3):118–122, 2006.

[6] M. Lopez, J. Whalley, P. Robbins, and R. Lister. Relationships between reading, tracing and writing skills in introductory programming. In *Proceeding of the Fourth International Workshop on Computing Education Research*, pages 101–112, 2008.

[7] A. Petersen, M. Craig, and D. Zingaro. Reviewing CS1 exam question content. In *Proceedings of the 42nd ACM Technical Symposium on Computer Science Education*, pages 631–636, 2011.

[8] V. Ramalingam, D. LaBelle, and S. Wiedenbeck. Self-efficacy and mental models in learning to program. *SIGCSE Bulletin*, 36(3):171–175, 2004.

[9] C. Schulte and J. Bennedsen. What do teachers teach in introductory programming? In *Proceedings of the Second International Workshop on Computing Education Research*, pages 17–28, 2006.

[10] J. Sheard, A. Carbone, R. Lister, B. Simon, E. Thompson, and J. L. Whalley. Going solo to assess novice programmers. In *Proceedings of the 13th Annual Conference on Innovation and Technology in Computer Science Education*, pages 209–213, 2008.

[11] J. Sheard, Simon, A. Carbone, D. Chinn, M.-J. Laakso, T. Clear, M. de Raadt, D. D'Souza, J. Harland, R. Lister, A. Philpott, and G. Warburton. Exploring programming assessment instruments: A classification scheme for examination questions. In *Proceeding of the Seventh International Workshop on Computing Education Research*, pages 33–38, 2011.

[12] Simon and S. Snowdon. Explaining program code: Giving students the answer helps – but only just. In *Proceeding of the Seventh International Workshop on Computing Education Research*, pages 93–100, 2011.

[13] A. Venables, G. Tan, and R. Lister. A closer look at tracing, explaining and code writing skills in the novice programmer. In *Proceedings of the Fifth International Workshop on Computing Education Research Workshop*, pages 117–128, 2009.

[14] J. L. Whalley, R. Lister, E. Thompson, T. Clear, P. Robbins, P. K. A. Kumar, and C. Prasad. An Australasian study of reading and comprehension skills in novice programmers, using the Bloom and SOLO taxonomies. In *Proceedings of the 8th Austalian Conference on Computing Education*, pages 243–252, 2006.

Using Reflective Blogs for Pedagogical Feedback in CS1

Jeffrey A. Stone
Pennsylvania State University
200 University Drive
Schuylkill Haven, PA 17972
+1-570-385-6267
stonej@psu.edu

ABSTRACT
The use of weekly, reflective student blogs can be one method for collecting ongoing feedback about a CS1 course. Reflective blogs permit a continuous feedback loop that can be used for both formative and summative assessment of pedagogical innovations. This paper reports on a two-year qualitative study involving the use of reflective blogging in six sections of two CS1-style courses. Reflective blogs were used as a low stakes, non-intimidating vehicle whereby concerns, requests, and other course-related issues could be voiced by students. The resultant blog posts were used as an assessment and feedback mechanism for a parallel pedagogical transformation of the participating courses. This study demonstrates that reflective student blogs in CS1 can be a useful tool for instructional planning. However, faculty must be careful to avoid reactionary changes which move the course away from predefined learning outcomes.

Categories and Subject Descriptors
K.3.2 **[Computers and Education]**: Computer and Information Science Education – Computer Science Education.

General Terms
Human Factors.

Keywords
CS1, Reflection, Writing, PALMS.

1. INTRODUCTION
Evaluation of student learning in Computer Science I (CS1) courses is often based on traditional implements, such as coding projects, quizzes, and exams. While these tools often provide valid assessments of student skill sets and learning outcomes, they say little about how students actually *learn* over the course of a semester. This is especially important during the piloting of new pedagogical techniques. End-of-class surveys are often used as one method to assess the effectiveness of new pedagogy. However, surveys are usually limited in the depth of their response choices and are often a snapshot in time rather than a progressive, evolving feedback mechanism. A more qualitative assessment of student learning over the course of a semester is often difficult to record and analyze, especially for institutions with large CS1 sections and limited faculty resources.

Permission to make digital or hard copies of all or part of this work for personal or classroom use is granted without fee provided that copies are not made or distributed for profit or commercial advantage and that copies bear this notice and the full citation on the first page. To copy otherwise, or republish, to post on servers or to redistribute to lists, requires prior specific permission and/or a fee.
SIGCSE'12, February 29–March 3, 2012, Raleigh, North Carolina, USA.
Copyright 2012 ACM 978-1-4503-1098-7/12/02...$10.00.

The use of weekly, reflective student blogs can be one method for collecting ongoing qualitative feedback about a CS1 course. Reflective blogs permit a continuous feedback loop whereby new pedagogy can be evaluated and adjustments can be made. A low-stakes, private reflective blog can permit a more open and documented evaluation of in-class activities than a more public discussion. By providing a non-threatening environment for feedback, the use of reflective blogs can be a valuable data source for pedagogical assessment.

The use of reflective blogs also provides an opportunity for students to build their cognitive skills and self-awareness of their own learning processes. The increasing heterogeneity of student majors, experiences and backgrounds at many institutions has encouraged some educators and curricula committees to consider a more multidisciplinary outlook for CS1 [10]. As a result, producing graduates with both technological skills as well as so-called "soft" skills (e.g. oral and written communication, collaborative skills, lifelong learning skills) is an important concern for many CS departments. Reflective blogs provide one vehicle whereby students can exercise both their writing skills and the cognitive and soft skills thought necessary for future success.

This paper will report on a two-year study involving the use of reflective blogging in six sections of two CS1-style courses. The reflective blogs were intended to be a non-intimidating vehicle whereby concerns, requests, and other course-related issues could be voiced by students. The author also anticipated that the blog posts could be used as an ongoing feedback mechanism for a parallel pedagogical transformation of two CS1-style courses (the PALMS for CS1 project). A third purpose, outside the scope of this paper, was to implement a low-stakes exercise that would help students build their cognitive and reflective skills while maintaining the core learning outcomes of the course. The outcomes and thematic patterns associated with these blog postings will be discussed, along with their implications and their use in future CS1 development at the host institution. This research builds on other works which discuss the use of blogging in introductory CS (e.g. [1], [4], [7]) but focuses on the pedagogical enhancement possibilities offered by such blogs.

2. BACKGROUND
Writing is seen as an important part of Computer Science curricula, both in terms of national curricular guidelines [3] and in studies involving faculty and student writing [5]. In particular, the use of expressive/reflective writing has been associated with a growth in student understanding and *metacognitive* skills ([6], [13]). Metacognitive skills have long been recognized as an

important factor in student learning, allowing students to assess their learning methods and progress in order to correct deficiencies and build on successful experiences [14]. These ideas align with theories of constructivism, whereby learners integrate new knowledge into new or existing mental models through active learning exercises [9]. Such abilities are considered important as part of so-called "21st Century Skills" which place a premium on critical thinking, information synthesis, communication, and lifelong learning skills, among others [8].

The use of blogging in Computer and Information Science is also well-documented. Reflective blogs have been used as part of experiential learning activities [12], to promote student "buy-in" to the relevance of computing ethics [1], and to support reflective thoughts on game playing [14]. Reflective blogs can be considered a "writing to learn" (WTL) exercise – the use of small, expressive writing used by students to reflect on concepts and further their own metacognition and understanding [5]. As noted by McDermott et al [7] and others, reflective writing has challenges. Proper scaffolding must be provided to overcome the inherent difficulty many students face in reflection, and exercises must be structured to promote learning and pedagogical outcomes.

2.1 Reflection as Feedback

Reflection as a continuous feedback loop for pedagogy is a slippery slope. Faculty must be careful to "stay on course" towards the required course topics and learning outcomes. However, student feedback provided by the reflective blogs can be used to identify particularly challenging topics for the class and adjust daily pedagogy when possible. For example, if the vast majority of a week's blog posts describe difficulty in understanding one-dimensional arrays, the faculty member may decide to spend time reviewing the subject the following week in class, given sufficient flexibility in the schedule. The feedback students provide can also be used to identify the viability of pedagogical implements, such as homework projects, in-class examples, quizzes or exams, and in-class labs. The depth of feedback possible through reflective writing can provide more detailed evaluation of these implements than simple surveys. Student feedback can be an impetus for revision or enhancement of these implements in future semesters. The diversity of student groups from semester-to-semester makes snap judgments questionable, but patterns in the feedback may emerge over time.

2.2 The PALMS for CS1 Project

The study described here is part of a larger effort to transform the CS1 courses at the Penn State University, Schuylkill Campus. The PALMS (Problem-Oriented Animated Learning Modules) for CS1 project, previously explored in [11], is designed to make the CS1 course and its content more engaging and relevant for both majors and non-majors alike. The PALMS for CS1 project involves two learning modules which combine multimedia learning tools with integrated labs, projects, quizzes and exams. The first module (Weeks 1-4) addresses basic problem-solving and algorithms without C++ syntax. The second module (Weeks 5-15) focuses on structured programming with C++ and traditional CS1 topics. Both modules use animation, video, audio, and storytelling to engage the students and build the problem-solving skills of students. The modules are constructed in such a way as to show the applicability of CS concepts within multiple majors and problem domains.

The use of the reflective blogging mechanism in the PALMS for CS1 project helps the students see and chart their progress through critical self-analysis and reflection. The reflective blogs also provide a feedback mechanism for the instructor on the effectiveness of the PALMS for CS1 modules and the associated pedagogy used in class. The student posts reflect their thoughts on the course at that point in time; as a result, the posts allow the PALMS for CS1 project developers to identify areas for improvement and/or adjustment. The blog provides an outlet for students to voice concerns and frustrations that otherwise may not be expressed through verbal interaction. Summative assessment surveys for the PALMS for CS1 project are used, but analysis of these results is outside of this papers' scope (see [11] for a discussion of this analysis).

3. STUDY DESIGN

3.1 Methods and Procedures

Reflective blogs were utilized in six sections of two CS1-style courses over the 2009-2011 academic years. Two sections of the first course (CS121, offered once per year) were intended specifically for CS and Engineering majors. Four sections of the second course (CS101, offered twice each year) were designed as a quantitative elective for non-majors. Despite the different populations, the content between the two courses differed on only one topic (recursion). Each course met for three 50-minute sessions each week. The use of a control group was not feasible due to limited enrollments.

Students were asked to create a reflective blog entry at the end of each of the 15 weeks during the semester. The ANGEL Course Management System was used to record the blog entries via the "Discussion Forum" tool. The forum was set up as a "Private User Journal" so that only the student and the instructor would see the posts. The decision to isolate the posts was designed to allow each student to feel comfortable expressing his/her thoughts and to help avoid a follow-the-herd pattern from emerging. The use of ANGEL was chosen due to its already-heavy integration into the courses and therefore represents a data collection method of convenience.

Scaffolding was provided to help the students construct their reflective blog entries. Students were given instruction on the meaning of reflection and reflective writing, as well as guidelines for length (one-half page or more), time frame for submission (approximately 48 hours after the last class of the week) and for style. Four identical questions were posed to the students each week to guide their reflective post. The four questions asked the students what they feel they learned that week; what they enjoyed that week, whether in class or in homework; what they found to be challenging or frustrating that week; and their current confidence level in their abilities. Students were also encouraged to illustrate their points using specific examples.

The instructor was careful to point out that the blog entries were low stakes. In order to receive credit, students simply had to create the blog entry each week. In-class reminders to complete the assignment were given at the beginning and end of each class week. Students were not graded on the quality of their assignments, merely on the completion of the assignment each week. It was hoped that this low stakes policy would encourage deeper and more open reflective entries.

3.2 Profile of Participants

The study yielded 59 consenting participants or 59.6% of the total course enrollments (N=99). The participants were primarily male (50, or 84.7%) and White/Caucasian (39, or 66.1%). The majority self-reported themselves as Science, Technology, Engineering, or Mathematics (STEM) majors (47, or 79.7%). Ten of the reported STEM majors reported a CS major. In terms of academic class, the class was mostly split between freshmen (28, 48.3%, N=58) and sophomores (20, 34.5%) though a small group of juniors and seniors also participated (5, 8.6% each). In terms of course grades, 32 passed the course with a "C" or better (54.2%, N=59), 17 received a "D" or "F" (28.8%), and 10 (16.9%) withdrew before completing the course.

4. RESULTS

A total of 505 Reflective Blog Entries were analyzed for this study. This number indicates that not all students completed each of the 15 reflective blog entries requested of them. The end result was that only 57.1% of the maximum possible entries (885) were actually posted by students. The reflective blog entries ranged from 8-889 words with an average post of 183.9 words. The level of quality and length in the reflections varied, perhaps due to the low stakes nature of the assignment.

The entries were analyzed using NVivo 9 qualitative analysis software. Entries were first examined and manually coded based on week and the four original questions. Further coding of the entries was based on thematic patterns discovered via the blog entry analysis. The coding which emerged from the blog posting analysis is described in the following sections.

4.1 Student Confidence Levels

Each week, students were asked to discuss their current confidence level as part of the blog post. The blog posts were analyzed and coded based on the student's response. The coding involved five categories – *No Confidence*, *Neutral*, *Low Confidence*, *Confidence*, and *High Confidence*.

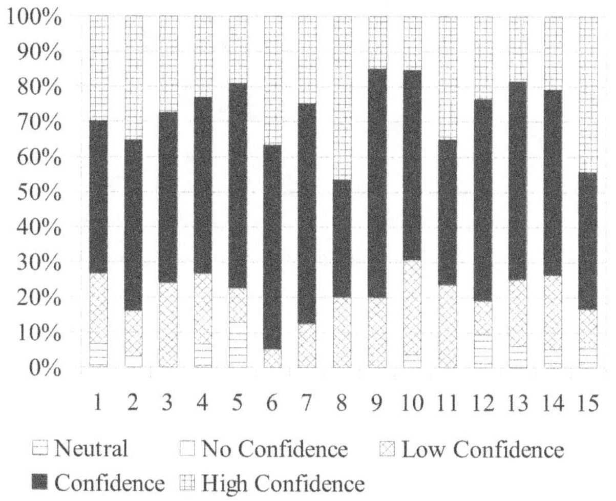

Figure 1. Confidence Level by Week, Weeks 1-15.

Figure 1 shows that most students reported *Confidence* throughout the semester, with the percentage of students reporting *Confidence* or *High Confidence* reaching a high point during Week 6 (the second week of C++) and a low point during Week 10 (the first week of one-dimensional arrays). The Week 10 drop is followed, however, by a percentage increase in both Weeks 11 and 12. During these weeks a greater class focus was placed on arrays and for loops; structures were also introduced in Week 12.

There was fluctuation in all coding categories over time, as to be expected – as new topics come along, students may naturally feel some apprehension. Ideally, over time, that apprehension should ease. The percentage of posts reporting *Confidence* or *High Confidence* at the end of Week 15 was encouraging, as it suggested a level of positive expectations for the high stakes final exam to follow.

Analysis of the blog content revealed that students who started the course with *Confidence* or *High Confidence* tended to remain confident throughout the semester. While some movement between these two categories was evident, these students' posts tended to be more positive than those from students reporting limited or nonexistent confidence. Two examples are as follows:

> *"My confidence level has been boosted a large amount in the past few weeks which I attribute to experience from projects as well as my learning experiences in class."*

> *"I am very confident in myself, and I am confident that I will always be able to get my program working because I can identify the problem way before the program is due and ask questions about what may be causing it to not work properly."*

Unfortunately, analysis of the blog content also revealed that those students who started with "Low Confidence" or "No Confidence" were unlikely to build confidence over the course of the semester. Many of these students either failed to complete the class or did so with a low grade. Notable among these were senior non-majors who chose CS101 as an alternative to a Math requirement. These students started the course with the perception that the course was difficult. This perception did not change over the course of the semester, despite the use of tutors and other assistance. The following is indicative of these confidence reports:

> *"At this point I don't think I am ever going to be confident with C++. I came to realization that Psych majors and C++ do not mix very well. I decided that I will just continue working very hard on my labs with <anonymous> and hopefully that will be enough to get through this class."*

Comments such as these suggest that the PALMS for CS1 project materials may not be having the desired effect on non-majors (i.e. engagement and materials to promote success). This pattern also suggests that more resources may be necessary to both engage and support students who enter the course with lower confidence.

4.2 Student Frustrations

Each week, students were asked to discuss their frustrations as part of the blog post. These frustrations could be in-class examples, projects, concepts, or any other issue which impeded the students' learning and enjoyment. The blog posts were analyzed and coded based on the student responses. The resultant coding involved five categories – *Course Topics*, *Quizzes and Exams*, *Personal Issues*, *Projects and Labs*, and *None*.

Frequency analysis of the post codes reveal that *Projects and Labs* were most often reported as the "frustrating" part of the week (34.5%, N=359). The fact that *Projects and Labs* ranks first was expected, as these activities involve the greatest portion of the course grade (approximately 50%) and often the greatest time investment for students. This category rank was followed by *Course Topics* (18.9%) and *Quizzes and Exams* (18.4%). *None* was reported by 15.6% of student posts. Only 12.5% reported *Personal Issues* as a "frustration" for the week.

The most commonly cited *Course Topics* for "frustration" were C++ syntax (20.6%, N=68) and algorithm construction (17.6%). Specific topics, such as loops, functions, and if statements, were cited less frequently. Frustration with C++ syntax was a consistent theme in the posts, specifically with detecting errors which impeded progress on labs and projects. For example:

> *"Something that was frustrating was that I was getting errors on the lab and I didn't know why."*
>
> *"I knew exactly what I wanted and needed to do but for some reason could not actually put it into the process."*

While many students expressed frustration about the amount of time spent deciphering cryptic C++ compiler messages, others were frustrated more by the time spent in figuring out the algorithm necessary to solve the problem. The vast majority of these posts mentioned difficulty in solving the problem using the desired implementation tools – such as arrays, functions, and strings – rather than in deciphering the problem itself.

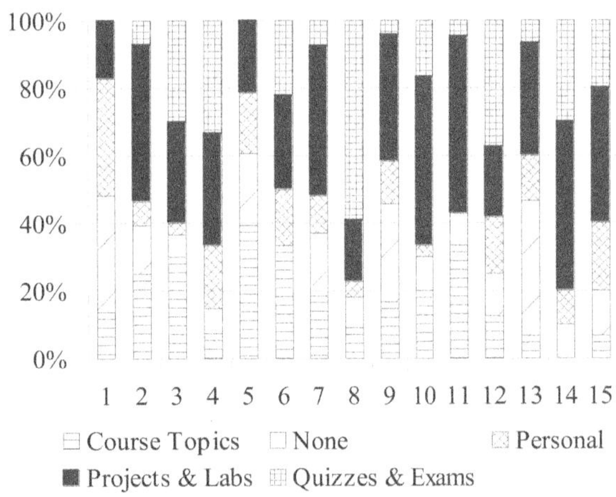

Figure 2. Frustrations by Week, Weeks 1-15.

An examination of the reported frustrations by week (see Figure 2) shows that the percentage reports for *Quizzes and Exams* spike in those weeks where an in-class quiz or exam is held, as can be expected. Many "frustrated" posts during these weeks decried the amount of material required to be absorbed for the quiz or exam and/or stated a lack of confidence in their performance. Weeks 2, 7, and 10 exhibit percentage spikes for *Projects and Labs*. To place this in perspective, Week 2 involves the first set of graded labs in the course; Week 7 involves the first projects which heavily integrate user-defined functions; and Week 10 involves the first project on one-dimensional arrays.

4.3 Student Engagement

Each week, students were asked to reflect on what they felt was enjoyable or "fun" during the past week. These "fun" things could be in-class examples, projects, concepts, or any other issue which enhanced the students' learning and enjoyment. The blog posts were analyzed and coded based on the student responses. The resultant coding involved eight categories with at least 10 coding references – *Course Topics*, *Getting Help, Good Grades, In-Class Examples*, *Problem-Solving and Algorithms*, *Project Time in Class*, *Projects and Labs*, and *None*.

Frequency analysis of the post codes reveal that *Course Topics* were most often reported as the "fun" part of the week (30.8%, N=312) followed closely by *Projects and Labs* (30.5%). The categories with the next highest amount of coding were *In-Class Examples* (11.2%) and *Problem-Solving and Algorithms* (9.9%). all other categories received less than 7% each. The most commonly cited *Course Topics* for "fun" was the use of the RAPTOR flowcharting tool [2] (44.8%, N=96; Weeks 1-4 only) and algorithms (17.6%). The next most frequent codings were conditional selection and repetition, tied at 12.5% of the posts.

An examination of the four most frequently reported "fun" items by week (see Figure 3) shows an interesting pattern in Weeks 1-4. The first four weeks of these courses are designed to introduce students to problem-solving techniques and algorithmic concepts independent of C++ syntax. Projects during this time are completed using pseudocode algorithms and RAPTOR. Figure 3 indicates an almost inverse relationship between *Course Topics* and *Projects and Labs* during the first four weeks – as course projects and labs were assigned, they were more often described as "fun" than the particular course topic they exercised. This relationship, coupled with the apparent enthusiasm for RAPTOR mentioned in the preceding paragraph, suggests that students are enjoying the implementation tool (RAPTOR) and hands-on work more that the specific course topic itself during Weeks 1-4.

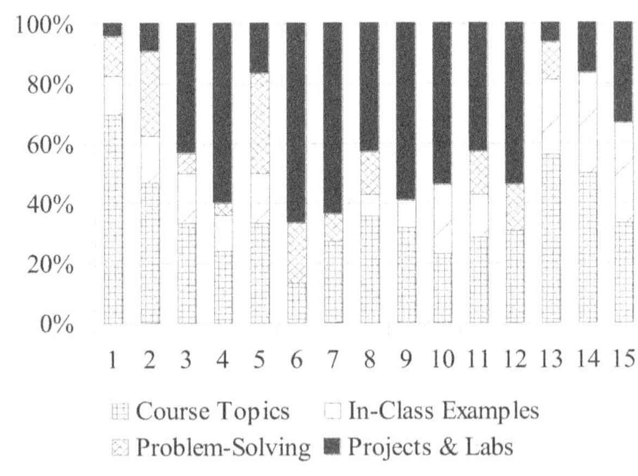

Figure 3. Enjoyment by Week, Weeks 1-15.

For the C++ portion of the course (Weeks 5-15) *Projects and Labs* are the predominant "fun" reported by students. Only during Weeks 13-15 does the percentage of *Course Topics* coding exceed the percentage of *Projects and Labs* coding. Weeks 13-15 usually involve the introduction of structures and file processing. It is also during this time that *In-Class Examples* have their highest percentage of "fun" coding, perhaps due to the larger scope of example that these topics provide. Analysis of the blog posts suggest students tended to focus on getting the project/lab done rather than "learning a specific topic", so much so that the two can be considered synonymous in the minds of many students.

Another pattern that emerged from the "fun" coding was the thrill of seeing a program work – in other words, applying the concepts learned in class to a particular problem and then seeing if your solution works. The satisfaction associated with successfully creating a program was often associated with a recognition that learning had occurred. Some examples:

> *"I really find the labs fun and enjoying. I find it satisfying to see my program work correctly after each lab is done. It allows me to know that I'm performing each task correctly and that I'm learning more and more as each week passes."*

> *"The highest point of this past week for me was Friday's Lab. I was able to create a working program on the fly and it just went to show how much I actually understood."*

5. DISCUSSION

Reflective blog postings in CS1 can provide opportunities for making significant pedagogical adjustments. Examples of near-term changes for the course sections in this study included moving the due date of "difficult" assignments, the increased use of in-class examples, increased attention to particular course topics, and additional time for student Q&A in class. For example, in more than one semester user-defined functions proved to be troublesome early in the C++ portion of the course. Initially, the author was able to adjust his course instruction to greater emphasize this topic early on and to reinforce it throughout the remainder of the semester. In future semesters, this difficulty was anticipated and the course was planned with this additional emphasis in mind. In this sense, the blogs served as a formative assessment tool for the course pedagogy.

Course projects and labs were one significant area in which the reflective blog postings made a long-term impact. The first year of this study coincided with the piloting of the PALMS for CS1 project's C++ materials (Module 2) in these courses. Less than 10 of the 505 blog posts mentioned the multimedia aspect of PALMS for CS1 Module 2 (all the posts were positive). Far greater mention was made of the PALMS for CS1 Module 2 projects, labs and in-class examples. As previously stated, course projects and labs represent the major portion of the course grade and a significant time investment for students. The "frustration" and "engagement" results provided feedback that has helped the author revise existing projects and create new ones.

Students were quick to point out the challenges, perceived difficulty or ease, and feelings about the projects and labs from week to week. For example:

> *"What was frustrating for me is how complicated that the project was this week. I feel like this project was a huge jump in difficulty from the last one, and I feel that it could have been made easier, or saved for a later project."*

Comments such as these were helpful in revising those projects where a significant amount of feedback was given. Revisions through more detailed instructions, more scaffolding, or through the correction of errors were performed for subsequent semesters. More positive comments helped to recognize which projects were engaging and accessible for students. For example:

> *"This week I found the hangman lab to be enjoyable. I found it to be enjoyable because it really did a lot and it was playing a game. This makes this lab become more real to me because someone might actually want to use this lab to make a hangman computer game."*

> *"Something I found interesting this week was the wind power lab. I was initially considering environmental engineering as my major, so i am obviously interested in that type of thing. Being able to apply programming to something you like makes it more enjoyable."*

Feedback such as this reaffirms the utility of specific projects and provides guidance for the creation of new ones. This feedback is helpful, considering the PALMS for CS1 project places an emphasis on student engagement for success [11].

The themes expressed in the analysis of student "confidence" suggest that more work is needed to support those students who enter the course with lesser confidence in their abilities and those who struggle along the way. Assistive measures resulting from the weekly blog feedback has primarily involved directed office hour sessions with students and faculty pairing of weaker students with stronger students for project work. Fortunately, the availability of tutors in recent semesters has helped with this problem, but more work needs to be done.

5.1 Study Challenges

The biggest challenge involved with this project was time. Qualitative analysis of the reflective blog entries requires a significant investment of time for coding and analysis. This method of data collection is more challenging than quantitative methods, but can be far more descriptive and compelling. However, other commitments may make this type of data collection prohibitive for some faculty.

Another significant challenge involved the coding of the responses themselves. While many students provided keywords in their posts which made coding straightforward (e.g. "My confidence going into the final is high"), some entries required some level of subjective judgment based on analysis of the overall entry content (e.g. "My confidence level, as of right now, is okay"). The level of subjectivity inherent in this analysis requires careful examination of the blog postings as well as prior knowledge of qualitative techniques.

Another significant challenge involved the student post content. Some students chose to write paragraph-style posts (as directed) while others simply had bullet lists with a phrase response. Some students frequently used IM-speak and others have difficulty with spelling and grammar. Students were notified of the expectations and issues more than once in each semester, but these problems still occurred in varying degrees each semester.

5.2 Future Directions

Future plans for this study involves examining the growth in cognitive and reflective skills of students over the course of a semester. This will involve a more formal assessment of the blog posts using an assessment rubric adapted from the one described in the author's prior work [12]. Changes will also be made to the initial "prompt" questions provided to students. It is hoped that these changes in questions will facilitate more in-depth and reflective feedback from students.

6. CONCLUSION

The study described in this paper demonstrates that reflective student blogs in CS1 can be a useful tool for instructional planning. By providing a low stakes, comfortable outlet for students to express their thoughts, valuable feedback about pedagogical innovations and week-to-week instruction can be obtained. Faculty can then apply this feedback to make both immediate changes in instruction as well as changes for future CS1 sections. However, faculty must be careful to avoid reactionary changes which move the course away from predefined learning outcomes.

7. ACKNOWLEDGEMENTS

The author would like to acknowledge the funding support of the Penn State Schuylkill Advisory Board. The author would also like to thank the many faculty and students whose feedback has been integral to the development of the PALMS for CS1 project. Finally, the author would like to thank the many reviewers of this paper for their insightful and constructive feedback.

8. REFERENCES

[1] Applin, A. 2006. A learner-centered approach to teaching ethics in computing. In *Proceedings of the 37th SIGCSE technical symposium on Computer science education (SIGCSE '06)*. ACM, New York, NY, USA, 530-534.

[2] Carlisle, M. C. 2009. Raptor: a visual programming environment for teaching object-oriented programming. *J. Comput. Small Coll.* 24, 4 (Apr. 2009), 275-281.

[3] Computing Curricula 2001. *Journal of Educational Resources in Computing.* 1, 3es (Sep. 2001), 1.

[4] Fekete, A., Kay, J., Kingston, J. and Wimalaratne, K. 2000. Supporting reflection in introductory computer science. In *Proceedings of the thirty-first SIGCSE technical symposium on Computer science education (SIGCSE '00)*, Susan Haller (Ed.). ACM, New York, NY, USA, 144-148.

[5] Hoffman, M., Dansdill, y. and Herscovici, D. 2006. Bridging writing to learn and writing in the discipline in computer science education. In *Proceedings of the 37th SIGCSE technical symposium on Computer science education (SIGCSE '06)*. ACM, New York, NY, USA, 117-121.

[6] Jamieson, L. H. 2002. Service learning in computer science and engineering. In *Proceedings of the 33rd SIGCSE Technical Symposium on Computer Science Education* (*SIGCSE '02*). ACM, New York, NY, 133-134.

[7] McDermott, R., Brindley, G. and Eccleston, G. 2010. Developing tools to encourage reflection in first year students blogs. In *Proceedings of the fifteenth annual conference on Innovation and technology in computer science education (ITiCSE '10)*. ACM, New York, NY, USA, 147-151.

[8] Partnership for 21st Century Skills. 2008. *21st century skills, education and competitiveness: A resource and policy guide*. Tucson, AZ.

[9] Piaget, J. 1972. *The Principles of Genetic Epistemology*. New York, Basic Books.

[10] Sahami, M., Guzdial, M., McGettrick, A. and Roach, S. 2011. Setting the stage for computing curricula 2013: computer science -- report from the ACM/IEEE-CS joint task force. In *Proceedings of the 42nd ACM technical symposium on Computer science education (SIGCSE '11)*. ACM, New York, NY, USA, 161-162..

[11] Jeffrey A. Stone and Tricia K. Clark. 2011. The impact of problem-oriented animated learning modules in a CS1-style course. In *Proceedings of the 42nd ACM technical symposium on Computer science education (SIGCSE '11)*. ACM, New York, NY, USA, 51-56.

[12] Jeffrey A. Stone and Elinor M. Madigan. 2007. Integrating reflective writing in CS/IS. *SIGCSE Bull. 39*, 2 (June 2007), 42-45.

[13] Yussen, S. 1985. The role of meta-cognition in contemporary theories of cognitive development. *Metacognition, Cognition and Human Performance* (D. Forrest-Pressley (ed)).

[14] Zagal, J. and Bruckman, A.. 2007. GameLog: fostering reflective gameplaying for learning. In *Proceedings of the 2007 ACM SIGGRAPH symposium on Video games (Sandbox '07)*. ACM, New York, NY, USA, 31-38.

Participation Patterns in Student Teams

Vreda Pieterse
Department of Computer Science
University of Pretoria
Pretoria, South Africa
vreda.pieterse@up.ac.za

Lisa Thompson
Department of Information Science
University of Pretoria
Pretoria, South Africa
lisa.thompson@up.ac.za

Linda Marshall
Department of Computer Science
University of Pretoria
Pretoria, South Africa
lmarshall@cs.up.ac.za

Dina M. Venter
SPSS Training and Technical Consultancy
Olrac-SPS (formerly SPSS South Africa)
Johannesburg, South Africa
dina@olsps.com

ABSTRACT

We describe a process that we applied for teaching teamwork in a Software Engineering module. Our objective with this process was to create opportunities for our students to experience some of the problems of working in a group before they formed teams in which they had to work for the rest of the year.

The process entails expecting students to work on well defined assignments for short periods in teams where risk factors were induced. Through experiencing these short bursts of intense team tribulation students are prepared to handle difficult events and situations in their teams.

We describe the design and implementation of this process. We report on changes in the levels of participation of the students during the process. We offer our explanation of possible factors that may have caused the observed variations.

Categories and Subject Descriptors

D.2.9 [**Software Engineering**]: Management—*Programming Teams*; K.3.2 [**Computers and Education**]: Computers and Information Science Education; K.6.1 [**Management of Computing and Information Systems**]: Project and People Management—*Staffing, Training*

General Terms

Management, Human Factors

Keywords

Team Formation, Teaching Teamwork, Soft Skills

Permission to make digital or hard copies of all or part of this work for personal or classroom use is granted without fee provided that copies are not made or distributed for profit or commercial advantage and that copies bear this notice and the full citation on the first page. To copy otherwise, to republish, to post on servers or to redistribute to lists, requires prior specific permission and/or a fee.
SIGCSE'12, February 29–March 3, 2012, Raleigh, North Carolina, USA.
Copyright 2012 ACM 978-1-4503-1098-7/12/02 ...$10.00.

1. INTRODUCTION

Apart from being an important skill required by industry for Software Engineering, teamwork is extensively applied in educational settings to support collaborative learning in all disciplines. Carter [4] emphasised the importance of teaching soft skills to our students as they are valued as much as technical skills. The occurrence of social loafing is seen as a common problem in student teams [1]. In our previous work [13], we describe diligent isolation as the opposite of social loafing and deem it equally problematic.

A process, which we call *rocking the boat* (RTB), was applied to maximise the probability of occurrence of these problems. By doing this, we exposed the students to situations where they could learn social skills that are required for teamwork. We expected that students would make errors related to inexperience within teams and that they would learn from these mistakes. However, the long term negative impact that may be caused by such errors, was obviated.

2. THEORY UNDERLYING RTB

2.1 Group development stages

Tuckman [15] designed one of the most cited models of small group development in the 1960s. The model's universal applicability and continuing use is recognised [3].

The four stages identified in the model are *Forming, Storming, Norming* and *Performing*. The theory states that a team can only reach its performing stage after moving though all the previous stages. The storming phase is usually characterised by conflict. During the norming stage, the conflict is resolved by establishing group norms.

2.2 Team size

Many problems can arise in large teams. One of which is the increased occurrence of social loafing [1, 9]. Another problem is increased difficulty in the coordination of interaction and collaboration [6, 2]. Steenkamp [14] cautions that student team size should not exceed five members. The negative issues often associated with increased group size have been seen to impact negatively on the performance of a team.

2.3 Academic alignment

In our experience, the distribution of the academic ability of team members may influence levels of participation and consequently, team success. A team where the members are homogeneous in terms of academic abilities, skills and goals is said to be *academically aligned* [13]. McKinney and Denton [11] observed higher occurrences of conflict experienced in teams with unbalanced skills.

2.4 Participation levels

When working in teams the participation level of individuals differ. We observed four levels of participation.

The term **diligent isolate** is used to refer to an individualistic member who relies only on himself/herself to complete the tasks at hand [13]. A diligent isolate sees others as ineffective and incapable [8] and as a result may discourage the participation of other members [12].

We use the term **insightful shaper** to refer to a member who takes a great deal of responsibility to ensure that the required work gets done and usually works harder than is expected. Unlike a diligent isolate who is usually unwilling to delegate some of the work, an insightful shaper succeeds in motivating and allowing all team members to participate.

We use the term **compliant worker** to refer to an individual who is likely to accept the decisions of others without consideration. This is usually done to avoid conflict or extra work. A compliant worker routinely does what is expected, but lacks initiative.

The term **social loafer** refers to an individual whose contribution is perceived to be inferior to that of others in a team. The social loafer delivers less than is required. They sometimes take credit for work done by the rest of the team.

We acknowledge that the level of participation of an individual is dependent on many factors and may change from one situation to another. The level of participation of an individual is on a continuum between social loafing on the one extreme and diligent isolation on the other.

3. SETTING

This research was conducted during the first six weeks of a SE module presented at the University of Pretoria in compliance with the requirements of the Ethics Committee of the university [16].

The module is presented on third year level. There were 64 students registered for the module. In this module the students are required to form teams in which they work on a year long fairly large industry based software product.

Before work on the project commenced, RTB was applied. During the implementation of RTB the students were expected to create the deliverables associated with the waterfall model of software development. This was required for a project with fairly large scope.

RTB was implemented in four rounds. Students were expected to work in teams that were assigned by the lecturers. New teams were assigned for each round. Each time ten teams, each with six or seven members, were formed. For each round all teams had to complete the same assignment. For each following round the deliverables of the previous round served as the specifications for the round. All teams had to use the same model solution of the previous round. Each round also had clearly specified deliverables.

Table 1: Risk factors induced in the four rounds

Risk Factor	Round			
	1	2	3	4
Large teams	++	++	++	++
Instability	++	++	+	++
Large project scope	+	+	+	++
Academic diversity	o	o	−	++
Lack of Experience	++	+	o	−

4. THE DESIGN OF RTB

RTB was designed to instigate the prevalence of unequal participation levels. The students were forced to deal with it and, through experience, learn how to avoid it. The process we designed and applied to achieve this was dubbed *rocking the boat*. This is a metaphorical description of the most prominent feature of this process, namely the unsettling of the student teams.

We base the design of RTB on our understanding of the levels of student participation as described in Section 2.4 as well as factors that contribute to these phenomena that were mentioned in Sections 2.2 and 2.3. With RTB we intend to create multiple storming stages and norming opportunities as described in Section 2.1 to facilitate the acquisition of the skills needed to move into the performing stage.

The storming stage of team development requires reasons for conflict. We achieve this through the introduction of factors known to contribute to team conflict. The intention is to expose the students to as many situations as possible, where they are forced to learn conflict resolution skills. We also provide a structured method of reflection as a norming opportunity in the form of peer reviews.

The deliberate creation of intense discomfort in teams may appear to be contrary to positive psychology theory that posits the maximisation of *flow experiences* [5]. However, it should be noted that these potentially negative experiences are applied in small bursts and are coupled with structured norming opportunities. We believe that these experiences facilitate the development of social skills enabling students to work more effectively in teams. If successful, this can lead to an increase in flow experiences in the months that follow after RTB.

4.1 Risk factors

The essence of RTB is the introduction of risk factors to maximise opportunities to learn teamwork skills. The different risk factors are introduced to varying degrees as shown in Table 1.

For every round the students were assigned to teams of six or seven members. These teams were deliberately larger than the ideal. By doing this we introduced the same high risk to all teams in all the rounds.

Koppenhaver et al [10] associated the occurrence of change of team members with instability. They identified instability as being detrimental to team performance. In all rounds, except the third round, all the students were assigned to teams with members that they had not worked with before. In the third round some pairs who had previously worked together were assigned to the same team.

The project scope has a significant impact on team performance [1]. Therefore, we used a project with substantial scope. We introduced high risk in all the rounds with the final round (the implementation phase) deemed slightly higher than the first three rounds.

The risk factor of academic diversity was different from round to round and is discussed in more detail in Section 5.

The risk factor of lack of experience was maximal at the beginning and declined over the rounds owing the fact that students gain experience through their participation in RTB.

4.2 Peer reviews

At the end of each round the students were expected to complete a peer review. The main purpose of the peer reviews was to provide a structured opportunity to reflect on their teamwork experiences of the round. Drake et al [7] report that students learn a great deal by reflecting on themselves as individuals within a team environment.

The questions that they had to answer were intended to guide them to reflect on their own contributions as well as those of the other members. These questions were exactly the same for all four rounds.

Firstly they were asked to select one of the following options to describe their participation:

- The members of my team should be aware that I have worked hard.
- The members of my team may think that I have slacked.

They were required to give a reason for their selection in a written paragraph. Next they were required to reflect on their own and their peers' commitment to the team by ranking their team members (including themselves) in order of dedication to the project. Further, they had to evaluate each member's contribution quantitatively as well as qualitatively.

By doing this exercise the students could compare their own contribution to those of the other members. Such reflection should reveal possible disparities and may also create more appreciation for work others may have done. The data that is analysed in Section 6 originated from these peer reviews.

5. THE IMPLEMENTATION OF RTB

5.1 Round 1

Members were allocated randomly. According to Bacon et al [2], random allocation creates an equal chance of teams being functional or dysfunctional. While there may be other factors contributing to this dysfunction resulting from random allocation of members to teams, we consider only the academic diversity risk factor in this context.

As can be seen in Table 1 the risk factors of large teams, and of instability was maximally introduced in this round. Through random allocation a moderate chance of having academic diversity was also introduced.

These teams worked together for two weeks. They were expected to produce a team portfolio by the end of the first week and a requirement specification document by the end of the second week.

5.2 Round 2

Again, the members were allocated largely randomly. We ensured that no two members in any team of the second round had worked together in the first round. Apart from lack of experience, the risk factors induced in this round were the same as those for the first round.

These teams were expected to produce an architectural design for the system within a week.

5.3 Round 3

We created teams with members that had similar levels of participation. We used their answers to the first question of the peer reviews (discussed in Section 4.2) to classify the students into categories in terms of their level of participation described in Section 2.4. These teams were faced with new social challenges. A team of diligent isolates was challenged by being placed in a situation where their team members would be less inclined to accept their decisions without offering their own opinions. Thus, they would not be able to dominate as usual. A team of social loafers was challenged by removing the opportunity to be carried. These students, who usually depend on others to prescribe what needs to be done, were placed in a situation where everybody would be inclined to wait for someone else to take the initiative.

We ended up with four teams that had entirely new team mates, and five teams that each contained one pair who had previously worked together, and one team with two such pairs. Therefore, the instability risk factor for these teams was slightly less than in the other rounds.

In our experience we observed a trend where the participation levels of students correlates with their academic abilities; diligent isolates tend to be academically strong while social loafers tend to be weaker. Therefore, the team allocation, based only on participation levels, lead to the creation of teams that were more likely to be academically aligned than in the previous two rounds.

The teams were expected to compile a detailed design specification for the project according to a model architectural design that was compiled by the teaching staff.

5.4 Round 4

We used the content of the first peer evaluation combined with the evaluation of the first assignment to form teams with inter-team balance. All the teams that were formed had similar internal structure.

Each student was classified using two orthogonal classifications, one according to his/her level of participation (leader/worker/slacker) and one according to his/her academic ability (strong/average/weak). We used this classification to assign diverse members to all teams. The resulting teams consisted mainly of two members in each class of each of the two orthogonal classifications. This team allocation resulted in the introduction of maximalty in all risk factors.

These teams were expected to implement a working prototype of the system with functionality showing proof of concept of the most important aspects as required by the given detailed design that was the outcome of the previous round. They had two weeks to complete this assignment.

6. DATA ANALYSIS

Within the interpretive paradigm, we used the information provided by the students in the peer reviews. We used the responses to the same questions that were used to allocate teams in the third round (See Section 5.3).

Classification of students into the categories described in Section 2.4 was done by two of the authors. Together we read each comment and based on this, classified each student into one of the categories per round.

While doing this we gained deeper insight into the nature of the categories. Two days later we revisited our analyses. Without looking at our initial classification, we repeated the process using the same method. Then we compared the two sets of results. In each case where there was a difference, we reconsidered the classification and made a final decision.

The following is an example of a comment that was made by a student whom we classified as a diligent isolate:

> *I was lenient on there submissions, and fixed all there faults, adn sacrificed my own sleep and stress levels to get the work in on time.*[1]

The distinction between diligent isolates and insightful shapers was not always clear. For example we had difficulty in deciding where to classify the following:

> *I provided most of the work*

Owing to the brevity of the quote it was unclear whether or not he/she took over or was assigned most of the work. We eventually classified this student as a diligent isolate.

In some cases the classification of an insightful shaper was obvious as can be seen in the following example:

> *I was partly responsible with bringing the group together and dividing up tasks. I also helped other people out when i had completed my assigned section.*

The following quote by a compliant worker fits our definition very well:

> *I did all tasks that were delegated to me.*

Sometimes the tone of the comments guided our decisions. For instance an insightful shaper might say *I did what **I said** I would do*, whereas a compliant worker might say *I did what **they said** I should do.*

There were different reasons for classifying a social loafer. Sometimes they offered excuses. In other cases they admitted that they could have done better as can be seen in the following:

> *I didn't have access to a computer the whole weekend, therefore I couldn't do everything I was supposed to.*

> *The task I was assigned to do was too much work*

The following comment is interesting:

> *I was supposed to be helping for the development of the android application and nothing was working so I was told leave it as a result, so instead of just sitting back and saying nothing is working, I decided to help my group members who were implementing the HQ system.*

It reinforces our theory that sometimes diligent isolate participation levels cause more social loafing. Because this student experienced difficulty with his task, he was told not to bother. A student placed in such a position may opt out. Such a student is carried by the rest of the team. However, in this case he/she voluntarily assisted with a different task and was consequently classified as a compliant worker.

[1]Note that most of our students are not English-speaking and the quotes are verbatim

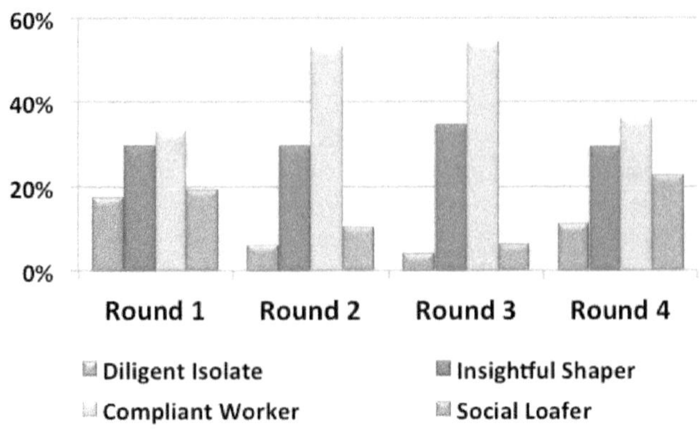

Figure 1: Classification of Respondents in the Different Rounds

7. LEVELS OF PARTICIPATION

Figure 1 shows the proportions of the respondents that were classified according to each of the participation levels during each of the experimental rounds.

The proportions of both diligent isolate and social loafer decreased from round one to round three and then increased from round three to round four. The round four proportion of diligent isolates is smaller than that of round one while the opposite is true for the proportion of social loafers. The proportions of insightful shapers did not vary much across the four rounds while the proportions of compliant workers remained the largest in every round.

Round two produced considerably fewer diligent isolates than round one. Consistent with our belief that the presence of diligent isolates causes other members to become social loafers, the proportion of social loafers also decreased.

The proportion of diligent isolates is the largest overall in round one. The most likely explanation is that it is a consequence of inexperience.

Compared to round one, the teams in round two exhibited a better composition regarding the proportions of diligent isolates, insightful shapers, compliant workers and social loafers. This happened despite the fact that both these rounds had (apart from lack of experience) the same risk factors built into them. A possible explanation is that the experience they gained during the first round enabled them to rectify some of the mistakes they had made previously.

Evaluating the proportions of the different levels of participation in round three, it is apparent that these teams were the most successful. This is the round where students with a propensity for similar levels of participation were clustered together. We anticipated that groups consisting of social loafers may not function effectively and also that a team consisting of diligent isolates may generate such extreme conflict that it will be dysfunctional. The success demonstrated during the third round was contrary to our expectations. A possible explanation is that these teams were likely to be academically aligned. Another factor that could have contributed to this success is that risk factors were lower.

The final round had the largest proportion of social loafers. This could serve as an explanation for why the teams were the least successful in this round. This came as no surprise since it was in this round that all the risk factors were maximised with members being academically unaligned as well as diverse in terms of their displayed levels of participation in previous rounds. Compared to the third round, the proportion of diligent isolates also increased considerably in this round.

The higher level of success demonstrated in the third round where academic alignment was probable and the lower level of success demonstrated in the final round where members were academically unaligned, confirms our theory that academic diversity within teams is a prominent factor that can foster the occurrence of diligent isolates and, consequently, social loafers [13].

8. PATTERNS OF PARTICIPATION

We observed that the participation level of most of the individual students tended to change from round to round. This confirms our premise that the level of participation is situational. 10.3% of all the classifications (21.0% of respondents) across the 4 Rounds were diligent isolate, 30.9% (58.1% of respondents) were insightful shaper, 43.8% were compliant worker and 14.9% (37.1% of respondents) were social loafer. The percentages of respondents add up to more than 100% since each respondent could have been classified four times as well as differently in each of the individual rounds.

8.1 Diligent Isolate

In our setting, diligent isolates were relatively scarce and were not consistently classified as such. Only 21.0% ($n = 13$) of the respondents were involved in the 20 classifications of diligent isolate. No student was a diligent isolate in more than two of the rounds while six students were classified as diligent isolates in one round only.

It seems that where the risk factors were the highest students were more inclined towards diligent isolation. For instance the following comments were given by the same student who was a diligent isolate in the first and the last rounds but a compliant worker in the middle rounds:

> ***Round 1:*** *As the team leader I organized the meetings, looked that all tasks were delivered on time and in the correct format and that the information in it was correct. Next to the mentioned duties, I had to the use-cases and did more use-case narratives than the others.*
>
> ***Round 2:*** *Worked the entire Saturday completing all of my tasks.*
>
> ***Round 3:*** *Worked on the 3 phases of Database design: Data Model Design, Logical Design and Physical Design.*
>
> ***Round 4:*** *Was part of everything of the system, but delivered the Client subsystem almost single handedly*

8.2 Insightful Shaper

58.1% ($n = 36$) of the respondents were involved in the 60 classifications of insightful shaper. One student was an insightful shaper in all rounds while none of the six classified as insightful shapers in three of the rounds were social loafers at any stage. The other levels of participation of the 29 students who were insightful shapers in one or two of the rounds varied across the board.

It seems that becoming an insightful shaper is related to maturity and/or experience. For example the following remarks were given by a student who was classified as a compliant worker in the first round but became an insightful shaper in the subsequent rounds.

> ***Round 1:*** *I basically did what was required and that on its own proves that i didn't slack and i worked to make sure the input i made was very correct.*
>
> ***Round 2:*** *I have done what was required from me and i also offered to help out other people.*
>
> ***Round 3:*** *I did what was required and i also helped other peole to do their work. I also helped in compiling the final document.*
>
> ***Round 4:*** *I worked under the presure that was present and did the parts that were required from my side and i helped out as we were one member short.*

It is possible that the experience and reflection offered by RTB contributed to this student realising that supporting the other members in the team is beneficial.

8.3 Compliant Worker

In our setting the occurrence of compliant workers is the highest. 75.8% ($n = 47$) of the respondents were involved in the 85 classifications of compliant worker. Although the participation levels of some of these students varied across the board, the tendency to be classified as social loafers in some of the rounds was higher than to be classified as a diligent isolate. Only four of these students were classified as diligent isolates at any stage while nine were classified as social loafers at some stage. Five students were classified compliant workers in all of the rounds.

The individual students who had fewer variations in their classifications in the different rounds were classified as compliant worker most of the time. This is an indication that compliant worker behaviour is less likely to be influenced by different situations.

The following remarks were provided by a consistent compliant worker:

> ***Round 1:*** *I did everything that I was required to do and I would submit my work on time.*
>
> ***Round 2:*** *I have put all the effort to do my work.*
>
> ***Round 3:*** *I did what I was required to do*
>
> ***Round 4:*** *I have done what I was required to do*

8.4 Social Loafer

37.1% ($n = 23$) of the respondents were involved in the 29 classifications of social loafer. No student was classified as a social loafer in more than two of the rounds. Seventeen students were classified as social loafers in only one round while six were classified as social loafers in two rounds. These students had a higher tendency to be classified as compliant workers than as insightful shapers or as diligent isolates in the rounds where they were not classified as social loafers. Thirteen out of the seventeen who were classified as social loafers in only one round were classified as compliant workers in most of the other rounds.

It is interesting to observe that the participation patterns of the classifications of social loafers reflects the same high level of fluctuations that is found in the classifications of diligent isolates. These classifications seem to be more likely to be influenced by the situational factors than the classifications of insightful shapers and compliant workers.

The following comments were given by an individual who was a social loafer in the first and last rounds, but a insightful shaper in the middle two rounds. In the two rounds where the teams experienced higher risks, this student slacked, whereas he was an asset to his team on the other two rounds.

> ***Round 1:*** *We could not find time to meet as a group and discuss since I am not full-time on campus.*
>
> ***Round 2:*** *I was always the first one to finish my part and always offer to help whoever was struggling.*
>
> ***Round 3:*** *I was always the first one to finish my tasks and always offer my services to anyone who was lacking behind.*
>
> ***Round 4:*** *We started coding the system a bit late and we could not have enough time to work together as a group.*

9. CONCLUSION AND FUTURE WORK

RTB provided intense experiential learning opportunities for our students. By unsettling the student teams from round to round, they were able to discover their strengths and weaknesses. Peer reviews were used to force the students to reflect on the functioning of their teams. Their responses enhanced our insight into the patterns of their participation.

We established that participation levels change with team composition, hence it is wrong to assume that a student will always participate at the same level. Where the risk factors were higher, the occurrence of diligent isolation and social loafing increased. Diligent isolation and social loafing seem to be more likely to be influenced by situational factors while compliant workers and insightful shapers tended to be more consistent in their levels of participation. We believe that further investigation and the incorporation of more data may lead to more trustworthy results.

RTB can be used to establish a positive attitude to group work. Care must be taken not use RTB too often or over too long a period as its effectiveness may by compromised.

Insight regarding the causes and effects of diligent isolation and social loafing can be used to assist students to be more functional in group work. A deeper understanding of the apparent mutually conducive relation between social loafing and diligent isolation may help students to avoid the occurrence thereof. Research into these phenomena in other disciplines could be valuable as it is likely to be equally applicable to group work in any discipline.

10. REFERENCES

[1] P. Aggarwal and C. L. O'Brien. Social loafing on group projects. *Journal of Marketing Education*, 30(3):255–264, 2008.

[2] D. R. Bacon, K. A. Stewart, and W. S. Silver. Lessons from the best and worst student team experiences: How a teacher can make the difference. *Journal of Management Education*, 23(5):467–488, 1999.

[3] D. A. Bonebright. 40 years of storming: a historical review of Tuckman's model of small group development. *Human Resource Development International*, 13(1):111–120, 2010.

[4] L. Carter. Ideas for adding soft skills education to service learning and capstone courses for computer science students. In *Proceedings of the 42nd ACM technical symposium on Computer science education*, SIGCSE '11, pages 517–522, New York, NY, USA, 2011. ACM.

[5] M. Csíkszentmihályi. *Flow: The Psychology of Optimal Experience*. HarperCollins, New York, 2008.

[6] L. A. Curral, R. H. Forrester, J. F. Dawson, and M. A. West. It's what you do and the way that you do it: Team task, team size, and innovation-related group processes. *European Journal of Work and Organizational Psychology*, 10(2):187 – 204, 2001.

[7] R. Drake, G. Goldsmith, and R. Strachan. A novel approach to teaching teamwork. *Teaching in Higher Education*, 11(1):33 – 46, 2006.

[8] T. Feldman Barr, A. L. Dixon, and J. B. Gassenheimer. Exploring the "lone wolf" phenomenon in student teams. *Journal of Marketing Education*, 27(1):81–90, 2005.

[9] P. Kelly. Achieving desirable group-work outcomes through the group allocation process. *Team Performance Management*, 14(1/2):22 – 38, 2008.

[10] G. D. Koppenhaver and C. B. Shrader. Structuring the classroom for performance: Cooperative learning with instructor-assigned teams. *Decision Sciences Journal of Innovative Education*, 1(1):1–21, 2003.

[11] D. McKinney and L. F. Denton. Affective assessment of team skills in agile CS1 labs: the good, the bad, and the ugly. In *Proceedings of the 36th SIGCSE technical symposium on Computer science education*, SIGCSE '05, pages 465–469, New York, NY, USA, 2005. ACM.

[12] E. Pfaff and P. Huddleston. Does it matter if I hate teamwork? What impacts student attitudes toward teamwork. *Journal of Marketing Education*, 25(1):37–45, 2003.

[13] V. Pieterse and L. Thompson. Academic alignment to reduce the presence of 'social loafers' and 'diligent isolates' in student teams. *Teaching in Higher Education*, 15(4):355–367, 2010.

[14] A. L. Steenkamp. A standards-based approach to team-based student projects in an information technology curriculum. In *Proceedings of the International Academy for Information Management (IAIM)*, 17th International Conference on Informatics Education Research (ICIER), pages 54 – 62, 2004.

[15] B. W. Tuckman. Developmental sequence in small groups. *Psychological Bulletin*, 63(6):384 – 399, 1965.

[16] University of Pretoria: Committee for Research Ethics and Integrity. Guidelines for responsible research: Policy and procedures, July 2007. Retrieved December 1, 2011 from `http://www.ais.up.ac.za/research/docs/guidelines_ethics.pdf`.

Application of Non-programming Focused Treisman-style Workshops in Introductory Computer Science

Alan C. Jamieson*
St. Mary's College of Maryland
18952 E. Fisher Rd
St. Mary's City, Maryland 20686
acjamieson@smcm.edu

Lindsay H. Jamieson† ‡
St. Mary's College of Maryland
18952 E. Fisher Rd
St. Mary's City, Maryland 20686
lhjamieson@smcm.edu

Angela C. Johnson§
St. Mary's College of Maryland
18952 E. Fisher Rd
St. Mary's City, Maryland 20686
acjohnson@smcm.edu

ABSTRACT

In the 1960s and 70s, Uri Treisman developed a specific style of workshops to encourage the retention of underrepresented minority students in Calculus courses at the University of California, Berkley. Since that time, workshops based on the Treisman model have been successfully implemented across the United States and have resulted in more underrepresented minority students successfully completing Calculus. Some attempts have been made to translate the Treisman model to Introductory Computer Science, but all previous attempts have been focused on programming skills. However, one of the student assumptions that deter women and underrepresented minorities from attempting a major or minor in Computer Science is that a computer scientist is purely a solitary programmer [11]. In this paper, we discuss a specific two year pilot program of non-programming focused Treisman-style workshops in conjunction with a Introductory Computer Science course.

Categories and Subject Descriptors

K.3.2 [**Computing Milieux**]: Computers and Education—*Computer and Information Science Education*

General Terms

Design, Human Factors

Keywords

Diversity, Treisman-style Workshops, CS1

*Department of Mathematics and Computer Science
†Department of Mathematics and Computer Science
‡Corresponding Author
§Department of Educational Studies

Permission to make digital or hard copies of all or part of this work for personal or classroom use is granted without fee provided that copies are not made or distributed for profit or commercial advantage and that copies bear this notice and the full citation on the first page. To copy otherwise, to republish, to post on servers or to redistribute to lists, requires prior specific permission and/or a fee.
SIGCSE'12, February 29–March 3, 2012, Raleigh, North Carolina, USA.
Copyright 2012 ACM 978-1-4503-1098-7/12/02 ...$10.00.

1. INTRODUCTION

The problem of encouraging women and underrepresented minority (URM) students to continue in computer science courses is well studied. We define URM as women and non-Asian minority men based on the information in the latest Taulbee survey as described by Zweben [12]. One way to attempt to improve the retention of women and underrepresented minority students is to adapt proven methodologies from other disciplines to work in Computer Science (CS) courses. We are specifically adapting Treisman-style workshops which work extremely well in encouraging underrepresented minority students to succeed in Calculus courses and continue in Mathematics majors to work with Introductory Computer Science courses. Our approach is to remove the complication of programming from the equation and focus the workshops on general CS and problem solving ideas. In this way we can attempt to mitigate the idea that pursuing a degree in Computer Science will end with the student writing code, alone, in front of a computer screen which is the belief of many women and underrepresented minority students [11].

Our CS Triesman-style workshop pilot was run at St. Mary's College of Maryland (SMCM), a four-year public liberal arts college with 2000 students and a residential campus.

The paper is organized in the following way. We start with background information on Treisman-style workshops as well as the history of Treisman-style workshops at SMCM. We follow with a discussion of how we organized our Computer Science Emerging Scholars Program, followed by our results and a brief concluding section.

2. A HISTORY OF TREISMAN-STYLE WORKSHOPS

Uri Treisman developed a specific style of workshops in the 1960s and 70s at University of California, Berkley, with the philosophy "not to 'fix the students,' but rather to change at least a small part of the university environment, by making it more welcoming, both socially and academically".[2] These workshops were the result of observations by Treisman of the work habits of successful and unsuccessful students in calculus courses [10]. Specifically, Treisman was attempting to ascertain the reasons for failure among minority students in freshman calculus. In observing the study habits of various ethnicities of calculus students, Treisman realized that African American students' academic lives were quite sepa-

Table 1: Demographic Breakdown for COSC120 courses from 2007-2010 - Female

Year	White	Black	Asian	Hispanic	American Indian	Unknown race	Total women
2007	17	7	2	2	0	2	30
2008	16	4	2	1	0	2	25
2009	21	2	0	1	0	0	24
2010	35	5	3	2	2	0	47

rate from their social interactions with peers while Chinese American students had integrated their interest in mathematics with their social lives [2, 10].

Over the past 30 years, Treisman-style workshops have been replicated at various institutions across the United States. The results of these programs include students who participate in the workshops achieving significantly higher grades and graduations rates [1, 6, 9]. These workshops also increased the number of underrepresented minority students completing both mathematics and calculus-based majors [3, 8, 9].

Treisman-style workshops are typically designed as a weekly or twice-weekly enrichment course where students are given a worksheet with problems that are loosely based on the content going on in the main course (Calculus 1 & 2, CS 1). These are problems that are more challenging than the homework assigned in the main course, but still related to the course material. Students attending the workshop are encouraged to work with the TAs and their peers to work through the problems. The workshop sessions are designed to foster a social environment where the students develop friendships and a comfort with their peers. It is important to note that these workshops are not designed to be just another recitation session, nor are they designed to be remedial [10].

3. TREISMAN-STYLE WORKSHOPS IN COMPUTER SCIENCE

Taking the Treisman-style workshop model and applying it in the Computer Science curriculum is not a new concept. There are two existing programs in the United States: University of Washington, Tacoma [5] and a combination of Treisman-style workshops and Peer-Led Team Learning at several universities including the University of Wisconsin-Madison and Duke University [7]. The combination programs discussed in [7] focus primarily on the programming portion of Computer Science with strategies for students to improve their programming skills being the primary goal of the workshops. The program at the University of Washington, Tacoma focuses on programming skills and program design problems [5, 4].

4. TREISMAN-STYLE WORKSHOPS AT ST. MARY'S COLLEGE OF MARYLAND

In 2005, Dr. David Kung, Dr. Katherine Socha and Dr. Angela Johnson began the Emerging Scholars Program (ESP) in Mathematics at St. Mary's College of Maryland. This is a 1-credit seminar consisting of Treisman-style workshops run in conjunction with Calculus I and Calculus II. Since the implementation of the program, the percentage of minority students who pass Calculus I has increased from 20% to 69%. Additionally, while 20% passed Calculus I before the program began, none earned a grade higher than C,

Table 2: Demographic Breakdown for COSC120 courses from 2007-2010 - Male

Year	White	Black	Asian	Hispanic	Unknown race	Total men
2007	38	4	0	0	0	42
2008	36	2	1	0	1	40
2009	29	5	1	2	2	39
2010	30	5	3	0	2	40

while the current percentage of African-Americans earning an A or B is 46%. Currently, this seminar occurs in both the Fall and Spring semesters with approximately 16 participants each semester pulled from Calculus I and Calculus II. After 5 years of seminars, and 60 students, 14 of the participants became Mathematics majors and one became a Computer Science major. Over half of the students have a major or an intended major in a STEM field.

5. TREISMAN-STYLE WORKSHOPS IN COMPUTER SCIENCE AT ST. MARY'S COLLEGE OF MARYLAND

Building on the success of the ESP in Mathematics, a computer science equivalent was started in Fall 2009. The Introduction to Computer Science course (COSC120) at St. Mary's College of Maryland can be used to fulfill the general education requirement in Mathematics as well as the entry point to the Computer Science major and minor. Because of this, the students taking COSC120 have a varying level of interest in Computer Science and comfort with Computer Science. There will also be some students who are taking COSC120 out of a fear of Calculus and/or a belief that Computer Science will be easier than Calculus. COSC120 in its current form has been offered since 2001 with varying enrollments from 40 in the 2001-2002 academic year to 87 in the 2010-2011 academic year. The demographic breakdown of COSC120 from 2007-2010 is shown in Tables 1 and 2. The demographic breakdown of Computer Science majors at SMCM from 2008-2012 is shown in Table 3. As you can see from Tables 1 and 2, the number of men and women taking COSC120 is roughly equal, with women actually outnumbering men in 2010. However, Table 3 shows that the percentage of women and students from underrepresented groups completing the major is much less than that of white men. Note that the percentage of graduates who are women and/or from underrepresented groups is expected to be much higher in 2012.

6. COMPUTER SCIENCE EMERGING SCHOLARS PROGRAM AT SMCM

In our workshop program, we pull the focus from programming specifics to general concepts in order to show students

Table 3: Demographic Breakdown of Computer Science majors at SMCM from 2008-2012

Graduation Year	Female	Under-represented minorities	Total graduates
2008	2	1	12
2009	1	0	13
2010	2	1	10
2011	1	2	11
2012 (expected)	7	4	20

that there is more to Computer Science as a field than just programming ability. Our Emerging Scholars Program is designed to look at various CS1 concepts in the abstract to reinforce the concepts presented in the course. Additionally, our goal is that the students will be able to see that working with others is a great way to develop innovative solutions to problems. The workshop is set up as a 1-credit course with a credit/no credit grading system. Students are assessed on participation.

During each two-hour workshop (meeting twice a week), the students are given a worksheet that presents interesting questions relating to a topic in CS1. Topics include Boolean logic, algorithm development, loop structures, ethics, discrete mathematics and game playing. An example 16-week topic list for ESP is listed as Table 4. In addition, we provide a social atmosphere where students feel free to interact with their TA's (former workshop participants beginning this year) and fellow participants as peers. This is especially important as we specifically target first year students. Our efforts in this aspect are intended to engender the sense of community crucial to the development of the cohort. Even something as simple as providing snacks and drinks can foster an informal atmosphere away from the formality of a classic lecture.

Several of the topics in the workshop also support SMCM's Core Curriculum. For instance, our worksheet on history, where students have to present an oral report on several important computer scientists (Anita Borg, Adm. Grace Hopper, etc.) has them practice their oral communication skills and information literacy skills. We also present them with topics and problems from courses further along in the CS curriculum. For instance, during the week for Boolean logic, we will have them do some elementary exercises in Digital Logic presented in the Computer Architecture course.

As an example of worksheets for the topics covered in the workshop, we present here versions of our worksheets for the Logic Puzzles and Problem Solving, Algorithm Development, and Modular Arithmetic topics.

Logic Puzzles and Problem Solving

1. **Monty Hall Problem**: Suppose you're on a game show and you're given the choice of three doors. Behind one door is a car; behind the others, goats. The car and the goats were placed randomly behind the doors before the show. The rules of the game show are as follows: After you have chosen a door, the door remains closed for the time being. The game show host, Monty Hall, who knows what is behind the doors, now has to open one of the two remaining doors, and the door he opens must have a goat behind it. If both remaining doors have goats behind them, he chooses one randomly. After Monty Hall opens a door with a goat, he will ask yo to decide whether you want to stay with your first choice or to switch to the last remaining door.

   Imagine that you chose Door 1 and the host opens Door 3, which has a goat. He then asks you, "Do you want to switch to Door Number 2?" Is it to your advantage to change your choice?

2. **Prisoner's Dilemma**: Two suspects are arrested by the police. The police have insufficient evidence for a conviction, and, having separated both prisoners, visit each of them to offer the same deal. If one testifies (defects from the other) for the prosecution against the other and the other remains silent (cooperates with the other), the betrayer goes free and the silent accomplice receives the full 10-year sentence. If both remain silent, both prisoners are sentenced to only six months in jail for a minor charge. If each betrays the other, each receives a five-year sentence. Each prisoner must choose to betray the other or to remain silent. Each one is assured that the other would not know about the betrayal before the end of the investigation. How should the prisoners act?

3. **Matching pennies** The game is played between two players, Player A and Player B. Each player has a penny and must secretly turn the penny to heads or tails. The players then reveal their choice simultaneously. If the pennies match (both heads or both tails), Player A receives one dollar from Player B (+1 for A, -1 for B). If the pennies do not match (one heads and one tails), Player B receives one dollar from Player A (-1 for A, +1 for B).

   How do you walk away with the most money?

Algorithms Worksheet

1. Write out an algorithm for creating the LEGO object you're given. Assume that your partner has all of the LEGO blocks he or she may need.

2. Exchange your algorithm with your partner and attempt to recreate your partner's object.

3. Compare your results with the original. What went well? What didn't go so hot?

Modular Arithmetic

1. **Candy Box Problem**: All UPCs have a checksum which makes sure that they are valid. The formula for the UPC works like this $3x_1 + x_2 + 3x_3 + x_4 + 3x_5 + x_6 + 3x_7 + x_8 + 3x_9 + x_{10} + 3x_{11} + x_{12}$ should be a multiple of 10 where x_i is the ith number in the UPC. Go get a Candy Box from the TA. You will see that someone has tampered with the UPC so that a number is now missing. Before you can open the box, you need to calculate the missing number. Once you've calculated your number, check it on another box of the same candy.

2. **Clock Math**: You have a friend who is studying abroad in Australia. You'd like to talk to your friend

Table 4: Example 16-week ESP Topic List

Week	Topic
1	History of CS
2	Logic Puzzles and Problem Solving
3	Classic Logic Problems (Monty Hall Problem, Prisoner's Dilemma, etc.)
4	Algorithm Development
5	Basic Arithmetic Functions (including modulo)
6	Classes and Objects
7	Strategy Games
8	Boolean Logic
9	Conditional Branching
10	Functions and Procedures
11	Ethics
12	String Manipulation
13	Discrete Mathematics
14	Recursion
15	Graph Theory
16	What's Next in CS?

over Skype, but you're not sure when to call. You know that Australia is 14 hours ahead of St. Mary's. Your Mom taught you that it's impolite to call someone before 9AM or after 9PM unless it's a dire emergency. You'd like to get some sleep. What times should you try to call your friend?

3. **Secret Code**: The Caesar Cipher is created by doing the following:

```
ABCDEFGHIJKLMNOPQRSTUVWXYZ
CDEFGHIJKLMNOPQRSTUVWXYZAB
```

In this case, the number associated with the Cipher is 2 meaning that A = C (the third letter of the alphabet. If your message was: HELLO WORLD, in this cipher, it would be written as JGNNQ YQTNF. Using the number 11 as the Cipher, decipher the following phrases:

```
SPWWZ HZCWO
DNSLPQPC SLWW
NZXAFEPC DNTPYNP TD QFY
```

Your turn! Choose a cipher, then encrypt a message. Write your message on the white board. Now try to crack the cipher for other groups messages.

4. **Splitting Numbers**: You are given a 5 digit number. Develop and algorithm for splitting off and printing out the individual digits in the number. For instance:

```
Enter a number: 34672
Digits: 3 4 6 7 2
```

Do you know enough to program that algorithm? What more do you need? Could you rewrite the algorithm into something that you could actually program?

7. RUNNING THE PROGRAM

At SMCM, we begin our recruitment of potential workshop participants during the summer after first-year students have committed to attending St. Mary's. In collaboration with our admissions office staff, we send out a first set of invitations targeted at first-year URM students with an indicated interest in STEM fields or economics. If the students are interested in joining the program, they email a short application back to the coordinating faculty member.

Later in the summer, after the first-year students have registered for classes, the coordinating faculty member gathers demographic information about first-year students enrolled in CS1. Those students who were not targeted by the original set of invitations will be sent invitations at this time. If there is space (we typically have a 16 student limit on this workshop), the coordinating faculty member will visit the CS1 classes during the first week of classes to talk about the workshop and do some in-person recruitment of students.

Teaching assistants for the workshop are selected from previous participants when available. During the first two years of the program, this was not possible as there were no students eligible to be a teaching assistant under our college policies. Instead, we used junior URM students who were doing well in our program. In the third year, we have begun to utilize previous ESP participants.

The TAs handle running the workshops with faculty supervision. The coordinating faculty member is responsible for setting the schedule for the semester, organizing any social activities (trips, weekend activities, etc.) and developing the worksheets. The TAs are in charge of making sure that the workshops stay focused as well as working with the students as they develop their solutions. The TAs also support the students in answering questions about concepts presented in class, completing assignments and preparing for exams.

8. RESULTS

In order to evaluate the effects of the ESP workshops, we administer an attitude survey at the beginning and end of the semester. This survey is based on the Fenema-Sherman Attitude Scales altered to query for Computer Science at-

Table 5: Grade distribution by race, 2007-08

	URM	White students
A	40%	66%
B	35%	13%
C	10%	13%
D,F	15%	5%

Table 6: Grade distribution by race, 2009-2010

	URM	White students
A	42%	75%
B	27%	17%
C	31%	7%
D,F		1%

titude. We also track attendance on the assumption that one way underrepresented students indicate that something is awry in the social dynamics they are experiencing in a class is by not attending the class. Additionally we look at grades achieved during CS1 and which students continue in the CS major or minor.

After two years of piloting the program, participation did not have any significant effects on changes in students' attitudes in computer science. Data was gathered on student attitudes towards success in computer science (whether they would be proud to let others know of their success), their beliefs about the discipline of computer science (for instance, beliefs that it is an open-ended discipline requiring creativity), their confidence in their ability to handle computer science materials and in their technical skills with computers, their interest and persistence in computer science and beliefs that it will be useful to them personally, and their attitudes towards working with others to solve computer science problems. Students who participated in the Emerging Scholars Program showed virtually no differences from non-participants in either their initial attitudes on each of these scales or in their changes in attitudes across the semester. Although this may change as more students participate in Emerging Scholars, it tentatively suggests that whatever the dynamics which have been responsible for low computer science participation by women and underrepresented minority students at St. Mary's in the past, attitudes towards computer science were not a central component, nor, as the persistence rates above indicate, are those attitudes a component in students' persistence decisions. These results suggest that, as Treisman said, there is no need to "fix" the students' attitudes towards computer science; rather, we need to fix our program to make it comfortable for all kinds of students.

The goal of the CSESP program is to increase the number of underrepresented minorities majoring in computer sci-

Table 7: All COSC120 students: Number who continue on in CS classes

	Total number	Continued to CS2 (p<=.01)	Continued to CS3 (p<=.05)
Not in ESP	130	39 (30%)	23 (18%)
In ESP	15	11 (73%)	6 (40%)

Table 8: URM COSC120 students: Number who continue on in CS classes

	Total number	Continued to CS2 (p<=.10)	Continued to CS3 (p<=.10)
Not in ESP	15	3 (20%)	1 (7%)
In ESP	5	3 (60%)	2 (40%)

Table 9: Female COSC120 students: Number who continue on in CS classes

	Total number	Continued to CS2 (p<=.01)	Continued to CS3
Not in ESP	59	14 (24%)	8 (14%)
In ESP	9	6 (67%)	3 (33%)

ence. At this point, none of the program participants has been enrolled in college long enough to graduate; thus, we have defined retention as continuing on to the next computer science courses, CS2 and CS3. We are also interested in studying whether program participation leads to higher grades among URM students, as happened in the St. Mary's College math ESP program which inspired this problem. Due to ethical considerations, our research design is quasi-experimental; because of the evidence from other Treisman-style workshops, we felt from the beginning that participating in CSESP would benefit students, and so we were unwilling to randomly assign some interested students to CSESP but deny its benefits to other interested students. Our comparison groups are non-comparable. Some members of the non-CSESP group were invited to participate in CSESP but declined, suggesting that they may have been less motivated or less interested in continuing in CS from the outset. Other members of the non-CSESP group are not under-represented in CS, suggesting that they may feel more comfortable in CS settings than CSESP participants. We analyzed rates of persistence and grade distributions using chi-square tests in SPSS, comparing rates of persistence to CS2 and to CS3 with participation in CS1; we report the Pearson chi-square significance.

When comparing the grades earned in CS1 before and after implementation of CSESP, there was not a distinct change in distribution (as seen in Tables 5 and 6). The major impact that these workshops have had is in the retention of women and URMs in computer science. The percentage of students in underrepresented groups who participate in CSESP and continue to CS2 and CS3 is much higher than students who don't participate in CSESP (as seen in Tables 7 and 8). This is especially evident in the number of women and students from underrepresented minorities who continue on to CS3 (as seen in Tables 8 and 9). Additionally, the grades for underrepresented minorities who participate in CSESP are much higher than for those students who do not participate in CSESP (as seen in Table 10). Despite the differences between comparison groups, and given the small size of the CSESP sample, these results are striking. Continuation rates to CS2 in the largest comparison (CSESP students with all other students in CS1) were significant at the .001 level.

Table 10: Grade distribution of URM students by CSESP participation, 2009-2010

	URM students in ESP	URM students not in ESP
A	4 (80%)	4 (27%)
B	1 (20%)	4 (27%)
C	0	6 (40%)
Withdrew	0	1 (7%)

We take these numbers with a grain of salt; we assume that some of the non-persisters in all groups (including the CSESP group) were never interested in continuing past CS1. Nonetheless, the persistence rates are remarkable given the overall dismal record of CS programs in retaining women and non-Asian men of color as well as the poor record of our institution in particular. Our evaluation proceeded on the assumption that, given the fact that SMCM is designated as the Honors College for the State of Maryland, our students are pre-selected for their high academic motivation, and so there were as many highly-motivated URM students in CS classes before the institution of CSESP as there are now. Thus, we are comfortable attributing the dramatically higher retention rates of URM students to program participation. While it is possible that the changes could be attributed to a sudden change in the number of motivated URM students, participation in CSESP is a much more likely explanation.

9. CONCLUSION

In the two years of the pilot CSESP, we have seen some very exciting results. Women and underrepresented minority students who participate in CSESP are significantly more likely than their peers to succeed in CS1 and continue toward a computer science major. This should result in a continuation of the increase in majors shown in Table 3 with a diversity more consistent with that of our student body.

Based on the results enumerated above, we are working to make the CSESP a regular course in our catalog and expand the program in various ways. Our first expansion would be to create a set of workshops in conjunction with the CS2 course. Ideally, this would serve to support the students who participate in the CSESP during CS1 as they work through CS2. Additionally, we would encourage those students who seem at risk of not succeeding in CS2 to find additional support by participating in the CSESP.

In the future, we would like to explore expanding the CSESP to other similar colleges and universities. This would allow us to expand the sample size and verify that the results that we have seen are not a result of the SMCM environment. We would then proceed to adapt the program to colleges and universities that are not similar to ours to analyze the potential of the program regardless of the institution type.

10. ACKNOWLEDGMENTS

The authors would like to thank the reviewers for their helpful suggestions on improvements for this paper.

11. REFERENCES

[1] B. B. Alexander, A. C. Burda, and Y. Hwang. Final formative feedback report: Wisconsin emerging scholars program. Technical report, Mat222, University of Wisconsin, LEAD Center, 1995.

[2] R. Asera. Calculus and community: A history of the emerging scholars program. Technical report, National Task Force on Minority High Achievement, College Board., 2001.

[3] M. V. Bonsangue. An efficacy study of the calculus workshop model. *CBMS Issues in Mathematics Educaiton*, 4:117–137, 1994.

[4] D. Chinn and K. Martin. Problem-based learning in computer science. *JCSC*, 21(1):239–245, 2005.

[5] D. Chinn, C. Spencer, and K. Martin. Problem solving and student performance in data structures and algorithms. In *ITiCSE '07*, pages 241–245, Dundee, Scotland, UK, June 23-27, 2007 2007.

[6] R. Fullilove and U. Treisman. Mathematics achievement among african-american undergraduates at the univeristy of california, berkley: An evaluation of the mathematics workshop program. *Journal of Negro Education*, 59:463–478, 1990.

[7] S. Horwitz and S. Rodger. Using peer-led team learning to increase participation and success of under-represented groups in introductory computer science. In *SIGCSE '09*, pages 163–167, Chattanooga, TN, USA, March 3-7, 2009 2009.

[8] T. Murphy, K. Stafford, and P. McCreary. Subsequent course and degree paths of students in treisman-style workshop calculus programs. *Journal of Women and Minorities in Science and Engineering*, 4:382–396, 1998.

[9] U. Treisman. Developing the next generation of mathematicians. a lecture presented at the 1991 annual meeting of the maa held in san francisco, california, january 1991. 1 videocassette (NTSC; 1/2 inch; VHS) (45 min.), January 1991.

[10] U. Treisman. Studying students studying calculus: A look at the lives of minority mathematics students in college. *College Mathematics Journal*, 23:362–372, 1992.

[11] S. Yardi and A. Bruckman. What is computing? bridging the gap between teenagers' perceptions and graduate students' experiences. In *ICER '07*, pages 39–49, Atlanta, GA, USA, September 15-16, 2007 2007.

[12] S. Zweben. Undergraduate cs enrollment continues rising; doctoral production drops. *Comput. Res. News*, 22(3), 2010.

Collaboration Across the Curriculum: A Disciplined Approach to Developing Team Skills

Ben Coleman
Moravian College
1200 Main Street
Bethlehem, PA 18018
coleman@cs.moravian.edu

Matthew Lang
Moravian College
1200 Main Street
Bethlehem, PA 18018
lang@cs.moravian.edu

ABSTRACT

Improving communication and collaborative skills of computer science students has been a priority in the community for some time. We present our philosophy, collaboration across the curriculum, which moves beyond existing individual courses or course units to teach collaboration skills in a pervasive manner. In our approach, concepts are introduced and skills are developed throughout the computer science curriculum—from CS1 to a capstone experience. Students are provided with opportunities to exercise skills in reflective environments that eventually mirror real-world experiences, and technical course content is not compromised.

We argue for this system and provide details about how collaboration across the curriculum is accomplished at a small liberal arts college.

Categories and Subject Descriptors

K.3.2 [**Computers and Education**]: Computer and Information Science Education

General Terms

Human Factors

Keywords

Collaboration, Teamwork, Curriculum, Communication

1. INTRODUCTION

Whether the message comes from the corporate world [1, 24] or our colleagues in academia [8, 25], there is a demand for students with better communication and teams skills. The general goal of teaching communication skills is not unique to computer science; many schools have embraced Communication Across the Curriculum (CXC) or Communication in Disciplines (CID) [5, 20] as requirements for all students. Both programs develop interpersonal communication and public speaking, and though they differ in their implementations, the emphasis of both programs is on teaching communication skills throughout multiple courses.

Although these programs do not directly address collaboration skills, the strength of CXC and CID is their deliberate approach to skill development *across the curriculum*. Both programs emphasize a progressive approach to developing students' abilities where later courses build upon ideas learned in earlier courses.

Since collaboration encompasses such a wide range of skills —from interpersonal communication and conflict resolution to team planning and division of labor—it is unreasonable to expect students to master collaboration in a single course. For students to truly learn to work in teams, collaboration needs to be considered a curricular goal, and our effort should be to determine appropriate places in the curriculum to introduce new collaborative skills.

We propose collaboration across the curriculum as an intentional approach to teaching team skills to students. In this system students are introduced to collaboration concepts at points in the curriculum that match their stage of development. Students in the introductory curriculum learn basic communication and collaboration skills in pairs. Based on these skills, students at the sophomore and junior level are assigned carefully planned-out experiences in group settings. Finally, in the senior capstone course students are expected to synthesize their previous experiences as they collaborate on a large-scale, semester-long project.

Throughout the curriculum, collaboration is taught following Kolb's [12] model of learning by providing students opportunities to experience, reflect upon, hypothesize about, and plan their collaborations. Through repetition across the curriculum that builds upon prior experience, students have time to absorb these collaboration concepts and develop their skills.

Because our approach spreads this material across the curriculum, it allows collaboration to be taught in a way that supports individual course content rather than replacing it. Through simple restructuring of in-class activities, laboratory activities, and programming assignments, students learn to collaborate as they learn course content.

The community has generated significant literature about teaching collaboration and teamwork. We recognize its importance in Section 2 and recommend that this work be used in the system we propose. Section 3 presents our philosophy for teaching collaboration across the curriculum and Sec-

Permission to make digital or hard copies of all or part of this work for personal or classroom use is granted without fee provided that copies are not made or distributed for profit or commercial advantage and that copies bear this notice and the full citation on the first page. To copy otherwise, to republish, to post on servers or to redistribute to lists, requires prior specific permission and/or a fee.
SIGCSE'12, February 29–March 3, 2012, Raleigh, North Carolina, USA.
Copyright 2012 ACM 978-1-4503-1098-7/12/02 ...$10.00.

tion 4 describes how we implemented this framework within our computer science major. We conclude by discussing the results of our approach in Section 5.

2. RELATED WORK

We propose that students should learn collaboration skills through multiple experiences across the entire curriculum. There is a large body of work that documents the design of *individual experiences* (*e.g.*, courses, workshops, etc.) and effective instruction for *specific skills* related to collaboration, and we utilize this work in our curriculum-wide approach.

Within the computing disciplines, various groups have developed resources to support teaching the communication skills that form the basis of collaborative skills. For example, Carter et al. [4] have developed model curriculum and syllabi to teach communication skills in Software Engineering courses. Similarly, Smith et al. [32] describe a set of activities to help teach students soft skills such controlling and using emotion and employing appropriate language in business communications. Blume et al. [16] provide a collection of workshops to help students communicate with team members more effectively. Finally, Norback et al. [27] describe a web-based system to teach communication skills.

A variety of authors have written about techniques to support teams in individual courses. Although the work of Oakley et al. [23] was originally described in terms of cooperative learning, their ideas work equally well for traditional teams. In their paper, they provide a thorough discussion of team concepts and issues as well as a collection of materials to assist faculty. Similarly, Brown and Dobbie [3] discuss a tutorial to help students learn team skills. A variety of authors have written about aspects of forming teams and characteristics that affect team success [6, 17, 28]. Kurkovsky [13] describes four roles the instructor should role play during a group project. Finally, Smarkusky and Smith [30] describe an approach to teaching collaboration skills where communication skills are included as learning objectives in CS1/2 to prepare students for group work in later classes.

Instructors interested in utilizing a formal process for team interactions have a few options. "The TEAM Handbook" [26] describes a commonly-used system within corporations. In an academic context, Hilburn [9] discusses how to use the "Team Software Process" originally described by Humphrey [10]. Others, including Smarkusky et al. [29, 30] provide collections of modules or workshops to help students learn group skills.

Techniques to evaluate teams are an important area of research. Smith and Smarkusky [31] and Smarkusky et al. [29] provide a thorough coverage of evaluation principles and supply a variety of matrices to evaluate groups. Brown and Dobbie [3] discuss ways to directly and indirectly assess a team. Stone and Madigan [33] discuss the use of reflective writing to teach communication and provide a useful rubric for grading.

Tuckman [35] describes the classic stages of any group: form, storming, norming, and performing, and Largent [15] discusses how these apply in an Agile team.

Extreme programming and the Agile process are popular paradigms in introductory courses. McKinney and Denton [18] use pair programming in the introductory sequence, and they discuss guidelines for making this technique effective as well as ways to assess students. Teles and Tolla de Oliveira [34] describe efforts to include communication skills across the curriculum and in a course on Agile development.

2.1 Collaborative Learning Pedogogies

Many popular alternatives to lecture-driven instruction use team-based systems to improve student learning. When these systems are used, students learn collaboration skills as a consequence of the team-based environment. However, this learning is a side-effect of the environment rather than a goal. Still, the evidence for their effectiveness in student learning makes them appealing, and they can can be used within our proposed model.

In the Problem-Based Learning (PBL) model of learning, students work in teams to solve problems during class sessions. Newman and Faulkner [22] describe a variation called Open-Ended Group Projects where the problems collectively form a large software project

In Peer-Led Team Learning (PLTL) small groups of students learn along side a student peer that recently completed the course. Murphy et al. [21] and Biggers et al. [2] describe lessons learned using this approach.

Popular in science classrooms, Process-Oriented Guided Inquiry Learning (POGIL) is a variation of PBL. The difference is that POGIL activities are more highly scripted; students construct an understanding of the material by answering questions that guide them through the learning cycle. Recently, Kussmaul [14] has developed activities that introduce POGIL in computer science classrooms.

For a comparison of these techniques, see the survey by Eberlein et al. [7].

3. COLLABORATION ACROSS THE CURRICULUM

Like writing or speaking well, collaboration must be developed throughout a student's undergraduate career as a department effort. As educators, we must be intentional about how and when we introduce, develop, and expect mastery by our students of the relevant skills. Therefore, we propose a curriculum-wide approach to developing collaboration skills: collaboration across the curriculum.

We describe our philosophy at different stages in the curriculum. In required courses, we introduce concepts of collaboration at appropriate places and then build upon these experiences later in the curriculum—both in required and elective courses. Consequently, students have the opportunity to see that the development of collaboration skills is part of the natural progression through the major—much like their ability to design and implement efficient algorithms or utilize abstraction to build complex systems.

Along the way, we carefully balance individual learning of course content with collaborative experiences by recognizing that skills can be learned without group experiences. Finally, whenever possible we assess and evaluate the student's reflection and analysis of a collaboration rather than the product of the collaboration.

At all levels of the curriculum, collaborative elements share a foundation in Kolb's model [12]: as students are exposed to new ideas, they are given opportunities to practice the skills, and are regularly asked to reflect upon their performance and plan for future experiences.

Effective collaboration requires communication, interpersonal, and conflict-resolution skills. Beyond these elements, students must learn individual abilities—recognizing their own strengths and weaknesses, trusting in the competence of others, committing themselves to team goals, and accommodating differing personal values and ideas—and subsequently learn to use these tools to create team environments in which members act in a coordinated manner, communicate with one another, share decisions, resolve conflicts, and produce collectively-built products [11, 19].

The development of collaboration begins by laying foundations in CS1 and CS2. However, in the introductory curriculum it is also important that students *individually* learn foundational principles. Combined with the fact that these courses already contain numerous requirements, the inclusion of collaboration skills presents a challenge. To balance these competing needs, we believe the introductory curriculum should teach basic communication skills and have multiple small-scale interactions. We recommend that these interactions be structured so that they meet the following guidelines:

- **Supervised assignments** either assigned in class or in a laboratory give teams mutual accountability.
- Assignments that revolve around a **single concept** provide student teams with a shared understanding of their task.
- **Pair-programming** limits the complexity of the team mechanics and results in a collectively-produced product.
- Time is set aside for **reflective discussion** of team experiences, so that elements that drive team success are highlighted.

The students that succeed in the introductory level have demonstrated a competency with basic programming techniques and are better prepared for traditional team-based programming. As they continue through the curriculum, we should build upon their success to further develop their collaboration skills. The focus of this development should be in required courses, as this guarantees that all students see the material. However, it is also important that students gain experience with collaboration in elective courses. Thus, our efforts should be tailored to the course and its place in the major.

Regardless of the course, students at this level are not necessarily ready for truly independent team work. When given open-ended projects with loosely-defined deliverable products, students tend to revert to a "group work" mentality: project elements are divided—most likely unequally—among group members who work independently and the final product of the group is simply the collection of their individual products.

Experiences at this level should be highly-structured but allow students to apply the skills learned in the introductory courses:

- **Clearly-defined specifications** provide team members with a shared understanding of the team's product and **objective rubrics** provide students with a shared understanding of success.
- Assignments should provide opportunities for real collaboration, but be **limited in duration** so that teams can incorporate feedback in future assignments.
- **Individual work products** like write-ups or experience reports allow instructors to assess individual skills and provide students with opportunities for honest peer-review.

As students gain experience, the quantity of scaffolding can be reduced and the size of projects can increase. The key point is that by planning how the experience changes throughout the curriculum, students have the opportunity to build upon success and truly learn collaborative skills.

After multiple such experiences, students are prepared to explore higher-level frameworks and paradigms of collaboration in a capstone course. In this course their prior experience allows them to appreciate how new techniques contribute to a team process.

3.1 A Deliberate Approach

Though none of the elements described above are necessarily novel, the program-wide decision to purposefully and deliberately introduce and develop collaborative skills *across the curriculum* is not one that appears in the literature.

If, as a community, we believe that collaborative skills are an essential element to a computer science education, we need to intentionally structure our course activities to support the development of this skill, that—like technical topics—courses should be linked in their development of this skill, and that departments and programs should decide *as a whole* how collaborative skills should be emphasized at different points in their curricula.

The approaches described in Section 2 will certainly be a part of these efforts; they have proven valuable enough to be supported by and of interest to the community. In fact, some of the ideas presented by others are part of the implementation of our philosophy.

4. OUR IMPLEMENTATION

We implemented a collaboration across the curriculum program at a small liberal arts college. Because of a limited variety of programs within the college, the development of most "soft skills" came from within the computer science program. Additionally, the college uses a unit system where a major contains twelve courses. Three of these courses (Calculus I and II and Discrete Mathematics) already lie outside of the computer science program. As a result, we could not require students to take courses that specifically address additional objectives, nor could we relax the technical objectives of existing courses.

Fortunately, the effects of these constraints aligned with our philosophy. Our implementation follows the model we propose, builds on the work presented in Section 2, and, as described in Section 5, has been successful in building collaboration skills in our students.

4.1 Introductory Courses

The process of developing collaborative skills begins immediately in the introductory CS1/CS2 sequence. However, before we can actively engage students in collaborative work, we need to break them out of thinking that collaboration is unethical—an idea many incoming freshmen learned in their high schools. In the introductory courses we *encourage* the students to work together on all assignments except tests, and we spend time in class helping them understand what responsible collaboration means. In addition, we actively practice paired-programming in our closed labs—again with instruction about how to work effectively with a partner. Combined with frequent in-class activities using active, group-based learning, students come to see the value of collaboration.

To discourage leeching, tests and the final are worth 40% of the overall grade; it is difficult to do well in the course without learning the material. The active nature of the class sessions also makes it obvious which students are coasting.

Closed laboratory activities are structured like POGIL [14] activities. Working in pairs, students are presented with a problem of the week, typically based on a simple game. Solving the problem is done by writing a small program to simulate the game and collect data. Before they begin, each pair explores the problem by hand and predicts the final outcome. After they collect data, they comment on their results and their original prediction.

Each week, classroom time is set aside as a weekly review session. During these sessions, students are asked to reflect upon positive and negative aspects of working in groups and plan how to leverage successes and avoid failures in future collaborative experiences.

The strength of this approach is that in-class activities, closed-labs, and homework assignments provide multiple collaborative experiences for students. Through in-class discussions and reflective writings, we prompt the students to reflect on their experiences, hypothesize alternative approaches, and plan for future collaborations. Students are then able to test their plans in next week's lab, tomorrow's class, or on the homework due Wednesday. This gives students an opportunity for multiple iterations through the learning cycle and to begin learning how to collaborate effectively.

4.2 Core Curriculum

During the second year, students have three additional courses they are required to take, two in the first semester and one in the second. These courses allow us to plan experiences that build upon the skills learned in CS1/CS2. In elective courses, experiences must be crafted to allow for students with differing levels of exposure to working in teams.

In the first two required courses, Algorithms and Data Structures and Computer Organization, students are given a series of team-based programming projects. Prior to the assignment of the first project, students learn about Tuckman's [35] theory of groups. After each project, students are asked to reflect about their group experience and relate it to Tuckman's theory. Since these courses are not about designing software, the specifications for these projects are very detailed. Further, the projects are short enough to reduce the complexity of the collaborative effort.

Students are graded on individually-produced write-ups that describe the process of creating the program as well as their team experience. Like CS1 and CS2, in-class reflection of team experiences follows project deadlines and students are given individual and collective feedback through their write-ups.

The third required course, an Introduction to Software Engineering, helps students begin the transition from highly-structured projects to a more open-ended system where students must make design decisions, split up work, and handle the inevitable conflicts between team members.

The course is designed around a semester-long project with several regular checkpoints. Deliverables, including a proposal, various stages of design documents, and implementation, are due at points throughout the semester. Teams receive feedback related to the technical aspects of their project through these deliverables. Teams are also required to have regular informal meetings with the instructor. Though technical topics are discussed in these meetings, students are also asked to assess the functioning of their team and are given direction and feedback from the instructor. These regular meetings allow students to see how the dynamics and mechanics of their teams are within their control and provide them with tools necessary to function successfully on an open-ended project.

Although the intermediate deliverables are important, a large part of a student's grade on this project is based on the analysis of the team experience. This prevents students from ignoring the team aspect of the project.

Students are also given a series of individual labs throughout the semester. These assignments develop and assess a student's software engineering skills as well as provide students with individual control of their final grade in the course.

Together, these three required courses introduce students to the major themes of collaborative software development. Based on these experiences, students are prepared for a set of elective courses that, in addition to the content goals, include a department-mandated requirement to further the students' development of collaboration skills. We provide two examples that illustrate the range of possibilities.

4.3 Elective Courses

Game Programming is a senior-level elective where student pairs implement a video game of their design. The learning objectives of the course focus on good software design, and each team must negotiate the design process for various aspects of their game. In-class discussions feature the relationship between good design and effective collaboration.

As the course progresses through various elements of game programming (*e.g.*, coordinate systems, agent behavior models, efficiency issues, collision detection, graph algorithms, path planning, etc.), team projects are given corresponding checkpoints. Instructor meetings with each team at checkpoints help monitor the progress of each group's collaboration. A group's final assessment, while dominated by the quality of their product, includes a significant element where students evaluate the collaboration.

In Artificial Intelligence, students complete a traditional semester-long research project in teams of three or four. The course attracts students with a wide range of technical experience (from freshmen to seniors), and groups are assigned by the instructor to ensure that each group reflects this diversity. While the research projects themselves are open-ended, the progression of each project is carefully scripted. Regular assessment of team performance occurs via in-class discussion, regular team meetings with the instructor, and periodic peer-review.

4.4 Capstone Experience

After multiple experiences in a structured setting, our students are ready for a "real" team experience. During their last semester of study, students are required to take a course titled "System Design and Implementation." As the capstone experience for students in the major, this course requires students to pull together ideas and skills from across the curriculum. Thus, it is perfectly positioned for the students to demonstrate mastery of the collaboration skills they have learned earlier in the curriculum and allow them to practice further team skills.

To further their theoretical understanding of software development via collaboration, students learn about a variety of software development frameworks and practices. Our goal is to expose students to a breadth of techniques and have them think about how the techniques contribute to software development. Students are assigned a variety of readings on advanced software methodologies such as refactoring, code review, and version control, and they prepare short reflective journal entries on each reading. These writing assignments form a basis for discussion in class.

As the students are learning these practices, they are introduced to the collaborative project for the course. Our goal is to provide the students with experience working on a software project with real clients and customers. In its current offering, students are developing education-related software for an NSF-funded research consortium. Through this project, students are exposed to all aspects of the software process—from requirements elicitation to testing. All phases of development are completed by teams of students.

Because our graduating class sizes are small (typically five to ten), students participate on multiple teams simultaneously. Through these teams, the students experience different aspects of team development because they are assigned roles in the teams based on their strengths. The instructor for the course assigns students to tasks, and by the end of the semester, each student is the team lead for at least one task.

By mixing conceptual material from the texts and hands-on tasks for the project, students gain a deeper appreciation for the content of the course. Students may appreciate the ideas behind version control patterns, but they truly understand them after they resolve conflicts or inadvertently break the build. In many cases, students try different approaches to collaborative work simply because the discussion of content naturally includes conversation about how to apply the material to current tasks. In other situations, students are required to apply new skills. For example, regular code reviews are mandated by the instructor, and the evaluation frequently results in refactoring assignments for one or more teams.

Because the primary learning objective for the course is the *collaborative process* of creating software, students are never graded on whether tasks are completed successfully. Instead, grades are based on self-evaluation and peer review. The final paper for the course asks the students to reflect on their experience with the project. By acknowledging various successes and failures during the semester, students gain context for the material of the course as well as their contribution to collaborative development. Along with this reflective paper, students submit a log of their efforts on the project during the semester as well as a peer evaluation of the contributions of the other students.

5. RESULTS AND DISCUSSION

Measuring whether students learn to collaborate is difficult, and at a school with only five to ten graduates per year, size confounds assessment. However, the principles used to guide the implementation of this curricular objective are informed by research both within and outside the CS education community. Further, anecdotal evidence indicates that our approach is working. Since we implemented this system, the students in the senior capstone are more successful at team work. They are better prepared for the day-to-day interactions with peers, allowing the course to cover more advanced topics in software engineering. In a reflective writing assignment at the end of the semester, the students identify team skills as a useful product of the course. In addition, recent graduates indicate they are better prepared for collaborative efforts in the workplace than their peers from other institutions:

- One student reports that his collaborative experiences in college were instrumental in obtaining a job, saying, "teamwork is what they look for most of all, and Moravian's technique obviously facilitated growth in that direction."
- Another student reports that utilizing skills such as pair-programming and code-review allowed him to integrate quickly into the team while a peer from another school struggled to get beyond a "solo programmer" approach.
- Another student reports that not only is his supervisor impressed with the refactoring he performs, but that he has helped other, more senior developers adopt these techniques.

For students to truly understand how to work on a team, they need to learn and practice collaboration in multiple courses, similar to how CXC and CID teach communication skills or Writing Across the Curriculum programs teach writing. We must think intentionally about appropriate places in the curriculum to introduce collaboration skills and recognize that, particularly at the introductory level, these skills are best learned using activities other than traditional group programming experiences. Regardless of the actual activity, students should be forced to reflect upon their experience, and faculty should utilize both peer-evaluation and reflective writing to evaluate each student's performance in the group rather than the final product. Finally, the actual use of group work should be crafted to support the students' stage of development with collaboration. Students are ready for open-ended projects at the senior level, but until then scaffolding should be in place.

We described our approach, but each school needs to shape collaboration across the curriculum to fit their program.

6. REFERENCES

[1] A. Begel and B. Simon. Struggles of new college graduates in their first software development job. In *Proceedings of the 39th SIGCSE technical symposium on Computer science education*, SIGCSE '08, pages 226–230, New York, NY, USA, 2008. ACM.

[2] M. Biggers, T. Yilmaz, and M. Sweat. Using collaborative, modified peer led team learning to improve student success and retention in intro cs. *SIGCSE Bull.*, 41:9–13, March 2009.

[3] J. Brown and G. Dobbie. Supporting and evaluating team dynamics in group projects. *SIGCSE Bull.*, 31:281–285, March 1999.

[4] M. Carter, M. Vouk, G. Gannod, J. Burge, P. Anderson, and M. Hoffman. Communication genres: Integrating communication into the software engineering curriculum. In *Proceedings of the 24th IEEE-CS Conference on Software Engineering Education and Training*, pages 22–24, 2011.

[5] D. P. Dannels and A. L. H. Gaffney. Communication across the curriculum and in the disciplines: A call for scholarly cross-curricular advocacy. *Communication Education*, 58(1):124–153, 2009.

[6] K. Deibel. Team formation methods for increasing interaction during in-class group work. *SIGCSE Bull.*, 37:291–295, June 2005.

[7] T. Eberlein, J. Kampmeier, V. Minderhout, R. S. Moog, T. Platt, P. Varma-Nelson, and H. B. White. Pedagogies of engagement in science. *Biochemistry and Molecular Biology Education*, 36(4):262–273, 2008.

[8] P. Gruba and R. Al-Mahmood. Strategies for communication skills development. In *Proceedings of the sixth conference on Australasian computing education - Volume 30*, ACE '04, pages 101–107, Darlinghurst, Australia, Australia, 2004. Australian Computer Society, Inc.

[9] T. B. Hilburn. Teams need a process! *SIGCSE Bull.*, 32:53–56, July 2000.

[10] W. S. Humphrey. *Introduction ot the Team Software Process.* Addison-Wesley, 2000.

[11] J. R. Katzenbach and D. K. Smith. The discipline of teams. *Harvard Business Review*, pages 111–120, March-April 1993.

[12] D. A. Kolb. *Experiential Learning: Experience as the source of learning and development.* Prentice Hall, Eaglewood Cliffs, NJ, 1984.

[13] S. Kurkovsky. Four roles of instructor in software engineering projects. *SIGCSE Bull.*, 40:354–354, June 2008.

[14] C. Kussmaul. Process-oriented guided inquiry learning (pogil) for entrepreneurship. In *Proceedings of the National Collegiate Inventors and Innovators Alliance 15th Annual Conference*, 2011.

[15] D. L. Largent. Getting and staying agile. *XRDS*, 17:38–41, September 2010.

[16] B. Lil, R. Baecker, C. Collins, and A. Donohue. A "communication skills for computer scientist" course. *SIGCSE Bull.*, 41:65–69, July 2009.

[17] R. Lingard and E. Berry. Teaching teamwork skills in software engineering based on an understanding of factors affecting group performance. *Frontiers in Education, Annual*, 2:S3G1–6, 2002.

[18] D. McKinney and L. F. Denton. Developing collaborative skills early in the cs curriculum in a laboratory environment. *SIGCSE Bull.*, 38:138–142, March 2006.

[19] S. Mickan and S. Rodger. Characteristics of effective teams: a literature review. *Austrailian Health Review*, 23(3):201–208, 2000.

[20] P. C. Miller. Communication across the curriculum: An annotated list of research. National Association of National Association of Communication Centers (NACC) webpage, 2007. Retrieved August 23, 2011 from `http://www.usm.edu/speakingcenter/NACC/resources.html`.

[21] C. Murphy, R. Powell, K. Parton, and A. Cannon. Lessons learned from a PLTL-CS program. In *Proceedings of the 42nd ACM technical symposium on Computer science education*, SIGCSE '11, pages 207–212, New York, NY, USA, 2011. ACM.

[22] I. Newman, M. Daniels, and X. Faulkner. Open ended group projects a 'tool' for more effective teaching. In *Proceedings of the fifth Australasian conference on Computing education - Volume 20*, ACE '03, pages 95–103, Darlinghurst, Australia, Australia, 2003. Australian Computer Society, Inc.

[23] B. Oakley, R. M. Felder, R. Brent, and I. Elhajj. Turning student groups into effective teams. *Journal of Student Centered Learning*, 2(1), 2004.

[24] D. J. Reifer. Educating software engineers: an industry viewpoint. *SIGSOFT Softw. Eng. Notes*, 30:8–9, May 2005.

[25] S. Ruff and M. Carter. Communication learning outcomes from software engineering professionals: a basis for teaching communication in the engineering curriculum. In *Proceedings of the 39th IEEE international conference on Frontiers in education conference*, FIE'09, pages 1271–1276, Piscataway, NJ, USA, 2009. IEEE Press.

[26] P. R. Scholtes, B. L. Joiner, and barbara J. Steibel. *The TEAM Handbook.* Ariel Inc., 2003.

[27] J. Shaul Norback, D. C. Llewellyn, J. Donnell, and T. Govindaraj. Using a web-based system to integrate workplace communication skills into engineering curriculum. In *Proceedings of the Frontiers in Education Conference, 2001. 31st Annual - Volume 02*, Washington, DC, USA, 2001. IEEE Computer Society.

[28] J. Sheridan-Ross. Practical tips for engaging students in team formation for multi-discipline computing projects. *SIGCSE Bull.*, 39:360–360, June 2007.

[29] D. Smarkusky, R. Dempsey, J. Ludka, and F. de Quillettes. Enhancing team knowledge: instruction vs. experience. *SIGCSE Bull.*, 37:460–464, February 2005.

[30] D. L. Smarkusky and H. H. Smith. Team projects throughout the curriculum: course management, teaching initiatives and outreach. *J. Comput. Small Coll.*, 19:119–129, May 2004.

[31] H. H. Smith, III and D. L. Smarkusky. Competency matrices for peer assessment of individuals in team projects. In *Proceedings of the 6th conference on Information technology education*, SIGITE '05, pages 155–162, New York, NY, USA, 2005. ACM.

[32] W. J. Smith, F. Bélanger, T. L. Lewis, and K. Honaker. Training to persist in computing careers. *SIGCSE Bull.*, 39:119–120, December 2007.

[33] J. A. Stone and E. M. Madigan. Integrating reflective writing in cs/is. *SIGCSE Bull.*, 39:42–45, June 2007.

[34] V. M. a. Teles and C. E. Tolla de Oliveira. Reviewing the curriculum of software engineering undergraduate courses to incorporate communication and interpersonal skills teaching. In *Proceedings of the 16th Conference on Software Engineering Education and Training*, pages 158–, Washington, DC, USA, 2003. IEEE Computer Society.

[35] B. W. Tuckman and M. A. Jensen. Stages of small-group development revisited. *Group & Organization Studies*, pages 419–427, 1977.

App Inventor for Android: Report from a Summer Camp

Krishnendu Roy
Department of Mathematics and Computer Science
Valdosta State University
1500 N. Patterson St.
Valdosta, GA 31698
kroy@valdosta.edu

ABSTRACT

Google's App Inventor for Android (AIA) is the newest visual "blocks" programming language designed to introduce students to programming through creation of mobile applications (apps). AIA opens up the world of mobile apps to novice programmers. Success stories of using AIA to introduce college students to programming exist.

We used AIA in computing summer camps for high school students that we offer at our university. This paper is an experience report about using AIA in our camps. We provide a detailed description of designing our camps with AIA including the process of selecting and setting-up an Android device and instructional materials that we developed and made available to everyone. We evaluated our camps through surveys to determine the effects on the students. We found that there was mostly a slight increase in the favorable disposition towards computing. We also share our successes with using AIA and what still needs improvement for wider use.

Categories and Subject Descriptors

K.3.2 [**Computer and Information Science Education**]; D.1.7 [**Visual Programming**]

General Terms

Design, Human Factors, Languages

Keywords

App Inventor, Android, Summer Camp, Outreach

1. INTRODUCTION

The struggle of computing related disciplines like computers science and information systems to attract undergraduate students in recent years is a well-documented problem. The first seven years of the last decade saw a steep decline in computing-student enrollment, especially females and minorities [3, 4]. In the past three years which saw an increase in undergraduate computing student enrollment as well as graduation, this trend reversed somewhat [4]. However, there is still a long way to go to reach the levels seen in 2001 – 02 in terms of student enrollment, percentage of female students, and percentage of minority students[1]. In the next eight years the female undergraduate student population is expected to grow by as much as 18%, and the undergraduate population for minorities is expected to grow by 3%, 24%, and 37% for American Indians, African Americans, and Hispanics respectively [24]. In the light of these statistics, the fact that computing disciplines traditionally struggle to attract females and minorities does not bode well.

Unlike most other science subjects, middle and high schools often do not cover computing in any structured manner. School students on the other hand develop interest in computing at an young age if they are exposed to it in an engaging way [2, 11]. Computer scientists are trying to address this challenge in various ways, one of which is the development of several sophisticated Initial Learning Environments (ILEs) like Alice, Scratch, Lego Mindstorms NXT, and Greenfoot [5, 13, 16]. Alice, Lego Mindstorms NXT, and Scratch are all visual "blocks" programming language, and were really successful in lowering the barrier of initial entry to programming.

Leveraging these ILEs and other technologies like wearable computing [14], many organizations designed outreach programs geared towards middle and high schoolers. These outreach programs included summer camps and workshops [1, 14, 18, 20, 21, 27], after-school and weekend enrichment programs [7, 20], and workshops and courses for middle and high school teachers [8, 15, 22]. These efforts are definitely a step forward towards filling-up the vacuum of exposure to computing that many school students currently witness.

A new entrant in the field of ILEs is Google's App Inventor for Android (AIA) [28]. Just like Scratch and Alice, AIA offers a visual "blocks" programming environment where students can create applications (apps) just by dragging and connecting various blocks that look and act like puzzle pieces. However, unlike Scratch and Alice the target device for running the apps is not a computer but any An-

Permission to make digital or hard copies of all or part of this work for personal or classroom use is granted without fee provided that copies are not made or distributed for profit or commercial advantage and that copies bear this notice and the full citation on the first page. To copy otherwise, to republish, to post on servers or to redistribute to lists, requires prior specific permission and/or a fee.
SIGCSE'12, February 29—March 3, 2012, Raleigh, North Carolina, USA
Copyright 2012 ACM 978-1-4503-1098-7/12/02 ...$10.00.

[1]Female and minority students were 17.5% and 27.7% respectively of the undergraduate computing student population in 2001 – 02. In 2010 – 11 female and minority students accounted for 13.4% and 26.1% respectively.

droid based smartphone/tablet. AIA opens up the rapidly exploding field of mobile applications development as a tool for introducing computing. Multiple universities used AIA in introductory computer science courses in 2010 – 11 [23]. However, to the best of our knowledge before the summer of 2011 no summer camp used AIA.

We organized computing summer camps for middle and high school students at Valdosta State University[2], a public regional university in southern Georgia in summer of 2010. We received seed funding from Georgia Institute of Technology's "Georgia Computes!"[3] project. We continued offering these camps in 2011. In 2011 we decided to give AIA a try in our high school camps. Overall, we had a positive experience with AIA in our camps, and in this paper we report our experience. Our main goal in this paper is to present the organizational aspects of offering a camp using AIA. This paper is not intended for learning AIA. In the next section we present our reasons to offer camps using AIA. Section 3 describes the design of our camps in details. Through pre-camp and post-camp surveys, we evaluated the effectiveness of the camps in raising the student's impression about computing. Our camps were mostly successful in that regard and Section 4 briefly presents the results. While using AIA we noted several of its strengths as well as areas where more attention is needed. In Section 5 we share them.

2. MOTIVATIONS FOR USING AIA

Many highly successful summer camps used Scratch, Alice, or Lego Mindstorms NXT as their main ILE. Hence, the question "Why one wants to use AIA?" as a complement/supplement to one of the other ILEs begs some discussion. The main reason is because of the increasing usage of smartphones and other hand-held devices like tablets among teens, especially females and minorities.

Nielsen recently published results from their Mobile Youth Around the World survey [25]. In this survey they found that one-third of the 15 – 24 year old population in USA own a smartphone. More interestingly, USA is the only country where among youths, more females own smartphones than males. Among the 15 – 24 year old US smartphone users, 83% use smartphones for advanced data services beyond calls and text messages and for a quarter of them their smartphone is their primary device of Internet access. If we consider the general population's smartphone ownership, Nielsen's survey pointed out that smartphone ownership is higher among minority groups – 45% among Asians, Hispanics, and Pacific Islanders, and 33% among African Americans [26]. Some of the interesting statistics specifically about teen smartphone usage in USA are that 94% of teens owning smartphones are advanced data services users. There was an increase not only in the number of teen smartphone users, but in their data consumption level as well. Data consumption increased four-fold for teen males and five-fold among teen females in just one year. App downloads among teens witnessed an increase of 12% in 2010. Pew Research Center published results from their Pew Internet and American Life Project in July 2011 [19], and their results show very similar trends. Not only are teens using smartphones like never before, their teachers are also utilizing mobile learning to deliver various contents from mathematics to vocabulary using mobile devices [9, 12, 29]. In fact researchers in the field of mobile learning project that every student in USA will have access to a mobile device for learning purposes within five years [9]. With this explosion of smartphone usage among teens, we should not overlook smartphones as a key device for introducing computing. This was our primary motivation to look in to mobile apps development for our summer camps.

We also had some secondary motivations to offer apps development in our camps. As reported in [1], we also faced *repeat campers problem*, and had to offer new activities to attract previous year's campers. Additionally, extrapolating from the Nielsen's survey, we also felt that campers, especially females, might perceive smartphones and apps as being more gender neutral just like wearable computing [14] as opposed to something like Lego NXT robots.

Android is one of the three main smartphone operating systems (OS), the other two being Apple's iOS and RIM Blackberry's OS. Android has the largest smartphone OS market share now, and saw a tremendous growth in the last two years while iOS' share remained steady and Blackberry's OS' share dropped [19, 26]. iOS still dominates the tablet market due to the great success of iPads. However with most of the major pc manufacturers releasing Android tablets in the past one year, Android devices have started catching up. Android is an open platform unlike iOS and Blackberry. Many hardware manufacturers produce Android devices. The diversity of Android devices both in terms of capability and price increased a lot in the past one year. ILEs that look and feel like Scratch and Alice but can develop apps for Android and iOS are not common. Gamesalad[4] is a contender for developing iOS apps, however it runs only on Macs which our department does not have. AIA on the other hand runs on all platforms. Hence, when we were looking for a mobile-ILE, AIA was our only option.

We offered two one-week-long high school camps. AIA was one of the two ILEs that we used the other being Lego NXT. Everyday the campers worked with AIA during the morning and Lego NXT in the afternoon session. In this paper we will concentrate only on our experience with AIA.

3. ORGANIZATION OF THE AIA CAMP

3.1 AIA Lab Setup

Setting up a computer lab for using any other ILE like Alice or Scratch is trivial, it just involves installing the required software. However, setting up a lab for activities involving AIA is not so trivial, especially if you consider selecting and procuring Android devices. We devoted considerable effort to figure out the most appropriate Android device for our purpose and then installed software based on that decision. Here we briefly summarize our decision process.

The AIA software comes bundled with a Java based Android smartphone emulator. The emulator is quite capable and is a good option if budget is limited. However we strongly be-

[2]`www.valdosta.edu/computingcamp`

[3]`http://gacomputes.cc.gatech.edu/`

[4]`www.gamesalad.com`

lieve that for an outreach activity like ours, we must provide smartphones so that the campers can run their creations on smartphones instantaneously. With a device with haptic feedback, the campers can literally not only touch but feel their creations. We think this makes a camper's experience more impressive. Keeping this in mind, we decided to buy Android devices.

3.1.1 Android Device Selection

Numerous Android devices are currently available which makes selecting a device confusing. The first decision we made was that we will buy a tablet and not a phone. We made that decision because of the following reasons:

(a) Some of the major carriers do not sell smartphones without any service contract.

(b) Others who do offer Android smartphones without any service contract (eg. Google's Nexus S phone from Sprint) charge an amount which is more than that of a tablet.

(c) We assumed that the apps our campers will create in the limited time will be basic apps which do not use phone-specific features like voice-calls and text messages.

(d) By buying a tablet we gain more screen area and perhaps better audio quality considering that the tablet's speakers are usually better than that of smartphones because of the larger form factor of the device.

Once we made the decision of buying a tablet, our choice came down to either Samsung Galaxy Tab or Motorola Xoom as not many Android tablets were available in March of 2011. Currently many Android tablets are available including Samsung Galaxy Tab 10.1, Asus Transformer, and Amazon Kindle Fire just to name a few. We picked Samsung Galaxy tab as it had some features like haptic feedback which Motorola Xoom did not. With haptic feedback you can make your device physically vibrate, something useful to have while designing even basic games. Almost all smartphones have this feature while most of the tablets do not. Galaxy Tab's size was a little smaller than Xoom which we thought will be easier for our campers to handle.

After we selected the device, before we bought them, we looked in to two issues:

(i) The device is capable of installing third-party apps which are not from Android Market (the main repository for Android apps). This step is important because there are some Android smartphones like HTC Aria, HTC Inspire, and LG Phoenix which have the option of installing apps from unknown sources removed by the phone carrier who is selling them. If this is the case, there will be problems while trying to install an app created in AIA. The easiest way to know whether this option is there or not is to navigate to *Applications* under *Settings* and make sure the option "*Unknown Sources*" is present. One can press *Menu* (one of the four hardware buttons present on any Android smartphone) → *Settings* → *Applications* to check this. Google's AIA setup guide web page[5] has figures that can serve as a further guide.

[5]http://www.appinventorbeta.com/learn/setup/phone.html

Table 1: Our AIA Video Tutorials and the Concepts Introduced

Tutorial	Concepts Introduced
Basic Drum Set	*C1:* Sequence *C2:* Event-driven programming
Advanced Drum Set	*C3:* Boolean values
Basic Pong Game	*C4:* Random number *C5:* if-then-else *C6:* Boolean conditions
Keeping Score in Pong	*C7:* Variables *C8:* Initialization and increment of variables *C9:* Datatype conversion
Baby Catch Game	*C10:* Procedures/methods

(ii) AIA requires Android Debug Bridge (ADB) drivers for interfacing with the device. It can be hard to find the ADB driver for a particular phone or tablet as often it comes packaged with different pieces of softwares. For example, HTC's syncing software contains the ADB driver while for Samsung, their Mobile Innovator development software contains the ADB driver. In our experience, to identify and download the ADB driver, one should first look in to the website *The App Inventor Repository* which contains a list of devices and the link to the drivers[6] and is updated frequently. We ensured that this driver is available for the tablets we were planning to buy.

3.1.2 AIA Software Setup

In our experience, resolving the two issues that we described in the previous section makes setting up AIA straight forward. One needs to install Java, the AIA software, and the ADB driver for the device and ensure that the firewall (if any) is not blocking any of those software. Google's AIA website has a detailed guide[5] about this.

3.2 Instructional Materials

AIA is still under development with regular additions of new features. For example Google added a new feature – *Advanced* programming block in *Blocks Editor* during our second camp. Since AIA is still at the initial development stage, not many instructional resources are available, especially for a brief fast-paced learning environment like ours. So we developed our own project-based learning model to introduce computational concepts through AIA.

We created five video tutorials to cover many of the basic computational ideas like if-then-else, variables, boolean conditions etc. The first two tutorials created a drum app. The third and the fourth tutorial created a pong game with score-keeping. The last tutorial created another game where a baby is catching a ball falling from the top. The tutorials covered concepts which were increasingly complex. Table 1 lists all the five apps that we created, and for each one of them lists the concepts introduced in that tutorial for the first time. We tried to introduce most of the basic computational concepts and covered several of them like if-then-else in multiple tutorials. A notable absence in the list of con-

[6]http://www.theairepository.info/faq/troubleshooting/graybutton

Table 2: Brief Description of the Apps Our Campers Created

	App Name	Description
A1.	Animal Friends	App displays several animals touching any of which makes the corresponding animal sound
A2.	Tekno Blocks	Extension of the pong game to create the classic brick-breaker game
A3.	Banana Blast	Another version of classic brick-breaker game where bananas replace bricks
A4.	Tennis	A two player game where each player controls a tennis player on the screen
A5.	On The Farm	Displays several different farm animals who make corresponding sounds when clicked
A6.	Button Click	A game where the objective is to tap a button as many times as possible in a minute
A7.	Light Saber	A light saber making different noises if the tablet is shaken vigorously
A8.	Hold your breath	A timer app to time how long someone can hold their breath
A9.	Shooting Game	Variation of the classic asteroid arcade game where fantasy characters replace asteroids
A10.	Big Piano	A 14 key fully functional piano

cepts is loops. This does not mean our campers did not learn about loops, we introduced them to loops during the very first day when they worked with Lego NXT.

We kept the length of these tutorials short. The shortest one (basic drum-set) is roughly seven and half minutes long and the longest one (baby catch game) is seventeen and half minutes long. Additionally, we divided all the tutorials in to smaller parts which were at most five minutes long. Each part corresponded to some intermediate programming step/unit. For example the pong game which had three main visual components - a ball, a paddle, and a start button had five parts in the tutorial. The first part to create the screen layout of the app, the second part to create the code corresponding to the start button, the third part to make the paddle move on touch, the fourth part to make the ball bounce off of the wall, and the last part to make the ball bounce off when it hits the paddle.

While designing the materials we decided that the camp will involve very little lecturing from the instructors. Instead, we wanted the campers to learn these concepts on their own. In order to facilitate self-paced project-based learning, we posted these video tutorials online, gave each camper a headphone, and asked them to follow the tutorials on their own. All these tutorials are available on Youtube[7] as a playlist. We also have them available on our website[8] as Flash videos for any one who needs to download them for offline use.

We asked the campers to follow the first two tutorials (basic and advanced drum set) on the first morning of the camp and the third and the fourth tutorials (pong game with score) on the second morning and create those apps. Even though we allowed them to follow the tutorials at their own pace most of them took similar amounts of time. The last tutorial was an optional one, but most of them completed that one as well. Then, we asked the campers, working in groups of two, to create a group-app over the Wednesday and Thursday morning. The Friday morning was devoted to finishing up and recording a small video clip displaying their project. We used these clips during the parent demonstration.

The campers' creations in both the camps were impressive, especially considering the fact that two-thirds of them had no programming experience and that they had a total of four mornings to learn AIA and then work on the apps. Our campers created ten group apps in total. Table 2 lists all the apps with a very brief description.

[7] `http://www.youtube.com/playlist?list=PL2D27126F35E50A1B`

[8] `http://www.valdosta.edu/~kroy/ai-tutorials.html`

4. EVALUATION

Our main goals were to introduce the campers to computational thinking and programming and to stimulate their interest in computing in general. We had fourteen and eight high schoolers in our first and second camp respectively. Our camps received seed funding from "Georgia Computes!" project. One of the requirements of that funding is to administer the pre and post camp surveys developed by the "Georgia Computes!". Hence, we used the results of these surveys as one of the ways to evaluate our camp. However, these surveys are about the entire camp which includes AIA and Lego NXT. So the results of these surveys are reflective of the effectiveness of both AIA and Lego NXT. Campers answered several questions using a standard five-point scale.

Table 3: Results from Pre/Post Camp Survey

	Camp 1		Camp 2	
Question	Pre	Post	Pre	Post
I am good at computing	3.92	4.17	3.50	3.33
I like computing	4.38	4.42	4.33	4.00
I know more than my friends about computers	3.85	3.92	3.33	3.50
I am interested in a career in computing	3.33	3.75	3.33	3.33
Women can have jobs in computing	4.69	4.85	4.67	4.50
Men can have jobs in computing	4.69	4.62	4.67	4.50
Computer jobs are boring	2.00	2.00	2.50	2.50

Table 3 lists the mean of the pre-camp and the post-camp responses. It shows that most of our campers came in with a favorable attitude towards computing. Among the first camp's participants there was a slight increase in the favorable disposition towards computing. In the second camp, we saw a decrease in some cases. We believe one possible reason for this might be the fact that none of the campers in the second camp except for one had any prior programming experience, and hence before the camp most of them had a vague idea about what computing actually means.

Table 4: Concept Usage by Apps

Concepts	Apps									
	A1	A2	A3	A4	A5	A6	A7	A8	A9	A10
C1	✓	✓	✓	✓	✓	✓	✓	✓	✓	✓
C2	✓	✓	✓	✓	✓	✓	✓	✓	✓	✓
C3	✓	✓	✓	✓	✓	✓	✓	✓	✓	✓
C4			✓	✓					✓	
C5		✓	✓	✓	✓	✓	✓	✓	✓	
C6		✓	✓	✓	✓	✓	✓	✓	✓	
C7		✓	✓	✓	✓	✓		✓	✓	
C8		✓		✓	✓	✓		✓	✓	
C9		✓	✓	✓	✓	✓		✓	✓	
C10		✓							✓	

We also analyzed the group apps that the campers created (A1 - A10 of Table 2) to estimate how many of the concepts (*C1 - C10*) listed in Table 1 did the campers actually use. The campers had freedom in creating their apps, so some of them needed to apply all the concepts listed in Table 1 while others used only a few. Table 4 presents our concept-usage matrix which shows almost all the apps incorporated most of the concepts. This indicates that high school students can very quickly learn the basic computational ideas through AIA and apply them meaningfully to create apps.

5. OUR IMPRESSION OF AIA

In this section we present some of our thoughts about AIA. AIA is still in its beta stage and new users might experience the initial setup related problems as mentioned in [6]. In January of 2012 Google will make it open-source and the newly created Center for Mobile Learning at MIT will take over the development [10, 17]. This means AIA will see a lot of development in future and will benefit from the expertize of the researchers who have developed Scratch. For brevity, we do not make any direct connection between our observations listed here and our experience of using AIA.

5.1 What Works

(a) AIA is the best of both worlds - Scratch/Alice and Lego NXT. In Scratch and Alice students create virtual animations, games, and stories[9]. Using Lego NXT students create robots that involves physical interaction. In AIA students can create many things that are possible in Scratch/Alice, but can now include physical interactions like touching and dragging.

(b) Transitioning-in to AIA from Scratch and even Alice is very smooth because of the similar look-and-feel. Hence, AIA complements existing Scratch and Alice users' learning experience.

(c) Transitioning-out from AIA to developing applications using Java and Android SDK is possible. AIA has a feature called *Java Bridge* which allows users to use AIA components in Java programs of Android SDK. This means a teacher can use AIA to introduce students to programming logic in a relatively simple way, and once the students gain sufficient maturity, they can transfer that knowledge directly to traditional programming. Many colleges and universities' introductory CS courses are based on Java. The high school AP CS courses are also based on Java programming. Hence, we feel this smooth transitioning-out feature of AIA is useful.

[9]Technically, using Picoboards with Scratch let users create a Scratch project which can have physical interaction like sound and light sensing, but this is not widely popular.

5.2 What Needs Improvement

(a) Scratch and Greenfoot have project galleries which allow social interaction and peer sharing among its users. We feel AIA needs a similar app gallery as well through which students can share their apps easily.

(b) AIA needs an easily available media library like Scratch. While introducing students to programming for the first time, it is imperative to ensure they do not have to spend a lot of time searching for suitable image and sound files.

(c) The AIA website needs a detailed centralized web page about what devices work and how. One of the main attractions of AIA is being able to connect a phone and test out a newly created app right away. If a students fails to figure out how to make a device to work with AIA, then that depreciates the entire experience.

(d) While working with AIA, at any instant either two or three windows are open depending on whether the user is using the emulator or not. We feel there should be some effort in somehow integrating these windows and come up with a single-window user-interface design with all the key components always visible.

(e) AIA should make execution more visible just like Scratch where executing code blocks have a white outline to denote that they are active.

(f) AIA should incorporate the feature of downloading a particular code-block-fragment from one app and uploading it to another app, something akin to exporting and importing *sprites* in Scratch.

(g) In Scratch double-clicking any block not connected to any other block executes just that block. A similar feature in AIA will help novice learners a lot.

6. CONCLUSIONS

AIA is an effective tool to introduce novice programmers to programming. Just like Scratch and Alice this tool has a visual way to create programs and hence lowers the barriers of initial entry to programming. But beyond that, since AIA connects a programmer to the world of mobile apps, this is the ideal tool to appeal to the interests of today's youth. There can be difficulties in initially making a phone or a tablet to connect to AIA, but that is something which is solvable. Overall, our experience of using AIA was a positive one and we intend to continue using AIA in future for high school and even middle school summer camps.

7. ACKNOWLEDGMENTS

We thank Stacy N. Mills and Deborah Stone for helping us run the camps. We also thank Barbara Ericson, Director, Computing Outreach at Georgia Institute of Technology for her support and advice in designing these camps.

8. REFERENCES

[1] J. C. Adams. Scratching middle schoolers' creative itch. In *Proc. of SIGCSE Technical Symposium on Computer Science Education*, pages 356–360, 2010.

[2] J. Aresnault, S. Godsoe, C. Holden, and J. Vetelino. Integration of sensors into secondary school classrooms. In *Proc. of IEEE Frontiers in Educ.*, 2005.

[3] J. M. Cohoon. Must there be so few?: including women in CS. In *Proc. of International Conference on Software Engineering*, pages 668–674, 2003.

[4] Computing Research Association. 2011. Taulbee Survey 2009-2010. Retrieved December 5, 2011 from http://www.cra.org/resources/taulbee/

[5] S. Cooper. The design of alice. *Trans. Comput. Educ.*, 10(4):15:1–15:16, Nov. 2010.

[6] D. Pogue. 2010. D.I.Y. Tool for Apps Needs Work. Retrieved December 5, 2011 from http://www.nytimes.com/2010/08/12/technology/personaltech/12pogue.html?pagewanted=1

[7] Z. Dodds and L. Karp. The evolution of a computational outreach program to secondary school students. In *Proc. of SIGCSE Technical Symposium on Computer Science Education*, pages 448–452, 2006.

[8] D. L. Dunn, R. G. Strader, and M. M. Pickard. Camps on a shoestring: how we survived a summer. In *Proc. of SIGCSE Technical Symposium on Computer Science Education*, pages 383–388, 2011.

[9] GoKnow.Com. 2011. Retrieved December 5, 2011 from http://goknow.com/index.html?pg=about

[10] Google Reasearch Blog. 2011. A new MIT center for mobile learning, with support from Google. Retrieved December 5, 2011 from http://googleresearch.blogspot.com/2011/08/new-mit-center-for-mobile-learning-with.html

[11] P. Hylton and W. Otoupal. Preparing urban secondary school students for entry into engineering and technology programs. In *Proc. of IEEE Conference on Frontiers in Education*, 2005.

[12] V. Kalloo, Kinshuk, and P. Mohan. Personalized game based mobile learning to assist high school students with mathematics. In *Proc. of IEEE International Conference on Advanced Learning Technologies*, pages 485–487, 2010.

[13] M. Koelling. The greenfoot programming environment. *Trans. Comput. Educ.*, 10(4):14:1–14:21, Nov. 2010.

[14] W. W. Y. Lau, G. Ngai, S. C. F. Chan, and J. C. Y. Cheung. Learning programming through fashion and design: a pilot summer course in wearable computing for middle school students. In *Proc. of SIGCSE Technical Symposium on Computer Science Education*, pages 504–508, 2009.

[15] J. Liu, C.-H. Lin, E. P. Hasson, and Z. D. Barnett. Introducing computer science to K-12 through a summer computing workshop for teachers. In *Proc. of SIGCSE Technical Symposium on Computer Science Education*, pages 389–394, 2011.

[16] J. Maloney, M. Resnick, N. Rusk, B. Silverman, and E. Eastmond. The scratch programming language and environment. *Trans. Comput. Educ.*, 10(4):16:1–16:15, Nov. 2010.

[17] MIT Media Relations. 2011. MIT Launches New Center for Mobile Learning. Retrieved December 5, 2011 from http://web.mit.edu/press/2011/mit-launches-new-center-for-mobile-learning.html

[18] Y. Ouyang and K. Hayden. A technology infused science summer camp to prepare student leaders in 8th grade classrooms. In *Proc. of SIGCSE Technical Symposium on Computer Science Education*, pages 229–233, 2010.

[19] Pew Research Center. 2011. Pew Internet & American Life Project. Retrieved December 5, 2011 from http://pewinternet.org/Reports/2011/Smartphones/Section-1/Overview-of-smartphone-adoption.aspx

[20] I. Pivkina, E. Pontelli, R. Jensen, and J. Haebe. Young women in computing: lessons learned from an educational & outreach program. In *Proc. of SIGCSE Technical Symposium on Computer Science Education*, pages 509–513, 2009.

[21] L. Pollock, K. McCoy, S. Carberry, N. Hundigopal, and X. You. Increasing high school girls' self confidence and awareness of CS through a positive summer experience. In *Proc. of SIGCSE Technical Symposium on Computer Science Education*, pages 185–189, 2004.

[22] S. H. Rodger, J. Hayes, G. Lezin, H. Qin, D. Nelson, R. Tucker, M. Lopez, S. Cooper, W. Dann, and D. Slater. Engaging middle school teachers and students with Alice in a diverse set of subjects. In *Proc. of SIGCSE Technical Symposium on Computer Science Education*, pages 271–275, 2009.

[23] E. Spertus, M. L. Chang, P. Gestwicki, and D. Wolber. Novel approaches to CS 0 with app inventor for android. In *Proc. of SIGCSE Technical Symposium on Computer Science Education*, pages 325–326, Milwaukee, Wisconsin, USA, 2010.

[24] The Chronicle of Higher Education: Almanac of Higher Education. 2011. Forecast for Growth on Campuses: More Women, Minorities. Retrieved December 5, 2011 from http://chronicle.com/article/Forecast-for-Growth-on/128272/

[25] The Nielsen Company. 2010. Mobile Youth Around the World. Retrieved December 5, 2011 from http://www.nielsen.com/content/dam/corporate/us/en/reports-downloads/2010%20Reports/Nielsen-Mobile-Youth-Around-The-World-Dec-2010.pdf

[26] The Nielsen Company. 2011. Among Mobile Phone Users, Hispanics, Asians are Most-Likely Smartphone Owners in the U.S. Retrieved December 5, 2011 from http://blog.nielsen.com/nielsenwire/consumer/among-mobile-phone-users-hispanics-asians-are-most-likely-smartphone-owners-in-the-u-s/

[27] H. C. Webb and M. B. Rosson. Exploring careers while learning Alice 3d: a summer camp for middle school girls. In *Proc. of SIGCSE Technical Symposium on Computer Science Education*, pages 377–382, 2011.

[28] D. Wolber. App inventor and real-world motivation. In *Proc. of SIGCSE Technical Symposium on Computer Science Education*, pages 601–606, Dallas, TX, USA, 2011.

[29] L. Wong and C. Looi. Mobile-assisted vocabulary learning in real-life setting for primary school students: Two case studies. In *Proc. of IEEE International Conference on Wireless, Mobile, and Ubiquitous Technologies in Education*, pages 88–95, 2010.

Effective and Sustainable Computing Summer Camps

Barbara Ericson
Georgia Institute of Technology
801 Atlantic Drive
Atlanta, GA 30332
+1-404 385-2107
ericson@cc.gatech.edu

Tom McKlin
The Findings Group
1201 Clairmont Road
Decatur, GA 30030
+1-404.633.9005
tom@thefindingsgroup.com

ABSTRACT

Summer camps are a popular form of outreach for colleges and universities. But, it is not enough to offer computing summer camps and hope that students like them. The camps should be effective by some measure, such as broadening participation by underrepresented groups and/or increasing learning. Summer camps should also be financially sustainable, so that institutions can continue to offer them regularly. The summer camps at Georgia Tech have become effective and financially sustainable. This paper presents the rationale for our camps, the evaluation results that demonstrate positive attitude changes and increases in learning, and the business model that makes them financially sustainable. It also reports on the evaluation results from seven other colleges and universities in Georgia that offered computing summer camps during the summer of 2011 with assistance from Georgia Tech.

Categories and Subject Descriptors

K.3.2 [**Computers and Education**]: Computer and Information Science Education – *computer science education, information systems education, Self-assessment*

General Terms

Measurement, Documentation, Design, Economics, Reliability, Experimentation, Human Factors, Languages, Verification

Keywords

Summer Camps, Gender and Diversity Issues, Outreach, Cell Phone Programming, App Inventor, PicoCrickets, Scratch, Alice, and Robots.

1. INTRODUCTION

The outreach efforts at Georgia Tech were designed to improve access to computing, increase students' knowledge of computing concepts, and change students' attitudes about computing. One of our goals is to introduce computing in ways that directly contradict the negative stereotypes about computing. We show that computing is social, interesting, and creative.

To prove that computing can be social we have students work in pairs and present their finished projects. To prove that computing can be interesting and creative we have students create: a musical pickle with PicoCrickets, spin art with LEGO NXT kits, a plane with a LEGO WeDo kit that controls a virtual plane in Scratch, a movie in Alice, or their own cell phone app using App Inventor. These are just a few of the projects from this summer. We do short demonstrations of new concepts and then let students create their own projects based on the new concepts.

Another of our goals is to increase the diversity of students in computing. We engage girls and young women by holding computing workshops with the Girl Scouts and Cool Girls. We attract underrepresented minorities through our summer camps and workshops with local schools. The College of Computing offers teacher workshops, weekend workshops for students, competitions, a lending library, visits to campus, and summer camps [3]. This paper focuses on our computing summer camps.

2. RELATED WORK

Some colleges and universities run computing summer camps, and many of these camps have shown some positive changes in attitudes about computing and/or self-reported knowledge of computing [1, 2, 4-10, 13-15]. Most of these camps are supported by grants or corporate donations and are not financially self-sustaining [4-10, 13-15].

The published literature shows at least one institution that has been offering self-sustaining camps and has reported statistically significant evidence of learning. Joel Adams of Calvin College has been running computing camps since 2003 [1]. Since 2004 he has run two single-sex camps for middle school students that are self-sustaining. In his 2009 camps he asked students to rate their knowledge of programming both at the beginning and end of the camp. He reported a statistically significant positive change in the girl's self rating [2]. Can we go beyond self-report? We would like to have summer camps that have a measurable impact on learning.

In this paper, we describe Georgia Tech's summer camps. Our model has evolved over the seven years that we have offered these camps. We present evidence that Georgia Tech's camps reach a large range of students (4th – 12th grade), result in statistically significant positive changes in attitudes towards computing, show objective and statistically significant evidence of learning, and are profitable. In addition, other computing summer camps that Georgia Tech helped start have also shown statistically significant positive changes in attitudes towards computing.

3. GEORGIA TECH'S CAMPS

Since 2009 we have offered 8 weeks of computing summer day camps. Given the constraints of Georgia Tech's summer semester, 8 weeks of camps are all that is feasible. These camps initially were not financially self-sustaining, but after adding camps for younger students, they have become profitable. Finding space to run the camps was an issue for years until we received dedicated space for our outreach program in the College of Computing Building in 2010. The space includes a classroom that can hold 24 students, a smaller room for robot courses, and a workroom for our equipment such as laptops, robot kits, and spare parts.

Permission to make digital or hard copies of all or part of this work for personal or classroom use is granted without fee provided that copies are not made or distributed for profit or commercial advantage and that copies bear this notice and the full citation on the first page. To copy otherwise, or republish, to post on servers or to redistribute to lists, requires prior specific permission and/or a fee.
SIGCSE'12, February 29–March 3, 2012, Raleigh, North Carolina, USA.
Copyright 2012 ACM 978-1-4503-1098-7/12/02...$10.00.

3.1 Details from our 2011 Camps

Camp instruction was from 9am to 3pm each day, except Wednesday afternoon when the students went to the pool. We did a scavenger hunt so that the students could see more of the campus. On the last day we had a parent show so that the students could show off their creations. Parents are given flyers about computing from CSTA, Dot Diva, and NCWIT.

We use CS Unplugged and/or kinesthetic learning activities every day to give students exposure to more computing concepts and to provide a break from working at the computer. CS Unplugged (see http://www.csunplugged.org/) activities introduce computing concepts such as error detection and correction and binary numbers. Kinesthetic learning activities include flowchart hopscotch and a Boolean game.

We pair expensive items like robots with free software like Scratch and Alice so that if students enjoy what they are doing at camp they can continue learning at home. See Table 1 for the materials used during each week of the summer camps. We have a different focus for each week of the camp so that students can attend more than one week of the camp and also attend for multiple years.

Table 1. Summer Camp Content

Middle 1	PicoCrickets and Scratch
Middle 2	LEGO NXT and Alice
High 1	App Inventor on Google Android Phones
High 2	LEGO NXT, LEGO Tetrix and Alice
Elem 1	Scratch, Pleo robots, and WeDo robots
Elem 2	Scratch and LEGO NXT – Simulations and Science
Elem 3	Scratch and LEGO NXT – Music
Elem 4	Scratch and LEGO NXT – Storytelling

See http://coweb.cc.gatech.edu/ice-gt/1485 and then click on the link for each week of camp in order to see the pictures from that week and a detailed agenda for each day. There are also links to instructions for our projects. Sections 3.1.1 to 3.1.8 give more detail on the items we use in our summer camps.

3.1.1 PicoCricket kits

A PicoCricket kit is an arts and crafts kit for the digital age. Students enjoyed creating a musical pickle and testing their reaction time using drag-and-drop programming. For more information see http://www.picocricket.com/.

Figure 1. Musical pickle with PicoCrickets

3.1.2 Scratch

Scratch is free software from MIT. Students enjoyed creating 2D animations, interactive art, music, and games using drag-and-drop programming. See http://scratch.mit.edu/ for more information.

3.1.3 LEGO NXT kits

LEGO NXT kits allowed students to construct a variety of projects such as a flipping gymnast and spin art using drag-and-drop programming. See http://www.legoeducation.us/ for more information. See http://nxtprograms.com/projects1.html for project ideas.

3.1.4 Alice

Alice is free software from CMU. Students enjoyed creating their own short movies using drag-and-drop programming. See http://www.alice.org for more information.

3.1.5 App Inventor for Android Devices

App Inventor is free software from Google. Students enjoyed creating apps for mobile devices including mole mash and a quiz using drag-and-drop programming. For more information see http://www.appinventorbeta.com/about/.

3.1.6 LEGO Textrix kits

LEGO Textrix kits are intended for high school students. Students enjoyed creating sturdier and more complicated robots. Tetrix can be programmed using NXT-G or RobotC. For more information see http://www.legoeducation.us.

3.1.7 Pleo robots

A Pleo is a baby dinosaur robot that you can program by specifying how to move parts on a timeline. Students enjoyed making it wag its tail, bow, or beg. For more information see http://www.pleoworld.com/Home.aspx.

3.1.8 LEGO WeDo kits

LEGO WeDo kits are smaller than the NXT kits and are intended for younger students. Students enjoyed creating a top spinner and a hungry alligator. The kits can be programmed using Scratch. For more information see http://www.legoeducation.us/.

Figure 2. LEGO WeDo top spinner

4. EVALUATION

We use paired pre and post surveys to evaluate the camps. For each statement, a five point Likert scale was used with 1 being strongly disagree and 5 being strongly agree. We usually see positive changes in attitudes for most of these items. But, due to space constraints we are only reporting the significant changes in this paper. All of our surveys ask students to rate their agreement or disagreement with the following 8 statements.

1. Computers are fun.
2. Programming is hard.
3. Girls can have jobs in computing (HS uses Women)
4. Boys can have jobs in computing (HS uses Men)
5. Computing jobs are boring (MS and HS survey uses Computer jobs are boring)
6. I am good at computing
7. I like computing
8. I know more than my friends about computing

Our complete pre and post surveys and other information about our computing summer camps such as sample forms and flyers are available at http://coweb.cc.gatech.edu/ice-gt/1091. Overall, the camps resulted in several statistically significant positive changes as shown in Table 2.

Table 2. Evaluation Results Overall

Statement	N	Pre/Post Mean	Paired t-test	Effect size
2. Programming is hard	169	2.78/2.56	.007**	0.21
6. I am good at computing	168	3.8/3.96	.032*	0.16
7. I like computing	168	4.4/4.55	.07†	0.14
8. I know more than my friends about computing	170	3.44/3.69	.002**	0.24

** p<.01, * p<.05, † p <.1

Our theory is that the ease of drag-and-drop programming helps reduce the assumption that programming is hard (Statement 2). By exposing students to computing in the camps we are seeing a significant change in their confidence in their abilities (Statements 6 and 8), and, a smaller change in how much they enjoy computing (Statement 7).

If we disaggregate by gender we get some interesting results. Girls rate computers as less fun on the post test (but not statistically significantly). Girls initially rate the statement, "Programming is hard" at about the same level as boys (girls = 2.74, boys = 2.77). However, girls experience a much larger and statistically significant shift in disagreement with this statement than the boys. That is, girls are more likely than boys to disagree with the statement that "Programming is hard" after the camp. Boys show a statistically significant improvement in "I am good at computing" while girls do not. Boys also have a statistically significant improvement in "I know more than my friends about computing". This is consistent with other work that shows that boys have higher confidence in computing than girls [12].

Table 3. Evaluation Results by Gender

Statement	Girls (n=39)	Boys (n=118)
1. Computers are fun	4.72/4.62	4.51/4.69†
2. Programming is hard	2.74/2.26*	2.77/2.6†
6. I am good at computing	3.89/3.92	3.81/4.03*
8. I know more than my friends about computing	3.21/3.46†	3.49/3.74*

** p<.01, * p<.05, † p <.1

Disaggregating by race/ethnicity shows that the summer camps resulted in statistically significant changes in attitudes for black students, but not for white students. We didn't find any statistically significant changes for other races.

Table 4. Evaluation Results by Race/Ethnicity

Statement	Pre/Post Black (n=67)	Pre/Post White (n=54)
1. Computers are fun	4.48/4.79*	4.54/4.56
2. Programming is hard	2.79/2.32**	2.72/2.66
6. I am good at computing	3.8/4.09*	3.79/3.94
7. I like computing	4.37/4.66*	4.54/4.48
8. I know more than my friends about computing	3.21/3.66**	3.54/3.76

** p<.01, * p<.05, † p <.1

Overall, the program has brought about significant changes in student attitudes among two important populations: females and black students.

5. EVALUATION OF SEEDED CAMPS

As part of Georgia Computes!, our National Science Foundation Broadening Participation in Computing grant, we have been providing "seed" money and training to help 11 other colleges and universities in Georgia start computing summer camps since 2007. The "seed" money is up to $5,000 per application and is used to buy equipment for the camps. We awarded 3-4 of these grants per year. These camps are intended to be self-sustaining. Of the 11 other colleges and universities that have received "seed" money only seven offered computing summer camps in 2011. These camps did result in several statistically significant changes in attitudes towards computing as shown in Table 5.

Table 5. Evaluation Results for Seeded Camps

Statement	N	Pre/Post Mean	Paired t-test	Effect size
3. Girls can do computing	307	4.22/4.34	.011*	0.06
6. I am good at computing	312	3.69/3.99	.000**	0.20
7. I like computing	311	4.25/4.41	.000**	0.05
8. I know more than my friends about computing	311	3.45/3.66	.000**	0.20

6. MEASURING LEARNING

In 2011 we administered a 10 question multiple choice test on Scratch or Alice at the beginning and end of each camp for 7 of the 8 camps at Georgia Tech. We didn't try to measure learning at the App Inventor camp since it was our first time running a camp using App Inventor. See http://coweb.cc.gatech.edu/ice-gt/1091 for the tests and answer keys.

The first question in the Scratch test asked the student to select the category for a block. Questions 2-6 asked the student to match a Scratch script to a computing concept such as a loop, handling an event, conditional execution, modifying a variable, or sending a message. Questions 7-10 required the student to determine the result of executing a script. Table 6 shows statistically significant changes from pre to post on 7 of the 10 questions. The number of students who took both the pre and post Scratch test was 106. There was no significant difference in results by gender or race.

Table 6. Scratch Test Results

Question	% Correct		t-test	Effect size
	Pre	Post		
1. Category	74%	92%	.000**	0.27
2. Loop	34%	55%	.002**	0.21
3. Event	17%	25%	.107	0.11
4. Variable	25%	48%	.000**	0.24
5. Message	24%	36%	.055†	0.13
6. Conditional	11%	29%	.001**	0.23
7. Animation	44%	72%	.000**	0.28
8. Drawing a square	35%	58%	.000**	0.24
9. Conditional test	38%	53%	.025*	0.15
10. Drawing a triangle	17%	25%	.147	0.1

** p<.01, * p<.05, † p <.1

The first question in the Alice test asked how many objects were in an object tree. Questions 2-5 asked the student to match an image from Alice to a computing concept such as executing a method, setting a property, executing a function, changing a variable, and creating an object. Questions 6-10 asked the student to read an Alice program and determine the result. Table 7 shows statistically significant changes from pre to post on 4 of the 10 questions. We administered the Alice test in a middle school and a high school camp. However, two responses on the middle school test were mistakenly mapped to one answer so we couldn't use that data. The number of students who took both the pre and post Alice test in the high school camp was 16. Due to the small sample size significant differences were not detected across race or gender.

Table 7. Alice Test Results

Question	% Correct		t-test	Effect size
	Pre	Post		
1. Num objects	16%	13%	1.00	0.00
2. Method	11%	38%	0.02*	0.559
3. Field	11%	6%	0.333	0.25
4. Num objects from a class	26%	63%	0.02*	0.559
5. Creating an object	58%	94%	0.004**	0.661
6. Which object turns 180?	74%	88%	0.333	0.25
7. What happens at the same time?	47%	75%	0.041*	0.5
8. Conditional test	53%	69%	0.104	0.408
9. Nested loop count?	26%	25%	0.58	0.144
10. While loop test	32%	38%	1.00	0.00

** p<.01, * p<.05, † p <.1

Please note that we include effect size along with t-test *p* values in Tables 2, 5, 6 and 7. The APA Task Force on Statistical Inference requests that authors "always provide some effect-size estimate when reporting a *p* value." [16]. Effect sizes describe the magnitude of statistical findings and also allow researchers to conduct meta-analyses across similar studies.

To understand the magnitude of the Georgia Computes effect sizes, we looked to similar literature on computer science education programs, but found no reported effect sizes. We did, however, find effect sizes for research in Out-of-School-Time math programs [11]. The effect sizes in the computing summer camps appear to be comparable to the Out-of-School-Time math programs of longer duration [11].

7. ANOTHER LOOK AT EFFECTIVNESS

There are many ways to consider a camp's "effectiveness" besides learning. One measure of the impact of our summer camps is the number of students that return each year. We had 30 (17%) students return from 2010. Of the 30 returning students 13 were female (43%) and 20 were underrepresented minorities (67%).

A different indicator of the effectiveness of the camps is the popularity of our elementary student one-day workshops. Last fall we started offering one Saturday workshop most months. These workshops are $25 per person for a three-hour workshop, which more than covers our costs. We scheduled 3 of these workshops for the fall of 2011 and all sessions filled just two days after registration began. We added an afternoon session for each date and most of these filled as well.

Yet another measure of the effectiveness of the camps is how many students major in computing after attending the camps. We know of at least 3 students who majored in computing at Georgia Tech after attending our summer camps. One was a black male, one a white female, and one was an Asian female. However, we only know about them because they self-identified. We hope to do a more formal study of past camp participants in the future.

7.1 History of the Camps

We started with 2 weeks of introductory computing camps for high school students (rising 9th-12th graders) in 2004. Our goal was to give more high school students exposure to computer science in order to entice more of them into the field. We especially targeted females and underrepresented minorities. The high school camps were popular, with 65 students attending each year, but they didn't bring in enough income to cover expenses.

In 2006 we added 3 weeks of camp for middle school students, in an attempt to make the camps financially sustainable. We have found that parents are willing to pay a higher fee for middle school student camps than for high school student camps, since high school students don't need day-care and can work during the summer. With the addition of 3 weeks of camps for middle school students the camps broke even.

In 2009 we added camps for elementary school students due to requests from parents and to bring in additional income. We charged the same fee for the elementary school students as for the middle school students. Since adding the camps for elementary schools students, the camps have become able. In 2011 we had a profit of $15,649 from the camps.

Table 8. Number of students, number of weeks per year, ages

Year	04	05	06	07	08	09	10	11
students	65	65	90	85	167	177	202	181
# weeks	2	2	5	5	8	8	8	8
ages	HS	HS	HS MS	HS MS	HS MS	HS MS ES	HS MS ES	HS MS ES

7.2 The 2011 Camps

The number of students who attended each camp varied from 15 to 30 with an average of 22 students. The last week of summer camp is always the hardest to fill since students like to have some time off before school starts again. The percentage of female students varied from nearly 15% to 50% with an average of 28.2%. The percentage of underrepresented minority students varied from 50% to 75% with an average of 61.3%. The total number of students was 181, however 36 (19%) of the students attended more than one week of camp. Of the students who attended more than one week of camp 10 (27%) were female and 26 (72%) were black (see Table 2).

Table 9. Camp attendance gender and minority percentages

Camp	Total	% female	% minorities	# days
Middle 1	20	15	75	5
Middle 2	30	33.3	60	5
High 1	24	20.8	50	5
High 2	18	33.3	55.6	4*
Elem 1	25	28	68	4*
Elem 2	27	14.8	74.1	5
Elem 3	22	50	50	5
Elem 4	15	33.3	53.3	5
Total	**181**	**28.2 avg**	**61.3**	

*Some camps were 4 days instead of 5 due to the July 4th holiday.

7.3 Summer Camp Income

Each applicant pays the camp fee (see Table 3) and a non-refundable fee of $15 for each application to help cover administrative costs. In 2011, we had 181 applications for a total of $2,715 in application fees. We gave scholarships to 29 students who paid a reduced fee of $75 per camp. Scholarships are based on either the student being on free or reduced lunch or if the family income is less than $35,000 a year. Other organizations at Georgia Tech that have run summer camps for many years recommended charging at least $75 for students who received a scholarship. They found that if the camp was free the students would not show for the camp, or would come late.

Table 10. Income from the camp fees

Camp	Fee	# Full Fee	# at $75	Total
Middle 1	$285	15	5	$4,650
Middle 2	$285	26	4	$7,710
High 1	$185	22	2	$4,220
High 2	$148	17	1	$2,591
Elem 1	$228	19	6	$4,782
Elem 2	$285	20	7	$6,225
Elem 3	$285	18	4	$5,430
Elem 4	$285	15	0	$4,275
Total		**152**	**29**	**$39,883**

The gross income from the summer camps was $39,883 + $2,715 = $42,598.

7.4 Summer Camp Expenses

To create sustainable summer camps, it's important to consider expenses seriously. For example, we do not use university faculty to run our camps—they are simply too expensive, and volunteers cannot be relied upon every year. We hire local teachers instead who have attended our teacher workshops. Teachers often are looking for work during the summer, have experience working with students in the camp age range, and we want them to try out innovative ways to introduce computing. Teachers who have led our summer camps have been much more likely to incorporate new approaches in their regular classes.

We provided lunch and a t-shirt for each student. We pay teachers $240 a day. We hired 2 high school students to assist at a rate of $8.00 an hour. These students were NCWIT aspiration award winners or had already worked with our outreach program. We also hired one undergraduate student assistant at $16 an hour. This student had also already worked with our outreach program. We covered parking for the teacher and student assistants. We bought supplies such as name tags, pens, pencils, batteries, wristbands, a first aid kit and extra LEGO parts. See Table 11 for more information on the expenses.

Table 11. Summer Camp Expenses

Expense Type	Total
Teacher Leader	$8,640
Parking	$78
High school assistants	$4,269
Undergraduate assistant	$4,256
Lunch	$7,412
T-shirts	$1,736
Supplies	$558
Total	**$26,949**

The total profit from the camps was $42,598 - $26,949 = $15,649.

7.5 Other Expenses to Consider

Our administrative staff worked about 15-20 hours a week on the summer camps during the eight weeks of camp. They also spent about 10 hours a week processing applications for 9 weeks. Thus the administrative costs were $3,000 for the 8 weeks of summer camps and about $2,000 in administrative costs for processing the applications. The total administrative costs were about $5,000. But, our administrative costs were covered by our National Science Foundation (NSF) Broadening Participation in Computing (BPC) grant so we didn't count this expense.

The computers we used were originally purchased as part of our National Science Foundation Broadening Participation in computing grant in 2007. We did not include them as an expense. If we bought 30 computers at about $1,000 each and use them for 4 years the cost per year would be $7,500 per year. We will use the profit from the camps to replace these computers over time.

We also didn't include the cost of our robotic kits or cell phones in our expenses. Ten of the PicoCricket kits were a gift from Microsoft. Twenty Android cell phones were a gift from Google. The rest of our equipment came from an Atlanta Women's

Foundation grant or from income from the camps from last year. Organizations could start with elementary and middle school summer camps using free software like Scratch and Alice and use the profit to buy additional equipment.

Even after considering administrative costs of approximately $5,000 and computer costs of $7,500 the camps would still have made a profit of $3,149.

8. CONCLUSIONS

Summer camps are an important way for computer science programs to engage pre-college students. But, we want to reach more than one summer's set of students, and we want to continue offering summer camps even when the grant funding ends. We also want summer camps that really work to encourage more students, and especially more diverse students, to study computing.

Georgia Tech's summer camps have developed over seven years into a model that is both effective and financially sustainable. The camps produce positive changes in attitudes towards computing and measurable gains in learning. The camps are especially effective at changing the attitudes of female and black students, two important underrepresented groups in computing. We offer here our model, in some detail, so that other institutions can create similar effective and financially sustainable camps. For more information, including agendas, timelines, pictures, projects, flyers, tips, and forms, see http://coweb.cc.gatech.edu/ice-gt/1485.

We recommend that colleges and universities thinking of starting computing summer camps start with camps for elementary or middle school students using free software such as Scratch and Alice. Profits from these camps can be used to add additional equipment such as robot kits or cell phones.

9. ACKNOWLEDGMENTS

Our thanks to the NSF Broadening Participation in Computing Program for support (award CNS-0634629 and CNS-0940394). All opinions reflected in this paper are those of the authors and not necessarily those of NSF. We also thank the Atlanta Women's Foundation, Microsoft, and Google for their support.

10. REFERENCES

[1] Adams, J. 2007. Alice, Middle Schoolers & The Imaginary Worlds Camps. *Proceedings of the 38th SIGCSE technical symposium on Computer science education*, Covington, Kentucky, USA, pp.307-311.

[2] Adams, J. 2010. Scratching Middle Schoolers' Creative Itch. *Proceedings of the 41st SIGCSE technical symposium on Computer science education*, Milwaukee, Wisconsin,USA, pp.356-360.

[3] Bruckman, A., Biggers, M., Ericson, B., McKlin, T., Dimond, J., DiSalvo, B., Hewner, M., Ni, L., and Yardi, S. 2009 Georgia Computes! Improving the Computing Education Pipeline. *Proceedings of the 40th SIGCSE technical symposium on Computer science education*, Chattanooga, Tennessee, USA, pp. 86-90.

[4] Craig, M. and Horton, D. Gr8 Designs for Gr8 Girls: A Middle-School Program and Its Evaluation, *Proceedings of the 40th SIGCSE technical symposium on Computer science education*, Chattanooga, Tennessee, USA, pp 221 – 225

[5] Doerschuk, P., Jiangjiang, L., Mann, J., 2007. Pilot Summer Camps in Computing for Middle School Girls: From Organization Through Assessment, *ITiCSE'07*, June 23–27, 2007, Dundee, Scotland, United Kingdom

[6] Dunn, D., Strader, R., and Pickard, M. 2011. Camps on a Shoestring: How We Survived a Summer, *Proceedings of the 42nd SIGCSE technical symposium on Computer science education*, Dallas, Texas,USA, pp.383-388

[7] Franklin, D., Conrad, P., Aldana, G., Hough, S. 2011. Animal Tlatoque: Attracting Middle School Students to Computing through Culturally-Relevant Themes. *Proceedings of the 42nd SIGCSE technical symposium on Computer science education*, Dallas, Texas,USA, pp.453-458

[8] Groth, D., Lauer, B., Hu, H., and Lee H. 2008. Improving Computer Science Diversity through Summer Camps. *Proceedings of the 39th SIGCSE technical symposium on Computer science education*, Portland, Oregon,USA, pp.180-181

[9] Hardnett, C. 2007. Gaming for Middle School Students: Building Virtual Worlds. *Proceedings of the 3rd international conference on Game development in computer science education*, Miami, Florida, USA, pp. 21-25.

[10] Lau, W., Ngai, G., Chan, S., and Cheung J. 2009. Learning Programming through Fashion and Design: A Pilot Summer Course in Wearable Computing for Middle School Students", *Proceedings of the 40th SIGCSE technical symposium on Computer science education.* Chattanooga, Tennessee, pp 504 – 508

[11] Lauer, P., Akiba, M., Wilkerson, S. B., Apthorp, H. S., Snow, D., and Martin-Glenn, M. L. 2006. *Out-of-School-Time Programs: A Meta-Analysis of Effects for At-Risk Students. Review of Education Research, 76*(2), 275-313.

[12] Margolis, J. and Fisher, A., 2002 Unlocking the Clubhouse - Women in Computing, The MIT Press, Cambridge, Massachusetts

[13] Pivkina, I., Pontelli, E., Jensen, R., Haebe, J. 2009. Young Women in Computing: Lessons Learned from an Educational & Outreach Program. *Proceedings of the 40th SIGCSE technical symposium on Computer science education*, Chattanooga, Tennessee,USA, pp.509-513

[14] Pollock, L., McCoy, K., Carberry, S., Hundigopal, N., You, X. 2004 Increasing High School Girls' Self Confidence and Awareness of CS through a Positive Summer Experience. *Proceedings of the 35th SIGCSE technical symposium on Computer science education*, Norfolk, Virginia,, USA, pp.185-189.

[15] Webb, H., and Rosson, M. 2011. Exploring Careers While Learning Alice 3D: A Summer Camp for Middle School Girls. *Proceedings of the 42nd SIGCSE technical symposium on Computer science education*, Dallas, Texas,USA, pp.377-382.

[16] Wilkinson, L., & Task Force on Statistical Inference. 1999. Statistical methods in psychology journals: Guidelines and explanations, *American Psychologist, 54*, 594-604.

A Summer Science Experience with Computer Graphics for Secondary Students

Timothy A. Davis
School of Computing
Clemson University
Clemson, SC 29634
tadavis@cs.clemson.edu

ABSTRACT

This paper describes the principles, implementation, and results of a weeklong summer science course for junior high and high school students interested in computer science. To motivate and foster interest and creativity in students, while providing adequate complexity to introduce programming concepts and techniques, we used programming projects in computer graphics as the main learning tool. Included in our discussion are experiences across three course offerings, as well as detailed course assignments.

Categories and Subject Descriptors

K.3.2: Computer and Information Science Education.

General Terms

Algorithms, Design.

Keywords

K-12 Education, Problem-based Instruction, Image Processing, τέχνη.

1. INTRODUCTION

The Summer Science and Academic Enrichment Program at Clemson University offers a two-week college experience for 7th through 12th grade students who are interested in learning first-hand about college life. Students live in campus dormitories, eat at university dining facilities, and participate in recreational activities. They also have access to faculty and career counselors to help guide them in critical pre-college decision-making. Most importantly, however, students attend specialized short courses in topics such as chemistry, bioengineering, psychology, theater, and computer science.

Permission to make digital or hard copies of all or part of this work for personal or classroom use is granted without fee provided that copies are not made or distributed for profit or commercial advantage and that copies bear this notice and the full citation on the first page. To copy otherwise, or republish, to post on servers or to redistribute to lists, requires prior specific permission and/or a fee.
SIGCSE'12, February 29–March 3, 2012, Raleigh, North Carolina, USA.
Copyright 2012 ACM 978-1-4503-1098-7/12/02...$10.00.

While such programs are not new and indeed, are offered at many universities, questions remain as to how to teach such short courses in an effective and engaging way. The computer science course is often taught as a short version of a typical CS1 class, i.e., introductory programming. Although some students can take a programming course in secondary school, many have not and thus their experience is not that of a computer scientist, but of a computer user (e.g., navigating the internet and using third-party software). Many students are unprepared to advance from computer user to computer scientist, especially before college; therefore, care must be taken to facilitate the transition. Specifically, course material must be relevant, engaging, and accessible to students in order for the course to be successful.

One way to achieve this goal is to incorporate an application of interest to the students. With the explosion of gaming, computer-animated movies, internet imagery, and other exciting visual elements in entertainment, a combination of computer graphics and image processing is an obvious choice. Further, we have some experience in using graphics in problem-based learning in our undergraduate curriculum. Over the past five years, we have redesigned our freshman and sophomore computer science courses to leverage problem-based instruction in the domain of computer-generated visual media through the NSF-supported τέχνη project [4]. We believe that computer graphics is a natural and effective problem domain to exploit for instruction since it is not only compelling and relevant to students, but also inherently possesses a rich set of problem types of varying complexity naturally suited to problem-based learning [3,5], the solutions of which can be evaluated quickly through visual feedback.

Utilizing computer graphics to teach introductory computer science courses at the college level [2,7] and for K-12 [1,8,9] has been published previously. Some have reported success with summer camp instruction [6], though they tend to rely on Alice or a proprietary system. For this work we use a standard C/Linux environment for all coursework and assignments since this approach is consistent with our entry-level courses.

Section 2 describes the design of the short course, while Section 3 details the class assignments and presents student results. Section 4 provides a discussion of the work presented including lessons learned, and Section 5 presents a conclusion and possible future directions.

2. COURSE DESIGN

In the summer program, the term of a short course may vary from one to two weeks, though most courses are offered for just one week to allow students the opportunity to experience a broad range of topics. With such a short timespan for a class, designing a course that provides students with a meaningful experience can be challenging. Specifically, we would like students to learn within a realistic class setting of an introductory computer science course, and to complete the course with a sense of enthusiasm to pursue the discipline further in college.

The standard schedule for a one-week course in this program involves a three-hour class meeting each day, including lab time for hands-on training. For our computer science course, this time was divided into short lecture periods, each followed by a hands-on lab. In this way, students could immediately apply what they learned in class with the help of the instructor and lab assistant. By design, the lecture classroom and computer lab were not co-located, which forced students to break away from the interactive computer sessions during lecture.

The lab assignments consisted of C programming problems in computer graphics and image processing. Due to the nature of the course, the assignments were necessarily straightforward. The majority of the programs, however, were open-ended so that the best students were challenged, and the average students were provided with a pathway to the highest level of success which he or she was capable of achieving. This approach also allowed students to add personal touches or design as they desired, as the graphics problems lend themselves to artistic input.

The goals of the course were to teach basic concepts of programming, including variables, looping, and logical flow control. Additionally, we wanted to teach basic navigation in Linux along the way. Each of the seven programming assignments were designed to re-enforce concepts covered in class, with all but the first using graphics or image processing.

3. PROGRAMMING PROJECTS

The following subsections describe the programming projects in detail, along with code and example images where applicable. Many of the projects build upon previous assignments, which aided in skills acquisition.

3.1 Project 1: Hello, World!

The first project was a simple text output program to introduce students to text editing, compilation, and navigation in the operating system. Additionally, students learned how to redirect output from the program to a file, which would become more important in later assignments where image data was captured in a similar fashion. Other optional portions of this assignment involved changing the output message and repeating it a given number of times. While students could easily duplicate the code to achieve repetitive output, the process of doing so led to a discussion of generalizing this procedure with the use of looping statements.

```
#include <stdio.h>

int main ()

{
   int ct;
   int R, G, B;    /* red, green, blue */

   /* ppm header */
   printf ("P3\n");          /* ppm code */
   printf ("500 500\n");     /* width height */
   printf ("255\n");         /* max color value */

   R = 255; G = 0; B = 0;

   for (ct = 0; ct < 250000; ct++) {

      /* output single pixel */
      printf ("%d %d %d\n", R, G, B);
   }
}
```

Figure 1: Image Creation Code

3.2 Project 2: Image Creation

For this project, students wrote a short program to output an image consisting of a single color (see Figure 1). Dealing with pixels naturally lends itself to looping; therefore, this assignment allowed for an introductory discussion of looping techniques. Additionally, information about color components and their storage in an image file were also given. As in our freshman and sophomore courses, we used **ppm** image files for their simplicity.

Once students wrote the simple program to output the pixels, they compiled and ran the executable, redirecting the output to a **ppm** file for later viewing. Additional enhancements the students could perform included changing the color of the image, producing an image that was half one color and half another, changing the resolution of the image, and experimenting with nested looping. This final enhancement was significant since we originally introduced pixel iteration as a single **for** loop, spanning all 250,000 pixels (i.e., 500 x 500 resolution), as in Figure 1. Changing the resolution simply involved modifying the height and width information found in the **ppm** header, as well as the loop termination value. The split-color image (Figure 2) was also easily produced by creating two separate **for** loops, each with its own color.

3.3 Project 3: Image Fade

Once the students were able to write a program to output pixel data that could be captured to an image file, they were ready to introduce additional logic to manipulate the pixels before output. At this point, students were required to use nested looping such that their pixel calculations could be performed in either a column or row-based fashion to produce a horizontal or vertical fade, respectively (see Figures 3 and 4 for code and an image using horizontal fade). Students were encouraged to try different colors and to alter the direction of the fade effect.

Figure 2: Project 2 Split Image

```
#include <stdio.h>

int main ()

{
   int row, column;
   int R, G, B;

   printf ("P3\n");
   printf ("500 500\n");
   printf ("255\n");

   R = 255; G = 255; B = 255;   /* start with white */

   for (row = 0; row < 500; row++) {

      for (column = 0; column < 500; column++) {

         printf ("%d %d %d\n",
                 (int) (R * (1 - column / 500.0)),
                 (int) (G * (1 - column / 500.0)),
                 (int) (B * (1 - column / 500.0)));
      }
   }
}
```

Figure 3: Horizontal Fade Code

Figure 4: Horizontal Fade

3.4 Project 4: Flag Day

At this stage, students were ready to create a simple image that was meaningful. After a brief lecture on methods for using looping to produce various results, we transitioned to an interactive problem-based learning session showing various flags and discussing how to produce their stripes, blocks, and diagonals in an image. This session involved modifying code in front of the class and allowing them to view the results. As students asked about changing different parts of the program, we modified the code directly to show the effect.

Once the students were in the lab, we asked them to find a flag image on the internet they would like to produce. For the most part, simple flags with two or three stripes were chosen, similar to the image shown in Figure 2; however, even these flags posed a challenge to some students. An optional part of the assignment asked students to create another flag or other shapes, such as squares and rectangles. From these shapes, students could output other images of their choosing.

3.5 Project 5: Grayscale

For this assignment, students read in each pixel of a color image file, converted it to grayscale, then output the pixel to another file, according to the following conversion equation:

```
gray = 0.3 * red + 0.59 * green + 0.11 * blue;
```

Once again, we used I/O redirection for simplicity since it allowed us to read and write files without using specialized C functions; instead, we could just use `printf()` and `scanf()` (see Figure 5). An optional portion of this project asked students to alter their program to handle image files of arbitrary size. This modification required that the program read and store resolution information needed for the output file.

```
#include <stdio.h>

int main ()

{
   int row, column;
   int R, G, B;
   int gray;

   printf ("P3\n");
   printf ("500 500\n");
   printf ("255\n");

   /* read ppm header from input file */
   scanf ("%*s %*d %*d %*d");

   for (row = 0; row < 500; row++) {

      for (column = 0; column < 500; column++) {

         /* read pixel from input file */
         scanf ("%d %d %d", &R, &G, &B);

         /* convert pixel to grayscale */
         gray = 0.3 * R + 0.59 * G + 0.11 * B;

         /* print gray pixel to output file */
         printf ("%d %d %d\n", gray, gray, gray);
      }
   }
}
```

Figure 5: Grayscale Code

Figure 6: Frame from *Kung Fu Panda*, copyright DreamWorks Animation

As shown in Figure 6, we chose to use a single frame from *Kung Fu Panda* as our sample image. Although this choice was trivial technically, it served to engage the students as they felt they were working on something real and familiar. As this assignment was given on the third day of class, this excitement motivated the students as they progressed toward more difficult projects.

3.6 Project 6: Color Replacement

This programming assignment required students to read in an image file, as in the previous assignment, and replace a particular color range with another color. This replacement was accomplished by a simple color channel swap of red and blue, and introduced logic control using an `if-else` statement with a compound condition. The specifications for the program stated that if the pixel values for red and green were above 220 and 200, respectively, the channel swap should be performed (see Figure 7). Once again, the *Kung Fu Panda* image was used, with the result being the sky changing from yellow to blue. Optional parts of this assignment asked the students to try to change the color of the leaves in the image as well. To do so, students would be required to analyze pixel colors using an image display program, such as `xv`, typically found in Linux environments.

3.7 Project 7: Image Compositing

Our next topic in class covered bluescreen compositing in movie production, which was not only relevant and engaging to the students, but was useful as a motivating problem for the final program. Students were asked to composite a bluescreen photographic image with a computer-generated background. To obtain the bluescreen images, each student was photographed in front of a bluescreen located in our Digital Production Arts studio. The blue pixels of the image were to be replaced with pixels generated for the fade effect in Project 3 (see Figure 8 for code and Figure 9 for sample student work with vertical fade). The blue replacement algorithm is remarkably simple and the students particularly enjoyed this project since it involved working with actual photographs of themselves. As an optional exercise, students could composite their flag designs from Project 4 in the background.

```
#include <stdio.h>

int main ()

{
   int row, column;
   int R, G, B;

   printf ("P3\n");
   printf ("500 500\n");
   printf ("255\n");

   /* read ppm header from input file */
   scanf ("%*s %*d %*d %*d");

   for (row = 0; row < 500; row++) {

      for (column = 0; column < 500; column++) {

         /* read pixel from input file */
         scanf ("%d %d %d", &R, &G, &B);

         if (R > 220 && G > 200)
         {
            /* swap channels if in range */
            printf ("%d %d %d\n", B, G, R);
         }

         else
         {
            /* otherwise, print unchanged pixel */
            printf ("%d %d %d\n", R, G, B);
         }
      }
   }
}
```

Figure 7: Color Replacement Code

```
#include <stdio.h>

int main ()

{
   int row, column;
   int R, G, B;

   printf ("P3\n");
   printf ("500 500\n");
   printf ("255\n");

   scanf ("%*s %*d %*d %*d");

   for (row = 0; row < 500; row++) {

      for (column = 0; column < 500; column++) {

         scanf ("%d %d %d", &R, &G, &B);

         if (B > R && B > G)  /* replace blue */
         {
            R = 255; G = 255; B = 255;
            printf ("%d %d %d\n",
                    (int) (R * (1 - row / 500.0)),
                    (int) (G * (1 - row / 500.0)),
                    (int) (B * (1 - row / 500.0)));
         }

         else
         {
            printf ("%d %d %d\n", R, G, B);
         }
      }
   }
}
```

Figure 8: Image Compositing Code

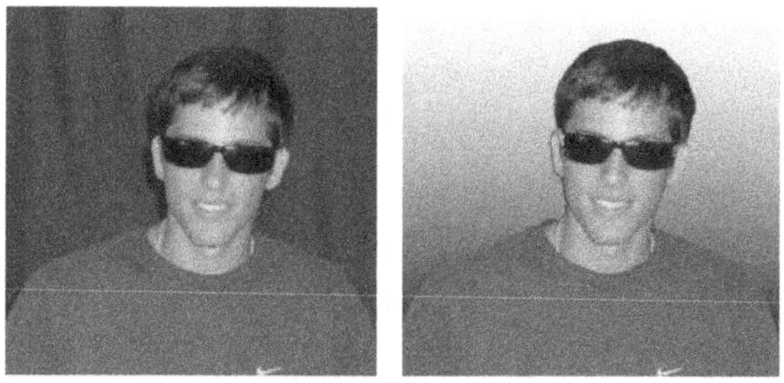

Figure 9: Horizontal Fade: Bluescreen Image (left); Composited Image (right)

4. DISCUSSION

This short course was offered three times during the course of one summer and was one of the most popular courses in the Summer Science Program. The students' experiences with the class, which follows our τέχνη approach to regular courses in terms of philosophy and implementation, have been generally positive and effective. Allowing students to implement graphically based problems is engaging and motivating, as evidenced through student pride in their final projects.

The course in its current scope, however, was unusually limited due to several factors:

- The course ran for only one week, which was a severely short period of time for beginners to learn about computer science and programming, as many students need time and experience to understand the concepts fully.

- Since students only had access to the computers during lab sessions, no projects could be assigned outside of the confines of our three-hour course. Nor could students experiment on their own or review the day's work. This situation not only precluded instruction of more advanced concepts, richer environments, and tools such as debuggers, but also limited student synthesis of the material.

- The student demographics in each of the sessions was much broader than anticipated, with student grade levels ranging from rising 8th graders to rising 12th graders. Additionally, some students were participating in the program because they were advanced students, while others were in attendance as borderline special needs students; thus, students varied widely in background and maturity level.

While these factors may seem extreme upon first glance, they are probably not unique across such summer programs, which tend to be condensed by design and intended to serve a broad range of students. Given these considerations, the most effective approach, as outlined above, was to provide basic assignments with opportunities for advanced students to explore further. Nearly every student completed all of the assignments, though some students required significantly more assistance than others. In any case, the graphical nature of the projects seemed to be universally engaging across the wide variety of students in the course, which is expected given the proliferation of computer-generated imagery throughout the world.

5. CONCLUSION

The goal of this paper is to present a useful approach to teaching introductory computer science to secondary students in a short summer course. Undoubtedly, many approaches exist, each with its own advantages and challenges. Following the approach outlined here involves no particular specialized packages, niche languages, or supplementary instructor training; instead, a standard Linux environment with a C compiler is all that is required. The approach follows our τέχνη program, which has been successfully used at Clemson University over the past eight years, and satisfies the broader goal of providing students with a substantive experience of an entry-level computer science course. Further, the class can be modified or expanded with additional modules or topics to fit the particular needs of a given program.

In future offerings of the course, we would like to replace the first assignment with one that contains visual aspects. Additionally, we would endeavor to enhance the final assignment to perform true compositing using two separate images rather than generating a portion of the image within the program. Finally, we would hope to provide ways to allow students access to the university computers after hours for additional experience.

6. ACKNOWLEDGMENTS

Work referenced in this paper was supported in part by the CISE Directorate of the U.S. National Science Foundation under awards EIA-0305318 and EAE-0722313.

7. REFERENCES

[1] Adams, J. C. Alice, middle schoolers & the imaginary worlds camps. *SIGCSE Bulletin*, 39(1), 2007, 307-311.

[2] Burger, K. R. Teaching two-dimensional array concepts in Java with image processing examples. *SIGCSE Bulletin*, 35(1), 2003, 205-209.

[3] Cunningham, S. Graphical problem solving and visual communication in the beginning computer graphics course. *SIGCSE Bulletin*, 34(1), 2002, 181-185.

[4] Davis, T. A., Geist, R. M., Matzko, S., and Westall, J. M. TEXNH: Trial phase for the new curriculum, *SIGCSE Bulletin*, 39(1), 2007, 415-419.

[5] Duch, B., Gron, S., and Allen, D. The power of problem-based learning. Stylus Publishing, LLC, Sterling, VA, 2001.

[6] Ericson, B., Guzdial, M., and Biggers, M. Improving secondary CS education: progress and problems. *SIGCSE Bulletin*, 39(1), 2007, 298-301.

[7] Fell, H. J., and Proulx, V. K. Exploring Martian planetary images: C++ exercises for CS1. *SIGCSE Bulletin*, 29(1), 1997, 30-34.

[8] Frost, D. Fourth grade computer science. *SIGCSE Bulletin*, 39(1), 2007, 302-306.

[9] Rodger, S. H., Hayes, J., Gaetjens, L., Qin, H., Nelson, D., and Tucker, R. Engaging middle school teachers and students with Alice in a diverse set of subjects. *SIGCSE Bulletin*, 41(1), 2009, 271-275.

Integrating UX with Scrum in an Undergraduate Software Development Project

Chase Felker, Radka Slamova, Janet Davis
Dept. of Computer Science
Grinnell College
Grinnell, IA 50112, USA
<felkerch, slamovar, davisjan>@grinnell.edu

ABSTRACT

We report our experiences using the Scrum agile software development method in an undergraduate user-centered web development project. Our chief contributions are to report on using Scrum in a summer research setting as distinct from academic-year coursework and to consider the integration of Scrum and user experience (UX) development methods in a learning environment. Our experience with combining Scrum and UX was positive: this methodology gave our project a clear structure, kept us motivated, and focused us on developing a usable final product. We discuss our adaptations of Scrum to UX development and to the summer research setting, along with challenges we faced and lessons learned, to inform students and faculty who wish to apply such methods in future projects.

Categories and Subject Descriptors

D.2.9 [**Software Engineering**]: Management.. H5.2 [**Information Interfaces**]: User Interfaces – *user-centered design.* K.3.2 [**Computers and Education**]: Computer and information science education – *computer science education.*

General Terms

Management, Human Factors.

Keywords

Agile development, Scrum, user experience, user-centered design, undergraduate research.

1. INTRODUCTION

While agile software development practices have become popular in professional environments, relatively little literature examines how learners can use agile methodologies in a non-professional setting. Moreover, published reports of combining user experience (UX) with agile development have focused on industry rather than academic settings. In this paper, we report on our experiences with combining the Scrum agile software development method with UX methods to improve the user experience of a local food co-op's website. Our approach integrated design and UX evaluation with software implementation in the context of a student summer research project.

Permission to make digital or hard copies of all or part of this work for personal or classroom use is granted without fee provided that copies are not made or distributed for profit or commercial advantage and that copies bear this notice and the full citation on the first page. To copy otherwise, or republish, to post on servers or to redistribute to lists, requires prior specific permission and/or a fee.
SIGCSE'12, February 29–March 3, 2012, Raleigh, North Carolina, USA.
Copyright 2012 ACM 978-1-4503-1098-7/12/02...$10.00.

In the next two sections, we explain our context and then describe how professional software developers have used Scrum alone and in combination with UX methods. In turn, we clarify how we modified Scrum for the undergraduate research setting and how we integrated Scrum with UX. Finally, we present benefits and challenges of our approach, arguing that Scrum can effectively be integrated with UX in our setting despite difficulties with estimating tasks. While some challenges remain, Scrum methodology gave our project a clear structure, kept us motivated, and focused us on developing a usable final product.

2. CONTEXT

Our software development project aimed to improve the user experience of the Grinnell Local Foods Co-op website. The Co-op is a student-run organization at a small liberal arts college that helps community members buy a variety of seasonal produce from local farmers each month during the school year. The Co-op links 7 farmers with about 250 members. The website was created to facilitate local food sales through the Co-op. The essential features include three interfaces: for members to browse the available produce and place their orders, for farmers to post their inventory, and for coordinators to manage orders. The existing website was difficult to use: members had to place orders by viewing the entire inventory on a single page; they had difficulties with editing orders; and they sometimes accidentally ordered sold-out items. Our major goal was to implement a shopping basket feature and any other high priority features identified by coordinators, members, and farmers.

We revised the website as part of a Mentored Advanced Project, a faculty-directed summer research project at Grinnell College. During the summer, two students worked closely with a faculty advisor for about 40 hours per week for 10 consecutive weeks.

Both students spent the first two weeks of the summer learning Scrum, PHP, MySQL, HTML, CSS, and revision control tools. During the next weeks, we continued to allocate learning time as we transitioned into fixing bugs and refactoring the website. Half way through the summer, we felt confident enough in PHP to start building new, complex pages, like the shopping basket page. By the end of the 9th week, we finished major coding and began reflecting on our experience in a final paper.

We built on the work of students from a Human-Computer Interaction class taught by the project advisor during the spring semester preceding our research. One team member was a student in this class; the other was not. The Human-Computer Interaction class conducted a single iteration of Hartson and Pyla 's UX development "Wheel" process [7] to redesign the Grinnell Local Foods Co-op website. The class first conducted an in-depth contextual inquiry, during which students interviewed farmers, members, and organizers about their role in the Co-op and observed users' interactions with the website. Data from the contextual inquiry were then summarized in a Work Activity Affinity Diagram [3,7], which helped the class develop models and requirements for the new website. The class also created a high-fidelity prototype of a revised website and tested the with several participants.

3. PRIOR WORK

3.1 Scrum

Scrum [13] is a popular agile software development methodology that "concentrates on how the Team members should function in order to produce the system flexibly in a constantly changing environment" [1, p. 27]. In contrast to the "waterfall method" of designing and detailing implementations at the start of the project, Scrum assumes that the project will change as the software develops. Scrum Teams work in short, fixed-length cycles called Sprints, typically two weeks to one month in length. At the end of each Sprint, the software is potentially shippable and all work that the Team committed to do at the start of the Sprint is done [5].

In Scrum, there are three major roles: The Product Owner, the Team, and the ScrumMaster [5]. The Product Owner assesses development items' business value and prioritizes them in a spreadsheet called the Product Backlog. The Product Owner thus shapes the direction of the project by specifying what is developed and when. The Team is a multi-skilled group of five to ten people who build the product. The ScrumMaster manages the project on a macro-level to make sure that none of the Team members is blocked on a task and Scrum is used effectively.

Scrum sets aside about 10 percent of the overall time for processes such as Sprint Planning, Review, and Retrospectives [5]. Before the start of each Sprint, the Team holds a Sprint Planning meeting where it selects the highest priority items to be completed in the next Sprint, plans how they will be implemented in detail, and estimates how long each will take. New items may not be added to the Sprint in progress.

Several structures help the Team to stay on track. The Sprint Backlog categorizes tasks as "Not started, In progress, Done, Blocked." The Burndown Chart graphs the number of hours that the Team needs to complete the Sprint. Finally, the Daily Scrum requires the Team and ScrumMaster to review the past day's tasks, coordinate on the coming day's tasks, and get help on blocked tasks.

At the end of each Sprint, the Team holds a Review where it shows work that has been completed and receives feedback on it. Following the Review is the Retrospective, where the Team reflects on what practices from that week should be sustained and what should be improved [5].

Scrum's structure helps the Team be flexible, operate at a sustainable pace, and maintain a multi-skilled team [5].

Recent work has addressed Scrum and other agile software development methods in the context of undergraduate education (e.g., [6, 8, 10, 15, 16]). However, all of the cited articles consider agile methods in the context of traditional courses rather than an intensely mentored summer research experience. Only one article discusses Scrum in particular [15], and none consider the relationship between software development and UX development.

3.2 UX Development

User experience (UX) encompasses the usefulness of a product, usability of a product, and emotional impact of the product on the user. Key aspects of UX include user satisfaction, ease-of-use, effectiveness, learnability, and retainability [7,14].

Beyond the structure of the UX Wheel [7], several existing UX practices contributed to our project:

Paper prototypes allow user interface designs to be tested before they are implemented in software [7,14]. Paper prototypes are easier to create and change than software, and they can help identify major usability problems before undergoing the costs of implementation. Because paper prototypes do not include computation, one of the designers must play the role of "computer" to operate the paper prototype.

Formative UX evaluation guides design by uncovering major impediments to usability [7,14]. Representative users participate remotely or in person, in a large group or individually, and at any point in the design process. Participants perform a set of tasks and think aloud to reveal their intentions and reactions so that the UX developers can understand usability problems.

The Rapid Iterative Testing and Evaluation (RITE) method facilitates formative UX evaluation by allowing the designer to make changes to prototypes as soon as problems are identified. By allowing greater flexibility to address problems and test proposed solutions within a single session, RITE minimizes the number of participants needed to uncover major usability problems and is therefore much more efficient [7,11].

Brief, regular tests are recommended by usability expert Steve Krug. He recommends that developers schedule UX tests even before knowing what they will be testing to produce a short list of the most essential problems with the current product [9, pg 28].

3.3 Integrating UX and agile development

Several industry professionals have reported on their experiences integrating UX development with agile software development [2,4,12]. Most report significant challenges. Even in companies that already support UX practices, UX experts and software experts often work in separate groups, and UX groups have difficulty adjusting to an agile methodology. For example, Paypal's UX Teams reported surprise at the fast-changing schedule of programmers and experienced uneven work loads. In order for the workload to become manageable, UX Teams adopted Scrum, with their own Product Owners and Backlogs, and learned to design a sprint ahead of the developers [4].

Theoretically, the major road block to integrating UX and agile development comes from tension between the incrementalism of agile processes and the holistic nature of some UX processes. In particular, contextual inquiry is a process of discovery that should be undertaken early in a project [3]. Rannikko suggests that while UX and Agile are not mutually exclusive, they need to make compromises [12]. Specifically, he suggests that comprehensive studies such as contextual inquiry should be completed before agile development begins. During agile development, both UX tasks and development tasks can be completed incrementally [12].

4. OUR USE OF SCRUM + UX

4.1 Scrum Practices

We significantly modified the major roles of Scrum. The Product Owner was a Co-op coordinator, the small Team consisted of two undergraduates, and the ScrumMaster was the faculty advisor. The Team was atypical in that it was smaller than normal (just two vs. 5-10 developers [5]), and its members were not experienced software developers. Our ScrumMaster was likely more involved with details than is typical; this was partially because our project was a learning experience and the faculty advisor had greater expertise than the Team. Our Product Owner differed significantly. As a coordinator for the Co-op she clearly had extensive experience with the site, but she took a comparatively hands off approach to the Product Owner role. As she held a full-time summer internship in another state, she was not present at any UX evaluations and her availability was quite limited. We spoke with her through Skype once per week during our

Sprint Review where we told her what we did, demoed what was done, prioritized new items with her, and received her approval for what we would do next week; she was not available to address further questions during Sprint Planning.

Although we modified Scrum roles, we closely followed the structure of Scrum. We maintained a Sprint Backlog with notecards on a white board, maintained a Burndown Chart, had Daily Scrums, and followed other Scrum processes. During the week, Team members averaged about six hours per day on Sprint work. Our multi-skilled Team programmed together much of the time. At the end of each Sprint, we had a Review where we met (online) with our Product Owner and demoed our finished tasks. A Retrospective always followed the Review. During the Sprint Planning meetings, the Team decided what tasks to commit to in the next Sprint, and then extensively planned and estimated all these tasks. These planning meetings lasted about 10 percent of the Sprint length, as suggested in the Scrum Primer [5].

We decided on one-week Sprints, a cycle shorter than the typical two to four weeks [5]. Choosing Sprint length was a challenge, which we will discuss in section 6.2. Although we followed Scrum's structure for the majority of the project, three weeks were not proper Sprints: for the first two weeks, we focused on learning Scrum and development tools, developing the Product Backlog and reviewing existing materials. We spent the final week preparing a project report.

Finally, our use of Scrum was unusual because we combined it with UX. This led us to separate "definitions of done" [5] for software and UX development tasks, along with other changes discussed below.

4.2 Combining UX with Scrum

Integrating UX with Scrum felt natural for our Team, since we were new to software development. Lacking any existing software development culture, there were no conflicts when introducing Scrum. Because our small Team did both UX and software development, collaborating across separate UX and software Teams was not a problem.

As noted earlier, Rannikko recommends that contextual inquiry be completed prior to starting software development [12]. Fortunately, we were able to rely on the results of the contextual inquiry completed by the Human-Computer Interaction class the previous semester. All the other UX development was completed during Sprints within the Scrum structure, consistent with Rannikko's recommendations [12].

During our Sprint Planning meetings, we determined whether we wanted to conduct a UX test that week, per Krug's advice to evaluate regularly [9, p. 27]. As our tests were always towards the end of the Sprint, and because we would test new features designed or implemented during that Sprint, we did not always know at the time of Sprint Planning exactly what we would be testing. A task during our Sprint would be to plan the evaluation session and write tasks for the participants to complete. We also included design and prototyping tasks in our Sprint Planning.

We conducted three formative UX evaluations: results from the evaluation were intended to improve the design rather than to draw conclusions about the system. The first two tests involved paper prototyping the login process and the ordering system, and the third tested these features after they were implemented. We spent about half a Sprint for each evaluation of a paper prototype, including sketching designs, creating the prototype, conducting a pilot test to discover obvious problems with the prototype or tasks, conducting the sessions, modifying the prototypes, and debriefing. While Krug advises that regular usability testing requires little more than half a day [9], he assumes developers are testing existing software.

Using the RITE method [11] gave us the flexibility to modify the prototypes and tasks between test sessions. We always made some modifications: no two participants worked with exactly the same tasks and system. Our tests lasted 30 minutes, and we allowed an additional 30 minutes between participants to either modify the prototype or change the tasks.

We also did frequent informal tests with the Product Owner where she both looked at sketches and experimented with implemented features. However, because of her remote location, she did not participate in testing paper prototypes or observe UX tests with participants acting as Co-op members.

5. BENEFITS

5.1 Benefits of Scrum

We benefited from the clear structure and motivation that Scrum supplies. At the start of the project, even small tasks were daunting due to our inexperience with PHP and other tools. Scrum helped by forcing us to plan out items for a set period of time, break them down into smaller tasks, and specify in detail what they would involve so we could estimate them accurately. Our Product Backlog provided constant temptation to work on one of the many other things that could be improved on the site, but Scrum strategies such as the Burndown Chart helped us stay on task. As work on a newly added item would not be reflected in the chart, we were motivated to only work on tasks we committed to do at the beginning of the Sprint. The Sprint Retrospectives and Reviews were a good learning opportunity; in fact all of our Recommended Strategies came from Retrospective discussions.

We did not have to deviate significantly from overall Scrum's structure to use it in a learning environment instead of a professional development setting. The project advisor easily assumed the role of ScrumMaster: her focus was to make sure we were not blocked on tasks rather than to micromanage our work. The Daily Scrum gave the advisor a reason to come in every day to check on student progress. As Hart observes, "frequent interactions help prevent small problems from snowballing into larger delays" [6]. The Team benefited from a daily deadline, since knowing that the advisor would come in at 1:30 gave motivation to accomplish something every day. This helped to give our Sprints a sustainable pace compared to previous school projects. When we deployed our code, there was no need for a "hardening Sprint" dedicated just to fixing bugs that were not caught during the Sprints. We attribute this to Scrum's emphasis on having a working system at all times.

5.2 Benefits of UX Design and Evaluation

Scrum emphasizes integrating the Product Owner into development. This is compatible with the user-centered design philosophy of involving users in all stages of development. However, the Product Owner is only one person and may not be able to represent the perspectives of all users. The UX process enabled many insights that, as individuals, the Scrum Team had overlooked. The Contextual Inquiry helped us set initial priorities. For example, we knew from the first day that everyone thought the ordering process on the old system needed to be fixed. UX evaluation of paper prototypes gave us confidence that we would implement a usable system. These tests were an effective and fast way to compare different design possibilities.

UX testing was always an effective deadline. Our paper prototypes or implementations needed to be complete enough to test. We paid our participants for 30 minute sessions, so we knew that we had to put some thought into what to test during that time.

Participants in the third UX test caught bugs that we had overlooked; for example our search feature would work only when the user pressed enter instead of the form submit button because of the way we displayed "Search produce" in the text box. This test also pointed out the most urgent items from our large Product Backlog that should be addressed before the site went live.

6. CHALLENGES

We faced several challenges related to the role of the Product Owner, Sprint planning, Sprint progress, and incorporating UX development.

6.1 A Different Role of Product Owner

Different Location and Constrained Time. One of our biggest challenges was trying to use Scrum as it is described in the literature while not having a fully committed Product Owner. Because our Product Owner could not watch our UX tests, she sometimes disagreed with our Team about users' needs. Moreover, we had difficulty remotely sharing our work with her due to erratic Internet connections. Our Product Owner was also not available to answer questions at any time, which forced us to make important decisions, like aborting a Sprint, without her.

Lack of Real Ownership. Our Product Owner did not have a real ownership of our project because she did not pay us to do the project, and it was not even her idea to do the project. Because we were paid by the school, not by the Local Foods Co-op, our Product Owner was grateful for any improvements we did on the website and felt it would be inappropriate for her to pressure us to work harder. Even when we did not finish our Sprint, she was grateful for our work and did not criticize our time management. In general, our Product Owner did not have high expectations for us and rarely offered constructive feedback or asked us to improve our work.

Assuming Some Responsibilities of Product Owner. Because our Product Owner was not able to take on all typical responsibilities, our ScrumMaster and Team members took over some of the tasks of a Product Owner, including updating Product Backlog and directing Sprint Review. Moreover, we made decisions such as aborting a Sprint by group consensus, when those decisions should have been made by the Product Owner.

6.2 Sprint Planning

Sprint length. We had a hard time deciding whether our Sprints should last one week or two weeks.

Two-week Sprints, which are more typical, give time to complete larger Product Backlog items and allow more room for error in estimating individual tasks. However, we would have had only three full Sprints during the summer, and thus would not experience Scrum as an iterative process. Another disadvantage was that the Team's inexperience made it difficult to estimate future tasks using skills the Team had not yet learned.

We decided instead to use one-week sprints, which enabled us to reflect on our Scrum experience on a weekly basis and thus to quickly adjust our planning to how long different kinds of tasks usually took. The negative consequence of doing one-week Sprints was that we sometimes failed to present a working system at the end of the Sprint because some tasks required more than a week of work.

Time estimates. Our greatest challenge during Sprint Planning Meetings was estimating how long different tasks would take. Although the Scrum Primer claimed that groups usually become accurate at estimating tasks within four weeks, we had problems coming up with realistic time estimates during the whole summer. We especially struggled with estimating time for complicated tasks, tasks that required learning a new skill, and tasks involving the use of CSS. We also constantly underestimated how long complicated tasks would take, usually because we failed to think of all things that needed to be done for the task to be complete or because we did not allocate enough time for instances when we got stuck. Furthermore, many of our tasks were different from those of professional software developers. Unlike in typical practice, Team members had to learn new web development tools and UX methods, and also wrote a research paper.

Another challenge was to set a minimum time estimate for our tasks. We decided that estimating less than 30 minutes for a task would be risky because, if we ended up getting stuck on the task, the time to complete the task would end up being many times longer than our time estimate. Thirty minutes was a strategic overestimate for most of the tasks that we hoped would balance out the time spent on unpredictably hard tasks.

Planning too much vs. too little. We had difficulty finding a healthy balance between planning tasks in excessive detail and not planning them well enough. Not breaking tasks into small pieces usually resulted in leaving something important out and thus underestimating how long it would take to complete a task. Planning tasks in great detail, on the other hand, usually resulted in a 4-hour long Sprint Planning Meeting and a Sprint Backlog overflowing with 30-minute task cards. By breaking complex tasks into smaller pieces during Sprint Planning, we usually avoided leaving something out, but we also sometimes spent more time planning a task than it would take to complete it.

New Functionality vs. Refactoring and Fixing Old Bugs. Because we were building on an existing website, one of our challenges was to decide how much time we wanted to spend improving the existing code and how much time we wanted to devote to creating a new functionality. Working with the previous website was difficult because code was duplicated and had inconsistent variable names and the code files were not organized in any way. During our project, we struggled to find a balance between making the code beautiful but never get any new features done versus suffering with the code as it was and focusing totally on implementing new features.

6.3 Sprint Progress

Doing Easy Tasks First - A Misleading Burndown Chart. The line of our Burndown Chart usually showed great progress during the first day of the Sprint and then leveled off during the next days of the Sprint, hardly ever reaching the desired "0 hours of work left" at the end of the Sprint. Seeing this pattern, we usually became overoptimistic during the first Daily Scrum of each Sprint and assumed that we would finish the Sprint without problems.

It took us several Sprints to realize that we appeared so productive after the first day of the Sprint not because we got a lot of work done, but because we picked the easiest, overestimated, 30-minute tasks first and we left the harder, underestimated tasks for the later stages of the Sprint. Thus, our curve would inevitably stop running steeply downwards as soon as we started working on the more complicated tasks, which were often underestimated.

Sprints Interrupted by Weekend. One reason why we tended to start with short and easy tasks was because we started our Sprints on Fridays and wanted to finish some tasks before leaving for the weekend. If we picked a complicated task on Friday, we would not complete it that day and have to remember it on Monday. Ideally we would have started our Sprints on Mondays, but we had to accommodate our Product Owner in scheduling the Sprint Review and Planning sessions.

6.4 Prototyping and UX Evaluation

Balancing UX and Implementation Work. We found it hard to decide which of our features needed to be paper prototyped and evaluated given our limited time. To provide a good user experience, we would ideally evaluate all of our features using sketches and paper prototypes before implementing them, and again after implementing them. However, UX evaluation took time away from implementation because we did not have separate UX and development Teams; both members of our Team needed to contribute to creating, testing, and evaluating prototypes.

When to design and test. We followed the parallel track development model that recommends conducting UX testing a Sprint ahead of implementation (Nodder & Nielsen, as cited in [12]). Although this model helped us successfully combine design with implementation for most of the summer, we wasted some time at the end of the summer when we did not get to implement a feature that we carefully designed a Sprint ahead.

Estimating UX Tasks. Guessing how long a design task would take was difficult because design tasks were more open-ended than coding tasks, and it was less obvious when we were done.

7. LESSONS LEARNED

Sprint Retrospectives exposed many lessons along the way, in addition to those synthesized at the end of the project. We relate lessons learned to communication with the Product Owner, Sprint Planning, Sprint progress, Retrospective, and Integrating UX.

7.1 Communication with Product Owner

Only demo things that are done. This rule is part of the Scrum Primer [5], but it was challenging for our group to stick to it when our new CSS markup was almost done and we wanted to show it to our Product Owner. Not showing a new feature until it is done motivates the Team to finish the task properly.

Do not arrange UX testing and client meeting on the same day. Scrum philosophy is to work at a "sustainable pace," and dealing with several users and a Product Owner in one day is exhausting.

7.2 Sprint Planning

Allocate time for learning. This practice will save time in the long run. We failed to allocate time for learning CSS at the beginning of the summer research, hoping to find quick solutions to our CSS problems. Because we did not understand how CSS works, we always spent much more time on tasks involving CSS than we predicted. By contrast, we did allocate time for learning PHP. Before diving into bug fixes and writing our own code, we spent several days reading about the basics of PHP and trying to understand existing code. Because we understood PHP quite well before we started using it, we were able to resolve PHP problems much more quickly than CSS problems.

Plan each task in detail. When we underestimated tasks during Sprint Planning, it was often because we did not think though all aspects of the task. Though extensive planning can be time-consuming, it let us estimate tasks more realistically.

Allocate time for developing a multi-skilled Team. As noted earlier, Scrum's philosophy is to encourage a development of a multi-skilled Team [5]. It was beneficial for each Team member to mentor the other, one having greater programming experience and the other skills in prototyping and user testing. By the end of the summer, both Team members were able to write website code and run UX evaluations.

Maintain a balance of UX and software development. We found it useful to include both refactoring and prototyping tasks in a single Sprint because when we got stuck on a coding task, we could still work on something different. In Sprints that did not require any prototyping or refactoring, we made sure to include smaller coding tasks (e.g., bug fixes) in case we got stuck.

Plan how to test code as part of Sprint Planning meeting. Planning tests in advance helped us set standards for our code and also helped us budget enough time for testing.

7.3 Sprint Progress

Use your definition of "done." This strategy will help you stay on task and know when it is time to move on to the next task.

Start your Sprint on Monday. We found that starting a Sprint on Friday led us to pick short tasks on Friday because we were afraid we would not finish larger tasks before the weekend. Having the weekend in the middle of our Sprint disrupted the sustainable pace of our Sprints.

Decide on an exact time when the Sprint ends. At first, the last day of the Sprint was hectic because we would continue working on new tasks until the start of the Sprint Review. It was tempting to work some extra time on the last day of the Sprint to finish all our tasks, but doing so made us exhausted, hungry, and stressed, which goes against Scrum's philosophy of sustainable work pace. Deciding to end our Sprint mid-day left a buffer for planning the review meeting and ensuring our work was ready to demo.

7.4 Retrospectives

Make time for retrospectives. Unfortunately, Scrum Teams often omit the Retrospective [5]. But retrospectives are key for allowing the Team time to reflect and improve their process. Our Sprint Retrospectives were incredibly useful. They helped us realize what we needed to change in order to be more successful in the next Sprints. In fact, most of the points in this section are taken from our Sprint Retrospective notes. Retrospectives were the primary time when we would purposefully step back and reflect on what should be changed.

7.5 Integrating Scrum and UX

Complete the Contextual Inquiry beforehand. Having the results of a recent contextual inquiry was incredibly helpful and allowed us to focus solely on design and implementation.

Create your own definition of "done" for UX-related tasks. Having a definition of done is a standard Scrum practice. Because our design tasks were very different from our coding tasks, it was helpful to have a different definition of "done" for design and implementation tasks.

Design a Sprint ahead of implementation. Designing just a Sprint before implementation for the most part prevented us from designing features we would never have time to implement.

Limit time for design. Design tasks are open-ended; judging when a sketch or prototype is complete is difficult. As inexperienced designers, we decided to allocate a certain amount of time to spend on design. Once that time was exhausted, we deferred further decisions until the evaluation.

Schedule testing before you know what you will test. Because of our short Sprints, we usually created our paper prototypes and task cards only days before the actual tests. However, participants usually want to know more than 2 days in advance that they are invited to a UX evaluation. Following the advice of Krug [9], we recruited participants and set up sessions with them before we knew what we would evaluate. This strategy originally sounded risky to us, but ended up working surprisingly well.

Allocate twice as much time for UX evaluation as sessions will actually take. Doubling the testing time during Sprint Planning will allow for adjusting the prototype between the participants and will leave enough time for setup.

Allow separate time for pilot testing and debriefing. Having task cards for pilot testing before the evaluation sessions and debriefing after the sessions are over will ensure that you allocate enough time for these important tasks.

The RITE method helps you get the most out of evaluation. RITE worked especially well when we were testing our paper prototypes because many of the things that confused the participants were easy to change and there was no point in keeping them the same. For example, after we found that participants overlooked our warnings, it made sense to write the warnings in a different position on the page and to test whether these changes will help. Thanks to RITE, we were able to greatly improve our designs with only 3-4 participants per evaluation.

If evaluating a working system, allocate at least an hour between participants. Changing software is usually more time-consuming than changing a paper prototype.

Test for as long as you are paying for. Pilot tests sometimes showed us that our tasks did not fill the 30-minute period that we would pay our participants for. We created more tasks so that the session would take at least 30 minutes, and we decided which tasks were optional if we were running out of time. Every minute with a participant can lead to discovering another problem or design idea, so concluding the session early would be a missed opportunity to discover something new and a waste of money.

Debrief right after UX tests. Reflecting on our results from UX evaluations right after the last session worked well because we still remembered most of our participants' comments and reactions. Debriefing early ensured that even Team members who could not take notes during the session could still contribute.

8. CONCLUSION

We learned that Scrum can successfully be used to guide user-centered software development in an undergraduate summer research project. We benefited most from Scrum's clear structure. Many of our "lessons learned" came from Sprint Retrospectives. Sprint Planning forced us to think about what each task entailed, and short, iterative cycles helped us maintain a sustainable pace. Integrating UX methods into our software development process was not that difficult, and it provided us with several benefits: it helped us to prioritize desirable features and choose among competing designs; it revealed usability problems prior to implementation; and it even uncovered some bugs. Our completed software is being used by the organization for which it was developed, and users are pleased with the results.

The project was not without its challenges. We had to significantly adjust Scrum since we did not have a committed Product Owner or a long time to work on the project. We also had to replan constantly, leave many Sprints incomplete, and even abort a Sprint, largely because we failed to accurately estimate many tasks and our one-week Sprints left little room for error. If Scrum is to be used in a learning environment, the Team needs to create ample task cards for learning and may wish to schedule longer Sprints despite having fewer Sprints.

We hope that our lessons learned will inform future undergraduate summer projects that aim to develop usable software.

9. ACKNOWLEDGMENTS

We thank the Grinnell Local Foods Co-op organizers and members for their cooperation and enthusiasm, our user study participants for their time and reflections, computer science summer research students and faculty for their insights, Grinnell College Writing Lab staff for proof-reading our paper, and Grinnell College for its financial support.

10. REFERENCES

[1] Abrahamsson, P., Salo, O., Ronkainen, J., Warsta, J.. Agile software development methods. Retrieved September 1, 2011 from http://www.vtt.fi/inf/pdf/publications/2002/P478.pdf

[2] ACM case study. UX design and agile: A natural fit? Communications of the ACM 54, 1 (January 2011), 54-60.

[3] Beyer, H. and Holtzblatt, K.. 1998. Contextual Design: Defining Customer-Centered Systems. San Diego, CA: Academic Press.

[4] Budwig, M., Jeong, S., Kelkar, K. When User Experience Meets Agile: A Case Study. 2009. In Extended Abstracts on Human Factors in Computing Systems (CHI EA 2009), Boston, MA, April 4-9, 2009, 3075-3083.

[5] Deemer, P. and Benefield, G. The Scrum Primer. Retrieved September 1, 2011 from http://www.rallydev.com/documents/scrumprimer.pdf

[6] Hart, D. 2010. Supporting agile processes in software engineering courses. Journal of Computing Sciences in Colleges, 25, 6, 136-143.

[7] Hartson, R. and Pyla, P. 2012. The UXBook: Process and guidelines for ensuring a quality user experience. San Francisco, CA: Morgan Kauffman.

[8] Kessler, R. and Dykman, N. 2007. Integrating traditional and agile processes in the classroom. In Proceedings of the Annual Technical Symposium on Computer Science Education (SIGCSE '07), Covington, KY, March 7-10, 2007, 312-316.

[9] Krug, S. 2010. Rocket Surgery Made Easy. Berkeley, CA: New Riders.

[10] Lu, B., and DeClue, T. 2011. Teaching agile methodology in a software engineering capstone course. Journal of Computing Sciences in Colleges, 26, 5, 293-299.

[11] Medlock, M.C., Wixon, D., Terrano, M., Romero, R., and Fulton, B. 2002. Using the RITE Method to improve products: a definition and a case study. Presented at the Usability Professionals Association, Orlando, FL, July 2002. Retrieved July 22, 2011 from http://www.microsoft.com/download/en/details.aspx?id=20940

[12] Rannikko, P. User-Centered Design in Agile Software Development. Retrieved 1 September 2011 from http://www.pirkkarannikko.com/agile-ucd.html

[13] Rising, L., and Janoff, N. S. 2000. The Scrum software development process for small teams. IEEE Software (July/August 2000), 2-8.

[14] Rogers, S., Sharp, H., and Preece, J. 2011. Interaction Design: Beyond Human-Computer Interaction, 3/e. John Wiley & Sons.

[15] Scharff, C. and Verma, R. 2010. Scrum to support mobile application development projects in a just-in-time learning context. In Proceedings of the 2010 ICSE Workshop on Cooperative and Human Aspects of Software Engineering (CHASE '10), Cape Town, South Africa, May 2, 2010.

[16] Sherrell, L. B. and Robertson, J. J. 2006. Pair programming and agile software development: Experiences in a college setting. Journal of Computing Sciences in Colleges, 22, 2, 145-153

Using WReSTT in SE Courses: An Empirical Study

Peter J. Clarke, Jairo Pava, Debra Davis and Frank Hernandez
School of Computing and Information Sciences
Florida International University
Miami, FL 33199, USA
{clarkep,jpava001,dledavis,fhern006}@cis.fiu.edu

Tariq M. King
Department of Computer Science
North Dakota State University
Fargo, ND 58108, USA
tariq.king@ndsu.edu

ABSTRACT

There continues to be a lack of adequate training for students in software testing techniques and tools at most academic institutions. Several educators and researchers have investigated innovative approaches that integrate testing into programming and software engineering (SE) courses with some success. The main problems are getting other educators to adopt their approaches and ensuring students continue to use the techniques they learned in previous courses.

In this paper we present a study that evaluates a non-intrusive approach to integrating software testing techniques and tools in SE courses. The study uses a *Web-Based Repository of Software Testing Tools* (WReSTT) that contains tutorials on software testing concepts and tools. The results of the study show that (1) students who use WReSTT in the classroom can improve their understanding and use of testing techniques and tools, (2) students find WReSTT a useful learning resource, and (3) the collaborative learning environment motivates students to complete assignments.

Categories and Subject Descriptors

K.3.2 [**Computer and Information Science Education**]: Miscellaneous

General Terms

Experimentation

Keywords

Software Testing, Unit testing, Repository, Collaborative Learning

1. INTRODUCTION

Integrating software testing in the curricula of many undergraduate computer science (CS) and information technology (IT) programs continues to be challenge. Although testing is one of the major approaches used to produce quality software [3], students get little or no training in the use of adequate testing techniques and tools. Several educators have investigated the integration of testing in CS1 and CS2 courses with success [5, 6, 7, 11] using various innovative techniques. However, anecdotal evidence suggests that subsequent courses in the curricula do not enforce the testing approaches taught in the earlier courses. This is one of the main reasons why we have elected to use a non-intrusive approach to integrating software testing techniques and tools in SE and upper-level programming courses.

There have also been several attempts to improve the testing content in the courses later in the curricula [10, 12, 13, 15]. This is of particular importance since software engineering and computer programming are expected to be two of the fastest growing occupations in the USA[1]. Although more academic institutions are offering software engineering (SE) courses, a great deal more needs to be done in order to adequately expose students to software testing and associated tools [14]. Using a non-intrusive approach to integrating software testing and testing tools into SE courses significantly reduces the need for the instructor to change the existing syllabus, assignments or projects. We expect our approach will lead to wider adoption of the use of testing tools in SE and upper-level programming courses.

The work presented in this paper builds on the work by Clarke et al. [1, 2] on the *Web-Based Repository of Software Testing Tools* - (WReSTT), an online repository of learning resources, to support software testing pedagogy. The initial presentation [1] describes the first version (V1) of WReSTT which primarily contains tutorials on how to setup and use software testing tools. Based on student feedback from WReSTT V1, a second version (V2) of WReSTT, was developed using a more user-friendly interface and included a component that utilized collaborative learning techniques [2]. Results from previous preliminary studies were used to guide the development of WReSTT V2.

In this paper we describe the recent improvements to WReSTT and the results of the first comprehensive study on the impact WReSTT has on students' conceptual understanding and use of software testing techniques and tools. The main contributions of the paper are as follows:

1. Extensions of WReSTT, specifically the instructors' and administrators' interface for course management.
2. Results of a study to show the: (1) impact WReSTT has on students' knowledge of software testing concepts and tools; (2) usability of WReSTT as a learning resource; and (3) impact the collaborative learning

Permission to make digital or hard copies of all or part of this work for personal or classroom use is granted without fee provided that copies are not made or distributed for profit or commercial advantage and that copies bear this notice and the full citation on the first page. To copy otherwise, to republish, to post on servers or to redistribute to lists, requires prior specific permission and/or a fee.
SIGCSE'12, February 29–March 3, 2012, Raleigh, North Carolina, USA.
Copyright 2012 ACM 978-1-4503-1098-7/12/02 ...$10.00.

[1]http://www.bls.gov/oco/ocos303.htm#outlook

environment has on motivating students to complete tasks.

The remainder of the paper is organized as follows. Section 2 presents the work most closely related to studies on using online resources in software testing pedagogy. Section 3 presents a brief overview of WReSTT and recent updates. Section 4 describes the study and we conclude in Section 5.

2. RELATED WORK

There are several online resources to support teaching and learning software testing concepts, skills, and other aspects of SE course curricula. In this section, we provide information on other web-based software testing learning repositories and pedagogical approaches being used to integrate testing in SE and CS programming courses.

2.1 Online Resources

The Software Quality Engineering Research Group (SoftQual) at the University of Calgary has developed lab courseware that seeks to teach students practical software testing skills [10]. The SoftQual repository [20] is freely available online, and consists of several labs on various testing topics. In each lab, students are introduced to the objectives and given instructions that familiarize them with the activity to be performed [10]. Tools used to support the SoftQual labs include Bugzilla, JUnit, CodeCover, CodeLipse, Rational Functional Tester, and MuClipse [10, 20].

WebIDE [23] is a web-based development environment that seeks to introduce SE best practices at an early stage in a student's educational career. The current version of the tool focuses on Test-Driven Learning (TDL) through small iterative examples. Users can browse labs by programming language (C, Java). The WebIDE environment incorporates a lockstep mechanism that requires students to write examples and tests before solutions [6, 23]. Instructors can also write their own labs according to an SE approach of choice, build custom evaluators, and provide detailed error messages to students.

The Repository for Open Software Education (ROSE) [17] is an education-friendly, open-source repository designed for SE courses. Although the repository is general-purpose, it provides details on the test-related artifacts associated with the projects. These details include the availability and specific format of automated unit and acceptance tests, as well as the inclusion of test plans and requirements documentation [15, 17]. Other online resources are described by Clarke et al. [2].

There are some similarities between WReSTT and the aforementioned repositories, however the differences are: (1) WReSTT focuses on tutorials for testing tools, and (2) WReSTT supports a collaborative learning model where students perform team activities and obtain virtual points in a social networking-like environment.

2.2 Studies

Garousi [10] discusses the experience of using the SoftQual Testing Lab Courseware [20] in a fourth-year undergraduate Software Reliability and Testing Course. The class consisted of 27 students, and there was a single TA to help the instructor with grading the students' lab solutions. Garousi [10] states that the students found the lab exercises very useful and beneficial for learning. Students' comments on each lab are also documented in the experience report, and provide evidence that the SoftQual testing labs are effective for teaching software testing skills.

Dvornik [6] performed a pilot study on using WebIDE in two sections of a CS0 course, where the topic was Android Development. The following hypothesis was examined in the study: Students using WebIDE will perform better on programming tasks than those using the traditional static labs. Students were randomly assigned to control and experimental (WebIDE) groups and validation was performed to ensure that the programming experience of each group was equivalent. The results of the study showed that: (1) students were more likely to successfully complete their Android application with WebIDE than with a traditional development environment; and (2) among students with prior programming experience, students who used WebIDE wrote better automated unit tests than those who did not use WebIDE.

Meneely et al. [15] reported their lessons learned from integrating some project artifacts available in ROSE into an undergraduate SE course. The course included a 2-hour lab session once a week to provide students with hands-on experience through tutorials and other teaching activities. Use of the iTrust project [18] was successful, and the authors emphasized that the value of ROSE is in alleviating the difficulty of finding these types of education-friendly open-source projects for use in SE courses.

Clarke et el. [1, 2] preformed two preliminary studies related to the two implementations of WReSTT (V1 and V2). The first study [1] reported on attempts to integrate the use of testing tools into CS2 and SE courses using a non-intrusive approach. This study provided information that WReSTT V1 would have a greater impact on student learning in SE courses than in CS2 courses. In the CS2 course the instructor would have to change his/her syllabus and labs in order for students to participate in WreSTT V1. The results of the second study [2], although preliminary, showed that WReSTT V2 had an impact of team work and students' understanding on testing and testing tools.

3. WRESTT

In this section we provide a more detailed overview of WReSTT and describe recent updates made to improve the course management component.

3.1 Overview of WReSTT

As previously stated, WReSTT [24] provides students access to learning resources to support their pedagogical needs in the area of software testing. WReSTT V1 [1] initially contained mainly testing tool tutorials. These tutorials include: *JUnit* [9] - a unit testing framework, *SWAT* [22] - Simple Web Automation Toolkit, and *Cobertura* [4] - a code coverage tool, among others. Clarke et al. [1] provide a more complete description of WReSTT V1.

WReSTT V2 was developed to support collaborative learning by allowing students to work together in teams and earn virtual points. Unlike WReSTT V1, V2 includes tutorials and quizzes on the core concepts of software testing and no tutorials on testing tools. WReSTT V2 allows students to be grouped into virtual learning teams, which can then compete for points based on the collaborative completion of quizzes and other knowledge assessment tasks. Points translate to in-class extra credit at the discretion of the course instructor. In addition, the student interface was redesigned

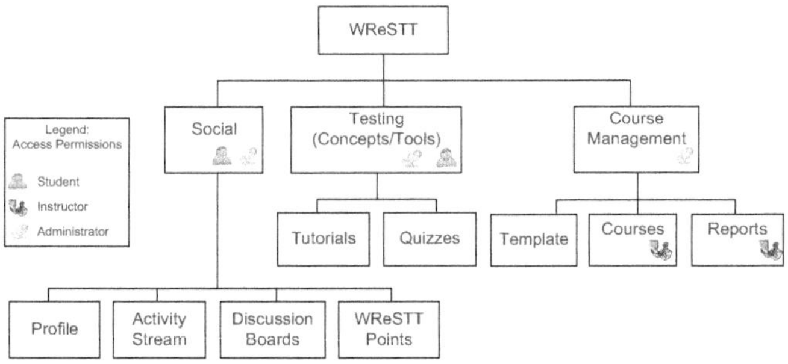

Figure 1: Partial block diagram of WReSTT V2.

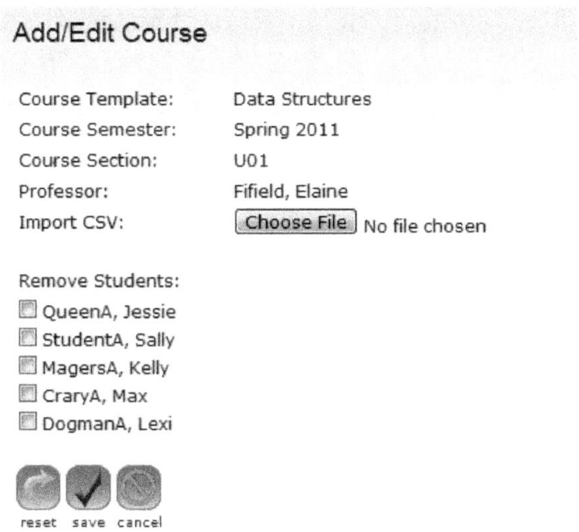

Figure 2: Instructor's interface to edit course.

to provide students with the look and feel of a social networking application e.g., Facebook [8]. The social aspect of WReSTT V2 provides students with the ability to create a profile, monitor the learning progress of classmates, post comments to the discussion boards, and identify which students have acquired the most points. The partial block diagram in Figure 1 shows the social and testing components of WReSTT V2.

3.2 Course Management

During the 2011 spring semester a team of students in the Senior Project class worked on improving the features in WReSTT V2. The project team was led by *Jairo Pava* (second author of this paper) and two other students *Dionny Santiago* and *Yesenia Sosa*. The main objectives of the project were to (1) develop the functionality for an administrator to create and manage courses (2) create an interface for instructors to upload and manage students in their classes, and (3) to test the new and existing functionality of WReSTT V2. The new course management component of WReSTT V2 is shown on the right of Figure 1. The legend on the left shows the access permissions for each user. For example, the instructor can access individual courses and the reports for those courses. Note that the access permissions for a block are used in its sub-blocks in addition to any new permissions.

The course management component provides an administrator with the ability to create course templates which can then be used to assign an instructor to a course. Once an instructor is assigned a course, that instructor can upload students into the course using a comma separated value (csv) file, the interface is shown in Figure 2. After uploading the course roster the instructor can then assign students to the various virtual teams. During the course, the instructor can access statistics such as the time spent on WReSTT, time spent per tutorial, and time spent per quiz. The instructor can also download the number of virtual points per student for the semester.

4. EMPIRICAL STUDY

In this section we present the various components of the study including the objectives, the methods used, the results and a discussion of the results. The results of the study were based on data collected using a pre/posttest and a student survey.

4.1 Objectives of Sudy

Most of the work published on WReSTT included preliminary or informal studies on the impact WReSTT has on students in SE and programming classes. This is the first study that uses the appropriate statistical methods to determine how beneficial it is to use WReSTT in SE courses. The objectives of this study are as follows:

Objective 1: Determine if the use of the resources in WReSTT improve the students' knowledge of software testing and their knowledge of software testing tools.

Objective 2: Determine whether students find WReSTT a useful and easy to use learning resource.

Objective 3: Determine if the use of a collaborative learning environment in WReSTT motivates students to complete the assigned tasks.

4.2 Methods

Sample: The students who participated in the study were recruited from the Spring and Summer 2011 *CEN 4010 Software Engineering I* courses at Florida International University. The groups were taught by two different instructors following the same syllabus. A total of 48 subjects (23 from the Spring semester and 25 from the Summer semester) participated in the study. Students from the Spring semester were assigned to the control group and students from the Summer semester were the treatment group.

Measurement: Two instruments, a pre/posttest (test) and survey, were used to collect the data for the study. Test instruments given to both the Spring and Summer classes were used to measure the students' knowledge of testing concepts, online software testing resources and testing tools. The test instrument is shown in Appendix A and consists of eight questions. Questions 1 and 2 focused on the objective of program testing and the use of testing techniques to create input values to test a simple method. Questions 3 and 4 focused on the students' knowledge and proficiency in using software testing tools. Questions 5 and 6 were used to determine if the students were aware of online testing resources and the type of learning materials that are available in these resources. Questions 7 and 8 addressed the importance of testing in programming assignments.

The survey instrument consists of thirty questions divided into five sections. Section 1 consisted of one question to de-

Q	Overall Reaction to Websites	N	V1 M (SD)	V2 M (SD)
2	Overall, I am satisfied with how easy it is to use the website	24	3.75 (1.1)	4.17 (0.9)
3	It is simple to use the website	24	3.71 (1.0)	4.04 (1.0)
4	I feel comfortable using the website	24	3.75 (1.0)	4.13 (0.8)
5	It was easy to learn to use the website	23	3.91 (1.0)	4.17 (1.0)
6	I believe I became productive quickly using the website.	23	3.83 (0.9)	3.87 (1.1)
7	The information (such as online help, on-page messages, and other documentation) provided with the web site is clear	22	3.59 (1.0)	3.86 (1.0)
8	It is easy to find the information I need	23	3.61 (1.0)	3.50 (0.8)
9	The information is effective in helping me complete the tasks and scenarios	23	3.83 (1.0)	4.00 (1.0)
10	The interface of the website is pleasant	24	3.54 (1.2)	4.17 (1.1)
11	I like using the interface of this website	24	3.42 (1.1)	3.96 (1.2)
12	The website has all the functions and capabilities I expect it to have	24	3.38 (1.0)	3.63 (1.2)
13	I believe that the website helped me earn a better grade	23	3.70 (0.9)	3.92 (.09)
14	I would recommend the website to fellow students	24	3.79 (0.9)	4.17 (0.9)
15	Overall I am satisfied with the website	24	3.63 (0.8)	4.13 (0.9)

Table 1: Students' mean scores (standard deviations) in Section 2 of the survey measuring their overall reactions to WReSTT versions 1 and 2.

termine if the students knew of any other online resource besides WReSTT. Section 2 focused on comparing the students' experiences with using WReSTT V1 and WReSTT V2 and consisted of 14 questions (Q2 - Q15), see Table 1. Section 3 consisted of 6 questions (Q16 - Q21) that focused on testing related questions in the context of using WReSTT, see Table 2. Section 4 focused on collaborative learning in the context of WReSTT V2 and consisted of 5 questions (Q22 - Q26), see Table 3. The questions in Section 2 of the survey were adapted from Tullis and Albert [21, pg. 140]. The following Likert scale was used in the survey: *1 = Strongly Disagree, 2 = Disagree, 3 = Neither agree nor Disagree, 4 = Agree, 5 = Strongly Agree.*

Design: The pre/posttest component of the study was conducted on two different groups from two different semesters (Spring and Summer). The pretest was administered prior to the testing part of the CEN 4010 course, i.e., prior to week 8 of the semester, and the posttest was administered at the end of the semester. The students were advised that the pre/posttests were optional and would not impact their grades.

The survey was administered only to the CEN 4010 group at the end of the Summer 2011 semester. The students participating in the study were required to register on WReSTT V1 prior to week 8 of the semester. The instructor then registered the students on WReSTT V2 in week 10 and assigned them to virtual teams, which were the same teams they were assigned to for the course project. The students were given two weeks to become familiar with WReSTT V1 before they received access to V2. Prior to taking the survey, the students were made aware of the virtual points they earned by participating in the activities for WReSTT V2.

Q	Testing Related Questions	N	M (SD)
16	The tutorials in WReSTT helped me to better understand testing concepts	24	4.33 (0.7)
17	The tutorials in WReSTT helped me to better understand how to use unit testing tools.	24	4.17 (0.7)
18	The tutorials in WReSTT helped me to better understand how to use code coverage testing tools.	24	3.54 (1.0)
19	The tutorials in WReSTT helped me to better understand how to use functional testing tools.	21	3.33 (1.0)
20	The number of tutorials in WReSTT is adequate	24	4.33 (1.0)
21	I would have used testing tools in my project if WReSTT did not exist.	23	2.91 (1.2)

Table 2: Students' mean scores (standard deviations) in Section 3 of the survey measuring perception of the usefulness of testing tutorials in WReSTT.

Q	Collaborative Learning Related Questions	N	M (SD)
22	The use of virtual points in WReSTT V2 encouraged me to visit the website and complete the tasks	24	4.67 (0.8)
23	The use of virtual points in WReSTT V2 encouraged my team to visit the website and complete the tasks	24	4.71 (0.6)
24	The event stream showing the activities of the other members in the class encouraged me to complete my tasks in WReSTT V2	24	4.38 (0.9)
25	The event stream showing the activities of the other members in the class encouraged my team to complete my tasks in WReSTT V2	24	4.50 (0.8)
26	Our team devised a plan to get the maximum number of points in WReSTT V2.	23	3.96 (1.3)

Table 3: Students' mean scores (standard deviation) of the survey measuring usefulness of the collaborative learning environment in WReSTT

4.3 Results and Analysis

To evaluate the effects using WReSTT on students' knowledge and understanding software testing techniques and tools, students were administered a pretest, prior to software testing being covered in class, and a posttest at the end of each semester. For each assessment, students were given a score indicating their performance on the test. A 2 (semester) x 2 (test) ANOVA [16] revealed a main effect of the test ($F(1,46) = 13.56$, $p < .01$), with students performing better on the posttest ($M = 12.27$, $SD = 10.5$) than the pretest. ($M = 7.19$, $SD = 5.1$). Results also revealed a main effect of semester ($F(1,46) = 40.40$, $p < .01$), with students performing better in the Summer semester ($M = 13.78$, $SD = 7.5$) than the Spring semester. ($M = 5.33$, $SD = 4.9$).

Results also found a significant interaction between semes-

		Pre-test		Post-test	
Semester	N	Mean	SD	Mean	SD
Spring	23	6.22	4.1	4.43	5.6
Summer	25	8.08	6.3	19.48	8.7

Table 4: Students' mean scores and standard deviations on the software testing pre- and post-tests in the spring and summer semesters.

ter and test ($F(1,46) = 25.47$, $p < .01$). As can be seen in Table 4, students from the Summer term, but not the Spring term, tended to perform better on the posttest than the pretest. Follow-up analyses revealed a significant difference between pre/posttest scores in the Summer ($t(24) = -5.01$, $p < .01$), but not in the Spring.

There was an increase in the number of students that were able to identify different testing tools (Appendix A, Q. 4), in the Summer semester from 7/25 to 22/25, there was no change in the Spring semester, 5/23. In addition, during the project presentations at the end of the Summer semester every student team demonstrated the use of at least one testing tool. No student team in the Spring semester demonstrated the use of any testing tool. There was also an increase in the number of students that were able to apply testing techniques (Appendix A, Q. 2) in the Summer semester from 1 to 12, versus the Spring semester from 1 to 3.

Students in the experimental group (Summer semester) were additionally administered a survey at the end of the semester designed to assess their perception of the ease of use and usefulness of WReSTT. A total of 24 students participated in the survey. In Section 1 of the survey 28% of students (N=18) indicated that they had previously used a learning resource other than WReSTT to learn about software testing, while 72% indicated no use of additional resources. Students' overall reactions to both versions of WReSTT were positive, with mean scores on questions in Section 2 of the survey above 3.38 for V1 of the website and above 3.50 for V2. Mean scores for each question in Section 2 for both versions can be found in Table 1.

To compare student reactions to WReSTT V1 and V2, students' responses to each question in Section 2 were analyzed using the Wilcoxon Signed-Ranks Test [19]. Results revealed, for those students whose responses varied, a significant difference between the students' reactions to the two versions of the website for questions 2 ($z=-2.23$, $p<.05$), 4 ($z=-2.07$, $p<.05$), 10 ($z=-2.82$, $p<.01$), 11 ($z=-2.70$, $p<.01$), and 15 ($z=-2.47$, $p<.01$), where students indicated a preference for WReSTT V2 over V1.

Students' perceptions of the usefulness of the tutorials available in WReSTT were also positive, with mean scores above 3.30 for all questions in Section 3. Students' responses to question 21, asking whether they would have used testing tools if WReSTT had not existed, indicated that many would not ($M = 2.91$, $SD = 1.2$). Mean scores for each question in Section 3 can be found in Table 2. Students further indicated that the use of a collaborative learning environment in WReSTT was a motivating factor in their learning, with mean scores above 3.95 on questions 22 through 25 in Section 3 of the survey, see Table 3.

4.4 Discussion

Objective 1. Results indicate that the use of WReSTT as a teaching tool for students learning software testing can significantly improve their understanding and use of software testing techniques and tools. Students in the Summer semester, who used WReSTT, performed significantly better on their post-tests than students in the Spring semester, who did not use WReSTT. There was no significant difference between their pre-test scores, indicating that this difference was not due to differences in students' knowledge before taking the course or the semester. One confounding variable, however, is the possible effect of the instructor. The Spring and Summer courses were taught by different instructors, which may have influenced the results. We plan to repeat the study using the same instructor for the control and treatment groups.

Objective 2. Results indicate that students do find WReSTT a useful resource for learning software testing techniques and tools. Specifically, students indicated that the tutorials in WReSTT helped them understand both software testing concepts and tools, and that there are a sufficient number of tutorials in WReSTT. Students also indicated that both versions of WReSTT helped them complete course tasks and earn a better grade in the class. Regarding ease of use, students indicated that both versions of WReSTT are easy to use and pleasant, and they would recommend use of the sites to other students.

Objective 3. Results indicate that students do find that the use of a collaborative learning environment in WReSTT motivates them to complete assignments. Specifically, students reported that the use of virtual points and event streaming encouraged them and their fellow team members to complete tasks in WReSTT.

5. CONCLUDING REMARKS

In this paper we described the recent updates made to the *Web-Based Repository of Software Testing Tools* (WReSTT) and the results from the first comprehensive study to determine the impact WReSTT has on testing pedagogy. The study was performed using two software engineering (SE) classes, Spring and Summer 2011. The results showed that (1) the use of WReSTT as a teaching tool can significantly improve the students' understanding and use of software testing techniques and tools; (2) students find WReSTT as a useful learning resource for learning software testing techniques and tools; and (3) students find using WReSTT as a collaborative learning environment motivates them to complete assignments. We plan to perform additional studies at different academic institutions to further validate our results.

6. ACKNOWLEDGMENTS

This work was supported in part by the National Science Foundation under grants DUE-0736833 (FIU) and DUE-0736771 (FAMU). We would like to thank Dionny Santiago and Yesenia Sosa for their work on WReSTT V2. We also appreciate the insightful comments provided by the reviewers on how to improve the paper.

7. REFERENCES

[1] P. J. Clarke, A. A. Allen, T. M. King, E. L. Jones, and P. Natesan. Using a web-based repository to integrate testing tools into programming courses. In *Proceedings of the ACM OOPSLA 2010 Companion*, SPLASH '10, pages 193–200, New York, NY, USA, 2010. ACM.

[2] P. J. Clarke, J. Pava, Y. Wu, and T. M. King. Collaborative web-based learning of testing tools in se courses. In *Proceedings of the 42nd SIGCSE Conference*, pages 147–152, New York, NY, USA, 2011. ACM.

[3] CNSS. Software 2015: A national software strategy to ensure u.s. security and competitiveness. Technical report, Center for National Software Studies, 2005.

[4] Cobertura Team. Cobertura, May 2010. `http://cobertura.sourceforge.net/`.

[5] C. Desai, D. S. Janzen, and J. Clements. Implications of integrating test-driven development into cs1/cs2 curricula. *SIGCSE Bull.*, 41(1):148–152, 2009.

[6] T. Dvornik, D. Janzen, J. Clements, and O. Dekhtyar. Supporting introductory test-driven labs with WebIDE. In *In Proceedings of the 24th IEEE-CS CSEET Conference*, pages 51 –60, may 2011.

[7] S. H. Edwards. Using software testing to move students from trial-and-error to reflection-in-action. In *Proceedings of the 35th SIGCSE Conference*, pages 26–30, New York, NY, USA, 2004. ACM.

[8] Facebook Team. Facebook, 2011. `http://www.facebook.com/`.

[9] E. Gamma and K. Beck. JUnit, 2008. `http://www.junit.org/`.

[10] V. Garousi. An open modern software testing laboratory courseware - an experience report. In *In Proceedings of the 23rd IEEE CSEET Conference*, pages 177 –184, March 2010.

[11] D. S. Janzen and H. Saiedian. Test-driven learning: intrinsic integration of testing into the cs/se curriculum. *SIGCSE Bull.*, 38(1):254–258, 2006.

[12] E. L. Jones. Integrating testing into the curriculum — arsenic in small doses. *SIGCSE Bull.*, 33(1):337–341, 2001.

[13] C. Kaner. Center for software testing education and research (CSTER), 2010. `http://www.testingeducation.org/`.

[14] T. C. Lethbridge, J. Diaz-Herrera, R. J. J. LeBlanc, and J. B. Thompson. Improving software practice through education: Challenges and future trends. In *FOSE '07: 2007 Future of Software Engineering*, pages 12–28, Washington, DC, USA, 2007. IEEE Computer Society.

[15] A. Meneely, L. Williams, and E. F. Gehringer. Rose: a repository of education-friendly open-source projects. In *In Proceedings of the 13th ITiCSE Conference*, ITiCSE '08, pages 7–11, New York, NY, USA, 2008. ACM.

[16] J. Neter, W. Wasserman, and M. H. Kutner. *Applied linear statistical models*. Irwin Press, Boston, 1990.

[17] Realsearch Group. ROSE: Repository for Open Software Education, 2011. `http://realsearchgroup.com/rose/`.

[18] Realsearch Research Group. iTrust, 2011. `http://agile.csc.ncsu.edu/iTrust/`.

[19] S. Siegel and N. J. Castellan. *Nonparametric Statistics for the Behavioral Sciences*. McGraw-Hill, New York, second edition, 1988.

[20] Software Quality Engineering Research Group (SoftQual). SoftQual Repository of Software Testing Laboratory Courseware, 2011. `http://www.softqual.ucalgary.ca/projects/testing_labs/`.

[21] T. Tullis and B. Albert. *Measuring the User Experience: Collecting, Analyzing, and Presenting Usability Metrics*. Elsevier: Morgan Kaufmann, 2008.

[22] Ultimate Software. SWAT, 2009. `http://sourceforge.net/projects/ulti-swat/`.

[23] WebIDE Development Team. WebIDE Labs, 2011. `http://web-ide.org`.

[24] WReSTT Team. Web-based Repository for Software Testing Tools, 2010. `http://wrestt.cis.fiu.edu/`.

APPENDIX

A. PRETEST/POSTTEST

This test will NOT impact your course grade.

ID Number (DO NOT use your name):

1. What is the main objective of program testing?

2.(a) Identify all the testing techniques you have used to create test cases:

(b) Write test cases to test the code provided below. Identify the testing technique used to generate the test case.

```
//Method to withdraw money from a bank account
//The following variables are defined as follows:
//requiredMin = 50.0 and balance = 100;
public void withdraw (double amount) {
  if ((balance - amount) < requiredMin)
   System.out.println("Insufficient funds");
  else
   balance = balance - amount;}
```

Input Value	Expected Output Values			Testing Technique
amount	amount	balance	requiredMin	

3. Have you ever used tools to support testing of programs? Circle your answer: Yes No

4. If you have answered "Yes" to Question (3), answer the following questions:

a. List the names of the tools you have used:

b. List one tool in each of the following categories that you have used and indicate your level of proficiency corresponding to each tool on a scale of 1 - 5 with, *1 = barely competent* and *5 = extremely proficient*:

	Category	*Tool(s)*	*Proficiency*
i	Unit Testing		
ii	Functional Testing		
iii	Code Coverage		

5. Do you know of any online resources that provide information on software testing? Yes No

6. If you have answered "Yes" to Question (5), answer the following questions:

a. State the names of online resources.

b. State the type of materials (notes, lab exercises, tutorials etc.) found at each resource listed above.

7. How beneficial do you think it is to use tools to support testing of your programming assignments? Use a scale of 1 - 5 with *1 = Not beneficial* and *5 = Extremely beneficial*

8. If you answered 2 or above to Question (7), state one reason for your answer.

Understanding the Tenets of Agile Software Engineering: Lecturing, Exploration and Critical Thinking

Shvetha Soundararajan, Amine Chigani and James D. Arthur
Department of Computer Science
Virginia Tech
Blacksburg, VA 24061, USA
{shvetha, achigani, arthur}@vt.edu

ABSTRACT
The use of agile principles and practices in software development is becoming a powerful force in today's workplace. In our quest to develop better products, therefore, it is imperative that we strive to learn and understand the application of agile methods, principles and techniques to the software development enterprise. Unfortunately, in many educational institutions, courses and projects that emphasize agile software development are minimal. At best, students have only limited exposure to the agile philosophy, principles and practices at the graduate and undergraduate levels of education. In an effort to address this concern, we offered an advanced graduate-level course entitled "Agile Software Engineering" in the Department of Computer Science at Virginia Tech. The primary objectives of the course were to introduce the values, principles and practices underlying the agile philosophy, and to do so in an atmosphere that encourages debate and critical thinking. The course was designed around three central components: (1) teaching the essentials of how one develops a product within an agile framework, (2) having invited talks by notable industry experts, and (3) having students present and discuss current agile research topics and issues. This paper describes our experiences during the offering of that course, and in particular, the unique perspectives of the class instructor, the teaching assistant and a student who was enrolled in the course.

Categories and Subject Descriptors
D.2 [**Software Engineering**], K.3.2 [**Computer Science Education**]: Computer and Information Science Education – *computer science education*

General Terms
Design, Documentation, Management, Theory

Keywords
Agile Instruction and Education, Exploring Agile Tenets, Agile Software Development, Agile Applicability, Software Engineering Education, Pedagogy

Permission to make digital or hard copies of all or part of this work for personal or classroom use is granted without fee provided that copies are not made or distributed for profit or commercial advantage and that copies bear this notice and the full citation on the first page. To copy otherwise, or republish, to post on servers or to redistribute to lists, requires prior specific permission and/or a fee.
SIGCSE'12, February 29–March 3, 2012, Raleigh, North Carolina, USA.
Copyright 2012 ACM 978-1-4503-1098-7/12/02...$10.00.

1. INTRODUCTION
The software development process systematically begins by identifying, specifying and baselining user requirements and then proceeds to the architecting, design, implementation, testing and maintenance phases. Traditional software development methodologies such as the Waterfall model [1] and the Spiral model [2] have helped reduce the chaotic state of software development by focusing on extensive planning, comprehensive documentation and gathering and specifying user requirements upfront. In the last two decades, however, many development teams have realized that these traditional approaches to software development are not suitable for all contexts [3, 4]. The traditional approaches, which are process-centric, are found to be inadequate and expensive for development efforts that have to address rapidly changing requirements. Government and industry stakeholders are increasingly required to innovate and respond to emerging needs. Hence, requirements are subjected to constant change in the form of refining existing requirements or adding new ones [5, 6]. This phenomenon is called *requirements drift* [5, 6]. Conventional methodologies attempt to foresee requirements and create a system architecture upfront in order to accommodate current and future needs. However, when previously unidentified requirements surface, the baselined system architecture may no longer accommodate the implementation of those requirements [7]. The cost of modifying the architecture, and in turn the code, in order to accommodate requirements identified late during the development lifecycle is substantial [2].

To accommodate change and address uncertainty, teams involved in software development are embracing the notion of agility [6]. Currently, the number of organizations adopting agile methods is increasing - some of the reasons being *(1) the ability to accommodate change throughout the development lifecycle, (2) improved quality, (3) greater return on investment, (4) shorter development periods, (5) improved customer satisfaction, (6) better team morale, (7) reduced waste* and *(8) better predictability* [7-10]. Therefore, it is essential for software engineers to understand the tenets of the agile philosophy.

We, the members of the Department of Computer Science at Virginia Tech, are dedicated to grooming the next generation of Software Engineers. Hence, the department offers courses representing core areas in Software Engineering and current research foci to better prepare our students for success in the Software Engineering arena. With agile software development becoming more widely used, we realize that instruction and exploration of agile tenets within an academic setting is essential. Since it is easier to propose special-topic courses at the graduate-level, we offered an advanced graduate-level course entitled "Agile Software Engineering."

1.1. Course Objectives

Instruction and exploration are integral components of an effective learning process. We designed our course, therefore, to place *equal importance* on both, and in particular, while addressing the many facets of agile software development. The principal objectives that guided course development were:

1. To introduce the agile philosophy, values, principles and practices
2. To develop a firm understanding of what constitutes agility, and how and why it differs from conventional Software Engineering
3. To think critically about the benefits and limitations in application of agile principles and practices.

The first objective focuses on the motivation, rationale and fundamentals underlying the agile approach. The second objective emphasizes a more in-depth study of agility and the rudiments of critical thinking within an agile framework. Finally, the third objective stresses exploration and reasoning about the *raison d'être* of the agile approach to software development.

1.2. Course Design

The advanced graduate-level Agile Software Engineering course was designed for graduate students who already understood conventional software engineering models and practices. To our delight, more than half of the students had been or were currently working in industry. The course was designed around three principal components: (1) the essentials of how one develops a product within an agile framework, (2) in-class presentations by industry experts, and (3) presentations by students to showcase current research topics and issues. The former two components focused more on instruction and the latter on exploration. During all three of the above, discussion, questions and debate were *highly encouraged.* In addition to the presentations, the students were also assigned research papers and in-class 'mini-exams.'

Table 1. Class Details

Pre-requisites	▪ Graduate–level Software Engineering Course or ▪ Graduate–level Software Design and Quality Course or ▪ Comparable Software Engineering experience	
Number of students at the doctoral and masters degree level	Doctoral 8	Masters 2
Number of students with industry work experience	7	
Number of students with prior experience in agile development	2	
Guiding Manuscript	"Agile Software Development Methods: Review and Analysis", Pekka Abrahamsson, Outi Salo, Jussi Ronkainen & Juhani Warsta, ESPOO 2002, VTT Pub	

Table 1 outlines additional course details, e.g., pre-requisites, enrollment, background knowledge of the students, and other details.

We realize that for students to fully understand and appreciate the concepts of Agile Software Engineering, they should apply agile methods. In a classroom setting, this can be achieved to some extent by involving the students in a semester-long project. However, due to time constraints, we did not include a project component to this course. We envision the future offerings of this course will include a semester-long project component.

The remainder of this paper is organized as follows. Section 2 provides an overview of experiences from the perspectives of the instructor, the teaching assistant and a student who took the course. Section 3 summarizes students' responses to prominent issues that emerged during class discussions. To encourage critical thinking and exploration, student responses had to be prepared in the form of research papers. In Section 4, we present the results from the end-semester course evaluation surveys. Finally, Section 5 summarizes our efforts and observations.

2. EXPERIENCES

In this section, we have included the experiences of the course staff (the instructor and the teaching assistant) and a student who participated in the course. These experiences, recorded from three different perspectives, discuss the extent to which the course objectives were achieved and outline the lessons learned.

2.1. Instructor's Perspective

The overarching objective of the course was to introduce the values, principles and practices underlying the agile philosophy, and to do so in an atmosphere that encourages debate and critical thinking.

The Basics: The goal for the initial portion of the course was to introduce the students to the agile tenets. More specifically, we wanted the student to (a) develop an understanding of what comprised the agile philosophy and software development approach, (b) gain an appreciation as to why it is needed, and (c) evolve a questioning mindset that encouraged critical thinking. The latter was particularly important because we wanted the students to develop their own perceptions as to how agile differed from the more conventional software development models and processes. We began by introducing the Agile Manifesto [11] and discussing the values it espoused. From this point, I provided presentations outlining Scrum [12], eXtreme Programming (XP) [12, 13] and Lean [14]. For each, the underlying principles, practices and activities were introduced. Throughout the presentations, questions were asked, and discussions ensued, that focused on comparisons among the methods, and on their similarities and differences with the more conventional development methodologies. To further immerse the students in the 'ways of agile,' each was required to identify, investigate and present an additional aspect of the agile software development approach. It is my opinion that while the presentations provided foundational knowledge, the discussions, debates, and student presentations were the tools that began cultivating their (the students) aptitude for critical thinking.

Invited Speakers: Three speakers from industry were invited to present and discuss their experiences with agile software development. The first speaker was Keith Lang who manages the development of Vanguard's Investment Product website. Of particular interest to the students was how they (the Vanguard Agile development teams) were able to have four concurrent agile development efforts, all of which were synchronized to produce a single product. Mr. Lang recounted his experiences in managing various software development efforts. The second speaker was Dr. Jason Lee who works for Meridium Corporation, and in particular, has helped integrate their agile practices with those practices fundamental to usability engineering [15]. A substantial amount of discussion revolved around how two seemingly independent processes could be integrated into a single set of complementary practices. The students were skeptical, but Dr. Lee was convincing. The third invited speaker was Dr. Ahmed Sidky, an Agile Consultant at TenPearls. Having consulted around the world, Dr. Sidky introduced the class to cultural issues and how they can and do impact the Agile Coaching process [16]. His presentation and insights provided a glimpse of agility rarely found in books or papers. Finally, we were fortunate to have Dr. Todd Stevens attend many class periods, and provide his comments on the topic '*de jour*.' Dr. Stevens, a Blacksburg resident, has worked with several agile teams, managing their agile development processes. Throughout the semester, he would provide a 'real world' perspective on issues and questions, and often challenged the students to think more critically.

From a pedagogical perspective, these people reinforced the theory of Agility through discussions of actual industry practices. The students expressed their appreciation of this fact in the many complimentary comments that followed.

Research Presentations: As a third component of the course, students were required to identify, present and critique published research papers focusing on some critical aspect of Agility. The Research Presentations helped expand the students' perspectives as to what are the important issues facing the agile community, and forced them (or provided them with the opportunity) to *analyze* current research efforts, *critique* the results, and then *defend* their assessment.

Research Papers: On a final note, throughout the semester, when (selected) questions arose for which there was no apparent answer, the students were asked to compose a 3-4 page research paper that responded to each question. Part of that task was to identify and cite supporting documents that confirmed their reasoning. This, too, was an activity intended to broaden each student's understanding of the agile philosophy, and to encourage critical thought.

2.2. Teaching Assistant's Perspective

I am a graduate student researcher in the field of Agile Software Engineering and I worked as the Teaching Assistant (TA) for the advanced graduate-level Agile Software Engineering course. My responsibilities as the TA included (1) instruction, (2) assisting with grading assignments, and (3) facilitating and leading class discussions.

The course was an excellent opportunity for me to hone my teaching skills. I delivered two lectures to (1) introduce the agile philosophy, its values and principles, and (2) provide an overview of some of the agile methods endorsed by the agile community. Additionally, I facilitated class discussions and offered insights and opinions about topics including, but not limited to, agile methods, current research trends and issues faced by the agile community.

I am a proponent of the agile philosophy. When I started my research in the field of agile software development nearly five years ago, I embraced the agile philosophy almost immediately. I expected the same from my fellow graduate students enrolled in the course. I was surprised to know that most of them were reluctant to accept the notion of agility. Though more than half of the number of students enrolled in the course had prior Software Engineering industry experience, only two of them had worked for organizations that had transitioned to an agile environment. This contributed significantly to their skepticism. For example, the students found the concept of minimal documentation hard to believe and accept. The class discussions at the beginning of the semester were almost confrontational. More than once, the whole class period was consumed by the discussions that would leave no time for the instructor to proceed with his topic for the day. As the semester progressed, however, the students began to appreciate and embrace the agile philosophy. I could observe that the discussions became more complimentary. The transition was reflected not only in the class discussions but also in their answers to questions in exams and assignments.

Dr. Ahmed Sidky was invited to present his experiences as an agile coach. During his presentation, he mentioned that the people of an organization ready to transition to agile are usually skeptical about the concept of agility to start with, and embrace the idea gradually. It was surprising to see the same trend in an academic setting.

My doctoral research involves assessing the collective 'goodness' of agile methods adopted by organizations [17]. We have developed an underlying structured framework to guide the assessment process. The design and construction of the framework revolves around the identification of agile objectives, principles that govern the achievement of those objectives, and practices that help implement those principles. Our discussions in class regarding Capability Maturity Model Integration (CMMI), the difficulties in applying it in an agile environment, the advantages and disadvantages of Capability Maturity Model (CMM) and CMMI with respect to agility, provided excellent insights and helped refine the design of the framework mentioned above. I presented my research to the class and received constructive feedback.

At Virginia Tech, students are required to evaluate their course instructors and teaching assistants at the end of each semester. An analysis of the student responses revealed that they found my insights valuable. What gives me greater pleasure than positive student evaluation results (outlined in Section 4) is that the students now embrace agility and have begun applying the agile philosophy in their work.

With the number of organizations transitioning to agile increasing, there is a need for agile education in colleges and universities. Courses such as these expose students to the concept of agility and prepare them to adopt and apply the agile philosophy in industry settings.

2.3. A Student's Perspective

The primary goal of taking the course was to learn the methods agile practitioners prescribe for developing software systems. As a doctoral student conducting research in architectures for network-centric systems of systems, which require process-oriented, plan-driven approaches in their development, I came into the course with two presumptions. First, I was doubtful about the ability of agile methods to scale to accommodate the needs of large-scale systems. Second, I was unsure how *agilists* claim to develop quality software without architecting for these qualities early on in the life cycle.

The experience from the course was both challenging and rewarding at the same time. The main challenge I faced consisted of my inability to reconcile my training and experience in conventional software engineering with the practices of agile methods. More specifically, one of the issues raised in many discussions in class was that of scalability. Being aware of the complexity of large-scale software development efforts, which is often characterized by multi-team, multi-system, and multi-year development aspects, it was problematic for me to see the applicability of agile practices such as small teams, non-emphasis on documentation and short life cycles in a large development effort.

In spite of this challenge, the experience in the course was stimulating in many ways. The course proved to be an excellent opportunity to widen my understanding and increase my appreciation of agile methods.

First, assignments were structured to engage our analytical thinking to explore the opportunities and the limitations of agile methods. They focused on wide areas of agile for which we prepared a short paper and a presentation to discuss our findings. This component of the course allowed me to reconcile my architecture experience with some of the agile practices and incorporate these new findings into my own work. This component of the course also encouraged me to write a position paper about agile and architecture that I presented in the Software Architecture Technology UserR Network (SATURN) Conference 2010 [18].

The second reason why this course was a successful experience is the fact that it changed my perspective about agile. In fact, I currently apply basic agile values and principles in conducting my own research work. Participating in this seminar made me understand that agile is a way of thinking rather than it is a set of practices. As a result, I have since become engaged within the architecture community in discussions about how we can bring the two domains together. Specifically, I advocate the use of four agile practices into architecture development. These practices include:

- User stories, which describe the functional capabilities that the system architecture must provide and which can be mapped to quality scenarios;
- Quality scenarios, which describe one or more quality characteristics of the system (e.g., maintainability, interoperability and usability);
- The "architecture wall" concept, which is literally the wall used to post and organize index cards and post-it notes describing the architecturally-relevant capabilities and their corresponding architectural blueprints; and
- Architectural refactoring, which refers to the way index cards and post-it notes are shifted around in a structured manner to ensure the integrity of the existing relationships among the user stories, among quality scenarios and between stories and quality scenarios.

Finally, my experience in this course gave me the chance to realize that, although practitioners from both sides of the fence (conventional and agile) see software development form different prisms, the two approaches can be complimentary. This is evidenced by the effect this course had on my own work, and by the emergence of several initiatives to reconcile between extreme interpretations of agile philosophy and traditional software development approaches.

The potential of agile methods is promising, as they have shown value and wide adoption in practice. Therefore, incorporating these methods in the computing curriculum, by offering courses such as this one, is fundamental to the success of next generation software engineering practitioners and researchers.

3. PROMOTING CRITICAL AND CREATIVE THINKING

As mentioned previously, class discussions formed an integral part of the course throughout the semester. The students were encouraged to critique agile methods, analyze their current state, discuss research issues and suggest solutions. During these discussions, some issues were brought to the forefront time and time again. These were important issues that the students knew were addressed in the conventional Software Engineering approaches. Therefore, the discussions were often about "*How are these issues addressed in the agile approach?*" In order to urge on the students' critical thinking, we selected three of the major issues and assigned them as research papers. The students were expected to write a short paper (3-4 page) addressing the issue. Critical thinking also enabled them to be creative in their solution approaches. In the following paragraphs, we discuss the assigned questions, the underlying issues, the students' thought process in outlining solutions and our observations.

Question 1: Government and contracting organizations expect agile organizations to meet the same Capability Maturity Model Integration (CMMI) [19] measurement standards as organizations employing a plan-driven development process. If we wanted a CMMI-like approach to measuring the capability of an agile organization [20], what Key Process Areas (KPAs) and measurement indicators would you define?

Issue: CMMI focuses on assessing an organization's process and process artifacts. On the other hand, agile Software Development places emphasis on assessing the working software or product.

Students' thought process: The students understood the essence of CMMI. They performed a comparative analysis of CMMI and the agile philosophy. Ways to strike a balance between the two were described.

Observations: We identified three approaches that the students suggested in order to nurture a symbiotic relationship between the agile philosophy and CMMI. They are outlined below:

- Identify KPAs from CMMI that are relevant to the agile environment, e.g., the Project Planning KPA. Modify the assessment criteria and the expected artifacts such that agility is not compromised.
- Attempting to force-fit agile to CMMI, or watering down CMMI to suit an agile environment, is not an effective solu-

tion. Develop a completely new set of KPAs that are modeled along the lines of the KPAs in CMMI, but that reflect the agile approach to Software Engineering.
- In analyzing the advantages and disadvantages of both CMMI and agile methods, it is imperative to develop a hybrid approach that provides the best of both worlds. More specifically, we should develop new KPAs and also modify existing KPAs that are suitable to an agile environment.

Question 2: How do we scale agile methods to fit larger scale systems development? Or more specifically, what are some of the issues that would have to be addressed to achieve scalability?

Issue: Agile methods were intended for small-scale systems.

Students' thought process: For larger scale systems, the students had a mental model of a conventional Software Engineering approach like the Waterfall model. They compared the agile approach to software engineering to the conventional approach and identified areas that they thought were crucial to scalability.

Observations: The students most often identified the need for comprehensive documentation, team size and system complexity as being at odds with existing agile practices. They also suggested ways to scale the identified factors.

Question 3: To what extent do agile methods address the maintenance activity?

Issue: Very little information is revealed concerning to what extent the agile Methodologies address the post-development maintenance activity.

Students' thought process: In conventional software engineering approaches, maintenance is portrayed as a downstream development activity. Some of the students perceived maintenance in this conventional sense. Others envisioned maintenance as a part of the agile development process itself.

Observations: The students focused primarily on the two approaches given below:
- Maintenance is integrated within the agile software development process. Certain artifacts developed during the process assists with maintenance within agile software development.
- Maintenance should be considered as a downstream development activity. After the product is developed, maintenance on that product should be supported.

4. ASSESSMENT

Students at Virginia Tech are requested to complete end semester course evaluation surveys to evaluate the courses, the course instructors and the teaching assistants. These surveys help course staff gauge the extent to which course objectives are met. In this section, we summarize the results for some of the questions from the surveys.

90% of the students enrolled in the course completed the surveys. The survey questions primarily involve providing descriptive answers or Likert scale measures.

We introduced the agile philosophy, the values and principles stated in the manifesto, and provided an overview of some of the agile methods endorsed by the agile community. These introductory lectures enabled the students to embrace the concept of agility and to realize that there are alternative ways of developing quality software, on time, within budget and of value to the customers. The students developed an understanding that they were no longer constrained by a conventional "waterfall-like" approach to developing software. We encouraged students to reason about how and why the agile software development paradigm differs from the conventional Software Engineering. When asked about the most valuable aspects of this course, one of the students responded by saying that "*it taught me to get rid of constraints*". Another student mentioned that the most valuable component of the course was "*learning about agile methods and comparing (it) to conventional Software Engineering*".

We recognize that agile philosophy is not the panacea for the issues that we face in the field of software development. We do question the suitability of agile methods for developing larger scale and mission and life critical systems. Hence, we wanted the students also to think critically about the benefits and limitations in applying the concept of agility. Class discussions and research paper assignments helped students hone their creativity and critical thinking. From the surveys, we determined that most students found the class discussions and the research paper assignments to be the most valuable components in this course.

All of the respondents indicated that their gains from the course pertaining to (1) knowledge of principles, theories and techniques, (2) logical thinking and problem solving ability, and (3) appreciation of the subject matter and the field, was average or greater than average. Figure 1 summarizes the results from the survey questions addressing course gains.

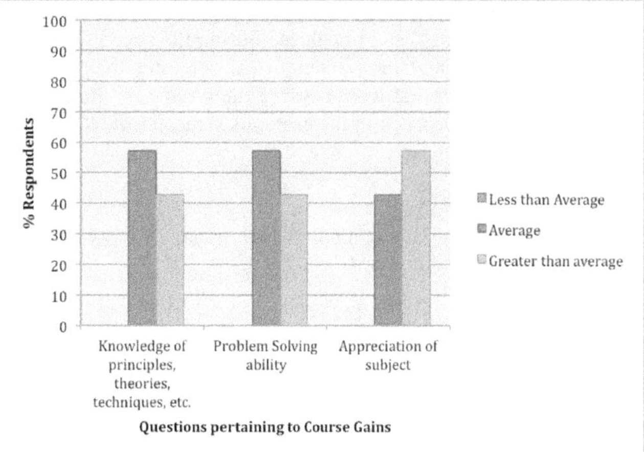

Figure 1. Summary of survey results for questions pertaining to course gains.

More than 70% of the students who completed the surveys had found the degree to which the subject matter was made stimulating or relevant to be "excellent." Most of the respondents (71%) recognized the values of the assignments to be "excellent". In summary, we received significantly positive feedback from the students. Based on the survey responses and the students' feedback, we are of the opinion that we have largely achieved what we set out to do (with respect to the course objectives) when we designed the course.

5. CONCLUSIONS

The intent of the course was to provide an understanding of Agile Software Engineering by studying the basics, questioning the principles and practices, and formulating reasoned opinions through critical thinking. We designed the course to include research presentations, talks by industry experts, class discussions and research paper assignments. Since most of the students had prior industry work experience, they were skeptical about the utility and effectiveness of agile methods. However, over the semester, we could observe that the students had begun to understand and appreciate the notion of agility. We could also perceive the evolution of critical thought as the semester progressed.

The students were required to complete the end-semester student evaluation surveys. Nine out of the ten students in the class completed the surveys. They all indicated that the course objectives were met. They also found the class discussions and research papers to have been the most valuable components of the course.

The agile philosophy has emerged from the experiences of several software engineering practitioners, and hence, its adoption has been predominantly in industry settings. Research in academia involving agile software development has been minimal. Therefore, students are receiving only minimal exposure to agile methods in the classroom environment. We conjecture that courses such as the Agile Software Engineering class we offered, can bridge the gap between industry and academia, and prepare budding software engineers to adopt and effectively apply agile concepts when they enter the software and systems development industry. In the future, we envision offering this course over two semesters. In the first semester, we plan to follow the course design outlined in this paper to help students understand the agile philosophy, principles, and practices. During the second semester, we propose to engage the students in a semester-long software development project that would enable them to apply the concepts of agility that they learned in the previous semester.

REFERENCES

[1] W. W. Royce, "Managing the development of large software systems," in *IEEE WESCON*, 1970, pp. 1-9.

[2] B. W. Boehm, "A Spiral Model of Software Development and Enhancement," *Computer,* vol. 21, pp. 61-72, 1988.

[3] R. S. Pressman, *Software Engineering: A Practitioner's Approach*, 6 ed.: McGraw - Hill International Edition, 2005.

[4] R. McCauley, "Agile development methods poised to upset status quo," *SIGCSE Bull.,* vol. 33, pp. 14-15, 2001.

[5] P. Henderson, "Why Large IT Projects Fail," 2006.

[6] A. A. Noureddine, M. Damodaran, and S. Younes, "A Framework for Harnessing the Best of Both Worlds in Software Project Management: Agile and Traditional," in *Information Systems Education Conference 2009*, Washington D.C, 2009.

[7] S. Soundararajan and J. Arthur, "A Soft-Structured Agile Framework for Larger Scale Systems Development," in *16th Annual IEEE International Conference and Workshops on Engineering of Computer-Based Systems (ECBS)*, San Francisco, 2009, pp. 187-195

[8] A. Sidky and J. Arthur, "Determining the Applicability of Agile Practices to Mission and Life-Critical Systems," presented at the Proceedings of the 31st IEEE Software Engineering Workshop, 2007.

[9] C. Schwaber, "The Truth About Agile Proceses - Frank Answers to Frequently Asked Questions," Forrester Research, 2007.

[10] J. Bergin, J. Caristi, Y. Dubinsky, O. Hazzan, and L. Williams, "Teaching software development methods: the case of extreme programming," in *Proceedings of the 35th SIGCSE technical symposium on Computer science education*, Norfolk, Virginia, USA, 2004, pp. 448-449.

[11] K. Beck, M. Beedle, A. v. Bennekum, A. Cockburn, W. Cunningham, M. Fowler, J. Grenning, J. Highsmith, A. Hunt, R. Jeffries, J. Kern, B. Marick, R. C. Martin, S. Mellor, K. Schwaber, J. Sutherland, and D. Thomas. (2001). *Manifesto for Agile Software Development.* Available: http://www.agilemanifesto.org

[12] P. Abrahamsson, O. Salo, J. Ronkainen, and J. Warsta, *Agile Software Development Methods: Review and Analysis.* Finland: VTT Publications, 2002.

[13] K. Beck and C. Andres, *Extreme Programming Explained: Embrace Change*, 2 ed.: Addison-Wesley Professional, 2004.

[14] M. Poppendieck and T. Poppendieck, *Lean Software Development: An Agile Toolkit*: Addison Wesley, 2003.

[15] J. C. Lee, D. Scott McCrickard, and K. T. Stevens, "Examining the Foundations of Agile Usability with eXtreme Scenario-Based Design," in *Proc. of Agile Conference, 2009. AGILE '09.*, 2009, pp. 3-10.

[16] G. Smith and A. Sidky, *Becoming Agile in an imperfect world.* Greenwich, CT 06830: Manning Publications Co., 2009.

[17] S. Soundararajan and J. D. Arthur, "A Structured Framework for Assessing the "Goodness" of Agile Methods," in *18th IEEE International Conference and Workshops on Engineering of Computer Based Systems (ECBS)*, Las Vegas, 2011, pp. 14-23.

[18] A. Chigani, "Agile Architecting: Using Agile Principles to Agilitize the Architecting Process," in *6th Software Architecture Technology User Network Conference (SATURN 2010)*, Minneapolis, MN, 2010.

[19] S. K. Land, *Jumpstart CMM/CMMI software process improvement: Using IEEE software engineering standards.* Hoboken, NJ: Wiley, 2005.

[20] H. Glazer, J. Dalton, D. Anderson, M. Konrad, and S. Shrum, "CMMI or Agile: Why Not Embrace Both!," 2008.

CS Principles: Piloting a National Course

Owen Astrachan
Duke University
ola@cs.duke.edu

Ralph Morelli
Trinity College
rmorelli@trincoll.edu

Dwight Barnette
Virginia Tech
barnette@cs.vt.edu

Jeff Gray
U. Alabama
gray@cs.ua.edu

Chinma Uche
GHA Math Science
cuche@crec.org

Bill Cowles
Booker T. Washington HS
william.cowles@mps.k12.al.us

Rebecca Dovi
Patrick Henry HS
rdovi@hcps.us

SUMMARY

Reports on a new national course designed to be an Advanced Placement course in Computer Science have been reported in [1-3]. This course has been designed from first principles to be taught nationwide at both the secondary and post-secondary levels. As part of this joint NSF/College Board project, 11 high schools are partnered with 10 colleges to teach the course, be part of a national initiative to test assessment items, and to help validate the curriculum framework that is the basis for the course and project.

The traditional Advanced Placement (AP) Computer Science program is intended to reflect enough of a common core of a first semester or year of university-level computer science so that placement or credit can be awarded for work done before college. This special session is a report of the second stage of pilot that is designed to lead to a national standard and a new, additional AP exam in the next five years. This course will not replace the traditional, CS1-oriented AP exam, but will be a new national introduction to Computer Science.

Categories and Subject Descriptors

K.3.2 [**Computer and Information Science Education**]: Computer Science Education

General Terms

Standardization, Human Factors

Keywords

Computer Science Education

1. BACKGROUND

The CS Principles course is the national lever by which we hope to move high school computing. This is a national project, with an advisory board of roughly thirty scientists and educators who are developing a new, rigorous introduction to computer science. The process guiding the development and implementation of the CS Principles course has been reported previously [1] and documents about the course and its 2010-2011 pilots are available from[4].

Copyright is held by the author/owner(s).
SIGCSE'12, February 29–March 3, 2012, Raleigh, North Carolina, USA.
ACM 978-1-4503-1098-7/12/02.

The CS Principles course was piloted at five colleges and universities in 2010-2011. This special session is a report on the second pilot, in which 10 new colleges are partnered with 11 high schools to deliver a course that reflects a modified curricular framework that resulted from an analysis of the first pilot and a national survey that was completed in May of 2011. A third, national pilot to more widely test the assessment being developed will take place in 2012-2013.

2. OBJECTIVES AND ORGANIZATION

This session is devoted to providing information about the CS Principles course as it is being taught and assessed during the 2011-2012 academic year. In addition to reporting on how the curricular framework is being taught at different schools, including the open choice of programming language that is part of the foundation on which CS Principles is built, we will report on the trial of a prototype national assessment being used in this pilot. Results of the delivery of this online assessment will be part of the session.

Three of the special session presenters are leading a college or university pilot of the CS Principles course, partnered with a near-by high school in delivering the course. Two of these three are members of the NMSI (National Math Science Initiative) [5]. Each of these presenters will be partnered with the high school teacher in presenting information about the courses they teach. The seven other Pilot II school instructor/teacher pairs will be in the audience to help answer questions and provide feedback during the part of the special session intended for feedback from the audience.

3. INTRODUCTION (ASTRACHAN)

Owen Astrachan is the PI of the CS Principles project. He will provide an overview of the goals of the pilots, what the curriculum framework covers, and the differences between the Pilot I and Pilot II project.

4. PER-SITE OVERVIEWS (SESSION PRESENTERS)

Each of the college/high school pairs will present for 10-15 minutes about how they are addressing the goals of the CS Principles project: broadening participation, encouraging a view of computer science that goes far beyond programming, and delivering a rich and profound course that exemplifies the national framework specified in [6]. The presenters will cover how they have implemented a course in which the big ideas that have been revised over the past year to include: big data, modeling, and simulation, the Internet, and cyber-security. The pairs will alsodiscuss what programming language and platform they have adopted and how that could be part of a portfolio-based assessment being designed for administration in 2012-2013.

5. AUDIENCE AND EXPECTATIONS

Questions relating to the new (AP) CS Principles course and pilot will have wide-ranging interest among SIGCSE attendees at both the post-secondary and K-12 level. All participants in Pilot II will be available to answer questions posed by the audience and framed by the session moderator.

6. REFERENCES

[1] O. Astrachan, T. Barnes, D. D. Garcia, J. Paul, B. Simon, and L. Snyder, "CS principles: piloting a new course at national scale," presented at the Proceedings of the 42nd ACM technical symposium on Computer science education, Dallas, TX, USA, 2011.

[2] O. Astrachan, K. Haynie, C. Stephenson, L. Diaz, and A. Briggs, "Re-imagining the first year of computing," presented at the Proceedings of the 41st ACM technical symposium on Computer science education, Milwaukee, Wisconsin, USA, 2010.

[3] O. Astrachan, J. Cuny, C. Stephenson, and C. Wilson, "The CS10K Project: Mobilizing the Community to Transform High School Computing," *Proceedings of the SIGCSE Symposium,* 2011 2011.

[4] (2011). *CS Principles.* Available: http://www.csprinciples.org

[5] N. M. S. I. (NMSI). Available: http://www.nationalmathandscience.org/

[6] O. Astrachan, A. Briggs, and C. P. Commission. (2011). *Big Ideas and Computational Thinking Practices.* Available: http://www.csprinciples.org

Fun, Phone, and the Future

Microsoft XNA Game Studio, Windows Phone, and Kinect SDK

Pat Yongpradit
Springbrook High School
201 Valley Brook Drive
Silver Spring, MD 20904
patyongpradit@live.com

ABSTRACT

Microsoft XNA Game Studio and C# provide the basis of an advanced high school or introductory post-secondary game development computer science course. Game development is serious computer science. The curriculum tools enable students to create games, simulations, and applications for the PC, Xbox 360, Windows Phone, and Kinect that expand students' skills in complex logic, object oriented programming (OOP), advanced algorithms, and data structures.

Categories and Subject Descriptors

K.3.2 Computer and Information Science Education

General Terms

Algorithms, Design, Human Factors, Languages

Keywords

Game development, C#, XNA, curriculum, Windows Phone, Kinect, mobile development, XNA Game Studio

1. SUMMARY

XNA game development appeals to students on many levels; it stimulates creativity, employs the latest tools and gadgets, delivers fun, and it provides the means for students to express their personal values and the power to make a difference. Microsoft XNA Game Studio can be used to create games, simulations, and applications for the PC, Xbox 360, Windows Phone, and Kinect.

In this session, attendees will:

- See demonstrations of Kinect and Windows Phone programming.
- Preview recently released XNA/C# programming curriculum materials that combines advanced computer science learning with the latest Microsoft technologies.
- Participate in game development projects.

Copyright is held by the author/owner(s).
SIGCSE'12, February 29–March 3, 2012, Raleigh, North Carolina, USA.
ACM 978-1-4503-1098-7/12/02.

Educators will value the two semesters of clustered, topic-centered lessons. A holistic approach builds skills and knowledge to enable students to analyze and design strategies to address real-world scenarios and projects. *Game Development with XNA: Semester 1* [1] is a semester-long curriculum created specifically as a high school capstone course for students who have previously studied computer science during one or two years of introductory and/or advanced high school courses. Students will build upon their foundational programming knowledge and skills by designing and implementing games and simulations that utilize input and output, involve complex logic, and apply object oriented programming (OOP), advanced algorithms, and data structures in independent and team projects.

Students can test the boundaries of their imagination and explore innovative ways of interacting with devices by creating programs for the Kinect sensor. Games or mobile applications can be sold in a global marketplace through Microsoft's free student developer program. The new curriculum was designed to inspire students to learn advanced programming skills, design exciting games, and create simulations that will help solve the world's toughest problems such as those presented in the Microsoft Imagine Cup.

Both the curriculum and the software are free and easily downloaded. The teacher-created and classroom-tested resources included lesson plans, video tutorials, creative projects with solution files, and various assessment tools. An online community group provides support for teachers working with the curriculum, software, and hardware.

2. OBJECTIVE

Learn how to deliver core and advanced computer science concepts, promote deep algorithmic thinking, and make computer science relevant through engaging learning experiences such as:

- Creating games for social causes using XNA Game Studio
- Developing and submitting an app for the Windows Phone
- Programming with the Kinect Sensor Software Development Kit

3. OUTLINE

- Introduction (5 min)
- Tour of XNA Game Studio IDE, Windows Phone, and Kinect programming (15)
- Demonstration of student projects and curriculum (10)
- Attendee interaction/ participation in programming and testing (30)
- Questions (15 min)

4. EXPECTATIONS

The intended audience for this session is high school CS teachers who are looking for ideas and resources for an advanced CS course and university instructors of typical introductory CS programming courses.

Attendees can expect to:

- Learn about XNA and C# as it relates to development for games, Windows Phone, and the Kinect game controller.
- Learn about the XNA game development curriculum: *Game Development with XNA: Semester 1.*
- Experience programming for the Windows Phone and Kinect.
- Experiment with the Phone and Kinect sensor.

SUITABILITY

This topic is most suitable for a Special Session because of the interactive nature of the delivery of the content. Attendees will be invited to get up out of their seats to participate with both the programming and user-interface devices.

This session will model effective classroom strategies for introducing and teaching game development.

5. REFERENCES

[1] Microsoft. 2011. Game Development with XNA: Semester 1 and Semester 2. Retrieved Sept 6, 2011 from http://www.microsoft.com/education/facultyconnection/precollegiate

Building an Open, Large-Scale Research Data Repository of Initial Programming Student Behaviour

Michael Kölling
University of Kent
Canterbury
UK
mik@kent.ac.uk

Ian Utting
University of Kent
Canterbury
UK
I.A.Utting@kent.ac.uk

SUMMARY

Many initiatives in improving initial learning of programming are based on gut instinct, guesswork, or localised experiences. Gathering real data as a basis for interventions and development work is rare, and doing so on a large scale is hard.

The BlueJ environment is currently being instrumented to allow users to opt in to a large scale research data acquisition project, which is intended to collect data useful to a wide variety of educational programming researchers.

The BlueJ project and its development team are ideally placed to collect such data: The development team has working contacts to various educational research groups, and the annual users of BlueJ number in the millions, with users in almost all parts of the world. This scale of deployment of BlueJ, and hence the volume and diversity of the data which can be gathered, are unique in the history of such investigations, and present a significant opportunity for researchers.

It is intended to provide open access to this data to any interested research project. We expect that the availability of a large scale, real world data set documenting the behaviour of learners of programming will enable a wide variety of investigations that were previously impractical.

This session aims at presenting the ideas so far, and getting input from interested researchers about the design of the data collection details.

Categories and Subject Descriptors

K.3.2 [**Computing Milieux**]: Computer and Information Science Education – *Computer science education.*

General Terms

Measurement, Experimentation.

Keywords

CS1, student behaviour, initial programming, BlueJ, data collection.

Copyright is held by the author/owner(s).
SIGCSE'12, February 29–March 3, 2012, Raleigh, North Carolina, USA.
ACM 978-1-4503-1098-7/12/02.

1. OVERALL OBJECTIVES

The main objectives of the session are two-fold:

- To inform educational programming researchers of this project and the resulting opportunities for large scale, data-driven programing education research; and
- To gather input for the design of the data gathering exercise, including the kind of data to be collected, possible research questions, and practical considerations.

The session will introduce the facilities which have been developed to gather data about beginners' behaviour in learning to program using Java and BlueJ. The theoretical opportunities of the availability of a large scale data set of student programming behaviour are significant, and have the potential to inform many different kinds of further research and development. However, details of the type of data being collected place constraints on the research questions which can be addressed.

While a framework for the data gathering is in the prototyping stage, details in many respects have not been fixed. Input from researchers potentially interested in such a data set is sought here, to ensure that as many users as possible can participate in the collection process, and that data is gathered that is useful to address a wide variety of diverse research questions.

This session gives researchers the chance to influence the type of data being collected and the mechanisms which facilitate the collection. Apart from the data design, important practical, political and ethical questions have to be addressed to make this project feasible. These include:

- How to deal with dissemination and installation in home and lab settings, including dealing with firewalls and locked-down systems.
- How to ensure anonymisation of data.
- How to enable longitudinal studies with anonymous data.
- How to gather informed consent, including how to disseminate all relevant information.
- How to enable local studies to add additional contextual (possibly personal) data to the centralised anonymous data.
- How to manage access to the data repository.

Input is sought in this session on all of these areas. We will also look at how contextual data can be gathered locally about subsets of the students using the system to complement the central anonymous data, and how these data sets can be combined to enrich the possible research.

2. OUTLINE OF THE SESSION

The session will start with a presentation of work undertaken to date, a description of the collection framework prototype, and a list of issues identified to far. The majority of the time will be dedicated to a structured discussion of the areas where input from the community is sought.

- Presentation of the data gathering framework; technical details and practical considerations
- Discussion of technical aspects: type of data gathered, technical issues
- Discussion of potential research questions that can be addressed using the data set
- Discussion of political and ethical considerations, and solutions to address them
- Description and discussion of a framework for additional contextual data gathering
- Discussion of managing access to the research data
- Discussion of the process from here: How to get and stay involved

3. EXPECTATIONS

The intended audience is Computer Science Education researchers with an interest in investigating beginning students' interactions with the environment in which they are learning to program.

We expect that the availability of a large set of research data can inform many different research questions, improve the quality of existing research and enable the investigation of new research questions. Making this data openly available to any interested research group creates the potential of wide ranging impact. As such, we expect that this project, if successful, can be of significant benefit to the CS Education community as a whole.

The success, however, depends on the extent to which practical and contextual issues are addressed in the project. It is expected that this session contributes fundamentally to ensuring that the research design is able to gather the right data and address the right questions for many independent research groups.

We expect that attendees will leave with an understanding of how the data-gathering framework could be useful in their research, at both world-wide and classroom-scale. We also expect that attendees will form the nucleus of a developing community around this data.

4. SUITABILITY FOR A SPECIAL SESSION

This session describes a technical work-in-progress which is intended to serve the CS Education research community. To ensure maximum usefulness, the project now depends in direct input and involvement of education researchers in our community.

The intention of this session is to form a community around this work based on the attendees' research questions. As such, it needs time for initial presentation of the framework, but mainly scope for discussion of what the emerging community needs. This time for discussion is not available in a traditional paper presentation, and the possibility of forming a community is not possible with a poster presentation.

The special session format is the only format that allows the type and scope of presentation and discussion required for these goals.

Assigning Student Programming Pairs Based on their Mental Model Consistency: An Initial Investigation

Alex Radermacher
North Dakota State University
IACC Bldg., Room 258
Fargo, ND, 58102
701-231-8562
alex.radermacher@ndsu.edu

Gursimran Walia
North Dakota State University
IACC Bldg., Room 258B3
Fargo, ND, 58102
701-231-8185
gursimran.walia@ndsu.edu

Richard Rummelt
North Dakota State University
IACC Bldg., Room 258B3
Fargo, ND, 58102
701-231-8194
richard.rummelt@ndsu.edu

ABSTRACT

Pair Programming has been shown to be beneficial to student learning. Much research has been conducted to effectively create student pairs when using pair programming in introductory computer science courses. This paper reports results of research investigating the effectiveness of pairing students based on their mental model consistency. Prior research has found a strong correlation between mental model consistency and performance in introductory computer programming courses. Evaluating students' mental models helps to provide insights into how students approach problem solving and may indicate how to effectively pair students to improve their programming ability and learning. The results from an empirical study conducted to investigate these effects indicate that mental model consistency is a predictor of student success in an introductory programming course. Future goals of this research are to fully evaluate all possible pairing arrangements and to produce tests that can be used to evaluate mental model consistency for other computer science concepts.

Categories and Subject Descriptors

K.3.2 [**Computer and Information Science Education**]: Computer Science Education.

General Terms

Measurement, Performance, Experimentation, Human Factors

Keywords

Computer Programming, Pair Programming, Mental Model, Mental Model Consistency, Empirical Study

1. INTRODUCTION

Educators have struggled with finding the best methods to educate new programmers and have attempted multiple approaches to solve this problem [5]. Numerous researchers have evaluated the use of pair programming in introductory programming courses and have found several benefits such as improvements in the quality of student work and an increase in the retention of students in programming classes [14, 20]. Additional studies have also shown that students are receptive to learning with pair programming and that pair programming improves students' confidence in their work [16].

Although pair programming is beneficial to students, there are still questions on how it should be implemented in order to maximize the student learning. Many pair programming studies related to evaluating the pair arrangements have focused on pair compatibility and have examined the effects of personality on compatibility [9, 18, 21]. The results of these studies indicate that student pairs may be more compatible if they share a similar work ethic, or have a dissimilar Myers Briggs perceiving functions. Additionally, multiple researchers have concluded that pairing students with similar levels of ability will produce more compatible pairs [4, 10]. However, very little research has actually examined the effectiveness of different pairing strategies on student learning outcomes. Previous studies have found that pairing individuals with similar confidence levels [19] and that pairing individuals with dissimilar temperaments [18] leads to pairs that produce higher quality work, but did not examine the effects of such pairings on the individual students in those pairs. One recent study determined that pairing students by similarity in ability improved learning outcomes for the bottom quartile of students, but was not more effective otherwise [2].

Measuring how pair programming affects individual learning can be difficult to measure. One issue is that when pair programming is used in a programming course, there are few assessments of individual ability, usually only midterm and final exams. Additionally, even though the work produced by a pair is generally of higher quality than that of an individual [20], it has not been determined if using pair programming helps all students to learn more than if they had worked individually. Because new students may have no previous programming experience, it is difficult to establish a baseline measurement of their performance in order to measure growth.

One possible solution to this problem is to evaluate students' mental model consistency at the onset of the semester to establish a baseline for their performance. A mental model is person's mental representation of a concept that it used to "describe, explain, and predict events in their environment" [3]. Previous research has indicated that there is a correlation between student mental model consistency and performance in an introductory computer science course [1, 6]. Because the test used to evaluate mental model consistency can be completed by students without prior programming experience, it can establish a baseline

Permission to make digital or hard copies of all or part of this work for personal or classroom use is granted without fee provided that copies are not made or distributed for profit or commercial advantage and that copies bear this notice and the full citation on the first page. To copy otherwise, or republish, to post on servers or to redistribute to lists, requires prior specific permission and/or a fee.
SIGCSE'12, February 29–March 3, 2012, Raleigh, North Carolina, USA.
Copyright 2012 ACM 978-1-4503-1098-7/12/02...$10.00.

expectation for performance as well as measure student growth. Further information on mental models can be found in Section 2.

This paper reports the results from an empirical study that was conducted to determine if mental model consistency is correlated with student performance when pair programming was used and whether or not certain pair combinations were more effective at shifting students towards a greater degree of mental model consistency. The results of this research indicate that when pair programming is used, there is a correlation between mental model consistency and student performance. Also, it appears as though certain consistency-based pairs are more effective than others, but there was insufficient data to indicate that the results were statistically significant with a high level of confidence.

The remainder of this paper is structured as follows. Section 2 provides background information on the assessment methods used in research along with a more detailed description of mental models. Section 3 describes the design of the empirical study that was conducted to investigate the effects of pair programming on changes in mental model consistency. Section 4 describes the data analysis and results. Section 5 discusses the threats to validity. Section 6 discusses the results based on the analysis performed in Section 4. Section 7 concludes the paper and provides a summary of future research direction.

2. BACKGROUND AND RELATED WORK

A mental model is a cognitive science term used to describe the cognitive representation of knowledge in the mind of an individual. Individuals use these models that they construct in order to reason [8, 15]. Similarly, novice programmers construct mental models that allow them to understand programming concepts such as variable assignment [11] and recursion [7, 17]. These researchers have also noted that the students often construct non-viable mental models which represent a flawed or incomplete understanding of a particular concept.

Ma, et al. found that at the end of the semester of an introductory programming course, only 17% of students held viable mental models for reference assignment [11] and that even after specifically developing a technique to assist students in developing viable mental models, 50% of students still held non-viable mental models [12]. Götschi, et al. found that over 50% of students held non-viable mental models for recursion [7].

Dehnadi, et al. conducted studies to investigate the students' mental model consistency, i.e., the tendency for a student to use the same mental model to solve a series of problems [5, 6]. The researchers developed twelve questions about variable assignment with multiple choice answers corresponding to different mental models of variable assignment. The most interesting result from the initial study was that students, who consistently used the same mental model, even if it was incorrect, tended to perform better than those students who used multiple different mental models [5, 6]. They also reported that students who migrated from an inconsistent to a consistent mental model when taking the test for a second time performed better than students who remained inconsistent in their mental model use.

Several follow-up studies were conducted to provide additional support to the original findings. Results from these studies are reported by Bornat, et al. [1]. After analyzing the results of these additional studies, the authors stated that the predictive ability of the mental model consistency test did not seem to be as accurate as it had originally appeared. However, it was determined that the test was not effective at predicting success for students who had already taken a programming course. Another factor that may explain the decrease in prediction ability is that in one study a large number of subjects dropped the course before the end of the study. Based on the results from this study, it is likely that these were the students with the lowest performance.

Mental models have also been evaluated in the context of groups and teams. Cannon-Bowers et al. examined how team decision making was affected by shared mental models between team members [3]. Mathieu, et al. examined the differences between task and team mental models [13]. Their research showed a correlation between both shared-task and shared-team mental models and team performance. Therefore, team members must share an understanding for the tasks that they will complete and must have similar conceptions of how the team should operate.

Based on the above study findings, the authors of this paper hypothesized that pair programming may be an effective method of migrating students towards greater mental model consistency. The general assumption was that regardless of how students were paired, two students would be able to develop viable mental models more quickly than if they were to work individually. It was also presumed that if one member of the pair possessed the correct mental model, then he or she would be able to share it with the other member of the pair.

3. STUDY DESIGN

The purpose of this study is to evaluate the effects of pair programming on student mental model migration and to determine if pairing students with certain mental models is more effective in improving student learning.

This experiment is a control-group design in which students took a mental model test at the beginning of the semester. Afterwards, students were randomly placed into one of three groups:

a. A homogenous group where both members exhibited mental model inconsistency.
b. A homogenous group where both members exhibited mental model consistency.
c. A heterogeneous group where one member exhibited mental model consistency and the other member exhibited mental model inconsistency.

Students' mental model consistency was measured based on their responses to the test developed by Dehnadi, et al. [6]. Next, students were randomly assigned a partner within that group. Then, the student pairs completed the same laboratory assignments during the first four weeks. After this the students were re-tested using the same mental-model test in order to evaluate changes in the consistency and viability of their mental. The students were then evaluated on the laboratory assignments and the exams during the course of the semester. The details of the study are provided in the following sections.

3.1 Research Questions:

The following research questions were investigated in this study:

Research Question 1: Is mental model consistency an accurate predictor of success when pair programming is used in an introductory programming course?

Research Question 2: Do students who migrate towards greater mental model consistency perform better than students who do not undergo such migration?

Research Question 3: Are certain pairing arrangements more effective at migrating students towards greater mental model consistency than other consistency-based pairing arrangements?

3.2 Indcpendent and Dependent Variables

The experiment manipulated the following independent variables:

a) *Mental Model Consistency*: The tendency for a subject to use the same mental model to solve similar problems.

b) *Pair Arrangement*: The pair group type that the subject was placed into.

We also measured the following dependent variables:

a) *Total Grade*: The final grade received by the subject, including the grades on exams and programming exercises.

b) *Exam Grades*: The grade received on midterm or final exam.

c) *Mental Model Migration*: Whether or not a subject migrated towards a more consistent mental model.

3.3 Study Subjects and Course Assignments

The participating subjects in this study were 83 students enrolled in CS1- Introductory Computer Programming Course at XXXX. Previous research shows that the mental model test is more effective at predicting student's success when, the subjects have little or no programming experience. The students who indicated that they had taken a previous programming course at a college level were excluded from analysis. Subjects working in pairs completed the programming exercises related to variable assignment, evaluating conditions, string manipulation, looping, and object oriented programming concepts during the semester.

4.4 Study Procedure

The experiment steps are discussed as follows:

a) *Step 1 – Test Subjects for Mental Model Consistency:* The students from the CS1 course were evaluated to determine their mental model. On the first day of the class, students were surveyed on their previous experience with programming or programming courses and were given a test devised by Dehnadi et al., to evaluate their mental model. Eleven (11) students had taken a college-level programming course in the past were placed in a separate group (and excluded from analysis) because the original researchers had discovered that their mental model test was not effective at predicting the student's success when applied to students with previous programming experience.

b) *Step 2 - Pair Subjects Based on Mental Model Consistency*: Subjects were randomly paired into one of three groups. The first group included student pairs where both the students had an inconsistent mental model (I-I). The second group included student pairs where one of the subjects had a consistent mental model while the other subject had an inconsistent mental model (I-C). The third group included student pairs where both the students had a consistent mental model (C-C). Students were randomly paired within each group in order to minimize the sources of potential bias. The researchers of this study chose to use these groups as there was no existing evidence to suggest than any particular pairing arrangement would be more effective than any of the others.

An attempt was made to keep the sizes of the groups relatively balanced in order to provide for better statistical analysis possibilities. Table 1 provides a brief description of the different levels of mental model consistency of the subjects who took the test and the number of students belonging to each level. The three subjects who left their answer sheet blank were treated as inconsistent for the purpose of group assignment.

After examining the pairs, a total of six mental model-based pairings were observed (described in Table 2). Table 2 also shows the total number of pairs belonging to each pairing arrangement. The random distribution of subjects was done because the researchers did not have any preconceptions about which pairing arrangements would be most effective.

c) *Step 3 – Students Work on Programming Exercises*: The subjects worked on programming exercises in their assigned pairs for the duration of the course. The grades for these programming exercises and exams were collected.

d) *Step 4 – Re-test subjects for Mental Model Consistency*: After four weeks, subjects were given the same test that was used in Step 1 to determine whether or not they had migrated towards greater mental model consistency. This re-test was given after students had been given two lectures about variable assignment. Because the original researchers had found that there were not large shifts in students' mental model consistency after four weeks into the course, no further reevaluations were performed [5].

e) *Step 5 – Evaluate Changes in Mental Model Consistency*: Subjects and pairing groups were evaluated to determine if certain pairing arrangements resulted in a higher tendency to migrate subject towards mental model consistency. Two types of mental model migrations analyzed in this study included: the migration from an inconsistent to a consistent mental model, and the migration from a consistently incorrect mental model to consistently correct mental model.

f) *Step 6 – Evaluate Performance of Subjects*: Subjects completed a midterm examination, the final exam, and eventually the course. Statistical analysis was performed on the grade subjects received on the midterm examination, the final exam, and the final grade received in the course.

Table 1. Mental Model Categories and Descriptions

Mental Model	Description	Number of Subjects
Consistent Correct(CC)	The correct approach was used for all or almost all questions.	10
Consistent Incorrect(CI)	The same incorrect approach was used for all or almost all questions.	19
Somewhat Inconsistent(SI)	Two or three different approaches were used across all questions.	27
Highly Inconsistent(HI)	More than three different approaches were used across all questions.	13

Table 2: Mental-Model Based Pairing Arrangements

Mental-Model-Based Pairs	Number
Inconsistent and Inconsistent (I-I): A pair where both subjects exhibit mental model inconsistency.	**11 pairs**
Inconsistent and Consistent Incorrect (I-CI): A pair where one subject exhibits mental model inconsistency and the other subject exhibits mental model consistency, but does not use the correct mental model.	**6 pairs**
Inconsistent and Consistent Correct (I-CC): A pair where one subjects exhibits mental model inconsistency and the other subject exhibits mental model consistency and uses the correct mental model.	**4 pairs**
Consistent Incorrect and Consistent Incorrect (CI-CI): A pair where both subjects exhibit mental model consistency but neither uses the correct mental model.	**6 pairs**
Consistent Incorrect and Consistent Correct (CI-CC): A pair where both subjects exhibit mental model consistency but only one of the subjects uses the correct mental model.	**7 pairs**
Consistent Correct and Consistent Correct (CC-CC): A pair where both subjects exhibit mental model consistency and both subjects use the correct mental model.	**1 pair**

3.4 Data Collection and Evaluation Criterion

Student performances on lab assignments and tests (including mid-term and final examinations) were analyzed to study the effects of the mental-model-based pairings on the students' performance and on the changes in their mental models.

This was also done so that a direct comparison could be made with the results from the original study to determine if the mental models were still as *accurate* at predicting the likelihood of a student to pass the course when pair programming is implemented. The final course grades for subjects in the study were also analyzed, so the correlation between mental model and final course grade are also presented in Section 4.

4. DATA ANALYSIS AND RESULTS

This presents an analysis of the data to provide answers to the research questions posed in Section 3.1.

4.1 Predictive Ability of Mental Models

Subjects' pair performances on lab assignments and their individual performances on tests (including mid-term and final examinations) were analyzed to determine if the mental model test administered at the beginning of the semester was an accurate predictor of subject performance in the course.

Table 3 shows the mean midterm exam scores and mean total course grades (all exams and programming exercises) for different mental model groups based on the results from the initial mental model test. The results show that while there is almost no difference in performance between subjects classified as highly inconsistent (HI) and subjects classified as somewhat inconsistent (SI). The results of a two-sample t-test show that there is no statistical difference between these groups in terms of course grade (p = .047) and nearly no statistical difference in the midterm exam grades (p = .131).

Table 3. Grades Across Mental Model Groups

Mental Model Types	Midterm Exam	Total Grade
Highly Inconsistent: HI	53.8	491.3
Slightly Inconsistent: SI	54.5	490.0
Inconsistent: I	54.3	490.4
Consistently Incorrect: CI	58.3	503.5
Consistently Correct: CC	70.8	541.8
Consistent: C	62.3	516.3

Similar analysis was performed to determine whether the performance of one mental model group was significantly better than another. Based on the results of a two-sample t-test, the subjects who had exhibited mental model consistency on initial test performed better in the course than the subjects who exhibited inconsistency with near statistical significance (p = .087). When examining the data more closely, it was determined that one outlier may have been heavily influencing the results of this test. The subject in question had tested consistent correct on the first test, but had regressed to consistent incorrect when re-tested. When this subject was removed from analysis, the results were significant (p = .022). Statistically significant results were also observed when comparing midterm exam scores between the two groups (p = .008). However, the CI group alone did not perform significantly better than the I group (p = .133) indicating that the CC group improved the overall scores significantly.

Additional analysis was performed on the results from the re-test of student mental model consistency (Step 4). The results of a two-sample t-test indicated that, once again, the subjects with mental model consistency (CI and CC) performed better than subjects with inconsistency on both the midterm exam (p = .001) and overall course grade (p = .005).. However, because large number of subjects classified with mental model inconsistency (HI and SI) on the second test had dropped the course, the researchers do not feel these results are strong.

When evaluating differences in performance between the CI subjects and CC subjects, researchers found that the subjects with the correct mental model (CC) after the second test performed significantly better than the subjects who merely showed consistency (CI) on both the midterm exam and overall course grade (p = .001, p = .005, respectively). The results from the initial test did not show a statistically significant difference when examining the total grade (p = .158), but are significant for the midterm exam (p = .005). These results indicate that significant performance gaps exist between the different groups.

4.2 Effects of Mental Model Migration

Researchers also analyzed student performance data to determine whether or not subjects who migrated towards greater consistency or correctness performed better than subjects who did not undergo any migration. The first four rows in Table 4 show the migration results for inconsistent subjects who migrated to using consistently using a particular mental model. The bottom two rows show the migration results for subjects who migrated from consistently using an incorrect model to consistently using the correct mental model.

The top two rows of Table 5 shows that subjects that begin consistently using the same mental model scored 11 points higher

Table 4. Mental Model Migration Results

Pair Arrangement	Migration to Consistency / Correctness	No Migration	Total
I – I	16	2	18
I – CI	3	2	5
I – CC	3	1	4
I – C	6	3	9
CI – CI	5	6	11
CI – CC	4	3	7

on average on the midterm than subjects who remained inconsistent. These subjects also had a higher final grade, but researchers do not believe this result is meaningful as few subjects who did not undergo migration completed the course. Based on the results of a two-sample t-test, subjects who exhibited mental model inconsistency on the initial test, but had migrated to mental model consistency before the re-test scored higher on the midterm exam than subjects who did not undergo migration (p = .030). There were not a sufficient number of data points to analyze final grade, because the majority of subjects that did not migrate to consistently using the same mental model dropped the course before the end of the semester.

Table 5. Exam Scores and Total Grade Based on Mental Model Migration

Mental Model Migration	Midterm Exam	Final Exam	Total Grade
Migration from I to C	57.0	52.5	496.2
No Migration from I to C	46.0	39.0	470.0
Migration from CI to CC	64.8	61.7	527.2
No migration from CI to CC	54.3	48.9	485.2

Similarly, the bottom two rows of Table shows the results of exams and the final course grade for subjects who consistently used an incorrect mental model (CI) and either migrated to using correct model (CC) or did not undergo migration before the second mental model test. The results from a two-sample t-test also showed that the subjects exhibiting mental model consistency, but using an incorrect mental model on the initial test (CI), and who transitioned to using the correct mental model (CC) before the re-test scored higher on the midterm than subjects who did not begin to use the correct mental model (p = .041). When comparing these groups based on the final exam and total grade for the course, the results showed near statistical significant (p = .058, p = .065 respectively).

4.3 Using the Pair Programming to Improve Students' Mental Model Consistency

To determine whether or not certain consistency-based pairs were more effective at migrating subjects towards greater mental model consistency, additional statistical analysis was performed. Table 4 shows the migration rates from inconsistency to consistency for each pair arrangement. Subjects in the I-I group showed the largest percentage chance of migration, but the migration rate was greater than 60% for all groups.

A chi-square test was performed to determine if there was a statistical association between the different treatments and migration towards consistency. No combination of comparisons showed statistical significance, but this result is likely due to the small sample sizes. Similar analysis was also performed to evaluate migration for consistent incorrect subjects towards using the correct mental model. Table 4 also shows migration rates for these subjects and indicates that both pair arrangements had a similar migration rate. Once again, no statistical significance was found between the two pair arrangements.

5. THREATS TO VALIDITY

This section attempts to address some of the threats to validity that may have affected the results of this research.

First, attendance was not taken during this course, so it is possible that whether or not subjects attended lectures had some influence on the tendency to undergo mental model migration. There was also a case where a subject who had originally tested as exhibiting mental model consistency and using the correct mental model, regressed to using an incorrect mental model on the re-test. This indicates that it is possible for a subject to blindly guess the correct mental model. A large number of the subjects who exhibited mental model consistency associated with poor performance dropped the course before taking the final. This made accurate analysis of performance on the final exam impossible and may also weaken the strength of our conclusions.

6. DISCUSSION OF RESULTS

Research Question 1: The purpose of the first question was to determine if the mental model consistency test could still provide an accurate prediction of student success if pair programming were used rather than requiring students to work individually.

The results provide good support for the effectiveness of the test, indicating a statistically significant difference in both final course grade and midterm exam score between subjects exhibiting consistency and inconsistency. Additionally, the results also provide partial support to indicate that subjects who consistently use the correct mental model (CC) will perform better than subjects who consistently use an incorrect mental model (CI). Based on these findings, it is concluded that the mental model test developed by Dehnadi is able to provide some prediction of success when pair programming is used [6, 5].

Research Question 2: This question was concerned with determining whether subjects migrating towards greater mental model consistency or using the correct mental model would perform better than subjects who did not undergo such migration.

In both cases, a migration towards greater consistency or using the correct mental model resulted in better performance on the midterm exam with statistical significance. When comparing subjects in the Consistent Incorrect group who had migrated to using the correct model with those who had not, there was near statistical significance in terms of overall course grade. It is suspected that this is due to the lowest performing subjects, who had not undergone migration, dropping the course. These findings are also in accordance with previous research by Dehnadi, et al. that suggests migration is correlated with success [5].

Research Question 3: This question was intended to determine whether certain combinations of pairs based on mental model consistency were more effective than others at migrating students towards greater consistency or using the correct mental model.

The results from this study do not indicate that one group is more effective than any other, but due to the low number of data points, it is difficult to completely dismiss the possibility. When extrapolating the data, it was found that pairing two inconsistent subjects (I-I) was preferable to pairing an inconsistent subject with a consistent subject (I-C). This suggests that further experimentation is necessary. Based on these results, there is not sufficient evidence to suggest that one pairing arrangement is more effective than another, or not using pair programming at all.

7. CONCLUSION AND FUTURE WORK

The results of this study provides support to encourage further studies, particularly to increase the number of data points in order to determine which pairing strategies are most effective. In future, we are also determined to improve our ability to assess subjects' individual learning outcomes often and earlier in the semester.

It is also possible for students to perform well in the initial weeks of the course and struggle with more difficult topics. Forming a viable mental model for variable assignment is important to grasp concepts introduced later in the course, but a good understanding of variable assignment does not always indicate that a student will form viable mental models for concepts such as iteration. Developing a mental model test for iteration would allow for researchers to examine correlations between consistency for variable assignment and other concepts. It would also provide a second potential measure for assessing student performance.

Additional future work includes developing a more general test for mental model consistency. The test developed by Dehnadi and Bornat is ineffective if given to students with prior programming experience and may not work if students lack a mathematical background in Algebra. One solution may be a test where students determine the next symbol in sequence of colored shapes.

8. REFERENCES

[1] R. Bornat, S. Dehnadi, and Simon. 2008. Mental models, consistency and programming aptitude. In *Proceedings of the tenth conference on Australasian computing education*, S. Hamilton and M. Hamilton (Eds.), Vol. 78. Australian Computer Society, Inc., Darlinghurst, Australia, 53-61.

[2] G. Braught, J. MacCormick, and T. Wahls. 2010. The benefits of pairing by ability. In *Proceedings of the 41st ACM technical symposium on Computer science education* (SIGCSE '10). ACM, New York, NY, USA, 249-253.

[3] J. A. Cannon-Bowers, E. Salas, S. A. Converse. 1993. In *Individual and Group Decision Making*. N. J. Castellan Jr. (Eds.). Lawrence Erlbaum, Hillside, NJ, USA, 221-246.

[4] E.A. Chaparro, A. Yuksel, P. Romero, and S. Bryant. 2005. Factors affecting the perceived effectiveness of pair programming in higher education. In *Psychology of Programming Interest Group 17th Workshop*, 5-18.

[5] S. Dehnadi and R. Bornat. 2006. The camel has two humps. Middlesex University Working Paper, http://www.cs.mdx.ac.uk/research/PhDArea/saeed/

[6] S. Dehnadi. 2006. Testing programming aptitude. In *Proceedings of the Psychology of Programming Interest Group 18th Annual Workshop,* 22-37.

[7] T. Götschi, I. Sanders, and V. Galpin. 2003. Mental models of recursion. *SIGCSE Bull.* 35, 1 (January 2003), 346-350.

[8] P. Johnson-Laird. 1983. *Mental Models*. Cambridge University Press, Cambridge, MA, USA.

[9] N. Katira, L. Williams, E. Wiebe, C. Miller, S. Balik, and E. Gehringer. 2004. On understanding compatibility of student pair programmers. In *Proceedings of the 35th SIGCSE technical symposium on Computer science education* (SIGCSE '04). ACM, New York, NY, USA, 7-11.

[10] N. Katira, L. Williams, and J. Osborne. 2005. Towards increasing the compatibility of student pair programmers. In *Proceedings of the 27th international conference on Software engineering* (ICSE '05). ACM, New York, NY, USA, 625-626.

[11] L. Ma, J. Ferguson, M. Roper, and M. Wood. 2007. Investigating the viability of mental models held by novice programmers. In *Proceedings of the 38th SIGCSE technical symposium on Computer science education* (SIGCSE '07). ACM, New York, NY, USA, 499-503.

[12] L. Ma, J. D. Ferguson, M. Roper, I. Ross, and M. Wood. 2008. Using cognitive conflict and visualisation to improve mental models held by novice programmers. In *Proceedings of the 39th SIGCSE technical symposium on Computer science education*. ACM, New York, NY, USA, 342-346.

[13] J. E. Mathieu, T.S. Heffner, G. F. Goodwin, E. Salas, and J. A. Cannon-Bowers. 2000. The influence of shared metnal models on team process and performance. In *Journal of Applied Psychology*, 85, 273-283.

[14] C. McDowell, L. Werner, H. Bullock, and J. Fernald. 2002. The effects of pair-programming on performance in an introductory programming course. *SIGCSE Bull.* 34, 1, 38-42.

[15] D. Norman. Some observatiosn on mental models. In *Mental Models*. D. Gentner and A. Stevens (Eds.). Lawrence Erlbaum, Hillside, NJ, USA,

[16] A. Radermacher and G. Walia. 2011. Investigating the effective implementation of pair programming: an empirical investigation. In *Proceedings of the 42nd ACM technical symposium on Computer science education* (SIGCSE '11). ACM, New York, NY, USA, 655-660.

[17] T. L. Scholtz and I. Sanders. 2010. Mental models of recursion: investigating students' understanding of recursion. In *Proceedings of the fifteenth annual conference on Innovation and technology in computer science education* (ITiCSE '10). ACM, New York, NY, USA, 103-107.

[18] P. Sfetsos, I. Stamelos, L. Angelis, and I. Deligiannis. 2009. An experimental investigation of personality types impact on pair effectiveness in pair programming. *Empirical Softw. Engg.* 14, 2 (April 2009), 187-226.

[19] L. Thomas, M. Ratcliffe, and A. Robertson. 2003. Code warriors and code-a-phobes: a study in attitude and pair programming. In *Proceedings of the 34th SIGCSE technical symposium on Computer science education* (SIGCSE '03). ACM, New York, NY, USA, 363-367.

[20] L. Williams, E. Wiebe, K. Yang, M. Ferzli, and C. Miller. 2002. In support of pair programming in the introductory computer science course. In *Computer Science Education*, 12, 3 (September 2002), 197-212.

[21] L. Williams, L. Layman, J. Osborne, and N. Katira. 2006. Examining the Compatibility of Student Pair Programmers. In *Proceedings of the conference on AGILE 2006* (. IEEE Computer Society, Washington, DC, USA, 411-420.

Group Whiteboards and Modeler/Customer Teams: Getting Closer to Industrial-Style Collaboration in a Classroom

David Socha
Computing and Software Systems
University of Washington Bothell
Bothell, WA, USA
dsocha@uwb.edu

ABSTRACT

This paper reports on two simple innovations that helped create a more authentic and engaging modeling experience in an undergraduate Analysis and Design course: (a) having each team of students act both as modelers for another team, and as customers for another team, and (b) providing each team with their own whiteboard. The results from their use throughout the course, and for a single use of the whiteboards in a Computing Technology and Public Policy course, were quite positive. They resulted in a qualitatively different experience noticeable both to the instructors and the students. While some students were initially reluctant to use the whiteboards, by the end of the course most students were enthusiastic about their use.

Categories and Subject Descriptors

K.3.2 [Computers and Education]: Computers and Information Science Education—Computer Science Education

General Terms

Design, Documentation, Human Factors.

Keywords

Analysis, Collaboration, Customers, Diagramming, Design, Groupwork, Modeling, Software, Teaching, Teams, Whiteboards

1. INTRODUCTION

This paper describes two techniques developed to create richer, more industrial-like interactions between "modelers" and "customers" in *CSS 370: Analysis and Design*, a core undergraduate course taught in the Computing and Software Systems (CSS) program at the University of Washington Bothell. In this 10-week course, CSS students learn about modeling: how to create and use a wide variety of business and software models by designing a software-enabled product.

Modeling is an iterative process, where modelers alternate between interacting with customers and working among themselves. When meeting with customers, modelers ask questions and use a wide variety of business and software models to explore, validate, and co-evolve their and their customers' understanding of the system under design. Back in their office, modelers use these insights to create and modify models reflecting key aspects of the product's desirability, feasibility, and viability [4] and to generate more questions for their customers.

This course had been designed to expose students to a wide variety of business and software models. It emphasized the usefulness of communication and abstraction in modeling. Students were exposed to a CASE tool, and required to create a substantial document containing a business plan and a set of software models that could, if needed, be "thrown over the wall" to a separate development team. The course emphasized the modeling process, how different models can help understand different aspects of customer needs, project size, risks, costs, etc., and how models relate to each other.

Historically in this course, each student worked on two projects in parallel throughout the quarter. The first was an instructor defined case study designed to help students learn about and practice each type of artifact. Students were grouped in teams of 4-5 students. In each class period, the instructor would describe one type of artifact. The students' homework was to create an example of that artifact for the case study. In the next class, students would circulate their examples within their team and get peer reviews and critique from their team members. This process generated far more examples of good and bad artifacts than the instructor could, and provided good fodder for class wide discussions. This helped students gain insights into the modeling artifacts and process.

The second project was an individual or pair project done outside of class time. Each student was required to deliver a complete and coherent business plan (delivered halfway through the quarter), and set of software models (delivered at the end of the quarter) for their project. These documents allowed instructors to assess each student's understanding of the individual artifacts, as well as their ability to weave the artifacts together into a coherent whole.

I taught this course for the first time in winter 2011 and saw an opportunity to experiment with creating an even richer and more realistic modeling interaction between modelers and customers. Reflecting upon the differences between this class and high-performing teams in industry, two differences stood out.

One is that the students were designing a system for themselves. There was no separation between modeler and customer. This led to some odd results, like students "assuming away" problems instead of having to deal with customer constraints. While students did have the peer review process, and some worked in

Permission to make digital or hard copies of all or part of this work for personal or classroom use is granted without fee provided that copies are not made or distributed for profit or commercial advantage and that copies bear this notice and the full citation on the first page. To copy otherwise, or republish, to post on servers or to redistribute to lists, requires prior specific permission and/or a fee.
SIGCSE'12, February 29–March 3, 2012, Raleigh, North Carolina, USA.
Copyright 2012 ACM 978-1-4503-1098-7/12/02...$10.00.

pairs on their large delivery, there was less chance to explore how modeling works when interacting with customers. My 19-years of experience in industry inclined me to believe that in many cases modeling (the verb) is as, or more, important than the model artifacts (the nouns). As Scott Ambler puts it, "*one of the primary reasons you model is to help improve communication*" [1].

Another difference between university settings and industry is that industry modelers in high-performing teams often have dedicated team rooms with abundant whiteboard space and walls covered with a rich set of artifacts and visual indicators relating to the work at hand. The whiteboards are a key tool for co-creating understanding, and are one of the most highly valued tools in agile teams [3]. The wall artifacts provide a highly visible and shared form of team memory and awareness, helping them focus on what matters. These enhance distributed cognition and sense making.

University classrooms, in contrast, tend to be sparsely and generically furnished with minimal equipment arranged for presentation mode (see Figure 1). They bear no project artifacts.

What would be a minimal set of changes we could make to the classroom in order to get better modeler and customer interactions?

This paper discusses some changes we made to the Spring 2011 instance of CSS 370 in order to address this question, and how well these changes worked.

2. BACKGROUND

How could we create more authentic modeler and customer interactions in a classroom? What provisions are most important for this?

Scott Ambler's 2002 book *Agile Modeling* lists 13 qualities that are important for effective agile modeling [1]. The left column of Table 1 lists these in priority order. The right column contains my informal assessment of how prevalent these qualities are in a typical university classroom.

Only 4 of these 13 qualities (see ✓s) are readily available in most classrooms. The top 2 qualities "dedicated space" and "significant whiteboard space" are *rarely* available. What does this mean for us as educators? How can we get these in our classrooms?

Many practitioners also agree on the value of whiteboards. In a 2007 study of the effectiveness and importance of 38 different agile practices (covering development, modeling and documentation, testing and quality, and management and organization) whiteboard sketching ranked as the most used (92.7% of respondents) and most useful (85.5%) [2].

In a 2011 study, Whiteboard sketches and Documentation tied as the 5th (of 15) most frequent technique for communicating with stakeholders (following Email, Face-to-face, End-of-iteration demos, and Repository of shared artifacts) [3].

Practitioners view whiteboards are a key agile modeling tool.

Educators have used at least two strategies to create more authentic modeler and customer interactions. Some use a project based course with larger teams so that students need to have this type of interaction with each other in order to successfully deliver their project [10][11], [12]. Some use a variety of different types of customers, ranging from other students to real customers [5], [7], [9].

3. COURSE DESIGN

My hypothesis was that students would learn more about modeling, and become more effective modelers, if they:

Table 1. Qualities for effective agile-modeling, in priority order, and an informal assessment of their availability in university classrooms.

Quality	In most classrooms?
Dedicated space	No; room must be left clean and in standard setup for next class
Significant whiteboard space	Not for 10 teams
Digital camera	✓ Yes via cell phones, though resolution may be less than optimal
Modeling supplies	✓ Inexpensive to provide
Bookshelf or storage cabinet	No
Large table	Rarely
Computer	✓ Usually at least one per team
Chairs	✓ Yes
Wall space to attach paper	Some, but must be cleared at end of class
Projector	One per room, not per team
Reference books	No
Food	Rarely
Toys	Rarely

1. Designed a product for other people
2. Met in person with their customers for significant times each week
3. Iterated frequently with their customers
4. Acted as both modelers, and the customers of modelers
5. Used a shareable model that everyone could see and edit concurrently

The experiment described in this paper introduces two synergistic changes: (1) each team acted both as a modeling team for another team, and as a customer team for a different team, and (2) each team had their own whiteboard to use in their modeling and design discussions. These are described in the next two sub-sections.

Note that in this paper the terms "modeler" and "designer" are used interchangeably.

3.1 Modeler and Customer Roles

How could we provide each of the 10 modeler teams with their own customer with whom they could have frequent design discussions? Designing a product for an external customer would solve our first problem, but external customers generally are not available for in-person weekly discussions, and the students would not get the benefit of acting as both modelers and customers. So, it would help if the customers were in the class.

A single customer in the class, such as a faculty member, would not work because I wanted each modeler team to have a significant amount of 1-on-1 time (at least 30 minutes per week) with their customer team. One person cannot do this for 10 teams.

Our solution was for each team to play both "modeler" and "customer" throughout the course. Here are the details.

In the first day of class, after covering the basic logistics for the course, I grouped the students into 10 teams of 3-4 students.

I then covered the essence of a 30-second pitch for a product or service concept, supplemented by readings on this. The assignment for the second day was for each student to come up with a 30-second pitch for a product or service concept of their choosing within a set of predefined constraints.

At the beginning of the second day of class, I explained that each team would choose one product from their 30-second pitches, but they would not be designing that product. Instead, they would be the "customer" team for this product. The product would be designed by the "modeler" team to their "left". Likewise, each team would be the "modeler" team for the "customer" team to their "right". Thus, Team 2 was the customer for Team 1 and the modeler for Team 3. Notice that whenever Team 2 interacted with Team 1, Team 2 was in the customer role. Likewise, whenever Team 2 interacted with Team 3, Team 2 was in the modeler role. This helped students keep clear on which role they were playing.

Each of the even-numbered teams then had 30 minutes during which to get together with their modeler team, deliver their 30-second project-concept pitches, and decide what product they would co-design. Then the odd-numbered teams assumed the customer role and did the same with the team to their "left".

This pattern continued for the rest of the quarter: each Wednesday each modeler team had at least 30 minutes to work with their customers, presenting and evolving models, asking and answering questions, and otherwise exploring the system they were designing. These were noisy sessions.

3.2 Effective Classroom Setting

The other major dilemma was how to provide the students with an effective set of tools for highly collaborative and interactive design discussions. Here is what we did with respect to the 15 qualities that Scott Ambler views as important for effective agile modeling (see Table 1).

Dedicated space. Could we provide dedicated space for each team, so they could adorn their space with the types of visual indicators and artifacts that are common for highly effective software development teams? Not when classrooms are shared by many classes throughout the day. Different classes have different needs for the use of the spaces and the arrangement of the furniture.

Significant whiteboard space. Could we provide each team with significant whiteboard space? In a previous industry job I had used inexpensive melamine board to create floor-to-ceiling whiteboards covering most of the walls of an entire office, two conference rooms, and one workspace.

How could I get even close to replicating this in a classroom? Classrooms have a limited supply of whiteboards, typically on one wall. Even if I were to cover all the walls with whiteboards, what about the wall of windows? And what about the students grouped in the center of the classroom with no easy wall access?

I happened to have some 4x4 foot sheets of melamine board at home. What if I provided one for each student team? The 4x4 foot sheets were awkward to carry, so what about 3x4 foot sheets? After the first week of the course, I went to Home Depot and purchased 5 sheets of melamine board. Home Depot cut each sheet into 2 3x4 foot and 2 2x2 foot boards (see Figure 2). For $75, I got 10 3x4 foot and 10 2x2 foot whiteboards.

On Monday, at the start of class, I asked for one person from each team to come with me and led them up to a lab where I had stashed the boards. I gave one board to each of the 10 teams. This was theirs, for creating shared artifacts during the discussions within their own team, or with another customer or modeler team.

Each team was responsible for bringing their whiteboard to class, and returning it to the lab storage area after class.

Digital camera. Most students have cell phones that take photos, so they had access to digital cameras for recording any models they wanted to view later. I also had a higher resolution camera (12 MB) that some students borrowed for larger or more detailed images.

Modeling supplies. We provided sticky notes, index cards, fat markers, painter's tape, whiteboard erasers, and whiteboard markers. One student supplemented these with colored pencils.

Bookshelf or storage cabinet. We had none.

Large table and **chairs.** Most of our classrooms have flat floors with movable chairs and tables (see Figure 1), so students could rearrange tables to create larger surfaces or open areas. They could not, however, leave materials on the work surfaces between classes.

Computer. Most students own laptops, so each team had at least one available.

Wall space to attach paper. The walls were never used for the student projects. In some ways, the portable 3x4 whiteboards acted as a surrogate for "wall space". Some teams left their sketches on their whiteboards so they could continue working on them later. Some teams put sticky notes or taped paper onto their whiteboard. No team used the walls or whiteboards for any persistent project status or information radiator.

Projector. The single, ceiling-mounted projector was never used by any team as part of their discussions.

Reference books. We had no reference books beyond the course textbooks or materials that students brought with them.

Food. Food was allowed in the rooms, but not provided. Students were responsible for clearing up after themselves.

Toys. We had no toys.

Figure 1: typical classroom at UW Bothell.

Figure 2: Converting 4x8 foot melamine boards into 2 3x4 foot and 2 2x2 foot boards.

4. RESULTS

The results discussed in this paper are qualitative and anecdotal. This paper is more of an experience report, then a well-crafted scientific experiment. Section 4.1 discusses the instructor's observations. Student observations follow in Section 4.2. Section 4.3 discusses the results of a fellow faculty member briefly using the whiteboards in his class.

4.1 My Observations

This bait and switch technique (having students come up with a product concept, and then forcing them to be the customer for that product instead of designing it themselves) caused some surprise and disappointment for students keen on building their concept. The students, however, soon came to appreciate the arrangement.

Whiteboards. The impact of the whiteboards was noticeable on the first day of use. I use a small chime to get students' attention during group exercises. The class typically quiets within moments.

This was not the case the first time the students were working with their whiteboards. After hitting the chime, the noise barely changed. The students had ignored my request to be quiet! This was my first indication that the whiteboards were working.

I quickly noticed that having the students' work visible on the whiteboards allowed me to walk around the room and offer suggestions, point out flaws, give praise, ask questions, and coach the students. What a delight!

Several teams initially had problems with the arrangement of their whiteboards. When flat on the desk, with seven or eight people gathered around, the text and drawings would be upside down for some. This made it more difficult to read and modify. Leaning the whiteboard against a window or wall and using the windowsill or a table to support its bottom fixed this problem.

One team had the whiteboard propped up in a way that only two people could access it at the time. Once the desks were moved out of the way, everyone on the team could write at the same time.

One team preferred using the 2x2 foot whiteboards, because they were easier to move around.

Modeler and customer interactions. The use of separate modelers and customer roles seemed to work well. Forcing the students to design for someone else dramatically reduced the amount that students assumed away any ambiguities. Instead, they took their questions to their customer team. They pondered what their customer team really wanted, formulated questions for their customer team, wished they had more time with their customer team, met with their customer team outside of class, and sent their customer team materials before meetings.

Dedicating a substantial portion of each Wednesday's class to these modeler-customer sessions allowed the students to iteratively refine their understanding and their models about the system they were designing. It also allowed the instructor to wander around the classroom, observe the interactions and dynamics, and coach.

Modeler and customer teams had some problems. Some teams felt their customers had unrealistic expectations. One customer team asked for major design changes in the third week of class. One modeler team took 3 iterations, 3 weeks, before the customer team was satisfied that the modeler team understood what the customers were asking for. These were significant lessons, and provided fodder for class discussions about modeler-customer interactions.

This division of modeler and customer teams seemed to increase the authenticity of the design interactions and the requirements and models they generated.

Figure 3 illustrates the type of engaged conversation that happened when a modeler team and a customer team interacted around their whiteboard. This level of engagement was typical in this class after the whiteboards were introduced. (It was higher than in the previous quarter without whiteboard use.)

Figure 4 shows the variety of simple agile modeling tools used by the teams: whiteboard, whiteboard markers and eraser, sticky notes, 3x5 cards, printed notes and documents, notebooks, pens, digital camera, computer (black, at top) and, of course, people.

Figure 3: Modelers and customers dicussing their design.

Figure 4: Multiple agile modeling tools in action.

4.2 Students' Observations

By the fourth week, 15 of the 34 students had written unsolicited remarks about the whiteboards in their weekly online learning logs. The most negative comments were from the 1st week of use "*I'm not sure if the whiteboards really helped us that much, but certainly some groups got plenty out of them,*" and "*I think the white board was of a little help.*"

The rest of the comments were very positive, ranging from "*Our use of whiteboards this time around was pretty useful. [...] The use of whiteboards in our meeting with other group members/our customer allowed us to give everyone a visual picture of how we planned to implement our website.*" to "*I loved the whiteboards!!*"

There also were some comments about the interactions between customers and modelers. They painted a similar picture to my personal observations, as discussed in section 4.1. Unfortunately, I did not think of asking them to write more about these interactions.

I did think to ask about the whiteboards. At the end of the 4th week I gave an optional prompt for their weekly learning log: write about how the whiteboards were, or were not, working for them.

14 of the 34 students wrote to this prompt. All were enthusiastic about the whiteboards:

- *In the beginning, I actually loathed the idea of using whiteboards. I felt it was unnecessary and made collaboration more complicated. I was so use to just designating someone in the group as a scribe rather than having a picture of the group notes on the board. [...] I now love the use of whiteboards. It helps to clear up confusions and misconceptions. It also makes communication more equal because everyone can contribute to the whiteboard.*

- *At first I was skeptical about how effective this approach would be. Little did I know how vital they would become in our team meetings.*
- *Our team dynamic has been improved. Everyone is very engaged in the conversation and is actively working with everyone else.*
- *The large surface area of the whiteboards is its greatest advantage. Being large enough, everyone can see what is going on and can make changes simultaneously. [...] Another advantage to having the whiteboards is the ability to erase, edit, and modify easily. A simple swipe of the hand easily clears out sections that need to be changed.*
- *The whiteboards help our group maintain our focus and provide us with a nice visual aid to keep track of where we have already been. It has also made it easier to visually keep our selves "in" the conversation, not getting lost in the mass of 6-8 people all talking at the same time.*
- *there are times where it is easier to just draw it then explain it*
- *Working on the mix of paper cards and whiteboard was tremendous experience that gave us a chance to sketch FOUR UI prototypes for less than 20 minutes.*
- *I am considering getting my own white board to use at home.*
- *I hadn't realized just how many ideas could be generated during this meeting until they were all written out on the board in front of me.*
- *One of the agile principles is to have rapid feedback amongst your team members and customers. The whiteboard enables this because, once again, all the information is available for everyone to view. As such, it enables people to quickly view and interpret the information. With that, they are able to quickly voice their opinions and concerns and make approach suggestions.*
- *The whiteboard allows not just one individual to write down ideas but welcomes all members to contribute. This not only helps speed up the brainstorming process but also enriches and improves it as a whole.*

By the end of the course, 21 of the 34 students had written comments in their learning logs about whiteboards. All but one of the comments were very positive.

Some students even suggested using whiteboards in other classes:

- *I hope it does catch on in other classes, as we're often expected to collaborate without such a tool to facilitate collaboration, and we resort to Google Docs and other tools even in situations where a whiteboard is better suited.*
- *In future classes, I'll be sure to make the suggestion to utilize whiteboards for group discussions if the instructor is not already aware of its many benefits.*

The only limitations that students noted were that whiteboards have limited physical space, support less concurrency than Google Docs, and may not be suitable for final versions of artifacts.

Some groups started to use multiple 3x4 foot whiteboards (at which point I bought more). One group took a different approach:

> *[We used the 32 feet of on-the-wall] white board in front of the class which helped tremendously, as the larger space, allowing everyone to stand up and be part of the writing.*

One team borrowed the whiteboards outside of class:

> *[We] used many of the large and small white boards to develop multiple models and use cases as well as improve upon some of the models that we already had. [... This] has been the most productive use of our time.*

4.3 Using Whiteboards in a Different Course

In the fourth week, I had a chance conversation with a colleague, Mark Kochanski, about the whiteboards. Mark borrowed my 2x2 foot whiteboards for use in his Computing Technology and Public Policy class. Mark noted that [8]:

> *The reaction was immediate and generally positive. [...]As an instructor, I saw more and richer interaction than without the use of these "whiteboards".*

Mark observed that whiteboards:

- *provided a central work product that students could focus on and in a simpler and more accessible form than laptops and paper-and-pencil*
- *forced groups to create a work product out of the discussion*
- *allowed mini presentations by each group about the discussion to be more formal and organized*
- *could be erased and managed easier than flipcharts*
- *can be captured by mobile phone camera for later use*

5. DISCUSSION

As described in previous sections, having each team act as both a modeler team and a customer team, and providing each team with its own whiteboard(s) seem to provide benefits. The students were more engaged, with more enthusiastic class interactions. The conversations between modelers and customers were more authentic. Students had insights because of their role as modelers, and insights because of their roles as customers.

I was surprised at how enthusiastic students were about the whiteboards, and that students independently came up with the recommendation of using them in other classes.

Having the customer teams and modeler teams interact through the medium of the whiteboard and other simple modeling tools is a synergistic thing to watch. Many of the students remarked on how effective the simple tools were for many of the activities are doing. At times, students would move particular diagrams into Visio for persistence or into Google Docs for sharing within their team and with their customer team outside of class.

Despite the lack of a dedicated room and walls to adorn with project artifacts, the changes we made in the Analysis and Design course created a modeling experience closer to what I was familiar with from my years of industrial experience.

Using the simplest modeling tools possible also makes pedagogical sense for these students new to modeling. It simplified the modeling experience while enhancing their collaboration. At this point in their training, it is important for them to learn how and when to use these different models, to see how the different models interact in real-time, and to enable quick feedback both from other modelers and their customers. These were the types of lessons I was focused on teaching.

Scott Ambler suggests another reason to use simple modeling tools; he speculates that using simple tools leads to simpler designs [1]. I have no data to support this.

I believe that quick feedback, including being able to quickly change a model, is especially important, not only for learning how to model but for doing modeling effectively. It speeds the process of creating understanding. It helps students coach each other. It was not uncommon for students to correct each other's syntax or usage as they were drawing particular models. As Alastair Cockburn notes, face-to-face at a whiteboard provides the richest communication channel and results in the highest communication effectiveness [6].

My observations, the students' reactions and writings, and the use in the Computing Technology and Public Policy class all indicate that team whiteboards provide a simple and effective tool for dramatically raising the level of interaction among students.

These changes did, however, introduce some problems. A long-standing tension in this course is how to have a project-based course where students truly embrace their project, and instructors get good assessments of individual students' competence with creating and understanding all of the artifacts and integrating them into a complete and coherent business and design document. Can students as individuals do what they are doing in their group? Moving from individual or pair projects to a project developed by 6-8 students from both modeler and customer teams make this more difficult. Quizzes and exams are a weak vehicle for this.

These changes also may diminish the students' ability to carry their projects (previously done individually or in pairs) into a capstone or entrepreneurial experience. Historically, many students have done this. Having multiple authors from both teams raises issues of ownership of the initial analysis and design work.

The techniques described in this paper provide additional tools to augment those already in an instructor's toolbox. Many of the lessons from this paper may apply across a wide set of domains across and beyond software systems.

6. THE FUTURE

Interest in having teams act in the modeler and customer roles, and in using team whiteboards is spreading. In spring 2011, UW Bothell administrators borrowed my whiteboards for a half-day working session. Mark Kochanski has continued refining and experimenting with the modeler/customer team roles and whiteboards while teaching the autumn 2011 instance of our Analysis and Design course. In autumn 2011 Skip Walter, who teaches a Human-Centered Design course at UW Seattle, used a variant of the modeler/customer roles in one class session where each student team "pitched" their product concepts first to another team acting as "design consultants", and then to another team acting as "venture capitalists". This allowed each student team to get feedback on how well they communicated their product concepts to each of these particular audiences, as well as get insights from the other team. After noticing the popularity of the whiteboards, the Computing and Software Systems program purchased many more 3x4 foot whiteboards for student use in our computer labs. Students continue to use these whiteboards as they work on homework and projects outside of class.

Some open questions are (a) how to measure the effectiveness of the whiteboards and the modeler/customer roles, and (b) does use of these approaches better prepare students for later design activities? Mark and I are working on studying these types of questions, and hope to start collecting some data this academic year.

Group whiteboards have arrived at UW Bothell, and we look forward to seeing how they spread.

7. ACKNOWLEDGMENTS

I thank Mark Kochanski for his insights into CSS 370 (he has taught the course multiple times) and for helping direct me toward workable changes. Jeff McKenna and Mary Hausladen contributed their insights from years of industrial experience as I rethought and modified the course. Elizabeth Davis was a great sounding board for my ideas.

8. REFERENCES

[1] Ambler, S.W. 2002. *Agile Modeling*, John Wiley and Sons, New York, NY.

[2] Ambler, S.W. 2007. *Agile Adoption Rate Survey Results: March 2007*. Retrieved August 28, 2011 from http://www.ambysoft.com/surveys/agileMarch2007.html

[3] Ambler, S.W. 2011. *Agile Teams Mini-Survey Results: April/May 2011*. Retrieved August 28, 2011 from http://www.ambysoft.com/surveys/agileTeams2011.html

[4] Brown, T. 2009. *Change by Design*. Harper Business, New York, NY.

[5] Callele, D., and Makaroff, D. 2006. Teaching Requirements Engineering to an Unsuspecting Audience. In *Proceedings of the 37th SIGCSE technical symposium on Computer science education* (Houston, Texas, USA, March 1-5, 2006). SIGCSE'06. ACM, New York, NY, 433-437. DOI= http://doi.acm.org/10.1145/1121341.1121475.

[6] Cockburn, A. 2002. *Agile Software Development*. Addison Wesley Longman, Inc., Reading, MA.

[7] Coppit D., and HaddoxSchatz J. M. 2005. Large Team Projects in Software Engineering Courses. In *Proceedings of the 37th SIGCSE technical symposium on Computer science education* (St. Louis, Missouri, USA, February 23-27, 2005). SIGCSE'05. ACM, New York, NY, 137-141. DOI= http://doi.acm.org/10.1145/1047344.1047400.

[8] Kochanski, M. 2011. Not All Learning Technology is High-Tech. Retrieved August 28, 2011 from https://faculty.washington.edu/markk/node/433

[9] Khmelevsky, Y. 2009. SW development projects in academia. In *Proceedings of the 14th Western Canadian Conference on Computing Education* (Burnaby, British Columbia, Canada, May 01-02, 2009). WCCCE '09. ACM, New York, NY, 60-64. DOI= http://doi.acm.org/10.1145/1536274.1536292.

[10] Socha, D., Razmov, V., and Davis, E. 2003. Teaching Reflective Skills in an Engineering Course. In *Proceedings of the 2003 ASEE Annual Conference & Exposition* (Nashville, Tennessee, June 2003).

[11] Tomayko, J. E. 1991. Teaching Software Development in a Studio Environment. *ACM SIGCSE Bulletin*, 23, 1 (Mar. 1991). ACM, New York, NY, 300-303. DOI= http://doi.acm.org/10.1145/107005.107070.

[12] Tuya, J., and García-Fanjul, J. 1999. Teaching Requirements Analysis by Means of Student Collaboration. In *29th Annual Frontiers in Education Conference* (San Juan, Puerto Rico, November 10-13, 1999) . FIE '99. 11–15. DOI= http://dx.doi.org/10.1109/FIE.1999.839227

Is There Service in Computing Service Learning?

Randy Connolly
Dept. Computer Science & Information Systems
Mount Royal University
4825 Mount Royal Gate SW,
Calgary, AB, Canada T3E 6K6
403-440-6061
rconnolly@mtroyal.ca

ABSTRACT

A variety of researchers have advocated for service learning projects in post-secondary computing programs. While these projects can achieve important disciplinary outcomes for the students, what has been under examined is the benefit that these projects have for the service recipients and their community. This paper argues that since service learning projects are meant to benefit both student donors and community recipients, we must examine much more carefully how computing service projects interact with all the social actors affected by the projects. Taking such an approach will require recognizing that ICT by itself will not improve or increase democracy, equality, social inclusion, or any other social good. Analogous to the experience of foreign aid recipients in the developing world, some service learning projects may actually do more harm than good. The paper concludes by providing some sample computer learning projects that are oriented more strongly towards achieving true service for the recipients.

Categories and Subject Descriptors

K.3.2 [Computers and Education]: Computer & Information Science Education – computer science education.

K.4.2 [Computers and Society]: Social Issues.

General Terms

Design, Experimentation.

Keywords

CS Education, Service Learning, Social Issues, Pedagogy.

1. INTRODUCTION

"Good intentions may do as much harm as malevolence if they lack understanding." – Camus [9]

One of the most heartening developments in the educational pedagogy of the 1990s was the (re)discovery of service learning. Seen by its advocates as a way to reengage the young with civic values ostensibly lost [22, 33], service learning is a "teaching and learning strategy that integrates meaningful community service with instruction and reflection to enrich the learning experience, teach civic responsibility, and strengthen communities" [34]. Service learning is very much rooted in American intellectual history, with many of its early advocates harkening back to a long tradition of youth service in the United States [32], as well as a wide variety of service-oriented government legislation, such as the Depression-era Civilian Conservation Corps, to the 1964 Volunteers in Service to America, to the more recent National Community Service Act and the President's Council on Service and Civic Participation. Indeed one could even stretch the American emphasis on youth volunteerism back to the Calvinist roots of America's initial theological covenant [30].[1]

Perhaps due to this historical resonance, service learning has been widely and enthusiastically adopted in the United States. More than half of all high schools and over 900 higher education institutions in the United States use service learning in their curriculum [7]. In the past decade, a wide variety of service-learning experiments in computing education have been reported. In the context of computing education, service learning has been praised in particular for providing an ideal active-learning environment that gives students practical experience with real-world clients. Christensen *et al* have provided a concise statement of the perceived benefits of service learning for computing students: that students are able to "experience a real IT environment," that they are "able to add this experience to their resumes," and that they can "feel good about … [their] contribution" [10].

But what is often under-argued is the benefit to the community in computing service learning. It is typically assumed in published accounts on computing service learning that by providing free labor for a non-profit organization, service learning projects are by definition of benefit to the recipients. The rest of this paper will provide some critiques of this stance and will argue that, analogous to the experience encountered by foreign aid recipients in the developing world, some service-learning projects may, despite the best of intentions, actually be harmful for the recipients and/or their surrounding community. The paper will also describe some alternative sample service-learning projects in an endeavor to re-inject some of the original social justice perspectives that were at the heart of the initial service-learning movement [27, 31, 38]. In other words, this paper attempts to

Permission to make digital or hard copies of all or part of this work for personal or classroom use is granted without fee provided that copies are not made or distributed for profit or commercial advantage and that copies bear this notice and the full citation on the first page. To copy otherwise, or republish, to post on servers or to redistribute to lists, requires prior specific permission and/or a fee.
SIGCSE'12, February 29–March 3, 2012, Raleigh, North Carolina, USA.
Copyright 2012 ACM 978-1-4503-1098-7/12/02...$10.00.

[1] Of course, nothing in the definition of service learning would prevent its adoption in other countries and cultures (see, for instance, [2]). Nonetheless, the vast majority of the service learning literature is from authors teaching within the United States.

move the attention of computing service learning away from its benefits for our students and toward the different ways we can make service learning more beneficial to the wider community. That is, following Valentine's computing education taxonomy, the intent of this paper is to "generate debate on an issue … among the broader [computer science educators] community" [46].

2. CATEGORIZING COMPUTING SERVICE LEARNING

Like almost any widely-adopted educational approach, a wide variety of practices are grouped under the service-learning umbrella. Furco [15] has described a continuum to capture the many different flavors of educational experiential service programs (See Figure 1).

Figure 1. Service Learning Continuum

These three service programs differ in their principle beneficiary, their focus, and their explicit educational purpose (see Table 1). Community service, according to this categorization, is primarily focused on the service and the benefits being provided to the recipients; students receive some indirect benefits such as awareness of others in their community and the satisfaction that comes from helping others. With service-based internships, by contrast, the focus is on student learning outcomes and thus the students are the primary beneficiary of the service activity. True service learning, according to Furco's continuum, is the attempt to balance the approaches of the other two so that both the community recipient and the student provider receive roughly equal benefits [14].

Table 1 – Service Perspectives

	Community Service	**Service Learning**	**Service-Based Internship**
Primary Beneficiary	Recipient	Recipient and Provider	Provider
Primary Orientation	Service	Service and Learning	Learning
Primary Purpose	Social justice and civic development	Civic and academic development	Career and academic development

So where do most reported computing service learning programs fall in this continuum? It is this paper's contention that there is a definite tendency toward adopting the internship approach. This claim is perhaps debatable in the sense that what is internship to this author may be understood as true service learning by the original authors. Nonetheless, some computing service learning programs can uncontroversially be categorized as lying on the internship side of the continuum. For instance Tan and Phillips [43] reports a service-learning project in which students created a variety of software systems for corporate clients. It hopefully is not uncharitable to say that this type of service-learning is really not that different from traditional forms of experiential learning such as co-ops, work-terms, and real-world capstone projects. While there is nothing wrong with such a student-driven purpose, one of the key hopes motivating the adoption of service-learning is that the student will gain some type of civic-mindedness through his or her service learning experience [6, 20, 33, 35]. Using the terminology of sociology and political science, many advocates of service learning have argued that it will increase the *social capital* of the participating students as well as broaden participation with, and deepen the commitment to, the surrounding civil society. This civic orientation is one of the key stated differences between internships and service learning.

Rather than providing services to businesses, most computing service-learning programs examined for this paper do attempt to satisfy the civic goals of service learning by selecting recipients within the non-profit sector. Some authors seem to provide mainly a functional justification for utilizing this sector; that is, they advocate non-profit recipients not for justice or civic reasons but because they are smaller organizations whose needs fit a single semester better and because there is a large supply of non-profit organizations that require computing help [24, 41, 45]. Other authors, however, do advocate for non-profit service recipients because this aligns the project with the community orientation of the larger service learning pedagogy. Reported non-profit recipients in the computing service learning literature include schools or other education organizations [10, 12, 17, 25], governments [44], charitable organizations [2, 5, 37, 39, 40, 41, 49], and the developing world [4]. Typical reported service projects are websites [2, 4, 17, 39, 44], databases [40, 41, 43, 44, 49] and hardware or software support [4, 10, 37, 42].

Where, then, do these types of free computer consulting projects for non-profit organizations fall on the service continuum? Certainly the authors of these studies observe that these projects provide the student with helpful computing and non-computing learning outcomes, such as experience working with real-world clients, exposure to work-place ethical issues, better understanding of the different aspects of the computing curriculum, practical experience in a team environment, improving communication skills, putting practical experience on their resumes, as well as the "'feel good' aspect" [39] of the work. Most of these purported outcomes are simply deduced from the nature of the work. A few authors have attempted to measure them by asking the students whether these skills have improved [2, 12, 17, 25, 40] or by asking the student to write a personal reflection on their experience [4, 21, 44, 49]. But since all of the above cited learning outcomes (except perhaps the "feel good" aspects) can also be achieved by traditional experiential internship programs, where then is the service in these types of projects?

3. FINDING THE SERVICE IN COMPUTING SERVICE LEARNING

As previously mentioned, service learning is distinguished from traditional experiential internship programs by a roughly equal focus on the service recipient and the student provider. The existing computer service learning literature appears to have a very strong emphasis on the perceived student benefits. The computing service learning literature is not alone in this regard. Abes, Jackson, and James [1] found in their review of the wider service learning literature that the main motivation for teachers and faculty in adopting service learning is the perception that it improves student learning. Maybach [28] observed that "in reality, the current paradigm of service learning is focused almost exclusively on the growth of the individual student providers" and that the "effects of the service provided, however, are very rarely researched." Butin [6] in his evaluation of K-16 service programs more strongly claims that "there is considerably less evidence that service learning has provided much benefit for the recipients."

How then does the literature on computing service learning perceive its community benefits? Almost without exception, all the computing papers examined for this study assume (directly or indirectly) that by providing free computer consulting work for non-profit organizations, they are, by definition providing a valuable community service. This is perhaps a natural assumption. We computing professionals and professors often make the assumption that ICT is ultimately a social good and hence providing free ICT consulting is by definition a social good as well. This assumption lies at the heart of the computing service learning literature. It substantially ignores the complexities involved in the interrelationship between computing technology and the social world in which it is embedded [11]. In the messy real world, what might seem beneficial to a profit or non-profit organization might not be beneficial to all its employees or its clients. What might, for instance, seem beneficial to an organization at $time_0$ might not be so at $time_N$ after on-going support costs are factored into the cost-benefit equation. Rosmaitia [39] is one of the few authors in the computing service learning literature that recognizes that this "asymmetry problem" (i.e., the problem that the benefits to the student provider may far exceed the benefits to the recipient) is one that needs to be addressed in any service learning project.

As we saw earlier, many of the computing service learning projects involve the creation of web sites for organizations and this activity is treated as an unambiguous social good. But the real costs of a web site, like with any software development project lie not in its initial development but in its ongoing maintenance and support [23]. While some service learning projects endeavor to train the recipients so that they can do the support themselves in the future [4, 44], these student-created web sites can also shift the agencies' limited resources away from their main organizational purpose to instead support and upgrade the new technological system. As Cameron [8] has noted in a non-computing service learning context, rather "than enhancing the shelter's ability to service its constituency, the student placements actually drain the organization's resources."

Providing web sites for an organization (such as a school) might also have complex unexpected consequences that are not unambiguously good. Brooks [4], for instance, notes that his students, in their computing service learning project in rural Peru, experience how computing technology can "truly be a force for positive change in people's lives," and then uses as his example of such a phenomenon the fact the school children in the village were no longer rushing outside to play sports during school breaks but were instead rushing to surf the internet. Similarly, providing web sites for teachers is by no means always beneficial for teachers (who have to spend additional time learning new technologies) or for the students' cognitive and academic performance [13, 47].

Even when the provision of free software to a non-profit organization benefits the organization, it might not benefit its employees or its clients. Bruce and Reisner [5], for instance, describe a service learning project in which the students created a mobile application to be used by visitors to an arboretum. While this project may indeed have been beneficial to the arboretum and its clients, what was left unexamined was the effect this student service project might have had on the arboretum's employees or volunteers in that existing tour guides potentially may have been made redundant and unnecessary due to the new software. Tan and Phillips [44] report a service learning project in which their students created a database that allows the university to monitor and report on absences amongst the student body; while such a project may benefit the university, there was no evaluation of the potential ethical issues of increasing the university's monitoring and tracking abilities. Finally, providing free ICT work might benefit an organization but hurt the wider community. For instance, by providing free used computers in a less developed geographic area [4, 42], the end result may actually undermine local expertise by depressing local price conditions and thereby make it difficult for local startups to economically compete against the free options. Interestingly, this is a frequently observed effect of certain types of foreign aid [36].

The comparison between foreign aid and computer service learning is a relevant one. In the 1950s and 1960s, so-called modernization theory was the dominant paradigm in international economics, comparative political science, as well as across a variety of international organizations such as the United Nations and the World Bank. Following the success of the US Marshall Plan in rebuilding the war-shattered economies of Western Europe, the modernization project supporters believed that countries in the less developed world could "catch up" to those in the developed world through the infusion of capital, modern technology, and western expertise [29]. Unfortunately modernization theory ended up being a failed project, both academically and in terms of real-world outcomes. Twenty years of development projects did not result in any significant relative "catch up" with developed countries in standards of living or in economic growth; indeed by some measures the gap between the developed and non-developed world widened during that time. In the academic arena, modernization theory has largely been discredited and replaced by alternative theoretic approaches to development, such as dependency theory, neo-liberalism, and neo-institutionalism [26]. All of these alternate approaches to development highlight how the typical modernization approaches (especially technology infusions) of the 1950s and 1960s tended to reinforce existing power relations and thereby had little impact on improving the relative imbalance between the developed and non-developed world nor did they ameliorate the conditions for the poor within the countries subjected to "modernization."

A very similar problem can be seen in many well-intentioned but unsuccessful attempts to address the so-called "digital divide." In these updated versions of modernization, communities or people lacking ICT were provided with it in the hope that it would be the catalyst to improving their standard of living by providing them with a tool for self-betterment. Naive efforts that do not significantly involve the recipients or take their social context into account have largely been unsuccessful in architecting transformations because, as Warschauer [48] noted, "ICT does not exist as an external variable to be injected from the outside to bring about certain results."

In other words, both the modernization project and many digital divide projects failed because they were predicated on a key faulty sociological assumption, one that is also evidently shared by the computing service learning literature. Modernization and digital divide advocates were committed to a type of technological determinism, in that they believed that technology is the primary agent of social change [18]. As computer professionals, we perhaps naturally assume that technology in general, and computing in particular, has a transformative effect on individuals, organizations, and society. The computing service literature contains a similar latent teleology that technologies are autonomous change agents, "that such agents can affect positive and sustained transformations, that such transformations are promoted by the more powerful for the less powerful … and that all individuals involved in such a transaction benefit from it" [6]. This is an assumption about social agency that is in general not shared by historians, sociologists, and other specialists in the Science, Technology, and Society (STS) research field [11].

It is this paper's contention that when we blithely assume that providing free computer help to non-profit organizations is by definition a social and community good, we are making an analogous error to the modernization planners of the 1950s and 1960s or many digital divide efforts of the late 1990s. When one assumes that providing ICT consulting, installing hardware, or setting up websites or databases will inevitably help the recipients and the wider community, it is often because one is also committed to the belief that ICT technology is transformative and (almost) always beneficial. If we are interested in truly providing services that benefit the recipients, the first step towards that goal should be the jettisoning of this belief and replacing it with a more sophisticated and contemporary social theory, one that recognizes that technologies exist within an institutional and social context and it is this context that determines how or if new technologies alter power relationships and social structures. Thus, the method for creating true computing service projects is not to inject ICT into non-profit organizations, but instead to carefully study the social structures and the relationships within and between the organization and its surrounding social actors beforehand. That is, we need to see how ICT might be used to make the organization, its employees, and its community more equitable, just, and socially inclusive [48]. This will require that those setting up computer service learning projects focus quite a bit less on student disciplinary learning outcomes and quite a bit more on achieving true service for the recipient social actors involved in the service project. The next section will provide some practical suggestions to help in this regard.

4. ADDING TRUE SERVICE

As Buton has noted [6], "service learning is both potentially transformative and repressive." It is this paper's contention that many of the reported service learning projects may perhaps unwittingly not always be beneficial for either the service recipient or the broader community. As well, by focusing almost exclusively on disciplinary student outcomes, these computing service learning projects have not realized the potential transformative effect of service learning. Robinson [38] notes that service learning programs that are limited to short-term work in non-profit organizations provides "poor training for critical citizenship, political reasoning, or social transformation." Niemi *et al* [35], in their evaluation of the political and participatory impact of high school service learning, found that the hoped-for long-term civic mindedness outcome was only achieved when service learning was prefaced with political and social contextualization and when the service work was explicitly tied to political or social justice goals. When such explicit social and political instruction is absent, service learning becomes "a kind of voluntary bandaiding of social problems that not only ignores the causes of social problems but lets off the hook those responsible for the problem" [20]. Various service learning researchers have argued that successful service learning projects need to move beyond service learning as charity and instead embrace service learning as justice [27, 38].

Such an advocacy orientation might, at first glance, seem too political for a computer science course. Yet Goldweber *et al* [16] have argued that computing students are very much motivated by a desire to benefit society and that explicitly embracing that desire may in reality be a key way to increase enrollments in computing disciplines. Just because we are "only" computing professionals, it doesn't mean that such an explicit social justice approach cannot be added to our service learning projects. Twenty years ago teaching ethics was considered the exclusive purview of philosophy departments, and yet today almost 90% of computer science programs include computing ethics instruction and that instruction is almost always provided by computer science faculty [16]. Simply by prefacing computing service learning projects with instruction in the complexities between technology and society and by showing how computing can improve or distort power relations between individuals, groups, and institutions, there is a chance that our students will gain more than just disciplinary computing outcomes from their service learning experience.

Similarly, if we are going to make use of service learning projects, we, as teachers, need to pay closer attention to the social and political outcomes of such projects and perhaps only approve of ones that are oriented more explicitly to maximizing social justice for a wider range of community actors. Perhaps one important way that this can be accomplished is by reversing or integrating the recipient and provider roles, an approach that has been used successfully in some innovative service programs [28]. Rather than treat non-profit organizations as clients for computing consulting, why not, for instance, have homeless individuals teach our students about the difficulties of finding vital government and charitable services in the new internet- and mobile-only environment when one doesn't own a cell phone or a computer. The students could then work with the homeless to show them how to find free internet-enabled computing and how to use web search for locating those services. Alternately, the students could set up those services via an informational kiosk in a homeless shelter; the students would also work together with the shelter's clients so that they could themselves operate the kiosk in the future. In this type of so-called border-crossing [19] service-learning project, the student is simultaneously learning from as well as empowering the recipient.

Another type of justice-oriented service project might be one in which the student works with people who have become unemployed due to ICT-enabled outsourcing. Again, the recipient can teach the student about the social reality of ICT advances, while the student can help the recipient by, for instance, together setting up an online resume/portfolio and making use of online job boards. Another example of a border-crossing service project would be one in which students collaborate with employees working within environments in which the employees are being electronically monitored. Once again, students could learn from the recipients about the potentially disciplinary nature of ICT advances [3] and then help the recipients in setting up encryption systems on their personal computer devices or how to make use of free online services that are less vulnerable to employee monitoring. This last example is of course potentially quite controversial since employers have legal, and often legitimate reasons for electronically monitoring their employees; nonetheless, working with such a luminal case may provide the most important lessons in the civic implications of real-world computing.

Setting up these types of computer service learning projects would be significantly more challenging than the usual ICT projects for non-profit organizations. As Mitchell [31] notes, involving students in social change projects is more difficult than traditional internship-style approaches and that professors "may need to work outside traditional non-profits and community-based organizations to partner with groups actively working to change systems and structures." For instance, there are agencies that do work with the homeless and the unemployed; similarly, unions and other employee organizations could facilitate these types of projects.

5. CONCLUSION

It is this paper's contention that computing service learning has been too preoccupied with the students' attainment of disciplinary outcomes. One of the consequences of this preoccupation has been a lack of critical awareness of the effect that computing projects have on their recipients. By re-orienting computing service learning towards the community recipients in a social-justice manner, our students can actually make a positive difference to their community as well as transform their understanding of the social implications of computing. As Maybach has noted [28], without "an accountability for or an understanding of the needs of the individuals in the urban community, the effects of service-learning projects may indeed be viewed as malevolent by the very individuals whose lives the service was intended to enhance, despite the best of intentions."

6. ACKNOWLEDGMENTS

The author would like to thank Amber Settle, Michael Goldweber, Rick Homkes, and Patrick Perri for providing helpful feedback on earlier drafts of this paper.

7. REFERENCES

[1] Abes, E. S., Jackson, G., and Jones, S. R. 2002. Factors That Motivate and Deter Faculty Use of Service Learning. *Michigan Journal of Community Service Learning* 9 (1).

[2] Al-Khalifa, H. S. 2010. Overcoming Gender Segregation in Service Learning Projects: A Case from Saudi Arabia. In *SIGITE '10: Proceedings of the 11th SIGITE technical symposium on information technology education.*

[3] Ball, K. and Wilson, D. C. 2000. Power, Control and Computer-based Performance Monitoring. *Organization Studies* 21 (3).

[4] Brooks, C. H. 2008. Community Connections: Lessons Learned Developing and Maintaining a Computer Science Service-Learning Program. In *SIGCSE '08: Proceedings of the 39th SIGCSE technical symposium on computer science education.*

[5] Bruce, R. and Reiser, S. 2006. Aligning Learning Objectives with Service-Learning Outcomes in a Mobile Computing Application. In *ACM-SE' 44: Proceedings of the 44th annual Southeast regional conference.*

[6] Butin, D. W. 2003. Of What Use Is It? Multiple Conceptualizations of Service Learning Within Education. *Teachers College Record* 105 (9).

[7] Butin, D. W. 2006. The Limits of Service-Learning in Higher Education. *Review of Higher Education* 29 (4).

[8] Cameron, S. D. 2010. *Getting Wisdom: The Transformative Power of Community Service Learning.* J.W. McConnell Family Foundation.

[9] Camus, A. 1948. *The Plague.* Trans. S. Gilbert. Penguin Books.

[10] Christensen, K., *et al* 2006. CSE Volunteers: A Service Learning Program to Provide IT Support to the Hillsborough County School District. In *SIGCSE '06: Proceedings of the 37th SIGCSE technical symposium on computer science education.*

[11] Connolly, R. 2011. Beyond Good and Evil Impacts: Rethinking the Social Issues Components in Our Computing Curricula. In *ITiCSE '11: Proceedings of the 16th annual conference on Innovation and technology in computer science education.*

[12] Egan, M. A. and Johnson, M. 2010. Service Learning In Introductory Computer Science. In *ITiCSE '10: Proceedings of the 15th annual conference on Innovation and technology in computer science education.*

[13] Fuchs, T. and Woessmann, L. 2004. Computers and Student Learning: Bivariate and Multivariate Evidence on the Availability and Use of Computers at Home and At School. *CESIFO Working Paper 1321.*

[14] Furco, A. 1996. Service-Learning: A Balanced Approach to Experiential Education. *Expanding Boundaries: Service and Learning.* Corporation for National Service.

[15] Furco, A. 2002. Is Service-Learning Really Better than Community Service?" *Service-Learning: The Essence of the Pedagogy.* Ed. Furco, A. and Billig, S. H. Information Age Publishing.

[16] Goldweber, M. *et al* 2011. Enhancing the Social Issues Components in our Computing Curriculum: Computing for the Social Good. *ACM Inroads* 2 (1).

[17] Guthrie, G. and C. J. Navarrete 2004. Service-Learning Impact on IS Students in a Web Development Course. *Information Systems Education Journal* 2 (12).

[18] Hagopian, F. 2000. Political Development, Revisited. *Comparative Political Studies* 33 (6/7).

[19] Hayes, E. and Cuban, S. 1997. Border Pedagogy: A Critical Framework for Service-Learning. *Michigan Journal of Community Service Learning* 4 (1).

[20] Herzberg, B. 1994. Community Service and Critical Teaching. *College Composition and Communication* 45 (3).

[21] Homkes, R. Assessing IT Service-Learning. 2008. In *SIGITE '08: Proceedings of the 9th SIGITE technical symposium on information technology education.*

[22] Kahne, J. and Westheimer, J. 1996. In the Service of What? The Politics of Service Learning. *The Phi Delta Kappan* 77 (9).

[23] Larman, C. 2004. *Agile & Iterative Development: A Manager's Guide.* Addison Wesley.

[24] Lazar, J. and Lazar, D. 2002. Service-Learning Partnerships in the Information Systems Curriculum. *Managing IT/community partnerships in the 21st century.* Ed. Lazar, J. Idea Group Inc.

[25] Linos, P. K., Herman, S., and Lally, J. 2003. A Service-Learning Program for Computer Science and Software Engineering. In *ITiCSE '03: Proceedings of the 8th annual conference on Innovation and technology in computer science education.*

[26] Martinussen, J. 1997. Society, State & Market: A Guide to Competing Theories of Development. Zed Books.

[27] Marullo, S. and Edwards, B. 2000. From Charity to Justice: The Potential of University-Community Collaboration for Social Change. *American Behavioral Scientist* 43 (5).

[28] Maybach, C. W. 1996. Investigating Urban Community Needs: Service Learning From a Social Justice Perspective. *Education and urban Society* 28 (2).

[29] McKay, J. 2004. Reassessing Development Theory: Modernization and Beyond. *Key Issues In Development.* Ed. Kingsbury, D. *et al.* Palgrave Macmillan.

[30] Miller, P. 1956. *Errand into the Wilderness.* Harvard University Press.

[31] Mitchell, T. D. 2008. Traditional vs. Critical Service-Learning: Engaging the Literature to Differentiate Two Models. *Michigan Journal of Community Service Learning* 14 (2).

[32] Morton, K. and Saltmarsh, J. 1997. Addams, Day, and Dewey: The Emergence of Community Service in American Culture. *Michigan Journal of Community Service Learning* 4 (1).

[33] Myers-Lipton, S. J. 1998. Effect of a Comprehensive Service-Learning Program on College Students' Civic Responsibility. *Teaching Sociology* 26 (4).

[34] National Service Learning Clearinghouse. 2011. What is Service Learning? Retrieved November 29, 2011 from http://www.servicelearning.org/what-is-service-learning.

[35] Niemi, R. G. *et al. 2*000. Community Service by High School Students: A Cure for Civic Ills? *Political Behavior* 22 (1).

[36] Pankaj, A. K. 2005. Revisiting Foreign Aid Theories. *International Studies* 42 (2).

[37] Purewal, T. S., Bennett, C., and Maier, F. 2007. Embracing the Social Relevance: Computing, Ethics and the Community. In *SIGCSE '07: Proceedings of the 38th SIGCSE technical symposium on Computer science education.*

[38] Robinson, T. 2000. Service Learning as Justice Advocacy. *PS: Political Science and Politics* 33 (3).

[39] Rosmaita, B. J. 2007. Making Service Learning Accessible to Computer Scientists. In *SIGCSE '07: Proceedings of the 38th SIGCSE technical symposium on computer science education.*

[40] Sanderson, P. and Vollmar, K. 2000. A Primer for Applying Service Learning to Computer Science. In *SIGCSE '00: Proceedings of the 31st SIGCSE technical symposium on Computer science education.*

[41] Scorce, R. A. 2010. Perspectives Concerning the Utilization of Service Learning Projects For a Computer Science Course. *Journal of Computing Sciences in Colleges* 25 (3).

[42] Stanley, T. D. and Colton, D. 2009. Six Years of Sustainable IT Service Learning. In *SIGITE '09: Proceedings of the 10th SIGITE technical symposium on information technology education.*

[43] Tan, J. and Phillips, J. 2005. Incorporating Service Learning into Computer Science Courses. *Journal of Computing Sciences in Colleges* 20 (4).

[44] Traynor, C. and McKenna, M. 2003. Service Learning Models Connecting Computer Science to the Community. *ACM SIGCSE Bulletin* 35 (4).

[45] Tucker M. L. *et al.* 1998. Community Service Learning Increases Communication Skills Across the Business Curriculum. *Business Communication Quarterly* 61 (2).

[46] Valentine, D. W. 2004. CS Educational Research: A Meta-Analysis of SIGCSE Technical Symposium Proceedings. In *SIGCSE '04: Proceedings of the 35th SIGCSE technical symposium on Computer science education.*

[47] Vigdor, J. and Ladd, H. 2010. Scaling the Digital Divide: Home Computer Technology and Student Achievement. *National Center for Analysis of Longitudinal Data in Education Research.* Working Paper 48.

[48] Warschauer, M. 2003. *Technology and Social Inclusion: Rethinking the Digital Divide.* MIT Press.

[49] Webster, L. D. and Mirielli, E. J. 2007. Student Reflections on an Academic Service Learning Experience in a Computer Science Classroom. In *SIGITE '07: Proceedings of the 8th SIGITE technical symposium on information technology education.*

Computer Science in NZ High Schools: The First Year of the New Standards

Tim Bell
Department of Computer Science and Software Engineering
University of Canterbury
New Zealand
+64 3 364-2987
tim.bell@canterbury.ac.nz

Peter Andreae
School of Engineering and Computer Science
Victoria University of Wellington
New Zealand
+64 4 463-5834
peter.andreae@ecs.vuw.ac.nz

Anthony Robins
Computer Science Department
University of Otago
New Zealand
+64 3 479-8314
anthony@cs.otago.ac.nz

ABSTRACT

Computer science became available as a nationally assessed topic in NZ schools for the first time in 2011. We review the introduction of computer science as a formal topic, including the level of adoption, issues that have arisen in the process of introducing it, and work that has been undertaken to address those issues.

Categories and Subject Descriptors

K.3.2 [**Computers and Education**]: Computer and Information Science Education – *curriculum.*

General Terms: Experimentation

Keywords: Computer science education, curriculum, high school, teachers.

1. INTRODUCTION

New Zealand (NZ) high schools are able to teach computer science as a formal topic that is defined in a national standard from February 2011, with more new material being phased in during 2012 and 2013. Despite the standards being new, and older programming standards still being available, over 1400 students in 49 schools have already registered for the new computer science standards.

The introduction of computer science into the high school curriculum has raised many issues, including teacher preparation, course design, and how computer science should be positioned with respect to other computing subjects. In this paper we describe the process for choosing material for the high school curriculum, look at how teachers were prepared for the changes, and reflect on the lessons learned now that the subject is actually being taught.

Until 2011, computer science as a discipline had not been available formally in the NZ high school curriculum. As a result of work done in 2008, the Ministry of Education commissioned a review of computing in schools, and new topics were introduced for the "National Certificate of Educational Achievement" (NCEA) that gave computing a higher status (previously it had been associated with less academic topics), and significantly, included topics from computer science beyond programming. The standards were developed in a compressed timeframe within a larger review of all existing NCEA standards across all curriculum areas, and the first standards were offered in 2011.

The term "Digital Technologies" was chosen to describe the general area of computing in schools. It has five "strands" that cover a range of aspects of computing as a tool and computing as a discipline: Digital Information, Digital Infrastructure, Digital media, Electronics, and Programming and Computer Science. It is the "Programming and Computer Science" strand that we focus on in this paper.

This is the first time computer science has been available formally for high school students in NZ, and represents a significant change in direction. More details about the new standards and how they came about can be found in [1].

While there are strong reasons for introducing computer science into schools urgently, its introduction has also raised issues and put pressure on teachers and schools as they struggle to make such significant changes in a short time. In the following we examine the new material, review its reception, and discuss the issues that have come up in the process.

2. CONTEXT OF COMPUTING EDUCATION IN NEW ZEALAND

The population of New Zealand is around 4.4 million people, which is very close to the median population of the US states (the 2010 median state population is 4.3 million for Kentucky). Because New Zealand is relatively small, is independent, and has a unified education system under the control of the Ministry of Education, the country is able to introduce innovations in education relatively quickly. In the case of computer science, a formal proposal for teaching computer science in high schools was made in 2009, and it was accepted and developed in time to be taught in schools in 2011.

Schooling in New Zealand is generally divided into primary ("Year 1" to "Year 8"), and secondary ("Year 9" to "Year 13", often referred to as high school). The main school leaving qualification for students is the "National Certificate of Educational Achievement" (NCEA), which is the main focus in Years 11 to 13 of high school for most students. The NCEA qualification is flexible, and can be endorsed in various ways depending on combinations of standards that students pass.

The standards used for *assessing* NCEA in years 11 to 13 are categorised into levels 1 to 3, and confusingly, the curriculum on

Permission to make digital or hard copies of all or part of this work for personal or classroom use is granted without fee provided that copies are not made or distributed for profit or commercial advantage and that copies bear this notice and the full citation on the first page. To copy otherwise, or republish, to post on servers or to redistribute to lists, requires prior specific permission and/or a fee.

SIGCSE'12, February 29-March 3, 2012, Raleigh, North Carolina, USA.

Copyright 2012 ACM 978-1-4503-1098-7/12/02...$10.00.

which *teaching* is based is referred to as levels 6 to 8. In 2011, the new standards offered are at level 1, so they will mainly be taken by year 11 students, and are taught based on level 6 of the curriculum.

NCEA allows schools to put together courses to suit local interests and the needs of students, based on a selection of assessment "standards" (note that the standards only specify the content that is to be assessed; this obviously influences what is taught, but there is a separation in principle). Students gain credits by achieving the standards, which are generally worth 3 or more credits each. One credit corresponds to about 10 hours total of teaching, homework and assessment. Several standards are grouped together for a course to make up about 18 to 24 credits; 120 credits corresponds to a full workload in a year. The combinations of standards are flexible, so (for example), a computing course might combine a programming standard with a web page standard to investigate web programming, but the same programming standard might be combined with an electronics standard to explore robotics or embedded systems. Full details of the requirements for NCEA are available from www.nzqa.govt.nz/qualifications-standards/qualifications/ncea/.

There are two types of standards: *unit* standards, and *achievement* standards. Unit standards are competency based, having a simple pass/fail outcome, and are generally associated with a skill that a student can either demonstrate or not. Achievement standards can be passed at three levels: Achieved (A), Merit (M), and Excellence (E). *Achievement* standards tend to be favoured by more academically-oriented students, and are important for gaining entrance to university and applying for scholarships. Unit standards are primarily associated with Polytechnics and Private Training Establishments, but high schools have been able to offer many of them.

Prior to 2011 the only standards available in computing were *unit* standards, and tended to be focused on using the computer as a tool rather than the discipline of computing and developing new systems – the titles of unit standards include "Produce simple desktop published documents using templates", "Produce a spreadsheet from instructions using supplied data" and "Find information using the Internet". Some programming unit standards have been available e.g. "Create and use simple command sequences in a computer language" (a level 1 standard), and "Create a computer program to provide a solution" (level 3). However, these standards do not expose students to the richness of the discipline of computer science. One key change is that some of the new standards introduce topics from computer science (such as algorithms and HCI) rather than just programming, and the new programming standards are more rigorous than the old unit standards.

It was significant that the old standards were *unit* standards. These are perceived as lower status and are not attractive to more academically oriented students. This contributed to the low image of computing among NZ secondary students. An important goal of having *achievement* standards is to put the subject on a par with subjects such as math and physics. They will also allow top students to gain results that reflect excellence in computing.

The level 2 and 3 standards will be progressively introduced in 2012 and 2013 respectively, so the first students to have done the new standards will be applying for university in 2014, and graduating from university around 2017.

Note that the New Zealand school year starts in February (the end of summer), and student results are released in January of the following year, so this report is focused on the design of the new standards and the issues surrounding their introduction to schools late in the first year of teaching for the new standards. Student performance in the standards will not be known until early in 2012, at which point a student focused review will be possible.

3. PURPOSE OF CS IN HIGH SCHOOLS

Significant factors in the declining interest in CS amongst school students in western countries include the widespread misunderstanding of the subject and the career [6, 7], and the confusion of the discipline of computing with learning how to use the computer as a tool.

The changes in computing in NZ high schools are intended to counter these misunderstandings by providing students with a broad overview of the kinds of topics and issues that are dealt with in computer science. Although it will also provide somewhat better preparation for careers, including university studies, this is a secondary goal, especially because there is considerable choice about how the subject is taught and therefore different students will have covered different areas [2].

Tied in with this is the idea of having relatively few standards in computer science. It would be easy to assume that having a lot of credits for computer science courses would give them more credibility or better prepare students for university, but it can have the opposite effect: students who don't understand what CS is are less likely to risk committing to an entire course on the topic, whereas if it is a small component of other courses, they are more likely to be exposed to it even if they regard it as an uninteresting part of an otherwise interesting course. Currently there are 9 credits (90 hours) available in level 1 Programming and Computer Science, so to make up the typical 18 to 24 credits (180 to 240 hours) for a course, schools will have to combine computer science with other topics such as web design or electronics.

Another important reason to keep the amount of content fairly light is that universities currently accept students with little or no computing background, so if some students who happened to do CS at high school had done up to three substantial years on the topic, this could create a diversity of incoming students that would be difficult to cater for. If the first year university course starts with introductory programming then the specialist students would be bored, and if it assumes three years of CS background, it would be beyond what less-prepared students could handle. The net effect could be to significantly *reduce* the number of students taking CS at university level!

Importantly, starting small enabled the topics to be deployed quickly, reducing the time needed for teacher training, developing supporting resources, and administrating a larger programme.

In the long-term when CS has become well established at high school this may become less of an issue, in the same way that students who intend to take physics at university level would be expected to have a substantial background from high school.

Because the term "computer science" is often misunderstood, it has been a challenge to keep it visible in the standards. At one stage the standards were simply called "Programming", reflecting a view that programming was the main topic studied in computer science. At every step of the way, the university representatives ensured that the strand remained titled "Programming and Computer Science".

4. NEW ACHIEVEMENT STANDARDS

The new Programming and Computer Science standards available at level 1 (for year 11 students) in 2011 are:

- AS91074 (Demonstrate understanding of basic concepts from computer science)
- AS91075 (Construct a plan for a basic computer program for a specified task)
- AS91076 (Construct a basic computer program for a specified task)

The official source for these standards is the New Zealand Qualifications Authority (NZQA); all Digital Technologies standards can be accessed from http://www.nzqa.govt.nz/ncea/assessment/search.do?query=Digital+Technologies&view=all&level=01. The three standards listed above have been formally approved and are being used in 2011.

AS91074 introduces three main concepts from computer science that can be summarized briefly as: algorithms and their cost for a problem of size *n*, characteristics of programming languages, and usability of user interfaces. AS91075 and AS91076 cover the design and implementation of computer programs respectively. Each of these standards is allocated 3 credits, which corresponds to about 30 hours of student work.

Level 2 standards follows the same pattern as level 1 i.e. one standard on concepts from computer science, and two on design and implementation of programs, and have the working labels 2.44, 2.45, 2.46. At level 3 the standards (currently 3.44, 3.45, 3.46) become considerably broader; these ones are still in draft form.

The standards dealing with computer science concepts were chosen so that students would be exposed to ideas that are both fundamental but also unexpected. For example, AS91074 includes evaluating algorithms for different size problems. It does *not* require students to implement algorithms, but simply to measure them. For example, they might be given two programs that implement selection sort and quicksort, and time how long they take on various size lists. The resulting graph would expose the quadratic vs. *n*log*n* behaviour, without using that terminology. It would be reasonable for students to understand how selection sort works by watching animations or physical demonstrations, and they might even be able to understand the principle of quicksort, but the key concept being taught is that the wrong algorithm can be significantly slower than a carefully chosen one.

Level 2 (2.44) addresses bit-level representation of data, the evaluation of user interfaces, and data encoding strategies such as compression and encryption (again, not implementation, but the *effect* of such systems, such as the sizes of compressed files).

At level 3 (3.44) a range of topics is offered based on the range in the ACM computer science curricula (such as formal syntax rules for programming languages, network communication protocols, intelligent systems), and students can choose one to explore. The process of choosing a topic from computer science makes the students face the breadth of topics that might be covered, and exploring one in detail enables them to investigate something that they find particularly appealing.

The standards each address several key concepts from computer science that are accessible to the students, teachable by teachers without a strong CS background (with appropriate resource support) and will build an appreciation for a range of fundamental topics across computer science. One issue with introducing topics such as those listed above is that they need to have the scope carefully defined so that a school student with a limited background in computing could tackle them. Fortunately there are many resources available to help with this, and a major project has identified hundreds of such resources of an appropriate level to make it easy for teachers to understand and teach the topics [3].

The other two standards at each level address programming. For level 1 and 2, they are split into two parts: designing a program for a task, and implementing the design as a program. Level 1 addresses tasks that involve input and output, and can be expressed as a single procedure (or method/function) program using sequence, selection and iteration, but only require simple data (no arrays, lists, or structures). Level 2 addresses multiple procedure programs that also use sequential data. The "design" standards (AS91075/1.45 and 2.45) involve producing a design which can be written in informal English, pseudocode, or a graphical format. The "implementation" standards involve constructing a working program in a programming language and testing and debugging it. This split is somewhat controversial, and the reasons for it and the problems with it will be discussed in a later section. At level 3, the design and coding are combined into a single (larger) standard (3.46) that requires programs that use procedures with parameters and files. At level 3, students must use a text-based programming language; at levels 1 and 2, drag-and-drop languages are allowed (and encouraged at level 1). The other standard (3.45) at level 3 addresses software engineering practices, using a disciplined development process and appropriate tools and practices.

The computer science standards (AS91074, 2.44 and 3.44) are assessed "externally" (by markers from outside the school), while the other standards are "internal" (assessed by teachers within each school). For most subjects external assessment is through end-of-year exams, but for various reasons of resourcing and policy the computer science standards (similar to other externally assessed technology standards) are assessed by students submitting a portfolio of up to 14 pages of work. This project style of assessment means that the topics need to be sufficiently broad that students can do individualized projects. For example, for HCI, students could perform a simple evaluation of an interface that they use personally (such as their own mobile phone or a home alarm system), rather than being given a particular interface to evaluate. This supports the goal of exposing students to a breadth of CS topics and seeing CS in action in everyday life, but it makes it difficult to assess particular skills, such as converting binary numbers, which could more easily be tested in a traditional exam.

It is generally preferred that the portfolio for an external assessment of a standard be based around a theme chosen by the student and/or teacher, which gives it coherency and makes it relevant to the local context. This can be a challenge for some standards, but for the 2.44 computer science standard, almost any digital system will have components that illustrate the three areas covered (storing bits, encoding information and an interface). For example, an MP3 player might be advertised as "2 GB", use AAC coding, and have a 5-button interface; or a digital camera might have a 24-bit sensor, use JPEG coding, and have an on-screen menu system. A student would be expected to choose a device, and demonstrate their knowledge of (say) representing data using bits by explaining the implications of 2 GB storage or a 24-bit sensor. This is more meaningful than an exam question that asks "Convert 00101100 to decimal", but it does rely on teachers and students coming up with individual, engaging projects that cover all the requirements of the standards.

By August 2011, most student registrations for standards were complete, and 3,197 students had enrolled for at least one of the Programming and Computer Science standards. (To put this in perspective, there are typically about 63,000 students in Year 11 [4]). The relative numbers of enrolments and offerings of the three standards are becoming clear, as shown in Figure 1. The program implementation standard is clearly the most popular, possibly because it is well understood, but there is significant interest in the computer science standard, which has about 50% of the enrolments of the programming standard. These statistics can be regarded as representing "early adopters", as the documentation and support for the standards wasn't complete until after the school year started, so there was some risk for a school committing to the standards, and no compulsion to do so.

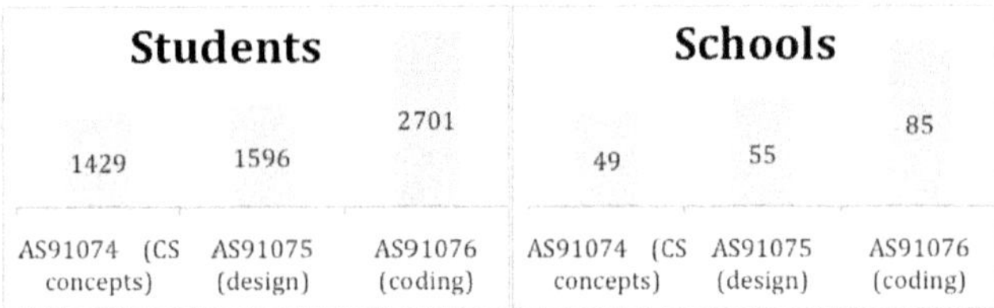

Figure 1. Relative registrations for the level 1 Programming and CS standards, from preliminary data of August 2011

Although it is possible to do the computer science standard without programming, only 11% of students have done this to date. 36% of programming students are taking computer science, and so a significant proportion are now being exposed to the deeper ideas behind programming.

5. SPLIT PROGRAMMING STANDARDS

As described earlier, programming has been split across two standards at each level. The standards are "Construct a plan for a [basic/advanced] computer program for a specified task" and "Construct a [basic/advanced] computer program for a specified task." Level 1 is "basic" and level 2 is "advanced", although the latter is still fairly introductory by university standards. There has been considerable debate over whether or not the split between design and implementation is appropriate, and implementing the split standards highlighted issues and problems that were not intended when they were written.

One reason for a split is purely political: as a general policy, the ministry officials' strong guidance was that each standard should be 3 or 4 credits, corresponding to 30 or 40 hours of learning and assessment time. Given that a first course in programming is typically several times larger than this, to get a reasonable number of hours on the topic it would need to be spread across more than one standard.

A second reason for a split is to make it easier for teachers who are teaching a broad course across several strands of digital technologies to include at least some component of programming and computer science. For example, it is more likely that a small programming standard could be included in an embedded electronics course or a digital media course. For such teachers, especially those without a background in programming or computer science, a single large standard might have been perceived as too much of a commitment.

A pedagogical reason for the particular split into "design" and "implementation" was to emphasise the importance of design by having half the credits associated with the design process. This was intended to counter the tendency of new programmers to jump into coding without thinking carefully, and to spend all their time attempting to modify their program until it works. A second pedagogical argument for this split is that many students find the design aspect particularly difficult when they start programming and need large amounts of help. Since students either get all the credits for a standard or none, splitting the standards in this way means that a student who failed the design component could be provided with a design outline which would still allow them to attempt the implementation standard to get part of the credits, and gain some appreciation for what programming is about.

A counterargument is that at this level students should be able to design *and* implement simple programs, so that making it possible to do just the implementation standard will lead to students who have experienced a very limited and inadequate version of "programming".

It is important to remember that the standards are for assessment, and do not specify how the topic should be taught, so it was expected that both topics (design and implementation) would be taught in an intertwined fashion, even though the split makes it possible for a school to teach design or implementation standards in isolation. Teaching implementation in isolation appears to have happened: 45% of the students have registered for the implementation standard but not the design standard. Only 3% of students registered for program design but not program implementation, which indicates that where design is taught it is usually followed by implementation. Because not all teaching is required to be assessed, it is possible (although unlikely) that both aspects are being taught but not assessed in these cases. It will be valuable to investigate what has happened with such students, and also find out if this is simply a transient effect as schools start by offering just one standard in the first year that the standards exist.

Another issue with splitting programming is that even where both parts were taught, teachers and resource writers have had some pressure from technology advisors (Ministry of Education officials) not to duplicate content between standards. This leads to the perverse situation of classes doing algorithm design for one task, then being given a separate algorithm for a separate task to write an actual program. This is a completely unintended side effect of the design vs. programming split and needs to be addressed by ensuring that the technology advisors (who need not be computing specialists) understand the standards better.

These issues are the subject of ongoing debate that will inevitably be informed by the outcomes of the first year experience.

6. PREPARING TEACHERS

Teacher training is crucial to the successful delivery of computer science, and a designated teacher preparation program is ideal [5].

Many of the areas covered by the new Digital Technologies standards were already being taught in schools (such as word processing, spreadsheets, databases, video/audio editing, desktop publishing and web design) and others were not uncommon (such as network administration, electronics and programming). However, almost none of the computer science topics (such as algorithm complexity, HCI, compression/encryption encoding, and intelligent systems) have been taught in NZ schools. The complete lack of experience in these topics, and widespread inexperience with programming made it clear very early that providing training for teachers would be essential so that they could deliver the courses confidently. The introduction of computer science in NZ has covered a relatively small amount of material (the new computer science standard corresponds to just 15% of one course per year), so it has been possible to get (some) teachers prepared with relatively informal training.

The teachers themselves organized a new national association called the "New Zealand Association for Computing, Digital and Information Technology Teachers" (NZACDITT), which began in March 2009, and from the start played a key role in teacher preparation and advocacy. Teachers were able to share ideas, resources and concerns through a discussion group and a website, as well as local and national meetings. Inevitably, conflicting views exist about how the new standards should develop and how teachers should be supported, and these have occupied a lot of the energy of the group. However, there has also been a lot of peer support, sharing of resources and organizing of "PD" (professional development) events done by the group, and a lot has been achieved in its very short history.

An informal survey was run in late 2010 through NZACDITT to see how well prepared teachers felt for the changes in 2011. The survey showed a high level of interest in the new Digital Technologies standards: of the 106 respondents, 91% reported that they would be using some of the new standards in 2011 for their year 11 classes, 5% were unsure, and 5% did not plan to use any.

The most popular standards that teachers anticipated using were concepts of information management, producing a digital outcome e.g. word processor document, and producing a digital media outcome e.g. video (91% for each). The less popular standards were two topics on infrastructure e.g. components of a computer (35% and 16%), and three on electronics (6%, 6% and 5%). 55% of teachers planned to use the standard on "basic concepts from computer science", with the two programming standards for design and implementation polling at 53% and 66% respectively. The survey also asked "Do you feel you will be ready to teach Digital Technologies in 2011?", to which 42% responded "yes", 22% "no", and 37% were unsure. The survey identified that teachers were particularly interested in being given "exciting lessons and lots of exercises", "a simplified structured programme", and "a glossary of terms".

Although in principle teachers should create locally relevant programs themselves, it is clear that, at least initially, it is helpful to be told exactly what to do. Because the topics are unfamiliar and the standards are new, teachers will be concerned that they might teach material that doesn't match the expectations of the standards. Thus strong guidance provides security for teachers that they are doing the right thing for their students.

Initially a lot of work was put into simply giving teachers confidence that they could get up to speed on these topics. Seeing terms like "encryption" and "intelligent systems" is daunting for someone who has come from a less technical background, yet the level at which these need to be taught can be done using relatively simple material that is abundantly available online and relates to everyday experience [3].

As an example, some teachers have balked at teaching the topic of "compression", yet developed enthusiasm once they learned that it involved activities like measuring the size of MP3 files, comparing the compression on different types of files (rock music, classical music, silence), and pondering the consequences of having to store all music in an uncompressed format. At university level students would be expected to understand what is happening inside the files, but because the goal of the new standards is to expose students to the scope of computer science, the focus is on exploring how the great ideas in computer science are used in daily life. Of course, some understanding is valuable, and teachers are referred to many resources designed to help non-specialists to understand the principles at work.

Some teachers had already been teaching programming in a variety of languages, so there was reasonable peer support for this, but the change in standards brought an opportunity to re-think which programming language should be taught. The new standards can be covered by most programming languages, but Python and Scratch emerged as popular choices, and teachers asked for training in these languages. At level 2, Python is emerging as a popular language, particularly for those who haven't offered programming in the past.

Many other computing teachers had not been teaching programming, and found the prospect daunting. Many teachers attended workshops on programming delivered by university faculty to show the teachers what was required for the standards, and to give them some experience with programming. While some teachers coped with the programming well, others found it difficult, and it became clear that substantially more professional development support would be necessary to bring all computing teachers to the level required for teaching to these standards.

Even teachers who were confident in programming needed support with terminology; for example, the level 1 programming standard requires the use of different types, and one teacher was unsure if Scratch had types (in fact, it has at least integers, strings, and Booleans in expressions, although digging deeper one finds that type errors are silently ignored!)

There are 7 computer science departments in NZ universities, and they have cooperated to support teachers who want to get up to speed with the new material. Each university has a local contact person who can provide direct support to local teachers. In addition, over the last year they have provided dozens of sessions at teacher conferences, training days, and workshops to first teach the teachers at the level that the students will be learning, and then give them confidence to explore the topics further.

A key project has been a joint venture between the seven university CS departments and the Ministry of Education, who have put up matching funds to generate an extensive list of resources for teaching computer science. The guide to resources, focused on the Programming and CS standards, is published through the NZACDITT website (they can be viewed at http://nzacditt.org.nz/project/programming-and-cs). The search for resources has produced hundreds of on-line sites that have (usually) free material teaching CS concepts [3]. To avoid overwhelming teachers, the resource guide begins with an "Our Picks" section which highlights a small number of resources that are particularly appropriate. There are also lesson plans provided as a starting point for teachers who want even more specific guidance, and these have proved popular.

One concern for the future is that there has been no indication from the Colleges of Education of changes in the teacher education programmes to support the new Digital Technologies standards. In the longer term, it is essential that they support the preparation of teachers for this area.

Long term efforts will need to include relevant training for new teachers, and re-training for existing teachers who don't have a CS background. CS has been placed in the technology area; half of the technology teachers in NZ are over 50 years old, and will have varying levels of motivation to re-train at that stage of their career. However, upcoming retirements mean that there is an opportunity to recruit new teachers with more appropriate skills.

7. ISSUES ARISING AND CONCLUSIONS

Computer science has been introduced into NZ schools in just two years from planning to implementation. The high pace has meant a lot of pressure for all concerned and inevitably the structure isn't as polished as it might be, but the relatively high levels of adoption reflect a strong interest in delivering the subject in schools. Government departments have been hard pressed to deliver supporting material in such a short time, and teacher training organizations are yet to adapt to the new standards, but this has been balanced by high levels of support for teachers from peers, universities and industry organizations. Such support is more haphazard and not always ideal, but it comes with a level of enthusiasm that provides some compensation for a lack of official programmes.

The normal process would be having a body of knowledge written before the standards are developed; because of the haste, these ended up being developed in tandem. While this led to some uncertainty as each changed by being informed by the other, it also meant that there was flexibility so that each could be fine-tuned to work better in practice.

The difficulty of developing resources (exemplars and sample assessments) to support the teaching was severely underestimated, mainly because it was a brand new topic, and the usual source of resource writers – teachers – did not have the experience to produce good resources in the short time frame. The late provision of these resources (long after the promised time and well after the teaching year had started) has been a source of great frustration and complaint by teachers.

Staff from many of the universities ran professional development (PD) workshops in various parts of the country. Although these were not enough, either in time or coverage of the country, the combination of this PD, existing expertise and teacher peer support, particularly in larger schools where there were more teachers with a broader background, meant that a relatively large number of students had access to the new material. Smaller schools and those further from the main centres found it harder to get up to speed with the new material. Good PD is strongly in the interests of both universities and industry, and partnership arrangements with the Ministry of Education have arisen from this motivation.

Given these problems, it is clear that the decision to aim for a smaller introduction to computer science, rather than a full three year programme, was critical. In particular, the PD barrier would have been insurmountable with a full programme – it would take years to prepare teachers who were fully qualified in CS.

One effect of the compressed timeframe was that some of the decisions made are controversial and may not work as intended. It is important that these decisions are revisited in a short timeframe, as soon as there is data from actual teaching practice.

Despite the huge pressures on writers and teachers alike caused by the rapid introduction, it still seems well worthwhile taking the short window of opportunity that opened in 2009, even if it will take some time to iron out the problems and spread it through a wider number of schools. The path chosen is one of "learning on the job", which provides opportunities for some students earlier, and means that resources are developed that meet real and immediate needs. It also prevented the proposed changes getting bogged down in the development process, which could have ultimately resulted in no change.

Having computer science, and computing in general, as a part of the "Technology" part of the NZ curriculum has raised issues because of having similar structures imposed on computing as those used for food technology and materials technology. In principle there are many similarities, such as designing for clients, but in practice the nature of the "materials" is quite different, and this has lead to some awkward compromises.

In the process of introducing this new topic to NZ schools, much has been learned, the attitudes of many teachers and officials have changed, and universities and industry have become much more engaged with schools. The success of the changes will be easier to judge when the first year results are released in January 2012, and the real effect will take several years to observe. In the meantime, work continues at a high pace and in spite of scarce resourcing, to equip teachers as best as possible to get students excited about programming and computer science.

8. ACKNOWLEDGEMENTS

Linda Pettigrew has provided us with helpful insights based on her discussions with teachers. We are grateful to NZACDITT, Natcoll, John Creighton, Geoff Gibbs and Scott Telfer for providing statistics relating to the adoption of the standards.

9. REFERENCES

[1] Bell, T., Andreae, P. and Lambert, L. (2010) *Computer Science in New Zealand High Schools.* Brisbane, Australia: 12th Australasian Computing Education Conference (ACE 2010), 18-21 Jan 2010. In Australian Computer Science Communications, 32, 2, 15-22.

[2] DTEP (2009), Outcomes from Digital Technologies Expert Panel / Ministry of Education Process, and Recommendations of the Digital Technologies Expert Panel (DTEP), retrieved from http://www.techlink.org.nz/curriculum-support/tks/resources/Outcomes-from-DTEP.pdf, August 2011

[3] Murugesh, S., Bell, T. and McGrath, A. (2010) *A Review of Computer Science Resources to Support NCEA.* Dunedin, New Zealand: 1st Annual Conference of Computing and Information Technology Research and Education NZ (CITRENZ2010), 6-9 Jul 2010. In Proceedings of the 1st Annual Conference of Computing and Information Technology Research and Education NZ, 173-181.

[4] NZQA (2011), Annual Report on NCEA & New Zealand Scholarship Data & Statistics (2010), May 2011, retrieved from http://www.nzqa.govt.nz/assets/About-us/Publications/ncea-annualreport-2010.pdf, August 2011

[5] Ragonis, N., Hazzan, O. & Gal-Ezer, J. (2010), A survey of computer science teacher preparation programs in Israel tells us: computer science deserves a designated high school teacher preparation!, *in* Gary Lewandowski; Steven A. Wolfman; Thomas J. Cortina & Ellen Lowenfeld Walker, ed., *SIGCSE* , ACM, pp. 401-405.

[6] Tucker, A.B. (2010). K-12 computer science: aspirations, realities and challenges. In: J. Hromkovic, R. Královic, J. Vahrenhold (Eds.): ISSEP 2010, LNCS, 5941, 22–34.

[7] Woratschek and Lenox (2009). Student Attitudes and Perceptions Regarding Computing and its Related Disciplines. *Information Systems Education Journal*, 7 (58). http://isedj.org/7/58/

Web Science: Expanding the Notion of Computer Science

Su White
Electronics and Computer Science
University of Southampton
UK
+44 23 8059 4471
saw@ecs.soton.ac.uk

Michalis N Vafopoulos
Aristotle University of Thessaloniki
Thessaloniki
Greece
+30 23 1038 3619
vaf@aegean.gr

ABSTRACT

This paper discusses the role and place of Web Science in the computing disciplines. It provides an account of work which has been established towards defining an initial curriculum for Web Science. It presents and analyses plans for future curriculum developments utilizing novel methods to support and elaborate curriculum definition and review. The findings of a desk survey of Web Science education are presented. The paper then recommends future activities which may help determine whether we should expand the notion of computer science.

Categories and Subject Descriptors

K.3.2 [**Computers and Education**]: Computer and Information Science Education – *Computer Science Education, Curriculum.*

General Terms

Documentation, Design, Human Factors, Standardization.

Keywords

Co-creation, Co-evolution, Computing Curriculum, Educational Repository, Inter-disciplinarity, Negotiated Curriculum, Web Science Curriculum, Web Science Education.

1. INTRODUCTION

This paper considers what place Web Science might occupy within the family of the computing disciplines. Initially defined as "the science of decentralized information systems", the coherent case for Web Science as a discipline is presented by Berners-Lee et al in 2006 [7, 8]. Having established itself as a rapidly evolving and fundamentally interdisciplinary field of study [13, 20] explorations and discussions of the relationship between Web Science and computer science have been initiated [14, 17, 21].

Since 2006 a series of curriculum development workshops have taken place and a number of institutions have begun to teach Web Science at masters and undergraduate level. Postgraduate Summer Schools have been organized and seminar series established. Perspectives and understandings of Web Science have also been integrated into established courses, typically as a perspective which demonstrates current theoretical advances and furnishes examples of contemporary practice. A Web Science curriculum categorization exercise has been undertaken [24, 25] (Table 1) and collaborations have been formed to define and agree a Web Science curriculum [26].

Permission to make digital or hard copies of all or part of this work for personal or classroom use is granted without fee provided that copies are not made or distributed for profit or commercial advantage and that copies bear this notice and the full citation on the first page. To copy otherwise, or republish, to post on servers or to redistribute to lists, requires prior specific permission and/or a fee.
SIGCSE'12, February 29–March 3, 2012, Raleigh, North Carolina, USA
Copyright 2012 ACM 978-1-4503-1098-7/12/02...$10.00.

The practice of established computing disciplines is to define and evolve subject definitions as formal recommendations for model curricula. Typically published by professional bodies like the ACM, these provide definitions of the aims and objectives of their curricula. Content is influenced by reflections, public discussion, and the de-facto realization of programs of study across universities and colleges worldwide. Faculty regularly report insights to communities like SIGCSE on changes whose impact ranges across individual topic areas, whole courses and programs.

The rest of this paper tracks the emergence of Web Science. It presents an account of a preliminary definition of the Web Science body of knowledge and associated curriculum initiatives. It considers the background to recent changes in the ACM curriculum family. It compares the emerging Web Science curricula with the various computing curricula to provide evidence to take this discussion further.

Questions necessarily arise: is it true, as Shneiderman claims in The Communications of the ACM [21], that *Web Science signals a whole new way of thinking about computer science*? Does Web Science have any chance of being recognized, when, as Hendler et al. point out [14], its only place in the ACM taxonomy is under *'miscellaneous'*? Can communities like SIGCSE agree a place for Web Science in existing curricula, either as a specialism or in its own right? Is it time to expand our notions of computer science?

2. WHAT IS WEB SCIENCE?

Web Science as a coherent area of study was brought formally to academic and public attention in 2006 with publications [7, 8] and the official launch of the Web Science Research Initiative. Today the formal Web Science agenda is driven through the Web Science Trust and the annual Web Science conference which since 2011 has been formally supported by the ACM. Web Science incorporates the quest to build an organized body of knowledge which can help make sense of the Web in an increasingly connected world. It is the study of an engineered technology (the Web) and the inter-related impacts of that technology on human, social and organizational domains. The study of Web Science is fundamentally interdisciplinary since it incorporates enquiring into what constitutes the Web, alongside how and why practices and organizations have emerged from, or are modified by, the wider interaction of society with the Web. As Berners-Lee et al point out in their 2006 monograph 'A Framework for Web Science" [8], Web Science, like computer science, is partly analytic but also synthetic.

It must be emphasized that Web Science is much more than the study of web technologies. The web ecosystem in its own right forms an important and coherent area of study. Web Science is of particular interest to members of the computing disciplines because it is in many ways like information science; it brings together science, technology and engineering with social, human and organizational sciences. However, we observe Web Scientists practicing in many different established disciplines. Some have originated in the computing disciplines others are found in independent disciplines utilizing their computing-related insights, expertise or perspective as core part of their subject specialism.

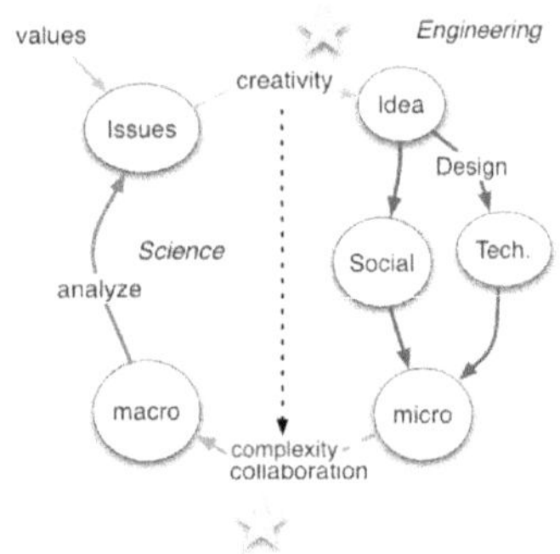

Figure 1. Berners-Lee's science and engineering approach with magic [5] modified to show complexity and collaboration

The complexity and inter-disciplinarity of Web Science has been represented by Berners-Lee as a process in which social and engineering factors are both present [5, 8]. This was first described by Berners-Lee et al and then subsequently developed into graphical form (figure 1). The inter-disciplinarity of Web Science has been the subject of ongoing discussion [13, 14, 20]. It is manifested in the range of perspectives presented in papers at the Web Science conference, and in the variety of different viewpoints and specialisms which are observed in the various Web Science programs of study which are underway and represented at the annual Web Science curriculum workshop. Embracing inter-disciplinarity presents particular problems for course designers; discussed below and in subsequent sections.

Hendler et al. in their 2008 CACM paper 'Web Science an Interdisciplinary Approach' opened the discussion on the place of Web Science in relationship to computer science [14]. They point out that the constraints of the ACM taxonomy reduces web scientists who research and publish in the computing disciplines to categorizing their work as *'miscellaneous'*. They point out this is despite the fact that the Web is: "the most used and one of the most transformative applications in the history of computing, even of human communications. It has changed how those in academia teach, communicate, publish, and do research. In industry, it has not only created an entire sector (or, arguably, multiple sectors) but affected the communications and delivery of services across the entire industrial spectrum. In government, it has changed not only the nature of how governments communicate with their citizens but also how these populations communicate".

In Sections 3, the extent of Web Science in the curriculum is identified and analyzed. The details have been consolidated from a survey (https://www.isurvey.soton.ac.uk/2290) conducted in the spring of 2011, Web Science Curriculum workshop discussion and individual enquiry. Section 4 presents the findings of a desk survey which compares the development of the current ACM curriculum family with the emergence the Web Science field of study and associated developments towards establishing an agreed Web Science curriculum. It examines example programs and courses, and identifies current views on the broader issues of curriculum definition. The final section considers how Web Science might therefore impact computer science and the family of computing disciplines.

3. WEB SCIENCE IN THE CURRICULUM

Currently there are approximately 20 Web Science courses worldwide with the majority at postgraduate level. Only a few undergraduate programs exist; more are emerging. Web Science courses are however sometimes offered as electives or as additional specialisms outside the mainstream curriculum. Although not exhaustive, the Web Science Trust maintains a list of taught programs demonstrating different ways in which Web Science can be nuanced (http://webscience.org/study.html).

3.1 The Web Science Curriculum

Since its inception, the Web Science Research Initiative and subsequently the Web Science Trust have convened annual workshops to discuss the contents and the formal definition of the Web Science Curriculum. Institutions who have been early in developing and offering programs of study in Web Science have pooled their expertise. One outcome has been the definition of a Web Science Subject Categorization (WSSC). This work was initially developed via a wiki hosted by the Web Science Trust. During 2011 it became available for public access (http://webscience.org/2010/wssc.html). The categorization can be applied to academic publications in Web Science, but a core part can also be used to define the boundaries of the Web Science body of knowledge. It is of particular use as a step towards curriculum definition. Working predominantly from existing definitions used by the World Wide Web Conference (W3C) and Web Science Conference a team of collaborators led by Michalis Vafopoulos created a framework for Web Science Subject Categorization [24, 25]. The definitions are linked to matching categories in computing, mathematics, economics sociology and political sciences. Table 1, at the end of the paper presents an abridged version.

Underpinning the Web Science Subject Categorization, is a model of the Web as an application that runs on the Internet the successful technical progress of which is crucial to the Web's universal role. It is vital for innovation that the Internet and the Web work together but advance independently [6]. Readers reviewing the subject categorization will recognize topics which also belong within the curriculum of their specialist area. The topic headings may equate to whole courses or form part of the contemporary understanding of the specialism. However it is also clear that the topics are all part of an individual whole which incorporates the particular multi-disciplinary and inter-disciplinary perspectives which are essential to Web Science.

Category (A) categorizes publications concerned with instructional and research exposition, conference proceedings and collections of papers. It is not directly relevant to the teaching body of knowledge – although teaching and research methods do have a role; see section 5. The web history and methodology category (B) includes web history, related biographies and epistemological and theoretical models of the web as an artifact. The Web Technologies (C) category addresses the underlying infrastructure (web milieux and basic web architecture) and the major enabling technologies for each Web era, namely Web 2.0, Semantic Web/Linked Data and Web of Things. Much of the debate within the Web Science curriculum community has focused on understanding the differences between a technologically-led perspective and a more interdisciplinary unified approach which is claimed for Web Science. Another area of contemporary interest concerns the class of scale-free networks. This area, massively analyzed and used in various disciplines and applications during the last five years, was initially identified through the analysis of real data gathered from Internet and Web networks [4]. The web analysis category (D) covers the mathematical methods applied in analyzing and exploring the Web. The web society category (E) covers topics which represent a range of human, social and organizational science perspectives: economic and business analysis; social engagement and social science; personal engagement and psychology; philosophy; law and politics and governance. This category reflects currently dominant associated specialisms and will inevitably change and evolve. It is also the area which institutions will use most selectively reflecting the expertise of departments and faculty who are hosting and leading specific teaching programs.

Like computer science teachers, Web Science teachers are developing expertise and understandings about effective ways in which to communicate the nuances of the discipline to learners, especially when seeking to explain the ways in which Web Science is distinctive from the study of web technologies. Specifically, the study of the Web and philosophy has been emerged in the framework of the PhiloWeb series of conferences (http://web-and-philosophy.org/). Initial definitions encompassing existence, time and space in the web may become particularly useful in building the principles of web didactics. These factors impact on Teaching the Web, category (F) covers knowledge related to educational approaches for Web Science at pre-college, undergraduate and graduate levels.

3.2 Web Science Teaching Today

In order to extend and refine our understanding of the extent and nature of Web Science education, a brief survey across the Web Science community (https://www.isurvey.soton.ac.uk/2290) was conducted. Ten respondents rated teaching practices against the Web Science Subject Categorization (WSSC) shown in Table 1. For the purposes of the survey, categories A (general) and F (teaching) were excluded although it is recognized that both are relevant to broader discussions of the curriculum. Interim analysis of the responses to the survey were reported to the 2011 Web Science conference [26]. The survey used the WSCC as a starting point for the body of knowledge. Responses largely confirmed a good match with interests and concerns of established teaching programs. Inevitably linguistic differences mean that detail of such understanding is best agreed via face-to-face conversations such as workshop and committee discussions. Since that time the number of respondents has increased, and the findings have remained broadly consistent. We will continue to gather this data from different communities worldwide, adjusting questions slightly to reflect particular understandings or teaching approaches which predominate in different education systems.

Listed programs at undergraduate and masters level are run in Europe and the United States, although it is known that universities in Brazil, Pakistan, Korea and China are also actively teaching Web Science. Undergraduate programs are typically hosted in institutions where a number of faculty have established research in Web Science and thus, there also exists an established stream of postgraduate research students in the area. Furthermore many teachers are already integrating Web Science perspectives into the established software engineering, computer science, information technology and information science curriculum as they incorporate current examples and emerging ideas. There is also evidence that students, at postgraduate and undergraduate level, introduce Web Science into their studies by choosing project and dissertation topics which fall within Web Science.

3.3 An example of a Web Science Program

Figure 2 shows an example structure of a Web Science masters program taught in Southampton. The program has now been taught for three years to a small cohort (~20). Students begin with a broad range of prior experience across science, technology and the human and social sciences, around 25% are CS graduates. UK students specialize from their first year of undergraduate study. The program has attracted approximately 50% female students (compared to around 10% in CS). The educational approach reflects the view that the web is a technical engineered artifact which is co-created and co-evolves. The course is highly participative using the students' prior experience as a resource to enable each participant to develop their own but shared understanding of the interdisciplinary nature of the web. It incorporated activities and resources which are co-created.

An undergraduate degree in Web Science is planned but it is unlikely to differ radically from this basic structure. There are differences between US and European educational systems which might affect such implementations. The program shown has been developed over four years, and is now teaching its third cohort. The team of faculty who designed the course, and who now teach the modules, purposefully included Web Scientists who are not computer scientists and there is active input from an industrial advisory panel. Content has been revised, reorganized and restructured in light of feedback from increasingly multidisciplinary cohorts of students. Although visualized as a progression, apart from the capstone experience all components of the program are present as threads running through the taught sessions delivered over two consecutive semesters.

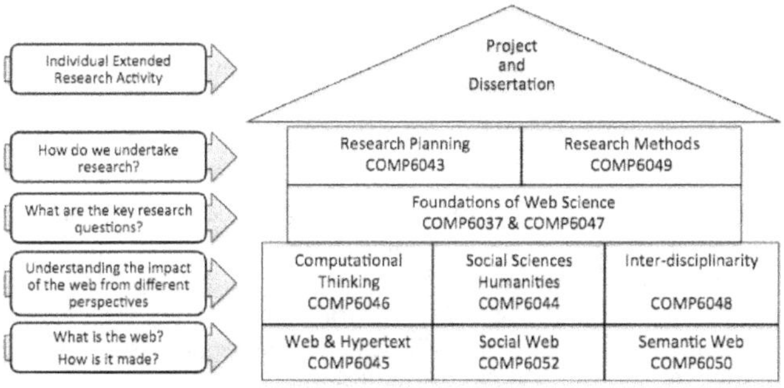

Figure 2 example of course content and approach

The diagram incorporates an acknowledgement of the need for interdisciplinary underpinnings to themselves support the foundations of Web Science. Research methods are emphasized for a number of reasons. i) Web scientists work at the frontiers of knowledge and understanding so research skills are relevant to every possible outcome in terms of career progression; ii) It ensures that the teaching moves beyond the simple descriptive and theoretical, enabling the students to experience inter-disciplinarity rather than encountering it as a static concept; iii) Research activities provide an authentic vehicle of the critical and analytical thinking, communication, interpersonal and team skills.

The masters attracts a mix of home and international students. We offer both Web Science and Web Technology (see flow diagram at http://webscience.ecs.soton.ac.uk). International students overwhelmingly opt for web technology; a subject known and understood in their home countries, although some ambitious international students who intend to progress to PhD have chosen Web Science. The web technology program takes a strong technological/software engineering approach, and only one module (Hypertext and Web Technologies for Masters) is common across the two programs. Currently Web Science students normally progress to PhD studentships, but our industrial panel represents a wide range of companies, suggesting that future work destinations will incorporate specialist consultancies alongside names already familiar from business and IT.

4. THE ACM CURRICULUM FAMILY

It is widely acknowledged that the focus and curriculum content in the family of computing disciplines is constantly evolving. External change inevitably triggers educational and curricula responses. Occasionally, when the disjunction becomes large, individual institutions undertake wholesale revision such as the recent changes at Stanford which Sahami et al. report in their 2010 paper [18]. The SIGCSE community provides a forum for sharing innovations, consolidating learning across our community of practice and providing additional communication channels between faculty and professional bodies.

The ACM has established a systematic program which draws on expertise from across the community and works to consolidate the learning into a coherent form manifested as formal models of various different recommended curricula [1, 2, 12, 15, 22]. Preparation for the Computing Curricula 2013 is now underway [19] which it is intended will build on previous model curricula [2, 3]. The rolling program of revisions demands time and effort, but it is a necessary response to the reality of our discipline areas. The nature of this overhead was emphasized in 2011 when the ACM/IEEE Task Force reported to SIGCSE "The development of curricular guidelines in computer science is particularly challenging given the rapid evolution and expansion of the field. Moreover, the growing diversity of topics in computer science and the integration of computing with other disciplines create additional challenges and opportunities in defining computing curricula" [19]

The ACM has sought to define curriculum recommendations since the 1960s and recognizes the diversity of computing disciplines with its 2005 overview volume [1]. It establishes its rationale in its opening words: "Computing has dramatically influenced progress in science, engineering, business, and many other areas of human endeavor. In today's world, nearly everyone needs to use computers, and many will want to study computing in some form". It identifies a family of disciplines which may grow or change in time (figure 3). CC2005 anticipates that other curriculum volumes would be needed for emerging disciplines.

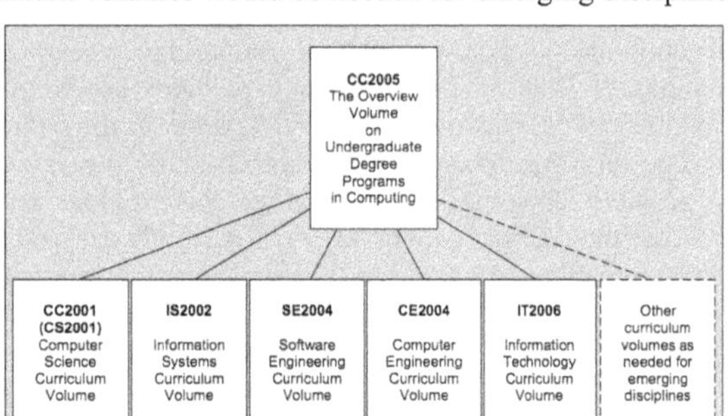

Figure 3. CC2005: the family of computing disciplines [1]

4.1 Web Science In The Curricula

A review of computing curriculum 2005 and specialist curricula within the computing family was undertaken. CC2005 provided the starting point. Subsequently specific model curricula were examined (figure 3), computer engineering and software engineering models, deemed most distant from Web Science, were excluded leaving computer science [2], information technology [15]and information science [12, 22]. The comparison items were course areas, topics and specific bodies of knowledge.

Examining the computing problem space in CC2005, p16 [1] confirmed that Web Science could have a place in the family. Topic areas for the computing family are identified as Organizational Issues and Information Spaces; Applications Technologies; Software Methods and Technologies; Systems Infrastructure; and Computer Hardware and Architecture. Of the 17 specific relevant non-computing topics identified in CC2005, 12 were deemed to also be part of Web Science, overlapping directly with IT and IS. When considering computing topics the pattern was repeated, of the 40 potential topics, 37 were deemed relevant to Web Science, again consistent with IT and IS. Next, specific model curricula all published at later dates, were examined.

- In IT2006 nine of the 13 Body of Knowledge (BOK) items map to Web Science, of the remainder there is some overlap (equivalent to approximately 75% of the suggested hours).
- In CS2008 looking at the core, only three of the 14 areas had near complete overlap, however many of the others are to be found in parts in the WSSC.
- In IS2010 four of the seven topic areas in Information Systems Specific knowledge were deemed relevant to Web Science, with overlap in the remaining areas. All of the computer areas identified were consistent with Web Science.
- MSIS2006 looked at masters degrees. It defined constituent courses rather than a body of knowledge. All of the courses had overlap with Web Science, but the focus was different, suggesting, like IT an overlap of more than 50%

New concepts introduced into MSIS2006 (business processes; emerging technologies; globalization; human computer interactions; and the impacts of digitization) were all considered relevant to Web Science. Similarly all items in the list of recent advances itemized by IT2008 were considered to be at the core of Web Science. Besides the overlap, there is a large part of the WSSC which is not found in any computing family curricula.

Little previous work exists discussing the role of Web Science in the computing curriculum. Riera's 2009 Web Science conference paper argues for Web Science to be added to the family of computer-related curriculum [17]. Riera presents four distinct focus area though which the computing curricula has progressed, each of which persists today; the computer systems; computer networks; web technologies and 'webiety' i.e. web[soc]iety. The paper argues that each member of the family of computing disciplines occupied a different space across these focus area, and Web Science should occupy the next space.

The sustained emergence of new methods and tools, never mind the interdisciplinary science of the web also challenge the traditional methods with which we define and publish model curricula. Community approaches to curriculum development already exists; in computer science CITIDEL is a repository of existing syllabi (http://www.citidel.org/) that enables designers of new courses to understand how others have approached the problem [23]. A community wiki was used in IS (http://blogsandwikis.bentley.edu/iscurriculum/) to help develop the curriculum dynamically [22] . A detailed account of a project to dynamically create and establish a Web Science curriculum were presented to the Web Science conference in 2011 [26]. The Web Science Curriculum Development project proposes a bottom up approach to drive curriculum definition, using the actual teaching materials collected in a community repository as the basis to iteratively negotiate and refine the definition of the curriculum. This is consistent with work by Cassells et al. on using a computing ontology [10]. Reservations voiced by Mitchel and Lutter [16] are to some extent answered by the findings of

Dicheva and Dichev who argue for the strength of the repository-led approach [11]. The approach of the Web Science Curriculum Development Project proposes a means to begin co-creating and defining the body of knowledge, and identifying the actual focus of real courses. That body of knowledge will be more detailed when there are more courses, more students and larger cohorts.

5. FUTURE WEB SCIENCE CURRICULA

More work is needed to agree whether Web Science has a place in the family of computing disciplines, and if so, at what level. An initial examination suggests that Web Science may have a place. Current practice shows far more postgraduate specialisms in Web Science than undergraduate. We might therefore expect the specification of a model curriculum for Web Science to follow the pattern established by information systems in their recent recommendations [12, 22] where the model for masters preceded that for undergraduates, but we might also usefully debate whether Web Science is an undergraduate topic. Three factors which may be influential in distinguishing degrees are i) emphasis on the mathematical and theoretical, often a strong signature in many European degrees; ii) early specialization in subject area – often typical in courses derived from UK roots; iii) broad foundation with later specialization – more typical of North American models. These factors are likely to influence the curriculum content, but may also determine whether a subject is most commonly found at undergraduate or post-graduate level.

The introduction of Web Science into the computing curriculum would add further complexity to discussions on the place of computational thinking introduced by Wing in 2006 [27]. The definitions of Web Science make clear the need to differentiate between the science of the web, and the underlying methods tools and technologies so often manifested as components of the computer science and IT curricula. There are many emerging, perhaps transient specialisms or sub-fields for example forensic computing or cyber-security, often historical artifacts which are able to capture the imagination of potential students, but Web Science is more than a historical artifact. Web Science covers much ground that is beyond the traditional focus of computing disciplines, with attendant implications for teaching and curriculum. This inter-disciplinarity of Web Science raises issues of the relationship between epistemological paradigms, cognitive approaches, and practical application first noted by Biglan [9]. The contribution by Halford et al. in 'Manifesto for Web Science?' articulates some of these interdisciplinary challenges [15]. These perspectives are particularly relevant to the CC2005 listed 'performance capabilities of graduates'. Web Science graduates would expect to perform more strongly in Biglan's soft applied area – suggesting a need to nuance the theory versus application differentiation used in the CC2005 problem space definition.

Web Science has a particular role in preparing graduates for jobs which do not yet exist. Although we may not be able to predict future job titles, we might predict that understanding the science of the web could be a crucial for employees and researchers of the future. Familiarity with a discipline which continues to emerge new technological solutions, business models and to augment and evolve human and social interactions can enable graduates to have the capacity to respond to future change. Developing the knowledge, skills and understandings which are concomitant with Web Science will be a powerful personal resource. Web Science within computing might also shift the gender balance and total skill set of computing graduates, a change which would be most noticeable in computer science. Ongoing debate needs to be scheduled and we should seriously consider expanding our notions of the study of computing.

6. ACKNOWLEDGMENTS

We would like to thank participants in the Web Science Curriculum Development Project, participants in the Web Science curriculum workshops and reviewers for feedback. Frank McCown for comments the first draft and Hugh Davis for ongoing criticisms. Michalis Vafopoulos received assistance developing WSSC from Ioannis Antoniou and Anastasia Dimou, Aristotle University of Thessaloniki, George Metakides, University of Patras, Leslie Carr, University of Southampton, Jacek Kopecky, The Open University and Kieron O'Hara, Web Science Trust, UK

7. REFERENCES

[1] ACM/AIS/IEEE-CS Joint Task Force for Computing Curricula. 2005. *Computing Curricula 2005: The Overview Report.*

[2] ACM/IEEE-CS Joint Interim Review Task Force. 2008. *Computer Science Curriculum 2008: An Interim Revision of CS 2001, Report from the Interim Review Task Force.*

[3] ACM/IEEE-CS Joint Task Force on Computing Curricula. 2001. *Computing Curricula 2001: Computer Science.*

[4] Barabási, A.-L. and Albert, R. October 15, 1999 1999. Emergence of Scaling in Random Networks. *Science*, 286 (5439), 509-512.

[5] Berners-Lee, T. 2007 The Process of Designing Things in a Very Large Space: Keynote Presentation http://www.W3.org/2007/Talks/0509-www-Keynote-Tbl/. *In Proceedings of the WWW2007*, (Banff, Alberta, Canada).

[6] Berners-Lee, T. 2010. Long Live the Web: A Call for Continued Open Standards and Neutrality. *Scientific American*, November 22 2010.

[7] Berners-Lee, T., Hall, W., Hendler, J., Shadbolt, N. and Weitzner, D. J. 11 August 2006. Creating a Science of the Web. *Science*, 313 (5788), 769 - 771.

[8] Berners-Lee, T., Hall, W., Hendler, J. A., O'Hara, K., Shadbolt, N. and Weitzner, D. J. 2006. A Framework for Web Science. *Foundations and Trends® in Web Science*, 1 (1), 1:130.

[9] Biglan, A. 1973. Relationships between Subject Matter Characteristics and the Structure and Output of University Departments. *Journal of Applied Psychology*, 57 (3), 204–213.

[10] Cassel, L. N., Davies, G., LeBlanc, R., Snyder, L. and Topi, H. June 23-27 2008. Using a Computing Ontology as a Foundation for Curriculum Development. *In Proceedings of the SW-EL'08 Sixth International Workshop on Ontologies and Semantic Web for E-Learning in conjunction with ITS 2008* (Montreal, Canada).

[11] Dicheva, D. and Dichev, C. 2010. Finding Resources and Collaborators within Digital Collections. *In Proceedings of the International Conference on Web Intelligence and Intelligent Agent Technology*, (Toronto, Canada.).

[12] Gorgone, J. T., Gray, P., Stohr, E. A., Valacich, J. S. and Wigand, R. T. 2006. MSIS 2006: Model Curriculum and Guidelines for Graduate Degree Programs in Information Systems. *SIGCSE Bulletin*, 38 (2), 121-196.

[13] Halford, S., Pope, C. and Carr, L. April 26-27th, 2010, 2010. A Manifesto for Web Science? *In Proceedings of the WebSci10: Extending the Frontiers of Society On-Line*, (Raleigh, NC: US.).

[14] Hendler, J., Shadbolt, N., Hall, W., Berners-Lee, T. and Weitzner, D. 2008. Web Science: An Interdisciplinary

Approach to Understanding the Web. *Communications of the ACM*, 51 (7), 60-69.

[15] Lunt, B. M., Ekstrom, J. J., Gorka, S., Hislop, G., Kamali, R., Lawson, E., LeBlanc, R., Miller, J. and Reichgelt, H. 2008. *Information Technology 2008: Curriculum Guidelines for Undergraduate Degree Programs in Information Technology*.

[16] Mitchell, S. M. and Lutters, W. G. 2006. Assessing the Value of Computer Science Course Material Repositories. *In Proceedings of the The19th Conference on Software Engineering Education and Training Workshops*

[17] Riera, D. 2009. Web Science: A New Computer-Related Curriculum. *In Proceedings of the WebSci'09: Society On-Line*, (Athens, Greece).

[18] Sahami, M., Aiken, A. and Zelenski, J. 2010. Expanding the Frontiers of Computer Science: Designing a Curriculum to Reflect a Diverse Field. *In Proceedings of the 41st ACM technical symposium on Computer Science Education*, (Milwaukee, Wisconsin, USA),47-51.

[19] Sahami, M., Guzdial, M., McGettrick, A. and Roach, S. 2011. Setting the Stage for Computing Curricula 2013: Computer Science -- Report from the ACM/IEEE-CS Joint Task Force. *In Proceedings of the 42nd ACM Technical Symposium on Computer science education*, (Dallas, TX).

[20] Shadbolt, N. and Berners-Lee, T. 2008. Web Science Emerges. *Scientific American*, 299 (4), 76.

[21] Shneiderman, B. 2007. Web Science: A Provocative Invitation to Computer Science. *Communications of the ACM*, 50 (6), 25-27.

[22] Topi, H., Valacich, J. S., Wright, R. T., Kaiser, K., Jay F Nunamaker, J., Sipior, J. C. and Gert Jan de Vreede. 2010. *IS2010: Curriculum Guidelines for Undergraduate Degree Programs in Information Systems*

[23] Tungare, M., Yu, X., Cameron, W., Teng, G., Pérez-Quiñones, M. A., Cassel, L., Fan, W. and Edward A. Fox. March 07-11 2007. Towards a Syllabus Repository for Computer Science Courses. *In Proceedings of the 38th SIGCSE Technical Symposium on Computer Science Education*, (Covington, Kentucky, USA).

[24] Vafopoulos, M. Web Science Subject Categorization (WSSC) Web Science Trust http://webscience.org/2010/wssc.html

[25] Vafopoulos, M. May 16-18 2011. The Web Science Subject Categorization (WSSC). *In Proceedings of the ACM WebSci '11*, (Koblenz, Germany).

[26] White, S., Croitoru, M., Bazan, S., Cerri, S., Davis, H. C., Jonquet, C., Prini, G., Scharffe, F., Staab, S., Tiropanis, T. and Vafopoulos, M. May 16-18 2011. Negotiating the Web Science Curriculum Development through Shared Educational Artefacts. *In Proceedings of the ACM WebSci '11*, (Koblenz, Germany).

[27] Wing, J. M. 2006. Computational Thinking. *Communications of the ACM*, 49 (3), 33-35.

Table 1. An abridged representation of the Web Science Subject Categorization.
NB: The full version at http://webscience.org/2010/wssc.html also specifies level 3 headings

<table>
<tr><td colspan="2">A General – not concerned with course content</td></tr>
<tr><td>B. Web History and Methodology
B.1 General Web History and Methodology
B.2 Web History
Web Forerunners; Biographies and related stories
B.3 Web Science Theory and Epistemology
Two Magics of Web Science; Actor Network Theory</td><td rowspan="3">E. Web Society
E.1a Economics
Goods in the Web; The Web economy; Antitrust Issues and Policies in the Web; Intellectual property and digital rights management; Web-based economic development
E.1b Business
E-commerce Business models in the Web; Advertising in the Web; sponsored search
E.2 Social Engagement and Social Science
Social networks; Mass phenomena; Collective intelligence; Peer production; Globalization; Systems; Social structures and processes; Virtual communities, groups and identity; Social capital and power inequality in the Web; On-line lives, intergenerational differences; Mass media
E.3 Personal Engagement and Psychology
System Psychology and Behavior; Child and adolescent psychiatry; Tele-working
E.4 Philosophy
Philosophy of information; Objects; Reference and Cognition in the Web; Ethics in the Web
E.5 Law
Intellectual Property in the Web; Digital Rights Management; Digital crime; Laws for Web access; Antitrust Law
E.6 Politics and Governance
Political science; E-Government; E-Politics; E-Democracy; Policy and Regulation; Web Governance; Privacy; Trust; Security; Network neutrality; E-Inclusion</td></tr>
<tr><td>C. Web Technologies
C.1 General Web Technologies
C.2 Web Milieux
Document technologies; Hypertext technologies; Internet technologies; Mobile Web technologies; Grid and Cloud computing technologies
C.3 Basic Web Architecture
HTTP and related technologies; URIs; HTML; XML; CSS and related technologies; Interfaces and Browsers; Servers Web Services
C.4 Web 2.0 technologies
C.5 Semantic Web/Linked Data
Metadata; Knowledge Representation; Ontology Languages; Linked Data; Natural Language Processing; Provenance systems in the Web
C.6 Internet/Web of Things</td></tr>
<tr><td>D. Web Analysis
D.1 General Web Analysis
D.2 Mathematical Methods of Web analysis
Web data sampling and analytics; Logic and Inference in the Web; Statistical Inference in the Web; Statistical Analysis of the Web; Web as a Complex System; Graphs; Networks; Mathematical methods for describing Web services; Crawling; Indexing and Searching; Data Mining; Information Retrieval and Machine Learning; Other Algorithms for the Web</td></tr>
<tr><td colspan="2">F - Teaching the web – not concerned with course content – under discussion and development</td></tr>
</table>

Educating the Educator Through Computation: What GIS Can Do For Computer Science

John Barr[*]
Ithaca College
401A Williams Hall
Ithaca, NY 14850, U.S.A.
barr@ithaca.edu

Ali Erkan[†]
Ithaca College
401B Williams Hall
Ithaca, NY 14850, U.S.A.
aerkan@ithaca.edu

ABSTRACT

Our institution is currently investing in the process-oriented methods of integrative learning to prepare students for a world that is not partitioned along disciplinary boundaries. Our departmental contribution to this investment is an initiative called "Educating the Educator" where we teach computational processes and computational thinking to colleagues from non-computational fields. Specifically, we designed a system where non-computational faculty members (along with undergraduates) enroll in an introductory, multidisciplinary, open source Geographic Information System (GIS) course to experience integrative learning as students. The faculty participants are subsequently required to integrate their newly acquired expertise with their own disciplinary teaching and research; the necessary time commitment is compensated by a three-credit teaching load reallocation. Our hypothesis is that increasing the general faculty's appreciation of computation (in the context of integrative learning) is an indirect yet effective and scalable way to reach a wider group of students to convey our fundamental disciplinary message: computing is more than programming and computing empowers people.

Categories and Subject Descriptors

K.3.2 [**Computer and Information Science Education**]: Curriculum, Computer Science Education
; J.2 [**Physical Sciences and Engineering**]: []

General Terms

Experimentation

Keywords

GIS, computational thinking, integrative learning, education

---

[*]Associate Professor of Computer Science.

[†]Associate Professor of Computer Science.

Permission to make digital or hard copies of all or part of this work for personal or classroom use is granted without fee provided that copies are not made or distributed for profit or commercial advantage and that copies bear this notice and the full citation on the first page. To copy otherwise, to republish, to post on servers or to redistribute to lists, requires prior specific permission and/or a fee.
SIGCSE'12, February 29–March 3, 2012, Raleigh, North Carolina, USA.
Copyright 2012 ACM 978-1-4503-1098-7/12/02 ...$10.00.

1. BACKGROUND

Like many institutions of higher education, Ithaca College is facing a changing academic landscape. During the past three years, our campus community has been engaged in discussions to determine ways in which we can adapt to these changes and address the associated challenges. The concept of integrative learning [20, 10] emerged as one of the leading themes to invigorate our institution and to make use of the teaching/scholarship potential lying at the intersections of our existing divisions. As a computer science (CS) department, we have always pointed out that computational tools are an intrinsic part of many disciplines. We are now able to advocate that computing is an integrative force *across* disciplines; that is, our problem-solving processes form a common thread between different fields.

As an illustration of this centrality and a contribution to our institutional priorities, we decided to create an integrative learning experience based on computation, subject to four considerations:

- **Process-oriented nature of integrative learning**: We did not want to swap content with other disciplines and we did not want to solve their problems for them. We wanted to expose computational paradigms to non-computational scholars to empower them as problem solvers in their own worlds.

- **Computational thinking**: Our field is more than programming [4, 5, 12, 17, 7]. We wanted to show the importance of CS within the standard forms of inquiry of a liberal education environment.

- **Multiple classifications of scholarship**: The discovery, integration, application, and teaching dimensions of scholarship (as defined by Boyer in [3]) is used to define faculty expectations at numerous institutions such as Ithaca College. In order to increase the dissemination of our work, we preferred to operate within the Boyer model so that adopting faculty members can justify the value of their participation in formal terms.

- **Institutional utilization of computers**: Even in academic institutions, many people use computers primarily as word-processors, spreadsheets, email clients, and browsers. We wanted to illustrate that the utility of computers can be extended into more general forms of data processing, modeling, analysis, and number crunching without having a CS degree.

The idea that met all these considerations took the form of a project called "Educating the Educator" (EtE) whose goal was officially stated as *"training non-computational faculty members in computation (in general) and GIS (in particular) so that they can be more effective scholars in their own fields."* Our choice of GIS over other tools around which we have designed successful service courses was also influenced by our assessment of our campus needs. Currently, many departments, ranging from marketing to religion, are in need of spatial data processing; they naturally prefer GIS expertise over scripting, Matlab, etc.

This paper is an outline of our work and a report of our first year experiences. In section 2, we provide a brief description of GIS. The project, as well as its timeline, is presented in section 3. Section 4 reviews the concepts that allow us to conduct "stealth CS education" in the context of GIS while section 5 reports our preparatory work (Fall 2009, Fall 2010) and first trial (Spring 2011). Future work regarding GIS as well as how we envision our efforts will feed into our college-wide general education initiatives are outlined in our conclusions in section 6.

2. WHAT IS GIS?

A Geographic Information System (GIS) allows people to work with data explicitly associated with locations on earth via a precise geo-coordinate system. However, the functions of a GIS are broader and more sophisticated than an electronic map. A GIS is a visual (and typically relational) database designed to work with multiple sources of data to reveal insights missing in single layer representations. Its architecture also allows spatial data to be kept in a centralized location (i.e. on a computer server) for remote/shared access over the Internet.

Figure 1 is an illustration of typical GIS functionality where the land-usage, elevation, parcels, streets, and customer information of a particular region are arranged into separate layers for planning purposes. Our interest in GIS is on its use to enable process oriented integration between different disciplines. For example, GIS layers can connect sociological, political, economic, and religious data/information expressed in map form; queries can then be issued to explore the presence of previously undetected spatial, temporal, and causal connections between these layers. The "What is GIS" chapter of [22] (showing Sir Frances Drake's circumvention of the world) and Patrick Rael's application of GIS in his "The Civil War Era" class at Bowdoin College [19] (to shed light on Abraham Lincoln's election in 1860) provide accessible and concrete examples of this approach; a growing number of edited texts reveal the associated scholarship potential [16, 9, 6, 2].

Currently, the most popular GIS system is ArcGIS which is a commercial package with a robust scripting language, extensive analysis/visualization tools, on-line models, and spatial databases. Unfortunately, it requires thousands of dollars for annual licensing fees. A number of alternative (and cheaper) commercial solutions exist, but their market presence has recently been diminishing. There is, fortunately, a growing number of reliable open source zero-cost options for experimentation [23]. One open source system called GRASS[1], in particular, comes with a well-established textbook that is currently in its third edition [15]. Another called QGIS[2] benefits from a vibrant user community. Many run on all major platforms.

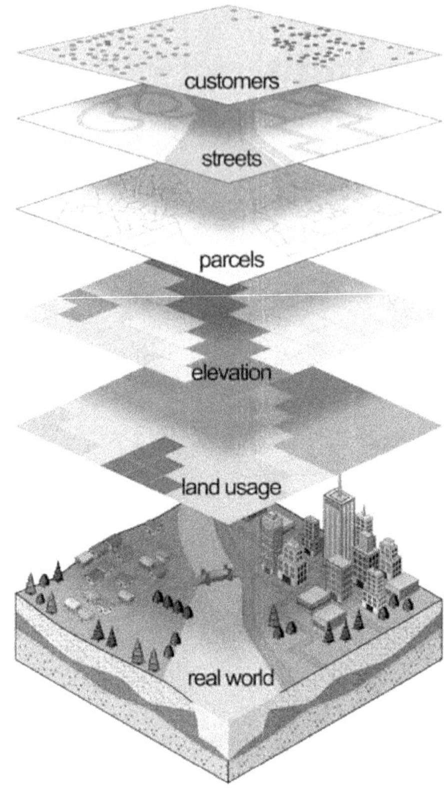

Figure 1: *The multi-layer representation of an area through the GIS framework.*

3. EDUCATING THE EDUCATOR

The "Educating the Educator" project is centered around an introductory, multi-disciplinary, and open source GIS course for a hybrid audience of students and faculty. Upon completion, the enrolled faculty members are expected to apply their GIS skills to a new or ongoing scholarship project in their own discipline. Each semester the course is offered, three seats are reserved for faculty members which are filled via a competitive proposal-based process. The time required to learn and apply the material is provided by a three credit teaching load reduction, financed by our faculty development office. The course was first offered during Spring 2011; the second iteration will take place during Spring 2012. Figure 2 is the timeline of the first two years, outlining instructional, scholarship, and teaching activities associated with the project.

Faculty participants are carefully chosen. Participants do not need experience in GIS but they must have research interests amenable to its use. They must show promise for concrete outcomes such as papers and/or grant applications. Finally participants must also be open to interdisciplinary research (specifically along the Boyer dimensions [3]) since integration is the over-arching goal of the campus-wide initiative.

The course and the support system are designed to provide

[1]http://grass.fbk.eu

[2]http://qgis.org

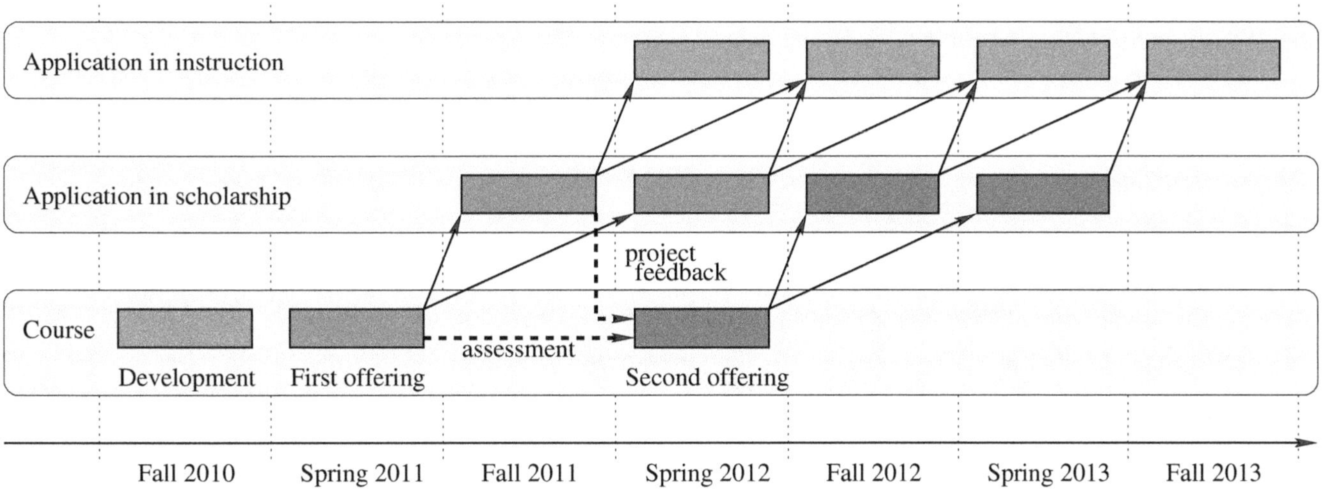

Figure 2: *The three year schedule for the "Educating the Educator" project is best outlined by three distinct timelines corresponding to when the GIS course is taught as well as when scholarship and instructional integration is anticipated. Participating faculty members occupy seats in the GIS course during Spring 2011 and Spring 2012. The first window of opportunity for GIS based scholarship for the first three participating faculty members are Fall 2011 and Spring 2012, as indicated with the left-most two boxes in the "Application in scholarship" band. Spring 2012 is also when GIS can trickle its way into the courses taught by the participating faculty members, as indicated with the left-most box in the "Application in instruction" band.*

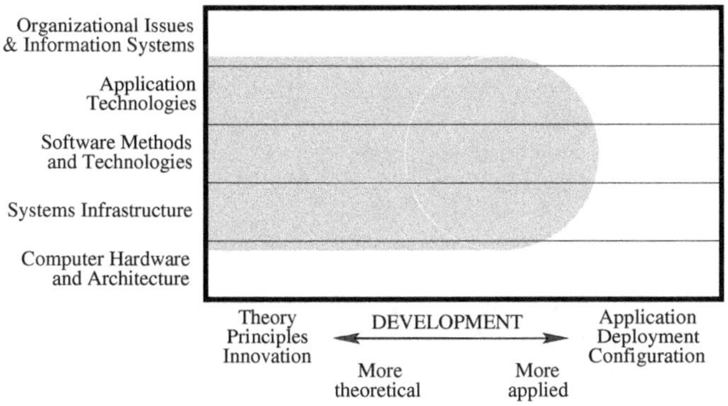

Figure 3: *The two dimensional representation of the problem space for the various well-established computing degrees as well as the particular footprint of computer science within this space; please refer to [21] for the footprints of four other degrees.*

the necessary conceptual understanding and skills to enable participants to successfully embed computation into their research. The productivity of this research, in turn, serves as a form of assessment on the effectiveness of the project. Specifically, if the course and support system truly manages to empower participants, then we expect to see an increase in the participants' scholarship that involves GIS.

4. CS IN GIS

As we were choosing a topic for our integrative learning initiative, we assessed the computing concepts and processes afforded by each of our options. Of all the options that fulfilled the constraints listed in section 1, we wanted one that would allow us to conduct "stealth CS education" where participants would practice and learn the foundational elements of our discipline as a side-effect. GIS is typically associated with Environmental Studies or related natural/life sciences; therefore, surveys of conventional introductory GIS books do not immediately reveal the overlap between GIS and CS. However, as we approached GIS from a CS angle, we realized that we have a convenient and natural context for exposing computationally significant concepts in three ways:

- **Computing landscape**: The "Computing Curricula 2005: The Overview Report" [21, page 16] document breaks down the general computing landscape into five distinctly defined areas: Computer Engineering, Computer Science, Information Systems, Information Technology, and Software Engineering. The problem space of each area is also mapped into a two-dimensional representation of "content" vs "development"; figure 3, for example, shows the focus area of CS. With respect to this framework, GIS are wide and deep enough to serve as a survey for systematic exposure to computing. For example, students are introduced to organizational issues and information systems (by examining, for example, how a GIS could be incorporated into the archaeological dig process, simplifying data collection, preservation, and display), application technologies (the GIS itself), software methods and technologies (the embedded scripting language of the chosen GIS), system infrastructure (the client/server model of distributed data and computation via the creation of a map whose parts and database reside on widely separated machines), and computer hardware and architecture (file systems, network connections, data collection devices).
- **Computational thinking**: Abstraction is at the core of computational thinking since it allows us to draw the line between what we consider to be significant and insignificant. A focus on significant elements, in turn, leads to simpler representations and more precise problem definitions.

Multi-dimensionality:	Attribute tables, coordinate systems
Function/mappings:	Statistical computations, geographic projections, continuous-to-ordinal data conversions
Algebra:	Boolean values/operations (and, or, not), set values/operations (intersect, union, negate), relational tables/operations (e.g. joins, relates)
Indirection:	Maps' inclusion of pointers to spatial data (rather than the actual data) for clear separation between data maintenance and use
Data representation:	Binary numbers, vectors, vector based images, raster based images
Data types:	`ints`, `floats`, `Booleans`, text, binary large objects (BLOBs)
Metadata:	Higher level information associated with spatial data that are excluded from geo-processing
Algorithmic thinking:	Spatial analysis, functional decomposition, computational consequence of reordering join sequences, network operations
Encapsulation:	Map layers stored in separate objects

Figure 4: *Computing techniques, concepts, and elements found in GIS.*

The architecture and operation of a GIS strongly hinges on the idea of abstraction. For example, every terrestrial entity that a GIS can represent (regardless of its shape, size, complexity, etc) is built on three types of abstractions: points, lines, and polygons (collectively referred to as "features"). A combination of features for a particular type of information leads to the "layer" abstraction. For example, the top layer in figure 1 illustrates customer information using point features while the second layer illustrates street information using line features. A collection of layers define the "map" abstraction. For students who have never done computation, coming to terms with such representations might actually amount to a threshold concept [13, 14] and reveal much about our approach to problem solving.

- **Computational concepts**: A GIS is rich in techniques, concepts, and calculations that directly set the stage for their official coverage in introductory CS courses (such as CS1, CS2, Discrete Math, etc.) Figure 4 presents the specific computational concepts exposed through a GIS course categorized by their corresponding CS concept. We see that even without the introduction of scripting, many of the recommended concepts for introductory CS courses (as described in "Computing Curricula 2001" [1, figure 7-1, page 27]) are present, to some degree, in a GIS course.

Because of low-enrollments (as experienced by many institutions), we have not yet had a statistically significant number of students take a CS1 course after taking our GIS course. However, we hypothesize (supported by anecdotal evidence) that a pre-programming exposure to these three categories of information would very much help us in teaching formal CS. Given the sparsity of published research on integrating GIS and CS (we were only able to find [24, 8, 11]), we think that this is a promising avenue to be explored once enrollments are back up.

5. PREPARATIONS AND FIRST TRIAL

Our first venture into GIS occurred during the Fall 2009 semester when the Environmental Science and Anthropology departments of our college asked us to accommodate their students' spatial data processing needs. We offered a conventional GIS course, using [18] as the required textbook. After a few weeks of instruction, we realized that a CS-centric perspective would have greater utility even for students who are not interested in pursuing a CS major/minor. Despite being hidden by a "spatial data processing skin", many of the concepts and skills associated with GIS are indeed deeply computational. Nevertheless, even without being able to do the necessary corrections, we administered a survey at the end of the semester to probe whether we were going in the right direction; the results are summarized in figure 5a. The 4.4 (out of 6) average for "quality of the educational experience" was indicative of our own learning experience. The 3.8 for "value of the material for your major" was somewhat surprising since the course had actually been designed for the needs of the enrolled majors. What we considered encouraging (and perhaps unexpected) was the 4.5 average for "encouragement of critical thinking," especially because we had not actually shifted our instruction to a CS-centric version. Most of our lectures during that semester had in fact been skill oriented.

During the Fall 2010 semester, we designed our new open source GIS course as the center of our Educating the Educator initiative. After a survey of the available systems, we decided not to use GRASS[3] which is arguably the most powerful and stable open source option available (as of 2011). Instead, we opted for QGIS[4] which (i) has a sufficient set of features to support an introductory course, (ii) has a very supportive user community, and (iii) is able to function as a front-end to GRASS if the needs of the students were to exceed the features provided by QGIS. Since there was no textbook for a multi-disciplinary GIS course based on open source software, we produced our own material which ranged from water-shed analysis to spatial social justice matters.

The relevant portion of the student statements collected at the ended of the semester (including the three faculty members) are shown in figure 5b. For the repeated statements of "**Encouragement of critical thinking**," "**Value of course for major**," and "**Overall quality of educa-**

[3]`http://grass.fbk.eu`
[4]`http://qgis.org`

GIS, Fall 2009	Ave	6=E	5=G	4=AA	3=A	2=BA	1=P	0=U	#1	#2	#3	#4	#5	#6	#7	#8	#9	#10	#11	#12	#13
Encouragement of critical thinking	4.5	1	7	2	3	0	0	0	4	5	5	3	3	6	3	4	5	5	5	5	5
Value of course for major	3.8	3	1	2	5	2	0	0	2	6	6	3	3	4	3	3	3	5	4	2	6
Overall quality of the educational experience	4.4	1	6	4	1	1	0	0	4	4	5	2	5	6	4	3	5	4	5	5	5

(a) Fall 2009 student statements

GIS, Spring 2011	Ave	6=E	5=G	4=AA	3=A	2=BA	1=P	0=U	#1	#2	#3	#4	#5	#6	#7	#8	#9	#10	#11
Encouragement of critical thinking	5.9	10	1	0	0	0	0	0	6	6	6	6	6	6	6	6	6	6	5
Value of course for major	5.2	6	3	0	2	0	0	0	6	6	6	5	6	6	3	5	5	3	6
Value of course for computing competence	5.2	5	4	1	1	0	0	0	5.5	5	6	4	6	5	3	5	6	6	6
Suitability of QGIS for spatial data processing	5.3	5	4	2	0	0	0	0	4.5	5	6	5	6	6	4	5	6	6	5
Value of class time for learning the material	5.3	4	5	1	0	0	0	0		6	6	5	5	5	4	6	5	6	5
Value of final project for learning the material	5.5	6	4	1	0	0	0	0	6	5	6	5	6	6	6	6	5	4	5
Overall quality of the educational experience	5.7	8	3	0	0	0	0	0	6	6	6	5	6	6	6	6	6	5	5

(b) Spring 2011 student statements

Figure 5: *Fall 2009 (13 students) vs Spring 2011 (11 students, three of whom are faculty members) student statements based on a seven level Likert scale:* ***0*** $\rightarrow$ ***unacceptable****,* ***1*** $\rightarrow$ ***bad****,* ***2*** $\rightarrow$ ***below average****,* ***3*** $\rightarrow$ ***average****,* ***4*** $\rightarrow$ ***above average****,* ***5*** $\rightarrow$ ***good****, and* ***6*** $\rightarrow$ ***excellent****. The statements that were repeated in both years are typeset in bold letters. The two boxes on the right are the raw student responses. The two middle boxes are histogram representations of the student responses where non-zero values are displayed with a blue background (for viewing convenience).*

tional experience," the average student responses went up by $\frac{5.9-4.5}{6} \approx 23\%$, $\frac{5.2-3.8}{6} \approx 23\%$, and $\frac{5.7-4.4}{6} \approx 22\%$ respectively. Since none of the students (faculty and undergraduate) had any association with CS and since the Spring 2011 course was more computational than Fall 2009, this was encouraging. Furthermore, when asked whether the course had raised the students' interest in CS, seven (of 11) responded with a "yes" while the remaining four choose "somewhat"; that is, every single participant registered increased interest in our discipline.

In terms of scholarship, the participating faculty members applied what they had learned in three different directions:

- **Scholarship**: The faculty member from the History Department used GIS to illustrate his findings as he reanalyzed historic data to remap racial violence in the late-19th century south. Since his findings are yet to be published, we omit the details.

- **Teaching**: The faculty member from the Religion and Philosophy department choose to map out the locations of news stories based on Abrahamic religions, as reported in the New York Times, within a two months window. Even though her results were mostly visual (i.e. she did not have significant results for analysis), her project created an interesting context regarding one of the most fundamental abstractions in a GIS: features. As outlined in section 2, GIS systems represent every terrestrial entity with one of three abstractions: points, lines, and polygons. When reporting the locations associated with Abrahamic religions, the need for tight coupling between pairs or triples of features surfaced. For example, if a story is based in Seattle but addresses an area in the Middle East, then the geographic representation needs to place a point on Seattle, a polygon over the middle east, and a line to connect the two. In addition to triggering a rich conversation on abstraction, we also stumbled upon an intuitive context in which we could have discussed "structs" (and even "classes") since "structs" (and "classes") are aggregates of simpler types.

- **Professional**: The faculty member from the Occupational Therapy department choose to map out membership, district, and event locations of the New York State Occupational Therapy Association (NYSOTA). Furthermore, based on the observation that professional events are scheduled in places that require excessive driving, she was able to propose new locations for these event to reduce the costs.

Finally, for completeness, below are the titles of the projects completed by students:

- Hennepin County Restaurants and Leisure Correlated with Sports Epicenters
- Understanding a FLLT Conservation Area through a QGIS Lens
- Urban Hip hop Youth Movement In NYC 80's-90's
- Mapping the ICNL Newfield Plots: A Crash-Course in Remote Sensing
- Does Behavior Affect Functional Habitat Use in Muskrat (Ondatra Zibethicus)?
- Green House Gas Emissions From Ithaca College
- Research into the Dynamics of Rome's Public Transport
- Sahelian Desertification: Climate Change vs. Human Interaction and its Effects on Annual Rainfall and Land Cover in Sudan

6. CONCLUSION

As we have outlined so far, the 'Educating the Educator" initiative was about integrative learning to highlight process oriented exchanges between different disciplines. Since we believe that CS is rich in processes and methods that can be utilized beyond our disciplinary boundaries, we used GIS to "spread the word". As we educate faculty members in this manner, we hypothesize that what they learn from us will empower them in their own fields and make them better problem solvers, especially as everyone now has to deal with greater amounts of data. We also hypothesized that when faculty members have a different and more contemporary look on CS, it is only a matter of time until their perspective trickles down to their students.

We think that the idea of educating the educator is an unexplored territory with tremendous potential. If we can make just a handful of faculty members more productive in their fields, we will then, indirectly, gain the interest of their students, especially as computational activities are worked into the instruction of a wider range of disciplines.

Finally (and most significantly), during a period when CS departments in at least some schools run the risk of being downsized or closed, we want to make it known that upper level administrators have other options. Our institution realized that computing is too important to be measured strictly with enrollment numbers and allowed us to be creative. The very nature of our discipline is integrative and we have the skills, interest, and knowledge to make the rest of our campus stronger. We think this is a message worth propagating.

7. ACKNOWLEDGMENTS

The authors thank Ithaca College for generously providing the faculty development funding needed to get this project off the ground.

8. REFERENCES

[1] Computing curricula 2001: Computer science, December 2001. Final Report.

[2] D. J. Bodenhamer, J. Corrigan, and T. M. Harris, editors. *The Spatial Humanities: GIS and the Future of Humanities Scholarship.* Indiana University Press, 2010. ISBN-13: 978-0253222176.

[3] E. L. Boyer. *Scholarship Reconsidered: Priorities of the Professoriate,* chapter 2. San Francisco: Jossey-Bass, 1990.

[4] P. Curzon, J. Peckham, H. Taylor, A. Settle, and E. Roberts. Computational thinking (ct): On weaving it in. In *ITiCSE '09: Proceedings of the 14th annual ACM SIGCSE conference on Innovation and technology in computer science education,* pages 201–202, New York, NY, USA, 2009. ACM.

[5] P. J. Denning. The profession of it beyond computational thinking. *Commun. ACM,* 52(6):28–30, 2009.

[6] M. Greengrass and L. Hughes, editors. *The Virtual Representation of the Past (Digital Research in the Arts and Humanities).* Ashgate, 2008.

[7] M. Guzdial. Education paving the way for computational thinking. *Commun. ACM,* 51(8):25–27, 2008.

[8] S. Hambrusch, C. Hoffmann, J. T. Korb, M. Haugan, and A. L. Hosking. A multidisciplinary approach towards computational thinking for science majors. In *SIGCSE '09: Proceedings of the 40th ACM technical symposium on Computer science education,* pages 183–187, New York, NY, USA, 2009. ACM.

[9] A. Hillier and A. K. Knowles, editors. *Placing History: How Maps, Spatial Data, and GIS Are Changing Historical Scholarship.* ESRI Press, 2008. ISBN-13: 978-1589480131.

[10] M. T. Huber, P. Hutchings, and R. Gale. Integrative learning for liberal education. *Peer Review,* 7(4):4–7, 2005.

[11] Y. Khmelevsky, L. Burge, M. Govorov, and G. Hains. Distance learning components in CS and GIS courses. In *Proceedings of the 16th Western Canadian Conference on Computing Education,* WCCCE '11, pages 17–21, New York, NY, USA, 2011. ACM.

[12] J. J. Lu and G. H. Fletcher. Thinking about computational thinking. In *SIGCSE '09: Proceedings of the 40th ACM technical symposium on Computer science education,* pages 260–264, New York, NY, USA, 2009. ACM.

[13] J. H. F. Meyer and R. Land. Threshold concepts and troublesome knowledge (1): linkages to ways of thinking and practising within the disciplines. In C. Rust, editor, *Improving Student Learning - Ten Years.* Oxford, 2003.

[14] J. H. F. Meyer and R. Land. Threshold concepts and troublesome knowledge (1): Epistemological considerations and a conceptual framework for teaching and learning. *Higher Education,* 49(3):373–388, 2005.

[15] M. Neteler and H. Mitasova. *Open Source GIS: A GRASS GIS Approach.* Springer, 2007.

[16] A. Okabe, editor. *GIS-based Studies in the Humanities and Social Sciences.* CRC Press, 2005.

[17] J. Peckham, L. L. Harlow, D. A. Stuart, B. Silver, H. Mederer, and P. D. Stephenson. Broadening participation in computing: issues and challenges. In *ITiCSE '07: Proceedings of the 12th annual SIGCSE conference on Innovation and technology in computer science education,* pages 9–13, New York, NY, USA, 2007. ACM.

[18] M. Price. *Mastering ArcGIS.* McGraw-Hill, 4th edition, 2010.

[19] P. Rael. Mapping new visions of history with GIS. Bowdoin College: `http://www.bowdoin.edu/news/archives/1academicnews/001962.shtml`.

[20] C. G. Schneider. Liberal education and integrative learning. *Issues in Integrative Studies,* (21), 2003.

[21] R. Shackelford, A. McGettrick, R. Sloan, H. Topi, G. Davies, R. Kamali, J. Cross, J. Impagliazzo, R. LeBlanc, and B. Lunt. Computing curricula 2005: The overview report. *SIGCSE Bull.,* 38(1):456–457, 2006.

[22] D. S. Sinton and J. J. Lund, editors. *Understanding Place: GIS and Mapping Across the Curriculum.* ESRI Press, 2006.

[23] S. Steinigera and E. Bocherb. An overview on current free and open source desktop GIS developments. *International Journal of Geographical Information Science,* 23(10):1345–1370, October 2009. DOI: 10.1080/13658810802634956.

[24] W. Zhang and T. Beaubouef. Geographic information systems: real world applications for computer science. *SIGCSE Bull.,* 40(2):124–127, 2008.

An Experience Report: On the Use of Multimedia Pre-Instruction and Just-in-Time Teaching in a CS1 Course

Paul Carter
Department of Computer Science
University of British Columbia
Vancouver, BC
Canada
pcarter@cs.ubc.ca

ABSTRACT

We describe an experience using online multimedia instruction and just-in-time teaching in an introductory programming course. Survey data has shown that students are strongly in favour of the approach. A series of screencasts was developed to replace the traditional lecture component of the course. Students were asked to review a small number of screencasts before each class and were assessed on their comprehension at the start of class using a series of "clicker" questions. A just-in-time mini-lecture was provided in response to the initial assessment, on an as-needed basis. The remaining class time was devoted to small-group exercises.

Categories and Subject Descriptors

K.3.2 [**Computer and Information Science Education**]: Computer Science Education

General Terms

Human Factors

Keywords

Multimedia instruction, screencasts, JiTT, peer instruction, CS1, pedagogy

1. INTRODUCTION

We describe an experience that combines just-in-time teaching (JiTT) [8] with peer instruction (PI) [4, 7] in an introductory computing course for engineering students at a large research-intensive university. This paper describes the continuation of a preliminary experience reported in [3]. In this earlier work, we described the use of these pedagogical techniques during a one-week module of the course. After favourable results, we now report on the application of these methods on a broader scale.

Permission to make digital or hard copies of all or part of this work for personal or classroom use is granted without fee provided that copies are not made or distributed for profit or commercial advantage and that copies bear this notice and the full citation on the first page. To copy otherwise, to republish, to post on servers or to redistribute to lists, requires prior specific permission and/or a fee.
SIGCSE'12, February 29–March 3, 2012, Raleigh, North Carolina, USA.
Copyright 2012 ACM 978-1-4503-1098-7/12/02 ...$10.00.

In brief, JiTT uses online learning and assessment technologies to supplement in-class activities. Typically, students engage in some kind of pre-class activity, such as textbook readings, coupled with web-based assessments. These assessments allow the instructor to focus subsequent class time on concepts that students find particularly difficult.

Traditional lecture is significantly reduced, allowing time for active learning exercises during class. PI is an example of one such learning activity in which students are presented with concept problems. These problems typically take the form of multiple choice questions that are answered using an electronic response system ("clickers") or a simple show of hands. Students first vote on an answer that they arrive at on their own. Assuming that there is some level of disagreement among students, they are invited to discuss their answers with neighbours and vote again. These assessments allow the lecture to be further tailored to student learning.

The use of JiTT and PI in Computer Science is not new. However, JiTT appears not to have been widely adopted in this discipline. Bailey et al. [2] reported on the use of JiTT in a CS0 course where students were asked to complete reading assignments and warm-up exercises as a form of pre-instruction. Davis [5] noted positive experiences with JiTT in systems and design courses. Pargas [9] reported on the use of PI in a sophomore-level data structures and algorithms course. Astrachan [1] used small programming assignments, that focussed on algorithmic problem solving, with online unit tests as a pre-instruction activity with JiTT. Simon et al. [11] report on one possible adaptation of PI to CS1 and CS1.5 courses while Porter et al. [10] reflect on their experiences utilizing PI in a variety of computing courses at different institutions.

We report on three significant departures from the traditional JiTT/PI approach. First, we use online screencasts to supplement textbook material as the form of pre-instruction, rather than textbook material alone. Second, rather than web based pre-class assessments, assessments are conducted at the start of class using clicker technology. Third, rather than the exclusive use of multiple choice questions during peer instruction, we use a mix of multiple choice, short answer, code reading and code writing questions.

A survey was conducted which indicated students very strongly support this approach.

2. THE COURSE

The course under consideration is taught at a large, research-intensive university. It provides an introduction to software development in C with applications in data acquisition and analysis for engineering students. The course is co-taught by the departments of Computer Science and Electrical & Computer Engineering and has an enrolment of over 800 students each winter session. Students are distributed fairly evenly across four sections, two in each term. The first eight weeks of the course are taught by Computer Science and the experience reported in this paper was conducted exclusively during that portion of the course.

The pedagogy described here was introduced in response to perceived student disengagement with a more traditional approach to lectures. In this study we assess student reaction to the use of JiTT and PI in the fall of 2009 and spring of 2010, with the modifications described below. We also report on minor modifications made in subsequent terms.

3. MODIFICATIONS TO JITT

In this section we report on three significant modifications that were made to the traditional JiTT/PI approach.

3.1 Pre-instruction through screencasts

In the typical JiTT approach described by Novak et al. [8], students are assigned pre-instruction activities in the form of textbook readings. These readings are coupled with web-based assessments that students must complete *before* coming to class. The results of this assessment are then used to help the instructor, in the following class, target concepts that students have found difficult.

Given the dynamic nature of program execution, we believe that students are likely to learn more effectively when multimedia presentations are used to complement static text. Stelzer et al. [13] reported on the comparative efficacy of multimedia presentations and textbook readings as a form of pre-instruction in an introductory physics course. They determined that students who received multimedia instruction performed significantly better on immediate post-tests and on tests of retention conducted two weeks later.

There have also been studies to show that students do not make appropriate use of textbooks as a form of pre-instruction. Stelzer et al. [13] report that even when textbook reading prior to class is encouraged with the use of pre-class assessments, about 70% of students admitted to "rarely" or "never" reading the textbook. Simon et al. [11] in their investigation of the use of PI in an introductory computing course also asked whether students read the textbook before class. They report that less than 40% of students indicated that they read the text before class "most or all of the time". Reports such as these suggest that students are using intuition, rather than knowledge gained from pre-instruction, to answer pre-class or in-class assessments.

In the present study, a series of 29 multimedia screencasts was developed and presented to students as the primary form of pre-instruction. Each screencast is between 2 and 15 minutes in duration (average approximately 7 minutes) and consists of a screen capture of a PowerPoint presentation with animations, voice over and closed-captioning. The goal of the screencasts is to present students with foundational material that they can reasonably be expected to learn on their own. Students were asked to watch up to 4 screencasts prior to each class. In addition to watching screencasts, students were pointed to relevant sections of the textbook.

3.2 Assessment of learning from pre-instruction activities

Rather than developing web-based assessments that students take before coming to class, a series of clicker questions was administered at the start of class to determine students' preparedness. The immediate feedback from clicker questions allowed the instructor to deliver mini-lectures on an as-needed basis. Students were first asked to respond individually to questions that were posed. After approximately 75% of the class clicked in a response, a short warning (typically 20-30 seconds) was given before closing the initial vote. In cases where less than about 80% of the class chose the correct answer, students were invited to form groups with neighbours to discuss why they selected their particular answer. It is important to note that students were not shown the result of the initial vote. After a period of discussion, students voted again. The result of the poll was then shared with the class. The instructor provided a brief justification for the correct answer and explained why the more popular incorrect answer(s) were incorrect. An open question & answer session followed to clear up any remaining misconceptions. This initial assessment activity typically took between 15 and 30 minutes of class time.

3.3 Peer instruction activities

Using the traditional PI approach, activities usually centre around multiple-choice questions that target students' conceptual understanding of the material. Simon et al. [11] report on the challenge of developing such questions for introductory CS courses and on determining their efficacy in assessing conceptual understanding. We have found multiple choice questions to be effective in generating student discussion and as a means for assessing student preparedness for class, as noted in section 3.2. However, multiple choice questions comprise only one assessment mechanism used in course examinations at our institution. We also felt that, rather than develop a bank of multiple choice concept questions that are aligned with course learning goals, it was easier to develop free-form questions that align with those goals.

The disadvantage to using free-form questions, of course, is that it is much harder to assess the impact that peer interaction has on student learning. Simon et al. [11] present data that measures the *normalized gain* that results from students discussing answers to multiple choice concept questions. This data provides valuable insight into the benefits of PI. With free-form answers, where there is no "before and after discussion" comparison to make, it is much harder to assess the impact of students discussing their ideas with each other.

Our peer instruction activities consist of a range of questions that are representative of the kinds of questions that could be asked on examinations, and some that go beyond what would normally be asked under exam conditions. After the assessment activity described in section 3.2 is complete, students are provided with a worksheet that outlines learning activities for the rest of the class period. Students work through the activities in groups of no more than 3 people. These groups are self-selected and normally consist of the people sitting in proximity. Students are instructed that no one in the group is to proceed to the next question until everyone in the group understands the solution to the current question. There are typically more exercises on a worksheet than can be completed during class. Any remaining exercises are left as (unmarked) homework.

While students work on examples, the instructor and a TA walk around the class asking and answering questions. The instructor's ability to "un-tether" from the front of the room allows barriers to be broken down between instructor and students. This is particularly important when working with first year students at a large institution where such students are often unsure how to approach their professors.

When the instructor notices that a majority of students have completed a particular question, a sample solution is presented. Sometimes this is done interactively, with the instructor prompting the students for input. Given that the students have already had a chance to construct their own solutions, differences between the solution presented by the instructor and those generated by the students can lead to productive discussion during which the relative merits of different solutions are investigated. Solutions to questions that are not presented in class are posted online after class.

In the first two offerings of the course that used this approach (fall 2009 and spring 2010), we were concerned that some students did not fully engage with these in-class activities. Given that there were approximately 200 people in the room for each lecture session, it was very difficult to monitor time-on-task for each group of students. In response to this concern, we introduced the use of carbonless copy paper in the fall of 2010. A book of copy paper was included in the course pack so that students did not have to go to any additional effort to obtain it. Students were asked to write answers to all worksheet problems on the copy paper. Each student was expected to have their own record of the solution arrived at by the group. At the end of class, students deposited one copy of their work into a hand-in box and took the other copy away with them. Students received participation credit for submitting any reasonable effort, whether correct or not, at completing the worksheet. The copy paper allowed us to monitor student participation without the overwhelming task of having to return work to the students. It also seemed to eliminate the incidence of students showing up at the start of class to get participation marks for responding to clicker questions and then disappearing!

4. CLICKER QUESTIONS

As mentioned above, clicker questions are used at the start of class as a means of assessing student comprehension of concepts delivered in the screencasts. The results of these assessments are used to determine the need for mini-lectures or further discussion on certain topics. As an example, the following question was asked in the spring of 2010 at the start of a class that focussed on iteration:

> What is the output from the code segment shown below?

```
int count = 0;

while( count < 3 ) {
    count++;
    printf( "%d", count );
}
```

A. 0 B. 123 C. 0123 D. 1 E. 1234

On the first vote, without any discussion with neighbours, 85% of the class chose the correct answer. It's important to note that while an earlier class had addressed the concept of loops in the context of flowcharts, there had been absolutely no discussion in class of the syntax used to represent loops. The only instruction provided on this topic was in the screencasts and textbook. This is an example of a question where peer discussion and a second vote were not deemed necessary.

The following question provides an example where discussion and a second vote was required:

> What value of `data` will cause the following loop to terminate?

```
while( data != 2 || data != 4 ) {
    ...
}
```

A. 2 B. 4 C. 0 D. no such value exists

On the first vote, only 46% of the class chose the correct answer while 44% chose option C. Students were not shown the result of the first vote but were invited to discuss their answer with neighbours and then vote again. On the second vote, 75% of the class chose the correct answer. This led to further instructor-led discussion on Boolean logic and infinite loops.

5. WORKSHEET QUESTIONS

In this section we expand on the types of questions that were included on worksheets. The worksheets were designed to pick up where the screencasts and clicker questions left off, and to gradually guide the students towards more complex problems. Worksheets typically started with basic code comprehension questions. For example, students might be asked to draw a flowchart to model a given code segment. Other questions ask students to hand-trace a given code segment and track the value of variables. More advanced code comprehension questions ask students to "explain in plain English" the overall purpose of a given code segment. Such questions and their relationship with code tracing and writing skills have been studied extensively by Lister et al. [6]. Finally, worksheets conclude with code writing questions of increasing difficulty.

6. ANALYSIS

6.1 Student reaction

In this section we examine student reaction to the JiTT/PI approach, their use of the screencasts and their attendance at class. A survey was conducted in the fall of 2009 immediately after the 8 week segment of the course in which this study occurred. The results are presented in Table 1. All of the statements in this table were prefaced with the following: *With reference to the first eight weeks of the course only, please indicate the extent to which you agree or disagree with the following statement.* Students were asked to respond using a Likert-like scale: Strongly Agree (SA), Agree (A), Disagree (D), Strongly Disagree (SD). Students were

Table 1: Survey Results

Statement	SA	A	D	SD	DNWTA	NR
I believe the teaching methods used in this course are effective in helping me learn the concepts presented	62.9% (48.3%)	31.4% (47.5%)	2.1% (2.5%)	0.6% (0.5%)	0.9% (1.0%)	2.1% (0.2%)
I would prefer that this course be taught using a traditional lecture format rather than having online screencasts and in-class problem sets	3.6% (2.2%)	7.5% (5.7%)	23.1% (42.6%)	62.9% (46.1%)	1.2% (3.2%)	1.8% (0.2%)
The online screencasts help me to learn basic concepts on my own	48.5% (42.6%)	47.0% (51.5%)	2.1% (3.7%)	0.3% (1.0%)	0.3% (0.2%)	1.8% (1.0%)
I believe I am more engaged in my APSC 160 class period than in other classes I'm taking this term that use a more traditional lecture format	49.7% (44.6%)	34.7% (43.3%)	7.5% (7.6%)	1.5% (0.2%)	3.9% (3.7%)	2.7% (0.5%)

also given the option of selecting *I do not wish to answer* (DNWTA). In addition, some students did not provide any response to some or all of the questions (NR). Of the approximately 450 students registered in the course, we received responses from 335. Students received a very small amount of course credit for participating. We see overwhelming support for the approach with over 94% of students either agreeing or strongly agreeing with the statement: *I believe that the teaching methods used in this course are effective in helping me learn the concepts presented.* As shown in Table 1, responses to other questions also demonstrate strong support from students.

Notably, this was the second time we ran a survey containing these questions. The earlier survey was conducted after 4 weeks to try to get a sense of how things were going. At that time over 400 students responded. The lower response rate to the survey after week 8 is unfortunate and is possibly due to the fact that students did not see the benefit of responding to it again. The figures in brackets in Table 1 show the results of the survey after week 4. Comparison with week 8 data shows that student opinions appear to have gained strength as the term progressed, with a higher percentage of those responding choosing SA or SD in most cases. It was encouraging to see the shift towards those responses that more strongly support the JiTT/PI approach to teaching and learning. One possibility is that, as the term progressed, students became more comfortable with this unfamiliar mode of instruction.

The surveys also allowed for free-form comments which provide some insight into the student perspective:

> "I loved the screencast format of the lectures. It required a little bit of extra responsibility to watch the screencasts, but the outcome was great."

This student makes the important observation that the approach requires more from students in terms of preparedness for class than the typical lecture approproach. Students cannot expect to benefit from class activities without having primed themselves for the in-class exercises.

> "The reason why the method used during the first 8 weeks was so effective for me was because I was able to talk to other students around me in order to get help."

This student identifies some of the benefits of peer instruction. Students were often reminded of the benefits of studying with peers both in and out of the classroom.

> "I like how you can replay a section you don't understand."

> "The simple screencasts were great for reviewing for the midterm as well as learning new concepts."

These comments highlight the fact that one of the benefits of screencasts is that they can be watched repeatedly. In addition to watching just before class, some students use them for review just before exams.

6.2 Student use of screencasts

As previously noted, other studies have shown that students often fail to engage with pre-instruction activities when those activities amount to reading the textbook [11], even when pre-class assessments aim to enforce it [13]. In this section we attempt to determine the extent to which students make use of the screencasts. This data was collected in the spring of 2010. At the end of the first 8 weeks of the course, we obtained a summary of the number of times each student had accessed each screencast. Data for 4 of the screencasts was not available due to an error in the way they had been posted to webCT. The data we obtained enabled us to determine how many of the screencasts each student had accessed at least once. Note that by "accessed" we mean that the student clicked on the link to download the file - we have no way of knowing to what extent the student made appropriate use of the screencast. We found that just over 75% of the class accessed at least 20 of the 25 screencasts for which we had data. We find this very encouraging when compared to other studies, mentioned above, that indicate very low, self-reported rates at which students complete pre-class readings. Note that this data doesn't tell us exactly *when*, during the eight week period, each student accessed each screencast; only that the screencast was accessed at some point. One possibility is that some students watched the screencasts just before the midterm exam, for example.

6.3 Attendance at class

As a by-product of using clickers at the start of each class, we have a snapshot of how many people were in attendance. During the fall of 2009, the average attendance rate was an impressive 91%. The lowest attendance rate was 81% and this occurred the day after the midterm exam (essentially, the last class of the first eight weeks of the course). Students earned up to 5% of their final course grade for participation in class. We believe this to be a strong motivator. Attendance in the spring of 2010 was lower, averaging 82%. One factor that may have influenced the lower attendance rate in the spring is that we reduced the weight on the particpation component from 5% to 3%.

7. INSTRUCTOR REFLECTIONS

We have seen that students appear to make good use of multimedia screencasts as a means of pre-instruction with JiTT. However, the development of screencasts is not without significant cost in terms of time. The screencasts described in this study were developed during a sabbatical year. However, we emphasize our pilot study [3] which suggests that these techniques can be effectively employed in isolated modules. Those considering applying this approach to their own courses need not feel that screencasts have to be developed for the entire course before progress can be made.

An additional challenge to the use of screencasts is that they cannot be edited as easily as a set of lecture notes or slides. It is therefore recommended that the course be evolved to a point where content is fairly stable before screencasts are developed.

While we do not have data to demonstrate learning gains over more traditional approaches, we did not see large scale differences over previous years' grade distributions. Others have reported that multimedia pre-instruction had a modest positive effect on exam performance. It was suggested that "benefits they may have received from the multimedia-based prelectures could have been offset by students devoting less time to studying for the exams" [12]. Given the many demands on student time, it is possible that we're playing a zero sum game. If learning is made more efficient in one course, students divert their extra time to other courses that are perceived to be more demanding. A comment from one student on our survey:

> "I feel I learned more with far less effort than I would have in a traditional lecture course."

indeed suggests that some students may have put less effort into the course than a course with a more traditional lecture approach.

In spite of the challenges, the approach yields many benefits. We have clearly received strong support from students. The use of PI allows students to experience first-hand their ability to learn from each other. Class periods tend to be animated and lively, and attendance levels are extremely good. Given that the instructor is free to walk around the room, undesirable behaviours that can sometimes be seen in the relative anonymity of large, traditional lecture halls are virtually eliminated. From the instructor perspective, we found class time to be far more enjoyable when considerable time is spent working with small groups of students rather than lecturing to the class as a whole. With introductory material dealt with using pre-instruction activities, classes can be tailored to the needs of the particular group of students taking the course at the time.

8. CONCLUSION

We have described an experience with multimedia screencasts, as a form of pre-instruction with JiTT. We have shown benefits in terms of high attendance at class, good use of pre-instructional materials by students and positive student reaction to the pedagogy. Modifications to the traditional JiTT approach have been presented that we believe are effective in the context of our introductory programming course for engineers. Although we do not have data to demonstrate improved student learning, we believe that the approach has not been detrimental. Survey data has shown that students are strongly in favour of the approach.

9. ACKNOWLEDGMENTS

This study was conducted with support from the Carl Wieman Science Education Initiative at the University of British Columbia.

I would like to express my thanks to Ben Yu who, at the time, was a Science Teaching and Learning Fellow with the Department of Computer Science, for help in administering surveys. I'd also like to acknowledge Leah Macfadyen, Skylight Research Associate and Michelle Lamberson, Director of the Centre for Teaching, Learning and Technology at UBC for arranging to provide me with data on student access to screencasts. Finally, thanks to Jackie Stewart, Department of Chemistry, who introduced me to the use of carbonless paper for conducting in-class activities.

10. REFERENCES

[1] O. Astrachan. Non-competitive programming contest problems as the basis for just-in-time teaching. In *Frontiers in Education, 2004. FIE 2004. 34th Annual*, pages T3H/20 – T3H/24 Vol. 1, Oct. 2004.

[2] T. Bailey and J. Forbes. Just-in-time teaching for CS0. In *SIGCSE '05: Proceedings of the 36th SIGCSE technical symposium on Computer science education*, pages 366–370, New York, NY, USA, 2005. ACM.

[3] P. Carter. An experiment with online instruction and active learning in an introductory computing course for engineers: JiTT meets CS1. In *Proceedings of the 14th Western Canadian Conference on Computing Education*, WCCCE '09, pages 103–108, New York, NY, USA, 2009. ACM.

[4] C. H. Crouch and E. Mazur. Peer instruction: Ten years of experience and results. *American Journal of Physics*, 69(9):970–977, September 2001.

[5] J. Davis. Experiences with just-in-time teaching in systems and design courses. In *Proceedings of the 40th ACM technical symposium on Computer science education*, SIGCSE '09, pages 71–75, New York, NY, USA, 2009. ACM.

[6] R. Lister, C. Fidge, and D. Teague. Further evidence of a relationship between explaining, tracing and writing skills in introductory programming. In *Proceedings of the 14th annual ACM SIGCSE conference on Innovation and technology in computer science education*, ITiCSE '09, pages 161–165, New York, NY, USA, 2009. ACM.

[7] E. Mazur. *Peer Instruction: A User's Manual.* Prentice Hall, New Jersey, 1997.

[8] G. M. Novak, E. T. Patterson, A. D. Gavrin, and W. Christian. *Just-In-Time Teaching: Blending Active*

Learning with Web Technology. Prentice Hall, New Jersey, 1999.

[9] R. P. Pargas. Reducing lecture and increasing student activity in large computer science courses. In *ITICSE '06: Proceedings of the 11th annual SIGCSE conference on Innovation and technology in computer science education*, pages 3–7, New York, NY, USA, 2006. ACM.

[10] L. Porter, C. Bailey Lee, B. Simon, Q. Cutts, and D. Zingaro. Experience report: a multi-classroom report on the value of peer instruction. In *Proceedings of the 16th annual joint conference on Innovation and technology in computer science education*, ITiCSE '11, pages 138–142, New York, NY, USA, 2011. ACM.

[11] B. Simon, M. Kohanfars, J. Lee, K. Tamayo, and Q. Cutts. Experience report: peer instruction in introductory computing. In *Proceedings of the 41st ACM technical symposium on Computer science education*, SIGCSE '10, pages 341–345, New York, NY, USA, 2010. ACM.

[12] T. Stelzer, D. T. Brookes, G. Gladding, and J. P. Mestre. Impact of multimedia learning modules on an introductory course on electricity and magnetism. *American Journal of Physics*, 78(7):755–759, 2010.

[13] T. Stelzer, G. Gladding, J. P. Mestre, and D. T. Brookes. Comparing the efficacy of multimedia modules with traditional textbooks for learning introductory physics content. *American Journal of Physics*, 77(2):184–190, 2009.

Using JiTT in a Database Course

Alexandra Martinez
Escuela de Ciencias de la Computación e Informática
Universidad de Costa Rica
San José, Costa Rica
alexandra.martinez@ecci.ucr.ac.cr

ABSTRACT

This paper describes our experience using the *Just-in-Time Teaching* (JiTT) technique in an undergraduate database course for computer science majors during two semesters. JiTT was implemented by giving the students reading assignments and asking them to complete web-based reading tests the day before class, so that the teacher could detect weaknesses in students' understanding of the material and adjust the lesson plan just in time for the next day class. Based on surveys as well as on exams and course grades, we found a significant improvement on the students' interest in the course and learning of the material.

Categories and Subject Descriptors

H.2.0 [**Database Management**]: General; K.3.2 [**Computers and Education**]: Computer and Information Science Education—*computer science education*

General Terms

Experimentation, Human Factors

Keywords

Database, Just in Time teaching, Active Learning, Instructional Technologies, Web-based Techniques, Classroom Management, Experience Report

1. INTRODUCTION

Just-in-Time Teaching (JiTT) was developed by Novak, Patterson, Gavrin, and Christian [14] as a pedagogical strategy to help nontraditional students improve their learning [16]. The key idea behind JiTT is to build a link between in-class and out-of-class activities through preparatory web-based assignments, which are known as "warm-ups" or "JiTT exercises" [16]. JiTT warm-ups usually consist in assigning some reading material to the students and asking them to complete a short online assignment, due a few hours before class. The teacher then plans for the upcoming class based on the student responses to the assignment. According to Novak and Patterson [13], JiTT exhibits two unique characteristics: (*i*) students go to class ready to actively participate in the different classroom activities, and (*ii*) students have a feeling of ownership since classroom activities are tailored to their needs. Previous experiences on the use of JiTT in Computer Science have been described in [7, 5, 12, 1].

Peer Instruction (PI) [10, 9, 17], on the other hand, is an interactive teaching technique that engages students through classroom activities including concept tests and discussions with fellow students. PI has been successfully combined with JiTT in the past [17, 5, 1]. An extensive discussion on combining JiTT with Peer Instruction can be found in [17].

Both JiTT and PI are part of a broader approach for teaching and learning called *Active Learning* [2]. McConnell [12] describes Active Learning as the use of techniques that involve students in the learning process, rather than listening to a lecture in a passive way. Students can actively learn by reading, writing, discussing, solving a problem, or responding to challenging questions [11, 12]. Active Learning has been shown to improve student comprehension and retention of material [4], as well as to increase student motivation and higher order thinking [12, 2]. Active Learning techniques have been successfully used in Computer Science courses, as reported in [11, 15, 4, 6, 5, 8, 3].

Davis [7] describes her experience with JiTT as a new instructor of systems and design courses, in particular, Operating Systems, Networking, Software Design, and Human-Computer Interaction. She used JiTT to increase student preparation and engagement in courses that featured a large reading component. Two approaches were presented: the first one was based on discussion questions emailed by students about the assigned readings, whereas the second was based on warm-up exercises prepared by the instructor. She states that the second approach was more work intensive (on the instructor's side) than the first one, but points out that warm-ups helped students to tie reading and thinking out of class with work on design problems in class.

Carter [5] reports on an experiment that combined JiTT with Peer Instruction in an introductory computing course for engineering students. The experiment lasted one week and consisted of asking students to review a series of online screencasts before class, assessing them on that material at the beginning of class, and then providing a just in time lecture as needed. Student feedback, gathered through a

Permission to make digital or hard copies of all or part of this work for personal or classroom use is granted without fee provided that copies are not made or distributed for profit or commercial advantage and that copies bear this notice and the full citation on the first page. To copy otherwise, to republish, to post on servers or to redistribute to lists, requires prior specific permission and/or a fee.
SIGCSE'12, February 29–March 3, 2012, Raleigh, North Carolina, USA.
Copyright 2012 ACM 978-1-4503-1098-7/12/02 ...$10.00.

survey, was positive. However, the impact on student learning was difficult to assess due to the short time students experienced with this technique.

Bailey and Forbes [1] present an implementation of JiTT and Peer Instruction in an introductory computer science course. They emphasize on the feedback loop between out-of-class work (web component) and classroom component as a key element of the JiTT strategy. Their web component consisted of warm-up exercises, course web pages, and assessment exercises (homework and laboratory assignments). The classroom component consisted of lectures, laboratory sessions, and in-class student activities. Based on a qualitative assessment, they reported that students were satisfied with the strategy but one of the main complaints was the amount of out-of-class work.

McConnell [12] suggests the use of pre-class online quizzes (through course management software) as a mechanism to determine whether students are understanding the content of reading assignments. He adds that the results of such quizzes can inform the instructor of topics that students found easy or difficult, allowing the instructor to shape the lecture or activities in the classroom.

Crouch and Mazur [9] found that changing from traditional instruction (i.e., pure lecturing) to Peer Instruction caused students' scores on a post-test to improve dramatically over scores from the same pretest, and their performance on traditional quantitative problems improved as well. These results are not dependent on a particular instructor. They also indicated that when enough effort is put into motivating students, their reactions to PI are generally positive.

Mazur and Watkins [17] identified the following benefits from a combined use of JiTT and PI: it provides opportunities for teachers and students to recognize background knowledge, it helps students develop discussion and reading for understanding skills, it helps students develop better metacognitive skills as they check their own understanding during pre-class reading and in-class questions, it personalizes the large classroom, it enables students to achieve greater conceptual learning gains, and it also helps diminish gender gaps in student learning.

This paper reports on our experience using JiTT in an undergraduate database course for two semesters and three course sections. The rest of the paper is organized as follows. Section 2 describes the author's motivation for using JiTT. Section 3 presents the methodology. Section 4 shows the results of the assessment. And Section 5 concludes the paper and outlines our plans for future work.

2. MOTIVATION

The first time the author taught the Database 1 course, she resorted to lecturing as her teaching methodology, which did not allow for much interaction with the students. She used to prepare the lessons based on the textbook's content to be *covered*, and little did she realize about the concepts students were struggling with until it was too late (when grading midterm or final exams). The results of this teaching approach were very clear by the end of the semester: some students failing the course, some dropping, and a general low performance on final course grades (median was 8 out of 10). Even worse, a third of the students formally surveyed by the Department indicated that they lowered their interest in the course because of the teacher, and the teacher was rated with a barely acceptable grade (7 out of 10) by the students who took the survey.

This led the teacher to question and rethink her teaching approach, get acquainted with novel pedagogical strategies, and start experimenting with some of them in her courses. In particular, the idea of using JiTT came after attending a talk on Peer Instruction and JiTT by Eric Mazur from Harvard University. The first attempt to incorporate JiTT in the database course was not as successful as expected, mainly due to the type of questions used in warm-ups. In the second attempt, the type of warm-up questions was changed based on feedback gathered from students as well as new ideas learned from LASPAU's program *The University in the 21st Century: from Teaching to Learning*, and it turned out to be a more successful experience (the teacher's grade increased to 9 and students' performance on final course grades also increased to a median of 9).

3. METHODOLOGY

3.1 The Course Context

The Databases 1 course is a 4-credit-hour mandatory course in the 3rd year of the Bachelor of Science's program, in the Department of Computer and Information Science at the University of Costa Rica. This course provides students with the necessary concepts to design, implement, and manipulate relational databases. It also offers an introduction to object-relational databases.

The course is offered every semester, and we usually open one or two sections per semester, with an average enrollment of 18 students each. The class meets twice a week for one hour and fifty minutes during 16 weeks, for a total of 64 hours of class in a semester. The textbook used in the course is Elmasri's and Navathe's *Fundamentals of Database Systems*, fifth edition, and a course-support booklet written by a colleague at my university.

We use Moodle as our online course platform since it has been used at our department for several years and our students are familiar with it. Moodle is a Course Management System that helps educators create online learning sites. Among other features, it allows students to fill out online questionnaires, which is how we managed our JiTT warm-ups.

3.2 First Implementation

The first implementation of JiTT in the course was during the second semester of 2010, when the author was teaching two sections of the course. There were 18 students registered in Section 1 and 14 students in Section 2. In this implementation, 5% of the final course grade consisted of JiTT warm-ups, and the rest of the grade consisted in exams, quizzes, homeworks and project. We used a total of six JiTT warm-ups this semester.

3.2.1 Out-of-class component

The preparatory out-of-class component consisted of a series of "reading tests" (this is how we called the JiTT warm-ups). Each reading test required students to read a chapter from the textbook (or course booklet, alternatively) and then asked students to complete a web-based test available in our Moodle platform (we used Moodle's questionnaire module for this purpose). All reading tests were due the day before class, usually at 3 p.m., in order to give the teacher enough time to read over the student's responses and adjust the next lesson accordingly.

All web-based tests had a similar structure: they contained three multiple-choice or short-answer questions plus one free-form/open question which was always the same: "Formulate questions about those parts of the reading that you did not understand or got confused about". Grading of the first three questions was based on technical correctness while grading of the fourth one was based on effort. Although students might not have understood all the material, the technical questions were very straightforward to answer; they basically just verified that the student indeed read the material. The advantage of this approach was that grading was simple and did not impose a major burden on the teacher since it was possible to leverage Moodle's automated grading scheme for the first three questions, leaving only the last open question for the teacher to grade. The disadvantage was that multiple-choice and short-answer questions made it easy for students to cheat and did not foster students to think deeper about the material. Because they were asked very simple questions just to check if they actually did the reading, many resorted to do a superficial reading just looking for the answers to the questions, which did not meet the objective of the assignment: to prepare them for the in-class activities.

3.2.2 In-class component

The in-class component was partly organized around student common misconceptions or difficulties, extracted from the warm-ups submitted by students. Emphasis was given to in-class discussion and cooperative learning activities. Many students were certainly engaged in the class activities prepared in a JiTT fashion, but there were still occasions when some students looked clue-less or just not-engaged. We believe this may have occurred due to a superficial or disconnected reading of the material by the students (facilitated by the type of questions in the reading tests), which did not prepare them for the in-class discussions and exercises.

Although the original aim of the teacher was to use JiTT throughout the entire course, in fact it could only be used six times in the semester, mainly due to the amount of preparation required on the teacher's side. This did not leave much room to experiment with different in-class activities. Consequently, the rest of the classes had to be planned without students' input, effectively yielding a mixed instructional approach that semester.

3.3 Second Implementation

The second implementation was during the first semester of 2011, when the author was teaching only *one* section of the course, but a particularly large one (with 32 students). In this implementation, 10% of the final course grade consisted of JiTT warm-ups, while the rest of the grade was distributed among exams, quizzes, homeworks, and project. A total of nine JiTT warm-ups were used this semester.

3.3.1 Out-of-class component

In the second implementation, the out-of-class component also consisted of a series of "reading tests' due the day before class. However, these tests differed from those used in the first implementation in two ways. First, the type of questions used were no longer multiple-choice or short-answer questions but rather free-form/open (essay-like) questions. Second, the tests could no longer be graded in an automated way by Moodle (due to the lack of a unique correct answer), making it necessary to grade all questions manually.

The new structure of the web-based tests consisted of two *technical* essay questions plus a third free-form/open question which was always the same: "What doubts or questions do you have about the reading? If you do not have questions, write what you found most useful and relevant from the reading for your personal learning." Grading of the first two questions was based on technical soundness (not necessarily correctness), while grading of the third one was based on effort. This time the grading job was delegated to the Teaching Assistant since it was very time-consuming. However, the teacher still glanced at the students' answers (especially the last one) in order to detect misconceptions or unclear points and be able to plan the next lesson accordingly. The advantages of using only essay type of questions were that it discouraged students from cheating (a straight copy from another student's answers was easily detected), helped them think deeper about the material (requiring higher order thinking skills), and prepared them better for the in-class activities.

3.3.2 In-class component

The in-class component was mainly organized around student common misconceptions or difficulties, extracted from warm-ups. Emphasis was given to *peer instruction* as an in-class strategy (introduced this semester), but old strategies like discussion and cooperative learning were used as well. This semester we were able to use nine JiTT warm-ups, an increase of 50% with respect to the previous semester.

4. ASSESSMENT RESULTS

Our experience with JiTT was assessed from the students' point of view and from the teacher's point of view. The student's perspective was gathered through surveys whereas the teacher's perspective was based on student grades as well as observed strengths and limitations.

4.1 The Students' Perspective

4.1.1 Assessment of JiTT

An informal web-based survey created by the teacher was given to students across the three sections where JiTT was implemented (second semester of 2010 and first semester of 2011). Participation in the survey was voluntary and anonymous. In the first implementation of JiTT, the survey was conducted in December 2010 and had a total of 29 participants. In the second implementation, the survey was conducted in July 2011 and had a total of 27 participants. Most questions in the survey were multiple-choice type but had an additional field where students could write comments (not mandatory).

Two questions in the survey were related to JiTT. The first one was "When you individually read the material before class and come to class with a basic knowledge on the subject, does your learning improve, not change, or worsen compared to when you do not read the material in advance and are faced with it for the first time in class?". Table 1 summarizes student responses. We observe from this table that a vast majority of students believe that their learning improves when they prepare for class by reading the material in advance. This provides support for JiTT, since it advocates for pre-class reading assignments as a way to prepare students for in-class activities. The following are representative positive comments from students:

> One comes to class with an idea of what is going to be explained, and gets more out of the class.

> I think it improves because what we really do in class is to clear doubts and more time is devoted to this.

Some negative aspects commented by students were:

> The problem arises when I read the material just to get over the test, because I have read only what I need to answer the questions but I have not learned anything.

> It depends on the subject, in some cases it is good to read in advance, but in other cases, especially when the reading is very complex, it is better to go to class, understand and then read.

The second question was: "Do you think that reading tests are an effective way of verifying that a student did the assigned reading?". The student's responses are summarized in Table 2. This table evidences the fact that in our first implementation of JiTT, the type of questions used on the reading tests facilitated cheating among students, therefore students felt that the reading tests were not an effective means to check whether they (or their classmates) did the reading. On the other hand, Table 2 also shows that the student perception changed for the second implementation of JiTT, where a higher percent of students believed the reading tests were effective. The following are sample student comments from the first implementation:

> I heard of many who copied the answers, so I don't know how effective they really are...

> No, because one can see the questions and find the answers in the book without reading.

And here are comments from the second implementation (the last comment reveals an issue with grading that will be discussed in section 4.2):

> Of course, since many of the questions required comprehension of the whole reading, for example, when asked to compare X vs Y and give reasons.

> Yes they are, since they encourage (and require) the student to read the material and study in advance.

> Not if they are graded... I consider it wrong that students get evaluated on material that has not yet been seen in class; for which they have not gotten their questions answered... It would be better if students got a high mark just for submitting the assignment, restricting it to answers that make sense despite not being 100% correct.

Table 1: Learning improvement from warm-ups.

	1st Implementation	2nd Implementation
Improve	100%	89%
Not change	0%	11%
Worsen	0%	0%

Table 2: Effectiveness of reading tests.

	1st Implementation	2nd Implementation
Yes	62%	78%
No	38%	22%
Blank	0%	0%

4.1.2 Integral Assessment of the Course

Every semester, our department runs an official survey to evaluate each of the courses taught during that semester. Participation in the survey is anonymous. In order to ensure high participation from students, the survey is applied during class time but teachers are not allowed to be present. We used these surveys to assess the benefits of JiTT.

The survey data from 2009 served as a control group when analyzing the effects of JiTT in the course, since the teacher did not use JiTT during that semester. A total of 18 students took the survey in 2009 (11 from Section 1 and 7 from Section 2), 25 in 2010 (13 from Section 1 and 12 from Section 2) and 16 in 2011 (all from Section 1). Although the questions in this survey were not specific to any course, we believe that some questions can relate to the inclusion of JiTT in our course. Next we present the more relevant results from this survey.

Table 3 summarizes the student responses to the question "Your teacher has managed to develop in you an attitude towards the course such that...(*i*) At the beginning I had no interest and still don't have, (*ii*) At the beginning I had no interest but now I have, (*iii*) At the beginning I had interest but it has decreased, (*ii*) At the beginning I had interest and it remains the same, (*ii*) At the beginning I had interest and it has increased". We can observe from Table 3 that in the two semesters when JiTT was used, none of the students showed a decrease in their interest for the course, whereas in the control group there were 5 out of 18 students (corresponding to a 28%) showing this behavior. Also, when comparing data from the control and experimental groups (JiTT implementations) in the last row of the table, we observe that a higher percentage of students reported a growth in their interest when JiTT was used.

Table 4 summarizes the student answers to the question "Is the teaching process in this course suitable?". When looking at the last row in Table 4, we observe an increase in the percentage of students who strongly agreed that the teaching process was suitable, from the control group to the experimental group. Also, none of the students from the experimental groups strongly disagreed that the teaching process was suitable, and only a small percentage disagreed.

Table 5 summarizes the student answers to the question "Using a scale of 1 to 10, with 1 being the lowest score and 10 the highest, in general, what rating would you give to the performance of the teacher in the course?". We observe from Table 5 that the median teacher rating increased from the control group to the first implementation of JiTT and remained the same for second implementation. The semesters

Table 3: Evolution of student interest.

	Control (2009)		1st Implementation		2nd Implementation
	Section 1	Section 2	Section 1	Section 2	Section 1
Had no interest and still don't have it	0%	0%	0%	0%	6%
Had no interest but now I have	0%	0%	15%	0%	0%
Had interest but has decreased	9%	57%	0%	0%	6%
Had interest and remains same	64%	43%	46%	42%	50%
Had interest and has increased	27%	0%	39%	58%	38%

Table 4: Assessment of the teaching process.

	Control (2009)		1st Implementation		2nd Implementation
	Section 1	Section 2	Section 1	Section 2	Section 1
Strongly disagree	9.1%	0%	0%	0%	0%
Disagree	27.3%	0%	15.4%	0%	6.2%
Neither agree nor disagree	18.2%	28.6%	0%	0%	12.5%
Agree	18.2%	28.5%	30.8%	25%	25%
Strongly agree	27.2%	42.9%	53.8%	75%	56.3%
Not sure	0%	0%	0%	0%	0%

Table 5: Teacher rating by the students.

	Control	1st Implement.	2nd Implement.
Median	7.0	9.0	9.0
IQR	1.0	1.0	2.0

Table 6: Comparison of final course grades.

	Control	1st Implement.	2nd Implement.
Median	8.0	8.5	9.0
IQR	1.5	1.5	1.0

Table 7: Comparison of overall exam grades.

	Control	1st Implement.	2nd Implement.
Median	7.1	7.8	8.4
IQR	1.6	2.0	1.8

where the teacher attained good ratings coincide with those where JiTT was used, which may be an indicative that students have a better perception of a teacher who uses JiTT because of the interaction, feedback, and personalization of the teaching process enabled by JiTT.

4.2 The Teacher's Perspective

The teacher used two quantitative instruments to evaluate the effectiveness of using JiTT in the course: exam grades and final course grades. Although final grades could be thought to subsume exam grades, that is not exactly true since a significant part of the course grade comes from a team-based project, and would not necessarily reflect the level of individual learning achieved by a student. Therefore, we analyzed both grades separately.

Table 6 shows the median and IQR (interquartile range) of the students' final course grades for the control group and for the two experimental groups (where JiTT was used). Grades from students dropping the course were not considered. Two different t-test were performed: one test compared final grades from the control group with those from the first implementation group, and the other test compared final grades from the control group with those from the second implementation group. Even though the first t-test yielded no significant difference between the two samples, the second t-test produced a P-value of 0.01 using a two-tailed t-test under an equal variances assumption ($F = 1.47$, $P = 0.15$). These results show a positive effect of the use of JiTT on the students' performance in the course.

To assess the effectiveness of JiTT on a more individual base, Table 7 shows the median and IQR of the students' exam grades, for the control group as well as for the two experimental groups. Grades from students dropping the course were not considered. Two t-test were performed: one comparing the exam grades from the control group with those from the first implementation group, and another one comparing exam grades from the control group with those from the second implementation group. The first t-test yielded no significant difference between the two samples, but the second produced a P-value less than 0.01 using a two-tailed t-test under an equal variances assumption ($F = 1.15$, $P = 0.35$). This result shows that students' individual performance on exams improved when using JiTT in the course.

The teacher also made a qualitative assessment on the strengths and limitations of the use of JiTT, based on her experience. The main strengths found were that students: (*i*) were more engaged in class, (*ii*) asked more interesting/advanced questions that enriched class discussion, and (*iii*) were able to take on a more active role in class (e.g., tackling problems and offering solutions). Another strength is that it enables the teacher to know her students' learning needs and abilities, and do something about it at the right time. Also, the fact that the teacher tailors her lessons based on students answers to JiTT warm-ups, helps the teacher to stay connected to the students. Furthermore, the use of open-ended (essay-type) questions in JiTT warm-ups not only fosters creative and critical thinking in students, but also helps students organize their ideas, draw connections, and clarify their thinking through writing (a key idea behind the "writing-to-learn" model).

The major limitation encountered was the large amount of time spent in designing good questions for JiTT warm-ups, reading students answers, and preparing for the next-day lesson. Although the second time some tasks were easier (e.g., designing questions), the total effort required was still high (student questions and problems were different from previous semesters, thus keeping preparation time invariable). We also faced some problems with the grading of JiTT warm-ups. First, the Teaching Assistant had a high expectation on students answers to reading tests and therefore was strongly penalizing mistakes. This was addressed by restating to the TA that grading of reading tests had to be more lenient than grading of other coursework (e.g., quizzes or homeworks) due to the fact that students were being asked questions on subjects that had not yet been studied in class. Second, grading rules became rather subjective and unclear because in order to be fair we wanted to take into account the effort made by the student, the evidence shown by the student that she indeed did the reading, and the ability to approach a correct/good answer. This was more a discomfort on the teacher's side than a real problem on the TA's side, but a solution is still needed.

5. CONCLUSION AND FUTURE WORK

The JiTT technique was employed for teaching an entry-level database course for Computer Science majors. It was applied by assigning readings and performing online warm-ups the day before class. This activity not only allowed students to get prepared for class, but also allowed the teacher to assess the students' understanding of the readings. Based on experiments performed along two semesters, and compared to a previous control group, the technique was shown to be successful in improving the learning of the students. This was verified by a significant improvement on the exams grades and final grades.

In the future, we plan to explore the use of different grading schemes for the warm-ups since some students pointed out in the surveys that the reading tests were graded too strictly, and they suggested that we gave credits for effort in all the questions. We would like to explore this idea but first we need to address issues related to plagiarism, and potential decrease in the quality of the reading and thinking made by the students (which will defeat the purpose of JiTT). We also plan on incorporating other teaching strategies that combine well with JiTT, such as Peer Instruction (already in use), and increasing the number of JiTT warm-ups in the course.

6. REFERENCES

[1] T. Bailey and J. Forbes. Just-in-Time Teaching for CS0. In *Proceedings of the 36th SIGCSE technical symposium on Computer science education*, SIGCSE '05, pages 366–370, New York, NY, USA, 2005. ACM.

[2] C. C. Bonwell and J. A. Eison. *Active Learning: Creating Excitement in the Classroom. ASHE ERIC Higher Education Report No. 1.* The George Washington University, School of Education and Human Development, Washington D.C., USA, 1st edition, 1991.

[3] M. Boyeena and P. Goteti. Promoting active learning through case driven approach: An empirical study on database course. In *Students' Technology Symposium (TechSym), 2010 IEEE*, pages 191 –195, april 2010.

[4] T. Briggs. Techniques for Active Learning in CS Courses. *J. Comput. Small Coll.*, 21:156–165, December 2005.

[5] P. Carter. An experiment with online instruction and active learning in an introductory computing course for engineers: JiTT meets CS1. In *Proceedings of the 14th Western Canadian Conference on Computing Education*, WCCCE '09, pages 103–108, New York, NY, USA, 2009. ACM.

[6] D. Cordes and A. Parrish. Active learning in computer science: impacting student behavior. In *Frontiers in Education, 2002. FIE 2002. 32nd Annual*, volume 1, pages T2A–1 – T2A–5 vol.1, 2002.

[7] J. Davis. Experiences with Just-in-Time Teaching in Systems and Design Courses. In *Proceedings of the 40th ACM technical symposium on Computer science education*, SIGCSE '09, pages 71–75, New York, NY, USA, 2009. ACM.

[8] S. Ludi, S. Natarajan, and T. Reichlmayr. An Introductory Software Engineering Course that Facilitates Active Learning. In *Proceedings of the 36th SIGCSE technical symposium on Computer science education*, SIGCSE '05, pages 302–306, New York, NY, USA, 2005. ACM.

[9] C. Crouch and E. Mazur. Peer Instruction: Ten years of experience and results. In *American Journal of Physics*, 69:970–977, 2001. ACM.

[10] E. Mazur. *Peer Instruction: A User's Manual.* Series in Educational Innovation. Prentice Hall, Upper Saddle River, NJ, 1997.

[11] J. J. McConnell. Active learning and its use in Computer Science. In *Proceedings of the 1st conference on Integrating technology into computer science education*, ITiCSE '96, pages 52–54, New York, NY, USA, 1996. ACM.

[12] J. J. McConnell. Active and Cooperative Learning: Tips and Tricks (Part I). *SIGCSE Bull.*, 37:27–30, June 2005.

[13] G. Novak and E. Patterson. An Introduction to Just-in-Time Teaching (JiTT). In S. Simkins and M. Maier, editors, *Just in Time Teaching Across the Disciplines*, pages 3–24. Stylus Publishing, 2009.

[14] G. M. Novak, A. Gavrin, and C. Wolfgang. *Just-in-Time Teaching: Blending Active Learning with Web Technology.* Prentice Hall PTR, Upper Saddle River, NJ, USA, 1st edition, 1999.

[15] S. Pollard and R. C. Duvall. Everything I Needed to Know About Teaching I Learned in Kindergarten: Bringing Elementary Education Techniques to Undergraduate Computer Science Classes. In *Proceedings of the 37th SIGCSE technical symposium on Computer science education*, SIGCSE '06, pages 224–228, New York, NY, USA, 2006. ACM.

[16] S. Simkins, M. Maier, and J. Rhem. *Just-in-Time Teaching: Across the Disciplines, and Across the Academy.* Stylus Publishing, Sterling, VA, USA, 1st edition, 2009.

[17] E. Mazur and J. Watkins. Just-in-Time Teaching and Peer Instruction. In S. Simkins and M. Maier, editors, *Just in Time Teaching Across the Disciplines*, pages 39–62. Stylus Publishing, 2009.

Process Oriented Guided Inquiry Learning (POGIL) for Computer Science

Clifton Kussmaul
Muhlenberg College
2400 Chew St
Allentown, PA 18104-5586 USA
1-484-664-3352
kussmaul@muhlenberg.edu

ABSTRACT

This paper describes an ongoing project to develop activities for computer science (CS) using process oriented guided inquiry learning (POGIL). First, it reviews relevant background on effective learning and POGIL, compares POGIL to other forms of active learning, and describes the potential of POGIL for CS. Second, it describes a sample POGIL activity, including the structure and contents, student and facilitator actions during the activity, and how activities are designed. Third, it summarizes current progress and plans for a NSF TUES project to development POGIL materials for CS. Finally, it discusses student feedback and future directions.

Categories and Subject Descriptors

K.3.1 [Computers and Education]: Computer Uses in Education – Collaborative learning. K.3.2 [Computers and Education]: Computer and Information Science Education – Computer science education.

General Terms

Algorithms, Experimentation.

Keywords

active learning, algorithms, communication, data structures, experience report, inquiry learning, POGIL, software engineering, teams.

1. INTRODUCTION

To improve student learning, enthusiasm, and retention, especially in science, technology, engineering, and mathematics (STEM) areas, educators have developed a wide variety of approaches to engage students, enhance learning, and emphasize attitudes and skills in addition to knowledge (often rote).

This paper describes an ongoing project to develop a set of process oriented guided inquiry learning (POGIL) activities focused on computer science, including topics in data structures and algorithms (DS&A) and software engineering (SE). First, it reviews relevant background on effective learning and POGIL, compares POGIL to other forms of active learning, and describes the potential of POGIL for CS. Second, it describes a sample POGIL activity, including the structure and contents, student and facilitator actions during the activity, and how activities are designed. Third, it summarizes current progress and plans for a project to development POGIL materials for CS. Finally, it discusses student feedback and future directions.

Permission to make digital or hard copies of all or part of this work for personal or classroom use is granted without fee provided that copies are not made or distributed for profit or commercial advantage and that copies bear this notice and the full citation on the first page. To copy otherwise, or republish, to post on servers or to redistribute to lists, requires prior specific permission and/or a fee.
SIGCSE'12, February 29-March 3, 2012, Raleigh,North Carolina, USA.
Copyright 2012 ACM 978-1-4503-1098-7/12/02...$10.00.

2. BACKGROUND

2.1 Active Learning in CS

Active learning is not new in CS education, and experiences have been reported in a variety of papers; a few are summarized below. Baldwin [3] described experiences, benefits, and pitfalls with discovery learning, which broadly refers to learning through self-teaching. McConnell [17] discussed active and collaborative learning (ACL) in CS, in a four part series that reviewed the benefits of ACL and describes a set of ACL activities, associated risks and ways of addressing them, characteristics of and techniques to promote effective groups, and activity design tips. Gonzalez [10] reported on CS1 sections where each session was roughly 1/3 discussion, 1/3 lecture, and 1/3 ACL. Students from ACL sections did significantly better in CS2 than peers from traditional sections. Beck and Chizhik [4] reported a CS1 course where students spent roughly half of class on ACL exercises. Students in the ACL section did significantly better than peers in a traditional section, and that effect was found for both genders and a variety of majors. Sowell and colleagues [21] [22] describe experiences with active learning in CS3, a software development course, and a systems software course, including sample exercises, lessons learned, and qualitative and quantitative results; in general, student grades and course evaluations improved.

Not surprisingly, CS faculty often explore ways to use technology to improve or supplement ACL (e.g. [2], [20]). Although there is an obvious risk of adding unneeded technology, there is also the potential to develop tools that could benefit other disciplines.

2.2 POGIL

POGIL is based on learning science (e.g. [24]), and shares characteristics with other forms of active, discovery, and inquiry-based learning (e.g. [8]). As described below, POGIL combines effective learning practices in ways that are synergistic.

In POGIL, teams of learners (typically 3-5) work on scripted inquiry activities and investigations designed to help them construct their own knowledge, often by modeling the original processes of discovery and research [18]. The teams follow processes with specific roles, steps, and reports that help students develop process skills and encourage individual responsibility and meta-cognition. The instructor serves as an active facilitator, not a lecturer or passive observer; active facilitation is a key aspect of POGIL. POGIL activities and processes are designed to achieve specific learning objectives; typically an activity is designed to focus on 1-2 (disciplinary) concepts and 1-2 process skills. The POGIL Project (www.pogil.org) offers a set of workshops to help faculty learn about POGIL theory and practice, including how to facilitate, evaluate, and develop POGIL activities.

POGIL activities generally follow a *learning cycle* with 3 phases [1]. In *exploration*, students look for trends or patterns in data they have collected or that is provided, and generate and test hypotheses to help understand or explain the data. In *concept invention*, the trends, patterns, or hypotheses are used to define a new concept or term; importantly, students have constructed understanding before the concept is introduced. In *application*, the new concept is applied in other situations or contexts to help students generalize its meaning and applicability. Thus, the scripted activity provides information and asks questions to guide students through the learning cycle and help them develop process and learning skills. (Alternatively, some POGIL activities introduce a concept, and follow it with application and exploration.)

Designing effective POGIL activities can be time-consuming, but supporting resources are available [11]. Generally, the author first identifies learning objectives and the focus of the activity. For examples, teams could analyze data, derive equations, or explore the behavior of a physical system. Next, the author creates a sequence of *key questions* that guide teams through the inquiry process. Finally, the author identifies and develops supporting information, such as prerequisites, glossary of terms, references, handouts, and subsequent assignments or projects.

Activities involve three types of key questions. *Directed questions* have definite answers, are based on material available to students, and provide a foundation for later parts of the activity. *Convergent questions* may have multiple answers, and require teams to analyze and synthesize information to reach non-obvious conclusions. *Divergent questions* are open-ended, do not have right or wrong answers, and may lead teams and individual students in different directions.

POGIL has been developed and validated over the last 15 years. POGIL has been used extensively in chemistry, and also in materials science and engineering [7], and CS [6], although POGIL does not yet appear to be well known in CS. Multiple studies have found that POGIL significantly improves student performance, particularly for average and below-average students. (e.g. [9], [13], [16]). Table 1 below summarizes data from 3 different experiments (in chemistry courses). In each case it compares final grade distributions between a lecture-based version of the course format and a later POGIL-based version.

Table 1: Summary of Experimental Data

#	format	%A	%B	%C	%D,W,F	statistics
1	pre: lecture	19	33	26	22	$\chi2=40.9$
	post: POGIL	24	40	26	10	$\alpha<0.005$
2	pre: lecture	20	20	27	33	$\chi2=70.1$
	post: POGIL	29	35	24	12	$\alpha<0.01$
3	pre: lecture	12	19	16	53	$\chi2=19.1$
	post: POGIL	9	32	31	28	$\alpha<0.005$

3. POGIL for CS

POGIL has particular potential for CS education. Software development is largely a problem-solving activity since background information is usually available, and POGIL helps students to develop their problem-solving abilities. Teams are important to most IT organizations, and POGIL helps students to develop important team process skills. POGIL also encourages students to collaborate and learn from each other rather than focusing on an instructor. In chemistry and other disciplines, effective POGIL activities seem to be adopted and adapted by other instructors and at other institutions. Thus, POGIL may provide useful models for reusable materials in CS education, where such reuse appears to be problematic.

POGIL also presents some distinct challenges for CS. Currently, not many effective POGIL activities exist in CS; thus, faculty need to invest significant time and effort developing them. CS courses and curricula are more varied than in chemistry, and portions of the content change more rapidly, making it more difficult to adopt or adapt materials at other institutions.

3.1 Sample Activity – Queues & Stacks

This section describes activity *Queues & Stacks (Q&S)*, which introduces queues and stacks, to show what a typical activity looks like, and what the facilitator and students do during class. It also describes common variations and some of the underlying motivations. The full activity is available online [15].

At the start of Q&S, the facilitator spends a minute or two providing motivation and background, and then distributes the activity to the student teams. Teams can be formed in many ways, e.g. at random, by ability (strong students together, weaker students together), or by student choice. The following sections contain text from the activity (in italics), followed by elaboration and discussion. For brevity, some text has been simplified, and some sections have been omitted (see notes below).

3.1.1 Introduction

As computer scientists, we study ***data structures*** *– ways to organize & structure data. Implementing a data structure has pedagogical value, but as good (lazy?) computer scientists, we don't want to re-implement a familiar data structure for every situation. Instead, we want to design an* ***abstract data type (ADT)*** *that captures the key ideas of a data structure and can be used in many different situations.*

This activity will give you some experience analyzing requirements and designing ADTs. In particular, you will investigate ***queues*** *and* ***stacks****. Before you start, complete the form below to assign a role to each person.*

Q&S uses the following roles:

- *Manager*: keeps track of time and makes sure everyone contributes appropriately.
- *Recorder*: records all answers and questions, so team members and the facilitator have accurate notes.
- *Speaker*: speaks on behalf of the team to the facilitator, other teams, or the entire class.

These roles are typical, but POGIL activities might have a variety of roles; for example, an activity involving equipment might have a *Technician*. Roles help provide multiple perspectives and ensure that all team members contribute. Students rotate roles for each activity, but teams usually stay together for a set of activities.

3.1.2 Queues - Real World

Consider the following situations:

- *People standing in a checkout line at a store.*
- *Suitcases or packages on a conveyor belt.*
- *Phone callers waiting on hold.*
- *Documents waiting to be printed on a printer.*

1. (2 min) All of these situations have some common characteristics. Identify 2 other similar situations.

2. (3 min) These are all examples of ***queues****. Summarize their key common characteristics in 2-4 sentences.*

3. (2 min) List any variations or exceptions to these characteristics. Review status with the facilitator before continuing.

Each team begins to work through the questions. Each question has an estimated duration to help teams manage time. The facilitator circulates around the classroom to monitor progress, clarify questions, and help address problems; teams are not expected to complete activities unassisted. These three questions focus on the *exploration* phase of the learning cycle. Question 2 is *convergent* (most teams will have similar answers); when most teams have answered it, the facilitator might take a minute or two and ask teams to report their answers, particularly if there are differences between teams. Question 3 is *divergent* (answers may vary), and provides an opportunity for faster teams to consider new ideas while slower teams catch up.

3.1.3 Queues – Abstract Data Types

Queues are often described as ***First-In, First-Out (FIFO)*** *or* ***Last-In, Last-Out (LILO)****.*

4. (3 min) Based on the key characteristics of queues that you identified above, ***list 4-5 key operations*** *for a queue ADT, and* ***rank them*** *by importance (1=high, 5=low).*

5. (5 min) Define a ***method signature*** *for each queue operation (starting with the most important) including an appropriate name, input parameters, and return types. You may include constructors, although Java interfaces do not normally specify constructors.*

```
public interface Queue<T> {
   public Queue<T>(int maxSize);

}
```

6. (2 min) Compare your queue interface with the set of operations listed in your textbook, the Java API, or Wikipedia. Summarize any differences, insights, or questions.

These questions are *convergent*, and focus on the *concept invention* phase of the learning cycle. When most teams have finished question 4, the facilitator might have teams report or post answers, and discuss any differences or questions that arise. As teams work on question 5, the facilitator might help teams review constructors, interfaces, and generics, as needed. If only a few students need help, they may receive it from teammates; if several teams need help, the facilitator might stop the activity to review key concepts with the entire class, or even postpone the activity until a later date. Thus, by monitoring team progress on the activity, the facilitator can quickly identify and address problems.

The activity uses syntax from the Java programming language and the JUnit testing framework, but could be adapted readily to other languages and frameworks, or pseudo-code.

3.1.4 Queues – Unit Testing

7. (5 min) Describe ***unit tests*** *to verify the behavior of the above queue methods. Focus on the most important or error-prone methods.* ***Each person*** *should work on* ***a different method****. Do not write JUnit tests; instead, use the* ***Unit Test Worksheet*** *for each method. Here is an example:*

Class: *Queue*
Signature*: public Queue<T>(int maxSize);*

Pre	*Inputs*	*Expected Result*	*Post*
none	*maxSize <= 0*	*Exception*	
none	*maxSize > 0*	*Queue object*	*check size*

8. (3 min) As a team, review the set of tests you developed, and adjust as necessary. Summarize your insights and questions. If there is time, reflect on ways that your team could have developed the unit tests more efficiently. Review with the facilitator before continuing.

Question 7 is *convergent*, and focuses on the *application* phase of the learning cycle, since students must apply their new concepts (of queues) in a different content (unit testing). Question 8 is more *divergent* and encourages teams to reflect on what they have learned and how their team functioned. As students and teams work on these questions, the facilitator might help teams review unit test concepts. If time permits, the instructor might also encourage students to consult with students working on similar methods in other teams. Again, this enables the facilitator to quickly identify and respond to problems.

The next three sections of the activity (not shown here) take a similar approach to stacks. This helps students recognize that the process of analysis, design, and testing can be applied to many different situations. Queues are introduced before stacks since the latter are often less intuitive. However, since stacks are easier to implement, the activity considers array implementations of stacks before queues.

3.1.5 Stacks – Array Implementation

A stack ADT can be implemented in multiple ways; you will see several approaches. For now, we will consider how to implement a stack using an array, e.g.:

```
public interface Stack<T> {
   // field(s)
   private T [] data;

   // constructor - allocate data
   public Stack<T>(int size) {
      this.data = (T[]) new Object[size];
   }
   // methods
}
```

9. (3 min) Assume we have an empty stack. ***Show the contents of the data array after each operation****. If you use additional fields (e.g. to keep track of positions in the array), add a column for each one and show how its value changes.*

	private T [] data				*other fields*		
Operation	*[0]*	*[1]*	*[2]*	*[3]*			
a. Create new data structure.							
b. Add 'A'.							
c. Add 'B'.							
d. Remove value.							
e. Insert 'C'.							
f. Get current size.							
g. Remove value.							
h. Insert 'D'.							

10. (3 min) For each stack method, write a complete English sentence to describe ***how it could be implemented*** *using an array, and its* ***O() performance****. Hint: None of the methods should be O(N).*

11. (2 min) Summarize the pros & cons of implementing a stack with an array. Review with the facilitator before continuing.

In one sense, question 9 prompts students to *apply* their new understanding of stacks, but in another sense it prompts them to *explore* array implementation as part of a new learning cycle. (Such overlap is not uncommon.) Question 10 leads students towards *formation* of an implementation approach which would likely be *applied* in a subsequent programming assignment. Question 11 prompts students to reflect on their learning.

The final section of the activity (not shown here) considers array implementation of queues, generally following the approach for stacks. As before, this helps students learn that similar processes can be applied in different situations. The facilitator might need to help students recognize some of the differences between stacks and queues, and how to address them efficiently.

3.1.6 Next Steps

Usually, teams finish the entire POGIL activity during class, where the facilitator is available to monitor progress and provide assistance if necessary. In some cases, teams may need to complete an activity outside of class.

A POGIL activity is usually followed by assignments, assessments, or other tasks to help solidify and/or assess student learning. For the Q&S activity, this might include:

- A written report summarizing what the team did and learned in the activity. This might be drafted by the Recorder and reviewed by other students.
- An individual peer assessment to help identify and correct problems within a team.
- A short quiz at the start of the next class meeting.
- Unit tests for the stack and queue interfaces.
- Array implementations of a stack and/or queue.

4. Project Plan

This section summarizes current progress and plans for a project to development POGIL materials for CS, supported by the National Science Foundation (NSF) Transforming Undergraduate Education in STEM (TUES) program. This project leverages the successful POGIL approach, extends it to CS, and explores some new directions that could benefit POGIL in other fields. Specifically, this project is developing, refining, validating, and disseminating two sets of 8-10 POGIL activities for CS. Set A focuses on data structures & algorithms (DS&A), including queues & stacks, lists, hash tables, recursion, searching, and sorting. Set B focuses on software engineering (SE) including project scheduling (e.g. work breakdown structures, Gantt charts, critical path), estimation (e.g. story points), project budgeting and financial planning, and elements of the unified modeling language (UML).

These activities are packaged as a set of handouts containing background information and questions, including space to write answers. Each activity packet contains appropriate supporting materials, such as worksheets, code samples, references, and rubrics. Each packet also contains overview information for facilitators, such as learning objectives, prerequisites, directions to prepare the activity, notes for facilitating, a brief history of the activity, and planned or suggested improvements.

As the activities are developed, they are reviewed by chemistry faculty with extensive POGIL experience, and by CS faculty who have completed introductory POGIL workshops and plan to use POGIL in their classrooms. An assessment expert guides and support more detailed assessment plans and activities. As activities are refined and validated, they are disseminated to the broader CS education community through papers, conference presentations, workshops, and a website [15].

Thus, this project seeks to produce materials for adoption by other CS faculty, and thereby improve the quality of CS education, and particularly for average and below average students. The project also seeks to identify and foster a POGIL community within CS. Table 2 summarizes the project timeline.

Table 2: Project Timeline
(AY=academic year; PA = POGIL activity)

Timeframe	PI & co-PIs	CS Collaborators
2011 Summer	plan assessment create/refine PAs	POGIL training review PAs
2011-12 AY	pilot/refine PAs show: talks	review/pilot PAs evaluate (baseline)
2012 Summer	create/refine PAs	review/refine PAs
2012-13 AY	refine PAs push: workshops	evaluate (baseline/treatment)
2013 Summer	create/refine PAs	create/refine PAs
2013-14 AY	refine PAs push: talks/workshops	evaluate (treatment) pilot/refine PAs

4.1 Project Status

To date, the project has drafted, piloted, and revised the following POGIL activities [15]:

A. Data Structures & Algorithms
   1. Searching (linear & binary)
   2. Queues & Stacks
   3. Linked Lists
   4. Sorting (mergesort & quicksort)

B. Software Engineering
   1. Project Scheduling (PERT, critical path)
   2. UML Use Case & Activity Diagrams
   3. UML Data Diagrams & CRC Cards

C. Programming Constructs & Techniques
   1. Unit Testing (JUnit)
   2. Error Handling & Exceptions
   3. Reading & Writing Files
   4. Inheritance

D. Other
   1. Teams & Roles (introductory)
   2. Mind Mapping
   3. Sequence Analysis (bioinformatics)

The programming construct activities involve specific syntax for Java and JUnit, but could be translated for other programming languages. The other activities would require only minor changes for other languages.

4.2 Assessment Plan

Table 3 summarizes the project assessment plan, which will be revised and expanded during 2011-2012, with assistance from an assessment expert. SIR-II is the Student Instructional Report II™ [5], and TDS is the Team Diagnostic Survey [23].

Table 3: Project Assessment Plan

	Goal	Techniques(s)
Students	Improve student learning outcomes.	Average grades. Qualitative assessment of selected assignments.
	Improve student affective outcomes.	Current (e.g. SIR-II), existing (e.g. TDS), & custom instruments.
	Improve student recruiting & retention.	Course enrollments & major/minor counts.
PIs & Collaborators	Develop & refine PAs.	Quarterly activity reports, peer review, interviews.
	Improve faculty affective outcomes.	Reflection, interviews.
	Enhance PAs with technology (FOSS).	Quarterly activity reports, peer review, interviews.
	Raise awareness (talks/papers/workshops).	Quarterly activity reports, interviews.
Other	Foster community for POGIL in CS.	Talk/workshop attendance & evaluation forms.

5. CONCLUSIONS

POGIL is based on learning science and has a proven track record in other disciplines. There are a variety of materials to help faculty develop and improve POGIL materials (e.g. [11] [12] [18]). POGIL classrooms are very different from lecture-based classrooms, but POGIL shares characteristics with other forms of active, discovery, and inquiry-based learning, so that faculty familiar with such approaches should not have difficulty adapting to POGIL.

5.1 Student Feedback

During 2009-2010 the author developed POGIL and other active learning activities [14] for a graduate course (roughly 20 students) on genetic algorithms, neural networks, and fuzzy systems [19]. The activities were presented as slides which were later posted for students to review. This reduced paper use and made it easier to tweak activities during class by adding steps or providing more information, and to manage the activity's pace.

At the end of the course, students were asked to briefly describe their experiences. The responses included recurring themes. Students were initially uncertain about an unfamiliar teaching and learning style, but then realized that they had mastered concepts and acquired useful process skills. Students also had some difficulty understanding the instructor's spoken language; however, individual teams could discuss the activity in the language(s) they preferred. For example:

> *Group discussions & exchanging ideas with other groups is a better one. This makes us think about it in a better way. As you come to each group to talk, we can clarify our doubts by discussing it with you. And you encourage us to think more about the topic.*

5.2 Future Directions

Future directions for this work include developing and revising more POGIL activities, extended and adapting them for courses and faculty at other institutions (including high schools and community colleges), developing POGIL activities in other areas of computer science and related disciplines, and working to develop a community of faculty using POGIL in computer science. We also hope to explore the potential of tools, such as wikis (e.g. TikiWiki) and learning management systems (e.g. Moodle), to help scale activities to larger courses and a broader community. Effective use of such tools could help the facilitator to monitor team progress, and enable student teams to more readily summarize and compare their results and conclusions.

6. ACKNOWLEDGMENTS

Thanks to the National Science Foundation (TUES program) under grant DUE-1044679, and to US-India Educational Foundation (USIEF) for a Fulbright-Nehru teaching award that provided opportunities and other support for this work.

7. REFERENCES

[1] Abraham, M. R. 2005. Inquiry and the learning cycle approach. In: Pienta, N. J., Cooper, M. M., Greenbowe, T. J., eds. *Chemists' Guide to Effective Teaching*. Upper Saddle River, NJ: Prentice Hall; 41–52.

[2] Anderson, R., Anderson, R., Davis, K. M., Linnell, N., Prince, C., and Razmov, V. 2007. Supporting active learning and example based instruction with classroom technology. *Proceedings of the 38th SIGCSE Technical Symposium on Computer Science Education*. ACM, New York, NY, 69–73. DOI=http://doi.acm.org/10.1145/1227310.1227338.

[3] Baldwin, D. 1996. Discovery learning in computer science. In: *Proceedings of the 27th SIGCSE Technical Symposium on Computer Science Education*. ACM, New York, NY, 222-226. DOI=http://dx.doi.org/10.1145/236462.236544.

[4] Beck, L. L., Chizhik, A. W. 2008. An experimental study of cooperative learning in CS1. In *Proceedings of the 39th SIGCSE Technical Symposium on Computer Science Education*. ACM, New York, NY, 205–209. DOI=http://doi.acm.org/10.1145/1352135.1352208.

[5] Centra, John A. 2006. *The Student Instructional Report II™: Its Development, Uses and Supporting Research*. Educational Testing Service (ETS). Retrieved Nov 8, 2011 from http://www1.ets.org/Media/Products/SIR_II/pdf/53228_sirII_white_paper.pdf

[6] De Palma, A. 2005. Engaging students through the guided-inquiry cycle. In: *Proceedings of Redesigning Pedagogy: Research, Policy, Practice*. National Institute of Education, Nanyang Technological University, Singapore.

[7] Douglas, E. P., Chiu, C. 2009. Use of guided inquiry as an active learning technique in engineering. In: *Proceedings of the 2009 Research in Engineering Education Symposium*. Palm Cove, Queensland, Australia.

[8] Eberlein, T., Kampmeier, J., Minderhout, V., et al. 2008. Pedagogies of engagement in science. *Biochemistry and Molecular Biology Education*. 36(4):262-273.

[9] Farrell, J. J., Moog, R. S., Spencer, J. N. 1999. A guided-inquiry general chemistry course. *Journal of Chemical Education*. 76(4):570.

[10] Gonzalez, G. 2006. A systematic approach to active and cooperative learning in CS1 and its effects on CS2. In *Proceedings of the 37th SIGCSE Technical Symposium on Computer Science Education*. ACM, New York, NY, 133–137. DOI= http://doi.acm.org/10.1145/1121341.1121386.

[11] Hanson, D. M. 2005. Designing process-oriented guided-inquiry activities. In: Beyerlein, S. W., Apple, D. K., eds. *Faculty Guidebook - A Comprehensive Tool for Improving Faculty Performance*. 2nd ed. Pacific Crest.

[12] Hanson, D. M. 2006. *Instructor's Guide to Process-Oriented Guided-Inquiry Learning*. Lisle, IL: Pacific Crest.

[13] Hanson, D. M., Wolfskill, T. 2000. Process workshops - A new model for instruction. *Journal of Chemical Education*. 77(1):120.

[14] Kussmaul, C. 2011. Process oriented guided inquiry learning for soft computing. *International Conference on Advances in Computing & Communication (ACC)*, Kochi, Kerala, India.

[15] Kussmaul, C. 2011. *CS-POGIL: Process Oriented Guided Inquiry Learning in Computer Science*. Retrieved Nov 8, 2011 from http://cspogil.org.

[16] Lewis, S. E., Lewis, J. E. 2005. Departing from lectures: An evaluation of a peer-led guided inquiry alternative. *Journal of Chemical Education*. 82(1):135.

[17] McConnell, Jeffrey J. 2005. Active and cooperative learning: tips and tricks (part I). *ACM SIGCSE Bulletin* 37 (June): 27–30. DOI= http://doi.acm.org/10.1145/1083431.1083457.

[18] Moog, R. S., Spencer, J. N. eds. 2008. *Process-Oriented Guided Inquiry Learning (POGIL)*. Oxford University Press, USA.

[19] Munakata, T. 2008. *Fundamentals of the New Artificial Intelligence: Neural, Evolutionary, Fuzzy and More*. 2nd ed. Springer.

[20] Schweitzer, D., and Brown, W. 2007. Interactive visualization for the active learning classroom. In *Proceedings of the 38th SIGCSE Technical Symposium on Computer Science Education*. ACM, New York, NY, 208–212. DOI= http://doi.acm.org/10.1145/1227310.1227384

[21] Sowell, R., Chen, Y., Buhler, J., Goldman, S. A., Grimm, C., and Goldman, K. J.. 2010. Experiences with active learning in CS 3. *Journal of Computing Sciences in Colleges* 25 (May): 173–179.

[22] Sowell, R., Gill, C., Chamberlain, R. D., Grimm, C., Goldman, K. J., and Tranel, M. 2010. The active-learning transformation: a case study in software development and systems software courses. *Journal of Computing Sciences in Colleges* 25 (May): 165–172.

[23] Wageman, R. et al. 2005. Team Diagnostic Survey. *The Journal of Applied Behavioral Science*. 41, 4 (Dec. 2005), 373 -398.

[24] Zull, J. 2002. *The Art of Changing the Brain: Enriching the Practice of Teaching by Exploring the Biology of Learning*. 1st ed. Stylus Publishing.

Integrating Communication Skills into the Computer Science Curriculum

Katrina Falkner
School of Computer Science
The University of Adelaide
Adelaide, South Australia, Australia, 5005
katrina.falkner@adelaide.edu.au

Nickolas J.G. Falkner
School of Computer Science
The University of Adelaide
Adelaide, South Australia, Australia, 5005
nickolas.falkner@adelaide.edu.au

ABSTRACT

Computer Science majors must be able to communicate effectively. Industry surveys identify the development of communication and critical thinking skills as key to the reform of the higher education sector. However, academics are challenged by time and discipline content pressures, as well as a lack of familiarity with the teaching and assessment of communication skills content. There is considerable existing work in the area of communication skills development, positioned both in terms of curriculum guidelines for effective communication skills development, and example communication skills activities. However, this research is deficient in detailed, contextualised methodologies and frameworks for the development of communication skills within the Computer Science curriculum. We present a new methodology, building upon well established theoretical frameworks, designed to assist academics in the development of communication skills activities integrated with discipline content across the curriculum. We illustrate this methodology in the design of a CS1/CS2 communication skills course.

Categories and Subject Descriptors

K.3 [**Computers & Education**]: Computers and Information Science Education

General Terms

Human Factors

Keywords

Communication Skills, Curriculum Design, CS1/CS2

1. INTRODUCTION

Academics and industry bodies both recognise that Computer Science students are characteristically grouped at the middle and lower end of the spectrum of communication skills. The 2009 Australian Learning and Teaching Council (ALTC) report, *Managing Educational Change in the ICT discipline at the Tertiary Education Level*, identifies the teaching of personal skills, including communication of all kinds, as a key area for curriculum reform in the sector [15]. Employers identified communication and problem-solving skills as the areas most in need for improvement.

Communication skills are crucial to the careers of Computer Science graduates. Graduates tend to be more successful when they demonstrate good communication skills and the ability to communicate clearly within a broad range of settings [8]. The increasingly inter-disciplinary and international nature of the Computer Science industry requires professionals to be able to communicate clearly with clients and colleagues, beyond the simple need to produce clear and understandable software and software documentation. Pomykalski [23] states 'the inability to write and think critically put information systems professionals at risk of being left behind in a rapidly changing technological environment'.

The development of communication skills is more than the development of effective writing and presentation skills for communicating with peers. A professional must learn to communicate within the language of their discipline, and to also communicate in the language used by readers or listeners outside of the discipline. Communication, both spoken and written, is a crucial tool in the development of critical thinking skills and in support of the development of discipline knowledge. Emig [6] discusses the broader underpinnings of the relationship between writing and learning, drawing our attention to the established belief that higher cognitive functions develop most fully when supported by communications activities.

Why do Computer Science students rarely receive the degree of training in communication skills development that is called for by both academic and industry groups? Very few Computer Science curricula include a core course that incorporates the development of communication skills in the context of computer science and, where these courses do exist, the focus of these courses is on general writing skills, rather than oral skills or professional communication skills [18, 10]. An increasingly crowded curriculum leaves little room for the development of non-technical areas [19].

We introduce a new methodology for the development of communication skills within the Computer Science curriculum, building upon well established theoretical frameworks for understanding and designing communication skills activities. We extend these approaches through a methodology for (a) identification of communication skills activities that provide depth and breadth in skill development, and (b) their composition and integration with discipline content and as-

Permission to make digital or hard copies of all or part of this work for personal or classroom use is granted without fee provided that copies are not made or distributed for profit or commercial advantage and that copies bear this notice and the full citation on the first page. To copy otherwise, to republish, to post on servers or to redistribute to lists, requires prior specific permission and/or a fee.
SIGCSE'12, February 29–March 3, 2012, Raleigh, North Carolina, USA.
Copyright 2012 ACM 978-1-4503-1098-7/12/02 ...$10.00.

sessment activities. To demonstrate our new methodology, we provide several examples of extended and new activities and demonstrate their inclusion in an integrated curriculum.

2. RELATED WORK

The ability for students to reflect upon the need for communication skills in their future careers is key to their learning. Placing the teaching of communication skills within a discipline context is more engaging and crucial in the long term recollection and application of these skills [1]. Several studies have reported on Communication Skills courses designed for the Computer Science context, both as independent courses [14, 12] and through integrating communication skills content within an existing course [4, 16, 21, 22]. Independent courses, the majority, are often tangentially placed within the discipline context, and fail to include discipline-specific tasks. Students are, therefore, unable to relate the writing activities directly to their experiences of the discipline [12], missing an opportunity to express information about their discipline in new and productive ways.

Kay [14] introduces a dedicated communication skills course for Computer Scientists that contains a wide range of communications activities including technical writing, oral presentations and writing for electronic media. Kay proposes the inclusion of a specialised technical context through the construction of a simple prototype software system around which example assignments can be framed. Michael [21] builds upon Kay's work to identify the strategies required in constructing an integrated communication skills course for Computer Scientists. Fell *et al* [7] identify a set of writing assignments that may be used from introductory to advanced courses. Several authors have defined course structures for specific discipline courses, including data structures [13] and junior programming [21]. Pollock [22] discusses the structure of a graduate level course with an emphasis on writing for developing research skills, while Derrick [3] presents strategies for efficient assessment within a similar context.

In this paper, we move beyond the definition of a single communications skill activity or course, to present a methodology for the construction of communication skills curricula for the Computer Science discipline. Fell *et al* [7] present a summary of writing in CS courses, and examples of integrating communication skills components within common discipline assignments in introductory and advanced programming courses. Kussmaul [17] develops a methodology for developing communication skills based on Agile methods.

Dugan and Polanski [5] present a taxonomy of writing tasks, defined by writing for learning, writing for academic communication, and writing for industrial communication, and a general guide to incorporating writing into any computer science course. This taxonomy can be used to select a specific subset of writing tasks appropriate for the purpose and experience of the students. Taffe [25] identifies three categories of writing within Computer Science: writing to develop facility with the language of the discipline; writing to explain results of a study; and writing as a process of clarification. Despite their contribution, these studies neglect the perspective of developing communication skills in both depth and breadth across the curriculum.

Perhaps the most successful approaches to teaching communication skills are those based on Fulwiler and Young's Writing Across the Curriculum (WAC) [9]. WAC describes an approach whereby writing is integrated across all courses within the curriculum, and used as an active learning approach to facilitate the development of both non-technical and technical skills. The WAC model is based on the following principles:

- writing is the responsibility of the entire academic community,
- writing must be integrated across departmental boundaries,
- writing instruction must be continuous during all four years of undergraduate education,
- writing promotes learning, and
- students begin to communicate effectively within an academic discipline only by practising the conventions of that discipline.

The consistent integration throughout a curriculum, based on WAC, identifies communication as a *requirement* of the discipline. Further, it allows students to experience the learning impact of communication and assists them in adopting communication as a learning tool. Teaching communication in context encourages students to use the direct explication of writing skills to develop an awareness of, and habitual use of, communication, both in general and in discipline specific communication.

Consistent integration of communication skills promotes opportunities for practice and reflective development; it is well recognised that practise is a crucial component in the process towards achieving expertise in an area [24] and this is no different in the development of communication skills. Further, the development of expertise in communication promotes the development of discipline expertise: students' understanding of the discipline content associated with communication tasks correlates to the degree of practise, and number of tasks undertaken [2].

3. PROPOSED METHODOLOGY

We build upon, and extend, the well established framework of WAC and the categorisation work of Taffe to define a methodology for understanding and designing communication skills curricula. This new methodology enables academics to identify activities that demonstrate depth and breadth in communication skills development. A matrix assists academics in the selection and appropriate composition of activities, with an accompanying series of principles that assist academics in integration with discipline content.

3.1 Theoretical Foundations

Developing facility with the language of Computer Science requires two areas of focus: learning to understand and apply the technical concepts introduced, and learning to communicate these concepts in both specialised and ordinary language in ways appropriate to the audience. Writing to explain the results of a study incorporates the more formal communications tasks undertaken by discipline professionals, including user documentation, performance reports and software documentation, as well as more informal communications, such as presentations, program summaries and discussions. It is this category that is commonly integrated into the Computer Science curriculum.

Table 1: A Matrix for Communication Skills Activity Identification.

depth	Developing Facility	Explanation and Description	Clarification
WTL	Reflections (journals, blogs), Question posing	One Minute Activities (designs, program summaries), forum postings, email	Reflections (journals, blogs); One Minute Activities (concept summaries, essays); Question posing
WID	Concept Maps; Glossaries; Resume; Thesis Statement; Experimental Descriptions; Citation	Portfolios; Project Reports; User Documentation; Essays; APIs; Online Documentation; Demonstrations	Project Proposals; Thesis Statement; Article Reviews; Program Comparisons; Program Summaries; Meeting minutes; Group discussion and debates
CDC	Innovation Report; Performance Report; Lab Reports; Presentations		

WAC programs typically promote the use of Writing to Learn (WTL) activities: informal writing assignments that enable *students* to analyse and develop key concepts presented in a course. This is in contrast to Writing in the Discipline (WID) activities, which model the formal communication required for *professionals* within a discipline. Incorporating both WTL and WID tasks within a curriculum is necessary as the capacity built through the completion of WTL activities leads to the ability to successfully attempt WID activities [20].

3.2 Developing Curricula

Our methodology combines the categorisations introduced by WAC and Taffe to develop a matrix of communication skills categories that guide the inclusion of communication skills activities within the Computer Science curriculum (Table 1). The matrix acts as a curriculum mapping tool that can be used to ascertain expected depth and breadth in exposure to communication skills development within a curriculum. In addition to the categories of WTL and WID, we define a new category, Communicating Discipline Content (CDC), which represents the deepest level of communication within the discipline while, concurrently, enabling students to model the full range of Computer Science communication skills.

Table 1 illustrates both the classification of communication skills activities when combining both categorisations and how these activities may be combined to achieve both depth and breadth. When both categorisations are viewed together, with the appropriate classification of activities, we are able to identify more precisely the aspect of skill development that is being addressed. For example, using this matrix, we are able to identify that although the selection of *reflections* and *user documentation* provide depth through the development from WTL to WID, they are each addressing a different form of Computer Science communication, and hence the desired bridging between activities is not achieved. Similarly, the combination of an *experimental description*, *performance report*, and *program summary* can be combined to demonstrate the spectrum of discipline communication skills. This particular combination of WID activities, however, we can identify as more appropriate for an advanced course where students have had prior opportunity to develop their expertise through informal WTL activities.

Our matrix enables faculty to determine a target aspect of skill development: how we can design courses to provide the intended depth, breadth, or combination, that is intended. For example, the selection of *reflections* as an activity can be combined with a *concept map* in order to provide deep *development of facility* with the discipline language. Similar activities are represented at different points within the matrix, for example the classification of *one-minutes activities*. This demonstrates the utility of a single activity in developing multiple skill areas - and the importance of recognising these activities as such so that they can be framed and assessed appropriately.

We identify four communication skills activities within the CDC category: *innovation report*, *performance report*, *laboratory report* and *presentation*. These activities represent the culmination of skill development in terms of depth gained through experience in WTL and WID activities, and span Taffe's categories.

3.3 Guiding Principles

We identify four principles to guide both the selection of activities from the provided matrix, and their integration with discipline courses.

1. Link communication skills activities with discipline activities and course objectives to provide motivation, engagement and active learning.
2. Bridge informal to formal activities, to enable modeling of communication via informal activities and application within the discipline to provide a professional perspective.
3. Use a range of activities that reflect the different types of writing undertaken by Computer Science professionals, including the kind of communication involved (as per Taffe), and communicating for a range of audiences, a range of mediums and levels of interactivity.
4. Use self- and peer-assessment where appropriate to engage students further in the reflection and review process, and provide opportunities for informal grading and feedback.

The principles we define assist faculty to identify communication skills activities that work with their existing discipline content or assessment tasks. Gribbin advises that one 'need look no further than the course objectives stated in the syllabus' when designing communication skills activities [11]. This statement makes a direct connection between each writing or speaking activity and the discipline objective that it is supporting. Communication skills activities are complementary to discipline content; they are designed to aid understanding of the discipline content, engaging the

Table 2: An Example Curriculum.

	Developing Facility	Explanation and Description	Clarification
WTL	Reflections (blogs)	One Minute Activities (designs, program summaries)	Reflections (blogs); One Minute Activities (concept summaries)
WID	Glossaries; Citation	APIs; Online Documentation;	Group discussion and debates
CDC	Innovation Report; Performance Report; Presentations		

students through their independent study and assignment work to explore further the discipline concepts.

Many discipline academics are also reluctant to adopt significant communication skills assignments in their courses because of the perceived time required for assessment and evaluation of these assignments [11]. However, not all communications assignments require formal grading. Peer review is a commonly used form of assessment for informal learning activities, providing the valuable components of assessment and feedback, while further encouraging analysis and reflection within the class.

3.4 Implementation

To demonstrate our methodology, we define the activities and structure of a pilot communication skills course designed to be taught in an integrated fashion across two discipline courses - an introductory programming course and a data structures course[1]. We apply our methodology in both the selection of activities (as illustrated in Table 2), and in their integration with discipline content.

We can immediately identify the need to include several WTL activities, as these activities will serve as the bedrock for future communication skill development, and will enable students to develop good learning behaviours built around communication. However, it is also necessary to include aligned WID activities to encourage skill development within the discipline, developing communication skills and enabling deeper learning of discipline concepts. The course structure culminates with the inclusion of CDC activities, to provide a unifying activity within the discipline combining all forms of Computer Science communication. Detailed assessment criteria, in the form of rubrics, are provided for each activity, with an emphasis on understanding assessment criteria integrated into the assessment of all activities.

3.4.1 Developing Facility

Personal *reflections* in a journal or blog enable students to write freely about their study experiences, their transition to tertiary study and the associated assessment practices. In the context of developing facility, reflections encourage students to learn and use the language of their discipline and study environment.

The *glossary* activities require weekly contributions to an online collaborative glossary, with each student required to contribute one new entry, or add discussion to an existing entry each week with appropriate citation for all sources, contributing an element of peer review and feedback. This activity provides practice in the use of language within the discipline, through the development of a discipline tool that can be used throughout the remainder of their studies.

[1]In our case study, the communication skills course exists as a separate course as it is undertaken by a specialised cohort of international students, from multiple prior institutions, however, these activities could be as easily embedded directly into the discipline courses.

3.4.2 Explanation and Description

Informal *One Minute Activities* require students to complete a small communications task prior to, or during, class that is related to a concept or assessment task from their discipline courses. In the context of explanation and description, we focus on the use of small design tasks or program summaries, primarily targetting the understanding of fundamental programming concepts and the application of those concepts through the development and analysis of brief code segments [26]. Again, peer review and feedback can be incorporated to provide regular, informal feedback and opportunities for reflection.

- Write a pseudo-code description of the following algorithm: ...
- Explain the design of the algorithm that you have developed for this assignment...

Building upon the One Minute Activities, we define a combined *API* and *online documentation* WID activity, involving the development of detailed online Application Programming Interface (API) documentation for a Java class that students had developed in their introductory programming course. Students were required to use the Javadoc environment to develop their API documentation, and were asked to provide a psuedo-formal algorithm description for each method in their class, identifying any special cases and providing an explanation of data used in the method. Students were also asked to provide several examples of the usage of each method, highlighting special cases. This activity enabled students to develop a better understanding of object oriented design and the algorithms they had designed and implemented.

3.4.3 Clarification

Reflections and One Minute Activities are also used for their ability to aid clarification. In their regular reflections, students are able to move beyond use of the discipline language to clarification of concepts, aiding by self review of their reflections each week to observe their own development. In this context, concept summaries are adopted as the One Minute Activity, again influenced by Zobel [26]. For this subset of One Minute Activities, we integrated a group discussion element to mimic professional behaviour, bridging directly from WTL to WID.

- Select a section of your textbook (less than 1 page) and identify the five main points.
- Take the five main points you constructed earlier and rewrite the section without looking at it.
- Select a section from your textbook (1-2 pages) and summarise it in 500 words. Repeat this using 400 words, then 300 words and finally 100 words. Which is the best version?

3.4.4 Communicating Discipline Content

Our new CDC category highlights discipline activities that build further upon the skills developed in WTL and WID, combining skills chosen from the range of developing facility through to clarification. In our course structure, we adopt three activities to illustrate CSC: the *innovation report*, *performance report* and *presentations*. These activities effectively act as *capstone* experiences in relation to the development of communication skills, enabling students to further develop and also evaluate their skill development.

Perhaps the most engaging of the communication skills activities, the Innovation Report requires students to research and write a report on an innovative technology of their choice. Demonstrating the creativity and breadth within Computer Science, this assignment asked students to identify a new innovation, provide evidence of the innovative nature and give a brief description of how this innovation might change our world. The Innovation Report enables students to develop their research skills within their discipline, and requires them to master discipline concepts in order to understand their innovation. The Innovation Report provides the opportunity for students to demonstrate each category of language skill: facility, explanation and description and clarification, and through its extension in the presentation skills activity (below) utilises multiple communication mediums. Sample topics were provided to the students, including: the influence of cloud computing on high performance computing, nanocomputing, touch screen devices, and the integration of technology into every day items.

Presentation activities are included throughout the course structure, typically building upon the One Minute Activities embedded throughout. These presentations enabled students to further embed the skills associated with those homework activities through the use of several communication mediums, whilst also acknowledging the student preference for a specific communication medium. In addition, we included two more substantial presentations, the first on a discipline topic of the students' choice, enabling students to build familiarity in the use of formal presentation tools and structure, and the second a presentation on their Innovation Report. This second presentation employed the same presentation tools, structure, and assessment criteria. In this presentation, students were also asked to complete peer-assessment for one other student. Building from the feedback from their WTL presentation enabled students to reflect upon their own assessment and assessment criteria.

The performance analysis report requires students to analyse, compare and report on the complexity analysis of two data structures studied in their discipline course. This activity again provides elements from developing facility to clarification, in that it consists of several sub-activities: starting with the identification of their hypothesis - *verification of algorithmic complexity*, the design of a series of experiments to test their hypothesis, the design and completion of a test code suite to undertake their experiments and the final write-up of all of the stages along with the analysis of their results. This activity was designed to develop understanding of complexity analysis (typically a challenging topic for our students), the process of performance analysis, as well as models for documenting performance information.

3.5 Findings

In our analysis we explore the impact of continual exposure of communication skills development in a pilot study, following the first cohort who have taken this course and subsequently graduated. Students found the activities in the communication skills course to be more challenging than those they had previously undertaken in general communications skills courses. This is unsurprising, in that our expectations were greater: students are developing discipline knowledge concurrently with facility with communication. However, students also found these activities more rewarding and helpful in developing their understanding of discipline content. Perhaps the best way to analyse the impact of the communication skills activities is to ascertain whether the students involved in the course felt the impact of the course activities on their communication skills and their understanding of discipline content. It is worth noting here that these students are international students undertaking their first semester of study, and as such are unfamiliar with both informal and formal communication in English. Within the Reflections exercise, students wrote freely about their experiences, and reflected upon both the changes to their learning and understanding of appropriate study skills:

> *This week I started to prepare my performance analysis report. It was my first time to do write this kind of report. It is much harder. I needed to test more and analysis the programs much deeper. It was a good way for me to understand the programs what I need to analysis.*
>
> *All the week, every classmate are working on the practical exercises. It is really a hard work for a newcomer student. Frequently, I think I have mastered the knowledge after took the lecture, however, once I'm in practice in front of the computer, I found it's not quite as I thought before. Even more, I can not run a program. I believe that is the main difference between practice and merely thinking.*

We have been able to observe the performance and behaviour of this pilot group across their program of study. Course Coordinators for the related discipline courses have reported increased facility by these students in understanding assessment tasks and completing language-rich assessments. Final examination questions for these courses were classified as either mathematical or linguistic, based on whether the question could be solved using a mathematical solving method, or required deeper understanding and discussion of concepts. Students who had undertaken the communications skills activities achieved better performance in the linguistic questions than previous cohorts, as they were able extract more information from the question and then provide an answer in a way that matched more appropriately the assessment criteria of the question. There were fewer examples of repetition from the course notes than had been seen previously. The results achieved by this initial cohort have indicated that exposure to integrated communication skills activities is of benefit. In their commencing year, these students represented approximately 25% of overall enrolments in undergraduate Computer Science programs (N=134). In general, the load pass rate for domestic Computer Science students within our institution is 83%, and for international students, 79%. The students from our cohort, also international students, demonstrated a load pass rate of 89% over the duration of their studies. However, there is considerable research to be undertaken before any true correlation can be identified. It is not surprising that students who are exposed to greater opportunities for communication skill development are able to perform to a higher standard in communication skills tasks. We intend to pursue a larger scale study using our methodology, applied to a broader range of students, exploring the usefulness of our methodology for Computer Science academics and impact upon student success.

4. CONCLUSIONS

Communication skills has been identified as a crucial skill area for Computer Scientists, both in the professional day to day activities and in the development of critical thinking and analysis skills. This paper presents a methodology for the development of communication skills curricula within Computer Science that encourages the use of communication skills activities throughout discipline curricula to facilitate both the development of discipline and professional skills. We present several examples of communication skills activities developed using our methodology, in the context of a communication skills course aligned with introductory Computer Science content.

5. REFERENCES

[1] J. Bransford. *How people learn: brain, mind, experience and school.* Washington, D.C.L National Academy Press, 2000.

[2] M. Collins. Using short pieces of writing (microthemes) to improve student learning. In *Teaching tips: innovations in undergraduate science instruction*, pages 7–8. Arlington, VA: National Science Teachers Association Press, 2004.

[3] E. Derrick. Tools for student engagement that facilitate development of communication skills. In *Advances in Computer, Information and Systems Sciences, and Engineering*, pages 481–483, 2006.

[4] H. Drury and C. Taylor. Providing the discipline context for skills development: report on the production of an interactive video for oral and visual communication in the biological sciences. In *Proceedings of HERDSA*, 1999.

[5] R. Dugan and V. Polanski. Writing for computer science: A taxonomy of writing tasks and general advice. *Journal of Computing Sciences in Colleges*, 21(6):191–203, June 2006.

[6] J. Emig. Writing as a mode of learning. *College Composition and Communication*, 28(2):122–128, 1977.

[7] H. Fell, V. Prouix, and J. Casey. Writing across the computer science curriculum. In *Proceedings of SIGCSE*, pages 204–209, 1996.

[8] P. Forsyth. Writing to inform - and impress. *Engineering Management*, 14(4):40, 2004.

[9] T. Fulwiler and A. Young. *Language Connections: Writing and Reading Across the Curriculum.* National Council of Tearchers of English, Urbana, Illinois, 1982.

[10] E. Giangrande. Communication skills in the CS curriculum. *Journal of Computing Sciences in Colleges*, 24(4):74–79, 2009.

[11] W. Gribbin. Writing across the curriculum: Assignments and evaluation. *The Clearing House*, 64(6):365–368, 1991.

[12] P. Gruba and H. Søndergaard. A constructivist approach to communication skills instruction in computer science. *Computer Science Education*, 11(3):203–219, 2001.

[13] J. Hartman. Writing to learn and communicate in a data structures course. *ACM SIGCSE Bulletin*, 21(1):32–36, February 1989.

[14] D. Kay. Computer scientists can teach writing: An upper division course for computer science majors. In *Proceedings of SIGCSE*, pages 117–120, 1998.

[15] T. Koppi and F. Naghdy. *Managing educational change in the ICT discipline at the tertiary education level.* Australian Learning and Teaching Council, 2009.

[16] Y. Korsarts, A. Fischback, J. Rufinus, J. Utell, and S.-L. Yoon. Developing oral and written communication skills in undergraduate computer science and information systems curriculum. In *Proceedings of ISECON*, pages 1–10, 2009.

[17] C. Kussmaul. Using Agile development methods to improve student writing. *Journal of Computing in Small Colleges*, 20(3):148–156, 2005.

[18] G. McDonald and M. McDonald. Developing oral communication skills of computer science undergraduates. In *Proceedings of SIGCSE*, pages 279–282, 1993.

[19] H. McGregor, S. Saunders, K. Fry, and E. Tayler. Designing a system for the development of communication abilities within an engineering context. *Australian Journal of Communication*, 27:83–94.

[20] S. McLeod and E. Maimon. Clearing the air: WAC myths and realities. *College English*, 62(5):573–583, 2000.

[21] M. Michael. Fostering and assessing communication skills in the computer science context. In *Proceedings of SIGCSE*, pages 119–123, 2000.

[22] L. Pollock. Integrating an intensive experience with communication skills development into a computer science course. *SIGCSE Bulletin*, 33(1):287–291, 2001.

[23] J. Pomykalski. Teaching systems analysis and design as a writing-intensive course. *Information Systems Education Journal*, 4(70):1–10, September 2006.

[24] S. Sonnentag. Expertise in professional software design: A process study. *Journal of Applied Psychology*, 83(5):703–715, 1998.

[25] W. Taffe. Writing in the computer science curriculum. *Writing Across the Curriculum*, 1(1):17–22, June 1989.

[26] J. Zobel. *Writing for Computer Science.* Springer-Verlag, 2004.

'Explain in Plain English' Questions: Implications for Teaching

Laurie Murphy
Pacific Lutheran University
Tacoma, Washington
lmurphy@plu.edu

Renée McCauley
College of Charleston
Charleston, SC 29424
mccauleyr@cofc.edu

Sue Fitzgerald
Metropolitan State University
St. Paul, MN 55106
sue.fitzgerald@metrostate.edu

ABSTRACT
This paper reports on the replication of a study of novice programmers, looking for relationships between ability to 'explain in plain English' the meaning of a code segment and success in writing code later in the semester. This study explores the question in a different learning environment and qualitatively evaluates 'explain in plain English' responses to identify implications for teaching. Statistical results from this study are similar to those of the earlier work. Results highlight students' fragile knowledge, particularly for students excluded from the primary analyses by a set of screening questions, and suggest the need for assessment and instruction of basic concepts later into the term than instructors are likely to expect.

Categories and Subject Descriptors
K.3.2 [**Computing Milieux**]: Computers and Education - Computer and Information Science Education

General Terms
Human Factors

Keywords
Computer science education research, qualitative research methods, mixed methods, explain in plain English.

1. INTRODUCTION
Computer science faculty members have long been baffled by the difficulty many novices have when learning to program. Data exist to support the assertion that, after completing their introductory programming courses, many intermediate students can neither read nor write code [6, 11]. In an effort to explain this phenomenon, Whalley et al. [14] hypothesized that "a vital step toward being able to write programs is the capacity to read a piece of code and describe [its function]." Building on this notion, Lopez et al. [10] found a correlation between student ability to explain a piece of code using plain English and their ability to write similar code. Lopez et al. suggested that there is a hierarchy of programming related tasks. "Knowledge of programming constructs forms the bottom of the hierarchy, with 'explain in plain English', Parson's puzzles and the tracing of iterative code forming one or more intermediate levels in the hierarchy."

In 2011, Corney, Lister and Teague (CLT) [3] performed a longitudinal study of novice programmers, looking for relationships between ability to 'explain in plain English' the meaning of a code segment, and success in writing code later in the semester. CLT found that students who could not correctly explain code early in the term were more likely to have difficulty writing code throughout the remainder of the semester. This paper reports preliminary findings of a replication of the CLT project designed to determine if similar results would be observed in a different environment. Additionally, this study extends the work of CLT by qualitatively evaluating students' 'explain in plain English' responses to identify implications for teaching. It is part of a larger study aimed at assessing the impact of teaching students to explain code over the course of a semester.

Results highlight students' fragile knowledge and suggest the need for assessment and instruction of basic concepts later into the term than instructors are likely to expect. Context and pedagogic practice appear to play a positive role in encouraging relational reasoning. Statistical results from this smaller study are similar to those of CLT [3], This work also examines the performance of students excluded from the primary analyses by a set of basic screening questions.

This paper is organized as follows: Section 2 summarizes the background research. Section 3 gives details of the methodology of this study. The findings are specified in Section 4. Teaching implications are addressed in Section 5. Finally, Section 6 presents suggestions for future work.

2. BACKGROUND
A series of recent studies have investigated the relationship between novice programmers' ability to write and explain code [7, 8, 9, 10, 13, 14]. These studies are characterized by their use of 'explain in plain English' questions, which present students with a code segment and require them to provide a brief, natural language description of what the code segment accomplishes. (See [5] for the complete list of 'explain in plain English' questions with solutions.) Responses to questions were analyzed in terms of the Structure of the Observed Learning Outcome (SOLO) taxonomy developed by John Biggs and Kevin Collis [1, 2]. Table 1 lists the SOLO reasoning categories with a brief description of how explanations of code segments could be categorized (adapted from [14]).

Lopez et al. [10] showed a link between *relational reasoning* and an ability to write code. These results were confirmed in replication studies [7, 8, 13].

The studies discussed above are similar in that they all elicited student responses at the end of the semester, and the 'explain in plain English' questions involved iteration and arrays.

CLT, however, attempted to assess relational reasoning among novices earlier in the term, prior to the introduction of loops. They investigated loop-less code to determine if relational reasoning was a factor in understanding this type of code segment. They identified code that swaps the contents of two variables as

Permission to make digital or hard copies of all or part of this work for personal or classroom use is granted without fee provided that copies are not made or distributed for profit or commercial advantage and that copies bear this notice and the full citation on the first page. To copy otherwise, or republish, to post on servers or to redistribute to lists, requires prior specific permission and/or a fee.
SIGCSE'12, February 29–March 3, 2012, Rayleigh, NC, USA.
Copyright 2012 ACM 978-1-4503-1098-7/12/02...$10.00.

the simplest piece of non-iterative code requiring relational reasoning and used swapping to see if students would struggle with 'explain in plain English' questions as subjects had in earlier studies using loops and arrays. The CLT study involved novice programmers in an introductory programming course who were given non-graded tests during weeks 3 and 5 of semester. The students were told that the test results would be used to guide future teaching. Like earlier 'explain in plain English' studies, data was also collected at the end of the term.

Table 1. SOLO Reasoning Categories

Category	Description
Relational	Provides a summary of what the code does in terms of the code's purpose.
Multistructural	A line-by-line description is provided of all the code.
Unistructural	Provides a description for only one portion of the code
Prestructural	Substantially lacks knowledge of constructs or is unrelated to the question

One of the 'explain in plain English' questions given to students at week 3 presented code that swapped two values. (See Appendix for the test questions.) CLT found that students who could not correctly explain, at week 3, that the code accomplished a swap, performed worse throughout the rest of the semester on various tasks (writing a swap, explaining a sort, explaining code that computed the product of even numbers, tracing a swap, writing code to reverse a string) than students who could explain a swap.

At week 5, participants were asked to write code that swapped two variables. CLT found that students who could not write a swap, at week 5, performed worse on various tasks (explaining a sort, explaining code that computed the product of even numbers, tracing a swap, writing code to reverse a string) throughout the remainder of the semester. Another week 5 question asked students to explain a sort. They found that students who could not explain a sort at week 5 performed consistently worse on later tasks (writing a swap, explaining code that computed the product of even numbers, tracing a swap, writing code to reverse a string) than students who could explain a sort.

CLT suggest that, very early on in the semester, introductory students divide into two groups, those who can think relationally and those who cannot. They suggest that this is the result of current pedagogic practice, not an innate weakness of students.

3. METHODOLOGY

This study adapted CLT's study [3] for use with introductory Java students at a small liberal arts university in the United States by translating their test questions from Python to Java. The questions were given in graded assessments during the spring 2011 semester. When the graded tests were returned the test questions were reviewed by the teacher and the importance of understanding the questions was emphasized. (Revised questions are included in the Appendix.)

3.1 Participants

Participants were 29 undergraduate students (12 female, 17 male) enrolled in a traditional "objects later" introductory Java programming course. Following the process conducted in CLT, data from eleven participants were eliminated from the quantitative analyses due to failure to correctly answer three screening questions (questions 1 through 3 on Test 1, see Appendix). Responses from two other students who did not complete all three question sets were also excluded from the quantitative analysis.

Data from 16 participants were analyzed quantitatively and data from all 29 were considered qualitatively.

3.2 Data Collection

CLT administered their ungraded tests at weeks 3 and 5 and at the end of the semester as part of the final exam. To conserve limited class time and encourage students to respond to the questions seriously, the current study incorporated all study questions into regular graded assessments. CLT's Test 1 questions were added to an exam during the third week of the term, Test 2 questions were added to a quiz during week six, and Test 3 questions were included in an exam given at week nine of a 15 week semester. The research study questions made up 5% of the total points possible for each of the exams, and 25% of the points on the quiz. Although Test 3 was administered before the end of the semester, students in the current study had completed all of the material addressed in those questions by week nine of the term.

3.3 Data Coding

From the students' perspective, the study questions were graded like all other questions on the assessment and they received partial credit in some cases. For analysis purposes, researchers discussed each of the partially correct responses and came to a consensus as to whether they should be counted as correct or incorrect. These were then used to replicate the quantitative analysis presented in the CLT study that found correlations between answers on different test questions.

We also conducted qualitative analyses on some of the test questions. This paper describes our assessment of the 'explain in plain English' exercises from Test 1 which required students to "explain a swap of two variables" and Test 2 which required students to "explain a sort of three values". Test 1 'explain a swap' questions were categorized based on the types of errors students made. We categorized Test 2 'explain a sort' answers according to the SOLO taxonomy based on previous work by Whalley et al. [14] (see Table 1). Responses to this question were categorized independently by two researchers. Three researchers worked together to come to consensus on the appropriate categorization of all responses. These results are discussed in 4.2.

4. FINDINGS

4.1 Quantitative Analysis

This section summarizes this study's quantitative results and compares them with those found in CLT [3]. Due to the small sample size, the numbers are not statistically significant. However, they are indicative of trends similar to those found by CLT. Below we refer to this study's results using SS, for Small Study.

4.1.1 Screening

CLT used the first three questions on Test 1, those designed to assess students' understanding of variables, assignment and simple tracing, as screening questions for their study. Students who did not answer all three screening questions correctly (144, or 63% of their students) were eliminated from the statistical analysis. The argument for doing this was to screen students who did not understand the necessary foundational concepts required to understand swapping. This is similar to excluding subjects who do not have an adequate understanding of English from a study where the questions are posed in English.

For comparison, we used the same procedure of removing students who could not answer the screening questions (11, or 41%) from our analysis. Tables 2-4 compare results from the two studies.

Table 2 shows similar results for students who passed the screening questions in both studies, with our SS students performing somewhat better on the three explanation questions (swap, sort and product of evens) and string reversal, but slightly lower on writing a swap.

Table 2. The percentage of students who answered each question correctly

Question		SS n=16	CLT n=83
Test 1	Explain a swap	63%	47%
Test 2	Write a swap	69%	73%
	Explain a sort of 3 variables	69%	48%
Test 3	MCQ, explain the product of even nums	94%	76%
	Trace a swap	88%	89%
	Write code to reverse a string	75%	59%

4.1.2 Explain a Swap

Table 3 compares the performance of students who could correctly explain a swap on Test 1 with those who could not for each institution. It shows how many in each group correctly answered the subsequent test questions. For example, only 33% of the small study (SS) students who were initially unable to explain a swap were able to write a swap on Test 2. Again, results between the two studies are similar. The most notable differences are on the Test 2 questions for students who could not explain a swap on Test 1; a lower percentage of the SS students were able to write a swap while more were able to explain a sort than those in the CLT study. This may be due in part to the fact that the Test 1 questions were reviewed and the importance of being able to understand and explain code was emphasized when the tests were returned to the SS students.

4.1.3 Write a Swap

Table 4 compares the performance of students who were able to write a swap on Test 2 with those who could not, again showing the percentage that were able to correctly answer subsequent questions. Here the performance for the SS students who incorrectly wrote the swapping code is considerably better than that found by CLT. Again, this suggests that reviewing and emphasizing earlier questions may improve student understanding. Differences in the timing of the tests and the nature of the assessments (graded vs. ungraded) may also have been factors.

4.1.4 Impact of Early Confusion about Variables

Students from our study who did not appear to understand swapping early in the term were able to recover fairly well. This led us to wonder about the students who had been screened from the statistical analysis early on, those who appeared to be confused about fundamental concepts such as variables and assignment. How did they fare as the term progressed?

Table 5 compares SS students who were unable to answer all three screening questions correctly on Test 1 with those who could. Here we see that these students not only did much worse at explaining a swap on Test 1, but that they also continued to struggle with swapping and sorting on Test 2. They seemed to recover somewhat on Test 3 on the 'explaining a product' question, although this question was multiple choice, and particularly on tracing a swap. However, they performed much worse than students who answered the screening questions correctly when it came to altering a loop to reverse a string.

4.2 Qualitative Analysis

As noted above, students were tested in weeks 3, 6 and 9 to see if their ability to explain the purpose of code segments was related to their ability to write code correctly. We took a closer look at several test questions to see what patterns emerged.

The following subsections present a qualitative analysis of the ways in which students went wrong on the two early 'explain in plain English' questions. They reveal misconceptions that appear to impede students' early attempts at relational reasoning.

Table 3. The performance of students, broken down according to the Test 1 'explain a swap' question

Test 1 Explain a swap		SS Wrong (n=6)	SS Right (n=10)	CLT Wrong (n=44)	CLT Right (n=39)	CLT χ^2 test
Test 2	Write a swap	33%	90%	57%	92%	p = 0.001
	Explain a sort of 3 variables	67%	70%	36%	62%	p = 0.03
Test 3	MCQ, explain the product of even nums	83%	100%	64%	90%	p = 0.01
	Trace a swap	83%	90%	82%	97%	p = 0.03
	Write code to reverse a string	50%	90%	41%	79%	p = 0.001

Table 4. The performance of students, broken down according to the Test 2 'write a swap' question

Test 2 Write a swap		SS Wrong (n=5)	SS Right (n=11)	CLT Wrong (n=22)	CLT Right (n=61)	CLT χ^2 test
Test 2	Explain a sort of 3 variables	40%	82%	14%	61%	p = 0.001
Test 3	MCQ, explain the product of even nums	100%	91%	59%	82%	p = 0.03
	Trace a swap	80%	91%	68%	97%	p = 0.001
	Write code to reverse a string	60%	82%	27%	70%	p = 0.001

Table 5. The performance of students, broken down according to the Test 1 screening questions (n = 27)

Test 1 Screening Questions		SS Wrong (n=11)	SS Right (n=16)
Test 1	Explain a swap	27%	63%
Test 2	Write a swap	18%	69%
	Explain a sort of 3 variables	18%	69%
Test 3	MCQ, explain the product of even nums	73%	94%
	Trace a swap	82%	88%
	Write code to reverse a string	27%	75%

4.2.1 Explain a Swap

We examined the most vulnerable students, those who could not pass the screening questions. Of the 13 students who did not answer all three screening questions correctly (including the two students who did not take all three tests), we observed the following about their answers to the 'explain a swap' question on Test 1:

- Four answered the question correctly. Closer inspection revealed that three of those students only missed one screening question, suggesting they likely did have a reasonably good grasp of variables and assignment and probably just made a careless mistake.
- Three of them indicated that the swap caused all three variables to be equal, which, interestingly, is what the screening questions they answered incorrectly actually did. These students were attempting to grasp the code on a relational level, but probably did not trace the code with example values in order to be sure of its actual purpose.
- Three left the question blank or gave incomplete or incomprehensible responses, suggesting a complete lack of understanding, even though an example swap using different variables was explained just above.
- Two said the statements restored the variables to their original values, ignoring the instructions that stated "NOTE: Tell what the second set of three lines of code do all by themselves. Do NOT think of those second three lines as being executed after the first three lines of code."
- One appeared to believe that assignments happened from left to right, given the following response: *The second set of data states that a = c once program begins because it assigns a->b, b->c, c->a*

Of the students who passed the screening questions, 10 of the 16 correctly described a swap, although one of them provided a multistructural (line-by-line) explanation as well. Errors included:

- Three students gave incorrect multistructural responses that simply described the code line-by-line. E.g., *a is assigned the value in b then b is assigned the value in c then c is assigned the value in a.*
- One gave a unistructural description, stating the code's purpose was to assign the value of c.
- One thought the code assigned the same value to all three variables.
- One gave a nonsensical answer.

Overall, the screening questions appear to have effectively identified those students who had a good understanding of variables and assignment. However, they also appear to have unnecessarily excluded some students. A slightly less stringent threshold for exclusion is indicated.

4.2.2 Explain a Sort

On Test 2, students were asked to explain a sorting code segment. We analyzed this test question by categorizing each answer as relational, multistructural, unistructural or prestructural using the SOLO taxonomy [1]. Whalley et al [14] performed a similar analysis on their data using the definitions given in Table 1.

Two researchers categorized student responses to this test question. Later all three authors negotiated these categorizations to consensus. Although the researchers reached consensus, it must be noted that the exact meanings of the SOLO designations of prestructural, unistructural, multistructural and relational as applied to computer programming are open to interpretation.

Table 6 summarizes the categorization of the 27 student answers using the SOLO taxonomy. The table shows the number of answers which fall into each category as well as the percentage of answers falling into each category. The vast majority were relational (70%); the students provided a summary of what the code did in terms of its purpose, although only 58% of these answers were correct as shown in the right column of Table 6. All prestructural and unistructural answers were incorrect as were most of the multistructural answers.

Table 6. SOLO categorization of answers to 'Explain a Sort'

Category	Number (%)	Correct (%)
Relational	19 (70%)	11 (58%)
Multistructural	4 (15%)	1 (25%)
Unistructural	3 (11%)	0 (0%)
Prestructural	1 (4%)	0 (0%)

Students went wrong in a number of ways.

- Many provided a plain English explanation but incorrectly deduced the purpose of the code.

  It prints the variable y1, y2, & y3 values in reverse order [Relational]

  It assigns y1 the highest value of the three variables [Relational]

  It prints y3 first, then the y2, finally the y1 because each step allowed a swap [Multistructural]

  To print y2 first, y2 second the[n] y1 [Unistructural]
- A few provided code instead of plain English [Prestructural]
- Some answers were correct and explained in plain English, but still reflected a step-by-step understanding

  The code prints y1, y2, & y3 after having made y1 hold the largest value, y3 the smallest and y2 the in between value. [Multistructural]
- Yet other answers were partially correct but subtly wrong, describing only part of the answer:

  It swaps the smaller values of two variables [Unistructural]
- Sadly, a few were simply incomplete.

  swap y1 and y2 when [Unistructural]

5. IMPLICATIONS FOR TEACHING

For some disciplines, introductory courses cover loosely related topics over a term, which means a misconception about one topic is unlikely to impede students' understanding of later material. The cumulative nature of programming, however, means that early misunderstandings can have disastrous consequences later in the course. 'Explain in plain English' questions appear to be an effective means for gauging students' level of abstract thinking.

We discuss here some possible implications of our findings on teaching practice.

5.1 Role of context and review

For students who demonstrated an understanding of variables and assignment, CLT found statistically significant correlations between ability to explain a swap at week 3 and write a swap at week 5, with performance on those tasks and on other programming tasks later in the term. Although analysis for statistical significance was not possible for this study, similar trends were seen for SS. At both institutions students who were able to explain swapping and sorting performed better later in the term. However, SS students who were *not* able to explain a swap appear to have recovered and performed better than the CLT group as the term progressed.

While our results should be viewed cautiously due to the small dataset, they suggest that pedagogic practice and context may somewhat mitigate difficulties for those students who catch on to the basics (i.e., variables and assignment) early in the term. Not only were the early swapping questions reviewed and emphasized for the SS students, but their overall learning context is also highly supportive; these students attend very small classes (15-25 students) held in a computer classroom that facilitates hands on practice, much of it done in pairs. They also participate in weekly two hour lab sessions conducted by the instructor and an undergraduate TA. Despite these advantages, for students who do not understand the basic concepts at week 3, recovering and succeeding in the course appears to be difficult.

5.2 Applying innovative teaching practice to identify and address fragile knowledge

As teachers we often assume that students understand the basics, particularly as the course progresses. However, the test data reveal confusion about basic concepts well into the semester, and suggest explanation questions could be useful for identifying students with fragile knowledge early in the term. Such students could be encouraged to visit tutors or directed to online visualizations or video podcasts to help them master these basic concepts. Common errors should be addressed explicitly and could be used in paired or small group discussions or as distracters for multiple-choice questions. These MCQs could be presented in the context of *Just in Time Teaching* [12] as a way of assessing students' understanding of basic concepts before covering more advanced concepts during class; or using *Peer Instruction* [4], which gives students an opportunity to discuss their responses in small groups as a way of challenging potentially faulty mental models.

6. FUTURE WORK

This work was conducted in the context of a larger study designed to examine the impact of exposing students to 'explain in plain English' questions over a term. In addition to the results reported here, students in this study were also given a set of more complex 'explain in plain English' questions involving loops and arrays on their final exam. Their performance on those questions, and on code writing questions, will be compared with those of students from earlier semesters at the same institution who were not given 'explain in plain English' test questions throughout the term.

'Explain in plain English' questions may well prove to be an effective way to gauge the point at which student thinking moves from concrete to abstract. A study of the impact of innovative teaching practices such as Just in Time Teaching or Peer Instruction in combination with 'explain in plain English' questions may shed light on students' ability to overcome early misconceptions.

7. ACKNOWLEDGMENTS

We extend our thanks to Raymond Lister for so generously sharing his problem sets.

8. REFERENCES

[1] Biggs, J. & Collis, K. 1982. *Evaluating the quality of learning: The SOLO taxonomy (Structure of the Observed Learning Outcome)*. Academic Press, New York, NY.

[2] Biggs, J. SOLO Taxonomy. Retrieved May 6, 2011 from http://www.johnbiggs.com.au/solo_taxonomy.html

[3] Corney, M., Lister, R. & Teague, D. 2011. Early relational reasoning and the novice programmer: Swapping as the "Hello World" of relational reasoning. *Proceedings of the 13th ACE Conference* (ACE '11). Australian Computing Society.

[4] Crouch, C. H. & Mazur, E. 2001. Peer instruction: Ten years of experience and results. *American Journal of Physics* 69.

[5] Lister, R. Explain in Plain English Questions: Examples and Answers. 2010. Retrieved May 19, 2011 from http://www.staff.it.uts.edu.au/~raymond/braceletace2010.

[6] Lister R., Adams, E. S., Fitzgerald, S., Fone, W., Hamer, J., Lindholm, M., McCartney, R., Moström, E., Sanders, K., Seppälä, O., Simon, B., Thomas, L. 2004. A multi- national study of reading and tracing skills in novice programmers. *SIGCSE Bull.* 36,4 (December 2004), 119-150.

[7] Lister, R., Clear, T., Simon, Bouvier, D. J., Carter, P., Eckerdal, A., Jacková, J., Lopez, M., McCartney, R., Robbins, P., Seppälä, O., & Thompson, E. 2009. Naturally occurring data as research instrument: analyzing examination responses to study the novice programmer. *SIGCSE Bulletin* 41:4, 156-173.

[8] Lister, R., Fidge C. & Teague, D. 2009. Further evidence of a relationship between explaining, tracing and writing skills in introductory programming. In Proceedings *of the14th Annual ITiCSE Conference* (ITiCSE '09). 161-165.

[9] Lister, R., Simon, B., Thompson, E., Whalley, J. & Prasad, C. 2006. Not seeing the forest for the trees: Novice programmers and the SOLO taxonomy, in *Proceedings of the 11th Annual ITiCSE Conference* (ITiCSE '06), 118-122.

[10] Lopez, M., Whalley, J., Robbins, P., & Lister, R. 2008. Relationships between reading, tracing and writing skills in introductory programming, in *Proceedings of the* 4th *ICER Workshop* (ICER'08), 101-112.

[11] McCracken, M., Almstrum, V., Diaz, D., Guzdial, M., Hagen, D., Kolikant, Y., Laxer, K., Thomas, L., Utting, I., & Wilusz, T. 2001. A multi-national, multi-institutional study of assessment of programming skills of first-year CS students. *SIGCSE Bull.* 33, 4 (December 2001), 125-140.

[12] Novak, G., Gavrin, A. & Wolfgang, C. 1999. Just-in-Time Teaching: Blending Active Learning with Web Technology, Prentice Hall, Upper Saddle River, NJ.

[13] Venables, A., Tan, G., & Lister, R. 2009. A closer look at tracing, explaining and code writing skills in the novice programmer. *Proceedings of the ICER Workshop* (ICER'09), 117-128.

[14] Whalley, J., Lister, R., Thompson, E., Clear, T., Robbins, P., Kumar, P. & Prasard, C. 2006. An Australasian Study of Reading and Comprehension Skills in Novice Programmers, using the Bloom and SOLO Taxonomies. In *Proceedings of the 8th ACE Conference* (ACE'06), 243-252.

APPENDIX

TEST 1
(Adapted from Corney, Lister & Teague, Exam 1 Spring 2011 at 3 weeks)

For the questions below, you may write down any work on this exam paper, except in the answer boxes. Write ONLY your answer in the answer boxes. (5 points)

1. In the boxes provided below, write the values in the variables after the following code has been executed:

   `r = 2;   s = 4;   r = s;`   *{Displayed vertically here to save space.}*

2. In the boxes provided below, write the values in the variables after the following code has been executed:

   `P = 1;   q = 8;   p = q;   q = p;`   *{Displayed vertically here to save space.}*

3. In the boxes provided below, write the values in the int variables after the following code has been executed:

   `x = 5;   y = 3;   z = 7;` *{Displayed vertically here to save space.}*

   `x = z;   y = x;   z = y;`

4. The purpose of the following three lines of code is swap the values in variables a and b:

   `c = a;   a = b;   b = c;` *{Displayed vertically here to save space.}*

   The three lines of code below are the same as the lines above, but in a different order:

   `a = b;   b = c;   c = a;` *{Displayed vertically here to save space.}*

   In one sentence that you should write in the box below, describe the purpose of those second set of three lines. NOTE: Tell what the second set of three lines of code do all by themselves. Do NOT think of those second three lines as being executed after the first three lines of code.

   {BOX OMITTED}

5. *{QUESTION OMITTED –same swap as above for variables i, j and k}*

TEST 2
(Adapted from Corney, Lister & Teague, Quiz 3 Spring 2011 at 6 weeks)

1. (2 point) Suppose you have two integer variables, called `p` and `q`. **In the box below write code to swap the values in those two variables**. You may declare and use any extra variables required to make the swap. Give each extra variable a meaningful name that reflects its purpose. *{BOX OMITTED}*
2. (1 point) *{QUESTION OMITTED – tracing a simple nested if}*
3. (2 points) If you were asked to describe the purpose of the code below, a good answer would be "*It prints the smaller of the two values stored in the variables* `a` *and* `b`".

```
if (a < b) System.out.print(a);
else   System.out.print(b);
```

In one sentence that you should write in the empty box below, describe the purpose of the following code.

Do **NOT** give a line-by-line description of what the code does. Instead, tell us the purpose of the code, like the purpose given for the code in the above example (i.e. "*It prints the smaller of the two values stored in the variables* `a` *and* `b`").

Assume that the variables y1, y2 and y3 are all variables with integer values.

In each of the three boxes that contain sentences beginning with "`Code to swap the values` ...",assume that appropriate code is provided instead of the box – do **NOT** write that code.

```
if (y1 < y2)
    [Code to swap the values in y1 and y2 goes here.]
if (y2 < y3)
    [Code to swap the values in y2 and y3 goes here.]
if (y1 < y2)
    [Code to swap the values in y1 and y2 goes here.]
System.out.println(y1);
System.out.println(y2);
System.out.println(y3);
```
{BOX OMITTED}

TEST 3
(Adapted from Corney, Lister & Teague, Exam 2 Spring 2011 at 9 weeks)

1. (2 points) Which best describes the purpose of the following function definition? You may assume the method has access to the `Scanner` object `keyboard`.

```
public static intdoSomethingWithNumbers( ) {
        int total = 1;
        System.out.print("Please input an integer: ");
        response = keyboard.nextInt();
        while (response != 0) {
                if (response % 2 == 0)
                    total = total * response;
                System.out.print("Please input an integer: ");
                response = keyboard.nextInt();
        }
        return total;
}
```

   a) It does not do anything as the body of the while loop never executes
   b) It returns the product of all numbers entered
   c) It returns the product of all even numbers entered
   d) It returns the product of all odd numbers entered

2. (1 point) What do the variables **value1**,**value2** and **value3** hold after the following Java code is executed? Assume that they are all int variables.

```
value1 = 10; value2 = 15; value3 = value1; value1 = value2;
value2 = value3;
```

   {Code displayed horizontally here to save space. Labeled boxes for answers omitted}

3. (2 points) The following Java code copies a string:

```
String source = "the cat sat on the mat";
String target = "";
for (inti = 0; i<source.length(); i++)
        target = target + source.charAt(i);
```

Rewrite this code snippet so the target string contains the source string in reverse. E.g., "abc" becomes "cba". *{BOX OMITTED}*

The Impact of Question Generation Activities on Performance

Andrew Luxton-Reilly, Daniel Bertinshaw, Paul Denny, Beryl Plimmer, Robert Sheehan
The University of Auckland
Auckland, New Zealand
andrew|daniel|paul|beryl|robert-s@cs.auckland.ac.nz

ABSTRACT

Recent interest in student-centric pedagogies have resulted in the development of numerous tools that support student generated questions. Previous evaluations of such tools have reported strong correlations between student participation and exam performance, yet the level of student engagement with other learning activities in the course is a potential confounding factor. We show such correlations may be explained by other factors, and we undertake a deeper analysis that reveals evidence of the positive impact question-generation activities have on student performance.

Categories and Subject Descriptors

K.3.2 [**Computers and Education**]: Computer and Information Science Education—*computer science education*

General Terms

Design, Human Factors

Keywords

StudySieve, question-generation, student generated, user generated content, question posing, free-response, contributing student pedagogy, constructive evaluation

1. INTRODUCTION

Increasingly, educators are exploring the use of pedagogies that involve student generated content [3]. In such pedagogies, technology plays a central role in facilitating the interaction between students [12]. It is therefore important that evaluation of techonology used in education goes beyond simple correlational studies to investigate *impact.*

One promising pedagogy requires students to generate exam-style questions and corresponding sample solutions. The questions are peer-reviewed and may be used by other students for drill-and-practice [15]. A number of purpose-built tools have been designed to support this approach [2, 21, 20, 19, 6, 16, 8, 13].

Permission to make digital or hard copies of all or part of this work for personal or classroom use is granted without fee provided that copies are not made or distributed for profit or commercial advantage and that copies bear this notice and the full citation on the first page. To copy otherwise, to republish, to post on servers or to redistribute to lists, requires prior specific permission and/or a fee.
SIGCSE'12, February 29–March 3, 2012, Raleigh, North Carolina, USA.
Copyright 2012 ACM 978-1-4503-1098-7/12/02 ...$10.00.

Evaluations of these tools have shown positive correlations between activity and performance [2, 7, 5, 13, 19]. However, this effect could be an epiphenomenon, occurring because "good" students who work hard during a course are more involved in all course-related activities (e.g. attending lectures, participating in tutorials, studying from textbooks) than weaker students.

In this paper we show that correlations between question-generation activity and performance may be explained by other factors, but deeper analysis of question-generation data reveals evidence that these activities do have a positive impact on performance.

2. RELATED WORK

Formal studies under controlled conditions have shown question generation to be an effective learning activity that results in improved test performance [1, 9]. In a review of studies in which students were taught to generate questions, Rosenshine et al. [18] describe how the act of generating questions does not directly improve understanding, but instead requires students to engage in tasks (such as reflecting on their understanding, searching relevant texts and combining information) that help improve comprehension.

Studies showing that student generated questions were not universally effective [4, 14] led researchers to focus on the specific content of the student generated questions compared to the questions used for assessment.

A study by Frase and Schwartz [11] found that question-generation activity resulted in improved recall in subsequent tests, but the recall effects were localized to content that was related to the generated questions. A later study by Foos et al. [10] confirmed these findings. A significant improvement in exam performance was observed for students who generated questions, but *only on questions with the same topic as the questions they generated.* The authors conclude that "generating potential test questions while preparing for an examination is a very effective technique leading to the highest performance on the material targeted by those test questions" [10, pg. 575].

A number of online tools have been developed by Computer Science educators to support pedagogies involving questions, answers and evaluations contributed by students. However, the numerous intrinsic and extrinsic influences on learning make it difficult to evaluate the impact of such interventions on student learning [17].

Studies of QPPA [21], Concerto [13], PeerWise [7, 5], QSIA [2] and ExamNet [19] have attempted to address the impact of the intervention on student performance by focusing on the relationship between student activity and performance. In studies involving Concerto [13], QSIA [2] and PeerWise [5], an attempt is made to control for prior ability. However, none of the studies compare the level of student engagement in question generation activities with *other* activities in the same course. In other words, they don't measure the level of engagement and ability of students in the context in which the tools are used.

In this paper we investigate the relationship between activity and performance by focusing on two research questions:

- RQ1. Is the correlation between activity and performance a suitable indicator of the effectiveness of a tool?
- RQ2. Do students who use an online tool to author questions on a given topic perform better on similar topics in an exam?

3. METHODOLOGY

StudySieve [16] is an online tool designed to support student generated free-response questions. Students in two undergraduate courses (CS111 and CS105) taught at The University of Auckland were required to use StudySieve to create questions and answers for a small percentage of their final grade. Archival coursework data and the logs of StudySieve use were analysed after the courses were complete. The courses involved in this study, and the analysis of the data are described below.

CS111 — Mastering Cyberspace: An Introduction to Practical Computing is a large service course (404 students) that provides non-majors with an introduction to computing concepts and their practical application. The coursework involves weekly laboratory sessions and a mid-semester test held in week 6. Students were required to author 1 question and answer 5 questions prior to the mid-semester test to receive 0.5% of their final grade.

CS105 — Principles of Computer Science provides an introduction to data structures and algorithms using Java. This course is normally taken by Computer Science majors after completing an introduction to programming. The course was taught in the summer semester 2011 to a class of 50 students.

Course	Students	Activity Requirements	% final
CS111	404	1 question, 5 answers	0.5%
CS105	50	5 questions, 5 answers	2.5%

Table 1: Summary of courses and StudySieve activity requirements.

3.1 Relationship between activity and performance

Students using StudySieve were required to submit a minimum number of questions and answers for a portion of their final mark, but there was no maximum imposed on activity. Some students contributed more questions and answers than required for their assessment. Students also provided feedback to their peers by contributing comments (which are not required nor assessed). In this study we use the number of questions, number of answers and number of comments as three different measures of activity. Since we are investigating the relationship between activity and exam performance, any student that did not sit the final exam was excluded from the study. Section 4.1 reports on simple correlations between activity measures and exam performance. Section 4.2 reports on correlations between activity and exam performance when controlling for prior knowledge, and Section 4.3 reports on correlations between StudySieve activity and performance when controlling for student ability within the same course.

3.2 Relationship between question authoring and performance in related exam questions

To investigate the relationship between authoring a question on a specific topic and exam scores for that topic, we first categorized the student generated questions according to the topics described in the course outline for each course. The question repository contained some student generated questions that were related to more than one topic, so it was not possible to code questions into mutually exclusive categories. For example, the following question submitted by a student in the CS105 course relates to both **big-O** and **binary trees**

> *What are the best case and worst case big-O running times for retrieving an element in a binary tree? Give an example of a sequence of items that would produce each of these big-O running times.*

The process used to classify and analyse the student generated questions are described below.

3.2.1 CS111

Students in the CS111 course generated 350 questions. Two authors categorized each question in the CS111 repository, working together to classify the first ten questions. After some initial discussion about coding boundaries, the remainder of the questions were coded individually. Since a single question may be related to multiple topics, the categorization was performed as a sequence of independent coding tasks. For each topic, every question was examined and coded as either relating to that topic or not. The inter-rater reliability was calculated for each coding task using Cohen's Kappa and substantial agreement was found for most topics (kappa ranged from .630–.966). In cases of coding disagreement, the questions were discussed until agreement was reached. Table 2 lists the topics and the number of student generated questions related to each topic.

Subsequently, we turned to the questions used in the mid-semester test and attempted to identify the student generated questions that were related to the instructor questions. During this process, it became apparant that the coding scheme used to classify student generated questions in CS111 was too coarse. The content covered in CS111 is broad and shallow, resulting in a lack of cohesive related knowledge within topics. For example: questions about Moore's Law and questions asking "What does RAM stand for?" are both classified as Hardware, but are not related questions (e.g. knowledge of Moore's law has no bearing on knowledge of hardware acronyms such as RAM).

Each question in the test was classified according to one of the topics, and all student generated questions belonging to that topic were examined to determine if they were closely related. This resulted in a small set of student generated

Topic	N
Bits and Bytes	48
Standards	16
Hardware	39
Software	22
Internet infrastructure	17
World-Wide Web	19
Email and Forums	17
Blogs and Wikis	19
Word processing	38
Digital images	10
PowerPoint	15
Acronyms	18
HTML/CSS	69
Other	1
Irrelevant	1

Table 2: Topics used to classify student generated questions in CS111

questions that were related to the material assessed in 18 of the 20 test questions. In two cases (a question about web caches and a question about file formats), there were no student generated questions that covered similar material.

For each of the test questions, we divided the students into those who *had* authored a related question (AQ), and those who *had not* authored a related question (NQ). Within each group (AQ and NQ) we calculated the percentage of students correctly answering the question. If the act of generating a question improves subsequent performance on related questions, as claimed by Foos et al. [10], then we would expect to see a higher percentage of students in the AQ group answering a given test question correctly compared with the NQ group. Section 4.4.1 reports the results of this analysis.

3.2.2 CS105

The topics covered in the CS105 course are conceptually more cohesive than those in CS111. student generated questions contributed to the CS105 repository (166 in total) were classified into topics identified from the course outline. To classify questions that involved multiple topics, each topic was considered independently, and questions were coded as either relating to the topic or being unrelated. The inter-rater reliability was calculated for each coding task using Cohen's Kappa and an acceptable level of agreement was found (kappa ranged between .652–.957). In cases of coding disagreement the questions were discussed until agreement was reached. Table 3 lists the topics and the number of student generated questions related to each topic.

The questions used in the final exam were also classified using the topics extracted from the course outline. In the CS105 course, the questions generated by students in each topic were all deemed to be relevant to the corresponding exam questions. All topics were assessed in the exam, except file reading/writing, sorting and ADTs which were assessed during a mid-semester test.

For each question in the final exam, we compared the results of the students who had generated a related question (AQ) with those students who had not generated a related question (NQ). Section 4.4.2 reports the results of this analysis.

Topics	N
Multi-dimensional arrays	5
File reading/writing	8
Exceptions	12
Sorting	28
Recursion	22
Big O	41
ADT	8
Lists	15
Stacks	18
Queues	5
Binary Tree	16
Binary Search Tree	12
Hash table	13
Other	7

Table 3: Number of questions related to each topic in the CS105 curriculum.

4. RESULTS

4.1 Relationship between Activity and Performance

As described in Section 3.1, three measures of activity are used to investigate the relationship between student use of StudySieve and performance on final exams: number of questions created, number of questions answered, and number of comments contributed. Since the distribution of the data is not normal, Spearman's Rho is used to calculate the correlation between exam score and each of number of questions, number of answers and number of comments. For each correlation, a two-tailed significance test was conducted. In almost all cases, a significant positive weak correlation was observed as shown in Table 4.

Activity measure	CS111 (N=371)		CS105 (N=45)	
	ρ	p	ρ	p
No. of questions	.27**	.000	.40*	.007
No. of answers	.31**	.000	.28	.064
No. of comments	.10*	.049	.38*	.011

* 0.05 significance level (2-tailed)
** 0.01 significance level (2-tailed)

Table 4: Correlations between activity and exam scores for the CS111 course (N=371) and the CS105 course (N=45).

The significant and positive correlations between activity and performance present in both courses are consistent with previous studies involving similar tools [21, 13, 7, 5, 2, 19].

4.2 Relationship between activity and performance, controlling for prior knowledge

Almost all students enrolled in the summer semester CS105 course have completed a year of study at The University of Auckland, so their grade point average (GPA) can be used as a surrogate measure of prior knowledge and cognitive ability (although the GPA was not available for 6 students). A partial correlation was calculated between activity and exam score, using GPA as a control. The results show that the number of comments contributed by students is significantly correlated with exam performance, even when controlling for prior ability. Table 5 summarizes the results of the partial correlation. This is consistent with findings from studies involving QSIA [2], ExamNet [19] and PeerWise [5].

Activity measure	r	p
Number of questions	.07	.663
Number of answers	.19	.244
Number of comments	.36*	.025

* 0.05 significance level

Table 5: Results of the partial correlation between activity and exam score when controlling for grade point average in the CS105 course (N=39).

4.3 Relationship between activity and performance, controlling for student ability

In CS105, students also completed a number of programming assignments. The total marks for assignments are strongly correlated with exam scores (ρ=.73, p<.001). We believe that the assignment marks provide an excellent measure of how "good" the student is (where "good" is interpreted as the combination of ability and effort over a sustained time period).

A partial correlation was performed between activity and exam score, using the assignment marks as a control for student ability with material relevant to the course. No significant correlations were found between activity and exam score once assignment marks were taken into account. Although the StudySieve activity is significantly correlated with exam performance, this correlation can be entirely explained by how well students did in the assignments. Table 6 summarizes the results from the partial correlation.

Activity measure	r	p
Number of questions	-.18	.243
Number of answers	-.17	.261
Number of comments	.06	.700

Table 6: Partial correlations between StudySieve activity and exam score in the CS105 course, controlling for total assignment marks (N=45)

Similarly in the CS111 course, correlations between activity and performance can be explained by controlling for engagement with other course-related activities. Students in CS111 attend weekly laboratories that focus on the practical application of theory learned in lectures. The total marks obtained from laboratories (i.e. the sum of weekly laboratory marks) is strongly correlated with exam score (ρ=.62, p<.001), and each of the StudySieve activity metrics: number of questions (ρ=.56, p<.001), number of answers (ρ=.55, p<.001) and number of comments (ρ=.27, p<.001).

A partial correlation was performed between activity and exam score, using the laboratory marks as a control for student ability with material relevant to the course. No significant correlations were found between activity and exam score once laboratory marks were taken into account. Table 7 summarizes the results from the partial correlation.

As with the CS105 course, the correlations between StudySieve activity and exam score are explained by using marks for other coursework activity as a surrogate measure of student ability in the context of a specific course.

Activity measure	r	p
Number of questions	-.020	.701
Number of answers	-.025	.635
Number of comments	-.047	.368

Table 7: Partial correlations between StudySieve activity and exam score in the CS111 course, controlling for total assignment marks (N=371)

4.4 Relationship between question authoring and exam performance in related topics

Although correlations between activity and exam score are easily explained by other metrics of student ability within a course, the research from educational psychology shows that question-generation activities generally improve exam performance on related questions [10]. In this section we focus on the impact of student question-generation activities on *related* test and exam questions.

4.4.1 CS111 questions

Since the CS111 course covers a broad range of unrelated topics, the number of student generated questions related to a given test question is reasonably small, and is not enough to perform statistical tests on individual topics. Of the 20 questions used in the mid-semester test, 2 of the questions had no related student generated questions. Students who authored a question on a related topic performed better than students who did not author a related question in 14 of the 18 remaining questions.

If the question-generation activity had no impact on exam performance, then we would expect the same percentage of students who *had* authored a related question (AQ) to select the correct answer compared with students who *had not* authored (NQ) a related question. The binomial test is used to determine the likelihood of the AQ group exceeding the NQ group in correctly answering test questions. The results indicate that the chances of the AQ group exceeding the NQ group in 14 of 18 cases due to random variation is small (p=0.012). We can conclude that the question-generation activity is likely to have had a positive effect on the exam performance of related questions.

4.4.2 CS105 questions

All the questions used in the CS105 exam were short-answer questions, requiring students to write an explanation, perform a calculation, or write a solution in the form of a Java method. Student performance on each exam question was analysed using a Mann-Whitney U test to determine if any significant difference existed between the marks of students who authored a related question compared with the marks of students who did not author a related question. In three of the exam questions — Big-O, Stacks and Hash tables — a significant difference was observed, but no difference was observed for the other question topics. This suggests that authoring a question about Big-O, Stacks or Hash tables resulted in improved exam performance on those topics. Table 9 summarizes the results.

One possible threat to the validity of this finding is that students may simply be writing questions about topics in

MCQ Topic in test	N	%AQ	%NQ	AQ>NQ
Binary numbers	28	.93	.81	✓
Binary prefixes	2	.50	.71	
Hardware components	22	.91	.89	✓
Moore's law	3	1.0	.68	✓
Software licenses	4	.50	.47	✓
TCP	4	1.0	.86	✓
Internet infrastructure	4	.25	.11	✓
Email protocols	9	.56	.53	✓
Email	4	.50	.48	✓
Blogs	6	.50	.63	
Wikis	8	.38	.51	
WWW history	6	.83	.77	✓
WWW infrastructure	0	NA	.79	NA
ASCII	11	.18	.43	
Standards	0	NA	.60	NA
Image size	6	1.0	.62	✓
PowerPoint criticism	6	.67	.46	✓
PowerPoint advice	7	.71	.59	✓
CGI	1	1.0	.26	✓
CGI	1	1.0	.43	✓

Table 8: Number of student generated questions in CS111 related to each mid-semester test question, and percentage of students answering each question correctly, divided into those who authored a related question (AQ) and those who did not author a related question (NQ).

which they are already knowledgeable. In this case, the difference between author and non-author groups is due to previous knowledge and has no direct impact on performance. Although this threat is impossible to reject entirely, students authored questions *after* they had completed an assignment on that topic, so it is possible to compare the related assignment marks to determine whether students chose to author questions on topics in which they were more knowledgeable than other students.

Assignment 3 had five questions related to Big-O performance analysis. We extracted the marks for these five questions and used a Mann-Whitney U test to compare the assignment marks of students who had generated a question on Big-O (μ=3.45) with the assignment marks of students who did not author a question on Big-O (μ=3.25). The results indicate that there is no significant difference between the groups (p=.321).

This suggests that students in both groups performed equally on questions involving Big-O prior to the use of StudySieve. The students who used StudySieve to generate a question on Big-O subsequently performed better on that topic during a final exam. Although this does not prove a causal relationship between question generation and performance increase in related exam questions, it provides some evidence of such an effect.

A similar analysis was performed with the Stacks topic, however the data is less rich. Assignment 4 had a single question related to stacks which was graded on a coarse scale (between 0 and 2 with increments of 0.5), and fewer students authored questions related to stacks. We used the marks from the relevant question in assignment 4 and applied a Mann-Whitney U test to compare the assignment

	(AQ)		(NQ)		
Topic	N	Mean	N	Mean	p
Multi-dim. arrays	5	4.80	40	5.15	.625
Exceptions	11	6.82	34	6.27	.645
Recursion	18	6.83	27	6.52	.780
Big-O	27	8.26	18	6.67	.021*
Lists	12	7.58	33	7.70	.744
Stacks	13	7.38	32	5.06	.031*
Queues	4	3.75	41	5.20	.593
Binary Tree	13	5.42	32	5.31	.679
Binary Search Tree	9	10.00	36	8.78	.097
Hash Table	12	17.00	33	11.38	.001**

* — significant at 0.05 level
** — significant at 0.01 level

Table 9: Comparison of the students who authored a question related to a given exam question (AQ) with students who did not author a question related to a given exam question (NQ) for the CS105 course.

marks of students who had generated a question on stacks (μ=1.57) with the assignment marks of students who did not author a question on stacks (μ=1.05). The results indicate that there is no significant difference between the groups (p=.081), although the p-value is much smaller than in the previous analysis.

Unfortunately, none of the assignment questions related to Hash Tables, so we have no variable to use as a control for that topic.

5. DISCUSSION AND CONCLUSIONS

Although positive correlations between activity and exam performance can be explained by the level of student ability in a given course, we have demonstrated that the act of question-generation has a positive impact on performance in related exam questions.

It is difficult to evaluate the impact of interventions in real teaching contexts due to the myriad of factors, both internal and external, that impact on student performance. The correlational findings in this paper mirror those of previous studies with a variety of related tools, providing strong evidence that activity with these tools is reliably correlated with exam performance. Although correlational studies are a good starting point in the evaluation of teaching interventions, the evaluation should not end there.

Intuitively, we might expect that the best students in the class would be actively involved in any learning opportunities that are offered. Conversely, the weaker students are less likely to take advantage of opportunies to engage in the kind of self-directed study that these question-generation tools provide. The findings of this study support such intuitions. Correlations between activity and exam performance can be explained by the level of student ability within the context of a course.

Integrating results from controlled studies in educational psychology has proved fertile in this study. We have shown that findings from studies of question-generation activity conducted under controlled conditions in psychology are transferrable to the domain of Computer Science, using online tool support. The act of question-generation has a positive impact on performance in related exam questions.

That some of the topics in the CS105 course show positive effects of question-generation activity while others do not warrants further investigation. While question-generation has been shown to improve performance on related exam questions, it is unclear exactly how similar the questions must be.

The vast majority of questions generated by students in the CS105 course tended to focus on concepts, or understanding code by tracing. Few questions asked students to write code for a solution. On the other hand, several of the actual exam questions required students to write fragments of code. This was the case for the exam questions that covered the topics of multi-dimensional arrays, lists, queues and binary trees. It may be that the questions authored by students on these topics, which represent 4 of the 7 topics listed in Table 9 for which a significant result was not found, were different enough in style that we do not see any measurable effects.

Both courses in this study placed fairly modest requirements on students in terms of their participation. Students were asked to author just 1 question in the CS111 course, and 5 in the CS105 course. As a result, most students did not produce many questions on any specific topic. Even in CS105, few students wrote more than one or two questions on the same topic. It may be that greater levels of authorship will produce more significant results, and this is something that we plan to investigate in the future.

We hope as a result of this study, education researchers involved in evaluations of technology push beyond correlational studies to focus on the ways in which interventions impact on students.

6. REFERENCES

[1] M. E. D. A. André and T. H. Anderson. The development and evaluation of a self-questioning study technique. *Reading Research Quarterly*, 14(4):605–623, 1979.

[2] M. Barak and S. Rafaeli. On-line question-posing and peer-assessment as means for web-based knowledge sharing in learning. *International Journal of Human-Computer Studies*, 61:84–103, 2004.

[3] B. Collis and J. Moonen. *An on-going journey: Technology as a learning workbench.* University of Twente, Enschede, The Netherlands., 2005.

[4] P. R. Denner and J. P. Rickards. A developmental comparison of the effects of provided and generated questions on text recall. *Contemporary Educational Psychology*, 12(2):135 – 146, 1987.

[5] P. Denny, B. Hanks, and B. Simon. Peerwise: replication study of a student-collaborative self-testing web service in a U.S. setting. In *SIGCSE '10: Proceedings of the 41st ACM technical symposium on Computer science education*, pages 421–425, New York, NY, USA, 2010. ACM.

[6] P. Denny, A. Luxton-Reilly, and J. Hamer. Student use of the PeerWise system. In *ITiCSE '08: Proceedings of the 13th annual SIGCSE conference on Innovation and Technology in Computer Science Education*, pages 73–77, Madrid, Spain, 2008. ACM.

[7] P. Denny, A. Luxton-Reilly, and B. Simon. Evaluating a new exam question: Parsons problems. In *ICER '08: Proceeding of the fourth international workshop on Computing education research*, pages 113–124, New York, NY, USA, 2008. ACM.

[8] P. Denny, A. Luxton-Reilly, E. Tempero, and J. Hendrickx. Codewrite: supporting student-driven practice of java. In *Proceedings of the 42nd ACM technical symposium on Computer science education*, SIGCSE '11, pages 471–476, New York, NY, USA, 2011. ACM.

[9] P. W. Foos. Effects of student-written questions on student test performance. *Teaching of Psychology*, 16(2):77–78, 1989.

[10] P. W. Foos, J. J. Mora, and S. Tkacz. Student study techniques and the generation effect. *Journal of Educational Psychology*, 86(4):567–576, Dec 1994.

[11] L. T. Frase and B. J. Schwartz. Effect of question production and answering on prose recall. *Journal of Educational Psychology*, 67(5):628–635, 1975.

[12] J. Hamer, H. C. Purchase, A. Luxton-Reilly, and J. Sheard. Tools for "contributing student learning". In *Proceedings of the 2010 ITiCSE working group reports on Working group reports*, ITiCSE-WGR '10, pages 1–14, New York, NY, USA, 2010. ACM.

[13] Y. Hirai and A. Hazeyama. A learning support system based on question-posing and its evaluation. *Creating, Connecting and Collaborating through Computing, International Conference on*, 0:178–184, 2007.

[14] J. R. Lehman and K. M. Lehman. The relative effects of experimenter and subject generated questions on learning from museum case exhibits. *Journal of Research in Science Teaching*, 21(9):931–935, Dec. 1984.

[15] A. Luxton-Reilly and P. Denny. Constructive evaluation: a pedagogy of student-contributed assessment. *Computer Science Education*, 20:145–167, 2010.

[16] A. Luxton-Reilly, P. Denny, B. Plimmer, and D. Bertinshaw. Supporting student-generated free-response questions. In *Proceedings of the 16th annual joint conference on Innovation and technology in computer science education*, ITiCSE '11, pages 153–157, New York, NY, USA, 2011. ACM.

[17] T. C. Reeves. Design research from a technology perspective. In J. van den Akker, K. Gravemeijer, S. McKenney, and N. Nieveen, editors, *Education Design Research*, pages 52–66. Routledge, 2006.

[18] B. Rosenshine, C. Meister, and S. Chapman. Teaching students to generate questions: A review of the intervention studies. *Review of Educational Research*, 66(2):181–221, Summer 1996.

[19] E. V. Wilson. Examnet asynchronous learning network: augmenting face-to-face courses with student-developed exam questions. *Computers & Education*, 42(1):87 – 107, 2004.

[20] F.-Y. Yu. Scaffolding student-generated questions: Design and development of a customizable online learning system. *Computers in Human Behaviour*, 25:1129–1138, 2009.

[21] F.-Y. Yu, Y.-H. Liu, and T.-W. Chan. A web-based learning system for question-posing and peer assessment. *Innovations in Education and Teaching International*, 42(4):337–348, 2005.

Understanding NSF Funding Opportunities

Victor Piotrowski
National Science Foundation
Division of Undergraduate Education
vpiotrow@nsf.gov

D. Suzanne Westbrook
National Science Foundation
Division of Undergraduate Education
swestbro@nsf.gov

Mimi McClure
National Science Foundation
Office of Cyberinfrastructure
mmcclure@nsf.gov

Jeff Forbes, Harriet Taylor
National Science Foundation
Directorate of Computer and Information Science and Engineering
jforbes@nsf.gov , htaylor@nsf.gov

SUMMARY

This session highlights programs in the National Science Foundation's Division of Undergraduate Education, Office of Cyberinfrastructure and Directorate of Computer and Information Science and Engineering. The focus is on providing descriptions of several programs of interest to college faculty and discussing the requirements and guidelines for programs in these areas. It includes a description of the proposal and review processes as well as strategies for writing competitive proposals. Participants are encouraged to discuss procedural issues with the presenters.

Categories and Subject Descriptors

K.3.2 Computer and Information Science Education

General Terms

Documentation.

Keywords

Grants, awards, proposals, National Science Foundation, education.

1. OVERALL OBJECTIVE, AUDIENCE, SUITABILITY

NSF supports projects to improve education in science, technology, engineering, and mathematics through several programs in its Education and Human Resources (EHR) directorate, as well as in its research directorates, including Computer and Information Science and Engineering (CISE) and the Office of Cyberinfrastructure (OCI). This forum presents a description of some education-related programs in OCI and the EHR and CISE directorates, and enables faculty to interact with the presenters concerning specific project ideas that could be appropriate for the various programs. This type of forum is best suited to a special session to encourage audience interaction and for making connections between faculty and NSF program directors.

2. SESSION OUTLINE

Each of the following programs will be described and questions from the audience are encouraged. Complete details about the programs can be found on the NSF websites for the Division of Undergraduate Education (DUE) [1], the Directorate for Computer & Information Science & Engineering (CISE) [2], and the Office of Cyberinfrastructure (OCI) [3].

Copyright is held by the author/owner(s).
SIGCSE'12, February 29–March 3, 2012, Raleigh, North Carolina,USA.
ACM 978-1-4503-1098-7/12/02.

2.1 Advanced Technological Education (ATE)

ATE is a program specifically geared for community colleges, or for four-year schools working closely with community colleges. This program focuses on improvement in the "education of science and engineering technicians at the undergraduate and the secondary school levels. [2]" Specific technological fields include computer and information technology, cybersecurity, forensics, and telecommunications.

2.2 Transforming Undergraduate Education in STEM (TUES)

TUES supports innovation in student learning in the classroom, and improvements in educational practice. Particular emphasis in TUES is on creating new learning materials and strategies, developing faculty expertise, implementing education innovations, assessing student achievement, and conducting research on undergraduate STEM education. The NSF showcase presents innovative TUES projects.

2.3 Cyberinfrastructure Training, Education, Advancement, and Mentoring (CI-TEAM)

The programs of OCI offer significant educational elements. One program in particular, CI-TEAM, is focused on the education and workforce development needed to prepare our citizens for success. OCI serves directly under the Office of the Director of the NSF, and thus is not a part of any other directorate. OCI supports research and development of the cyberinfrastructure (CI) needed to support a cyber-enabled and scientific society, and the education and training required to sustain and support the CI. The current foci are on big data, HPC (high performance computing), and virtual organizations including attention to the development of networks, software, security, and algorithms to support the above. In all of our efforts we collaborate across NSF and with other government agencies as our work is highly interdisciplinary in nature.

2.4 Federal Cyber Service: Scholarships for Service (SFS)

This program seeks to increase the number of qualified students entering information assurance and computer security and to increase the capacity of the US higher education enterprise to continue to produce professionals in these fields. The SFS program is has two tracks: (1) the Scholarship Track that provides funding for scholarships to students in information assurance and computer security, and (2) the Capacity Building Track that provides funding for professional development of information assurance and computer security faculty and for the development of academic programs in these fields.

2.5 Information Technology Experiences for Students and Teachers (ITEST)

While there are four main components to ITEST, the two most likely to be of interest are youth-based projects for students in K-12, and comprehensive projects for K-12 teachers and students. "It is anticipated that projects funded under the ITEST program will not only increase interest in IT through the creation of effective student education programs in both school and non-school contexts, but also maintain interest through supportive activities that include parental involvement, career exploration, externships, research, and multi-year programs."

Two other programs in the Division of Research on Learning in Formal and Informal Settings (DRL) for supporting K-12 students and teachers are Informal Science Education (ISE) and Discovery Research K-12 (DRK-12). These will both be briefly covered.

2.6 Research Experiences for Undergraduates Sites (REU Sites)

Research experience is one of the most effective ways of attracting talented undergraduates to, and retaining them in careers in science and engineering, including careers in teaching and research. The REU Sites program aims to provide appropriate and valuable educational experiences for cohorts of 8-10 undergraduate students in the summer through participation in research and professional development activities. REU projects involve students, most who are from other than the host institution, in meaningful ways in ongoing research programs or in research projects specifically designed for the REU program. REU projects feature high-quality interaction of students with faculty and/or other research mentors and access to appropriate facilities and professional development opportunities.

2.7 Research Experiences for Teachers in Engineering and Computer Science (RET Sites)

The RET Sites program provides support for the active participation of in-service and pre-service K-12 STEM teachers and community college faculty in ongoing engineering and computer science research. Institutions build bridges with their communities through hosting a cohort of 10-15 teachers for summer research and ongoing community activities during the school year. Encouraging active participation of K-12 educators and community college faculty in research is an excellent way to

roaden and increase the capacity of the teacher pool in the U. S. to teach engineering and computer science concepts to their students and to encourage students to pursue engineering and computer science careers.

2.8 Computing Education for the 21st Century (CE21)

The CE21 program goals are to (1) increase the number and diversity of K-14 students and teachers who develop and practice computational competencies in a variety of contexts; and (2) increase the number and diversity of early postsecondary students who are engaged and have the background in computing necessary to successfully pursue degrees in computing-related and computationally-intensive fields of study. CE21 projects must contribute to the creation of a rich research base that informs our understanding of effective teaching and learning in computing and draw on partnerships among the computing and teaching and learning communities, institutions of learning, including primary, secondary and post-secondary institutions and organizations, and other stakeholders. CE21 projects can achieve these goals by developing new instructional materials and interventions, develop and evaluate efforts to enhance computing teaching expertise, or implement and test promising interventions at scale.

2.9 STEM Talent Expansion Program (STEP)

STEP grants fall into two categories of activities. Type 1 activities are aimed at implementing recruitment or retention strategies that will lead to a measurable increase in the number of students obtaining STEM degrees in baccalaureate or associate degree programs or completing credits toward transfer to a baccalaureate degree program in STEM fields at community colleges. Type 2 activities focus on educational research on factors affecting associate or baccalaureate degree attainment in STEM.

3. WRITING COMPETITIVE PROPOSALS

NSF programs are quite competitive but there are simple strategies you should be aware of when writing proposals to improve your chances of success. First and foremost, read the Program Solicitation carefully. Your goal is to help reviewers quickly understand *what* you intend to do and that you have given sufficient thought of *how* you intend to do it. Organize the proposal to address the essential components described in the solicitation. Use headings, boldface and bulleted lists to help the reader quickly understand the organization of the proposals. Address each point thoroughly but succinctly. And finally, start well before the submission deadline. Include sufficient lead time to allow colleagues to provide feedback and for your research office to approve the proposal. Specific directions for completing your proposal can be found online [4].

4. REFERENCES

[1] http://nsf.gov/div/index.jsp?div=DUE

[2] http://nsf.gov/dir/index.jsp?org=CISE

[3] http://nsf.gov/dir/index.jsp?org=OCI

[4] http://nsf.gov/funding/preparing/

Teaching Outside the Text

Renee Ciezki
Estrella Mountain Community College
Division of Instructional Computing
3000 N. Dysart Road
Avondale, Arizona 85392
+1.623.935.8000
renee.ciezki@estrellamountain.edu

Barbara Ericson
Institute for Computing Education
College of Computing
Georgia Institute of Technology
Atlanta, Georgia
+1.404.385.2107
ericson@cc.gatech.edu

Robert Glen Martin
School for the Talented and Gifted
1201 East Eighth Street, Suite 302
Dallas, TX 75203
+1.972.925.6311
martinrg@sbcglobal.net

Lester Wainwright (Moderator)
Charlottesville High School
1400 Melbourne Road
Charlottesville, VA 22901
+1.434.245.2410
wainwrl1@ccs.k12.va.us

Summary

We know that students bring diverse experiences and an assortment of learning styles into our classrooms. We greet them and hand out a syllabus listing the required textbook(s). One size does not fit all when it comes to textbooks. In this session, participants will discover teaching activities that can be used to supplement any computer science textbook. These activities include human modeling and role playing, interactive whiteboard activities, case studies, class projects, games, and more.

By exploring "extra" activities not found in most textbooks, participants will learn how these hands-on, interesting and fun activities can help students understand the topics listed in the AP Computer Science A Course Description: Object-oriented Program Design, Program Implementation, Program Analysis, Standard Data Structures, Standard Algorithms, and Computing in Context.

Student attention spans seem to be getting shorter. The panelists found themselves spending more and more time searching for and/or developing supplemental resources in efforts to reach and retain students. Members of the AP Computer Science-A Development Committee will share these resources and lead a discussion of proven strategies and lesson ideas for teaching outside the textbook.

Categories and Subject Descriptors

K.3.2 [**Computers and Education**]: Computer and Information Science Education – *computer science education, curriculum, information systems education*

General Terms

Algorithms, Management, Design

Keywords

Curricular resources, pedagogy

Copyright is held by the author/owner(s).
SIGCSE'12, February 29–March 3, 2012, Raleigh, North Carolina, USA.
ACM 978-1-4503-1098-7/12/02.

1. Renee Ciezki

First impressions are important, and we have all formed long-lasting opinions based on them. The first week of class is a critical time to capture students' interest and to convince them that the study of computer science can be both fun and attainable. Renee will describe some early activities that get students involved and lay a foundation for success. She will also share ideas for presenting and reinforcing computer science concepts using stories and simple objects.

2. Barbara Ericson

Barbara has had the unique experience of teaching computer science to a wide range of students—from 4th graders to undergraduate students. She will discuss a variety of programming environments and will share activities that can be done without computers.

3. Robert Glen Martin

Glen has developed numerous lessons aimed at first-year computer science students, and he freely shares them with other instructors. He offers a variety of labs, based on the GridWorld case study and environment that are classroom-ready and contain complete instructions, all handouts, starter projects, and answer keys. In addition to his own work with GridWorld, Glen will present resources for teaching standard algorithms.

4. Lester Wainwright

Pair programming and special assessment strategies foster collaboration and help students feel connected to their classmates and to the course content. Lester will discuss ways to encourage practice and will lead the discussion with participants.

Computer Engineering Review Task Force Report

John Impagliazzo (Moderator)
Hofstra University
Hempstead, New York 11549 USA
+1.516.463.6774
John.Impagliazzo@Hofstra.edu

Susan Conry
Clarkson University
Potsdam, New York 13699 USA
+1.315.268.6510
conry@clarkson.edu

Eric Durant
Milwaukee School of Engineering
Milwaukee, Wisconsin 53202 USA
+1.414.277.7439
durant@msoe.edu

Andrew McGettrick
University of Strathclyde
Glasgow, G1 1XQ, Scotland, UK
+44.(0)141.552.4400
Andrew.McGettrick@cis.strath.ac.uk

Mitch Thornton
Southern Methodist University
Dallas, Texas 75205 USA
+1.214.768.1371
mitch@lyle.smu.edu

Timothy Wilson
Embry-Riddle Aeronautical University
Daytona Beach, Florida 32114 USA
+1.386.226.6994
Timothy.Wilson@erau.edu

SUMMARY

In early 2011, the ACM and the IEEE Computer Society (IEEE/CS) created the CE2004 Review Task Force (RTF) and charged it with the task of reviewing and determining the extent to which the document "Curriculum Guidelines for Undergraduate Degree Programs in Computer Engineering," produced 2004 December 12 and known as CE2004 [1] required revisions. The RTF submitted a report to both societies in July of 2011. The report summarized a survey of academic and industry constituents conducted by the RTF. It recommended keeping the structure and the vast majority of the content of the original CE2004 document. However, it also recommended that contemporary topics should be strengthened or added while de-emphasizing other topics that appeared to be waning from the curricular mainstream of computer engineering. Additionally, the RTF recommended that the two societies form a joint special-purpose committee to update and edit the earlier document and to seek input and review from the computer engineering industrial and academic communities through presentations and workshops co-located at major conferences. The presenters of this special session were members of the 2011 RTF and two presenters were members of the original curricular task force from 2004. The presentation will provide insights in the RTF findings and thoughts on how a future computer engineering report might evolve.

Categories and Subject Descriptors

K.3.2 [Computers and Education]: Computers and Information Science Education – *Curriculum*

Copyright is held by the author/owner(s).
SIGCSE'12, February 29–March 3, 2012, Raleigh, North Carolina, USA.
ACM 978-1-4503-1098-7/12/02.

General Terms

Standardization, Human factors

Keywords

Computer engineering, curricular report, education, ACM, IEEE Computer Society

1. OVERALL OBJECTIVE

The primary objective of this session is to present to the computing community the progress made by ACM and the IEEE/CS in transforming the existing "Curriculum Guidelines for Undergraduate Degree Programs in Computer Engineering," also known as CE2004 to a new and contemporary report. A secondary objective is to solicit input from the computing community on ways to improve the existing report so that it is current and reflects the state-of-the-art of the practice of computer engineering. The presenters from both ACM and IEEE/CS represent all six members of the RTF.

The RTF developed and sent survey invitations to 20,000 industry and academic constituents in the computer engineering field. The RTF also contacted some ABET industry program evaluators to solicit their input. In all, the TF received 14 industry responses and 263 academic responses. Although the survey default was anonymity, respondents had the option of providing contact information in case they were interested in having further input on the revisions; 10 industry and 51 academic respondents provided contact information. Some new or expanded technical skill suggestions derived from the survey included areas of networking, software engineering agile methods and tools, embedded system design, parallel programming, and hardware/software co-design.

The RTF found that the majority of what the constituencies believe is important is already covered well in CE2004. However, the RTF did identify significant deviations that could guide the revision process toward a document that is appropriately forward looking given the continuing changes in the computer engineering landscape.

The RTF recommended that a team of volunteers lead the revision effort beginning in fall of 2011 with interim updates as necessary. The RTF largely affirmed the contents of CE2004 compiled nearly a decade ago. However, the RTF recognized that several advances have occurred during that time. It recommended that the societies form a new core research and writing special committee of eight to twelve members derived from ACM and IEEE/CS members to include representatives from academia, industry, government, and community college groups. The special committee should make key drafts of their revisions available to a wide constituency, including all respondents to the survey who expressed interest in having further input. The special committee should make efforts to include key conferences from outside of the United States.

2. OUTLINE OF SESSION

The session includes some introductory remarks and an overview of the project by the session moderator. The five remaining participants will present individual presentations surrounding the work of the task force. A robust interaction with the audience will be an integral part of the session. The presenters will distribute summary handouts during the session. Presentations are as follows.

Dr. John Impagliazzo, a member and principal co-author of CE2004 committee and RTF member, will present a brief overview of the CE2004 document. He will describe the evolution and components of the 2004 report and focus on its body of knowledge.

Dr. Eric Durant, the de facto leader of the RTF, will summarize the six-month activities of the group. He will focus on the organization of the task-force challenges and the strategies used to overcome them.

Dr. Mitch Thornton, RTF member, will continue the discussion on the work of the RTF. He will focus on the results of the surveys and contrast the suggestions received from industry with those received from academia.

Dr. Tim Wilson, RTF member, will discuss the activities of the special committee formed jointly by ACM and IEEE/CS. He will address the trials the group is facing or will face and highlight the actions the special committee plans to take to meet those challenges.

Dr. Susan Conry, chair of the Engineering Accreditation Commission of ABET and RTF member, will discuss how the computer engineering curriculum complements the current ABET criteria. She will highlight the essential elements of the criteria and show how the new curriculum satisfies those criteria.

Dr. Andrew McGettrick, a member of the CE2004 committee, chair of the ACM Education Board, and RTF member, will describe the way ahead and the activities expected to take place over the next two years.

3. EXPECTATIONS

The expected audience is computing educators who have an interest in computing curricula, particularly as it affects the computer engineering field. Audience participants will acquire greater familiarity with ACM and IEEE/CS joint efforts to produce an updated coherent document that benefits a large component of the computing field. The presenters will elicit feedback from the audience via a brief survey on a few topics to enhance the quality of the final report.

4. SUITABILITY

This presentation reflects a report of an effort that is a work-in-progress. The outcome of the effort will be an updated, contemporary curriculum recommendation endorsed jointly by the ACM and the IEEE/CS. Since the work is in a state of transition, it is more suitable as a special session rather than a panel or a paper on the summary of results. Indeed, suggestions and written commentary from the audience will receive full consideration by the joint special committee.

ACKNOWLEDGEMENTS

The presenters acknowledge the encouragement received from the ACM Education Board and the IEEE/CS Educational Activities Board. It also acknowledges the efforts of all members of the RTF.

REFERENCE

[1] D. Soldan. 2004. "Curriculum Guidelines for Undergraduate Degree Programs in Computer Engineering," CE2004. Retrieved 2011 August 23 from http://www.acm.org/education/education/curric_vols/CE-Final-Report.pdf

Social Sensitivity and Classroom Team Projects: An Empirical Investigation

Lisa Bender, Gursimran Walia,
Krishna Kambhampaty, Kendall E. Nygard
North Dakota State University
Computer Science Dept. 2740
Fargo, ND 58108
+1 701-231-8562
{lisa.l.bender, gursimran.walia, k.kambhampaty, kendall.nygard} @ ndsu.edu

Travis E. Nygard
Ripon College
300 Steward Street
Ripon, WI 54971
+1 920-748-8783
NygardT@ripon.edu

ABSTRACT

Team work is the norm in major development projects and industry is continually striving to improve team effectiveness. Researchers have established that teams with high levels of social sensitivity tend to perform well when completing a variety of specific collaborative tasks. Social sensitivity is the personal ability to perceive, understand, and respect the feelings and viewpoints of others, and it is reliably measurable. However, the tasks in recent research have been primarily short term, requiring only hours to finish, whereas major project teams work together for longer durations and on complex tasks. Our claim is that, social sensitivity can be a key component in predicting the performance of teams that carry out major projects. Our goal is to determine if previous research, which was not focused on students or professionals in scientific or technical fields, is germane for people in computing disciplines. This paper reports the results from an empirical study that investigates whether social sensitivity is correlated with the performance of student teams on large semester-long projects. The overall result supports our claim that the team social sensitivity is highly correlated with successful team performance. It suggests, therefore, that educators in computer-related disciplines, as well as computer professionals in the workforce, should take the concept of social sensitivity seriously as an aid or obstacle to productivity.

Categories and Subject Descriptors

K.3.2 [**Computer and Information Science Education**]: Computer Science Education.

General Terms

Measurement, Performance, Experimentation, Human Factors

Keywords

Computer Science, Collaboration, Social Sensitivity, Teams, Empirical Study

Permission to make digital or hard copies of all or part of this work for personal or classroom use is granted without fee provided that copies are not made or distributed for profit or commercial advantage and that copies bear this notice and the full citation on the first page. To copy otherwise, or republish, to post on servers or to redistribute to lists, requires prior specific permission and/or a fee.
SIGCSE'12, February 29–March 3, 2012, Raleigh, North Carolina, USA.
Copyright 2012 ACM 978-1-4503-1098-7/12/02...$10.00.

1. INTRODUCTION

Team work has become increasingly important in today's world. Individual work is also highly valued, but as the world grows more complex, projects also grow more complex. They tend to have objectives that involve many sophisticated tasks and require the collective work of individuals to accomplish. This is especially true for computer scientists and software engineers who work in the area of software development. Complex projects require people to interact with each other as well as with computing technologies. Project development processes are often difficult due to the complexity of the technologies, as well as the complexity of social interactions between the project team members. Previous research asserts that the ability to use soft skills to navigate interpersonal relationships and negotiate social interactions is critical to team success [10, 19]. With current academic standards and curricula, many students graduate with the technical, hard skills that they need, but they often lack necessary soft skills that are critical to team success [28]. Begel and Simon studied recent college graduates who were hired by Microsoft and found that while the new hires generally did well, there were numerous problems with communication and collaboration with others [6]. Soft skills are not only important to teamwork, but also to education. Researchers note that interpersonal and small-group skills are essential to positive cooperative learning [1].

One factor that can greatly influence collaborative team performance is team composition. Much research has been done on team composition, but no single attribute stands out as key to superior performance. Intriguing questions were raised by a recent group intelligence study, which established that group intelligence depends less on how smart individual group members are and more on team dynamics, including how well team members collaborate [33]. These researchers found that social sensitivity made the largest contribution to a group's overall intelligence and was a primary predictor of team effectiveness in accomplishing short-term tasks. Social sensitivity is defined as the personal ability to perceive and understand the mind and mood of others. Our primary research goal is to determine if the connection between social sensitivity and team performance extends to students or professionals in computing fields who carry out longer-term tasks within major projects.

We conducted an empirical study that investigated the effect of social sensitivity on the performance of project teams consisting of computer science and management information system students who worked on semester-long projects. These student projects were completed in multiple stages, each building upon previous work. The results indicate that social sensitivity maybe key to success for these team projects, and suggest that social sensitivity would likewise be key in the success of complex projects, such as those carried out by software development teams.

The remainder of this paper is structured as follows. Section 2 provides background information on team formation research, social sensitivity, and tests for social sensitivity. Section 3 describes the design of the empirical study that was conducted to investigate the effects of social sensitivity on team performance. Section 4 describes the data analysis and results. Section 5 discusses the threats to validity. Section 6 provides a discussion of the results based on the analysis performed in Section 4. Section 7 concludes the paper and provides a summary of future research.

2. BACKGROUND AND RELATED WORK

The prominence of collaboration in the computing industry has created the need to study how to form highly effective teams. West [4] notes that effective teams complete projects quickly, develop and deliver cost-effective products, maintain high quality, have low stress levels, have high team member satisfaction, and promote innovation. He also notes that although effective teams can benefit a project, teamwork is not automatically beneficial. A major team-related factor that can affect project performance is the interaction of individual personalities. Other factors affecting the project performance include team communication, cooperation, and coordination [9, 14]. One of the main factors contributing to poor performance is project team composition [19]. This suggests that management needs to form teams wisely.

There are many factors to consider when forming teams, and their impact on team composition has been widely studied. An increasing number of educators use many criteria to form teams such as gender, race, prior class or work experience, personality, problem solving style, and/or grade point average [21]. Within Software Engineering field, some of the factors include the effects of personality composition [16, 27], team member abilities [4, 15], team roles [4, 7, 8, 12], diversity [25], shared mental models [19, 22], and team member satisfaction [19]. Chan et al. [10] suggests that soft skills are the primary factor that should be considered for achieving good project performance. They argue that higher levels of soft skills within the team facilitate the application development skills and domain knowledge skills necessary to achieve good project performance. In the spirit of this study, our work has produced new knowledge by taking a soft skill that Chan et al did not interrogate (i.e., social sensitivity) and investigated how it affects the team performance.

Social Sensitivity is the ability to correctly understand the feelings and viewpoints of people [17]. It has also been defined as "*the ability to understand and manage people*" [31]. Salovey and Mayer [26] view social sensitivity as an element of emotional intelligence and identify some of the characteristics of socially intelligent people to include the ability to admit mistakes, to accept others for who they are, to enhance other's moods, to be social problem solvers, to be flexible thinkers, and to have an interest in the world at large. They also recognize that the appraisal and expression of emotion often takes place on a nonverbal level. The ability to perceive nonverbal expression insures smoother interpersonal cooperation. By perceiving, empathizing, and then responding appropriately, people experience greater satisfaction, more positive emotions, and lower stress. Such positive emotions aid in creative thinking and enable flexibility in arriving at alternatives to problems. These characteristics suggest that high levels of social sensitivity could be a benefit for teams.

Every person has a certain level of social sensitivity, but there is evidence that people who choose technical careers have less of it on average than the population at large [2]. More specifically, Baron-Cohen et al. [2] produced evidence that suggests that engineers, mathematicians, physicists, and computer scientists are typically less socially sensitive than their peers in the humanities, arts, and social sciences. They suggest that people in these technical disciplines have more difficulty decoding what others are thinking and feeling. Although this research did not address teams specifically, it suggests to us that teams of technical people may be challenged in the area of social sensitivity.

Our study is not the first to address the relationship between social sensitivity and teamwork, but the duration and complexity of our project make it unique. A major inspiration for our study comes from the work of Woolley et al. [33]; a recent study on social sensitivity that established a correlation between social sensitivity and effective teamwork. They describe a group general effectiveness or collective intelligence that predicts group performance and is grounded in how well groups interact and work together. Another interesting result from this study was that team performance was not driven by the intelligence of individuals on the teams; group cohesion, motivation, or satisfaction. The tasks in their study were short-term contrived tasks requiring hours, rather than months, to complete. Thus, those team members had little opportunity to develop longer-term working patterns. Our study extends this research by interrogating the effects of social sensitivity on teams that worked together for longer durations—the better part of an academic semester—and produced a complex series of deliverables during that time. In many ways our study closely approximates a real working environment.

In order to proceed with our study, we needed an accurate test to determine an individual's level of social sensitivity. There are several methods for testing social sensitivity. The one we chose to use is referred to as the "Reading the Mind in the Eyes" test which was created and validated by Baron-Cohen et al. [3]. This test gauges the accuracy of individuals in judging someone's emotional state by looking at their eyes. A subject is presented with a series of 36 photographs of the eye-area of actors. For each photograph, the subjects are asked to choose which of four adjectives best-describes how the person in the photograph is feeling. This test was originally developed to measure an 'advanced theory of mind' in adults, which is the ability to identify mental states in oneself or another person. The test has been found to have test-retest reliability [18]. Alternative techniques for measuring social sensitivity, such as the George Washington Social Intelligence Test [30] and the Vineland Social Maturity Scale [5] were rejected due to reported inaccuracies or the inclusion of factors irrelevant to our research [24, 29].

3. STUDY DESIGN

The study was designed to analyze the relationship between the social sensitivity of student teams and the quality of work in computer science team projects. This study investigates whether the student teams with higher average social sensitivity were positively correlated with their actual performance on the project, as measured by grades.

This study used a randomized experimental design in which participants were tested to determine their social sensitivity scores and were then randomly assigned to teams of three participants each. Each team worked together to complete a major semester-long project on an ethical issue related to current computer technology in society. The project deliverables were evaluated to score the student team's performance on the project. The details of the study are provided in the following subsections.

3.1 Study Goals and Hypotheses

Using the Goal Question Metric (GQM) approach [5], the following goals and hypotheses were formulated.

Goal 1: *Analyze* student's social sensitivity scores *for the purpose of* evaluation *with respect to* their team project performance.

> ***Hypothesis 1:*** Student teams with higher average social sensitivity scores perform significantly better on the project.

Goal 2: *Analyze* student's social sensitivity levels *for the purpose of* characterizing their effect *with respect to* the increase in the team project performance.

> ***Hypothesis 2:*** Student teams with differing average scores of social sensitivity have significant differences in their team performance scores.

3.2 Independent and Dependent Variables

The experiment manipulated the following independent variable:

a) ***Social Sensitivity Score***: Each participant completed the "Reading the Mind in the Eyes" test [3] in order to determine their individual social sensitivity score.

The following dependent variable was measured:

a) ***Team Performance***: This measure includes the total points earned by each team—the sum of scores on four project deliverables submitted throughout the semester.

3.3 Participating Subjects

The participant subjects were ninety-eight graduate and undergraduate computer science and management of information systems students enrolled in the Social Implications of Computing course at large public university. Seventy-six students (17 out of 18 females and 59 out of 80 males) chose to participate in the study. The course required the students to work together on a project involving a multi-vocal response to an ethical issue related to the world of computer science and technology.

3.4 Artifacts

Each of the thirty-four teams produced a project proposal document for a different computer-related ethical topic. The key concept was that each individual in the group was required to adopt a distinct viewpoint that corresponded to a stakeholder. Rather than writing as a single voice trying to answer the ethical question posed in the proposal, the group members represented diverse views on their topic. The consequences of alternative actions were traced to their logical conclusions and evaluated with regard to their impact on other stakeholders. One goal of having the students working together as a team was to help them to *understand* perspectives other than their own, and, through discussions, to produce a final presentation and essay that contains ideas that would not have been articulated by working independently. The students met throughout the semester to develop their instructor-approved topics and produced an interim report, a final report, and a final project presentation.

3.5 Experimental Procedure

The study steps are as follows:

a) ***Step 1 – Test Subjects for Social Sensitivity:*** The "Reading the Mind in the Eyes" test [3] was administered at the beginning of the semester to measure each subject's social sensitivity. A glossary was provided that contained a definition and sample sentence for each of the emotion word selection choices used in the test. The basis for the glossary was provided by the work of Baron-Cohen et al. [3]. The purpose of the glossary was to ensure that participants had a clear understanding of the definitions of words. The students were encouraged to read through the glossary prior to the test and to refer to it as needed during the test. The survey was administered online and the completed responses were analyzed for correctness. Individual social sensitivity scores were based on the number of correct responses.

b) ***Step 2 – Forming Student Teams***: Subjects were randomly assigned to teams of three students each. A total of 34 teams were formed. Because one student dropped the course, by the end of the semester 33 teams had three students each and one team had two students.

c) ***Step 3 – Actualizing Team Projects***: The students worked in teams on specific semester-long projects. Each team produced a project proposal, an interim report, a final report, and a final presentation. Most groups chose a topic from a list of ideas provided by the instructor, although students could pursue any topic that was approved by the instructor. After the project was approved, the teams performed the necessary research to write a project proposal due February 28. The proposal required them to articulate ethical questions that they planned to investigate, justify the questions' importance, identify major stakeholders and ethical values, specify their research methods, and plan the project. Half way through the semester, each team submitted an interim progress report (due April 11) that described the project goal, objectives, and scope, employed research methods, used evidence to support ethical viewpoints, and evaluated potential stakeholder actions. Near the semester end, each team gave an oral presentation (due April 29-May6) on their project and submitted a final written report (due May 6).

d) ***Step 4 – Evaluating Team Projects***: Scores were determined for each deliverable using detailed rubrics to structure the grading. All grading was done by the same person. All members of a team received the same score for each assignment. The team performance (i.e., *the total team score*) was measured by summing each team's score from all the four deliverables.

e) ***Step 5 – Peer-Self Evaluations***: After each deliverable, the subjects completed an evaluation of each of their team members as well as themselves. As identified in the literature (e.g., [24, 25]), the following ten candidate characteristics of an effective team member were included: focusing on the tasks, being dependable, responsibility sharing, listening, questioning, discussing, research and information sharing, individual performance, brainstorming, and group teamwork. Subjects rated each of the ten attributes on a 5-point Likert scale (4 –Excellent, 3 – Good, 2 – Average, 1 – Poor, and 0 –

Fail) and provided comments. These results were captured to help researchers better understand the results.

f) ***Step 6 – Post-Study Survey:*** A nineteen-question survey was administered to the students at the end of the semester. The post-study survey collected data regarding the self-perceived effectiveness of each team, including whether members felt valued; if the team cooperated, communicated, and interacted well; if effective feedback occurred among team members; if conflict existed and how it was resolved; and what the quality was of the team work environment overall.

3.6 Data Collection and Evaluation Criterion

Because this study investigates the impact of social sensitivity on team performance, only teams that had at least two team members consenting to participate in the study were included in our analysis; and only the consenting team member's social sensitivity scores and team performance scores were collected. After this elimination process, 28 out of 34 teams remained in the study.

Individual student social sensitivity test scores for each of the 76 participating subjects are shown in Figure 1. The social sensitivity (SS) scores range from a minimum of 9 to a maximum of 32, with most subjects scoring in the range of 19 to 25. Interestingly, our mean sample score of 22.59 was lower than the general population sample score of 26.2 reported by Baron-Cohen et al [3]. Team average SS scores were also calculated. The average team SS scores range from a minimum of 12 to a maximum of 29, with the most of subjects scoring in the range of 19 to 25.

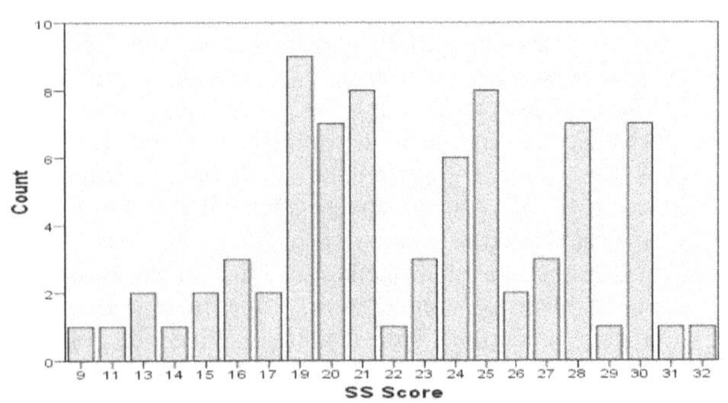

Figure 1. Individual Social Sensitivity Scores.

Student team performances on the four project deliverables were summed into a final project score for use in the analysis of the impact of the team's average SS on the final project team scores.

4. DATA ANALYSIS AND RESULTS

This section provides analysis of the quantitative data that includes student's social sensitivity scores and their team's project performance. This section is organized around the two hypotheses presented in Section 3.1. An alpha value of 0.05 was used for all statistical analysis and r^2 value of 0.30 was used for correlations.

4.1 Analysis of the Effect of Social Sensitivity (SS) on Team's Project Performance

This section analyzes the connection between the student's SS and their performance on the team project. Because each team consisted of two to three subjects, and the SS data from Step 1 was individual data, the individual SS scores were combined into one team score. The SS score of each team was calculated by averaging the individual team member's SS scores. The performance of each team (i.e., *total team score*), while developing their projects, was calculated by combining the scores on each of the four deliverables. This analysis was performed for each of the 28 teams.

Figure 2 plots each team's average SS scores against their total team project score. To test hypothesis 1, we ran a linear regression test to see whether the average SS scores of a team were positively correlated to the team's performance (i.e., total team score). The results show that the team SS score had a significant positive correlation with the total team score ($p = 0.001$; Pearson's $R = 0.383$; $r^2 = 0.16$). Additional testing was also performed to determine if there were any outliers, and the results confirmed that there were no outliers.

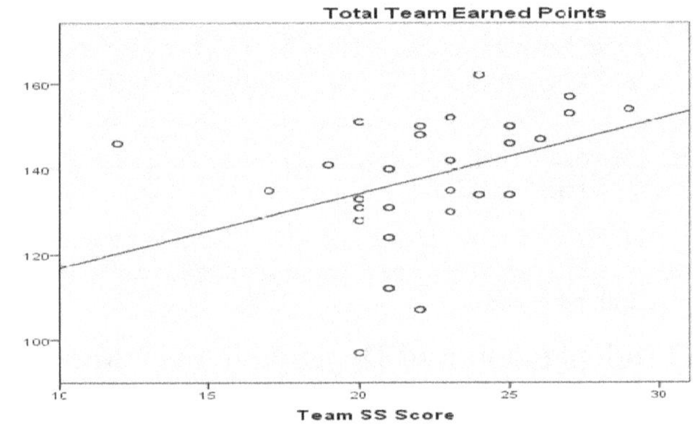

Figure 2. Effect of Social Sensitivity on the Team Performance.

We also analyzed whether the team SS scores were correlated with the team performance on each of the four deliverables. The results showed that the team SS scores had a strong and significant positive correlation with their performance on the project proposal ($p=0.004$), interim report ($p=0.003$), and final report ($p=0.05$). The result, however, did not show a significant correlation between teams' average SS and performance on the final presentation ($p=0.382$).

In order to better understand the results, the individual SS scores (shown in Figure 1) were also analyzed to evaluate their relationship to the performance of the teams. The results show that individual SS also had a significant positive correlation with the total team score ($p = 0.009$; Pearson's $R = 0.297$; $r^2 = 0.09$). Based on these results, the teams with higher average SS performed significantly better on their project.

4.2 Analysis of Student Teams with Differing Average Levels of Social Sensitivity

The results reported in Section 4.1 indicate that the *individual* SS and the *team* SS scores were positively correlated with team performance. We performed further analysis to determine the cut-offs points in order to gain insights into the level of social sensitivity required to produce a significantly higher level of team performance.

We determined these cutoff points by analyzing the performance of the teams at multiple levels of team SS. Clusters of teams were set at different ranges on the SS scale. The mean team scores for each cluster were then calculated and analyzed. The results are shown in Figure 3 and are explained below.

As shown in Figure 2, there were only 2 teams with a SS score below 18 (the mid-point of the SS scale), and no team had a SS score greater than 29. Therefore, we used a SS scale of 19-29. We divided teams into three different clusters, such that a roughly equal number of teams belonged to each. Using this process, three different SS Level clusters (19-21; 22-24; and 25-29) were formed. Next, the mean performance of the teams in each of the three SS clusters was calculated. An independent samples-t test was then performed to determine whether there was a significant difference in the mean performance of teams. The result shows that the teams with SS scores ranging from 22-24 performed significantly better than the teams whose SS scores ranged from 19-21 ($p = 0.03$). Similarly, the teams with SS scores ranging from 25-29 performed significantly better than the teams with SS scores of 22-24. These results are shown in the top section of Figure 3.

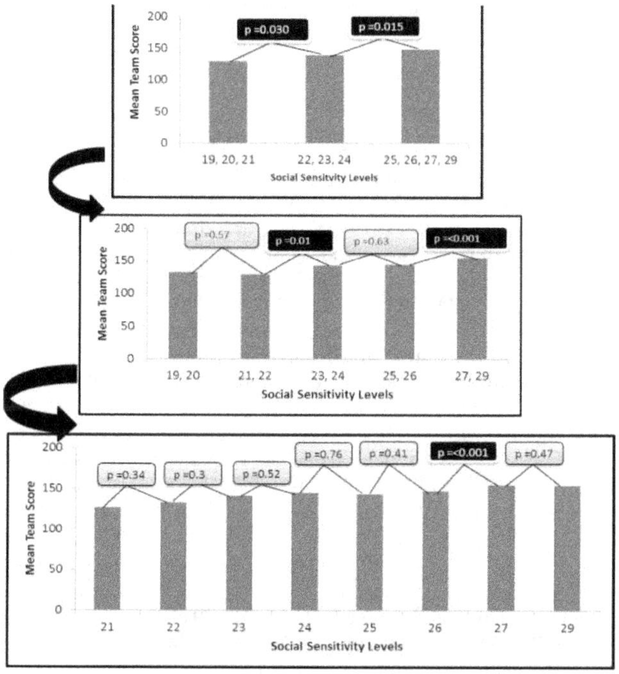

Figure 3. Team Performance at Different SS Levels

Performing further analysis of these results, we created smaller SS clusters. Using the same analytical process, we compared the mean performance of teams in each of these SS groups. These results are shown in the middle section of Figure 3. The independent samples t-test showed that teams with SS scores of 23 and 24 performed significantly better than teams with lower SS scores ($p = 0.01$) and that the teams with SS scores of 27 and 29 were better than teams with lower SS scores ($p < 0.001$).

Continuing this analysis for fine-grained SS scores in this study (as shown in the bottom section of Figure 3), we found that a SS of 27 resulted in significantly better team performance, and that SS scores beyond 27 does not result in significantly higher team performance. We note that there were not an equal number of teams in each of the fine-grained SS groups, and this could have an impact on our results.

5. THREAT TO VALIDITY

Although the results of this study are encouraging, there are certain threats to validity that exist. One such threat is language proficiency. Approximately fifty percent of the students in the course are international students. Even though each of these students has passed an English proficiency exam, some could have struggled with the language. To improve construct validity in the "Reading the Mind in the Eyes" test, a glossary was provided that contained a definition and sample sentence for each of the word selection choices used in the test. Students were encouraged to read through the glossary before they took the test and refer to it as necessary during the test. However, because the students were not supervised while taking the test, we do not know how extensively the glossary was used. Feedback from students suggests that some groups struggled with language barriers as well, which could be a confounding factor that hinders success.

6. DISCUSSION OF RESULTS

Our fundamental finding is that SS is a good predictor of team performance carrying out major student team projects with complex tasks and multiple deliverables over long periods of time. This extends previous research that showed that SS had high impact on teams accomplishing well defined short-term relatively simple tasks. Task complexity is an important factor in team performance because the difficulty of the task can impact the success of the team [20]. Complex tasks within large projects have many opportunities for errors and they can be hard to identify. Such projects can easily create a stressful environment for students which can hinder team performance (e.g. impaired decision making, decreased speed and accuracy of task performance) by adversely affecting team coordination and ability to engage in team activities. These difficulties can ultimately discourage a team. The factor of project duration on team performance comes into play as team members become more intertwined and interdependent, the impact of one member's lapse can disrupt the entire team's performance. The longer the team works together, the more intertwined they are likely to become.

Another interesting finding in our study is that it is supports Baron-Cohen's assertion that engineers, mathematicians, physicists, and computer scientists are, generally, less socially sensitive. The participants in our survey are all majoring in scientific or technical disciplines and their mean SS score of 22.59 was lower than the original general population sample mean SS score of 26.2 of Baron-Cohen et al [3]. This suggests that these students find it more difficult to perceive and understand the feelings and viewpoints of others. An awareness of this can help educators better recognize reasons behind team difficulties and help students focus on techniques for managing that social deficit.

Yet another finding is that there is a significant correlation between SS and team performance on the first three deliverables of the project, but not on the last deliverable (i.e. the project presentation). One possible reason for this is that a more collaborative effort was needed to create the three written documents; whereas the presentation was based on the final report and the team members likely partitioned the presentation and worked independently to each produce their own portion. During the actual presentation, most groups had each member take turns where each member spoke sequentially, one after another. The independent performance of this task may have diminished the effect of the SS factor on the performance of this last deliverable.

7. CONCLUSION AND FUTURE WORK

Our results establish that the performance of teams is positively correlated with the SS of members. This is valuable knowledge for managers and educators. Although we recognize that teams need members with the correct skill set and knowledge, by using SS as an additional input, more effective teams can be composed.

Using quantitative data related to work in teams, our work demonstrates compelling correlations between SS and performance on group projects. These correlations tempt us to assert that high SS causes high performance. We expect that our future work with qualitative analysis will support this connection. We have extensive qualitative data from study participants that relates to their experiences working on the teams, and we hope that these will be useful for teasing how SS impacted groups on practical levels. We know that some groups faced interpersonal challenges, and we plan to investigate whether such challenges were better-overcome in teams with socially-sensitive individuals.

Assuming that SS is a cause rather than simply correlated with team success, then this type of research raises many exciting questions of interest to people across academia. How much SS is needed for success? Can SS be learned? Authors such as Anthony Mersino have published techniques for improving emotional intelligence [23]. If these techniques can be effectively applied to improve SS, then team performance can also be improved. In any case, it is our hope that a greater understanding of SS will result in better learning experiences in the college classroom, better productivity of software engineering teams, and ultimately better relationships between all humans.

8. REFERENCES

[1] Bacon, D.R., Stewart, K.A., and Silver, W.S. 1999. Lessons from the Best and Worst Student Team Experiences: How a Teacher Can Make the Difference. *Journal of Management Education.* 23, 467-488.

[2] Baron-Cohen, S., Bolton, P., Wheelwright, S., Scahill, V., Short, L., Mead, G., and Smith, A. 1998. Autism occurs more often in families of physicists, engineers, and mathematicians. *Autism.* 2, 296-301.

[3] Baron-Cohen, S., Wheelwright, S., Hill, J., Raste, Y., and Plumb, I. 2001. The 'Reading the Mind in the Eyes' Test Revised Version: A Study with Normal Adults, and Adults with Asperger Syndrome or High-functioning Autism. *Child Journal of Psychology and Psychiatry*, 42, 2, 241-251,.

[4] Barrick, M.R., Stewart, G.L., Neubert, M.J., and Mount, M.K. 1998. Relating Member Ability and Personality to Work-Team Processes and Team Effectiveness. *Journal of Applied Pshchology.* 83, 377-391.

[5] Basili, V.R., Caldiera, G., and Rombach, H.D. 1994. *The Goal Question Metric Approach.* Technical Report. Department of Computer Science, University of Maryland.

[6] Begel, A. and Simon, B. 2008. Struggles of new college graduates in their first software development job. In *Proceedings of the 39th SIGCSE technical symposium on Computer science education* (Portland, OR, USA, 2008). ACM.

[7] Belbin, M. 1993. Team Roles at Work. Butterworth-Heinemann, Oxford.

[8] Beranek, G., Zuser, W., and Grechenig, T. 2005. Functional Group Roles in Software Engineering Teams. In *HSSE'05* (St. Louis Missouri USA, May 2005), 1-5.

[9] Bradley, J.H. and Hebert, F.J. 1997. The effect of personality type on team performance. *Journal of Management Development.* 16, 5, 337-353.

[10] Chan, C.L., Jiang, J.J., and Klein, G. 2008. Team Task Skills as a Facilitator for Application and Development Skills. *IEEE Transactions On Engineering Management.* 55, 3 (Aug. 2008), 434-441.

[11] Cohen, S.G. and Bailey, D.E. 1997. What Makes Teams Work: Group Effectiveness Research from the Shop Floor to the Executive Suite. *Journal of Management.* 23, 3, 239-290.

[12] Dubinsky, Y. and Hazzan, O. 2006. Using Roles Scheme to Derive Software Project Metrics. *Journal of Systems Architecture.* 52, 11 (Nov. 2006), 693-699.

[13] Dukerich, J.M. 2002. Leadership, team building, and team member characteristics in high performance project teams. *Engineering Management Journal.* Dec. 2002.

[14] Faraj, S. and Sproull, L. 2000. Coordinating expertise in software development teams. *Management Science.* 46, 12 (De. 2000), 1554-1568.

[15] Felder, R. and Brent, R.. 2001. Effective strategies for cooperative learning. *Journal of Cooperation & Collaboration in College Teaching.* 10, 69-75.

[16] Gorla, N. and Wah Lam, Y. 2004. Who Should Work With Whom? 2004. *Communications of the ACM.* 47, 6 (Jun. 2004), 79-82.

[17] Greenspan, S. 1981. Defining childhood social competence. *Advances in Special Education.* 3, 1-39.

[18] Hallerback, M.U., Lugnegard, T., Hjarthag, F., and Gillberg. C. 2009. *Cognitive neuropsychiatry*, 14 (Mar. 2009), 127-143.

[19] Ikonen, M. and Kurhila, J. 2009. Discovering High-Impact Success Factors in Capstone Software Projects. In *SIGITE'09* (Fairfax, Virginia, USA, October 2009), 235-244.

[20] Langan-Fox, J., Cooper, C.L., and Klimoski, R.J. Research Companion to theDysfunctional Workplace: Management Challenges and Symptoms (New Horizons in Management). Edward Elgar Publishing. Camberly, UK.

[21] Lewis, T.S. and Smith, W.J. 2008. Creating High Performing Software Engineering Teams: The Impact of Problem Solving Style Dominance On Group Conflict and Performance. 24, 2, 121-130.

[22] Mathieu, J.E., Heffner, T.S., Goodwin, G.F., Salas, E., and Cannon-Bowers, J.A. 2000. The Influence of Shared Mental Models on Team Process and Performance. *Journal of Applied Psychology*, 85, 2 (Apr. 2000), 273-283.

[23] Mersino, A. 2007. Emotional Intelligence for Project Managers. *American Management Association*, New York.

[24] Pedrini, D.T. and Pedrini, B.C. Vineland Social Maturity Scale Profile. Retrieved August 18, 2011 from http://www.eric.ed.gov/PDFS/ED079342.pdf.

[25] Pieterse, V., Kourie, D., and Sonnekus, I. 2006. Software Engineering Team Diversity and Performance. In *Proceedings of annual SAICSIT 204* (Somerset West South Africa 2006), 180-186.

[26] Salovey, P. and Mayer, J.D. 1990. Emotional Intelligence. *Imagination, Cognition, and Personality.* 9, 3, 185-211.

[27] Shen, S., Prior, S.D., White, A.S., and Karamanoglu, M. 2007. Using Personality Type Differences to Form Engineering Design Teams. *Engineering Education.* 2, 2, 54-66.

[28] Smarkusky, D., Dempsey, r., Ludka, J., and de Quillettes, F. 2005. In SIGCSE '05 (St. Louis, Missouri USA, Feb. 2005).

[29] Sternberg, R.J. *Handbook of intelligence, 2nd ed.* 2000. (359-379). Cambridge, U.K.: Cambridge University Press.

[30] Strang, R. 1930. Measures of Social Intelligence, *American Journal of Sociology*, 36, 2, 263-269.

[31] Thorndike, R.L. and Stein, S. 1937. An Evaluation of the Attempts to Measure Social Intelligence. *Psychological Bulletin*, 34, 5 (May 1937), 275-284.

[32] West, M.A. 2004. *Effective teamwork: practical lessons from organizational research.* Malden, MA: Wiley-Blackwell, 9-14.

[33] Woolley, A.W., Chabris, C.F., Pentland, A., Hashmi, N., and Malone,T.W. 2010. Evidence for a Collective Intelligence Factor in the Performance of Human Groups. *Science 2010.* ePub ahead of print doi10.1126/science.1193147

Taming Complexity in Large Scale System Projects

Shimon Schocken
Efi Arazi School of Computer Science
IDC Herzliya
P.O.B. 167 Herzliya, Israel 46150
972-9-952-7231
shimon@idc.ac.il

ABSTRACT

Engaging students in large system development projects is an important educational objective, since it exposes design and programming challenges that come to play only with scale. Alas, large scale system projects can be monstrously complex – to the extent of being infeasible in academic settings. We describe a set of principles and a framework that enable students to develop large-scale systems, e.g. a complete hardware platform or a compiler, in several semester weeks.

Categories and Subject Descriptors

B.6.3 [**Logic Design**]: Design Aids – *Hardware description languages, Simulation.*

C.0 [**Computer Systems Organization: General**]: *Hardware / software interfaces, System architectures, Systems specification methodology*

K.3.2 [**Computers and Education**]: Computer and Information Science Education – *Computer Science Education.*

General Terms

Design, Languages.

Keywords

Software Engineering, Compilers/Programming Languages & Paradigms, Experience Report, Active Learning, Hardware Simulation, Modularity, Abstraction, Software Development, Tools, Architecture/Hardware.

1. INTRODUCTION

As computers and networks become more complex and specialized, students increasingly lose sight of the big picture, failing to comprehend how hardware and software systems work together, as one enterprise. In order to address this problem, we developed a course [1] and a book [2] that provide a synthetic, hands-on view of applied computer science, as it unfolds in the process of building a general-purpose computer system – hardware and software – in one semester. All the course materials, software tools and projects are available on the web, freely and in open source [3].

Our approach is based on a series of hands-on hardware and software construction projects, leading to the creation of a simple, yet sur prisingly powerful, computer system. The hardware projects (building a CPU, RAM, and an overall computer platform called *Hack*) are implemented in a simple hardware description language. The software projects (building an assembler, virtual machine, and a compiler for a simple Java-like language called *Jack*) can be done in any programming language. Toward the course's end, the students use Jack to write a mini OS and develop some cool application, the popular choice being interactive computer games. This explains the "*From Nand to Tetris*" title under which the course is typically offered.

How can we squeeze so much work into a single one-semester course? This is the central question that the paper seeks to answer. We describe the various design techniques and pedagogical principles that we used to ease and streamline the students' workload in the course, as they build the computer from the ground up. Some of these techniques, and certainly all the principles, can inform the planning of any large-scale system project, in and out of academia. In particular, we describe four guiding design principles, and illustrate how they can be used to contain development complexity: modularity, abstraction, staging, and focus. We end the paper with general comments about designing and planning large-scale system projects in the context of CS education.

The paper includes many references to a web site [3] where readers can find and use all the software tools and project materials mentioned in the text.

2. MODULARITY

The construction of the Hack/Jack platform is broken into five hardware development projects and seven software development projects, entailing roughly 14 weeks of instruction. Each hardware project guides the students through a gradual construction of a family of related chips, ordered by growing complexity. Every chip in the architecture – *Xor* gate, *Adder*, *ALU*, etc., is specified by a small suite consisting of an HDL (Hardware Description Language) file stub, a test script, and a compare file – all given to the student. The student's task is to edit and extend the supplied stub file into working HDL code (see Figures 1a-b). This code, in turn, can be simulated and tested on a hardware simulator, supplied in the course web site [3]. The exact contract for each chip development is as follows: "when loading your HDL implementation into the hardware simulator and testing

Permission to make digital or hard copies of all or part of this work for personal or classroom use is granted without fee provided that copies are not made or distributed for profit or commercial advantage and that copies bear this notice and the full citation on the first page. To copy otherwise, or republish, to post on servers or to redistribute to lists, requires prior specific permission and/or a fee.
SIGCSE'12, February 29–March 3, 2012, Raleigh, North Carolina, USA.
Copyright 2012 ACM 978-1-4503-1098-7/12/02...$10.00.

it using the supplied test script, the simulator should generate the same outputs listed in the supplied compare file." The simulator compares the actual and the desired outputs automatically, as a side-effect of evaluating the chip's logic.

Altogether, the Hack hardware platform comprises 33 chips. The chips are constructed gradually, and bottom up, starting with elementary *Nand.hdl* chips and ending a few weeks later with the final *Computer.hdl* chip. Let us describe the first few rungs in this construction. Using a given *Nand* gate (the only "given" artifact in the course), the student is guided to build a *Not* gate; using *Not* and *Nand* gates, an *And* gate is built; using *Not* and *And* gates, an *Or* gate is built; using *Or*, *And*, and *Not* gates, a *Multiplexor* is built, and so on. At the end of this recursive ascent – divided into five projects and five semester weeks – a simple Von Neumann platform emerges. This platform is called *Hack*.

Special care and several design iterations were needed to turn *Hack* into a highly modular and succinct architecture. As a result, each chip in the architecture consists of just a few lower-level chip parts, and, correspondingly, can be implemented with just a few lines of HDL code. The most complex chip – the *CPU* – can be implemented with 17 lines of HDL code. The top-most chip – the *Computer* itself – is implemented with three lines of code, specifying the connectivity of the three lower-level chips of which it is made: *CPU*, *RAM*, and *ROM*.

Students routinely build this hardware platform in five semester weeks. Next, they move on to build the computer's software hierarchy, whose development is broken into seven projects. Each software project is specified by an API describing several classes, each consisting of a handful of methods (most students implement our API's using Java, C#, Python, and Perl). For example, the Assembler API includes a *Parser* class (8 methods), a *CodeGenerator* class (3 methods), and a *SymbolTable* class (4 methods). As with the hardware projects, the students are not told "go build an assembler." Rather, they are given a detailed blueprint and a plan of action that walks them through a staged development of each API, from simple to complex methods. In each step, they are guided to unit-test their work with supplied test files.

To summarize, the course atoms are chips and methods. The course web site provides a complete description and specification of each atom, in the form of API's and test scripts; the student's task is to follow proposed implementation plans and build and integrate these atoms into a full-blown computer system. Note that the students are not engaged in any design tasks, as all the chip and class API's are given, along with the necessary unit-testing files. Working from given design documents is extremely important on pedagogical grounds, as we argue later in the paper.

The course normally engages students who took only introductory CS courses. That students with limited programming experience and no hardware background can build this computer in one semester is a triumph of modular design and unit-testing. Equally important is an *abstract* view of the task at hand, as we now turn to explore.

3. ABSTRACTION

We believe that *abstraction* holds the key to containing complexity. With that in mind, we view a computer system as a set of abstractions [4]. A module's abstraction specifies precisely and unambiguously what the module ought to do when presented with certain inputs. For example, the abstraction of a *Xor* gate is a *Xor* truth table; the abstractions of more complex chips are specified using less structured but equally concise functional statements. In a similar fashion, the abstractions of software

```
CHIP Add16 {
   IN a[16], b[16];  // 16-bit inputs
   OUT out[16];      // 16-bit sum a + b
   // Computes the 16-bit sum a + b according to the rules of
   // binary addition. The most significant carry bit is ignored.
}
```

Figure 1a. Typical HDL "stub file", specifying a 16-bit adder abstraction

```
CHIP Add16 {
  IN a[16], b[16];  // 16-bit inputs
  OUT out[16];      // 16-bit sum of a + b
  // Computes the 16-bit sum a + b according to the rules of
  // binary addition. The most significant carry bit is ignored.
  PARTS:
    FullAdder (a = a[0], b = b[0], c = 0, sum = out[1], carry = c0);
    FullAdder (a = a[1], b = b[1], c = c0, sum = out[1], carry = c1);
    FullAdder (a = a[2], b = b[2], c = c1, sum = out[2], carry = c2);
    ...
    FullAdder (a = a[15], b = b[15], c = c14, sum = out[15]);
}
```

Figure 1b. Implementation of the chip abstraction from Figure 1a. This classic design is based on 16 "full-adders" (Fig. 1c below), each contributing one bit to the sum and propagating its carry bit to the next adder (the least significant carry bit is set to 0; the most significant carry bit is ignored). In HDL, each line describes a lower-level chip part, along with its connections to other chip parts. Inter-chip connections (e.g. c0, c1, c2, ...) are declared as needed.

```
CHIP FullAdder {
   IN a, b, c;        // 1-bit inputs
   OUT sum,carry; // 1-bit outputs: right bit of a+b+c and the carry
   PARTS:
   HalfAdder (a = a, b = b, sum = sum1, carry = carry1);
   HalfAdder (a = c, b = sum1, sum = sum, carry = carry2);
   HalfAdder (a = carry1, b = carry2, sum = carry);
}

CHIP HalfAdder {
   IN a, b;            // 1-bit inputs
   OUT sum, carry;  // 1-bit outputs: right bit of a+b and the carry
   PARTS:
   Xor (a = a, b = b, out = sum);
   And (a = a, b = b, out = carry);
}
```

Figure 1c. Possible implementations of the chip parts from Figure 1b; Each chip is made of lower-level chips, all the way down to Nand gates (not shown here)

modules are statements of their intended function. For example, the *advance*() method of the assembler's *Parser* module is abstracted as follows: "reads the next command from the input and makes it the current command; should be called only if *hasMoreCommands*() is true; initially there is no current command".

The bonds that enable abstractions to interact with each other and with external test programs are agreed-upon input and output argument names. Thus, these names must also be part of the abstraction's specification. The separation of *abstraction* (the "what") from *implementation* (the "how") is of course a hallmark of sound system design [5,6]. Our course illustrates the benefits of this principle in a vivid and hands on fashion. Let us give an example, taken from the domain of hardware design. We begin with a brief overview of how the hardware simulator works.

Consider the 16-bit adder implementation shown in Figure 1b. To test this adder, one loads the file *Add16.hdl* into the hardware simulator. The simulator then starts parsing the loaded HDL code. When the simulator encounters the name of a lower-level chip part, say *FullAdder*, it searches the user's directory for a file named *FullAdder.hdl*. If such a file is found, the simulator recurses to parse its HDL code, all the way down to the *Nand* gates level. Once the entire parse tree is thus constructed, the simulator begins evaluating the chip logic. This is done either interactively, using test values supplied by the user via the simulator's GUI, or batch-style, by reading test values from a supplied test script. In either case, the simulator binds the chip's input variables to the test values and percolates the results through the parse tree, all the way up to the chip's output variables.

A few years ago, when we implemented the hardware simulator in Java and prepared the hardware projects, we observed that each chip abstraction (e.g. *FullAdder*) can be implemented in at least two different ways: as an HDL program, stored in, say, a *FullAdder.hdl* file, and also as a Java class, stored in a *FullAdder.class* file. Both implementations realize – albeit in remarkably different ways – the same abstraction, delivering precisely the same chip functionality. Exploiting this duality, we've augmented the hardware simulator with a library of 33 Java classes, each implementing the specified function of one member of the *Hack* chip set. This was done in order to speed up the simulator's operation and compensate for missing chip parts.

Here is an example of how this dual functionality comes to play: suppose we use the hardware simulator to evaluate the *Add16.hdl* chip implementation shown in Figure 1b, consisting of 16 inter-connected and lower-level *FullAdder* chip parts. What should the simulator do if, in the course of this top-down evaluation process, it fails to find the corresponding *FullAdder.hdl* file in the user's directory? The simplest solution would have been to halt with an "unknown chip part: *FullAdder*" exception. Yet our simulator is more forgiving: when it fails to find *FullAdder.hdl* in the user's directory, it automatically reverts to using the services of its built-in *FullAdder.class* file, without forestalling the evaluation of the parent chip. In general, the functionality of any missing *X.hdl* file is automatically delivered by a corresponding *X.class*, if such is available in the simulator's built-in chips library.

This convention had far-reaching implications on the course delivery. Although the standard course entails building the entire hardware platform from the ground up, the built-in "java chips" enable the freedom of building this platform in any desired scope and order. Operationally, HDL code written by students may well include missing chip part implementations, either because the instructor decided to exclude them from the project or because the student had trouble implementing them. This void will have no impact on simulating and testing the parent chip: built-in Java chips will automatically kick in to stand for any missing parts in the implementation. In fact, when developing any given chip in the context of some hardware projects, it makes sense to intentionally ignore HDL implementations of requisite lower-level chips developed in previous projects. This way, the student is assured to use proven built-in Java chips, without having to worry about old bugs creeping into the current work.

We note in passing that the hardware simulator is completely independent of the *Hack* platform. Different people can design and simulate different hardware platforms and chip sets, as needed. Further, if they wish to run behavioral simulation of their platforms and test their design before they set out to implement them in HDL – either partially or completely – they can write their own library of built-in Java chips, and add the library to the simulator's environment. The simulator's software is open source, and is specifically built to support the design and implementation of different hardware architectures, not just *Hack*.

Behavioral simulation ended up being a crucial element of our course. It serves to decouple not only hardware projects from each other, but also the development of individual chips within each project. It enables instructors to pick and choose which chips they want their students to implement, in any desired order, without having to develop all the chips "below" them. And, it enables students who get stuck with some chip implementation to leave it aside and go on with the rest of the project. Looking back, all these benefits emanated from insisting that chip abstraction should be completely separate from its implementation. Adhering to this single design principle radically transformed our course. Such is the power of abstraction.

4. STAGING

In and by itself, a modular design is a static artifact; it is not a plan of action. In order to turn the design into an executable artifact, an implementation plan must be articulated. We believe that seeing such plans, and understating their pros and cons by actually following them, is an important part of computer science education.

Good implementation plans are typically *staged*. The general staging strategy is based on decomposition: when seeking a solution S to a given problem P, it is usually better to start by solving a reduced problem P', and then extending its solution S' into the final solution S. In some cases, the reduction from P to P' is straightforward, and so is the extension of S' to S. In other cases, the stages must be contrived with care and foresight. We now give two examples of this strategy, as they come to play in the course.

The first example is the development of an assembler for the Hack assembly language [2]. The implementation plan is three-staged, as follows. First, the students are guided to develop a basic assembler (S') that can handle programs without labels (P'). This is a fairly straightforward task – one simply translates symbolic mnemonics into their binary equivalents, using the machine language specification. Next, the students are walked through the implementation of an API designed to build and use a symbol table. Finally, and using this added functionality, the students extend their basic assembler into a final assembler (S) capable of handling any assembly program, with or without symbols (P).

In this case, the P→P' reduction and the S'→S extension are relatively straightforward. And yet even here, as always, the architect must exercise care and foresight. First, the API of the basic solution must be planned from the outset in a manner that facilitates a smooth transition to the final solution; ideally, the basic API of S' should become a subset of the final API of S. Second, the separation to stages must be supported by test files (e.g. assembly programs with and without symbols) and by a staged unit-testing plan. All these elements must be put in place by the system architect before development ensues.

The second example is the development of a compiler for Jack, the high-level language of the Hack/Jack platform. Jack is an object-based language with a Java-like syntax. Following the Java/C# paradigm, Jack code is compiled into an interim VM language, designed to operate on a stack-based virtual machine. There are two alternatives for executing the resulting VM programs. One can either execute them directly, using a supplied VM simulator available in the course web site [3], or one can translate them further, into native Hack code, and then run the resulting binary code on the Hack computer built previously. Our VM model and simulator are described in detail in [7].

This two-tiered compilation scheme implies a two-tiered compiler: from Jack to the interim VM language, and then from the VM language to assembly. The development of this compiler is broken into four separate projects and four semester weeks. Let us focus on the top tier of the compiler (sometimes called *front-end*), whose operation is illustrated in Figure 2. This tier is designed to translate source Jack code into target VM code. The translation task consists of two main sub-tasks: parsing the source code into some canonic representation, and then generating target code from the representation. Note that parsing depends only on the grammar of the source language, while code generation depends only on the grammar of the target language.

Normally, a compiler performs both tasks in the same run: a compilation engine parses the source code and generates target code on the fly. And yet from a software development standpoint, writing such a compiler is a major effort. With that in mind, we broke the development into two separate projects: first, the students implement a supplied *Parser* API; next, they implement a supplied *CodeGenerator* API. The division of the original problem P into sub-problems P1 and P2 required the introduction of an interim link that enables the transition from sub-solution S1 to sub-solution S2. As usual, each sub-solution must be planned, developed and unit-tested in isolation.

The link that we've introduced to connect the two stages is an XML representation of Jack semantics. Using a brief spec on how Jack grammar can be expressed in XML [2, p. 207], the students are guided to write a *Parser* program that takes a Jack file and generates from it a corresponding XML file.

The next project guides the students through the process of converting the XML representation into a stream of VM commands. This is done by an algorithm that performs a depth-

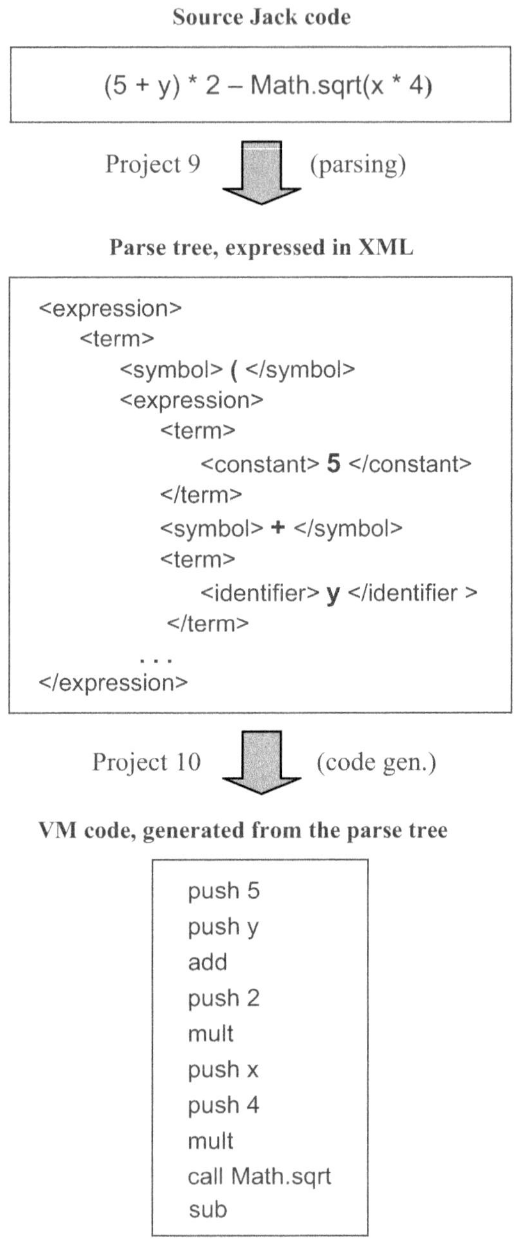

Figure 2. High-level Jack code (top) is compiled into VM code (bottom). The XML code in the middle is an intermediate artifact, designed to decouple the translator's development into two separate and stand-alone projects.

first traversal of the XML code, generating VM commands on the fly (note that the XML file is essentially a parse tree, slanted horizontally). For example, when reaching a terminal XML node of the form `<constant> 5 </constant>`, the algorithm outputs "`push 5`"; when backtracking into an interim node of the form `<symbol> + </symbol>`, the algorithm outputs "`add`", and so on. This process emits a VM program, as seen in the bottom of Figure 2. The VM program can then be loaded and executed on the VM simulator, or translated further into assembly (the latter translation is carried out by the compiler's "back-end", whose development entails two additional projects, not described here).

To summarize the development of the compiler's front-end, one project deals with translating a Jack program into XML; the subsequent project deals with translating the XML into executable VM code. At this point, though, the XML scaffolding has served its purpose, and can be removed from the scene. Thus, in the last part of the project, the students modify the compilation engine developed in the previous project, replacing the logic that generated static XML code with logic that generates executable VM code. Thus, the design of the basic compiler is essentially morphed into the design of the final compiler.

At the end, of course, a compiler is a compiler is a compiler. All the effort described in this section – staging, unit-testing, XML representation, morphing – is invested in order to tame the development's complexity and ration the student's workload into a manageable series of homework assignments. Needles to say, there is an important lesson here: modular and staged design also promotes the development of high quality software [5], and a carefully planned set of homework assignments is quite similar to a well-planned set of programming sub-tasks.

5. FOCUS

Constructing a general-purpose computer from first principles is a humongous undertaking; accomplishing this task in one semester requires some concessions. With that in mind, our approach is based on four simplifying principles: no exceptions, no efficiency, no special features, no design uncertainty.

No exceptions: throughout the projects, it is deliberately and explicitly assumed that all inputs are error-free. For example, when writing the assembler or the compiler, we assume that the source files that the translators have to process contain only valid Hack and Jack code, respectively; there is no need to write error checking and messaging code. In a similar fashion, when we develop the *Add16* chip or the *ALU*, we explicitly ignore overflow; there is no need to design special logic and circuitry to handle this exception.

We believe that ignoring exceptions – if done openly and explicitly – is perfectly acceptable. The act of analyzing and documenting missing or wanting features in one's implementation is an important exercise, educating for honesty and precision.

No efficiency: Some of our hardware and software designs are inefficient. For example, consider how we build a RAM chip. First, we build an 8-register RAM. Next, we assemble eight such chips with direct addressing logic to build a 64-register RAM. Next, we assemble eight such chips to build a 512-register RAM. Three similar steps later we end up with the 16K memory chip required for the Hack computer. The resulting RAM design is elegant, but far from optimized. In the context of this course though, this is acceptable: striving for elegance is no less important than striving for efficiency, and in most cases both pursuits lead to the same end.

How manifest is the inherent inefficiency of the Hack/Jack platform? When we set out to design this platform several years ago, we defined our efficiency lower bound as follows: we wish to design a computer that will be sufficiently fast to execute interactive graphics and animation programs without visible delays. This goal has been achieved: hundreds of computer games like *Tetris* and *Space Invaders* were already developed in the Jack language by students and self-learners. Following compilation, these programs run smoothly on the Hack platform (for example, see [8]).

No special features: It would be nice to have a fancy ALU that supports floating point arithmetic; it would be nice if the high level language featured more data types; it would be nice if the compiler had error diagnostics; it would be nice if the virtual machine were optimized; it would be nice is the operating system supported a file system; it would be nice to write a Scheme interpreter over the Hack platform; it would be nice to write a C compiler; and wouldn't it be nice if two Hack machines could communicate over the Internet? The list of "nice to haves" goes on and on. Every one of these suggestions provides an excellent pretext for a fruitful and lively class discussion and advanced projects.

No design uncertainty: In this course, all the software designs are given. The students are not asked to design anything – they "merely" have to implement the supplied HDL stub files and APIs. We believe that except for software design courses, students should not be asked to design systems. Our experience shows that college students, as well as entry-level programmers, are not sufficiently mature to engage in design; letting them loose on a non-trivial design task can cause more damage than benefit. License to design a system should be given only after one has reviewed, understood, and implemented, many examples of good designs. Thus, discussing and implementing good designs – either by creating or borrowing them – should be a central part of our teaching mission.

Taken together, the limited treatment of exceptions, efficiency, and special features serves an important educational purpose: it focuses the students' minds on the big picture. One of the major goals in this course is to expose great ideas and gems in applied computer science, as they unfold in hands-on implementations. This level of engagement requires focus and concentration that cannot be achieved without setting explicit limits on scope and resolution.

6. DISCUSSION

Since we've made the course materials freely available on the web, thousands of students from India, China, Africa, and western countries have built the Hack/Jack computer system. This learning experience took place in traditional academic settings as well as in self-organized study groups, ranging from Harvard University to the University of the People. The vast majority of the students who complete this course know nothing about hardware or compilation upon starting their journey. And yet many of them are happy campers, expressing publicly the joy and satisfaction they experience building the machine.

In addition to regular students, the course is taken by many self-learners, having nothing but intellectual curiosity and pursuit of knowledge to motivate their work (for a typical self-organized course site using our course materials, see [9]). This, for us, is indirect evidence that complexity has been tamed, or at least contained. This could not have been accomplished without the four critical success factors described in this paper: modularity, abstraction, staging, and focus. It's important to note that none of these elements is a natural or obvious feature of the system that one seeks to develop. Rather, they must be contrived and articulated by the system architect [10].

In our case, and in the case of many readers of this article, the architect is also the course instructor, toiling to prepare his or her course materials. Too often, we spend huge amounts of time on polishing our lectures, rather than on creating innovative projects and challenging problem sets. We believe that in computer science, the balance should be reversed: learning and competence are internalized by doing, not by attending lectures.

When we do give our students challenging programming projects, our execution often leaves much to be desired. The project's goal is obscure, instructions are not clearly stated, design and API's are sloppy shod or entirely missing, neither unit-testing nor implementation plans are given. Too often, the project statement is a little more than "Here is a story about an airline reservation system. Now go build it." Such project preparation is not only unfair to the students, it may well turn them into sloppy engineers.

We believe that good engineering is good education [11]. We hope that our course provides a step in that direction.

Acknowledgement: I am indebted to Noam Nisan, whose brilliance and mastery of computer science made all this possible, and to Mark Armbrust, who manages the course's Q&A forum with equal measures of rigor and generosity. I am also grateful to our former students Yaron Ukrainitz and Yannai Gonczarowski, programming wizards and chief developers of the TECS software suite.

7. REFERENCES

[1] Schocken, S., Nisan, N. Armoni, M. 2009. A Synthesis Course in Hardware Architecture, Compilers, and Software Engineering, *SIGCSE 2009* Proceedings.

[2] Nisan, N., Schocken, S. 2005. *The Elements of Computing Systems*. Cambridge, MA: MIT Press.

[3] Nisan, N., Schocken, S. 2005. *TECS Course Web Site*. www.idc.ac.il/tecs

[4] Kramer, J. 2007. Is abstraction the key to computing?, *Communications of the ACM*, Vol. 50, No. 4, pp. 37-42.

[5] Meyer, B. 2000. Object-Oriented Software Construction, *Prentice-Hall*.

[6] Hazzan, O. and Tomayko, J. 2005. Reflection and Abstraction Processes in the Learning of the Human Aspects of Software Engineering, *IEEE Computer* 38(6), pp. 39-45.

[7] Schocken, S. 2009. Virtual machines: abstraction and implementation, *ITiCSE 2009* Proceedings.

[8] Tetris game example on the Jack/Hack Platform: http://tinyurl.com/4yxmoyv

[9] A do-it-yourself CS course, based on the approach, developed and administered by Parag Shah: http://tinyurl.com/3jotumk

[10] Parnas, D.L. 1972. On the criteria to be used in decomposing systems into modules. *Communications of the ACM*, Vol. 15 Issue 12, Dec. 1972.

[11] Carey, K. 2010. Decoding the value of computer science education, *The Chronicle of Higher Education*, Nov. 2010.

An Approach for Evaluating FOSS Projects for Student Participation

Heidi J. C. Ellis
Western New England University
1215 Wilbraham Rd.
Springfield, MA 01119
00-1-413-782-1748
ellis@wne.edu

Michelle Purcell
Drexel University
3141 Chestnut St
Philadelphia, PA 19104
00-1-215-895-2179
mjw23@drexel.edu

Gregory W. Hislop
Drexel University
3141 Chestnut St
Philadelphia, PA 19104
00-1-215-895-2179
hislop@drexel.edu

ABSTRACT
Free and Open Source Software (FOSS) offers a transparent development environment and community in which to involve students. Students can learn much about software development and professionalism by contributing to an on-going project. However, the number of FOSS projects is very large and there is a wide range of size, complexity, domains, and communities, making selection of an ideal project for students difficult. This paper addresses the need for guidance when selecting a FOSS project for student involvement by presenting an approach for FOSS project selection based on clearly identified criteria. The approach is based on several years of experience involving students in FOSS projects.

Categories and Subject Descriptors
K.3.2 [**Computers and Education**]: Computer and Information Science Education – *Computer science education.*

General Terms
Management, Human Factors.

Keywords
Free and open source software, computing education, student projects

1. PROBLEM STATEMENT
The use of free and open source software (FOSS) in academia is growing as instructors realize the rich learning environment offered by the transparency of the development process and artifacts. FOSS projects may be used to support a wide variety of learning objectives. Such projects are frequently used as a tool to teach computing topics such cryptography [1], distributed software development [2], operating systems [3], and robotics [4]. Frequently, FOSS code is used as a base for learning [5-6].

This paper focuses on the direct participation of students in FOSS projects that involves making some form of contribution to the project. Several recent efforts have involved students in FOSS projects within the classroom [7-14]. While these reports of student learning in FOSS projects are positive, many instructors are cautious in adopting this approach. FOSS projects can be complex and may present learning challenges to both instructors and students including:

- presence of a large, complex code base
- use of different or new programming languages
- use of a variety of development tools
- understanding of community interactions
- scheduling of deliverables with FOSS calendar

While some recent work has provided guidance to instructors desiring to involve students in FOSS projects [15, 16], approaches to identifying appropriate FOSS projects and selecting reasonable assignments is an ongoing issue. This paper attempts to address this problem by providing a framework of evaluation criteria that can be used to determine approachable FOSS projects that may support student involvement.

1.1 Open Source Culture and Tools
In order for instructors to provide entre for students into FOSS projects, instructors must understand the FOSS culture and tools used. There are several excellent books that cover the open source culture [17-19]. A discussion of the steps that may be taken to involve students in FOSS projects from the perspectives of the FOSS and academic communities is included in [15].

There are three major resources that instructors may find helpful when involving students in FOSS projects. The first is the TeachingOpenSource [20] community which was established to aid instructors who desire to involve students in FOSS projects. The second are forges. A software forge such as sourceforge.net is a platform that supports collaborative software development. In addition, a forge will typically host many independent projects. Lastly, ohloh.net is a site that collects, collates and analyzes data from multiple FOSS projects. Ohloh provides information about the landscape of FOSS projects, allowing one to search and compare FOSS projects by project type, language and other characteristics.

One of the most important aspects for instructors to remember when involving students in FOSS projects is the principle of "giving back". FOSS instructors must identify ways that students can make contributions to projects that are useful to the FOSS community. This is essential to supporting the community and provides an important life lesson to students.

Permission to make digital or hard copies of all or part of this work for personal or classroom use is granted without fee provided that copies are not made or distributed for profit or commercial advantage and that copies bear this notice and the full citation on the first page. To copy otherwise, or republish, to post on servers or to redistribute to lists, requires prior specific permission and/or a fee.
SIGCSE'12, February 29–March 3, 2012, Raleigh, North Carolina, USA.
Copyright 2012 ACM 978-1-4503-1098-7/12/02...$10.00.

2. KEY EVALUATION ASPECTS

From the instructor's perspective, there are several obvious characteristics of FOSS projects that can be used to evaluate the "fit" of a FOSS project for use with a class. These aspects include the suitability of FOSS project opportunities to support student assignments, platform used, programming language(s) used, development environment, and perhaps hardware requirements. These aspects tend to be well-understood by instructors and the fit of the project easily assessed based on these characteristics.

However, since the student will be involved in an ongoing FOSS project, the health, personality, and approachability of the project itself must be understood. Several recent research efforts have resulted in models for assessing the health of a FOSS project.

An early work by Crowston et al. [21] describes a set of measures of success for FOSS projects that include user satisfaction and involvement, product quality, software process, age of the project, number of developers and their satisfaction, and the number of downloads. Hahn et al. [22] identify the ability to attract volunteers and to organize contributions as a success factor for FOSS projects. Weiss [23] describes a model for measuring the success of FOSS projects based on the popularity of the project on the Web. The approach mines search engine knowledge to determine the popularity of a project. Beaver et al. [24] describe a model based on existing FOSS project data that uses agents to simulate behavior of developers. The model is intended to predict the success of the FOSS project based on individual contributions, actions of developers, and popularity and performance of the project. English and Schweik [25] describe a classification of FOSS projects based on characteristics of how the project was founded and its' growth pattern afterwards.

While these efforts provide insight into the workings of FOSS projects, their complexity typically prohibits their use in identifying FOSS projects for possible student participation. Callaway [26] has created a metric based on product and development features that assigns points to various FOSS project features including bundling, libraries, source control, releases, documentation, licensing and more. The drawback to this method is that it is time-intensive. However, this might be a good exercise for students to do once a project has been selected. Below we suggest a straightforward approach for instructors to use to select FOSS projects appropriate for student involvement.

3. A MODEL FOR EVALUATING FOSS PROJECTS

The first step in selecting a FOSS project is to identify a set of potential projects. One way to do this is to browse a forge such as sourceforge.net, launchpad.net, or gitorious.org. Ohloh provides a project profile for a FOSS project including programming language used, commit history, history of the codebase and more.

Begin by identifying a set of five or six potential projects. Once this set has been identified, select three of the most interesting. You may return to this set and choose another project if one in the subset does not meet the criteria at any phase.

An overview of the evaluation model is shown in Figure 1. The model evolved out of several years of experience involving students in FOSS projects and includes evaluation criteria for three important aspects of FOSS projects. A FOSS project's **viability** is essential to supporting student learning. The project must have an active community that is engaged in ongoing development. Student participation is dependent on the **approachability** of the project. The project should have an identifiable on-ramp for new participants and describe how new contributors may join the community and make contributions. A third important aspect is that of **suitability.** The project must provide appropriate learning experiences for the course as well as a sufficient number of learning opportunities.

	Viability	Approach-ability	Suitability
Mission Critical Criteria	- Size/Scale/ Complexity - Activity - Active Community	- Clear On-Ramp	- Appropriate Artifacts - Contributor Support
2nd-ary Criteria	- Domain - Maturity - User Support - Roadmap	- Contribution Types - Openness to Contributions - Student Friendliness	- Product Description - Platform - Development Features

Figure 1. FOSS Evaluation Criteria.

The model differentiates between two levels of criteria. **Mission Critical** criteria are characteristics of the FOSS project that must be present in order to support student success. **Secondary Criteria** are criteria that contribute to the success of student experiences, however a FOSS project may fail to meet one or two of these criteria and still be a viable project for student participation.

The model is intended to be applied in a top-down fashion where the **critical** aspects are evaluated first. This allows instructors to more easily weed out projects that are infeasible for student involvement.

In the following sections, we describe each of the three evaluation aspects and their criteria. We tag each criterion as being either mission critical or secondary and provide general guidelines for how to determine whether a criterion has been met.

3.1 Viability

This set of criteria is intended to help identify the maturity, stability and future prospects of a FOSS project. These criteria help identify projects that are still in very initial stages of development, very complex projects, dormant projects, and projects that lack sufficient development community. Much of the data used in this evaluation may be obtained from the project web site, Ohloh.org., or SourceForge.net.

Size/Scale/Complexity (critical) – An ideal project should be neither overly simple nor overly complex. Students do not need to understand the entire project, however they should be able to understand a subset of the project. One quick measure of size is LOC. For instance, smaller FOSS projects include the Maven Eclipse Plugin at 96 KLOC and the Eclipse Checkstyle Plugin at 60 KLOC. A medium size FOSS project that has been used successfully in classes by the authors is OpenMRS which has 213 KLOC. Larger projects include Chromium at 5 MLOC and Mozilla at 5.3 MLOC.

However, LOC does not provide insight into the architecture of the project, nor its modularity. Larger projects such as Mozilla may use a plug-in architecture that supports small student code contributions. Therefore, observation of the design provides insight into the modularity and complexity of the project.

Another indication of project complexity is the number of committers on the project. A reasonable number is at least six committers working on the project within the last 12 months. If a project is much smaller than this, the project may not be sufficiently mature to provide a rich learning environment. If the project is larger, the complexity of the code (and development environment) may present a barrier to student learning.

Activity (critical) - The project should be reasonably active. Ten commits per month is minimally acceptable and 30 commits or more per month, on average, would be favorable. Looking back a year or more will provide an understanding of the pattern of commits. This data can be retrieved from Ohloh.net.

Community (critical) – In order to support student learning, the project must have an active user community. While it is difficult to quantitatively evaluate the activity of a user community, some indicators of community health include a regular history of project downloads and documentation updates over time, current activity on user mailing lists, and testimonials on the project web site.

It is also important to observe the recency of the activity. Are there lags between updates? Are there current questions that have not been answered on forums or lists? What is the IRC activity? What is the recent history of downloads? All of these will provide insight into the community activity.

Domain (secondary) - The domain of the application may have an impact on student learning. Some FOSS projects require a lot of domain knowledge. For instance, gaming software likely presents less of a learning curve to students than software to process data from nuclear magnetic resonance experiments.

Maturity (secondary) – The project should have at least one stable production release. Projects that lack this may not have the organization to support student learning. SourceForge.net provides a *status* feature that indicates releases and Ohloh.net provides an *analysis summary* that provides information on the stability of the code base.

User support (secondary) – The project should have clear instructions for downloading, installing and using the project. Other evidence of user support includes FAQs, forums, and lists for users. Such support for users of the project gives some indication of responsiveness of developers to users and to activity in the project. The quality of end-user documentation also provides insight into the maturity of the project.

Roadmap for the future (secondary) – Does the project have a roadmap or blueprint for future development? Student learning is best supported by projects that have a roadmap that includes new feature development, a method for users to submit new feature requests and a process for identifying how new features are prioritized.

3.2 Approachability

In addition to a project being viable, in order to successfully support student participation, the project must be approachable by students. It must have sufficient documentation and guidance for students, and the community must also be welcoming for new contributors. Specific criteria for determining project approachability include:

On-ramp (critical) - The project must have an identifiable "on-ramp" for new contributors to become involved and to learn. The project should contain instructions for how to join the community and first steps toward making a contribution. Some projects may even have on-ramp instructions aimed specifically for students. We suggest the following 3-point scale for evaluating on-ramp:

- Insufficient-Few or no pointers on how to get involved.
- Sufficient--Suggestions about how to get involved other than contributing money with accompanying high-level instructions.
- Ideal -Obvious link to get started, list of suggestions for things to do and detailed instructions.

Contribution types (secondary) - Does the project contain opportunity for multiple types of contributions (documentation, requirements, testing, debugging, coding, etc)? Clearly, the project should include opportunities for the type of contribution that fits the class.

Openness to contributions (secondary) – Acceptance of a student contribution to a project provides valuable affirmation to student learning. Determine whether the project accepts external patches. Ask how to get student work committed or look to see if the community has a description of how contributions are accepted or whether a "committer" is identified. A project that never commits any of the code from outside the core community members is likely to not accept new contributions from students which may negatively affect student motivation.

Student-friendliness (secondary) – An ideal project for student involvement is one that welcomes and values student contributions. One easy gauge of the student-friendliness of a project is if the community members moderate the tone of communication. Review developer mailing lists and archives and sit in on an IRC conversation to gauge tone. If developers are getting "flamed" that will have a negative effect on student motivation.

3.3 Suitability

The suitability of a FOSS project depends a large part on the course and its content. Instructors should reflect on the learning objectives for the course and the types of activities that could be undertaken as well as the types of contributions that students could make. For instance, a course on technical writing would be a good fit for a FOSS community that needs developer or user documentation written. Similarly, a web-based FOSS project might serve as a good project for a usability course.

Appropriate artifacts (critical) – FOSS projects offer a wealth of different types of contributions that may serve as a base for student work. For instance, many FOSS projects need documentation written, testing performed, or designs created, in addition to code contributions. In order for a particular FOSS project to be suitable for a class, appropriate artifacts for students to both study and contribute to must exist in that FOSS project. Therefore, a FOSS project being evaluated for use in a course on technical writing should provide multiple opportunities for students to contribute documentation.

Contributor support (critical) – The ideal FOSS project for student participation is one that contains a high volume of guidance for students as they learn. The project should contain information on how the project is administered and managed. Communication tools such as IRC and lists should be clearly documented and developers should have a web presence. The operating processes such as the process for getting a change committed, feature selection and approval, and feature status should be well documented. In addition, the questions posed on IRC, lists, and forums should have supportive and timely responses.

Product description (secondary) – In order for a project to support student participation, students must be able to understand the purpose of the project. Does the project clearly describe the product? Can students understand the intended uses of the product?

Platform (secondary) – What software and hardware platform does the FOSS project run on? Are resources available to support these platforms? Typically instructors desire a platform with which students are familiar.

Development features (secondary) – Some classes may be dependent on features of the actual FOSS project code including:

- **Programming language** – Students may find it easier to participate in a project that uses a programming language familiar to them. FOSS projects may use more than one programming language so when you get to actual assignments, review that the programming language is a good fit.
- **Development environment** – Similar to programming language, students may find it easier to participate in a project that uses tools and a development environment with which they are familiar. This criterion may be less important than the programming language but for large projects, the development environment can be quite complex.
- **Supporting technologies** – Does the project depend on additional software packages such as databases or libraries? The presence of additional technologies adds to the complexity of a project and may create a steeper learning curve for students.

3.4 Other Considerations

In addition to the criteria described in the previous three sections, there are several characteristics of projects that should be considered:

Sizzle-factor – How attractive is the project to students? Projects that students find more appealing (e.g., games) may provide greater motivation to students. Projects with a humanitarian focus may provide motivation for students [8, 10, 11].

Long-term prospects – Most instructors teach a similar set of courses from term to term and from year to year. Selection of a project that has the possibility of supporting student participation for future terms and years may reduce instructor preparation time and effort for future courses.

Ownership - Does the project hold the possibility for being able to create a sense of "ownership" for students? Is this a project that students will want to follow during future development? Creating a sense of project ownership in students may also increase student motivation and learning.

4. APPLICATION OF THE APPROACH

In this section, we show how the evaluation approach described in the previous section is applied to example projects. Given the variety of courses that may desire to involve students in FOSS projects and the possible variety in topics, we do not provide concrete rubrics for evaluating each criterion. Instead, we suggest that each criterion be rated on a one-to-three scale where one indicates that the criterion is lacking in the FOSS project and three indicates full support for the criterion by the FOSS project. The general approach is:

1. Evaluate the **mission critical** criteria first. A scale of less than a two on any of these criteria should remove the FOSS project from consideration.
2. Evaluate the **secondary** criteria on a scale from one to three. A score of above 20 for the **secondary** criteria indicates a viable project. Projects that score below 20 should be examined to determine if the low-scoring criteria will negatively impact student involvement.

The first evaluation is of the Mifos microfinance application, which provides a framework of functionality for institutions including client management; portfolio management; and loan tracking, supporting 28 microfinance institutions. Three sites were used during the assessment including the Mifos site (http://mifos.org/), the Mifos SourceForge site (http://sourceforge.net/projects/mifos/), and the Ohloh page on Mifos (http://www.ohloh.net/p/mifos).

Critical Criteria

	R'ting	Rationale
Viability		
Size/scale/ complexity	2	Design is documented and appears modular. Domain appears within comprehension needed for bug fix.
Activity	2	Spiky activity—1382 in Feb but 19 in August.
Community	3	However, some of developer list questions seem unaddressed. Steady download activity over last year. Over last 12 months ranged between 550 and 850.last year between 600-850. However, drops to under 400 in August.
Approachability		
Clear on-ramp	3	Obvious links to get started, detailed instructions.
Suitability		
Appropriate Artifacts	3	Useful documentation on coding standards and how to submit patches as well as how to setup development environment.
Contributor Support	2	Communication tools documented. However, developers are not always available to help answer immediate-need questions by IRC. Forums are supportive with generally timely response, a few development list questions seemed unanswered.

Figure 2. Evaluation of Mission Critical Criteria for Mifos.

Figure 2 above shows the result of step 1, evaluation of the mission critical criteria. The figure shows both the numeric evaluation as well as comments that provide some rationale for the rating. Based on the results of the evaluation, the Mifos application fulfills all of the mission critical criteria. The strong positive aspects of Mifos include a clear on-ramp for new contributors including instructions and the presence of useful documentation on coding standards and how to submit patches.

As none of the mission critical criteria rank less than a two (see Figure 2), the secondary criteria are then evaluated. Figure 3 shows the result of the evaluation.

Secondary Criteria		
	R'ting	Rationale
Viability		
Domain	2	Microfinance application reasonably understandable. Students should be able to contribute simple bug. However, some bugs might be more difficult.
Maturity	3	Yes-version 2.1.5
User Support	3	FAQs are available as well as user support on mailing lists. User manual and deployment toolkit exist.
Roadmap	2	Technical roadmap exists and feature submittal process exists, but new features are not yet prioritized into most recent overall roadmap.
Approachability		
Contribution Types	3	Multiple types of contribution available as well as opportunities for bug fixes.
Openness to Contributions	3	Yes, the process is documented on how to submit bug fixes.
Student Friendliness	3	No indication of flaming and the community is helpful on developer and user lists.
Suitability		
Product Description	3	There are recommended microfinance readings, case studies of MIFOS deployed, video, and demo server available for learning about the product. Students should have basic understanding of domain.
Platform	3	Development environment based on FOSS and could be set up on Windows or Mac machine. No special software or hardware resources needed.
Development Features	1	programming language (Java) and development environment (Eclipse, Maven) and somewhat familiarity with the supporting technologies (mySQL, Jetty, J2EE).
Secondary Total:	26	

Figure 3. Evaluation of Secondary Criteria for Mifos.

The evaluation results shown in Figure 3 appear to indicate that Mifos is a very good project for student involvement. Mifos is a mature project with stable releases and good user and developer support. There are multiple ways that students can contribute to the project and the community is open to student participation. The domain is understandable by students and the development platform requires no special resources.

In order to demonstrate evaluation of a project that may have potential, yet is not yet ready for student involvement, Figure 4 shows the evaluation of the Mission Critical criteria for Sigmah. Sigmah is a Humanitarian Project Management application (http://www.sigmah.org/). Upon first look, Simgah is appealing based on its size and complexity and level of activity. However, the number of product downloads are few and the user guide is only available in French which could indicate a small user base. This also makes it difficult for students to understand the project, especially since most of the demonstration site is also in French.

Critical Criteria		
	Rating	Rationale
Viability		
Size/scale/ complexity	3	124 KLOC. Modular design
Activity	3	Average around 60 per month in the last year.
Community	1	War downloads since first release on Jun 21 only 45, responses are timely and supportive, user base at moment seems small
Approachability		
Clear on-ramp	2	Minimum provided, no coding guidelines.
Suitability		
Appropriate Artifacts	2	Testing and coding needed. Other opportunities unclear.
Contributor Support	2	Developers communicate via google groups, very timely response, but no IRC

Figure 4. Evaluation of Mission Critical Criteria for Sigmah.

It should be noted, however, that this project may evolve to be one that could support student involvement. The project is relatively young, the domain is reasonably understandable by students, and the development team has already provided some good resources to help developers get started. In addition, a web search reveals that Sigmah has 12 non-governmental organizations in France on their steering committee which could indicate a stable future for the project. This project may pick up momentum and be one where student involvement can make a real difference.

5. CONCLUSION

This paper presents an approach for evaluating FOSS projects for student involvement and contribution to the project. Criteria that impact student involvement in a project are identified and a set of Mission Critical criteria that must be fulfilled are presented. The Mifos microfinance and the Sigmah humanitarian project management software are used as examples to demonstrate the utility of the approach. The model and approach described in the paper evolved out of several years of experience involving students in FOSS projects and is flexible to support differing types of student participation including fixing bugs, writing code, writing documentation, testing, and more.

6. ACKNOWLEDGMENTS

This material is based on work supported by the National Science Foundation under Grants DUE-0958204, DUE-0940893, and DUE-0940925. Any opinions, findings and conclusions or recommendations expressed in this material are those of the author(s) and do not necessarily reflect the views of the National Science Foundation (NSF). We would also like to thank Drexel students Andrew Hagner, Benjamin Kos, and Jon Thompson for applying the model to FOSS projects.

7. REFERENCES

[1] McAndrew, A. 2008. "Teaching cryptography with open-source software, *Proceedings of the 39th SIGCSE technical symposium on Computer science education, SIGCSE '08,* pp. 325—329, doi =http://doi.acm.org/10.1145/1352135.1352247.

[2] Meneely, A. and Williams, L., 2009. "On preparing students for distributed software development with a synchronous, collaborative development platform," *SIGCSE Bull.*, Vol. 41, No. 1. Mar. 2009, pp. 529--533, doi = http://doi.acm.org/10.1145/1539024.1509047

[3] Nieh, J. and Vaill, C. 2005. "Experiences teaching operating systems using virtual platforms and linux," *SIGCSE Bull.*, Vol. 37, No. 1, Feb. 20005, pp. 520--524, doi = http://doi.acm.org/10.1145/1047124.1047508

[4] Nickens, G. V., Tira-Thompson, E. J., Humphries, T. and Touretzky, D. S., 2009. "An inexpensive hand-eye system for undergraduate robotics instruction," *SIGCSE Bull.*, Vol. 41, No 1, Mar. 2009, pp.423--427, doi = http://doi.acm.org/10.1145/1539024.1509016

[5] Petrenko, M., Poshyvanyk, D., Rajlich,V., and Buchta, J., 2007. "Teaching Software Evolution in Open Source," *IEEE Computer*, Vol. 40, No. 11, pp. 25-31

[6] Liu, P. L., 2008. "Using open-source robocode as a Java programming assignment," *SIGCSE Bull.*, Vol. 40, No 4., Nov. 2008, pp. 63--67, doi =http://doi.acm.org/10.1145/1473195.1473222

[7] Pedroni, M., Bay, T., Oriol, M., Pedroni, A., 2007. "Open Source Projects in Programming Courses", *ACM SIGCSE Bulletin*, Vol 39, No 1., pp. 454-458.

[8] Ellis, H.J.C., Morelli, R.A., de Lanerolle, T., 2007. "Holistic Software Engineering Education Based on an Open Source Project," *20th Annual Conference on Software Engineering Education and Training*, pp. 327-335.

[9] Hepting, D. H., Peng, L., Maciag, T. J., Gerhard, D., and Maguire, B. 2008. "Creating synergy between usability courses and open source software projects," *SIGCSE Bull.*, Vol. 40, No. 2, June 2008, pp. 120-123, doi = http://doi.acm.org/10.1145/1383602.1383649

[10] Hislop, G.W., Ellis, H.J.C., and Morelli, R.A., 2009. "Evaluating Student Experiences in Developing Software for Humanity", *ACM SIGCSE Bulletin - ITiCSE,* Vol 41, No 3., pp. 263-267.

[11] Morelli, R. A., Tucker, A., Danner, N., De Lanerolle, T R., Ellis, H. J. C., et al, 2009. "Revitalizing computing education through free and open source software for humanity", *CACM,* Vol. 52, No 8., pp. 67-75.

[12] Morelli, R. A., and De Lanerolle, T. R., "FOSS 101: Engaging introductory students in the open source movement," 2009. *ACM SIGCSE Bulletin - SIGCSE '09,* Vol. 41, No 1., pp. 311-315.

[13] Marmorstein, R., 2011. "Open source contribution as an effective software engineering class project," Proceedings of the 16th annual joint conference on Innovation and technology in computer science education, ITiCSE '11 Darmstadt, Germany, pp. 268-272. doi = http://doi.acm.org/10.1145/1999747.1999823

[14] Yue, K.B., Damania, Z., Nilekani, R. and Abeysekera, K., 2011. "The use of free and open source software in real-world capstone projects," J. Comput. Sci. Coll., Vol. 26, No. 4, pp. 85-92.

[15] Ellis, H.J.C., Hislop, G.W., Chua, M., and Dziallas, S., 2011."How to Involve Students in FOSS Projects," *41st Annual Frontiers in Education Conference, 2011. FIE 2011,* October 2011.

[16] Professors Open Source Summer Experience, http://www.communityleadershipteam.org/posse/ retrieved 8/10/11.

[17] Raymond, E., 1999. "The Cathedral and the Bazaar", *Knowledge, Technology & Policy,* Vol 12, No 3, pp. 23-49.

[18] Feller, J., Fitzgerald, B., Understanding Open Source Software Development, Pearson Education, 2001.

[19] Fogel, K., 2005. Producing Op Producing Open Source Software, How to Run a Successful Free Software Project, Retrieved 8/20/11 from: http://producingoss.com/en/index.html

[20] teachingopensource.com

[21] Crowston, K., Annabi, H., and Howison, J., 2003. "Defining Open Source Project Success," In *Proceedings of the 24th Int.l Conference on Information Systems,* ICIS, Seattle.

[22] Hahn, J., Moon, J.Y., and Zhang, C., "Emergence of New Project Teams from Open Source Software Developer Networks: Impact of Prior Collaboration Ties,"2008. *Information Systems Research,* Vol. 19, No. 3, pp. 369-391. DOI: 10.1287/isre.1080.0192

[23] Weiss, D., "Measuring Success of Open Source Projects Using Web Search Engines," 2005. *The First International Conference on Open Source Systems OSS2005: Open Source Systems*, Geneva, Italy, pp. 93-99.

[24] Beaver, J.M., Cui, X. St Charles, J. L. and Potok, T. E., 2009. "Modeling success in FLOSS project groups," *Proceedings of the 5th International Conference on Predictor Models in Software Engineering, PROMISE '09,* Vancouver, British Columbia, Canada, pp. 16:1--16:8. doi = http://doi.acm.org/10.1145/1540438.1540461

[25] English, R., Schweik, C. M., "Identifying Success and Tragedy of FLOSS Commons: A Preliminary Classification of Sourceforge.net Projects, 2007. " *First International Workshop on Emerging Trends in FLOSS Research and Development (FLOSS'07: ICSE Workshops 2007)* Minneapolis, Minnesota, May 20-May 26.

[26] Callaway, T., "How to Tell if a FLOSS Project is Doomed to Fail," http://www.theopensourceway.org/wiki/How_to_tell_if_a_FLOSS_project_is_doomed_to_FAIL retrieved 8/10/11.

Integrating Computing into Middle School Disciplines Through Projects *

Susan Rodger
Duke University
Durham, NC USA
rodger@cs.duke.edu

Melissa Dalis
Duke University
Durham, NC USA
melissa.dalis@duke.edu

Chitra Gadwal
UMBC
Baltimore, MD USA
cgadwa1@umbc.edu

Jenna Hayes
Duke University
Durham, NC USA
jlynnehayes@gmail.com

Peggy Li
Duke University
Durham, NC USA
peggy.li@duke.edu

Liz Liang
Duke University
Durham, NC USA
lizliang217@gmail.com

ABSTRACT

For four years we have been integrating computing into a variety of middle school disciplines via the Alice programing language. Early on we focused on creating curriculum materials for teachers to use in teaching the basic programming and animation concepts. This paper describes our efforts over the past two years in creating model projects for students to build in all disciplines, and our most recent focus on science and mathematics projects. For science we have introduced experiments in Alice and the tools needed for them. In mathematics we have created projects to increase their understanding of programming and to use the projects to increase their understanding of mathematics. We also discuss our efforts in workshops to teach K-12 teachers Alice and an analysis of the teachers' lesson plans and worlds developed in the most recent workshop.

Categories and Subject Descriptors

K.3.2 [**Computing Milieux**]: Computers and Education-Computer and Information Science Education

General Terms

Human Factors

Keywords

Alice, virtual worlds, K-12 education, middle school, introductory computer science

*The work of these authors are supported by the National Science Foundation grants ESI-0624642 and DRL-1031351, IBM Faculty Awards and CRA DREU awards

Permission to make digital or hard copies of all or part of this work for personal or classroom use is granted without fee provided that copies are not made or distributed for profit or commercial advantage and that copies bear this notice and the full citation on the first page. To copy otherwise, to republish, to post on servers or to redistribute to lists, requires prior specific permission and/or a fee.
SIGCSE'12, February 29–March 3, 2012, Raleigh, North Carolina, USA.
Copyright 2012 ACM 978-1-4503-1098-7/12/02 ...$10.00.

1. INTRODUCTION

A report conducted by the Association for Computing Machinery (ACM) and the Computer Science Teachers Association (CSTA) revealed that computer science education in the United States K-12 classrooms is at a crisis[1]. Although middle school students (grades 6-8) use computers for many tasks at home and at school, the majority of them never quite understand what computer science is and how it relates to problem solving. Their exposure to computers in school is most likely with spreadsheets, word processors and media presentation tools. Few high schools have a computer science course and even fewer middle schools offer a computer science course, a crucial time when students are starting to think about careers.

One difficulty in the adoption of computer science is the lack of standards. The CSTA and ACM have developed a model curriculum for K-12 computer science [20] that is now under revision in addition to several model curriculum documents such as the Level I course which is recommended for students in grades K-8 [10].

The lack of exposure to computer science at the K-12 level leads to few students choosing computer science as a career in college. The NCWIT scorecard[14] mentions future problems in the United States, that the U.S. Bureau of Labor Statistics predicts that the U.S. will only be able to fill about one-third of technology jobs in 2018 with U.S. Citizens. There are efforts to increase the number of K-12 students exposed to computing such as the 10,000 teachers project [7], and a new proposed AP CS Principles Course[4]. Many projects targeting middle school include CS Unplugged [5], Alice [2, 3, 8], Scratch [19] and Greenfoot [11].

Our project focuses on using Alice, a 3D virtual worlds programming environment, to integrate computing into K-12. A study using Alice with college students[13] showed improvement in students' performance in CS 1, retention within computer science and attitudes towards computer science. We have been teaching Alice, since 2002 at Duke University in several courses and in outreach programs to K-12 students and have seen first hand the excitement Alice brings to students. Based on our success in outreach programs, we began teaching Alice programming to middle school teachers in all disciplines. Alice is attractive to middle and high school students because they can easily create interactive animated games and stories. As it is difficult to insert a new course into a middle school curriculum, we are integrating computing into middle schools by training teachers to use Alice for student projects in their disciplines.

This paper describes our efforts over the past two years to create sample projects for specific disciplines to show teachers how students can use Alice for projects in middle school. Most of these projects include tutorials for students to build them as a sample project in learning Alice. The majority of these projects are in math and science, but we also describe projects for other disciplines and general projects. We also include an analysis of the teachers lesson plans and worlds developed in our 2011 workshop.

2. BACKGROUND

We have run Alice workshops since 2005 and specifically targeting middle school and high school teachers since 2008 training over 150 teachers. In 2008 and 2009 we developed a wide range of Alice tutorials on both computer science topics and animation topics [18, 17, 6]. The computer science topic tutorials included if statements, events, variables, functions, random numbers, lists, and inheritance. The animation tutorials included moving the camera, creating lighting effects, creating scene changes, modifying objects with textures, and creating people you know using pictures. Working with the teachers led to creating template worlds and objects they could use. In particular we created a series of quiz template worlds to make it easier for teachers to create a quiz world.

The main feedback from teachers in our 2009 and 2010 one-week summer workshops were a need for a large number of sample Alice projects and longer workshops. Thus in summers 2010 and 2011 we developed a large number of model projects for many disciplines, with the largest number for mathematics and science. The majority of the projects include a tutorial. In Summer 2011 we ran a two-week Alice workshop for teachers and spent the extra week in helping them to develop lesson plans.

3. SCIENCE PROJECTS

Alice can play a helpful role in the middle school science classroom. The link between the physical and life sciences and computing is already acknowledged in the curriculum objectives for middle school science. For example, units in the 8th grade North Carolina Standard Course of Study (NCSCS)[16] for Science include "Using Technology to Study our World" and "Technology for a better tomorrow". A goal common to both units is to learn how to use software to view and process data for communication. Many of the other units have sections where Alice can fill in as a model.

An interactive model can also be used to collect data. Many times the concept being presented has no experiment that can easily be done in a classroom; Alice can provide an interactive alternative for collecting data. Beyond teaching concrete facts, science curriculums aim to develop skills in students that will help them in understanding the scientific data. In fact, the NCSCS in science states that the achievement of "scientific literacy" is the primary goal of the science curriculum. Being able to create and read the visualizations of data used in scientific articles is a core part of their mission. Being able to analyze data using visualizations is an important skill that Alice allows students to learn easily.

One challenge to producing models, especially scientific, in Alice is the need for accurate objects. There are a lack of objects in the Alice gallery that are suited for teaching some areas of science. Earth science and ecosystems are easier because these types of objects are well represented in the Alice library. Other subjects such as genetics need objects made before one can easily create a model. We had to repurpose ordinary geometric shapes in some of our science worlds.

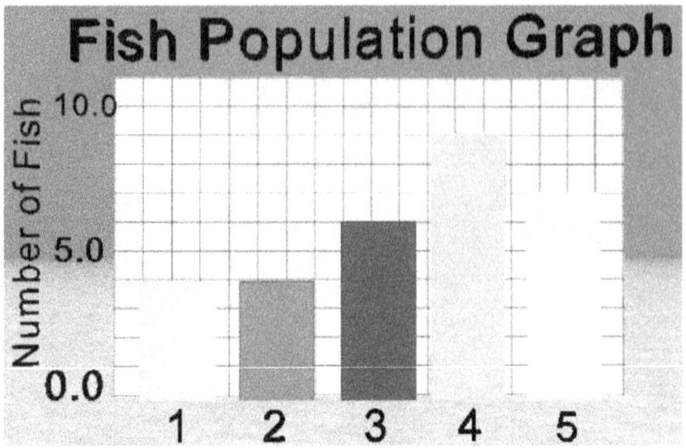

Figure 1: BarChart of Fish Rounds

3.1 Experiments

We surveyed science teachers on how to integrate Alice into science classes. From their responses we focused on examples in earth science.

To visualize the data, we created a bar chart in Alice. The bar chart uses rectangles that resize height to indicate value. The bars can be put together in a list to form a bar chart that animates changing values by increasing or decreasing the height of the rectangles. The list can be created with data a user already has or by collecting the data in an experiment.

The motivation for our first example world came from a biology teacher and focuses on population change. There is an activity where students simulate and record the changing population of fish in the pond originally using goldfish crackers. Alice provides a way to simulate the population of fish, but also will allow the data to be collected and visualized in the same program. By changing the numbers of fish that are taken from the pond, students can see how populations change. Instead of recording the numbers by hand, the numbers are saved into a growing list in Alice. When more and more fish are taken, eventually the population stops increasing and begans to quickly subside - a model for unsustainable fishing - that they can quickly see both visually but also in the bar chart that is automatically created in the end. Figure 1 shows a resulting bar chart after 5 rounds of collection.

This bar chart became the model for a more general bar chart object. We created a tutorial to show how to create a bar chart in any world as well as a template world that one can start with that already contains a bar chart.

For another example, we created an atmosphere world that uses two animating bars, one for temperature and one for pressure. We chose the atmosphere primarily because it was a topic that multiple teachers in the survey mentioned. It is also a topic that would be greatly enhanced by data visualization. Since the layers are differentiated by how temperature behaves in relation to altitude, it is important to differentiate how pressure and temperature behave differently. As the scientist advances through the different layers of earth's atmosphere, students are able to learn about each layer as well as visually appreciate how the two variables of interest change.

The data for the world is stored in three different lists in the world-temperature, pressure, and altitude. We obtained the data for the world by combining NASA, UK's Discovering Antarctic Organization, and Portland State University models. Ideally, special charting objects would be in the Alice library. The Alice team has plans to create a 3D Bar-Chart Object to add to the Alice library.

We sent these worlds to the teachers for feedback. In general, the feedback from the five teachers that responded was positive. One of the teachers suggested expanding the atmosphere world to include the different layers of the earth so that it could be used for two different units.

3.2 Models of Tiny Objects

There is a need for interactive models in the science classroom to help conceptualize objects that are either too small or too large to be practically demonstrated in the classroom. Alice's ability to easily produce interactive animations means that with the right mix of objects from Alice's library and creativity, these models can be created using Alice.

An example to help visualize concepts that are too small to see physically in a classroom is an interactive Alice world for a lac operon model. Many middle school and high school biology textbooks classically use the lac operon as an example for gene regulation. Our world uses differently colored geometric shapes to represent enzymes and molecules inside the cell. Two sliders marked "Lactose" and "Glucose" allow students to experiment with the lactose and glucose levels independently and observe how that changes the interaction of molecules in the cell and ultimately affect the rate the lactase gene is transcribed.

4. MATH PROJECTS

We describe several interactive Alice projects for middle school math. Students use them to practice a math concept. We built tutorials for each of these to encourage students to build the worlds. Then students will be integrating mathematics while learning programming concepts.

4.1 Algebra/Function

Danica McKeller writes books for girls to better understand math concepts. She uses examples that girls can relate to. One of the ideas we took from her book [12] was her functions factory. She describes it as putting a food product into a factory and it comes out differently. She relates this to how one would plug in x into an algebraic expression and get a different answer.

We integrated this concept into a world. We used ice cream as the x value that goes into the factory or algebraic expression, and comes out the factory with a different ice cream flavor. In the world, the x value, coefficient, constant, and the wrong answer choices are generated randomly. Ten rounds are played. If all ten rounds are correct the reward is a life time supply of ice cream.

In building the world one can modify the number of questions the player must answer and the amount of questions they need to get correct. They can change the type of equation; instead of doing algebraic expressions they could do something simpler. Another change is to add negative numbers to the world. Changing x-value, coefficient, and constant to generate random numbers that can be negative will make the world more difficult and once they play they can get practice working with negative numbers. According to the NCSCS, this tutorial fulfills grade 8 learning object 5.01 which includes developing and understanding the concept of a function.

4.2 Energizer Exercises

Energizers for middle school address the high rise of obesity in America. More teachers are trying to implement exercise and learning at the same time. One of our teachers uses Math Middle-School Energizers [15] in her classes. At our workshop she was able to recreate one of the energizers in Alice and we recreated one as well that we describe here.

An operations computations Alice world teaches NCSCS grade 6 learning objective 1.04 and grade 7 1.02. Both include fluency in addition, subtraction, multiplication, and division of numbers. The student/teacher can choose which operation they want by clicking on the symbol. Then random numbers are generated and the problem is displayed. For 10 seconds you must complete the physical activity that corresponds with the operation. Then the player will be prompted to answer the question. For addition the physical activity associated with it is hitting the drums, subtraction is knee lifts, multiplication is twist, and division is running in place.

4.3 Plotting Points

We created a math world for plotting points based on an idea from a teacher. The player has to click and drag points onto the graph at the correct coordinate. There is one invisible object in the world, a pair of axes, which are aligned with the axes on the grid. To check what coordinates the points are at, they are compared to their relation to the axes. The program uses a formula to convert the units in Alice to units on the graph. The coordinates which the player is required to plot are stored as variables. This makes it very easy if a teacher wanted to change the points or make them random.

We created two additional worlds to expand on checking the coordinates of a point. The first world, shows the student how to plot a line. First, they are given an equation for the line in slope-intercept form. The teacher in the world gives a short explanation of how to use an equation to plot a point, and then asks what the y-intercept of the line should be. If they answer correctly, they must click on the first point and move it to the y-intercept and click ok. Then the teacher asks what the slope is and the player must type it in. The player then has to plot what the next point should be using the slope. If both points are plotted correctly, the line is drawn, which goes through the two points. The world can be modified to plot as many lines as the teacher chooses. They can also easily change the equations which are stored using variables. This automatically changes the equation that is displayed, what numbers must be typed in, and what points must be plotted. They can also change how much instruction is given for each equation. If fewer instructions are wanted, the teacher does not explain how slope intercept form works at the beginning, and instead of having to type in the numbers, the player is only required to plot the two points of each line.

Another example world we created teaches students how to use a scatter plot to predict future data. It starts out

Figure 2: Collecting Data for Bike Plot

Figure 3: Percentage Discounts

with a biker riding down the street. The player clicks on the clock four times during the ride to collect data as shown in Figure 2. Each time the clock is clicked, the time and the biker's current position are recorded and displayed on the screen. Then a graph is displayed, on which the player is required to plot each of the four points. Once all four of the points have been correctly plotted, the player has to use a best fit line to figure out how far the biker could travel in other amounts of time. In this problem, the student gets to see and interact with the bike ride as opposed to just reading the story problem in a textbook.

4.4 Percentages

The Alice world in Figure 3 teaches students how to apply percentage discounts to whole numbers. In this world, there are about eight toys either on a table, hanging on the wall, or under the table. One at a time each toy tells the player, what their original price is and what their percent discount is. The player must calculate the new price and enter it in when prompted to. Each toy's original price is random and the discount starts at 10% and increases with each new toy.

4.5 Distributive Property

A world on the distributive property allows students to practice expanding simple expressions and corresponds to Competency Goal 5: Objective 5.01 of the NCSCS for grade 6 mathematics. A factored expression in the form a(bx+c) is displayed, where a, b, and c are random integers ranging from -10 to 10 (although these specific minimum and maximum values can be easily changed). The student must determine whether another displayed expression is the correct expansion of a(bx+c); the correct answer is (a*b)x+(a*c). However, by changing the sign (positive or negative) of a*b and a*c, the student must also be careful with signs when multiplying numbers.

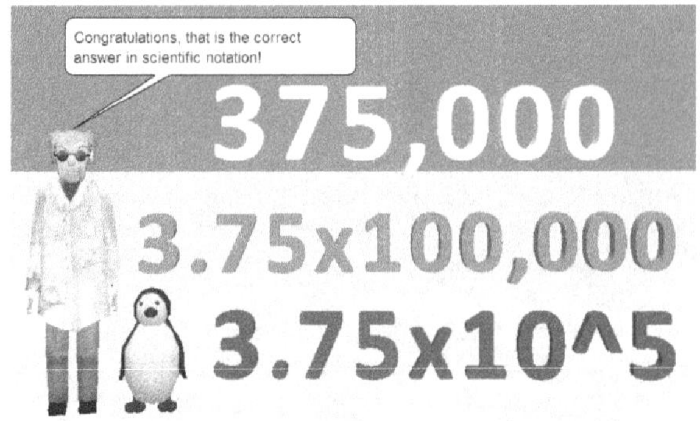

Figure 4: Scientific Notation

4.6 Reducing Fractions

This world helps students practice reducing fractions to lowest common terms. A fraction is displayed and the student must fully reduce this fraction; the fraction is guaranteed to always have a reduced form with a denominator not equal to 1 (final answer is not an integer). To input the answer, the student clicks the numerator or denominator of an adjacently displayed fraction to increment its value by 1 (for example, 1 becomes 2 when clicked, 8 becomes 9, and 9 becomes 1 again) and checks the answer when ready. The numerator and denominator are both single-digit random integers, but the range can be changed.

4.7 Scientific Notation

The world in Figure /refscinotation both explains and provides a chance to practice writing numbers in scientific notation. A mad scientist and penguin review the definition and format of scientific notation and demonstrate using an example. During the practice portion, the student is shown a number in standard form and is prompted to convert it to scientific notation, but can get a hint where the number is displayed in product form.

4.8 Multiplication Table

This world is an interactive (0-10)x(0-10) multiplication table in Alice. The world starts with an empty table and repeatedly asks multiplication problems. When a user enters a correct answer it is entered into the table. Every time a player plays the game, the questions are asked in a different random order. When a player gets the question right the first guess, the number turns green and red if it's wrong. The player is prompted for the answer until he gets it right, types "answer" to skip to see the answer, or "end" to end the game.

4.9 Balancing the Scales

This world tests a player's knowledge of inequalities. Two types of arithmetic expressions (addition, subtraction, multiplication, division, negative numbers, fractions, etc.) are placed onto the scale and asked for evaluation. The player

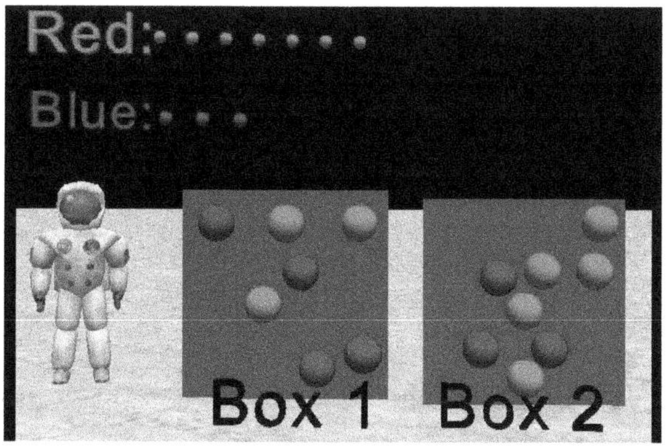

Figure 5: Random Sampling

has to decide if the first expression is greater than, less than or equal to the second expression.

4.10 Sampling

By using the classic red and blue marble approach, this world shown in Figure 5 demonstrates two important types of sampling introduced in a statistics class: simple random sampling and stratified random sampling. The player can choose which type of sampling he wants to see, and the red and blue balls are collected at the top of a screen in a sort of bar graph. Extensions for this in this exercises inquire about many of the associated probabilities.

4.11 Card Game Set

We created an Alice world on the classic SET game. There are 27 cards in the game, each with 3 attributes: color (red, green, or blue), number (1, 2, or 3) and shape (oval, squiggle, or rectangle). A SET is a collection of 3 of these cards such that all 3 cards are all the same or all different in each of the 3 categories. This game can be used as an early introduction to set theory, combinatorics, randomness, and probability.

4.12 Card Game War

We created an Alice world on the classic card game of War. Players 1 and 2 press the 1 and 2 buttons, respectively, to draw their card, and the player with the higher card wins both. If the two players draw cards of the same value, then there is a war. This game can be used for probability purposes in the classroom.

4.13 Choosing Randomly

An Alice world created to help teachers randomly choose students from a class. The students are displayed with girl and boy bodies with photos of their heads instead of the ones given in Alice. A player can either choose to sample a specified number of people all at once, or he can choose to sample them one at a time and pressing the "+1" button in corner to add another student to the sample. One can insert pictures of people they know for the students.

5. OTHER PROJECT WORLDS

We describe worlds helpful for other disciplines. For history, we created a sample world on the history of the Brooklyn Bridge. A student could use the tutorial of the world as a guideline to build a world on a different topic. Similarly for language arts we created a sample tutorial to show students how to create an interactive book report. For Spanish we created a sample world to to make banana bread. Instructions are given in Spanish to ask the user to put specific ingredients in a certain order into a mixing bowl. These items must be clicked and dragged into the bowl in that order.

Several of our tutorials are sample games. One is an adventure game in which the user has several items they need to find and cannot advance until they have found a specific item. One game to catch a ball in mitt shows how to build a score and integrate it in. One game is a boat racing against time that shows how to build a timer and to integrate it in.

6. MASTERY LEVEL OF TEACHERS

In the summer of 2011 we held a two-week Alice workshop attended by 26 K-12 teachers. The first part was Alice instruction and the second part was working with them to develop Alice worlds and Alice lesson plans. The teachers produced 32 different Alice example worlds and corresponding lesson plans. After the workshop their worlds were analyzed by examining the concepts they used in their worlds and examining their lesson plans for their planned usage of the world.

The teachers managed to pick up a significant number of Alice concepts. Of the 98 total basic Alice features determined by us, 69 different Alice features were used by the attendees in their worlds. These concepts include events, properties, methods, functions, programming logic, dummy objects and sound recording. On average, 20.78 features were used in each of the Alice worlds built, though advanced interactive worlds contain as many as 46 different Alice features and basic Alice worlds contain as few as 7 total concepts.

The worlds and corresponding lesson plans, were tallied based on academic subject area, the corresponding lesson type, and the number of Alice concepts used. The subject areas of the teachers were Business Technology, Computer Applications, English, ESL, Fine Art, Foreign Language, Math, Physical Education, Science, and Social Studies.

Here are the results. Of the 32 example worlds tallied, 12 Alice lesson plans state that their world will be an example for a future project or part of a technology course. 11 worlds created are for interactive games. These come with lesson plans that either express some interest in letting students build their own Alice worlds, or only plan to let students play one of the teachers Alice pre-built games. The final 9 Alice worlds built by the attendees use primarily animation elements and either come with a lesson plan that specifies using Alice only as an informative presentation, or includes a lesson plan that does not provide any coherent academic purpose.

Nearly one-third of the Alice worlds built by attendees were designed for technology and multimedia classes. Of the lesson plans counted, those from Business Technology and Computer Applications show the most interest in using Alice as a primary teaching tool. Despite this interest, however, those teacher's worlds use some of the fewest Alice features. In the Business Technology category, the average number of feature used per world was 16, whereas the average number of features used across the board was 20.78. Within the group of Business Technology teachers who plan on building Alice worlds, the average number of features used per world was 13.67. Amongst the Computer Applications teachers, the average number of features used per world was 17.

Among attendees from different subject areas, math teachers showed the greatest knack for using Alice programming features. Of the 10 Alice worlds built in the math subject area, the average number of features used per world was 25.8. This was the highest average amongst worlds from all the different subject areas. However, out of these 10 Alice worlds, only 1 includes a lesson plan that involves having students build their own Alice game. 6 out of 10 math worlds were advanced Alice games built for students to play. A close analysis of the coding from the interactive game math worlds show that many teachers who created worlds in math were able to use more programming concepts. In addition, math teachers were able to apply Alice features to a number of different math concepts. These concepts include using a number line, division, systems of equations, and finding number subsets.

Other teaching areas that showed interest in teaching Alice are language arts, ESL, foreign language, and science. Teachers from these subject areas are primarily interested in using Alice as a supplementary tool to generate interest in an existing course topic.

Overall, teachers who built interactive games used the highest total number of Alice Concepts per world. The average features used in this category is 29.33 out of the total average 20.78. Worlds that teach students to build their own Alice worlds averaged 20.81 features per world. The remaining 8 teachers who built presentation-only worlds show the least likelihood of continuing to use Alice extensively in the classroom except as a lecture tool.

7. CONCLUSIONS

Using feedback from teachers we have created over sixty Alice tutorials and projects to integrate computing into middle school. They are available on our web site [9]. Every attendee in our 2011 workshop created a functioning Alice world and lesson plan, with most creating a world advanced enough to successfully convey an academic topic relevant to their field of teaching. Teachers expressed positive feedback on continuing to use Alice in the coming school year. From our experience, the best way to integrate computing into middle school is through technology teachers, getting them to work with teachers in other disciplines. Involving math teachers with technology teachers would likely lead to a deeper experience in programming.

8. ADDITIONAL AUTHORS

Additional authors: Francine Wolfe (Benedictine College, Atchinson, KS, email: `wolf1267@ravens.benedictine.edu`) and Wenhui Zhang (Duke University, Durham, NC, email: `wenhui.zhang@duke.edu`).

9. REFERENCES

[1] ACM and CSTA. Running on empty: The failure to teach k-12 computer science in the digital age, 2010. www.acm.org/Runningonempty/.

[2] Alice. website, 2011. Retrieved September 1, 2011 from http://alice.org.

[3] Alice Symposium June 2009. website, 2009. Retrieved September 1, 2011 from http://www.cs.duke.edu/csed/aliceSymposium2009.

[4] College Board. CS principles, 2011. Retrieved September 1, 2011 from http://csprinciples.org.

[5] Computer Science Unplugged. website, 2011. Retrieved September 1, 2011 from http://csunplugged.org.

[6] S. Cooper, W. Dann, D. Lewis, P. Lawhead, S. Rodger, M. Schep, and R. Stalvey. A pre-college professional development program. In *The 16th Annual Conference on Innovation and Technology in Computer Science Education (ITiCSE 2011)*, pages 188–192, 2011.

[7] J. Cuny. Finding 10,000 teachers. In *CSTA Voice, 5, 6*, pages 1–2, Jan 2010.

[8] W. Dann, S. Cooper, and R. Pausch. *Learning to Program with Alice, Third Edition.* Pearson, Prentice Hall, 2011.

[9] Duke University Adventures in Alice Programming. website, 2011. Retrieved September 1, 2011 from http://www.cs.duke.edu/csed/alice/aliceInSchools.

[10] D. Frost, A. Verno, D. Burkhart, M. Hutton, and K. North. A model curriculum for k-12 computer science, level i objectives and outcomes, 2009. CSTA Curriculum Document.

[11] Greenfoot. website, 2011. Retrieved September 1, 2011 from http://greenfoot.org.

[12] D. McKellar. *Hot X: Algebra Exposed.* Hudson Street Press, 2010.

[13] B. Moskal, D. Lurie, and S. Cooper. Evaluating the effectiveness of a new instructional approach. In *Thirty-Fifth SIGCSE Technical Symposium on Computer Science Education*, pages 75–9, 2004.

[14] National Center for Women & IT. Ncwit scorecard 2011: A report on the status of women in information technology, 2011.

[15] North Carolina Department of Public Instruction. Math middle-school energizers - classroom-based physical activities, July 2006.

[16] North Carolina Standard Course of Study. website, 2011. Retrieved September 1, 2011 from http://www.ncpublicschools.org/curriculum.

[17] S. H. Rodger, M. Bashford, L. Dyck, J. Hayes, L. Liang, D. Nelson, and H. Qin. Enhancing k-12 education with alice programming adventures. In *The 15th Annual Conference on Innovation and Technology in Computer Science Education (ITiCSE 2010)*, pages 234–238, 2010.

[18] S. H. Rodger, J. Hayes, G. Lezin, H. Qin, D. Nelson, R. Tucker, M. Lopez, S. Cooper, W. Dann, and D. Slater. Engaging middle school teachers and students with Alice in a diverse set of subjects. In *Fourtieth SIGCSE Technical Symposium on Computer Science Education*, pages 271–275, 2009.

[19] Scratch. website, 2011. Retrieved September 1, 2011 from http://scratch.mit.edu.

[20] A. Tucker, F. Deek, J. Jones, D. McCowan, C. Stephenson, and A. Verno. A model curriculum for k-12 computer science: Final report of the acm k-12 task force curriculum, 2cd edition, 2006.

Children Learning Computer Science Concepts via Alice Game-Programming

Linda Werner
University of California
Santa Cruz, CA
linda@soe.ucsc.edu

Shannon Campe
ETR Associates
Scotts Valley, CA
shannonc@etr.org

Jill Denner
ETR Associates
Scotts Valley, CA
jilld@etr.org

ABSTRACT
Programming environments that incorporate drag-and-drop methods and many pre-defined objects and operations are being widely used in K-12 settings. But can middle school students learn complex computer science concepts by using these programming environments when computer science is not the focus of the course? In this paper, we describe a semester-long game-programming course where 325 middle school students used Alice. We report on our analysis of 231 final games where we measured the frequency of successful execution of programming constructs. Our results show that many games exhibit successful uses of high level computer science concepts such as student-created abstractions, concurrent execution, and event handlers.We discuss the implications of these results for designing effective game programming courses for young students.

Categories and Subject Descriptors
K.3.2 [Computers and Education]: Computer and Information Science Education – *Computer science education.* D.3.3 [Programming Languages]: Language Constructs and Features

General Terms
Experimentation, Languages, Measurement

Keywords
Assessment, Game-Programming, Middle School, Pair Programming, Alice

1. INTRODUCTION
Widely used initial programming environments like Alice and Scratch use drag-and-drop methods and provide many pre-defined objects and operations. Researchers and educators at the K-12 level are hopeful that these environments will teach computer science (CS) even when being used in other subject areas such as math, physics, biology, earth science, history, and language arts [12]. Since CS is not (yet) one of the K-12 core topics [4], using these programming environments in the core curriculum holds promise for introducing CS concepts to a broader and more diverse group of students. But there is little research on whether students as young as those in middle school will learn complex computer science concepts from using Alice when CS is not the focus of the course. In this paper, we describe a game-programming course called iGame that involved 325 middle school students using Alice across four semesters (in and after school). iGame was part of a study where we addressed many research questions including the following:

- What are the CS concepts that are accessible with Alice programming constructs?
- What are the Alice programming constructs that are used by middle school students making games without required game specifications?
- Which of these programming constructs are used successfully by middle school students?

To address these research questions, we reviewed a subset (approximately 20) of student-created games to identify the CS concepts that are accessible, and then analyzed all 231 games by counting the frequency of inclusion and successful execution of these programming constructs. In this paper, we first discuss prior related work, followed by a description of the iGame course including participant demographics, procedures of the study, and the game analysis process. Next, we list the results of the analysis of the games and discuss these results. The paper concludes with a discussion of future work.

2. PRIOR WORK
Studies of programming environments for K-12 audiences focus primarily on psychological and educational factors, with less attention to the software engineering perspective [11]. Two edited books from the late 1980s include research on how novices learn to program [13][10]. It has only been in recent years that we have seen studies of what students learn when using programming environments designed for youth such as Alice, Scratch, Kodu, Stagecast Creator, and Agent Sheets. We briefly describe some of the relevant findings from these studies.

Kelleher et al worked with Alice 2.0 and Storytelling Alice, a version of Alice developed to motivate young women to program. She reported that young women using Storytelling Alice and Alice were equally successful at learning basic programming constructs [6]. A large study of high school students in Taiwan found that Alice was more effective at teaching comprehension of fundamental programming concepts than C++[16]. Maloney et al [9] analyzed 536 Scratch projects created by youth aged 8-18 during an 18-month period at an after-school community center. Approximately 20% of the projects had no 'scripts,' meaning no programming. Of the remaining 425 projects, 88% exhibit scripts running in parallel, and more than 50% included user interaction and the use of looping constructs. Another study of Scratch use among 5th grade students found that the most common programming concepts included Boolean expression, conditions, and loops. Less frequent were variables and events [2]. Stolee and

Permission to make digital or hard copies of all or part of this work for personal or classroom use is granted without fee provided that copies are not made or distributed for profit or commercial advantage and that copies bear this notice and the full citation on the first page. To copy otherwise, or republish, to post on servers or to redistribute to lists, requires prior specific permission and/or a fee.
SIGCSE'12, February 29–March 3, 2012, Raleigh, North Carolina, USA.
Copyright 2012 ACM 978-1-4503-1098-7/12/02...$10.00.

Fristoe [14] analyzed 346 Kodu programs created by Xbox users and shared on the Xbox Live Community and reported on program constructs that represent understanding of CS concepts. The age range of these Kodu programmers' is unknown. Rodger et al [12] analyzed all Alice programs created by approximately 35 middle school students who attended one of a series of one-week summer camps. These researchers measured CS topics used in the programs. They also included a few programming patterns in their list of constructs: timer and score. Unfortunately, they reported no details about whether the constructs used in these programs, which mapped to specific CS topics, were on executable program paths (i.e., "reachable"). Werner et al [17] analyzed 23 Alice games created by middle school aged children enrolled in a summer camp. They reported on programming construct use representative of specific CS concepts including those exhibiting abstraction and various methods of program flow control necessary for algorithmic design. They reported high use of event handlers and parallelism but again did not report if these constructs were found in reachable code. Denner et al [5] analyzed 108 Stagecast Creator games created by primarily low income Latina middle school girls for evidence of characteristics in three categories: programming, organizing and documenting, and designing for usability. They report 82% of the programs exhibited conditional execution, 36% exhibited parallel execution, 41% had no unreachable code, but only 4% of the program used global variables. Koh et al [7] developed an automatic method to semantically analyze AgentSheets programs, another programming environment used in K-12, producing a 'computational thinking pattern graph' for each program. These graphs can be superimposed on one another to allow for visual comparison of the corresponding programs. They have used this method to analyze approximately 2500 student projects looking for patterns such as counting, generating, absorption, collision, etc, but there are no published reports of their analysis of this large set of programs.

The studies reviewed above provide some indication of the kinds of programming constructs and the CS concepts that are accessible with these types of programming environments. The current paper extends this prior work by looking not only at which programming constructs are used, but whether they are used successfully, and whether they were provided by the programming environment or created by the students.

Some of the prior studies of programming environments designed for youth focused on making games, while others used other types of projects. However, there is enough evidence to suggest that programming a game holds particular promise for engaging students in higher order thinking and comprehension [5][3][15]. Therefore, in the current study, we focus on programming games.

3. iGAME

3.1 Participants

The games described in this paper were collected over 2 years as part of a study of how game creation and pair programming can promote computational thinking in middle school students. A total of 325 students with parental consent voluntarily participated in study classes at seven public schools along the central California coast. Here we report on 231 games created individually or as part of a programming pair. In year 1, 90 students participated in after-school classes, and in year 2, 37 participated in after-school and 198 in elective, in-school technology classes.

Of the 325 students, 37% were female; they ranged in age from 10-14 years (mean=12), 45% were white, 37% were Latino/a, 73% spoke English or primarily English at home. Among the 274 for whom we had parent report, 27% had mothers with educational levels of high school or lower, and 38% of mothers had completed a university degree (since mothers are more likely to complete the consent forms, we rely on their educational levels).

3.2 Procedure

Two of the programming environments in the Alice series developed at Carnegie Mellon University were used in our study. In year 1, students used Storytelling Alice (SA), and in year 2 they used Alice 2.2 due to the limited use of PCs (which is necessary to run SA) at our partner schools. In the rest of this paper we will refer to both SA and Alice 2.2 as Alice unless it is necessary to distinguish between the two. Alice allows users to control characters in 3D environments using drag-and-drop programming and using a language that is closely related to Java and many other modern imperative programming languages. Most code is written in the methods of objects that have properties that store state and functions that return values. Each property, method, and function is attached to an object, with World being the global object. The event system in Alice is primarily used to handle user interactions, such as mouse clicks, although it can also handle in-World events, such as a change in a variable's value.

Classes were randomly assigned to a pair programming or solo programming condition. Pairs and individual students engaged with CS concepts in a three-stage acquisition progression called Use-Modify-Create [8] over approximately 20 hours during a semester. In the first half of the semester, pairs and individual students worked through a series of self-paced instructional exercises built to provide scaffolding, which we call "challenges." During the last half of the course, the students freely designed and developed their own games. Figure 1 shows the Alice programming environment and a student-created game titled "Wizard Duel" where wizards throw lightning bolts and fire balls at each other to acquire points to win. Most students completed 8 to 10 challenges, though some completed all 17. In our courses where pair programming was used, two students shared one computer to both work through the challenges and create their game, with one driving (controlling the mouse and keyboard) and the other navigating (checking for bugs, consulting resources, and providing input). Students were asked to reverse roles approximately every 20 minutes. In our courses where pair programming was not used, each student worked individually on the challenges and their game.

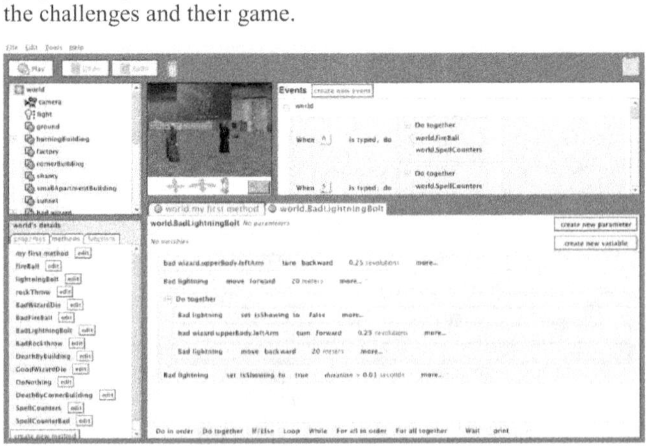

Figure 1: Student-created 'Wizard Duel' game.

3.3 Game analysis process

Five undergraduate CS students were trained to examine the 231 games (66 SA games and 165 Alice 2.2 games) and count programming constructs the middle school students used, and which use resulted in no failures. Our analysis is similar to that done by Rodger et al [12] of Alice programs, Maloney et al [9] of Scratch programs, and Stolee and Fristoe [14] of Kodu programs with one big difference: we look for **reachable** (i.e., on a path that is executable) instances of important programming constructs. Only one of the studies described in Section 2, the study by Denner et al [5] of 108 Stagecast Creator programs created by middle school students, looked at issues of reachability. They found 59% of the Stagecast programs contained unreachable code. From our experience teaching middle school students other programming environments, we found it common that students would include code that is never executed. For this study, if the Alice construct is reachable, then we determine whether execution of that construct causes abnormal program termination. All games were analyzed by at least two of the five undergraduate students and all discrepancies were discussed until unanimous agreement was reached, or the discrepancy was resolved by one of the authors. If we were only looking for the presence of these constructs and not reachability, this analysis could be automated. Due to determining whether the constructs in the abstraction and modeling category were created by the student/pair ('student-created') and testing if the instance of each reachable construct in each category did not cause abnormal program termination when executed ('no failure'), human observation was required.

4. RESULTS AND DISCUSSION

The important programming constructs in our analysis are divided into three categories: abstraction and modeling (see Table 1), control structures (see Table 2), and event handlers (see Table 3).

Table 1. Abstraction and Modeling constructs

Construct	# (%) student-created	# (%) reached	of # reached, #(%) no failure
Methods *student created only*	164 (71%)	138 (60%)	135 (98%)
Parameters *student created only*	1 (0.4%)	1 (0.4%)	1 (100%)
Functions	1 (0.4%)	106 (46%)	100 (94%)
Variables non-list	72 (31%)	62 (27%)	53 (86%)
Variables list	9 (4%)	5 (2%)	4 (80%)

Table 2. Control Structure constructs

Construct	# (%) reached	of # reached, #(%) no failure
If/else using variable or function in Boolean expression	67 (29%)	63 (94%)
If/else using true/false in Boolean expression	14 (6%)	8 (57%)
Nested if/else	17 (7%)	15 (88%)
Loop	32 (14%)	27 (84%)
While	38 (17%)	32 (84%)
Do in order	54 (23%)	50 (93%)
Do together	145 (63%)	136 (94%)
For all in order	2 (1%)	1 (50%)
For all together	4 (2%)	4 (100%)

Table 3. Event Handler constructs

Construct	# (%) reached	of # reached, #(%) no failure
Method other than 'my first method' at start	37 (16%)	32 (87%)
When a NUMBER is typed	28 (12%)	27 (96%)
When a LETTER is typed	101 (44%)	98 (97%)
When SPACE is typed	39 (17%)	39 (100%)
When ENTER is typed	13 (6%)	13 (100%)
When SINGLE ARROW is typed	34 (15%)	31 (91%)
When ANY KEY is typed	6 (3%)	2 (33%)
When the mouse is clicked on object	102 (44%)	99 (97%)
Let ARROW KEYS move object	100 (44%)	100 (100%)
Let MOUSE move list object	1 (0.4%)	1 (100%)
While something is true	10 (4%)	9 (90%)
When something becomes true	38 (17%)	36 (95%)
When a variable changes	2 (1%)	1 (50%)
Let the MOUSE orient the camera	0 (0%)	0 (0%)
Let the MOUSE move the camera	8 (4%)	8 (100%)

Tables 1, 2, and 3 list the programming constructs for each category, the number of games for which an instance of that programming construct was 'student-created', 'reached', and 'reached with no failure', and the percentages of the total number of programs for each of those conditions. For the abstraction and modeling constructs, we report data for all three categories ('student-created', 'reached, 'reached with no failure). For control structure and event handler constructs, we report data for only two categories, 'reached' and 'reached with no failure.' Only these two categories are important for control structures because students don't 'create' these constructs; they take existing instructions and program them to execute actions in their games. For event handler constructs, Alice provides handlers; students only have to select and use them correctly.

It is important to note that only instances of 'Methods' and 'Parameters' that were student-created (see Table 1) were counted. All students experimented with the set of built-in methods ('move', 'turn', 'resize', 'say', 'play sound', 'move to', etc.) and common parameters of these methods ('duration', 'style', etc.) that come standard in all gallery objects. We were interested in whether or not a game has a student-created method (at the global level or local to an object) and any student-created parameters. We found that the majority (71%) of games contained a student-created method; in 60% of the games a student-created method was reachable; and in 98% of the games where at least one student-created method was reachable, it executed without failure.

Only one Alice 2.2 game contained a student-created method with a parameter. With student-created parameters, very complex abstractions are possible. This topic was covered, with other topics, in the last challenge; it is not surprising there are limited examples of this construct in the games since many students did not work through a number of the latter challenges. The lack of exposure to latter challenges and limited practice to repeat use of the construct was also evident in the creation and use of functions. Students used built-in functions that were reachable in almost half of the games (46%). Of the games with a reachable built-in function, 94% of them executed without failing. Only one student created their own function using Alice 2.2 but it was not used on an executable program path. Figure 2 shows program code from a student game containing the most commonly found use of a built-in function - to implement collision detection in Alice. There was a large difference in the percentage of games containing the use of functions between SA (used in year 1) and Alice 2.2 (used in year 2). 33% of the SA games used functions but 51% of the Alice 2.2 games used functions. The reason for this difference may be due to the addition of a required challenge that taught the proximity function into the year 2 curriculum. Figure 3 shows another example of the use of the proximity function (to execute a method containing multiple instructions).

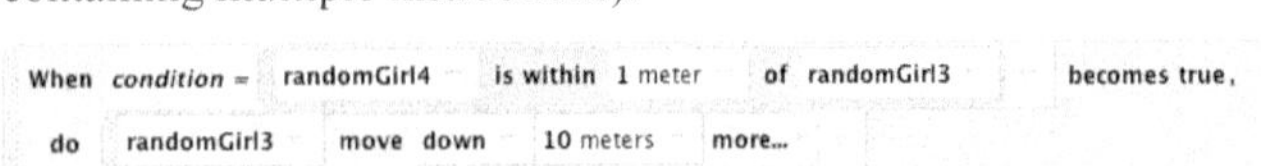

Figure 2: An event handler with a built-in proximity function.

Students often created their own non-list variables (32% of the games had at least one instance) and 27% of the games used either their own or built-in non-list variables in reachable code. Non-list variables were used without failure in 85% of those games in which they were found in reachable code. Students often used non-list variables to implement patterns such as counters and timers in their games. This is another area where there was a large difference between games created using Alice 2.2 and SA due to making a formerly optional challenge a required one in year 2: 32% of the Alice 2.2 games (year 2) contained one or more uses of non-list variables; only 15% of the SA games (year 1) contained one or more uses of non-list variables. Only a few games contained successfully-used student-created or built-in variable lists. More often, students repeated code segments for each individual object rather than building a list of objects and using the special list processing constructs of 'For all together' or 'For all in order'.

Students frequently used If/Else conditional statements using variables or functions in the Boolean expression (29% of the games with at least one of these statements in reachable code, 94% of those successfully used). The If/Else conditional statements using true or false in the Boolean expression were not frequently used. If an instance of this was found in a student's program and there were no instructions to execute in the body of the If/Else statement, it was counted as an unsuccessful use. 43% of the uses of this construct were unsuccessful. Our hypothesis is that the student tried to use this construct, couldn't figure it out or changed their mind around its use, but didn't remove it from their program because the presence of this construct did not affect execution.

More uses of looping constructs were found in year 2 Alice 2.2 games (17% for the loop construct, 21% for the while construct) than in year 1 SA games (6% for the loop construct, 6% for the while construct). This is likely a result of students programming more 'timers' in their games which typically include the use of a while loop and a non-list variable. This difference could have been due to moving the challenge that taught timers to earlier in the curriculum for year 2.

At least one instance of the 'Do together' parallel computing construct was found in most games: 63% of the games had at least one reachable instance and 94% of those games have a use that is successful. This is suggestive of the ease of use of the parallel programming construct, 'Do together'. Students appear to understand its use and want to use it to produce desired game effects. Less commonly used was the 'Do in order' sequential processing construct. Sequential instruction execution is the default mode of execution. The 'Do in order' construct is required in those instances when only one instruction is allowed, such as an instruction in the body of an If/Else instruction or an instruction in an event handler. Students could create a method and place a call to the new method in those instances.

Most of the students used some kind of event handler in their games with successful execution (85%). The most commonly used events were "when a letter is typed" (present in 44% of the games, 97% of the games where it is present execute the construct instance without failure), "when a mouse is clicked on an object" (44%, 97%) and "let arrow keys move object" (44%, 100%). Figure 3 shows the student game "Bunny Run," with the use of a 'while something is true' event. In this example, the student wants the game to be over when any of the hawks fly close to the rabbit. We did not see many uses of this type of event handler; only nine games used this successfully. This is an example of a very engaging game, that does not include the use of explicit conditional statements (ie., If/Else) or variables of which we may expect to see in games. Some of the games (16%) also contained code that calls a different method when their game starts (method other than 'My first method' when program starts). None of our instructional materials demonstrate these ideas. These uses may be representative of how some students are intrepid users of computer technology and discover new and interesting ways to control their games in different ways.

One result that holds for almost all Alice programming constructs: if a student used a programming construct, it was generally used correctly. This result is important because "it will save other researchers ... from doing this type of laborious analysis when automated analysis could suffice.[1]"

Rodger et al [12] reported that 100% of their students used built-in methods in their programs but not quite 50% of their students created methods. Our numbers reflect a higher percentage of student-created method use. Rodger's summer camps were only one week long which may have contributed to the differences found in students creating methods. However, this can't account

[1] These quoted words are thanks to an anonymous reviewer.

for the differences in student-created function use or list variable use. Approximately 60% of their students used built-in functions and almost 15% of their students created their own functions. Forty-five percent of their students created lists and 40% used instructions for list processing. These topics were covered in Rodger's summer camps. Our students did not create and use their own functions and did not create and use list variables. Perhaps these differences are because these two topics were covered in latter challenges that most students did not complete. Further study needs to be done to confirm this hypothesis. We are in the process of determining the number of challenges completed by each student so we can know whether the number and specific constructs within the challenges affects the programming constructs a student used in their game.

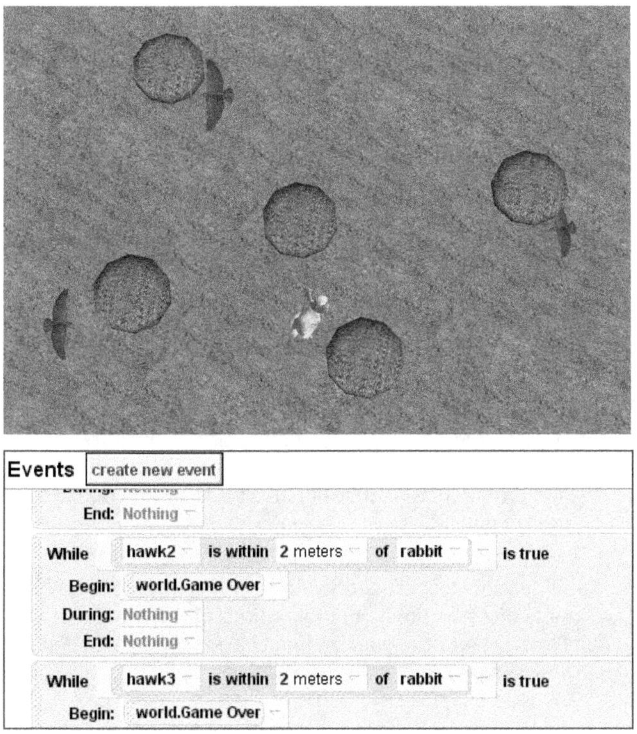

Figure 3. 'Bunny Run' student game with 'while something is true' event.

5. CONCLUSIONS AND FUTURE WORK

Elective technology computer game design courses for middle school students are a promising strategy to introduce CS concepts to a broad population. The findings show that students demonstrated an understanding of a range of computer science concepts that include abstraction and modeling, control structures, and event handlers, while using Alice to make games. The most common constructs were methods, functions, and events. Surprisingly, there were few differences between the use and successful use of constructs, suggesting that if something was in the program, it was generally used correctly.

Based on prior research [13], we expected that making games in Alice would engage students in key features of programming, such as extensive control structures for sequential, conditional, and parallel execution; both global and local variables; abstractions via the use of methods and functions; and event handling for mouse clicks and key input. And indeed, many of the games incorporated elements that represent these complex programming concepts. Almost one-third of the programs used variables, almost one half used functions, but only one of these programs contained a student-created function. Creating functions and using them, as well as creating methods with parameters, are complex concepts that were included in challenges along with the instructions for using other programming constructs. The findings suggest that some of the examples or the specific focus we placed on certain constructs in some of the challenges were not clear to the students, or did not help them program their game ideas. We are in the process of analyzing the game mechanics students chose. Even if not fully operational, those choices will help us learn more about what to include in the curriculum and how to teach this age group

Our results build on prior studies that show middle school students are able to use programming constructs that exhibit complex CS concepts such as abstraction, but struggle with variable initialization, looping, conditionals, pointers, and recursion. This study extends prior research on the use of programming concepts in computer game design courses because we analyzed the creation, use in reachable code, and execution without failure, of programming constructs. Almost all of the prior research focused on syntactic analysis but not on whether the programming constructs were executable, or executable without failure. Future studies that compare students working with different programming environments are needed to determine whether some types of programming constructs are used more frequently because they are the easiest to learn in Alice, because they satisfied conditions for a 'good game' (user input, clear instructions, engaging narrative), or because they were used more frequently in the sample games and challenges.

The simple counts of programming constructs reported in this paper is only a first step in our research on what students are learning while programming a game in Alice. Our broader focus is on the definition and assessment of computational thinking in middle school, in which the use and understanding of programming constructs is one small part [1]. To this end, we are also looking at the students' games for evidence of programming patterns (i.e., combinations of programming constructs) and game mechanics. We have identified a number of non-contiguous sequences of programming constructs that when present in an Alice program indicate a higher abstraction, similar to the work by Koh et al [7]. A few examples of these Alice patterns are counters, timers, and collision detection. We have also identified a number of game mechanics in the students' games such as navigation, collection, and timed challenge. It is possible that the mechanic might inform what students learn for their games and, therefore, determines how computationally "complex" (i.e., constructs/patterns used) the game is. The ideas a student has for their 'dream' game are very motivational for a student's learning. If we can determine what students want to design, then we can identify programming constructs necessary to implement the game mechanics and patterns for those 'dream' games. This process should drive curriculum development.

6. ACKNOWLEDGMENTS

Our thanks go to the teachers and administrators at our seven schools, specifically Anne Guerrero, Shelly Laschkewitsch, Don Jacobs, Sue Seibolt, Karen Snedeker, Susan Rivas, and Katie Ziparo. Thanks also to teaching assistants, Will Park and Joanne Sanchez; and to Eloy Ortiz and Pat Rex, whose vital support was necessary to run this program. Thanks to all of the students who participated. Finally, thanks to our undergraduate researchers Dominic Arcamone, Melanie Dickinson, Steven Butkus, Anthony Lim, and Kimberly Shannon who analyzed the students' games.

This research is partially funded by a grant from NSF 0909733 "The Development of Computational Thinking among Middle School Students Creating Computer Games." Any opinions, findings, conclusions or recommendations expressed in this material are those of the authors and do not necessarily reflect the views of the National Science Foundation.

7. REFERENCES

[1] Barr, V. and Stephenson, C., 2011. Bringing computational thinking to K-12: what is Involved and what is the role of the computer science education community? ACM Inroads 2(1), 48-54.

[2] Baytak, A. & Land, S.M., 2011. Advancing elementary-school girls' programming through game design. International Journal of Gender, Science, and Technology, 3(1).

[3] Carbonero, M., Szafron, D., Cutumisu, M., & Schaeffer, J., 2010. Computer-game construction A gender-neutral attractor to computing science. Computesr & Education, 55, 1098-1111.

[4] Cooper, S., Pérez, L.C.and Rainey, D., 2010. K--12 computational learning. Communications of the ACM, 53(11), 27-29.

[5] Denner, J., Werner, L. and Ortiz, E., 2012. Computer games created by middle school girls: Can they be used to measure understanding of computer science concepts? Computers & Education, 58(1), 240-249.

[6] Kelleher, C., Pausch, R. and Kiesler, S., 2007. Storytelling Alice motivates middle school girls to learn computer programming. In Proceedings of the SIGCHI conference on Human factors in computing systems. ACM, New York, NY, USA, 1455-1464.

[7] Koh, K.H., Basawapatna, A., Bennett, V., Repenning, A., 2010. Towards the automatic recognition of computational thinking for adaptive visual language learning. IEEE Symposium on Visual Languages and Human Centric Computing, pp. 59-66.

[8] Lee, L., Martin, F., Denner, J., Coulter, B., Allan, W., Erickson, J., Malyn-Smith, J., and Werner, L., 2011. Computational thinking for youth in practice. ACM Inroads 2(1), 32-37.

[9] Maloney, J.H., Peppler, K., Kafai, Y., Resnick, M. and Rusk, N., 2008. Programming by choice: urban youth learning programming with Scratch. In Proceedings of the 39th SIGCSE technical symposium on Computer science education. ACM, New York, NY, USA, 367-371.

[10] Mayer, R.E., 1988. Teaching and learning computer programming: Multiple research perspectives. Psychology Press.

[11] Robins, A., Rountree, J., & Rountree, N., 2003. Learning and teaching programming: A review. Computer Science Education, 13(2), 137-172.

[12] Rodger, S., Hayes, J., Lezin, G., Qin, H., Nelson, D., Tucker, R., Lopez, M., Cooper, S., Dann, W. and Slater, D., 2009. Engaging middle school teachers and students with Alice in a diverse set of subjects. In Proceedings of the 40th ACM technical symposium on Computer science education. ACM, New York, NY, USA, 271-275.

[13] Soloway, E. and Spohrer, J., 1989. Studying the Novice Programmer. Mahwah, NJ: Erlbaum.

[14] Stolee, K. and Fristoe, T., 2011. Expressing computer science concepts through Kodu game lab. In Proceedings of the 42nd ACM technical symposium on Computer science education. ACM, New York, NY, USA, 99-104.

[15] Vos, N., van der Meijden, H., & Denessen, E., 2011. Effects of constructing versus playing an educational game on student motivation and deep learning strategy use. Computers & Education, 56(1), 127-137.

[16] Wang, T., Mei, W., Lin, S., Chiu, S., & Lin, J., 2009. Teaching programming concepts to high school students with Alice. 39th ASEE/IEEE Frontiers in Education Conference, San Antonio, TX.

[17] Werner, L., Denner, J., Bliesner, M.and Rex, P., 2009. Can middle-schoolers use Storytelling Alice to make games?: results of a pilot study. In Proceedings of the 4th International Conference on Foundations of Digital Games. ACM, New York, NY, USA, 207-214.

The Writers' Workshop for Youth Programmers

Digital Storytelling with Scratch in Middle School Classrooms

Quinn Burke
University of Pennsylvania
Graduate School of Education
Philadelphia, PA
215-990-8879
burkew@dolphin.upenn.edu

Yasmin B. Kafai
University of Pennsylvania
Graduate School of Education
Philadelphia, PA
215-746-3468
kafai@gse.upenn.edu

ABSTRACT

This study investigates the potential to introduce basic programming concepts to middle school children within the context of a classroom writing-workshop. In this paper we describe how students drafted, revised, and published their own digital stories using the introductory programming language Scratch and in the process learned fundamental CS concepts as well as the wider connection between programming and writing as interrelated processes of composition.

Categories and Subject Descriptors

K.3.2 [**Computing & Information Science Education**]: Computer Science and Education, Curriculum, Literacy

General Terms: Design, Human Factors, Languages

Keywords: Computer Science education, Scratch, programming, digital storytelling

1. INTRODUCTION & RATIONALE

With the current efforts to broaden participation in computing and introduce computational literacy on the K-12 level [19], there is a need for educational approaches and models that connect to existing curricular practices. According to the recent report from the Association of Computing Machinery, *Running On Empty* [24], less than two-thirds of K-12 schools in the country offer any form of standardized CS-based curricula. While organizations like the ACM and Computer Science Teachers Association (CSTA) continue to push for such standards on the state level, this study takes an alternative route to getting CS more immediately into the classroom. Building upon previous research teaching programming in terms of storytelling [3; 15], this paper introduces the writers' workshop model [4] as a means to facilitate a particular *process* by which youth can learn programming during the school-day and within core-curricula subject matter.

The widespread growth of the writing workshop on the K-12 level can be traced to the seminal publication of Calkins' [4] *The Art of Teaching Writing*. Promoting a communal setting over solitary endeavor and stressing writing as a perpetual process and not

Simply the finished product, the writing workshop opened composition as a form of personal expression available to all children. Such a shift was nothing less than a sea-change on the K-12 level, as over the vast majority of the 20th century, writing was a discipline in which the finished product garnered far more attention than the process by which it was created [21]. Yet as Calkins' own mentor Donald Murray cautioned educators about the craft: "Writing might be magical—but it's not magic. It's a process, a rational series of decisions and steps that every writer makes and takes, no matter what the length, the deadline, even the genre…" [10]. Writing does not simply magically appear nor is it an elite skill limited to a select few based on gene-pools. It is a learned process that can always be further honed and developed through personal reflection, endeavor, and shared experience.

Much like writing three decades ago, computer programming still faces this myth of the "magical". Studies [14; 18] suggest, one of the primary reasons for the declining enrollment and lack of diversity within CS as a major is based upon this perception that the field is meant for only a select few who happen to be inherently skilled at it. As DiSalvo and Bruckman [8] point out about their recent efforts to broaden and diversify student interest in the field, "computer science itself is not that difficult—but wanting to learn it is" (p. 27). Efforts to demystify programming through activities like game design [7] and storytelling [15] have been successful in introducing children to CS at earlier ages. However, because these approaches' main emphasis have been centered upon the learning of programming (with game design and storytelling playing only a secondary, "prop" role), they have been relegated to afterschool or summer club activities in which children self-select to participate (often based upon a pre-existing interest in learning computer science). Meanwhile within the classroom, the overwhelming majority of K-12 student continue to remain only vaguely aware of programming as a utilitarian tool, while educators remain wary of attempting to introduce yet another subject into curricula already stretched tight by high-stakes test prep and accountability measures.

Here we propose a different approach that leverages some of the previous successes we have had using storytelling to teach programming [3] but now brings to bear particular alignment to state standards in language arts instruction. Our study takes place in the context of a school-day classroom using the structure of a writing workshop as a means to (a) facilitate a deliberate process by which children can learn computer programming, and (b) leverage the professional knowledge of K-12 educators in traditional English/ language arts classrooms to better integrate programming into core-content classroom activities. With a class middle school students, we conducted a two-month long writing workshop that focused on generating one's own digital stories using the programming language Scratch. Our focus was two-fold: first, to what extent can the existing English/ language arts frameworks be used to tie the composition process to digital storytelling in Scratch? And second, how do the Scratch designs incorporate both narrative and programming elements and to what extent do students can students appreciate such overlap?

Permission to make digital or hard copies of all or part of this work for personal or classroom use is granted without fee provided that copies are not made or distributed for profit or commercial advantage and that copies bear this notice and the full citation on the first page. To copy otherwise, or republish, to post on servers or to redistribute to lists, requires prior specific permission and/or a fee.
SIGCSE'12, February 29–March 3, 2012, Raleigh, North Carolina, USA.
Copyright 2012 ACM 978-1-4503-1098-7/12/02...$10.00.

2. BACKGROUND

The pedagogical underpinnings of the writers workshop draw on extensive research from community of practice [16] and communities of learners [2] in which individuals develop their composition skills based on three crucial elements: (1) authentic practice; (2) finished product, and (3) collaborative support. In his review of literature focusing on the connection between learning programming and general problem solving skills, Palumbo [20] likewise stresses the need for K-12 programming instruction to be developed through a series of stages, in which the task is meaningful to participants, and feedback is mutual and continuous. While early introductory programming languages such as Logo had success in entering school classrooms in the early 1980s, such success was short-lived in part due to a lack of authentic practices and products which tied such learning to wider problem solving skills.

2.1 Authentic practice

In "Thick Authenticity: New Media and Authentic Learning", Shaffer and Resnick [23] posit that digital media has the opportunity to create learning environments for children that are at once (1) personal, (2) real world, (3) disciplinary, and (4) assessable. However, too often instruction using computers and digital media is simply "teaching computers" as opposed to teaching through the computer. Consequently while children may have in-depth knowledge of a wide range of digital media applications, there may be a severe lack in understanding how such media relate to each other and to oneself for personal expression. Likewise, in terms of writing, learning parts of speech and the structure of sentences without any designated purpose beyond grammar acquisition fails to produce effective writers [17]. The writing workshop provides an alternative environment to learning composition, in which narratives are generated not based upon knowledge acquisition but upon personal reflection and individual expression.

2.2 Finished product

Learning through-design ties back to project-based learning which itself is based upon the Constructionist model in which students simultaneously learn new information and design a product which reflects such learning [11; 12]. Previous studies exploring storytelling and programming through the constructionist model [15; 26] focus on using stories as a means to make coding more accessible and palpable to children. However in both cases, the value of storytelling as the finished product was only considered in terms of its ability to interest children in programming, and there was little consideration how the story genre offered a viable link between the discipline of programming and the discipline of writing. While code is certainly a valuable skill, using digital storytelling simply as a way to draw kids into programming neglects to take into account the full and rich ways such storytelling can also be used to develop children's sense of narrative structure. As Sandy Hayes points out, "Students don't have to produce standardized writing to meet writing standards" [10]. Programming-as-storytelling in the setting of a writing workshop represents one such potential "unstandardized" format that deserves further exploration in schools.

2.3 Collaborative support

Black's research [1] on teens' fan fiction writing suggests that when youth can find an environment where writing acts as a social outlet, a collaborative process, and a means for personal expression, their output can be both prodigious and notable in both style and content. Writing—a process which K-12 schools still regularly struggle to make creative, personal, and collaborative—took on a far more interactive nature in a forum outside of the classroom. Our study here builds directly on Black's research, examining the various multi-media projects children share and comment upon on another file-sharing website, http://www.scratch.mit.edu. While not traditional pen-and-paper compositions, the programming projects children write and share using the Scratch website are very much digital "texts" incorporating words, images, and sounds to produce a wide variety of stories, games, and animations. Students not only have the opportunity to share their digital stories with each in the workshop but within the wider Scratch community, which currently has over 800,000 registered members and nearly 2 million uploaded projects.

In terms of combining authentic practice and collaborative support with a constructionist learning model, we find that a number of other recent efforts such as Glitch testers [8] and Scratch-based Collaboration Challenges [13] use these same principles in setting up successful educational projects. Yet what we are proposing with the writing workshop for programmers is a K-12 pedagogical model that has potential to introduce coding in core academic subject matters, align with state standards.

3. The Writers-Workshop for Middle School

Participants

For seven weeks in the Fall of 2010, we set up 11 writing workshop sessions in an elective course using Scratch at an urban public middle school located in West Philadelphia. Ten students—all boys, ages twelve to fourteen—participated in the writing workshops and were representative of the schools' diverse population of African-American, Caucasian, and Latino children. In total, we collected eleven projects (one participant created two stories) by the end of the program.

Choice Elective & Alignment with State Academic Standards

Over the course of the seven weeks, every Choice session would open with a brief "mini-lesson" [5] emphasizing a particular element of effective composition (such as characterization, foreshadowing, setting a scene) which would likewise be tied to learning a particular coding procedure in Scratch (e.g., using the broadcast feature to establish dialogue, importing external images, using loops to standardize behavior). Every mini-lesson was supported by anywhere from one to three sample digital stories selected from the Scratch website, which exemplified a particular storytelling element or genre of storytelling (e.g., mystery, action/ adventure) featured within the lesson. This not only grounded the lessons in practical application but offered an excellent segue to examining the actual coding scripts of the projects, exploring exactly how the sample story creators achieved a particular effect with the Scratch programming language. All lesson plans were aligned to Pennsylvania state standards Reading, Writing, Listening, and Speaking on the 8th grade level and supported by the school's junior-high literacy instructor Mrs. Steinberg, who offered feedback rubrics and pre-writing activities from her own classes which were based on her use of Calkins' [5]text.

	Subject:	Grade(s)	Course
	Content Area: ELA	5th – 7th	Scratch *Choice*

TU. 11/9

Standards: 1.9.7.A; 1.9.7.B;

Obj: *The objective for the initial session is for kids to (a) get acquainted with the basic features of Scratch & (b) start generating ideas for their own stories*

Materials: Laptops w/ Scratch

Pre-Class Activity: Kids should enter the club &begin getting out to laptops, accessing the software

Lesson: After introducing yourselves & your backgrounds, focus on initially

- Introducing the 3 panels of Scratch & getting a sample sprite to move & speak
- Ensuring the kids have Scratch as a download on their laptops
- Briefly discuss creating stories w/ Scratch & demo 2 sample projects
  - My Scratch Story (traditional) http://scratch.mit.edu/projects/idigcows/123644
  - Harry Potter & the Monster Under the Bed (much more intricate) http://scratch.mit.edu/projects/mizzy42/11516

Activities: start playing with Scratch

Writing Activity:

Closure: Review the basic 3 panels over the final 5 mins. & introduce the Scratch website (http://scratch.mit.edu) for those who are able/ would like to work from home

Assessment: No formal assessment but take note—are kids paying attention? Engaged?

Assignment: Start thinking about your own story ideas—come in with 2 ideas for next week!

Figure 1: Lesson from the outset of the workshop, created within the template recommended by the Philadelphia School District and aligned to PA academic standards

The workshop followed five stages over the seven weeks, which, while distinct, did have some overlap from week to week depending on individual student progress:

- **Pre-writing/ Planning *(Weeks 1-2)*:** Every participant generated 3-4 "seed ideas" [5] and entered these into their Writer's Notebook, which they then reviewed with us for feedback.
- **Drafting *(Weeks 2-3)*:** Once students had discussed their seed ideas with us, they proceeded to sketch out their ideas using storyboards. Using a pencil, kids drew out their individual shots with the knowledge that these screen-by-screen renderings would act as a "roadmap" for their compositions.
- **Revising *(Weeks 3-6)*:** Once their Storyboards had officially been approved (sessions 3 & 4), the middle-schoolers began to compose their actual digital stories. All participants utilized both a "bottom up" and "top-down" approach to composing their stories, in which the former refers to creating anew in Scratch, while the latter involved sampling others' projects and repurposing the code for their own projects. The majority of participants leaned more to "bottom up" composition, particularly over weeks 3-4 of the *Choice* class.
- **Editing *(Week 6)*:** The briefest stage of the 5, students made final revisions based on comments they had received online as well as during weeks 6-7 of class. Many of the edits were simply "fine-tuning" in terms of correcting spelling and grammar in characters' dialogue or trouble-shooting the programmed behavior of a coded sprite.
- **Publishing *(Weeks 6-7)*:** All students posted to the Scratch website again over the final two weeks of the workshop; over the final day, students presented their final projects to their classmates in terms of plot and characterization as well as in terms of the underlying code operating their digital stories.

4. DATA ANALYSIS

During the workshop, we collected a variety of data sources:

CS attitudes pre/post surveys: Adapted from a Georgia Tech's computer science attitudes survey developed by Lijun Ni and Mark Guzdial (http://coweb.cc.gatech.edu/ mediaComp-teach/16), pre-and post-surveys were given to all participants in the study gauging their familiarity and attitudes to digital media, their sense of their own storytelling and computer capabilities, and their own attitudes toward working collaboratively and creatively.

Field Note Observations: Collected daily and transcribed within a twenty-four period, they were subsequently coded thematically capturing particular usage trends across the workshop.

Video Footage: All sessions were videotaped in their entirety with select sections transcribed for the sake of better capturing a moment-by-moment understanding of how students use the software in the workshop. All post-session interviews with students were video-taped and transcribed.

Scratch Project (artifact) analysis: All Scratch projects were periodically collected over the duration of the program (a minimum of three times per project) and subsequently examined in terms of their staged storylines and underlying coding scripts. All projects were also analyzed in regard to their programming blocks using *Scrape* technology, a tool developed by RiverSound Media (http://happyanalyzing.com).

Post-Interviews: At the program's end, all students participated in 5-10 minute interviews gauging their experience in the classroom. As with the field note observations, these interviews were subsequently coded thematically.

5. FINDINGS

Over the course of the workshop, students learned both the fundamentals of programming and storytelling, and this is charted here in terms of the products (digital stories) they programmed, the processes (debugging and revising) they utilized, and their overall perceptions of the workshop at its close.

5.1 Product

In terms of product, 9 out of the 10 participants generated a complete digital story, entailing multiple characters, settings, and plot stages. Each finished project also entailed a number of key coding concepts not simply characteristic of Scratch but of all programming languages—from Java to C++ —clearly indicating that over the workshop's eleven sessions the middle school students not only composed their own digital stories in the software but also learned and applied some key fundamentals programming concepts in the process.

The chart that follows highlights some of the programming concepts students used in the creation of their stories as well as the frequency of use:

Table 1: Types & frequency of programming concepts utilized

Programming Concept	% of Projects Utilizing the Concept	Frequency per Project
Coordination & Synchronization	100%	8.8
Threads (Parallel Execution)	100%	1.6
Loops	90%	2.5
Event-Handling	100%	1.5 inputs per project
Boolean Logic	20%	1.6
Conditional Statements	30%	1.7
Variables	10%	.3

One such story was Darryl's crayfish tale (below) which was based on a real-life experience in which he won a salt-water crayfish at school but ended up killing the poor animal with tap water.

Figure 2: Darryl's whimsical project "Crayfish" depicting the creature's untimely end

Though Daryl's digital story is brief (approximately a minute-and-half long), it took over ten hours to program and the coding scripts he utilized were very much characteristic of those of his peers in the classroom. Like the wider class, Daryl relied heavily on the use of costume changes and dialogue between characters to propel his story forward. Also like his peers, Daryl's project made use of a single input key (in his case, the green "go" flag in the upper right-hand corner), which once clicked, set the story in motion to its conclusion. Unlike a number of his classmates, Daryl's project demonstrated more intricate programming through his use of the "broadcast" command which allowed for his story's programmed objects to trigger the behavior of other objects, precluding the need of timed intervals to coordinate events.

5.2 Process

These commonalities among projects in terms of code are not unsurprising given that all students followed the same process in the classroom, learning code through storytelling. All ten participants had a strong sense of the stages of writing. This was the expectation—having met with Mrs. Steinberg the month prior to the workshop, she assured me the students went through these stages of composition whether they were composing a poem, a graphic novel, or an expository essay. However, even more than their familiarity with the stages of writing, the middle-school students' familiarity with the elements of writing—particularly the elements of creative fiction—offered a particularly useful scaffold as means to introduce the basic elements of Scratch over the first two weeks of the workshop. Couching the use of Scratch in terms of common language arts concepts such as rising action and static versus dynamic characterization proved remarkably effective in acquainting (or in some cases, reacquainting) the students to the Scratch programming language. Simply being able to describe basic elements of programming in writing terminology eased participants' unfamiliarity with the coding process.

Table 3: Addressing the CS language "barrier" through analogous terminology

Writing Term	Programming Term
Protagonist/ Antagonist	"sprites"
Drafting	"design"
Revising	"debugging"
Character Motivation	coding "parameters"

"Oh yeah, I understand 'round' versus 'flat' characters," Marcus remarked with some surprise when I explained during session #3 how flat "stock" characters' programmed behavior could be "looped" while the protagonist's more dynamic (and thus "round") behavior would be far less repetitive. Accordingly, children learned to program Scratch sprites based on a particular character's motivations. In this sense, literary elements such characterization and setting served not only as a means to introduce programming terminology, but also acted as the vehicle through which children learned how to program. In the case of 8th grader Marcus' fantasy basketball game, protagonist and NBA star Tim Hardaway had a diverse, linear-based coding sequence, timed out in intervals. Meanwhile antagonist Lebron James's coded sprite (below) had limited programmed behavior that was far less varied and entirely looped, typical of characterization that is both flat and static in nature.

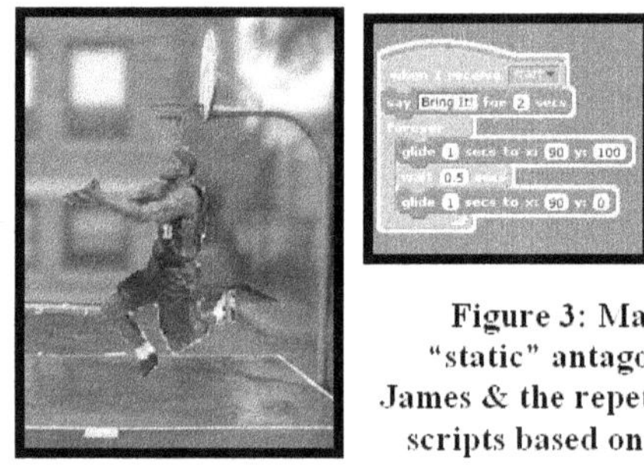

Figure 3: Marcus's "static" antagonist Lebron James & the repetitive coding scripts based on his motivation

5.2.1 Brainstorming & Outlining

As indicated in the planning guide and sample lesson above, students began to map out their digital stories in Scratch over sessions #3 and 4 of the workshop. Generally, students relied on three different sources to generate ideas for their potential digital stories (none of which were mutually exclusive):

- **writer's notebook**: distributed by Mrs. Steinberg to every 7th and 8th grader, the black-and-white speckled pad is the mandated starting point for any composition in her classes. Intended as a place to simply write down ideas, students need to generate at least three potential ideas before they opt for any single one—a requirement which was maintained for the workshop as well.
- **Sprite cache:** an assortment of various character images, ranging from people to animals to alphabet letters are stored within the Scratch software; users can click upon these stocked folders to import various sprites into a project.
- **popular culture:** while the term "popular culture" encompasses an innumerable array of source-material, here it refers to those images that students searched out over the Internet, saved to their laptops, and imported into Scratch as image files (JPEGs typically); learning this process over session #3, many students grew very excited as it allowed them to utilize figures from their own favorite stories and games as their lead characters.

While students eagerly imported and tinkered with various Sprites from both the web and Scratch caches over the first two weeks, getting them to commit to a set narrative via the storyboards proved to be a real challenge, though this challenge was not necessarily an unexpected one. Previous studies utilizing storyboards for Scratch-based narratives [3; 6] likewise found some measure of children's resistance to using storyboards, partially due to an unwillingness to commit to a single narrative and partially due to participants' reluctance to return to pencil-and-paper after having begun to compose digitally. "Aw, come on, I already know what I want" protested Darrell over session #4 upon learning that all participants needed a completed storyboard before proceeding with their digital stories. While Darrell already felt confident he knew his narrative pathway without help from the storyboard, other participants were uncertain about which captions they should sketch out as the key passages to their storylines. And still others—despite repeated mollification that the storyboards were a mere outline—worried their pencil-and paper renderings were going to be critiqued for a lack of artistry. Yet, despite these issues, as expected, the storyboards did get all of the students actually verbalizing their ideas aloud through the process of putting them to paper, and they did provide a discernible end-point to the composition process—namely, the resolution of the narrative. All participants had completed and submitted their storyboards by session #5. The shortest storyboard consisted of a mere 3 captions while the longest extended to 7 captions, with 5 captions as the most common length.

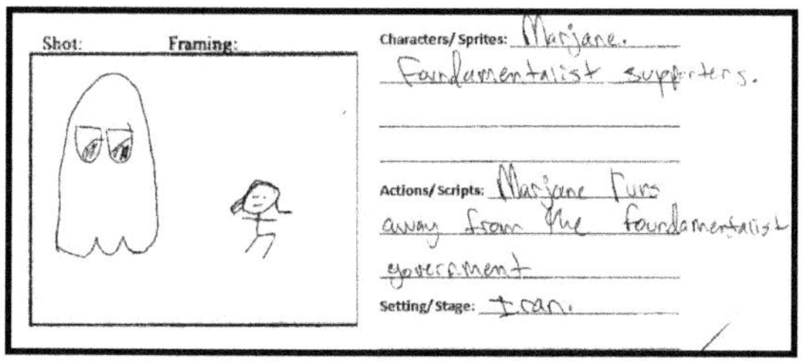

Figure 4: Sample caption from Carlos' Scratch version of *Persepolis*

5.2.2 Drafting, Feedback, & Revising

As an outline, the storyboards served as the student's raw "roadmap" and was the first piece they submitted and received formal feedback by way of written comments on the paper itself. While three of the storyboard submissions were fairly perfunctory, including only an absolute minimal amount of detail, the remaining seven were well-organized and well utilized the side-space alongside the caption box to explain *the who?* (character/ sprites), *the what?* (actions/ scripts), and *the where?* (settings/ stages) of each progressing scene.

Following these notes on the storyboard submissions, feedback over the next three sessions was more informal, including comments and suggestions on individual student projects as the group worked independently on them. The entire class participated in ten-minute "gallery walk" midway through the workshop, leaving their laptops open to their in-the-works projects and then walking the room with their peers, sampling each others' stories and asking questions based on what they viewed thus far. To a degree, the projects students had prepared for the gallery walk served as their initial drafts; however, no participant had actually completed his digital story at this point, which made giving constructive feedback more difficult for the students. Students largely commented on the appearance of each other's characters (e.g., "cool costume", "nice look") but had a difficult time providing more substantial feedback about elements like plot development and characterization. "So what's supposed to happen here?" 8th grader Todd asked of his friend's Greg's project during the gallery walk, unable to offer much more given that he was entirely uncertain where the narrative was actually heading.

More directed feedback came from us as instructors during the next session when all students posted their draft projects at the Scratch website. Using the anonymous username "SLA_User" and with storyboards in hand, we reviewed each project based upon what had been uploaded to the Scratch website thus far and what the remaining captions on the storyboard indicated should happen next. Using the "Comments" feature on the website, we posted brief observations, small items of encouragements, and occasional questions. Given the character-limit of the Comments box as well as the decidedly "non-academic" nature of the website, we opted to keep the comments succinct and casual; the goal was not to exhaust the students with a "to do" list but rather engage them with the prospect of sharing their work with wider audiences online.

5.3 Perceptions

Based on the post-survey, 70% of respondents agreed or strongly agreed that the storyboard helped them create their stories; 70% agreed or strongly agreed that they learned more about computing during the workshop, while 80% indicated they learned more about storytelling during the workshop; 70% agreed or strongly agreed that they felt better at computing based on the workshop; 90% agreed or strongly agreed that they had enjoyed the workshop experience; and 70% agreed or strongly agreed that anyone can be a good storyteller in Scratch if he or she works hard at it.

In post-interviews, it was storytelling that occupied much of the one-on-one feedback from students, with multiple middle-schoolers stressing the importance of the storyboards in ensuring they had a particular idea in mind for their Scratch project. "Scratch can do almost anything," explained Daryl in his post-interview, "It has hundreds of controls, hundreds of images and you can even take ones of the Internet.... And so, all you need to do is have a focus."

6. DISCUSSION

Returning to our research questions, it is clear that the writing workshop setting alongside the school's existing language arts standards proved to be not only an effective framework for facilitating middle school children's digital composition within Scratch, but also underscored the wider connection between coding and writing as interrelated processes of composition. Digital storytelling in Scratch—particularly in terms of the workshop's focus on characterization and plot analysis—offers a new medium through which children can exercise the composition skills they learned within traditional literacy classrooms while also offering the mutual benefit of introducing coding at earlier ages.

However, as evident in Table #1 above, certain coding bricks in the storytelling workshop—namely, conditionals, Boolean Logic, and Variables—were not widely used. These coding scripts are characteristic of games in which there are no fixed outcomes, and such scripts are simply not integral to linear narratives. Therefore participants did not learn much about these essential coding concepts over the seven weeks of the workshop. This finding is not an indictment of the usage of storytelling to introduce programming, but rather a caveat that while the writing-workshop model offers certain advantages in introducing coding to children, its products only represent the end-result of a certain type of programming. Moving forward, we are interested in expanding the parameters of the workshop to have youth compose interactive stories, which will not only introduce a wider range of programming variables but offer further insight on the intersection of narrative and game-making in digital media [22].

In terms of future workshops, there is also very much the need to explore (and make more explicit) the intersection between coding and narrative composition as they relate to computational thinking in the classroom [19; 25]. The workshop we designed and enacted largely held storytelling and coding apart as separate entities—each integral to and serving the same end goal—but introduced separately nonetheless. Computational thinking, which emphasizes the practical and *creative* functionality of algorithms, offers a potential new lens for accentuating the connection between coding and writing, both of which attempt to articulate a precise input in order to facilitate a particular output. *Make* magazine's recent partnership with the National Writing Project [9] is based upon such a premise, creating a series of workshops for literacy teachers that emphasize their role as "makers" within the classroom and student writing as a tangible "product" in which the technical and creative are inextricably intertwined. As systematically coded images and sounds placed in aesthetic juxtaposition, digital stories in Scratch are likewise "products" that embody both the technical and the creative elements of composition and offer a broader conception of what "writing" with computers may look like in the 21st century.

This said, while it is crucial to broaden K-12 schools' conception of literacy as well as make computer science more interdisciplinary in nature, it is equally important to be mindful of the respective disciplines out of which this workshop originated and the potential limitations of our study for instructors in these disciplines. In the discipline of English/ language arts, literacy instructors first and foremost need the designated time to enact such a weekly workshop, as well as a population of students familiar enough with the stages of writing to be capable of comfortably following them in terms of Scratch storytelling. In the discipline of computer science, CS instructors may well appreciate the Constructionist nature of the workshop, yet there still needs to be a continued push to ensure that programming enters schools primarily through statewide academic standards specific to CS (and not simply technology). For them, this study represents an alternative—and hopefully only temporary—route to getting CS into the K-12 classroom.

7. REFERENCES

[1] Black, R.W. 2008. *Adolescents and Online Fan Fiction*. New York: Peter Lang.

[2] Brown, A., and Campione, J. 1994. Guided discovery in a community of learners. In K. McGilly (Ed.), *Classroom Lessons: Integrating Cognitive Theory and Classroom Practice* (pp. 229-290). Cambridge, MA: MIT Press.

[3] Burke, Q. and Kafai, Y.B. 2010. Programming and storytelling: Opportunities for learning about coding and composition. In *Proceedings of the 9th International Conference on Interaction Design and Children Conference 2010* (Barcelona, Spain, June 09-11), pp. 348-51.

[4] Calkins, L. 1986. *The Art of Teaching Writing*. Portsmouth, NH: Heinemann.

[5] Calkins, L. 1994. *The Art of Teaching Writing* (2nd Ed.). Portsmouth, NH: Heinemann.

[6] Costa, N. 2009. Animating Aesop's Fables. *Teachers Network*. Retrieved August 12, 2011 from http://teachers network.org/grantwinners/Teachnet09NancyCosta.htm.

[7] Denner, J., Werner, L., Bean, S. and Campe, S. 2005. The girls creating games program: Strategies for engaging middle-school girls in information technology. *Frontiers: A Journal of Women Studies*, 26, 1, 90-98.

[8] DiSalvo, B. and Bruckman, A. 2011. From interests to values. *Communications of the ACM*, 54, 8 (Aug 2011), 27-29.

[9] Dougherty, D. 2010. Teachers as makers. *O'Reilly Radar* (December 11, 2010. Retreived August 23, 2011 from http://radar.oreilly.com/2010/12/teachers-as-makers.html.

[10] Feinberg, B. 2007. The Lucy Calkins Project. *Education Next*, *7*, 3, 26-31.

[11] Harel, I., and Papert, S. 1990. Software design as a learning environment. *Interactive Learning Environments,* 1, 1–32.

[12] Kafai, Y. B. 2005. The classroom as living laboratory: Design-based research for understanding,comparing, and evaluating learning science through design. *Educational Technology,* 45, 28–33.

[13] Kafai, Y.B., Fields, D.A., Burke, Q. 2011 (accepted). Collaborative agency in youth online creative production in Scratch. In. *Proceedings of the 19th International Conference on Computers in Education* (Chiang Mai, Thailand, Nov 28 – Dec 2).

[14] Kelleher,C. and Pausch, R. 2005. Lowering the barriers to programming: A taxonomy of programming environments and languages for novice programmers. *ACM Computing Surveys*, 37, 2, 83-137.

[15] Kelleher,C. and Pausch, R. 2007. Using storytelling to motivate programming. *Communications of the ACM*, 50, 7, 59-64.

[16] Lave, J., and Wenger, E. 1991. *Situated Learning: Legitimate peripheral participation*. Cambridge, England: Cambridge University Press.

[17] Lensmire, T. 1994. *When Children Write: Critical Re-visions of the Writing Workshop*. New York: Teachers College Press.

[18] McGrath-Cohoon, J. and Asprey, W. (Eds.) 2006. *Women and Information Technology: Research on Under-representation*. Cambridge, MA: MIT Press.

[19] National Research Council. 2010. *Report of a Workshop on the Scope and Nature of Computational Thinking*. Washington, DC: National Academies Press.

[20] Palumbo, D.B. 1990. Programming language/problem-solving research: A review of relevant issues," *Review of Educational Research*, 60, 1, 65–89.

[21] Resnick, L.B. 1987. *Education and learning to think*. Washington, DC: National Academy Press.

[22] Robertson, J. and Good, J. 2005. Story creation in virtual game worlds. *Communications of the ACM*, 48, 1, 61-65.

[23] Shaffer, D. W., and Resnick, M. 1999. Thick authenticity: New media and authentic learning. *Journal of Interactive Learning Research,* 10, 2, 195-215.

[24] Wilson, C., Sudol, L., Stephenson, C., and Stehlik, M. 2010. *Running on Empty: The Failure to Teach K–12 Computer Science in the Digital Age*. ACM. DOI = http://www.acm.org/runningonempty/fullreport.pdf.

[25] Wing, J.M. 2006. Computational thinking. *Communications of the ACM*, 49, 3, 33-35.Texas

[26] Wolz, U., Ouyang, Y., Leutenegger, S.T. 2011. Scratching the subject surface. In *Proceedings of the 42nd ACM Technical Symposium on Computer Science Education*. (Dallas, TX, March 09-12). ACM, New York, NY, 48-90.

A Software Craftsman's Approach to Data Structures

Matti Luukkainen, Arto Vihavainen, Thomas Vikberg
University of Helsinki
Department of Computer Science
P.O. Box 68 (Gustaf Hällströmin katu 2b)
Fi-00014 University of Helsinki
{ mluukkai, avihavai, tvikberg }@cs.helsinki.fi

ABSTRACT

Data Structures (CS2) courses and course books do not usually put much emphasis in the process of how a data structure is engineered or invented. Instead, algorithms are readily given, and the main focus is in the mathematical complexity analysis of the algorithms. We present an alternative approach on presenting data structures using worked examples, i.e., by explicitly displaying the process that leads to the invention and creation of a data stucture and its algorithms. Our approach is heavily backed up by some of the best programming practices advocated by the Agile and Software Craftsmanship communities. It brings the often mathematically oriented CS2 course closer to modern software engineering and practical problem solving, without a need for compromise in proofs and analysis.

Categories and Subject Descriptors

K.3.2 [**Computers and Education**]: Computer and Information Science Education *Computer Science Education*

General Terms

Algorithms, Design, Experimentation, Verification

Keywords

data structures, software engineering best practices, worked example, instructional design

1. INTRODUCTION

Data Structures (CS2) is the cornerstone course of most computer science curriculums. It usually covers principles of algorithm analysis, stacks, queues, linked lists, set implementations (binary search trees and hash tables), sorting algorithms and graphs. The course is usually taken at a later part of the first year or during the second year after students have acquired basic programming and mathematics knowledge.

Most CS2 course books, such as the books by Aho et. al. [2], Cormen et. al. [9] and Sedgewick [16], take a traditional, procedural pseudocode based approach to presenting the algorithms. A growing number of books where pseudocode is replaced with a real programming language exists, see e.g. [11, 18], but the traditional pseudocode-based approach dominates most of the CS2 courses.

A typical CS2 course implementation introduces one data structure at a time. The data structure and its algorithms are usually covered step by step as follows. First, the need of a data structure is motivated and the algorithms for the data structure are given as pseudocode. Then, the behavior of the algorithms are visualized and clarified by simulations, and finally, the complexity and correctness of the algorithms are analyzed formally.

There are several problems in this approach. As the data structures and related algorithms are presented as given, the students do not have the opportunity to discover the data structures themselves. Instead of just showing what a data structure is and how it works, it would be more enlightening to see the actual process of how a data structure is engineered step by step from scratch. In literature this type of explicitly thought out teaching process is often referred to as *worked example* [7]. Worked examples are often used in the cognitive apprenticeship [8] based learning methods that have recently had many successful applications in teaching programming (see e.g. [5, 7, 13, 17]).

Another problem is related to the way in which pseudocode (or real programming language code) is used in course books. Algorithms are often written as big monolithical entities, where variables follow a single letter naming convention. This writing style is taxing to a beginner since bad variable naming does not give much of a hint on the purpose of the variables, and the algorithms do not bear any structure that would make their intention more explicit. Simply put, the traditional approach of presenting algorithms does not take into account the limitations of human' cognitive architecture, which sets limits on how many *concepts* the working memory can hold at a time [7].

Unnecessary cognitive load is not the only problem of the pseudocode style used in CS2 courses and course books. Many algorithms of data structures have some common logic, however given pseudocode usually repeats the common parts of the logic. Thus, the pseudocode used in CS2 breaks many of the long known best practices of software engineering such as *don't repeat yourself* (no copy-paste code), *use short methods*, *use simple focused classes*, and *use descriptive names* (see eg. [12, 14]).

The importance of these best practices have lately been heavily advocated by some of the Agile Software Engineering methods, especially Extreme Programming [4] and the Software Craftsmanship community [15, 12, 14].

Permission to make digital or hard copies of all or part of this work for personal or classroom use is granted without fee provided that copies are not made or distributed for profit or commercial advantage and that copies bear this notice and the full citation on the first page. To copy otherwise, to republish, to post on servers or to redistribute to lists, requires prior specific permission and/or a fee.
SIGCSE'12, February 29–March 3, 2012, Raleigh, North Carolina, USA.
Copyright 2012 ACM 978-1-4503-1098-7/12/02 ...$10.00.

At least in our university the courses with emphasis in software engineering such as the introductory programming (CS1) are also putting more and more emphasis on the best pracices. Our results indicate that instruction in CS2 benefits from taking good programming practices into account.

The rest of this paper is organized as follows. In section 2, we describe Software Craftsman's approach to data structures, an approach based on worked examples backed heavily by some of the best practices advocated by the Software Craftsmanship and Agile Software Engineering communities. Section 3 gives excerpts of a worked example where a hash table is developed from scratch. Section 4 evaluates the effectiveness of the approach from the students' point of view in contrast to traditional lectures, and section 5 concludes the paper.

2. A SOFTWARE CRAFTSMAN'S APPROACH TO DATA STRUCTURES

In our approach a data structure and its related algorithms are presented in the worked example manner where the actual data structure is engineered step by step from scratch, starting by giving a motivation for the data structure, e.g. a problem, and finishing in a detailed implementation. Instead of pseudocode, a concrete programming language is used (in our case we utilize Java as it is the language in our CS1 courses).

Data structures are engineered using *Test-driven development* [3], a discipline where tests are written before the actual code. Test-driven development is well suited for implementing data structures as it puts lots of emphasis on the interface design of the actual code to be written [1].

Engineering a data structure proceeds in small steps. First an intermediate step is identified and a few tests are written for it. Then the actual code that passes the tests is written. When tests pass, the next step is to write another test that leads one step closer to the solution.

However, if one notices that the code that was written is not clean, i.e., it breaks some of the best programming practices, the code is *refactored* to a clean form. Refactoring means the process where the internal structure of the code is altered but its interface and behavior remain unaltered [10]. In order to efficiently do refactoring, it is essential that the tests are automated, for example, by using a test framework. As we use Java, a natural choice for the test framework has been JUnit [3].

By using clean code principles in expressing algorithms we believe that the understandability of the algorithms is also increased. Using meaningful variable names and splitting algorithms into manageable pieces is expected to ease the students' task of grasping the abstract ideas behind the algorithms.

3. AN EXAMPLE: A HASH TABLE

In this example, we demonstrate our approach by implementing a simple student register, where the information of a student (student number, list of course registrations and grades, etc.) can be quickly retrieved by using the students' name. Information on a student is encapsulated to class `Student` (details omitted), and the name used as a search key is assumed to be a `String`.

We start by defining an interface that the student register data structure is supposed to implement:

```
public interface StudentRegister {
  void add(Student student);
  Student find(String name);
}
```

There are two operations; one for adding a student and one for finding a student based on a name.

Next we define the basic behavior of what is expected from a student register. The behavior is defined in terms of JUnit tests:

```
@Test
public void addedStudentIsFound() {
  Student jones = new Student("Jones");
  studentReg.add(jones);
  assertEquals(jones, studentReg.find("Jones") );
}

@Test
public void nonExistingStudentIsNotInRegister() {
  assertEquals(null, studentReg.find("Kennedy") );
}
```

In JUnit, each test is defined as a method annotated with `@Test`. Each test is designed to test one simple functionality, and the name of the test method documents its purpose. Execution of a test starts by setting up the state that is expected to hold before the testable behavior is executed. After the state has been set, the testable behavior is executed and the result is verified, typically with the `assert`-family of methods. Tests are run and results can be analyzed automatically, either by "pressing a button" in an IDE or by running a command line script.

In the tests above it is assumed that the variable `studentReg` refers to the hash table under test and that it is empty before the test methods are executed. The first test, `addedStudentIsFound` starts by creating a student object and adding it to the hash table. Then the `find`-method, that is being tested, is called and the result is verified. The second test, `nonExistingStudentIsNotInRegister`, verifies that the register does not attempt to return a student that is not in the register.

Starting the implementation

As the University of Helsinki has roughly 39000 students, it could be possible to store all student-objects in an array of roughly equal size. An idea is to define a mapping from each student to an array index:

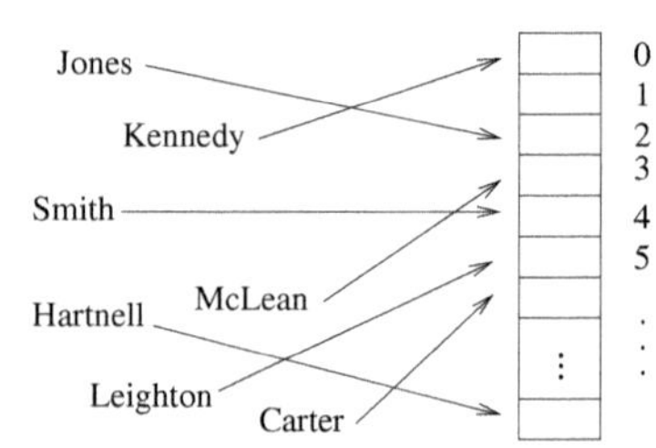

Since the data structure is a hash table, we will name and define our initial implementation of the interface as follows:

```
public class RegisterHashTable
              implements StudentRegister {
  private Student[] students;

  public RegisterHashTable(int size) {
    students = new Student[size];
  }
```

```
  public void add(Student student) {
  }

  public Student find(String name) {
    return null;
  }
}
```

We define the size of the hash table to be a constant `SIZE` for testing. In JUnit the test setup is done in a method annotated with `@Before`. The method is executed before each test is run, so all the tests start with an empty hash table:

```
@Before
public void setUp() {
  studentReg = new RegisterHashTable(SIZE);
}
```

The idea of the hash table is to map a key (now a `String` representing the student's name) to an index of an array. A simple but not very efficient mapping can be defined first:

```
public void add(Student student) {
  students[0] = student;
}

public Student find(String name) {
  if ( students[0]==null ||
       !students[0].getName().equals(name) )
    return null;

  return students[0];
}
```

This simple implementation that maps each student to the position 0 of the table is enough to get the current tests to pass. In test-driven development, it is a very common technique to first do a hardcoded or "quick and dirty" implementation to make the tests pass and only after that to sit back and think about a more elaborate solution.

It is ugly to first use the method `getName` and then `equals` to compare a students' name to a given name. Following the *tell, don't ask* -principle [12], we simplify this by adding a method `nameEquals` to class Student:

```
public Student find(String name) {
  if ( students[0]==null ||
       !students[0].nameEquals(name) )
    return null;

  return students[0];
}
```

A better hash function

Next step is to introduce a test which adds two students to the hash table. That test forces us to consider the mapping of students to different indices:

```
@Test
public void ifTwoAddedBothAreFound(){
  Student jones = new Student("Jones");
  Student smith = new Student("Smith");

  studentReg.add(jones);
  studentReg.add(smith);

  assertEquals(jones, studentReg.find("Jones") );
  assertEquals(smith, studentReg.find("Smith") );
}
```

A simple approach for calculating a hash value is to sum up the ascii codes of the characters in the name string, and then take modulo base the hash table size of the sum:

```
public void add(Student student) {
  int index = 0;
  for (int i = 0; i < student.getName().length(); i++) {
    index += student.getName().charAt(i);
  }
  index = index % students.length;

  students[index] = student;
}

public Student find(String name) {
  int index = 0;
  for (int i = 0; i < name.length(); i++) {
    index += name.charAt(i);
  }
  index = index % students.length;

  if ( students[index]==null ||
    !students[index].nameEquals(name)) )
  return null;

  return students[index];
}
```

The implementation passes the tests. However, one notices that the hash function is calculated (copy-pasted!) in two different places. This violates the *do not repeat yourself* principle and, if left in the code, most probably will cause all sorts of problems later, for example if the logic of the hash function calculation needs to be changed. So we decide to refactor the copy-paste code to a separate method:

```
public void add(Student student) {
  int index = hashCode(student.getName());
  students[index] = student;
}

public Student find(String name) {
  int index = hashCode(name);

  if ( students[index]==null ||
      !students[index].nameEquals(name) )
    return null;

  return students[index];
}

private int hashCode(String name) {
  int index = 0;
  for (int i = 0; i < name.length(); i++) {
    index += name.charAt(i);
  }
  return index % students.length;
}
```

Tests are run immediately to ensure that refactoring has not broken the code.

Method `add` can be further simplified by replacing the temporary `index` value by the method call:

```
public void add(Student student) {
   students[ hashCode(student.getName()) ] = student;
}
```

Hash collisions

Next we create a test for a boundary case where more students are added to the register than there is space in the backing table. This makes it evident that in the case of *hash collisions*, an information loss prevention strategy is needed:

```
@Test
public void ifManyAddedEachIsFound(){
  List<Student> students = buildAListOf(SIZE + 1);
  for (Student student : students)
    studentReg.add(student);

  for (Student student : students) {
    assertEquals(student,
                 studentReg.find(student.getName()));
  }
}
```

The test uses a method `buildAListOf(int numberOfStudents)`, which generates a given number of student objects and returns those in a List. In the above example, students in the generated list are added to the hash table, after which the existence of all students is tested.

The test above does not pass which forces us to think of another solution. The idea of chaining the objects to linked lists is introduced. All objects that have the same hash value are entered into a linked list in the corresponding position of the hash table:

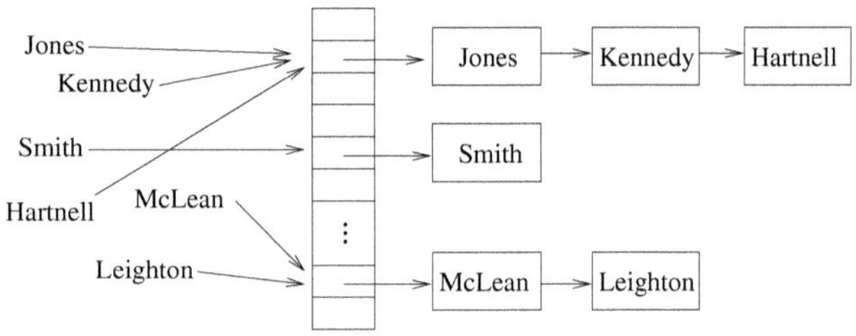

Collision chains are implemented with Java's `LinkedList` data structure, which has been covered in an earlier part of the course, and the hash table is declared to hold lists. Methods `add` and `find` are changed correspondingly. The hash function remains the same as it is simply used to select the right list in each case.

```
private LinkedList<Student>[] students;

public RegisterHashTable(int size) {
   students = new LinkedList[size];
   for (int i = 0; i < students.length; i++)
      students[i] = new LinkedList<Student>();
}

public void add(Student student) {
   students[ hashCode(student.getName()) ].add(student);
}

public Student find(String name) {
  for (Student student : students[ hashCode(name) ]) {
    if ( student.getName().equals(name) )
      return student;
  }
  return null;
}
```

After doing the modifications, tests are run and we discover that they now pass.

Separating hash function calculation from hash table

Our hash function implementation uses the well known *division method* [9] for calculating the hash value. There exists also other types of hash functions. In our solution the hash table operations (adding and finding elements), and the calculation of the hash value, are tightly coupled since both are defined in the same class. In other words, the class is not very focused, and has too many responsibilities. This can be problematic if we would like to have alternative approaches for calculating the hash value. The modifiability of our current solution is not optimal due to a class with too many responsibilities.

A good solution to the problem is again refactoring. Calculating the hash value should be extracted to a class of its own. We start the process by writing tests to the hash function:

```
@Before
public void setUp() {
  hasher = new Hasher(SIZE);
}

@Test
public void stringGetsAlwaysSameHashValue() {
  assertEquals( hasher.hash("Jones"),
                hasher.hash("Jones") );
}
```

The class implementing the hash function is called `Hasher`, and the method to calculate the hash value is `hash`.

The next step is to create a class that passes the test. We simply take the method of our previous approach and perform some renaming:

```
public class Hasher {
  private int sizeOfHashTable;

  public Hasher(int size) {
    this.sizeOfHashTable = size;
  }

  public int hash(String string) {
    int value = 0;
    for (int i = 0; i < string.length(); i++)
      value += string.charAt(i);

    return value % sizeOfHashTable;
  }
}
```

The simple test passes. The next step is to plug a hash-object into the hash table:

```
public class RegisterHashTable
               implements StudentRegister {

  private LinkedList<Student>[] students;
  private Hasher hasher;

  public RegisterHashTable(int size) {
    hasher = new Hasher(size);
    students = new LinkedList[size];
    for (int i = 0; i < students.length; i++)
      students[i] = new LinkedList<Student>();
  }

  public void add(Student student) {
    students[ hasher.hash(student.getName()) ].add(student);
  }

  public Student find(String name) {
    for (Student student : students[ hasher.hash(name) ] ) {
      if ( student.nameEquals(name) )
        return student;
    }
    return null;
  }
}
```

Strengthening the hash function

All tests pass, and the basic functionality of the hash table is now ready. However, we have some doubts about our hash function. Let us first clarify the structure of the function. We notice that two separate tasks, mapping a string to integer and calculating the hash value based on an integer are currently mixed within one method. Let us refactor the string to integer mapping and hash value calculation to separate methods:

```
public int hash(String string) {
  return hashValue( stringToInteger(string) );
}

protected int hashValue(int value) {
  return value % sizeOfHashTable;
}

protected int stringToInteger(String string) {
  int value = 0;
  for (int i = 0; i < string.length(); i++)
    value += string.charAt(i);

  return value;
}
```

Tests pass after the refactoring, so we can go on. The integer that represents a string is calculated as a sum of ascii codes. This is not a good strategy if the hash table is big as only a small range of hash table indices are used when hashed strings are relatively short. A better schema is to scale up character ascii values based on their position in the string by multiplying them with a suitable prime [6]:

```
private int stringToInteger(String string) {
  int value = 0;
  int multiplier = 1;
  for (int i = 0; i < string.length(); i++) {
     value += string.charAt(i)*multiplier;
     multiplier *= PRIME;
  }
  return value;
}
```

Interestingly this change breaks some of our tests! We quickly discover that the problem is that in some situations the array index becomes negative. With a little bit of analysis, for example by using a debugger, we notice that the cause of the error is integer overflow in method **stringToInteger**.

The problem is fixed by returning the absolute value of the string to integer mapping:

```
private int stringToInteger(String string) {
   // ...
   return Math.abs(value);
}
```

This fixes the problems and all tests pass. We want to prevent this type of accidents by adding a test that checks that calculated hash values are within the expected range[1]:

```
@Test
public void valueWithinRange() {
  String string = "";
  for (int i = 0; i < 1000; i++) {
    string += "a";
    assertTrue( hasher.hash(string) >= 0 &&
                hasher.hash(string) < hashTableSize);
  }
}
```

[1]More representative input sets can be easily generated but are omitted due to space limitations.

Further modificationas

Due to size limitations we can't show the complete example here. The hash table example that was done in the lecture was continued with defining another type of hash function, *the multiplication method* [9]. The extension was done by extending the class **Hasher**. The only change needed was to override the method that calculates the hash value:

```
public class HashMultiply extends Hasher {
  protected int hashValue(int value) {
    return (int) ( sizeOfHashTable *
                   fractionPart(value * GOLDEN_RATIO) );
  }
}
```

Thanks to the good structure of the solution, it was extremely easy to implement an alternative version of the hash table that uses a different type of hash function.

The lecture was continued by reflecting on what was done from an algorithmical perspective and by performing a complexity analysis of the algorithm. The implementation was also polished, e.g. user friendly creation patterns were created by introducing static factory methods.

4. THE USE AND EFFECTIVENESS OF THE APPROACH

The worked example style of presenting data structures and algorithms was applied at the Data Structures course at the University of Helsinki for the first time in Spring 2011. The participants of the course were mainly first year Computer Science majors. The course lasts one term and consists of 4 hours of lectures each week with both programming and non-programming take-home assignments.

The following data structures were covered using the worked example style: stack, singly linked list, binary search tree, hash tables with chaining, open hashing, merge sort and quick sort. Besides just showing the program code, an overhead projector was heavily used in the worked example style of lectures to illustrate and reflect on what was being done. Traditional pseudocode representation of the data structures was also available in handouts, but was not explicitly covered during the worked example lectures.

The rest of the data structures in the course (queue, double linked lists, heap and graphs) were covered in a traditional way. Besides presenting various algorithms and data structures, the course included basics of algorithm analysis. Each of these three parts took roughly one third of the lecturing time of the course.

In order to measure the effectiveness of worked example style of lectures, the students were asked to fill an anonymous survey that asked which lecturing approach the students prefer from a learning point of view. The results are shown in the table below (total number of answers was 52).

Opinion	Percentage
Worked examples much better	44.2 %
Worked examples slightly better	34.6 %
Both equal	5.8%
Traditional lectures slightly better	3.8 %
Traditional lectures much better	5.8 %
No opinion	5.8 %

Altogether 78.8 % of the students thought that the worked example style supports learning better and only 9.6 % preferred the traditional format. Thus students clearly preferred the renewed lecturing approach.

It is somewhat hard to estimate the effect of our approach to the overall learning. Results from both the mid-term exam and the final exam were somewhat better than a year ago when all the lectures were traditional[2]. Pass rate of the course in Spring 2011 was 79 %, while in Spring 2010 it was 71 % – a clear improvement. However, other factors may also have been involved.

Many students gave direct verbal and textual feedback about the lectures. The majority of the feedback was positive, but some semi-critical opinions were also received, eg.:

Programming in the lectures helps to grasp the ideas of the algorithms a bit better compared to pseudocode or readily made program code. However, there is not much difference since programming in lectures proceeds quite quickly and there is not too much time to discuss why the particular solutions were selected in implementing the algorithms. To the lecturer the selections may seem obvious, but for a novice it is not clear why some choices are favoured over some others since the "blind alleys" where a novice programmer often finds herself are not explored.

This is clearly a good comment, and it would certainly be beneficial to discuss more alternative implementation strategies during the lectures e.g. by contrasting the "well engineered" solutions with the more problematic approaches that some students end up with.

5. CONCLUSIONS

Traditional pseudocode-oriented CS2-courses have quite often switched students from "software engineering mode", promoted in programming and software engineering courses, to "algorithmics mode". In the algorithmics mode, all good programming practices are often forgotten, and the focus in programming is getting correct end results. Because of the focus in end results, and not in the process, the code written in CS2 courses is often quality-wise poor from software engineering point of view.

We proposed an alternative approach to conducting CS2 lectures. The approach builds on the ideas of worked examples, i.e., instead of just presenting the solutions, the process that leads to the solution is shown in a step-by-step manner. Instead of using pseudocode, the approach uses a real programming language with best programming practices to illustrate the engineering process of a data structure.

Our aim is to bridge the gap between software engineering practices and the more theory-oriented field of data structures and algorithms, and to demonstrate students that they actually benefit from writing well structured, automatically tested, and maintainable code.

The following anonymous feedback summarizes the purpose and benefits of our approach quite well:

Programming during the lectures is a good idea. Not only because of the illustrative power, but also the "hidden agenda" of repeatedly showing the benefits of good programming habits such as automatic tests, refactoring and programming against interfaces. The more students get inspiration and examples of good practices, the more likely it is that they will also pursue those in the future.

During the lectures we guide the students through problem-solving sessions, from motivating the need of a data structure all the way up to a concrete solution. By doing this several times for different data structures, we hope to give a student the means to act herself in similar problem solving contexts. Best programming practices are utilized in the process since those promote the understandability of the solutions by good naming and separation of concerns.

[2]The lecturer and course content was same in both course instances.

6. ACKNOWLEDGMENTS

We thank Jaakko "gndi" Kurhila and Matti "mpa" Paksula for their invaluable contributions.

7. REFERENCES

[1] J. Adams. Test-driven data structures: revitalizing CS2. In *Proc. of the 40th ACM technical symposium on Computer science education*, SIGCSE '09, 2009.

[2] A. V. Aho, J. E. Hopcroft, and J. Ullman. *Data Structures and Algorithms*. Addison-Wesley Longman Publishing Co., Inc., 1983.

[3] K. Beck. *Test Driven Development: By Example*. Addison-Wesley, 2002.

[4] K. Beck and C. Andres. *Extreme Programming Explained: Embrace Change (2nd Edition)*. Addison-Wesley Professional, 2004.

[5] T. R. Black. Helping novice programming students succeed. *J. Comput. Small Coll.*, 22(2):109–114, 2006.

[6] J. Bloch. *Effective Java (2nd Edition) (The Java Series)*. Prentice Hall, 2008.

[7] M. E. Caspersen and J. Bennedsen. Instructional design of a programming course: a learning theoretic approach. In *ICER '07: Proc. of the 3rd international workshop on Computing education research*, 2007.

[8] A. Collins, J. S. Brown, and A. Holum. Cognitive apprenticeship: making thinking visible. *American Educator*, 6:38–46, 1991.

[9] T. Cormen, C. Leiserson, R. Rivest, and C. Stein. *Introduction to Algorithms, 3rd edition*. The MIT Press, 2009.

[10] M. Fowler, K. Beck, J. Brant, W. Opdyke, and D. Roberts. *Refactoring: Improving the Design of Existing Code*. Addison-Wesley Professional, 1999.

[11] M. T. Goodrich and R. Tamassia. *Data structures and algorithm analysis in C++, 5th edition*. Wiley, 2010.

[12] A. Hunt and D. Thomas. *The Pragmatic Programmer: From Journeyman to Master*. Addison-Wesley Professional, 1999.

[13] M. Kölling and D. J. Barnes. Enhancing apprentice-based learning of Java. In *SIGCSE '04: Proc. of the 35th technical symposium on Computer science education*, 2004.

[14] R. C. Martin. *Clean Code: A Handbook of Agile Software Craftsmanship*. Prentice Hall, 2008.

[15] P. McBreen. *Software Craftsmanship: The New Imperative*. Prentice Hall, 2001.

[16] R. Sedgewick and K. Wayne. *Algorithms, 4th edition*. Addison-Wesley, 2011.

[17] A. Vihavainen, M. Paksula, and M. Luukkainen. Extreme apprenticeship method in teaching programming for beginners. In *Proc. of the 42nd ACM technical symposium on Computer science education*, SIGCSE '11, 2011.

[18] M. A. Weiss. *Data Structures & Problem Solving Using Java, 4 th edition*. Addison-Wesley, 2009.

Jutge.org: An Educational Programming Judge*

Omer Giménez
Google Inc.

Jordi Petit
Universitat Politècnica de Catalunya
contact@jutge.org

Salvador Roura
Universitat Politècnica de Catalunya

ABSTRACT

Jutge.org is an open access educational online programming judge where students can try to solve more than 800 problems using 22 programming languages. The verdict of their solutions is computed using exhaustive test sets run under time, memory and security restrictions. By contrast to many popular online judges, Jutge.org is designed for students and instructors: On one hand, the problem repository is mainly aimed to beginners, with a clear organization and gradding. On the other hand, the system is designed as a virtual learning environment where instructors can administer their own courses, manage their roster of students and tutors, add problems, attach documents, create lists of problems, assignments, contests and exams. This paper presents Jutge.org and offers some case studies of courses using it.

Categories and Subject Descriptors

D.m [**Software**]: Miscellaneous

General Terms

Tools, Experiences, Active learning, Instructional technologies.

1. INTRODUCTION

It is a well established fact that practice is fundamental to learn computer programming. Whether at secondary, high school or university level, instructors assign programming problems to beginner students in order to help them acquire this skill.

These problems often require devising an algorithm and writing a program that, given some inputs, produces the corresponding outputs. Most of these problems put their emphasis on understanding rather than on technical knowledge: the problems are not solved through some "magic" command, but, rather, on thinking how to algorithmically combine a few basic instructions and data structures that appear in just about any modern programming language.

For instructors, correcting programming assignments is tedious and error-prone. However, due to their nature, programming problems are ideal candidates for automated assessment. A review on automatic assessment of programing problems can be found in [10] and recent experiences include [9, 13, 15].

That said, the current running horses of automatic correction systems are the *online judges* in the Internet. Online judges are web based systems that offer a repository of programming problems and a way to submit solutions to these problems in order to obtain a verdict on their behaviour when run on different public and private data sets. Some fine and popular online judges include UVa [6], Timus [4], Sphere [3], CodeChef [1], TopCoder [5], ...

However, the main purpose of the aforesaid systems is to help their users to train themselves for several types of contests, such as the ACM ICPC or, even, to help companies recruiting programmers (TopCoder). As a consequence, these judges are competitively oriented, and the difficulty of most of their problems ranges from advanced to very difficult. Even though experiences with competitive learning have been reported [14, 16], overall these sites are not adequate for beginners and do not provide much help for their instructors.

In order to remedy this situation, we present Jutge.org, our online judge built with an educative aim.

Jutge.org innovates in a number of aspects. First, and in contrast to other online judges, Jutge.org is designed both for students and instructors. Integrating in a coherent way ideas from both traditional online judges and from learning management systems as Moodle [2], instructors can manage their own courses, add their own problems, attach documents, create assignment lists, monitor the progress of the students, update rosters of students and tutors and interact with them. Second, the repository of problems at Jutge.org is clearly organized by topics and graded by difficulty. The problem collection enables a systematic progress, largely independent of the programming language of choice. Thus, instructors can tailor their programming courses using a large base of problems according to their needs and preferences.

The paper is organized as follows: First, we sketch the interface of Jutge.org, showing its main resources and presenting two scenarios. Then we survey its architecture, stressing security concerns. Next, we present its repository of graded problems. Finally, we describe our experience using the system in several settings, draw some conclusions, and advance ideas towards future work.

Jutge.org is can be found at https://www.jutge.org and has an open access policy. Jutge.org is free and will remain free for all students and tutors. Currently, Jutge.org is also free for instructors. All features can be tried without registering using the demo account.

*This work has partially been supported by the Spanish project FORMALISM (TIN2007-66523) and by the UPC innovation project "Disseny i implantació de les assignatures de programació als nous Graus d'Enginyeria Informàtica".

*The spelling of Jutge.org follows Catalan, not English.

Permission to make digital or hard copies of all or part of this work for personal or classroom use is granted without fee provided that copies are not made or distributed for profit or commercial advantage and that copies bear this notice and the full citation on the first page. To copy otherwise, to republish, to post on servers or to redistribute to lists, requires prior specific permission and/or a fee.
SIGCSE'12, February 29–March 3, 2012, Raleigh, North Carolina, USA.
Copyright 2012 ACM 978-1-4503-1098-7/12/02 ...$10.00.

2. INTERFACE

In order to present the possibilities of Jutge.org, we first introduce the main types of users and the main teaching resources available at Jutge.org; then, we present two typical scenarios of use.

2.1 Types of users and teaching resources

Users in Jutge.org can have (not mutually exclusive) different roles: *Students*, *Tutors*, *Instructors* and *Administrators*.

The main resource of Jutge.org are *problems*. Problems are identified by a unique short code and consist of a problem statement that describes the task to perform, some public test cases (sample input and sample output) and some private test cases. For instance, problem P29212 is titled "Modular exponentiation" and can be found at https://www.jutge.org/problems/P29212.

Most of the problems can be solved in any programming language that has been set up in the judge. Currently, 22 programming languages with 31 different compilers are available. These include[1] C++, C, Java, Python, Scheme, Pascal, ...

Almost all problem statements in Jutge.org are offered in English. As Jutge.org supports multilingual problems, most problems are also offered in Catalan or in Spanish (or both). Statements are available in HTML, PDF and PS.

The teaching resources of Jutge.org are primarily organized in *courses*. Also, courses can contain *lists of problems*. For instance "Algorithms" is a public course that contains a list called "Divide and conquer" that, in turn, contains several problems including "Modular exponentiation". A problem can be in many lists and a list can be in many courses. For instance, "Modular exponentiation" is also in the "Problems on Mathematics" course. Moreover, courses can contain *documents* in HTML format.

In addition, instructors can also add problems, and organize *exams* and *contests* within courses. Scripting is also possible by the way of *webservices*. Because of space reasons, these features will not be much discussed in this paper; see [8] for technical details.

2.2 First scenario: Standalone user

Let us consider the following scenario: Some user —let's call her Lisa— wishes to use Jutge.org to learn to program or, maybe, to improve her programming skills.

In order to use Jutge.org, Lisa first creates her account. Once logged in, Lisa will find that the system already offers her some public courses and some public lists of problems (see Section 4.1). As any other user, she can enroll any of those courses.

After browsing the contents of the public courses, Lisa can try to solve a problem. To do so, Lisa reads the problem statement and considers its sample test cases. At this point, Lisa designs and develops a solution for the problem in her own computer, compiling it, and validating it using the sample test cases and other test cases that she can think about herself. Finally, Lisa uploads the source code file to the online judge, which returns its verdict, typically in less than five seconds.

In order to emit a verdict, the engine of the online judge tests the solution submitted by Lisa using a set of private test cases. Possible verdicts include "Accepted", "Wrong answer", "Execution error", and others[1].

Lisa can submit to the judge as many solutions as desired. There is just a reasonable limitation in the number of allowed submissions in order to dissuade users from using the judge as an online compiler. All the submitted source code and associated verdicts together with satellite data as submission date are stored in the judge so that Lisa can retrieve them later.

[1] See https://www.jutge.org/documentation/compilers for the complete list of compilers and .../verdicts for the complete list of verdicts.

In addition to the capacities related to submitting and retrieving solutions (which are more or less similar to other online judges available), Lisa can update her profile, enroll and un-enroll courses, browse the courses, lists, documents, exams and problems...

2.3 Second scenario: An universitary course

We consider now another typical scenario where Prof. Oak is responsible for an introductory course to programming at her university for the next semester. 400 students (including Carla) will take her course, and a dozen of teachers (including Bob) will also assist her during the laboratory sessions. Prof. Oak is convinced that recursion is very important, so her course will emphasize it.

In order to set up her course using Jutge.org, Prof. Oak will get an account with instructor privileges and proceed as follows:

First, Prof. Oak will create a new course, "CS1 2011" say. Then, she will create some lists of problems and will populate them with the public problems already offered by Jutge.org according to her preferences. The system already offers so many problems that she does not need to create new problems on her own. Her course may contain, for instance, some lists called "Introduction", "Procedures", "Recursion" and "Backtracking" in accordance to the course syllabus. As she has already prepared some notes she plans to distribute, she will place them in new documents, or will link them from these documents. At this point, she is ready to invite all her students by providing their official email address at the university. All invited students will receive an email stating that they can enroll the "CS1 2011" course. Naturally, only the invited users are allowed to join her course. In the same way, Prof. Oak will also invite her assistant teachers, who will be designated as tutors for this course.

All through the semester, Prof. Oak can freely modify the information contained in her course. These updates will be seen in real time by all her students and tutors.

At some point, it may happen that Carla has some doubt about a particular problem that she is not able to solve. So Carla contacts Bob my email to state her difficulties and ask for help. In order to help students, tutors can use a special feature of Jutge.org called *supervision*: Supervision enables Bob to impersonate Carla's account and access her problems and submissions related to the "CS1 2011" course. By looking to her submissions and inspecting her code, Bob can spot her mistakes, answer her doubts and offer further guidance.

Note that, because of privacy issues, a tutor can only supervise students that have enrolled his courses and, moreover, supervision is limited to the problems that this course contains. Moreover, during supervision, the supervisor tutor cannot perform any action on behalf of the supervised student.

We pursue our scenario by imagining that, at some point, Prof. Oak wants to gather data on the overall progress of her students. To help her, Jutge.org offers a wealth of diagrams and statistics such as the ones shown in Figure 2.3.

Additionally, Prof. Oak is able to create exams or contests for the students in her course and Jutge.org also offers her other minor but practical functionalities that alleviate her administrative burden. For instance, the solutions that the students submit during the exams are easily distributed to the tutors, so that they can grade those solutions according to their own method.

We finish our scenario by noting that, on the next year, Prof. Oak could again be responsible for the same course but, of course, with different students. So, she will only need to copy "CS1 2011" to a new course "CS1 2012", invite a new roster of students and, maybe, new tutors. After this copy, the lists and documents are preserved but, naturally, can be further modified.

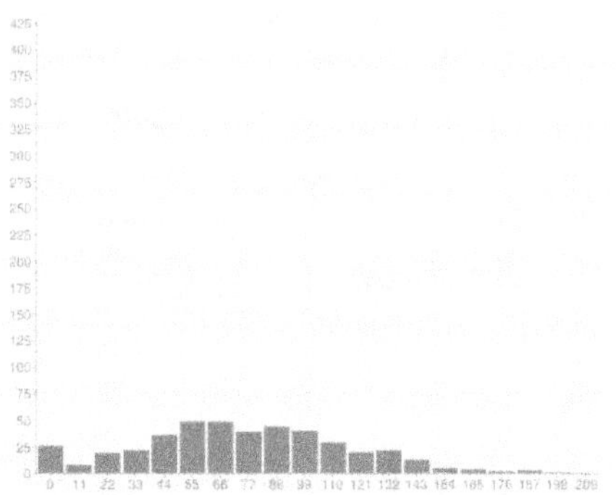

(a) Histogram of solved problems by students. Hor. axis: number of problems; vert. axis: number of students.

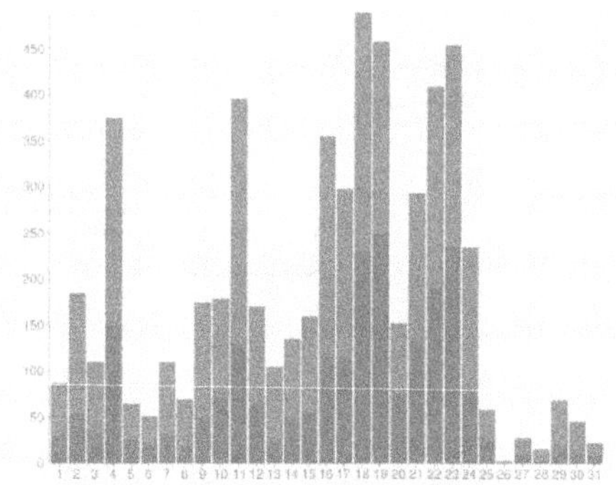

(b) Number of submissions for each day of May 2011. Green: accepted submissions; red: rejected submissions.

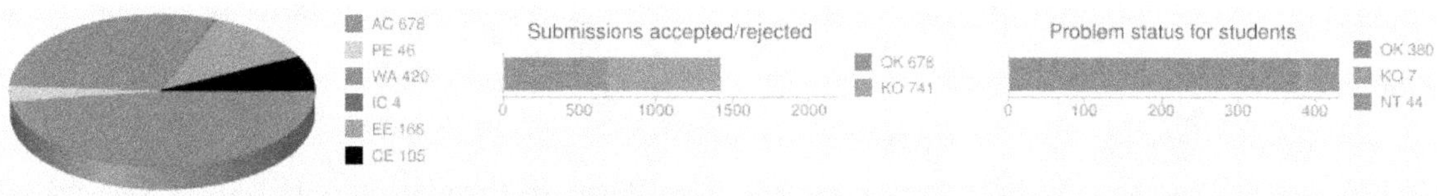

(c) Results for problem P67723 (Euclides algorithm): At left, distribution of verdicts; at center, proportion of accepted/rejected submissions; at right, number of students with the problem accepted (OK), rejected (KO) and not tried (NT).

The actual data in the three subfigures corresponds to the "Programació 1" course during spring 2011 at FIB.

Figure 1: Some diagrams that Jutge.org offers to instructors.

3. ARCHITECTURE AND SECURITY

In this section we survey the architecture on which the Jutge.org system is built, which is largely dependant on the possible attacks such a system must deal with, the requirement to offer verdicts in almost real time, and the need to make such a system scalable.

3.1 Security concerns

As any IT system, an online judge must cope with several threats. However, unlike many other systems, an online judge will welcome all users to submit their potentially malicious codes and execute them on their behalf. A nice analysis on the risks of such environments can be found in [11]; these include: Forcing a high compilation time, consuming resources at compilation time, accessing restricted information, misusing the network, modifying or harming the testing environment, circumventing the time measurement, exploiting covert channels, misusing additional services, and exploiting bugs in the OS.

Consequently, our system must provide a secure execution environment to execute arbitrary programs written in a myriad of programming languages without comprising the stability of the system nor its confidential information.

3.2 Efficiency and scalability

Users expect online judges to emit their verdicts in almost real time. In our case, we aim to correct almost all submissions in less than ten seconds. Such a rate can be considered standard.

In order to guarantee these correction rates as the number of users increases, we have designed a distributed system that is scalable by adding more servers to it. Here, a key problem is that our resources only allow adding servers from time to time and, because of this, these servers will have different speeds and capacities: we cannot consider that all of them are equal and, so, CPU time limits cannot be fixed in advance. In any case, users should not be aware of these differences.

3.3 Infrastructure and network architecture

The current Jutge.org infrastructure contains six Linux servers. One of these servers (the master or gateway) is the one that is used as the front-end: it offers the web, stores the database and maintains the submissions queue. The other servers are the back-end and are used as slave machines to process submissions. A separate backup and monitoring system is kept.

The overall distributed architecture is shown in Figure 2.

The master is directly connected to the Internet. For security reasons, the slaves are only connected to the master using a private network. In this way, slaves do not have a direct Internet access.

Moreover, the slaves do not process the submissions on their own, but rather rely on different virtual machines that are periodically restarted from scratch using inmutable disks. Each slave machine runs as many virtual machines as cores it has. Also, these slaves are used as a firewall to make more difficult escaping from the virtual machines they provide.

3.4 Correction of a submission

Users submit their submissions from the web server. These are sent to the queue manager, which will dispatch them to the virtual machines and return their correction.

According to some parameters that influence the priority of the submissions (e.g., exam submissions must be corrected before regular ones) and the load of the slaves machines, the queue manager sends the submissions to the virtual machines in the slave machines as soon as possible. In fact, the queue manager not only sends the actual submission, but also some related data as the problem test cases and the reference solution. In any case, each virtual machine just corrects one submission at a time.

Once in a virtual machine, submissions are corrected according to a *driver* that depends on the problem type. Roughly, the standard driver computes the verdict of the submission in two phases:

1. In the first phase, the reference solution is checked for correctness. That is, it is compiled and executed on all the test

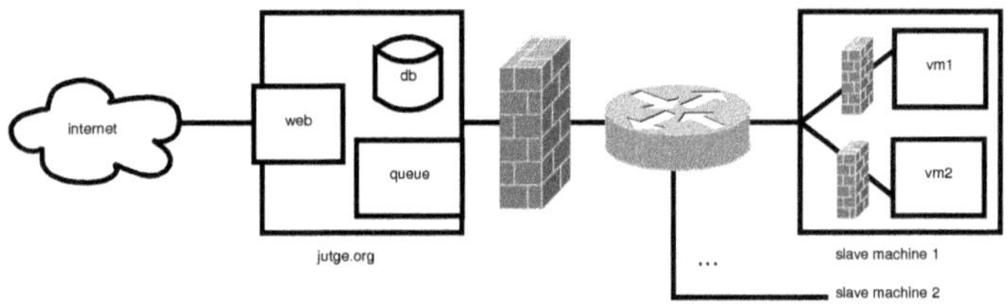

Figure 2: Network architecture and security

cases. In the event the reference solution did not work, an "*Internal error*" verdict would be issued. During the execution of the reference solution, CPU timings, wall-clock timings and memory measurements are performed.

2. Then, in the second phase, the submitted solution is checked for correctness as follows: First, the submission is compiled; in case of an error, the verdict is "*Compilation Error*", and the complete error will be reported to the user. If compilation succeeds, the compiled program is executed, as many times as test cases the problem has. If any of these executions aborts, the verdict is "*Execution Error*", together with a short explanation of the cause of the error (segmentation fault, CPU time exceeded, etc.). If not, then all the produced outputs are checked against the correct outputs (Section 4.3 gives more details in the possible ways to do it). If the checking is as expected, then the verdict is "*Accepted: Test cases passed*". If some of the files differ, then an additional check is performed to guess whether the differences are only minor (spaces or carriage returns, lower or upper case differences, etc.), in which case the verdict is "*Presentation error*". If this relaxation does not account for the output difference, then the verdict is "*Wrong answer*".

3.5 Secure environment

In order to protect the integrity of the system, all the above mentioned executions of programs (including compilation steps) are performed in a sandbox environment that includes switching to a low-privilege nobody user, limiting file system access by a chroot jail, monitoring system calls and using setrlimits (similar in spirit to [17]), and restricting CPU-time, clock-time and memory usage.

The queue manager waits the correction of the virtual machine. If it takes too long, an error is reported to the administrator (failure or possible attack) and the machine is rebooted. In case of success, the verdict and its related information is stored in the database.

Ideally, once a virtual machine has corrected a submission, this virtual machine would be rebooted. However, rebooting after each correction takes too much time and our experience restoring machines from a frozen state is negative. So we resort to just killing all nobody processes and only rebooting machines after a dozen of corrections so as to amortize the reboot time.

All connections use SSH or HTTPS. The only step that requires root privileges is the switch to the chrooted and unprivileged user environment, which is done with a setuid program.

4. THE PROBLEMS

Most of the problems publicly available in Jutge.org have been written by the authors in order to teach their respective courses at Universitat Politècnica de Catalunya (UPC). Many of these problems are at introductory and medium levels, while the average level of the problems in other online judges as UVA and SPOJ is much higher. This reflects that Jutge.org is an educative online judge.

In this section, we first present the problem collections publicly available. We then survey which kinds of problems exist.

4.1 Problem collection

Right now, Jutge.org contains more than 800 problems publicly available. These problems are organized in the following courses:

Learning to program: This course is aimed to students who want to learn programming from scratch using an imperative language. This course is further organized in different graded lists: Introduction, First loops, Loops inside loops, First procedures, Recursivity, Sequences, Consolidation I, Unidimensional arrays, Multidimensional arrays, Tuples, Fundamental algorithms, and Consolidation II.

Algorithms: This course is a continuation of the previous one, placing its emphasis on the use of data structures and the application of basic algorithmic techniques. It currently contains the following lists: Backtracking (Subsets), Backtracking (Permutations), Backtracking (Consolidation), Dynamic programming (1), Binary search, Divide and conquer, Sets and maps, Stacks, Queues and priority queues, Greedy algorithms, Graph algorithms, Parsing problems, More backtracking, Brute force, Dynamic programming (2), and Other problems.

Problems from the OIE contests: This course gathers all problems used in the Spanish Olympiads (see Section 5). Thus, the problems in this course are oriented towards users with some programming experience and their difficulty ranges from easy to hard.

Problems from the UPC contests: This course gathers all problems used in the programming contests organized by the Universitat Politècnica de Catalunya (UPC) to train and select students to participate in the ACM ICPC contests. Thus, the problems in this course require some knowledge on algorithms and sound programming. This course contains most of the more difficult problems in this judge.

Problems from the FME Contests: This course gathers all problems used in the programming contests organized at the Facultat de Matemàtiques i Estadística (FME) among the students of a second semestral course on algorithms. The problems in this course also require some knowledge on algorithms and programming but are, in general, easier than those of the UPC contests.

Problems on Mathematics and **Problems on Physics:** These courses include problems related to mathematics and physics. They are still under development. Their goal is to provide interest on programming to people in these areas.

Many of the problems have been tested extensively by UPC students during the latest five years. As a consequence, we are quite confident about their statements, solutions and test cases.

4.2 IO problems versus procedural problems

Many online judges follow the UVa model and ask for programs that read some input and write some output depending on that input. Other judges, as TopCoder, ask for some class or function with a fixed interface on their arguments.

Jutge.org offers both approaches. Most of the problems follow the IO model, but other problems explicitly ask for a conformant function or class. Indeed, procedures, functions and classes are a fundamental concept taught in introductory courses.

For instance, problem P22654 asks to write a C++ procedure `void decompose(int n, int& h, int& m, int& s);` that, given a quantity of seconds n, computes how many hours h, minutes m and seconds s it represents. Likewise, problem P48763 asks to implement some methods for a *Clock* class.

Problems that ask to write a particular function also may arise when the problem setter wants to check that an efficient sublinear solution has been used. For instance, dichotomic search (P81966).

In any case, in order to test candidate solutions to these problems, the problem setter must write a client program that will call the function written by the student. A difficulty we face with this type of problems is that both their statement and their associated client programs must take into account the target programming language.

4.3 Checkers

Most problem statements on online judges are written in an unambiguous way, specifying the set of valid inputs and their corresponding unique correct outputs. The validation process of a submission is easy: the outputs of each test case produced by a candidate solutions must exactly match the outputs produced by the reference solution. As said in Section 3.4, when the differences are only minor a "*Presentation error*" verdict is reported.

In Jutge.org, most of the problems are also of this type, but the system also offers some variations (internally implemented by *checkers*) that we survey below.

Lousy checkers. In many cases, enforcing a strict format of the output is unnecessary. The problem setter may not care whether words must be separated by one space, two spaces or a blank line. Likewise, the case of the letters may not matter. Problems whose output should take into account these considerations use the *lousy checker*. So, the effect of this checker is turning "*Presentation error*" verdicts into "*Accepted*" ones.

Elastic checkers. In many enumerative problems, the order of the output is also irrelevant, provided it contains all what it must contain but not more. For instance, problem P79494 asks for a list of all possible completions of a sudoku puzzle. Here, the order in which all solutions are written is not essential and, in fact, forcing a particular order would complicate the statement and negatively affect the creativity of the student. Analogously, in problem P18957, where all subsets of $\{1, ..., n\}$ must be printed, the order in which these 2^n subsets are written is not important and, furthermore, the order in which the elements of each subset are written is also irrelevant.

To handle this type of problems, Jutge.org offers *elastic checkers* that, given a specification of the separators of the elements, take these considerations into account. We note that these checkers can also report "*Presentation errors*" by default.

Epsilon checker. In some types of mathematical problems, floating point precision can be an issue. In some cases, these issues render some problems too unstable to be written (for instance, *are three given points aligned?*). In other cases, when the output of a problem is a floating point number, an approximation can be tolerated. To address this issue, the *epsilon checker*, given an ε value, tolerates and absolute error of ε between the values in the reference output and the candidate output. For instance, problem P37619 asks to compute the sine of an angle using Taylor series.

External checkers. In some problems, solutions are not unique. For instance, the Minimum Spanning Tree problem can have many optimal solutions for each weighted graph given as input. Jutge.org offers a powerful way to check the output for this type of problems using *external checkers*. An external checker is another program (written by the problem setter) that, given an input of the problem and given the output of a candidate solution on that input, decides whether this solution is correct or not. For instance, in the case of the MST, the checker would first read the weighted graph, then compute the weight of a MST using its own solution; afterwards, it would read the edges listed by the output of the candidate solution and, finally, would check that these exists, that they really form a spanning tree and, that the sum of their weights equals the one found by the reference solution. P43694 is such a problem.

5. EXPERIENCE

In this section we describe several case studies using the system.

5.1 Programació-1

Jutge.org is an evolution of our previous experience with the "Jutge de P1", an online judge specially aimed for and restricted to the students of the course Programació-1 taught at Facultat d'Informàtica de Barcelona (FIB). P1 is a first-year, compulsory, one semester programming course that assumes no previous knowledge on computers in general nor programming in particular. In average, 400 students take this course each semester.

A detailed account on the experience organizing P1 using the judge during six semesters was given in [12]. The main characteristic of this course is its very strong emphasis placed in solving programming problems. Indeed, the fundamental objective of P1 was stated as: *"a student passing P1 must be able to confidently code correct, readable programs solving problems of elementary difficulty"*. All P1 exams were online.

Consequently, this course required, on the one hand, an extensive problem collection, carefully selected and ordered, and on the other hand, a fully automatic judge to validate in real time the programs submitted by the students. Our opinion is that using an on-line judge offers several advantages for such a course:

- As a learning tool, it is a useful device to learn programming, since it contains an extensive list of exercises, automatically evaluates the solutions submitted by students throughout the course and gives an immediate verdict about their correctness (relying in very exhaustive test cases).
- As a tool for helping on the evaluation process, the on-line judge makes it possible to grade students precisely in the competence that they must acquire, that is, solving simple programming problems. This includes reading and understanding the statement of a problem, thinking about an algorithm solving it, coding it, and checking that it works. In addition, the judge is objective and unbiased.
- As a tool for monitoring students progress, the on-line judge provides a source of objective, untainted data from a hitherto unknown depth to us. The instructors can easily access this data, both as global statistics on all students enrolled, or as particular data restricted to a particular student or programming problem.

With respect to the observed results, [12] shows that there is a clear correlation between the amount of problems the students solve and the grades they obtain; also, that a great majority of the students that solve the laboratory and homework problems pass the course. Unfortunately, the data collected on the on-line judge made clear that the effort that most students dedicated to the course was far from the workload required according to the number of ECTS credits. As a sad but logical result, a high number of those students failed P1.

5.2 Courses on algorithms

Similarly, Jutge.org has also been used for students in their second year/course of studies, emphasizing a syllabus more related to data structures and algorithms. In particular, Anàlisi i Disseny d'Algorismes and Estructures de Dades i Algorismes at FIB and

Informàtica-2 and Algorísmia at FME. In these courses, about a third of the grade is based on an online exam using the judge.

5.3 Various competitive experiences

While Jutge.org emphasises education, it can also be used as an online system to organize programming contests.

The most visible event hosted by Jutge.org is the organization since 2007 of the Olimpiada Informática Española (OIE), which is an annual programming contest open to students in Spanish high schools. The OIE is organized in two rounds: In the first round, contestants participate in an online contest organized via the Internet. In the second round, the top 25 students are invited to participate, in-place, in a final contest. The four OIE champions represent Spain at the International Olympiad in Informatics. Participants in the OIE also use Jutge.org in order to train themselves, access the problems of the past years and practice in warm-up contests. For historical reasons, OIE participants use another web front-end (olimpiada-informatica.org) to access our online judge.

Our system has also been used since 2003 to train and select the students from our university (UPC) that participate in the regional ACM ICPC contests. Analogously, the Universitat Pompeu Fabra has recently used Jutge.org in order to organize their contests.

5.4 Promotion of CS in 2ary and high school

The authors of Jutge.org are also involved in courses that promote computer science and computational thinking at secondary and high school levels. Recently, three such courses have taken place, sponsored by the Joves i Ciència program of Catalunya-Caixa, whose mission is to enhance the scientific activity of young students with interest, motivation and talent for science. These are intensive courses targeted to high school students with top performance but with no (or minimal) experience in programming. The courses take place for one week just at the beginning or the end of the school summer holidays and are taught by university professors with the help of university students.

The syllabus of these courses is similar to the one that we have described for P1, probably with less width and depth, but combining a strongly practical approach with a minimal theory to guarantee scientific rigour. Their development is purposely set under an entertaining mood.

The feedback received by the Joves i Ciència program after these courses is that the students are very satisfied with the experience and specially appreciate its practical approach. Not surprisingly, some of them find the course too intense, while others enjoy such an intensive course.

6. CONCLUSION

In this paper we have surveyed the resources, the functionality and the implementation of Jutge.org, an online judge specially built with an educative aim. We have also related it to various teaching experiences.

Built on a base of more the 800 clearly organized and graded problems, the main features of Jutge.org for instructors are the automation of the correction process, the creation and maintenance of their own courses and rosters, the management of their assignment lists, and the access to instant information about the progress of their students. The main features of Jutge.org for students are the possibility to enroll in their instructor courses and in public courses, to get instant feedback on their solutions, and to practice with many different programming languages.

The different experiences we have reported include the instruction of two massive courses (a first programming course and a course on basic algorithms and data structures) that have involved thousands of university students, the instruction of intensive courses to promote computer science among high school students, and the organization of several events, such as internal university contests and the Spanish Olympiads in informatics. These experiences, which already account for half a million of submissions, confirm the flexibility, robustness and reliability of Jutge.org.

For the near future, further system deployment is envisaged. On one hand, we are considering the use of cloud resources to distribute our correction load. On the other hand, we are working towards data mining the most discriminative and small data sets for each problem, based on the many wrong submissions we have historically received. We expect that distilling and offering these highly discriminative inputs to students and tutors would boost their productivity.

Finally, we would like to mention that Jutge.org has recently been extended in order to support formal verification techniques to assist teaching in logic circuit design [7].

7. REFERENCES

[1] CodeChef. http://www.codechef.com.

[2] Moodle. http://moodle.org.

[3] Sphere Online Judge. http://www.spoj.pl.

[4] Timus Online Judge. http://acm.timus.ru.

[5] TopCoder. http://www.topcoder.com.

[6] UVa Online Judge. http://http://uva.onlinejudge.org.

[7] J. Carmona, J. Cortadella, J. de San Pedro, and J. Petit. Integrating formal verification in an on-line judge for e-learning digital circuit design. In *Proc. of the 43rd ACM Technical Symposium on Computer Science Education (SIGCSE-2012)*, 2012.

[8] A. Caterineu and J. Petit. Jutge.org: Instructor's Guide. http://www.jutge.org/documentation/guide.pdf, 2011.

[9] B. Cheang, A. Kurnia, A. Lim, and W.-C. Oon. On automated grading of programming assignments in an academic institution. *Computers & Education*, 41(2):121–131, 2003.

[10] C. Douce, D. Livingstone, and J. Orwell. Automatic test-based assessment of programming: A review. *ACM Journal on Educational Resources in Computing*, 5(3), 2005.

[11] M. Forišek. Security of Programming Contest Systems. In V. Dagiene and R. Mittermeir, editors, *Information Technologies at School*, pages 553–563, 2006.

[12] O. Giménez, J. Petit, and S. Roura. Programació 1: A pure problem-oriented approach for a CS1 course. In C. Hermann, T. Lauer, T. Ottmann, and M. Welte, editors, *Proc. of the Informatics Education Europe IV (IEE-2009)*, pages 185–192, Freiburg, 2009.

[13] M. Joy, N. Griffiths, and R. Boyatt. The BOSS online submission and assessment system. *ACM Journal on Educational Resources in Computing*, 5(3), 2005.

[14] A. Kosowski, M. Malafiejski, and T. Noinski. Application of an online judge & contester system in academic tuition. In *ICWL'07*, pages 343–354, 2007.

[15] A. Kurnia, A. Lim, and B. Cheang. Online judge. *Computers & Education*, pages 299–315, 2001.

[16] M. Revilla, S. Manzoor, and R. Liu. Competitive learning in informatics: The UVa online judge experience. *Olympiads in Informatics*, 2:131–148, 2008.

[17] B. Yee et al. Native client: A sandbox for portable, untrusted x86 native code. In *Proceedings of the IEEE Symposium on Security and Privacy*, 2009.

Integrating Formal Verification in an Online Judge for e-Learning Logic Circuit Design *

Javier de San Pedro, Josep Carmona, Jordi Cortadella, and Jordi Petit
Departament de Llenguatges i Sistemes Informàtics, Universitat Politècnica de Catalunya
Barcelona, Spain
jspedro@lsi.upc.edu, jcarmona@lsi.upc.edu, jordicf@lsi.upc.edu, jpetit@lsi.upc.edu

ABSTRACT

This paper investigates the use of formal verification techniques to create online judges that can assist in teaching logic circuit design. Formal verification not only contributes to give an exact assessment about correctness, but also saves the instructor the tedious task of designing test cases. The paper explains how formal verification has been integrated in an online judge. It also describes the courseware created for a course on logic circuits and the successful experience of using it in a one-week summer course with students from secondary and high school.

Categories and Subject Descriptors

K.3.1 [**Computers and Education**]: Computer Uses in Education—*computer-assisted instruction*; B.6.3 [**Logic Design**]: Design Aids—*hardware description languages, verification*

General Terms

Algorithms, Design, Human factors

Keywords

Formal verification, logic circuit design, online judge, Verilog

1. INTRODUCTION

Most bachelor programs in Computer Science/Engineering include some course on designing logic circuits. At the time students take this course, they are usually familiar with basic programming concepts in some high-level language and have some knowledge about good programming practices: simplicity, cost, modularity, re-usability, etc. Most of their programming skills have been obtained by trying to solve many programming problems of increasing difficulty.

One of the most important decisions in creating a course syllabus on logic design is to choose the formalism to specify and describe circuits. In a similar way as students are exposed to programming by using high-level languages (e.g., C, C++, Java) and automatic tools (compilers) to translate a program into machine language, we strongly advocate for using a similar approach when designing circuits [17, 19]. This approach is not as disruptive as it looks when compared with the modern practice in industry today. Designers describe their circuits with *Hardware Description Languages* (HDL) and implement their circuits using CAD tools that automatically generate logic netlists [12]. The netlists are later transformed into layouts using physical synthesis tools. Indeed, as the time of assembly language passed long ago and common programming continuously evolves towards more abstract paradigms, the time of schematic capture has also passed and circuit design has evolved towards a more reliable and productive methodology based on HDLs.

Another important issue when creating a course on logic circuits is designing a set of problems that enables students to apply the theoretical concepts they learn to practical problems, and how to handle the assessment of these problems. Drawing a parallelism with our experience on computer programming, we advocate for the use of a collection of problems of increasing difficulty and the use of a online judge to automatically correct their solutions. Online judges have a variety of advantages that make them appealing for modern teaching methodologies: permanent and immediate assessment, adaptation to the progress of each student, more productivity, etc. See [5, 13] for an overview on online programming judges.

This paper introduces a novel online judge that uses formal verification to automatically correct problems on logic circuit design. Some features of this judge make it unique among the existing ones:

- Circuits are described using a HDL.
- Correctness is proved for all possible input stimuli by using formal verification techniques and tools.
- No test cases have to be designed to assess about correctness.
- When an incorrect circuit is submitted, the judge provides a counterexample trace for which the circuit behavior differs from the expected one.

These features have been implemented in Jutge.org, a open access educational online programming judge that already offers 800 programming problems [10] using several programming languages. Thanks to the new innovative correction engine, Jutge.org currently offers an introductory course of digital circuit design that includes a large variety of assignments on logic design, from simple combinational circuits to complex sequential controllers, all carefully orga-

*This work has partially been supported by the Spanish project FORMALISM (TIN2007-66523) and by the Catalan Government (SGR 2009-1137).

Permission to make digital or hard copies of all or part of this work for personal or classroom use is granted without fee provided that copies are not made or distributed for profit or commercial advantage and that copies bear this notice and the full citation on the first page. To copy otherwise, to republish, to post on servers or to redistribute to lists, requires prior specific permission and/or a fee.
SIGCSE'12, February 29–March 3, 2012, Raleigh, North Carolina, USA.
Copyright 2012 ACM 978-1-4503-1098-7/12/02 ...$10.00.

nized and sorted by difficulty. About 60 new problems on circuits can now be solved in Verilog, other HDLs being under preparation.

An approach that shares the main objectives of this paper was proposed in [8], where students can submit their design with LogicFlash [9], a graphic tool for schematic capture. Combinational circuits are checked by generating all possible input patterns. Sequential circuits are checked by generating a set of test patterns that cover all the state transitions of an automaton designed by the instructor. That approach suffers from various problems: (1) the cost of checking correctness becomes prohibitive for large circuits (e.g. a 32-bit adder), (2) many sequential circuits (e.g., counters, shift registers, sequential arithmetic circuits, register files, etc) cannot be practically described with automata and, (3) the coverage of all state transitions in an automaton does not guarantee correctness for all possible input traces. In contrast, the approach we present is able to handle circuits of medium complexity. For example, circuits that generate the Fibonacci series (8-bit numbers) or compute the greatest common divisor using Euclid's algorithm (6-bit numbers) have been proved (or disproved) to be correct. The verification of a simple 8-bit CPU with more than 30 internal flip-flops is also possible.

The paper is organized as follows. To start, as preliminaries, we overview HDLs. Afterwards, we present a guided tour that presents our courseware and its use. Then, we explain which formal verification techniques we apply to assess the correction of the candidate solutions and we show their implementation and integration in Jutge.org. Finally, we describe our experience using the system in a one-week summer course with talented high-school students, draw some conclusions, and advance ideas towards future work.

2. PRELIMINARIES: HDLS

The design, simulation, synthesis and verification of hardware devices can be accomplished by the use of a Hardware Description Language (HDL) [15].

The primitives of a HDL can describe the structure and behavior of logic circuits. In contrast to programming languages, HDLs incorporate three aspects that make them suitable for describing hardware:

1. *Notion of time*: the language provides statements to support time and delays of the components.
2. *Concurrency/Parallelism*: the semantics of the language is inherently concurrent, i.e., different components of the system are assumed to operate in parallel.
3. *Simulation capabilities*: circuit specifications can be validated by designing *testbenches*, i.e., modules that instantiate the design and monitor the reaction to a set of input stimuli. This capability contributes to gain confidence on the design's intended function, but also enables *architectural exploration*, i.e., evaluating and comparing different implementations of the same circuit.

Verilog [18] and VHDL [3] are the most popular HDLs used in logic circuit design. Verilog has been chosen for the on-line judge, however an extension to VHDL would also be feasible by using the appropriate synthesis tools.

Verilog. The primitives provided by Verilog allow different descriptions of the functionality of a circuit. *Structural* models are used to described hierarchical netlists of logic gates or instances of other modules. *Dataflow* models are used to describe combinational logic by means of different types of operators (logical, arithmetic, relational, bit-wise, etc). Finally, *behavioral* models are used to describe the functionality using primitives similar to those

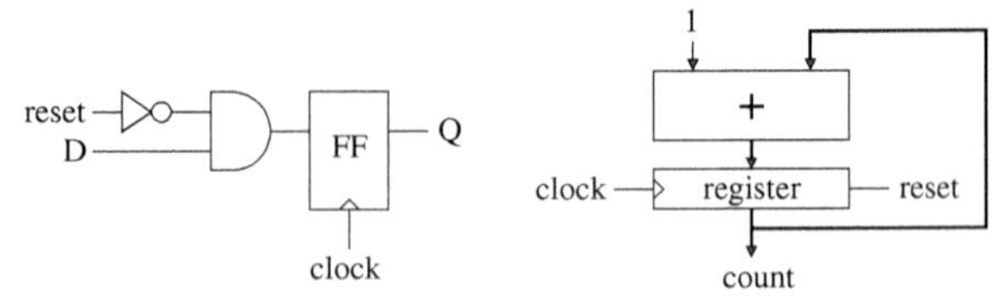

Figure 1: Circuits inferred by the description of a flip-flop and an n-bit counter with synchronous reset.

provided in programming languages (conditional, looping, concurrency, etc).

The syntax of Verilog is similar to the C programming language, also very popular both in education and industry. A Verilog design consists of a hierarchy of modules, where modules may communicate through input and output ports. A module can contain a combination of the following: net/variable declarations, concurrent and sequential statement blocks, and instances of other modules.

Below we can see a structural description of a full adder. The circuit has three inputs (*a*, *b* and *cin*) and two outputs (*sum* and *cout*) and contains a set of logic gates (*xor*, *and*, *or*) connected to the inputs, outputs and wires.

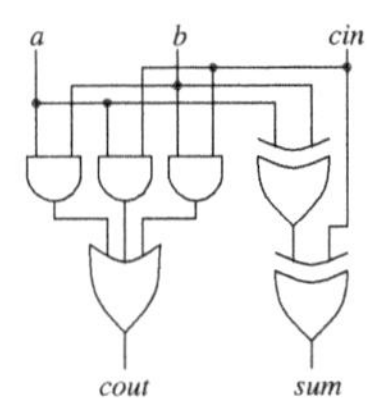


```
module full_adder (a, b, cin, sum, cout);
  input a, b, cin;
  output sum, cout;
  wire x1, x2, x3;
  xor (sum, a, b, cin);
  and (x1, a, b);
  and (x2, a, cin);
  and (x3, b, cin);
  or (cout, x1, x2, x3);
endmodule
```

An implementation with the same behavior can be described with a dataflow model using logic equations, as shown below.

```
module full_adder (a, b, cin, sum, cout);
  input a, b, cin;
  output sum, cout;
  assign sum = a ^ b ^ cin;
  assign cout = a & b | cin & (a | b);
endmodule
```

For sequential systems, Verilog provides the *always* statement, commonly used to model the behavior of memory elements triggered by signal events. This is the statement typically used to describe flip-flops and latches in sequential circuits. For example, the next two examples illustrate how the behavior of a flip-flop and an n-bit counter with synchronous reset can be modeled using the *always* statement.

```
// flip-flop behavior
always @(posedge clock)
  if ( reset ) Q <= 0;
  else Q <= D;
```

```
// counter behavior
always @(posedge clock)
  if ( reset ) count <= 0;
  else count <= count + 1;
```

A Verilog compiler would automatically infer the logic gates and flip-flops to implement the behavior described above. Possible netlists derived by the compiler are shown in Fig. 1. The circuits could be later simplified by CAD tools that would automatically propagate the constants at the inputs and eliminate the redundant logic gates.

Synthesizable HDL. Both Verilog and VHDL have language subsets declared as *synthesizable* [2], meaning that CAD tools can automatically infer circuit structures that implement the specified functionality. Typically, the synthesizable subset includes the structural and dataflow models of the language. Whereas some complex operators (such as multiplication or division) may not always be included, addition/subtraction, relational and bit-wise operators are always included. The synthesizable subset is the one used by the students and the online judge to design and verify the circuits.

Besides various commercial tools, there are several open-source Verilog compilers/simulators. We have used Icarus Verilog [20].

3. GUIDED TOUR

This section offers a guided tour to the course on logic circuit design and the new judge engine that we have created. We encourage the reader to follow these steps in his/her web browser.

The course is available at Jutge.org, an open access educational online programming judge [10]. In order to access it, users can log in at https://www.jutge.org using the demo account or freely registering their own account. Afterwards, users should enroll the "*Introduction to Digital Circuit Design*" course in the Courses section. At this point, users can access its 60 problems (identified with a short hash code) and organized in the following lists:

Combinational circuits: Simple controllers, multiplexers, voting systems, priority encoders, properties on numbers, ...

Arithmetic circuits: Starts from 1-bit adders/comparators and progresses to n-bit adder/subtractors, comparators, incrementers and small ALUs.

Sequential circuits: Includes various up/down counters, sequence recognizers, simple control circuits (e.g., a traffic-light controller) and some sequential arithmetic (e.g., a generator of Fibonacci series or a calculator of the GCD using Euclid's algorithm).

A simple CPU: The design is split in four components (ALU, datapath, program counter and control unit) that are finally connected to create a complete 8-bit CPU with small instruction/data memories.

As an example, consider problem X12983 (the second problem in the Arithmetic Circuits list), which asks for the implementation of a full adder.

To solve this problem, a student could write an implementation either in structural form (using logic gates) or in dataflow form (using logic equations), such as the ones presented in the previous section for the module *full_adder*. In either case, these descriptions can be automatically synthesized into circuits that can be later verified for correctness.

To validate the implementation, our student would submit this piece of code to the judge, which would produce a verdict in a few seconds. Typical verdicts include "*Compilation error*", "*Accepted*", or "*Wrong answer*". In the case of the latest, the judge would also offer a set of values for the input ports that causes such wrong answer.

In order to test the correctness of a student's implementation, the problem setter has provided a *golden model* that will be never be disclosed to the students. This model can be at any level of abstraction, e.g., using arithmetic operators. For instance, this is the actual golden model provided for the full adder problem:

```
module full_adder (a, b, cin, sum, cout);
  input a, b, cin;
  output sum, cout;
  assign {cout, sum} = a + b + cin;
endmodule
```

After solving the previous problem, our student could tackle problem X84292, which asks for an N-bit adder. A possible implementation could use an array of N instances of full adders:

```
module adder (A, B, cin, SUM, cout);
  parameter N = 16;
  input [N-1:0] A, B;
  input cin;
  output [N-1:0] SUM;
  output cout;
  wire [N-1:1] carry;
  full_adder FA[N-1:0] (A, B, {carry,cin}, SUM, {cout,carry});
endmodule
```

The flow is similar for sequential circuits. For example, the problem X05944 proposes the design of a (*mod 3*)-counter that generates the sequence $0, 1, 2, 0, 1, 2, \cdots$. The golden model implements the counter using a behavioral conditional statement:

```
module mod3_counter (count, clk, rst);
  input clk, rst;
  output reg [1:0] count;
  always @(posedge clk)
    if (rst | (count == 2)) count <= 0;
    else count <= count + 1;
endmodule
```

Let us assume the student misunderstands the specification of the problem and implements a conventional (*mod 4*)-counter with a 2-bit adder and a register as follows:

```
module mod3_counter(count, clk, rst);
  input clk, rst;
  output [1:0] count;
  wire [1:0] next_count;
  wire cout;
  adder #(2) _add_ (count, 1, 0, next_count, cout);
  register #(2) _reg_ (next_count, count, clk, rst);
endmodule
```

In this case, the judge will report a *"Wrong answer"*. More interestingly, the judge will also provide *the shortest trace* from the initial state to an erroneous state. This trace will be reported in textual and graphical form, as shown in Fig. 2, where the circle indicates the unexpected value according to the specification of the problem.

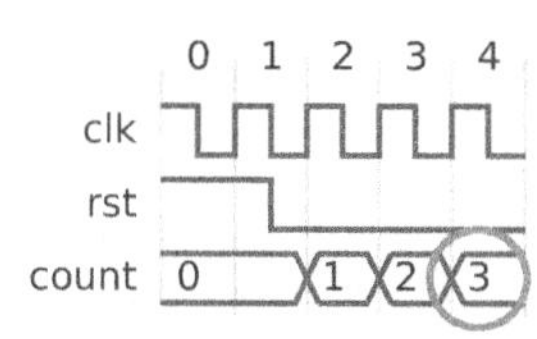

Figure 2: Waveform report for the mod3_counter circuit.

In the next two sections a detailed explanation on the underlying theory and techniques is provided for the interested reader.

4. FORMAL VERIFICATION

Testing shows the presence, not the absence of bugs.
E.W. Dijkstra.

Although simulation may provide insights on the correctness of a circuit, one cannot have an absolute guarantee of its correctness unless the circuit is exercised with *all possible input stimuli*. This requirement makes simulation inviable for the verification of circuits with medium/large complexity.

In the last three decades, there has been a significant progress in Boolean reasoning methods for equivalence checking. Two main techniques have been proposed to symbolically enumerate all possible states of a circuit: Binary Decision Diagrams (BDD) [4] and

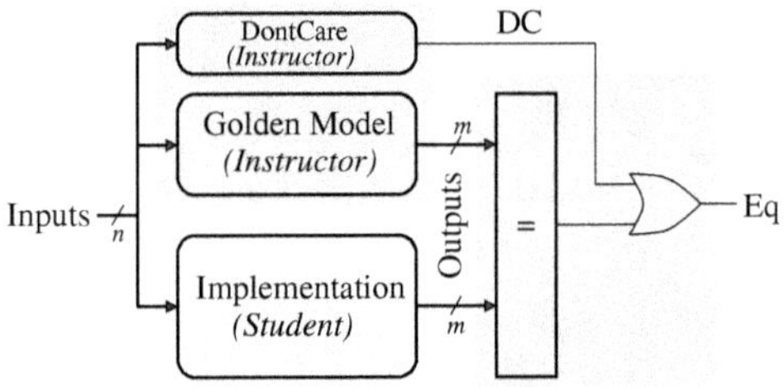

Figure 3: Miter created to verify sequential equivalence.

SAT solvers [11]. Still, the methods for the equivalence checking of sequential machines can only handle small circuits (e.g., few dozens of state variables) when the internal sequential elements of the two circuits (golden model and implementation) are different. When the sequential structure is the same, the problem can be reduced to combinational equivalence checking [14].

Unfortunately, the problem we are facing needs to prove, in general, the equivalence of sequential machines that are internally different, since the states variables of the golden model may differ from the ones used by the student. They may have different number of flip-flops, state encoding and initial state.

Golden model vs. implementation. The equivalence of the two circuits is checked by creating a *miter*, as shown in Fig. 3. A miter is a circuit that is derived from the two original circuits, inserting a comparator to compare the outputs of the two circuits. The circuits are equivalent when the output of the miter, *Eq*, is proved to be a tautology (always at 1).

In case of combinational circuits, equivalence is reduced to a satisfiability problem, i.e., finding an assignment that contradicts *Eq*. If it does not exist, the circuits are equivalent.

In case of sequential circuits, all the reachable states of the miter must be visited using all the possible input stimuli. This is a much costly task and symbolic techniques (e.g., using BDDs) are often used to mitigate the state explosion problem.

In our case, we have chosen an open-source tool that has become state-of-the-art in the verification community: *NuSMV* [6]. NuSMV is a symbolic model checker [7] that can verify circuit properties specified in temporal logic [16]. For the verification of sequential equivalence, NuSMV receives the miter circuit and the invariant property that "*Eq must always be true*".

Don't cares. In different situations, equivalence does not need to be strict. For example, before the two circuits are reset, the observed behavior may differ. Two circuits transferring data do not need to show the same output while the "*valid*" bit is not asserted.

For such cases, the miter can be enhanced with an auxiliary circuit (DontCare in Fig. 3) that masks the equivalence of the outputs when they do not need to be equivalent. The DontCare circuit must be provided by the instructor together with the golden model. More specifically, the *don't care* conditions (DC) can be specified for each individual output of the circuit (not shown in the figure).

Error traces. Under the unsatisfactory case that the implementation is not equivalent to the golden model, formal verification tools can provide a valuable feedback to the student: a counterexample that disproves the equivalence of the circuits. In case of a combinational circuit, the counterexample is simply an assignment to the inputs for which the outputs differ. In case of sequential circuits, the tool can report a trace of input stimuli that drives the erroneous circuit from the initial state to the state that produces the unexpected output. Typically, sequential verifiers are capable of generating the shortest trace to an error condition.

```
MODULE example(a)
VAR r: boolean;
ASSIGN next(r) := !(a | r);
```

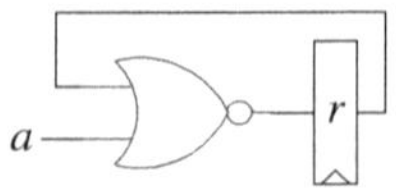

Figure 4: NuSMV model for a simple circuit.

5. VERIFICATION PROCESS

5.1 Overall flow

Verification starts by first synthesizing the Verilog models. For this, we use Icarus Verilog [20], which transforms the model into an internal hierarchical representation. Icarus Verilog can also be customized with plugins that can access the internal representation and generate other models. This is the strategy we have used to generate NuSMV models from Verilog.

Once the model provided by the student has been transformed into a NuSMV module, it is combined with the golden model provided by the instructor to create the miter circuit shown in Fig. 3. We next provide more details on the verification flow.

5.2 Conversion to NuSMV model

NuSMV has a modeling language for finite systems that can describe the sequential behavior of Boolean signals. Figure 4 depicts a simple example of a circuit with one input signal (*a*) and one output signal (*r*), where the output signal is also a state variable (declaration of `VAR`). The `ASSIGN` statement describes the behavior of each signal assigning a Boolean expression. When the behavior is sequential, `next(`*r*`)` is used to denote the value of the signal at the *next* cycle. More details about the NuSMV language can be found in [6, 1].

The circuit internal representation of Icarus Verilog is a hypergraph, where the nodes represent the synthesized components and the hyperedges represent the wires connecting the components.

The nodes can represent logic gates or special modules from a *Library of Parametrized Modules* (LPMs) performing higher level functions (e.g., integer addition, register, ...). The LPMs are assumed to be implemented with pre-designed logic blocks for each target technology.

Let us illustrate the conversion to NuSMV with a the example below, that models a counter with a control signal (*inc*) that indicates when the value of the counter must be incremented.

```
module counter(clk, rst, inc, count);
  input clk, rst, inc;
  output reg [1:0] count;
  always @(posedge clk)
    if (rst) count <= 0;
    else if (inc) count <= count + 1;
endmodule
```

Icarus Verilog will produce an internal representation as the one shown in Fig. 5. The ports from the original module are represented by ellipsis. Additionally, two LPMs have been synthesized: a register and an adder. The hyperedges are represented by the circles between nodes.

This representation corresponds to the schematic shown in Fig. 6 with an *N*-bit counter and one additional connection of the *inc* port to the Chip Enable (CE) port of the register.

By traversing the graph backward from the output ports and state variables, it is possible to reach the driver of each signal in the circuit and derive the expressions that determine their behavior.

The NuSMV model is generated by traversing the graph and using the following conversion rules:

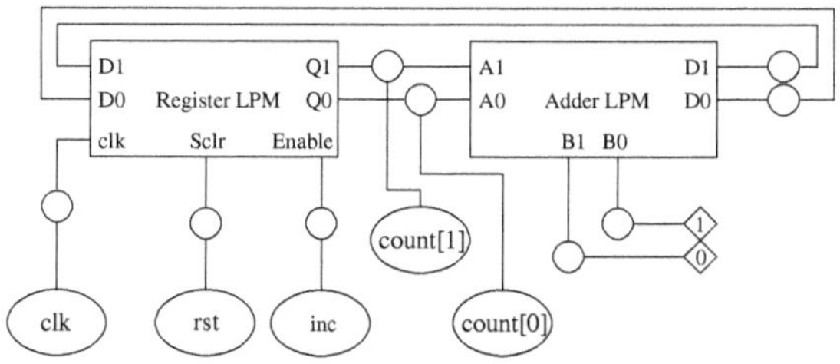

Figure 5: Icarus internal graph for the counter circuit.

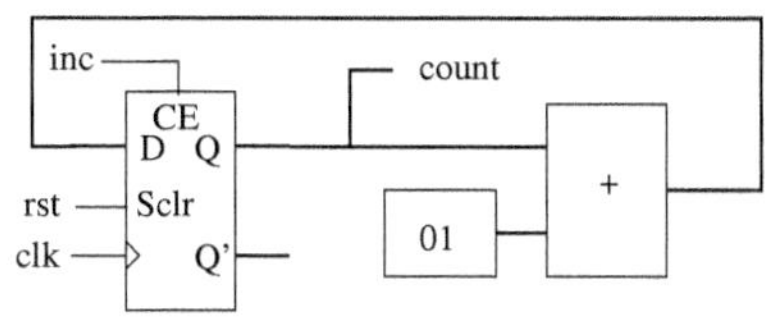

Figure 6: Schematic for the counter circuit.

1. Verilog modules are converted into NuSMV modules and input ports are converted into module parameters.

2. Instances inside a module are converted into NuSMV instances, and the real argument expressions that are passed to those instances are generated by graph traversal.

3. Output ports are converted into `define` statements, and their expressions are calculated by graph traversal. Other generated expressions can then refer to these definitions as if they were NuSMV output parameters.

By using the previous transformation rules, the following NuSMV model is obtained for the counter:

```
MODULE counter(inc, rst)
VAR
    ff: lpm_register (add.Q, inc , rst );
    add: lpm_adder(ff.Q, 0b2_01);
DEFINE
    count := ff.Q;
```

5.3 Generation of the miter

Once both NuSMV models have been generated, the miter module is generated by adding a comparator of all the output ports. The miter is the top NuSMV module that will be subject to verification.

At this stage, the property for verification is also generated. The property is an invariant that guarantees that *Eq* is always asserted after the circuit has been reset.

LPM definitions are also included as NuSMV modules. These definitions are instanced from a manually created set of NuSMV modules for each of the possible LPMs. For example, the definition of the *lpm_register* with support for synchronous clear and chip enable signals (like the one in Fig. 5) is the following:

```
MODULE lpm_register(Data, Sclr, Enable)
VAR     Q : word[< register_size >];
ASSIGN  next(Q) := case
    Sclr : 0;          -- If clear is raised
    Enable : Data;     -- If chip enabled
    TRUE : Q;          -- Otherwise, keep current value
  esac;
```

An important observation is that the NuSMV models ignore the clock signal. The reason for that is because the circuits to be verified are assumed to have a single clock that triggers all sequential elements on the rising edge. In this way, the NuSMV model can safely assume that the implicit clock of the system corresponds to the common clock used in the Verilog models.

5.4 Verification and error diagnosis

After executing the top model with the miter, NuSMV gives an answer stating whether the requested property is asserted. In case it is not asserted, NuSMV also emits an error diagnosis by providing a counterexample trace of the input stimuli that drive the circuit from the initial state to another state in which the outputs differ.

Since the structure of the NuSMV model is isomorphic to that of the original circuit, the system can easily generate an equivalent trace in Verilog-like syntax and a graphical representation as a waveform, as shown in Fig. 2.

5.5 Integration in Jutge.org

The verification process previously presented has been integrated in Jutge.org. Internally, Jutge.org is designed as a distributed master-slave system, with a master computer that offers the web server, stores the database and keeps the submission queue, and several slave servers that host the different virtual machines that perform the actual correction tasks under a secure environment [10]. In order to correct a submission, a slave machine receives the problem description (including the golden model), the candidate solution and a driver module, which guides the compilation, execution and checking process to produce a verdict.

Thanks to the modular architecture of Jutge.org, extending the system to accommodate problems on circuits has been an easy task. On the back-end (subsystem that corrects submissions), it was only needed to create a new driver to guide the correction of problems on circuits. This driver implements all of the validation steps as detailed in this section. On the front-end (web interface), it was just necessary to add some features to offer a nice display of the information computed together with the verdict as, for instance, the error traces and waveforms.

6. A SUMMER COURSE ON CIRCUITS

The courseware we have described was first used in an intensive, one-week summer course (7 hours/day) on logic circuit design during July 2011. There were 26 students from secondary and high-school (mostly 16/17-year old) that had no previous knowledge about circuit design. The course was sponsored by the Joves i Ciència program of CatalunyaCaixa, whose mission is to enhance the scientific activity of young students with interest, motivation and talent for science.

The main goal of the course was to expose the students to logic design and to exercise their capabilities of logic reasoning by posing challenging problems. Given the origin of the students, there was no special intention of teaching a particular methodology for circuit design, although some common strategies were introduced during the lectures to help them in solving exercises. Except for short periods of time in which some expository lectures were taught (not longer than one hour per day), the students were spending most of the time solving problems on their computers and testing them with the online judge.

Few of the students managed to complete the CPU, whereas most of the students could complete several sequential circuits of different complexity. Interestingly, a few students also worked at night from home with the online judge, even after such an exhausting working day.

Students were free to select their favorite exercises depending on their skills and confidence of success. At the end of the course, 3 students could solve more than 50 exercises, 3 students between 40 and 49 exercises, 13 students between 30 and 39, and 7 students between 20 and 29.

The online judge was essential to achieve a high design productivity that would not have been possible with only the assistance of the 2 or 3 instructors that were permanently in the lecture room. The bandwidth provided by the judge and the assessment delivered by the formal verification tool (counterexamples in erroneous circuits) contributed to have an environment that could continuously help the students without the need of an instructor.

Schematics were rarely used during the course, mostly on the first day to provide the intuitive sense that the components of a circuit are connected with wires. After that, some block diagrams were shown when necessary. The logic gates were introduced on the first day. After a couple of simple exercises, combinational logic was always specified with Boolean equations.

At the end of the course, the students filled up a survey and showed a very high satisfaction with the use of Verilog and the online judge for learning logic circuit design.

On the negative side, we observed that the feedback provided by the judge was so informative that the students were too eager to submit the solution to the judge even before simulating and validating the correctness. While this aspect was not important for the main goals of the course (logic reasoning), it should be taken into account for Bachelor's courses, in which a design methodology including simulation should be stimulated.

7. CONCLUSIONS

While using formal verification to fully prove software correctness is still a utopia, it is becoming a common successful practice in hardware design. In this paper we have shown that it is possible to build an introductory course on digital circuit design around a collection of problems that are automatically corrected by an online judge without test cases. The introduction of formal verification methods in online judges provides a novel paradigm that contributes to broaden the use of such tools in particular and of e-learning techniques in general.

For introductory courses, in which the complexity of the circuits is still small, formal verification can be effectively used to handle a large variety of design examples. This paradigm starts hitting the state explosion wall when the number of state variables of the circuit increases. In these cases, divide-and-conquer schemes to design and verify smaller components of the system can still be used. However, we will have to resort to more conventional approaches based on the simulation of test cases when formal verification cannot go that far, which is the classical approach used today in online judges for programming courses and contests.

The time required by an instructor to write a problem on circuits with formal verification is much less than the time to write programming problems. In both cases the correct solution must be written, but in the former case, there is no need to write an extensive test set as in the latter.

The experience in using this courseware in a one-week intensive summer course with talented high-school students has shown a remarkable productivity in designing different types of circuits with growing complexity, from simple combinational circuits to complex state machines, including a small CPU.

As future work, we are planning to enhance the online judge with the evaluation of different metrics that can assess on the quality and/or suitability of the solution. The number of logic gates or the logic depth of the circuit can be calculated to give a quality metric on complexity and delay. This metric can be compared with the one of the golden model and provide feedback to the student in case a low-quality design has been submitted. For example, if a student designs a slow ripple carry adder when a fast carry-lookahead adder was requested, the judge would report that a circuit with excessive logic depth has been submitted.

8. REFERENCES

[1] NuSMV v2.5 User Manual. http://nusmv.fbk.eu.

[2] J. Bhasker. *Verilog HDL Synthesis: A Practical Primer*. Star Galaxy Publishing, 1998.

[3] J. Bhasker. *A VHDL Primer*. Prentice Hall, third edition, 1999.

[4] R. E. Bryant. Graph-based algorithms for boolean function manipulation. *IEEE Trans. Computers*, 35(8):677–691, 1986.

[5] B. Cheang, A. Kurnia, A. Lim, and W.-C. Oon. On automated grading of programming assignments in an academic institution. *Computers & Education*, 41(2):121–131, 2003.

[6] A. Cimatti et al. NuSMV2: An OpenSource Tool for Symbolic Model Checking. In *Proc. International Conference on Computer-Aided Verification (CAV 2002)*, volume 2404 of *LNCS*. Springer, July 2002.

[7] E. M. Clarke, O. Grumberg, and D. Peled. *Model checking*. MIT Press, 2001.

[8] M. Damm, F. Bauer, and G. Zucker. Solving Digital Logic Assignments with Automatic Verification in SCORM Modules. In *International Conference on Interactive Computer-Aided Learning (ICL)*, pages 359–363, 2009.

[9] M. Damm, B. Klauer, and K. Waldschmidt. LogiFlash - A Flash-based Logic-Simulator for Educational Purposes. In *World Conference on Educational Multimedia, Hypermedia and Telecommunications*, pages 748–750, 2003.

[10] O. Giménez, J. Petit, and S. Roura. Jutge.org: An educational programming judge. In *Proc. of the 43rd ACM Technical Symposium on Computer Science Education (SIGCSE-2012)*, 2012.

[11] E. I. Goldberg, M. R. Prasad, and R. K. Brayton. Using SAT for combinational equivalence checking. In *Proceedings of the Conference on Design, Automation and Test in Europe (DATE)*, pages 114–121, 2001.

[12] D. Jansen. *The Electronic Design Automation Handbook*. Kluwer Academic Publishers, 2003.

[13] M. Joy, N. Griffiths, and R. Boyatt. The BOSS online submission and assessment system. *ACM Journal on Educational Resources in Computing*, 5(3), 2005.

[14] A. Kuehlmann and C. A. J. van Eijk. *Combinational and sequential equivalence checking*, pages 343–372. Kluwer Academic Publishers, 2002.

[15] J. P. Mermet. *Fundamentals and Standards in Hardware Description Languages*. Kluwer Academic Publishers, Norwell, MA, USA, 1993.

[16] A. Pnueli. The temporal logic of programs. In *FOCS*, pages 46–57. IEEE, 1977.

[17] A. Sagahyroon and M. Massoumi. On the use of hardware description languages in teaching VLSI design courses. In *Proceedings of the 26th Annual Frontiers in Education (FIE)*, volume 2, pages 713–716, 1996.

[18] D. E. Thomas and P. Moorby. *The Verilog hardware description language*. Kluwer, third edition, 1996.

[19] Z. Vranesic and S. Brown. Use of HDLs in teaching of computer hardware courses. In *Workshop on Computer Architecture Education (WCAE)*, 2003.

[20] S. Williams. Icarus Verilog. http://iverilog.icarus.com.

Computing For STEM Majors: Enhancing Non CS Majors' Computing Skills[1]

Joel C. Adams   Randall J. Pruim
Department of Computer Science
Calvin College
Grand Rapids, MI 49546
1-616-526-8666
{adams, rpruim}@calvin.edu

ABSTRACT

One of the challenges facing the U.S. technological workforce is that as fewer students take computing courses, fewer college graduates are being prepared for computing careers. Besides trying to attract more CS majors, another approach is to (i) design a computing curriculum that appeals to students and faculty from other (non-CS) disciplines, (ii) use special scholarships to attract students to that curriculum, and (iii) sponsor faculty development workshops for non-CS departments. In this paper, we detail this approach, using a new introductory course oriented to science majors, and scholarships funded by the National Science Foundation Scholarships for Science, Technology, Engineering, and Mathematics (NSF S-STEM) program to motivate non-CS majors to take CS courses. We also present several success stories that this approach has produced in its first two years.

Categories and Subject Descriptors

K.3.2 [**Computers and Education**]: Computer and Information Science Education – *computer science education.*

General Terms

Economics, Experimentation, Human Factors.

Keywords

Computing, curriculum, NSF, scholarships, sciences, S-STEM.

1. INTRODUCTION

Between 2002 and 2009, the number of U.S. college students graduating with a major in computer science programs declined precipitously [3], as shown in Figure 1. Reasons for this decline include a variety of societal factors, such as negative stereotypes associated with computer science (CS), a persistent myth that the computing jobs were all being off-shored, and other factors [2].

Although the numbers increased in 2010, the number of bachelors degrees awarded remained below 8,000 students, and was just 58% of the 2002 number. (2011 numbers were not yet available.)

Permission to make digital or hard copies of all or part of this work for personal or classroom use is granted without fee provided that copies are not made or distributed for profit or commercial advantage and that copies bear this notice and the full citation on the first page. To copy otherwise, or republish, to post on servers or to redistribute to lists, requires prior specific permission and/or a fee.
SIGCSE'12, February 29–March 3, 2012, Raleigh, North Carolina, USA. Copyright 2012 ACM 978-1-4503-1098-7/12/02...$10.00.

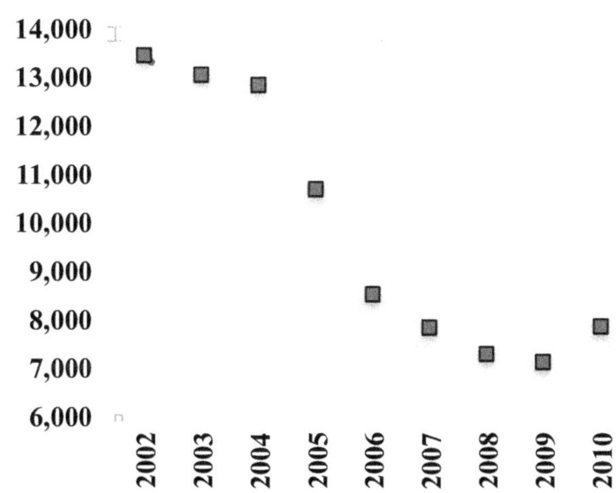

Figure 1. U.S. CS Bachelors Degrees By Year (Taulbee)

This decline in college graduates with computing expertise comes at a time when there is increased demand in the U.S. economy for computing professionals with current technical skills, especially in the areas of software engineering and networking [8].

To increase the number of college graduates with computing expertise, we have been pursuing a 2-pronged strategy:

1. We have been promoting the computer science major by various means, including videos showing alumni using their computing skills in socially relevant ways, publicizing the reality of the careers market for software engineers, and so on.
2. We have been encouraging students from other majors to take computing courses, as a way to help them bring the power of the computer to their discipline, in order to improve their post-graduation marketability. For example, if a student is a physics major, we work to convince her that acquiring additional computing expertise will make her a *better physicist.*

For better or worse, many U.S. computing professionals do not hold a degree in computer science. Instead, many professionals completed their bachelors in another area that required them to take computing courses. Then, after graduation, they discovered that their computing skills held the key to a satisfying career. If our proverbial physics major has taken computing courses and she can find work as a physicist, that's great; if not, she can likely pursue a satisfying career as a computing professional.

1. This work supported in part by NSF S-STEM grant #0850228.

In this paper, we focus on the second "prong" of our strategy, specifically students majoring in non-CS STEM disciplines. Many of these students have an established affinity for computing, many STEM major programs require their students to take an introductory CS course, most STEM students have the quantitative skills to succeed in subsequent CS courses, and CS is clearly useful for their disciplines.

In the next section, we describe curricular changes we have implemented as part of this strategy. In section 3, we describe special scholarships we offer for such students. In section 4, we discuss challenges and successes that we have encountered. Section 5 presents our conclusions.

2. CURRICULUM CHANGES

One challenge in promoting computing to different disciplines is to avoid the appearance that one is trying to "poach" their majors.

To engage our target audience of STEM majors and avoid this political pitfall, we decided to do two things:

1. Construct a new introductory course oriented around STEM problems; and
2. Construct a new minor program, designed to appeal to students (and faculty) from STEM disciplines.

In the rest of this section, we detail these two curricular changes.

2.1 A New Introductory Course

Computing is increasingly being applied to different disciplines, ranging from STEM areas to the digital arts and humanities. If majors from computer science, and other STEM disciplines are in the same introductory computing (CS1) classroom, it can be a challenge to teach and motivate the students who have such varied interests. The issue is that if the problems being presented and solved in the course are of interest to one discipline (e.g., computer science), then those problems may not be especially interesting or motivating to the students from other disciplines (e.g., biology, physics). Finding problems that appeal to a wide audience is challenging.

One could imagine building separate introductory computing courses for computational biology, computational chemistry, computational physics, and so on. At a small college, this is impractical. However, it is feasible to construct a new introductory course that uses computing to solve problems from different STEM disciplines. For example, we might introduce expressions and assignment statements in the context of computing gravitational forces, introduce string processing in the context of a genomics problem, and so on. Different problems will appeal to different students, with something for everyone.

We began by convening an open meeting with STEM faculty members interested in computing, to get their input on what their student majors needed to learn about computing. The two most surprising results were that our mathematicians wanted students to learn Python, and our chemists wanted students to gain basic Linux system administration skills, including being able to perform source-code software installations.

From this feedback, we designed CS 106 *Introduction to Scientific Modeling and Computation*. An important consideration for us was that students completing this course should be able to continue on to and be successful in our CS2 course. To accomplish this, we gave this new course the same student learning outcomes as our "normal" CS1 course, and chose [4] as our course text. The course has the syllabus given in Table 1:

Table 1. CS 106 Syllabus

Week	Topic
1	Introduction to programming, algorithms
2	Using built-in classes (lists)
3	Types: numbers, strings, tuples, ...
4	Numeric & Boolean expressions; calling functions
5	String operations, expressions, formatting
6	For loops
7	If statements
8	While loops
9	User-defined functions
10	User-defined classes
11	Inheritance
12	Exception handling
13	Dictionaries
14+	Complete and present final projects

The weekly course format consists of 3 hours of lecture, a 2-hour hands-on laboratory exercise in which students are free to work in groups, and a programming assignment that students are to complete individually to apply that week's concepts.

As can be seen at the end of Table 1, each student completes an open-ended individual course project, in which they apply their new computational skills to a problem from their discipline.

Before teaching the course for the first time, we sponsored faculty development workshops for our STEM faculty, in which we introduced them to Python and the course's content, giving them hands-on experience with what their students would be learning. As a result of these experiences, our physics department is now beginning to incorporate significant computation into their upper-level courses, building on the knowledge and skills their students acquire in CS 106.

Because we are a small institution, we can only offer the course once per year. To get students started, we chose the Fall semester. Figure 2 presents the annual course enrollments thus far:

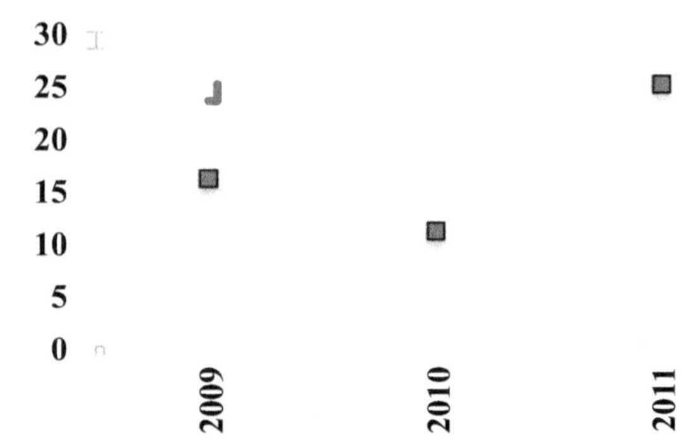

Figure 2. CS 106 Course Enrollment By Year

While noisy, the enrollment trend is positive, as word of mouth circulates about the course and more STEM faculty advisors begin advising their students to take the course.

First-year STEM students often have very full schedules, taking one or more science courses (which include weekly lab exercises), the introductory calculus sequence, and general education courses. As a result, it can be difficult for first year students to fit a technical course like CS 106 into their schedule. To illustrate, in 2011, taking the course were: 1 first-year student, 11 sophomores, 9 juniors, and 4 seniors. By contrast, the vast majority of the students in our "normal" CS1 course are first-year students.

We have had some outstanding success stories (see below), which are helping other STEM students see how programming skills can be beneficial to science students. As a result, positive word of mouth about the course is building among the students.

We are also beginning to see some of these CS 106 students continue to our CS2 course, in which they generally do very well; and on through our new minor program, which we describe next.

2.2 A New Minor

At small colleges where overall enrollment numbers are fixed, the number of student majors is a zero-sum game: more majors in department A means fewer majors in department B, and if department B's enrollments drop too low, the administration may see it as a candidate for budget reductions. A collegial campus can be disrupted if one department appears to be "poaching" other departments' majors.

By contrast, a *minor program*, consisting of 18-24 semester hours of coursework, is generally non-threatening to other departments, since it does not reduce their number of majors. Moreover, if a minor is perceived as beneficial to that major discipline, those departments may even promote it to their students. Our STEM faculty are quite aware that much of the cutting-edge work in their disciplines involves computing, so they were very supportive of the idea of a minor program that would help their students integrate computing with their disciplines.

With their input, we constructed a new *Scientific Computation and Modeling* (SCM) minor, in which students from STEM fields would take computer science courses and apply computing to their disciplines. This minor's requirements consist of:

1. One of our introductory courses (our normal CS1 course or the new CS 106 course): 4 semester hours.
2. Our CS2 course: 4 sem. hrs.
3. An introductory (100-level) database course: 1 sem. hr.
4. Two intermediate or advanced (200- or 300-level) CS courses: 6-7 sem. hrs.
5. Any other STEM course that has #1 as a prerequisite (i.e., that includes a significant computational component): 3-4 sem. hrs. Note that these can also be CS courses.
6. An approved investigatory project (e.g., a capstone project, a research/investigations course, an internship, etc.) that involves significant STEM programming: 0-4 sem. hrs.

The SCM minor thus totals 18-24 semester hours, depending on exactly how a student completes its requirements. This minor is a very new program; so we only have one student officially registered for it at the moment (a senior chemistry major), but there may be others pursuing it who have not yet formally registered. We believe that it will grow in popularity as we and other STEM departments work at promoting it.

It is worth mentioning that this basic structure could serve as a model for other interdisciplinary computing minor programs (e.g., digital arts and humanities, social sciences, etc.).

3. SCHOLARSHIPS

One approach to addressing the shortfall of computing skills is to offer scholarships to students willing to major in computer science [1]. This approach may reward the limited number of students interested in studying computer science, but many talented students never consider majoring in computer science, even with the lure of a scholarship [6]. The negative societal factors associated with computing are such that many students self-select themselves out of consideration for such scholarships.

Because of this, we decided to take a broader approach. In 2009, we wrote a successful NSF grant proposal to offer merit- and need-based scholarships to any student from a STEM major who was willing to integrate science and computing. To provide flexibility, the requirements are quite simple: a student must (i) take a sequence of computing courses, and (ii) find a way to integrate computing with science. A student might accomplish this in the following ways:

- Be a STEM major and pursue the Scientific Computation and Modeling minor.
- Be a STEM major, pursue a computer science minor, and have a clear plan to integrate the two (via one or more course projects, research experiences, or other means).
- Be a computer science or information systems major and a science major or minor, with a clear plan to integrate the two.
- Pursue our ABET-accredited BCS major (which requires extra science), with a clear plan to integrate CS and science.

Students are not limited to these four options, but can design their own approach, which they specify as part of the application process. The scholarship applications are reviewed and are awarded by an interdisciplinary faculty committee.

The majority of these scholarships were given to incoming first-year students, with automatic renewal so long as the student makes progress on their plan and funds remain available. The range of awards has been \$4,000 to \$8,000 per year, with different students receiving different amounts based on financial need. So far, this program has been quite successful at attracting students to computing: Figure 3 shows the number of students to whom we have awarded scholarships by major the first two years:

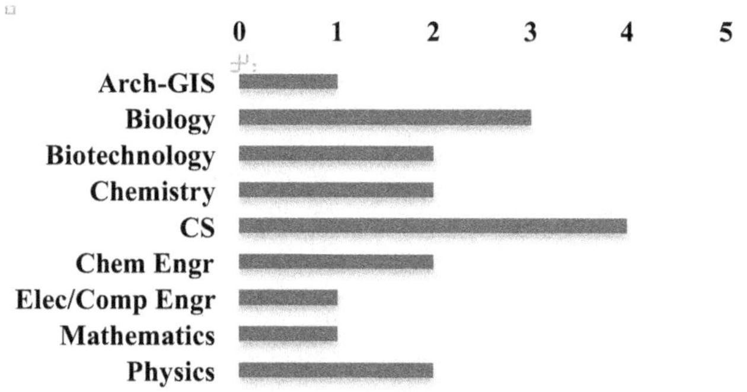

Figure 3: Total S-STEM Scholarships By Major (2 Years)

33% of these scholarships have gone to females; 67% to males. While this female percentage is lower than we would like, it is much higher than our percentage of female CS majors, who have enjoyed having more female classmates in their CS courses.

The scholarships have also been a recruiting tool for our college: Roughly 70% of the prospective students to whom we have offered scholarships have accepted them and enrolled in our programs. Several have indicated that these scholarships were a key factor in their decision to attend our college.

For a variety of reasons, some good candidates for these scholarships do not apply for them before arriving at college. They may not have had any significant computing experience in high school, or they may not have heard about the scholarships, or various other reasons. For the sake of these students, we do not award all of these scholarships to prospective students. Instead, we try to reserve a few each year for already-enrolled students who show computational aptitude, as an incentive for them to further develop those abilities.

Additional information about our program is available from our scholarship program's website [7].

4. DISCUSSION

Our approach of using curriculum change plus scholarships as incentives for science students to study computing has produced both challenges and successes. In this section, we discuss them.

4.1 Challenges

4.1.1 Discipline-Specific Challenges

Our original intent was to attract students from a wide range of STEM disciplines to computing. This has proven to be easier in some disciplines than others.

For example, the 'E' in STEM stands for engineering. Since all engineering students are required to take one computing course (and electrical engineers are required to take two), they would appear to be excellent candidates for acquiring more advanced computing skills. However, the curriculum of an ABET-accredited undergraduate engineering program is very full. At our college, a typical engineering major has just 1 or 2 elective courses in her entire four-year program; her program prescribes all the rest of her courses. As a result, most engineering students have been unable to take many computing courses beyond what their major requires, unless they arrive with many Advanced Placement (AP) or other college credits. Because of this, only one engineering student has been able to construct a credible plan to take the additional computing courses needed to be eligible for one of our scholarships.

4.1.2 More CS Majors?

When we wrote the NSF S-STEM grant proposal, there was some disagreement within our CS department about our strategy. Some felt that we should just focus on recruiting CS majors – that every scholarship given to a non-CS major was a lost CS major. In a time of shrinking college budgets and academic deans reviewing program efficiencies, this was a serious concern.

However, it was pointed out that some colleges giving CS-only NSF scholarships found they "had to scramble a bit to find enough eligible students to use the scholarship money" [6]. Moreover, that was in 2002-2005, and CS enrollments were much higher at that time than they were in 2009, as Figure 1 shows.

It was also noted that while our proposed approach might not increase the number of CS majors as much as possible, it would increase the number of students taking CS courses, most of which had plenty of room to accommodate more students. The proposed approach would thus improve the CS department's classroom efficiency, if not the number of CS majors.

It was also argued that this represented an opportunity to market our discipline to other departments. That is, if it was true that studying CS would make science students better scientists, then the science students taking our courses would be more capable scientists than their peers who did not take our courses, and thus become unofficial ambassadors in their departments for us.

Finally, it was pointed out that our BCS majors would be eligible for these scholarships with almost no additional requirements.

These arguments were sufficient to convince the naysayers to give this approach a try. As seen in Figure 3, CS has received a plurality of the scholarships thus far, and all of these have been to outstanding incoming students. Our approach has thus increased the number of CS majors by a few students per year.

However, the real benefit of giving 14 scholarships to non-CS majors has been to get these students to take CS courses they would not otherwise have taken. The best of these students have returned to their departments and used their newfound computing skills to accomplish things there that would have been impossible otherwise. In the process, these students have shown the faculty and other students in their home departments the value that CS courses and programming skills can provide to their disciplines. In the next section, we present a few of these students' stories.

4.1.3 Sustainability?

It is fair to ask whether our approach is sustainable after the NSF grant that funds our scholarships expires. We believe our approach may be sustainable, provided a critical mass of non-CS students and faculty experience the value computing *within their disciplines*, sufficient to make it self-sustaining. In the next section, we present stories that suggest this may be happening.

4.2 Success Stories

Our college has a strong summer undergraduate research program, where the benefits of our approach have appeared most directly.

4.2.1 Abby and Ben

In Fall 2010, Abby was a first year Biology major whose advisor recommended she take CS 106. Ben was a senior BioTech major and SCM minor who had taken CS 106 as a sophomore, the first year it was offered. Both are recipients of our NSF scholarships.

In summer 2011, both were hired as undergraduate research assistants on a computational biology project. The project was to use a matrix assisted laser desorption/ionization time of flight (MALDI-TOF) mass spectrum analyzer to study various structures, ranging from individual proteins to individual bacteria to colonies of bacteria. This machine uses lasers to bombard a bio-substance, which then flies apart, allowing spectral analysis. The results of this analysis are recorded as numbers in text files, which can be processed via software applications.

The MALDI-TOF manufacturer provides software to process these files, but the functionality of this software is too limited to answer the research questions Ben and Abby were investigating.

However, drawing on their CS 106 experience (including agile development techniques like pair programming), Abby and Ben co-wrote Python programs to process the MALDI-TOF output files, compute answers to research questions, and auto-generate full-color graphical spectra to visualize the mass spectrometry results. Thanks to their CS 106 programming skills, their research group was able to answer biological research questions that they could not answer using the manufacturer's software. Their research is being submitted to a prominent biology journal.

4.2.2 *Daniel*

Daniel was a first year student in 2010 who received one of our NSF scholarships. Since he was interested in both CS and physics, he decided to take our traditional CS1 (Java) course rather than CS 106. One of the lab exercises in this course is an image processing exercise, in which students learn how to implement Photoshop-style effects (e.g., gray scale, blur, sepia tint, etc.) for altering digital photographs.

In the spring 2011 semester, Daniel continued in both CS and physics. In our CS2 course, he learned about C++, memory management, and how to build and use elementary data structures. Following this course, he decided that he liked both CS and physics, so he would double-major in both disciplines.

During summer 2011, Daniel was hired as an undergraduate research assistant in our astronomy research group. The projects included identifying previously unknown astronomical bodies, ranging from asteroids and comets to planetoids and variable stars. For example, variable stars had traditionally been identified by manually inspecting photographs of the same region of the sky on different nights, and for each star in the photograph, comparing its appearance in different photographs, to determine visually if its appearance had changed, indicating it was a variable star. During the previous 3 years, a total of 33 variable stars had been identified through this manual inspection process.

Using his CS1 image-processing project and the knowledge of data structures he gained from CS2, Daniel wrote a program that automated this process, iterating through different regions of the sky, and for a given region, scanning different photos of that region to identify likely variable stars. The stars identified by his program must be subsequently validated by a human, but Daniel's program has greatly accelerated the output of this research group: During summer 2011, his program identified over 80 variable stars – more than twice as many stars in 10 weeks as had been identified in the previous 3 years.

The faculty member leading Dan's research group says they are "trying to learn how to drink from a fire hose" – that Dan's program is producing results faster than they can deal with them. Needless to say, this is a nice problem to have. These results are being submitted to the International Variable Star Index (see *www.aavso.org/vsx/*), as well as a leading astronomy journal.

4.2.3 *Erin*

Erin was a junior Business-Mathematics major who took CS 106 in Fall 2010 to satisfy her mathematics cognate requirement. In late June 2011, she sent the following e-mail to her instructor:

> *Hi Professor _____,*
>
> *I just wanted to tell you thank you for your wonderful teaching last fall. I didn't realize how handy my computer programming skills would be, but I currently have an internship at an insurance company and on the first day they were having me learn a computer programming language called SAS. I have never used it before, but I picked it up quite quickly because I understand if statements, for loops, and all that fun stuff. I have recalled things from CS 106 everyday that have helped me to do my job well. I would be lost without you!*

Through her internship, Erin discovered that even introductory programming skills are beneficial and can open unexpected doors. Dissemination of this and our other success stories is helping to create a positive "buzz" on our campus and change the image of computing.

4.2.4 *Luke*

In Fall 2010, Luke was a senior physics major who, despite having several friends who were CS majors, was not especially interested in computing. As a result, he put off taking any CS courses until his senior year, when he took CS 106.

In summer 2010, Luke had been an undergraduate researcher in the same Astronomy group that Daniel joined in summer 2011. Luke's research was on galaxy clusters, specifically trying to determine which galaxies are *actually* clustered, as opposed to galaxies that *appear* to be clustered when viewed through the limited vantage point of a single telescope.

To solve this problem, Luke turned to NASA's Extra-galactic Database (NED, see *ned.ipac.caltech.edu*), which contains data on the distances to particular galaxies. In Luke's words:

> *The data that we get back from NED is in a rather unusable form; there is lots of extra information, duplicate information, and information on galaxies that we don't care about.*
>
> *This is where my CS106 project came in. I used python code to take the raw NED download, and to turn it into something useful. My code dealt with the many complications of filtering out the uninteresting and duplicate data, and turning the data into a format that we could use.*
>
> *I then actually used the data I got from NED this summer. We had distance data on around 1000 galaxies, and due to my CS106 work, we were able to add in information on about 500 more (... an increase of around 50%!!).*
>
> *The information that we gleaned from NED helped us better identify which galaxies were actually part of the clusters we were studying, and has worked its way into a paragraph of my paper in prep. So my python code was actually really scientifically useful; I was able to make progress on my research while learning in class.*

As in Erin's case, this feedback came in an unsolicited e-mail from Luke to his CS 106 instructor (who is not one of this paper's authors). Students like Luke and Erin are discovering – to their surprise – that programming is "actually ... useful", opening doors and enabling them to do things they could not do before.

4.2.5 *Our Physics & Astronomy Department*

For some years, our Department of Physics and Astronomy has been aware that they needed to incorporate more computation into their Physics curriculum. While the faculty development workshops described in section 2.1 introduced them to Python and CS 106, these workshops did not provide them with a strategy for how to integrate computation into their courses.

During summer 2011, they held their own workshop focused on computational physics, led by Dr. Ruben Landau of Oregon State University. Dr. Landau was able to introduce them to numerous computational physics examples and numerical methods from the Python version of his book [5]. He was also able to give them practical advice on how to use Python in physics. Since Dr. Landau "spoke their language", he was able to answer their questions about computational physics pedagogy in a way that we as computer scientists could not.

Thanks to this workshop, our physicists now have a wide assortment of computational examples they can use in their courses, a plan for incorporating them across the physics curriculum, and a newfound enthusiasm for computing. We expect this to further raise the interest in CS among their majors.

4.2.6 Other Successes

Space limitations prevent us from presenting other successes in detail, but we will summarize them here.

In summer 2011, we hosted a workshop on computational biology for our Biology department, taught by Dr. Jeffrey Krause and Dr. Gloria Rendon, computational biologists from the Shodor Educational Foundation (see *www.shodor.org*) and the National Center for Supercomputing Applications (see *www.ncsa.illinois.edu*), respectively. This workshop was well attended, and provided our Biology faculty with new ideas for integrating computational modeling into the biology curriculum.

Three of our scholarship recipients have graduated – a biologist, a biotechnologist, and an archeology+GIS major. The biologist and biotechnologist are either in or entering graduate programs in computational biology; the third graduate is working in a library and volunteering his GIS skills to the New Jersey Museum.

As shown in Figure 3, we have also awarded scholarships the past two years to strong incoming students planning to be CS majors. At present, these students are still young, but they show much potential and we anticipate great things from them.

5. CONCLUSIONS

The demand for college graduates with advanced computing skills far exceeds the supply, and it seems likely to do so for the foreseeable future. At the same time, many college students continue to choose majors where there are limited career opportunities, comparatively speaking.

To remedy this situation, we recommend a 2-pronged approach that can be summarized as follows:

1. Promote the discipline of computer science through all possible means.
2. Find ways to encourage non-CS majors to take CS courses.

In this paper, we have presented our strategy for the second "prong", specifically how to attract science students to take additional CS courses, given their quantitative strengths.

Our strategy includes the following elements:

- Curriculum change:
  - Creating a new introductory computing course that solves problems of interest to students in the sciences.
  - Creating a new minor program for non-CS STEM students willing to mix CS and their discipline.
- Financial incentives: NSF S-STEM scholarships for students willing to integrate computing and science.
- Faculty development workshops for STEM faculty.

While only in its second year, we already have several successes with this program: Enrollments in our new CS 106 course are increasing. Non-CS students have used new computing skills to improve their post-baccalaureate career options through summer internships and undergraduate research experiences. Non-CS faculty members have become increasingly aware of how computing can improve both their teaching and their research, and have participated in discipline-specific workshops on computing. More science students are studying computing, improving our faculty-student ratios (making our administration happy). Strong CS majors have joined our program, raising standards for their peers and improving department morale.

Computing is ubiquitous today, and students have many different interests. If we can encourage non-CS students to acquire computing skills beyond those taught in a typical 'computer literacy' course, they may – like some of the students listed in Section 4.2 – be surprised at how useful those skills are, whether in doing research or in the workplace. If we can attract students early enough in their academic careers, some of them may discover an unsuspected delight in the science of computing and problem solving, and continue on to more advanced courses. If we can build a critical mass of non-CS students who are interested in developing technology, rather than just consuming it, we believe our approach can become self-sustaining, and we have presented evidence that this may be happening.

We hope that our experience will provide a useful model for other CS departments, and that this report will encourage them to reach out and build bridges to their colleagues in other departments. We look forward to reading their reports.

6. ACKNOWLEDGMENTS

We gratefully acknowledge the support of the National Science Foundation and the Howard Hughes Medical Institute. Without their help, these events reported here would not have occurred.

7. REFERENCES

[1] G. Callaghan, J. C. Little, C. Morell, R. Sabin, and S. Sorkin, "Scholarships for the Computing Sciences: Panel Discussion", *Journal of Computing Sciences in Colleges*, (20)3, Feb 2005, pp. 171-172..

[2] L. Carter, Why students with an apparent aptitude for computer science don't choose to major in computer science, *Proc. 37th SIGCSE Technical Symposium on Computer Science Education*, March 2006, 27-31. DOI= http://doi.acm.org/10.1145/1121341.1121352.

[3] Computing Research Associates, *CRA Taulbee Survey Archive*. Online, http://archive.cra.org/statistics/. Accessed August 2011.

[4] M. Goldwasser and D. Letscher, *Object-Oriented Programming in Python*, Pearson / Prentice Hall, 2008.

[5] R. Landau, *A Survey of Computational Physics*, Princeton University Press (Java version), 2012. Python version online: http://physics.orst.edu/~rubin/Books/eBookWorking/index.html. Accessed August 2011.

[6] C. Martincic and D. Carlson, "The NSF CSEMS Grant Program: Our Experience With The Proposal Process And Program Execution", *Journal of Computing Sciences in Colleges*, (19)1, Oct 2003, pp. 73-82.

[7] R. Pruim, *NSF Scholarships*, Online: http://www.calvin.edu/isri/nsf-scholarships/index.html, Accessed August 2011.

[8] U.S. Bureau of Labor Statistics, *Occupational Outlook Handbook (OOH), 2010-11 Edition*, Online: http://www.bls.gov/oco/, Accessed August 2011.

Operations Research: Broadening Computer Science In A Liberal Arts College

Barbara Anthony
Southwestern University
1001 East University Avenue
Georgetown, TX 78626
anthonyb@southwestern.edu

ABSTRACT

Operations research, while not traditionally taught at many small or liberal arts colleges, can be a significant asset to the offerings of a computer science department. Often seen as a discipline at the intersection of mathematics, computer science, business, and engineering, it has great interdisciplinary potential and practical appeal, allowing for recruitment of students who may not consider taking a CS0 or CS1 course. A special topics course in operations research was offered by the computer science department at Southwestern University as an upper-level elective, and it was also cross-listed as a business and mathematics elective. Not only did the course benefit computer science majors who appreciated the applications and different perspectives, but it provided a means for the department to serve a wider population, increased interdisciplinary education, and resulted in a filled-to-capacity upper-level course in computer science for the first time in recent memory. This course is now being considered as a permanent elective that will interest computer science majors and minors as well as draw in students from disciplines across campus. For departments with limited faculty resources for teaching non-major courses, offering an operations research course provides an alternative that simultaneously serves the department and the campus as a whole.

Categories and Subject Descriptors

K.3.2 [**Computers and Education**]: Computer and Information Science Education

General Terms

Experimentation, Management

Keywords

computer science education, interdisciplinary, liberal arts, non-majors, operations research, outreach

Permission to make digital or hard copies of all or part of this work for personal or classroom use is granted without fee provided that copies are not made or distributed for profit or commercial advantage and that copies bear this notice and the full citation on the first page. To copy otherwise, to republish, to post on servers or to redistribute to lists, requires prior specific permission and/or a fee.
SIGCSE'12, February 29–March 3, 2012, Raleigh, North Carolina, USA.
Copyright 2012 ACM 978-1-4503-1098-7/12/02 ...$10.00.

1. INTRODUCTION

While larger universities may be facing a boom in computer science enrollments [19], smaller liberal arts colleges do not always experience the same trends [12]. Furthermore, at some liberal arts colleges, the question arises: does computer science have a place in a liberal arts education, and if so, what should its role be [17]? Liberal arts colleges aim to provide both breadth and depth, exposing students to a wide variety of disciplines and topics, as well as delving into their chosen major. Sometimes it is equally important to recruit students to take one or two classes in the discipline as it is to recruit majors or minors.

A variety of strategies have been tried to recruit students, but many of them have focused on getting students into the major or minor by having a broad CS0 or using CS1 as a recruiting tool [16]. While our CS0 course is marketed to all students, and our CS1 course requires no previous programming experience, we have had limited success with that approach at Southwestern University. All mathematics majors are required to take CS1, but few choose to take additional computer science courses. We do not have the faculty resources that some larger institutions have to teach additional courses that are geared towards non-majors, nor a large enough student body to have different versions of CS1 based on the audience.

Interdisciplinary courses and programs are strongly encouraged at many liberal arts institutions. Such ventures have been attempted and studied, including examples such as a "CS0++ course [combining] CS with statistics, ecology, and the philosophy and history of science" [10], and through "interdisciplinary application tracks [including] bioinformatics, computer information systems, geographic information technology, and human computer interaction" [18]. While courses of that type show promise as entry points for potential majors and minors, there is still room in the curriculum for students who are willing to consider a computer science course, but for various reasons do not want to take CS0 or CS1. Various universities have offered what are typically upper-level courses in computer science to students without the standard prerequisites, including "open AI" [14] and a database course designed for non-majors [11]. In part due to the large number of business majors at Southwestern University, we saw the potential for an upper-level elective in operations research, that could be cross-listed under business, computer science, and mathematics.

Operations research was a natural choice in our situation due to existing faculty member expertise, but there are other motivations for its selection which make it worth considering

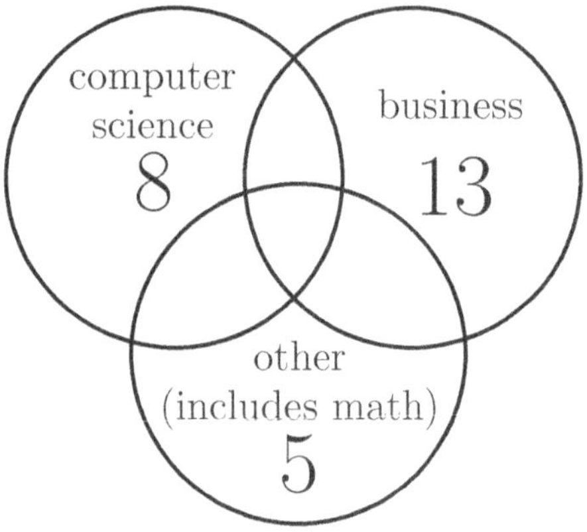

Figure 1: Class enrollment by major in Fall 2010; there were a few major/minor pairs, but no double majors.

by other colleges. At Southwestern University, since Computer Science and Mathematics are a combined department, with some faculty teaching in both disciplines, many students are aware that a number of the courses can be quite beneficial to students of either major. Some colleges where departments typically operate more independently may benefit from similar cross-listing. Recently, Macalester College introduced a course sequence in computational science which they have found beneficial in linking computer science not only to mathematics but also to the other sciences [15].

Integrating operations research with computer science is hardly unique. Carnegie Mellon University and Georgia Institute of Technology both have PhD programs in Algorithms, Combinatorics and Optimization which include the departments/schools/colleges of computer science, mathematics, and either business (operations research group) or industrial and systems engineering [2, 5]. Yet the offering of operations research is far from standard in undergraduate computer science curricula.

2. COURSE CONTENT AND STRUCTURE

2.1 Prerequisites

Teaching an upper-level course across disciplines requires careful planning, especially when there is no common core of mathematics or computer science courses that all students must take (as there might be at an engineering school). Mathematics majors at Southwestern University are required to take CS1, computer science majors have mathematics requirements including calculus and linear algebra, while business majors typically take statistics and calculus. Thus, to make this course truly accessible to students in all three majors, we could not require courses that otherwise might have been desirable prerequisites, such as linear algebra, algorithms, or even CS1. Actual enrollment numbers from the different majors are illustrated in Figure 1. Within each of the three majors, one or two students had a declared minor in one of the other listed majors.

A prerequisite of junior standing was used as a common way of ensuring a certain level of maturity of the student; case-by-case exceptions were made for a few students, primarily computer science majors. More important than the official prerequisites in guiding the appropriate self-selection of the course were email descriptions of the course, posted information on departmental bulletin boards, and informational presentations given in targeted courses, including the business capstone. Students were advised that they would need to be able to perform calculations (calculators or computers allowed), would need to use some software but would not need to know a programming language, and would be expected to consider problems from real-world perspectives and write for both general and technical audiences.

2.2 Resources

Numerous resources are available regarding operations research. Some of the materials that were most useful for this course came from INFORMS (Institute for Operations Research and the Management Sciences), and its Forum on Education [4]. The 2010 INFORMS Annual Meeting session on "The First Undergraduate OR Course" included a presentation by Martonosi of Harvey Mudd College. Her talk recognized that students may encounter operations research only once in their undergraduate career and they can be shown "both the power of O.R. to solve complex, real-world problems and its rich theoretical underpinnings" [13]. The operations research literature also talks about the value of 'real-world' projects, whether as one component of a course or as the focus of a capstone course in a program where the "OR-affiliated faculty includes members from the Departments of Mathematical Sciences, Management, Computer Science, and Economics and Geography" [8].

While there are some good, traditional choices for a textbook for a first course in operations research, they may assume the students have a particular background. Books aimed at business students may have a more spreadsheet-based design, focusing on the use of Excel without providing the same theoretical understanding. Other texts assume a programming or mathematical background that is often limited to either computer science or mathematics majors. For this course, *Schaum's Outline of Theory and Problems of Operations Research* [9] was chosen. It is intended more as a reference with a compendium of solved problems, highlighting the main ideas in a much briefer manner than a traditional text. Additionally, it allowed more freedom to select topics and order them as desired, without as much dependence on previous chapters. The relatively low cost as compared to most textbooks was also a factor in its favor. As is the norm for books from this series, all problems in the book are solved, so homework assignments pulled straight from the text do not work. In our case, many homework problems were devised independently, some were taken from other sources, and some required students to either arrive at the same answer as the text using software, or to provide a detailed written explanation of the answer and justification of the steps. Many students can benefit from practicing their technical written and explanatory skills, and when the answer is provided, it reduces complaints about points being deducted in spite of achieving the correct numerical solution.

A variety of software is available for solving linear and integer programs, both on a small scale and for commercial applications. Since many college students are familiar with Microsoft Office products, using the Excel Solver Add-In by Frontline Systems [1] that is included with the Windows version of Excel (a Mac version is available for download) provides a low barrier to entry. The GNU Linear Programming Kit (GLPK) [3] is a powerful package, capable of accepting a variety of input formats, but is often more intimidating to students without a computer science background. Google Docs Spreadsheet also provides a Solver [6], but with far fewer features (in particular, no sensitivity analysis). Note that while the options all provide subsets of the same numerical information, the terminology used differs; to mitigate this potential source of confusion for students, instructors can use this opportunity to talk about how names develop, simultaneous discoveries, and how applications can affect naming conventions. For some courses and students, it may be appropriate to have students write their own solver implementing the simplex method, among other algorithms.

Table 1: Major Topics Covered

Major Topics Covered
Mathematical Modeling
Graphical Solutions of Linear Programs
Simplex Method
Duality and Sensitivity Analysis
Integer Programming
Transportation Algorithm
Assignment Problem
Traveling Salesman Problem
Network Analysis
Maximum Flow and Minimum Cut
Project Planning

2.3 Integrating the Students and the Material

As a special topics elective that does not serve as a prerequisite for future courses, there was some degree of freedom in the material covered in this operations research course. Keeping in mind the audience, it was designed so that all students would benefit, regardless of their background in algorithms, real-world case studies, and proofs. Certainly linear and integer programming would be included in an operations research course. The term *programming* alone leads to interesting discussions about the histories of computer science and operations research, as many student (regardless of their major) associate the word programming with programming languages. The course also provides numerous opportunities to reiterate that computer science is far more than 'just' programming. Solving linear programs by the simplex method is one of the earlier algorithms introduced in the course, though the graphical technique for lower-dimension problems is also introduced. Students also encounter duality early in the semester, and gain an understanding of the economic interpretation of the dual and that the dual is a powerful concept elsewhere in computer science. The dual aids in the study of sensitivity analysis, which also leads to questions about the accuracy of data and assumptions.

Throughout the study of various types of linear programs, the necessity of exact terminology was evident. Naturally, binary numbers were familiar to computer science and mathematics majors, yet their utility in ensuring certain constraints (such as exactly one of these five situations must happen) was novel to many. Having to think about variables and numbers as being binary, integer, or general, as well as the importance of non-negativity constraints, gave new significance to those terms. Likewise, the word *or* can be ambiguous or context-dependent in English as to whether or not it is an exclusive or, yet has a precise meaning in the realm of computer science. The importance of word choice was evident when students had to translate between word problems and systems of equations.

Sometimes computer scientists think of trees as so fundamental to their work that they forget that what they think of as a tree is not an innate concept for much of the world. Branch and bound techniques for integer programming provide a memorable example of how a tree can be used in storing relevant information and making decisions in a relatively efficient way. Yet, at the same time, these problems quickly illustrate the potential complexity of integer programming, making the exponential growth abundantly clear.

Algorithms were familiar to all students to various extents, though perhaps not by that terminology or with much thought about runtime or resource usage. Throughout the semester, students saw a variety of algorithms, with varying degrees of difficulties in implementation, explanation, and motivation. For instance, understanding the simplex algorithm in two dimensions leads to reasonable intuition about why it succeeds for problems with many more variables. It provides the rationale behind the steps in the manipulation of the linear equations, but does not generally make the solution trivial, whether the student is calculating it by hand or writing a program to complete the steps. Degenerate cases and ambiguous procedures (such as tie-breaking) show up and illustrate the need for handling all cases. Students who had previously taken an algorithms course were reminded of the variety of algorithms available for network analysis problems, and how a graph representation of a problem can be useful. All students saw that the edges on a graph and associated numerical values can have a variety of meanings, among them measures of capacity or speed, indicators of quantity shipped or used, or indicating precedence for project planning.

The Traveling Salesman Problem (TSP), a familiar topic in algorithms and complexity courses in computer science, can be introduced from a different perspective in operations research. First, cover the assignment problem which has a simple solution procedure (the Hungarian Method) and obvious applications. From there, proceed to the TSP, and show that a solution to the assignment problem may (but does not have to) satisfy the TSP constraints. Then, apply branch and bound strategies to either require or preclude one of the assignments. For students who have already learned that TSP is NP-hard, it is often revealing to see that two straightforward procedures can be combined to solve the TSP, yet the growth of the branch and bound tree presents an obvious challenge, illustrating the hardness of the problem in a more concrete manner. A listing of the major topics and the order in which they were covered is provided in Table 1.

Mathematics and computer science majors both have substantial experience with proofs, but often find them rather unrelated to the applications. However, in this course they were provided with more examples where the proofs were necessary to truly understand the algorithms and solve the problems. For instance, with the simplex method, even with the correct intuition that optimal solutions occur only at the corners, or on boundaries/faces between optimal corners, a proof is still necessary. While the proof is not that difficult, it is also not trivial, and provides students with an example where it is easy to see how the proof develops. As both mathematics and computer science majors at Southwestern University take linear algebra, they were provided with more examples of how linear algebra has both theoretical and applied or practical uses.

Generally, each group of majors brought a somewhat different set of strengths to this course. Mathematics majors were the group most familiar with using geometry to solve problems, despite its relevance in computer science. Yet they were often the least likely to be comfortable with the applications, and applying what had been proved to real-world problems. Business majors were comfortable with case studies with real problems, including picking out which information was pertinent, but often struggled with translating that information into equations when needed. To varying degrees, all groups of students struggled with letting the algorithm do its work to find an optimal solution rather than trying to either seed it with a perceived good value or adding constraints that were not truly part of the problem but 'seemed logical'. To that end, it was useful when the instructor could provide specific, realistic counterexamples to these inaccurate assumptions, enabling students to develop that skill as the semester progressed.

As mentioned, different software options were available for students to use, primarily the glpsol solver in the GLPK, and Excel's Solver. Both were used for in-class demonstrations. Interestingly, while Excel was familiar to the majority of the business majors, there were computer science majors who had not previously used it. Not surprisingly, most students quickly mastered the necessary tasks in Excel. Several computer science majors observed that portions of Excel were intuitive because it prompts the user that one of the inputs to the sumproduct function should be an array. The computer science majors are quite familiar with the concept of an array, and were easily able to explain it to some of their classmates. The particularities of the various file formats required by glpsol reinforced (especially for the non-computer science majors) that a computer can only understand syntax which it has been programmed to accept, and reminded the computer science majors of how they should think about their design choices and what a parser has to be able to handle.

2.4 Group Project: Case Study

All students were required to complete a semester-long group project, a case study, modified from one used at Harvey Mudd College. Due to the composition of the class, each group of approximately four students was required to have at least one computer science major/minor, and at least two business major/minors. With that requirement, students were allowed to self-select their groups. The mixed nature of the groups was intended to provide different perspectives and background knowledge, and to ensure that at least one student would be comfortable using glpsol if the size of the problems warranted, as the built-in Microsoft Excel Solver limits users to 200 changeable cells or decision variables.

To ensure adequate progress throughout the semester, there were several intermediate deadlines. Selection of groups was completed within the first weeks of the semester. A multi-page proposal about the problem, the work completed, and the outline of future progress was due one-third of the way through the semester. At this time, students were provided substantial feedback about their decisions thus far, given advice about factors they should consider that they had not, and guided where necessary to ensure that the scope of the project was reasonable given the constraints of the semester. Halfway through the semester, each student in each group had to meet with another student to discuss the status of their project, with the listener writing up a brief status report and providing additional feedback. In this way, each group collectively got feedback not only from the instructor but from (typically) four of their peers, and had to choose how to reconcile the potentially conflicting recommendations. A final portfolio was due at the end of the semester, which had to include both a brief executive summary (aimed at a non-technical manager) as well as a full technical report, complete with recommendations, acknowledged limitations, and sensitivity analysis. Students recognized throughout the semester that some assumptions had to be made, and some data was likely to be inexact, gaining a better appreciation of why sensitivity analysis is important. Many also experienced the potentially undesirable effects of adding constraints because it seems like they will be necessary in the final solution, only to discover that linear programming does best when given the freedom to find optimal solutions given only the true constraints.

Students were provided with some topic suggestions, but were free to select their own, which all groups did. Some students chose projects that were relevant to the campus or the community, such as equipping the redesigned athletic training room, or how the local food pantry should distribute items to satisfy nutritional and taste requirements while serving the needs of clients. Other groups thought about problems related to their jobs and hobbies, including stocking a bar and constructing the ideal basketball team with a salary cap. Students were sometimes creative and usually successful in finding information relevant to their problem, and the campus offices and community organizations seemed willing to provide what they needed. For instance, a group whose project involved the location of materials in the library was able to get data about the number of times each item in the collection had been checked out in various recent time intervals. While students were not required to implement their solution (due to logistical constraints), in some courses that may be an option, and it may be possible to work directly with campus or community organizations, though that might be more appropriate for a capstone course. Students potentially can continue or expand their projects as independent studies in subsequent semesters; as many of the students graduated at the end of the semester, none took advantage of that opportunity this time.

3. COURSE HISTORY AND LOGISTICS

The idea of offering an operations research course at Southwestern University was first conceived when the author used operations research techniques to solve a recurring scheduling problem on campus [7]. Each fall, approximately 30 first-year seminars are taught, and each seminar has an orientation to the library, as well as some other common modules. Typically this scheduling had been done by hand by administrative staff, on an ad hoc basis. Since it is fairly straightforward to devise the appropriate integer program to find an optimal solution to scheduling these modules, incorporating the desires of the faculty and the librarians as well as space limitations as constraints, we volunteered to do so, using a Java program to efficiently write out all the constraints in an appropriate format that could be handled by the solvers in the GNU Linear Programming Kit. The results were well-received, and provided a means of sharing some applications of computer science beyond the games, popular software, or web-based applications that many typically consider.

Some assignments were designed to target the students' different majors. For instance, students could either solve several examples of the transportation problem by hand using the transportation simplex algorithm, or they could work from prototype code to implement the missing details. In either case, students would become familiar with the steps of the algorithm; as would be expected, only computer science majors chose the code, but some business majors did discuss some of the ideas of the code and what was involved with their peers outside of the classroom. While part of the motivation may have been determining perceived fairness of the options, it reinforced the idea that computers are great tools to automate repetitive processes, yet can only do what the programmers specify. Due to the nature of cross-listing at Southwestern University, students can designate the course as business, computer science, or math, and make changes retroactively, so we could not require students to complete particular assignments or enroll based on their major, as is often done in various universities (for instance, with a course that is both undergraduate and graduate level). While perhaps a desirable option, careful assignment design and targeting can help most students select the variant that is most appropriate for them. Likewise, such differentiated assignments can help ensure that the course is rigorous enough for each major yet mindful of the different backgrounds and expectations of the students in each major.

3.1 Students: Recruiting and Enrollment

The first key to success in this course was having buy-in from all of the departments. As mentioned, when computer science and mathematics are a combined department, communication between those faculty is easy. In our case, the business program readily recognized the value of this course, did not have anyone in their department who was excited about teaching it themselves, and had an abundance of students so there were no concerns about this course affecting the size of their elective courses. In fact, they invited us to use their internal channels (bulletin boards, departmental listservs, etc.) to share information with potential students.

The second factor involves the students. While students will often take a cross-listed course taught by a faculty member in their discipline, a business major can be understandably reticent about taking a course taught by a computer science faculty member. In our case, it helped immensely that we had a few business majors who had taken one or more computer science classes, who became the champions of the operations research course to their fellow business majors. Additionally, students generally like to have their friends in classes, so this course provided a way for computer science majors to encourage others to take the course in a way they typically can not. Finally, since students were provided evidence that operations research techniques had been used successfully to solve a campus problem (scheduling first-year seminar modules) the course was more appealing.

Courses at Southwestern University are typically capped at 25 students, but computer science classes are often smaller. It is not unusual to have upper-level elective courses have single digit enrollment. In part because of the promotion of the special topics course, all the available spaces filled during preregistration, and we allowed a few students to enroll above the cap, knowing that there are typically some registration changes during the first week of the semester. The semester ended with 26 students completing the course, and only one student dropping after the first week of classes. Computer science majors and minors made up a substantial percentage of the course, but were not the majority. Enrolled students listed majors in accounting, business, computer science, economics, mathematics, and sociology. Having a full class is good for increasing awareness of the discipline to students, faculty, and advisors on campus, and is also viewed favorably by the administration. It is unlikely that Southwestern University course sizes will change by an order of magnitude, but the course has the potential to scale for larger class sizes, especially since much of the group work is done independently of the instructor.

3.2 Feedback and Evaluation

The first time teaching a course is rarely perfect, and this course proved no exception. Despite being aware of the mathematics cross-listing, there was the business major who expressed irritation at having to do arithmetic in the simplex method. There were the computer science majors who wanted to deal only with the abstracted versions of the problems and did not like having to consider constraints such as the impossibility of placing half of a person in one location and half in another. Some students also thought that homework should be evaluated only based on the procedure, not if they also got the correct answer, and were reminded that they would like the engineers building bridges to get the numbers correct. Yet, typical of many courses, for each student who disliked a particular topic, project, or aspect of the course, there was another who rated it favorably, whether it was the number/style of assignments, the software available to use, the group project, or the textbook. Some of the students who were searching for jobs after graduation noted that the group project and other more realistic problems solved during the semester were useful talking points during their interviews. Recent graduates have since noted the applicability of this material in their jobs.

The final grade distribution was fairly typical for an upper-level elective, and students of all majors were equally likely to succeed. In fact, the percentage of students receiving an A or A- in the course was identical for both computer science and business majors, at slightly more than one-third of each group, and similar for math majors (the smallest group). The proportions of students receiving the lowest grades were also comparable. The suggestion that seems the most useful for future offerings is to make more direct connections with specific topics covered in the required business curriculum, as was done for the computer science and math courses. More handouts were provided in this course than typical, in part because of the varied backgrounds of the students, and this minor change seemed to help some students feel more comfortable. Likewise, because some of the students had the perceived advantage of having had exams in other courses written by the same instructor, an optional review session was held before the midterm exam. While the direct benefit of these features is hard to measure, and may be negligible, it seems worthwhile to do in this situation, and will be retained in future years. Repeated offerings could provide additional data and a larger sample size for more extensive evaluation.

3.3 Future Plans

While this course was initially offered as a one-time special topics course, its success and a current campus-wide interdisciplinary focus make it a prime candidate to become a regularly-offered elective. Over the next year, when the department reviews its elective offerings, it seems likely that Operations Research will be added to the offerings, and a typically low-enrollment elective will revert to independent study status. A permanent cross-listing of the course as both Computer Science and Mathematics is almost certain. Discussions will take place with the Business department to see about a continued cross-listing that will allow Operations Research to count as one of the free electives in the major, as it did as a special topics course. It may be possible to co-teach the course with a member of the Business faculty, allowing for more of a tie-in with other Business courses or some collaborative projects. Finally, options similar to cross-listing but that allow for differentiated assignments (mandatory as opposed to self-selected) based on students' majors may be worth exploring.

4. CONCLUSIONS

While CS0, CS1, and dedicated non-majors courses will continue to provide the majority of access and recruiting into computer science, there are other viable options for some schools to consider. In particular, liberal arts colleges with relatively low enrollment in computer science as compared to some other disciplines, particularly business, may find offering an operations research course to be beneficial to both majors and non-majors, and the campus as a whole. Especially at small colleges, it seems that favorable word of mouth about courses within a discipline can have a substantial impact on which electives and distribution courses students choose to take, and interdisciplinary courses with limited prerequisites that students can take with their friends are often popular. Note that this course is not expected to have a noticeable and direct impact on the number of majors and minors, nor was it intended to; it has a prerequisite of junior standing and is targeted at students who have declared particular majors (business, computer science, and/or mathematics). Rather, the goal is to serve the majors and minors, while providing another opportunity for students to explore computer science. Preliminary feedback at Southwestern University suggests that the course strengthened the curriculum for majors and non-majors alike, as students saw connections between computer science and other disciplines.

5. ACKNOWLEDGEMENTS

Thanks to Susan Martonosi from Harvey Mudd College for sharing the materials from her Introduction to Operations Research course, in particular the idea and details for the group project case study.

6. REFERENCES

[1] FrontlineSolvers: Developers of the Excel solver. `http://www.solver.com/`.

[2] Georgia Tech's Ph.D. program in algorithms, combinatorics, and optimization. Retrieved August 12, 2011 from `http://www.aco.gatech.edu/`.

[3] GLPK (GNU linear programming kit). `http://www.gnu.org/software/glpk/`.

[4] INFORMS forum on education. Retrieved August 12, 2011 from `http://www.informs.org/Community/INFORM-ED`.

[5] Program in algorithms, combinatorics and optimization at Carnegie Mellon University. Retrieved August 12, 2011 from `http://aco.math.cmu.edu/index.html`.

[6] Using solve : Tools. Retrieved August 12, 2011 from `http://docs.google.com/support/bin/answer.py?hl=en&answer=139704&topic=15158`.

[7] B. M. Anthony. Scheduling of first-year seminar modules. Unpublished technical report.

[8] A. P. Armacost and J. K. Lowe. Operations research capstone course: A project-based process of discovery and application. *INFORMS Trans. Ed.*, 3(2):1–25, 2003.

[9] R. Bronson and G. Naadimuthu. *Schaum's Outline of Theory and Problems of Operations Research*. McGraw-Hill, 1997.

[10] J. B. Cushing, R. Weiss, and Y. Moritani. CS0++ broadening computer science at the entry level: interdisciplinary science and computer science. *J. Computing Sciences in Colleges*, 23:51–57, December 2007.

[11] D. Goelman. Databases, non-majors and collaborative learning: a ternary relationships. In *Proceedings of the 13th annual conference on Innovation and Technology in Computer Science Education*, ITiCSE '08, pages 27–31, New York, NY, USA, 2008. ACM.

[12] M. Goldweber. TauRUs: a "Taulbee survey" for the rest of us. *ACM Inroads*, 2:38–42, May 2011.

[13] S. Martonosi. The first (and often only) O.R. course: Something for everyone. INFORMS Annual Meeting, Austin, TX, November 2010.

[14] M. Merzbacher. Open artificial intelligence - one course for all. *SIGCSE Bull.*, 33:110–113, February 2001.

[15] G. M. Schneider. Computational science as an interdisciplinary bridge. In *Proceedings of the Thirtieth SIGCSE Technical Symposium on Computer Science Education*, SIGCSE '99, pages 141–145, 1999.

[16] T. Urness and E. Manley. Building a thriving CS program at a small liberal arts college. *J. Computing Sciences in Colleges*, 26:268–274, May 2011.

[17] H. M. Walker and C. Kelemen. Computer science and the liberal arts: A philosophical examination. *Trans. Comput. Educ.*, 10:1–10, March 2010.

[18] M. Zhang, E. Lundak, C.-C. Lin, T. Gegg-Harrison, and J. Francioni. Interdisciplinary application tracks in an undergraduate computer science curriculum. In *Proceedings of the Thirty-Eighth SIGCSE Technical Symposium on Computer Science Education*, SIGCSE '07, pages 425–429, 2007.

[19] S. Zweben. Undergraduate CS degree production rises; doctoral production steady: 2009-2010 Taulbee survey. *Computing Research News*, 23(3), May 2011.

Beyond Competency: A Context-Driven CSO Course

Jeff Cramer
Computer Science and Engineering
Taylor University
Upland, IN 46989
765 998 4684
jcramer@cse.taylor.edu

Bill Toll
Computer Science and Engineering
Taylor University
Upland, IN 46989
765 998 4931
btoll@cse.taylor.edu

ABSTRACT
In the process of revising our general education course, which is required of a large fraction of students, we attempted to answer the question "What should a graduate of a liberal arts university understand about computational technology?" As computing technology has impacted and created drastic change in nearly all aspects of everyday life, university students may know more about narrow areas of technology but the true impact on their lives cannot be understood without an appreciation for the nature and limitations of the technology. This paper presents a set of assumptions about the impact of technology on individuals and society and describes elements of a computing context designed to enable students to critically evaluate the technology that has such an impact on their lives. Assessment of the approach indicates that students are more aware of the impact of technology and the importance of an understanding of the technology.

Categories and Subject Descriptors
K.3.2 [**Computer and Information Science Education**]: Computer science education, Curriculum, Information systems education

K.4.2 [**Social Issues**]: Abuse and crime involving computers

K.7.4 [**Professional Ethics**]: Ethical dilemmas

General Terms
Measurement, Design

Keywords
Computer Science education, Non-majors, Liberal arts

1. INTRODUCTION
The authors received an internal grant to continue a process of revising the general education computing course at Taylor University. This course is required of all majors except for those offered by Computer Science and Engineering and Elementary Education majors, who have their own required course. Many schools refer to these computer classes as technological "competency" or "literacy". Jane Turk recognized that these terms can be broadened [1], but there is still a need to replace these terms with something larger. For several years our course has increasingly focused on a broader picture than competency and literacy.

Various approaches have been investigated to design and deliver a computing course that promotes an understanding of computation and its role in society. Many papers available in the literature discuss application to majors, [2] as example. Others address courses designed for a more general audience such as ours [3], [4], [5], [6], [7], [8]. Some papers seem to fall into a category that is somewhere between a major specific course and a general education requirement [9]. A helpful view of the difference between such courses was presented in a discussion of computer science education in China through the distinction of professional computing from fundamental computing [10].

While there is much in common in the approaches discussed in the literature, a model was needed for our environment of a course for nearly all students at a selective liberal arts university. Several discussions and two brainstorming sessions were conducted with a variety of faculty and staff in an attempt to answer our key question "What should a graduate of a liberal arts university understand about computational technology?" The interactions reinforced the instructors' views of the direction the course should take and helped formulate a design for the course that could successfully match expectations. The input also clarified to the instructors that students in a liberal arts setting must learn more about computing than just tool using. They must learn to evaluate the effects of technology on self and society.

The word "context" captures the vision for what the course should be. We are convinced that the course can be successful only by careful, continuous attention to the idea of ***context*** presented throughout the course. The understanding of the importance of developing the proper context within which such courses are taught has been recognized [11], [12].

2. DEFINITION OF CONTEXT
A liberal arts education requires students to gain an understanding of the world around them. Technology is a major part of this world and therefore must be understood. Put another way, educated people cannot have a fully informed view of the world if they do not understand the way technology is integrated into so much of it. The twentieth century philosopher, Martin Heidegger [13] reminds us that to view technology as simply a tool is only partially correct. There is something else going on with technology when we use it. He referred to this as the essence of technology. Thus, part of the context of technology is

Permission to make digital or hard copies of all or part of this work for personal or classroom use is granted without fee provided that copies are not made or distributed for profit or commercial advantage and that copies bear this notice and the full citation on the first page. To copy otherwise, or republish, to post on servers or to redistribute to lists, requires prior specific permission and/or a fee.
SIGCSE'12, February 29–March 3, 2012, Raleigh, North Carolina, USA.
Copyright 2012 ACM 978-1-4503-1098-7/12/02...$10.00.

understanding how it effects our view of the world when we use it.

For the purpose of course development the word "context" was defined as the set of fundamental concepts

- within which computing technology exists
- that must be considered to understand and evaluate the interaction of technology with society and individuals
- that allow an educated person to function in the contemporary world

Assumptions were developed so that specific elements of context could be defined and described. The list was derived through conversations between the course instructors as they tried to understand the areas of context that our students are lacking. These assumptions are:

1. As computing technology becomes more complex and hidden
   - students understand less about how the world functions
   - the student's worldview is impacted by technology in ways that are not recognized and, therefore, not critically evaluated

2. Computing technology creates an alternate view of the world where societal structure and human relationships have different meanings than in previous generations.

3. If the way in which computing technology impacts every aspect of life is not understood, it is impossible to have a full concept of what it means to be human.

4. Technology is so intertwined with contemporary life that ethical issues are more easily hidden. A person who does not have some understanding of technology cannot understand ethical issues.

5. Education now includes reading, writing, arithmetic, and computation. Less emphasis is placed on the traditional three pillars due to the supposed power of computation.

6. The availability of google, wikipedia, and similar resources provides quick surface-level answers to almost any question, especially technical how-to questions. While this approach offers solutions to immediate problems, it forms an inadequate knowledge base for a liberally educated person.

7. General education computing courses aimed at competency and literacy foster the above paradigms rather than critically analyzing them.

8. Although the above assumptions emphasize a broad view of computing, students need to learn what tools are available and how to use them.

3. COURSE MODIFICATIONS

The course has undergone a series of modifications. For several years the course has stressed the examination of technology's impact on society to include negative aspects and unintended consequences. These concepts fit well with the revised course and are continued in a somewhat modified manner. It is important to state that discussion emphasizes such issues but that we do not judge that computing technology is "bad", but rather to counteract common assumptions that all aspects of technology are "good". As Neil Postman [14] said, the benefits of technology are obvious; therefore we should look more closely at the negative effects. The course has included, and continues to include, material from Neil Postman as well as Nicholas Carr [15] as required readings.

Some material is presented with strong statements in order to gain the attention of the students. For example, the course web page begins with the following quote from Jacques Ellul [16]:

> "Prepare them to live in technology and at the same time against technology . . . to develop a critical awareness of the modern world"

The course has also emphasized ethics applied to computing and technology, including an introduction to ethical theory.

3.1 FALL 2008 – SPRING 2009

The first change made to the course was between fall 2008 and spring 2009 when the class sections and sizes were modified to allow for a team-teaching approach. In fall 2008 the course was taught in 5 sections of 45 students each on a Tuesday/Thursday schedule. Beginning in the spring 2009 semester the course was changed to meet in two large groups of 120 each on Tuesday and then broken into four smaller groups of 60 each on Thursday. Lab times remained the same for both semesters. This format change allowed for more lecture style and lab demo material to be covered on Tuesdays, and for discussion and interaction on Thursday. An interesting effect was that even though the class sizes were larger, because the students moved from a large lecture hall on Tuesday to a smaller classroom on Thursday, the 60 student sections seemed small in comparison and facilitated an acceptable amount of interaction and discussion.

3.2 FALL 2009

Major modifications were incorporated beginning in the fall semester, 2009. Students were introduced to our concept of a context driven course. Lectures, labs, and course readings were designed to emphasize the context of computing in the students' world.

The idea of computing context and its relation to a liberal arts education is mentioned and acknowledged in nearly ever class session. Each lab includes an introduction section placing the tool and/or the topic of the lab in the broad context presented in the course. Students are provided with an explanation of why the particular topic is valuable to learn.

Labs are designed as much as possible to convey more than one idea. For example, three labs are devoted to the use of different tools (spreadsheet, database, and web forms) but also illustrate concepts of data structures and their impact. The first lab of this set requires manipulating data and answering certain questions about student registration information. The second lab explores the use of a database with the same data while discussing additional questions that can be easily answered due to increased structure in the data. The third lab utilizes a provided database and web server software to generate responses to queries from a student created web form.

Guest lectures are utilized to stress context and provide relevance to topics. The University Director of Technology Services discusses bandwidth and related issues that are important to students.

The Department offers an "add-on" curriculum in Systems (analysis, design, etc.). The Director of the Systems program presents material on "what is a system?" and "what does it mean to approach a problem from a systems perspective?"

Students in a web application development course (from our department) speak to the class on the topic, "What every graduate of a liberal arts university should understand about the Internet."

Throughout the semester, students are able to move from seeing only the benefits of computational technology and the usefulness of computer applications, to critically analyzing the effects on self and society. They are given a chance to put computational technology in a proper context with their world.

3.3 FALL 2011

As with most computer science courses, the modifications are ongoing. This fall the labs have moved to a cloud computing environment. Instead of using PhotoShop, we are using pixlr.com. Instead of traditional web design with Adobe Dreamweaver, we are using WordPress. Instead of Microsoft Office, we are using Google Docs. The goal is to meet the students where they actually live—online. Like the rest of the course, students will be asked to evaluate both benefits and problems with cloud computing.

4. CONTEXT DRIVEN CONTENT

As course modifications continue, context remains the driving force. There is sometimes conflict between what students think they need to know, and what the instructors want them to learn. By placing course topics in context, students are better able to see why they are doing what's asked of them. For example, the context for students while working through the section on programming and algorithmic thinking is not that every student will become a programmer. They are asked to understand that this is what a computer scientist does, how a computer scientist thinks, and what is possible in software development. Part of the context of computational computing is knowing what is possible and what is not—removing the "magic" from what a computer is doing.

The instructors believe that course modifications, past and future, serve the purpose of the course if they are designed and taught with context in mind.

4.1 ELEMENTS

In order to map "context" to course structure and material, elements of the context that can be related to course activity were identified.

Beyond the aspects of ethics and the relationship of technology and society discussed above, the elements in very broad terms are:

- nature of computation – algorithm processes, concepts of complexity, practical and theoretical limits on what is reasonable to compute
- systems mindset
- data can be organized – the method of organization impacts what can be accomplished easily and efficiently
- ethical theories to support application
- history of computing and technology – the way in which technology has developed has had its own impact on
- tools – an educated person knows what tools are available and should not be intimidated by new hardware and software
- technological literacy – basic ideas of hardware and software, including speed issues, cloud computing, and virtual machines

4.2 TOPICS

A list of topics was developed from the context elements. The approach used is that topics are organized into "context ingredients". As in a recipe prepared by a master chef, it is possible to taste the individual ingredients but the true flavor of the course is determined by the combination of the ingredients.

Topic categories are:

- Ethics and society
    - ethics – theory and application
    - intellectual property
    - societal impact
    - appropriate technology
    - computing to support non-profit endeavors
- Data organization
    - structuring of data
    - spreadsheets
    - database
- Information
    - web pages – construction, design
    - information context
    - interaction with data through web interfaces
- Computation
    - limits on power
    - algorithmic thinking – including concepts of complexity
    - systems thinking – what is a system?
    - programming – to provide understanding of process, not practical skills

4.3 EXAMPLES

To further explain the course design, we provide the following examples of topics that are taught to develop an understanding of context with students.

A. Ethics

Computers (especially when networked) allow people and organizations to do things that couldn't be done in the past. They also allow for the same things to be done in different ways. Students are taught to think about the ethical issues arising from such change.

Graduates of a liberal arts university should be able to analyze computer ethics issues as they arise and be able to respond to them in an informed way. Students are taught a basic overview of ethical theory and asked to respond to case studies and other readings of ethical issues in computing.

Students are introduced to the ideas of employee monitoring, privacy, intellectual property, theft, and even human relations in a social networking environment.

This section of the course concludes with a book discussion related to computational technology and society. Neil Postman's *Technopoly*, and Nicholas Carr's *The Shallows: What the Internet is Doing to Our Brains*, are two books that have been used. Because the students meet twice a week, once in a large group, and another time in a smaller section, we are able to facilitate an open atmosphere of discussion.

B. Data

Graduates of a liberal arts university should know that the manner in which data is organized affects what can be done with the data. Students are given some realistic student enrollment data in spreadsheet form and directed to answer some questions about the data that require spreadsheet manipulation.

In a later lab, the rows of the spreadsheet are divided into database tables. Students are asked to answer questions that would be difficult in spreadsheet format but are easy with database organization.

In the next lab, students have designed a web form using Dreamweaver to query a provided data base and server application. Although writing SQL is not stressed, students are shown the SQL statement generated by their query along with the results.

C. Computational efficiency

Graduates of a liberal arts university should be aware that some problems are "harder" to solve, in an algorithmic complexity way, than others. To illustrate this point, an interactive lecture is presented where the professor guesses a number between 1 and 1000 with no more than 10 guesses using binary search. The next problem considered is one where students schedule a time to meet for lunch in groups of 2, then in groups of 3, etc. Students are convinced that adding one more person to the discussion doubles the amount of work. These types of problems are described as logarithmic $O(\lg N)$ and exponential $O(2^N)$ although most of the students do not grasp the mathematics involved.

D. Algorithmic thinking

Graduates of a liberal arts university should have some understanding of algorithmic approaches to problem solving. Students complete a "programming" lab where a game is played to move a character to light a lightbulb. Students choose and order operations such as turn right, move forward, jump in order to accomplish the task. The selected steps are not executed until after all are selected.

There are a limited number of locations to store the steps. Therefore, functions in the form of a group of icons representing steps are needed. The concept of procedural abstraction to simplify problem solving is discussed in this context.

5. ASSESSMENT

In order to assess the impact of the newly redesigned course on students, a survey was given at the end of each semester from fall 2008 to spring 2010. The same 17 questions were asked using a five-point Likert scale of Strongly Disagree, Disagree, Undecided, Agree, Strongly Agree.

The goal of this survey was to discover whether students had an increased understanding of the purpose of the course and whether they were satisfied with what they had learned. Our reasoning for this measurement of student perceptions was based on two ideas; 1) students will learn more if they believe they have a clear understanding of the purpose of the course, and 2) increased student satisfaction represents a positive improvement in the learning that takes place, especially in a campus-wide, general education course, where motivation is an important factor. The data gathered represents 100% participation among the 220+ students each semester.

The seven questions most pertinent to this paper are listed in Table 1 below. They were used to measure, across five semesters, student perceptions of the value of the course.

Table 1. Survey Questions

1. I have a better understanding of the relationship between technology and society.
2. This class is about understanding the role of computation in today's society.
3. This course caused me to rethink my personal use of technology.
4. This course is necessary at Taylor University.
5. I am better prepared to interact with computers and technology in the future because of this course.
6. *My attitude towards this course at the beginning of the semester was that it would be valuable.
7. *My attitude towards this course at the end of the semester was that it was valuable.

* No data for fall 2008

5.1 Results

It is important to note that this course was redesigned over the course of several semesters. The fall 2008 semester represents the last time the course was taught as-is without any modifications.

During the next three semesters, new ideas were implemented into the course. In the second semester, spring 2009, besides changing class sizes and format, the idea of context was becoming a part of the course. But it wasn't until fall 2009 and spring 2010 that the emphasis of context was intentionally introduced as the overarching idea. The survey results continued to show an increase in the students' perceptions that they understood the purpose of the course and were increasing their satisfaction. Some highlights across all five semesters follow:

An indicator that students are satisfied with the course can be found in the results from survey item 4. From fall 2008 to spring 2010 students increased their perception that this course is useful for students at Taylor University. The 19% increase moved from 41% to 60% of the students responding with Agree or Strongly Agree. A side benefit of this response could be that students will speak positively of the course to their peers and help change the perspective that this is a competency course.

Students also showed an increase in the perception that learning about ethical issues with technology and society was valuable. Survey item 3 measured this positive result.

Most notably there was a positive increase in the two questions, items 6 and 7, which asked about the students perceptions of the course at the beginning of the semester and then at the end. (Note: we have data for this response for only four semesters.) In the response to, "My attitude towards this course at the beginning of the semester was that it would be valuable," 31% chose Agree or Strongly Agree in spring 2009 compared to 39% in fall 2010. Likewise, for the response about their attitude at the end of the semester the responses were 53% and 64% respectively. This shows that students are moving in the right direction in a two-fold way. First, students are increasing each semester in their perceptions that this course will be valuable, as well as increasing in the final outcome that it was indeed valuable. Secondly, Agree/Strongly Agree responses increased from the beginning of the semester to the end from 39% to 64%--a 25% increase.

5.2 Assessment Conclusion

The responses to the survey indicate that as the idea of context was introduced into the course, students increased their perception that the course was valuable. When the course was revised to be centered around context, students shared the perception of being more satisfied and having a better understanding of its purpose. Improving student satisfaction is a good beginning towards increasing the learning outcomes for this course. It is our belief that students are increasing in their understanding that this course is relevant and fitting in a liberal arts education.

6. REFERENCES

[1] Turk, J. 2010. Computer Literacy as Life Skills for a eb 2.0 World. In *Proceedings of the 41st SIGCSE Technical Symposium on Computer Science Education*, 417-422.

[2] Purewal, T. S., Bennett, C., Maier, F. 2007. Embracing the Social Relevance: Computing, Ethics and the Community. In *Proceedings of the 38th SIGCSE Technical Symposium on Computer Science Education*, 556-560.

[3] Barr, J., Cooper, S., Goldweber, M., Walker, H. 2010. What Everyone Needs to Know About Computation (panel). In *Proceedings of the 41st SIGCSE Technical Symposium on Computer Science Education*, 127-128.

[4] Burns, B. 2005. A New Approach to Computer Science in the Liberal Arts. *Journal of Computing in Small Colleges,* 20, 68-77.

[5] Cliburn, D. C. 2006. A CS0 Course for the Liberal Arts. In *Proceedings of the 37th SIGCSE Technical Symposium on Computer Science Education*, 77-81.

[6] Giangrande, E. 2008. Computing for the 21st Century. *Journal of Computing Sciences in Colleges*, 23, 31-36.

[7] Turk, J., Wiley, S. 1997. Teaching Social and Ethical Issues in the Literacy Course. In *Proceedings of the 28th SIGCSE Technical Symposium on Computer Science Education*, 10-14.

[8] Zimmerman, B. 2004. Content and Laboratories of a Computing Science Course for Non-Majors in the 21st Century. *Journal of Computing in Small Colleges*, 19, 68-77.

[9] Guzdial, M., Forte, A. 2005. Design Process for a Non-majors Computing Course. *Proceedings of the 36th SIGCSE Technical Symposium on Computer Science Education*, 361-365.

[10] Zhang, M., Lo, V. M. 2010. Undergraduate Computer Science Education in China. In *Proceedings of the 41st SIGCSE Technical Symposium on Computer Science Education*, 396-400.

[11] Martin, F. G., Kuhn, S. 2006. Computing in Context: Integrating an Embedded Computing Project into a Course on Ethical and Societal Issues. In *Proceedings of the 37th SIGCSE Technical Symposium on Computer Science Education*, 525-529.

[12] Pasternak, A., Vahrenhold, J. 2010. Braided Teaching in Secondary CS Education: Contexts, Continuity, and the Role of Programming. In *Proceedings of the 41st SIGCSE Technical Symposium on Computer Science Education*, 204-208.

[13] Heidegger, M. (1977). *The question concerning technology, and other essays*. New York: Harper & Row.

[14] Postman, N., *Technopoly: The Surrender of Culture to Technology*, New York, Vintage Books, 1993.

[15] Carr, N., *The shallows: What the Internet is Doing to our Brains*, W W Norton & Co Inc. 2011.

[16] Ellul, J., & Vanderburg, W. H. (2004). *Perspectives on our age: Jacques Ellul speaks on his life and work.* Toronto: House of Anansi Press.

Nifty Assignments

Nick Parlante, Julie Zelenski
(moderators)
Stanford University
nick.parlante@cs.stanford.edu
zelenski@cs.stanford.edu

Joshua T. Guerin
University of Kentucky
jtguer2@uky.edu

Dave O'Hallaron
Carnegie Mellon University
droh@cs.cmu.edu

Stephen Davies
University of Mary Washington
stephen@umw.edu

Debby Keen
University of Kentucky
keen@cs.uky.edu

Kevin Wayne
Princeton University
wayne@princeton.edu

Zachary Kurmas
Grand Valley State University
kurmasz@gvsu.edu

Daniel Zingaro
University of Toronto
daniel.zingaro@utoronto.ca

Categories and Subject Descriptors
K.3.0 [**Computers and Education**]: General.

General Terms
Algorithms, Design, Languages.

Keywords
Education, assignments, homeworks, examples, repository, library, nifty, pedagogy.

Introduction
I fiddle with topics in the syllabus, edit demos and presentations and entertain myself with fun slide transitions. And yet, inevitably, I must accept that most of what my students learn and remember from my course comes from the assignments. Great assignments are hard to dream up and time-consuming to develop. With that in mind, the Nifty Assignments session is all about promoting and sharing the ideas and ready-to-use materials of successful assignments.

Each presenter will introduce their assignment, give a quick demo, and describe its niche in the curriculum and its strengths and weaknesses. The presentations (and the descriptions below) merely introduce each assignment. A key part of Nifty Assignments is the mundane but vital role of distributing the materials – handouts, data files, starter code – that make each assignment ready to adopt. The Nifty Assignments home page, **http://nifty.stanford.edu**, gathers all the assignments and makes them and their support materials freely available.

If you have an assignment that works well and would be of interest to the CSE community, please consider applying to present at Nifty Assignments. See the nifty.stanford.edu home page for more information.

Nick's standing ACM editorial: a large part of the value of Nifty Assignments is that all the materials are on the internet for anyone to see without screening people (or search engines!) out by some affiliation or login. In keeping with the ACM's mission to promote Computer Science, the ACM should raise funds in some other way, such as by charging authors. The ACM materials should be simply and freely available on the internet.

Copyright is held by the author/owner(s).
SIGCSE'12, February 29–March 3, 2012, Raleigh, North Carolina, USA.
ACM 978-1-4503-1098-7/12/02.

Exploring Loops with Sounds (CS1) - Daniel Zingaro
A typical early CS1 assignment has students use loops to solve small programming problems. Rather than relying on variations of string or array problems, this assignment has students loop through sound objects to perform interesting transformations on those sounds.

Students begin by writing a function to remove vocals from music. The technique is particularly simple, relying on a crude generalization of how music is recorded. Importantly, the function is a pure loop function, with no if-statements or booleans. Since public domain vocals are difficult to find, I provide students with wav files whose vocals can be removed with varying levels of success.

Following this warm-up, students write functions to fade-in and fade-out a sound, then compose these functions in order to add both types of fades in a single call. Finally, building on what was learned about fading, students write a function to make a sound move from left to right in the stereo field. Subtle but important differences between fading and panning lead to an understanding of the use of helper functions to avoid code duplication.

With a suitable abstraction of sounds and samples, each function can be written in around fifteen lines of code. The assignment gives students practice with loops, processing sequences, and function composition. Students should be encouraged to experiment with the vocal-removal algorithm. Students with interest in sound-editing may wish to create songs, adding vocals in various ways to see how well the algorithm can remove them.

Plucking a Guitar String (CS1) - Kevin Wayne
Simulate the plucking of a guitar string with the Karplus-Strong algorithm and transform your laptop into a musical instrument. The assignment illustrates a basic programming construct (a data type that stores a sequence of values), takes advantage of a fundamental computer science concept (digital audio represents sound as a sequence of amplitudes), and shows the role of computation in an important application (physically-modeled sound synthesis).

Karplus-Strong models the vibration of a guitar string with a remarkably simple process: Maintain a buffer of amplitudes; then, repeatedly delete the first amplitude from the front of the buffer and append the average of the first two amplitudes to the end of the buffer. The size of the buffer determines the frequency of the guitar string.

To represent a guitar, you will create many guitar strings (of different frequencies), process keystrokes to identify which strings get plucked, superpose the resulting sound waves, and sonify the results. The key data structure needed to perform the Karplus-String simulation efficiently is a ring buffer (bounded queue).

The assignment is designed for late use in a CS1 (or very early use in a CS2) curriculum. It relies on a real-time audio library with an extremely simple API — we have developed versions in both Java and Python. There are numerous opportunities for creativity, enrichment, and inspiration: perform a musical piece on your laptop, plot the sound wave as the user plays the keyboard guitar, or modify the Karplus-Strong update rule to design a new instrument

Tournament Uno (CS1) - Stephen Davies

One of the difficulties a CS1 instructor faces is the large gap in incoming skill sets. Some students are taking the course as a true introduction to programming, while others have been self-taught hackers for years. How can an instructor truly challenge the programming-savvy while at the same time not overwhelming novices with an overly complex assignment?

One way is by introducing good-spirited competition within the class. Uno! is a simple but popular card game known around the world. The complexity involved in simply following the rules is modest, but there are a surprising number of choices players unconsciously make as they play. (Should I match the up card's rank, or color? Should I play my wild card now or hold it? Does the person in the lead come immediately after me, and would it be wise to use a penalty card on them? What should I change the color to? etc.)

This nifty assignment comes equipped with a Java simulator program that can simulate thousands of consecutive Uno! games in seconds. Only one thing is missing: the pluggable strategy method for each player. Students formulate their strategies and write code to choose which card to play, which are then plugged into the simulator and compete against each other in a bracket-style tournament. It's surprising how motivating it is to even the most advanced students to try and reach the Final Four!

A PPM Image Editor (CS1-CS2) - Joshua T. Guerin and Debby Keen

Undergraduates often come into introductory-level computer science courses with expectations that match their past, multimedia-heavy computing experiences. Thus, programming assignments with graphical elements are often a favorite for intro-level CS courses. However, many commonly used programming environments don't facilitate easy use of computer graphics. Even in the case where simple graphics libraries are available, they are generally language (and platform) dependent and often favor a "black-box" style of coding that doesn't encourage a deep, low-level understanding of the underlying algorithms or data structures.

The PPM image format offers instructors a powerful tool for grounding graphics assignments in the real world. The PPM specification allows for ASCII representation of an uncompressed image, making image-editing possible in the language and platform of the instructor's choice, without the need for external libraries. Students can create seemingly advanced tools using simple (CS1 or CS2) level control and data structures. Students gain the experience of creating interesting image filters from scratch, as well as a deeper understanding of the underlying algorithms and representations used to manipulate images.

In our teaching resource package we have provided several example filters from which the instructor can choose, including pixel-level effects: color inversion, black and white / grayscale conversion, adjustment of brightness/contrast/noise, and image-level effects such as flipping and blurring.

Igel Ärgern (CS2) - Zachary Kurmas

Igel Ärgern is a simple and fun German board game whose name is commonly translated as "Hedgehogs in a Hurry". This board game makes for an excellent CS2 project because (1) it brings together many CS2 topics (two-dimensional arrays, stacks, inheritance, polymorphism, design, GUI, etc.), (2) it has an unusually large number of rule variations, and (3) the finished product is a real, published game that both adults and children enjoy playing.

The main idea of the game is that players race their four hedgehogs across the board; however, there are two challenges: (1) Hedgehogs can stack on top of each other; and only the top hedgehog in the stack may move. (2) There are obstacles (denoted by black squares) on the board. The rules suggest many different behaviors for these obstacles (concrete blocks, pits, etc.). Implementing different behaviors for the obstacles provides the students an interesting exercise in inheritance and polymorphism.

In addition to different obstacle behavior, there are many other rule variations that that can be used to either modify the project from semester to semester or to encourage student creativity.

The current version of this project is designed as a large, six-week semester project with no starter code; however, it can easily be scaled down into one or more smaller projects (e.g., by providing the GUI and having the students implement the game logic only).

Binary Bomb (CS3+) - Dave O'Hallaron

A *binary bomb* is a device that makes it fun for students to learn assembly language. The scenario is that the nefarious Dr Evil has planted a bunch of *bombs* on our system. We ask the students to help us defeat Dr. Evil by defusing one of these bombs.

A *bomb* is a C program that consists of *phases*. Each phase expects the student to type some string. Typing the correct string *defuses* the phase. Otherwise the bomb *explodes* by printing "Boom." In either case, the bomb sends the string to a server, which validates it, awarding points for each defused phase and deducting for each explosion. The server displays statistics for each bomb on a real time scoreboard. The twist is that students get only a binary executable. To defuse their bomb, they must reverse-engineer this binary, understanding the assembly code for each phase.

The bomb is beautiful in many ways. Although we don't expect intro courses to adopt this particular lab, it can teach us a lot about designing good assignments. The bomb is *fun*, turning a dry topic into a game. The bomb requires *reverse engineering*, a type of thinking that gives deep insight and forces students to learn tools like debuggers. The bomb is *polymorphic*. Each student gets a unique autogenerated bomb, which helps reduce cheating. The bomb is *interactive*. Students love to see their peers' progress on the real-time scoreboard. The bomb is *autograded*, scaling to classes of arbitrary size.

Update on the CS Principles Project

Owen Astrachan
Duke University
Durham, NC
ola@cs.duke.edu

Amy Briggs
Middlebury College
Middlebury, VT
briggs@middlebury.edu

Jan Cuny
National Science Foundation
Arlington, VA
jcuny@nsf.gov

Lien Diaz
College Board
New York, NY
ldiaz@collegeboard.org

Chris Stephenson
Computer Science Teachers Association
New York, NY
cstephenson@csta.acm.org

SUMMARY

The CS Principles Project is a collaborative effort to develop a new introductory course in computer science, accessible to all students. Computer Science educators at all levels have worked together on the development of the new curriculum under the direction of the College Board with support from the National Science Foundation. This special session provides an opportunity for the CS Principles project leaders to report on recent updates and new directions, and to engage in discussion on all aspects of the project with SIGCSE participants.

Categories and Subject Descriptors

K.3.2 [**Computer and Information Science Education**] *Computer science education, Curriculum*

General Terms

Management, Design, Experimentation.

Keywords

Computer Science Education, K-12 Curriculum, CS Principles, Computational Thinking.

1. INTRODUCTION (ASTRACHAN)

The Computer Science Principles project [1] is a collaborative effort—sponsored by the NSF and led by a large group of computer science faculty working together with the College Board—to design and teach a new introductory course in computer science, accessible to all students. A primary goal is for this course to become a new AP offering in addition to the current CS AP A course and examination. Previous SIGCSE panels and special sessions [2, 3, 4] have provided opportunities for project leaders and affiliated individuals to engage the SIGCSE community in meaningful discussion about the direction of the project. This special session brings together project leaders to report on the current status of the project and next steps, as well as continue to gather feedback from the SIGCSE community.

Two elements of the next directions include the development of prototype exam questions, and the investigation of performance-based assessment. The current round of course pilots in 2011-12 will be testing the set of prototype exam questions developed by members of the project team. Project leaders anticipate an additional round of course piloting in 2012-13 that will include performance-based assessment with a portfolio component.

Owen Astrachan is PI of the CS Principles project and co-chair of the CS Principles Commission. He has led the course development process as well as outreach efforts to involve computer science educators at all levels in ensuring the success of the CS Principles project.

2. CURRICULUM REVISIONS (BRIGGS)

CS Principles is designed to be engaging, accessible, rigorous, and most of all inspiring. It is meant—as are all AP courses—to be both a high school course and an introductory college course. It teaches programming, but is not programming centric. The course is intended to introduce a broad audience of students to the content, practices, thinking, and skills that are central to computing. The Big Ideas underlying the course design include Creativity, Abstraction, Data, Algorithms, Programming, the Internet, and the global impacts of computing. These content areas have been paired with computational thinking practices in order to develop a set of student learning objectives.

This special session will provide an opportunity for SIGCSE participants to discuss recent changes to the CS Principles curriculum and how those changes are being reflected in the prototype assessments currently being developed.

Amy Briggs is co-PI of the CS Principles project and co-chair of the CS Principles Commission. She has led the recent revision process on the CS Principles curriculum framework.

Copyright is held by the author/owner(s).
SIGCSE'12, February 29–March 3, 2012, Raleigh, North Carolina, USA.
ACM 978-1-4503-1098-7/12/02.

3. NSF INVOLVEMENT (CUNY)

The Computer and Information Science and Engineering (CISE) Directorate at the National Science Foundation aims to ensure a computationally competent 21st Century workforce ready to lead the global economy in both computing-related and computing-intensive fields. To create and sustain such a workforce, CISE launched its CE21 Program, which focuses on the teaching and learning of computing in diverse, K-14 student populations. CE21 has supported the development of a framework for the new CS Principles course. With CE21 support, it was piloted at the college level in 2010-2011 and in 2011-2012 at both the high school and the college levels.

CE21 hopes to develop an academic community and research base that will enable the widespread adoption of the CS Principles course. At the 2- and 4-year college level, CE21 will fund the development and evaluation of curricula, course materials, assessments, and alternative delivery mechanisms. It will also fund K-12/university collaborations that work to get CS Principles into high schools through the design, piloting, and assessment of pre-service and in-service teacher training, professional development and ongoing support of computer science high school teachers. Finally CE21 will fund studies into the scaling of successful interventions for widespread impact. Ultimately, CISE hopes that CE21 will catalyze a larger community effort that will ensure that all students have the opportunity to develop interest and competencies that could lead to careers in computing-related and computing-intensive fields.

Jan Cuny from the National Science Foundation provides a governmental perspective as the program manager for the Computing Education for the 21st Century (CE21) Program that focuses on K-14 education and has supported the development of the CS Principles course.

4. COLLEGE BOARD UPDATE (DIAZ)

In Spring 2011 the College Board reached out to the computer science education community for input on the CS Principles curriculum framework. Approximately 120 college and university department chairs and faculty completed a lengthy survey on the draft curriculum framework. At the same time, approximately 80 department chairs or their designees sent letters of attestation to the College Board, signaling a level of endorsement that has provided great momentum to the project as it moves forward.

CS Principles was piloted at five colleges and universities during the 2010-11 academic year. During 2011-12 it is being piloted at 11 high schools that are partnered with a college or university to offer a CS Principles course. These schools are widely dispersed throughout the country. The College Board will be expanding the project over the next few years and working in cooperation with the NSF CS10K and CE21 programs to bring the CS Principles curriculum to more schools and more students.

Lien Diaz is a Director of Curriculum and Content Development at the College Board AP Program. She coordinates and oversees all aspects of the CS Principles course development process, including curriculum development, piloting, and assessment development.

5. CSTA PERSPECTIVE (STEPHENSON)

The CS Principles project is national in scope and leverages College Board's Advanced Placement program to facilitate widespread changes in high school curricula at a national level. These changes must be accompanied by corresponding changes at the college/university level. At this session we will share how different constituencies within the CS community are becoming involved and are working together to further this initiative.

Chris Stephenson is executive director of CSTA and a member of the CS Priniples Commission. She spearheads the active involvement of high school teachers and policy makers in supporting the CS Principles project.

6. AUDIENCE AND EXPECTATIONS

This special session is intended to report on the current status and future directions of the CS Principles project. This major effort will be of interest to all computer science educators at all levels. Each of the session leaders is a leader of some aspect of the CS Principles project and can report on recent developments. After brief remarks by the session leaders, thirty minutes will be available for discussion with audience members.

7. REFERENCES

[1] CS Principles website: http://csprinciples.org.

[2] *The CS10K Project: Mobilizing the Community to Transform High School Computing.* Astrachan, Cuny, Stephenson, Wilson. Proceedings of SIGCSE 2011, 85-86.

[3] *Re-Imagining the First Year of Computing.* Astrachan, Haynie, Stephenson, Diaz, Briggs, Proceedings of SIGCSE 2010, 329-330.

[4] *Advanced Placement Computer Science: The Future of Tracking the First Year of Computing.* Astrachan, Walker, Stephenson, Diaz, Cuny. Proceedings of SIGCSE 2009, 397-398.

Implementing Evidence-based Practices Makes a Difference in Female Undergraduate Enrollments

Wendy DuBow
(Moderator)
National Center for Women & IT (NCWIT)
University of Colorado
303.492.5462
wendy.dubow@colorado.edu

Elizabeth Litzler
Center for Workforce Development
University of Washington
206.543.4810
elitzler@uw.edu

Maureen Biggers
School of Informatics & Computing
Indiana University
Bloomington, IN
812.856-0739
biggersm@indiana.edu

Mike Erlinger
Computer Science
Harvey Mudd College
Claremont, CA
909.621-8912
mike@cs.hmc.edu

SUMMARY

While many computing departments may be aware there are "promising" and "proven" practices for recruiting and retaining female students, there seems to be a drive to try new and novel approaches rather than use what is known, or strongly suspected, to be effective. Developing a diverse student body is a long-term multi-faceted process that includes active recruitment, inclusive pedagogy, meaningful curriculum and necessitates student, faculty and institutional support, as well as assessment of progress [1,2,3]. Given all the moving parts and intrinsic challenges of enacting change, departments could make it easier on themselves - and very likely achieve better results - if they intentionally and systematically used practices that have been shown to be effective.

This panel will present the rationale for implementing evidence-based practices to increase female enrollments in undergraduate computing departments, and share evidence of successes. Wendy DuBow will examine the concept of evidence-based practices as well as describe briefly the research-based approaches taken by the National Center for Women & Information Technology (NCWIT) to identify the evidence-based practices an academic institution could use and distribute easy-to-use materials explaining such practices. Elizabeth Litzler will supplement this rationale by sharing compelling evaluation data that show that academic departments that implement a variety of evidence-based practices and actively seek to increase their female enrollments actually do see increases. Maureen Biggers will describe her department's recent efforts to increase female undergraduates at Indiana University, which enabled them to double the number of new female majors. Mike Erlinger will discuss Harvey Mudd's recent successes in attracting more Computer Science majors overall, including a large percentage of female students.

Categories and Subject Descriptors

K.3.2 Computer and Information Science Education

General Terms

Measurement, Human Factors

Keywords

Broadening Participation, Gender, Diversity, Evidence-based Practices, Women

Copyright is held by the author/owner(s).
SIGCSE'12, February 29–March 3, 2012, Raleigh, North Carolina, USA.
ACM 978-1-4503-1098-7/12/02.

1. WENDY DUBOW

The moderator will explain the advantages of implementing evidence-based practices. As a member of the social science team at NCWIT, she understands the process by which recruitment and retention practices are identified by NCWIT as evidence-based and as holding promise of effectiveness. As NCWIT's internal evaluator, she has collected evaluation data from hundreds of stakeholders, including computer science faculty and high-school teachers, about the usefulness of NCWIT's readable descriptions of promising practices and practical suggestions for implementation.

2. ELIZABETH LITZLER

Evaluation evidence from academic departments indicates that use of evidence-based practices disseminated by NCWIT is positively correlated with an increased percentage of females enrolled in computing at a given institution. This presentation will describe the statistical findings from an analysis of undergraduate computing enrollments at a subset of NCWIT Academic Alliance institutions. In addition, the presenter will share information about the breadth of use of evidence-based practices, and the effects of being influenced by more than one practice. This presentation will provide a broad overview of the impact of evidence-based practices, generally, and will lead into presentations by faculty members who have implemented specific evidence-based practices.

The presenter is NCWIT's external evaluator and has been involved with the evaluation of the organization and its programs for five years. She has social science expertise in quantitative analysis and methodology.

3. MAUREEN BIGGERS

As Assistant Dean for Diversity and Education in the School of Informatics at Indiana University, Maureen Biggers led the adoption of several best practices that promote a systemic change model which, according to NCWIT, will lead to increased enrollment and retention of women [4]. In 2009, the department set a goal to double the number of undergraduate women in two years, and within 18 months had achieved that goal. Initiatives focused on curricular reform at the introductory level, collecting data to identify top influencers for enrolling in the introductory courses and then using that information to develop strategic recruiting initiatives [5], and a bi-monthly Collegium focusing on faculty pedagogy as it relates to student success, image, and retention of students [6,7]. Enrollment in the school continues to grow, with female undergraduate computer science and informatics majors increasing at a rate of 41%, and males increasing by 16%.

4. MIKE ERLINGER

The computer science department at Harvey Mudd College (HMC) attacked the problem of both attracting and keeping women as computer science (CS) majors with a multi-aspect approach that included the following:

- Changing the College-required computer science course from a focus on programming to a focus on both the principles of CS and social impacts of CS. For years, this class has been required of all HMC students. While programming is still a significant part of the course, the emphasis is no longer on programming. Also, this class is staffed in a way that students see faculty (female and male) who have different research interests. This approach implements some of NCWIT's Promising Practices, e.g., "How Can You Re-Engineer Your Undergraduate Program to Increase Women's Representation in Computing? Small Steps Toward Systemic Change (Case Study 1)" [8].
- Providing the opportunity for all incoming women to attend Grace Hopper. Post-attendance surveys indicate that this opportunity has changed the perspective of the attendees about computer science and its place in society.
- Providing summer research opportunities for women after their first year. While their education and experiences usually have not prepared them to do CS research, we make an effort to involve young women in projects in a way that they are productive and emerge with a better understanding of computer science. [9]

At HMC, students do not choose their major until their sophomore year. Thus, the above activities are not restricted to those who have already decided on CS. Rather, through these activities we hope to both increase the number of women majors and increase the understanding of CS among all HMC students.

Two other features of HMC have also contributed to the growth in women CS majors. First, the college has increased the number of women students on campus overall. Second, one-third of the nine computer science faculty members are women.

This panelist will discuss results from surveys related to the number of women computer science majors and the effects of Grace Hopper Celebration attendance on changes in computer science attitudes by the attendees.

5. ACKNOWLEDGEMENTS

The authors thank the National Science Foundation for support under award CNS-0813956, NCWIT's Strategic Partner Microsoft, and Investment Partners Avaya, Pfizer, and Bank of America. Data collection for the NCWIT external evaluation would not have been possible without the cooperation and commitment of the representatives of the Academic Alliance institutions. All opinions reflected in this paper are those of the authors and not necessarily those of the National Science Foundation.

6. REFERENCES

[1] Ely, D. 1990. Conditions that facilitate the implementation of educational technology innovations. *Journal of Research on Computing in Education*, 23(2), 298-305.

[2] "Education Systemic Change Tools." National School Board Association. Retrieved August 31, 2011 from http://www.nsba.org/sbot/toolkit/edsctls.html

[3] Cohoon, J.M., Thompson, L.D., Goodall, J., Dohrman, R. & Litzler, E. 2010. Consultants on Systemic Reform for Gender Balance. In *Proceedings of the 41st ACM Technical Symposium on Computer Science Education* (Milwaukee, WI, USA, March 10-13, 2010). SIGCSE 2010. ACM, New York, NY, 554-555. DOI= http://doi.acm.org/10.1145/1734263.1734447

[4] Barker, L.J. & Cohoon, J.M. How Can You Re-Engineer Your Undergraduate Program to Increase Women's Representation in Computing? Small Steps Toward Systemic Change. NCWIT, Boulder, CO. http://www.ncwit.org/reengineerundergrad

[5] Strategic Planning for Recruiting Women into Undergraduate Computing: High Yield in the Short Term. NCWIT, Boulder, CO. http://www.ncwit.org/recruitingworkbook

[6] Barker, L. and Cohoon, J. Key Practices for Retaining Undergraduates in Computing. NCWIT, Boulder, CO. http://www.ncwit.org/retainundergrads

[7] Communicating for Change: Persuade Colleagues to Get on Board. NCWIT, Boulder, CO. http://www.ncwit.org/commchange

[8] Barker, L.J. & Cohoon, J.M. How Can You Re-Engineer Your Undergraduate Program to Increase Women's Representation in Computing? Small Steps Toward Systemic Change. NCWIT, Boulder, CO. http://www.ncwit.org/reengineerundergrad

[9] NCWIT Academic Alliance & CRA-W. REU-In-A-Box: Expanding the Pool of Computing Researchers. NCWIT, Boulder, CO. http://www.ncwit.org/reubox

Life Two Years After a Game Programming Course: Longitudinal Viewpoints on K-12 Outreach

Antti-Jussi Lakanen, Ville Isomöttönen, Vesa Lappalainen
Department of Mathematical Information Technology
University of Jyväskylä, Finland
{antti-jussi.lakanen, ville.isomottonen, vesal}@jyu.fi

ABSTRACT

In our faculty we have run week-long K-12 game programming courses now for three summers. In this paper we investigate what programming-related activities students do after they take a course, and what factors in the students' background relate to post-course programming. We also investigate a possible change in the students' interest towards higher education science studies. We find that most students continue programming after the course and that their interest towards science studies keeps increasing. In student background we observed some indicative trends, but did not find reliable explaining factors related to post-course programming or increased interest towards science studies.

Categories and Subject Descriptors

K.3.2. [**Computers and education**]: Computers and Information Science Education—*Computer Science Education*

General Terms

Experimentation, Human Factors

Keywords

K-12, outreach, game programming, recruitment, long-term impacts

1. INTRODUCTION

Educators and IT professionals agree that the need for computing professionals will increase in the future. At the same time the academic world witnessed a steep student decline in computer science during the past decade[1]. This disparity resulted in the wide range of strategies and activities that aim to engage young people in studying computer science and information technology at the higher education level; see for example [1, 4]. These efforts are often referred to as K-12 outreach.

In our faculty we have hosted week-long game programming courses for youngsters aged between 11–17 years. With these events we want to not only give a positive image of the field and industry, but also emphasize the connection between creating computer games and real-world problems in information technology. To date we have arranged eleven course instances with 233 participants during the summers 2009–2011.

In this paper we present a study that investigates the courses' effects on participants' interest in higher education science studies and the continuance of programming-related activities. Specifically, we are interested in the long-term impact of this kind of summer event. Our approach was to conduct and analyze three separate surveys: a pre-, a post-, and a longitudinal follow-up survey.

2. RELATED WORK

Many institutions have arranged (summer) events where middle and high school aged students can get acquainted with computers and computing [3, 6, 7, 9, 10]. These events have been based on game programming (e.g. [7]), programming with robots (e.g. [6].), contests involving a wide range of computing activities (e.g. [9]), etc. The common feature seems to be that students can work in an explorative manner and that social and collaborative aspects of computing are deliberately included. In general, experiences from these events are very positive, showing students' enjoyment and a positive change in students' attitudes towards computer science.

From a research perspective, there are several critical aspects concerning the students' positive responses. For example, computing events tend to attract students who are already engaged in computers and who thereby already posses a positive attitude towards science (especially computer science) studies. In this connection, Culley [2] suggests that boys who are into computer games are more likely to engage in programming. Without differentiating between boys and girls, this is perhaps evident in [6] where many of the 10th graders were experienced with games but not with programming prior to the three day event, where programming was one aspect of study. Promisingly, quite many of these students (16 %) suggested that more about programming languages could have been included in the event.

The literature also suggests that self-selected events outside school give better student responses if compared to or-

[1]The decline reversed towards the end of the decade. According to CRA, starting from 2008 there has been an upward trend in the number of undergraduate students majoring in computer science in U.S. schools [5].

Permission to make digital or hard copies of all or part of this work for personal or classroom use is granted without fee provided that copies are not made or distributed for profit or commercial advantage and that copies bear this notice and the full citation on the first page. To copy otherwise, to republish, to post on servers or to redistribute to lists, requires prior specific permission and/or a fee.
SIGCSE'12, February 29–March 3, 2012, Raleigh, North Carolina, USA.
Copyright 2012 ACM 978-1-4503-1098-7/12/02 ...$10.00.

dinary school surveying, as noticed in [11]. This is also evident in a study where we find an impression of school-devised rather than self-selected participation, and where an increase in students' interests towards IT as a career was not that clear [12]. It is worth noting that the study by Schulte and Knobelsdorf [13] indicates the difficulty of attitudinal and conceptual change when students hold problematic self-images and conceptions of CS.

Overall, the critical aspects above suggest that students' background should be explicated when considering the impact of computing events devised to attract youngsters to the field. Stone and Kitlan [15] refer to families, peers, and K-12 system as factors affecting the students' perceptions. They underline that students already possess a view of computing at the time of entering college level studies, for which they emphasize collaboration between K-12 teachers, K-12 study advisors, and university faculties. Interestingly, they found an indication of K-12 system teachers and study advisers not affecting students' computing perceptions in an expected way, which points to the difficulty of understanding how students form their perceptions.

Positive student responses are usually collected right at the end of the events, but it is acknowledged (e.g. [3, 9, 11]) that more studies are needed to clarify long-term effects. Some indications of the long-term effects exist. We find that some authors report how schools start to continuously engage in IT-related events [3], which is likely to indicate a growing interest towards computing activities. Sivilotti and Laugel [14] point out that exposing students in particular to a programming language enables students to independently continue their computing hobby. We found encouraging evidence of the positive long-term impact of outreach events principally in the context of science education, see [8].

The present paper is motivated from the need for longitudinal studies where also students' background is explicated in relation to their responses. We report K-12 students' responses as to whether they had continued programming hobby after our week-long game programming course. We also asked these students about their computer usage at home in order to understand how such background factors might affect their interests.

3. THE STUDY

3.1 Context of the study

The study was conducted in conjunction with game programming summer courses for teenagers, as a part of the faculty's outreach program. During the summers 2009–2011 altogether 233 youngsters participated in eleven different course instances. The events are organized and advertised by the faculty staff, and the students register for the courses without K-12 system coordination. These five-day events consisted of lectures and teaching basic programming skills (8 hours), game design (3 hours), game development using *Jypeli* programming library[2] and C# language (12 hours), and showcasing (2 hours). *Jypeli* is an event-driven library to handle collisions, user input, and physics, so that a simple program can be written without loops and if-sentences. *Jypeli* was developed at our department to allow beginner programmers to start with real programming tools instead of tools made just for teaching. The course concept and *Jypeli* library are presented in more detail in [7].

[2]See `https://trac.cc.jyu.fi/projects/npo/wiki/about`

The results in the present paper concern the students who participated in any of those courses between 2009–2010. On top of the data collected during the courses we contacted these students with a follow-up survey to include longitudinal viewpoints. Because of the longitudinal nature of this study the students of the summer 2011 are not included in the numbers.

3.2 Research questions and survey description

Our study is framed around three research questions that are described below.

- RQ1: Does a student continue programming games or programs after a week-long game programming course?
- RQ2: Are there any background factors that characterize those who have continued programming after the course?
- RQ3: Does interest towards higher education science studies increase (in 1–2 years) after the course?

By science studies we refer to STEM fields, which include e.g. computer science, mathematics and physics. In the questionnaires these three disciplines were listed as examples.

The study consisted of three separate surveys:

- one made on the first day of each course, later referred to as a pre-survey,
- one made on the last day of each course, later referred to as a post-survey, and
- a longitudinal follow-up survey made 1–2 years after the course, depending on when the student participated in the course. This is later referred to as a follow-up survey.

Table 1: Follow-up survey questions

	Question	Scale	RQ
Q1	I have made games or programs after the course	Y/N	RQ1
Q2	I have modified someone else's code	Y/N	RQ1
Q3	If made/modified code, I have used *Jypeli*	Y/N	RQ1
Q4	After the course I have... (multiple choices; see section 4)	Y/N	RQ1
Q5	I am going to apply for science studies	Likert 1–5	RQ3
Q6	I would attend an advanced follow-up course	Likert 1–5	RQ3
Q7	The number of computers at home	#	RQ2
Q8	I use my mobile phone to... (multiple choices; see section 4)	Y/N	RQ2

Table 2: Programming-related activities after the course

After the course I have...	n	%
read the course material	32	21.3
read some other study material, electronic or written	31	20.7
gone to the course website (wiki)	31	20.7
read programming forums	19	12.7
written to programming forums	8	5.3
joined some programming-related Facebook group	4	2.7

In the pre-survey we collected quantitative data, like the students' basic background information, game-playing habits, earlier programming experience, and game design experience. In addition, we asked why the students chose to attend the course and whether they will choose voluntary CS courses in their curriculum[3] and plans to go for science studies in the future. Some other data, that is not included in the present analysis, was also collected. These included conceptions of easy and hard things in programming, skills needed in programming, etc.

In the post-survey we concentrated on overall contentment, impressions of the lessons and assignments, course usefulness, and changes in eagerness towards science studies.

The follow-up survey collected numeric data about how students had continued their hobby, the students' future plans regarding science studies, and their computer usage at home. The survey sheet was sent to 150 students by mail. Altogether 58 students (39 %) returned the survey. The questions in Table 1 are addressed in the present paper. Followed by the question is the scale and the research question that we try to answer.

In addition to the questions Q7 and Q8 in Table 1, we can address the research question RQ2 from many perspectives by reflecting the results of the follow-up survey against the pre- and post-survey answers. Overall, we note that the follow-up survey is our main focus in this paper.

4. RESULTS

4.1 Programming activities after the course

The majority of respondents had somehow continued their journey in the world of programming. In Table 3 we have crosstabbed the first two questions (Q1, Q2). The table shows that $38/58 \approx 65.5\%$ have either made their own games or modified someone else's game or program while 20 did neither.

Table 3: Programming after the course

		Q2 No	Q2 Yes
Q1	No	20	6
	Yes	10	22

[3]In Finnish National Core Curriculum for Basic Education there are no dedicated CS courses, but municipalities have freedom to add CS to curricula locally.

The students had been active in the area of programming also in other ways. Table 2 gives frequencies of the simple Yes/No questions (Q4). Please note that students had a chance to pick zero or more answers from the options.

During the courses the participants used *Jypeli* game programming library [7], but no more than 20 students ($\approx 34\%$) continued to use *Jypeli* after the course (Q3). This suggests that they either got to know or were already familiar with some other programming tools and continued using them.

By combining the information from the first four questions (Q1–Q4) we found that overall $53/58 \approx 91.3\%$ of the respondents had either programmed or done something related to programming, which is a surprisingly high number.

4.2 Background of programmers

Next we wanted to investigate the background of the students who had programmed or edited program code after the course (see Q1 and Q2 above). Earlier programming experience does correlate a little (.345 Pearson correlation, .01 significance level) to making games after the course (see Figure 1). It is certainly notable that more than half (57 %) of the students who had *none* or *little programming experience* had continued programming 1–2 years after the course.

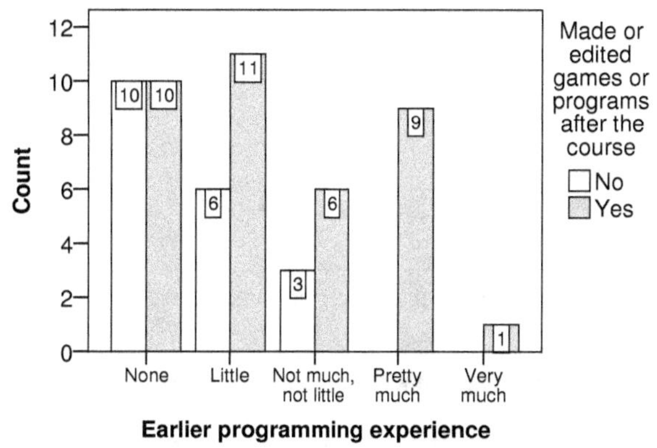

Figure 1: Pre-course vs post-course programming

The multiple choice question about the reasons to take the course, as asked in the pre-survey, is crosstabbed with the question about post-course programming in Table 4. Please note that students had a chance to pick zero or more answers from the options. There are a couple of viewpoints worth mentioning. If a friend or parents told the student to take the course, he or she probably did not continue programming after the course. Correspondingly, own free will is an important factor that keeps the hobby going. For example, if a student had plans to be a professional programmer, or was just interested in games in general, he probably did continue programming afterwards. Again, taking the course "just for fun" often leads to making games or programs later on. We acknowledge that the answers are from small groups of individuals with no statistical reliability, but they give a signal about the motivators and background factors when it comes to continuing in the world of computing after a week-long programming camp.

We also examined whether the students' general impression of the course at the time of the post-survey correlated with the post-course programming. This did not give statistically reliable results. Roughly speaking, however, the

Table 4: I came to the course because... vs post-course programming

	Programmed Yes	No
I want to learn to program	30 (68 %)	14
I'm interested in computer games	27 (64 %)	15
Programming may become my profession	15 (79 %)	4
I wanted to do something fun	10 (67 %)	5
My friend came along	8 (67 %)	4
I didn't want to spend the whole summer on holiday	5 (83 %)	1
I'm interested in natural sciences	5 (63 %)	3
My parents told me to	4 (31 %)	9
I wanted to do something useful	1 (50 %)	1
Of my friend's recommendation	1 (33 %)	2

students who liked the course most have also been active after the course (see Figure 2).

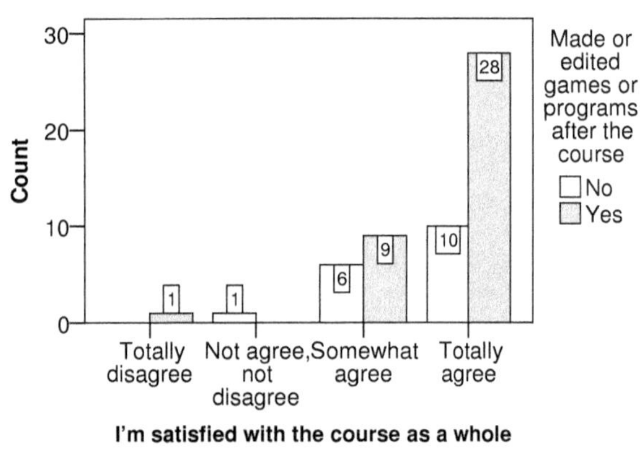

Figure 2: Overall satisfaction vs post-course programming

4.3 Interest towards science studies

One of the most interesting viewpoints of the follow-up survey was the attraction the youngsters demonstrated towards studying science in higher education, and if the numbers had changed somehow during the years. The follow-up survey gave a mean of 3.83 with 1.06 standard deviation (see Figure 3).

The same question (Q5) was asked also in the pre- and post-surveys. The pre-survey ($n = 140$) gave 3.16 (SD = 1.19) and the post-survey ($n = 140$) 3.41 (SD = 1.16) on average which would suggest that the interest towards science studies had risen 0.67 points on average from the pre-survey to the time of follow-up survey.

In Table 5 we focus on the group who filled both pre- and follow-up surveys[4]. We have crosstabbed the question Q5 from the pre- and the follow-up survey. Numbers 1–5 indicate the answers on a regular *Likert* scale, 1 meaning "totally disagree", 5 "totally agree". We call this matrix A.

[4]Some students who answered the follow-up survey did not answer this question in the pre-survey, dropping n down to 51.

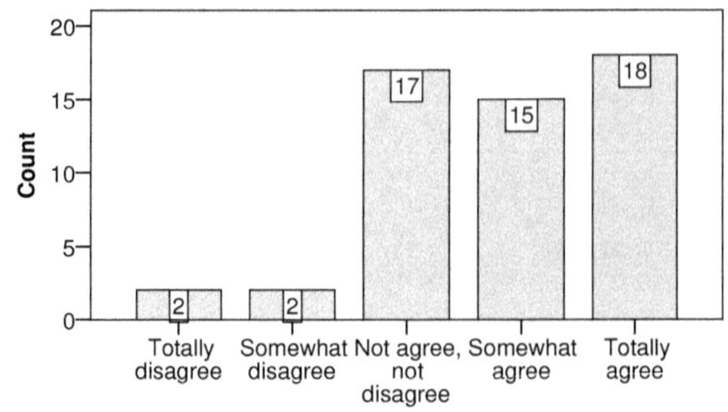

Figure 3: I am going to apply for science studies

Table 5: I am going to apply for science studies: pre vs. follow-up

		Follow-up survey 1	2	3	4	5
	1	*1*	0	**2**	**1**	0
	2	0	*1*	**4**	**2**	**2**
Pre-survey	3	0	0	*6*	**4**	**3**
	4	0	0	4	*5*	**6**
	5	0	0	1	2	*7*

The upper triangular matrix gives the cases where the student has given the *same* or *greater* value in the follow-up survey than in the pre-survey. On 24 cases the student gave a greater value in the follow-up (figures boldfaced) and on 20 cases the same (figures italicized). On seven cases the student reported that his/her interest has dropped one or two steps. We notice that the students who lowered their values are those who initially gave a high grade (4 or 5), while the increase in values has taken place with those who first gave a low value.

We calculate the mean of change with simply

$$(\sum_{i=1}^{5}\sum_{j=1}^{5}(j-i)a_{ij})/n$$

where i denotes a row, j a column in matrix A, and n is the sum of the elements. The sum is 29 and n being 51 gives us an increase of $29/51 \approx 0.57$; the mean rose from 3.35 to 3.92 and standard deviation declined from 1.20 to 0.97 in this population. On the other hand, there is no statistically significant correlation between overall satisfaction with the course in the post-survey and the students' interest towards science studies in the follow-up survey. This is somewhat surprising, and suggests that participating in the course in general may be linked to increased interest towards science studies — whether a student liked the course or not. This, however, is a matter of further study.

Quite many students said they would like to attend an advanced course (see Figure 4). At this point we do not offer one, but actually 28 of 150 students of the years 2009–2010 did later attend a second – or even third – time, making the course a follow-up for themselves[5]. Some of these students continued with the games they had started ear-

[5]Majority of the students discussed here re-attended during the summer 2011. The follow-up survey data includes only one student who had taken the course more than once.

lier while some wanted to make an all-new game with more advanced features. This is a good indicator of the interest towards continuing the programming hobby, and also hints about the students' eagerness towards science studies. A minor correlation between questions Q6: "I would attend an advanced follow-up course" and Q5: "I am going to apply for science studies" was found (.313 Pearson correlation, .05 significance level).

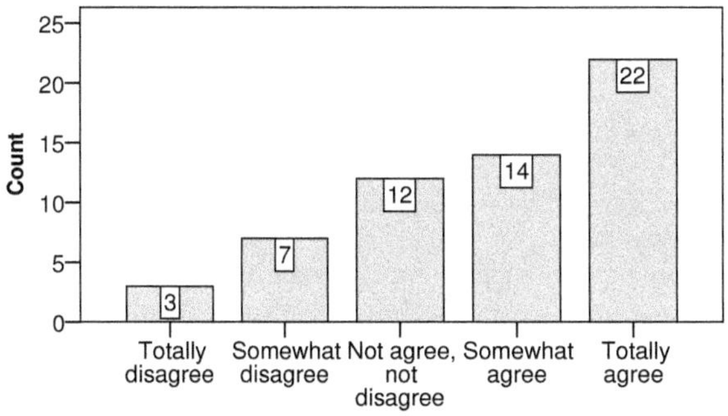

Figure 4: I would attend a follow-up course

4.4 Computer and mobile phone usage

On average the respondent had 3.6 computers (see Figure 5). The number of computers runs on the x-axis. The most common count of computers is two but almost as common is to have four computers. Some even have ten computers. None of the students said they do *not* have computers at home. In our data set the number of computers at homes does not correlate to making games afterwards nor interest towards science studies. Here we note that in today's homes in Finland it's quite common to have, not only one, but several computers[6]. Therefore youngsters can easily have access to them and begin developing their own computer games instead of just playing games.

We also asked the students about their mobile phone usage (Q8). To summarize, 44 students (76 %) play mobile games, 42 (72 %) take photos, 37 (64 %) listens to music, 34 (59 %) use calendar, and 29 (50 %) use web browser. We did not find any way these numbers could further illuminate our results above. For example, diversity in the phone usage did not correlate with the students' post-course programming or intrests towards science studies.

5. DISCUSSION AND CONCLUSIONS

In this study we examined students' programming-related activities after a week-long game programming course for beginners. The participants were middle school students, mostly aged between 12–16 years. We also examined whether certain background factors characterize the students who continue to program after the course. Furthermore, we investigated a possible change in the students' interest towards higher education science studies.

[6]A study by Statistics Finland show a rapid increase in the number of computers per household in Finland, suggesting a trend towards a siutation where each member of a household has a personal computer. Source: `http://www.stat.fi/til/sutivi/2010/sutivi_2010_2010-10-26_kat_001_fi.html`.

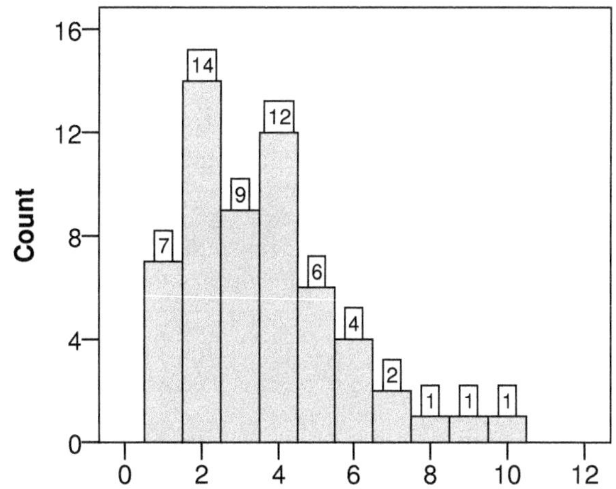

Figure 5: How many computers do students have at their homes

With regard to the research question RQ1, we found that almost all follow-up survey respondents (over 90 %) had done some activities related to programming. More than 65 % had actually made games or at least edited source code. Also, majority of those students who had no earlier programming experience did continue programming, which is a very promising result. The students mostly used some other tools than the ones used during the courses, which indicates that the students are willing to explore new ways of creating games and programs.

Concerning the research question RQ2, we did not find statistically significant background factors with respect to the question about post-course programming. This suggests that students with different backgrounds can be inspired by the course and continue to program games. However, there is some hint that attending the course voluntarily (in contrast with, e.g., being forced by parents) tends to lead to making games or other programs later on.

Finally, with respect to the research question RQ3, we found that the students' interest towards science studies had increased after the course. On a five-step Likert scale (1 meaning the lowest, 5 the highest) the respondents gave an average of 3.83 in the follow-up survey. From the first day of the course until the follow-up survey the interest among the respondents rose 0.57 points on average. This is not (statistically) related to satisfaction with the course nor pre-course programming experience. For the educators and faculty members struggling with student decline this is a promising result, suggesting that kids with different backgrounds and previous knowledge can become inspired about science during and after attending an outreach event.

In the surveys of this study we did not specify the exact meaning of the word *programming* to the students. Therefore, we do not have detailed information about what type of programming the students had done. A matter of further study is *what kind* of programming exercises students do after a course, e.g., games, web programming, or some other types of programs. This information could yield a better understanding of the relationship between the students' post-course activities and background factors.

Our future work also includes a deeper study about student's conceptions of the term *programming*, and what they perceive to be programming-related activities.

6. ACKNOWLEDGEMENTS

This study and the programming course presented in this paper were partly funded by Technology Industries of Finland Centennial Foundation. We wish to thank the developers of Jypeli library Tero Jäntti, Tomi Karppinen, Janne Nikkanen, Simo Haatainen, and Tuukka Puranen.

7. REFERENCES

[1] T. Bell, P. Curzon, Q. Cutts, V. Dagiene, and B. Haberman. Introducing students to computer science with programmes that don't emphasise programming. In *Proceedings of the 16th annual joint conference on Innovation and technology in computer science education*, ITiCSE '11, pages 391–391, New York, NY, 2011. ACM.

[2] L. Culley. *Gender equity and computing in secondary schools: issues and strategies for teachers*, pages 147–159. Taylor & Francis, Bristol, PA, USA, 1993.

[3] M. A. L. Egan and T. Lederman. The impact of IMPACT: Assessing students' perceptions after a day of computer exploration. In *Proceedings of the 16th annual joint conference on Innovation and technology in computer science education*, ITiCSE '11, pages 318–322, New York, NY, 2011. ACM.

[4] R. Garlick and E. C. Cankaya. Using alice in CS1: A quantitative experiment. In *ITiCSE '10: Proceedings of the fifteenth annual conference on Innovation and technology in computer science education*, pages 165–168, New York, NY, 2010. ACM.

[5] M. Green and P. Harsha. Computer science majors significantly increase for the second year in a row. CRA. Press release, March 2010. `http://www.cra.org/uploads/documents/resources/taulbee/CRA-Taulbee-PR-2010-Final.pdf`.

[6] M. Huggard and C. M. Goldrick. Incentivising students to pursue computer science programmes. In *ASEE/IEEE Frontiers in Education Conference, 36th Annual*, pages S4C–3. IEEE, 2006.

[7] V. Isomöttönen, A.-J. Lakanen, and V. Lappalainen. K-12 game programming course concept using textual programming. In *Proceedings of the 42nd ACM technical symposium on Computer science education*, SIGCSE '11, pages 459–464, New York, NY, 2011. ACM.

[8] D. G. Markowitz. Evaluation of the long-term impact of a university high school summer science program on students' interest and perceived abilities in science. *Journal of Science Education and Technology*, 13(3):395–407, 2004.

[9] B. R. Maxim and B. S. Elenbogen. Attracting k-12 students to study computing. In *ASEE/IEEE Frontiers in Education Conference, 39th Annual*, pages M1H–1. IEEE, 2009.

[10] B. R. Maxim, W. I. Grosky, and J. P. Baugh. Work in progress - introducing information technology through game design. In *ASEE/IEEE Frontiers in Education Conference, 37th Annual*, pages T1B–1. IEEE, 2007.

[11] P. Moorman and E. Johnson. Still a stranger here: Attitudes among secondary school students towards computer science. In *Proceedings of the 8th annual conference on Innovation and technology in computer science education*, ITiCSE '03, pages 193–197, New York, NY, 2003. ACM.

[12] G. B. Randolph and D. O. Owen. Attracting communities and students to IT with a community service web contest. In *Proceedings of the 9th ACM SIGITE conference on Information technology education*, SIGITE '08, pages 77–80, New York, NY, 2008. ACM.

[13] C. Schulte and M. Knobelsdorf. Attitudes towards computer science-computing experiences as a starting point and barrier to computer science. In *ICER '07: Proceedings of the third international workshop on Computing education research*, pages 27–38, New York, NY, 2007. ACM.

[14] P. A. G. Sivilotti and S. A. Laugel. Scratching the surface of advanced topics in software engineering: A workshop module for middle school students. In *Proceedings of the 39th SIGCSE technical symposium on Computer science education*, SIGCSE '08, pages 291–295, New York, NY, 2008. ACM.

[15] J. A. Stone and D. P. Kitlan. Factors impacting student perceptions of computing and CIS majors. *J. Comput. Small Coll.*, 25:156–163, January 2010.

Reflections on Outreach Programs in CS Classes: Learning Objectives for "Unplugged" Activities

Renate Thies
Cusanus-Gymnasium Erkelenz and
Technische Universität Dortmund
44227 Dortmund, Germany
renate.thies@cs.tu-dortmund.de

Jan Vahrenhold
Technische Universität Dortmund
Faculty of Computer Science
44227 Dortmund, Germany
jan.vahrenhold@cs.tu-dortmund.de

ABSTRACT

To provide a unified view of any scientific field, outreach programs need to realistically portray the subject in question. Consequently, topics and methods actually taught in Computer Science courses should to be touched upon in Computer Science outreach programs or, conversely, elements from successful Computer Science outreach programs can be used to enrich established courses in Computer Science.

We follow up on the latter aspect and investigate how outreach material might be used as a teaching resource in lower secondary Computer Science. In particular, we extract and classify learning objectives from the activities of the well-received *Computer Science Unplugged* program. Based upon this classification, we comment on where and to which extent these activities can be used to enrich teaching Computer Science in secondary education.

Categories and Subject Descriptors: K.3.2 [Computers and Education]: Computer and Information Science Education

General Terms: Design, Theory.

Keywords: Outreach Programs, Learning Objectives, Taxonomy, Computer Science Unplugged.

1. INTRODUCTION

Despite domestic and global economy crises, the recent past has seen a steadily increasing demand for Information Technology and Computer Science professionals. Yet this demand is neither reflected in increasing enrollment numbers or the recognition of Computer Science as a subject worth full curriculum credit in secondary education — see, e.g., a current ACM/CSTA report on this crisis [25]. To alleviate this imbalance, the Computer Science Education community has leveraged a variety of outreach programs designed to spark the interest in computer science as a subject of study and to convince students, parents, and policymakers that studying Computer Science prepares for entering the academic and non-academic workforce at a high level.

Permission to make digital or hard copies of all or part of this work for personal or classroom use is granted without fee provided that copies are not made or distributed for profit or commercial advantage and that copies bear this notice and the full citation on the first page. To copy otherwise, to republish, to post on servers or to redistribute to lists, requires prior specific permission and/or a fee.
SIGCSE'12, February 29–March 3, 2012, Raleigh, North Carolina, USA.
Copyright 2012 ACM 978-1-4503-1098-7/12/02 ...$10.00.

Recent studies [9, 24] show that outreach programs can significantly influence the attitude towards Computer Science.

Given the enthusiasm about the success of outreach activities that is visible from discussion groups (such as the `cs-unplugged-sharing` Google group) and web sites of a variety of outreach programs (see Section 2) it seems like a natural step to try to carry over this momentum to Computer Science classrooms or at least to try to establish teaching units based upon outreach activities. Unfortunately, the only evaluation so far of such an attempt is rather discouraging: Feaster *et al.* [13] report that a high-school course based upon the *Computer Science Unplugged* program had "no statistically significant impact on [...] perceived content understanding" [13, p. 248] and raise the question of determining how and how not to use such programs in class.

To address this question, we present a formalized perspective on assessing the use of outreach-based teaching units in secondary education. In particular, we evaluate the activities in *Computer Science Unplugged* with respect to learning objectives and classify these objectives according to Bloom's revised taxonomy [3]. The resulting classification sheds some light on the contrast between the above-mentioned study of Feaster *et al.* [13] and the observation that outreach is rather effective when directed at middle schoolers [1, 9, 24].

2. OUTREACH PROGRAMS

There are several approaches to classifying outreach programs, e.g., according to whether or not programming is the main focus [4]. For the purpose of this paper, however, we distinguish between three types of outreach programs: (i) programs that incorporate human factors to debunk stereotypes about people in Computer Science, (ii) programs that aim at presenting Computer Science as a "serious" subject, and (iii) programs that let participants interactively explore Computer Science topics at an appropriate level. In case of a hybrid form, we assign the program to the category that is stressed most in the program's description.

Human-Factor Based Outreach Programs.

While the success of almost any human-human interaction (such as outreach) heavily relies on the personality of the people presenting, there are some programs that are explicitly designed to showcase that people in Computer Science are not what negative stereotypes seem to suggest. Incidentally, most of these programs are directed towards underrepresented groups where role models seem of particular importance. Examples include the *Digital Divas* [19], *CS Girls Rock* [17], and a variety of "roadshow" programs presented at the SIGCSE 2009 workshop on "Roadshow Roadmap: Getting Started with K-12 Outreach". In a different line of approaches Computer Science professionals are paired with groups of high-school students to provide them with an inside view of the "real world" in Computing – see, e.g., the "Computer Science, Academia and Industry" program [27].

By design, these outreach programs have a strong focus on presenting role models and debunking stereotypes. Consequently, these programs vary quite a lot with the people presenting, and thus no "standardized" material is available which could be used as teaching material and from which learning objective could be extracted.

Competitive Outreach Programs.

According to Wing, two messages need to be delivered to a pre-college audience: "Intellectually challenging and engaging scientific problems remain to be understood and solved [in Computer Science] [...] [and] one can major in Computer Science and do anything." [26, p. 35]. Put differently, it is important to present Computer Science as a discipline as intellectually challenging and engaging as traditional STEM subjects. In this light, competitive programs such as International and National Olympiads in Informatics, the Beaver Contest [10], or various robotics activities such as the (Junior) *FIRST*® LEGO® League have been established. While outreach using the Olympiads clearly is retention-oriented and directed towards a pre-college audience that has a more than average proficiency in Computer Science already, the Beaver Contest and its national variants and the robotics programs are comprised of challenges designed for different age groups in middle and high school.

It seems that the very nature of these programs, namely being competitive, implies that they can be used very well as a motivation for and assessment of teaching units. As mentioned above, however, our study aims at investigating which outreach material can be used as *teaching* material in unmodified form. At least from a theoretical if not idealistic point of view, using the challenges from these activities verbatim as teaching material would be undesirable "teaching to the test". Also, based upon the first author's experience as an advisor of students participating in such contests and as a former member of the challenge committee of the German Beaver contest, we point out that using challenges as "highlights" at the end of teaching units or projects (as reported by in-service teachers) most often serves reinforcement purposes, and these heavily depend on what has been taught before in the respective teaching unit. Thus, we refrain from trying to extract learning objectives from these challenges.

Interactive outreach programs.

An interactive outreach program provides the participants with hands-on activities. We do not further distinguish by duration (such a program's duration may range from a short workshop to multi-day summer camp) but by whether these programs are centered around a computing (programming) environment or not. Programming-related outreach programs are based upon programming languages or environments that stem from courses offered in tertiary education (Alice [11], for instance originally was used for a Virtual Reality course) or have been designed to specifically prepare for courses or at least constructs taught in secondary or tertiary education (examples include Greenfoot [18], DrScheme/Racket [14], and Scratch [20]).

What is noteworthy about this type of outreach program is that by design there is an obvious and direct correspondence between the content of the outreach program and what is being taught in school or college. Thus, at least in principle, it is possible to select a learning objective, e.g., "students understand that objects communicate by sending messages" or "students can apply loop structures to iteratively solve problems", from the corresponding course and use the outreach program towards a target-group adjusted version of this learning objective.

In contrast to this, other outreach programs intentionally do not use programming environments (or computers, for that matter). Probably the best known representative of this kind of programs is *Computer Science Unplugged* [5], but there are other programs along the same lines [7, 9, 16, 21]. Curzon *et al.* [8] compare the *Computer Science Unplugged*, *cs4fn* and *CSInside* projects and conclude that the activities in all these projects are "effective as an outreach and teaching resource" [8, p. 94]. Due to the prominent standing of *Computer Science Unplugged*, the availability of extensive material, and the fact that several recent studies focus of the effects of *Computer Science Unplugged*, we chose *Computer Science Unplugged* as the focus of our study.

3. BLOOM'S REVISED TAXONOMY

As mentioned above, we aim at classifying outreach activities that present topics in Computer Science according to learning objectives. Despite some shortcomings (see also the *Summary and Evaluation* part of Section 4), Bloom's *Taxonomy of Educational Objectives* [6] for the dimension of *cognitive processes* still is the predominant taxonomy for the assessment of learning objective in Computer Science — see, e.g., the recent report by Fuller *et al.* [15] and the study by Starr *et al.* [23]. Our classification of learning objectives is based upon a revision of Bloom's *Taxonomy of Educational Objectives* as proposed by Anderson *et al.* [3]. This taxonomy adds a *knowledge dimension* and has been used previously in (self-)assessment in Computer Science – see, e.g., the recent report by Alaoutinen and Smolander [2] and the references therein.

The revised taxonomy is used to classify learning objectives according to two orthogonal dimensions: The *knowledge dimension* subdivided into four types of knowledge of increasing complexity [3, p. 46]: *factual* knowledge ("basic elements students must know to be acquainted with a discipline or solve problems in it"), *conceptual* knowledge ("interrelationships among the basic elements within a larger structures [...]"), *procedural* knowledge ("how to do something, methods of inquiry, and criteria for using skills, algorithms, techniques, and methods"), and *metacognitive* knowledge ("knowledge of cognition in general as well as awareness and knowledge of one's own cognition"). The *cognitive process dimension* is subdivided into six types of increasingly more complex cognitive processes [3, p. 67f.]: to *remember* ("retrieve relevant knowledge from long-term memory"), to *understand* ("construct meaning from instructional messages [...]"), to *apply* ("carry out or use a procedure [...]"), to *analyze* ("break material into its constituent parts and determine how the parts relate to one another or to an overall structure or purpose"), to *evaluate* ("make judgements based on criteria and standards"), and to *create* ("put elements together to form a coherent or functional whole; reorganize elements into a new pattern or structure").

4. LEARNING OBJECTIVES IN COMPUTER SCIENCE UNPLUGGED

In contrast to material designed for classroom use, outreach material is designed with a different purpose (namely outreach) in mind and thus cannot be expected to explicitly list learning objectives. Even though, most *Computer Science Unplugged* activities contain guidelines and comments for instructors. Based upon these guidelines and the teaching experience of the first author (a formally trained in-service computer science teacher who uses *Computer Science Unplugged* activities in middle school and runs dissemination workshops for other teachers), we extracted and classified learning objectives for all twelve activities in the revised[1] *Computer Science Unplugged* book [5]. Due to space constraints we detail the results for selected activities and give a summary for the remaining activities (see Figure 4).

Since the activities in *Computer Science Unplugged* were not – at least not initially – designed to serve as teaching material it may very well be the case that some objectives were intended but not written down by the authors. Nevertheless, our analysis works under the assumption that a learning objective needs to be substantiated by what is explicitly contained in the activity's description. Without such an assumption the extraction and classification of learning objectives would be subject to interpretation effects and thus not reproducible. To err on the positive side, we decided that – when in doubt – to assign an objective to the more complex of two categories in either dimension.

We illustrate the range of degrees to which learning objectives can be extracted with three examples. The first example (Activity 11) illustrates peculiarities in classifying learning objectives related to algorithms. The second and third examples present two activities that allow for a rich collection of learning objectives (Activity 6) or barely scratch the surface of a topic and thus allow for (and require) follow-up activities to be designed by the teacher (Activity 10).

Example 1: Finite-State Automata.

The goal of Activity 11 [5, pp. 86–100] is to let children discover finite-state automata by playing a treasure hunt game in which they can travel between islands (states) using either of two friendly pirate ships (state transitions) whose destination islands are not revealed until after boarding. The game ends upon finding Treasure Island (final state). During the game, some children represent an island each and offer and reveal directions (state transitions) while the remaining children traverse the map. This activity's description substantiates the following learning objectives (see Figure 1)

(i) Students are able to reconstruct (part of) the map by playing the game.

Evidence: "Use your map to keep track of where you are going and which ship you have travelled on." [5, p. 87]

Classification: The learning objective comprises knowledge of basic terminology and specific details (but no more) and thus falls into the *factual knowledge* category. To achieve the objective, students must "execute a given procedure"[2], thus the objective falls into the *apply* category.

(ii) Students become acquainted with a representation of a finite-state automaton.

Evidence: "Here is a more complicated version of the same idea of representing a map. [[Finite state automaton shown.]] [. . .] You can make up a variety of games and puzzles based upon this idea of finite-state automata." [5, p. 97]

Classification: The learning objective comprises knowledge of a model and thus falls into the *conceptual knowledge* category. To achieve the objective, students must "change from one form of representation to another" (possibly generalizing), thus the objective falls into the *understand* category.

(iii) Students experience that it is possible to infer the representation of a finite-state automaton from a given, valid sequence of transitions.

Evidence: "[[Description of a coin toss game]] There is a very simple 'map' that will describe the sequence of coin tosses. See if you can figure it out. (Hint: it has just four 'islands')" [5, p. 98]

Classification: The learning objective comprises knowledge of a model and thus falls into the *conceptual knowledge* category. To achieve the objective, students must "parse" and "deconstruct" the given sequence, thus the objective falls into the *analyze* category.

Given that the third learning objective in fact requires the students to run algorithms devised by themselves, one might ask why this does not result in a classification as *procedural knowledge*. The reason for this is that the instructions *as given in the activity* neither indicate how to obtain the desired solution nor provide means (e.g., other example strings) for the students to verify whether their result is right or wrong. Even if one is working under the assumption that learning is done in a constructivist way, obtaining procedural knowledge requires that students have a strong chance of eventually fulfilling the learning objective.

Similarly, even though the learning objective involves writing down the description of a finite-state automaton, the cognitive process is not to "devise a procedure" or to "invent a product" (*create*) but to "break material into its constituent parts" [the four states are given to the students] and to "determine how the parts relate to one another" (*analyze*).

Knowledge \ Cognitive Processes	Remember	Understand	Apply	Analyze	Evaluate	Create
Factual			(i)			
Conceptual		(ii)		(iii)		
Procedural						
Meta-cognitive						

Figure 1: Classifications for *Finite-State Automata.*

[1]The original edition and the web site contain more activities. Based upon interaction with of one of the authors (T. Bell) we decided to work with the revised version which contains less but didactically more elaborate activities.

[2]The operators used for classifying cognitive processes refer to the synopsis of Anderson *et al.* [3, p. 67f.]

Example 2: Searching Algorithms.

While *Computer Science Unplugged* has a strong focus on algorithms, not all learning objectives related to algorithms can be classified as comprising *procedural knowledge* since the activities (see above) may "only" involve carrying out an algorithm but do not *explicitly* aim at a deeper understanding of the procedure. In contrast, Activity 6 [5, pp. 45–63] is one of activities that contains the most explicit algorithmic content of all activities. In this activity, students play a variant of *Battleships* with three different sets of rules and are led to discover different ways of searching in unordered and ordered sets. Each player has a hidden and unique sheet with 26 ships at positions A–Z where each ship has a unique number and announces the number of one of these ships. The goal of this turn-based game is to quickly identify the position at which a ship with the given number is located on the opponent's sheet. This activity's description substantiates the following learning objectives (see Figure 2):

(i) Students discover linear search by playing *Battleships* with sheets in which the ships are given unordered.

Evidence: "Now take turns to guess where your partner's ship is. [...] This method is called 'linear search', because it involves going through all the positions, one by one." [5, p. 47]

Classification: The learning objective comprises knowledge of subject-specific skills and algorithms (*procedural knowledge*). The cognitive process involved is to "draw a logical conclusion from the presented information" (*understand*).

(ii) Students discover the disadvantages of linear search.

Evidence: "What were the scores? What would be the minimum and maximum scores possible?" [5, p. 47]

Classification: The learning objective comprises absolute knowledge of specific details (*factual knowledge*) without relation to lower bounds or models of computation. The cognitive process involved is to "abstract a general theme or major point(s)" (*understand*).

(iii) Students discover binary search by playing *Battleships* with sheets in which the ships are ordered by their numbers.

Evidence: "The best strategy is always to choose the middle ship of the section that must have the selected ship. [...] If this strategy is applied how many shots will it take to find a ship? [...] This method is called 'binary search', because it divides the problem into two parts." [5, p. 48]

Classification: The learning objective comprises knowledge of subject-specific skills and algorithms (*procedural knowledge*). As the algorithm is explained and reinforced, the cognitive process involved is more complex than for the "linear search" learning objective, namely to "apply a procedure to a familiar task" (*apply*).

(iv) Students discover the advantages of binary search as compared to linear search.

The knowledge dimension of this learning objective is the same as in (ii) while the cognitive process involved is to "judge which of two methods is the best way to solve a given problem" (*evaluating*).

(v) Students discover hashing (with separate chaining) by playing *Battleships* with sheets in which the ships are hashed to one of ten buckets by the last digit in the sum-of-digits in the ship's number.

[Even though it seems as if students learn to apply a hashing algorithm, the activity and thus this learning objective comprises neither a formal or generalized description of hashing nor addresses the concept of a collision and its resolution. For this reason the classification of this learning objective is the same as the classification of (i) and less complex than the classification of (iii).]

(vi) Students discover the advantages of hashing by considering which ships are "easy" and "hard" to locate.

[See learning objective (iv).]

(vii) Students gain an understanding about when to use which searching algorithm.

Evidence: "Which of the three searching processes is fastest? Why? What are the advantages of each of the three different ways of searching?" [5, p. 49]

Classification: The learning objective comprises knowledge of "criteria for determining when to use appropriate procedures" [3, p. 46] (*procedural knowledge*) and involves the cognitive processes of "differentiating" and "selecting" (*analyze*).

Knowledge \ Cognitive Processes	Remember	Understand	Apply	Analyze	Evaluate	Create
Factual		(ii)			(iv), (vi)	
Conceptual						
Procedural		(i), (v)	(iii)	(vii)		
Meta-cognitive						

Figure 2: Classifications for *Searching Algorithms*.

Example 3: Routing and Deadlock in Networks.

As mentioned above, we decided to be as objective as possible by working with the activities as given and not with what one could possibly teach based upon these activities. One activity whose description substantiates only very few learning objectives but that leaves a lot of possibilities for follow-up teaching (this is even mentioned in the description) is Activity 10 [5, p. 81–83] (note that this description is significantly shorter than the previous descriptions). In this activity, students simulate passing messages or tokens in a certain network topology by passing around labelled oranges according to two basic rules ("an orange can only be passed to a neighbor", "no person may have more than two oranges at any given time"). The game ends if no person has two oranges with different labels. This activity's description substantiates the following learning objectives (see Figure 3):

(i) Students realize that there are problems that cannot be solved by greedily approaching isolated problems but by cooperatively working towards the goal.

Evidence: "Children will quickly find that if they are 'greedy' [...] then the group might not be able to attain its goal. It may be necessary to emphasize that individuals don't 'win' the game, but that the puzzle is solved when everyone has their oranges." [5, p. 82]

Classification: The learning objective comprises knowledge of subject-specific methods (working greedily or working cooperatively, *procedural knowledge*) and involves the cognitive process of "concluding" (*understand*). [Again, no explicit algorithm is given which could be understood or carried out.]

(ii) Students become acquainted with the concepts of *routing* and *deadlocks* and their relation to networks.

Evidence: "Routing, congestion and deadlock can present frustrating problems in many different networks. Just think of your favourite rush-hour traffic! [...] Sometimes when the computers are 'down' in businesses (such as banks) the problem is caused by a communication network deadlock. Designing networks so that routing is easy and efficient and congestion is minimized is a difficult problem faced by many kinds of engineers." [5, p. 83]

Classification: The learning objective comprises knowledge of "interrelationships between basic elements [...] that enable them to function together" [3, p. 46] (*conceptual knowledge*) and involves the cognitive process of "construct[ing] a cause-and-effect-model of a system" (*understand*).

Knowledge \ Cognitive Processes	Remember	Understand	Apply	Analyze	Evaluate	Create
Factual						
Conceptual		(ii)				
Procedural		(i)				
Meta-cognitive						

Figure 3: Classifications for *Routing and Deadlocks.*

Summary and Evaluation.

The classification of all twelve activities in the *Computer Science Unplugged* book results in the matrix in Figure 4:

Knowledge \ Cognitive Processes	Remember	Understand	Apply	Analyze	Evaluate	Create
Factual	2, 4	6	1, 11		6, 7	
Conceptual	9	2, 7, 8, 10, 11, 12		1, 11		
Procedural		3, 4, 6, 10	2, 3, 4, 6, 7, 8	1, 6, 9		
Meta-cognitive						

Figure 4: Classification by activity numbers.

Keeping in mind that *Computer Science Unplugged* was not designed for *teaching*, we comment on this matrix.

First of all, the absence of learning objectives on the *metacognitive* level is undesirable but easy to explain. Metacognitive knowledge includes *strategic knowledge*, i.e., "knowledge of general strategies for learning, thinking, and problem solving" [3, p. 56], and this being a central component envisioned for *Computational Thinking* [26] would be highly desirable to address while teaching. However, according to Piaget [22] students progress to the "formal operational stage" at about 12 years of age. Also, since the activities are designed to rarely last more than one hour and thus do not allow for extensive in-depth discussion and repetitions, it is almost impossible to achieve learning objectives related to metacognitive knowledge, especially not for the younger part of the audience the activities are designed for.

The second comment relates to the *cognitive process* dimension where we note a clustering in the lower half of the scale. On one hand, this serves as an excellent formal explanation for the success of *Computer Science Unplugged* in outreach: there is no cognitive inhibition threshold. In addition to this, learning objectives in almost every activity are spatially close in the matrix, i.e., one can move from one learning objective to the next without jumping levels in both dimensions. On the other hand, the cognitive processes of "analyzing" and "evaluating" are addressed explicitly in only four and two out of twelve activities, respectively, and the process of "creating" is absent. Since these cognitive processes tend to become even more relevant in high school, our classification may also contribute towards explaining the "limited success" [13] of using *Computer Science Unplugged* as teaching material in high school.

It has been observed by Fuller *et al.* [15] that the linear ordering of the cognitive processes may not always be appropriate in Computer Science and Algorithms in particular – see [15] for an alternative, two-dimensional variant of this dimension. Regardless of the particular ordering, however, the widespread absence of "evaluate" and "create" processes still is a significant impediment to reaching the teaching goals set forth for higher secondary education in general. An additional drawback is that these processes not only significantly shape the internal view of Computer Science as envisioned in Computational Thinking but are also crucial for the external reception of the field: "Our competence is judged not by our ability to explain principles, but by the quality of what we do." [12, p. 18].

5. CONCLUSIONS

We have presented a formal description and classification of learning objectives that can be extracted from the *Computer Science Unplugged* activities. Our findings are threefold: Based upon our classification, we can – on a formal level – explain and support the success of *Computer Science Unplugged* when used for the outreach purpose it was designed for. Similarly, the classifications indicate that the activities can be used very well for introductory purposes in class. However, the classifications also seem to imply that the use of *Computer Science Unplugged* activities *in unmodified form* for something they were *not* constructed for, i.e., in lieu of fully-fledged teaching material or as stand-alone teaching units, is somewhat limited since the learning objectives do not fully cover the cognitive processes and types of knowledge desirable for secondary education and for a comprehensive representation of the field [12, 26].

Based upon the above observations, we are currently implementing and evaluating a new approach to teaching Computer Science in lower secondary education that tries to build upon the (literally speaking) momentum attributed to kinesthetic activities. While designing this approach, we revisited established teaching units and used the classification summarized in Figure 4 to determine where to carefully weave in parts of *Computer Science Unplugged* activities.

6. REFERENCES

[1] J. C. Adams. Alice, middle schoolers & the imaginary worlds camps. In *Proc. 38th SIGCSE Technical Symp. on Computer Science Education*, pages 307–311, 2007.

[2] S. Alaoutinen and K. Smolander. Student self-assessment in a programming course using bloom's revised taxonomy. In *Proc. 15th Annual SIGCSE Conf. on Innovation and Technology in Computer Science Education, ITiCSE 2010*, pages 155–159, 2010.

[3] L. W. Anderson, D. R. Krathwohl, P. W. Airasian, K. A. Cruikshank, R. E. Mayer, P. R. Pintrich, J. Raths, and M. C. Wittrock, editors. *A Taxonomy for Learning, Teaching, and Assessing: A Revision of* Bloom's Taxonomy of Educational Objectives. *Abridged Edition.* Longman, New York, 2001.

[4] T. Bell, P. Curzon, Q. Cutts, V. Dagienė, and B. Haberman. Introducing students to computer science with programmes that don't emphasise programming. In *Proc. 16th Annual Joint Conf. on Innovation and Technology in Computer Science Education, ITiCSE 2011*, page 391, 2011.

[5] T. Bell, I. H. Witten, M. Fellows, and R. Adams. *Computer science unplugged. an enrichment and extension programme for primary-aged children.* Unplugged, Canterbury, 2002.

[6] B. S. Bloom (ed.), M. D. Engelhart, E. J. Furst, W. H. Hill, and D. R. Krathwohl. *Taxonomy of Educational Objectives: Handbook I: Cognitive Domain.* McKay, New York, 1956.

[7] P. Curzon. Keynote talk: Serious fun in computer science. In *Proc. 12th Annual SIGCSE Conf. on Innovation and Technology in Computer Science Education, ITiCSE 2007*, page 1, 2007.

[8] P. Curzon, P. W. McOwan, Q. I. Cutts, and T. Bell. Enthusing & inspiring with reusable kinaesthetic activities. In *Proc. 14th Annual SIGCSE Conf. on Innovation and Technology in Computer Science Education, ITiCSE 2009*, pages 94–98, 2009.

[9] Q. I. Cutts, M. I. Brown, L. Kemp, and C. Matheson. Enthusing and informing potential computer science students and their teachers. In *Proc. 12th Annual SIGCSE Conf. on Innovation and Technology in Computer Science Education, ITiCSE 2007*, pages 196–200, 2007.

[10] V. Dagienė. Information technology contests – introduction to computer science in an attractive way. *Informatics in Education*, 5(1):37–46, 2006.

[11] W. P. Dann, S. Cooper, and R. Pausch. *Learning to Program with Alice.* Pearson Education, London, UK, 2nd ed., 2009.

[12] P. J. Denning. Great principles of computing. *Comm. ACM*, 46(11):15–20, Nov. 2003.

[13] Y. Feaster, L. Segars, S. K. Wahba, and J. O. Hallstrom. Teaching CS unplugged in the High School (with limited success). In *Proc. 16th Annual Joint Conf. on Innovation and Technology in Computer Science Education, ITiCSE 2011*, pages 248–252, 2011.

[14] M. Felleisen, R. B. Findler, M. Flatt, and S. Krishnamurthi. The TeachScheme! project: Computing and programming for every student. *Computer Science Education*, 14(1):55–77, 2004.

[15] U. Fuller, C. G. Johnson, T. Ahoniemi, D. Cukierman, I. Hernán-Losada, J. Jackova, E. Lahtinen, T. L. Lewis, D. M. Thompson, C. Riedesel, and E. Thompson. Developing a computer science-specific learning taxonomy. *ACM SIGCSE Bulletin*, 39(4):152–170, Dec. 2007.

[16] J. Gallenbacher. *Abenteuer Informatik. IT zum Anfassen - von Routenplaner bis Online-Banking.* Spektrum-Verlag, Wiesbaden, 2nd ed., 2008. In German.

[17] S. Graham and C. Latulipe. CS girls rock: Sparking interest in computer science and debunking the stereotypes. In *Proc. 34th SIGCSE Technical Symp. on Computer Science Education*, pages 322–326, 2003.

[18] M. Kölling. The Greenfoot programming environment. *ACM Transactions on Computing Education*, 10(4), Nov. 2010. Article 14, 21 pages.

[19] C. Lang, A. Craig, J. Fisher, and H. Forgasz. Creating digital divas: Scaffolding perception change through secondary school and university alliances. In *Proc. 15th Annual SIGCSE Conf. on Innovation and Technology in Computer Science Education, ITiCSE 2010*, pages 38–42, 2010.

[20] J. H. Maloney, K. Peppler, Y. Kafai, M. Resnick, and N. Rusk. Programming by choice: urban youth learning programming with scratch. In *Proc. 39th SIGCSE Technical Symposium on Computer Science Education*, pages 367–371. 2008.

[21] R. Mittermeir, E. Bischof, and K. Hodnigg. Showing core-concepts of informatics to kids and their teachers. In *Teaching Fundamentals Concepts of Informatics, 4th International Conf. on Informatics in Secondary Schools – Evolution and Perspectives, ISSEP 2010*, volume 5090 of *Lecture Notes in Computer Science*, pages 143–154, Berlin, 2010. Springer.

[22] J. Piaget. *The Psychology of Intelligence.* Routledge Chapman & Hall, London/New York, 2nd ed., 2001.

[23] C. W. Starr, B. Manaris, and R. H. Stalvey. Bloom's taxonomy revisited: Specifying assessable learning objectives in computer science. In *Proc. 39th SIGCSE Technical Symposium on Computer Science Education*, pages 261–265. 2008.

[24] R. Taub, M. Ben-Ari, and M. Armoni. The effect of CS unplugged on middle-school students' views of CS. In *Proc. 14th Annual SIGCSE Conf. on Innovation and Technology in Computer Science Education, ITiCSE 2009*, pages 99–103, 2009.

[25] C. Wilson, L. A. Sudol, C. Stephenson, and M. Stehlik. Running on empty: The failure to teach K-12 computer science in the digital age. Association for Computing Machinery / Computer Science Teachers Association, 2010. Also available via `http://www.acm.org/Runningonempty`.

[26] J. M. Wing. Computational thinking. *Comm. ACM*, 49(3):33–35, Mar. 2006.

[27] C. Yehezkel and B. Haberman. Bridging the gap between school computing and the "real world". In *Informatics Education – The Bridge between Using and Understanding Computers International Conference on Informatics in Secondary Schools – Evolution and Perspectives, ISSEP 2006*, volume 4226 of *Lecture Notes in Computer Science*, pages 38–47, Berlin, 2006. Springer.

Weaving a Tapestry: Creating a Satellite Workshop to Support HS CS Teachers in Attracting and Engaging Students

Ambareen Siraj, Martha J. Kosa, Summer-Mistine Olmstead
Tennessee Technological University
Department of Computer Science
110 University Drive
Cookeville, TN 38505
{ASiraj, MJKosa}@tntech.edu; SMOlmstead21@students.tntech.edu

ABSTRACT

In this paper, we describe the Tennessee Technological University (TTU) Tapestry Workshop for high school (HS) teachers. The Tapestry Workshop initiative - a collaborative partnership between TTU, the University of Virginia (UVA) and HS teachers - shares strategies, practices, and innovative ideas for teaching Computer Science (CS) effectively. This three-day professional development workshop utilized informational, technical, networking, activity-, and discussion-oriented sessions geared towards attracting and engaging a diverse body of CS students. The workshop was a worthwhile professional development activity for both the organizers and attendees and contributed to the initiation of a local HS CS program.

Categories and Subject Descriptors

K.3.2 [**Computer and Information Science Education**]: Computer science education

General Terms

Design, Management, Human Factors.

Keywords

CS Education Community, K-12 outreach, High School Computer Science, AP CS

1. INTRODUCTION

Computing technologies are integral to our lives today and will be more so in the future. As a result, computer scientists will be in the highest demand of all the science, technology, engineering and math disciplines soon, according to the Federal Bureau of Labor Statistics' Occupational Outlook Handbook [8]. The College Board reports a decade of continuing low contributions to the CS HS pipeline compared to other STEM disciplines [11]. One initiative to address this challenge originated from UVA, the project Teachers Attracting Girls (TAG) to High School Computer Science (HS CS) [32], a BPC-LSA NSF project by principal investigators Drs. James and Joanne Cohoon [4]. In partnership with UVA, the TTU Tapestry Workshop is a collaborative effort to increase the pipeline production of middle and high school students into college CS programs. The workshop provided a professional development opportunity to high school CS teachers so that they can effectively recruit and retain a diverse body of students in computing. In this paper, we describe the planning, organization, and evaluation of the three-day TTU Tapestry Workshop. The common goals of the TTU Tapestry and UVA TAG/Tapestry workshops include training teachers to:

- Attract more and diverse students into high school CS classes,
- Influence the perceptions of students, parents, guidance counselors, administrators, and other teachers about the importance of CS courses and the opportunities they provide,
- Engage students in different CS related activities.

The workshop also provided opportunities for teachers to:

- Interact and network with national experts and college faculty on teaching and diversity practices,
- Explore activities for gaining the interest of all students,
- Form a network of like-minded people for ongoing curriculum discussion and development.

As part of the collaboration, we were provided with guidance, support, and resources to offer this satellite workshop for educators across the nation to effectively attract and engage a larger and more diverse body of students. Section 2 highlights related work in the area of CS professional development workshops for HS educators. Section 3 discusses the planning process. Section 4 describes workshop logistics. Section 5 identifies the primary interests of workshop attendees and the agenda. Section 6 summarizes the sessions and relates attendee interests to session contents. Section 7 shares evaluation results. Section 8 describes dissemination efforts. Section 9 discusses future work. Finally section 10 concludes.

2. RELATED WORK

Computing workshop initiatives focusing on educator needs include Computer Science for High School (CS4HS), Computer Science Unplugged, "Computational Thinking for the Sciences", Summer Institute for Advanced Placement Computer Science (APCS), the Georgia Computes! Alliance, "Introducing Computer Science to K-12 through a Summer Computing Workshop for Teachers", Exploring Computer Science (ECS), and Duke University workshops for Alice, Peer Led Team Learning, and Social Networks [6, 5, 1, 16, 7, 22, 15, 31].

Permission to make digital or hard copies of all or part of this work for personal or classroom use is granted without fee provided that copies are not made or distributed for profit or commercial advantage and that copies bear this notice and the full citation on the first page. To copy otherwise, or republish, to post on servers or to redistribute to lists, requires prior specific permission and/or a fee.
SIGCSE'12, February 29–March 3, 2012, Raleigh, North Carolina, USA.
Copyright 2012 ACM 978-1-4503-1098-7/12/02...$10.00.

CS4HS is a Google initiative advancing CS and computational thinking in middle and high schools through regional short workshops in the US, Canada, Africa, Middle East, and Europe. Computer Science Unplugged offers techniques for the positive promotion of the computing discipline - without using computers. "Computational Thinking for the Sciences" was a three-day workshop for high school science and mathematics teachers using simulation and other activities to emphasize the relationships between computer science and the natural sciences and mathematics. The Computer Science Equity Alliance focusing on the Los Angeles Unified School District (LAUSD) held a Summer Institute for APCS from 2004 to 2007 providing students with instruction and development and educators a collaboration opportunity. "Georgia Computes!" hosted faculty workshops offering resources for teaching CS1 with media computation, engineering, and robotics. "Introducing Computer Science to K-12 through A Summer Computing Workshop for Teachers" was a one-week effort to expose computer, technology, math and science teachers to computing concepts using Alice and Scratch [9, 25]. ECS works to expand computer science in the LAUSD. ECS also strives to increase participation from the African-American, Latino, and females. Dr. Susan Rodger (Duke University) has been involved in workshops, including Alice, Peer Led Team Learning, and Social Networks. In 2011, the Tapestry initiative by UVA [32] extended to two satellite sites, one at the University of Delaware [14] and ours at TTU.

3. PLANNING

We learned about the TAG workshops when PI Dr. Joanne Cohoon shared information at the 2010 Grace Hopper Celebration of Women in Computing. UVA was soliciting applications from universities to host satellite sites for the Tapestry workshops. Although we always understood the need for more efforts to increase the pipeline for CS professionals, we did not have the resources to begin. This call for participation was our opportunity We applied formally online, articulating our need and strategy. We were later notified that TTU will be the first satellite site to offer the workshop in the summer of 2011; the University of Delaware would organize another later in the summer.

We were first invited to attend a one-day training workshop, where the UVA organizers shared their previous workshop experiences. They articulated their goals and expectations, and shared their workshop structure, techniques, and resources. They also presented specific guidelines for financial support that UVA would provide through the NSF grant, and discussed the limitations and other potential funding sources. Financial support from UVA through NSF would provide the cost of meals, campus lodging for two nights, and stipends of $1000 each for the participants.

We expected to receive a "Workshop in a Box" product; what we received instead was a "Do it Yourself Box" customizable process with resources, advice, lessons learned, shared experiences, and financial assistance. In retrospect, we appreciate that the organization and content of our workshop was left to our discretion so that we could customize the workshop content to match the needs of our attendees. After the training, we had approximately five months to plan for the workshop. As necessary, we contacted the UVA organizers to address our questions and concerns.

4. LOGISTICS

The TTU Tapestry workshop targeted teachers of CS/computer technology, school administrators, and counselors from regional high schools, because HS CS education is nearly nonexistent in our immediate area. In order to get started, we needed to inform community leaders, in addition to the teachers and potential CS teachers, to gain their support. That is why in addition to the nationwide solicitation for workshop participants, we especially invited our county school board directors, our area high school principal, and teachers to attend the workshop.

Day 1	
8:30 AM	Registration, Breakfast, & Socialization
10:00 AM	Welcome
10:30 AM	Keynote: Creating Computer Science for All Students
11:30 AM	Ice Breaking
12:00 PM	Lunch
12:45 PM	CS Resources for Teachers and Students
1:45 PM	Gender and Computing
3:00 PM	Break
3:30 PM	AP CS Principles Review
4:15 PM	Promising Practices
5:00 PM	End of Day 1
6:30 PM	Dinner Get-Together
Day 2	
8:30 AM	Breakfast & Socializing
9:30 AM	Opening
9:45 AM	STEM Center Resources
10:00 AM	Rethinking CS1
11:15 AM	Break
11:30 AM	Teaching ALL!
12:15 PM	Lunch
1:00 PM	Recruiting for Diversity
2:00 PM	CS Summer Camps
3:00 PM	Break
3:30 PM	Attracting K-12 Traditional and Special Needs Students to Computing using Kodu, CS Unplugged, and Lego Robots
4:15 PM	Teaching High School Computer Science as if the Rest of the World Existed
5:00 PM	End of Day 2
6:30 PM	Dinner Get-Together
Day 3	
8:30 AM	Breakfast & Socializing
9:30 AM	Opening
9:45 AM	Nifty Programming
10:30 AM	Break
10:45 AM	Promising Practices
11:30 AM	We're Technical Women
12:15 PM	Lunch
1:00 PM	Brain Storming & Networking
2:00 PM	Assessment
3:00 PM	End of Day 3

Figure 1: Tapestry Workshop Agenda

A web presence (http://www.ttutapestry.org) was immediately established with the workshop's goals and agenda. Next, the workshop was nationally advertised to teachers via the CSTA newsletter and mailing lists, SIGCSE, social networking sites, word-of-mouth to fellow educators, and our departmental website. For regional advertisement, the TTU STEM Center bulletin board and the local newspaper were used. Approval from the Institutional Review Board (IRB) for the Protection of Human Subjects at TTU was obtained before any data collection and evaluation. Applications from potential attendees were collected through an online form.

We received approximately fifty applications; thirty attendees were selected, based on school demographics, current teaching assignments, aspirations, and expectations. They came from Tennessee, Alabama, Georgia, Florida, North Carolina, Virginia, Ohio, Pennsylvania, New Jersey, and California.

The workshop was held at the new TTU Millard Oakley STEM Center for the Teaching and Learning of Science, Technology, Engineering and Mathematics [33]. We strived to treat the teachers as honored guests, following advice from the UVA organizers.

5. CONTENT

The workshop sessions were planned and structured to achieve the goals of the TAG workshops and to meet the expectations of the attendees. To understand their expectations, specific questions were asked on the application forms. Based on our understanding of the profiles of TTU Tapestry workshop attendees, we identified three groups of teachers with diverse primary interests:

- ***Founders:***
  - This group of teachers was seeking advice in initiating CS courses in their schools;
- ***Recruiters:***
  - This group of teachers had initiated CS courses in their schools and was seeking advice in recruiting more and diverse members;
- ***Retainers:***
  - This group of experienced CS teachers was seeking advice in offering advanced CS courses and retaining the students in those advanced classes.

Thus, we designed our workshop to be an ensemble of diverse sessions to satisfy the needs of all three groups. Fifteen speakers were invited to conduct the sessions shown in Figure 1.

6. SESSIONS

The keynote for Tapestry was by ACM Distinguished Speaker Dr. Mark Guzdial from Georgia Tech, who presented "Creating Computer Science for All Students", describing the need to develop new kinds of classes and new kinds of approaches to teaching CS to meet the growing needs of both non-computing and computing majors.

The remainder of the workshop consisted of fourteen informational, technical, networking, activity-, and discussion-oriented sessions. The following briefly summarizes the sessions. Table 1 shows how each session related to the three different teacher groups.

6.1 CS Resources for Teachers and Students

Barbara Ericson, Director of Computing Outreach for the Institute for Computing Education (ICE) for the College of Computing at Georgia Tech, presented a variety of resources for teachers and students. Computer Science Unplugged, as previously mentioned, offers methods for computer science concepts without the use of computers. The University of California at Berkeley provides a collection of kinesthetic learning activities (KLA) [21]. Georgia Tech hosts the Institute of Computing Education Distance Education Portal [20]. The free programming resources include Lightbot, Scratch, Alice, Media Computation, GridWorld, CodingBat, Practice-It, and App Inventor [4, 25, 9, 23, 18, 17, 30, 3].

6.2 Gender and Computing

The HS education community is fundamental to the solution of the gender inequality. UVA's Dr. Joanne Cohoon introduced the attendees to gender issue awareness in CS. She discussed issues in gender and computing through data on diversity in HS and college CS and highlighted the gap in females in computing with the following examples. While 57% of 2008 bachelor degree holders were women, only 18% of computer and information sciences undergraduate degrees were awarded to women. In 2011, the College Board reported that the percentage of females intending to major in computer science was much lower than in other STEM fields Only 19 % of computer science AP exam-takers were female.

Table 1. Tapestry Session Interests

	Founding a CS Program	Recruiting and Diversity	Retention
CS Resources for Teachers and Students	√		√
Gender & Computing	√	√	
AP CS Principles Overview	√	√	√
Promising Practices	√	√	√
Rethinking CS1		√	√
Teaching ALL!		√	√
Recruiting for Diversity	√	√	
CS Summer Camps		√	√
Attracting K-12 Traditional and Special Needs Students to Computing		√	
Nifty Programming			√
We're Technical Women	√	√	√
Brainstorming & Networking	√	√	√

6.3 AP CS Principles Overview

Dr. Martha Kosa introduced the AP CS Principles initiative; the official title was "CS Principles: Who, What, Where, When, Why?" She first discussed the NCWIT brochure "America's Got Talent (But Not Enough Is Going into Computer Science)" [2], and then the problems with the current AP CS course [12]. The Passion, Beauty, Joy, Awe (PBJA) movement [29] and the CS10K project [13] converged with other ideas to lead to the initiative. Five university faculty members, including Dan Garcia (UC-Berkeley) and Larry Snyder (University of Washington), piloted courses during the 2010-2011 year. Kosa chose creativity from the 7 Big Ideas [10] as her theme. She found computational examples of textual and graphical creativity in the exploration of words, emotions, and facts, including an emotional search engine [19]. Then she quickly showed Garcia's first day abstraction lesson and Snyder's "Bits of Color" lesson, where art was the motivator. Next, she highlighted the beauty and usefulness of algorithms, with simple recursive art and Snyder's steganography lesson. Finally, she displayed anecdotes from female computing teachers and professionals as encouragement.

6.4 Promising Practices

Each day of the workshop, there was a session called "Promising Practices". Each session was led by an experienced CS HS teacher (Robert Luciano, Scott Portnoff, and Seth Reichelson from PA, CA, and FL, respectively), who had attended previous TAG workshops. They all teachers shared how they had significantly improved recruitment, retention, and engagement in their classes using knowledge and insight gained in TAG workshops. They also shared strategies, practices, active learning activities, and ideas that worked well in their classes.

6.5 Rethinking CS 1

Dr. James Cohoon showcased inspiring perspectives on CS1, opening with examples of poems from students. At UVA, CS1X is an introductory course which is designed for students with no prior experience level; it is also designed to be attractive to underrepresented groups.

6.6 Teaching ALL!

Dr. Ambareen Siraj presented this session on tips and techniques to reach out to all students in a diverse group. This session pointed out how teachers often appear to be unconsciously gender-biased in teaching and how it negatively affects students. It shared ways to practice equitable teaching in class where members of all groups share the same opportunities and the same constraints with full participation. The teachers were informed about different forms of bias and participated in group exercises where they identified such bias and worked to eliminate it. The session also illustrated how to use gender-neutral language in classroom instruction, create assignments that are not gender sensitive, and deal with stereotypical notions about CS.

6.7 Recruiting for Diversity

Dr. Joanne Cohoon introduced active recruiting messages for more and diverse students. Cohoon provided effective, positive messages addressing students and their influencers, which can be readily utilized by educators. Successful communication techniques were offered. Such as using appealing messages, avoiding stereotype perpetuation, and tailoring for target audiences of students, parents, or counselors. Common student objections to CS were listed, as well as techniques for overcoming them, including helpful assets, such as the NCWIT Award for Aspirations in Computing.

6.8 CS Summer Camps

Dr. Zhijiang Dong from Middle Tennessee State University (MTSU) shared his experiences with the NSF-funded multi-institutional Partners in Innovation in Information Technology (PIIT) project for CS summer camps for HS students [24]. With a capacity of 20 students for each camp and priority given to underrepresented students, three one-week camps are offered in Alice, robotics, and multimedia.

6.9 Attracting K-12 Traditional and Special Needs Students to Computing

Doctoral student Taha Ben Brahim, from Auburn University, described a K-12 CS outreach program targeted especially for special needs students, as well as traditional students. The program uses Kodu, CS Unplugged, and Lego Robots to successfully generate interests among such a diverse body of students.

6.10 Nifty Programming

Dr. Mark Boshart of TTU shared examples of intriguing programming assignments, such as the Mastermind game and a maze solver, that he had found to be effective in teaching CS concepts. For each assignment, he explained the alignment of assignment tasks with curriculum topics.

6.11 We're Technical Women

The title of this session was inspired by the "We Are Technical Women" video from the Anita Borg Institute. Four TTU women (two CS alumni and two current CS students) spoke in this panel discussion. They have taken different, unique paths in their career journey. One alumna currently works in industry, while the other one works in academia. One of the students is a senior undergraduate, and the other one is pursuing her master's degree. Each panel member shared her own journey and perspective, covering the following topics: her high school computing experience, the impact of that experience on her college major, her mentors/teachers and their influences, her career/college experience, and her current position.

The purpose of this session was to convey to the HS teachers how influential they can be in students' lives. Through the stories told, the teachers were once more reminded of the deep appreciation of their responsibility and job.

6.12 Brainstorming and Networking

The brainstorming session was organized to articulate and integrate ideas from the attendees based on the following pre-workshop questions:

- Are there any classroom assignment examples that you will particularly recommend for others?
- Are there any classroom instructional practices that you will particularly recommend for others?
- Are there any experiments that you tried in class but will recommend others NOT to try?
- If you have recruiting experience in CS classes, what has worked for you?

The survey results were summarized and presented to all attendees to provide an opportunity to discuss further and to solicit additional comments, concerns, and ideas. In addition, the attendees were divided into the Founders, Recruiters, and Retainers groups, as mentioned in Section 5. Each group discussed their individual perspectives, experiences, and lessons learned from the workshop on the challenge at hand and produced a group report on ideas and solutions to address the challenge. Each group then presented their findings to the audience for feedback. At the end, a final summary of the brainstorming session was shared with the audience.

7. EVALUATION

Each attendee completed a post-workshop survey. Due to space limitations, we focus on only two parts. The first major part involved rating the following eight workshop elements:

W1. Material will help me attract more students
W2. Help me attract diverse (girls or minority) students
W3. Help me persuade decision makers about importance of CS
W4. Logistics were well done
W5. Former workshop participants talking about their experiences was useful.
W6. NCWIT materials will be very useful.
W7. Compares favorably with other teacher workshops
W8. Would recommend to other HS CS teachers

Figure 2 summarizes the ratings. The one teacher who responded to W7 with "Moderately Disagree" commented that the workshop was actually much better than most other HS workshops.

The second major part involved rating the fourteen individual sessions, with the same ratings as in Figure 2. "Strongly Disagree" appeared in some ratings, but it appeared very infrequently, with at most 2 participants giving that rating in any session. "Moderately Disagree" also appeared infrequently. The total of "Moderately Agree" and "Strongly Agree" for every session was at least 72%, with 9 totals equaling 100%. The top six sessions, with respect to the "Strongly Agree" numbers, were as follows: Promising Practices, AP CS Principles Overview, Teaching ALL, Recruiting for Diversity, and We're Technical Women.

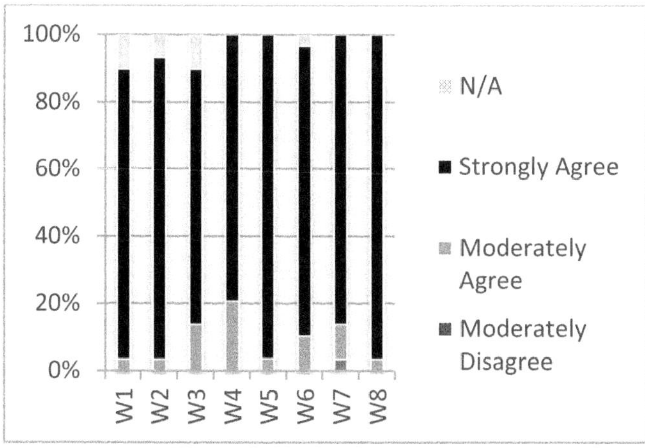

Figure 2: Evaluation Results

The attendees had more gender diversity than the typical college CS classroom; slightly less than half were female. They responded most favorably to information that they could immediately use in their classes, especially the tips for recruiting students. Immediate use was hard to achieve because approximately 50% of the attendees had taught CS for two years or less, and approximately 30% had no CS teaching experience. Many comments requested more hands-on activities and a less intense daily schedule. To summarize, the attendees perceived that the workshop was a worthwhile professional development activity. On a last note, we asked the attendees if they would consider returning to similar workshops if no stipend were offered. Surprisingly, almost 40% said that they would, and 25% (most likely, regional attendees) even expressed a willingness to pay a reasonable registration fee to attend such a workshop at TTU.

8. DISSEMINATION

Throughout the workshop, all presentations, materials for classroom activities, and resources were collected and integrated. For example, NCWIT provided printed resources for CS teachers, such as Promising Practices, Talking Points, Programs-in-a-Box, workbooks, guides, outreach ideas, reports, papers, and statistics, all designed to help recruit and retain CS students. The session contents were made publicly accessible via the website http://www.csc.tntech.edu/tapestry/agenda.html for any interested HS CS teachers, not just the attendees. Another initiative was to create a social networking (Facebook) group called CS@HS Tapestry for communication and sharing of experiences among all participants at all locations. This group was created because we wanted this community of teachers to remain connected even after the workshops were over. And they are. Periodically, members share news, resources, and experiences. The link to this open Facebook community is http://www.facebook.com/groups/107753865985279/.

9. LESSONS LEARNED AND FUTURE WORK

This was the first project where we:

- Collaborated with experts in this area, primarily UVA faculty and PIs for the TAG projects,
- Learned about organizing such professional development workshops and resources for initiating HS CS programs, recruiting, and retaining more and diverse groups of CS students,
- Provided teaching resources to CS HS teachers to attract and engage CS students.

From an organizational perspective, we underestimated the amount of time necessary to prepare for the workshop. Two faculty (Siraj and Kosa) organized it, with help from our departmental administrative assistant and three volunteer students (including coauthor Olmstead).

Early establishment of a Web presence and targeted advertising in multiple locations were effective in publicizing the workshop. The ACM Distinguished Speakers Program and early identification of participant expectations and needs, leading to customization of the workshop content, were instrumental in the success of the workshop. We plan to offer similar workshops biannually. In future workshops, we plan to include more interactive and discussion-oriented sessions and more time for networking. Possible avenues to seek funding for future workshops would be Google's CS4HS program, NSF, and NCWIT. At the least, we will have the support of the TTU STEM Center to conduct single-day workshops for regional CS teachers.

10. CONCLUSION

The Tapestry workshop turned out to be a great experience for us, motivating work towards improving K-12 CS education. Since the Tapestry workshop, TTU has become a member of the NCWIT Academic Alliance [27] and an Affiliate of the NCWIT Award for Aspirations in Computing [28]. We will be hosting the NCWIT Award for Aspirations in Computing for Tennessee sometime in Spring 2012. Additionally, we are working with the TTU administration to offer scholarships to winners of the NCWIT-Tennessee Award for Aspirations in Computing.

The TTU Tapestry workshop inspired county school board administrators to offer CS courses at our local high school for the first time, in the fall of 2011. The school hired a new CS instructor (a workshop participant). It is also providing professional development opportunities to a mathematics teacher to acquire skills in teaching CS.

CS is rarely taught in Tennessee high schools. Tennessee, like the rest of the US, must go much further to improve CS education. It is not going to happen overnight, but everything has to start somewhere. Global changes start locally.

ACKNOWLEDGMENTS

Our sincere gratitude goes to Drs. Joanne and James Cohoon. We are thankful for their mentorship, guidance and financial support. We also thank Dr. Catherine Brawner (Research Triangle Educational Consultants), who evaluated the workshop. We are grateful to the TTU Millard Oakley STEM Center for the wonderful workshop location. Special thanks go to Cody Easley for development of the website, Valerie Nash for ensuring compliance with TTU policies and procedures, and Layton McDaniel for help during the workshop. Last but not least, we acknowledge and appreciate all the workshop attendees, whose interest, time, and effort made this workshop a success. After all, they are the real weavers of this Tapestry!

11. REFERENCES

[1] S.I. Ahamed, Brylow, D., Ge, R., Madiraju, P., Merrill, S. J., Struble, C.A., and Early, J.P. 2010. Computational Thinking for the Sciences: A Three Day Workshop for High School Teachers. In Proceedings of the 41st ACM Technical Symposium on Computer Science Education (Milwaukee, Wisconsin, USA, March 10-13, 2010). SIGCSE'10. ACM, New York, NY, 42-46. DOI=http://doi.acm.org/10.1145/1734263.1734277.

[2] America's Got Talent: But Not Enough is Going Into Computer Science. http://www.ncwit.org/resources.csprinciples.html.

[3] App Inventor. http://appinventor.googlelabs.com.

[4] Armor Games, Light-Bot. http://armorgames.com/play/6061/light-bot-20.

[5] T. Bell, I. Witten, and M. Fellows. Computer Science Unplugged. http://csunplugged.org.

[6] Blum, L. and Cortina, T.J. 2007. CS4HS: An Outreach Program for High School CS Teachers. In Proceedings of the 38th SIGCSE Technical Symposium on Computer Science Education (Covington, Kentucky, USA, March 07-11, 2007). SIGSE '07. ACM, New York, NY, 9-23.

[7] Bruckman, A., Biggers, M., Ericson, B., McKlin, T., Dimond, J., DiSalvo, B., Hewner, M., Ni, L., and Yardi, S. 2009. "Georgia computes!": Improving the Computing Education Pipeline. In Proceedings of the 40th ACM Technical Symposium on Computer Science Education (Chattanooga, TN, USA, March 04-07, 2009). SIGCSE'09. ACM, New York, NY, 86-90. DOI=http://doi.acm.org/10.1145/1508865.1508899.

[8] Bureau of Labor Statistics. U.S. Department of Labor. 2010. Occupational Outlook Handbook, 2010-11 Edition, Computer Software Engineers and Computer Programmers. DOI=http://www.bls.gov/oco/ocos303.htm.

[9] Carnegie Mellon University, Alice. http://www.alice.org.

[10] The College Board. "Computer Science: Principles. Computational Thinking Practices. Big Ideas, Key Concepts, and Supporting Concepts." http://csprinciples.org/docs/Practices+BigIdeas-08-05-11.pdf.

[11] The College Board, Association of Computing Machinery.

[12] The College Board of AP Computer Science A Course Description. http://apcentral.collegeboard.com/apc/public/repository/ap-computer-science-course-description.pdf.

[13] CS 10K Initiative. http://www.csprinciples.org.docs/Practices+BigIdea-08-05-11.pdf.

[14] Department of Computer and Information Sciences, University of Delaware. UDo.CS2011: A Workshop for High School Computer Science Teachers. http://www.eecis.udel.edu/~pollock/UDoCS.

[15] Exploring Computer Science. http://www.exploringcs.org.

[16] J. Goode. 2010. Connecting K-16 Curriculum & Policy: Making Computer Science Engaging, Accessible, and Hospitable for Underrepresented Students. In Proceedings of the 41st ACM Technical Symposium on Computer Science Education (Milwaukee, Wisconsin, USA, March 10-13, 2010). SIGCSE'10. ACM, New York, NY, 22-26. DOI=http://doi.acm.org/10.1145/1734272.

[17] Greenfoot. http://www.greenfoot.org.

[18] GridWorld. http://www.horstmann.com/gridworld/.

[19] Jonathan Harris and Sep Kamvar. We Feel Fine. http://wefeelfine.org.ICE Distance Education Portal. http://ice-web.cc.gatech.edu/dl/.

[20] ICE Distance Learning Portal. http://ice.cc.gatech.edu/dl/.

[21] Kinesthetic Learning Activities. http://people.cs.ubc.ca/~kla/.

[22] Jiangjiang Liu, Cheng-Hsien Lin, Ethan Philip Hasson, and Zebulun David Barnett. 2011. Introducing computer science to K-12 through a summer computing workshop for teachers. In Proceedings of the 42nd ACM technical symposium on Computer science education (SIGCSE '11). ACM, New York, NY, USA, 389-394. DOI=10.1145/1953163.1953277 http://doi.acm.org/10.1145/1953163.1953277.

[23] Media Computation Teachers Website. http://mediacomputation.org.

[24] Middle Tennessee State University Partners for Innovation in Information Technology (PIIT). http://frank.mtsu.edu/~piit.

[25] MIT Media Lab, Scratch. http://scratch.mit.edu.

[26] National Science Foundation. DOI=http://nsf.gov/awardsearch/showAward.do?AwardNumber=1042452.

[27] NCWIT. http://www.ncwit.org/alliance.academic.php.

[28] NCWIT Aspirations in Computing. https://awardportal.ncwit.org/comps.state.php?competitionId=68&action=details.

[29] Passion, Beauty, Joy, and Awe. http://www.computingportal.org/node/3954.

[30] Practice-It. http://webster.cs.washington.edu:8080/practiceit/.

[31] Susan Rodger's Home Page. http://cs.duke.edu/~rodger/.

[32] TAG Workshops: Teachers Attracting Girls to Computing. http://www.cs.virginia.edu/~cohoon/tagworkshops.

[33] Tennessee Technological University. Millard Oakley STEM Center. http://www.tntech.edu/stem/about/.

Who AM I? Understanding High School Computer Science Teachers' Professional Identity

Lijun Ni & Mark Guzdial
School of Interactive Computing
Georgia Institute of Technology
85 5th Street NW
Atlanta, GA, 30332-0760
{lijun, guzdial} @cc.gatech.edu

ABSTRACT

Quality computer science (CS) teachers are critical for secondary computing education. In addition to increasing the number of high school (HS) CS teachers, there is a great need for supporting those teachers to grow and stay as committed, effective teachers. Recent literature on teacher education suggests that teachers' sense of commitment and (other aspects of) teaching profession is tightly linked with their teacher identity. However, the current educational system in the U.S. does not provide typical contexts for teachers to build a sense of identity as CS teachers. This study is intended to gain an initial understanding of CS teachers' perceptions about their own professional identity and potential factors that might contribute to these perceptions. Our findings indicate that current HS teachers teaching CS courses do not necessarily identify themselves as CS teachers. They have different perceptions related to CS teaching. Four kinds of factors can contribute to these perceptions: teachers' educational background and certification, CS curriculum and department hierarchy, availability of CS teacher community, and teachers' perceptions about the field of CS.

Categories and Subject Descriptors

K.3.2 [**Computers and Education**]: Computer and Information Science Education–*computer science education.*

General Terms

Design, Experimentation, Theory.

Keywords

HS CS Teacher, CS Teacher Identity, Professional Development, Community

1. INTRODUCTION

To achieve quality CS education, we need quality CS teachers. The reality is: Too few high schools in the U.S. have computing/CS teachers with formal CS training and many schools do not have CS teacher at all [19]. In addition to the need for increasing the number of CS teachers, there is also the need for supporting those teachers we have recruited and trained to become better teachers and continue teaching CS.

Permission to make digital or hard copies of all or part of this work for personal or classroom use is granted without fee provided that copies are not made or distributed for profit or commercial advantage and that copies bear this notice and the full citation on the first page. To copy otherwise, or republish, to post on servers or to redistribute to lists, requires prior specific permission and/or a fee.
SIGCSE'12, February 29-March 3, 2012, Raleigh, NC, USA.
Copyright 2012 ACM 978-1-4503-1098-7/12/02…$10.00.

In secondary education, we are facing a big challenge of sustaining teachers overall [16]. Teacher turnover is significantly high and especially beginning teacher attrition is a serious problem [11]. Based on an analysis from the National Center for Education Statistics, it is estimated that almost a third of America's teachers leave the teaching profession sometime during the first three years of teaching, and almost half leave within five years [12]. In CS education, we are working on preparing more CS teachers. The NSF CS/10K project is aimed at preparing 10,000 CS teachers by 2015 [6]. Looking forward to 2015, we have 10,000 well prepared teachers including many beginning teachers. If similar teacher turnover rate happens to these CS teachers, we are going to lose around half of them by 2020. Therefore, a key question for us is: how can we sustain those good CS teachers we have recruited, trained and hired?

Much recent literature on teacher education highlights the importance of teachers developing a professional identity as teachers of a specific subject [2, 3]. This literature suggests that a strong sense of teacher identity is a major indicator or feature of committed, quality teachers [4, 5, 7]. Researchers have also identified contextual factors that significantly influence teachers' identity such as educational background, pre-service training and school culture [2,]. For HS CS teachers, it could be a big issue to establish professional identity under the current educational system, without consistent certificate standards and with computing usually excluded from the core curriculum [8, 19]. In the U.S., there is no CS background requirement or consistent certificate process specifically for CS teaching as teachers in some other counties do [17]. HS CS teachers usually do not have a computing department they can belong to, in contrast to most post-secondary computing faculty or secondary teachers teaching subjects under the core curriculum. We will offer more discussion about these challenges in the next section. In brief, the current secondary education system in the U.S. does not provide *typical* contexts for teachers to build a sense of identity as CS teachers. Then, what kind of identity do our current HS CS teachers hold?

This study is intended to gain an initial understanding of CS teachers' perceptions about their own professional identity and potential factors that might contribute to these perceptions. The two research questions explored in this study are: 1. What kind of professional identities do current HS CS teachers hold? 2. What influences teachers' sense of identity as a CS teacher?

2. THEORTETICAL FRAMEWORK

2.1 Teacher Identity Matters

Teacher identity theory offers a particular conceptual lens for us to understand the issue of teacher commitment and retention. Teacher (professional) identity is broadly defined as being recognized as a certain kind of teacher by self or others [2, 3, 9]. It reflects a subtle dimension of the complex and ongoing process through which teachers get to know themselves, their students, and the subject matter they teach [4]. The emerging literature on teacher identity suggests that identity reveals a set of values, beliefs and goals that shape how teachers makes sense of their own teaching experiences and thereby influences the way teachers teach, the way they develop as teachers, and their attitudes toward educational changes [3]. For example, Margolis et al [14] found that teachers who did not value CS as a priority for students to learn would not be willing to invest energy to recruit students into CS courses. Especially, teacher identity is central to sustaining motivation, efficacy, job satisfaction and commitment, and these attributes are crucial in determining whether teachers leave or stay in the profession [5, 7]. For example, Hong [10] found that dropout teachers indicated more negative aspects of their teacher identity. The essential roles of teacher identity inspire us to look at the professional identity that HS CS teachers bring into their teaching, which has the potential to offer insights for supporting and sustaining CS teachers.

2.2 Challenges of Building Professional Identity for HS CS Teachers

For HS CS teachers, the evolving, young nature of the computing field and its educational practice adds a few challenges of its own to the general list of challenges for HS teachers to building their sense of professional identity as CS teachers.

First, the relative newness and evolving nature of the computing field itself brings big challenges for teachers to identify the subject matter they are teaching. The study of CS as a scientific discipline is often confused with other uses of computing technology within education, such as computer applications and educational technology [8]. Second, the current certification situation makes it more difficult for teachers to identify themselves as CS teachers. In many states, a CS teaching certificate is not required in order to teach CS. Teachers with little or no CS training are frequently assigned to teach CS courses. Where certification requirements do exist, they often have no connection to CS content [19]. Moreover, CS courses are often offered in different programs (mainly Business or Math), which do not treat CS as an individual academic discipline. Such a confusing situation makes it difficult for teachers to identify what they are teaching and what kind of teachers they are. Third, since there are still very few CS teachers, these teachers are especially isolated. This kind of isolation might prevent them from building a sense of belonging and affiliation with other CS teachers.

Considering the above challenges, it can be a big issue for teachers to build a sense of identity as CS teachers. In this paper, we would like to understand what kind of professional identities current CS teachers bring into their teaching. In addition to teachers' self-identification (e.g., as a CS teacher or not), we examine specific features of their identity to further understand what they mean by saying "I'm (not) a CS teacher". Informed by the theoretical framework of social identity [18], mathematics identities [15] and science teacher identity [13], we specifically look at the following three aspects of their teacher identity:

- Attitudes and values

This element involves teachers' attitudes and values related to teaching CS, e.g., their sense of values of learning and teaching CS, and confidence in their own abilities to teach CS.

- Motivation and commitment

This element examines teachers' motivational dimension related to their CS teaching, especially their motivation to strive to teach well, to continue teaching CS, and to grow the CS program.

- Sense of belonging/affiliation

This element examines teachers' sense of awareness and ownership of being a member of a certain social group related to their teaching in CS (e.g., a member of a CS teacher community).

3. STUDY METHOD

3.1 Data Collection

One major method in teacher identity research is called narrative inquiry [1]. This method suggests that researchers examine teacher identity through interviewing teachers and then analyzing teachers' narrations on their teaching experiences. In this study, we conducted semi-structured interviews with nine HS CS teachers in Atlanta, who taught at least one of the introductory CS courses listed in the computing pathway (the Georgia computing curriculum.) All these teachers were teaching at least some form of CS involving introductory programming. Before the interview, they completed a demographic questionnaire.

The interview lasted around 60-90 minutes. Interview questions were framed by the three aspects of teacher identity features introduced above. We asked participants to introduce themselves and what they were teach, to tell the stories of how they started teaching CS, how they felt about their teaching, and challenges they faced in teaching CS. Interview transcripts were analyzed in terms of the sense of identity teachers perceived and what contributed to those perceptions. The process of analysis is a conceptual qualitative discourse analysis focusing on the experiences, feelings, and beliefs described by the participants [1].

3.2 Participant Background

Eight of the nine participants came from public schools and one teacher taught at a private school. Their CS teaching experience varied from 2 years to over 10 years, and their school accommodated from less than 500 students to over 2000 students. In the public schools, CS courses were offered in the Business program under the Career, Technical and Agricultural Education (CTAE) department. In the private school, CS courses were offered in the Business and Computer Technology department, which served students similarly to the Business program in public schools. Therefore, there was no big difference in terms of where CS courses were offered among these schools.

Table 1 Participant Professional Backgrounds

Teacher	Educational Background	Certificate
Alex	Electrical Engineering; Management	Technology Education; Business Education
Becky	CIS	Business Education
Bob	CIS; Math Education	Technology Education; Business Education
Ryan	Political Science; Leadership	N/A
Cindy	Math Education	Math Education
John	CS and Math; Math Education	Math Education
Pat	Business	Business Education
May	Management; Elementary Education	Business Education
Rose	Business Education	Business Education

Table 1 lists these teachers' professional background information. All the teacher names mentioned in this paper are pseudonyms. Only three teachers held a computing related degree: one in CS and two in CIS (Computer Information Systems). As to certification status, Ryan did not pursue a teacher certificate since that was not required in a private school. Six of the remaining eight teachers got a Business Education certificate, which allowed them to teach CS courses. Both of the two teachers holding a Math degree got a Math Education certificate and belonged to the Math department. The six teachers holding a Business Education certificate belonged to the Business department in their schools.

4. FINDINGS

This section first presents how the participants self-identified themselves as teachers in different subjects with different identity features. The second part of this section reports how the participants explained their perceptions as teachers in different subjects: what different background aspects and other factors contributed to their self-perceptions as a CS teacher (or not).

4.1 Perceived (CS) Teacher Identity: Self-Identification and Identity Features

The participants were explicitly asked to introduce themselves and clarify their own teacher identity. Overall, these nine teachers self-identified themselves either as a CS teacher, as a Business teacher, or as both a CS teacher and teacher in another subject (Math or Business). Section 4.1.1 - 4.1.3 present information about these three kinds of teacher identities with (varied) identity features indicated by these teachers, such as their confidence in teaching CS, their beliefs in the values of learning CS, their motivation to seek professional development and commitment in teaching CS.

4.1.1 I'm a CS Teacher

Four teachers saw themselves as CS teachers: Alex, Becky, Bob and Ryan. They used words like "computer science teacher", "computer teacher", and "programming teacher" to introduce themselves. In particular, Ryan called himself a programming teacher and explained that he didn't label himself as a CS teacher to avoid confusion about the meaning of CS teacher.

> [Ryan]: "I would lump myself more as a Programming teacher, because that is most of my courses... I think people don't understand what it means to be a [CS] teacher. It means different things to different people. In the past when I've said that, people want to talk about typing... That's a skill, but it's not what I'm teaching actually."

These teachers understood the broad scope of the field of CS and believed the values for students to learn CS. However, not all of them were committed to CS teaching since it was not in the core curriculum. One teacher (Alex), who was teaching mainly CS, explicitly expressed a sense of crisis as a CS teacher, which drove him to preparing a Math Education certificate for job security.

> [Alex]: "High schools are much more interested in the core subjects: Math, English, Science, and Social Studies, which have the graduation test... They're much more interested in those than the Career Technology classes [including CS]. So, I just took the Math test because I wanted to make sure that I could find a job in a school that I might want to go to."

Three of them felt they were confident in teaching CS courses with a few years of teaching experience. Meanwhile, another teacher, Becky, was still struggling with how to teach CS well. Even if she held a background in CIS and had been teaching CS for several years, she did not feel confident. She perceived CS as hard to teach for a couple of reasons.

> [Becky]: "I struggle with giving everyone the material and being able to explain it... I struggle with how to be creative. I have a problem with trying to make the programs have meaning to them... It is hard to teach. It's hard knowing how to teach it... It's hard to explain... I would have to definitely update my skills... When I look at kids' codes, they think I should know it as soon as I look at it... I have to study it just like they do."

We also saw another common feature among these four teachers, who self-identified as a CS teacher: they all saw the evolving nature of CS and would like to learn more to keep updated and teach these courses better. In addition, since they were isolated, they all wanted to keep connected and collaborate with other teachers to address challenges in teaching CS.

> [Ryan]: "The most difficult thing has been when machines don't quite handle the software interface and it changes. Also, I had some issues with language and paradigm shifts from procedural to object-oriented. It was an interesting journey of trying to navigate that. That would have been probably better done if I had initiated more contact with other teachers and had a group to work wit. It's so important to have a group of peers you have collaboration with."

4.1.2 Mixed: I'm a CS and X Teacher

Three teachers identified themselves as teachers in both CS and another subject: Cindy, John and Pat. Cindy was a Math and CS teacher, seeing CS as part of Math. John saw himself as both a CS and Math teacher, but more passionate in CS. Pat claimed she was a Business teacher as well as a CS teacher.

• Cindy: "I'm a Math teacher" & "CS is Applied Math."

Cindy reported herself teaching both (one) Math and (three) CS courses, but she was really a Math teacher since she believed that CS was part of Math. Also, she would like to stay teaching Math instead of moving to teaching all CS.

> [Cindy]: "I am a Math certified teacher, so I am a Math teacher who teaches [CS]. I really think that [CS] is a Math course. It's like Applied Math. You're applying what you know in Math to that... I want to stay in the Math area as well. I don't want to go all the way over to that other side, because I was trained to be a Math teacher."

Considering CS as part of Math, she used lots of Math problems as examples to be solved by programming in her CS courses. For example, she asked the students to turn the quadratic formula or the distance formula into a Java statement, or asking them to take a 2D matrix and figure out a magic square by writing a code.

• John: "I'm a Math and CS teacher, but I'm a better Math teacher."

John identified himself as a Math and CS teacher, but emphasized that he was more passionate about teaching CS. He studied Math as well to help himself to better understand CS topics.

> [John]: "I would introduce myself as a Math and CS teacher... I'm definitely more passionate about teaching CS. I enjoy teaching CS... The main reason I'm not teaching it

full-time is, there isn't really a place where I could make that a full-time job... CS was my first choice as a major. I ended up adding a Math degree so I would be a little bit more likely to understand some complex topics in CS."

However, he believed he was a better Math teacher due to the isolation of CS teachers, while the Math teacher community was available to him.

[John]: "Even though I feel like I know CS better than Math and I'm more passionate about it, I still think I'm a better Math teacher, just because I've had so much support. Whenever I have problems, I can talk with the people that I work with, who have taught for many years in Math. Every day, I'm eating lunch with Math teachers. So, we can talk about our problems. With CS, I've got nobody to talk to."

- **Pat: "I'm the only Marketing teacher and I'm also the only CS teacher."**

This teacher saw herself as both a Marketing (part of Business) and CS teacher. She was striving to teach an individual CS course instead of sessions with CS and Business combined.

[Pat]: "This semester, I teach one section of Beginning Programming in a class combined with a section of Intermediate Programming, and one section of Marketing Principles. Next semester, I look to include a class where I might see Beginning Programming, Intermediate Programming, and AP CS in one class, Marketing Principles and Sales and Promotion in one class at one time."

- **Teacher isolation and sense of affiliation/community**

All these three teachers reported the issue of (CS) teacher isolation and perceived the lack of a sense of affiliation. They expressed the desire to connect with other CS teachers. However, they did not see some Business teachers as their peers who they could collaborate with.

[Cindy]: "I don't have many colleagues in the county that I can turn to… I've sat and talked to people… They all have their own way of wanting to do things [in CS]... We have a lot of people who are Business teachers with no idea what they're doing with this class. I'm hoping to meet more people that I can collaborate with and that are more like-minded to my style of teaching so that I can get more ideas."

Another teacher, Pat, further pointed out that putting some Business teachers who did not want to teach CS into the CS education community hurt the program.

[Pat]: "One of the biggest problems is that [CS] has been lumped in with Business and many of these teachers want nothing to do with CS. [They] consider it too hard to learn, don't have the background to be effective in it, and want to go back to keyboarding and computer applications. They hurt the program because they 'have' to teach… If a teacher wants to learn it and teach it they can-- but so many don't."

4.1.3 I'm a Business Teacher

The remaining two teachers (May and Rose) saw themselves as Business teachers. With a Business Education certificate, they saw their main responsibility in teaching Business, no matter if they were teaching mainly CS (May) or only one CS course (Rose).

Both of them saw learning computing or CS as important to every student. However, May was struggling with differentiating computer applications from computing or CS. Overall, she saw computing as being able to operate the computer (e.g., creating a Word document), while CS was advanced programming and was only for those smart students.

[May]: "I think, [CS] is more for really, really smart people... If I have to go take this CS degree, it's going to be really hard… I think CS is a much higher level… When I say computing, I think of computing as being able to operate the computer, being able to type a Word document, being able to use the Internet… I believe most students can successfully take and complete Computing in the Modern World, but it takes a little higher level of intelligence to complete the Programming and AP CS."

May reported that although she was isolated as the only one who taught CS courses, she felt confident in teaching those courses. First, she gained confidence in the process of teaching every year. Second, she felt the general resources she could access from the CTAE department in her local county and the state was sufficient for her. She was not looking for further learning and collaboration opportunities from other teachers.

Another Business teacher, Rose, was also confident about teaching Computing in the Modern World, the only CS course she was teaching. In particular, Rose was comfortable with her school not offering more programming courses for students interested in CS. She believed that other Business courses can meet students' need instead.

[Rose]: "I think that most of our students, who have been interested in [CS] and have asked about it, truly do have a desire to learn [CS]. They were really disappointed that we're not offering it… They truly want it, and I think they've settled for Business classes... I think as an overall department, they flow well together, because there is some interrelated stuff... Some students who want to go into programming might want to own their own business. So, Business Essentials would be great for them, because it teaches them entrepreneurship and the skills behind the scenes that they may need to start their own business."

4.1.4 Summary of Self-Identity by Teachers

The above sections presented how the participants self-identified themselves as teachers in different subjects. Overall, these teachers all taught more or less some form of CS, but they were different in terms of their confidence and commitment, and their sense of the need for learning and CS teacher community.

4.2 Influencing Factors

This section presents how teachers explained their own perceptions as a CS teacher or teacher in another subject. Overall, four kinds of factors contributed to these teachers' self-identity related to their teaching in CS (with at least two teachers reported similarly): their educational background and certification, CS curriculum and department hierarchy, availability of CS teacher community, and teachers' perceptions about the field of CS.

4.2.1 Educational Background and Certification

First of all, these teachers relied on their own educational background to identify themselves as teachers in a specific subject. For example, Bob identified himself as a CS teacher with his computing background. In contrast, Rose saw herself as a Business teacher since her major was Business Education.

[Rose]: "Well, I identify myself more as Business Education [teacher]. I teach Accounting, also. I've taught

> Computer Applications and Programming. So, really my degree is not in [CS]. It's in Business Education. So, that's just my identity."

Beyond self-identification, teachers' personal educational background could also influence specific aspects of their identity and likely their teaching practices as well. As presented in Section 4.1.2, Cindy felt more comfortable with teaching Math. She felt she could "get a good handle on Math" since she was more familiar with Math. She also saw CS as part of Math and used Math problems in her programming courses. Moreover, she would like to continue teaching Math even if she enjoyed teaching CS.

Similarly to educational background, teachers used the certificate(s) they held as one kind of criteria for self-identification. For example, both May and Rose believed that they were Business teacher since that was what they were certified for.

Certificates also determine the path teachers came into CS teaching, which also influenced how other entities (e.g., the local county and local school) identified the teacher in related subjects. For example, Bob was seen as an Engineering teacher due to his first certificate in Technology Education, which determined the courses assigned to him and his professional development requirements. In fact, Bob was always interested in teaching CS. He was confused with which certificate would allow him to teach CS courses and thus experienced a devious path to CS teaching.

> [Bob]: "I had my Technology Education certification first... I originally thought Technology Education would encompass the Computer classes. It wasn't until I got into the school system that I found out that [CS] was under Business... [I then did the Business Education certificate] because I wanted to teach the [CS] classes."

Similar to Bob, since there was no specific certificate for CS teachers, John got a Math Education certificate as the route to teaching CS. He had started teaching Math before he was able to teach CS. He was still seen as a Math teacher by his students since he worked in the Math department and his classroom was also physically located on the Math hall.

4.2.2 CS Curriculum and Department Hierarchy

Participants also reported that CS curriculum and department hierarchy influenced their identity related to CS teaching. Here, CS curriculum and department hierarchy refer to what courses are offered under which part of the secondary curriculum and thereby under which department/academic unit. In Georgia, CS courses were offered under the same unit (Business and CS program under the CTAE department). These courses were electives. Such situation could prevent students, administrators as well as teachers seeing the values of these courses. Meanwhile, by putting CS under Business, some Business teachers who were not interested in teaching these technical courses had to teach these courses. These teachers likely did not value what they were teaching and were not motivated to teach these courses. As we will discuss in the next section, this situation can also hurt the sense of community of those isolated but more motivated CS teachers.

4.2.3 Availability of CS Teacher Community

As we can see from section 4.1, most of these teachers expressed a sense of need to learn to teach CS better, including all the four CS teachers and the three mixed subject teachers listed above. As usually there were no other CS teachers in their local schools, these teachers were isolated. The lack of peers and community did not only prevent learning opportunities among CS teachers, but also hurt these teachers' feelings about themselves. They felt that they did not have peers or colleagues like themselves at their schools. As presented above, Pat was complaining that teachers who did not care about CS hurt the whole community of CS teachers. Cindy was looking for teachers with similar mindsets for collaboration, who did not see CS as computer applications and did not teach programming like teaching applications.

In addition to the sense of belonging/affiliation, the lack of community/peers also influenced other aspects of teacher identity. As presented above, John felt he was a better Math teacher than a CS teacher due to the lack of support from peer CS teachers.

4.2.4 Teachers' Perceptions of the Subject (CS)

The participants also held different perceptions about the field of CS and CS education. These perceptions influenced specific aspects of their teacher identity in CS teaching, such as their beliefs in the values of CS, their confidence in teaching CS, the need for learning and CS teacher communities.

First, they had different definitions about computing and CS. Most teachers saw the values of CS for students and broadly defined CS or computing as problem-solving using computers. However, the two Business teachers saw learning computing as learning about operating computers. So, they recognized the values of learning 'computing' for every student. Meanwhile, they narrowly defined CS as being only about programming and was only for smart students.

Secondly, some teachers were concerned about the rapidly changing nature of the CS field. That influenced how they felt about teaching CS and the need for continual learning. As presented above, Becky perceived that CS was hard to teach. She clearly saw the need for updating her own knowledge and skills. Similarly, Ryan and Cindy also understood that CS was an evolving and broad field, and felt they needed to learn with peer CS teachers. In contrast, the two Business teachers (May and Rose) were confident in their current teaching and did not indicate a strong sense of need for continual learning.

5. SUMMARY AND DISCUSSION

5.1 Summary of Findings

This study is a first step to look at how current HS CS teachers identified themselves and felt about their teaching in CS. From this study, we have found that these CS teachers held different teacher identities with varied features related to their motivation and commitment in teaching CS. Some of these teachers were not committed to teaching CS, or not confident. Some held narrow views about CS and therefore its values. They were all isolated and most of them were looking for learning opportunities and communities specifically for CS teachers.

Results from this study indicate four factors influencing these teachers' perceptions about their identity related to CS teaching: teachers' educational background and certification, CS curriculum and department hierarchy, availability of CS teacher community, and teachers' perceptions about the field of CS. These four aspects are not individual factors and can interact with each other.

First, it is natural for a teacher to pursue a certificate in his/her own major. We can see an overall match between teachers' educational background and the certificate (s) they hold. Second, the structural aspect of secondary CS education determines the academic nature of CS (curriculum). In Georgia, CS is under Business. Teachers usually need a Business Education certificate to teach CS. Such an administrative context can cause other issues for CS education. For example, CS courses as electives can hurt the value of CS and lose student interest. This can then lead to fewer students, fewer CS courses offered, and fewer CS teachers needed. Such ripple effect can cause the isolation of CS teachers. Third, teachers' perceptions about CS influence their sense of the need for learning and what kind of community they want to join. With different understandings about things like what is CS, who should learn CS, what are the goals of CS courses, they can form different opinions about themselves and who count as their peers.

5.2 Implications for CS Teacher Professional Development

The findings from this study suggest a need for helping current HS teachers build a sense of professional identity as a CS teacher, in order to sustain and foster these teachers as committed, quality CS teachers. This is not a unique need for preparing CS teachers. As Alsup [1] concluded in her book, *Teacher Identity Discourses*, "Beginning teachers need a teacher education that provides them with opportunities to develop satisfying professional identities, so that they can live and work in challenging institutional environments." As we discussed earlier, the unique challenges for CS teacher professional development are tightly linked with the evolving, young nature of the computing field and the structural context for computing education. As computing educators, we need to recognize and work on how to address these challenges.

It is obvious that the structural aspects of CS education under the current educational system, such as curriculum standards and certificate requirements, are critical in determining other aspects of CS education including our CS teachers' knowledge, motivation, commitment as well as their teaching practices. However, it is hard to change those aspects. Meanwhile, our findings also indicate that many CS teachers are isolated and lack of support and learning opportunities while they feel the need for learning. Therefore, it can be one way to offer support for those existing CS teachers and influence their own sense of identity by creating a community of local CS teachers where they can learn and support each other and change their perceptions of CS, CS teaching and themselves as a (CS) teacher.

5.3 Future Work

After gaining an initial understanding of HS CS teachers' identity and potential influencing factors, we are currently conducting a study exploring how to support CS teachers' identity development, through a professional development program with a focus on promoting teacher learning and community building. We are expecting to further our understanding of ways to change teachers' identity into more committed CS teachers.

6. ACKNOWLEDGMENTS

We would like to thank all the teacher participants. This work is supported by NSF Grant No. 0829601. Any opinions, findings, and conclusions or recommendations expressed in this material are those of the author(s) and do not necessarily reflect the views of the National Science Foundation.

7. REFERENCE

[1] Alsup, J. *Teacher Identity Discourses: Negotiating Personal and Professional Spaces*. Routledge, USA, 2006.

[2] Beauchamp, C. and Thomas, L.2009. Understanding teacher identity: An overview of issues in the literature and implications for teacher education. *Cambridge Journal of Education*, 39, (2), 175-189.

[3] Beijaard, D., Meijer, P. C. and Verloop, N. 2004. Reconsidering research on teachers' professional identity. *Teaching and Teacher Education*, 20(2), 107-128.

[4] Cardelle-Elawar, M., Irwin, L., Lizarraga, S. d. A. and Lusia, M. 2007. A cross cultural analysis of motivational factors that influence teacher identity. *Electronic Journal of Research in Educational Psychology.* 5 (3), 565-592.

[5] Chan, W. Y., Lau, S., Nie, Y., Lim, S., and Hogan, D. 2008. Organizational and personal predictors of teacher commitment: The mediating role of teacher efficacy and identification with school. *American Educational Research Journal*, 45 (3), 597-630.

[6] Cuny, J. 2010. Finding 10,000 teachers: Transforming high school computer science. *The CSTA Voice*, 5 (6), 1-2.

[7] Day, K., Stobart, A., Sammons, G., and Stobart, P. 2006. The Personal and Professional Selves of Teachers: Stable and Unstable Identities. *British Educational Research Journal*, 32 (4), 601-616.

[8] Ericson, B., Armoni, M., Gal-Ezer, J., Seehorn, D., Stephenson, C. and Trees, F. 2008. *Ensuring exemplary teaching in an essential discipline: Addressing the crisis in computer science teacher certification*. Final Report of the CSTA Teacher Certification Task Force. ACM.

[9] Gee, J. P. 2001. Identity as an analytic lens for research in education. *Review of Research in Education*, 25, 99-125.

[10] Hong, J. Y. 2010. Pre-service and beginning teachers' professional identity and its relation to dropping out of the profession. *Teaching and Teacher Education*, 26 (8), 1530-1543.

[11] Ingersoll, R. M. 2001. Teacher Turnover and Teacher Shortages: An Organizational Analysis. *American Educational Research Journal*, 38 (3), 499-534.

[12] Ingersoll, R. M. 2002. The Teacher Shortage: A Case of Wrong Diagnosis and Wrong Prescription. *NASSP Bulletin*, 86 (631), 16-31.

[13] Luehmann, A. L. 2007. Identity development as a lens to science teacher preparation. *Science Education*, 91 (5), 822-839.

[14] Margolis, J., Estrella, R., Goode, J., Holme, J. J. and Nao, K. 2008. *Stuck in the Shallow End: Education, Race, and Computing*. MIT Press.

[15] Martin, D. B.2000. *Mathematics Success and Failure Among African-American Youth: The Roles of Sociohistorical Context, Community Forces, School Influence, and Individual Agency.* Routledge.

[16] NCTAF. 2002. *Unraveling the "teacher shortage" problem: Teacher retention is the key.* National Commission on Teaching and America's Future (NCTAF).

[17] Orit, H., Judith, G.-E. and Lenore, B. 2008. A model for high school computer science education: the four key elements that make it! In *Proceedings of the 39th SIGCSE Technical Symposium on Computer Science Education*. ACM.

[18] Pennington, M. C. 2002. Teacher identity in TESOL. In *Proceedings of the Quality in Teacher Education Seminar.* London, UK.

[19] Wilson, C., Sudol, L. A., Stehlik, M. and Stephenson, C. 2010. *Running On Empty: The Failure to Teach K-12 Computer Science in the Digital Age.* ACM.

Introducing Parallelism and Concurrency in the Data Structures Course

Dan Grossman Ruth E. Anderson
Dept. of Computer Science & Engineering
University of Washington
Seattle, WA, USA
djg@cs.washington.edu rea@cs.washington.edu

ABSTRACT

We report on our experience integrating a three-week introduction to multithreading in a required data structures course for second-year computer science majors. We emphasize a distinction between parallelism and concurrency that teaches students to use extra processors effectively and enforce mutual exclusion correctly. The material fits naturally in the data structures course by having the same mix of algorithms, programming, and asymptotic analysis as the conventional, single-threaded part of the course.

Our department has used this unit for 1.5 years and will do so indefinitely. We report feedback from students, multiple instructors for the course, and students in a later course that uses threads. We developed a full set of course materials that have been adapted for use by instructors in various courses at five other institutions so far.

Categories and Subject Descriptors

K.3.2 [**Computers and Education**]: Computer and Information Science Education – *computer science education, curriculum*

General Terms

Algorithms, Experimentation

Keywords

Parallelism, Concurrency, Data Structures, Fork-Join, Mutual Exclusion, Undergraduate Curriculum

1. INTRODUCTION

As multiprocessors become increasingly common across the computing landscape, there is widespread interest in expanding coverage of threads, parallelism, concurrency, synchronization, etc. in undergraduate computer science curricula. However, as described in a recent exploration of the subject [3], there is not yet consensus on where in the curriculum to introduce these topics and what fundamental concepts are most important. In the near term, many institutions may find it equally unrealistic to, on the one hand, modify many courses so that multithreading pervades the curriculum or, on the other hand, add an entire required course. Instead, our approach has been to use *part* of a required lower-level course, roughly three weeks, to introduce topics like threads in such a way that various advanced courses, such as computer architecture, operating systems, databases, algorithms, graphics, and many others, can rely on them.

This paper reports on our successful experience introducing parallelism and concurrency into our department's required data structures course. Since Spring 2010, five instructors, ourselves included, have taught the course, with a range of background in parallelism from none to moderate and teaching experience from graduate student to senior faculty. Success requires no more experience than what is already needed to teach data structures – if you can learn topics like B-Trees and Dijkstra's Shortest-Path Algorithm well enough to teach them, then you can learn everything in our unit. All our materials are freely available and have already been adapted by instructors at five other institutions.

The central pedagogic theme is a clear distinction between *parallelism* – using extra computational resources to solve a problem faster – and *concurrency* – correctly and efficiently managing access to shared resources. We start with parallelism and divide-and-conquer fork-join algorithms before introducing the more difficult concurrency topics such as race conditions and deadlock. Just like in the rest of the data structures course, the material covers programming constructs and pragmatics (in Java, though language choice is not crucial), algorithms, asymptotic complexity, and constant-factor overheads. We emphasize fundamental problems like computing a reduction (e.g., a sum) over an array in parallel or ensuring an API enforces mutual exclusion. Given only three weeks, we focus on shared-memory programming, leaving message passing and distributed programming for more advanced elective courses.

Our goals in sharing our experience are to:

- Convince others that a data structures course is a very natural place in a computer science curriculum to make room for a general introduction to parallelism and concurrency. The topics rely on and reinforce core ideas already in the course.
- Elucidate parallelism versus concurrency as a core theme.
- Encourage adoption of our materials, including reading notes, slides, sample homework and exam questions, and a programming project.
- Share mostly-positive feedback from students, instructors, and students in a later course (namely operating systems).

Permission to make digital or hard copies of all or part of this work for personal or classroom use is granted without fee provided that copies are not made or distributed for profit or commercial advantage and that copies bear this notice and the full citation on the first page. To copy otherwise, or republish, to post on servers or to redistribute to lists, requires prior specific permission and/or a fee.
SIGCSE'12, February 29–March 3, 2012, Raleigh, North Carolina, USA.
Copyright 2012 ACM 978-1-4503-1098-7/12/02...$10.00.

With these goals, the rest of the paper largely describes the course-unit content and motivation (Section 3) after a brief primer on our larger curriculum context (Section 2). We then discuss why data structures is a great fit for the material (Section 4). Section 5 shares feedback from various stakeholders: students, instructors, and those who have adapted the materials at other institutions. Section 6 discusses related work. Section 7 describes the freely available materials and concludes.

The materials described in this paper are actively maintained at [10].

2. CURRICULUM CONTEXT

To put our three-week curriculum unit in context, this section briefly describes our other low-level courses in general and the data structures course in particular. However, the unit should fit well somewhere in most computer science curricula.

Our university is on a ten-week quarter system, with most computer science courses (including data structures) having three 50-minute lectures and one 50-minute recitation section per week. The data structures course ranges in size from 30 – 100 students and is a pre-requisite for most advanced courses. It comes after a two-quarter introductory programming sequence and a discrete structures course (boolean and first-order logic, induction, finite-state machines, sets and relations, undecidability, etc.). Other low-level courses, not pre-requisites for data structures, cover lower levels of abstraction (C, assembly, binary); hardware design; probability, statistics and P vs. NP; programming languages; and software design and implementation.

The data structures course is fairly conventional, building on the initial coverage of stacks, queues, and binary search trees in the introductory courses. The course covers asymptotic complexity, priority queues, balanced search trees (AVL trees, B-Trees), hashing, sorting, graphs, and graph algorithms. To make room for multithreading, we reduced coverage of amortization and removed more obscure priority-queue implementations, disjoint-sets (union/find), and network flow, some of which will move to an advanced elective algorithms course. The course has (Java) programming and paper-and-pencil homework exercises. The parallelism and concurrency unit comes late in the course.

3. CONTENT AND MOTIVATION

This section describes the core concepts covered by our materials. The unit includes 8-10 hours of instruction, two homework assignments, and a programming project.

3.1 Introduction to Multithreading

To introduce the unit, we identify the key assumption made in prior courses that is false and that we will remove: one thing happens at a time (sequential execution). Given multiple threads of execution, we can cover three main questions:

- What are some programming techniques for creating and controlling threads and letting them communicate?
- How can parallel algorithms run faster (asymptotically and/or in practice) than sequential algorithms?
- How must software be written differently so that multiple threads can access the same resources without error?

The second question above is about *parallelism*, using multiple computational resources effectively. A canonical example is using P processors to sum n numbers in time $O(n/P + \log n)$. The third question is about *concurrency*, correctly and efficiently managing access to shared resources. A canonical example is a dictionary (e.g., a hash table) that allows lookup operations from multiple threads simultaneously but ensures that insert operations occur only while all simultaneous operations wait. This distinction pervades the entire unit, and all issues of concurrency (the more difficult topic) are delayed until the second half after students are more comfortable with threads and parallel algorithms.

After introducing the basic notions of parallelism and concurrency, we then cover the *shared-memory* model: each thread has its own call-stack and control flow, but heap objects are potentially shared (though it is good style to share very few). *Communication* occurs when threads have references to the same memory, one writes, and another reads. Students have little trouble grasping this model. Correctness always requires *coordination*. For the parallelism portion, the only coordination (i.e., synchronization) primitive we use is *join*: one thread waits unless/until another thread terminates. We briefly mention other models (message-passing, dataflow, data parallelism), but, due to time constraints and a less natural fit in the course, do not revisit them.

3.2 Basic Fork-Join Parallelism

Shared-memory basics are all one needs to discuss our canonical example of how to use P threads (imagine P=4) to sum an array. A natural pseudocode algorithm is roughly:

```
int sum(int[] arr, int P) {
 int[] answers = new int[P];
 int len = arr.length;
 for(int i=0; i < P; i++)
   create a thread to sum from
   arr[i*len/P] to arr[(i+1)*len/P]
   sequentially; put result in answers[i]
 wait by joining on each of the P threads
 return the sum of the P values in answers
}
```

Implementing this solution in a language like Java requires some more code such as creating Thread objects and storing them in an array so that the waiting step can iteratively join on each thread, but the pseudocode is enough to demonstrate three key points:

- Interthread communication occurs using variables `arr` (read by the helper threads) and `answers` (written by the helper threads).
- The waiting step is essential coordination for reading the correct answers. Conversely, if we join on each thread (waiting for it to finish) right after creating it, then we get the correct answer, but the threads never run in parallel.
- If P processors are available, we can expect the algorithm to run approximately P times faster than a sequential algorithm, but there is some overhead from using threads.

More interestingly, we then argue that *this style of parallel programming has serious weaknesses that we can fix via divide-and-conquer recursion*, an approach we use for the rest of the parallelism section. These weaknesses include:

- The approach assumes we know how many processors are available, but we often do not. Other threads may already be running or the operating system may be using processors for other programs. If P is set to 4 but only 3 processors are available, this algorithm will likely run 1.5x slower than if P is set to 3. The number of processors available might even change while the algorithm is running.

- Though unlikely with a simple operation like sum, different subproblems might take different amounts of time (a load imbalance) and we will end up waiting for the slow portion while other processors sit idle.

The elegant-if-counterintuitive solution to these problems is to use recursion to create many more threads than processors, relying on the underlying scheduler to assign the threads to processors as they become available. In pseudocode:

```
int sum(int[] arr) {
  return sumRange(arr,0,arr.length);
}
int sumRange(int[] arr, int lo, int hi) {
  if(hi-lo < CUTOFF) //e.g., CUTOFF=500
    sum range sequentially and return it
  int mid = (hi+lo)/2;
  create thread to compute
      sumRange(arr,mid,hi) and store answer
  int leftAns = sumRange(arr,lo,mid);
  join on thread created above
  return leftAns + answer from other thread
}
```

This algorithm creates an implicit tree of recursive calls. Each node has two children where one child is a new thread. So after n levels of recursion, we have 2^n threads. We analyze this style of algorithm in Section 3.3.

While there are some programming details for using this style in Java (we spend a recitation section on them), they are less burdensome than most threaded programming. However, one should *not* use Java's built-in threads for this style of algorithm; they were not engineered for many threads doing small pieces of work. Instead, Java's ForkJoin Framework [8] was created exactly for this scenario and provides an asymptotically optimal expected-time guarantee (see Section 3.3).

The Java ForkJoin Framework is in the standard library of Java 7 (package java.util.concurrent) and is available for download for Java 6. Our materials give detailed stand-alone instructions for using the library, which is important because students using our materials need only a few methods from three classes whereas the full framework supports sophisticated industrial-strength use. No special hardware is needed, though having at least 4 cores makes parts of the project more meaningful.

Many other languages have similar frameworks (based on the pioneering work of Cilk [2]), including Intel's Cilk+ and Thread Building Blocks for C++ [6] and Microsoft's Task Parallel Library [9] for C#. In the near future, we hope to partner with instructors using languages other than Java to produce adapted versions of the materials. Such adaptation should be entirely straightforward because we use only basic features.

3.3 Analyzing Parallel Programs

Learning to use asymptotic complexity to analyze the efficiency of algorithms is a key component of our data structures course and parallelism should be treated analogously. Fortunately, the fork-join style makes this easy.

We analyze a parallel algorithm in terms of *work* and *span*. Work is the time it would take one processor to complete the task, and span is the time it would take an infinite number of processors. Span is not infinitesimal because computational dependencies must be respected and it takes $O(1)$ time to create a thread. We can define a conceptual directed acyclic graph of the computation where each node is $O(1)$ unit of work and each edge indicates a dependency where the source must complete before the destination can begin. Then work is the total number of nodes and span is the longest path in the graph. Analyzing our recursive array-sum algorithm for an array of size n reveals it has $O(n)$ work and $O(\log n)$ span.

But how is that useful when we have P processors and P is neither one nor infinite? Using techniques best left to an advanced course, the fork-join framework implementation provides an expected-time guarantee of $O(work/P + span)$. We do teach why this guarantee is within a constant factor of optimal: ignoring caching effects, P processors cannot do more than P times better than one processor nor can they do better than an infinite number of processors.

Switching to a sequential algorithm when the recursive problem size drops below a cutoff such as 500 is a key practical technique that does not change the asymptotic complexity. In terms of the computational DAG, the array-sum algorithm produces a binary tree of threads and this cut-off trims out the bottom nine layers of the DAG, i.e., almost all the threads, with the span still logarithmic in the array size.

Finally, we study Amdahl's Law, which analyzes a program's speed-up as you add more processors under the basic assumptions that (1) part of the program parallelizes perfectly ($O(1)$ span) and (2) the rest gets no benefit from more processors (inherently sequential). Amdahl's Law is three lines of simple algebra, but its negative ramifications (e.g., to get 100x speed-up from 256 processors, you must be able to parallelize more than 99% of a program's execution) are best appreciated by having students plot some curves that it implies.

3.4 More Parallel Algorithms

The array-sum example in Section 3.2 is an example of a *reduction*, which means a single result is produced from a collection using an associative (but not necessarily commutative) operator. Many computations are reductions, such as finding the maximum or finding the left-most (or right-most) element satisfying a property. One could program a reduction pattern once and for all by taking in a function object or closure for the associative operation, but we believe students benefit from first writing several reductions manually.

Even simpler than reductions are *maps*, in which a new collection is produced by applying an operation independently to each element of an input collection. Maps and reductions are the workhorses of parallel programming, so we emphasize them. Tying back into a discussion of data structures, we also note that arrays and balanced trees are more suitable for parallelization than ordinary linked lists.

But stopping here leaves the misimpression that what can be parallelized is only what is "obvious" when, in fact, just as non-obvious data structures can provide exponential speed-ups in sequential code, non-obvious parallelization techniques can provide exponential parallelism.

The core "fancy" algorithm we choose to discuss is for *parallel prefix-sum* [7]. The prefix-sum problem is to take an `int[] in` and produce an `int[] out` where `out[i]` is the sum of `in[0]..in[i]`. An $O(n)$ sequential solution is suitable for a CS1 exam since `out[i]=in[i]+out[i-1]`. A surprising parallel version with $O(n)$ work and $O(\log n)$ span works with two passes over the data, with the first building a clever intermediate data structure.

The prefix-sum algorithm in turn can be used as the key trick in implementing a *parallel pack* operation, in which we create an array `out` that has no empty spaces and contains exactly those elements of an array `in` satisfying some property (e.g., "greater than x"). Finding the elements is a trivial map operation; packing them into an array without spaces in parallel is not.

Lastly, parallel pack is the key algorithm we need for a parallel version of quicksort that has $O(n \log n)$ work and $O(\log^2 n)$ span, which requires parallelizing quicksort's partitioning step.

These "fancy" algorithms show that parallelism is not always obvious and that a key technique in algorithm design (sequential or parallel!) is to use known algorithms as subroutines. Our reading notes and lecture slides explain the algorithms in detail. We believe these algorithms are as elegant as any sequential material that may need to be excised to make room, and they take at most one lecture.

3.5 Concurrency, Mutual Exclusion, Locks

We then completely shift focus to concurrent access of shared data structures and the need for mutual exclusion, noting that the parallelism portion used algorithms where threads never tried to access the same data simultaneously. The concurrency portion of the material takes slightly more time than parallelism, but we describe it in less depth in this paper due to space constraints and since our approach is more conventional. We focus on using locks in general and Java's `synchronized` statement in particular to define critical sections that are the right size: neither too small for correctness nor too large to provide efficient concurrent access.

We focus on two distinct programming errors that are often muddled because both are called, "race conditions." *Data races* occur when two threads read/write or write/write the same object field without being ordered by synchronization. For reasons discussed at the end of the unit, data races are, except for expert use, always wrong in any program even if they seem right [1]. But preventing data races is not enough. *Bad interleavings*, also known as higher-level races, result from critical sections that are misplaced or too small for preserving application behavior. What is "bad" depends on the program. For example, if a stack *peek* operation is implemented in terms of a synchronized *pop* followed by a separately synchronized *push*, there are no data races but other threads may still see an illegal intermediate state of the stack. Having students identify bad interleavings and the errors that result is a rich source of homework problems. We use concurrent access to data structures as examples throughout this section.

3.6 Concurrency Programming Guidelines

Locks are notoriously difficult to use correctly, so teaching what locks are and why they are needed is setting up students to repeat all the common mistakes. We advocate teaching students guidelines for sticking to known-to-work concurrency idioms. Frankly, this material is a bit dry and students may not be ready to appreciate it, but we hope they will be able to refer back to it when using locks after the course. Our guidelines are not novel (see, for example, Chapter 1 of [5]), but students need to know about them. They include ideas like: share among threads as few objects as possible, mutate as few objects as possible (cf. functional programming), have a consistent locking protocol, and start with coarse-grained locking and then identify where thread contention occurs.

3.7 Remaining Concurrency Topics

Using locks to enforce mutual exclusion and avoid both data races and bad interleavings is the core skill we impart, but four remaining topics complete our introduction to concurrency:

- Deadlock and techniques for avoiding it
- Readers/writer locks to allow simultaneous read-only access
- Passive waiting for a condition to change and the canonical example of using condition variables to implement a buffer. (Warning: condition variables are surprisingly difficult to use correctly, but some notion of passive waiting is important.)
- Memory-model basics: programs with data races cannot be reasoned about in terms of possible interleavings [1]

3.8 Cross-Cutting Themes on Coverage

The list of topics in our three-week unit is carefully designed to cover only some of the basics "every computer scientist should know" from a particular perspective:

- It separates parallelism and concurrency, while emphasizing the similarities and differences by teaching them adjacently. In the real world, one often must deal with parallelism and concurrency together, but pedagogy is often best when it separates concepts that are combined and confused in practice. Parallelism is easier, so we do it first.
- It focuses entirely on the programmer's view: We *use* threads, locks, and fork-join. We do not *implement* them.
- We leave to other courses all issues related to scheduling.
- We do not cover distributed computing issues, notably latency and fault tolerance.

This focus gives a common foundation on which diverse advanced courses (O/S, distributed programming, networks, databases, graphics, computer architecture, etc.) can build, and it gives students the background to understand non-sequential programs (e.g., at summer internships).

4. THE DATA STRUCTURES FIT

Perhaps our most surprising conclusion is that the data structures course is a great fit for introducing parallelism and concurrency, since this is not (at least yet) common practice. Hopefully the previous section demonstrates our belief that our curriculum unit fits in data structures just as well as the graph algorithms unit, the sorting unit, etc. In this section, we briefly give a high-level view of why this fit works so well and then describe specific topic-level synergies with other course units.

At a high level, the data structures course teaches students to (1) reason asymptotically in terms of abstract models, (2) appreciate the interplay between theory and practice (connecting algorithms to code and analysis to execution time), (3) use well-known conceptual building blocks they would be unlikely to reinvent (e.g., trees with guaranteed balance) and that can be exponentially (in the technical sense) better than naïve approaches, and (4) to separate data structure interface from implementation and to appreciate that narrower interfaces can allow more flexible implementations. Our parallel and concurrency topics reinforce all these outcomes: (1) work, span, and Amdahl's Law are asymptotic ideas, (2) homework assignments consider both algorithms and coding details, (3) non-obvious algorithms provide exponential parallel speedup, and, (4) thread-safe APIs demand an even more careful consideration of interfaces and how operations may interfere with each other. In short, an introduction to threads benefits from the same mix of algorithms, programming models, implementation, and theoretical analysis that is often unique to the data structures course.

On a more detailed level, there are many nice connections with conventional topics from sequential data structures; we give a few examples. Students have just learned divide-and-conquer sequential algorithms and how to reason asymptotically, so divide-and-conquer parallel algorithms reinforce the same concepts. Constant-factor issues are perfectly analogous: A particularly nice connection is showing how in practice sequential quicksort implementations switch to an $O(n^2)$ sort for small n, exactly like parallel algorithms switch to sequential variants below a cutoff. Using a DAG to define work and span demonstrates another application of graphs. For concurrency, data structures like queues and hash tables provide most of the canonical examples for bad interleavings. Revisiting previous data structure abstractions and considering thread safety is fun and timely. A bounded buffer is a queue that blocks instead of raising exceptions when it is empty or full. Hash tables that are rarely changed can motivate readers/writer locks.

5. FEEDBACK FROM STAKEHOLDERS

As of fall 2011, the course has been taught six times so far at UW by five different instructors. Over 250 students at UW have taken the course since Spring 2010. In addition, instructors at five other universities have adapted these materials for their use. We have not performed a broad evaluation or formal learning outcomes assessment, but we can report on our current experience based on feedback from students and instructors.

5.1 Students

Students taking the course were all Computer Science or Computer Engineering majors. The course was a required course, and a prerequisite for many other courses.

Student interest – Overall, students seemed to enjoy the parallelism and concurrency material. In Winter 2011, during the last week of the quarter, students were given an in-class free response survey to gauge their impressions of the course material (N=84, out of 94 enrolled). Responses were coded to identify how often parallelism and concurrency topics were mentioned. For comparison, the number of occurrences of data structures and other topics are also listed (some students mentioned multiple items in their response). In response to "What is the most **important** thing you learned in this course?" 29 students (35%) mentioned parallelism and concurrency topics, 57 students (68%) mentioned data structures topics, and 15 students mentioned other overarching topics like "Big-O" or "Everything". When asked "What is the most **interesting** thing you learned in this course?", 57 students (68%) listed parallelism and concurrency topics. Complete data for this one-time survey appears in Table 1. Overall, it seems that students consider parallelism and concurrency a substantial and interesting part of the course, on par with other core concepts like data structures and asymptotic complexity.

Table 1. Number of student responses mentioning various topics in response to the questions "*What was the most [X] thing you learned in this course?*" (N=84)

X	Parallelism/ Concurrency	Data Structures	Other	No Answer
Important	29 (35%)	57 (68%)	15 (18%)	0
Interesting	57 (68%)	34 (40%)	2 (2%)	0
Surprising	40 (48%)	33 (39%)	13 (15%)	1
Fun	26 (31%)	41 (49%)	19 (23%)	1

Student learning - As one data point on how well students learned the new material, we examined the final exam scores of students in Spring 2010 and Winter 2011. In Spring 2010 (N=32), the first quarter the course was offered, students performed slightly better on the data structures questions (85%) than on the parallelism and concurrency questions (77%). In Winter 2011 (N=94) their performance on both types of questions was comparable (87%). In both quarters, students performed slightly better on the parallelism questions than on the concurrency questions. Although this is only one data point, it concurs with the general feeling of instructors that students were able to learn the material and that the concurrency material was more challenging for students than the parallelism material.

5.2 Instructors

One of the authors developed the course materials and taught the course for the first time in Spring 2010. For the next four quarters, four different instructors (three faculty members, one graduate student) taught the course. These other instructors had experience teaching data structures, but all were unfamiliar with most or all of the parallelism and concurrency material prior to preparing for the course. All instructors indicated that their teaching evaluations were similar to those they normally received in other courses.

Usefulness of provided materials - All four instructors used the provided slides and reading notes and found them to be an important resource for students. Instructors used a combination of the provided written homework problems and made up their own. One instructor felt that the provided project (see Section 7) was too large and trimmed it down. Another instructor created his own project.

Course pace and structure - Multiple instructors found that teaching the concurrency programming guidelines content (Section 3.6) was unexciting. One instructor planned to de-emphasize this and the advanced concurrency material (Section 3.7) in the future, partially because he felt pressed for time. In the context of 10-week quarters, some instructors felt that the material was somewhat rushed, which can lead to a more superficial coverage of some advanced data structures topics. The instructors felt concurrency material was more challenging for students than parallelism, though both were important.

5.3 Students in Later Courses

One reason to teach parallelism and concurrency in an early and required course is so that later courses can assume and build on that material. We are just starting to see students in upper level courses who have taken a version of the data structures course containing the parallelism and concurrency unit. In Spring 2011, out of 38 students enrolled in operating systems, 20 of them had seen concurrency in the data structures course. As a preliminary effort to gauge the impact of teaching parallelism and concurrency early, in the last week of Spring quarter 2011, we conducted a voluntary web survey of students enrolled in operating systems. Nine of those 20 students responded to our survey. When asked if they felt that their experience with parallelism and concurrency in data structures helped them in operating systems, 4 of the 9 viewed the previous material as "1-Indispensible!", 4 viewed it as "2-Fairly useful", and 1 student did not answer (none listed it as "3-A little useful" or "4-Not very useful"). Student views on the usefulness of previous coverage of specific concurrency topics (those most relevant to operating systems) are shown in Table 2.

Table 2. Student responses to "*For each of the following topics, did seeing the material in data structures help your understanding of material in operating systems*?" (N = 9)

Topics	Incredibly useful	Fairly useful	A little useful	Not very useful	I do not remember seeing this
Threads	3	4	1	1	0
Race conditions / data races	6	2	0	0	1
Mutual exclusion / locks	4	4	0	0	1
Deadlock	3	3	2	0	1

5.4 Instructors at Other Institutions

In the last year, faculty at five other institutions have adapted our materials for their use. The materials were used/adapted for CS2 courses and as introductory materials for advanced parallelism/concurrency courses (course links are at [10]). All five instructors found the materials useful and when recently polled informed us that they will use the materials again.

6. RELATED WORK

A 2010 ITiCSE working group explored the issue of integrating parallelism into computer science curricula in great detail, providing a range of references on potential content and approaches that have been tried [3]. Our approach to fork-join parallelism based on recursive algorithms and work/span has been long advocated by parallel-programming leaders such as Charles Leisersen and Guy Blelloch. Cormen et al. [4] offers a more advanced and high-level take on fork-join parallelism (but no mutual exclusion). Similarly, our approach to concurrency and mutual exclusion is by no means new. What we have added is a self-contained pedagogy for teaching parallelism and concurrency adjacently and as a natural fit in a lower-level data structures course.

7. OBTAINING THE MATERIALS

All our materials have been separated from the particulars of our data structures course, and we actively maintain them (fixing errors, improving explanations, etc.) [10]. All materials are open and free, and we have posted all the sources so others can develop their own extracts or extensions. We have developed:

- Written reading notes for students (and instructors!) that cover all the material, about 65 pages in total. Some other institutions have used these as-is in lieu of a textbook while others have developed a subset to match their needs better.
- Lecture slides (PowerPoint), paper-and-pencil homework exercises, and sample exam questions
- A programming project using parallelism to (at least in theory) more quickly process real U.S. census data. A simple GUI (provided) makes the program fun to explore.

Based on our positive experiences using these materials in our data structures course over the past 1.5 years, we encourage others to consider adapting them to their own context.

8. REFERENCES

[1] Adve, S. V. & Boehm, H-J. 2010. Memory models: a case for rethinking parallel languages and hardware. *Communications of the. ACM* 53, 8 (August 2010), 90-101.

[2] Blumofe, R. D., Joerg, C.F., Kuszmaul, B. C., Leiserson, C. E., Randall, K. H., & Zhou, Y. 1995. Cilk: an efficient multithreaded runtime system. In *ACM SIGPLAN Symposium on principles and practice of parallel programming*, 207-216. See also: http://software.intel.com/en-us/articles/intel-cilk-plus/

[3] Brown, R., Shoop, E., Adams, J., Clifton, C., Gardner, M., Haupt, M., & Hinsbeeck, P. 2010. Strategies for preparing computer science students for the multicore world. In *Proc. of the 2010 ITiCSE working group reports*, 97-115.

[4] Cormen, T., Leiserson, C., Rivest, R. & Stein, C. 2009. *Introduction to Algorithms*, 3rd Edition, The MIT Press.

[5] Goetz, B. & Peierls, T. et al. 2006. *Java Concurrency in Practice*. Addison Wesley.

[6] Intel Threading Building Blocks, http://threadingbuildingblocks.org/

[7] Ladner, R. E.; Fischer, M. J. 1980. Parallel prefix computation. *Journal of the ACM* 27, 4 (October 1980), 831–838.

[8] Lea, D. 2000. A Java fork/join framework. In *Proc.of the ACM 2000 conference on Java Grande*, 36-43. See also: http://g.oswego.edu/dl/concurrency-interest/

[9] Leijen, D., Schulte, W., & Burckhardt, S. 2009. The design of a task parallel library. In *ACM SIGPLAN conference on object oriented programming systems languages and applications*, 227-242. See also: http://msdn.microsoft.com/en-us/library/dd460717.aspx

[10] Current version of the materials: http:// www.cs.washington.edu/homes/djg/teachingMaterials

Exploring Concurrency Using The Parallel Analysis Tool

Brian Rague
Weber State University
Computer Science Dept
Ogden, UT, 84408
801.626.7377
brague @ weber.edu

ABSTRACT

Laboratory work in the CS classroom is intended to solidify essential concepts and core design principles. Because of recent advances and the widespread adoption of multicore technologies, one area of investigation that has become increasingly important across all levels of CS instruction is parallel computing. This paper describes the initial version of the Parallel Analysis Tool (PAT), a pedagogical tool designed to assist undergraduate students in visualizing concurrency and effectively connecting parallel processing to applied coding strategies. The PAT is a complete Java development environment, with an emphasis on (1) helping students to identify appropriate code locations where parallelization can be applied and (2) allowing students to subsequently examine the practical performance tradeoffs of these parallelization decisions in a laboratory setting. The Parallel Quotient (PQ), a fundamental dimensionless metric generated by the PAT, supports the student's conceptual understanding and analysis of the relative benefits of employing various parallel programming strategies.

Categories and Subject Descriptors

D.1.3 [**Programming Techniques**]: Concurrent Programming -- Parallel Programming

General Terms

Algorithms, Design.

Keywords

parallelism, visual tool, program analysis, parallel concepts, parallel perceptions, model

1. INTRODUCTION

The prevalence of multicore processors and parallel platforms has made concurrency a fundamental, necessary component of CS instruction. The growing importance of concurrency in the classroom is a recent trend recognized in the ACM CS2008 Curriculum Update, which states "the increased emphasis on concurrency will not be a passing fashion but rather it represents a fundamental shift towards greater attention to concurrency matters" [3].

Permission to make digital or hard copies of all or part of this work for personal or classroom use is granted without fee provided that copies are not made or distributed for profit or commercial advantage and that copies bear this notice and the full citation on the first page. To copy otherwise, or republish, to post on servers or to redistribute to lists, requires prior specific permission and/or a fee.
SIGCSE'12, February 29–March 3, 2012, Raleigh, North Carolina, USA.
Copyright 2012 ACM 978-1-4503-1098-7/12/02...$10.00.

Development environments have traditionally supported student experiential laboratory investigations into program design and development, with a primary emphasis on constructing syntactically correct code and effectively incorporating sequential control structures to meet program requirements. Student familiarity with the standard three-pane visual interface can be leveraged for the purposes of introducing and exploring this essential next level of program design: parallelism.

This paper describes the development and operation of a Java-based software visualization tool created especially for the classroom to help connect students with the special challenges associated with conceptualizing parallel programs and identifying concurrency in code. This Parallel Analysis Tool (PAT) offers the instructor of parallel computing an engaging laboratory platform by which students can rapidly acquire a hands-on appreciation of the tradeoffs related to parallelizing selected code sections of a traditional sequential program.

At the visual interface level, the PAT displays editable Java source code and generates a corresponding UML Activity diagram [9], an artifact used frequently in software engineering. More importantly, the PAT provides students an experimental environment in which immediate feedback in the form of real-time measurements of program speedup help to improve the student's ability to recognize optimal locations for introducing concurrency into code.

2. TOOLS FOR PARALLEL INSTRUCTION

Integrated circuit manufacturers like Intel and AMD not only produce multicore chips for commodity computational devices, but also provide extensive curriculum support for undergraduate courses focused on parallel architecture and programming [10]. Research in multicore computer architectures continues to move forward, though many challenging issues still remain [4][6]. Davis [7] constructed a top ten list of the key problems confronting multicore development; programming methodology was listed as the number one issue. Although it is generally recognized that most programmers do not have the necessary background in concurrency design to fully utilize the current multicore architectures [8], tools and environments customized for parallel application development can help alleviate the challenge that both software engineers and computer science students confront when attempting to produce reliable and efficient parallel programs.

To assist in the instruction of parallel concepts, various visual tools such as those described by Stasko [22], Kurtz [15], Carr [2], and Bi [1] have been used to investigate the behavior of threads and processes in running programs. The Parallel Studio recently released by Intel enhances the developer's tool suite with a threading assistant, threading error checker, and threading performance profiler.

However, these tools are designed primarily for students and professionals that have "previous exposure to classical concurrency issues at the operating system level and basic knowledge of computer networks" [5]. The implication is that students are not equipped to comprehend or correctly manage parallel processes until sufficiently conversant with system level software. Regarding parallelism using threads, Carr [2] states: "(1) multithreaded programming requires a new mindset; (2) the behavior of a multithreaded program is dynamic, making debugging very difficult; (3) proper synchronization is more difficult than anticipated; and (4) programming interfaces are usually more complex than necessary, causing students to spend time in learning the system details rather than the fundamentals."

Lee has stated outright that because of the inherent unreliability of thread behavior between program executions, the thread model may not be best for parallel application design: "Threads are seriously flawed as a computation model because they are wildly non-deterministic." To program parallel systems, Lee proposes a novel coordination language with a visual syntax layered above and orthogonal to an established programming language providing mundane, low-level functionality [16].

Indeed, threads currently represent the de facto primitive for programmers delving into parallel application code, and so a parallel computing course often equates to a detailed treatment of low-level system constructs like threads. At the same time, discussion about various modes of conceptual "thinking" has swirled around the topic of how best to prepare a student for future success in computer science [18]. Tools used in classroom laboratory settings should not only advance the student's experience with implementation techniques, but also expose the student to novel ways of abstracting broad computing problems.

In contrast to visual interfaces that monitor thread behavior, the Parallel Analysis Tool presented here provides a view that displays the parallel program adjacent to a corresponding Activity Diagram, a software development artifact from the UML. Coupling code with a corresponding diagram clearly outlining the program structure and purpose *within the same view* keeps the student mindful of the high-level programming task. This unique design perspective allows the PAT to be utilized in courses ranging from introductory programming to advanced software engineering.

The PAT also does not require the student to instrument the original program with extra programming statements or preprocessor directives. PAT operation is controlled strictly through code comments. The philosophy is to allow the code to execute "as is," unencumbered by additional syntactic bindings to the monitoring tool which might interfere with the overall behavior and flow of the program. For pedagogical reasons alone, it is beneficial for student comprehension of parallel behavior if additional programming commands unrelated to the code's original objectives are avoided. In the case of a CS1 level student learning a new programming language, it is especially critical that only native statements from that language occupy the learner's attention, even when parallel analysis is being applied to the codebase by a software tool dynamically behind the scenes.

3. THE PARALLEL ANALYSIS TOOL

Visual analysis software for parallel computing predominantly targets the time capture and rendering of multithreaded activities, highlighting the interaction among various synchronization objects (e.g., mutexes) and simultaneously executing threads. Thread management does not provide a complete picture of parallel design. Within the context of a comprehensive CS curriculum, presenting the low-level thread model to beginning CS1 students would most likely prove distracting and confusing since the rudimentary idea of a "process" as it relates to programming has not yet been firmly established in the mind of the student taking an introductory *Fundamentals of Programming* course. This section discusses the development and operation of the Parallel Analysis Tool, a pedagogical tool designed to assist undergraduate students at all levels in visualizing concurrency and effectively connecting parallel processing to applied coding strategies.

3.1 PAT Design

The use of instructional multimedia or software is commonplace and widely accepted in teaching environments [14][17]. The pedagogical principles driving the design and development of the PAT are rooted in assisting instructors with the laboratory component of a parallel programming module by offering an alternative hands-on approach for students to observe and experiment with the practical effects of applying concurrency to actual running code. The main objective of the PAT design effort was to distill core information about parallel program design and performance into a compact visual interface format immediately intelligible to the CS student. A single CS1 appropriate performance metric that imparted the most information about the quality of the concurrency effort was employed.

Various measures can be used to evaluate parallel programs [19][23]. When comparing sequential and parallel performance for a single application or kernel, the number of primary interest is often the speedup factor $S(p; n)$, defined in Equation 1 as the ratio of sequential execution time to parallel execution time:

$$S(p,n) = \frac{\textit{Sequential Execution Time}}{\textit{Parallel Execution Time}} \qquad (1)$$

The variable p is the number of processors, n is a measure of the "size" of the program, and it is assumed that the "best" sequential algorithm is used for this relative analysis.

When scalability is factored in, the speedup computation assumes different forms depending on constraints such as constant problem size, constant parallel execution time, or memory availability. Although speedup is a useful measure which encourages the student programmer to increase the percentage of viable parallelizable code wherever possible, it abstracts away critical program design issues that are valid topics of study for CS students.

Developing parallel programs requires a working knowledge of both architecture and algorithms. As stated by Janssen and Nielsen [11], practitioners of parallel program design and implementation must consider the "major obstacles to achieving linear speedups. . . such as communication overhead and load imbalance." Sivasubramaniam [21] aptly describes the difference between linear speedup and real execution time as the sum of algorithmic overhead and interaction overhead. CS students would be well served by a performance metric or expression which opens discussion about both algorithmic overhead issues (inherently serial code, balanced task management) and interaction overhead (contention, latency, synchronization, resource management, and cache effects.)

A theoretical measure more suitable to the student and pedagogical needs of the CS classroom is the parallel computation/communication ratio which will be referred to as the parallel quotient (PQ):

$$PQ(p,n) = \frac{t_{comp}(p,n)}{t_{comm}(p,n)} \quad (2)$$

The PQ can be assumed as roughly proportional to speedup since increased communication overhead will tend to degrade speedup whereas increasing the time dedicated to concurrent computation relative to communication will lead to improved speedup:

$$PQ(p,n) \propto S(p,n) \quad (3)$$

Note that PQ and the speedup factor are both functions of p and n. The execution time of a parallel program is the sum of t_{comp} and t_{comm}, and for classroom discussion purposes both algorithmic and interaction overhead can be viewed as contributors to t_{comm}.

The PQ number can be interpreted as a measure of the *quality* of the parallelization effort. A high PQ would suggest that parallelization is generally effective and essentially the right course of action. A low PQ suggests possible diminishing returns through parallelization. CS students could benefit from the summary feedback provided by a single metric, which promptly conveys the benefits or drawbacks of a particular parallel design strategy without miring the student in detailed analysis. Essentially, code parallelization choices which increase the PQ are reinforced.

A PQ number could be determined not only for an entire application, but also for select sections of code. One of the challenges confronting the student programmer is identifying which parts of the code are good candidates for parallelization. By monitoring PQ values for code sections that possess inherent parallelization such as loops, the student will gain familiarity and confidence with the paradigm of parallel thinking.

If required, there will be ample time to introduce the student to threading concepts and detailed synchronization mechanisms such as semaphores and mutexes later in the CS course or program. The reductionist PQ analysis described here seeks to initially expose the CS student to important high level parallel design concepts, providing a counterbalance to the adoption of a rigid approach in which only sequential thinking is applied to computing problems.

The challenge facing the CS student is one of *recognition*: given a programming model and underlying parallel architecture, which sections of code are good concurrency candidates? Any tool assisting students at this level of analysis should foster this recognition skill, reinforcing the student's parallelization choices with straightforward feedback measures. The PQ number described earlier offers a simple scalar measurement generated by the PAT. The PAT also provides the student a visualization format motivated by the UML Activity diagrams typically employed in software engineering.

In brief, the Activity diagram provides a "flow-chart" perspective of a computational process, with the important addition of synchronization bars that join or fork several actions. This visual notation helps to solidify the student's conceptualization of a set of parallel processes, and terms such as "fork" and "join" could potentially open further discussion about detailed topics related to processes and threads. Also, given the various preferred learning modalities of student populations, the visual component of the PAT will offer a different perspective of parallel code behavior.

As a representative example adapted from Kaminsky [12] and used to illustrate PAT functionality, CS students may be asked to model the basic flow of a program that determines if an integer is prime using the trial division algorithm. In the first version of this program listed in Figure 1, this prime test routine will be applied sequentially to a series of eight very large prime numbers, resulting in a relatively lengthy execution time (approx. 5.8 secs on a 2.59 GHz dual quad-core AMD Opteron server with 15.9 GB of RAM).

```
public class ParallelTest {

   static int n = 8; // Number of input values
   static long[] inputValues = new long[n];

   public static void main(String args[]) {

     long t1 = System.currentTimeMillis();

     /* Set Input Values */
     inputValues[0] = 1000000000000037L;
     inputValues[1] = 1000000000000091L;
     ...more input values

     /* Test for Prime */
     for(int i = 0; i < n; i++)
     {
    isPrime(inputValues[i]);
     }

     /* Display program duration */
     long t2 = System.currentTimeMillis();
     System.out.println("Running Time:" + (t2-t1) + "
msecs");
   }

   private static boolean isPrime(long x)
   {
    ...trial division algorithm...
   }
}
```

Figure 1: Prime Test Sequential Program

Students examining the code example in Figure 1 may identify the loop that performs the prime test as a good candidate for concurrency since a significant amount of computation time is devoted to determining if a given number is prime. Similarly, students may regard the array initialization section as a reasonable place to apply parallelization because each separate statement within that section is performed independently. The PAT is designed to allow CS students to rapidly investigate the validity of their parallel design decisions by using empirical execution times of both the sequential and parallel versions of the program to calculate experimental speedup and thus generate a feedback PQ value.

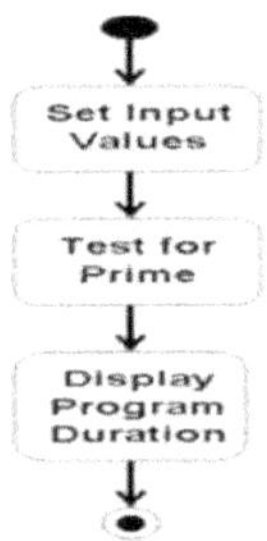

Figure 2: Activity Diagram for Prime Test Program

Figure 2 shows the associated Activity diagram in which the labels for each activity correspond to the commented sections in the main method of the program displayed in Figure 1.

3.2 PAT Operation

The PAT is fundamentally a source code translator and execution environment written in Java. The PAT converts a Java sequential program with specialized annotations into a Java parallel program that utilizes the openly available Parallel Java Library developed at the Rochester Institute of Technology by Alan Kaminsky [13]. Parallel Java is described as an API and middleware for parallel programming in 100% Java on SMP parallel computers, cluster parallel computers, and hybrid SMP/cluster parallel computers.

The startup screen shown in Figure 3 and the functional diagram illustrated in Figure 4 provide a comprehensive portrait of the component parts and features of the PAT design.

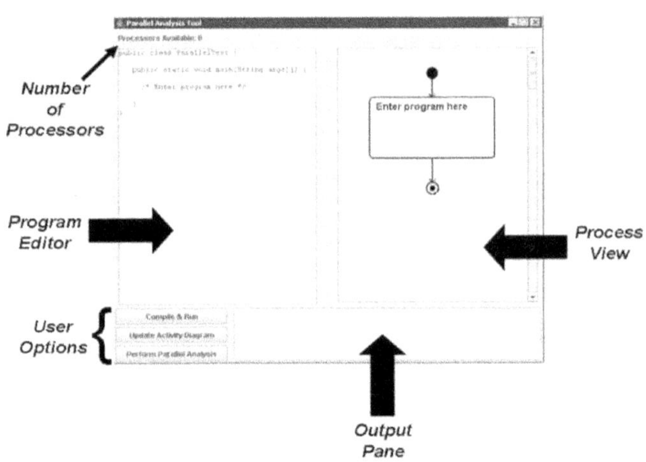

Figure 3: PAT User Interface

On startup, the PAT detects the number of available processors on the host platform and displays that value just underneath the title bar. This vital piece of information makes the user/student aware of the primary parameter of the underlying parallel architecture and provides important context for subsequent analysis in which program performance is measured as a function of the number of processors appropriated for the parallel computation.

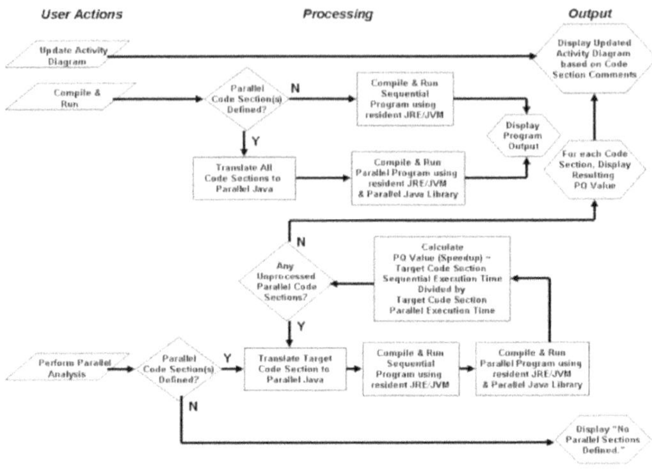

Figure 4: PAT Functional Diagram

The three user option functions located in the lower-left section of the PAT user interface are listed down the left hand side of Figure 4. The *Update Activity Diagram* function simply updates the current activity diagram in the Process View pane of the PAT. As mentioned earlier, the activity labels are obtained from the comments preceding each code section in the main method. The PAT provides basic Java compile-and-run capabilities, generating program results in the Output Pane of the user interface. If specific code sections are marked by the programmer for parallelization (to be described below), the PAT *Compile & Run* option performs a translation of all these program sections to valid Parallel Java source code prior to compiling and executing this auto-generated parallel program.

The *Perform Parallel Analysis* option activates the core functional capability of the PAT, resulting in the calculation and display of PQ values. Before outlining how the PAT conducts parallel analysis, the technique by which the programmer identifies parallel code sections will be described. A straightforward annotation mechanism is used to indicate code sections to be translated to Parallel Java. This approach is motivated by the tagging strategies and metadata facility used in languages like Java and C#, and to some extent the pragmas that drive parallel compilation in OpenMP. Figure 5 gives an example of the annotation structure recognized by the PAT.

```
/* P=8 Test for Prime */
 for(int i = 0; i < n; i++)
 {
isPrime(inputValues[i]);
 }
```

Figure 5: PAT Annotation Defining Parallel Code Sections

In this example, the prime number test loop from Figure 1 is selected by the programmer as a viable candidate for parallelization. Within the comment line that immediately precedes the loop, a **P=8** notation is prepended to the comment as shown in Figure 5. The meaning of this additional text is straightforward for the CS student: *use a total of eight processors to parallelize the for-loop immediately following the annotated comment line.* In general, the specialized PAT annotation that triggers translation of code sections to Parallel Java is **P = *n*** where *n* is the number of processors to be employed during parallel execution of the code section.

Currently, the PAT supports two types of code structures that respond to the parallel annotation: 1) for-loop, and 2) sequence of statements delimited by curly braces. Future versions of the software can extend the translation capabilities such that other programmatic parallelizations (translations) can be realized, but the two code sections listed above were more than sufficient to allow students ample opportunities to experiment with and understand proper application of parallel concepts in the context of working programs. Syntactic constraints regarding the proper placement of the annotated comment line with respect to the targeted parallel code section did not impede student progress when using the tool. Informative error messages that guide students in diagnosing annotation problems are an integral part of the PAT.

Returning to the *Perform Parallel Analysis* function depicted in Figure 4, the Java regular expression API routines are used to parse the original source code for occurrences of parallel section annotations. If no annotations exist in the program, then an appropriate "No Parallel Sections Defined" message is displayed in the Output Pane. If one or more parallel sections are indicated, then the PAT performs the following steps for each individual section:

1. Translate Target Code Section to Parallel Java: Using parsing routines and the scaffolding provided by static code fragments, the PAT assembles Parallel Java source using the original source code, the number of processors specified in the parallel annotation, and the actual number of physical processors/cores. Figure 6 lists the Parallel Java code generated after PAT source translation of the code section given in Figure 5. Note that a team of eight threads is created and activated, with each thread assigned to a single execution of the program statements defined by the run method [13]. If the student specified sixteen processors (**P=16**) rather than eight, then each of the eight real processor threads would be assigned two tasks, which would be reflected in code as a change in the upper limit of the Parallel Java for-loop from one to two: `for(int k = 0;k < 2; k++)`.

```
// Begin program timing
SeqStartTime8061 = System.nanoTime();
    /* P=8 Test for Prime */
new ParallelTeam(8).execute (new ParallelRegion()
{
public void run()
{
int index = getThreadIndex();
for(int k = 0; k < 1; k++) {
int i = k * 8 + index;
    isPrime(inputValues[i]);
}}});
// End program timing
SeqStartTime8062 = System.nanoTime();
```

Figure 6: PAT Translation to Parallel Java

2. Compile and Run Sequential Program: Prior to executing the original sequential program, the PAT instruments the source code with two timing statements in order to calculate an execution time estimate for the program. Figure 7 shows the resulting sequential code after injecting timing commands both immediately before and after the code section of Figure 5. These statements utilize the Java nanosecond timer to provide a measure of the overall sequential execution time used in the calculation of the PQ value.

```
// Begin program timing
SeqStartTime8061 = System.nanoTime();
    /* P=8 Test for Prime */
    for(int i = 0; i < n; i++)
    {
    isPrime(inputValues[i]);
    }
// End program timing
SeqStartTime8062= System.nanoTime();
```

Figure 7: PAT Instrumentation with Timing Statements

3. Compile and Run Parallel Program: Note that the parallel code section in Figure 6 is flanked with timing statements similar to those in the sequential code in Figure 7. These statements utilize the Java nanosecond timer to provide a measure of the overall execution time of this parallel section. The parallel execution time acquired by the PAT is used in the calculation of the PQ value.

4. Calculate the PQ Value: Given both the sequential execution time and parallel execution time of the code section of interest, a PQ value (speedup) can be calculated for this section using Equation 1.

After the previous steps are performed for each individually annotated code section, the PAT activity diagram in the Process View is updated with the calculated PQ value (see Figure 8).

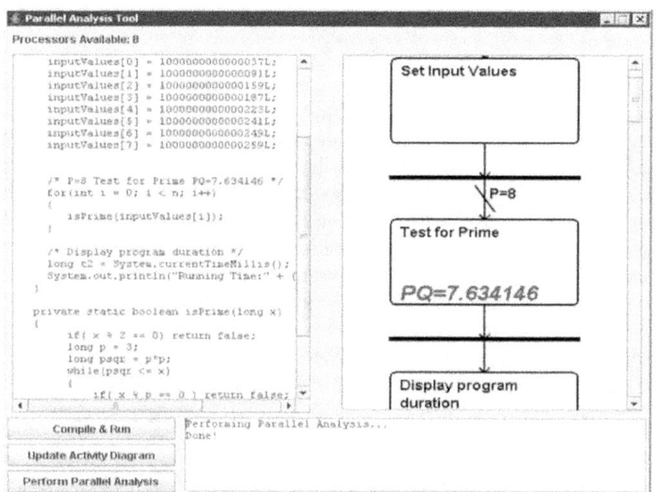

Figure 8: PAT after Parallel Analysis

In this way, students can receive timely feedback on the quality of the parallelization effort using the PQ performance metric described earlier. To reinforce the classroom discussion about modeling parallel processes, note the activity diagram corresponding to the parallel section is updated using an appropriate join, fork, and customized shorthand notation indicating that eight processors have been recruited for the execution of this code section.

4. PAT IN THE CLASSROOM

The PAT has been employed as an intervention in a prior educational study [20]. As part of that study, thirty-one students enrolled in an undergraduate introductory *Fundamentals of Programming* class were assigned exercises (available on request) which focused on performing experiments with the PAT software. In one exercise, for a given code section students were asked to adjust the number of processors and note the effect on the resulting PQ value. Through analysis of these recorded data, students were to recommend the optimum number of processors to use for the specific target code section running on the class host server. By emphasizing the broad interplay of both software and hardware in the empirical results, this exercise reinforces the importance of considering both algorithm and architecture in parallel design.

In a second exercise, students are confronted with the reality that parallelizing certain sections of code may yield disappointing results. Students must analyze the situation in which a parallel strategy is applied to a collection of very fast initialization statements. In this case, the time investment for thread setup and overhead significantly overwhelms any nominal performance gains attained by parallelizing statements with extremely short execution times. The contrast in the magnitude of the PQ number communicates the important message that indiscriminate use of concurrency is a viable concern when designing parallel programs. The extremely low PQ value that results when parallelizing eight very fast initialization statements among eight processors illustrates the subtle distinctions the student must make when practicing the art of finding concurrency in code.

5. SUMMARY

The Parallel Analysis Tool (PAT) described in this paper offers a unique variation on the traditional development environment used in introductory programming classrooms. The primary intention of this software tool is to cultivate and hone the student's ability to find concurrency directly within Java source code. Student users can also experiment with parallel performance in real time by directly utilizing multicore resources available in the underlying platform. Students are able to specify the number of processors to be recruited for a parallel task, and are able to rapidly assess the quality of their concurrency strategies through a speedup metric called the PQ value. By transforming specific code sections from sequential to parallel and examining the influence on overall program performance, students are able to experience firsthand a shared-memory model process called *incremental parallelization*, by which a sequential program is converted into a viable parallel program one block of code at a time.

The PAT as currently constructed can be expanded, both in usage and functionality. The laboratory exercises described above require that students work with pre-existing code rather than develop their own. Regarding specific program structure analysis, at present the PAT targets two types of parallel code constructs: for-loop parallelism, and explicit task (functional) parallelism. These two programming structures encompass a wide variety of potential entry points in which parallelism may be introduced into code. The PAT can be enhanced to also include shared task lists or other resources, and to allow for the identification of critical sections. Exclusively utilized on SMP platforms, the PAT's migration to message passing systems has yet to be explored.

6. REFERENCES

[1] Bi, Y. and Beidler, J. 2007. "A Visual Tool for Teaching Multithreading in Java." *Journal of Computing Sciences in Colleges*.

[2] Carr, S. et al. 2003. "ThreadMentor: A Pedagogical Tool for Multithreaded Programming." *ACM Journal of Educational Resources*, 3, 1 (March, 2003), 1-30.

[3] Computer Science Curriculum 2008: An Interim Revision of CS 2001, Interim Review Task Force, IEEE Computer Society, ACM. http://www.acm.org/education/curricula.

[4] Constantinou, T., et al. 2005. "Performance implications of single thread migration on a chip multi-core." *ACM SIGARCH Computer Architecture News*, 80-91.

[5] Cunha, J.C. et al. 1998. "An Integrated Course on Parallel and Distributed Processing." *SIGCSE*.

[6] Darringer, J. A. 2007. "Multi-core design automation challenges." *Proceedings of the annual conference on Design Automation*, 760-764.

[7] Davis, A. 2007. "Top Ten List of Multi-Core Problems." Slides by permission. Multi-Core Discussion Colloquium. University of Utah.

[8] Feng, W. and Pavan, B. 2009. "Tools and Environments for Multicore and Many-Core Architectures." *Computer*, 26-27.

[9] Fowler, M. 2003. *UML Distilled: A Brief Guide to the Standard Object Modeling Language*, Addison-Wesley.

[10] Intel Higher Education Curriculum Forum. Retrieved 8/1/11: http://www.intel.com/education/highered/Multicore/Multicore.htm

[11] Janssen, C.L. and Nielsen, I.M.B. 2008. *Parallel Computing in Quantum Chemistry*, CRC Press.

[12] Kaminsky, A. 2010. *Building Parallel Programs*, Course Technology, Boston.

[13] Kaminsky, A. Parallel Java Library. Retrieved 8/1/11 from Rochester Institute of Technology – Dept. of Computer Science: http://www.cs.rit.edu/~ark/pj.shtml

[14] Kozielska, M. 2000. "Educational Computer Programs in Learning in Physics by Action." *Education Media International*, 37, 3, 161-166.

[15] Kurtz, B.L. 1998. "A Concurrency Simulator Designed for Sophomore-level Instruction." *SIGCSE*.

[16] Lee, E. A. 2006. "The Problem with Threads." *Computer*.

[17] Mbarika, V.W.A. 2003. "A Multimedia Case Study Approach to Communicate IT Concepts at the Graduate Level." *Journal of SMET Education*, 4, 1 & 2, 28-36.

[18] McMaster, K., Rague, B., and Anderson, N. 2010. "Integrating Mathematical Thinking, Abstract Thinking, and Computational Thinking." *Frontiers in Education Conference*.

[19] Quinn, M.J. 2004. *Parallel Programming in C with MPI and OpenMP*, McGraw-Hill, New York.

[20] Rague, B. 2011. "Measuring CS1 Perceptions of Parallelism." *Frontiers in Education Conference*.

[21] Sivasubramaniam, A., et al. 1993. "An Approach to Scalability Study of Shared Memory Parallel Systems." Technical Report GIT-CC-93/62.

[22] Stasko, J.T. 1995. "The PARADE Environment for Visualizing Parallel Program Executions: a Progress Report." Technical Report GIT-GVU-95-03.

[23] Wilkinson, B., and Allen, M. 2005. *Parallel Programming*, 2nd ed., Pearson Prentice-Hall.

Virtual Clusters for Parallel and Distributed Education

Elizabeth Shoop
Macalester College
shoop@macalester.edu

Richard Brown
St. Olaf Collage
rab@stolaf.edu

Eric Biggers
Macalester College
ebiggers@macalester.edu

Malcolm Kane
Macalester College
mknae2@macalester.edu

Devry Lin
Macalester College
tlin@macalester.edu

Maura Warner
Macalester College
mwarner@macalester.edu

ABSTRACT

The reality of multicore machines as a standard and the prevalence of distributed cloud computing has signaled a need for parallel and distributed computing to become integrated into the computer science curriculum. At the same time, operating system virtualization has become a common technique with open standard tools available to any practitioners. Virtual machines (VMs) installed on available computer lab resources can be used to simulate high-performance cluster computing environments. This paper describes two such virtual clusters in use at small colleges, demonstrates their effectiveness for parallel computing education, and provides information about how to obtain the VMs for use in an educational lab setting. We have used these clusters to introduce parallelism into several courses in our undergraduate curriculum.

Categories and Subject Descriptors

K.3.2 Computer and Information Science Education.

General Terms

Performance, Experimentation.

Keywords

Virtual Machines, Virtual Clusters, Parallel and Distributed Computing Education.

1. INTRODUCTION

Parallelism has become commonplace in the computing industry. Not only do corporations build and maintain their own clusters and supercomputers, but cluster time can be purchased from such service providers as Amazon Web Services, Rackspace, and Microsoft Azure. To prepare graduates for this situation, teaching parallel and distributed computing concepts to students across the curriculum is gaining interest and momentum among faculty. Many colleges and universities lack the resources to construct a dedicated Beowulf-style cluster for use in computer science (CS) classes.

However, since typical teaching assignments at educational institutions tend to require hardware capacity (enough machines for students in labs) rather than throughput, powerful hardware in the form of individual workstations is already on campus and in use by CS students. Since that hardware may sit largely idle and unused during nights and weekends and between major assignment due-dates, it represents a computation resource that can be used for parallel and distributed computing, thanks to the advent of virtual machines [1], [2] [3].

A common workhorse powering the burgeoning use of parallelism in industry is the virtual cluster. The aforementioned service providers – Amazon Net Services, etc. – rent virtual cluster time to clients. Although virtual clusters most commonly appear in industry, there is no reason why they cannot be utilized in an educational setting as well. A virtual cluster is relatively easy to construct and can be built without the purchase of any new equipment or software. A CS department in need of a cluster now has the option of networking their underutilized machines to create a virtual Beowulf cluster to capture otherwise unused computing capacity and more fully leverage existing hardware investments [1]. The possibility of student management provides another layer of educational opportunity: virtual cluster implementation and maintenance gives students hands-on learning experience with operating systems, networking, and system administration. Finally, the presence of a virtual cluster on-site can help to encourage students and faculty to incorporate more distributed and cluster computing in coursework and projects, thus supporting those students in learning the principles of parallelism and concurrency they will need in their careers [4][5].

These clusters can be constructed using virtual machines running on lab computers around campus. KVM, VMWare and VirtualBox are popular virtualization software packages. There are many cluster resource managers and schedulers available for free; open-source versions of the parallel Message-Passing Interface (MPI) are easy to acquire. A virtual cluster can be built by students, for students, in CS labs using the equipment that CS departments already own. In this paper, we will discuss the configuration and performance of two virtual clusters being used for enhancing computer science education: the MistRider cluster at Saint Olaf College, and the Selkie cluster at Macalester College. We will present the architecture of the Saint Olaf MistRider virtual cluster, then describe how we benchmarked the performance of several cluster configurations to assess virtualization overhead in terms of system performance. We will move on to the architecture and configuration of the Selkie cluster, and examine the overhead produced on the physical host machines in the computer lab to assess the impact of heavy load on the virtual cluster on student use of the lab machines, presenting a comprehensive picture of the functionality and feasibility of virtual clusters in a college setting. We have made the virtual machine images available for educational use along with support materials and instructional materials, and we report

Permission to make digital or hard copies of all or part of this work for personal or classroom use is granted without fee provided that copies are not made or distributed for profit or commercial advantage and that copies bear this notice and the full citation on the first page. To copy otherwise, or republish, to post on servers or to redistribute to lists, requires prior specific permission and/or a fee.
SIGCSE '12, February 29 –March 3, 2012, Raleigh, North Carolina, USA.
Copyright 2012 ACM 978-1-4503-1098-7/12/02...$10.00.

on lessons we have learned while developing and maintaining these clusters and using them for coursework.

2. UPDATE: THE MISTRIDER CLUSTER

In a 2009 paper [6], one of us described the MistRider cluster at St. Olaf, a 37-node Linux cluster implemented on Linux classroom and laboratory machines using KVM virtualization to implement the cluster nodes. Whereas many earlier clusters on laboratories involved rebooting physical machines to form a temporary dedicated cluster system, and an earlier cluster involving virtualization placed the cluster nodes on the host operating system (which provides the base system resources for virtualization) and the interactive user's sessions on a guest or virtual operating system (booted on guest virtual machines created using the host system's resources), MistRider located the cluster nodes systems as guests, and general-purpose classroom and lab processes in the host operating system. The MistRider design matched the core purpose of those classroom and lab machines as the primary computing resources for CS courses and projects, while providing a cluster computing resource sufficient for educational uses.

Beowulf cluster computing, in which high-performance clusters are constructed from commodity hardware and open-source software, had thrived and grown since it's inception about 20 years earlier. During that timespan, specially designed "supercomputers" were largely replaced by clusters as the primary platform for high-performance computing, to the extent that the great majority of the fastest computing systems (as listed on the TOP 500 list at www.top500.org) were cluster systems. In [6], we proposed various curricular applications of cluster computing, both as an example of system architecture and as a platform for data-intensive scalable computing using the open-source Hadoop framework for the map-reduce parallel computing pattern [7]. We argued that Hadoop's fault tolerance, particularly its ability to recover from losses of nodes, would provide robust map-reduce computations on the virtual cluster, where unsuspecting novice students might power-cycle a classroom or laboratory machine without realizing that it would mean crashing a node in a virtual cluster. We highlighted uses of Hadoop in an upper-level Parallel Computing Systems course, and in a Scheme-based introductory course in which a strategically simplified interface inspired by [8] made Hadoop computations accessible to beginning programmers.

2.1 Experience with MistRider Cluster

After nearly four years of usage, the MistRider cluster has served us very well. Here, we observe several aspects of our experience.

Reliability. The system, still our largest cluster on campus, has proven to be remarkably reliable -- the up-front investment in collaboration with our IT department led to a system with high availability and low ongoing maintenance. Our student cluster managers, who do not have root access on the host operating system, can create or destroy virtual machines and launch or shut down virtual operating system kernels for the cluster at will. When upgrading the host operating system, our IT staff needs only update or relaunch a small number of scripts and set some permissions in order to give the cluster managers all the access they need to develop and operate the virtual cluster. Once early configuration was finalized, we have experienced no difficulties with our TRUNCed networking, in which two virtual networks operate over a single network line through a single network card. One of those networks is controlled by the IT department for use by the host operating system; the other virtual network is controlled by student cluster managers for the virtual cluster.

MistRider is our workhorse. Our strategy of favoring Hadoop computations on this cluster for robustness via fault tolerance has worked very well. In fact, we have continued to launch Hadoop jobs without having to re-upload data at times when over 50% of the computers were down for maintenance.

Capacity. Of course, it remains possible to overwhelm the MistRider resources. When a Hadoop computation presses on the capacity of the MistRider system (e.g., an analysis of Wikipedia with all of its history), we have sometimes observed some performance degradation in the host operating system, noticable mostly by host-system "power users." However, this is largely a sign that a cluster application has too large a scale for our 37-node cluster, and several users with such applications have appropriately migrated to larger resources elsewhere.

Student cluster management. Our strategy of using undergraduate students exclusively as our cluster managers has worked very well. We currently have a team of four cluster managers with various degrees of experience, which provides us with a succession of well-trained cluster managers as the seniors graduate, and which constitutes a sufficient critical mass to address emerging needs as they arise. In six years of student cluster management (three with MistRider), we have only had to shut down or reboot a cluster once, when a water-related emergency occurred one New Years Eve.

The success of our student cluster management experience has largely been due to the good fortune of strong, interested students, careful selection among them, and supervision that focuses on setting direction and policy and seeking out needed resources. Our cluster managers have been chief collaborators in our undergraduate research program, with an attitude of helpfulness and (when appropriate) mentoring. They have consistently been among our lead undergraduate researchers themselves. However, administrative support and the availability of resources has also been essential. The ability to pay cluster managers (at the normal rate) using student work funds and the great willingness of our IT staff to assist with our projects, mostly by loaning equipment and answering questions, has proven invaluable.

Impact on curriculum. Our use of the MistRider cluster to support curriculum has been amplified and expanded due to our grant-funded collaborative CSinParallel project to develop modular materials for teaching parallelism, which began in 2010. In particular, our early software that enabled Scheme CS1 students to launch Hadoop jobs with potentially large data evolved into the WebMapReduce (WMR) interface [9] (webmapreduce.sourceforge.org). Nowadays, every introductory CS student at both of our institutions learns about map-reduce parallel computations through hands-on exercises with WMR, and upper-class students also use WMR either as a practical tool for map-reduce computations or as a precursor to programming Hadoop directly. MistRider also serves many of our advanced parallel computation teaching and project needs, for example MPI programming, in our (now larger) Parallel Computing Systems elective.

MistRider had significant impact in Macalester's CS curriculum as well, providing remote service for WMR and other cluster computations before Macalester built its own virtual cluster, Selkie.

Some new directions. We now implement our admin or "head" nodes as virtual systems, on separate server hardware networked to the MistRider cluster nodes. We learned this lesson the hard way: a disk crash at an unfortunate time led to many hours of reconstruction work that can be avoided by simply booting a checkpointed virtual operating-system kernel image on different physical hardware. This virtual server strategy is also convenient for running multiple services on the same physical hardware.

We are now branching out to create interdisciplinary applications of parallel computing, each with a customized user interface for a particular "client" in another field. The fact that we dare this initiative with users who may have reluctance about technology indicates the confidence we have in the reliability of the MistRider platform and the consistent quality of our student cluster management team.

2.2 Analysis of MistRider Performance

We have carried out a performance analysis of the MistRider system, comparing the virtual system with TRUNCed networking against the same virtual cluster but with a (second) dedicated physical network, and against a physical cluster (no virtualization) with the same configuration. We will summarize this work here; see [10] for a complete treatment.

2.2.1 HPCC Benchmarks

The High Performance Computing Challenge (HPCC) [11] benchmark suite brings together seven previously existing performance tests, for a widely recognized comprehensive test of cluster system performance. The names of the tests suggest the types of computation they assess: High Performance Linpack (HPL); parallel matrix transpose (PTRANS); memory bandwidth (STREAM); matrix multiply (DGEMM); Fast Fourier Transform (FFTE); random access (RandomAccess); and network bandwidth and latency (b_eff). Each component benchmark measures real-world application performance in terms of spatial and temporal locality of memory access.

2.2.2 Summary of Results

The MistRider cluster with virtualization performed comparably to an identically configured cluster in CPU and memory performance on HPL, PTRANS, and Random Access, but network bandwidth and latency suffered considerably under KVM virtualization, at least using our commodity networking hardware. We note, however, that if input-output memory management units become standard on network interface cards, we anticipate that virtualization overhead for networking may be eliminated altogether.

3. REPORT: ADDITIONAL VIRTUAL CLUSTER

Because the St. Olaf MistRider cluster was successful for use in classes and for teaching students about virtual machines and creating and maintaining clusters, we capitalized on the St. Olaf experience and built a second virtual cluster at Macalester College. In this case, the hardware platforms were Apple iMacs in two computing labs shared by the Mathematics, Statistics, and Computer Science Department. One lab has 16 mid-2010 models, and the other has 28 new mid-2011 models. We called the cluster Selkie, named for a creature in Scottish mythology.

3.1 Technical Specifications

When ordering the iMac machines we were careful to get the quad-core models, just as St. Olaf had. We also found that 8 GB of RAM was useful, so that each VM and host could use 4 GB each. This was an increase from St. Olaf's configuration– Mathematics and Computer Science student researchers using our host lab machines seemed to need the extra memory when running Mathematica computations and during web application development work using IDEs such as eclipse and ItelliJ. The 16 mid-2010 models have a 1 TB hard drive, and each of the 28 mid-2011 models have a 500GB hard drive.

We used the VirtualBox product (http://www.virtualbox.org/) for our virtual machines because it runs on Mac OS X and it is open source and freely available. Our current OS configuration on each VM is Ubuntu linux Server version 10.04. Each VM is approximately 1GB, representing the space used for the OS, software installed, and home directories for users. VirtualBox enables file systems on the host to be mounted in the VM, so we created a file called /cluster on each host that was then mounted on the VM (in VirtualBox this is called file sharing). This file space is necessary for using Hadoop for map-reduce computations. Each VM is configured to use 4GB of RAM and 2 CPUs (virtual box has settings for these) and is given its own IP address.

Each VM has the following software installed for use in parallel and distributed computing: Hadoop [7], OpenMPI [12], and TORQUE [13]. Like all beowulf-style clusters, one VM is different because it is designated for the 'head' node (we followed Mistrider's model and make that virtual also). This is where students will submit MPI jobs to TORQUE for scheduling and run Hadoop jobs. The software installed on this VM is specific for the head node of the cluster, and includes WebMapReduce, a tool for enabling the use of map-reduce in all level of the curriculum [9]. The rest of the VMs represent 'exec', or execute nodes in the cluster, and have the appropriate software installed for them to execute Hadoop and MPI jobs. Thus, we have made two VMs available, one for the head node and one for all of the exec nodes.

We have successfully used the Selkie virtual cluster to execute large Hadoop map-reduce computations and to submit and execute several MPI examples that we use in the upper-level parallel and distributed computing course. Throughout a full semester, Math and CS students were able to use the host portion of these machines for their coursework and projects with little effect on their work. In the next section, we examine empirically whether the heavily used running VMs have an effect on the experience of students using the host machines in the labs.

3.2 Usability Tests

It is important to know whether the cluster running virtually on computer lab machines will have deleterious effects on the user experience of students using the host machines during class or open lab times. In our labs, students use the computers for a great deal of different activities, ranging from using tools such as Mathematica, Matlab, and R for various mathematical computations, to software development using IDEs such as eclipse, and to general Web surfing and Web application use. We devised a series of tests to determine the extent to which parallel and distributed high-performance computations being run on the virtual cluster affect the students using the host machines in the lab. Our goal was to run benchmarks or tests that significantly taxed the virtual cluster and simultaneously run two types of example tests on the physical host iMacs: 1) a typical set of Mathematica calculations and 2) a network performance benchmark suite. The former is an example of a compute-bound computation that likely surpasses what students might perform when working on homework, and the latter would give us an understanding of how the network, and thus the typical applications that use the network, will be affected by the virtual cluster's simultaneous use of the network.

The computations that we used on the virtual cluster to tax it were:

- The HPCC benchmarks used for performance testing of the St. Olaf mistrider virtual cluster.
- The b_eff_io benchmark [14], designed to measure the efficiency of a cluster or high performance computer when running a program using a large number of Message Passing Interface (MPI) input/ouput (IO) routines. In the case of our cluster, all nodes are writing through to local disk on the host machines, thus using this resource of the host.
- A typical Hadoop word count application using approximately 300 books from Project Gutenberg as input (http://www.gutenberg.org/). We use Hadoop via the WebMapReduce interface for several activities and homework in our introductory CS1 course.

These were chosen to represent typical to extreme uses of our cluster by students when working on lab exercises or homework in advanced or introductory courses.

The computations that we used on the host iMac machines to demonstrate their performance were:

- A Mathematica benchmark maintained by Karl Unterkofler on https://homepages.fhv.at/ku/karl/timings80.html. This benchmark consists of a series of typical calculations, such as finding the factorial of 10 million, summations, factorizations, integrations, and determining eigenvalues of matrices.
- The set of network performance benchmarks found at www.netperf.org (netperf tests). These tests measure 1) the time to send and receive data between two machines (also called stream performance); and 2) The time to send a request and receive a response (also called a transaction time) with and without connection time included. In our case we ran the tests using TCP, a commonly used network packet protocol, and measured times to send/receive between two of the iMacs in our lab.

The Mathematica benchmark consists of 16 computations whose CPU times are recorded and added together to produce an overall number of seconds. While the performance on one non-loaded host is interesting to note, we were primarily concerned with the differences between running the tests on an unloaded host and running them on that same host when the virtual cluster was in heavy use.

The netperf benchmarks consist of 5 tests whose elapsed time in seconds is defined using a command-line option:

1. A TCP 'stream' test, in which buffers of data are sent by one host using the system's send() request, and received by a second host. Overall network throughput, measured in bits per second, is reported.
2. A TCP 'sendfile' test, in which the data is sent using the system's sendfile() request, but is otherwise the same as the 'stream' test. Because the sendfile() function will use the file system's buffer cache, this test should be slightly faster on most systems.
3. A TCP 'maerts' test, which is exactly like the stream test, but data is sent in the opposite direction from the stream test (maerts is stream backwards).
4. A TCP request/response test, is a synchronous, one transaction at a time test in which many transaction are requested and responded to between two hosts, and a transaction rate is reported in transactions per second, along with a rough estimate of the percent of the CPU utilized for the test.
5. A TCP connect/request/response test is similar to the above test, but a transaction includes a connection time as well as request and response time.

We ran these tests in order (specifically 2,1,3,4,5 above) using two hosts on an unloaded virtual cluster and when the virtual cluster was in heavy use. Running these in order means that different tasks were taking place on the virtual machines on those hosts when each test was being run, though we were able to run the netperf tests for particular times that corresponded to each test being run on the cluster. The numbers between hosts on an unloaded cluster represent the performance of the network in the building where the machines are being used, and the numbers when the cluster is in use should represent the degradation in network performance on the host due to the resources the virtual machine is using on the host.

3.3 Experiments

What follows is a description of how we conducted our tests, running HPCC, b_eff_io, and Hadoop on the virtual cluster while running the Mathematica benchmark or the netperf tests on host iMac machines. We used a cluster of 15 virtual nodes for the following tests.

We ran the HPCC suite with the goal, not of maxing out the memory on every node, but rather of producing significant load while running the job for roughly 30 minutes. We initially ran the suite and found that with the default values, HPCC ran for an adequate duration and produced a consistent CPU load of 100% and memory load of approximately 4% on every compute node in Selkie. HPL and PTRANS ran with a matrix size of 14080 and process grids of 5x6 (chosen because we used a cluster of 15 2-CPU nodes).

Since the HPCC suite consists of many benchmarks, some of which are very processor- and memory-intensive, and some of which are very network-intensive, we decided to run netperf individually against every portion of the HPCC suite, insofar as that was possible. We therefore created five scripts that ran the netperf benchmarks for fixed amounts of time, each script corresponding to a specific HPCC benchmark, and then manually ran them at the appropriate time as the HPCC suite progressed. Specifically, we ran netperf against MPIRandomAccess, MPIRandomAccess_LCG, LatencyBandwidth, and HPL. Our fifth script ran against a collection of small, very rapid benchmarks in the HPCC suite, including PTRANS (about 40 seconds) and MPIFFT (about 20 seconds). Because it was running against such a wide variety of tests, we have not included it in our results, but we have retained the data. We replicated this test five times.

We similarly ran the Mathematica benchmarks five times against each portion of the HPCC suite and averaged those values together.

Our goal for the b_eff_io benchmarks was to produce significant load on the cluster for a sufficient amount of time. The b_eff_io benchmark requires that users input the available memory of each compute node, and the maximum total memory available to the entire cluster, as its goal is to max the system out with MPI IO routines. We found that giving b_eff_io the node memory size of 1024MB and a total system memory of 15360MB produced a job that used the cluster heavily and ran for about 30 minutes, an ideal length of time for collecting data from benchmarks on the host iMacs. We ran the netperf suite concurrently with the b_eff_io benchmark, running each netperf test for five minutes, which gave a total running time of 25 minutes. Since b_eff_io produced consistent load on the compute nodes' CPUs and memory and the Mathematica benchmarks takes about a minute to run, we ran the Mathematica benchmarks five times during two runs of b_eff_io.

Our running of Hadoop on the cluster was as follows: to produce sufficient load on the cluster, we ran two concurrent word count jobs through Hadoop using the Web Map Reduce interface, resubmitting each job as soon as it completed. Word counting is the "hello, world" of Hadoop, a simple, standard job for testing out a new Hadoop setup or starting students off on learning to use the framework. For input, we used a group of 293 ebooks from Project Gutenberg. We produced a consistent load on every node of between 60% and 100%. Load was mostly between 90% and 100%, although when one of the jobs completed, load on three or four of the nodes would sometimes dip down to 60% or 70% for perhaps 60 seconds during job resubmission. Load on the cluster was, however, mostly between 90% and 100%. This approximates a typical workload of Hadoop use by students because Hadoop attempts to schedule its jobs in such a way that the available nodes in a cluster are being used efficiently and to full capacity.

3.4 Results

Here we report on how the programs running on the hosts fared when the cluster was inactive and when loaded as described in the previous section.

The most informative netperf result was the output of the TCP STREAM test. We found that the TCP MAERTS test mirrored the STREAM results almost exactly, as did the SENDFILE test. The Request/Response tests are not particularly germane, as they don't really tell us much about the change in user experience, so we omit the data here (it is available from the authors).

The netperf STREAM results appear in Fig. 1. In this figure, the HPCC tests that run more than one minute are separated out, since we were able to run netperf tests while each one was running. The best throughput was, as expected, obtained when no jobs were running on Selkie, at about 11.73x10^6 bytes per second (Bps). The worst performance was obtained during the HPL (High-Performance Linpack) benchmark portion of the HPC Challenge suite: 9.51x10^6 Bps, 81% of average performance with no traffic on the cluster. A 19% loss of bandwidth is by no means insignificant, but it is certainly not prohibitive. Student researchers working on the host machines did not complain of significant slowdown in their Internet connections, nor did they report any issues with their software development projects during network-intensive benchmarking on Selkie. Torrent downloads would probably be disrupted by large amounts of network traffic from the cluster, but usual (and legal) student use of the lab machines did not appear to be adversely affected by the decreased bandwidth.

With no jobs on the cluster, our Mathematica benchmarks ran for an average of 54.31 seconds (see Fig 2). The High-Performance Linpack (HPL) test from the HPCC benchmark suite tended to slow Mathematica down the most, running for an average of 88.56 seconds. That is a 63% increase in running time, which is significant. Running a Hadoop job that produced significant load on the cluster, however, produced an average running time increase of only 26%.

It is clear that running large cluster jobs can have a significant effect on CPU-heavy work such as Mathematica on the host machines. Larger, longer-running jobs run by mathematics, computer science, or statistics students will be noticeably affected by significant work on Selkie.

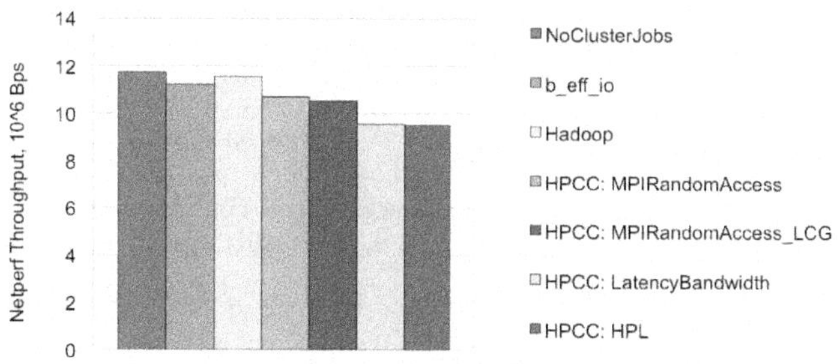

Figure 1. Network throughput between hosts with and without virtual cluster activity

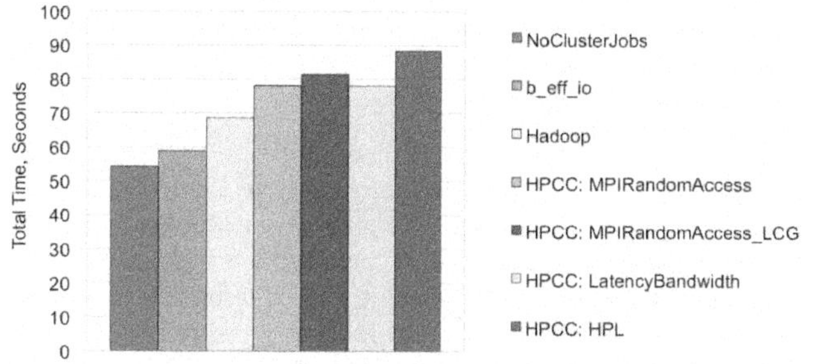

Figure 2. Mathematica benchmark times on a host, with and without virtual cluster activity

However, use of interactive software packages or the running of smaller programs on the lab machines will likely not suffer unduly, although there will likely be some slowdown (anecdotal evidence from student researchers running large software packages such as IntelliJ IDEA and Firebug suggest that this sort of day-to-day student work does not suffer unduly as a result of heavy load on the cluster).

It may be necessary to only run large cluster jobs after hours, or to produce some sort of sign-up sheet or cluster schedule to avoid undue load on the host machines. However, fixes like these are easily implemented with a scheduler like TORQUE and perfectly reasonable. Small jobs running on the cluster, however, will likely have little to no impact on students working in the computer labs, so it is doubtful that in-class activities on the cluster would pose a problem. The HPCC suite consistently loaded both processors on all compute nodes at around 100%, Hadoop likewise. More reasonably sized programs written and run by students in a course on parallelism did not have the same effect on host performance.

3.5 Lessons Learned

Next we describe several somewhat technical details and lessons we learned while creating the Selkie cluster. We first and foremost advise that you start small with a few nodes in your cluster and work your way up to creating larger clusters. We have further detailed instructions for cluster setup that we have documented as we learned to do this– they can be found on http://selkie.macalester.edu.

Regarding the host machines, though we upgraded the memory to 8 GB, this may not be strictly necessary, depending on how you use the machines. However, the cost for upgrading memory is not prohibitive, so it could be quite worth the price. An account with admin privileges is needed to install VirtualBox on the hosts and to set up fixed IP addresses for each host (we created a separate account for this purpose, which could be restricted to IT staff).

The VM for the head node of the cluster is a workhorse, so we found it desirable to use a host that was not one of the machines in our public lab, but rather an additional machine that the managers of the cluster have access to and control over at any time (in the same manner as was done for MistRider).

For networking, each VM needs to be given its own IP address. For both maintenance and administration, we found it easiest to assign these manually and configure each VM to be on the same subnet. This enabled us to easily use the Ganglia tool (http://ganglia.sourceforge.net/) for visualizing the state of the cluster, which we found very helpful. The VM IP address also needs to be on the same subnet as the host (a VirtualBox requirement).

For taking care of tasks needed to run on each host or all of the exec VMs, we found the tool called clusterssh to be very useful (http://sourceforge.net/projects/clusterssh/; available for install in linux using aptget). This can run on any machine and opens ssh terminal windows to a list of machines. In one you type commands that get executed in all the open terminals to the other machines. For example, each VM for the 'execute' nodes must be given a new MAC address and have its IP address configured using VirtualBox. Using the VirtualBox GUI to do this on each host can be time consuming– we found it helpful to use the command line VboxManage tool for these tasks through clusterssh. VboxManage and clusterssh can be used this way for other management of all VMs in tandem, including configuring the 'hostnames' file and starting up each VM. One prerequisite task that this does not work for is setting up ssh for passwordless access on each VM, which is needed for clusterssh and running the TORQUE job scheduler.

We also found that it was easier to have NFS and NIS (required for a beowulf cluster and TORQUE) to be initialized after setting up the MAC addresses and IP addresses and starting each VM and properly configuring a 'hostnames' file for all nodes in the cluster. When the VM was initially configured to start NFS and NIS immediately on boot, the initial VM has the wrong hostnames file, causing NFS and NIS to be unable to locate the machines in the cluster. The VMs we provide now have NFS and NIS initially not set to start on boot. These VMs also contain an iso file for Ubuntu linux server, since cluster nodes do not need to have a GUI for user logins– each VM is run in what VirtualBox calls 'headless' mode, where ssh is the only access.

4. AVAILABILITY OF VMS, MATERIALS

The virtual machines for the head node and the execution nodes are available for download at ftp://selkie.macalester.edu. The files are in the Open Virtualization Format, which enables them to be used by a number of different virtualization vendors. We also provide instructions for using them to set up a cluster, along with scripts that have streamlined the process of configuring them on the hosts with the IP addresses unique to an institution's computing environment. Each Ubuntu linux VM has OpenMPI, TORQUE, Hadoop, and WebMapReduce installed. These are tools we have used while developing course modules for parallel computing in a variety of courses, most prominently at the introductory level [17]. These course modules are available for use at http://csinparallel.org.

5. CONCLUSION

In conclusion, a virtual cluster can be a good way to harness the power of your computer labs for using parallel and distributed computing examples in courses. By simply getting quad-core models with at least 500GB of disk and 4-8 GB of memory when you next update your lab machines, you can create a virtual cluster that has many uses in courses and as a platform for student training in system administration and maintenance.

6. REFERENCES

[1] A. Gaspar, S. Langevin, and W. Armitage, "Virtualization Technologies in the Undergraduate IT Curriculum," *IT Professional*, vol. 9, no. 4, pp. 10-17, 2007.

[2] A. Goscinski and A. Wong, "Performance evaluation of the concurrent execution of NAS parallel benchmarks with BYTE sequential benchmarks on a cluster," in *Parallel and Distributed Systems, 2005. Proceedings. 11th International Conference on*, vol. 1, pp. 313-319 Vol. 1, 2005.

[3] M. Bergman, J. Funston, and P. Glifeather-Crowley, "Low-cost compute clusters in virtualized environments," *Journal of Comuting Sciences in Colleges*, vol. 25, no. 1, pp. 159-166, Oct. 2009.

[4] R. Brown et al., "Strategies for preparing computer science students for the multicore world," in *Proceedings of the 2010 ITiCSE working group reports on Working group reports - ITiCSE-WGR '10*, p. 97, 2010.

[5] "NSF/IEEE-TCPP Curriculum Initiative on Parallel and Distributed Computing – Core Topics for Undergraduates." [Online]. Available: http://www.cs.gsu.edu/~tcpp/curriculum/index.php. [Accessed: 02-Sep-2011].

[6] R. A. Brown, "Hadoop at home: large-scale computing at a small college," in *Proceedings of the 40th ACM technical symposium on Computer science education*, pp. 106-110, 2009.

[7] "Apache Hadoop Project." [Online]. Available: http://hadoop.apache.org/. [Accessed: 01-Sep-2011].

[8] M. Johnson, R. H. Liao, A. Rasmussen, R. Sridharan, D. Garcia, and B. K. Harvey, *Infusing Parallelism into Introductory Computer Science Curriculum using MapReduce*. EECS Department, University of California, Berkeley, 2008.

[9] P. Garrity, T. Yates, R. Brown, and E. Shoop, "WebMapReduce: an accessible and adaptable tool for teaching map-reduce computing," in *Proceedings of the 42nd ACM technical symposium on Computer science education - SIGCSE '11*, p. 183, 2011.

[10] E. Johnson, P. Garrity, T. Yates, and R. Brown, "Performance of a Virtual Cluster in a General-Purpose Teaching Laboratory," in *IEEE Cluster Conference*, p. to appear, 2011.

[11] P. Luszczek et al., "Introduction to the HPC Challenge Benchmark Suite," Lawrence Berkeley National Laboratory, LBNL Paper LBNL-57493, 2005. Retreived from http://www.escholarship.org/uc/item/6sv079jp, 03-Sep-2011.

[12] "Open MPI: Open Source High Performance Computing." [Online]. Available: http://www.open-mpi.org/. [Accessed: 03-Sep-2011].

[13] "TORQUE Resource Manager." [Online]. Available: http://www.clusterresources.com/products/torque-resource-manager.php. [Accessed: 02-Sep-2011].

[14] R. Rabenseifner, "Effective I/O Bandwidth (b_eff_io) Benchmark." [Online]. Available: https://fs.hlrs.de/projects/par/mpi//b_eff_io/. [Accessed: 19-Aug-2011].

[15] R. Brown and E. Shoop, "Modules in community: injecting more parallelism into the computer science curriculum," in *Proceedings of the 42nd ACM technical symposium on Computer science education - SIGCSE '11*, p. 447, 2011.

Cross Teaching Parallelism and Ray Tracing: A Project-based Approach to Teaching Applied Parallel Computing

Chris Lupo
Computer Science Department
Cal Poly
San Luis Obispo, California, USA
clupo@calpoly.edu

Zoë J. Wood
Computer Science Department
Cal Poly
San Luis Obispo, California, USA
zwood@calpoly.edu

Christine Victorino
Department of Education
University of California
Santa Barbara, California, USA
cvictorino@education.ucsb.edu

ABSTRACT

Massively parallel *Graphics Processing Unit* (GPU) hardware has become increasingly powerful, available and affordable. Software tools have also advanced to the point that programmers can write general purpose parallel programs that take advantage of the large number of compute cores available in the hardware. With literally hundreds of compute cores available on a single device, program performance can increase by orders of magnitude. We believe that introducing students to the concepts of parallel programming for massively parallel hardware is of increasing importance in an undergraduate computer science curriculum. Furthermore, we believe that students learn best when given projects that reflect real problems in computer science.

This paper describes the experience of integrating two undergraduate computer science courses to enhance student learning in parallel computing concepts. In this cross teaching experience we structured the integration of the courses such that students studying parallel computing worked with students studying advanced rendering for approximately 30% of the quarter long courses. Working in teams on a joint project, both groups of students were able to see the application of parallelization to an existing software project with both the benefits and complications exposed early in the curriculum of both courses. Motivating projects and performance gains are discussed, as well as student survey data on the effectiveness of the learning outcomes. Both performance and survey data indicate a positive gain from the cross teaching experience.

Categories and Subject Descriptors

K.3 [**Computers and Education**]: Computer and Information Science Education; D.1.3 [**Programming Techniques**]: Concurrent Programming—*Parallel Programming*; D.2.8 [**Software Engineering**]: Metrics—*Performance Measures*; I.3 [**Computing Methodologies**]: Computer Graphics

General Terms

Design, Performance

Keywords

GPU, CUDA, Graphics

Permission to make digital or hard copies of all or part of this work for personal or classroom use is granted without fee provided that copies are not made or distributed for profit or commercial advantage and that copies bear this notice and the full citation on the first page. To copy otherwise, to republish, to post on servers or to redistribute to lists, requires prior specific permission and/or a fee.
SIGCSE'12, February 29–March 3, 2012, Raleigh, North Carolina, USA.
Copyright 2012 ACM 978-1-4503-1098-7/12/02 ...$10.00.

1. INTRODUCTION

Multicore and many-core systems have become increasingly available in a variety of compute platforms; from high-performance compute systems, to traditional workstations, to mobile devices and embedded systems. This prevalence of parallel computing hardware has increased demand for computer science graduates with a skill set that includes parallel and concurrent programming.

Likewise, there is always a demand for students who have experience with real world industrial settings, such as working in a team where team members have diverse skill sets. Thus, for three weeks of a ten week quarter, we sought to combine the lectures and lab assignments of two distinct upper division courses, CPE 458: Applied Parallel Computing and CPE/CSC 473: Advanced Rendering Techniques, in order to cross teach the material of both courses.

The material covered in the advanced rendering course primarily focuses on student's development of a large individual software project, specifically a ray tracer. This computer graphics project involves developing a large code base and complex algorithms to render (or draw) a geometric scene. The focus of the course is on rendering algorithms, however, ray tracing is an application that can benefit from parallelism, thus it was a natural pairing for this cross teaching experience.

1.1 Pedagogical Motivation

By cross teaching the courses, we sought to expose the distinct student populations to relevant course material and a team development experience, while not sacrificing their in-depth learning of each individual sub-field of computer science. Specifically, we sought to expose the students in the rendering course to the potential of speeding up their code using parallel programming and to likewise expose the parallel computing students to a large real software project in need of parallelization. The experience exposed each group of students to a different sub-field of computer science and more importantly exposed those students to a scenario where they were required to share their learning with one another in concrete cross course projects.

1.2 Setting

Teaching students effective multicore programming is a challenge even with a relatively small number of cores [2]. However, recent *Graphics Processing Unit* (GPU) implementations allow a programmer access to hundreds of compute cores on a single device [10]. The cost of these devices has become affordable to many academic institutions for deployment in computer laboratories and GPU technology can be used effectively for general purpose computing [8, 12].

NVIDIA Corporation, one of the leading designers of GPU systems, has developed a program for universities to incorporate their *Compute Unified Device Architecture* (CUDA) technology into computer science curricula. California Polytechnic State University in San Luis Obispo, where the work described in this paper was performed, is part of NVIDIA's CUDA Teaching Center program [9].

Graphics computations are well suited to GPU computing, so the integration of an applied parallel computing course with an emphasis on GPU computing and an advanced rendering course can occur quite naturally. With this in mind, for the 4–6th week of the quarter, the two courses were joined together for lectures, labs and project assignments.

1.3 Research Methodology

Our research method for evaluating the contribution of cross teaching the two courses involved two measures, student surveys and student project performance. All students were required to submit two surveys, pre-cross teaching and post. These surveys were used to evaluate student's self-reported progress with learning outcomes and attitude towards the course material. In addition, students were required to submit lab reports documenting the change in the performance of their software. Students were required to profile and optimize their projects on the CPU and measure time performance with various test cases and then to profile and optimize their solution using CUDA and GPU computing.

1.4 Contributions

- We present our experience in integrating an applied parallel computing course and an advanced rendering course to provide students with a real-world application of parallel computing.
- We present performance data from students in the courses demonstrating the performance gain for the software projects.
- We present student survey data on the effectiveness of this integrated course structure in learning parallel computing and advanced rendering concepts.

2. COURSE STRUCTURE

Two senior-level computer science courses were cross taught for 30% of the Spring quarter of 2011 (weeks 4–6 of the ten-week quarter). Each course had approximately 35 students in senior or graduate standing. The courses were CPE 458: Applied Parallel Computing and CPE/CSC 473: Advanced Rendering Techniques.

2.1 Applied Parallel Computing

Taught by Professor Lupo, the applied parallel computing course used the CUDA development environment as the setting to teach parallel applications. Specifically, parallelism was taught using NVIDIA GeForce 470 GPUs, each having 448 compute cores. GPUs utilize a *Single-Program Multiple-Data* (SPMD) architecture where a single program thread is executed in parallel on multiple processing units. This architecture is similar to SIMD architectures where a single instruction is executed in parallel. However, the GPU does not guarantee instruction level synchronization across compute cores.

The learning outcomes of the applied parallel computing course include:

- Analyze applications that benefit from massive amounts of parallelism.
- Become familiar with contemporary parallel programming paradigms and the systems on which they are used.
- Gain significant experience with GPU computing hardware and programming models, with specific emphasis on NVIDIA's CUDA architecture.
- Analyze and measure performance of modern parallel computing systems.
- Analyze the impact of communication latency and resource contention on throughput.
- Master basic parallel computation with the CUDA programming model.

Prior to being integrated with the other course, students in the applied parallel computing course were assigned a project to implement parallel matrix multiplication. The goals of the initial project were to familiarize the students with the language features and development tools necessary to parallelize applications to run on a GPU, and to gain experience identifying portions of a program to parallelize to improve performance. The assignment had three deliverables;

1. a high performance sequential implementation on a modern CPU,
2. a parallel implementation using OpenMP on a multi-core CPU with eight cores, and
3. a working implementation on a NVIDIA GeForce GTX 470 GPU using the CUDA architecture.

Students were allowed to work on this project in teams of two students.

Figure 1 shows the average class results of both runtime and overall speedup for the matrix multiplication project. Speedup is relative to the sequential CPU runtime. The average performance improvement of the GPU implementation was 27.2 times faster than the average sequential execution time. Some teams had a speedup of greater than 50, and every team saw performance improvement.

This project helped ensure that the students in the applied parallel computing course knew the basics of parallelizing a program for execution on a GPU prior to being integrated with students in the other course.

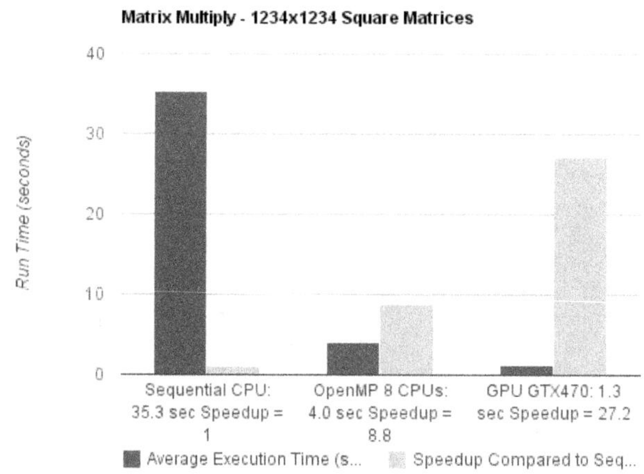

Figure 1: Matrix multiplication project results from CPE 458 prior to cross teaching.

2.2 Advanced Rendering

Taught by Professor Wood, the learning outcomes of the advanced rendering course include:

- Master basic ray tracing algorithms (camera transformations, intersections, lighting, geometry transforms, anti-aliasing, shadows, reflection, and refraction)
- Exposure to global illumination algorithms (including Monte-Carlo ray tracing and photon mapping)
- Develop large software project in C++
- Develop an individual rendering project beyond the class ray tracer
- Excite students about topics related to rendering and computer graphics

Prior to being integrated with the other course, students in the advanced rendering course were assigned a project to begin their ray tracer program, written from scratch in C++. This initial software developed by the students was the core code to be used throughout the quarter, including during the cross teaching of parallelism. The students software at the point of integration, included the ability to:

1. parse a Pov-Ray formatted scene file and construct appropriate data structures to represent the camera, lights and any scene geometry
2. complete a ray-cast and intersection with spheres and planes
3. write out result images in a standard image format (e.g. bmp or png)

2.3 Cross Teaching Experience

During the three week cross teaching experience, lectures were shared between the two faculty, Professor Lupo and Wood and covered a brief exposure to background information and new material to both student groups. Students formed teams of at least two and at most three members, with each team consisting of at least one student from each course in order to complete the required cross course projects. Teams met during one of two lab times to work together on their two main joint assignments during the cross teaching experience.

We defined specific learning outcomes for the students for the cross teaching experience (see Appendix A) and our general goals included encouraging students to:

- Practice team-work and collaboration
- Build upon and enhance initial software together as a team
- Create software extensible by a team
- Share knowledge in teams including members with different backgrounds and expertise
- See the benefit of parallel programming on ray tracing
- Experience pair programming
- Experience another teacher's style

2.4 Cross Teaching Student Projects

Students from both courses were assigned two large lab assignments to be completed in teams. In general these projects were intended to allow the students to develop a ray tracer which off-loaded geometry intersections to the GPU to speedup rendering times. Students from the two different courses were expected to help one another with understanding ray tracing and CUDA. It is worth noting that the two student groups had significantly less exposure to the alternate course material (approximately 3 weeks versus a single background lecture). This created a situation where students relied on one another to teach each other specifics about CUDA and ray tracing.

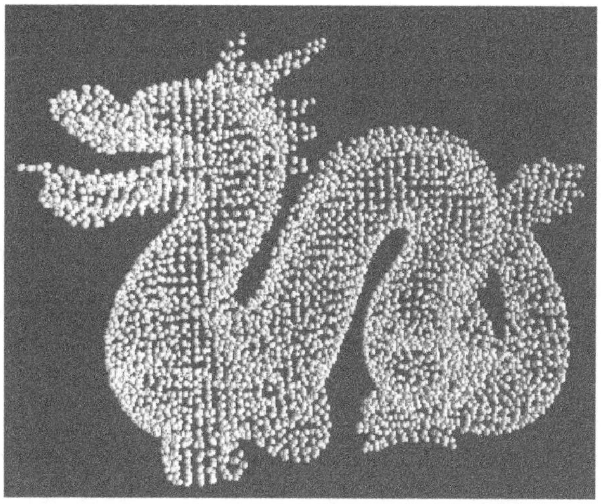

Figure 2: A ray traced rendering of the dragon model with approximately five thousand spheres.

2.4.1 Lab 1: Ray Tracing with CUDA

The initial project that students were assigned was designed to acquaint the advanced rendering students with the compute power of the GPU and the versatility of the CUDA framework and vice-versa to expose applied parallel programming students to the realities of applying CUDA to a real-world application. At a high level, the first ray cast in a ray tracing algorithm is highly parallel in that little synchronization is needed between threads, and is scalable enough to run on hundreds or thousands of cores at once.

Students were given a variety of large scenes with 5,000 to 36,000 spheres and asked to render an image of 640 by 480 pixels using their existing ray tracers. Rendering such a scene with non-optimized CPU code took an average of 6 minutes for the largest scene (with some team's code taking

35 minutes to complete the render). See Figure 2 for an example of 5,000 sphere model.

Students were required to take their existing CPU code and:

1. profile their code to determine the function or functions where the largest percentage of execution time is spent,
2. optimize their CPU code (for example through in-lining, etc. where appropriate)
3. prepare their code for the GPU,
4. outsource intersection tests to the GPU
5. compile the results, and
6. measure the speedup of the GPU implementation.

For this portion of the project, the students were given considerable guidance on how to approach the design so that they could focus on how to parallelize the intersection testing portion of their ray tracers.

A primary educational objective was for students to use a systems engineering approach to look at where their code could best be optimized for parallel execution through the use of profiling and to educate students about the power of profiling.

2.4.2 Lab 2: Triangle Intersections and Anti-aliasing

For this second portion of the project, students were given less guidance so they could have the experience of designing a parallel implementation based on their existing knowledge and experience. This portion of the project was also team-based, with students continuing to work with their established teams.

The students continued with building a ray tracer on both the CPU and GPU. Teams were required to add code to their implementations to intersect rays with triangles and add anti-aliasing to their code (super-sampling of 4 more stratified sampled rays per pixel).

Task assignments were given such that team members would add to their existing skill sets and learn new material rather than repeating procedures they had already learned prior to the course integration. In doing so, it was also recommended that students in each team teach their other team members to reinforce what each student had already learned prior to the course integration.

To best integrate the team's knowledge, in a pair programming style, the applied parallel computing student member(s) of the teams were tasked with writing the triangle intersection routine for the CPU. The advanced rendering team member(s) were tasked with writing the GPU version of the triangle intersection code. The CPU implementation is used for reference execution speed and profiling of the code to determine which functions should be outsourced to the GPU. Outsourcing of triangle intersection tests to the GPU was a requirement of this portion of the project, and each team's implementation was required to handle input files that have both a mix of triangles and spheres. Students were also required to add anti-aliasing to their implementations.

Each team had to test and profile their code with both the CPU only implementation, and the CUDA implementation that outsourced intersections to the GPU. Measurement of speedup of rendering for a given input file with a large number of triangles and spheres was required in the final report for the project.

Figure 3: A ray traced rendering of the Stanford Bunny model with 70K triangles and 36K spheres.

2.5 Student Project Results

Students were able to complete the assigned projects and achieve impressive speedups of their rendering times. Lab assignments required students to render various high resolution models, for example a 70,000 triangle model of the 'Stanford Bunny' (see Figure 3). All final images were required to be 640 by 480 pixels. Figures 2 and 3 show examples of the renders produced by student's code. For Lab 1, students were required to render a bunny model that included 36,000 spheres. Team's results varied but time improvements from off loading sphere intersections to the GPU resulted in time improvements from 6 times faster to 1000 times faster, with the average speed up of 354 times faster rendering.

For the second lab which included models that featured both triangles and spheres, CPU timings to render the 70,000 triangle bunny model, called 'bunny jumbo', averaged 19.6 minutes (with teams times ranging from around 7 minutes to 40 minutes). Allowing students to see that such a simple setting with a single complex model, required such long render times motivated them to parallelize their code to help speedup run times. After off loading the triangle intersections to the GPU, teams on average only had to wait 14.4 seconds for the 'bunny jumbo' file to render. This represents an average speed up of 82 times faster. This lesson was further emphasized when students added anti-aliasing to their program (adding 4 rays per pixel). Anti-aliasing creates much smoother, aesthetically pleasing images but adding four times as many rays resulted in average CPU run times of 91 minutes! However, with the use of the GPU the same rendering on average took 44.2 seconds for a team pairwise average speedup of 204 times faster. Figure 4 shows a scatter plot of different teams' speedups of the average CPU time versus each team's GPU timings for the anti-aliasing portion of Lab 2. There were 18 teams in the combined class. However, one team was unable to finish their anti-aliasing

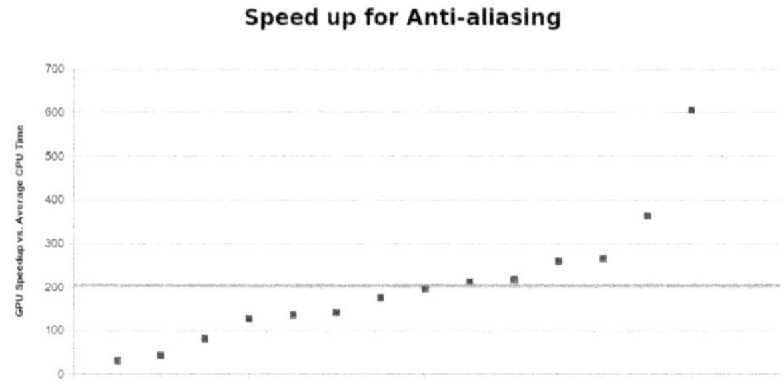

Figure 4: Scatter plot of student teams' render time speedup for the anti-aliasing portion of Lab 2. Note that students obtained impressive speedups on average of 204 times faster.

Table 1: Data for pairs of learning outcomes from pre and post survey results, surveyed before and after course integration. A two-tailed paired-samples t-test indicated positive significant gains on all learning outcomes, except for learning outcomes three and four.

pair	Pre Mean	Post Mean	t	df	Sig. (< .001)
LO1	2.09	4.04	-9.858	44	.00
LO2	1.67	3.24	-8.453	44	.00
LO3	3.8	4.18	-1.828	44	.07
LO4	4.27	4.00	1.219	44	.23
LO5	3.4	4.38	-4.896	44	.00
LO6	2.82	4.04	-5.500	44	.00
LO7	2.91	4.16	-5.442	42	.00
LO8	2.66	4.39	-8.162	43	.00
LO9	3.02	4.13	-5.976	44	.00
LO10	2.84	3.82	-4.149	43	.00

implementation on the GPU, and three teams were unable to get CPU run times due to their implementations taking too long to run prior to the assignment being submitted.

These impressive improvements to performance illustrate the successful migration of the student's CPU code to the GPU. In the post-survey, 97% of the students reported that their ray tracer was significantly faster using parallelism and that they were able to create images of substantially more complex scenes in reasonable amounts of time using parallelism. In addition, 91% felt they were able to enhance the realistic appearance of their output using anti-aliasing without a substantial time penalty using parallelism. Finally, 46.7% reported that they were interested in doing a final project related to parallelism and ray tracing after the cross teaching experience.

3. RESULTS AND CONCLUSION

Specific learning outcomes were designed to assess the course integration experience. Pre- and post-surveys examined the extent to which students achieved these learning outcomes on a five-point Likert-type scale (i.e., 1- Strongly Disagree, 2 - Disagree, 3 - Neither Agree nor Disagree, 4 - Agree, 5 - Strongly Agree). Using a two-tailed paired-samples t-test to compare pre- and post-survey means, results indicated that eight of the ten learning outcomes had positive, significant increases in the mean from pre-course integration to post-course integration ($p < .001$). All learning outcomes are listed in Appendix A. See Table 3 for details.

Both the performance gains achieved by students in their program and the survey data analysis all point to very positive outcomes from the cross teaching of the two courses. Students were uniformly able to see large speedups in their code using parallelization and students were able to cross over their knowledge from each individual course and gain valuable knowledge from one another about two distinct subfields of computer science. In addition, we feel the experience allowed us to achieve all of our general goals of the cross teaching experience, such as working in a team that required sharing knowledge with teammates, experiencing pair programming and another teacher's style.

More importantly, their experience of having their code be expanded by a classmate and needing to explain individual knowledge in a team setting gave students a hand-on experience often found in the computer science industry. From the post survey, some of the student's comments include: "Great "real world" experience." and "I enjoyed the experience of working with another student with different knowledge from another related course and combining it to create something cool."

Of course the cross teaching of the two different courses was not without its complications. As one student said: "I think the results that came from both joint labs were super amazing. Being able to see how implementing certain areas of code would affect performance was very informative. I suggest a more streamlined integration into the joint labs. This means preparing the initial ray tracers with parallelism in mind, and earlier coverage of CUDA for 458 students."

In the end the students had the first hand chance to experience much of what is difficult about real world projects. Their starting code was not perfect (it was written in C++ and needed to be converted to C) and the team members had different strengths (with one team member being better prepared for the CUDA aspects of the lab, while the other student had a better understanding of the ray tracer code).

As faculty, there are small modifications we could make to the lab assignments and team balancing that would further enhance the students learning, but overall, working together required everyone to expand their knowledge, which was the desired effect. In the future we hope to continue our collaboration of sharing course content and allowing the students to experience the joy of teaching one another. One improvement we could make in our analysis of the cross-teaching would be the inclusion of a pre and post cross teaching academic quiz related to the desired learning outcomes.

4. RELATED WORK

The teaching of parallel computing in computer science with a motivating application is certainly not a new endeavor. In 1992, Kitchen et al. described the use of game playing as a technique for teaching parallel computing concepts [4]. In 1995, Nevison described an approach to teaching parallelism in which each course in the curriculum provides a small contribution to the overall objective of understanding parallel computing [7]. More recently, Rebbi describes a project-oriented course in computational physics to teach parallel computing concepts [13]. In 2008, Breen et al. describe the use of ray tracing as an example application to introduce what they refer to as "embarrassingly parallel" computing [1]. In 2011, Ortiz described the teaching of concurrency oriented programming with the Erlang language [11].

Many computer science educators are in general agreement that the SIMD model is an important component of parallel computing education, and that many-cored GPU technology is a cost-effective way for universities to provide powerful compute hardware to students for hands-on experimentation [5, 14, 15, 16].

An entire course curriculum based on GPU computing and the CUDA model was developed into a textbook by Kirk and Hwu in 2010 [3]. Developing a ray tracer in CUDA is described in considerable detail in a collection of papers presented in a recent book collection [6].

The cross teaching experience described in this paper is complementary to prior research, and may be successfully employed in a variety of courses in which faculty recognize an opportunity for students to learn about parallel computing.

As far as we know, this is the first time that two distinct upper division computer science courses were combined to teach these concepts, with students expected to master the distinct course concepts in depth while working on a related project in the alternate sub-field.

APPENDIX

A. LEARNING OUTCOMES

Learning outcomes for the cross-teaching experience included:

1. Understand and apply basic ray tracing algorithms (e.g., camera transformations, intersections, shadows, reflections).
2. Identify global illumination algorithms (e.g., Monte Carlo ray tracing, photon mapping).
3. Able to develop a software project in C++.
4. Interested in topics related to rendering and computer graphics.
5. Able to analyze applications that benefit from parallelism.
6. Identify contemporary parallel programming paradigms and the systems on which they are used.
7. Identify GPU computing hardware and programming models (e.g., NVIDIA's CUDA architecture).
8. Able to conduct basic parallel computation with the CUDA programming model.
9. Able to analyze and measure performance of modern parallel computing systems.
10. Able to determine the impact of communication latency and resource contention on throughput.

B. ACKNOWLEDGMENTS

We would especially like to thank Bob Somers and Chris Gibson for their service as teaching assistants. Their help in preparing our combined laboratory assignments and working with the students was incredibly valuable. We also thank Cal Poly's Computer Science Department for supporting us in this educational experiment, and handling the scheduling of our two courses. Additionally, we are also thankful to NVIDIA Corporation for the CUDA Teaching Center program and their support in helping us bring CUDA and GPU computing into Cal Poly's curriculum.

C. REFERENCES

[1] B. J. Breen, C. E. Weidert, J. F. Lindner, L. M. Walker, K. Kelly, and E. Heidtmann. Invitation to embarrassingly parallel computing. *American Journal of Physics*, 76(4):347–352, 2008.

[2] T. Chen, Q. Shi, J. Wang, and N. Bao. Multicore challenge in pervasive computing education. In *Grid and Pervasive Computing Workshops, 2008. GPC Workshops '08. The 3rd International Conference on*, pages 310 –315, May 2008.

[3] D. B. Kirk and W. mei W. Hwu. *Programming Massively Parallel Processors*. Morgan Kaufmann, 2010.

[4] A. T. Kitchen, N. C. Schaller, and P. T. Tymann. Game playing as a technique for teaching parallel computing concepts. *SIGCSE Bull.*, 24:35–38, September 1992.

[5] A. Marowka. Think parallel: Teaching parallel programming today. *Distributed Systems Online, IEEE*, 9(8):1, August 2008.

[6] W. mei W. Hwu. *GPU Computing Gems, Emerald Edition*. Morgan Kaufmann, 2011.

[7] C. H. Nevison. Parallel computing in the undergraduate curriculum. *Computer*, 28(12):51 –56, December 1995.

[8] J. Nickolls and W. J. Dally. The GPU computing era. *Micro, IEEE*, 30(2):56 –69, March-April 2010.

[9] NVIDIA Corporation. CUDA Teaching Center Program. `http://research.nvidia.com/content/cuda-teaching-center-ctc-program`.

[10] NVIDIA Corporation. Supercomputing with NVIDIA Tesla. `http://www.nvidia.com/object/tesla_computing_solutions.html`.

[11] A. Ortiz. Teaching concurrency-oriented programming with erlang. In *Proceedings of the 42nd ACM technical symposium on Computer science education*, SIGCSE '11, pages 195–200, New York, NY, USA, 2011. ACM.

[12] J. D. Owens, D. Luebke, N. Govindaraju, M. Harris, J. Krüger, A. Lefohn, and T. J. Purcell. A survey of general-purpose computation on graphics hardware. *Computer Graphics Forum*, 26(1):80–113, 2007.

[13] C. Rebbi. A project-oriented course in computational physics: Algorithms, parallel computing, and graphics. *American Journal of Physics*, 76(4):314–320, 2008.

[14] S. Rivoire. A breadth-first course in multicore and manycore programming. In *Proceedings of the 41st ACM Technical Symposium on Computer Science education*, SIGCSE '10, pages 214–218, New York, NY, USA, 2010. ACM.

[15] C. Sadowski, T. Ball, J. Bishop, S. Burckhardt, G. Gopalakrishnan, J. Mayo, M. Musuvathi, S. Qadeer, and S. Toub. Practical parallel and concurrent programming. In *Proceedings of the 42nd ACM technical symposium on Computer science education*, SIGCSE '11, pages 189–194, New York, NY, USA, 2011. ACM.

[16] G. Wolffe and C. Trefftz. Teaching parallel computing: new possibilities. *Journal of Computing Sciences in Colleges*, 25:21–28, October 2009.

Cabana: A Cross-platform Mobile Development System

Paul E. Dickson
Hampshire College
School of Cognitive Science
893 West St.
Amherst, MA 01002, USA
pdickson@hampshire.edu

ABSTRACT

Mobile application development is a hot topic in computer science education, and debate rages over which platform to develop on and what software to use for development. Cabana is a web-based application designed to enable development on multiple mobile platforms and to make application development easier. It uses an approach to application programming based on a wiring diagram that is supplemented with the ability to program directly using JavaScript. It is an ideal choice for application development in introductory computer science courses and for upper-level courses where the focus is on application design and not application programming. This paper introduces Cabana and describes its use in two different computer science courses.

Categories and Subject Descriptors

K.3.2 [**Computers and Education**]: Computer and Information Science EducationComputer Science Education; D.1.7 [**Programming Techniques**]: Visual Programming

General Terms

Design, Languages

Keywords

Cabana, iPhone, Android, AppInventor, Xcode, Mobile Devices, apps, Smartphone

1. INTRODUCTION

Mobile device application development is a hot topic and to judge by the number of papers published about mobile development [1, 2, 3, 4, 5, 6, 7, 9, 11], a growing part of computer science education. Students are excited about and are asking for courses in it and faculty are scrambling to build those courses. Departments see mobile application development as a way to attract new students to computer science while providing a fertile environment for teaching fundamental computer science topics like memory management, networking, human-computer interaction, etc. The question is usually not whether a course should be offered in a computer science department but whether mobile application development should be integrated into existing courses or be a stand-alone course.

Many questions remain to be answered, one of the biggest being which platform to develop on. Apple has a free university program but this requires the school to own Apple hardware and sign a licensing agreements. Android is free to develop on but does not have the same application market as Apple [8]. Blackberry and other platforms exist but they have the same problem as iOS and Android: once you decide to develop for one platform you are locked into it unless you want to learn a second environment. Another choice would be to develop web applications using HTML5, which would run on all platforms, but in that case students would be taking a web design course and not a mobile applications course. In this paper we discuss Cabana, a piece of software for developing mobile applications that currently creates mobile web applications that can run on any smartphone browser and that will soon be able to create native applications for both iPhone and Android.

Cabana was developed by Department of Behavior and Logic, Inc. (DOBL) and is currently in beta testing. It is available at https://www.cabanaapp.com/. We used it in classes at Hampshire College for an academic year as it progressed from alpha to beta testing. Cabana is designed to make app development easier and uses an approach based on a wiring diagram for linking different code modules together. Cabana comes with a set of code modules that give basic programming functionality (if-then statements, for loops, counters, etc.) but also allows the user to create modules where the functionality is defined using JavaScript.

Our experience with Cabana has been that it is far easier to use in a classroom environment than is Apple's Xcode and that it makes mobile application development accessible to even a CS0 audience. We have found that it makes it possible to build a course that focuses on mobile application development and not on learning to program in a specific SDK. Cabana is a web-based application and therefore is cross-platform and it includes a simulator. It requires no hardware to be acquired since the web applications can be tested on any mobile device with a browser, something many students and faculty already own.

In this paper we describe how Cabana works and provide examples of the development environment. We also discuss how Cabana functioned in the classroom, both its strengths and weaknesses. We make the case that Cabana should be

Permission to make digital or hard copies of all or part of this work for personal or classroom use is granted without fee provided that copies are not made or distributed for profit or commercial advantage and that copies bear this notice and the full citation on the first page. To copy otherwise, to republish, to post on servers or to redistribute to lists, requires prior specific permission and/or a fee.
SIGCSE'12, February 29–March 3, 2012, Raleigh, North Carolina, USA.
Copyright 2012 ACM 978-1-4503-1098-7/12/02 ...$10.00.

considered as an alternative method for developing mobile applications and not that it is the only solution.

2. RELATED WORK

A lot of ground work has been done with regard to development of courses that include mobile application development. This work has not led to any type of a consensus though because of factors of environment and the goals of the courses. A snapshot of the approaches to mobile application development and the strengths and weaknesses of each gives a good background as to why it is so hard to determine the best platform and environment to use.

Rogers [9] and Ivanov [4] did a great job of describing what is required to teach an iPhone development course. They describe the process of becoming a part of the Apple University program and what is required in terms of hardware and software. Ivanov in particular describes some of the issues of working with a developing platform and describes the problems created when Apple updated Xcode and iOS part way through the semester, changing Xcode functionality and portions of the SDK requiring revisions of the course plan. Some of the difficulties in learning the iOS SDK and Xcode environment including the need to learn Objective-C and Cocoa Touch are also discussed.

The question of whether to work on the Android platform instead of Apple's iOS has also been covered [2, 3]. Whereas Goadrich et al. [3] simply describe the benefits of one platform versus another, Fenwick et al. [2] encourage movement away from iOS because of how locked a platform it is. Both make the argument that a platform choice should be influenced by what hardware is present on campus. Good points are made about cost of development on given platforms, programming language restrictions, software requirements, etc. Fenwick et al. make the additional comparison to mobile web applications and describe the attractiveness of their being platform independent while mentioning that this does make it harder, in some cases impossible, to access on device hardware like GPS, sound, camera, etc. This is not to say that iOS and Android are the only platforms, as Mahmoud et al. [7] have done great work building a toolkit to make teaching mobile application development on the Blackberry easier and have shown how to integrate Blackberry development into a large number of courses.

Substantial work has also gone into making mobile application development easier. Wolber [11] describes Google's App Inventor and how it can be used to teach mobile application development and focuses on how easy and accessible App Inventor makes programming applications for Android. Great detail is given to the block programming method used that does not require/allow the user to write code. Using App Inventor for introductory courses has become sufficiently mainstream to have been discussed at SIGCSE in 2010 [10].

Others have focused primarily on how application development can be used to motivate students in a standard computer science curriculum [5, 6]. Kurkovsky [5] talks about using mobile game development to motivate computer science topics. He emphasizes how the mobile devices get students excited and give them a platform that helps them to connect concepts like computer networking, database management, etc. to the real world. Loveland [6] talks about integrating Android development into a human-computer interaction course. She talks about doing web development using the Google Web Toolkit to develop applications and then running those applications on an Android simulator.

3. BACKGROUND

Our initial decision to do application development in the classroom was in Fall 2009 when we decided to use iOS as the platform for a video game development course [1]. We were led to this decision to use the iPhone as a platform for a variety of reasons, the most important being that it would excite our students and limit the scope of games they could create and because we are primarily an Apple-based campus. Our approach to preparing the course was similar to that of Ivanov and Rogers [4, 9].

While students liked the course and felt like they learned a lot, they and the faculty found that the iOS platform got in the way of teaching video game design. With Apple updating Xcode 3 times during the semester, the class became experts in installing the latest 5GB download. Also, references and tutorials were often out of date within a month of being written, making it a constant scramble to try to keep course material up to date. Concepts as simple as flipping between different screens could take upwards of an hour to describe and demonstrate in class because of the amount of back end coding and SDK knowledge required. This meant that the course ended up being a 50% iOS and 50% game design course. That is not to say that students do not gain a lot from exposure to a real-world environment where platforms can change rapidly but instead to point out that the this was not the education in video game design we were hoping to give to our students in this course.

With this in mind, we started looking for a new development platform for our video game design course and for the mobile application course that we wanted to develop that would focus on design and human-computer interaction and not on programming. We did not seriously consider moving to Android because our students are primarily Apple based. In the three courses we have now taught that used mobile devices, we have averaged 1-2 students per course who have had an Android compared with the 85% who own iPhones or iTouches. We did not want to shift to a web-based application development platform that would be as much for web development as mobile development because we felt we would lose student interest if we did not have a tight mobile focus.

This led to our collaboration with DOBL, a company cofounded by one of our alumni. DOBL was developing an application that was intended to make it easier to build mobile applications and that would enable users to develop for multiple mobile platforms. They did not intend to have their applications compile cross-platform but instead to be module based so when you were developing for iOS you would include the iOS touch module whereas when developing for Android you would include the Android touch module. This seemed to be the best option for us since we hoped it would give us the ease of programming found with App Inventor while still enabling us to interact with the Apple devices our students primarily have.

4. CABANA

By the time we started working with Cabana it had become a browser-based application. We alpha tested it in our first class that used it and early beta tested it in our second. For much of this time, our students were the only users working with Cabana. The specific details of our classroom experiences using Cabana are described after a description of how Cabana works.

The best way of showing the Cabana environment is to build a simple application in Cabana. We will do this in two parts; first we will build an application that flips between screens by pressing buttons; next we will add a JavaScript node that implements the Pythagorean theorem. The first application was chosen to demonstrate Cabana since the simple flipping between screens took an hour to teach during class using Xcode and iOS but only about 5 minutes in Cabana. The applications are kept to the minimum with no effort put into styling or formatting in order to keep them simple.

4.1 Screen-flipping Application

When starting an application in Cabana, you are asked to choose between a multi-screen application and a single-screen application and whether you want it to be landscape or portrait. We chose a multi-screen portrait application and the software opened a view similar to that seen in Figure 1. The left side of the screen gives an overview of the application and the right side contains information and components that can be added to the interface on the left. All Cabana applications begin with a start screen and then shift to the application screen. We added a second screen and drew lines between the screens that control movement between them and labeled Forward and Back. The names represent actions that can be called from the code so that when the action forward is called in the application screen, the application will shift to the added screen.

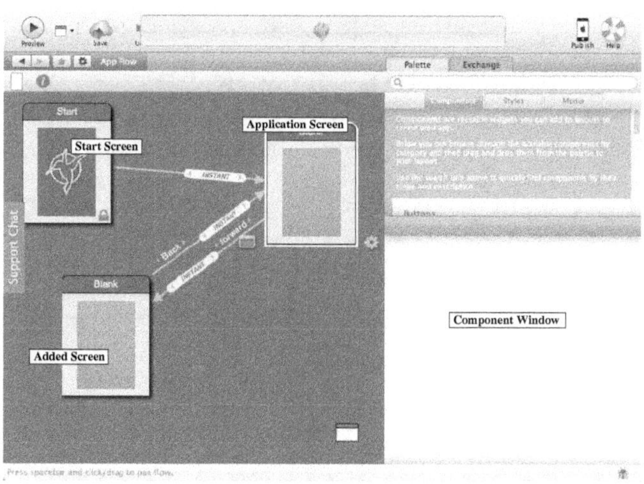

Figure 1: Overall application flow.

The user then interacts with a specific screen by double clicking on it to get an enlargement (Figure 2). A list of components on the right gives the user options of different objects that can be added to the screen like the button we have added. All components are dragged from the component list to the desired location on the screen. Below the list of components appears a list of options that can be set for a given component that has been added to the screen.

Since we want to use the button to jump from the application screen to the added screen, we need to link it to the

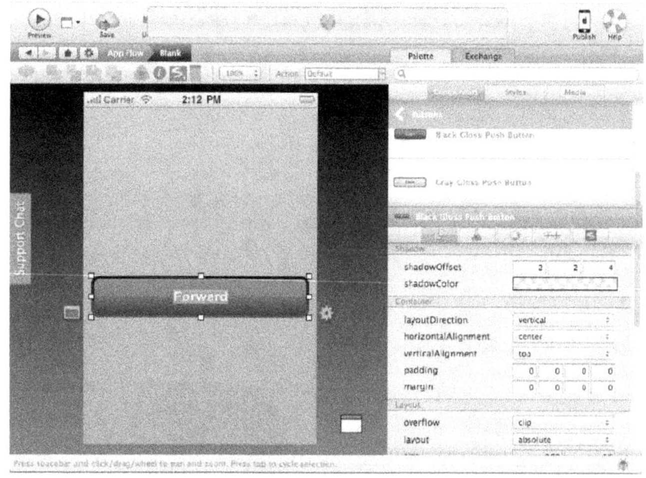

Figure 2: Screen layout with Cabana tools.

code that controls the application. We do this by clicking on the rectangular symbol at the lower left corner of the item (the button in Figure 2) we wish to punch through to our wiring diagram (Figure 3). All Cabana logic and control is handled by wiring diagrams. Again, the components (nodes) are available on the right side of the screen and the wiring is shown on the left. The large box is the wiring for the button and the smaller box is a node that we have added that fires an action, in this case calling forward to send us to the added screen. This is accomplished by connecting the touched signal on the button box to the fire signal on the action box. We specify that the action to run is forward by connecting forward to the action to fire input on the action box. This is all that is required to create an application that shifts from one screen to another with a button push. The application can be previewed or published with a push of a button. Demonstrating this process takes about 5 minutes versus the approximately 60 minutes needed for Xcode. Some of the reasons this takes so long in Xcode is that new files need to be created for the new screen, code needs to be written that relies on a solid knowledge of the iOS SDK, and the code needs to be linked into the interface builder.

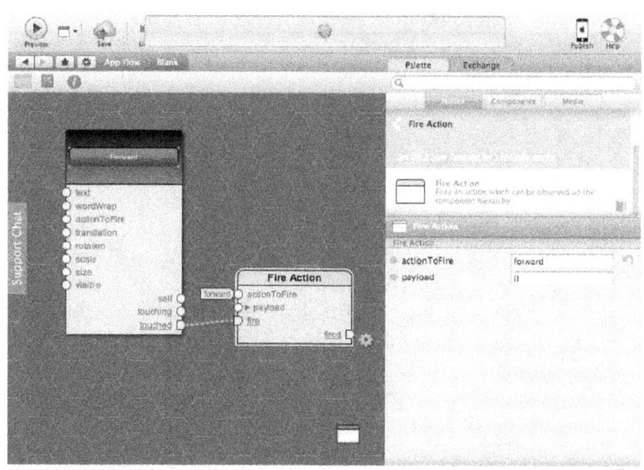

Figure 3: Wiring diagram with Cabana tools.

4.2 Pythagorean Theorem Application

The example of building an application to run the Pythagorean theorem is given to show how JavaScript nodes function. The basic layout of the application was created by dragging and dropping the desired fields onto the screen (Figure 4). Each component is punched through to the wiring diagram (Figure 5). The text written into each text field and the signal from the buttons touched are linked to the sampleNode, which is a custom JavaScript node, and its result is connected to the display text area. The inputs and outputs of the JavaScript node are specified in the JavaScript node (Figure 6).

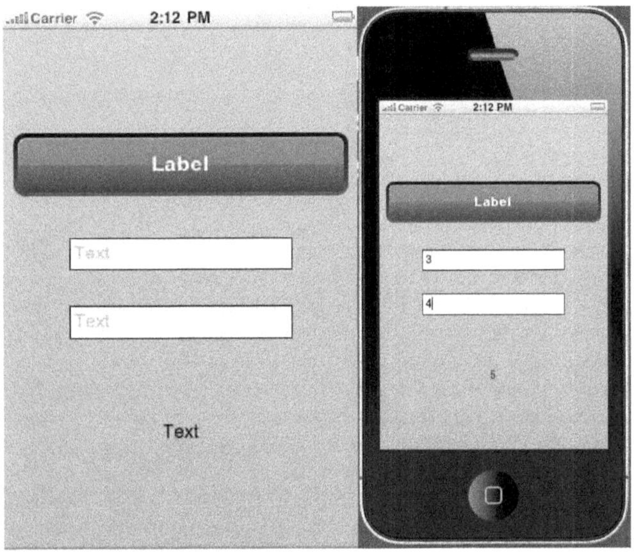

Figure 4: Enlarged screen layout and application preview.

By double clicking the JavaScript node, users enter an editing node that enables them to label the node and write JavaScript to specify how that node will work. Figure 6 shows an enlargement of this editing window with the top being where the control is specified while the bottom specifies the input and output types. Inputs and outputs are defined as either signals or data where the data is specified by data type. The function of the node is defined using standard JavaScript; sample output of this application can be found in Figure 4.

5. COURSES

The decision to use Cabana in our video game development course was made in Spring 2010 when DOBL assured us that it would be ready by the start of Fall 2010. We had a student intern with DOBL over the summer of 2010 to ensure that we would have an on-site expert for the system. As a result of our experiences using Cabana in the video game design course, we next decided to use it for our inaugural mobile application course.

One point to consider is the makeup of computer science courses at Hampshire College. We do not have set majors so there is no way to guarantee student background for our classes. Even though these courses are upper level, the only restriction placed upon students is that they must have had at least one programming course. This means that some

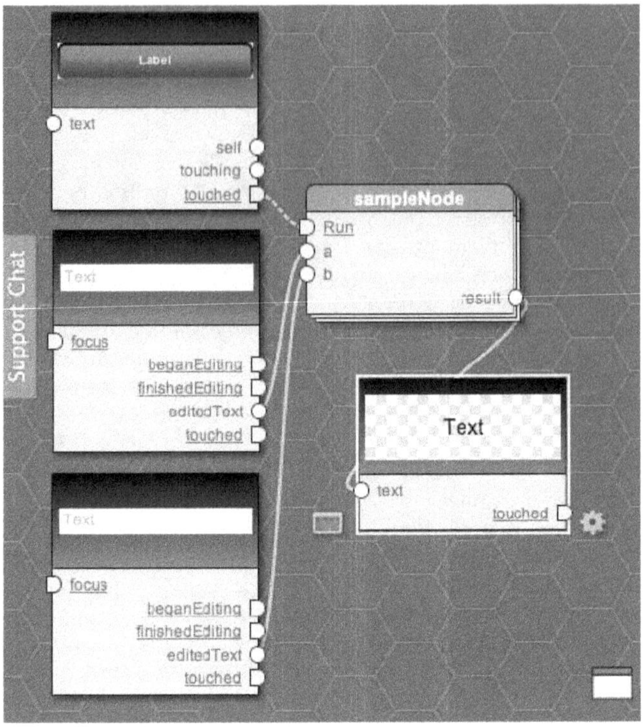

Figure 5: Enlarged wiring diagram with JavaScript node.

of the students in these courses have only a high school programming background while others have nearly complete computer science majors. This has a large effect on the work and expectations for our classes.

5.1 Video Game Development

We began the semester with an early alpha version of Cabana and with only our student who had interned at DOBL having a good handle on how Cabana worked. Cabana being in early alpha testing had a large number of bugs and large parts of it were rewritten during the semester. Whenever bugs were discovered, DOBL quickly worked to fix them for us.

Cabana was not a complete success for this game development course. Cabana is intended for making applications and not games and so support for high-level graphics, quick responses, character spawners, etc. did not exist. Also, large-scale revisions of Cabana often broke code that had been written by students weeks earlier. These difficulties were not that different from those experienced with iOS and Xcode, which are also under constant refinement. Students did seem to pick up Cabana far faster than they had iOS and Xcode the previous semester and this enabled us to focus the course more fully on video games.

Despite the setbacks, Cabana was not a complete failure. At the end of the video game design course that used Xcode, only 2 of 5 student groups within the class had games that could be played on the iPhone. At the end of the semester using Cabana, 4 out of 5 groups had working games. While many of the students complained about the constant updates and bugs within Cabana, all who had done equivalent work with iOS found that Cabana, although frustrating, was enormously easier to use than Xcode.

Figure 6: JavaScript node code.

5.2 Mobile Application Development

Based on our experience with Cabana in the game development course, we decided to use it for our mobile application course. The fact that Cabana was moving into beta testing and that mobile applications are its intended market suggested that we would have greater success. The focus of the mobile application course was on the development process and human-computer interaction and not on the details of programming mobile applications, though students would be expected to do this. Roughly one-third of the students in the mobile application course had taken the video game design course the semester before and had experience with Cabana.

Cabana turned out to be a huge success for this course. Students found it easy to work and develop with Cabana. The wiring-based logic was a little complicated for students to pick up at first but soon became second nature. Our students were able to rapidly build application and test them. With the ease of building simple applications, our students were able to build Tamagotchis in under a week. This made it possible for the focus to be on high-level design and not debugging. Even our novice programmers were able to build mobile applications rapidly.

The entire process of using Cabana was not completely smooth. Bugs still existed that caused failures with correctly written code. Also, a couple of changes were made to Cabana even though it was in beta, which caused previously working applications to break part way through the semester.

This course was only made possible by Cabana. Without the ability to rapidly create a prototype that Cabana provides, the course would never have been able to focus on high-level concepts. Equally, without the ease of use, quite a few students would have been unable to complete their final projects: all but one student had a successful final project. The final projects show the ability to polish applications with Cabana (Figure 7).

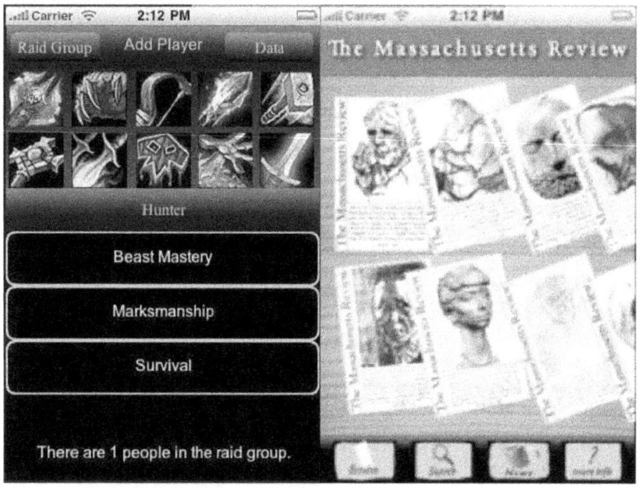

Figure 7: Final project mobile application samples.

6. DISCUSSION

Cabana is a program for developing mobile applications and the best way to see where Cabana fits into application development is to compare it with the major alternatives. As seen in Table 1, Cabana is the only development environment for mobile applications that is capable of creating web-based mobile applications and hence cross-platform applications. While other methods of creating mobile web applications exist (for example, developing with Google Web Toolkit), Cabana is the only one that we know of that is only oriented toward creating mobile applications. As of right now Cabana does not enable a user to create native applications but that will be changing soon. Like App Inventor, Cabana is easy to learn and to use and does not require the user to learn a large amount of the device SDK. The downside to this is that Cabana, like App Inventor, does not give the developer full control over the device.

	Web	Native	Device	Easy	Control
Cabana	Yes	Soon	Yes	Yes	Partial
iOS	No	Yes	Yes	No	Yes
Android	No	Yes	Yes	No	Yes
App Inventor	No	Yes	Yes	Yes	Partial
Other Native	No	Yes	Yes	No	Yes

Table 1: Comparison of mobile application developing environments. Web: create web-based applications, Native: create native applications, Device: have access to device hardware, Easy: easy to get started for a novice, Control: provides programmer with full control over device though SDK, Other Native: developing native applications for another platform.

All of this suggests that the focus of the project needs to be considered when deciding whether to use Cabana. If the goal is to look into data transfer between devices or processor management within the scope of a limited device, then choosing to develop for iOS, Android, or another platform using its native environment makes the most sense. Equally, if the goal is to expose students to a new platform and what it is like to develop in a real-world environment with its limitation, then native application development again makes the most sense.

Cabana eliminates a lot of the low-level work, such as provisioning devices, that is necessary for native development and makes it easy for beginners to begin developing mobile applications. Like App Inventor, Cabana provides an environment that novices can quickly grasp but unlike App Inventor it does not limit development to one platform. Cabana's cross-platform nature also makes it ideal for environments with more than a single mobile platform and may enable a school to avoid purchasing a class set of any particular mobile device.

Cabana is ideal for courses where the focus in on interface design because rapid prototyping enables students to quickly build, test, and revise designs. It provides an interface that easily enables users to build attractive interfaces but still gives the user the power to build complicated programs.

The combination of wiring diagram and JavaScript node creation for application functionality makes it accessible to all levels of programmer. For the novice, nodes exist that perform functions like addition and subtraction and others that provide logic like if statements. Experienced programmers who prefer to write code can simply write JavaScript nodes that include all of their logic and avoid having to try to use the nodes. This gives Cabana an advantage over App Inventor since you are not restricted to a novice-centered programming environment like App Inventor's block language and an advantage over native environment programming since programming background is not required.

Cabana is not perfect and is at the time of this publication still not completely established. Some functionality is still changing though this does not differ greatly from our experience developing under iOS. Also, although wiring nodes together to build programs provides an easy entry into logic and algorithm design for some students, others, including some students who can program easily, never fully grasp it.

One final point for consideration is cost. Developing for Android be it directly or using App Inventor is free. Apple has an educational program that allows schools to develop for iOS for free. DOBL has not yet finalized a pricing model for Cabana but plans to have both a free plan and an educational discount. The free plan will likely limit the number of projects that can be worked on and application publication. The educational discount is likely to be the free plan with fewer restrictions and also free.

7. CONCLUSIONS

A lot of choices have to be made when deciding what approach to take for developing mobile applications. Cabana provides a cross-platform environment for developing cross-platform mobile applications. It is accessible to novice students and powerful enough to enable experienced students to create impressive applications. It does not provide students with the level of control they would have developing in a native environment but does provide enough control for most applications. We found it to be extremely useful in the classroom and recommend its use both in introductory courses and courses focused on high-level design.

8. ACKNOWLEDGMENTS

Thanks to DOBL for providing Cabana for use in our classes and for providing consistent timely development of features as we needed them.

9. REFERENCES

[1] Paul E. Dickson. Experiences building a college video game design course. *J. Comput. Small Coll.*, 25(6):104–110, 2010.

[2] James B. Fenwick, Jr., Barry L. Kurtz, and Joel Hollingsworth. Teaching mobile computing and developing software to support computer science education. In *Proceedings of the 42nd ACM technical symposium on Computer science education*, SIGCSE '11, pages 589–594, New York, NY, USA, 2011. ACM.

[3] Mark H. Goadrich and Michael P. Rogers. Smart smartphone development: ios versus android. In *Proceedings of the 42nd ACM technical symposium on Computer science education*, SIGCSE '11, pages 607–612, New York, NY, USA, 2011. ACM.

[4] Lubomir Ivanov. The i-phone/i-pad course: a small college perspective. *J. Comput. Sci. Coll.*, 26:142–148, June 2011.

[5] Stan Kurkovsky. Engaging students through mobile game development. *SIGCSE Bull.*, 41:44–48, March 2009.

[6] Susan Loveland. Human computer interaction that reaches beyond desktop applications. In *Proceedings of the 42nd ACM technical symposium on Computer science education*, SIGCSE '11, pages 595–600, New York, NY, USA, 2011. ACM.

[7] Qusay H. Mahmoud, Thanh Ngo, Razieh Niazi, Pawel Popowicz, Robert Sydoryshyn, Matthew Wilks, and Dave Dietz. An academic kit for integrating mobile devices into the cs curriculum. *SIGCSE Bull.*, 41:40–44, July 2009.

[8] Elinor Mills. Report: Android app market growing faster than iphone apps. http://reviews.cnet.com/8301-13970_7-20032228-78.html, Oct 2011.

[9] Michael P. Rogers. Wrong number: avoiding the hidden perils in iphone development. *J. Comput. Small Coll.*, 25:300–305, May 2010.

[10] Ellen Spertus, Mark L. Chang, Paul Gestwicki, and David Wolber. Novel approaches to cs 0 with app inventor for android. In *Proceedings of the 41st ACM technical symposium on Computer science education*, SIGCSE '10, pages 325–326, New York, NY, USA, 2010. ACM.

[11] David Wolber. App inventor and real-world motivation. In *Proceedings of the 42nd ACM technical symposium on Computer science education*, SIGCSE '11, pages 601–606, New York, NY, USA, 2011. ACM.

Mobile Apps for the Greater Good: A Socially Relevant Approach to Software Engineering

V. Paúl Pauca
Department of Computer Science
Wake Forest University
Winston-Salem, NC 27109
paucavp@wfu.edu

Richard T. Guy
Department of Computer Science
University of Toronto
Toronto, Ontario M5S 3G4
guy@cs.toronto.edu

ABSTRACT

Socially relevant computing has recently been proposed as a way to reinvigorate interest in computer science. By appealing to students' interest in helping others, socially relevant computing aims to give students life-changing experiential learning not typically achieved in the classroom, while providing software that benefits society at large. For the last two years, the Wake Forest University Computer Science Department has been using mobile device programming, agile methods, and real-world, socially relevant projects for teaching software engineering in a liberal arts Computer Science curricula. We report on the teaching methods, student experiences, and products delivered by this approach. In particular, one of these products, VERBAL VICTOR, is now a commercial and social entrepreneurship success in the field of assistive technology for communication disabilities.

Categories and Subject Descriptors

K.3.0 [**Computers and Education**]: General

General Terms

Design, Human Factors

Keywords

socially relevant computing, teaching software engineering, mobile computing

1. INTRODUCTION

Software engineering design is often used as a capstone course in the computer science curriculum [4, 10]. Working in groups, students are expected to supplement their knowledge and creativity with software engineering principles to tackle meaningful design problems. The practical implementation of this course can be often challenging. First, software engineering material often differs from other courses in the computer science curriculum due to its heightened emphasis of open-ended problems. Often, the student is not able to appreciate the true challenges of engineering software and can easily trivialize the material at hand. Second, emphasizing well-written requirements and other artifacts is tedious and even the best students can find it boring and unnecessarily laborious. Third, meaningful design problems are hard to find. Sample problems or case studies found in the literature are often trivial, unoriginal, or simply uninteresting for most students. Moreover, the lack of a real client perpetuates the expectation that software produced in class will never be really used or tested outside of the classroom. As a result, students often lack motivation to do well and sometimes get by with mediocre work.

In the last two of years of teaching software engineering at Wake Forest University, we have found that leveraging current interest in mobile device programming and agile methods, and focusing on challenging problems that directly benefiting society can have a tremendous impact in students' performance and motivation throughout the course. By collaborating with teachers and speech language pathologists at a local school for children with disabilities, we have been able to identify software engineering problems and real users who can test and benefit from the software produced in class. Open-ended problems of social relevance are presented to the students who must put their knowledge and creativity into the design and implementation of systems that solve problems of interest to society at large.

This approach to computer science education was labeled socially relevant computing by Buckley, Nordlinger, and Subramanian [3]. They employ this term to refer to the use of real-world problems with high social value in the computer science curricula. In this approach, students are challenged to grapple with problems of societal and interpersonal relevance, focusing on learning computing for a cause, rather than as an end in and of itself. The key idea is to attract students who may not otherwise see computer science as an alternative to social sciences and the humanities. We apply the same idea to students who are already enrolled in computer science, but who may not understand how a software engineering course relates to their coursework.

In this paper, we describe our approach for teaching software engineering within the context of recent work on agile methodology [1, 7, 10] and, specifically, socially relevant computing [3]. We describe the Scrum-based course structure that we utilized to emphasize deliverable products for specific, outside clients. In addition, we discuss some of the projects that emerged from two iterations of the course, including one product, VERBAL VICTOR, that has enjoyed success on Apple's App Store.

Permission to make digital or hard copies of all or part of this work for personal or classroom use is granted without fee provided that copies are not made or distributed for profit or commercial advantage and that copies bear this notice and the full citation on the first page. To copy otherwise, to republish, to post on servers or to redistribute to lists, requires prior specific permission and/or a fee.
SIGCSE'12, February 29–March 3, 2012, Raleigh, North Carolina, USA.
Copyright 2012 ACM 978-1-4503-1098-7/12/02 ...$10.00.

2. BACKGROUND

2.1 Technology for Disabilities

The field of assistive technology for disabilities is a rich source for real-world problems of great social value. Assistive devices for communication and speech disabilities is a field dominated by expensive, single-purpose devices aimed at assisting people with various communication needs. These so-called augmentative and alternative communication (AAC) devices vary significantly in power and sophistication.

Electronic AAC devices present the user with a selection of action buttons (overlaid with symbols) to choose from. Typically, when the user chooses a particular action, the device plays an appropriate sound for the selected action. For example, to indicate he is thirsty and wants a drink, a user would press on the button showing a cup. The device then plays a pre-recorded sound such as "I am thirsty." The majority of affordable AAC devices (less than $400) give users a small number of options (e.g. four buttons in the Hip Talker). If the desired button is not present, then the user or caretaker needs to switch symbols (typically printed in paper and laminated for durability) or go through the time-consuming process of creating new content from scratch. More high tech AAC systems, such as the DynaVox Vmax+ employ touch screen and computer technology and are advertised for all age ranges, cognitive abilities, and skill levels, but their cost is prohibitive (~$7000) for many families.

2.2 Mobile Devices

The availability of programmable built-in cameras and other sensors is enabling the use of smart devices as *data gathering and processing tools* for a variety of medical and other applications. Not surprisingly, the advent and ubiquity of smart mobile devices is reshaping the world of AAC devices for a variety of disabilities. Smart phones and tablet computers represent a modern device whose image contrasts favorably with the stigma of a dedicated assistive technology. Kane et al. [9] examined mobile computing use by people with visual and motor disabilities and found that mass-market devices with accessibility features were preferred by several participants for their lower cost and for the freedom they offer from reliance on makers of specialized hardware.

2.3 Verbal Victor

VERBAL VICTOR is an app developed by computer science students at Wake Forest University that turns the iPhone or iPad into an AAC system. Originating from one of our software engineering projects in the first iteration of our course (see AUGCOMM in section 4), VERBAL VICTOR is becoming a popular alternative to traditional AAC devices. Since its first release in January of 2011, it has been downloaded over 2500 times, as of October of 2011. Two updates to the original version were released in March, 2011. The current version is a universal app for both iPhone and iPad platforms (see Figure 1). VERBAL VICTOR is one of the success stories that have occurred as a result of our approach to teaching software engineering.

VERBAL VICTOR represents an important bridge between the two iterations of our course. The students identified a gap between AAC devices on the market and the capabilities offered by smart phone technology. In contrast to the DynaVox Vmax+, VERBAL VICTOR was targeted to people with poor fine motor control and emerging cognitive skills.

(a) iPod Touch

(b) iPad

Figure 1: AAC system based on iPhone and iPad.

The philosophy is to avoid a one-size-fits-all solution to communication disabilities. By focusing on a specific target population, VERBAL VICTOR is able to better satisfy the needs of this audience, while keeping the price low ($7 App Store). Figures 2 and 3 show screenshots of the user and administrator modes in the iPhone.

Figure 2: Reconfigurable user interface (iPhone).

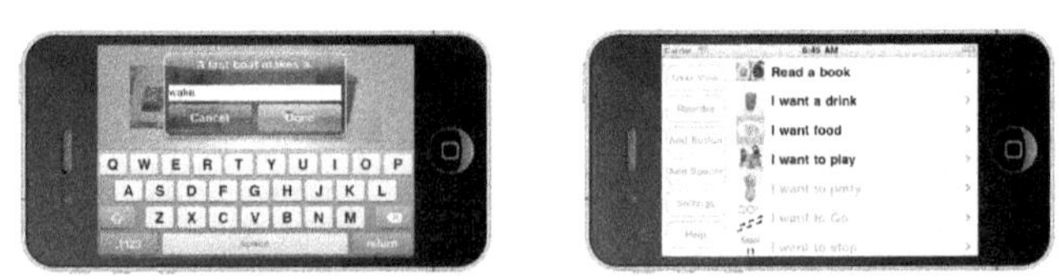

Figure 3: Gesture control protected administrator view.

VERBAL VICTOR also exemplifies the interesting collaborations that have emerged as a result of this work. The entrepreneurship program at Wake Forest University found value in this product as a way for students to think concretely about social entrepreneurship. Two computer science students involved with the development of AUGCOMM were offered summer internships to take the application to market. Other collaborations emphasizing the greater impact of research and educational components of this work are ongoing.

3. METHODOLOGY

3.1 Approach

Mobile app development is a topic of current interest to a wide student audience. Mobile devices are pervasive in popular culture and mobile development confers a democratized software business experience. App stores offer a well-defined pipeline to bring products to market without the additional costs incurred in the traditional way of publishing and advertising software. By focusing on mobile development, we offer students the chance to publish working software in reasonable time without losing focus.

From a pedagogical standpoint, mobile development also introduces a large framework against which students must program. The specialized sensory and networking aspects of mobile development mean that third-party applications rely on features of an SDK. User-generated code must conform to pre-defined design patterns, e.g. model-view-controller (MVC). Students gain the experience of entering a project "mid-stream" which more accurately represents software engineering in the wild. Working with a pre-existing code base took on new importance for participants in the second offering of our course, as some teams chose to extend and augment a project from the previous year.

Teaching through real-world problems dovetails with the opportunity for students to see mobile development projects through to final products. The desire for societal impact has been implicated as a reason for the significantly higher graduation rate in social sciences as compared to Computer Science [2]. The great disparity between popular and assistive technology and the capability to bridge these two through the use of mobile devices offers the perfect opportunity to reach out to students' interest in philanthropy and service [8]. Moreover, getting to know and working with people and children with disabilities and their families can give students a unique and invaluable experience not typically associated with the Computer Science curricula. Our focus is therefore on accessibility applications as a means to motivate Computer Science students as they learn traditional course material, knowing that a successful project might very well have a positive impact for someone else.

Agile software development has gained increased attention in software engineering courses over the last decade, see e.g. [1, 6, 10, 11] with generally positive outcomes. Agile methods were evolved by practitioners working in the software industry and its usage is becoming mainstream. Hazam and Dubinsky [7] offer ten arguments as to why agile techniques should be taught in academia. Our motivation for focusing on agile methods includes the inherent uncertainty and changing nature of open-ended problems in software for assistive purposes and the increasing relevance of agile methods in actual practice.

3.2 Course Structure

Our software engineering course was structured around the development of mobile apps with social benefit for actual clients and users in the community, and this was communicated to the students from the start. A successful project would produce a reasonable prototype that the client would find valuable. In the first year, a few applications were suggested, including the development of an AAC device for children with emerging communication skills, but students were allowed to look for their own project ideas within the Wake Forest campus community. Based on the success achieved with the AAC project (see VERBAL VICTOR in section 2.3) and a close relationship with a local school for children with disabilities, all projects in the second year were required to focus on technology for disabilities.

Course material aimed to facilitate the successful completion of student projects. First, students spent a significant amount of time in the first two weeks familiarizing themselves with mobile device (i.e. iPhone / iPad) programming, Objective-C, event-driven programming, and the XCode IDE. This was done through lectures, in-class student presentations, and tutorials involving small sample problems. Learning event-driven programming and using existing built-in frameworks and design patterns was perhaps one of the key difficulties faced by students used to writing most of their code from scratch.

Two weeks into the course, the Scrum methodology [12] was introduced to set clear short-term goals, help manage team effort, and enable a timely delivery of software artifacts. Students were required to understand and use product backlogs to organize and prioritize client-specified features. Development was organized in a sequence of two-week sprints. Sprint planning meetings were conducted at the beginning of each sprint (i) to select product backlog items according to the team's current capacity (number of hours available to be devoted to the project in the current sprint), and (ii) to break down each item into individual tasks and team members responsible for these tasks. The resulting sprint backlog contained fixed requirements for the current sprint. In addition, students were required to keep daily updates of their work, resulting in appropriate burndown charts. At the end of each sprint, teams were required to make presentations specifying the status of their project, what did or did not work, what difficulties they found, and how these could be ameliorated. This approach gave the students a chance to learn from their mistakes. Deemer *et al.*'s [5] online book was invaluable in providing the students with concrete examples of how product backlogs, sprint backlogs, and burndown charts were to be specified. Google Docs was the student's tool of choice for keeping track of text documents and burndown charts.

Version control tools were introduced after the first sprint. In particular, we set up a remote Subversion repository where teams could share their work without interfering with each other. Before this, students had experienced the difficulties and hassle of sharing code by email or even Dropbox and readily welcome Subversion into the development process. Students understood the process of branching and tagging in a practical way, and provided software deliverables for each sprint in the form of tags in the repository.

Development in iOS is heavily dependent on the understanding of design patterns, particularly the MVC pattern. The separation between model, controller, and view is difficult to grasp when dealing with XCode, Interface Builder and related tools. As a result, a significant amount of time was devoted to understanding and implementing MVC and other design patterns independently of the XCode IDE. This was done as part of lecture, homework assignments, and quizzes using languages familiar to the students such as

GNU C++ and Java in either Windows or Linux environments. Other patterns studied closely included Delegate, Adapter, Bridge, Abstract Factory, and Strategy patterns. Students were also introduced to design through UML diagrams and use cases and required to employ these tools in the iterative and incremental evolution of their projects.

Classical software engineering material typically reviewed in early chapters of most introductory textbooks was covered in the second half of the course. This material included topics such as software testing, processes, models and lifecycle, quality, and CMMI. At the end of the course, students were required to make a final presentation, showing the client-guided evolution of their projects throughout the course.

Throughout the course, students were required to approach their client with prototypes and design decisions. The sometimes shifting requirements and an evolving understanding of the problem at hand fit nicely with the biweekly scrum layout of the course calendar.

4. RESULTS

4.1 Software Projects in the First Year

Four software projects were developed in our first year of teaching the course: AugComm, PlantCatalog, FreeASL, and WakeTour. Three of these projects are highlighted next.

4.1.1 AugComm

AugComm is an AAC app developed for a child whose SuperTalker device (see Figure ??(b)) broke after a year of use. The team developing Augcomm visited the child's school and met with one of his parents, his teacher, and his speech therapist. The product backlog was started based on this initial interaction. The team kept close communication with the child's parent and interacted with the teacher at various times during the semester.

A prototype ready for testing was developed midway through the course. The prototype was loaded on the teacher's iPhone and tested with the child and his classmates. Feedback obtained from the teacher was invaluable for introducing, validating, and eliminating multiple features and design decisions. AugComm later provided the basis for Verbal Victor.

4.1.2 PlantCatalog

PlantCatalog is an app for cataloging trees and was developed for field biology work that originated as a need in the Biology Department at Wake Forest. The team developing this app met with a Biology professor whose conservation research work requires trees to be identified and mapped in the field. The students started with a basic navigation controller and Google maps that a user could annotate via GPS and the touch screen. Midway through the semester, the students found out that, in addition to the type of tree, estimating the tree's height and width was an important consideration for calculating carbon content. In subsequent iterations, the students developed a way to use the iPhone as a height measuring device using the built-in accelerometer.

4.1.3 FreeASL

FreeASL is an app developed for the purpose of learning American Sign Language (ASL). The client in this case was a special education teacher proficient in ASL. The students developed a prototype that enabled the user to type in basic phrases which were then matched with appropriate video clips showing how to sign the phrase in ASL. Subsequent iterations included a remote server containing a searchable database of sample video clips showing appropriate hand movement for commonly used phrases. The teacher collaborating with the team was able to provide much of the content used in the app. In this case, requirements and product functionality was determined by the type of media made available to the group through the ASL teacher. FreeASL was subsequently released in the AppStore, and the group later aggregated the short videos by categories and released them on Youtube.

4.2 Software Projects in the Second Year

Due to the success and close relationships with potential clients achieved with Verbal Victor, students in the second year were asked to focus on apps for helping children with physical and cognitive disabilities. Five apps were developed by the end of the semester: Chatting Victor, Scanning Victor, Schedule Victor, iTraceShapes, and ShapesAndSounds. The first four projects are highlighted next.

4.2.1 Chatting Victor & Scanning Victor

Both of these apps used AugComm as the starting code base and implement AAC systems. Chatting Victor enables a user to construct basic sentences for children with more advanced communication skills. This functionality is often provided by higher end AAC devices such as the Dynavox Vmax+ (see Figure ??(d)). Scanning Victor scans over available options displayed on the screen, pausing for a few seconds over each option. By tapping anywhere on the touch screen, the user selects the option currently being scanned. This enables users who may not have the required strength or hand dexterity to communicate. A special education teacher was the client for these projects and the applications were developed with specific users in mind. In particular, Scanning Victor was designed for a child with severe cerebral palsy with poor vision and motor control.

4.2.2 Schedule Victor

This app implements a reward-based schedule board for children with autism. Schedule boards consist of symbols denoting specific tasks to be accomplished in order and are often used to help organize a child's activities. The students worked with local speech therapists who provided significant guidance and expertise in the implementation of the schedule board. The main idea of Schedule Victor was to enable the therapist or parents to arrange appropriate star-based rewards for well-accomplished activities.

4.2.3 iTraceShapes

This app uses music and video to motivate children to learn to trace shapes and improve their fine motor control. The basic idea was provided by the parent of a child with special needs and the target audience were children with focus attention problems, such autism. The students spent a great deal of time prototyping and testing this idea, finally converging into a working app. iTraceShapes allows parents or therapists to select a child's favorite song (e.g. Elmo's song) to play while the child is correctly tracing a

Num	Item	Volunteer	Priority	Estimate of Value	Initial Estimate of Effort	% Completed
R16	Add delete button functionality	TG	1	10	4	100.00%
R17	Try to streamline communication by giving admin direct access to augcom	TG	4	8	1	100.00%
R18	Fix swipe	Harry	1	10	3	100.00%
R19	Add settings button to admin screen	Eddie	1	10	4	100.00%
R19.1	- Add num buttons (2,4,6) to settings	Eddie	3	9	2	100.00%
R19.2	- Add password chooser and hint (does not need to be secret)	Eddie	5	5	2	100.00%
R20	Admin list updates on changes	TG	2	6	2	100.00%
R21	Add password query to the admin entrance.	TG	1	5	3	66.67%
R22	Add database of users		4	10	0	
R23	Allow grouping of buttons by user		4	10	0	
R24	Allow reording of the buttons		4	8	0	
R25	Slightly reduce button sizes	TG	5	4	1	100.00%
R26	Use addNewList to talk to admin	TG	5	6	1	100.00%
R27	Fix bug: swipe overrides two finger touch	Harry	2	10	1	100.00%
R28	Fix bug: play can be hit when recording and recording can be hit when playing	Harry	1	10	1	100.00%
			Total hours		25	Hours per Day
				Ideal hours per day	1.75	Acumulate Hours

Figure 4: Sample sprint backlog from the AugComm project in year one.

shape shown in the screen and to pause when the child stops tracing. After a shape has been been traced a user-specified number of times, then the child's favorite video is played (e.g. Elmo ABC in Youtube).

iTraceShapes is currently being tested with a few children with autism spectrum and other disabilities.

4.3 Usage of Scrum

The Scrum methodology was used both years with positive results. Students responded well to the two-week sprint deadlines and milestones, producing documentation and software artifacts in a timely manner while adjusting to changing demands on their finished product. Figure 4 shows a sample sprint backlog generated by one of the teams in the first year. Figure 5 shows the corresponding burndown chart. However, not all elements of the Scrum methodology worked as expected. In particular, the daily scrum did not work very well due to the large variance in students' course and work schedules.

5. CONCLUSIONS AND FINAL REMARKS

In this paper, we have presented an approach to software engineering education that uses real world problems originating from the field of assistive technology for people and children with disabilities. This course has been successfully taught at Wake Forest University for the last two years and emphasizes learning and practical use of agile methods for project management and development [6]. Student evaluations were positive and interest in the applications and related material continued after the completion of the course. In particular, 12% of students in the first year and 30% of students in the second year are continuing to work on apps for disabilities either through independent studies or individual work.

Connections and opportunities for multidisciplinary collaboration continue to expand. iTraceShapes will soon be released in the App Store and research and development of Chatting Victor and Scanning Victor continues. Two business students also expressed interest in collaboration and performed an initial study of the application market. Additionally, highly promising student-driven collaborations with machine learning experts have begun. There is a great opportunity to continue to infuse assistive technology with modern computer science tools, bridging the gap created by the development of expensive specialized hardware over the last few decades. We believe that social relevance can be further integrated into the computer science curricula, helping attract a more diverse group of student earlier on.

Teaching software engineering through socially relevant software also introduces special challenges, especially for students who are able to produce an application that they plan to distribute. Most universities, including our own, require that intellectual property developed using university resources be signed over to the university itself. Teachers must carefully consider the relationship between student projects and the university, especially where royalties are concerned.

6. ACKNOWLEDGMENTS

The authors wish to thank students at Wake Forest University and teachers, therapists, and parents at the Centers for Exceptional Children who helped make the course and related projects a reality. In particular, we wish to thank Mike Britt, the Executive Director of the Centers for Exceptional Children and Carol Kirby, Principal of the Children's Center for the Physically Disabled, for opening up their schools to our students and providing time to their teachers and therapists to work with our various student groups. Martha Farrow, a teacher at the Children's Center for the Physically Disabled, gave invaluable feedback, energy and dedication into the development of Verbal Victor. Kristine Drum and Amalie Harris, speech language pathologists at the Special Children's School, provided great support during the second year. Finally, the success of Verbal Victor

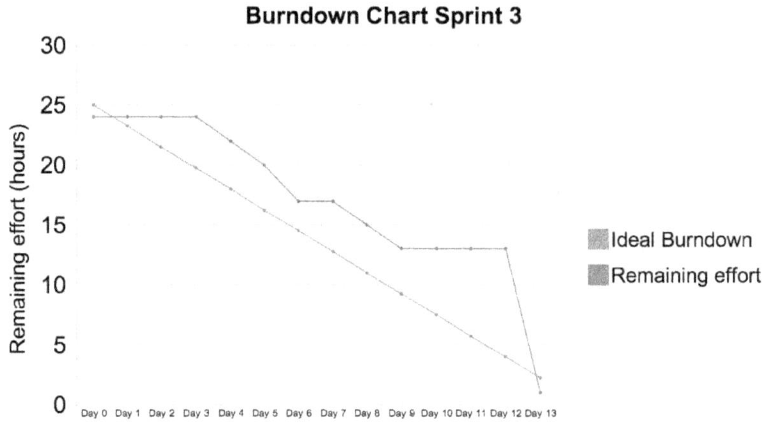

Figure 5: Sample burndown chart from the AugComm project in year one.

would not have been possible without the support of the Office of Entrepreneurship and Dr. Betsy Gatewood through various summer internships.

7. REFERENCES

[1] M. I. Alfonso and A. Botia. An iterative and agile process model for teaching software engineering. In *Proceedings of the 18th Conference on Software Engineering Education & Training*, pages 9–16, Washington, DC, USA, 2005. IEEE Computer Society.

[2] M. Buckley, H. Kershner, K. Schindler, C. Alphonce, and J. Braswell. Benefits of using socially-relevant projects in computer science and engineering education. In *Proceedings of the 35th SIGCSE technical symposium on Computer science education*, SIGCSE '04, pages 482–486, New York, NY, USA, 2004. ACM.

[3] M. Buckley, J. Nordinger, and D. Subramanian. Socially relevant computing. In *SIGCSE '08 Proc. of the 39th SIGCSE technical symposium on Computer science education*, SIGCSE '08, pages 347–351, New York, NY, USA, 2008. ACM.

[4] A. T. Chamillard and K. A. Braun. The software engineering capstone: structure and tradeoffs. In *Proceedings of the 33rd SIGCSE technical symposium on Computer science education*, SIGCSE '02, pages 227–231, New York, NY, USA, 2002. ACM.

[5] P. Deemer, G. Benefield, C. Larman, and B. Vodde. *The Scrum Primer*. 2010.

[6] Y. Dubinsky and O. Hazzan. A framework for teaching software development methods. *Computer Science Education*, 15(4):275–296, 2005.

[7] O. Hazzan and Y. Dubinsky. Why software engineering programs should teach agile software development. *SIGSOFT Softw. Eng. Notes*, 32:1–3, March 2007.

[8] R. Huntley. *The world according to Y: inside the new adult generation*. Allen Unwin, 2006.

[9] S. K. Kane, C. Jayant, J. O. Wobbrock, and R. E. Ladner. Freedom to roam: A study of mobile device adoption and accessibility for people with visual and motor disabilities. *Proc. ASSETS*, pages 115–122, 2009.

[10] B. Lu and T. DeClue. Teaching agile methodology in a software engineering capstone course. *J. Comput. Sci. Coll.*, 26:293–299, May 2011.

[11] T. Reichlmayr. The agile approach in an undergraduate software engineering course project. In *33rd ASEE/IEEE Frontiers in Education Conference*, pages 13–18, 2003.

[12] K. Schwaber and M. Beedle. *Agile software development with Scrum*. Prentice Hall, 2002.

Using Mobile Phone Programming to Teach Java and Advanced Programming to Computer Scientists

Derek Riley
University of Wisconsin-Parkside
Kenosha, WI
rileyd@uwp.edu

ABSTRACT

In this work an approach employing the Android mobile phone platform in an upper division computer science course to teach Java programming and other advanced computer science topics is presented. Mobile phones are growing influences in the computing market, but their strengths and popularity are rarely exploited in computer science classrooms. The aim of the course is to harness this enthusiasm to improve fluency in the Java language to afford an opportunity to learn how to work on large, complex projects and to enhance the students' preparedness for the job market. The ideas presented in this work could be adapted for improving learning in many courses across the computing curriculum.

Categories and Subject Descriptors: K.3.2 [Computer and Information Science Education]: Curriculum, Computer science education

General Terms: Human Factors, Design

Keywords: Java,Android,Education,Course.

1. INTRODUCTION

The recent revolution in mobile computing has taken computing out of the office and into pockets around the world, and the market segment is projected to continue growth [9]. Having grown up using mobile phones, students find the transition to smart phones to be natural. They enthusiastically master smart phone user interfaces and applications, so it seems that students with an interest in programming will be highly motivated to learn how to program smart phones. Harnessing this enthusiasm in upper-division computer science courses can potentially improve the learning of core computing topics as well as improve the preparedness of students for the job market. In this work I present a course designed to teach the Java language and object oriented programming to upperclassmen using the Android platform.

There are several platforms in the mobile device community. The Android platform was chosen because it is open source, it has a large community of active developers, and its development can be done using any operating system, therefore eliminating the need to buy Apple computers (as is required for iOS development) [6]. Android is especially well-suited for use in the computer science classroom because it utilizes many features of the Java programming language and provides a plug-in for integration with Eclipse [2] including an emulation environment called the Android Virtual Device (AVD), which eliminates the need to have the actual mobile devices to do basic development [1]. However, many students already own and use Android-based mobile devices, so they can be easily used if students desire to pursue programming of more advanced features not implemented in the AVD.

The goal of the course presented in this paper is to use Android as a platform to teach upperclassmen computer science students the Java language. The students in CSCI 3033 at Middle Tennessee State University (MTSU) numbered twenty-eight: twenty-six were computer science majors and two were math majors. Many only had used C/C++ previously, and this course was their first exposure to learning a new programming language.

Android has been used previously as a platform in mobile device courses [7, 5, 10], but given the newness of the platform, no textbook currently exists to teach Java or any other upper-division courses using Android examples. Further, most Java language textbooks are intended for CS1/CS2 courses, so they are not easily adapted for an upper-division course. The concepts presented in this paper could be adapted for use in other upper level CS courses such as networking, event-driven programming, parallel programming, game design, graphics, databases, and more.

Writing simple applications from scratch using the Android platform requires proficiency in OO concepts, event-driven programming, and the Android architecture, so the learning curve for Android is steep enough to keep most students from learning it on their own. Further, only about two-thirds of the students in the MTSU course had taken upper-level courses such as operating systems, networking, or algorithms, so many topics were covered in the course in addition to the Android material to enable the students to utilize some of the advanced Android features they chose to explore while learning Java.

The contributions of this work are twofold. First, I present an extensible course to bridge the gap between C++ and Java using Android while demonstrating the course's efficacy. The course is designed to overcome the aforemen-

Permission to make digital or hard copies of all or part of this work for personal or classroom use is granted without fee provided that copies are not made or distributed for profit or commercial advantage and that copies bear this notice and the full citation on the first page. To copy otherwise, to republish, to post on servers or to redistribute to lists, requires prior specific permission and/or a fee.
SIGCSE'12, February 29–March 3, 2012, Raleigh, North Carolina, USA.
Copyright 2012 ACM 978-1-4503-1098-7/12/02 ...$10.00.

tioned challenges by covering a breadth of computing topics to soften the Android learning curve and cater to a wide variety of computing backgrounds. The course also attempts to use relatable and realistic projects to motivate students without causing them to be overwhelmed by the challenges of learning a new language.

The second contribution is a proposed curriculum consisting of targeted individual and group projects designed to teach a variety of programming concepts for Android. Several examples of student group projects are presented to demonstrate student capabilities at this level. A post-course survey shows that students view the instructional approach favorably with regard to learning Java programming skills. The survey also indicates that students to feel more prepared for what they are likely to encounter in their future careers as a result of this course.

2. THE COURSE

This section describes the goals and design of CSCI 3033. The course is is typically taken by upperclassmen enrollees who need to fulfill a language breadth requirement, but it is not required for any academic major or minor program of study. The C++ language is used as the primary language for most undergraduate Computer Science courses at MTSU; the only prerequisites for this course are CS1 and CS2.

2.1 Goals

The main goal of CSCI 3033 is to teach students how to become competent Java developers, which includes proficiency in OO programming topics, the use of libraries, and much more. Because of the potentially varied background of the students in the course, it was necessary to cover a wide variety of topics from the basics of the Java programming environment to more advanced topics such as multithreading and event-driven programming. Another pedagogical priority was success for all students regardless of their programming background, together with student exposure to large, real-world software challenges.

Key CSCI 3033 topics reinforced with programming assignments or examples included inheritance, polymorphism, interfaces, exception handling, streams, files, and collections. Additionally, it was expected that students would acquire a basic understanding of GUI programming and the core Android API. More challenging topics such as multithreading, event-driven programming, networking, XML, and graphics were incorporated as time permitted. Lastly, it was important for best software engineering practices to be a common thread of all course presentations and assignments.

Assessment of the course goals was accomplished by a midterm exam, several individual programming assignments, a final, cumulative project, and a post-semester survey. I posit that these tools were adequate for assessing the individual student performance.

2.2 Course Design

The course was split into five units according to the aforementioned goals: Java introduction, OO programming, Android introduction, advanced Android, and software engineering. Because of the variation in student background, special care was taken to select examples that were motivating, realistic, and allowed the students some creative freedom.

Unit 1 (One Week) The first unit was an introduction to the basic syntax of Java. Throughout this unit command-line programming was used to help teach the basics of the Java programming environment without the use of an IDE. Unit 1 focused on the differences between Java and C++, and programming assignments were designed to introduce students to the compilation and running environment. By the end of this unit students were able to write, compile, and run Java applications consisting of a couple of simple classes.

Unit 2 (Three Weeks) The second course unit explored object-oriented programming (OOP) with inheritance, polymorphism, libraries, and packages, presented in one or two class periods each. Most students were previously familiar with OOP, but a few non-traditional or transfer students were not. OOP concepts are reinforced through many in class examples, individual programming assignments, and homework problems.

The concepts of Java interfaces, exception handling, files, streams, collections, and the Java API and class libraries were also included in Unit 2. The non-Android components of the Trainster programming assignment (described in Section 3.1) were presented using only command-line interactions. Other topics explored in Unit 2 include the Eclipse IDE, Javadoc documentation, UML class diagrams, and UML object diagrams. A midterm examination was administered after this unit to access student knowledge of the Java basics.

Unit 3 (Two Weeks) The third unit introduced the Android operating system and programming environment. Students began by participating in a lab to create an Android tip calculator application using a single class and simple user interface. Most of the code for this project was provided by the instructor. Concepts of event-driven programming, operating systems, and GUI objects and layouts are discussed using this and other Android examples.

The Trainster code developed in Unit 2 was re-implemented for the Android environment with some added functionality and GUI features as described in Section 3.1. After students successfully implemented their individual Trainster projects, they formed groups to brainstorm ideas for the their final project.

Unit 4 (One Week) This next unit includes lectures on more advanced Android and Java concepts such as threads, intents (interprocess communication), libraries, sensors, GPS, and more. The students proposed, planned, and began the development of their final projects during this time (as described in Section 3.2), so lectures were tailored to the topics required for the wide variety of proposed projects.

Unit 5 (Seven Weeks) As the students developed their final projects, lectures concentrated on the concepts of debugging, design patterns, testing, project management, and effective presentations. Time was also devoted to examining software documentation, external libraries, intellectual property, open source licenses, and other topics. Students were required to give project update presentations, and the class was encouraged to share code and suggest improvements to each others' projects. The Android platform introduced many real-world programming examples that required students to put software engineering theory into practice and work as a collaborative development group.

3. ANDROID PROJECTS

Two major projects were used in CSCI 3033: one individual project (Trainster) and one group project. The individual Trainster project required the students to develop an application that stores and calculates Body Mass Index (BMI) data for use by a personal trainer. The group projects were unique with each group required to propose, design, and create their own Android application.

3.1 Trainster Project

The Trainster project consisted of a series of smaller, incremental projects designed to teach basic Java syntax; these projects were completed in the first half of the semester. Upon completion, Trainster is a software application that a personal trainer (at a gym) could use for storing information about clients. The specific learning outcomes of Trainster related to the topics of inheritance, polymorphism, exception handling, and basic Android application programming. The project was divided into three phases to correspond to the concepts discussed in lectures.

Phase 1: Simple BMI Students wrote an application to calculate a person's BMI given a height (in inches) and weight (in pounds) as shown in (1). This phase of the project only required command-line programming, to ensure student focus on Java syntax and good programming techniques. The result of the BMI calculation is a floating-point value that crudely indicates the status of an individual's heath and is categorized using Table 3.1 [4]. Students were required to create an object to contain the client's name, height, weight, BMI, and category.

$$BMI_E = \frac{703 * weight}{height^2} \tag{1}$$

BMI	Category
<18.5	Underweight
18.5-25	Normal
25-30	Overweight
>30	Obese

Table 1: BMI categorizations

Phase 2: OO Extension For this phase of the project, students used inheritance and polymorphism, permitting application users to enter, calculate, and save clients' BMI data with both English and metric units. The BMI calculation for metric units is similar (2) to the English calculation, so the students were required to create an abstract 'Body' class as well as 'English' and 'Metric' subclasses that inherit from the 'Body' superclass and overload a calculate() method.

Phase 2 also required sorting a list of clients in order to expose students to Java data structures. During this phase of the project students were also introduced to the Eclipse IDE [2]. The OO phase of the project also only required command-line programming to allow students to focus on the OO concepts.

$$BMI_M = \frac{weight}{height^2} \tag{2}$$

Phase 3: Android Application In the final phase of the project the students were required to create an Android application that allowed users to enter multiple clients, including name, height, weight, and units (English or metric). Students used the Java classes developed in Phase 2 and were required to use exception handling to ensure robustness. Students were encouraged (but not required) to serialize their objects to save state in the event that the application was interrupted.

Phase 3 also introduced students to Android GUI programming concepts, using EditText and TextView objects as well as buttons, XML layouts, and views. Students were required to create a main screen to allow the user to enter data as well as a second screen to allow users to view the clients. This satisfied learning outcomes related to the concepts of emulators, event-driven programming, Activities (threads), and file systems. A screen shot of an example version of the application is shown in Figure 1. Students were required to design their own GUI using the XML layout editor included in the Eclipse ADT plugin.

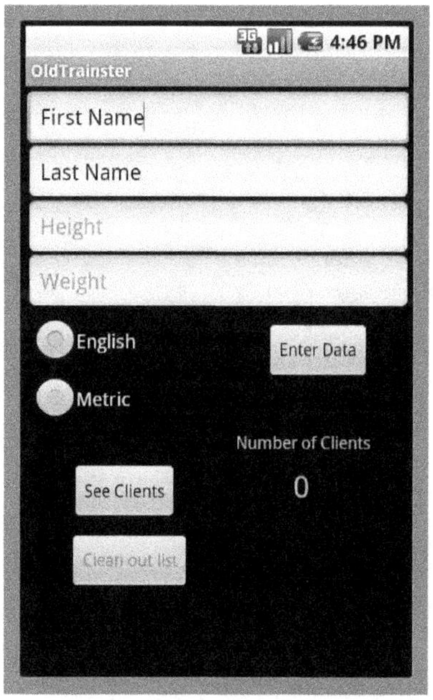

Figure 1: Personal trainer Android application

3.2 Group Project

Few programming projects in the real world allow programmers to work exclusively on their own, so exposure to group projects is a critical part of any programmer's education [8]. I was particularly interested in developing team programming skills while students learned Java to integrate this experience with OO programming practices.

Near the midpoint of the semester, students presented proposed ideas for Android-based applications to their peers. During the proposal presentations, the class was encouraged to brainstorm, suggest improvements, and highlight challenges in each others' ideas. The students were given time in class to meet with each other and form groups (on their own). One week after forming teams students were required to present the details of their proposed projects and generate initial requirements documents including preliminary UML diagrams. The initial presentations were intended to allow students to 'dream big' while the second presentations were intended to force the students to impose realistic goals and distill plans into a practical form from their initial ideas.

The requirements for the project were intentionally open to encourage creativity. Guidelines required that all projects demonstrated Java fluency and incorporated at least one of the following topics: networking, multithreading, databases, sensors (GPS, accelerometer, etc), or advanced graphics.

Two more presentations were required of the project teams: a mid project presentation and a final presentation. In both, students were required to present working prototypes, discuss challenges, and highlight obstacles. In the final presentation the students were also required to present their testing scheme, project documentation, and to summarize the experience. During all presentations, students were asked to critique and suggest improvements for others' projects.

4. EXPERIENCE

A post-course survey (see Figure 2) was conducted to assess various aspects of the course from the student perspective. The survey was completed by 26 students (35% were third-year and 65% were fourth-year or beyond). The results of this survey are summarized in Section 4.4.

Anonymous post course survey (for research/course development use only)

Overall GPA at MTSU (estimated) _______ GPA in CS (estimated) _______

Class standing	Sophomore		Junior	Senior
Rate your Java expertise before taking this course	None	Little	Some	Expert
Rate your Java expertise after taking this course	None	Little	Some	Expert
Rate your feeling of preparedness for the job market prior to the course	None	Little	Some	Ready
Rate your feeling of preparedness for the job market after this course	None	Little	Some	Ready
Rate the effectiveness of the Trainster application for teaching Java concepts	Poor	OK	Good	Great
Rate the effectiveness of the Trainster application for teaching Android basics	Poor	OK	Good	Great
Rate the effectiveness of the group project for teaching Java concepts	Poor	OK	Good	Great
Rate the effectiveness of using Android to teach Java	Poor	OK	Good	Great
Rate your Android expertise after taking this course	None	Little	Some	Expert

Please use the back of this sheet to provide suggestions or other comments

Figure 2: Post-semester survey

4.1 Trainster Project

The Trainster project is an effective project to introduce Java because it illustrates the utility of OO programming and code reuse using Java. Given the students' varied programming backgrounds, forcing them to use OO concepts and start with command-line programming appeared to equalize student abilities. Enhancements for programming assignments, such as using more efficient data structures, sorting, and file manipulation, were encouraged (but not required) to challenge the more advanced programmers.

Grades on the early phases of Trainster were lower than the grades for the later phases of the project, most likely due to the differences in OO programming understanding and ability. The students who struggled with the basics of OO programming mostly caught up by the later phases of the project because they re-implemented what they had written earlier so it would utilize the OO concepts correctly and work for the later phases of the project.

Student survey responses demonstrated a favorable attitude toward code reuse and code refactoring. Other comments expressed pleasure with a project that allowed for some creative freedom. When asked to rate the effectiveness of the Trainster application in teaching Java concepts no student rated it this as 'Poor', 19% of students rated it 'OK', 54% rated it 'Good', and 27% rated it 'Great'.

Student survey responses associated with Phase 3 of the Trainster project indicated a favorable attitude toward working on a project that had obvious real-world applications. When students were asked to rate the effectiveness of the Trainster application for teaching the Android basics, no students rated this 'Poor', 12% of students rated it 'OK', 54% rated it 'Good', and 34% rated it 'Great'.

Students also remarked the project was easy to understand, grade expectations were clear, and it was nice to be able to take creative liberties with the assignment. The best projects were demonstrated in class. The students appeared enthusiastic during these demonstrations, creating a positive competitive environment.

4.2 Group Project

Team programming was an opportunity for students to use Java and apply OO design in a group setting. Students related well to mobile phone applications, perhaps because most use such applications regularly in daily life. To foster creative ideas for the team projects, one class period was used to brainstorm and discuss ideas as a class. Students were told to prepare for the class by talking to teammates to propose specific applications. The current popularity of Android applications together with student creativity generated more good ideas than there were teams to implement them. The variety of applications reflected the variety of student interest.

A common characteristic of initially proposed projects was that they tended to be overly ambitious for the limited duration of the class, but this too can be an important lesson. Students were required to show how the proposed application was significantly different than existing applications in order to encourage students to research before writing code. Example projects are presented in Section 4.3.

Grades for the final projects were generally quite good (mostly 'A's or 'B's). A large part of the grade (60%) was for planning, proposing, and presenting the work, while the actual code represented the other 40%. The 60% weighting was intended to encourage students to hone communication skills and enhance the collaborative environment. All submitted projects were fully functional, with several exhibiting more functionality than initially proposed. Some groups did not implement every proposed requirement, but all projects demonstrated adequate proficiency with the Java language and Android platform.

Students indicated in the post-course survey that they enjoyed having the opportunity to learn Java using the Android group project. The survey asked students to rate the effectiveness of the group project for teaching Java concepts. No students rated this 'Poor', 4% of students rated it 'OK', 23% rated it 'Good', and 73% rated it 'Great'.

Students also mentioned that they enjoyed the ability to work in teams where the strengths of each student could be leveraged and they could choose a project of interest. They claimed to spend much more time on their projects than they have in previous CS courses, and felt that the time spent was enjoyable. Lastly, students indicated that they enjoyed the collaborative environment of the class and were surprised by how much they learned from each other through their presentations, discussions, and other in class interactions.

4.3 Example Projects

The team projects ranged from clever utility applications to games to entertainment applications. The vast majority of the projects had positive outcomes because the students were self-motivated and encouraged by each other to create useful, functional applications. Some of the best projects required hundreds of programming hours and several thousand lines of code. A few projects created by the students are explained briefly below.

Figure 3: Audio recording application

Audio recorder- This application allows users to record audio, encode it into MP3, and save notes in the audio using timestamps. The application also utilizes voice-to-text libraries, permitting users to name their recordings based on what is said in the recording. Figure 3 shows a screen shot of the recording screen of the application.

Wiring Diagram Generator- This utility application for car audio enthusiasts allows users to select a configuration of speakers, amplifier, and impedence to create a custom color-coded wiring diagram. The application also provides the user with other calculators to determine the wiring gauge necessary and capacitor required for a specific installation. Figure 4 shows a screen shot of an example wiring diagram.

Tap the duck game This game randomly generates sprites (small duck images) that fly around the screen and entice the user to tap them, at which time they disappear. The sprites bounce around the screen quickly, but with varying speeds, and the program keeps track of how many sprites the user taps in a limited amount of time. The sprites also switch directions when reaching a boundary, and it supports multiple game layers.

This application is especially sophisticated because the students had to incorporate 2D graphics programming as well as design their own game engine using multithreading for performance reasons. A screen shot of the application can be seen in Figure 5.

Wheelchair trainer This application assists wheelchair users in training for athletic events by keeping maintaining

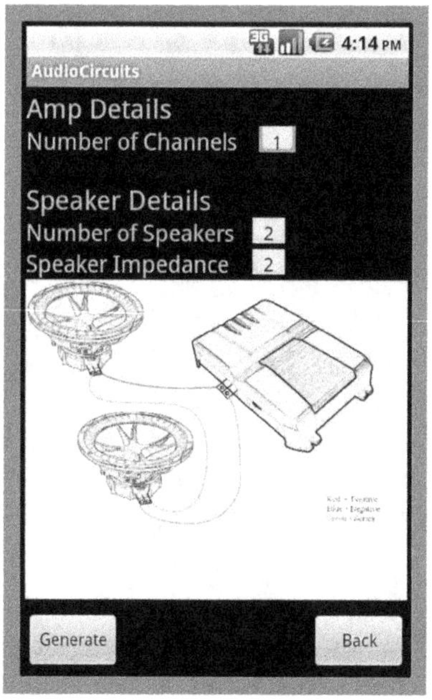

Figure 4: Wiring diagram generator for car audio

the number of pushes made and the distance traveled over time. The application uses the Android device accelerometer to track the force of pushes and the GPS to measure the distance traveled. Data is recorded so the user can compare training runs. A sensitivity adjustment was included to account for the manner in which different road surfaces and different wheel types affect accelerometer readings. A screen shot of this application can be seen in Figure 6.

4.4 Evaluation

The primary goal of the course was to teach students how to become competent Java developers. The post-course survey asked students to rate their Java expertise before and after the course. 69% of students rated their before course Java expertise as 'None', 23% rated their expertise 'Little', 8% rated it 'Some', and no students considered themselves an 'Expert'. No students rated their post-course expertise as 'None' or 'Little', 46% rated it 'Some', and 54% considered themselves an 'Expert'.

To assess the impact of Android students were asked to rate the effectiveness of using Android to teach Java concepts. No student rated this 'Poor', 12% of students rated it 'OK', 42% rated it 'Good', and 46% rated it 'Great'. One student wrote a comment that he learned Java concepts using Android that he felt that he would not have learned in a traditional Java course.

One of the challenges of computer science education in the internet age is the availability of online solutions to common programming assignments. While some Android software is available online, most of the applications are closed-source, so students learn to use developer websites and forums to collaborate with other programmers instead of just copying them. Another advantage of using Android for projects is that students inherently incorporate creativity into their own projects making plagiarism obvious.

In the post-semester survey students were asked to rate their feeling of preparedness for the job market prior to and

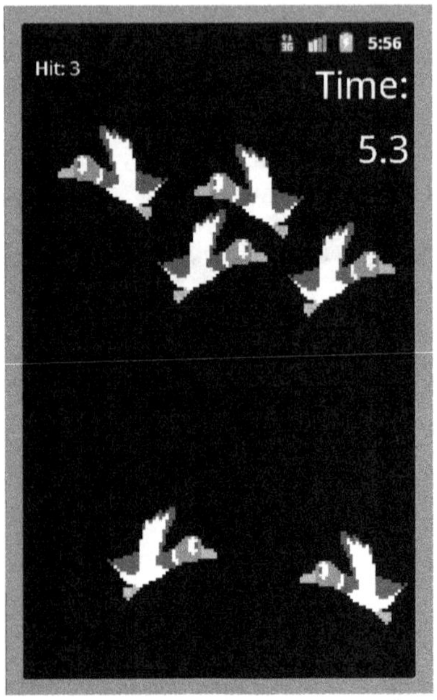

Figure 5: Tap the duck game screen shot

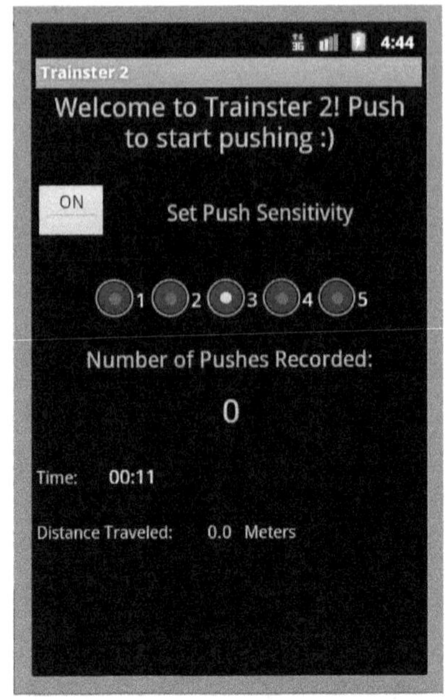

Figure 6: Wheelchair training application

after the course. 19% of students rated their pre-course preparedness as 'None', 35% rated it 'Little', 38% rated it 'Some', and 8% of students considered themselves 'Ready'. No students rated their post-course preparedness as 'None', 4% of students rated it 'Little', 31% rated it as 'Some', and 65% considered themselves 'Ready'.

5. CONCLUSIONS

This paper presents a course designed to teach C/C++ programmers how to develop OO Java software using the Android mobile operating system platform. The course is designed to accommodate students from a wide variety of programming backgrounds and to harness their creativity and enthusiasm for programming mobile phones in order to enhance learning outcomes. According to [3] approximately 30 percent of CS departments use C/C++ as the language for CS1/CS2; this suggests that approaches such as the one described could be applicable to such institutions. Further, Android can be used as a platform to teach other upper-division computing courses such as operating systems, networking, parallel programming, graphics, and others.

There are several challenges of incorporating Android into an established course. First, class time must be spent discussing the nuances of the operating system and visualization that are specific to Android, which takes away from the time for other topics. Another challenge of this approach is the ever-changing landscape of mobile operating systems. The Android plug-in and libraries are constantly changing, so the course and computer labs must be kept up to date to incorporate the changes. Another challenge was created by the so-called digital divide because some students were unfamiliar with mobile devices, and therefore, they did not feel motivated to use them in the course. Despite these challenges, this course has demonstrated that incorporation of Android programming into courses requires little investment beyond time, so I posit that Android is an effective platform for teaching Java and selected programming concepts.

6. REFERENCES

[1] The Android developers website, 2011.

[2] The Eclipse Foundation, 2011.

[3] S. Davies, J. A. Polack-Wahl, and K. Anewalt. A snapshot of current practices in teaching the introductory programming sequence. In *Proceedings of the 42nd ACM technical symposium on Computer science education*, SIGCSE, pages 625–630, 2011.

[4] G. Eknoyan. Adolphe quetelet (1796–1874)–the average man and indices of obesity. *Nephrol. Dial. Transplant*, 23(1):47–51, 2008.

[5] J. B. Fenwick, Jr., B. L. Kurtz, and J. Hollingsworth. Teaching mobile computing and developing software to support computer science education. In *Proceedings of the 42nd ACM technical symposium on Computer science education*, SIGCSE, pages 589–594, 2011.

[6] M. Goadrich and M. Rogers. Smart smartphone development: iOS versus Android. In *SIGCSE*, volume 42, 2011.

[7] V. Matos and R. Grasser. Building applications for the Android OS mobile platform: a primer and course materials. *J. Comput. Small Coll.*, 26:23–29, October 2010.

[8] S. Rebelsky and C. Flynt. Real-world program design in CS2: the roles of a large-scale, multi-group class project. In *SIGCSE*, volume 32, 2000.

[9] M. Stanley. *The Mobile Internet Report*, December 2009.

[10] D. Wolber. App inventor and real-world motivation. In *Proceedings of the 42nd ACM technical symposium on Computer science education*, SIGCSE, pages 601–606, 2011.

RoboLIFT: Engaging CS2 Students with Testable, Automatically Evaluated Android Applications

Anthony Allevato and Stephen H. Edwards
Department of Computer Science
Virginia Tech
114 McBryde Hall, MC 0106
Blacksburg, VA 24061
allevato@vt.edu, edwards@cs.vt.edu

ABSTRACT

Making computer science assignments interesting and relevant is a constant challenge for instructors of introductory courses. Android has become popular in these courses to take advantage of the increasing popularity of smartphones and mobile "apps." This has been shown to increase student engagement but it is only the first step, and we must continue to provide support for teaching methodologies that we have used in the past, such as test-driven development and automated assessment. We have developed RoboLIFT, a library that makes unit testing of Android applications approachable for students. Furthermore, by supporting existing automated grading techniques, we are able to sustain large student enrollments, and we evaluate the effects that using Android has had on student performance.

Categories and Subject Descriptors

K.3.2 [**Computers and Education**]: Computer and Information Science Education; D.2.2 [**Software Engineering**]: Design Tools and Techniques—user interfaces; D.2.5 [**Software Engineering**]: Testing and Debugging—testing tools.

General Terms

Design, Verification.

Keywords

Android, mobile development, smartphone, tablet, apps, test-driven development, TDD, JUnit, test-first coding, graphical user interfaces, GUI.

1. INTRODUCTION

A frequent challenge at the early levels of computer science education is creating programming assignments that are relevant and current, engage the students and keep their interest, and still cover the fundamental topics taught in the course.

The CS2 course at Virginia Tech focuses on data structures and software design, which are abstract topics that require a strong motivation for students at the early levels to understand and appreciate. One attempt at such motivation has been to introduce students at this stage to graphical user interfaces (GUIs), allowing them to explore the data management aspects of the course by wrapping them inside interesting and interactive applications. We also use this as a rationale for introducing students to design patterns such as *observer* and *model-view-controller*.

Permission to make digital or hard copies of all or part of this work for personal or classroom use is granted without fee provided that copies are not made or distributed for profit or commercial advantage and that copies bear this notice and the full citation on the first page. To copy otherwise, or republish, to post on servers or to redistribute to lists, requires prior specific permission and/or a fee.
SIGCSE'12, February 29–March 3, 2012, Raleigh, North Carolina, USA.
Copyright 2012 ACM 978-1-4503-1098-7/12/02...$10.00.

We wish to underscore, however, that the additions made to the CS2 course were *not* intended to transform it into a GUI programming and design course. Rather, students are introduced to event-driven programming and taught how to develop very rudimentary GUIs as a way of illustrating the potential real-world applications of lower-level data structures.

Until now we have taught students how to design and implement GUIs for standard desktop applications using the Java Swing framework. The use of these sorts of applications, however, has been decreasing as the computing industry and markets shift toward web-based applications and mobile "apps." We have found success in our CS1 course in recent years by transitioning to web-based applications using CloudSpace [9], and we wished to explore the possibilities of making similar improvements to CS2.

We determined that Google's Android mobile platform is a strong fit for our curriculum, thanks to a number of compelling factors: Android development uses the Java programming language, which our CS1 and CS2 courses already teach; developing simple but interesting Android applications does not require an advanced understanding of computer science, and students upon reaching CS2 should have the maturity to tackle such topics; and the Android platform has a strong market presence, ensuring that we are teaching our students a skill set that they can successfully apply in their career after completing the program.

Many educators have made similar evaluations and begun using Android in their early computer science courses, and they have seen an increase in student excitement as a result [5, 6]. However, much of the work done so far does not describe solutions to problems beyond just getting students to write Android applications, such as how to manage test-driven development and automated assessment. Since we at Virginia Tech extensively apply these concepts in our courses, we were obligated to ensure that we did not sacrifice any of our existing practices during a transition to a new platform.

2. STUDENT DEVELOPMENT PROCESS

Students at Virginia Tech start out in the CS1 course using BlueJ [1] as the preferred development environment. The CS2 course "graduates" students to Eclipse, in order to build their experience with a more mature environment that they are likely to encounter later in their careers. We feel that students at the beginning of this course have reached a point where they understand enough of the fundamentals that they can now use features such as auto-complete and quick fixes that Eclipse provides, but there has never been a specific feature or requirement of the work assigned in the course that compelled its use.

Developing for the Android platform provides a stronger rationale for this transition, because Google provides officially supported development tools for Eclipse. Students can therefore take advantage of a fully integrated development environment.

2.1 GUI Design Support

In previous offerings of the course that were taught using Swing, students were required to design their GUIs by writing Java code and using Swing's layout managers. Students often found this to be unnecessarily tedious, and real-world developers rarely do GUI development in this fashion. The state of the Swing WYSIWYG visual editor project for Eclipse has been somewhat uncertain in recent years, however, and its usage model and the resulting Java code that it generates make it an unsuitable tool for students learning GUIs for the first time.

The Android development tools for Eclipse, however, include a different WYSIWYG GUI designer that generates XML layout files used by the platform. Even though students who took our CloudSpace-based CS1 course are already familiar with writing HTML and XML-like markup for designing complex user interfaces, they are generally happy to find that they can prototype their Android GUIs even more quickly by using a visual tool. With limited time available to work on each project, speeding up the GUI design phase of the students' development cycle allows them to focus their attention on the more relevant data-oriented course topics that they are being asked to apply.

2.2 Test-Driven Development

The CS1 and CS2 courses at Virginia Tech place a great emphasis on test-driven development, requiring that students thoroughly test the solution code that they write by factoring test coverage into their scores on the programming projects [2]. We have seen that encouraging our students to write good unit tests incrementally greatly decreases the number of defects in their work [3].

When we originally added a Swing programming component to the CS2 course, we wanted to ensure that our students could continue to write comprehensive JUnit tests for GUI code. Such tests simulate user actions on a GUI and then make assertions about the state of the GUI components or the underlying data model. To this end, we developed LIFT, the Library for Interface Testing [8], for writing Swing-based unit tests. LIFT provides a clean interface with simple methods that students can call to interact with their GUI (for example, "click this button" or "drag the mouse from here to there"), and it also provides highly expressive filter-based component retrieval capabilities ("get the button that is enabled and has text 'OK'") using an API based on a "fluent interface" design [4].

In order to feel comfortable with a move from Swing to Android, it was important that we did not lose the successful testing approach that we had built up over the past few years. Android OS contains powerful runtime instrumentation features and a number of classes for writing unit tests, but these APIs are clearly designed with the professional programmer in mind rather than a beginning student. Methods for interacting with the GUI under test are scattered among a few different classes, and because the tests run on a separate thread from the GUI, the user must have a strong understanding Java's and Android's threading models in order to use them successfully.

```
EditText firstValue = getView(
    EditText.class, R.id.firstValue);
EditText secondValue = getView(
    EditText.class, R.id.secondValue);
TextView sumLabel = getView(
    TextView.class, R.id.sumLabel);
Button addButton = getView(
    Button.class, where.textIs("Add"));
```

Figure 1. Retrieving references to widgets for testing.

```
enterText(firstValue, "10");
enterText(secondValue, "20");
click(addButton);

assertEquals("Sum = 30",
    sumLabel.getText());
```

Figure 2. Interacting with user interface elements in a test case using RoboLIFT.

Therefore, we developed RoboLIFT, a port of the existing LIFT library to the Android platform, in order to provide the same simple interaction and component retrieval APIs for Android applications. RoboLIFT provides a testing interface nearly identical to that of the original LIFT library, with appropriate changes in nomenclature to better integrate with the terminology used by the Android platform (for example, "views" rather than "components").

Android applications consist of one (or more) *activity,* which represents (in most cases) a single screen and user interface with which the user can interact. Like the testing infrastructure native to Android OS, RoboLIFT treats the activity as the "unit" to be tested. By extending the generic `AndroidTestCase` class provided by RoboLIFT and passing the activity class as the generic type parameter (and, as an implementation detail, also including a no-argument constructor that passes the activity class to its superclass), students can make use of the testing methods that the library provides.

Figure 1 shows the generic `getView()` method that students can use to access the views and widgets in their layouts. The first three lines show the most common usage of this method, which takes as its parameters the `Class` object representing the type of the view to be retrieved and the identifier that the student assigned to the view. The class parameter acts as another check to ensure that the view that is retrieved is the correct type and also eliminates the need to explicitly downcast the reference that is returned.

The fourth line in Figure 1 illustrates how one might use a "fluent interface" filter instead of an identifier to retrieve a view. This feature is implemented in the same fashion as in the original LIFT library [8]. In most cases, students will use the simple identifier-based version of the `getView()` method; the fluent filters are more useful to instructors who may wish to write reference tests that retrieve views by some other criteria. Methods also exist to

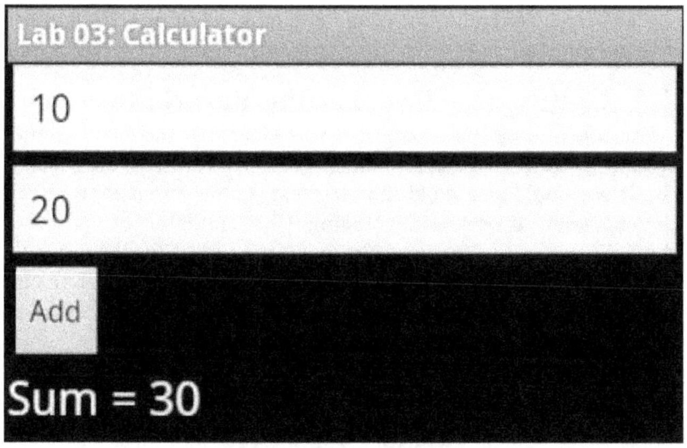

Figure 3. Visual feedback that the student sees when running the test case in Figure 2.

perform more powerful retrievals, such as retrieving a list of *all* views that satisfy a particular set of criteria.

RoboLIFT provides several easy-to-use methods for interacting with standard GUI widgets, such as `click()` and `enterText()`. An example of their usage is shown in Figure 2. These methods make it very easy for students to describe the actions that they want to perform and then use familiar JUnit assertions to check the state of their views or their underlying data model. If more elaborate touch input needs to be simulated (for example, a touch-drag-release sequence at specific coordinates on a view), methods such as `touchDown()`, `touchMove()`, `touchUp()` can be used to describe those actions. The major benefits to students are that these methods are significantly simpler than the corresponding Android instrumentation methods (which RoboLIFT uses internally), and they also hide the complex threading and synchronization issues that exist in Android GUI testing.

When students run their tests in the Android emulator, they are able to see them execute in real time and watch as widgets are clicked and text is typed into fields, just as if they were carrying out the actions themselves. The end result of such a test run is shown in Figure 3. Anecdotally, we have seen that many students resist unit testing and initially have difficulty appreciating its value. This kind of visual feedback is a great tool for overcoming those barriers because students can see a realistic mapping of the test code they write to the actions that it performs, they can easily re-execute a large batch of tests, and they can see how effortlessly the computer can automate the same tasks that they would otherwise have to carry out much more slowly by hand.

2.3 Skeleton Projects

For each Android-based assignment in the course, we provide students with a skeleton Eclipse project that they download and import into their workspace before they begin. Doing this might raise concerns that students are missing out on an important part of the Android development cycle, because creating such a project involves configuring a number of options such as the application name, package identifier, target SDK, minimum supported API version, and so forth. However, just as we stress that this is not a GUI design course, this also is not a dedicated Android programming course, so we relieve the students of the burden of setting up a complex Android manifest for each project.

Another motivating factor for providing skeleton projects is that the built-in Android project creation wizard in Eclipse encourages the creation of a separate project to contain the unit tests for an application. While this is a reasonable model to follow in real-world development, keeping the unit tests in the same project as the students' solution code simplifies their development process and the workflow required to submit their solutions. Bypassing this default behavior would require that students manually configure their project's manifest file to support unit tests. If students were asked to manually configure their projects to support testing, especially when many already resist testing, we would likely find that this would delay their use of TDD practices even further. Therefore, we do this configuration in advance in the skeleton projects so that they can start writing tests immediately, as they have in the previous course.

3. AUTOMATED ASSESSMENT

In many of our computer science courses, students submit their solutions and test code to Web-CAT [2] for automatic evaluation. Web-CAT builds their code, runs their own unit tests to determine the completeness of their testing based on the amount of code coverage achieved, and then runs their solution against a set of instructor-written reference tests to evaluate its correctness.

For a project that requires implementing a GUI, the process is essentially the same; however, instead of testing their solution by calling a predefined set of methods on classes that they wrote, we instead exercise their program by interacting with its GUI.

We wish for students to have the freedom to be creative with their designs, so we do not want to shackle them with strict requirements about their component hierarchy or the screen positioning of user interface elements. For Swing-based programs, we took advantage of the fact that each component can have associated with it an identifying "name" property, and we gave students a set of required components and their names that we would look up in reference tests.

We can achieve the same testing behavior for Android applications, since each view in a layout is given a unique identifier. When a student adds a view to a layout in the GUI editor, he or she can give that view a symbolic name, which is used to define an integer constant in the project's auto-generated `R.id` class. By giving students the names of the views that they are required to include in their layout, we can then look them up based on those names and interact with them.

3.1 Automating the Android Emulator

Our first approach was merely to automate the process that students use to run their own tests. A plug-in was developed for Web-CAT that takes the student's uploaded code, builds an Android application package, installs it onto an instance of the Android emulator that exists on the server, and then starts the tests inside the application and collects the results. This approach was initially desirable because it exactly mirrored the conditions under which students ran their tests, reducing the possibility that environmental differences might cause inconsistencies in the results. Care was taken to ensure that each grading cycle used a clean instance of the virtual device so that state left behind by submissions graded earlier would not affect those that came later.

However, it soon became apparent that automating the emulator would be problematic. The biggest hurdle to overcome was that the official Android emulator can be quite slow, even on modern hardware, and attempts to automate it were often unstable. In our experiments during the development of this course material, we found that Web-CAT would take between 2 and 3 minutes to grade even a simple submission with a trivial number of test cases. This time would only increase if we brought the number of tests up to the amount that students typically write and also included a similar number of thorough instructor-written tests.

Delays of this degree can cause logistical problems in large courses. In comparison, our students are accustomed to grading times of approximately 30 seconds for non-GUI Java programs, or possibly one minute for larger Swing-based GUI applications. Further exacerbating this problem is the fact that Web-CAT currently grades submissions sequentially, placing submissions in a single queue while one is being processed. Parallel clustered grading support is under development, but the performance issues associated with the emulator would require a large number of physical servers to take full advantage of such capabilities. Furthermore, having clustered grading would still do nothing to decrease the time needed to grade each individual submission. With an enrollment of approximately 150 students in CS2 in a typical semester, a heavy load on the server might have students waiting several hours for their results. Students value the (near) immediate feedback they receive, and take advantage of it to complete multiple edit/revise cycles during the time the assignment is open so that they can refine their solution as much as possible, and such substantial delays would be undesirable.

3.2 Bypassing the Emulator with Robolectric

In our search for possible ways to increase the speed of the emulator, we discovered a framework called Robolectric [7], which allows one to bypass the emulator completely and run unit tests in a local JVM in the same manner that plain (non-Android) Java unit tests would be run. Normally, Android code cannot run on a standard JVM, because Google uses its own custom Dalvik JVM for Android devices. In fact, the Android JAR file that developers use when building their code only contains stub classes and methods that throw runtime exceptions. Robolectric lets unit tests run locally by injecting a set of "shadow classes" that provide barebones implementations of many of the standard classes in the Android API with reasonable default behaviors.

By using Robolectric, unit tests for Android applications ran no more slowly than Swing unit tests using LIFT. In fact, if we compare a set of Swing-based tests to a similar set of Android-based tests, the Android tests would run *faster* because Robolectric does not actually render the user interface or use the local system's event queue to simulate inputs.

The fact that the application's GUI is never laid out or rendered also presented some initial challenges when using Robolectric during automated grading. This resulted in some code coverage problems (for example, the `onDraw()` method in a view was never executed) and some behavioral consistency issues arose when a student's code used the width or height of a view as a dependent variable in a calculation. Under Robolectric, all views had a width and height of zero, so if the student wrote a test case that clicked a location one-fourth of the way across a view, the test would have different behavior than if it ran in the emulator where view bounds were actually computed.

We addressed those situations by extending Robolectric's shadow classes to provide behavior that better mimicked the real behavior of Android on the emulator. After one semester of use, we have managed to fill many of these gaps based on the scenarios that students encountered during their time working on the programming assignments. However, there may be more such situations that could be revealed by using assignments of a different nature or with different GUI components than those that we have used so far. Our hope is that after a few semesters of use, we will have covered most of the common situations that students will encounter.

3.3 Uniting the Two Testing Paradigms

After considering these issues, it was clear that the right solution would be one that incorporated the best of both approaches. Students should be able to run their tests in the actual environment under which they are developing (the emulator or an actual Android device) in order to get satisfying visual feedback for the tests that they write. Then, Web-CAT should use Robolectric during grading to minimize delays in getting feedback to students.

To apply this strategy, we were required to implement two versions of the RoboLIFT API. One version of the library uses the native Android instrumentation classes built into the operating system to simulate interaction with the user interface, and this is the version that is given to students for running their tests on an emulator or device.

These instrumentation classes are not available to Robolectric, however. Instead, interaction must be simulated by calling various methods on the framework's augmented shadow classes, so we also have a second implementation of RoboLIFT that runs on Web-CAT with Robolectric. While this increases the maintenance required to keep them in sync and functionally equivalent, we still view it as the best way of balancing the different needs of student testing vs. automated testing.

4. CLASSROOM USAGE

In the first offering of the CS2 course that included Android (Summer 2011), we developed two new lab assignments and one new programming project that incorporated a wide range of Android user interface concepts to motivate the implementation and application of some fundamental data structures and design patterns.

The labs are self-contained, two-hour pair programming exercises that give students the opportunity to practice and apply the material that they learn in lecture. In the context of teaching Android GUI programming, we identified two major areas that we wanted students to be able to explore. First, students should be able to understand and use built-in widgets such as buttons and text fields to develop a simple user-interactive program, and the calculator example shown in Figure 3 is the final deliverable for that lab. A second lab teaches students how to subclass a view and override its rendering and touch-input methods to support more complex interactions.

One important aspect of the new lab material is that even though they are very simple applications, students must still implement a proper model-view-controller decomposition of the problem and must still write comprehensive tests for their code. Rather than sacrifice these notions due to limited time in labs, we feel that it is important that the students have as much reinforcement of these concepts as possible.

The larger programming project was an interactive maze solver, shown in Figure 4. It combines the concepts that students learned in lab and features standard button and text view widgets as well as a customized view where students must handle touch events and render the maze, which is represented by a two-dimensional array. The user of the application can draw the walls of the maze with his or her finger. Then, by clicking the "Solve Maze" button, the program searches the maze for a solution, showing the correct solution (if found) and any paths that were dead ends that required backtracking. Students were required to implement the search using a linked stack.

Figure 4. The Maze Solver project.

During the Fall 2011 term, we plan to introduce another Android-based project that takes advantage of some other unique features of the platform, such as Google Maps integration to display data of interest to the local community.

Additionally, students enrolled in a fall or spring offering of the course form three-member teams and develop group projects. Some general requirements are given in order to enforce the course objectives (for example, the project must incorporate some interesting, non-trivial data structures and a GUI), but beyond that the students are encouraged to be as creative as they like. It is our hope that the Android platform will spur even more creativity, and while it is certainly not a goal of the course, some students may wish to go as far as marketing their application at some point afterward.

5. EVALUATION

Our dataset includes Swing-based program submissions made in three offerings of the CS2 course during Spring 2010, Fall 2010, and Spring 2011, and Android-based submissions made during Summer 2011. Each student was allowed an unlimited number of submissions to each assignment before the due date, but only the final submission counted toward his or her grade (unless he or she asked that an earlier one be counted instead). There were 296 students who took the course during the semesters during which Swing was used, and 18 students who took the course when Android was the teaching platform.

Group	Mean	Std. Dev.
Swing		
Spring 2010	94.6	11.6
Fall 2010	98.4	5.0
Spring 2011	96.3	11.6
Across all semesters	96.4	10.5
Android		
Summer 2011	98.4	3.9

Table 1. Test coverage statistics for groups of assignment submissions.

In the Swing offerings of the course, students were given two programming projects that required them to implement a GUI. The assignment that most closely resembles the maze solver in terms of the design of the application and its educational goals is an image gallery implemented using a circular linked list. The primary goal of each of these assignments was to develop a linear linked data structure and then apply it by wrapping it in a GUI. Our analysis below compares student outcomes on these two assignments.

5.1 Test Coverage

One of the main objectives of our introductory CS courses is that students learn how to test their solution code thoroughly, which we evaluate by computing the amount of code coverage they achieve through their own testing. The coverage metric used for grading was computed as the sum of the student's statement coverage, decision coverage, and method coverage. In order to ensure that we have not fallen short of our goals as a side effect of introducing Android into the course, we compared students' test coverage from semesters during which Swing was used to the semester during which Android was used.

Table 1 shows the population statistics for student submissions grouped by platform and by semester. Across all final submissions to GUI assignments (N = 324), the average code coverage achieved was 96.5%. An analysis of variance did not indicate a statistically significant difference in the code coverage between the Swing and Android assignments ($F(1, 322) = 0.605$, $p = 0.437$). There was also no significant difference between semesters ($F(3, 320) = 2.57, p = 0.054$).

These results allow us to feel more comfortable that our students were able to write test cases for Android-based applications that were comparable in thoroughness and rigorousness to those that students have been writing for Swing-based applications.

5.2 Program Correctness

The next metric we examined was program correctness (Table 2), which is evaluated by running a set of instructor-written reference tests on the student's solution. The percentage of these tests that passed is reported to the student, and a limited number of hints are provided that describe areas where the student's solution (and therefore testing) need work.

Across all final submissions to GUI assignments (N = 324), the average pass rate achieved against instructor-provided reference tests was 93.7%. An analysis of variance did not indicate a significant difference between the Swing and Android assignments ($F(1, 322) = 0.0774$, $p = 0.781$), nor was there a

Group	Mean	Std. Dev.
Swing		
Spring 2010	92.8	13.3
Fall 2010	95.1	11.2
Spring 2011	93.1	16.1
Across all semesters	93.7	13.6
Android		
Summer 2011	94.6	11.7

Table 2. Reference test correctness statistics for groups of assignment submissions.

significant difference between semesters ($F(3, 320) = 0.617$, $p = 0.605$).

Based on these results, we also feel comfortable that students had no more difficulty writing *correct* code that satisfied the program requirements when using Android as the teaching platform than students did when using Swing.

5.3 Student Opinions

After the due date for each programming project, Web-CAT releases an optional survey to students that asks their opinions of the assignment, focusing on gauging engagement and frustration. The surveys ask students to rate facets of the assignment on a 1–10 scale and then provide detailed opinions in a free response. With an enrollment of only 18 students for the first Android offering, we were unable to get a sufficient number of responses for meaningful quantitative analysis. Based on the submitted answers to the free response questions, however, those who did respond seemed to appreciate the use of Android in class and found it motivating and exciting. Less favorable comments were focused on the parts of the assignments that dealt with low-level data structures rather than any difficulties caused by the choice of platform.

A particularly good point was made by one student who expressed that while the skeleton projects were useful to help get started, it would have been useful to see the complete project creation process from scratch as well, in order to better understand what goes into the configuration of an Android application. Our belief is that the final group project in the fall and spring offerings of the course is a suitable place for this to occur, since students will be making decisions about the application name, package structure, and other choices normally given to them in the skeleton.

6. FUTURE WORK

For reasons of simplicity, both in programming and testing, the projects assigned in the course consist of a single Android activity. RoboLIFT would benefit from being able to fully support testing applications comprising multiple activities as well. Currently, each activity can already be tested as a separate self-contained unit. Imagine, however, that activity A contains a button that displays activity B when clicked. In order to achieve full code coverage, we would need to provide a convenient API that allows them to make the assertion "did activity B start?" after clicking the appropriate button in activity A.

RoboLIFT currently supports basic interactions such as touching views, selecting menu items, and simulating keyboard input. We are currently working to add support for other user interface elements such as spinners and modal dialogs so that students can design even more advanced user interfaces and still be able to test them rigorously.

Lastly, we would like to find ways of using other features unique to mobile devices in our assignments, such as camera integration, multi-touch interaction and motion sensors. However, the emulator currently restricts what is possible and we want to ensure that students who do not own an Android device are not left out. Efforts are currently underway to obtain a small number of phones and tablets for student use but our large enrollments make it infeasible to provide one for every student. It is our hope again that, until then, students who have devices of their own will use the group project as an opportunity to creatively explore some of these features, and we will encourage them to do so.

7. REFERENCES

[1] BlueJ, 2011. *BlueJ – The interactive Java environment.* http://www.bluej.org

[2] Edwards, S. H. 2003. Rethinking computer science education from a test-first perspective. In *OOPSLA '03 Companion of the 18th Annual ACM SIGPLAN Conference on Object-Oriented Programming, Systems, Languages, and Applications* (San Diego, California, June 9–11, 2003). OOPSLA '03. ACM, New York, NY, 148–155. DOI=http://doi.acm.org/10.1145/949344.949390.

[3] Edwards, S. H. 2004. Using software testing to move students from trial-and-error to reflection-in-action. In *Proceedings of the 35th Annual SIGCSE technical symposium on Computer science education* (Norfolk, Virginia, March 3–7, 2004). SIGCSE '04. ACM, New York, NY, 26-30. DOI= http://doi.acm.org/10.1145/971300.971312.

[4] Fowler, M. 2005. *FluentInterface.* http://martinfowler.com/bliki/FluentInterface.html

[5] Goadrich, M., Jadud, M., and Jennings, J. 2011. Exploring the use of Android in CS2. In *SmartPhones in the Curriculum Workshop (SMACK 2011) of the 2011 24th Conference on Software Engineering Education and Training* (Honolulu, Hawaii, May 22–24, 2011).

[6] Heckman, S., Horton, T. B., and Sherriff, M. 2011. Teaching second-level Java and software engineering with Android. In *2011 24th Conference on Software Engineering Education and Training* (Honolulu, Hawaii, May 22–24, 2011). CSEE&T '11, 540–542.

[7] Robolectric, 2011. *Robolectric: Unit test your Android application.* http://www.robolectric.org

[8] Snyder, J., Edwards, S. H., and Pérez-Quiñones, M. A. 2011. LIFT: taking GUI unit testing to new heights. In *Proceedings of the 42nd ACM technical symposium on Computer science education* (Dallas, Texas, March 9–12, 2011). SIGCSE '11. ACM, New York, NY, 643–648. DOI= http://doi.acm.org/10.1145/1953163.1953343.

[9] Woods, M., Back, G., and Edwards, S. 2010. An infrastructure for teaching CS1 in the cloud. In *Proceedings of the 2010 ASEE Southeast Section Conference,* Blacksburg, Virginia, April 2010.

Highway Data and Map Visualizations for Educational Use

James D. Teresco
Siena College
515 Loudon Rd.
Loudonville, NY, USA
jteresco@siena.edu

ABSTRACT

It is often a challenge to find interesting and appropriate data sets to use as examples to demonstrate graph data structures and algorithms. Goals for the data are often conflicting. The data should include examples small enough to work through in a class example by hand, but some large enough to demonstrate important behaviors of a structure or algorithm. Data should be freely available in a convenient format and should have some real-world relevance. Visualization of the data and results computed from it is helpful.

This paper describes a collection of graph data sets generated from the Clinched Highway Mapping Project's highway data and some examples of their use in undergraduate courses on data structures and algorithms. The source data, the process used to convert the data into a more useful format, some examples of its use, and a visualization tool using the Google Maps API, are described.

Categories and Subject Descriptors

K.3.2 [**Computer and Information Science Education**]: Computer science education; E.1 [**Data Structures**]: Graphs and networks; G.2.2 [**Graph Theory**]: Graph algorithms

General Terms

Algorithms

Keywords

Pedagogical tools, Graph data structures, Algorithm visualization, Google Maps API.

1. INTRODUCTION

Both students and instructors enjoy class examples and assignments that have both relevance to a real problem and an interactive and visual component [6]. The challenge is often in finding appropriate data sets. This paper describes a collection of data sets representing highway data that can be used to help study graph and other structures and algorithms. The project's motivation was to improve upon an often-used example when studying Dijkstra's algorithm for computing single-source shortest paths on a graph. A small number of vertices represent places (e.g., cities, airports, intersections, rooms), and edges represent the cost in distance or time to travel from one to the other. Figure 1 (top) shows such an example graph.

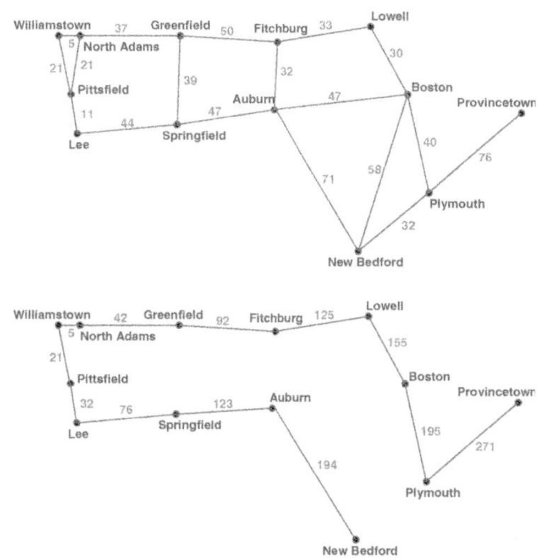

Figure 1: Top: a simple graph of towns in Massachusetts that can be used to demonstrate graph structures and algorithms. Bottom: Computed single-source shortest paths from Williamstown.

The graph has some appealing characteristics. It has some basis in reality. An adjacency matrix or adjacency list representation can be drawn by the instructor or students during class. Algorithms such as Dijkstra's Algorithm can be traced to completion (Figure 1, bottom), step-by-step at the start, and more quickly once students have the basic idea.

A somewhat larger and more interesting data set previously used by the author includes 466 segments of highways in the United States Interstate highway system gathered from an old Rand McNally road atlas. Each entry is defined by the two town names at the endpoints, the name of the highway connecting the two, and the distance in miles between them. For example,

```
albany_ny binghamton_ny I-88 142
```

Permission to make digital or hard copies of all or part of this work for personal or classroom use is granted without fee provided that copies are not made or distributed for profit or commercial advantage and that copies bear this notice and the full citation on the first page. To copy otherwise, to republish, to post on servers or to redistribute to lists, requires prior specific permission and/or a fee.
SIGCSE'12, February 29–March 3, 2012, Raleigh, North Carolina, USA.
Copyright 2012 ACM 978-1-4503-1098-7/12/02 ...$10.00.

indicates that I-88 connects Albany, New York, with Binghamton, New York, over a distance of 142 miles.

This data set is too large to study manually, but small enough to serve as a good data set for testing a laboratory or homework program. While this data could be visualized in an abstract graph form, it lacks any information about where the towns at the graph vertices are located.

This paper describes a collection of data sets that are similar in spirit to the above examples, but with some important advantages. This data is extracted from the Clinched Highway Mapping (CHM) project [9]. The vertices represent places (usually intersections) and the edges represent roads connecting those places. Place data consists of a name and a latitude-longitude pair that allows the places to be plotted on a map. Each data set represents one or more highway systems in North America or Europe, ranging in size from a few dozen vertices and edges up to over one hundred thousand. The smaller data sets can be used in class examples or for debugging programs, while the larger sets can be used to test programs more thoroughly, and to analyze their performance meaningfully.

The CHM project is described in more detail in Section 2. Section 3 details the CHM data and how it is converted into formats more convenient for academic use. In Section 4, the mapping system, based on the Google Maps API [2], is described. Examples of data sets and their uses are presented in Section 5. Finally, some concluding remarks and ideas for future extensions are discussed in Section 6.

2. THE CLINCHED HIGHWAY MAPPING PROJECT

The CHM project, created and managed by Timothy Reichard, allows users to track segments of highways on which they have traveled (or, in "roadgeek" terminology, "clinched"). They can compare their travels to fellow users and generate maps of their travels. Users submit a list of highway segments they have clinched, specifying the highway by name and region specifier, and the endpoints of the segment they have traveled. The project began with the Interstate highway system in the United States, but has expanded to include many other national and state/provincial highway systems in North America and Europe. The highway systems in the project are constantly being expanded and existing systems are being updated, corrected, and enhanced by a small team of volunteer collaborators (including the author).

2.1 CHM Project Data Granularity

A key feature of the CHM project is the granularity of the data used to represent the highways. Which intersections should be included in the description of a highway? In the early stages of the project, this decision was quite easy. The only highways represented were the U.S. Interstates, and the only way to enter or exit these highways is at a freeway interchange or a highway terminus. A CHM user could specify their clinched segments by the interchange numbers (or, state or international boundary or other terminus) for each highway. Interchanges are usually located every few miles, so the straight lines connecting interchanges form a reasonable approximation of the shape and length of the highway. Some exceptions exist, such as interchanges 2 and 3 of Interstate 90 in Massachusetts (Figure 2). They are 30.3 miles of driving distance apart along a road that winds

Figure 2: The straight line connecting interchanges 2 and 3 of I-90 in Massachusetts. The direct distance is 28.29 miles, but the actual driving distance is two miles longer as the road winds through mountains.

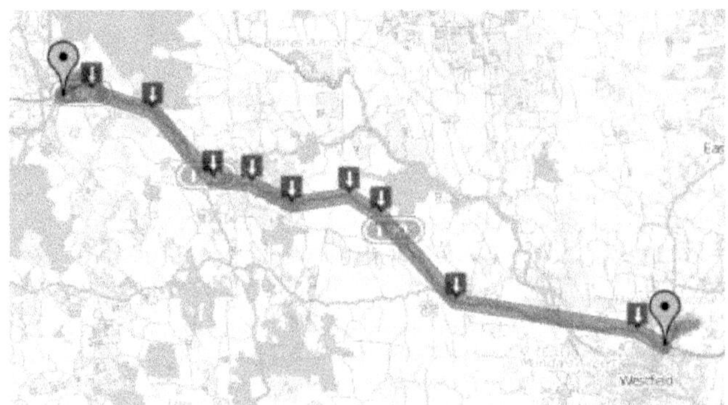

Figure 3: The route between interchanges 2 and 3 of I-90 in Massachusetts after adding "shaping" points to improve the approximation of the road. The distance via shaping points is 30.1 miles.

its way over and through the Berkshire Mountains, but the straight line distance is only 28.29 miles.

When the CHM project was expanded beyond limited access roads to include those with numerous "at-grade" intersections, new decisions were needed. Guidelines were developed to determine which intersections to use to define a route (called *waypoints* in the project's terminology), and how to name those points. It would be impractical to attempt to include every intersection, especially for longer routes and routes through urban areas, nor would it add much value to the project. Most travelers will enter and exit the highways at major intersections. On average, waypoints are spaced less than two miles apart.

Support for "hidden" waypoints was also added, allowing more accurate highway segment lengths and maps for curved road segments. These are points that are generally not useful to CHM users as potential endpoints of a traveled segment but which significantly improve the accuracy of the approximated route. For example, the segment between interchanges 2 and 3 of I-90 in Massachusetts has 9 hidden waypoints, as shown in Figure 3, which increase its approximated length to 30.1 miles.

For the purposes of CHM users, the waypoints are found using the project's Highway Browser, which plots all of the waypoints for a route within a given region using the Google Maps API. But for CHM collaborators and for the purposes of the project described here, a more detailed look at how the data is gathered and stored is necessary.

2.2 Gathering CHM Data

CHM collaborators create route descriptions by specifying a list of waypoints, gathered using a range of sources and tools[1]. In many cases, it is as simple (and at times, tedious) as centering an online map on the desired waypoint and copying a URL that represents the waypoint to the highway's waypoint list. Care is taken to use only freely-available map data in this process. Since most Google Maps data is copyrighted, routes gathered could be considered an inappropriate derivative work. Therefore, routes are generally plotted from maps in the OpenStreetMap project [7] or government satellite or topographic imagery.

2.3 CHM Data Formats

The underlying CHM data is contained in a number of plain-text files. First, a CSV-format *system file* lists the routes that make up a highway system (e.g., the U.S. Interstates, the New York state numbered highways, the German autobahn system). Entries have the format

```
usany;NY;NY5;;;;ny.ny005
usany;NY;NY52;Bus;Bea;Beacon, NY;ny.ny052busbea
usany;NY;NY114;;Gre;Greenport, NY;ny.ny114gre
```

where the 7 semicolon-separated entries represent (1) the internal CHM system name – in this case, `usany`, which is the New York state numbered highways, (2) the region name – usually a standard abbreviation for the state or province, sometimes a country, (3) the route name – `NY5` means New York route 5, (4) a banner – usually empty, could be `Bus` to represent a business route as in the second entry above, `Alt` for an alternate route, `Byp` for a bypass route, etc., (5) an abbreviation – usually empty but used to distinguish between multiple routes with the same number and/or banner within a region, (6) a city – when an abbreviation is used, a human-readable place name corresponding to that abbreviation, and (7) a waypoint file name – the name of the file that contains the waypoint data for the route.

A *waypoint file* lists the points that comprise a single route. For example, the file `ny.ny005.wpt` which describes New York state route 5, includes the lines shown in Figure 4.

Each line represents one waypoint by specifying a waypoint name, which must be unique within a route, and an OpenStreetMap URL that centers on the waypoint, from which only the the latitude and longitude entries in the query string are important. Waypoint names that begin with a '+' are treated as hidden waypoints.

3. CONVERTING CHM DATA

This collection of files works well for the CHM project, but is not convenient for the project described here. The waypoints in different files need to be matched up by coordinates and edges need to be added for adjacent waypoints within a route to create a graph.

[1]See `http://cmap.m-plex.com/docs/sources.php`

3.1 Creating an Initial Graph

An author-developed Java program is used to create a graph in memory that represents the highways in one or more CHM systems, optionally restricted by region. The basic idea is simple – for each waypoint file, a graph vertex is created at each waypoint, and a graph edge is created connecting each pair of consecutive waypoints, labeled with the name of the route being processed.

Graph vertex labels usually take the form

```
NY5@ChaDr 42.929044 -74.175761
```

where the name is the route name followed by `@` and the waypoint name from the route's list. Edges are defined by their vertex endpoints and are labeled with the name of the highway connecting them. Edge lengths are not stored, as they can be computed as needed from endpoint coordinates.

However, there are complications to consider even as the initial graph is being created:

- Intersecting highways will each have a waypoint for the other. These will have the same (or at least very nearly the same) coordinates and must be represented by a single graph vertex.
- Highways often overlap each other for part of their routings (sometimes called a "concurrency" or a "multiplex"). For example, Interstates 80 and 90 share the same roadway between western Indiana and central Ohio. Vertices and edges along a concurrency should represent the points and segments of all concurrent highways, but each should exist only once in the graph.

Vertex and edge labels representing multiple routes are handled by adding the information from the new highway to the appropriate vertex or edge as each highway is processed. Vertex labels, however, can end up being quite complex using this approach. When a waypoint corresponding to an already-existing vertex is encountered, the vertex label is extended to include information about the new highway that visits that location. For example, a simple intersection between two highways, `NY5` and `NY103`, would be given the label `NY5@NY103&NY103@NY5`. A number of techniques are applied to simplify such labels. This one would be simplified to `NY5/NY103`. Even after applying several simplifications, each of which looks for a pattern, some waypoints remain unsimplified and have fairly long labels. Each highway encountered that has a segment connecting the same two vertices results in an augmentation of the corresponding edge's label with the new highway's name.

3.2 Graph Data File Formats

After simplifications have been applied, the in-memory representation of a graph is written to a file. The file format is straightforward and reasonably easy to read back in to a graph structure. The file consists of three sections: (*i*) one line containing the number of vertices $|V|$ and edges $|E|$ in the file, (*ii*) $|V|$ lines specifying vertices with a waypoint label and the point's coordinates, and (*iii*) $|E|$ lines specifying the edges, with two vertex numbers (determined by their order in the vertex list section of the file) and an edge label specifying the routes that traverse this edge. For example, the file that includes all CHM-plotted highways within the state of New York looks like this:

```
NY67_W http://www.openstreetmap.org/?lat=42.956689&lon=-74.239748
GuyParkAve http://www.openstreetmap.org/?lat=42.955041&lon=-74.220500
NY30/67 http://www.openstreetmap.org/?lat=42.937480&lon=-74.192777
ChaDr http://www.openstreetmap.org/?lat=42.929044&lon=-74.175761
```

Figure 4: Waypoint data file entries for New York state highway 5 near Amsterdam. The entire route consists of 234 waypoints of this form.

```
8260 9189
I-78@NJ/NY 40.727649 -74.021244
I-78@HudSt 40.723714 -74.007908
... 8257 more vertex entries ...
NY878@AtlBeaBr 40.596304 -73.736973
0 1 I-78
2 3 I-81
... 9186 more edge entries ...
8258 8259 NY878
```

4. HIGHWAY DATA EXAMINER

Perhaps the most desirable feature of the data sets created by this project is the ability to visualize them in map form using a tool called the *Highway Data Examiner (HDX)*. HDX is built upon the Google Maps API. It can visualize both the graph data itself and the results of computations that use the data.

Google provides a number of application programmer interfaces to access their mapping capabilities, including one that allows embedding of a map into a web page using JavaScript. Developers must obtain an API key from Google to use the Google Maps API[2], but the service is free for non-commercial use. The HDX web-based viewer is available for use by instructors, so instructors (and students) need not obtain an API key or even do any JavaScript programming unless they wish to host and possibly extend HDX at their own site, or wish to develop other Google Maps applications.

Since its release in 2005, the Google Maps API has been used in countless web sites, including some whose primary purpose is educational. Some are focused on web development (e.g.,[5]), while others use the maps as a tool in a course (e.g., [4, 8]).

4.1 Using the Google Maps API

HDX uses several Google Maps API JavaScript objects and methods[3]. The map itself is displayed in an HTML `div` with `id="map"` by constructing a `GMap2` object

```
map = new GMap2(document.getElementById("map"),
        { mapTypes: [mapMapnik, mapOsmarender] });
```

The `mapTypes` parameter directs the `GMap2` to include OpenStreetMap map images in addition to the default map images from Google. A desired waypoint (graph vertex) at latitude `lat` and longitude `lon` with is added to `map` as follows:

```
marker = new GMarker(new GLatLng(lat, lon));
map.addOverlay(marker);
marker.bindInfoWindowHtml(markerinfo);
```

where `markerinfo` is the HTML to be displayed when a user clicks the marker on the map. A line connecting waypoints, representing a graph edge or a path among a collection of waypoints is added as a `GPolyline` object:

```
conn = new GPolyline(edgePts, "#0000FF", 10, 0.4);
map.addOverlay(conn);
```

where `edgePts` is an array of `GLatLng` representing the coordinates of the points along the path, and the remaining parameters indicate that the line should be blue, have a width of 10, and a transparency of 0.4. These objects are created and destroyed over the life of a map as different graphs or routes or other items are displayed.

4.2 Using HDX

HDX is launched by visiting the appropriate URL, `http://courses.teresco.org/chm/viewer/`, specifying either a query string parameter or using a file selector on the page to choose the data file to be visualized.

HDX has two plotting modes intended for student and instructor use. Graph mode (Figure 5, top), which is invoked when a file with a `.gra` extension is specified, plots all waypoints and connections between them. Clicking on a waypoint's marker brings up its name, waypoint number, and coordinates. Graph mode is also appropriate for waypoint-only displays by specifying 0 edges. Path mode (Figure 5, center), which is invoked when a file with a `.pth` extension is specified, plots the waypoints in the file with connections drawn between successive points. This mode is suitable for viewing route paths computed using programs such as implementations of Dijkstra's Algorithm.

5. PEDAGOGICAL USES

As with many related projects (e.g., [3]), the motivation for this project is pedagogical. Here, the project began as part of a Data Structures assignment to compute single-source shortest paths using Dijkstra's Algorithm [10]. Students were provided with data sets that were predecessors of those described here and a framework of a Java program that they were required to complete. Their tasks included adding methods to read and parse a graph data file to create an appropriate in-memory representation, to traverse the graph to compute various statistics about the data, to output the waypoints in the graph, and to compute the shortest path between any two waypoints. Students were encouraged, but not required, to use an existing graph implementation in the "structure package" software that comes with Bailey's free textbook [1]. The granularity of the data was ideal for such a project – not so small that it would be considered a "toy" data set, but not so large as to be overwhelming. The fact that students were not only using and programming a very relevant algorithm, but they were generating meaningful results in a context similar to those produced by tools they use regularly made it a very compelling assignment.

[2]The API key is optional in Version 3 of the Google Maps JavaScript API, so instructors and students will be able to install HDX on their own servers without obtaining a key once HDX has been updated to use the new API.

[3]The description here refers to the Google Maps API V2.

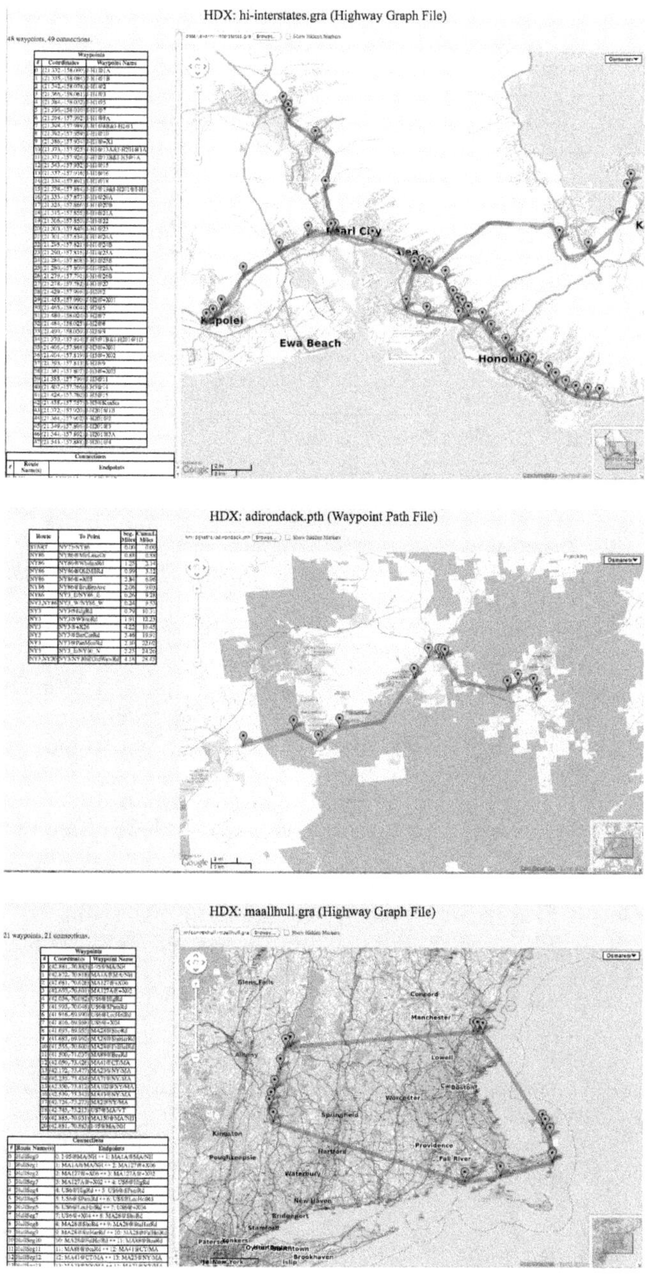

Figure 5: HDX examples. Top: graph mode view of the Hawaii Interstate highways. The raw file contents are shown on the left. Center: path mode view of a computed routing between Tupper Lake and Lake Placid, New York. Route name, waypoint, and distance information about the route shown is on the left. Hidden waypoints are not shown as markers in either case, but may be displayed by selecting the "Show Hidden Markers" toggle. Bottom: a graph mode visualization of a computed convex hull of the vertices at all waypoints in Massachusetts.

The project was expanded for use in an Analysis of Algorithms course [11, 12] to provide some class examples (e.g., Figure 5, bottom, shows a computed convex hull) and an expanded assignment to compute shortest paths.

In each case, students had the ability to visualize the results of their programs using an earlier version of the Google Maps-based viewer. Students did not take advantage of this as frequently as hoped, mainly because of the awkward procedure required at the time. Students needed to create their output files, upload them to a repository on the viewer's web server, then visit an appropriate URL in their browser to see their results. The current version of HDX eliminates the need to upload result files by providing a file selector that allows students to plot data from a file on their local computer in just one step.

5.1 Available Data Sets

The CHM project is constantly expanding to include new highway systems in different parts of the world, and improving the quality of the data in existing systems. This data can then be converted to graph form for use in this project. As an added bonus, the conversion process often points to potential errors and omissions in the CHM data, improving the data for both projects' purposes.

Table 1 shows many of the graphs that have been created and which are available for use in examples and assignments at the time of this writing. While all of these sets represent the same type of data, their sizes and other other characteristics vary widely. The range of sizes is especially important in an academic setting. The smallest data sets can be used to trace through an algorithm manually or to aid in debugging of programs. The moderately sized sets can be good for realistic examples and to test programs that perform correctly for small data sets. The largest sets can be used to test scalability of implementations and to help with performance analysis studies. The data sets also vary in spatial scale, density, and connectivity. The latter can be especially important for testing special cases of some algorithms. For example, systems that include highways on islands not connected by bridges to the mainland will include multiple disconnected components (ferry routes are not plotted).

6. CONCLUSIONS AND FUTURE WORK

The data sets and mapping capabilities described have been used for class examples and assignments in two courses. The system allowed students to work with real-world data and provided a capability for them to visualize their results. The assignments led to interesting discussions about what would be needed to extend to more fine-grained data, to add time estimates in addition to distances, and how routes could be converted to reliable turn-by-turn directions.

The number and quality of data sets has been increased significantly, and HDX is now much easier to use. The system will continue to be used in the author's courses and is available for use elsewhere. HDX works quite well for smaller data (up to a several hundred `Gmarkers` and `GPolylines`), but initial display and manipulation of maps with too many items added bogs down the Google Maps implementation. More efficient operation on larger sets is being investigated.

A second graph data organization is being developed that will make graph data more compact and visualizations less dense. Hidden waypoints are very helpful for improving the accuracy of routes. However, for the purposes of a graph in

Table 1: **Available CHM-based graph data sets.**

Data set	$\|V\|$	$\|E\|$
de-interstates: Delaware Interstate highways	26	24
hi-interstates: Hawaii Interstate highways	48	49
canyt: Yukon territorial highway system	351	354
hiall: All plotted highways in Hawaii	549	576
usact: Connecticut state highway system	1524	1751
usama: Massachusetts state highway system	1828	2099
maall: All plotted highways in Massachusetts	2284	2759
usapa: Pennsylvania state highway system	6691	6499
nyall: All plotted highways in New York	8260	9189
manyall: All plotted highways in New York and Massachusetts	10,468	11,906
canada-all: All plotted highways in Canada	16,177	16,436
usai: United States Interstate highway system	21,554	21,505
usaus: United States U.S. highway system	57,281	58,625
usanational: All plotted national highway system routes in the United States	82,362	86,041
usa-all: All plotted (state and national) highways in the United States	160,928	174,157
uscanada-all: All plotted highways in the United States and Canada	177,089	190,593

this project, they are almost always waypoints represented by a vertex of degree 2 and would be unlikely to be meaningful. Such hidden waypoints and the extra edges they induce between visible points can be collapsed into a single edge with the hidden waypoint positions stored in a list associated with that edge. This requires a new graph data structure and file format, and corresponding changes both to programs that use the data, and to HDX.

A longer-term goal for the project is to use the data and an enhanced viewer to implement interactive visualizations of algorithms that operate on these data sets. Adding, removing, and changing the colors and sizes of the `GMarker` and `GPolyline` objects on the map as an algorithm proceeds could enhance student understanding of the algorithm. The range of sizes of the data sets will again be a strength, as small sets can be used to trace through step-by-step interactive visualizations while larger sets would be more appropriate for an automated overview showing progress on a larger scale. This would be similar to the visualization described in [3], but making use of the wide range of data sizes and the additional information (i.e., route names for edge labels) available with the processed CHM data.

7. ACKNOWLEDGMENTS

Thank you to CHM Project leader Tim Reichard and the project collaborators for use of their highway data. Some of the JavaScript code in HDX is based heavily on CHM programs written by Reichard. Thank you to the anonymous reviewers whose feedback helped to improve this paper. And finally, thank you to the students in the Fall 2009 COMSC 211 Data Structures course at Mount Holyoke College and the Spring 2011 CSIS 385 Analysis of Algorithms students at Siena College for their patience and feedback.

8. REFERENCES

[1] D. A. Bailey. *Java Structures, Data Structures in Java for the Principled Programmer.* $\sqrt{7}$ edition, 2007. `http://www.cs.williams.edu/~bailey/JavaStructures/Welcome.html`.

[2] Google Maps API reference. `http://code.google.com/apis/maps/`, 2010.

[3] V. Karavirta. Real-world, student selectable data for education – learning graph algorithms. In *Proceedings of the IADIS International Conference Cognition and Exploratory Learning in Digital Age*, pages 129–136, Timisoara, Romania, October 2010.

[4] D. J. Malan. Reinventing CS50. In *Proceedings of the 41st ACM technical symposium on Computer science education*, SIGCSE '10, pages 152–156, New York, NY, USA, 2010. ACM.

[5] J. McGookey. "Mashup in a day," a mashup lesson plan. Grand Valley State University Technical Library, Paper 56, 2009. `http://scholarworks.gvsu.edu/cistechlib/56`.

[6] T. L. Naps, G. Rössling, V. Almstrum, W. Dann, R. Fleischer, C. Hundhausen, A. Korhonen, L. Malmi, M. McNally, S. Rodger, and J. A. Velázquez-Iturbide. Exploring the role of visualization and engagement in computer science education. *SIGCSE Bull.*, 35:131–152, June 2003.

[7] OpenStreetMap: the free wiki world map. `http://www.openstreetmap.org/`, 2010.

[8] Y. Ouyang, M. Lehmann, K. Hayden, and D. Kilb. Opportunities presented when developing learning resources for middle schoolers. *J. Comput. Small Coll.*, 24(4):144–150, 2009.

[9] T. Reichard. The clinched highway mapping project. `http://cmap.m-plex.com/`, 2010.

[10] J. D. Teresco. A Dijkstra's algorithm shortest path assignment using the Google Maps API: poster session. *J. Comput. Small Coll.*, 25(6):253–255, 2010.

[11] J. D. Teresco. Graph algorithms using highway mapping data and the Google Maps API. Poster, 2011. SIGCSE 2011, The 42nd ACM Technical Symposium on Computer Science Education.

[12] J. D. Teresco. Using the Google Maps API with highway mapping data as a pedagogical tool: demonstration session. *J. Comput. Small Coll.*, 26(6):58–60, 2011.

Experiments with Algorithm Visualization Tool Development

Michael C. Orsega
Department of Computer Science
The University of West Georgia
Carrollton, GA
morsega@westga.edu

Bradley T. Vander Zanden
Department of Electrical Engineering and Computer Science
The University of Tennessee
Knoxville, TN
bvz@eecs.utk.edu

Christopher H. Skinner
Department of Educational Psychology and Counseling
The University of Tennessee
Knoxville, TN
cskinne1@utk.edu

ABSTRACT

This paper presents the initial stages of a teaching tool named iSketchmate, intended for instructor use during lecture. iSketchmate allows users to create and manipulate splay trees through an animated GUI. It improves upon existing tools by providing (1) the ability to begin with any user-defined tree, (2) a history mechanism so tree operations can be repeated or changed, and (3) finer-grained animation within each operation so instructors may give further descriptions at intermediate steps within any given operation. Experiments showed iSketchmate users could produce significantly more diagrams and these diagrams were significantly more accurate than those made with pencil and paper.

Categories and Subject Descriptors

K.3.1 [**Computer Uses in Education**]: Computer-assisted instruction (CAI); E.1 [**Data Structures**]: Trees

General Terms

Algorithms, Experimentation, Human Factors

Keywords

iSketchmate

1. INTRODUCTION

When presenting complex algorithms such as splay-tree operations, instructors often draw diagrams on a whiteboard to help explain the concepts they are presenting. In introductory computer science data structures courses, instructors may use the whiteboard to diagram splay trees because the whiteboard is extremely flexible, allowing them to draw any image they desire. However, the whiteboard also has a number of drawbacks that could be addressed with a properly written computer-aided drawing tool. The instructors using a whiteboard cannot produce smooth animations that show how rotations can be used to rebalance a tree or revert to a previous state of the tree to answer student questions without re-drawing the tree. Drawing and re-drawing trees using a whiteboard also takes time and instructors may make errors when drawing these trees. Thus, when using a whiteboard the instructor must focus on performing the operations correctly and drawing the trees accurately, as well as describing clearly the manipulations they are performing on the trees.

Some instructional animation applications for splay trees currently exist. However, they provide a limited set of controls and, as discussed in the related work section, do not give the instructor all the functionality necessary when teaching splay-tree concepts. We have created a computer program named iSketchmate, intended to alleviate these problems with the whiteboard and the current animation applications. iSketchmate allows instructors to quickly create any splay tree that they like and then perform a series of operations on that tree. Additionally, iSketchmate gives the user the ability to view the history of operations and revert back to a previous version of the tree. At that time, the instructor can either demonstrate the operations again, or choose a new set of operations to demonstrate. During this entire process, the program will be doing the calculations so the instructor is ensured of correct results, thus freeing the instructor to concentrate more on describing the operations clearly and less on drawing the diagram accurately.

2. RELATED WORK

Instructors have long made use of diagrams and animations to help clarify complex operations in many fields. But the question remains as to how useful these images are for the students. Mayer et al. studied the value of dual views (e.g., images paired with textual information to describe complex, mechanical systems). They found that illustrations do help to improve the recall of explanative information [8]. Extending this work, researchers experimented with animations and their usefulness [9]. These studies showed that animations were helpful as a means of creating a connection between the concepts and the application of the concepts. Their results also showed that students learn better from text and images rather than simply text alone.

Permission to make digital or hard copies of all or part of this work for personal or classroom use is granted without fee provided that copies are not made or distributed for profit or commercial advantage and that copies bear this notice and the full citation on the first page. To copy otherwise, to republish, to post on servers or to redistribute to lists, requires prior specific permission and/or a fee.

SIGCSE'12, February 29–March 3, 2012, Raleigh, North Carolina, USA.

Copyright 2012 ACM 978-1-4503-1098-7/12/02 ...$10.00.

Work by Palmiter and Elkerton showed mixed results when using animations. They provided users with a set of instructions for performing a task. Some of the users were additionally shown an animated demonstration [11]. When tested immediately following the instruction, the subjects who saw the animation performed better and stated that they enjoyed the experience better than those who received only text. On the whole the studies suggest that presenting concepts using animated illustrations does no harm and may do some good, especially if a way is found to actively involve students in the animation process. It is also clear that instructors are likely to continue to convey concepts by drawing and transforming diagrams, and that providing helpful tools to assist them is a useful goal.

Currently there are a number of general graphical editing tools that can be used to create presentations. Software tools such as Microsoft PowerPoint give the user the ability to design splay-tree images and simulate animation by creating multiple images on different slides. Adobe Flash provides the ability to create animations with primitive shapes like boxes and lines. However, the creation of these images is time consuming. The reason for the awkwardness of creating animated images using these tools is they do not contain specific knowledge about the instructional domain of splay trees and therefore cannot provide time-saving sketching, manipulation or animation assistance for the instructor.

A number of academic tools have been created to address some of the shortcomings of these commercial systems [1, 15, 10, 4, 3]. These systems provide the ability to share slides with students in a real-time environment through the use of PDAs, laptops and tablet PCs. Presentation slides and notes can be saved and replayed later for student review. However, once again these systems lack detailed knowledge of the subject material, in our case splay trees, and cannot provide additional time-saving assistance to instructors when lecturing.

There are also a variety of tools available that have some of the same characteristics as iSketchmate. The majority of these tools appear as either a standalone Java application or a Java applet embedded into a web page. Examples of these applications are Growing Tree [14], Java Models [5], Splay Tree Applet [6], and TRAKLA2 [7].

All of these tools provide users with a set of controls for selecting splay-tree operations and for navigating through the animations. All allow users to delete or find a value in a splay tree. Java Models, Growing Tree, and TRAKLA2 give users the ability to insert any value they wish and to control the speed of the animation. However these three begin with a random, pre-populated tree, which is helpful for quickly getting started with some examples, but the user cannot start with a predefined tree. Growing Tree begins with an empty tree; however it also provides a mechanism to generate a random splay tree to work on.

Two other applications, JAWAA [12] and ANIMAL [13] allow for easy drag and drop creation of animations, but have little knowledge of the algorithms involved. This gives the user the power to create nice animations, but does not provide for standard built-in operations depending on the specific data structure. This means that operations that are not permissible by the structure can be demonstrated by the user, such as removing a node from the middle of a stack or queue.

New York University's "Binary Search Tree Visualization" [2], also begins with a pre-populated tree and allows for any value to be inserted, deleted or found. The unique part of this tool is the way it presents the algorithm's steps in a comic strip-like form. That is, the initial tree is displayed and the user selects an operation. Next a set of forward and backward controls is enabled which allow the user to scroll through the steps of the operation. Although this tool does not employ animation, it does provide a snapshot of the tree at each step, along with a textual description. Users are also able to step back in the process to see previous versions of the tree.

None of the programs we have found allow the user to create a custom, pre-populated splay tree. The user can insert the desired values and then perform a set of manipulations to a tree in order to eventually obtain the desired values and structure; however this takes some practice and can be very time consuming. The lack of this feature makes it difficult and time-consuming for instructors to use a specific tree that they are interested in and can force them to work with a tree with which they are not comfortable. Also, with the exception of Binary Search Tree Visualization, none of the tools provide the ability to revert the tree back to a previous state or to replay an operation. This means that during lecture, if a student is confused and asks a question, the instructor cannot easily go back to redo the operation.

3. DESCRIPTION OF ISKETCHMATE

iSketchmate is designed to assist instructors when lecturing to a class or helping a student during one-on-one interaction. It is a standalone Java application comprised of three different window panes: a design pane, an animate pane and a revert pane.

3.1 The Design Pane

The design pane came about from informal discussions with a variety of instructors and students. From these discussions we identified several types of trees that instructors would be likely to create:

1. Splay trees created by adding nodes, one at a time.
2. Random splay trees created either with or without a specified number of nodes and/or a range of node values.
3. Splay trees created by providing a specified list of node values in a particular sequence. This tree differs from the type in item 1 because the entire tree should be shown at once, without showing the steps required to create each node.
4. Specific, complete splay trees that may be illustrated in a textbook.

Some of the current splay-tree tools allow users to create the first two types of trees but none of them give the user the ability to create the last two types of trees. iSketchmate's design pane allows all four types of trees to be created.

We initially envisioned allowing users to sketch a tree, much as they would on a whiteboard. However, after investigations with several prototypes, we found that trees can be constructed more quickly using the keyboard and simply tabbing between nodes. We also found that users were most comfortable filling in each level of a tree before proceeding

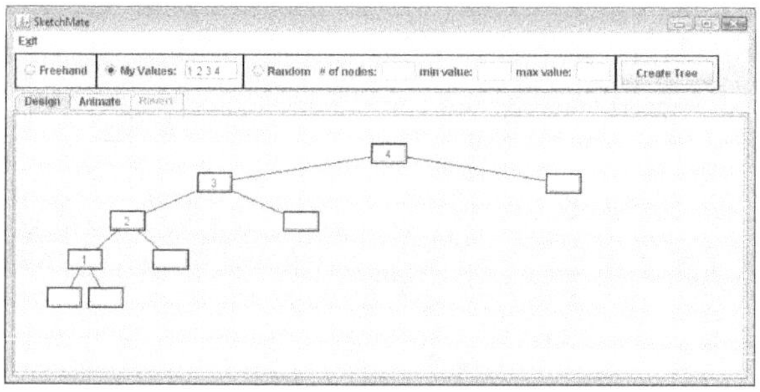

Figure 1: iSketchmate's design pane

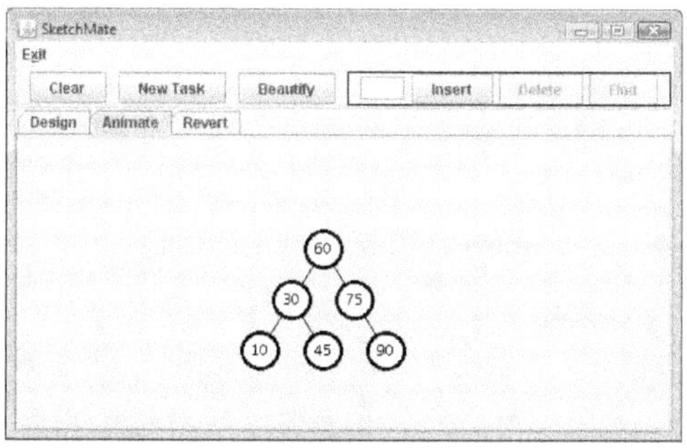

Figure 2: iSketchmate's animate pane.

to the next level (i.e., a breadth-first traversal). The design pane that ultimately evolved is shown in Figure 1.

An interesting interaction with the design pane occurs when the user wants to duplicate a splay tree, such as one illustrated in a textbook. Initially a single text box representing the root of the tree is presented. As soon as the user types a value into this text box, two more text boxes are displayed: one for the root's left child and one for its right child. The user can then use the tab key to navigate to the next node. Once again, as a value is entered in this new node, two new text boxes are created for this node's children. Subsequent presses of the tab key will visit the nodes in an order-level (breadth-first) traversal. Additionally, the up arrow key will shift the focus to the current node's parent and the down arrow will move to the current node's left child. This type and tab navigation technique has proven efficient and well-liked by test subjects.

3.2 The Animate Pane

After creating a tree using the design pane, users can use the animate pane, (see Figure 2), to perform three different types of splay-tree operations: insert, delete, find. After the user chooses a particular operation, the actions needed to perform this operation, such as locating a node or splaying a node to the root, are shown as a sequence of animations. iSketchmate currently pauses at the end of each animated action, which gives the instructor a chance to insert commentary that explains what is happening.

For example, when performing a rotation that will detach a subtree from a node, a pause is inserted just after the subtree becomes detached (see Figure 3) allowing the instructor to explain why the subtree was detached and to describe the next rotational step.

iSketchmate also gives an instructor the ability to prompt the class for what the next step will be, thus increasing student interaction. While some other existing tools give the user the ability to pause the animation, our user testing suggests that the animations themselves are too course-grained. In particular, existing animation tools move multiple parts of the tree simultaneously and we have found that doing so tends to be overwhelming to the viewer, and that it is better to move single pieces of the tree sequentially.

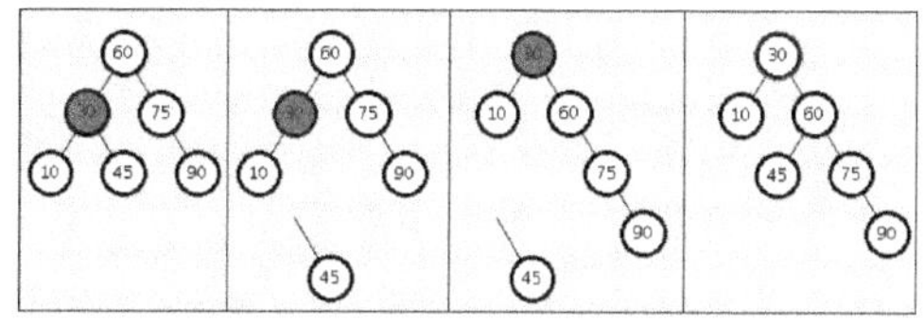

Figure 3: The steps necessary to perform the zig operation on the node with value 30. Frame 1: Initial tree. Frame 2: Right subtree is detached. Frame 3: Node 30 is rotated right. Frame 4: Subtree is reattached as a left child of 60.

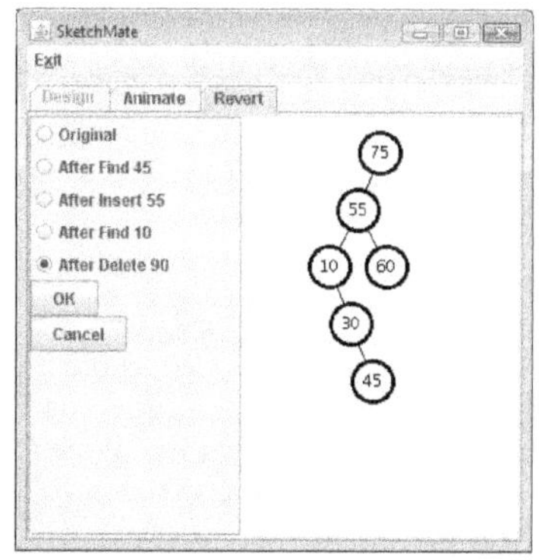

Figure 4: iSketchmate's revert pane

3.3 The Revert Pane

Another unique feature of iSketchmate is the revert pane, (see Figure 4). Each time an operation is performed in the animate pane, the operation and the resulting tree are saved and can later be displayed in the revert pane. The operations that have been performed on the tree are listed along the left side of the window as radio buttons. When the user selects one of the operations, the tree that resulted from that operation is shown on the pane to the right. The instructor can then request that that version of the tree be restored to the animate pane.

This display of historical operations leads to some interesting uses. The most obvious use, and the reason why this pane was created, was so that instructors could revert back to a previous state of the tree for further discussion. It is likely that an instructor may be demonstrating an example and a student in the class either wants to see the demonstration again or perhaps would like to see a different operation performed on that tree in its previous state. In either of these cases, the instructor can simply click this pane, select a previous version of the tree, and return to the animate pane to demonstrate the operation.

Another use of this pane could be at the end of the demonstration, as a review of the steps performed. This is especially useful when beginning with an empty tree and then showing the state of the tree after inserting values one at a time. The instructor can go through the demonstration and at the end switch over to the revert pane. The instructor can then sequentially click the radio buttons to show the students how the tree changed with each insertion.

4. THE EXPERIMENTS

To validate iSketchmate's utility to instructors, we conducted two experiments. The first experiment compared iSketchmate with paper and pencil during the preparation of a lecture. The second experiment compared iSketchmate with the whiteboard when instructors had to draw diagrams to respond to incidental questions about the splay tree material they were presenting. Both experiments compared the efficiency and accuracy of using iSketchmate versus the typical tool used by an instructor (i.e., paper and pencil or the whiteboard).

4.1 Experiment I

In the first experiment, we evaluated iSketchmate relative to paper and pencil in the preparation of splay-tree examples to be used for lecture. The experiment used a within-subjects, post-test only design. We gave participants a list of trees and operations to perform on those trees and asked them to work through the examples using iSketchmate and paper and pencil. The hypotheses were that participants would be able to prepare more examples using iSketchmate and that those examples would be more accurate than those created with paper and pencil.

4.1.1 Subjects, setting and materials

We recruited 25 students from an upper level undergraduate / graduate course in the Computer Science Department. Although splay-tree content was not addressed in this course, all participants were familiar with this data structure. Participants received extra credit in the course for participating in the study.

The experiment took place using the computers in a Computer Science lab on campus. All machines had a Pentium 4 processor with 1 GB of RAM and were running the Debian operating system. Participants were provided a copy of the iSketchmate program on a USB drive.

Additionally, experimenters developed one set of 18 specific splay-tree tasks. Each of the 18 splay-tree tasks consisted of first copying the picture of the tree from the exercise and then performing 3 or 4 individual operations: insert, delete, or find. Although this study could have been run with a series of operations on the same splay tree (e.g., 1 splay tree with 60 sequential operations), operations within each task were limited to 3 - 4 so that participant errors would not be propagated for more than a few operations. These procedures allowed us to preserve the integrity of our experiment as participants were more likely to be working with the trees we intended them to work with, as opposed to tree they may have developed following numerous sequential errors. Additionally, structuring tasks in this manner allowed us to score operation accuracy similarly to grading a multi-step math problem where individual operations can be marked as correct if they are performed correctly in light of previous errors.

4.1.2 Design and analysis

A within-subjects, post-test only design was used to test for differences on accuracy and efficiency of splay-tree operations prepared using iSketchmate (experimental condition) and paper and pencil (control condition). To control for sequence effects, condition order was counterbalanced across participants. The dependent variables included the number of operations completed in 15 minutes and the percentage of completed operations that were correct. For each participant the final operation was not scored for accuracy unless it was completed. Paired samples t-tests were used to test for significant differences across dependent variables. All differences were considered significant at the $\rho < 0.05$ level.

Table 1: Experiment I Summary Data. SD is the standard deviation.

	Mean	SD
Num completed (iSketchmate)	39.44	6.131
Num completed (paper/pencil)	25.84	5.893
% completed correctly (iSketchmate)	.99121	0.017
% completed correctly (paper/pencil)	.71225	0.201

4.1.3 Procedures

Participants met in a lab classroom and were given a brief, 10-minute overview of splay trees. For those participants working first with iSketchmate, the experimenter used iSketchmate to present the overview. For those working with paper and pencil first, the experimenter used the whiteboard to present the overview. This initial review covered basic single and double rotations in a splay tree and how these rotations are used in insert, delete and find operations.

Following the review, participants were allotted 15 minutes to work on the 18 splay-tree tasks using either iSketchmate or paper and pencil. Participants were asked to complete these tasks as quickly and accurately as possible. After completing the tasks using the first tool, the experimenter provided a second, shorter review (about 2 minutes), of a single rotation using the other tool (either whiteboard or iSketchmate). Participants were then given 15 additional minutes to complete the identical splay-tree tasks using the second tool.

4.1.4 Results and Discussion

The means and standard deviations across groups and dependent variables are shown in Table 1. As predicted, both measures showed a significant difference between the group using iSketchmate and those using paper and pencil. Specifically, participants using iSketchmate completed more operations ($t(24) = 10.213$, $\rho < .001$) and had a higher percent correct ($t(24) = 7.027$, $\rho < .001$).

Results showed participants completed about 2.6 operations per minute (39.44/15) with iSketchmate, but only about 1.7 (25.84/15) operations per minute with paper and pencil. These results suggest instructors will be able to prepare lecture material more efficiently using iSketchmate as opposed to drawing them using paper and pencil. Perhaps more importantly, diagrams prepared with iSketchmate were almost always accurate (less than 1% errors). The errors that were created were always due to the participant miscopying the tree. By contrast, almost 30% of the diagrams prepared using paper and pencil were wrong. These results suggest that instructors using iSketchmate may prepare better lecture examples that do not confuse students with inaccurate diagrams.

4.2 Experiment II

Experiment II was designed to simulate a lecture environment where each participant from Experiment I was asked to deliver a presentation on a provided splay-tree operation. A between-subjects, post-test only design was used with participants randomly assigned to either a iSketchmate or whiteboard condition. After delivering the initial presentation, participants were asked follow-up questions. To simulate the incidental questions that students may ask during a lecture, participants were not given these follow-up questions ahead of time. Dependent variables included the accuracy of their responses to the questions and the number of seconds required to respond to each incidental question. The hypotheses were that participants using iSketchmate would answer the questions more quickly and more accurately.

4.2.1 *Subjects, setting, and materials*

The participants in Experiment II were the same as those in Experiment I. The presentations were given in one of three different, empty classrooms, depending on availability. Participants were provided with either a computer running the iSketchmate program or a whiteboard, marker, and eraser.

4.2.2 *Design and analysis*

A between-subjects, post-test only design was used to test for differences across groups when responding to incidental questions in an analogue lecture environment. Participants responded using either iSketchmate or the whiteboard. The dependent variables were the number of seconds to complete both the second and third (incidental) operations and the accuracy of the resulting trees. Directional t-tests were used to test for significant differences across dependent variables with Bonferroni corrections used to control experiment-wise error rates. All differences were considered significant at the $\rho < 0.05$ level.

4.2.3 *Procedures*

After the participants completed the first experiment where they used both iSketchmate and paper and pencil, they were randomly assigned to deliver their presentations using either iSketchmate (experimental group) or the whiteboard (control group). All were given the same splay tree and asked to prepare the same presentation showing the splay operations necessary to insert a value into the tree. They were also told to be prepared to answer additional questions about the tree, but were not told the specific questions ahead of time. Within one week of the first experiment, each participant scheduled an individual appointment to come back and deliver their presentation. After completing their presentation, which lasted roughly 5 to 10 minutes, we attempted to simulate what might happen in a classroom and asked the participant to go back to the original tree and show the steps necessary to insert a different value into the tree. When this insertion was complete, we asked them to show the steps needed to insert a third value into the original tree.

After each question was asked, the primary experimenter used a stopwatch and recorded the number of seconds required for the participants to draw and describe the operation. Operationally accuracy was based solely on the final diagram, not the verbal descriptions. As in Experiment I, partial credit was awarded when splay steps were performed correctly in light of previous errors. The computer saved iSketchmate diagrams and a video-recorder was used to collect permanent products, which were used to score whiteboard responses. A second experimenter independently scored 50% of the responses using the videotape records. Interscorer agreement was calculated for the number of seconds to respond and the resulting trees. Results showed interscorer agreement was 100% for operations completed accurately and 100% for number of seconds to complete an operation (within 2 seconds). These data suggest that student responses were scored consistently.

Table 2: Experiment II Summary Data

	Mean	SD
Splay ops correct (iSketchmate)	5.00	0.000
Splay ops correct (whiteboard)	1.75	0.754
Demo time (seconds) (iSketchmate)	166.46	17.376
Demo time (seconds) (whiteboard)	611.92	111.226

4.2.4 *Results and Discussion*

The means and standard deviations for operation completion times and accuracy rates are included in Table 2. As expected, participants using iSketchmate completed more of their splay operations correctly ($t(23) = 15.574$, $\rho < .001$) and completed them in less time ($t(23) = 4.117$, $\rho < .001$).

These results show that on average participants presenting with iSketchmate responded to each question in less than 1.5 minutes whereas those presenting with the whiteboard required over 5 minutes to respond to each question. Furthermore, participant diagrams were always correct when using iSketchmate, but only 35% were accurate when using the whiteboard.

Extrapolating these data to a 10-minute question-and-answer session following a lecture shows that using iSketchmate would allow our participants to respond to seven student questions and each response would be accurate. However, using the whiteboard our participants would have been able to respond to only two questions and at least one of the diagrams would be wrong, which would likely hinder student learning. Thus the instructor using iSketchmate can leverage its efficiency by addressing more student questions, and address them more clearly with accurate diagrams.

5. GENERAL DISCUSSION

The results of these initial experiments are encouraging. We feel we have succeeded in creating a tool that helps an instructor prepare for lectures more quickly and more accurately. Also, the instructor using this tool to help deliver the lecture will be able to both present animations of the operations as they take place and create the animations quickly, easily, and most importantly, accurately. iSketchmate's accuracy is important because when instructors accidentally draw an incorrect tree, students are likely to become frustrated and confused. Additionally, some students may have to unlearn concepts that they accidentally acquired while viewing the incorrect tree. Since iSketchmate always produces the correct result, students will always be taught the correct way to perform splay-tree operations.

iSketchmate's accuracy also comes into play when the instructors are asked follow-up questions because while it is easy to prepare a lecture with predefined examples, students often pose questions that the instructor may not have considered. In these cases, instructors using iSketchmate can rest assured that they will always perform the steps for the algorithm correctly, and therefore correctly answer the questions, no matter what question is asked.

Finally we stress that participants were given only 10 minutes as both a review of splay trees and an orientation to iSketchmate. We believe that most instructors would be willing to make a 10 minute investment in learning such a tool, given the increased efficiency and correctness of the results.

6. FUTURE RESEARCH

The biggest external validity limitation with these experiments was the use of students, as opposed to instructors. By selecting upper-level undergraduate and graduate students, we hoped our participants were familiar with splay trees and had some degree of presentation experience. However, those who regularly teach splay trees may have been able to complete the preparation and presentation tasks more quickly and more accurately. Additionally, in Experiment II we used analogue conditions to mimic students asking unexpected questions in class. Participants responded to experimenter-developed, pre-planned questions in a room with only the primary experimenter present. Future researchers could address these external validity limitations by running similar studies with professors or instructors serving as participants in their typical classrooms when responding to unplanned student-generated questions (i.e., generalization across participants, settings, and tasks).

Future work will also continue extending the program to work with other data structures. We selected splay trees because they contain more involved operations, but an easy extension is to adapt it for binary search trees. Other extensions could be constructed for other tree structures such as AVL trees and red-black trees. We want to be sure that each structure is thoroughly constructed, tested, and verified before moving ahead. Eventually we would like to see other non-tree structures implemented.

7. CONCLUSIONS

In this paper we described an instructional program that we have created, iSketchmate, which helps instructors draw and manipulate splay trees in a lecture setting. We also described two experiments that compared iSketchmate with the traditional lecturer tools, paper and pencil or the whiteboard. Results from the experiments showed that using iSketchmate helped improve the efficiency of both preparing for lecture and for presenting splay-tree material. The experimental results also showed that the trees produced by iSketchmate were more accurate than those completed with either paper and pencil or the whiteboard. The results suggest that iSketchmate lessens the cognitive burden on instructors who are presenting material about splay trees, thus allowing them to focus more of their attention on the students and their presentation. The results also suggest that instructors can use iSketchmate to present more splay-tree examples and to do so having confidence that their examples are correct.

8. REFERENCES

[1] R. Anderson, R. Anderson, B. Simon, S. A. Wolfman, T. VanDeGrift, and K. Yasuhara. Experiences with a tablet pc based lecture presentation system in computer science courses. In *SIGCSE '04: Proceedings of the 35th SIGCSE technical symposium on Computer science education*, pages 56–60, New York, NY, USA, 2004. ACM Press.

[2] H. Biermann and R. Cole. Comic strips for algorithm visualization. Technical report, 1999.

[3] C. Buckalew and A. Porter. The lecturer's assistant. In *SIGCSE '94: Proceedings of the twenty-fifth SIGCSE symposium on Computer science education*, pages 193–197, New York, NY, USA, 1994. ACM Press.

[4] J. Dan R. Olsen, T. Taufer, and J. A. Fails. Screencrayons: annotating anything. In *UIST '04: Proceedings of the 17th annual ACM symposium on User interface software and technology*, pages 165–174, New York, NY, USA, 2004. ACM Press.

[5] A. Gogeshvili. Java models, 2002. Retrieved November 29, 2011 from http://webdiis.unizar.es/asignaturas/EDA/AVLTree/avltree.html.

[6] D. Ierardi and T.-W. Li. Splay tree applet, 1996. Retrieved November 29, 2011 from http://www.ibr.cs.tu-bs.de/courses/ss98/audii/applets/BST/SplayTree-Example.html.

[7] L. Malmi, V. Karavirta, A. Korhonen, J. Nikander, O. Seppala, and P. Silvasti. Visual algorithm simulation exercise system with automatic assessment: Trakla2. In *Informatics in Education*, page 048, 2004.

[8] R. E. Mayer. Systematic thinking fostered by illustrations in scientific text. *Journal of Educational Psychology*, 81(2):240–246, 1989.

[9] R. E. Mayer and V. K. Sims. For whom is a picture worth a thousand words? extensions of a dual-coding theory of multimedia learning. *Journal of Educational Psychology*, 86(3):389–401, 1994.

[10] B. A. Myers, H. Stiel, and R. Gargiulo. Collaboration using multiple pdas connected to a pc. In *CSCW '98: Proceedings of the 1998 ACM conference on Computer supported cooperative work*, pages 285–294, New York, NY, USA, 1998. ACM Press.

[11] S. Palmiter and J. Elkerton. An evaluation of animated demonstrations of learning computer-based tasks. In *CHI '91: Proceedings of the SIGCHI conference on Human factors in computing systems*, pages 257–263, New York, NY, USA, 1991. ACM Press.

[12] W. C. Pierson and S. H. Rodger. Web-based animation of data structures using jawaa. In *SIGCSE '98: Proceedings of the twenty-ninth SIGCSE technical symposium on Computer science education*, pages 267–271, New York, NY, USA, 1998. ACM Press.

[13] G. Rößling and B. Freisleben. Animal: A system for supporting multiple roles in algorithm animation, 2002.

[14] C. Sanders, B. Segewick, and K. Wayne. Growing tree, 2002. Retrieved November 29, 2011 from http://introcs.cs.princeton.edu/GrowingTree/GT.jnlp.

[15] M. Wilkerson, W. G. Griswold, and B. Simon. Ubiquitous presenter: increasing student access and control in a digital lecturing environment. In *SIGCSE '05: Proceedings of the 36th SIGCSE technical symposium on Computer science education*, pages 116–120, New York, NY, USA, 2005. ACM Press.

CSTutor: A Pen-Based Tutor for Data Structure Visualization

Sarah Buchanan
University of Central Florida
4000 Central Florida Blvd.
Orlando, Fl 32816
sarahb@cs.ucf.edu

Brandon Ochs
University of Central Florida
4000 Central Florida Blvd.
Orlando, Fl 32816
brandonochs@knights.ucf.edu

Joseph J. LaViola Jr.
University of Central Florida
4000 Central Florida Blvd.
Orlando, Fl 32816
jjl@eecs.ucf.edu

ABSTRACT

We present CSTutor, a sketch-based interface designed to help students understand data structures. It currently supports Linked Lists, Binary Search Trees, AVL Trees, and Heaps, and creates an environment in which a user's sketched diagram and code are combined seamlessly. In each of the data structure modes, the user can naturally sketch a data structure on the canvas just as they would on the white board. CSTutor analyzes the user's diagrams in real time, and automatically generates code in a separate code view to reflect any changes the user has made. Additionally, the code can also be edited and any new code changes animate the data structure drawn on the canvas. The connection between the data structure drawn on the canvas and the code implementation is intended to bridge the gap between the conceptual diagram of a data structure and the actual implementation. We also present the results of a perceived usefulness survey. The results of the study indicate that the majority of students would find CSTutor helpful for learning data structures.

Categories and Subject Descriptors

K.3.1 [**Computers and Education**]: Computer-assisted instruction (CAI)

General Terms

Algorithms, Human Factors, Experimentation

Keywords

Sketch-based input, data structures, visualization, animation

1. INTRODUCTION

Instructors in Computer Science generally present new data structures using Powerpoint presentations or drawings on a whiteboard combined with pseudo-code. Usually an instructor will have to draw several instances of a diagram to explain an operation. This can be troublesome for multiple reasons. First, students may not understand which piece of pseudo-code pertains to which change in the diagram. Second, it is often time consuming and difficult for instructors to draw each instance of the diagram. We designed CSTutor (see Figure 1) with the goal of bridging the gap between the conceptual diagram of a data structure and the actual implementation.

In addition to diagrams, algorithm visualization tools are used by students and instructors as a supplemental learning aid. However, studies have shown that algorithm visualization alone does not improve a student's level of learning; it is the level of student engagement with the algorithm visualization that is effective [5]. In addition, many existing systems are not practical for use in the classroom or by students because creating the data structures and animations is too time consuming. These systems are not flexible enough to support creating and editing examples on the fly.

To facilitate a more unified approach to learning and to address the issues above, we developed CSTutor, a novel, pen-based application for data structure visualization that combines sketching, animating and coding of data structures. The intended users of CSTutor are students in a beginning data structures and algorithms class (CS1 at the University of Central Florida). The system lets the user sketch elements of a data structure and perform operations on them through the recognition of handwritten symbols and gestures. Once a gesture is recognized the operation on

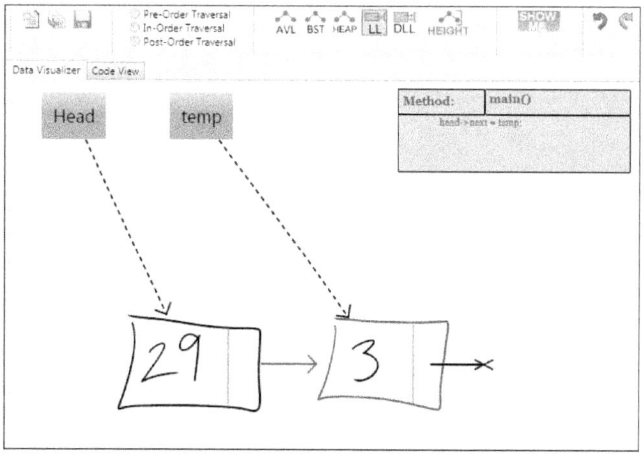

Figure 1: A screenshot of the sketching area in Linked List mode after nodes 29 and 3 are added.

Permission to make digital or hard copies of all or part of this work for personal or classroom use is granted without fee provided that copies are not made or distributed for profit or commercial advantage and that copies bear this notice and the full citation on the first page. To copy otherwise, to republish, to post on servers or to redistribute to lists, requires prior specific permission and/or a fee.
SIGCSE'12, February 29–March 3, 2012, Raleigh, North Carolina, USA.
Copyright 2012 ACM 978-1-4503-1098-7/12/02 ...$10.00.

the data structure is animated while simultaneously adding automatically generated code to the code view. In addition, the code can be edited and any new code changes animate the drawing in real time. In other words, if the user sketches changes to the diagram, the code will dynamically change, and if the user edits the code, the diagram will animate and update itself. The data structures represented in CSTutor (Linked List, Doubly Linked List, Binary Search Tree, Heap, and AVL Tree) were chosen specifically because they are the most basic data structures taught in introductory computer science classes.

In order to gauge the usefulness of CSTutor in aiding CS1 students before incorporating this tool into the curriculum, we conducted a perceived usefulness survey. The tool was demonstrated to 88 students at the end of their CS1 class as a way to review the data structures before the final exam. A video demonstrating how CSTutor can be used to teach data structures can be found here: `http://youtu.be/uEja_cxrGCg`.

2. RELATED WORK

Many data structure visualization and animation tools have been developed over the past 30 years, without gaining much success in the classroom. Of these tools, Tango and XTango were some of the earliest algorithm animation systems that became popular in the early 1990's. XTango was similar in nature to what CSTutor accomplishes in that it attempts to aid computer science students in understanding algorithms through animation [12]. The difference with CSTutor, however, is that we created an environment where users can quickly and easily create their own data structures by sketching them. Additionally, CSTutor lets users create custom functions to manipulate the data structure and watch how their code interacts with it.

Two of the most widely used software visualization tools in use today are JGrasp and Jeliot, which focus heavily on debugging code rather than understanding the concepts of data structures. JGrasp is a comprehensive IDE that generates visualizations as needed from the user's actual program during routine development [2]. It differs from our system in that it focuses on creating visualizations from the user's code, while we create code from a sketch-based diagram and modify the diagram with edits made to the code. Jeliot [8] is similar to JGrasp, however it focuses on beginning concepts such as expression evaluation and assignment of variables, whereas our system focuses on core data structures such as trees and linked lists.

JHAVEPOP [4] is another teaching tool which focuses soley on linked lists by presenting specific linked list problems to solve, and then graphically displaying their results. The focus of this program is very similar to CSTutor, however we wanted to take this idea further by creating a system that can be used to teach users about multiple data structures with an interactive pen-based interface.

In addition, JAWAA and TRAKLA are algorithm animation tools that have had positive results in the classroom. JAWAA is a web-based algorithm animation scripting language that allows students to print animation commands from their own programs [1]. In contrast to CSTutor, JAWAA requires the students to have knowledge of what they want the animation to do, whereas CSTutor creates the animations behind the scenes and does not require the user to enter any special print commands. With TRAKLA students can solve algorithm problems with a drag and drop interface and then are provided automatic assessment [7]. CSTutor differs from TRAKLA since it has an interactive pen-based interface as well as a source code component.

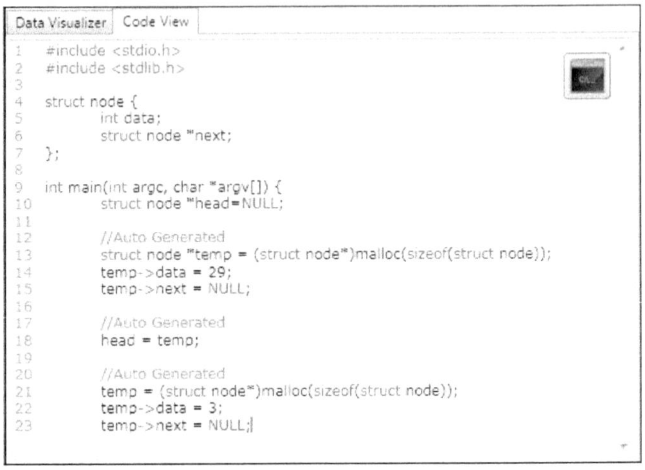

Figure 2: The code area in Linked List mode after nodes 29 and 3 are added to the list.

There have been several pen-based tools developed for learning and entering information in the computer science domain. SketchUML and Tahuti are sketch-based tools for UML class diagrams [6, 10]. GraphPad is a web-based software system that lets the instructor and students interact electronically during class on Tablet PCs. Students can also submit solutions to graph problems and receive feedback [9]. CSTutor is different from GraphPad in that GraphPad does not incorporate the code implementation of the data structure and does not use animation, whereas CSTutor does both. The system presented in [14] is a pen-based flowchart recognition system that recognizes flowchart components and generates runnable C code. This is similar to CSTutor in that it recognizes ink and then generates code, however it is not applicable to data structures and does not reflect changes to the code in any way in the sketched diagram. To the best of our knowledge, CSTutor is the first pen-based application that incorporates animation and coding, designed for aiding Computer Science students in understanding data structures.

3. CSTUTOR USER INTERFACE

CSTutor has two main views that users are able to switch between. The default view is a canvas (see Figure 1) which has been designed to look and feel like pen and paper that provides feedback in an unobtrusive way. The buttons on the screen are minimalistic, and all of the commands are given through gestures where possible. Running alongside this is the code view area, which gives the user a scaffold since any sketched data structure generates corresponding code, giving students a head start in writing various data structure operations. The code view behaves just like a typical IDE by highlighting keywords and providing compile and debug information. However what sets CSTutor apart from a typical compiler is that any updates to the code will actually impact the data structure in the canvas, and the user can step through the animation to see how their code impacts the data structure.

The sketching area for CSTutor is built on Microsoft's InkCanvas, and uses both gesture and character recognition. Gestures are detected by using the iStraw algorithm [13] for cusp detection in combination with heuristics defining each gesture. We found this to be a significant improvement over Microsoft's built in gesture recognizer, which was not only inaccurate at times but also limited us to use a pre-defined gesture set which was not appropriate for our application. We aim to model the gestures after what is normally done on pen and paper. For instance, circling a value when sketching a Binary Search Tree node is what is normally done on pen and paper, thus the completion of the circle gesture is what alerts the system that a new node has been added to the tree.

3.1 Sketching Area

The user is able to choose between the different data structures, which allows us to limit the available gestures to only what operations are available for the current data structure. In order to keep the UI as natural as possible, a combination of several basic gestures are used for each interaction mode. Linked Lists and Doubly Linked Lists use a combination of rectangle, line, and scribble erase gestures. For the trees (Binary Search Tree, Heap and AVL Tree) a combination of circle, arrow, tap, and scribble erase gestures are used. All of the gestural operations that we have chosen are based on how a professor would teach these concepts using a diagram, and the content comes from a variety of course lectures and textbooks [11].

Additional pointers to nodes are represented as blue rectangles on the canvas. The head pointer remains static for each different data structure to emphasize that it is necessary to have a pointer to the beginning. The temp pointer box is also always there as a temporary pointer to any new nodes, or nodes that are being modified. The user can use a line gesture to connect any of these pointers to different nodes. For example, changing which node the head points to is useful for inserting a node to the front of a linked list, and changing which node the temp pointer is pointed to can be useful for deleting a node in these data structures. In addition, any pointers the user creates in their code appear on the canvas as blue rectangles with the corresponding variable names.

3.2 Code Area

Any sketch created in the canvas always creates a section of code in order to show the connection between the diagram and any code changes. When a sketch is completed, the corresponding code is simultaneously added to the main method in the code area (see Figure 2) and is also shown in an information box in the user's sketch area (see Figure 1). The auto-generated code is meant to demonstrate how memory works, and is not the modular code you would see in a program. Users can edit the auto-generated code, add their own functions and operations, compile and run the code, and step through the resulting changes to the diagram. Compiler output is also displayed in the user's code area, and any warning or error messages are shown.

The Show Me button is important for animating the user's compiled code and is used to iterate through the animations step by step. Each step in the animation has the potential to create new nodes, delete existing nodes, or move the connections of any of the nodes or pointers.

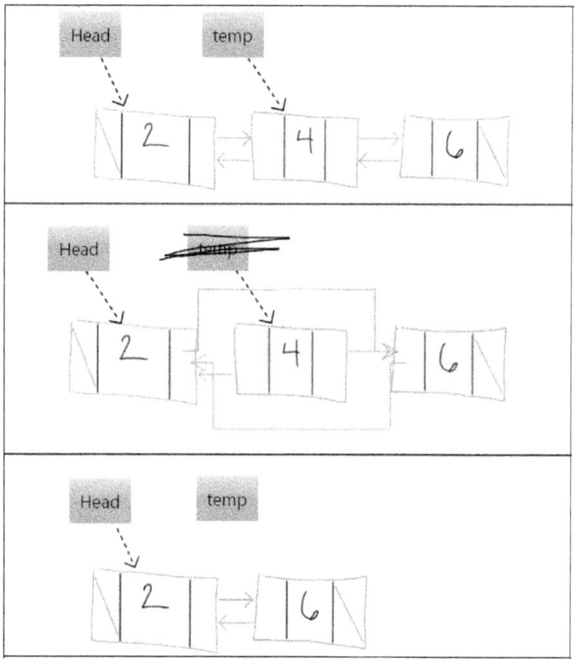

Figure 3: The steps required to delete a node from a Doubly Linked List: (1) Assign temp to the node to be deleted, (2) bypass the node to be deleted, (3) free the node pointed to by temp.

3.3 Interaction Modes

3.3.1 Linked List and Doubly Linked List

The sketching area is designed to allow the user to do the same operations on the data structure through sketching as they can through code. They can create nodes, connect and disconnect nodes, assign/un-assign pointers to nodes, delete nodes and pointers, and update the data and next values. For example, a linked list node is created by writing the value of the node and then boxing that region in with a rectangle. When the rectangle gesture is completed, the surrounded strokes are sent to an online recognizer that analyzes the user's handwriting to determine the numerical value. After the node is drawn it is translated and scaled to make room for subsequent sketches. Then, a small box is drawn within the node to represent the allocated memory for a pointer to the next node. A null pointer stroke is also added to this memory field for nodes where the next link is null (see Figure 1). Sketching a node on the canvas also affects the code in the code window, and generates code that does the following: (1) allocates a node in memory, (2) assigns a value to that node, and (3) sets the node's next value to null.

For operations such as delete, instead of the user simply scratching out a node we enforce that the user goes through each step they would have to implement in code using gestures in the canvas (see Figure 3). For example, the temp pointer first needs to be assigned to the node being deleted by drawing a line to the node from the temp pointer box. Secondly, the neighboring nodes need to be linked to each other to bypass the deleted node. Finally, the node pointed to by temp can be freed by using a scratch out gesture on the temp node and the node is deleted from memory. These steps would create the following code:

```
temp = head->next;
head->next = head->next->next;
head->next->next->prev = head;
free(temp);
```

We designed the Linked List and Doubly Linked List interaction modes to require that the lists be connected, or at least that all nodes are accessible by a pointer, to demonstrate memory leaks to the user. For example, if a user creates their first node without connecting it to the temp or head pointer, any future nodes will not be added and the user is shown a warning message. Additionally, in the delete example above, if the user bypasses the node they wish to delete without first assigning temp to that node, then temp is automatically assigned to that node. This rule is presented in [11], and says that access must be preserved to all nodes that will be needed later in the solution of a problem.

3.3.2 *Binary Search Trees*

Tree nodes are created by writing the value of the node and then circling that number, which sends the surrounded strokes to an online recognizer, just as with the Linked List mode. After the node is drawn it is dynamically arranged on the canvas and lines are drawn to each child node if the children are not null (see Figure 4). Similar to the Linked List mode, sketching a new node with a value of 5 creates the following code:

```
temp =
(struct node*)malloc(sizeof(struct node));
temp->data = 5;
temp->left = NULL;
temp->right = NULL;
head = insert(head, temp);
```

Note that since inserting into the tree requires more than a single line of code, we have abstracted the insert code into its own function and we hide it from the user's code window. We chose to hide the implementation of insert from the user so that they can code their own insert function and visualize it on the canvas.

We initially supported having a newly created node moved to the correct position in the tree automatically. However, we want to ensure that students know how to insert a node according to the binary search tree property, so we make sure the user sketches the node in the proper area of the tree. If the node is added to the correct position, it is colored green. Otherwise, if the node is in an incorrect position the strokes are colored red and the user cannot make additional operations on the tree until the offending node is scribbled out (see Figure 4).

In addition to inserting new nodes in the tree, the user can delete a node by scratching out the node. Since insertion and deletion are the main operations made to a binary search tree, gestural operations (e.g., circle for creating nodes and scribble erase for deleting nodes) are provided for them and any other operations on the tree must be implemented in the user's code.

3.3.3 *Heaps*

The heap data structure we support is a minimum binary heap, since this data structure is taught in entry level Computer Science courses. The heap is displayed in the same manner as the Binary Search Tree, with an additional array

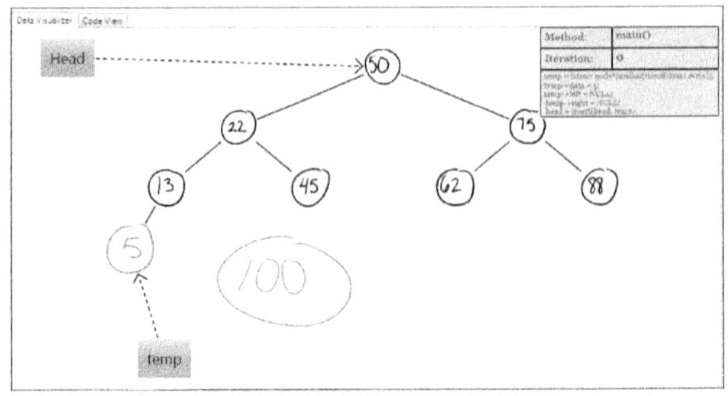

Figure 4: The sketching area in Binary Search Tree mode. Node 5 was added to the correct location and is colored green, whereas node 100 was added to the incorrect location and it is colored red.

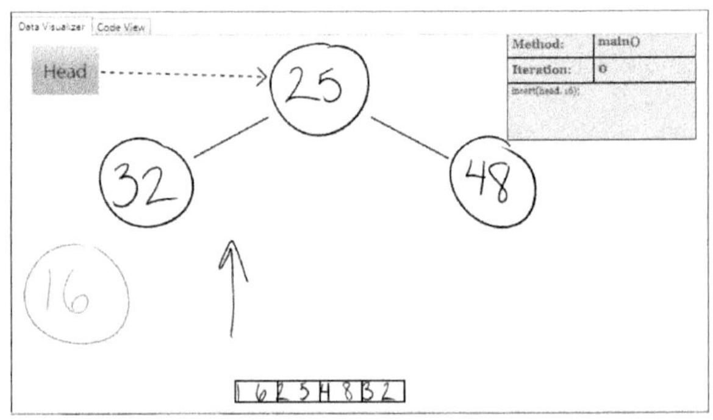

Figure 5: The sketching area in heap mode. Node 16 has just been added to the heap, and the up arrow gesture has been performed to swap 16 with its parent node. Beneath the heap the current state of the array is shown.

underneath that is updated after each operation. Although a binary heap is usually visualized as a tree, it is generally implemented using an array [11], thus it is necessary to show the heap and array at the same time (see Figure 5).

The main operations performed on a heap are inserting new nodes and removing the minimum element. Since there are many steps for the insert and remove minimum operations, we have abstracted both into their own functions, just like the insert operation in Binary Search Tree mode.

Similar to the Binary Search Tree mode, if the node is added to the correct spot (the next open leaf node), the node is colored green, otherwise it is red. If the node that is inserted is less than its parent, then a percolate up function is recursively called, so that the node can continue to swap locations with its parent until it is in its correct location in the tree. Originally, the swap operations were animated immediately, so the node would be swapped up the tree without any user input. However, since many exams ask the student to show each step in an insert heap operation, we make the user draw an up arrow gesture for each necessary swap up, and a down arrow gesture for each swap down (see Figure 5).

The second operation supported in heap mode is to remove the minimum node, which is done with a scribble erase gesture on the root of the tree. Once this node is removed, it must be replaced with the last leaf node in the tree. Since we want to ensure that the user knows which node to select as a replacement, we require a tap gesture next to the replacement node. If the wrong node is selected it is colored red, and the program will wait until the correct node is selected before finally animating the swap. Once the root is replaced, it must be swapped with its children until the root becomes the minimum element in the tree if it is not already. After each operation on the heap, the array underneath the tree is updated to reflect the current state of the heap data structure as it exists in memory.

3.3.4 AVL Trees

Many students often struggle with understanding the conceptual operations on AVL trees as well as their implementation. One common approach to teaching AVL trees is to teach the conceptual operations on an AVL tree diagram before delving into the code implementation. Some examples of conceptual operations that are taught are identifying the balance factor, determining if a rotation is needed, determining what kind of rotation is needed, and finally what the tree should look like after it has been rotated. In a classroom setting all of these operations are initially presented without the code and are still difficult to understand. Once the code is presented many students become even more confused with the recursive implementation. CSTutor adds guidance to help with understanding conceptual operations and delving into the code.

When a user is sketching an AVL tree in CSTutor and a rotation is needed, the user cannot continue sketching until the rotation is completed. A single rotation is completed with an arrow gesture in the required direction, and once the correct gesture is done the tree animates to reflect the changes of the rotation. Since a double rotation is simply a call to two consecutive single rotations, we enforce that the user makes two arrow gestures for a double rotation and the user can visualize each single rotation separately to see specifically what the code is doing. We designed CSTutor to force students to actively rotate the tree with arrow gestures, instead of allowing users to passively observe the AVL tree animations to promote active learning.

4. INITIAL ASSESSMENT

Before incorporating CSTutor into the curriculum for a semester long user study, we demonstrated its capabilities to a CS1 class. CSTutor was presented to 88 students prior to the final exam. Approximately 30 minutes were dedicated to showing review problems for each of the following data structures: Linked Lists, Binary Search Trees, Minimum Heaps, and AVL Trees, followed by 5 minutes for questions and 10 minutes to complete the questionnaire. The students' feedback was based off of this review which covered two examples of how to use each data structure, focusing on both diagram and code changes. Students were also shown how their code changes could be animated and traced through step by step in the sketching view. The review was conducted using an HP tc4400 Tablet PC connected to a projector. After the review session we asked the students to assess the perceived usefulness [3] of CSTutor, and to think about how it could have impacted their ability to learn the course material. The questionnaire consisted of 10 statements on a Likert scale with options: (1) Strongly Disagree, through (7) Strongly Agree.

The results of the survey are shown in Figure 6 and indicate that students found that CSTutor would be generally useful in learning data structures. Questions 7 through 10 show that students felt CSTutor would be useful for the variety of data structures presented, but did not prefer one over another. Question 6 had the lowest average, indicating that students did not feel as strongly about CSTutor helping to find bugs compared to its other features.

We also asked two open response questions: (1) "Do you feel that using CSTutor would be useful in better understanding how some data structures (i.e. Linked Lists, Binary Search Trees, Heaps, and AVL Trees) are implemented? If so, how? If not, why not", and (2) "What changes would you like to see made to CSTutor to make it better?"

The answers to the open response questions were also positive. Most students (61 students) commented that visualizing operations on the data structures would help them. For example, some students said that: "Seeing the code visually with the animation makes connecting a concept to code a lot easier", "I think it would be very useful for AVL trees, because rotations are hard to visualize", "As a visual learner,

Table 1: The CSTutor Perceived Usefulness questions given to students.

	Student Assessment Questions
Q1	CSTutor would have helped me with the material in CS1.
Q2	CSTutor would help me understand how each step in a program is working.
Q3	CSTutor would enable me to complete my homework assignments more quickly.
Q4	Animating what I'm coding would help me understand data structures better.
Q5	Auto-generating code while sketching a diagram would help me understand the relationship between the diagram and the code.
Q6	CSTutor would help me find errors in a program.
Q7	CSTutor would help me understand the implementation of Linked Lists better.
Q8	CSTutor would help me understand the implementation of Binary Search Trees better.
Q9	CSTutor would help me understand the implementation of Heaps better.
Q10	CSTutor would help me understand the implementation of AVL Trees better.

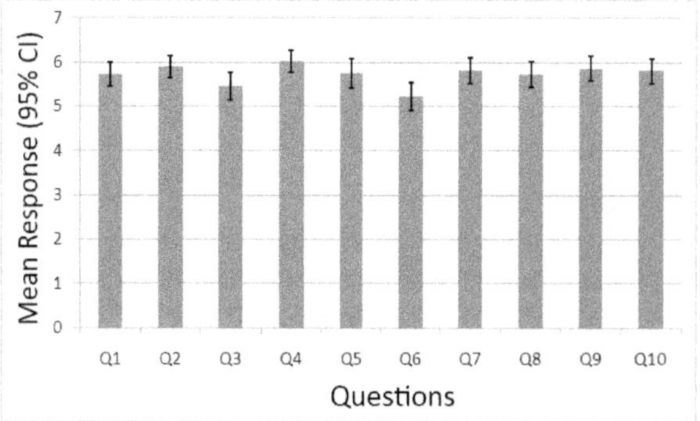

Figure 6: The average results of the Likert scale questions shown with the confidence intervals.

it is helpful for me to literally see what a function is doing. I feel it helps show why you need to do some things, like allocating memory, or making a temp pointer", and "Yes, being able to see the data structure in a visual, interactive way makes coming up with the actual code easier."

Four students had negative open response comments about CSTutor. For example, students commented "I don't really think this would be very useful. This would turn students into being lazy", "Sometimes you might not know what the software is doing", and "No, it mirrors the way it was taught. Therefore, it cannot help to better understand the subject."

Another four students felt that they understood the material enough without the tool, but that it might help other students who are visual learners. For example, one student commented "I feel it would help with generating code, but I don't find the material in CS1 too difficult. Would definitely help with intro to linked lists for someone with little knowledge of how pointers work." Ten students had neutral responses, and the remaining nine students left the open response blank.

There were also many useful suggestions in the second free response question. Some examples include, adding additional data types, giving more feedback for compiler or run-time errors, and more feedback if the user does something wrong.

5. FUTURE WORK

In the future we would like to make CSTutor more robust to user errors and provide more pedagogical feedback. Although users can visualize many logical mistakes by watching the animations of their functions, errors that cause the program to crash (such as infinite loops and referencing null pointers) are hard to determine without tracing through the code. We would like to allow the capability to more intelligently alert the user of these types of errors, instead of simply showing the compiler output. We would also like to give the user the option of using different programming languages, so that CSTutor can be used outside of CS1 at UCF. In addition, the current automatically generated code needs to be refined so that it demonstrates how memory works as well as proper programming abstraction. Ultimately we would like to incorporate all additional data structures and algorithms seen in CS1 and CS2. In the near future we are going to conduct a semester long user study in a CS1 class examining the effects of using CSTutor on students' understanding and learning of data structures.

6. CONCLUSION

We have presented CSTutor, a pen-based tool for dynamic visualization of data structures. CSTutor provides support for Linked Lists, Doubly Linked Lists, Binary Search Trees, AVL Trees and Heaps and visualizes their operations directly on the canvas. Users can input each data structure and operation using pen-based techniques and CSTutor recognizes the user's handwriting using character recognition. In addition, the user can input functions on the data structure in code and visualize their functions that operate on their sketches. We also conducted an informal user study, where we found the data structures and animations were well liked by the participants indicating formal semester long evaluations are required.

7. ACKNOWLEDGEMENTS

This work is supported in part by NSF CAREER award IIS-0845921 and NSF awards IIS-0856045 and CCF-1012056.

8. REFERENCES

[1] A. Akingbade, T. Finley, D. Jackson, P. Patel, and S. H. Rodger. Jawaa: easy web-based animation from cs 0 to advanced cs courses. *SIGCSE Bull.*, 35:162–166, January 2003.

[2] J. H. Cross, II, T. D. Hendrix, J. Jain, and L. A. Barowski. Dynamic object viewers for data structures. In *Proceedings of the 38th SIGCSE technical symposium on Computer science education*, SIGCSE '07, pages 4–8, New York, NY, USA, 2007. ACM.

[3] F. D. Davis. Perceived usefulness, perceived ease of use, and user acceptance of information technology. *MIS Quarterly*, 13:319–340, September 1989.

[4] D. Furcy. Jhavepop: visualizing linked-list operations in c++ and java. *J. Comput. Small Coll.*, 25:32–41, October 2009.

[5] S. Grissom, M. F. McNally, and T. Naps. Algorithm visualization in cs education: comparing levels of student engagement. In *Proceedings of the 2003 ACM symposium on Software visualization*, SoftVis '03, pages 87–94, New York, NY, USA, 2003. ACM.

[6] T. Hammond and R. Davis. Tahuti: a geometrical sketch recognition system for uml class diagrams. In *ACM SIGGRAPH 2006 Courses*, SIGGRAPH '06, New York, NY, USA, 2006. ACM.

[7] L. Malmi and A. Korhonen. Automatic feedback and resubmissions as learning aid. In *Advanced Learning Technologies, 2004. Proceedings. IEEE International Conference on*, pages 186 – 190, aug.-1 sept. 2004.

[8] A. Moreno, N. Myller, E. Sutinen, and M. Ben-Ari. Visualizing programs with jeliot 3. In *Proceedings of the working conference on Advanced visual interfaces*, AVI '04, pages 373–376, New York, NY, USA, 2004. ACM.

[9] R. P. Pargas and S. Bryfczynski. Using ink to expose students' thought processes in cs2/cs7. *SIGCSE Bull.*, 41:168–172, March 2009.

[10] L. Qiu. Sketchuml: The design of a sketch-based tool for uml class diagrams. In *Proceedings of World Conference on Educational Multimedia, Hypermedia and Telecommunications*, ED-MEDIA, 2007.

[11] T. A. Standish. *Data Structures, Algorithms, and Software Principles in C.* Addison-Wesley, Reading, Massachusetts, 1995.

[12] J. Stasko. Animating algorithms with xtango. *SIGACT News*, 23:67–71, May 1992.

[13] Y. Xiong and J. J. LaViola, Jr. Revisiting shortstraw: improving corner finding in sketch-based interfaces. In *Proceedings of the 6th Eurographics Symposium on Sketch-Based Interfaces and Modeling*, SBIM '09, pages 101–108, New York, NY, USA, 2009. ACM.

[14] Z. Yuan, H. Pan, and L. Zhang. A novel pen-based flowchart recognition system for programming teaching. In E. Leung, F. Wang, L. Miao, J. Zhao, and J. He, editors, *Advances in Blended Learning*, volume 5328 of *Lecture Notes in Computer Science*, pages 55–64. Springer Berlin / Heidelberg, 2008.

ECvisual: A Visualization Tool for Elliptic Curve Based Ciphers

Jun Tao, Jun Ma
Department of Computer Science
Michigan Technological University
Houghton, MI
{junt,junm}@mtu.edu

Melissa Keranen
Department of Mathematical Sciences
Michigan Technological University
Houghton, MI
msjukuri@mtu.edu

Jean Mayo
Ching-Kuang Shene
Department of Computer Science
Michigan Technological University
Houghton, MI
{jmayo,shene}@mtu.edu

ABSTRACT

This paper describes a visualization tool ECvisual that helps students understand and instructors teach elliptic curve based ciphers. This tool permits the user to visualize elliptic curves over the real field and over a finite field of prime order, perform arithmetic operations, do encryption and decryption, and convert plaintext to a point on an elliptic curve. The demo mode of ECvisual can be used for classroom presentation and self-study. With the practice mode, the user may go through steps in finite field computations, encryption, decryption and plaintext conversion. The user may compute the output for each operation check each answer for correctness. This helps students understand the primitive operations and how they are used in an elliptic curve cipher. The opportunity for self-study provides an instructor greater flexibility in selecting a lecture pace for this detail-filled material. Classroom evaluation was positive and very encouraging.

Categories and Subject Descriptors

K.3.2 [**Computers and Education**]: Computer and Information Science Education—*Computer science education, information systems education*

General Terms

Algorithms, Security

Keywords

Cryptography, visualization

1. INTRODUCTION

Modern cryptography research started in the late 1960's, and was quickly developed into a significant field in mathematics and computer science. Landmark textbooks and handbooks appeared [5, 7, 8, 9] and schools began offering courses in cryptography. Due to the increasing interests in network/data security, the CS education community also started to add cryptography into the CS curricula. The demographics of the students taking these courses may cause challenges for educators. While CS students have difficulty dealing with the sophisticated mathematics that the cryptosystems are built upon, Mathematics majors often get lost in the details of the complicated algorithms.

Well-designed pedagogical tools can be used to help alleviate these problems and enhance the learning both inside and outside of the classroom. In recent years, we saw a flood of visualization tools published; however, they are mainly on teaching security (*e.g.*, [11, 12]) with some on cryptography (*e.g.*, [3, 10, 14, 15]). We could not find visualization tools for the elliptic curve based ciphers even though this type of cipher is becoming more important in practice. Thus, we chose to develop ECvisual to fulfill our needs and at the same time contribute to the CS education community. ECvisual is flexible in that it can be used as a demonstration tool in class and also be made available to students to use as a self-study tutorial for them to explore on their own. ECvisual is part of a larger project to provide visualization tools to help address the challenges of teaching cryptography.

ECvisual was used in a junior-level introductory cryptography course. The evaluation showed that it was effective and computer science and mathematics related students rated ECvisual highly although there were small variations among different disciplines. On the other hand, reactions from other students were somewhat different, and further investigation would be needed to determine the cause.

In the following, Section 2 provides the background of our cryptography course, Section 3 presents our visualization tool, Section 4 is a detailed study of our findings from a classroom evaluation, and Section 5 is our conclusion.

2. COURSE INFORMATION

ECvisual was used in a cryptography course, MA3203 Introduction to Cryptography, that was offered out of the Department of Mathematical Sciences at Michigan Technological University. It is a Junior level course that gives a basic introduction to the field of Cryptography. Our course covers classical cryptography, the Data Encryption Standard (DES), the Advanced Encryption Standard (AES), the RSA

Permission to make digital or hard copies of all or part of this work for personal or classroom use is granted without fee provided that copies are not made or distributed for profit or commercial advantage and that copies bear this notice and the full citation on the first page. To copy otherwise, to republish, to post on servers or to redistribute to lists, requires prior specific permission and/or a fee.
SIGCSE'12, February 29–March 3, 2012, Raleigh, North Carolina, USA.
Copyright 2012 ACM 978-1-4503-1098-7/12/02 ...$10.00.

algorithm, discrete logarithms, hash functions, and elliptic curve cryptography. For each cryptosystem, we study how it was designed, why it works, how one may attack the system, and how it has been used in practice. One of the more recent advances in cryptography was the development of elliptic curve versions for many cryptosystems. The course ends with a study of elliptic curves and how they may be applied in the field of cryptography. The major topic studied is an elliptic curve based ElGamal cryptosystem.

The course is geared towards Mathematics majors, but typically the majority of students are not Math majors, and many of them are Computer Science majors. In this particular semester, the course consisted of 17 Computer Science majors, 9 Mathematics majors, and 12 from other majors.

ECvisual was used extensively in class to complement the lecture. The instructor first introduced the concept of an elliptic curve to the class. ECvisual was used to demonstrate what the graph of a typical elliptic curve looks like. It allowed the instructor to demonstrate both the addition law and the associative law graphically. The instructor then introduced elliptic curves modulo a prime, p. Here, ECvisual was used to demonstrate the addition of points in the field, and it was also used to show the subgroup of any particular point. When the elliptic curve version of the ElGamal cryptosystem was introduced in class, the instructor used ECvisual to demonstrate the algorithm as well as the method used to covert plaintext to a point on the elliptic curve.

In addition to the benefits for demonstration, ECvisual also has practice components built in to allow students to work with elliptic curves on their own. ECvisual was made available to students to download on their own computer. With ECvisual, one is able to practice adding points on the curve, converting plaintext to a point on the curve, encrypting, and decrypting points.

After the students had access to the software for a week, the instructor distributed a survey to the class. Extra credit was offered to anyone who used the software and completed the survey.

3. SOFTWARE DESCRIPTION

ECvisual is designed to help instructors teach and students learn the elliptic curve based ElGamal cryptosystem. It supports Linux, MacOS and Windows. ECvisual has two subsystems, one over the real field and the other over a finite field of order p. Due to screen space limitation, p is restricted to no more than 17. ECvisual has two operation modes: the demo mode and the practice mode. The demo mode may be used by instructors for classroom demonstration and by students to visualize the detail of computations. The practice mode is designed to help students go through the computations step-by-step and perform self-study. Thus, a student may use the practice mode to step through a computation procedure, fill in the answers, and check for correctness.

ECvisual has three pages, the Table page, the Curves page, and the Finite Field page. When ECvisual starts, the Table page is shown, and this is where the elliptic curve formula is set. One can define a particular curve to work with by choosing appropriate parameters on this page (Section 3.2). The continuous elliptic curve is shown on the Curves page (Section 3.1). The Finite Field page illustrates the finite field of an elliptic curve (Section 3.2). This page also includes encryption and decryption (Section 3.3) and plaintext to elliptic curve point conversion algorithms (Section 3.4).

3.1 The Elliptic Curve Group over Reals

This component provides the user with an opportunity to practice and visualize the elliptic curve group over the real number field. The user selects an elliptic curve by supplying the a and b in $y^2 = x^3 + ax + b$. Then, ECvisual draws the curve, allows the user to zoom in and out, selects two points P and Q, computes the intersection point of the line PQ and the curve (*i.e.*, −(P+Q)), and shows P+Q.

To visualize the associative law, the user clicks on the Associative Law button, picks three points P, Q and R, and ECvisual displays intermediate computations showing P+Q+R = (P+Q)+R = P+(Q+R) (Figure 1). Thus, the user should be able to easily learn the abstract idea via visualization.

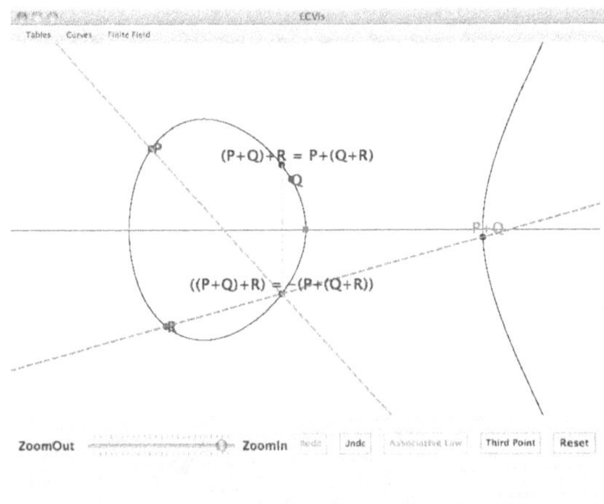

Figure 1: The Elliptic Curve Associative Law

3.2 The Elliptic Curve Group over a Finite Field

The elliptic curve group over finite field $\mathbf{Z}_p$ component helps students visualize and practice elliptic curve computations over a finite field of prime order. The user supplies a prime number $p > 3$ and the parameters a and b in $y^2 = x^3 + ax + b$, where $4a^3 + 27b^2 \neq 0$ must hold. Then, the system displays a grid and all points on the curve with the identity element marked as inf at the center of each edge of the grid (Figure 2).

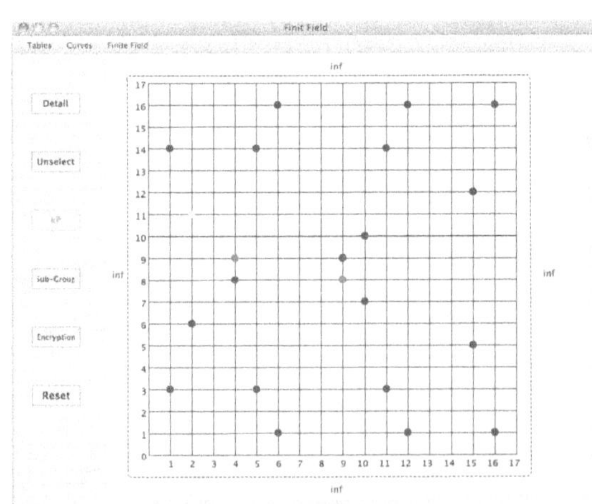

Figure 2: An Elliptic Curve Over a Finite Field: $y^2 = x^3 + 3x + 5$ (mod 17)

The user may click on the Table button to show the additive, multiplicative, and additive and multiplicative inverse tables (Figure 3).

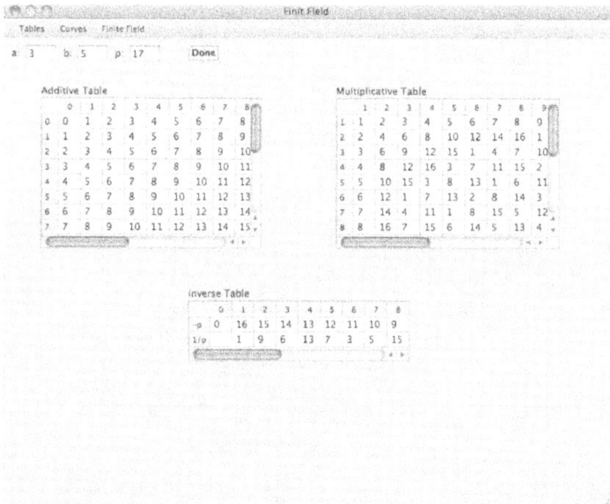

Figure 3: Addition, Multiplication, and Inverse Tables Over a Finite Field: $y^2 = x^3 + 3x + 5$ (mod 17)

The Detail button (Figure 2) on the left panel brings up the **Detail Computation** window with which the user can practice computations on an elliptic curve. For example, the user may click on two points, which are shown in red and whose values are shown in the **Detail Computation** window as P and Q in the order of selection (Figure 4). Initially, all fields other than P and Q are blank. The user may choose Run, Step or Practice. The Run button asks the system to compute P + Q and displays all intermediate results such as $y_2 - y_1$, $x_2 - x_1$, the multiplicative inverse of $x_2 - x_1$ (*i.e.*, $(x_2 - x_1)^{-1}$), the slope λ of the line PQ, the x-coordinate of the intersection point of line PQ and the elliptic curve, and the corresponding y-coordinate. The point P + Q is shown in yellow.

The user may select Step to step through the computation. In this case, the user fills in the result one-by-one with the help of the computation tables (Figure 3), and the system verifies the input and displays **Correct!** if the answer is a correct one. The user may also select Practice and fill in *all* answers. The system then verifies all input and displays **Correct!** if all of them are correct. Incorrect answers are highlighted and **Wrong!** is displayed.

With this environment, the user may try to find a subgroup of prime order by repeatedly computing P, 2P = P+P, etc until $(n-1)$P is the identity. This can be performed by clicking on the kP button on the left panel. ECvisual is also able to find and display *all* subgroups of prime order by clicking on the Sub-Group button. Each subsequent click on the Sub-Group button will cycle through the prime order subgroups one-by-one. Thus, the user may step through these subgroups to choose an appropriate one for encryption. The preferable subgroup is the one with maximum prime order. Figure 5 shows a subgroup of order 23 with the edges showing the generation order of this subgroup.

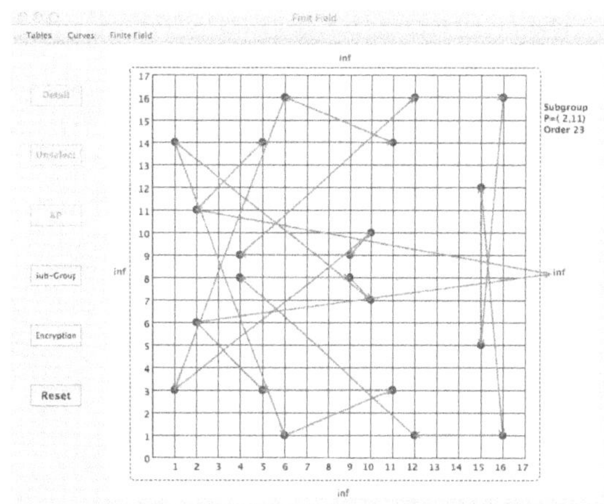

Figure 5: A Subgroup of Order 23 Starting with $(2, 11)$: $y^2 = x^3 + 3x + 5$ (mod 17)

3.3 Encryption and Decryption

Once a maximum prime order subgroup is found, the p in $\mathbf{Z}_p$, the equation of the chosen elliptic curve, and the point P and its order n are the public domain parameters. After this, the user may practice encryption and decryption easily by clicking on the Encryption button. This brings up the **Encryption & Decryption** window. For example, the user may select a private key d randomly in the interval $[0, n-1]$ and compute the public key Q= dP. The sender represents the text by a point M on the elliptic curve, selects randomly a number k in $[1, n-1]$, computes $C_1 = k$P and C_2 =M+kQ, and sends (C_1, C_2) to the recipient. The recipient uses her private key d to compute $dC_1 = d(k\text{P}) = k(d\text{P}) = k\text{Q}$, and, hence, recovers M= $C_2 - k$Q. In this way, elliptic curve encryption and decryption can be practiced easily with the visualization/practice system.

Figure 6 shows an encryption practice session. The system selects point P and a subgroup of maximum prime order, and allows the user to select a private key and fill in intermediate results. Again, the system will tell the user whether his/her computation is correct or wrong.

3.4 Plaintext to Elliptic Curve Point

Converting a plaintext to a point on an elliptic curve is not very trivial and requires larger p to be "practical." Hence, this component is independent of the remaining components because large p is impractical for visualization. ECvisual uses the Koblitz method [6]. Figure 7 shows a demonstration session of the Koblitz technique.

4. EVALUATION

The ECvisual survey consists of two components, a set of nine questions and 13 write-in comments. The nine questions are listed in Table 1. Choices available are 5:strongly

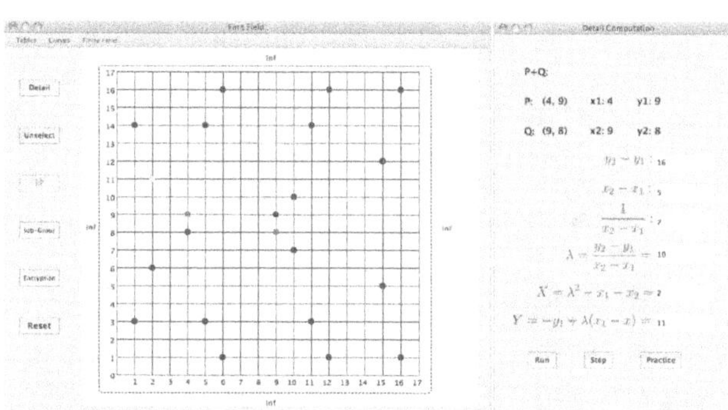

Figure 4: Compute $(2, 11) = (4, 9) + (9, 8)$

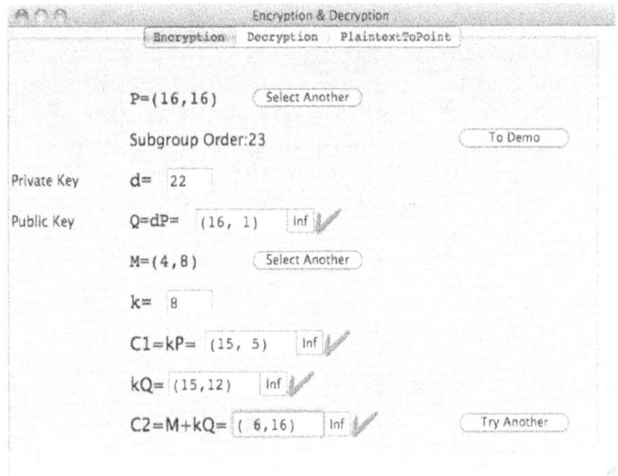

Figure 6: Encryption Practice: $y^2 = x^3 + 3x + 5 \pmod{17}$

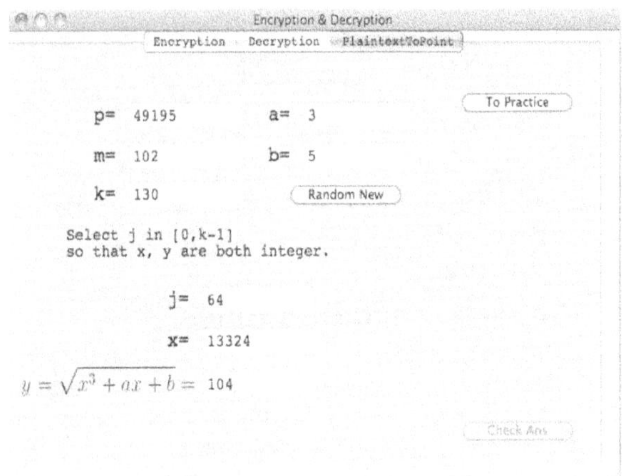

Figure 7: Plaintext to Elliptic Curve Point

agree, 4:agree, 3:neutral, 2:disagree, and 1:strongly disagree. Because we intend to study the impact of ECvisual on multiple disciplines, students were asked to fill in their disciplines. We collected 31 survey forms of which two were invalid. The distribution of majors is as follows: 3 in computer network and system administration (CNSA), 5 in computer and electrical engineering (CpE), 13 in computer science (CS), 5 in mathematics (Math), 1 in materials engineering, 1 in biological science, and 1 undeclared. The last three are grouped into the Other category.

4.1 General Discussion

Table 2 shows the mean and standard deviation of each question. In general, reactions to ECvisual are positive. The highest score of 4.2 with a small standard deviation of 0.5 was given to Q1, indicating that students agreed highly that ECvisual helped them understand what an elliptic curve is. Q4, Q5 and Q9 received the same score of 3.9, suggesting that ECvisual enhanced self-study and the course, and helped students understand the arithmetic on an elliptic curve. The remaining five questions were rated approximately the same (*i.e.*, 3.6 and 3.7) with slightly larger standard deviation. Thus, student reactions are mixed although the general trend is still in the positive side.

Correlations among student responses are high. The highest correlation is between Q2 and Q6 (0.87), which means students learned elliptic curve representations with the demo mode and practice mode. The lowest correlations 0.61 are between Q1 and Q8, and between Q1 and Q9. Overall, students answered questions in a rather similar pattern.

Table 3 shows the effect sizes (*i.e.*, Cohen's d [1, 4]) among questions. We noted that the mean of Q1 (4.2) is very different from those of Q2, Q3, Q6 and Q8 (3.6) with effect sizes no less than 0.8. Additionally, effect sizes among Q2, Q3, Q6 and Q8 are very small. Therefore, student responses to Q2, Q3, Q6 and Q8 are nearly identical, and significantly different from responses to Q1. The effect sizes between Q1 and Q4 (0.44) and Q1 and Q5 (0.36) are moderate, indicating responses to Q1 and Q4, and those to Q1 and Q5 are moderately different. Moreover, the effect size between Q4 and Q5 is zero, suggesting students answered these two questions nearly identically. Consequently, students liked ECvisual for elliptic curve arithmetic and for self-study. It is interesting to point out that, except for Q1, effect sizes of Q8 and other questions are very small (0) to moderate (0.52). This indicates that except for Q1, students ratings of Q8 and other questions are not very different. The effect sizes between Q9 and Q1 and between Q9 and Q8 are moderate (0.5); but, effect sizes between Q9 and other questions are very small (0.05) to moderate (0.4). Hence, except for Q1 and Q8, students rated other questions similar to Q9.

In summary, we found students felt that ECvisual helped them understand elliptic curves and their arithmetic, and also helped self-study.

4.2 Discipline Specific Discussion

Because the class has students from more than five disciplines, it is very helpful to understand the differences among these groups. Table 4 shows summary statistics by disciplines. On average, CS students rated ECvisual the highest

Table 1: Survey Questions

Number	Question
Q1	ECvisual's demo mode helped me understand what an elliptic curve is
Q2	ECvisual's demo mode helped me understand how to represent plaintext as a point on an elliptic curve
Q3	ECvisual's demo mode helped me understand how to encrypt and decrypt using elliptic curve version of the ElGamal cryptosystem
Q4	ECvisual's demo mode was helpful for my self-study
Q5	ECvisual's practice mode helped me understand how to add points on an elliptic curve
Q6	ECvisual's practice mode helped me understand how to represent plaintext as a point on an elliptic curve
Q7	I understand the elliptic curve version of the ElGamal cryptosystem more after I was able to use ECvisual
Q8	By using ECvisual I was able to identify the parts of the elliptic curve version of the ElGamal cryptosystem that I do not understand
Q9	ECvisual enhanced the course.

Table 2: Mean and Standard Deviation

	Q1	Q2	Q3	Q4	Q5	Q6	Q7	Q8	Q9
Mean	4.2	3.6	3.6	3.9	3.9	3.6	3.7	3.6	3.9
S.Dev	0.5	0.9	0.7	0.7	0.8	0.9	0.8	0.7	0.7

Table 3: Effect Sizes Among Questions

	Q2	Q3	Q4	Q5	Q6	Q7	Q8	Q9
Q1	0.80	0.89	0.44	0.36	0.87	0.70	1.02	0.51
Q2		0.02	-0.30	-0.40	0.08	-0.10	0.09	-0.30
Q3			-0.40	-0.40	0.07	-0.20	0.08	-0.40
Q4				-0.00	0.44	0.24	0.50	0.05
Q5					0.46	0.27	0.52	0.09
Q6						-0.20	0.00	-0.40
Q7							0.24	-0.20
Q8								-0.50

(3.85) with the smallest standard deviation (0.21). Slightly lower is from CpE students (3.82) with a slightly larger standard deviation (0.34), meaning CpE student responses were not as concentrated as those of CS students. Both CNSA and Math students rated ECvisual similarly; but, CNSA has a smaller standard deviation. Students in Other rated ECvisual lower with the largest standard deviation.

Table 4: Discipline-Specific Summary Statistics

	Q1	Q2	Q3	Q4	Q5	Q6	Q7	Q8	Q9
CNSA	4.0	3.3	3.7	3.7	3.7	3.7	4.0	3.7	4.0
CpE	4.2	3.8	3.6	4.2	4.0	3.4	3.6	3.4	4.2
CS	4.2	3.6	3.8	4.0	3.9	3.6	4.0	3.7	3.8
Math	4.2	3.4	3.4	3.8	4.2	4.0	3.4	3.6	4.0
Other	4.0	4.0	3.3	3.3	3.7	2.7	3.0	3.0	3.0

	CNSA	CpE	CS	Math	Other
Mean	3.74	3.82	3.85	3.78	3.33
S.Dev	0.22	0.34	0.21	0.34	0.47

Table 5 has the correlation coefficient and effect size of each discipline pair. The correlation between CS and CNSA (0.69) is the highest, followed by the correlation between CS and CpE (0.67). This suggests that ratings by CS, CpE and CNSA students are reasonably similar; however, the correlation between CNSA and CpE is smaller (0.31). On the other hand, correlation between CpE and Math and correlation between CpE and Other are slightly larger than 0.5. The correlation between Other and CNSA is -0.27, indicating students in these two disciplines rated ECvisual oppositely.

Table 5: Discipline-Specific Correlation/Effect Size

Numbers are presented as correlation (effect size)

	CpE	CS	Math	Other
CNSA	0.31 (-0.30)	0.69 (-0.55)	0.36 (-0.14)	-0.27 (1.17)
CpE		0.67 (-0.11)	0.53 (0.14)	0.52 (1.26)
CS			0.43 (0.28)	0.36 (1.51)
Math				0.10 (1.15)

The effect sizes of Other and other disciplines are rather large, suggesting students in Other rated ECvisual very differently from mathematics and computer related disciplines. The correlation (0.69) and effect size (-0.55) between CSNA and CS are moderate, indicating individual question ratings may still have a moderate difference. Other effect sizes are small, and rating differences are insignificant.

Given these findings, we may conclude that students in computer related disciplines (*i.e.*, CSNA, CS and CpE) rated ECvisual similarly, Math students have their own somewhat different view about the effectiveness of ECvisual, and students in Other have a significantly different feeling. But, we should keep in mind that sample size of the Other category is small and further investigation would be needed. This raises questions to be addressed in the future: (1) are there discipline differences in the use of visualization tools? (2) what are the causes of these differences? and (3) how can we address these differences?

4.3 Student Comments

The set of 13 write-in questions is designed to allow students to make suggestions which can be used for future development. We focus on the following issues: (1) whether elliptic curves modulo p for $p \leq 17$ is good enough, (2) whether the representation of the identity element (infinity) is intuitive, (3) whether the representation of subgroups of prime order is useful, (4) whether the elliptic curve version of the ElGamal cipher needs improvement, (5) the evaluation of the demo and practice modes, (6) frequency of using ECvisual for self-study, and (7) software installation problems.

Student comments showed that the $p \leq 17$ restriction is sufficient for understanding the concepts. Only a few mentioned p should be much larger to be "realistic". However, this is impractical because screen asset is not enough for large p visualization. One way to somewhat overcome this restriction would be adding a zooming capability and allowing the user to mouse over to see the details such as coordinates of a point.

There were no very negative comments on the design of ECvisual. Typical comments were "It is easy to use", "Perfect, except for the $p \leq 17$ thing", "Good design, easy to follow and very helpful in learning the system" and "Simple and to the point." Some issues were raised. Major ones were (1) should support $p > 17$ as mentioned earlier, (2) should use symbols and notations exactly the same as in the textbook, (3) finite field computation tables should always be visible and available rather than putting them under a tab, and (4) providing comments and descriptions for each step would be more user friendly and more convenient.

Students were very positive about the identity element and subgroups visualization. Some indicated "the identity element helped me understand exactly how infinity was represented" while one student believed the identity element should only be above the top edge. Comments for the subgroups of prime order were nearly all positive. Students said "It was very clear and useful", "I like that it lights up all the dots, a very useful setup", and "I like being able to cycle through subgroups and orders". Again, some students wished to have step-by-step comments and descriptions so that they can follow the flow easier.

The practice mode was also very welcome with comments like "The practice mode is also good. If an answer is wrong there will be a big warning sign to inform you", "The practice mode helped check that you are doing the work correctly, so that is useful", "The practice mode works well and allows for some user interaction", and "Good to check answers. It is useful to be able to switch between practice and demo".

Because the students only had a week to play with ECvisual before taking this survey, the frequency of using this tool is not very high. Most of them used the tool a few times, and a few of them played with the tool "quite often". In general, they used ECvisual when they were solving problems, checking for some details, forgot the inner working of the algorithm, and used it for practice and further understanding. Since the encryption and decryption algorithms are simple once the concepts of finite fields and elliptic curves are understood, we are not surprised by the fact that a few students only used it once or twice, or did not use it at all. As a result, some students said this component is useful or somewhat useful. Students did not report any installation issues, although three of them complained about system crashes.

In summary, with the statistics and student comments presented above, we believe ECvisual has fulfilled its purpose, helping students learn and the instructor teach the ElGamal cryptosystem based on elliptic curves over finite fields. With the comments and suggestions, we should be able to improve ECvisual significantly in the near future.

5. CONCLUSION

The above presented a visualization tool ECvisual for teaching and learning elliptic curve groups over the real field and over a finite field of prime order, and the ElGamal cryptosystem based on elliptic curves. With ECvisual instructors are able to present all the details and inner working of these algorithms. It also helps students see the "flow" of each algorithm, learn the concepts about elliptic curves, and practice the computation steps using the practice mode.

Our evaluation results showed that ECvisual was effective in classroom presentation and for student self-study. Students in this class were in five disciplines with computer science majors being the largest. We also investigated the impact of ECvisual on each group. Our findings indicated that the computer science related group reacted to ECvisual in the most positive way. The non-CS and non-Math majors reacted to ECvisual slightly differently, but the sample size of this group is very small. It is interesting to point out that the same trend was observed in our earlier DESvisual study [15]. Whether this is a disciplinary difference is not clear at this point and further investigation is required. However, the positive impact of ECvisual on computer science students learning is undeniable.

ECvisual is a part of larger development project of cryptography visualization tools. In the near future, ECvisual will be extended in a number of ways. The most needed extensions are (1) the support of larger finite field (*i.e.*, larger p) and better ways of navigation and visualization, (2) a better visualization for the finite field grid, perhaps automatically adjusting the maximum value of p by a detection of screen size and permitting zooming, (3) a better operation scheme that allows the user to mouse over the finite field grid to show the coordinates of each point, (4) a better design so that the finite field tables are always visible and available, (5) a better hint, comment, and error reporting feature so that the user can retrieve the needed hints and comments easily for self-study, and (6) a library to support elliptic curve cryptosystems based programming assignments. Moreover, we plan to design a class library with which student programs may turn on or off the visualization feature without extra instrumentation so that the visual aid may also be used as a debugging tool. In other words, ECvisual becomes the front-end of a larger system that supports programming and visualization. This technique was used in ThreadMentor successfully [2, 13].

Prototypes of DESvisual and ECvisual and classroom evaluation forms are available at the following URL:

`http://www.cs.mtu.edu/~shene/NSF-4.`

6. REFERENCES

[1] M. Borenstein, L. V. Hedges, J. P. T. Higgins, and H. R. Rothstein. *Introduction to Meta-Analysis.* Wiley, 2009.

[2] S. Carr, J. Mayo, and C.-K. Shene. ThreadMentor: A pedagogical tool for multithreaded programming. *ACM Journal on Educational Recourses in Computing*, 3(1), March 2003.

[3] G. Cattaneo, D. D. Santis, and U. F. Petrillo. Visualization of cryptographic protocols with grace. *Journal of Visual Languages & Computing*, 19:258–290, 2008.

[4] J. Cohen. *Statistical Power Analysis for the Behavioral Sciences.* Lawrence Earlbaum Associates, Hillsdale, NJ, second edition, 1988.

[5] D. E. R. Denning. *Cryptography and Data Security.* Addison-Wesley, 1982.

[6] N. Koblitz. Elliptic curve cryptosystems. *Mathematics of Computation*, 48(177):203–209, January 1987.

[7] A. J. Menezes, P. C. V. Oorschot, and S. A. Vanstone. *Handbook of Applied Cryptography.* CRC Press, 1996.

[8] A. Salomaa. *Public-Key Cryptography.* Springer-Verlag, 1992.

[9] B. Schneier. *Applied Cryptography: Protocols, Algorithms, and Source Code in C.* Wiley, second edition, 1995.

[10] D. Schweitzer and L. Baird. The design and use of interactive visualization applets for teaching ciphers. In *Proceedings of the 7th IEEE Workshop on Information Assurance.* IEEE, June 2006.

[11] D. Schweitzer and L. Baird. Grasp: A visualization tool for teaching security protocols. In *Proceedings of the 11th Colloquium for Information Systems Security Education*, 2006.

[12] D. Schweitzer and W. Brown. Using visualization to teach security. *Journal of Computing Sciences in College*, 24(5):143–150, May 2009.

[13] C.-K. Shene. Multithreaded Programming with ThreadMentor: A Tutorial, 2001. `http://www.cs.mtu.edu/~shene/NSF-3/e-Book/index.html`.

[14] X. Simms and H. Chi. Enhancing cryptography education via visualization tools. In *ACM Southeast Regional Conference*, pages 344–345. ACM, March 2011.

[15] J. Tao, J. Ma, M. Keranen, J. Mayo, and C.-K. Shene. DESvisual: A visualization tool for the des cipher. *Journal of Computing Sciences in College*, 27(1):74–80, 2011.

Rediscovering the Passion, Beauty, Joy, and Awe: Making Computing Fun Again, part 5

Daniel D. Garcia (moderator)
University of California, Berkeley
777 Soda Hall
Berkeley, CA 94720
+1 (510) 517-4041
ddgarcia@cs.berkeley.edu

Barbara Ericson
Georgia Institute of Technology
801 Atlantic Drive
Atlanta, GA, 30332
+1 (404) 385-2107
ericson@cc.gatech.edu

Joanna Goode
College of Education
University of Oregon
Eugene, OR 97403-5277
+1 (541) 346-2826
goodej@uoregon.edu

Colleen Lewis
Graduate School of Education
University of California, Berkeley
Berkeley, CA 94720
+1 (510) 388-7215
colleenl@cs.berkeley.edu

Categories and Subject Descriptors
K.3.2 [**Computer and Information Science Education**]: Computer science education

General Terms
Experimentation

Keywords
Computer science education

1. SUMMARY

In 2006, computing education was suffering from a crisis – enrollments were dropping sharply at universities and colleges across the United States, and interest in computing from high school and middle school students was waning significantly. At the 2007 SIGCSE Symposium, the ACM Education Board organized a special session to explore the underlying causes [4]. In his keynote at the same conference, Grady Booch exhorted us to share the "passion, beauty, joy and awe" (PBJA) of computing [3]. This led to a series of room-packed sessions at the following four SIGCSE symposia to explore that idea from different angles [7, 8, 9, 12]. They have provided a forum for sharing:

- **What we've done**: Highlighting successful PBJA initiatives the presenters have undertaken or seen and wish to celebrate.
- **What we should do (curriculum)**: Pointing out where our curriculum is lacking in PBJA, and how to fix it.
- **How we should do it (pedagogy)**: Sharing how a change in attitude / focus / etc. can make strides to improving PBJA.

Fortunately, enrollments have been continually rising, and there are colleges where the numbers are so strong (returning to historic highs), that some claim the crisis is over [14, 15]. Some point to "the Facebook Factor" as the source of inspiration for many young students, claiming this is a "Sputnik moment" [13]. Many dispute this, however, citing statistics that indicate under-represented students have not returned, and continuing negative connotations about the field [1]. This PBJA "movement" was born out of this enrollment crisis, but is not tied to it. There is always value in sharing novel best practices and advocating techniques that make computing fun.

In the past, we tried to gather educators who brought a wide variety of perspectives (e.g., in 2010 we heard from international, domestic, high school, university and industrial representatives). At recent sessions, we've shifted from that "breadth-first" model to a "depth-first" one. This year we have invited three educators who have worked tirelessly toward broadening participation of computing to underrepresented groups. The hope with this panel is to be able to explore best practices in outreach, in terms of extolling the PBJA of computing.

2. BARBARA ERICSON

Georgia Tech's *Institute for Computing Education* has been working to increase the quantity and diversity of computing students since 2004 [10]. We offer computing summer camps for 4th - 12th grade students, hold competitions for Scratch, Alice, and Advanced Placement Computer Science, offer weekend workshops with youth-serving organizations (Girls Scouts, Cool Girls), work with after-school programs, and run teacher workshops. We have tried many approaches for introducing computing including Lightbot 2.0, Scratch, Alice, CS Unplugged, LEGO robots, PicoCrickets, IPRE robots, App Inventor, Greenfoot, Pleo robots, and Media Computation. We introduce hundreds of students to computing each year. We will present a summary of the results from our outreach events and show a few student-created projects. We also have a distance-learning website with step-by-step video instructions of our projects [11].

Copyright is held by the author/owner(s).
SIGCSE'12, February 29–March 3, 2012, Raleigh, North Carolina, USA.
ACM 978-1-4503-1098-7/12/02.

3. JOANNA GOODE

Exploring Computer Science (ECS) is a yearlong introductory computer science course aimed at broadening participation in computing [6]. It has been used with high school students in Los Angeles Unified School District (LAUSD), the second-largest school district in the country. The driving focus of our curriculum is an inquiry-based approach to teaching and learning. The research-based instructional design is central to the course's curricular materials and accompanying professional development. This approach advocates a student-centered learning community that embraces and integrates student's experiences, cultural backgrounds, and knowledge of community as central to the introduction of computer science theories and applications. To help teachers develop and hone instructional strategies aligned with inquiry and equity, we offer ongoing professional development workshops and an on-site coaching program. We have learned that the focus on pedagogy is as important as the CS content of the curriculum. ECS is now being offered to over 2000, mostly African American and Latino/a students in over 26 LAUSD schools. About 40% of enrolled students are girls. We are scaling up throughout the state of California and supporting efforts in other states and Puerto Rico. LAUSD students who have taken this class in the past three years report increased engagement, interest, problem-solving skills, and indicate an increased likelihood of learning more computer science in the future.

4. COLLEEN LEWIS

In our outreach efforts at UC Berkeley, we are embracing both re-use and innovation. In collaboration with a fellow graduate student, we founded a program to support the pipeline of undergraduate women in computing majors at UC Berkeley. The program, *CS KickStart*, is a one-week intensive program to recruit and support female freshmen who are interested in computer science, but have no prior experience with it [5]. CS KickStart is directly based upon the *Schnupperstudium* outreach program at ETH Zurich [16] and uses curriculum developed at Georgia Tech [10]. Beyond re-use, we have developed curriculum for a middle school outreach program that is being used at numerous schools in the San Francisco Bay area, and the curriculum has been requested by more than 30 educators worldwide. It was also used as a starting point for our *Beauty and Joy of Computing* AP CS Principles pilot course [2]. We will share our experience with these outreach initiatives to meet the needs of local students.

5. REFERENCES

[1] ACM, WGBH. Interim report. *New Image for Computing*. April, 2009. `www.acm.org/membership/NIC.pdf`

[2] The Beauty and Joy of Computing website. `bjc.berkeley.edu`

[3] Booch, G. 2007. Readn', writ'n, 'rithmetic… and code'n. *SIGCSE Bull.* 39, 1 (Mar. 2007), 197-197. `doi.acm.org/10.1145/1227504.1227380`

[4] Cassel, L., McGettrick, A., Guzdial, M., and Roberts, E. 2007. The current crisis in computing: what are the real issues?. In *Proceedings of the 38th SIGCSE Technical Symposium on CS Education* (Covington, KY, USA, March 07-11, 2007). SIGCSE '07. ACM, New York, NY, 329-330. `doi.acm.org/10.1145/1227310.1227426`.

[5] CS Kickstart website. `cs-kickstart.berkeley.edu`

[6] Exploring Computer Science (ECS) website [daily instruction plans available]. `www.exploringcs.org`

[7] Garcia, D. D., Cutler, R., Dodds, Z., Roberts, E., and Young, A. 2009. Rediscovering the passion, beauty, joy, and awe: making computing fun again, continued. In *Proceedings of the 40th ACM Technical Symposium on CS Education* (Chattanooga, TN, USA, March 04-07, 2009). SIGCSE '09. ACM, New York, NY, 65-66. `doi.acm.org/10.1145/1508865.1508889`

[8] Garcia, D. D., Chapman, G., Hazzan, O., Johnson, M., and Sudol, L. A. 2010. Rediscovering the passion, beauty, joy, and awe: making computing fun again, part 3. In *Proceedings of the 41st ACM Technical Symposium on CS Education* (Milwaukee, WI, USA, March 10 - 13, 2010). SIGCSE '10. ACM, New York, NY, 394-395. `doi.acm.org/10.1145/1734263.1734399`

[9] Garcia, D. D., Hutton, M. F., Lemon, E., and Paley, J. 2011. Rediscovering the passion, beauty, joy, and awe: making computing fun again, part 4. In *Proceedings of the 42nd ACM technical symposium on Computer science education* (SIGCSE '11). ACM, New York, NY, USA, 613-614. `doi.acm.org/10.1145/1953163.1953332`

[10] Institute for Computing Education (ICE) website. `coweb.cc.gatech.edu/ice-gt`

[11] ICE Distance Education website. `ice-web.cc.gatech.edu/dl`

[12] McGettrick, A., Roberts, E., Garcia, D. D., and Stevenson, C. 2008. Rediscovering the passion, beauty, joy and awe: making computing fun again. In *Proceedings of the 39th SIGCSE Technical Symposium on Computer Science Education* (Portland, OR, USA, March 12 - 15, 2008). SIGCSE '08. ACM, New York, NY, 217-218. `doi.acm.org/10.1145/1352135.1352213`

[13] NY Times. *Computer Studies Made Cool, on Film and Now on Campus*. `www.nytimes.com/2011/06/11/technology/11computing.html`

[14] NY Times. *CS Programs Make a Comeback in Enrollment*. `www.nytimes.com/2009/03/17/science/17comp.html`

[15] Reges, S. Email to SIGCSE-members mailing list. *enrollment crisis over?* 2009-05-21.

[16] Women in CS Forum website. `www.frauen.inf.ethz.ch`

Promoting Student-Centered Learning with POGIL

Helen H. Hu
Westminster College
Salt Lake City, UT, 84105
hhu@westminstercollege.edu

Clifton Kussmaul
Muhlenberg College
Allentown, PA 18104
kussmaul@muhlenberg.edu

SUMMARY

POGIL (Process Oriented Guided Inquiry Learning) is a type of learning based on the principle that students learn more when they construct their own understanding. Rather than teaching by telling, POGIL instructors provide activities that guide students to discover concepts on their own. Students work in groups, encouraging them to discuss their findings with their peers. Not only do students learn the material better, but the very process of discovery teaches them to be better problem solvers. This special session will provide SIGCSE attendees the opportunity to experience a POGIL activity for themselves. The presenters will share guided inquiry activities tested in our classrooms. We will discuss ways that POGIL may be used to transform computer science classes at all levels, from high school to graduate-level classes, from small schools to large universities.

Categories and Subject Descriptors

K.3.2 [**Computing Milieux**]: Computers and Education-Computer and Information Science Education[Computer science education]

General Terms

Design, Experimentation

Keywords

active learning, cooperative learning, POGIL, teams

1. OVERALL SESSION OBJECTIVE

Process Oriented Guided Inquiry Learning, or POGIL, is a proven learning method that encourages students to learn coursework material in cooperative groups [6]. Instead of passively listening to a traditional lecture, POGIL students work together in groups on specifically designed activities that guide students to discover principles on their own. For example, instead of being told in lecture that a return statement ends the execution of a method, students might be asked what happens if two lines in their program are reversed (so that a line of code appears after the return statement). When students discover these concepts for themselves, they remember them better.

Copyright is held by the author/owner(s).
SIGCSE'12, February 29–March 3, 2012, Raleigh, North Carolina, USA.
ACM 978-1-4503-1098-7/12/02.

5 minutes	*Introduction to POGIL*
20 minutes	*Hands-on Activity*: Experince POGIL as Students Would
10 minutes	*Our Experiences with POGIL*: Introduction to Programming (Hu) Data Structures & Algorithms (Kussmaul) Software Engineering (Kussmaul)
10 minutes	*Using POGIL in Your Classroom*: Tips on Facilitating Using Existing POGIL Activities Writing Your Own POGIL Activities
30 minutes	Q&A Discussion

Research has shown that students learn course content better in POGIL classrooms, with more students earning A's and B's [5]. At both small colleges and large universities, the percentage of failing students was halved in POGIL classrooms [8]. Students themselves prefer POGIL over traditional lectures [2]. POGIL has been used successfully in chemistry classrooms at secondary schools, high schools, small colleges and large universities since the 1990s. More recently, it has been used in biology, engineering, mathematics, and computer science (*e.g.*, [1]). The POGIL Project (www.pogil.org) provides a variety of resources, including workshops to help faculty learn about POGIL practice and theory.

The leaders of this special session have used POGIL with an Introductory Programming class for Scientists, a Data Structures and Algorithms class, a Software Engineering class, and a Soft Computing class for graduate students [3]. We have also incorporated POGIL materials as one class period exercises in other Computer Science classes. One of us (Kussmaul) is the PI on a NSF TUES grant to develop and disseminate POGIL activities for Data Structures and Algorithms and for Software Engineering, and we are actively seeking collaborators to review and evaluate POGIL activities.

This special session will include a hands-on activity to allow audience members to experience POGIL for themselves. The presenters will share our POGIL materials and experiences with the audience and discuss tips for using POGIL in the classroom.

2. OUTLINE OF THE SESSION

In this special session, we will start with a five minute introduction on POGIL and its effectiveness. Next, we will break the audience into small groups to work through a

POGIL activity and experience POGIL as students would. Afterwards, each presenter will speak on how POGIL has worked in our classrooms, and we will share links to our POGIL materials with the audience. We will then provide tips on how to be a good POGIL facilitator, how to write your own POGIL materials, and different ways POGIL can be used in the classroom. The session will conclude with a question and answer discussion.

2.1 Helen Hu

Since 2005, I have co-taught an introductory programming class for scientists with a chemistry professor and POGIL enthusiast [7]. In our Scientific Computing course, students are assigned pre-activity questions before class. During class, students work through POGIL activities that are a mix of critical thinking questions and python programming. Each activity ends with some programming assignments to be completed for homework before the next class period. I have found my POGIL students learn programming fundamentals better than my students in my traditional CS 1 course. While initially a POGIL activity appears to require more class time than a lecture on the same material, students master the concepts better and thus progress through more advanced material quicker than students in a traditional classroom. POGIL activities have the additional benefit of promoting student-to-student interaction, requiring students to work together to succeed. Having seen all these benefits firsthand, I have started incorporating POGIL activities in my otherwise traditionally taught Computer Science classes.

During this special session, I will provide a web link to my POGIL activities. While all the Scientific Computing POGIL activities have been written with scientific applications, most include several modules that could be incorporated without changes to any CS 1 course. However, I have also learned from my POGIL experiences that a skilled facilitator is key to students learning the material. During this special session, I will share tips on how an instructor should monitor and question student teams during the activities, in ways that encourage deeper thought in the right direction.

2.2 Clifton Kussmaul

My first experience with POGIL was in Neural Networks and Fuzzy Systems, a master's level computer science course at the University of Kerala, in south India. It took considerable time to develop the activities, and often I had to adjust them during class sessions. An end-of-course survey showed that students were uncertain at first about POGIL, since it was quite different from the familiar lecture format, but over time most students recognized that they were mastering concepts more effectively and acquiring useful process skills. Furthermore, teams could communicate in their native language rather than having to translate to and from English. More recently, I have used POGIL in Computer Science II, Software Engineering, and other courses [4] at Muhlenberg College, a small liberal arts college. Developing activities becomes easier with practice, although it still takes considerable effort to refine activities to the point that other faculty could adopt or adapt them in their own classrooms. As part of the NSF TUES project, I am sharing these activities with colleagues at other institutions, including some high school CS teachers, and we will be formally evaluating the activities in future years. As we pilot and refine activities, we post them to http://cspogil.org.

3. EXPECTATIONS

This special session should appeal to anyone interested in incorporating more active learning in their classrooms. Attendees will experience how students discover computer science principles for themselves while working through POGIL exercises. They will learn how POGIL has been used in CS classrooms, how to access POGIL materials and get involved in the NSF project, and how to learn more through POGIL workshops and regional meetings.

4. REFERENCES

[1] E. Douglas and C. Chiu. Use of guided inquiry as an active learning technique in engineering. In *Proceedings of the 2009 Research in Engineering Education Symposium*, Palm Cove, Queensland, Australia, 2009.

[2] D. Hanson and T. Wolfskill. Process workshops - a new model for instruction. *J. Chem. Educ.*, 77:120–130, 2000.

[3] C. Kussmaul. Process oriented guided inquiry learning for soft computing. In *International Conference on Advances in Computing & Communication (ACC)*, Kochi, India, 2011.

[4] C. Kussmaul. Process oriented guided inquiry learning (POGIL) for computer science. In *Proceedings of the SIGCSE Technical Symposium on Computer Science Education*, Raleigh, NC, USA, 2012.

[5] G. McKnight. Effectiveness of POGIL. Retrieved September 1, 2011 from http://www.pogil.org/about/effectiveness.

[6] R. Moog and J. N. Spencer, editors. *Process-Oriented Guided Inquiry Learning (POGIL)*. Oxford University Press, 2008.

[7] T. Shepherd. Using computational studies to promote interdisciplinary learning. Invited Talk at the NORM ACS Regional Meeting, June 2008.

[8] A. Straumanis and E. Simons. Assessment of student learning in POGIL organic chemistry. In *Abstracts of papers of the American Chemical Society*, volume 231, March 2006.

Teaching Secure Coding-
Report from Summit on Education in Secure Software

Blair Taylor (moderator)
Towson University
btaylor@towson.edu

Matt Bishop
University of California Davis
bishop@cs.ucdavis.edu

Diana Burley
George Washington University
dburley@gwu.edu

Steve Cooper
Stanford University
coopers@cs.stanford.edu

Ron Dodge
United States Military Academy
Ron.Dodge@usma.edu

Robert Seacord
Carnegie Mellon University/SEI
rcs@cert.org

Categories and Subject Descriptors
D.2.4 [**Software**]: Software/Program Verification - *reliability*

K.3.2 [**Computers and Education**]: Computer and Information Science Education – *computer science education*

General Terms
Reliability, Security

Keywords
Secure Coding

1. SUMMARY
Software is critical to life in the 21st century. It drives financial, medical, and government computer systems as well as systems that provide critical infrastructures in areas such as transportation, energy, networking, and telecommunications. As the number and severity of attacks that exploit software vulnerabilities increase, writing reliable, robust, and secure programs will substantially improve the ability of systems and infrastructure to resist such attacks. Education plays a critical role in addressing cybersecurity challenges of the future, such as designing curricula that integrate principles and practices of secure programming into educational programs.

To help guide this process, the National Science Foundation Directorates of Computer and Information Science and Engineering (CISE) and Education and Human Resources (EHR) jointly sponsored the Summit on Education in Secure Software (SESS), held in Washington, DC in October, 2010. The goal of the summit was to develop roadmaps showing how best to educate students and current professionals on robust, secure programming concepts and practices, and to identify both the resources required and the problems that had to be overcome.

The Summit made 10 specific recommendations, developed from the roadmaps:

1. Increase the number of faculty who understand the importance of secure programming principles, and will require students to practice them.
2. Provide faculty support for the inclusion of security content through clinics, labs, and other curricular resources.
3. Establish professional development opportunities for college faculty, non-computer science professionals, and K-12 educators to heighten their awareness and understanding of secure programming principles.
4. Integrate computer security content into existing technical (e.g. programming) and non-technical (e.g. English) courses to reach students across disciplines.
5. Require at least one computer security course for all college students:
    a. For CS students focus on technical topics such as how to apply the principles of secure design to a variety of applications.
    b. For non-CS students focus on raising awareness of basic ideas of computer security.
6. Encourage partnerships and collaborative curriculum development that leverages industry and government needs, resources, and tools.
7. Promote collaborative problem solving and solution sharing across organizational (e.g. corporate) boundaries.
8. Use innovative teaching methods to strengthen the foundation of computer security knowledge across a variety of student constituencies.
9. Develop metrics to assess progress toward meeting the educational goals specified in the roadmaps presented in this document.
10. Highlight the role that computer security professionals should play in key business decision-making processes.

The goal of this session is to share some of the key findings and challenges identified by the summit and to actively engage the community in the discussions. Each of the speakers participated in the summit and brings a unique viewpoint to the session.

2. MATT BISHOP
Matt Bishop is on the faculty of the Department of Computer Science at the University of California at Davis. His main research area is the analysis of vulnerabilities in computer

Copyright is held by the author/owner(s).
SIGCSE'12, February 29–March 3, 2012, Raleigh, North Carolina, USA.
ACM 978-1-4503-1098-7/12/02.

systems, including modeling them, building tools to detect vulnerabilities, and ameliorating or eliminating them. He has participated in numerous studies of computer systems, including as one of the co-PIs of the California Top-to-Bottom Review of electronic voting systems certified for use in that state. He helped organize, and chaired the first two USENIX UNIX Security workshops. He is active in information assurance education, and has presented tutorials at SANS, USENIX, and other conferences. His textbook, *Computer Security: Art and Science*, was published in December 2002 by Addison-Wesley Professional. **As co-organizer of the Summit and a co-author of the Summit report, he will present the foundation for the session discussion by describing the importance of robust coding.**

3. DIANA BURLEY

Diana Burley is an Associate Professor in the Graduate School of Education and Human Development at the George Washington University. She is also a board member of the GW Cyber Security Policy and Research Institute (CSPRI). Prior to joining GW, Dr. Burley served as a Program Director in the Directorate for Education and Human Resources at The National Science Foundation (NSF). While at NSF, she served as the lead Program Director for the Federal Cyber Service: Scholarship for Service (SFS) program. **As a co-organizer of the Summit and co-author of the report, Diana will describe the goals and outcomes of the summit.**

4. STEVE COOPER

Steve Cooper is an Associate Professor in the Computer Science Department at Stanford University. He formerly taught at Purdue University and Saint Joseph's University. Steve worked in NSF's Division of Undergraduate Education, within its Education and Human Resources Directorate as a program manager, and worked on the CCLI, ATE, NSDL, SFS, and S-STEM programs. Steve also serves as Chairman of the Board of Directors for the Computer Science Teachers Association. In addition to his extensive work with Alice, his current research includes the creation of a serious game to teach secure coding practices to novice programmers. (This work is supported in part by NSF – 1022557.) **For the past three years, Steve has led a series of Working Groups at ITICSE towards creating a series of curricular guidelines for IA programs [2, 3] and will link these results to the summit.**

5. RON DODGE

Ron Dodge has served for over 23 years in the United States Army. Currently he is an Associate Professor permanently stationed at the United States Military Academy and the Associate Dean for Information and Education Technology. Ron is the vice-chair for the Colloquium for Information Systems Security Education (CISSE), Secretary for the IFIP TC 11.8 working group on Information Security Education, and on the executive committee for the Institute for Information Infrastructure Protection. Ron has spent the last 10 years developing innovative methods to teach and train Cyber Security and Assurance. **In addition to offering a viewpoint from a military institution, Ron will address the role that security in general and secure software development in particular will play in Computing Curriculum 2013.**

6. ROBERT SEACORD

Robert Seacord manages the Secure Coding Initiative at CERT, located in Carnegie Mellon's Software Engineering Institute (SEI). CERT, among other security related activities, regularly analyzes software vulnerability reports and assesses the risk to the Internet and other critical infrastructure. Robert is an adjunct professor in the Carnegie Mellon University School of Computer Science and in the Information Networking Institute. His principal areas of expertise include software security, C, C++, and Java-programming languages, component-based development, graphical interface design, and human factors. His books include: Secure Coding in C and C++, The CERT C Secure Coding Standard, The CERT Oracle Secure Coding Standard for Java (SEI Series in Software Engineering). **Robert will discuss the ongoing work and resources available at CERT in the area of secure software education.**

7. BLAIR TAYLOR (moderator)

Blair Taylor is a Clinical Assistant Professor in the Department of Computer and Information Sciences at Towson University and is the PI for the NSF-funded Security Injections @ Towson project. *Security injections* are strategically-placed security-related modules for existing undergraduate classes. (This work is supported by NSF – 0817267.) Blair has experience in information assurance education and two and four-year computer science articulation. **Blair will serve as moderator of the session.**

8. REFERENCES

[1] Burley, D and Bishop, M. 2011. Summit on Education in Secure Software Final Report. http://nob.cs.ucdavis.edu/bishop/notes/2010-sess/2010-sess.pdf

[2] Cooper, S., Nickell, C., Piotrowski, V., Oldfield, B., Abdallah, A., Bishop, M., Caelli, B., Dark, M., Hawthorne, E., Hoffman, L., Pérez, L., Pfleeger, C., Raines, R., Schou, C., and Brynielsson, J. 2010. An exploration of the current state of information assurance education. SIGCSE Bull. 41, 4 (January 2010), 109-125. DOI=10.1145/1709424.1709457

[3] Cooper, S., Nickell, C., Pérez, L., Oldfield, B., Brynielsson, J., Gökce, A., Hawthorne, E., Klee, K., Lawrence, A., and Wetzel, S. 2010. Towards information assurance (IA) curricular guidelines. In Proceedings of the 2010 ITiCSE working group reports on Working group reports (ITiCSE-WGR '10), Alison Clear and Lori Russell Dag (Eds.). ACM, New York, NY, USA, 49-64. DOI=10.1145/1971681.1971686

Starting with Ubicomp: Using the SenseBoard to Introduce Computing

Mike Richards
Centre for Research in Computing
The Open University
Milton Keynes, UK
+44 (0)1908 654023
m.richards@open.ac.uk

Marian Petre
Centre for Research in Computing
The Open University
Milton Keynes, UK
+44 (0) 1908 653373
m.petre@open.ac.uk

Arosha K. Bandara
Centre for Research in Computing
The Open University
Milton Keynes, UK
+44 (0) 1908 653545
a.k.bandara@open.ac.uk

ABSTRACT

In this paper, we describe a new undergraduate module for novice students conducted entirely through distance learning: *My Digital Life* (TU100). The module has been designed to lower the barriers to creating programs that interact with the world; TU100's materials have been designed to excite, encourage, reassure and support learners who explore the novel topic of ubiquitous computing through playful experimentation. It introduces the fundamentals of computing by giving students the capability for programming a device, the SenseBoard, which has built-in input/output and sensors. Programming is done in Sense, an extension of Scratch, which scaffolds programming and reduces the syntax burden. TU100 has taken inspiration from childhood learning and commercial product design to produce compelling, yet academically rigorous study materials.

Categories and Subject Descriptors

K.3.2 [Computer and Information Science Education]: *Computer science education, Curriculum, Literacy*; D.3.m PROGRAMMING LANGUAGES; D.2.6 [Programming Environments]: Interactive environments.

General Terms

Experimentation, Human Factors, Languages.

Keywords

Computer Science education, distance education, ubiquitous computing, SenseBoard, Sense, programming

1. MOTIVATION

The world of computing has changed: it is increasingly ubiquitous. Computers are becoming part of numerous manufactured objects that populate our everyday lives. Ten years ago there was no Facebook or Twitter. Fifteen years ago broadband access to the internet in the home was an unimaginable luxury. Just twenty years ago people still had to buy their books, music and feature films from a high street shop. The digital revolution might still be young, but it has arguably brought about the biggest change in our lifestyles in the last two hundred years. The ubiquitous computer of tomorrow promises, or perhaps threatens, to change the world beyond recognition.

Permission to make digital or hard copies of all or part of this work for personal or classroom use is granted without fee provided that copies are not made or distributed for profit or commercial advantage and that copies bear this notice and the full citation on the first page. To copy otherwise, or republish, to post on servers or to redistribute to lists, requires prior specific permission and/or a fee.
SIGCSE'12, February 29–March 3, 2012, Raleigh, North Carolina, USA.
Copyright 2012 ACM 978-1-4503-1098-7/12/02...$10.00.

Yet our students still often come to us with a vision of 'computing' limited to working with end-user applications such as Microsoft Office.

Our response is *My Digital Life* (TU100), an introductory module designed to align their understanding of the computing discipline with their experience of ubiquitous computing in the world.

TU100 makes powerful concepts and capabilities available to learners as their first academic experience of the discipline, in order to engage their attention while introducing fundamentals. Students are given hands-on experience of designing, building and programming the small, ubiquitous computers that will become increasingly common over the next decade. TU100 is designed in the tradition of efforts such as Alice [1, 4, 5] and Scratch [7, 8, 17], which prioritise hands-on demonstration of what computing can do, use scaffolding and libraries to give even beginners access to powerful programming elements, use programming to generate visible effects of interest to students, and hence captivate the imagination of learners in order to widen engagement in the discipline. TU100 considers the 'big picture', too, and gives students a conceptual framework for understanding and considering the profound technological, economic, political and ethical changes brought about by information technology.

The paper provides a broad introduction to TU100, outlining some of the challenges and experiences that shaped it, describing the key elements of the module, and summarizing early evidence of impact with students.

2. OVERVIEW OF *'MY DIGITAL LIFE'*

My Digital Life (TU100) is an undergraduate module for novice students conducted entirely through distance learning. (An introduction to the Open University and its model of distance education is given in the Appendix.) Beginning in October 2011, the module will be presented twice a year, with an anticipated cohort of some **5,250 students** per year. TU100 comprises 1/6 of the credits needed for an undergraduate degree. The workload is approximately 20 hours per week for a period of 30 weeks. Most OU students are part-time learners, and TU100 will be the only module they will be studying.

TU100 has been designed as a single point of entry for students wishing to complete a degree in computing or information technology, possibly in combination with another subject such as mathematics or business. Our intention was to provide a module for anyone who wishes to know about and use modern technology, whatever their own specialist subject.

3. CHALLENGES AND LESSONS

TU100 has been designed to address a number of explicit pedagogic challenges: improving the learning experience by reducing programming barriers, introducing fundamentals of ubicomp while also developing core academic skills, and realizing the OU philosophy through playful learning.

3.1 Reducing the obstacle of programming

Despite a number of differing approaches, previous introductory programming modules at the OU have not proved to be entirely satisfactory; a sizeable proportion of students either failed the related assessment, or were disinclined to continue to study programming. Many of these students would withdraw from studying computing entirely. Student feedback revealed a number of causes:

- Almost all conventional languages require students to passively learn a large amount of material before they can begin writing and understanding even the simplest of programs;
- Students with no background in programming were frustrated by the pedantic syntax and cryptic naming conventions used in written programming languages;
- Novices have trouble understanding program flow and were often unable to debug their applications, a problem made worse by inadequate debuggers;
- Students who had previous experience with, or a natural aptitude for, programming were able to complete all the programming activities but found them trivial;
- Our chosen language, JavaScript (along with most other small, relatively simply languages) is not suited to developing interesting, media-rich applications that will engage novices.

Of course, TU100 is not our first attempt to mitigate the programming barrier. Between 1999 and 2006 the OU ran a successful Level 2 module that introduced programming using Smalltalk. The module's approach to Smalltalk was called LearningWorks [21]: which incorporated a large collection of small activities that built on one another. For introductory activities, students directly manipulated software objects using their mouse, instead of typing commands. As students' confidence and skills grew, typed commands were introduced alongside the graphical interface, until students were ready to begin using a conventional programming environment.

The module's success in teaching programming rested substantially on this notion of building from one thing to the next, from immediate, direct manipulation to alternative forms of interaction, from concrete activities to programming concepts.

Lesson 1: Segue between skills.

3.2 Ubicomp and critical thinking

As part of its social remit to widen participation in education, the OU does not set *any* prerequisites or admissions requirements for study at level one; our admissions are 'open' to anyone who wants to learn. Although the majority of beginner students have some formal qualifications, many have none, and most have no background in their chosen subjects. Therefore OU level-one modules must include some fundamental skills development, especially in the areas of numeracy, literacy and academic skills.

Any introduction to computing and information technology risks overwhelming newcomers with a colossal amount of disparate information. TU100 overcomes this by using a strong narrative thread which runs throughout the module: *our relationship with digital technologies*. It begins by considering personal experience of familiar technology and ends by discussing how technologies are transforming our world. It takes students on a journey from the origins of information technology through to the familiar computers of today, and on to tomorrow's radical technologies. The aim is to introduce computing concepts while also developing students' intellectual skills.

The beginning of the module explores fundamental yet familiar technological concepts such as the PC, the mobile telephone and conventional broadcast media. At the same time, students are eased into patterns of study that they will continue to use throughout TU100; they take notes, summarise short pieces of text and contribute to online surveys (such as their use of digital media) and to online discussion groups.

The remainder of the first half of the module introduces the concept of ubiquitous computing in the context of the previously-explored technologies. Students first experience ubicomp by reading Weiser's genesis paper [19]; not only developing their research skills, but also (hopefully) experiencing the excitement of seeing a fundamental technological change described for the first time. Once they are familiar with the concepts of ubicomp, students explore the enabling technologies of sensors and location-based services in more detail.

Once students have a sound understanding of technological concepts, they move on to the social implications of new technologies. The emphasis in the second half of the module switches toward the core academic skills of fact-finding and argumentation. Once again the discussion begins with familiar technologies such as email and social media.

The latter part of the module has an explicitly activist approach. Students are encouraged to express their own opinions on a range of contemporary issues, using a range of resources to summarise the issue, present a point of view, or develop counter-arguments. Topics as diverse as the possible effects of video games on childhood development, the role of social media in politics and the impact of new technologies in the developing world are discussed. Amongst other activities, students are asked to take part in a debate on a topical issue (such as the role of copyright in the digital age), to measure their internet connection speed to help map the roll-out of broadband internet access across Britain and to research and publicise organisations overcoming digital exclusion around the world.

Lesson 2: Use a clear narrative thread to guide the learning journey.

3.3 Playful learning

The OU philosophy embraces life-long learning, which means striving to realize education that is fun, engaging, and fulfilling, as well as effective in conventional terms of academic achievement. Our philosophy of 'openness' to learners means re-assessing assumptions and expectations about students (who may have no previous qualifications, or many), designing learning experiences that are hands-on and accessible, and emphasizing relevance and play. The design of TU100 was informed by previous research and experience.

Our experience in robotics for children [14, 16] and in studies of what children do on their computers after school [12] provided useful insights, not least into the impact on learning of motivational technologies such as robots and online social networks. Children in informal contexts learn by tinkering: examining and modifying existing artefacts to make new variants.

They learn by trying things out. When they engage with a new environment, children go straight to the examples; they don't bother with tutorials, if they can have a conversation instead.

As summarized in [12]: "The environments that appear to be successful with children are those offering useful instructive examples as a springboard to things they actually want to do; that provide immediacy of results and effects, that provide a forum for sharing and publishing successes; and that offer 'room for growth' by considerable progression beyond the basics to more advanced concepts and tools." Computing is a routine part of play for contemporary children; our challenge was to make play a routine part of learning computing.

Lesson 3: Enable tinkering.

4. KEY INGREDIENTS

TU100 takes on board the challenges and lessons, and strives to harness the excitement of ubiquitous computing as a means to motivate students and give them a concrete awareness of the potential of the discipline, while introducing them to the fundamentals of computing. The module has been designed to lower the barriers to creating programs that interact with the world; the SenseBoard, our 'lab in a box', has been designed to facilitate playful experimentation.

This section describes the key ingredients of the module:

- the *SenseBoard*, a programmable hardware device designed for ubiquitous applications;
- *Sense*, a media-rich programming environment that extends Scratch for ubiquitous applications using the SenseBoard;
- the *study materials*, a structured collection of texts and learning activities designed for distance learning.

4.1 The SenseBoard

The SenseBoard is a tethered device based around the Arduino microcontroller. The concept of a programmable hardware device for novices is not new; the PicoBoard [13] was developed precisely for this purpose and similar microcontroller boards have been used successfully in teaching [15]. However, the PicoBoard has no outputs (LEDs or motors) limiting its usefulness for designing ubiquitous devices and it is relatively expensive in the UK. An alternative was to use Phidgets [6] or Arduino [2, 3] kits, which are widely used in ubiquitous applications and electronics courses. Their intimidating 'breadboard' appearance and the need to understand basic circuits and to wire in connections and components precluded their use with novice students.

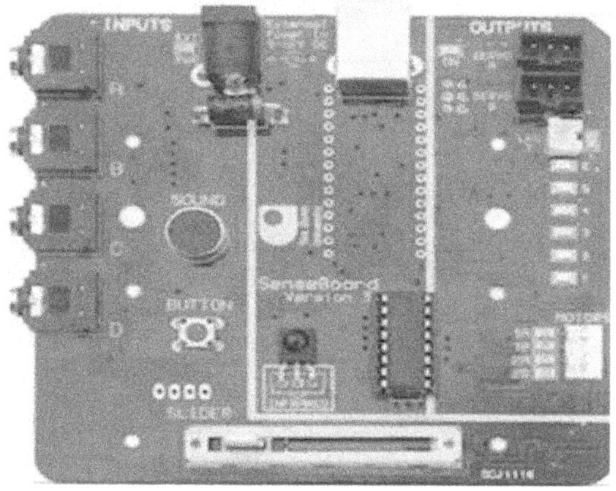

Figure 1: The SenseBoard

In contrast, the SenseBoard (Figure 1) provides a basic repertoire of 'plug and play' functionality. The design of the SenseBoard aimed to broadly replicate the functionality of the PicoBoard as well as adding output devices. The SenseBoard has a number of devices on board, including a slider, a pushbutton switch and a bank of 6 LEDs. It is supplied with the necessary USB cable, a set of plug-in sensors, a motor and a plug-in infrared LED.

The usefulness of an 'experiment kit' that allowed students to build their own ubicomp devices was unarguable, but it could only be justified if it would not place an undue financial burden on the university or the student. This necessitated developing a low-cost, yet powerful experiment kit. After several iterations of the design, the final cost of a boxed SenseBoard kit is approximately US$70 when ordered in bulk.

Figure 2: The SenseBoard box.

The SenseBoard is made more attractive by consumer-quality packaging (Figure 2). Early anxieties were expressed that students unfamiliar with electronic components would find the SenseBoard unappealing or even frightening. Students might be afraid of breaking delicate components, or of receiving an electric shock during handling of the board. Some concerns could be addressed in the design of the SenseBoard itself, by using oversized, robust connectors and ensuring a high quality of finish closer to that of a consumer product than a bare electronics board.

Further reassurance was provided by packaging the board in a manner used for toys rather than that used for electronic components. The kits are delivered in an especially designed, robust cardboard box that can be reused for storing and organizing projects. Every part of the kit is individually boxed in clearly labeled and illustrated packaging so they can be identified immediately as and when they are needed.

The kit is further supported with a dedicated website that includes step-by-step set-up guides, diagnostic software, frequently asked question pages, online videos demonstrating how to set up the kit and what it can achieve as well as a telephone technical helpdesk.

4.2 Sense

For TU100 we chose to adopt and extend the Scratch language [17]. Scratch is a media-rich programming environment notable for its clear programming structure. Individual program blocks (e.g. if-else statements, logical operators and variables) can only be assembled in meaningful (not necessarily correct) ways, and this removes some of the major frustrations experienced by previous students. Scratch:

- Explicitly shows the flow of programs;
- Replaces cryptic naming conventions with simple, obvious names;
- Largely removes the need for syntax;
- Offers immediate feedback;
- Supports media-rich applications.

Although Scratch is not a language in industrial use, it provides students with all the basic skills needed to succeed in most common programming languages – without having to worry about syntax. It also builds students' confidence in their own abilities by allowing them to develop systems quickly. Scratch has proved extremely popular with educators and students alike [7, 8]. Although Scratch was clearly designed for children, our user tests demonstrated that Scratch appeals to adults as well; we were surprised by their enthusiasm.

Nevertheless, Scratch was not ideal for our purposes:

- It lacked some of the richer programming concepts (such as string comparisons) required by the computing curriculum;
- Scratch exists within a closed sandbox environment without the networked support which was necessary for teaching ubiquitous computing.

Sense [18] addresses these needs by adding a number of features:

- New operators for string and list manipulation, and file i/o;
- Constructs for reading data from internet data sources (such as RSS feeds);
- Ability to write data to an internet data repository (a web service hosted by the OU) and read it back as an RSS feed;
- Ability to read inputs from Sense board and control outputs;
- Ability to include in-line comments in programs – allowing students to develop the skill of documenting their code.

Students engage with Sense through a large number of activities, most of which last less than half an hour. The activities are designed to reinforce the learning found in the other module materials, and demonstrate how smart devices and ubiquitous technology can be used in authentic situations. Activities are tightly constrained and come with sample solutions. Students can choose to complete an activity without assistance, or use one of a number of methods of support:

- Step-by-step instructions on completing the activity;
- Partial programs: complex or tedious parts of the program are provided;
- Exploded programs: the program is broken into individual blocks, the student must assemble them in the correct order;
- Sample solutions: the complete program can be examined;
- Screencasts: narrated video showing how to complete an activity.

Every activity is supplied with a completed solution. If a student has failed to complete the current activity for any reason (most commonly lack of time rather than lack of skill) they can begin the next activity using the provided solution, rather than spending yet more time trying to catch up with their peers. All activities come with suggestions for extension and improvement, which will guide interested students to develop their skills further.

Two example activities are the weather clock and the whereabouts clock. As well as recording and displaying data, the SenseBoard and motors can be used to create large, highly visible, physical displays illustrating aspects of ubiquitous computing.

The weather clock reads and displays weather forecast data from a public RSS feed. The program parses the feed for particular weather data and uses that information to display the appropriate weather symbol on the Sense Stage. At the same time the motor rotates an indicator hand to a matching symbol on a clock-face like display which the student will have constructed from paper.

A similar idea underlies the whereabouts clock, inspired by the Harry Potter books and work conducted at Microsoft Research Cambridge [20]. This project relies on a common feed shared by a group of students which holds the status of each student; (at work, online, unavailable, etc.). Students change their status inside Sense by clicking onscreen buttons, and their status is immediately updated on the feed. Each user has their own whereabouts clock which periodically polls the RSS feed and indicates each person's status using a moving pointer.

5. STUDY MATERIALS

TU100 is divided into 29 week-long 'parts'. Each part is comprised of a core teaching text (delivered in print or online) as well as associated learning activities. The majority of materials have been developed especially for TU100, encompassing printed texts, electronic documents, video and DVDs. Approximately half of TU100's study material is delivered electronically. Generally, material discussing fundamental concepts (such as the history of computing, or network technologies) which are less likely to date has been delivered as print items, whilst rapidly changing topics have been designed for electronic delivery.

5.1 Printed documents

TU100's printed materials have been designed to appeal to new students, with widely-spaced text with wide margins that allow students to add their own notes. The materials are full colour, printed on heavy stock and illustrated throughout, in six softbound volumes. Early parts of the module contain prominent signposts informing students how long they should expect to spend studying a section. These signposts are gradually reduced as students learn the essential skills of managing their own studies. Marginal icons are used at points where students require additional resources (such as their SenseBoard, the OU library or one of the module DVDs), to help students organize their studies.

High-quality printed materials are comparatively expensive and less flexible than electronic delivery; however our experience is that many newcomers are attracted and reassured by books. Printed texts have a higher perceived value than online materials. Most students keep their study materials after completing a module, both in order to continue to refer to them and to share them with other people.

5.2 Online material

TU100 students have access to a dedicated website based around an online calendar telling them what should be studied and when. The calendar links to every resource needed to complete the module including electronic copies of the teaching materials, the activities, videos and the online conferencing system.

Electronic copies of all teaching materials are available which can be read online through a web browser, or studied offline in HTML, PDF or ePub (electronic book) format. Amazon's Kindle format will be supported at a future date.

Students submit assessment materials as word-processed documents through an assignment portal from where they are collected by their tutor. The document is marked and commented inside a word processor before being returned to the same portal and the student notified.

Students are also expected to complete self-assessment activities on the TU100 website. These activities take the form of multiple choice, single-word answer, single-sentence or drag-and-drop exercises which provide immediate feedback about the student's progress. Electronic self-assessment activities are improving continually, with increasingly complex activities being developed across the university.

5.3 Online conferencing

The OU has been an enthusiastic user of online conferencing and is a major contributor to the Moodle discussion software. TU100 students have access to a number of discussion fora. First, they share a discussion group with a group of about 20 students moderated by their personal tutor which is used to coordinate activities that require students to share programs, constructively criticize one another's work and complete group activities building a large project.

Second, students have access to a technical support forum where they can ask for assistance with some aspect of the TU100 software from fellow students, tutors and members of the module team. The module team will run occasional online conferences; these chats not only attempt to overcome any perceived isolation experienced by distance learners, but also allow the module team to address any concerns raised by students without waiting for end-of-module feedback. Many distance students find it important to 'engage with the experts': to interact with the people who create the modules.

Finally, students have a so-called 'café conference' where they can talk among themselves about almost any issue.

As well as these asynchronous conferences, TU100 provides tutors with Blackboard Inc.'s Elluminate *Live!*® conferencing software which allows them to create synchronous conferences. Tutors may, if they choose, run short online tutorials exploring an aspect of the module, a Sense masterclass or a question-and-answer session. The module team has provided a list of sample Elluminate tutorials, but tutors are encouraged to create and share their own tutorials with one another. Synchronous tutorials are especially popular with tutors who have widely dispersed students, such as those in rural Scotland and those with a large number of students serving in the armed forces.

Although TU100 will not be making formal use of social media such as Facebook or Twitter, we fully expect students to follow their predecessors in creating self-supported 'study groups' to offer mutual support. Whilst these groups cannot be moderated by the OU, students are made aware of the consequences of sharing assessment solutions with one another.

5.4 Broadcast-quality video

The OU has a long history of educational programming which has continued for TU100. Specially-commissioned video supporting teaching materials gives OU students unique access to individuals, companies and locations that they could not obtain for themselves or in conventional universities. Video helps make explicit otherwise complex technical or philosophical materials and serves to break up large amounts of teaching text. TU100's videos include access to Microsoft Research laboratories, Google, an interview with Alan Kay, a fieldtrip to Nepal exploring issues of the digital divide, clean power generation for cloud computing in Iceland and an interview with one of the founders of Wikileaks. TU100 videos are available in low resolution and high definition over the internet and in conventional PAL resolution on the module DVDs.

5.5 Further learning resources

As well as the core TU100 materials supplied directly to students and those found on the TU100 website itself, the module uses a number of other resources.

5.5.1 Library resources

Students have remote access to the Open University library collection, and through it, to a wide range of journals, collections and citation lists. A number of activities in the module demonstrate how to use the library to find and download technical journal articles and to cite materials appropriately.

5.5.2 Technical support

If students encounter problems using Sense and the SenseBoard they are first guided to support pages found on the TU100 website which provide a set of diagnostic tests they can complete to identify and resolve issues. If these tests fail, students can telephone or email technical support staff who have been trained in setting up Sense and the SenseBoard.

In the event that technical support cannot resolve a software problem, the issue is referred to the module team so that a bug fix can be implemented. Faulty SenseBoards are replaced at no expense to the student and are returned to the board supplier so that any manufacturing defects can be identified and eliminated.

5.5.3 Employment resources

Rather than learning for the sake of it, the majority of OU students are learning to improve career prospects. In association with the OU employment group, TU100 provides two week-long online workshops where students can receive advice about improving their employability. Video interviews have been recorded with major employers including Google, Opera and CCP Interactive that give light-hearted, useful information about how to apply for technology jobs and what it is like to work in the field.

6. OPEN SOURCE LEARNING

The OU has been a strong proponent of sharing learning materials and technologies with individuals and other institutions. Sense is freely available as an open-source project. The SenseBoard specification is also freely available in the public domain. At present, the OU cannot supply SenseBoards to other users, but SenseBoards can be built either individually or mass manufactured without paying any licence fee to the OU.

TU100 video materials will be available for free reuse on iTunesU [10] and through YouTube [11]. Some TU100 materials are also available for free reuse through the OU's OpenLearn website [9].

7. DOES IT WORK?

We have tested the materials – and especially the SenseBoard and Sense – with a range of prospective users, from teenagers to retirees, from complete novices through hobbyists to computing professionals. So far, in terms of empowering novices to create interesting effects with low overheads, the outcome has been reliable: new users are able to produce a working program during their first session with the SenseBoard and Sense in under 20 minutes. They often start with the SenseBoard equivalent of 'Hello, world' – making the LEDs light up in a pretty pattern. And they don't stop with their first program. Novice and near-expert users alike tend to carry on tinkering. When they realize that the input from the sensors on their board can be aggregated with that from other students via the internet – wherever those students may be – they are struck by possibility: "Oh, so that means that I could…"

Early indications (less than one month into the first presentation) are that students have engaged enthusiastically with Sense and the SenseBoard. If anything, we underestimated their enthusiasm to begin using the novel technologies. Although we provided many introductory activities, it quickly became clear that many students were designing, creating and sharing their own projects. Before any Sense teaching had taken place, more than 200 projects had been announced on the student fora, many offered as downloads to other students. The most common projects were recreations of early arcade video games, perhaps reflecting the age of our students and the rich multimedia potential of Sense. Students requested and received advice about all aspects of game programming, including discussions of complex mathematics and how to increase performance.

A large number of student projects are under development. The most 'conventional' include video game controllers and simple weather stations, but other projects include a sound-controlled tea maker and a remote sensor for detecting paranormal activity. Each of these activities has been suggested by a student who has received encouragement and support from fellow students. We hope that this collaboration and community spirit continue.

We wanted to teach entry-level computing in a way that could compete with students' rich experiences of computing in the 'real world', e.g.: gaming, social networks, multi-media, web sites. So we mimic the characteristics of that *ad hoc* exposure: starting with 'cool ideas' that capture the imagination, reducing barriers, using commercial product design to package it compellingly. The result has attracted interest from educators at all levels, from policy-makers and from researchers. The typical reaction to the SenseBoard is: "Where can I get one?"

8. ACKNOWLEDGMENTS

We thank Garry Bulmer, Robert Seaton and Ian Cameron for their work developing the SenseBoard hardware and software. Our thanks also to the Scratch team at MIT for all of their encouragement and help in bringing Scratch's ethos to adult learners. Sense was developed for the OU by John Daniels and Dave Cleal of Syntropy Ltd. We also thank the hundreds of people around the world who gave their time during our interviews and location shoots, and the colleagues who contributed to TU100.

9. REFERENCES

1. *Alice*, Carnegie-Mellon University: http://www.alice.org/ (accessed 28 August 2011)
2. *Arduino*: http://www.arduino.cc (accessed 28 August 2011)
3. Buechley, L., Eisenberg, M., Catchen, J., Crockett, A. (2008) *The LilyPad Arduino: Using computational textiles to investigate engagement, aesthetics, and diversity in computer science education.* CHI 2008, ACM Press, 423-432.
4. Conway, M., Audia, S., Burnette, T., Cosgrove, D., Christiansen, K, Deline, R., Durbin, J., Gossweiler, R., Kogi, S., Long, C., Mallory, B., Miale, S., Monkaitis, K., Patten, J., Pierce, J., Schochet, J., Staak, D., Stearns, B., Stoakley, R., Sturgill, C., Viega, J., White, J., Williams, G., and Pausch, R. (2000) *Alice: Lessons learned from building a 3D system for novices.* CHI 2000, ACM Press, 486-493.
5. Cooper, S., Dann, W., Pausch, R. (2003) *Teaching objects-first in introductory computer science.* SIGCSE, ACM Press, 191-195.
6. Greenberg, S., Fitchett, C. (2001) *Phidgets: Easy development of physical interfaces through physical widgets.* User Interface Software and Technology (UIST'01), ACM Press, 209-218.
7. Malan, D.J., Leitner H.H. (2007) *Scratch for budding computer scientists.* SIGCSE'07, ACM Press, 223-227.
8. Maloney, J., Resnick, M., Rusk, N., Silverman, B., Eastmond, E. (2010) *The Scratch programming language and environment.* ACM Transactions on Computing Education, 10 (4): 1-15.
9. *OpenLearn at the Open University*: http://openlearn.open.ac.uk/ (accessed 28 August 2011)
10. *The Open University on iTunes*: http://open.edu/itunes/ (accessed 28 August 2011)
11. *The Open University on YouTube*: http://www.youtube.com/user/TheOpenUniversity (accessed 28 August 2011)
12. Petre, M., Blackwell, A. (2007) *Children as unwitting end-user programmers.* IEEE Symposium on Visual Languages and Human-Centric Computing (VL/HCC'07), 239-242.
13. *PicoBoard:* http://www.picocricket.com/picoboard.html (accessed 28 August 2011)
14. Price, B., Hirst, A., Johnson, J., Petre, M., Richards, M. (2002) *Using robotics for teaching computing, science, and engineering at a distance.* 5th IASTED International Conference on Computers and Advanced Technology in Education (CATE), 54-159.
15. Richards, M., Woodthorpe, J. (2009) *Introducing TU100 'My Digital Life': Ubiquitous computing in a distance learning environment.* UbiComp 2009.
16. *RoboFesta*: http://www.robofesta-europe.org/britain/ (accessed 28 August 2011)
17. *Scratch at MIT*: http://scratch.mit.edu (accessed 28 August 2011)
18. *Sense at the Open University*: http://sense.open.ac.uk/ (accessed 28 August 2011)
19. Weiser, M. (1991) *The computer for the 21st century*, Scientific American, 3, 94-104.
20. *Whereabouts clock, Microsoft Research Cambridge:* http://research.microsoft.com/en-us/groups/sds/whereaboutsclock.pdf (accessed 28 August 2011)
21. Woodman, M., Griffiths, R., Macgregor, M., Holland, S. (1999) *OU LearningWorks: A Customized Programming Environment for Smalltalk Modules.* ICSE'99, 638-641.

Appendix: Introduction to the OU

With more than 250,000 active students, the Open University (OU) is the UK's largest university. Originally founded in the late 1960s to exploit the possibilities of broadcasting to bring higher education to those who had been unable to attend conventional universities, the OU has continued to be at the forefront of technological developments in education.

The OU offers independently-audited qualifications ranging from introductory certificates, through bachelors, postgraduate degrees and doctorates, as well as a range of recognized professional certifications. The OU was conceived as a distance education institution, and all OU undergraduate students continue to study at a distance.

Most modules use printed and online self-study materials that have been designed especially for distance students. The development of new modules may take several years; with materials undergoing rigorous quality assurance procedures in terms of readability, consistency and accessibility to disabled students – as well as developmental testing with target users, and critical reading by external experts. Quality comes at a price; developing a module of this calibre may cost several million pounds.

Students are assessed throughout their period of study, via self-assessment online materials and by periodic formal assessment which is sent to a part-time member of the university staff for marking. Modules may include a final project, which requires the student to use a number of skills learned in the module.

Every OU student belongs to a 'tutorial group' that is run by a part-time, fully-trained 'Associate Lecturer'; who in turn is supported by regional 'Staff Tutors' and by central academic staff at the university's main campus in Milton Keynes. This scalable approach allows the OU to teach very large cohorts of students (some modules may have in excess of 10,000 students during each presentation), whilst ensuring that individual students can receive personalized, professional support and engage in a student community.

Improving First-year Success and Retention through Interest-Based CS0 Courses

Michael Haungs, Christopher Clark, John Clements, David Janzen
Computer Science
California Polytechnic
1 Grand Ave
San Luis Obispo, CA 93407
{mhaungs,cmclark,clements,djanzen}@calpoly.edu

ABSTRACT

Many computer science programs suffer from low student retention rates. At Cal Poly San Luis Obispo, academic performance and retention rates among first-year computer science students are among the lowest on campus.

In order to remedy this, we have developed a new CS0 course featuring different "tracks" that students can choose from (e.g. robotics, gaming, music, mobile apps). This allows students to learn the basics of programming, teamwork, and college-level study in a domain that is of personal interest. In addition, the course relies on classic Project-based Learning (PBL) approaches as well as a focus on both academic and non-academic factors shown to increase student retention.

Initial assessment demonstrates positive results in the form of increased academic performance in post CS0 courses and student retention.

Categories and Subject Descriptors

K.3.2 [**Computers and Education**]: Computer and Information Science Education—*Computer Science Education*

General Terms

Experimental

Keywords

CS0, CS1, Cornerstone, motivation, self-efficacy

1. INTRODUCTION

The ubiquity of computing in modern society is no longer in doubt. Communication, transportation, education, business, medicine, and entertainment are all, to a certain extent, applications of computing systems. However, despite the rise of computers in our everyday lives, the number of students, and in particular females and minorities, studying computer science as undergraduates has not kept pace with our society's need to train computer engineers and scientists. Further compounding this issue is the fact that many computer science programs suffer from low student retention rates[5]. At Cal Poly, academic performance and retention rates among first-year computer science students are among the lowest on campus. These problems forced us to take a serious look at the goals of our introductory curriculum, and ways in which it could be dramatically reshaped.

1.1 Non-Academic Factors

Typically, the main focus of first-year freshman computer science courses is to build academic proficiency in introductory material. While academic success is correlated to increased student retention, certain non-academic factors also strongly affect it. Examples of non-academic factors may include but are not limited to student confidence, program culture, time management, etc.

Evidence of the effects of non-academic factors can be found in a recent study by ACT[1], that reported a strong correlation between non-academic factors and student success and retention [12]. Their recommendations for improving student retention are complementary with cornerstone, project-based learning initiatives prevalent in the literature and are aligned with our own observations.[2]

Carnegie Mellon University (CMU) greatly increased their enrollment and retention of women in CS [8] by improving several non-academic factors. In particular, they changed the culture of the program, placed it in a social context, closed the experience gap, dealt with student confidence issues, and emphasized the importance of good teaching and faculty-student relationships.

Also of significance are the achievements made at Harvey Mudd College, where a combination of a breadth-first approach to the CS1 course, interaction with computing professionals, and research experiences were used as a means to increase participation in CS [1]. Notably, enrollment of women in CS at Harvey Mudd rose from 11% to 50% from the years 2003 to 2007.

Working in groups has also shown to improve performance. Observations by Williams [15] show increases in academic performance when Pair Programming is used in a CS1 course.

Permission to make digital or hard copies of all or part of this work for personal or classroom use is granted without fee provided that copies are not made or distributed for profit or commercial advantage and that copies bear this notice and the full citation on the first page. To copy otherwise, to republish, to post on servers or to redistribute to lists, requires prior specific permission and/or a fee.
SIGCSE'12, February 29–March 3, 2012, Raleigh, North Carolina, USA.
Copyright 2012 ACM 978-1-4503-1098-7/12/02 ...$10.00.

[1]ACT is an independent, non-for-profit organization specializing in education and workforce development improvement. Historically, ACT stood for "American College Testing".

[2]In the rest of this paper, we use the term *non-academic factors* as defined in ACT's report.

Project Based Learning (PBL) has also been shown as a valid technique for improving learning and academic success [2].

Like CMU and Harvey Mudd, we chose an integrated approach to our CS retention issues where in addition to building a firm grasp of elementary programming concepts, including software testing and development methods, we aim to improve the following non-academic factors: *a student's academic-related skills, academic self-confidence, achievement motivation, and social support and involvement.*

1.2 Interest-Based Tracks

In addition to these proven measures, we embarked upon an experiment in the form of interest-based "tracks."

For the last several years, the CS department has taught an elective Gaming-focused course [10], where students both inside and outside of Computer Science work in teams to build games of their own design. Students in these classes reported that nearly all students characterized computer science as collaborative, multi-disciplinary, and creative.

Building on this success, we decided to expand this to all of our first-year students. Bearing in mind that not all students would be interested in gaming, though, we decided to offer four parallel tracks, each one focused on a different domain. Each of these tracks focuses student attention on applications of Computer Science outside the traditional CS "box," illustrating the interdisciplinary nature of the major and allowing them to work with others outside of the class.

In our first iteration, these tracks included Mobile Applications, Robotics, Gaming, and Music. Each student, upon enrolling, was required to rank these tracks according to their interest level. Students were enrolled in the classes based on these rankings, thus allowing them to self-select their learning communities. The resulting classes feature students that predominantly have higher interest in the course's topic. The authors are not aware of any other computer science program that offers this choice to its first-year students.

In the next section, we describe the course framework common to all versions of the course, regardless of theme. Following this framework, we describe the first four versions of the course offered. Next, we highlight how the organization of the course helps us focus on certain non-academic factors shown to be strongly correlated to improved retention. We then provide our initial assessment of the success of the course. Last, we discuss plans we have for future course improvement.

2. CSC 123 CURRICULUM

Historically, Cal Poly's computer science department has taught an introductory course sequence that is spread across three quarters in the first year of study. Named "Fundamentals of Computer Science" (CSC 101, CSC 102 and CSC 103), the 3 courses cover basics of computer programming in procedural and object-oriented styles, with students working primarily in C and Java. The new course, CSC 123, is taken before CSC 101 and hence shifts the existing sequence back one quarter.

2.1 Common CSC 123 Framework

The tracks all started with a common set of goals, as follows:

Equal participation All course versions will ensure there is balanced participation in the course for students of all programming backgrounds. This will be accomplished by picking projects that are familiar to almost all students (e.g. game design or music), but don't have obvious solutions, allow for creative solutions, and in which prior programming experience is not a significant advantage to student success in the course.

Basic Learning Outcomes All course versions will ensure that students completing the course will have learned certain fundamentals of computer programming, e.g. datatypes, loops, etc.

Software Development Process All course versions will require students to complete a large project. In doing so, students will follow a software development process that includes iterative design, implementation, and testing.

Team-based Learning All course versions will have students working in teams to complete their projects. Team sizes will range from 4-6 students. To provide students with initial guidance on how to function within a team, a short lecture and workshop will be conducted.

Grading Scheme All course versions will use the same set of deliverables and grading rubric on project demonstrations, presentations, reports, and exams. For exams, half of the exam questions will be common to all course versions (see Figure 1 for an example), while the other half will be specific to the application theme.

Student Mentoring All course versions will use a formal student mentoring system in which outside of lecture and lab hours, upper year students will lead workshops on programming within application themes. To improve culture within the program (a known problem for retention as stated by Crenshaw [6]), mentors will be trained to maximize participation from all students and help foster a working community.

Applications with External Clients All course versions will have an external client, typically outside the discipline of computing, who will provide high level direction on the project in terms of its use in the respective discipline.

2.2 Specific CSC 123 Themes

The four initial themes of CSC 123 offered during the Fall quarter, 2010, are given below. As described in the previous section, the different versions of the course have common learning objectives, structure, and desired outcomes. The application themes were used to motivate students. For example, the Computing in Robotics theme taught students about robotics and their use in marine biology. In programming and preparing robots for real ocean deployments and working alongside biologists, engineering students were exposed to situations that they would not otherwise experience in CS. Combined with the fact that application themes were

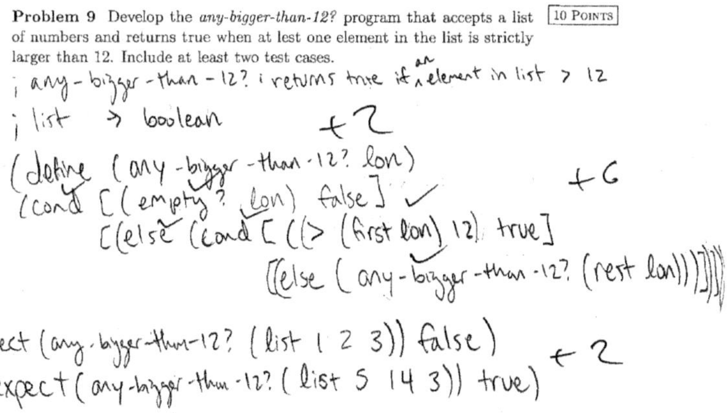
Problem 9 Develop the *any-bigger-than-12?* program that accepts a list of numbers and returns true when at lest one element in the list is strictly larger than 12. Include at least two test cases. 10 POINTS

```
; any-bigger-than-12? ; returns true if an element in list > 12
; list -> boolean                                   +2
(define (any-bigger-than-12? lon)                    +6
  (cond [(empty? lon) false]
        [else (cond [((> (first lon) 12) true]
                     [else (any-bigger-than-12? (rest lon))])]))

(checkexpect (any-bigger-than-12? (list 1 2 3)) false)    +2
(check-expect (any-bigger-than-12? (list 5 14 3)) true)
```

Figure 1: A question and student answer taken from the final exam from the music section of CSC 123. Students in that section programmed in Racket.

preselected by students, it is hoped that the students' motivation toward this course and the field of computing itself will be dramatically increased. Here are the class descriptions of the four different themes given to the students:

Theme 1: Mobile Computing Explore computing and software development by creating apps for Android-based smart phones. Students will work in teams to imagine, design, prototype, build, test, and launch apps for the Android market. Students will gain hands-on experience with the languages and tools needed to build Android apps, and they will test their apps on Android phones.

Theme 2: Computing in Robotics Explore computing and software development by designing a controller and mission planner for an autonomous underwater robot. Students will learn background on underwater robotics and its application to biology, oceanography and marine archaeology. After learning basic underwater robot control, students will deploy robots in Avila Bay California from our lab on the pier. Students will then work in teams to imagine, design, prototype, build, and test their own robot controller and mission planner via real ocean deployments.

Theme 3: Computing in Gaming Explore computing and software development by creating a full featured web-based computer game. This course includes an overview of the development process of games and an introduction to gaming fundamentals: logic, story and game play. The course will focus on design, teamwork, and using an iterative development process. Students will learn basic programming skills in order to develop a simple 2D game using a scripting language (such as Actionscript).

Theme 4: Computing in Music Students will write programs that generate music. Early compositions will focus on the elements of western harmony. Later ones will allow students to explore timbre and digital sound processing. Students will work collaboratively in teams to design, develop, and test their programs and compositions. The course will focus on design, teamwork, and the use of an iterative development process. The course is intended to be an enjoyable introduction to both computer science and elementary composition.

2.3 Stressing Non-Academic Factors in CSC 123

As mentioned in Section 2.1, we have common, basic learning outcomes in all themes of CSC 123. The goal of these outcomes are to increase the students ability to succeed in future CS courses by giving them a firm foundation in basic programming fundamentals. One key aspect to building up student academic skill is the fact that we do not assume any prior programming experience (clearly stated in the course description and syllabus) which helps us to:

1. provide students new to CS a non-threatening, confidence building environment to learn the basics,
2. give students who have learned poor programming habits an opportunity to correct them,
3. and allow students with prior experience an opportunity to practice their knowledge in order to gain mastery.[3]

While academic proficiency is very important to overall student success, a recent meta-study, [12], found that certain non-academic factors are key to student success as well. The factors we considered and built into our course are the ones that are most strongly related to student success. They are academic-related skills, academic self-confidence, social support, and achievement motivation. We describe each and the role the play in our course below.

2.3.1 Academic-Related Skills

Academic-related skills refer to the ability a student has to form good study habits, manage their time, take good notes, and use academic resources, such as the campus library and computer labs. We develop these skills in our students in three ways. First, we provide access to upper year student mentors who have developed successful study habits to meet

[3] A common technique used in the Kumon method of teaching.

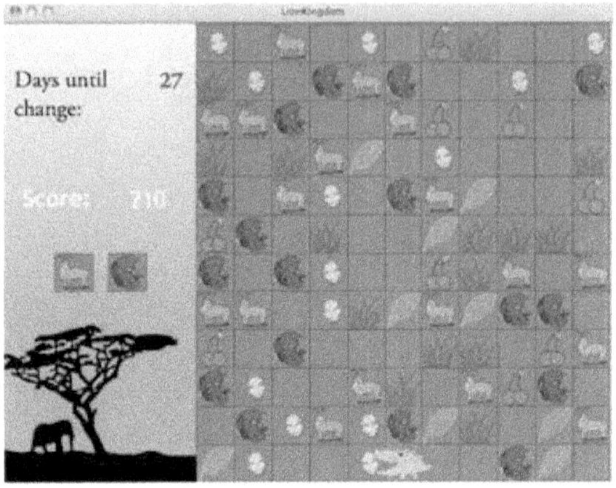

Figure 2: Lion Kingdom, an original game programmed and designed by CSC123 students.

with CSC123 students regularly and help them prepare for upcoming milestones and exams. [13] and [4] demonstrate how effective this type of mentoring can be. Second, we expose our students to a wide variety of assessment techniques typically found in college courses to help them make the transition from high school forms of assessment providing them with the experiences they need to better understand how to acclimate to college academic life. In [9], they found that difficulty adjusting to college life was a factor in poor retention and that activities that smooth this transition are beneficial. In lecture, we discuss good study habits [14], how to plan their time for upcoming class deliverables, and highlight resources available to them.

2.3.2 Academic Self-Confidence

Academic self-confidence refers to how successful a student feels they are (or can be) in an academic environment. Students with a low-level of confidence tend to procrastinate or avoid academically challenging activities. In the worst case, it can lead to changing majors, academic dishonesty, or dropping out of college [9, 3]. We attempt a number of ways to boost academic self-confidence. First, we chose topics that most students are already familiar with regardless of their academic background. Contrast the types of discussion that can occur on the first day in a class on introductory Java versus a course on video games. While students with no prior programming experience would feel intimidated in the former, they are quite able to participate in the latter. Figure 2 shows "Lion Kingdom", a game created by a group of students where 4 of the 5 team members had no programming experience.

Our courses include hands-on labs that build student programming skills and confidence as they incrementally master topics within the course domain. Students use both pedagogical and professional development environments. For instance, students in the music version use DrRacket, and students in the mobile version use App Inventor for Android, Eclipse with Java and the Android SDK, and WebIDE [7], an NSF-sponsored lab environment created by two of the authors.

Our courses also stress learning a software development process and applying software best practices such as test-driven development (e.g, [11]). This gives students the tools

Figure 3: An Android application for skiers complete with instant, online updating of ski conditions.

they need to tackle the type of challenging programming activities they will encounter in later courses. Often, having a clear starting point to a project is all a student needs to feel confident about completing the project.[4] Figure 3 shows a final project done in the mobile development section of CSC 123. While, initially the task to create such an application seemed daunting, the students were carefully led through a process with intermediate milestones to tackle the problem in a productive manner. The first project milestone involved creating a vision and scope, feature list, and user interface mockups for the proposed app. Each student was provided an Android phone, allowing them to explore apps in the Android Market. As a result, every student could contribute to the project idea from the very beginning, regardless of prior programming experience. Subsequent milestones involved development status presentations, testing, product demos, and reflections on the software development experience.

2.3.3 Social Support

For the purpose of student retention, it is important that students feel connected to their institution, faculty, peers, and campus activities [12]. To help foster a feeling of connectedness, we have students work in teams, provide upper-level student mentoring, require the students to attend relevant technical talks on campus, and arrange for a wide variety of student clubs to come talk the students. The benefits of student team support are well-documented in the literature.

2.3.4 Achievement Motivation

Achievement motivation describes the level at which a student wants to be successful in the class and major. In lecture in CSC 123, we spend time providing a"big picture" view of computer science and how it will allow them to work in a wide variety of industries and make real-world contributions through multi-disciplinary collaborations. CSC123 was constructed to reflect this view. Students are able to work with peers on a substantial quarter-long project in a context they self-selected. For the robotics students, they were able to launch in actual Autonomous Underwater Vehicle (AUV), Figure 4, and have it navigate to predetermined waypoints.

At the end of the course, CSC 123 students present their work to both students in their section and students from other CSC123 sections. We found this activity builds camaraderie within sections and a healthy competition between sections.

[4]To quote Mary Poppins, "Once begun, half done."

Figure 4: The AUV, programmed by Calpoly CS freshmen, at Avila Bay.

Grade	Fall 2009 %	Winter 2011 %	Difference
A	28.51%	38.99%	10.48%
B	30.12%	30.82%	0.70%
C	16.87%	15.72%	-1.14%
D	9.24%	3.77%	-5.46%
F/W	15.26%	10.69%	-4.57%

Table 1: Performance in CSC 101 (123 majors)

3. ASSESSMENT

We empirically studied the impact of the CSC 123 course by analyzing student grades and enrollments in first-year courses.

3.1 Grades

The first null hypothesis N_1 was that students taking CSC 123 would perform the same in first year computing courses as in the previous year without CSC 123. The independent variable was students taking CSC 123. The dependent variables were final grades in CSC 101 and CSC 102 in the *typical* quarter (i.e. on the normal schedule when students are expected to take the course). The control group consisted of all students who took CSC 101 and CSC 102 in Fall 2009 and Winter 2010 respectively. The experimental group was all students who took CSC 123, CSC 101, and CSC 102 in Fall 2010, Winter 2011, and Spring 2011 respectively. There were no substantial differences in the material covered in CSC 101 and CSC 102 between the two years, other than the introduction of CSC 123 which moved the typical CSC 101 and CSC 102 sequence from Fall/Winter quarters to Winter/Spring.

A total of 249 students took CSC 101 in Fall 2009, and 209 students took CSC 101 in Winter 2011. Of the 209 Winter 2011 students, 159 or 76.1% also took CSC 123 (i.e. they were computer science, software engineering, or computer engineering majors). Table 1 reports the percentage of students earning A's (A and A-), B's (B+, B, B-), C's (C+, C, C-), D's (D+, D, D-), and F/W (failing or withdrew from course) for the offering of CSC 101 which is *typical*, or on schedule, for Computer Science, Software Engineering, and Computer Engineering Majors. This data indicates that the number of students earning A's in CSC 101 increased by over 10%, while the number of students failing CSC 101 decreased by over 4%. These differences were both statistically significant using the chi-squared test at a 5% significance level. The Fall 2009 numbers include all students who took CSC 101 (CSC/SE/CPE majors and non-majors), whereas the Winter 2011 numbers include only the students who took both CSC 123 and CSC 101 (i.e. only CSC/SE/CPE majors). For comparison, Table 2 reports the differences when including all students, majors and non-majors, in both Fall 2009 and Winter 2010. The differences are similar.

Grade	Fall 2009 %	Winter 2011 %	Difference
A	28.51%	38.38%	9.76%
B	30.12%	32.54%	2.42%
C	16.87%	14.35%	-2.51%
D	9.24%	3.83%	-5.41%
F/W	15.26%	11.00%	-4.26%

Table 2: Performance in CSC 101 (all students)

Grade	Winter 2010 %	Spring 2011 %	Difference
A	33.68%	28.36%	-5.33%
B	28.95%	36.57%	7.62%
C	20.00%	24.63%	4.63%
D	10.00%	5.22%	-4.78%
F/W	7.37%	5.22%	-2.14%

Table 3: Performance in CSC 102 (123 students)

Grade	Winter 2010 %	Spring 2011 %	Difference
A	33.68%	29.89%	-3.79%
B	28.95%	34.24%	5.29%
C	20.00%	23.91%	3.91%
D	10.00%	5.98%	-4.02%
F/W	7.37%	5.98%	-1.39%

Table 4: Performance in CSC 102 (all students)

A total of 190 students took CSC 102 in Winter 2010, and 184 students took CSC 102 in Spring 2011. Of the 184 Spring 2011 students, 134 or 72.8% also took CSC 123 (i.e. were computer science, software engineering, or computer engineering majors). Table 3 reports results from CSC 102, comparing Winter 2010 and Spring 2011, the *typical* quarters for CSC/SE/CPE majors. Similar to CSC101, fewer students who took 123 failed CSC102. However, unlike CSC101, fewer students who took 123 received A's. Similar results are seen in Table 4 which reports all students, majors and non-majors in CSC102.

Although students who took CSC 123 performed significantly better in CSC 101 than students who did not take CSC 123, we are unable to reject the null hypothesis and claim that students performed better in first-year courses when they take CSC 123.

3.2 Retention

The second null hypothesis N_2 was that students taking CSC 123 would enroll in the second first year computing course (CSC 102) at the same rate as in the previous year without CSC 123. The independent variable was students taking CSC 123. The dependent variable was students in CSC 102 as a percentage of students in CSC 101 in the previous quarter for the *typical* quarter (i.e. on the normal schedule when students are expected to take the course).

The control and experimental groups were the same as for the previous section.

In the control group, 190 students took CSC 102 in Winter 2010 following the 249 students who took CSC 101 in Fall 2009, for a rate of 76.31%. In the experimental group, 184 students took CSC 102 in Spring 2011 following the 209 students who took CSC 101 in Winter 2011, for a rate of 88.04%. In addition, only five of the 205 students who took CSC 123 have elected to change to non-computing majors. We are still waiting on official numbers for the previous years for comparison. Although time will tell if CSC 123 improves retention to graduation, this almost 12% increase in CSC 102 enrollment rates is encouraging.

4. CONCLUSIONS

Our work is still unfinished; we have yet to see the effect of our experiment on students in the existing "103" class that ends the historical first-year sequence, and must instead rely on our impressions, and the reports of our students.

Fortunately, those impressions and reports are positive ones! We are now gearing up for the second iteration of the class, and we've added another track–visual arts–to our existing ones. We consider our experiment a success, and look forward to hearing from others who adopt our approach.

5. ACKNOWLEDGEMENTS

Our work is supported from a variety of sources. We would like to acknowledge Ignatios Vakalis, our department chair, for his vision and commitment to enable these new courses.

The mobile sections used Android phones and labs that were created with support from a Google Faculty Research Award. In addition, the WebIDE system is supported by the National Science Foundation. This material is based upon work supported by the National Science Foundation under Grant No. 0942488. Any opinions, findings, and conclusions or recommendations expressed in this material are those of the author(s) and do not necessarily reflect the views of the National Science Foundation.

Last, we would like to recognize Patricia Marin and John T. Yun, Associate Professors at UC Santa Barbara, for their continued effort in helping us collect first-year assessment data.

6. REFERENCES

[1] O. Alvarado and Z. Dodds. Women in cs: An evaluation of three promising practices. In *SIGCSE*, 2010.

[2] M. Barg, A. Fekete, T. Greening, O. Hollands, J. Kay, and J. Kingston. Problem-based learning for foundation computer science courses. *Computer Science Education*, 10(2):109–128, 2000.

[3] M. Besterfield-Sacre, C. Atman, and L. Shuman. Characteristics of freshmen engineering students: Models for determining student attrition in engineering. *Journal of Engineering Education*, pages 139–149, 1997.

[4] H. Carver, L. Henderson, and et al. Increased retention of early computer science and software engineering students using pair programming. *20th Conference on Software Engineering Education and Training*, pages 115–122, 2007.

[5] J. Coheen and L.-Y. Chen. Migrating out of computer science. *Computing Research News.*, 15(2), 2003.

[6] Crenshaw, Metcalf, Chambers, and Thakkar. A case study of retention practices at the university of illinois at urbana-champaign. In *Proceedings of the 39th ACM technical symposium on computer science education*, pages 412–416, 2008.

[7] T. Dvornik, D. Janzen, J. Clements, and O. Dekhtyar. Supporting introductory test-driven labs with webide. In *Software Engineering Education and Training (CSEE T), 2011 24th IEEE-CS Conference on*, pages 51 –60, may 2011.

[8] A. Fisher and J. Margolis. Unlocking the clubhouse: The carnigie mellon experience. *SIGSCE Bulletin*, 34(2), 2002.

[9] J. Goldfinch and M. Hughes. Skills, learning styles and success of first-year undergraduates. *Active Learning in Higher Education*, 8(3), 2007.

[10] M. Haungs, J. Clements, and D. Janzen. Improving engineering education through creativity, collaboration, and context in a first year course. In *American Society for Engineering Education (ASEE) Annual Conference*, Pittsburgh, PA, 2008.

[11] D. Janzen and H. Saiedian. Test-driven development: Concepts, taxonomy, and future direction. *IEEE Computer*, 40(2):43–50, 2005.

[12] V. Lotkowski, S. Robbins, and R. Noeth. The role of academic and non-academic factors in improving college retention. ACT Policy Report, www.act.org/research/policy/index.html, 2004.

[13] M. Marszalek, A. Snauffer, S. Good, G. Hein, and A. Monte. Mentors improve the college experience of engineering undergraduates. *Proceedings of the 2005 35th ASEE/IEEE Frontiers in Education Conference*, 2005.

[14] W. Pauk. *How to Study in College*. Houghton Mifflin Company, 2000.

[15] L. Williams, E. Wiebe, K. Yang, M. Ferzli, and C. Miller. In support of pair programming in the introductory computer science course. *Computer Science Education*, 12(3):197–202, 2002.

Reshaping the Image of Computer Science in Only Fifteen Minutes (of Class) a Week

Sara Sprenkle
Washington and Lee University
Lexington, VA 24450
sprenkles@wlu.edu

Shannon Duvall
Elon University
Elon, NC
sduvall2@elon.edu

ABSTRACT

Low undergraduate enrollments in computer science will not meet the future demand of employers. Some reasons for the low enrollments are computer science's nerdy image, lack of understanding of the field, and low motivation for learning programming. We propose to change the image of computer science by exposing students to applications of computing and its impact on their lives through reading and discussing recent news articles in 15 minutes of class. We call this component of our courses the *Broader Issues* in computer science. In this paper, we present our motivation for the Broader Issues component, how we implemented the component in CS0 and CS1 courses, and our evaluation of the component, including student reactions to and impact of the component.

Categories and Subject Descriptors

K.3.2 [**Computer and Information Science Education**]: Computer Science Education

General Terms

Human Factors

Keywords

computer science education, introductory course, teaching methods

1. INTRODUCTION

Enrollments of undergraduates in computer science have declined since the dot-com bust [22, 2]. More recently, enrollments are starting to increase, but current enrollments will not meet the future demands of employers [7]. Low enrollment is partially attributed to the image of computer science as nerdy and limited to programming [8, 10]. Women in particular are more interested in computer science when they see the field in terms of real-world applications that benefit mankind [10]. Some groups are working to change computer science's image, with initiatives aimed at motivating the study of computer science(e.g., [21, 11]) and busting the nerd stereotype (e.g., [3]), but these approaches have not necessarily been integrated into the computer science curriculum. Often the real-world issues are only discussed in an ethics unit rather than integrated into the core topics of programming and algorithms.

We propose to change the image of computer science by *exposing students to applications of computing and its impact on their lives through reading and discussing recent news articles in 15 minutes of class time.* We call this component of our courses the *Broader Issues* in computer science.

The Broader Issues component has several goals. First, **the articles should help students put abstract class material into real-world context.** Reading and discussing news articles is an easy way to introduce the human element and relevance to society in an established course. We are careful to choose articles that directly connect to the class material so that the articles help the students see the large-scale application of their small-scale assignments. Tedford used a similar idea in her data structures class, where students worked on large projects that relate to current events [19]. Our approach is based on a similar goal—helping students connect real life with abstract course material—but is easier to implement in any course with less time constraints.

Secondly, **articles should show the broad range of computer science applications and opportunities**. In a study of high school girls, Jepson and Perl found that two reasons girls do not choose to study computer science is that there are not enough computer scientist role models and that the girls do not know much about the field of computing [12]. One way to appeal to women in computer science classes is to "humanize" the course [4]. That is, women are more engaged in material that has an obvious connection with people's lives because "they are not interested in computing for the sake of computing" [10]. News articles are an easy and unintimidating way to learn about the breadth of the field and its diverse role models.

Thirdly, the addition of the Broader Issues component should **improve students' written and oral communication skills**. Students write a short summary of each article. Low-stakes writing assignments allow students to practice focused, analytical writing—without high grading costs [9]. Furthermore, Waite et al. advocate a "Conversational Classroom," citing that their course was more successful when classroom discussion was encouraged [24]. Students

Permission to make digital or hard copies of all or part of this work for personal or classroom use is granted without fee provided that copies are not made or distributed for profit or commercial advantage and that copies bear this notice and the full citation on the first page. To copy otherwise, to republish, to post on servers or to redistribute to lists, requires prior specific permission and/or a fee.
SIGCSE'12, February 29–March 3, 2012, Raleigh, North Carolina, USA.
Copyright 2012 ACM 978-1-4503-1098-7/12/02 ...$10.00.

learned to engage one another's opinions and ideas as well as reflect on their own. Including the Broader Issues component in class allowed us to create a conversational classroom. Students have time to read the article, research more information if they are interested, write about their opinions on the issue, and read the opinions of others before coming to class to discuss the article. As a result, class discussions are a lively exchange of ideas and a time for students to draw parallels from the reading to their other course work and articles. The discussion atmosphere also encourages students to open up to one another and gel as a group, warding off the typical competitive and intimidating atmosphere.

The last and perhaps most important goal for the Broader Issues class component is **to expose students to how a computer scientist thinks and feels about current issues**. The articles we use in the class highlight the issues we are naturally interested in as computer scientists. In class discussions we can model the thinking process we use to evaluate the information in the article. Learning "disciplinary thinking" has been argued to be more important in a course than the memorization of facts or the explanation of concepts [5, 13]. Gaining computing skills is only one aspect of class, and students "should learn to think as a member of a particular disciplinary community and to be familiar with the types of debates in which members engage" [5]. Furthermore, several groups designing curriculum guidelines recommend covering social and ethical issues [6, 14], which naturally come up when discussing recent news articles.

The remainder of this paper is organized as follows: Section 2 describes our implementation of the component in CS0 and CS1 courses; Section 3 describes our evaluation of the approach and presents the results; and in Section 4, we make recommendations and conclusions for others who are interested in integrating this component into their courses.

2. COURSE ACTIVITIES AND LOGISTICS

The Broader Issues component of the class consisted of three parts: reading, writing analyses, and discussing the articles in class. These activities happened on a weekly basis. We discuss the approach as we applied it in CS0 and CS1 courses, but we believe a similar approach can be taken in other courses as well.

2.1 Articles

We selected articles that were relevant to the course, were easy to read and short (generally taking less than fifteen minutes to read), covered a variety of topics, were not narrowly focused, and that we believed students would find interesting.

The articles frequently came from news sources such as Wired, ACM Communications, or ACM TechNews. After colleagues learned about our use of articles, they sent articles that they liked and/or had discussed in class. For some topics, we chose several articles that had different angles on the week's topic and may interest different students. For example, students could choose between two articles on the topic of environmental monitoring: a more technical one on volcanoes and a less technical one on zebras. Students looking for a more challenging read or who were more interested in volcanoes than zebras could read the more technical article.

We scheduled reading articles when they were timely (e.g., electronic voting near election days) and near relevant course material. For example, in CS1, we read a DARPA Urban Challenge article after covering `if` statements. Students are thrilled to read from a real-world researcher, "We were just one IF [statement] away from success" [23]. The article also emphasizes the importance of testing and debugging, supporting our requirement for demonstrating good testing in their submitted assignments.

Examples of our articles can be found at
`http://computersciencenews.blogspot.com/`.

2.2 Short Writing Assignments

During our study, students wrote summaries as comments on a blog so that other students could read their entries and students would get experience using a blog. The summaries had to contain the following information for full credit:

- How interesting this article is on a scale of 0 to 9
- The three most important points in the article(s)
- How the article affected your understanding of CS and how computing relates to other areas
- How the article relates to our course
- One question for class discussion

Writing serves several purposes. First, we can verify that the student read the article. Second, students practice writing, which many colleges emphasize, especially in the sciences. Third, we can see if the students understood the relationship between the article and the class. Fourth, we get input from students on what would make for interesting discussion. Fifth, if discussion lulls, we can ask specific students about points in their blog.

2.3 In-class Discussions

During class, we posed several questions, students volunteered answers, and discussion usually flowed from there. To facilitate discussion, we tried to maintain a balance so that no student dominated the conversation. We posed new questions when discussion waned, sometimes played devil's advocate, and always tried to challenge the students' thinking.

In the CS1 classes, we also had small group (3-4 students) discussions. The purpose of the small groups was to encourage shy students to participate. The instructor chose the small groups before class, arranging different groups each week in various ways, such as randomly, using the modulo operator, by gender, by year, by article read, or by opinion.

The articles sparked discussion on issues traditionally discussed in introductory computer courses, such as efficiency and cost tradeoffs and testing challenges, but also unexpected topics, such as usability, privacy, security, ethics, and economic and social policies. Students did not expect to discuss such issues in a computer science course, but found they could relate their experiences and expertise from other areas to their computer science course.

2.4 Grading

Students were evaluated on their blog entry and their participation in class discussion. The blog entry was weighted more than participation because students could participate in discussion without reading the article. We graded blog entries based on their clarity, understanding, thoughtfulness, English grammar, and completeness. The blogs were quick to read and to grade, and it was usually evident if the students were making connections between the articles and the course content. For the discussion grading, students were usually given full credit for participation if they said something during discussion. Even though the Broader Issues were worth less than 10% of the students' course grade, the students still took the assignments seriously.

2.5 Extra Credit

We gave students some extra-credit opportunities based on the Broader Issues component. Students could find new articles that interested them, summarize them, and write about how they found the article and why it interested them. While some of the articles students found were too narrow to be used for the class, many of these extra-credit articles can be assigned in the current or future classes.

3. EVALUATION AND OBSERVATIONS

In this section, we describe our methodology for evaluation and provide quantitative and anecdotal evidence of the effectiveness of including the Broader Issues in our courses.

3.1 Methodology

We evaluated our approach in one CS0 course and five CS1 courses at two small liberal arts universities. All classes were small and populated mostly with students who were not planning to major in computer science but rather were completing a general education requirement or elective.

We used two surveys to evaluate our approach. At the beginning of the semester, students completed a survey about their backgrounds, their perceptions of computer science, what computer science majors do after graduation, and how computer science related to their lives, if at all. At the end of the semester, the students completed an anonymous evaluation, where they rated various parts of the Broader Issues component of the course and reflected on their changed perceptions of computing. In addition, part of the students' written assignment was to rate their interest in that week's article. We used this information to help identify trends for what types of articles would be most engaging in future courses.

The objective of the surveys are to evaluate the effectiveness of our approach, in particular:

- how interested are the students in the articles' topics?
- how interested are the students in the small group and class discussions of the articles?
- how much time do students spend reading the articles and writing summaries?
- what effect do the article assignments have on the students' writing and communication skills, their understanding of computer science, their ability to think computationally, and their perceptions of computer science?

3.2 Results

We gathered both statistical and anecdotal evidence to see if our goals for the Broader Issues component were being met.

3.2.1 Logistics of Readings and Discussions

The majority of students rated the quality of readings and large class discussions as "very good" or "excellent". However, students found that small-group discussions were mediocre. We believe that the classes were too small to merit breakout groups, and smaller group sizes may have made some students feel pressured to carry the conversation.

Students were very engaged in class discussions and enjoyed that aspect of class. A peer evaluator for one CS1 class lecture said, "Throughout both phases of this Broader Issues component [small and class discussions], it was obvious that the students had read and understood the articles, and that they were genuinely interested in the material. Again, the discussion and debate was lively and fun."

While a few students responded that they felt too much time was spent on class discussions, the majority of students would prefer more time. We feel that the fifteen minutes per week was just right: enough to engage lively discussion without sacrificing other course content. As one student commented, it's a good thing to leave them wanting more!

All students reported spending on average an hour or less reading and summarizing the articles; CS0 students all reported spending less than 30 minutes. Some of the CS1 articles were more technical and, therefore, more challenging to read and summarize. Students reported that they would like more emphasis on the discussion in class as well as more weight on this component in their final grades.

Women comprised half of the CS0 students but less than one-third of the CS1 students. In both courses women responded well to the Broader Issues component, writing thoughtful blog entries and participating in discussion. In personal communication, one woman math major in CS1 credited the Broader Issues as her reason for continuing on to the next computer science course.

The following quotes from students further illustrate their enthusiasm for the Broader Issues component:

- "This was my favorite part of the class!"
- "I thought the readings were always good and pretty interesting and they were a nice break from the programming."
- "It was good that we kept up to date with the latest news in the computing world."

3.2.2 Article Interest

Most students rated their overall interest in the articles as either "very good" or "excellent". No individual article in CS1 scored on average less than 5.5 on a scale of 0 to 9, and most were higher. CS1 students found the articles on Privacy and Security in Facebook [18], the One Laptop Per Child project [16], the DARPA Urban Challenge [23], and the AI system Watson [20] the most interesting, averaging over 8. CS0 students were most interested in the articles on Electronic Voting [17], the One Laptop Per Child project [1], and Steganography and Terrorism [15]. Even if students were not interested in an article, they often recognized its value, as evidenced in a student's blog entry: "While the article is worth reading, I did not find it to be interesting." The following student quotes show that most did in fact find the articles interesting as well as worthwhile.

- "The articles regarding steganography and the XO laptop were really relevant and interesting, a rare combination."

- "I really enjoyed the articles. It was interesting to see how computing really effects [sic] our lives in current times, and the discussions were also a nice change from the regular lecture."

3.2.3 Communication and Writing Skills

While it is not clear that the students improved in terms of grammar, the students' quality of answers to discussion questions improved over the course of the semester. They were better able to compare articles and draw conclusions at the end of the semester. In addition, the students were able to more clearly and precisely construct their answers.

Students often wrote thoughtful entries that revealed more about themselves than we would typically expect in a class. However, students did not appreciate being evaluated on English grammar and clarity in a computer science course. Since the study, we have tried requiring a Word document or hand-written response rather than the blog format, and students were more careful with their grammar and did not resent being evaluated on grammar.

While some articles generated more interest than others, each discussion was lively and there was never a problem getting most students to participate. Since some students are naturally more opinionated and outspoken than others, ensuring that everyone had a chance to be heard in 15 minutes often presented a challenge. Small-group discussions were employed to include everyone but were only mildly successful. Shy students still often hung back from the discussion, while the other students preferred the larger group setting. Small group discussions worked best when the groups felt safer (such as grouping by gender) and when the small group discussion had an agenda (e.g., they had to prepare to debate other small groups). We were pleased to find that students had civil discussions: even when there were dissenting opinions, the students were never rude.

3.2.4 Impact on Understanding of Computer Science

The CS0 and CS1 student responses differed most widely about how the articles impacted their understanding of computer science. In the CS1 classes, 63% rated the articles' impact as "excellent" or "very good" and only 15% rated it as "fair" or "poor". In CS0, however, only 19% of students rated the articles' impact as "excellent" or "very good" while 48% rated it as "fair" or "poor". We believe there are several reasons for this. First, the CS0 course is a non-programming breadth course: most topics are fairly easy to understand and the course is designed to show the variety of topics in computing. The CS1 course, however, is an introductory programming course and the Broader Issues component is the only connection in the class between the programming topics and their wider applications. It is not surprising that the articles make a bigger impact on the CS1 students' understanding of computer science.

However, students did not always make the expected connections to the articles. For example, late in the semester some CS1 students thought the answer to the "relevance" question was "they probably used this week's data structure to implement this program." While that may be true, we were often looking for a more specific connection to our class's concepts. For example, the Facebook article discussed how Facebook uses frequencies in its algorithms [18], and we had calculated frequencies in a recent assignment. Furthermore, some students talked about how complicated Facebook's algorithms are. We wanted to take the mystery and difficulty out of these applications, hoping they could see that an algorithm in a recent assignment could be scaled up to do something similar to Facebook's algorithm. In addition, some, students did not critically analyze the article and could not draw conclusions beyond what the author concluded, making their grade on the writing portion lower. We used class discussion to address these misunderstandings.

In the following quotes, students comment on the impact of the articles and discussions on their understanding of computer science.

- "I love this part of the course. It's nice how this part allows you to see real-life examples of what you do in class."
- "I thought it was a great element because it made the material we are learning more real to me."
- "I truly enjoyed this component of the class and it definitely served to put some perspective on the things we were doing in lab and learning about in class."

3.2.5 Computational Thinking

Perhaps the most difficult goal to assess was students' learning to think like computer scientists. Computational thinking starts with showing students how conceptual constructs relate to interesting, real-world, challenging problems [25]. Ultimately we would like the students to approach their own problem-solving using computing concepts like design, abstraction, and efficiency that they learn in class. Certainly the goal of computational thinking is beyond the grasp of many non-majors after one course in computing. We did, however, find some students in each class that seemed especially intrigued by the Broader Issues component of class. Sometimes, students would write long blog entries on everything the article made them think about. Some students would get interested and follow links or find related articles to the given topic. In two separate classes, a student who stopped coming to class and turning in assignments still read articles and posted blog entries. Sometimes, we would walk into class and students were already discussing the week's article, the students would leave class talking about it, or they mentioned talking to other students not in the class about the article.

In general, even if a student was struggling with the course content, the readings and participating in class discussion would bring them back into their comfort zone. They enjoyed making connections between course content and an article. For example, many students are thrilled that the `If` statement is mentioned in the DARPA Urban Challenge article [23], that Excel 2007 was released with a bug involving binary numbers, and that the One Laptop Per Child project uses Linux and Python.

Perhaps most compelling are the insights of some students. For example, after reading articles about the One Laptop Per Child (OLPC) project and gender differences in computing, one student drew a parallel between the two that amazed us. He stated that the OLPC project's biggest challenge is that the local leaders fear the change it represents—a shift in power. He then hypothesized a similar fear in traditional computer scientists that, consciously or not, may keep them from greater efforts to diversify computing.

Other survey responses lead us to believe that students are learning more about what problems interest computer scientists and what the field of computing is really like.

- "Computer scientists aren't sitting around programming machine language but are instead involved in a wide variety of topics solving problems in just about every field."
- "I now realize that Computer Science is an interactive field that affects everything we do, even voting."
- "I can now identify the reaches of computer science in society, and I also found computer science to be fascinating since it is in essence another way of thinking, something which is beneficial in any field."
- "In some sense, computer science is perhaps the most pure of the sciences, simply asking 'what is the most efficient, most precise, overall best way to solve any given problem?' regardless of what that problem actually is."

3.2.6 *Perceptions of Computer Science*

As expected, at the beginning of the course, students had a variety of perceptions about computer science. Many mentioned that they use computers and applications daily, that computer scientists program, and that computer science majors become programmers. A few who had taken computer science courses before mentioned algorithms and problem-solving. Some advanced math and science majors mentioned how programming would help them in their research or coursework. At the end of the course, however, it was clear that the Broader Issues component of class had indeed broadened their perceptions of the field, as evidenced by the following quotes.

- "Throughout the course I have become aware of the many possibilities and applications that computer science and programming provide. I never would have known that I could have a basic understanding of the programming behind automated cars or wireless sensor networks just by learning basic for loops and if statements in Python."
- On Voting: "I think that this article changed my views on computing. I entered this class with little to no knowledge of computing and the informational age. I am shocked to find that such programs can be uploaded so quickly into a supposedly 'airtight' system."
- "The Broader Issues portion of our course, however, has brought me to the realization that there is much more to the Computer Scientist than meets the eye... I typically think of Computer Scientists as people who create programs for their own profit, but the 'One Laptop Per Child' article proved otherwise."

It is clear to us that the Broader Issues component of class met the goals we had set. In the next section, we provide more details on lessons learned from our experience and possible pitfalls of our approach.

4. LESSONS LEARNED AND CONCLUSION

Reading and discussing computer science news stories for a relatively short time in class each week is admittedly a simple idea. However, it has made a significant impact in our students' first experience with computer science. With little administrative work, little devoted classtime, and little extra effort from the students, the students are finding the diversity, impact, and excitement of the field. We highly recommend that others introduce this type of element into their computer science courses, and to help, we have compiled some advice based on our experiences.

First, begin keeping a log of interesting articles (starting with our repository, if you wish). When you come across an interesting news event, write the link as well as a few keywords of how the article connects to your course. Soon you will have plenty of articles to get started. You do not need to have all the articles in place at the beginning of a course—you or your students may find new ones during the semester. In addition, we have a blog containing articles that we found interesting and/or have used in class: `http://computersciencenews.blogspot.com`.

We graded blog entries using a points rubric. While grading was done quickly, it can be even faster using a "check" system. Give checks for satisfactory/typical work, a check-minus for unsatisfactory work, a check-plus for exemplary work, and a 0 for incomplete. In addition, not every blog needs to be graded for every student every week. Random sampling for grading tends to work well since the blog posting is due each week. It is also unclear whether the discussion portion of the component needs to be graded. For the study, we graded based simply on attendance or participation. Since neither of these were a problem in class, that part of the grading can probably be dropped.

As discussion facilitator, you have to balance letting students lead the discussion and preventing tangents. You also have to play devil's advocate sometimes and support opinions that you don't believe. It is helpful for the students if they know that your contribution to the conversation is not what you personally believe but rather fodder for discussion. Many students feel uncomfortable contradicting a professor unless they are specifically instructed that it is the correct thing to do.

Small group discussions were not as effective as class discussions in some cases, which may be caused by our small class size. Larger classes may find the small group forum effective. Small groups worked best for preparing students to take specific roles or argue certain opinions within the class discussion. This is also an easy way to start a discussion when students are reluctant to talk. Assigning a small group of students a role or opinion also forces a student to think and argue from a new perspective.

5. REFERENCES

[1] Little laptop a hit in rural Peru. `http://www.cnn.com/2007/WORLD/americas/12/24/laptop.village.ap/`, Dec. 2007.

[2] Bachelor's and associate's degrees awarded in computer sciences, by sex, 1985–2005. `http://www.nsf.gov/statistics/wmpd/figc-2.htm`, 2008.

[3] Nerd girls: Breaking the stigmas and stereotypes of women in engineering.

http://www.nerdgirls.org/public/index.html, 2011.

[4] D. Blank and D. Kumar. Patterns of curriculum design. In L. Cassel and R. Reis, editors, *Informatics, Curricula, and Teaching Methods*, pages 77 – 86. Kluwer Academic Publishers, 2003.

[5] R. Boyle and M. Clark. CS++: Content is not enough. In *Proceedings of the Technical Symposium on Computer Science Education (SIGCSE)*, volume 36, pages 422–426, March 2004.

[6] Cassel, L., et. al. Computer science curriculum 2008: An interim revision of CS 2001. Report from the interim review task force, 2008.

[7] C. I. O. Council. Forecast of future labor supply and demand. http://cio-nii.defense.gov/initiatives/netgenerationguide/supply_demand.html, Apr. 2010.

[8] C. Dean. Computer science takes steps to bring women to the fold. http://www.nytimes.com/2007/04/17/science/17comp.html, Apr. 2007.

[9] P. Elbow. *High Stakes and Low Stakes in Assigning and Responding to Writing*. Jossey-Bass, 1997.

[10] S. Graham and C. Latulipe. CS girls rock: sparking interest in computer science and debunking the stereotypes. In *SIGCSE Bulletin*, pages 322–326, 2003.

[11] K. T. N. Hartness. Working to change perceptions. *Journal of Computing Sciences in Colleges*, 26:259–267, May 2011.

[12] A. Jepson and T. Perl. Priming the pipeline. *SIGCSE Bulletin*, 34(2):36–39, 2002.

[13] J. A. Langer, C. Confer, and M. Sawyer. Teaching disciplinary thinking in academic coursework. In J. Mangineri and C. Block, editors, *Creating Powerful Thinking in Teachers and Students*, pages 81 – 109. Harcourt Brace, 1994.

[14] Liberal Arts Computer Science Consortium. A 2007 model curriculum for a liberal arts degree in computer science. *Journal on Educational Resources in Computing*, 7, June 2007.

[15] K. Maney. Bin Laden's messages could be hiding in plain sight. http://www.usatoday.com/tech/columnist/2001/12/19/maney.htm, Dec. 2001.

[16] D. Pogue. Laptop with a mission widens its audience. http://www.nytimes.com/2007/10/04/technology/circuits/04pogue.html, Oct. 2007.

[17] T. Riordan. Researchers reveal 'extremely serious' vulnerabilities in e-voting machines. http://www.princeton.edu/main/news/archive/S15/81/65023/index.xml, Sept. 2006.

[18] J. Smith. Facebook's news feed knows what you did last summer. http://www.insidefacebook.com/2007/10/29/facebook's-news-feed-knows-what-you-did-last-summer/, Oct. 2007.

[19] P. Tedford. Using current events as a teaching tool for an undergraduate data structures course. *Journal of Computing Sciences in Colleges*, 18:50–55, April 2003.

[20] C. Thompson. What is I.B.M.'s Watson? http://www.nytimes.com/2010/06/20/magazine/20Computer-t.html, June 2010.

[21] University of Washington Computer Science and Engineering. Why Choose CSE? http://www.cs.washington.edu/WhyCSE, 2011.

[22] J. Vesgo. Enrollments and degree production at US CS departments drop further in 2006-07. *Computing Research News*, Mar. 2008.

[23] J. Voelcker. Autonomous vehicles complete DARPA urban challenge. http://www.spectrum.ieee.org/nov07/5717, Nov. 2007.

[24] W. M. Waite, M. H. Jackson, and A. Diwan. The conversational classroom. *SIGCSE Bulletin*, 35(1):127–131, 2003.

[25] J. M. Wing. Computational thinking. *Communications of the ACM*, 49:33–35, March 2006.

Experiences Teaching MapReduce in the Cloud

Ariel Rabkin, Charles Reiss, Randy Katz, David Patterson
{asrabkin,charles,randy,pattrsn}@cs.berkeley.edu
Electrical Engineering and Computer Science Department
University of California, Berkeley

ABSTRACT

We describe our experiences teaching MapReduce in a large undergraduate lecture course using public cloud services. Using the cloud, every student could carry out scalability benchmarking assignments on realistic hardware, which would have been impossible otherwise. Over two semesters, over 500 students took our course. We believe this is the first large-scale demonstration that it is feasible to use pay-as-you-go billing in the Cloud for a large undergraduate course. Modest instructor effort was sufficient to prevent students from overspending. Average per-pupil expenses in the Cloud were under $45, less than half our available grant funding. Students were excited by the assignment: 90% said they thought it should be retained in future course offerings.

Categories and Subject Descriptors

K.3.2 [**Computer and Information Science Education**]: Computer science education—*Human Factors*

General Terms

Economics, Management, Measurement

Keywords

Cloud computing, Education, MapReduce

1. INTRODUCTION

Cloud computing is a major and disruptive change in how computing services are delivered. The term "cloud" has unfortunately been used for several different related concepts. In this paper, we refer to what is sometimes called a "public cloud" — a service that allows large quantities of computational resources to be allocated in a pay-as-you-go manner with minimal prior arrangement [1]. This change is beginning to percolate into the undergraduate curriculum. Many universities are now offering courses that cover MapReduce [5] and related distributed execution systems [9, 8, 2]. These courses prepare students for a world in which large-scale distributed "big data" processing is routine. In contrast, the change in billing models caused by cloud computing has not yet had overt impact on undergraduate instruction.

This paper describes an effort to integrate the cloud into lower-division courses, allowing new kinds of assignments. For the last year, we have used Amazon's public Elastic Compute Cloud, EC2, as a platform for the MapReduce unit in our introductory machine organization course at UC Berkeley. This course is ordinarily taken by students in their third or fourth semester. The Fall term had 170 students; the Spring had 320.

To make the course more relevant to current computing challenges, we made parallelism a central theme. We wanted to emphasize parallelism at all levels, from the inherently parallel nature of hardware logic blocks through multicore systems and all the way up to warehouse-sized shared-nothing clusters. Data-flow frameworks like MapReduce are the most successful parallel programming model for commodity hardware clusters. These frameworks embody solutions to many of the fundamental challenges of coarse-grain parallelism: handling failures, dividing up work into independent chunks, handling inconsistent performance across the cluster, and so on.

Clouds make the cost, and therefore the efficiency, of computing explicit. For many instructors and pupils, this will be a novel environment. For others, though, it will be seen as a reversion to a pre-PC era, in which students were given quotas for the computing resources available to them. There is an important distinction, however: in the cloud, users choose whether to consume resources sequentially or in parallel. This choice offers a tradeoff between efficiency and time-to-completion, which was not generally visible in the mainframe era but which is a significant aspect of parallel computing, and an important lesson we sought to teach.

1.1 Instructional Goals

We were driven to use a public cloud by the conjunction of several instructional goals. First, we thought the experience of using public cloud infrastructure and seeing the actual dollar cost of compute resources would be a valuable one for students. Second, we wanted students to experience running and debugging distributed MapReduce jobs on a significantly-sized cluster. Given the size of our student body, using purely university IT resources would have imposed unacceptable infrastructure costs. Last, we wanted students to evaluate the performance of MapReduce jobs and see the speedup from parallelism. This requires isolation from other students, which is difficult to achieve without

Permission to make digital or hard copies of all or part of this work for personal or classroom use is granted without fee provided that copies are not made or distributed for profit or commercial advantage and that copies bear this notice and the full citation on the first page. To copy otherwise, to republish, to post on servers or to redistribute to lists, requires prior specific permission and/or a fee.
SIGCSE'12, February 29–March 3, 2012, Raleigh, North Carolina, USA.
Copyright 2012 ACM 978-1-4503-1098-7/12/02 ...$10.00.

the public cloud. (Cloud providers such as Amazon Web Services offer virtualized platforms with consistent performance. This gives customers predictable value-for-money. While the consistency is not perfect, it is good enough for many practical purposes, including ours.)

1.2 Research Questions and Methods

The focus of this paper is on the opportunities and challenges offered by the cloud, rather than on teaching big data, parallelism, or MapReduce. We answer three research questions: Can we effectively manage cloud costs in a large introductory class, given current billing models? Can we use rented cloud hardware to demonstrate principles of parallelism using MapReduce? What difficulties do lower-division students confront when using current industry-grade tools like Hadoop on EC2?

We use instructional costs, student survey results, and the average quality of graded student work to evaluate the success of our course. As we will show, using the cloud worked well. Costs were moderate; students were happy. We made mistakes along the way, particularly in terms of preparing students for "big data" programming. We describe the lessons we learned and what we intend to do differently going forward. We focus on the second offering of the course, in the Spring, which was larger, better documented, and benefited from the experience of the first offering.

During the Spring semester, we administered three surveys to students: one over the Winter break before the course, once in the middle of the semester, and once at the end of the term. The first and last surveys are relevant to this paper. At the time of the opening survey, we had email addresses for two-thirds of the students who would ultimately enroll. Of these, 80% responded. The final survey had responses from half the enrolled students.

2. RELATED WORK

Several schools are now teaching MapReduce as part of their undergraduate curricula. Here, we summarize these efforts and contrast them with our own.

In the Spring of 2007, the University of Washington taught an experimental course covering Hadoop for upper-division undergraduates [9]. (This course has since become a regular offering.) The emphasis was on the use of Hadoop (the standard open-source MapReduce implementation) to solve practical problems at large scale. Students spend several weeks on a large project. In contrast, we are teaching lower-division undergraduates, in a machine organization course that includes MapReduce as just one unit.

Both Tufts and the University of Maryland have offered "big data" courses with a strong focus on MapReduce and related technologies [4, 10]. Maryland has made use of EC2 for this purpose. As with UW, this was in the context of a small upper-division class, with MapReduce, not pricing or parallelism, being the focus.

UC Berkeley has experimented with integrating Hadoop MapReduce very early into the curriculum, covering it briefly in the initial programming course. This course is taught in Scheme, not Java, using a custom-written Scheme-to-MapReduce glue library [8]. Performance tuning is a non-goal, as is understanding the mechanisms behind parallel execution.

Even small schools have been able to cover Hadoop. St. Olaf College has a Hadoop cluster, managed by student volunteers and used in several courses [2]. The cited paper is notable for the suggestion that schools should explore "obtaining 'cloud' resources on demand." Our paper represents a large-scale demonstration and evaluation of that possibility. Subsequent effort at St. Olaf has been directed towards simplifying Hadoop, hiding the details from students [6]. As with Berkeley's introductory class, considerable effort was made to have students write MapReduce programs in Scheme, hiding the Hadoop Java APIs and command-line job submission. We took the opposite approach, exposing students to the real industrial tools and documentation.

Harvard has experimented with using EC2 to provide compute resources to their introductory CS course [11]. Students, though, are completely insulated from provisioning and billing. Effectively, the Cloud is used as a scalable replacement for local IT infrastructure, rather than to allow assignments that could not have been taught otherwise.

3. COURSE DESIGN

We wanted students to understand the sort of data processing that cloud computing makes available. Accordingly, we designed our assignments to be sufficiently compute-intensive that it would be obvious why one would want to rent computing resources rather than use one's own machines. We choose data processing tasks (rather than, for example, a web application use case) because the cost and time benefits of parallelizing are more apparent here. Data processing assignments give students a clear metric for efficiency: cost per gigabyte of input.

It was important to us that, as much as practical, students used the same tools that professionals use. One reason was permitting more direct application of the assignment to student's own processing tasks. Another is that we did not want students to form the impression that performance anomalies and debugging challenges were the consequence of us providing only a "student-quality" framework. We wanted students to understand that these are pervasive issues when dealing with real distributed systems. Further, using standard tools will reduce the maintenance burden on future course staff.

Originally, our MapReduce assignments used C to match other assignments in the course. This relied on Hadoop's language-neutral "streaming" mode[1], which executes an external program for each Map and Reduce task. This caused several problems; as we discuss below, debugging in this environment was a significant challenge. While not a formal prerequisite, most students taking our course had some experience in Java or a C-like language. Hence, we switched from C to Java for the Spring offering of the course. This permitted our assignments to use Hadoop's better-supported Java API.

Our course had four two-week project assignments, a two-hour lab and three hours of lecture per week. Projects had an intermediate milestone deadline to help students start early. We assigned short problem sets for homework and had two written exams. Students were assessed primarily on their projects and the exams. Most labs served as tutorials for the project assignments. For the MapReduce project we had one (Fall semester) or two (Spring) such labs for the MapReduce and cloud computing unit. For the labs, students were permitted partners, but the projects were done individually.

[1] `http://hadoop.apache.org/common/docs/r0.20.0/streaming.html`

Sem.	Lines of Code	Description	Dataset Size (bytes)	Corpus
FS	0	Lab: performance measurement, introduction to EC2 tools	20,000 MB (F); 8,000 MB (S)	Wikipedia (F); Usenet (S)
F	~ 50	Project: PageRank [12] in C, using Hadoop Streaming locally and then on EC2	650 MB	Web graph
S	~ 10	Lab: writing MapReduce programs in Java, running locally	34 MB	Usenet
S	~ 50	Project: computing a text-comparison metric locally and then on EC2	8,000 MB	Usenet

Table 1: Assignments used. F= Fall, S=Spring, FS = both

We designed our MapReduce unit around a set of related text-processing assignments, characterized by simple algorithms to be executed on big data. We strove for assignments that would be slightly more complex than the usual "word count"-style examples for MapReduce, but that would not overly tax students' nascent Java programming skills. Table 1 summarizes these assignments.[2]

In both semesters, our assignments culminated with a project. This required students to write a small data processing program and run it on a large data set. We had students run their program in the cloud, vary the number of (virtual) machines used, and measure the scale-up. The data set their programs ran across was chosen to be as large as practical while requiring less than a half-hour of time waiting for programs to complete.

In the Fall semester, the text corpus was the link graph (pairs of source and destination web pages) from a circa 1999 crawl of CS department webpages, derived from the Stanford WebBase project [7]. In the Spring, we used subsets of the Westbury lab corpus of Usenet messages [13]. In both cases, we pre-loaded a copy of the data in the cloud where it could be quickly accessed.

All assignments, both lab and project, came with conceptual questions as well as coding. We asked students, for instance, to compute how much money they had spent, and what price this was per unit of work. This was intended to draw students' attention to the economic aspects of cloud computing. Since cloud computing costs scale linearly with computational resources, increased cost per unit work makes it clear when students are seeing less than ideal speedup.

In the Spring, we added a lab where students developed some small MapReduce programs (using the Hadoop Java API) and ran them locally using Hadoop MapReduce's single-process mode. We provided students with a complete word count implementation and instructed them to use it as a template for the two MapReduce programs assigned in the lab: counting the number of documents containing each word (instead of the number of times each word appears) and constructing an inverted index from the source text. We supplied a subset of the Usenet corpus for both cases.

4. EVALUATION

This section evaluates our experience in several dimensions. We emphasize cost management, not because it is the most important goal, but because it is tied directly to our core goal of using the cloud for lower-division instruction. When using the public cloud, the cost per student becomes visible to both instructors and pupils in a way that is not currently common in computer science. We also evaluate the quality of student work and reported student satisfaction. These demonstrate that using the cloud provided sufficiently consistent performance to allow students to see parallel speedup.

In both semesters, we provided students with scripts to launch a Hadoop MapReduce cluster on Amazon's Elastic Compute Cloud (EC2) and run programs on it. These scripts were responsible for the necessary accounting, access control, and billing. They were based on Cloudera's Hadoop scripts [3], modified to access our shared account and integrated with the local user account structure in our environment for accounting.

4.1 Payment Models

Amazon and other Infrastructure-as-a-service cloud providers use a post-paid billing model. Users supply a credit card number when they create their accounts. Users then use the provider's API, command line tools, or web interface to request resources, which are then made available. At the end of every month, users' credit cards are billed for the previous month's usage. There is no way for users to impose a cutoff beyond which further requests will be denied. The Cloud unit of our course was funded by an education grant from Amazon Web Services. Even so, Amazon requires a payment card for each account, which will be billed if usage exceeds the amount of the grant.

Our grant was for \$100 per student per semester, the standard size offered by Amazon. From our research experience, we knew that cloud usage could easily exceed expectation. We anticipated that most of our usage would occur shortly before the deadline. We wanted to have enough slack in our budget to ensure that we would not exhaust the budget in this pre-deadline peak. We also wanted to reserve some funds so that students who made mistakes and needed extra resources could still complete the assignment.

One approach would have been to have a separate Amazon grant allocation per student. Doing this would have required students to supply their own credit card, if they exceeded the grant. We thought this was inappropriate. Students agreed: In the Fall semester, we surveyed the students on whether they would be comfortable signing up for an EC2 account with their credit card for backup billing.

The full wording of the question was as follows: *Amazon Web Services is set up for companies rather than for students, so the way you get an account is to get an activation key (which we have) and then supply a credit card number as a backup in case you exceed your initial allocation. We think you'll only use 20% of your allocation for both your lab and*

[2]These can be obtained via `http://www-inst.eecs.berkeley.edu/~cs61c/archives.html`

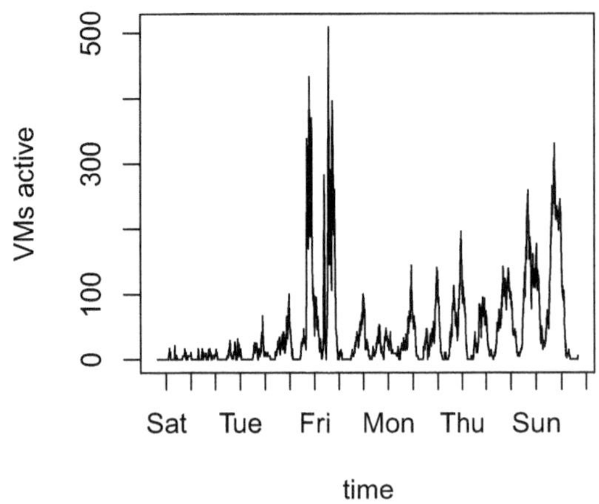

Figure 1: Number of active virtual machines on our course account in the Spring semester over time. The peak (over 500 virtual machines) occurs during the day the lab assignment was given. The second peak is the project due date.

your project, so we think no one will get close to exhausting their allocation.

Approximately a third of students responded; half of these said they would not be willing to risk their own money. Consequently, we chose to have a single Amazon account for the class, with subaccounts for each student. This decision required us to create our own wrapper scripts for all the tools we expected students to need.

4.2 Provisioning

Obtaining the computing resources for our course was not simply a matter of signing up online as cloud computing is traditionally imagined. All our usage went through one account with Amazon. Amazon requires approval for an account to run more than twenty virtual machines, and these approvals are usually granted as a matter of course. Amazon is much more reluctant to approve large requests over a thousand machines, especially without strong evidence of an ability to pay for sustained usage at that scale.

The potential peak for our assignment was approximately 3000 virtual machines (9 VMs per student and 320 students). We worried that if most of the class worked on the assignment simultaneously near the deadline, we might actually hit the limit. We asked Amazon to increase our limit, but we only received capacity for about a third of our maximum usage. So we crossed our fingers, hoped that a sufficient number of students who do the assignment early, and accepted the thousand-instance limit. Happily, this posed no problem in practice, as Figure 1 shows.

In the Spring, peak instantaneous usage was around 500 8-core virtual machines: we instructed students to time their programs on two cluster sizes, 5 and 9 machines, and compare the timings. Obtaining and managing a similarly capable physical cluster would have been much more expensive.

We conclude that using a cloud computing provider was effective in supplying students with large compute resources for short periods. Even though we had many hundreds of students and most students did their work close to deadlines, no one ran out of machines. The cost was relatively modest, around \$45 per student in the Spring and around \$25 per student in the Fall. In the Fall, with limited experience, we opted for medium-size instances, with 2 cores each. In the Spring, we decided that it was worth the expense to give students experience with modern datacenter-standard hardware, and used 8-core machines.

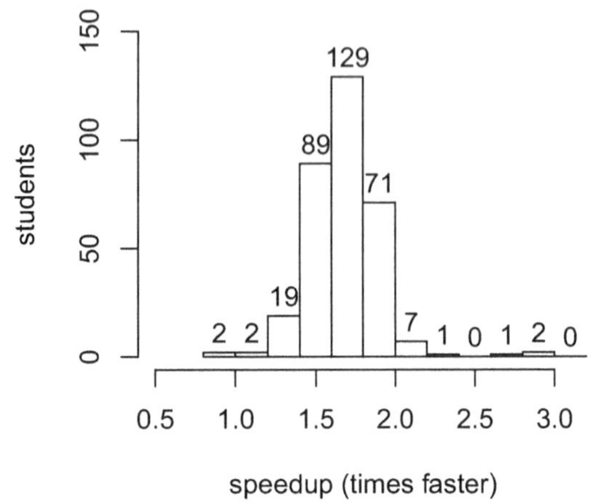

Figure 2: Speedups observed by students. Most students saw a substantial but sub-linear speedup, as desired.

4.3 Experiencing Parallelism and Big Data

Figure 2 plots the reported parallel speedups observed by students. Most students saw more than a 1.5 speedup when they increased their cluster sizes by a factor of 1.8; few saw more than 2. Seeing this speedup was a good result. Most students saw a sizable but sublinear speedup, the right expectation to have for parallelism in general. That some students saw anomalous speedup is also useful pedagogically. Performance variation in clouds (or other distributed systems) is an important and inevitable fact. Students benefit from seeing that it happened to them or their classmates at least some of the time.

The overall quality of student work impressed us. In the Spring, 75% of student projects passed all our test cases; many more failed only due to minor bugs that could have been caught with more testing. This shows that students were able to cope with the MapReduce programming model.

4.4 Student Satisfaction

We now turn to quantitative evaluation of how well our course ran in terms of student satisfaction. At the end of the Spring semester, we administered a survey to our class. We asked students to rank the four class projects in terms of value. The four projects were MapReduce, writing a MIPS emulator in C, writing an optimized matrix-multiply program, and designing a pipelined processor at the logic-gate level. The second and fourth of these are routine and well-debugged class projects, with the last of these usually being very popular.

Thirty percent of students thought MapReduce was the most valuable, and another thirty percent listed it as second-most-valuable. The MapReduce assignment came in second, overall. We conclude that students are enthusiastic about the assignment, even given its rough edges and challenges.

We asked students explicitly whether they would advocate keeping or replacing the project. 45% of students suggested keeping unequivocally, and another 47% marked "There are pros and cons, but better to keep it." Only 8% marked "better to drop" or "definitely drop."

Several students thought that the project was valuable to them professionally. One student commented "Too many employers are looking at Cloud Computing for it to be dropped from the curriculum - it's good to give students at least an intro to the subject." Another noted that "employers at job fairs really seemed to like it!"

The students who were dissatisfied primarily focused on programming language issues. A minority of students struggled because they had only minimal Java proficiency coming in. This was not a universal problem; many students had comments like "I didn't know Java, and though I missed points for a few small things, the project was overall definitely still worth it."

5. LESSONS LEARNED

On the whole, our experiment with using the public cloud for undergraduate core courses worked well. Even so, we learned several negative lessons. This section describes those lessons and what we intend to do differently in future offerings of the course.

5.1 Debugging

One of our pedagogic goals was to have students experience real-world big data programming and debugging. In the Fall 2010, using C, several students received a very pointed lesson in the importance of local testing and defensive programming. Buggy C programs often fail with segmentation faults. Locally, these can be diagnosed with a debugger such as GDB. But when the C program is run inside Hadoop, there is no opportunity to do so. Hadoop Streaming provides poor diagnostics for programs that fail without outputting an error message. Hence, troubleshooting can be difficult, even for experienced course staff.

In the Spring, using Java, debugging was easier. Typically, when Map or Reduce tasks fail, a stack trace is recorded in the logs. This meant that staff, at least, could work out where student programs had gone awry. Students had difficulties, though. Reading and understanding stack traces is not a skill that is emphasized or taught in our introductory programming courses. Nor did students previously have to cope with test cycles measured in minutes, rather than seconds. Forcing students into a more demanding (and realistic) debugging scenario thus exposed a gap in their previous CS education that we tried to remedy as best we could.

This problem was exacerbated by the linguistic fragmentation of the early undergraduate curriculum in our school: there is no imperative language that students were required to know, coming in to the class. This meant that students were challenged by both the cloud program and unfamiliar programming languages. As of Fall 2011, our introductory course has switched to Python, which we could reasonably use for this assignment. This switch would also reduce the confusion caused by Hadoop's sometimes-idiosyncratic and unevenly-documented Java APIs. We expect the difficulty of Python debugging to be comparable to Java.

5.2 Efficiency

In both semesters, the staff coded and tested a simple implementation before releasing the assignment to students. We used this to estimate performance, both in choosing the data set size to assign students as well as to announce the performance they should expect. In the Spring, many students produced solutions that were more than a factor of two slower. Although our reference implementation was not specially optimized, the simple MapReduce programs we had the students write are sensitive to overheads from object creation, autoboxing (Java's automatic wrapping of primitive values in objects), string parsing, and string/number conversions. Students whose programs did more of these than our reference implementation (for example, keeping a counter in an Integer instead of an int or splitting a string in an inner loop) were correct but much slower. A small number of students made poor data-structure choices, resulting in run-times quadratic in the number of words in an input record (representing a Usenet message). Since we were targeting a run time of around 15 minutes, the financial effect of students' programs running even two or three times slower than our reference implementation was substantial.

Here again, a large-scale assignment in the cloud showed both us and the students a previously unsuspected gap in their prior experience. After we became aware of the slow program problem, we supplied a non-trivial local test dataset and told students what run time they should expect on it. We also gave a brief list of ways to make programs faster for students who were interested in doing so: avoiding object creation, reducing the number of generated map output keys, and so on.

In future offerings, we will spend more time advising students on how to debug in distributed contexts and how to program in a performance-conscious manner. Performance issues fit naturally into a computer organization course, so this strikes us as a good use of class time.

5.3 Waste

Inefficiency was not the major driver of costs; waste was. Some students accidentally left virtual machines running idle. We had mitigated the risk of this by configuring our scripts to automatically shutdown virtual machines after a time delay, though initially, we did not always enable this feature. Early versions of the staff-supplied wrapper scripts had a bug and would occasionally fail to terminate virtual machines when students requested it.

A much larger problem was that some students would rerun their entire experiment after any technical glitch or mistake. This repetition was responsible for the outliers seen in Figure 3. Our management scripts were only available on the campus hosts, so students seeking to use the cloud from home would log into campus, rather than running directly from home. These students were generally not aware of tools like GNU Screen that would let them maintain their session on the instructional machines after a network failure. Also, students assumed incorrectly that they could not continue using their existing EC2 session when they reconnected.

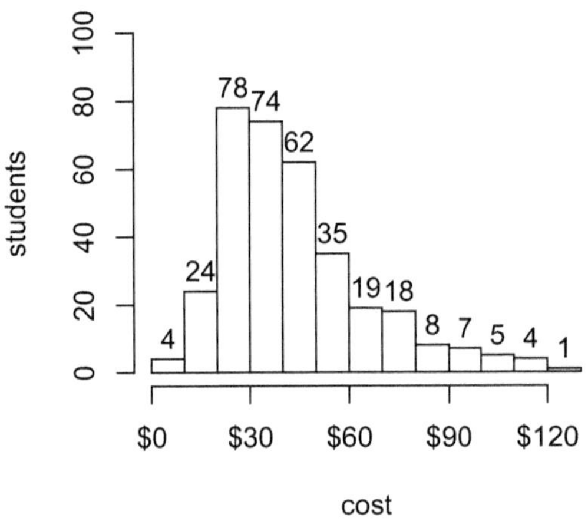

Figure 3: Histogram of estimated Spring semester EC2 usage per student.

Consequently, many students would start a fresh set of virtual machines (killing the old ones) each time they experienced a problem. Since EC2 charges for at least an hour each time a virtual machine is started, this could get expensive quickly. Some students who did not experience these glitches made different errors that lead them to restart machines unnecessarily — for example, assuming that each run of their program required a fresh cluster.

6. CONCLUSIONS

Today's cloud billing options are not ideally adapted to academic needs. Ideally, each student would have a balance of cloud credits issued by staff, and their accounts would be suspended if the limit is exceeded. Students should be unable to view each others' work or terminate virtual machines belonging to other students. Course staff should be able to use standard industry tools, without needing to modify them to prevent abuse. We understand that vendors, particularly Amazon, are working to introduce new billing models more appropriate for classroom use. This issue may therefore be resolved soon.

Even so, our experience was a success overall. Though current cloud billing models posed some difficulties, per-pupil costs were not a problem. In the Spring version of our course, we only spent $45 per student on average, less than half the standard grant, or $15000 total. This is small compared to the overall instructional cost of the course. The per-pupil cost is comparable to a textbook.

The vast majority of students were conscientious about costs. They were generally careful to not waste computing resources. The ones who were careless were usually quick to respond when notified that they had accidentally kept instances running. Cost management was a small fraction of the staff time for the assignment.

The course also succeeded in pedagogic terms. Students had the opportunity to exercise their programming and debugging skills in a new and challenging environment. They were able to experience parallel performance at a scale that would have been unthinkable without the cloud. And they were able to experience cutting-edge tools that helped them grow professionally.

Our course let every student in a large course run their programs on comparatively large clusters of modern hardware, without scheduling or resource contention. This experience would have been infeasible without the public cloud. Students enjoyed the ability to run at a "real" scale with real tools. Student evaluation was very positive of using Hadoop, even despite rough edges and difficulty.

Acknowledgements

Our course was funded by an Amazon Web Services instructional grant.

7. REFERENCES

[1] M. Armbrust, A. Fox, R. Griffith, A. Joseph, R. Katz, A. Konwinski, G. Lee, D. Patterson, A. Rabkin, et al. Above the Clouds: A Berkeley View of Cloud Computing. Technical Report 2009-28, UC Berkeley, 2009.

[2] R. A. Brown. Hadoop at home: large-scale computing at a small college. In *SIGCSE*, 2009.

[3] Cloudera, inc. Configuring and Running CDH Cloud Scripts. Retrieved August 31, 2011 from `https://ccp.cloudera.com/display/CDH2DOC/Configuring+and+Running+CDH+Cloud+Scripts`, 2011.

[4] A. Couch. Comp150 CPA. Retrieved August 21, 2011 from `http://www.cs.tufts.edu/comp/150CPA/`, 2011.

[5] J. Dean and S. Ghemawat. MapReduce: Simplified Data Processing on Large Clusters. *Commun. ACM*, Volume 51(Issue 1):107–113, 2008.

[6] P. Garrity, T. Yates, R. Brown, and E. Shoop. WebMapReduce: an accessible and adaptable tool for teaching map-reduce computing. In *SIGCSE*, 2011.

[7] J. Hirai, S. Raghavan, H. Garcia-Molina, and H. Paepcke. WebBase: A repository of web pages. In *WWW*, May 2000.

[8] M. Johnson, R. H. Liao, A. Rasmussen, R. Sridharan, D. D. Garcia, and B. Harvey. Infusing Parallelism into Introductory Computer Science Curriculum using MapReduce. Technical Report EECS-2008-34, UC Berkeley, 2008.

[9] A. Kimball, S. Michels-Slettvet, and C. Bisciglia. Cluster computing for web-scale data processing. In *SIGCSE*, 2008.

[10] J. Lin. Data-Intensive Information Processing Applications. Retrieved August 21, 2011 from `http://www.umiacs.umd.edu/~jimmylin/cloud-2010-Spring/info.html`, 2011.

[11] D. J. Malan. Moving cs50 into the cloud. *J. Comput. Small Coll.*, 25:111–120, June 2010.

[12] L. Page, S. Brin, R. Motwani, and T. Winograd. The PageRank Citation Ranking: Bringing Order to the Web. Technical report, Stanford Digital Library Technologies Project, 1998.

[13] C. Shaoul and C. Westbury. A usenet corpus. Retrieved August 21, 2011 from `http://www.psych.ualberta.ca/~westburylab/downloads/usenetcorpus.download.html`, May 2011.

Developing Microlabs Using Google Web Toolkit

Barry L Kurtz
Appalachian State University
Computer Science Department
Boone, NC 28608
(828) 262-7008
blk@cs.appstate.edu

James B Fenwick Jr.
Appalachian State University
Computer Science Department
Boone, NC 28608
(828) 262-2708
jbf@cs.appstate.edu

Philip Meznar
Appalachian State University
Computer Science Department
Boone, NC 28608
(828) 262-2370
meznarp@appstate.edu

ABSTRACT

Closed labs have become a common feature in computer science education because they provide hands-on experience in a supervised setting. Microlabs extend this approach into the lecture format with very short hands-on activities in the "middle of the lecture." The programming microlab approach was developed for a distributed computing course that integrated all levels of parallelism (multicore, cluster, and grid). Since that time we have developed logical microlabs where students solve conceptual problems that do not involve programming. These are integrated into a Microlab Learning Cycle. We want our microlabs to be usable with a wide variety of computing devices, including tablets. After experimenting with different development environments we have adopted the Google Web Toolkit (GWT). After presenting the current status of our activities, we discuss future directions for microlab development. This work is supported, in part, by three National Science Foundation grants.

Categories and Subject Descriptors K.3.2 [Computer and Information Science Education] Computer Science Education

General Terms Human Factors

Keywords Active learning, automated grading, web development

1. APPROACHES TO ACTIVE LEARNING

The Learning Cycle was developed by Robert Karplus in the 1960s as part of the Science Curriculum Improvement Study [1]. The Learning Cycle model of instruction is used by many POGIL (Process Oriented Guided Inquiry Learning) projects in the STEM disciplines [2]. This model of instruction has three phases:

- Exploration – after a very minimal introduction to the topic students are asked to explore a particular problem and see if they can discover a solution. This is guided discovery in the sense that as students work on the problem they receive feedback that guides them towards a correct solution.
- Invention – once students have experienced trying to solve one or more problems in the target topic, the instructor, supported by the textbook or other learning resources, introduces the topic formally, as is commonly done in lecture today.
- Application – Once the students are introduced to the topic both experientially (the exploration phase) and formally (the invention phase) they apply this knowledge to related problems in the domain. For computer science students this often means writing a program or methods in a program that allows the computer to solve problems in the target domain.

Permission to make digital or hard copies of all or part of this work for personal or classroom use is granted without fee provided that copies are not made or distributed for profit or commercial advantage and that copies bear this notice and the full citation on the first page. To copy otherwise, or republish, to post on servers or to redistribute to lists, requires prior specific permission and/or a fee.
SIGCSE'12, February 29–March 3, 2012, Raleigh, North Carolina, USA.
Copyright 2012 ACM 978-1-4503-1098-7/12/02...$10.00.

Over the last several years many papers [3, 4, 5] have been published reporting on the Tablet PC as an effective learning tool during lecture. Kurtz and Fenwick, authors on this paper, have also used tablet PCs in the classroom and found it to be an effective means of active learning [6]. Typically a logical problem is presented to students to solve as part of a lecture presentation. Students ink their solutions on the tablet and submit them anonymously for review by the instructor. The instructor selects and displays one or two student submissions for further discussion before moving on to the next topic. A major limitation of this approach is that only a few students receive direct feedback on the solutions submitted. In our approach of using logical microlabs during lecture every student receives individualized feedback and can submit solutions multiple times.

One widely used tool to teach introductory programming is CodingBat [7]; it is similar to our programming microlab approach. [8] reports on using "Proglets" to teach first year programming in Java; this approach focuses the student's attention onto a very specific topic with minimal overhead for the student. One of the most successful tools in Computer Science education is the development of JFLAP to help teach formal language theory. This tool, which is similar to our logical microlab approach, has been used successfully in a large number of universities [9].

A variation of the closed lab is a testing environment where students have to complete small program components under strictly monitored and possibly timed conditions. Ken Bowles [10] at the University of California San Diego (UCSD) introduced the use of drills and programming quizzes to support instruction in UCSD Pascal in the CS1 course. Kurtz has used this approach at three universities: the University of California Irvine, New Mexico State University [11], and Appalachian State University [12].

2. WHAT IS A MICROLAB?

Both logical microlabs and programming microlabs share several common characteristics: they are a 5-15 minute activity that occurs during lecture, students can work individually or in pairs, answers are submitted to an automated grading system, students are given constructive feedback if the submitted solution is not correct, and students can submit modified solutions for evaluation.

2.1 Logical microlabs

A logical microlab asks students to solve a conceptual problem in computer science. The problem does not involve any programming. Solutions are entered graphically and submitted for evaluation. To illustrate this process consider the following microlab where a student is asked to build a binary search tree (BST) given the postorder traversal (see Figures 1-3).

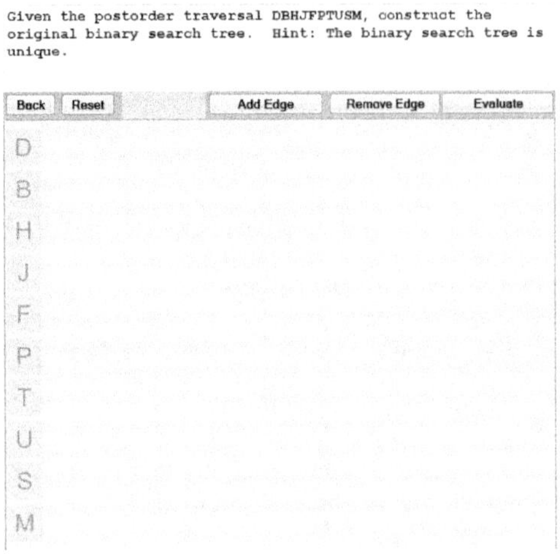

Figure 1: Initial Screen

A student drags and drops the nodes on the screen into positions to form a binary tree and adds edges as appropriate. This microlab has been used on a variety of devices including laptops, netbooks, and tablets; this is unlike tablet PCs that must support inking on the screen. When the student clicks evaluate the system first checks that the structure that has been built is a tree and every node has been included. If so, the system proceeds to evaluate the correctness of the response and provide appropriate feedback. If there is an error the system attempts to guide the student towards a correct solution as seen in Figure 2.

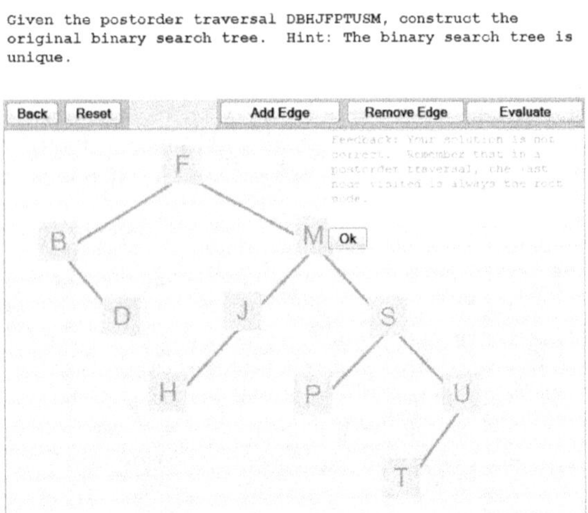

Figure 2: Feedback after first attempt: Your solution is not correct. Remember that in a postorder traversal, the last node visited is always the root node.

The student appears to follow this advice and submits a second solution; the results are shown in Figure 3. By comparing the given traversals the student finds that there is a problem with the nodes H and J. On a third attempt the student finds the correct tree and is given a congratulatory message.

If students do not find a correct solution in the allotted time, the instructor asks them to stop working on the problem and return to lecture mode. All attempts are saved by the system so that students can complete the problem outside of class. We have found that if students are given full credit for solutions submitted by the start of the next lecture period, they are willing to go back to lecture mode even when not finished

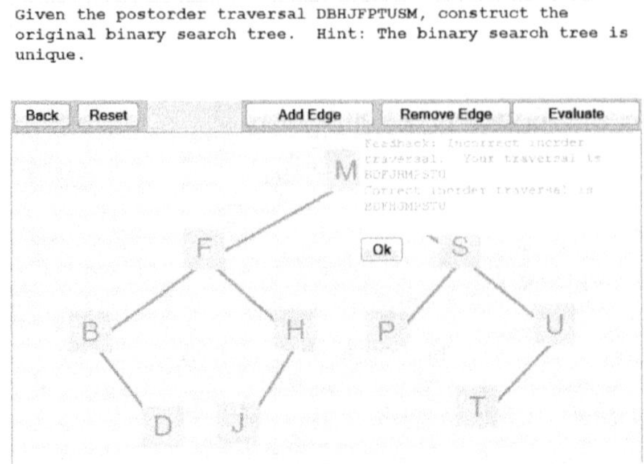

Figure 3: Feedback on second attempt: Incorrect inorder traversal. Your traversal is BDFJHMPSTU. Correct inorder traversal is BDFHJMPSTU.

2.2 Programming microlabs

The programming microlab often is directly related to a logical microlab on the same topic. After allowing students to work on the logical microlab shown above, the instructor with student input may develop a recursive algorithm in pseudocode to solve the problem of building a BST from a postorder traversal. To make this algorithm concrete in a particular programming language the problem needs to be expressed using appropriate structures. For building the tree introduced in the logical microlab it is decided that each node contains a single alphabetic character and that a traversal is represented as a string of characters. A Node class needs to be developed that allows construction of a binary tree with a unique root node.

The programming microlab to write a buildBST method that given the postorder traversal as a String returns the root node of the completed tree. This is a nontrivial method, but if a pseudocode algorithm has been developed during lecture it is possible to introduce the problem as a microlab. The microlab testing environment provides all necessary components, such as the Node class and the testing framework, so the student can concentrate on completing the given method. The skeleton program that is given to the students for the buildBST method is shown in Figure 4.

```
Node buildBST(String postorder){
  // write the code for the base case of an empty tree
  // create root, the last node in the postorder traversal
  // write the code for the base case for a tree with one node
  //count the number of nodes in the left subtree
  // create the postorder traversal of the left subtree
  // build the left subtree using recursion
  // create the postorder traversal of the right subtree
  // build the right subtree using recursion
  // return the root of the tree
}
```

Figure 4: Skeleton code for buildBST

The solution for this method varies depending on how the instructor wants to handle the Node class. There are two common choices:

- Make the Node class an inner class with public fields that can be accessed directly using the dot notation
- Make the Node class with private fields that uses getter/setter methods to change values in the Node fields

The solution shown in Figure 5 uses the getter/setter approach.

```
Node buildBST(String postorder){
  // write the code for the base case of an empty tree
  if(postorder.length()==0) return null;
  // create root, the last node in the postorder traversal
  char rootValue = postorder.charAt(postorder.length()-1);
  Node root = new Node(rootValue);
  // write the code for the base case for a tree with one node
  if(postorder.length()==1) return root;
  //count the number of nodes in the left subtree
  int countLeft = 0;
  for(int j = 0; j < postorder.length(); j++)
    if(postorder.charAt(j) < rootValue) countLeft++;
  // create the postorder traversal of the left subtree
  String leftPostorder = postorder.substring(0, countLeft);
  //build the left subtree using recursion
  root.setLeft(buildBST(leftPostorder));
  // create the postorder traversal of the right subtree
  String rightPostorder =
        postorder.substring(countLeft, postorder.length()-1);
  //build the right subtree using recursion
  root.setRight(buildBST(rightPostorder));
  return root;
}
```

Figure 5: A correct solution for buildBST

It would be very challenging for even the best students in the class to complete this method in 15 minutes. The string operations alone are a source of difficulty. So it is very important that students be allowed to complete the microlab outside of class and still receive full credit for completion.

It is natural to ask why even use a programming microlab to introduce this programming problem; why not just assign it as a program? Our experience with the programming microlab approach provides two answers to this question:

- During the 15 minutes allowed for the microlab during lecture the instructor can provide guidance and clarification for the entire group to get them on the right track; for the microlab shown above a quick review of appropriate String methods might be beneficial.
- By providing the testing framework and submission deadline students can complete this programming activity quickly (about 2 days) that might have required a week to complete as a "do it from scratch" programming assignment.

2.3 The Microlab Learning Cycle

The microlab learning cycle assumes there is a logical microlab and programming microlab associated with the topic being studied, such as building a BST based on a postorder traversal shown previously.

- The exploration phase uses a logical microlab that allows students to investigate the problem domain as they search for a solution to a particular problem or set of problems.
- The invention phase is like "normal" lecture where the instructor introduces any formal notation, representation or algorithms for the topic being studied.
- One of the activities in the application phase is a programming microlab that allows students to develop computer programs or program components to solve problems in the target domain.

3. DEVELOPMENT ENVIRONMENT

3.1 Initial Development

The original programming microlab environment, called WAGS (Web-based Automated Grading System), was developed on a Linux server to support instruction in parallel and distributed computing. Two language environments were supported: Java for threads and C for OpenMP and MPI. This system worked well for desktop computers or full feature laptop computers.

Logical microlabs were first developed during the summer of 2010. We needed a platform that allowed development of rich Internet applications across a variety of platforms. We initially decided to use JavaFX because of our student developers' familiarity with Java. As tablets became increasingly popular we needed an environment that would run on these platforms. We were not surprised that JavaFX does not run on iPads but we were surprised to find it does not run on Android due to the fact Google uses its own version of the Java Virtual Machine. We searched to find a new development environment and selected the Google Web Toolkit.

3.2 Current Development

Google Web Toolkit (GWT) is a development toolkit for building and optimizing complex browser-based applications [13]. Its goal is to enable productive development of high-performance web applications without the developer having to be an expert in browser quirks, XMLHttpRequest, and JavaScript. GWT is used by many products at Google, including Google Wave and the new version of AdWords. It is open source, completely free, and used by thousands of developers around the world.

The major GWT components include:

- GWT Java-to-JavaScript Compiler: translates the Java programming language to the JavaScript programming language.
- GWT Development Mode: Allows the developers to run and execute GWT applications in development mode (the app runs as Java in the JVM without compiling to JavaScript). Development mode is supported through the use of a native-code plugin called the Google Web Toolkit Developer Plugin for most popular browsers.
- JRE emulation library: JavaScript implementations of the commonly used classes in the Java standard class library (such as most of the java.lang package classes and a subset of the java.util package classes).
- GWT Web UI class library: A set of custom interfaces and classes for creating widgets.

The heart of GWT is the Java-to-JavaScript Compiler, allowing a developer to write rich web applications in Java. Upon compilation the developer can choose different modes detailing the readability and efficiency of the created JavaScript. Furthermore, the compiler will create different permutations of the code to handle some of the quirks that arise from differences in browsers.

GWT provides different approaches to common web application functions. In the current iteration of microlab development the logical microlabs are deployed on Google's App Engine servers, while the programming microlabs are deployed on a Linux machine running Apache. This and the natural differences between logical and programming microlabs created many opportunities to become familiar with the multiple approaches offered by GWT for GUI creation, client-server interaction, and data persistence.

Logical and programming microlabs require interfaces with different strengths. Logical microlabs require dynamic widgets with drag and drop capability, while programming microlabs are more static as most work is done through a text editor. Thus the programming microlab interfaces were created using UiBinder, a GWT utility that allows for a declarative GUI creation while also simplifying the creation of handlers for the different widgets (from either the GWT or Java libraries). In essence, UiBinder allows the developer to graft HTML and CSS into their application. The more dynamically-oriented logical microlab interfaces were created programmatically, allowing for greater dexterity in handling the drag-and-drop nature of the widgets.

A typical programming microlab involves a skeleton method or methods that are provided to the students. Each student completes the methods and submits them for evaluation. The testing framework contains other methods representing a correct solution of the microlab. The entire program is compiled, and, if successful, the output of the corresponding methods is shown to the student to provide feedback. Figure 6 shows a student submitting one of the exercises – the student code is shown on the left, and the evaluation is displayed on the right.

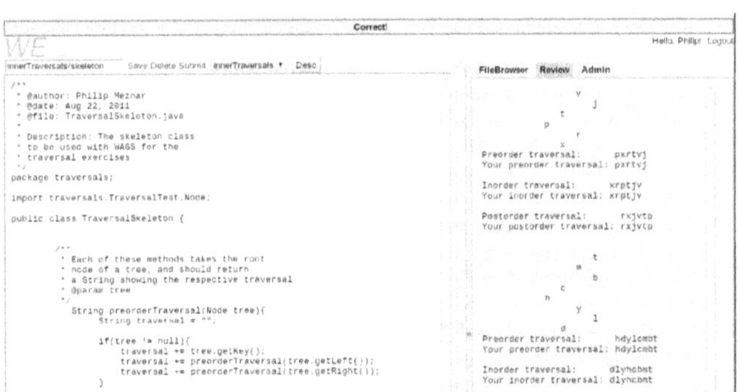

Figure 6: A typical student screen

Google offers application hosting on their App Engine Servers. This provides a very scalable architecture along with use of Google's database system, the DataStore. Thus, choice of deployment environment affects many other aspects of the application.

GWT provides different methods of client-server interaction for use in different deployment environments. This flexibility creates an easy method of storing and retrieving exercises, files, submissions, and a list of successful completions to the microlabs regardless of server structure. The logical microlabs use GWT's RPC functionality, which allows the programmer to easily write both the client and server code in Java along with granting easy access to the DataStore.

The programming microlabs currently employ GWT's RequestBuilder class, which provides an easy interface and encapsulation for handling HTTP get and post requests. Under both methods GWT handles the asynchronous network calls, again easing the development process.

GWT is a prime development environment for microlabs because of its ease and flexibility of use. If the developer is not that familiar with JavaScript, using UiBinder and RequestBuilder allows a developer to still use HTML, CSS, and server-side language skills. Or, the developer can use the Google App Engine, allowing you to create your entire application without having to leave your favorite Java IDE. If the developer has no preference, GWT can be used to fit development around the purpose of your application – it provides you with many easy to use tools, making it simple to have the right tool for the job.

In short, GWT allows for the easy creation of diverse microlabs that can be run simultaneously in a classroom on many different platforms while providing individualized and automated feedback and grading.

4. CLASSROOM EXPERIENCE

Detailed examples of the early programming microlabs for the distributed computing course appear in [14] and are not repeated here. We do review the evaluation of these microlabs and then discuss our recent classroom experiences.

4.1 Teaching Distributed Computing

There were ten programming microlabs used when teaching Java threads, five when teaching OpenMP, seven when teaching MPI, and two when teaching grid computing. A few microlabs had two separate activities that were graded independently. There were 31 microlab grades spread throughout the course; each component was graded on a satisfactory/not satisfactory basis. If a student did not finish a microlab during the allotted time, the student could complete it after class and check it off the next lecture period. Eighty four percent of students earned 90% or higher on the microlabs; the remaining students earned between 80 to 90%. These success rates are much higher than other course activities. The most frequent cause for not completing a microlab was absenteeism during the lecture that introduced the lab activities.

In the course evaluation students were asked to agree or disagree with the statement: The microlabs helped me understand the lecture materials. The results appear in Table 1; it can be seen that students reacted very positively to the use of microlabs. When asked in a free-form question "What was the best part of the course?" 50% of students explicitly said the microlabs.

Table 1: Evaluation Results

The microlabs helped me understand the lecture materials.					
Topic	**SD**	**D**	**N**	**A**	**SA**
Threads	0.0	0.0	0.0	33.3	66.7
OpenMP	0.0	0.0	0.0	66.7	33.3
MPI	0.0	0.0	0.0	50.0	50.0
Web Services	0.0	0.0	33.3	33.3	33.3
SD(strongly disagree),D(disagree),N(neutral),A(agree),SA(strongly agree)					

4.2 Teaching Data Structures

Our first set of micolab pairs (logical and programming) are aimed at the data structures course since this course, unlike distributed computing, is required for all students in accredited programs. The target domain involved binary trees and tree traversals. There are four activities with microlab support for this section of instruction.

1. Perform binary tree traversals
2. Build a Binary Search Tree (BST) by inserting a sequence of nodes into an initially empty tree
3. Build a BST given the postorder traversal (described earlier)
4. Build a general binary tree given the preorder and inorder traversals

The primary objective of these topics is to have students develop recursive algorithms to solve problems involving binary trees. The students use a logical microlab to explore the concept followed by lecture that formally introduces the concept and then a programming microlab to develop functional code. Our testing so far has been in Java but the software could be adapted to other object-oriented programming environments such as C++ and C#.

Figure 7 shows a student running one of the logical microlabs that teach tree traversals. This is a very short microlab usually completed in less than a minute for each given tree. There are a variety of trees used in the various microlabs for the three traversals investigated: preorder, inorder, and postorder. Two levels of help are provided. In the extended help mode, which is used first, the student is informed node-by-node when an error is made and asked to make a different choice. In the normal help mode, shown below in Figure 7, the student must complete the entire traversal before the answer is evaluated.

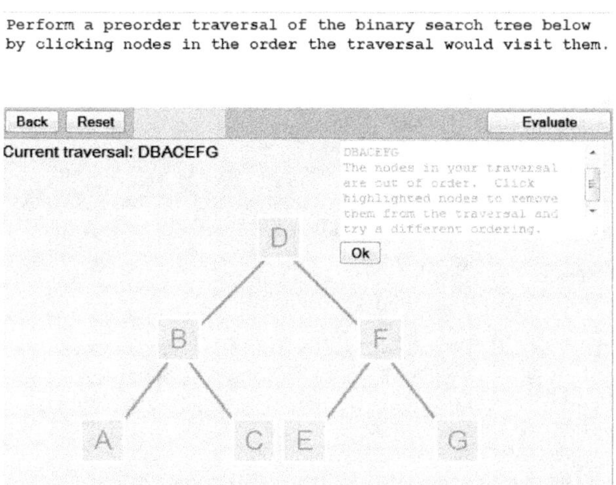

Figure 7: Logical microlab for preorder traversal

The programming microlabs associated with these activities involve writing the traversal algorithms. Students are required to write the node values to the console when visited. The testing environment is able to capture this data and compare it with correct methods to provide the students with useful feedback.

In Fall 2011 we used the four binary trees and traversals lab pairs in a data structures class at Appalachian State University. Each of the four topics (traversals, build a BST based on insertions, build a BST based on a postorder traversal, build a general binary tree based on preorder and inorder traverals) was presented during one lecture period (50 minutes) where students first completed the logical microlab activities, the instructor discussed strategies and guided students towards a pseudocode algorithm, and then students started the programming microlab. Both microlabs could be accessed and finished outside of class.

One of the exam questions asked the students to draw the BST after inserting the values 71, 42, 38, 61, 22, 51, 53, 52, 16 into an empty tree, find the height of the tree, then perform preorder, inorder, and postorder traversals of the tree. With this data there was no right subtree of the root. Of the 19 students who answered this question, 17 drew the correct tree, 15 had the correct height (the other four were off by one), and 12 students had all three traversals correct (many others missed a single item).

Table 2 shows the results of a survey given after completing all microlab activities. Values ranged from 1 representing a negative response to 5 representing a positive response.

Table 2: Survey Results

Question	Value
How well did you understand the algorithms necessary to solve problems involving binary trees?	4.0
How much did this activity improve your understanding of binary tree algorithms?	3.2
How thought-provoking did you find the logical microlabs?	3.6
How thought-provoking did you find the programming microlabs?	3.1
Were the logical microlabs easy to follow?	4.1
Were the programming microlabs easy to follow?	2.7
How valuable did you find the experience of using the microlabs for learning the material?	3.7
How well do you feel able to apply what you've learned from these microlabs?	3.7
In comparison to learning the material from lecture, how effective did you find the microlabs as a learning experience?	3.1
How clear were the instructions of each exercise?	3.5
How helpful were the microlabs about binary tree traversals?	3.4
How helpful were the microlabs to build a Binary Search Tree (BST) given a sequence of insertions into an empty tree?	3.2
How helpful were the microlabs to build a BST given the post order traversal?	3.5
How helpful were the microlabs to build a general binary tree given the preorder traversal and in order traversal?	3.5
How helpful was the microlab feedback for correct and incorrect answers?	3.1
How helpful was it to complete the logical microlab before attempting the programming microlab?	3.7

In general the logical microlabs were better received than the programming microlabs. A typical response to an open-ended question was "I like dragging and dropping things, those are fun." The programming microlabs were more challenging and often elicited more negative responses. Students preferred to work in offline environment such as Eclipse and not use the WAGS editor as indicated by the comment "The graphical representations were fun and helpful, but the WAGS editor and problem moving between WAGS and Eclipse caused problems for the programs."

The logical microlabs recorded each attempt submitted for evaluation. As students progressed through the sequence of activities they were able to solve problems with fewer attempts. For example, on the fourth and final activity to build a BST based on a postorder traversal, sixty percent of the students found the correct tree on their first submission. We have noticed one behavior with the programming microlabs that caused some concern. The better students complete the microlabs with the fewest compiles, typically two or three. We have had other students who use a "try this, try that" approach. They have many more compiles (sometime 20 or 30) and very little time between each compile. In the future we plan to consider a grade based on the number of attempts before a solution is found (fewer attempts equals better grade). Students will be given a reasonable number of attempts (say 12) before any penalty is incurred.

5. FUTURE DEVELOPMENT

The WAGS editor used a rich text area to display the methods the students were editing. Currently, rich text areas are not accessible on an iPad, limiting the distribution of the system. Furthermore, while the students were only required to alter one or more methods for the lab, they were given access to the entire class, enabling them to create unexpected errors. WAGS is being updated to use a text area, enabling editing on iPads and other mobile devices, as well as parsing the class file so only the appropriate methods are editable by students. We will test this revised system in a CS2 class at the end of the Fall semester 2011.

The Data Structure Tool that was used to develop the logical microlabs associated with binary trees can be used to develop other topics related to data structures. We plan to add "Add Node" and "Remove Node" operations. Other problem domains that we plan to develop include list structures, heaps, and graphs.

The same drag/drop and connect interface can be used in many other computer science domains, including finite state automata and digital logic. Whenever possible we will adapt existing software tools to the GWT environment. For example, the highly successful JFLAP program developed with NSF sponsorship is developed in Java. Since GWT applications are developed in Java, this will be one of the first applications we will attempt to port to GWT.

We also plan to develop microlabs appropriate for introductory courses. We currently use the Head First Design Patterns book [15] in our introductory software engineering course. The authors use Code Magnets (inspired by refrigerator magnets) to ask the reader to rearrange a sequence of coding steps or activities or diagram components to solve a particular problem. We will adapt this approach to the conceptual development of algorithms in introductory level courses. These logical microlabs will allow students to think conceptually about formulating an algorithm without having to worry about getting the character-by-character syntax correct. The follow-up programming microlabs will allow students to fully implement the algorithm after they know it is logically correct.

6. ACKNOWLEDGMENTS

This work has been supported in part by three NSF grants: Modern Distributed Computing Education (DUE0737355), Developing Software and Methodologies for eBook/Browsers to Enhance Learning (DUE1044572), and Transforming Computer Science Education with Microlabs (DUE1122752).

7. REFERENCES

[1] Fuller, Robert G. (editor), "A Love of Discovery: Science Education – The Second Career of Robert Karplus", Kluwer Academic/Plenum Publishers, 2002, chapter 4

[2] POGIL: Process Oriented Guided Inquiry Learning; www.pogil.org

[3] R. Anderson, R. Anderson, K. Davis, N. Linnell, C.Prince, V. Razmov, "Supporting Active Learning and Example Based Instruction with Classroom Technology", SIGCSE 2007

[4] M. Wilkerson, W. Griswold, B. Simon, "Ubiquitous Presenter: Increasing Student Access and Control in a Digital Lecturing Environment," SIGCSE 2005

[5] T. Denning, W. Griswold, B. Simon, M. Wilkerson, "Multimodal Communication in the Classroom: What does it mean for us?," SIGCSE 2006

[6] B. Kurtz, J. Fenwick, C. Ellsworth, "Using Podcasts and Tablet PCs in Computer Science" Proceedings of the 45th ACM Southeast Conference, Winston-Salem NC, March 2007.

[7] CodingBat – Online Code Practice http://codingbat.com/

[8] C. Edmondson, "Proglets for First-Year Programming in Java," Inroads, SIGCSE Bulletin, Vol 41, Number 2, June 2009, pp 108-112

[9] Susan H. Rodger, Eric Wiebe, Kyung Min Lee, Chris Morgan, Kareem Omar, Jonathan Su, "Increasing engagement in automata theory with JFLAP", SIGCSE Bulletin Volume 41 Issue 1, March 2009

[10] K. Bowles, A CS1 course based on Stand-Alone Microcomputers, SIGCSE Bulletin, Vol. 9, No. 1, February 1978, 125-127

[11] B. Kurtz, H. Pfeiffer, "Developing Programming Quizzes to Support Instruction in Abstract Data Types", SIGCSE Bulletin, Vol. 21, No. 1, February 1989, pp. 66-70

[12] C. Ellsworth, B. Kurtz, J. Fenwick, "The Quiver system", SIGCSE 2004 Technical Symposium on Computer Science Education, Norfolk VA, 2004, pp. 205-209

[13] Google Web Toolkit http://code.google.com/webtoolkit/

[14] B. Kurtz, R. Tashakkori, J. Helfert, M. Sage, Using Microlabs to Teach Modern Distributed Computing, Technical Symposium on Computer Science Education, Milwaukee, WI 2010

[15] Elisabeth Freeman, Eric Freeman, Bert Bates, Kathy Sierra, "Head First Design Patterns", O'Reilly Media; 1st edition, November 1, 2004

Teaching Operating Systems Using Android

Jeremy Andrus
Dept of Computer Science
Columbia University
New York, NY
jeremya@cs.columbia.edu

Jason Nieh
Dept of Computer Science
Columbia University
New York, NY
nieh@cs.columbia.edu

ABSTRACT

The computing landscape is shifting towards mobile devices. To learn about operating systems, it is increasingly important for students to gain hands-on kernel programming experience in these environments, which are quite different from traditional desktops and servers. We present our work at Columbia University to teach operating systems using Android, an open, commercially supported software platform increasingly used on mobile and embedded devices. We introduce a series of five Android kernel programming projects suitable for a one semester introductory operating systems course. Each project teaches a core operating system concept infused with Android or mobile device specific context, such as Android specific process relationships, use of sensors, and design considerations for resource constrained mobile devices. We also introduce an Android virtual laboratory based on virtual appliances, distributed version control, and live demonstrations which gives students hands-on Android experience, with minimal computing infrastructure. We have used these Android kernel programming projects and the Android virtual lab to teach an introductory operating systems course. Although this was our first time teaching the course using Android, over 80% of students surveyed enjoyed using Android and the majority of students preferred Android to traditional desktop development.

Categories and Subject Descriptors: D.4.0 [Operating Systems]: General; K.3.1 [Computers and Education]: Computer Uses in Education–distance learning; K.3.2 [Computers and Education]: Computer and Information Science Education–computer science education

General Terms: Design, Experimentation, Human Factors

Keywords: Operating Systems, Android, Mobile Devices

1. INTRODUCTION

Hands-on learning through programming projects plays a key role in computer science education, and hands-on kernel programming projects are especially important in the area of operating systems (OS). Many approaches to designing these kernel programming projects have been proposed and implemented. Several pedagogical OSes exist [4,13,14] where students fill in or build missing subsystems. In recent years, many institutions have also begun using Linux to teach OS [1, 6, 11]. All these solutions focus primarily on desktop or server environments, whether physical or virtual.

The computing landscape, however, is shifting. The dominant computing platform is becoming the mobile device [5, 15]. The real-world constraints and operating environment of mobile devices are quite different from traditional desktop or server computers. It is important for students to learn in this new environment, and its prevalence and popularity can be used to create engaging programming projects.

We present our work using Android to teach OS through hands-on kernel programming projects. We chose Android for several reasons. First, as a production system it enables students to learn about real-world OS issues which are hard to glean from simplified pedagogical projects. Second, since Android is based on the open-source Linux kernel, students can leverage a wealth of Linux tools and documentation. Third, Android's use of the Linux kernel provides a familiar transition path from courses already using Linux to teach OS. Fourth, Android is the fastest growing mobile platform to date, and its popularity makes it of tremendous interest to students. Fifth, Android is open-source which allows exploration of a complete production system including the OS kernel, user space libraries, and a graphical user environment written in Java. Sixth, as a commercial platform, Android continues to be developed and improved which naturally evolves the platform as a pedagogical tool, enabling students to learn in a modern context. Finally, as a commercial platform, there is no need for us to maintain or update Android or any of its development tools. This allows us to focus limited resources on teaching rather than time consuming in-house OS development.

To facilitate our use of Android to teach OS, we created an Android virtual lab where students learn about operating systems using both emulated and physical mobile devices. We manage the complexity of device cross-compilation and production kernel development tools by providing a virtual appliance pre-configured with all the software tools necessary to develop an Android Linux kernel. A virtual appliance can be readily deployed, downloaded and used by students without the installation or configuration necessary to deploy Android development tools natively on their personal computers. Additionally, our Android virtual lab uses a distributed version control system and live demonstration infrastructure to develop, distribute, submit and grade homework projects. Our use of the Android emulator in con-

Permission to make digital or hard copies of all or part of this work for personal or classroom use is granted without fee provided that copies are not made or distributed for profit or commercial advantage and that copies bear this notice and the full citation on the first page. To copy otherwise, to republish, to post on servers or to redistribute to lists, requires prior specific permission and/or a fee.
SIGCSE'12, February 29–March 3, 2012, Raleigh, North Carolina, USA.
Copyright 2012 ACM 978-1-4503-1098-7/12/02 ...$10.00.

junction with this infrastructure allows remote and distance learning students to take full advantage of our Android virtual lab, while also facilitating close collaboration with on-campus students using physical mobile devices.

Students work in groups to complete five Android Linux kernel programming projects. These projects require students to read and understand core Android Linux components, and then either modify or add components as required. The projects build in complexity, and cover various important OS topics: (1) system calls and process based on the unique process hierarchy of an Android device, (2) synchronization where a global resource such as the orientation sensor is shared amongst many processes, (3) scheduling by exploiting Android's single-application usage model to increase device responsiveness, (4) virtual memory and the exact size and nature of Android's inter-process shared memory, and (5) file systems with automatic geo-tagging.

We successfully used Android in a 100 student introductory OS course at Columbia University. Over 80% of students surveyed enjoyed applying OS concepts to the Android platform, and the majority of students preferred Android over traditional desktop development.

2. ANDROID VIRTUAL LAB

Central to any OS development lab is universal access to proper development tools for all students. Our Android virtual lab provides each student with a pre-configured VMware virtual appliance containing all the Android and Linux development tools necessary to complete each programming project. The set of tools includes all tools necessary to boot and test a real device as well as the Android SDK comprising the Android emulator, a tool to create virtual devices, and a device debug GUI tool. We also include a cross-compilation toolchain, Android's Bionic C library, and several shell scripts to mitigate the complexity of embedded development.

Although Android development tools are available for a wide variety of platforms, we provide a pre-configured virtual appliance for four important reasons. First, we avoid mistakes or incompatibilities in development tool installation. For example, when the course was offered, the Android development tools did not support Mac OS 10.6, Mac OS versions prior to 10.4, or Linux distributions other than Ubuntu. Students may also use non-standard PC configurations which would put unnecessary management burden on the instructional staff. Second, the virtual appliance can be used as a safety net for students who corrupt their development tool installation or experience complete system failure. The VMware Workstation snapshot feature can be used to make incremental backups of student work and any changes they make to the development environment. A snapshot is also an easy way for students to begin a homework assignment from a known good configuration. Third, by pre-configuring all of the development tools, we avoid complicated cross-compilation setup by providing simple, standard Makefiles and shell scripts for both kernel and user-level development. The Android SDK is designed primarily for GUI application development not kernel development, so some configuration of the compiler and Android runtime libraries is necessary. A standardized environment allows us to provide simple Makefile examples for user-level test programs and simple Linux kernel cross-compilation instructions. Finally, the virtual appliance gives us freedom to customize both the tools and the Android user space. Customizing the Android user space allows us to create more engaging projects as well as to overcome deficiencies in development tools. We use a customized version of the Android emulator which enables students to use the *Sensor Simulator* program from OpenIntents [12] to inject orientation and acceleration data into the emulator by interacting with a 3D model of a phone instead of manually entering numbers into a shell prompt. We also use a custom device drawing library to support the kernel scheduling project described in Section 3.3.

To manage homework project preparation, distribution, submission and grading, we use the Git distributed version control system, already used by Android and Linux for source code version control. Each homework assignment consists of a single Git repository that typically contains a complete Linux kernel tree, template user-space projects as necessary, any additional tools needed to complete the assignment, and a Makefile used to prepare the student's emulator or device for project development. Instructional staff prepare each project repository and push it to a central Git server. The repository is then replicated such that all student groups are given access to their own private repository on the Git server. The central Git server also facilitates distributed group collaboration even when one or more students are remote or distance learning students.

To maximize grading efficiency, we extend the previously developed concept of live demonstrations [7]. Three or four student groups are assigned an hour long demo time slot. During the first 20-30 minutes, all student groups perform a complete clone of their homework submission Git repository, cross-compile the Linux kernel for their mobile device, and install and boot the new kernel. In the last 30-40 minutes, the staff meets individually with each group. During this time, groups demonstrate functionality required by the homework, further explain their solution methodology, and participate in a basic code review. This time helps instructional staff to better understand the group's submission, correct common mistakes, and see how group members contributed to an assignment. Live demos also provide opportunities for instructional staff to explain solutions which can facilitate a more complete understanding of difficult and challenging assignments.

Our Android virtual lab is designed to support remote or distance learning students, though such students may only have access to the emulator and not a real Android device. These students can still participate in demonstrations using freely available screen-sharing applications such as *Skype*, *join.me* or *VNC*.

3. KERNEL PROJECTS

Using our Android virtual lab, students work in groups to complete five kernel programming projects. These projects require students to read, understand, and modify core Linux components. While some projects require writing a simple user space test program, students are never required to compile the entire Android code base or write any GUI applications. The five projects focus on five important OS concepts, and infuse Android or mobile device specific investigation into the assignment. The five areas covered by the assignments are: system calls and processes, synchronization, scheduling, virtual memory, and file systems. Corresponding Android-related topics incorporated in these areas are: the *zygote* process and Java worker threads, device sensors, display-prioritized scheduling, multi-process working set via copy-on-write shared memory, and location aware file systems.

The assignments progress in complexity, building not only on OS principles learned in earlier assignments, but also on Android specific knowledge gained. For example, the first assignment requires students to investigate the Android process tree and note how all GUI programs are children of a process named zygote. In a subsequent homework, they investigate the cross-process memory sharing method used by the zygote to save system RAM. We formalize each project's Android and mobile device investigation by asking students to answer a small number of questions designed to make them reflect on how the particular OS concept was applied in the context of an Android or mobile device.

All assignments are intended to keep students focused on the OS principles being taught, and designed such that a group of two or three students can complete them with no prior kernel or Android experience. We provide detailed step-by-step instructions on cross-compiling and device or emulator use. Android specific aspects of the assignments are presented as practical application of the core principle, and most of the Linux kernel modifications necessary to complete the assignments are contained in architecture independent code. Thus, the solution complexity remains manageable and homework setup and prerequisite topic knowledge is kept to a minimum, yet students engage with a complex, real-world system.

3.1 System Calls and Processes

The first project lays the groundwork for future projects as students investigate the primary application abstraction, the process, and its primary interface into the kernel, the system call. Our focus in this assignment is process creation, termination, properties, and relationships in the context of a mobile device. In completing this assignment, students also gain an understanding of kernel data structures, such as linked lists, and their APIs. All subsequent assignments require students to be intimately familiar with these concepts.

Students write a new system call which returns the system process tree in DFS order. This involves modifying architecture specific system call entry points, manipulating and traversing the kernel data structures representing processes and threads, and managing data transfer to and from the kernel. To test the system call, they write a simple user space application to invoke this new system call and print out the process tree similar to the UNIX *ps* utility.

The system call allows students to examine Android's process tree and application startup method, which provide insight into a key system design that drives the entire Java-based user environment. Java applications are interpreted in the *Dalvik* virtual machine, and are represented in the OS as processes which are children of a special process called the zygote. The Dalvik virtual machine starts several worker threads for each application to handle things like input events and garbage collection. Thus, the process tree of Android devices shows not only the relationship between the *init* process and its children, but also the relationship that all Java applications have to the zygote and the symmetry of their component threads.

Students investigate the zygote process using their test program, and are asked to reason why an embedded or mobile system might use such a process. This reflection is designed to connect the pedagogical concept of process creation using copy-on-write memory to a real-world mobile device with memory and disk constraints. Benefits of the zygote include faster application startup time, and cross-process memory sharing of core library code and static data.

The Android emulator enables remote or distance learning students taking the class to complete this assignment without a physical device. The Android emulator provides a complete machine emulation in which a standard version of the Android runtime is installed and run. Thus, remote or distance learning students can investigate the Android process tree using the emulator in the same way on-campus students use real devices.

3.2 Synchronization

The second project focuses on synchronization, a critical aspect of a modern multi-tasking OS. The wealth of sensors available on modern mobile devices provides an excellent pedagogical vehicle to demonstrate real-world applications of synchronizing concurrent or interleaved access to a single resource. In completing this assignment, students also gain an appreciation for manipulating and interacting with embedded system sensors.

Students implement a novel synchronization primitive, the *orientation event*, which allows multiple processes to block until the mobile device has been put into a particular orientation. For example, a process can block until the phone is placed face down on a table. To accomplish this, they first write a user space daemon which reads device orientation through a standard Android hardware abstraction library, and then passes the data into the kernel through a new system call. The orientation event interface is implemented as a set of three new system calls: `orientevt_open`, `orientevt_close`, and `orientevt_wait`. The daemon process passing device orientation into the kernel functions as the signal which wakes up any blocked process. Students test this new interface by writing several small test programs. Each test program forks multiple children, and each child process blocks on an orientation event opened by its parent. When the device is moved within the range of the desired orientation, all child processes should be unblocked.

Orientation and acceleration sensors are an integral part of the mobile device experience, and incorporating them into a synchronization project gives students an experience that desktop or server machines cannot provide. The ability for multiple processes to wait for a device to enter a particular orientation or acceleration profile has many possibilities in real-world user applications and system services such as interactive game controls and pre-fall system shutdown.

As students investigate sensor-based synchronization on Android, they are also exposed to real device interaction using a hardware abstraction layer. This interaction necessarily includes basic understanding and manipulation of sensor data. We provide several helper functions to keep the students focused on the primary topic of synchronization, however the exposure to real-world device data is a valuable experience which can be directly applied in the workforce.

The Android emulator provides the ability for remote or distance learning students to complete this assignment without a physical device. We provide a modified version of the Android emulator, a daemon process to run on the emulator, and a Java-based host application which simulates [12] a mobile device using a 3D wire-frame model. As students manipulate the model in the Java application, orientation information is sent to the daemon process which updates emulator state. The Android hardware abstraction layer reads this emulator state. In this way, remote students can have a similar experience to on-campus students

3.3 Scheduling

The third project focuses on scheduling. Mobile devices generally operate as a single user environment, and thus have significantly different scheduling requirements from desktop or server machines. For example, Android users typically view a single application at a time, not multiple applications in multiple windows.

In what is one of the most challenging projects, students write a new scheduling policy for the Linux kernel. This is the first assignment which requires students to manipulate a substantial portion of core Linux kernel code. To mitigate the daunting task of implementing a new scheduler, we leverage the modular scheduling framework in Linux which provides several examples of self-contained schedulers. We encourage students to use these existing schedulers as templates. The new scheduling policy trades fairness and throughput for responsiveness, a key metric in mobile devices. We call our new scheduler, "Display Boosted Multi-level Container" (*DBMC*) scheduling, and the primary objective of this scheduler is to "boost" the priority of foreground applications. Since mobile devices typically display a single application at at time, boosting the priority of this single, foreground, application decreases its execution time and increases the apparent device responsiveness.

To support DBMC scheduling, we made a small (15 line) change to the Android user space environment that leverages the Android application usage and security model. In contrast with desktop Linux systems, Android only allows a single application to use the display at a time. While multiple applications can run simultaneously, only one draws on the screen. When an application is installed onto an Android device, a unique user ID is generated and assigned to the application. The application is always run using these unique credentials. We wrote a simple, 15-line patch to a core Android drawing library, `libsurfaceflinger.so`, which informs the kernel of the process ID of the application currently drawing on the screen. Students use the unique user ID associated with the process to easily assign the associated threads and processes to a single scheduling entity, the container. The container is used for scheduling so that the priority boost is applied to all of the threads and processes of the foreground application.

Students are asked to run Android using their new scheduler and consider what qualitative impact there is on system performance compared to the existing Linux scheduler. A correct solution implemented on the Google ADP1 booted the GUI 5–10 seconds faster than the standard Linux kernel, but initialized the network and cellular connections significantly slower. Students are also asked to reflect on this scheduler's impact on graphics-intensive games where process starvation can occur and overall game play can suffer.

The Android emulator provides a similarly satisfying experience for remote and distance learning students. The same modified drawing library is used in the emulator. A correct solution implemented on the emulator booted the GUI faster, and made the entire UI qualitatively more usable and responsive.

3.4 Virtual Memory

The fourth project explores memory management, a critical aspect of mobile device OSes, with a focus on virtual memory and paging Using a mobile device to investigate virtual memory and paging highlights real-world system constraints and provides a unique platform to investigate creative solutions in memory sharing and allocation.

Students write a new monitoring mechanism to track the working set of specified processes, and a new system call to extract the recorded data. The working set is defined as the set of pages accessed (read or write) by a process during some time period. To test this mechanism, students add a set of processes to the monitoring mechanism, and then write a user space program that invokes the new system call and displays usage information for each process.

Here we follow up the investigation of the zygote process seen in the first project as discussed in Section 3.1. This process loads several libraries and Java classes, pre-initializes Dalvik virtual machine state, and listens on a socket for connections from a client. To start a Java application, Android connects to the zygote socket and requests that the process fork. The child begins executing Java code at a particular method of a specified class, and the parent resumes listening on the socket. When the child forks, all memory mapped by the parent is shared copy-on-write with the child. This includes all loaded libraries and initialized Dalvik virtual machine state. This is drastically different from a traditional desktop or server where processes are spawned from a shell or init process that has little or nothing in common with the application being started.

Students use their working set monitor to investigate the cross-process shared memory of the zygote and its children. We define the set of pages originally mapped by the zygote as the, "Android working set." Students use their user space utility to calculate the intersection of the Android working set with the working set of each zygote child process. For simplicity, we assume that no process un-maps or re-maps a region of memory originally mapped by the zygote; this allows us to use the virtual addresses returned by our new system call without needing a more complicated virtual to physical address mapping. By investigating the unique implementation of a zygote process, students gain an appreciation for the memory constraints of a real device and can measure the effectiveness of Android's zygote solution for reducing memory usage.

The Android emulator provides the ability for remote or distance learning students to complete this assignment without a physical device. The assignment does not require the use of any physical device features.

3.5 File Systems

The final project focuses on file systems. Similar to virtual memory, file systems tend to be large and complex pieces of code, so we have students implement extensions to an existing file system code base. This assignment requires students to gain practical understanding of how the virtual file system (VFS) infrastructure is designed, which is the key file system abstraction layer that every file system designer needs to understand. In addition to the file abstraction, students are exposed to issues that arise in real-world systems, such as the endian-ness of permanent data storage, data consistency and reliability, and embedded data retrieval.

Students modify an existing disk-based file system to automatically include GPS information so that this information can be used by any application. We refer to this as the geo-tagged file system. All files and directories in a geo-tagged file system include embedded location information in the form of latitude and longitude values. Students write a new system call and user-level daemon to inform the kernel of the current device location, which is retrieved from the GPS sensor via the Android hardware abstraction library similar to the one used in the second project discussed in Section 3.2. Students then modify the `ext2` file system to retrieve the last known location data and update a file or directory every time it is created or modified. Students test the geo-tagged file system by writing a second system call to retrieve the embedded location data for a given pathname. This assignment brings together several topics from earlier homework assignments including system calls, synchronization, and sensor data management. As a more advanced challenge, students can implement VFS layer interfaces which would allow any disk-based file system to implement the geo-tagging.

While it is possible to use a GPS sensor with a desktop or laptop system, the integration of location services in a mobile device is much more engaging, and exposes the student to real-world issues of sensor data reliability and permanent storage. In addition to the actual device location returned by the hardware abstraction layer, we also ask students to store the relative "age" of the location data (the number of seconds since the location was last updated in the kernel). This provides a basic confidence metric that can be used when later retrieving a file's location.

Students discover the practicality of their solution as they create a file system image which contains at least three files with unique location data. Students can have fun visiting different places while keeping track of exactly where they were with a simple shell command on their phone such as: `echo "HERE" > `date +"%s"`.txt`.

The Android emulator provides an emulated GPS sensor, allowing remote and distance learning students to fully participate in the assignment. The emulated location is accessed using the same hardware abstraction layer library used on the real device, and can be updated using the emulator's debug interface. The Android development tools also provide a graphical utility which can update the emulator's location by reading `.kml` files generated in Google Earth. Thus remote and distance learning students can take a virtual trip using Google Earth and save files in their geo-tagged file system from each location they visit.

4. EXPERIENCES

We used Android as the homework project platform in an introductory course on operating systems at Columbia University in Fall 2010. This was the first time we taught the entire course using Android devices and Android-kernel projects. Despite our mistakes and mis-steps, the overall response from students was overwhelmingly positive. Approximately one hundred students enrolled in the course, and we asked all of them to complete evaluation surveys at the end of the course. Sixty percent of the students completed the survey. Figure 1 shows the results. Of those students who completed the survey, 80% said they enjoyed using Android in the course. Most students who completed the survey said Android was both helpful in learning OS concepts

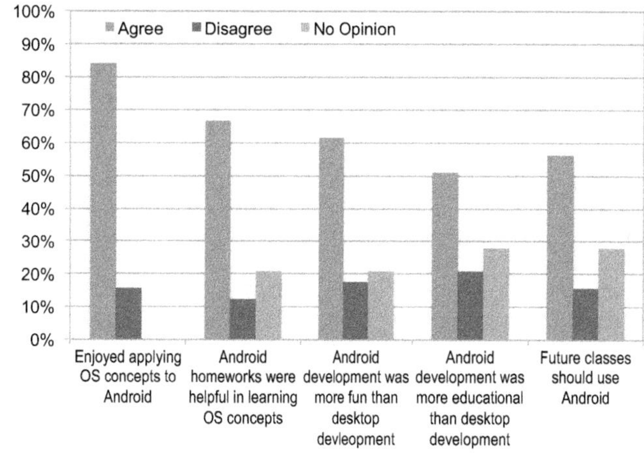

Figure 1: OS Course Survey Results

and more fun than traditional desktop development; students preferred Android to traditional desktop development by a ratio of 3 to 1. In addition, not more than 21% of the students actively disagreed with any given survey question.

Students were also asked to comment on what they enjoyed the most and what they enjoyed the least about the course. Students found the Android kernel projects fun, exciting, engaging and educational. They also appreciated the practical skills gained from their experience. When asked the question, "What did you like best about using Android for this course?" students responded with:

- *"The practicality of it,"*
- *"More fun and exciting,"*
- *"It's more like real work, not just homework,"*
- *"Increased curiosity about mobile platforms,"*
- *"Using a modern system,"*
- *"All sensor related assignments were fun."*

Negative feedback was concentrated around the speed of the emulator and debugging of the embedded systems (emulator and mobile device). Students felt that the emulator was too slow, and that debugging an embedded kernel was overly complicated. Unfortunately, the speed of the emulator is directly correlated to the speed of the laptop on which it is run, and because the mobile device uses an ARM processor the instruction set must be emulated which is a slow process. In the future, as SMP support for ARM is integrated into QEMU, and as laptop processor speeds increase, it should be possible to speed up the emulator. Debugging an embedded system is an inherently complicated task, and simplifying the process is not easy. One approach to this problem is to create more explicit and detailed instructions on the use of Android and kernel level debugging techniques. such as the use of `/proc/last_kmsg` which stores the kernel log message buffer of the last booted kernel and can be used to diagnose the previous kernel crash. It also may be possible to provide hardware-modified devices that expose either a JTAG connection for low-level debugging, or a serial port for simplified kernel debugging. The Google ADP1, for example, exposes serial RX/TX pins on its *ExtUSB* connector.

Finally, although students had some difficulty with device debugging, the overall experience using Android as the homework project platform in our introductory OS course was positive. Students not only learned the OS principles being taught, but also gained valuable real-world skills such as practical device debugging and embedded code development. We have already heard from students who were able to directly apply the skills they learned in this course to a professional job or internship opportunity.

5. RELATED WORK

In recent years, courses using the Linux kernel for OS programming projects have become increasingly popular [1, 6, 8, 11]. However, these approaches focus primarily on Linux desktop and server environments and provide no hands-on experience with mobile platforms. Lawson *et al* [9] describe a single programming project where students modify a Linux kernel designed to run on an iPod. However, this single project does not incorporate any mobile device specific pedagogy and does not provide a rigorous, project-based curriculum for understanding OS principles in the context of mobile platforms. The BabyOS [10] and embedded XINU [3] projects focus on embedded systems, but lack the real-world applicability of a production Linux kernel. Furthermore, because Android is based on the Linux kernel, our approach provides a straightforward transition path for courses that already use the Linux kernel to incorporate the mobile and embedded concepts embodied in our Android projects. Our approach provides a mapping of structured Linux kernel programming projects onto the Android platform where students gain insight into real-world systems and learn practical skills immediately applicable in today's job market.

Various pedagogical OSes have also been developed [4, 13, 14], but none of them offer students practical experience or insight into modern mobile platforms. Atkin *et al* [2] developed a pedagogical OS focused on portability and mobility. However, all programming projects are done at user level in a simulator, and do not offer the engaging, real-world experience of using a popular, mobile computing platform such as Android on real mobile devices.

Several institutions offer courses in mobile application development [16] . These courses focus on mobile application APIs, and do not teach OS concepts. They offer no insight into the lower-level software infrastructure of mobile platforms on which applications run. In contrast, our method of using Android to teach OS provides students with a real understanding of how things work under the covers as embodied by the unique OS environment created by the Linux kernel running on a mobile device.

6. CONCLUSIONS

We have developed a series of hands-on Android Linux kernel programming projects designed to immerse students in a mobile computing environment while simultaneously teaching core OS principles. The projects progressively introduce OS principles and mobile computing, and implicitly teach students about real-world embedded device development. We use key aspects of modern mobile devices, such as orientation sensors, to enrich the hands-on experience and increase student engagement.

We created an Android virtual lab where both on campus and remote students complete Android Linux kernel programming projects using an emulator or mobile device. We also leverage a distributed version control system and live demonstration infrastructure for homework design, distribution, submission, and grading. Our experience with 100 students using Android to teach OS demonstrates that students enjoy using mobile devices while learning OS principles, and appreciate the practical skills they gain.

7. ACKNOWLEDGEMENTS

This work was supported in part by NSF grants CNS-1018355, CNS-0914845, and CNS-0905246, and a Google Research Award.

8. REFERENCES

[1] C. L. Anderson and M. Nguyen. A Survey of Contemporary Instructional Operating Systems for use in Undergraduate Courses. *Journal of Computing Sciences in Colleges*, 21:183–190, October 2005.

[2] B. Atkin and E. G. Sirer. PortOS: An Educational Operating System for the Post-PC Environment. In *Proceedings of the 33rd ACM Technical Symposium on Computer Science Education*, SIGCSE '02, pages 116–120, New York, NY, USA, 2002. ACM.

[3] D. Brylow. An Experimental Laboratory Environment for Teaching Embedded Operating Systems. In *Proceedings of the 39th ACM Technical Symposium on Computer Science Education*, SIGCSE '08, pages 192–196, New York, NY, USA, 2008. ACM.

[4] R. Cox, C. Frey, X. Yu, N. Zeldovich, and A. Clements. Xv6 – A Simple Unix-like Teaching Operating System. http://pdos.csail.mit.edu/6.828/xv6/.

[5] Deloitte Development, LLC. Deloitte Predictions for the Technology, Media and Telecommunications Sector, 2011. http://www.deloitte.com/us/telecompredictions2011.

[6] R. Hess and P. Paulson. Linux Kernel Projects for an Undergraduate Operating Systems Course. In *Proceedings of the 41st ACM Technical Symposium on Computer Science Education*, SIGCSE'10, pages 485–489, New York, NY, USA, 2010. ACM.

[7] O. Laadan, J. Nieh, and N. Viennot. Teaching Operating Systems Using Virtual Appliances and Distributed Version Control. In *Proceedings of the 41st ACM Technical Symposium on Computer Science Education*, SIGCSE'10, pages 480–484, March 2010.

[8] O. Laadan, J. Nieh, and N. Viennot. Structured Linux Kernel Projects for Teaching Operating Systems Concepts. In *Proceedings of the 42nd ACM Technical Symposium on Computer Science Education*, SIGCSE'11, pages 287–292, March 2011.

[9] B. Lawson and L. Barnett. Using iPodLinux in an Introductory OS Course. In *Proceedings of the 39th ACM Technical Symposium on Computer Science Education*, SIGCSE '08, pages 182–186, New York, NY, USA, 2008. ACM.

[10] H. Liu, X. Chen, and Y. Gong. BabyOS: A Fresh Start. In *Proceedings of the 38th ACM Technical Symposium on Computer Science Education*, SIGCSE '07, pages 566–570, New York, NY, USA, 2007. ACM.

[11] J. Nieh and C. Vaill. Experiences Teaching Operating Systems Using Virtual Platforms and Linux. In *Proceedings of the 36th ACM Technical Symposium on Computer Science Education*, SIGCSE '05, pages 520–524, New York, NY, USA, 2005. ACM.

[12] OpenIntents. SensorSimulator – openintents – Sensor Simulator for simulating sensor data in real time. – Make Android applications work together. – Google Project Hosting. http://code.google.com/p/openintents/wiki/SensorSimulator.

[13] B. Pfaff, A. Romano, and G. Back. The Pintos Instructional Operating System Kernel. In *Proceedings of the 40th ACM Technical Symposium on Computer Science Education*, SIGCSE '09, pages 453–457, New York, NY, USA, 2009. ACM.

[14] A. S. Tanenbaum. A UNIX Clone with Source Code for Operating Systems Courses. *SIGOPS Operating Systems Review*, 21:20–29, January 1987.

[15] Wikipedia. Mobile Device – Wikipedia, the free encyclopedia. http://en.wikipedia.org/wiki/Handheld_device.

[16] E. Woyke. iPhone and Android Apps 101. http://www.forbes.com/2008/11/11/mobile-apps-colleges-tech-wire-cx_ew_1111mobileapps.html.

Open Educational Resources in Computer Science Teaching

Christo Dichev
Computer Science Department
Winston Salem State University
Winston Salem, NC
dichevc@wssu.edu

Darina Dicheva
Computer Science Department
Winston Salem State University
Winston Salem, NC
dichevad@wssu.edu

ABSTRACT

Open content and open access to resources are important factors in the innovation of Computer Science education. This paper presents a study aimed at gaining an understanding of the needs of Computer Science educators in terms of Open Educational Resources (OER): what kind of resources they need, when they need them, how they use them, and what are the barriers and the enablers for using OER The results of the study are compared and analyzed in the context of the popular OER sites. The work contributes to the research on OER utilization and discovery.

Categories and Subject Descriptors

K.3.2 [**Computers and Education**]: Computer and Information Science Education; H.3.5 [**Information Storage and Retrieval**] On-line Information Services

General Terms

Design, Human Factors

Keywords

Open Education, Open Content, Open Educational Resources

1. INTRODUCTION

The vision of open content educational material on the Web, has attracted substantial attention [1]. Open educational resources (OER) include instructional materials, tools, and media used for teaching and learning that are free from copyright restrictions or are publicly licensed for anyone to use, adapt, and redistribute. One of the challenges facing Open Education is that while the open content grows in popularity and we witness the proliferation of repositories and portals for OER content, it becomes more difficult for potential users to find the content they need.

In this open but competitive environment one obvious question is how OER portals can attract educators and make them use the available content. A derived question is what type of resources the repositories should host and how they should structure and support exploration of their sites. Many aspects, from structuring OER metadata to tuning OER search engines, are factors in ensuring matches between OER and educators who might utilize and benefit from them. Among those, the most problematic is the "finding-getting-using" challenge faced by educators seeking open content. In this relation, one unconventional viewpoint that may become useful is to look at the content itself as a sort of commodity. This brings a market perspective, in a sense of viewing the offered content as a marketplace of competing products. As a result, the value of the repository itself, in particular its capability in helping users find the right content is the proper differentiator and value proposition to the educator [2].

This new viewpoint not only suggests a market perspective but also opens it to the corresponding solutions provided in this area. One idea that we found relevant and promising is the Christensen's "jobs-to-be-done marketing" theory [3,4]. This theory states that people buy products and services *to get jobs done*. It holds that products are successful when they connect with a circumstance – with a job that customers find themselves needing to get done. The job-to-be-done model in OER context implies going beyond the conventional practice and trying to see whether there are 'jobs' desired by educators that fit to the OER niche. For example, in OER context the model suggests finding the answers of questions, such as: What types of teaching materials are in high demand? Is finding code examples matching subject X, a need experienced by a large population of Computer Science teachers? Is finding content that matches a specific learning goal a frequent task for certain category of instructors?

The "job-to-be-done" approach is motivated and intended for the market economy. It may seem that this view is inconsistent with the open education movement, which aims at an environment freed from the constraints of copyright and monetary exchange. However, "selling more goods" is a viable driving objective in this environment despite the Creative Commons licensing scheme that enables authors to give away their material for use while having the option to retain certain rights. Selling is used here not in its traditional sense, but in the sense of utilization of the offered 'open' goods. Open educational sites do take some actions to attract more users: they count the number of visits, the number of downloads, etc. The open and monetary based educational sectors compete for users' attention. This implies that the "job-to-be-done" point of view is consistent with the open educational environment. It suggests (1) focusing on understanding the jobs that involve use of open educational repositories, and (2) improving repositories' functional, social, and affective dimensions so that they serve their users better.

Permission to make digital or hard copies of all or part of this work for personal or classroom use is granted without fee provided that copies are not made or distributed for profit or commercial advantage and that copies bear this notice and the full citation on the first page. To copy otherwise, or republish, to post on servers or to redistribute to lists, requires prior specific permission and/or a fee.
SIGCSE'12, February 29–March 3, 2012, Raleigh, North Carolina, USA.
Copyright 2012 ACM 978-1-4503-1098-7/12/02...$10.00.

Motivated by these observations, we conducted a study to (1) better understand for what needs/type of jobs Computer Science teachers seek OER, and (2) provide insights about OER design decisions that can address these need. Only by understanding the Computer Science teaching needs deeply and in their variety can the OER community begin to address these needs.

2. THE STUDY

The purpose of this study was to gather an empirical insight of the potential and the possible impact of OER on Computer Science teaching. In order to understand the instructors' needs and how the current and future OER meet (should meet) those needs, we conducted a survey. A key motivational factor backing up the survey was the Christensen's model. Accordingly, the job not the user was in the focus of the survey. We especially tried to avoid questions related to the specifics of user-OER interactions. Our understanding is that the specifics should be derived from understanding and explicating of the "jobs-to-be-done" needs. The central set of questions that emerged as guiding directions for the survey were as follows:

- What kind of OER are most needed?
- When are OER most needed?
- How are OER used?

2.1 The Survey

Data was collected through questionnaire[1], distributed to Computer Science instructors via email. The questionnaire was sent to about 3000 teachers via email including SIGCSE, UK OER, and OCW/OER research mailing lists, selected departments, and individual emails. Only 315 instructors (less than 15%) responded. A sizeable number of them - 103, didn't complete the survey stating that they have never used OER content. In order to diversify the survey results we gathered data from various university categories: research universities (31%) and predominantly teaching universities, including HBCU and Community Colleges (69%). The list of survey participants includes instructors from various geographic regions: North America (168), Europe (71), Africa (45) and South America (31).

The three central questions were translated into 10 survey questions, clarifying and detailing the points of the central set. The top five questions were multiple choice - multiple answer, while the remaining ones were open ended.

2.1.1 Multiple-Choice Section

Question 1. *Which of the following criteria for selecting material (resources) for your teaching do you consider essential: (a) Completeness of coverage of the topic; (b) Level of complexity (difficulty); (c) Level of detail; (d) The programming language it is based on; (e) The textbook it is related to; (f) Level of illustration by examples; (g) Recency (currency); (h) Popularity; (i) The quality of content; (j) The quality of layout; (k) The institution/author it originates from; (l) Any other criteria you consider important but not listed above?*

The aim of the first question was to obtain indicators about which criteria matter most when instructors select OER content. The outcome of this question indicates that the quality of content is the dominating criterion, while the level of illustration by examples, the level of complexity, and the level of detail play almost as important role as the completeness of coverage of the topic.

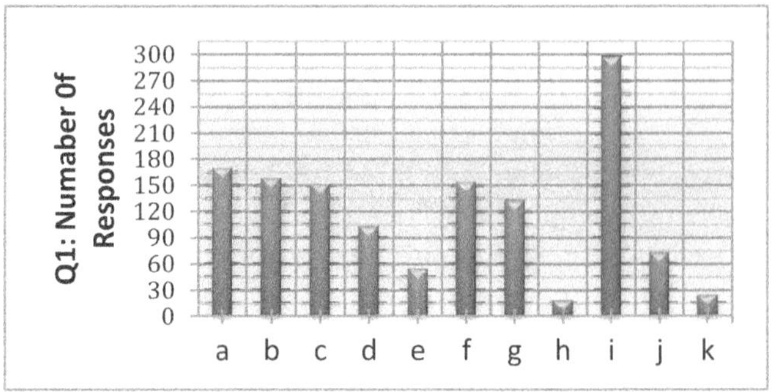

This result is in disagreement with the current trend of OER repositories to focus on structuring the hosted resources based on topicality, with less attention to the other facets of the resources. Besides the listed criteria, some survey participants proposed the granularity, the license, the programming language, and the sequence of topics as additional factors in resource selection.

Question 2. *The availability of which of the following resource types do you find most useful in your teaching practice? (a) Lecture notes; (b) PowerPoint slides; (c) Code examples; (d) Assignments/ projects; (e) Tests; (f) Problems; (g) Solutions; (h) Reading lists; (i) Textbooks; (j) Syllabi; (k) Videos; (l) Any other types you consider important but not listed above?*

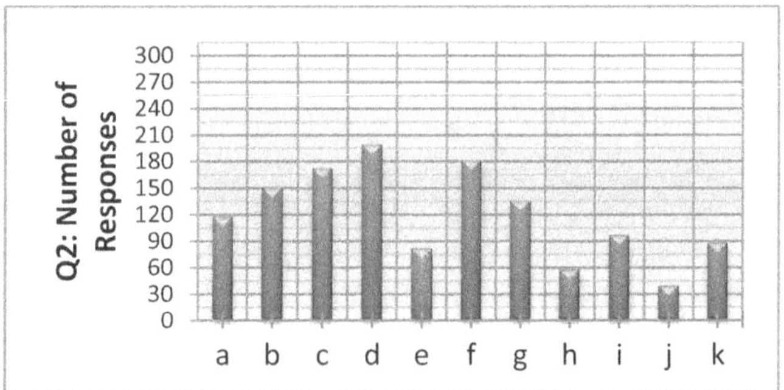

The purpose of this question was to get an insight about the type of teaching material that an instructor typically needs and thus to provide guidance for a better balance of the hosted OER content. The outcome of the question attests that for Computer Science teachers the need for assignments, code examples, and problems is higher than the need for PowerPoint slides. This fact is also in conflict with the major type of teaching content provided on OER sites. In addition to the listed resource types, the participants proposed: images, animations, cartoons, simulations, audio podcast, journal articles, and blogs as helpful in their practice.

If we name the most frequent and challenging task faced by the teachers in terms of OER utilization as "find my needed content", then the purpose of the first two questions was to explicate the criteria and the content types characterizing "my needed content", while the next questions targeted the condition of its use.

Question 3. *When do you (would you) consider using open educational content in your teaching practice: When (a) Designing a new course; (b) Updating course material; (c) There is no adequate textbook or supplemental material available; (d) Covering novel (emerging) topics; (e) Explaining/clarifying a concept; (f) Teaching new concepts skills; (g) Any other cases?*

[1] http://iiscs.wssu.edu/drupal/?q=node/1641

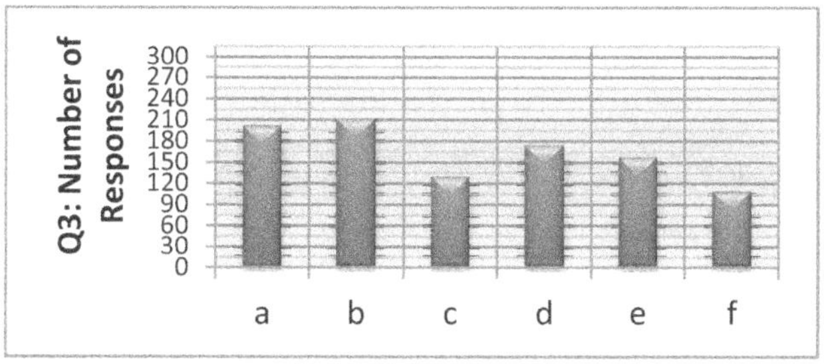

The results of this question point out that teachers turn to OER most frequently when they have to design or update their courses, when clarifying new concepts or when they need to cover novel topics. While the current OER trend is to organize and provide the teaching content in terms of courses, the result implies a need of structures facilitating an access to finer-grain components and accompanying units. For example, teachers should be able to find out whether a specific concept is covered in a particular lecture without going through each slide. In many cases OER repositories don't provide an appropriate framework for exploring various facets and details of the hosted information.

Question 4. *How do you (would you) use open educational content: (a) As it is published; (b) By adapting it to fit my context; (c) By incorporating pieces of open content into my own material; (d) By remixing pieces of open content?*

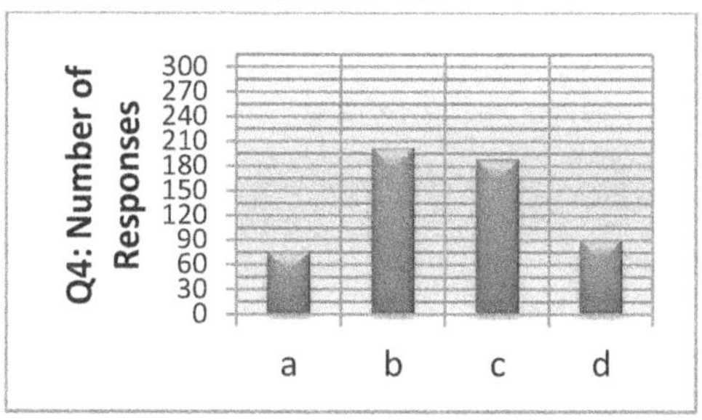

The answers to this question signal that users need not only access to the content at different levels of granularity but also in interoperable formats. They need pieces from various lecture notes, along with pieces from PowerPoint slides, assignments and tests. Adapting, incorporating and remixing content requires modularization and compatible formats and grain size.

Question 5. *Open educational content for which of the following kinds of computer science disciplines (topics) do you consider more needed?: (a) Established; (b) Fast changing; (c) Emerging?*

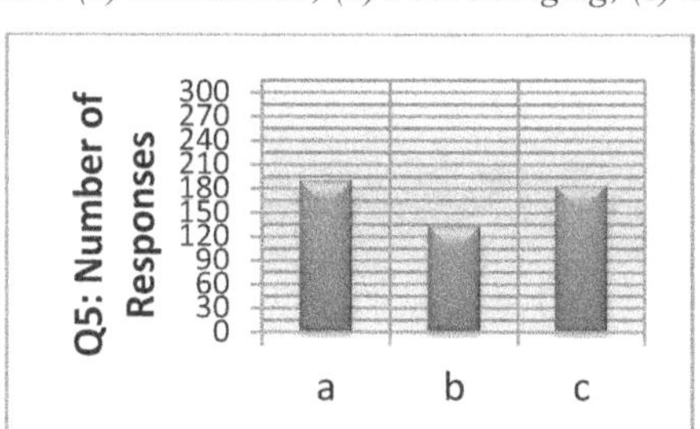

This question targets the category of disciplines ranging from established to emergent, where the need for OER is most evident. The expressed views on this question are mixed. The dominating opinion is that the established topics are most appropriate for OER, followed by the emerging and fast changing topics. According to the answers, educational content in emerging and fast changing disciplines are in proportional demand with established disciplines but in reality the former are almost not existent in the current OER repositories.

2.1.2 Open Ended Section

The purpose of the last section containing five open ended questions was to gather qualitative information about the level of awareness and use of OER, the perceived obstacles, potential facilitators and the type of tasks that the teachers would like to accomplish with the help of OER. One way to make OER a viable alternative for the job "find material for my teaching" is to reduce the barriers and foster the enablers for using them. The following two questions are set to capture some emerging patterns regarding the barriers and enablers to OER use.

Question 6. *What are the most significant barriers to the use of open educational content in teaching?*

The responses to this question can be summarized in a keyword style as follows: *finding, customizing, availability, awareness, access, quality, and license.* Several groups of semantically equivalent answers emerged from the 211 responses to the question. The aggregated meaning of the answers in each group was summarized in a single statement serving as a message carrier for the group responses. The following is a list of such summaries for the groups that contain more than five answers. (Some actual answers are given in italics as supportive illustrations.)

- Difficulty of finding OER content matching specific context (87 respondents).
  Finding suitable material of high quality (often this takes an amount of time comparable to producing one's own materials)
  Time to search
  Finding content appropriate for my audience
- Difficulty of customizing the content to local conditions and the instructor's approach (41 respondents).
  Teachers may have their own style (regarding structure, preferred sub-topics, level of detail, layout) and thus are afraid of re-using existing content
  Difference in the style and terminology used
- Availability and variety of OER content (23 respondents).
  Lack of availability for many subjects and lack of variety in what is available
  Lack of good open content
- Assurance of quality (16).
  Uncertainty about quality of OER
  Time that should be taken in checking it for accuracy
- Awareness of the existence of OER content (14).
  I didn't even know open educational content was available
  Awareness of OER is still limited
- Incompatible open content licenses (11).
  The fear that it might, in error, include some copyrighted sources
  Restrictive open licences (use of ND clause in Creative Commons licences)
- Attitude, recognition and publicity (9 respondents).
  Attitudes of instructors and administrators
  Culture of "charity" rather than sharing
  I think many colleagues are far too protective against their own material

- Worry that "free" means "bad quality" (7 respondents).
Most people seem to believe that if it's really open, it must be (a) unsupported or (b) incomplete or (c) out-of-date

  I believe the biggest barrier to be attitude ~ the notion that "free" or "open" (to many) has the stigma of being not as high in quality or as supported

- Availability of a centralized database containing OER that can be conveniently searched (5 respondents).
Find a good repository where you can use and adapt specific content.

The dominating obstacle reported by participants, which amounts to 41% of the responses was the effort needed to find appropriate content. The second major barrier (19% of the responses) was the work needed for adaptation and the third one (11% of the responses) was the availability of appropriate resources. Among the answers not included in the above groups but worth mentioning are: the language barrier for non-English speaking instructors, worry that materials won't persist, and poor metadata. Previous research on OER utilization has identified finding relevant resources as a significant obstacle [5]. The results of our survey confirmed yet again that it is the most significant barrier for effective use of OER.

Question 7. *If there are any enablers that you believe could increase the adoption of open educational content in teaching, please list them below with a brief explanation.*

The responses to this question can be summarized by the following terms: *finding, central repository, publicity, trust, broader coverage, collaborative tools, clear licenses and accessibility.* As before, several groups were identified within the 203 answers to the question. The groups containing more than five answers are summarized below.

- Improved tools for searching and finding relevant content (79 respondents).
Less time to find and change content relevant to my subject
Really good search capability
The only thing that would help would be to make it easier to locate, and have some type of vetting system
A rating system that would enable one to find the good stuff quickly
Filtering searches by topic, nature of exercise (e.g., lab, homework offline, programming assignment, etc.), environment (operating system, application software)

- Central repository for sharing and reviewing OER materials (76 respondents).
Central repository of links to OER material in different institutes
A central repository of content, with syllabi for various courses
More globally accepted sites to share educational content (there are many yes, but is there really a place that everybody knows?)
ACM/SIGCSE sponsored repository for Computer Science material

- Publicity and exposure of successful OER utilization (33 respondents).
Help documentation, examples of successful adoption with tips and hints
More exposure/advertisement to users

- Quality verification and establishment of public trust (18 respondents).
Reviews of open materials in a way that administrators would give credit
Include peer evaluation and establishment of public trust

- Broader course and topic coverage (13 respondents)..
Greater choice of courses and lectures
Continued growth of the practice so that more is available

- Tools for collaborative OER content creation (11 respondents).
A collaborative resource to produce and distribute educational content,
Increasing the use of interactive collaborative tools

- Explicit, unambiguous copyright rules (9 respondents).
Clearer use of licenses to establish what one is or is not allowed to do
Clear copyright/license/usage rules and standards (type Wikipedia/Media)

- Improved accessibility to OER materials (6 respondents).
Better accessibility of the content ...

The top two enablers that were identified are "improved tools for searching and finding" (39%) and "centralized OER repositories" (37%). These enablers are related as the availability of central repositories in general improves resource findability. The next major enabler (16%) is publicity of the OER resources and their usage, followed by tools for collaborative OER creation (9%). Among the enablers shared by several respondents but not listed in the above groups are the metadata and recognition of the value of reusing OER.

The next question was intended to identify the most desirable tasks that can be achieved assuming the existence of relevant resource discoverability tools.

Question 8. *Consider tasks such as:*
"Find a set of PowerPoint slides matching syllabus X"
"Find PowerPoint slides similar to the material in resource X"

Can you list some other tasks that are not addressed by the current resource discovery services but with possible positive impact on open content use?

As before, the 108 received answers were grouped by meaning:

- Find resource [of type X] on topic Y [of level/competency Z] (48 respondents).
Find PowerPoint slides that explain concept C
Find code examples for lecture X (junior level)
Find an assignment reinforcing concept X

- Browse by category X [refine by category Y] [refined by category Z] (26 respondents)
Search the content inside the code examples for examples in java illustrating a given concept
Search for a course of a specific level, or from a specific university or from a specific author, based on a specific language

- Find resource [of type X] to be incorporated in resource Y [of topic Z] [of type U] [of level/competency V] (14 respondents).
Find a set of pictures illustrating topic X discussed in resource Y ...
Find tests applicable to this course ...

- Find alternative content to the resource X (12 respondents).
  Find alternative materials for this part of the course
- Find resources [of type X] matching syllabus Y [satisfying course goal Z] (8 respondents).
  Find textbook type materials matching this syllabus

This open ended question was not expressed in terms of the functionality of the current search tools. Rather it was formulated in a way to provoke participants to respond with a "wish list" of features, which if made available would benefit teachers. The huge multiplicity of the ways users describe "their content" reflects varying needs and also explains the bulk of resource discovery techniques proposed by the participants. On the top of the wish list were tools for finding resources satisfying multiple constrains (44% of the respondents) and browsing by multiple categories/refinements (24% of the respondents).

Question 9. *Have you ever used open educational content in your teaching practice?*

More than one third of the respondents (123) reported that they have never used OER. This number becomes even more disproportional if we add the 103 individuals who declined to participate in the survey because they have never used OER.

Question 10. *How many institutions (sites) offering open educational content do you know of?*

The majority of respondents reported that they know one or two sites (typically including MIT OpenCourseWare). At the other end were the 34 participants that knew a dozen or more OER sites.

2.2 What is the Reality?

The low use of OER from Computer Science educators signals that the level of understanding of who the users are and what they need is insufficient. This fact motivated us to carry out two additional studies focused on existing OER sites in order to identify some reasons for this phenomenon.

The goal of the first study was to collect some evidence on the coverage of Computer Science topics by OER sites and how easy it is to find open content on selected topics. We picked a set of introductory and upper-level courses following the latest ACM Curriculum Recommendation (http://www.acm.org/education/curricula/ComputerScience2008.pdf), namely: Analysis of Algorithms, Artificial Intelligence, Computer Architecture, Computer Networks, Database Management, Introduction to Programming, Operating Systems, Programming Languages, and Software Engineering, assuming a lecture level as a granularity criterion for the results. From each of those introductory or core courses we selected topics and searched for resources that can be used as lecture plans or notes (see Table 1). In addition, we included elective type courses and more advanced subjects (see the last seven rows in Table 1) in order to weigh the availability of more specific against more conventional Computer Science OER material. We used Google's advanced search to narrow down the results to materials licensed under a Creative Commons Attribution. For comparison with the open web search we repeated the search experiment with twelve OER sites providing Computer Science materials, namely: MIT OpenCourseWare, Connexions, CITIDEL, The Open University OpenLearn, OpenCourseWare Consortium, OER Commons, Merlot (general repository with OER content), NSDL, Wikibooks, SOFIA, EDNA, and UCI OpenCourseWare. We used again Google's advanced search but this time to localize the search within the corresponding domain, which resulted in twelve search sessions triggered by queries such as "operating systems synchronization java site:merlot.org".

Table 1. Results of Google and OER search on selected topics

No	Search Keywords	Found Relevant	
		Google	**OER**
1	analysis algorithms spanning trees	0	0
2	artificial intelligence reasoning systems	0	0
3	computer architecture pipelining	1	3
4	computer networks congestion control	1	6
5	database management normalization	1	9
6	data structures binary trees	2	3
7	introduction programming java inheritance	1	3
8	operating systems synchronization java	1	1
9	programming languages data types	1	0
10	software engineering agile development	1	4
11	artificial intelligence definite clause grammars	0	0
12	e-commerce web services	0	0
13	hardware media security blue-ray prm	0	0
14	information system security access matrix model	0	0
15	information system security public key infrastructure	0	0
16	web programming php arrays	3	2
17	web programming xml xpath	0	0

The results showed that the coverage of the selected core and introductory Computer Science courses is quite low - around 2.5 (average) resources per topic. The coverage of elective Computer Science courses and advanced topics is even lower - 0.4 (average) resources per topic. This fact is in contrast with the outcome derived from the survey responses attesting that greater topic coverage is one of the enablers of effective OER use. The latter results also indicate a disturbing imbalance: almost no OER materials were found for emerging disciplines, where instructors need even stronger support since recent advances are typically not covered in textbooks. This study identified additional factors that do not meet the expectations of the survey responders. With a few exceptions, the twelve OER sites are institutional repositories that do not provide support for resubmitting derivative work. The majority of OER repositories do not collect user reviews/comments on the quality of the resources hosted on their sites and do not provide support for social/community recognition (e.g. rating) of resources.

The purpose of the second study was to analyze further the points of disagreement between the survey results and OER sites hosting Computer Science resources. Our first observation was that from the 13,000 courses published by 150 universities [6] only 21 sites provide Computer Science related materials: MIT Open CourseWare, Connexions, OERCommons, CITIDEL, UCI (OpenCourseWare), Stanford School Engineering Everywhere, Webcast.berkeley, VideoLectues.NET, EDNA, MERLOT, The Open University, OpenLearn, University of Michigan, SOFIA, Intel's Academic Community, University of Southern Queensland, Notre Dame OpenCourseWare, University of Massachusetts Boston, Utah Valley University, and Weber State

University. Each of the last four sites hosts a single course. The ability to tell at a glance if particular content is a good match for a specific teaching activity is a critical feature for efficient selection of adequate resources. As one respondent reported "*I can't afford to spend even 3 minutes evaluating each resource in a list. If it takes that long, it is often faster to just write my own.*"

In general, resource metadata does not meet the expectation outlined in the survey responses. Merlot supports perhaps the richest metadata set that includes *material type, date added, date modified, description, author, submitter, peer reviews, audience, language, copyright, source code, accessible information available, cost, creative commons*. Most problematic here is the license related metadata. In the majority of the examined cases the provided information was "copyright: *yes*", "creative commons: *unsure*". This fact along with the *cost* related metadata is in contradiction with the OER philosophy. With respect to metadata, OER Commons supports the following set: *abstract, author, subject, institution name, collection, grade level, course type, languages, material type* and *media format*. However, key criteria related to the quality of content (e.g. indication for peer evaluation) or recency, are missing. MIT Open Courseware supports a comparable although implicit metadata set. The metadata provided by the remaining sites is limited, typically a subset of the following list: *author, title, summary/subject, level* and *year of submission*. Some sites support tagging (OpenLearn) or comments (Merlot). The OER resources vary greatly in their depth and target audience. Most of the metadata in the repositories however is about the content itself, and not about its use, which would enable a more efficient selection decision.

In terms of resource type availability, only MIT Open Courseware provides adequate collection of resource types: lecture notes, videos, audio lectures, assignments, exams, solutions, projects, examples, study material, online textbooks, syllabus and interactive demonstrations. It provides also visual means to easily locate the relevant resource types. Unfortunately, those types are distributed unevenly among different resources. For example, we found only one lecture accompanied by an interactive demonstration, one course with a syllabus and another one with an online textbook. Also, program examples if available are not directly accessible. According to the survey assignments, program examples, problems and solutions are the most needed resource types. However, there are only few repositories offering (a limited amount) of those resource types. For example, in Merlot from the 70 resources under category "Programming" only 15 have code examples, and from the 15 resources under the category "User Interfaces" only 1 has code examples. As to the assignments, we were able to locate only four assignments in total. Surprisingly, in Connexions among the 19,034 reusable modules there were no PowerPoint slides, assignments, code examples, problems, solutions or tests for Computer Science topics. Some sites, such as Webcast.Berkeley or VideoLectues.net offer only video materials. Regarding resource recency only five sites offer fresh content. For example, CITIDEL hasn't gotten many updates in the last 5 years.

As indicated by the survey, poor support for finding relevant content was seen as a major barrier, while providing adequate tools for finding such content was reported as a major enabler. In this context, there is a significant gap between the desired and actual support. The best example in terms of resource discoverability is probably Connexions, which offers multiple browse and search options. The site allows browsing by subject, title, author, keyword, popularity, language, revision date, institution, all collections, and keyword search that can be narrowed to a specified subject, collection, title, and author. In a similar fashion, OER Commons supports searching by subject area, grade level, resource type, and by tags/keywords. On the other hand, CITIDEL allows users to search by communities and collections, titles, authors, subjects, date and alphabetically. However, the navigation is inflexible and clumsy.

In a nutshell, current OER repositories are falling short of meeting users' expectations in terms of adequate support for finding needed content. Somewhat unexpected was the fact that desired and not so uncommon search strategies such as "find more like this" are not provided by any of the examined sites.

3. CONCLUSION

Looking for appropriate resources is a frequent job in the teaching practice. OER represent a new "org chart" for dissemination and use of educational resources and the new solutions should not be constrained by old paradigms. The studies we conducted reveal a gap between the views of the potential OER consumers and the solutions offered by the OER providers. A disagreement was identified in several aspects with sometimes unexpected mismatch between the reality and the expectations. Just a great volume of open content is not sufficient. It should come in a variety of depth, details, levels and grain-size. It should support different teaching activities, different selection criteria, and be easy findable and adaptable. Although examples of successful OER utilization are not isolated phenomena, there is a low level of awareness about existing OER. Reducing the gap between the needs of the OER consumers and the solutions offered by the OER providers will bring benefits to Computer Science educators and help them to deal with ever fast changing and emerging subjects.

Our further research agenda includes evaluating the impact of the growing OER content on teaching practice and on learning outcomes, and situating OER within the broader picture of changing models of Computer Science education.

4. ACKNOWLEDGMENTS

This material is based upon work supported by the NSF Grant No. DUE-1044224 "NSDL: Social Bookmarking for Digital Libraries: Improving Resource Sharing and Discoverability".

5. REFERENCES

[1] Downes, S. 2007. Models for Sustainable Open Educational Resources. *Interdisciplinary Journal of Knowledge and Learning Objects, 3,* 29-44.

[2] Identifying the "Job" for OER Repositories, Retrieved August 17, 2011 http://saulnier.typepad.com/learning_technology/2011/04/identifying-the-job-for-oer-repositories.html.

[3] Christensen, C. M. 2010. Integrating Around the Job to Be Done. *Harvard Business School Module Note, 611-004.*

[4] Christensen, C., Donovan T. 2002. If You View the Customer's World in Terms of Products and Features Rather Than Jobs That Need to Be Done, You'll Miss the Target. *Optimize Magazine* 46 (June 2002).

[5] Dichev C., Bhattarai B., Clonch C., Dicheva D. 2011. Towards Better Discoverability and Use of Open Content. In *Proceedings of S3T'11*, Springer Verlag, AICS101, 195-203.

[6] Muramatsu B. 2011. Transforming OpenCourseWare into Open Courseware (http://conference.ocwconsortium.org/ index.php/ 2011/cambridge/paper/view/131 papers/).

Emergent Themes in a UI Design Hybrid-Studio Course

Yolanda Jacobs Reimer
Computer Science
University of Montana
Missoula, MT
reimer@cs.umt.edu

Katherine Cennamo
Learning Sciences and Technologies
Virginia Tech
Blacksburg, VA
cennamo@vt.edu

Sarah A. Douglas
Computer Science
University of Oregon
Eugene, OR
douglas@cs.uoregon.edu

ABSTRACT

The goal of our research and teaching collaboration has been to learn more about how key aspects of pedagogy commonly incorporated in architecture and industrial design classes might positively impact the teaching of user interface (UI) design within a standard computer science curriculum. Toward that end, we studied a number of studio design courses, developed a set of curriculum guidelines, and analyzed the effectiveness of these guidelines as implemented in a UI design course. We discovered three emergent themes: 1) students need early and constant reminders that design is an iterative process involving user feedback and testing; 2) instructor modeling is critical; and 3) technology needs to be carefully managed at critical junctures throughout the class.

Categories and Subject Descriptors

K.3.2 [**Computer and Information Science Education**]: *Computer science education, Curriculum.*

General Terms

Design, Measurement, Human Factors.

Keywords

Studio-based learning, user interface design, computer science education research, design critiques.

1. INTRODUCTION

The studio environment for teaching and learning has long been used in schools of architecture, art and industrial design. Although details vary, typical studio classes involve dedicated desk space for students, longer meeting periods with instructors and peers, and regular engagement in design critiques (crits). Educators are drawn to this method of teaching, in part, because of its collaborative, team-based nature, and because of its potential to foster creativity [1]. In a recent trend, computer science educators have been investigating how aspects of the studio method might be translated to their own field. Positive impacts on self-confidence and peer learning [7], as well as content mastery and programming achievement [6] are indicated.

Permission to make digital or hard copies of all or part of this work for personal or classroom use is granted without fee provided that copies are not made or distributed for profit or commercial advantage and that copies bear this notice and the full citation on the first page. To copy otherwise, or republish, to post on servers or to redistribute to lists, requires prior specific permission and/or a fee.
SIGCSE'12, February 29–March 3, 2012, Raleigh, North Carolina, USA.
Copyright 2012 ACM 978-1-4503-1098-7/12/02...$10.00.

As researchers also interested in questions of how critical aspects of the studio might be transferred to other disciplines, the goal of our three-year collaboration among three Universities has been to discover what defines the studio method and how key aspects of its pedagogy and environment might positively affect the teaching of user interface (UI) design within a standard computer science curriculum. Using case study research methodology [10], we collected and analyzed a wide range of qualitative data from courses in architecture, industrial design and HCI, resulting in a detailed case description of each studio classroom. During our fall 2009 annual meeting, faculty members from these disciplines and educational research developed a list of 43 initial guidelines through cross case analysis of our five studio cases, which we subsequently categorized in groups of surface structure, pedagogy, epistemology, and community of practice [13].

Following this meeting, the educational researchers involved in this work reviewed the list of guidelines to identify supporting data from the five cases. In some instances, particular guidelines were modified slightly to more closely reflect the evidence in the data. Concurrent with the development of this set of guidelines, the HCI instructors modified their courses to better reflect some principles that seemed lacking in their current class structure. We then collected and analyzed data from each course to determine which modifications were most effective, which modifications were in need of improvement, and the impact of these changes on participants.

Positioned within this larger research context, the work we present here describes the classroom experience and evaluation of one of these UI design courses taught during the spring of 2010. We refer to this course as a *hybrid*-studio course because we are not teaching a full-time studio course, but instead have added studio "units" in the form of design crits into an HCI course bounded in space and time by a standard computer science curriculum. Using our guidelines development work, we initiated a number of changes to the way we had been teaching the UI design course previously. Some of these changes included:

1. Streamlined lecture content and scheduling changes to allow more room for modeling, examples, and discussion.
2. More opportunities to discuss the studio concept with students to facilitate understanding.
3. Promotion of quicker, more changeable designs.

When assessing the effectiveness of these changes and the course in general, we noticed a number of emergent trends or themes we focus on throughout the remainder of this paper. In particular, we discovered that students need constant reminders that design is an iterative process rather than a static construct, instructor modeling is critical, and technology needs to be carefully managed at a number of critical junctures throughout the class. These trends and the evidence we use to justify them extends earlier work [1].

2. RELATED WORK AND BACKGROUND

The allure of the studio as a learning environment and the promises that it seems intrinsically to hold continue to attract researchers to the question of how studios can be integrated into various levels and fields of the computer science curriculum. Some have focused on human-computer interaction design courses and offer concrete examples of how curriculum, schedules, workspaces and assignments might best complement teaching with the studio method [5,12], while others have adapted the studio model for use in earlier CS1 and CS2 courses [6,7]. The studio model has also been integrated over the span of multiple semesters to address long-standing gaps in the typical software engineering education [11], and its peer review aspect has been shown to have a positive impact on student confidence and attitudes in a game design course [3]. Indeed, while many academics continue to pursue this method of teaching, some venturing so far as to offer an entire CS degree that is studio-based [2], the professional world also realizes the potential benefits of this approach in agile software development [14].

Despite a general intuition that studio-based instruction has many advantages over a traditional approach and empirical studies that attempt to illustrate some of these [6,7], challenges facing the studio method remain [15]. A strength of our contribution to this body of work is the varied perspectives and viewpoints of our research team and the extensive data set we have accumulated over multiple years and numerous course offerings.

3. RESEARCH METHOD

During the spring of 2010, the user interface design course reported on in this study had 10 undergraduate and 3 graduate students registered. Only one of the students (an undergraduate) was female. All students received a passing grade in the class with the exception of two undergraduates, one of whom dropped the class about half-way through. The class met two times a week, 80 minutes at a time, for 14+ weeks. There were four group-based project assignments plus a final presentation throughout the semester. All projects included a written report and an in-class design critique (crit). Students were expected to present the state of their current work during crits, open the discussion up to questions and review, and incorporate feedback into subsequent projects as applicable. The final course grade was determined based on these projects, two individual in-class quizzes, individual sketch-outs and class participation. During this offering of the course, all projects revolved around the same assigned design challenge as follows:

Project 1: Low-fidelity design of an interactive, information kiosk for the University bookstore.

Project 2: Iterative design (of project 1) and heuristic evaluation [8].

Project 3: High-fidelity prototype implementation of design.

Project 4: Usability testing with real users.

Final project/presentation: Visual narrative reflecting on semester-long design.

Lincoln and Guba [9] coined the term "trustworthiness" to talk about reliability and validity in qualitative research, and our attempts at trustworthiness focused on gathering a wide range of data that has allowed us to see alternative explanations and dimensions to the analysis. As such, we collected different types of data over an extended period of time (an entire semester) that included: Course documents (syllabus, project handouts), instructor reflections on the course, videotapes of relevant course sessions, student reflections made after each major course project, and student pre- and post-course survey results. These various kinds of data were used to "triangulate" or corroborate the themes and conjectures that arose through our analyses.

This data was analyzed in multiple ways. Since the online surveys contained both closed and open-ended questions, we were able to look at and report on student responses both quantitatively and qualitatively. In some cases, students first answered a closed-ended question that had limited responses, and then they elaborated on their selection with open-ended remarks. In these instances, we provide quantitative results first and then further examine comments to see why students answered the way they did. In other cases, we were also able to compare reactions from the beginning of the course to the end of the course by asking the same questions on both pre- and post-course questionnaires. Student reflections to given prompts turned in with each project assignment also provided a rich source of information. We looked at these written responses carefully and noted when trends became obvious. From there, sample comments were extracted as appropriate, and we quantified how often students mentioned critical aspects. Finally, we were able to review videotapes taken during select class sessions and transcribe oral exchanges to support the emergent trends we were seeing and sensing.

4. EMERGENT THEMES

4.1 Design is About Process, Interaction

One of the first emergent themes we recognized, and one that proved overarching to the others, was that many students seem to have a misconception of what design is when they first begin the course. When asked on a preliminary survey: "*How knowledgeable do you consider yourself to be about design?*", 83.3% said "somewhat" (see Table 1). Despite the high percentage of students who claimed design knowledge, when asked to elaborate on their experiences, many described concepts associated with implementation, software applications, website design and graphics design. There was very little mention of iteration, or the importance of user feedback and testing, which seems to indicate that initially students do not understand critical aspects of design as a *process*. Remarks from students who answered 'somewhat' included:

- *"I ran my own company for a few years ... and built databases for small to medium sized companies and some large companies also. I worked with Access 97 and later versions"*
- *"Web design, logo design, strong photoshop and illustrator background."*
- *"I do graphic design primarily for small nonprofit organizations, mostly web design and print material. I also have taken classes in engineering and CAD. I consider myself a design enthusiast."*

How knowledgeable do you consider yourself to be about design?	Beginning of semester *n=12*	End of semester *n=10*
Very	8%	40%
Somewhat	83%	60%
Not at all	8%	0%

Table 1. Students' perception of own design knowledge.

When asked the same question at the end of the semester, again as shown in Table 1, students were more confident in their own design knowledge, and the comments they provided suggest that the course helped them acquire a better sense of what design really is. As seen from sample remarks below, students seem to have a better grasp of design as iterative process where user feedback is key.

- *"We covered one full iteration of the design process. From initial rough designs, fleshing out to more realistic screens, usability testing, implementation, and user testing, this class provided a ton of experience. Working with the same team throughout the entire process helped to experience a more realistic scenario."*
- *"I was able to work at every roll in a design team from UI designer, programmer, and tester. I gained experience in designing a system at multiple levels of refinement. I participated in UI testing playing all roles in the testing process including note taking, test administration, and timing/ setup. I gained experience in GOMs evaluation. Participating in the design crits was especially useful."*
- *"Designing through the early stages through several iterations all the way through user testing. While condensed to one sentence this class had a lot to teach."*
- *"I participated in several iterations of a design. One big iteration toward the end of the class. I learned about working in a team and about doing my own work. I also learned something about user interface design."*

These results indicate to us the importance of early discussions that focus on what the process of design is all about. As we see from the following emergent themes, modeling, providing in-class examples, and finding ways to separate design from implementation are all critical steps towards achieving this. The earlier students understand design as a process, the quicker they are able to practice it effectively, the more opportunities they have for iteration, and the more they will ultimately learn.

4.2 Modeling is Critical

A second emergent theme that quickly became apparent after making changes to our spring 2010 UI design course was that in-class modeling exercises seemed to have a positive impact on the students in a number of ways. By providing them with examples of how one might identify, sketch, and design solutions to everyday problems, students were able to more readily understand that low-fidelity sketches are quick yet useful and easily accessible early in design, and that design challenges and solutions are essentially everywhere and not necessarily limited to software interfaces.

One of the first instances of integrating a modeling exercise early in the curriculum involved the instructor presenting a design challenge she had recently encountered at the local airport. Depicting this problem with a simple hand-drawn sketch and discussing it with the class, the instructor was able to show that one need not be an artist to effectively illustrate design, and that challenges are ubiquitous in the world we live in and they often relate to much more than just software programs. Once the design problem was shown and discussed, the instructor used the same medium to illustrate her solution (see Figure 1). In this particular case, the instructor's solution included changing the location of airline and TSA check-in agents, and re-directing the overall flow of customer traffic. A key result of this exercise was that students were suddenly "provided" with both the tools and the freedom they needed to start working and thinking immediately about design. This simple exercise debunked the notion that design is difficult, removed, and inaccessible.

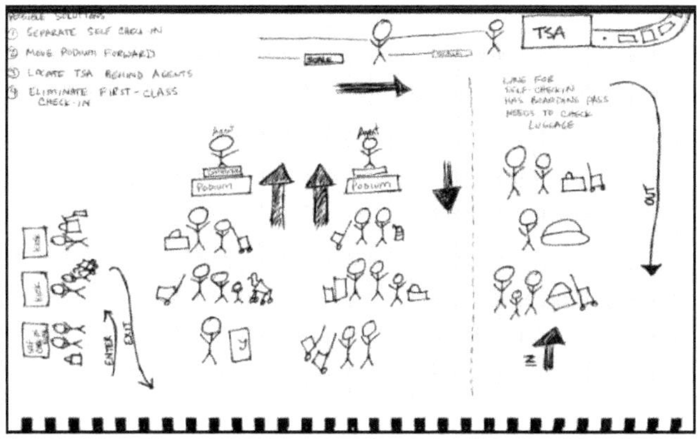

Figure 1. Instructor's hand-drawn solution to design problem.

As a follow-up to the problem/solution exercise modeled by the instructor, students were given a homework assignment whereby they had to identify a design challenge in the world, sketch up the problem as well as a solution, and be prepared to present it to the class. Figure 2 shows one student's solution to a problem he discovered with the wiring of light switch locations in his apartment. As shown, he was able to effectively communicate a solution by mimicking the instructor's use of low-fidelity sketches. Most importantly, this student became empowered to seek out design challenges and to begin thinking about how he might resolve them. This is the first critical learning moment in design.

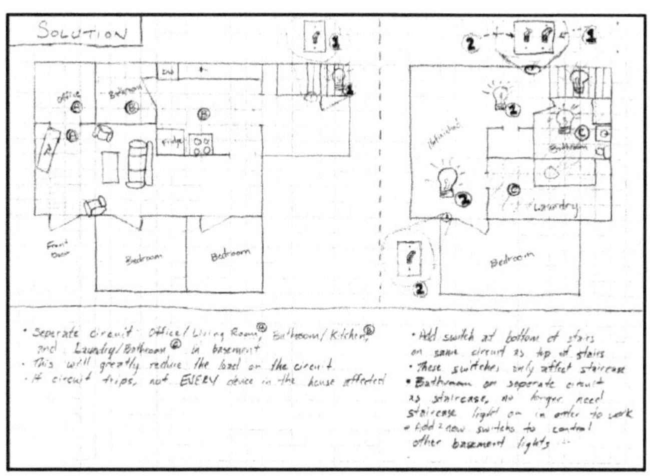

Figure 2. Student solution to discovered design problem.

Another new modeling exercise that proved quite effective was the in-class design of a kiosk to supply packaging materials in the campus center post office. Students were asked to visit the site on their own time and observe the people that flowed through the space and any physical constraints associated with the area. They were also asked to think about the kind of functionality that such a kiosk should support. Then, together as a class, we began our design discussion with three main questions: *Who are our users?*, *What kind of physical constraints (location) are we designing for?*, and *What functionality should our system support?* One student even took pictures of the space to share with the group during our design discussion.

Toward the end of the first day of this in-class exercise, the discussion turned to functional requirements for the packaging kiosk and the appropriate level at which they should be defined in early design. It quickly became apparent to the instructor that students did not clearly understand this issue and they were both confused and frustrated by it, especially given that they were also working on something similar at home as part of their first group assignment. The instructor was able to capitalize on this, work up new teaching points for the follow-up day of discussion and make these points using the in-class exercise rather than the design homework. Because the discussion remained focused on the in-class example, students were free to express confusion about something they did not necessarily "own", yet they were also able to apply what they were learning to their homework. This alleviated preoccupation with what was needed to get a good grade and re-positioned it instead on critical learning concepts.

During the second day of this in-class exercise, after the discussion of functional requirements concluded, the class was divided into four groups of three. The instructor handed out rolls of blank poster paper and markers, and asked each group to begin designing a specific part of the system that we had been discussing. This was one of the moments in the semester where the classroom energy and dynamic most closely resembled a traditional studio as observed in architecture and ID disciplines. Students talked and sketched within their group for about 25 minutes, after which they taped their designs to the wall and explained their work to the rest of the class for about 5 minutes more per group. One example of a group sketch is shown in Figure 3.

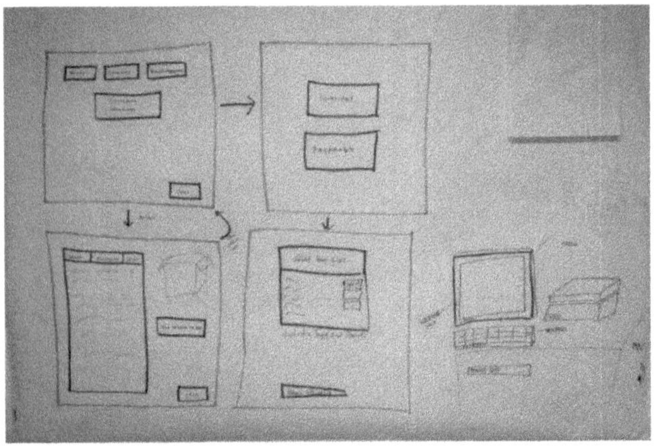

Figure 3. One student group sketch of shipping kiosk.

The second part of this exercise, once again, reminded students that low-fidelity sketches are an effective way to illustrate ideas, particularly early in the process, and it gave them a first taste of what to expect during upcoming design crits. Students recognized that they would be expected to explain and justify the decisions they made, and they quickly understood the types of questions and comments that would typically follow from their peers and the class instructor.

While we were able to sense the positive impact of modeling by gauging the response and energy of the class, additional qualitative evidence is also found in student responses to questions we asked them to reflect on as they completed the first design project: "*What exercises/events/activities have we had in class thus far that have helped you improve your designs? How and why have they helped (be specific)?*" Eleven of 13 responses included mention of an in-class exercise or an assignment that was modeled by the instructor. Samples include:

- *"The in-class design crit session using the in-class designs was by far the most helpful activity. It was hard to know exactly what the process of designing involved until I participated in it and received feedback from the instructor."*
- *"The exercise that we did in class where we designed the packaging material dispenser was the most helpful [...]. The first exercise helped by giving me a good idea of what sort of feedback we might be getting and what sort of features were well liked by the group."*
- *"I think the in-class sessions (sketch-outs, "mini" design crits, etc.) helped to clarify exactly what was expected of us. In particular, the post office kiosk sketch-out helped me think about how to generate new ideas. For each new design, I tried to think of reasons why that particular design was BOTH good and bad, and then tried to come up with ways to improve the design."*

4.3 Separate Design from Implementation

The third and perhaps most important trend we witnessed in teaching the UI design course is that computer science students often have a difficult time separating design from implementation. A typical sequence of projects in our courses involves multiple rounds of iterative design, followed by high-fidelity prototype implementation. We believe it is critical that students create at least one interactive prototype of their designs so they can fully experience usability testing with end-users. This testing is often the "Aha moment" of the class for many students, which is why we have been reluctant to eliminate the prototyping and testing exercises altogether. However, upon looking more closely at the data gathered from our classes, we realize that creating a clearer separation between design and implementation is necessary.

4.3.1 Impending implementation limits ideation

From the earliest stages of the class, many students fixate on whether or not they will eventually have to implement their design ideas. This often results in students feeling afraid or intimidated by the technical nature of the impending implementation and they may reject good design ideas very early in the process, right at the time when they should be generating many different, creative possibilities. Student questions like: *"Are we taking into account how easy it would be to make the changes that we're suggesting?"*, and *"Are we supposed to implement this?"*, taken from class videotape analysis, are commonplace. This preoccupation with implementation is natural given that it is the focus of most of the other courses computer science students are required to take. They are largely unused to thinking about interface design in-and-of itself. Although it is certainly important that CS students are aware of technical limitations when designing so they can avoid creating impractical solutions, this often interferes with their ability to "think outside the box" and generate the most creative, novel, and useful designs.

This problem we highlight—the tension between conceptualizing many creative design ideas at the outset coupled with the knowledge that eventually some sort of implementation may be required—is also noticed by some of the students themselves. At the end of the semester when reflecting back on the entire design-implement-evaluate development cycle they just engaged in, one student notes: "*I was surprised by how heavily design decisions were influenced by implementation. Once a method of implementation is chosen, many nifty designs get tossed out because they'd be too hard to code.*" Another admits that feedback gathered later in the process may not be as welcome when students have to program the system, as captured by the sentiment: "*The last design crit had less of an impact on this project's design because we had to make so many concessions when actually implementing the system.*" Sadly, the end result is that students' creative processes are often staunched when they realize the limitations that surround their own ability to implement what they imagine: "*The inspiration I had at the beginning of the project was mostly ruled to be impractical for a few reasons.*"

4.3.2 Computer technology can impede early design

Another factor that often seems to hamper the process of early design is the use of computer graphics programs (like PowerPoint) to generate preliminary sketches. When students rely on computer technology too early in the design process, their work is often more "fixed", they tend to generate fewer ideas, and they are less likely to react openly and incorporate feedback and suggested changes. Because of this, we have made a concerted effort to either mandate or strongly encourage students to use simple hand-drawn sketches for their earliest design projects.

Despite these warnings, one of the four teams in this class still proceeded to create their initial design graphics using the computer, and a member of another team commented on his Project 1 reflection: "*Sometimes I caught myself wondering, 'Why pencil-and-paper drawings? Isn't this a computer science class?'*" This reluctance to use early hand-drawn sketches to capture design ideas is quite possibly linked, once again, to a preoccupation with coding and implementation. It seems as though students are too eager and focused on implementing their designs, even when they are very cursory, rather than understanding and being fully engaged in the process of early iteration.

Another student comment made after the second class project, which involved modifying preliminary designs based on feedback, illustrates further danger associated with relying on software to generate designs: "*...because I'm the best at bending PowerPoint to my will in the groups, changes to the design after the initial stage came through me...*" In our classes, design is intended to be a deeply collaborative activity with all members of a team participating equally, but this feedback shows how practical aspects of time, resources, and materials often undermine this objective.

4.3.3 Implementation frustrates

Although there can be negative impacts of impending implementation on the process of early design, as just outlined, it remains critical that students experience usability testing firsthand. Regardless of how many times an instructor or classroom peers provide feedback based on screen designs, the lessons students learn by observing actual users interact with a prototype of their system are extremely powerful. However, given this end goal, during the implementation phases of this class we repeatedly stress that prototypes only need to *look* functional. It is not necessary for them to work completely or to be entire robust in order to have a successful testing experience. In fact, developing complete systems during the prototyping stage goes against standard tenets of User-Centered Design where feedback from users is solicited early and often so that subsequent changes are easier to incorporate [4]. Because of this, shortcuts are encouraged in the implementation phase and program functionality is often "dummied-up" as long as it does not interfere with the appearance of system interaction.

One example we often provide to explain this concept to students is to imagine that their system has a user login screen. When a test subject enters a username and password, which the system appears to then accept, it does not mean that a backend database should be created and used for validation as it would in a real program. From the user's perspective, the difference would not likely be noticed anyway, and the point of the class is to focus on the design of the function, not the programming constructs used to implement it.

However, despite our best efforts to convince them otherwise, many students still conceive of this as a UI programming class, and they often end up frustrated with the lack of time needed to create systems to the level they are used to. Some students are particularly unwilling to accept these constraints because it goes against the grain of so many of their other CS courses where complete and secure programming techniques are the focus. The following comments taken from student reflections after the high-fidelity prototyping phase of a class project illustrate the palpability of their frustration with these kind of time and programming constraints.

"I like writing code and wish I could write more sql and vba code to get more functionality into the project."

"I wish we had more time to actually implement the system itself, instead of just making more of a slide show linked with buttons. [...], but I do understand that this class is based on the user interface design and not the coding."

"Writing screens for the implementation was ten times more time consuming than making lifeless screenshots as we did for Project 2."

We also discovered that finding a common prototyping language that everyone in the group is familiar with and can effectively contribute to is problematic. Many teams relied on PowerPoint for their high-fidelity prototype, which the instructor suggested as a possibility in that most students have used it before and it removes much of the temptation to over-program the design. However, this seemed to exacerbate the students' frustration with the limited functionality of their prototypes, as indicated by these additional comments.

"Because I implemented this in MS PPT, there were some limiting factors."

"I would have like to program this in a reasonable programming language instead of an interactive PowerPoint..."

"This project was fairly difficult to collaborate on because it was a PowerPoint file. We ran into a lot of difficulties with compatibility between machines..."

"We had a number of problems with PowerPoint..."

Lastly, we see some students express disappointment after the implementation phase of the class that further indicates the difficulty they have accepting that the course was fundamentally about design, not programming. For example, one student opines, *"It just seems somewhat pointless to have invested the hours to do the testing, the hours to compile the results, and the hours to write up our conclusions regarding the results to simply let the project doe at this point"* while another says *"I kind of wish we went all the way in this project."* While these sentiments confirm that students are often deeply invested in their work and motivated enough to want to take it further, it also shows how difficult it is to break the deeply ingrained notion that upper division CS courses must revolve around implementation and that the design and evaluation of a system is somehow not enough.

5. CONCLUSIONS

After making changes to a hybrid-studio HCI course that revolves around iterative design, peer critiques, prototyping and evaluation, we discovered a number of important trends. First, students coming into the class seem to lack a fundamental understanding of what design is. They often equate it to programming, website creation, or graphics rather than an iterative process requiring multiple rounds of user feedback and testing. Modeling the process of design in-class for students turns out to have a critical impact. Students need to be shown how to identify and understand design challenges, analyze them, generate multiple ideas to resolve those problems, and communicate their solutions in a way that encourages feedback for subsequent iterations. Students must also be encouraged to think creatively and outside the box during early design, and to create as many ideas as possible before settling on the best one.

While incorporation of technology is expected in most computer science courses, we also see how it must be carefully managed by the instructor in the case of user interface design. In particular, students should be required to develop preliminary sketches with pen and paper. If computer graphics programs are relied upon too early in the process, creativity and a willingness to evolve designs may be negatively impacted. Furthermore, instructors should also work hard to increase the separation between the process of design and that of implementation. On the one hand, students tend to limit their creative ideas during the design phase due to their concern over impending implementation; on the other hand, their subsequent implementation often falls short as well in that they simply lack the necessary time or expertise to prototype the system fully. Perhaps most critically, students may end up frustrated by this dichotomy and develop negative feelings associated with the process of design in general.

While we recognize the importance of having students prototype some portion of their designs so they can experience usability testing with actual users, there are ways to minimize the impact on design creativity. Ideally a full semester course could focus first on design only, followed by a second semester course focusing on prototype implementation and evaluation. Given that this sequence is unlikely to fit in most CS curriculums, another possibility is to teach key aspects of UI design within other programming classes, or even to co-link courses to meld these aspects together as appropriate. In our ongoing work, we hope to investigate further the effect of some of these suggestions.

6. ACKNOWLEDGMENTS

We wish to thank Matthew Hagedal for his help with the data analysis phase of this research. This work is supported by the National Science Foundation (NSF) Grant Nos. 0725145, 0725290, and 0725215. Opinions expressed are those of the authors and do not necessarily reflect the views of the entire research team or the NSF. For more information, see: http://www.studiocollaborative.soe.vt.edu.

7. REFERENCES

[1] Cennamo, K., Douglas, S.A., Vernon, M., Brandt, C., Scott, B., Reimer, Y., & McGrath, M. (2011). Promoting Creativity in the Computer Science Design Studio. *Proc. SIGCSE 2011*, pp. 649-654.

[2] Docherty, M., Sutton, P., Brereton, M., Kaplan, S. (2001). An innovative design and studio-based CS degree. *Proc. SIGCSE 2001*, pp. 233-237.

[3] Estey, A., Long, J., Gooch, B., and Gooch, A.A. (2010). Investigating studio-based learning in a course on game design. *Proc. FDG 2010*, pp. 64-71.

[4] Gould, J.D. (1988). How to design usable systems (excerpt). In R. Baecker, J. Grudin, W. Buxton, & S. Greenberg (Eds.), Readings in human-computer interaction, toward the year 2000, 93–121. New York, NY: Morgan-Kaufman.

[5] Greenberg, S. (2008). Embedding a design studio course in a conventional Computer Science program. P. Kotzé, W. Wong, J. Jorge, A. Dix and P. Silva (eds): Creativity and HCI: From Experience to Design in Education - Selected Contributions from HCIEd 2007.

[6] Hendrix, D., Myneni, L., Narayanan, H., and Ross, M. (2010). Implementing studio-based learning in CS2. *Proc. SIGCSE 2010*, pp. 505-509.

[7] Hundhausen, C., Agrawal, A., Fairbrother, D., and Trevisan, M. (2010). Does studio-based instruction work in CS 1? An empirical comparison with a traditional approach. *Proc. SIGCSE 2010*, pp. 500-504.

[8] Lewis, C., and Rieman, J. (1993). Task-centered user interface design: A practical introduction. Available at: http://hcibib.org/tcuid/

[9] Lincoln, Y. S., & Guba, E. G. (1985). *Naturalistic inquiry*. Beverly Hills, CA: Sage.

[10] Merriam, S. B. (1998). *Qualitative research and case study applications in education*. San Francisco: Jossey-Bass.

[11] Nurkkala, T., and Brandle, S. (2011). Software studio: teaching professional software engineering. *Proc. SIGCSE 2011*, pp. 153-158.

[12] Reimer, Y., and Douglas, S. (2003). Teaching HCI design with the studio approach. *Computer Science Education* 13, 3, 191-205.

[13] Shaffer, D. W. (2007). Learning in design. In R.A. Lesh, J.J. Kaput & E. Hamilton (Eds), *Foundations for the future in mathematics education* , pp. 99-126. Mahwah, NJ: Erlbaum.

[14] Ungar, J. M., and White, J. A. (2008). Agile user-centered design: enter the design studio – a case study. *Proc. CHI 2008*, pp. 2167-2177.

[15] Williams, A., Ostwald, M., and Askland, H.H. (2010). The design studio, models of creativity and the education of future designers. *Proc. DESIRE 2010*, pp. 131-137.

A Multilevel, Multidimensional Undergraduate Course and Lab Experience on Embedded Multimedia Systems

Dimitrios Charalampidis
Electrical Engineering Department
University of New Orleans
New Orleans, LA 70148, U.S.A
1-504-280-7415
dcharala@uno.edu

James Haralambides
Dept. of Math and Computer Science
Barry University
Miami Shores, FL 33161
1-305-899-3286
jharalambides@mail.barry.edu

ABSTRACT

Traditional curricular structures can be fragmented in the sense that course inter-relationships or links between theories, methodologies, and practices, are not immediately recognized by the students. The completion of the course puzzle and the integration of course knowledge usually become evident only after graduation. In this paper, we describe a course/lab implementation that has offered students a unique opportunity to experience the full spectrum of course elements, namely, fundamentals of theory, algorithmic design, hardware design and simulation, and implementation and testing on programmable logic devices all within a single framework.

The course/lab design has been a collaborative effort between the Dept. of Electrical Engr. (EE) at the University of New Orleans (UNO) and the Dept. of Math and Computer Science (CS) at Barry University (BU). This has helped ensure that the course/ lab offerings can be implemented successfully in diverse environments.

Categories and Subject Descriptors

K.3.2 [Computer and Information Science Education]: Computer science education, D.4.7 [Organization and Design]: Real-time systems and embedded systems

General Terms

Algorithms, Design, Experimentation, Theory.

Keywords

Multimedia applications, embedded systems, image and signal processing, multi-level and multi-dimensional course design.

1. INTRODUCTION

Embedded systems have increasingly become part of our lives in applications that include smart homes, cell phones, medical devices, and automotive systems to name a few. The rapid growth of the field has increased the demand for professionals with skills in the design and implementation processes for such systems. Academic institutions have recognized the challenges this trend presents and have introduced specialized programs or course and lab entities that offer students the opportunity to engage in research and educational activities in the field [1, 6].

Permission to make digital or hard copies of all or part of this work for personal or classroom use is granted without fee provided that copies are not made or distributed for profit or commercial advantage and that copies bear this notice and the full citation on the first page. To copy otherwise, or republish, to post on servers or to redistribute to lists, requires prior specific permission and/or a fee.
SIGCSE'12, February 29–March 3, 2012, Raleigh, North Carolina, USA.
Copyright 2012 ACM 978-1-4503-1098-7/12/02...$10.00.

While there are a good number of course and lab entities that teach the design of embedded systems and explore their possible interfaces with relevant computing disciplines [3, 4, 7], we believe that many approaches are unidirectional or limited in scope. The majority of courses are designed to offer a hands-on approach on a subject area studied earlier, are exclusively project-based, or focus on the fundamentals of embedded systems design alone.

We have designed and implemented a course/lab entity that integrates the active learning process (see Figure 1) of the subject area(s) (multimedia applications for signal and image processing) to the development of software and hardware designs for carefully selected applications, to the implementation and testing of such on programmable logic devices (FPGAs). The uniqueness of the course design lies in the fact that it provides a single framework for students to experience all elements of education and research: a) fundamentals of theory in the subject areas of digital design, signal processing, and image processing, b) algorithmic design with the support of integrated development environments (IDEs), hardware design and simulation using hardware description languages (VHDL), and embedded design on programmable logic devices (Xilinx FPGA boards).

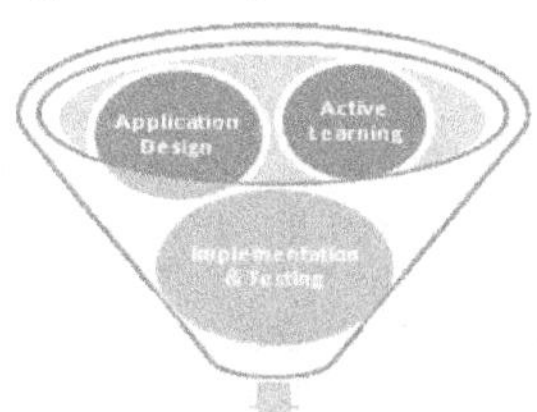

Figure 1. Learn, Design, Build

It is not necessarily the amount of information or the set of techniques used that makes the difference. We have placed a strong emphasis on the integration of the following parameters: a) Modularity, b) Adaptability, c) Multi-Dimensionality, d) Cohesiveness, and e) Breadth (see also Figure 2).

Modularity is the objective of many course designs as it allows for the adoption of materials according to the needs of a particular institution, a student body, or an instructor's area of expertise. Modularity does not guarantee *adaptability* unless the modules themselves are designed to allow for variation in content, academic level, and student backgrounds and interests. The course material was developed using a modular approach both in terms of detail level and topics range. A list of modules includes: Digital Design, Signal Processing, Image Processing, Hardware Design using VHDL, and Embedded Systems Design. Additional modules were developed for course projects and research topics (for example, edge detection or speech synthesis). The level of detail and the extension of content coverage at each of the collaborating institutions varied based on the academic programs and the class composition. While a more in-depth approach was taken by the CS department at BU on digital design and a lesser emphasis was placed on the intrinsic details of signal processing for Computer Information Students at the same institution, the roles were reversed for the EE department at UNO. The autonomous nature of the majority of modules allows for the expandability of the course to include alternative computing disciplines such as neural networks, pattern recognition, and power.

A *multi-dimensional* course explores the synergies among a number of disciplines within the computing field. Multi-disciplinary synergies must be brought forth naturally to discourage fragmentation in the learning process. Therefore, in addition to offering multi-disciplinary modules, the instructors paid special attention to provide a seamless transition between these modules and between different topics within the same module using an interconnecting theme (*cohesive property*). For instance, the theme for signal processing was audio synthesis. Students were introduced to fundamental theory, such as discrete signals and the frequency domain, and more advanced topics such as poles/zeros, and their relation to sound synthesis. Regarding the hardware aspects of the design, students emphasized the behavioral rather than the structural modeling approach.

Breadth measures the width of the theory-to-implementation range. We have implemented a *multi-level* course/lab design that reaches all elements of the range, namely, fundamentals of theory, algorithmic design, hardware design and optimization, simulation and testing, and implementation and performance evaluation.

In addition to the successful integration of the aforementioned parameters, the course/lab must be realizable. Challenges relate to faculty expertise necessary for such multi-faceted designs and to infrastructure, namely, software and hardware resources and associated costs [10, 11]. The instructors have used a variety of tools and resources ranging from commercial hardware platforms (Xilinx development boards) to professional software suites (Visual Studio Professional, Matlab, Xilinx ISE Design Suite) to freeware or public domain applications (Octave, Freemat, Visual Studio Express, Xilinx Webpack). A fully functional course/lab can be designed with minimal expenses as effective learning can take place with the exclusive use of freeware or public domain applications. Yet, certain software and hardware environments may enhance the learning experience. Embedding student designs require the use of a hardware platform. Educational boards (for example, Xilinx development boards) can be purchased at academic pricing (<$100/board). As students may share hardware equipment in group projects, the total course/lab cost is very affordable for most if not all institution budgets.

The course/lab has been offered for two years as a collaborative effort at both UNO (Dept. of Electrical Engineering) and BU (Dept. of Math and Computer Science). The diverse student population between the institutions has been used as a measure of success and applicability in non-uniform environments.

2. RELATED WORK

A number of institutions have introduced course/lab structures that deal with embedded systems education. An extensive study for the undergraduate curriculum is found in [5]. Curricular areas explored are mostly hardware related in subject areas such as microcontrollers, system-on-chip, critical systems, and robotics.

A joint effort (Nexos project) between Marquette University and University of Buffalo resulted in course materials and a supporting lab for hands-on projects in embedded systems courses [7]. Recommendations are made for low cost software and hardware solutions to support the course infrastructure.

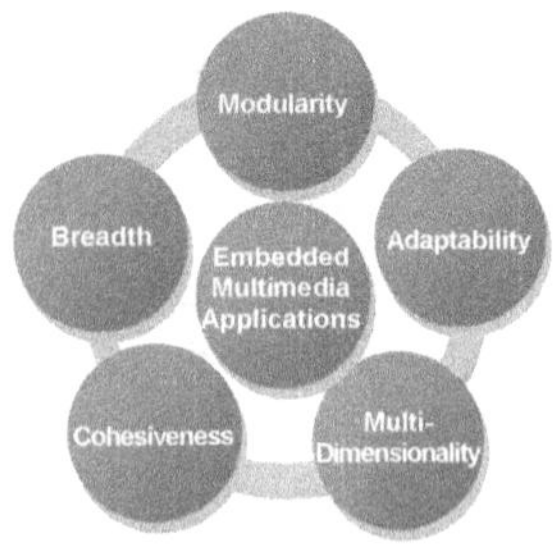

Figure 2. The integration of course parameters

Interdisciplinary approaches can be classified into two main categories: a) those that attempt to relate multiple subject areas [8], and b) those that generate synergies among diverse student populations to facilitate enhanced learning [9]. The former approach still operates on a limited subset of computing fields while the second produces synergies on a relatively static course structure.

3. COURSE STRUCTURE/MODULES

Students enrolled in the class ranged from sophomore to senior and majored in Computer Science or Computer Information Sciences (BU) and Electrical Engineering (UNO). Course and lab content in areas that include signal and image processing, HDL, and embedded design make this course more appropriate for upper-level undergraduates. The course/lab sessions were offered three times a week at BU (1 hour each) and twice (1½ hour each) or once (3 hours) at UNO. Due to the need for more in-depth lab sessions, students showed a preference towards fewer, longer sessions.

The multidisciplinary nature of the course is supported by the selection of its modules: a) digital design, b) embedded system design (VHDL), c) signal processing, and d) image processing. A careful selection of topics and applications (e.g., medical image processing, music synthesis, and speech processing) is essential in order to enhance module cohesion. Based on the student population, the instructor at BU explored the first two subject areas at greater detail while the instructor at UNO dedicated more time on the latter two. To avoid fragmentation, topics in these subject areas were integrated through lab and homework assignments, software/hardware simulations, and projects. All materials used in the course were produced by the CS and EE instructors.

The multidimensional course structure has been achieved with the use of course materials and tools that range from theoretical concepts, to algorithmic designs, to hardware implementations, simulations, and embedding in programmable logic devices (FPGAs). Digital design deals with theoretical concepts (Boolean algebra, algebraic simplification, and finite state machines), yet it emphasizes the design of hardware systems. VHDL has many similarities to high level programming languages [2]. As such, it supports algorithmic design, and at the same time it is an excellent integration vehicle for linking a theoretical design to its hardware implementation. Signal processing and image processing are two areas that place a strong emphasis on theoretical concepts. Nevertheless, it is highly desirable for efficiency purposes to embed algorithms in these areas to hardware devices. FPGA boards (Spartan 3e) and supporting software tools (Xilinx ISE Development Suite) offered the means to do just that in the lab. The structure of course components is shown in detail in Figure 3.

Topics in the digital design segment follow a sequence that leads to block design. The selection reflects components which the instructors believe are essential to understand the concepts and lead to implementation of these designs in the abstract level supported by VHDL. Thus, the emphasis has been placed in the behavioral description of hardware components, their timing requirements, and the finite state machines that simulate them.

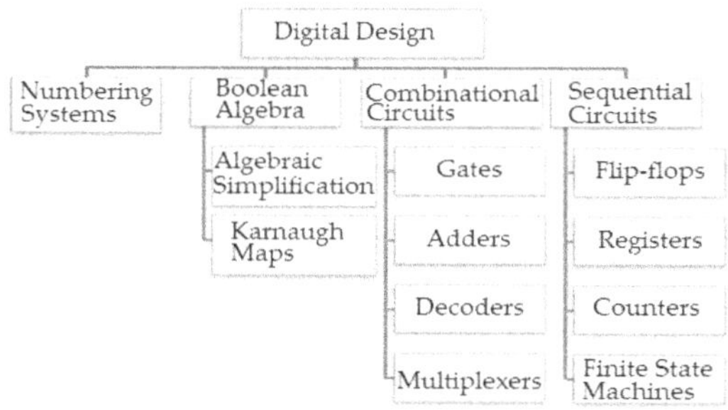

a) Digital Design

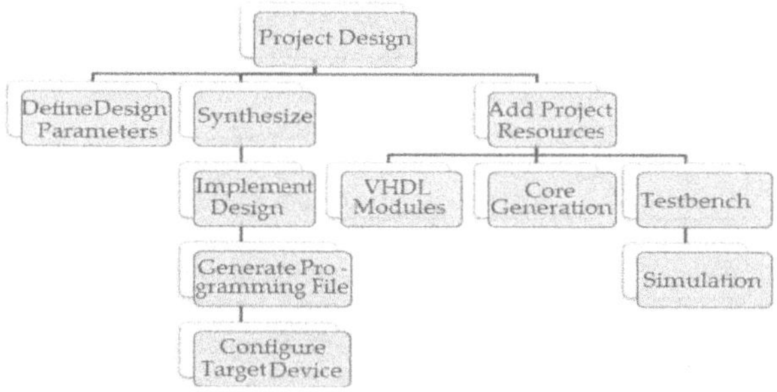

b) Embedded Design using VHDL

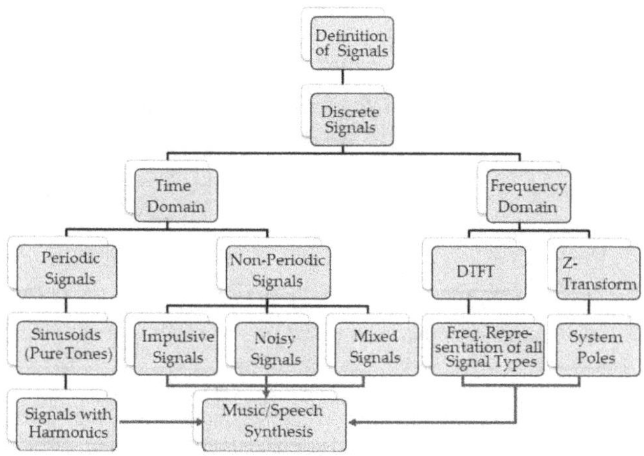

c) Signal Processing

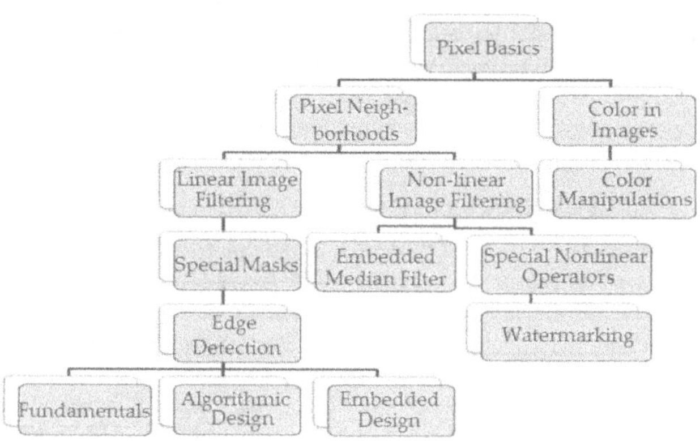

d) Image Processing

Figure 3. Structure of course components

All UNO students had background knowledge of the subject area and covered the topics depicted in Figure 3.a in the form of a review. Varying student backgrounds at BU led to a more in-depth coverage of all areas. Key digital components were designed and simultaneously implemented in VHDL and were mainly studied in terms of their interfaces and behaviors. Full coverage of the hierarchy was realized.

VHDL has been the hardware description language of choice for embedded designs in assignments and class projects. Most students in both institutions had minimal or no background knowledge in this area. Coverage focused on: a) fundamental programming structures (assignment, selection, iteration) and its similarities and differences to corresponding high-level programming languages and: b) modeling of hardware devices exploring the notions of "processes" and "concurrency". This course segment was covered in alternating fashion with digital design to offer a hands-on approach. The instructors observed that the combination of digital design concepts, VHDL implementation, and embedding design using programmable logic devices (Spartan 3E boards) results in a steeper learning curve and generates student enthusiasm.

The topics covered within the signal processing area lead towards specific goals, namely, music and speech synthesis. Initially, the module provides basic definitions of signals and their properties. It continues with a reference to specific signals of interest such as sinusoids and other periodic signals, impulsive and noisy signals. The selection of these types of signal is essential to show their inherent relationship to speech and music. The particular module structure allows students to acquire specialized, yet complete comprehension of all the signal processing materials necessary to integrate all component areas and applications studied.

The instructors chose different subsets of the hierarchy to better match their respective student population. For example, since UNO students had already acquired some fundamental knowledge on the subject area, the UNO instructor covered all specialized topics of the hierarchy. For example, more information was presented about systems and system properties, so that students could learn more about noisy signals, the frequency domain, Z-transform, transfer functions, transfer function poles and the relationship of the above to sound, and in particular speech synthesis. BU students had no prior knowledge in the subject areas. As such, the instructor at BU selected a subset of the hierarchy that focused on discrete signals, the time and frequency domain in general, and periodic (sinusoids) and non-periodic signals (impulsive and noisy signals) that lead to music synthesis.

Both student bodies had limited background knowledge in the image processing subject area. Coverage focused on topics that are fundamental but necessary for practically any image processing application. For example linear and non-linear filtering algorithms are used in edge detection, feature extraction, image restoration, and image enhancement. Color image processing is important for image representation as well as hardware-based processing (physical storage in relation to color depth).

4. ASSIGNED PROJECTS

The instructors carefully selected and designed the assigned projects with the purpose of strengthening the course objectives, i.e., to provide a multi-level/dimensional course/lab experience and to expose students to research concepts. All projects required that students had acquired knowledge from different course components (digital systems, embedded design, and signal/speech processing or image processing), and involved students in algorithmic development, design, implementation, and testing. Although the projects were not designed to produce novel research results, they were closely associated to research areas, such as sound synthesis, and image enhancement. Descriptions for four sample projects are presented next.

4.1 Project 1 – Sound Synthesis

The objective of the project was to synthesize musical instrument sounds with using a computer keyboard connected to the Spartan 3E board, and the on-board digital-to-analog converter (DAC). Students had to write VHDL code to produce weighted sums of sinusoids/harmonics that represented the instrument tones. Sample waveforms for instrument tones were collected from the Internet. Prior to implementation, students had to simulate sound synthesis using a software tool (e.g. Octave) to acquire experience with the audio synthesis process. Sinusoid samples had to be stored in FPGA memory, and keyboard keys were used to determine the instrument's tone (pitch). The weighted sums of sinusoids had to be send to the DAC and played back using external speakers. The instructors provided generic VHDL codes for controlling the keyboard and the DAC. Students had to learn the associated theory of digital systems, embedded design, and sound synthesis, work on the algorithmic design of harmonic generation using a software tool, implement their design on embedded systems using VHDL, and simulate/test their design using the Xilinx development tools.

4.2 Project 2 – Morphing

The objective of this project was to implement a system that dynamically transitions between two faces, and displays the morphing results on a computer monitor using the VGA port of the FPGA board. Students were asked to learn the associated theory of digital systems, embedded design, and image processing, work on the algorithmic design using Matlab, or Octave, simulate/test their design, and implement their design on FPGAs. VHDL code was written to calculate a pixel-wise weighted sum between two images and to perform half-toning. The VGA controller on the Spartan 3E board supports only 3-bit color images, and 1-bit monochrome images. In order to create the impression of more than two gray levels in a binary image, pixels were converted into blocks of 0s and 1s using the following 4×4 binary masks depending on their intensity:

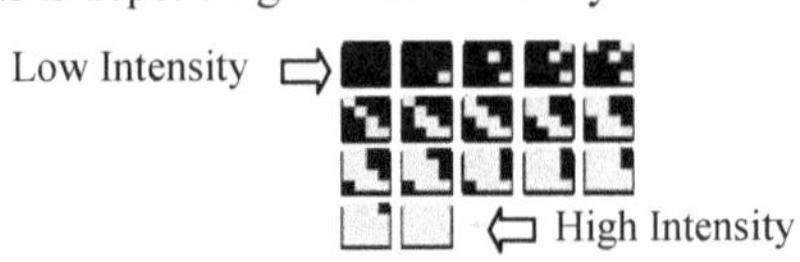

The instructors provided VHDL code for pixel display on a monitor. A half-toning example is presented next.

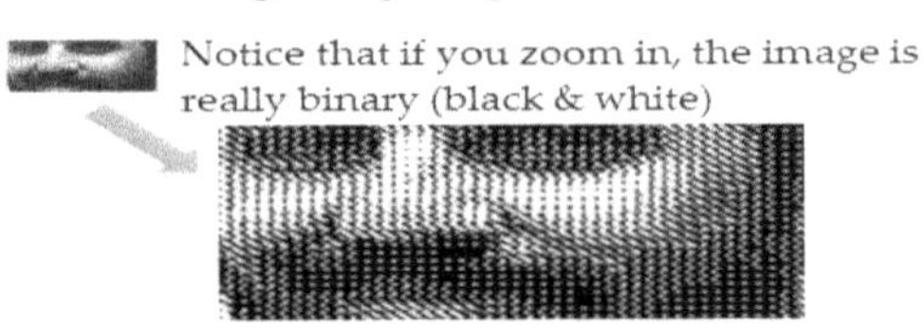

An example of morphing at different stages is presented below:

4.3 Project 3 – Embossing

The objective of this project was to design and implement an algorithm to perform image embossing. Students were asked to display the embossing results on a computer monitor, using the Spartan 3E board's VGA port. Students were asked to write VHDL code to find vertical edges by subtracting a pixel from its horizontal neighbor, and then add a constant to the resulted image. As in the case of morphing, students had to implement half-toning, and display the original and processed images on the monitor. An example of an original image and the associated embossed and half-toned embossed images are shown below.

Original *Embossed* *Embossed-Halftoned*

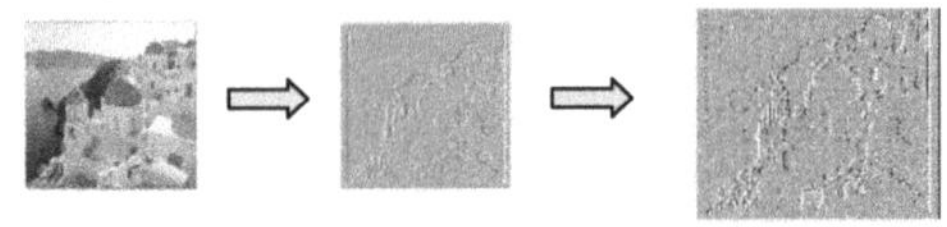

4.4 Project 4 – Edge Detection

The objective of this project was to design and implement an algorithm to perform edge detection on 3-bit color images. Similarly to projects 2 and 3, students had to learn the associated theory of both digital systems and image processing, and work on the algorithmic design, embedded system design and implementation, and simulation/testing. Students were asked to write code in a programming language of their choice to reduce the color depth an input color image to 3-bit RGB representation (1 bit/channel), and VHDL code for computing pixel intensity differences horizontally and vertically for neighboring pixels in a single pass. The original and processed images were displayed on the monitor. An example of an original and a 3-bit color images, and the edge detection results are shown next.

Original Image 3-bit color Edge detection

5. PUBLICITY AND DISSEMINATION

The dissemination process is based on the creation and dynamic update of a web site (http://fs.uno.edu/dcharala/CCLI) that includes class materials (such as lectures, projects, and software/documentation) and advertisement of this web site to affiliated universities. It includes presentation and publication of experiences to conference proceedings. The instructors have been involved in a number of activities that enhance the visibility of the project such as participation in the STEM Annual Symposium (2 years, BU), interaction with prospective high school students through university organized activities, intra-university career service activities, and dissemination of information to wider audiences (module availability, project demonstrations).

6. ASSESSMENT

As part of the NSF/CCLI project, assessment efforts measured the success of the course objectives, and overall project activities, including the development of educational materials, the dissemination of project outcomes, and the evaluation instruments used. This section concentrates on the assessment results directly associated to the course/lab objectives. Several evaluation instruments were developed by the instructors and course evaluator, including surveys and face-to-face student interviews. Assessment data were collected for two course offerings per institution, namely for Spring 2010 (Year 1) and for Spring 2011 (Year 2). An assessment summary is presented next.

6.1 Research Elements

BU: Continuous feedback on research activities was obtained during lectures and on-campus interviews. Student responses for one of the relevant questions are presented in Table 1. This data was collected for both years toward the end of the semester. Note that O/NR indicates "Other/No Response".

Table 1. Student responses to question 1

Question	Year	1	2	1	2	1	2	1	2
		Yes		A little		No		O/ NR	
Did you have opportunities to conduct research on topics/ apps/projects discussed in class?	***BU***	6	6	1	0	0	0	3	0
	UNO	20	5	0	7	0	1	0	1

Students demonstrated levels of enthusiasm for their involvement in the 2nd and 3rd Annual STEM symposiums where they presented comprehensive project results and finalized embedded designs. During both years, students presented their project work to departmental seminars. Most students considered hands-on project related research activities to be quite challenging. They reported the need for extended involvement and assistance in hardware design. Final reviews received by students revealed a better understanding of research activities than early ones. Tabular results for the first year include literature reviews, search engines, and tutorial websites. Second year results demonstrate a uniform perception of research involvement for all students.

UNO: During both offerings, research elements were introduced by reference during lectures, via presentation of appropriate modules, or through projects. During the second year, students were assigned a project on image watermarking, for which they had to implement and reproduce results based on one of the instructor's research papers. The project was provided in the form of a module and included introductory information about watermarking and clustering, questions to access students' knowledge of the particular topic, specific project deliverables, and references. Student responses (see Table 1) confirmed their involvement to research activities.

6.2 Multi-dimensional/level course structure

6.2.1 Student feedback

Students liked the fact that knowledge from different topics is combined to design, implement, and evaluate their work. They enjoy the immediate integration of theoretical concepts, to algorithmic designs, to hardware implementations, all during the same lecture/lab assignment.

Based on evaluation feedback and instructor observations, student background is important in determining an optimal module sequence, and depth and duration of coverage. UNO students were able to realize the connection between the theory and applications relatively early in the semester. The reason is that signal/image processing concepts were presented after a quick review on digital design, as they already possessed knowledge of the subject area. BU students concentrated on digital design and VHDL for a longer period of time. As a result, they experienced a concept-application association, only upon introduction of signal/image processing materials.

BU: Surveys addressing the multidimensional and the balanced multilevel nature of the course were distributed toward the end of the semester for both years and are presented in table 2. Students developed a better perception a module inter-relations upon successful completion of all project activities. Most students, having limited background in hardware, found project activities related to hardware description languages and embedded design quite challenging. During the second year the instructor provided a more extensive study of hardware components. Additionally, certain project modules were prepared and provided to students ahead of time. This allowed students to concentrate on the algorithmic mapping aspects of their projects more. Student feedback received at the end of the second year indicated a uniform perception of a balanced, multi-level/disciplinary nature for the course.

UNO: Data collected during both years (table 2) revealed that the majority of students agreed that the final project brought together the multidimensional/integrative knowledge acquired, and that the course provides a good balance between the different course elements. Few students preferred to be further exposed to hardware implementation, less exposed to theory, or have a smoother transition between software and hardware. Such concerns were addressed during the second year, when the instructor restructured the course lectures and increased the number of in-class software/hardware-related demonstrations to provide a smoother transition between the software and hardware elements. A larger number of lectures were dedicated to the detailed description of hardware tools and implementations, especially those relevant to the final project. Fewer lectures were dedicated to course content associated to the review of pre-requisite knowledge (such as digital systems).

In the second year, the course involved an assortment of lectures and labs, and was offered for 90-minutes, twice-a-week. The instructor provided students extensive assistance with software and hardware tools. However, several of these activities took place outside regular class time. During the first year, the 3-hour/once-a-week offering of the course, allowed an easier implementation of a lab setting during class time. In order to retain the 3-hour/per week course setting, so that this course does not differ from other UNO electives, an optimal course setting may include a 2 hour lecture taking place twice a week, accompanied by a 1 hour lab offered at alternating weeks.

Table 2. Student responses to questions 2 and 3

Question	Year	1	2	1	2	1	2	1	2
		Yes		A little		No		O/ NR	
Does the project bring together knowledge acquired on digital design, VHDL, & signal/image proc. (integrative experience)?	***BU***	6	6	0	0	0	0	4	0
	UNO	14	14	0	0	0	0	7	0
Has the course provided a balanced mix of theory, design, hardware implementation (multidimensional)?	***BU***	2	6	6	0	0	0	2	0
	UNO	12	13	0	0	7	1	2	0

6.2.2 Course content

The multidimensional nature was supported by the following course modules and associated disciplines: a) Digital Design M1: Combinational Logic, M2: sequential logic, b) Image Processing - M3: Fundamentals of Theory, M4: Edge Detection (M4.1: Theory, M4.2: Algorithmic Design, and M4.3: Embedded Design), M5: Median Filters (theory and embedded design), c) Signal Processing - M6: Fundamentals of Theory, d) Embedded Design - M7: VHDL, M8: Software User Guide. Modules M1, M2, M3, M4.1, and M6 emphasize theory and algorithmic methodologies. Module 4.2 emphasizes algorithmic design. Modules M4.3, M7 and M8 emphasize embedded design. Module M5 covers the full spectrum of theory, algorithmic design, and embedded design. Class lectures and homework assignments emphasize the algorithmic aspect of the course (mainly image and signal processing algorithmic design). Lab assignments and projects emphasized the implementation (FPGA programming) and testing (simulation and verification of embedded design) aspects of the course.

The course modules prepared by the instructors were found to be helpful. In certain cases, the modular and content structure of new courses depends on student backgrounds and interests. The collaborative nature of the project assisted in determining such parameters. Interaction between the collaborating institutions has led to the development of appropriate course materials for wider audiences. This conjecture is supported by student feedback with respect to the appropriateness and difficulty level of course content as it relates to their background level and interest.

BU: The survey results presented in table 3 regarding the course materials were collected for both years after homework assignment 1 (third question), after homework assignment 3 and the introduction of signal/image processing fundamentals (second question), and at the end of the semester (first question). A strong majority of students found class materials to be readily available and helpful towards homework/lab and project activities.

Table 3. Student responses to questions 3 and 4

Question	Year	1	2	1	2	1	2
		Yes		No		O/ NR	
Were you provided with sufficient materials and background info to start working on the project?	***BU***	7	6	1	0	2	0
	UNO	16	14	0	0	5	0
Does the class together with homework/lab assignments offer an integrative experience about software, hardware, and hands-on experience?		4	6	2	0	4	0
Do you feel that the class lessons provided a good foundation to complete the homework?		8	5	0	1	2	0

UNO: The results presented in table 3 indicate that the vast majority of the students felt that the materials prepared by the instructors, in addition to the information presented during the lectures, was sufficient to start working on the project. Responses from 5 students that took the class during the first year indicated that developed code was provided to students by the instructors. Additionally, students completed a survey that directly assesses how well the four main course topics were covered. The results are summarized in table 4. The vast majority of students indicated for both years that the course objectives were achieved as either very well (in most cases) or well.

Table 4. Course objectives evaluations for UNO

Attempts: 18 (Year 1), 14 (Year 2): How well were these course objectives achieved? very well (5), well (4), acceptably (3), poorly (2), failed (1) Students completing this course will learn:

	Intro to VHDL		Intro to Image Processing		Intro to Signal Processing		FPGA/other hardware topics	
	Year 1	**Year 2**	**Year 1**	**Year 2**	**Year 1**	**Year 2**	**Year 1**	**Year 2**
5	66.7%	50%	55.6%	57.1%	61.1%	42.9%	61.1%	14.3%
4	22.2%	28.6%	44.4%	42.9%	33.3%	42.9%	33.3%	71.4%
3	11.1%	21.4%	0%	0%	5.6%	14.3%	5.6%	14.3%
2	0%	0%	0%	0%	0%	0%	0%	0%
1	0%	0%	0%	0%	0%	0%	0%	0%

7. CONCLUSIONS

Education in embedded systems has expanded greatly over the years. Many course/lab offerings address the issues of modularity and interdisciplinary methodologies in order to enhance the effectiveness of the course for wider audiences. Nevertheless, most such designs remain focused on a small subset of computing subject areas or follow a static prerequisite curricular structure that limits the attractiveness of the course to students in hardware related fields.

We have implemented a multi-level/disciplinary course and lab structure that integrates active learning in the subject areas of signal and image processing, algorithmic and hardware design, and embedded system design. The uniqueness of the approach is based on a number of parameters: a) the course is autonomous in that it requires minimal background knowledge, b) students learn all concepts and design methodologies and engage in design and implementation activities in a single framework, c) carefully selected applications and unifying themes provide high levels of cohesion for the course's constituent components, and d) the course is adaptable to address different student backgrounds and interests.

8. ACKNOWLEDGMENTS

This work was supported in part by the National Science Foundation/CCLI program (DUE-0836806 and DUE-0836828).

9. REFERENCES

[1] Association for Computing Machinery. Computing Curricula 2005. http://www.acm.org/education/curricula-recommendations.

[2] IEEE Design Automation Standards Committee (2008) Std 1076-2008, IEEE Standard VHDL Language Reference Manual, IEEE, New York, NY, USA.

[3] Belarin, F., Chiodo, M., Hsieh, H., Jureska, A., Lavagno, L., Passerone, C., Sangiovanni-Vincentelli, A., Sentovich, E., Suzuki, K., and Tabbara, B. 1997. *Hardware-Software Co-Design of Embedded System: The POLIS Approach*, Norwell, MA: Kluwer.

[4] Chu, P. P. 2008. FPGA Prototyping by VHDL Examples: Xilinx Spartan-3 Version, Wiley-Interscience.

[5] Koopman, Choset, Gandhi, et.al. Undergraduate embedded system education at Carnegie Mellon. *Transactions on Embedded Computing Systems*, 4(3):500–528, 2005.

[6] Grimheden, M., Torngren, M., 2005. What is Embedded Systems and How Should It Be Taught? *ACM Trans. on Embedded Computing Systems (TECS)*, 4(3): 633–651, ACM Press, NY, 2005.

[7] Brylow, D., Ramamurthy, B., 2008. Nexos: A Next Generation Embedded Systems Laboratory. *Proceedings of the 2008 Workshop on Embedded Systems Education* (Atlanta, Georgia, October 23, 2008).

[8] Hamrita, T. K., Potter, W. D., and Bishop, B., 2005. Robotics, microcontroller and embedded systems education initiatives: An interdisciplinary approach. *International Journal of Engineering Education*, 21(4):730–738, 2005.

[9] Valino, J. R., Czernikowski, R. S., Interdisciplinary Teaming as an Effective Method to Teach Real-Time and Embedded Systems Courses. *Proceedings of the 2008 Workshop on Embedded Systems Education* (Atlanta, Georgia, October 23, 2008).

[10] Mitra, T. 2006. Challenges in Designing Embedded Systems Courses. *Proceedings of the 2006 Workshop on Embedded Systems Education* (Atlanta, Georgia, October 23, 2006).

[11] Falk Salewski, F., 2006. Hardware Platform Design Decisions in Embedded Systems - A Systematic Teaching Approach. *Proceedings of the 2006 Workshop on Embedded Systems Education* (Atlanta, Georgia, October 23, 2006).

Effective Closed Labs in Early CS Courses: Lessons from Eight Terms of Action Research

Elizabeth Patitsas
University of Toronto & University of British Columbia
40 St George St.
Toronto ON M5S 2E4
patitsas@cs.utoronto.ca

Steven Wolfman
University of British Columbia
2366 Main Mall
Vancouver BC V6T 1Z4
wolf@cs.ubc.ca

ABSTRACT

We report on best practices we have established to teach first-year computer science students in closed laboratories, founded on over three years of action research in a large introductory discrete mathematics and digital logic course. Our practices have resulted in statistically significant improvements in student and teaching assistant perception of the labs. Specifically, we discuss our practices of streamlining labs to reduce load on students that is extraneous to the lab's learning goals; establishing a positive first impression for students and TAs in the early weeks of the term; and effectively managing the teaching staff, including weekly preparation meetings for TAs using and a gradual, iterative curriculum development cycle that engages all stakeholders in the course.

Categories and Subject Descriptors

K.3.2 [**Computers and Information Science Education**]: Pedagogy, education research

General Terms

Design, management

Keywords

Computer science education, curriculum development, curriculum evaluation, teaching assistants, labs, survey

1. INTRODUCTION AND MOTIVATION

The practice of having students taught in a laboratory setting, known as "closed laboratories"[1], "labs", or "practicals", came to prominence in the 1990s after the Denning report [3] recommended them. Among other hopes, CS educators believed these labs might dramatically improve interest in and perception of CS [13].

Unfortunately, a closed laboratory can also dissuade students from continuing in a major [12], as we also experienced. Specifically, if students perceive that a laboratory does not contribute to their learning, they are less likely to persist in the program [12]. Four years ago, students in our introductory discrete mathematics and hardware course complained of irrelevant and confusing subject matter, ill-prepared teaching assistants, and difficult yet unenlightening labs. The following year, we began our research to improve the course's laboratory component.

In this paper, we present key practices developed from our successful 3.5-year iterative refinement and assessment program for the course's closed labs. This paper is a follow-up to our previous one [14] and focuses on our high-level findings, including an additional year of data collection and analysis. Our changes aimed to improve student perception of the quality and relevance of labs. Our recommended practices therefore improve students' self-perceived learning and satisfaction with labs.[2]

The three sets of best practices we recommend in the remainder of this paper stand out from among many interventions we have attempted in meeting several criteria: (1) we have substantial longitudinal evidence to support their efficacy, (2) they generalize beyond the idiosyncrasies of our first-year discrete mathematics/digital logic course, and (3) they scale well to large courses.

1.1 Related Work

Deacon and Hajek [5] performed a six-semester study of student perceptions of the value of university physics labs. They found the four greatest factors on student perception were: pressure to complete labs within the allotted time, quality of the information in the written lab manuals, help provided by the teaching staff, and students' level of preparedness. Our work agrees with their findings: we found streamlining labs to reduce time pressure and clarify the written lab manuals and pre-lab work to be vitally important, as was effectively managing and preparing the teaching staff so they could be more effective in helping students.

[1]We define a closed lab as a structured problem-solving session in a university facility—usually with specialized equipment—that is: required, synchronous, collocated, and facilitated.

[2]Consistent with the literature on student perception of learning [6] and our own observations, we do not believe that these changes have negatively impacted student learning, but we have only anecdotal evidence of positive impact.

Permission to make digital or hard copies of all or part of this work for personal or classroom use is granted without fee provided that copies are not made or distributed for profit or commercial advantage and that copies bear this notice and the full citation on the first page. To copy otherwise, to republish, to post on servers or to redistribute to lists, requires prior specific permission and/or a fee.
SIGCSE'12, February 29–March 3, 2012, Raleigh, North Carolina, USA.
Copyright 2012 ACM 978-1-4503-1098-7/12/02 ...$10.00.

Iterative curriculum development has played a central role here. Jones [9] lists five conditions that promote and sustain changes in the curriculum, all of which are satisfied in our work: mutual trust amongst stake-holders; committed and consistent leadership; proceeding with a non-threatening, incremental pace of change; professional development for academic staff; and effective motivation of curriculum developers. The best practices presented in this paper pertain only to the first four of these conditions, and assume motivation for improving labs for students and teaching staff.

2. CONTEXT OF THE COURSE

Our first-year course at the University of British Columbia has a hybrid curriculum of discrete mathematics and digital logic. Lectures topics include finite state machines, propositional and predicate logic, proofs, and some digital logic; however, the labs focus on digital logic, both simulated and physical. The course is a pre-requisite to the second year theory and systems courses, and takes our CS1 as a co-requisite. Approximately 300 students take the course annually, mostly first-year CS students.

The weekly lab sessions are two-hours long, and capped at 25 students. A pair of teaching assistants (TAs) run each session. Labwork is divided into "pre-lab" work, to be completed before arriving at the lab and graded upon arrival, and "in-lab" work, to be completed during the lab session and graded as it is completed.[3].

The course is taught by 1–3 instructors and about 7–15 TAs. Roughly half the TAs are undergraduates who excelled in the course themselves. The remaining (graduate) TAs typically have strong backgrounds in discrete mathematics but weaker backgrounds in digital logic, particularly breadboarding. Together the authors (a TA and an instructor) were on the course staff during every term of our research except one.

3. OUR APPROACH TO THE LABS

In action research, we act simultaneously as designers, instructors, and assessors of the course. With our iterative approach, our curriculum development and assessment methodology evolve over time. As such, we give here a brief description of the key long-term structures responsible for curriculum development and assessment of the labs' success. Where iterative changes are important in later sections, we mention them explicitly.

We solicited formal and informal feedback from all involved stakeholders. We gather informal, ad hoc feedback through talking to students, TAs and instructors. Our formal instruments now include surveying students after each lab and at the end of the term, and surveying TAs at the end of the term. Additional supporting data came from instruments focused on other parts of the course, particularly the mid-term and final course evaluations. These observations are used to inform the next cycle of development of the research, following the action research process to cyclically plan, act, observe, and reflect [11].

The weekly surveys occur at the end of the labs. We began this in summer 2010, the fourth term of this project. Students rate the following on a 5-point Likert scale:

Q1: I had enough time to work on this lab.

Q2: The written instructions were clear and well-written.

Q3: The lab was relevant to the lecture material.

Q4-7: The lab was {interesting | challenging | rewarding | fun}.

Q8: The lab was an effective learning exercise.

And then there are two open-ended questions:

Q9: What did you like most about the lab?

Q10: How do you think the lab could be best improved?

The end of term surveys for the students and TAs are analogous, and ask about how the labs went over the full course of the term. We started these surveys in spring 2009. The questions for the students are:

Q1-3: The {labs | pre-labs | challenge questions} contributed to my understanding of the course material.

Q4: The labs were related to the rest of the course material.

Q5: The labs were marked fairly.

Q6-10: The labs were {interesting | challenging | rewarding | fun | well-organized}.

Q11-12: I liked working with the {Magic Box[4]|circuit simulator[5]}

After Q3, Q5, Q10 and Q12, students had open-ended comment boxes inviting them "Feel free to comment on any of the above questions:", to elaborate on how they had answered the quantitative questions. There are then three additional open-ended questions:

Q13: What were your {favourite|least favourite} labs? Why?

Q14: How well did the labs integrate into the lectures? Did the labs help you understand the lectures?

Q15: The labs were intended to be done in pairs. Did you work in a pair? A group of three? How was this for you?

Q16: Do you have any other comments or suggestions about the labs? Did you like them?

For the end of term TA survey, some questions were reworded to ask for their perception of how the students found the labs (e.g. "The labs contributed to my students' understanding of the course material"). At this time, TAs also annotate copies of the terms' labs, commenting on what went well and what should be changed for the next term. Revisiting the labs this way also focuses TAs' survey responses.

The weekly student surveys are analyzed on a weekly basis, with summaries made of the qualitative feedback. The end of term surveys are analyzed at the end of every term; quantitative trends are examined across terms, and qualitative feedback are encoded for comparison between terms.

4. LESSONS FOR EFFECTIVE LABS

In this section, we present three sets of lessons (best practices) for effective labs. We ground the lessons by describing how they arose in our practice and provide the evidence—both quantitative and qualitative—that convinced us of their importance.

[3]The labs also feature optional bonus questions at the end, called "challenge problems"

[4]the breadboarding kits

[5]Until the end of 2010: TKGate; afterwards: Logisim

4.1 Streamline Labs

Lesson: Streamline labs to reduce the extraneous load [4] of the students.

In the weekly student surveys, we found that whether students "had enough time to work on this lab" was a crucial factor in their satisfaction, a statistically significant predictor of how "fun", "interesting", and "rewarding" the lab would be perceived. To give students enough time on the labs, we streamlined them in several ways: crafting a usable grading scheme that makes the students' goals clear (section 4.1.1), clarifying and hewing to our own intended learning goals (section 4.1.2), and eliminating obstacles that contributed to none of these goals (section 4.1.3).

One change we made to the labs early in this process was to reduce their length: aiming for labs to take 100 minutes to complete in the two-hour lab sessions [14]. This shift reduced the stress on students and TAs, allowing them to focus on the lab at hand, rather than the pressures of time.

4.1.1 *Clarify the Grading Scheme*

Lesson: Design the grading scheme to be clear, public, and accepted by all stakeholders.

Unclear lab grading schemes are frustrating for students and correspond with increased attrition rates [12]. When we began our changes to the labs in 2008, the grading schemes for the labs were private to the TAs and heterogeneous across labs. Informal feedback from students and staff meeting comments from TAs indicated the scheme was unclear to both parties and disorganized; students wasted valuable lab time (theirs and the TAs') worrying about grading issues.

Thus, we began clearly marking required tasks in each lab by prefacing them with a bold "**TODO:**". We continued streamlining the grading scheme (in 2009) by standardizing on a single, public rubric for all labs.

In the new rubric, TAs graded students holistically, with the goal of promoting analysis and creativity in the labs, and had levels such as *"Students completed the lab with clear analysis that is consistent with their data... [and] show[ed] creativity and insight... that goes beyond expectations."* and *"Students completed some significant part of the lab ... On questioning by the TA about specific cases with incomplete work or rough analysis, the students indicate a plan for polishing the work given significantly more resources."*

However, TAs found the scheme difficult to interpret and apply consistently, and they pushed back strongly. Many TAs began grading for completion instead. This was a lesson for us: that all stakeholders *must* be involved and motivated in changes to the labs.

As a compromise between our goals and practical usability, six of the eight points in the labs are now for completion of the tasks labeled "**TODO:**" (including one point for the weekly survey); the other two points of eight remain targeted at analysis and creativity.

With continued feedback from students and TAs, these latter two points became more clearly defined, first as lists of suggested tasks and eventually as two "further analysis questions", each marked with a "**TODO (further analysis):**". These pose open-ended design and analytical questions about students' work. These questions require students to reflect on their work—such as comparing and contrasting circuit designs, thinking about applications of their work, or relating different concepts they had used.

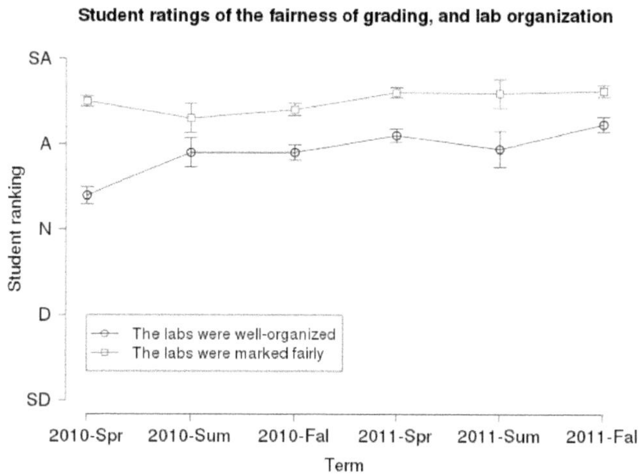

Figure 1: The holistic scheme was used in the first shown term; subsequent terms used the "further analysis question" approach and its revisions.

The further analysis questions fulfill our goals of promoting higher-level thinking in the lab by engaging students in analysis and design. They fit into the consistent format of the lab; making grading less subjective and more practical for TAs, and clear to students. TAs also indicate that they enjoy these "further analysis questions", as they lead to deeper discussions with students. And as shown in Figure 1, students rate the labs as more organized than in 2009, when we began with the analysis marks. More significantly, surveyed TAs now statistically significantly agree more with "I felt comfortable marking my students."

4.1.2 *Write the lab to its goals*

Lesson: In writing a lab, first decide the intended tasks of the lab. Then write the lab to support these tasks, avoiding interesting details that are irrelevant to the lab's goals.

An unexpected result of labeling all gradable tasks as one of "**TODO (pre-lab):**", "**TODO:**", or "**TODO (further analysis):**" was to shift our lab design paradigm to a goal-oriented one, a long-advocated but oft-overlooked style [15, 7]. When writing new labs, or revising old ones, we began to write our labs by *first* deciding what each of the ten TODO tasks should be – and *then* writing up the rest of the lab to support those tasks.

A result of the new goal-oriented design was labs that were more focused, and more streamlined. We produced labs with less text, particularly "seductive detail": i.e. material that is interesting but not relevant to the instructional goal. It was thus clearer to students what was expected of them, and these expectations were better scaffolded [14]. Indeed, work in the education literature has shown us that "seductive detail" decreases learning [10].

As we reduce text, we have found it valuable to illustrate the labs with more figures and sometimes links to helpful animations. The increased use of diagrams has been particularly helpful for our students with poor English comprehension skills, traditionally the weakest group of students in the labs. To help this group, we have also used readability indices as a guide for improving either entire labs, or sections of labs, for readability. End of term survey data from the TAs on "the labs were well-written" has had statistically significant improvement since 2009.

With less text in the lab manuals, we also began adding whitespace after each TODO task for students to fill in their own work. We have been generous in the amount of whitespace we give students, and have found that they appreciate having enough space to do their work in the manual directly. We have also made a point of making the whitespace proportional to the amount of work expected for the TODO task, further communicating our expectations to the students.

We also worked to cut extraneous activities. We previously reported trying "discussion periods" to encourage group discussion in each lab section [14], but we later cut these due to the amount of time they required.

4.1.3 Reduce Extraneous Difficulties

Lesson: With each lab's goals identified, you can now search for, and defuse, the sources of greatest pain for students that are unconnected to your goals.

Just as we worked to reduce extraneous *words* in the lab writeup [14], we have also begun focusing on reducing extraneous *difficulties*. We now regularly search out and address sources of "pain" for students that do not advance our learning goals. We discover these problems from students—who are vocal about problematic elements in survey responses and informal discussions, sometimes about difficulties that contribute little to learning—and from TAs—who we ask weekly about particular or unusual difficulties students have.

Central to our efforts has been to improve the lab equipment and its management: a breadboarding kit known as "The Magic Box" and a circuit simulator.

As we have described previously, students initially bought their "Magic Boxes", but we switched to lab-owned and managed kits [14]. Our survey data now show a dramatic positive shift in student perception. Rather than wanting to get (and feeling disappointed for not getting) their "money's worth", students were free to enjoy breadboarding for what it was. In student surveys, the visual, immediate feedback of the "blinking lights" is a commonly praised by the students.

We saw a similar shift in 2010 when we changed circuit simulators from TKGate [2] to Logisim [1]. As shown in Figure 2[6], TKGate was not very popular, particularly in comparison to the Magic Box. With the switch to Logisim in 2010W2, we saw a dramatic jump in student ratings of the circuit simulator. Both students and TAs prefer Logisim for its better usability, pared-down interface, and compatibility with multiple operating systems.

We are now looking at improving the breadboarding experience. Students often complain of the difficulty of reading the labels on the 74LS series chips, particularly when they search through boxes of unsorted chips. We plan to simplify this by painting over the most commonly used chips' labels to colour-code them. Presently, we do this for an early lab exercise, where students are given "mystery chips" with the labels painted over, and they are tasked with identifying the chips. Afterwards, the students have a tendency to hoard

[6]For more of our data, see `http://www.cs.toronto.edu/~patitsas/sigcse/sigcse2012_appendix.html`

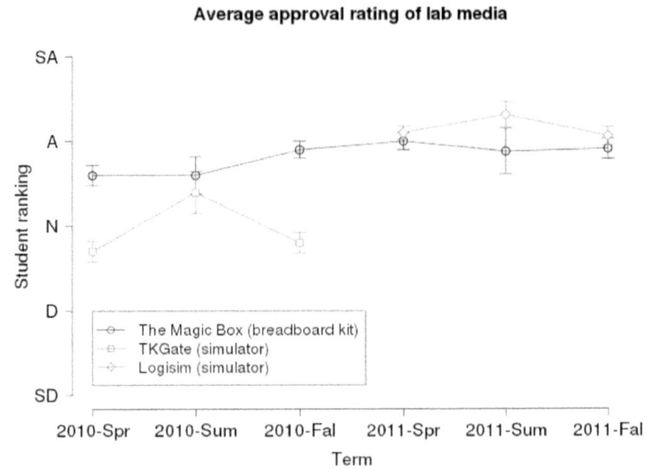

Figure 2: End of term student survey responses to "I liked working with the {Magic Box|circuit simulator}", showing a jump from TKGate to Logisim.

the painted chips for use in later labs, finding these easier to use than the provided magnifying glasses!

4.2 Making a Positive First Impression

Lesson: Identify and reduce extraneous complexity in the earlier weeks, allowing students to focus on the tasks at hand.

Student and TA feedback indicated the importance of making the first lab of the term welcoming to students, setting an expectation that labs would be fun, creative, and exploratory. As we noted in previous work [14], we had introduced a scaled-down version of the last lab—an exploration of a working CPU simulation—as the first lab of the term, with the aim of telling an overarching story in the course. Unfortunately, we found that a fully functional CPU in the first lab overwhelmed students.

Based on TA feedback, we tried moving the introductory lab on the CPU to the second week, returning the first lab of the term to being an introduction to basic logic gates. Complaints continued about the introductory CPU lab even after pushing it back a week – one TA wrote that *"[My least favourite lab was] CPU simulation, lab 3 or 4. very vague and students didn't know what they're doing."*

From discussions with students and TAs, it emerged that the problem was the overwhelming nature of a complete CPU. Working with TAs, we produced a stripped-down version of an ALU, as shown in Figure 3. Students still got a taste of the story of the course, and this version has gotten no complaints from students in the after-lab survey unlike previous terms, where it was a common student complaint.

Meanwhile, our first lab of the term, that on basic logic gates, was getting complaints that it did not give them enough training in how to use the breadboards, nor was a gentle enough introduction. For example, one TA wrote in the end of term survey, *"debugging huge magic box circuits was no fun. we could spend some time in the first a couple of labs to make sure students learn how to build circuits step by step. Perhaps, we can have an example circuit building step by step guide."* – and student feedback agreed: *"Make the*

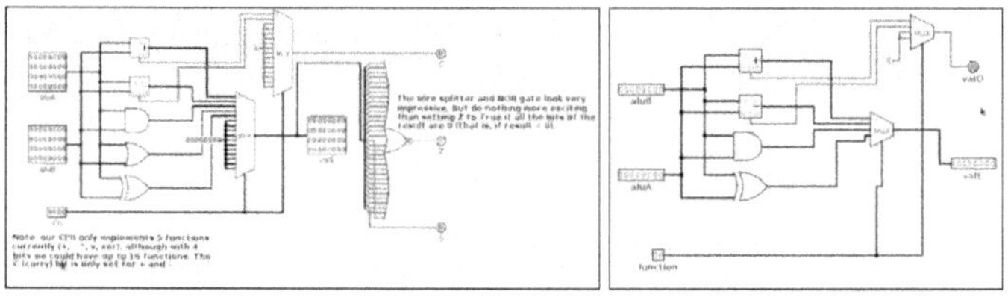

Figure 3: On the left, the complex Y86 ALU module from spring 2010; on the right, the pared down ALU from summer 2010. Both are too small to read details but still illustrate why the former was too confusing for students early in their first term.

labs more accessible, as in, try teaching with simpler circuits and approaches. The current labs are like following a step by step instruction of an overly complex manual which you can follow but not understand." The students had a clear preference for starting off breadboarding, since as one student wrote, *"The Magic Box is very tactile and rewarding."*

After an extended conversation about this with a few students, the lab coordinator wrote up a new introductory lab, giving students a gentler learning curve, illustrating most key steps with photos, and harnessing the students' motivation to play with the oft-praised "blinking LEDs". The new lab also featured an icebreaker activity, and greater opportunities for students to collaborate in the lab.

After adding the newer, gentler introduction to breadboarding in fall 2010, we saw a noticeable improvement in how students ranked the breadboarding kits, as shown in Figure 2. TA feedback is that students are now more comfortable with breadboarding, although work remains on how to better equip our students with debugging skills. Student feedback about the lab was overwhelmingly positive: *"I really liked the introduction and the ice breaker as we got to know the TA's and the other students in the class. I also liked learning how to use the clock to control LED's"* and *"[My favourite part was] Bread boarding. I enjoyed wiring up our own system of flashing lights."*

4.3 Improving Organization of TAs

Lesson: Prepare TAs together to establish a consistent level of preparation, and a community of support amongst the teaching staff.

As noted in previous work, we have found it critical to hold weekly meetings of the lab TAs—separate from our full staff meetings—wherein they complete the upcoming lab as if they were students and discuss how they plan to teach it [14]. Our analysis of TA and student survey data now reinforces the importance of this decision. As one TA noted in the TA survey, *"the lab TA meetings shortened the amount of prep time I needed to prepare for each lab"*—useful for managing the limited hours TAs have to work. These meetings ensure all TAs prepare to at least a consistent, sufficient level.

Furthermore, better-prepared TAs need less time to figure out complications or difficult problems in the lab and more time facilitating students' work. The community that the weekly lab TA meetings foster is hugely important for knowledge transfer between TAs, not only improving the teaching experience for them, but giving them support to grow as teachers. This supports greater "pull transfer" between TAs, which is known to be more important in knowledge transfer between educators [8].

The TAs were overall quite satisfied, and in the TA survey, would readily provide examples of enjoying themselves. Some examples include: *"Definitely challenging, and a large amount of work, but rewarding after having talked to some of the students at the end of the term."* and *"It was fun to build the counter[7] in two different ways, and comparing the two really helped the students' understanding."*

The lab TA meetings initially lasted one hour per week but later expanded to an hour and a half. Meetings early in the term often stretch to two hours to accommodate the greater training overhead. Even with the expanded time-slot, some TAs remain hungry for longer meetings; e.g. *"I would have liked more discussion on the further analysis questions in the lab meetings."* Practically, however, we recognize the need to achieve the goals of these expensive—in staff time—meetings efficiently and see this as future work.

Another lesson we learned painfully was that the instructors must communicate the vital importance and *mandatory* nature of these meetings early to lab TAs. Before we made this a matter of routine, absenteeism was a problem, but the lab coordinator (always a TA for us, and often an undergraduate TA) lacked the authority to enforce attendance. On the other hand, the intentional absence of the *instructors* at these sessions—besides saving instructor time—also encouraged TAs to provide candid feedback that never arose at full staff meetings.

Since refining the process of running the weekly meetings, we have found the course to run more smoothly for TAs and instructors, and students rate the labs as being more organized in the end-of-term surveys. As we see in Figure 1, students rate "The labs were well-organized" statistically significantly higher now. Furthermore, the end of term TA surveys have had significant gains in how interesting and fun they find the labs, how useful they find the meetings, and how comfortable they feel marking their students.

4.3.1 *Improve Organization* for *TAs*

Lesson: Establish a development cycle which is iterative, and incorporates feedback from all stakeholders in the course.

TA preparation is doomed to failure when the labs themselves are ill-prepared. We have therefore established a careful intra- and inter-term cycle of preparation and development on the labs. At the intra-term level, the timeline is driven by the need to post the lab manual at least one week in advance of the first lab session that uses it, so that students can practically complete the pre-lab work and to communicate that the pre-lab requirement is serious. At the inter-term level, we incorporate feedback from students, TAs, and instructors into iterative improvements in each lab and the arc of the labs as a whole.

A TA in the role of "lab coordinator" manages the curriculum development cycle. We have established a repository of documents for the coordinator to aide in this process: two—one aimed at planning development and one at managing TAs—lay out key tasks and timelines, and a third documents the history of feedback and comments on labs. The coordinator also updates these documents each term.

[7] A type of digital circuit used for counting.

The cycle of development and management proceeds as follows. Students write a short survey about their impressions of the lab as they complete it. At the next lab TA meeting, the lab coordinator debriefs the TAs about the lab[8]. The lab coordinator uses these data and their own notes when redrafting the lab for the next term. The coordinator sends an early draft to the instructor, for feedback and to ensure the lab is in harmony with the instructor's vision for the course[9]. Next, at the weekly lab meeting, the TAs give feedback that leads to further revisions, which both improves the lab and gives the TAs a sense of ownership. To accommodate that revision cycle, the meeting is two weeks before the lab is first used, or one week before the deadline for posting the lab. Students then write the lab, and the cycle begins again. Any given lab meeting sits at two points on this cycle: prospective and retrospective.

5. CONCLUSIONS

After 3.5 years of action research on this course, we have learnt three sets of generalizable lessons about the management and teaching of closed laboratories. Our changes have statistically significantly improved student perception of the labs, including self-reported learning. Further, the lab teaching assistants also report higher satisfaction and better preparation to teach the labs.

The first set of lessons is *to streamline the labs to reduce the extraneous load on the students.* This includes cutting down lab manuals in terms of words, particularly "seductive detail". In writing a lab, first identify its goals and the tasks to satisfy them. Then, write the rest of the lab instructions to support those goals, avoiding extraneous detail. Having identified the goals in each lab, search for and defuse the sources of greatest pain for students that are unconnected to those goals. Design the grading scheme to guide students' work toward the labs' goals; to admit clear and consistent interpretation by all stakeholders (students, TAs, and instructors); and to be acceptable in practice by those stakeholders. And, as with other elements of the course, eliminate extraneous complexity in grading.

Our second group of lessons is *to particularly target the earlier weeks* to start students and TAs on better footing and establish the desired atmosphere in the labs. Start students off gently—for us, introducing the equipment—in a way that promotes creativity and exploration. We found specifically that previewing the full story of the course early in the term could work, but only with aggressive simplification and careful attention to student motivation.

Our final set of lessons was *to effectively manage the teaching staff.* Prepare TAs together every week, creating a community of support for the teaching staff. This intra-term cycle of preparation can also form an integral part of the inter-term curriculum development cycle. Between terms, establish an iterative development cycle that incorporates feedback from all stakeholders in the course, ensuring long-term buy-in and success of curriculum development efforts.

6. ACKNOWLEDGMENTS

We would like to thank all the students, TAs, lab coordinators, and instructors associated with this course over the course of this project. Our work would not be possible without their feedback and participation. The first author was funded partly by the CS Science Education Initiative, and the Natural Sciences and Engineering Research Council.

[8]The lab coordinator also runs one or more labs for first-hand experience and to get informal feedback from students.
[9]The draft is often accompanied by advice about how to link the course of the labs to the course of the lectures.

7. REFERENCES

[1] Logisim. http://ozark.hendrix.edu/ burch/logisim/.

[2] TKGate. http://www.tkgate.org.

[3] D. E. Comer, D. Gries, M. C. Mulder, A. Tucker, A. J. Turner, and P. R. Young. Computing as a discipline. *Commun. ACM*, 32:9–23, January 1989.

[4] T. de Jong. Cognitive load theory, educational research, and instructional design: some food for thought. *Instructional Science*, 38:105–134, 2010. 10.1007/s11251-009-9110-0.

[5] C. Deacon and A. Hajek. Student perceptions of the value of physics laboratories. *International Journal of Science Education*, 33(7):943–977, 2011.

[6] D. Dunning, K. Johnson, J. Ehrlinger, and J. Kruger. Why people fail to recognize their own incompetence. *Current Directions in Psychological Science*, 12(3):83–87, 2003.

[7] A. Fekete and A. Greening. Designing closed laboratories for a computer science course. *SIGCSE Bull.*, 28:295–299, March 1996.

[8] S. Fincher and J. Tenenberg. Warren's question. In *Proceedings of the third international workshop on Computing education research*, ICER '07, pages 51–60, New York, NY, USA, 2007. ACM.

[9] E. A. Jones. Special issue: Transforming the curriculum: Preparing students for a changing world. *ASHE-ERIC Higher Education Report*, 29(3):1–101, 2002.

[10] R. E. Mayer, E. Griffith, I. T. N. Jurkowitz, and D. Rothman. Increased interestingness of extraneous details in a multimedia science presentation leads to decreased learning. *Journal of experimental psychology Applied*, 14(4):329–339, 2008.

[11] R. O'Brien. An overview of the methodological approach of action research. *Theory and Practice of Action Research*, 1998. English version.

[12] C. O'Neal, M. Wright, C. Cook, T. Perorazio, and J. Purkiss. The impact of teaching assistants on student retention in the sciences: Lessons for TA training. *Journal of College Science Teaching*, 36(5):24–29, 2007.

[13] B. C. Parker and J. D. McGregor. A goal-oriented approach to laboratory development and implementation. In *Proceedings of the twenty-sixth SIGCSE technical symposium on Computer science education*, SIGCSE '95, pages 92–96, New York, NY, USA, 1995. ACM.

[14] E. Patitsas, K. Voll, M. Crowley, and S. Wolfman. Circuits and logic in the lab: toward a coherent picture of computation. In *WCCCE '10: Proceedings of the 15th Western Canadian Conference on Computing Education*, pages 1–5, New York, NY, USA, 2010. ACM.

[15] B. E. Walvoord, V. J. Anderson, T. A. Angelo, and V. J. Anderson. *Effective Grading: A Tool for Learning and Assessment.* Jossey-Bass, 1998.

What Do Students Learn About Programming From Game, Music Video, And Storytelling Projects?

Joel C. Adams Andrew R. Webster
Department of Computer Science
Calvin College
Grand Rapids, MI 49546
1-616-526-8666

{adams, arw7}@calvin.edu

ABSTRACT

Drag-and-drop learning environments like Alice (*alice.org*) and Scratch (*scratch.mit.edu*) eliminate syntax errors, making them attractive as ways to introduce programming concepts to students. Alice is closely associated with storytelling, Scratch was designed for creating music videos, and both can be used to create games. Having had students create each kind of project, we began to wonder: Do students learn different things creating games compared to music videos or stories? What programming constructs do students actually *use* (and hence learn well enough to be able to *apply*)? To answer these questions, we conducted a quantitative analysis of a collection of over 300 different student projects created using these tools. In examining different kinds of projects, we found significant differences in how frequently the students creating those projects used variables, if statements, loops, and dialog constructs.

Categories and Subject Descriptors

D.2.6 [**Software**]: Programming Environments – *graphical environments, integrated environments*; D.3.3 [**Programming Languages**]: Language Constructs – *control structures*; K.3.2 [**Computers and Education**]: Computer and Information Science Education – *computer science education.*

General Terms

Design, Experimentation, Human Factors, Languages.

Keywords

Alice, games, genres, music videos, projects, Scratch, storytelling.

1. INTRODUCTION

Each July since 2003, the lead author has directed the Imaginary Worlds Camps, an outreach effort designed to introduce middle and high school students to basic programming concepts. Campers were expected to arrive at camp with a computing project in mind, which the camp helped them bring to fruition.

Permission to make digital or hard copies of all or part of this work for personal or classroom use is granted without fee provided that copies are not made or distributed for profit or commercial advantage and that copies bear this notice and the full citation on the first page. To copy otherwise, or republish, to post on servers or to redistribute to lists, requires prior specific permission and/or a fee.
SIGCSE'12, February 29–March 3, 2012, Raleigh, North Carolina, USA. Copyright 2012 ACM 978-1-4503-1098-7/12/02...$10.00.

From 2003-2007, we used Alice [4] as our teaching environment. Campers were told they would be creating a computer-generated movie, so they should bring a story they wanted to animate [1].

From 2008-2011, we used Scratch [7] as our teaching environment. Campers were told they could create a music video or game: If they wanted to create a video, they were to bring a song to the camp; to create game, they were to bring an idea for their game. The vast majority of our students – male and female – chose to create games rather than music videos [2].

One of the goals of our outreach was to introduce these students to the basic concepts of programming, so that these concepts would be familiar if they subsequently took an AP or college CS course. (Another goal was to make it *fun* so that these students *would* subsequently take an AP or college CS course.) We therefore kept our camp syllabus quite consistent through the years, showing the students how to use each tool's abstraction mechanism, variables, types, expressions, loop statements, if statements, and other basic features. Students thus received instruction in the same basic concepts regardless of which year they attended the camp.

However, as we shifted from storytelling projects to (mostly) game projects, we noticed that the campers were asking different questions than before. For example, with storytelling projects, students rarely (if ever) needed to know how an if statement worked or how to construct a Boolean expression. But with game projects, virtually every student seemed to need to know about such topics. It seemed as though game projects were forcing the students to apply programming language concepts that the storytelling (and music video) projects did not.

Bloom's Taxonomy [3] differentiates several different levels of understanding. The lowest three levels can be summarized as:

1. *Knows.* The student can recall or recognize information, ideas, and principles in the approximate form they were learned.
2. *Comprehends.* The student can comprehend, translate, or interpret information based on prior learning.
3. *Applies.* The student can select, transfer, and use data and principles to solve a problem or task with minimal direction.

One of the strengths of project-based learning is that it forces students to move from the first level of merely "knowing" concepts through the second level of comprehension and on to the third level of being able to use and *apply* those concepts – a deeper level of understanding than mere "book learning".

Games, music videos, and storytelling projects can be thought of as different genres of projects, or *project-genres*. Since the works in different literary genres can have different characteristics, we decided to perform a quantitative analysis of our students' projects, to see if there were indeed significant differences in the frequency with which our students applied different programming language constructs in different project-genres

Our study differs from previous studies in a variety of ways. [5] performed a coarse-grained analysis of the projects from the Scratch website. [6] compared Scratch to Logo using student surveys rather than the programs they wrote. [8] studied a group of Scratch programs and compared their structures to accepted computer science practice. Our work differs from these works by performing a fine-grained analysis of the programming constructs used in student projects from across different project-genres.

2. PROCEDURE

From 2004-2011, a total of 322 students attended our camps and created projects. Of these projects, 209 were Alice 2.0 story-telling projects, 103 were Scratch 1.4 game projects, and 10 were Scratch 1.4 music video projects.

We studied these projects in three steps:

1. We recorded research questions in which we were interested.
2. We collected the data needed to answer our questions by counting measurable properties of the projects.
3. We analyzed the data collected in step 2, testing for statistical significance.

In the rest of this section, we detail steps 2 and 3. To avoid presenting them twice, we present our research questions in section 3, along with our results.

2.1 Data Collection

To answer our research questions, we began by constructing a spreadsheet to store the properties of our students' projects. In this spreadsheet, we created entries for each student project containing the age of its creator and his/her gender, its genre (game, music video, or storytelling), and entries for each language construct being counted. These included:

- variable declarations
- if statements
- loop statements: both counting loops (e.g., for loops) and more general condition-controlled loops (e.g., while loops)
- subprogram definitions: user-defined methods in Alice, and *when I receive <message>* stacks in Scratch

We also counted the invocations of certain predefined animation constructs that both Alice and Scratch provide, such as *move* commands, *wait* commands, and dialog commands (e.g., *say* or *think*). We also counted some specific objects that are commonly used in Alice projects, such as fire animations.

Collecting this data from 322 projects was a formidable challenge, so we wrote a variety of scripts to automate the collection of the process, plus unit tests and test files to validate those scripts.

Writing these scripts introduced several challenges. For example, different projects were of different lengths, so to make our comparisons fair, we normalized our results by computing the number of occurrences of each construct per 100 lines of code in a given project. Challenges specific to Alice projects included:

- Each Alice world, its methods, its objects, their methods, etc. are stored in a plethora of XML files. Rather than recreate Alice's entire XML schema to parse these files, we found it easier to open a project and use Alice's *File > Export Code For Printing* mechanism to dump its methods to a single HTML file, which we could then easily process with a script.
- Some Alice objects contain non-standard but predefined methods that are difficult to distinguish from user-defined subprograms. Fortunately, the Alice Gallery lists each object's predefined non-standard methods, and the *Export Code For Printing* operation let us choose which methods to print, so we were able to use this mechanism to only export methods defined by our students.

Challenges specific to Scratch projects included:

- Scratch files store some attributes in binary format and other attributes in text format. To determine this structure, we had to delve into Scratch's source code and trace the logic of the methods it used to read in a Scratch project. Since Scratch is written in Squeak (see *squeak.org*), this was nontrivial.
- Scratch's *(shift) File > Write Project Summary* and *File > Write Multiple Project Summaries* mechanisms provide useful statistics about a given Scratch project, including counts of the number of sprites, the number of stage costumes, the number of occurrences of a particular block, and so on. But they do not provide a count of variables used in the project, so we modified Scratch's (Squeak) code to also provide this information.

Once we had solved each challenge, we used our scripts to collect the data needed to answer our research questions.

2.2 Data Analysis

Our scripts generated the raw data needed to answer our research questions. For example, to compare the number of if statements used in games to the number of if statements used in music videos, one script generated a list of the numbers of if statements used in each game project, and another script generated a list of the numbers of if statements used in each music video project.

To determine whether the differences in the resulting lists were statistically significant, we used the statistical tools in Excel's *Data Analysis* package to perform unmatched T-tests on the lists.

3. RESULTS AND DISCUSSION

In this section, we present our research questions and the answers we were able to find. In each case, we formulated a null hypothesis and tried to reject it. For example, when investigating whether there were significant differences in the number of variables used in the different kinds of projects (see section 3.1), our null hypothesis was that there would be no significant difference in the number of variables used in gaming projects, music video projects, or story-telling projects.

Where many studies use a p-value of 0.05 as a threshold for statistical significance, we chose a stronger threshold of 0.01, to increase the confidence levels of our conclusions.

3.1 Variable Declarations

We were interested in seeing if there were significant differences in the numbers of variables used in the different project-genres. In Alice, we counted both local variable and parameter declarations; in Scratch, we counted both local and global variables. Figure 1 shows the normalized average number of variable declarations in each kind of project:

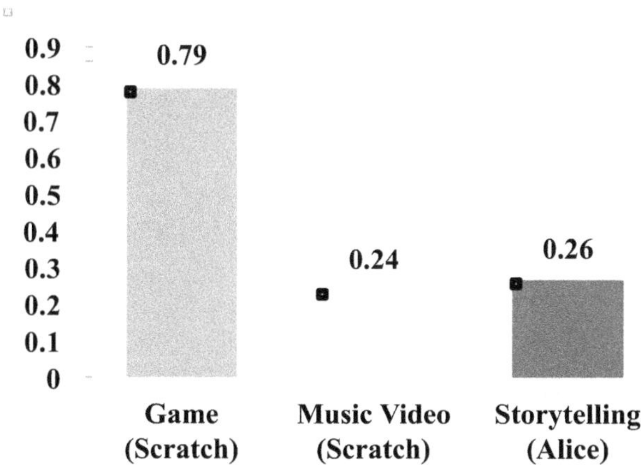

Figure 1. Variable Declarations Per 100 Lines of Code

Students doing game projects declared significantly more variables than music video projects ($p = 5.4e\text{-}7$) or storytelling projects ($p = 1.54e\text{-}7$). There was no significant difference in the number of variables used in music video projects compared to storytelling projects ($p = 0.71$).

Since not all projects used variables, we also examined what percentage of each kind of project used them. Figure 2 shows the percentage of each kind of project that declared at least 1 variable:

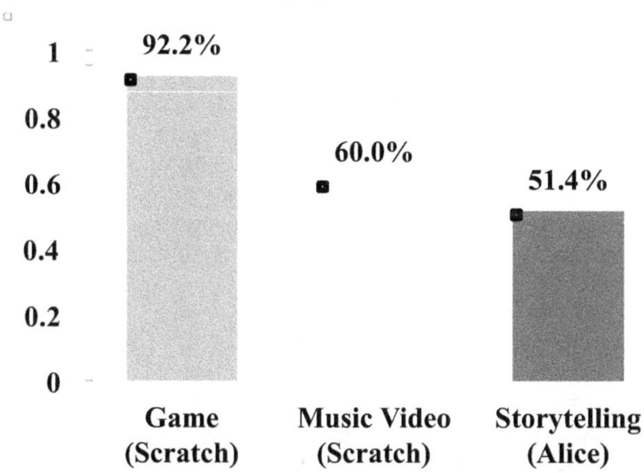

Figure 2. Percentage of Projects Using Variables

Although the chart shows a 32.2% difference between gaming projects and music video projects, this difference was not significant ($p = 0.082$). As mentioned previously, just 10 of 113 scratch projects were music videos, so this is likely due to our small sample size of music videos.

However, we did find that significantly more students used variables when creating game projects, compared to those creating storytelling projects ($p = 2.095e\text{-}18$).

The difference in variable use between music videos and storytelling projects was not significant ($p = 0.629$).

These results suggest that gaming is the best of these three project-genres for teaching students about variables. The reason is that for many games, the game must *remember* specific information (e.g., the player's score, a character's health, and so on), naturally motivating the use of variables. Our results suggest there is less need for such "remembering" in music video and storytelling projects.

3.2 If Statements

We were also interested in seeing if there were significant differences in the number of if statements used in the different projects-genres. Figure 3 shows the normalized average number of if statements in each kind of project:

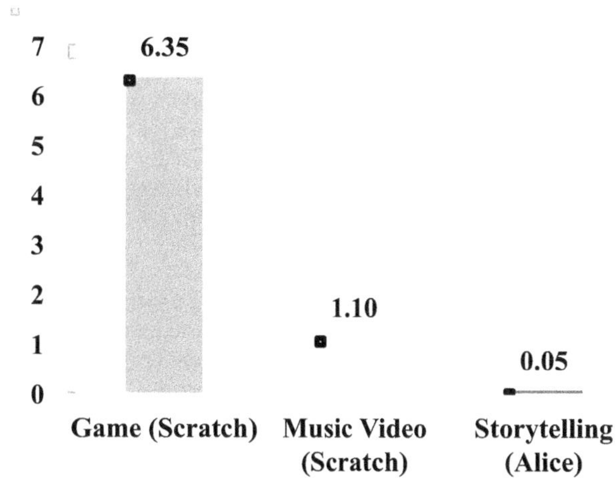

Figure 3. If Statements Per 100 Lines of Code

We found that students creating game projects declared significantly more if statements than students doing music videos ($p = 1.25e\text{-}7$) or storytelling projects ($p = 7.09e\text{-}37$). Students also used more if statements when creating music videos than when creating storytelling projects, but this difference was not significant ($p = 0.070$); again, likely due to small sample size.

We did not find this pattern to be surprising, as most music videos and stories have a linear narrative structure in which the branching behavior provided by an if statement is less useful. (So-called "Choose Your Own Adventure" stories are an exception, since they have a non-linear, interactive structure.) By contrast, games are full of conditional logic that define how gameplay unfolds (e.g., If Pac Man is touching a ghost ...).

3.3 Loop Statements

We also wanted to see if there were significant differences in the numbers of loop statements used in the different project-genres. Figure 4 shows the normalized average number of loop statements in each kind of project:

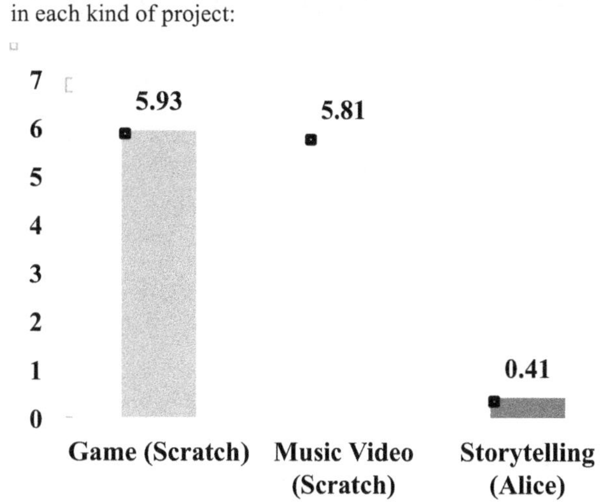

Figure 4. Loop Statements Per 100 Lines of Code

We found no significant difference in the number of loop statements used in game projects compared to music videos (p = 0.951); however there were significant differences between games and storytelling projects (p = 1.1e-5), and music videos and storytelling projects (p = 0.0064).

This high use of loops in music videos was quite surprising, as our previous results had led us to expect that music videos would be more similar to storytelling projects than games. In looking over the projects, it appears that the kinds of animations used in music videos (e.g., characters dancing to the music) tend to repeat the same movements, motivating the use of loops. By contrast, the kinds of animations used in storytelling projects tend to follow a linear storyline, in which repetition is less useful.

3.4 Subprograms

Since abstraction is such an important part of programming, we originally planned to compare the extent to which students used abstraction in game, music video, and storytelling projects.

However, the abstraction mechanisms in Alice and Scratch are quire different. Where Alice 2 provides fully parameterized methods, Scratch 1.4 provides message broadcasts and handlers for those messages. As we reflected on these differences, we felt it was impossible to do a fair comparison of the two mechanisms. We therefore limited our analysis to game vs. music video projects; we did not find any significant differences (p = 0.25) in average number of subprograms in these projects.

3.5 Program Length

We also compared the lengths of the different kinds of projects, in terms of the total lines of code. Figure 5 presents our results:

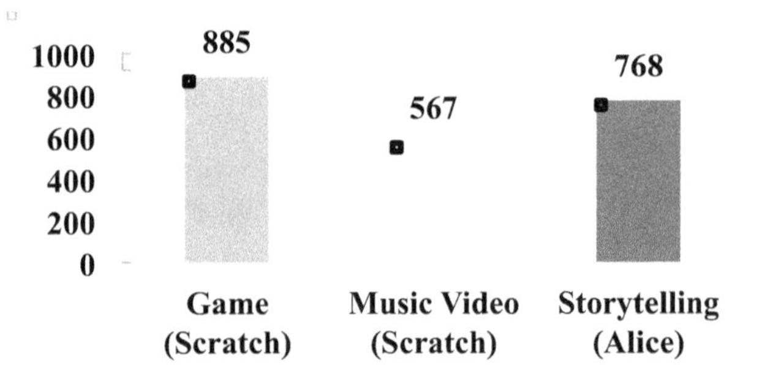

Figure 5. Average Project Length (Lines of Code)

As can be seen, game projects are on average the longest. The difference between games and music videos is significant (p = 0.0014). However, the difference between games and storytelling projects was not significant (p = 0.083); nor was the difference between music videos and storytelling projects (p = 0.136).

From this, we conclude that students find all three of these kinds of projects sufficiently motivating to write lengthy projects. Music videos may be shorter because they tend to be simpler than games; and compared to storytelling projects, more of their behaviors can be achieved using loops, as discussed in section 3.3.

3.6 Dialog

Both Alice and Scratch provide *say* and *think* constructs that display a character's speech and thoughts, respectively. We found significant differences in how often these messages get used in the different project-genres, as shown in Figure 6:

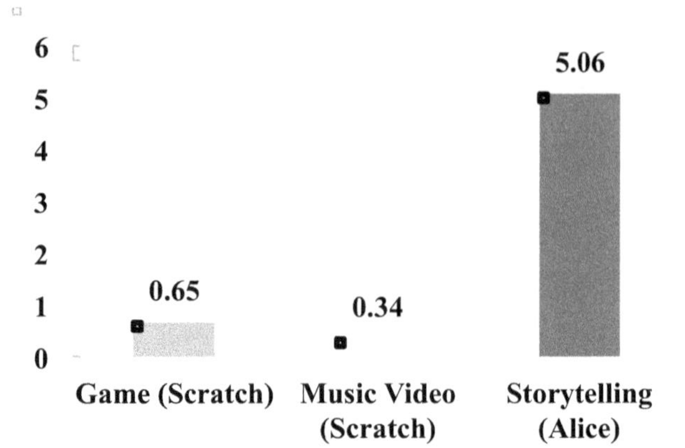

Figure 6. *Say* + *Think* Constructs Per 100 Lines of Code

Figure 6 shows that students creating storytelling projects employ much more dialog than students creating games or music videos. These differences were significant, as shown in Table 1:

Table 1. Significance of Differences in Figure 6

Dialog Difference In...	P-Value	Significant?
Games vs. Music Videos	0.392	No
Games vs. Storytelling	**1.1e-46**	**Yes**
Music Videos vs. Storytelling	**8.24e-10**	**Yes**

These differences are noteworthy: where dialog makes up less than 1% of the statements in games and music videos, it makes up over 5% of the statements in storytelling projects. When one considers that a student must also type the string a character is saying or thinking – one of the few times a student must type in Alice or Scratch – this suggests that students creating story-telling projects spend non-trivial amounts of time creating dialog

3.7 Age Differences

We examined whether age made any difference in the complexity of our students' projects. For younger students (11 and 12) vs. older students (13 and 14), we examined the number of variables, if statements, loop statements, subprograms, objects (in Alice) or sprites (in Scratch), and lines of code used in each kind of project. Of these, the only significant difference was that in Alice projects, older students used more lines of code than younger students (p = 4.15e-5), as shown in Figure 7:

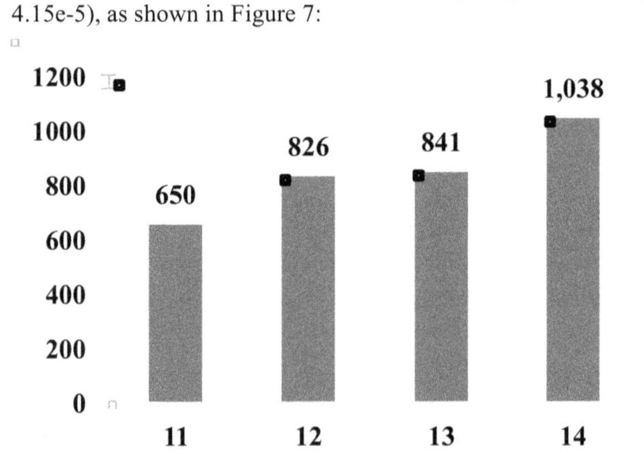

Figure 7. Lines of Code in Alice Projects by Age

We had expected older students' projects to differ from younger students' projects in more ways than project length.

Another age-related finding was that in gaming projects, older students used Scratch's *pick random number* block significantly more than younger students (p = 0.0083), as seen in Figure 8:

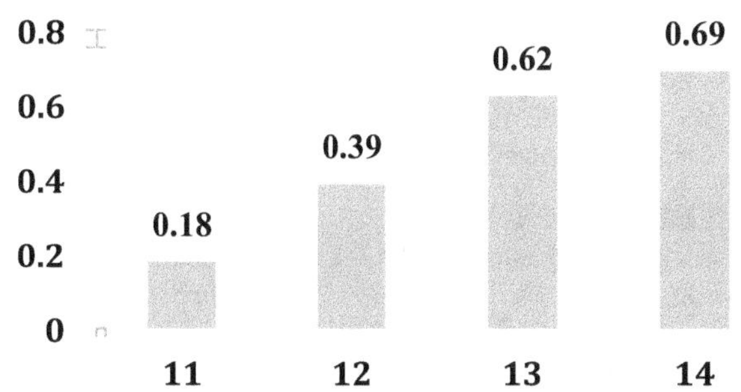

Figure 8. Use of *pick random* Per 100 Lines of Code by Age

We taught our Scratch students about randomness as a way to make games less predictable. Figure 8 suggests that our students' ability to actually make use of this concept of randomness improved with their age.

3.8 Gender Differences

We compared boys' and girls' projects using a number of metrics, including the number of variables, the number of if statements, the number of loop statements, the number of subprograms, the number of objects or sprites, and the number of lines of code per project. There were differences: e.g., boys' projects had more lines of code on average than girls' projects; however, none of these differences were statistically significant.

Three areas where we found statistically significant differences were (in Scratch) the choice of looping constructs; and (in Alice) the number of *say* messages and the number of fire animations.

3.8.1 Choice of Loops

As we saw in section 3.3, the students creating games and music videos used more loops than the students creating storytelling projects. Since Scratch provides four different kinds of loops, we decided to see if there were any gender preferences for these loops. Figure 9 shows what we discovered:

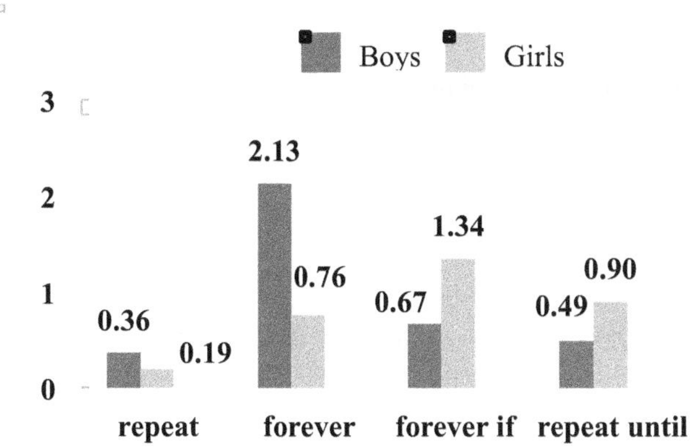

Figure 9. Loops Per 100 Lines of Scratch Code by Loop Type

Note that boys used the conceptually simpler loops (*repeat n times* and *forever*) more frequently, while girls used the conditional loops (*forever if* and *repeat until*). These latter loops are more complex because they require the construction of Boolean expressions. We speculate that the girls might be using the more sophisticated loops more frequently because girls are typically developmentally ahead of boys at these ages.

Of these four different loop statements, only the difference in boys' vs. girls' use of the *forever* loop was statistically significant, as can be seen in Table 2:

Table 2. Gender Preference Significance in Figure 9

Loop	Boys vs. Girls P-Value	Significant?
repeat n times	0.276	No
forever	**2.4e-7**	**Yes**
forever if	0.082	No
repeat until	0.109	No

3.8.2 Use of Dialog Messages

During our Alice camps, it appeared to us that our girls' stories featured more dialog than our boys' stories, so we counted the number of *say* and *think* messages each used. Figure 10 presents the normalized averages for each gender:

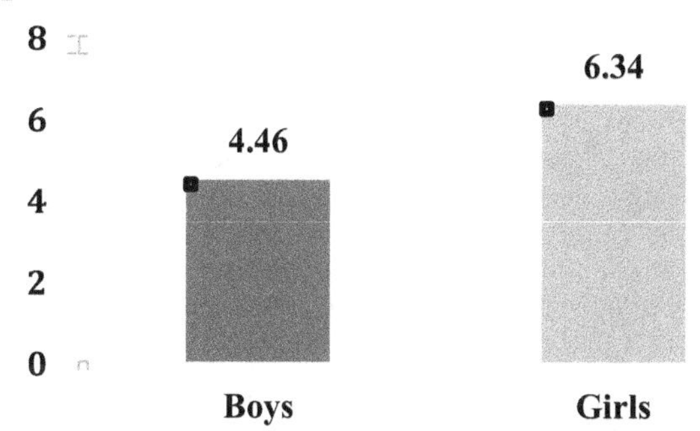

Figure 10. Dialog Messages Per 100 Lines of Alice Code

This difference was significant (p = 3.67e-5); girls' used significantly more dialog in their stories than boys.

3.8.3 Use of Fire Animations

In teaching students to use Alice, we never demonstrated fire animations. However, they seemed to be very popular so we decided to count them. Figure 11 presents the results of this count:

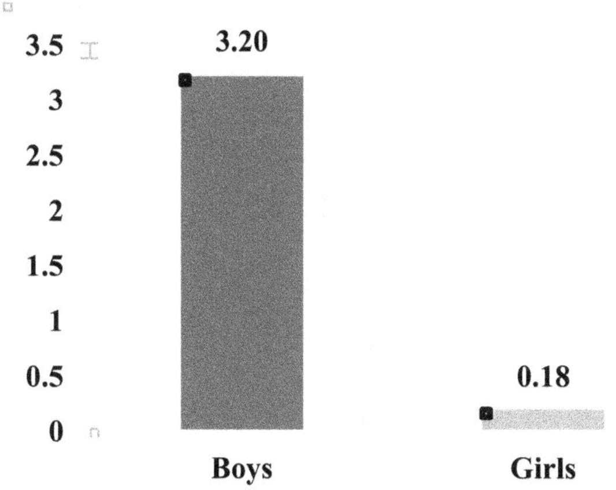

Figure 11. Average Fire Animations Per Alice Project

The average boys' story has more than three fire animations; the average girls' story has nearly zero. This significant difference (p = 1.81e-9), suggests further differences in what story elements boys and girls find interesting: most fire animations represented explosions or similar events associated with "action" movies.

Regardless of whether one attributes these differences to nature or nurture, Figures 10 and 11 imply that the genders differ markedly in the kinds of stories they find appealing. Even at these young ages, boys favor "action" elements, while girls favor dialog.

We also examined whether age was a factor in the boys' use of fire animations. There was no significant difference (p = 0.384) in the number of fire animations used by younger vs. older boys.

4. CONCLUSIONS

Games, music videos, and storytelling assignments represent different project-genres. We have examined a group of over 300 open-ended projects from these genres created by middle school students in our summer camps. Each camp was designed to introduce students to the same basic computing concepts: variables and expressions, if statements, loops, subprograms, and objects, as well as domain-specific animation concepts.

Quantitative analysis of our students' projects suggests that these project-genres motivate students to *use* (i.e., learn well enough to *apply*) quite different things. Figure 12 summarizes some of the interesting and significant differences we found.

The three groups of results in Figure 12 may be viewed as the *profiles* of the average projects in these three project-genres. Students creating games used the most variables, if statements, and loops. Students creating music videos used nearly as many loops as games, but far fewer variables and if statements. Students creating story-telling projects used the fewest loops, variables, and if statements, but made the most use of dialog.

We conclude that these project-genres differ markedly in what they motivate students to learn to use. For example, if students can easily create storytelling projects without using any repetition, conditional logic, or Boolean algebra, they are unlikely to reach the 3rd level of Bloom's Taxonomy with respect to these concepts (unless artificially required to do so). By contrast, gaming projects require students to use these concepts, and thus provide intrinsic motivation for students to learn them.

We hope that this report will catalyze other studies on project-genres and what they teach, perhaps using tools such as Greenfoot (*www.greenfoot.org*), Kodu (*fuse.microsoft.com/kodu*), Processing (*processing.org*), or others. We would especially like to see a study profiling game (or music video) projects in Alice and storytelling projects in Scratch, to see how those profiles compare to our results from Figure 12. We look forward to these studies.

5. ACKNOWLEDGMENTS

This work was made possible by support from the Computer Science Department and Science Division of Calvin College.

6. REFERENCES

[1] J. Adams (2007) Alice, Middle Schoolers, and the Imaginary Worlds Camps, *38st SIGCSE Technical Symposium*, Covington, KY, 307-311

[2] J. Adams (2010) Scratching Middle Schoolers' Creative Itch,. *41st SIGCSE Technical Symposium*, Milwaukee, WI, 356-360.

[3] J. Buckley and C. Exton (2003) Blooms' Taxonomy: A Framework for Assessing Programmers' Knowledge of Software Systems, *11th IEEE International Workshop on Program Comprehension*, Portland, OR, 165-174.

[4] S. Cooper, W. Dann, and R. Pausch, Teaching Objects-first In Introductory Computer Science, *34th SIGCSE Technical Symposium*, Reno, NV, 191-195.

[5] A. Dahotre, Y. Zhang, and C. Scaffidi, (2010) A Qualitative Study of Animation Programming in the Wild. *ACM-IEEE 4th International Symposium on Empirical Software Engineering and Measurement*, Bolzano-Bozen, Italy, 1-10.

[6] C. Lewis, How Programming Environment Shapes Perception, Learning and Goals: Logo vs. Scratch, *41st SIGCSE Technical Symposium*, Milwaukee, WI, 346-350.

[7] J. Maloney, K. Peppler, Y. Kafai, M. Resnick, and N. Rusk, (2008). Programming by Choice: Urban Youth Learning Programming with Scratch. *39th SIGCSE Technical Symposium*, Portland, OR, 367-371.

[8] O. Meerbaum-Salant, M. Armoni, and M. Ben-Ari, Habits of Programming in Scratch, *16th ITiCSE Conference*, Darmstadt, Germany, 168-172.

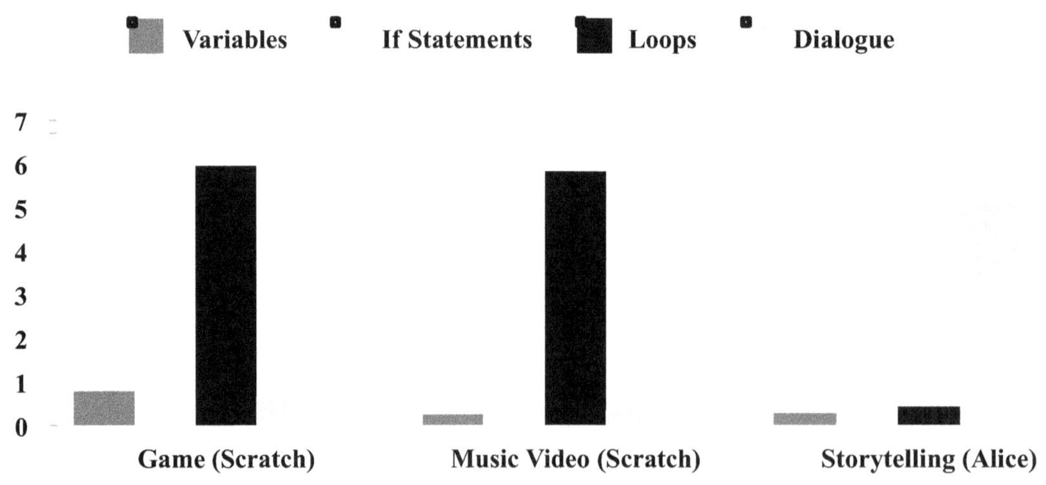

Figure 12. Use of Programming Constructs in Game, Music Video, and Storytelling Projects (Per 100 Lines of Code)

Bayesian Network Analysis of Computer Science Grade Distributions

Adam Anthony
Baldwin-Wallace College
275 Eastland Rd.
Berea, Ohio 44017
apanthon@bw.edu

Mitch Raney
Baldwin-Wallace College
275 Eastland Rd.
Berea, Ohio 44017
mraney@mail.bw.edu

ABSTRACT

Time to completion is a major factor in determining the total cost of a college degree. In an effort to reduce the number of students taking more than four years to complete a degree, we propose the use of Bayesian networks to predict student grades, given past performance in prerequisite courses. This is an intuitive approach because the necessary structure of any Bayesian network must be a directed acyclic graph, which is also the case for prerequisite graphs. We demonstrate that building a Bayesian network directly from the prerequisite graph results in effective predictions, and demonstrate a few applications of the resulting network in areas of identifying struggling students and deciding upon which courses a department should allocate tutoring resources. We find that many of our observations agree with what has long been considered conventional wisdom in computer science education.

Categories and Subject Descriptors

K.3.2 [**Computer and Information Science Education**]: Computer science education; I.2.6 [**Learning**]: Parameter Learning

General Terms

Experimentation

Keywords

Bayesian Network, Course Prerequisites, Grade Prediction

1. INTRODUCTION

There has recently been national attention on the time to completion of a Bachelor's degree and its impact on the high cost of post-secondary education[1]. Time to completion is a definite cause of concern for computer science majors because a single academic failure early in the program may result in registering for additional semesters beyond four years of study when no relevant courses can be taken until the failed prerequisite is completed satisfactorily. Our research focuses primarily on the task of addressing potential semester overflows by identifying key points in a student's academic experience in which extra care should be taken to ensure that adequate progress is made on their academic plan.

Computer science curricula are characterized by their strong prerequisite structures. It was our intention to investigate the justification of these structures in a statistical way by interpreting them as a Bayesian network. This is intuitive in the sense that the primary structure of a Bayesian network is a directed acyclic graph (DAG), just as the prerequisite structure of a major degree program must also necessarily be a DAG. Our hypothesis was that if such a network could make effective predictions, then it could be applied in novel ways to improve retention and student success by identifying critical courses on an individual, personalized basis for each student such that the student would overall be more likely to remain in the major and be successful.

An example of one simple way that students can be assisted is in the identification of courses in which they may struggle. If it is likely that the student will fail a course, it would be in that student's best interest to either seek tutoring on the subject, if the course must be taken, or avoid the course altogether if possible. Rather than focusing on avoiding difficult situations, we believe that with adequate information, students can be motivated to understand their personal strengths and weaknesses and to then allocate their time and effort appropriately so that they will be most successful.

What we have found is that the statistics do match our intuition in many cases, and that we can make effective predictions about student grades by training a model on past data collected for students who have already completed the program. We also implemented a forward-chaining prediction algorithm that projects a student's performance forward in a rough chronological order from any point of completion within the curriculum. This analysis allows us to ask and begin to answer questions about how to identify students who may leave the major, when to initiate tutoring, and whether some prerequisite links are justified or not. In the remainder of the paper, we first look at prior work, then explain how our data was collected, refined, and used to create a Bayesian network to be used for predicting student grades. We then present and discuss a number of experimental results obtained by applying the network in various ways.

Permission to make digital or hard copies of all or part of this work for personal or classroom use is granted without fee provided that copies are not made or distributed for profit or commercial advantage and that copies bear this notice and the full citation on the first page. To copy otherwise, to republish, to post on servers or to redistribute to lists, requires prior specific permission and/or a fee.
SIGCSE'12, February 29–March 3, 2012, Raleigh, North Carolina, USA.
Copyright 2012 ACM 978-1-4503-1098-7/12/02 ...$10.00.

2. RELATED WORK

There are many related articles in the area of applying Bayesian network analysis to the task of analyzing the learning process, particularly in the realm of intelligent tutoring systems. Much of the work involves the construction of networks for specific learning tasks, typically within an assessment framework[6, 8]. In these models, nodes are learning objectives for a specialized subject area, rather than courses, and arcs are defined in an application-specific manner, using expert knowledge. There has also been a great deal of research in the Education literature, though most of the literature involved predicting success based on secondary education data and entrance exam scores, rather than current post-secondary coursework performance (see, for example, [2, 4]).

The most similar work in this area was by Dekhtyar et al. [3], who developed a Bayesian network structure based on a combination of course prerequisites and expert knowledge. Their assumption was that prerequisites are limited by a need to create programs that can be completed within a limited time span (e.g., 4 years or 8 semesters). They applied their network to the task of selecting electives at the point where their computer science curriculum's core was completed (Programming I, Data Structures, Software Engineering, Discrete Math, Calculus I).

Our approach differs significantly from theirs. First, we believe that the prerequisite structure alone is sufficient in many curricula because additional dependencies are often captured indirectly via prerequisite chains and 'gateway' courses that must be completed before most high level courses may be registered. Second, while predicting performance in electives given core performance is a useful application of Bayesian networks, and our approach does consider such scenarios, it is also useful to analyze scenarios earlier in the curriculum where we might be able to catch problems and solve them through a combination of schedule revision and/or tutoring. In short, we believe that while the approach we take is not novel, the analysis and application that we take with this approach is novel, and the observations that we have made will have value to the computer science education community.

3. APPROACH

As mentioned above, our approach to grade prediction in the computer science major was implemented using Bayesian networks. There are a number of quality software packages available freely online that were sufficient for our needs. The package we selected was Weka, a popular and comprehensive machine learning tool from the University of Waikito [5] that includes powerful Bayes net creation, inference and experimentation tools. With the proper software in place, the next task was to gather and prepare a sufficient data set for training and evaluation.

We requested, from our school's registration and records office, anonymized grade data for all students taking any course with a CSC prefix from the last 12 years (when the institution began recording grades under the current system). As with any real-world data set, we quickly discovered some major consistency problems. First, we had to allow missing values in the data set because not every course is required of all students, and also because we felt it was worthwhile to include students who only completed part of the major, such as those who opted for a computer science minor. Second, the distribution of students in the different courses was inconsistent with what we would expect from a typical CS program. For example, we had 274 students in total, but only 11 had taken our current offering of CSC-245, a data structures course that is required of all majors. What we quickly realized was that the data covered three separate degree programs, which we ultimately addressed by splitting the data into three separate data sets based on the year in which each student entered the program.

Typically, having three distinct sets would be an advantage in an analysis such as this, because we could validate our results in multiple scenarios. However, the most recent program is merely an iterative change from its predecessor, so that both data sets only cover a small time period—3 years and 1 year, respectively. Therefore, we only had 37 students in the degree program effective from 2006 to 2009 and from 2009 to 2010. Furthermore, the students in the 2009 to 2010 data set all had several unknown values because we have not had any students graduate from that program at this time. The net result of these problems is that the most recent collections of students with the most up-to-date curricula are inadequate for effective prediction and evaluation.

The positive outcome from this data processing was that within our degree program from 1998 to 2005 was a solid core of students who had completed the program, and provided adequate volume for statistical predictions. Our final data set was gathered from this set and consisted of 226 students in various stages of completion in the program. The variety of completion points was useful in evaluating and analyzing student performance within the major. While this data set was adequate for significant analysis, we still hope to work with larger institutions in the future so that we can repeat the tests using a larger volume of students.

With the data collected, processed and cleaned, the next task was to format it in the .ARFF format supported by WEKA and build a Bayesian network that could be used to make predictions. As stated above, this project was inspired by the realization that, in majors such as computer science, a complex pre-requisite structure is already a well-formed DAG and is thus instantly translatable to a Bayesian network. We hypothesized that if a Bayesian network formed from the prerequisite structure was an effective predictor of future academic performance, then the prerequisite paths would be well justified, and if it was a poor predictor then we might be able to gain insight as to which course sequences seem to pose problems, and compare that to our professional intuition about the sequences.

We ultimately produced the Bayesian network pictured in Figure 1. Table 1 provides course titles for each course number seen in the networks. All of the variables in each of the conditional probability tables were discrete (A,B,C,D,F), and so the associated conditional probabilities for each value were computed in the standard way using frequency counts, as detailed in Chapter 14 of Artificial Intelligence: A Modern Approach [7].

4. METHODOLOGY

To evaluate the effectiveness of the Bayes Network approach, we conducted several tests, some of which could be useful in identifying critical groups of students. In the following experiments, results are averaged using 100-fold cross-validation, unless the number of students available for the test is less than 100, in which case leave-one-out cross validation was performed.

As a baseline for comparison, we used a model in which, for each course, the most frequently awarded grade would be the default prediction for every student. In other words, the model makes the assumption that all courses are mutually independent of one another. This is a sensible baseline, because in the absence of all external knowledge about a student, this is the most reasonable attempt at making an effective prediction. Prediction performance using this technique can be seen in Section 5 in Table 1

The next test we performed was the classic form of analysis with a Bayesian network. This was done by taking a subset of students as a test set, and learning the Bayesian model with the remaining training set. Then, withholding grading data for exactly one class in the test set, grades were predicted for that class for each student. This type of test is useful because it is generally performed when making predictions with Bayesian networks and thus gives us a clear impression of whether our data and approach are sufficient for a detailed analysis. Prediction performance using this technique can also be seen in Section 5 in Table 1

Unfortunately, this classic style of Bayesian network evaluation has few applications if our goal is to analyze curricula. Predictions are not worthwhile if students have already completed the entire curriculum, and it is illogical to suppose that a prerequisite course has not been completed when a later course has been finished. One advantage of Bayesian networks is that they are robust in the case of multiple unknown values. Multiple unknowns are iteratively predicted by sampling a value for every node in the network for which all of its conditionally dependent values are known. In each iteration, the sampled value is assigned to its respective node as being 'known,' and the process continues until all nodes are given a value.

In principle, this method for predicting multiple unknowns can be for any subset of course grades. However, if we restrict the possible known/unknown partitioning of course grades to those which are chronologically appropriate, then the prediction process can actually be seen as a simulation of a student's completion of the program. For example, suppose that we are interested in predicting future performance of incoming Freshmen. In this particular degree program, a typical Freshman would take CSC-150 (Fundamentals of Computer Science), CSC-210 (Programming I), and CSC-215 (Digital Topics), which, combined as a sequence, form a foundational knowledge base. Our prediction would be performed by selecting the training set and excluding from the test set all grades but the four courses mentioned above. Then, the next course in the sequence would be individually predicted for each student, and this predicted value would then be added to a new copy of the test set data. This process is repeated using the new test set until every course has a predicted value. Precluding any variation in how students schedule courses due to timing, work, or personal constraints, this process produces a reasonable projection of a student's performance over time.

This chronologically-ordered prediction process can be augmented and applied in several ways, such as analyzing the expected performance of students who prematurely departed the major. This and other applications are discussed in more detail in the next section, within the context of the completed analysis.

5. RESULTS

Table 1 shows the performance of the Bayes network in predicting student grades for an individual course, given grades in all other courses. Also included is the baseline performance of predicting grades for each course, independent of all other courses. Academic intuition is validated in this case, since all courses accurately predict student grades at least as well as the independent prediction in all cases, and in several cases, the performance is significantly better. One particularly successful instance is with CSC-260, which covers both linear and non-linear data structures. The grades are distributed fairly well in this course, with the independent predictor correct only 30% of the time, but when prerequisite dependencies are considered, performance is increased to 77%. In the case of CSC 330, the independent predictor had a performance of 0%. This was an artifact of a small sample size combined with very close frequency counts for two grade values and procedural tie-breaking in the Weka software. We would expect that this value would be non-zero if a larger sample were obtained, or if random tie-breaking were implemented.

Many papers, including Dekhtyar et al.'s [3], also reduced the number of categories for each course from (A,B,C,D,F) to (Good, Pass, Fail) in order to reduce the complexity and increase prediction performance. We don't entirely agree with this simplification because students do have a significant interest in whether they might receive an A or a B in a course. However, we noticed a similar trend in our misclassified results that shows that our predictions, while in some cases low, were often incorrect by one letter grade. Figure 2 shows the collected predictions for all students in all courses. In each grade category except for D and F, the most frequently predicted grade was the actual grade for that category, and the next most frequent selection was always an adjacent value. In the case of D and F, we find that our Bayesian network seems optimistic. We believe that this is actually a trend in the data. It is plausible to believe that students with a recurring pattern of failure would not continue in the program, so that predicting subsequent F grades would not be rational. A similar trend is seen for D grades, although D grades are predicted correctly more often than the analysis correctly predicts F grades.

There are several ways to apply the chronological analysis technique in which we iteratively predict a student's grades one at a time in an order that would be typical of a real student. The first one that we looked at was analyzing the expected performance of students who did not complete a major or minor. We identified these students as any who completed the entrance sequence of CSC-150, CSC-210 and CSC-215, but no other CSC courses. We then applied the chronological analysis and projected all remaining grades for students with only those first three courses given as known variables.

Table 2 details the results when students were partitioned into three sets: students who dropped (DROP), the complementary set for the dropped students (NDROP), and their union (ALL). The average GPA of the ALL group provides a benchmark by which we can evaluate the other two groups (The actual average GPA for all students, regardless of their level of completion, was 2.68. It is less use-

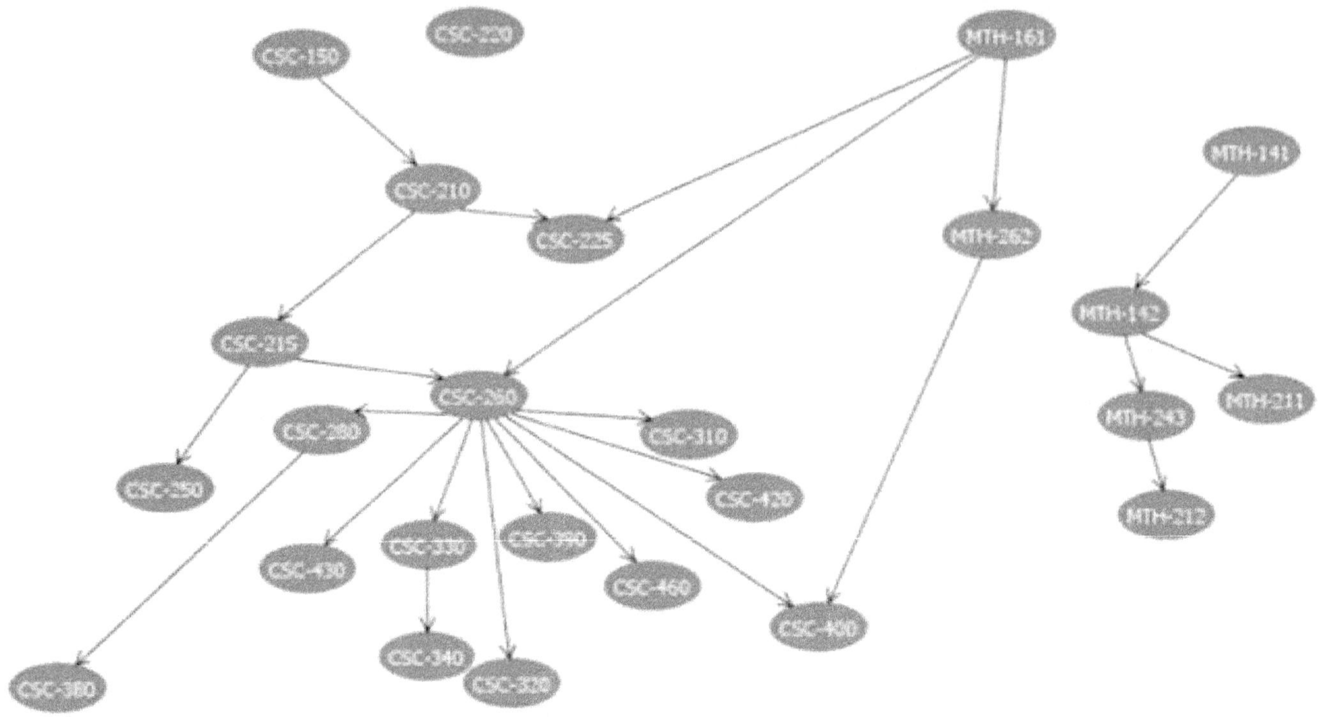

Figure 1: Bayesian network constructed using the prerequisite structure defined in our 1998–2005 curriculum.

Course Title	Course #	# Students	# Parent Nodes	Bayes' Net	Independent
Fundamentals of Computer Science	CSC-150	226	0	53.3937	41.5929
Computer Science I	CSC-210	221	1	51.5837	32.1267
Digital Topics (Basic Circuits and Architecture)	CSC-215	216	1	53.2407	36.5741
Fundamentals of Distributed Systems	CSC-220	76	0	48.6842	48.6842
Information Systems I	CSC-225	129	2	56.5891	39.5349
Multimedia Programming	CSC-250	26	1	46.1538	38.4615
Computer Science II (5 Credits, incl. data structures)	CSC-260	53	2	77.3585	30.1887
Database I	CSC-280	91	1	48.3516	38.4615
Computer Architecture	CSC-320	55.5556	1	46.6667	51.111
Web Programming I	CSC-330	15	1	60.0	0
Web Programming II	CSC-340	8	1	75.0	62.5
Database II	CSC-380	24	1	54.1667	45.8333
Compiler Design	CSC-390	30	1	66.6667	50
Operating Systems	CSC-400	42	2	76.1905	42.8571
Formal Languages	CSC-420	13	1	84.6514	53.8462
Algorithms	CSC-430	8	1	87.5	62.5
Systems Analysis and Design	CSC-460	67	1	38.806	31.3433
Discrete Math I	MTH-161	164	0	51.8293	24.3902
Calculus I	MTH-141	102	0	38.2353	31.3725
Calculus II	MTH-142	48	1	68.75	52.0833
Linear Algebra	MTH-211	21	1	57.1429	42.8571
Differential Equations	MTH-212	9	1	44.4444	44.4444
Calculus III	MTH-243	28	1	57.1429	53.5714
Discrete Math II	MTH-262	59	1	57.6271	33.8983

Table 1: Basic Bayesian prediction of student grades in which one course is withheld and the remaining are used to predict student scores for that individual course. Results are averaged over 100 folds of cross-validation.

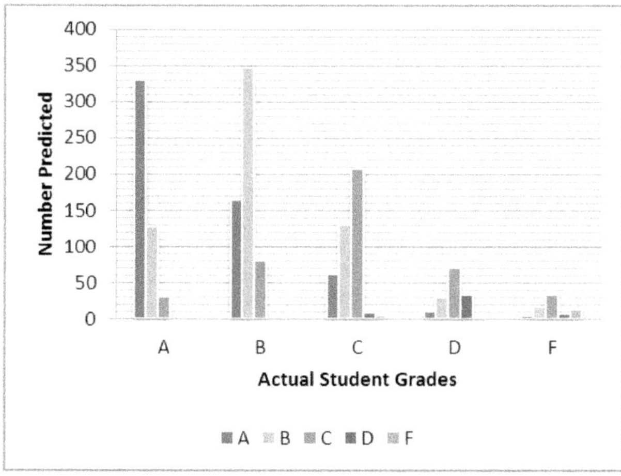

Figure 2: Frequency of predicted values for each actual grade given. Values are collected for all students over all courses.

	Average	Std. Dev.	Above ALL
DROP	2.831628	0.254866 (0.21,0.21)	42%
NDROP	2.935642	0.233443 (0.12,0.26)	64%
ALL	2.907407	0.244068 (0.22,0.27)	60%

Table 2: Average GPA performance when projecting students' grades past the introductory sequence. Values in Parentheses next to the standard deviations indicate the percentage of students in each group one standard deviation above or below the mean. The final column gives the percentage of students in each group who outperformed the average value in the ALL group.

ful, due to prediction-inflation as discussed above). First, it should be noted that the students in the DROP set do have a lower average GPA, and students in NDROP have a slightly higher GPA. This would confirm, as is generally believed, that many students who are projected to perform poorly will drop the major. What is somewhat surprising is the fact that 42% of students who dropped the major were projected to perform above average. Combined with the observation above, that grade predictions tend to be very close to the actual student's grade when earning a C or better, we conclude that it is likely that those 42% of students who dropped the major, had they stayed, would have performed very well. Unfortunately, our analysis was only conducted on computer science majors, so we have little frame of reference as to whether this is an unusually high number of talented students who dropped the major. However, it certainly identifies a large group of students whose retention would have a significant impact on computer science enrollments.

Another question is what can be done to help these students? Is there a point in the curriculum at which we can provide effective tutoring to increase the overall GPA? Applying the same method as above, we generated a new data set in which each student has a varying chance (10% up to 90%) of increasing their grade in one or both of CSC-210 and CSC-215 by a letter grade. Our first two experiments supposed that a tutoring program would be initiated for either CSC-210 or CSC-215. In both cases, we found that when the chance of increasing a grade through tutoring was 60% or higher, the average projected GPA for the students in the DROP set rose to 2.91, which is better than the average GPA for all students. The impact of raising the single grade on a student's GPA is 0.04 points, so this increase does include expected increased performance in later, non-tutored courses. If a program were initiated in both courses, the expected average score after 50% effectiveness is approximately 3.0, which is higher than for the students in the NDROP set.

There are two perspectives to keep in mind with this result. First, the students we identified as having dropped the major were in this group, so 42% of the tutored students were considered above average, and may not seek tutoring in real life. Second, this experiment assumes that increasing a student's grade alters their characteristics such that their future behavior would be similar to that of a high-quality student. This may not be a fair assumption. Regardless, we conclude that providing resources for effective tutoring early in the major (which is provided at many institutions) is justifiable in the sense that it can help give under-achieving students a better chance of being successful in future courses.

6. FUTURE WORK

We would like to extend this work to run on a larger data set, perhaps obtained collaboratively from a larger institution. We also believe that there are other majors on our campus that have a prerequisite structure with sufficient complexity to perform the same analysis. We would also be interested in digging deeper to obtain external predictors, as other studies have done, such as test scores and high school GPA. It would also be interesting to investigate the drop-rates for other majors to see if 42% would be considered a large number of students dropping the major.

One experiment that we performed, but omitted, was predicting course grades by learning a dependency structure, rather than specifying it as a fixed prerequisite structure. Most instances of this experiment produced useless results in which the algorithm added 'backward' dependencies in which higher level courses were identified as being parents of lower level courses. In the context of basic unbounded prediction, this actually makes sense: if you were to perform well in a 400-level class, it is safe to say that you probably fared well in the lower-level class. But as far as providing us useful information for applying to curriculum analysis and design, the outcome is not meaningful. Furthermore, whereas one could expect improved performance under this method, the performance was more often lower than when using the fixed prerequisite structure, and in some cases was even worse in predicting grades than the independent predictor. One observation we noticed, though, was that the structure learning process routinely added mathematics courses as prerequisites to certain computer science courses.

We have preliminary results that are consistent with the presumption that prerequisite relations do not capture all beneficial course orderings, but only the most important [3]. One compelling example we obtained from the structure learning experiments was to add MTH-211 (Linear Algebra) as a parent to CSC-260, and MTH-212 (Differential Equations) as a parent to CSC-430 (Algorithms), the prediction accuracy for the respective CSC courses increased from 77.3% to 83% for CSC-260 and from 87.5% to 100% for CSC-430. We hypothesize that while there could potentially be improvement in accuracy by adding additional prerequisite dependencies, the most significant of those dependencies are likely already identified in the prerequisite structure, while lesser dependencies are omitted because the ordering of coursework must be somewhat flexible.

However, it would be interesting to see what subtle effects exist between different course orderings, but to effectively find interesting orderings, we would have to modify the typical Bayes net structure learning algorithm, since it is implemented to allow dependencies in any direction. One could develop a restricted algorithm that prevents certain dependencies from being added. For example, a course may not have an arc to another if the former is a descendant of the latter in the original prerequisite graph. Another possible restriction heuristic would be to disallow arcs between courses with a higher order course number (e.g., from a 300 level course to a 200 level course).

7. CONCLUSION

In this paper, we have shown that the prerequisite structure of a computer science curriculum does have predictive power when treated as a Bayesian network. We demonstrated a selection of analysis techniques that are revealing in terms of curriculum analysis. Many of our observations are consistent with conventional wisdom in computer science education, such as which courses benefit students the most when tutoring is offered. In the future, we hope to continue this research and to delve more deeply into the various aspects of computer science curricula.

8. ACKNOWLEDGMENTS

Marie desJardins from the department of Computer Science and Electrical Engineering at the University of Maryland Baltimore County provided some useful insights that led to the chrnonological analysis technique.

9. REFERENCES

[1] L. Alexander. The three-year solution. *Newsweek, Retrieved from http://www. newsweek. com/id/218183*, October 2009.

[2] J. V. D'Agostino and S. M. Bonner. High School Exit Exam Scores and University Performance. *Educational Assessment*, 14(1):25–37, 2009.

[3] A. Dekhtyar, J. Goldsmith, H. Li, and B. Young. The Bayesian advisor project: modeling academic advising. Technical report, University of Kentucky Dept. of Computer Science Technical Report TR 323, 2001.

[4] P. J. Donnelly. *Examining Pre-College Academic Variables: Investigating Future College Success.* PhD thesis, 2010.

[5] M. Hall, E. Frank, G. Holmes, B. Pfahringer, P. Reutemann, and I. H. Witten. The WEKA data mining software: An update. *SIGKDD Explorations*, 11(1), 2009.

[6] Z. A. Pardos, N. T. Heffernan, B. Anderson, C. L. Heffernan, and W. P. Schools. Using fine-grained skill models to fit student performance with Bayesian networks. *Handbook of Educational Data Mining*, pages 417+, 2010.

[7] S. Russell and P. Norvig. *Artificial Intelligence A Modern Approach.* Pearson, third edition, 2010.

[8] R. Zwick and L. Lenaburg. Using Discrete Loss Functions and Weighted Kappa for Classification: An Illustration Based on Bayesian Network Analysis. *Journal of Educational and Behavioral Statistics*, 34(2):190–200, 2009.

Through the Looking Glass: Talking about the World with Visualization

Fernanda Viégas and Martin Wattenberg
Google's "Big Picture" Visualization Research Group
Cambridge, Massachusetts
fm@hint.fm

Abstract

Data visualization has historically been accessible only to the elite in academia, business, and government. It was "serious" technology, created by experts for experts. In recent years, however, web-based visualizations--ranging from political art projects to news stories--have reached audiences of millions.

What will this new era of data transparency look like--and what are the implications for technologists who work with data? To help answer this question, we report on recent research into public data analysis and visualization. Some of our results come from Many Eyes, a "living laboratory" web site where people may upload their own data, create interactive visualizations, and carry on conversations. We'll also show how the art world has embraced visualization. We'll discuss the future of visual literacy and what it means for a world where visualizations are a part of political discussions, citizen activism, religious discussions, game playing, and educational exchanges.

Categories and Subject Descriptors

K.3.2 [**Computers and Education**]: Computer and Information Science Education – *Computer science education*

General Terms

Experimentation

Copyright is held by the author/owner(s).
SIGCSE'12, February 29–March 3, 2012, Raleigh, North Carolina, USA.
ACM 978-1-4503-1098-7/12/02.

SIGCSE 2012 Workshops

Using Social Networking to Improve Student Learning Through Classroom Salon

John Barr, *Ithaca College*
Ananda Gunawardena, *Carnegie Mellon University*

This workshop introduces an innovative social collaboration tool called Classroom Salon (CLS). Developed at Carnegie Mellon University, CLS is a combination of electronic books, social networks, and analytic tools. With CLS, instructors can upload documents, create social groups, and monitor student activities. Students can annotate documents, answer questions, and communicate in a social networks context. Students learn through participation in social networks while instructors use the tools built into CLS to easily and effectively analyze their participation. The workshop covers extant social networks, introduces CLS web-based software (nothing to install) and demonstrates the use of CLS to help students master critical skills such as code review, debugging, and reading documentation. Participants will create Salons, learn how to use them in their courses, and learn how to use the built-in tools to analyze student activities. A laptop with wifi is mandatory.

ACM Categories & Descriptors: K.3.1; K.3.2

Keywords: Social Networking, Collaborative Documents, Assessment

Challenges and Opportunities in Conducting Educational Research in the Computer Science Classroom: How to Collect Empirical Evidence to Assess Whether Students Really Learned

Aman Yadav, *Purdue University*
John Tim Korb, *Purdue University*

This workshop will provide CS educators with tools to conduct educational research. Primary objectives of this workshop are: (1) learn basic principles of educational research; (2) learn about educational research designs: qualitative vs. quantitative; experimental vs. quasi-experimental; case studies, survey; and (3) to practice designing research. This workshop will help participants make informed decisions when faced with limitations of educational research and collect empirical evidence about what works in the classroom. In addition, we will also discuss how to develop robust student outcome measures, such as surveys and tests.

ACM Categories & Descriptors: K.3.1

C++11 in Parallel

Joseph E. Hummel, *University of California, Irvine*

As hardware designers turn to multi-core CPUs and GPUs, software developers must embrace parallel programming to increase performance. No single approach has yet established itself as the right way to develop parallel software. However, C++ has long been used for performance-oriented work, and it s a safe bet that any viable approach involves C++. This position has been strengthened by ratification of the new C++0x standard, officially referred to as C++11 . This workshop will introduce the new features of C++11 related to parallel programming, including type inference, lambda expressions, closures, multithreading support, and thread-local storage. The workshop will close with brief discussion of other technologies, including Intel TBB, ArBB, Cilk Plus, and Microsoft PPL, AAL, AMP. This is a laptop optional workshop.

ACM Categories & Descriptors: D.1.3; D.3.3

Keywords: C++, C++0x, C++11, concurrency, asynchronous and parallel programming, multithreading, parallelism

The Absolute Beginner's Guide to JUnit in the Classroom

Stephen H. Edwards, *Virginia Tech*
Manuel A. Perez-Quinones, *Virginia Tech*

Software testing has become popular in introductory courses, but many educators are unfamiliar with how to write software tests or how they might be used in the classroom. This workshop provides a practical introduction to JUnit for educators. JUnit is the Java testing framework that is most commonly used in the classroom. Participants will learn how to write and run JUnit test cases; how-to s for common classroom uses (as a behavioral addition to an assignment specification, as part of manual grading, as part of automated grading, as a student-written activity, etc.); and common solutions to tricky classroom problems (testing standard input/output, randomness, main programs, assignments with lots of design freedom, assertions, and code that calls exit()). Laptop recommended.

ACM Categories & Descriptors: D.2.5; D.1.5; K.3.2

Keywords: software testing, test-driven development, test-first coding, Java, programming assignments, automated assessment

Student Scrums

Tom Reichlmayr, *Rochester Institute of Technology*

Over the past ten years Agile software development practices have grown in acceptance and have gained a solid foothold in commercial software development. Our students are entering the workforce with an increasing percentage of companies that are using Agile processes and practices in the development of their products and services. The most widely used Agile project management framework is Scrum. Scrum has a well defined approach for organizing and controlling a software development project. It is almost always implemented in combination with Agile software development practices, but is flexible enough to even be used for managing non-software projects. Selecting Scrum as the framework for student team projects has the advantage of introducing software process at a level of ceremony that both captures foundational software engineering practices and is manageable within the constraints of a class or capstone project.

Copyright is held by the author/owner(s).
SIGCSE'12, February 29–March 3, 2012, Raleigh, North Carolina, USA.
ACM 978-1-4503-1098-7/12/02

This workshop will introduce participants to the components of the Scrum framework with activities designed to demonstrate the flexibility of Scrum to support a diverse set of course learning outcomes at all levels of the curriculum. Laptop optional

ACM Categories & Descriptors: K.6.3; D.2.1

Keywords: Scrum, user stories, acceptance testing, Agile software development, teams, project planning, estimation, tracking

Reviewing NSF Proposals: Learn about Effective Proposal Writing via the Review Process

Sue C. Fitzgerald, *National Science Foundation*
Guy-Alain Amoussou, *National Science Foundation*

This workshop focuses on the NSF proposal review process. Via close examination of the review process, participants gain an understanding of how to write good reviews and how to improve their own proposal writing. The workshop covers the following topic areas: the proposal review process from submission of a proposal to award or decline; elements of a good review; NSF merit criteria (intellectual merit and broader impacts); elements of a good proposal; and how to volunteer to review proposals. The workshop uses a structured guided-interactive methodology to lead participants through each topic by introducing related issues, engaging participants in group exercises designed to explore and share their understanding of the issues, and then providing some expert opinion on these issues. Good and bad examples and a Top Ten List of Do s and Don t s will be provided. The intended audience is faculty members at two-year and four year colleges and universities who wish to better understand the NSF review process and/or those who are seeking NSF funding in support of undergraduate education. Participants will include people with little or no proposal reviewing experience, novice proposal writers, and those with more experience who seek to improve their proposal writing and/or reviewing skills. Laptop optional.

ACM Categories & Descriptors: K.3.2

Keywords: Funding, National Science Foundation, grants, proposal writing, reviewing grant proposals

A Hands-On Comparison of iOS vs. Android

Michael Rogers, *Northwest Missouri State University*
Mark Goadrich, *Centenary College of Louisiana*

This workshop is designed for faculty, considering teaching a course in mobile app development, who are unsure as to whether they should use iOS, Android, or both. To help them make an educated decision, in this workshop participants will build one app, to implement the game Pig, in both platforms. By so doing, they will be able to make a head-to-head comparison of the respective development environments, languages, and frameworks, guided by experienced instructors. Participants will need to bring (or share) a recent-vintage MacBook Pro / MacBook Air, with Xcode, Eclipse, and appropriate SDKs, installed prior to the workshop. Details, including installation instructions, may be found at androidios.goadrich.com. Laptop Required.

ACM Categories & Descriptors: D.2.0

Keywords: Mobile Computing, iOS, Android

Killing 3 Birds with One Course: Service Learning, Professional Writing, and Project Management

Joseph Mertz, *Carnegie Mellon University*
Scott McElfresh, *Wake Forest University*
Steven Andrianoff, *St. Bonaventure University*
Jennifer Dempsey, *St. Bonaventure University*

Service learning is a great idea, but can be fraught with problems. We have taken an alternative to the project-course approach. Instead of team-based system-development, we use a student-consultant model. Students individually consult with a nonprofit. Each student leads a small technology project that brings about sustainable change in an organization, while developing analysis, planning, and communication skills. One instructor can manage 30 clients a semester, and we have had nearly 400 to date. Our clients are happy and recruit others. In this session we will share our tricks and help attendees adapt them to their situations: managing a large number of partnerships, helping students develop leadership and communication skills, and assessing their performance. A student presenter will describe her consulting experience.

ACM Categories & Descriptors: K.3.2; K.4.0

Keywords: Service Learning, Leadership, Professional Practice, Consulting, Project Course, Capstone Course

Computer Science Unplugged, Robotics, and Outreach Activities

Tim Bell, *University of Canterbury*
Daniela Marghitu, *Auburn University*
Lynn Lambert, *Christopher Newport University*

You ve been asked to talk to an elementary or high school class about Computer Science, but how can you ensure that the talk is engaging? Or perhaps you re trying to introduce a concept from Computer Science to a school group, but you want a fun way to get the class engaged. This workshop is a hands-on introduction to Computer Science Unplugged (www.csunplugged.org), a widely used set of kinesthetic, fun activities that cover many core areas of computer science without using high technology. We will explore how to use the activities in a variety of situations, including combining them with robotics activities, and explore some novel applications. Attendees will receive a CD with a copy of a handbook for teachers and a collection of videos demonstrating the activities.

ACM Categories & Descriptors: K.3.2

Keywords: Outreach, high school

Introduction to Using FPGAs in the Computer Science Curriculum

William M. Jones, *Coastal Carolina University*
D. Brian Larkins, *Coastal Carolina University*

One of the challenges in modern curriculum design is balancing between breadth and depth of topics while simultaneously reinforcing the interconnections among topics in the field. To

Copyright is held by the author/owner(s).
SIGCSE'12, February 29–March 3, 2012, Raleigh, North Carolina, USA.
ACM 978-1-4503-1098-7/12/02

address these challenges, faculty are often forced to approximate real-world systems, sometimes at the expense of any hands-on experience. We have integrated field-programming gate array (FPGA) systems first used in our hardware-based courses into several higher-level systems and applications courses. This allows us to leverage student familiarity with a hands-on, flexible hardware platform and also strengthen the relationships between different subfields within computer science. In this workshop, we present participants with guided hands-on activities for making use of FPGAs in common computer science courses such as digital logic design, computer organization and programming, and compiler construction. Laptop required.

ACM Categories & Descriptors: K.3.2

Keywords: FPGA, Education, Curriculum, Hardware Platform

Helping Students Become Better Communicators

Janet E. Burge, *Miami University*
Paul V. Anderson, *Miami University*
Gerald C. Gannod, *Miami University*
Michael Carter, *North Carolina State University*
Deanna Dannels, *North Carolina State University*
Margaret Heil, *North Carolina State University*
Mladen Vouk, *North Carolina State University*

To be successful, CS and SE graduates need strong communication skills (writing, speaking, and teaming), particularly within their discipline. Students exercise these skills during their classes but are not always given explicit domain-specific instruction on these skills, instead relying on instruction provided outside the program. CS and SE faculty are not always comfortable in evaluating these aspects of their assignments and are often unhappy with the results. In this workshop we will lead sessions on teaching writing, speaking, and teaming; situating assignments in workplace-scenarios (to motivate students); and writing communication rubrics that convey faculty expectations to students and support evaluation of student work. For more information, see www.muohio.edu/sigcse_workshop11. A laptop is recommended but not mandatory for this workshop.

ACM Categories & Descriptors: K.3.2

Keywords: Writing, Speaking, Teaming, Communication

ROS for Educators: Teaching with the Robot Operating System and Microsoft Kinect

Michael Ferguson, *Willow Garage*
Julian Mason, *Duke University*
Sharon Gower Small, *Siena College*
Zachary Dodds, *Harvey Mudd College*

The Microsoft Kinect and Willow Garage's Robot Operating System (ROS) are changing the way robots are developed. Together, these tools can enable today's CS educators to provide richer and more research-representative experiences with robots and perception. This hands-on workshop will introduce ROS and showcase two pilot courses taught using ROS and the Kinect. Four 20-minute talks will intersperse with participants' hands-on development of Python programs on low-cost Kinect-equipped robots and the ARDrone quadcopter. This workshop is intended for all college-level CS educators interested in robotics or embodied AI. First-time ROS/Kinect users are particularly welcome! Laptops and robots will be provided. See http://www.ros.org/wiki/Courses/sigcse2012. Laptops optional.

ACM Categories & Descriptors: I.2.9; K.3.2

Keywords: Robotics, Robot Operating System, ROS, Kinect, course design

Board Game Project Ideas for CS 1 and CS 2

Zachary Kurmas, *Grand Valley State University*
James Vanderhyde, *Benedictine College*

Participants will have fun learning and playing relatively unknown board games that are especially suitable for programming projects. We will present games where (1) all players can view the same screen, (2) the board is reasonably simple to program, and (3) there are several elements of the game that relate strongly to a common CS 1, CS 2, or discrete math topic. After we explain the rules and highlight the CS-related elements of the games, participants will have the opportunity to play the games, ask questions, and suggest rule variations that will improve the resulting programming project. See http://www.cis.gvsu.edu/~kurmasz/GamesWorkshop/ for more details and a list of games that may be presented. Laptop Optional.

ACM Categories & Descriptors: K.3.2

Keywords: Games

A Taste of Linked Data and the Semantic Web

David Hyland-Wood, *University of Mary Washington*
Marsha Zaidman, *University of Mary Washington*

The Web has created a global information space of linked documents. The Semantic Web creates an information space of linked data from multiple sources. Information can be mined from the interlinking of available datasets by a distributed query language known as SPARQL, the SQL equivalent for the Semantic Web. Participants will understand and appreciate the role of linked data on the Semantic Web; be able to model, represent, and interpret simple linked data applications; complete exercises that create simple Linked Data models; appreciate the benefits of Linked Data over relational database modeling; be aware of successful commercial applications of linked Data;be directed to resources that facilitate incorporation of this material into their courses. WiFi/Laptop Required.

ACM Categories & Descriptors: H.2.8; D.m

Keywords: Semantic Web, Linked Data

Teaching with Greenfoot and the Kinect: A Novel Way to Engage Beginners

Michael Kölling, *University of Kent*
Neil Brown, *University of Kent*

The Microsoft Kinect is a sensor module that allows accurate tracking of humans moving in front of it. Greenfoot is an introductory Java programming environment that makes it easy to

Copyright is held by the author/owner(s).
SIGCSE'12, February 29–March 3, 2012, Raleigh, North Carolina, USA.
ACM 978-1-4503-1098-7/12/02

create animated graphical projects. By combining Greenfoot and the Kinect students can write programs where the user s body is used for input. Users interact with games by waving their hands, jumping, running, dancing, ... These kinds of programs are incredibly good fun and engage target groups who would not normally be interested in programming. The workshop is aimed at teachers of introductory programming courses (high school/university) who have some programming experience and want to incorporate new kinds of projects into their teaching. Laptop recommended but not required. Kinect hardware will be provided.

ACM Categories & Descriptors: K.3.2

Keywords: Introductory programming; Greenfoot; Kinect

Intellectual Property Law Basics for Computer Science Instructors

David G. Kay, *University of California, Irvine*

Increasingly the practice of computing involves legal issues. Patenting algorithms, domain name poaching, downloading music, and re-using' HTML and graphics from web sites all raise questions of intellectual property (IP) law (which includes patents, copyrights, trade secrets, and trademarks). In the classroom, computer science educators often confront questions that have legal ramifications. The presenter, who is both a computer scientist and a lawyer, will introduce the basics of intellectual property law to give instructors a framework for recognizing the issues, answering students' questions, debunking the most egregious misconceptions about IP, and understanding generally how the law and computing interact. All CS educators are welcome; no computer is required.

ACM Categories & Descriptors: copyrights

Keywords: trade secrets

Teaching and Learning Computing via Social Gaming with Pex4Fun

Nikolai Tillmann, *Microsoft Research*
Jonathan de Halleux, *Microsoft Research*
Tao Xie, *North Carolina State University*
Judith Bishop, *Microsoft Research*

Pex4Fun (pexforfun.com) is a web-based serious gaming environment for teaching computing at many levels, from high school all the way through graduate courses. Unique to the

Pex4Fun experience is a cloud-based program evaluation engine based on dynamic symbolic execution and SMT-solving, which provides customized feedback to the student and automated grading for the teacher. Thus, Pex4Fun connects teachers, curriculum authors, and students in a social experience, tracking and streaming progress updates in real time. In particular, Pex4Fun finds interesting and unexpected input values that help students understand what their code is actually doing. The real fun starts with coding duels where students write code to implement a teacher's specification. Pex4Fun finds any discrepancies in behavior between the student's code and the specification. Then based on the reported discrepancies, the student improves his or her code towards the specification. Pex4Fun can be used to develop interesting, engaging, and demanding class materials on mathematics, algorithms, programming languages, or problem solving in general. A teacher can use an integrated wiki to author these class materials for students to work through. This workshop involves creating and teaching course materials at Pex4Fun. Participants should bring a laptop computer. The intended audience includes all levels of CS educators who are interested in integrating educational technology in their teaching environments.

ACM Categories & Descriptors: D.2.3; D.2.5; D.2.6

Keywords: Programming, Social Gaming, Dynamic Symbolic Execution, Testing, Debugging

Welcome to Makerland: A First Cultural Immersion into Open Source Communities

Mel Chua, *Purdue University*
Sebastian Dziallas, *Franklin W. Olin College of Engineering*
Heidi J. C. Ellis, *Western New England University*
Gregory W. Hislop, *Drexel University*
Karl R. Wurst, *Worcester State University*

Participating in free and open source (FOSS) software communities provides students with authentic learning while supplying instructors with a wide variety of educational opportunities including coding, testing, documentation, professionalism and more. However, instructors may be unfamiliar with how FOSS communities work and therefore may be reluctant to involve students in such communities. This workshop is a subset of material used in Red Hat's Professors' Open Source Summer Experience (http://communityleadershipteam.org/posse) workshop, now in its third year of successfully providing a ramp to FOSS projects for instructors. These instructors have demonstrated success in involving their students in FOSS communities where students have contributed code, interface design, and more. Intended audience: Computing educators at the college or high school level interested in involving students in open source software projects in any capacity (testing, coding, documentation, design, project management, observational shadowing of a large-scale project, etc). The workshop may also be of interest to pre-high school computing educators and members of the open source community. No experience with open source communities or contribution is necessary.

ACM Categories & Descriptors: K.3.2

Keywords: open source, service learning, cognitive apprenticeship, communities of practice

Computational Art and Creative Coding: Teaching CS1 with Processing

Ira Greenberg, *Southern Methodist University*
Deepak Kumar, *Bryn Mawr College*
Dianna Xu, *Bryn Mawr College*

This workshop showcases a new approach to teaching CS1 using computational art as a context. Participants will be introduced to the Processing programming language and environment, designed for the construction of 2D and 3D visual forms. Its IDE is light-

Copyright is held by the author/owner(s).
SIGCSE'12, February 29–March 3, 2012, Raleigh, North Carolina, USA.
ACM 978-1-4503-1098-7/12/02

weight, but well-suited for the rapid proto-typing needed for dynamic visual work. We hope to bring the excitement, creativity, and innovation fostered by Processing into the computer science education community. Instructors of all experience levels are welcome. Hands-on portion of the workshop will enable participants to explore Processing and create visual effects on the fly. Course materials and handouts detailing the software, curriculum, and teaching resources will be given out. All participants will need to bring their own laptops.

ACM Categories & Descriptors: K.3.2

Keywords: CS1, computer science, education, pedagogy, creative computation, creative coding, art, visual portfolio, Processing

AP CS Principles and the Beauty and Joy of Computing Curriculum

Daniel D. Garcia, *University of California, Berkeley*
Brian Harvey, *University of California, Berkeley*
Tiffany Barnes, *University of North Carolina, Charlotte*
Luke Segars, *University of California, Berkeley*
Eugene Lemon, *Ralph J Bunche High School*
Sean Morris, *Albany High School*
Josh Paley, *Henry M. Gunn High School*

The Beauty and Joy of Computing (BJC) is an introductory computer science curriculum developed at the University of California, Berkeley (and adapted at the University of North Carolina, Charlotte), intended for high school juniors through university non-majors. It was used in two of the five initial pilot programs for the AP CS Principles course being developed by the College Board and the National Science Foundation. Our overall goal is to support the CS10K project by preparing instructors to teach the AP CS Principles course through the BJC curriculum. In this workshop, we will share our experiences as instructors of the course at the university and high school level, provide a glimpse into a typical week of the course, and share details of NSF-funded summer professional development opportunities.

ACM Categories & Descriptors: K.3.2

Keywords: Beauty and Joy of Computing, Advanced Placement Computer Science Principles, AP CS Principles, BYOB, Build Your Own Blocks

Peer Instruction in the CS Classroom: A Hands-On Introduction

Daniel Zingaro, *University of Toronto*
Cynthia Bailey-Lee, *University of California, San Diego*
John Glick, *University of San Diego*
Leo Porter, *Skidmore College*
Beth Simon, *University of California, San Diego*

We introduce participants to Peer Instruction (PI): an active learning technique applicable to the teaching of many subjects, including CS. In PI, Students work together to exchange perspectives and answer challenging conceptual questions, and are supported by short teaching segments. We will introduce and motivate PI, demonstrate its use in combination with a clicker system, and show that PI is much more than the use of clickers. Participants will work in groups to develop new PI questions addressing challenges to their students' learning, and discuss numerous pedagogical benefits conferred through PI. Instructors interested in increasing engagement in any CS course may attend. Participants are encouraged to bring current lecture materials. Laptop optional

ACM Categories & Descriptors: K.3.2

Keywords: peer instruction, active learning

Incorporating Software Architecture in the Computer Science Curriculum

Martin L. Barrett, *East Tennessee State University*
Steve Chenoweth, *Rose-Hulman Institute of Technology*
Larry Jones, *Software Engineering Institute*
Amine Chigani, *Virginia Tech*
Ayse Bener, *Ryerson University*
Mei-Huei Tang, *Gannon University*

This workshop introduces software architecture concepts and their incorporation into computer science and software engineering curricula. Participants will learn techniques used in industry to specify quality attributes critical to architecture and use those attributes to drive the system structure using common architectural styles. Exercises will demonstrate these techniques and explore pedagogical uses of the techniques in CS and SE classes. Sample computer science curricula with courses that integrate workshop material will be presented. Presenters will lead a brainstorming session to help participants develop practical methods for using the material in their courses. Participants will become part of a community of educators sharing educational resources in software architecture.

ACM Categories & Descriptors: D.2.11

Keywords: Software Architecture

Parallelism and Concurrency for Data-Structures & Algorithms Courses

Robert A. Chesebrough, *Intel Corporation*
Johnnie W. Baker, *Kent State University*

This workshop is inspired by Dan Grossman s SIGCSE 2011 workshop on Data Abstractions. We also review C/C++ conversions of the original Java-based materials and will also include material from the Parallel Algorithms course at Kent State. The workshop will appeal to data-structure and algorithms course instructors. Workshop topics will include divide and conquer approaches, work sharing concepts, and a scoped locking scheme in OpenMP for C++ classes. This material is driven via core data-structure examples (queues, sorting, reductions, etc.) and using a Fork/Join Framework found in OpenMP and Intel® Cilk Plus and Intel® Threading Building Blocks. Participants will write parallel programs and test them on the Intel® Many-core Testing Lab. Laptop Required. Laptop is required.

ACM Categories & Descriptors: D.1.3

Keywords: Data Structures, Algorithms, C++, OpenMP, Intel® Cilk Plus, Intel® Threading Building Blocks

Copyright is held by the author/owner(s).
SIGCSE'12, February 29–March 3, 2012, Raleigh, North Carolina, USA.
ACM 978-1-4503-1098-7/12/02

ARTSI Robotics Roadshow-in-a-Box: Turnkey Solution for Providing Robotics Workshops to Middle and High School Students

Monica Anderson, *The University of Alabama*
David Touretzky, *Carnegie Mellon University*
Chutima Boonthum-Denecke, *Hampton University*

In this half-day tutorial, we will introduce the ARTSI Robotics Roadshow-in-a-Box (RRIB) , a single point resource for those getting started in robotics outreach. The RRIB is a kit which contains robots, software and prepared materials for providing robotics workshops for middle and high school students that focuses on showing computer scientists as problem solvers and not just programmers through activities with a larger context. The RRIB fills a need for materials that are accessible to those who may have limited knowledge of robotics or limited experience in middle school outreach, whether that is undergraduate students or faculty researchers who might have limited outreach experience or preparation time. Laptop Required.

ACM Categories & Descriptors: K.3.1

Keywords: Robotics, Middle School

Program by Design: From Animations to Data Structures

Kathi Fisler, *WPI*
Stephen Bloch, *Adelphi University*

We present the Program by Design introductory CS curriculum through the lenses of graphics, animations, algebra, and data structures. Animations programming is popular for CS1, but many such curricula lack clean paths into CS2. Program by Design is different. Using and reinforcing concepts from algebra, students learn to write animations (including standard topics such as model/view separation and event-handling), then move seamlessly into working with structured data, lists, trees, and objects. The curriculum emphasizes design, testing, and writing maintainable programs, without losing the engagement of animations. The workshop uses lectures and hands-on exercises to provide high-school and college teachers an overview of the approach. See www.programbydesign.org. Laptop Optional.

ACM Categories & Descriptors: K.3.2; D.2.2

Keywords: Introductory computing curricula, programming with animations, test-driven design, object-oriented programming

CS Outreach with App Inventor

Michelle Friend, *Stanford University*
Jeff Gray, *University of Alabama*

Mobile phone programming can provide teens an authentic and engaging hook into computer science. With App Inventor, developed by Google and moved to MIT, programming Android apps is as easy as clicking blocks together. App Inventor has been used successfully in after school programs, roadshows, summer camps, teacher workshops, and computer science classrooms from middle school through college. Participants will get an overview of App Inventor including project ideas and sample student code, hear outreach planning suggestions, write programs, develop outreach plans, and see how the Java Bridge helps transition from App Inventor to Java. Please bring a laptop with App Inventor. Even the most time-stretched professor or teacher can encourage students in computer science with App Inventor.

ACM Categories & Descriptors: K.3.2

Keywords: Outreach, Mobile, K-12

Making Mathematical Reasoning Fun: Tool-Assisted, Collaborative Techniques

Jason O. Hallstrom, *Clemson University*
Joe Hollingsworth, *Indiana University Southeast*
Joan Krone, *Denison University*
Murali Sitaraman, *Clemson University*

Is it possible to excite students about learning the mathematical principles that underlie high-quality software? Can we teach them to apply these principles using modern software tools? Can this be accomplished without displacing existing content? In each case, the answer is a resounding yes but it takes the right set of pedagogical principles, teaching tools, and classroom exercises. This hands-on laboratory will introduce a set of principles, tools, and exercises that have proven to work. By adopting one content module at a time, educators will better prepare students to reason rigorously about the software they develop and maintain. The workshop will introduce a series of independent content modules that can be introduced in any course where mathematical reasoning might be taught from introductory programming and software engineering to data structures and algorithms. They are designed to supplement, rather than replace, existing course materials. Fees for this workshop will be covered for a limited number of attendees through an NSF award; limited travel support is also available. A laptop is required to participate.

ACM Categories & Descriptors: K.3.2

Keywords: Analytical reasoning, interface specifications, contract programming, formal methods, learning tools

Snap! (Build Your Own Blocks)

Brian Harvey, *University of California, Berkeley*
Daniel Garcia, *University of California, Berkeley*
Josh Paley, *Henry M. Gunn High School*
Luke Segars, *University of California, Berkeley*

This workshop is for high school and college teachers of general-interest (CS 0') computer science courses. It presents the programming environment used in two of the five initial AP CS Principles pilot courses. Snap! (Build Your Own Blocks) is a free , graphical, drag-and- drop extension to the Scratch programming language. Scratch, designed for 8-14 year olds, models programs as "scripts" without names, arguments, or return values. Snap! supports older learners (14-20) by adding named procedures (thus recursion), procedures as data (thus higher order functions) structured lists, and sprites as first class objects with inheritance. Participants will learn Snap! through discussion, programming exercises, and exploration. See http://snap.berkeley.edufor details. Laptop required.

Copyright is held by the author/owner(s).
SIGCSE'12, February 29–March 3, 2012, Raleigh, North Carolina, USA.
ACM 978-1-4503-1098-7/12/02

ACM Categories & Descriptors: graphical

Keywords: drag-and-drop extension to the Scratch programming language. Scratch

Circuits and Microcontrollers in Computer Organization Laboratories

Marge M. Coahran, *Dickinson College*
Janet Davis, *Grinnell College*

This workshop will introduce a set of hands-on laboratory activities appropriate for a first Computer Organization course. Participants will work with real equipment: first implementing elementary digital circuits with TTL logic chips, and then programming AVR microcontrollers in assembly to drive fun accessories such as LEDs and speakers. Participants will not take equipment home afterwards, but will receive parts lists and vendor information. The workshop is intended for educators with little electronics background who are interested in incorporating electronics laboratories into their courses. Laptops (Linux, Mac, or Windows) will provide the programming environment for the AVRs. Free software will be available before the workshop. Participants will work in pairs. Laptop recommended.

ACM Categories & Descriptors: K.3.2

Keywords: Computer organization laboratories, digital circuits, assembly language, AVR microcontroller

Web Development with Python and Django

Ariel Ortiz, *Tecnológico de Monterrey, Campus Estado de México*

Many instructors have already discovered the joy of teaching programming using the Python programming language. Now it s time to take Python to the next level. This workshop will introduce Django, an open source Python web framework that saves you time and makes web development fun. It s aimed at Computer Science instructors who want to teach how to build elegant web applications with minimal fuss. Django follows the Model-View-Controller (MVC) architectural pattern. Its goal is to ease the creation of complex, database-driven websites. Django emphasizes reusability and pluggability of components, rapid development, and the principle of DRY (Don t Repeat Yourself). Python is used throughout, even for settings, files, and data models. Topics that will be covered during the workshop include: setup and configuration, template language, and database integration through object-relational mapping. Participants should have some familiarity with Python, HTML and SQL. Laptop Required.

ACM Categories & Descriptors: K.3.2; C.2.4

Keywords: Python, Django, MVC, Web development

Improving the Accessibility of Computing Enrichment Programs

Richard Ladner, *University of Washington*
Karen Alkoby, *Gallaudet University*
Jeff Bigham, *University of Rochester*
Stephanie Ludi, *Rochester Institute of Technology*
Daniela Marghitu, *Auburn University*
Andreas Stefik, *University of Southern Illinois, Edwardsville*

Many wonderful enrichment programs have been created to introduce young people to computing, but with little attention to making them accessible to students with disabilities. In this workshop participants will learn from practitioners who have introduced computing and programming to young people with disabilities. They will also learn first-hand from students with disabilities about their needs in learning programming. There will be breakout sessions for participants to apply what they have learned to improve existing enrichment programs such as Alice, Arduino, Scratch, Kodu, App Inventor, Greenfoot, Lego Mindstorms, Processing, and Computer Science Unplugged.

ACM Categories & Descriptors: K.3.2

Keywords: Disability, Computing Enrichment, Programming

Enhancing Student Interest by Extending Graphics Applications

Samuel A. Rebelsky, *Grinnell College*

Computer science teachers strive for new examples and problems to interest millenials. The Media Computation approach has proven successful in attracting students in contexts from community colleges to R1 universities students are clearly excited by writing programs that make images. In this workshop, we show how to go a step further and have write scripts and plug-ins in Python for open-source graphics programs such as the GNU Image Manipulation Program and Inkscape, open source alternatives to Photoshop and Illustrator. With this approach, students not only make images, they also write filters and features that they can share with others, even with non-programmers. For example, students have written filters that fractalize vector graphics or that turn images into something that looks like stained glass. The ability to make programs that others will use is particularly motivational. We will explore ways in which students can interact with both Inkscape and GIMP, from working with interactive programming consoles to writing plug-ins that can easily be shared with others. We will also consider the ways in which different models of image making can be used to motivate the major programming paradigms. The approach has been used with Python, Scheme, and C and for everything from a one-week module to a full course.

ACM Categories & Descriptors: K.3.2

Keywords: Novice programming, Python, GNU Image Manipulation Program, Inkscape, Open Source

Copyright is held by the author/owner(s).
SIGCSE'12, February 29–March 3, 2012, Raleigh, North Carolina, USA.
ACM 978-1-4503-1098-7/12/02.

Engage Your Students By Teaching Programming Using Only Mobile Devices with TouchDevelop

Nikolai Tillmann, *Microsoft Research*
MichaB Moskal, *Microsoft Research*
Jonathan de Halleux, *Microsoft Research*
Manuel Fähndrich, *Microsoft Research*
Tao Xie, *North Carolina State University*

We are experiencing a technology shift: Powerful and easy-to-use touchscreen-based mobile devices like smartphones and tablets are becoming more prevalent than traditional PCs and laptops. We propose that computer programming, and thus teaching of programming, can and should be done directly on the mobile devices themselves, without the need for a separate PC or laptop to write code. In this workshop, participants will learn about developing software directly on smartphones without a PC using TouchDevelop, a novel application creation environment on Windows Phone 7 from Microsoft Research (http://touchdevelop.com). Its typed, structured programming language is built around the idea of only using a touchscreen as the input device to author code. A semi-structured code editor makes it easy to navigate between different syntax elements. By inferring types and mining previously written programs, the editor provides highly predictive auto-completion suggestions to the user. The language provides built-in primitives that make it easy to access the rich sensor data available on a mobile device. Programming on mobile devices engages students in new ways, allowing them to access and manipulate programmatically their most personal digital data such as pictures, videos, and music. Programming on smartphones which we carry around with us at all times means instant gratification for students, as they can show their games and applications to their friends, and it means that students can do their homework or additional practicing at all times. For this workshop, a laptop is optional; Windows Phone 7 devices will be provided for exercises.

ACM Categories & Descriptors: D.2.3; D.2.11; D.2.6

Keywords: Programming, Mobile Devices, Touchscreen, Cloud, Type inference

CS in Parallel: Modules for Adding Parallel Computing to CS Courses, from CS2 to Theory of Computation

Richard A. Brown, *St. Olaf College*
Elizabeth Shoop, *Macalester College*

Parallel computing with more and more cores is here to stay. This workshop presents four independent, class-tested, primarily hands-on modules for incrementally adding parallelism in undergraduate CS courses, each requiring 1 to 3 class days and versatile for diverse courses and curricula: parallelizing loops and sharing memory on Intel's Manycore Testing lab (for a second CS course or for computer organization); parallel web crawler in Java or C++ (second CS course); parallel sorting (algorithms); À-calculus theory for communicating sequential processes (theory of computation). Workshop materials provided, drawn from CSinParallel.org. Intended audience: CS instructors. Laptop recommended (Windows, Mac, Linux).

Copyright is held by the author/owner(s).
SIGCSE'12, February 29–March 3, 2012, Raleigh, North Carolina, USA.
ACM 978-1-4503-1098-7/12/02

ACM Categories & Descriptors: K.3.2; D.1.3

Keywords: CS education, education, parallelism, parallel computing, multicore, parallel programming, scalability, curriculum, parallel sorting, pi-calculus, CSP, OpenMP, computer organization, Java, C++

Listening to Linked Lists: Using Multimedia to Learn Data Structures

Mark Guzdial, *Georgia Institute of Technology*
Barbara Ericson, *Georgia Institute of Technology*

Everybody teaches linked lists, with homework like implementing duplicate, weave, and reverse. When those nodes contain strings or numbers, these are pretty boring assignments. When these nodes contain music (MIDI), these operations are composing music, which can then be played. This workshop shows how to use music, images, and sounds to teach the basic data structures, including linked lists, circular linked lists, stacks, queues, and trees. These pieces can then be tied together through the use of simulations to generate animated movies. We will be using Java, though many of the methods can also be used in Python.

ACM Categories & Descriptors: K.3.2

Keywords: Linked lists, data structures, multimedia, media computation

Puzzle-Based Learning: Introducing Critical Thinking and Problem Solving for Computer Science and Engineering

Raja Sooriamurthi, *Carnegie Mellon University*
Nickolas Falkner, *University of Adelaide*
Zbigniew Michalewicz, *University of Adelaide*

Puzzle-based learning (PBL) is an emerging model of teaching critical thinking and problem solving. Today s market place needs skilled graduates capable of solving real problems of innovation in a changing environment. While solving puzzles is innately fun, companies such as Google and Yahoo also use puzzles to assess the creative problem solving skills of potential employees. In this interactive workshop we will examine a range of puzzles, games, and general problem solving strategies. Participants will emerge with the needed pedagogical foundation to offer a full course on PBL or to include it as part of another course. Currently 40+ institutions around the world are offering courses based on PBL. More details are available at www.PuzzleBasedLearning.edu.au. Laptop optional.

ACM Categories & Descriptors: A.0; G.0

Keywords: pedagogy, critical thinking

SIGCSE 2012 Posters

Using Reflection to Enhance Feedback for Automated Grading

Carl Alphonce, *University at Buffalo*
Joseph LeGasse, *Meritain Health*

Feedback serves a critical role in the learning process. For formative assessment to be effective in supporting a student s learning, feedback must be provided in a timely fashion (so a student can derive benefit while engaging in the learning activity), it must be consistent across multiple submissions of the same student as well as across submissions by different students, and it must be of high quality (i.e. it must give students guidance as to how to improve their submission). In this poster we present a small library of Java classes which aid the writing automated tests for assessing the design of student programming exercises. Through its use of reflection we can allow more free-form assignments, and can provide feedback on both program functionality and design.

ACM Categories & Descriptors: K.3.2

Keywords: Automated testing, reflection, automated feedback

The Cross-Curriculum Mobile Computing Labware for CS

Kai Qian, *Southern Polytechnic State University*
Dan Lo, *Southern Polytechnic State University*
Yi Pan, *Georgia State University*
Yanqing Zhang, *Georgia State University*
Xiaolin Hu, *Georgia State University*
Liang Hong, *Tennessee State University*

Advanced mobile devices such as smart phones and tablets have become a part of daily lives for digital native students today. The integration of mobile computing with these devices into multiple courses in computer science (CS) curriculum will connect the education to leading-edge information technologies, motivate and engage students in CS learning, fill in the gap with IT industry needs, and help faculties build strong expertise on modern mobile computing. Meanwhile, the hands-on experience with mobile computing will supply the students with a better understanding of the classical CS concepts. In this paper, we propose to develop a cross-curriculum labware based on the Android platform to introduce the knowledge and practice of a wide range of CS subjects with smart phones and tablets.

ACM Categories & Descriptors: D.3.3

Keywords: Mobile computing, Android, Mobile device, Labware.

Copyright is held by the author/owner(s).
SIGCSE'12, February 29–March 3, 2012, Raleigh, North Carolina, USA.
ACM 978-1-4503-1098-7/12/02.

Merging Healthcare and Technology: A Multi-Disciplinary Health Information Technology (HIT) Curriculum

Elizabeth V. Howard, *Miami University – Middletown*
Jill E. Courte, *Miami University – Hamilton*
Donna M. Evans, *Miami University – Middletown*
Marilyn Anderson, *Miami University - Middletown*

Please be patient with us as we move to our new computer system is a common sign at healthcare providers offices. Mandates from the federal government are merging the fields of healthcare and information technology and experts predict a significant increase in jobs related to Health Information Technology (HIT). In this poster session, we will share our new HIT curriculum (Bachelor of Science in Information Technology with a major in Health Information Technology) along with the process followed to develop this curriculum. Developed in collaboration with nursing educators and in consultation with HIT professionals, this unique multi-disciplinary program blends technology and healthcare to prepare students for a wide variety of opportunities in the evolving field of HIT.

ACM Categories & Descriptors: K.0

Keywords: Health Information Technology;New Curriculum;Multidisciplinary

An Integrated Introduction to Network Protocols and Cryptography to High School Students

William M. Mongan, *Drexel University*

We describe our experience in teaching an integrated module in networks, mathematics, and cryptography, suitable for high school students. The objective is to design a lesson with minimal prerequisite background and a varying degree of programming experience, with an aim towards exciting students early on about computing. Students create and implement a chat program protocol and a minimal RSA algorithm implementation, and implement a brute force algorithm to recover each other's private key. Depending on student experience, scaffolding can be provided to assist with the programming, and advanced topics are possible as extensions to this lesson. We hope that this lesson can be taught as an interdisciplinary unit in math and computer science classes.

ACM Categories & Descriptors: C.2.2; K.3.2

Keywords: Networking, Education

A PC-based Robot for Learning Computer Vision and Advanced Programming

Xuzhou Chen, *Fitchburg State University*
Nadimpalli V.R. Mahadev, *Fitchburg State University*

In this paper, we describe an approach of using a PC based robot (PCRob) for teaching advanced topic course in pattern recognition and computer vision. Unlike most of the robots where only the microprocessors are used, the robot we design and build uses mini

PC and off-the-shelf peripherals to provide the computing power in order to process some functionalities such as image processing and pattern recognition.

ACM Categories & Descriptors: I.2.5; K.3.2

Keywords: Robot; Robotic programming, Pattern recognition, Speech recognition

Girls Gather for Computer Science (G2CS)

Shereen Khoja, *Pacific University*
Juliet Brosing, *Pacific University*
Camille Wainwright, *Pacific University*
Jeffrey Barlow, *Pacific University*

Girls Gather for Computer Science (G2CS) is an innovative computer science summer camp for middle school girls. The goal of the camp is to change how girls experience computer science by placing them in an all-female environment where they explore computer science in a fun and interactive way. Girls are exposed to female role models while middle school teachers and parents are educated about the issues facing women in technology fields. Each week of the camp has a different theme: web development, robotics, programming with Alice, and computer hardware and the camp includes field trips to local technology companies such as Intel and Vernier Software & Technology. Campers use a closed social networking site to communicate and share ideas, and continue to use this site after the camp is over. This provides the girls with a supporting community that will continue to foster their interest in computer science even after the camp has ended. Oregon Public Broadcasting (OPB) partnered with us to produce the camp website, a 10 minute video of the camp, 5 interviews with professional female computer scientists, and online interactive games that teach computer science concepts. The project includes a ten-year study to follow the progress of the campers. Initial assessment of G2CS shows that it had a positive and significant impact on the participants.

ACM Categories & Descriptors: K.3.2

Keywords: Summer Camp, Women in CS

Debuggems to Assess Student Learning in E-Textiles

Deborah A. Fields, *University of Pennsylvania*
Kristin A. Searle, *University of Pennsylvania*
Yasmin B. Kafai, *University of Pennsylvania*
Hannah S. Min, *University of Pennsylvania*

One challenge in assessing students engineering and programming designs is that the problems are difficult to evaluate with pencil and paper. Projects with multiple types of designs (circuitry, coding, aesthetics) can go wrong in many ways (Resnick, Berg, & Eisenberg, 2000). Identifying, debugging, and solving these problems is at the crux of being able to design computational and material projects. In this poster we analyze high school students collaborative engagement with a series of isomorphic deconstruction kits (debuggems) developed to assess their learning of coding, circuit design and creation (through sewing) in e-textiles with the LilyPad Arduino. The debuggem was designed based on our observations of common challenges that students faced when designing their own e-textiles projects during 4-week workshops. We videotaped ten students collaborating in pairs as they worked to turn on LEDs in a project strategically designed with problems in poor crafting, non-functional circuitry design and insufficient coding. Analysis includes what problems students struggled the most to solve and common types of problem solving strategies used. The debuggem was successful in that it revealed common problems, allowed for multiple solutions, and capitalized on collaborative learning. As hoped, all students solved most problems but no group solved every problem in the time allotted without help; student pairs also came up with multiple solutions. The findings indicate that deconstruction kits are not only promising tools for evaluating students learning of designing with e-textiles but also valuable learning tools, especially when peer collaboration is taken into account.

ACM Categories & Descriptors: K.3.0

Keywords: E-textiles, programming, assessment

Mediascripting: Teaching Introductory CS by Through Interactive Graphics Scripting

Janet Davis, *Grinnell College*
Samuel A. Rebelsky, *Grinnell College*
Jerod Weinman, *Grinnell College*

upswing, Computer science teachers continue to strive for new examples and problems to interest millenials. The Media Computation approach (Guzdial 2003) has proven successful in attracting students in contexts from community colleges to R1 universities students are clearly excited by writing programs that make images. In this project, take Media Computing in new directions: we have students build images by interactively scripting an application, which means that they can more easily experiment and mix work that they create by hand and work that they create by programming ; we work collaboratively with studio art faculty, so students build works that must meet underlying design criteria; we teach using the workshop approach, so most classes involve students working in small teams on a set of problems; and we use a multi-paradigm approach students make images using functional, declarative, imperative, and object-oriented techniques. This approach has proven quite successful our enrollments are up (at least 33% in CS1, 50% in CS2). We are attracting more women (now 1/3 of our students). And comparative data suggest that our students gain significantly more confidence in their abilities than do student in other introductory science courses.

ACM Categories & Descriptors: K.3.2

Keywords: Novice programming, Media Computation, Multi-paradigm programming

Do Faculty Recognize the Difference Between Computer Science and Information Technology?: A Survey of Liberal Arts Faculty

Hannah Fidoten, *Knox College*
Jaime Spacco, *Knox College*

Copyright is held by the author/owner(s).
SIGCSE'12, February 29–March 3, 2012, Raleigh, North Carolina, USA.
ACM 978-1-4503-1098-7/12/02.

We asked all of the liberal arts faculty who advise undergraduates on course selection at the 14 colleges in the Associated Colleges of the Midwest a series of questions regarding their perceptions of the personality traits of Computer Science (CS) students, topics they think are covered in CS classes, and their overall impressions of CS. Our goal was to test empirically the hypothesis that many non-CS faculty are unaware of the differences between CS and Information Technology (IT). We received over 200 survey responses, which revealed that, among non-CS faculty, 10% disagree or are neutral that CS should even be part of a liberal arts curriculum, 9% think that CS students are taught to fix printers and other peripherals, and 35% believe that CS students are taught to use Microsoft Word and Excel in their courses. Our results also revealed that 60% of CS faculty believe that men are more interested in CS than are women (although we did not ask why they believe this to be the case). Overall, while we found statistically significant differences between the answers given by CS and non-CS faculty, the overall evidence suggests that the majority of non-CS faculty in the Associated Colleges of the Midwest have a good understanding of CS.

ACM Categories & Descriptors: K.3.2

Keywords: survey, cs ed research

Interdisciplinary Travel Courses in Computer Science

Paige H. Meeker, *Presbyterian College*

In today s world, many students are being encouraged not only to participate in class work and internships, but to travel and gain experiential knowledge. At Presbyterian College, students are required to complete either a research/internship class or an experiential/travel class as a part of their general education requirements. Computer science students were often going on trips with other departments to fulfill this need. This poster explores a course offered at Presbyterian College in May, 2010, which took students from our Physics and Computer Science department behind the scenes of Kennedy Space Center and Walt Disney World. It will include information both about course content and about the cost and overhead involved in planning such a course.

ACM Categories & Descriptors: A.m

Keywords: New Course Topics, Travel

User Type Clustering to Refine Search and Browse for Educational Resources

Monika Akbar, *Virginia Tech*
Clifford A. Shaffer, *Virginia Tech*

Educational portals such as Algoviz.org contain rich information resources, and a key concern is directing the users to specific resources that are of interest to them. While AlgoViz has significant traffic, we cannot count on active user participation in the form of explicit ratings of individual resources. Often called a "cold-start" problem, this scenario is well-known in community-based websites. Lacking active user data, we instead use log data to deduce user trends. We describe our techniques for clustering users based on the log data. We show how this cluster analysis can be used to refine searching and browsing within AlgoViz. Our approach has the potential to be useful for a wide range of educational resource portals.

ACM Categories & Descriptors: H.4.0; K.3.0

Keywords: Information Systems, CS Ed Research

A Comprehensive CS Curriculum Revision, Implementation, and Analysis

Steven Huss-Lederman, *Beloit College*

In 2005, the Beloit College Computer Science Program began a complete revision of its courses and curriculum facing usual issues: limited staff, declining enrollments, and the Computing Curricula 2001 document. We used ½ semester, ½ unit courses to address the diverse areas with limited courses allowing multiple entry points by interest and knowledge level and flexibility for non-majors; however, it did present scheduling and staffing issues. After two years of experience, we revised our ideas to recombine some ½ unit courses to allow larger projects, stacked courses where students at different levels took courses together, and instituted a two year capstone experience that combined material from several classes. The poster will provide details and an opportunity to exchange ideas.

ACM Categories & Descriptors: K.3.2

Keywords: Curricular revision

Developing an Interdisciplinary Health Informatics Security and Privacy Program

Xiaohong Yuan, *North Carolina A&T State University*
Jinsheng Xu, *North Carolina A&T State University*
Kossi Edoh, *North Carolina A&T State University*
Hong Wang, *North Carolina A&T State University*

Health informatics is one of the nation s largest growth industries. With the government's increasing interest in electronic health records and growing investment by healthcare organizations in technology, there is a large demand for a health informatics and health information technology workforce. To protect health information systems, it is highly important for health informatics professionals to be well educated and trained in information assurance, and to understand the many concerns of security, privacy, integrity and reliability. This poster describes our project of developing a new interdisciplinary program of Bachelor of Science in Computer Science (BSCS) concentration in Health Informatics Security and Privacy (HISP) at North Carolina A&T State University (NC A&T SU). To establish this program, we are developing a new course on health information systems in the Department of Computer Science, a new course on Mathematics for Health Informatics in the Department of Mathematics, and modifying an existing course in the Department of Management. We are also developing three course modules on health informatics security and privacy: Health Information Assurance and Security, Access Control in Healthcare Information Systems, and XML Security in Health Information Systems. These course modules will be integrated in the existing computer security and information assurance courses in the Department of Computer

Copyright is held by the author/owner(s).
SIGCSE'12, February 29–March 3, 2012, Raleigh, North Carolina, USA.
ACM 978-1-4503-1098-7/12/02.

Science. The BSCS concentration in HISP curriculum as well as project plan will also be described in this poster.

ACM Categories & Descriptors: E.3; H.0; J.3

Keywords: Health Information Systems, Health Informatics, Information Security and Privacy

A Team Software Development Course Featuring iPad Programming

Robert E. England, *Transylvania University*

This poster describes a new upper level undergraduate computer science course in team software development, featuring the Apple iPad as the development platform. The course draws from a wide range of state-of-the-art topics in software development theory and practice, including use of Apple s extensive software development Cocoa Touch framework for its mobile devices, advanced Object-Oriented Programming, gang of four Design Patterns, and traditional Software Engineering practices, including accountability to external clients and public presentation of results. The course was developed at Transylvania University, a small Liberal Arts college of approximately 1200 students, and it was taught there during the Fall 2010 semester.

ACM Categories & Descriptors: K.3.1

Keywords: iPad, Xcode, mobile computing, team project, interface programming

The Role of Belonging in Engagement, Retention and Persistence in Computer Science

Nanette Veilleux, *Simmons College*
Rebecca Bates, *Minnesota State University*
Diane Jones, *University of Washington*
Cheryl Allendoerfer, *University of Washington*
Joy Crawford, *University of Washington*

Retaining students in computer science (CS) majors has been a persistent topic among CS educators for almost two decades. Discussion and research has largely focused on improving student engagement in the academic experience in order to provide a more welcoming and compelling introduction to the field. Research has identified a wide variety of factors affecting student engagement in general, which in turn affects key outcomes including academic achievement, retention and persistence. Feeling connected to a community and sense of belonging can substantially influence student engagement. Our study suggests that this sense of belonging can also help mitigate student perceptions that influence them to be discouraged, especially about their ability to succeed, and leave computer science. In particular, support from extra-curricular as well as academic communities may lead students to perceive that ability is not a binary, fixed constraint, but a malleable gradient that can be influenced by factors within the student s control.

ACM Categories & Descriptors: K.3.2

Keywords: Computer Science Education, Retention, Persistence

Streamlining Project Setup in Eclipse for Both Time-Constrained and Large-Scale Assignments

Ellen Boyd, *Virginia Tech*
Anthony Allevato, *Virginia Tech*

Many introductory computer science courses include regular lab sessions that require students to develop short programs that relate to corresponding lecture material. Logistical tasks required for assignment completion, such as project setup and submission, impose certain burdens on students and instructors. Due to time constraints, instructors frequently provide starter files or skeleton projects for students to import into their workspace at the beginning of each lab so that they can feasibly complete the assignment in the required time. Setting up projects in Eclipse to include these files and dependencies still consumes significant time during these labs, however. To eliminate the time spent trying to fix project configuration issues, we have developed a plug-in for Eclipse that allows students directly from within the IDE to download and import multi-file projects corresponding to individual lab assignments. The projects will be automatically imported into the student s workspace and will be correctly configured and linked to any required dependencies. The plug-in can also be employed with large-scale programming assignments; as assignments increase in complexity, they may require a non-trivial amount of extra configuration before students can begin work on their solution. With this plug-in, students can now focus primarily on the problem-solving aspect of their work and accomplish all necessary tasks, from initial project configuration to final delivery, without leaving the Eclipse IDE and interrupting their workflow.

ACM Categories & Descriptors: K.3.2; D.2.6

Keywords: Eclipse, IDE, labs, project configuration

A Customizable Platform for Classroom Collaboration Using Mobile Devices

Stephen B. Hughes, *University of Northern Iowa*
J Ben Schafer, *University of Northern Iowa*
Aaron Mangel, *University of Northern Iowa*
Sean Fredericksen, *University of Northern Iowa*

One of the major perceived barriers to the adoption of Classroom Response Systems, a.k.a. clickers , is limited interactivity. Students using dedicated clicker hardware are often only able to provide basic multiple choice or simple numeric responses. The accessibility and flexibility of smartphones make them an intriguing platform for managing some of the shortfalls of traditional classroom response systems. This approach not only leverages a resource that a growing number of students already own, but also aims to enhance the effectiveness of the system by tapping into the robust interaction capabilities that these devices afford. This poster will describe a smartphone implementation of a classroom response system and discuss efforts to extend the basic clicker interaction model.

ACM Categories & Descriptors: K.3.1

Keywords: Collective Interaction, Classroom Response Systems, Computer Supported Collaborative Learning

Copyright is held by the author/owner(s).
SIGCSE'12, February 29–March 3, 2012, Raleigh, North Carolina, USA.
ACM 978-1-4503-1098-7/12/02.

Explaining the Dynamic Structure and Behavior of Java Programs Using a Visual Debugger

Demian Lessa, *University at Buffalo*
Bharat Jayaraman, *University at Buffalo*

An important challenge in teaching object-oriented (OO) programming and methodology in introductory Computer Science courses is explaining the run-time of OO programs. This is largely due to the OO methodology, which encourages the use of features such as polymorphism and design patterns, resulting in object interactions and control flow that are hard to grasp, especially for novice programmers. We present an approach to program comprehension in which students use storyboards and visual debugging to build a clear mental model of the dynamic behavior of OO programs. In this context, a storyboard consists of a sequence of figures representing run-time aspects of interest (e.g. states or interactions) and an explanatory narrative in terms of OO concepts and source elements. The selected visual debugger must render execution histories and run-time states using visual notations consistent with the OO methodology (e.g., objects, member fields, method calls within object contexts). Instructors create storyboards using figures exported from the debugger and incorporate them in course materials. Further, storyboards included in specifications of programming assignments alongside test cases provide students with a detailed account of their programs' run-time at interesting points in execution. By executing their programs under the visual debugger, students can compare the observed run-time states with those illustrated in the storyboards and effectively assess the behavioral correctness of their programs. Hence, the combined use of storyboards and visual debugging can benefit students during the coding phase by guiding them towards writing code that closely adheres to the OO methodology from the outset.

ACM Categories & Descriptors: D.1.5;D.2.5; K.3.2

Keywords: Visual Debugging, Program Comprehension, Storyboard

Using FPGA Systems Across the Computer Science Curriculum

D. Brian Larkins, *Coastal Carolina University*
H. Erin Rickard, *Coastal Carolina University*
William M. Jones, *Coastal Carolina University*

The field of computer science is continuously growing, requiring curriculum developers to make numerous tradeoffs between depth and breadth with every advance. Faculty must look for new ways to communicate more concepts within a fixed number of contact hours as well as employ techniques that underscore interrelated concepts over multiple courses. With this poster, we present the use of field-programmable gate arrays (FPGAs) as a flexible hardware system that may be modified to suit the needs of a wide variety of classes. While FPGA devices are a natural fit for teaching hardware concepts in organization and architecture classes, we feel that they can also be used in a variety of roles within a number of other courses. We describe our work integrating FPGA curriculum modules into several courses in the CS curriculum: organization and architecture, compiler construction, robotics, operating systems, security, and image processing. We believe that by using these devices in several courses, students gain greater familiarity with a hands-on, reconfigurable hardware platform and can leverage this experience throughout their coursework. This approach is consonant with recent trends that emphasize the importance of students being able to reason about the end-to-end operation of an entire system and helps strengthen the relationships between different subfields within computer science. We describe both the changes made to our curriculum and the effectiveness of our approach.

ACM Categories & Descriptors: K.3.2

Keywords: FPGA, Education, Curriculum, Hardware Platforms

Maximizing Content Learning for Deaf Students and English as a Second Language Students

Raja S. Kushalnagar, *Rochester Institute of Technology*
Joeseph S. Stanislow, *Rochester Institute of Technology*

The introductory programming college course is usually difficult for many new students, as they struggle to master basic programming concepts and to develop logically correct programs. Surveys in college have estimated that around 30 percent of these students drop out or fail it. These tasks are even more difficult for Deaf and Hard of Hearing (DHH) students, even when provided with accessible visual translations through sign language interpreters or real-time captions. We have extended the idea of traditional audio capture and transmission accessible technology devices by developing and testing use of smart phones as multimedia recording devices to record multiple videos and stream them to the deaf or hard of hearing student. We call this approach multiple video perspectives.

ACM Categories & Descriptors: H.5.1

Keywords: Educational Learning; Multimedia Interfaces

All-in-One Virtualized Laboratory

Shamsi Moussavi, MassBay Community College
Giuseppe Sena, MassBay Community College

Laboratory-based courses--the corner stone of Computer Science programs in our community college--have been difficult to manage due to the shortage of lab space, available equipment, and basic infrastructures. This has meant that for the past few years, we have not been able to offer certain courses that allow students administrative privileges in order to complete their assignments, such as Web Server Administration course. We wanted to be able to offer a number of courses requiring various systems, levels of functionality, and networking set up in one laboratory. We researched and experimented with different virtualized systems. Specifically, we looked at the use of VMs in CS courses and laboratories. Through use of virtualization technology we implemented multiple VMs (one for each course) on each computer in a laboratory. Each VM was set up for specific course requirement; hence, multiple courses were offered simultaneously in one laboratory. In designing the laboratory, we were also careful not to adversely affect the security of college's computer network. Therefore, the virtualized laboratory was separated from the college's computer network. This approach not only provided

Copyright is held by the author/owner(s).
SIGCSE'12, February 29–March 3, 2012, Raleigh, North Carolina, USA.
ACM 978-1-4503-1098-7/12/02.

the capabilities that we were looking for, but can also be used in future to provide easier access to students, even from outside the school network.

ACM Categories & Descriptors: K.3.1

Keywords: Virtual Machines, Computer networking, Virtualization software, lab-based courses, access to underlying OS, higher privileges for access

Recursive Thinkers and Doers in Cs1

Joseph A. Cottam, *Indiana University*
Suzanne Menzel, *Indiana University*

Computer scientists require a precise and complete understanding of recursion. Earlier work has indicated that recursion merits attention in CS1 [2]. We present a simple test question that, when used in a final exam for three courses over two semesters, is shown to significantly predict student performance on the final. To evaluate student responses, we present an evaluation rubric that directly reveals common misconceptions about recursion and recursive procedures.

ACM Categories & Descriptors: K.3.2

Keywords: CS1/2, recursion, programming aptitude, concept inventory

Computing in Context: Video Scenarios for Recognizing and Utilizing Basic Computing Constructs

Madalene Spezialetti, *Trinity College*

This poster presents a tool for providing novice students with a context in which to develop the ability to identify problems and patterns for their solutions by using video scenarios. A video scenario is a short film (typically 2-7 minutes) which has an extemporaneous feel. Each video depicts individuals facing a particular problem that can be helped through a computing solution. A selection of video scenarios is presented which is specifically designed to cultivate the problem identification and solution formulation skills of novice programmers by focusing on problems which can be solved using basic computing constructs. The videos can be used in a wide variety of settings and are suitable for use at the middle school, high school and college levels.

ACM Categories & Descriptors: K.3.2

Keywords: video in education, programming constructs, introductory computing

Programming Board-Game Strategies in the Introductory CS Sequence

Ivona Bezakova, *Rochester Institute of Technology*
James Heliotis, *Rochester Institute of Technology*
Sean Strout, *Rochester Institute of Technology*
Adam Oest, *Rochester Institute of Technology*
Paul Solt, *Rochester Institute of Technology*

Board games provide a natural context for the use of basic data structures and search algorithms taught in a typical introductory CS sequence. Unlike traditionally used programming assignments where students implement the actual game, we provide the game engine' and ask the students to implement player strategies. The engine graphically displays the current state of the game and cyclically calls the individual player strategies to perform their moves. The students need to apply the same algorithms as if programming the rule checker for the game. And with the added strategy component

ACM Categories & Descriptors: E.1; F.2.2; K.3.2

Keywords: leaving space for continued improvements and experimentation. The poster describes the game we used last academic year

Copyright is held by the author/owner(s).
SIGCSE'12, February 29–March 3, 2012, Raleigh, North Carolina,USA.
ACM 978-1-4503-1098-7/12/02.

SIGCSE 2012 Posters II

Implementing and Assessing a Blended CS1 Course

John J. Wright, *Juniata College*

Whether we like it or not, college administrations and students are increasingly looking for online courses. K-12 schools are increasingly using online content and blending it with standard content. One of the bridges for us between traditional course delivery and online delivery is the blended course. This approach seems well suited to computer science, which often requires work in labs or with specialized equipment or software. It takes the approach of reversing that which is traditionally lecture and assignments, making classes more interactive and students less passive. This poster seeks input on a blended implementation of CS1 and a subsequent SoTL project to test the effectiveness of offering this course in a blended format.

ACM Categories & Descriptors: K.3.2

Keywords: Blended Learning, CS1

Designing with Projects in Mind: An Approach for Creating Authentic (and Manageable) Programming Projects

Scott Alexander Turner, *University of North Carolina at Pembroke*

Creating programming projects that engage students has been a continual challenge in computer science. Ideally, programming projects should require student to reflect upon and apply programming concepts and help them develop creativity, problem-solving, and other skills for the workplace. The use of real-world problems is one possible solution to the issue but it comes at the cost of increased complexity, size, and burden on the instructor. One approach to reducing these costs is to design (or redesign) programs, developed as part of a research agenda, for use as student projects. Designing these programs for flexibility, adding extra, student-appropriate, feedback and identifying portions of the code that could become interesting student projects helps support both research and classroom learning at the same time. By explicitly designing with projects in mind, instructors can control the complexity and size of these real-world problems and can, potentially, create a platform that can support multiple types of student assignments. This poster describes the experience of redesigning a UML diagramming tool to implement this idea and provides examples of the design decisions made, lessons learned during the process, and other programs that could be used in a similar fashion. Future work includes evaluating the students reaction to the projects and whether enough support is being provided.

ACM Categories & Descriptors: K.3.2

Keywords: Situated Learning, Problem-based learning (PBL), Real-World Problem, Computer Science Education

Copyright is held by the author/owner(s).
SIGCSE'12, February 29–March 3, 2012, Raleigh, North Carolina, USA.
ACM 978-1-4503-1098-7/12/02.

Integrating Elementary Computational Modeling and Programming Principles

Jose M. Garrido, *Kennesaw State University*

We propose an approach to introduce computational models and basic programming principles in an integrated manner and as early as possible in the computing curricula. Our goal is to help educate students of computer science, mathematics, and the various science disciplines, in computational modeling. For this, we have developed a sequence of four courses in computational modeling, the first of which integrates computational modeling with programming principles and includes elementary numerical methods for solving the models. This entry-level course is described and a URL is provided with details of the four courses. Developing a computational model of a problem includes formulating the mathematical representation and implementing it by applying Computer Science concepts, principles and methods.

ACM Categories & Descriptors: I.6.5

Keywords: computational modeling

RoboLIFT: Simple GUI-Based Unit Testing of Student-Written Android Applications

Anthony Allevato, *Virginia Tech*
Stephen H. Edwards, *Virginia Tech*

Many computer science educators have adopted test-driven development practices in their introductory computer science courses, as a way of encouraging incremental development and decreasing defects in student code. This practice is straightforward for basic data-driven objects, but making unit testing of GUI applications approachable for students poses a larger challenge. We have previously addressed this problem for Swing applications by developing LIFT, a library that allows students to easily write JUnit tests for Swing interfaces. Since then, we have transitioned away from Swing to Android as the development platform in CS2 to better motivate and excite our students about their assignments. To fully support this change, we had to ensure that our students could fully test the GUI portions of their solutions on that platform as well. The Android operating system has significant built-in support for GUI testing, but the standard API is too complex for students to use. In order to address this, we developed RoboLIFT, a framework that eases the task of writing concise and complete unit tests for Android applications. Furthermore, RoboLIFT also has support for automated grading on the Web-CAT automated assessment system, so even if instructors do not require their students to follow test-driven development practices, they can still enjoy the benefits of automated grading by writing correctness tests that use RoboLIFT to exercise the students graphical user interfaces.

ACM Categories & Descriptors: K.3.2; D.2.2; D.2.5

Keywords: Android, mobile development, smartphone, tablet, apps, test-driven development, TDD, JUnit, test-first coding, graphical user interfaces, GUI

OpenDSA: A Creative Commons Active-ebook

Eric Fouh, *Virginia Tech*
Maoyuan Sun, *Virginia Tech*
Clifford Shaffer, *Virginia Tech*

OpenDSA is an open-source, community-based effort to create a complete active-eBook for Data Structures and Algorithms courses at the undergraduate level. Active-eBooks go beyond hypertextbooks, being a close integration of text and images with interactive visualizations and assessment activities. They solve two major problems: The difficulty of conveying dynamic process with static media, and the need by students to have many practice exercises and immediate feedback. Development in HTML5/JavaScript allows maximum portability. OpenDSA will proceed with broad participation from the algorithm visualization community. Focusing on reuse of materials, instructors can pick and choose content and modify as desired.

ACM Categories & Descriptors: K.3.1

Keywords: Data Structures, Assessment, Instructional Technologies

Active Learning in Computer Science Education Using Meta-Cognition

Murali Mani, *University of Michigan, Flint*
Quamrul Mazumder, *University of Michigan, Flint*

Courses that involve problem solving provide an opportunity to incorporate meta-cognition as an active learning strategy, where students reflect on their confidence levels on their solutions to problems. As compared to other typically used active learning strategies, meta-cognition provides concrete and comprehensive feedback about the students learning. The data about confidence levels is potentially useful to both the instructor and the student: an instructor can utilize the data about confidence levels as a second measure of student learning (this is in addition to the scores obtained); a student gets valuable feedback with regards to his/her own comprehension of the topics when he/she examines the confidence levels. We have incorporated meta-cognition techniques in four computer science courses over two semesters at University of Michigan, Flint, including CS1, and also graduate level courses. By analyzing the data obtained, we are able to infer conclusions about (a) How correlated are the scores obtained to the confidence levels reported (b) Is meta-cognition assisting in learning, and (c) Are students more satisfied with a course that incorporates meta-cognition.

ACM Categories & Descriptors: K.3.2

Keywords: meta-cognition, active learning, experiential learning

Dynamic Programming Across the CS Curriculum

Yana Kortsarts, *Widener University*
Vasily Kolchenko, *New York City College of Technology The City University of New York*

Copyright is held by the author/owner(s).
SIGCSE'12, February 29–March 3, 2012, Raleigh, North Carolina, USA.
ACM 978-1-4503-1098-7/12/02.

Dynamic programming is one of the important algorithmic techniques often not appropriately covered in the core undergraduate CS courses, and there is no sufficient emphasize on application of advanced techniques to practical problems. As a result, students are not becoming fully familiar with this extremely important concept. We present our experience in integrating dynamic programming algorithmic technique in various core and elective undergraduate computer science courses, such as introductory programming, cryptography and bioinformatics. Examples are based on the real world scenarios and motivate students to learn in order to solve practical problems. The reported work was partially funded by the National Science Foundation, NSF CPATH award # 0939120 and NSF I3 award # 0930242

ACM Categories & Descriptors: K.3.2

Keywords: Bioinformatics, Dynamic Programming, Cryptology

50 Ways to be A FOSSer: Simple Ways to Involve Students & Faculty

Clif Kussmaul, *Muhlenberg College*
Heidi J. C. Ellis, *Western New England University*
Gregory W. Hislop, *Drexel University*

Participating in free and open source software (FOSS) has numerous benefits for students (and faculty), and there is increasing interest in encouraging such participation. There is a broad range of possible contributions to FOSS projects including documentation, testing, coding, and more. This range allows people with a variety of backgrounds, including little or no CS background, to contribute to a FOSS project. This poster describes the status of a project to identify and categorize learning activities that contribute to FOSS. During Spring 2011, an NSF-sponsored workshop on student participation in humanitarian FOSS for the SoftHum project brought together a group of experienced FOSS developers, faculty, and students. One result of this workshop was a list of nearly 100 learning activities that could contribute to FOSS projects and provide meaningful experiences for students and faculty. We were surprised by the variety of results. Some of the activities have been used successfully or are variations of familiar learning activities; others are ideas that seem promising but require further development and validation. We are experimenting with individual activities, and seeking colleagues interested in doing likewise. We are also mapping the learning activities onto Computer Science Curriculum 2008 to make it easier for faculty to identify relevant activities and map them to course or program learning objectives. The poster briefly summarizes relevant background, describe the process used to identify appropriate activities and provide examples of activities and their mappings.

ACM Categories & Descriptors: K.3.2; D.2.0

Keywords: active learning, communication, experience report, free & open source software

Teaching Computer Science and Programming Concepts Using LEGO NXT and TETRIX Robotics, and Computer Science Unplugged Activities

Daniela Marghitu, *Auburn University*
Taha Ben Brahim, *Auburn University*
John Weaver, *Auburn University*

Auburn University s Robo Camp K12 outreach program integrates various robotics platforms to maximize students critical thinking and creativity development. This work presents how robotics could be used to teach students computer science concepts and skills through implementing the Computer Science Unplugged (CSU) activities. CSU provide an insightful learning environment where students learn computer science concepts through some playful, coordinated and stress free activities. Implementing such activities using robots resulted in multiple benefits: 1) students acquired advanced computer science notions without undergoing the high stress levels associated with such activities and 2) students maintained high levels of motivation and concentration during the entire six weeks of the camp.

ACM Categories & Descriptors: J.0

Keywords: K12, Computational Thinking, Robotics

Using POGIL to Teach Students to be Better Problem Solvers

Helen H. Hu, *Westminster College*

POGIL is a learning method that encourages students to learn coursework material in cooperative groups. Instead of passively listening to a traditional lecture, POGIL students work together on activities that guide students to discover programming concepts and algorithms for themselves. For example, instead of being told in lecture that a return statement ends the execution of a method, students might be asked what happens if two lines in their program are reversed (so that a line of code appears after the return statement). This emphasis on the process of discovery teaches students to become better problem solvers. POGIL has been used for over 15 years in science classrooms, where studies have shown it to be more effective than traditional lectures, measured both in student mastery of the material and in student retention. This poster provides examples of how traditional programming assignments can be transformed into POGIL lessons that emphasize problem solving and critical thinking skills. A POGIL activity on loops has students working through iterations of Newton s method by hand before writing the code. Critical thinking questions guide students to manipulate the code to experiment with infinite loops, initialization statements and conditionals. Two other activities on recursion and writing pseudocode are detailed on the poster. Information on facilitating a POGIL activity and writing your own POGIL activities can be found online at http://pogil.org/resources. Additional examples of computer science POGIL activities can be found at http://cspogil.org.

ACM Categories & Descriptors: K.3.2

Keywords: cooperative learning, problem solving, active learning, POGIL, teams

Developing a Gaming Concentration in the Computer Science Curriculum at an Hbcu

Jinghua Zhang, *Winston-Salem State University*
Elva J. Jones, *Winston-Salem State University*

Copyright is held by the author/owner(s).
SIGCSE'12, February 29–March 3, 2012, Raleigh, North Carolina, USA.
ACM 978-1-4503-1098-7/12/02.

We propose a unique gaming concentration to reenergize computer science(CS) education at Winston-Salem State University (WSSU), an HBCU. Nationally, many gaming concentration programs in the CS curriculum have been successfully developed. Nevertheless, to our knowledge, none has been established at any of the HBCUs. The proposed gaming concentration aims to educate minority students with the skills necessary to participate as computer scientists in a game development team and other software development projects. The concentration will help the enrollment and retention of underrepresented students and increase the quality of graduates in this field. A successful gaming concentration at WSSU will advance the knowledge in developing curricula for HBCUs and other minority institutions.

ACM Categories & Descriptors: K.3.2

Keywords: Curriculum, Gaming Concentration Program

OOSSIE: An Open Source Software Defined Radio (SDR) Toolset for Education and Research

Jason Snyder, *Virginia Tech*

OSSIE is an open source SDR project created for education and research. When used as a teaching example, OSSIE provides lessons about open source and systems development. It is also an ideal platform for a variety of projects, from capstone studies to theses. A series of labs introduces new users to the software and quickly illustrate key SDR concepts and practices. Included components and waveforms provide excellent examples and allow for the simple creation of new waveform applications. The waveform workshop allows SDR developers to concentrate on the signal processing aspects of OSSIE software development by automatically generating code necessary for interfacing with the OSSIE Core Framework. Finally, the Core Framework provides an ideal platform for SDR and signal processing research.

ACM Categories & Descriptors: K.3.2

Keywords: Software Defined Radio, Software Engineering

Implementing a Communication-Intensive Core Course in a CS Curriculum: A Survey of Methods

Jean H. French, *Coastal Carolina University*

While a focus on programming and mathematical skills is second nature to computer science faculty, perhaps equally important should be the recognition of the need for students to master communication skills. This poster presents the measured results of various methods used in the implementation of a communication-intensive core course into a CS curriculum at a small liberal arts university. The communication intensive core course is a CS1 introduction to computer science which is required to implement both oral and written assignments. Five key areas of success were implemented to help support the communication-intensive CS curriculum. They are: (1) communication skills need to be integrated within the CS curriculum, (2) communication skills should begin to be developed early in the student's academic career, (3) communication skills include a broad range of categories, (4) communication skills need to be supported by feedback, and (5) communication skills can be taught in the CS curriculum without sacrificing CS content. The results are provided on a four-point scale and focus on both student success and grading complexity. Scores are provided for each of the methods used since the course was first implemented in 2007. Such a comprehensive evaluation aims to assist in determining which methods are best suited for implementing a core communication that stresses continuous improvement in communication skills.

ACM Categories & Descriptors: K.3.2

Keywords: Communication skills, oral communication skills, written communication skills, accreditation, curriculum

The Reflective Mentor: Charting Undergraduates Responses to Computer Science Service Learning

Quinn Burke, *University of Pennsylvania*
Yasmin B. Kafai, *University of Pennsylvania*
Jean Griffin, *University of Pennsylvania*
Rita M. Powell, *University of Pennsylvania*
Michele Grab, *University of Pennsylvania*
Susan B. Davidson, *University of Pennsylvania*
Joseph S. Sun, *University of Pennsylvania*

Community service courses are often where undergraduates make connections between academic content and practical computer science applications, build bridges between the university and the community, and ultimately increase access to technology in such communities. In this poster we report on our efforts supported by a NSF Broadening Participation in Computing grant to design, implement, and evaluate a service-learning course based on a cascading mentoring model linking together the faculty

ACM Categories & Descriptors: administration

Keywords: broadening participation in computing, community service, mentoring

Teaching Cryptography Using Hands-On Labs

Li Yang, *University of Tennessee at Chattanooga*
Joseph Kizza, *University of Tennessee at Chattanooga*
Andy Wang, *Southern Polytechnic State University*
Chung-Han Chen, *Tuskegee University*

Abstract: Teaching cryptography is essential in undergraduate information assurance (IA) education as it is an indispensable component in the IA knowledge domain and plays a key role in ensuring information confidentiality, integrity and availability. Hands-on method in cryptography is a good approach to achieve this as it engages students in real-world settings, which will inspire creativity of students and train them to adapt cryptographic solutions to emerging areas. We design a collection of labs which allow students to gain hands-on experiences with cryptographic algorithms, especially increasing student awareness of possible threats and attacks to various cryptographic techniques. The developed hands-on exercises tied with each cryptography topic teach students both cryptographic algorithm and vulnerabilities. In each exercise students experience cryptographic techniques and its possible threats and attacks. In other words, students learn and understand both strength and weakness of each cryptography technique. Our labs cover topics of encryption, digital signature, key management, etc. These labs can be plugged into courses at different levels from CS1 to senior courses such as network security, security management, etc. Our approach enriches experiential learning materials in cryptography. Our effort contributes to cryptography courseware development and IA education in terms of hands-on exercises. The hands-on labs can be adopted in various levels of undergraduate Computer Science (CS) and IA courses. Hands-on labs are available at http://cryptolabs.info/.

ACM Categories & Descriptors: D.4.6

Keywords: Cryptography, Hands-on labs

From Drawing to Programming: Attracting Middle-School Students to Programming Through Self-Disclosing Code

Pelle Hall, *Grinnell College*
Andrew Hirakawa, *Grinnell College*
Jennelle Nystrom, *Grinnell College*
Samuel A. Rebelsky, *Grinnell College*

Consider a middle-school student playing with a computer. What does she do? She may chat with friends. She may surf the Web. She may even play a few games. But she is also likely to make things with drawing programs, word processors, or other applications that make things. Can one leverage that creativity to encourage her to want to learn to program? Projects from Alice (Moskal et al. 2004) to Scratch (Maloney et al. 2010) have certainly shown that tools that tie creativity and programming can encourage students to think algorithmically. Despite the success of these programs, there is still room for new models that link children s artistic interests with programming. In this project, we explore the link between creativity and programming through a different model, one in which the drawing application self discloses underlying commands (DiGiano & Eisenberg 1995). As students draw images with the GNU Image Manipulation Program, a Photoshop-like application, a small window displays code that represents their actions. For example, when they draw a line, a draw line command appears that includes the coordinates of the line; when they change brushes, a set brush command appears that includes the name of the brush. Eventually, students refer to these commands to redraw their figures, to copy their figures, and to change their figures. Slowly they move from copying and pasting code, to modifying, to writing their own instructions, and beyond.

ACM Categories & Descriptors: K.3.2

Keywords: Novice programming, Self-disclosing code, GNU Image Manipulation Program

Proposed Revisions to the Social and Professional Knowledge Area for CS2013

Carol Spradling, *Northwest Missouri State University*
Florence Appel, *Saint Xavier University*
Elizabeth Hawthorne, *Union County College*

Copyright is held by the author/owner(s).
SIGCSE'12, February 29–March 3, 2012, Raleigh, North Carolina, USA.
ACM 978-1-4503-1098-7/12/02.

The ACM/IEEE-CS 2001/2008 computer science curricular guidelines are in the process of being updated and the strawman version of CS2013 will be unveiled at SIGCSE 2012. Inclusion of the ethical, societal and professional responsibility issues dates back to Computing Curricula 1991. This poster session will present the revised Social and Professional issues knowledge area and provide a means for any SIGCSE community member to provide feedback directly to SIGCAS and the CS2013 steering committee. Specific core and elective knowledge units, topics and learning outcomes will be delineated. The current state of the discipline and the profession were examined to provide contemporary guidance for the education of ethical behavior, professional practice and societal impact for computer science majors.

ACM Categories & Descriptors: K.3.2

A Better API for Java Reflection

Zalia Shams, *Virginia Tech*
Stephen H. Edwards, *Virginia Tech*

Instructors often write reference tests to evaluate student programs. In Java, reference tests should be independent of submitted solutions as they are run against all student submissions. Otherwise, they may even fail to compile against some solutions. Reflection is a useful feature for writing code without compile-time dependencies, which is valuable for writing software tools that inspect code. However, educators avoid using reflection as code written using Java s Reflection API is complex, unintuitive and verbose. We present ReflectionSupport, a library that enables one to write reflection-based code in concise, simple and readable fashion. It helps educators write reference tests without compile-time dependencies of solutions and develop educational tools such as automated graders.

ACM Categories & Descriptors: D.2.5

Keywords: Test-driven development, automated assessment, software testing, programming assignments, test coverage, reflection, bytecode transformation.

Hands-On Labs for A Mini-Course on Mobile Application Development

Qusay H. Mahmoud, *University of Guelph*
Nicholas Mair, *University of Guelph*
Younis Mohamed, *University of Guelph*
Sunny Dhillon, *University of Guelph*

In this poster we present a set of hands-on labs for a mini-course on mobile application development that can be used as a lab component of any Computing course. The labs revolve around a single theme whereby students experiment with designing and developing the user interface, interaction model, and inter-connectivity of a mobile application for Google Scholar; the developed application can be deployed on a variety of mobile platforms, including BlackBerry, Android, and iPhone devices (smartphones and tablets). Students learn about mobile programming models and cross-platform development and appreciate the unique opportunities such devices offer, but also become aware of the development challenges they present. For more information, please visit: http://cmer.uoguelph.ca.

ACM Categories & Descriptors: D.2.6

Keywords: Mobile Application Development, Cross-Platform Development, Hands-on Labs, Mobile Computing

CEOPH Evaluation, Evolution, and Archival Storage

Vicki L. Almstrum, *Strayer University, North Austin Campus*
Barbara Boucher Owens, *Southwestern University*
Mary Z. Last, *Computing Educators Oral History Project*
Deepa Muralidhar, *North Gwinnett High School*

This poster presents recent progress with the Computing Educators Oral History Project (CEOHP). To provide context, the poster includes a brief history of CEOHP and a summary of the interviews currently in the collection (a total of twenty-six completed interviews at the end of 2011). During Evaluation efforts in 2009 and 2010, a series of face-to-face and on-line qualitative interviews provided feedback about the CEOHP website, including its organization, content, and usability by target groups. The Evolution process incorporated ideas generated during Evaluation to improve both quality and consistency of the collection elements and the CEOHP website. In the Archival Storage process, all completed interviews in the CEOHP collection are being submitted to the prestigious Charles Babbage Institute for permanent indexing and archiving. These archival steps will become part of CEOHP s standard processing procedures, so each interview added to the CEOHP collection will be archived by the Charles Babbage Institute, guaranteeing that these materials will survive far into the future. This poster describes major steps, challenges, and achievements in the areas of Evaluation, Evolution, and Archival Storage, as well as the spiral nature of these activities as part of the on-going process of growing a collection such as CEOHP.

ACM Categories & Descriptors: K.2;K.3.2; K.7.0

Keywords: Gender, Equity, Careers, Oral History, Life Stories, Evaluation, Pedagogy

CodeTrainer Teacher Authoring System: Facilitating User-Created Content in an Intelligent Tutoring System

Christy L. McGuire, *Tutor Technologies, Inc.*
Thomas K. Harris, *Tutor Technologies, Inc.*
Jonathan Steinhart, *Tutor Technologies, Inc.*
Leigh Ann Sudol-DeLyser, *Carnegie Mellon University*

With grant funding from the National Science Foundation, we are developing the CodeTrainer Content Authoring System, a mechanism that allows educators to create and contribute their own curriculum content and align that content with the features of our larger intelligent tutoring system, CodeTrainer. Through a series of user studies, we evaluated the needs of computer science educators for both curriculum content and appropriate user interface. Results from these studies indicate that computer science educators would find CodeTrainer a useful tool, and

Copyright is held by the author/owner(s).
SIGCSE'12, February 29–March 3, 2012, Raleigh, North Carolina, USA.
ACM 978-1-4503-1098-7/12/02.

offered suggestions for improving the usability. This material is based upon work supported by the National Science Foundation under Grant No. 1113692.

ACM Categories & Descriptors: H.5.2

Keywords: Intelligent Tutoring Systems, Interactive Learning Environments, Adaptive Learning, Content Authoring, Authoring Tool, Computer Science Education

Comparing Feature Sets Within Visual and Command Line Environments and Their Effect on Novice Programming

Edward Dillon, *University of Alabama*
Monica Anderson, *University of Alabama*
Marcus Brown, *University of Alabama*

Improving the novice s experience with programming may be key to retaining more students interested in Computer Science. Programming environments is an area that lacks comprehensive study. Some entry-level sequences prefer visual environments while others tout the benefits of command line environments. In either case, there is little more than anecdotal evidence to support either choice. We present a novel categorization of programming tools based on assistive features that predict the usefulness of programming environments for novices. This categorization is supported by a controlled study that measured the differences in engagement, efficiency, comprehension, and usability. We found that the extremes of assistive features are problematic regardless of prior programming experience.

ACM Categories & Descriptors: K.3.2; H.5.2

Keywords: Assistive Features, Novice Programming, Learning

Exploring Connected Worlds

Jeffrey Forbes, *Duke University*

The widespread use of online social networks provides a particularly compelling domain for introducing computer science techniques and concepts to undergraduate students. As part of the HarambeeNet project, I developed a new course on the Science of Networks that explores the interconnectivity of social, technological, and natural entities. Students in the course learn fundamental techniques from graph and game theory to analyze network structure and behavior. Material for the course was developed and refined through a survey of exemplar courses, workshops, and faculty learning communities all focused on network science. The poster describes the course framework, provides some example assignment and lecture material, and presents some lessons learned.

ACM Categories & Descriptors: K.3.2

Keywords: network science, social networks, non-majors

Copyright is held by the author/owner(s).
SIGCSE'12, February 29–March 3, 2012, Raleigh, North Carolina,USA.
ACM 978-1-4503-1098-7/12/02.

SIGCSE 2012 Birds-of-a-Feather Abstracts

CS Unplugged, Outreach and CS Kinesthetic Activities

Tim Bell, *University of Canterbury*
Lynn Lambert, *Christopher Newport University*
Daniela Marghitu, *Auburn University*

Outreach activities including CS Unplugged demonstrate computer science concepts at schools and public venues based around kinesthetic activities rather than hands-on computer use. CS Unplugged is a global project that has shared many such activities for children to adults using no technology, including how binary numbers represent words, images and sound, routing and deadlock, public/private key encryption, and others. These and other effective outreach programs can combat the idea that computer science = programming or, worse, keyboarding; and can educate the public, interest students, and recruit majors. Many people have used these activities, and adapted them for their own culture or outreach purposes. Come share your outreach ideas and experiences with such activities. Employers, researchers and teachers have noted the need for effective outreach to ensure that students and the public be exposed to, and understand what Computer Science is. CS Unplugged is a collection of activities that are accessible to a general audience, need no technology, are fun, and cover many core areas of computer science. The focus of this session will be discussing activities that introduce computer science concepts and way of thinking, and that are consistent with Jeanette Wing's Computational Thinking. The session is intended to allow exchanging ideas about effective outreach in the community, in K-12, and even non-major classes. There are many variations of these activities, and it is valuable to get practitioners together to share their successes and not-so-successful events so that others can benefit from them.

ACM Categories & Descriptors: K.3.2 **Keywords:** outreach

Infusing Software Assurance and Secure Coding into Introductory CS Courses

Elizabeth K. Hawthorne, *Union County College*
Nancy R. Mead, *Carnegie Mellon University*
Mark A. Ardis, *Stevens Institute of Technology*
Carol A. Sledge, *Carnegie Mellon University*

Nearly every facet of modern society depends heavily on highly complex software systems. The business, energy, transportation, education, communication, government, and defense communities rely on software to function, and software is an intrinsic part of our personal lives. Teaching software assurance and secure coding practices are significant challenges currently facing computer science educators. The Strawman version of the CS2013 curricular volume recognizes this vital need and has included a new knowledge area to specifically address software and information assurance in undergraduate computer science education. Also recognizing the importance of the software assurance discipline for protecting national infrastructures and systems, the U.S. Department of Homeland Security (DHS) has identified the growing need for skilled practitioners in this area. At the direction of the DHS, the Software Engineering Institute at Carnegie Mellon University initiated the Software Assurance Curriculum Project. Session leaders will share curricular materials from this project and will facilitate active discussion centered on infusing software assurance into introductory computer science courses at two-year and four-year colleges and universities. The latest curricular volume published September 2011 will be distributed at the session and includes a review of related curricula, outcomes and body of knowledge, expected background of target audiences, and outlines of six courses. These curricular materials are also available online at: www.sei.cmu.edu/library/abstracts/reports/11tr017.cfm.

Copyright is held by the author/owner(s).
SIGCSE'12, February 29–March 3, 2012, Raleigh, North Carolina, USA.
ACM 978-1-4503-1098-7/12/02.

ACM Categories & Descriptors: D.2.0

Keywords: software assurance, secure coding, information assurance, computer security, curriculum, computer science

Web-Cat User Group

Stephen H. Edwards, *Virginia Tech*

Web-CAT is the most widely used open-source automated grading system, with about 10, 000 users at over 65 institutions worldwide. Its plug-in architecture supports extensibility, with plug-ins for Java (including Objectdraw, JTF, Swing, and Android), C++, Python, Haskell, and more. It is also a powerful tool for educational research data collection. It supports a wide variety of assessment strategies, but is famous for grading students on how well they test their own code. Web-CAT won the 2006 Premier Award, recognizing high-quality, non-commercial courseware for engineering education. This BOF will allow existing users and new adopters to meet, share experiences, and talk about what works and what doesn t. Information on getting started quickly with Web-CAT will also be provided.

ACM Categories & Descriptors: K.3.2; D.1.5

Keywords: software testing, test-driven development, test-first coding, Java, programming assignments, automated assessment

Teaching Open Source: Involving Students in Free and Open Source Software (FOSS) Project Communities

Sebastian Dziallas, *Franklin W. Olin College of Engineering*
Heidi J. C. Ellis, *Western New England University*
Mel Chua, *Purdue University*
Steven Huss-Lederman, *Beloit College*
Karl R. Wurst, *Worcester State University*

Involving students from a wide range of backgrounds in Free and Open Source Software (FOSS) project communities gets them a hands-on, portfolio-building experience in the creation of a real-world project while simultaneously building their institution's public profile. The Teaching Open Source (http://teachingopensource.org) community is an emergent (3 year old) group working on scaffolding to bridge the cultural differences between academic and FOSS communities of practice. Join us to share questions, challenges, and triumphs of incorporating

FOSS participation into existing and new curricula as well support resources for doing so. Alumni and current members of the POSSE (Professors' Open Source Summer Experience, http://communityleadershipteam.org/posse) will attend in mentorship roles. Faculty attendance at the SIGCSE 2010 BoF on Teaching Open Source (TOS) indicates that student involvement in FOSS projects is a teaching and learning approach of interest for many faculty members. The transparency of both artifacts and process make FOSS an attractive real-world experience that enhances peer learning and intrinsic motivation for a diversity of courses, from introductory, interdisciplinary, and non-major classes to software engineering core offerings and senior capstones. However, such student participation involves a significant learning curve and effort on the part of the faculty member, and support structures for faculty are still maturing. 2011-2012 marks the 3rd academic year the TOS community has explored this realm together, and the past year has seen the emergence of more best practices, support resources, and curricular material. Community members are starting to design cross-institutional research on the impact of FOSS participation on students. BoF attendees will be encouraged to ask questions, network, and take advantage of the TOS community as a support structure for their own courses and projects. The audience is expected to consist of instructors who 1) are interested in learning how to get started in involving students in FOSS projects; or 2) have involved students in FOSS projects and are looking for better ways to facilitate student learning within FOSS projects.

ACM Categories & Descriptors: K.3.2

Keywords: FOSS, open source, teaching open source, communities of practice

AP CS Principles and the 'Beauty and Joy of Computing' Curriculum

Brian Harvey, *University of California*
Tiffany Barnes, *University of North Carolina*
Luke Segars, *University of California*

The College Board's guidelines for the coming AP CS Principles course are broad enough to allow many different interpretations. In particular, different courses have different levels of technical depth. The "Beauty and Joy of Computing" curriculum, used by two of the initial five pilot sites, aims high, with recursion and higher order functions included in the programming half of the course. This session is for high school or college level instructors considering teaching an AP CS Principles course and interested in using the BJC curriculum, and/or the Snap! (formerly BYOB) visual programming language used in the curriculum. See http://bjc.berkeley.edu for the curriculum and http://snap.berkeley.edu for the language.

ACM Categories & Descriptors: K.3.2

Keywords: AP CS Principles; recursion; higher order functions; Snap!; BJC

Copyright is held by the author/owner(s).
SIGCSE'12, February 29–March 3, 2012, Raleigh, North Carolina, USA.
ACM 978-1-4503-1098-7/12/02.

Teaching Track Faculty in CS

Daniel D. Garcia, *University of California, Berkeley*
Jody Paul, *Metropolitan State College of Denver*
Mark Sherriff, *University of Virginia*

Many computer science departments have chosen to hire faculty to teach in a teaching-track position that parallels the standard tenure-track position, providing the possibility of promotion, longer-term contracts, and higher pay for excellence in teaching and service. This birds-of-a-feather is designed to gather educators who are currently in such a position to share their experiences as members of the faculty of their departments and schools, and to provide opportunities for schools considering such positions to gather information.

ACM Categories & Descriptors: K.3.2

Keywords: Teaching Track Faculty, Lecturer with Security of Employment, Professor of the Practice

A Town Meeting: SIGSCE Committee on Expanding the Women-In-Computing Community

Gloria Childress Townsend, *DePauw University*

In January 2004, we organized the second SIGCSE Committee ("Expanding the Women-in-Computing Community"). Our annual Town Meeting provides dissemination of information concerning successful gender issues projects, along with group discussion and brainstorming, in order to create committee goals for the coming year. We select projects to highlight through listserv communication and through our connections with NCWIT, ABI, ACM-W, CRA-W, etc. This year we will highlight the new NSF Broadening Participation in Computing grant -- a grant that encompasses projects we presented in previous BOFs and a grant that builds on an alliance among ACM-W, ABI and NCWIT.

ACM Categories & Descriptors: K.4.2 Social Issues

Keywords: gender issues

Sharing Incremental Approaches for Adding Parallelism to CS Curricula

Richard A. Brown, *St. Olaf College*
Elizabeth Shoop, *Macalester College*
Joel C. Adams, *Calvin College*
David P. Bunde, *Knox College*
Jens Mache, *Lewis & Clark College*
Paul F. Steinberg, *Intel Corporation*
Matthew Wolf, *Georgia Institute of Technology*
Michael Wrinn, *Intel Corporation*

Recent industry changes, including multi-core processors, cloud computing, and GPU programming, increase the need to teach parallelism to CS undergraduates. But few CS programs can afford to add new courses or greatly alter syllabi, and the large parallelism body of knowledge relates to many courses. Participants in this BOF will share incremental approaches for adding parallelism to undergraduate CS curricula, where students study parallel computing in brief units. This networking event/ brainstorming session/ swap meet will bring together:

people with sharable parallelism expository readings, hands-on exercises, tech support ideas, etc.;

people wishing to include such materials in their courses; and people curious about incremental approaches to teaching parallel computing.

ACM Categories & Descriptors: K.3.2; D.1.3

Keywords: CS education, education, parallelism, parallel computing, multicore, GPGPU, accelerators, cloud computing, distributed computing, distributed programming, parallel programming, Beowulf clusters, map-reduce, data-intensive, scalability, curriculum

Computer Science: Small Department Initiative

James Jerkofsky, *Walsh University*
Cathy Bareiss, *Olivet Nazarene University*

Faculty in small departments (perhaps 3 FTE, perhaps only 1 or 2, &) face special situations both challenges and strengths. In this BOF, members will have a chance to talk about both. Challenges include maintaining a well-rounded curriculum and attracting students. Strengths include a close relationship with other members of the department and majors. These and other topics are open for discussion; the specific topics will be based upon the composition and interests of the group assembled.

ACM Categories & Descriptors: A.m

Keywords: small department, small department initiative

Teaching with Alice

Don Slater, *Carnegie Mellon University*
Wanda Dann, *Carnegie Mellon University*
Steve Cooper, *Stanford University*

This session is for anyone currently using Alice 2.2 and / or thinking about using Alice 3, or exploring the possibility of using Alice in his or her curriculum. The discussion leaders and experienced Alice instructors will share teaching strategies, tips, and tricks with each other and those new to Alice. The session provides an arena for sharing Alice instructional materials and ideas for courses at all educational levels. This is an opportunity to share assignments and pointers to web sites where collections of instructional materials, such as syllabi, student projects, exams, and other resources are available.

ACM Categories & Descriptors: K.3.2

Keywords: Alice, Alice 2.2, Alice 3.0, Education

Identifying Effective Pedagogical Practices for Commenting Computer Source Code

Peter J. DePasquale, *The College of New Jersey*
Michael E. Locasto, *University of Calgary*
Lisa C. Kaczmarczyk, *Independent Assessment Consultant*

Few, if any, pedagogical practices exist for helping students embrace best practices in writing software documentation, particularly source code comments. Although instructors often stress the importance of good commenting, two problems exist. First, it can be difficult to actually define these best practices, and second, it can be difficult to grade or assess students application of such methods/practices. This Birds-of-a-Feather session focuses on capturing for dissemination a concrete list of code commenting best practices used by the attendees as they teach their classes. We will aim to facilitate the development of commenting best practices by collecting the experiences and suggestions of the BOF attendees into a concrete list of practices and initiatives (and we plan to post this to our publicly accessible project wiki). Additionally, we plan to report on our progress in creating and deploying the COMTOR system, an NSF-funded project that supports feedback to students and grading capabilities for instructors of student source code comments.

Copyright is held by the author/owner(s).
SIGCSE'12, February 29–March 3, 2012, Raleigh, North Carolina, USA.
ACM 978-1-4503-1098-7/12/02.

ACM Categories & Descriptors: D.1.0; K.3.1

Keywords: Commenting, Source Code, Pedagogy

Design of a Computer Security Teaching and Research Laboratory

Jeffrey L. Duffany, *Universidad del Turabo*
Afredo Cuz, *Polytechnic Uuniversity of Puerto Rico*

Design of a Computer Security Teaching and Research Laboratory Jeffrey L. Duffany, Ph.D., Universidad del Turabo Alfredo Cruz, Ph.D., Politechnic University of Puerto Rico To enhance the learning process a certain amount of hands-on experience is desirable to supplement the theory portion of computer security-related courses. This includes courses in information assurance, database security, computer security and computer forensics, among others. Many classrooms designed for teaching computer programming have personal computers for use by each student. Some universities have dedicated laboratories. These labs and classrooms can be expensive to maintain and upgrade and this may be done by a separate IT department. There are budget constraints and political issues that must be addressed between the school, faculty and university administration. Because of these constraints, many schools and universities may be lacking in their lab resources for teaching computer security. This situation could be improved in many cases with little financial investment. This presentation is based on sharing the experience of professors that are currently teaching these courses to graduate and undergraduate students. These professors will present ideas on specific hardware and software that can be used to develop a computer security lab or to enhance a classroom environment, with an emphasis on free and open source software, operating systems and the use of virtual machines.

ACM Categories & Descriptors: K.6.5

Keywords: computer security

Student ICTD Research and Service Learning Abroad

Joseph Mertz, *Carnegie Mellon University*
Ralph Morelli, *Trinity College*
Ruth E. Anderson, *University of Washington*

This BOF is a chance for information sharing among faculty interested in involving students in ICTD research and/or service learning toward cultural and economic development globally. It takes a lot to get students out into the field. Challenges include developing partnerships, negotiating agreements, vetting the safety of destinations, identifying sources of funding, navigating the logistics of immunizations, visas, accommodations and flights to less-traveled places, reassuring parents as to the wisdom of their child's participation, managing development partner expectations, advising students' activities, and many more. This BOF will provide a venue for sharing experiences, information, and identifying potential new collaborations.

ACM Categories & Descriptors: K.3.2; K.4.0

Keywords: Service Learning, Global Learning, ICTD, ICT4D, Internships, Field Research

Imaging College Educators

Jerod Weinman, *Grinnell College*
Ellen Walker, *Hiram College*

Within computing, the imaging field includes computer vision, image understanding, and image processing. While much research and teaching is done at the graduate level, the typical imaging educator at an undergraduate institution is the only specialist in his or her department. This BOF brings together educators who currently teach imaging courses or may be interested in expanding curricular offerings. We will emphasize sharing best practices, ideas, and resources as well as building a network for continued cooperation. Discussion topics may include course organization, assignments and projects, and lecture aids or other materials. Our network will include a mailing list for participants to ask questions and share ideas about imaging pedagogy and other means of sharing course materials.

ACM Categories & Descriptors: K.3.2

Keywords: computer vision, image processing

Let's Talk Social Media

Kimberly D. Voll, *University of British Columbia*

Our students are the social media generation, touting Facebook, Google+, and even Twitter accounts as a matter of course. Providing rich, highly integrated environments, social media systems are a template for community and connection. In contrast, CS education is via singular modalities: lectures, textbooks, labs, discussions, et cetera, that share no active or social connection (you cannot +1 a lecture, for example, share a passage of a text with a classmate, or pull up a view that truly integrates a course and its community). But now we have the technology to create learning environments that share the same rich, multimedia experience as the popular social media sites. What should this look like? How do we start? What have you tried? We ll open with a brief overview of the leading social media tools for those unfamiliar, then proceed straight to an open discussion.

ACM Categories & Descriptors: K.3.2

Keywords: social media; education

Copyright is held by the author/owner(s).
SIGCSE'12, February 29–March 3, 2012, Raleigh, North Carolina, USA.
ACM 978-1-4503-1098-7/12/02.

Program By Design: Teachscheme/Reachjava

Viera K. Proulx, *Northeastern University*
Stephen Bloch, *Adelphi University*

Program by Design is a new name for the comprehensive introduction to programming at all levels that began with TeachScheme/ReachJava. This unconventional introductory computing curriculum covers both functional and the object-oriented program design in a systematic design-based style, enforcing test-first design from the beginning. The Bootstrap curriculum makes programming and algebra exciting for children ages 11-15. Special libraries support the design of interactive graphics-based games, musical explorations, client-server and mobile computing. We invite you to come and meet those who have used the curriculum, learn about new additions, libraries, bring in your experiences with the curriculum, show your projects, or ask questions about how it works and how you can use it. This work is sponsored by two NSF DUE CCLI grants: Redesigning Introductory Computing: The Design Discipline, Grant #00618543, and Integrating Test Design into Computing Curriculum from the Beginning, Grant #0920182.

ACM Categories & Descriptors: D.1.0

Keywords: CS1/2, Curriculum Issues, K-12 Instruction, Object-Oriented Issues

CSTA Chapters: Supporting Your Local Computer Science Educators

Frances P. Trees, *Rutgers. The State University of New Jersey*
Helen Hu, *Westminster College*
Chinma Uche, *Greater Hartford Academy of Mathematics and Science*

As part of its commitment to developing a strong community of computer science educators, the Computer Science Teachers Association (CSTA) supports the development of regional CSTA chapters. A CSTA chapter is a local branch of CSTA designed to facilitate discussion of local issues, provision of member services at the local level, and to promote CSTA membership on the national level [1]. This BOF will provide a platform for the discussion of CSTA chapter formation and for the sharing of successful chapter activities.

ACM Categories & Descriptors: A.m

Keywords: K-12 CS Education, K-12, outreach

Revitalizing Computing Camp and Outreach: How Do We Engage Teenagers in Cool Technology?

Kristine S. Nagel, *Georgia Gwinnett College*
Evelyn Brannock, *Georgia Gwinnett College*
Robert Lutz, *Georgia Gwinnett College*

Tech Camps are popular outreach tools to interest teens in computing programs and technology careers. One of the biggest obstacles is how to make Tech Camp cool and inviting for teenagers. How do we grab the attention of students to enroll? Once at camp, how do we engage teens with computing as a creative tool with relevancy to their lives? It is summer; subject areas must be entertaining and relevant. Can we stay ahead of the tech-savvy teens with our budget constraints? Robots and storytelling have long been used; how do we innovate and spark interest, throughout the year? The purpose of this BOF is to share ideas, such as App Inventor for Android to create apps, including text messaging, encouraging students to incorporate their own creative graphics, and using tablet devices.

ACM Categories & Descriptors: **K.3.0**

Keywords: K-12 Outreach, visual programming, game programming, creativity, feeding pipeline

Active eTextbooks for CS: What Should They Be?

Clifford A. Shaffer, *Virginia Tech*

What should the textbook of tomorrow look like in a world of ubiquitous access to computing? Hypertextbooks have proved difficult to create and been fundamentally passive experiences. Commercial eBooks are merely books printed on an electronic screen instead of paper. New technologies such as HTML5 make it feasible to develop interactive applications that integrate with web services to provide a rich, pedagogically effective learning environment compatible with a range of computing platforms. We seek to generate discussion by participants to describe what they hope to see in online textbooks in the near future, and what resources and support would be required for them to adopt such a thing into their own courses.

ACM Categories & Descriptors: **E.1; E.2; K.3.2**

Keywords: Active Electronic Textbooks, Data Structure and Algorithm Visualizations, Algorithm Animation, Courseware

Enriching Computing Instruction with Studio-Based Learning

N. Hari Narayanan, *Auburn University*
Martha Crosby, *University of Hawaii at Manoa*
Dean Hendrix, *Auburn University*
Christopher Hundhausen, *Washington State University*

This BOF is related to the Special Session Transforming the CS Classroom with Studio-Based Learning (SBL). SBL promotes learning in a collaborative context by having students construct, present, review and refine their work with the guidance of peers and teachers. A team of CS educators and education experts have been implementing and evaluating SBL in CS courses over the past five years. The BOF will introduce SBL to the SIGCSE audience, and engage them in a discussion of the potential of, evidence for, and practical advice regarding SBL as an instructional approach that can motivate as well as teach students. Discussions will include war stories' from teachers who have adopted the approach in their courses and hands-on activities to help participants apply SBL to their courses.'

ACM Categories & Descriptors: **K.3.1; K.3.2**

Keywords: Design Crits, Evaluation, Pedagogy, Studio-Based Learning

Copyright is held by the author/owner(s).
SIGCSE'12, February 29–March 3, 2012, Raleigh, North Carolina, USA.
ACM 978-1-4503-1098-7/12/02.

AP CS A - Sharing Teaching Strategies and Curricular Ideas

Lester L. Wainwright, *Charlottesville High School*
Renee Ciezki, *Estrella Mountain Community College*
Robert G. Martin, *School of the Talented and Gifted*

This BOF will provide an opportunity for high school and college faculty to discuss the AP CS A curriculum and to explore possibilities for collaborations and outreach activities between high schools and colleges.

ACM Categories & Descriptors: **A.1**

Keywords: AP CS A

Regional Celebrations of Women in Computing (WiC) - Best Practices

Jodi Tims, *Baldwin-Wallace College*
Ellen Walker, *Hiram College*
Rachelle Kristof Hippler, *Bowling Greens State University Firelands College*

Regional celebrations are locally organized, professional conferences modeled after the Grace Hopper Celebration of Women in Computing (GHC). This BOF allows people who have organized or would like to organize such a conference to get together to share successes and challenges. Attendees that have hosted a regional celebration should bring a un-poster (i.e. 8.5 x 11 flyer, 30 copies) that highlights their conference features and/or shares lessons learned. The leaders plan to divide the time between the 5 major areas of conference planning: program, sponsorship, publicity/communications, registration, and site/logistics.

ACM Categories & Descriptors: **K.m**

Keywords: Women in Computing

Hacking and the Security Curriculum: Building Community

Richard S. Weiss, *The Evergreen State College*
Michael E. Locasto, *University of Calgary*
Jens Mache, *Lewis & Clark College*

Incorporating information security into the undergraduate curriculum continues to be a topic of interest to SIGCSE attendees. The purpose of this BOF is to help sustain the existing community of educators and researchers interested in bringing ethical hacking skills and an understanding of security into the classroom and relating these topics to the foundations of Computer Science. We would like to bring our colleagues together to share pedagogical practices, stories of hacking and how to use them to inspire our students and communicate complex concepts in computer science and security. We also plan to discuss our own experiences, practices and ongoing efforts (e.g., our infosec teaching experiences, the SISMAT program, EDURange and the dissemination of infosec interactive exercises). SISMAT is one of many alternatives for teaching cybersecurity to undergraduates. It is based on the Hacker Curriculum and includes a two-week summer intensive program, a research component and an internship. A description can be viewed at http://www.ists.dartmouth.edu/events/sismat/. An education in computer science can be an important resource in nurturing future leaders in cybersecurity, but only if we enable a community of educators willing to share approaches. This was highlighted by Sally Finch's keynote speech in 2010. At our BOF last year, several people had stories to share, and we plan to focus on that.

ACM Categories & Descriptors: C.2.0

Keywords: hacker curriculum, community, cybersecurity, teaching, education

Flipping the Classroom

Barry Brown, *Sierra College*

In a flipped classroom, students watch or listen to the lecture at home and do homework in the classroom. The classroom becomes much more interactive and the educator has ample opportunity to provide individualized guidance when it's most needed. The watch-at-home content can include recorded lectures, demonstration videos, adaptive quizzes, or anything in between. Come share your experiences developing "flip" material, learn from others what's involved, and find out whether it's working to improve success and retention.

ACM Categories & Descriptors: K.3.1: Distance learning; Computer-assisted instruction (CAI)

Keywords: education

Using Social Networks to Engage Computer Science Students

Semmy Purewal, *UNC Asheville*
Owen Astrachan, *Duke University*
David Brown, *Pellissippi State Community College*
Jeffrey Forbes, *Duke University*

Social Networking continues to be a popular past-time among high school and college students. In this birds of a feather session, we will share ideas on integrating social networking topics into computer science courses at the introductory and non-major levels. Additionally we will discuss approaches to integrating social network programming into upper level courses. Finally we will attempt to address the following questions: will social networking draw new students into the computing disciplines the way that video games did in the previous generation? Will it attract new types of students with different expectations? Is social networking just a fad that will have no effect on Computer Science programs? Or is social networking a topic that is better left to other academic disciplines?

ACM Categories & Descriptors: K.3.2

Keywords: Social Networks, Computer Science Education, Student Engagement

Digital Humanities: Reaching Out to the Other Culture

Robert E. Beck, *Villanova University*

This discussion will connect instructors who are reaching out to their colleagues in the humanities to discover areas of collaboration. It focuses on what these disciplines have to contribute to our knowledge of computing and how computational thinking informs these disciplines. One goal is to lay the foundation for a more general program of study in digital humanities that would reach students who would like to see how computing could enhance their work in history, literature, anthropology, or philosophy, for example.

ACM Categories & Descriptors: J.5

Keywords: Digital humanities; interdisciplinary computing

A Multimedia and Liberal Arts Approach to a First Course in Programming and Its Crossover Potential for Computer Science and the Arts

Trish Cornez, *University of Redlands*
Richard Cornez, *University of Redlands*

Attracting computer science students in a liberal arts setting serves to enhance the background and breadth of the class of professional programmers. There is a segment of the student population that is talented and artistic, but may not be aware of the interplay between computer science and the arts or computer science and mathematics and the sciences. Students are acculturated in a visual, interactive, and interdisciplinary world. This BOF will provide a platform for a discussion on how multimedia can be integrated in beginning level computing courses. Discussions will focus on attributes of conventional and unconventional first languages and explore a liberal arts approach to integrate disciplines both scientific and artistic. We envision discussions relevant to (a) mathematicians visualizing processes using multimedia and algorithms, (b) physicists using game programming to explore physical and virtual worlds, (c) computer scientists and behavioral scientists collaborating on responsive systems, (d) musicians, artists, and computer scientists creating computational art. The audience is expected to consist of faculty looking at nontraditional approaches to a first course in programming. Faculty with an aim to attract students to computer science studies will find this discussion useful. Those who feel their curriculum to be too narrowly focused and wish to broaden their curriculum to include the humanities and interdisciplinary approaches to computer science will find like-minded peers to communicate with.

ACM Categories & Descriptors: D.0

Keywords: Multimedia, Arts, Technology

Teaching with App Inventor for Android

Hal Abelson, *Massachusetts Institute of Technology*
David Wolber, *University of San Francisco*
Ralph Morelli, *Trinity College*
Jeff Gray, *University of Alabama*
Chinma Uche, *Greater Hartford Academy of Math and Science*

App Inventor for Android is a visual blocks language for building mobile apps. Like Scratch, the language s drag-and-drop blocks interface significantly lowers the barrier to entry. Beginners can immediately build apps that interface with mobile technology (e.g., GPS, Text-to-speech, SMS Texting) and build apps that have a real-world impact. App Inventor has great potential for increasing interest in programming and attracting women and other

Copyright is held by the author/owner(s).
SIGCSE'12, February 29–March 3, 2012, Raleigh, North Carolina, USA.
ACM 978-1-4503-1098-7/12/02.

underrepresented groups to computer science. Students learn by tinkering with their most beloved devices, phones and tablets, and even novices can create apps in an exciting and intuitive environment. App Inventor is relevant to teachers from middle school through the university level who are interested in a highly motivating method of teaching programming. In this BoF, we will discuss the language, its future in K-12 and university education, and its new home at the MIT Center for Mobile Learning.

ACM Categories & Descriptors: D.3.0; K.3.2

Keywords: Mobile computing, Computer Science Education

Technology That Educators of Computing Hail (TECH): Come, Share Your Favorites!

Daniel D. Garcia, *University of California, Berkeley*
Luke Segars, *University of California, Berkeley*

The pace of technology for use in computing education is staggering. In the last five years, the following tools / websites have completely transformed our teaching: Piazza, Google Docs, YouTube, Doodle and whenisgood.net, Skype and Google Hangout, and Khan Academy among others. Hardware has also played a part we love our Zoom H2 digital voice recorder (for recording CD-quality lecture audio), Blue Yeti USB mike (for audio/videoconferences), and iClickers (for engaging students in class). Do you wish you could easily share your favorites? Want to find out what the others know that you don t? Have a tool you ve built and want to get some users? Come to this BOF! We ll also show the TECH website we ve built that attempts to collect all of these tools in one place.

ACM Categories & Descriptors: K.3.2

Keywords: Tools, Technologies and Tools

Motivating CS1/2 Students with the Android Platform

John Lewis, *Virginia Tech*
Anthony Allevato, *Virginia Tech*
Stephen Edwards, *Virginia Tech*

The use of Android in computing courses is growing. Students find it engaging because it offers a unique opportunity to develop Java apps for mobile devices. Android offers opportunities and challenges in a teaching environment, especially in CS1 and CS2. As a professional-level platform, it incorporates many design idioms that may require students to learn advanced language features earlier. It also introduces logistical complications in setting up development tools and code projects. Existing approaches to software testing and automated grading also must be adapted. This BOF will gather educators interested in using Android in their courses, focusing on issues that arise when balancing the need to teach fundamental concepts with the complexities required to accomplish basic tasks on the Android platform. We look forward to sharing assignments, resources, techniques, and experiences with others interested in Android.

ACM Categories & Descriptors: D.1.5

Keywords: Android, mobile platforms

Copyright is held by the author/owner(s).
SIGCSE'12, February 29–March 3, 2012, Raleigh, North Carolina, USA.
ACM 978-1-4503-1098-7/12/02.

Interdisciplinary Database Collaborations

Suzanne W. Dietrich, *Arizona State University*
Don Goelman, *Villanova University*

Databases play a major role across many disciplines for the storage and retrieval of information. Many database educators are establishing collaborations with colleagues representing a diverse spectrum of interests, for both research and pedagogical purposes. Further, the range of cooperating disciplines is expanding, as evidenced by the emergence of new fields such as computational journalism, as well as by the proliferation of discipline-specific dialects of XML. The goal of this Birds-of-a-Feather session is to bring database educators together to share their experiences on interdisciplinary collaborations in an open dialogue that is fostered by this format.

ACM Categories & Descriptors: H.2.4

Keywords: Databases, Interdisciplinary

Google Summer of Code and Google Code-In Bof

Carol Smith, *Google, Inc.*

Google Summer of Code is the outreach program aimed at getting university students involved in a 3-month online internship working in open source software development. Google Code-in is the contest aimed at involving 13-18 year olds in open source software development, documentation translation, outreach, research, and more. I will be discussing both programs at this BoF and encouraging students and teachers to get involved. We'll open the forum for discussion amongst the attendees about how to participate, how to get the word out, and answer any questions they may have.

ACM Categories & Descriptors: K.3.0

Keywords: education, open source

Building Partnerships Across the CS Education Spectrum

Chris Stephenson, *Computer Science Teachers Association*
Steve Cooper, *Stanford University*
Don Yanek, *Northside College Prep High School*
Jeff Gray, *The University of Alabama*

Over the last five years, CSTA has built a solid outreach and teacher support network through the work of its chapters and Leadership Cohort. This network has also become a major source of active partnerships between K-12 teachers, their schools, and colleagues from colleges, universities, and industry. The goal of this BOF is to provide concrete examples and suggestions for SIGCSE members interested in building these kinds of partnerships.

ACM Categories & Descriptors: K.3.2

Keywords: K-12 Outreach, Partnerships

Engaging the Community with Mobile App Projects

William Turkett, *Wake Forest University*
Paúl Pauca, *Wake Forest University*
Joel Hollingsworth, *Elon University*

As the popularity of mobile devices surges, more and more organizations are looking to exploit the novel interaction methods of mobile devices to re-deploy legacy software or to develop innovative new applications. Many organizations are looking to nearby universities for expertise in this area. At the same time, mobile computing has become increasingly integrated within courses in CS departments. Historically, capstone courses and other advanced electives have resulted in the production of non-trivial software artifacts. This BOF will provide a platform for discussion of how the use of mobile app platforms in such courses can allow for the development of meaningful software projects that engage with and give back to the community and provide rich opportunities for service learning.

ACM Categories & Descriptors: K.4.0

Keywords: Outreach, Software Engineering

Have Class, Will Travel

Paige H. Meeker, *Presbyterian College*

At many schools, various disciplines offer travel courses to enhance the knowledge of the student. How can we introduce such courses to computer science departments across the country? This BOF will provide a time of sharing ideas for such courses and discuss travel courses that have been successfully taught. This will include not only the material for the course but also discussion concerning the additional planning overhead that must be considered when traveling cost, insurance, itinerary, safety, etc.

ACM Categories & Descriptors: A.m

Keywords: New Course Topics, Travel

Integration of Experiential Learning and Teaching: Beyond the Walls of the Classroom, Techniques, Challenges and Merits

Arshia A. Khan, *College of St. Scholastica*
Tammy Lichtenberg, *College of St. Scholastica*
Rishika Dhody, *College of St. Scholastica*
Joel Poualeu, *College of St. Scholastica*

Integration of Experiential learning and teaching: -Beyond the walls of the classroom, techniques, challenges and merits Arshia Khan, College of St. Scholastica Tammy Lichtenberg, College of St. Scholastica John Woosle, Southeastern Louisiana University Rishika Dhody, College of St. Scholastica Joel Poualeu, College of St. Scholastica Integration of experiential learning is critical in the field of computer science. It makes science education more rigorous, relevant, and extends the learning beyond the academic walls by engaging students in real world experiences and enforcing active learning. Engaging students in real world experiences is the new pedagogical method of active learning. Connecting theoretical concepts to real world applications will strengthen skills and knowledge (McLaughlin, 2010). Technology is evolving over night and the job requirements are extremely volatile. Educators in the field of computer science have a challenging task of staying abreast with the technology and market needs while self learning the new technologies. One way of staying a breast with the changing needs is to rely on the businesses for input on what should be taught and using them to extend the learning into the real world through experiential learning. The gap between academia and industry can potentially be reduced by interweaving experiential learning with regular classroom activities. This session will involve faculty and business leaders and employees, discussing various mechanisms of involving and collaborating with businesses in an attempt to bring real world simulations and experiences in a classroom. The techniques, challenges and merits of experiential learning will be discussed along with communication and other soft skills that are not covered in textbooks but can only be learned by experiential learning. Internships are one form of experiential learning. Business collaborations provide opportunities to bring awareness of market requirements and means of achieving experiential learning.

ACM Categories & Descriptors: A.0

Keywords: Experiential Learning

Copyright is held by the author/owner(s).
SIGCSE'12, February 29–March 3, 2012, Raleigh, North Carolina, USA.
ACM 978-1-4503-1098-7/12/02.

SIGCSE 2012 SRC Graduate Student Research Abstracts

Deduced Social Networks for Educational Portal

Monika Akbar, *Virginia Tech*

Educational portals mostly rely on resources. Combining an online community and analyzing and harnessing the user trends can provide users with more information on how others succeed in the vast information space. The AlgoViz Portal collects metadata on Algorithm Visualizations and provides community support. We show how logs can be used to discover latent relationships between users, deducing an implicit social network. Clustering of the log data allows us to find different page-viewing patterns, giving us an idea about the different groups of users and their information seeking behavior.

Student Adherence to Test-First Programming in the Classroom

Kevin Buffardi, *Virginia Tech*

Virginia Tech employed Web-CAT, an automated testing tool, for several years in CS1 and CS2 classes to introduce and reinforce Test-Driven Design (TDD). Our concern over some students not accepting or adhering to test-first principles drew attention to the need to identify these students' behaviors and the consequential impact on their programs. Our research used Web-CAT data to analyze snapshots of students' work-in-progress to identify testing and development patterns of those not adhering to TDD. Analysis also focused on the relationship between TDD adherence and several measurements of code quality. Based on the results, we drew inferences on possible strategies to improve acceptance and adherence to TDD.

Computing Computational Thinking

Kyu Han Koh, *University of Colorado at Boulder*

Visual programming with game/simulation creation is one of common approaches to raise computer science interests in K-12 education. Several research papers indicate that motivational benefits of visual programming learning are successfully brought to computer science education, but still it is not clear what kinds of knowledge students have actually learned through making games and/or simulations. In this research, a method to analyze the semantic meaning of visual programming is provided to support educational benefits of visual programming in computer science education.

CipherXRay: Exposing Cryptographic Operations and Secrets from Binay Execution

Xin Li, *George Mason University*

We focus on the technical feasibility of exposing the cryptographic operations and secrets from the execution of a potentially obfuscated binary executable. We build CipherXRay upon one of the defining characteristics of all good cryptographic algorithms - the avalanche effect. CipherXRay is able to not only reliably identify the cryptographic operations, but also accurately pinpoint the location, size and boundary of the input buffer, the output buffer and the cryptographic key buffer. We have evaluated CipherXRay with OpenSSL, KeePassX, Kraken malware and a number of third party programs with built-in compression and checksum. Our results demonstrate that current implementations of cryptographic algorithms achieve virtually no secrecy if their execution can be monitored.

An Analysis of Optimizing Power-Performance on Multi-core CPUs

Vijayalakshmi Saravanan, *Ryerson University*

Our thesis proposal is to investigate the optimum power/performance of multi-core processors. This state-of-the-art report is examined in two different architectures such as multi-thread and multi-core in terms of power and performance gains: (a) to find the optimum number of processor cores in such architectures based on instructions per cycle (IPC) and (b) to present an efficient buffered LR (Left-Right) algorithm for pipeline stall reduction which reduces the power consumption and maximizes the CPU utilization (i.e., throughput). We describe the experimental setup and simulators required to verify the results and then propose a benchmark for the design of multi-core processors.

Dynamic Test Input Generation for Database Applications to Achieve High Mutation Score

Tanmoy Sarkar, *Iowa State University*

Traditionally automatic generation of test inputs focuses on achieving high block or branch coverage and then assessing the adequacy of the generated test inputs is done by mutation testing. It is a technique where typical programming errors are replicated by modifying actual program and then checking whether (or to what extent) a test suite can distinguish between the actual program and its modified version. The modified versions are referred to as the mutants. Mutation testing of test suits for database applications presents an interesting and important challenge. Database applications consists of complex programming constructs as in typical applications and also consists of embedded SQL queries in various application paths. Mutants in such applications can be realized by not only modifying original program but also by modifying the embedded SQL queries. The objective of mutation testing in database applications, therefore, to check whether a given test suit can distinguish the actual application from its mutants. While mutation testing for typical program and for SQL queries exist, research in the field of mutation testing for database applications which combines both these aspects is still in a state of infancy. In this work, we propose to address the problem of mutation testing for database application by developing an automated test case generation technique which not only will provide high degree of branch coverage but also will achieve high SQL mutation score.

Using Refactoring to Achieve Quality Without A Name

M. Edward Wilborne, III, *North Carolina State University*

Mapping Christopher Alexanderís fifteen principles of good design to Martin Fowlerís behavior preserving code transformations, known as Refactoring, may result in code that has Alexander's "quality without a name". This research will provide programmers a guide to improving the quality of object oriented code without the program resorting to making random refactorings.

SIGCSE 2012 SRC Undergraduate Student Research Abstracts

Evaluating Relevance Metrics for Search in Personalized Network Spaces

Anthony Bentancur, *University of North Carolina at Charlotte*

In Personalized Network Spaces (PNets) people have access to an abundant amount of that originates from people and devices embedded within the surrounding environment. Users and applications that utilize information in these settings require the ability to get information about the "here" and "now", exhibiting tight spatiotemporal integration. We propose Gander, a personalized search engine that allows users to perform search of the "here" and "now" in the "here" and "now"; in other words, Gander supports dynamic search of the rapidly changing environment without reliance on a centralized index or connection to the Internet. The contribution of this work is the creation and evaluation of Gander relevance metrics that describe desirable spatiotemporal properties of data, and are used to order the search results for presentation to the search user. In this work, I create two new relevance metrics and evaluate their effectiveness in ordering results by incorporating them into Gander queries that are executed over a PNets environment. The two relevance metrics that I designed and implemented rank results for a search query for amusement park rides in order of: 1) rides that the user has not ridden and 2) rides near a bench. The NDCG values from evaluating these two relevance metrics were around .70 and .80 respectively. Our results, measured in terms of Normalized Discounted Cumulative Gain, show that our spatiotemporal relevance metrics provide high degrees of utility to Gander users.

Exploring Text-Based Analysis of Test-Case Dependencies of Web Applications

Camille Cobb, *Washington and Lee University*

Test cases formulated from user sessions of a web application often depend on what happened in a previous session to the shared, persistent application state. When ordering test suites, these dependencies must be maintained to avoid predominantly executing error code. This work explores the feasibility of computing dependencies directly from the test cases. We propose a novel text-based analysis of the URL requests. Our exploratory study of URL requests to five deployed web applications suggests that resources contain textual clues useful for estimating test-case dependencies. The results provide a foundation to implement a test-case dependency model that uses a text-based analysis approach to identify dependencies and an arranger that uses the model to automatically order test suites.

Improving the Flexibility of JFLAP through Presentation of Explicit Formal Definitions and Symbol Alphabets

Julian Genkins, *Duke University*

Java Formal Languages and Automata Package (JFLAP) is a software visualization suite focused on the canonical concepts of a course in Formal Languages and Automata (FLA) Theory. The software eases the construction, modification, and testing of FLA algorithms and machines, catalyzing learning. Recent additions to JFLAP include a formal definition component which highlights the elements that formally underlie a given automata or grammar. This includes a panel corresponding to any symbol alphabets associated with a formal definition which allows for more varied, complex definitions while retaining backwards compatibility. This new system makes explicit much of the work previously done implicitly by JFLAP, encouraging greater user interaction and providing more rapid, productive feedback.

Using Static Analysis to Evaluate Student Code

Alexandra Johnson, *Carnegie Mellon University*

The automated assessment of student code is beneficial both for the learners and for the course staff. Students benefit from the immediate feedback and reduction of metacognitive requirements of early programming assignments, while course staff reclaim hours of tedious grading. Although important, current implementations of assessment tend to be course grained and focus more on the functionality (or lack thereof) of a solution than the knowledge a student has demonstrated. In this work we evaluate the use of a static analysis technique, abstract syntax trees, combined with JUnit testing to award partial credit to incorrect program solutions. Results show a significant improvement with the use of ASTs in automated program assessment.

Teaching Computer Science Concepts Through Educational Games Using Social Aspects Within Peers

Javier Olaya, *Kean University*

The demand of computer science is growing and unfortunately the early college students are avoiding this degree. Production of Computer Science degrees are declining and the consequences are low participation of under-represented groups. The largest group currently is women and this is a loss to the computer science field. The students that come straight to university with no experience in programming have more difficulty accomplishing computer science assignments. Therefore, it is necessary for these students to find ways to enhance their learning. This research assesses the effectiveness of learning computer science lessons through an educational game.

Cloud Filter

Mateus Oliveira *The College of New Jersey*

Cloud Filter is a research project conducted at the University of Calgary that serves to question the security capabilities of cloud services. The primary issue that we targeted is the lack of fine-grain filtering of data storage. Services, such as Amazon S3, limit users to only a handful of locations where data can be stored. We suspect that this is because these cloud services do not have the hardware capabilities to support this security mechanism to all of its users. To test our hypothesis, we created our own Cloud Filtering Linux Kernel Module to implement this location control management.

Metaphor: A Declarative Approach to Computational Art

Jaimie Sauls, *University of Arizona*

Computer science is misrepresented as a science and such misperceptions may contribute to students' negative views and reluctance to join this field of study. The Laboratory for Computer Science creates online lessons for high school students that introduce computing theories in an interactive way. This study examines how students' perceptions of computer science change upon completion of these labs. The focus is on the students' perspective of computer science and their place in the field irrespective of their identification with a specific minority group. Identifying whether the stigmas or stereotypes are present with the students that experience these lessons and whether a deeper knowledge of the underlying theories in computer science will change these views is the goal.

Modeling the Power Consumption of Computer Systems with Graphics Processing Units (GPUs)

Stephanie Schmidt, *Sonoma State University*

To help optimize computer systemsí energy efficiency, researchers have developed models relating these systems instantaneous power consumption to resource utilization metrics available in software. Existing power models assume the major consumers of dynamic power are the central processing unit (CPU), memory and disk. The increased use of graphics processing units (GPUs) for general-purpose computing compromises this assumption. Therefore, models that exclude the GPU may significantly mispredict power consumption. I built full-system power models for two GPU-equipped machines in order to test this hypothesis. This research is the first to quantify: the inaccuracy of traditional high-level system power models for GPU workloads; the benefits of including GPU metrics in a full-system power model when applied to both GPU and non-GPU workloads; and the sensitivity of the model to the specific choice of GPU metrics.

Four-dimensional mapping with mobile robotics and RGB-D sensors

Tanner Schmidt, *Duke University*

Mapping with mobile robots in both two and three dimensions has been an active area research and has produced many great results. However, the environments in which robots operate are often dynamic. Adding time as a fourth dimension to the mapping problem allows robotic systems to track changes in their surroundings. This can be accomplished via extension the octree data structure, by inserting a map between parent nodes and their children such that the subtree of a given node at any point in time can be accessed by selecting from the map the node that was valid at that time. This method is efficient in that it does not increase the depth of the octree. This data structure can then be queried to determine the state of the environment in the past or to analyze changes to the map.

Experimentally Exploring Algorithmic Descriptions of Three-Dimensional Geometry

Elizabeth Skiba, *SUNY Geneseo*

GUI based software is the traditional tool for describing complex geometry, however I hypothesize that algorithmic descriptions are superior for reasons including their ability to reuse pieces of geometry. I designed an experiment to compare three geometry description tools. Descriptions were generated manually, through the use of a GUI, and algorithmically. I specifically investigate their strengths and weaknesses when changing a pre-existing geometry. I measured a ratio of initial size of the description to size of a change to that description. Results suggest that algorithmic description has significant advantages over other methods of describing changes to geometry.

PICS: Platform Independent Cloud Scripting

Kelly Smith, *Slippery Rock University*

Previous work in minimizing the inherent difficulties of parallel programming has yielded three popular methods for automated, scaled parallelization: OpenMP, MPI, and CUDA. This research borrows much of its philosophy from these methods, adds parallel language constructs to JavaScript, and provides a general-purpose framework for spawning algorithms to a heterogeneous, platform-independent cloud of processing entities including mobile devices. Currently the cloud consists of clients on the following platforms: Windows, Linux, OSX, Android, and any modern web browser. Initial results have been encouraging, and this framework has proven to be effective in bringing parallel computing to untapped computing resources.

Modular Program Design and Verification in RESOLVE

Daniel Welch, Denison University

In 2003, Sir Charles Anthony Hoare issued a challenge to the computing community at large to construct a verifying compiler. To answer this challenge, a language named RESOLVE was developed to not only achieve the goal of verification, but also create a language supportive of modular, reuse-oriented, software design principles. To determine the developmental state of RESOLVE in relation to this vision, we implement Kruskal's minimum spanning tree algorithm as proof of concept. This algorithm, due to its reliance of multiple components, presents an opportunity to test RESOLVE's new verifier and compiler on a sufficiently complicated project.

Matching XML Schema Documents

William West, *The College of New Jersey*

With the dynamic nature of databases, there is a growing need to re-organize and combine sets of data. While the combination of two or more data sets is often done manually, this can become a costly and time-consuming process. Thus, automatic methods of database schema matching become necessary. XML is unique in its use of a tree-like structure and strictly defined element, hence requiring its own matching algorithms to achieve optimal accuracy. In this paper, we focus on developing an XML schema matcher in Java. A schema matching framework is outlined in detail, using two standard XSD schemas as examples. We find that through the use of existing Java libraries and external APIs, a custom and fully functional XML schema matcher can be successfully developed in Java.

Author Index

join today!

SIGCSE & ACM

www.acm.org/sigcse www.acm.org

The **ACM Special Interest Group on Computer Science Education** (SIGCSE) provides a forum for educators to discuss the problems concerned with the development, implementation, and/or evaluation of computing programs, curricula, and courses, as well as syllabi, laboratories, and other elements of teaching and pedagogy. SIGCSE features an annual technical symposium and additional conferences on educational issues and research. Members receive an electronic quarterly newsletter (*SIGCSE Bulletin*) and an annual compilation of conference proceedings on CD. Members also receive *ACM Inroads*, a quarterly magazine.

The **Association for Computing Machinery** (ACM) is an educational and scientific computing society which works to advance computing as a science and a profession. Benefits include subscriptions to *Communications of the ACM*, *MemberNet*, *TechNews* and *CareerNews*, full and unlimited access to thousands of online courses and books, discounts on conferences and the option to subscribe to the ACM Digital Library.

- ❑ SIGCSE (ACM Member) .... $ 25
- ❑ SIGCSE (ACM Student Member & Non-ACM Student Member) .... $ 8
- ❑ SIGCSE (Non-ACM Member) .... $ 25
- ❑ ACM Professional Membership ($99) & SIGCSE ($25) $124
- ❑ ACM Professional Membership ($99) & SIGCSE ($25) & ACM Digital Library ($99) $223
- ❑ ACM Student Membership ($19) & SIGCSE ($8) .... $ 27
- ❑ Expedited Air for *Communications of the ACM* (outside N. America) .... $ 54

payment information

Name ____________________

ACM Member # ____________________

Mailing Address ____________________

____

City/State/Province ____________________

ZIP/Postal Code/Country ____________________

Email ____________________

Mobile Phone ____________________

Fax ____________________

Mailing List Restriction
ACM occasionally makes its mailing list available to computer-related organizations, educational institutions and sister societies. All email addresses remain strictly confidential. Check one of the following if you wish to restrict the use of your name:

- o ACM announcements only
- o ACM and other sister society announcements
- o ACM subscription and renewal notices only

Credit Card Type: ❑ AMEX ❑ VISA ❑ MC

Credit Card # ____________________

Exp. Date ____________________

Signature ____________________

Make check or money order payable to ACM, Inc

ACM accepts U.S. dollars or equivalent in foreign currency. Prices include surface delivery charge. Expedited Air Service, which is a partial air freight delivery service, is available outside North America. Contact ACM for more information.

Questions? Contact:
ACM Headquarters
2 Penn Plaza, Suite 701
New York, NY 10121-0701
voice: 212-626-0500
fax: 212-944-1318
email: acmhelp@acm.org

Remit to:
ACM
General Post Office
P.O. Box 30777
New York, NY 10087-0777

SIGAPP12

www.acm.org/joinsigs

Association for Computing Machinery

Advancing Computing as a Science & Profession

www.ingramcontent.com/pod-product-compliance
Lightning Source LLC
LaVergne TN
LVHW082344011026
849160LV00024B/1044
9781450310987